A SHAKESPEAREAN GENEALOGY

This chart reflects Shakespeare's history plays and is thus not historically accurate. Many descendants of Henry II and Edward III are omitted. On occasion, Shakespeare combined or simply invented historical figures. These deviations from fact are explained in the notes.

In the chart, the names of Kings and Queens are printed in capitals, and the dates of their reigns are printed in bold. The names of characters appearing in the plays are underlined.

Henry
d. 1183

Edward, Prince of
Wales 1330–1376

RICHARD II
1367–1400
(1377–99)

William of
Hatfield

Lionel, Duke of
Clarence 1338–1368

Philippa
m. Edmund
Mortimer, Earl
of March

RICHARD I
1157–1199
(1189–99)

Philip Faulconbridge*
(Richard Plantagenet)

John of Gaunt,
Duke of Lancaster
1340–1399
m. Blanche of
Lancaster
m. Constance of
Castile
m. Katherine
Swynford

HENRY IV
1367–1413
(1399–1413)

Thomas Beaufort,
Duke of Exeter
1377–1427

Henry Beaufort,
Bishop of Winchester
1375–1447

John Beaufort,
Earl of Somerset
1372–1409

Joan Beaufort
m. Ralph Neville,
Earl of
Westmoreland

HENRY II
1133–1189
(1154–89)
m. Eleanor
of Aquitaine
d. 1204

Geoffrey, d. 1186
m. Constance
of Brittany

Arthur
1187–1203

JOHN 1167–1216
(1199–1216)

HENRY III
1207–1272
(1216–72)

EDWARD I
1239–1307
(1272–1307)

EDWARD II
1284–1327
(1307–27)

Edmund of Langley,
Duke of York
1341–1402

Edward, Duke of
Aumerle d. 1415

Richard, Earl
of Cambridge
d. 1415 m. Anne
Mortimer (above)

EDWARD III
1312–1377
(1327–77)
m. Philippa of
Hainault

Thomas of
Woodstock, Duke of
Gloucester 1355–1397

Anne

Eleanor
m. Alfonso VIII,
King of Castile

Blanche, d. 1252
m. Louis VIII
of France

William of
Windsor

*Philip Faulconbridge, the bastard son of Richard I, had no historical existence. Such a character appears in the play *The Life and Death of King John* and is referred to in passing in Holinshed's *Chronicles*.

† In the character of Edmund Mortimer, Shakespeare combines two historical figures. The Edmund Mortimer who married Catrin, daughter of Owain Glyndŵr, was the grandson of Lionel, Duke of Clarence, and the younger brother of Roger, Earl of March. He died in 1409. Shakespeare combines him with his nephew, the Edmund Mortimer recognized by Richard II as his heir (d. 1424). This second Edmund was the brother of Anne Mortimer and the uncle of Richard Plantagenet.

‡ The character of the Duke of Somerset combines Henry Beaufort with his younger brother Edmund (d. 1471), who succeeded him as Duke.

- Elizabeth Mortimer ("Kate") m. Henry Percy ("Hotspur") 1364–1403
  - Henry, Earl of Northumberland 1394–1455

- EDWARD IV 1442–1483 (1461–83) m. Elizabeth Woodville d. 1492
  - EDWARD V 1470–1483 (1483)
  - Richard, Duke of York 1472–1483
  - Elizabeth of York 1465–1503 m. HENRY VII (below)

- Edmund, Earl of Rutland 1443–1460

- Edmund Mortimer†

- George, Duke of Clarence 1449–1478 m. Isabel Neville (below)

- Anne Mortimer m. Richard, Earl of Cambridge (below)
  - Richard Plantagenet, Duke of York 1411–1460 m. Cicely Neville (below)
    - RICHARD III 1452–1485 (1483–85) m. Anne Neville (below)

- HENRY V 1387–1422 (1413–22) m. Catherine 1401–1437
  - HENRY VI 1421–1471 (1422–61) m. Margaret of Anjou d. 1482
    - Edward, Prince of Wales 1453–1471 m. Anne Neville (below)

- Thomas, Duke of Clarence d. 1421

- John of Lancaster, Duke of Bedford 1389–1435

- Arthur m. Catherine of Aragon (below)

- Margaret m. James IV of Scotland
  - James V of Scotland
    - Mary, Queen of Scots
      - JAMES I 1566–1625 (1603–25)

- Humphrey, Duke of Gloucester 1391–1447 m. Eleanor Cobham d. 1454

- John Beaufort, Duke of Somerset 1403–1444
  - Margaret Beaufort m. Edmund Tudor, Earl of Richmond
    - HENRY VII 1457–1509 (1485–1509) m. Elizabeth of York (above)

- HENRY VIII 1491–1547 (1509–47) m. Catherine of Aragon
  - MARY I 1516–1558 (1553–58) m. Philip of Spain

  m. Anne Boleyn
  - ELIZABETH I 1533–1603 (1558–1603)

- Edmund Beaufort, Duke of Somerset 1406–1455
  - Henry Beaufort, Duke of Somerset 1436–1464‡

  m. Jane Seymour
  - EDWARD VI 1537–1553 (1547–53)

  m. Anne of Cleves
  m. Katherine Howard
  m. Katherine Parr

- Richard Neville, Earl of Salisbury 1400–1460
  - Richard Neville, Earl of Warwick 1428–1471
    - Isabel Neville d. 1476 m. George, Duke of Clarence (above)
    - Anne Neville d. 1485 m. Edward, Prince of Wales (above) m. RICHARD III (above)
  - John Neville, Marquess of Montague d. 1471

- Cicely Neville m. Richard Plantagenet, Duke of York (above)

- Mary m. Charles Brandon
  - Frances
    - Jane Grey 1537–1554

- Humphrey, Duke of Buckingham 1402–1460
  - Humphrey Stafford d. 1455
    - Henry, Duke of Buckingham 1454?–1483
      - Edward, Duke of Buckingham 1478–1521

Richard II, 1377–99   Richard was the eldest son of Edward the Black Prince, himself the eldest son of King Edward III, who ruled England from 1327 to 1377. When the Black Prince died in battle in France in 1376, Richard became the legitimate heir to the throne. He ruled from Edward's death in 1377 until he was deposed in 1399 by Henry Bolingbroke, the eldest son of John of Gaunt, Duke of Lancaster. Because he was the fourth son of Edward III, Gaunt and his Lancastrian descendants had weaker hereditary claims to the throne than did Richard. When deposed, Richard had no children to succeed him, but he recognized Edmund Mortimer, Fifth Earl of March, as his heir presumptive. This Mortimer was descended from Lionel, Duke of Clarence, the third son of Edward III, and therefore also had stronger hereditary claims to the throne than did Bolingbroke. Shakespeare combined this Mortimer with his uncle Edmund Mortimer, who married Owain Glyndŵr's daughter.

Henry IV, 1399–1413   Henry Bolingbroke, eldest son of John of Gaunt, seized the throne from Richard II in 1399. When Henry died in 1413, he was succeeded by his eldest son, Prince Hal, who became Henry V.

Henry V, 1413–22   Henry V became king in 1413 and reigned until his death in 1422. He was succeeded by his son, Henry VI.

Henry VI, 1422–61   Henry VI was less than one year old when he succeeded his father, Henry V. In the young king's minority, his uncle Humphrey, Duke of Gloucester, was named Lord Protector, and the kingdom was ruled by an aristocratic council. Henry VI assumed personal authority in 1437. He was deposed in 1461 by his third cousin, who was crowned Edward IV. Henry was murdered in 1471.

Edward IV, 1461–83   Edward, the eldest son of Richard, Duke of York, seized the throne from Henry VI in 1461. His Yorkist claim to the throne derived from his grandmother, Anne Mortimer, who was descended from Lionel, third son of Edward III, and was sister to that Edmund Mortimer recognized by Richard II as his heir presumptive; Edward IV's grandfather, Richard, Earl of Cambridge, was the son of Edmund of Langley, fifth son of Edward III. Edward IV reigned until his death in 1483. His heir was his eldest son (Edward), but the throne was usurped by his brother Richard, Duke of Gloucester.

Richard III, 1483–85   Richard III was the youngeer brother of Edward IV. After the death of Edward IV in 1483, Richard prevented the coronation of Edward V with a claim of illegitimacy and succeeded to the throne himself. Edward and his younger brother, Richard, Duke of York, were murdered in the Tower of London. Richard III was killed at the Battle of Bosworth Field in 1485, and the kingdom fell to the victor, Henry Tudor, Earl of Richmond.

Henry VII, 1485–1509   Henry Tudor seized the throne from Richard III in 1485. He was descended from John of Gaunt by John's third marriage, with Catherine Swynford. He married Elizabeth, daughter of Edward IV, uniting the houses of Lancaster and York. He died in 1509 and was succeeded by his son, Henry VIII.

Henry VIII, 1509–47   Henry was the second son of Henry VII. His older brother, Arthur, died in 1502. Henry VIII's first wife was Catherine of Aragon, who bore his daughter Mary. His second wife, Anne Boleyn, was the mother of Elizabeth. His third wife, Jane Seymour, bore him a son, who succeeded to the throne as Edward VI after Henry VIII died in 1547.

Edward VI, 1547–53   Edward VI was nine years old when he became king. From 1547 to 1549, the realm was governed by a Lord Protector, the Duke of Somerset; power then passed to John Dudley, Duke of Northumberland. When Edward VI died in 1553, Northumberland attempted unsuccessfully to prevent the succession of Mary Tudor by installing as queen his daughter-in-law, Lady Jane Grey, a great-granddaughter of Henry VII.

Mary I, 1553–58   Mary, daughter of Henry VIII and his first wife, Catherine of Aragon, came to the throne in 1553. She married King Philip of Spain but died childless. She was succeeded by her half sister, Elizabeth.

Elizabeth I, 1558–1603   Elizabeth, the daughter of Henry VIII and his second wife, Anne Boleyn, became queen after the death of her half sister, Mary, in 1558. She ruled until her death in 1603. She was succeeded by her cousin James.

James I, 1603–1625   James VI of Scotland became James I of England in 1603. His claim to the throne of England derived from his great-grandmother, Margaret Tudor, a daughter of Henry VII who married James IV of Scotland. James ruled England and Scotland until his death in 1625; he was succeeded by his son, Charles I.

THE NORTON SHAKESPEARE

THIRD EDITION

Volume I
Early Plays and Poems

TEXTUAL EDITORS

DAVID M. BERGERON, University of Kansas, *The Winter's Tale*

THOMAS CARTELLI, Muhlenberg College, *Richard III*

DERMOT CAVANAGH, University of Edinburgh, *King John*

PATRICK CHENEY, Pennsylvania State University, *Venus and Adonis, The Rape of Lucrece, The Passionate Pilgrim, The Phoenix and Turtle,* and *Attributed Poems*

LINE COTTEGNIES, Université Sorbonne Nouvelle—Paris 3, *2 Henry IV*

HANNAH CRAWFORTH, King's College London, *The Two Noble Kinsmen*

TRUDI L. DARBY, King's College London, *Much Ado About Nothing*

ANTHONY B. DAWSON, University of British Columbia, *Hamlet*

MATTHEW DIMMOCK, University of Sussex, *2 Henry VI*

PASCALE DROUET, University of Poitiers, *Henry VIII*

LUKAS ERNE, University of Geneva, *A Midsummer Night's Dream*

JENNIFER FORSYTH, Kutztown University, *1 Henry VI*

EUGENE GIDDENS, Anglia Ruskin University, *Timon of Athens*

SUZANNE GOSSETT, Loyola University Chicago, *All's Well That Ends Well*

GRACE IOPPOLO, University of Reading, *King Lear*

JANE KINGSLEY-SMITH, University of Roehampton, *Love's Labor's Lost*

JAMES A. KNAPP, Loyola University Chicago, *The Comedy of Errors*

JESSE M. LANDER, University of Notre Dame, *1 Henry IV*

LYNNE MAGNUSSON, University of Toronto, *The Sonnets* and *A Lover's Complaint*

HOWARD MARCHITELLO, Rutgers University—Camden, *Henry V*

LEAH S. MARCUS, Vanderbilt University, *As You Like It* and *The Merchant of Venice*

CLARE McMANUS, University of Roehampton, *Othello*

GORDON McMULLAN, King's College London, *Romeo and Juliet*

GRETCHEN E. MINTON, Montana State University, *Troilus and Cressida*

ROBERT S. MIOLA, Loyola University Maryland, *Macbeth*

HELEN OSTOVICH, McMaster University, *The Merry Wives of Windsor*

GAIL KERN PASTER, Folger Shakespeare Library, *Twelfth Night*

LOIS POTTER, University of Delaware, *Pericles*

NATHALIE RIVÈRE DE CARLES, University of Toulouse—Jean Jaurès, *The Two Gentlemen of Verona*

WILLIAM H. SHERMAN, University of York, *The Tempest*

CATHY SHRANK, University of Sheffield, *Coriolanus*

JAMES R. SIEMON, Boston University, *Julius Caesar*

CATHERINE SILVERSTONE, Queen Mary University of London, *Titus Andronicus*

MATTHEW STEGGLE, Sheffield Hallam University, *Measure for Measure*

ALAN STEWART, Columbia University, *Richard II*

HOLGER SCHOTT SYME, University of Toronto, *Edward III* and *Sir Thomas More*

NEIL TAYLOR, University of Roehampton, *3 Henry VI*

ANN THOMPSON, King's College London, *Cymbeline*

VIRGINIA MASON VAUGHAN, Clark University, *Antony and Cleopatra*

SARAH WERNER, Folger Shakespeare Library, *The Taming of the Shrew*

The Theater of Shakespeare's Time, HOLGER SCHOTT SYME, University of Toronto
Performance Notes, BRETT GAMBOA, Dartmouth College

THE NORTON SHAKESPEARE

THIRD EDITION

Volume I
Early Plays and Poems

Stephen Greenblatt, *General Editor*
HARVARD UNIVERSITY

Walter Cohen
UNIVERSITY OF MICHIGAN

Suzanne Gossett, *General Textual Editor*
LOYOLA UNIVERSITY CHICAGO (EMERITA)

Jean E. Howard
COLUMBIA UNIVERSITY

Katharine Eisaman Maus
UNIVERSITY OF VIRGINIA

Gordon McMullan, *General Textual Editor*
KING'S COLLEGE LONDON

W · W · NORTON & COMPANY · NEW YORK · LONDON

W. W. Norton & Company has been independent since its founding in 1923, when William Warder Norton and Mary D. Herter Norton first published lectures delivered at the People's Institute, the adult education division of New York City's Cooper Union. The firm soon expanded its program beyond the Institute, publishing books by celebrated academics from America and abroad. By mid-century, the two major pillars of Norton's publishing program—trade books and college texts—were firmly established. In the 1950s, the Norton family transferred control of the company to its employees, and today—with a staff of 400 and a comparable number of trade, college, and professional titles published each year—W. W. Norton & Company stands as the largest and oldest publishing house owned wholly by its employees.

Editor: Julia Reidhead
Managing Editor, College: Marian Johnson
Associate Editor: Emily Stuart
Manuscript Editors: Harry Haskell, Alice Vigliani
Media Editor: Carly Fraser Doria
Media Project Editor: Kristin Sheerin
Production Manager: Eric Pier-Hocking
Digital Production: Mateus Texeira, Colleen Caffrey
Marketing Manager, Literature: Kim Bowers
Photo Editor: Trish Marx
Composition: Westchester Book Company
Manufacturing: LSC Communications

The Library of Congress has catalogued the full edition as follows:
Shakespeare, William, 1564–1616.
The Norton Shakespeare / Stephen Greenblatt, General Editor, Harvard
University; Walter Cohen, University of Michigan; Suzanne Gossett, General
Textual Editor, Loyola University Chicago (Emerita); Jean E. Howard, Columbia
University; Katharine Eisaman Maus, University of Virginia; Gordon McMullan,
General Textual Editor, King's College London.—Third edition.
pages cm
Includes bibliographical references and index.
ISBN 978-0-393-93499-1 (hardcover)
I. Greenblatt, Stephen, 1943– editor.   II. Cohen, Walter, 1949– editor.
III. Gossett, Suzanne, editor. IV. Howard, Jean E. (Jean Elizabeth), 1948– editor.
V. Maus, Katharine Eisaman, 1955– editor.   VI. McMullan, Gordon,
1962– editor.   VII. Title.
PR2754.G74 2015
822.3'3—dc23

2015018869

This edition: ISBN 978-0-393-93857-9

W. W. Norton & Company, Inc., 500 Fifth Avenue, New York, NY 10110-0017
wwnorton.com

W.W. Norton & company Ltd., 15 Carlisle Street, London W1D 3BS

3 4 5 6 7 8 9 0

Contents

Additional works, media, contextual materials, and bibliographies
are available in the Digital Edition

Appendices

Contents by Genre

Comedies

Histories

Tragedies

Poems

Contents by Date of First Publication

Most of the composition dates of Shakespeare's plays and poems are conjectural. The dates of first known publication are given here. However, since the first quarto of *Hamlet* was only discovered in 1823, and only one copy of the first quarto of *Titus Andronicus* survives, it may well be that early editions of which we are unaware did in fact exist, and some may even turn up yet. At first many of Shakespeare's plays were published anonymously; once he was famous and successful, quite a few plays and some poems whose authorship is either rejected or currently under dispute were advertised with his name (or the initials W.S.). Other plays published anonymously are believed by some scholars to be all or in part by Shakespeare. The earliest published text of a given play is not necessarily the fullest or most authoritative, so while *The Norton Shakespeare* includes editions of all such texts in the Digital Edition, the earliest publication is not always chosen to represent the play in the print edition. The following list includes those plays and poems found in *The Norton Shakespeare*.

Illustrations

Preface

This Third Edition of *The Norton Shakespeare* is both a continuation and a new beginning. Readers who have already found the format of the printed book and its editorial apparatus to their liking will get what they are looking for. The emphasis continues to be on the pleasure of reading, with a particular attention to undergraduates who may be encountering Shakespeare for the first time. "If then you do not like him," wrote Shakespeare's first editors almost four hundred years ago, "surely you are in some manifest danger not to understand him." We have from the start made every effort, through the glosses, notes, introductions, and other materials, to facilitate understanding and hence to enhance liking. We are careful not to overburden Shakespeare's words with explication or to crowd the page with distracting commentary. The clear, uncluttered, single-column format is designed to encourage absorption. But we try to offer enough help to allow the beauty and the luminous intelligence of these stupendous works to shine.

We have in this edition carefully revised each of our introductions (including the long General Introduction) and reviewed every one of our notes and glosses, altering and adding where appropriate. Our goal has been to hold onto what our readers have told us works well, but also to update the introductions, bibliographies, filmographies, and other materials to reflect current scholarship, shifting emphases, and newly released films. An entirely new feature of this edition is an illuminating Performance Note, by Brett Gamboa (Dartmouth College), that accompanies each of the plays. These notes describe the particular and recurrent theatrical challenges with which actors and directors have grappled in mounting any given work. The strategies devised over the centuries in response to these challenges are a fascinating point of entry into critical issues of interpretation. The notes are also an invaluable guide to what audiences should look for when they attend a new production.

From its inception, *The Norton Shakespeare* has paid exceptionally close attention to the accuracy as well as the accessibility of the texts and, in particular, to the challenge posed by those plays that exist in multiple substantive versions. For the Third Edition, all of Shakespeare's plays and poems have been newly edited, from scratch, by an international team of leading textual scholars. This hugely ambitious and complex undertaking has been based on the principle of single-text editing— that is, where more than one early authoritative text of a given play has survived, rather than merging them into one (as has been traditionally done), we have edited each text in its own right. We thereby offer the reader texts as close as possible to the original versions as read by Shakespeare's contemporaries. A lively and accessible new General Textual Introduction fully articulates this principle, explores the nature of the documents that have come down to us from Shakespeare's own time, and explains in detail the editorial practices on which this new text of the complete works is meticulously based.

Approximately half of Shakespeare's plays appeared both in small-format versions (quartos), printed in the playwright's own lifetime, and in the large-format First Folio (1623), published seven years after his death. As early as the eighteenth century, careful readers began to notice that there were differences, sometimes minor and sometimes quite significant, between these printings of the same plays. Starting with the landmark Shakespeare editions of Alexander Pope (1723) and Lewis Theobald (1733), editors initiated the practice of blending the different versions together, picking and choosing as their taste dictated or as they imagined that Shakespeare would have done, had he himself produced a definitive text. Hence, for example, the two distinct texts of *King Lear* were routinely fashioned into a single text, with editors combining lines that appear only in one or the other early version and choosing among hundreds of variant readings.

From its inception, *The Norton Shakespeare* rejected this editorial method (known as "conflation"). We have continued in the current print edition our hallmark practice of offering, on facing pages, the 1608 Quarto text of *King Lear* and the substantial revision of the play as printed in the First Folio (1623). While each version may be read independently—we have provided glosses and footnotes for each—the significant points of difference between the two are immediately apparent and available for comparison. It is thus possible to watch in extraordinarily sharp focus changes in the early modern text of one of Shakespeare's greatest plays. We recognize at the same time that a combined text, in one form or another, has long served as the *King Lear* upon which innumerable performances of the play have been based and on which a huge body of literary criticism has been written. Hence in addition to providing the Quarto and Folio texts, we wanted to offer readers a version of this great tragedy that combines the two without entirely erasing their differences. The solution that we provide in these pages is what in the first two editions of *The Norton Shakespeare* we used in the comparable case of *Hamlet*. We print the Folio text of *King Lear*, but we have moved the lines that are solely in the Quarto into the body of the play. In doing so, however, we did not want simply to produce a conflated version. We have therefore indented the Q-only passages, printed them in a slightly different typeface, and numbered them in such a way as to make clear their provenance. We call this a "scars-and-stitches" solution, since, though still eminently readable and enjoyable, it clearly marks the points of insertion and difference.

The Norton Shakespeare, then, includes three separate texts of *King Lear*. The reader can compare them, analyze the role of editors in constructing the texts we now call Shakespeare's, explore in detail the kinds of decisions that playwrights, editors, and printers make and remake, witness firsthand the historical transformation of what might at first glance seem fixed and unchanging. We offer extraordinary access to this supremely brilliant, difficult, compelling play.

Hamlet, the other great tragedy at the very center of Shakespeare's achievement, similarly exists in multiple versions: the 1604 Second Quarto (Q2), the longest of the early editions; the 1623 Folio text (F), which lacks some 200 lines found in Q2 but includes more than 70 lines not found there; and, casting a fascinating light on the more familiar version of the tragedy, the drastically different First Quarto (Q1, the so-called Bad Quarto). As in the case of *Lear,* editors for centuries have routinely conflated the Q2 and F *Hamlets*.

The realities of bookbinding—not to mention our recognition of the limited time in the typical undergraduate syllabus—preclude our offering in the print edition four *Hamlets* (Q1, Q2, F, and combined) to parallel the three *Lears*. What we have provided in these pages instead is a new incarnation of the solution we came up with in the first two editions of *The Norton Shakespeare*. While basing our *Hamlet* on the Q2 text, we have moved the Folio passages, among which are some of the tragedy's most famous lines, into the body of the play. But, as with the "scars-and-stitches" *Lear*, we have made it possible for readers who are interested to see what has been added.

The growing interest in the possibility of teaching the First Quarto of *Hamlet* has also led us to add that strange text, in fully glossed and annotated form, alongside the more familiar version of Shakespeare's most famous tragedy. Readers can wonder at a *Hamlet* in which the hero muses "To be, or not to be—ay, there's the point," and they can see how drastically one theater troupe in Shakespeare's own time probably cut the play for performance.

These and other changes all serve to keep *The Norton Shakespeare* fresh and current. But this Third Edition, as I have already suggested, is much more than a careful revision and updating. It is a thoroughgoing rethinking both of the entire Shakespeare corpus and of the whole way in which Shakespeare is experienced by contemporary readers. For the purposes of this preface, a single feature of the newly edited text should be emphasized: it was created not only for the print edition, but also for a new and exciting Digital Edition. From its inception the print edition featured both the Quarto and the Folio texts of *King Lear,* and we have now added the First Quarto of *Hamlet.* Our Digital Edition makes available fully glossed and annotated Quarto and Folio versions of the plays—fifteen in all—for which more than one early authoritative text exists, thereby offering the reader access to these plays as they were first experienced by Shakespeare's contemporaries. This means not only the two versions of *Lear,* which can be viewed in side-by-side scrolling format for comparison as well as individually, and not only the three versions of *Hamlet.* It also means multiple versions, with fascinating variants, of such beloved, centrally important plays as *Romeo and Juliet, Othello, Richard II, Richard III, Henry V, Love's Labor's Lost,* and *A Midsummer Night's Dream.* There are Quarto and Folio versions as well of *2* and *3 Henry VI, Titus Andronicus, 2 Henry IV, The Merry Wives of Windsor,* and *Troilus and Cressida.* The Digital Edition also offers an appendix of selected scenes from a number of multiple-version plays, presented side-by-side so that they can easily be compared for teaching purposes. For anyone interested in Shakespeare's practices of composition and revision and in the fascinating process through which his plays, passing through the printing house, have managed to reach us, the digital *Norton Shakespeare* is an unprecedented resource.

Links to the widely respected *Norton Facsimile of the First Folio of Shakespeare,* edited by Charlton Hinman, and to quarto facsimile pages make it possible for readers to see for themselves the original materials with which the editors have been working to create this new text of the complete works.

In the digital *Norton Shakespeare* we also include for the first time an edition of the full text of *Sir Thomas More,* a multi-authored play, unpublished in the period, whose manuscript includes a section in Shakespeare's own hand, the only surviving one of its kind. We also include an edition of *Edward III,* another play of which Shakespeare appears to have been part-author. Both texts are interesting as examples of the collaborative nature of much Elizabethan and Jacobean theater, a collaboration reflected as well in the late plays *Pericles, Henry VIII, The Two Noble Kinsmen,* the lost *Cardenio,* and—more debatably—such works as *1 Henry VI, Titus Andronicus,* and *Timon of Athens.*

This extraordinary wealth of texts, all complete with introductions, notes, and glosses, has been made possible by the vastness of the digital space. That space has allowed us to supplement the useful aids in the print edition—including maps, genealogies, a glossary, a short bibliography, a timeline, and a selection of key documents—with further resources. For the Digital Edition, the volume editors have created expanded bibliographies for the study of Shakespeare's works, and Misha Teramura (Harvard University), who edited and glossed the documents in the print text, has assembled and edited a larger archive of Tudor and Stuart documents relevant to Shakespeare and his theater world.

The remarkable expansion of texts is only the beginning. The resources of the Digital Edition have made possible innovations that were, until very recently, only a teacher's idle daydreams. Shakespeare scholars have long understood that the decisions editors make—for example, choosing one variant over another, or adding stage directions, or making consistent the multiple speech prefixes often used for a single character—can affect the meaning of the plays. But on the printed page it has been difficult to call attention to the significance of these decisions without interrupting the flow of the reading experience, while the long lists of textual variants printed at the ends of plays are so much raw data, rarely consulted or understood by anyone but experts. Now, by clicking a marginal icon, readers can summon illuminating Textual Comments for each play, written by the textual editor, that focus on textual-editing decision points influencing interpretation. It is possible for all interested readers now to understand textual cruxes and to see—and, for that matter, to call into question—key editorial choices.

Similarly, a crucially important dimension of Shakespeare's texts, as everyone grasps, is that they were originally intended for performance. Hence the brief discussion in the General Introduction of the theatrical scene Shakespeare encountered and helped to transform is now greatly enriched in "The Theater of Shakespeare's Time," a lively and original essay by Holger Schott Syme (University of Toronto). Syme conjures up a fiercely competitive world of multiple theater companies and rival venues, all scrambling for plays that will survive the attention of the government censor and lure crowds of spectators to part with their pennies.

Performance is obviously not only a matter of historical interest. It remains, for most of us and certainly for our students, central to the full experience of the plays. But, without overfreighting the page, it has been difficult to highlight this dimension in the printed book. Descriptions of famous performances, from Garrick to the present, rarely capture the significance of key interpretive choices by actors or directors. Now clicking on marginal icons keyed to particular moments in the texts allows one to read incisive and insightful Performance Comments that supplement the Performance Note preceding each play. These comments, by Brett Gamboa, highlight passages that are particularly famous challenges in performance and explore how a director or actor's interpretive choices affect meaning. Taken individually, the Performance Comments call attention to specific decisions that must be made in the realization of a play; taken together, they constitute a brilliant exploration of the performative dimensions of Shakespeare's art.

The performative dimension is enhanced by two further features of the Digital Edition. First, there are recordings of all of the songs—66 of them—in the plays, from the award-winning *Shakespeare's Songbook* audio companion by Ross Duffin. It is now possible for readers to take in fully the pervasive presence of music in Shakespeare's plays, something that the printed stage direction "*Music*" cannot hope to do. Second, there are over eight hours of spoken-word audio of key passages and scenes and those that pose particular challenges to readers. These have been specially recorded for the Digital Edition by the highly regarded company, Actors from the London Stage. With a simple click it is now possible for readers to hear the words on the page come alive in the voices of gifted actors.

The digital *Norton Shakespeare* brings together in one place an unparalleled array of resources for understanding and enjoying Shakespeare. These resources are not the primitive accumulation of materials, of dubious utility or reliability, which often makes the web an untrustworthy guide. Rather, each of the texts and other material has received the same careful scholarly and pedagogical attention that has made the print edition a success. But we are aware that different readers will have different interests and needs, often varying from time to time. The reading experience of the Digital Edition, including the visibility of icons, line numbers, glosses, and notes, can be easily customized, so that with a click readers can either "quiet" the page or access Norton's abundant reading help. The Digital Edition platform provides customizable highlighting, annotating, and comment-sharing tools that facilitate active reading.

The publisher also provides instructors with a wealth of free resources beyond the Digital Edition. An Instructor Resource Disc created for the new edition features the more than eight hours of spoken-word audio recorded by Actors from the London Stage, 150 songs, and over 100 images from the book in both JPEG and PowerPoint for easy classroom presentation. The images are available for download on the publisher's instructor resource page, wwnorton.com/instructors. In addition, the Norton Shakespeare YouTube channel brings together a carefully curated and regularly updated collection of the best of the web's Shakespeare video resources, allowing instructors to easily show clips from stage and film in class.

The extraordinary labor of love that has led to this new and revised edition of *The Norton Shakespeare* has involved a large number of collaborators. The volume editors owe a substantial debt of thanks to the readers of the earlier editions. Our readers have formed a large, engaged community, and their endorsements, observations, and suggestions for revision and expansion have proved invaluable. We have also profited from the highly detailed reviews of each individual feature of the edition commissioned by the publisher and performed with exemplary seriousness by many of our most esteemed professional colleagues.

At the very center of the Third Edition is the newly edited text of the Complete Works, an enormous, exhaustive, and exhausting enterprise. We wish to acknowledge with deepest gratitude the extraordinary labors of our gifted team of textual editors, listed on the title-page spread, led with an exemplary blend of discipline, patience, intellectual seriousness, and scholarly rigor by Gordon McMullan and Suzanne Gossett.

The *Norton Shakespeare* editors have had the valuable—indeed, indispensable—support of our publisher and a host of undergraduate and graduate research assistants, colleagues, friends, and family, whose names we gratefully note in the Acknowledgments that follow. All of these companions have helped us find in this long collective enterprise what the "Dedicatorie Epistle" to the First Folio promises to its readers: delight. We make the same promise to the readers of our edition and invite them to continue the great Shakespearean collaboration.

STEPHEN GREENBLATT
CAMBRIDGE, MASSACHUSETTS

Volume Editors' Acknowledgments

The creation of this edition has drawn heavily on the resources, experience, and skill of its remarkable publisher, W. W. Norton. Norton's record of success in academic publishing has sometimes made it seem like a giant, akin to the multinational corporations that dominate the publishing world, but it is in fact the only major publishing house that is employee-owned. Our principal guide has been our brilliant editor Julia Reidhead, whose calm intelligence, common sense, and steady focus have been essential in enabling us to reach our goal. With this Third Edition, we were blessed once again with the indispensable judgment and project-editorial expertise of Marian Johnson, managing editor, college department, as well as scrupulous manuscript editing by Alice Vigliani and Harry Haskell. Carly Fraser Doria, literature media editor, skillfully guided us through the new waters of the Digital Edition, following Cliff Landesman's innovative lead. Assistant editor Emily Stuart managed with remarkable skill and graciousness the complexities of manuscript preparation and review. Kim Yi, managing editor, digital media, and Kristin Sheerin, digital project editor, oversaw the monumental checking and proofing of files. In addition, we are deeply grateful to Cara Folkman, media assistant editor; JoAnn Simony and Elizabeth Audley, digital file coordinators; Eric Pier-Hocking, production manager; and Debra Morton Hoyt, corporate art director, who, along with designer Timothy Hsu, created our Ortelius-inspired cover design. Thanks also to Mary Jo Mecca for design and construction of the jester hat. For invaluable help in creating the Digital Edition, we would like to thank Jane Chu and Colleen Caffrey, digital designers, and Mateus Teixiera and Kristian Sanford, digital production.

The editors have, in addition, had the valuable—indeed, indispensable—support of a host of undergraduate and graduate research assistants, colleagues, friends, and family. Even a partial listing of those to whom we owe our heartfelt thanks is very long, but we are all fortunate enough to live in congenial and supportive environments, and the edition has been part of our lives for a long time. We owe special thanks for sustained dedication and learning to our colleagues, friends, and principal assistants:

Stephen Greenblatt wishes to thank his talented research assistants at Harvard, including Maria Devlin, Seth Herbst, Rhema Hokama, David Nee, Elizabeth Weckhurst, Benjamin Woodring, Catherine Woodring, and, above all, Misha Teramura. In addition, he is grateful for valuable assistance from Rebecca Cook and Aubrey Everett, along with advice and counsel from many friends, colleagues, and students. Thanks also go to C. Edward McGee (University of Waterloo), Barbara D. Palmer (late of the University of Mary Washington), Sylvia Thomas (the Yorkshire Archaeological Society), and John M. Wasson (late of Washington State University). He acknowledges a special and enduring debt to Ramie Targoff (Brandeis University).

Walter Cohen wishes to thank Marjorie Levinson (University of Michigan).

Jean Howard would like to acknowledge the help of each of her excellent research assistants at Columbia University: Bryan Lowrance, John Kuhn, Alexander Paulsson Lash, Chris McKeen, and especially Emily Shortslef, whose scholarly contributions have been indispensable and impeccable and whose good cheer is astonishingly unflagging.

We gratefully acknowledge the reviewers who provided thoughtful critiques for particular plays or of the project as a whole: Bernadette Andrea (University of Texas at San Antonio), John M. Archer (New York University), Oliver Arnold (University of California–Berkeley), Amanda Bailey (University of Connecticut), JoAnn D. Barbour

(Texas Woman's University), Catherine Belsey (Swansea University), Barbara Bono (University at Buffalo), Michael D. Bristol (McGill University), Karen Britland (University of Wisconsin–Madison), James C. Bulman (Allegheny College), William C. Carroll (Boston University), Kent Cartwright (University of Maryland, College Park), Joseph Cerami (Texas A&M University), Julie Crawford (Columbia University), Jonathan Crewe (Dartmouth College), Stephen Deng (Michigan State University), Christy Desmet (University of Georgia), Donald R. Dickson (Texas A&M University), Mario DiGangi (Graduate Center of the City University of New York), Tobias Doering (University of Munich), Frances Dolan (University of California–Davis), John Drakakis (University of Stirling), Heather Dubrow (Fordham University), Holly Dugan (George Washington University), Amy E. Earhart (Texas A&M University), Katherine E. Eggert (University of Colorado–Boulder), Lars D. Engle (University of Tulsa), Christopher John Fitter (Rutgers University), Mary Floyd-Wilson (University of North Carolina–Chapel Hill), Susan Caroline Frye (University of Wyoming), Brett Gamboa (Dartmouth College), Evelyn Gajowski (University of Nevada, Las Vegas), Hugh Hartridge Grady, Jr. (Arcadia University), Kenneth Gross (University of Rochester), Elizabeth Hanson (Queen's University), Jonathan Gil Harris (George Washington University), Michael Hattaway (New York University), Diana Henderson (Massachusetts Institute of Technology), Terence Allan Hoagwood (Texas A&M University), Lucia Kristina Hodgson (Texas A&M University), Peter Holbrook (The University of Queensland), Peter Holland (University of Notre Dame), John W. Huntington (University of Illinois at Chicago), Lorna Hutson (University of St. Andrews), Coppélia Kahn (Brown University), Jeffrey Knapp (University of California–Berkeley), Yu Jin Ko (Wellesley College), Paul A. Kottman (The New School), Bryon Lew (Trent University), Genevieve Love (Colorado College), Julia R. Lupton (University of California–Irvine), Ellen MacKay (Indiana University), Cristina Malcolmson (Bates College), Lawrence G. Manley (Yale University), Steven Mentz (St. John's University), Erin Minear (College of William and Mary), Arash Moradi (Shiraz University), Ian Moulton (Arizona State University), Steven Mullaney (University of Michigan), Cyrus Mulready (State University of New York–New Paltz), Karen Newman (Brown University), Mary A. O'Farrell (Texas A&M University), Laurie E. Osborne (Colby College), Simon Palfrey (Oxford University), Garry Partridge (Texas A&M University), Thomas Pendleton (Iona College), Peter G. Platt (Barnard College), Christopher Pye (Williams College), Phyllis R. Rackin (University of Pennsylvania), Sally Robinson (Texas A&M University), Mary Beth Rose (University of Illinois at Chicago), Suparna Roychoudhury (Mount Holyoke College), Elizabeth D. Samet (United States Military Academy at West Point), Melissa E. Sanchez (University of Pennsylvania), Michael Schoenfeldt (University of Michigan), Laurie J. Shannon (Northwestern University), Jyotsna Singh (Michigan State University), Elizabeth Spiller (Florida State University), Tiffany Stern (Oxford University), Richard Strier (University of Chicago), Ayanna Thompson (George Washington University), Douglas Trevor (University of Michigan), Henry S. Turner (Rutgers University), Brian Walsh (Yale University), Tiffany Jo Werth (Simon Fraser University), Adam Zucker (University of Massachusetts).

General Textual Editors' Acknowledgments

First and foremost, we are grateful to Stephen Greenblatt for inviting us to imagine, and then to create, a wholly new text of Shakespeare for the Third Edition of *The Norton Shakespeare*; to the volume editors—Jean Howard, Katharine Maus, and Walter Cohen—for working closely with us and for supporting the single text–editing principle we adopted; and to Julia Reidhead, the edition's publisher, for her gracious engagement and direction at every stage. And of course we are hugely grateful to the remarkable team of editors with whom we have worked, all of whom, without exception, accepted the invitation with alacrity, edited superbly, completed their work in timely fashion, and tolerated the necessary processes stemming from the need to ensure that each individual play functions both in its own right and as part of the edition as a whole. We want to thank and acknowledge them all. We also wish to thank Lacey Conley, who provided invaluable research assistance at crucial moments in the creation of the text. None of this would have been possible without the indefatigable work of the team at Norton. Marian Johnson, managing editor, college, provided invaluable wisdom and care for the newly edited text. Cliff Landesman's enthusiasm for the project and his willingness to explore—and help us understand—the digital possibilities were invaluable. Carly Fraser Doria and Emily Stuart responded with remarkable generosity, patience, and professionalism to our requests and anxieties. And we are particularly grateful to Norton's copy editors, Alice Vigliani and Harry Haskell, for their wonderfully precise work on the texts of the plays.

Editors tend to fight like cats in a sack over the choices they make when editing Shakespeare—they did this in the eighteenth century, and they try their best to keep up the tradition today—yet they also know that they are in fact highly mutually dependent, and it matters a great deal to us to note that we have had a second set of collaborators in the creation of this new text, none of whom has had actual direct involvement in *The Norton Shakespeare*, Third Edition—due in some cases to working on equivalent editions for other presses—but without whose textual and critical work we could not have acquired the knowledge we needed to create this edition. These include David Bevington, Peter Blayney, A. R. Braunmuller, R. A. Foakes, John Jowett, David Scott Kastan, Laurie Maguire, Sonia Massai, Eric Rasmussen, Tiffany Stern, Gary Taylor, Stanley Wells, and Martin Wiggins. And we would like in particular to acknowledge our considerable debt to Richard Proudfoot, who mentored us both in the fine art of editing and whose knowledge of the Shakespearean text and generosity with that knowledge are unsurpassed. We should acknowledge too certain key resources without which our editorial work would have been, practically speaking, impossible: these include the British Library's remarkable Shakespeare in Quarto website and the online text and facsimiles provided by the Internet Shakespeare Edition (a remarkable enterprise led by the generous and endlessly energetic Michael Best).

Finally, we should also note that any edition of Shakespeare is merely one in a very long line, and all modern Shakespearean editors are indebted to the extraordinary work of the earliest toilers in the field—from Shakespeare's friends Heminges and Condell assembling the First Folio and thus providing the crucial basis for all subsequent work on the Shakespeare canon, to the anonymous editors of the Second, Third, and Fourth Folios, to the crucial work of Rowe, Capell, Pope, Johnson, Theobald, and their successors in the eighteenth, nineteenth, and twentieth centuries. How they did any of it without word-processing software and the resources of the Internet we cannot for the life of us figure out.

GORDON MCMULLAN and SUZANNE GOSSETT

General Introduction

STEPHEN GREENBLATT

"He was not of an age, but for all time!"

There are writers whose greatness is recognized only long after they have vanished from the earth. There are writers championed by a coterie of devoted followers who tend the flame of admiration against the cold world's indifference. There are writers beloved in their native land but despised abroad, and others neglected at home yet celebrated on distant shores. Shakespeare is none of these. His genius was recognized almost immediately. The famous words with which we have begun were written by his friend and rival Ben Jonson. They have been echoed innumerable times, across the centuries, across national and linguistic boundaries, across the demarcation lines of race and class, religion and ideology. Shakespeare belongs not simply to a particular culture—English culture of the late sixteenth and early seventeenth centuries—but to world culture, the dense network of constraints and entitlements, dreams and practices that help to make us fully human. Indeed, so absolute is Shakespeare's achievement that he has himself come to seem like great creating nature. His works embody the imagination's power to transcend time-bound beliefs and assumptions, particular historical circumstances, and specific artistic conventions. If we should ever be asked as a species to bring forward one artist who has most fully expressed the human condition, we could with confidence elect Shakespeare to speak for us. As it is, when we do ask ourselves the most fundamental questions about life—about love and hatred, ambition, desire, and fear, the demand for justice and the longing for a second chance—we repeatedly turn to Shakespeare for the words we wish to hear.

The near-worship Shakespeare inspires is one of the salient facts about his art. But we must at the same time acknowledge that this art is the product of peculiar historical circumstances and specific conventions, four centuries distant from our own. The acknowledgment is important because Shakespeare the working dramatist did not typically lay claim to the transcendent, visionary truths attributed to him by his most fervent admirers; his characters more modestly say, in the words of the magician Prospero, that their project was "to please" (*The Tempest*, Epilogue, line 13). The starting point, and perhaps the ending point as well, in any encounter with Shakespeare is simply to enjoy him, to savor his imaginative richness, to take pleasure in his infinite delight in language.

"If then you do not like him," Shakespeare's first editors wrote in 1623, "surely you are in some manifest danger not to understand him." Over the years, accommodations have been devised to make liking Shakespeare easier for everyone. When aspects of his language began to seem difficult, texts were published with notes and glosses. When the historical events he depicted receded into obscurity, explanatory introductions were written. When the stage sank to melodrama and light opera, Shakespeare made his appearance in suitably revised dress. When the populace had a craving for hippodrama, plays performed entirely on horseback, *Hamlet* was dutifully rewritten and mounted. When audiences went mad for realism, live frogs croaked in productions of *A Midsummer Night's Dream*. When the stage was stripped

1

bare and given over to stark exhibitions of sadistic cruelty, Shakespeare was our contemporary. And when the theater ceded some of its cultural centrality to radio, film, and television, Shakespeare moved effortlessly to Hollywood and the sound stages of the BBC.

This virtually universal appeal is one of the most astonishing features of the Shakespeare phenomenon: plays that were performed before glittering courts thrive in junior high school auditoriums; enemies set on destroying one another laugh at the same jokes and weep at the same catastrophes; some of the richest and most complex English verse ever written migrates with spectacular success into German and Italian, Hindi, Swahili, and Japanese. Is there a single, stable, continuous object that underlies all of these migrations and metamorphoses? Certainly not. The global diffusion and long life of Shakespeare's works depend on their extraordinary malleability, their protean capacity to elude definition and escape secure possession. His art is the supreme manifestation of the mobility of culture. At the same time, this art is not without identifiable shared features: across centuries and continents, family resemblances link many of the wildly diverse manifestations of plays such as *Romeo and Juliet, Hamlet,* and *Twelfth Night.* Moreover, if there is no clear limit or end point, there is a reasonably clear beginning, the England of the late sixteenth and early seventeenth centuries, when the plays and poems collected in *The Norton Shakespeare* made their first appearance.

An art virtually without end or limit but with an identifiable, localized, historical origin: Shakespeare's achievement defies the facile opposition between transcendent and time-bound. It is not necessary to choose between an account of Shakespeare as the scion of a particular culture and an account of him as a universal genius who created works that continually renew themselves across national and generational boundaries. On the contrary: crucial clues to understanding his art's remarkable power to soar beyond the time and place of its origin lie in the very soil from which that art sprang.

Shakespeare's World

Life and Death

Life expectancy at birth in early modern England was exceedingly low by our standards: under thirty years, compared with over seventy today. Infant mortality rates were extraordinarily high, and it is estimated that in the poorer parishes of London only about half the children survived to the age of fifteen, while the children of aristocrats fared only a little better. In such circumstances, some parents must have developed a certain detachment—one of Shakespeare's contemporaries writes of losing "some three or four children"—but there are many expressions of intense grief, so that we cannot assume that the frequency of death hardened people to loss or made it routine.

Still, the spectacle of death, along with that other great threshold experience, birth, must have been far more familiar to Shakespeare and his contemporaries than to ourselves. There was no equivalent in early modern England to our hospitals, and most births and deaths occurred at home. Physical means for the alleviation of pain and suffering were extremely limited—alcohol might dull the terror, but it was hardly an effective anesthetic—and medical treatment was generally both expensive and worthless, more likely to intensify suffering than to lead to a cure. This was a world without a concept of antiseptics, with little actual understanding of disease, with few effective ways of treating earaches or venereal disease, let alone the more terrible instances of what Shakespeare calls "the thousand natural shocks that flesh is heir to."

The worst of these shocks was the bubonic plague, which repeatedly ravaged England, and particularly English towns, until the third quarter of the seventeenth

1609.

From the 24
to the 31.   there
Died in London, the Liberties,   364
the out parishes, & the pesthouse
whereof of the Plague————— 177
Christned in all those places—— 123
Parishes clear   parishes infec.   48

Bill recording plague deaths in London, 1609.

century. The plague was terrifyingly sudden in its onset, rapid in its spread, and almost invariably lethal. Physicians were helpless in the face of the epidemic, though they prescribed amulets, preservatives, and sweet-smelling substances (on the theory that the plague was carried by noxious vapors). In the plague-ridden year of 1564, the year of Shakespeare's birth, some 254 people died in his native Stratford-upon-Avon, out of a total population of 800. The year before, some 20,000 Londoners are thought to have died; in 1593, almost 15,000; in 1603, 36,000, or over a sixth of the city's inhabitants. The social effects of these horrible visitations were severe: looting, violence, and despair, along with an intensification of the age's perennial poverty, unemployment, and food shortages. The London plague regulations of 1583, reissued with modifications in later epidemics, ordered that the infected and their households should be locked in their homes for a month; that the streets should be kept clean; that vagrants should be expelled; and that funerals and plays (as occasions in which large numbers of people gathered and infection could be spread) should be restricted or banned entirely. Comparable restrictions were not placed on gatherings for religious observance, since it was hoped that God would heed the desperate prayers of his suffering people.

The plague, then, had a direct and immediate impact on Shakespeare's own profession. City officials kept records of the weekly number of plague deaths; when these surpassed a certain number, the theaters were peremptorily closed. The basic idea was not only to prevent contagion but also to avoid making an angry God still angrier with the spectacle of idleness. While restricting public assemblies may in fact have slowed the epidemic, other public policies in times of plague, such as killing the cats and dogs, may have made matters worse (since the disease was spread not by these animals but by the fleas that bred on the black rats that infested the poorer neighborhoods). Moreover, the playing companies, driven out of London by the closing of the theaters, may have carried plague to the provincial towns.

Even in good times, when the plague was dormant and the weather favorable for farming, the food supply in England was precarious. A few successive bad harvests, such as occurred in the mid-1590s, could cause serious hardship, even starvation. Not surprisingly, the poor bore the brunt of the burden: inflation, low wages, and rent increases left large numbers of people with very little cushion against disaster. Further, at its best, the diet of most people seems to have been seriously deficient. The lower classes then, as throughout most of history, subsisted on one or two foodstuffs, usually low in protein. The upper classes disdained green vegetables and milk and gorged themselves on meat. Illnesses that we now trace to vitamin deficiencies were rampant. Some but not much relief from pain was provided by the beer that Elizabethans, including children, drank almost incessantly. (Home brewing aside, enough beer was sold in England for every man, woman, and child to have consumed forty gallons a year.)

Wealth

Despite rampant disease, the population of England in Shakespeare's lifetime grew steadily, from approximately 3,060,000 in 1564 to 4,060,000 in 1600 and 4,510,000 in 1616. Though the death rate was more than twice what it is in England today, the birthrate was almost three times the current figure. London's population in particular soared, from 60,000 in 1520 to 120,000 in 1550, 200,000 in 1600, and 375,000 a half-century later, making it the largest and fastest-growing city not only in England but in all of Europe. Every year in the first half of the seventeenth century, about 10,000 people migrated to London from other parts of England—wages in London tended to be around 50 percent higher than in the rest of the country—and it is estimated that one in eight English people lived in London at some point in their lives. The economic viability of Shakespeare's profession was closely linked to this extraordinary demographic boom: between 1567 and 1642, theater historians have estimated, the London playhouses were paid anywhere between 50 and 75 million visits.

As these visits to the theater indicate, in the capital city and elsewhere a substantial number of English men and women, despite hardships that were never very distant, had money to spend. After the disorder and dynastic wars of the fifteenth century, England in the sixteenth and early seventeenth centuries was for the most part a nation at peace, and with peace came a measure of enterprise and prosperity: the landowning classes busied themselves building great houses, planting orchards and hop gardens, draining marshlands, bringing untilled acreage under cultivation. The artisans and laborers who actually accomplished these tasks, though they were generally paid very little, often managed to accumulate something, as did the small freeholding farmers, the yeomen, who are repeatedly celebrated in the period as the backbone of English national independence and well-being. William Harrison's *Description of Britain* (1577) lovingly itemizes the yeoman's precious possessions: "fair garnish of pewter on his cupboard, with so much more odd vessel going about the house, three or four featherbeds, so many coverlets and carpets of tapestry, a silver salt [cellar], a bowl for wine (if not a whole nest) and a dozen of spoons." There are comparable accounts of the hard-earned acquisitions of the city dwellers—masters and apprentices in small workshops, shipbuilders, wool merchants, cloth makers, chandlers, tradesmen, shopkeepers, along with lawyers, apothecaries, schoolteachers, scriveners, and the like—whose pennies from time to time enriched the coffers of the players.

The chief source of England's wealth in the sixteenth century was its textile industry, an industry that depended on a steady supply of wool. The market for English textiles was not only domestic. In 1565, woolen cloth alone made up more than three-fourths of England's exports. (The remainder consisted mostly of other textiles and raw wool, with some trade in lead, tin, grain, and skins.) The Company of Merchant Adventurers carried cloth not only to nearby countries like France, Holland, and Germany but also to distant ports on the Baltic and Mediterranean, establishing links with Russia and Morocco (each took about 2 percent of London's cloth in 1597–98). English lead and tin, as well as fabrics, were sold in Tuscany and Turkey, and merchants found a market for Newcastle coal on the island of Malta. In the latter half of the century, London, which handled more than 85 percent of all exports, regularly shipped abroad more than 100,000 woolen cloths a year, at a value of at least £750,000. This figure does not include the increasingly important and profitable trade in so-called New Draperies, including textiles that went by such exotic names as bombazines, callamancoes, damazellas, damizes, mockadoes, and virgenatoes. When the Earl of Kent in *King Lear* insults Oswald as a "filthy, worsted-stocking knave" (2.2.14–15) or when the aristocratic Biron in *Love's Labor's Lost* declares that he will give up "taffeta phrases, silken terms precise, / Three-piled hyperboles" and woo henceforth "in russet 'yeas,' and honest kersey 'noes'" (5.2.407–08, 414), Shakespeare is assuming that a substantial portion of his audience will be alert to the social significance of fabric.

There is amusing confirmation of this alertness from an unexpected source: the report of a visit made to the Fortune playhouse in London in 1614 by a foreigner, Father Orazio Busino, the chaplain of the Venetian embassy. Father Busino neglected to mention the name of the play he saw, but like many foreigners, he was powerfully struck by the presence of gorgeously dressed women in the audience. In Venice, there was a special gallery for courtesans, but socially respectable women would not have been permitted to attend plays, as they could in England. In London, not only could middle- and upper-class women go to the theater, but they could also wear masks and mingle freely with male spectators and women of ill repute. The bemused cleric was uncertain about the ambiguous social situation in which he found himself:

> These theaters are frequented by a number of respectable and handsome ladies, who come freely and seat themselves among the men without the slightest hesitation. On the evening in question his Excellency and the Secretary were pleased to play me a trick by placing me amongst a bevy of young women. Scarcely was I seated ere a very elegant dame, but in a mask, came and placed herself beside me. . . . She asked me for my address both in French and English; and, on my turning a deaf ear, she determined to honor me by showing me some fine diamonds on her fingers, repeatedly taking off not fewer than three gloves, which were worn one over the other. . . . This lady's bodice was of yellow satin richly embroidered, her petticoat of gold tissue with stripes, her robe of red velvet with a raised pile, lined with yellow muslin with broad stripes of pure gold. She wore an apron of point lace of various patterns: her head-tire was highly perfumed, and the collar of white satin beneath the delicately-wrought ruff struck me as extremely pretty.

Father Busino may have turned a deaf ear on this "elegant dame" but not a blind eye: his description of her dress is worthy of a fashion designer and conveys something of the virtual clothes cult that prevailed in England in the late sixteenth and early seventeenth centuries, a cult whose major shrine, outside the royal court, was the theater.

Imports, Patents, and Monopolies

England produced some luxury goods, but the clothing on the backs of the most fashionable theatergoers was likely to have come from abroad. By the late sixteenth century, the English were importing substantial quantities of silks, satins, velvets, embroidery, gold and silver lace, and other costly items to satisfy the extravagant tastes of the elite and of those who aspired to dress like the elite. The government tried to put a check on the sartorial ambitions of the upwardly mobile by passing sumptuary laws—that is, laws restricting to the ranks of the aristocracy the right to wear certain of the most precious fabrics. But the very existence of these laws, in practice almost impossible to enforce, only reveals the scope and significance of the perceived problem.

Sumptuary laws were in part a conservative attempt to protect the existing social order from upstarts. Social mobility was not widely viewed as a positive virtue, and moralists repeatedly urged people to stay in their place. Conspicuous consumption that was tolerated, even admired, in the aristocratic elite was denounced as sinful and monstrous in less exalted social circles. English authorities were also deeply concerned throughout the period about the effects of a taste for luxury goods on the balance of trade. One of the principal English imports was wine: the "sherris" whose virtues Falstaff extols in *2 Henry IV* came from Xeres in Spain; the malmsey in which poor Clarence is drowned in *Richard III* was probably made in Greece or in the Canary Islands (from whence came Sir Toby Belch's "cup of canary" in *Twelfth Night*); and the "flagon of rhenish" that Yorick in *Hamlet* had once poured on the Gravedigger's head came from the Rhine region of Germany. Other imports included canvas, linen, fish, olive oil, sugar, molasses, dates, oranges and lemons, figs, raisins, almonds, capers, indigo, ostrich feathers, and that increasingly popular drug tobacco.

Joint stock companies were established to import goods for the burgeoning English market. The Merchant Venturers of the City of Bristol (established in 1552) handled great shipments of Spanish sack, the light, dry wine that largely displaced the vintages of Bordeaux and Burgundy when trade with France was disrupted by war. The Muscovy Company (established in 1555) traded English cloth and manufactured goods for Russian furs, oil, and beeswax. The Venice Company and the Turkey Company— uniting in 1593 to form the wealthy Levant Company—brought silk and spices home from Aleppo and carpets from Constantinople. The East India Company (founded in 1600), with its agent at Bantam in Java, brought pepper, cloves, nutmeg, and other spices from East Asia, along with indigo, cotton textiles, sugar, and saltpeter from India. English privateers "imported" American products, especially sugar, fish, and hides, in huge quantities, along with more precious cargoes. In 1592, a privateering expedition principally funded by Sir Walter Ralegh captured a huge Portuguese carrack (sailing ship), the *Madre de Dios,* in the Azores and brought it back to Dartmouth. The ship, the largest that had ever entered any English port, held 536 tons of pepper, cloves, cinnamon, cochineal, mace, civet, musk, ambergris, and nutmeg, as well as jewels, gold, ebony, carpets, and silks. Before order could be established, the English seamen began to pillage this immensely rich prize, and witnesses said they could smell the spices on all the streets around the harbor. Such piratical expeditions were rarely officially sanctioned by the state, but the Queen had in fact privately invested £1,800, for which she received about £80,000.

In the years of war with Spain, 1586–1604, the goods captured by the privateers annually amounted to 10–15 percent of the total value of England's imports. But organized theft alone could not solve England's balance-of-trade problems. Statesmen were particularly worried that the nation's natural wealth was slipping away in exchange for unnecessary things. In his *Discourse of the Commonweal* (1549), the prominent humanist Sir Thomas Smith exclaims against the importation of such trifles as mirrors, paper, laces, gloves, pins, inkhorns, tennis balls, puppets, and playing cards. And more than a century later, the same fear that England was trading its riches for trifles and wasting away in idleness was expressed by the Bristol merchant John Cary. The solution, Cary argues in "An Essay on the State of England in Relation to Its Trade" (1695),

Forging a magnet, 1600. The metal on the anvil is aligned North/South (Septentrio/Auster). From *De Magnete* by William Gilbert.

is to expand productive domestic employment. "People are or may be the Wealth of a Nation," he writes, "yet it must be where you find Employment for them, else they are a Burden to it, as the Idle Drone is maintained by the Industry of the laborious Bee, so are all those who live by their Dependence on others, as Players, Ale-House Keepers, Common Fiddlers, and such like, but more particularly Beggars, who never set themselves to work."

Stage players, all too typically associated here with vagabonds and other idle drones, could have replied in their defense that they not only labored in their vocation but also exported their skills abroad: English actors routinely performed on the Continent. But their labor was not regarded as a productive contribution to the national wealth, and plays were in truth no solution to the trade imbalances that worried authorities.

The government attempted to stem the flow of gold overseas by establishing a patent system initially designed to encourage skilled foreigners to settle in England by granting them exclusive rights to produce particular wares by a patented method. Patents were granted for such things as the making of hard white soap (1561), ovens and furnaces (1563), window glass (1567), sailcloths (1574), drinking glasses (1574), sulfur, brimstone, and oil (1577), armor and horse harness (1587), starch (1588), white writing paper made from rags (1589), aqua vitae and vinegar (1594), playing cards (1598), and mathematical instruments (1598).

By the early seventeenth century, English men and women were working in a variety of new industries like soap making, pin making, knife making, and the brewing of alegar and beeregar (ale- and beer-based vinegar). But although the ostensible purpose of the government's economic policy was to increase the wealth of England, encourage technical innovation, and provide employment for the poor, the effect of patents was often the enrichment of a few and the hounding of poor competitors by wealthy monopolists, a group that soon extended well beyond foreign-born entrepreneurs to the favorites of the monarch who vied for the huge profits to be made. "If I had a monopoly out" on folly, the Fool in *King Lear* protests, glancing at the "lords and great men" around him, "they would have part in't." The passage appears only in the Quarto version of the play (*History of King Lear* 4.140–41); it may have been cut for political reasons from the Folio. For the issue of monopolies provoked bitter criticism and parliamentary debate for decades. In 1601, Elizabeth was prevailed upon to revoke a number of the most hated monopolies, including aqua vitae and vinegar, bottles, brushes, fish livers, the coarse sailcloth known as poldavis and mildernix, pots, salt, and starch. The whole system was revoked during the reign of James I by an act of Parliament.

Haves and Have-Nots

When in the 1560s Elizabeth's ambassador to France, Sir Thomas Smith, wrote a description of England, he saw the commonwealth as divided into four sorts of people: "gentlemen, citizens, yeomen artificers, and laborers." At the forefront of the class of gentlemen was the monarch, followed by a very small group of nobles—dukes, marquesses, earls, viscounts, and barons—who either inherited their exalted titles, as the eldest male heirs of their families, or were granted them by the monarch. Under Elizabeth, this aristocratic peerage numbered between 50 and 60 individuals; James's promotions increased the number to nearer 130. Strictly speaking, Smith notes, the younger sons of the nobility were only entitled to be called "esquires," but in common speech they were also called "lords."

Below this tiny cadre of aristocrats in the social hierarchy of gentry were the knights, a title of honor conferred by the monarch, and below them were the "simple gentlemen." Who was a gentleman? According to Smith, "whoever studieth the laws of the realm, who studieth in the universities, who professeth liberal sciences, and to be short, who can live idly and without manual labor, and will bear the port, charge and countenance of a gentleman, he shall be called master . . . and shall be taken for a gentleman." To "live idly and without manual labor": where in Spain, for example, the crucial mark of a gentleman was "blood," in England it was "idleness," in the sense of sufficient income to afford an education and to maintain a social position without having to work with one's hands.

For Smith, the class of gentlemen was far and away the most important in the kingdom. Below were two groups that had at least some social standing and claim to authority: the citizens, or burgesses, those who held positions of importance and responsibility in their cities, and yeomen, farmers with land and a measure of economic independence. At the bottom of the social order was what Smith calls "the fourth sort of men which do not rule." The great mass of ordinary people have, Smith writes, "no voice nor authority in our commonwealth, and no account is made of them but only to be ruled." Still, even they can bear some responsibility, he notes, since they serve on juries and are named to such positions as churchwarden and constable.

In everyday practice, as modern social historians have observed, the English tended to divide the population not into four distinct classes but into two: a very small empowered group—the "richer" or "wiser" or "better" sort—and all the rest who were without much social standing or power, the "poorer" or "ruder" or "meaner" sort. References to the "middle sort of people" remain relatively rare until after Shakespeare's lifetime; these people are absorbed into the rulers or the ruled, depending on speaker and context.

The source of wealth for most of the ruling class, and the essential measure of social status, was land ownership, and changes to the social structure in the sixteenth and seventeenth centuries were largely driven by the land market. The property that passed into private hands as the Tudors and early Stuarts sold off confiscated monastic estates and then their own crown lands for ready cash amounted to nearly a quarter of all the land in England. At the same time, the buying and selling of private estates was on the rise throughout the period. Land was bought up not only by established landowners seeking to enlarge their estates but also by successful merchants, manufacturers, and urban professionals; even if the taint of vulgar money-making lingered around such figures, their heirs would be taken for true gentlemen. The rate of turnover in land ownership was great; in many counties, well over half the gentle families in 1640 had appeared since the end of the fifteenth century. The class that Smith called "simple gentlemen" was expanding rapidly: in the fifteenth century, they had held no more than a quarter of the land in the country, but by the later seventeenth, they controlled almost half. Over the same period, the land held by the great aristocratic magnates held steady at 15–20 percent of the total.

Riot and Disorder

London was a violent place in the first half of Shakespeare's career. There were thirty-five riots in the city in the years 1581–1602, twelve of them in the volatile month of June 1595. These included protests against the deeply unpopular Lord Mayor Sir John Spencer, attempts to release prisoners, anti-alien riots, and incidents of "popular market regulation." There is an unforgettable depiction of a popular uprising in *Coriolanus*, along with many other glimpses in Shakespeare's works, including Jack Cade's grotesque rebellion in *2 Henry VI*, the plebeian violence in *Julius Caesar*, and Laertes' "riotous head" in *Hamlet*.

The London rioters were mostly drawn from the large mass of poor and discontented apprentices who typically chose as their scapegoats foreigners, prostitutes, and gentlemen's servingmen. Theaters were very often the site of the social confrontations that sparked disorder. For two days running in June 1584, disputes between apprentices and gentlemen triggered riots outside the Curtain Theater involving up to a thousand participants. On one occasion, a gentleman was said to have exclaimed that "the apprentice was but a rascal, and some there were little better than rogues that took upon them the name of gentlemen, and said the prentices were but the scum of the world." These occasions culminated in attacks by the apprentices on London's law schools, the Inns of Court.

The most notorious and predictable incidents of disorder came on Shrove Tuesday (the Tuesday before the beginning of Lent), a traditional day of misrule when apprentices ran riot. Shrove Tuesday disturbances involved attacks by mobs of young men on the brothels of the South Bank, in the vicinity of the Globe and other public theaters. The city authorities took precautions to keep these disturbances from getting completely out of control, but evidently did not regard them as serious threats to public order.

Of much greater concern throughout the Tudor and early Stuart years were the frequent incidents of rural rioting. Though in *The Winter's Tale* Shakespeare provides a richly comic portrayal of a rural sheepshearing festival, the increasingly intensive production of wool had its grim side. When a character in Thomas More's *Utopia* (1516) complains that "the sheep are eating the people," he is referring to the practice of enclosure: throughout the sixteenth and early seventeenth centuries, many acres of croplands once farmed in common by rural communities were fenced in by wealthy landowners and turned into pasturage. The ensuing misery, displacement, and food shortages led to repeated protests, some of them violent and bloody, along with a series of government proclamations, but the process of enclosure was not reversed. The protests were at their height during Shakespeare's career: in the years 1590–1610, the frequency of anti-enclosure rioting doubled from what it had been earlier in Elizabeth's reign.

Although they often became violent, anti-enclosure riots were usually directed not against individuals but against property. Villagers—sometimes several hundred, often fewer than a dozen—gathered to tear down newly planted hedges. The event often took place in a carnival atmosphere, with songs and drinking, that did not prevent the participants from acting with a good deal of political canniness and forethought. Especially in the Jacobean period, it was common for participants to establish a fund for legal defense before commencing their assault on the hedges. Women were frequently involved, and on a number of occasions wives alone participated in the destruction of the enclosure, since there was a widespread, though erroneous, belief that married women acting without the knowledge of their husbands were immune from prosecution. In fact, the powerful Court of Star Chamber consistently ruled that both the wives and their husbands should be punished.

Although Stratford was never the scene of serious rioting, enclosure controversies turned violent more than once in Shakespeare's lifetime. In January 1601, Shakespeare's friend Richard Quiney and others leveled the hedges of Sir Edward Greville, lord of Stratford manor. Quiney was elected bailiff of Stratford in September of that year but did not live to enjoy the office for long. He died from a blow to the head struck by one of Greville's men in a tavern brawl. Greville, responsible for the administration of justice, neglected to punish the murderer.

There was further violence in January 1615, when William Combe's men threw to the ground two local aldermen who were filling in a ditch by which Combe was enclosing common fields near Stratford. The task of filling in the offending ditch was completed the next day by the women and children of Stratford. Combe's enclosure scheme was eventually stopped in the courts. Though he owned land whose value would have been affected by this controversy, Shakespeare took no active role in it, since he had previously come to a private settlement with the enclosers insuring him against personal loss.

Most incidents of rural rioting were small, localized affairs, and with good reason: when confined to the village community, riot was a misdemeanor; when it spread outward to include multiple communities, it became treason, punishable by death. The greatest of

The Peddler. From Jost Amman, *The Book of Trades* (1568).

the anti-enclosure riots, those in which hundreds of individuals from a large area participated, commonly took place on the eve of full-scale regional rebellions. The largest of these disturbances, Kett's Rebellion, involved some 16,000 peasants, artisans, and townspeople who rose up in 1549 under the leadership of a Norfolk tanner and landowner, Robert Kett, to protest economic exploitation. The agrarian revolts in Shakespeare's lifetime were on a much smaller scale. In the abortive Oxfordshire Rebellion of 1596, a carpenter named Bartholomew Steer attempted to organize a rising against the hated enclosures. The optimistic Steer allegedly promised his followers that "it was but a month's work to overrun England" and informed them "that the commons long since in Spain did rise and kill all gentlemen . . . and since that time have lived merrily there." Steer expected several hundred men to join him on Enslow Hill on November 21, 1596, for the start of the rising; no more than twenty showed up. They were captured, imprisoned, and tortured. Several were executed, but Steer apparently cheated the hangman by dying in prison.

Rebellions, most often triggered by hunger and oppression, continued into the reign of James I. The Midland Revolt of 1607, which may be reflected in *Coriolanus,* consisted of a string of agrarian risings in the counties of Northamptonshire, Warwickshire, and Leicestershire, involving assemblies of up to five thousand rebels in various places. The best known of their leaders was John Reynolds, called "Captain Powch," because of the pouch he wore, whose magical contents were supposed to defend the rebels from harm. (According to the chronicler Edmund Howes, when Reynolds was captured and the pouch opened, it contained "only a piece of green cheese.") The rebels, who were called by themselves and others both "Levelers" and "Diggers," insisted that they had no quarrel with the King but only sought an end to injurious enclosures. But Robert Wilkinson, who preached a sermon against the leaders at their trial, credited them with the intention to "level all states as they leveled banks and ditches." Most of the rebels got off relatively lightly, but, along with other ringleaders, Captain Powch was executed.

The Legal Status of Women

English women were not under the full range of crushing constraints that afflicted women in some countries in Europe. Foreign visitors were struck by their relative freedom, as shown, for example, by the fact that respectable women could venture unchaperoned into the streets and attend the theater. Yet while England was ruled for over forty years by a powerful woman, the great majority of women in the kingdom had very restricted social, economic, and legal standing. To be sure, a tiny number of influential aristocratic women, such as the formidable Countess of Shrewsbury, Bess of Hardwick, wielded considerable power. But, these rare exceptions aside, women were denied any rightful claim to institutional authority or personal autonomy. When Sir Thomas Smith thinks of how he should describe his country's social order, he declares that "we do reject women, as those whom nature hath made to keep home and to nourish their family and children, and not to meddle with matters abroad, nor to bear office in a city or commonwealth." Then, with a kind of glance over his shoulder, he makes an exception of those few for whom "the blood is respected, not the age nor the sex": for example, the Queen.

Single women, whether widowed or unmarried, could, if they were of full age, inherit and administer land, make a will, sign a contract, possess property, sue and be sued, without a male guardian or proxy. But married women had no such rights under English common law, the system of law based on court decisions rather than on codified written laws. Early modern writings about women and the family constantly return to a political model of domination and submission, in which the husband and father justly rules over wife and children as the monarch rules over the state. The husband's dominance in the family was the justification for the common-law rule that prohibited married women from possessing property, administering land, signing contracts, or bringing lawsuits in their own names: married women were described as legally "covered" by their husbands. Yet this conception of a woman's role conveniently ignores the fact that a *majority* of the adult women at any time in Shakespeare's England were not married. They were either widows or spinsters (a term that was not yet pejorative), and thus for the most part managed their own affairs. Even within marriage, women typically had more control over certain spheres than moralizing writers on the family cared to admit. For example, village wives oversaw the production of eggs, cheese, and beer, and sold these goods in the market. As seamstresses, pawnbrokers, second-hand clothing dealers, peddlers and the like—activities not controlled by the all-male craft guilds—women managed to acquire some economic power of their own, and, of course, they participated as well in the unregulated, black-market economy of the age and in the underworld of thievery and prostitution.

Women were not in practice as bereft of property as, according to English common law, they should have been. Demographic studies indicate that the inheritance system called primogeniture, the orderly transmission of property from father to eldest male heir, was more often an unfulfilled wish than a reality. Some 40 percent of marriages failed to produce a son, and in such circumstances fathers often left their land to their daughters, rather than to brothers, nephews, or male cousins. In many families, the father died before his male heir was old enough to inherit property, leaving the land, at least temporarily, in the hands of the mother. And while they were less likely than their brothers to inherit land ("real property"), daughters normally inherited a substantial share of their parents' personal property (cash and movables).

In fact, the legal restrictions upon women, though severe in Shakespeare's time, actually worsened in subsequent decades. English common law was significantly less egalitarian in its approach to wives and daughters than were alternative legal codes (manorial, civil, and ecclesiastical) still in place in the late sixteenth century. The eventual triumph of common law stripped women of many traditional rights, slowly driving them out of economically productive trades and businesses.

Limited though it was, the economic freedom of Elizabethan and Jacobean women far exceeded their political and social freedom—the opportunity to receive a grammar school or university education, to hold office in church or state, to have a voice in public debates, or even simply to speak their mind fully and openly in ordinary conversation. Women who asserted their views too vigorously risked being perceived as shrewish and labeled "scolds." Both urban and rural communities had a horror of scolds. In the Elizabethan period, such women came to be regarded as a threat to public order, to be dealt with by the local authorities. The preferred methods of correction included public humiliation—of the sort Katherina endures in *The Taming of the Shrew*—and such physical abuse as slapping, bridling with a bit or muzzle, and half-drowning by means of a contraption called the "cucking stool" (or "ducking stool"). This latter punishment originated in the Middle Ages, but its use spread in the sixteenth century, when it became almost exclusively a punishment for women. From 1560 onward, cucking stools were built or renovated in many English provincial towns; between 1560 and 1600, the contraptions were installed by rivers or ponds in Norwich, Bridport, Shrewsbury, Kingston-upon-Thames, Marlborough, Devizes, Clitheroe, Thornbury, and Great Yarmouth.

Such punishment was usually intensified by a procession through the town to the sound of "rough music," the banging together of pots and pans. The same cruel festivity accompanied the "carting" or "riding" of those accused of being whores. In some parts of the country, villagers also took the law into their own hands, publicly shaming women who married men much younger than themselves or who beat or otherwise domineered over their husbands. One characteristic form of these charivaris, or rituals of shaming, was known in the West Country as the Skimmington Ride. Villagers would rouse the offending couple from bed with rough music and stage a raucous pageant in which a man, holding a distaff, would ride backward on a donkey, while his "wife" (another man dressed as a woman) struck him with a ladle. In these cases, the collective ridicule and indignation were evidently directed at least as much at the henpecked husband as at his transgressive wife.

Women and Print

Books published for a female audience surged in popularity in the late sixteenth century, reflecting an increase in female literacy. (It is striking how many of Shakespeare's women are shown reading.) This increase is probably linked to a Protestant longing for direct access to the Scriptures, and the new books marketed specifically for women included devotional manuals and works of religious instruction. But there were also practical guides to such subjects as female education (for example, Giovanni Bruto's *Necessary, Fit, and Convenient Education of a Young Gentlewoman*, 1598), midwifery (James Guillemeau's *Child-birth; or, the Happy Delivery of Women*, 1612), needlework (Federico di Vinciolo's *New and Singular Patterns and Works of Linen*, 1591), cooking (Thomas Dawson's *The Good Housewife's Jewel*, 1587), gardening (Pierre Erondelle's *The French Garden*, 1605), and married life (Patrick Hanney's *A Happy Husband; or, Directions for a Maid to Choose Her Mate*, 1619). As the authors' names suggest, many of these works were translations, and almost all were written by men.

Starting in the 1570s, writers and their publishers increasingly addressed works of recreational literature (romance, fiction, and poetry) partially or even exclusively to women. Some books, such as Robert Greene's *Mamillia, a Mirror or Looking-Glass for the Ladies of England* (1583), directly specified in the title their desired audience. Others, such as Sir Philip Sidney's influential and popular romance *Arcadia* (1590–93), solicited female readership in their dedicatory epistles. The ranks of Sidney's followers eventually included his own niece, Mary Wroth, whose romance *Urania* was published in 1621.

In the literature of Shakespeare's time, women readers were not only wooed but also frequently railed at, in a continuation of a popular polemical genre that had long inspired heated charges and countercharges. Both sides in the polemic generally agreed that it was the duty of women to be chaste, dutiful, and modest in demeanor; the argument was whether women fulfilled or fell short of this proper role. Ironically, then, a modern reader is more likely to find inspiring accounts of courageous women not in the books written in defense of female virtue but in attacks on those who refused to be silent and obedient.

The most famous English skirmish in this controversy took place in a rash of pamphlets at the end of Shakespeare's life. Joseph Swetnam's crude *Arraignment of Lewd, Idle, Froward, and Unconstant Women* (1615) provoked three fierce responses attributed to women: Rachel Speght's *A Muzzle for Melastomus*, Esther Sowernam's *Esther Hath Hang'd Haman*, and Constantia Munda's *Worming of a Mad Dog*, all in 1617. There was also an anonymous play, *Swetnam the Woman-Hater Arraigned by Women* (first performed around 1618), in which Swetnam, depicted as a braggart and a lecher, is put on trial by women and made to recant his misogynistic lies.

Prior to the Swetnam controversy, only one English woman, writing under the pseudonym "Jane Anger," had published a defense of women (*Jane Anger Her Protection for Women*, 1589). Learned women writers in the sixteenth century tended not to become involved in public debate but rather to undertake a project to which it was difficult for even obdurately chauvinistic males to object: the translation of devotional literature into English. Thomas More's daughter Margaret More Roper translated Erasmus (*A Devout Treatise upon the Pater Noster*, 1524); Francis Bacon's mother, Anne Cooke Bacon, translated Bishop John Jewel (*An Apology or Answer in Defence of the Church of England*, 1564); Anne Locke Prowse, a friend of John Knox, translated the *Sermons of John Calvin* in 1560; and Mary Sidney, the Countess of Pembroke, completed the metrical version of the Psalms that her brother Sir Philip

Sidney had begun. Elizabeth Tudor (the future queen) herself translated, at the age of eleven, Marguerite de Navarre's *Le Miroir de l'âme pécheresse* (*The Glass of the Sinful Soul*, 1544). The translation was dedicated to her stepmother, Katherine Parr, herself the author of a frequently reprinted book of prayers.

There was in the sixteenth and early seventeenth centuries a social stigma attached to print. Far from celebrating publication, authors, and particularly female authors, often apologized for exposing themselves to the public gaze. Nonetheless, a number of women ventured in print beyond pious translations. Some, including Elizabeth Tyrwhitt, Anne Dowriche, Isabella Whitney, Mary Sidney, and Aemilia Lanyer, composed and published their own poems. Aemilia Lanyer's *Salve Deus Rex Judaeorum*, published in 1611, is a poem in praise of virtuous women, from Eve and the Virgin Mary to her noble patron, the Countess of Cumberland. "A Description of Cookeham," appended to the poem, is one of the first English country house poems, a celebration in verse of an aristocrat's rural estate.

The first Tudor woman to translate a play was the learned Jane Lumley, who composed an English version of Euripides' *Iphigenia at Aulis* (ca. 1550). The first known original play in English by a woman was by Elizabeth Cary, Viscountess Falkland, whose *Tragedy of Mariam, the Fair Queen of Jewry* was published in 1613. This remarkable play, which was not intended to be performed, includes speeches in defense of women's equality, though the most powerful of these is spoken by the villainous Salome, who schemes to divorce her husband and marry her lover. Cary, who bore

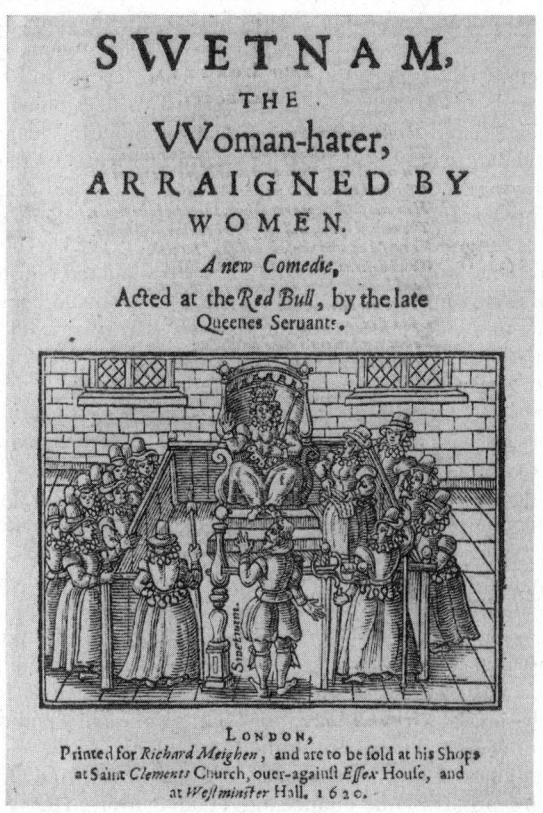

Title page of *Swetnam the Woman-Hater, Arraigned by Women* (1620), a play written in response to Joseph Swetnam's *The Arraignment of Lewd, Idle, Forward, and Unconstant Women* (1615); the woodcut depicts the trial of Swetnam in act 4.

eleven children, herself had a deeply troubled marriage, which effectively came to an end in 1625 when, defying her husband's staunchly Protestant family, she openly converted to Catholicism. Her biography was written by one of her four daughters, all of whom became nuns.

Henry VIII and the English Reformation

There had long been serious ideological and institutional tensions in the religious life of England, but officially, at least, England in the early sixteenth century had a single religion, Catholicism, whose acknowledged head was the pope in Rome. In 1517, drawing upon long-standing currents of dissent, Martin Luther, an Augustinian monk and professor of theology at the University of Wittenberg, challenged the authority of the pope and attacked several key doctrines of the Catholic Church. According to Luther, the Church, with its elaborate hierarchical structure centered in Rome, its rich monasteries and convents, and its enormous political influence, had become hopelessly corrupt, a conspiracy of venal priests who manipulated popular superstitions to enrich themselves and amass worldly power. Luther began by vehemently attacking the sale of indulgences—certificates promising the remission of punishments to be suffered in the afterlife by souls sent to purgatory to expiate their sins. These indulgences were a fraud, he argued; purgatory itself had no foundation in the Bible, which in his view was the only legitimate source of religious truth. Christians would be saved not by scrupulously following the ritual practices fostered by the Catholic Church—observing fast days, reciting the ancient Latin prayers, endowing chantries to say prayers for the dead, and so on—but by faith and faith alone.

This challenge, which came to be known as the Reformation, spread and gathered force, especially in northern Europe, where major leaders like the Swiss pastor Ulrich Zwingli and the French theologian John Calvin established institutional structures and elaborated various and sometimes conflicting doctrinal principles. Calvin, whose thought came to be particularly influential in England, emphasized the obligation of governments to implement God's will in the world. He advanced too the doctrine of predestination, by which, as he put it, "God adopts some to hope of life and sentences others to eternal death." God's "secret election" of the saved made Calvin uncomfortable, but his study of the Scriptures had led him to conclude that "only a small number, out of an incalculable multitude, should obtain salvation." It might seem that such a conclusion would lead to passivity or even despair, but for Calvin predestination was a mystery bound up with faith, confidence, and an active engagement in the fashioning of a Christian community.

The Reformation had a direct and powerful impact on those territories, especially in northern Europe, where it gained control. Monasteries, many of them fabulously wealthy, were sacked, their possessions and extensive landholdings seized by princes or sold off to the highest bidder; the monks and nuns, expelled from their cloisters, were encouraged to break their vows of chastity and find spouses, as Luther and his wife, a former nun, had done. In the great cathedrals and in hundreds of smaller churches and chapels, the elaborate altarpieces, bejeweled crucifixes, crystal reliquaries holding the bones of saints, and venerated statues and paintings were attacked as "idols" and often defaced or destroyed. Protestant congregations continued, for the most part, to celebrate the most sacred Christian ritual, the Eucharist, or Lord's Supper, but they did so in a profoundly different spirit from that of the Catholic Church—more as commemoration than as miracle—and they now prayed not in the ancient liturgical Latin but in the vernacular.

The Reformation was at first vigorously resisted in England. Indeed, with the support of his ardently Catholic chancellor, Thomas More, Henry VIII personally wrote (or at least lent his name to) a vehement, often scatological attack on Luther's character and views, an attack for which the pope granted him the honorific title "Defender of the Faith." Protestant writings, including translations of the Scriptures into English, were seized by officials of the church and state and burned. Protestants who made their views known were persecuted, driven to flee the country, or arrested, put on trial, and burned at the stake. But the situation changed drastically and decisively when in 1527 Henry decided to seek an annulment from his first wife, Catherine of Aragon, in order to marry Anne Boleyn.

Catherine had given birth to six children, but since only a daughter, Mary, survived infancy, Henry did not have the son he craved. Then as now, the Catholic Church did not ordinarily grant divorce, but Henry's lawyers argued on technical grounds that the marriage was invalid (and therefore, by extension, that Mary was illegitimate and hence unable to inherit the throne). Matters of this kind were far less doctrinal than diplomatic: Catherine, the daughter of Ferdinand of Aragon and Isabella of Castile, had powerful allies in Rome, and the pope ruled against Henry's petition. A series of momentous events followed, as England lurched away from the Church of Rome. In 1531, Henry charged the entire clergy of England with having usurped royal authority in the administration of canon law (the ecclesiastical law that governed faith, discipline, and morals, including such matters as divorce). Under extreme pressure, including the threat of mass confiscations and imprisonment, the Convocation of the Clergy begged for pardon, made a donation to the royal coffers of over £100,000, and admitted that the King was "supreme head of the English Church and clergy" (modified by the rider "as far as the law of Christ allows"). On May 15 of the next year, the convocation submitted to the demand that the King be the final arbiter of canon law; on the next day, Thomas More resigned his post.

In 1533, Henry's marriage to Catherine was officially declared null and void, and on June 1 Anne Boleyn was crowned queen (a coronation Shakespeare depicts in his late play *Henry VIII*). The King was promptly excommunicated by Pope Clement VII. In the following year, the parliamentary Act of Succession confirmed the effects of the annulment and required an oath from all adult male subjects confirming the new dynastic settlement. Thomas More and John Fisher, the Bishop of Rochester, were among the small number who refused. The Act of Supremacy, passed later in the year, formally declared the King to be "Supreme Head of the Church in England" and again required an oath to this effect. In 1535 and 1536, further acts made it treasonous to refuse the oath of royal supremacy or, as More had tried to do, to remain silent. The first victims were three Carthusian monks who rejected the oath—"How could the King, a layman," said one of them, "be Head of the Church of

The Pope as Antichrist riding the Beast of the Apocalypse. From *Fiery Trial of God's Saints* (1611; author unknown).

England?"—and in May 1535, they were duly hanged, drawn, and quartered. A few weeks later, Fisher and More were convicted and beheaded. Between 1536 and 1539, the monasteries were suppressed and their vast wealth seized by the crown.

Royal defiance of the authority of Rome was a key element in the Reformation but did not by itself constitute the establishment of Protestantism in England. On the contrary, in the same year that Fisher and More were martyred for their adherence to Roman Catholicism, twenty-five Protestants, members of a sect known as Anabaptists, were burned for heresy on a single day. Through most of his reign, Henry remained an equal-opportunity persecutor, ruthless to Catholics loyal to Rome but also hostile to some of those who espoused Reformation ideas, though many of these ideas gradually established themselves on English soil.

Even when Henry was eager to do so, it proved impossible to eradicate Protestantism, as it would later prove impossible for his successors to eradicate Catholicism. In large part this tenacity arose from the passionate, often suicidal heroism of men and women who felt that their souls' salvation depended on the precise character of their Christianity. It arose too from a mid-fifteenth-century technological innovation that made it almost impossible to suppress unwelcome ideas: the printing press. Early Protestants quickly grasped that with a few clandestine presses they could defy the Catholic authorities and flood the country with their texts. "How many printing presses there be in the world," wrote the Protestant polemicist John Foxe, "so many blockhouses there be against the high castle" of the pope in Rome, "so that either the pope must abolish knowledge and printing or printing at length will root him out." By the century's end, it was the Catholics who were using the clandestine press to propagate their beliefs in the face of Protestant persecution.

The greatest insurrection of the Tudor age was not over food, taxation, or land but over religion. On Sunday, October 1, 1536, stirred up by their vicar, the traditionalist parishioners of Louth in Lincolnshire, in the north of England, rose up in defiance of the ecclesiastical delegation sent to enforce royal supremacy. The rapidly spreading rebellion, which became known as the Pilgrimage of Grace, was led by the lawyer Robert Aske. The city of Lincoln fell to the rebels on October 6, and though it was soon retaken by royal forces, the rebels seized cities and fortifications throughout Yorkshire, Durham, Northumberland, Cumberland, Westmoreland, and northern Lancashire. Carlisle, Newcastle, and a few castles were all that were left to the King in the north. The Pilgrims soon numbered 40,000, led by some of the region's most prominent noblemen. The Duke of Norfolk, representing the crown, was forced to negotiate a truce, with a promise to support the rebels' demands that the King restore the monasteries, shore up the regional economy, suppress heresy, and dismiss his evil advisers. The Pilgrims kept the peace for the rest of 1536, on the naive assumption that their demands would be met. But Henry moved suddenly early in 1537 to impose order and capture the ringleaders; 130 people, including lords, knights, heads of religious houses, and, of course, Robert Aske, were executed.

In 1549, two years after the death of Henry VIII, the west and north of England were the sites of further unsuccessful risings for the restoration of Catholicism. The Western Rising is striking for its blend of Catholic universalism and intense regionalism among people who did not yet regard themselves as English. One of the rebels' articles, protesting against the imposition of the English Bible and religious service, declares, "We the Cornish men (whereof certain of us understand no English) utterly refuse this new English." The rebels besieged but failed to take the city of Exeter. As with almost all Tudor rebellions, the number of those executed in the aftermath of the failed rising was far greater than those killed in actual hostilities.

The Children of Henry VIII: Edward, Mary, and Elizabeth

Upon Henry's death in 1547, his ten-year-old son, Edward VI, came to the throne, with his maternal uncle Edward Seymour named as Duke of Somerset and Lord

Protector (regent while the King was still a minor). Both Edward and his uncle were staunch Protestants, and reformers hastened to transform the English church accordingly. During Edward's reign, Archbishop Thomas Cranmer formulated the forty-two articles of religion that became the core of Anglican orthodoxy and wrote the first Book of Common Prayer, which was officially adopted in 1549 as the basis of English worship services.

Somerset fell from power in 1549 and was replaced as Lord Protector by John Dudley, later Duke of Northumberland. When Edward fell seriously ill, probably of tuberculosis, Northumberland persuaded him to sign a will depriving his half-sisters Mary (the daughter of Catherine of Aragon) and Elizabeth (the daughter of Anne Boleyn) of their claim to royal succession. The Lord Protector was scheming to have his daughter-in-law, the Protestant Lady Jane Grey, a great-granddaughter of Henry VII, ascend to the throne. But when Edward died in 1553, Mary marshaled support, quickly secured the crown from Lady Jane (who had been titular queen for nine days), and had Lady Jane executed, along with her husband and Northumberland.

Queen Mary immediately took steps to return her kingdom to Roman Catholicism. Though she was unable to get Parliament to agree to return church lands seized under Henry VIII, she restored the Catholic Mass, once again affirmed the authority of the pope, and put down a rebellion that sought to depose her. Seconded by her ardently Catholic husband, Philip II, King of Spain, she initiated a series of religious persecutions that earned her (from her enemies) the name "Bloody Mary." Hundreds of Protestants took refuge abroad in cities such as Calvin's Geneva; almost three hundred less fortunate Protestants were condemned as heretics and burned at the stake.

Mary died childless in 1558, and her younger half-sister Elizabeth became queen. Elizabeth's succession had been by no means assured. For if Protestants regarded the marriage of Henry VIII to Catherine as invalid and hence deemed Mary illegitimate, so Catholics regarded his marriage to Anne Boleyn as invalid and deemed Elizabeth illegitimate. Henry VIII himself seemed to support both views, since only

The Family of Henry VIII: An Allegory of the Tudor Succession, by Lucas de Heere (ca. 1572). Henry, in the middle, is flanked by Mary to his right, and Edward and Elizabeth to his left.

three years after divorcing Catherine, he beheaded Anne Boleyn on charges of treason and adultery and urged Parliament to invalidate the marriage. Moreover, though
during her sister's reign Elizabeth outwardly complied with the official Catholic
religious observance, Mary and her advisers were deeply suspicious, and the young
princess's life was in grave danger. Poised and circumspect, Elizabeth warily evaded
the traps that were set for her. As she ascended the throne, her actions were scrutinized for some indication of the country's future course. During her coronation procession, when a girl in an allegorical pageant presented her with a Bible in English
translation—banned under Mary's reign—Elizabeth kissed the book, held it up reverently, and laid it to her breast; when the abbot and monks of Westminster Abbey
came to greet her in broad daylight with candles (a symbol of Catholic devotion) in
their hands, she briskly dismissed them with the telling words "Away with those
torches! We can see well enough." England had returned to the Reformation.

Many English men and women, of all classes, remained inwardly loyal to the old
Catholic faith; Shakespeare's father and mother may well have been among these.
But English authorities under Elizabeth moved steadily, if cautiously, toward ensuring at least an outward conformity to the official Protestant settlement. Recusants,
those who refused to attend regular Sunday services in their parish churches, were
fined heavily. Anyone who wished to receive a university degree, to be ordained as a
priest in the Church of England, or to be named as an officer of the state had to swear
an oath to the royal supremacy. Commissioners were sent throughout the land to
confirm that religious services were following the officially approved liturgy and to
investigate any reported backsliding into Catholic practice or, alternatively, any
attempts to introduce more radical reforms than the Queen and her bishops had chosen to embrace. For many of the Protestant exiles who streamed back to England
were eager not only to undo the damage Mary had done but to carry the Reformation
much further. They sought to dismantle the church hierarchy, to purge the calendar
of folk customs deemed pagan and the church service of ritual practices deemed
superstitious, to dress the clergy in simple garb, and, at the extreme edge, to smash
"idolatrous" statues, crucifixes, and altarpieces. Pressing for a stricter code of life
and a simplified system of worship, the religious radicals came to be called Puritans.
Throughout her long reign, however, Elizabeth herself remained cautiously conservative and determined to hold in check what she regarded as the religious zealotry of
Catholics, on the one side, and Puritans, on the other.

Shakespeare's plays tap into the ongoing confessional tensions: "sometimes," Maria
in *Twelfth Night* says of the sober, festivity-hating steward Malvolio, "he is a kind of
puritan" (2.3.129). But the plays tend to avoid the risks of direct engagement: "The devil
a puritan that he is, or anything constantly," Maria adds a moment later, "but a time-
pleaser" (2.3.135–36). *The Winter's Tale* features a statue that comes to life—exactly
the kind of magical image that Protestant polemicists excoriated as Catholic superstition and idolatry—but the play is set in the pre-Christian world of the Delphic Oracle.
And as if this careful distancing might not be enough, the play's ruler goes out of his
way to pronounce the wonder legitimate: "If this be magic, let it be an art / Lawful as
eating" (5.3.110–11).

In the space of a single lifetime, England had gone officially from Roman Catholicism, to Catholicism under the supreme headship of the English king, to a guarded
Protestantism, to a more radical Protestantism, to a renewed and aggressive Roman
Catholicism, and finally to Protestantism again. Each of these shifts was accompanied by danger, persecution, and death. It was enough to make some people wary. Or
skeptical. Or extremely agile.

The English Bible

Luther had undertaken a fundamental critique of the Catholic Church's sacramental
system, a critique founded on the twin principles of salvation by faith alone (*sola fide*)

and the absolute primacy of the Bible (*sola scriptura*). *Sola fide* contrasted faith with "works," by which was meant primarily the whole elaborate system of rituals sanctified, conducted, or directed by the priests. Protestants proposed to modify or reinterpret many of these rituals or, as with the rituals associated with purgatory, to abolish them altogether. *Sola scriptura* required direct lay access to the Bible, which meant in practice the widespread availability of vernacular translations. The Roman Catholic Church had not always and everywhere opposed such translations, but it generally preferred that the populace encounter the Scriptures through the interpretations of the priests, trained to read the Latin translation known as the Vulgate. In times of great conflict, this preference for clerical mediation hardened into outright prohibition of vernacular translation and into persecution and book burning.

Zealous Protestants set out, in the teeth of fierce opposition, to put the Bible into the hands of the laity. A remarkable translation of the New Testament, by an English Lutheran named William Tyndale, was printed on the Continent and smuggled into England in 1525; Tyndale's translation of the Pentateuch, the first five books of the Hebrew Bible, followed in 1530. Many copies of these translations were seized and burned, as was the translator himself, but the printing press made it extremely difficult for authorities to eradicate books for which there was a passionate demand. The English Bible was a force that could not be suppressed, and it became, in its various forms, the single most important book of the sixteenth century.

Tyndale's translation was completed by an associate, Miles Coverdale, whose rendering of the Psalms proved to be particularly influential. Their joint labor was the basis for the Great Bible (1539), the first authorized version of the Bible in English, a copy of which was ordered to be placed in every church in the kingdom. With the accession of Edward VI, many editions of the Bible followed, but the process was sharply reversed when Mary came to the throne in 1553. Along with people condemned as heretics, English Bibles were burned in great bonfires.

Marian persecution was indirectly responsible for what would become the most popular as well as most scholarly English Bible, the translation known as the Geneva Bible (1560), prepared, with extensive, learned, and often fiercely polemical marginal notes, by English exiles in Calvin's Geneva and widely diffused in England after Elizabeth came to the throne. In addition, Elizabethan church authorities ordered a careful revision of the Great Bible, and this version, known as the Bishops' Bible (1568), was the one read in the churches. The success of the Geneva Bible in particular prompted those Elizabethan Catholics who now in turn found themselves in exile to bring out a vernacular translation of their own in order to counter the Protestant readings and glosses. This Catholic translation, the so-called Rheims Bible (1582), may have been known to Shakespeare, but he seems to have been far better acquainted with the Geneva Bible, and he would also have repeatedly heard the Bishops' Bible read aloud. Scholars have identified over three hundred references to the Bible in Shakespeare's work; in one version or another, the Scriptures had a powerful impact on his imagination.

A Female Monarch in a Male World

In the last year of Mary's reign, 1558, the Scottish Calvinist minister John Knox thundered against what he called "the monstrous regiment of women." When the Protestant Elizabeth came to the throne the following year, Knox and his religious brethren were less inclined to denounce female rulers, but in England as elsewhere in Europe there remained a widespread conviction that women were unsuited to wield power over men. Many men seem to have regarded the capacity for rational thought as exclusively male; women, they assumed, were led only by their passions. While gentlemen mastered the arts of rhetoric and warfare, gentlewomen were expected to display the virtues of silence and good housekeeping. Among upper-class males, the will to dominate others was acceptable and indeed admired; the same will in women was condemned as a grotesque and dangerous aberration.

The Armada portrait: note Elizabeth's hand on the globe.

Apologists for the Queen countered these prejudices by appealing to historical precedent and legal theory. History offered inspiring examples of just female rulers, notably Deborah, the biblical prophetess who judged Israel. In the legal sphere, crown lawyers advanced the theory of "the king's two bodies." As England's crowned head, Elizabeth's person was mystically divided between her mortal "body natural" and the immortal "body politic." While the queen's natural body was inevitably subject to the failings of human flesh, the body politic was timeless and perfect. In political terms, therefore, Elizabeth's sex was a matter of no consequence, a thing indifferent.

Elizabeth, who had received a fine humanist education and an extended, dangerous lesson in the art of survival, made it immediately clear that she intended to rule in more than name only. She assembled a group of trustworthy advisers, foremost among them William Cecil (later named Lord Burghley), but she insisted on making many of the crucial decisions herself. Like many Renaissance monarchs, Elizabeth was drawn to the idea of royal absolutism, the theory that ultimate power was properly concentrated in her person and indeed that God had appointed her to be his deputy in the kingdom. Opposition to her rule, in this view, was not only a political act but also a kind of impiety, a blasphemous grudging against the will of God. Apologists for absolutism contended that God commands obedience even to manifestly wicked rulers whom he has sent to punish the sinfulness of humankind. Such arguments were routinely made in speeches and political tracts and from the pulpits of churches, where they were incorporated into the Book of Homilies, which clergymen were required to read out to their congregations.

In reality, Elizabeth's power was not absolute. The government had a network of spies, informers, and agents provocateurs, but it lacked a standing army, a national police force, an efficient system of communication, and an extensive bureaucracy. Above all, the Queen had limited financial resources and needed to turn periodically to an independent and often recalcitrant Parliament, which by long tradition had the sole right to levy taxes and to grant subsidies. Members of the House of Commons were elected from their boroughs, not appointed by the monarch, and though the Queen had considerable influence over their decisions, she could by no means dictate policy. Under these constraints, Elizabeth ruled through a combination of adroit political maneuvering and imperious command, all the while enhancing her authority in the eyes of both court and country by means of an extraordinary cult of love.

"We all loved her," Elizabeth's godson Sir John Harington wrote, with just a touch of irony, a few years after the Queen's death, "for she said she loved us." Ambassadors, courtiers, and parliamentarians all submitted to Elizabeth's cult of love, in which the Queen's gender was transformed from a potential liability into a significant asset. Those who approached her generally did so on their knees and were expected to address her with extravagant compliments fashioned from the period's most passionate love poetry; she in turn spoke, when it suited her to do so, in the language of love poetry. The court moved in an atmosphere of romance, with music, dancing, plays, and the elaborate, fancy-dress entertainments called masques. The Queen adorned herself in gorgeous clothes and rich jewels. When she went on one of her summer "progresses," ceremonial journeys through her land, she looked like an exotic, sacred image in a religious cult of love, and her noble hosts virtually bankrupted themselves to lavish upon her the costliest pleasures. England's leading artists, such as the poet Edmund Spenser and the painter Nicholas Hilliard, enlisted themselves in the celebration of Elizabeth's mystery, likening her to the goddesses of classical mythology: Diana, Astraea, Phoebe, Flora. Her cult drew its power from cultural discourses that ranged from the secular (her courtiers could pine for her as a chaste, unattainable maiden) to the sacred (the veneration that under Catholicism had been due to the Virgin Mary could now be directed toward England's semidivine queen).

There was a sober, even grim aspect to these poetical fantasies: Elizabeth was brilliant at playing one dangerous faction off against another, now turning her gracious smiles on one favorite, now honoring his hated rival, now suddenly looking elsewhere and raising an obscure upstart to royal favor. And when she was disobeyed or when she felt that her prerogatives had been challenged, she was capable of an anger that, as Harington put it, "left no doubtings whose daughter she was." Thus when Sir Walter Ralegh, one of the Queen's glittering favorites, married without her knowledge or consent, he found himself promptly imprisoned in the Tower of London. And when the Protestant polemicist John Stubbs ventured to publish a pamphlet stridently denouncing the Queen's proposed marriage to the French Catholic Duke of Alençon, Stubbs and his publisher were arrested and had their right hands chopped off. (After receiving the blow, the now prudent Stubbs lifted his hat with his remaining hand and cried, "God save the Queen!")

The Queen's marriage negotiations were a particularly fraught issue. When she came to the throne at twenty-five years old, speculation about a suitable match, already widespread, intensified and remained for decades at a fever pitch, for the stakes were high. If Elizabeth died childless, the Tudor line would come to an end. The nearest heir was her cousin Mary, Queen of Scots, a Catholic whose claim was supported by France and by the papacy and whose penchant for sexual and political intrigue confirmed the worst fears of English Protestants. The obvious way to avert the nightmare was for Elizabeth to marry and produce an heir, and the pressure upon her to do so was intense.

More than the royal succession hinged on the question of the Queen's marriage; Elizabeth's perceived eligibility was a vital factor in the complex machinations of international diplomacy. A dynastic marriage between the Queen of England and a foreign ruler would forge an alliance powerful enough to alter the balance of power in Europe. The English court hosted a steady stream of ambassadors from kings and princes eager to win the hand of the royal maiden, and Elizabeth, who prided herself on speaking fluent French and Italian (and on reading Latin and Greek), played her romantic part with exemplary skill, sighing and spinning the negotiations out for months and even years. Most probably, she never meant to marry any of her numerous foreign (and domestic) suitors. Such a decisive act would have meant the end of her independence, as well as the end of the marriage game by which she played one power off against another. One day she would seem to be on the verge of accepting a proposal; the next, she would vow never to forsake her virginity. "She is a princess," the French ambassador remarked, "who can act any part she pleases."

The Kingdom in Danger

Beset by Catholic and Protestant extremists, Elizabeth contrived to forge a moderate compromise that enabled her realm to avert the massacres and civil wars that poisoned France and other countries on the Continent. But menace was never far off, and there were constant fears of conspiracy, rebellion, and assassination. Many of the fears swirled around Mary, Queen of Scots, who had been driven from her own kingdom in 1568 by a powerful faction of rebellious nobles and had taken refuge in England. Her presence, under a kind of house arrest, was a source of intense anxiety and helped generate continual rumors of plots. Some of these plots were real enough, others imaginary, still others traps set in motion by the secret agents of the government's intelligence service under the direction of Sir Francis Walsingham. The situation worsened greatly after Spanish imperial armies invaded the Netherlands in order to stamp out Protestant rebels (1567), after the St. Bartholomew's Day Massacre of Protestants (Huguenots) in France (1572), and after the assassination there of Europe's other major Protestant leader, William of Orange (1584).

The Queen's life seemed to be in even greater danger after the proclamation of Pope Gregory XIII in 1580 that the assassination of the great heretic Elizabeth (who had been excommunicated a decade before) would not constitute a mortal sin. The immediate effect of the proclamation was to make existence more difficult for English Catholics, most of whom were loyal to the Queen but who fell under grave suspicion. Suspicion was intensified by the clandestine presence of English Jesuits, trained at seminaries abroad and smuggled back into England to serve the Roman Catholic cause. When Elizabeth's spymaster Walsingham unearthed an assassination plot in the correspondence between the Queen of Scots and the Catholic Anthony Babington, the wretched Mary's fate was sealed. After vacillating, a very reluctant Elizabeth signed the death warrant in February 1587, and her cousin was beheaded.

The long-anticipated military confrontation with Catholic Spain was now unavoidable. Elizabeth learned that Philip II, her former brother-in-law and onetime suitor, was preparing to send an enormous fleet against her island realm. It was to sail to the Netherlands, where a Spanish army would be waiting to embark and invade England. Barring its way was England's small fleet of well-armed and highly maneuverable fighting vessels, backed up by ships from the merchant navy. The Invincible Armada reached English waters in July 1588, only to be routed in one of the most famous and decisive naval battles in European history. Then, in what many viewed as an act of God on behalf of Protestant England, the Spanish fleet was dispersed and all but destroyed by violent storms.

As England braced itself to withstand the invasion that never came, Elizabeth appeared in person to review a detachment of soldiers assembled at Tilbury. Dressed in a white gown and a silver breastplate, she declared that though some among her councillors had urged her not to appear before a large crowd of armed men, she would never fail to trust the loyalty of her faithful and loving subjects. Nor did she fear the Spanish armies. "I know I have the body of a weak and feeble woman," Elizabeth declared, "but I have the heart and stomach of a king, and of England too." In this celebrated speech, Elizabeth displayed many of her most memorable qualities: her self-consciously histrionic command of grand public occasion, her subtle blending of magniloquent rhetoric and the language of love, her strategic appropriation of traditionally masculine qualities, and her great personal courage. "We princes," she once remarked, "are set on stages in the sight and view of all the world."

The English and Otherness

Shakespeare's London had a large population of resident aliens, mainly artisans and merchants and their families, from Portugal, Italy, Spain, Germany, and above all France and the Netherlands. Many of these people were Protestant refugees, and they were accorded some legal and economic protection by the government. But they were not always welcomed by the local populace. Throughout the sixteenth century, London was the site of repeated demonstrations and, on occasion, bloody riots against the communities of foreign artisans, who were accused of taking jobs away from Englishmen. There was widespread hostility as well toward the Welsh, the Scots, and especially the Irish, whom the English had for centuries been struggling unsuccessfully to subdue. The kings of England claimed to be rulers of Ireland, but in reality they effectively controlled only a small area known as the Pale, extending north from Dublin. The great majority of the Irish people remained stubbornly Catholic and, despite endlessly reiterated English repression, burning of villages, destruction of crops, and massacres, incorrigibly independent.

Shakespeare's *Henry V* (1598–99) seems to invite the audience to celebrate the conjoined heroism of English, Welsh, Scots, and Irish soldiers all fighting together as a "band of brothers" against the French. But such a way of imagining the national community must be set against the tensions and conflicting interests that often set these brothers at each other's throats. As Shakespeare's King Henry realizes, a feared or hated foreign enemy helps at least to mask these tensions, and indeed, in the face of the Spanish Armada, even the bitter gulf between Catholic and Protestant Englishmen seemed to narrow significantly. But the patriotic alliance was only temporary.

Another way of partially masking the sharp differences in language, belief, and custom among the peoples of the British Isles was to group these people together in contrast to the Jews. Medieval England's Jewish population, the recurrent object of persecution, extortion, and massacre, had been officially expelled by King Edward I in 1290. Therefore few if any of Shakespeare's contemporaries would have encountered on English soil Jews who openly practiced their religion. Elizabethan England probably did, however, harbor a small number of so-called Marranos, Spanish or Portuguese Jews who had officially converted to Christianity but secretly continued to observe Jewish practices. One of those suspected to be Marranos was Elizabeth's own physician, Roderigo Lopez, who was tried in 1594 for an alleged plot to poison the Queen. Convicted and condemned to the hideous execution reserved for traitors, Lopez went to his death, in the words of the Elizabethan historian

A Jewish man depicted poisoning a well. From Pierre Boaistuau, *Certain Secret Wonders of Nature* (1569).

William Camden, "affirming that he loved the Queen as well as he loved Jesus Christ; which coming from a man of the Jewish profession moved no small laughter in the standers-by." It is difficult to gauge the meaning here of the phrase "the Jewish profession," used to describe a man who never as far as we know professed Judaism, just as it is difficult to gauge the meaning of the crowd's cruel laughter.

Elizabethans appear to have been fascinated by Jews and Judaism but quite uncertain whether the terms referred to a people, a foreign nation, a set of strange practices, a living faith, a defunct religion, a villainous conspiracy, or a messianic inheritance. Protestant reformers brooded deeply on the Hebraic origins of Christianity; government officials ordered the arrest of those "suspected to be Jews"; villagers paid pennies to itinerant fortune-tellers who claimed to be descended from Abraham or masters of cabalistic mysteries; and London playgoers, perhaps including some who laughed at Lopez on the scaffold, enjoyed the spectacle of the downfall of the wicked Barabas in Christopher Marlowe's *Jew of Malta* (ca. 1589) and the forced conversion of Shylock in Shakespeare's *Merchant of Venice* (1596–97). Jews were not officially permitted to resettle in England until the middle of the seventeenth century, and even then their legal status was ambiguous.

Shakespeare's England also had a small African population whose skin color was the subject of pseudo-scientific speculation and theological debate. Some Elizabethans believed that Africans' blackness resulted from the climate of the regions in which they lived, where, as one traveler put it, they were "so scorched and vexed with the heat of the sun, that in many places they curse it when it riseth." Others held that blackness was a curse inherited from their forefather Chus, the son of Ham, who had, according to Genesis, wickedly exposed the nakedness of the drunken Noah. George Best, a proponent of this theory of inherited skin color, reported that "I myself have seen an Ethiopian as black as coal brought into England, who taking a fair English woman to wife, begat a son in all respects as black as the father was, although England were his native country, and an English woman his mother: whereby it seemeth this blackness proceedeth rather of some natural infection of that man."

As the word "infection" suggests, Elizabethans frequently regarded blackness as a physical defect, though the blacks who lived in England and Scotland throughout the sixteenth century were also treated as exotic curiosities. At his marriage to Anne of Denmark, James I entertained his bride and her family by commanding four naked black youths to dance before him in the snow. (The youths died of exposure shortly afterward.) In 1594, in the festivities celebrating the baptism of James's son, a "Black-Moor" entered pulling an elabo-

Man with head beneath his shoulders. From a Spanish edition of Mandeville's *Travels*. See *Othello* 1.3.144–45: "and men whose heads / Grew beneath their shoulders." Such men were frequently reported by medieval travelers to the East.

rately decorated chariot that was, in the original plan, supposed to be drawn in by a lion. There was a black trumpeter in the courts of Henry VII and Henry VIII, while Elizabeth had at least two black servants, one an entertainer and the other a page. Africans became increasingly popular as servants in aristocratic and gentle households in the last decades of the sixteenth century.

Some of these Africans were almost certainly slaves, though the legal status of slavery in England was ambiguous. In Cartwright's Case (1569), the court ruled "that England was too Pure an Air for Slaves to breathe in," but there is evidence that black slaves were owned in Elizabethan and Jacobean England. Moreover, by the mid-sixteenth century, the English had become involved in the profitable trade that carried African slaves to the New World. In 1562, John Hawkins embarked on his first slaving voyage, transporting some three hundred blacks from the Guinea coast to Hispaniola, where they were sold for £10,000. Elizabeth is reported to have said of this venture that it was "detestable, and would call down the Vengeance of Heaven upon the Undertakers." Nevertheless, she invested in Hawkins's subsequent voyages and loaned him ships.

English men and women of the sixteenth century experienced an unprecedented increase in knowledge of the world beyond their island, for a number of reasons. Religious persecution compelled both Catholics and Protestants to live abroad; wealthy gentlemen (and, in at least a few cases, ladies) traveled in France and Italy to view the famous cultural monuments; merchants published accounts of distant lands such as Turkey, Morocco, and Russia; and military and trading ventures took English ships to still more distant shores. In 1496, a Venetian tradesman living in Bristol, John Cabot, was granted a license by Henry VII to sail on a voyage of exploration; with his son Sebastian, he discovered Newfoundland and Nova Scotia. Remarkable feats of seamanship and reconnaissance soon followed: on his ship the *Golden Hind,* Sir Francis Drake circumnavigated the globe in 1579 and laid claim to California on behalf of the Queen; a few years later, a ship commanded by Thomas Cavendish also completed a circumnavigation. Sir Martin Frobisher explored bleak Baffin Island in search of a Northwest Passage to the Orient; Sir John Davis explored the west coast of Greenland and discovered the Falkland Islands off the coast of Argentina; Sir Walter Ralegh ventured up the Orinoco Delta, in what is now Venezuela, in search of the mythical land of El Dorado. Accounts of these and other exploits were collected by a clergyman and promoter of empire, Richard Hakluyt, and published as *The Principal Navigations* (1589; expanded edition 1599).

"To seek new worlds for gold, for praise, for glory," as Ralegh characterized such enterprises, was not for the faint of heart: Drake, Cavendish, Frobisher, and Hawkins all died at sea, as did huge numbers of those who sailed under their command. Elizabethans sensible enough to stay at home could do more than read written accounts of their fellow countrymen's far-reaching voyages. Expeditions brought back native plants (including, most famously, tobacco), animals, cultural artifacts, and, on occasion, samples of the native peoples themselves, most often seized against their will. There were exhibitions in London of a kidnapped Eskimo with his kayak and of Native Virginians with their canoes. Most of these miserable captives, violently uprooted and vulnerable to European diseases, quickly perished, but even in death they were evidently valuable property: when the English will not give one small coin "to relieve a lame beggar," one of the characters in *The Tempest* wryly remarks, "they will lay out ten to see a dead Indian" (2.2.30–31).

Perhaps most nations learn to define what they are by defining what they are not. This negative self-definition is, in any case, what Elizabethans seemed constantly to be doing, in travel books, sermons, political speeches, civic pageants, public exhibitions, and theatrical spectacles of otherness. The extraordinary variety of these exercises (which include public executions and urban riots, as well as more benign forms of curiosity) suggests that the boundaries of national identity were by no means clear and unequivocal. Even peoples whom English writers routinely, viciously stigmatize

An Indian dance. From Thomas Hariot, *A Brief and True Report of the New Found Land of Virginia* (1590).

as irreducibly alien—Italians, Indians, Turks, and Jews—have a surprising instability in the Elizabethan imagination and may appear for brief, intense moments as powerful models to be admired and emulated before they resume their place as emblems of despised otherness.

James I and the Union of the Crowns

Though under great pressure to do so, the aging Elizabeth steadfastly refused to name her successor. It became increasingly apparent, however, that it would be James Stuart, the son of Mary, Queen of Scots, and by the time Elizabeth's health began to fail, several of her principal advisers, including her chief minister, Robert Cecil, had been for several years in secret correspondence with him in Edinburgh. Crowned King James VI of Scotland in 1567 when he was but one year old, Mary's son had been raised as a Protestant by his powerful guardians, and in 1589 he married a Protestant princess, Anne of Denmark. When Elizabeth died on March 24, 1603, English officials reported that on her deathbed the Queen had named James to succeed her.

Upon his accession, James—now styled James VI of Scotland and James I of England—made plain his intention to unite his two kingdoms. As he told Parliament in 1604, "What God hath conjoined then, let no man separate. I am the husband, and all of the whole isle is my lawful wife; I am the head and it is my body; I am the

Funeral procession of Queen Elizabeth. From a watercolor sketch by an unknown artist (1603).

shepherd and it is my flock." But the flock was less perfectly united than James optimistically envisioned: English and Scottish were sharply distinct identities, as were Welsh and Cornish and other peoples who were incorporated, with varying degrees of willingness, into the realm.

Fearing that to change the name of the kingdom would invalidate all laws and institutions established under the name of England, a fear that was partly real and partly a cover for anti-Scots prejudice, Parliament balked at James's desire to be called "King of Great Britain" and resisted the unionist legislation that would have made Great Britain a legal reality. Though the English initially rejoiced at the peaceful transition from Elizabeth to her successor, there was a rising tide of resentment against James's advancement of Scots friends and his creation of new knighthoods. Lower down the social ladder, English and Scots occasionally clashed violently on the streets: in July 1603, James issued a proclamation against Scottish "insolencies," and in April 1604, he ordered the arrest of "swaggerers" waylaying Scots in London. The ensuing years did not bring the amity and docile obedience for which James hoped, and, though the navy now flew the Union Jack, combining the Scottish cross of St. Andrew and the English cross of St. George, the unification of the kingdoms remained throughout his reign an unfulfilled ambition.

Unfulfilled as well were James's lifelong dreams of ruling as an absolute monarch. Crown lawyers throughout Europe had long argued that a king, by virtue of his power to make law, must necessarily be above law. But in England sovereignty was identified not with the king alone or with the people alone but with the "King in Parliament." Against his absolutist ambitions, James faced the crucial power to raise taxes that was vested not in the monarch but in the elected members of the Parliament. He faced as well a theory of republicanism that traced its roots back to ancient Rome and that prided itself on its steadfast and, if necessary, violent resistance to tyranny. Shakespeare's fascination with monarchy is apparent throughout his work, but in his Roman plays in particular, as well as in his long poem *The Rape of Lucrece*, he manifests an intense imaginative interest in the idea of a republic.

The Jacobean Court

With James as with Elizabeth, the royal court was the center of diplomacy, ambition, intrigue, and an intense jockeying for social position. As always in monarchies, proximity to the king's person was a central mark of favor, so that access to the royal bedchamber was one of the highest aims of the powerful, scheming lords who followed James from his sprawling London palace at Whitehall to the hunting lodges and country estates to which he loved to retreat. A coveted office, in the Jacobean as in the Tudor court, was the Groom of the Stool, the person who supervised the disposal of the king's wastes. The officeholder was close to the king at one of his most exposed and vulnerable moments and enjoyed the further privilege of sleeping on a pallet at the foot of the royal bed and assisting the monarch in putting on the royal under-shirt. Another, slightly less privileged official, the Gentleman of the Robes, dressed the king in his doublet and outer garments.

The royal lifestyle was increasingly expensive. Unlike Elizabeth, James had to maintain separate households for his queen and for the heir apparent, Prince Henry. (Upon Henry's death at the age of eighteen in 1612, his younger brother, Prince Charles, became heir, eventually succeeding his father in 1625.) James was also extremely generous to his friends, amassing his own huge debts in the course of pay-ing off theirs. As early as 1605, he told his principal adviser that "it is a horror to me to think of the height of my place, the greatness of my debts, and the smallness of my means." This smallness notwithstanding, James continued to lavish gifts upon hand-some favorites such as the Earl of Somerset, Robert Carr, and the Duke of Bucking-ham, George Villiers.

The attachment James formed for these favorites was highly romantic. "God so love me," the King wrote to Buckingham, "as I desire only to live in the world for your sake, and that I had rather live banished in any part of the earth with you than live a sorrow-ful widow's life without you." Such sentiments, not surprisingly, gave rise to widespread rumors of homosexual activities at court. The rumors are certainly plausible, though the surviving evidence of same-sex relationships, at court or elsewhere, is extremely dif-ficult to interpret. A statute of 1533 made "the detestable and abominable vice of bug-gery committed with mankind or beast" a felony punishable by death. (English law

declined to recognize or criminalize lesbian acts.) The effect of the dra-conian laws against sodomy seems to have been to reduce actual prose-cutions to the barest minimum: for the next hundred years, there are no known cases of trials resulting in a death sentence for homosexual activity alone. If the legal record is therefore unreliable as an index of the extent of homosexual relations, the literary record (including, most famously, the majority of Shake-speare's sonnets) is equally opaque. Any poetic avowal of male-male love may simply be a formal expression of affection based on classical models, or, alternatively, it may be an expres-sion of passionate physical and spiri-tual love. The interpretive difficulty is compounded by the absence in the period of any clear reference to a homosexual "identity," though there are many references to same-sex acts and feelings. What is clear is that male friendships at the court of James and elsewhere were suffused with eroticism, at once exciting and threatening, that subsequent peri-ods policed more anxiously.

James I. Attributed to John De Critz the Elder (ca. 1606).

In addition to the extravagant expenditures on his favorites, James

Two Young Men. By Crispin van den Broeck.

was also the patron of ever more elaborate feasts and masques. Shakespeare's work provides a small glimpse of these in *The Tempest,* with its exotic banquet and its "majestic vision" of mythological goddesses and dancing nymphs and reapers. The actual Jacobean court masques, designed by the great architect, painter, and engineer Inigo Jones, were spectacular, fantastic, technically ingenious, and staggeringly costly celebrations of regal magnificence. With their exquisite costumes and their elegant blend of music, dancing, and poetry, the masques, generally performed by the noble lords and ladies of the court, were deliberately ephemeral exercises in conspicuous expenditure and consumption: by tradition, at the end of the performance, the private audience would rush forward and tear to pieces the gorgeous scenery. And though masques were enormously sophisticated entertainments, often on rather esoteric allegorical themes, they could on occasion collapse into grotesque excess. In a letter of 1606, Sir John Harington describes a masque in honor of the visiting Danish king in which the participants, no doubt toasting their royal majesties, had had too much to drink. A lady playing the part of the Queen of Sheba attempted to present precious gifts, "but, forgetting the steps arising to the canopy, overset her caskets into his Danish Majesty's lap. . . . His Majesty then got up and would dance with the Queen of Sheba; but he fell down and humbled himself before her, and was carried to an inner chamber and laid on a bed." Meanwhile, Harington writes, the masque continued with a pageant of Faith, Hope, and Charity, but Charity could barely keep her balance, while Hope and Faith "were both sick and spewing in the lower hall." This was, we can hope, not a typical occasion.

While the English seem initially to have welcomed James's free-spending ways as a change from the parsimoniousness of Queen Elizabeth, they were dismayed by its consequences. Elizabeth had died owing £400,000. In 1608, the royal debt had risen to £1,400,000 and was increasing by £140,000 a year. The money to pay off this debt, or at least to keep it under control, was raised by various means. These included customs farming (leasing the right to collect customs duties to private individuals); the highly unpopular impositions (duties on the import of nonnecessities, such as spices, silks, and currants); the sale of crown lands; the sale of baronetcies; and appeals to an increasingly grudging and recalcitrant Parliament. In 1614, Parliament demanded an end to impositions before it would relieve the King and was angrily dissolved without completing its business.

James's Religious Policy and the Persecution of Witches

Before his accession to the English throne, the King had made known his view of Puritans, the general name for a variety of Protestant sects that were agitating for a radical reform of the church, the overthrow of its conservative hierarchy of bishops, and the rejection of a large number of traditional rituals and practices. In a book he wrote, *Basilikon Doron* (1599), James denounced "brainsick and heady preachers" who were prepared "to let King, people, law and all be trod underfoot." Yet he was not entirely unwilling to consider religious reforms. In religion, as in foreign policy, he was above all concerned to maintain peace.

On his way south to claim the throne of England in 1603, James was presented with the Millenary Petition (signed by one thousand ministers), which urged him as "our physician" to heal the disease of lingering "popish" ceremonies. He responded by calling a conference on the ceremonies of the Church of England, which duly took place at Hampton Court Palace in January 1604. The delegates who spoke for reform were moderates, and there was little in the outcome to satisfy Puritans. Nevertheless, while the Church of England continued to cling to such remnants of the Catholic past as wedding rings, square caps, bishops, and Christmas, the conference did produce some reform in the area of ecclesiastical discipline. It also authorized a new English translation of the Bible, known as the King James Bible, which was printed in 1611, too late to have been extensively used by Shakespeare. Along with Shakespeare's works, the King James Bible has probably had the profoundest influence on the subsequent history of English literature.

Having arranged this compromise, James saw his main task as ensuring conformity. He promulgated the 1604 Canons (the first definitive code of canon law since the Reformation), which required all ministers to subscribe to three articles. The first affirmed royal supremacy; the second confirmed that there was nothing in the Book of Common Prayer "contrary to the Word of God" and required ministers to use only the authorized services; the third asserted that the central tenets of the Church of England

The "swimming" of a suspected witch.

were "agreeable to the Word of God." There were strong objections to the second and third articles from those of Puritan leanings inside and outside the House of Commons. In the end, many ministers refused to conform or subscribe to the articles, but only about ninety of them, or 1 percent of the clergy, were deprived of their livings. In its theology and composition, the Church of England was little changed from what it had been under Elizabeth. In hindsight, what is most striking are the ominous signs of growing religious divisions that would by the 1640s burst forth in civil war and the execution of James's son Charles.

James seems to have taken seriously the official claims to the sacredness of kingship, and he certainly took seriously his own theories of religion and politics, which he had printed for the edification of his people. He was convinced that Satan, perpetually warring against God and His representatives on earth, was continually plotting against him. James thought moreover that he possessed special insight into Satan's wicked agents, the witches, and in 1597, while King of Scotland, he published his *Demonology,* a learned exposition of their malign threat to his godly rule. Hundreds of witches, he believed, were involved in a 1589 conspiracy to kill him by raising storms at sea when he was sailing home from Denmark with his new bride.

In the 1590s, Scotland embarked on a virulent witch craze of the kind that had since the fifteenth century repeatedly afflicted France, Switzerland, and Germany, where many thousands of women (and a much smaller number of men) were caught in a nightmarish web of wild accusations. Tortured into making lurid confessions of infant cannibalism, night flying, and sexual intercourse with the devil at huge, orgiastic "witches' Sabbaths," the victims had little chance to defend themselves and were routinely burned at the stake.

In England too there were witchcraft prosecutions, though on a much smaller scale and with significant differences in the nature of the accusations and the judicial procedures. Witch trials began in England in the 1540s; statutes against witchcraft were enacted in 1542, 1563, and 1604. English law did not allow judicial torture, stipulated lesser punishments in cases of "white magic," and mandated jury trials. Juries acquitted more than half of the defendants in witchcraft trials; in Essex, where the judicial records are particularly extensive, some 24 percent of those accused were executed, while the remainder of those convicted were pilloried and imprisoned or sentenced and reprieved. The accused were generally charged with *maleficium,* an evil deed—usually harming neighbors, causing destructive storms, or killing farm animals—but not with worshipping Satan.

After 1603, when James came to the English throne, he somewhat moderated his enthusiasm for the judicial murder of witches, for the most part defenseless, poor women resented by their neighbors. Though he did nothing to mitigate the ferocity of the ongoing witch hunts in his native Scotland, he did not try to institute Scottish-style persecutions and trials in his new realm. This relative waning of persecutorial eagerness principally reflects the differences between England and Scotland, but it may also bespeak some small, nascent skepticism on James's part about the quality of evidence brought against the accused and about the reliability of the "confessions" extracted from them. It is sobering to reflect that plays like Shakespeare's *Macbeth* (1606), Thomas Middleton's *Witch* (before 1616), and Thomas Dekker, John Ford, and William Rowley's *Witch of Edmonton* (1621) seem to be less the allies of skepticism than the exploiters of fear.

The Playing Field

Cosmic Spectacles

The first permanent, freestanding public theaters in England date only from Shakespeare's own lifetime: a London playhouse, the Red Lion, is mentioned in 1567, and

James Burbage's playhouse, The Theatre, was built in 1576. (The innovative use of these new stages, crucial to a full understanding of Shakespeare's achievement, is discussed in a separate essay in this volume, by the theater historian Holger Schott Syme.) But it is quite misleading to identify English drama exclusively with these specially constructed playhouses, for in fact there was a rich and vital theatrical tradition in England stretching back for centuries. Many towns in late medieval England were the sites of annual festivals that mounted elaborate cycles of plays depicting the great biblical stories, from the creation of the world to Christ's Passion and its miraculous aftermath. Most of these plays have been lost, but the surviving cycles, such as those from York, are magnificent and complex works of art. They are sometimes called "mystery plays," either because they were performed by the guilds of various crafts (known as "mysteries") or, more likely, because they represented the mysteries of the faith. The cycles were most often performed on the annual feast day instituted in the early fourteenth century in honor of the Corpus Christi, the sacrament of the Lord's Supper, which is perhaps the greatest of these religious mysteries.

The Feast of Corpus Christi, celebrated on the Thursday following Trinity Sunday, helped give the play cycles their extraordinary cultural resonance, but it also contributed to their downfall. For along with the specifically liturgical plays traditionally performed by religious confraternities and the "saints' plays," which depicted miraculous events in the lives of individual holy men and women, the mystery cycles were closely identified with the Catholic Church. Protestant authorities in the sixteenth century, eager to eradicate all remnants of popular Catholic piety, moved to suppress the annual procession of the Host, with its gorgeous banners, pageant carts, and cycle of visionary plays. In 1548, the Feast of Corpus Christi was abolished. Towns that continued to perform the mysteries were under increasing pressure to abandon them. It is sometimes said that the cycles were already dying out from neglect, but recent research has shown that many towns and their guilds were extremely reluctant to give them up. Desperate offers to strip away any traces of Catholic doctrine and to submit the play scripts to the authorities for their approval met with unbending opposition from the government. In 1576, the courts gave York permission to perform its cycle but only if

> in the said play no pageant be used or set forth wherein the Majesty of God the Father, God the Son, or God the Holy Ghost or the administration of either the Sacraments of baptism or of the Lord's Supper be counterfeited or represented, or anything played which tend to the maintenance of superstition and idolatry or which be contrary to the laws of God . . . or of the realm.

Such "permission" was tantamount to an outright ban. The local officials in the city of Norwich, proud of their St. George and the Dragon play, asked if they could at least parade the dragon costume through the streets, but even this modest request was refused. It is likely that as a young man Shakespeare had seen some of these plays: when Hamlet says of a noisy, strutting theatrical performance that it "out-Herods Herod," he is alluding to the famously bombastic role of Herod of Jewry in the mystery plays. But by the century's end, the cycles were no longer performed by live actors in great civic celebrations. They survived, if at all, in the debased form of puppet shows.

Early English theater was by no means restricted to these civic and religious festivals. Payments to professional and amateur performers appear in early records of towns and aristocratic households, though the Latin terms—*ministralli, histriones, mimi, lusores,* and so forth—are not used with great consistency and make it difficult to distinguish among minstrels, jugglers, stage players, and other entertainers. Performers acted in town halls and the halls of guilds and aristocratic mansions, on scaffolds erected in town squares and marketplaces, on pageant wagons in the streets, and in inn yards. By the fifteenth century, and probably earlier, there were organized companies of players traveling under noble patronage. Such companies earned a living providing amusement, while enhancing the prestige of the patron.

Panorama of London, showing two theaters, both round and both flying flags: a flying flag indicated that a performance was in progress. The Globe is in the foreground, and the Hope, or Beargarden, is to the left.

A description of a provincial performance in the late sixteenth century, written by one R. Willis, provides a glimpse of what seems to have been the usual procedure:

> In the City of Gloucester the manner is (as I think it is in other like corporations) that when the Players of Interludes come to town, they first attend the Mayor to inform him what nobleman's servant they are, and so to get license for their public playing; and if the Mayor like the Actors, or would show respect to their Lord and Master, he appoints them to play their first play before himself and the Aldermen and common Council of the City and that is called the Mayor's play, where everyone that will come in without money, the Mayor giving the players a reward as he thinks fit to show respect unto them.

In addition to their take from this "first play," the players would almost certainly have supplemented their income by performing in halls and inn yards, where they could on some occasions charge an admission fee. It was no doubt a precarious existence.

The "Interludes" mentioned in Willis's description of the Gloucester performances are likely plays that were, in effect, staged dialogues on religious, moral, and political themes. Such works could, like the mysteries, be associated with Catholicism, but they were also used in the sixteenth century to convey polemical Protestant messages, and they reached outside the religious sphere to address secular concerns as well. Henry Medwall's *Fulgens and Lucrece* (ca. 1490–1501), for example, pits a wealthy but dissolute nobleman against a virtuous public servant of humble origins, while John Heywood's *Play of the Weather* (ca. 1525–33) stages a debate among social rivals, including a gentleman, a merchant, a forest ranger, and two millers. The structure of such plays reflects the training in argumentation that students received in Tudor schools and, in particular, the sustained practice in examining all sides of a difficult question. Some of Shakespeare's amazing ability to look at critical issues from multiple perspectives may be traced back to this practice and the dramatic interludes it helped to inspire.

Another major form of theater that flourished in England in the fifteenth century and continued on into the sixteenth was the morality play. Like the mysteries, moralities addressed questions of the ultimate fate of the soul. They did so, however, not by rehearsing scriptural stories but by dramatizing allegories of spiritual struggle. Typically, a person named Human or Mankind or Youth is faced with a choice between a pious life in the company of such associates as Mercy, Discretion, and Good Deeds and a dissolute life among riotous companions like Lust or Mischief. Plays like *Mankind* (ca. 1465–70) and *Everyman* (ca. 1495) show how powerful these unpromising-sounding dramas could be, in part because of the extraordinary comic vitality of the evil character, or the Vice, and in part because of the poignancy and terror of an individual's encounter with death. Shakespeare clearly grasped this power. The hunchbacked Duke of Gloucester in *Richard III* gleefully likens himself to "the formal Vice, Iniquity." And when Othello wavers between Desdemona and Iago (himself a Vice figure), his anguished dilemma echoes the fateful choice repeatedly faced by the troubled, vulnerable protagonists of the moralities.

If such plays sound a bit like sermons, it is because they were. Clerics and actors shared some of the same rhetorical skills. It would be misleading to regard church-going and playgoing as comparable entertainments, but in attacking the stage, ministers often seemed to regard the professional players as dangerous rivals. "To leave a Sermon to go to a Play," warned the preacher John Stoughton, "is to forsake the Church of God; to betake oneself to the Synagogue of Satan, to fall from Heaven to Hell." The players themselves were generally too discreet to rise to the challenge; it would have been foolhardy to present the theater as the church's direct competitor. Yet in its moral intensity and its command of impassioned language, the stage frequently emulates and outdoes the pulpit.

Music and Dance

Playacting took its place alongside other forms of public expression and entertainment as well. Perhaps the most important, from the perspective of the theater, were music and dance, since these were directly and repeatedly incorporated into plays. Many plays, comedies and tragedies alike, include occasions that call upon the characters to dance: hence Beatrice and Benedict join the other masked guests at the dance in *Much Ado About Nothing*; in *Twelfth Night,* the befuddled Sir Andrew, at the instigation of the drunken Sir Toby Belch, displays his skill, such as it is, in capering; Romeo and Juliet first see each other at the Capulet ball; the witches dance in a ring around the hideous caldron and perform an "antic round" to cheer Macbeth's spirits; and, in one of Shakespeare's strangest and most wonderful scenes, the drunken Antony in *Antony and Cleopatra* joins hands with Caesar, Enobarbus, Pompey, and others to dance "the Egyptian Bacchanals."

Moreover, virtually all plays in the period, including Shakespeare's, apparently ended with a dance. Brushing off the theatrical gore and changing their expressions from woe to pleasure, the actors in plays like *Romeo and Juliet* and *Julius Caesar* would presumably have received the audience's applause and then bid for a second round of applause by performing a stately pavane or a lively jig. The vogue may have begun to wane in the early seventeenth century, but only to give way to other post-play entertainments, such as the improvisation game known as "themes" where someone in the audience would shout out a theme or question (for example, "Why barks that dog?") and the actor would come up with an extempore response. (The clown Robert Armin, who played the Fool in *King Lear*, was apparently an expert at this game.) Jigs, with their comical leaping dance steps often accompanied by scurrilous ballads, remained popular enough to draw not only large crowds but also official disapproval. A court order of 1612 complained about the "cut-purses and other lewd and ill-disposed persons" who flocked to the theater at the end of every play to be entertained by "lewd jigs, songs, and dances." The players were warned to suppress these disreputable entertainments on pain of imprisonment.

The displays of dancing onstage clearly reflected a widespread popular interest in dancing outside the walls of the playhouse as well. Renaissance intellectuals conjured up visions of the universe as a great cosmic dance, poets figured relations between men and women in terms of popular dance steps, stern moralists denounced dancing as an incitement to filthy lewdness, and, perhaps as significant, men of all classes evidently spent a great deal of time worrying about how shapely their legs looked in tights and how gracefully they could leap. Shakespeare assumes that his audience will be quite familiar with a variety of dances. "For, hear me, Hero," Beatrice tells her friend, "wooing, wedding, and repenting is as a Scotch jig, a measure, and a cinquepace" (*Much Ado About Nothing* 2.1.61–62). Her speech dwells on the comparison a bit, teasing out its implications, but it still does not make much sense if you do not already know something about the dances and perhaps occasionally venture to perform them yourself.

Closely linked to dancing and even more central to the stage was music, both instrumental and vocal. In the early sixteenth century, the Reformation had been disastrous for sacred music: many church organs were destroyed, choir schools were closed, the glorious polyphonic liturgies sung in the monasteries were suppressed. But by the latter part of the century, new perspectives were reinvigorating English music. Latin Masses were reset in English, and tunes were written for newly translated, metrical psalms. More important for the theater, styles of secular music were developed that emphasized music's link to humanist eloquence, its ability to heighten and to rival rhetorically powerful texts.

This link is particularly evident in vocal music, at which Elizabethan composers excelled. Renowned composers William Byrd, Thomas Morley, John Dowland, and others wrote a rich profusion of madrigals (part songs for two to eight voices unaccompanied) and ayres (songs for solo voice, generally accompanied by the lute). These works, along with hymns, popular ballads, rounds, catches, and other forms of song, enjoyed immense popularity, not only in the royal court, where musical skill was regarded as an important accomplishment, and in aristocratic households, where professional musicians were employed as entertainers, but also in less exalted social circles. In his *Plain and Easy Introduction to Practical Music* (1597), Morley tells a

Frans Hals, *The Clown with the Lute* (1625).

story of social humiliation at a failure to perform that suggests that a well-educated Elizabethan was expected to be able to sing at sight. Even if this is an exaggeration in the interest of book sales, there is evidence of impressively widespread musical literacy, reflected in a splendid array of music for the lute, viol, recorder, harp, and virginal, as well as the marvelous vocal music.

Whether it is the aristocratic Orsino luxuriating in the dying fall of an exquisite melody or bully Bottom craving "the tongs and the bones," Shakespeare's characters frequently call for music. They also repeatedly give voice to the age's conviction that there was a deep relation between musical harmony and the harmonies of the well-ordered individual and state. "The man that hath no music in himself," warns Lorenzo in *The Merchant of Venice,* "nor is not moved with concord of sweet sounds, / Is fit for treasons, stratagems, and spoils" (5.1.83–85). This conviction in turn reflects a still deeper link between musical harmony and the divinely created harmony of the cosmos. When Ulysses in *Troilus and Cressida* wishes to convey the image of universal chaos, he speaks of the untuning of a string (1.3.108–09).

The playing companies must have regularly employed trained musicians, and many actors (like the actor who in playing Pandarus in *Troilus and Cressida* is supposed to accompany himself on the lute) must have possessed musical skill. When Shakespeare's company began to use an indoor theater, the Blackfriars, as a second venue, it became famous for its orchestra, and, among other composers, the King's Musician, Robert Johnson, seems to have written songs for the actors to sing. Unfortunately, we possess the original settings for very few of Shakespeare's songs, possibly because many of them may have been set to popular tunes of the time that everyone knew and no one bothered to write down.

Alternative Entertainments

Plays, music, and dancing were by no means the only shows in town. There were jousts, tournaments, royal entries, religious processions, pageants in honor of newly installed civic officials or ambassadors arriving from abroad; wedding masques, court masques, and costumed entertainments known as "disguisings" or "mummings"; juggling acts, fortune-tellers, exhibitions of swordsmanship, mountebanks, folk healers, storytellers, magic shows; bearbaiting, bullbaiting, cockfighting, and other blood sports; folk festivals such as Maying, the Feast of Fools, Carnival, and Whitsun Ales. For several years, Elizabethan Londoners were delighted by a trained animal—Banks's Horse—that performed elaborate dance steps and could, it was thought, do arithmetic and answer questions. And there was always the grim but compelling spectacle of public shaming, mutilation, and execution.

Most English towns had stocks and whipping posts. Drunks, fraudulent merchants, adulterers, and quarrelers could be placed in carts or mounted backward on asses and paraded through the streets for crowds to jeer and throw refuse at. Women accused of being scolds, as we have already remarked, could be publicly muzzled by an iron device called a "brank" or tied to a cucking stool and dunked in the river. Convicted criminals could have their ears cut off, their noses slit, their foreheads branded. Public beheadings (generally reserved for the elite) and hangings were common. Those convicted of treason were sentenced to be "hanged by the neck, and being alive cut down, and your privy members to be cut off, and your bowels to be taken out of your belly and there burned, you being alive."

Shakespeare occasionally takes note of these alternative entertainments: at the end of *Macbeth,* for example, with his enemies closing in on him, the doomed tyrant declares, "They have tied me to a stake. I cannot fly, / But bearlike I must fight the course" (5.7.1–2). The audience is reminded then that it is witnessing the human equivalent of a popular spectacle—a bear chained to a stake and attacked by fierce dogs—that they could have paid to watch at an arena near the Globe. And when, a few moments later, Macduff enters carrying Macbeth's head, the audience is seeing the theatrical equiva-

An Elizabethan hanging.

lent of the execution of criminals and traitors that they could have also watched in the flesh, as it were, nearby. In a different key, the audiences who paid to see *A Midsummer Night's Dream* or *The Winter's Tale* got to enjoy the comic spectacle of a Maying and a Whitsun Pastoral, while the spectators of *The Tempest* could gawk at what the Folio list of characters calls a "savage and deformed slave" and to enjoy an aristocratic magician's wedding masque in honor of his daughter.

The Enemies of the Stage

In 1624, a touring company of players arrived in Norwich and requested permission to perform. Permission was denied, but the municipal authorities, "in regard of the honorable respect which this City beareth to the right honorable the Lord Chamberlain," gave the players twenty shillings to get out of town. Throughout the sixteenth and early seventeenth centuries, there are many similar records of civic officials prohibiting performances and then, to appease a powerful patron, paying the actors to take their skills elsewhere. As early as the 1570s, there is evidence that the London authorities, while mindful of the players' influential protectors, were energetically trying to drive the theater out of the city.

Why should what we now regard as one of the undisputed glories of the age have aroused so much hostility? One answer, curiously enough, is traffic: plays drew large audiences—the public theaters could accommodate thousands—and residents objected to the crowds, the noise, and the crush of carriages. Other, more serious concerns were public health and crime. It was thought that numerous diseases, including the dreaded bubonic plague, were spread by noxious odors, and the packed playhouses were obvious breeding grounds for infection. (Patrons often tried to protect themselves by sniffing nosegays or stuffing cloves into their nostrils.) The large crowds drew pickpockets, cutpurses, and other scoundrels. On more than one occasion, if Shakespeare's fellow actor Will Kemp may be believed, pickpockets, caught in the act during a performance, were tied to a post onstage "for all people to wonder at." The theater was, moreover, a well-known haunt of prostitutes and, it was alleged, a place where innocent

Syphilis victim in tub. Frontispiece to the play *Cornelianum Dolium* (1638), possibly written by Thomas Randolph. The tub inscription translates as "I sit on the throne of love, I suffer in the tub"; and the banner as "Farewell, O sexual pleasures and lusts."

maids were seduced and respectable matrons corrupted. It was darkly rumored that "chambers and secret places" adjoined the theater galleries, and in any case, taverns, disreputable inns, and whorehouses were close at hand.

There were other charges as well. Plays in the public, outdoor amphitheaters were performed in the afternoon and therefore drew people, especially the young, away from their work. They were schools of idleness, luring apprentices from their trades, law students from their studies, housewives from their kitchens, and potentially pious souls from the sober meditations to which they might otherwise devote themselves. Wasting their time and money on disreputable shows, citizens exposed themselves to sexual provocation and outright political sedition. Even when the content of plays was morally exemplary—and, of course, few plays were so gratifyingly high-minded—the theater itself, in the eyes of most mayors and aldermen, was inherently disorderly.

The attack on the stage by civic officials was echoed and intensified by many of the age's moralists and religious leaders, especially those associated with Puritanism. While English Protestants earlier in the sixteenth century had attempted to counter the Catholic mystery cycles and saints' plays by mounting their own doctrinally correct dramas, by the century's end a fairly widespread consensus, even among those mildly sympathetic toward the theater, held that the stage and the pulpit were in tension with one another. After 1591, a ban on Sunday performances was strictly enforced, and in 1606, Parliament passed an act imposing a hefty fine of £10 on any person who shall "in any stage-play, interlude, show, May-game, or pageant, jestingly or profanely speak or use the holy name of God, or of Christ Jesus, or of the Holy Ghost, or of the Trinity (which are not to be spoken but with fear and reverence)." If changes in the printed texts are a reliable indication, the players seem to have complied at least to some degree with the ruling. The Folio (1623) text of *Richard III,* for example, omits the Quarto's (1597) four uses of "zounds" (for "God's wounds"), along with a mention of "Christ's dear blood shed for our grievous sins"; "God's my judge" in *The Merchant of Venice* becomes "well I know"; "By Jesu" in *Henry V* becomes a very proper "I say"; and in all the plays, "God" is from time to time metamorphosed to "Jove."

But for some of the theater's more extreme critics, these modest expurgations were tiny bandages on a gaping wound. In his huge book *Histriomastix* (1633), William Prynne regurgitates a half-century of frenzied attacks on the "sinful, heathenish, lewd, ungodly Spectacles." In the eyes of Prynne and his fellow antitheatricalists, stage plays were part of a demonic tangle of obscene practices proliferating like a cancer in the body of society. It is "manifest to all men's judgments," he writes, that effeminate mixed dancing, dicing, stage-plays, lascivious pictures, wanton fashions, face-painting, health-drinking, long hair, love-locks, periwigs, women's curling, powdering and cutting of their hair, bonfires, New-year's gifts, May-games, amorous pastorals, lascivious effeminate music, excessive laughter, luxurious disorderly Christmas-keeping, mummeries . . . [are] wicked, unchristian pastimes.

Given the anxious emphasis on effeminacy, it is not surprising that denunciations of this kind obsessively focused on the use of boy actors to play the female parts. The enemies of the stage charged that theatrical transvestism excited illicit sexual desires, both heterosexual and homosexual.

Since cross-dressing violated a biblical prohibition (Deuteronomy 22:5), religious antitheatricalists attacked it as wicked regardless of its erotic charge; indeed, they often seemed to consider any act of impersonation as inherently wicked. In their view, the theater itself was Satan's domain. Thus a Cambridge scholar, John Greene, reports the sad fate of "a Christian woman" who went to the theater to see a play: "She entered in well and sound, but she returned and came forth possessed of the devil. Whereupon certain godly brethren demanded Satan how he durst be so bold, as to enter into her a Christian. Whereto he answered, that *he found her in his own house,* and therefore took possession of her as his own" (italics in original). When the "godly brethren" came to power in the mid-seventeenth century, with the overthrow of Charles I, they saw to it that the playhouses, shut down in 1642 at the onset of the Civil War, remained closed. Public theater did not resume until the restoration of the monarchy in 1660.

Faced with enemies among civic officials and religious leaders, Elizabethan and Jacobean playing companies relied on the protection of their powerful patrons. As the liveried servants of aristocrats or of the monarch, the players could refute the charge that they were mere vagabonds, and they claimed, as a convenient legal fiction, that their public performances were necessary rehearsals in anticipation of those occasions when they would be called upon to entertain their noble masters. But harassment by the mayor and aldermen of the City of London—an area roughly one mile square, defined by the old Roman walls—continued unabated, and the players were forced to build their theaters outside the immediate jurisdiction of these authorities, either in the suburbs or in the areas known as the "liberties." A liberty was a piece of land within the City of London itself that was not directly subject to the authority of the Lord Mayor. The most significant liberty from the point of view of the theater was the area near St. Paul's Cathedral called "the Blackfriars," where, until the dissolution of the monasteries in 1538, there had been a Dominican priory. It was here that in 1608 Shakespeare's company, then called the King's Men, took over an indoor playhouse in which they performed during the winter months, reserving the open-air Globe in the suburb of Southwark for the warmer months.

Censorship and Regulation

In addition to those authorities who campaigned to shut down the theater, there were others whose task was to oversee, regulate, and censor it. Given the outright hostility of the former, the latter may have seemed to the London players equivocal allies rather than enemies. After all, plays that passed the censor were at least licensed to be performed and hence conceded to have some limited legitimacy. In April 1559, at the very start of her reign, Queen Elizabeth drafted a proposal that for the first time envisaged a system for the prior review and regulation of plays throughout her kingdom:

The Queen's Majesty doth straightly forbid all manner interludes to be played either openly or privately, except the same be notified beforehand, and licensed within any city or town corporate, by the mayor or other chief officers of the same, and within any shire, by such as shall be lieutenants for the Queen's Majesty in the same shire, or by two of the Justices of Peace inhabiting within that part of the shire where any shall be played. . . . And for instruction to every of the said officers, her Majesty doth likewise charge every of them, as they will answer: that they permit none to be played wherein either matters of religion or of the governance of the estate of the commonweal shall be handled or treated upon, but by men of authority, learning and wisdom, nor to be handled before any audience, but of grave and discreet persons.

This proposal, which may not have been formally enacted, makes an important distinction between those who are entitled to address sensitive issues of religion and politics—authors "of authority, learning and wisdom" addressing audiences "of grave and discreet persons"—and those who are forbidden to do so.

The London public theater, with its playwrights who were the sons of glovers, shoemakers, and bricklayers and its audiences in which the privileged classes mingled with rowdy apprentices, masked women, and servants, was clearly not a place to which the government wished to grant freedom of expression. In 1581, the Master of the Revels, an official in the Lord Chamberlain's department whose role had hitherto been to provide entertainment at court, was given an expanded commission. Sir Edmund Tilney, the functionary who held the office, was authorized

to warn, command, and appoint in all places within this our Realm of England, as well within franchises and liberties as without, all and every player or players with their playmakers, either belonging to any nobleman or otherwise . . . to appear before him with all such plays, tragedies, comedies, or shows as they shall in readiness or mean to set forth, and them to recite before our said Servant or his sufficient deputy, whom we ordain, appoint, and authorize by these presents of all such shows, plays, players, and playmakers, together with their playing places, to order and reform, authorize and put down, as shall be thought meet or unmeet unto himself or his said deputy in that behalf.

What emerged from this commission was in effect a national system of regulation and censorship. One of its consequences was to restrict virtually all licensed theater to the handful of authorized London-based playing companies. These companies would have to submit their plays for official scrutiny, but in return they received implicit, and on occasion explicit, protection against the continued fierce opposition of the local authorities. Plays reviewed and allowed by the Master of the Revels had been deemed fit to be performed before the monarch; how could mere aldermen legitimately claim that such plays should be banned as seditious?

The key question, of course, is how carefully the Master of the Revels scrutinized the plays brought before him either to hear or, more often from the 1590s onward, to peruse. What was Tilney, who served in the office until his death in 1610, or his successor, Sir George Buc, who served from 1610 to 1621, looking for? What did they insist be cut before they would release what was known as the "allowed copy," the only version licensed for performance? Unfortunately, the office books of the Master of the Revels in Shakespeare's time have been lost; what survives is a handful of scripts on which Tilney, Buc, and their assistants jotted their instructions. These suggest that the readings were rather painstaking, with careful attention paid to possible religious, political, and diplomatic repercussions. References, direct or strongly implied, to any living Christian prince or any important English nobleman, gentleman, or government official were particularly sensitive and likely to be struck. Renaissance political life was highly personalized; people in power were exceptionally alert to insult and zealously patrolled the boundaries of their prestige and reputation.

Moreover, the censors knew that audiences and readers were quite adept at applying theatrical representations distanced in time and space to their own world. At a time of riots against resident foreigners, Tilney read *Sir Thomas More,* a play in which Shakespeare probably had a hand, and instructed the players to cut scenes that, though set in

1517, might have had an uncomfortable contemporary resonance. "Leave out the insurrection wholly," Tilney's note reads, "and the cause thereof and begin with Sir Thomas More at the Mayor's sessions, with a report afterwards of his good service done being sheriff of London upon a mutiny against the Lombards only by a short report and not otherwise at your own perils. E. Tilney." Of course, as Tilney knew perfectly well, most plays succeed precisely by mirroring, if only obliquely, their own times, but this particular reflection evidently seemed to him too dangerous or provocative.

The topical significance of a play depends in large measure on the particular moment in which it is performed, and on certain features of the performance—for example, a striking resemblance between one of the characters and a well-known public figure—that the script itself will not necessarily disclose to us at this great distance, or even disclosed to the censor at the time. Hence the Master of the Revels noted angrily of one play performed in 1632 that "there were diverse personated so naturally, both of lords and others of the court, that I took it ill." Hence too a play that was deemed allowable when it was first written and performed could return, like a nightmare, to disturb a different place and time. The most famous instance of such a return involves Shakespeare, for on the day before the Earl of Essex's attempted coup against Queen Elizabeth in 1601, someone paid the Lord Chamberlain's Men (Shakespeare's company at the time) forty shillings to revive their old play about the deposition and murder of Richard II. "I am Richard II," the Queen declared. "Know ye not that?" However distressed she was by this performance, the Queen significantly did not take out her wrath on the players: neither the playwright nor his company was punished, nor was the Master of the Revels criticized for allowing the play in the first place. It was Essex and several of his key supporters, including the man who commissioned the performance, who lost their heads.

Evidence suggests that the Master of the Revels often regarded himself not as the strict censor of the theater but as its friendly guardian, charged with averting catastrophes. He was a bureaucrat concerned less with subversive ideas per se than with potential trouble. That is, there is no record of a dramatist being called to account for his heterodox beliefs; rather, plays were censored if they risked offending influential people, including important foreign allies, or if they threatened to cause public disorder by exacerbating religious or other controversies. The distinction is not a stable one, but it helps to explain the intellectual boldness, power, and freedom of a censored theater in a society in which the perceived enemies of the state were treated mercilessly. Shakespeare could have Lear articulate a searing indictment of social injustice—

> Robes and furred gowns hide all. Plate sins with gold,
> And the strong lance of justice hurtless breaks.
> Arm it in rags, a pigmy's straw does pierce it.
> (4.5.159–61)

—and evidently neither the Master of the Revels nor the courtiers in their robes and furred gowns protested. But when the Spanish ambassador complained about Thomas Middleton's anti-Spanish allegory *A Game at Chess*, performed at the Globe in 1624, the whole theater was shut down, the players were arrested, and the King professed to be furious at his official for licensing the play in the first place and allowing it to be performed for nine consecutive days.

In addition to the system for the licensing of plays for performance, there was a system for the licensing of plays for publication. At the start of Shakespeare's career, such press licensing was the responsibility of the Court of High Commission, headed by the Archbishop of Canterbury and the Bishop of London. Their deputies, a panel of junior clerics, were supposed to review the manuscripts, granting licenses to those worthy of publication and rejecting any they deemed "heretical, seditious, or unseemly for Christian ears." Without a license, the Stationers' Company, the guild of the book trade, was not supposed to register a manuscript for publication. In practice, as various complaints and attempts to close loopholes attest, some playbooks were printed without a license. In 1607, the system was significantly revised when Sir George Buc began to license plays for the press. When Buc succeeded to the post of Master of the Revels in 1610, the powers to license plays for the stage and the page were vested in one man.

Theatrical Innovations

The theater continued to flourish under this system of regulation after Shakespeare's death in 1616; by the 1630s, as many as five playhouses were operating daily in London. When the theater reemerged in 1660 after the eighteen-year hiatus imposed by Puritan rule, it quickly resumed its cultural importance, but not without a number of significant changes. Major innovations in staging resulted principally from continental influences on the English artists who accompanied the court of Charles II into exile in France, where they supplied it with masques and other theatrical entertainments.

The institutional conditions and business practices of the two companies chartered by Charles after the Restoration in 1660 also differed from those of Shakespeare's theater. In place of the more collective practice of Shakespeare's company, the Restoration theaters were controlled by celebrated actor-managers who not only assigned themselves starring roles, in both comedy and tragedy, but also assumed sole responsibility for many business decisions, including the setting of their colleagues' salaries. At the same time, the power of the actor-manager, great as it was, was limited by the new importance of outside capital. No longer was the theater, with all of its properties from script to costumes, owned by the "sharers," that is, by those actors who held shares in the joint stock company. Instead, entrepreneurs would raise capital for increasingly fantastic sets and stage machinery that could cost as much as £3,000, an astronomical sum, for a single production. This investment in turn not only influenced the kinds of new plays written for the theater but helped to transform old plays that were revived, including Shakespeare's.

In his diary entry for August 24, 1661, Samuel Pepys notes that he has been "to the Opera, and there saw Hamlet, Prince of Denmark, done with scenes very well, but above all, Betterton did the prince's part beyond imagination." This is Thomas Betterton's first review, as it were, and it is typical of the enthusiasm he would inspire throughout his fifty-year career on the London stage. Pepys's brief and scattered remarks on the plays he voraciously attended in the 1660s are precious because they are among the few records from the period of concrete and immediate responses to theatrical performances. Modern readers might miss the significance of Pepys's phrase "done with scenes": this production of Hamlet was only the third play to use the movable sets first introduced to England by its producer, William Davenant. The central historical fact that makes the productions of this period so exciting is that public theater had been banned altogether for eighteen years until the Restoration of Charles II.

A brief discussion of theatrical developments in the Restoration period will enable us at least to glance longingly at a vast subject that lies outside the scope of this introduction: the rich performance history that extends from Shakespeare's time to our own, involving tens of thousands of productions and adaptations for theater, opera, dance, Broadway musicals, and of course films. The scale of this history is vast in space as well as time: already in the late sixteenth and early seventeenth centuries, troupes of English actors performed as far afield as Poland and Bohemia.

While producing masques at the court of Charles I, the poet William Davenant had become an expert on stage scenery, and when the theaters reopened, he set to work on converting an indoor tennis court into a new kind of theater. He designed a broad open platform like that of the Elizabethan stage, but at the back of this platform he added or expanded a space, framed by a proscenium arch, in which scenes could be displayed. These elaborately painted scenes could be moved on and off, using grooves on the floor. The perspective effect for a spectator of one central painted panel with two "wings" on either side was that of three sides of a room. This effect anticipated that of the familiar "picture frame" stage, developed fully in the nineteenth century, and began a subtle shift in theater away from the elaborate verbal descriptions that are so central to Shakespeare and toward the evocative visual poetry of the set designer's art.

Another convention of Shakespeare's stage, the use of boy actors for female roles, gave way to the more complete illusion of women playing women's parts. The King issued a decree in 1662 forcefully permitting, if not requiring, the use of actresses. The royal decree is couched in the language of social and moral reform: the introduction of actresses will require the "reformation" of scurrilous and profane passages in plays, and this in turn will help forestall some of the objections that shut the theaters down in 1642. In reality, male theater audiences, composed of a narrower range of courtiers and aristocrats than in Shakespeare's time, met this intended reform with the assumption that the new actresses were fair game sexually; most actresses (with the partial exception of those who married male members of their troupes) were regarded as, or actually became, whores. But despite the social stigma, and the fact that their salaries were predictably lower than those of their male counterparts, the stage saw some formidable female stars by the 1680s.

The first recorded appearance of an actress was that of a Desdemona in December 1660. Betterton's Ophelia in 1661 was Mary Saunderson (ca. 1637–1712), who became Mrs. Betterton a year later. The most famous Ophelia of the period was Susanna Mountfort, who appeared in that role for the first time at the age of fifteen in 1705. The performance by Mountfort that became legendary occurred in 1720, after a disappointment in love, or so it was said, had driven her mad. Hearing that *Hamlet* was being performed, Mountfort escaped from her keepers and reached the theater, where she concealed herself until the scene in which Ophelia enters in her state of insanity. At this point, Mountfort rushed onto the stage and, in the words of a contemporary, "was in truth Ophelia herself, to the amazement of the performers and the astonishment of the audience."

David Garrick and George Anne Bellamy in a celebrated production of *Romeo and Juliet* at Drury Lane, London. Engraving after a painting by Benjamin Wilson (1753).

That the character Ophelia became increasingly and decisively identified with the mad scene owes something to this occurrence, but it is also a consequence of the text used for Restoration performances of *Hamlet.* Having received the performance rights to a good number of Shakespeare's plays, Davenant altered them for the stage in the 1660s, and many of these acting versions remained in use for generations. In the case of *Hamlet,* neither Davenant nor his successors did what they so often did with other plays by Shakespeare, that is, alter the plot radically and interpolate other material. But many of the lines were cut or "improved." The cuts included most of Ophelia's sane speeches, such as her spirited retort to Laertes' moralizing; what remained made her part almost entirely an emblem of "female love melancholy."

Thomas Betterton (1635–1710), the prototype of the actor-manager, who would be the dominant figure in Shakespeare interpretation and in the English theater generally through the nineteenth century, made Hamlet his premier role. A contemporary who saw his last performance in the part (at the age of seventy-four, a rather old Prince of Denmark) wrote that to *read* Shakespeare's play was to encounter "dry, incoherent, & broken sentences," but that to see Betterton was to "prove" that the play was written "correctly." Spectators especially admired his reaction to the Ghost's appearance in the Queen's bedchamber: "his Countenance . . . thro' the violent and sudden Emotions of Amazement and Horror, turn[ed] instantly on the Sight of his fathers Spirit, as pale as his Neckcloath, when every Article of his Body seem's affected with a Tremor inexpressible." A piece of stage business in this scene, Betterton's upsetting his chair on the Ghost's entrance, became so thoroughly identified with the part that later productions were censured if the actor left it out. This business could very well have been handed down from Richard Burbage, the star of Shakespeare's original production, for Davenant, who had coached Betterton in the role, had known the performances of Joseph Taylor, who had succeeded Burbage in it. It is strangely gratifying to notice that Hamlets on stage and screen still occasionally upset their chairs.

Shakespeare's Life and Art

Playwrights, even hugely successful playwrights, were not ordinarily the objects of popular curiosity in early modern England. Many plays in this period were issued without the name of the author—there was no equivalent to our copyright system, and publishers were not required to specify on their title pages who wrote the texts they printed. Only occasionally were there significant exceptions, motivated by the pursuit of profit. Though by 1597 seven of Shakespeare's plays had been printed, the title pages did not identify him as the author. Beginning in 1598 Shakespeare's name, spelled in various ways, began to appear, and indeed several plays almost certainly not written by him were printed with his name. His name—Shakespeare, Shake-speare, Shakspeare, Shaxberd, Shakespere, and the like—had evidently begun to sell plays. During his lifetime more published plays were attributed to Shakespeare than to any other contemporary dramatist.

But this marketplace interest did not extend to the details of his life. It is both revealing and frustrating that the First Folio editors, John Heminges and Henry Condell—who knew Shakespeare well—were virtually silent about their friend's personal history. Though they included the author's picture, they did not bother to include his birth and death dates, his marital status, the names of his surviving children, his intellectual and social affiliations, his endearing or annoying quirks of character, let alone anything more psychologically revealing, such as the "table talk" carefully recorded by followers of Martin Luther. Shakespeare may have been a very private man, but, as he was dead when the edition was produced, it is unlikely to have been his own wishes that dictated the omissions. The editors evidently assumed that the potential buyers of the book—and this was an expensive commercial venture—would not be particularly interested in what we would now regard as essential biographical details.

Such presumed indifference is, in all likelihood, chiefly a reflection of Shakespeare's modest origins. He flew below the radar of ordinary Elizabethan and Jacobean social curiosity. In the wake of the death of the poet Sir Philip Sidney, Fulke Greville wrote a fascinating biography of his friend, but Sidney was a dashing aristocrat, linked by birth and marriage to the great families of the realm, and he died tragically of a wound he received on the battlefield. Writers of a less exalted station did not excite the same interest, unless, like Ben Jonson, they cultivated an extravagant public persona, or, like another of Shakespeare's contemporaries, Christopher Marlowe, they ran afoul of the authorities and got themselves murdered. The fact that there are no police reports, Privy Council orders, indictments, or postmortem inquests about Shakespeare, as there are about Marlowe, tells us something significant about Shakespeare's life—he possessed a gift for staying out of trouble—but it is not the kind of detail on which biographers thrive.

Yet Elizabethan England was a record-keeping society, and centuries of archival labor have turned up a substantial number of traces of its greatest playwright and his family. By themselves the traces would have relatively little interest, but in the light of Shakespeare's plays and poems, they have come to seem like precious relics and manage to achieve a considerable resonance.

Shakespeare's Family

William Shakespeare's grandfather, Richard, farmed land by the village of Snitterfield, near the small, pleasant market town of Stratford-upon-Avon, about ninety-six miles northwest of London. The playwright's father, John, moved in the mid-sixteenth century to Stratford, where he became a successful glover, landowner, moneylender, and dealer in wool and other agricultural goods. In or about 1557, he married Mary Arden, the daughter of a prosperous and well-connected farmer from the same area, Robert Arden of Wilmcote.

John Shakespeare was evidently highly esteemed by his fellow townspeople, for he held a series of important posts in local government. In 1556, he was appointed ale taster, an office reserved for "able persons and discreet," in 1558 was sworn in as a constable, and in 1561 was elected as one of the town's fourteen burgesses. As burgess, John served as one of the two chamberlains, responsible for administering borough property and revenues. In 1567, he was elected bailiff, Stratford's highest elective office and the equivalent of mayor. Though John Shakespeare signed all official documents with a cross or other sign, it is likely, though not certain, that he knew how to read and write. Mary, who also signed documents only with her mark, is less likely to have been literate.

According to the parish registers, which recorded baptisms and burials, the Shakespeares had eight children, four daughters and four sons, beginning with a daughter, Joan, born in 1558. A second daughter, Margaret, was born in December 1562 and died a few months later. William Shakespeare ("Gulielmus, filius Johannes Shakespeare"), their first son, was baptized on April 26, 1564. Since there was usually a few days' lapse between birth and baptism, it is conventional to celebrate Shakespeare's birthday on April 23, which happens to coincide with the Feast of St. George, England's patron saint, and with the day of Shakespeare's death fifty-two years later.

William Shakespeare had three younger brothers, Gilbert, Richard, and Edmund, and two younger sisters, Joan and Anne. (It was often the custom to recycle a name, so the first-born Joan must have died before the birth in 1569 of another daughter christened Joan, the only one of the girls to survive childhood.) Gilbert, who died in his forty-fifth year in 1612, is described in legal records as a Stratford haberdasher; Edmund followed William to London and became a professional actor, though evidently of no

Southeast Prospect of Stratford-upon-Avon, 1746. From *Gentleman's Magazine* (December 1792).

particular repute. He was only twenty-eight when he died in 1607 and was given an expensive funeral, perhaps paid for by his successful older brother.

At the high point of his public career, John Shakespeare, the father of this substantial family, applied to the Herald's College for a coat of arms, which would have marked his (and his family's) elevation from the ranks of substantial middle-class citizenry to that of the gentry. But the application went nowhere, for soon after he initiated what would have been a costly petitioning process, John apparently fell on hard times. The decline must have begun when William was still living at home, a boy of twelve or thirteen. From 1576 onward, John Shakespeare stopped attending council meetings. He became caught up in costly lawsuits, started mortgaging his land, and incurred substantial debts. In 1586, he was finally replaced on the council; in 1592, he was one of nine Stratford men listed as absenting themselves from church out of fear of being arrested for debt.

The reason for the reversal in John Shakespeare's fortunes is unknown. Some have speculated that it may have stemmed from adherence to Catholicism, since those who remained loyal to the old faith were subject to increasingly vigorous and costly discrimination. But if John Shakespeare was a Catholic, as seems possible, it would not necessarily explain his decline, since other Catholics (and Puritans) in Elizabethan Stratford and elsewhere managed to hold on to their offices. In any case, his fall from prosperity and local power, whatever its cause, was not absolute. In 1601, the last year of his life, his name was included among those qualified to speak on behalf of Stratford's rights. And he was by that time entitled to bear a coat of arms, for in 1596, some twenty years after the application to the Herald's office had been initiated, it was successfully renewed. There is no record of who paid for the bureaucratic procedures that made the grant possible, but it is likely to have been John's oldest son, William, by that time a highly successful London playwright. By elevating his father, he would have made himself a gentleman as well.

Education

Stratford was a small provincial town, but it had long been the site of an excellent free school, originally established by the church in the thirteenth century. The main purpose of such schools in the Middle Ages had been to train prospective clerics; since many aristocrats could neither read nor write, literacy by itself conferred no special distinction and was not routinely viewed as desirable. But the situation began to change markedly in the sixteenth century. Protestantism placed a far greater emphasis upon lay literacy: for the sake of salvation, it was crucially important to be intimately acquainted with the Holy Book, and printing made that book readily available. Schools became less strictly bound up with training for the church and more linked to the general acquisition of "literature," in the sense both of literacy and of cultural knowledge. In keeping with this new emphasis on reading and with humanist educational reform, the school was reorganized during the reign of Edward VI (1547–53). School records from the period have not survived, but it is almost certain that William Shakespeare attended the King's New School, as it was renamed in Edward's honor.

Scholars have painstakingly reconstructed the curriculum of schools of this kind and have even turned up the names and rather impressive credentials of the schoolmasters who taught at the King's New School when Shakespeare was of school age. (The principal teacher at that time was Thomas Jenkins, an Oxford graduate, who received £20 a year and a rent-free house.) A child's education in Elizabethan England began at age four or five with two years at what was called the "petty school," attached to the main grammar school. The little scholars carried a "hornbook," a sheet of paper or parchment framed in wood and covered, for protection, with a transparent layer of horn. On the paper was written the alphabet and the Lord's Prayer, which were reproduced as well in the slightly more advanced *ABC with the Catechism,* a combination primer and rudimentary religious guide.

After students demonstrated some ability to read, education for most girls came to a halt, but boys could go on, at about age seven, to the grammar school. Shakespeare's images of the experience are not particularly cheerful. In his famous account of the Seven Ages of Man, Jaques in *As You Like It* describes

> the whining schoolboy with his satchel
> And shining morning face, creeping like snail
> Unwillingly to school.
>
> (2.7.145–47)

The schoolboy would have crept quite early: the day began at 6:00 A.M. in summer and 7:00 A.M. in winter and continued until 5:00 P.M., with very few breaks or holidays.

At the core of the curriculum was the study of Latin, the mastery of which was in effect a prolonged male puberty rite involving much discipline and pain as well as pleasure. A late sixteenth-century Dutchman (whose name fittingly was Batty)

The Cholmondeley Ladies (ca. 1600–1610). Artist unknown. This striking image brings to mind Shakespeare's fascination with twinship, both identical (notably in *The Comedy of Errors*) and fraternal (in *Twelfth Night*).

proposed that God had created the human buttocks so that they could be severely beaten without risking permanent injury. Such thoughts dominated the pedagogy of the age, so that even an able young scholar, as we might imagine Shakespeare to have been, could scarcely have escaped recurrent flogging.

Shakespeare evidently reaped some rewards for the miseries he probably endured: his works are laced with echoes of many of the great Latin texts taught in grammar schools. One of his earliest comedies, *The Comedy of Errors,* is a brilliant variation on a theme by the Roman playwright Plautus, whom Elizabethan schoolchildren often performed as well as read; and one of his earliest tragedies, *Titus Andronicus,* is heavily indebted to Seneca. These are among the most visible of the classical influences that are often more subtly and pervasively interfused in Shakespeare's works. He seems to have had a particular fondness for *Aesop's Fables,* Apuleius's *Golden Ass,* and above all Ovid's *Metamorphoses.* His learned contemporary Ben Jonson remarked that Shakespeare had "small Latin and less Greek," but from this distance what is striking is not the limits of Shakespeare's learning but rather the unpretentious ease, intelligence, and gusto with which he draws upon what he must have first encountered as laborious study.

Traces of a Life

In November 1582, William Shakespeare, at the age of eighteen, married twenty-six-year-old Anne Hathaway, who came from the village of Shottery near Stratford. Their first daughter, Susanna, was baptized six months later. This circumstance, along with the fact that Anne was eight years Will's senior, has given rise to a mountain of speculation, all the more lurid precisely because there is no further evidence. Shakespeare depicts in several plays situations in which marriage is precipitated by a pregnancy, but he also registers, in *Measure for Measure* (1.2.133ff), the Elizabethan belief that a "true contract" of marriage could be legitimately made and then consummated simply by the mutual vows of the couple in the presence of witnesses.

On February 2, 1585, the twins Hamnet and Judith Shakespeare were baptized in Stratford. Hamnet died at the age of eleven, when his father was already living for much of the year in London as a successful playwright. These are Shakespeare's only known children, though in the mid-seventeenth century the playwright and impresario William Davenant hinted that he was Shakespeare's bastard son. Since people did not ordinarily advertise their illegitimacy, the claim, though impossible to verify, at least suggests the unusual strength of Shakespeare's posthumous reputation.

William Shakespeare's father, John, died in 1601; his mother died seven years later. They would have had the satisfaction of witnessing their eldest son's prosperity, and not only from a distance, for in 1597 William purchased New Place, the second-largest house in Stratford. In 1607, the playwright's daughter Susanna married a successful and well-known physician, John Hall. The next year, the Halls had a daughter, Elizabeth, Shakespeare's first grandchild. In 1616, the year of Shakespeare's death, his daughter Judith married a vintner, Thomas Quiney, with whom she had three children. Shakespeare's widow, Anne, died in 1623, at the age of sixty-seven. His first-born, Susanna, died at the age of sixty-six in 1649, the year that King Charles I was beheaded by the parliamentary army. Judith lived through Cromwell's Protectorate and on to the Restoration of the monarchy; she died in February 1662, at the age of seventy-seven. By the end of the century, the line of Shakespeare's direct heirs was extinct.

Patient digging in the archives has turned up other traces of Shakespeare's life as a family man and a man of means: assessments, small fines, real estate deeds, minor actions in court to collect debts. In addition to his fine Stratford house and a large garden and cottage facing it, Shakespeare bought substantial parcels of land in the vicinity. When in *The Tempest* the wedding celebration conjures up a vision of "barns and garners never empty," Shakespeare could have been glancing at what the legal documents record as his own "tithes of corn, grain, blade, and hay" in the fields near

Stratford. At some point after 1610, Shakespeare seems to have begun to shift his attention from the London stage to his Stratford properties, though the term "retirement" implies a more decisive and definitive break than appears to have been the case. By 1613, when the Globe Theater burned down during a performance of Shakespeare and Fletcher's *Henry VIII*, Shakespeare was probably residing for the most part in Stratford, but he retained his financial interest in the rebuilt playhouse and probably continued to have some links to his theatrical colleagues. Still, by this point, his career as a playwright was substantially over. Legal documents from his last years show him concerned to protect his real estate interests in Stratford.

A half-century after Shakespeare's death, a Stratford vicar and physician, John Ward, noted in his diary that Shakespeare and his fellow poets Michael Drayton and Ben Jonson "had a merry meeting, and it seems drank too hard, for Shakespeare died of a fever there contracted." It is not inconceivable that Shakespeare's last illness was somehow linked, if only coincidentally, to the festivities on the occasion of the wedding in February 1616 of his daughter Judith (who was still alive when Ward made his diary entry). In any case, on March 25, 1616, Shakespeare revised his will, and on April 23 he died. Two days later, he was buried in the chancel of Holy Trinity Church beneath a stone bearing an epitaph he is said to have devised:

> Good friend for Jesus' sake forbear,
> To dig the dust enclosed here:
> Blest be the man that spares these stones,
> And curst be he that moves my bones.

The verses are hardly among Shakespeare's finest, but they seem to have been effective: though bones were routinely dug up to make room for others—a fate imagined with unforgettable intensity in the graveyard scene in *Hamlet*—his own remains were undisturbed. Like other vestiges of sixteenth- and early seventeenth-century Stratford, Shakespeare's grave has for centuries now been the object of a tourist industry that borders on a religious cult.

Shakespeare's will has been examined with an intensity befitting this cult; every provision and formulaic phrase, no matter how minor or conventional, has borne a heavy weight of interpretation, none more so than the sole bequest to his wife, Anne, of "my second-best bed." Scholars have pointed out that Anne would in any case have been provided for by custom and that the terms are not necessarily a deliberate slight, but the absence of the customary words "my loving wife" or "my well-beloved wife" is difficult to ignore.

Portrait of the Playwright as Young Provincial

The great problem with the surviving traces of Shakespeare's life is not that they are few but that they are unspectacular. Christopher Marlowe was a double or triple agent, accused of brawling, sodomy, and atheism. Ben Jonson, who somehow clambered up from bricklayer's apprentice to classical scholar, served in the army in Flanders, killed a fellow actor in a duel, converted to Catholicism in prison in 1598, and returned to the Church of England in 1610. Provincial real estate investments and the second-best bed cannot compete with such adventurous lives. Indeed, the relative ordinariness of Shakespeare's social background and life has contributed to a persistent current of speculation that the glover's son from Stratford-upon-Avon was not in fact the author of the plays attributed to him.

The anti-Stratfordians, as those who deny Shakespeare's authorship are sometimes called, almost always propose as the real author someone who came from a higher social class and received a more prestigious education. Francis Bacon, the Earl of Oxford, the Earl of Southampton, even Queen Elizabeth, have been advanced, among many others, as glamorous candidates for the role of clandestine playwright. Several famous people, including Mark Twain and Sigmund Freud, have espoused these theories, though very few scholars have joined them. Since Shakespeare was quite well known in his own time as the author of the plays that bear his name, there would need to have been an extraordinary conspiracy to conceal the identity of the real master who (the theory goes) disdained to appear in the vulgarity of print or on the public stage. Like many conspiracy theories, the extreme implausibility of this one seems only to increase the fervent conviction of its advocates.

To the charge that a middle-class author from a small town could not have imagined the lives of kings and nobles, one can respond by citing the exceptional qualities that Ben Jonson praised in Shakespeare: "excellent *Phantsie*; brave notions, and gentle expressions." Even in ordinary mortals, the human imagination is a strange faculty; in Shakespeare, it seems to have been uncannily powerful, working its mysterious, transforming effects on everything it touched. His imagination was intensely engaged by what he found in books. He seems throughout his life to have been an intense, voracious reader, and it is fascinating to witness his creative encounters with Raphael Holinshed's *Chronicles of England, Scotland, and Ireland*, Plutarch's *Lives of the Noble Grecians and Romans*, Ovid's *Metamorphoses*, Montaigne's *Essays*, and the Bible, to name only some of his favorite books. But books were clearly not the only objects of Shakespeare's attention; like most artists, he drew upon the whole range of his life experiences.

To those accustomed to instant telecommunication, photography, film, and digital media, that range might seem narrowly circumscribed, but in fact something like the opposite was the case. Though we inhabit a vast virtual world, our experiential world is deliberately reduced, carefully screened, and tightly delimited. Most of us are born, sicken, and die in special institutions set apart from everyday life. We have invented means to quiet toothaches, heal wounds, and put us to sleep through painful surgeries. Those we condemn as criminals are penned up and punished behind high, windowless walls. We scarcely ever see our political representatives in person, and when we vote, we enter small, private booths. We take our entertainments most often in the dark or in the privacy of our homes, and those homes are generally walled off from the homes of others. Our meat bears little or no visible relation to the animal from which it comes; the slaughtering and butchering is discretely done out of sight. Our wastes disappear down drains; our rubbish is collected and disposed of; we live and move about in a well-lit, heavily policed, massively controlled environment.

None of this was the case in Shakespeare's world. Virtually anyone who grew up in the late sixteenth century would have had occasion to hear the sharp cries of childbirth and the groans of dying. There were a small number of hospitals and lazar houses (for lepers), but for the most part the sick, the maimed, and the mad mingled with everyone else in the crowded, muddy streets. The sufferings attendant on ordinary life were inescapable, and very few palliatives were available. (There were limits to the oblivion that the strongest ale could bring.) Malefactors, as we have seen, were most often punished in public, often hideously. There was nothing remotely equivalent to our taste for privacy. Servants were ubiquitous, and it was a rare person who had the privilege or perhaps the inclination to escape into solitude. Guests at an inn would often find themselves sharing a room or even a bed with a complete stranger. Smells and tastes—in a world without flush toilets and refrigeration—were intense, and so too were colors, for Elizabethans of any means favored vividly dyed and elaborately worked clothing. There were no streetlights, and the days faded into nights that were pitch dark and often dangerous.

Nothing here is particular to Shakespeare's biography; these were the conditions in this period of everyone's life. And what would astonish or appall us, if we were suddenly carried back into the past, would simply have been taken for granted as the way things are by most of those born into that world. But Shakespeare seems precisely not to have taken anything for granted: he seems to have carefully noted everything, from the carter who urinates in the chimney and complains of his fleabites (*1 Henry IV* 2.1.19–20) to the mad beggar who sticks sprigs of rosemary into his numbed arms (*King Lear* 2.2.177–79) to the merchant who keeps his money locked up in a desk that is covered with a Turkish tapestry (*Comedy of Errors* 4.1.103–04).

Shakespeare may have begun this practice of noting quite early in his life. When he was a very young boy—not quite four years old—his father was chosen by the Stratford council as the town bailiff. The bailiff of an Elizabethan town was a significant position; he served the borough as a justice of the peace and performed a variety of other functions, including coroner and clerk of the market. He dealt routinely with an unusually wide spectrum of local society, for on the one hand he distributed alms and on the other he negotiated with the lord of the manor. More to the point, for our purposes, the office was attended with considerable ceremony. The bailiff and his deputy were entitled to appear in public in furred gowns, attended by sergeants bearing maces before them. On Rogation Days (three days of prayer for the harvest, before Ascension Day), they would solemnly pace out the parish boundaries, and they would similarly walk in processions on market and fair days. On Sundays, the sergeants would accompany the bailiff to church, where he would sit with his wife in a front pew, and he would have a comparable seat of honor at sermons in the Guild Chapel. On special occasions, there would also be plays in the Guildhall, at which the bailiff would be seated in the front row.

On a precocious child (or even, for that matter, on an ordinary child), this ceremony must have had a significant impact. It would have conveyed irresistibly the power of clothes (the ceremonial gown of office) and of symbols (the mace) to transform identity as if by magic. It would have invested the official in question—Shakespeare's own father—with immense power, distinction, and importance, awakening what we may call a lifelong dream of high station. And perhaps, pulling slightly against this dream, it would have provoked an odd feeling that the father's clothes do not fit, a perception that the office is not the same as the man, and an intimate, firsthand knowledge that when the robes are put off, their wearer is inevitably glimpsed in a far different, less exalted light.

The honoring of the bailiff was only one of the political rituals that Shakespeare could easily have witnessed as a young man growing up in the provinces. As we have seen, Queen Elizabeth was fond of going on what were known as "progresses," triumphant ceremonial journeys around her kingdom. In 1574—when Shakespeare was ten years old—one of these progresses took her to Warwick, near Stratford-upon-Avon. The crowds that gathered to watch were participating in an elaborate celebration of charismatic power: the courtiers in their gorgeous clothes, the nervous local officials bedecked in velvets and silks, and at the center, carried in a special litter like a bejeweled icon, the virgin queen. The Queen cultivated this charisma, taking over in effect some of the iconography associated with the worship of the Virgin Mary, but she was also paradoxically fond of calling attention to the fact that she was after all quite human. For example, on this occasion at Warwick, after the trembling Recorder, presumably a local civil official of high standing, had made his official welcoming speech, Elizabeth offered her hand to him to be kissed: "Come hither, little Recorder," she said. "It was told me that you would be afraid to look upon me or to speak boldly; but you were not so afraid of me as I was of you; and I now thank you for putting me in mind of my duty." Of course, the charm of this royal "confession" of nervousness depends on its manifest implausibility: it is, in effect, a theatrical performance of humility by someone with immense confidence in her own histrionic power.

A royal progress was not the only form of spectacular political activity that Shakespeare might well have seen in the 1570s; it is still more likely that he would have witnessed parliamentary elections, particularly since his father was qualified to vote. In 1571, 1572, 1575, and 1578, there were shire elections conducted in Warwick, elections that would certainly have attracted well over a thousand voters. These were often memorable events: large crowds came together; there was usually heavy drinking and carnivalesque festivity; and at the same time, there was enacted, in a very different register from that of the monarchy, a ritual of empowerment. The people, those entitled to vote by virtue of meeting the property and residence requirements, chose their own representatives by giving their votes—their voices—to candidates for office. Here, legislative sovereignty was conferred not by God but by the consent of the community, a consent marked by shouts and applause.

Recent cultural historians have been so fascinated by the evident links between the spectacles of the absolutist monarchy and the theater that they have largely ignored the significance of this alternative public arena, one that generated intense excitement throughout the country. A child who was a spectator at a parliamentary election in the 1570s might well have found the occasion enormously compelling. It is striking, in any case, how often the adult Shakespeare returns to scenes of mass consent, and striking too how much the theater depends on assembling crowds and soliciting popular acclamation.

The most frequent occasions for the gathering together of crowds were neither elections nor theatrical performances, but rather the religious services that all Elizabethans were expected to attend at least once a week. (Recurrent absences were noted and investigated.) Protestant spokesmen routinely condemned the Catholic Mass as a form of perverse theatrical performance: a "play of sacred miracles," a "wonderful pageant," a "devil Theater." The Catholic Mass, as it had been celebrated for centuries, was outlawed, and with it a range of other Catholic rites. On occasion those rites were still practiced in secret, at considerable danger, and it is possible that Shakespeare could have been among those present. He was certainly present at the services of the English Church, whose ceremonies led by berobed priests, guided by the resonant prose of the Book of Common Prayer, and held in settings whose magnificence continues to astonish us, had their own intense histrionic power.

The young Shakespeare, whether true believer or skeptic or something in between ("So have I heard, and do in part believe it," says Hamlet's friend Horatio [1.1.164]), might have carried away from such ceremonies several impressions: an intimation of immense, cosmic forces that may impinge upon human life; a heightened understanding of the power of language to form and exalt the spirit; an awareness of intense, even murderous competition and rivalry among competing rituals; and perhaps a sense of the longing to believe that may be awakened and shaped in large crowds.

I have placed Shakespeare himself in each of these scenes—which together sketch the root conditions of the Elizabethan theater—because some people have found it difficult to conceive how this one man, with his provincial origins and his restricted range of experience, could have so rapidly and completely mastered the central imaginative themes of his times. Moreover, it is sometimes difficult to grasp how seeming abstractions such as market society, monarchical state, and theological doctrine were actually experienced directly by distinct individuals. Shakespeare's plays were social and collective events, but they also bore the stamp of a particular artist, one endowed with a remarkable capacity to craft lifelike illusions, a daring willingness to articulate an original vision, and a loving command, at once precise and generous, of language. These plays are stitched together from shared cultural experiences, inherited dramatic devices, and the pungent vernacular of the day, but we should not lose sight of the extent to which they articulate an intensely personal vision, a bold shaping of the available materials. Four centuries of feverish biographical speculation, much of it foolish, bear witness to a basic intuition: the richness of these plays, their inexhaustible openness, is the consequence not only of the auspicious collective conditions of the culture but also of someone's exceptional skill, inventiveness, and courage at taking those conditions and making of them something rich and strange.

The Theater of the Nation

What precisely were the collective conditions disclosed by the spectacles that Shakespeare would likely have witnessed? First, the growth of Stratford-upon-Avon, the bustling market town of which John Shakespeare was bailiff, is a small version of a momentous sixteenth-century development that made Shakespeare's career possible: the making of an urban "public." That development obviously depended on adequate numbers; the period experienced a rapid and still unexplained growth in population. With it came an expansion and elaboration of market relations: markets became less periodic, more continuous, and more abstract—centered, that is, not on the familiar materiality of goods but on the liquidity of capital and goods. In practical terms, this meant that it was possible to conceive of the theater not only as festive entertainment for special events—Lord Mayor's pageants, visiting princes, seasonal festivals, and the like—but as a permanent, year-round business venture. The venture relied on revenues from admission—it was an innovation of this period to have money advanced in the expectation of pleasure rather than offered to servants afterward as a reward—and counted on habitual playgoing, with a concomitant demand for new plays from competing theater companies: "But that's all one, our play is done," sings the Clown at the end of *Twelfth Night* and adds a glance toward the next afternoon's proceeds: "And we'll strive to please you every day" (5.1.393–94).

Second, the royal progress is an instance of what the anthropologist Clifford Geertz has called the Theater State, a state that manifests its power and meaning in exemplary public performances. Professional companies of players, like the one Shakespeare belonged to, understood well that they existed in relation to this Theater State and would, if they were fortunate, be called upon to serve it. Unlike Ben Jonson, Shakespeare did not, as far as we know, write royal entertainments on commission, but his plays were frequently performed before Queen Elizabeth and then before King James and Queen Anne, along with their courtiers and privileged guests. There are many fascinating glimpses of these performances, including a letter from Walter Cope to Robert Cecil, early in James's reign. "Burbage is come," Cope writes, referring to the leading actor of Shakespeare's company, "and says there is no new play that the Queen hath not seen, but they have revived an old one, called *Love's Labor's Lost*, which for wit and mirth he says will please her exceedingly. And this is appointed to be played tomorrow night at my Lord of Southampton's." Not only would such theatrical performances have given great pleasure—evidently, the Queen had already exhausted the company's new offerings—but they conferred prestige upon those who commanded them and those in whose honor they were mounted.

Monarchical power in the period was deeply allied to spectacular manifestations of the ruler's glory and disciplinary authority. The symbology of power depended on regal magnificence, reward, punishment, and pardon, all of which were heavily theatricalized. Indeed, the conspicuous public display does not simply serve the interests of power; on many occasions in the period, power seemed to exist in order to make pageantry possible, as if the nation's identity were only fully realized in theatrical performance. It would be easy to exaggerate this perception: the subjects of Queen Elizabeth and King James were acutely aware of the distinction between shadow and substance. But they were fascinated by the political magic through which shadows could be taken for substantial realities, and the ruling elite was largely complicit in the formation and celebration of a charismatic absolutism. At the same time, the claims of the monarch who professes herself or himself to be not the representative of the nation but its embodiment were set against the counterclaims of the House of Commons. And this institution too, as we have glimpsed, had its own theatrical rituals, centered on the crowd whose shouts of approval, in heavily stage-managed elections, chose the individuals who would stand for the polity and participate in deliberations held in a hall whose resemblance to a theater did not escape contemporary notice.

Third, in outlawing the Catholic Mass and banning the medieval mystery plays, along with pilgrimages and other rituals associated with holy shrines and sacred images, English Protestant authorities hoped to hold a monopoly on religious observances. But they inevitably left some people, perhaps substantial numbers of them, mourning what they had lost. Playing companies could satisfy at least some of the popular longings and appropriate aspects of the social energy no longer allowed a theological outlet. That is, official attacks on certain Catholic practices made it more possible for the public theater to appropriate and exploit their allure. Hence, for example, the plays that celebrated the solemn miracle of the Catholic Mass were banned, along with the most elaborate church vestments, but in *The Winter's Tale* Dion can speak in awe of what he witnessed at Apollo's temple:

> I shall report,
> For most it caught me, the celestial habits—
> Methinks I so should term them—and the reverence
> Of the grave wearers. Oh, the sacrifice!
> How ceremonious, solemn, and unearthly
> It was i'th' off'ring!
>
> (3.1.3–8)

And at the play's end, the statue of the innocent mother breathes, comes to life, and embraces her child.

The theater in Shakespeare's time, then, is intimately bound up with all three crucial cultural formations: market society, the Theater State, and the church. But it is important to note that the institution is not *identified* with any of them. The theater may be a market phenomenon, but it is repeatedly and bitterly attacked as the enemy of diligent, sober, productive economic activity. Civic authorities generally regarded the theater as a pestilential nuisance, a parasite on the body of the commonwealth, a temptation to students, apprentices, housewives, even respectable merchants to leave their serious business and lapse into idleness and waste. That waste, it might be argued, could be partially recuperated if it went for the glorification of a guild or the entertainment of an important dignitary, but the only group regularly profiting from the theater were the players and their disreputable associates.

For his part, Shakespeare made a handsome profit from the commodification of theatrical entertainment, but he seems never to have written "city comedy"—plays set in London and more or less explicitly concerned with market relations—and his characters express deep reservations about the power of money and commerce: "That smooth-faced gentleman, tickling commodity," Philip the Bastard observes in *King John*, "wins of all, / Of kings, of beggars, old men, young men, maids" (2.1.569–73). We could argue that the smooth-faced gentleman is none other than Shakespeare himself, for his drama famously mingles kings and clowns, princesses and panderers. But the mingling is set against a romantic current of social conservatism: in *Twelfth Night*, the aristocratic heiress Olivia falls in love with someone who appears far beneath her in wealth and social station, but it is revealed that he (and his sister Viola) are of noble blood; in *The Winter's Tale*, Leontes' daughter Perdita is raised as a shepherdess, but her noble nature shines through her humble upbringing, and she marries the Prince of Bohemia; the strange island maiden with whom Ferdinand, son of the King of Naples, falls madly in love in *The Tempest* turns out to be the daughter of the rightful Duke of Milan. Shakespeare pushes against this conservative logic in *All's Well That Ends Well*, but the noble young Bertram violently resists the unequal match thrust upon him by the King, and the play's mood is notoriously uneasy.

Similarly, Shakespeare's theater may have been patronized and protected by the monarchy—after 1603, his company received a royal patent and was known as the King's Men—but the two institutions were by no means identical in their interests or their ethos. To be sure, *Richard III* and *Macbeth* incorporate aspects of royal propaganda, but given the realities of censorship, Shakespeare's plays, and the period's drama as a whole, are surprisingly independent and complex in their political vision. There is, in any case, a certain inherent tension between kings and player kings: Elizabeth and James may both have likened themselves to actors onstage, but they were loath to admit their dependence on the applause and money, freely given or freely withheld, of the audience. The charismatic monarch insists that the sacredness of authority resides in the body of the ruler, not in a costume that may be worn and then discarded by an actor. Kings are not *representations* of power—or do not admit that they are—but claim to be the thing itself. The government institution that was actually based on the idea of representation, Parliament, had theatrical elements, as we have seen, but it significantly excluded any audience from its deliberations. And Shakespeare's oblique portraits of parliamentary representatives, the ancient Roman tribunes Sicinius Velutus and Junius Brutus in *Coriolanus*, are anything but flattering.

Finally, the theater drew significant energy from the liturgy and rituals of the late medieval church, but as Shakespeare's contemporaries widely remarked, the playhouse and the church were scarcely natural allies. Not only did the theater represent a potential competitor to worship services, and not only did ministers rail against prostitution and other vices associated with playgoing, but theatrical representation itself, even when ostensibly pious, seemed to many to empty out whatever it presented, turning substance into mere show. The theater could and did use the period's deep currents of religious feeling, but it had to do so carefully and with an awareness of conflicting interests.

Shakespeare Comes to London

How did Shakespeare decide to turn his prodigious talents to the stage? When did he make his way to London? How did he get his start? Concerning these and similar questions we have a mountain of speculation but no secure answers. There is not a single surviving record of Shakespeare's existence from 1585, when his twins were baptized in Stratford church, until 1592, when a rival London playwright made an envious remark about him. In the late seventeenth century, the delightfully eccentric collector of gossip John Aubrey was informed that prior to moving to London the young Shakespeare had been a schoolteacher in the country. Aubrey also recorded a story that Shakespeare had been a rather unusual apprentice butcher: "When he killed a calf, he would do it in a high style, and make a speech."

These and other legends, including one that has Shakespeare whipped for poaching game, fill the void until the unmistakable reference in Robert Greene's *Groatsworth of Wit Bought with a Million of Repentance* (1592). An inspired hack writer with a university education, a penchant for self-dramatization, a taste for wild living, and a strong streak of resentment, Greene, in his early thirties, was dying in poverty when he penned his last farewell, piously urging his fellow dramatists Christopher Marlowe, Thomas Nashe, and George Peele to abandon the wicked stage before they were brought low, as he had been, by a new arrival: "For there is an upstart crow, beautified with our feathers, that with his 'Tiger's heart wrapped in player's hide' supposes he is as well able to bombast out a blank verse as the best of you, and, being an absolute *Johannes Factotum*, is in his own conceit the only Shake-scene in a country." If "Shake-scene" is not enough to identify the object of his attack, Greene parodies a line from Shakespeare's early play *3 Henry VI*: "O tiger's heart wrapped in a woman's hide" (1.4.137). Greene is accusing Shakespeare of being an upstart, a plagiarist, an egomaniacal jack-of-all-trades—and, above all perhaps, a popular success.

By 1592, then, Shakespeare had already arrived on the highly competitive London theatrical scene. He was successful enough to be attacked by Greene and, a few months later, defended by Henry Chettle, another hack writer who had seen Greene's manuscript through the press (or, some scholars speculate, had written the attack himself and passed it off as the dying Greene's). Chettle expresses his regret that he did not suppress Greene's diatribe and spare Shakespeare "because myself have seen his demeanor no less civil than he excellent in the quality he professes." Besides, Chettle adds, "divers of worship have reported his uprightness of dealing, which argues his honesty and his facetious [polished] grace in writing that approves his art." "Divers of worship": not only was Shakespeare established as an accomplished writer and actor, but he evidently had aroused the attention and the approbation of several socially prominent people. In Elizabethan England, aristocratic patronage, with the money, protection, and prestige it alone could provide, was probably a professional writer's most important asset.

This patronage, or at least Shakespeare's quest for it, is most visible in the dedications in 1593 and 1594 of his narrative poems *Venus and Adonis* and *The Rape of Lucrece* to the young nobleman Henry Wriothesley, Earl of Southampton. It may be glimpsed as well, perhaps, in the sonnets, with their extraordinary adoration of the fair youth, though the identity of that youth has never been determined. What return Shakespeare got for his exquisite offerings is likewise unknown. We do know that among wits and gallants, the narrative poems won Shakespeare a fine reputation as an immensely stylish and accomplished poet. An amateur play performed at Cambridge University at the end of the sixteenth century, *The Return from Parnassus,* makes fun of this vogue, as a foolish character effusively declares, "I'll worship sweet Mr. Shakespeare, and to honor him will lay his *Venus and Adonis* under my pillow." Many readers at the time may have done so: the poem went through sixteen editions before 1640, more than any other work by Shakespeare.

Patronage was crucially important not only for individual artists but also for the actors, playwrights, and investors who pooled their resources to form professional theater companies. The public playhouses had enemies, especially among civic and religious authorities, who wished greatly to curb performances or to ban them altogether. An Act of Parliament of 1572 included players among those classified as vagabonds, threatening them therefore with the horrible punishments meted out to those regarded as economic parasites. The players' escape route was to be nominally enrolled as apprentices in guilds, as if they were learning to be goldsmiths or grocers rather than actors. Alternatively, as we have noted, they could be officially listed as the servants of high-ranking noblemen.

When Shakespeare came to London, presumably in the late 1580s, there were more than a half-dozen of these companies operating under the patronage of various aristocrats. We do not know for which of these companies, several of which had toured in Stratford, he originally worked, nor whether he began, as legend has it, by holding gentlemen's horses outside the theater or by serving as a prompter's assistant and then graduated to acting and playwriting. Shakespeare is listed among the actors in Ben Jonson's *Every Man in His Humor* (performed in 1598) and *Sejanus* (performed in 1603), but we do not know for certain what roles he played, nor are there records of any of his other performances. Tradition has it that he played Adam in *As You Like It* and the Ghost in *Hamlet,* but he was clearly not one of the leading actors of the day.

Shakespeare may initially have been associated with the company of Ferdinando Stanley, Lord Strange; that company included actors with whom Shakespeare was later linked. Or he may have belonged to the Earl of Pembroke's Men, since there is evidence that they performed *The Taming of a Shrew* and a version of *3 Henry VI.* At any event, by 1594, Shakespeare was a member of the Chamberlain's Men, for his name, along with those of Will Kemp and Richard Burbage, appears on a record of those "servants to the Lord Chamberlain" paid for performance at the royal palace at Greenwich on December 26 and 28. Shakespeare stayed with this company, which during the reign of King James received royal patronage and became the King's Men, for the rest of his career.

Many playwrights in Shakespeare's time worked freelance, moving from company to company as opportunities arose, collaborating on projects, adding scenes to old plays, scrambling from one enterprise to another. But certain playwrights, among them the most successful, wrote for a single company, often agreeing contractually to give that company exclusive rights to their theatrical works. Shakespeare seems to have followed such a pattern. For the Chamberlain's Men, later the King's Men, he wrote an average of two plays per year. His company initially performed in The Theatre, a playhouse built in 1576 by an entrepreneurial actor and trained craftsman, James Burbage, the father of the actor Richard, who was to perform many of Shakespeare's greatest roles. When in 1597 their lease on this playhouse expired, the Chamberlain's Men passed through a difficult time, but they formed a joint stock company, raising sufficient capital to lease a site and put up a splendid new playhouse in the suburb of Southwark, on the south bank of the Thames. This playhouse, the Globe, opened in 1599. Shakespeare is listed in the legal agreement as one of the principal investors, and when the company began to use Blackfriars as their indoor playhouse around 1610, he was a major shareholder in that theater as well. The Chamberlain's Men dominated the theater scene, and the shares were quite valuable. Then as now, the theater was an extremely risky enterprise—most of those who wrote plays and performed in them made pathetically little money—but Shakespeare was a notable exception. The fine house in Stratford and the coat of arms he succeeded in acquiring were among the fruits of his multiple mastery, as actor, playwright, and investor of the London stage.

Edward Alleyn. Artist unknown. Alleyn was the great tragic actor of the Admiral's Men (the principal rival to Shakespeare's company). He was famous especially for playing the major characters of Christopher Marlowe.

The Shakespearean Trajectory

Though Shakespeare's England was in many ways a record-keeping society, no reliable record survives that details the performances, year by year, in the London theaters. Every play had to be licensed by the Master of the Revels, but the records kept by the relevant government officials from 1579 to 1621 have not survived. A major theatrical entrepreneur, Philip Henslowe, kept a careful account of his expenditures, including what he paid for the scripts he commissioned, but unfortunately Henslowe's main business was with the Rose and the Fortune theaters and not with the playhouses at which Shakespeare's company performed. A comparable ledger must have been kept by the shareholders of the Chamberlain's Men, but it has not survived. Shakespeare himself apparently did not undertake to preserve all his writings for posterity, let alone to clarify the chronology of his works or to specify which plays he wrote alone and which with collaborators.

The principal source for Shakespeare's works is the 1623 Folio volume of *Mr. William Shakespeares Comedies, Histories, & Tragedies.* The world owes this work,

IF YOV KNOW NOT ME,
You know no body.
OR,
The troubles of Queene ELIZABETH.

LONDON.
Printed by B.A. and T.F. for Nathanaell Butter. 1 6 3 2.

Title page of *If You Know Not Me, You Know Nobody; or, the Troubles of Queen Elizabeth* (1632).

lovingly edited after his death by two of the playwright's friends, an incalculable debt: without it, nearly half of Shakespeare's plays, including many of his greatest masterpieces, would have been lost forever. The edition does not, however, include any of Shakespeare's nondramatic poems, and it omits four plays in which Shakespeare is now thought to have had a significant hand, *Edward III, Pericles, Cardenio,* and *The Two Noble Kinsmen,* along with his probable contribution to the multiauthored *Sir Thomas More.* (A number of other plays were attributed to Shakespeare, both before and after his death, but scholars have not generally accepted any of these into the established canon.) Moreover, the Folio edition does not print the plays in chronological order, nor does it attempt to establish a chronology. We do not know how much time would normally have elapsed between the writing of a play and its first performance, nor, with a few exceptions, do we know with any certainty the month or even the year of the first performance of any of Shakespeare's plays. The quarto editions of those plays that were published during Shakespeare's lifetime obviously establish a date by which we know a given play had been written, but they give us little more than an end point, because there was likely to be a substantial though indeterminate gap between the first performance of a play and its publication.

With enormous patience and ingenuity, however, scholars have gradually assembled a considerable archive of evidence, both external and internal, for dating the composition of the plays. Besides actual publication, the external evidence includes explicit reference to a play, a record of its performance, or (as in the case of Greene's attack on the "upstart crow") the quoting of a line, though all of these can be maddeningly ambiguous. The most important single piece of external evidence appears in 1598 in *Palladis Tamia,* a long book of jumbled reflections by the churchman Francis Meres that includes a survey of the contemporary literary scene. Meres finds that "the sweet, witty soul of Ovid lives in mellifluous and honey-tongued Shakespeare, witness his *Venus and Adonis,* his *Lucrece,* his sugared Sonnets among his private friends, etc." Meres goes on to list Shakespeare's accomplishments as a playwright as well:

> As Plautus and Seneca are accounted the best for Comedy and Tragedy among the Latins: so Shakespeare among the English is the most excellent in both kinds for the stage; for Comedy, witness his *Gentlemen of Verona,* his *Errors,* his *Love labors lost,* his *Love labors won,* his *Midsummers night dream,* & his *Merchant of Venice:* for Tragedy his *Richard the 2, Richard the 3, Henry the 4, King John, Titus Andronicus* and his *Romeo and Juliet.*

Meres thus provides a date by which twelve of Shakespeare's plays had definitely appeared (including one, *Love's Labor's Won,* that appears either to have been lost or to be known to us by a different title). Unfortunately, Meres provides no clues about the order of appearance of these plays, and there are no other comparable lists.

Faced with the limitations of the external evidence, scholars have turned to a bewildering array of internal evidence, ranging from datable sources and topical allusions on the one hand to evolving stylistic features (ratio of verse to prose, percentage of rhyme to blank verse, colloquialisms, use of extended similes, and the like) on the other. Thus, for example, a cluster of plays with a high percentage of rhymed verse may follow closely upon Shakespeare's writing of the rhymed poems *Venus and Adonis* and *The Rape of Lucrece* and therefore be datable to 1594–95. Similarly, vocabulary overlap probably indicates proximity in composition, so if four or five plays share relatively "rare" vocabulary, it is likely that they were written in roughly the same period. Again, there seems to be a pattern in Shakespeare's use of colloquialisms, with a steady increase from *As You Like It* (1599–1600) to *Coriolanus* (1608), followed in the late romances by a retreat from the colloquial.

Ongoing computer analysis should provide further guidance in the future, though the precise order of the plays, still very much in dispute, is never likely to be settled to universal satisfaction. Still, certain broad patterns are now widely accepted. These patterns can be readily grasped in *The Norton Shakespeare*, which presents the plays according to our best estimate of their chronological order.

Shakespeare began his career, probably in the early 1590s, by writing both comedies and history plays. The attack by Greene suggests that he made his mark with the series of theatrically vital, occasionally brilliant, and often crude plays based on the foreign and domestic broils that erupted during the unhappy reign of the Lancastrian Henry VI. Modern readers and audiences are more likely to find the first sustained evidence of unusual power in *Richard III* (ca. 1592), a play that combines a richly imagined central character, a dazzling command of histrionic rhetoric, and an overarching moral vision of English history.

At virtually the same time that he was setting his stamp on the genre of the history play, Shakespeare was writing his first—or first surviving—comedies. Here, there are even fewer signs than in the histories of an apprenticeship. *The Comedy of Errors*, one of his early works in this genre, already displays a rare command of the resources of comedy: mistaken identity, madcap confusion, and the threat of disaster, giving way in the end to reconciliation, recovery, and love. Shakespeare's other comedies from the first half of the 1590s, *The Two Gentlemen of Verona*, *The Taming of the Shrew*, and *Love's Labor's Lost*, are no less remarkable for their sophisticated variations on familiar comic themes, their inexhaustible rhetorical inventiveness, and their poignant intimation, in the midst of festive celebration, of loss.

Successful as are these early histories and comedies, and indicative of an extraordinary theatrical talent, Shakespeare's achievement in the later 1590s would still have been all but impossible to foresee. Starting with *A Midsummer Night's Dream* (1595–96), Shakespeare wrote an unprecedented series of romantic comedies—*The Merchant of Venice*, *Much Ado About Nothing*, *The Merry Wives of Windsor*, *As You Like It*, and *Twelfth Night* (1600–1601)—whose poetic richness and emotional complexity remain unmatched. In the same period, he wrote a sequence of profoundly searching and ambitious history plays—*Richard II*, *1* and *2 Henry IV*, and *Henry V*—which together explore the death throes of feudal England and the birth of the modern nation-state ruled by a charismatic monarch. Both the comedies and histories of this period are marked by their capaciousness, their ability to absorb characters who press up against the outermost boundaries of the genre: the comedy *The Merchant of Venice* somehow contains the figure, at once nightmarish and poignant, of Shylock, while the *Henry IV* plays, with their somber vision of crisis in the family and the state, bring to the stage one of England's greatest comic characters, Falstaff.

If in the mid- to late 1590s Shakespeare reached the summit of his art in two major genres, he also manifested a lively interest in a third. As early as 1592–93, he wrote the crudely violent tragedy *Titus Andronicus*, the first of several plays on themes from Roman history, and a few years later, in *Richard II*, he created in the protagonist a figure who achieves by the play's close the stature of a tragic hero. In the same year that Shakespeare wrote the wonderfully farcical "Pyramus and Thisbe" scene in *A Midsummer Night's Dream*, he probably also wrote the deeply tragic realization of the same story in *Romeo and Juliet*. But once again, the lyric anguish of *Romeo and Juliet* and the tormented self-revelation of *Richard II*, extraordinary as they are, could not have led anyone to predict the next phase of Shakespeare's career, the great tragic dramas that poured forth in the early years of the seventeenth century: *Hamlet, Othello, King Lear, Macbeth, Antony and Cleopatra*, and *Coriolanus*. These plays, written between 1600 and 1608, seem to mark a major shift in sensibility, an existential and metaphysical darkening that many readers think must have drawn upon a deep personal anguish, perhaps caused by the decline and death of Shakespeare's father, John, in 1601.

Whatever the truth of these speculations—and we have no direct, personal testimony either to support or to undermine them—there appears to have occurred in the same period a shift as well in Shakespeare's comic sensibility. The comedies written between 1601 and 1607, *Troilus and Cressida, Measure for Measure*, and *All's Well That Ends Well*, are sufficiently different from the earlier comedies—more biting in tone, more uneasy with comic conventions, more ruthlessly questioning of the values of the characters and the resolutions of the plots—that they led many twentieth-century scholars to classify them as "problem plays" or "dark comedies." This category has recently begun to fall out of favor, since Shakespeare criticism is perfectly happy to demonstrate that *all* of the plays are "problem plays." But there is another group of plays, among the last Shakespeare wrote, that continue to constitute a distinct category. *Pericles, Cymbeline, The Winter's Tale*, and *The Tempest*—written between 1607 and 1611, when the playwright had developed a remarkably fluid, dreamlike sense of plot and a poetic style that could veer, apparently effortlessly, from the tortured to the ineffably sweet—have been known since the late nineteenth century as the "romances." These plays share an interest in the moral and emotional life less of the adolescents who dominate the earlier comedies than of their parents. The romances are deeply concerned with patterns of loss and recovery, suffering and redemption, despair and renewal. They have seemed to many critics to constitute a deliberate conclusion to a career that began in histories and comedies and passed through the dark and tormented tragedies.

One effect of the practice of printing Shakespeare's plays in a reconstructed chronological order, as this edition does, is to produce a kind of authorial plot, a progress from youthful exuberance and a heroic grappling with history, through psychological anguish and radical doubt, to a mature serenity built upon an understanding of loss. The ordering of Shakespeare's "complete works" in this way reconstitutes the figure of the author as the beloved hero of his own, lived romance. There are numerous reasons to treat this romance with considerable skepticism: the precise order of the plays remains in dispute, the obsessions of the earliest plays crisscross with those of the last, the drama is a collaborative art form, and the relation between authorial consciousness and theatrical representation is murky. Yet a longing to identify Shakespeare's personal trajectory, to chart his psychic and spiritual as well as professional progress, is all but irresistible.

The Fetishism of Dress

Whatever the personal resonance of Shakespeare's own life, his art is deeply enmeshed in the collective hopes, fears, and fantasies of his time. For example, throughout his plays, Shakespeare draws heavily upon his culture's investment in costume, symbols of authority, visible signs of status—the fetishism of dress he must have witnessed from early childhood. Disguise in his drama is often assumed to be incredibly effective: when Henry V borrows a cloak, when Portia dresses in a jurist's

robes, when Viola puts on a young man's suit, it is as if each has become unrecogniz-
able, as if identity resided in clothing. At the end of *Twelfth Night,* even though Viola's true identity has been disclosed, Orsino continues to call her Cesario; he will do
so, he says, until she resumes her maid's garments, for only then will she be transformed into a woman:

> Cesario, come—
> For so you shall be while you are a man—
> But when in other habits you are seen,
> Orsino's mistress and his fancy's queen.
> (5.1.371–74)

The pinnacle of this fetishism of costume is the royal crown, for whose identity-
conferring power men are willing to die, but the principle is everywhere, from the
filthy blanket that transforms Edgar into Poor Tom to the coxcomb that is the badge
of the licensed fool. Antonio, wishing to express his utter contempt, spits on Shylock's "Jewish gaberdine," as if the clothing were the essence of the man; Kent, pouring insults on the loathsome Oswald, calls him a "filthy worsted-stocking knave"; and
innocent Imogen, learning that her husband has ordered her murder, thinks of herself as an expensive cast-off dress, destined to be ripped at the seams:

> Poor I am stale, a garment out of fashion,
> And for I am richer than to hang by th' walls,
> I must be ripped: to pieces with me.
> (*Cymbeline* 3.4.50–52)

What can be said, thought, felt in this culture seems deeply dependent on the
clothes one wears—clothes that one is, in effect, *permitted* or *compelled* to wear,
since there is little freedom in dress. Shakespearean drama occasionally represents
something like such freedom: after all, Viola in *Twelfth Night* chooses to put off her
"maiden weeds," as does Rosalind, who declares, "We'll have a swashing and a martial outside" (*As You Like It* 1.3.116). But these choices are characteristically made
under the pressure of desperate circumstances, here shipwreck and exile. Part of the
charm of Shakespeare's heroines is their ability to transform distress into an opportunity for self-fashioning, but the plays often suggest that there is less autonomy than
meets the eye. What looks like an escape from cultural determinism may be only a
deeper form of constraint. We may take, as an allegorical emblem of this constraint,
the transformation of the beggar Christopher Sly in the playful Induction to *The
Taming of the Shrew* into a nobleman. The transformation seems to suggest that you
are free to make of yourself whatever you choose to be—the play begins with the
drunken Sly claiming the dignity of his pedigree ("Look in the Chronicles" [Induc-
tion 1.3–4])—but in fact he is only the subject of the mischievous lord's experiment,
designed to demonstrate the interwovenness of clothing and identity. "What think
you," the lord asks his huntsman,

> if he were conveyed to bed,
> Wrapped in sweet clothes, rings put upon his fingers,
> A most delicious banquet by his bed,
> And brave attendants near him when he wakes—
> Would not the beggar then forget himself?

To which the huntsman replies, in words that underscore the powerlessness of the
drunken beggar, "Believe me, lord, I think he cannot choose" (Induction 1.33–38).
Petruccio's taming of Katherina is similarly constructed around an imposition of
identity, an imposition closely bound up with the right to wear certain articles of clothing. When the haberdasher arrives with a fashionable lady's hat, Petruccio refuses it
over his wife's vehement objections: "This doth fit the time, / And gentlewomen wear
such caps as these." "When you are gentle," Petruccio replies, "you shall have one, too, /

And not till then" (4.3.70–73). At the play's close, Petruccio demonstrates his authority
by commanding his tamed wife to throw down her cap: "Off with that bauble; throw
it underfoot" (5.2.122). Here as elsewhere in Shakespeare, acts of robing and disrob-
ing are intensely charged, a charge that culminates in the trappings of monarchy.
When Richard II, in a scene that was probably censored during the reign of Elizabeth
from the stage as well as the printed text, is divested of his crown and scepter, he
experiences the loss as the eradication of his name, the symbolic melting away of his
identity:

> Alack the heavy day,
> That I have worn so many winters out
> And know not now what name to call myself.
> Oh, that I were a mockery king of snow,
> Standing before the sun of Bolingbroke
> To melt myself away in water-drops.
> (4.1.250–55)

When Lear tears off his regal "lendings" in order to reduce himself to the nakedness of the Bedlam beggar, he is expressing not only his radical loss of social identity
but the breakdown of his psychic order as well, expressing therefore his reduction to
the condition of the "poor bare forked animal" that is the primal form of undifferen-
tiated existence. And when Cleopatra determines to kill herself in order to escape
public humiliation in Rome, she magnificently affirms her essential being by array-
ing herself as she had once done to encounter Antony:

> Show me, my women, like a queen. Go, fetch
> My best attires. I am again for Cydnus
> To meet Mark Antony.
> (5.2.226–28)

Such scenes are a remarkable intensification of the everyday symbolic practice of
Renaissance English culture, its characteristically deep and knowing commitment to
illusion: "I know perfectly well that the woman in her crown and jewels and gorgeous
gown is an aging, irascible, and fallible mortal—she herself virtually admits as
much—yet I profess that she is the virgin queen, timelessly beautiful, wise, and just."
Shakespeare understood how close this willed illusion was to the spirit of the theater, to the actors' ability to work on what the chorus in *Henry V* calls the "imaginary
forces" of the audience. But there is throughout Shakespeare's works a counterintu-
ition that, while it does not exactly overturn this illusion, renders it poignant, vulnerable, fraught. The "masculine usurp'd attire" that is donned by Viola, Rosalind,
Portia, Jessica, and other Shakespeare heroines alters what they can say and do,
reveals important aspects of their character, and changes their destiny, but it is, all
the same, not theirs and not all of who they are. They have, the plays insist, natures
that are neither transformed nor altogether concealed by their dress: "Pray God
defend me," exclaims the frightened Viola. "A little thing would make me tell them
how much I lack of a man" (*Twelfth Night* 3.4.271–72).

The Paradoxes of Identity

The gap between costume and identity is not simply a matter of what women supposedly lack; virtually all of Shakespeare's major characters, men and women, convey
the sense of both a *self-division* and an *inward expansion*. The belief in a complex
inward realm beyond costumes and status is a striking inversion of the clothes
cult: we know perfectly well that the characters have no inner lives apart from
what we see on the stage, and yet we believe that they continue to exist when we do
not see them, that they exist apart from their represented words and actions, that
they have hidden dimensions. How is this conviction aroused and sustained? In part,

it is the effect of what the characters themselves say: "My grief lies all within," Richard II tells Bolingbroke,

> And these external manner of laments
> Are merely shadows to the unseen grief
> That swells with silence in the tortured soul.
> (4.1.288–91)

Similarly, Hamlet, dismissing the significance of his outward garments, declares, "I have that within which passes show— / These but the trappings and the suits of woe" (1.2.85–86). And the distinction between inward and outward is reinforced throughout this play and elsewhere by an unprecedented use of the aside and the soliloquy.

The soliloquy is a continual reminder in Shakespeare that the inner life is by no means transparent to one's surrounding world. Prince Hal seems open and easy with his mates in Eastcheap, but he has a hidden reservoir of disgust:

> I know you all, and will a while uphold
> The unyoked humor of your idleness.
> Yet herein will I imitate the sun,
> Who doth permit the base contagious clouds
> To smother up his beauty from the world,
> That, when he please again to be himself,
> Being wanted he may be more wondered at
> By breaking through the foul and ugly mists
> Of vapors that did seem to strangle him.
> (*I Henry IV* 1.2.170–78)

"When he please again to be himself": the line implies that identity is a matter of free choice—you decide how much of yourself you wish to disclose—but Shakespeare employs other devices that suggest more elusive and intractable layers of inwardness. There is a peculiar, recurrent lack of fit between costume and character, in fools as in princes, that is not simply a matter of disguise and disclosure. If Hal's true identity is partially "smothered" in the tavern, it is not completely revealed either in his soldier's armor or in his royal robes, nor do his asides reach the bedrock of unimpeachable self-understanding.

Identity in Shakespeare repeatedly slips away from the characters themselves, as it does from Richard II after the deposition scene and from Lear after he has given away his land and from Macbeth after he has gained the crown. The slippage does not mean that they retreat into silence; rather, they embark on an experimental, difficult fashioning of themselves and the world, most often through role-playing. "I cannot do it," says the deposed and imprisoned Richard II. "Yet I'll hammer't out" (5.5.5). This could serve as the motto for many Shakespearean characters: Viola becomes Cesario, Rosalind calls herself Ganymede, Kent becomes Caius, Edgar presents himself as Poor Tom, Hamlet plays the madman that he has partly become, Hal pretends that he is his father and a highwayman and Hotspur and even himself. Even in comedy, these ventures into alternate identities are rarely matters of choice; in tragedy, they are always undertaken under pressure and compulsion. And often enough it is not a matter of role-playing at all, but of a drastic transformation whose extreme emblem is the harrowing madness of Lear and of Leontes.

There is a moment in *Richard II* in which the deposed king asks for a mirror and then, after musing on his reflection, throws it to the ground. The shattering of the glass serves to remind us not only of the fragility of identity in Shakespeare but of its characteristic appearance in fragmentary mirror images. The plays continually generate alternative reflections, identities that intersect with, underscore, echo, or otherwise set off that of the principal character. Hence, Desdemona and Iago are not only important figures in Othello's world—they also seem to embody partially realized aspects of himself; Falstaff and Hotspur play a comparable role in relation to Prince Hal, Fortinbras and Horatio in relation to Hamlet, Gloucester and the Fool in relation to Lear, and so forth. In many of these plays, the complementary and contrasting characters figure in subplots, subtly interwoven with the play's main plot and illuminating its concerns. The note so conspicuously sounded by Fortinbras at the close of *Hamlet*—what the hero might have been, "had he been put on"—is heard repeatedly in Shakespeare and contributes to the overwhelming intensity, poignancy, and complexity of the characters. This is a world in which outward appearance is everything and nothing, in which individuation is at once sharply etched and continually blurred, in which the victims of fate are haunted by the ghosts of the possible, in which everything is simultaneously as it must be and as it need not have been.

Are these alternatives signs of a struggle between contradictory and irreconcilable perspectives in Shakespeare? In certain plays—notably, *Measure for Measure, All's Well That Ends Well, Coriolanus,* and *Troilus and Cressida*—the tension seems both high and entirely unresolved. But Shakespearean contradictions are more often reminiscent of the capacious spirit of Montaigne, who refused any systematic order that would betray his sense of reality. Thus, individual characters are immensely important in Shakespeare—he is justly celebrated for his unmatched skill in the invention of particular dramatic identities, marked with distinct speech patterns, manifested in social status, and confirmed by costume and gesture—but the principle of individuation is not the rock on which his theatrical art is founded. After the masks are stripped away, the pretenses exposed, the claims of the ego shattered, there is a mysterious remainder; as the shamed but irrepressible Paroles declares in *All's Well That Ends Well,* "Simply the thing I am / Shall make me live" (4.3.316–17). Again and again the audience is made to sense a deeper energy, a source of power that at once discharges itself in individual characters and seems to sweep right through them.

The Poet of Nature

In *The Birth of Tragedy,* Nietzsche called a comparable source of energy that he found in Greek tragedy "Dionysos." But the god's name, conjuring up Bacchic frenzy, does not seem appropriate to Shakespeare. In the late seventeenth and eighteenth centuries, it was more plausibly called Nature: "The world must be peopled," says the delightful Benedict in *Much Ado About Nothing* (2.3.213), and there are frequent invocations elsewhere of the happy, generative power that brings couples together—

> Jack shall have Jill,
> Naught shall go ill,
> The man shall have his mare again, and all shall be well.
> (*A Midsummer Night's Dream* 3.2.461–63)

—and the melancholy, destructive power that brings all living things to the grave: "Golden lads and girls all must, / As chimney-sweepers, come to dust" (*Cymbeline* 4.2.261–62).

But the celebration of Shakespeare as a poet of nature—often coupled with an inane celebration of his supposedly "natural" (that is, untutored) genius—has its distinct limitations. For Shakespearean art brilliantly interrogates the "natural," refusing to take for granted precisely what the celebrants think is most secure. His comedies are endlessly inventive in showing that love is not simply natural: the playful hint of bestiality in the line quoted above, "the man shall have his mare again" (from a play in which the Queen of the Fairies falls in love with an ass-headed laborer), lightly unsettles the boundaries between the natural and the perverse. These boundaries are called into question throughout Shakespeare's work, from the cross-dressing and erotic crosscurrents that deliciously complicate the lives of the characters in *Twelfth Night* and *As You Like It* to the terrifying violence that wells up from the heart of the family in *King Lear* or from the sweet intimacy of sexual desire in *Othello*. Even the boundary between life and death is not secure, as the ghosts in *Julius Caesar, Hamlet,* and *Macbeth* attest, while the principle of natural death (given its most eloquent articulation by old Hamlet's murderer, Claudius!) is repeatedly tainted and disrupted.

Disrupted too is the idea of order that constantly makes its claim, most insistently in the history plays. Scholars have observed the presence in Shakespeare's works of the so-called Tudor myth—the ideological justification of the ruling dynasty as a restoration of national order after a cycle of tragic violence. The violence, Tudor apologists claimed, was divine punishment unleashed after the deposition of the anointed king, Richard II, for God will not tolerate violations of the sanctified order. Traces of this propaganda certainly exist in the histories—Shakespeare may, for all we know, have personally subscribed to its premises—but a closer scrutiny of his plays has disclosed so many ironic reservations and qualifications and subversions as to call into question any straightforward adherence to a political line. The plays manifest a profound fascination with the monarchy and with the ambitions of the aristocracy, but the fascination is never simply endorsement. There is always at least the hint of a slippage between the great figures, whether admirable or monstrous, who stand at the pinnacle of authority and the vast, miscellaneous mass of soldiers, scriveners, ostlers, poets, whores, gardeners, thieves, weavers, shepherds, country gentlemen, sturdy beggars, and the like who make up the commonwealth. And the idea of order, though eloquently articulated (most memorably by Ulysses in *Troilus and Cressida*), is always shadowed by a relentless spirit of irony.

The Play of Language

If neither the individual nor nature nor order will serve, can we find a single comprehensive name for the underlying force in Shakespeare's work? Certainly not. The work is too protean and capacious. But much of the energy that surges through this astonishing body of plays and poems is closely linked to the power of language. Shakespeare was the supreme product of a rhetorical culture, a culture steeped in the arts of persuasion and verbal expressiveness. In 1512, the great Dutch humanist Erasmus published a work called *De copia* that taught its readers how to cultivate "copiousness," verbal richness, in discourse. (Erasmus obligingly provides, as a sample, a list of 144 different ways of saying "Thank you for your letter.") Recommended modes of variation include putting the subject of an argument into fictional form, as well as the use of synonym, substitution, paraphrase, metaphor, metonymy, synecdoche, hyperbole, diminution, and a host of other figures of speech. To change emotional tone, he suggests trying *ironia, interrogatio, admiratio, dubitatio, abominatio*—the possibilities seem infinite.

In Renaissance England, certain syntactic forms or patterns of words known as "figures" (also called "schemes") were shaped and repeated in order to confer beauty or heighten expressive power. Figures were usually known by their Greek and Latin names, though in an Elizabethan rhetorical manual, *The Art of English Poesy,* George Puttenham made a valiant if short-lived attempt to give them English equivalents, such as "*Hyperbole,* or the Overreacher," "*Ironia,* or the Dry Mock," and "*Ploce,* or the Doubler." Those who received a grammar school education throughout Europe at almost any point between the Roman Empire and the eighteenth century probably knew by heart the names of up to one hundred such figures, just as they knew by heart their multiplication tables. According to one scholar's count, Shakespeare knew and made use of about two hundred.

As certain grotesquely inflated Renaissance texts attest, lessons from *De copia* and similar rhetorical guides could encourage mere prolixity and verbal self-display. But though he shared his culture's delight in rhetorical complexity, Shakespeare always understood how to swoop from baroque sophistication to breathtaking simplicity. Moreover, he grasped early in his career how to use figures of speech, tone, and rhythm not only to provide emphasis and elegant variety but also to articulate the inner lives of his characters. Take, for example, these lines from *Othello,* where, as scholars have noted, Shakespeare deftly combines four common rhetorical figures—*anaphora, parison, isocolon,* and *epistrophe*—to depict with painful vividness Othello's psychological torment:

> By the world,
> I think my wife be honest, and think she is not;
> I think that thou art just, and think thou art not.
> I'll have some proof.
>
> (3.3.380–83)

Anaphora is simply the repetition of a word at the beginning of a sequence of sentences or clauses ("I/I"). *Parison* is the correspondence of word to word within adjacent sentences or clauses, either by direct repetition ("think/think") or by the matching of noun with noun, verb with verb ("wife/thou"; "be/art"). *Isocolon* gives exactly the same length to corresponding clauses ("and think she is not/and think thou art not"), and *epistrophe* is the mirror image of *anaphora,* in that it is the repetition of a word at the end of a sequence of sentences or clauses ("not/not"). Do we need to know the Greek names for these figures in order to grasp the effectiveness of Othello's lines? Of course not. But Shakespeare and his contemporaries, convinced that rhetoric provided the most natural and powerful means by which feelings could be conveyed to readers and listeners, were trained in an analytical language that helped at once to promote and to account for this effectiveness. In his 1593 edition of *The Garden of Eloquence,* Henry Peacham remarks that *epistrophe* "serveth to leave a word of importance in the end of a sentence, that it may the longer hold the sound in the mind of the hearer," and in *Directions for Speech and Style* (ca. 1599), John Hoskins notes that *anaphora* "beats upon one thing to cause the quicker feeling in the audience."

Shakespeare also shared with his contemporaries a keen understanding of the ways that rhetorical devices could be used not only to express powerful feelings but to hide them: after all, the artist who created Othello also created Iago, Richard III, and Lady Macbeth. He could deftly skewer the rhetorical affectations of Polonius in *Hamlet* or the pedant Holofernes in *Love's Labor's Lost.* He could deploy stylistic variations to mark the boundaries not of different individuals but of different social realms; in *A Midsummer Night's Dream,* for example, the blank verse of Duke Theseus is played off against the rhymed couplets of the well-born young lovers, and both in turn contrast with the prose spoken by the artisans. At the same time that he thus marks boundaries between both individuals and groups, Shakespeare shows a remarkable ability to establish unifying patterns of imagery that knit together the diverse strands of his plot and suggest subtle links among characters who may be scarcely aware of how much they share with one another.

One of the hidden links in Shakespeare's own works is the frequent use he makes of a somewhat unusual rhetorical figure called *hendiadys.* An example from the Roman poet Virgil is the phrase *pateris libamus et auro,* "we drink from cups and gold" (*Georgics* 2.192). Rather than serving as an adjective or a dependent noun, as in "golden cups" or "cups of gold," the word "gold" serves as a substantive joined to another substantive, "cups," by a conjunction, "and." Shakespeare uses the figure over three hundred times in all, and since it does not appear in ancient or medieval lists of tropes and schemes and is treated only briefly by English rhetoricians, he may have come upon it directly in Virgil. *Hendiadys* literally means "one through two," though Shakespeare's versions often make us quickly, perhaps only subliminally, aware of the complexity of what ordinarily passes for straightforward perceptions. When Othello, in his suicide speech, invokes the memory of "a malignant and a turbaned Turk," the figure of speech at once associates enmity with cultural difference and keeps them slightly apart. And when Macbeth speaks of his "strange and self-abuse," the *hendiadys* seems briefly to hold both "strange" and "self" up for scrutiny. It would be foolish to make too much of any single feature in Shakespeare's varied and diverse creative achievement, and yet this curious rhetorical scheme has something of the quality of a fingerprint.

But all of his immense rhetorical gifts, though rich, beautiful, and supremely useful, do not adequately convey Shakespeare's relation to language, which is less strictly functional than a total immersion in the arts of persuasion may imply. An Erasmian admiration for copiousness cannot fully explain Shakespeare's astonishing vocabulary of some 25,000 words. (His closest rival among the great English poets of the period was John Milton, with about 12,000 words, and most major writers, let alone ordinary people, have much smaller vocabularies.) This immense word hoard, it is worth noting, was not the result of scanning a dictionary; in the late sixteenth century, there were no large-scale English dictionaries of the kind to which we are now accustomed. Shakespeare seems to have absorbed new words from virtually every discursive realm he ever encountered, and he experimented boldly and tirelessly with them. These experiments were facilitated by a flexibility in grammar, orthography, and diction that the more orderly, regularized English of the later seventeenth and eighteenth centuries suppressed.

Owing in part to the number of dialects in London, pronunciation was variable, and there were many opportunities for phonetic association between words: the words "bear," "barn," "bier," "bourn" "born," and "barne" could all sound like one another. Homonyms were given greater scope by the fact that the same word could be spelled so many different ways—Christopher Marlowe's name appears in the records as Marlowe, Marloe, Marlen, Marlyne, Merlin, Marley, Marlye, Morley, and Morle—and by the fact that a word's grammatical function could easily shift, from noun to verb, verb to adjective, and so forth. Since grammar and punctuation did not insist on relations of coordination and subordination, loose, nonsyntactic sentences were common, and etymologies were used to forge surprising or playful relations between distant words.

It would seem inherently risky for a popular playwright to employ a vocabulary so far in excess of what most mortals could possibly possess, but Shakespeare evidently counted on his audience's linguistic curiosity and adventurousness, just as he counted on its general and broad-based rhetorical competence. He was also usually careful to provide a context that in effect explained or translated his more arcane terms. For example, when Macbeth reflects with horror on his murderous hands, he shudderingly imagines that even the sea could not wash away the blood; on the contrary, his bloodstained hand, he says, "will rather / The multitudinous seas incarnadine." The meaning of the unfamiliar word "incarnadine" is explained by the next line: "Making the green one red" (2.2.64–66).

What is most striking is not the abstruseness or novelty of Shakespeare's language but its extraordinary vitality, a quality that the playwright seemed to pursue with a kind of passionate recklessness. Perhaps Samuel Johnson was looking in the right direction when he complained that the "quibble," or pun, was "the fatal Cleopatra for which [Shakespeare] lost the world, and was content to lose it." For the power that continually discharges itself throughout the plays, at once constituting and unsettling everything it touches, is the polymorphous power of language, language that seems both costume and that which lies beneath the costume, personal identity and that which challenges the merely personal, nature and that which enables us to name nature and thereby distance ourselves from it.

Shakespeare's language has an overpowering exuberance and generosity that often resembles the experience of love. Consider, for example, Oberon's description in *A Midsummer Night's Dream* of the moment when he saw Cupid shoot his arrow at the fair vestal: "Thou rememberest," he asks Puck,

> Since once I sat upon a promontory
> And heard a mermaid on a dolphin's back
> Uttering such dulcet and harmonious breath
> That the rude sea grew civil at her song

> And certain stars shot madly from their spheres
> To hear the sea-maid's music?
>
> (2.1.148–54)

Here, Oberon's composition of place, lightly alluding to a classical emblem, is infused with a fantastically lush verbal brilliance. This brilliance, the result of masterful alliterative and rhythmical technique, seems gratuitous; that is, it does not advance the plot, but rather exhibits a capacity for display and self-delight that extends from the fairies to the playwright who has created them. The rich music of Oberon's words imitates the "dulcet and harmonious breath" he is intent on recalling, breath that has, in his account, an oddly contradictory effect: it is at once a principle of order, so that the rude sea is becalmed like a lower-class mob made civil by a skilled orator, and a principle of disorder, so that celestial bodies in their fixed spheres are thrown into mad confusion. And this contradictory effect, so intimately bound up with an inexplicable, supererogatory, and intensely erotic verbal magic, is a key to *A Midsummer Night's Dream,* with its exquisite blend of confusion and discipline, lunacy and hierarchical ceremony.

The fairies in this comedy seem to embody a pervasive sense found throughout Shakespeare's work that there is something uncanny about language, something that is not quite human, at least in the conventional and circumscribed sense of the human that dominates waking experience. In the comedies, this intuition is alarming but ultimately benign: Oberon and his followers trip through the great house at the play's close, blessing the bride-beds and warding off the nightmares that lurk in marriage and parenthood. But there is in Shakespeare an alternative, darker vision of the uncanniness of language, a vision also embodied in creatures that test the limits of the human—not the fairies of *A Midsummer Night's Dream* but the weird sisters of *Macbeth.* When in the tragedy's opening scene the witches chant, "Fair is foul, and foul is fair," they unsettle through the simplest and most radical act of linguistic equation (x is y) the fundamental distinctions through which a moral order is established. And when Macbeth appears onstage a few minutes later, his first words unconsciously echo what we have just heard from the witches' mouths: "So foul and fair a day I have not seen" (1.3.39). What is the meaning of this linguistic "unconscious"? On the face of things, Macbeth presumably means only that the day of fair victory is also a day of foul weather, but the fact that he echoes the witches (something that we hear but that he cannot know) intimates an occult link between them, even before their direct encounter. It is difficult, perhaps impossible, to specify exactly what this link signifies—generations of emboldened critics have tried without notable success—but we can at least affirm that its secret lair is in the play's language, like a half-buried pun whose full articulation will entail the murder of Duncan, the ravaging of his kingdom, and Macbeth's own destruction.

Macbeth is haunted by half-buried puns, equivocations, and ambiguous grammatical constructions known as amphibologies. They manifest themselves most obviously in the words of the witches, from the opening exchanges to the fraudulent assurances that deceive Macbeth at the close, but they are also present in his most intimate and private reflections, as in his tortured broodings about his proposed act of treason:

> If it were done when 'tis done, then 'twere well
> It were done quickly. If th'assassination
> Could trammel up the consequence and catch
> With his surcease success—that but this blow
> Might be the be-all and the end-all!—here,
> But here, upon this bank and shoal of time,
> We'd jump the life to come.
>
> (1.7.1–7)

The dream is to reach a secure and decisive end, to catch as in a net (hence "trammel up") all of the slippery, unforeseen, and uncontrollable consequences of regicide, to hobble time as one might hobble a horse (another sense of "trammel up"), to stop the flow ("success") of events, to be, as Macbeth later puts it, "settled." But Macbeth's words themselves slip away from the closure he seeks; they slide into one another, trip over themselves, twist and double back and swerve into precisely the sickening uncertainties their speaker most wishes to avoid. And if we sense a barely discernible note of comedy in Macbeth's tortured language, a discordant playing with the senses of the word "done" and the hint of a childish tongue twister in the phrase "catch / With his surcease success," we are in touch with a dark pleasure to which Shakespeare was all his life addicted.

Look again at the couplet from *Cymbeline:* "Golden lads and girls all must, / As chimney-sweepers, come to dust." The playwright who insinuated a pun into the solemn dirge is the same playwright whose tragic heroine in *Antony and Cleopatra,* pulling the bleeding body of her dying lover into the pyramid, says, "Our strength is all gone into heaviness" (4.15.34). He is the playwright whose Juliet, finding herself alone on the stage, says, "My dismal scene I needs must act alone" (*Romeo and Juliet* 4.3.19), and the playwright who can follow the long, wrenching periodic sentence that Othello speaks, just before he stabs himself, with the remark "O bloody period!" (5.2.349). The point is not merely the presence of puns in the midst of tragedy (as there are stabs of pain in the midst of Shakespearean comedy); it is rather the streak of wildness that they so deliberately disclose, the sublimely indecorous linguistic energy of which Shakespeare was at once the towering master and the most obedient, worshipful servant.

From Page to Stage: Shakespeare at Work

Shakespeare's extraordinary imaginative and linguistic power left its mark, like a personal signature, on everything he wrote. But his plays became the property of the theatrical company in which he was a shareholder. The company could choose to sell its plays to printers who might hope to profit if the public was eager to read as well as to watch a popular hit. But relatively few plays excited that level of public interest. Moreover, playing companies did not always think it was in their interest to have their scripts circulating in print, at least while the plays were actively in repertory: players evidently feared competition from rival companies and thought that reading might dampen playgoing. Plays were on occasion printed quickly, in order to take advantage of their popularity, but they were most often sold to the printers when the theaters were temporarily closed by plague, or when the company was in need of capital (four of Shakespeare's plays were published in 1600, presumably to raise money to pay the debts incurred in building the new Globe), or when a play had grown too old to revive profitably. There is no conclusive evidence that Shakespeare disagreed with this professional caution. There was clearly a market for his plays in print as well as onstage, and he himself may have taken pride in what he wrote as suitable for reading as well as viewing. But unlike Jonson, who took the radical step of rewriting his own plays for publication in the 1616 folio of his *Works,* Shakespeare evidently never undertook to constitute his plays as a canon. If in the sonnets he imagines his verse achieving a symbolic immortality, this dream apparently did not extend to his plays, at least through the medium of print.

Moreover, there is no evidence that Shakespeare had an interest in asserting authorial rights over his scripts, or that he or any other working English playwright had a public "standing," legal or otherwise, from which to do so. (Jonson was ridiculed for his presumption.) There is no indication whatever that he could, for example, veto changes in his scripts or block interpolated scenes or withdraw a play from production if a particular interpretation, addition, or revision did not please him. To be sure, in his advice to the players, Hamlet urges that those who play the clowns "speak no more than is set down for them," but—apart from the question of whether the prince speaks for the playwright—the play-within-the-play in *Hamlet* is precisely an instance of a script altered to suit a particular occasion. It seems likely that Shakespeare would have routinely accepted the possibility of such alterations. Moreover, he would of necessity have routinely accepted the possibility, and in certain cases the virtual inevitability, of cuts in order to stage his plays in the two to two and one-half hours that was the normal performing time. There is an imaginative generosity in many of Shakespeare's scripts, as if he were deliberately offering his fellow actors more than they could use on any one occasion and hence giving them abundant materials with which to reconceive and revivify each play again and again, as they or their audiences liked it. The Elizabethan theater, like most theater in our own time, was a collaborative enterprise, and the collaboration almost certainly extended to decisions about selection, trimming, shifts of emphasis, and minor or major revision.

Writing for the theater for Shakespeare was never simply a matter of sitting alone at his desk and putting words on paper; it was a social process as well as individual act. We do not know the extent to which this process frustrated him; in Sonnet 66 he writes of "art made tongue-tied by authority." Shakespeare may have been forced on occasion to cut lines and even whole scenes to which he was attached; shifting political circumstances may have occasioned rewriting, possibly against his will; or his fellow players may have insisted that they could not successfully perform what he had written, compelling him to make changes he did not welcome. But compromise and collaboration are part of what it means to be in the theater, and Shakespeare was, supremely, a man of the theater.

As a man of the theater, Shakespeare understood that whatever he set down on paper was not the end of the story. It would inevitably be shaped by the words he spoke to his fellow actors and by their own ideas concerning emphasis, stage business, tone, pacing, possible cuts, and so forth. It could be modified too by the intervention of the government censor or by intimations that some powerful figure might take offense at something in the script. To the extent that the agreed-upon alterations were ever written down, they were recorded in the promptbook used for a particular performance, and that promptbook could in turn be modified for a subsequent performance in a different setting.

For many years, it was thought that Shakespeare himself did little or no revising. Some recent editors have argued persuasively that there are many signs of authorial revision, even wholesale rewriting. But there is no sign that Shakespeare sought through such revision to bring each of his plays to its "perfect," "final" form. On the contrary, many of the revisions seem to indicate that the scripts remained open texts that the playwright and his company expected to add to, cut, and rewrite as the occasion demanded.

Ralph Waldo Emerson once compared Shakespeare and his contemporary Francis Bacon in terms of the relative "finish" of their work. All of Bacon's work, wrote Emerson, "lies along the ground, a vast unfinished city." Each of Shakespeare's dramas, by contrast, "is perfect, hath an immortal integrity. To make Bacon's work complete, he must live to the end of the world." Recent scholarship suggests that Shakespeare was more like Bacon than Emerson thought. Neither the Folio nor the quarto texts of Shakespeare's plays bear the seal of final authorial intention, the mark of decisive closure that has served, at least ideally, as the guarantee of textual authenticity. We want to believe, as we read the text, "This is the play as Shakespeare himself wanted it read," but there is no license for such a reassuring sentiment. To be "not of an age, but for all time" means in Shakespeare's case not that the plays have achieved a static perfection, but that they are creatively, inexhaustibly unfinished.

The Status of the Artist

That we have been so eager to link certain admired scripts to a single known playwright is closely related to changes in the status of artists in the Renaissance, changes that led to a heightened interest in the hand of the individual creator. Like medieval painting, medieval drama gives us few clues as to the particular individuals who fashioned the objects we admire. We know something about the places in which these objects were made, the circumstances that enabled their creation, the spaces in which they were placed, but relatively little about the particular artists themselves. It is easy to imagine a wealthy patron or a civic authority in the late Middle Ages commissioning a play on a particular subject (appropriate, for example, to a seasonal ritual, a religious observance, or a political festivity) and specifying the date, place, and length of the performance, the number of actors, even the costumes to be used, but it is more difficult to imagine him specifying a particular playwright and still less insisting that the entire play be written by this dramatist alone. Only with the Renaissance do we find a growing insistence on the name of the maker, the signature that heightens the value and even the meaning of the work by implying that it is the emanation of a single, distinct shaping consciousness.

In the case of Renaissance painting, we know that this signature does not necessarily mean that every stroke was made by the master. Some of the work, possibly the greater part of it, may have been done by assistants, with only the faces and a few finishing touches from the hand of the illustrious artist to whom the work is confidently attributed. As the skill of individual masters became more explicitly valued, contracts began to specify how much was to come from the brush of the principal painter. Consider, for example, the Italian painter Luca Signorelli's contract of 1499 for frescoes in Orvieto Cathedral:

> The said master Luca is bound and promises to paint [1] all the figures to be done on the said vault, and [2] especially the faces and all the parts of the figures from the middle of each figure upwards, and [3] that no painting should be done on it without Luca himself being present. . . . And it is agreed [4] that all the mixing of colors should be done by the said master Luca himself.

Such a contract at once reflects a serious cash interest in the characteristic achievement of a particular artist and a conviction that this achievement is compatible with the presence of other hands, provided those hands are subordinate, in the finished work. For paintings on a smaller scale, it was more possible to commission an exclusive performance. Thus the contract for a small altarpiece by Signorelli's great teacher, Piero della Francesca, specifies that "no painter may put his hand to the brush other than Piero himself."

There is no record of any comparable concern for exclusivity in the English theater. Unfortunately, the contracts that Shakespeare and his fellow dramatists almost certainly signed have not, with one significant exception, survived. But plays written for the professional theater are by their nature an even more explicitly collective art form than paintings; they depend for their full realization on the collaboration of others, and that collaboration may well extend to the fashioning of the script. It seems that some authors may simply have been responsible for providing plots that others then dramatized; still others were hired to "mend" old plays or to supply prologues, epilogues, or songs. A particular playwright's name came to be attached to a certain identifiable style—a characteristic set of plot devices, a marked rhetorical range, a tonality of character—but this name may refer in effect more to a certain product associated with a particular playing company than to the individual artist who may or may not have written most of the script. The one contract whose details do survive, that entered into by Richard Brome and the actors and owners of the Salisbury Court Theater in 1635, does not stipulate that Brome's plays must be written by him alone or even that he must be responsible for a certain specifiable proportion of each script. Rather, it specifies that the playwright "should not nor would write any play or any part of a play to any other players or playhouse, but apply all his study and endeavors therein for the benefit of the said company of the said playhouse." The Salisbury Court players want rights to everything Brome writes for the stage; the issue is not that the plays associated with his name be exclusively *his* but rather that he be exclusively *theirs*.

Recent textual scholarship, then, has been moving steadily away from a conception of Shakespeare's plays as direct, unmediated emanations from the mind of the author and toward a conception of them as working scripts, composed and continually reshaped as part of a collaborative commercial enterprise in competition with other, similar enterprises. One consequence has been the progressive weakening of the idea of the solitary, inspired genius, in the sense fashioned by Romanticism and figured splendidly in the statue of Shakespeare in the public gardens in Germany's Weimar, the city of Goethe and Schiller: the poet, with his sensitive, expressive face and high domed forehead sitting alone and brooding, a skull at his feet, a long-stemmed rose in his crotch. In place of this projection of German Romanticism, we have now a playwright and sometime actor who is also (to his considerable financial advantage) a major shareholder in the company—the Chamberlain's Men, later the King's Men—to which he loyally supplies for most of his career an average of two plays per year.

As a shareholder Shakespeare had to concern himself with such matters as economic cycles, lists of plague deaths, the cost of costumes, government censorship, city ordinances, the hiring and firing of personnel, and innumerable other factors that affected his enterprise. Practical considerations did not merely affect the context of his writing for the stage; they also shaped the form of what he wrote. His plays were not monuments, fixed in every detail and immobilized forever. They were like living beings, destined to change as a condition for their very survival.

One of the very first biographical mentions of Shakespeare, in the Reverend Thomas Fuller's *History of the Worthies of England* (1662), seems to have grasped this principle of mobility. Fuller reports—or imagines—the "wit-combats" that Shakespeare and Jonson had at the Mermaid Tavern:

> which two I behold like a Spanish great galleon and an English man of war; Master Jonson (like the former) was built far higher in learning, solid but slow in his performances. Shakespeare, with the English man of war, lesser in bulk, but lighter in sailing, could turn with all tides, tack about, and take advantage of all winds by the quickness of his wit and invention.

The encounters Fuller describes may be apocryphal, but to "turn with all tides, tack about, and take advantage of all winds" is a canny description of the highly mobile texts that Shakespeare fashioned and bequeathed to posterity.

Conjuring Shakespeare

The Elizabethan and Jacobean public had an interest in reading plays as well as seeing them. There was a lively market in such texts, often rushed into print to catch public excitement, and there is even evidence that at certain performances it was possible for audiences at the playhouse to purchase a copy of the very play they were watching.

Shakespeare's attitude to this market is unclear. Unlike Ben Jonson, he never personally edited and oversaw the publication of his plays, either individually or as a collection, but he may, for all we know, have imagined some day doing so. Perhaps death simply overtook him before he reached that goal. Certainly the Folio editors, though they were themselves fellow actors, thought of his plays as literary works. In 1623, seven years after the playwright's death, Heminges and Condell believed they could sell copies of their expensive collection of Shakespeare's plays—"What euer you do," they urge their readers, "buy"—by insisting that their texts were "as he conceiued them."

"As he conceived them": potential readers in the early seventeenth century then were already interested in access to Shakespeare's "conceits"—his "wit," his imagination, and his creative power—and were willing to assign a high value to the products of his particular, identifiable skill, one distinguishable from that of his company and of his rival playwrights. After all, Jonson's dedicatory poem in the Folio praises Shakespeare not as the playwright of the incomparable King's Men but as the equal of Aeschylus, Sophocles, and Euripides. And if we now see Shakespeare's dramaturgy in the context of his contemporaries and of a collective artistic practice, readers continue to have little difficulty recognizing that most of the plays attached to his name tower over those of his rivals.

The First Folio included an engraving purporting to show what Shakespeare looked like, but in the little poem that accompanied this image Jonson urged the reader to "look / Not on his Picture, but his Book." The words on the page then should conjure up the author himself; they should ideally give the reader unmediated access to the astonishing forge of imaginative power that was the mind of the dramatist. Such is the vision—at its core closely related to the preservation of the divinely inspired text in the great scriptural religions—that has driven many of the great editors who have for centuries produced successive editions of Shakespeare's works. The vision was not yet fully formed in the First Folio, for Heminges and Condell still felt obliged to apologize to their noble patrons for dedicating to them a collection of mere "trifles." But by the eighteenth century, there were no longer any ritual apologies for Shakespeare; instead, there was growing recognition of the supreme artistic importance of his works.

At the same time, from the eighteenth century onward, there was growing recognition of the uncertain, conflicting, and in some cases corrupt state of the surviving texts. Every conceivable step, it was thought, must be undertaken to correct mistakes, strip away corruptions, and return the texts to their pure and unsullied form. Noticing that there were multiple texts of fully half of the plays and noticing too that these texts often contain significant variants, editors routinely conflated the distinct versions into a single text in an attempt to reconstruct the ideal, definitive, complete, and perfect copy that they imagined Shakespeare must have aspired to and eventually reached for each of his plays. In doing so they succeeded in producing something that Shakespeare himself never wrote.

Heminges and Condell, who knew the author and had access to at least some of his manuscripts, lamented the fact that Shakespeare did not live "to have set forth and overseen his own writings." But even had he done so—or, alternatively, even if a cache of his manuscripts were discovered in a Warwickshire attic tomorrow—all of the editorial problems would not be solved, though the textual landscape would change, nor would all of the levels of mediation be swept away. The written word has strange powers: it seems to hold onto something of the very life of the person who has written it, but it also seems to pry that life loose from the writer, exposing it to vagaries of history and chance quite independent of those to which the writer was personally subject. Moreover, with the passing of centuries, the language itself and the whole frame of reference within which language and symbols are understood have decisively changed. The most learned modern scholar still lives at a huge experiential remove from Shakespeare's world and, even holding a precious copy of the First Folio in hand, cannot escape having to read across a vast chasm of time what is, after all, an edited text. The rest of us cannot so much as indulge in the fantasy of direct access: our eyes inevitably wander to the glosses and the explanatory notes.

Abandoning the dream of direct access to Shakespeare's final and definitive intentions is not a cause for despair, nor should it lead us to throw our hands up and declare that one text is as good as another. What it does is to encourage us to be actively interested in the editorial principles that underlie the particular edition that we are using. It is said that the great artist Brueghel once told an inquisitive connoisseur who had come to his studio, "Keep your nose out of my paintings; the smell of the paint will poison you." In the case of Shakespeare, it is increasingly important to bring one's nose close to the page, as it were, and sniff the ink. More precisely, it is important to understand the rationale for the choices that the editors have made.

The rationale behind *The Norton Shakespeare* is described at length in the Textual Introduction to this volume. What should be stressed here is the fact that

Shakespeare was the master of the unfinished, the perpetually open. The notion of finding a perfectly fixed text of one of his plays, the copy that he directly handed over to the printer as his "final" version, goes against everything we know about his personal practice and about Elizabethan and Jacobean theater. Shakespeare wrote his plays to be performed by professional players in a range of different settings, at different times, and before different publics. The project required considerable flexibility. As a working playwright, he seems to have thought about the creation of "parts" or roles, often with specific actors in mind though always with the understanding that the personnel might change. Taken all together, of course, the parts made up a whole, but both the individual pieces and the larger structure they formed were and have remained open. The editors of *The Norton Shakespeare* have tried to record and preserve this openness.

Speaking only for myself, I will confess a further ambition: I would like to meet Shakespeare in person. I think that throughout his career Shakespeare produced in effect detachable parts of himself, parts that derived from his personhood (his social relationships, his acquired knowledge, his temperament, his memories, his inner life, and so forth) but that moved independently in the world. He created out of himself hundreds of secondary agents, his characters, some of whom seem even to float free of the particular narrative structures in which they perform their given roles and to take on an agency we ordinarily reserve for biological persons. As an artist he literally gave his life to these agents, transferring his personal energies to them.

I do not mean that Shakespeare's characters are all self-portraits in the sense of referring back to his individual existence (though some of them almost certainly do). I mean rather that Shakespeare's life is, in an unusually intense and vivid way, in his works. And therefore when I open the printed book or scroll through the Digital Edition, I feel his eerie presence and want to call out, with the words Ben Jonson wrote in his dedicatory poem to the First Folio, "My Shakespeare, rise!"

General Textual Introduction

GORDON McMULLAN AND SUZANNE GOSSETT

Most people read an edition of Shakespeare's plays and poems because they want to read the plays and poems, not because they wish to dwell on the material origins of the texts they are reading—where the texts came from, how the manuscripts looked, who printed them, for whom they were printed, how the publishing practices of the English Renaissance made them what they are. Yet attention to the text itself is, we believe, an integral part of understanding the meaning of Shakespeare's works, considerably enhancing the pleasure of the reading experience. Seeing Shakespeare in the theater, reading Shakespeare on the page: both can offer extraordinary, multiply layered experiences of entertainment and intellectual uplift, a sense of unparalleled access to the past, and often simply a great deal of fun. We have edited the text of Shakespeare with these pleasures, and the reader's choices, in mind, and we wish to share with you a sense of the further levels of engagement that close attention to the origins of the text itself can bring.

For us, first and foremost, the *textual* is inseparable from the *critical*. That is, the "themes" we locate in Shakespeare, the sense of the place of the plays and poems in Shakespeare's world and in our own, the ways in which these remarkable writings require us to reflect on being human, on being gendered, on living in community, on having an ethnicity and a class status, all have their foundation in the words we read— and if we don't know whether the words we are reading are the "right" ones, or if we don't have the tools to reflect on the challenges presented by the very idea of "right" words, then we may miss out on key aspects of the Shakespearean experience. The fantasies of the "anti-Stratfordians" (people who claim Shakespeare's works were written by one or another equally implausible candidate) serve to remind us of the obsession of our age with Shakespearean *authenticity,* with the urge to ensure that the Shakespeare we see performed, or that we read or study, is the *real* Shakespeare, the *authentic* Shakespeare. The primary question we address in our textual introduction is central to this debate—"How authentic is the text I am reading?"—and in order to do this we need to reflect on two things: on the nature of the Shakespearean text and on the complex idea of "authenticity." Once we have done that, we can begin to explain some of the decisions we made in editing the texts that together form *The Norton Shakespeare.*

The "Authentic" Shakespeare

For centuries, playgoers and readers had two questions answered for them in advance: which plays and poems to read as "Shakespeare's" (the reader logically assumed that if a play or poem was in the "complete works," then it was Shakespeare's, and if not, not), and, beyond that, which *text* of a given Shakespeare play or poem to read. This second question might seem odd. Surely there is only one *Hamlet* and that is the *Hamlet* Shakespeare wrote? Yet not only does more than one authoritative text of certain plays (above all, as it happens, of *Hamlet*) exist, some of which are very different from each other, but the word "authoritative" raises a third question—notably, "On what grounds do we decide that a printed text is close to what Shakespeare actually wrote?" Moreover, the first of these questions is itself not straightforward. The boundaries of the Shakespeare canon—those texts accepted as being written in whole or in part by Shakespeare—have always been porous. Neither *Pericles* nor *The Two Noble Kinsmen,* for instance, was included in the First Folio, yet both have long been attributed to Shakespeare (in each case, as it happens, to Shakespeare working jointly with another playwright, as pretty much all his fellow Elizabethan and Jacobean playwrights did), and both are now invariably included in "Complete Works" editions. Some plays have been considered part of the Shakespeare canon for far less time. *Edward III,* for instance, now appears in editions as a "Shakespeare and others" play, where a couple of decades ago it did not. Times change, evidence surfaces, and methods of attributing authorship develop. As a result, other plays continue to hover at the edges of the canon. At the time of writing, the newest contender for inclusion is a celebrated play by Thomas Kyd called *The Spanish Tragedy,* for which, it is suggested, Shakespeare supplied extra scenes, capitalizing on the play's success. *The Spanish Tragedy* does not appear in the present edition of *The Norton Shakespeare,* but if in due course we are sufficiently convinced by the arguments for its inclusion, then in it will come. What the French thinker Jacques Derrida called "the logic of the supplement" operates here: each time you add something to a volume called "Complete" you make it *more* complete, but the fact that you needed to add something to complete a volume already claiming to be "complete" has the effect of undermining the very possibility of completeness. For editors of Shakespeare, this is unavoidable—and to be celebrated, not resented.

It is not only the *external* borders of the Shakespeare canon that are fluid; the *internal* borders too—the choice of words within a given play or poem—have never, to the surprise of many readers, been firmly fixed. Shakespeare lovers are aware, perhaps, that Hamlet's flesh is too "solid," "sullied," or "sallied," depending on which version of the play one reads; they may also have wondered which of two "others"—"the base Judean" or "the base Indian"—is the one to which Othello really means to compare himself just before his suicide; but they may not realize that these celebrated instances of Shakespearean textual choice are part of a much broader canvas of instabilities, uncertainties, and options. This means that not only the choice of play, but the choice of *text* of that play, affects the reader's experience of Shakespeare.

The key question arising here is that of the "right" reading, the "authentic" reading, a status usually taken to require a direct relationship to the author. The mental adjustment needed is to accept that, quite often, there may be either *no* "right" reading or *more than one*. We cannot ever know exactly what Shakespeare wrote because (with one limited, debated exception) we do not have the holograph manuscript (a manuscript in his own handwriting) of any of his plays or poems. Shakespeare's own manuscripts of the plays in the First Folio or in the various quartos that predate the Folio have not survived, and so editors are unable to do the one thing they would most like to be able to do, which is to compare what Shakespeare actually wrote with what was printed. The apparent exception is the lines in the surviving manuscript of *Sir Thomas More* that are largely accepted as being in Shakespeare's hand—but, maddeningly, this is the one play in the Shakespeare canon as currently constituted that never found its way into print in the late sixteenth or early seventeenth century. So, even in the case of the one brief section of extant manuscript generally thought to be in Shakespeare's hand, we cannot make a direct comparison between what was written and what was printed.

It was long believed that Shakespeare never revised his texts (a myth prompted by the prefatory material to the First Folio) and therefore that there must have been one, and only one, lost master original from which all subsequent texts derive. But further complicating the notion of the "authentic Shakespeare" is the existence of short, variant quarto texts of several plays. Because certain of these are noticeably inferior to the Folio (or, sometimes, to a fuller quarto) text of the same play, they were traditionally referred to as "bad quartos." In recent years, scholars have sought to replace the unhelpful connotations of "bad" with neutral descriptive terms such as "short quartos," but the point of origin of these texts remains unclear. Are they "authentic"? One long-standing argument has it that they are "reported" texts, the product of "pirate" printers who sat a handful of actors down and persuaded them to recall not only their own lines but the entire play—this, it is claimed, explains the discrepancy in quality between the lines of certain characters in these quartos (e.g., Mercutio in the First Quarto of *Romeo and Juliet,* whose lines are nearly identical to those in the much fuller Second Quarto) and those of others. These quartos vary considerably, from the brief, highly problematic quarto of *The Merry Wives of Windsor* to the much more independent and interpretively convincing First Quarto of *Hamlet.* It has sometimes been proposed that these quartos may represent Shakespeare's early drafts. A further possibility, championed recently as a development of increasing editorial openness to the possibility that Shakespeare did occasionally revise his own work, is that the short quartos represent "theatrical" versions of the plays, whereas the lengthy Folio texts represent more overtly "literary" versions designed with readers in mind. It may be that we will never fully understand how these quartos came to be so different from the fuller, ostensibly more authoritative versions in the First Folio and elsewhere, but it seems essential to present them in all their intriguing difference. Our editorial principles and the technology we adopt in this edition allow us to include fully edited versions of all these quartos, so that the reader may understand the complexity of deciding what constitutes "authentic" Shakespeare.

The Text in the Print House

One reason it is hard to know what Shakespeare actually wrote is that all early modern printed texts include interpretations, adjustments, and misreadings of the manuscripts on which they are based (which may have been the author's own or a neater scribal copy), as well as mechanical errors made by the compositors in the process of setting the type for printing. Moreover, workers in the Renaissance print house did not simply transfer the words passively from writer to reader; they actively intervened in what they printed. There was no fixed way to spell words in Shakespeare's day—Shakespeare himself spelled his own name differently at different times when signing documents—and compositors made the most of this irregularity to even out or "justify" the line they were setting (for example, by adding or removing a final "e" on an individual word). Similarly, there was no sense that the printer's duty was to print exactly what he found in the manuscript with which he was working. On the contrary, since early modern play manuscripts typically included little or no punctuation, it was the job of the compositor setting the type to add punctuation so as to enable and enhance the reader's experience. One of the most misleading of Shakespearean myths, one prevalent among actors even today, is the claim that the punctuation in the First Folio expresses "Shakespeare's instructions to actors": those theater professionals who have carefully timed their pauses and breaths according to the arrangement of commas and semicolons in the First Folio may be sad to learn that they are almost certainly basing their practice on the habits of Compositor A or Compositor J (since we almost never know the names of the workers in the print houses, compositors are usually referred to by letter).

To understand how the printing process affected the texts we read, it helps to know how the two principal formats in which Shakespeare's plays were printed—folio and quarto—were put together. A folio is made up of standard-sized sheets of paper printed with two pages on each side, then folded in half and assembled with several other such folded sheets inserted inside each other to form a "gathering" or "quire"; these gatherings are then stitched together to form the book. A quarto is made of the same standard-sized sheets of paper but is printed with four pages on each side and then folded twice (so that it is a quarter the size of the original sheet and half the size of a folio); each set of four leaves is either stitched together with other sets or inserted into a number of others to form a gathering as with a folio; the gatherings are then sewn through the central fold to form a book (which is why, very occasionally, you might come across a book where some of the pages need cutting apart if the print is to be read; the folding of the sheet to form eight pages will always require two edges to be cut after binding). Try folding a sheet of paper and you will see how this works. If you write the page numbers from one to eight on the folded sheet and then unfold it again, you will see that pages 1, 4, 5, and 8 (the "outer forme") are on one side and 2, 3, 6, and 7 (the "inner forme") are on the other, and that only some pages on each side are printed consecutively. (Scholars in fact tend to specify locations in early printed texts not by page numbers, which are notoriously unreliable in books from Shakespeare's day, but by what are called "signatures," which express the physical construction of the book—that is, the number of leaves collected together as a gathering and the number of gatherings that make up the book. Thus B2, or B2r, signifies the front side—recto—of the second sheet in gathering B, while C3v means the reverse side—verso—of the third sheet in gathering C.) A compositor setting either an inner or an outer form was thus not setting the type in the order of the plot, and you can imagine the loss of understanding this might produce at moments of complication in the text, even in an experienced professional. And then of course there is the Elizabethan equivalent of the coffee break to consider: one compositor would at times take over from another and carry on setting the type, and you can see where this has happened because the new compositor has different habits—his own preferences for abbreviating speech prefixes, say—and in a context where there are two characters with similar names he might misunderstand the speech prefix for the one and set it as the other, thus attributing a speech to the wrong speaker—all of which makes it that much harder to determine the nature of the manuscript from which the compositors were working.

If you look at the illustration on the next page, you can see a visual summary of the print workers' tasks. In the right foreground a boy is examining a forme (the frame into which the type is locked for printing) that has been set with type; he seems to be doing a last check against the manuscript while waiting for the forme to be placed in the press. To the far left, a pair of compositors is setting type from typecases, with the manuscript copy from which they are working stuck to the wall in front of them; behind them, a worker is replacing used type into a typecase arranged alphabetically and vertically ("upper-case" letters, i.e., capitals, at the top, "lower-case" below); to his right, a bespectacled proofreader checks an as-yet-uncorrected sheet against copy; in the background, a figure who is just possibly a woman (there is evidence that women worked in, and sometimes even, as printers' widows, owned, print houses) is using absorbent, wool-stuffed leather balls to apply ink to the forme before it is placed on the bed of the press; and, finally, the pressman pulls the bar across to lower the central weight of the press onto the conjunction of inked type and blank paper and thus imprint the sheet.

The first sheet pulled would be handed to the proofreader for checking, and he would mark errors for correction; when he finished, the press would be stopped, the (now very inky) type adjusted to make the corrections, and the process would then continue. The pressman would, however, keep printing sheets during the twenty minutes it might take the proofreader to work through the proof, and those uncorrected sheets (a hundred or so) would be stacked together indiscriminately with the corrected ones in the overall print run (which was 1,200 or so copies in the case of the First Folio), not separated or discarded. The result is that early printed books are a blend of uncorrected and corrected sheets, and no individual copy of a book such

Unknown engraver, after Stradanus (Jan van der Straet), *Invention of Book Printing,* from *Nova reperta* (New inventions and discoveries of modern times; ca. 1599–1603).

as the Folio is likely to be exactly the same as any other, given the random distribution of uncorrected sheets. If you look closely at the list of textual variants to this edition, you will see that editors sometimes note when they have selected a corrected reading from a copy of the base text other than the primary one from which they are working.

One printing-house factor likely to affect the text was the need for print workers to "cast off," that is, to work out how many lines of a given manuscript would fit on a printed page, and to make pencil annotations in the manuscript to mark where page breaks would fall in print. Occasionally mistakes would be made, and you can see in the printed text where either a compositor has realized that he still has a lot of words to set but little space to play with, and so keeps everything tight, or where he is, by contrast, running out of words yet still has a fair amount of page to fill, and so deploys white space, printers' ornaments, and the like. For examples of these composition strategies, see pages 80 and 81.

of Romeo and Iuliet.

On Thurſday next be married to the Countie.

  Iu.: Tell me not Frier that thou hearſt of it,
Vnleſſe thou tell me how we may preuent it.
Giue me ſome ſudden counſell : els behold
Twixt my extreames and me, this bloodie Knife
Shall play the Vmpeere, arbitrating that
Which the Commiſsion of thy yeares and arte
Could to no iſſue of true honour bring.
Speake not, be briefe : for I deſire to die,
If what thou ſpeakſt, ſpeake not of remedie.

  Fr : Stay *Iuliet*, I doo ſpie a kinde of hope,
VVhich craues as deſperate an execution,
As that is deſperate we would preuent.
If rather than to marrie Countie *Paris*
Thou haſt the ſtrength or will to ſlay thy ſelfe,
Tis not vnlike that thou wilt vndertake
A thing like death to chyde away this ſhame,
That coapſt with death it ſelfe to flye from blame.
And if thou dooſt, Ile giue thee remedie,

  Iul : Oh bid me leape (rather than marrie *Paris*)
From off the battlements of yonder tower :
Or chaine me to ſome ſteepie mountaines top,
VVhere roaring Beares and ſauage Lions are :
Or ſhut me nightly in a Charnell-houſe,
VVith reekie ſhankes, and yeolow chaples ſculls :
Or lay me in tombe with one new dead :
Things that to heare them namde haue made me tremble ;
And I will doo it without feare or doubt,
To keep my ſelfe a faithfull vnſtaind VVife
To my deere Lord, my deereſt *Romeo*.

  Fr : Hold *Iuliet*, hie thee home, get thee to bed,
Let not thy Nurſe lye with thee in thy Chamber :
And when thou art alone, take thou this Violl,
And this diſtilled Liquor drinke thou off :
VVhen preſently through all thy veynes ſhall run
A dull and heauie ſlumber, which ſhall ſeaze

H 3

Each

Q1 *Romeo and Juliet*, H3r. An example of a "tight" page where the casting-off seems to have been efficient.

The excellent Tragedie

Each yitall spirit: for no Pulse shall keepe
His naturall progresse, but surcease to beate:
No signe of breath shall testifie thou liust,
And in this borrowed likenes of shrunke death,
Thou shalt remaine full two and fortie houres.
And when thou art laid in thy Kindreds Vault,
Ile send in hast to *Mantua* to thy Lord,
And he shall come and take thee from thy graue.

    Iul: Frier I goe, be sure thou send for my deare *Romeo.*

                                 Exeunt.

Enter olde Capolet, his Wife, Nurse, and
Seruingman.

    Capo: Where are you sirra?
    Ser: Heere forsooth.
    Capo: Goe, prouide me twentie cunning Cookes.
    Ser: I warrant you Sir, let me alone for that, Ile knowe
them by licking their fingers.
    Capo: How canst thou know them so?
    Ser: Ah Sir, tis an ill Cooke cannot licke his owne fin-
gers.
    Capo: Well get you gone.

                  Exit Seruingman.

But wheres this Head-strong?
    Moth: Shees gone (my Lord) to Frier *Laurence* Cell
To be confest.
    Capo: Ah, he may hap to doo some good of her,
A headstrong selfewild harlotrie it is.

                         Enter

Q1 *Romeo and Juliet,* H3v. An example of a "loose" page—note the white space and use of the ornament.

These moments of professional adjustment necessarily affect the texts we have inherited, and a close look at the early printed page may explain why lines that seem metrically regular have been set as prose, say, or as fragmented verse lines. Here from the First Quarto of *King Lear* is an example of verse lines that have been squeezed into prose in order to save space:

The Hiſtorie of King Lear.

like a riotous Inne;epicuriſme, and luſt make more like a tauerne
or brothell, then a great pallace; the ſhame it ſelfe doth ſpeake
for inſtant remedie: be thou deſired by her, that elſe will take the
thing ſheebegs, a little to diſquantitie your traine, and the remainder that ſhall ſtill depend, to bee ſuch men as may beſort
your age, that know themſelues and you.

Lear. Darkenes,and Deuils! ſaddle my horſes, call my traine
together; degenerate baſtard, ile not trouble thee; yet haue I left
a daughter.

Gon. You ſtrike my people;and your diſordred rabble,make
ſeruants of their betters,   *Enter Duke.*

Lear. We that too late repent. O ſir,are you come?is it your
will that wee prepare any horſes?ingratitude!thou marble har-
ted fiend, more hideous when thou ſheweſt thee in a child,then
the Sea-monſter: deteſted kite, thou liſt my traine, and men of
choiſe and rareſt parts, that all particulars of dutie knowe, and
in the moſt exaƈt regard, ſupport the worſhips of their name?O
moſt ſmall fault, how vgly did'ſt thou in *Cordelia* ſhewe, that
like an engine wrencht my frame of nature from the fixt place;
drew from my heart all loue,and added to the gall. O *Lear!Lear!*
beat at this gate that let thy folly in, and thy deere iudgement
out; goe,goe, my people.

Duke, My Lord,I am giltles,as I am ignorant.

Lear. It may be ſo my Lord: harke *Nature*,heare deere God-
deſſe; ſuſpend thy purpoſe, if thou did'ſt intend to make this
creature fruitful,into her wombe conuey ſterility; drie vp in hir
the organs of increaſe,and from her derogate body neuer ſpring
a babe to honour her; if ſhee muſt teeme, create her childe of
ſpleene, that it may liue and bee a thourt diſſeatur'd torment to
her; let it ſtampe wrinckles in her brow of youth; with accent
teares , fret channels in her cheeks;turne all her mothers paines
and benefits to laughter and contempt, that ſhee may feele,that
ſhe may feele, how ſharper then a ſerpents tooth it is, to haue a
thankleſſe child; goe, goe, my people.

Duke. Now Gods that we adore, whereof comes this !

Gon. Neuer afflict your ſelfe to know the cauſe, but let his
diſpoſition haue that ſcope that dotage giues it.

Lear. What,fiftie of my followers at a clap,within a fortnight?

      D 2   *Duke.*

Q1 *King Lear*, D2r

And here from the First Quarto of *Henry V* is an example of prose that has been set as rough verse (notice how the first word of each line of Fluellen's speeches is capitalized) in order to stretch it out to fill the available space:

of Henry the fift.

So hath he sworne the like to me.
 K. How think you *Flewellen*,is it lawfull he keep his oath?
 Fl. And it please your maiefty,tis lawful he keep his vow.
If he be periur'd once,he is as arrant a beggerly knaue,
As treads vpon too blacke shues.
 Kin. His enemy may be a gentleman of worth.
 Flew. And if he be as good a gentleman as Lucifer
And Belzebub,and the diuel himfelfe,
Tis meete he keepe his vowe.
 Kin. Well firrha keep your word.
Vnder what Captain serueft thou?
 Soul. Vnder Captaine *Gower*.
 Flew. Captaine *Gower* is a good Captaine
And hath good littrature in the warres.
 Kin. Go call him hither.
 Soul. I will my Lord.

           Exit fouldier.

 Kin. Captain *Flewellen*,when *Alonfon* and I was
Downe together,*I* tooke this gloue off from his helmet,
Here *Flewellen*, weare it. If any do challenge it,
He is a friend of *Alonfons*,
And an enemy to mee.
 Fle. Your maieftie doth me as great a fauour
As can be defired in the harts of his fubiects.
I would fee that man now that fhould chalenge this gloue:
And it pleafe God of his grace,*I* would but fee him,
That is all.
 Kin. *Flewellen* knowft thou Captaine *Gower*?
 Fle. Captaine *Gower* is my friend.
And if it like your maieftie,*I* know him very well.
 Kin. Go call him hither.
 Flew. *I* will and it fhall pleafe your maieftie.
 Kin. Follow *Flewellen* clofely at the heeles,
The gloue he weares, it was the fouldiers:
      F 2   *It*

Q1 *Henry V*, F2r

Understanding these print-house procedures clarifies how at each stage of the printing process error and variety may be introduced: at the stage of "casting off," at the stage of setting the type from manuscript (especially if the writer had difficult handwriting), at the stages of proofreading and press correction, and in the assembly of corrected and uncorrected sheets into the book itself. Clearly, we need to be wary of assuming that the material features of the early texts unconditionally transmit "authorial intention."

What Kind of Edition Is This?

Editions always exist for readers. There is no more fundamental question for an editor than "For whom am I editing?" because the answer determines very substantially the nature of the edition produced. No edition can be designed for every imaginable reader; on the contrary, specific kinds of editing are done with specific sets of readers in mind. "Diplomatic" editions, for instance, are designed for scholars: they reproduce all the features of the original text without correction or alteration, but for most readers they would make for an unappealing reading experience. An "old-spelling" edition is another possibility: it is edited (that is, an editor has emended the text where error is apparent and included other aids to reading, such as stage directions), but it remains in the spelling (and, perhaps, the punctuation) of Shakespeare's day and is thus again likely to be difficult going for most contemporary readers. Modern-spelling editions are designed to make early modern texts as accessible as possible: the editor makes necessary corrections to the text, adds stage directions where they are needed to clarify the action, makes consistent certain variable features of the original, and modernizes the spelling and punctuation of those texts (while keeping a close eye on moments when the modernizing of spelling or punctuation might change the actual meaning). It is this latter course—the modern-spelling edition designed to offer maximum accessibility for contemporary readers—that *The Norton Shakespeare* adopts, but with certain developments and enhancements and with a specific set of principles for editorial choice.

We—the team of editors who together created this edition—have edited the works of Shakespeare—that is, the existing early texts—from scratch on the basis of a set of principles known as "single-text editing." The first two editions of *The Norton Shakespeare* were based on the text created in 1986 for Oxford University Press—a groundbreaking edition that transformed the modern editing of Shakespeare—but editorial practice has changed since that time, and Norton has created a new text for the present moment. This text is new both in its physical construction and in its theoretical underpinnings.

First, this, the Third Edition of *The Norton Shakespeare*, is "born digital." That is, we have taken the opportunity offered by the interactive ebook format to offer readers and classroom teachers an unprecedented set of options that will allow them to engage with, not just be passive recipients of, the words before them. The Digital Edition allows readers to open textual and performance comments by clicking on icons in the margin next to the line they are reading; to toggle from the text to a facsimile of the original printed folio or quarto; to hear all the songs scattered through the plays; and to listen to eight hours of selected scenes read by professional actors. In addition, readers can view the Quarto and Folio versions of *King Lear* side by side, scrolling as they choose; side-by-side viewing is also available for selected scenes from six plays and for two versions of a sonnet. Readers using the print and electronic editions in combination will be able to move between thumbing through the printed book and navigating the ebook not only for added portability but also in order to find additional versions of fifteen plays plus many enhancements, not least a selection of Textual Comments designed to underline the interconnections of textual decisions and the meaning of the plays.

Second, this edition adopts a new approach to the Shakespearean text, one made possible in part by the opportunities offered by the digital platform. Our underlying editorial principle has been, at its simplest, to edit the *text,* not the *work.* Let us explain what we mean by this with reference in particular to the plays (though there are similar issues with the sonnets). Shakespeare's plays exist in imperfect ways— none of them ideal, none of them perfectly representing what Shakespeare wrote or what his first audiences heard. Editors have always recognized that these surviving printed texts vary in their origins, though all must bear in some way "traces" of the original literary works that Shakespeare wrote out with quill and paper. Lying behind the surviving texts are, variously, authorial drafts, "fair" or scribal copies, theatrical promptbooks, and occasionally unfinished materials—often a mixture of more than one of these. One older editorial tradition sought to address the imperfections present in the texts as a result of this variable provenance by reconstructing, to a greater or lesser extent, an imagined original, creating an edition that—drawing on their professional knowledge of the writing habits of Shakespeare and his contemporaries, of Elizabethan handwriting, and of the printing process—the editors believed to be nearer to what Shakespeare and his audiences would have known or wanted than the actual surviving text with its flaws and imperfections. Of course editors need to correct many of those flaws and imperfections: to give readers a comprehensible reading experience, you must address errors and other distractions. But we believe it is not necessary or even desirable to try to reconstruct a "perfect" work that may never have existed in this form. Consequently, we have made the decision not to do what editors have normally done for centuries, which is to emend at will by merging the differing elements of distinct early texts of a given play, but rather to provide carefully considered editions of each of the early authoritative texts of works for which more than one such text survives. Similarly, in dealing with plays for which only one text survives, we have stayed as close as possible to that text when sense can be made of it, not adopting a traditional emendation if it appears to us to be the product of editorial preference rather than necessary for sense. In other words, we have chosen to edit the *texts* we actually have, not the *play* or the *poem* we do not, to accept uncertainty, and to exercise a certain skepticism toward earlier claims that sometimes made the editor seem a substitute for Shakespeare.

As we have noted, this edition was "born digital"—that is, we set out to invert the prior hierarchy of page and screen by creating an edition that would reach its fullest potential in digital form. Both the print and the digital editions are, in different ways, "complete works." The print volume includes all the poems, some of which exist in various manuscripts and others in print; there is usually only one form of each of these, though we include the entire *Passionate Pilgrim,* which was falsely ascribed to Shakespeare alone but does include some of his poems in variant forms. It—the print volume—includes all the plays too, providing one text for each play (except for *Hamlet,* for which we offer two editions, the First Quarto and a text merging the Second Quarto with materials from the Folio, and *King Lear,* for which we offer editions of the Quarto and the Folio, plus a merged text including all materials in both: for an account of the inclusion of these merged editions, or "conflations," in an edition based on single-text editing principles, see page 87, below. In deciding which of several texts to include in the bound volume we have used a pragmatic and flexible measure. Rather than (as has been done in the past) claiming to be able to determine and present the text that was Shakespeare's "original" version—or his "final" version, or the one that the company probably performed—we have in the case of plays that exist in significantly different texts printed the text that is most complete and apparently most finished. This often means the text in the First Folio, where about half the plays appear for the first time in the only text we have. But when—as, for example, in the case of *Romeo and Juliet* or of *1 Henry IV*—the Folio text is itself derived from a good quarto, we choose that earlier quarto as the base text from which our print edition is created.

We encourage readers to work with both versions, digital and print, to gain the most possible from *The Norton Shakespeare*. Editing Shakespeare digitally enables us to offer readers the opportunity to read, compare, and contrast the two (or, in the case of *Hamlet*, three) early texts of each of the plays for which multiple texts exist. Whether the plays exist in one substantive text or several, we have taken the same approach to the editing—modernizing spelling and punctuation on principles that are consistent across the edition, providing additional stage directions where they are required to clarify the action, and trusting the original text wherever possible, emending only where absolutely necessary and not "reconstructing" material in addition to that provided by the surviving texts.

The primary impact of these choices is, naturally, on those plays for which more than one early substantive text exists. For instance, we provide (in the Digital Edition) edited texts of Quarto *Othello* and Folio *Othello*—two different texts representing, we believe, two subtly different plays. Even when two separate early texts are nearly identical, the differences can be fascinating. Thus, in *Othello,* the female protagonist, Desdemona, infuriates her father by marrying an older man who is both black and a convert from Islam. Her father, who initially voices a series of racist reasons for assuming that Othello had brainwashed his daughter into eloping with him, sees her as shy and almost worryingly asexual (she has shown no interest in the eligible men he has introduced her to), but Othello's narrative of the process by which he wooed her suggests that she is more actively aware of her sexuality than her father believes: "My story being done, / She gave me for my pains a world of sighs. / [. . .] She thanked me / And bade me, if I had a friend that loved her, / I should but teach him how to tell my story, / And that would woo her" (Q 1.3.145–46, 150–53).

> She gaue me for my paines a world of sighes;
> She swore Ifaith twas strange,twas passing strange;
> Twas pittifull,twas wondrous pittifull;

Q1 *Othello*, C3v

So the Quarto. The slightly later Folio version of the play alters one key word: "My story being done, / She gave me for my pains a world of kisses" (F 1.3.158–59).

> She gaue me for my paines a world of kisses:
> She swore in faith 'twas strange : 'twas passing strange,
> 'Twas pittifull : 'twas wondrous pittifull.

F *Othello*, ss5v

Thus there are two equally coherent versions of the same line, different in one small but significant way. By providing editions of both texts, we avoid the necessity of preferring the one reading over the other (male editors have typically preferred "sighs," just as the editorial tradition seems generally to assume, in the phrasing of inserted stage directions, that men kiss women, not that women and men kiss each other), and we open up for our readers a degree of choice—to read the Quarto with its sighing Desdemona or the Folio with its more ardent, kissing Desdemona—and their decision about which version to read will impact the way they see the tragedy unfolding and thus their interpretation of the play. In this way, the study of the material features of the text and of the meaning of the play are inseparable.

This tiny difference between Quarto *Othello* and Folio *Othello* may represent revised authorial intention or some incidental external influence; we cannot know for certain. But there is a category of difference between Quarto and Folio that reminds us that when we read Shakespeare's plays we are dealing with the substantially collaborative process that is theatrical production—and thus with texts that have in various ways gone through the performance process. The severe reduction in Emilia's and Desdemona's parts in act 4 of Quarto *Othello*—the cutting, for instance, of the "Willow Song" that Desdemona sings before she goes to bed for the last time or of Emilia's wry lines about husbands—may be due not to authorial choice, a decision on Shakespeare's part to reduce the prominence of the women at this late stage of the play, but to theatrical necessity, that is, the presumed absence from the King's Men at one point of boy actors with sufficient singing ability or stamina. Often we can only guess at the reasons for such changes, but the point is that they are very often material and environmental, not intentional in the sense of being deliberate changes made for artistic reasons by the author. Yet they cannot be dismissed simply as "inauthentic," not only because we do not know Shakespeare's role at such moments but also because all staged plays are necessarily constructed through collaborative engagement between text and actor. Furthermore, for readers and playgoers across subsequent centuries, these renegotiated texts, offering evidence of multiple inputs for a range of practical reasons, were the "real" Shakespeare. Knowing about the practical processes of playwriting, performance, and printing enables the reader to gain a fuller understanding of the nature of the Shakespearean text as an expression of the highly socialized process of dramatic creativity.

We have noted in passing that, across the centuries, the borders of the Shakespeare canon have been fluid. For a century and a half, the *King Lear* that audiences saw in the theater was not Shakespeare's *King Lear* as we know it, but an adaptation of the play created by Irish poet and playwright Nahum Tate in the late seventeenth century that radically cut and altered the original, even providing a happy ending that suited the theatrical expectations of the day but looks to us bewilderingly inappropriate. Once the popularity of the Tate version had faded, the *King Lear* that audiences began to see reverted to "Shakespeare's *King Lear*"—or, rather, to a particular version of that play, one that editors (and directors) assembled from the two markedly different early texts, Quarto and Folio, by including as many of the different lines as possible from each and merging or "conflating" them into a play a few hundred lines longer than either of the early texts. The paradox is obvious—in the process of trying to present the reader with a "Shakespearean" text, editors produced a text different from either of the ones for which Shakespeare was responsible—yet for readers from the mid-nineteenth to the late twentieth centuries, this elongated version of *King Lear* was the one they read and grew to know and love as "Shakespeare's" play.

This history underpins the decision of *The Norton Shakespeare* to include, alongside editions of the early texts of *Hamlet* and *King Lear*, a further, "scars and stitches" conflated edition of each—that is, an edition of each play that, by way of indentation and a distinctive yet quiet difference in font, makes the process of conflation visible without intruding excessively on the pleasure of the reading experience. We provide these multiple options because they will enable readers to see how these texts changed, developed, and were remade across time. In the case of *King Lear*, it is very possible that Shakespeare was involved in reworking his tragedy a couple of years after he had first written it and it had gone into regular production, and readers can reflect on that dynamic process by comparing the two early versions; equally, they can choose to read the "scars and stitches" edition, which both replicates the experience of nineteenth- and twentieth-century readers who came to know the play through traditional conflated editions and makes visible the process through which that conflation was achieved. Thus in the Digital Edition we offer three versions of *King Lear*—and four of *Hamlet*—so as to enable readers to witness the dynamic and contingent processes that go into the bringing-into-the-present of Shakespeare's plays.

"Single-Text Editing" and the Treatment of Error

The Norton Shakespeare seeks to minimize intervention by the editor, but there are nonetheless occasions when the editor must assist the reader in making sense of the text and where it is not immediately obvious how to do so. In order to explain our decision making at such moments, we will offer some examples. Readers will see that for all texts in this edition, both print and digital, we offer in the Digital Edition a set of Textual Variants, compressed notes in which editors mark each moment where the edited version is in some way different from the "base text," that is, from the original quarto or folio text from which the edition is formed, specifying where the preferred word or other feature originates—from another early text, or from the editorial tradition, or from our own choice. No edition of a Shakespeare play can simply present the exact words of its base text, because no early text is free from error or complication. How many times, after all, reading a modern printed book, have you spotted errors, omissions, or typos? Even with the vast technological transformations since Shakespeare's death, the printing process remains flawed; so you would expect that any text printed in (or somewhat after) Shakespeare's day—created on a manually operated press using fiddly metal type set by hand in wooden frames, in often cramped conditions, using toxic ink, and always under pressure to speed up the process to keep the business afloat—would include a fair number of such errors. As we have noted, the print-house workers were actively involved in the creation of the Shakespearean text, an involvement that is by no means limited to error—but human error is inevitable and pervasive.

Consequently, editors working on the basis of single-text editing must always balance their commitment to the text against the possibility of error. Our basic premise is that the editor should not attempt to alter or "improve"—by following a different text, the editorial tradition, or her own informed invention—any reading that can make sense, even if that meaning seems a little strained. While such difficulties may arise from print-house errors, they may instead be signs of the semantic or syntactical differences between our current version of the English language and that of the late sixteenth and early seventeenth centuries. Single-text editing compels editors— and their readers—to make an effort to understand the given text, rather than to slide into something apparently more familiar. This is known as the principle of the "harder reading" (in Latin, *lectio difficilior*), and it expresses our urge not to risk obliterating the powerful specificity and difference of Shakespeare's works, even as it remains the editor's task to address error when it is undoubtedly present.

The multiplicity of early authoritative texts sometimes confronts the editor adhering to single-text-editing principles with difficult decisions. For example, at one point in the Folio text of *Troilus and Cressida*, Thersites is abusing Patroclus: "Let thy bloud be thy direction till thy death," he sneers, "then, if she that laies thee out sayes thou art a fair coarse [i.e., corpse], I'll be sworne and sworne upon't, she never shrowded any but Lazars." The earlier Quarto reads the central section as follows: "if she that layes thee out sayes thou art not a fair course," and it seems clear that the Folio corrects the Quarto reading, since the "not" makes nonsense of the meaning ("You'll be so ugly by the time you die that if the person laying out your corpse says you're beautiful then the only possible conclusion would be that the dead bodies she usually buries must all be lepers"). The editor therefore emends by removing the "not" from her Quarto edition on the grounds that while single-text editing normally requires her to maintain differences between cognate texts—that is, between texts of the same play that have reached us through different processes of transmission— she must not do this at the expense of sense.

By contrast, the two texts of *King Lear* provide a fine instance of the presence or absence of a word—again, as it happens, "not"—offering equal sense in two cognate texts. At the very end of the long first scene in the Folio, Lear's daughters Goneril and Regan talk together about their aging father's increasingly erratic behavior, and

Goneril notes that "the obseruation we haue made of it hath beene little"—an expression of regret for not taking notice of these mood swings before they led to the current crisis:

> **G*on*.** You fee how full of changes his age is, the ob-
> feruation we haue made of it hath beene little:he alwaies
> lou'd our Sifter moft, and with what poore iudgement he
> hath now caft her off, appeares too groffely.

F *King Lear*, qq3r

In the Quarto, however, Goneril notes that "the obseruation we haue made of it hath *not* bin little" (our italics)—that is, that the sisters have in fact been aware of the problem for quite a while:

> *G*on**. You fee how full of changes his age is the obferuation we
> haue made of it hath not bin little; hee alwaies loued our fifter
> moft, and with what poore iudgement hee hath now caft her
> off, appeares too groffe.

Q1 *King Lear*, C1r

It is this earlier version that is invariably chosen by conflating editors and is thus the reading that those who already know *King Lear* will recognize. Yet it is not the only meaningful option. Both readings make sense, even if one is less familiar, and the advantage of single-text editing is that the editor is not forced to choose one option and thus to dilute the possibilities for meaning on both page and stage.

We briefly mentioned earlier one of the best-known cruxes in *Othello*, the moment at which the protagonist, just prior to his suicide, compares himself to a racial other who also failed to recognize the extraordinary value of what he had until he lost it. In the Quarto, the lines read "one whose hand, / Like the base *Indian*, threw a pearle away, / Richer then all his Tribe"; this has, marginally, been the version preferred by editors across time:

> Perplext in the extreame ; of one whofe hand,
> Like the bafe *Indian*, threw a pearle away,
> Richer then all his Tribe: of one whofe fubdued eyes,

Q1 *Othello*, N2r

In the Folio, the lines read "one, whose hand / (Like the base Iudean) threw a Pearle away / Richer then all his Tribe"—the "Judean" here probably being associated with Christ's betrayer, Judas Iscariot, and thus, for Shakespeare's audiences, with Jews in general:

> Perplexed in the extreame : Of one, whofe hand
> (Like the bafe Iudean) threw a Pearle away
> Richer then all his Tribe: Of one, whofe fubdu'd Eyes,

F *Othello*, vv5v

Note two elements here. First, the punctuation differs; neither version can be said to be either *better* or *more authorial* than the other in this regard (the parentheses in the Folio, for instance, are probably the preference of the King's company scribe, Ralph Crane, who transcribed several plays for inclusion in the Folio). Second, the difference between "*Indian*" and "Iudean" could be attributed to two kinds of easy error: a misreading of a scratchy secretary-hand "i" for "e" (or vice versa)—

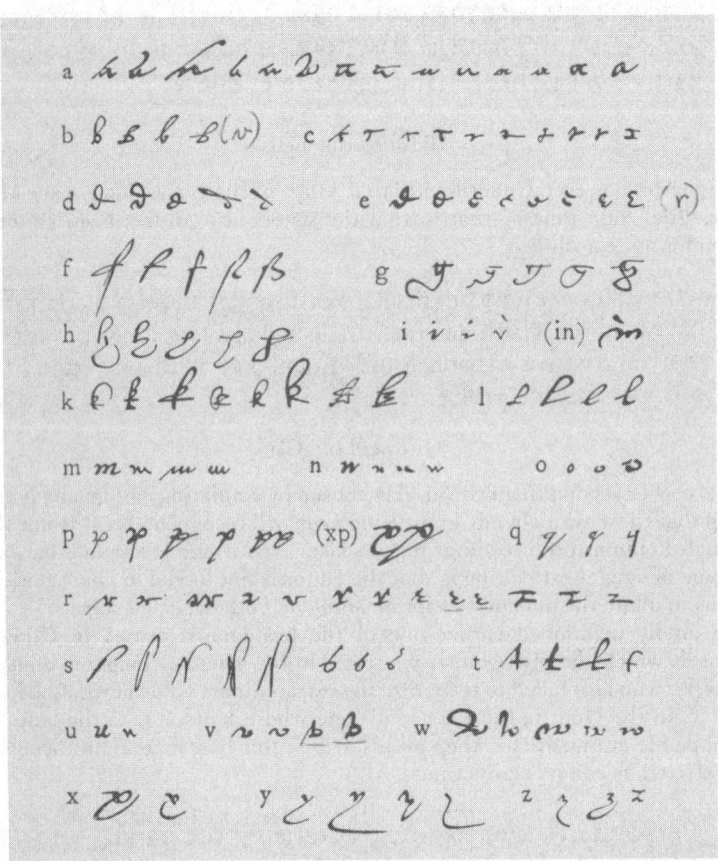

Sample minuscules in secretary hand from Ronald B. McKerrow, *An Introduction to Bibliography for Literary Students*, Oxford 1927.

—and an accidental inversion of the individual type "n" for "u" (or vice versa) by the compositor. The vice versas underline the impossibility of deciding which is "correct," and the presence in *The Norton Shakespeare* of editions of both early texts removes the need for the imposition of editorial preference.

Single-text editing thus seeks to minimize editorial intervention while remaining aware of the needs of the reader and offering clarification (e.g., in the form of expanded or inserted stage directions, which we mark with square brackets) of action, speaker, or other elements of the original that may delay the reader's progress through the play. For these pragmatic reasons, we have chosen to maintain certain traditional overarching elements that could be considered to run counter to the theory of single-text editing. An instance is our division of almost all play texts into acts and scenes, an editorial practice that dates back to the eighteenth century. Such neat divisions are by no means always present in the base texts—either in the Folio, which is not always consistent or precise in its divisions (*Love's Labor's Lost,* for instance, has two different acts marked "*Actus Quartus*"; Folio *Hamlet* stops marking act divisions after act 2), or in the various quartos, many of which either mark scene divisions only or offer no divisions or numbers at all. Act divisions only became fully formalized with the development of indoor playhouses, where the necessity of trimming the candles every half-hour or so required breaks in the action; they thus apply far less to Elizabethan plays than to Jacobean. Our working premise for this edition, however, is that many of our readers will wish to locate scholarly discussions of these plays by critics who, almost without exception, cite speeches by act and scene number; thus, we offer act and scene numbers for all main texts and reserve scene divisions only for a handful of quartos that do not fall into the usual divisions.

The single-text editor's task is not necessarily more straightforward when she is dealing with plays with only one early authoritative text. One of the key questions anyone editing on single-text-editing principles has to ask is when to emend and when to leave alone. An instance comes in *All's Well That Ends Well*, which opens (in our modernized version) with this stage direction:

> *Enter young* BERTRAM, *Count of Roussillon, his mother* [*the Dowager* COUNTESS], *and* HELEN, *Lord* LAFEU, *all in black.*

The *"and"* seems to be in an odd place here; that is, you might expect it to be positioned between "HELEN" and "*Lord*," completing the list. Yet it comes instead between "*Mother*" and "HELEN." Is this simply a mistake by the compositor? It could easily be. Often, editors simply move the *"and"* to what seems to be the logical place between "HELEN" and "*Lord*." But what if there is a different logic to its positioning? It might be that Shakespeare is using the conjunction to separate two pairs: to connect Bertram and his mother on the one hand, and Helen and Lafeu on the other. Equally, the *"and"* might serve to connect the Countess and Helen, a connection that proves particularly resilient in the action to follow. Rather than limit the possibilities, we leave the stage direction as it is in the Folio, simply modernizing and standardizing the names and clarifying (with "dowager") that the Countess is the widow of Bertram's father. A theater director might wish to think about the staging options this stage direction offers.

All of these editorial challenges inevitably require the creation of something hybrid, something impure, despite the earnest intentions of the regularizing editor. Editing is always negotiation, and it is always compromise. This does not mean it is slapdash or arbitrary; on the contrary, it must be exceptionally precise, requiring a level of patience and concentration that is not everyone's forte. The paradox for editors is that the outcome of good work—words or lines or stage directions that took a great deal of experience, research, and agonizing to establish—will be simply, and rightly, invisible to the reader. In this, the editor's lot is not so very different—structurally, if not creatively—from that of the collaborating playwright. Effective collaboration is about effacing the joins between the work of different contributors—we presume that Shakespeare and Fletcher, composing *Henry VIII* and *The Two Noble Kinsmen* together, would not have wanted audience members to register when the writing of a given scene switched from the one to the other—and the quiet collaboration across time that is the work of the editor ought by definition to be hidden, at least in the case of editions created for the general reader and the advanced student who do not want or need the intrusion of the mediator.

Shakespeare and the Multiplication of Meaning

Most people, reading a Shakespeare poem or play, have in mind the question "What did Shakespeare mean here?" as they reflect on the words, especially if the words are not easy to make sense of. Despite the profound ways in which the Romantic construction of authorship as a process of untrammeled, transcendent individual inspiration has been questioned and deconstructed over the last half-century, the general understanding of the processes of writing, as of all forms of creativity, remains firmly bound up with ideas of intention, of textual "ownership," of the creative artist as "author"— that is, as the sole source of "authority" in respect of the form and meaning of a given text. We have tried in this introduction to suggest that the meanings of Shakespeare's plays and poems have a wider range of starting points, emerge from a more complex, varied, and fascinating creative base, than simply what the poet himself "meant"—in other words, that Shakespearean "authenticity" is a multivalent concept, one that includes at its core what the author meant but also a range of other, contiguous collaborations, negotiations, and origins for meaning. The Shakespearean text is fluid and multiple, and the nature of the engagement of both editor and reader with that text should, we believe, follow suit. We have much to gain by being open to the increased possibilities this transformed understanding can bring. The very words themselves are, in so many ways, unfixed in their meanings; the ways through which they came into the public domain in Shakespeare's own day—in manuscript, on the stage, in the various print formats available to those seeking to profit from publication—are also multiple; and the ways in which the plays and poems have been presented and re-presented in subsequent centuries make "multiple" seem a gross understatement. Shakespeare seems to have re-thought and re-imagined his own writings; his colleagues in the King's Men negotiated and adapted his work to suit conditions; publishers printed it in a range of ways, official and unofficial, working with Shakespeare himself on the poems if not on the plays (we have no evidence that Shakespeare—unlike his friend and rival Ben Jonson—oversaw the printing of his plays, whereas he clearly did pay attention to the publication of his poems), and his former colleagues gathered most, though not all, of the plays into a single, rather grandiose Folio in 1623, initiating the long tradition of editing the works to make them available for the "great variety of readers." *The Norton Shakespeare* offers its readers a set of options for reading and understanding Shakespeare that makes the most both of the digital technologies and of the editorial practices of the present, giving the reader choices—of text, of taxonomy, of glossarial support—and in the process providing the means for a new generation actively to discover, engage with, learn from, and—above all—be thrilled and moved by these astonishing works in all their fabulous multiplicity.

The Theater of Shakespeare's Time

HOLGER SCHOTT SYME

Early modern London was a theatrical city like no other, as the travel writer Fynes Moryson proudly proclaimed: "as there be, in my opinion, more plays in London than in all parts of the world I have seen, so do these players or comedians excel all others in the world." Moryson wrote just after Shakespeare's death, around 1619, but the world of playacting he described had thrived in and around England's capital long before Shakespeare arrived there. The decades between 1567, when the first theater built in England since the Romans opened its doors, and 1642, when playacting was prohibited by Parliament, saw an unprecedented and still unparalleled flourishing of theatrical artistry. Moryson's account emphasizes not just the quality of London's actors, but also the sheer quantity of plays on offer: as far as he was concerned, there was more theater in the city than anywhere else in the world. The historical record bears out his impression. English acting companies, driven by a constant hunger for new work, kept dozens of dramatists busy writing a staggering number of plays—more than 2,500 works, of which just over 500 survive. Theaters sprang up all around London in the 1570s. Throughout Shakespeare's career, there were never fewer than four acting venues in operation; some years, up to nine theaters were competing for audiences. Different spaces and different companies catered to different tastes and income brackets: the tiny indoor location of the Boys of St. Paul's, an acting company of youths, could accommodate fewer than 100 of the wealthy courtiers and law students who were their typical spectators; the Swan Theater, on the other hand, the largest of the open-air venues that were the most common type of theater in Shakespeare's London, had room for over 3,000 people from all social backgrounds. The theater was rich and varied, an engine of artistic experiment and a place where traditions flourished; it was an art form both elite and popular; it provided entertainment for kings and queens even as their governments worried that it was difficult to control, attracting large and boisterous crowds and posing a threat to public health during plague outbreaks.

In London, theater was everywhere. But *what* was it? Who performed it, where, under what circumstances, using what methods and techniques, and for whom?

History

Before we can approach these questions, a few words about historical evidence are in order. Theater is a transitory art, not designed to leave behind lasting records or traces; it is, as Shakespeare never tired of noting, a kind of dream. In Shakespeare's time, it was a pursuit about which the government cared only intermittently, and was therefore rarely the subject of official recordkeeping. Much of what we know about playhouses and acting companies derives from squabbles over money and the lawsuits that followed. What information survives is just enough to make theater historians realize how much has been lost. For instance, with few exceptions, we do not know who performed which roles. We cannot name a single character Shakespeare played. Even for the most famous actors of the age, we can list at most a handful of parts. Nor do we

93

know how popular most of Shakespeare's plays were. His history plays, more than his tragedies or comedies, sold well as books—but did they do as well on stage? We would like to think so, but without attendance records, we cannot know for sure. *Much Ado About Nothing* was never reprinted on its own after its initial publication in 1600. Does that mean it was a theatrical flop too? Probably not—else why print it at all? But we cannot be certain.

One extant document contains a tremendous amount of information: Philip Henslowe's business record, known as his *Diary*. Henslowe was a financier who owned three theaters and served as a financial manager of sorts for the acting companies that rented his venues. The *Diary* includes performance records from 1592 through 1597, mostly for the Lord Admiral's Men. It allows us to get a sense of this company's business practices, its repertory of plays, its inventory of props and costumes, and its dealings with playwrights and artisans. And the *Diary* makes us realize just how many plays have disappeared: it mentions about 280 titles, of which at most 31 survive.

This may all sound rather depressing, as if the story of Shakespeare's theater were ultimately irretrievable. But it is not. We can interpret archaeological discoveries; extrapolate from extant records such as Henslowe's or the accounts of court officials; trace contemporary responses to the theater in letters, diaries, satires, and polemics; and study plays and their stage directions to understand what features playwrights expected in playhouses and how they intended to use them. We can make the most of what survives to construct a tentative and careful, but not baseless, narrative of what this world may have been like.

Playhouses

Theater in Shakespeare's London was predominantly an outdoor activity. Most playhouses were open-air spaces much larger than the few indoor venues. The building simply called The Theatre, in the suburb of Shoreditch, north of the City of London, created a model in 1576 that many playhouses would follow for the next forty years. It was a fourteen-sided polygonal structure, nearly round, with an external diameter of about seventy-two feet; audiences stood in the open yard or sat in one of three galleries. There was probably a permanent stage, which thrust out into the yard, with the galleries behind it serving as a balcony over the performance area and, where they were walled off, providing a backstage area (the "tiring house" in early modern terminology). The Theatre may not have had a roof over its stage. The Rose Theater in Southwark, across the Thames from the City of London, was built without such a roof in 1587; one was added during renovations in 1592. The shape of the stage also changed over time: archaeological excavations have shown that the Rose's original stage was relatively shallow, not extending far into the yard. In 1592, the space was redesigned to allow the stage to thrust out farther, creating a deeper playing area surrounded by standing spectators on three sides. This model would be followed in later playhouses, but whereas the Rose's stage (and probably those of other early theaters as well) tapered toward the front, later ones were rectangular and thus quite large. Judging from the erosion around the stage area in the excavated Rose, audiences responded with enthusiasm to the new configuration, pressing as close to the action as possible.

This first generation of playhouses also included The Theatre's close neighbor in Shoreditch, the Curtain, built in 1577 and named not after a stage curtain, which these theaters did not have, but after its location, the "Curtain Estate." The Theatre, the Curtain, and the Rose resembled one another in size and shape and had room for 2,000–2,500 spectators. The next generation of theaters did not depart from the earlier model in shape, but anticipated larger crowds. The Swan (1595), the Globe (1599), and the last outdoor theater erected in London, the Hope (1613), had a capacity of about 3,000. They were impressive buildings not just because of their size but

This view of London's northern suburbs shows the Curtain playhouse (the three-story polygonal structure with the flag on the left). It aptly illustrates the almost rural location of these early theaters: the Curtain stands adjacent to farmhouses and windmills.

also because they were beautifully decorated, as foreign visitors reported. Johannes de Witt, a Dutchman, described the Swan in 1596 as an "amphitheater of obvious beauty," admiring its wooden columns painted to look like marble.

Although some of the later playhouses modified the formula set by The Theatre, all the open-air venues shared a common spatial and social logic. They all separated their audience into those standing in the yard (the "groundlings" or "understanders"), who paid a penny to enter the theater, and those who sat in one of the galleries, paying two pennies for the lower level or three for the upper levels, where the benches had cushions. The most exclusive seats, at sixpence, were in the "lords' rooms," probably located in the sections of the galleries closest to the stage, and possibly in the balcony over the stage. Fashionable gallants and wealthy show-offs could also sit on the stage itself, paying an additional sixpence for a stool. Neither the "lords' rooms" nor the stools onstage gave the best view of the play, but they provided unparalleled opportunities to put fancy clothes on display: these were seats for being seen. Stage-sitting was often satirized as a vain and foolish habit, and the groundlings evidently objected to the rich fops blocking their view. As Shakespeare's contemporary Thomas Dekker describes the scene at one of the outdoor theaters, the "scarecrows in the yard hoot at you, hiss at you, spit at you, yea, throw dirt even in your teeth: 'tis most Gentlemanlike patience to endure all this, and to laugh at the silly animals."

The theaters, though hierarchically structured, were unusually inclusive: audience members from all social spheres could gain admission and enjoy the same spectacles. Social hierarchies became dangerously porous in this shared space, as Dekker's stage-sitters experienced firsthand: the commoners in the yard could hurl abuse and even dirt at the gentle and noble audience members onstage. Lords had to suffer close proximity with their social inferiors. However, the playhouses' inclusiveness had limits, too: the poor and royalty were unlikely to enter a theater. Neither Queen Elizabeth I nor King James I ever did.

Purpose-built theaters were not the only places where plays were performed. From the mid-1570s on, four inns also regularly hosted acting companies: the Bell, the Bull, the Cross Keys, and the Bell Savage. Only one of them, the Bell, seems to have had an indoor hall for play performances; the others had yards in which a stage could be erected. These yards had open galleries to give guests access to rooms on the upper floors, so that the overall structure of the auditorium was similar to the theaters: an open yard surrounded by galleries, at least some of which would have had benches. Unlike the theaters, however, which stood in the suburbs surrounding London, the inns were within or just outside the city walls. This location made them favored acting sites in the winter, when the roads were unpredictable and the days

A Victorian photograph of the Elizabethan galleried yard of the White Hart Inn in Southwark, similar to the layout of the inns used for performing plays.

were short, making it difficult for audience members to return to the City before the gates were shut at nightfall. But the inns irked London authorities. No venues other than churches allowed for the assembly of as many people as inn yards did, and play performances could attract particularly unruly crowds. For the authorities, these places created a threat of public disorder right in the heart of the City, and for over two decades, Lord Mayors and aldermen made intermittent attempts to shut down acting at the inns. It seems they succeeded by 1596, since references to regular performances in those venues cease after that year.

No adult acting company regularly performed in an indoor space in London between 1576 and 1610. There were a number of such venues, though, notably a very small theater near St. Paul's Cathedral, with room for only a select few, and a somewhat larger space inside the former Blackfriars friary. Both were active in the 1570s and 1580s, when two children's companies used them—acting troupes made up of choirboys from the royal chapels and St. Paul's Cathedral. By the time Shakespeare arrived in London, however, the old Blackfriars had closed, and neither space was used during the 1590s. But the boys' companies started performing again around the turn of the century, acting exclusively indoors.

This reemergence lies behind the conversation between Rosencrantz and Hamlet about the "eyrie of children" that produce plays mocking "the common stages." Although the boys' companies could not seriously jeopardize the adult troupes' economic success, their reappearance around 1600 apparently made their grown-up competitors look unfashionable among the trendiest patrons. Exclusivity was the hallmark of these companies and their indoor theaters, which were referred to as "private" playhouses; unlike the "common" theaters, these venues kept the wider world out both architecturally and socially. Entrance fees were much higher, probably starting at sixpence (the price of the costliest seats in the open-air theaters) and going up to over two shillings.

The boys also performed less frequently than the adult companies. They made the most of their elite status, thriving on satirical plays and a willingness to court controversy that sometimes landed them in hot water with persons of influence. Their financial situation was as unstable as their favor with the authorities. When King James, in March 1608, shut down the children's company that was using a recently constructed theater inside the former Blackfriars monastery, he unwittingly made theater history. Soon thereafter, the decades-old division between outdoor adult and indoor boys' companies came to an end. In 1610, near the end of Shakespeare's career, the King's Men adopted the Blackfriars as a second venue. Even after that, however, most audiences would still have experienced plays in the outdoor playhouses that remained the most popular, accessible, and visible acting venues in and around London.

Companies and Repertories

What was an acting company in Shakespeare's time? Formally, a group of players serving a noble patron. A law of 1572 had forced performers to find official sponsors to avoid legal prosecution as "vagrants" and "masterless men." That is why the troupe with which Shakespeare was associated for most of his documented career was first known as the Lord Chamberlain's Servants, and after 1603 as the King's Servants: these actors were officially servants of the Lord Chamberlain (the member of the Privy Council in charge of the royal household), and later of King James I. (Modern scholars generally refer to these companies as the Lord Chamberlain's Men and the King's Men.) All companies resident in London for at least part of the year were associated with high-ranking noblemen. After 1603, most of these troupes came under royal patronage, formally serving the King, the Queen, or a member of their family.

In all likelihood, the connection between patrons and companies was fairly loose, although the players technically formed part of their patrons' households. Take the example of James's son-in-law, the Count Palatine: his troupe, the Palsgrave's Men, operated under that name from 1613 to 1632, although their supposed patron only lived in England for a few months from 1612 to 1613. Links may have been closer where companies were sponsored by nobles of lower rank, as was common throughout the kingdom. Dozens of these groups appear in contemporary records. They toured the towns, cities, and stately homes surrounding their lords' seats, returning at Christmas to entertain families and guests. Whether they visited London is unclear, as is the question of what plays they performed; but some of them were so active on the road that they probably traveled to the country's biggest city as well.

What most defined a company were its leading members: the actors who would typically take on all major roles and who jointly owned the troupe's stock of costumes, props, and, crucially, play scripts. There were between six and a dozen of these "sharers." They not only formed the heart of any acting company, but also had an immediate financial interest in its success, as they divided the weekly profits among themselves. But there was more to a troupe of actors than its sharers. When the King's Men received their royal patent, or license, in 1603, the document not only identified the nine sharers (Shakespeare among them) as "servants" of James I, but also recognized that those servants required further "associates" to stage plays. These hired actors could in some cases be as closely associated with a company as the sharers. John Sincklo, for example, was a member of the Chamberlain's Men for most of their existence and is mentioned by name in the stage directions to three of Shakespeare's plays. He was apparently an extraordinarily thin man and is often linked with very skinny characters—in 1 Henry IV he played the Beadle whom Doll Tearsheet calls a "thin man in a censer." Sincklo was a fixture of Chamberlain's Men productions for playwrights and audiences alike, and an integral part of their identity. Yet despite this status,

Sincklo continued to be an employee rather than an owner of the company for the rest of his recorded life.

The theatrical power of one other set of actors likewise outstripped their institutional power within the company: the male youths who played all female roles. These "boys"—in reality, adolescents who would not have started acting before they were twelve or thirteen and sometimes continued into their early twenties—were associated with the companies as sharers' apprentices. In effect, therefore, none of the actors who played Shakespeare's great female roles, from Tamora to Lady Macbeth to Hermione, were officially members of an acting troupe; rather, they belonged to a sharer's household. Each boy was contracted to serve his master for at least seven years, in return for instruction, room, and board. But officially, they would not have been in training as actors, since there was no guild for actors (and thus no official training available). Instead, they formally became apprentices in the trade governed by the guild to which their master belonged. For example, John Heminges, one of the leading sharers in Shakespeare's troupe, was a member of the Company of Grocers, the guild that oversaw that trade. Over thirty years, he had about ten apprentices. Since Heminges did not actually work as a grocer, these youths were probably boy actors, being trained as stage performers. If they completed their term, though, they could pay a fee and become "freemen" of the Company of Grocers and citizens of London— positions that came with many legal advantages and privileges. Although many boy actors did not become leading men, the social status they gained by formally completing an apprenticeship left them free to make their way in life after their careers as players had ended.

Although increasingly integrated into London's social life over the course of Shakespeare's career, most acting companies also spent part of the year touring market towns and stately homes. Acting was frowned upon if not strictly forbidden in London during Lent, the forty days or so before Easter, and companies had to go elsewhere to secure an income then; there was also a long-standing custom of traveling during the summer, when days were longer and roads more reliable (see the map of touring routes in the map appendix, below). Many companies only knew this itinerant existence, and it was their

Money was collected in small, round earthenware containers that had to be smashed after a performance. Many fragments of these were found during the excavation of the Rose playhouse.

work that the young Shakespeare may have seen in Stratford. But around the time he began working as a theater professional some companies had started to regard London as their home. By the 1590s, that group included Lord Strange's Men, the Admiral's Men, and the Earl of Pembroke's Men. They established long-term relationships with the owners of playhouses where they performed more or less permanently. The Admiral's Men became associated with the Rose and later the Fortune, both theaters belonging to Philip Henslowe. The Chamberlain's Men, founded in 1594, started at The Theatre, owned by James Burbage (whose son Richard would soon emerge as the troupe's young star). Pembroke's Men may have been the resident company at the Swan once that playhouse opened in 1595. A further troupe probably occupied the Curtain. By 1599 yet another company, the Earl of Derby's Men, took up residence at the Boar's Head. In fact, so many acting troupes performed in London that there were never fewer than four venues in operation during Shakespeare's career, and in some years the city sustained nine theaters.

The proprietors of most of those playhouses rented their buildings to the actors for a share of the revenues: half the takings from the galleries belonged to the landlord, while the sharers in the company retained all income from the yard and the other half of the takings from the galleries. Troupes and theater owners thus divided profits as well as risk: if a play flopped, the landlord also lost income, just as he gained from popular offerings. Some owners, Henslowe in particular, acted as the company's financial manager, keeping stock of belongings and conducting transactions on the actors' behalf.

Despite the great variety of playhouses and acting companies, or perhaps because of it, some venues developed specific profiles. This happened surprisingly early in the history of London theater. Writing in 1579, the antitheatrical polemicist Stephen Gosson excluded some plays from his general criticism, praising two "shown at the Bull"; two others "usually brought into the Theater"; and especially "the two prose books played at the Bell Savage, where you shall find never a word without wit, never a line without pith, never a letter placed in vain." Within a few years of opening, then, two of the inns and The Theatre were already known for specific plays one could expect to see there—whereas the four venues Gosson does not mention may have staged precisely the kinds of plays of which he disapproved.

All the same, few playhouses or acting companies were famous exclusively for a handful of titles or a particular kind of drama. The repertories of most troupes, including the Chamberlain's Men and King's Men, were inclusive in their approach to themes and genres and combined old favorites with new and potentially challenging material. The King's Men's 1603 patent describes them as performing not only "comedies, tragedies, histories"—the kinds of plays we might expect from Shakespeare's company—but also "interludes, morals, pastorals." Shakespeare's works do not represent all these categories, and they likely do not represent the full range of shows his troupe staged. If Henslowe's *Diary* is a reliable model, companies commissioned ten to twenty plays each year, and new plays dominated their repertory. If a play failed to draw crowds, it disappeared quickly. If it had staying power, it would remain in circulation for a while, but few became recognized classics destined to be revived every couple of years. In general, it seems that audiences enjoyed periodically reencountering older scripts, but had a more voracious appetite for fresh material—although old stories might frequently return in novel versions. Companies would produce their own take on plays from competing repertories: the Admiral's Men paid Ben Jonson in 1602 for a script about Richard III, for instance; and the Chamberlain's Men bought Jonson's *Every Man in His Humor* in 1598, probably hoping to capitalize on a 1597 hit at the Rose, George Chapman's *Comedy of Humors*. Even a single troupe's repertory might feature multiple plays drawn from the same stories or materials. The King's Men owned another *Richard II* play, which they staged at the Globe in April 1611—within weeks of performances of *Macbeth*, *Cymbeline*, and *The Winter's Tale*. Of those three Shakespearean offerings, the latter two were then still quite new; but *Macbeth* would have been a revival, an indication that it was a success when first performed.

The repertory system required daily turnover. Staging the same play for days at a time, let alone for weeks, was practically unheard of. The nine consecutive performances of Thomas Middleton's *A Game at Chess* at the Globe in 1624 were described as extraordinary at the time—nowadays, of course, a run of nine nights would be notable for its brevity. We can get a glimpse of what a typical selection of shows would have looked like in Shakespeare's company from Henslowe's *Diary*, which contains the only surviving sample of the Chamberlain's Men's repertory (staged in collaboration with the Admiral's Men in June 1594):

MON 3 June	*Hesther and Ahasuerus*
TUE 4 June	*The Jew of Malta*
WED 5 June	*Titus Andronicus*

THU 6 June	*Cutlack*
SAT 8 June	*Belin Dun*
SUN 9 June	*Hamlet*
MON 10 June	*Hesther and Ahasuerus*
TUE 11 June	*The Taming of a Shrew*
WED 12 June	*Titus Andronicus*
THU 13 June	*The Jew of Malta*

The two companies performed seven different plays in ten days. Of those, two were tragedies based on fictional plots (*The Jew of Malta* and *Titus Andronicus*), two were tragedies set in the distant northern European past (*Cutlack* and *Hamlet*—the latter not Shakespeare's version), one was a biblical drama (*Hesther and Ahasuerus*), one was a history or tragedy drawn from the English chronicles (*Belin Dun*, about a highwayman hanged by King Henry I), and one was a comedy (*The Taming of a Shrew*—again, not Shakespeare's). One play was brand-new (*Belin Dun*); one recent (*Titus Andronicus*, first performed in January 1594); two quite old (*The Jew of Malta* and *The Taming of a Shrew* were probably written before 1590); and we know nothing about the others.

The two companies' combined offerings constitute a representative mixture of old and new; of different geographical settings and historical periods; of tragic, heroic, moral, and comedic entertainments. Variety was a predictable feature of any company's stock of plays. Predictability, however, was not. For theatergoers keen to see a performance of *Titus* after its successful June 5 outing, finding out when the play was going to be mounted next was neither easy nor straightforward (we now know that their next chance would have come on June 12). They may have relied on word of mouth, as the actors commonly announced the next day's play at the end of a show; they might have encountered the players marching through the City in the morning hours, advertising that day's performance; or they may have read the news on one of the playbills posted daily all over the City to inform audiences what was being staged where. But would-be spectators had to keep their eyes peeled: while repertories responded to popular demand, they did not follow an easily foreseeable schedule. Since *Titus* did well, it would certainly be back onstage soon. But exactly when was uncertain.

Why Shakespeare's Company Was Different

The playhouse in which the Chamberlain's Men and the King's Men performed after 1599, the Globe, was a unique building project. In 1597 James Burbage's lease for the land on which The Theatre stood ran out, and a year later the Chamberlain's Men were forced to vacate the premises and move to the neighboring Curtain. The building itself, however, still belonged to Burbage, and after his death in 1597, to his sons Cuthbert and Richard, the latter Shakespeare's fellow sharer. The Burbages therefore took the extraordinary step of having a carpenter dismantle the structure and use the salvaged timber to build a new playhouse. This would be erected on a plot of land on the other side of London, south of the river and across the street from Henslowe's Rose Theater. This new theater, the Globe, would be significantly bigger than its predecessor. As archaeological digs have revealed, it was probably a sixteen-sided polygon with a diameter of about eighty-five feet, nearly fourteen feet more than The Theatre's. It was operational by September 1599, when the Swiss traveler Thomas Platter saw a performance of *Julius Caesar* at what he called "the straw-thatched house"—almost certainly the Globe, which had a thatched roof over the galleries and stage.

Opening a new playhouse right next to the small and aging Rose might look like an aggressive gesture on the Burbages' part, bringing the Chamberlain's Men into direct competition with the Admiral's Men. In such a turf-war narrative, Burbage and company look like history's winners: Henslowe and his son-in-law Edward Alleyn almost immediately started building a new playhouse elsewhere. The Admiral's Men abandoned the Rose in 1600 and moved into their new home, the Fortune, in Clerkenwell, northwest of the City and far away from the Globe. But there is no reason to think that a desire to ramp up competition motivated the Burbages' decision. For one thing, this kind of thinking would have been out of step with the general atmosphere of mutual respect among London's acting companies. For another, the very speed with which Henslowe and Alleyn acted supports a different story. In fact, the Burbages may have chosen the Southwark location because they knew that Henslowe had started to look for a suitable site for a new playhouse and that the Admiral's Men would soon leave their old home.

What made the Globe a remarkable project was neither its builders' allegedly aggressive approach to the theatrical marketplace nor its size or design, which were no more impressive than the Swan's. The Globe was unique for the way it was financed: it belonged not to a separate landlord, but to members of the acting company itself.

How did this come about? It may be that when the Burbages decided to move their playhouse in 1598, they did not have sufficient funds for that enterprise. In 1596, their father had spent the very large sum of £600 to transform a medieval hall inside the former Blackfriars monastery into a theater. The purpose of this investment is uncertain: the doomed lease negotiations for The Theatre had not yet begun, so James Burbage might have been trying to expand his activities as a theater owner rather than replace his old playhouse. He had only been his son's company's landlord for a little over a year when he bought the Blackfriars, and may very well have had another company in mind for the new space. Whatever the case, the new venue was the largest indoor performance space in London, and probably the first hall theater designed for an adult company. But the undertaking failed. Almost instantly, a group of wealthy inhabitants of the Blackfriars precinct successfully protested against the plan. The composition of that group is enlightening: it contained Lord Hunsdon, the patron of Shakespeare's company; and Hunsdon's recently deceased father had tried to buy part of the same property Burbage was after the year before. If the new playhouse was meant for the Chamberlain's Men, it is certainly strange that both these patrons of the company attempted to prevent its construction.

In any event, the property was not a viable alternative when Richard Burbage and his fellows lost The Theatre. Whether for financial reasons or because neither Cuthbert nor Richard Burbage wanted to play the role of theater owner and landlord, the brothers devised a solution that would for the first time put a venue mostly in actors' hands. Half the enterprise belonged to the Burbages (since they contributed the timber from The Theatre), but the remaining 50 percent was divided equally among five of the seven or eight remaining sharers in the Chamberlain's Men: John Heminges, William Kemp, Augustine Phillips, Thomas Pope, and William Shakespeare. At Christmas 1598, this consortium signed the lease for the plot of land in Southwark. They subsequently covered the construction costs of £700, exactly what The Theatre had cost to build in 1576.

Having a playhouse owned by the majority of the sharers in an acting company was a unique business model. These sharers now were responsible for the upkeep of the building, but they also, as landlords, received a portion of the entire revenue from every show (the Globe used the same rental agreement as the Rose, splitting performance income between landlords and actors). Beyond economics, the agreement created an unparalleled strong bond between these actors and their venue. It practically ensured that the Globe became their default home, and that its joint owners would remain members of the same acting company. The Globe was made for the Chamberlain's Men—but the Chamberlain's Men, in a sense, were also made by the Globe.

What happened to the Blackfriars property in the meantime? It stood empty for three years; and then, in 1600, it became an active theater after all. That year, Richard Burbage, clearly unwilling to adopt his father's or Henslowe's business model, leased

This section of Wenceslaus Hollar's 1647 "Long View" of London, drawn from South-wark, shows the Globe in its rebuilt state. The Globe is the round building in the middle, misidentified as a "Beere bayting" arena. The round building to its right, mislabeled "The Globe," is in fact the Hope playhouse, which by the 1620s was used exclusively as a bearbaiting venue.

the Blackfriars venue outright to the manager of a boys' acting company—for a flat annual fee of £40, and for twenty-one years. No revenue sharing, no managerial services: Burbage washed his hands of his father's failed endeavor. (The boys' company did not face the same opposition as the 1596 venture, perhaps because it performed as rarely as once a week, or because it represented a more up-market kind of playing.)

Eventually, the Blackfriars would become the King's Men's second venue: they probably started performing plays there sometime in 1610, at the very end of Shakespeare's career. But neither the company nor the Burbages were in any rush to move indoors. In 1604, the boys' company's manager tried to return the building to them and cut the twenty-one-year lease short, but the Burbages were uninterested. Only after the King forced out the children's troupe in 1608 did they agree to terminate the lease. The brothers owned the property and certainly had no financial incentive to search for investors. And yet the Burbages immediately turned the Blackfriars into another shared venture, splitting costs and revenues equally among themselves, one outsider, and four King's Men's sharers, including Shakespeare. The idea here was evidently not to maximize personal gain, but to enhance the company's profile—and its leaders' fortunes.

Within a decade, the Blackfriars turned into *the* place for new, fashionable plays. But during Shakespeare's lifetime, it never outshone the older outdoor space. For the first years of the new theater's existence, references to King's Men plays mention only the Globe; prominent audience members, including foreign princes, still visited the open-air venue; and in 1613, the company emphatically reaffirmed its commitment to its traditional playhouse. That year, the building's cost-effective thatched roof caught

Paulus wharfe

A different section of Hollar's panorama shows the Blackfriars precinct across the river from the Globe and Hope theaters. Just left off the center, next to the spire of St. Bride's Church, the long roof with two tall chimneys marks the probable location of the Blackfriars theater.

fire during the first performance of Shakespeare and Fletcher's *Henry VIII.* The Globe burned down, leaving the King's Men with only an indoor theater at their disposal. However, instead of redefining themselves as the Blackfriars company, they extended their lease on the Southwark plot, invested the enormous sum of £1,400, and rebuilt their playhouse—with decorations that made it, in the words of an eyewitness, "the fairest that ever was in England." This time, the galleries and stage had tiled roofs.

If the Chamberlain's/King's Men were unique in forming such a strong interconnection between actors and theaters, they also benefited from the unusual privilege of having an in-house playwright. No other company in the 1590s seems to have had a sharer who could also provide, on average, two plays a year. In addition, Shakespeare apparently performed other tasks for his company that would normally have been farmed out to hired dramatists, which included writing new scenes for old plays. The sheets in the *Sir Thomas More* manuscript that are probably in Shakespeare's handwriting are one example: there, he provided a long scene for a collaboratively authored text that needed major patching to be stageable. There is also evidence that additions to Thomas Kyd's *Spanish Tragedy* first printed in 1602 are by Shakespeare; if so, he wrote them for a Chamberlain's Men revival of this early classic (originally staged around 1587). The role of Hieronimo in the play was one of Richard Burbage's star turns, so we know the script found its way into the company's repertory at some point in the late 1590s or early 1600s.

Although the Chamberlain's Men were unusually fortunate to have Shakespeare as a sharer, we should not overestimate his place in their repertory. He was no Thomas Dekker, the dramatist who between 1597 and 1603 wrote or coauthored 41 new plays for a range of companies. Nor was Shakespeare as productive as Thomas Heywood, who claimed to have authored or cowritten more than 220 plays in a career spanning forty years. Given a need for at least ten fresh scripts a year, Shakespeare's contributions to his company's repertory were valuable, even indispensable—but they could never make up more than a fraction of the new material commissioned every year. Even if demand for new plays slowed in the 1620s, after the King's Men had accumulated a stock of reliably popular offerings, those of Shakespeare's works that had proved their lasting appeal would always be part of a much larger set of scripts. And the company treated Shakespeare's plays much like other authors' works, hiring play-wrights to spruce up the old texts and make them newly exciting for audiences; in Shakespeare's case, it was Thomas Middleton who revised *Measure for Measure*, *Macbeth*, and possibly others.

At Court

Thinking of theater as a commercial enterprise taking place in venues accessible to all who paid the price of admission means leaving out one important aspect of early modern theater: private performances for aristocratic audiences. Companies were occasionally paid to stage their plays inside the London houses of noble clients, but such interactions with the highest social ranks were intermittent and unpredict-able. The court, on the other hand, annually required actors to provide entertain-ments during lengthy revels between Christmas and Twelfth Night, and usually at Shrovetide (the three days before Ash Wednesday). Under Elizabeth I, there was only one court, her own, and theatrical activities were limited to those two holiday periods. With the ascension of James I, however, the number of royal courts multiplied—besides the King's own, Queen Anne, Prince Henry, and later Prince Charles also maintained courts with their own occasions for entertainment—and playing was no longer limited to holidays. The records show that the royally sponsored adult companies could be sum-moned to one of the palaces at any time. Officially, the courts' desire for theater justified the actors' need to play all year round in public venues, despite the City authorities' con-cerns: companies constantly had to rehearse and try out plays in front of live audiences so they could be ready to perform whenever a royal patron needed them.

The person in charge of organizing royal entertainments was the Master of the Revels, an officer who worked for the Lord Chamberlain. Under Elizabeth, the office was held by Sir Edmund Tilney. His job was not an easy one: he was responsible for choosing the appropriate companies and plays from the multitude available in London. In his early years, Tilney's approach seemed scattershot, with up to seven different troupes playing at court per season. The sheer complexity of keeping that many com-panies organized may have led to the foundation of an elite troupe under Elizabeth's own patronage, the Queen's Men, who dominated court entertainments for a few years after 1583. In 1594, the Master of the Revels apparently undertook a second effort to streamline holiday performances, this time relying not on a single troupe, but on a pair—and his superior, the Lord Chamberlain, adopted one of those compa-nies as his own. For five years thereafter, Tilney could draw on two consistently excellent groups of actors, the Chamberlain's Men and the Admiral's Men.

As in 1583, though, this approach gave the Queen's revels a rather different com-plexion from the popular theaters. The Queen's Men were the leading company for about ten years after their creation, but other troupes eventually reappeared in the court season. Similarly, Shakespeare's company and their colleagues at the Rose were prominent but far from alone in London, and their competitors also turned up on Tilney's payroll again before long. Derby's Men, Worcester's Men, Hertford's Men, and the boys' companies all performed at court within a few years of the establish-ment of the Lord Chamberlain's troupe in 1594. Tilney's tenure as Master of the Revels was marked by repeated, ultimately futile efforts to limit actors' access to courtly employment—efforts seemingly designed to shut out the unrestrained variety of the public theatrical marketplace.

Under James I, the Lord Chamberlain's office finally acknowledged the size and diversity of London's theater world. Abandoning the model of a separate set of privileged companies with access to the court, the crown instead brought all major London companies gradually under royal patronage. By 1615, five adult troupes were being officially sponsored by members of James's family. Only those companies were asked to perform at court, but they were probably also the only acting outfits remaining in London: there were not enough playhouses to accommodate more than five permanent adult companies.

Even if the diversity of companies performing at court came to reflect the situation in the public playhouses over the course of Shakespeare's career, the repertory the actors drew on for their courtly performances remained distinct in surprising ways. We might expect that kings and queens, princes, ambassadors, and wealthy courtiers would have made for the most discerning and demanding audience imaginable, but the records tell a different story. Often, the plays staged at court were already several years old; by the 1610s, Revels playlists begin to feel like compilations of the classics that had their place in every company's repertory but could not normally compete with the appeal of new material. The court's, or the Master of the Revels', taste was broadly on the conservative side.

Though the records list almost no specific play titles from Elizabeth's reign, those surviving from James's time suggest that the King and his inner circle liked their Shakespeare well aged. In 1604, there were *A Midsummer Night's Dream*, nine years old; *The Merry Wives of Windsor*, seven years old; and *The Comedy of Errors*, over ten years old. The next year, we have recorded performances of *Henry V*, six or seven years after its first staging; and of *The Merchant of Venice*, at least seven years old, but performed twice within three days in James's presence in February 1605. These were the typical Shakespearean offerings. Exceptions occurred, including the still-new *Tempest* and *Winter's Tale* in November 1611, but for the most part, the Master of the Revels assembled an unadventurous repertory in which certain favorites often reappear. *Twelfth Night*, *The Winter's Tale*, *Othello*, and *1 Henry IV* show up every few years, as do some of Ben Jonson's plays (*Volpone* and *The Alchemist* in particular) and titles whose continued popularity at court now seems puzzling (such as the anonymous *Greene's Tu Quoque* and *The Merry Devil of Edmonton*). A company that performed for the royal households as often as did the King's Men must have adjusted to their courtly audience's expectations to some degree, and may therefore have been less quick to follow the latest artistic fashions than a company less in demand at court. But even so, Shakespeare and his fellows probably saw acting for their royal patrons as quite a different challenge from playing for London audiences. And in spite of the unquestionable importance of their connection to the royal household, the fact that they performed publicly far more frequently and depended on the income from those performances probably meant that their day-to-day activities were less influenced by the preferences of the court than we might imagine.

The Regulation of Playing and Its Failures

Organizing court entertainments was the most important aspect of the Master of the Revels' job, but he had another major responsibility: the licensing of new plays. Every script had to be submitted to him for approval, and only manuscripts bearing his license and signature were allowed to be performed. In their censorship activities, Tilney and his successors concentrated mainly on three concerns: no actual persons could be slandered or attacked; plays had to steer clear of incendiary topics and language; and, after a law banning profanity onstage had been passed in 1606, actors were no longer allowed to utter oaths using the name of God in any form. In the main, though, the Master of the Revels was not the acting companies' antagonist. For instance, Tilney did not simply reject *Sir Thomas More*, although he found the play objectionable on a number of counts; instead, he suggested changes that would enable him to give the players his license.

That relatively benign mode of control could quickly shift into an aggressive register when the players crossed a line. Companies that staged plays without first having them licensed, if discovered, were severely reprimanded. Stricter actions followed whenever a performance offended a person of high rank and influence. Playhouses were sometimes shut down as a consequence, and actors and playwrights found themselves in prison while under investigation. When these perceived transgressions happened (and they happened infrequently), the state was typically unable to explain what had gone wrong, especially if the play had been licensed. Playwrights would routinely offer the likeliest theory: the actors had ad-libbed, adding content the Master of the Revels had not seen and the author(s) had not written. There was certainly a kernel of truth to those defenses. Live performance is invariably different from the script on which it is based. But although that insight was not unknown to Shakespeare's contemporaries, it never seemed to affect the official system of licensing, which continued to operate unchanged throughout the early modern period.

Beyond the licensing requirements, there are few signs that the state took any sustained interest in regulating the theatrical marketplace, in London or elsewhere in the country. Nor were such efforts especially effective when they did occur. One of the most significant interventions took place in July 1597, apparently in response to a now-lost play, *The Isle of Dogs*, performed by Pembroke's Men at the Swan. This performance caused a massive scandal, landed some actors and the playwright Ben Jonson in jail under investigation for sedition, shut down all the theaters, and ruined Pembroke's Men financially. We do not know what made the play so offensive, but it must have been a serious trespass. The Privy Council's reaction to what it regarded as the players' "lewd and mutinous behaviour" was unprecedentedly severe; an order went out to stop all performances and have all playhouses demolished within three months. As telling as this order, though, is what happened next: almost nothing. The company was broken up, but no theaters were destroyed. Henslowe's *Diary* shows no signs that he was concerned about loss of income, and before long a new London-based company established itself in a new theater, the Boar's Head. For the next few years, the Privy Council attempted to control the number of troupes and playhouses in London, but every one of its annual letters to the local authorities expresses frustration about the inefficient implementation of the previous set of orders. No letters on the subject written after 1602 survive.

The Privy Council's general indifference to tightly regulating the theaters and its relatively hands-off attitude, even in the brief period when it adopted restrictive policies, did not align well with the wishes of the Lord Mayor and aldermen of the City, for whom the theaters posed a perennial challenge to public order. However, even the City authorities were not consistent in their opposition: they habitually relied on actors and playwrights for the annual civic entertainments, especially the Lord Mayor's pageants. Some aldermen befriended players, and actors participated in parish-level government (Shakespeare's colleagues Henry Condell and John Heminges were church wardens; Edward Alleyn and Philip Henslowe served as members of the vestry, or parish council, of St. Saviour's Church in Southwark). And although opposition to regular performances at the inns in the City was fairly consistent over twenty years, this policy may not have been the reason that all the large playhouses were built in the suburbs. Rather, high property prices and the scarcity of plots of land large enough for an amphitheater-style structure inside the densely packed City probably forced theater-builders to look beyond the city walls. Having large gathering places close to their gates but beyond their control vexed London authorities, but their anger may have been fueled by more than a simple desire to prohibit playacting: the theaters made a lot of money, and none of that income could be taxed by the City—despite the fact that the vast majority of playgoers would have been Londoners. The Mayor and his aldermen thus had many reasons for feeling aggrieved. Not only did they have to suffer the threat of riots and public disturbances sparked at the theaters, but they could not even collect fees and taxes in return.

The one cause that brought the interests of City and Privy Council together was also the single biggest economic threat to the acting companies, and the most frequent reason for playhouse closures: the plague. While the transmission of diseases was not well understood in early modern England, the authorities knew that crowds spread illness. Hence the government would order the theaters to shut whenever plague deaths reached a certain level (these figures had to be recorded and reported parish by parish every week). Sometimes, such closures were a precaution and did not last long. But on a number of occasions during Shakespeare's career, the theaters were closed for many months, with disastrous consequences for the London-based companies. A plague outbreak in 1593 halted performances for almost the entire year, forced all companies to tour, and caused a major reorganization of the theatrical landscape—out of which the Chamberlain's Men emerged as a new troupe formed from the fragments of its disbanded predecessors. At least as devastating was the horrific eruption of plague that shut down all playing in London from March 1603 to September 1604, and the less severe but longer episode that kept the theaters closed from August 1608 to the end of 1610. The first decade of James's reign was an especially chaotic and challenging time for the London companies, as there were lengthy plague closures even in the years when the playhouses were periodically open. If the world of London theater changed fundamentally after Shakespeare's retirement in 1613, the great watershed may not have been the introduction of multiple royal patrons or of new indoor performance venues, but instead the comparative stability offered by an extended period without plague outbreaks. In any case, it seems clear that the greatest threat to an acting company's fortunes was not the Privy Council, the censor, or local authorities, but a mysterious, unpredictable, and lethal disease.

Casting

We have already glimpsed some of the details of how an early modern acting company was put together: at its core were the sharers, the actors who jointly owned the troupe's assets; then there were a number of male youths, usually apprenticed to the sharers, who played women and children; and then there was a group of hired men, who had no financial stake in the group's success, as they were paid a set salary, although some (such as John Sincklo) stayed loyally with the same troupe. Beyond those actors, most London companies employed someone who functioned like a modern stage manager, the book-holder. That person was responsible for maintaining play scripts and organizing the backstage action during performances; he likely also acted as a prompter. Finally, there were employees who collected admission fees, cleaned the theater, and probably doubled as stagehands. Some of these workers were women, a female presence in an otherwise entirely male business.

Senior actors developed a degree of professional specialization. The most obvious experts were the clowns or fools, often among the most prominent members of any company. Richard Tarlton was the first of the great and famous Elizabethan clowns, and he was the Queen's Men's undisputed star until his death in 1588. Will Kemp, a sharer in the Chamberlain's Men as well as, for a short while, in the Globe, took over Tarlton's crown as the funniest man on English stages. After Kemp left the company in 1599, Robert Armin inherited his role as clown. The styles of these comedic performers differed, with Tarlton famed as an improviser and singer, Kemp known for his athleticism, and Armin for his subtler verbal wit, but they all had one thing in common: their responsibilities included the comic entertainments performed after plays

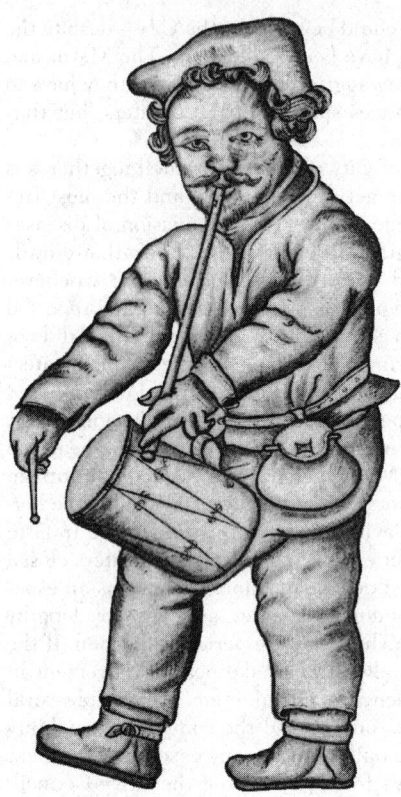

This portrait of Richard Tarlton, drawn by John Scottowe in or around 1588, shows Tarlton dressed as a jester, playing the tabor (a kind of drum) and pipe.

were done. Hence, they regularly appeared before audiences as themselves or as recognizable stage personae. They were certainly among the most readily identifiable faces of the company.

Unlike other roles, the clowns' parts in plays were often not fully scripted, and allowed for improvisation—the excessive use of which Hamlet criticizes when he tells the players to "let those that play your clowns speak no more than is set down for them." It is thus no coincidence that even as playwriting became a profession separate from acting, famous clowns still continued to be known as dramatists as well: Tarlton, Kemp, and Armin all wrote, as did John Shank, John Singer, and William Rowley. The line between the play and its performance, between the playwright's text and what the actors said and did, was particularly blurred in these performers' roles—and we should not assume that authors (or anyone else) found this especially troubling. It would be an error to read Hamlet's views as Shakespeare's, let alone the audience's: by all accounts, including Hamlet's, theatergoers enjoyed the clowns' ad-libbing and did not mind if such riffing delayed the progress of the play. We should, however, take seriously Hamlet's use of the plural "clowns." The company's specialist clown would never have been the only actor with comedic skills. Hamlet itself requires at least two clowns, the two gravediggers, even if Armin took on three of the plays' foolish roles and acted Polonius, Osric, and the first gravedigger (a casting choice the structure of the play allows). Twelfth Night, similarly, calls for a designated clown, but also needs another comically gifted actor as Sir Andrew Aguecheek. Shakespeare's company included a number of such performers. Thomas Pope, one of its founding sharers, had a reputation as a comedian, as did Richard Cowley, a hired man with the Chamberlain's Men who became a sharer in the King's Men.

If not all comic parts always went to the same performer, the same is true of dramatic leads. Two great tragic actors dominate all narratives of Shakespeare's stage: Edward Alleyn, the Admiral's Men's star, and Richard Burbage, the Chamberlain's and King's Men's leading player. Both rose to prominence in the 1590s. Alleyn, Burbage's senior by three years, gained fame first. However, although he led the longer life (Burbage died in 1619, Alleyn in 1626), his career as an actor lasted nowhere near as long as his colleague's: sometime before 1606, Alleyn retired from the stage to devote his attention to even more profitable ventures, whereas Burbage continued acting until his death. But even these two titans of the stage would not have taken the lead in every play: that is not how ensembles work. Alleyn certainly performed the title characters in Christopher Marlowe's Tamburlaine and Doctor Faustus and Barabas in The Jew of Malta, though he may not have originated those roles; beyond these, we know of five other parts in which he acted, four of them from lost plays. Burbage's list is not much longer. An elegy written shortly after his death laments that with him died characters that no other actor could bring to life as powerfully: "No more young Hamlet, old Hieronimo, / Kind Lear, the grievèd Moor." He was closely associated, then, with three of Shakespeare's plays and Kyd's *Spanish Tragedy*; notably, those works were at least ten years old when he died.

We might expect that Burbage, at the height of his fame, played all the largest parts, but the elegy suggests otherwise: Othello is a smaller role than Iago. What is more, when the Chamberlain's Men were established in 1594, Burbage was only twenty-five, the youngest sharer, and had not yet risen to the level of prominence he would later attain; and the company included other well-known actors: George Bryan, John Heminges, Augustine Phillips, and William Sly. Initially, Burbage's name would not have been the most recognizable among these, and even when his reputation ultimately eclipsed the others', he would—and could—not

A contemporary portrait of Richard Burbage. Burbage sometimes worked as a visual artist, and some scholars believe this painting to be a self-portrait.

have been the only choice for leads. Think of Shakespeare's plays from the mid-1590s: Burbage probably played Romeo, but what about *Richard II*? Would Burbage have been a better fit for the king or for the usurper Bolingbroke? In *The Merchant of Venice*, Shylock is the star turn nowadays, but Bassanio may have been the likelier role for Burbage, with older actors, like Bryan or Phillips, taking the roles of the other two male leads, Antonio and Shylock—or Thomas Pope, if Shylock was considered a comic part. Or take, as a final example, *Titus Andronicus*. Titus is the largest role, but Burbage may well have been a better fit for Aaron, a younger and more agile character.

Matching actors' ages to those of their characters, though, is a complicated business, and a casting consideration that was treated differently in Shakespeare's time from now. Burbage played Lear when he was no older than thirty-seven; and he was famous in the role of Hieronimo—an elderly father figure—by 1601, when he was just thirty-two. The same actor, then, might have acted the aged King Lear, "old Hieronimo," and "young Hamlet" within the span of a few days. And yet, despite this apparent disregard for verisimilitude, it was the supposedly lifelike quality of his acting that made Burbage famous. A writer in the 1660s reported on his ability to "wholly transfor[m] himself into his part, putting off himself with his clothes, as he never assumed himself again until the play was done." Part of Burbage's power was that he could seemingly become another person, even if that meant aging by decades. If the effect was a kind of make-believe, however, the means were an orator's, not those of modern psychological realism. What contemporary witnesses praise is Burbage's facility with speech, with finding the right vocal affect and the right quality of voice to express his character. As important was his aptitude at suiting his physical movement to the role, finding what were called the right "actions." That term probably referred to an elaborate arsenal of gestures and body positions that was systematic enough that audiences could read and make sense of actors' movements: putting a hand on the heart, holding one's face in one's hands, making a fist, and so on. Even if Burbage seemed able to go beyond conventions and give his actions an unusually personal or individual quality, though, it is clear that what seemed lifelike in Shakespeare's theater had little to do with a modern understanding of stage realism.

Burbage's specific talent may have been self-transformation; Alleyn, on the other hand, was known and remembered for his extraordinary stage presence. But both actors used a similar technical arsenal. Alleyn, like Burbage, was praised for his "excellent action"—as Thomas Nashe wrote in 1592, not even the greatest Roman actors "could ever perform more in action than famous Ned Alleyn." If Burbage disappeared into his roles, Alleyn was celebrated for the awe-inspiring quality he himself lent the characters he played. We do not know what his acting would have looked like onstage, but its outsized effect was not universally popular. Hamlet's criticism of players that "so strutted and bellowed" that "they imitated humanity so abominably" may refer to actors of Alleyn's ilk, perhaps an implicit statement that the Chamberlain's Men favored a different approach to performance. After Alleyn's death, in the reign of Charles I, the larger-than-life style associated with him was frowned upon by some writers and by spectators at some theaters. But there is no evidence that Burbage's brand of acting displaced Alleyn's within Shakespeare's lifetime. More probably, the two actors' particular aptitudes represented the pinnacles of two different but not incompatible acting techniques that in other players' work appeared in mixed forms. Both of these men were exceptional figures, after all. The Admiral's Men were not a company of many Alleyns, nor were the Chamberlain's Men a troupe of Burbages. What most performers and audiences probably understood "acting" (or "playing") to mean is captured vividly in these lines from *Richard III*:

> Come, cousin, canst thou quake, and change thy color,
> Murder thy breath in middle of a word,
> And then begin again, and stop again,
> As if thou wert distraught and mad with terror?

> (3.5.1–4)

What Richard is asking Buckingham here is whether he can act—and Buckingham replies that he can indeed "counterfeit the deep tragedian," in part because he can use the appropriate actions (looks, trembling, starts, smiles). Both characters describe a kind of performance that is highly codified, quite predictable, and not exactly lifelike; but both share the confidence that a talented actor can turn hackneyed gestures and tics into a convincing impression of reality.

If actors were capable of creating something like reality out of obvious fictions, and if those fictions could stretch to having an actor in his thirties play an old king one day and a young prince the next, then it cannot have been difficult for performers and audiences to come to terms with the widespread practice of doubling. All but the actors cast in the largest roles routinely played multiple characters, often leaving the stage as one person only to return shortly thereafter, wearing a new hat or a different cloak, as an entirely different character. Doubling meant that most early modern plays, although they may feature thirty or more characters, could be staged by around fourteen actors. In *The Merchant of Venice*, for example, the same player could take the parts of Old Gobbo, Tubal, the Jailer, and the Duke; or Morocco, Arragon, and the Duke—in either case, characters ranging widely in age and social status.

Like doubling, the casting of male youths in all female parts was a firmly established theatrical convention, though one that had less to do with pragmatic considerations than with a strong moral rationale. The idea of women putting their bodies on public display, even if fully clothed, was widely regarded as immoral and likened to prostitution. All-male casts were so deeply ingrained in English theatergoers' expectations that seeing actual women play female roles startled those who traveled abroad, where female actors were common. Some expressed their surprise that women could in fact act; others compared the Continental female performers critically to English boy players, whom they considered preferable not on moral but on artistic grounds. The women, these witnesses argued, played their characters too close to life, not artfully enough. A degree of artifice was as desirable in the boy actors' performances as in those delivered by the men. But as with the adult players, that artfulness did not diminish the potential impact of the show, as a famous account of a 1610 staging of *Othello* in Oxford attests. There, the scholar Henry Jackson recalls how Desdemona's death affected him: "although she always acted her whole part supremely well, yet when she was killed she was even more moving, for when she fell back upon the bed she implored the pity of the spectators by her very face." The boy player disappears behind the female pronouns, as if the artifice of the performance had become invisible. At the same time, Jackson registers that the body onstage, female or not, is not quite like a real corpse either; it responds to, and demands a response from, "the spectators." Yet, despite his recognition that the actor, or the character, is manipulating the audience's emotions, Jackson still responds emotionally and is in fact moved. The convention of using male youths for

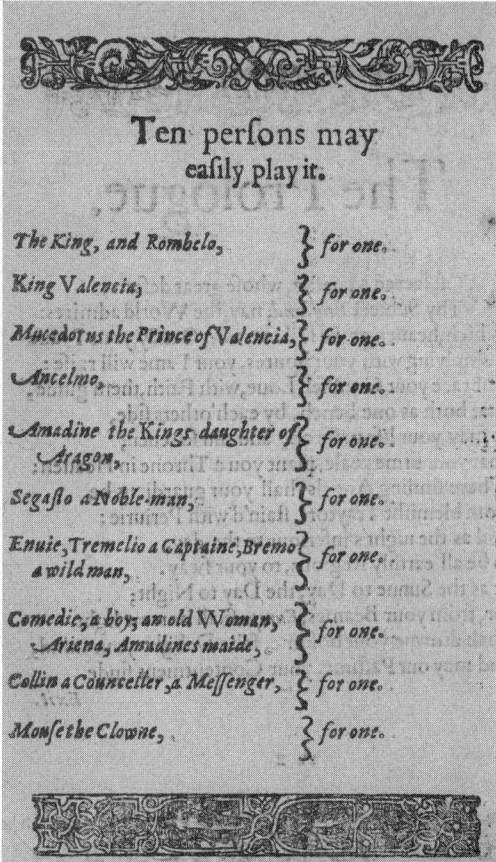

A chart from the second edition of the very popular anonymous play *Mucedorus* (1606), showing which actors can play more than one part.

female parts, then, was of a piece with the broader understanding of acting in Shakespeare's time as an art that deployed heightened artifice in order to create an affectively powerful semblance of real life.

Staging and Its Meanings

The staging of a new play in Shakespeare's time did not begin in a rehearsal room or in a theater, but in an actor's home. One of the first tasks of the company book-holder in readying a new script for performance was the preparation of the players' individual parts: each actor received only his own lines, along with the cues to which he was to respond and a handful of stage directions. Initially, then, most actors did not know who else was onstage with them, how many lines those other characters had, how much time passed between the scenes in which they appeared, or even who would give them their cues—nor what those characters said before the two or three words that made up the cue. Since companies performed together almost every day and actors often lived close to each other, informal discussions must have taken place to clarify relationships between characters, but any performer's primary duty would have been to learn

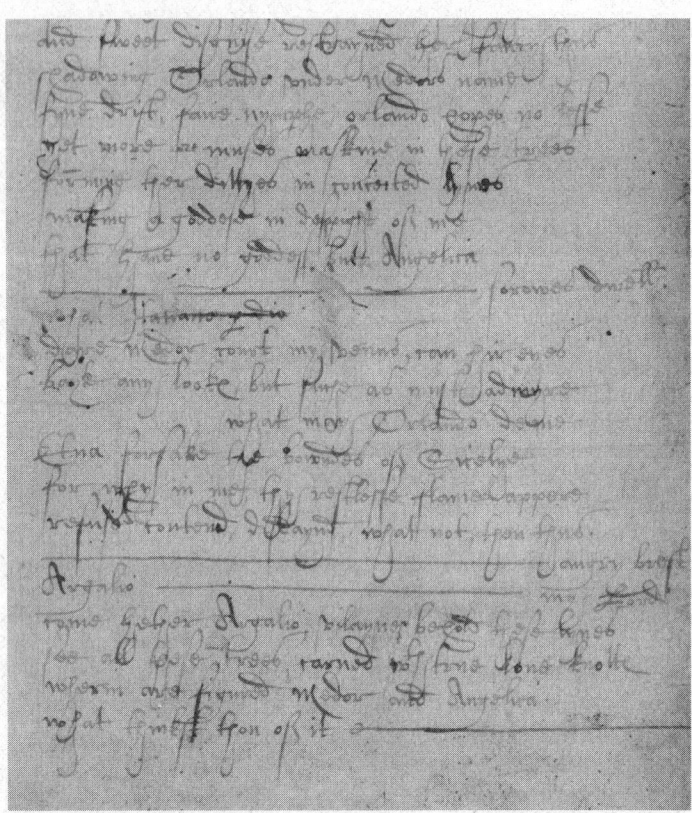

A section of Edward Alleyn's part for the role of Orlando in Robert Greene's *Orlando Furioso*. The long lines across the page mark breaks in Orlando's speech; at their end, the actor could find the cue for his next line.

his part in relative isolation, finding appropriate actions and intonations for his lines and memorizing cues. For leads, this was a formidable responsibility. Parts were written on strips of paper that were glued together to form a roll—which is why the terms "role" and "part" are synonymous. The scrolls for leads could reach remarkable length and heft. The one extant early modern part, Alleyn's copy of Orlando in Robert Greene's *Orlando Furioso*, is six inches wide and an impressive thirteen feet long, but its 530 lines probably did not overly tax an actor who had mastered more than 1,100 lines in *The Jew of Malta* and nearly 900 lines in the second part of *Tamburlaine*.

By Shakespeare's time, the solitary actor preparing his role could have predicted how the play would be staged with some certainty. The setup illustrated in the 1596 drawing of the Swan Theater is broadly representative of what a performer could expect in any venue: a rectangular, flat, largely empty stage; no sets in the modern sense, and few large furniture items; two pillars, probably set back from the edges of the stage by a few feet; at least two stage doors, and possibly a third in the center; and a balcony where scenes described as taking place "aloft" or "above" would be staged, though sections of it may also have offered additional audience seating, and part of it may have been used as a "music room." Even if there was no central stage door, there would have been an area between the two entrances that lay concealed behind an arras or a curtain that could be drawn to reveal pre-set tableaux, such as Hermione's statue in *The Winter's Tale*, Ferdinand and Miranda's chess game in *The Tempest*, or the caskets in *The Merchant of Venice*. There was also a trapdoor giving access to the space underneath the stage (sometimes called hell)—the place from which the ghost of Hamlet's father calls out to his son and his friends. In some theaters,

The interior of the Swan Theater, a sixteenth-century copy of a drawing by the Dutch traveler Johannes de Witt.

there was a pulley system that allowed objects, such as the figure of Jupiter in *Cymbeline*, to be lowered to the stage from the roof above it. That roof was often called the heavens, so that the stage as a whole represented a Christian microcosm, with hell, earth, and heaven enclosed in a round—*Hamlet*'s "distracted globe" or *Henry V*'s "wooden O."

This fairly stable, symbolically rich staging setup lent itself to an emblematic

The modern Globe on London's South Bank. This 1997 reconstruction is significantly larger than the original, but it captures the general idea of what an early modern theater may have looked like.

approach to performance. Figures appearing in the balcony are not always more powerful than those on the stage itself, but their position above could be dramatically exploited that way. When Tamora appears "aloft" alongside Saturninus in *Titus Andronicus*, for example, the staging suggests her elevation from prisoner of war to empress—a shift that officially does not take place until twenty lines later. The appearance of a prisoner and a foreigner in the location symbolically associated with supreme national power, however, also instantly signals how much of a topsy-turvy world Saturninus's Rome is about to become. This kind of visual logic of power returns in many plays that deal with the subjects of governance or rule: the descent of Richard II from the balcony to the stage when he surrenders to Bolingbroke is a particularly rich example. However, the emblematic use of the stage (where "above" means "powerful") could always be layered onto other modes of representation. In *Richard II*, the balcony also stands for an actual space "above," the battlements of Flint Castle; as the stage direction has it, Richard and his allies "enter on the walls." The stage to which he descends likewise is not simply "below" but also the "base court," the castle's lower court where Bolingbroke is waiting. From the perspective of the actor working with his part, the scene and its stage directions would have carried these various representational meanings—the text informed him both of Richard's movement from sun-like power to debasement before his enemy, and of the fact that the scene is taking place in two different locations in a castle. But the directions also had additional pragmatic value, as "on the walls" told the actor that he would have to enter on the balcony.

Stage directions such as these are explicit. Far more common are "internal" stage directions: textual references to actions characters perform. Often, these are straightforward: for instance, Bolingbroke's "there I throw my gage" in *Richard II*. But they can also be quite opaque. In *Hamlet*, when Polonius says, "Take this from this if this be otherwise," the line only tells the actor to perform some kind of gesture—he needs to indicate what "this" should be taken from what other "this" if Polonius is wrong. The most common interpretation is "my head from my shoulders" (indicated with appropriate gestures), but he may also be talking about his staff of office and his hand, or

A performance at the modern Globe.

his chain of office and his neck, or something else. The line requires actions to complete it, but it does not prescribe those actions.

Explicit and implicit stage directions allowed for a very short rehearsal period: they made it possible for the actor to conceive much of his performance alone. The text may not always tell him what to do, but it will often tell him when he needs to do *something*. However, there are also many cases where Shakespeare's plays seem to presuppose a good deal of back and forth between actors. For example, when Hamlet tells his mother to "leave wringing of your hands" in 3.4, the youth playing Gertrude would have needed to know to perform that action before Hamlet tells him to stop it—but there may have been no indication of this in his part. So while the part system allowed players to prepare for much, and while the established shape and features of playhouses by the 1590s made it possible for actors to anticipate many staging decisions before ever rehearsing a play, Shakespeare's texts also contain many instances where a successful performance depends on the players going beyond their individual parts.

Even if rehearsal periods were short, it is hard to imagine that the elaborate dumbshows, masques, and battle scenes featured in some plays were not carefully prepared. But rehearsal in the modern sense did not exist, mainly because the modern idea of character work did not exist. Renaissance actors did not spend long hours developing ideas about their characters' biographies, inner lives, or hidden feelings. Acting was primarily a physical and oratorical art and, in its conventionality, quite predetermined. What made any individual performance surprising and unpredictable were the specific effects achieved by bringing together a particular text with a conventionalized physical and vocal arsenal. But rehearsal also did not have to address many of the technological challenges that only came into being in the modern theater. In an outdoor venue without artificial lighting, actors do not need to hit their "marks"; an expansive stage lit only by sunlight allows for greater freedom of movement than one illuminated by an elaborate lighting design. Lastly, staging was determined in part by the architecture of the playhouses. Certain spots on stage worked especially well for certain set pieces. Soliloquies, for instance, were at their most powerful not when delivered front and center, but instead from a position farther away from the audience, off-center, and underneath the stage roof, which provided the greatest sense of acoustic intimacy. Therefore, an actor preparing a speech could predict with some certainty where onstage he would deliver it.

Of course there is more to staging a play than speaking lines and finding positions. Nowadays, sets are of paramount importance. In Shakespeare's time, they were all but nonexistent, except for some big-impact items: the Rose Theater owned a hell-mouth, probably covering the trapdoor, for devils to enter and exit in plays such as Marlowe's *Doctor Faustus*. Tombs, caves, and cages also appear in Henslowe's inventory, as do magical trees and severed heads. One other cost factor of modern productions, however, loomed similarly large in Shakespeare's time: costumes. Dresses in particular could be more expensive to commission than new plays, and companies maintained a rich stock of costumes; in 1598, the Admiral's Men owned at least eighty complete men's outfits. Most of these were generic items, but some were character-specific: "Harry the Fifth's velvet gown," "Longshanks' suit," or "Merlin's gown and cape."

What the actors wore was the most noteworthy visual aspect of staging. On a basic level, costumes identified characters. If the actor playing Tubal in *The Merchant of Venice* also played the jailor and the Duke, his three characters would have been distinguished initially and immediately by different garments. But costumes did more than facilitate identification. Dress signified social rank. It instantly allowed audiences to place characters, without having heard them speak or knowing anything else about them. More important, dress could set the scene: a nightgown signaled where and when an action took place; a forester's outfit told the audience to imagine a woodland setting; an innkeeper's costume moved the scene to a tavern. And dress denoted historical periods—as can be seen in Henry Peacham's famous illustration of *Titus Andronicus*. In this 1590s drawing, Titus's garments—Roman armor and a toga accessorized with a laurel wreath—immediately inform the viewer that this is a classical figure, and that the play is set in ancient Rome.

Yet Peacham's picture also shows that costume functioned in multiple registers on Shakespeare's stage. Titus wears Roman dress, and the short tunics of the three figures on the right also suggest quasiclassical costumes. But Tamora, on her knees in a flowing, embroidered gown and wearing a nonclassical crown, signifies less an ancient figure (Goth or Roman) than royalty. Her garments, unlike those of the characters beside her, are designed to situate her not in history, but in a particular social sphere. The outfits of the two leftmost characters follow a different logic yet again: they are Elizabethan soldiers, with breeches, halberds, and contemporary helmets. Their costume has no historical function; its sole purpose is to identify them as having a particular occupation. Dress, then, could signify in multiple, mutually contradictory ways at the same time on Shakespeare's stage. What Peacham's image

Henry Peacham's illustration of a scene from *Titus Andronicus* (ca. 1595).

suggests visually is that *Titus Andronicus*, while set in Rome, is also concerned with general questions of monarchic power and soldierly virtue. All three of those aspects of the play could be communicated through costume. If the picture portrays a kind of theater capable of sustaining anachronistic and logical contradictions in the pursuit of its thematic goals, it is representative of the broader, and pervasive, anachronism of Shakespearean drama, in which church bells ring and books rather than scrolls are read in *Julius Caesar*'s Rome, while the title character wears that most Elizabethan of male garments, a doublet. No matter how far back in historical time these plays were set, they also always took place in the present moment.

Audience members seem to have consumed a wide range of foods at the theater. Archaeologists found oyster shells, remnants of crab, and a large quantity of nutshells and fruit seeds at the Rose Theater site.

Impressive and expensive as the actors' costumes could be, their visual impact would necessarily have been lessened by the daylight playing conditions: performers were not isolated in space and light as they can be in modern theaters, but always competed for attention with the audience itself, with the equally splendid figures in the lords' rooms and on stage stools, and with whatever distracting things spectators chose to do while the play was in progress: play cards, smoke tobacco, solicit prostitutes (or johns). Aurally, too, Shakespeare's stage was not as insulated as a modern theater. Spectators were rowdier and more audibly present than audiences now. But the sounds of the city would also have infiltrated the open-air space: church bells, the noise of bears and hounds from the nearby bearbaiting arenas, the cries of street vendors, and perhaps even the sound of performances at neighboring playhouses might all have been heard. Going to a play in early modern London was never exclusively about the action and words onstage; it was always also about the theater itself, its temporary inhabitants, and the places where the theaters stood. Visually and aurally, the stage was in competition with the world, but it also found ways of integrating that world into its fictions.

Although the early modern theatrical experience was shaped by a host of immediate sensory perceptions, it equally depended on the audience's ability to refashion those impressions in their minds—even as plays insisted on drawing attention to the material reality of the stage. The Prologue to *Henry V* illustrates this condition perfectly. On the one hand, it mocks the apparent inadequacy of the theater, an "unworthy scaffold," a "cockpit" laughably ill suited to representing the "vasty fields of France"; it mercilessly reminds the audience where they are. At the same time, the Prologue also encourages the listeners to ignore all these carefully catalogued shortcomings and allow the play to work "on your imaginary forces," pleading with them to "piece out our imperfections with your thoughts." The Prologue seems to indulge in a risky game: it explains in detail why the theater should fail even as it dares the audience to make it work. But this risk lay at the heart of Shakespeare's theatrical art. We can detect it in the use of boy actors as much as in contradictory costuming choices and willful anachronisms. It found its most daring expression in the frequent use of narrative, seemingly the least theatrical form of writing. Antonio's tearful farewell to Bassanio in *The Merchant of Venice*; the deaths of the Dukes of Suffolk and York in *Henry V*; the reunion of Perdita and Leontes in *The Winter's Tale*; most remarkably, the death of as charismatic a character as Falstaff, in *Henry V*: again and again, Shakespeare chose to have events such as these reported by other characters rather than staging them before his spectators' eyes. In these scenes, the words and their demands on the audience's imagination do not just compete with what is visible, as they always did in the early modern playhouse. These narrations do more than that: they celebrate and rely on the power of words to take audiences out of the theater altogether, to transport them, without any visual aid whatsoever, to places and encounters that even the characters in the play itself only imagine.

And yet, despite placing such trust in language's capacity to transform reality, both the scenes and their author depended on their actors' ability to make audiences believe those words. If language's appeal to the imagination was meant to pull theatergoers out of their immediate sensory experience and into an engagement with a world of fiction, that goal could be achieved only by virtue of the very bodies, costumes, and props whose specific presence audiences were encouraged to transform into representations of an alternative reality. If a play worked, it enabled its viewers almost to forget the theaters whose splendor impressed so many visitors; allowed them to imagine for a moment that the words they heard did not come from a scroll of paper, that they had not been preapproved and licensed by a government official, purchased by a profit-hungry company, and written by a commercial playwright. Ultimately, then, in spite of the theater's undeniably powerful architectural, social, cultural, and visual presence in the lives of Shakespeare's contemporaries, its success in creating alternative, fictional worlds depended on an audience capable of understanding that all this splendor was not an end in itself. That is the marvelous paradox of Shakespeare's theater: it invested a great deal of goods, money, and physical labor in an effort to persuade people not to ignore those material realities altogether, but to use them as a means of accessing greater, still more wondrous, and wholly imaginary worlds beyond.

EARLY PLAYS
AND POEMS

The Two Gentlemen of Verona

Readers and playgoers have often found both startling and disconcerting the events that conclude *The Two Gentlemen of Verona*. Proteus, a young man thwarted in his love for Silvia, who loves Proteus's friend Valentine, says that since wooing her with words has not worked, he will follow the soldier's path and "love you gainst the nature of love—force ye" (5.4.58). At that moment, Valentine steps out of hiding and stops the attempted rape by denouncing Proteus as a treacherous friend. Overcome with remorse for the betrayal of Valentine, though not explicitly for his attempted sexual violence, Proteus begs forgiveness. Generously, Valentine says he is content. He then announces that he will give Silvia to Proteus as a sign of the renewal of the friendship between the two men. A near rape and the offer of a woman as an object of exchange between men—is this the stuff of comedy?

Apparently a number of directors, actors, and critics have thought not. In the mid-eighteenth century, it became common to cut Valentine's offer to give Silvia to his friend, a stage tradition that largely held until William Charles Macready, the famous actor and producer of Shakespeare's plays, reintroduced the lines in 1841. As late as 1952, however, Denis Carey's production at the Bristol Old Vic again deleted Valentine's offer. Some critics have been so certain Shakespeare could not have written the scene as it stands that they argued that it was altered in the playhouse. How do we explain why Shakespeare concluded his comedy with events that to many people have seemed so distasteful and so disconcerting?

One answer might be that Shakespeare was simply a young dramatist not fully in control of his craft. *The Two Gentlemen of Verona* is, after all, one of his earliest plays, perhaps the earliest. It bears marks of its early date of composition. It has, for example, the smallest cast of any of the plays. Many scenes contain only two or three speakers, as if Shakespeare had not yet mastered the skill of orchestrating a full complement of stage voices and bodies. It is marked as well by a number of plot inconsistencies and confusing details. Valentine and Proteus leave Verona to go to the Emperor's court, for example, but end up attaching themselves to the Duke of Milan—an important nobleman, certainly, but not the Emperor. Likewise, the geographical placement of some scenes is vague. The characters speak of Verona, Milan, Mantua, and Padua, but the names often are used interchangeably and seem collectively to be Shakespeare's shorthand for "Italy" rather than distinct places.

In other ways, however, the play is both an accomplished theatrical piece and a genuine precursor of many aspects of Shakespeare's later comic techniques and structures. The play features lovers whose fickle or thwarted passions lead them into all sorts of difficulties: treachery to friends, banishment, disguise. These difficulties get sorted out only after most of the drama's significant players decamp to a forest outside Milan. There, in a green world complete with a band of outlaws, the fickle Proteus reverts to his original love for Julia, Silvia's disapproving father forgoes his objections to Valentine, friendship is renewed between the two young men, the outlaws are pardoned and unworthy lovers dismissed. The utopian possibilities for social renewal in a world beyond the walls and customs of the city are celebrated in this play as they will later be in *A Midsummer Night's Dream*, *As You Like It*, and other Shakespearean romantic comedies of the 1590s. *Two Gentlemen* also contains the first of Shakespeare's cross-dressed heroines, the faithful Julia, who follows her fickle lover from Verona to Milan and then, as his page, accompanies him into the woods in his pursuit of Silvia. Male disguise allows Julia a freedom of action and movement not normally granted to early modern women, but, as was often to be the case in later Shakespearean comedies, this freedom has as its ultimate goal the heroine's embrace of marriage.

The excellence of much of the play, then, suggests that the difficulties many have experienced with the ending stem not from Shakespeare's relative inexperience as a dramatist, but rather from the subject matter of the play itself—that is, from Shakespeare's ambitious attempt to probe the relationship between two kinds of bonds: friendship between men and love between a man and a woman. In the Renaissance, each of these was a privileged relationship, but their relative worth was a matter for debate and disagreement. In staging his exploration of the claims of love and friendship, Shakespeare drew on two different sources. The first was a Spanish prose romance published in 1542, Jorge de Montemayor's *Diana Enamorada*. Translated into French in 1578 and into English in the 1580s, it was published in English in 1598. Shakespeare, then, could have read the story in French or in the unpublished English version. He could also have learned of it from an anonymous play performed at court in 1585, *The History of Felix and Philomena*, now lost.

The Montemayor romance focuses on a man's unfaithfulness in love. Don Felix leaves Felismena for Celia; Felismena pursues him in the guise of a page; Celia falls in love with the page and conveniently dies when the page rejects her. Shakespeare retains much of this material in the Proteus–Silvia–Julia triangle but adds the Valentine plot, probably drawn from the story of two friends, Titus and Gisippus, told by Boccaccio and then recounted in book 2, chapter 12, of Thomas Elyot's *Book of the Governor* (1531). In this story, Titus falls in love with the woman Gisippus is to marry, and Gisippus gives the woman to his friend. Later, Gisippus takes upon himself the blame for a murder Titus is wrongly accused of committing.

Male friendship ("Steadfast is the love based on inclination"). From Richard Brathwaite, *The English Gentleman*, 2nd edition (1633).

The story unabashedly advances the claims of heroic male friendship over other ties, including those of male–female love. Shakespeare's challenge in *The Two Gentlemen of Verona* is to join together aspects of these two stories. In his play, there are two pairs of lovers, not just a fickle Proteus figure moving between two women, and the close friendship between Valentine and Proteus is given a prominence equal to that of the male–female love stories.

In foregrounding the importance of male friendship, Shakespeare joined a long tradition of writers who celebrated such friendships, often comparing them favorably with the presumably more dangerous relationships men could have with women. In *The Governor*, for example, Elyot praised male friendship in terms that would be echoed in other early modern texts: "Verily it is a blessed and stable connection of sundry wills, making of two persons one in having and suffering. And therefore a friend is properly named of philosophers the other I. For that in them is but one mind and one possession and that which more is, a man more rejoiceth at his friend's good fortune than at his own" (book 2, chapter 11). The French essayist Michel de Montaigne, whose writings Shakespeare might have encountered in French before John Florio's English translation of 1603, also praised the friendship of equals as a mingling of souls so complete that no line divides them. By contrast, Sir Francis Bacon (who also wrote an essay in praise of friendship) in his essay "Of Love" captures the fear and disdain with which passionate love between men and women was often regarded: "In life it doth much mischief, sometimes like a siren, sometimes like a fury. You may observe that amongst all the great and worthy persons (whereof the memory remaineth, either ancient or recent) there is not one that hath been transported to the mad degree of love; which shows that great spirits and great business do keep out this weak passion."

The Two Gentlemen of Verona participates both in the celebration (and critique) of male friendship and in the comic deflation of male–female love. Several times male characters speak of the strange transformations of the self that passion for a woman can induce. Proteus, choosing to stay in Verona with Julia rather than follow his friend to Milan for an education in courtiership, speaks of his own choice disdainfully. Of Valentine he says:

> He after honor hunts, I after love.
> He leaves his friends to dignify them more;
> I leave myself, my friends, and all, for love.
> Thou, Julia, thou hast metamorphosed me:
> Made me neglect my studies, lose my time,
> War with good counsel, set the world at naught;
> Made wit with musing weak, heart sick with thought.
> (1.1.63–69)

The play is one of Shakespeare's first explorations of what it means to be transformed, or "metamorphosed," by love of a woman. Perhaps he took his cue from the Roman poet Ovid's vastly popular book the *Metamorphoses*, which contained numerous tales of people transformed by love. In Ovid, gods sometimes assume the shapes of mortals or of animals to pursue their beloved; or women turn into trees or flowers in their flight from unwanted amorous advances. In *The Two Gentlemen of Verona*, Proteus's name echoes that of the sea god who could change shape at will and who was thus often associated with a fickle nature. In the above passage Proteus is the one who first mentions being metamorphosed by love, but the play rings many changes on this idea. Sometimes the transformations wrought by love seem comic to others. Speed, for example, has excellent fun laughing at the strange transformations of his master, Valentine, who, in love with Silvia, begins to act like a perfect malcontent, "metamorphosed with a mistress" (2.1.27). A malcontent, here meaning someone made melancholy by love, was a stock figure in Renaissance literature and the visual arts, sometimes rendered comic by his disordered attire or his moody alienation from his fellow men.

Sometimes, however, in this play, love is shown to have more positive consequences. It leads to heroic feats such as Julia's daring cross-dressed journey in pursuit of Proteus, and to the outpouring of poetry and songs. However fickle Proteus's passion for Silvia shows him to be, it also moves him to offer her the gorgeous song "Who is Silvia? What is she / That all our swains commend her?" (4.2.37–38). In the movie *Shakespeare in Love*, in which scenes and speeches from *The Two Gentlemen of Verona* are used to indicate Shakespeare's promise as a writer of romantic comedy, this lyricism compels Viola de Lesseps, the aristocratic heroine, to fall in love with the youthful Shakespeare who wrote those verses. Within the play, Valentine, under the influence of love, is prepared to scale the walls of Silvia's tower to bear her away;

The love melancholic. Isaac Oliver, *Edward, First Lord Herbert of Cherbury* (1617).

however, not all the metamorphoses wrought by love are either comic or admirable. Love also makes men dangerous and hurtful. Under the influence of his fickle passions, Proteus abandons one woman for another, betrays Valentine's marriage plans to Silvia's father, and threatens to rape the woman he supposedly adores. Proteus speaks three soliloquies in *The Two Gentlemen of Verona* (2.4.188–210, 2.6.1–43, and 4.2.1–17), and in each he struggles with the confusion to which his mixed allegiances and desires have led him. Loving Silvia, he has betrayed Julia and betrayed Valentine, acknowledging that "I love his lady too too much, / And that's the reason I love him so little" (2.4.201–02). As moralists warned, the passion of man for woman can turn a man into a beast.

By contrast, friendship between men, though much compromised in this text, holds the promise of an ennobling intimacy. When Proteus and Valentine must part in the first scene, Proteus's language betrays the depth of his love for and dependence on his friend:

> Wilt thou be gone? Sweet Valentine, adieu.
> Think on thy Proteus when thou haply seest
> Some rare noteworthy object in thy travel.
> Wish me partaker in thy happiness
> When thou dost meet good hap; and in thy danger,
> If ever danger do environ thee,
> Commend thy grievance to my holy prayers;
> For I will be thy beadsman, Valentine.
>
> (1.1.11–18)

Here, the friend is imagined as "the other I," sharer of every joy, intimate of every thought. The delight with which Valentine later welcomes Proteus to the Duke's court and even his eventual offer of Silvia to his friend are signs of the potential depth of male bonds in the play and in early modern culture. In fact, to an early modern audience, Valentine's offer was perhaps not so shocking as it seems to contemporary audiences, but rather the unsurprising outcome of a social world that valued male friendship above most other forms of association.

But Valentine's gesture, of course, suggests the potential cost to women of these powerful male bonds. It neither serves their desires nor is made with their consent. By the way he creates the characters of Julia and Silvia, Shakespeare invites his audience to take them and their emotions seriously and makes it difficult to overlook the men's irresponsible and callous treatment of them. While Proteus is faithful neither to his male friend nor to his female beloved, the women are models of constant affection. Each, moreover, risks a good deal for her beloved. Julia courts public scandal by dressing as a boy and following Proteus to Milan; Silvia flees her father's court to follow the banished Valentine into the forest. Each, moreover, is respectful of her female rival.

Julia, in particular, is a complex figure, proud and silly in the scene in which she pretends not to want to read the letter her maid has brought her from Proteus (1.2), but impressively dignified when, disguised as a male page, she is faced with the task of being Proteus's messenger to Silvia (4.4). Asked by Silvia to describe Julia, the disguised woman says that Julia is of her color and height. She knows this, she claims, because once she wore Julia's clothes "to play the woman's part" (4.4.155) in a holiday pageant. Moreover, the part she played

> 'twas Ariadne, passioning
> For Theseus' perjury and unjust flight,
> Which I so lively acted with my tears
> That my poor mistress, movèd therewithal,
> Wept bitterly; and would I might be dead
> If I in thought felt not her very sorrow.
> (4.4.162–67)

Ariadne, of course, is an archetype of the betrayed woman. She helped her lover, Theseus, escape the man-eating Minotaur in the labyrinth on Crete, but then was abandoned by him on the island of Naxos. The abandoned Julia, so transformed by love and grief that she no longer can lay claim to her own name, finds a point of identification in Ariadne's grief and in imagining what "Julia" would have felt to see the enactment of Ariadne's story. This is a wonderfully complicated moment, a representation of a woman's grief and self-alienation and also her empathetic engagement with the story of another woman's grief. It at once reveals the cost, to women, of men's inconstancy and makes it difficult to accept that women should simply become the objects of exchange between male friends.

The nearly tragic consciousness here granted to Julia is countered in this play by the boisterous comic voices of Speed and Lance, two of Shakespeare's earliest and liveliest clowns. Their presence helps suggest that however complicated Shakespeare's exploration of the tension between love and friendship becomes, the outcome will not be fully tragic. Speed is a clever clown, excellent at puns and wordplay, devastatingly accurate in his parodic imitation of Valentine's lovesick behavior and clever enough to see, when his master cannot, that Silvia has induced Valentine to write a love letter to himself. Lance, who may have been added to the play in the later stages of composition, is a doltish clown whose command of the English language is remarkable mainly for its deficiencies. If Speed specializes in puns, the witty play on the double meaning of words, Lance specializes in malapropisms, the linguistic blunders by which one word is mistaken for another. He can, for example, when leaving home to follow his master to Milan, say that he has received his "proportion, like the prodigious son" (2.3.3), by which he means that he has received his portion, or inheritance, like the prodigal son in the

"I'll be sworn I have sat in the stocks for puddings he hath stolen" (4.4.26–27). From Geffrey Whitney, *A Choice of Emblems* (1586).

biblical story who received his inheritance and squandered it. In Lance's fractured English, nothing is communicated straightforwardly. He blunders into meaning, his linguistic mistakes turning the language of the learned and the witty on its head. In Lance's mouth, words become unfamiliar and unpredictable, always ready to yield up an obscene innuendo or to forge unlikely connections between different domains of meaning.

Lance's larger role in the play is as comically unsettling as his language. As was to be increasingly true of many of Shakespeare's low-life characters and subplots, his behavior mirrors and comments on the behavior of his "betters," but in a deflationary and unpredictable way. Lance's great love is for his dog, Crab. When he must leave for Milan, he is in an agony of grief because his dog, like a hard-hearted mistress, sheds no tears for his departure. "I think Crab my dog be the sourest-natured dog that lives. My mother weeping, my father wailing, my sister crying, our maid howling, our cat wringing her hands, and all our house in a great perplexity, yet did not this cruel-hearted cur shed one tear" (2.3.4–8). So deep is Lance's affection for his dog that when Crab, who in the end does accompany his master to Milan, disgraces himself by pissing under the Duke's table at a banquet, Lance takes the blame—and the subsequent punishment—upon himself. It is "the bit with the dog" that in *Shakespeare in Love* particularly wins the approval of Queen Elizabeth.

The highborn lovers, Proteus and Valentine, do not always show an equal devotion to their human mistresses. Lance's attachment threatens to expose both the element of absurdity lurking inside every grand passion and also the falsity of the assumption that only the wellborn are capable of self-sacrifice. In fact, Lance's affection for Crab shows just how many forms love can take, including affection that reaches across the line supposedly dividing one species from another, man from animal. Thomas Elyot, speaking of friends, claimed that their tie made "of two persons one." Lance's language about his dog expresses his feeling of just such an overwhelming and confusing intersubjective unity: "I am the dog. No, the dog is himself, and I am the dog. Oh, the dog is me, and I am myself" (2.3.19–20). Affection in this play takes many forms. However, when Lance contemplates marriage, his thoughts are less romantic than pragmatic. As Lance and Speed read a catalog of the qualities of Lance's beloved (3.1.267–350), Lance focuses on the practical: the woman's ability to fetch and carry, to sew, and to milk. And her faults, which are manifold, pale in his eyes beside her wealth. Set against the rarefied courtship rituals of his masters, Lance's pragmatism underscores the mundane aspects of the institution of marriage to which courtship will lead and beside which affection for a friend or a dog might seem more pleasurable.

Together the two clowns do much to increase the hilarity and confusion that permeate this early comedy: a play in which letters are only with great difficulty delivered to their receivers, love tokens given to one mistress are rerouted to another, and masculine affection proves remarkably fickle and unsteady. When something like order descends on this society, it does so in a locale where Lance does not go—the forest outside Milan. The initial scenes in the forest are striking in that they have the fairy-tale quality of a Robin Hood story come to life. Banished from Milan,

Valentine and Speed are beset by robbers in the forest; but these outlaws are so impressed with Valentine's bearing and his skill in languages that they make him captain of their forest band (4.1.54–66). Outside the town, living apart from women, the outlaws establish an alternative community where Valentine, despite his grief at being separated from Silvia, finds a measure of contentment. Several of Shakespeare's later comedies will depend on the contrast between the flawed life of town or court and the less fettered existence of rural spaces. *The Two Gentlemen of Verona* tries out this juxtaposition, contrasting to the betrayals and confusions of urban life and male-female courtship the straightforward male camaraderie of the forest.

The arrival of women and of Proteus, Valentine's friend-turned-rival, disrupts this harmonious male community as first Silvia appears, escorted by the timid Eglamour, and then Proteus, attended by Julia, disguised as his page. Suddenly, the potential for violence escalates as the frustrated Proteus threatens Silvia with rape, and both men lay claim to her affections. The disguised Julia can only watch. Just moments before Proteus, Silvia, and Julia arrived, Valentine had made a speech that obliquely suggests one way their encounter might end. Alone in the woods, Valentine describes how he can

> sit alone, unseen of any,
> And to the nightingale's complaining notes
> Tune my distresses and record my woes.
> (5.4.4–6)

By mentioning the nightingale, Valentine evokes a horrific tale of sexual violence. In a story made famous by Ovid in the *Metamorphoses,* the beautiful Philomela was raped by her brother-in-law, Tereus, and eventually transformed into a nightingale. The bird's song is so melancholy because it is a perpetual lament for Philomela's lost chastity.

As it turns out, no one undergoes Philomela's fate in *The Two Gentlemen of Verona.* Silvia escapes rape, just as Julia avoids Ariadne's fate when the fickle Proteus returns his affections to her. But the close of this early comedy, through its mythic allusions and flirtation with sexual violence, hints at the tragic endings that have narrowly been averted. In this regard, the play is not unlike *A Midsummer Night's Dream*, in which there is a properly comic ending with lover wedded to lover while the last act of that play includes an unintentionally comic enactment of the tragic story of Pyramus and Thisbe, lovers whose passion ended in death, not marriage. Though *Two Gentlemen* ends comically, with two marriages in prospect and male friendship restored, the violent and unexpected turnabouts in the play's concluding moments indicate the difficulty of joining a tale of heroic male friendship to a tale of romantic love between men and women. Especially for the women, the "happy" ending comes at a cost. The two marriages are arranged only after male friendship has been renewed and Valentine has offered—without consulting Silvia—to give his beloved to his friend. Though the two women get the men they have desired, Silvia never speaks again after she is offered to Proteus. Her response to all that has happened remains cloaked in silence, while Julia at the play's end is still in her male disguise (even though she has revealed her true identity). That disguise is both a reminder of the dangers she has encountered because of Proteus's fickleness and perhaps a hint that it is in the form of a boy that Julia is most pleasing to him. As we have seen, this ending since at least the eighteenth century has been controversial, perhaps because much of modern culture has come to value love between men and women over other kinds of emotional bonds. In the Renaissance, the matter was not so settled, a reminder of the different ways in which Shakespeare both is and is not our contemporary.

JEAN E. HOWARD

SELECTED BIBLIOGRAPHY

Demeter, Jason. "Pearls in Beauteous Ladies' Eyes: Shakespeare, Race, and Riots in the American Metropolis." *Journal of Narrative Theory* 41 (Fall 2011): 378–400. Analyzes how lines from *The Two Gentlemen of Verona* figured in commentary on American race relations in the 1960s and 1970s, and how Joseph Papp's 1971 musical version of the play used a multiracial cast in the context of pronounced racial tensions in New York City.

Fudge, Erica. "'The dog is himself': Humans, Animals, and Self-Control in *The Two Gentlemen of Verona*." *How to Do Things with Shakespeare: New Approaches, New Essays*. Ed. Laurie Maguire. Oxford: Blackwell, 2008. 185–209. Reading from within the emerging field of animal studies, Fudge argues that Lance's dog, Crab, pissing under a table, reveals the incivility against which humans (often unsuccessfully) define themselves.

Guy-Bray, Stephen. "Shakespeare and the Invention of the Heterosexual." *Early Modern Literary Studies* Special Issue 16 (October 2007): 12.1–28. http://purl. oclc.org/emls/si-16/brayshks.htm. Argues that in early modern culture homosociality is more important than married love and that heterosexuality, rather than being natural, has to be made up or constructed. *Two Gentlemen* shows how this works.

Hunt, Maurice. "Catholicism, Protestant Reformation, and *The Two Gentlemen of Verona*." *Shakespeare's Religious Allusiveness: Its Play and Tolerance*. Aldershot, Eng.: Ashgate, 2004. 1–17. Addresses the play's deployment of Catholic and Protestant images, metaphors, and concepts, arguing that the Catholic elements create a more memorable, lyric effect despite the play's apparent commitment to the triumph of Protestant ideas of conversion and companionate marriage.

Kiefer, Frederick. "Love Letters in *The Two Gentlemen of Verona*." *Shakespeare Studies* 18 (1986): 65–85. Explores the role of letters in the negotiation of love in *Two Gentlemen*, which contains more letters than any of Shakespeare's other comedies.

Masten, Jeffrey. "*The Two Gentlemen of Verona*." Vol. 3 of *A Companion to Shakespeare's Works: The Comedies*. Ed. Richard Dutton and Jean E. Howard. 4 vols. Oxford: Blackwell, 2003. 266–88. Argues against the idea that *Two Gentlemen* is an immature play because of its focus on male friendship rather than heterosexual love, and argues for male friendship as the abiding framework for Shakespeare's writing career.

Rivlen, Elizabeth. "Shakespeare's Apprenticeship: Performing Service in *The Comedy of Errors* and *The Two Gentlemen of Verona*." *The Aesthetics of Service in Early Modern England*. Evanston, IL: Northwestern UP, 2012. 27–51. Focuses on the ubiquity of servants in Shakespeare's early plays and their capacity not just to mirror but to alter elite identities.

Schlueter, June, ed. "*The Two Gentlemen of Verona*": *Critical Essays*. New York: Garland, 1996. Gathers eighteenth- and nineteenth-century comments on the play along with essays by twentieth-century critics and reviews of notable theater and television productions.

Shannon, Laurie. "The Early Modern Politics of Likeness." *Sovereign Amity: Figures of Friendship in Shakespearean Contexts*. Chicago: U of Chicago P, 2002. 17–53. Traces male friendship discourse from Cicero to Montaigne, showing its importance both for intimate relations between sovereign selves and also for its role in political discourse.

Slights, Camille Wells. "*The Two Gentlemen of Verona* and the Courtesy Book Tradition." *Shakespeare Studies* 16 (1983): 13–31. Argues that the play explores the fashioning of a Renaissance gentleman.

FILMS

A Spray of Plum Blossoms. 1931. Dir. Bu Wancang. China. 100 min. Set on a modern Cantonese military base, this silent film stars Ruan Lingyu, an icon of early Chinese cinema, as Julia. Highlights the intimate relationship between Julia and Silvia, with both women at times dressed in military uniforms.

The Two Gentlemen of Verona. 1983. Dir. Don Taylor. UK. 137 min. This BBC-TV version, in color, employs period music and elegant Italian settings in a performance that foregrounds the heterosexual love plot.

Shakespeare in Love. 1998. Dir. John Madden. USA. 123 min. Starring Gwyneth Paltrow and Joseph Fiennes. Includes scenes and speeches from *The Two Gentlemen of Verona* as examples of Shakespeare's early success with comedy and love lyric.

TEXTUAL INTRODUCTION

The Two Gentlemen of Verona is first mentioned in Francis Meres's list of Shakespeare's comedies and tragedies in his *Palladis Tamia* of 1598. "Shakespeare," Meres notes, "among the English is the most excellent in both kinds for the stage," adding, "for comedy, witness his Gentlemen of Verona." This, along with the play's elliptical composition and occasional lapses in dramatic coherence, has led editors and critics to agree that it is one of Shakespeare's very earliest works.

Textually speaking, the play is relatively straightforward. There is only one surviving early authoritative text—that printed in the 1623 First Folio (F)—and the issues an editor must address in presenting the play to the modern reader by and large require reflection not so much on complex cruxes as on the best ways to present certain moments in the action with the fullest clarity. That said, even the "best" of Shakespeare's play texts have been multiply mediated, and there are elements in the Folio text of *The Two Gentlemen of Verona* that make its origins less than entirely clear: editors remain divided over the nature of the underlying copy.

The play appears from certain features (e.g., a high proportion of parentheses enclosing subordinate clauses and "massed entries") to be one of several in the Folio that the interventionist King's Men scribe Ralph Crane transcribed in the early 1620s (which include *The Tempest, The Merry Wives of Windsor,* and *Measure for Measure,* plays with which *The Two Gentlemen of Verona* is grouped at the beginning of the First Folio). But what precisely was Crane transcribing? Suggestions have included a manuscript in Shakespeare's own hand (a holograph); an assemblage consisting of the "plot" (the outline of entries per scene that would have been pinned up within the tiring house) combined with the separate parts given to each actor; or a promptbook. Yet none of these alone would appear to account for all of the Folio text's inconsistencies, and the matter remains open—though editors generally think the promptbook hypothesis the least likely, presuming that many of the play's inconsistencies would necessarily have been resolved for performance and entrances indicated. In addition, the text seems to have been set by two, or perhaps three, compositors, each of whom appears to have introduced his own habits in terms of spelling, contractions, and the like (see Howard-Hill 1973).

For this edition, as for other *Norton Shakespeare* plays with massed entries, entry stage directions have been relocated as required for characters' actual entrances. At 1.3.0, for instance, F reads "*Enter Antonio and Panthino. Protheus.*" Here the initial SD becomes two distinct SDs: "*Enter* ANTONIO *and* PANTINO" (1.3.0) and, to make the action clear for the uninitiated reader, "*Enter* PROTEUS *with a letter, unaware of Antonio and Pantino's presence*" (1.3.43). (The Textual Variants note all emendations and relocations of such massed entry directions.) When Julia passes herself off as Sebastian, the page boy, and witnesses Proteus's betrayal, her cross-dressing needs to be precisely indicated from 4.2.25 on. Other clarifications include the attribution of a song to Proteus at 4.2.37 (see Digital Edition TC 9). Similarly, Turio has been replaced by a Servant at 2.4.112 (Digital Edition TC 6).

Characters' names have been modernized unless the context calls for the retention of the F spelling, e.g., at 1.3.67 (Digital Edition TC 4). Place-names in this play are at times rather loosely deployed and occasionally need rationalization: to reflect a coherent journey between Verona and Milan, for instance, the apparently erroneous mention of "Padua" (2.5.1) has been emended here to "Milan," a city for which modern English spelling has been retained except at 3.1.81 and 5.4.126, where "Milano" has been preferred for metrical reasons (Digital Edition TC 8).

NATHALIE RIVÈRE DE CARLES

TEXTUAL BIBLIOGRAPHY

Howard-Hill, T. H. "The Compositors of Shakespeare's Folio Comedies." *Studies in Bibliography* 26 (1973): 62–106.
Johnson, Samuel, ed. William Shakespeare, *Works* (London, 1745).
Pope, Alexander, ed. William Shakespeare, *Works*. 6 vols. (London, 1723–25).
Theobald, Lewis, ed. William Shakespeare, *Works*. 7 vols. (London, 1733).

PERFORMANCE NOTE

Faced with realizing the simple structure and flat characterizations of *The Two Gentlemen of Verona*, many productions affect an ironic distance to the play, revealing through their actors a wry awareness of the characters' thinness and romantic excesses. With or without such irony, productions frequently take antinaturalistic approaches to the play, indulging in its lyricism, stylizing the acting, and highlighting the main characters' naive exuberance to create an atmosphere of levity and inconsequence. Such approaches potentially lessen the human stakes of the play, thereby preventing the disturbing fifth-act events from spoiling the comic resolution; or conversely, they may deepen the impact of a rape scene staged with terrifying realism, rendering the "comic" ending richer and more unsettling for the wide chasm between generic expectations and dramatic reality. Other productions develop darker aspects throughout, introducing, for instance, Proteus as a sinister Byronic figure who competes enviously with Valentine or else presenting Sylvia's (or Proteus's) father as a chillingly realistic tyrant. Such choices develop depth in characters by destabilizing their archetypal roles, along with the play's generic identity, contributing to an audience's uncertainty about its resolution.

The roles of Proteus and Julia, in fact, require considerable versatility: one is alternately tender and ruthless, the other as equivocal as constant, and both cunning, witty, impassioned, and capable of deception. Productions might also pursue complexity by suggesting that Valentine's ego and condescension at least partly explain Proteus's betrayal, or that some homoerotic attraction inspires the rivalry for one or both. Meanwhile, Silvia can be exceptionally dignified or overly entitled; the outlaws mistreated gentlemen or unsavory convicts; and Lance can tinge the play with warmth or melancholy. Other considerations in performance include managing the play's notoriously difficult ending (see Digital Edition PC 2) and deciding whether and how to resolve its many inconsistencies—e.g., Proteus sails from one landlocked city to another; the Duke of Milan seems to think he—at least in the Folio text—is in Verona (3.1.81); and the play assigns the name "Sir Eglamour" to two different men who appear to have opposite characteristics, one of whom Sylvia praises for chivalry shortly before he abandons her in the forest (5.3.6–7).

Brett Gamboa

The Two Gentlemen of Verona

THE PERSONS OF THE PLAY

DUKE of Milan, father to Silvia
SILVIA, beloved of Valentine, daughter to the Duke
PROTEUS, a gentleman of Verona
LANCE, clownish servant to Proteus
VALENTINE, a gentleman of Verona
SPEED, clownish servant to Valentine
TURIO, a foolish rival to Valentine
ANTONIO, father to Proteus
PANTINO, servant to Antonio
JULIA, beloved of Proteus
LUCETTA, waiting-woman to Julia
EGLAMOUR, agent for Silvia in her escape
HOST, where Julia lodges

Three OUTLAWS with Valentine
SERVANT to the Duke
Musicians
Ursula, maid to Silvia

1.1

[*Enter*] VALENTINE[1] [*and*] PROTEUS.[2]

VALENTINE Cease to persuade, my loving Proteus.
Home-keeping youth have ever homely° wits.   *dull*
Were't not affection° chains thy tender° days   *love / young*
To the sweet glances of thy honored love,
5   I rather would entreat thy company
To see the wonders of the world abroad
Than, living dully sluggardized° at home,   *made lazy*
Wear out thy youth with shapeless° idleness.   *aimless*
But since thou lov'st, love still,° and thrive therein, *constantly*
10 Even as I would when I to love begin.
PROTEUS Wilt thou be gone? Sweet Valentine, adieu.
Think on thy Proteus when thou haply° seest   *by chance*
Some rare noteworthy object in thy travel.
Wish me partaker in thy happiness
15 When thou dost meet good hap;° and in thy danger, *fortune*
If ever danger do environ° thee,   *surround*
Commend° thy grievance to my holy prayers;   *Entrust*
For I will be thy beadsman,[3] Valentine.

1.1 Location: Presumably Verona, though we learn this only from the title.
1. St. Valentine is the patron saint of lovers; Valentine's name may thus indicate his role as faithful lover.
2. In classical mythology, a sea god who could change shape at will; the name suggests a fickle nature. In 1.1, Proteus is pronounced with three syllables; elsewhere in the play, often with two. In F, the names of all the characters who appear in a given scene are listed as it opens, even if they enter at a later point. This edition marks entrances when characters actually appear onstage. In this scene, Speed enters at line 70, though in F his entrance is not marked and his name is listed with that of Proteus and Valentine at the beginning of the scene.
3. One who prays (counts the beads of a rosary) for another's spiritual welfare.

	VALENTINE And on a love-book[4] pray for my success?	
20	PROTEUS Upon some book I love I'll pray for thee.	
	VALENTINE That's on some shallow story of deep love—	
	How young Leander crossed the Hellespont.[5]	
	PROTEUS That's a deep story of a deeper love,	
	For he was more than over-shoes[6] in love.	
25	VALENTINE 'Tis true, for you are over-boots in love,	
	And yet you never swam the Hellespont.	
	PROTEUS Over the boots? Nay, give me not the boots.°	*do not mock me*
	VALENTINE No, I will not, for it boots° thee not.	*profits*
	PROTEUS What?	
	VALENTINE To be in love, where scorn is bought with groans,	
30	Coy looks with heartsore sighs, one fading moment's mirth	
	With twenty watchful,° weary, tedious nights.	*wakeful*
	If haply won, perhaps a hapless° gain;	*an unlucky*
	If lost, why then a grievous labor won;	
	However,° but a folly bought with wit,	*Either way*
35	Or else a wit by folly vanquishèd.	
	PROTEUS So, by your circumstance,° you call me fool.	*lengthy discourse*
	VALENTINE So, by your circumstance,° I fear you'll prove.	*situation*
	PROTEUS 'Tis Love you cavil at.° I am not Love.	*find fault with*
	VALENTINE Love is your master, for he masters you;	
40	And he that is so yokèd by a fool	
	Methinks should not be chronicled for wise.	
	PROTEUS Yet writers say, "As in the sweetest bud,	
	The eating canker° dwells, so eating love	*harmful caterpillar*
	Inhabits in the finest wits of all."	
45	VALENTINE And writers say, "As the most forward bud	
	Is eaten by the canker ere it blow,°	*blossom*
	Even so by love the young and tender wit	
	Is turned to folly, blasting° in the bud,	*withering*
	Losing his verdure° even in the prime,°	*greenness / spring*
50	And all the fair effects of future hopes."	
	But wherefore waste I time to counsel thee	
	That art a votary[7] to fond° desire?	*foolish*
	Once more adieu. My father at the road°	*harbor*
	Expects my coming, there to see me shipped.[8]	
55	PROTEUS And thither will I bring thee, Valentine.	
	VALENTINE Sweet Proteus, no. Now let us take our leave.	
	To Milan let me hear from thee by letters	
	Of thy success° in love and what news else	*fortune (good or bad)*
	Betideth° here in absence of thy friend,	*Happens*
60	And I likewise will visit thee with mine.	
	PROTEUS All happiness bechance to thee in Milan.	
	VALENTINE As much to you at home; and so farewell.	

Exit.

PROTEUS   He after honor hunts, I after love.

---

4. A book about love (instead of a prayer book). Valentine is teasing Proteus for making love his religion.
5. In classical mythology, Leander drowned while swimming the Hellespont (a narrow strait of water in modern Turkey separating the Gallipoli peninsula from mainland Asia) to visit his love, Hero. Shakespeare probably had read in manuscript Christopher Marlowe's poem "Hero and Leander."

6. So deep as to cover the shoes (or boots); recklessly or excessively.
7. One devoted to a particular pursuit; one bound by vows to a religious life.
8. Although Verona and Milan are inland, Shakespeare writes of Verona as if it were located, like London, on a tidal river leading to the sea.

	He leaves his friends to dignify° them more;	*bring honor to*
65	I leave[9] myself, my friends, and all, for love.	
	Thou, Julia, thou hast metamorphosed° me:	*transformed*
	Made me neglect my studies, lose° my time,	*waste*
	War with good counsel, set the world at naught;°	*put no value on the world*
	Made wit with musing weak, heart sick with thought.°	*melancholy ideas*

[*Enter* SPEED.]

70 SPEED   Sir Proteus, save you.[1] Saw you my master?

PROTEUS   But now he parted hence to embark for Milan.

SPEED   Twenty to one, then, he is shipped already,
And I have played the sheep[2] in losing him.

PROTEUS   Indeed a sheep doth very often stray,

75 An if° the shepherd be a while away.   *An if = If*

SPEED   You conclude that my master is a shepherd, then, and
I a sheep?

PROTEUS   I do.

SPEED   Why, then, my horns are his horns,[3] whether I wake or

80 sleep.

PROTEUS   A silly answer, and fitting well a sheep.

SPEED   This proves me still a sheep.

PROTEUS   True, and thy master a shepherd.

SPEED   Nay, that I can deny by a circumstance.°   *argument*

85 PROTEUS   It shall go hard but I'll prove it by another.[4]

SPEED   The shepherd seeks the sheep and not the sheep the
shepherd; but I seek my master and my master seeks not me.
Therefore I am no sheep.

PROTEUS   The sheep for fodder follow the shepherd; the shep-

90 herd for food follows not the sheep. Thou for wages followest
thy master; thy master for wages follows not thee. Therefore
thou art a sheep.

SPEED   Such another proof will make me cry "baa."

PROTEUS   But dost thou hear? Gav'st thou my letter to Julia?

95 SPEED   Ay, sir. I, a lost mutton,° gave your letter to her, a laced   *sheep*
mutton,° and she, a laced mutton, gave me, a lost mutton,   *prostitute (slang)*
nothing for my labor.

PROTEUS   Here's too small a pasture for such store° of muttons.   *abundance*

SPEED   If the ground be overcharged,° you were best stick[5] her.   *overburdened*

100 PROTEUS   Nay, in that you are astray: 'twere best pound° you.   *empound; beat*

SPEED   Nay, sir, less than a pound shall serve me for carrying
your letter.

PROTEUS   You mistake. I mean the pound—a pinfold.°   *pen for stray animals*

SPEED   From a pound to a pin?[6] Fold it° over and over,   *Multiply*

105 'Tis threefold too little for carrying a letter to your lover.

PROTEUS   But what said she?

9. Textual Comment Editors since Pope have emended F's "I loue" to "I leave." Proteus's declaration that he will "leave" (neglect) everything else for love sets up a contrast between himself and Valentine, who "leaves" (departs) in order to bring honor to his friends. See Digital Edition TC 1.

1. Textual Comment Before 1606, when a parliamentary act prohibited actors from speaking the name of God or Christ, Speed's words of greeting here would have been "God save you." F has an apostrophe before "save," a trace of this deleted word. See Digital Edition TC 2.

2. Been foolish, with a pun on "ship." "Ship" and "sheep" were pronounced similarly.

3. As Speed's master, Valentine owns Speed's horns. Traditionally, the horns signified the cuckold and were attributed to men whose wives were unfaithful.

4. It shall fare ill with me unless I prove my claim by using another argument.

5. Stab or slaughter the extra sheep, with a pun on "stick" as meaning "have sexual intercourse with."

6. Proverbially, pins have little value (e.g., "not worth a pin"). Speed fears he is going to be paid too little for carrying the letter to Julia.

SPEED [*nodding, then saying*] Ay.°   *Yes*
PROTEUS Nod—ay? Why, that's "noddy."°   *a fool*
SPEED You mistook, sir! I say she did nod, and you ask me if
110   she did nod, and I say "Ay."
PROTEUS And that set together is "noddy."
SPEED Now you have taken the pains to set it together, take it
    for your pains.
PROTEUS No, no, you shall have it for bearing the letter.
115 SPEED Well, I perceive I must be fain° to bear with you.   *willing*
PROTEUS Why, sir, how do you bear with me?
SPEED Marry,[7] sir, the letter very orderly,° having nothing but   *dutifully*
    the word "noddy" for my pains.
PROTEUS Beshrew me° but you have a quick wit.   *Curse me (a mild oath)*
120 SPEED And yet it cannot overtake your slow purse.
PROTEUS Come, come, open the matter; in brief, what said she?
SPEED Open your purse that the money and the matter may
    be both at once delivered.
PROTEUS [*giving him money*] Well, sir, here is for your pain.
125   What said she?
SPEED Truly, sir, I think you'll hardly win her.[8]
PROTEUS Why? Couldst thou perceive so much from her?
SPEED Sir, I could perceive[9] nothing at all from her—no, not so
    much as a ducat[1] for delivering your letter. And being so hard°   *stingy; cold*
130   to me that brought your mind,° I fear she'll prove as hard to   *wishes*
    you in telling° your mind. Give her no token but stones,[2] for   *when you speak*
    she's as hard as steel.
PROTEUS What said she? Nothing?
SPEED No, not so much as "Take this for thy pains." To tes-
135   tify° your bounty, I thank you, you have testerned me;[3] in   *attest to*
    requital whereof, henceforth, carry your letters yourself!
    And so, sir, I'll commend you to my master.   [*Exit.*]
PROTEUS Go, go, be gone, to save your ship from wreck,
    Which cannot perish having thee aboard,
140   Being destined to a drier death on shore.[4]
    I must go send some better messenger.
    I fear my Julia would not deign° my lines,   *graciously accept*
    Receiving them from such a worthless post.°   *Exit.*   *messenger; blockhead*

1.2

Enter JULIA *and* LUCETTA.

JULIA But say, Lucetta, now we are alone,
    Wouldst thou then counsel me to fall in love?
LUCETTA Ay, madam, so you stumble not unheedfully.°   *carelessly*
JULIA Of all the fair resort° of gentlemen   *company*
5   That every day with parle° encounter me,   *talk*
    In thy opinion which is worthiest love?

---

7. A mild oath suggesting surprise, from the Virgin
Mary's name.
8. You'll have a hard time winning her.
9. Punning on an obsolete meaning of "perceive" as
"receive."
1. A coin worth about three shillings and sixpence, a
generous tip.

2. Precious stones; pebbles; perhaps also testicles.
token: love-gift.
3. Given me a testern, a coin worth much less than
the ducat Speed wanted.
4. *Which . . . shore:* alluding to the proverb "He that
is born to be hanged shall never be drowned."
1.2 Location: Out of doors, maybe in Julia's garden.

LUCETTA   Please you° repeat their names, I'll show my mind   *If you will*
  According to my shallow simple skill.
JULIA   What think'st thou of the fair Sir Eglamour?[1]
10 LUCETTA   As of a knight well spoken, neat,° and fine;   *elegant*
  But, were I you, he never should be mine.
JULIA   What think'st thou of the rich Mercatio?
LUCETTA   Well of his wealth; but of himself, so-so.
JULIA   What think'st thou of the gentle Proteus?
15 LUCETTA   Lord, Lord, to see what folly reigns in us.
JULIA   How now? What means this passion° at his name?   *outburst of emotion*
LUCETTA   Pardon, dear madam; 'tis a passing° shame   *great*
  That I, unworthy body as I am,
  Should censure° thus on lovely gentlemen.   *pass judgment*
20 JULIA   Why not on Proteus, as of all the rest?
LUCETTA   Then thus: of many good, I think him best.
JULIA   Your reason?
LUCETTA   I have no other but a woman's reason:
  I think him so because I think him so.
25 JULIA   And wouldst thou have me cast my love on him?
LUCETTA   Ay, if you thought your love not cast away.
JULIA   Why, he of all the rest hath never moved° me.   *proposed marriage to*
LUCETTA   Yet he of all the rest I think best loves ye.
JULIA   His little speaking shows his love but small.
30 LUCETTA   Fire that's closest kept° burns most of all.   *most enclosed*
JULIA   They do not love that do not show their love.
LUCETTA   Oh, they love least that let men know their love.
JULIA   I would I knew his mind.
LUCETTA   [*handing her Proteus' letter*]   Peruse this paper, madam.
35 JULIA   "To Julia." Say, from whom?
LUCETTA   That the contents will show.
JULIA   Say, say! Who gave it thee?
LUCETTA   Sir Valentine's page; and sent, I think, from Proteus.
  He would have given it you, but I, being in the way,
40   Did in your name receive it.[2] Pardon the fault, I pray.
JULIA   Now, by my modesty, a goodly broker!°   *go-between*
  Dare you presume to harbor wanton lines?°   *receive love letters*
  To whisper and conspire against my youth?
  Now trust me, 'tis an office° of great worth,   *position; duty*
45   And you an officer fit for the place.
  There! Take the paper! [*She gives* LUCETTA *the letter.*] See it
    be returned,
  Or else return no more into my sight.
LUCETTA   To plead for love deserves more fee than hate.
JULIA   Will ye be gone?
LUCETTA   That you may ruminate.°   *Exit.*   *meditate*
50 JULIA   And yet I would I had o'erlooked° the letter.   *examined*
  It were a shame to call her back again
  And pray her to° a fault for which I chid her.   *ask her to commit*
  What fool is she, that knows I am a maid
  And would not force the letter to my view?

---

1. Not the same Eglamour who assists Silvia in 4.3.
The name is found in medieval romances and by the
1590s seems to have acquired comic associations.

2. An inconsistency in the text. In 1.1, Speed said he
delivered the letter to Julia. He may have mistaken
Lucetta for Julia or lied to Proteus.

55	Since maids in modesty say "No" to that	
	Which they would have the profferer° construe "Ay."	*giver*
	Fie, fie, how wayward is this foolish Love	
	That, like a testy° babe, will scratch the nurse	*cranky*
	And presently,° all humbled, kiss the rod?[3]	*immediately after*
60	How churlishly I chid Lucetta hence,	
	When willingly I would have had her here?	
	How angerly I taught my brow to frown,	
	When inward joy enforced my heart to smile?	
	My penance is to call Lucetta back	
65	And ask remission for my folly past.	
	What ho! Lucetta!	

[*Enter* LUCETTA.]

LUCETTA   What would your ladyship?
JULIA   Is't near dinner-time?
LUCETTA   I would it were,
That you might kill° your stomach° on your meat   *expend / hunger; rage*
And not upon your maid.
[*She drops and picks up the letter.*][4]
JULIA   What is't that you
70   Took up so gingerly?°   *cautiously*
LUCETTA   Nothing.
JULIA   Why didst thou stoop, then?
LUCETTA   To take a paper up that I let fall.
JULIA   And is that paper nothing?
75   LUCETTA   Nothing concerning me.
JULIA   Then let it lie for those that it concerns.
LUCETTA   Madam, it will not lie where it concerns,
Unless it have a false interpreter.
JULIA   Some love of yours hath writ to you in rhyme.
80   LUCETTA   That I might sing it, madam, to a tune,
Give me a note. Your ladyship can set[5]—
JULIA   As little by such toys° as may be possible.   *trifles*
Best sing it to the tune of "Light o'love."[6]
LUCETTA   It is too heavy° for so light a tune.   *serious*
85   JULIA   Heavy? Belike it hath some burden,[7] then?
LUCETTA   Ay, and melodious were it, would you sing it.
JULIA   And why not you?
LUCETTA   I cannot reach so high.[8]
JULIA   Let's see your song. [*She tries to grab the letter.*][9] How
        now, minion?[1]
LUCETTA   Keep tune° there still. So you will sing it out.[2]   *in tune; in good humor*
90   And yet methinks I do not like this tune.[3]

---

3. Children sometimes had to kiss the stick with which they were beaten.
4. There is no indication in F of when Lucetta drops the letter that she here picks up. Some directors and editors assume that she drops it, either advisedly or inadvertently, before leaving the stage at line 49. To have her drop and immediately retrieve the letter, as here, may suggest that Lucetta is again trying to call her mistress's attention to it.
5. Set to music. Julia takes it to mean "set store by" or "give value to."
6. A popular song in Shakespeare's time.
7. Refrain; heavy load; perhaps punningly referring to the weight of a body during intercourse.

8. Sing so high a note; hope to win so high-ranking a lover.
9. TEXTUAL COMMENT The struggle between Julia and Lucetta fixes the attention of the audience on the letter, highlighting its importance in the play's erotic plotline. This edition adds stage directions to those implied in the dialogue to help readers follow the movements of this prop. See Digital Edition TC 3.
1. Hussy; with a possible pun on "minim," a musical term for a half note.
2. Finish singing it; come to the end of your anger.
3. Julia may have struck or threatened to strike Lucetta.

JULIA   You do not?

LUCETTA   No, madam, 'tis too sharp.°   high-pitched; bitter

JULIA   You, minion, are too saucy.

LUCETTA   Nay, now you are too flat°   low-pitched; blunt

95   And mar the concord° with too harsh a descant.°   harmony / melody
            There wanteth but a mean to fill your song.[4]

JULIA   The mean is drowned with your unruly bass.°   low notes; bad conduct

LUCETTA   Indeed, I bid the base for[5] Proteus.
                    [JULIA grabs the letter.]

JULIA   This babble shall not henceforth trouble me.

100   Here is a coil with protestation.°   fuss about a love vow
                    [She tears the letter and drops the pieces.]
                    [LUCETTA motions to pick them up.]
            Go, get you gone, and let the papers lie!
            You would be fing'ring them to anger me.

LUCETTA   [aside]   She makes it strange,° but she would be best   pretends not to care
            pleased
            To be so angered with another letter.   [Exit.]

105   JULIA   Nay, would I were so angered with the same.
                    [She picks up pieces of the letter.]
            O hateful hands to tear such loving words;
            Injurious wasps[6] to feed on such sweet honey
            And kill the bees that yield it with your stings!
            I'll kiss each several° paper for amends.   separate

110   Look, here is writ "kind Julia." Unkind Julia!
            As° in revenge of thy ingratitude   As if
            I throw thy name against the bruising stones,
            Trampling contemptuously on thy disdain.
            And here is writ "Love-wounded Proteus."

115   Poor wounded name, my bosom as a bed
            Shall lodge thee till thy wound be thoroughly healed;
            And thus I search° it with a sovereign° kiss.   probe; cleanse / healing
            But twice or thrice was "Proteus" written down.
            Be calm, good wind: blow not a word away

120   Till I have found each letter in the letter
            Except mine own name. That, some whirlwind bear
            Unto a ragged, fearful, hanging° rock   overhanging
            And throw it thence into the raging sea!
            Lo, here in one line is his name twice writ:

125   "Poor forlorn Proteus, passionate Proteus,
            To the sweet Julia"—that I'll tear away;
            And yet I will not, sith° so prettily   since
            He couples it to his complaining names.
            Thus will I fold them, one upon another:

130   Now kiss, embrace, contend, do what you will.[7]
                    [Enter LUCETTA.]

LUCETTA   Madam, dinner is ready and your father stays.°   waits

JULIA   Well, let us go.

LUCETTA   What, shall these papers lie like telltales here?

---

4. There lacks but a tenor part to complete your song. Her implication is that Julia lacks a man to fulfill her desires.
5. I sang the bass part for; I acted in the interests of (a phrase from the game called prisoner's base).
6. Referring to her hurtful fingers.
7. Julia uses sexually charged language when she suggests that the fragments of paper bearing her and Proteus's names might "couple," "kiss," "embrace," and "contend" (struggle against each other).

JULIA   If you respect° them, best to take them up.   *value*
135 LUCETTA   Nay, I was taken up° for laying them down.   *scolded*
    Yet here they shall not lie for° catching cold.   *for fear of*
        [*She picks up pieces of the letter.*]
    JULIA   I see you have a month's mind to° them.   *a strong desire for*
    LUCETTA   Ay, madam, you may say what sights you see;
    I see things, too, although you judge I wink.°   *close my eyes*
140 JULIA   Come, come, will't please you go?   *Exeunt.*

1.3

Enter ANTONIO *and* PANTINO.

ANTONIO   Tell me, Pantino, what sad° talk was that   *serious*
    Wherewith my brother held you in the cloister?°   *covered walk*
PANTINO   'Twas of his nephew Proteus, your son.
ANTONIO   Why, what of him?
PANTINO   He wondered that your lordship
5   Would suffer him to spend his youth at home
    While other men, of slender° reputation,   *insignificant*
    Put forth° their sons to seek preferment° out—   *Send / advancement*
    Some to the wars to try their fortune there;
    Some to discover islands far away;
10   Some to the studious universities.
    For any or for all these exercises
    He said that Proteus your son was meet,°   *fit*
    And did request me to importune° you   *beg*
    To let him spend his time no more at home,
15   Which would be great impeachment to his age°   *reproach in his old age*
    In having known no travel in his youth.
ANTONIO   Nor need'st thou much importune me to that
    Whereon this month I have been hammering.°   *thinking hard*
    I have considered well his loss of time,
20   And how he cannot be a perfect° man,   *complete*
    Not being tried and tutored in the world.
    Experience is by industry achieved,
    And perfected by the swift course of time.
    Then tell me—whither were I best to send him?
25   PANTINO   I think your lordship is not ignorant
    How his companion, youthful Valentine,
    Attends° the Emperor¹ in his royal court.   *Waits upon*
ANTONIO   I know it well.
PANTINO   'Twere good, I think, your lordship sent him thither.
30   There shall he practice° tilts and tournaments,   *take part in*
    Hear sweet discourse, converse with noblemen,
    And be in eye of° every exercise   *witness*
    Worthy his youth and nobleness of birth.
ANTONIO   I like thy counsel. Well hast thou advised,
35   And that thou mayst perceive how well I like it,
    The execution of it shall make known.
    Even with the speediest expedition,°   *swiftness*
    I will dispatch him to the Emperor's court.

1.3 Location: Antonio's house in Verona.
1. One of several inconsistencies in the plot. Proteus and Valentine are later shown at the court of the Duke of Milan, not at the Emperor's court. The references to Milan continue in 2.5.1, 3.1.81, and 5.4.126, but Milan had ever only been an imperial court in the fourth century C.E. Shakespeare is either inflating the political significance of the Duke of Milan's court or making a mistake.

PANTINO   Tomorrow, may it please you, Don Alfonso
40   With other gentlemen of good esteem
    Are journeying to salute the Emperor
    And to commend their service to his will.
ANTONIO   Good company—with them shall Proteus go.
    [*Enter* PROTEUS *with a letter, unaware of Antonio*
        and Pantino's presence.]
    And in good time!° Now will we break with him.[2]   *at the right moment*
45 PROTEUS   Sweet love, sweet lines, sweet life!
    Here is her hand, the agent of her heart.
    Here is her oath for love, her honor's pawn.°   *pledge*
    Oh, that our fathers would applaud our loves
    To seal our happiness with their consents.
50   O heavenly Julia!
ANTONIO   How now? What letter are you reading there?
PROTEUS   May't please your lordship, 'tis a word or two
    Of commendations° sent from Valentine,   *greetings*
    Delivered by a friend that came from him.
55 ANTONIO   Lend me the letter. Let me see what news.
PROTEUS   There is no news, my lord, but that he writes
    How happily he lives, how well beloved
    And daily gracèd° by the Emperor,   *honored*
    Wishing me with him, partner of his fortune.
60 ANTONIO   And how stand you affected° to his wish?   *disposed*
PROTEUS   As one relying on your lordship's will,
    And not depending on his friendly wish.
ANTONIO   My will is something sorted with° his wish.   *in agreement with*
    Muse° not that I thus suddenly proceed,   *Wonder*
65   For what I will, I will, and there an end.
    I am resolved that thou shalt spend some time
    With Valentinus[3] in the Emperor's court.
    What maintenance° he from his friends° receives,   *money / family*
    Like exhibition° thou shalt have from me.   *The same allowance*
70   Tomorrow be in readiness to go.
    Excuse it not,[4] for I am peremptory.°   *resolved*
PROTEUS   My lord, I cannot be so soon provided.°   *equipped*
    Please you deliberate a day or two.
ANTONIO   Look what° thou want'st shall be sent after thee.   *Whatever*
75   No more of stay: tomorrow thou must go!
    Come on, Pantino, you shall be employed
    To hasten on his expedition. [*Exeunt* ANTONIO *and* PANTINO.]
PROTEUS   Thus have I shunned the fire for fear of burning
    And drenched me in the sea where I am drowned.
80   I feared to show my father Julia's letter,
    Lest he should take exceptions° to my love,   *object*
    And with the vantage of mine own excuse[5]
    Hath he excepted most° against my love.   *raised most obstacles*
    Oh, how this spring of love resembleth
85   The uncertain glory of an April day,

2. Reveal the plan to him.
3. TEXTUAL COMMENT This is the only instance of
the spelling "Valentinus" in F. This use of Latin,
which was the primary diplomatic language in the
sixteenth century, may suggest that Antonio envisions a political purpose to Proteus's journey. See

Digital Edition TC 4.
4. Do not offer reasons why you should be excused
from this.
5. And by taking advantage of my lie (that the letter
came from Valentine).

Which now shows all the beauty of the sun,
And by and by a cloud takes all away!
[*Enter* PANTINO.]

PANTINO　Sir Proteus, your father calls for you.
He is in haste; therefore I pray you go.

90　PROTEUS　Why, this it is: my heart accords thereto,
And yet a thousand times it answers "No."[6]　　　*Exeunt.*

2.1

Enter VALENTINE *and* SPEED. [VALENTINE *drops*
a glove.]

SPEED　Sir, your glove.

VALENTINE　　　　　Not mine. My gloves are on.

SPEED　Why, then, this may be yours, for this is but one.[1]

VALENTINE　Ha? Let me see—ay, give it me, it's mine.
Sweet ornament that decks° a thing divine.　　　　　　*decorates*

5　Ah, Silvia, Silvia!

SPEED [*calling*]　Madam Silvia! Madam Silvia!

VALENTINE　How now, sirrah?[2]

SPEED　She is not within hearing, sir.

VALENTINE　Why, sir, who bade you call her?

10　SPEED　Your worship, sir, or else I mistook.

VALENTINE　Well, you'll still be° too forward.　　　　　*persist in being*

SPEED　And yet I was last chidden° for being too slow.　　*chided (scolded)*

VALENTINE　Go to,[3] sir. Tell me, do you know Madam Silvia?

SPEED　She that your worship loves?

15　VALENTINE　Why, how know you that I am in love?

SPEED　Marry, by these special marks: first, you have learned,
like Sir Proteus, to wreathe° your arms, like a malcontent;[4]　　*fold*
to relish° a love-song, like a robin-redbreast; to walk alone,　　*sing*
like one that had the pestilence;° to sigh, like a schoolboy　　*plague*
20　that had lost his ABC;° to weep, like a young wench that had　*primer; spelling book*
buried her grandam; to fast, like one that takes° diet; to　　*keeps to a*
watch,° like one that fears robbing; to speak puling,° like a　*lie awake / whiningly*
beggar at Hallowmas.[5] You were wont,° when you laughed,　*formerly accustomed*
to crow like a cock; when you walked, to walk like one of the
25　lions; when you fasted, it was presently° after dinner; when　　*immediately*
you looked sadly, it was for want of money. And now you are
metamorphosed with a mistress, that when I look on you I
can hardly think you my master.

VALENTINE　Are all these things perceived in me?

30　SPEED　They are all perceived without ye.°　　　　*in your appearance*

VALENTINE　Without me?[6] They cannot.

SPEED　Without you? Nay, that's certain, for without° you were　　*unless*
so simple, none else would.° But you are so without these fol-　*(perceive them)*
lies[7] that these follies are within you and shine through you

---

6. *my* . . . "*No*": suggesting that Proteus is divided
between desire to go and desire to stay. *accords thereto:*
agrees to it.
2.1 Location: Milan.
1. A pun—"one" could be pronounced like "on."
2. Fellow; a form of address to social inferiors.
3. Expression of impatience.

4. A person made melancholy and discontented by
love. Such people were often depicted with folded arms.
5. All Saints' Day, November 1, when it was customary to give charity to beggars.
6. Valentine has taken Speed to mean, "They are all
perceived when you are absent."
7. But you are so outwardly marked by these follies.

35 like the water in an urinal,° that not an eye that sees you but   *glass jar for urine*
is a physician to comment on your malady.
VALENTINE But tell me, dost thou know my lady Silvia?
SPEED She that you gaze on so as she sits at supper?
VALENTINE Hast thou observed that? Even she, I mean.
40 SPEED Why, sir, I know[8] her not.
VALENTINE Dost thou know her by my gazing on her, and yet
know'st her not?
SPEED Is she not hard-favored,° sir?   *ugly*
VALENTINE Not so fair, boy, as well-favored.°   *gracious; esteemed*
45 SPEED Sir, I know that well enough.
VALENTINE What dost thou know?
SPEED That she is not so fair as—of you—well favored.°   *looked on with favor*
VALENTINE I mean that her beauty is exquisite but her favor°   *graciousness*
infinite.
50 SPEED That's because the one is painted° and the other out of   *(with cosmetics)*
all count.[9]
VALENTINE How painted? And how out of count?
SPEED Marry, sir, so painted to make her fair that no man
counts of° her beauty.   *takes account of; values*
55 VALENTINE How esteem'st thou me? I account of her beauty.
SPEED You never saw her since she was deformed.[1]
VALENTINE How long hath she been deformed?
SPEED Ever since you loved her.
VALENTINE I have loved her ever since I saw her, and still I
60 see her beautiful.
SPEED If you love her, you cannot see her.
VALENTINE Why?
SPEED Because Love is blind. Oh, that you had mine eyes, or
your own eyes had the lights° they were wont to have when   *power to see clearly*
65 you chid at Sir Proteus for going ungartered![2]
VALENTINE What should I see then?
SPEED Your own present folly and her passing° deformity. For   *excessive*
he, being in love, could not see to garter his hose, and you,
being in love, cannot see to put on your hose.
70 VALENTINE Belike, boy, then you are in love, for last morning
you could not see to wipe my shoes.
SPEED True, sir! I was in love with my bed. I thank you, you
swinged° me for my love, which makes me the bolder to   *beat*
chide you for yours.
75 VALENTINE In conclusion, I stand affected to° her.   *in love with*
SPEED I would you were set[3] so your affection would cease.
VALENTINE Last night she enjoined° me to write some lines   *instructed*
to one she loves.
SPEED And have you?
80 VALENTINE I have.
SPEED Are they not lamely writ?
VALENTINE No, boy, but as well as I can do them.
[*Enter* SILVIA.]
Peace, here she comes.

---

8. Punning on "know" as meaning "to be sexually
familiar with."
9. *out of all count:* innumerable.
1. Altered (Speed implies that Valentine's love for
Silvia distorts his view of her).

2. Garters kept stockings from falling down. Going
"ungartered" was a traditional sign of love melancholy.
3. Seated; satisfied. Speed has interpreted "stand"
as carrying its bawdy connotation of "having an
erection."

SPEED [*aside*]   Oh, excellent motion!° Oh, exceeding puppet!°   *puppet show / (Silvia)*

85   Now will he interpret[4] to her!

VALENTINE   Madam and mistress, a thousand good-morrows.

SPEED [*aside*]   Oh, give° ye good e'en!° Here's a million of   *God give / evening*
manners.

SILVIA   Sir Valentine and servant,[5] to you two thousand.

90   SPEED [*aside*]   He should give her interest, and she gives it
him.[6]

VALENTINE   As you enjoined me, I have writ your letter
Unto the secret nameless friend of yours,
Which I was much unwilling to proceed in

95   But for my duty to your ladyship.
[*He gives her the letter.*]

SILVIA   I thank you, gentle servant. 'Tis very clerkly° done.   *like a scholar*

VALENTINE   Now trust me, madam, it came hardly off,°   *was not done easily*
For being ignorant to whom it goes
I writ at random, very doubtfully.

100   SILVIA   Perchance you think too much of so much pains?

VALENTINE   No, madam. So it stead° you, I will write,   *help*
Please you command a thousand times as much.
And yet—

SILVIA   A pretty period.° Well, I guess the sequel,°   *pause / what is next*

105   And yet I will not name it. And yet I care not.
And yet take this again. [*She offers him the letter.*] And yet I
thank you,
Meaning henceforth to trouble you no more.

SPEED [*aside*]   And yet you will. And yet another "yet."

VALENTINE   What means your ladyship? Do you not like it?

110   SILVIA   Yes, yes. The lines are very quaintly° writ,   *skillfully*
But, since unwillingly, take them again.
[*She offers him the letter again.*]
Nay, take them.

VALENTINE   Madam, they are for you.

SILVIA   Ay, ay. You writ them, sir, at my request,
But I will none of them. They are for you.

115   I would have had them writ more movingly.

VALENTINE   Please you, I'll write your ladyship another.

SILVIA   And when it's writ, for my sake read it over,
And if it please you, so. If not, why, so.

VALENTINE   If it please me, madam? What then?

120   SILVIA   Why if it please you, take it for your labor.
And so, good morrow, servant.   *Exit.*

SPEED [*aside*]   Oh, jest unseen, inscrutable, invisible
As a nose on a man's face or a weathercock on a steeple!
My master sues° to her, and she hath taught her suitor,   *appeals*

125   He being her pupil, to become her tutor.
Oh, excellent device!° Was there ever heard a better?   *trick*
That my master, being scribe, to himself should write the
letter?

VALENTINE   How now, sir? What are you reasoning with
yourself?

---

4. Provide commentary (as if in a puppet show).
5. In courtly love literature, a man devoted to a lady
is called her servant.

6. He should surpass her in compliments, but she
surpasses him.

SPEED   Nay, I was rhyming. 'Tis you that have the reason.
130 VALENTINE   To do what?
SPEED   To be a spokesman from Madam Silvia.
VALENTINE   To whom?
SPEED   To yourself. Why, she woos you by a figure.°   device; indirect means
VALENTINE   What figure?
135 SPEED   By a letter, I should say.
VALENTINE   Why, she hath not writ to me.
SPEED   What need she, when she hath made you write to
   yourself? Why, do you not perceive the jest?
VALENTINE   No, believe me.
140 SPEED   No believing you indeed, sir. But did you perceive her
   earnest?[7]
VALENTINE   She gave me none, except an angry word.
SPEED   Why, she hath given you a letter.
VALENTINE   That's the letter I writ to her friend.
145 SPEED   And that letter hath she delivered, and there an end.
VALENTINE   I would it were no worse.
SPEED   I'll warrant you, 'tis as well.
   For often have you writ to her, and she, in modesty,
   Or else for want of idle time, could not again reply;
150 Or fearing else some messenger that might her mind
      discover,
   Herself hath taught her love himself to write unto her lover!
   All this I speak in print,° for in print I found it.[8]   very precisely
   Why muse you, sir? 'Tis dinner-time.
VALENTINE   I have dined.°   (on love)
155 SPEED   Ay, but hearken, sir. Though the chameleon[9] Love can
   feed on the air, I am one that am nourished by my victuals
   and would fain° have meat. Oh, be not like your mistress: be   be eager to
   moved, be moved![1]   Exeunt.

2.2
Enter PROTEUS *and* JULIA.
PROTEUS   Have patience, gentle Julia.
JULIA   I must, where is no remedy.
PROTEUS   When possibly I can, I will return.
JULIA   If you turn not,° you will return the sooner.   are not unfaithful
5 [*She gives him a ring.*][1] Keep this remembrance for thy
   Julia's sake.
PROTEUS   Why, then, we'll make exchange. Here, take you this.
   [*He gives her a ring.*]
JULIA   And seal the bargain with a holy kiss.
   [*They kiss.*]
PROTEUS   Here is my hand for my true constancy.
   And when that hour o'erslips° me in the day   passes by
10 Wherein I sigh not, Julia, for thy sake,
   The next ensuing hour some foul mischance

7. To be serious. Valentine takes "perceive" to mean
"receive," and takes "earnest" to mean "pledge" or
"money given to seal a bargain."
8. Speed's reference to a printed speech probably
shouldn't be taken literally. More likely, he is making
fun of Valentine's inability to understand Silvia's
trick by stressing his own care with language.

9. A small lizard that can exist for long periods without food and was thought to feed on air.
1. Be kind; be induced (to eat).
2.2 Location: Probably Julia's house or garden.
1. The action in this scene resembles a betrothal ceremony, and thus in the Elizabethan period a legally
binding agreement to marry.

Torment me for my love's forgetfulness.

My father stays° my coming. Answer not.   *awaits*

The tide is now. [JULIA *weeps*.] Nay, not thy tide of tears.

15 That tide will stay° me longer than I should.   *delay*

Julia, farewell.   [*Exit* JULIA.]

      What, gone without a word?

Ay, so true love should do. It cannot speak,

For truth hath better deeds than words to grace° it.   *adorn*

    [*Enter* PANTINO.]

PANTINO   Sir Proteus, you are stayed for.

PROTEUS   Go. I come, I come.

20 Alas, this parting strikes poor lovers dumb.   *Exeunt.*

2.3

Enter LANCE[1] [*with his dog Crab*[2]].

LANCE   Nay, 'twill be this hour ere I have done weeping; all

the kind° of the Lances have this very fault. I have received   *family; kin*

my proportion,° like the prodigious[3] son, and am going with   *portion*

Sir Proteus to the Imperial's° court. I think Crab my dog be   *(for "Emperor's")*

5   the sourest-natured dog that lives.[4] My mother weeping, my

father wailing, my sister crying, our maid howling, our cat

wringing her hands, and all our house in a great perplexity,

yet did not this cruel-hearted cur shed one tear. He is a

stone, a very pebble-stone, and has no more pity in him than

10 a dog. A Jew would have wept to have seen our parting![5]

Why, my grandam, having no eyes,° look you, wept herself   *being blind*

blind at my parting. Nay, I'll show you the manner of it.[6]

This shoe is my father. No, this left shoe is my father. No,

no, this left shoe is my mother. Nay, that cannot be so nei-

15 ther. Yes, it is so, it is so: it hath the worser sole.[7] This shoe

with the hole[8] in it is my mother, and this my father. A ven-

geance on't: there 'tis.[9] Now, sir, this staff is my sister, for,

look you, she is as white as a lily and as small° as a wand.°   *slender / small stick*

This hat is Nan, our maid. I am the dog. No, the dog is him-

20 self, and I am the dog. Oh, the dog is me, and I am myself.

Ay, so, so. Now come I to my father: "Father, your blessing."

Now should not the shoe speak a word for weeping? Now

should I kiss my father—well, he weeps on. Now come I to

my mother: oh, that she could speak now, like a wood

25 woman![1] Well, I kiss her. Why, there 'tis: here's my mother's

breath[2] up and down.° Now come I to my sister: mark the   *exactly*

moan she makes.[3] Now the dog all this while sheds not a

2.3 Location: A street in Verona.

1. A shortened form of "Lancelot."

2. "Crab" may mean "crab apple" or a "crabbed, ill-tempered person."

3. Lance frequently confuses one word with another. His reference here is to the biblical parable of the prodigal son, who wastes his inheritance but is welcomed home again (Luke 15:11–32).

4. PERFORMANCE COMMENT Crab is quite often played by a real dog, adding an exciting potential for randomness and even sabotage. See Digital Edition PC 1.

5. Alluding to proverbs claiming that Jews and dogs lack pity.

6. Here Lance takes off his shoes to demonstrate the points in his following speech.

7. Punning on "soul" and alluding to medieval debates about whether women had souls.

8. Punning on "hole" as "female genitalia."

9. Presumably Lance is now satisfied with his positioning of the shoes.

1. TEXTUAL COMMENT F has "would-woman," a term that editors have long emended. This edition emends to "wood," meaning "mad" or "enraged, furious," which reflects Lance's description of his mother's grief at his departure. See Digital Edition TC 5.

2. Comparing the smelly shoe to his mother's breath.

3. Perhaps Lance makes his staff "moan" by swishing it in the air.

tear nor speaks a word; but see how I lay the dust with my
tears.
     [*Enter* PANTINO.]

30 PANTINO   Lance, away, away! Aboard! Thy master is shipped,
and thou art to post° after with oars.° What's the matter?   *hurry / in a rowboat*
Why weep'st thou, man? Away, ass, you'll lose° the tide if   *miss*
you tarry any longer.
LANCE   It is no matter if the tied[4] were lost, for it is the unkind-
35 est tied that ever any man tied.
PANTINO   What's the unkindest tide?
LANCE   Why, he that's tied here, Crab, my dog.
PANTINO   Tut, man! I mean thou'lt lose the flood,° and in los-   *miss the tide*
ing the flood, lose thy voyage, and in losing thy voyage, lose
40 thy master, and in losing thy master, lose thy service, and in
losing thy service— [LANCE *silences him.*] Why dost thou
stop my mouth?
LANCE   For fear thou shouldst lose thy tongue.
PANTINO   Where should I lose my tongue?
45 LANCE   In thy tale.
PANTINO   In thy tail!°   *rear end*
LANCE   Lose the tide, and the voyage, and the master, and the
service, and the tied. Why, man, if the river were dry, I am
able to fill it with my tears; if the wind were down, I could
50 drive the boat with my sighs.
PANTINO   Come, come away, man. I was sent to call° thee.   *summon*
LANCE   Sir, call me what thou dar'st!
PANTINO   Wilt thou go?
LANCE   Well, I will go.   *Exeunt.*

2.4

Enter VALENTINE, SILVIA, TURIO, *and* SPEED.

SILVIA   Servant!
VALENTINE   Mistress?
SPEED   Master, Sir Turio frowns on you.
VALENTINE   Ay, boy, it's for love.
5 SPEED   Not of you.
VALENTINE   Of my mistress, then.
SPEED   'Twere good you knocked° him.   [*Exit.*]   *struck*
SILVIA   Servant, you are sad.
VALENTINE   Indeed, madam, I seem so.
10 TURIO   Seem you that you are not?
VALENTINE   Haply° I do.   *Perhaps*
TURIO   So do counterfeits.
VALENTINE   So do you.
TURIO   What seem I that I am not?
15 VALENTINE   Wise.
TURIO   What instance° of the contrary?   *evidence*
VALENTINE   Your folly.
TURIO   And how quote° you my folly?   *detect; observe*
VALENTINE   I quote it in your jerkin.°   *short coat*

---

4. Taking "tide" for "tied," or one who is tied up, mean-   2.4 Location: The Duke's court in Milan.
ing Crab.

20 TURIO   My jerkin is a doublet.°   *jacket; couple or pair*
   VALENTINE   Well, then, I'll double your folly.
   TURIO   How?
   SILVIA   What, angry, Sir Turio? Do you change color?
   VALENTINE   Give him leave, madam; he is a kind of
25   chameleon.¹
   TURIO   That hath more mind to feed on your blood than live
   in your air.²
   VALENTINE   You have said, sir.
   TURIO   Ay, sir, and done, too, for this time.
30 VALENTINE   I know it well, sir. You always end ere you begin.
   SILVIA   A fine volley of words, gentlemen, and quickly shot
   off.
   VALENTINE   'Tis indeed, madam; we thank the giver.
   SILVIA   Who is that, servant?
35 VALENTINE   Yourself, sweet lady, for you gave° the fire. Sir   *spark*
   Turio borrows his wit from your ladyship's looks and spends
   what he borrows kindly° in your company.   *properly; naturally*
   TURIO   Sir, if you spend word for word with me, I shall make
   your wit bankrupt.
40 VALENTINE   I know it well, sir. You have an exchequer° of   *treasury*
   words and, I think, no other treasure to give your followers,
   for it appears by their bare liveries³ that they live by your
   bare° words.   *worthless*
        [*Enter the* DUKE *with a letter in his hand.*]
   SILVIA   No more, gentlemen, no more! Here comes my father.
45 DUKE   Now, daughter Silvia, you are hard beset.°   *set upon (by men)*
   —Sir Valentine, your father is in good health.
   What say you to a letter from your friends
   Of much good news?
   VALENTINE   My lord, I will be thankful
   To any happy messenger° from thence.   *bringer of happy news*
50 DUKE   Know ye Don Antonio, your countryman?
   VALENTINE   Ay, my good lord, I know the gentleman
   To be of worth and worthy estimation,
   And not without desert so well reputed.
   DUKE   Hath he not a son?
55 VALENTINE   Ay, my good lord, a son that well deserves
   The honor and regard of such a father.
   DUKE   You know him well?
   VALENTINE   I knew him as myself, for from our infancy
   We have conversed° and spent our hours together.   *kept company*
60 And though myself have been an idle truant,
   Omitting° the sweet benefit of time   *Neglecting*
   To clothe mine age° with angel-like perfection,   *adorn my years*
   Yet hath Sir Proteus, for that's his name,
   Made use and fair advantage of his days:
65 His years but young, but his experience old;
   His head unmellowed,° but his judgment ripe;   *without gray hair*
   And in a word, for far behind his worth

---

1. Chameleons can change color, perhaps suggesting   to 2.1.155), but Turio would rather drink Valentine's
that Turio is fickle in love.   blood.
2. Chameleons were supposed to live on air (see note   3. By their threadbare clothing.

Comes all the praises that I now bestow,
He is complete° in feature° and in mind,   *perfect / appearance*
70   With all good grace to grace a gentleman.
DUKE   Beshrew me, sir, but if he make this good,°   *proves this to be true*
He is as worthy for an empress' love
As meet° to be an emperor's counselor.   *fit*
Well, sir, this gentleman is come to me
75   With commendation from great potentates,°   *rulers; men of power*
And here he means to spend his time awhile.
I think 'tis no unwelcome news to you.
VALENTINE   Should I have wished a thing,° it had been he.   *anything*
DUKE   Welcome him, then, according to his worth.
80   —Silvia, I speak to you, and you, Sir Turio;
For Valentine, I need not cite° him to it.   *urge*
I will send him hither to you presently.   [*Exit.*]
VALENTINE   This is the gentleman I told your ladyship
Had come along with me, but that his mistress
85   Did hold his eyes locked in her crystal looks.
SILVIA   Belike that° now she hath enfranchised° them   *Perhaps / freed*
Upon some other pawn for fealty.[4]
VALENTINE   Nay, sure, I think she holds them prisoners still.
SILVIA   Nay, then he should be blind, and being blind
90   How could he see his way to seek out you?
VALENTINE   Why, lady, Love hath twenty pair of eyes.
TURIO   They say that Love hath not an eye at all.[5]
VALENTINE   To see such lovers, Turio, as yourself.
Upon a homely object, Love can wink.°   *close its eyes*
[*Enter* PROTEUS.]
95 SILVIA   Have done, have done! Here comes the gentleman.
VALENTINE   Welcome, dear Proteus! —Mistress, I beseech
you
Confirm his welcome with some special favor.
SILVIA   His worth is warrant for his welcome hither,
If this be he you oft have wished to hear from.
100 VALENTINE   Mistress, it is. Sweet lady, entertain him[6]
To be my fellow-servant to your ladyship.
SILVIA   Too low a mistress for so high° a servant.   *tall; distinguished*
PROTEUS   Not so, sweet lady, but too mean° a servant   *lowly*
To have a look of° such a worthy mistress.   *from*
105 VALENTINE   Leave off discourse of disability.°   *unworthiness*
Sweet lady, entertain him for your servant.
PROTEUS   My duty will I boast of, nothing else.
SILVIA   And duty never yet did want his meed.°   *lack his reward*
Servant, you are welcome to a worthless mistress.
110 PROTEUS   I'll die on° him that says so but yourself.   *die fighting*
SILVIA   That you are welcome?
PROTEUS   That you are worthless.
[*Enter* SERVANT.][7]

---

4. *Upon . . . fealty:* Because of some other lover's
pledge of faithful service.
5. Referring to the blindness of Cupid.
6. Take him into your service.
7. TEXTUAL COMMENT Even though F does not indi-

cate the entrance of a servant at this point and assigns
the following line to Turio, many editors have assumed
that a servant must enter here to bring the message
that Silvia's father would speak with her. See Digital
Edition TC 6.

SERVANT   Madam, my lord your father would speak with you.
SILVIA   I wait upon his pleasure.   [*Exit* SERVANT.]
                              —Come, Sir Turio;
       Go with me. —Once more, new servant, welcome.
115   I'll leave you to confer of° home affairs.   *talk about*
       When you have done, we look to hear from you.
PROTEUS   We'll both attend upon your ladyship.
                              [*Exeunt* SILVIA *and* TURIO.]
VALENTINE   Now tell me: how do all from whence you came?
PROTEUS   Your friends are well and have them much
       commended.°   *sent their regards*
VALENTINE   And how do yours?
120   PROTEUS   I left them all in health.
VALENTINE   How does your lady? And how thrives your love?
PROTEUS   My tales of love were wont to weary you:
       I know you joy not in a love-discourse.
VALENTINE   Ay, Proteus, but that life is altered now.
125   I have done penance for contemning° Love,   *despising*
       Whose high imperious thoughts have punished me
       With bitter fasts, with penitential groans,
       With nightly tears, and daily heartsore sighs.
       For in revenge of my contempt of love,
130   Love hath chased sleep from my enthrallèd° eyes   *enslaved*
       And made them watchers of mine own heart's sorrow.
       O gentle Proteus, Love's a mighty lord
       And hath so humbled me as° I confess   *that*
       There is no woe to° his correction,°   *equal to / punishment*
135   Nor to his service no such joy on earth.
       Now, no discourse, except it be of love!
       Now can I break my fast, dine, sup, and sleep
       Upon the very naked name of love.
PROTEUS   Enough! I read your fortune in your eye.
140   Was this the idol that you worship so?
VALENTINE   Even she; and is she not a heavenly saint?
PROTEUS   No, but she is an earthly paragon.°   *model without equal*
VALENTINE   Call her divine.
PROTEUS   I will not flatter her.
VALENTINE   Oh, flatter me; for Love delights in praises.
145   PROTEUS   When I was sick, you gave me bitter pills,
       And I must minister the like to you.
VALENTINE   Then speak the truth by° her; if not divine,   *about*
       Yet let her be a principality,°   *angel*
       Sovereign° to all the creatures on the earth.   *Superior*
PROTEUS   Except my mistress.
150   VALENTINE   Sweet, except not any,°   *make no exceptions*
       Except° thou wilt except against° my love.   *Unless / insult*
PROTEUS   Have I not reason to prefer° mine own?   *advance*
VALENTINE   And I will help thee to prefer her, too:
       She shall be dignified with this high honor,
155   To bear my lady's train, lest the base earth
       Should from her vesture° chance to steal a kiss   *garments*
       And, of so great a favor growing proud,
       Disdain to root° the summer-swelling flower   *receive the roots of*
       And make rough winter everlastingly.
160   PROTEUS   Why, Valentine, what braggartism° is this?   *excessive boasting*

VALENTINE Pardon me, Proteus; all I can is nothing
　　　To her[8] whose worth makes other worthies nothing.
　　　She is alone.°　　　　　　　　　　　　　　　　　　　　　*unique*
PROTEUS　　　　　Then let her alone.
VALENTINE Not for the world! Why, man, she is mine own,
165　And I as rich in having such a jewel
　　　As twenty seas, if all their sand were pearl,
　　　The water nectar, and the rocks pure gold.
　　　Forgive me that I do not dream on thee,°　　　　　*pay attention to you*
　　　Because thou seest me dote upon my love.
170　My foolish rival, that her father likes
　　　Only for° his possessions are so huge,　　　　　　*because*
　　　Is gone with her along, and I must after,
　　　For Love, thou know'st, is full of jealousy.
PROTEUS But she loves you?
175　VALENTINE Ay, and we are betrothed. Nay, more, our
　　　　　marriage hour,
　　　With all the cunning manner of our flight,
　　　Determined of:° how I must climb her window,　　*Decided upon*
　　　The ladder made of cords, and all the means
　　　Plotted and 'greed on for my happiness.
180　Good Proteus, go with me to my chamber
　　　In these affairs to aid me with thy counsel.
PROTEUS Go on before. I shall inquire you forth.°　　*seek you out*
　　　I must unto the road° to disembark　　　　　　　*harbor*
　　　Some necessaries that I needs must use,
185　And then I'll presently° attend you.　　　　　　　*at once*
VALENTINE Will you make haste?
PROTEUS I will.　　　　　　　　　　[*Exit* VALENTINE.]
　　　Even as one heat another heat expels,[9]
　　　Or as one nail by strength drives out another,
190　So the remembrance of my former love
　　　Is by° a newer object quite forgotten.　　　　　　*because of*
　　　Is it mine eye, or Valentine's praise,[1]
　　　Her true perfection, or my false transgression,
　　　That makes me, reasonless,° to reason thus?　　　*wrongly; without cause*
195　She is fair, and so is Julia that I love—
　　　That I did love, for now my love is thawed,
　　　Which like a waxen image 'gainst a fire
　　　Bears no impression of the thing it was.
　　　Methinks my zeal to° Valentine is cold,　　　　　*affection for*
200　And that I love him not as I was wont.
　　　Oh, but I love his lady too too much,
　　　And that's the reason I love him so little.
　　　How shall I dote on her with more advice°　　　　*upon more deliberation*
　　　That thus without advice begin to love her?
205　'Tis but her picture° I have yet beheld,　　　　　　*outer appearance*
　　　And that hath dazzlèd my reason's light.
　　　But when I look on her perfections,
　　　There is no reason but° I shall be blind.　　　　　*doubt that*

8. *all . . . her:* all I can say is nothing in comparison
with her.
9. Referring to a popular belief that the application
of heat takes away the pain of a burn.

1. Textual Comment F reads, "It is mine, or *Valen-
tines* praise?" which editors have long emended for
sense and for metrical regularity. See Digital Edition
TC 7.

If I can check my erring love, I will;
210   If not, to compass° her I'll use my skill.   *Exit.*   *win*

2.5

Enter SPEED *and* LANCE.

SPEED   Lance, by mine honesty, welcome to Milan.[1]

LANCE   Forswear° not thyself, sweet youth, for I am not wel-   *Perjure*
come. I reckon this always, that a man is never undone° till   *ruined*
he be hanged, nor never welcome to a place till some certain
5   shot° be paid, and the hostess say, "Welcome."   *tavern bill*

SPEED   Come on, you madcap. I'll to the alehouse with you
presently, where, for one shot of five pence, thou shalt have
five thousand welcomes. But, sirrah, how did thy master
part with Madam Julia?

10   LANCE   Marry, after they closed[2] in earnest, they parted very
fairly in jest.

SPEED   But shall she marry him?

LANCE   No.

SPEED   How, then? Shall he marry her?

15   LANCE   No, neither.

SPEED   What, are they broken?°   *no longer engaged*

LANCE   No. They are both as whole as a fish.[3]

SPEED   Why, then, how stands the matter with them?

LANCE   Marry, thus: when it stands well with him,[4] it stands
20   well with her.

SPEED   What an ass art thou! I understand thee not.

LANCE   What a block° art thou that thou canst not! My staff[5]   *stupid person*
understands me.

SPEED   What thou say'st?

25   LANCE   Ay, and what I do, too. Look thee, I'll but lean, and my
staff understands me.

SPEED   It stands under thee indeed.

LANCE   Why, "stand-under" and "under-stand" is all one.

SPEED   But tell me true: will't be a match?

30   LANCE   Ask my dog. If he say "Ay," it will; if he say "No," it
will; if he shake his tail and say nothing, it will.

SPEED   The conclusion is, then, that it will.

LANCE   Thou shalt never get such a secret from me but by a
parable.°   *an indirect speech*

35   SPEED   'Tis well that I get it so. But, Lance, how say'st thou[6]
that my master is become a notable lover?

LANCE   I never knew him otherwise.

SPEED   Than how?

LANCE   A notable lubber,° as thou reportest him to be.   *clumsy, stupid person*

40   SPEED   Why, thou whoreson[7] ass, thou mistak'st° me.   *misunderstand*

LANCE   Why, fool, I meant not thee; I meant thy master.[8]

2.5 Location: A street in Milan.
1. TEXTUAL COMMENT F reads "Padua," which is
probably an error, since the play's other references to
geography have Valentine and Proteus traveling to
and from Milan. See Digital Edition TC 8.
2. Came to an agreement; embraced.
3. Lance takes "broken" to mean "in pieces" and
replies with a proverb.
4. When it goes well with him; when he has an
erection.

5. A stick used when walking; also a euphemism for
"penis." During this dialogue Lance may play with
his staff, which he says "understands" (supports;
comprehends) him.
6. What can you say about the fact.
7. Literally, "son of a whore." A term of abuse frequently used in jest.
8. Punning on "mistake." Lance understood Speed
to mean "you misjudge me" or "you confuse me with
someone else."

SPEED   I tell thee my master is become a hot lover.

LANCE   Why, I tell thee I care not, though he burn himself in
love.[9] If thou wilt, go with me to the alehouse; if not, thou
45   art an Hebrew, a Jew, and not worth° the name of a   *worthy*
Christian.

SPEED   Why?

LANCE   Because thou hast not so much charity in thee as to
go to the ale[1] with a Christian. Wilt thou go?

50   SPEED   At thy service.   *Exeunt.*

2.6

Enter PROTEUS *alone.*

PROTEUS   To leave my Julia shall I be forsworn;°   *guilty of vow-breaking*
To love fair Silvia shall I be forsworn;
To wrong my friend I shall be much forsworn;
And e'en that power° which gave me first my oath   *(Love)*
5   Provokes me to this threefold perjury.
Love bade me swear, and Love bids me forswear;
O sweet-suggesting° Love, if thou hast sinned,   *sweetly seductive*
Teach me, thy tempted subject, to excuse it.
At first I did adore a twinkling star,
10   But now I worship a celestial sun.
Unheedful° vows may heedfully° be broken,   *Careless / advisedly*
And he wants° wit that wants resolvèd will°   *lacks / determination*
To learn° his wit t'exchange the bad for better.   *teach*
Fie, fie, unreverent tongue, to call her bad
15   Whose sovereignty so oft thou hast preferred°   *recommended*
With twenty thousand soul-confirming° oaths.   *soul-confirmed; devout*
I cannot leave° to love, and yet I do;   *cease*
But there I leave to love where I should love.
Julia I lose, and Valentine I lose;
20   If I keep them, I needs must lose myself;
If I lose them, thus find I by their loss
For Valentine, myself, for Julia, Silvia.[1]
I to myself am dearer than a friend,
For love is still° most precious in itself,   *always*
25   And Silvia—witness heaven that made her fair—
Shows Julia but° a swarthy Ethiop.[2]   *to be merely*
I will forget that Julia is alive,
Rem_memb'ring that my love to her is dead;
And Valentine I'll hold an enemy,
30   Aiming at Silvia as a sweeter friend.
I cannot now prove constant to myself
Without some treachery used to Valentine.
This night he meaneth with a corded° ladder   *rope*
To climb celestial Silvia's chamber window,
35   Myself in counsel, his competitor.[3]
Now presently I'll give her father notice
Of their disguising and pretended° flight,   *intended*

---

9. *burn himself in love:* be too passionate; suffer the
burning sensations of venereal disease.
1. Referring to a church-ale, a charitable festival at
which ale was sold in aid of the church or to relieve
the poor.
2.6 Location: The Duke's court in Milan.

1. Proteus claims that to hold on to his selfhood and
his love (Silvia), he must give up Julia and Valentine.
2. Ethiopian, or black African. The comparison rests
on a European idealization of female fairness or
whiteness.
3. Myself in on the secret as his partner.

Who, all enraged, will banish Valentine—
For Turio he intends shall wed his daughter.
40 But, Valentine being gone, I'll quickly cross°   *thwart*
By some sly trick blunt Turio's dull proceeding.
Love, lend me wings to make my purpose swift,
As thou hast lent me wit to plot this drift.°   *Exit.*   *scheme*

2.7
Enter JULIA *and* LUCETTA.

JULIA Counsel, Lucetta; gentle girl, assist me,
And e'en in kind love I do conjure° thee,   *entreat*
Who art the table° wherein all my thoughts   *notebook; tablet*
Are visibly charactered° and engraved,   *written*
5 To lesson° me and tell me some good mean°   *teach / way*
How with my honor I may undertake
A journey to my loving Proteus.
LUCETTA Alas, the way is wearisome and long.
JULIA A true-devoted pilgrim is not weary
10 To measure° kingdoms with his feeble steps;   *make his way through*
Much less shall she that hath Love's wings to fly,
And when the flight is made to one so dear,
Of such divine perfection, as Sir Proteus.
LUCETTA Better forbear till Proteus make return.
15 JULIA Oh, know'st thou not his looks are my soul's food?
Pity the dearth° that I have pinèd in   *famine*
By longing for that food so long a time.
Didst thou but know the inly° touch of love,   *inward*
Thou wouldst as soon go kindle fire with snow
20 As seek to quench the fire of love with words.
LUCETTA I do not seek to quench your love's hot fire,
But qualify° the fire's extreme rage,   *lessen*
Lest it should burn above the bounds of reason.
JULIA The more thou damm'st it up, the more it burns!
25 The current that with gentle murmur glides,
Thou know'st, being stopped, impatiently doth rage.
But when his fair course is not hinderèd,
He makes sweet music with th'enameled° stones,   *shiny*
Giving a gentle kiss to every sedge°   *plant*
30 He overtaketh in his pilgrimage;
And so by many winding nooks he strays
With willing sport to the wild ocean.
Then let me go and hinder not my course.
I'll be as patient as a gentle stream,
35 And make a pastime of each weary step
Till the last step have brought me to my love,
And there I'll rest as after much turmoil
A blessèd soul doth in Elysium.[1]
LUCETTA But in what habit° will you go along?   *clothing*
40 JULIA Not like a woman, for I would prevent°   *forestall*
The loose encounters of lascivious men.
Gentle Lucetta, fit° me with such weeds°   *equip / clothing*
As may beseem some well-reputed page.

2.7 Location: Julia's house.   1. In Greek mythology, the final abode, after
                                                 death, of blessed souls.

LUCETTA Why, then, your ladyship must cut your hair.

45 JULIA No, girl, I'll knit° it up in silken strings   *bind*
With twenty odd-conceited° true-love knots.[2]   *strangely devised*
To be fantastic° may become a youth   *fanciful*
Of greater time° than I shall show° to be.   *age / appear*

LUCETTA What fashion, madam, shall I make your breeches?

50 JULIA That fits as well as "Tell me, good my lord,
What compass° will you wear your farthingale?"[3]   *fullness*
Why, ev'n what fashion thou best likes, Lucetta.

LUCETTA You must needs have them with a codpiece,[4] madam.

JULIA Out, out,° Lucetta! That will be ill favored.°   *Not so / unbecoming*

55 LUCETTA A round hose,[5] madam, now's not worth a pin
Unless you have a codpiece to stick pins on.

JULIA Lucetta, as thou lov'st me, let me have
What thou think'st meet and is most mannerly.°   *seemly; modest*
But tell me, wench, how will the world repute me

60 For undertaking so unstaid° a journey?   *reckless*
I fear me it will make me scandalized.°   *disgraced*

LUCETTA If you think so, then stay at home and go not.

JULIA Nay, that I will not.

LUCETTA Then never dream on infamy, but go!

65 If Proteus like your journey when you come,
No matter who's displeased when you are gone:
I fear me he will scarce be pleased withal.°   *with it*

JULIA That is the least, Lucetta, of my fear.
A thousand oaths, an ocean of his tears,

70 And instances of infinite° of love   *an infinity*
Warrant me° welcome to my Proteus.   *Assure me I will be*

LUCETTA All these are servants to deceitful men.

JULIA Base men that use them to so base effect!
But truer stars did govern Proteus' birth:[6]

75 His words are bonds, his oaths are oracles,
His love sincere, his thoughts immaculate,
His tears pure messengers sent from his heart,
His heart as far from fraud as heaven from earth.

LUCETTA Pray heaven he prove so when you come to him.

80 JULIA Now, as thou lov'st me, do him not that wrong
To bear a hard opinion of his truth.
Only deserve my love by loving him,
And presently° go with me to my chamber   *at once*
To take a note of what I stand in need of

85 To furnish me upon my longing° journey.   *love-prompted*
All that is mine I leave at thy dispose,°   *in your care*
My goods, my lands, my reputation;
Only in lieu thereof dispatch me hence.°   *help me hurry away*
Come, answer not, but to it presently;

90 I am impatient of my tarriance.°   *Exeunt.*   *delay*

---

2. Ornamental ribbons supposed to symbolize love.
3. Hooped petticoat.
4. A pouch attached to the front of men's breeches, covering the genital area. In the Elizabethan period, codpieces could be elaborately decorated, as with pins (line 56).
5. Breeches fitting the legs and thighs tightly and puffed out at the hips.
6. The stars' position at one's birth supposedly determined one's character.

3.1

Enter DUKE, TURIO, [*and*] PROTEUS.

DUKE   Sir Turio, give us leave,° I pray, awhile;   *leave us alone*
    We have some secrets to confer about.   [*Exit* TURIO.]
    Now tell me, Proteus, what's your will with me?

PROTEUS   My gracious lord, that which I would discover°   *reveal*
5   The law of friendship bids me to conceal.
    But when I call to mind your gracious favors
    Done to me, undeserving as I am,
    My duty pricks° me on to utter that   *urges*
    Which else no worldly good should draw from me.
10   Know, worthy prince, Sir Valentine my friend
    This night intends to steal away your daughter.
    Myself am one made privy to the plot.
    I know you have determined to bestow her
    On Turio, whom your gentle daughter hates,
15   And should she thus be stol'n away from you,
    It would be much vexation to your age.
    Thus for my duty's sake I rather chose
    To cross° my friend in his intended drift°   *thwart / plan*
    Than by concealing it heap on your head
20   A pack of sorrows, which would press you down,
    Being unprevented,° to your timeless° grave.   *unstopped / early*

DUKE   Proteus, I thank thee for thine honest care,
    Which to requite° command me[1] while I live.   *repay*
    This love of theirs myself have often seen,
25   Haply° when they have judged me fast asleep,   *Perchance*
    And oftentimes have purposed to forbid
    Sir Valentine her company and my court.
    But fearing lest my jealous aim might err
    And so unworthily disgrace the man—
30   A rashness that I ever yet have shunned—
    I gave him gentle looks, thereby to find
    That which thyself hast now disclosed to me.
    And that thou mayst perceive my fear of this,
    Knowing that tender youth is soon suggested,°   *tempted*
35   I nightly lodge her in an upper tower,
    The key whereof myself have ever kept;
    And thence she cannot be conveyed away.

PROTEUS   Know, noble lord, they have devised a mean°   *plan*
    How he her chamber window will ascend
40   And with a corded ladder fetch her down,
    For which the youthful lover now is gone,
    And this way comes he with it presently,
    Where, if it please you, you may intercept him.
    But, good my lord, do it so cunningly
45   That my discovery° be not aimèd° at;   *disclosure / guessed*
    For love of you, not hate unto my friend,
    Hath made me publisher of this pretense.[2]

DUKE   Upon mine honor, he shall never know
    That I had any light° from thee of this.   *information*
        [*Enter* VALENTINE.]

3.1 Location: The Duke's court in Milan.   2. Has caused me to make this plan public.
1. Ask anything of me.

50 PROTEUS   Adieu, my lord. Sir Valentine is coming.
                                                    [*Exit* PROTEUS.]
DUKE   Sir Valentine, whither away so fast?[3]
VALENTINE   Please it° your grace, there is a messenger   *If it please*
    That stays° to bear my letters to my friends,   *waits*
    And I am going to deliver them.
55 DUKE   Be they of much import?
VALENTINE   The tenor° of them doth but signify   *general sense*
    My health and happy being at your court.
DUKE   Nay, then, no matter. Stay with me awhile.
    I am to break with thee of° some affairs   *disclose to you*
60   That touch me near, wherein thou must be secret.
    'Tis not unknown to thee that I have sought
    To match my friend Sir Turio to my daughter.
VALENTINE   I know it well, my lord, and sure the match
    Were° rich and honorable. Besides, the gentleman   *Would be*
65   Is full of virtue, bounty, worth, and qualities
    Beseeming° such a wife as your fair daughter.   *Suited to*
    Cannot your grace win her to fancy him?
DUKE   No, trust me: she is peevish, sullen, froward,°   *perverse*
    Proud, disobedient, stubborn, lacking duty,
70   Neither regarding° that she is my child   *taking into account*
    Nor fearing me as if I were her father.[4]
    And, may I say to thee, this pride of hers
    Upon advice° hath drawn my love from her,   *After consideration*
    And where° I thought the remnant° of mine age   *whereas / remainder*
75   Should have been cherished by her childlike duty,
    I now am full resolved to take a wife
    And turn her out to who will take her in.
    Then let her beauty be her wedding dower,
    For me and my possessions she esteems not.
80 VALENTINE   What would your grace have me to do in this?
DUKE   There is a lady in Milano[5] here
    Whom I affect,° but she is nice° and coy,   *love / hard to please*
    And naught esteems° my agèd eloquence.   *does not value*
    Now therefore would I have thee to my tutor—
85   For long agone° I have forgot° to court;   *ago / forgotten how*
    Besides, the fashion of the time is changed—
    How and which way I may bestow° myself   *conduct*
    To be regarded in her sun-bright eye.
VALENTINE   Win her with gifts if she respect° not words.   *heed*
90   Dumb jewels often in their silent kind°   *nature*
    More than quick words do move a woman's mind.
DUKE   But she did scorn a present that I sent her.
VALENTINE   A woman sometimes scorns what best contents her.
    Send her another: never give her o'er,
95   For scorn at first makes after-love the more.
    If she do frown, 'tis not in hate of you,
    But rather to beget more love in you.
    If she do chide, 'tis not to have you gone,

---

3. Valentine may be crossing the stage without noticing the Duke or starting to retreat on seeing him.
4. Nor respecting me as a father should be respected.
5. F reads "in Verona," another sign of inconsistency
in regard to the play's setting. In this line "Verona" is
replaced by "Milano" rather than "Milan" for greater
metrical regularity.

Forwhy° the fools° are mad if left alone.   *Because / (women)*
100 Take no repulse, whatever she doth say:
For° "Get you gone" she doth not mean "Away!"   *By*
Flatter and praise, commend, extol their graces;
Though ne'er so black,° say they have angels' faces.   *dark-complexioned*
That man that hath a tongue, I say, is no man
105 If with his tongue he cannot win a woman.
DUKE   But she I mean is promised by her friends
Unto a youthful gentleman of worth,
And kept severely from resort of men,
That no man hath access by day to her.
110 VALENTINE   Why, then, I would resort to her by night.
DUKE   Ay, but the doors be locked and keys kept safe,
That no man hath recourse to her by night.
VALENTINE   What lets but one may enter° at her window?   *hinders one from entering*
DUKE   Her chamber is aloft, far from the ground,
115 And built so shelving° that one cannot climb it   *projecting so far out*
Without apparant hazard of his life.
VALENTINE   Why, then, a ladder quaintly° made of cords   *skillfully*
To cast up, with a pair of anchoring hooks,
Would serve to scale another Hero's[6] tower,
120 So° bold Leander would adventure it.   *Provided*
DUKE   Now, as thou art a gentleman of blood,°   *well-born; passionate*
Advise me where I may have such a ladder.
VALENTINE   When would you use it? Pray, sir, tell me that.
DUKE   This very night. For Love is like a child
125 That longs for everything that he can come by.
VALENTINE   By seven o'clock I'll get you such a ladder.
DUKE   But hark thee! I will go to her alone.
How shall I best convey the ladder thither?
VALENTINE   It will be light, my lord, that you may bear it
130 Under a cloak that is of any length.
DUKE   A cloak as long as thine will serve the turn?
VALENTINE   Ay, my good lord.
DUKE   Then let me see thy cloak;
I'll get me one of such another length.
VALENTINE   Why, any cloak will serve the turn, my lord.
135 DUKE   How shall I fashion me to wear° a cloak?   *get used to wearing*
I pray thee, let me feel thy cloak upon me.
    [*He snatches the cloak and finds a rope ladder and a*
    letter hidden within.]
What letter is this same? What's here? "To Silvia"?
And here an engine° fit for my proceeding!   *instrument (the ladder)*
I'll be so bold to break the seal for once.
140 [*Reads.*] "My thoughts do harbor° with my Silvia nightly,   *dwell*
And slaves they are to me that send them flying.
Oh, could their master come and go as lightly,
Himself would lodge where senseless° they are lying.   *without feeling*
My herald° thoughts in thy pure bosom rest them   *message-bearing*
145 While I, their king, that thither them importune,°   *command*
Do curse the grace° that with such grace° hath blest   *good fortune / favor*
   them,

---

6. See note to 1.1.22. Hero, Leander's beloved, lived in a tower.

Because myself do want° my servant's fortune.   lack
I curse myself, for° they are sent by me,   because
That they should harbor where their lord should be."
150   What's here? "Silvia, this night I will enfranchise thee."
'Tis so! And here's the ladder for the purpose.
Why, Phaëton,[7] for° thou art Merops' son,   since
Wilt thou aspire to guide the heavenly car,
And with thy daring folly burn the world?
155   Wilt thou reach° stars because they shine on thee?   grasp at
Go, base intruder, overweening° slave,   presumptuous
Bestow thy fawning smiles on equal mates,°   mates of your own rank
And think my patience, more than thy desert,
Is privilege for° thy departure hence.   Allows
160   Thank me for this more than for all the favors
Which, all too much, I have bestowed on thee.
But if thou linger in my territories
Longer than swiftest expedition°   speed
Will give thee time to leave our royal court,
165   By heaven, my wrath shall far exceed the love
I ever bore my daughter or thyself!
Be gone. I will not hear thy vain excuse,
But, as thou lov'st thy life, make speed from hence.   [Exit.]
VALENTINE   And why not death, rather than living torment?
170   To die is to be banished from myself,
And Silvia is myself. Banished from her
Is self from self: a deadly banishment.
What light is light if Silvia be not seen?
What joy is joy if Silvia be not by?
175   Unless it be to think that she is by
And feed upon the shadow° of perfection.   image; memory
Except I be by Silvia in the night,
There is no music in the nightingale.
Unless I look on Silvia in the day,
180   There is no day for me to look upon.
She is my essence, and I leave° to be   cease
If I be not by her fair influence[8]
Fostered, illumined, cherished, kept alive.
I fly not death to fly his deadly doom:[9]
185   Tarry I here, I but attend on° death,   wait for
But fly I hence, I fly away from life.
                [Enter PROTEUS and LANCE.]
PROTEUS   Run, boy, run, run, and seek him out.
LANCE   So-ho! So-ho![1]
PROTEUS   What seest thou?
190   LANCE   Him we go to find. There's not a hair on 's head but 'tis
a Valentine.[2]

---

7. Famous in Greek mythology for his reckless ambition, Phaëton set the world on fire when he tried to drive the chariot of his father, Helios, the sun god. Phaëton's mother, Clymene, was married to Merops, not Helios, making Phaëton illegitimate. The rest of the line, naming Merops as Phaëton's father, may question Phaëton's status as the son of Helios (and so his ability to drive the sun god's chariot) or may be an ironic means of calling attention to his illegitimacy.

8. Alluding to the popular belief that the stars exert power, or "influence," over individuals.
9. I cannot escape death by fleeing the Duke's death sentence.
1. A cry in hare hunting and hawking.
2. Punning on "hare" and on Valentine's name. Every part, down to the "hair," of the creature he sees suggests a "valentine," or stereotypical lover.

PROTEUS Valentine?

VALENTINE No.

PROTEUS Who, then? His spirit?

195 VALENTINE Neither.

PROTEUS What, then?

VALENTINE Nothing.

LANCE Can nothing speak? Master, shall I strike?

PROTEUS Who wouldst thou strike?

200 LANCE Nothing.

PROTEUS Villain, forbear.

LANCE Why, sir, I'll strike nothing. I pray you—

PROTEUS Sirrah, I say forbear. —Friend Valentine, a word.

VALENTINE My ears are stopped and cannot hear good news,

205 So much of bad already hath possessed them.

PROTEUS Then in dumb silence will I bury mine,°   *(my news)*

    For they are harsh, untunable,° and bad.   *out of tune*

VALENTINE Is Silvia dead?

PROTEUS   No, Valentine!

VALENTINE No Valentine indeed for sacred Silvia.

    Hath she forsworn me?

210 PROTEUS   No, Valentine.

VALENTINE No Valentine, if Silvia have forsworn me.

    What is your news?

LANCE Sir, there is a proclamation that you are vanished.°   *(for "banished")*

PROTEUS That thou art banishèd—oh, that's the news—

215 From hence, from Silvia, and from me thy friend.

VALENTINE Oh, I have fed upon this woe already,

    And now excess of it will make me surfeit.°   *sicken*

    Doth Silvia know that I am banishèd?

PROTEUS Ay, ay, and she hath offered to the doom,°   *sentence*

220 Which unreversed stands in effectual force,[3]

    A sea of melting pearl, which some call tears.

    Those at her father's churlish feet she tendered;°   *offered*

    With them, upon her knees, her humble self,

    Wringing her hands, whose whiteness so became them

225 As if but now they waxèd° pale for woe.   *turned*

    But neither bended knees, pure hands held up,

    Sad sighs, deep groans, nor silver-shedding tears[4]

    Could penetrate her uncompassionate sire,

    But Valentine, if he be ta'en, must die.

230 Besides, her intercession chafed him so,

    When she for thy repeal° was suppliant,   *recall from exile*

    That to close° prison he commanded her,   *tightly enclosed*

    With many bitter threats of biding° there.   *staying permanently*

VALENTINE No more, unless the next word that thou speak'st

235 Have some malignant power upon my life.

    If so, I pray thee breathe it in mine ear,

    As ending anthem° of my endless dolor.°   *final hymn / grief*

PROTEUS Cease to lament for that° thou canst not help   *what*

    And study° help for that which thou lament'st.   *devise*

240 Time is the nurse and breeder of all good.

    Here, if thou stay, thou canst not see thy love;

---

3. Which, unless reversed, will be enforced.   4. Tears that flow like silver streams.

Besides, thy staying will abridge thy life.
Hope is a lover's staff; walk hence with that
And manage it° against despairing thoughts. *use it as a weapon*
245 Thy letters may be here, though thou art hence,
Which, being writ to me, shall be delivered
Even in the milk-white bosom of thy love.
The time now serves not to expostulate.° *complain; argue*
Come, I'll convey thee through the city gate,
250 And ere I part with thee confer at large° *discuss at length*
Of all that may concern thy love affairs.
As thou lov'st Silvia, though not for thyself,
Regard thy danger and along with me.
VALENTINE   I pray thee, Lance, an if° thou seest my boy, *an if = if*
255 Bid him make haste and meet me at the North Gate.
PROTEUS   Go, sirrah, find him out. —Come, Valentine.
VALENTINE   O my dear Silvia! Hapless Valentine!
　　　　　　[*Exeunt* PROTEUS *and* VALENTINE.]
LANCE   I am but a fool, look you, and yet I have the wit to
think my master is a kind of a knave. But that's all one,° *all right*
260 be but one knave.[5] He lives not now that knows me to be in
love; yet I am in love, but a team of horse shall not pluck that
from me, nor who 'tis I love; and yet 'tis a woman, but what
woman I will not tell myself; and yet 'tis a milkmaid; yet 'tis
not a maid,° for she hath had gossips;[6] yet 'tis a maid, for she *virgin*
265 is her master's maid and serves for wages. She hath more
qualities° than a water-spaniel,[7] which is much in a bare° *abilities / mere*
Christian. Here is the catalog of her condition. [*He produces
a paper.*] "*Imprimis*:[8] she can fetch and carry." —Why, a
horse can do no more. Nay, a horse cannot fetch, but only
270 carry. Therefore is she better than a jade.° "*Item*: she can *inferior horse*
milk." Look you, a sweet virtue in a maid with clean hands.
　　　　　　[*Enter* SPEED.]
SPEED   How now, Signor Lance? What news with your
mastership?
LANCE   With my master's ship? Why, it is at sea.
275 SPEED   Well, your old vice still: mistake the word.[9] What
news, then, in your paper?
LANCE   The black'st news that ever thou heard'st.
SPEED   Why, man? How black?
LANCE   Why, as black as ink.
280 SPEED   Let me read them.
LANCE   Fie on thee, jolt-head;° thou canst not read. *blockhead*
SPEED   Thou liest. I can.
LANCE   I will try thee. Tell me this: who begot thee?
SPEED   Marry, the son of my grandfather.
285 LANCE   O illiterate loiterer! It was the son of thy grandmother.
This proves that thou canst not read.
SPEED   Come, fool, come. Try me in thy paper.

---

5. If he is only moderately a rascal; only a knave in one area (love).
6. Women who attended at childbirth; people who served as sponsors at the baptism of a newborn child.
7. A dog used for hunting waterfowl.
8. The paper employs the language of official docu-

ments. "*Imprimis*," Latin for "in the first place," was used to begin inventories. "*Item*" (line 270), meaning "also," was used to introduce subsequent articles in a list.
9. *your . . . word:* your customary fault of making blunders with language.

LANCE [*giving* SPEED *the paper*]   There—and Saint Nicholas[1]
  be thy speed.°   *protection*
290 SPEED   "*Imprimis*: she can milk."
LANCE   Ay, that she can.
SPEED   "*Item*: she brews good ale."
LANCE   And thereof comes the proverb: "Blessing of your
  heart, you brew good ale."
295 SPEED   "*Item*: she can sew."
LANCE   That's as much as to say: "Can she so?"
SPEED   "*Item*: she can knit."
LANCE   What need a man care for a stock° with a wench   *dowry*
  when she can knit him a stock?°   *stocking*
300 SPEED   "*Item*: she can wash and scour."
LANCE   A special virtue, for then she need not be washed and
  scoured.[2]
SPEED   "*Item*: she can spin."
LANCE   Then may I set the world on wheels,° when she can   *take life easy*
305   spin for her living.
SPEED   "*Item*: she hath many nameless° virtues."   *inexpressible*
LANCE   That's as much as to say "bastard virtues," that indeed
  know not their fathers and therefore have no names.
SPEED   Here follow her vices.
310 LANCE   Close at the heels of her virtues.
SPEED   "*Item*: she is not to be fasting in respect of° her breath."   *on account of*
LANCE   Well, that fault may be mended with a breakfast.
  Read on.
SPEED   "*Item*: she hath a sweet mouth."[3]
315 LANCE   That makes amends for her sour breath.
SPEED   "*Item*: she doth talk in her sleep."
LANCE   It's no matter for that so she sleep not in her talk.
SPEED   "*Item*: she is slow in words."
LANCE   O villain, that set this down among her vices! To be
320   slow in words is a woman's only virtue. I pray thee, out
  with't, and place it for her chief virtue!
SPEED   "*Item*: she is proud."°   *haughty; lascivious*
LANCE   Out with that, too! It was Eve's legacy,[4] and cannot be
  ta'en from her.
325 SPEED   "*Item*: she hath no teeth."
LANCE   I care not for that neither, because I love crusts.
SPEED   "*Item*: she is curst."°   *shrewish*
LANCE   Well, the best is, she hath no teeth to bite.
SPEED   "*Item*: she will often praise° her liquor."   *appraise (by tasting)*
330 LANCE   If her liquor be good, she shall; if she will not, I will,
  for good things should be praised.
SPEED   "*Item*: she is too liberal."°   *bold; wanton*
LANCE   Of her tongue she cannot, for that's writ down she is
  slow of; of her purse she shall not, for that I'll keep shut.

---

1. The patron saint of schoolchildren and scholars.
2. *washed and scoured*: slang for "knocked down and
beaten."
3. A sweet tooth; a wanton nature.
4. In the Garden of Eden, Satan, in the form of a
serpent, tempted Eve, wife of the first man, Adam, to
eat fruit from the tree of knowledge of good and evil,
which God had forbidden humans to taste. Eve was
thus guilty of the sin of pride for disobeying God and
putting her will before his command. See Genesis
2:15–3:24.

335 Now, of another thing⁵ she may, and that cannot I help.
Well, proceed.
SPEED "*Item*: she hath more hair than wit, and more faults
than hairs, and more wealth than faults."
LANCE Stop there! I'll have her. She was mine and not mine
340 twice or thrice in that last article. Rehearse° that once more. Repeat
SPEED "*Item*: she hath more hair than wit—"
LANCE "More hair than wit." It may be. I'll prove it. The
cover of the salt hides the salt,° and therefore it is more° saltcellar / greater
than the salt; the hair that covers the wit is more than the
345 wit, for the greater hides the less. What's next?
SPEED "And more faults than hairs."
LANCE That's monstrous! Oh, that that were out!
SPEED "And more wealth than faults."
LANCE Why, that word makes the faults gracious.° Well, I'll pleasing
350 have her, and if it be a match—as nothing is impossible—
SPEED What then?
LANCE Why, then will I tell thee that thy master stays° for waits
thee at the North Gate.
SPEED For me?
355 LANCE For thee? Ay, who art thou? He hath stayed for a bet-
ter man than thee.
SPEED And must I go to him?
LANCE Thou must run to him, for thou hast stayed so long
that going° will scarce serve the turn. walking
360 SPEED Why didst not tell me sooner? Pox of⁶ your love letters!
[*Exit.*]
LANCE Now will he be swinged° for reading my letter. An beaten
unmannerly slave, that will thrust himself into secrets. I'll
after, to rejoice in the boy's correction. *Exit.*

3.2

Enter DUKE *and* TURIO.
DUKE Sir Turio, fear not but that she will love you
Now Valentine is banished from her sight.
TURIO Since his exile she hath despised me most,
Forsworn my company, and railed at me,
5 That° I am desperate° of obtaining her. So that / hopeless
DUKE This weak impress° of love is as a figure impression
Trenchèd° in ice, which with an hour's heat Cut
Dissolves to water and doth lose his form.
A little time will melt her frozen thoughts,
10 And worthless Valentine shall be forgot.
[*Enter* PROTEUS.]
How now, Sir Proteus? Is your countryman,
According to our proclamation, gone?
PROTEUS Gone, my good lord.
DUKE My daughter takes his going grievously?
15 PROTEUS A little time, my lord, will kill that grief.
DUKE So I believe, but Turio thinks not so.

---

5. "Purse" (line 334) and "another thing" were collo-   6. May disease take (a curse).
quial terms for "female genitalia."   3.2 Location: Scene continues.

Proteus, the good conceit° I hold of thee— *opinion*
For thou hast shown some sign of good desert—
Makes me the better° to confer with thee. *the more willing*

20 PROTEUS Longer than I prove loyal to your grace
Let me not live to look upon your grace.
DUKE Thou know'st how willingly I would effect
The match between Sir Turio and my daughter?
PROTEUS I do, my lord.

25 DUKE And also, I think, thou art not ignorant
How she opposes her° against my will? *herself*
PROTEUS She did, my lord, when Valentine was here.
DUKE Ay, and perversely she persevers so!
What might we do to make the girl forget

30 The love of Valentine, and love Sir Turio?
PROTEUS The best way is to slander Valentine
With falsehood, cowardice, and poor descent:
Three things that women highly hold in hate.
DUKE Ay, but she'll think that it is spoke in hate.

35 PROTEUS Ay, if his enemy deliver° it. *report*
Therefore it must with circumstance° be spoken *supporting detail*
By one whom she esteemeth as his friend.
DUKE Then you must undertake to slander him.
PROTEUS And that, my lord, I shall be loath to do.

40 'Tis an ill office for a gentleman,
Especially against his very° friend. *true*
DUKE Where your good word cannot advantage° him, *profit*
Your slander never can endamage° him; *harm*
Therefore the office is indifferent,° *neutral*

45 Being entreated to it by your friend.[1]
PROTEUS You have prevailed, my lord. If I can do it
By aught° that I can speak in his dispraise, *anything*
She shall not long continue love to him.
But say this weed° her love from Valentine: *uproot*

50 It follows not that she will love Sir Turio.
TURIO Therefore, as you unwind her love from him,
Lest it should ravel and be good to none,
You must provide to bottom it on me;[2]
Which must be done by praising me as much

55 As you in worth dispraise Sir Valentine.
DUKE And, Proteus, we dare trust you in this kind
Because we know, on Valentine's report,
You are already Love's firm votary,° *disciple*
And cannot soon revolt and change your mind.

60 Upon this warrant shall you have access
Where you with Silvia may confer at large—
For she is lumpish,° heavy, melancholy, *low-spirited*
And for your friend's sake will be glad of you—
Where you may temper° her, by your persuasion, *mold*

65 To hate young Valentine and love my friend.
PROTEUS As much as I can do, I will effect.
But you, Sir Turio, are not sharp enough:
You must lay lime[3] to tangle° her desires *capture*

---

1. Being asked to do it by a friend like me.   3. Birdlime, a sticky substance used to trap birds.
2. To wind it like a skein of thread upon me.

By wailful sonnets whose composèd° rhymes   *well-crafted*
70 Should be full fraught° with serviceable vows.[4]   *laden*
DUKE   Ay, much is the force of heaven-bred poesy.
PROTEUS   Say that upon the altar of her beauty
    You sacrifice your tears, your sighs, your heart;
    Write till your ink be dry, and with your tears
75 Moist it again, and frame some feeling line
    That may discover° such integrity.°   *reveal / sincerity*
    For Orpheus'[5] lute was strung with poets' sinews,°   *nerves*
    Whose golden touch could soften steel and stones,
    Make tigers tame and huge leviathans°   *whales*
80 Forsake unsounded deeps to dance on sands.
    After your dire-lamenting elegies,°   *love poems*
    Visit by night your lady's chamber window
    With some sweet consort;° to their instruments   *band of musicians*
    Tune° a deploring dump.° The night's dead silence   *Sing / sad melody*
85 Will well become such sweet-complaining grievance.
    This, or else nothing, will inherit° her.   *win*
DUKE   This discipline° shows thou hast been in love.   *instruction*
TURIO   And thy advice this night I'll put in practice.
    Therefore, sweet Proteus, my direction-giver,
90 Let us into the city presently
    To sort° some gentlemen well skilled in music.   *select*
    I have a sonnet that will serve the turn
    To give the onset° to thy good advice.   *start*
DUKE   About it, gentlemen.
95 PROTEUS   We'll wait upon your grace till after supper,
    And afterward determine our proceedings.
DUKE   Even now about it. I will pardon you.°   *Exeunt.*   *excuse you from service*

4.1

Enter certain OUTLAWS.
FIRST OUTLAW   Fellows, stand fast: I see a passenger.°   *traveler*
SECOND OUTLAW   If there be ten, shrink not, but down with 'em.
    [*Enter* VALENTINE *and* SPEED.]
THIRD OUTLAW   Stand,° sir, and throw us that° you have about ye.   *Halt / that which*
    If not, we'll make you sit and rifle° you.   *search*
5 SPEED [*to* VALENTINE]   Sir, we are undone! These are the
    villains
    That all the travelers do fear so much.
VALENTINE [*to the* OUTLAWS]   My friends—
FIRST OUTLAW   That's not so, sir! We are your enemies—
SECOND OUTLAW   Peace! We'll hear him.
10 THIRD OUTLAW   Ay, by my beard will we; for he is a proper° man.   *handsome*
VALENTINE   Then know that I have little wealth to lose.
    A man I am crossed with adversity.
    My riches are these poor habiliments°   *clothes*
    Of which, if you should here disfurnish° me,   *deprive*
15 You take the sum and substance that I have.
SECOND OUTLAW   Whither travel you?

---

4. Promises to be of service.
5. A figure in Greek mythology famous for his

entrancing music.
4.1 Location: A forest between Mantua and Milan.

VALENTINE   To Verona.

FIRST OUTLAW   Whence came you?

VALENTINE   From Milan.

20 THIRD OUTLAW   Have you long sojourned there?

VALENTINE   Some sixteen months,¹ and longer might have
    stayed
    If crooked° fortune had not thwarted me.   *evil*

FIRST OUTLAW   What, were you banished thence?

VALENTINE   I was.

SECOND OUTLAW   For what offense?

VALENTINE   For that which now torments me to rehearse:°   *tell*

25   I killed a man,² whose death I much repent,
    But yet I slew him manfully in fight,
    Without false vantage or base treachery.°   *unfair advantage*

SECOND OUTLAW   Why, ne'er repent it, if it were done so.
    But were you banished for so small a fault?

30 VALENTINE   I was, and held me glad of such a doom.°   *sentence*

FIRST OUTLAW   Have you the tongues?°   *skill in languages*

VALENTINE   My youthful travel therein made me happy,°   *fortunate; skilled*
    Or else I often had been miserable.

THIRD OUTLAW   By the bare scalp of Robin Hood's fat friar,°   *(Friar Tuck)*

35   This fellow were a king for our wild faction.°   *band*

FIRST OUTLAW   We'll have him! Sirs, a word.
        [OUTLAWS *talk apart.*]

SPEED [*to* VALENTINE]   Master, be one of them! It's an honor-
    able kind of thievery.

VALENTINE   Peace, villain.

40 FIRST OUTLAW [*to* VALENTINE]   Tell us this: have you anything
    to take to?³

VALENTINE   Nothing but my fortune.°   *luck*

THIRD OUTLAW   Know, then, that some of us are gentlemen,
    Such as the fury of ungoverned youth

45   Thrust from the company of awful° men.   *respectable*
    Myself was from Verona banishèd
    For practicing° to steal away a lady,   *plotting*
    An heir, and near allied unto the Duke.

SECOND OUTLAW   And I from Mantua, for a gentleman

50   Who, in my mood,° I stabbed unto the heart.   *anger*

FIRST OUTLAW   And I for suchlike petty crimes as these.
    But to the purpose, for we cite our faults
    That they may hold excused our lawless lives;
    And partly seeing you are beautified

55   With goodly shape, and by your own report
    A linguist and a man of such perfection
    As we do in our quality° much want—   *profession*

SECOND OUTLAW   Indeed, because you are a banished man,
    Therefore, above the rest,⁴ we parley° to you: *talk*

60   Are you content to be our general,

---

1. A claim not consonant with the play's overall time scheme. Either this is a textual inconsistency or Valentine is lying.
2. Why Valentine lies here is much debated. He may be protecting Silvia's reputation or trying to impress the outlaws.
3. Any way to support yourself.
4. For that above all other reasons.

To make a virtue of necessity
And live as we do in this wilderness?
THIRD OUTLAW   What say'st thou? Wilt thou be of our
    consort?°   *company*
Say "Ay," and be the captain of us all.
65   We'll do thee homage and be ruled by thee,
Love thee as our commander and our king.
FIRST OUTLAW   But if thou scorn our courtesy, thou diest.
SECOND OUTLAW   Thou shalt not live to brag what we have
    offered.
VALENTINE   I take your offer and will live with you,
70   Provided that you do no outrages
On silly° women or poor passengers.°   *defenseless / travelers*
THIRD OUTLAW   No, we detest such vile base practices.
Come, go with us, we'll bring thee to our crew°   *band of men*
And show thee all the treasure we have got,
75   Which, with ourselves, all rest at thy dispose.°   *Exeunt.*   *disposal*

4.2

Enter PROTEUS.
PROTEUS   Already have I been false to Valentine,
And now I must be as unjust to Turio.
Under the color° of commending him   *pretext*
I have access my own love to prefer.°   *advance*
5   But Silvia is too fair, too true, too holy
To be corrupted with my worthless gifts.
When I protest true loyalty to her,
She twits° me with my falsehood to my friend.   *reproaches*
When to her beauty I commend my vows,
10   She bids me think how I have been forsworn
In breaking faith with Julia, whom I loved.
And notwithstanding all her sudden quips,°   *sharp rebukes*
The least whereof would quell a lover's hope,
Yet, spaniel-like, the more she spurns my love,
15   The more it grows and fawneth on her still.
    [*Enter* TURIO *with Musicians.*]
But here comes Turio. Now must we to her window
And give some evening music to her ear.
TURIO   How now, Sir Proteus? Are you crept before us?
PROTEUS   Ay, gentle Turio, for you know that love
20   Will creep° in service where it cannot go.°   *crawl / walk*
TURIO   Ay, but I hope, sir, that you love not here.
PROTEUS   Sir, but I do, or else I would be hence.
TURIO   Who? Silvia?
PROTEUS   Ay, Silvia—for your sake.
TURIO   I thank you for your own.° [*to Musicians*] Now,   *own sake*
    gentlemen,
25   Let's tune, and to it lustily awhile.
    [*Enter* JULIA, *in page-boy's clothes, as Sebastian, and
    the* HOST. *They talk apart.*]
HOST   Now, my young guest, methinks you're alicholly;° I pray   *melancholy*
    you, why is it?

4.2 Location: Outside the Duke's palace under Silvia's window by moonlight.

JULIA Marry, mine host, because I cannot be merry.

HOST Come, we'll have you merry. I'll bring you where you
30 shall hear music and see the gentleman that you asked for.

JULIA But shall I hear him speak?

HOST Ay, that you shall.

JULIA That will be music.

HOST Hark, hark.[1]

35 JULIA Is he among these?

HOST Ay. But peace, let's hear 'em.

[Music.]

PROTEUS [sings][2] Who is Silvia? What is she
    That all our swains° commend her?   *lovers*
    Holy, fair, and wise is she.
40   The heaven such grace did lend her
    That she might admirèd be.

    Is she kind as she is fair?
    For beauty lives with kindness.
    Love° doth to her eyes repair°   *(Cupid) / pay a visit*
45   To help° him of his blindness,   *cure*
    And, being helped, inhabits there.

    Then to Silvia let us sing
    That Silvia is excelling.
    She excels each mortal thing
50   Upon the dull earth dwelling.
    To her let us garlands bring.

HOST How now? Are you sadder than you were before? How
do you, man? The music likes° you not?   *pleases*

JULIA You mistake; the musician likes me not.

55 HOST Why, my pretty youth?

JULIA He plays false,[3] father.

HOST How, out of tune on the strings?

JULIA Not so, but yet so false that he grieves my very heartstrings.

HOST You have a quick° ear.   *perceptive*

60 JULIA Ay, I would I were deaf; it makes me have a slow° heart. *heavy*

HOST I perceive you delight not in music.

JULIA Not a whit when it jars so.°   *is so discordant*

HOST Hark, what fine change° is in the music.   *modulation*

JULIA Ay, that "change" is the spite.

65 HOST You would have them always play but one thing?

JULIA I would always have one play but one thing. But, Host,
doth this Sir Proteus that we talk on often resort unto this
gentlewoman?

HOST I tell you what Lance, his man, told me: he loved her
70 out of all nick.°   *excessively*

JULIA Where is Lance?

HOST Gone to seek his dog, which tomorrow, by his master's
command, he must carry for a present to his lady.

JULIA Peace, stand aside. The company parts.

---

1. Probably music plays.
2. TEXTUAL COMMENT This song is not ascribed to
anyone in F, but Julia's later comments in lines 54–

58 suggest that it is Proteus who sings while playing
a stringed instrument. See Digital Edition TC 9.
3. Is unfaithful; plays out of tune.

75 PROTEUS   Sir Turio, fear not you. I will so plead
        That you shall say my cunning drift° excels.   *scheme*
    TURIO   Where meet we?
    PROTEUS   At Saint Gregory's[4] well.
    TURIO   Farewell.
                        [*Exeunt* TURIO *and Musicians.*]
            [*Enter* SILVIA *above.*°]   *(at her window)*
    PROTEUS   Madam, good even to your ladyship.
    SILVIA   I thank you for your music, gentlemen.
80   Who is that that spake?
    PROTEUS   One, lady, if you knew his pure heart's truth,
        You would quickly learn to know him by his voice.
    SILVIA   Sir Proteus, as I take it.
    PROTEUS   Sir Proteus, gentle lady, and your servant.
    SILVIA   What's your will?
85 PROTEUS   That I may compass yours.[5]
    SILVIA   You have your wish. My will is even this,
        That presently you hie° you home to bed.   *speed*
        Thou subtle, perjured, false, disloyal man,
        Think'st thou I am so shallow, so conceitless,°   *witless*
90   To be seducèd by thy flattery
        That hast deceived so many with thy vows?
        Return, return, and make thy love amends.
        For me—by this pale queen of night[6] I swear—
        I am so far from granting thy request
95   That I despise thee for thy wrongful suit,
        And by and by intend to chide myself
        Even for this time I spend in talking to thee.
    PROTEUS   I grant, sweet love, that I did love a lady,
        But she is dead.
    JULIA [*aside*]   'Twere false, if° I should speak it;   *even if*
100   For I am sure she is not burièd.
    SILVIA   Say that she be; yet Valentine, thy friend,
        Survives, to whom, thyself art witness,
        I am betrothed. And art thou not ashamed
        To wrong him with thy importunacy?°   *improper requests*
105 PROTEUS   I likewise hear that Valentine is dead.
    SILVIA   And so suppose am I, for in his grave,
        Assure thyself, my love is burièd.
    PROTEUS   Sweet lady, let me rake it from the earth.
    SILVIA   Go to thy lady's grave and call hers thence,
110   Or, at the least, in hers sepulcher° thine.   *bury*
    JULIA [*aside*]   He heard not that.
    PROTEUS   Madam, if your heart be so obdurate,°   *hardened*
        Vouchsafe° me yet your picture for my love,   *grant*
        The picture that is hanging in your chamber.
115   To that I'll speak, to that I'll sigh and weep;
        For since the substance of your perfect self

---

4. Patron saint of musicians and singers.
5. *compass:* win. Punning on "will." That I may win
your good will; that I may conquer your sexual desire.

6. The moon, imagined as Diana, goddess of
chastity.

Is else devoted,[7] I am but a shadow,°   *mere nothing*
And to your shadow° will I make true love.   *image*
JULIA [*aside*] If 'twere a substance, you would sure deceive it
120   And make it but a shadow, as I am.
SILVIA   I am very loath to be your idol, sir.
But since your falsehood shall become you well°   *make you fit*
To worship shadow and adore false shapes,
Send to me in the morning, and I'll send it.°   *(the picture)*
And so, good rest.   [*Exit.*]
125 PROTEUS   As wretches have o'ernight
That wait for execution in the morn.   [*Exit.*]
JULIA   Host, will you go?
HOST   By my halidom,° I was fast asleep.   *holy relic (an oath)*
JULIA   Pray you, where lies° Sir Proteus?   *lodges*
130 HOST   Marry, at my house. Trust me, I think 'tis almost day.
JULIA   Not so; but it hath been the longest night
That e'er I watched, and the most heaviest.°   [*Exeunt.*]   *saddest*

4.3

Enter EGLAMOUR.

EGLAMOUR   This is the hour that Madam Silvia
Entreated me to call and know her mind:
There's some great matter she'd employ me in.
Madam, madam!
[*Enter* SILVIA *above.*]
SILVIA   Who calls?
EGLAMOUR   Your servant and your friend;
5   One that attends your ladyship's command.
SILVIA   Sir Eglamour, a thousand times good morrow!
EGLAMOUR   As many, worthy lady, to yourself.
According to your ladyship's impose,°   *command*
I am thus early come to know what service
10   It is your pleasure to command me in.
SILVIA   O Eglamour, thou art a gentleman—
Think not I flatter, for I swear I do not—
Valiant, wise, remorseful,° well accomplished.   *compassionate*
Thou art not ignorant what dear goodwill
15   I bear unto the banished Valentine,
Nor how my father would enforce me marry
Vain Turio, whom my very soul abhors.
Thyself hast loved, and I have heard thee say
No grief did ever come so near thy heart
20   As when thy lady and thy true love died,
Upon whose grave thou vowed'st pure chastity.
Sir Eglamour, I would° to Valentine—   *would go*
To Mantua, where I hear he makes abode;
And for° the ways are dangerous to pass   *because*
25   I do desire thy worthy company,
Upon whose faith and honor I repose.°   *rely*
Urge not[1] my father's anger, Eglamour,

---

7. Is devoted to someone else.   1. Do not offer as an excuse.
4.3 Location: The same place, the next morning.

But think upon my grief, a lady's grief,
And on the justice of my flying hence
30 To keep me from a most unholy match,
Which heaven and fortune still° rewards with plagues.   *always*
I do desire thee, even from a heart
As full of sorrows as the sea of sands,
To bear me company and go with me;
35 If not, to hide what I have said to thee,
That I may venture to depart alone.
EGLAMOUR   Madam, I pity much your grievances,
Which, since I know they virtuously are placed,
I give consent to go along with you,
40 Recking° as little what betideth° me   *Caring / happens to*
As much I wish all good befortune° you.   *befall*
When will you go?
SILVIA   This evening coming.
EGLAMOUR   Where shall I meet you?
SILVIA   At Friar Patrick's cell,
Where I intend holy confession.
45 EGLAMOUR   I will not fail your ladyship.
Good morrow, gentle lady.
SILVIA   Good morrow, kind Sir Eglamour.   *Exeunt.*

4.4

Enter LANCE [*with his dog Crab*].

LANCE   When a man's servant shall play the cur° with him,   *act like a stupid dog*
look you, it goes hard. One that I brought up of° a puppy,   *from*
one that I saved from drowning when three or four of his
blind brothers and sisters went to it.° I have taught him even   *met their death*
5 as one would say precisely, "Thus I would teach a dog." I was
sent to deliver him as a present to Mistress Silvia from my
master, and I came no sooner into the dining chamber but
he steps me to[1] her trencher° and steals her capon's leg. Oh,   *wooden plate*
'tis a foul thing when a cur cannot keep° himself in all com-   *behave*
10 panies! I would have, as one should say, one that takes upon
him to be a dog indeed, to be, as it were, a dog at° all things.   *adept at*
If I had not had more wit than he, to take a fault upon me
that he did, I think verily he had been hanged for't; sure as I
live, he had suffered for't. You shall judge. He thrusts me
15 himself into the company of three or four gentleman-like
dogs under the Duke's table. He had not been there—bless
the mark[2]—a pissing while[3] but all the chamber smelt him.
"Out with the dog," says one; "What cur is that?" says
another; "Whip him out," says the third; "Hang him up,"
20 says the Duke. I, having been acquainted with the smell
before, knew it was Crab and goes me to the fellow that
whips the dogs: "Friend," quoth I, "you mean to whip the
dog?" "Ay, marry do I," quoth he. "You do him the more
wrong," quoth I, "'twas I did the thing you wot° of." He   *know*
25 makes me no more ado, but whips me out of the chamber.

4.4 Location: The same place, somewhat later.
1. *he steps me to:* he (the dog) steps forward to
Lance's embarrassment or to his detriment. Here and
in line 14, "thrusts me," Lance is describing the dog's

actions and their negative effect on himself.
2. An apology for offensive language.
3. Slang for "a very short time." Lance here employs
it literally.

How many masters would do this for his servant? Nay, I'll be
sworn I have sat in the stocks[4] for puddings[5] he hath stolen,
otherwise he had been executed! I have stood on the pillory[6]
for geese he hath killed, otherwise he had suffered for't! [*to*
30 *Crab*] Thou think'st not of this now. Nay, I remember the
trick you served me when I took my leave of Madam Silvia.
Did not I bid thee still mark° me, and do as I do? When didst   *watch*
thou see me heave up my leg and make water against a gentlewoman's farthingale?° Didst thou ever see me do such a   *hooped petticoat*
35 trick?

    [*Enter* PROTEUS *and* JULIA *as Sebastian.*]

PROTEUS [*to* JULIA]   Sebastian[7] is thy name? I like thee well
   And will employ thee in some service° presently.   *work; sexual business*
JULIA   In what you please; I'll do what I can.
PROTEUS   I hope thou wilt. [*to* LANCE] How now, you whore-
   son peasant,
40   Where have you been these two days loitering?
LANCE   Marry, sir, I carried Mistress Silvia the dog you
   bade me.
PROTEUS   And what says she to my little jewel?
LANCE   Marry, she says your dog was a cur, and tells you cur-
45   rish thanks is good enough for such a present.
PROTEUS   But she received my dog?
LANCE   No, indeed, did she not. Here have I brought him
   back again.
PROTEUS   What, didst thou offer her this from me?
50 LANCE   Ay, sir. The other squirrel[8] was stolen from me by the
   hangman's° boys in the marketplace, and then I offered her   *fit for the hangman*
   mine own, who is a dog as big as ten of yours, and therefore
   the gift the greater.
PROTEUS   Go, get thee hence and find my dog again,
55   Or ne'er return again into my sight.
   Away, I say! Stayest thou to vex me here?
   A slave that still an end° turns me to shame.   *always*

    [*Exit* LANCE *with Crab.*]

   —Sebastian, I have entertained thee
   Partly that I have need of such a youth
60   That can with some discretion do my business—
   For 'tis no trusting to yon foolish lout—
   But chiefly for thy face and thy behavior,
   Which, if my augury° deceive me not,   *fortune-telling skills*
   Witness good bringing-up, fortune, and truth.
65   Therefore know thou for this I entertain thee.
   Go presently, and take this ring with thee:
   Deliver it to Madam Silvia.
   She loved me well delivered° it to me.   *who gave*
JULIA   It seems you loved not her, to leave° her token.[9]   *part with*
   She is dead, belike?°   *perchance*

---

4. An instrument of punishment in which the offender
sat with feet clamped between two wooden planks
into which ankle holes had been cut.
5. Dishes made of animal intestines or stomachs
stuffed with meat and spices.
6. An instrument of punishment similar to the stocks.
One stood with head and hands clamped between

wooden planks.
7. A name sometimes associated with male homoeroticism and the arrow-pierced body of St. Sebastian.
8. A disparaging reference to the small dog Proteus
intended to give Silvia.
9. TEXTUAL COMMENT For a discussion of "love" and
"leave" in this line, see Digital Edition TC 1.

70 PROTEUS   Not so; I think she lives.

JULIA   Alas!

PROTEUS   Why dost thou cry, "Alas"?

JULIA   I cannot choose but pity her.

PROTEUS   Wherefore shouldst thou pity her?

75 JULIA   Because methinks that she loved you as well
    As you do love your lady Silvia.
    She dreams on him that has forgot her love;
    You dote on her that cares not for your love.
    'Tis pity love should be so contrary,
80   And thinking on it makes me cry, "Alas."

PROTEUS   Well, give her that ring, and therewithal°   *along with it*
    This letter. [*He points.*] That's her chamber. Tell my lady
    I claim the promise for her heavenly picture.
    Your message done, hie home unto my chamber,
85   Where thou shalt find me sad and solitary.   [*Exit.*]

JULIA   How many women would do such a message?
    Alas, poor Proteus, thou hast entertained
    A fox to be the shepherd of thy lambs!
    Alas, poor fool,[1] why do I pity him
90   That with his very heart despiseth me?
    Because he loves her, he despiseth me;
    Because I love him, I must pity him.
    This ring I gave him when he parted from me
    To bind him to remember my goodwill.
95   And now am I, unhappy messenger,
    To plead for that which I would not obtain,
    To carry that which I would have refused,
    To praise his faith which I would have dispraised.
    I am my master's true confirmèd love,
100   But cannot be true servant to my master
    Unless I prove false traitor to myself.
    Yet will I woo for him, but yet so coldly
    As, heaven it knows, I would not have him speed.°   *succeed*
       [*Enter* SILVIA, *attended by her maid Ursula.*]
    Gentlewoman, good day! I pray you, be my mean°   *agent; means*
105   To bring me where to speak with Madam Silvia.

SILVIA   What would you with her, if that I be she?

JULIA   If you be she, I do entreat your patience
    To hear me speak the message I am sent on.

SILVIA   From whom?

110 JULIA   From my master, Sir Proteus, madam.

SILVIA   Oh, he sends you for a picture?

JULIA   Ay, madam.

SILVIA   Ursula, bring my picture there.
       [*Ursula passes her the picture.*]
    Go, give your master this. Tell him from me
115   One Julia, that his changing thoughts forget,
    Would better fit his chamber than this shadow.°   *portrait*

JULIA [*handing* SILVIA *a letter*][2]   Madam, please you peruse
    this letter.

---

1. Julia is referring to herself.
2. Possibly the first letter is from Proteus to Julia. Whether Julia offers it to Silvia by mistake or deliberately (as she later seems deliberately to mistake two rings) is open to question.

    Pardon me, madam, I have unadvised°   *inadvertently*
    Delivered you a paper that I should not—
        [*She takes the letter back and gives* SILVIA *another.*]
120   This is the letter to your ladyship.
   SILVIA [*pointing at the first letter*]   I pray thee, let me look on
      that again.
   JULIA It may not be. Good madam, pardon me.
   SILVIA There, hold. I will not look upon your master's lines:
    I know they are stuffed with protestations
125   And full of new-found° oaths which he will break   *newly made*
    As easily as I do tear his paper.
        [*She tears the second letter.*]
   JULIA Madam, he sends your ladyship this ring.
   SILVIA The more shame for him that he sends it me,
    For I have heard him say a thousand times
130   His Julia gave it him at his departure.
    Though his false finger have profaned the ring,
    Mine shall not do his Julia so much wrong.
   JULIA She thanks you.
   SILVIA What say'st thou?
135   JULIA I thank you, madam, that you tender° her.   *show concern for*
    Poor gentlewoman, my master wrongs her much.
   SILVIA Dost thou know her?
   JULIA Almost as well as I do know myself.
    To think upon her woes I do protest
140   That I have wept a hundred several times.
   SILVIA Belike she thinks that Proteus hath forsook her?
   JULIA I think she doth, and that's her cause of sorrow.
   SILVIA Is she not passing° fair?   *exceedingly*
   JULIA She hath been fairer, madam, than she is.
145   When she did think my master loved her well,
    She, in my judgment, was as fair as you.
    But since she did neglect her looking glass
    And threw her sun-expelling mask[3] away,
    The air hath starved° the roses in her cheeks   *withered*
150   And pinched the lily tincture° of her face,   *white color*
    That now she is become as black as I.
   SILVIA How tall was she?
   JULIA About my stature: for at Pentecost,[4]
    When all our pageants of delight° were played,   *pleasing performances*
155   Our youth got me to play the woman's part,[5]
    And I was trimmed° in Madam Julia's gown,   *dressed*
    Which served me as fit, by all men's judgments,
    As if the garment had been made for me.
    Therefore I know she is about my height,
160   And at that time I made her weep a-good,°   *in earnest*
    For I did play a lamentable° part.   *pitiable*
    Madam, 'twas Ariadne, passioning
    For Theseus' perjury and unjust flight,[6]

---

3. A mask to block the sun worn by upper-class Englishwomen to preserve their light complexions.
4. Religious days seven weeks after Easter, when plays and theatrical pageants were staged in many English towns.

5. Act the female role, as boys conventionally did in the Elizabethan theater.
6. In Greek mythology, Ariadne hanged herself after she was abandoned by her lover, Theseus. *passioning:* sorrowing.

Which I so lively° acted with my tears   *convincingly*
165 That my poor mistress, movèd therewithal,
Wept bitterly; and would I might be dead
If I in thought felt not her very sorrow.
  SILVIA She is beholden to thee, gentle youth.
Alas, poor lady, desolate and left!
170 I weep myself to think upon thy words.
Here, youth: there is my purse. I give thee this
For thy sweet mistress' sake, because thou lov'st her.
Farewell.
  JULIA And she shall thank you for't if e'er you know her—
               [*Exit* SILVIA *with Ursula.*]
175 A virtuous gentlewoman, mild and beautiful!
I hope my master's suit will be but cold,°   *unsuccessful*
Since she respects my mistress' love so much.
Alas, how love can trifle with itself!
Here is her picture. Let me see. I think
180 If I had such a tire,° this face of mine   *headdress*
Were full as lovely as is this of hers;
And yet the painter flattered her a little,
Unless I flatter with myself too much.
Her hair is auburn, mine is perfect yellow:
185 If that be all the difference in his love,
I'll get me such a colored periwig.°   *wig*
Her eyes are gray as glass, and so are mine;
Ay, but her forehead's low, and mine's as high.[7]
What should it be that he respects° in her   *esteems*
190 But I can make respective° in myself,   *worthy of esteem*
If this fond Love were not a blinded god?
        [*She picks up the portrait.*]
Come, shadow, come, and take this shadow up,[8]
For 'tis thy rival. O thou senseless form,
Thou shalt be worshipped, kissed, loved, and adored!
195 And, were there sense° in his idolatry,   *reason*
My substance should be statue in thy stead.[9]
I'll use thee kindly for thy mistress' sake
That used me so; or else, by Jove I vow,
I should have scratched out your unseeing eyes
200 To make my master out of love with thee!   *Exit.*

5.1

Enter EGLAMOUR.

  EGLAMOUR The sun begins to gild the western sky,
And now it is about the very hour
That Silvia at Friar Patrick's cell should meet me.
She will not fail, for lovers break not hours,°   *appointments*
5 Unless it be to come before their time,
So much they spur their expedition.°   *hasten their progress*
    [*Enter* SILVIA.]
See where she comes. Lady, a happy evening!

---

7. Mine's as high as hers is low. High foreheads were considered a sign of beauty.
8. Probably addressing herself as a "shadow," or mere nothing, Julia means "pick up Silvia's portrait" or "take up the challenge posed by this woman."
9. My person ("substance") should be an idol ("statue") to Proteus rather than Silvia's picture.
5.1 Location: An abbey in Milan.

SILVIA   Amen, amen! Go on, good Eglamour,
    Out at the postern° by the abbey wall;   *back door or side door*
10 I fear I am attended° by some spies.   *followed*
EGLAMOUR   Fear not; the forest is not three leagues off;
    If we recover° that, we are sure° enough.   *Exeunt.*   *reach / safe*

5.2

Enter TURIO, PROTEUS, *and* JULIA *[as Sebastian].*

TURIO   Sir Proteus, what says Silvia to my suit?
PROTEUS   O sir, I find her milder than she was,
    And yet she takes exceptions at° your person.   *objects to*
TURIO   What? That my leg is too long?
5 PROTEUS   No, that it is too little.
TURIO   I'll wear a boot to make it somewhat rounder.
JULIA *[aside]*   But love will not be spurred to what it loathes.[1]
TURIO   What says she to my face?
PROTEUS   She says it is a fair one.
10 TURIO   Nay, then the wanton lies! My face is black.
PROTEUS   But pearls are fair; and the old saying is,
    "Black men are pearls in beauteous ladies' eyes."
JULIA *[aside]*   'Tis true, such pearls[2] as put out ladies' eyes,
    For I had rather wink° than look on them.   *shut my eyes*
15 TURIO   How likes she my discourse?
PROTEUS   Ill when you talk of war.
TURIO   But well when I discourse of love and peace?
JULIA *[aside]*   But better indeed when you hold your peace.
TURIO   What says she to my valor?
20 PROTEUS   O sir, she makes no doubt of that.
JULIA *[aside]*   She needs not when she knows it cowardice.
TURIO   What says she to my birth?
PROTEUS   That you are well derived.°   *descended*
JULIA *[aside]*   True: from a gentleman to a fool.
25 TURIO   Considers she my possessions?
PROTEUS   Oh, ay, and pities them.
TURIO   Wherefore?
JULIA *[aside]*   That such an ass should owe° them.   *own*
PROTEUS   That they are out by lease.°   *rented out*
    [Enter the DUKE.]
30 JULIA   Here comes the Duke.
DUKE   How now, Sir Proteus? How now, Turio?
    Which of you saw Eglamour of late?
TURIO   Not I.
PROTEUS   Nor I.
DUKE   Saw you my daughter?
PROTEUS   Neither.
DUKE   Why, then, she's fled unto that peasant° Valentine,   *rascal*
35 And Eglamour is in her company.
    'Tis true, for Friar Laurence[3] met them both

5.2 Location: The Duke's court in Milan.
1. F assigns this line to Proteus and lines 13 and 14
to Turio, but it makes more sense to assign them to
the disguised Julia, whose covert comments on the
words of Proteus and Turio provide the scene with
much of its humor.

2. Punning on the medical meaning of "pearl" as a
thin film or cataract growing over the eye.
3. Possibly a slip for "Friar Patrick," mentioned in
the preceding scene and at line 41 below, although
there may be more than one friar in the forest.

As he, in penance, wandered through the forest.
Him he knew well, and guessed that it was she,
But, being masked, he was not sure of it.
40　Besides, she did intend confession
At Patrick's cell this even, and there she was not.
These likelihoods confirm her flight from hence.
Therefore, I pray you, stand not to discourse,
But mount you presently and meet with me
45　Upon the rising of the mountain foot
That leads toward Mantua, whither they are fled.
Dispatch,° sweet gentlemen, and follow me.　　　[Exit.]　　　*Hurry*
TURIO　Why, this it is to be a peevish° girl　　　*silly; perverse*
That flies her fortune when it follows her.
50　I'll after, more to be revenged on Eglamour
Than for the love of reckless Silvia.　　　[Exit.]
PROTEUS　And I will follow, more for Silvia's love
Than hate of Eglamour that goes with her.　　　[Exit.]
JULIA　And I will follow, more to cross that love
55　Than hate for Silvia, that is gone for love.　　　[Exit.]

5.3
[*Enter*] OUTLAWS [*and*] SILVIA [*as their captive*].
FIRST OUTLAW　Come, come, be patient. We must bring you to
our captain.
SILVIA　A thousand more mischances than this one
Have learned° me how to brook° this patiently.　　　*taught / endure*
5　SECOND OUTLAW　Come, bring her away.
FIRST OUTLAW　Where is the gentleman that was with her?°　　　*(Eglamour)*
THIRD OUTLAW　Being nimble-footed, he hath outrun us,
But Moses and Valerius[1] follow him.
Go thou with her to the west end of the wood;
10　There is our captain. We'll follow him that's fled.
The thicket is beset;° he cannot scape.　　　*surrounded*
[*Exeunt* SECOND *and* THIRD OUTLAWS.]
FIRST OUTLAW　Come, I must bring you to our captain's cave.
Fear not; he bears an honorable mind
And will not use a woman lawlessly.
15　SILVIA　O Valentine, this I endure for thee!　　　*Exeunt.*

5.4
Enter VALENTINE.
VALENTINE　How use° doth breed a habit in a man!　　　*custom*
This shadowy desert,° unfrequented woods,　　　*uninhabited spot*
I better brook° than flourishing peopled towns.　　　*endure*
Here can I sit alone, unseen of any,
5　And to the nightingale's complaining notes[1]
Tune my distresses and record my woes.
O thou° that dost inhabit in my breast,　　　*(addressing Silvia)*
Leave not the mansion[2] so long tenantless
Lest, growing ruinous, the building fall

5.3 Location: At the frontiers of the Mantua forest.
1. Presumably, Moses and Valerius are fellow members of the outlaw band.
5.4 Location: Another part of the forest.

1. In classical mythology, Philomela was turned into a nightingale after Tereus raped her; her song is a lament.
2. Referring to his body as Silvia's home.

10   And leave no memory of what it was!
      Repair me with thy presence, Silvia!
      Thou gentle nymph, cherish thy forlorn swain.
           [*Shouts within.*]
      What hallooing? And what stir is this today?
      These are my mates, that make their wills their law,

15   Have° some unhappy passenger° in chase.   *Who have / traveler*
      They love me well, yet I have much to do
      To keep them from uncivil outrages.
      Withdraw thee, Valentine.
           [VALENTINE *hides. Enter* PROTEUS, SILVIA, *and* JULIA
           as Sebastian.]
                    Who's this comes here?
   PROTEUS   Madam, this service I have done for you—

20   Though you respect not aught your servant doth—
      To hazard life and rescue you from him
      That would have forced your honor° and your love.   *violated your chastity*
      Vouchsafe me for my meed° but one fair look!   *reward*
      A smaller boon° than this I cannot beg,   *request*

25   And less than this I am sure you cannot give.
   VALENTINE [*aside*]   How like a dream is this I see and hear!
      Love, lend me patience to forbear awhile.
   SILVIA   Oh, miserable, unhappy that I am!
   PROTEUS   Unhappy were you, madam, ere I came;

30   But by my coming I have made you happy.
   SILVIA   By thy approach° thou mak'st me most unhappy.   *amorous advances*
   JULIA [*aside*]   And me, when he approacheth to your presence.
   SILVIA   Had I been seizèd by a hungry lion
      I would have been a breakfast to the beast

35   Rather than have false Proteus rescue me.
      O heaven, be judge how I love Valentine,
      Whose life's as tender° to me as my soul.   *precious*
      And full as much, for more there cannot be,
      I do detest false perjured Proteus.

40   Therefore be gone; solicit me no more.
   PROTEUS   What dangerous action, stood it next to death,
      Would I not undergo for one calm° look!   *gentle*
      Oh, 'tis the curse in love, and still approved,°   *always confirmed*
      When women cannot love where they're beloved.

45 SILVIA   When Proteus cannot love where he's beloved!
      Read over Julia's heart, thy first best love,
      For whose dear sake thou didst then rend thy faith
      Into a thousand oaths, and all those oaths
      Descended into perjury° to love me!   *Were forsworn*

50   Thou hast no faith left now unless thou'dst two,[3]
      And that's far worse than none. Better have none
      Than plural faith, which is too much by one,
      Thou counterfeit° to thy true friend.   *deceiver; false friend*
   PROTEUS   In love
      Who respects friend?
   SILVIA   All men but Proteus.

---

3. You have no faithfulness left now unless you were to have two lovers (Julia and Silvia).

55　PROTEUS　Nay, if the gentle spirit of moving words
　　　　Can no way change you to a milder form,
　　　　I'll woo you like a soldier, at arm's end,°　　　　　　　　*at swordpoint*
　　　　And love you 'gainst the nature of love—force ye.
　　　　　　　[*He seizes her.*]
　　SILVIA　O heaven!
60　PROTEUS　I'll force thee yield to my desire.
　　VALENTINE [*stepping forward*]　Ruffian! Let go that rude
　　　　　uncivil touch,
　　　　Thou friend of an ill fashion!
　　PROTEUS　　　　　　　　　　Valentine!
　　VALENTINE　Thou common° friend—that's without faith or　　*superficial*
　　　　　love,
　　　　For such is a friend now. Treacherous man,
65　　Thou hast beguiled my hopes! Naught but mine eye
　　　　Could have persuaded me. Now I dare not say
　　　　I have one friend alive; thou wouldst disprove me.
　　　　Who should be trusted when one's right hand
　　　　Is perjured to the bosom?° Proteus,　　　　　　　　　*false to the heart*
70　　I am sorry I must never trust thee more,
　　　　But count the world a stranger for thy sake![4]
　　　　The private wound is deepest. O time most accursed,
　　　　'Mongst all foes that a friend should be the worst!
　　PROTEUS　My shame and guilt confounds me.
75　　Forgive me, Valentine. If hearty sorrow
　　　　Be a sufficient ransom for offense,
　　　　I tender't° here. I do as truly suffer　　　　　　　　　　*offer it*
　　　　As e'er I did commit.
　　VALENTINE　　　　　　Then I am paid,
　　　　And once again I do receive thee° honest.　　　　　　　*accept you as*
80　　Who by repentance is not satisfied
　　　　Is nor of heaven nor earth, for these are pleased;
　　　　By penitence th'Eternal's wrath's appeased.
　　　　And that my love may appear plain and free,
　　　　All that was mine in Silvia[5] I give thee.[6]
　　JULIA　O me unhappy!
　　　　　　[*She faints.*]
　　PROTEUS　　　　　　　Look to the boy.
85　VALENTINE　　　　　　　　　Why, boy!
　　　　Why, wag!° How now? What's the matter? Look up. Speak.　　*sweet boy*
　　JULIA　O good sir, my master charged me to deliver a ring to
　　　　Madam Silvia, which out of my neglect was never done.
　　PROTEUS　Where is that ring, boy?
　　JULIA　　　　　　　　　　Here 'tis. This is it.
　　　　　　[*She gives* PROTEUS *a ring.*]
90　PROTEUS　How? Let me see.
　　　　Why, this is the ring I gave to Julia!
　　JULIA　Oh, cry you mercy, sir; I have mistook!
　　　　　　[*She produces another ring.*]　This is the ring you sent to Silvia.

---

4. But cut myself off from the world (in disillusion-
ment) because of your treachery.
5. All my claims to Silvia; all that was mine, in the
person of Silvia; all the love I gave to Silvia.

6. PERFORMANCE COMMENT Each production's
approach to Valentine's offer can help condemn or
redeem him while either neutralizing or intensifying the
sequence's disturbing aspects. See Digital Edition PC 2.

PROTEUS　But how cam'st thou by this ring? At my depart
95　　I gave this unto Julia.
JULIA　And Julia herself did give it me—
　　　[*She reveals herself.*] And Julia herself hath brought it
　　　　hither.
PROTEUS　How? Julia?
JULIA　Behold her that gave aim to° all thy oaths　　　　*was the object of*
100　　And entertained 'em deeply in her heart.
　　　How oft hast thou with perjury cleft the root!°　　*bottom of her heart*
　　　O Proteus, let this habit° make thee blush!　　　　　　　*disguise*
　　　Be thou ashamed that I have took upon me
　　　Such an immodest raiment, if shame live
105　　In a disguise of love.[7]
　　　It is the lesser blot, modesty finds,
　　　Women to change their shapes° than men their minds.　*appearances; clothes*
PROTEUS　Than men their minds? 'Tis true. O heaven, were
　　　man
　　　But constant, he were perfect! That one error
110　　Fills him with faults, makes him run through all th'sins;
　　　Inconstancy falls off ere it begins.[8]
　　　What is in Silvia's face but I may spy
　　　More fresh in Julia's, with a constant° eye?　　　　　　*faithful*
VALENTINE　Come, come, a hand from either.
115　　Let me be blest to make this happy close.°　　　　*ending; union*
　　　'Twere pity two such friends should be long foes.
　　　　　　[JULIA *and* PROTEUS *join hands.*]
PROTEUS　Bear witness, heaven, I have my wish forever.
JULIA　And I mine.
　　　　　　[*Enter* OUTLAWS *with the* DUKE *and* TURIO *as their*
　　　　　　captives.]
OUTLAWS　　　　　A prize, a prize, a prize!
VALENTINE　Forbear, forbear, I say! It is my lord the Duke.
　　　　　　[OUTLAWS *release their captives.*]
120　　[*to the* DUKE] Your grace is welcome to a man disgraced:
　　　Banished Valentine.
DUKE　　　　　Sir Valentine?
TURIO　Yonder is Silvia, and Silvia's mine.
VALENTINE　Turio, give back,° or else embrace thy death!　　*stand back*
　　　Come not within the measure° of my wrath.　　　　　　　*reach*
125　　Do not name Silvia thine; if once again,
　　　Milano° shall not hold thee. Here she stands:　　　　　　*Milan*
　　　Take but possession of her with a touch—
　　　I dare thee but to breathe upon my love.
TURIO　Sir Valentine, I care not for her, I.
130　　I hold him but a fool that will endanger
　　　His body for a girl that loves him not.
　　　I claim her not, and therefore she is thine.
DUKE　The more degenerate and base art thou
　　　To make such means° for her as thou hast done　　　　*efforts*

---

7. *if . . . love:* if a disguise one wears for the sake of　　8. The inconstant man begins to deceive, or "fall
love can be considered shameful; if one who pretends　　off," even before he swears constancy.
to feel love is capable of feeling shame.

135 And leave her on such slight conditions.°	*trivial reasons*
—Now, by the honor of my ancestry,	
I do applaud thy spirit, Valentine,	
And think thee worthy of an empress' love.	
Know, then, I here forget all former griefs,°	*grievances*
140 Cancel all grudge, repeal° thee home again,	*recall*
Plead a new state in thy unrivaled merit,[9]	
To which I thus subscribe:° Sir Valentine,	*bear witness*
Thou art a gentleman, and well derived;	
Take thou thy Silvia, for thou hast deserved her.	
145 VALENTINE I thank your grace; the gift hath made me happy.	
I now beseech you, for your daughter's sake,	
To grant one boon° that I shall ask of you.	*favor*
DUKE I grant it for thine own, whate'er it be.	
VALENTINE These banished men that I have kept withal°	*lived with*
150 Are men endued with worthy qualities.	
Forgive them what they have committed here,	
And let them be recalled from their exile.	
They are reformèd, civil, full of good,	
And fit for great employment, worthy lord.	
155 DUKE Thou hast prevailed; I pardon them and thee.	
Dispose of them as thou know'st their deserts.	
—Come, let us go. We will include all jars°	*end all discord*
With triumphs,° mirth, and rare solemnity.°	*pageants / festivity*
VALENTINE And, as we walk along, I dare be bold	
160 With our discourse to make your grace to smile.	
What think you of this page, my lord?	
DUKE I think the boy hath grace in him; he blushes.	
VALENTINE I warrant you, my lord, more grace than boy.[1]	
DUKE What mean you by that saying?	
165 VALENTINE Please you, I'll tell you as we pass along,	
That you will wonder° what hath fortunèd.°	*marvel at / happened*
Come, Proteus, 'tis your penance but to hear	
The story of your loves discoverèd.°	*revealed*
That done, our day of marriage shall be yours,	
170 One feast, one house, one mutual happiness. *Exeunt.*	

---

9. Argue (that there is) a new situation created by your unparalleled merit.

1. He has more feminine charm ("grace") than male gender (that is, "he" is really a girl).

The Second Part of Henry the Sixth

What happens to a kingdom when the sitting monarch is too weak to rule effectively? Shakespeare explores this difficult problem in *2 Henry VI*, in which Henry, crowned when he was nine months old, never establishes control over his realm. As his assertive French wife, Margaret of Anjou, exclaims in exasperation to the Duke of Suffolk, who had wooed her for Henry:

> when in the city Tours
> Thou ran'st a tilt in honor of my love
> And stol'st away the ladies' hearts of France,
> I thought King Henry had resembled thee
> In courage, courtship, and proportion,
> But all his mind is bent to holiness
> To number Ave-Maries on his beads.
> (1.3.49–55)*

Margaret thought she would be marrying a chivalric hero, one adept at the arts of love and war; instead, she finds herself wed to an ineffective, pious man who elsewhere openly expresses his desire to live as a private person rather than as his country's king. Partly as a result of Henry's deficiencies, Margaret grows increasingly independent, conducting a love intrigue with Suffolk and openly defying her husband's wishes. Presented as a sexualized figure of gender disorder, Margaret is as powerful as her husband is weak. Margaret, however, represents but one of the threats to Henry's authority and the country's well-being. Lacking the strong hand of a powerful monarch to rein them in, Henry's nobles quarrel and threaten civil war, and eventually a group of rebellious commoners storm London, killing all who oppose them. The kingdom slides into chaos.

For modern audiences, *2 Henry VI* can seem strikingly contemporary. The chaos of civil war, bloody conflicts between warring political and religious groups, struggles over who can lay claim to a "homeland"—these are all-too-familiar aspects of twenty-first-century life. So, too, is the opportunism of political leaders who use chaotic conditions to further their own selfish interests rather than the common good. Indeed, any notion of promoting the common good is one of the most poignant casualties of the bloody strife unleashed in the course of the play.

In the early modern period, the king, standing at the top of the social order and invested with enormous responsibilities, was charged with guaranteeing the well-being of all his subjects. The symbolic head and heart of the body politic, the monarch was enjoined to rule wisely, to care for his subjects, and to take counsel from and exert control over the nobility. Many theories of kingship argued that monarchs had their authority from God; rebellion against a sitting monarch was a form of treason punishable by death. Given the centrality of the king to the health of the kingdom and its subjects, an evil or a weak king could have a disastrous impact on the realm. Tyrants—that is, kings who followed their passions, refused to take counsel, and ignored the welfare of their subjects—were anxiously discussed by the political thinkers of the period. Could they ever be overthrown? Must their tyranny be endured? In plays such as *Richard III* and *Macbeth*, Shakespeare dramatized such

---

* All quotations are taken from the edited text of the Folio, printed here. The Digital Edition includes edited texts of both the Folio and the Quarto.

181

Henry VI, depicted as a child, carried by the Earl of Warwick.

tyrant kings and in each case showed their deaths at the hands of high-placed subjects. Henry VI poses a different kind of danger. Rather than being an evil or personally ambitious monarch, he is simply ineffectual and weak, unable to control the ambition and selfish desires of his nobles or to see to the welfare of his subjects. In effect, 2 Henry VI explores what happens when a kingdom is left rudderless, graphically depicting the brutality let loose when the king is unable to assert his authority, commoners are set against nobles, and nobles begin to destroy one another.

2 Henry VI may well be the first English history play Shakespeare wrote. It has been dated as early as 1591 and exists in two distinct versions: a Quarto edition printed in 1594 entitled *The First Part of the Contention betwixt the Two Famous Houses of York and Lancaster* and a longer version printed in the First Folio in 1623 (for the differences between these two texts, see the Textual Introduction). Historically, the protracted broils depicted in this and the following play were known as the Wars of the Roses (1455–85) because the House of York, which staked its claim to England's throne through Lionel, Duke of Clarence, third son of Edward III, took a white rose for its emblem, while the House of Lancaster, which claimed the throne through John of Gaunt, fourth son of Edward III, became identified with the red rose. Together, 2 and 3 Henry VI explore the horror of a kingdom divided against itself.

When read, 2 Henry VI can seem chaotic, a series of violent acts carried out by a bewildering array of characters who rise to the forefront of attention only to disappear quickly from view. But the play is more carefully structured than may at first be apparent, and its dramatic effectiveness is registered in the many successful performances it has had since the middle of the twentieth century. For the first two acts, the strength of Humphrey, Duke of Gloucester, counterbalances the King's weakness. Since the King's youth, Duke Humphrey has served as Lord Protector of the realm and has striven to see the common people treated fairly and the quarreling nobles kept in check. The play reaches a decisive turning point in act 3 when Gloucester, driven from office by the Queen, Suffolk, York, and Cardinal Beaufort (who is also the Bishop of Winchester), is murdered. With Gloucester gone, no one can protect the King or the kingdom from the ambition of Richard, Duke of York, the most powerful of the nobles who would supplant Henry. From act 3 on, York and his minions dominate the action, countered primarily by the equally strong-willed Margaret. In the brutal struggles that follow upon Gloucester's death, one powerful figure after another suffers disgrace or death, including Cardinal Beaufort, Suffolk, and Somerset. York, however, does not fall but, like Margaret, moves with unnerving single-mindedness into the power vacuum created by the King's passivity.

To register in performance the disaster that has overtaken England, Shakespeare relentlessly focuses on the human bodies maimed, brutalized, and destroyed by the play's contending forces. The death of Gloucester is exemplary. In the Quarto version of the text, he is strangled onstage in his bed; in the Folio version of the play, his death occurs offstage. But in both texts, the corpse is eventually displayed to the audience while Warwick recites a grisly description of the state of the body. In contrast to the paleness of a man who has died peacefully, the good Duke's

> face is black and full of blood,
> His eyeballs further out than when he lived,
> Staring full ghastly like a strangled man;
> His hair upreared, his nostrils stretched with struggling,
> His hands abroad displayed, as one that grasped
> And tugged for life and was by strength subdued.
> Look on the sheets: his hair, you see, is sticking;
> His well-proportioned beard made rough and rugged,
> Like to the summer's corn by tempest lodged.
> It cannot be but he was murdered here;
> The least of all these signs were probable.
>
> (3.2.168–78)

This terrible inventory of the unnatural state of Gloucester's dead body highlights the marks of his futile struggle for life—the bulging eyes, the disordered hair and beard, the outstretched hands. Warwick's point is that these are *not* the signs of a soul weighed down by sin and unprepared for death, as is true of Cardinal Beaufort, whose death occurs in the next scene; rather, Gloucester's disordered corpse testifies to the horrific and untimely circumstances in which he died.

In this extremely violent play, many other bodies suffer indignity, pain, and death, and in performance the brutality can be overwhelming. In act 4, Suffolk, captured on his flight to France, is beheaded offstage by his captors. His body is then taken to England, where Queen Margaret, in one of the most macabre scenes in Shakespeare, carries his severed head around the court, lamenting her dead lover. Later, the rebels attacking London capture Lord Saye, a supporter of King Henry. After enumerating a catalog of his crimes, including the "crime" of literacy, the followers of Jack Cade, the chief rebel, behead Saye along with his son-in-law. Cade's followers then stick the severed heads on poles and carry them through the streets, grotesquely making them "kiss" at every corner. After five days of living in the woods without food have rendered him too famished to fight effectively, Jack Cade is himself beheaded and his head taken to the King. This is hardly an exhaustive list of the forms of violence depicted in the play. It does not, for example, take account of those slain in battle, such as Somerset, or of the shameful treatment Cade visits upon defeated enemies, such as Sir Humphrey Stafford and his brother, whose armor he strips from their corpses before he drags their bodies behind his horse toward London. England is being torn apart by civil war, and the severed heads and maimed bodies that litter the stage show the cost of this man-made disaster.

Some small portion of this violence stems from the monarch's authority to punish unruly or disobedient subjects. In Elizabethan England, traitors' heads were regularly displayed on London Bridge, and public executions were popular spectacles, showing the king's power over traitors and criminals. In 2 *Henry VI*, the most spectacular scene of public correction involves Eleanor Cobham, Gloucester's wife. A proud and ambitious woman who hopes to see her husband displace Henry as King of England, Cobham dabbles in the forbidden arts of witchcraft and conjuration, soliciting prophecies about the fate of the King and two of his nobles, Suffolk and Somerset. Such prophecies were considered politically dangerous because they caused uncertainty and unrest among the common people and could be used to foment sedition. They had been specifically banned by Henry VIII, Edward VI, and Elizabeth. Like many famous prophecies, those delivered to Eleanor Cobham are ambiguous. For example, "The duke yet lives that Henry shall depose / But him outlive and die a violent death" (1.4.29–30) can mean either that Henry shall depose a duke or that a duke shall depose Henry. Nor is it entirely clear who shall outlive whom and die a violent death. The ambiguity of such statements was exactly what rulers feared, since under the cover of a benign interpretation they could be used to predict and promote rebellion. For engaging in witchcraft and conjuration as well as for circulating such prophecies, Eleanor Cobham is first shamed—she must walk through London carrying a candle and wearing only a sheet, her crimes listed on a piece of paper pinned to her back—and then banished, and her confederates hanged and burned. The King here appears to be using sanctioned violence to punish dangerously seditious subjects.

Yet in much of the play, the state either fails to control violence or else uses it with questionable justice. Even Eleanor's case is more ambiguous than the above account suggests. She did undeniably dabble in witchcraft, yet she was urged on by people in the employ of Suffolk and the Cardinal, who wished through her acts to disgrace her innocent husband and dislodge him from power. Legally, Eleanor's punishment is just, yet it occurs in a context of chicanery and treachery that the King either does not or will not see until Gloucester, the chief prop of royal justice, has been removed. Between the discovery of Eleanor's witchcraft and her public shaming, the play shows the audience another troubling example of a ritual of justice. Earlier Peter Thump, an apprentice, had accused his master, Horner, of saying that the Duke of York—not Henry—was the rightful ruler of England. Thump had no proof but his own word, and Horner had no defense but denial. To resolve the issue, Gloucester orders a day of combat for the man and master: whoever wins the duel would be assumed to have spoken the truth. Such trials by combat were customary in adjudicating disputes among nobles. But the apprentice is terrified, having no experience with such contests or with the weapons commonly used in them: the sword or the lance. As it is dramatized, the trial by combat becomes a parody of justice. Rather than fighting with swords, the two contestants appear with sandbags attached to poles, and Horner is roaring drunk. It is under these conditions that the apprentice kills his master, and the King, who has now taken Gloucester's staff of office from him as the result of Eleanor's treason, seems satisfied that justice has prevailed. But the ludicrous nature of the drunken encounter threatens to empty such traditional rituals of their meaning and legitimacy.

With Gloucester's death, the King's fair and effective control of the machinery of justice and of violence is further compromised. Under the pressure of an enraged commons, Henry *does* banish Suffolk for his role in Gloucester's death, but the King cannot begin to contain the escalating stage violence. In the second half of the play, his loss of control is demonstrated by the spectacular rise to power of the lower-class rebel Jack Cade, one of York's minions. As he marches toward London, Cade boasts that the laws of England are to come from his mouth, and he arrogates to himself the right to kill whomever he chooses. The murder of Lord Saye, the death of the clerk of Chartham, the desecration of Stafford's body—these are a mere sampling of events in a brutal career, and the play does not shrink from showing what is cruel and arbitrary in Cade's brief reign of terror. Critics often take Shakespeare's representation of Cade as confirming Elizabethan fears about the dangers of popular rule.

Yet interpreting Cade and his actions is a complicated business. Does Shakespeare create this character simply to discredit popular rebellion, or does he use Cade to articulate the legitimate grievances of the common people and employ Cade's brutality as a disquieting mirror of the brutality of the ruling classes? Cade is not synonymous with "the commons" in this play. In the opening acts, while he is still in power, Gloucester is presented as a champion of the people and promotes a commonwealth in which the King and nobles care for the needs of the commoners and are responsive to their petitions. The people, in turn, seem confident that their views will be heard by those near the King. For example, in 1.3, three commoners wait with petitions for Gloucester: Peter Thump wishes to report his master's treasonous words about the Duke of York; another man complains that Cardinal Beaufort's man has unlawfully seized his land, house, and wife; a third protests that the Duke of Suffolk has enclosed the commons of Melford. (Enclosures—fencing in land once shared by many for growing food and grazing cattle—were a main cause of rural protest in the sixteenth and seventeenth centuries.) How these commoners behave as political agents registering grievances with those in power is revealing. First, the petitioners believe that they can get redress from the Lord Protector, the figure nearest the King himself. Second, they use peaceful means to obtain their desires. Third, they act from a position of loyalty to their King and his Lord Protector. Thump, in particular, puts himself at personal risk to report an act of treason against Henry. These figures hardly constitute a mob or a many-headed monster. Even when they become enraged by Gloucester's murder and demand the banishment of Suffolk, they couch their protest as a desire to protect the King rather than to seize power for themselves.

In 1.3, the petitioners are largely thwarted in their appeal for justice because they mistake Suffolk for Gloucester. Suffolk and the Queen are interested in dealing with York's supposed treason because they can use that accusation to prevent York from becoming Regent of France. They ignore the other petitions, one of which details a complaint against Suffolk himself. It is the nobles and not the commoners who fail to exercise their political duties responsibly. Timid and gullible and surrounded by selfish nobles like Suffolk, the King disregards the welfare and the needs of the common people, who are presented in this scene as loyal and orderly actors in a hierarchical commonwealth.

Cade enters the picture only when the one noble—Gloucester—who cares about maintaining this paternal relationship between the commons and the King is about to be killed. At the end of 3.1, York, in soliloquy, reveals his intention to use the army levied against Ireland to further his own political ends; in addition, he will employ the Kentishman Jack Cade as his stalking horse in his move to seize the crown. Cade will pretend to be John Mortimer, a claimant to the throne through the Yorkist line, in order to test the waters for York's own bid for power. Cade is thus never an entirely independent agent of the people; rather, he is at least in part the tool of an ambitious nobleman who employs him because he is stubborn, strong, and impervious to pain. York reports that in battle against the Irish, Cade

> fought so long till that his thighs with darts
> Were almost like a sharp-quilled porcupine;
> And in the end, being rescued, I have seen
> Him caper upright like a wild Morisco,
> Shaking the bloody darts as he his bells.
> (3.1.362–66)

Morris dancers tied bells to their legs, and these shook and jangled as they danced. The powerful image of the wounded Cade dancing depicts a man endowed with enormous spirit and physical strength. It is worth recalling that one of the most famous clowns of the 1590s, Will Kemp, who may have played the part of Cade, was himself a noted acrobat and dancer; in 1599, he left Shakespeare's company and did a celebrated morris dance from London to Norwich. Skilled and strong, Cade and Kemp suggest both what was feared and what was admired about hardhanded men, some of whom were employed in the London theater industry and some of whom would have been in the audience. In fact, the Cade scenes must have been powerfully charged, because out of this rebel's mouth—along with arbitrary brutality and pompous self-aggrandizement—issues a critique of social and economic inequality that, endowed with a long history, also spoke to living issues in the London of the 1590s.

Historically, Cade's rebellion occurred in 1450, but in portraying it Shakespeare draws on accounts of many instances of popular social protest. For example, he takes from Raphael Holinshed's *Chronicles of England, Scotland, and Ireland* (1587 edition) details from the Peasants' Revolt of 1381, in which rebels such as Wat Tyler burned London Bridge and attacked the Savoy (John of Gaunt's house) and the Inns of Court, both places of privilege that became a focus for lower-class anger. Other popular uprisings occurred in 1517, when apprentices on Ill May Day attacked foreign workers in the City of London; in 1549 (Kett's Rebellion); and in London itself throughout the 1590s. Between 1581 and 1602, there were numerous outbreaks of

Will Kemp doing his morris dance. From Kemp's *Nine Days' Wonder* (1600).

disorder in London directed against various forms of economic hardship, some of which stemmed from disruptions and changes in the English cloth trade that disadvantaged English weavers. Protests also occurred against the high price of commodities such as butter and fish, and against the granting of monopolies that put the sale of key goods, such as starch, in the hands of a small group. Apprentices were often involved in and blamed for these riots. Many of Cade's followers in *2 Henry VI* are artisans: weavers and butchers. Through Cade, their economic grievances find expression, along with the articulation of an alternative model of social and economic organization much more radically utopian than that implied in Gloucester's hierarchical paternalism.

This tradition of popular radicalism, whose roots went back at least to the fourteenth century, stressed that all men had been equally redeemed by Christ's blood and that there was as much nobility in the labor of an honest man as in the fine silks and the educated speech of a gentleman. A riddle common throughout Europe from the fourteenth century on—"When Adam delved and Eve span, who then was the gentleman?"—suggests the egalitarian purposes for which the Bible could be appropriated. The first man and woman, digging in the earth and spinning cloth, knew no distinctions of rank, simply the dignity of labor. Often, popular protest stressed the value of manual labor, as opposed to the idleness of the rich, and claimed the clouted shoe or hobnailed boot of the rural peasant and the leather apron of the urban laborer as valued emblems of their working lives.

The Cade scenes are filled with references to this egalitarian tradition. In 4.2, when the rebels first describe how Cade means to reform the commonwealth, they make clear that in their view working men, and only working men, should be magistrates and rulers. Referring to Scripture, the Second Rebel says: "and yet it is said, 'Labor in thy vocation,' which is as much to say as, 'Let the magistrates be laboring men'—and therefore should we be magistrates" (4.2.15–17). By contrast, the present nobility "scorn to go in leather aprons" (4.2.12) and have no respect for handicraftsmen. Part of Cade's success is that he is able to mobilize such artisan anger against the privileges of gentlemen, whether those be conferred by literacy or by inherited wealth. Much of Cade's violence is directed against those who can read and write, like the clerk of Chartham or Lord Saye. Literacy, whether defined as the ability to read or to read and write, was a privilege of the minority in Shakespeare's England—and a privilege that brought power in its wake. Cade was not alone in trusting oral exchanges rather than written documents because writing was often used by the powerful to oppress the poor, especially through deeds and other legal instruments that the unskilled could not read. This explains the logic of Cade's threat not only to kill all the lawyers but also to punish all those who wrote on parchment, that is, those in control of written documents. Not only would he release his followers from the tyranny of writing, but he also promises to increase their material well-being by providing cheap bread and high-quality beer and by insisting that all goods would be held in common and all men clothed in one livery.

It is hardly necessary to point out how often Cade contradicts himself in articulating his vision of a commonwealth of equals and how he undermines the utopian aspirations of the tradition of popular radicalism to which his words repeatedly refer. In his egalitarian commonwealth, Cade, of course, would be king, and from his mouth would come all the laws by which others would live. Women would have no rights in his commonwealth but would be fair game for rape and sexual abuse. Insisting on appropriating the ancient custom of noblemen to have the maidenheads of the women their servants or tenants were to marry, Cade says: "there shall not a maid be married but she shall pay to me her maidenhead" (4.7.110–11). In the Quarto version of the text, the sexual crimes enacted by Cade and his followers are even more extensively and vividly detailed than in the Folio. All told, the violence and arbitrary cruelty Cade repeatedly displays make him a frightening figure and one whom even his followers often recognize as a charlatan and a hypocrite.

Yet Cade's personal viciousness does not simply wipe away the power of the social critique to which he intermittently gives voice and which had a history extending far beyond this play. When Cade learns that Lord Saye has his horse covered with an elaborate cloth, he bluntly states a point of view that must have resonated with some in Shakespeare's audience: "Marry, thou oughtst not to let thy horse wear a cloak when honester men than thou go in their hose and doublets" (4.7.44–45). Moreover, Shakespeare gives plenty of evidence in the play that if many commoners feel anger and resentment toward the nobility, many nobility are in their turn full of contempt for the lower classes. Act 4, which is dominated by Cade, opens with the scene in which Suffolk is captured and questioned by the lieutenant of a ship. Furious that when he reveals himself as the Duke of Suffolk his captors do not free him immediately, Suffolk contemptuously attacks the lieutenant:

> Obscure and lousy swain! King Henry's blood,
> The honorable blood of Lancaster,
> Must not be shed by such a jaded groom.
> (4.1.50–52)

The lines underscore the truth of the second rebel's claim that the gentlemen of England do not have much respect for hardhanded men. Suffolk's disdain is especially ironic because the Whitmore who kills Cade himself claims to be a gentleman, and the lieutenant who condemns Suffolk carefully lists the crimes he has committed against the monarch and against his country: taking from the realm's treasury, making the Queen an adulteress, marrying Henry to an unworthy wife, colluding in Humphrey's death, and promoting the loss of France. Those on the ship are, in essence, putting Suffolk on trial—a trial fueled by their own anger at his insolence. Rather than answer the charges lodged against him, Suffolk chooses haughtily to stand on his class privilege and goes to his death.

This complicated political drama seems unequivocally to confirm only one principle: the absence of a strong and just king leaves the commonwealth at risk, but at risk not solely from its most disenfranchised members. Cade, who offers the most radical critique of social inequality, is personally vilified and discredited within the play; but it is arguable that the larger context for his grim saturnalia of violence is the

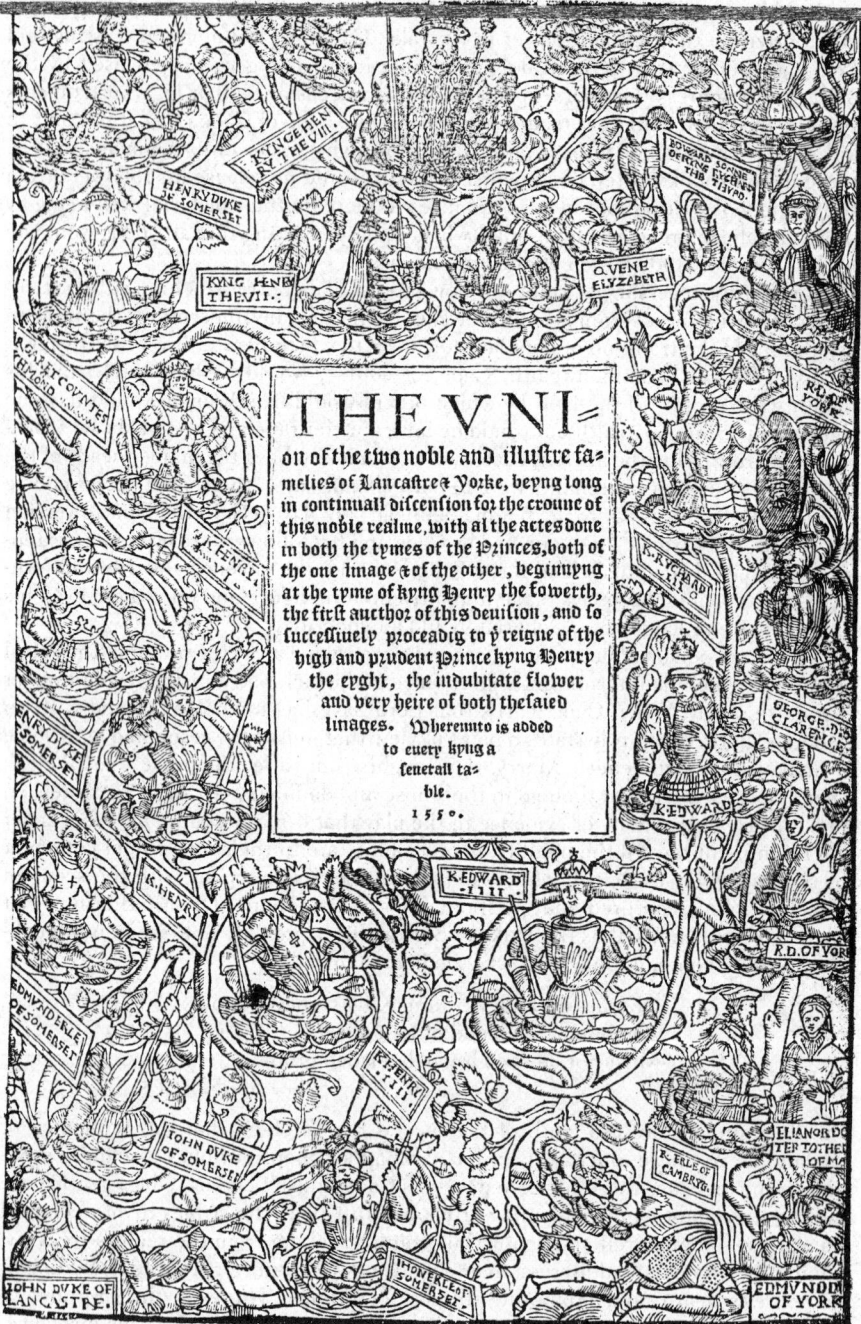

The houses of York and Lancaster depicted as two parts of a rosebush conjoined, by the marriage of Henry VII and Elizabeth of York, to form the Tudor dynasty. Title page to Edward Halle's (or Hall's) *Union of the Two Noble and Illustrious Families of Lancaster and York* (1550 edition).

unspeakable selfishness of the English nobles. Many of them—York, Suffolk, Winchester—are everything Cade accuses the nobility of being. Moreover, after the grisly murder of Gloucester, can it be thought that only the common people have the capacity for lawless violence? Though Cade is killed in this play, civil war does not vanish with his death, because the ambition and selfishness of these English nobles have not been contained. York still lives, and it will take Shakespeare another two plays to trace the destructive legacy of his ambition.

Some critics have suggested that given the venality of many of the nobles and the cruelty and hypocrisy of Cade, the play privileges the point of view of Alexander Iden, the landowning gentleman who kills Cade. Iden is well worth scrutiny. A property holder, a man who has built a brick wall around his garden, Iden also has charitable impulses. He "sends the poor well pleasèd from [his] gate" and at first does not want to fight with Cade, a "poor famished man" (4.10.21, 41). Does Iden's garden represent an English Eden? Shakespeare sounds several evocative notes through the creation of this figure. Iden conjures up the virtues of rural England as opposed to the values of the corrupt court or the rampaging urban artisans. And he anticipates the emergence of the bourgeois property holder as the backbone of the nation. But Iden is not the dominant force in the political landscape of the play, nor, despite his seeming independence, are his loyalties in doubt. When he learns who the poor famished man really is, Iden is glad to have killed Cade; and when he delivers the rebel's head to King Henry, he receives a knighthood in return. The independent property holder is certainly the King's man and no friend to those who would level the social order and make property common. How deeply Shakespeare—the man from rural Stratford who eventually became a major property holder in that town—idealized Iden, or replicated his political stance, is a matter for debate.

JEAN E. HOWARD

SELECTED BIBLIOGRAPHY

Cartelli, Thomas. "Suffolk and the Pirates: Disordered Relations in Shakespeare's 2 Henry VI." A Companion to Shakespeare's Works: The Histories. Ed. Richard Dutton and Jean E. Howard. Oxford: Blackwell, 2003. 325–43. Argues that aristocratic pride and self-interest, especially as embodied in the Duke of York and in Suffolk, are resisted by the Cade rebels and by the men who kill Suffolk. In the process, the Lieutenant and Whitmore, unlike Cade, become the idealized voice of the Commons.

Chartier, Roger. "Jack Cade, the Skin of a Dead Lamb, and the Hatred for Writing." Shakespeare Studies 34 (2006): 77–89. Examines Cade's preference, one shared by many medieval and early modern people, for the authority of the living voice over that of the written text.

Fitter, Chris. Radical Shakespeare: Politics and Stagecraft in the Early Career. London: Routledge, 2012. Argues for Shakespeare's radical political commitments as indicated in 2 Henry VI by how he handles the Jack Cade plot and alludes to ideas and practices favoring lower-class resistance to monarchical tyranny and aristocratic abuses.

Greenblatt, Stephen. "Murdering Peasants: Status, Genre, and the Representation of Rebellion." Representations 1 (1983): 1–29. Explores the difficulties of representing early modern popular insurrection and the ideological instability of such representations.

Hampton-Reeves, Stuart, and Carol Chillington Rutter. Shakespeare in Performance: The Henry VI Plays. Manchester: Manchester UP, 2006. Examines the production history of the Henry VI plays by the Royal Shakespeare Company and other companies since the 1950s.

Helgerson, Richard. "Staging Exclusion." *Forms of Nationhood: The Elizabethan Writing of England*. Chicago: U of Chicago P, 1992. 195–245. Argues that through a predominantly negative representation of Cade and through a focus on the consolidation of monarchical rule, Shakespeare was instrumental in disrupting the traditional link between the theater and popular revolt.

Howard, Jean E., and Phyllis Rackin. "*Henry VI, Part II*." *Engendering a Nation: A Feminist Account of Shakespeare's English Histories*. London: Routledge, 1997. 65–82. Examines the relationship between political disorder and gender disorder, with special attention paid to Queen Margaret, King Henry, Eleanor Cobham, and Jack Cade.

Hutson, Lorna. "Noises Off: Participatory Justice in *2 Henry VI*." *The Law in Shakespeare*. Ed. Constance Jordan and Karen Cunningham. Houndmills, Basingstoke, Hampshire: Palgrave Macmillan, 2007. 143–66. Argues that by the sixteenth century, English law depended both on increased recourse to forensic evidence and on continuing emphasis on the people's role in initiating and adjudicating prosecutions. Examines Warwick's speech over Duke Humphrey's body and the Commons' response as a utopian image of this process.

Knowles, Ronald. "The Farce of History: Miracle, Combat, and Rebellion in *2 Henry VI*." *Yearbook of English Studies* 21 (1991): 168–86. Examines the dramatic techniques of ironic juxtaposition, mirroring, and parody through which Shakespeare staged historical events and processes.

Patterson, Annabel. "The Peasant's Toe: Popular Culture and Popular Pressure." *Shakespeare and the Popular Voice*. Cambridge, MA: Blackwell, 1989. 32–51. Argues that there was a cultural tradition of popular protest in Shakespeare's England to which his representation of Jack Cade is indebted.

FILM

Henry VI, Part Two. 1983. Dir. Jane Howell. UK/USA. 211 mins. Sumptuously costumed but tepid BBC-TV production with Julia Foster as Margaret, David Burke as Gloucester, Peter Benson as Henry VI, and Trevor Peacock as Cade.

TEXTUAL INTRODUCTION

The First Folio of 1623 neatly records among its histories three parts of *Henry VI* running continuously. The full title of the middle play of the three is *The Second Part of Henry the Sixth, with the Death of the Good Duke Humphrey*. Although the Folio is presented by its compilers as authoritative, this was not the only version of the play we now call *2 Henry VI* in circulation in early modern England. In 1594, a Quarto version of the play had been printed that was around one-third shorter than the one in the Folio. This Quarto featured a more expansive title:

> *The First part of the Contention betwixt the two Famous Houses of York and Lancaster, with the Death of the good Duke Humphrey*

The play was published again in Quarto format in 1600 and then again in 1619, this time twinned with *The True Tragedy of Richard Duke of York and the Death of Good King Henry the Sixth* (now known as *3 Henry VI*) in a two-play volume titled *The Whole Contention betweene the two Famous Houses, Lancaster and Yorke, With the Tragical ends of the good Duke Humfrey, Richard Duke of York, and King Henry the Sixth*.

As this complicated textual history suggests, the relationship between the three parts of *Henry VI* is far less straightforward than the tidy sequence suggested by the Folio's list of contents. Scholars are divided over the extent of Shakespeare's authorship of *1 Henry VI* and its chronological relationship to *2* and *3 Henry VI*, with some believing that it postdates them (as the 1594 Quarto title suggests). A later date of composition for *1 Henry VI* would make *2 Henry VI* one of Shakespeare's very first plays for the professional stage.

The pronounced divergence in title and length between the two primary versions—the 1623 Folio (F) and the 1594 Quarto (Q)—of 2 *Henry VI* also suggests deeper differences. They too have vexed scholars, and a number of theories have been presented to explain the relationship between the two versions. It is generally agreed that the shorter Q is more obviously oriented toward performance. Often, its stage directions are far more elaborate and precise than those of the Folio, which can be rather vague—that *"Bolingbroke or Southwell"* reads the conjuring words in F 1.4; or that Cade enters in F 4.2 *"with infinite numbers."* This led scholars in the 1920s to make the influential suggestion that the Folio text (the version followed by most modern editions) was based on Shakespeare's own manuscript; by contrast, the Quarto was considered to be a faulty version of the Folio text, one perhaps based on a theatrical promptbook prepared for either a London or a touring performance, or on an incomplete memorial reconstruction of the play by one player or a group of players.

Yet there are differences between the Folio and the Quarto that are not easily explained by poor pirated reconstruction or the difference between theatrical promptbook and author's manuscript. The sequence of dramatic events is often more successful in the Quarto—for example, the shift of the reading of the Spirit's prophecies from 1.4.58–68 (F) to 2.1.145–55 (Q), or of Richard's battle with Somerset from before 5.2.65 (F) to the beginning of 5.2 (Q). The expansion of certain scenes (Q 4.7), the contraction of others (Q 3.2), and the subtle but distinct difference in Queen Margaret's role between the two versions also suggest deliberate crafting rather than the haphazard distortions one would associate with faulty memory.

In the past few decades, a shift in editorial approaches to Shakespeare has had important implications for the two versions of 2 *Henry VI*. There is increased awareness of the role of the playing company (actors, prompters) as well as the printing house (scribes, compositors) and the censor in creating the playtexts that remain, each of which complicates our notion of what is "Shakespearean." In the case of 2 *Henry VI*, the nature of the differences between the two versions requires that they be treated as distinct, coherent entities with divergent investments. This shift in editorial emphasis does not remove the possibility that the Quarto is in some part the product of memorial reconstruction, but it does suggest that Folio and Quarto are the products of different kinds of revision, with different and equally "authentic" histories. This realization undermines the earlier editorial impulse to conflate—to merge two versions of a given play into one—in an attempt to reach a "pure" Shakespearean original. Neither of the two texts of 2 *Henry VI* is necessarily "faulty."

In offering texts of both Folio and Quarto, *The Norton Shakespeare* provides an opportunity to read each individually and gain a sense of the differences as well as the similarities between the two. They have been approached as separate plays, and although the more elaborate stage directions of the Quarto have occasionally been used to explain the staging of the same scenes in the Folio, the differing order of events and varying length of scenes have been maintained; there has been no attempt to insert elements of one text into the other. The result is two plays, modernized in spelling and punctuation in line with *The Norton Shakespeare* editorial principles, that not only offer insights into an extraordinary dramatic creation—probably one of Shakespeare's first—but also reveal the forces bearing on playtexts as they took different courses from author to stage and into print.

MATTHEW DIMMOCK

TEXTUAL BIBLIOGRAPHY

Urkowitz, Steven. "'If I Mistake in Those Foundations Which I Build Upon': Alexander's Textual Analysis of *Henry VI* 2 and 3." *English Literary Renaissance* 18.2 (1998): 230–56.

PERFORMANCE NOTE

Seven star turns, nearly seventy speaking roles, and some striking contributions from otherwise minor characters make 2 *Henry VI* an inviting, demanding ensemble piece. Augmenting its casting challenges are stark transitions in tone and subject, from the political conspiring that debases Humphrey and Eleanor, to the carnival atmosphere of Cade's rebellion, to the martial tenor preceding the battle at St Albans. Productions often emphasize parallels implicit in the trifold structure (Humphrey's fall / Cade's rise; Cade's fall / York's rise) while striving to keep Henry, Margaret, and Suffolk from getting lodged in the background. According to the director's aim to engage the audience's sense of justice or relief as York moves to supplant Henry, York's soliloquies can reveal arrogant self-interest or patriotism, a traitor's cunning or a competent ruler's intelligence, while Henry's troubles at court can result from abundance of mercy or mere ineptitude. Margaret can weaken Henry's legitimacy by appearing too readily at ease in his intrigue-riddled court and flaunting her appetite for Suffolk before a naïve king, or she can remain fiercely loyal to her husband's cause while taking a more platonic refuge with Suffolk on account of Henry's religious devotion.

Any production's treatment of the commoners involves some interesting choices. Cade can be a socialist crusader or a monster, engaging his followers in valid rebellion or mindless anarchy. Some directors downplay the commoners' participation and relevance, particularly when adapting the trilogy in two parts; others enhance it by conceiving the audience as an interested party, sympathetic to or complicit in the commoners' impoverishment. Accordingly, the commoners might urge audiences at the play's opening/intermission to voice their dissent or else regard them as entitled oppressors. Other considerations in performance include the authenticity of the prophecies in 1.4, how persuasive York's arguments about lineage are in 2.2, and whether Gloucester's murder (and various other beheadings) occurs onstage or off.

Brett Gamboa

The Second Part of Henry the Sixth, with the Death of the Good Duke Humphrey

[THE PERSONS OF THE PLAY

KING HENRY the Sixth
QUEEN MARGARET
Humphrey, Duke of GLOUCESTER
Dame ELEANOR, Duchess of Gloucester
CARDINAL Beaufort, Bishop of Winchester
Marquess of SUFFOLK
Duke of SOMERSET
Duke of BUCKINGHAM
CLIFFORD
YOUNG CLIFFORD
VAUX

Richard, Duke of YORK
EDWARD, Earl of March, eldest son to York
RICHARD, son to York
Earl of SALISBURY
Earl of WARWICK, son to Salisbury

PETITIONERS
PETER Thump, the Armorer's man
Thomas HORNER, Armorer
PRENTICES
NEIGHBORS

Sir John HUME
MARGERY JORDAN, a witch
Roger BOLINGBROKE, a conjurer
SPIRIT

Sander SIMPCOX, a poor man
His WIFE
MAYOR of St Albans
BEADLE
TOWNSMEN

Sir John STANLEY
Sheriff and Officers of London
HERALD
Two MURDERERS
COMMONS

LIEUTENANT
MASTER
Master's MATE

Walter WHITMORE
Two GENTLEMEN, prisoners

Two REBELS
Jack CADE
DICK, a butcher
Smith, a WEAVER
SAWYER
MICHAEL
CLERK of Chartham
Sir Humphrey STAFFORD
William, BROTHER to Stafford
Lord SAYE
Lord SCALES
Matthew Gough
Alexander IDEN

MESSENGERS
POST
Citizens of London
Attendants, Falconers, Servants, Soldiers]

1.1 (Q 1.1)

Flourish° of trumpets, then hautboys.° Enter   *Fanfare / oboes*
KING HENRY, *Duke Humphrey [of* GLOUCESTER*],*
SALISBURY *[and]* WARWICK, *and [*CARDINAL*]*
Beaufort on the one side; QUEEN MARGARET,
SUFFOLK, *[and]* YORK, SOMERSET, *and* BUCKINGHAM
on the other.[1]

SUFFOLK *[kneeling]*   As by your high imperial majesty
  I had in charge° at my depart° for France   *was charged / departure*
  As procurator° to your excellence   *deputy*
  To marry Princess Margaret for your grace,°   *on your behalf*
5   So in the famous ancient city Tours,
  In presence of the Kings of France and Sicil,[2]
  The Dukes of Orléans, Calabre,° Bretagne, and Alençon,   *Calabria*
  Seven earls, twelve barons, and twenty reverend bishops,
  I have performed my task and was espoused,
10   And humbly now, upon my bended knee,
  In sight of England and her lordly peers,
  Deliver up my title in the Queen
  To your most gracious hands, that are the substance
  Of that great shadow° I did represent: *image (of royalty)*
15   The happiest° gift that ever marquess[3] gave,   *most fortunate; best*
  The fairest queen that ever king received.
KING HENRY   Suffolk, arise. Welcome, Queen Margaret.
  I can express no kinder° sign of love   *more natural*

1.1 Location: The palace, London.
1. TEXTUAL COMMENT Q's stage directions here are slightly different and more elaborate: King Henry enters with Duke Humphrey, Somerset and Buckingham, and Cardinal Beaufort, and at the other door York enters before Queen Margaret and Suffolk, who are then followed by Salisbury and Warwick. Q's directions may derive from a theatrical promptbook.

See Digital Edition TC 1 (Folio edited text).
2. Sicily. Queen Margaret's father, René, Duke of Anjou, was Sicily's king in name only.
3. A nobleman ranking below a duke and above an earl. In *1 Henry VI,* Suffolk holds the rank of earl; here, he appears as a marquess; later in this scene, Henry will make him a duke for his service as royal marriage broker.

Than this kind° kiss. O Lord that lends me life,   *affectionate*
20 Lend me a heart replete° with thankfulness,   *fully provided*
For thou hast given me in this beauteous face
A world of earthly blessings to my soul,
If sympathy° of love unite our thoughts.   *mutual feeling*
QUEEN MARGARET   Great King of England and my gracious
    lord,
25 The mutual conference° that my mind hath had—   *intimate talk*
By day, by night, waking and in my dreams,
In courtly company or at my beads°—   *while praying*
With you, mine alderliefest° sovereign,   *entirely most precious*
Makes me the bolder to salute my king
30 With ruder terms such as my wit affords
And overjoy of heart doth minister.°   *suggest*
KING HENRY   Her sight did ravish, but her grace in speech,
Her words y-clad° with wisdom's majesty,   *clad*
Makes me from wond'ring° fall to weeping joys,   *admiring*
35 Such is the fullness of my heart's content.
Lords, with one cheerful voice welcome my love.
ALL [*kneeling*]   Long live Queen Margaret, England's
    happiness.
QUEEN MARGARET   We thank you all.
        Flourish. [*They all rise.*]
SUFFOLK [*to* GLOUCESTER]   My lord Protector, so it please
    your grace,
40 Here are the articles of contracted peace
Between our sovereign and the French King Charles
For eighteen months concluded by consent.
GLOUCESTER [*reads*]   "*Imprimis:*° It is agreed between the   *First*
French King Charles and William de la Pole, Marquess of
45 Suffolk, ambassador for Henry, King of England, that the
said Henry shall espouse the Lady Margaret, daughter unto
René, King of Naples, Sicilia, and Jerusalem, and crown her
Queen of England ere the thirtieth of May next ensuing.
    Item:° That the duchy of Anjou and the county of Maine   *Likewise*
50 shall be released and delivered to the King her father—"
    [GLOUCESTER *lets the paper fall.*]
KING HENRY   Uncle, how now?
GLOUCESTER   Pardon me, gracious lord.
Some sudden qualm° hath struck me at the heart   *illness; fear*
And dimmed mine eyes that I can read no further.
KING HENRY   Uncle of Winchester, I pray read on.
55 CARDINAL [*reads*]   "*Item:* It is further agreed between them
that the duchies of Anjou and Maine shall be released and
delivered over to the King her father, and she sent over of°   *at*
the King of England's own proper° cost and charges, with-   *personal*
out having any dowry."
60 KING HENRY   They please us well. [*to* SUFFOLK] Lord
    Marquess, kneel down.
We here create thee the first Duke of Suffolk
And gird thee with the sword. —Cousin⁴ of York,
We here discharge your grace from being regent

---

4. A form of address customarily used by English monarchs to nobles.

I'th' parts° of France till term of eighteen months   *(English) regions*
65   Be full° expired. —Thanks, uncle Winchester,   *fully*
    Gloucester, York, Buckingham, Somerset,
    Salisbury, and Warwick;
    We thank you all for this great favor done
    In entertainment° to my princely Queen.   *welcome*
70   Come, let us in, and with all speed provide
    To see her coronation be performed.

               Exeunt KING HENRY, QUEEN MARGARET,
                and SUFFOLK. *The rest remain.*

GLOUCESTER   Brave peers of England, pillars of the state,
    To you Duke Humphrey must unload his grief,
    Your grief, the common grief of all the land.
75   What, did my brother Henry° spend his youth,   *Henry V*
    His valor, coin, and people in the wars;
    Did he so often lodge in open field
    In winter's cold and summer's parching heat,
    To conquer France, his true inheritance;[5]
80   And did my brother Bedford toil his wits
    To keep by policy° what Henry got?   *political skill*
    Have you yourselves, Somerset, Buckingham,
    Brave York, Salisbury, and victorious Warwick,
    Received deep scars in France and Normandy;
85   Or hath mine uncle Beaufort and myself,
    With all the learned Council of the realm,
    Studied so long, sat in the Council House
    Early and late, debating to and fro
    How France and Frenchmen might be kept in awe;°   *obedience*
90   And hath his highness in his infancy
    Crownèd in Paris in despite of foes—
    And shall these labors and these honors die?
    Shall Henry's conquest, Bedford's vigilance,
    Your deeds of war, and all our counsel die?
95   O peers of England, shameful is this league,
    Fatal this marriage, canceling your fame,
    Blotting your names from books of memory,
    Razing the characters° of your renown,   *Erasing the records*
    Defacing monuments of conquered France,
100   Undoing all, as° all had never been.   *as though*
CARDINAL   Nephew, what means this passionate discourse,
    This peroration° with such circumstance?[6]   *rhetorical speech*
    For France, 'tis ours, and we will keep it still.°   *always*
GLOUCESTER   Ay, uncle, we will keep it if we can;
105   But now it is impossible we should.
    Suffolk, the new-made duke that rules the roost,
    Hath given the duchy of Anjou and Maine
    Unto the poor King René, whose large style°   *exalted title*
    Agrees not with the leanness of his purse.
110 SALISBURY   Now, by the death of Him that died for all,[7]
    These counties were the keys of Normandy.
    But wherefore weeps Warwick, my valiant son?

5. England laid claim to France throughout the four-   1.1.85–90.
teenth century, and Henry V won the title "heir of   6. Such long-winded formality; so many details.
France" with the Treaty of Troyes in 1420. See *Henry V*   7. An oath equivalent to "by Christ's death."

WARWICK   For grief that they are past recovery.
For were there hope to conquer them again,
115   My sword should shed hot blood, mine eyes no tears.
Anjou and Maine? Myself did win them both—
Those provinces these arms of mine did conquer—
And are the cities that I got with wounds
Delivered up again with peaceful words?
120   *Mort Dieu!*[8]

YORK   For Suffolk's Duke, may he be suffocate,°   *choked (a pun)*
That dims the honor of this warlike isle!
France should have torn and rent my very heart
Before I would have yielded to this league.
125   I never read but° England's kings have had   *I have always read that*
Large sums of gold and dowries with their wives,
And our King Henry gives away his own
To match with° her that brings no vantages.°   *wed / profits (dowry)*

GLOUCESTER   A proper jest, and never heard before,
130   That Suffolk should demand a whole fifteenth[9]
For costs and charges in transporting her!
She should have stayed in France and starved in France
Before—

CARDINAL   My lord of Gloucester, now ye grow too hot;
135   It was the pleasure of my lord the King.

GLOUCESTER   My lord of Winchester, I know your mind.
'Tis not my speeches that you do mislike
But 'tis my presence that doth trouble ye.
Rancor will out. Proud prelate, in thy face
140   I see thy fury. If I longer stay
We shall begin our ancient bickerings.
—Lordings,° farewell, and say when I am gone   *My lords*
I prophesied France will be lost ere long.   *Exit.*

CARDINAL   So, there goes our Protector in a rage.
145   'Tis known to you he is mine enemy;
Nay, more, an enemy unto you all
And no great friend, I fear me, to the King.
Consider, lords, he is the next of blood[1]
And heir apparent to the English crown.
150   Had Henry got an empire by his marriage
And all the wealthy kingdoms of the west,[2]
There's reason he° should be displeased at it.   *(Gloucester)*
Look to it, lords: let not his smoothing° words   *flattering*
Bewitch your hearts. Be wise and circumspect.
155   What though the common people favor him,
Calling him "Humphrey, the good Duke of Gloucester,"
Clapping their hands and crying with loud voice
"Jesu maintain your royal excellence,"
With "God preserve the good Duke Humphrey!"
160   I fear me, lords, for all this flattering gloss°   *fair appearance*
He will be found a dangerous Protector.

BUCKINGHAM   Why should he, then, protect our sovereign,

---

8. God's death (French oath).
9. A tax of one-fifteenth of the value of personal
property.
1. Because Henry VI did not yet have children, the

heir to the throne was Gloucester, his father's brother.
2. An anachronistic reference to the European conquest of the Americas.

He being of age[3] to govern of himself?
—Cousin of Somerset, join you with me
165 And altogether with the Duke of Suffolk;
We'll quickly hoist° Duke Humphrey from his seat.   *remove*
CARDINAL   This weighty business will not brook° delay.   *permit*
I'll to the Duke of Suffolk presently.°   *Exit.*   *immediately*
SOMERSET   Cousin of Buckingham, though Humphrey's
pride
170 And greatness of his place be grief to us,
Yet let us watch the haughty Cardinal;
His insolence is more intolerable
Than all the princes' in the land beside.
If Gloucester be displaced, he'll be Protector.
175 BUCKINGHAM   Or° thou or I, Somerset, will be Protectors,   *Either*
Despite Duke Humphrey or the Cardinal.
                         Exeunt BUCKINGHAM *and* SOMERSET.
SALISBURY   Pride went before, ambition follows him.[4]
While these do labor for their own preferment°   *advancement*
Behooves it us to labor for the realm.
180 I never saw but Humphrey, Duke of Gloucester,
Did bear him like a noble gentleman.
Oft have I seen the haughty Cardinal,
More like a soldier than a man o'th' church,
As stout° and proud as° he were lord of all,   *arrogant / as if*
185 Swear like a ruffian and demean° himself   *conduct*
Unlike the ruler of a commonweal.
—Warwick, my son, the comfort of my age,
Thy deeds, thy plainness,° and thy housekeeping°   *honesty / hospitality*
Hath won the greatest favor of the commons
190 Excepting none but good Duke Humphrey.
—And, brother York,[5] thy acts in Ireland,
In bringing them to civil discipline,°   *civilized order*
Thy late exploits done in the heart of France
When thou wert regent for our sovereign,
195 Have made thee feared and honored of the people.
Join we together for the public good
In what we can to bridle° and suppress   *restrain*
The pride of Suffolk and the Cardinal
With Somerset's and Buckingham's ambition
200 And, as we may, cherish° Duke Humphrey's deeds   *encourage*
While they do tend° the profit of the land.   *promote*
WARWICK   So God help Warwick, as he loves the land
And common profit of his country.
YORK   And so says York, [*aside*] for he hath greatest cause.
205 SALISBURY   Then let's make haste away and look unto the
main.[6]
WARWICK   "Unto the main"? O father, Maine is lost—
That Maine, which by main° force Warwick did win   *overwhelming*

---

3. Henry VI being old enough. At the time represented in this scene, the historical King was twenty-four years old and Gloucester was no longer Protector. Shakespeare here as elsewhere alters his sources.
4. A variation on the proverb "Pride goes before and shame comes after." Salisbury seems to refer to the Cardinal, who exited first, as "pride" and to Buckingham and Somerset as "ambition."
5. York was actually Salisbury's brother-in-law, having married Salisbury's sister Cicely.
6. And consider the principal matter at stake. A gambling term, with subsequent puns on the several meanings of "main," including wordplay on "Maine," a French province lost in Suffolk's treaty.

And would have kept so long as breath did last!
"Main chance," father, you meant, but I meant Maine,
210 Which I will win from France or else be slain.

Exeunt WARWICK *and* SALISBURY.

YORK Anjou and Maine are given to the French,
Paris is lost, the state of Normandy
Stands on a tickle° point now they are gone;   an unstable
Suffolk concluded on the articles,
215 The peers agreed, and Henry was well pleased
To change two dukedoms for a duke's fair daughter.
I cannot blame them all: what is't to them?
'Tis thine[7] they give away and not their own.
Pirates may make cheap pennyworths of° their pillage   sell at a low price
220 And purchase friends and give to courtesans,°   prostitutes
Still° reveling like lords till all be gone,   Continually
While as the silly° owner of the goods   While the helpless
Weeps over them and wrings his hapless° hands   unlucky
And shakes his head and trembling stands aloof
225 While all is shared and all is borne away,
Ready to starve and dare not touch his own.
So York must sit and fret and bite his tongue
While his own lands are bargained for and sold.
Methinks the realms of England, France, and Ireland
230 Bear that proportion° to my flesh and blood   relation
As did the fatal brand Althaea burnt
Unto the prince's heart of Calydon.[8]
Anjou and Maine both given unto the French?
Cold° news for me: for I had hope of France   Unwelcome
235 Even as I have of fertile England's soil.
A day will come when York shall claim his own,
And therefore I will take the Nevilles' parts[9]
And make a show of love to proud Duke Humphrey,
And when I spy advantage,° claim the crown,   opportunity
240 For that's the golden mark° I seek to hit.   target
Nor shall proud Lancaster[1] usurp my right,
Nor hold the scepter in his childish fist,
Nor wear the diadem upon his head,
Whose church-like humors° fits not for a crown.   pious temperament
245 Then, York, be still awhile till time do serve.
Watch° thou, and wake when others be asleep   Stay awake
To pry into the secrets of the state,
Till Henry, surfeiting° in joys of love   sickened from excess
With his new bride and England's dear-bought queen,
250 And Humphrey with the peers be fall'n at jars.°   into contention
Then will I raise aloft the milk-white rose,[2]
With whose sweet smell the air shall be perfumed,
And in my standard° bear the arms of York   military flag
To grapple with the house of Lancaster;

---

7. It is your own (York is addressing himself and referring to his claim to the throne).
8. Althaea, mother of Meleager, Prince of Calydon, was told by the Fates that her son would live only as long as a log burning in the fire at his birth. She snatched the log from the flames; but later, when Meleager killed her brothers, Althaea returned the log to the fire and Meleager's heart stopped beating. See Ovid, *Metamorphoses* 8.
9. And therefore will I ally myself with Salisbury and Warwick.
1. Henry VI was also Duke of Lancaster.
2. The emblem of the Yorkists; the red rose was the Lancastrian emblem.

255 And, force perforce,° I'll make him yield the crown   *by violent coercion*
Whose bookish rule hath pulled fair England down.   *Exit.*

1.2 (Q 1.2)

Enter Duke Humphrey [of GLOUCESTER] *and his
wife,* ELEANOR.

ELEANOR   Why droops my lord like over-ripened corn°   *grain*
Hanging the head at Ceres' plenteous load?[1]
Why doth the great Duke Humphrey knit his brows
As frowning at the favors of the world?
5 Why are thine eyes fixed to the sullen earth,
Gazing on that which seems to dim thy sight?
What seest thou there? King Henry's diadem
Enchased° with all the honors of the world?   *Adorned*
If so, gaze on, and grovel on thy face[2]
10 Until thy head be circled with the same.
Put forth thy hand; reach at the glorious gold.
What, is't too short? I'll lengthen it with mine
And, having both together heaved° it up,   *raised*
We'll both together lift our heads to heaven
15 And never more abase our sight so low
As to vouchsafe° one glance unto the ground.   *grant*
GLOUCESTER   O Nell, sweet Nell, if thou dost love thy lord,
Banish the canker° of ambitious thoughts.   *ulcer*
And may that thought, when I imagine ill
20 Against my king and nephew, virtuous Henry,
Be my last breathing in this mortal world.
My troublous dreams this night° doth make me sad.   *this past night*
ELEANOR   What dreamed my lord? Tell me and I'll requite it
With sweet rehearsal° of my morning's dream.[3]   *recital*
25 GLOUCESTER   Methought this staff, mine office-badge° in   *symbol of my position*
court,
Was broke in twain—by whom, I have forgot,
But, as I think, it was by th' Cardinal—
And on the pieces of the broken wand
Were placed the heads of Edmund, Duke of Somerset,
30 And William de la Pole, first Duke of Suffolk.
This was my dream: what it doth bode God knows.
ELEANOR   Tut, this was nothing but an argument°   *a proof*
That he that breaks a stick of Gloucester's grove
Shall lose his head for his presumption.
35 But list° to me, my Humphrey, my sweet duke: *listen*
Methought I sat in seat of majesty
In the cathedral church of Westminster
And in that chair° where kings and queens were crowned,   *throne*
Where Henry and Dame Margaret kneeled to me
40 And on my head did set the diadem.
GLOUCESTER   Nay, Eleanor, then must I chide outright.
Presumptuous dame, ill-nurtured° Eleanor,   *ill-trained*
Art thou not second woman in the realm

1.2 Location: The Duke of Gloucester's house, London.
1. At the rich harvest of Ceres (the Roman goddess of agriculture and the harvest).
2. Crawl on the ground (perhaps to seek supernatural aid).
3. Morning dreams were popularly believed to be true.

And the Protector's wife, beloved of him?
45 Hast thou not worldly pleasure at command
Above the reach or compass of thy thought?
And wilt thou still be hammering° treachery   *devising*
To tumble down thy husband and thyself
From top of honor to disgrace's feet?
50 Away from me and let me hear no more.
ELEANOR   What, what, my lord? Are you so choleric°   *hot-tempered*
With Eleanor for telling but her dream?
Next time I'll keep my dreams unto myself
And not be checked.°   *rebuked*
55 GLOUCESTER   Nay, be not angry; I am pleased again.
       Enter MESSENGER.
MESSENGER   My lord Protector, 'tis his highness' pleasure
You do prepare to ride unto St Albans,
Whereas° the King and Queen do mean to hawk.   *Where*
GLOUCESTER   I go. —Come, Nell, thou wilt ride with us?
60 ELEANOR   Yes, my good lord, I'll follow presently.°   *immediately*
       Exeunt Duke Humphrey [of GLOUCESTER
                              and MESSENGER].
Follow I must; I cannot go before
While Gloucester bears this base° and humble mind.   *servile*
Were I a man, a duke and next of blood,
I would remove these tedious stumbling blocks
65 And smooth my way upon their headless necks
And, being a woman, I will not be slack
To play my part in Fortune's pageant.[4]
—Where are you there? Sir John![5] Nay, fear not, man;
We are alone: here's none but thee and I.
       Enter [Sir John] HUME.
70 HUME   Jesus preserve your royal majesty.
ELEANOR   What say'st thou? "Majesty"? I am but "grace."[6]
HUME   But by the grace of God and Hume's advice
Your grace's title shall be multiplied.
ELEANOR   What say'st thou, man? Hast thou as yet conferred
75 With Margery Jordan, the cunning witch,[7]
With Roger Bolingbroke, the conjurer?
And will they undertake to do me good?
HUME   This they have promised to show your highness:
A spirit, raised from depth of underground,
80 That shall make answer to such questions
As by your grace shall be propounded him.
ELEANOR   It is enough; I'll think upon the questions.
When from St Albans we do make return
We'll see these things effected to the full.
85 Here, Hume, take this reward; make merry, man,
With thy confederates in this weighty cause.   *Exit.*
HUME   Hume must make merry with the Duchess' gold;

---

4. In Roman mythology, the goddess Fortune symbolized the element of chance in human life and was often depicted with a rudder (as the pilot of destiny), wings, or a wheel. Here, Fortune is imagined as directing a medieval play ("pageant") or leading a ceremonial procession.

5. Priests were commonly addressed as "sir."
6. The appropriate title for a duchess.
7. Cunning women, sometimes prosecuted for witchcraft, were familiar village figures who made a living by telling fortunes, healing sicknesses, making love potions, and finding lost objects.

Marry,[8] and shall. But how now, Sir John Hume?
Seal up your lips and give no words but mum;
90 The business asketh silent secrecy.
Dame Eleanor gives gold to bring the witch:
Gold cannot come amiss, were she a devil.
Yet have I gold flies from another coast[9]—
I dare not say from the rich Cardinal
95 And from the great and new-made Duke of Suffolk,
Yet I do find it so; for, to be plain,
They, knowing Dame Eleanor's aspiring humor,°   *ambitious nature*
Have hired me to undermine the Duchess
And buzz° these conjurations in her brain.   *whisper*
100 They say, "A crafty knave does need no broker,"°   *middleman; agent*
Yet am I Suffolk and the Cardinal's broker.
Hume, if you take not heed, you shall go near
To call them both a pair of crafty knaves.
Well, so it stands; and thus I fear at last
105 Hume's knavery will be the Duchess' wrack,°   *ruin*
And her attainder° will be Humphrey's fall.   *conviction*
Sort° how it will, I shall have gold for all.   *Exit.*   *Turn out*

1.3 (Q 1.3)

Enter three or four PETITIONERS, [PETER] *the
Armorer's man° being one.*   *apprentice*

FIRST PETITIONER My masters, let's stand close. My lord Protector will come this way by and by, and then we may deliver
our supplications in the quill.°   *as a group*
SECOND PETITIONER Marry, the Lord protect him, for he's a
5 good man. Jesu bless him.
Enter SUFFOLK *and* QUEEN MARGARET.
FIRST PETITIONER Here 'a° comes, methinks, and the Queen   *he*
with him. I'll be the first, sure.[1]
SECOND PETITIONER Come back, fool. This is the Duke of
Suffolk, and not my lord Protector.
10 SUFFOLK How now, fellow?[2] Wouldst anything with me?
FIRST PETITIONER I pray, my lord, pardon me; I took ye for my
lord Protector.
QUEEN MARGARET "To my lord Protector"? Are your supplications to his lordship? Let me see them. [*She takes the peti-*
15 *tion of* FIRST PETITIONER.] What is thine?
FIRST PETITIONER Mine is, an't° please your grace, against   *if it*
John Goodman, my lord Cardinal's man, for keeping my
house and lands and wife and all from me.
SUFFOLK Thy wife too? That's some wrong indeed. [*to* SECOND
20 PETITIONER] What's yours? What's here? [*He reads.*] "Against
the Duke of Suffolk, for enclosing the commons[3] of Melford." How now, sir knave?

---

8. By the Virgin Mary (a mild oath).
9. I have gold that comes from another quarter.
1.3 Location: The palace, London.
1. In F, these lines are assigned to Peter, but lines
11–12 suggest they are spoken by the First Petitioner,
who here pushes himself forward to get the attention
of the Queen and Suffolk (whom he believes to be
Gloucester).

2. A common form of address to a social inferior.
3. Fencing in for private use land once used by the
entire community. The practice of enclosure, which
benefited landowners while forcing into poverty the
lower classes who had farmed the land, was a chronic
source of unrest in many regions in early modern
England.

SECOND PETITIONER Alas, sir, I am but a poor petitioner of
    our whole township.

25 PETER [*offering his petition*] Against my master Thomas Horner,
    for saying that the Duke of York was rightful heir to the
    crown.

QUEEN MARGARET What say'st thou? Did the Duke of York
    say he was rightful heir to the crown?

30 PETER That my mistress was? No, forsooth, my master said
    that he was, and that the King was an usurper.

SUFFOLK —Who is there?
        Enter a SERVANT.

Take this fellow in, and send for his master with a pursui-
vant° presently. [*to* PETER] We'll hear more of your matter   *an officer*
35 before the King.   *Exit.*

QUEEN MARGARET And as for you that love to be protected
    Under the wings of our Protector's grace,
    Begin your suits anew, and sue to him.
        [*She*] *tear[s] the supplication.*[4]
    Away, base cullions![5] —Suffolk, let them go.

40 ALL PETITIONERS Come, let's be gone.   *Exeunt.*

QUEEN MARGARET My lord of Suffolk, say, is this the guise,°   *custom*
    Is this the fashions, in the court of England?
    Is this the government of Britain's isle
    And this the royalty of Albion's° king?   *England's*
45 What, shall King Henry be a pupil still
    Under the surly Gloucester's governance?
    Am I a queen in title and in style°   *form of address*
    And must be made a subject to a duke?
    I tell thee, Pole, when in the city Tours
50 Thou ran'st a tilt[6] in honor of my love
    And stol'st away the ladies' hearts of France,
    I thought King Henry had resembled thee
    In courage, courtship,° and proportion,[7]   *courtly manners*
    But all his mind is bent to holiness
55 To number Ave-Maries on his beads.[8]
    His champions are the prophets and apostles,[9]
    His weapons holy saws° of sacred writ,   *sayings*
    His study is his tilt-yard,° and his loves   *jousting arena*
    Are brazen images of canonizèd saints.
60 I would the college of the cardinals
    Would choose him Pope and carry him to Rome
    And set the triple crown° upon his head: *papal crown*
    That were a state fit for his holiness.

SUFFOLK Madam, be patient. As I was cause
65 Your highness came to England, so will I
    In England work your grace's full content.

QUEEN MARGARET Beside the haughty° Protector have we   *arrogant*
    Beaufort

---

4. In Q, Suffolk is the one who "tears the papers."
This is one of the places where F gives more initiative
to Margaret than does Q.
5. Lowborn rascals. "Cullion" comes from the Italian word *coglioni*, meaning "testicles."
6. You took part in a jousting tournament.
7. Physical grace; physique.
8. Referring to a Roman Catholic devotion in which a

string of beads (a rosary) is used to keep track of
prayers said in a particular sequence. Among the
prayers are "Ave Maria," or "Hail Mary," addressed to
the Virgin Mary.
9. A champion stood in for the king at jousts and
tournaments. Margaret scornfully suggests that
Henry VI makes holy men rather than real warriors
his champions.

The imperious churchman, Somerset, Buckingham,
And grumbling York; and not the least of these
70 But can do more in England than the King.
SUFFOLK   And he of these that can do most of all
Cannot do more in England than the Nevilles:
Salisbury and Warwick are no simple peers.
QUEEN MARGARET   Not all these lords do vex me half so much
75 As that proud dame, the Lord Protector's wife.
She sweeps it through the court with troops of ladies
More like an empress than Duke Humphrey's wife:
Strangers in court do take her for the Queen.
She bears a duke's revenues on her back,°   *wears costly clothing*
80 And in her heart she scorns our poverty.
Shall I not live to be avenged on her?
Contemptuous° base-born callet° as she is,   *Despicable / whore*
She vaunted 'mongst her minions° t'other day   *followers*
The very train of her worst-wearing° gown   *poorest*
85 Was better worth° than all my father's lands   *worth more*
Till Suffolk gave two dukedoms° for his daughter.   *(Maine and Anjou)*
SUFFOLK   Madam, myself have limed a bush[1] for her
And placed a choir of such enticing birds
That she will light° to listen to the lays°   *perch / songs*
90 And never mount to trouble you again.
So let her rest; and, madam, list to me
For I am bold to counsel you in this:
Although we fancy not the Cardinal
Yet must we join with him and with the lords
95 Till we have brought Duke Humphrey in disgrace.
As for the Duke of York, this late complaint[2]
Will make but little for his benefit.
So one by one we'll weed them all at last
And you yourself shall steer the happy helm.
     Sound a sennet.° Enter KING HENRY, *Duke Humphrey*   *trumpet call*
     [*of* GLOUCESTER], CARDINAL, BUCKINGHAM, YORK,
     SALISBURY, WARWICK, *and* ELEANOR.
100 KING HENRY   For my part, noble lords, I care not which:
Or° Somerset or York, all's one to me.   *Either*
YORK   If York have ill demeaned° himself in France,   *conducted*
Then let him be denied the regentship.
SOMERSET   If Somerset be unworthy of the place,
105 Let York be regent; I will yield to him.
WARWICK   Whether your grace be worthy, yea or no,
Dispute not that; York is the worthier.
CARDINAL   Ambitious Warwick, let thy betters speak.
WARWICK   The Cardinal's not my better in the field.°   *in battle*
110 BUCKINGHAM   All in this presence are thy betters, Warwick.
WARWICK   Warwick may live to be the best of all.
SALISBURY   Peace, son. —And show some reason,
     Buckingham,
Why Somerset should be preferred in this.
QUEEN MARGARET   Because the King, forsooth,° will have it so.   *truly*

---

1. Have set a trap. Elizabethans caught birds by smearing bushes and twigs with a sticky substance known as
birdlime.

2. This recent complaint. Suffolk means that Peter's
claim against his master casts doubt on York's loyalty
to the King.

115   GLOUCESTER Madam, the King is old enough himself
    To give his censure.° These are no women's matters.   *judgment*
    QUEEN MARGARET If he be old enough, what needs your grace
    To be Protector of his excellence?
    GLOUCESTER Madam, I am Protector of the realm
120   And at his pleasure will resign my place.
    SUFFOLK Resign it, then, and leave thine insolence.
    Since thou wert king—as who is king but thou?—
    The commonwealth hath daily run to wrack,
    The Dauphin[3] hath prevailed beyond the seas,
125   And all the peers and nobles of the realm
    Have been as bondmen to thy sovereignty.
    CARDINAL The commons hast thou racked;° the clergy's bags   *overtaxed*
    Are lank and lean with thy extortions.
    SOMERSET Thy sumptuous buildings[4] and thy wife's attire
130   Have cost a mass of public treasury.
    BUCKINGHAM Thy cruelty in execution
    Upon offenders hath exceeded law
    And left thee to the mercy of the law.
    QUEEN MARGARET Thy sale of offices and towns in France,
135   If they were known, as the suspect° is great,   *suspicion*
    Would make thee quickly hop without thy head.[5]
            Exit Duke Humphrey [of GLOUCESTER*].*
        [QUEEN MARGARET *drops her fan.*][6]
    —Give me my fan. What, minion,° can ye not?   *hussy*
        She gives ELEANOR *a box on the ear.*
    I cry you mercy,° madam. Was it you?   *beg your pardon*
    ELEANOR Was't I? Yea, I it was, proud Frenchwoman!
140   Could I come near your beauty with my nails,
    I could set my ten commandments° in your face.   *(ten fingers)*
    KING HENRY Sweet aunt, be quiet; 'twas against her will.°   *unintentional*
    ELEANOR Against her will, good King? Look to't in time;
    She'll pamper thee and dandle° thee like a baby.   *toy with*
145   Though in this place most masters[7] wear no breeches,
    She shall not strike Dame Eleanor unrevenged!   *Exit.*
    BUCKINGHAM [*aside to* CARDINAL] Lord Cardinal, I will
      follow Eleanor
    And listen after Humphrey how he proceeds.
    She's tickled° now; her fume needs no spurs;   *vexed*
150   She'll gallop far enough to her destruction.   *Exit.*
        Enter Duke Humphrey [of GLOUCESTER*].*
    GLOUCESTER Now, lords, my choler being overblown°   *dispelled*
    With walking once about the quadrangle,
    I come to talk of commonwealth affairs.
    As for your spiteful false objections,
155   Prove them and I lie open to the law.
    But God in mercy so deal with my soul
    As I in duty love my king and country.
    But to the matter that we have in hand:

---

3. "Dauphin" was the title of the oldest son of the French King, but here it refers to the French King himself, Charles VII, and bears witness to the fact that England did not acknowledge Charles's right to the throne.
4. Probably a reference to Greenwich Palace. In

1437, Gloucester obtained a grant to expand the old manor, which he lent to Henry VI and Margaret for their honeymoon.
5. Proverbial expression meaning to be beheaded.
6. In Q, the Queen lets fall a glove, not a fan.
7. The one most in control (the Queen).

—I say, my sovereign, York is meetest° man *the most suitable*
160 To be your regent in the realm of France.
SUFFOLK Before we make election° give me leave *a choice*
To show some reason, of no little force,
That York is most unmeet of any man.
YORK I'll tell thee, Suffolk, why I am unmeet.
165 First, for° I cannot flatter thee in pride; *because*
Next, if I be appointed for the place,
My lord of Somerset will keep me here
Without discharge,° money, or furniture° *payment / equipment*
Till France be won into the Dauphin's hands.
170 Last time I danced attendance on his will[8]
Till Paris was besieged, famished, and lost.
WARWICK That can I witness, and a fouler fact° *deed*
Did never traitor in the land commit.
SUFFOLK Peace, headstrong Warwick.
175 WARWICK Image of pride, why should I hold my peace?
        Enter [HORNER, the] *armorer, and* [PETER,] *his man.*
SUFFOLK Because here is a man accused of treason.
Pray God the Duke of York excuse himself.
YORK Doth any one accuse York for a traitor?
KING HENRY What mean'st thou, Suffolk? Tell me, what are
        these?
180 SUFFOLK Please it your majesty, this is the man
That doth accuse his master of high treason.
His words were these: that Richard, Duke of York,
Was rightful heir unto the English crown,
And that your majesty was an usurper.
185 KING HENRY Say, man, were these thy words?
HORNER An't shall please your majesty, I never said nor thought
any such matter. God is my witness, I am falsely accused by
the villain.
PETER By these ten bones,° my lords, he did speak them to me *(ten fingers)*
190 in the garret one night as we were scouring my lord of York's
armor.
YORK Base dunghill villain and mechanical,° *manual laborer*
I'll have thy head for this thy traitor's speech!
I do beseech your royal majesty,
195 Let him have all the rigor of the law.
HORNER Alas, my lord, hang me if ever I spake the words. My
accuser is my prentice,° and when I did correct him for his *apprentice*
fault the other day he did vow upon his knees he would be
even with me. I have good witness of this; therefore I
200 beseech your majesty, do not cast away° an honest man for a *destroy*
villain's accusation.
KING HENRY Uncle, what shall we say to this in law?
GLOUCESTER This doom,° my lord, if I may judge: *judgment*
Let Somerset be regent o'er the French
205 Because in York this breeds suspicion;[9]
And let these have a day appointed them
For single combat in convenient place,

8. I did as he wished. York refers to events depicted France. See *1 Henry VI* 4.3.9–11.
in *1 Henry VI*, specifically to Somerset's failure to 9. Because this matter casts doubt on York's loyalty.
supply him with reinforcements during the wars in

For he hath witness of his servant's malice.
This is the law and this Duke Humphrey's doom.
210 SOMERSET   I humbly thank your royal majesty.
HORNER   And I accept the combat willingly.
PETER   Alas, my lord, I cannot fight; for God's sake, pity my
    case! The spite of man prevaileth against me. O Lord, have
    mercy upon me; I shall never be able to fight a blow. O Lord,
215 my heart!
GLOUCESTER   Sirrah,[1] or° you must fight or else be hanged.   *either*
KING HENRY   Away with them to prison, and the day
    Of combat shall be the last of the next month.
    Come, Somerset, we'll see thee sent away.

                                          Flourish. Exeunt.

1.4 (Q 1.4)

Enter the witch [MARGERY JORDAN], *the two priests*
[John HUME *and John Southwell], and [Roger]*
BOLINGBROKE.[1]

HUME   Come, my masters. The Duchess, I tell you, expects
    performance of your promises.
BOLINGBROKE   Master Hume, we are therefor° provided. Will   *for that purpose*
    her ladyship behold and hear our exorcisms?°   *conjuring of spirits*
5 HUME   Ay, what else? Fear you not her courage.
BOLINGBROKE   I have heard her reported to be a woman of an
    invincible spirit. But it shall be convenient, Master Hume,
    that you be by her aloft while we be busy below; and so, I
    pray you, go in God's name and leave us.   *Exit* HUME.
10 Mother Jordan, be you prostrate and grovel on the earth;
    John Southwell, read you and let us to our work.
            Enter ELEANOR [*and* HUME] *aloft.*
ELEANOR   Well said, my masters, and welcome all. To this
    gear,° the sooner the better.   *business*
BOLINGBROKE   Patience, good lady; wizards know their times.
15 Deep night, dark night, the silent of the night,
    The time of night when Troy was set on fire,[2]
    The time when screech owls cry and bandogs° howl   *chained watchdogs*
    And spirits walk and ghosts break up° their graves: *burst open*
    That time best fits the work we have in hand.
20 Madam, sit you and fear not; whom we raise
    We will make fast within a hallowed verge.°   *magic circle*
            Here [*they*] *do the ceremonies belonging*[3] *and make*
            the circle. BOLINGBROKE *or Southwell reads, "Conjuro*
            te,"[4] *&c. It thunders and lightens terribly; then the*
            SPIRIT *riseth.*
SPIRIT   *Adsum.*°   *I am here*
MARGERY JORDAN[5]   Asnath!

---

1. A common form of address to a social inferior.
1.4 Location: Gloucester's garden, London.
1. Neither Q nor F names John Southwell as one of
the two priests in this scene, but he is named in dialogue at line 11. Q has Eleanor enter at the beginning
of the scene; F has her enter aloft a few lines into the
scene. After Hume's exit at line 9, he must reenter
aloft at some point to attend Eleanor. This entry is
not marked, but having Hume reenter after line 11
leaves enough time for him to exit the stage at line 9
and make an entrance above.

2. Virgil's *Aeneid*, book 2, describes how the Greeks,
having entered Troy through treachery, set fire to the
ancient city.
3. The rituals necessary (for conjuring spirits).
4. I conjure you (Latin), the beginning of a spell.
5. TEXTUAL COMMENT One of the differences
between F's and Q's versions of this scene is the role
of Margery Jordan, whose prominence in F creates a
connection between women and witchcraft. See Digital Edition TC 2 (Folio edited text).

By the eternal God whose name and power
25   Thou tremblest at, answer that° I shall ask;   *what*
For till thou speak thou shalt not pass from hence.
SPIRIT   Ask what thou wilt—that° I had said and done!   *would that*
BOLINGBROKE [*reading*] "First, of the King: what shall of him
     become?"
SPIRIT   The duke yet lives that Henry shall depose
30   But him outlive and die a violent death.[7]
             [*Southwell writes the answers.*]
BOLINGBROKE "What fates await the Duke of Suffolk?"
SPIRIT   By water shall he die and take his end.
BOLINGBROKE "What shall befall the Duke of Somerset?"
SPIRIT   Let him shun castles.
35   Safer shall he be upon the sandy plains
Than where castles mounted° stand.   *on mountains*
Have done, for more I hardly can endure.
BOLINGBROKE Descend to darkness and the burning lake!
False° fiend, avoid!°   *Treacherous / be gone*
    Thunder and lightning.

                Exit SPIRIT.

    Enter the Duke of YORK *and the Duke of* BUCKINGHAM
    with their guard [*and Sir Humphrey* STAFFORD] *and*
    break in.

40 YORK   Lay hands upon these traitors and their trash!
   —Beldam,° I think we watched you at an inch.°   *Witch / closely*
   [*to* ELEANOR *above*] What, madam, are you there? The
     King and commonweal
   Are deeply indebted for this piece of pains.°   *your trouble*
   My lord Protector will, I doubt it not,
45   See you well guerdoned° for these good deserts.   *rewarded*
ELEANOR   Not half so bad as thine to England's King,
Injurious° Duke, that threatest where's no cause.   *Abusive*
BUCKINGHAM True, madam? None at all? [*He indicates papers.*]
    What call you this?
   —Away with them! Let them be clapped up close°   *imprisoned securely*
50 And kept asunder. —You, madam, shall with us.
   —Stafford, take her to thee.
            [*Exit* STAFFORD *to arrest* ELEANOR *above.*]
   —We'll see your trinkets here all forthcoming.[8]
   —All away.

        Exeunt [JORDAN, *Southwell,* BOLINGBROKE,
        and Guard below; STAFFORD, ELEANOR, *and*
                  HUME *above*].

YORK   Lord Buckingham, methinks you watched her well.
55   A pretty plot,° well chosen to build upon.   *trick; plot of ground*
Now pray, my lord, let's see the devil's writ.
What have we here?

---

6. An anagram of "Sathan," a variant form of "Satan." Demons were supposed to be invoked by anagrams.
7. *The . . . death:* Like many prophecies, this one is ambiguous. The syntax of the first line can mean that there lives a duke whom Henry shall depose or who shall depose Henry. The duke is probably York, who in *3 Henry VI* forces Henry to give the crown to York and his sons rather than to Henry's own son, thus symbolically deposing him. York, however, dies a violent death after the Battle of Wakefield, and Henry outlives him. But Henry also dies a violent death, murdered in the Tower of London by the Duke of York's son, Richard, Duke of Gloucester, who eventually becomes King Richard III.
8. We'll see that your worthless goods (the conjuring paraphernalia) are produced as evidence against you.

(*He reads.*) "The duke yet lives that Henry shall depose,
But him outlive, and die a violent death."
60 Why, this is just°   *precisely*
Aio, Aeacida, Romanos vincere posse.[9]
Well, to the rest—
"'Tell me what fate awaits the Duke of Suffolk?'
By water shall he die and take his end.
65 'What shall betide the Duke of Somerset?'
Let him shun castles;
Safer shall he be upon the sandy plains
Than where castles mounted stand."
—Come, come, my lords, these oracles
70 Are hardly° attained and hardly understood.   *with difficulty*
The King is now in progress towards St Albans;
With him the husband of this lovely lady.
Thither goes these news as fast as horse can carry them:
A sorry breakfast for my lord Protector.
75 BUCKINGHAM Your grace shall give me leave, my lord of York,
To be the post° in hope of his reward.   *messenger*
YORK At your pleasure, my good lord.   [*Exit* BUCKINGHAM.]
                                            —Who's within there, ho?
        Enter a Servingman.
Invite my lords of Salisbury and Warwick
To sup with me tomorrow night. Away.   *Exeunt.*

2.1 (Q 2.1)

        Enter KING HENRY, QUEEN MARGARET,
        Duke Humphrey [of GLOUCESTER], CARDINAL,
        and SUFFOLK, *with Falconers hallooing.*

QUEEN MARGARET Believe me, lords, for flying at the brook°   *hawking for waterfowl*
I saw not better sport these seven years' day;
Yet, by your leave, the wind was very high
And, ten to one, old Joan had not gone out.[1]
5 KING HENRY But what a point,[2] my lord, your falcon made,
And what a pitch° she flew above the rest!   *height*
To see how God in all his creatures works!
Yea, man and birds are fain° of climbing high.   *fond*
SUFFOLK No marvel, an it like° your majesty,   *if it please*
10 My lord Protector's hawks do tower so well;
They know their master loves to be aloft°   *to rule over others*
And bears his thoughts above his falcon's pitch.[3]
GLOUCESTER My lord, 'tis but a base ignoble mind
That mounts no higher than a bird can soar.
15 CARDINAL I thought as much: he would be above the clouds.
GLOUCESTER Ay, my lord Cardinal, how think you by that?
Were it not good your grace could fly to heaven?
KING HENRY The treasury of everlasting joy.
CARDINAL Thy heaven is on earth: thine eyes and thoughts

9. "I say that you, descendant of Aeacus, the Romans can conquer." A famously ambiguous response by an oracle to King Pyrrhus's question about whether he would conquer Rome.
2.1 Location: St Albans.
1. The hawk named "old Joan" would probably not have flown because of the high wind.
2. High position to which hawks fly to await prey.
3. Alluding to Gloucester's heraldic crest, which consisted of a falcon with a maiden's head. Suffolk is accusing Gloucester of overweening ambition.

20   Beat on° a crown, the treasure of thy heart,   *Think obsessively about*
     Pernicious Protector, dangerous peer,
     That smooth'st it so with° King and commonweal.   *Who so flatters*
GLOUCESTER   What, Cardinal? Is your priesthood grown
     peremptory?°   *imperious; impudent*
     Tantaene animis coelestibus irae?[4]
25   Churchmen so hot? Good uncle, hide such malice—
     With such holiness can you do it?
SUFFOLK   No malice, sir; no more than well becomes°   *is appropriate to*
     So good° a quarrel and so bad a peer.   *just*
GLOUCESTER   As who, my lord?
SUFFOLK   Why, as you, my lord,
30   An't like your lordly lord's Protectorship.
GLOUCESTER   Why, Suffolk, England knows thine insolence.
QUEEN MARGARET   And thy ambition, Gloucester.
KING HENRY   I prithee peace,
     Good Queen, and whet not on° these furious peers,   *do not encourage*
     For blessed are the peacemakers on earth.[5]
35 CARDINAL   Let me be blessed for the peace I make—
     [*aside to* GLOUCESTER] Against this proud Protector with
         my sword.
GLOUCESTER [*aside to* CARDINAL]   Faith, holy uncle, would't
     were come to that.
CARDINAL [*aside to* GLOUCESTER]   Marry, when thou dar'st.
GLOUCESTER [*aside to* CARDINAL]   Make up no factious
     numbers for the matter;[6]
40   In thine own person answer thy abuse.°   *insult; offense*
CARDINAL [*aside to* GLOUCESTER]   Ay, where thou dar'st not
     peep; and, if thou dar'st,
     This evening, on the east side of the grove—
KING HENRY   How now, my lords?
CARDINAL [*aloud*]   Believe me, cousin Gloucester,
     Had not your man put up° the fowl so suddenly,   *raised; startled*
     We had had more sport.
45   [*aside to* GLOUCESTER]   Come with thy two-hand sword.
GLOUCESTER   True, uncle.
     [*aside to* CARDINAL]   Are ye advised?° The east side of the grove.   *agreed*
CARDINAL [*aside to* GLOUCESTER]   I am with you.
KING HENRY   Why, how now, uncle Gloucester?
GLOUCESTER   Talking of hawking; nothing else, my lord.
     [*aside to* CARDINAL] Now, by God's mother, priest, I'll shave
         your crown[7] for this,
     Or all my fence° shall fail.   *skill in fencing*
50 CARDINAL [*aside to* GLOUCESTER]   *Medice te ipsum.*[8]
     Protector, see to't well; protect yourself.
KING HENRY   The winds grow high—so do your stomachs,°   *tempers*
     lords.
     How irksome is this music to my heart!
     When such strings jar,[9] what hope of harmony?

---

4. Quoting Virgil's *Aeneid* 1.11: "Can there be such
anger in heavenly minds?"
5. Quoting Jesus' Sermon on the Mount (Matthew
5:9).
6. Call in no supporters for this quarrel.

7. Alluding to a tonsure, or a shaved circular patch,
often seen on the heads of religious men.
8. "Physician, (heal) thyself" (see Luke 4:23).
9. When instruments such as these grow discordant.

55   I pray, my lords, let me compound° this strife.   *settle*
         *Enter [*TOWNSMAN*] crying, "A miracle!"*
     GLOUCESTER   What means this noise?
     —Fellow, what miracle dost thou proclaim?
     TOWNSMAN   A miracle, a miracle!
     SUFFOLK   Come to the King and tell him what miracle.
60   TOWNSMAN   Forsooth, a blind man at Saint Alban's shrine[1]
     Within this half hour hath received his sight—
     A man that ne'er saw in his life before.
     KING HENRY   Now God be praised, that to believing souls
     Gives light in darkness, comfort in despair!
         Enter the MAYOR *of St Albans and his brethren,*
         *bearing the man [*SIMPCOX*] between two in a*
         chair[, his WIFE *and* TOWNSMEN *following].*
65   CARDINAL   Here comes the townsmen on° procession   *in*
     To present your highness with the man.
     KING HENRY   Great is his comfort in this earthly vale,
     Although by his sight his sin be multiplied.[2]
     GLOUCESTER   Stand by, my masters; bring him near the King.
70   His highness' pleasure is to talk with him.
     KING HENRY   Good fellow, tell us here the circumstance
     That we for thee may glorify the Lord.
     What, hast thou been long blind and now restored?
     SIMPCOX   Born blind, an't please your grace.
75   WIFE   Ay, indeed was he.
     SUFFOLK   What woman is this?
     WIFE   His wife, an't like your worship.
     GLOUCESTER   Hadst thou been his mother, thou couldst have
     better told.
80   KING HENRY   Where wert thou born?
     SIMPCOX   At Berwick[3] in the north, an't like your grace.
     KING HENRY   Poor soul, God's goodness hath been great to
     thee.
     Let never day nor night unhallowed° pass,   *unblessed*
     But still° remember what the Lord hath done.   *continually*
85   QUEEN MARGARET   Tell me, good fellow, cam'st thou here by
     chance
     Or of devotion to this holy Shrine?
     SIMPCOX   God knows, of pure devotion, being called
     A hundred times, and oft'ner, in my sleep,
     By good Saint Alban, who said, "Simon, come;
90   Come offer° at my shrine, and I will help thee."   *make an offering*
     WIFE   Most true, forsooth, and many time and oft
     Myself have heard a voice to call him so.
     CARDINAL   What, art thou lame?
     SIMPCOX   Ay, God almighty help me.
     SUFFOLK   How cam'st thou so?
     SIMPCOX   A fall off of a tree.
     WIFE   A plum tree,[4] master.
95   GLOUCESTER   How long hast thou been blind?

---

1. A shrine to the first British martyr, who was   temptation.
beheaded by the Romans for giving sanctuary to   3. Town on the Scottish border, far from St Albans.
Christians.   4. Slang for "female thighs and genitals."
2. Although his sight will lead him into more

SIMPCOX   Oh, born so, master.
GLOUCESTER   What, and wouldst climb a tree?
SIMPCOX   But that° in all my life, when I was a youth.   *Only that once*
WIFE   Too true, and bought his climbing very dear.
GLOUCESTER   Mass,° thou loved'st plums well that wouldst   *By the mass (an oath)*
100   venture so.
SIMPCOX   Alas, good master, my wife desired some damsons°   *tiny plums; testicles*
       and made me climb, with danger of my life.
GLOUCESTER [*aside*]   A subtle knave, but yet it shall not serve.
       —Let me see thine eyes. Wink° now; now open them.   *Close your eyes*
105   In my opinion yet thou seest not well.
SIMPCOX   Yes, master, clear as day, I thank God and Saint
       Alban.
GLOUCESTER   Say'st thou me so? What color is this cloak of?
SIMPCOX   Red, master, red as blood.
110   GLOUCESTER   Why, that's well said. What color is my gown of?
SIMPCOX   Black, forsooth, coal-black as jet.°   *glossy black stone*
KING HENRY   Why, then thou know'st what color jet is of?
SUFFOLK   —And yet, I think, jet did he never see.
GLOUCESTER   But cloaks and gowns before this day a many.°   *a multitude*
115   WIFE   Never before this day, in all his life.
GLOUCESTER   —Tell me, sirrah, what's my name?
SIMPCOX   Alas, master, I know not.
GLOUCESTER [*pointing*]   What's his name?
SIMPCOX   I know not.
120   GLOUCESTER [*pointing*]   Nor his?
SIMPCOX   No indeed, master.
GLOUCESTER   What's thine own name?
SIMPCOX   Sander[5] Simpcox, an if it please you, master.
GLOUCESTER   Then, Sander, sit there, the lying'st knave
125   In Christendom. If thou hadst been born blind,
       Thou mightst as well have known all our names
       As thus to name the several colors we do wear.
       Sight may distinguish of colors, but suddenly
       To nominate° them all, it is impossible.   *name*
130   —My lords, Saint Alban here hath done a miracle;
       And would ye not think that cunning° to be great   *skill*
       That could restore this cripple to his legs again.
SIMPCOX   O master, that you could!
135   GLOUCESTER   My masters of St Albans, have you not beadles[6]
       in your town, and things called whips?
MAYOR   Yes, my lord, if it please your grace.
GLOUCESTER   Then send for one presently.°   *immediately*
MAYOR   —Sirrah, go fetch the beadle hither straight.
                              Exit [a TOWNSMAN].
GLOUCESTER   Now fetch me a stool hither by and by. —Now,
140   sirrah, if you mean to save yourself from whipping, leap me°   *for me*
       over this stool and run away.
SIMPCOX   Alas, master, I am not able to stand alone. You go
       about to torture me in vain.
                    Enter a BEADLE *with whips.*

---

5. Although he gives his name as "Sander Simpcox" here, at line 89, Simpcox refers to himself as "Simon." It has been proposed that "Sander" was the name of an actor who played the part of Simpcox, that his name entered Q at this point, and that this portion of F derives from Q.
6. Minor parish officials who administered punishment to vagabonds and those guilty of petty offenses.

GLOUCESTER   Well, sir, we must have you find your legs.
145   —Sirrah beadle, whip him till he leap over that same stool.
BEADLE   I will, my lord. —Come on, sirrah, off with your
  doublet quickly.
SIMPCOX   Alas, master, what shall I do? I am not able to stand.
        After the BEADLE *hath hit him once, he leaps over the*
        stool and runs away, and [TOWNSMEN] *follow and cry,*
        "A miracle!" [and exeunt].
KING HENRY   O God, seest thou this and bearest so long?
150 QUEEN MARGARET   It made me laugh to see the villain run.
GLOUCESTER   Follow the knave and take this drab° away.   *slut*
WIFE   Alas, sir, we did it for pure need.°   *out of utter poverty*
GLOUCESTER   Let them be whipped through every market town
  Till they come to Berwick from whence they came.
                  Exeunt [WIFE, BEADLE, MAYOR, *and*
                      remaining TOWNSMEN].
155 CARDINAL   Duke Humphrey has done a miracle today.
SUFFOLK   True—made the lame to leap and fly away.
GLOUCESTER   But you have done more miracles than I—
  You made in a day, my lord, whole towns to fly.[7]
        Enter BUCKINGHAM.
KING HENRY   What tidings with our cousin Buckingham?
160 BUCKINGHAM   Such as my heart doth tremble to unfold.
  A sort of naughty persons, lewdly bent[8]
  Under the countenance and confederacy°   *protection and complicity*
  Of Lady Eleanor, the Protector's wife,
  The ringleader and head of all this rout,
165   Have practiced° dangerously against your state,   *plotted*
  Dealing with witches and with conjurers
  Whom we have apprehended in the fact,°   *in the very act*
  Raising up wicked spirits from underground,
  Demanding of King Henry's life and death
170   And other° of your highness' Privy Council,   *other members*
  As more at large your grace shall understand.[9]
CARDINAL   And so, my lord Protector, by this means
  Your lady is forthcoming° yet at London.   *in custody*
  [*aside*] This news, I think, hath turned your weapon's
    edge;°   *blunted your sword*
175   'Tis like, my lord, you will not keep your hour.[1]
GLOUCESTER   Ambitious churchman, leave° to afflict my   *cease*
    heart.
  Sorrow and grief have vanquished all my powers
  And, vanquished as I am, I yield to thee
  Or to the meanest groom.°   *poorest servant*
180 KING HENRY   O God, what mischiefs work the wicked ones,
  Heaping confusion on their own heads thereby?
QUEEN MARGARET   Gloucester, see here the tainture° of thy nest;   *defilement*

---

7. Referring to the French towns that Suffolk gave
away when he arranged Henry's marriage to Margaret.
8. A gang of evil people, wickedly inclined.
9. TEXTUAL COMMENT In Q, the prophecies delivered
by the Spirit are read aloud by King Henry upon
Buckingham's news, rather than (as in F) by York at
Eleanor's arrest. The heightening of dramatic ten-

sion produced by having the King and Suffolk hear
their deaths prophesied suggests that Q may be a
performance-based version of the play. See Digital
Edition TC 3 (Folio edited text).
1. Appointment (for the duel previously arranged
between Gloucester and Cardinal Beaufort).

And look thyself be faultless, thou wert best.

GLOUCESTER Madam, for myself, to heaven I do appeal

185 How I have loved my king and commonweal;
And, for my wife, I know not how it stands.
Sorry I am to hear what I have heard.
Noble she is, but if she have forgot
Honor and virtue and conversed° with such   *consulted*

190 As, like to pitch,° defile nobility,   *dark, sticky substance*
I banish her my bed and company[2]
And give her as a prey to law and shame
That hath dishonored Gloucester's honest name.

KING HENRY Well, for this night we will repose us here;

195 Tomorrow toward London back again
To look into this business thoroughly
And call these foul offenders to their answers
And poise° the cause in Justice' equal scales,   *weigh*
Whose beam stands sure,[3] whose rightful cause prevails.

Flourish. Exeunt.

2.2 (Q 2.2)

Enter YORK, SALISBURY, *and* WARWICK.

YORK Now, my good lords of Salisbury and Warwick,
Our simple supper ended, give me leave
In this close walk° to satisfy myself   *secluded path*
In craving your opinion of my title,

5 Which is infallible, to England's crown.

SALISBURY My lord, I long to hear it at full.

WARWICK Sweet York, begin; and if thy claim be good,
The Nevilles are thy subjects to command.

YORK Then thus:[1]

10 Edward the Third, my lords, had seven sons:
The first, Edward the Black Prince, Prince of Wales;
The second, William of Hatfield; and the third,
Lionel, Duke of Clarence; next to whom
Was John of Gaunt, the Duke of Lancaster;

15 The fifth was Edmund Langley, Duke of York;
The sixth was Thomas of Woodstock, Duke of Gloucester;
William of Windsor was the seventh and last.
Edward the Black Prince died before his father
And left behind him Richard, his only son,

20 Who after Edward the Third's death reigned as king
Till Henry Bolingbroke, Duke of Lancaster,
The eldest son and heir of John of Gaunt,
Crowned by the name of Henry the Fourth,
Seized on the realm, deposed the rightful king,

25 Sent his poor queen to France from whence she came,
And him to Pomfret, where, as all you know,
Harmless Richard was murdered traitorously.

---

2. Echoing the language of church law, which permitted marital separation "from bed and board" in cases of adultery, heresy, and cruelty.
3. Whose bar (from which the two scales are suspended) is perfectly balanced and therefore allows accurate measurements.
2.2 Location: The Duke of York's garden, London.

1. TEXTUAL COMMENT York manipulates his family history to make his claim to the throne seem legitimate. His explanation is so long and complex that Warwick's rhetorical question at its conclusion, "What plain proceedings is more plain than this?" (line 53), is usually very funny in performance. See Digital Edition TC 4 (Folio edited text).

WARWICK   Father, the Duke hath told the truth;
    Thus got the house of Lancaster the crown.
30 YORK   Which now they hold by force and not by right;
    For Richard, the first son's heir, being dead,
    The issue of the next son should have reigned.
SALISBURY   But William of Hatfield died without an heir.
YORK   The third son, Duke of Clarence, from whose line
35 I claim the crown, had issue Philippe, a daughter,
    Who married Edmund Mortimer, Earl of March;[2]
    Edmund had issue, Roger, Earl of March;
    Roger had issue, Edmund, Anne, and Eleanor.
SALISBURY   This Edmund, in the reign of Bolingbroke,
40 As I have read, laid claim unto the crown
    And, but for Owain Glyndŵr, had been king,
    Who kept him in captivity till he died—
    But to the rest.
YORK   His eldest sister Anne,
    My mother, being heir unto the crown,
45 Married Richard, Earl of Cambridge, who was son
    To Edmund Langley, Edward the Third's fifth son.
    By her I claim the kingdom; she was heir
    To Roger, Earl of March, who was the son
    Of Edmund Mortimer, who married Philippe,
50 Sole daughter unto Lionel, Duke of Clarence.
    So, if the issue of the elder son
    Succeed before the younger, I am king.
WARWICK   What plain proceedings is more plain than this?
    Henry doth claim the crown from John of Gaunt,
55 The fourth son; York claims it from the third:
    Till Lionel's issue fails, his should not reign;
    It fails not yet, but flourishes in thee
    And in thy sons, fair slips of such a stock.[3]
    Then, father Salisbury, kneel we together
60 And in this private plot° be we the first   *plot of ground*
    That shall salute our rightful sovereign
    With honor of his birthright to the crown.
SALISBURY *and* WARWICK [*kneeling*]   Long live our sovereign
    Richard, England's king.
YORK   We thank you, lords. [*They rise.*] But I am not your king
65 Till I be crowned and that° my sword be stained   *until*
    With heart-blood of the house of Lancaster;
    And that's not suddenly to be performed
    But with advice° and silent secrecy.   *deliberation*
    Do you as I do in these dangerous days,
70 Wink at° the Duke of Suffolk's insolence,   *Ignore*
    At Beaufort's pride, at Somerset's ambition,
    At Buckingham, and all the crew of them,
    Till they have snared the shepherd of the flock,
    That virtuous prince, the good Duke Humphrey.

---

2. Like Raphael Holinshed and Edward Hall, whose chronicles Shakespeare used as sources for this play, Shakespeare conflates Edmund Mortimer, the fifth Earl of March, who was named heir to the throne by Richard II, with his uncle of the same name who was captured by Glyndŵr, a Welsh lord whom Shakespeare was later to depict in *1 Henry IV* as a rebel against the King. Although Shakespeare here says Glyndŵr kept Mortimer imprisoned until he died, in *1 Henry IV* he follows the chronicles in having Mortimer eventually marry Glyndŵr's daughter.
3. Fair cuttings of such a tree.

75 　'Tis that they seek; and they in seeking that
　　　Shall find their deaths, if York can prophesy.
　SALISBURY　My lord, break we off; we know your mind at full.
　WARWICK　My heart assures me that the Earl of Warwick
　　　Shall one day make the Duke of York a king.
80 　YORK　And, Neville, this I do assure myself:
　　　Richard shall live to make the Earl of Warwick
　　　The greatest man in England but the King.　　　*Exeunt.*

2.3 (Q 2.3)

Sound trumpets. Enter KING HENRY and state° to　　　persons of rank
banish the Duchess[: QUEEN MARGARET, GLOUCESTER,
the Dukes of SUFFOLK, BUCKINGHAM, and YORK, the
Earls of SALISBURY and WARWICK; and,] with Guard[,
ELEANOR, Margery JORDAN, John Southwell and John
HUME, two PRIESTS, and Roger BOLINGBROKE].[1]

　KING HENRY　Stand forth, Dame Eleanor Cobham,
　　　Gloucester's wife.
　　In sight of God and us your guilt is great.
　　Receive the sentence of the law for sin
　　Such as by God's book are adjudged to death.[2]
5 　—You four, from hence to prison back again;
　　From thence unto the place of execution.
　　The witch in Smithfield[3] shall be burnt to ashes,
　　And you three shall be strangled° on the gallows.　　　hanged
　　—You, madam, for° you are more nobly born,　　　because
10 　Despoilèd° of your honor in your life　　　Deprived
　　Shall, after three days' open penance done,
　　Live in your country here in banishment
　　With Sir John Stanley in the Isle of Man.[4]
　ELEANOR　Welcome is banishment; welcome were my death.
15 　GLOUCESTER　Eleanor, the law, thou seest, hath judged thee:
　　I cannot justify° whom the law condemns.　　　excuse
　　Mine eyes are full of tears, my heart of grief.
　　　　　[*Exeunt ELEANOR and prisoners, with Guard.*]
　　Ah, Humphrey, this dishonor in thine age
　　Will bring thy head with sorrow to the ground.
20 　—I beseech your majesty, give me leave to go;
　　Sorrow would° solace and mine age would ease.　　　desires
　KING HENRY　Stay, Humphrey, Duke of Gloucester. Ere
　　　thou go,
　　Give up thy staff.[5] Henry will to himself
　　Protector be, and God shall be my hope,
25 　My stay, my guide, and lantern to my feet.
　　And go in peace, Humphrey, no less beloved
　　Than when thou wert Protector to thy king.
　QUEEN MARGARET　I see no reason why a king of years°　　　who is of age
　　Should be to be° protected like a child.　　　need to be

2.3 Location: A London hall of justice.
1. F's stage direction simply reads "*Sound Trumpets.
Enter the King and State, with Guard to banish the
Duchess.*" Neither F nor Q mentions Jordan, the two
priests, or Bolingbroke, but F clearly requires them.
2. *Receive . . . death:* alluding to Exodus 22:18:
"Thou shalt not suffer a witch to live." At times

throughout Elizabeth's reign, witch hunts were conducted and laws against witchcraft strictly enforced.
3. Famous as the site in London where heretics were
burned.
4. An island off England's northwestern coast.
5. Emblem of his office as Protector.

30 God and King Henry govern England's realm!
—Give up your staff, sir, and the King his° realm. *the King's*

GLOUCESTER My staff? Here, noble Henry, is my staff:
As willingly do I the same resign
As ere° thy father Henry made it mine; *formerly*
35 And even as willingly at thy feet I leave it
As others would ambitiously receive it.
[*He lays down the staff.*]
Farewell, good King. When I am dead and gone
May honorable peace attend thy throne. *Exit.*

QUEEN MARGARET Why, now is Henry King and Margaret
Queen
40 And Humphrey, Duke of Gloucester, scarce himself,
That bears so shrewd a maim:[6] two pulls° at once; *pluckings; tugs*
His lady banished and a limb° lopped off. *(his staff)*
[*She picks up the staff and gives it to KING HENRY.*]
This staff of honor raught,° there let it stand *seized*
Where it best fits to be, in Henry's hand.
45 SUFFOLK Thus droops this lofty pine and hangs his sprays;° *branches*
Thus Eleanor's pride dies in her youngest days.° *in its youth*
YORK Lords, let him go. —Please it your majesty,
This is the day appointed for the combat,
And ready are the appellant° and defendant, *challenger*
50 The armorer and his man, to enter the lists,° *dueling area*
So please your highness to behold the fight.
QUEEN MARGARET Ay, good my lord; for purposely therefore
Left I the court to see this quarrel tried.
KING HENRY A° God's name, see the lists and all things fit; *In*
55 Here let them end it—and God defend the right!
YORK I never saw a fellow worse bestead,° *prepared*
Or more afraid to fight, than is the appellant,
The servant of this armorer, my lords.
Enter at one door the Armorer[, HORNER,] and his
NEIGHBORS, drinking to him so much that he is drunk;
and he enters with a drum before him and his staff
with a sandbag fastened to it; and at the other door his
man [PETER], with a drum and sandbag, and
PRENTICES drinking to him.
FIRST NEIGHBOR Here, neighbor Horner, I drink to you in a
60 cup of sack;° and fear not, neighbor, you shall do well enough. *sherry*
SECOND NEIGHBOR And here, neighbor, here's a cup of
charneco.° *port*
THIRD NEIGHBOR And here's a pot of good double° beer, neigh- *extra-strong*
bor: drink, and fear not your man.
65 HORNER [*accepting the offers of drink*] Let it come,° i'faith, *Pass it around*
and I'll pledge you all, and a fig[7] for Peter.
FIRST PRENTICE Here, Peter, I drink to thee, and be not afraid.
SECOND PRENTICE Be merry, Peter, and fear not thy master.
Fight for credit° of the prentices! *the honor*
70 PETER [*refusing the offers of drink*] I thank you all. Drink and
pray for me, I pray you, for I think I have taken my last

6. Who endures so painful a mutilation.
7. Slang for "vulva"; hence, an obscene insult. It was
typically accompanied by a gesture in which the
thumb was thrust between two closed fingers or into
the mouth.

draught in this world. Here, Robin, an if° I die, I give thee   *an if = if*
my apron; and Will, thou shalt have my hammer; and here,
Tom, take all the money that I have. O Lord bless me, I pray
75 God, for I am never able to deal with my master—he hath
learnt so much fence° already.   *fencing skill*

SALISBURY Come, leave your drinking and fall to blows.
—Sirrah, what's thy name?

PETER Peter, forsooth.

80 SALISBURY Peter? What more?

PETER Thump.

SALISBURY Thump? Then see thou thump thy master well.

HORNER Masters, I am come hither, as it were upon my man's
instigation, to prove him a knave and myself an honest man;
85 and, touching the Duke of York, I will take my death° I never   *stake my life on it*
meant him any ill, nor the King, nor the Queen; and there-
fore, Peter, have at thee° with a downright° blow.   *I come at thee / vertical*

YORK Dispatch; this knave's tongue begins to double.°   *to slur his words*
        Sound trumpets; alarum to the combatants.
        They fight, and PETER *strikes* HORNER *down.*

HORNER Hold, Peter, hold! I confess, I confess treason.
        [*He dies.*]

90 YORK Take away his weapon. —Fellow, thank God and the
good wine in thy master's way.°   *belly*

PETER O God, have I overcome mine enemies in this presence? O Peter, thou hast prevailed in right.

KING HENRY Go, take hence that traitor from our sight,
For by his death we do perceive his guilt,
95 And God in justice hath revealed to us
The truth and innocence of this poor fellow,
Which he° had thought to have murdered wrongfully.   *Whom he (Horner)*
—Come, fellow, follow us for thy reward.
                        Sound a flourish. Exeunt.

2.4 (Q 2.4)

Enter Duke Humphrey [of GLOUCESTER] *and his men,*
in mourning cloaks.[1]

GLOUCESTER Thus sometimes hath the brightest day a cloud;
And after summer evermore succeeds°   *follows*
Barren winter with his wrathful nipping° cold;   *biting*
So cares and joys abound as seasons fleet.°   *fly by*
5 Sirs, what's o'clock?

SERVANT Ten, my lord.

GLOUCESTER Ten is the hour that was appointed me
To watch the coming of my punished duchess;
Uneath° may she endure the flinty streets,   *Scarcely*
10 To tread them with her tender-feeling feet.
Sweet Nell, ill can thy noble mind abrook°   *endure*
The abject° people gazing on thy face   *lowborn*
With envious° looks, laughing at thy shame,   *spiteful*
That erst° did follow thy proud chariot wheels   *formerly*
15 When thou didst ride in triumph through the streets.
But soft, I think she comes, and I'll prepare

2.4 Location: A London street.
1. Hooded black garments worn to funerals to express sorrow.

My tear-stained eyes to see her miseries.

    Enter Duchess [ELEANOR] in a white sheet, a taper
    burning in her hand, [barefoot, with verses upon
    her back,]² with the Sheriff and Officers[, and
    Sir John STANLEY].

SERVANT   So please your grace, we'll take her° from the   *rescue her by force*
   Sheriff.

GLOUCESTER   No, stir not for your lives; let her pass by.

20   ELEANOR   Come you, my lord, to see my open shame?
   Now thou dost penance too. Look how they gaze!
   See how the giddy multitude do point
   And nod their heads and throw their eyes on thee.
   Ah, Gloucester, hide thee from their hateful° looks   *full of hate*
25   And, in thy closet° pent up, rue° my shame   *private chamber / grieve over*
   And ban° thine enemies, both mine and thine.   *curse*

GLOUCESTER   Be patient, gentle Nell; forget this grief.

ELEANOR   Ah, Gloucester, teach me to forget myself;
   For whilst I think I am thy married wife
30   And thou a prince, Protector of this land,
   Methinks I should not thus be led along,
   Mailed up³ in shame, with papers on my back,
   And followed with a rabble that rejoice
   To see my tears and hear my deep-fet groans.⁴
35   The ruthless flint doth cut my tender feet
   And, when I start,° the envious people laugh   *flinch*
   And bid me be advisèd how I tread—
   Ah, Humphrey, can I bear this shameful yoke?
   Trowest° thou that ere I'll look upon the world   *Believeth*
40   Or count them happy that° enjoys the sun?   *who*
   No: dark shall be my light and night my day;
   To think upon my pomp shall be my hell.
   Sometime I'll say, "I am Duke Humphrey's wife,
   And he a prince and ruler of the land;
45   Yet so he ruled and such a prince he was
   As he stood by whilst I, his forlorn duchess,
   Was made a wonder and a pointing stock°   *an object of scorn*
   To every idle rascal° follower."   *lowborn*
   But be thou mild and blush not at my shame,
50   Nor stir at nothing till the ax of death
   Hang over thee, as sure it shortly will.
   For Suffolk—he that can do all in all
   With her° that hateth thee and hates us all—   *(Margaret)*
   And York, and impious Beaufort, that false priest,
55   Have all limed bushes⁵ to betray thy wings
   And, fly thou how thou canst, they'll tangle thee.
   But fear not thou until thy foot be snared,
   Nor never seek prevention of° thy foes.   *safeguards against*

GLOUCESTER   Ah, Nell, forbear; thou aimest all awry.
60   I must offend before I be attainted;°   *condemned for treason*
   And had I twenty times so many foes,

---

2. Eleanor's offenses were presumably detailed in these verses.

3. Enveloped: a term from falconry that describes the condition of a hawk wrapped in cloth so as to prevent it from flying away.

4. Moans fetched from deep within me.

5. Coated bushes with birdlime (see note to 1.3.87).

And each of them had twenty times their power,
All these could not procure me any scathe°   harm
So long as I am loyal, true, and crimeless.
65   Wouldst have me rescue thee from this reproach?
Why, yet thy scandal were not wiped away,
But I in danger for the breach of law.
Thy greatest help is quiet, gentle Nell:
I pray thee sort° thy heart to patience.   adapt
70   These few days' wonder will be quickly worn.[6]
          Enter a HERALD.
HERALD   I summon your grace to his majesty's parliament,
holden° at Bury[7] the first of this next month.   to be held
GLOUCESTER   And my consent ne'er asked herein before?
This is close° dealing. —Well, I will be there.   secret
                          [*Exit* HERALD.]
75   —My Nell, I take my leave. —And, Master Sheriff,
Let not her penance exceed the King's commission.
SHERIFF   An't please your grace, here my commission stays,°   ends
And Sir John Stanley is appointed now
To take her with him to the Isle of Man.
80   GLOUCESTER   Must you, Sir John, protect° my lady here?   keep in custody
STANLEY   So am I given in charge, may't please your grace.
GLOUCESTER   Entreat° her not the worse, in that° I pray   Treat / just because
You use her well. The world may laugh again,
And I may live to do you kindness if you do it her.
85   And so, Sir John, farewell.
          [GLOUCESTER *begins to leave.*]
ELEANOR   What, gone, my lord, and bid me not farewell?
GLOUCESTER   Witness my tears—I cannot stay to speak.
                  Exit Duke Humphrey [of GLOUCESTER*].*
ELEANOR   Art thou gone, too? All comfort go with thee,
For none abides with me. My joy is death—
90   Death, at whose name I oft have been afeared
Because I wished this world's eternity.°   immortality on earth
—Stanley, I prithee go, and take me hence,
I care not whither, for I beg no favor;
Only convey me where thou art commanded.
95   STANLEY   Why, madam, that is to the Isle of Man,
There to be used according to your state.°   rank; condition
ELEANOR   That's bad enough, for I am but reproach;°   in a state of shame
And shall I then be used reproachfully?
STANLEY   Like to a duchess and Duke Humphrey's lady,
100   According to that state you shall be used.
ELEANOR   Sheriff, farewell, and better than I fare,
Although thou hast been conduct° of my shame.   conductor
SHERIFF   It is my office, and, madam, pardon me.
ELEANOR   Ay, ay, farewell; thy office is discharged.
                          [*Exit* SHERIFF.]
105   Come, Stanley, shall we go?
STANLEY   Madam, your penance done, throw off this sheet,
And go we to attire you for our journey.

6. What was marveled at for a few days will soon be   7. Bury St Edmunds, a town in Suffolk.
forgotten.

ELEANOR   My shame will not be shifted[8] with my sheet:
          No, it will hang upon my richest robes
110   And show itself, attire me how I can.
          Go, lead the way; I long to see my prison.   *Exeunt.*

3.1 (Q 3.1)

Sound a sennet. Enter KING [HENRY], QUEEN
[MARGARET], CARDINAL, SUFFOLK, YORK, BUCKINGHAM,
SALISBURY, *and* WARWICK *to the parliament.*

KING HENRY   I muse° my lord of Gloucester is not come.   *am surprised*
          'Tis not his wont° to be the hindmost man,   *habit*
          Whate'er occasion keeps him from us now.
QUEEN MARGARET   Can you not see, or will ye not observe
5   The strangeness of his altered countenance?
          With what a majesty he bears himself,
          How insolent of late he is become,
          How proud, how peremptory, and unlike himself?
          We know the time since° he was mild and affable,   *We remember when*
10   And if we did but glance a far-off look,
          Immediately he was upon his knee,
          That all the court admired him for° submission.   *was amazed at his*
          But meet him now, and be it in the morn
          When everyone will give the time of day,°   *say good morning*
15   He knits his brow and shows an angry eye
          And passeth by with stiff unbowèd knee,
          Disdaining° duty that to us belongs.   *Not paying*
          Small curs° are not regarded when they grin,°   *dogs / snarl; show teeth*
          But great men tremble when the lion roars—
20   And Humphrey is no little man in England.
          First, note that he is near you in descent
          And, should you fall, he is the next will mount.°   *mount the throne*
          Meseemeth then it is no policy,°   *not prudent*
          Respecting° what a rancorous mind he bears   *Considering*
25   And his advantage following your decease,
          That he should come about your royal person
          Or be admitted to your highness' council.
          By flattery hath he won the commons' hearts,
          And when he please to make commotion°   *incite rebellion*
30   'Tis to be feared they all will follow him.
          Now 'tis the spring, and weeds are shallow-rooted;
          Suffer° them now and they'll o'ergrow the garden   *Tolerate*
          And choke the herbs for want of husbandry.
          The reverent care I bear unto my lord
35   Made me collect° these dangers in the Duke.   *deduce*
          If it be fond,° call it a woman's fear;   *foolish*
          Which fear if better reasons can supplant,
          I will subscribe° and say I wronged the Duke.   *concur*
          —My lord of Suffolk, Buckingham, and York,
40   Reprove° my allegation if you can,   *Refute*
          Or else conclude my words effectual.°   *decisive*
SUFFOLK   Well hath your highness seen into this Duke;
          And had I first been put to speak my mind,

---

8. Changed, with a pun on "shifted" as meaning "put   3.1 Location: A great hall, Bury St Edmunds.
on new undergarments."

I think I should have told your grace's tale.
45 The Duchess by his subornation,°   *instigation*
    Upon my life, began her devilish practices;
    Or if he were not privy to those faults,°   *crimes*
    Yet by reputing° of his high descent,   *boasting*
    As next the King he was successive heir,
50 And such high vaunts° of his nobility,   *boasts*
    Did instigate the bedlam[1] brain-sick Duchess
    By wicked means to frame° our sovereign's fall.   *devise*
    Smooth runs the water where the brook is deep,
    And in his simple show° he harbors treason.   *outward appearance*
55 The fox barks not when he would steal the lamb.
    —No, no, my sovereign, Gloucester is a man
    Unsounded° yet and full of deep deceit.   *Unfathomed*
  CARDINAL   Did he not, contrary to form of law,
    Devise strange° deaths for small offenses done?   *cruel; illegal*
60 YORK   And did he not, in his protectorship,
    Levy great sums of money through the realm
    For soldiers' pay in France and never sent it,
    By means whereof the towns each day revolted?
  BUCKINGHAM   Tut, these are petty faults to° faults unknown   *compared to*
65 Which time will bring to light in smooth Duke Humphrey.
  KING HENRY   My lords, at once:° the care you have of us   *once and for all*
    To mow down thorns that would annoy our foot
    Is worthy praise, but shall I speak my conscience?
    Our kinsman Gloucester is as innocent
70 From meaning treason to our royal person
    As is the sucking lamb or harmless dove.
    The Duke is virtuous, mild, and too well given
    To dream on evil or to work my downfall.
  QUEEN MARGARET   Ah, what's more dangerous than this fond
    affiance?°   *foolish confidence*
75 Seems he a dove? His feathers are but borrowed,
    For he's disposèd as the hateful raven.
    Is he a lamb? His skin is surely lent him,
    For he's inclined as is the ravenous wolves.[2]
    Who cannot steal a shape that means deceit?[3]
80 Take heed, my lord; the welfare of us all
    Hangs on the cutting short that fraudful° man.   *treacherous*
        Enter SOMERSET.
  SOMERSET   All health unto my gracious sovereign.
  KING HENRY   Welcome, Lord Somerset. What news from
    France?
  SOMERSET   That all your interest in those territories
85 Is utterly bereft you. All is lost.
  KING HENRY   Cold news, Lord Somerset, but God's will be
    done.
  YORK [*aside*]   Cold news for me, for I had hope of France
    As firmly as I hope for fertile England.

---

1. Insane (a shortened form of "Bethlehem Hospital," a notorious asylum maintained by the City of London).
2. *Is he . . . wolves:* alluding to the Sermon on the Mount, which warns of "false prophets, which come to you in sheep's clothing, but inwardly they are ravening wolves" (Matthew 7:15).
3. Who that intends to deceive cannot assume an appropriate disguise?

Thus are my blossoms blasted° in the bud, | withered
90 And caterpillars eat my leaves away.
But I will remedy this gear° ere long, | business
Or sell my title for a glorious grave.

Enter Duke Humphrey [of GLOUCESTER].

GLOUCESTER   All happiness unto my lord the King.
Pardon, my liege, that I have stayed° so long. | delayed
95 SUFFOLK   Nay, Gloucester, know that thou art come too soon,
Unless thou wert more loyal than thou art.
I do arrest thee of high treason here.
GLOUCESTER   Well, Suffolk, thou shalt not see me blush,
Nor change my countenance for this arrest.
100 A heart unspotted is not easily daunted.
The purest spring is not so free from mud
As I am clear from treason to my sovereign.
Who can accuse me? Wherein am I guilty?
YORK   'Tis thought, my lord, that you took bribes of France
105 And, being Protector, stayed° the soldiers' pay, | withheld
By means whereof his highness hath lost France.
GLOUCESTER   Is it but thought so? What are they that think it?
I never robbed the soldiers of their pay,
Nor ever had one penny bribe from France.
110 So help me God, as I have watched the night°— | stayed up all night
Ay, night by night—in studying good for England,
That doit° that e'er I wrested from the King, | a coin of little value
Or any groat° I hoarded to my use, | a coin worth 4 pence
Be brought against me at my trial day.
115 No: many a pound of mine own proper store,° | personal fortune
Because I would not tax the needy commons,
Have I dispursèd° to the garrisons | paid
And never asked for restitution.
CARDINAL   It serves you well, my lord, to say so much.
120 GLOUCESTER   I say no more than truth, so help me God.
YORK   In your protectorship you did devise
Strange tortures for offenders, never heard of,
That° England was defamed by° tyranny. | So that / was infamous for
GLOUCESTER   Why, 'tis well known that whiles I was
Protector
125 Pity was all the fault that was in me,
For I should° melt at an offender's tears, | would
And lowly words were ransom for their fault.
Unless it were a bloody murderer
Or foul felonious° thief that fleeced poor passengers,° | wicked / travelers
130 I never gave them condign° punishment. | well-deserved
Murder indeed, that bloody sin, I tortured
Above the felon or what trespass else.[4]
SUFFOLK   My lord, these faults are easy,° quickly answered, | slight
But mightier crimes are laid unto your charge
135 Whereof you cannot easily purge yourself.
I do arrest you in his highness' name
And here commit you to my lord Cardinal
To keep until your further time of trial.

---

4. More than any other kind of crime.

KING HENRY My lord of Gloucester, 'tis my special hope
140　That you will clear yourself from all suspense°—　　　　　　　*suspicion*
　　My conscience tells me you are innocent.
　　GLOUCESTER Ah, gracious lord, these days are dangerous.
　　Virtue is choked with foul ambition,
　　And charity chased hence by rancor's hand;
145　Foul subornation⁵ is predominant,
　　And equity exiled° your highness' land.　　　　　　　　　　*exiled from*
　　I know their complot° is to have my life;　　　　　　　　　　　*plot*
　　And if my death might make this island happy
　　And prove the period° of their tyranny,　　　　　　　　　*mark the end*
150　I would expend it with all willingness.
　　But mine is made the prologue to their play,
　　For thousands more that yet suspect no peril
　　Will not conclude their plotted tragedy.
　　Beaufort's red sparkling eyes blab his heart's malice,
155　And Suffolk's cloudy brow his stormy hate;
　　Sharp Buckingham unburdens with his tongue
　　The envious load that lies upon his heart;
　　And dogged° York, that reaches at the moon,　　　*currish; determined*
　　Whose overweening° arm I have plucked back,　　　　　　　*arrogant*
160　By false accuse° doth level° at my life.　　　　　　*accusation / aim*
　　—And you, my sovereign lady, with the rest,
　　Causeless have laid disgraces on my head
　　And with your best endeavor have stirred up
　　My liefest liege° to be mine enemy.　　　　　　　*dearest sovereign*
165　Ay, all of you have laid your heads together—
　　Myself had notice of your conventicles°—　　　　　*secret meetings*
　　And all to make away my guiltless life.
　　I shall not want° false witness to condemn me,　　　　　　　*lack*
　　Nor store of treasons to augment my guilt.
170　The ancient proverb will be well effected:
　　"A staff is quickly found to beat a dog."
　　CARDINAL My liege, his railing is intolerable.
　　If those that care to keep your royal person
　　From treason's secret knife and traitor's rage
175　Be thus upbraided, chid, and rated at,°　　　　　　*berated; scolded*
　　And the offender granted scope of speech,
　　'Twill make them cool in zeal unto your grace.
　　SUFFOLK Hath he not twit° our sovereign lady here　　　　*upbraided*
　　With ignominious words, though clerkly couched,°　　*cleverly phrased*
180　As if she had subornèd some to swear
　　False allegations to o'erthrow his state?°　　　　　　*high position*
　　QUEEN MARGARET But I can give the loser leave to chide.
　　GLOUCESTER Far truer spoke than meant. I lose indeed—
　　Beshrew° the winners, for they played me false,　　　　　　*Curse*
185　And well such losers may have leave to speak.
　　BUCKINGHAM He'll wrest the sense° and hold us here all day.　*distort the meaning*
　　Lord Cardinal, he is your prisoner.
　　CARDINAL Sirs, take away the Duke and guard him sure.
　　GLOUCESTER Ah, thus King Henry throws away his crutch
190　Before his legs be firm to bear his body.
　　Thus is the shepherd beaten from thy side,

5. Instigating others to commit crimes, including perjury.

And wolves are gnarling° who shall gnaw thee first.　　　　　*snarling*
Ah, that my fear were false; ah, that it were!
For, good King Henry, thy decay° I fear.　　　　　　　　*ruin*
　　　　　　　Exit Duke Humphrey [of GLOUCESTER].
195　KING HENRY　My lords, what to your wisdoms seemeth best
　　　Do or undo as if ourself were here.
　　QUEEN MARGARET　What, will your highness leave the
　　　　parliament?
　　KING HENRY　Ay, Margaret. My heart is drowned with grief,
　　　Whose flood begins to flow within mine eyes,
200　My body round engirt° with misery;　　　　　　　　*encircled*
　　　For what's more miserable than discontent?
　　　Ah, uncle Humphrey, in thy face I see
　　　The map of honor, truth, and loyalty;
　　　And yet, good Humphrey, is the hour to come
205　That e'er I proved thee false or feared thy faith.°　*doubted your loyalty*
　　　What louring° star now envies thy estate　　　　　　*gloomy*
　　　That these great lords and Margaret our queen
　　　Do seek subversion of thy harmless life?
　　　Thou never didst them wrong, nor no man wrong.
210　And as the butcher takes away the calf,
　　　And binds the wretch, and beats it when it strays,
　　　Bearing it to the bloody slaughterhouse,
　　　Even so, remorseless, have they borne him hence;
　　　And as the dam° runs lowing up and down,　　　　　*mother*
215　Looking the way her harmless young one went,
　　　And can do naught but wail her darling's loss,
　　　Even so myself bewails good Gloucester's case
　　　With sad unhelpful tears, and with dimmed eyes
　　　Look after him, and cannot do him good,°　　　　*give him help*
220　So mighty are his vowèd enemies.
　　　His fortunes I will weep and 'twixt each groan
　　　Say, "Who's a traitor? Gloucester he is none."
　　　　　　　Exit [with SALISBURY *and* WARWICK].
　　QUEEN MARGARET　Free° lords, cold snow melts with the　*Noble*
　　　　sun's hot beams.
　　　Henry my lord is cold in great affairs,
225　Too full of foolish pity; and Gloucester's show
　　　Beguiles him as the mournful crocodile
　　　With sorrow snares relenting passengers,[6]
　　　Or as the snake, rolled in a flowering bank,
　　　With shining checkered slough° doth sting a child　*skin*
230　That for the beauty thinks it excellent.
　　　Believe me, lords, were none more wise than I,
　　　And yet herein I judge mine own wit good,
　　　This Gloucester should be quickly rid the world
　　　To rid us from the fear we have of him.
235　CARDINAL　That he should die is worthy policy;
　　　But yet we want a color° for his death.　　　　　　*pretext*
　　　'Tis meet he be condemned by course of law.
　　SUFFOLK　But in my mind that were no policy.
　　　The King will labor still° to save his life,　　　*continually*

---

6. Compassionate travelers. Sixteenth-century natural historians claimed that crocodiles moaned and wept in order to lure sympathetic humans to their death.

240	The commons haply° rise to save his life,	*perhaps*
	And yet we have but trivial argument,°	*evidence*
	More than mistrust,° that shows him worthy death.	*Other than suspicion*
	YORK So that, by this, you would not have him die?	
	SUFFOLK Ah, York, no man alive so fain° as I.	*willing*
245	YORK [*aside*] 'Tis York that hath more reason for his death.	
	—But, my lord Cardinal, and you, my lord of Suffolk,	
	Say as you think, and speak it from your souls:	
	Were't not all one an empty° eagle were set	*a hungry*
	To guard the chicken from a hungry kite°	*bird of prey*
250	As place Duke Humphrey for the King's Protector?	
	QUEEN MARGARET So the poor chicken should be sure of death.	
	SUFFOLK Madam, 'tis true; and were't not madness, then,	
	To make the fox surveyor° of the fold,	*guardian*
	Who being accused a crafty murderer,	
255	His guilt should be but idly posted over°	*foolishly ignored*
	Because his purpose is not executed?	
	No. Let him die in that he is a fox,	
	By nature proved an enemy to the flock,	
	Before his chaps° be stained with crimson blood,	*jaws*
260	As Humphrey proved, by reasons, to my liege.[7]	
	And do not stand on quillets° how to slay him;	*subtle distinctions*
	Be it by gins,° by snares, by subtlety,	*traps*
	Sleeping or waking, 'tis no matter how,	
	So he be dead; for that is good deceit°	*a good idea*
265	Which mates° him first that first intends deceit.	*checkmates; kills*
	QUEEN MARGARET Thrice-noble Suffolk, 'tis resolutely spoke.	
	SUFFOLK Not resolute, except° so much were done;	*unless*
	For things are often spoke and seldom meant.	
	But that° my heart accordeth with my tongue—	*to show that*
270	Seeing the deed is meritorious,	
	And to preserve my sovereign from his foe—	
	Say but the word, and I will be his priest.[8]	
	CARDINAL But I would have him dead, my lord of Suffolk,	
	Ere you can take due orders for a priest.[9]	
275	Say you consent and censure° well the deed,	*approve*
	And I'll provide his executioner;	
	I tender so the safety of my liege.	
	SUFFOLK Here is my hand; the deed is worthy doing.	
	QUEEN MARGARET And so say I.	
280	YORK And I. And now we three have spoke it,	
	It skills not greatly who impugns our doom.[1]	
	Enter a POST.	
	POST Great lords, from Ireland am I come amain°	*in haste*
	To signify that rebels there are up°	*up in arms*
	And put the Englishmen unto the sword.[2]	

7. Just as Humphrey proved (to be a fox or an enemy) to Henry.

8. I will kill him. Suffolk alludes to the priest's role in administering the sacrament of last rites to dying Christians.

9. Can become a priest; can arrange to have a priest there.

1. It doesn't matter who questions our decision.

2. TEXTUAL COMMENT Revolts in Ireland were a common occurrence during the 1590s. Here, Q specifies that the rebels are led by "the wild O'Neill," the name of an early fifteenth-century rebel, Owen O'Neill. The name may also allude to Hugh O'Neill, Earl of Tyrone, who had recently rebelled against the English in Ireland. See Digital Edition TC 5 (Folio edited text).

285 Send succors, lords, and stop the rage betime°   *promptly*
Before the wound do grow uncurable;
For, being green,° there is great hope of help.   *fresh*
CARDINAL A breach that craves a quick expedient stop.
What counsel give you in this weighty cause?
290 YORK That Somerset be sent as regent thither.
'Tis meet° that lucky ruler be employed—   *fit (said scornfully)*
Witness the fortune he hath had in France.
SOMERSET If York with all his far-fet° policy   *crafty*
Had been the regent there instead of me,
295 He never would have stayed in France so long.
YORK No, not to lose it all as thou hast done.
I rather would have lost my life betimes
Than bring a burden of dishonor home
By staying there so long till all were lost.
300 Show me one scar charactered° on thy skin;   *inscribed*
Men's flesh preserved so whole do seldom win.
QUEEN MARGARET Nay, then, this spark will prove a raging
    fire
If wind and fuel be brought to feed it with.
No more, good York; sweet Somerset be still.
305 Thy fortune, York, hadst thou been regent there,
Might happily° have proved far worse than his.   *perhaps*
YORK What, worse than naught? Nay, then a shame take all.
SOMERSET And in the number° thee, that wishest shame.   *among them*
CARDINAL My lord of York, try what your fortune is.
310 Th'uncivil kerns of Ireland³ are in arms
And temper clay° with blood of Englishmen.   *moisten the earth*
To Ireland will you lead a band of men
Collected choicely, from each county some,
And try your hap° against the Irishmen?   *luck*
315 YORK I will, my lord, so please his majesty.
SUFFOLK Why, our authority is his consent,
And what we do establish he confirms.
Then, noble York, take thou this task in hand.
YORK I am content. Provide me soldiers, lords,
320 Whiles I take order° for mine own affairs.   *arrange*
SUFFOLK A charge, Lord York, that I will see performed.
But now return we to the false Duke Humphrey.
CARDINAL No more of him; for I will deal with him
That henceforth he shall trouble us no more.⁴
325 And so break off; the day is almost spent.
—Lord Suffolk, you and I must talk of that event.
YORK My lord of Suffolk, within fourteen days
At Bristol I expect my soldiers,
For there I'll ship them all for Ireland.
330 SUFFOLK I'll see it truly done, my lord of York.
                              Exeunt [all but YORK].

---

3. Barbaric Irish foot soldiers or rebels. Kerns were the most numerous, poorest, and most lightly armed of the Irish soldiers who fought against the English during Elizabeth's reign. Many Elizabethan writers described the Irish as an inferior, uncivilized "race" and used the term "kern" to signify all Irish opponents of England.

4. TEXTUAL COMMENT While F emphasizes Cardinal Beaufort's leading role in Duke Humphrey's death, Q's version of this scene, which includes an exchange among York, Margaret, and Buckingham not included in F, gives Margaret more responsibility for urging his death. See Digital Edition TC 6 (Folio edited text).

YORK   Now, York, or never, steel thy fearful thoughts,
    And change misdoubt° to resolution.   *fear*
    Be that thou hop'st to be, or what thou art
    Resign to death; it is not worth th'enjoying.
335   Let pale-faced fear keep° with the mean-born° man   *dwell / lowborn*
    And find no harbor in a royal heart.
    Faster than springtime showers comes thought on thought,
    And not a thought but thinks on dignity.°   *high estate (kingship)*
    My brain, more busy than the laboring spider,
340   Weaves tedious° snares to trap mine enemies.   *laborious*
    Well, nobles, well: 'tis politicly done
    To send me packing with an host of men;
    I fear me° you but warm the starvèd° snake   *I am afraid / frozen*
    Who, cherished in your breasts, will sting your hearts.
345   'Twas men I lacked, and you will give them me;
    I take it kindly, yet be well assured
    You put sharp weapons in a madman's hands.
    Whiles I in Ireland nourish a mighty band,
    I will stir up in England some black storm
350   Shall blow ten thousand souls to heaven or hell;
    And this fell° tempest shall not cease to rage   *ferocious*
    Until the golden circuit° on my head,   *crown*
    Like to the glorious sun's transparent beams,
    Do calm the fury of this mad-bred flaw.[5]
355   And, for a minister° of my intent,   *an agent*
    I have seduced a headstrong Kentishman,
    John Cade of Ashford,
    To make commotion,° as full well he can,   *rebellion*
    Under the title of John Mortimer.[6]
360   In Ireland have I seen this stubborn Cade
    Oppose himself against a troop of kerns
    And fought so long till that his thighs with darts[7]
    Were almost like a sharp-quilled porcupine;
    And in the end, being rescued, I have seen
365   Him caper° upright like a wild Morisco,[8]   *leap*
    Shaking the bloody darts as he° his bells.   *as would the dancer*
    Full often, like a shag-haired[9] crafty kern,
    Hath he conversèd with the enemy
    And, undiscovered, come to me again
370   And given me notice of their villainies.
    This devil here shall be my substitute;
    For that° John Mortimer, which now is dead,   *Because*
    In face, in gait, in speech he doth resemble.
    By this I shall perceive the commons' mind,
375   How they affect° the house and claim of York.   *like*
    Say he be taken, racked,[1] and torturèd,

---

5. This storm ("flaw") created by madness.
6. The Mortimers are the family line by which York claims the crown. See York's account of his claim in 2.2.9–52.
7. Light spears or arrows, the weapons for which kerns were known.
8. A Moor who converted to Christianity; a morris dancer. Deriving from the Spanish word for "Moor," the morris dance was originally a Spanish dance that reenacted Christian battles with Moors. From the

fifteenth century, it was associated with English popular festivals and was usually performed by men with bells attached to their legs who carried sticks and wore costumes from English folklore.
9. Alluding to the popular notion that the Irish grew "glibs," or long, thick bangs, in order to disguise themselves and escape punishment for their crimes.
1. Tortured by having one's limbs fastened to a frame that stretched the body.

I know no pain they can inflict upon him
Will make him say I moved him to those arms.
Say that he thrive, as 'tis great like° he will,   *very likely*
380 Why, then, from Ireland come I with my strength
And reap the harvest which that rascal° sowed.   *base fellow*
For, Humphrey being dead, as he shall be,
And Henry put apart, the next for me.   *Exit.*

3.2 (Q 3.2)

Enter two or three [MURDERERS], *running over
the stage from the murder of Duke Humphrey
[of* GLOUCESTER].[1]

FIRST MURDERER Run to my lord of Suffolk; let him know
We have dispatched the Duke as he commanded.
SECOND MURDERER Oh, that it were to do![2] What have we
 done?
Didst ever hear a man so penitent?
  Enter SUFFOLK.
5 Here comes my lord.
SUFFOLK Now, sirs, have you dispatched this thing?
FIRST MURDERER Ay, my good lord, he's dead.
SUFFOLK Why, that's well said. Go get you to my house;
I will reward you for this venturous° deed.   *dangerous*
10 The King and all the peers are here at hand.
Have you laid fair° the bed? Is all things well   *rearranged*
According as I gave directions?
FIRST MURDERER 'Tis, my good lord.
SUFFOLK Away, be gone.   *Exeunt* [MURDERERS].
  Sound trumpets. Enter KING [HENRY], QUEEN
  [MARGARET], CARDINAL, [*and*] SOMERSET, *with
  Attendants.*
15 KING HENRY [*to* SUFFOLK] Go call our uncle to our presence
  straight;°   *immediately*
Say we intend to try his grace today
If° he be guilty, as 'tis publishèd.   *To find whether*
SUFFOLK I'll call him presently,° my noble lord. *Exit.* *at once*
KING HENRY Lords, take your places, and I pray you all
20 Proceed no straiter° 'gainst our uncle Gloucester *more severely*
Than from true evidence, of good esteem,°   *worthy of belief*
He be approved in practice culpable.°   *determined guilty*
QUEEN MARGARET God forbid any malice should prevail
That faultless may condemn a nobleman![3]
25 Pray God he may acquit him° of suspicion.   *himself*
KING HENRY I thank thee, Meg; these words content me
 much.
  Enter SUFFOLK.
How now? Why look'st thou pale? Why tremblest thou?
Where is our uncle? What's the matter, Suffolk?
SUFFOLK Dead in his bed, my lord; Gloucester is dead.
30 QUEEN MARGARET Marry, God forfend!°   *forbid*

3.2 Location: Gloucester's bedchamber and an
adjoining room of state, Bury St Edmunds.
1. In contrast to F's stage directions, Q indicates
that the actual smothering of Gloucester is shown

onstage.
2. Would that it were still to be done (so that it could
remain undone).
3. That may condemn a noble man who is blameless.

CARDINAL   God's secret judgment. I did dream tonight°   *last night*
   The Duke was dumb and could not speak a word.
        KING [HENRY] *swoons.*
QUEEN MARGARET   How fares my lord? Help, lords, the King
   is dead!
SOMERSET   Rear° up his body; wring him by the nose.[4]   *Raise*
35   QUEEN MARGARET   Run, go, help, help! O Henry, ope thine
   eyes.
SUFFOLK   He doth revive again. Madam, be patient.
KING HENRY   O heavenly God!
QUEEN MARGARET   How fares my gracious lord?
SUFFOLK   Comfort, my sovereign; gracious Henry, comfort.
KING HENRY   What, doth my lord of Suffolk comfort me?
40   Came he right now° to sing a raven's note[5]   *a moment ago*
   Whose dismal tune bereft° my vital powers,   *robbed me of*
   And thinks he that the chirping of a wren,
   By crying comfort from a hollow° breast,   *an insincere*
   Can chase away the first-conceivèd° sound?   *previously perceived*
45   Hide not thy poison with such sugared words.
      [SUFFOLK *offers to help* KING HENRY *rise.*]
   Lay not thy hands on me—forbear, I say!
   Their touch affrights me as a serpent's sting.
   Thou baleful messenger, out of my sight!
   Upon thy eyeballs murderous tyranny
50   Sits in grim majesty to fright the world.
   Look not upon me, for thine eyes are wounding;
   Yet do not go away; come, basilisk,[6]
   And kill the innocent gazer with thy sight.
   For in the shade° of death I shall find joy;   *shadow*
55   In life but double death, now Gloucester's dead.
QUEEN MARGARET   Why do you rate° my lord of Suffolk thus?   *chide*
   Although the Duke was enemy to him
   Yet he most Christian-like laments his death.
   And, for myself, foe as he was to me,
60   Might liquid tears or heart-offending° groans   *heart-wounding*
   Or blood-consuming[7] sighs recall his life,
   I would be blind with weeping, sick with groans,
   Look pale as primrose with blood-drinking sighs,
   And all to have the noble Duke alive.
65   What know I how the world may deem° of me?   *judge*
   For it is known we were but hollow friends;
   It may be judged I made the Duke away:
   So shall my name with slander's tongue be wounded,
   And prince's courts be filled with my reproach.
70   This get I by his death. Ay me, unhappy
   To be a queen and crowned with infamy.
KING HENRY   Ah, woe is me for Gloucester, wretched man.
QUEEN MARGARET   Be woe for me, more wretched than he is.
   What, dost thou turn away and hide thy face?
75   I am no loathsome leper—look on me!
   What? Art thou, like the adder, waxen deaf?[8]

4. This was thought to revive circulation and restore consciousness.
5. According to popular superstition, an omen of death.
6. A mythical reptile, hatched from a cock's egg, whose look was supposed to be fatal.
7. It was popularly believed that each sigh or groan drew a drop of blood from the heart.
8. Alluding to the belief that adders stopped up their ears to resist attempts to charm them.

Be poisonous too, and kill thy forlorn queen.
Is all thy comfort shut in Gloucester's tomb?
Why, then Queen Margaret was ne'er thy joy.
80 Erect his statue and worship it,
And make my image but an alehouse sign.⁹
Was I for this nigh wrecked upon the sea,
And twice by awkward° wind from England's bank°   *unfavorable / shore*
Drove back again unto my native clime?
85 What boded this but° well-forewarning wind   *but that*
Did seem to say, "Seek not a scorpion's nest,
Nor set no footing on this unkind shore"?
What did I then, but cursed the gentle gusts
And he that loosed them forth their brazen caves¹
90 And bid them blow towards England's blessed shore
Or turn our stern upon a dreadful rock?
Yet Aeolus would not be a murderer,
But left that hateful office unto thee.
The pretty vaulting° sea refused to drown me,   *bounding*
95 Knowing that thou wouldst have me drowned on shore
With tears as salt as sea through thy unkindness.
The splitting rocks cowered in the sinking sands²
And would not dash me with their ragged sides
Because thy flinty heart, more hard than they,
100 Might in thy palace perish° Margaret.   *destroy*
As far as I could ken° thy chalky cliffs,   *see*
When from thy shore the tempest beat us back,
I stood upon the hatches° in the storm,   *deck*
And, when the dusky sky began to rob
105 My earnest-gaping° sight of thy land's view,   *earnestly peering*
I took a costly jewel from my neck—
A heart it was, bound in with diamonds—
And threw it towards thy land. The sea received it,
And so I wished thy body might my heart;
110 And even with this I lost fair England's view,
And bid mine eyes be packing° with my heart,   *be gone*
And called them blind and dusky spectacles°   *instruments of sight*
For losing ken of Albion's° wishèd coast.   *England's*
How often have I tempted Suffolk's tongue—
115 The agent of thy foul inconstancy—
To sit and watch me, as Ascanius³ did
When he to madding° Dido would unfold   *going mad (with love)*
His father's acts, commenced in burning Troy!
Am I not witched like her? Or thou not false like him?
120 Ay me, I can no more!° Die, Margaret,   *my strength fails*
For Henry weeps that thou dost live so long.
          Noise within. Enter WARWICK, [SALISBURY,] *and*
          many COMMONS.⁴
WARWICK   It is reported, mighty sovereign,

9. Inns and shops in Elizabethan London were usually distinguished by signs bearing images rather
than words.
1. Referring to Aeolus, whom Zeus appointed ruler
of the winds, which he kept in caves. *brazen*: strong
(as brass).
2. Rocks that ordinarily break ships into pieces
crouched down fearfully in the sands where ships

usually sink.
3. In book 1 of the *Aeneid*, Venus sends Cupid in the
form of Ascanius, son of Aeneas, to bewitch Dido,
Queen of Carthage, and inflame her with love for
Aeneas.
4. Common people; those below the rank of gentleman.

That good Duke Humphrey traitorously is murdered
By Suffolk and the Cardinal Beaufort's means.
125 The commons, like an angry hive of bees
That want° their leader, scatter up and down   *lack*
And care not who they sting in his revenge.
Myself have calmed their spleenful° mutiny   *angry*
Until they hear the order° of his death.   *manner*
130 KING HENRY   That he is dead, good Warwick, 'tis too true,
But how he died God knows, not Henry.
Enter his chamber, view his breathless corpse,
And comment then upon° his sudden death.   *And then explain*
WARWICK   That shall I do, my liege. —Stay, Salisbury,
135 With the rude multitude till I return.
            [*Exeunt* WARWICK *at one door,* SALISBURY *and*
                        COMMONS *at another.*]⁵
KING HENRY   O thou that judgest all things, stay° my thoughts—   *restrain*
My thoughts that labor to persuade my soul
Some violent hands were laid on Humphrey's life.
If my suspect° be false, forgive me, God,   *suspicion*
140 For judgment only doth belong to thee.
Fain would I go to chafe his paly° lips   *pale*
With twenty thousand kisses and to drain°   *rain; let fall*
Upon his face an ocean of salt tears,
To tell my love unto his dumb deaf trunk,°   *body*
145 And with my fingers feel his hand, unfeeling.°   *which lacks feeling*
But all in vain are these mean obsequies,°   *funeral rites*
And to survey his dead and earthy image,
What were it but to make my sorrow greater?
            Bed put forth. [*Enter* WARWICK, *who draws the*
            curtains, showing Humphrey, Duke of GLOUCESTER,
            dead in his bed.]
WARWICK   Come hither, gracious sovereign; view this body.
150 KING HENRY   That is to see how deep my grave is made,
For with his soul fled all my worldly solace;
For, seeing him, I see my life° in death.   *that my life will end*
WARWICK   As surely as my soul intends to live
With that dread King° that took our state° upon him   *(Christ) / condition*
155 To free us from his Father's wrathful curse,
I do believe that violent hands were laid
Upon the life of this thrice-famèd° duke.   *very famous*
SUFFOLK   A dreadful oath, sworn with a solemn tongue!
What instance° gives Lord Warwick for his vow?   *evidence*
160 WARWICK   See how the blood is settled in his face.
Oft have I seen a timely-parted ghost⁶
Of ashy semblance, meager, pale, and bloodless,
Being all descended to the laboring heart,⁷
Who in the conflict that it holds with death
165 Attracts the same° for aidance° 'gainst the enemy,   *(the blood) / aid*
Which with the heart there cools and ne'er returneth
To blush and beautify the cheek again.

---

5. Although F does not specify an exit for Warwick, Salisbury, or the commons here, the dialogue suggests that all leave the stage, since Warwick returns at line 148 to reveal Gloucester's corpse, and Salisbury is given an entry at line 241.
6. The corpse of someone who died a natural death.
7. The blood having all drained into the palpitating heart.

But see, his face is black and full of blood,
His eyeballs further out than when he lived,
170 Staring full ghastly like a strangled man;
His hair upreared, his nostrils stretched with struggling,
His hands abroad displayed,° as one that grasped   *spread wide*
And tugged for life and was by strength subdued.
Look on the sheets: his hair, you see, is sticking;
175 His well-proportioned beard made rough and rugged,
Like to the summer's corn by tempest lodged.°   *beaten down*
It cannot be but he was murdered here;
The least of all these signs were probable.°   *sufficient proof*
SUFFOLK   Why, Warwick, who should do the Duke to death?
180 Myself and Beaufort had him in protection,
And we, I hope, sir, are no murderers.
WARWICK   But both of you were vowed Duke Humphrey's
        foes,
And you, forsooth, had the good Duke to keep.°   *guard*
'Tis like you would not feast him like a friend,
185 And 'tis well seen he found an enemy.
QUEEN MARGARET   Then you belike° suspect these noblemen   *perchance*
As guilty of Duke Humphrey's timeless° death?   *untimely*
WARWICK   Who finds the heifer dead and bleeding fresh
And sees fast° by a butcher with an ax   *near*
190 But will suspect 'twas he that made the slaughter?
Who finds the partridge in the puttock's° nest   *kite's (bird of prey)*
But may imagine how the bird was dead,°   *killed*
Although the kite soar with unbloodied beak?
Even so suspicious is this tragedy.
195 QUEEN MARGARET   Are you the butcher, Suffolk? Where's
        your knife?
Is Beaufort termed a kite? Where are his talons?
SUFFOLK   I wear no knife to slaughter sleeping men,
But here's a vengeful sword, rusted with ease,°   *lack of use*
That shall be scoured in his rancorous heart
200 That° slanders me with murder's crimson badge.   *Who*
—Say, if thou dar'st, proud lord of Warwickshire,
That I am faulty in Duke Humphrey's death.
WARWICK   What dares not Warwick, if false Suffolk dare him?
QUEEN MARGARET   He dares not calm his contumelious° spirit,   *insolent*
205 Nor cease to be an arrogant controller,°   *critic; slanderer*
Though Suffolk dare him twenty thousand times.
WARWICK   Madam, be still, with reverence may I say,
For every word you speak in his behalf
Is slander to your royal dignity.
210 SUFFOLK   Blunt-witted lord, ignoble in demeanor,
If ever lady wronged her lord so much,
Thy mother took into her blameful bed
Some stern° untutored churl, and noble stock   *rough*
Was graft with crab-tree slip, whose fruit thou art,[8]
215 And never of the Nevilles' noble race.

---

8. *noble . . . art:* into the trunk of a great tree was inserted a cutting, or "slip," from an inferior, wild one, and you are the result. The analogy puns on "stock" as meaning "an aristocratic line of descent" and implies that the pedigree has been tainted. "Noble stock" may also refer to the trunk of a noblewoman's body into which a worthless "slip," such as the penis of a low-born man, has been inserted.

WARWICK   But that the guilt of murder bucklers° thee   *shields*
    And I should rob the deathsman° of his fee,   *executioner*
    Quitting° thee thereby of ten thousand shames,   *Freeing*
    And that my sovereign's presence makes me mild,[9]
220   I would, false murderous coward, on thy knee
    Make thee beg pardon for thy passèd° speech,   *just uttered*
    And say it was thy mother that thou meant'st,
    That thou thyself wast born in bastardy,
    And after all this fearful homage° done,   *cowardly submission*
225   Give thee thy hire° and send thy soul to hell,   *reward*
    Pernicious bloodsucker of sleeping men!
SUFFOLK   Thou shalt be waking while I shed thy blood,
    If from this presence° thou dar'st go with me.   *(the King's presence)*
WARWICK   Away even now, or I will drag thee hence.
230   Unworthy though thou art, I'll cope° with thee   *fight*
    And do some service to Duke Humphrey's ghost.
                   Exeunt [SUFFOLK *and* WARWICK].
KING HENRY   What stronger breastplate than a heart
      untainted?
    Thrice is he armed that hath his quarrel just;
    And he but naked, though locked up in steel,°   *armored*
235   Whose conscience with injustice is corrupted.
            A noise within.
QUEEN MARGARET   What noise is this?
            Enter SUFFOLK *and* WARWICK *with their*
            weapons drawn.
KING HENRY   Why, how now, lords? Your wrathful weapons
      drawn
    Here in our presence? Dare you be so bold?
    Why, what tumultuous clamor have we here?
240 SUFFOLK   The traitorous Warwick with the men of Bury
    Set all upon me, mighty sovereign.
            Enter SALISBURY.
SALISBURY   Sirs, stand apart; the King shall know your mind.
    —Dread lord, the commons send you word by me,
    Unless Lord Suffolk straight be done to death,
245   Or banished° fair England's territories,   *banished from*
    They will by violence tear him from your palace
    And torture him with grievous lingering death.
    They say by him the good Duke Humphrey died;
    They say in him they fear your highness' death;
250   And mere° instinct of love and loyalty,   *pure*
    Free from a stubborn opposite° intent,   *antagonistic*
    As being thought to contradict your liking,[1]
    Makes them thus forward in° his banishment.   *insistent upon*
    They say, in care of your most royal person,
255   That if your highness should intend to sleep,
    And charge that no man should disturb your rest
    In pain of your dislike or pain of death,
    Yet not withstanding such a strait° edict,   *strict*
    Were there a serpent seen, with forkèd tongue,
260   That slyly glided towards your majesty,

9. It was illegal to draw weapons in the King's   1. That might be thought to contradict your wishes.
presence.

It were but necessary you were waked,

Lest being suffered° in that harmful slumber,   *permitted to remain*

The mortal worm° might make the sleep eternal.   *deadly serpent*

And therefore do they cry, though you forbid,

265 That they will guard you, whe'er° you will or no,   *whether*

From such fell° serpents as false Suffolk is,   *cruel*

With whose envenomèd and fatal sting

Your loving uncle, twenty times his worth,

They say, is shamefully bereft of life.

270 COMMONS (*within*)   An answer from the King, my lord of

Salisbury!

SUFFOLK   'Tis like° the commons, rude unpolished hinds,°   *probable / boors*

Could send such message to their sovereign!

But you, my lord, were glad to be employed,

275 To show how quaint° an orator you are.   *skilled*

But all the honor Salisbury hath won

Is that he was the lord ambassador

Sent from a sort° of tinkers² to the King.   *gang*

COMMONS (*within*)   An answer from the King, or we will all

280 break in!

KING HENRY   Go, Salisbury, and tell them all from me

I thank them for their tender loving care

And, had I not been cited° so by them,   *urged*

Yet did I purpose as they do entreat.

285 For sure, my thoughts do hourly prophesy

Mischance unto my state by Suffolk's means.

And therefore by His° majesty I swear   *(God's)*

Whose far unworthy deputy I am,

He shall not breathe° infection in this air   *breathe out; spread*

290 But three days longer, on the pain of death.

[*Exit* SALISBURY.]

QUEEN MARGARET   O Henry, let me plead for gentle° Suffolk.   *noble*

KING HENRY   Ungentle Queen to call him "gentle Suffolk."

No more I say! If thou dost plead for him,

Thou wilt but add increase unto my wrath.

295 Had I but said, I would have kept my word,

But when I swear, it is irrevocable.

[*to* SUFFOLK] If after three days' space thou here beest

found

On any ground that I am ruler of,

The world shall not be ransom for thy life.

300 —Come, Warwick, come; good Warwick, go with me;

I have great matters to impart to thee.

Exeunt [KING HENRY *and* WARWICK;

bed drawn back in].

QUEEN MARGARET   Mischance and sorrow go along with you!

Heart's discontent and sour affliction

Be playfellows to keep you company!

305 There's two of you—the devil make a third,

And threefold vengance tend upon your steps!

SUFFOLK   Cease, gentle Queen, these execrations

And let thy Suffolk take his heavy° leave.   *sorrowful*

---

2. Tinkers were usually itinerant pot menders and were synonymous with vagrants and gypsies.

QUEEN MARGARET Fie, coward woman³ and soft-hearted
　　　wretch!
310　　Hast thou not spirit to curse thine enemy?
　　SUFFOLK A plague upon them! Wherefore° should I curse　　　　　　　　*Why*
　　　them?
　　　Would curses kill, as doth the mandrake's groan,⁴
　　　I would invent as bitter searching° terms　　　　　　　　　　　　　　　*piercing*
　　　As curst, as harsh and horrible to hear,
315　　Delivered strongly through my fixèd° teeth　　　　　　　　　　　　*clenched*
　　　With full as many signs of deadly hate
　　　As lean-faced envy⁵ in her loathsome cave.
　　　My tongue should stumble in mine earnest words;
　　　Mine eyes should sparkle like the beaten flint;
320　　Mine hair be fixed on end, as one distract—
　　　Ay, every joint should seem to curse and ban,°　　　　　　　　*speak bitterly*
　　　And even now my burdened heart would break,
　　　Should I not curse them. Poison be their drink!
　　　Gall,° worse than gall, the daintiest that they taste!　　　*Bile (a bitter fluid)*
325　　Their sweetest shade a grove of cypress trees!⁶
　　　Their chiefest prospect° murdering basilisks!⁷　　　　　　　　　　　*view*
　　　Their softest touch as smart° as lizards' stings!　　　　　　　　　*sharp*
　　　Their music frightful as the serpent's hiss,
　　　And boding screech owls⁸ make the consort° full!　　　*group of musicians*
330　　All the foul terrors in dark-seated hell—
　　QUEEN MARGARET Enough, sweet Suffolk; thou torment'st
　　　thyself,
　　　And these dread curses, like the sun 'gainst glass,
　　　Or like an over-chargèd gun, recoil
　　　And turns the force of them upon thyself.
335　　SUFFOLK You bade me ban, and will you bid me leave?°　　　　　　*stop*
　　　Now, by the ground that I am banished from,
　　　Well could I curse away a winter's night,
　　　Though standing naked on a mountaintop
　　　Where biting cold would never let grass grow,
340　　And think it but a minute spent in sport.
　　QUEEN MARGARET Oh, let me entreat thee cease. Give me
　　　thy hand
　　　That I may dew it with my mournful tears;
　　　Nor let the rain of heaven wet this place
　　　To wash away my woeful monuments.°　　　　　　　　　*signs of grief (tears)*
345　　Oh, could this kiss be printed in thy hand
　　　That thou mightst think upon these° by the seal°　　　　　*(lips) / imprint*
　　　Through whom° a thousand sighs are breathed for thee.　*which (her lips)*
　　　So get thee gone, that I may know my grief;
　　　'Tis but surmised whiles thou art standing by
350　　As one that surfeits° thinking on a want.°　　　　　　　*gorges / famine*
　　　I will repeal thee° or, be well assured,　　　　　　　　　*win your recall*
　　　Adventure to be banishèd° myself—　　　　　　　　　　　*Risk banishment*

3. In calling Suffolk a woman, Margaret questions
his manhood. The pun in the next line on "spirit" as
meaning "semen" as well as "courage" continues
Margaret's assault on Suffolk's masculinity.
4. It was popularly believed that the mandrake—an
herb whose root was thought to resemble a man and
to grow wherever the semen of a man executed for
murder had fallen—killed humans with its dreadful
scream when it was uprooted.
5. Envy was traditionally described as an emaciated
woman. See Ovid, *Metamorphoses* 2.949ff.
6. From ancient times, trees associated with death.
Frequently planted in graveyards, their wood was
used for coffins.
7. See note to line 52 above.
8. Thought to be harbingers of death.

And banishèd I am, if but from thee.
Go, speak not to me; even now be gone.
355 Oh, go not yet! Even thus two friends condemned
Embrace, and kiss, and take ten thousand leaves,
Loather a hundred times to part than die.
Yet now farewell, and farewell life with thee.
SUFFOLK Thus is poor Suffolk ten times banishèd:
360 Once by the King and three times thrice by thee.
'Tis not the land I care for, wert thou thence:
A wilderness is populous enough,
So Suffolk had thy heavenly company.
For where thou art, there is the world itself,
365 With every several° pleasure in the world,   *distinct*
And where thou art not, desolation.
I can no more. Live thou to joy° thy life;   *enjoy*
Myself no joy in naught but that thou liv'st.
        Enter VAUX.
QUEEN MARGARET Whether goes Vaux so fast? What news,
        I prithee?
370 VAUX To signify unto his majesty
That Cardinal Beaufort is at point of death;
For suddenly a grievous sickness took him
That makes him gasp, and stare, and catch the air,
Blaspheming God and cursing men on earth.
375 Sometime he talks as if Duke Humphrey's ghost
Were by his side; sometime he calls the King
And whispers to his pillow, as to him,
The secrets of his over-chargèd° soul.   *overburdened*
And I am sent to tell his majesty
380 That even now he cries aloud for him.
QUEEN MARGARET Go tell this heavy message to the King.
        Exit [VAUX].
Ay me! What is this world? What news are these?
But wherefore grieve I at an hour's poor loss,[9]
Omitting° Suffolk's exile, my soul's treasure?   *Ignoring*
385 Why only, Suffolk, mourn I not for thee,
And with the southern clouds[1] contend in tears—
Theirs for the earth's increase, mine for my sorrows?
Now get thee hence. The King, thou know'st, is coming;
If thou be found by° me, thou art but dead.   *near*
390 SUFFOLK If I depart from thee, I cannot live.
And in thy sight to die, what were it else
But like a pleasant slumber in thy lap?[2]
Here could I breath my soul into the air
As mild and gentle as the cradle-babe
395 Dying with mother's dug° between its lips;   *nipple*
Where, from° thy sight, I should be raging mad,   *out of*
And cry out for thee to close up mine eyes,
To have thee with thy lips to stop my mouth;
So shouldst thou either turn° my flying soul   *return to me*

9. Alluding to the Cardinal's old age and suggesting
that he has in any case but a short time (an hour) to
live.
1. It was generally thought that rain came from the
south.
2. Punning on "die in thy lap" as meaning "have an
orgasm while in your embrace."

400   Or I should breathe it so into thy body,
       And then it lived in sweet Elysium.[3]
       To die by thee were but to die in jest;[4]
       From thee to die were torture more than death.
       Oh, let me stay, befall what may befall!
405 QUEEN MARGARET Away! Though parting be a fretful
        corrosive,°   *painful remedy*
       It is applièd to a deathful° wound.   *deadly*
       To France, sweet Suffolk! Let me hear from thee;
       For whereso'er thou art in this world's globe,
       I'll have an Iris[5] that shall find thee out.
410 SUFFOLK I go.
    QUEEN MARGARET And take my heart with thee.
    SUFFOLK A jewel locked into the woefullest cask°   *casket*
       That ever did contain a thing of worth.
       Even as a splitted bark,° so sunder° we: *boat / part*
       This way fall I to death.
415 QUEEN MARGARET   This way for me.
                       Exeunt [by different doors].

3.3 (Q 3.3)

Enter KING HENRY, SALISBURY *and* WARWICK, *to*
   CARDINAL *Beaufort, in bed[, raving and staring].*
KING HENRY How fares my lord? Speak, Beaufort, to thy
    sovereign.
    CARDINAL If thou beest Death, I'll give thee England's
    treasure—
    Enough to purchase such another island—
    So° thou wilt let me live and feel no pain.   *If*
5 KING HENRY Ah, what a sign it is of evil life
    Where Death's approach is seen so terrible.
    WARWICK Beaufort, it is thy sovereign speaks to thee.
    CARDINAL Bring me unto my trial when you will.
    Died he° not in his bed? Where should he die?   *(Gloucester)*
10   Can I make men live whe'er° they will or no?   *whether*
    Oh, torture me no more: I will confess.
    Alive again? Then show me where he is.
    I'll give a thousand pound to look upon him.
    He hath no eyes: the dust hath blinded them.
15   Comb down his hair—look, look, it stands upright,
    Like lime twigs[1] set to catch my wingèd soul!
    Give me some drink, and bid the apothecary
    Bring the strong poison that I bought of him.
    KING HENRY O thou eternal mover of the heavens,°   *(God)*
20   Look with a gentle eye upon this wretch.
    Oh, beat away the busy meddling fiend
    That lays strong siege unto this wretch's soul,
    And from his bosom purge this black despair.
    WARWICK See how the pangs of death do make him grin.° *bare his teeth*
25 SALISBURY Disturb him not; let him pass peaceably.

---

3. In classical mythology, the paradise where blessed
souls dwelled.
4. To die near you or by means of you is not really to
die (with a continuing pun on "die" as meaning "attain
orgasm").

5. In Greek mythology, Iris was a messenger of the
gods, particularly of Hera.
3.3 Location: The Cardinal's bedchamber, London.
1. Twigs smeared with birdlime. See note to 1.3.87.

KING HENRY   Peace to his soul, if God's good pleasure be.
  —Lord Cardinal, if thou think'st on heaven's bliss,
  Hold up thy hand; make signal of thy hope.
     [CARDINAL *dies.*]
  He dies and makes no sign. O God, forgive him.
30 WARWICK   So bad a death argues a monstrous life.
KING HENRY   Forbear to judge, for we are sinners all.
  Close up his eyes and draw the curtain close,
  And let us all to meditation.°   *Exeunt.*   *prayer*

4.1 (Q 4.1)

Alarum. Fight at sea. Ordnance° goes off. Enter   *Small cannon*
LIEUTENANT, [*the* MASTER *and Master's* MATE, *Walter*
WHITMORE, *and*] SUFFOLK[, *disguised, with two*
GENTLEMEN *as prisoners,*] *and others.*

LIEUTENANT   The gaudy, blabbing, and remorseful day[1]
  Is crept into the bosom of the sea,
  And now loud-howling wolves arouse the jades[2]
  That drag the tragic melancholy night,
5 Who, with their drowsy, slow, and flagging wings,
  Clip° dead men's graves, and from their misty jaws   *Embrace*
  Breathe foul contagious darkness in the air.
  Therefore bring forth the soldiers of our prize,°   *captured ship*
  For, whilst our pinnace° anchors in the Downs,[3]   *small ship*
10 Here shall they make their ransom on the sand,
  Or with their blood stain this discolored shore.[4]
  —Master, [*indicating* FIRST GENTLEMAN] this prisoner
    freely give I thee.
  —And thou that art his mate, make boot of this.[5] [*indicating*
  SECOND GENTLEMAN]
  —The other [*indicating* SUFFOLK], Walter Whitmore, is thy
    share.
15 FIRST GENTLEMAN   What is my ransom, master? Let me
    know.
MASTER   A thousand crowns, or else lay down your head.
MATE [*to* SECOND GENTLEMAN]   And so much shall you give,
    or off goes yours.
LIEUTENANT [*to both* GENTLEMEN]   What, think you much to
    pay two thousand crowns,
  And bear the name and port° of gentlemen?   *demeanor*
20 WHITMORE   Cut both the villains' throats! —For die you
    shall.
  The lives of those which we have lost in fight
  Be counterpoised° with such a petty sum?   *Be compensated*
FIRST GENTLEMAN   I'll give it, sir, and therefore spare my life.
SECOND GENTLEMAN   And so will I, and write home for it
    straight.
25 WHITMORE [*to* SUFFOLK]   I lost mine eye in laying the prize
    aboard,°   *boarding the ship*

4.1 Location: On the Kentish coast.
1. The garish, telltale (revealing secrets of the dark), and guilty day.
2. Usually worn-out cart horses; here, an allusion to the dragons of Hecate that, according to classical mythology, drew Night's chariot.
3. A sheltered area of the North Sea near the English Channel where ships could seek refuge.
4. Or discolor this shore with their blood.
5. Make a profit from (the ransom of) this second prisoner.

And therefore to revenge it shalt thou die—
And so should these, if I might have my will.

LIEUTENANT   Be not so rash. Take ransom; let him live.

SUFFOLK   Look on my George:[6] I am a gentleman.
30   Rate° me at what thou wilt, thou shalt be paid.   *Value*

WHITMORE   And so am I; my name is Walter[7] Whitmore.
[SUFFOLK *starts*.]
How now? Why starts thou? What, doth death affright?

SUFFOLK   Thy name affrights me, in whose sound is death.
A cunning man did calculate my birth,[8]
35   And told me that by "water" I should die.
Yet let not this make thee be bloody-minded;
Thy name is Gualtier,[9] being rightly sounded.

WHITMORE   Gualtier or Walter: which it is I care not.
Never yet did base dishonor blur our name
40   But with our sword we wiped away the blot.
Therefore, when merchant-like I sell revenge,
Broke be my sword, my arms° torn and defaced,   *coat of arms*
And I proclaimed a coward through the world.

SUFFOLK   Stay, Whitmore, for thy prisoner is a prince,
45   The Duke of Suffolk, William de la Pole.

WHITMORE   The Duke of Suffolk muffled up in rags?

SUFFOLK   Ay, but these rags are no part of the Duke.
Jove sometime went disguised, and why not I?

LIEUTENANT   But Jove was never slain as thou shalt be.

50   SUFFOLK   Obscure and lousy° swain! King Henry's blood,[1]   *lice-infested*
The honorable blood of Lancaster,
Must not be shed by such a jaded groom.[2]
Hast thou not kissed thy hand° and held my stirrup?   *(a gesture of servility)*
Bareheaded, plodded by my footcloth mule,[3]
55   And thought thee happy when I shook° my head?   *nodded*
How often hast thou waited at my cup,
Fed from my trencher,° kneeled down at the board,°   *platter / table*
When I have feasted with Queen Margaret?
Remember it, and let it make thee crestfall'n[4]—
60   Ay, and allay this thy abortive° pride.   *monstrous*
How in our voiding lobby° hast thou stood   *antechamber*
And duly waited for my coming forth?
This hand of mine hath writ° in thy behalf,   *written testimonials*
And therefore shall it charm° thy riotous tongue.   *silence*

65   WHITMORE   Speak, Captain, shall I stab the forlorn swain?°   *wretched peasant*

LIEUTENANT   First let my words stab him, as he hath me.

SUFFOLK   Base slave, thy words are blunt° and so art thou.   *harmless*

LIEUTENANT   Convey him hence, and on our longboat's side
Strike off his head.

SUFFOLK   Thou dar'st not for thy own.

70   LIEUTENANT   Pole?[5] Sir Pool? Lord?

---

6. Alluding to the image of St. George and the dragon on the insignia of the Order of the Garter, the highest order of English knighthood.
7. "Walter" was usually pronounced "water." The spirit Asnath, conjured by Roger Bolingbroke, had predicted that Suffolk should die by "water" (see 1.4.32).
8. An astrologer cast my horoscope.
9. French for "Walter."
1. A dubious claim: Suffolk's mother was a distant cousin to Henry VI.
2. Servant in charge of horses; contemptible fellow.
3. The animal used to bear the large, richly ornamented cloth displayed in royal processions.
4. Humble; deprived of a "crest" (coat of arms).
5. TEXTUAL COMMENT The following punning insults play on Suffolk's family name, which can be pronounced "pool" ("sink," i.e., dirty water). See Digital Edition TC 7 (Folio edited text).

Ay, kennel,° puddle, sink,° whose filth and dirt   *open gutter / cesspool*
Troubles the silver spring where England drinks;
Now will I dam up this thy yawning mouth
For swallowing the treasure of the realm.
75 Thy lips that kissed the Queen shall sweep the ground,
And thou that smiled'st at good Duke Humphrey's death
Against the senseless° winds shall grin in vain,   *unfeeling*
Who in contempt shall hiss at thee again.
And wedded be thou to the hags of hell
80 For daring to affy° a mighty lord   *betroth*
Unto the daughter of a worthless king,
Having neither subject, wealth, nor diadem.
By devilish policy art thou grown great
And like ambitious Sulla,[6] over-gorged
85 With gobbets° of thy mother's° bleeding heart.   *chunks / (England's)*
By thee Anjou and Maine were sold to France;
The false revolting° Normans through° thee   *rebellious / because of*
Disdain to call us lord, and Picardy
Hath slain their governors, surprised our forts,
90 And sent the ragged soldiers wounded home.
The princely Warwick and the Nevilles all,
Whose dreadful swords were never drawn in vain,
As hating thee, are rising up in arms;
And now the house of York, thrust from the crown
95 By shameful murder of a guiltless king[7]
And lofty, proud, encroaching tyranny,
Burns with revenging fire, whose hopeful colors
Advance° our half-faced sun,[8] striving to shine,   *Display*
Under the which is writ, "*Invitis nubibus.*"°   *In spite of clouds*
100 The commons here in Kent are up in arms,
And to conclude, reproach and beggary
Is crept into the palace of our king
And all by thee. —Away! Convey him hence.
SUFFOLK   Oh, that I were a god, to shoot forth thunder
105 Upon these paltry, servile, abject drudges!
Small things make base men proud. This villain here,
Being captain of a pinnace, threatens more
Than Bargulus, the strong Illyrian pirate.[9]
Drones° suck not eagles' blood, but rob beehives.   *Beetles; parasites*
110 It is impossible that I should die
By such a lowly vassal as thyself.
Thy words move rage and not remorse in me.
I go of message° from the Queen to France: *as messenger*
I charge thee waft° me safely 'cross the Channel.   *convey*
115 LIEUTENANT   Walter—
WHITMORE   Come, Suffolk, I must waft thee to thy death.
SUFFOLK   *Paene gelidus timor occupat artus.*[1]

---

6. The Roman dictator Lucius Cornelius Sulla (138–78 B.C.E.), notorious for drawing up lists of enemies whom he executed or banished.
7. Alluding to the deposition and murder of Richard II, which enabled the Lancastrian branch of the royal family to seize the throne. Shakespeare dramatizes these events in *Richard II*.
8. A sun emerging above clouds was the badge of Edward III and his successor, Richard II.

9. A reference to Bardylis, a fourth-century B.C.E. Illyrian king alluded to in Cicero's *De Officiis (On Public Duties)*, a text much used in Elizabethan schools. Some English translations of Cicero described him as a bandit, robber, or pirate.
1. Cold fear seizes my limbs almost entirely (perhaps alluding to Virgil, *Aeneid* 7.446; Lucan, *Pharsalia* 1.246; or both).

It is thee I fear—
WHITMORE   Thou shalt have cause to fear before I leave thee.
120   What, are ye daunted now? Now will ye stoop?
FIRST GENTLEMAN   My gracious lord, entreat him; speak
     him fair.
SUFFOLK   Suffolk's imperial tongue is stern and rough,
   Used to command, untaught to plead for favor.
   Far be it we should honor such as these
125   With humble suit: no, rather let my head
   Stoop to the block than these knees bow to any
   Save to the God of heaven and to my king,
   And sooner dance upon a bloody pole[2]
   Than stand uncovered to the vulgar groom.
130   True nobility is exempt from fear;
   More can I bear than you dare execute.
LIEUTENANT   Hale° him away, and let him talk no more.   *Drag*
SUFFOLK   Come, soldiers, show what cruelty ye can,
   That this my death may never be forgot.
135   Great men oft die by vile bezonians;[3]
   A Roman sworder and banditto° slave   *cutthroat and lawless*
   Murdered sweet Tully;[4] Brutus' bastard hand[5]
   Stabbed Julius Caesar; savage islanders
   Pompey the Great[6]—and Suffolk dies by pirates.
                Exit WHITMORE *with* SUFFOLK.
140   LIEUTENANT   And as for these whose ransom we have set,
   It is our pleasure one of them depart.
   [*to* SECOND GENTLEMAN] Therefore come you with us, and
     [*to his men, indicating* FIRST GENTLEMAN] let him go.
                Exeunt all but the FIRST GENTLEMAN.
        Enter WHITMORE, *with* [*Suffolk's*] *body* [*and
        severed head*].
WHITMORE   There let his head and lifeless body lie
   Until the Queen his mistress bury it.   *Exit.*
145   FIRST GENTLEMAN   Oh, barbarous and bloody spectacle!
   His body will I bear unto the King.
   If he revenge it not, yet will his friends;
   So will the Queen that living held him dear.
                [*Exit with body and head.*]

4.2 (Q 4.2)
Enter [*two* REBELS *carrying staves*].[1]
FIRST REBEL   Come and get thee a sword, though made of a
   lath;[2] they have been up° these two days.   *in revolt*

---

2. Punning on his name ("Pole") and on Elizabethan slang for "head" ("poll"), Suffolk alludes to the fact that heads of executed criminals were set upon poles in public places. Londoners would often pass by such poles as they crossed the bridge on their way to the theaters in Southwark.
3. Base fellows. From the Spanish word *bisoño*, meaning "recruit": foot soldiers were usually poor commoners.
4. *Tully*: The Roman orator Cicero, who was in fact murdered by Roman soldiers.
5. Brutus, who helped murder Caesar, was rumored to have been his illegitimate son.
6. Alluding either to Plutarch's claim that the Egyptians who murdered this Roman general were led by

one born on the island of Chios or to the tradition that Pompey was murdered on the island of Lesbos.
4.2 Location: Blackheath, Kent.
1. TEXTUAL COMMENT Staves are mentioned only in the Q stage directions and dialogue, and they may reflect performance. While Q names the rebels "George" and "Nick," and F as "Bevis" and "John Holland," this edition corrects what is probably a mistake in F (Bevis and Holland were probably actors who played these parts, not actual rebels in the time of Henry VI). Consequently, the characters here are called "First Rebel" and "Second Rebel." See Digital Edition TC 8 (Folio edited text).
2. A strip of wood commonly used as a sword or dagger by the Vice figure in English morality plays.

SECOND REBEL They have the more need to sleep now, then.

FIRST REBEL I tell thee, Jack Cade the clothier³ means to
5 dress the commonwealth, and turn it,⁴ and set a new nap
upon it.⁵

SECOND REBEL So he had need, for 'tis threadbare. Well, I say
it was never merry world in England since gentlemen came
up.°   *came into fashion*

10 FIRST REBEL Oh, miserable age! Virtue is not regarded in
handicraftsmen.°   *artisans*

SECOND REBEL The nobility think scorn to go in leather aprons.°   *(workers' attire)*

FIRST REBEL Nay, more: the King's Council are no good
workmen.

15 SECOND REBEL True; and yet it is said, "Labor in thy vocation," which is as much to say as, "Let the magistrates be
laboring men"—and therefore should we be magistrates.

FIRST REBEL Thou hast hit it. For there's no better sign of a
brave° mind than a hard° hand.   *fine / calloused*

20 SECOND REBEL I see them, I see them! There's Best's son, the
tanner of Wingham.

FIRST REBEL He shall have the skins of our enemies to make
dog's leather⁶ of.

SECOND REBEL And Dick the butcher.

25 FIRST REBEL Then is sin struck down like an ox, and iniquity's
throat cut like a calf.

SECOND REBEL And Smith the weaver.

FIRST REBEL Argo,⁷ their thread of life is spun.

SECOND REBEL Come, come; let's fall in with them.

Drum. Enter CADE, *Dick [the]* BUTCHER, *Smith the*
WEAVER, *and a* SAWYER, *with infinite numbers.*

30 CADE We, John Cade, so termed of° our supposed father—   *named for*

BUTCHER [*aside*] Or rather of stealing a cade° of herrings.   *barrel*

CADE For our enemies shall fall before us,⁸ inspired with the
spirit of putting down kings and princes. —Command
silence.

35 BUTCHER Silence!

CADE My father was a Mortimer—

BUTCHER [*aside*] He was an honest man and a good brick-
layer.⁹

CADE My mother a Plantagenet—

40 BUTCHER [*aside*] I knew her well; she was a midwife.

CADE My wife descended of the Lacys¹—

BUTCHER [*aside*] She was indeed a peddler's daughter and sold
many laces.

WEAVER [*aside*] But now of late, not able to travel with her
45 furred pack,² she washes bucks³ here at home.

CADE Therefore am I of an honorable house.

---

3. Clothiers, or textile workers, were involved in a
number of uprisings throughout the sixteenth century.
4. Turn it inside out (as a way of renewing old
cloth), with a secondary sense of inverting the social
hierarchy.
5. Improve its surface texture, probably by brushing
the outer fibers ("nap") of the cloth; reform it.
6. Inferior leather used in glove making.
7. A variant form of *ergo*, Latin for "therefore."
8. Borrowing biblical language and punning on the

Latin *cadere*, meaning "fall."
9. Punning on "Mortimer" and "mortarer" (meaning
"builder").
1. The family name of the earls of Lincoln.
2. Not able to travel with her peddler's pack made of
skins with the hair turned outward; not able to make
a living with her sexual organs.
3. She washes laundry; she absolves ("washes") cuckolds (husbands with horns, like bucks) of their shame
by helping them get even with their unfaithful wives.

BUTCHER [*aside*] Ay, by my faith, the field is honorable, and
there was he born, under a hedge; for his father had never a
house but the cage.°   *prison*

50 CADE Valiant I am.
WEAVER [*aside*] 'A° must needs, for beggary is valiant.[4]   *He*
CADE I am able to endure much.
BUTCHER [*aside*] No question of that, for I have seen him
whipped[5] three market days together.

55 CADE I fear neither sword nor fire.
WEAVER [*aside*] He need not fear the sword, for his coat is of
proof.[6]
BUTCHER [*aside*] But methinks he should stand in fear of fire,
being burnt i'th' hand for stealing of sheep.[7]

60 CADE Be brave, then, for your captain is brave and vows reformation. There shall be in England seven halfpenny loaves
sold for a penny, the three-hooped pot shall have ten hoops,[8]
and I will make it felony to drink small° beer. All the realm   *weak*
shall be in° common, and in Cheapside[9] shall my palfrey° go   *held in / saddle horse*

65 to grass; and when I am king, as king I will be—
ALL God save your majesty!
CADE I thank you, good people—there shall be no money; all
shall eat and drink on my score,° and I will apparel them all   *at my expense*
in one livery that they may agree like brothers and worship

70 me their lord.
BUTCHER The first thing we do, let's kill all the lawyers.
CADE Nay, that I mean to do. Is not this a lamentable thing,
that of the skin of an innocent lamb should be made parchment; that parchment, being scribbled o'er, should undo a

75 man? Some say the bee stings, but I say 'tis the bee's wax,°   *sealing wax*
for I did but seal[1] once to a thing, and I was never mine own
man since. —How now? Who's there?
              Enter [some, bringing in] a CLERK.
WEAVER The clerk of Chartham: he can write and read and
cast account.°   *do arithmetic*

80 CADE Oh, monstrous!
WEAVER We took him setting of boys' copies.[2]
CADE Here's a villain!
WEAVER He's a book in his pocket with red letters[3] in't.
CADE Nay, then he is a conjurer.

85 BUTCHER Nay, he can make obligations° and write court hand.[4]   *bonds*
CADE I am sorry for't. The man is a proper° man, of mine   *handsome*
honor; unless I find him guilty he shall not die. —Come
hither, sirrah, I must examine thee. What is thy name?
CLERK Emmanuel.

90 BUTCHER They use to write it on the top of letters.[5] —'Twill
go hard with you.

---

4. Worthy of praise; sturdy. The Weaver is referring
ironically to the fact that Elizabethan poor laws
made it illegal to give alms to able-bodied, or "valiant," beggars.
5. The usual punishment for vagabonds.
6. Impenetrable (from dirt?); well worn.
7. Thieves were branded on one hand with a "T" for
"thief."
8. "Hoops," or regularly spaced bands on pots, were
used for measuring. Cade means that for the price of
a three-hooped pot (about a quart), one will receive

over three times that amount.
9. Elizabethan London's chief commercial district.
1. Sign and seal (a legal document).
2. Preparing writing exercises for schoolboys. Village clerks often doubled as schoolmasters.
3. Alluding to the red printing in almanacs and
primers.
4. The script used for legal documents.
5. The name, which means "God is with us," commonly appeared on legal documents.

CADE Let me alone. Dost thou use to write thy name? Or hast
thou a mark[6] to thyself, like a honest plain-dealing man?

CLERK Sir, I thank God I have been so well brought up that I
95 can write my name.

ALL He hath confessed! Away with him! He's a villain and a
traitor.

CADE Away with him, I say! Hang him with his pen and inkhorn about his neck.   *Exit one with the* CLERK.

        Enter MICHAEL[, *a rebel*].[7]

100 MICHAEL Where's our general?

CADE Here I am, thou particular[8] fellow.

MICHAEL Fly, fly, fly! Sir Humphrey Stafford and his brother
are hard by with the King's forces.

CADE Stand, villain, stand, or I'll fell thee down. He shall be
105 encountered with a man as good as himself. He is but a
knight, is 'a?

MICHAEL No.[9]

CADE To equal him I will make myself a knight presently. [*He
kneels.*] Rise up, Sir John Mortimer. [*He rises.*] —Now, have
110 at him!

        Enter Sir Humphrey STAFFORD *and his* BROTHER,
        with drum and Soldiers.

STAFFORD Rebellious hinds,° the filth and scum of Kent,   *peasants*
Marked for the gallows, lay your weapons down!
Home to your cottages; forsake this groom.
The King is merciful if you revolt.°   *turn against Cade*

115 BROTHER But angry, wrathful, and inclined to blood
If you go forward; therefore yield, or die.

CADE As for these silken-coated slaves, I pass° not.   *care*
It is to you, good people, that I speak,
Over whom, in time to come, I hope to reign,
120 For I am rightful heir unto the crown.

STAFFORD Villain, thy father was a plasterer,
And thou thyself a shearman,[1] art thou not?

CADE And Adam was a gardener.

BROTHER   And what of that?

CADE Marry, this: Edmund Mortimer, Earl of March,
125 Married the Duke of Clarence' daughter, did he not?

STAFFORD Ay, sir.

CADE By her he had two children at one birth.

BROTHER That's false.

CADE Ay, there's the question; but I say 'tis true.
130 The elder of them being put to nurse
Was by a beggar-woman stol'n away
And, ignorant of his birth and parentage,
Became a bricklayer when he came to age.
His son am I; deny it if you can.

135 BUTCHER Nay, 'tis too true; therefore he shall be king.

WEAVER Sir, he made a chimney in my father's house, and the
bricks are alive at this day to testify it; therefore deny it not.

---

6. Those who were illiterate often "signed" documents by using distinctive marks.
7. Q calls this figure "Tom."
8. Private (as opposed to "general" in the previous
line).

9. No, nothing but a knight. The Messenger is replying to the negative implied in the prior sentence: "He
is nothing but a knight, is he?"
1. One who cuts the nap from cloth during its
manufacture.

STAFFORD   And will you credit this base drudge's words
That speaks he knows not what?

140 ALL   Ay, marry will we; therefore get ye gone.

BROTHER   Jack Cade, the Duke of York hath taught you this.

CADE [*aside*]   He lies, for I invented it myself. —Go to, sirrah.[2] Tell the King from me that for his father's sake, Henry
the Fifth, in whose time boys went to span-counter° for   *played a game of toss*

145 French crowns,[3] I am content he shall reign, but I'll be Protector over him.

BUTCHER   And, furthermore, we'll have the Lord Saye's[4] head
for selling the dukedom of Maine.

CADE   And good reason, for thereby is England maimed and

150 fain to go with a staff, but that my puissance° holds it up.   *power*
—Fellow kings, I tell you that that Lord Saye hath gelded the
commonwealth, and made it an eunuch, and—more than
that—he can speak French, and therefore he is a traitor.

STAFFORD   Oh, gross and miserable ignorance!

155 CADE   Nay, answer if you can. The Frenchmen are our enemies; go to, then. I ask but this: can he that speaks with the
tongue of an enemy be a good counselor, or no?

ALL   No, no—and therefore we'll have his head!

BROTHER   Well, seeing gentle words will not prevail,

160 Assail them with the army of the King.

STAFFORD   Herald, away, and throughout every town
Proclaim them traitors that are up with Cade,
That those which fly before the battle ends
May even in their wives' and children's sight

165 Be hanged up for° example at their doors;   *to make an*
And you that be the King's friends follow me.
               Exeunt [the STAFFORDS *and their soldiers].*

CADE   And you that love the commons, follow me!
Now show yourselves men; 'tis for liberty.
We will not leave one lord, one gentleman:

170 Spare none but such as go in clouted shoon,°   *hobnailed shoes*
For they are thrifty honest men, and such
As would, but that they dare not, take our parts.

BUTCHER   They are all in order, and march toward us.

CADE   But then are we in order when we are most out of

175 order.° Come, march forward!   [*Exeunt.*]   *rebellious*

4.3 (Q 4.3)

Alarums to the fight, wherein both the STAFFORDS *are
slain. Enter* CADE *and the rest.*

CADE   Where's Dick, the butcher of Ashford?

BUTCHER   Here, sir.

CADE   They fell before thee like sheep and oxen, and thou
behaved'st thyself as if thou hadst been in thine own

5 slaughterhouse. Therefore thus will I reward thee: the Lent

---

2. Term used to address inferiors.
3. Alluding to Henry V's conquest of France. "French
crowns" might refer to French coins, kings, kingdoms, or the bald heads that were symptomatic of the
venereal diseases blamed on the French.

4. *Lord Saye:* James Fiennes, Treasurer of England,
was associated with Suffolk in the loss of Anjou and
Maine.
4.3 Location: Scene continues.

shall be as long again as it is, and thou shalt have a license
to kill for a hundred lacking one.[1]

BUTCHER   I desire no more.

CADE   And, to speak truth, thou deserv'st no less.
[*He takes up Stafford's sword.*]

10   This monument of the victory will I bear, and the bodies
shall be dragged at my horse heels till I do come to London,
where we will have the Mayor's sword borne before us.

BUTCHER   If we mean to thrive and do good, break open the
gaols and let out the prisoners.

15   CADE   Fear not° that, I warrant thee. Come, let's march   *Don't worry about*
towards London.   *Exeunt.*

4.4 (Q 4.4)

Enter KING HENRY *with a supplication, and*
QUEEN MARGARET *with Suffolk's head,*
the Duke of BUCKINGHAM, *and the Lord* SAYE.

QUEEN MARGARET [*aside*]   Oft have I heard that grief
softens the mind
And makes it fearful and degenerate;
Think therefore on revenge, and cease to weep.
But who can cease to weep and look on this?

5   Here may his head lie on my throbbing breast,
But where's the body that I should embrace?

BUCKINGHAM   What answer makes your grace to the rebels'
supplication?

KING HENRY   I'll send some holy bishop to entreat,
For God forbid so many simple souls

10   Should perish by the sword. And I myself,
Rather than bloody war shall cut them short,
Will parley° with Jack Cade, their general.   *speak*
But stay, I'll read it over once again.

QUEEN MARGARET   Ah, barbarous villains! Hath this lovely face

15   Ruled like a wandering planet over me,[1]
And could it not enforce them to relent
That were unworthy to behold the same?

KING HENRY   Lord Saye, Jack Cade hath sworn to have thy
head.

SAYE   Ay, but I hope your highness shall have his.

20   KING HENRY   —How now, madam?
Still lamenting and mourning for Suffolk's death?
I fear me, love, if that I had been dead,
Thou wouldst not have mourned so much for me.

QUEEN MARGARET   No, my love, I should not mourn, but die
for thee.
Enter a MESSENGER.

25   KING HENRY   How now? What news? Why com'st thou in
such haste?

1. Butchers were not permitted to slaughter meat
during Lent (the forty-day period before Easter during which Christians were to avoid eating flesh)
except by special license to provide food for the ill.
Cade promises the Butcher that he will have such a
license and that Lent will be twice as long as it is

now. *thou . . . one:* You can kill ninety-nine animals,
or serve ninety-nine customers.
4.4 Location: The palace, London.
1. It was popularly believed that influences from the
stars ("wandering planets") determined the fate of
those born under them.

MESSENGER   The rebels are in Southwark.[2] Fly, my lord!
   Jack Cade proclaims himself Lord Mortimer,
   Descended from the Duke of Clarence' house,
   And calls your grace "usurper" openly,
30   And vows to crown himself in Westminster.
   His army is a ragged multitude
   Of hinds and peasants, rude and merciless.
   Sir Humphrey Stafford and his brother's death
   Hath given them heart and courage to proceed.
35   All scholars, lawyers, courtiers, gentlemen,
   They call false caterpillars° and intend their death.   *treacherous parasites*
KING HENRY   Oh, graceless° men! They know not what   *sinful*
   they do.[3]
BUCKINGHAM   My gracious lord, retire to Kenilworth°   *(a royal castle)*
   Until a power be raised to put them down.
40 QUEEN MARGARET   Ah, were the Duke of Suffolk now alive,
   These Kentish rebels would be soon appeased.°   *made peaceful*
KING HENRY   Lord Saye, the traitors hateth thee;
   Therefore away with us to Kenilworth.
SAYE   So might your grace's person be in danger:
45   The sight of me is odious in their eyes,
   And therefore in this city will I stay
   And live alone as secret as I may.
        Enter another MESSENGER.
MESSENGER   Jack Cade hath gotten London Bridge;
   The citizens fly and forsake their houses;
50   The rascal people, thirsting after prey,
   Join with the traitor, and they jointly swear
   To spoil° the city and your royal court.   *plunder*
BUCKINGHAM   Then linger not, my lord; away, take horse!
KING HENRY   Come, Margaret; God our hope will succor us.
55 QUEEN MARGARET [*aside*]   My hope is gone, now Suffolk is
   deceased.
KING HENRY [*to* SAYE]   Farewell, my lord. Trust not the
   Kentish rebels.
BUCKINGHAM [*to* SAYE]   Trust nobody, for fear you be
   betrayed.
SAYE   The trust I have is in mine innocence,
   And therefore am I bold and resolute.   *Exeunt.*

4.5 (Q 4.5)

Enter Lord SCALES *upon the Tower, walking. Then
enter two or three* CITIZENS *below.*

SCALES   How now? Is Jack Cade slain?
FIRST CITIZEN   No, my lord, nor likely to be slain, for they
   have won the bridge, killing all those that withstand them.
   The Lord Mayor craves aid of your honor from the Tower to
5   defend the city from the rebels.
SCALES   Such aid as I can spare you shall command,
   But I am troubled here with them myself;
   The rebels have assayed° to win the Tower.   *attempted*

2. A suburb of London (in Shakespeare's time, the site of brothels and theaters).
3. An echo of Jesus' words on the cross to those who crucified and mocked him. See Luke 23:34.
4.5 Location: The Tower, London.

But get you to Smithfield[1] and gather head,°   *raise forces*
10 And thither I will send you Matthew Gough.
Fight for your king, your country, and your lives!
And so farewell, for I must hence again.   *Exeunt.*

4.6 (Q 4.6)
Enter Jack CADE *and the rest, and strikes his staff on*
London Stone.[1]

CADE   Now is Mortimer lord of this city. And here, sitting
upon London Stone, I charge and command that, of the
city's cost, the Pissing Conduit[2] run nothing but claret wine
this first year of our reign. And now henceforward it shall be
5   treason for any that calls me other than Lord Mortimer.
     Enter a SOLDIER, *running.*
SOLDIER   Jack Cade! Jack Cade!
CADE   Knock him down there.
     They kill him.
BUTCHER   If this fellow be wise, he'll never call ye Jack Cade
more; I think he hath a very fair warning. [*He reads Soldier's*
10   *message.*] —My lord, there's an army gathered together in
Smithfield.
CADE   Come, then, let's go fight with them. But first, go and
set London Bridge on fire and, if you can, burn down the
Tower too. Come, let's away.   *Exeunt.*

4.7 (Q 4.7)
Alarums. Matthew Gough is slain, and all the rest.
Then enter Jack CADE *with his company.*

CADE   So, sirs, now go some and pull down the Savoy.[1] Others
to th'Inns of Court[2]—down with them all.
BUTCHER   I have a suit unto your lordship.
CADE   Be it a lordship, thou shalt have it for that word.
5 BUTCHER   Only that the laws of England may come out of
your mouth.
JOHN [*aside*]   Mass,[3] 'twill be sore° law, then, for he was thrust   *harsh*
in the mouth with a spear, and 'tis not whole yet.
WEAVER [*aside*]   Nay, John, it will be stinking law, for his
10   breath stinks with eating toasted cheese.
CADE   I have thought upon it; it shall be so. Away! Burn all
the records of the realm; my mouth shall be the Parliament
of England.
JOHN [*aside*]   Then we are like to have biting° statutes unless   *severe*
15   his teeth be pulled out.
CADE   And henceforward all things shall be in common.
     Enter a MESSENGER.
MESSENGER   My lord, a prize, a prize! Here's the Lord Saye
which sold the towns in France. He that made us pay one-

---

1. Area just outside London's walls and to the northwest.
4.6 Location: Cannon Street, London.
1. An ancient stone found in Cannon Street and famous as a London landmark.
2. The nickname for Little Conduit, a fountain used by lower-class Londoners as a water supply.
4.7 Location: Smithfield; London.

1. An anachronistic reference to the London residence of the Duke of Lancaster, which was burned down during a 1381 uprising and not rebuilt until 1505.
2. The buildings where London's lawyers were trained and lived.
3. *Mass:* a mild oath meaning "By the mass" (By the Holy Eucharist).

and-twenty fifteens and one shilling to the pound, the last
20 subsidy.[4]
    Enter a Rebel with the Lord SAYE.
CADE Well, he shall be beheaded for it ten times. Ah, thou
say, thou serge—nay, thou buckram lord![5] Now art thou
within point-blank° of our jurisdiction regal. What canst   *within reach*
thou answer to my majesty for giving up of Normandy unto
25 Mounsieur Basimecu,[6] the Dolphin of France? Be it known
unto thee by these presence,[7] even the presence of Lord
Mortimer, that I am the besom° that must sweep the court   *broom*
clean of such filth as thou art. Thou hast most traitorously
corrupted the youth of the realm in erecting a grammar
30 school; and whereas, before, our forefathers had no other
books but the score and the tally,[8] thou hast caused printing to be used, and, contrary to the King, his crown, and
dignity, thou hast built a paper mill.[9] It will be proved to
thy face that thou hast men about thee that usually talk of
35 a noun and a verb and such abominable words as no Christian ear can endure to hear. Thou hast appointed justices of
peace to call poor men before them about matters they
were not able to answer. Moreover, thou hast put them in
prison and, because they could not read,[1] thou hast hanged
40 them, when indeed only for that cause° they have been   *for that reason alone*
most worthy to live. Thou dost ride in a footcloth,[2] dost
thou not?
SAYE What of that?
CADE Marry, thou oughtst not to let thy horse wear a cloak
45 when honester men than thou go in° their hose and doublets.   *wear only*
BUTCHER And work in their shirt, too—as myself, for exam-
ple, that am a butcher.
SAYE —You men of Kent—
BUTCHER What say you of Kent?
50 SAYE Nothing but this: 'tis *bona terra, mala gens*.[3]
CADE Away with him, away with him! He speaks Latin.
SAYE Hear me but speak, and bear me where you will.
Kent, in the *Commentaries* Caesar writ,
Is termed the civil'st° place of all this isle;   *most civilized*
55 Sweet is the country because full of riches,
The people liberal,° valiant, active, wealthy—   *generous*
Which makes me hope you are not void of pity.
I sold not Maine; I lost not Normandy;
Yet to recover them would lose my life.
60 Justice with favor° have I always done;   *leniency*

---

4. He who made us pay very high personal property taxes in the last tax assessment. A "fifteen" was a levy of one-fifteenth of the property value; "twenty-one fifteens" would be a tax in excess of the value of the property itself.
5. Say was an expensive silk fabric, serge a durable woolen fabric often worn by the lower classes, and buckram a coarse linen also worn by the poor.
6. Punning on *baise mon cul*, French for "kiss my ass."
7. "These presents" was a legal term meaning "the present document," a phrase that begins many legal writings of the period. Cade, however, means "in the presence of the King, who declares the law."
8. A rudimentary device for keeping track of finan-

cial transactions. Sticks were marked, or "scored," split into two pieces, and then divided between the debtor and creditor. Each half was called a "tally."
9. Printing presses and paper mills were not in fact established in England until late in the fifteenth century. Under Elizabeth, they were subject to strict regulation.
1. Read Latin. By demonstrating reading knowledge of Latin, a person charged with a crime in early modern England could plead "benefit of clergy" and thereby be excused from hanging.
2. An ornamented cloth hung over the back of a horse and reaching to the ground on each side.
3. A good land, a bad people.

Prayers and tears have moved me, gifts could never.
When have I aught° exacted at your hands,   *anything*
Kent, to maintain the King, the realm, and you?
Large gifts have I bestowed on learnèd clerks°   *scholars*
65 Because my book preferred me to the King[4]
And, seeing ignorance is the curse of God,
Knowledge the wing wherewith we fly to heaven,
Unless you be possessed with devilish spirits,
You cannot but forbear to murder me.
70 This tongue hath parleyed unto° foreign kings   *negotiated with*
For your behoof°—   *behalf*
CADE   Tut, when struck'st thou one blow in the field?°   *battlefield*
SAYE   Great men have reaching hands;[5] oft have I struck
Those that I never saw, and struck them dead.
75 REBEL   O monstrous coward! What—to come behind folks?
SAYE   These cheeks are pale for watching for your good—
CADE   Give him a box o'th' ear, and that will make 'em red
again.
SAYE   Long sitting° to determine poor men's causes   *(as a judge)*
80 Hath made me full of sickness and diseases.
CADE   Ye shall have a hempen caudle,[6] then, and the help of
hatchet.°   *executioner's ax*
BUTCHER   Why dost thou quiver, man?
SAYE   The palsy, and not fear, provokes me.
85 CADE   Nay, he nods at us, as who should say, "I'll be even with
you." I'll see if his head will stand steadier on a pole, or no.
Take him away and behead him.
SAYE   Tell me wherein have I offended most?
Have I affected wealth or honor? Speak.
90 Are my chests filled up with extorted gold?
Is my apparel sumptuous to behold?
Whom have I injured, that ye seek my death?
These hands are free from guiltless bloodshedding,
This breast from harboring foul deceitful thoughts.
95 Oh, let me live!
CADE [*aside*]   I feel remorse in myself with his words, but I'll
bridle it. He shall die, an it be but for pleading so well for his
life. —Away with him! He has a familiar° under his tongue;   *demon*
he speaks not i'God's name. Go, take him away, I say, and
100 strike off his head presently,° and then break into his son-in-   *immediately*
law's house, Sir James Cromer, and strike off his head, and
bring them both upon two poles hither.
ALL   It shall be done.
SAYE   Ah, countrymen, if when you make your prayers
105 God should be so obdurate as yourselves,
How would it fare with your departed souls?
And therefore yet relent, and save my life.
CADE   Away with him, and do as I command ye!
                [*Exit one or two with the Lord* SAYE.]
The proudest peer in the realm shall not wear a head on his

4. Because my own education brought me to the attention of the King (and improved my social position).
5. A variation on the classical proverb "Kings have
long hands," suggesting that monarchs and influential

people such as Lord Saye have influence that causes
much to happen even when they are not present.
6. Caudle was a warm gruel, but "a hempen caudle"
was a slang term for "hangman's noose."

110 shoulders unless he pay me tribute; there shall not a maid
be married but she shall pay to me her maidenhead[7] ere they
have it; men shall hold of me *in capite*,[8] and we charge and
command that their wives be as free° as heart can wish or   *sexually available*
tongue can tell.

115 BUTCHER   My lord, when shall we go to Cheapside and take up
commodities upon our bills?[9]

CADE   Marry, presently.

ALL   Oh, brave!

*Enter one with the heads [of Lord Saye and Sir James
Cromer on poles].*

CADE   But is not this braver? Let them kiss one another, for
120 they loved well when they were alive. Now part them again,
lest they consult about the giving up of some more towns in
France. —Soldiers, defer the spoil° of the city until night;   *destruction; plunder*
for, with these borne before us instead of maces, will we
ride through the streets, and at every corner have them kiss.

125 Away!   *Exeunt.*

4.8 (Q 4.8)

Alarum and retreat. Enter again CADE *and all his
rabblement.*

CADE   Up Fish Street! Down Saint Magnus' Corner![1] Kill and
knock down! Throw them into Thames!

Sound a parley.

What noise is this I hear? Dare any be so bold to sound retreat
or parley when I command them kill?

Enter BUCKINGHAM *and old [Lord]* CLIFFORD.

5 BUCKINGHAM   Ay, here they be that dare and will disturb
thee!

Know, Cade, we come ambassadors from the King
Unto the commons, whom thou hast misled,
And here pronounce free pardon to them all
That will forsake thee and go home in peace.

10 CLIFFORD   What say ye, countrymen? Will ye relent
And yield to mercy whilst 'tis offered you,
Or let a rabble lead you to your deaths?
Who loves the King and will embrace his pardon,
Fling up his cap, and say, "God save his majesty."

15 Who hateth him and honors not his father,
Henry the Fifth, that made all France to quake,
Shake he his weapon at us° and pass by.   *Defy us*

ALL   God save the King! God save the King!

CADE   What, Buckingham and Clifford, are ye so brave?°   *arrogant*
20 —And you, base peasants, do ye believe him? Will you needs
be hanged with your pardons about your necks? Hath my
sword therefore broke through London gates that you

---

7. Alluding to a supposed feudal practice by which a
lord had the right to sleep with the bride of any of his
vassals on the night of her wedding.
8. A Latin phrase indicating property held by grant
directly from the king, with a pun on *caput* (Latin for
"head") as slang for "maidenhead."
9. TEXTUAL COMMENT And acquire goods on credit or
by means of our weapons ("bills"); and rape women,
punning on "commodity" as meaning "female sexual

organs" and "bills" as meaning "penises." Q extends
this scene to include two other incidents that heighten
Cade's brutality: the burning of London Bridge, and
Cade's mockery and execution of a Sergeant who asks
for justice after his wife was raped by a rebel. See Digital Edition TC 9 (Folio edited text).
4.8 Location: Smithfield; London.
1. Place at the northern end of London Bridge opposite Southwark.

should leave me at the White Hart[2] in Southwark? I thought
ye would never have given out° these arms till you had   *abandoned*
25   recovered your ancient freedom. But you are all recreants
and dastards° and delight to live in slavery to the nobility.   *traitors and cowards*
Let them break your backs with burdens, take your houses
over your heads, ravish your wives and daughters before
your faces. For me, I will make shift for one,° and so God's   *take care of myself*
30   curse light upon you all.
ALL   We'll follow Cade! We'll follow Cade!
CLIFFORD   Is Cade the son of Henry the Fifth
That thus you do exclaim you'll go with him?
Will he conduct you through the heart of France
35   And make the meanest° of you earls and dukes?   *lowest born*
Alas, he hath no home, no place to fly to,
Nor knows he how to live but by the spoil,
Unless by robbing of your friends and us.
Were't not a shame that whilst you live at jar,°   *at odds*
40   The fearful° French, whom you late vanquishèd,   *timid*
Should make a start° o'er seas and vanquish you?   *rouse themselves*
Methinks already in this civil broil
I see them lording it in London streets,
Crying *"Villiago!"*[3] unto all they meet.
45   Better ten thousand base-born Cades miscarry°   *meet disaster*
Than you should stoop unto a Frenchman's mercy.
To France, to France, and get what you have lost!
Spare England, for it is your native coast.
Henry hath money; you are strong and manly;
50   God on our side, doubt not of victory.
ALL   A Clifford!° A Clifford! We'll follow the King and   *To Clifford*
Clifford!
CADE [*aside*]   Was ever feather so lightly blown to and fro as
this multitude? The name of Henry the Fifth hales° them to   *draws*
55   an hundred mischiefs and makes them leave me desolate. I
see them lay their heads together to surprise° me. My sword   *capture*
make way for me, for here is no staying. —In despite of the
devils and hell, have through° the very middest of you! And   *here I come through*
heavens and honor be witness that no want of resolution in
60   me, but only my followers' base and ignominious treasons,
makes me betake me to my heels.   *Exit.*
BUCKINGHAM   What, is he fled? —Go some and follow him,
And he that brings his head unto the King
Shall have a thousand crowns for his reward.
                                    Exeunt some of them.
65   Follow me, soldiers, we'll devise a mean°   *way*
To reconcile you all unto the King.   *Exeunt.*

4.9 (Q 4.9)

Sound trumpets. Enter KING HENRY, QUEEN
MARGARET, *and* SOMERSET *on the terrace.*
KING HENRY   Was ever king that joyed° an earthly throne   *enjoyed*
And could command no more content than I?
No sooner was I crept out of my cradle

---

2. An inn, with a pun on the coward's "white heart"   3. A variation on the Italian word for "coward."
(because drained of its blood or spirit).   4.9 Location: Kenilworth Castle.

But I was made a king at nine months old.
5 Was never subject longed to be a king
As I do long and wish to be a subject.

Enter BUCKINGHAM *and* CLIFFORD.

BUCKINGHAM   Health and glad tidings to your majesty.
KING HENRY   Why, Buckingham, is the traitor Cade
surprised?
Or is he but retired to make him strong?

Enter multitudes with halters about their necks.[1]

10 CLIFFORD   He is fled, my lord, and all his powers do yield,
And humbly thus, with halters on their necks,
Expect° your highness' doom° of life or death.   *Await / sentence*
KING HENRY   Then heaven set ope° thy everlasting gates   *open*
To entertain my vows of thanks and praise.
15 —Soldiers, this day have you redeemed your lives,
And showed how well you love your prince and country.
Continue still° in this so good a mind,   *always*
And Henry, though he be infortunate,°   *unlucky*
Assure yourselves, will never be unkind.
20 And so with thanks and pardon to you all
I do dismiss you to your several countries.°   *different regions*
ALL   God save the King! God save the King!

Enter a MESSENGER.

MESSENGER   Please it your grace to be advertisèd°   *informed*
The Duke of York is newly come from Ireland,
25 And with a puissant and a mighty power
Of gallowglasses and stout kerns[2]
Is marching hitherward in proud array
And still proclaimeth, as he comes along,
His arms are only to remove from thee
30 The Duke of Somerset, whom he terms a traitor.
KING HENRY   Thus stands my state,° 'twixt Cade and York   *condition*
distressed,
Like to a ship that, having scaped a tempest,
Is straightway calm° and boarded with a pirate.   *becalmed*
But now is Cade driven back, his men dispersed,
35 And now is York in arms to second° him.   *support*
I pray thee, Buckingham, go and meet him,
And ask him what's the reason of these arms.
Tell him I'll send Duke Edmund° to the Tower;   *(Somerset)*
And, Somerset, we will commit thee thither
40 Until his army be dismissed from him.
SOMERSET   My lord, I'll yield myself to prison willingly,
Or unto death, to do my country good.
KING HENRY   In any case be not too rough in terms,°   *language*
For he is fierce and cannot brook° hard language.   *endure*
45 BUCKINGHAM   I will, my lord, and doubt not so to deal
As all things shall redound unto your good.
KING HENRY   Come, wife, let's in, and learn to govern better;
For yet° may England curse my wretched reign.   *up until now*

Flourish. Exeunt.

---

1. Cade's followers wore nooses as a sign of their
submission.
2. *gallowglasses:* professional Irish mercenary soldiers
who were usually armed with axes and rode on horseback. For *kerns,* see note to 3.1.310.

4.10 (Q 4.10)

Enter CADE.[1]

CADE Fie on ambitions! Fie on myself, that have a sword and
yet am ready to famish. These five days have I hid me in these
woods and durst not peep out, for all the country is laid° for   *set with traps*
me; but now am I so hungry that, if I might have a lease of my
5   life for a thousand years, I could stay° no longer. Wherefore   *delay*
on a brick wall have I climbed into this garden to see if I can
eat grass, or pick a salad another while, which is not amiss to
cool a man's stomach° this hot weather. And I think this word   *hunger; anger*
"salad" was born to do me good; for many a time, but for a
10   sallet,° my brain-pan had been cleft with a brown bill;[2] and   *helmet*
many a time, when I have been dry and bravely marching, it
hath served me instead of a quart pot to drink in; and now the
word "salad" must serve me to feed on.

Enter [Alexander] IDEN.

IDEN Lord, who would live turmoilèd° in the court   *harried*
15   And may enjoy such quiet walks as these?
This small inheritance my father left me
Contenteth me, and worth a monarchy.
I seek not to wax great by others' waning,
Or gather wealth I care not with what envy;
20   Sufficeth that° I have maintains my state,   *that what*
And sends the poor well pleasèd° from my gate.   *(with their alms)*

CADE Here's the lord of the soil come to seize me for a stray°   *trespasser*
for entering his fee-simple[3] without leave. —Ah, villain,
thou wilt betray me and get a thousand crowns of the King
25   by carrying my head to him; but I'll make thee eat iron like
an ostrich[4] and swallow my sword like a great pin, ere thou
and I part.

IDEN Why, rude companion,° whatsoe'er thou be,   *lowborn fellow*
I know thee not. Why, then, should I betray thee?
30   Is't not enough to break into my garden
And, like a thief, to come to rob my grounds,
Climbing my walls in spite of me the owner,
But thou wilt brave° me with these saucy terms?   *taunt*

CADE Brave thee? Ay, by the best blood that ever was
35   broached,° and beard° thee, too. Look on me well: I have ate   *shed / defy*
no meat these five days, yet come thou and thy five men,
an if I do not leave you all as dead as a doornail, I pray God
I may never eat grass more.

IDEN Nay, it shall ne'er be said, while England stands,
40   That Alexander Iden, an esquire of Kent,
Took odds° to combat a poor famished man.   *advantage*
Oppose thy steadfast gazing eyes to mine;
See if thou canst outface me with thy looks.
Set limb to limb, and thou art far the lesser;

4.10 Location: Alexander Iden's garden, in Kent.
1. Q's stage direction indicates that Jack Cade enters
at one door and Alexander Iden and his men at
another. Q's version of this scene is shorter than F's
and makes clear what F only implies: that Iden is
accompanied by attendants. The presence of these
figures makes Cade's offer to fight Iden seem the
more courageous. In Q, Iden enters unarmed, orders
one of his men to fetch his sword, and chivalrously

orders them to stand aside while he fights Cade. In F,
Iden presumably enters armed.
2. A long-handled weapon with an axlike blade. The
brown color is from blood or varnish.
3. Property that belonged forever to its owner and
his or her heirs; on it, stray animals could legally be
seized.
4. It was popularly believed that ostriches ate iron.

45   Thy hand is but a finger to my fist,
    Thy leg a stick comparèd with this truncheon.°   *thick staff (his leg)*
    My foot shall fight with all the strength thou hast,
    And if mine arm be heavèd in the air,
    Thy grave is digged already in the earth.
50   As for words, whose greatness answers words,[5]
    Let this my sword report what speech forbears.
   CADE   By my valor, the most complete° champion that ever I   *accomplished*
    heard. Steel, if thou turn the edge° or cut not out the burly-   *fail to cut*
    boned clown in chines° of beef ere thou sleep in thy sheath,   *roasts*
55   I beseech Jove on my knees thou mayst be turned to hobnails.
          Here they fight[; CADE falls].
    Oh, I am slain! Famine and no other hath slain me. Let ten
    thousand devils come against me, and give me but the ten
    meals I have lost, and I'd defy them all. Wither, garden, and
    be henceforth a burying place to all that do dwell in this
60   house, because the unconquered soul of Cade is fled.
   IDEN   Is't Cade that I have slain, that monstrous traitor?
    Sword, I will hallow thee for this thy deed,
    And hang thee o'er my tomb when I am dead.
    Ne'er shall this blood be wipèd from thy point,
65   But thou shalt wear it as a herald's coat
    To emblaze the honor that thy master got.[6]
   CADE   Iden, farewell, and be proud of thy victory. Tell Kent
    from me she hath lost her best man, and exhort all the world
    to be cowards. For I, that never feared any, am vanquished
70   by famine, not by valor.
          [He] dies.
   IDEN   How much thou wrong'st me, heaven be my judge.
    Die, damnèd wretch, the curse of her that bare thee!
    And as I thrust thy body in with my sword,[7]
    So wish I I might thrust thy soul to hell.
75   Hence will I drag thee headlong° by the heels   *head downward*
    Unto a dunghill which shall be thy grave,
    And there cut off thy most ungracious head,
    Which I will bear in triumph to the King,
    Leaving thy trunk for crows to feed upon.
          Exit [with the body].

5.1 (Q 5.1)

*Enter YORK and his army of Irish, with drum
and colors.*

   YORK   From Ireland thus comes York to claim his right
    And pluck the crown from feeble Henry's head.
    Ring bells aloud! Burn bonfires clear and bright
    To entertain° great England's lawful king!   *welcome*
5   Ah, *sancta maiestas!*° Who would not buy thee dear?   *sacred majesty*
    Let them obey that knows not how to rule;
    This hand was made to handle naught but gold.
    I cannot give due action to my words,

5. Obscure line. It may mean "As for words, I whose   killing Cade.
might more than matches your words."   7. As I thrust my sword into your body.
6. *But . . . got:* Just as a device on a herald's coat   **5.1** Location: The remainder of the play takes place
proclaims his lord's identity and status, so the blood   in an open field between St Albans and London.
on Iden's sword proclaims the fame he has won for

Except° a sword or scepter balance it.   *Unless*

10   A scepter shall it have, have I° a soul,   *as sure as I have*
     On which I'll toss the *fleur-de-lis* of France.[1]
           Enter BUCKINGHAM.
     [*aside*] Whom have we here? Buckingham to disturb me?
     The King hath sent him, sure. I must dissemble.

     BUCKINGHAM   York, if thou meanest well, I greet thee well.

15   YORK   Humphrey of Buckingham, I accept thy greeting.
     Art thou a messenger, or come of pleasure?

     BUCKINGHAM   A messenger from Henry, our dread liege,
     To know the reason of these arms° in peace;   *armed men*
     Or why thou, being a subject as I am,

20   Against thy oath and true allegiance sworn,
     Should raise so great a power without his leave,
     Or dare to bring thy force so near the court?

     YORK [*aside*]   Scarce can I speak, my choler is so great.
     Oh, I could hew up rocks and fight with flint,

25   I am so angry at these abject terms.°   *insulting words*
     And now, like Ajax Telamonius,[2]
     On sheep or oxen could I spend my fury.
     I am far better born than is the King,
     More like a king, more kingly in my thoughts;

30   But I must make fair weather° yet awhile   *pretend to be mild*
     Till Henry be more weak and I more strong.
     —Buckingham, I prithee pardon me
     That I have given no answer all this while;
     My mind was troubled with deep melancholy.

35   The cause why I have brought this army hither
     Is to remove proud Somerset from the King,
     Seditious to his grace and to the state.

     BUCKINGHAM   That is too much presumption on thy part;
     But if thy arms be to no other end,

40   The King hath yielded unto thy demand:
     The Duke of Somerset is in the Tower.

     YORK   Upon thine honor, is he prisoner?

     BUCKINGHAM   Upon mine honor, he is prisoner.

     YORK   Then, Buckingham, I do dismiss my powers.

45   —Soldiers, I thank you all; disperse yourselves.
     Meet me tomorrow in Saint George's Field;[3]
     You shall have pay and everything you wish.
                                    [*Exeunt Soldiers.*]
     [*to* BUCKINGHAM] And let my sovereign, virtuous Henry,
     Command° my eldest son—nay, all my sons—   *Demand*

50   As pledges of my fealty and love;
     I'll send them all as willing as I live.
     Lands, goods, horse, armor, anything I have
     Is his to use, so° Somerset may die.   *provided that*

     BUCKINGHAM   York, I commend this kind° submission.   *natural; proper*

55   We twain will go into his highness' tent.
           Enter KING HENRY *and Attendants.*

---

1. On which I'll impale the national emblem of   his Greek enemies.
France, the lily flower.   3. One of the main drill grounds for Elizabethan
2. A Greek hero of the Trojan War who went mad   militia, located south of the Thames.
and slaughtered a flock of sheep, taking them to be

KING HENRY   Buckingham, doth York intend no harm to us,
    That thus he marcheth with thee arm in arm?
YORK   In all submission and humility
    York doth present himself unto your highness.
60 KING HENRY   Then what intends these forces thou dost
      bring?
YORK   To heave the traitor Somerset from hence,
    And fight against that monstrous rebel Cade,
    Who since I heard to be discomfited.°   *defeated*
      Enter IDEN *with Cade's head.*
IDEN   If one so rude° and of so mean condition°   *uncultivated / low rank*
65   May pass into the presence of a king,
    Lo, I present your grace a traitor's head,
    The head of Cade, whom I in combat slew.
KING HENRY   The head of Cade? Great God, how just art
      Thou?
    Oh, let me view his visage, being dead,
70   That living wrought me such exceeding trouble.
    —Tell me, my friend, art thou the man that slew him?
IDEN   I was, an't like° your majesty.   *if it please*
KING HENRY   How art thou called? And what is thy degree?°   *rank*
IDEN   Alexander Iden, that's my name,
75   A poor esquire[4] of Kent that loves his king.
BUCKINGHAM   So please it you, my lord, 'twere not amiss
    He were created knight for his good service.
KING HENRY   Iden, kneel down.
        [IDEN *kneels and is knighted.*]
                  Rise up a knight.
        [IDEN *rises.*]
    We give thee for reward a thousand marks,
80   And will° that thou henceforth attend on us.   *command*
IDEN   May Iden live to merit such a bounty,
    And never live but true unto his liege.
      Enter QUEEN MARGARET *and* SOMERSET.
KING HENRY   See, Buckingham, Somerset comes with the
      Queen.
    Go bid her hide him quickly from the Duke.
85 QUEEN MARGARET   For thousand Yorks he shall not hide his
      head,
    But boldly stand and front° him to his face.   *confront*
YORK   How now? Is Somerset at liberty?
    Then, York, unloose thy long-imprisoned thoughts,
    And let thy tongue be equal with thy heart.
90   Shall I endure the sight of Somerset?
    False king, why hast thou broken faith with me,
    Knowing how hardly I can brook abuse?[5]
    "King" did I call thee? No, thou art not king,
    Not fit to govern and rule multitudes,
95   Which dar'st not, no, nor canst not rule a traitor.
    That head of thine doth not become a crown;
    Thy hand is made to grasp a palmer's° staff,   *pilgrim's*
    And not to grace an awful° princely scepter.   *awe-inspiring*

---

4. A member of the gentry ranking just below a knight.
5. Knowing with what difficulty I can tolerate deception.

That gold must round engirt these brows of mine,
100 Whose smile and frown, like to Achilles' spear,
Is able with the change to kill and cure.[6]
Here is a hand to hold a scepter up,
And with the same to act° controlling laws.   *enact*
Give place! By heaven, thou shalt rule no more
105 O'er him whom heaven created for thy ruler.
SOMERSET O monstrous traitor! I arrest thee, York,
Of capital treason 'gainst the King and crown.
Obey, audacious traitor! Kneel for grace.
YORK Wouldst have me kneel? First, let me ask of these
110 If they can brook I bow a knee to man.
—Sirrah, call in my sons to be my bail.   [*Exit Attendant.*]
—I know, ere they will have me go to ward,°   *into custody*
They'll pawn° their swords of° my enfranchisement.°   *pledge / for / freedom*
QUEEN MARGARET Call hither Clifford; bid him come amain°   *at once*
115 To say if that the bastard boys of York
Shall be the surety for their traitor father.
                               [*Exit* BUCKINGHAM.]
YORK O blood-bespotted Neapolitan,[7]
Outcast of Naples, England's bloody scourge!
The sons of York, thy betters in their birth,
120 Shall be their father's bail, and bane° to those   *destruction*
That for my surety will refuse the boys.
           Enter EDWARD *and* RICHARD.
See where they come. I'll warrant they'll make it good.
           Enter CLIFFORD [*and* YOUNG CLIFFORD].
QUEEN MARGARET And here comes Clifford to deny their
     bail.
CLIFFORD [*kneeling*] Health and all happiness to my lord the
     King.
     [*He rises.*]
125 YORK I thank thee, Clifford. Say, what news with thee?
Nay, do not fright us with an angry look;
We are thy sovereign. Clifford, kneel again.
For thy mistaking so, we pardon thee.
CLIFFORD This is my king, York: I do not mistake;
130 But thou mistakes me much to think I do.
—To Bedlam[8] with him! Is the man grown mad?
KING HENRY Ay, Clifford, a bedlam° and ambitious humor°   *mad / disposition*
Makes him oppose himself against his king.
CLIFFORD He is a traitor; let him to the Tower,
135 And chop away that factious pate° of his.   *rebellious head*
QUEEN MARGARET He is arrested, but will not obey.
His sons, he says, shall give their words for him.
YORK Will you not, sons?
EDWARD Ay, noble father, if our words will serve.
140 RICHARD And if words will not, then our weapons shall.
CLIFFORD Why, what a brood of traitors have we here!
YORK Look in a glass,° and call thy image so.   *mirror*

6. Telephus, wounded by Achilles' spear, was cured by rust from that same spear.
7. Margaret's father claimed the throne of Naples. Elizabethan writers typically associated Italy with sexual vice, criminality, and the evils of Roman Catholicism.
8. The shortened name of a London insane asylum. See note to 3.1.51.

I am thy king, and thou a false-heart traitor.
Call hither to the stake my two brave bears,
145 That with the very shaking of their chains
They may astonish these fell-lurking° curs.[9]   *savagely waiting*
Bid Salisbury and Warwick come to me.
> *Enter* WARWICK *and* SALISBURY.

CLIFFORD   Are these thy bears? We'll bait thy bears to death,
And manacle the bearherd° in their chains,   *bear keeper (York)*
150 If thou dar'st bring them to the baiting place.°   *bear pit*
RICHARD   Oft have I seen a hot o'er-weening° cur   *overconfident*
Run back and bite° because he was withheld,   *(his keeper)*
Who being suffered with° the bear's fell° paw,   *injured by / savage*
Hath clapped his tail between his legs and cried—
155 And such a piece of service will you do,
If you oppose yourselves° to match Lord Warwick.   *undertake*
CLIFFORD   Hence, heap of wrath, foul indigested lump,
As crooked in thy manners as thy shape.[1]
YORK   Nay, we shall heat you thoroughly anon.°   *soon*
160 CLIFFORD   Take heed, lest by your heat you burn yourselves.
KING HENRY   Why, Warwick, hath thy knee forgot to bow?
Old Salisbury, shame to thy silver hair,
Thou mad misleader of thy brainsick son!
What, wilt thou on thy deathbed play the ruffian,
165 And seek for sorrow with thy spectacles?°   *eyes; eyeglasses*
Oh, where is faith? Oh, where is loyalty?
If it be banished from the frosty head,
Where shall it find a harbor in the earth?
Wilt thou go dig a grave to find out° war,   *in seeking out*
170 And shame thine honorable age with blood?
Why art thou old and want'st° experience?   *lack*
Or wherefore dost abuse it if thou hast it?
For shame, in duty bend thy knee to me,
That bows unto the grave with mickle° age.   *much*
175 SALISBURY   My lord, I have considered with myself
The title of this most renownèd duke,
And in my conscience do repute his grace
The rightful heir to England's royal seat.
KING HENRY   Hast thou not sworn allegiance unto me?
180 SALISBURY   I have.
KING HENRY   Canst thou dispense with heaven for[2] such
    an oath?
SALISBURY   It is great sin to swear unto a sin,
But greater sin to keep a sinful oath.
Who can be bound by any solemn vow
185 To do a murderous deed, to rob a man,
To force a spotless virgin's chastity,
To reave° the orphan of his patrimony,   *bereave*
To wring the widow from her customed right,[3]

---

9. York refers to the Elizabethan sport of bearbaiting, in which a tame bear was chained to a stake and set upon with dogs. Warwick's family crest depicted a bear chained to a staff. See below, lines 202–03.
1. *foul . . . shape:* alluding to the belief that Richard of Gloucester was deformed from birth (he was a hunchback) and to the notion that bears are born as formless lumps and licked into shape by their mothers.

indigested: ill-formed. The recent discovery of Richard's skeleton reveals that he did indeed suffer from a severe spinal deformity.
2. Can you win dispensation from heaven for breaking.
3. Her traditional right to a portion of her husband's estate.

And have no other reason for this wrong
190 But that he was bound by a solemn oath?
QUEEN MARGARET   A subtle traitor needs no sophister.°   *expert in false reasoning*
KING HENRY   Call Buckingham, and bid him arm himself.
YORK   Call Buckingham and all the friends thou hast;
I am resolved for death and dignity.°   *(the crown)*
195 CLIFFORD   The first I warrant thee, if dreams prove true.
WARWICK   You were best to go to bed and dream again
To keep thee from the tempest of the field.
CLIFFORD   I am resolved to bear a greater storm
Than any thou canst conjure up today;
200 And that I'll write upon thy burgonet,°   *helmet*
Might I but know thee by thy house's badge.°   *family crest*
WARWICK   Now, by my father's badge, old Neville's crest,[4]
The rampant bear chained to the ragged° staff,   *jagged*
This day I'll wear aloft° my burgonet,   *on top of*
205 As on a mountaintop the cedar shows
That keeps his leaves in spite of any storm,
Even to affright thee with the view thereof.
CLIFFORD   And from thy burgonet I'll rend thy bear
And tread it underfoot with all contempt,
210 Despite the bearherd° that protects the bear.   *bear keeper (York)*
YOUNG CLIFFORD   And so to arms, victorious father,
To quell the rebels and their complices.°   *accomplices*
RICHARD   Fie, charity, for shame! Speak not in spite,
For you shall sup with Jesu Christ tonight.
215 YOUNG CLIFFORD   Foul stigmatic,[5] that's more than thou
canst tell.
RICHARD   If not in heaven, you'll surely sup in hell.   *Exeunt.*

5.2 (Q 5.2)

[*Alarum.*] *Enter* WARWICK.
WARWICK   Clifford of Cumberland, 'tis Warwick calls!
An if thou dost not hide thee from the bear
Now, when the angry trumpet sounds alarum
And dead° men's cries do fill the empty air,   *dying*
5 Clifford, I say, come forth and fight with me!
Proud northern lord, Clifford of Cumberland,
Warwick is hoarse with calling thee to arms.
Enter YORK.
How now, my noble lord? What, all afoot?°   *not on horseback*
YORK   The deadly-handed Clifford slew my steed;
10 But match to match I have encountered him,
And made a prey for carrion kites and crows
Even of the bonny beast he loved so well.
Enter CLIFFORD.
WARWICK   Of one or both of us the time is come.
YORK   Hold, Warwick; seek thee out some other chase,°   *game*
15 For I myself must hunt this deer to death.
WARWICK   Then nobly, York; 'tis for a crown thou fight'st.

---

4. The Neville badge was actually a bull. Warwick inherited the badge of a bear from his father-in-law, Richard Beauchamp.

5. One branded with the mark of crime, as Richard is "branded" with deformity.
5.2 Location: Scene continues.

—As I intend, Clifford, to thrive today,
It grieves my soul to leave thee unassailed.   *Exit* WARWICK.

CLIFFORD   What seest thou in me, York? Why dost thou
  pause?

20   YORK   With thy brave bearing° should I be in love,[1]   *fine appearance*
But that thou art so fast mine enemy.

CLIFFORD   Nor should thy prowess want° praise and esteem,   *lack*
But that 'tis shown ignobly and in treason.

YORK   So let it help me now against thy sword,

25   As I in justice and true right express it.

CLIFFORD   My soul and body on the action both.[2]

YORK   A dreadful lay!° Address° thee instantly.   *wager / Prepare*

CLIFFORD   *La fin couronne les oeuvres.*[3]
     [*They fight.* CLIFFORD *dies.*]

YORK   Thus war hath given thee peace, for thou art still.

30   Peace with his soul, heaven, if it be thy will.   [*Exit.*]
     Enter YOUNG CLIFFORD.

YOUNG CLIFFORD   Shame and confusion! All is on the rout,°   *in disorderly retreat*
Fear frames° disorder, and disorder wounds   *gives rise to*
Where it should guard. O war, thou son of hell
Whom angry heavens do make their minister,

35   Throw in the frozen° bosoms of our part°   *cowardly / faction*
Hot coals of vengeance! Let no soldier fly.
He that is truly dedicate° to war   *dedicated*
Hath no self-love; nor he that loves himself
Hath not essentially, but by circumstance,°   *merely by accident*
The name of valor.
     [*He sees his father's body.*]

40   Oh, let the vile world end,
And the premised° flames of the last day   *foreordained*
Knit earth and heaven together.
Now let the general trumpet blow his blast,[4]
Particularities° and petty sounds   *Individual affairs*

45   To cease! Wast thou ordained, dear father,
To lose thy youth in peace, and to achieve
The silver livery of advisèd° age,   *wise*
And, in thy reverence and thy chair-days,° thus   *old age*
To die in ruffian battle? Even at this sight

50   My heart is turned to stone, and while 'tis mine
It shall be stony. York not our old men spares;
No more will I their babes. Tears virginal
Shall be to me even as the dew to fire,[5]
And beauty, that the tyrant oft reclaims,°   *calms the tyrant*

55   Shall to my flaming wrath be oil and flax.
Henceforth I will not have to do with pity.
Meet I an infant of the house of York,

---

1. TEXTUAL COMMENT While F stresses Clifford and York's nobility and shared code of honor, Q's version of the fight between these men is more bitter in tone and in dialogue, setting up a total and irreparable division between the houses of Lancaster and York. See Digital Edition TC 10 (Folio edited text).
2. I wager both my soul and my body on the outcome of this fight ("action").
3. The end crowns the works (French).
4. Young Clifford is evoking doomsday, when a trumpet will summon everyone to judgment (see 1 Corinthians 15:52).
5. Dew was popularly believed to make fire burn more fiercely.

Into as many gobbets° will I cut it   *lumps of flesh*
As wild Medea young Absyrtus did.[6]

60   In cruelty will I seek out my fame.
Come, thou new ruin of old Clifford's house;
          [*He takes up his father's body.*]
As did Aeneas old Anchises bear,[7]
So bear I thee upon my manly shoulders.
But then Aeneas bare a living load

65   Nothing so heavy as these woes of mine.   [*Exit.*]
          Enter RICHARD *and* SOMERSET *to fight.* [SOMERSET
          is killed.]

RICHARD So, lie thou there,
For underneath an alehouse' paltry sign,
The Castle in St Albans, Somerset
Hath made the wizard famous in his death.[8]

70   Sword, hold thy temper;[9] heart, be wrathful still;
Priests pray for enemies, but princes kill.   [*Exit.*]
          Fight. Excursions.° *Enter* KING HENRY, QUEEN   *Skirmishes*
          MARGARET, *and others.*

QUEEN MARGARET Away, my lord! You are slow; for shame,
          away!
KING HENRY Can we outrun the heavens?° Good Margaret,   *escape our fate*
          stay.
QUEEN MARGARET What are you made of? You'll nor° fight   *neither*
          nor fly.

75   Now is it manhood, wisdom, and defense
To give the enemy way and to secure us°   *save ourselves*
By what° we can, which° can no more but fly.   *whatever means / who*
          Alarum afar off.
If you be ta'en, we then should see the bottom
Of all our fortunes; but if we haply scape°—   *by chance escape*

80   As well we may, if not° through your neglect—   *if we don't fail*
We shall to London get, where you are loved
And where this breach now in our fortunes made
May readily be stopped.
          Enter YOUNG CLIFFORD.

YOUNG CLIFFORD But that my heart's on future mischief set,

85   I would speak blasphemy ere° bid you fly;   *before I would*
But fly you must; uncurable discomfit°   *irreversible defeat*
Reigns in the hearts of all our present parts.°   *remaining forces*
Away for your relief! And we will live
To see their day and them our fortune give.[1]

90   Away, my lord, away!   *Exeunt.*

---

6. According to classical mythology, as Medea fled
over the sea with her lover, Jason, she murdered her
brother Absyrtus and scattered bits of his body on
the waves so that her father would stop to collect the
fragments and be delayed in his pursuit of her.
7. In Virgil's *Aeneid* 2.707–29, Aeneas carries his
aged father, Anchises, on his back in their escape
from the burning city of Troy.

8. Somerset's death under the sign of the Castle Inn
confirms the Spirit's warning that he shun castles
(see 1.4.34–36). *in his:* by his (Somerset's).
9. Retain the resiliency of steel.
1. *we . . . give:* we will survive to see a day of victory
like theirs and to make them suffer misfortunes like
ours.

5.3 (Q 5.3)

Alarum. Retreat. Enter YORK, [*his sons* EDWARD
and] RICHARD, WARWICK, *and Soldiers, with drum
and colors.*

YORK   Of Salisbury, who can report of him—
That winter° lion who in rage forgets   *aged*
Agèd contusions and all brush of time,[1]
And like a gallant in the brow° of youth   *prime*
5 Repairs° him with occasion?° This happy day   *Revives / action*
Is not itself, nor have we won one foot,
If Salisbury be lost.

RICHARD   My noble father,
Three times today I holp° him to his horse,   *helped*
Three times bestrid him;[2] thrice I led him off;
10 Persuaded him from any further act;
But still° where danger was, still there I met him   *always*
And, like rich hangings in a homely° house,   *humble*
So was his will in his old feeble body.

      Enter SALISBURY.

But, noble as he is, look where he comes.
15 SALISBURY   Now, by my sword, well hast thou fought today;
By th' mass so did we all. —I thank you, Richard.
God knows how long it is I have to live,
And it hath pleased him that three times today
You have defended me from imminent death.
20 Well, lords, we have not got that which we have:[3]
'Tis not enough our foes are this time fled,
Being opposites of such repairing nature.[4]

YORK   I know our safety is to follow them,
For, as I hear, the King is fled to London
25 To call a present court of parliament.
Let us pursue him ere the writs° go forth.   *summons to Parliament*
What says Lord Warwick? Shall we after them?

WARWICK   After them? Nay, before them, if we can!
Now, by my hand, lords, 'twas a glorious day!
30 St Albans' battle, won by famous York,
Shall be eternized° in all age to come.   *immortalized*
Sound drum and trumpets, and to London all—
And more such days as these to us befall!   *Exeunt.*

5.3 Location: Scene continues.
1. Bruises of old age and all assaults of time.
2. Stood over the fallen Salisbury to protect him.

3. We have not secured what we have won.
4. Since they are enemies who can quickly recover
what they have lost.

The Third Part of
Henry the Sixth

There are two Richards in 3 *Henry VI.* As the play begins, Richard of York is attempting to seize the English throne from Henry VI, the Lancastrian king. This Richard is killed at the end of the first act, and it is his tragic death to which the title of the Octavo version of the play refers: *The True Tragedy of Richard Duke of York and the Death of Good King Henry the Sixth.* The murdered duke, however, has four sons: Edward, Edmund (known as the Earl of Rutland), George, and Richard. This second Richard, who eventually acquires the title Duke of Gloucester, is a hunchback; and much of the play chronicles his attempts to continue his father's efforts to seize the English throne. Near the end of the play, this second Richard meditates on his condition:

> Then, since the heavens have shaped my body so,
> Let hell make crooked my mind to answer it.
> I have no brother, I am like no brother;
> And this word "love," which greybeards call divine,
> Be resident in men like one another
> And not in me. I am myself alone.
>
> (5.6.78–83)*

This chilling pronouncement places Richard outside kinship networks, even though his two older brothers, Edward and George, are very much alive; and it exempts him from ordinary bonds of human affection.

Claiming to know nothing of love, Richard blames his isolation on his misshapen body. He is not "like" other men, not even like his brothers, because heaven has formed his body crookedly. Richard's lines may be simply a convenient explanation for villainy, a justification for doing harm. He may, in fact, be playing on the commonly held assumption that a deformed body was the sign of a corrupted inner nature. Many people in the early modern period believed that an atypical body was God's way of marking a sinner. But the play complicates such assumptions. Richard seems less a born sinner than a man who willingly and willfully embraces villainy as a path to the crown he avidly seeks. In this passage he blames heaven for his body but actively invites hell to give him a crooked mind. Moreover, Richard's unusual body seems no impediment to his success. While he disclaims a lover's power, in the next play in this first tetralogy of history plays, *Richard III*, he successfully woos Lady Anne; and he is throughout a notable warrior and a master political strategist. Richard's crooked body and mind at times, indeed, seem less the singular attributes of one person and more a symbol of the time's deformity, the nature of which the play gradually unfolds.

3 *Henry VI* is one of the most ambitious of the early history plays associated with Shakespeare's name simply in terms of the span of historical matter it covers. It is in part a continuation of 2 *Henry VI*, in which Shakespeare began to dramatize the Wars of the Roses between the Lancastrian descendants of Edward III, who took the red rose for their symbol, and his Yorkist descendants, who claimed the white. In the struggles between these two branches of the family, the Yorkists asserted that Henry

*All quotations are taken from the edited text of the Folio, printed here. The Digital Edition includes edited texts of both the Folio and the Octavo.

VI's grandfather, Henry IV, had illegitimately usurped the throne from Richard II, the son of Edward III's oldest male offspring, Edward, the Black Prince. Even though the Lancastrians could claim the throne through John of Gaunt, Edward III's fourth son, the Yorkists felt that they had a superior claim as descendants of the third son, Lionel, Duke of Clarence, and his daughter Philippa. In 3 *Henry VI*, Shakespeare depicts many of the most significant military encounters stemming from the struggle between the two branches of the family, stretching from the Battle of Wakefield (1460), in which the Duke of York was captured and killed by the Lancastrian forces of Henry VI, to the Battle of Tewkesbury in 1471, in which Edward, the eldest son of Richard, Duke of York, decisively defeated the Lancastrian army. It is after the latter battle, and Richard, Duke of Gloucester's subsequent murder of Henry VI in the Tower of London, that the hunchbacked Richard speaks his chilling lines about having no father (in the Octavo version) and no brother (in both Octavo and Folio).

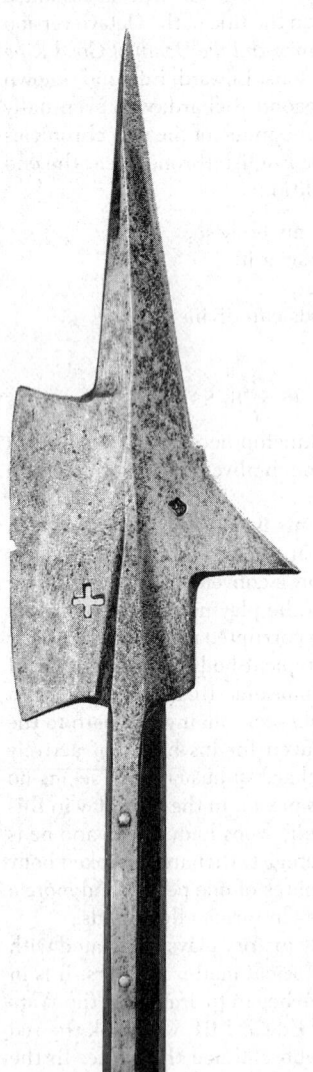

As with all his history plays, Shakespeare takes many liberties with the historical sources of 3 *Henry VI*, Raphael Holinshed's *Chronicles of England, Scotland, and Ireland* (1587 edition) and Edward Hall's *The Union of the Two Noble and Illustrious Families of Lancaster and York* (1548). Many historical events are simply omitted or conflated with other events, and aspects of the historical record are altered for dramatic or thematic purposes. For example, at the time of the Battle of Wakefield, at which Richard, Duke of York was killed, his son Richard was only seven years old. But in Shakespeare's play, he is a grown man who himself participates in the battle and after it vows revenge for his father's death. Moreover, that death is handled with grim originality. In Hall, Clifford decapitates York, then puts a paper crown on his severed head and presents it on a pole to Margaret, Henry VI's warlike queen. In Holinshed, Clifford verbally torments York before beheading him. But in none of the sources does Margaret dominate the scene as she does in Shakespeare's play. In 3 *Henry VI*, she taunts York ferociously and—a detail found in none of the sources—to wipe his tears gives him a handkerchief that has been dipped in the blood of Rutland, York's twelve-year-old son, who had been butchered by Clifford earlier in the same battle. Eventually both Margaret and Clifford stab York, and Margaret orders his head displayed on the gates of the city of York.

This scene of torture and torment displays the sovereign power that Margaret has assumed. Her husband too timid to fight successfully and her son's right to rule at stake, Margaret exults in rendering her great Yorkist adversary an abject victim of her hate. Yet the scene has unintended consequences. It recalls the medieval cycle drama in which Christ, mocked and crowned with thorns, takes on the sins of mankind at his crucifixion, and the napkin dipped in Rutland's blood becomes an emblem of the son's martyrdom, as well. The effect of the scene on a theater audience may be adduced from its effect on onstage bystand-

Seventeenth-century ornamental halberd from southern Germany.

ers. The tough Northumberland, witnessing York's suffering, twice declares himself moved to tears: "Beshrew me, but his passions moves me so / That hardly can I check my eyes from tears" (1.4.150–51) and "Had he been slaughter-man to all my kin / I should not for my life but weep with him / To see how inly sorrow gripes his soul" (1.4.169–71). York, enduring his suffering with manly fortitude mingled with manly sorrow for his murdered son, makes a pious end: "Open thy gate of mercy, gracious God, / My soul flies through these wounds to seek out thee" (1.4.177–78). It is largely this scene, vividly rendered as a visual and emotional spectacle, that justifies the Octavo text's designation of the play as *The True Tragedy of Richard Duke of York*. It also prepares for the abrupt reversal of political fortunes that is enacted at the play's conclusion. The Yorkists finally rout the Lancastrian army led by Margaret, and she, pleading for the life of her son, young Prince Edward, must watch as he is repeatedly stabbed, an ironic replay of Rutland's death and her indifference to Richard of York's grief. Rather than its agent, Margaret is now herself the victim of pitiless sovereign power.

We have further contemporary evidence of the scene's theatrical effectiveness. In September 1592, Robert Greene, a rival playwright, published *Greene's Groats-worth of Wit*, in which he makes fun of Shakespeare by parodying a line from this scene. Richard at one point exclaims of Margaret, "O tiger's heart wrapped in a woman's hide" (1.4.137). Greene writes of Shakespeare that "there is an upstart Crow, beautified with our feathers, that with his *Tiger's heart wrapt in a Player's hide*, supposes he is as well able to bombast out a blank verse as the best of you: and being an absolute *Johannes fac totum* [jack-of-all-trades], is in his own conceit the only Shake-scene in a country." Greene, who had a university education, clearly resented Shakespeare, who did not but who was nonetheless having considerable theatrical success. Greene accuses Shakespeare either of appropriating his work or of acting in his dramas ("beautified with our feathers") and of thinking too well of himself and his many theatrical skills. Particularly striking is Greene's own appropriation of Richard's line about Margaret to apply to Shakespeare. Implicitly, Greene suggests that there is something as unnatural and presumptuous in Shakespeare's theatrical ambition as in the cruelty and ambition of Henry's manlike queen. At the same time, this appropriative gesture pays tribute, however grudging, to Shakespeare's skill as a writer of memorable dialogue. Affronted by Shakespeare's success, Greene nonetheless grants his rival the homage of parody. The lines have another value as well. Although *3 Henry VI* was first printed in the short Octavo version of 1595, Greene's comments suggest that some version of the play—written by Shakespeare alone or in collaboration—had been staged or was circulating in manuscript by late summer of 1592.

This early play, then, may have brought Shakespeare contemporary notoriety. It certainly shows his boldness in adapting chronicle history to fit the requirements of the theater. And while some critics have seen *3 Henry VI* as flawed, evidencing Shakespeare's weariness with his dramatization of the Wars of the Roses or his inability to shape so much matter into coherent form, theatrical productions of this play attest to its viability on the stage. The vicious energies of hate and ambition that propel the play make its enactment an intense and exhausting experience. The vigorous stage battles, the soaring rhetorical duels between the contending factions, the centrality of the ruthless Margaret, the emergence of the alienated Richard, Duke of Gloucester as the brooding antihero—these are elements that, particularly in the post–World War II period, have led to many memorable productions, productions that emphasize a once-civil world spiraling vertiginously toward chaos.

But the play is also more than the sum of its memorable parts. When Richard asserts, "I am myself alone," his chosen isolation follows from the play's carefully orchestrated dramatization of the breakdown of social order, particularly as epitomized in the breakdown of family ties. From its inception, the Wars of the Roses, a continuing civil war, was also a family feud in that it pitted the Lancastrian and Yorkist descendants of Edward III against one another. But in the prior play, *2 Henry VI*, members of each family line and their followers typically remained loyal to their faction. Family lineage was a source of pride and identity. One sees this also in *1 Henry VI* in the idealized relationship between the English hero Lord Talbot and his son John. John aspires in all respects to emulate his father, and the two of them die together in battle defending England and the honor of their family name. In *3 Henry VI*, by contrast, family bonds are hideously fragile; and when they break, chaos ensues. Unflinching in its depiction of emotional and physical violence, the play examines the forms of monstrous individualism that emerge when the social identities provided by networks of kinship and feudal loyalty no longer exert their hold. In effect, *3 Henry VI* depicts the radical separation of self from defining social networks as a species of monstrosity.

The signal event in the play's treatment of the sundering of family bonds is King Henry's startling offer, at the beginning of act 1, to entail the crown to Richard, Duke of York in exchange for Henry's right to hold the throne during his lifetime. Henry has a son, Prince Edward, and his act negates his son's right to the throne. It also transforms the crown of England from a symbol of lineal succession into an alienable property. The immediate consequence is that Henry's supporters turn from him in disgust and his wife, Queen Margaret, proclaims:

> I here divorce myself
> Both from thy table, Henry, and thy bed
> Until that Act of Parliament be repealed
> Whereby my son is disinherited.
>
> (1.1.247–50)

Suddenly, Edward is *her* son, not Henry's; and soon thereafter she is raising an army to lead against the Yorkists. Many in the play describe Margaret's acts as unnatural, yet they follow from Henry's feckless negation of his role as guarantor of his son's succession. It was a truism of the early modern gender system that unmanly men, unnatural in their weakness, opened the door to a corresponding anomaly, the Amazonian manlike woman. Margaret is represented as such a figure, taking Henry's place both at the head of his army and also as champion of young Edward's lineal rights. Her authority in these roles stems directly from her socially sanctioned position as Henry's lawful wife and Edward's natural mother. Unlike Joan of Arc in *1 Henry VI*, who refuses to marry and from an early age pushes herself into the position of France's military champion, Margaret becomes a battlefield leader and her son's protector mainly as a consequence of Henry's failures. The ruthlessness that for so long makes her a successful military commander clashes with gendered expectations about women's gentle natures, but that ruthlessness also paradoxically reveals what masculine success looks like. Labeled monstrous when attained

Edward IV (1442–1483). Probably painted during his reign; artist unknown.

by a woman, her pitilessness is what Henry lacks and what leads to his death and the loss of the Lancastrian claim to the throne. Margaret is the only character to appear in all four of the early history plays associated with Shakespeare's name (*1, 2,* and *3 Henry VI* and *Richard III*), and she represents the tetralogy's most sustained exploration of what masculine power looks like when assumed by a woman as an extension of her roles as royal wife and mother. Her strengths contradict the patriarchal view that women are inherently weaker than men, and she uses her position to assert dominion both in the state and in the household.

Occasionally, especially in his early plays, Shakespeare wrote what Hereward T. Price called "mirror scenes," that is, scenes that are separate from the main line of plot development but that symbolically encapsulate, or mirror, some of the play's chief thematic concerns. In *3 Henry VI,* 2.5 is such a scene. Having given command of his army to Clifford and Margaret, Henry sits contemplatively upon a molehill while the Battle of Towton proceeds without him. Voicing his longing for the simplicity of a pastoral life, Henry suddenly sees a soldier carry onstage a man he has killed. It turns out to be the soldier's father, who was forced to serve with the Yorkist forces, while the son had been impressed into King Henry's service. The King then observes a second soldier carry onstage a man *he* has killed. It turns out to be the soldier's son. The scene schematically underscores one of the play's primary emblems of social disintegration: namely, the severing of bonds between father and son, son and father, leaving nothing to replace these bonds but individual rapaciousness. In both instances, the killers of the dead men have brought the bodies onstage to search them for money—"some store of crowns" (2.5.57) and "gold" (80). The ironic power of the scene is heightened, of course, because its central events are witnessed and lamented by King Henry, who has already disinherited his own son and as king is the symbolic fountainhead from which the familial disorder before him flows.

But the most interesting variation on the theme of dissevered families is embodied in the persons of Richard, Duke of York and his four sons: Edward, George, Richard, and Rutland. At the beginning of the play, the Yorks constitute an unusually integrated unit. Richard's sons support their father and urge him to seize the crown. Before he is captured at the Battle of Wakefield, Richard praises his offspring, assuming that in the battle "they have demeaned themselves / Like men born to renown by life or death" (1.4.7–8). At Wakefield, one of Richard's sons, the young Rutland, is killed. Just before the remaining three sons learn that their father has also died as a consequence of that battle, they praise him, as he has praised them. No one is more gracious than young Richard, who says, "Methinks 'tis prize enough to be his son" (2.1.20). At that moment, three suns appear in the heavens, each distinct, and then these suns join together. The pun on "suns/sons" seems to lead Edward to interpret this odd spectacle to mean that the three sons of Richard,

> Each one already blazing by our meeds,
> Should notwithstanding join our lights together
> And over-shine the earth as this the world.
>
> (2.1.36–38)

He then pledges to have three suns emblazoned on his shield.

As with all portents, the exact significance of this one is unclear. To Edward, it seems to imply the unwavering unity of the three sons of York. Yet Richard, who is to be as devastated as any of them by the news of their father's death, treats Edward's assertion that he will wear three suns on his shields as the occasion for a joke that distances him from his brother. "Nay, bear three daughters; by your leave I speak it, / You love the breeder better than the male" (2.1.41–42). With the death of the powerful patriarch, Richard, Duke of York, fraternal rivalry quickly replaces fraternal unity, and broken allegiances multiply. When Edward insists on marrying a commoner, the widow Lady Elizabeth Grey, Warwick, who is Edward's strongest supporter and who has been sent to France to secure a French bride for Edward, turns

"My ashes, as the phoenix, may bring forth / A bird that will revenge upon you all" (1.4.35–36). From Geffrey Whitney, *A Choice of Emblems* (1586).

against him in disgust. George temporarily abandons his brother, marries Warwick's daughter, and joins the Lancastrian cause. Richard, always outwardly loyal, privately vows to hack his way to the throne and displace both of his brothers in the process.

With ties of kinship and loyalty broken, nothing remains but the sheer exertion of individual will. Richard emerges as both the most fascinating and the most horrific character in the second half of the play because his will is indomitable and his desires unchecked by any moral constraints. The audience probably registers this fact most decisively during the bravura soliloquy that Richard speaks after he and George have watched—and obscenely commented upon—Edward's wooing of Lady Grey. Soliloquies, in which a character speaks to himself but is overheard by the theater audience, help create the illusion of interiority and inner subjectivity. Perhaps goaded by jealousy at the sight of Edward's successful wooing of Lady Grey, Richard in his soliloquy both reveals his frustrations and desires and hardheadedly maps a future course. In quick succession, he contemplates the number of people who before him have claims on the throne; resigns himself to seek instead the pleasures of courtship and love; despairs, since his atypical body prevents him from being loved; resolves therefore to seek the crown at any cost; and vows to change himself into any imaginable persona necessary to achieve his end. The soliloquy is long (3.2.124–95) and relentless. Richard tracks his argument like a bloodhound, registering his predicament with memorably vivid language:

> And yet I know not how to get the crown,
> For many lives stand between me and home,
> And I—like one lost in a thorny wood,
> That rents the thorns and is rent with the thorns,
> Seeking a way and straying from the way,
> Not knowing how to find the open air
> But toiling desperately to find it out—
> Torment myself to catch the English crown; . . .
> (3.2.172–79)

Struggle and frustration are evident in the repetitions of this passage. Seeking, straying, toiling, Richard is in constant motion, throwing himself against impossible barriers. The crown eludes him, yet he goes on. He is by turns attractive and frightening.

Many prototypes are drawn upon to create this distinctive character. His "individuality" does not emerge from nowhere but depends on Shakespeare's skillful appropriation of prior dramatic resources. Richard's characterization owes much, for example, to the striving, overreaching stage heroes created by Shakespeare's early rival Christopher Marlowe. Like Marlowe's Tamburlaine, Richard makes his heaven "to dream upon the crown" (3.2.168) and stops at nothing to achieve that goal. In part, he is also fashioned after the Vice figure from the medieval religious drama. The Vice was the character—often witty and quite disconcertingly entertaining— who embodied the principle of evil and tried to compel others to sin. Richard's witty asides, as much as his aggression and lack of scruple, reveal his kinship to the Vice.

Perhaps this character's strongest association, however, is with the figure of the stage machiavel, whom Richard himself evokes at the end of his soliloquy. The historical Niccolò Machiavelli was an Italian political philosopher whose influential book *The Prince* pragmatically rather than moralistically detailed the tactics and principles that made for successful government in the modern world. In the popular imagination, he came to stand for the hypocrisy and political cunning associated with Protestant England's symbolic enemy, Catholic Italy.

Sharing affinities with each of these figures but not fully modeled on any of them, Richard functions in Shakespeare's play to suggest what emerges when one no longer acknowledges the primacy of the identities constructed by the words "son" and "brother." In a society that defined people in terms of their place within family structures and social hierarchies, to separate oneself from those structures and hierarchies risked being read as monstrous and unnatural. Richard is riveting precisely because he seems so autonomous and so indifferent to the bonds and loyalties—to family and to king—that supposedly hold his society together and constrain the actions of its members. Though not the only one in the play whose ambition corrodes ties of blood and allegiance, Richard most fully epitomizes ambition's dehumanizing effects. He is a man without allegiances who uses his crooked body both as an excuse for his behavior and as a motivation to win his society's most glittering prize—the crown—by whatever means lies to hand.

Marriage is one way to incorporate individuals into social structures, but in 3 *Henry VI* the breakdown of social bonds is both caused and symbolized by its disorderly marriages. In the feudal world depicted in most of Shakespeare's early history plays, marriages in noble or monarchical families were primarily premised not on love but on dynastic convenience. Wives were chosen for the dowry or the territory or the alliances they brought with them. To marry for love was viewed as dangerous because it introduced irrational passion into what was supposed to be a rational choice and threatened the husband's control of himself and of his spouse. In marrying the widow Lady Grey, Edward makes such a passion-driven marriage and thereby nearly loses control of the kingdom. By his actions, he forfeits Warwick's loyalty and temporarily that of his brother George. King Henry had also made an irrational match in marrying the dowerless Margaret (see 2 *Henry VI* 1.1). In 3 *Henry VI*, this initial lack of control finds its consequence in Henry's inability to govern Margaret and in the increasingly topsy-turvy nature of their marriage.

The end of the play, however, refocuses on the marriage of Edward and Lady Grey to bring a tenuous and highly ironized sense of resolution to the play's action. In the final scene, King Edward admires the son to which his wife, now Queen Elizabeth, has given birth and invites his brothers Richard and Clarence to do the same. The ambience is domestic in a modern way. This is a marriage of affection more than utility. Edward calls the babe "Ned" (5.7.16) and his wife "Bess" (15), the nicknames suggesting intimacy. But if Edward thinks this cozy domesticity, so pleasing to him but so politically ill advised, can reestablish the Yorkist dynasty and center it on him and his descendants, the presence of Richard signals otherwise. Leaning down to kiss the babe, Richard says, "And that I love the tree from whence thou sprang'st, / Witness the loving kiss I give the fruit" (31–32). The tree he refers to is, of course, the family of York, the family tree from which he himself springs. But then, in an aside, he adds: "To say the truth, so Judas kissed his master / And cried, 'All hail!' whenas he meant all harm" (33–34). For Richard to cast himself as the betrayer of Christ bodes badly for the happy family: Edward, Ned, and Bess. To twenty-first-century audiences and theatergoers, the King's doting attention to his wife and son may make him seem quite modern and quite human. Yet viewed historically and in its dramatic context, the King's behavior also signals his weakness, his propensity to let his affections overrule his reason. Fixated on his Ned and his Bess, he seems oblivious to the threat posed by his alienated, thoroughly undomestic brother.

3 *Henry VI* ends, then, with a scene that underscores the tenuousness of Edward's purchase on power and threatens a renewal of civil war and family strife. The play's

imaginative landscape is dominated by those willful, monstrous individuals such as Richard and Margaret who thrive amid the chaos of a disintegrating society. Few can oppose them, most especially not "the good King Henry," a man disastrously unsuited to play a monarch's part. Hovering on the periphery of this play's action and killed before its final scene, Henry is gradually transformed into a mere observer of the public world around him. Saintly and detached, he comes to represent the antithesis of Richard's surging, self-centered ambition, finally serving almost as choric commentator and as prophet. He predicts, for example, that Henry, Earl of Richmond (later Henry VII) will be England's savior (4.6.68–76), and he predicts (5.6.37–43) that many will come to curse the hunchbacked Richard (later Richard III). But hope for release from Richard's evil lies far in the future, and Henry's increasing saintliness neither erases his responsibility for civil war nor solves the immediate problem of secular rule. Neither saints nor monsters are particularly suited to govern other men. Edward is neither and so seems more fit to rule; yet he is unable to control, or even to recognize, his brother's villainy. 3 Henry VI feels so grim because its compelling depiction of the unraveling of England's social fabric suggests little about how that fabric can once again be rewoven.

JEAN E. HOWARD

SELECTED BIBLIOGRAPHY

Bergeron, David. "The Play-Within-the-Play in 3 Henry VI." Tennessee Studies in Literature 22 (1977): 37–47. Examines four instances of Shakespeare's early use of the play within the play in 3 Henry VI.

Berman, Ronald. "Fathers and Sons in the Henry VI Plays." Shakespeare Quarterly 13 (1962): 487–97. Explores the disruption of relations between fathers and sons, kings and subjects under conditions of war and unstable monarchy.

Champion, Larry. "Developmental Structure in Shakespeare's Early Histories: The Perspective of 3 Henry VI." Studies in Philology 76 (1979): 218–38. Argues that the play reveals Shakespeare's increasing technical sophistication and mastery of dramatic structure.

Griffith, Huw. "Shakespeare, Pathos and Sovereign Violence: 3 Henry VI and King Lear." "Rapt in Secret Studies": Emerging Shakespeares. Ed. Daryl Chalk and Laurie Johnson. Newcastle upon Tyne: Cambridge Scholars Publishing, 2010. 91–111. Examines the speech of those who, like Rutland and York, are victims of pitiless sovereign violence in 3 Henry VI, arguing that such voices invite the audience to respond with empathy to human vulnerability.

Hunt, Maurice. "Unnaturalness in Shakespeare's 3 Henry VI." English Studies: A Journal of English Language and Literature 80 (1999): 146–67. Links Shakespeare's play to Thomas Sackville and Thomas Norton's earlier tragedy Gorboduc, as each explores the motif of unnatural behavior and its political consequences.

Kahn, Coppélia. "'The Shadow of the Male': Masculine Identity in the History Plays." Man's Estate: Masculine Identity in Shakespeare. Berkeley: U of California P, 1981. 47–81. Argues that in the early history plays masculine identity emerges primarily from emulation of or rivalry with the father.

Levine, Nina S. "Ruling Women and the Politics of Gender in 2 and 3 Henry VI." Women's Matters: Politics, Gender, and Nation in Shakespeare's Early History Plays. Newark: U of Delaware P, 1998. 68–96. Argues that in 3 Henry VI the misogyny surrounding Margaret's representation is tempered by her role in fighting for her son's succession to the throne and her defense of the English national interest.

Schwarz, Kathryn. "Fearful Simile: Stealing the Breech in Shakespeare's Chronicle Plays." Tough Love: Amazon Encounters in the English Renaissance. Durham, NC:

Duke UP, 2000. 79–107. Discusses the differently disruptive roles of Joan of Arc and Queen Margaret in *1, 2,* and *3 Henry VI,* arguing that Margaret, unlike Joan, gains her distinctive power to destroy patriarchal structures from working within the normative social roles of wife and mother.

Strohm, Paul. "York's Paper Crown: 'Bare Life' and Shakespeare's First Tragedy." *Journal of Medieval and Early Modern Studies* 36.1 (Winter 2006): 75–101. Explores *3 Henry VI* as Shakespeare's first tragedy in which Richard of York's mock coronation with a paper crown before his execution recalls medieval martyr drama and gives his death a significance Margaret cannot control.

Williams, Katherine Schapp. "Enabling Richard: The Rhetoric of Disability in *Richard III.*" *Disability Studies Quarterly* 29 (2009): www.dsq-sds.org. Explores the way Richard of Gloucester (later Richard III) uses his bodily difference as a source of power, thereby challenging premodern expectations about deformity as a mark of evil or of impotence.

Film

The Third Part of King Henry VI. 1983. Dir. Jane Howell. UK/USA. 211 min. A BBC-TV production with Julia Foster as Margaret and Peter Benson as a bookish and ineffectual Henry VI.

TEXTUAL INTRODUCTION

We know that some version of this play, whether it was written by Shakespeare alone or in collaboration, was being performed in 1592, probably at the Rose Theater. A printed version appeared in 1595, bearing the title *The true Tragedie of Richard Duke of Yorke, and the death of good King Henrie the Sixt, with the whole contention betweene the two Houses Lancaster and Yorke.* Because it was published in the small format known as octavo, this text is referred to here as "O." Two further editions of *The True Tragedy,* this time in the slightly larger quarto format (hence Q2 and Q3), appeared in 1600 and 1619, each slightly modifying its predecessor in a number of places but nevertheless recording what is essentially the same text.

A very different printed version of the play, this time entitled *The third Part of Henrie the Sixt, with the death of the Duke of Yorke,* appeared in 1623 in the posthumous collection of Shakespeare's works known as the First Folio. This version (F) is considerably longer than O (2,949 verse lines as opposed to 2,109). While the plot is virtually the same and the speeches sometimes close or even identical, there are hundreds of minor verbal variants throughout, and in places the dialogue and organization of the action are quite dissimilar. *3 Henry VI* subsequently went into three more editions, again with some very minor modifications—F2 in 1632, F3 in 1663, and F4 in 1685.

If an editor knew for certain the steps whereby a text such as O or F was transmitted from Shakespeare's pen to the printed page, it might be possible to identify with confidence which text should be the base text and then assess the relative merit of each variant reading from the other text. In the case of this play, however, the transmission of the texts is a puzzle. Almost all, but not all, modern editors have been convinced that peculiarities and inconsistencies in some of F's stage directions and speech prefixes indicate an author's working papers. If they are right, F's printers could have worked directly from a manuscript in Shakespeare's hand.

But the true nature of O, and its relation to F, have been debated since at least the late seventeenth century—and have yet to be resolved. A copy of O wasn't rediscovered until 1796, but, working from the Quarto and Folio texts, scholars soon divided into three camps: those, including Edmond Malone in 1790, who could not believe O really was by Shakespeare; those, including Alexander Pope in 1725, who thought it was

Shakespeare's first draft of what he later revised as F; and finally those, including Samuel Johnson in 1765, who thought that, despite its being published first and F being published twenty-eight years later, O's text in fact derived from the text that lies behind F.

In the twentieth century the idea took hold that Johnson was right and O is a "memorial reconstruction"—that is, the result of an attempt to recall the text of a play by someone who has either witnessed or appeared in it. O's "conspicuous passages of nonsense" and the fact that it "often severely fractures the verse" (these phrases come from Randall Martin's Oxford edition of 2008) are to be explained by memory lapses and mishearings on the part of the person or persons trying to reconstruct the F text.

All these theories take it for granted that O is inferior to F. Its compositor(s) certainly sometimes struggled to realize the text as blank verse, or even, occasionally, as verse at all. But this may well reflect difficulty with interpreting the manuscript serving as base text, rather than with the text embodied in that manuscript; this edition relines 213 of O's lines, about 10 percent of the text, in an attempt to release blank verse whenever possible—but it also has to reline 118 lines of F, and F had Q3 to refer to. As for passages of nonsense, they are few and far between. Indeed, Laurie Maguire has argued that O is a remarkably clear, consistent, and coherent text that shows no signs of having been a memorial reconstruction.

Those who support the memorial reconstruction theory attribute the attempt at remembering to one, or probably more, actors. But they are not agreed whether the actors were trying to recall the play behind F, or an abridged touring version of it, or a much earlier version that Shakespeare later revised to become the play behind F. In 2001 the Arden editors, Eric Rasmussen and John Cox, picking up an idea from Peter Blayney, tentatively wondered whether O might derive instead from a transcript of the play as performed (and therefore probably exhibiting cuts), which had been made by one of the actors for a friend, using a mixture of scripts and his memory (166).

Until recently, modern editors have assumed that their task was to select the extant early text closest to Shakespeare's hand and use it as their base text, while correcting any obvious errors (whatever their source, even if it be Shakespeare himself rather than a scribe or a promptbook holder or a printer's compositor). Since the 1980s, however, editors have increasingly come to accept that Shakespeare may have revised some of his plays and that two different texts might both, in part at least, be authoritative. Some editors have even argued that reported or other kinds of derivative texts could be regarded as having authority either as records of Elizabethan performances, say, or even simply as historical phenomena.

F is certainly a fuller text than O, and for that reason alone it is the version included in the print edition, but the Digital Edition also includes a text of O that has been edited according to the same principles—namely, that its readings are preserved wherever it is possible to argue that they make good sense.

NEIL TAYLOR

Textual Bibliography

Blayney, Peter W. N. "The Publication of Playbooks." *A New History of Early English Drama.* Ed. John D. Cox and David Scott Kastan. New York: Columbia UP, 1997. 383–422.

Cox, John, and Eric Rasmussen. "The Texts of *The True Tragedy* and *3 Henry VI.*" Introduction to *King Henry VI Part 3.* The Arden Shakespeare. London: Thomson, 2001. 148–76.

Maguire, Laurie E. *Shakespeare's Suspect Texts.* Cambridge: Cambridge UP, 1996.

Martin, Randall. "*The True Tragedy of Richard Duke of York* and *3 Henry VI*: Report and Revision." *Review of English Studies* 53 (2002): 8–30.

PERFORMANCE NOTE

Despite its uncertain protagonist, its near-comic compression of events, and its cloudy resolution, 3 Henry VI has a surprisingly successful stage history. The most compelling productions make strengths of apparent flaws, exploiting the play's episodic structure and thin characterizations to imply that regardless of which family comes to power, England's future is uncertain. Productions often stage scenic echoes that link spectacular atrocities on either side, affirming the similarities of the two families repeatedly displacing one another at the center of tragic scenes. Sometimes productions do choose sides, presenting incessant battles and self-serving ambitions to offset an attractively pious portrayal of Henry, or as background for the quandaries of a ruler who is ambivalent about power. Letting Henry emerge as a meditative choric figure in 2.5, or as a Christian archetype who rejects majesty and aggression before offering himself to his enemy, can heighten the sense of climax at his death. Other productions build psychological depth in Warwick, indicating that his role as kingmaker reflects not smug self-regard but deep desire for England's stability. Warwick's struggle to embrace whatever means to peace seems least objectionable thence becomes a source of sustained dramatic interest.

Richard and Margaret can also emerge as sites of sympathetic engagement, particularly when productions suggest that their pursuits of power and revenge stem from the prejudice and mockery each has endured at court. Additionally, audience awareness of Richard as the future Richard III inspires some directors to amplify his role as a comic Vice figure, often overshadowing deliberately weaker portrayals of Henry and Edward IV in the process. Productions also choose whether to stress York's nobility or ambition; whether Henry transcends or shrinks from earthly rule; whether Edward IV is a competent alternative to Henry or equally obtuse; and whether Richard and Margaret are characterized by sheer bloodlust or an extravagant sense of loyalty. They also make critical choices in representing Richard's deformities, motivating George's reversal in 5.1 and instilling irony or assurance at play's end. Additional dramaturgical considerations include managing the Octavo's stage directions (e.g., in scene 10, Clifford's entrance "*with an arrow in his neck*"); the appearance of "three suns" in 2.1; and deciding whether to transpose the civil wars to a contemporary setting.

Brett Gamboa

The Third Part of Henry the Sixth

[THE PERSONS OF THE PLAY

King HENRY the Sixth
Queen MARGARET of Anjou, his wife, and daughter to René, King of Naples and Sicily
PRINCE EDWARD, Prince of Wales, son to Henry and Margaret
Lord CLIFFORD
Duke of EXETER
Duke of SOMERSET
Earl of NORTHUMBERLAND
Earl of WESTMORLAND
Earl of OXFORD
Henry Tudor, Earl of Richmond
SOMERVILLE
HUNTSMAN
SON who has killed his father in battle

Richard Plantagenet, Duke of YORK
EDWARD, Earl of March, eldest son to York, later King Edward the Fourth
GEORGE, second son to York, later Duke of Clarence
RICHARD, third son to York, later Duke of Gloucester
Earl of RUTLAND, youngest son to York
SIR JOHN Mortimer, uncle to York
Sir Hugh Mortimer, brother to Sir John
ELIZABETH, Lady Grey, widow to Sir John Grey; later Queen Elizabeth and wife to
    King Edward the Fourth
Prince Edward of York, infant son of Edward and Elizabeth
Richard Neville, Earl of WARWICK
Marquess of MONTAGUE, brother to Warwick
Earl of Pembroke
Lord Stafford
Duke of NORFOLK
Lord HASTINGS
Sir William Stanley
Anthony Woodville, Lord RIVERS, brother to Lady Grey
LIEUTENANT of the Tower of London
Sir John MONTGOMERY
NOBLEMAN
TUTOR to Rutland
Nurse to Prince Edward of York
FATHER who has killed his son in battle
Three WATCHMEN

King LOUIS the Eleventh of France
Lady BONA of Savoy, sister-in-law to Louis
Lord Bourbon, a French admiral

MAYOR of York
Aldermen of York

Mayor of Coventry
Citizens of Coventry
SINKLO, a keeper
HUMFREY, a keeper
GABRIEL, a messenger
MESSENGERS
POSTS
Soldiers, Drummers, Trumpeters, Attendants]

1.1 (O Scene 1)

Alarum.° Enter [Richard] Plantagenet[, the Duke of   *Trumpet-call to arms*
YORK, *with his sons]* EDWARD *[and]* RICHARD*[, the*
Duke of] NORFOLK, *[the Marquess of]* MONTAGUE, *[his*
brother the Earl of] WARWICK, *and Soldiers.*

WARWICK   I wonder how the King escaped our hands!
YORK   While we pursued the horsemen of the North[1]
    He slyly stole away and left his men,
    Whereat the great lord of Northumberland,
5   Whose warlike ears could never brook retreat,[2]
    Cheered up the drooping army; and himself,
    Lord Clifford, and Lord Stafford all abreast
    Charged our main battle's° front and, breaking in,   *army's*
    Were by the swords of common soldiers slain.[3]
10   EDWARD   Lord Stafford's father, Duke of Buckingham,
    Is either slain or wounded dangerous.°   *dangerously*
    I cleft his beaver° with a downright° blow.   *helmet visor / vertical*
    That this is true, father, behold his blood.
MONTAGUE   And, brother,[4] here's the Earl of Wiltshire's blood,
15   Whom I encountered as the battles joined.
RICHARD *[throwing down the Duke of Somerset's head]*[5]
    Speak thou for me, and tell them what I did.
YORK   Richard hath best deserved of all my sons.
    —But is your grace dead, my lord of Somerset?
NORFOLK   Such hope have all the line of John of Gaunt.[6]
20   RICHARD   Thus do I hope to shake King Henry's head.
WARWICK   And so do I, victorious Prince of York.
    Before I see thee seated in that throne
    Which now the house of Lancaster usurps,
    I vow by heaven these eyes shall never close.
25   This is the palace of the fearful° King   *frightened*
    And this the regal seat: possess it, York,
    For this is thine and not King Henry's heirs'.
YORK   Assist me, then, sweet Warwick, and I will,
    For hither we have broken in by force.
30   NORFOLK   We'll all assist you; he that flies shall die.

1.1 Location: The Parliament House, London.
1. *horsemen . . . North:* cavalry from northern England.
2. Could never endure hearing the trumpet call signaling retreat.
3. Shakespeare names York (rather than a common soldier) as the person who killed Clifford at several points later in the play. *2 Henry VI)* dramatizes this death in 5.3.
4. The historical Montague was York's nephew. He was also, as Shakespeare suggests elsewhere in this play, Warwick's brother.
5. This Duke of Somerset was killed by Richard,

Duke of York, in the last act of *2 Henry VI* in front of an alehouse called The Castle. This fulfilled a warning given by a spirit that Somerset should shun castles. Like many prophecies, this one was ambiguous, referring to an alehouse rather than an actual castle. In *3 Henry VI,* another Duke of Somerset, son of the duke whom Richard slew, is featured as a character.
6. May all the descendants of John of Gaunt have the same fate. John of Gaunt held the title Duke of Lancaster; Somerset was his grandson, and Henry VI his great-grandson. The Yorkists contended that John of Gaunt's son Henry IV had usurped Richard II's crown.

YORK Thanks, gentle° Norfolk. Stay by me, my lords,   *noble*
  And, soldiers, stay and lodge by me this night.
    They go up [to the chair of state].
WARWICK And when the King comes, offer him no violence
  Unless he seek to thrust you out perforce.°   *by force*
35 YORK The Queen this day here holds her Parliament,
  But little thinks we shall be of her council.
  By words or blows here let us win our right.
RICHARD Armed as we are, let's stay within this house.
WARWICK The "Bloody Parliament" shall this be called
40 Unless Plantagenet, Duke of York, be king
  And bashful Henry deposed, whose cowardice
  Hath made us bywords° to our enemies.   *objects of scorn*
YORK Then leave me not. My lords, be resolute.
  I mean to take possession of my right.
45 WARWICK Neither the King nor he that loves him best,
  The proudest he that holds up° Lancaster,   *supports*
  Dares stir a wing if Warwick shake his bells.[7]
  I'll plant Plantagenet,[8] root him up who dares.
  Resolve thee, Richard: claim the English crown.
    Flourish.° Enter King HENRY *[the Sixth, Lord]*   *Trumpet fanfare*
    CLIFFORD, *[the Earl of]* NORTHUMBERLAND, *[the Earl*
    of] WESTMORLAND, *[the Duke of]* EXETER, *and the rest.*
50 HENRY My lords, look where the sturdy° rebel sits,   *stubborn*
  Even in the chair of state. Belike° he means,   *Probably*
  Backed by the power of Warwick, that false peer,
  To aspire unto the crown and reign as king.
  Earl of Northumberland, he slew thy father,
55 And thine, Lord Clifford, and you both have vowed revenge
  On him, his sons, his favorites, and his friends.
NORTHUMBERLAND If I be not, heavens be revenged on me.
CLIFFORD The hope thereof makes Clifford mourn in steel.[9]
WESTMORLAND What, shall we suffer this? Let's pluck him
  down.
60 My heart for anger burns; I cannot brook it.
HENRY Be patient, gentle Earl of Westmorland.
CLIFFORD Patience is for poltroons° such as he.   *cowards*
  He durst° not sit there had your father lived.   *dared*
  My gracious lord, here in the Parliament
65 Let us assail the family of York.
NORTHUMBERLAND Well hast thou spoken. Cousin,° be it so.   *Kinsman*
HENRY Ah, know you not the city° favors them   *(London)*
  And they have troops of soldiers at their beck?°   *absolute command*
WESTMORLAND But when the Duke is slain, they'll quickly fly.
70 HENRY Far be the thought of this from Henry's heart,
  To make a shambles° of the Parliament House.   *slaughterhouse*
  Cousin of Exeter, frowns, words, and threats
  Shall be the war that Henry means to use.
  —Thou factious° Duke of York, descend my throne   *rebellious*

7. *If Warwick makes a move.* Elizabethans attached bells to the legs of falcons in order to further frighten the falcon's prey; Warwick is comparing himself to such a threatening bird.
8. *Richard, Duke of York was also called Richard Plantagenet. The Plantagenets were the medieval* dynasty that began to rule England in 1154, when Henry II assumed the throne. The Yorkist and Lancastrian families were both descended from this dynasty.
9. In armor (rather than the black cloaks that were conventionally worn by mourners).

75 And kneel for grace and mercy at my feet.
I am thy sovereign.
YORK   I am thine.
EXETER   For shame, come down. He made thee Duke of York.
YORK   It was my inheritance, as the earldom[1] was.
EXETER   Thy father was a traitor to the crown.[2]
80 WARWICK   Exeter, thou art a traitor to the crown
In following this usurping Henry.
CLIFFORD   Whom should he follow but his natural king?
WARWICK   True, Clifford: that's Richard, Duke of York.
HENRY   And shall I stand, and thou sit in my throne?
85 YORK   It must and shall be so. Content thyself.
WARWICK   Be Duke of Lancaster; let him be King.
WESTMORLAND   He is both King and Duke of Lancaster,
And that the lord of Westmorland shall maintain.
WARWICK   And Warwick shall disprove it. You forget
90 That we are those which chased you from the field,
And slew your fathers, and with colors° spread   *flags*
Marched through the city to the palace gates.
NORTHUMBERLAND   Yes, Warwick, I remember it to my grief,
And, by his soul, thou and thy house shall rue it.
95 WESTMORLAND   Plantagenet, of thee and these thy sons,
Thy kinsmen, and thy friends, I'll have more lives
Than drops of blood were in my father's veins.
CLIFFORD   Urge it no more, lest that instead of words
I send thee, Warwick, such a messenger
100 As shall revenge his death before I stir.
WARWICK   Poor Clifford, how I scorn his worthless threats!
YORK   Will you we° show our title to the crown?   *Do you wish us to*
If not, our swords shall plead it in the field.
HENRY   What title hast thou, traitor, to the crown?
105 Thy father was, as thou art, Duke of York,[3]
Thy grandfather, Roger Mortimer, Earl of March.
I am the son of Henry the Fifth,
Who made the Dauphin[4] and the French to stoop
And seized upon their towns and provinces.
110 WARWICK   Talk not of France, sith° thou hast lost it all.   *since*
HENRY   The Lord Protector[5] lost it and not I:
When I was crowned I was but nine months old.
RICHARD   You are old enough now, and yet° methinks you lose.   *and even now*
Father, tear the crown from the usurper's head.
115 EDWARD   Sweet father, do so: set it on your head.
MONTAGUE   Good brother, as thou lov'st and honorest arms,
Let's fight it out and not stand caviling° thus.   *quibbling*
RICHARD   Sound drums and trumpets and the King will fly.
YORK   Sons, peace.
120 HENRY   Peace thou, and give King Henry leave° to speak.[6]   *permission*

---

1. The earldom of March, which York inherited from his mother and through which he claimed the throne.
2. York's father, the Earl of Cambridge, was executed for treason (see *Henry V* 2.2).
3. In fact, the historical York's father was not the Duke of York. York inherited that title from his uncle (Edward).
4. Title of the oldest son of the French king.
5. Humphrey, Duke of Gloucester, was Lord Protector during Henry VI's youth and, as such, had oversight of the king and kingdom. His downfall is dramatized in *2 Henry VI*.
6. In O, line 120 is assigned to Northumberland, and is then followed by four lines not included in F. See Textual Introduction for a discussion of the two textual forms (folio and octavo) in which *3 Henry VI* was first printed, and of the considerable differences between them.

WARWICK Plantagenet shall speak first. Hear him, lords,
And be you silent and attentive too,
For he that interrupts him shall not live.
HENRY Think'st thou that I will leave my kingly throne
125 Wherein my grandsire and my father sat?
No, first shall war unpeople this my realm.
Ay, and their colors, often borne in France,
And now in England to our heart's great sorrow,
Shall be my winding-sheet.° —Why faint you,⁷ lords?   *burial shroud*
130 My title's good, and better far than his.
WARWICK Prove it, Henry, and thou shalt be King.
HENRY Henry the Fourth by conquest got the crown.
YORK 'Twas by rebellion against his king.°   *(Richard II)*
HENRY [*aside*] I know not what to say: my title's weak.
135 —Tell me, may not a king adopt an heir?
YORK What then?
HENRY An if° he may, then am I lawful king: *An if=If*
For Richard, in the view of many lords,
Resigned the crown to Henry the Fourth,
140 Whose heir my father was, and I am his.
YORK He rose against him,° being° his sovereign,   *(Richard) / who was*
And made him to resign his crown perforce.
WARWICK Suppose, my lords, he did it unconstrained,
Think you 'twere prejudicial to his crown?°   *his claim to the throne*
145 EXETER No, for he could not so resign his crown
But° that the next heir should succeed and reign.   *Without ensuring*
HENRY Art thou against us, Duke of Exeter?
EXETER His° is the right, and therefore pardon me.   *(York's)*
YORK Why whisper you, my lords, and answer not?
150 EXETER My conscience tells me he is lawful king.
HENRY All will revolt from me and turn to him.
NORTHUMBERLAND Plantagenet, for all the claim thou lay'st,
Think not that Henry shall be so deposed.
WARWICK Deposed he shall be in despite° of all.   *spite*
155 NORTHUMBERLAND Thou art deceived: 'tis not thy southern
    power°   *army*
Of Essex, Norfolk, Suffolk, nor of Kent,
Which makes thee thus presumptuous and proud,
Can set the Duke up° in despite of me.   *(on the throne)*
CLIFFORD King Henry, be thy title right or wrong,
160 Lord Clifford vows to fight in thy defense.
May that ground gape and swallow me alive
Where I shall kneel to him that slew my father.
HENRY O Clifford, how thy words revive my heart!
YORK Henry of Lancaster, resign thy crown.
165 —What mutter you, or what conspire you, lords?
WARWICK Do right unto this princely Duke of York,
Or I will fill the house with armèd men
And over the chair of state where now he sits
Write up his title with usurping blood.⁸
        He stamps with his foot, and the Soldiers show
        themselves.

---

7. Why do you lose heart?
8. With the blood of Henry, whom Warwick considers a usurper.

170　HENRY　My lord of Warwick, hear but one word:
　　　Let me for this my lifetime reign as king.
　　YORK　Confirm the crown to me and to mine heirs,
　　　And thou shalt reign in quiet while thou liv'st.
　　HENRY　I am content. Richard Plantagenet,
175　　Enjoy the kingdom after my decease.
　　CLIFFORD　What wrong is this unto the Prince, your son!
　　WARWICK　What good is this to England and himself!
　　WESTMORLAND　Base, fearful, and despairing Henry!
　　CLIFFORD　How hast thou injured both thyself and us!
180　WESTMORLAND　I cannot stay to hear these articles.°　　　　　　　　terms of agreement
　　NORTHUMBERLAND　Nor I.
　　CLIFFORD [to NORTHUMBERLAND]　Come, cousin, let us tell
　　　the Queen these news.
　　WESTMORLAND　Farewell, faint-hearted and degenerate King,
　　　In whose cold blood no spark of honor bides.°　　　　　　　　　　lives
185　NORTHUMBERLAND　Be thou a prey unto the house of York
　　　And die in bands° for this unmanly deed.　　　　　　　　　　　fetters
　　CLIFFORD　In dreadful war mayst thou be overcome,
　　　Or live in peace abandoned and despised.
　　　　　　　　　　　[Exeunt CLIFFORD, NORTHUMBERLAND,
　　　　　　　　　　　　　WESTMORLAND, and their Soldiers.]⁹
　　WARWICK　Turn this way, Henry, and regard them not.
190　EXETER　They seek revenge and therefore will not yield.
　　HENRY　Ah, Exeter.
　　WARWICK　　　　　Why should you sigh, my lord?
　　HENRY　Not for myself, Lord Warwick, but my son,
　　　Whom I unnaturally shall disinherit.
　　　But be it as it may. [to YORK] I here entail°　　　　　　　　　bequeath
195　The crown to thee and to thine heirs forever,
　　　Conditionally that here thou take an oath
　　　To cease this civil war and, whilst I live,
　　　To honor me as thy king and sovereign,
　　　And neither by treason nor hostility
200　To seek to put me down and reign thyself.
　　YORK　This oath I willingly take and will perform.
　　WARWICK　Long live King Henry! Plantagenet, embrace him.
　　HENRY　And long live thou and these thy forward° sons.　　　　precocious
　　YORK　Now York and Lancaster are reconciled.
205　EXETER　Accursed be he that seeks to make them foes.
　　　　　　　　Sennet.¹ Here they come down.²
　　YORK　Farewell, my gracious lord; I'll to my castle.³
　　WARWICK　And I'll keep London with my soldiers.
　　NORFOLK　And I to Norfolk with my followers.
　　MONTAGUE　And I unto the sea, from whence I came.
　　　　　　　　　　　[Exeunt YORK, EDWARD, RICHARD, WARWICK,
　　　　　　　　　　　　　NORFOLK, MONTAGUE, and their Soldiers.]
210　HENRY　And I with grief and sorrow to the court.
　　　　　　　　Enter Queen [MARGARET and PRINCE EDWARD].

---

9. TEXTUAL COMMENT F provides no exit for these characters. Here and elsewhere the Folio text fails to indicate when certain characters enter or exit the stage, and the editor has to supply these directions. See Digital Edition TC 1 (Folio edited text).

1. Trumpet notes signaling a procession.
2. This line indicates that a "state," a chair or raised platform, might be required for the scene.
3. Sandal, located near Wakefield in Yorkshire.

EXETER Here comes the Queen, whose looks bewray° her anger.　　　　　*reveal*
　　　　I'll steal away.
HENRY　　　　Exeter, so will I.
MARGARET Nay, go not from me; I will follow thee.
HENRY Be patient, gentle Queen, and I will stay.
215　MARGARET Who can be patient in such extremes?
　　　　Ah, wretched man, would I had died a maid
　　　　And never seen thee, never borne thee son,
　　　　Seeing thou hast proved so unnatural a father.
　　　　Hath he deserved to lose his birthright thus?
220　　Hadst thou but loved him half so well as I,
　　　　Or felt that pain° which I did for him once,　　　　*(labor pains)*
　　　　Or nourished him as I did with my blood,
　　　　Thou wouldst have left thy dearest heart-blood there
　　　　Rather than have made that savage duke thine heir
225　　And disinherited thine only son.
　　PRINCE EDWARD Father, you cannot disinherit me.
　　　　If you be King, why should not I succeed?
　　HENRY Pardon me, Margaret; pardon me, sweet son:
　　　　The Earl of Warwick and the Duke enforced me.
230　MARGARET Enforced thee? Art thou King and wilt be forced?
　　　　I shame° to hear thee speak. Ah, timorous wretch,　　　*am ashamed*
　　　　Thou hast undone thyself, thy son, and me,
　　　　And given unto the house of York such head[4]
　　　　As thou shalt reign but by their sufferance.
235　　To entail him and his heirs unto the crown,
　　　　What is it but to make thy sepulcher
　　　　And creep into it far before thy time?
　　　　Warwick is Chancellor and the lord of Calais;
　　　　Stern Falconbridge commands the narrow seas;°　　　*(Straits of Dover)*
240　　The Duke° is made Protector of the realm;　　　　　　*(York)*
　　　　And yet shalt thou be safe? Such safety finds
　　　　The trembling lamb environèd° with wolves.　　　　*surrounded*
　　　　Had I been there, which am a silly° woman,　　　　*helpless*
　　　　The soldiers should have tossed me on their pikes°　*axlike weapons*
245　　Before I would have granted° to that act.　　　　*assented*
　　　　But thou preferr'st thy life before thine honor,
　　　　And, seeing thou dost, I here divorce myself
　　　　Both from thy table, Henry, and thy bed[5]
　　　　Until that Act of Parliament be repealed
250　　Whereby my son is disinherited.
　　　　The northern lords that have forsworn thy colors
　　　　Will follow mine if once they see them spread—
　　　　And spread they shall be, to thy foul disgrace
　　　　And utter ruin of the house of York.
255　　Thus do I leave thee. Come, son, let's away,
　　　　Our army is ready; come, we'll after them.
　　HENRY Stay, gentle Margaret, and hear me speak.
　　MARGARET Thou hast spoke too much already. Get thee gone.
　　HENRY Gentle son Edward, thou wilt stay me?°　　　　*stay with me*
260　MARGARET Ay, to be murdered by his enemies.

---

4. Such freedom to act. To give a horse its head means
to loosen its reins and let it go where it will.
5. *I here . . . bed:* echoing the language of church

law, which permitted marital separation "from bed
and board" in cases of adultery, heresy, and cruelty.

PRINCE EDWARD   When I return with victory from the field
    I'll see your grace; till then, I'll follow her.
MARGARET   Come, son, away. We may not linger thus.
              [Exeunt MARGARET *and* PRINCE EDWARD.]
HENRY   Poor Queen, how love to me and to her son
265   Hath made her break out into terms of rage.
    Revengèd may she be on that hateful duke,
    Whose haughty spirit, wingèd with desire,
    Will cost° my crown and, like an empty° eagle,   *cost (me) / a hungry*
    Tire° on the flesh of me and of my son.   *Feed ravenously*
270   The loss of those three lords torments my heart:
    I'll write unto them and entreat them fair.°   *courteously*
    Come, cousin, you shall be the messenger.
EXETER   And I, I hope, shall reconcile them all.
                   [Flourish.] Exeunt.

1.2 (O Scene 2)

Enter RICHARD, EDWARD, *and* MONTAGUE.

RICHARD   Brother, though I be youngest, give me leave.°   *allow me (to speak)*
EDWARD   No, I can better play the orator.
MONTAGUE   But I have reasons strong and forcible.
          Enter the Duke of YORK.
YORK   Why, how now, sons and brother, at a strife?
5   What is your quarrel? How began it first?
EDWARD   No quarrel but a slight contention.
YORK   About what?
RICHARD   About that which concerns your grace and us,
    The crown of England, father—which is yours.
10 YORK   Mine, boy? Not till King Henry be dead.
RICHARD   Your right depends not on his life or death.
EDWARD   Now you are heir; therefore enjoy it now.
    By giving the house of Lancaster leave to breathe,°   *permission to rest*
    It will outrun you, father, in the end.
15 YORK   I took an oath that he should quietly reign.
EDWARD   But for a kingdom any oath may be broken.
    I would break a thousand oaths to reign one year.
RICHARD   No, God forbid your grace should be forsworn.°   *perjured*
YORK   I shall be if I claim by open war.
20 RICHARD   I'll prove the contrary, if you'll hear me speak.
YORK   Thou canst not, son, it is impossible.
RICHARD   An oath is of no moment,° being not took   *consequence*
    Before a true and lawful magistrate
    That hath authority over him that swears.
25 Henry had none, but did usurp the place.
    Then, seeing 'twas he that made you to depose,°   *swear an oath*
    Your oath, my lord, is vain and frivolous.
    Therefore to arms! And, father, do but think
    How sweet a thing it is to wear a crown,
30 Within whose circuit° is Elysium[1]   *circumference*
    And all that poets feign° of bliss and joy.   *imagine*
    Why do we linger thus? I cannot rest

1.2 Location: York's castle, Sandal (in Yorkshire).
1. In classical mythology, the paradise where blessed souls dwelled.

Until the white rose that I wear be dyed
Even in the lukewarm blood of Henry's heart.

35 YORK Richard, enough. I will be king or die.
[*to* MONTAGUE] Brother, thou shalt to London presently°   *at once*
And whet° on Warwick to this enterprise.   *urge*
Thou, Richard, shalt to the Duke of Norfolk
And tell him privily° of our intent.   *secretly*
40 You, Edward, shall unto my lord Cobham,
With whom the Kentishmen will willingly rise;°   *rebel; take arms*
In them I trust, for they are soldiers
Witty, courteous, liberal, full of spirit.
While you are thus employed, what resteth more°   *what else remains*
45 But that I seek occasion how to rise,
And yet the King not privy to my drift,°   *aware of my intent*
Nor any of the house of Lancaster?
            Enter GABRIEL[*, a messenger*].²
But stay, what news? Why com'st thou in such post?°   *haste*
GABRIEL The Queen, with all the northern earls and lords,
50 Intend here to besiege you in your castle.
She is hard by with twenty thousand men,
And therefore fortify your hold,° my lord.   [*Exit.*]   *castle*
YORK Ay, with my sword. What, think'st thou that we fear them?
Edward and Richard, you shall stay with me.
55 My brother Montague shall post to London.
Let noble Warwick, Cobham, and the rest,
Whom we have left protectors of the King,
With powerful policy° strengthen themselves   *cunning*
And trust not simple Henry nor his oaths.
60 MONTAGUE Brother, I go. I'll win them, fear it not.
And thus most humbly I do take my leave. *Exit* MONTAGUE.
            Enter [SIR JOHN] *Mortimer and his brother*[*, Sir Hugh
            Mortimer*].
YORK Sir John and Sir Hugh Mortimer, mine uncles,
You are come to Sandal in a happy° hour.   *fortunate*
The army of the Queen mean to besiege us.
65 SIR JOHN She shall not need; we'll meet her in the field.
YORK What, with five thousand men?
RICHARD Ay, with five hundred, father, for a need.°   *if necessary*
A woman's general; what should we fear?
            A march afar off.
EDWARD I hear their drums. Let's set our men in order,
70 And issue forth and bid them battle straight.°   *at once*
YORK Five men to twenty: though the odds be great
I doubt not, uncle,³ of our victory.
Many a battle have I won in France
Whenas° the enemy hath been ten to one.   *When*
75 Why should I not now have the like success?
                                        Alarum. Exeunt.

---

2. TEXTUAL COMMENT In O, this character is described
simply as "*a Messenger.*" Some editors believe that
Gabriel may have been the name of the actor playing
the messenger. The same may be true of the keepers
called "*Sinklo*" and "*Humfrey*" at 3.1. This edition
retains Gabriel as the messenger's name. See Digital

Edition TC 2 (Folio edited text).
3. TEXTUAL COMMENT Some editors change "uncle" to
"uncles," since York has already addressed his uncles
Sir John and Sir Hugh Mortimer, but "uncle" makes
sense as well, given that York has spoken most recently
to Sir John. See Digital Edition TC 3 (Folio edited text).

1.3 (O Scene 3)

Enter [the Earl of] RUTLAND *and his* TUTOR.

RUTLAND Ah, whither shall I fly to scape° their hands?   escape
Ah, Tutor, look where bloody Clifford comes.

Enter CLIFFORD *[and Soldiers].*[1]

CLIFFORD Chaplain, away, thy priesthood saves thy life.
As for the brat of this accursèd duke,
5 Whose father slew my father, he shall die.

TUTOR And I, my lord, will bear him company.

CLIFFORD Soldiers, away with him.

TUTOR Ah, Clifford, murder not this innocent child,
Lest thou be hated both of° God and man.   by

*Exit [*TUTOR, *guarded by Soldiers].*

10 CLIFFORD How now? Is he dead already? Or is it fear
That makes him close his eyes? I'll open them.[2]

RUTLAND So looks the pent-up° lion o'er the wretch   caged
That trembles under his devouring paws;
And so he walks, insulting° o'er his prey,   scornfully triumphing
15 And so he comes to rend his limbs asunder.
Ah, gentle Clifford, kill me with thy sword
And not with such a cruel threat'ning look.
Sweet Clifford, hear me speak before I die:
I am too mean° a subject for thy wrath.   lowly
20 Be thou revenged on men and let me live.

CLIFFORD In vain thou speak'st, poor boy: my father's blood
Hath stopped the passage where thy words should enter.

RUTLAND Then let my father's blood open it again.
He is a man and, Clifford, cope° with him.   fight

25 CLIFFORD Had I thy brethren here, their lives and thine
Were not revenge sufficient for me.
No, if I digged up thy forefathers' graves
And hung their rotten coffins up in chains,
It could not slake° mine ire nor ease my heart.   lessen
30 The sight of any of the house of York
Is as a Fury[3] to torment my soul,
And till I root out their accursèd line
And leave not one alive, I live in hell.
Therefore—

35 RUTLAND Oh, let me pray before I take my death.
To thee I pray: sweet Clifford, pity me.

CLIFFORD Such pity as my rapier's point affords.

RUTLAND I never did thee harm; why wilt thou slay me?

CLIFFORD Thy father hath.

RUTLAND   But 'twas ere I was born.
40 Thou hast one son, for his sake pity me,
Lest in revenge thereof, sith° God is just,   since
He be as miserably slain as I.

1.3 Location: A battlefield between Sandal and Wake-field.
1. Although no F or O stage direction indicates whether any soldiers are present during this scene, Clifford's command at line 7 makes it clear that some, at least, escort the Tutor offstage. Some may remain to exit at the end of the scene with Rutland's body.
2. TEXTUAL COMMENT F has three lines here (ending

"alreadie?," "eyes?," and "them"), which may have been a printer's error. This edition produces the blank verse in which Shakespeare's early plays are usually composed—unrhymed lines of ten syllables each—by combining the three lines into two. See Digital Edition TC 4 (Folio edited text).
3. A goddess of vengeance.

Ah, let me live in prison all my days,
And when I give occasion of offense
45   Then let me die, for now thou hast no cause.
CLIFFORD   No cause?
Thy father slew my father; therefore die.
        [*He stabs him.*]
RUTLAND   *Di faciant laudis summa sit ista tuae.*[4]
        [*He dies.*]
CLIFFORD   Plantagenet, I come, Plantagenet!
50   And this, thy son's blood cleaving to my blade,
Shall rust upon my weapon till thy blood,
Congealed with this, do make me wipe off both!
                              Exit [*with Rutland's body*].

1.4 (O Scene 4)
Alarum. Enter Richard, Duke of YORK.

YORK The army of the Queen hath got° the field,	*won*
My uncles[1] both are slain in rescuing me,	
And all my followers to the eager foe	
Turn back° and fly like ships before the wind	*Turn their backs*
5 Or lambs pursued by hunger-starvèd wolves.	
My sons—God knows what hath bechancèd° them;	*happened to*
But this I know, they have demeaned° themselves	*conducted*
Like men born to renown by life or death.	
Three times did Richard make a lane to me	
10 And thrice cried, "Courage, father, fight it out!"	
And full as oft came Edward to my side	
With purple falchion° painted to the hilt	*curved sword*
In blood of those that had encountered him;	
And when the hardiest warriors did retire,	
15 Richard cried, "Charge, and give no foot of ground!"	
And cried, "A crown, or else a glorious tomb,	
A scepter, or an earthly sepulcher!"	
With this we charged again, but—out, alas!—	
We budged° again, as I have seen a swan	*gave way*
20 With bootless° labor swim against the tide	*fruitless*
And spend her strength with overmatching° waves.	*against too powerful*
A short alarum within.°	*offstage*
Ah, hark, the fatal followers do pursue,	
And I am faint and cannot fly their fury;	
And were I strong, I would not shun their fury.	
25 The sands° are numbered that makes up my life.	*(of the hourglass)*
Here must I stay, and here my life must end.	

Enter the Queen [MARGARET], CLIFFORD,
NORTHUMBERLAND, *the young* PRINCE [EDWARD],
and Soldiers.

Come, bloody Clifford, rough Northumberland,	
I dare your quenchless fury to more rage;	
I am your butt,° and I abide your shot.	*target (in archery)*
30 NORTHUMBERLAND Yield to our mercy, proud Plantagenet!	
CLIFFORD Ay, to such mercy as his ruthless arm	

---

4. "The gods grant that this may be the height of your   **1.4 Location:** Scene continues.
glory" (Ovid, *Heroides* 2.66).   1. Sir John and Sir Hugh Mortimer.

With downright payment[2] showed unto my father.
Now Phaëthon hath tumbled from his car[3]
And made an evening at the noontide prick.[4]
35 YORK   My ashes, as the phoenix,[5] may bring forth
A bird° that will revenge upon you all,   child
And in that hope I throw mine eyes to heaven
Scorning whate'er you can afflict me with.
Why come you not? What, multitudes, and fear?
40 CLIFFORD   So cowards fight when they can fly no further;
So doves do peck the falcon's piercing talons;
So desperate thieves, all hopeless of their lives,
Breathe out invectives° 'gainst the officers.   words of violence
YORK   O Clifford, but bethink thee once again
45 And in thy thought o'errun° my former time   review
And, if thou canst for blushing, view this face
And bite thy tongue that slanders him with cowardice
Whose frown hath made thee faint and fly ere this.
CLIFFORD   I will not bandy with thee word for word,
50 But buckler° with thee blows twice two for one.   join in close combat
      [He draws his sword.]
MARGARET   Hold, valiant Clifford, for a thousand causes
I would prolong a while the traitor's life.
Wrath makes him deaf. Speak thou, Northumberland.
NORTHUMBERLAND   Hold, Clifford, do not honor him so much
55 To prick thy finger, though to wound his heart.
What valor were it when a cur doth grin°   show its teeth
For one to thrust his hand between his teeth
When he might spurn° him with his foot away?   kick
It is war's prize to take all vantages,°   opportunities
60 And ten to one is no impeach of valor.[6]
      [They fight and take YORK.]
CLIFFORD   Ay, ay, so strives the woodcock with the gin.[7]
NORTHUMBERLAND   So doth the coney° struggle in the net.   rabbit
YORK   So triumph thieves upon their conquered booty;
So true° men yield, with robbers so o'ermatched.   honest
65 NORTHUMBERLAND   What would your grace have done unto
      him now?
MARGARET   Brave warriors, Clifford and Northumberland,
Come, make him stand upon this molehill here
That raught° at mountains with outstretched arms,   reached
Yet parted but° the shadow with his hand.   only
70 What, was it you that would be England's King?
Was't you that reveled in our Parliament
And made a preachment° of your high descent?   sermon
Where are your mess of° sons to back you now—   group of four
The wanton Edward and the lusty George?

75   And where's that valiant crookback° prodigy,°   *hunchback / marvel; monster*
      Dickie, your boy, that with his grumbling voice
      Was wont to cheer his dad in mutinies?
      Or with the rest, where is your darling Rutland?
      Look, York, I stained this napkin° with the blood   *handkerchief*
80   That valiant Clifford with his rapier's point
      Made issue from the bosom of the boy;
      And if thine eyes can water for his death
      I give thee this to dry thy cheeks withal.°   *with*
      Alas, poor York, but that I hate thee deadly
85   I should lament thy miserable state.
      I prithee grieve to make me merry, York.
      What, hath thy fiery heart so parched thine entrails°   *inner organs*
      That not a tear can fall for Rutland's death?
      Why art thou patient, man? Thou shouldst be mad,
90   And I to make thee mad do mock thee thus.
      Stamp, rave, and fret, that I may sing and dance.
      Thou wouldst be fee'd,° I see, to make me sport.   *paid*
      York cannot speak unless he wear a crown—
      A crown for York! And, lords, bow low to him.
95   Hold you his hands whilst I do set it on.
            [*She puts a paper crown on his head.*]
      Ay, marry, sir, now looks he like a king.
      Ay, this is he that took King Henry's chair,
      And this is he was his adopted heir.
      But how is it that great Plantagenet
100   Is crowned so soon and broke his solemn oath?
      As I bethink me, you should not be king
      Till our King Henry had shook hands with death.
      And will you pale° your head in Henry's glory   *enclose*
      And rob his temples of the diadem
105   Now in his life, against your holy oath?
      Oh, 'tis a fault too too unpardonable.
      Off with the crown, and with the crown his head,
      And whilst we breathe° take time to do him dead!°   *rest / kill him*
      CLIFFORD   That is my office, for my father's sake.
110   MARGARET   Nay, stay, let's hear the orisons° he makes.   *prayers*
      YORK   She-wolf of France, but worse than wolves of France,
      Whose tongue more poisons than the adder's tooth!
      How ill-beseeming° is it in thy sex   *unbecoming*
      To triumph like an Amazonian trull[8]
115   Upon their woes whom Fortune captivates.°   *subdues*
      But that° thy face is vizard-like,[9] unchanging,   *Were it not that*
      Made impudent with use of evil deeds,
      I would assay,° proud Queen, to make thee blush.   *attempt*
      To tell thee whence thou cam'st, of whom derived,
120   Were shame enough to shame thee, wert thou not shameless.
      Thy father bears the type° of King of Naples,   *title*
      Of both the Sicils,[1] and Jerusalem,

---

8. In the manner of an Amazonian whore. Amazons were a tribe of mythical warrior women who governed themselves and lived separate from men. Sometimes they were accused of sexual impropriety because to beget offspring they would mate with men they had conquered but did not marry.

9. Masklike; fixed in expression like the frontpiece of a helmet. Perhaps alluding to the practice of prostitutes, who wore masks.
1. Naples and Sicily (known as the Kingdom of the Two Sicilies).

Yet not so wealthy as an English yeoman.[2]
Hath that poor monarch taught thee to insult?
125 It needs not, nor it boots° thee not, proud Queen,   *profits*
Unless the adage° must be verified   *proverb*
That beggars mounted run their horse to death.
'Tis beauty that doth oft make women proud,
But God he knows thy share thereof is small.
130 'Tis virtue that doth make them most admired;
The contrary doth make thee wondered at.
'Tis government° that makes them seem divine;   *self-control*
The want thereof makes thee abominable.
Thou art as opposite to every good
135 As the Antipodes[3] are unto us,
Or as the South to the Septentrion.[4]
O tiger's heart wrapped in a woman's hide,
How couldst thou drain the lifeblood of the child
To bid the father wipe his eyes withal
140 And yet be seen to bear a woman's face?
Women are soft, mild, pitiful,° and flexible;   *full of pity*
Thou stern, obdurate, flinty, rough, remorseless.
Bidd'st thou me rage? Why, now thou hast thy wish.
Wouldst have me weep? Why, now thou hast thy will.
145 For raging wind blows up incessant showers,
And when the rage allays° the rain begins: *abates*
These tears are my sweet Rutland's obsequies,
And every drop cries vengeance for his death
'Gainst thee, fell° Clifford, and thee, false Frenchwoman!   *cruel*
150 NORTHUMBERLAND   Beshrew° me, but his passions moves me so   *Curse*
That hardly can I check my eyes from tears.
YORK   That face of his the hungry cannibals
Would not have touched, would not have stained with blood,
But you are more inhuman, more inexorable,
155 Oh, ten times more than tigers of Hyrcania.[5]
See, ruthless Queen, a hapless° father's tears.   *an unlucky*
This cloth thou dipped'st in blood of my sweet boy,
And I with tears do wash the blood away.
Keep thou the napkin and go boast of this,
160 And if thou tell'st the heavy° story right,   *sorrowful*
Upon my soul the hearers will shed tears.
Yea, even my foes will shed fast-falling tears
And say, "Alas, it was a piteous deed!"
There, take the crown, and with the crown my curse,
165 And in thy need such comfort come to thee
As now I reap at thy too cruel hand.
Hard-hearted Clifford, take me from the world;
My soul to heaven, my blood upon your heads!
NORTHUMBERLAND   Had he been slaughterman to all my kin
170 I should not for my life but weep with him
To see how inly° sorrow gripes° his soul.   *inward / seizes*
MARGARET   What, weeping-ripe,° my lord Northumberland?   *ready to weep*

---

2. Landowner below the rank of gentleman.   make up the Great Bear constellation.
3. People living on the opposite side of the world.   5. Region in ancient Persia known for the cruelty of
4. North. The word refers to the seven stars that   its tigers (see Virgil, *Aeneid* 4.366–67).

Think but upon the wrong he did us all
And that will quickly dry thy melting tears.
175 CLIFFORD [*stabbing* YORK]   Here's for my oath; here's for my
father's death!
MARGARET [*stabbing* YORK]   And here's to right our gentle-hearted
King!
YORK   Open thy gate of mercy, gracious God,
My soul flies through these wounds to seek out thee.
[*He dies.*]
MARGARET   Off with his head and set it on York gates,
180 So York may overlook the town of York.
Flourish. Exeunt [with Soldiers bearing out
York's body].

2.1 (O Scene 5)
A march. Enter EDWARD, RICHARD, *and their power.*
EDWARD   I wonder how our princely father scaped,
Or whether he be scaped away or no
From Clifford's and Northumberland's pursuit.
Had he been ta'en, we should have heard the news;
5 Had he been slain, we should have heard the news;
Or had he scaped, methinks we should have heard
The happy tidings of his good escape.
How fares my brother? Why is he so sad?
RICHARD   I cannot joy until I be resolved
10 Where our right valiant father is become.°   *has betaken himself*
I saw him in the battle range about
And watched him how he singled Clifford forth.
Methought he bore him in the thickest troop
As doth a lion in a herd of neat,°   *cattle*
15 Or as a bear encompassed round with dogs,
Who having pinched° a few and made them cry,   *bitten*
The rest stand all aloof and bark at him.
So fared our father with his enemies,
So fled his enemies my warlike father.
20 Methinks 'tis prize enough to be his son.
[*Three suns appear in the air.*]¹
See how the morning opes her golden gates
And takes her farewell of the glorious sun.
How well resembles it the prime of youth,
Trimmed° like a younker° prancing to his love!   *Dressed up / young man*
25 EDWARD   Dazzle mine eyes, or do I see three suns?
RICHARD   Three glorious suns, each one a perfect sun,
Not separated with the racking° clouds   *drifting*
But severed in a pale clear-shining sky.
See, see! They join, embrace, and seem to kiss,
30 As if they vowed some league inviolable.
Now are they but one lamp, one light, one sun.
In this the heaven figures° some event.   *prefigures*
EDWARD   'Tis wondrous strange, the like yet never heard of.
I think it cites° us, brother, to the field,   *summons*

2.1. Location: Fields near the border, or marches,
between Wales and England.
1. This stage direction, which appears only in O, suggests that the acting company that performed the play
would have had to have some kind of artificial "suns"
they used as properties for this scene.

35	That we, the sons of brave Plantagenet,	
	Each one already blazing by our meeds,°	*merits*
	Should notwithstanding join our lights together	
	And over-shine the earth as this° the world.	*this phenomenon*
	Whate'er it bodes, henceforward will I bear	
40	Upon my target three fair-shining suns.[2]	

RICHARD   Nay, bear three daughters; by your leave I speak it,
          You love the breeder° better than the male.   *childbearer; woman*

                    Enter [a MESSENGER,] blowing.[3]

          But what art thou whose heavy looks foretell
          Some dreadful story hanging on thy tongue?

45 MESSENGER   Ah, one that was a woeful looker-on
          Whenas° the noble Duke of York was slain,   *When*
          Your princely father and my loving lord.

    EDWARD   Oh, speak no more, for I have heard too much.

    RICHARD   Say how he died, for I will hear it all.

50 MESSENGER   Environèd° he was with many foes,   *Surrounded*
          And stood against them as the hope of Troy[4]
          Against the Greeks that would have entered Troy.
          But Hercules[5] himself must yield to odds,
          And many strokes, though with a little ax,
55   Hews down and fells the hardest-timbered oak.
          By many hands your father was subdued,
          But only slaughtered by the ireful° arm   *angry*
          Of unrelenting Clifford and the Queen,
          Who crowned the gracious Duke in high despite,°   *in great contempt*
60   Laughed in his face, and when with grief he wept,
          The ruthless Queen gave him to dry his cheeks
          A napkin steepèd in the harmless blood
          Of sweet young Rutland, by rough Clifford slain.
          And after many scorns, many foul taunts,
65   They took his head and on the gates of York
          They set the same, and there it doth remain,
          The saddest spectacle that e'er I viewed.   [*Exit.*]

    EDWARD   Sweet Duke of York, our prop to lean upon,
          Now thou art gone we have no staff, no stay.°   *support*
70   O Clifford, boist'rous° Clifford, thou hast slain   *savage*
          The flower of Europe for his chivalry,
          And treacherously hast thou vanquished him,
          For hand to hand he would have vanquished thee.
          Now my soul's palace° is become a prison;   *(my body)*
75   Ah, would she° break from hence, that this my body   *(my soul)*
          Might in the ground be closèd up in rest,
          For never henceforth shall I joy again,
          Never, oh, never, shall I see more joy.

    RICHARD   I cannot weep, for all my body's moisture
80   Scarce serves to quench my furnace-burning heart,
          Nor can my tongue unload my heart's great burden,
          For selfsame wind° that I should speak withal   *breath*

---

2. As elsewhere, Shakespeare here slightly changes his sources. In Holinshed's *Chronicles*, Edward chose the sun as his badge because he had seen three suns join in one before the Battle of Mortimer's Cross, which he won. *target*: shield.
3. Blowing a horn as messengers did to announce themselves.
4. *hope of Troy*: Hector, a mighty warrior in Homer's *Iliad*, who defended the city of Troy against Greek invaders.
5. A mythic hero of enormous physical strength and courage.

Is kindling coals that fires all my breast
And burns me up with flames that tears would quench.
85 To weep is to make less the depth of grief;
Tears then for babes, blows and revenge for me!
Richard, I bear thy name, I'll venge° thy death,   revenge
Or die renownèd by attempting it.
EDWARD   His name that valiant Duke hath left with thee;
90 His dukedom and his chair⁶ with me is left.
RICHARD   Nay, if thou be that princely eagle's bird,
Show thy descent by gazing 'gainst the sun:⁷
For "chair and dukedom," "throne and kingdom" say—
Either that is thine, or else thou wert not his.
        March. Enter WARWICK, [*the*] *Marquess* [*of*]
        MONTAGUE, *and their army.*
95 WARWICK   How now, fair lords? What fare?° What news abroad?   success
RICHARD   Great lord of Warwick, if we should recount
Our baleful° news, and at each word's deliverance   deadly
Stab poniards° in our flesh till all were told,   daggers
The words would add more anguish than the wounds.
100 O valiant lord, the Duke of York is slain.
EDWARD   O Warwick, Warwick! That Plantagenet
Which held thee dearly as his soul's redemption
Is by the stern Lord Clifford done to death.
WARWICK   Ten days ago I drowned these news in tears,
105 And now, to add more measure to your woes,
I come to tell you things sith° then befall'n.   since
After the bloody fray at Wakefield fought,
Where your brave father breathed his latest° gasp,   last
Tidings, as swiftly as the posts° could run,   messengers
110 Were brought me of your loss and his depart.°   death
I, then in London, keeper of the King,
Mustered my soldiers, gathered flocks of friends,
Marched toward Saint Albans to intercept the Queen,
Bearing the King in my behalf along;
115 For by my scouts I was advertisèd°   informed
That she was coming with a full intent
To dash our late° decree in Parliament   recent
Touching King Henry's oath and your succession.
Short tale to make, we at Saint Albans met,
120 Our battles° joined, and both sides fiercely fought.   armies
But whether 'twas the coldness of the King—
Who looked full gently on his warlike Queen—
That robbed my soldiers of their heated spleen,°   fiery passion
Or whether 'twas report of her success,
125 Or more than common fear of Clifford's rigor,
Who thunders to his captives blood and death,
I cannot judge. But to conclude with truth,
Their weapons like to lightning came and went;
Our soldiers', like the night-owl's lazy flight
130 Or like a lazy thresher with a flail,⁸

6. Seat of his authority as duke.
7. Eagles, described by Elizabethans as the king of birds, were supposed to be able to gaze unblinkingly at the sun.
8. Threshers beat grain from wheat with specially designed sticks, or "flails."

Fell gently down as if they struck their friends.
I cheered them up with justice of our cause,
With promise of high pay and great rewards,
But all in vain: they had no heart to fight,
135   And we, in them, no hope to win the day.
So that we fled, the King unto the Queen;
Lord George your brother, Norfolk, and myself
In haste, posthaste, are come to join with you;
For in the Marches° here we heard you were,   *Welsh borders*
140   Making another head° to fight again.   *Raising another army*

EDWARD   Where is the Duke of Norfolk, gentle Warwick?
And when came George from Burgundy to England?

WARWICK   Some six miles off the Duke is with the soldiers;
And for your brother, he was lately sent
145   From your kind aunt, Duchess of Burgundy,[9]
With aid of soldiers to this needful war.

RICHARD   'Twas odds, belike,[1] when valiant Warwick fled.
Oft have I heard his praises in pursuit,°   *(of enemies)*
But ne'er till now his scandal of retire.[2]

150 WARWICK   Nor now my scandal, Richard, dost thou hear,
For thou shalt know this strong right hand of mine
Can pluck the diadem from faint° Henry's head   *weak*
And wring the awful° scepter from his fist,   *awe-inspiring*
Were he as famous and as bold in war
155   As he is famed for mildness, peace, and prayer.

RICHARD   I know it well, Lord Warwick; blame me not.
'Tis love I bear thy glories makes me speak.
But in this troublous time what's to be done?
Shall we go throw away our coats of steel
160   And wrap our bodies in black mourning gowns,
Numb'ring our Ave-Maries with our beads?[3]
Or shall we on the helmets of our foes
Tell our devotion[4] with revengeful arms?
If for the last, say "Ay," and to it, lords.

165 WARWICK   Why, therefore Warwick came to seek you out,
And therefore comes my brother Montague.
Attend me, lords. The proud insulting Queen,
With Clifford and the haught° Northumberland,   *haughty*
And of their feather many more proud birds,
170   Have wrought° the easy-melting King like wax.   *worked on*
He swore consent to your succession,
His oath enrollèd° in the Parliament;   *officially recorded*
And now to London all the crew are gone
To frustrate both his oath and what beside
175   May make against° the house of Lancaster.   *be unfavorable to*
Their power, I think, is thirty thousand strong.
Now, if the help of Norfolk and myself,

---

9. According to the chronicles, both George and Richard were sent for safety to the court of Philip of Burgundy; his wife, the Duchess of Burgundy, whom Warwick mentions, was a granddaughter of John of Gaunt.
1. The odds must have been much against him.
2. Defamation or condemnation of him for retreating (from his enemies).

3. Rosary beads are used in Roman Catholic devotion for keeping track of the prayers one has said, including "Ave Marias" ("Hail Marys"), prayers addressed to the Virgin Mary.
4. Proclaim the object of our devotion (York), with a pun on "telling" as meaning "counting," which is what one does when saying the rosary.

With all the friends that thou, brave Earl of March,[5]
Amongst the loving Welshmen canst procure,
180   Will but amount to five-and-twenty thousand,
Why, *via*,° to London will we march,   *onward*
And once again bestride our foaming steeds,
And once again cry "Charge!" upon our foes,
But never once again turn back and fly.
185 RICHARD   Ay, now methinks I hear great Warwick speak.
Ne'er may he live to see a sunshine day
That cries "Retire!" if Warwick bid him stay.
EDWARD   Lord Warwick, on thy shoulder will I lean;
And when thou fail'st—as God forbid the hour—
190   Must Edward fall, which peril heaven forfend!°   *forbid*
WARWICK   No longer Earl of March, but Duke of York;
The next degree° is England's royal throne.   *step*
For King of England shalt thou be proclaimed
In every borough as we pass along;
195   And he that throws not up his cap for joy
Shall for the fault make forfeit of his head.
King Edward, valiant Richard, Montague,
Stay we no longer dreaming of renown,
But sound the trumpets and about our task.
200 RICHARD   Then, Clifford, were thy heart as hard as steel,
As thou hast shown it flinty by thy deeds,
I come to pierce it or to give thee mine.
EDWARD   Then strike up drums! God and Saint George° for us!   *patron saint of England*
    Enter a MESSENGER.
WARWICK   How now, what news?
205 MESSENGER   The Duke of Norfolk sends you word by me
The Queen is coming with a puissant° host   *powerful*
And craves your company for speedy counsel.
WARWICK   Why, then, it sorts.° Brave warriors, let's away.   *is fitting*
                                    Exeunt.

2.2 (O Scene 6)

Flourish. Enter the King [HENRY], *the Queen*
[MARGARET], CLIFFORD, NORTHUMBERLAND, *and*
young PRINCE [EDWARD], *with drum*° *and trumpets.*   *drummer*
MARGARET   Welcome, my lord, to this brave town of York.
Yonder's the head of that arch-enemy
That sought to be encompassed with your crown.
Doth not the object cheer your heart, my lord?
5 HENRY   Ay, as the rocks cheer them that fear their wrack°.   *(wreck)*
To see this sight it irks my very soul.
Withhold revenge, dear God—'tis not my fault,
Nor wittingly have I infringed my vow.
CLIFFORD   My gracious liege,° this too much lenity°   *sovereign / mildness*
10   And harmful pity must be laid aside.
To whom do lions cast their gentle looks?
Not to the beast that would usurp their den.
Whose hand is that the forest bear doth lick?
Not his that spoils° her young before her face.   *takes as prey*

5. The title by which Edward and his father before   and note to 1.1.78.
him laid claim to the throne of England. See line 191   2.2. Location: Before the walls of York.

15   Who scapes the lurking serpent's mortal sting?
Not he that sets his foot upon her back.
The smallest worm will turn, being trodden on,
And doves will peck in safeguard of their brood.
Ambitious York did level° at thy crown,   *aim*

20   Thou smiling while he knit his angry brows.
He, but a duke, would have his son a king
And raise° his issue° like a loving sire;   *raise in rank / offspring*
Thou, being a king, blessed with a goodly son,
Didst yield consent to disinherit him,

25   Which argued thee a most unloving father.
Unreasonable creatures° feed their young;   *animals*
And though man's face be fearful to their eyes,
Yet in protection of their tender ones,
Who hath not seen them, even with those wings

30   Which sometime they have used with fearful flight,
Make war with him that climbed unto their nest,
Offering their own lives in their young's defense?
For shame, my liege, make them your precedent.
Were it not pity that this goodly boy

35   Should lose his birthright by his father's fault,
And long hereafter say unto his child,
"What my great-grandfather and grandsire got
My careless father fondly° gave away"?   *foolishly*
Ah, what a shame were this! Look on the boy,

40   And let his manly face, which promiseth
Successful fortune, steel thy melting heart
To hold thine own and leave thine own with him.
HENRY   Full well hath Clifford played the orator,
Inferring° arguments of mighty force.   *Offering*

45   But, Clifford, tell me, didst thou never hear
That things ill got had ever bad success?°   *outcome*
And happy always was it for that son
Whose father for his hoarding went to hell?
I'll leave my son my virtuous deeds behind,

50   And would my father had left me no more.
For all the rest is held at such a rate°   *cost*
As brings a thousandfold more care to keep
Than in possession any jot of pleasure.
Ah, cousin York, would thy best friends did know

55   How it doth grieve me that thy head is here.
MARGARET   My lord, cheer up your spirits, our foes are nigh
And this soft courage makes your followers faint.°   *lose heart*
You promised knighthood to our forward° son—   *precocious*
Unsheathe your sword and dub¹ him presently.°   *at once*

60   Edward, kneel down.
HENRY   Edward Plantagenet, arise a knight,
And learn this lesson: draw thy sword in right.
PRINCE EDWARD   My gracious father, by your kingly leave,
I'll draw it as apparent° to the crown   *heir*

65   And in that quarrel° use it to the death.   *cause*
CLIFFORD   Why, that is spoken like a toward° prince.   *bold*

---

1. Confer the rank of knight by the ceremony of striking the shoulder with a sword.

Enter a MESSENGER.

MESSENGER   Royal commanders, be in readiness,
    For with a band of thirty thousand men
    Comes Warwick, backing of° the Duke of York,[2]   *supporting*
70   And in the towns as they do march along
    Proclaims him king, and many fly to him.
    Deraign your battle,° for they are at hand.   *Deploy your troops*
CLIFFORD   I would your highness would depart the field:
    The Queen hath best success when you are absent.
75 MARGARET   Ay, good my lord, and leave us to our fortune.
HENRY   Why, that's my fortune too; therefore I'll stay.
NORTHUMBERLAND   Be it with resolution, then, to fight.
PRINCE EDWARD   My royal father, cheer these noble lords
    And hearten those that fight in your defense.
80   Unsheathe your sword, good father; cry, "Saint George!"°   *England's patron saint*
        March. Enter EDWARD, WARWICK, RICHARD, [*his
        brother*] GEORGE, NORFOLK, MONTAGUE, *and Soldiers.*
EDWARD   Now, perjured Henry, wilt thou kneel for grace
    And set thy diadem upon my head,
    Or bide° the mortal° fortune of the field?   *wait for / fatal*
MARGARET   Go rate° thy minions,° proud insulting boy.   *chide / favorites*
85   Becomes it thee to be thus bold in terms
    Before thy sovereign and thy lawful king?
EDWARD   I am his king, and he should bow his knee.
    I was adopted heir by his consent,
    Since when his oath is broke; for as I hear,
90   You that are king, though he do wear the crown,
    Have caused him by new act of Parliament
    To blot out me and put his own son in.
CLIFFORD   And reason too:
    Who should succeed the father but the son?
95 RICHARD   Are you there, butcher? Oh, I cannot speak.
CLIFFORD   Ay, crookback, here I stand to answer thee,
    Or any he, the proudest of thy sort.°   *gang*
RICHARD   'Twas you that killed young Rutland, was it not?
CLIFFORD   Ay, and old York, and yet not satisfied.
100 RICHARD   For God's sake, lords, give signal to the fight.
WARWICK   What say'st thou, Henry? Wilt thou yield the crown?
MARGARET   Why, how now, long-tongued Warwick, dare you
        speak?
    When you and I met at Saint Albans last,
    Your legs did better service than your hands.
105 WARWICK   Then 'twas my turn to fly, and now 'tis thine.
CLIFFORD   You said so much before, and yet you fled.
WARWICK   'Twas not your valor, Clifford, drove me thence.
NORTHUMBERLAND   No, nor your manhood that durst make
        you stay.
RICHARD   Northumberland, I hold thee reverently.°   *in respect*
110   Break off the parley, for scarce I can refrain
    The execution of my big-swoll'n heart[3]
    Upon that Clifford, that cruel child-killer.

---

2. Edward has now assumed the title Duke of York   3. From acting passionately. Passions were supposed
after the death of his father.   to cause the heart to swell.

CLIFFORD I slew thy father: call'st thou him a child?		
RICHARD Ay, like a dastard° and a treacherous coward,		*base coward*
115	As thou didst kill our tender brother Rutland.	

CLIFFORD I slew thy father: call'st thou him a child?

RICHARD Ay, like a dastard° and a treacherous coward,   *base coward*

115 As thou didst kill our tender brother Rutland.

But ere sunset I'll make thee curse the deed.

HENRY Have done with words, my lords, and hear me speak.

MARGARET Defy them, then, or else hold close thy lips.

HENRY I prithee, give no limits to my tongue;

120 I am a king and privileged to speak.

CLIFFORD My liege, the wound that bred this meeting here

Cannot be cured by words; therefore, be still.

RICHARD Then, executioner, unsheathe thy sword.

By him that made us all, I am resolved

125 That Clifford's manhood lies upon his tongue.°   *exists only in words*

EDWARD Say, Henry, shall I have my right or no?

A thousand men have broke their fasts today

That ne'er shall dine unless thou yield the crown.

WARWICK If thou deny,° their blood upon thy head,   *refuse*

130 For York in justice puts his armor on.

PRINCE EDWARD If that be right which Warwick says is right,

There is no wrong, but everything is right.

RICHARD[4] Whoever got° thee, there thy mother stands,   *sired*

For well I wot° thou hast thy mother's tongue.   *know*

135 MARGARET But thou art neither like thy sire nor dam,

But like a foul misshapen stigmatic,[5]

Marked by the Destinies[6] to be avoided,

As venom° toads or lizards' dreadful stings.   *poisonous*

RICHARD Iron of Naples hid with English gilt,[7]

140 Whose father bears the title of a king

As if a channel° should be called the sea,   *gutter*

Sham'st thou not, knowing whence thou art extraught,°   *descended*

To let thy tongue detect° thy baseborn heart?   *reveal*

EDWARD A wisp of straw[8] were° worth a thousand crowns   *would be*

145 To make this shameless callet° know herself.   *whore*

Helen of Greece was fairer far than thou,

Although thy husband may be Menelaus,[9]

And ne'er was Agamemnon's brother° wronged   *(Menelaus)*

By that false woman as this king by thee.

150 His father° reveled in the heart of France   *(Henry V)*

And tamed the King and made the Dauphin[1] stoop,

And had he matched° according to his state°   *(Henry VI) wed / rank*

He might have kept that glory to this day.

But when he took a beggar to his bed

155 And graced thy poor sire with his bridal day,[2]

Even then that sunshine brewed a shower for him

---

4. TEXTUAL COMMENT F assigns these lines to War-wick, O to Richard. Margaret's reply suggests that O is correct and Richard is meant to speak these lines. See Digital Edition TC 5 (Folio edited text).
5. A deformed person; a criminal marked by means of an iron brand for his or her crime.
6. The Fates, three goddesses in classical mythology thought to determine the course of a person's life.
7. You cheap product of Naples, hiding under the gold veneer of an English marriage. Since Naples is synonymous in many Elizabethan texts with prostitution and venereal disease, "iron" may also refer to the metal noses worn by wealthy people to disguise the disfigur-

ing effects of syphilis.
8. Being made to wear or hold straw was a practice by which women were marked as scolds in public shaming rituals.
9. The Trojan War was said to have begun because the Greek Helen, the most beautiful woman in the world, betrayed her husband, Menelaus, and eloped with the Trojan warrior Paris.
1. The French king's oldest son, later Charles VII of France.
2. And brought honor to your impoverished father by marrying you.

That washed his father's fortunes forth of° France   *out of*
And heaped sedition on his crown at home.
For what hath broached this tumult but thy pride?
160   Hadst thou been meek, our title° still had slept,   *claim to the throne*
And we, in pity of the gentle King,
Had slipped° our claim until another age.   *postponed*
    GEORGE   But when we saw our sunshine made thy spring
And that thy summer bred us no increase,°   *harvest*
165   We set the ax to thy usurping root,
And though the edge hath something° hit ourselves,   *to some extent*
Yet know thou, since we have begun to strike,
We'll never leave till we have hewn thee down
Or bathed thy growing with our heated bloods.
170   EDWARD   And in this resolution I defy thee,
Not willing any longer conference,
Since thou denied'st the gentle King to speak.
Sound trumpets! Let our bloody colors wave,
And either victory or else a grave!
175   MARGARET   Stay, Edward.
    EDWARD   No, wrangling woman, we'll no longer stay.
These words will cost ten thousand lives this day.   *Exeunt.*

2.3 (O Scene 7)

Alarum. Excursions.° Enter WARWICK.[1]   *Skirmishes*
    WARWICK   Forespent° with toil, as runners with a race,   *Exhausted*
I lay me down a little while to breathe;°   *rest*
For strokes received and many blows repaid
Have robbed my strong-knit° sinews of their strength   *powerful*
5   And, spite of spite,° needs must I rest awhile.   *come what may*
      Enter EDWARD, *running.*
    EDWARD   Smile, gentle heaven, or strike, ungentle° death,   *ignoble*
For this world frowns and Edward's sun[2] is clouded.
    WARWICK   How now, my lord, what hap?° What hope of good?   *fortune*
      Enter GEORGE.
    GEORGE   Our hap is loss, our hope but sad despair,
10   Our ranks are broke, and ruin follows us.
What counsel give you? Whither shall we fly?
    EDWARD   Bootless° is flight: they follow us with wings,   *Useless*
And weak we are and cannot shun pursuit.
      Enter RICHARD.
    RICHARD   Ah, Warwick, why hast thou withdrawn thyself?
15   Thy brother's[3] blood the thirsty earth hath drunk,
Broached° with the steely point of Clifford's lance,   *Set flowing*
And in the very pangs of death he cried,
Like to a dismal clangor heard from far,
"Warwick, revenge! Brother, revenge my death!"
20   So underneath the belly of their steeds
That stained their fetlocks in his smoking° blood,   *steaming*
The noble gentleman gave up the ghost.
    WARWICK   Then let the earth be drunken with our blood.

2.3 Location: The remaining scenes in act 2 take place in the fields near York.
1. While Shakespeare does not specify the locale, the events in this and the following three scenes resemble those associated with a battle waged at Towton in Yorkshire in 1461.
2. Good fortune, alluding to the sun as Edward's emblem.
3. Warwick's half brother, the Bastard of Salisbury.

I'll kill my horse because I will not fly.
25 Why stand we like soft-hearted women here,
Wailing our losses whiles the foe doth rage,
And look upon,° as if the tragedy   *on*
Were played in jest by counterfeiting actors?
Here on my knee I vow to God above
30 I'll never pause again, never stand still,
Till either death hath closed these eyes of mine
Or fortune given me measure of revenge.
 EDWARD O Warwick, I do bend my knee with thine,
And in this vow do chain my soul to thine;
35 And, ere my knee rise from the earth's cold face,
I throw my hands, mine eyes, my heart to Thee,°   *(God)*
Thou setter-up and plucker-down of kings,[4]
Beseeching Thee, if with Thy will it stands°   *agrees*
That to my foes this body must be prey,
40 Yet that Thy brazen° gates of heaven may ope   *made of brass*
And give sweet passage to my sinful soul.
Now, lords, take leave until we meet again,
Where'er it be, in heaven or in earth.
 RICHARD Brother, give me thy hand, and, gentle° Warwick,   *noble*
45 Let me embrace thee in my weary arms.
I that did never weep now melt with woe
That winter should cut off our springtime so.
 WARWICK Away, away! Once more, sweet lords, farewell.
 GEORGE Yet let us all together to our troops
50 And give them leave° to fly that will not stay,   *permission*
And call them pillars that will stand to° us,   *by*
And, if we thrive, promise them such rewards
As victors wear at the Olympian games.[5]
This may plant courage in their quailing breasts,
55 For yet is hope of life and victory.
Forslow° no longer; make we hence amain.° *Exeunt.* *Delay / speedily*

2.4 (O Scene 8)
Excursions. Enter RICHARD *and* CLIFFORD.
 RICHARD Now, Clifford, I have singled thee alone.[1]
Suppose this arm is for the Duke of York,
And this for Rutland, both bound to revenge,
Wert thou environed with a brazen wall.
5 CLIFFORD Now, Richard, I am with thee here alone.
This is the hand that stabbed thy father York,
And this the hand that slew thy brother Rutland,
And here's the heart that triumphs in their death
And cheers these hands that slew thy sire and brother
10 To execute the like upon thyself.
And so, have at thee!
   They fight. WARWICK *comes.* CLIFFORD *flies.*
 RICHARD Nay, Warwick, single out some other chase,°   *prey*
For I myself will hunt this wolf to death. *Exeunt.*

---

4. Echoing a biblical description of God in Daniel
2:21. See also 3.3.157, where Margaret calls Warwick
the "setter-up and puller-down of kings."
5. The Olympic Games in ancient Greece were festi-

vals that included athletic contests. Victors were presented with garlands of olive leaves.
2.4
1. I have isolated you from the herd (a hunting term).

2.5 (O Scene 9)
Alarum. Enter King HENRY, *alone.*

HENRY   This battle fares like to the morning's war[1]
When dying clouds contend with growing light,
What time° the shepherd, blowing of° his nails,   *When / on*
Can neither call it perfect day nor night.

5   Now sways it this way, like a mighty sea
Forced by the tide to combat with the wind.
Now sways it that way, like the selfsame sea
Forced to retire by fury of the wind.
Sometime the flood prevails, and then the wind,

10   Now one the better, then another best,
Both tugging to be victors, breast to breast,
Yet neither conqueror nor conquerèd.
So is the equal poise° of this fell° war.   *balance / deadly*
Here on this molehill[2] will I sit me down.

15   To whom God will, there be the victory.
For Margaret, my queen, and Clifford too
Have chid me from the battle, swearing both
They prosper best of all when I am thence.
Would I were dead, if God's good will were so.

20   For what is in this world but grief and woe?
O God, methinks it were a happy life
To be no better than a homely swain,°   *simple shepherd*
To sit upon a hill, as I do now,
To carve out dials quaintly,° point by point,   *sundials artfully*

25   Thereby to see the minutes how they run:
How many makes the hour full complete,
How many hours brings about° the day,   *completes*
How many days will finish up the year,
How many years a mortal man may live.

30   When this is known, then to divide the times:
So many hours must I tend my flock,
So many hours must I take my rest,
So many hours must I contemplate,
So many hours must I sport myself,

35   So many days my ewes have been with young,
So many weeks ere the poor fools will ean,°   *give birth*
So many years ere I shall shear the fleece.
So minutes, hours, days, months, and years,
Passed over to the end they° were created,   *for which they*

40   Would bring white hairs unto a quiet grave.
Ah, what a life were this! How sweet, how lovely.
Gives not the hawthorn bush a sweeter shade
To shepherds looking on their silly° sheep   *innocent*
Than doth a rich embroidered canopy

45   To kings that fear their subjects' treachery?
Oh, yes, it doth, a thousandfold it doth.
And to conclude, the shepherd's homely curds,
His cold thin drink out of his leather bottle,
His wonted° sleep under a fresh tree's shade,   *customary*

2.5
1. In O, this fifty-four-line soliloquy is reduced to thirteen lines, perhaps shortened for performance.

2. See 1.4.67, where Richard, Duke of York is made to stand on a molehill before his death.

50   All which secure and sweetly he enjoys,
     Is far beyond a prince's delicates,°   *delicacies*
     His viands° sparkling in a golden cup,   *food*
     His body couchèd in a curious° bed,   *an ornate*
     When care, mistrust, and treason waits on him.
           Alarum. Enter a SON *that hath killed his father at one*
           door, and a FATHER *that hath killed his son at another*
           door[, with their bodies].[3]
55   SON [*coming forward*]   Ill blows the wind that profits nobody.
     This man, whom hand to hand I slew in fight,
     May be possessèd with some store of crowns,°   *coins*
     And I, that haply° take them from him now,   *by chance*
     May yet ere night yield both my life and them
60   To some man else, as this dead man doth me.
     Who's this? O God, it is my father's face,
     Whom in this conflict I unwares have killed.
     O heavy times, begetting such events!
     From London by the King was I pressed forth;[4]
65   My father, being the Earl of Warwick's man,°   *servant*
     Came on the part° of York, pressed by his master;   *side*
     And I, who at his hands received my life,
     Have by my hands of life bereavèd him.
     Pardon me, God, I knew not what I did,
70   And pardon, father, for I knew not thee.
     My tears shall wipe away these bloody marks,
     And no more words, till they have flowed their fill.
     HENRY   O piteous spectacle, O bloody times!
     Whiles lions war and battle for their dens,
75   Poor harmless lambs abide their enmity.
     Weep, wretched man; I'll aid thee tear for tear,
     And let our hearts and eyes, like civil war,
     Be blind with tears and break o'ercharged° with grief.   *overburdened*
     FATHER [*coming forward*]   Thou that so stoutly hath resisted me,
80   Give me thy gold, if thou hast any gold,
     For I have bought it with an hundred blows.
     But let me see, is this our foeman's° face?   *enemy's*
     Ah, no, no, no, it is mine only son!
     Ah, boy, if any life be left in thee,
85   Throw up thine eye. See, see what showers arise,
     Blown with the windy tempest of my heart,
     Upon thy wounds, that kills mine eye and heart.
     Oh, pity, God, this miserable age!
     What stratagems,° how fell,° how butcherly,   *violent acts / cruel*
90   Erroneous,° mutinous, and unnatural,   *Criminal*
     This deadly quarrel daily doth beget!
     O boy, thy father gave thee life too soon,
     And hath bereft thee of thy life too late!°   *recently*
     HENRY   Woe above woe, grief more than common grief!

---

3. F indicates a simultaneous entrance, at two different doors, of a "*Son that hath kill'd his Father*" and a
"*Father that hath kill'd his Son.*" O designates these
figures as simply "*First soldier, with a dead man in his
arms*" and "*another soldier, with a dead man,*" and gives
them entrances at lines 13 and 24, respectively, but
without mention of two doors. In O, the relationship

between the living and the dead is revealed through
the dialogue only.
4. Forcibly enlisted. Because England had no standing army until the latter half of the seventeenth century, many soldiers in Elizabethan England were
conscripts.

95   Oh, that my death would stay° these ruthful° deeds!   *stop / pitiful*
        Oh, pity, pity, gentle heaven, pity!
        The red rose and the white are on his face,
        The fatal colors of our striving houses;
        The one his purple blood right well resembles,
100   The other his pale cheeks methinks presenteth.
        Wither one rose and let the other flourish;
        If you contend, a thousand lives must wither.
   SON   How will my mother for a father's death
        Take on with° me and ne'er be satisfied!   *Rage against*
105 FATHER   How will my wife for slaughter of my son
        Shed seas of tears and ne'er be satisfied!
   HENRY   How will the country for these woeful chances°   *events*
        Misthink° the King and not be satisfied!   *Think ill of*
   SON   Was ever son so rued a father's death?
110 FATHER   Was ever father so bemoaned his son?
   HENRY   Was ever king so grieved for subjects' woe?
        Much is your sorrow; mine, ten times so much.
   SON   I'll bear thee hence, where I may weep my fill.
                              [Exit, carrying his father.]
   FATHER   These arms of mine shall be thy winding-sheet;°   *burial shroud*
115   My heart, sweet boy, shall be thy sepulcher,
        For from my heart thine image ne'er shall go;
        My sighing breast shall be thy funeral bell,
        And so obsequious° will thy father be   *dutiful in mourning*
        E'en for the loss of thee, having no more,
120   As Priam⁵ was for all his valiant sons.
        I'll bear thee hence, and let them fight that will,
        For I have murdered where I should not kill.
                            Exit[, carrying his son].
   HENRY   Sad-hearted men, much overgone° with care,   *overcome*
        Here sits a king more woeful than you are.
        Alarums. Excursions. Enter the Queen [MARGARET],
        the PRINCE [EDWARD], *and* EXETER.
125 PRINCE EDWARD   Fly, father, fly! For all your friends are fled,
        And Warwick rages like a chafèd° bull.   *an angered*
        Away, for death doth hold us in pursuit.
   MARGARET   Mount you, my lord, towards Berwick⁶ post amain.°   *ride speedily*
        Edward and Richard, like a brace° of greyhounds   *pair*
130   Having the fearful flying hare in sight,
        With fiery eyes sparkling for very wrath
        And bloody steel grasped in their ireful hands,
        Are at our backs, and therefore hence amain.°   *at full speed*
   EXETER   Away, for vengeance comes along with them!
135   Nay, stay not to expostulate;° make speed   *argue*
        Or else come after. I'll away before.
   HENRY   Nay, take me with thee, good sweet Exeter;
        Not that I fear to stay, but love to go
        Whither the Queen intends. Forward! Away!   *Exeunt.*

---

5. King of Troy during the Trojan War. His fifty sons, of whom Hector was one, were killed defending the city.

6. Berwick-upon-Tweed, a town in Northumberland near the Scottish border.

2.6 (O Scene 10)
A loud alarum. Enter CLIFFORD, *wounded.*

CLIFFORD   Here burns my candle out; ay, here it dies,
  Which whiles it lasted gave King Henry light.
  O Lancaster, I fear thy overthrow
  More than my body's parting with my soul.
5 My love and fear° glued many friends to thee,   *Love and fear of me*
  And now I fall. Thy tough commixtures[1] melts,
  Impairing Henry, strength'ning misproud° York.   *arrogant*
  And whither fly the gnats but to the sun?[2]
  And who shines now but Henry's enemies?
10 O Phoebus, hadst thou never given consent
  That Phaëthon[3] should check° thy fiery steeds,   *manage*
  Thy burning car° never had scorched the earth.   *chariot*
  And Henry, hadst thou swayed° as kings should do,   *ruled*
  Or as thy father and his father did,
15 Giving no ground unto the house of York,
  They never then had sprung like summer flies,
  I and ten thousand in this luckless realm
  Had left no mourning widows for our death,
  And thou this day hadst kept thy chair° in peace.   *throne*
20 For what doth cherish° weeds but gentle air?   *nurture*
  And what makes robbers bold but too much lenity?
  Bootless are plaints° and cureless are my wounds;   *Useless are pleas*
  No way to fly, no strength to hold out flight.
  The foe is merciless and will not pity,
25 For at their hands I have deserved no pity.
  The air hath got into my deadly wounds,
  And much effuse° of blood doth make me faint.   *effusion*
  Come, York and Richard, Warwick and the rest,
  I stabbed your fathers' bosoms; split my breast.
    Alarum and retreat. Enter EDWARD, WARWICK,
    RICHARD *and Soldiers,* MONTAGUE, *and* GEORGE.[4]
30 EDWARD   Now breathe we, lords; good fortune bids us pause
  And smooth the frowns of war with peaceful looks.
  Some troops pursue the bloody-minded Queen
  That led calm Henry, though he were a king,
  As doth a sail filled with a fretting° gust   *blowing fitfully*
35 Command an argosy° to stem° the waves.   *a merchant ship / resist*
  But think you, lords, that Clifford fled with them?
  WARWICK   No, 'tis impossible he should escape,
  For, though before his face I speak the words,
  Your brother Richard marked him for the grave,
40 And wheresoe'er he is, he's surely dead.
    CLIFFORD *groans.*
  RICHARD   Whose soul is that which takes her heavy leave?
  A deadly groan, like life and death's departing.
  See who it is.
  EDWARD   And now the battle's ended,

2.6
1. The compound of love and fear that I commanded.
2. Alluding to the sun as Edward's emblem. See note to 2.1.40.
3. The son of Phoebus, god of the sun. See note to 1.4.33.

4. Montague does not speak during the scene. Neither he nor George is indicated in O's stage directions, in which George speaks the same lines as in F. The peculiarity of listing these noble figures last may suggest that they were added as an afterthought.

If friend or foe, let him be gently used.

45 RICHARD   Revoke that doom° of mercy, for 'tis Clifford,   *sentence*
Who not contented that he lopped the branch
In hewing Rutland, when his leaves put forth,
But set his murd'ring knife unto the root
From whence that tender spray° did sweetly spring—   *shoot*
50 I mean our princely father, Duke of York.
WARWICK   From off the gates of York fetch down the head,
Your father's head, which Clifford placèd there;
Instead whereof let this supply the room.[5]
Measure for measure[6] must be answerèd.°   *given in return*
55 EDWARD   Bring forth that fatal screech owl to our house[7]
That nothing sung but death to us and ours;
Now death shall stop his dismal threat'ning sound
And his ill-boding° tongue no more shall speak.   *doom-promising*
WARWICK   I think his understanding is bereft.°   *destroyed*
60 —Speak, Clifford, dost thou know who speaks to thee?
—Dark cloudy death o'ershades his beams of life
And he nor° sees, nor hears us what we say.   *neither*
RICHARD   Oh, would he did, and so perhaps he doth.
'Tis but his policy to counterfeit
65 Because he would avoid such bitter taunts
Which in the time of death he gave our father.
GEORGE   If so thou think'st, vex him with eager° words.   *bitter*
RICHARD   Clifford, ask mercy and obtain no grace.
EDWARD   Clifford, repent in bootless penitence.
70 WARWICK   Clifford, devise excuses for thy faults—
GEORGE   While we devise fell° tortures for thy faults.   *cruel*
RICHARD   Thou didst love York, and I am son to York.
EDWARD   Thou pitied'st Rutland; I will pity thee.
GEORGE   Where's Captain Margaret to fence° you now?   *protect*
75 WARWICK   They mock thee, Clifford—swear as thou wast wont.
RICHARD   What, not an oath? Nay, then the world goes hard
When Clifford cannot spare his friends an oath.
I know by that he's dead, and, by my soul,
If this right hand would buy two hours' life,
80 That I in all despite might rail at him,
This hand° should chop it off and with the issuing blood   *(his left hand)*
Stifle° the villain whose unstanchèd° thirst   *Choke / insatiable*
York and young Rutland could not satisfy.
WARWICK   Ay, but he's dead. Off with the traitor's head
85 And rear it in the place your father's stands.
And now to London with triumphant march,
There to be crownèd England's royal King,
From whence shall Warwick cut the sea to France
And ask the Lady Bona[8] for thy queen.
90 So shalt thou sinew° both these lands together,   *tie firmly*
And having France thy friend, thou shalt not dread
The scattered foe that hopes to rise again,

---

5. Let Clifford's head take its place.
6. Alluding to the strict rule of justice described in Mark 4:24: "With what measure ye mete, it shall be measured unto you."
7. Bring forth that creature ominous to our house.

Screech owls were traditionally thought to be harbingers of death.
8. The sister-in-law of King Louis XI of France and daughter of Louis, Duke of Savoy.

For, though they cannot greatly sting to hurt,
Yet look to have them buzz to offend thine ears.
95 First will I see the coronation,
And then to Brittany I'll cross the sea
To effect this marriage, so it please my lord.
EDWARD   Even as thou wilt, sweet Warwick, let it be,
For in thy shoulder° do I build my seat,   with your support
100 And never will I undertake the thing
Wherein thy counsel and consent is wanting.
Richard, I will create thee Duke of Gloucester,
And George, of Clarence. Warwick as ourself
Shall do and undo as him pleaseth best.
105 RICHARD   Let me be Duke of Clarence, George of Gloucester;
For Gloucester's dukedom is too ominous.⁹
WARWICK   Tut, that's a foolish observation.
Richard, be Duke of Gloucester. Now to London,
To see these honors in possession.   *Exeunt.*

3.1 (O Scene 11)

Enter SINKLO *and* HUMFREY, *with crossbows in
their hands.*

SINKLO   Under this thick-grown brake° we'll shroud ourselves,   thicket
For through this laund° anon the deer will come   clearing
And in this covert will we make our stand,
Culling the principal° of all the deer.   Selecting the best
5 HUMFREY   I'll stay above the hill, so both may shoot.
SINKLO   That cannot be; the noise of thy crossbow
Will scare the herd, and so my shoot is lost.
Here stand we both and aim we at the best,°   as well as we can
And, for° the time shall not seem tedious,   so that
10 I'll tell thee what befell me on a day
In this self° place where now we mean to stand.   same
Enter the King [HENRY] with a prayer book.
HUMFREY   Here comes a man; let's stay till he be past.
[*They stand apart.*]
HENRY   From Scotland am I stol'n, even of° pure love,   out of
To greet mine own land with my wishful° sight.   longing
15 No, Harry, Harry, 'tis no land of thine;
Thy place is filled, thy scepter wrung from thee,
Thy balm washed off wherewith thou wast anointed.
No bending knee will call thee Caesar° now,   emperor
No humble suitors press to speak for right,°   beg for justice
20 No, not a man comes for redress of° thee.   from
For how can I help them, an not myself?
SINKLO   Ay, here's a deer whose skin's a keeper's fee.¹
This is the quondam° king; let's seize upon him.   former
HENRY   Let me embrace the sour adversaries,²
25 For wise men say it is the wisest course.

---

9. Referring to the fact that three previous Dukes of
Gloucester had suffered violent deaths.
3.1 Location: A forest in northern England near the
Scottish border.
1. Traditionally, hunters presented the horns and skin
of a captured deer to the park's gamekeeper.

2. TEXTUAL COMMENT Because this line's placement
of "adversaries" suggests that the stress would fall
(against usual practice and Shakespeare's typical use
of the word) on the second syllable (-vers-), editors have
occasionally emended F's "Aduersaries" to "adversities." See Digital Edition TC 6 (Folio edited text).

HUMFREY　Why linger we? Let us lay hands upon him.
SINKLO　Forbear awhile, we'll hear a little more.
HENRY　My Queen and son are gone to France for aid,
　And, as I hear, the great commanding Warwick
30　Is thither gone to crave the French King's sister
　To wife for Edward. If this news be true,
　Poor Queen and son, your labor is but lost,
　For Warwick is a subtle orator
　And Louis a prince soon won with moving words.
35　By this account, then, Margaret may win him,
　For she's a woman to be pitied much:
　Her sighs will make a batt'ry° in his breast;　*breach*
　Her tears will pierce into a marble heart;
　The tiger will be mild whiles she doth mourn;
40　And Nero[3] will be tainted° with remorse　*touched*
　To hear and see her plaints, her brinish° tears.　*salty*
　Ay, but she's come to beg, Warwick to give:
　She on his left side, craving aid for Henry;
　He on his right, asking a wife for Edward.
45　She weeps and says her Henry is deposed;
　He smiles and says his Edward is installed—
　That she, poor wretch, for grief can speak no more,
　Whiles Warwick tells his title,[4] smooths the wrong,
　Inferreth° arguments of mighty strength,　*Presents*
50　And in conclusion wins the King from her
　With promise of his sister and what else
　To strengthen and support King Edward's place.
　O Margaret, thus 'twill be, and thou, poor soul,
　Art then forsaken, as thou went'st forlorn.
55　HUMFREY [*coming forward*]　Say, what art thou[5] talk'st of
　　kings and queens?
HENRY　More than I seem, and less than I was born to:
　A man at least, for less I should not be,
　And men may talk of kings, and why not I?
HUMFREY　Ay, but thou talk'st as if thou wert a king.
60　HENRY　Why, so I am in mind, and that's enough.
HUMFREY　But if thou be a king, where is thy crown?
HENRY　My crown is in my heart, not on my head,
　Not decked with diamonds and Indian stones;°　*pearls*
　Nor to be seen: my crown is called content,
65　A crown it is that seldom kings enjoy.
HUMFREY　Well, if you be a king crowned with content,
　Your crown content and you must be contented
　To go along with us; for, as we think,
　You are the king King Edward hath deposed,
70　And we his subjects, sworn in all allegiance,
　Will apprehend you as his enemy.
HENRY　But did you never swear and break an oath?
HUMFREY　No, never such an oath, nor will not now.
HENRY　Where did you dwell when I was King of England?
75　HUMFREY　Here in this country, where we now remain.
HENRY　I was anointed King at nine months old,

---

3. A notoriously cruel Roman emperor.
4. While Warwick asserts Edward's claim to the
throne.
5. *what art thou*: what manner of person are you who.

My father and my grandfather were kings,
And you were sworn true subjects unto me—
And tell me, then, have you not broke your oaths?
80 SINKLO No, for we were subjects but° while you were king.   only
HENRY Why, am I dead? Do I not breathe a man?
Ah, simple men, you know not what you swear.
Look, as I blow this feather from my face
And as the air blows it to me again,
85 Obeying with° my wind when I do blow   Submitting to
And yielding to another when it blows,
Commanded always by the greater gust:
Such is the lightness° of you common men.   fickleness
But do not break your oaths, for of that sin
90 My mild entreaty shall not make you guilty.
Go where you will, the King shall be commanded;
And be you kings: command and I'll obey.
SINKLO We are true subjects to the King, King Edward.
HENRY So would you be again to Henry,
95 If he were seated as King Edward is.
SINKLO We charge you in God's name and the King's
To go with us unto the officers.
HENRY In God's name, lead; your king's name be obeyed,
And what God will, that let your king perform;
100 And what he will, I humbly yield unto.   *Exeunt.*

3.2 (O Scene 12)

Enter King EDWARD, [RICHARD, *Duke of*] *Gloucester,*
[GEORGE, *Duke of*] *Clarence,* [*and*] ELIZABETH[,
Lady Grey].

EDWARD Brother of Gloucester, at Saint Albans field
This lady's husband, Sir Richard Grey, was slain,
His land then seized on by the conqueror.
Her suit is now to repossess those lands,
5 Which we in justice cannot well deny
Because in quarrel of the house of York
The worthy gentleman did lose his life.
RICHARD Your highness shall do well to grant her suit;
It were dishonor to deny it her.
10 EDWARD It were no less, but yet I'll make a pause.
RICHARD [*aside to* GEORGE] Yea, is it so?
I see the lady hath a thing° to grant   (sexual) favor
Before the King will grant her humble suit.
GEORGE [*aside to* RICHARD] He knows the game; how true he
keeps the wind!¹
15 RICHARD [*aside to* GEORGE] Silence!
EDWARD Widow, we will consider of your suit;
And come some other time to know our mind.
ELIZABETH Right gracious lord, I cannot brook° delay.   tolerate
May it please your highness to resolve me now,

3.2 Location: The royal palace, London.
1. "The game" suggests the "sport" of hunting animals
or of pursuing sex partners, as well as the objects of
both pursuits. Hounds "keep the wind" by keeping the
prey against the wind so that it does not catch the scent
of the hunter and run away. George implies that
Edward pursues Elizabeth with similar skill. The following lines are full of sexual wordplay that George and
Richard clearly intend, but Elizabeth probably does not.

20 And what your pleasure° is shall satisfy me.   *will; sexual desire*

RICHARD [*aside to* GEORGE]   Ay, widow? Then I'll warrant° you   *guarantee*
all your lands,

An if° what pleases him shall pleasure you.   *An if = If*

Fight closer or, good faith, you'll catch a blow.[2]

GEORGE [*aside to* RICHARD]   I fear° her not, unless she chance   *fear for*
to fall.[3]

25 RICHARD [*aside to* GEORGE]   God forbid that, for he'll take
vantages.°   *opportunities*

EDWARD   How many children hast thou, widow? Tell me.

GEORGE [*aside to* RICHARD]   I think he means to beg a child
of her.[4]

RICHARD [*aside to* GEORGE]   Nay, then whip me: he'll rather
give her two.

ELIZABETH   Three, my most gracious lord.

30 RICHARD [*aside to* GEORGE]   You shall have four, if you'll be
ruled by him.

EDWARD   'Twere pity they should lose their father's lands.

ELIZABETH   Be pitiful, dread lord, and grant it, then.

EDWARD   Lords, give us leave;° I'll try this widow's wit.   *leave us alone*

RICHARD [*aside to* GEORGE]   Ay, good leave have you, for you
will have leave,

35 Till youth take leave and leave you to the crutch.[5]
[RICHARD *and* GEORGE *step aside.*]

EDWARD   Now tell me, madam, do you love your children?

ELIZABETH   Ay, full as dearly as I love myself.

EDWARD   And would you not do much to do them good?

ELIZABETH   To do them good I would sustain some harm.

40 EDWARD   Then get your husband's lands to do them good.

ELIZABETH   Therefore I came unto your majesty.

EDWARD   I'll tell you how these lands are to be got.

ELIZABETH   So shall you bind me to your highness' service.

EDWARD   What service wilt thou do me if I give them?

45 ELIZABETH   What you command that rests in me to do.

EDWARD   But you will take exceptions to my boon.°   *request*

ELIZABETH   No, gracious lord, except° I cannot do it.   *unless*

EDWARD   Ay, but thou canst do what I mean to ask.

ELIZABETH   Why, then, I will do what your grace commands.

50 RICHARD [*aside to* GEORGE]   He plies her hard, and much rain
wears the marble.

GEORGE [*aside to* RICHARD]   As red as fire? Nay, then, her wax
must melt.

ELIZABETH   Why stops my lord? Shall I not hear my task?

EDWARD   An easy task; 'tis but to love a king.

ELIZABETH   That's soon performed, because I am a subject.

55 EDWARD   Why, then, thy husband's lands I freely give thee.

ELIZABETH   I take my leave with many thousand thanks.

---

2. Fight nearer to avoid his thrusts. Conflating sexual slang and the language of dueling, Richard puns on "blow" as meaning both "hit" and "sexual thrust."
3. Stumble; submit to sex.
4. To ask her to bear him a child; to petition for guardianship of one of her children. English monarchs generated income by gaining control of wealthy orphans from the Court of Wards and Liveries and arranging their marriages in ways profitable to the monarch.
5. *Ay . . . crutch:* Yes, we will leave you alone, for you will take liberties (with Elizabeth) until your youth departs and leaves you walking on crutches (too old for love). The multiple puns in these lines include "crutch" as a play on "crotch."

RICHARD [*aside to* GEORGE]   The match is made; she seals it
  with a curtsy.
EDWARD   But stay thee, 'tis the fruits of love I mean.
ELIZABETH   The fruits of love I mean, my loving liege.
60 EDWARD   Ay, but, I fear me, in another sense.
  What love think'st thou I sue so much to get?
ELIZABETH   My love till death, my humble thanks, my prayers,
  That love which virtue begs and virtue grants.
EDWARD   No, by my troth, I did not mean such love.
65 ELIZABETH   Why, then, you mean not as I thought you did.
EDWARD   But now you partly may perceive my mind.
ELIZABETH   My mind will never grant what I perceive
  Your highness aims at, if I aim aright.°   *guess correctly*
EDWARD   To tell thee plain, I aim to lie with thee.
70 ELIZABETH   To tell you plain, I had rather lie in prison.
EDWARD   Why, then, thou shalt not have thy husband's lands.
ELIZABETH   Why, then, mine honesty° shall be my dower,   *chastity*
  For by that loss I will not purchase them.
EDWARD   Therein thou wrong'st thy children mightily.
75 ELIZABETH   Herein your highness wrongs both them and me.
  But, mighty lord, this merry inclination
  Accords not with the sadness° of my suit.   *seriousness*
  Please you dismiss me either with ay or no.
EDWARD   Ay, if thou wilt say "ay" to my request;
80   No, if thou dost say "no" to my demand.
ELIZABETH   Then no, my lord; my suit is at an end.
RICHARD [*aside to* GEORGE]   The widow likes him not; she
  knits her brows.
GEORGE [*aside to* RICHARD]   He is the bluntest wooer in
  Christendom.
EDWARD [*aside*]   Her looks doth argue° her replete with modesty,   *prove*
85   Her words doth show her wit incomparable,
  All her perfections challenge° sovereignty: *lay claim to*
  One way or other she is for a king,
  And she shall be my love, or else my queen.
  —Say that King Edward take thee for his queen?
90 ELIZABETH   'Tis better said than done, my gracious lord.
  I am a subject fit to jest withal,
  But far unfit to be a sovereign.
EDWARD   Sweet widow, by my state° I swear to thee   *kingship*
  I speak no more than what my soul intends,
95   And that is to enjoy thee for my love.
ELIZABETH   And that is more than I will yield unto.
  I know I am too mean to be your queen
  And yet too good to be your concubine.
EDWARD   You cavil,° widow; I did mean my queen.   *object frivolously*
100 ELIZABETH   'Twill grieve your grace my sons should call you
  father.
EDWARD   No more than when my daughters call thee mother.
  Thou art a widow and thou hast some children,
  And, by God's mother, I being but a bachelor,
  Have other some.° Why, 'tis a happy thing   *some others*
105   To be the father unto many sons.
  Answer no more, for thou shalt be my queen.

RICHARD [*aside to* GEORGE]   The ghostly father° now hath done   *holy priest*
    his shrift.[6]

GEORGE [*aside to* RICHARD]   When he was made a shriver,[7] 'twas
    for shift.[8]

EDWARD   Brothers, you muse° what chat we two have had.   *wonder*

110   RICHARD   The widow likes it not, for she looks very sad.

EDWARD   You'd think it strange if I should marry her.

GEORGE   To who, my lord?

EDWARD   Why, Clarence, to myself.

RICHARD   That would be ten days' wonder at the least.

GEORGE   That's a day longer than a wonder lasts.[9]

115   RICHARD   By so much is the wonder in extremes.°   *exceedingly great*

EDWARD   Well, jest on, brothers; I can tell you both
    Her suit is granted for her husband's lands.

           Enter a NOBLEMAN.

NOBLEMAN   My gracious lord, Henry your foe is taken
    And brought your prisoner to your palace gate.

120   EDWARD   See that he be conveyed unto the Tower,
    And go we, brothers, to the man that took him
    To question of his apprehension.
    Widow, go you along; lords, use her honorably.

           Exeunt all but RICHARD.

RICHARD   Ay, Edward will use women honorably.

125   Would he were wasted, marrow, bones, and all,[1]
    That from his loins no hopeful branch may spring
    To cross° me from the golden time I look for.   *keep*
    And yet, between my soul's desire and me—
    The lustful Edward's title burièd°—   *eliminated*

130   Is Clarence, Henry, and his son, young Edward,
    And all the unlooked-for° issue of their bodies   *unforeseen*
    To take their rooms,° ere I can place myself.   *places*
    A cold premeditation° for my purpose!   *A discouraging prospect*
    Why, then, I do but dream on sovereignty

135   Like one that stands upon a promontory
    And spies a far-off shore where he would tread,
    Wishing his foot were equal with his eye,[2]
    And chides the sea that sunders him from thence,
    Saying he'll lade° it dry to have his way.   *empty*

140   So do I wish° the crown, being so far off,   *wish for*
    And so I chide the means that keeps me from it,
    And so, I say, I'll cut the causes off,
    Flattering me with impossibilities.
    My eye's too quick, my heart o'erweens° too much,   *presumes*

145   Unless my hand and strength could equal them.
    Well, say there is no kingdom then for Richard:
    What other pleasure can the world afford?
    I'll make my heaven in a lady's lap
    And deck my body in gay ornaments

150   And witch° sweet ladies with my words and looks.   *bewitch*

---

6. Has heard her confession and given absolution.
7. A priest who hears confessions from sinners.
8. It was for a purpose; it was in order to gain access to her undergarments ("shift").
9. Referring to the proverbial expression "nine days' wonder," something that for a short while causes a sensation.

1. Would he were destroyed by disease. Elizabethan medical theory held that syphilis attacked the bones, affected male "mettle," or semen, and caused sterility.
2. Wishing he were able to attain what his eye sees.

O miserable thought, and more unlikely
Than to accomplish° twenty golden crowns!   obtain
Why, Love forswore° me in my mother's womb   abandoned
And, for° I should not deal in her soft laws,   so that
155   She did corrupt frail Nature with some bribe
To shrink mine arm up like a withered shrub,
To make an envious° mountain on my back,   a detested
Where sits deformity to mock my body;
To shape my legs of an unequal size,
160   To disproportion me in every part
Like to a chaos° or an unlicked bear whelp[3]   formless mass
That carries no impression like the dam[4]—
And am I then a man to be beloved?
O monstrous fault, to harbor such a thought!
165   Then, since this earth affords no joy to me
But to command, to check,° to o'erbear° such   rebuke / dominate
As are of better person° than myself,   appearance
I'll make my heaven to dream upon the crown
And, whiles I live, t'account this world but hell
170   Until my misshaped trunk that bears this head
Be round impalèd° with a glorious crown.   enclosed
And yet I know not how to get the crown,
For many lives stand between me and home,°   (my goal)
And I—like one lost in a thorny wood,
175   That rents° the thorns and is rent with the thorns,   rends
Seeking a way and straying from the way,
Not knowing how to find the open air
But toiling desperately to find it out—
Torment myself to catch the English crown;
180   And from that torment I will free myself
Or hew my way out with a bloody ax.
Why, I can smile and murder whiles I smile,
And cry "Content!" to that which grieves my heart,
And wet my cheeks with artificial tears,
185   And frame my face to all occasions.
I'll drown more sailors than the mermaid[5] shall;
I'll slay more gazers than the basilisk;[6]
I'll play the orator as well as Nestor,[7]
Deceive more slyly than Ulysses[8] could,
190   And, like a Sinon,[9] take another Troy.
I can add colors to the chameleon,[1]
Change shapes with Proteus[2] for advantages,
And set the murderous machiavel[3] to school.

---

3. Alluding to the popular belief that bears were born as formless lumps and licked into shape by their mothers.
4. That does not resemble its mother.
5. A fabulous marine monster, resembling a woman, who sang sweet songs to lure sailors onto the rocks and to their death.
6. A mythical reptile, hatched from a cock's egg, whose look was supposed to be fatal.
7. The Greek king and aged counselor present at the siege of Troy, famous for his skill in speech.
8. The Greek warrior famous for his cunning, hero of Homer's *Odyssey*.
9. Like a treacherous man. According to Virgil, Sinon's lies convinced the Trojans to accept as a gift the wooden horse in which the Greek soldiers who later sacked Troy were concealed.
1. A reptile able to change the color of its skin in order to blend into its surroundings.
2. A Greek sea god who was able to assume different shapes at will.
3. Niccolò Machiavelli (1469–1527), an Italian political philosopher popularly known in England as a depraved advocate of political cunning and ruthlessness.

Can I do this, and cannot get a crown?
195 Tut, were it farther off, I'll pluck it down.   *Exit.*

3.3 (O Scene 13)

Flourish. Enter LOUIS,[1] *the French King, his sister*
BONA, *his Admiral, called Bourbon,* PRINCE EDWARD,
Queen MARGARET, *and the Earl of* OXFORD. *Louis sits,*
and riseth up again.

LOUIS   Fair Queen of England, worthy Margaret,
     Sit down with us. It ill befits thy state
     And birth that thou shouldst stand while Louis doth sit.
MARGARET   No, mighty King of France: now Margaret
5   Must strike her sail° and learn awhile to serve   *humble herself*
     Where kings command. I was, I must confess,
     Great Albion's° Queen in former golden days,   *England's*
     But now mischance hath trod my title down
     And with dishonor laid me on the ground,
10   Where I must take like seat unto my fortune[2]
     And to my humble seat conform myself.
LOUIS   Why, say, fair Queen, whence springs this deep despair?
MARGARET   From such a cause as fills mine eyes with tears
     And stops my tongue, while heart is drowned in cares.
15 LOUIS   Whate'er it be, be thou still like thyself
     And sit thee by our side.
          [*He*] *seats her by him.*
                                        Yield not thy neck
     To Fortune's yoke, but let thy dauntless mind
     Still ride in triumph over all mischance.
     Be plain, Queen Margaret, and tell thy grief;
20   It shall be eased if France° can yield relief.   *the King of France*
MARGARET   Those gracious words revive my drooping thoughts
     And give my tongue-tied sorrows leave to speak.
     Now therefore be it known to noble Louis
     That Henry, sole possessor of my love,
25   Is, of° a king, become a banished man   *instead of*
     And forced to live in Scotland a forlorn,°   *an outcast*
     While proud ambitious Edward, Duke of York,
     Usurps the regal title and the seat
     Of England's true-anointed lawful king.
30   This is the cause that I, poor Margaret,
     With this my son, Prince Edward, Henry's heir,
     Am come to crave thy just and lawful aid.
     An if thou fail us, all our hope is done.
     Scotland hath will to help, but cannot help;
35   Our people and our peers are both misled;
     Our treasure seized, our soldiers put to flight,
     And, as thou seest, ourselves in heavy plight.
LOUIS   Renownèd Queen, with patience calm the storm
     While we bethink a means to break it off.
40 MARGARET   The more we stay° the stronger grows our foe.   *delay*

3.3 Location: The King's palace, France.
1. TEXTUAL COMMENT Probably pronounced like
"loose." F and O have "*Lewis.*" This edition modernizes words in languages other than English. See Digi-

tal Edition TC 7 (Folio edited text).
2. Where I must take a position in keeping with my
fortune.

LOUIS   The more I stay the more I'll succor thee.
MARGARET   Oh, but impatience waiteth on° true sorrow.   *attends*
    Enter WARWICK.
  And see where comes the breeder of my sorrow.
LOUIS   What's he approacheth boldly to our presence?
45 MARGARET   Our Earl of Warwick, Edward's greatest friend.
LOUIS   Welcome, brave Warwick. What brings thee to France?
    He descends. She ariseth.
MARGARET   Ay, now begins a second storm to rise,
  For this is he that moves both wind and tide.
WARWICK   From worthy Edward, King of Albion,
50   My lord and sovereign and thy vowèd friend,
  I come in kindness and unfeignèd love,
  First, to do greetings to thy royal person,
  And then to crave a league of amity,°   *friendship*
  And, lastly, to confirm that amity
55   With nuptial knot, if thou vouchsafe to grant
  That virtuous Lady Bona, thy fair sister,
  To England's King in lawful marriage.
MARGARET [*aside*]   If that go forward, Henry's hope is done.
WARWICK (*speaking to* BONA)   And, gracious madam, in our
  King's behalf
60   I am commanded, with your leave and favor,
  Humbly to kiss your hand and with my tongue
  To tell the passion of my sovereign's heart,
  Where fame, late ent'ring at his heedful ears,
  Hath placed thy beauty's image and thy virtue.
65 MARGARET   King Louis and Lady Bona, hear me speak
  Before you answer Warwick. His demand
  Springs not from Edward's well-meant honest love
  But from deceit, bred by necessity;
  For how can tyrants safely govern home
70   Unless abroad they purchase° great alliance?   *obtain*
  To prove him tyrant this reason may suffice:
  That Henry liveth still. But, were he dead,
  Yet here Prince Edward stands, King Henry's son.
  Look, therefore, Louis, that by this league and marriage
75   Thou draw not on thy danger and dishonor,
  For though usurpers sway the rule° awhile,   *wield power*
  Yet heavens are just and time suppresseth wrongs.
WARWICK   Injurious° Margaret.   *Insulting*
PRINCE EDWARD   And why not "Queen"?
WARWICK   Because thy father Henry did usurp,
80   And thou no more art prince than she is queen.
OXFORD   Then Warwick disannuls° great John of Gaunt,   *cancels*
  Which did subdue the greatest part of Spain,
  And after John of Gaunt, Henry the Fourth,
  Whose wisdom was a mirror to the wisest,
85   And after that wise prince, Henry the Fifth,
  Who by his prowess conquerèd all France:
  From these our Henry lineally descends.
WARWICK   Oxford, how haps it in this smooth discourse
  You told not how Henry the Sixth hath lost
90   All that which Henry the Fifth had gotten?
  Methinks these peers of France should smile at that.

But, for the rest, you tell a pedigree
Of threescore-and-two years,[3] a silly° time   *trifling*
To make prescription for a kingdom's worth.[4]

95 OXFORD   Why, Warwick, canst thou speak against thy liege,
Whom thou obeyed'st thirty-and-six years,
And not bewray° thy treason with a blush?   *reveal*

WARWICK   Can Oxford, that did ever fence the right,°   *defend justice*
Now buckler° falsehood with a pedigree?   *shield*
100 For shame, leave Henry and call Edward king.

OXFORD   Call him my king by whose injurious doom°   *insulting judgment*
My elder brother, the Lord Aubrey Vere,[5]
Was done to death? And, more than so, my father,
Even in the downfall° of his mellowed years   *decline*
105 When nature brought him to the door of death?
No, Warwick, no: while life upholds this arm,
This arm upholds the house of Lancaster.

WARWICK   And I the house of York.

LOUIS   Queen Margaret, Prince Edward, and Oxford,
110 Vouchsafe at our request to stand aside
While I use further conference° with Warwick.   *talk further*
They stand aloof.

MARGARET   Heavens grant that Warwick's words bewitch
him not.

LOUIS   Now, Warwick, tell me, even upon thy conscience,
Is Edward your true king? For I were loath
115 To link with him that were not lawful chosen.

WARWICK   Thereon I pawn my credit and mine honor.

LOUIS   But is he gracious in the people's eye?

WARWICK   The more that[6] Henry was unfortunate.°   *unlucky*

LOUIS   Then further: all dissembling set aside,
120 Tell me for truth the measure of his love
Unto our sister Bona.

WARWICK   Such it seems
As may beseem° a monarch like himself.   *befit*
Myself have often heard him say, and swear,
That this his love was an external plant
125 Whereof the root was fixed in virtue's ground,
The leaves and fruit maintained with beauty's sun,
Exempt from envy, but not from disdain,[7]
Unless the Lady Bona quit° his pain.°   *end / (by loving him)*

LOUIS   Now, sister, let us hear your firm resolve.
130 BONA   Your grant or your denial shall be mine.
([*She*] *speaks to* WARWICK.) Yet I confess that often ere this day,
When I have heard your King's desert° recounted   *merit*
Mine ear hath tempted judgment to desire.[8]

LOUIS   Then, Warwick, thus: our sister shall be Edward's.
135 And now forthwith shall articles be drawn
Touching the jointure° that your King must make,   *marriage settlement*

---

3. Meaning the sixty-two years between 1399, when Henry IV deposed Richard II, and 1461, when Henry VI was deposed by Edward.
4. To make a claim based on custom for something as valuable as a kingdom.
5. Eldest son of the twelfth Earl of Oxford, John de Vere. Both were executed for treason by the Yorkists

in 1462.
6. The more (gracious) because.
7. Exempt from malice, but not exempt from (being hurt by) her disdain for him.
8. What I heard tempted my judgment to desire Edward.

Which with her dowry shall be counterpoised.°   *equally balanced*
—Draw near, Queen Margaret, and be a witness
That Bona shall be wife to the English King.

140 PRINCE EDWARD   To Edward, but not to the English King.

MARGARET   Deceitful Warwick, it was thy device
By this alliance to make void my suit;
Before thy coming Louis was Henry's friend.

LOUIS   And still is friend to him and Margaret.

145 But if your title to the crown be weak,
As may appear by Edward's good success,
Then 'tis but reason that I be released
From giving aid, which late° I promisèd.   *recently*
Yet shall you have all kindness at my hand

150 That your estate requires and mine can yield.

WARWICK   Henry now lives in Scotland at his ease,
Where, having nothing, nothing can he lose.
And as for you yourself, our quondam° Queen,   *former*
You have a father able to maintain you,

155 And better 'twere you troubled him than France.°   *(Louis)*

MARGARET   Peace, impudent and shameless Warwick,
Proud setter-up and puller-down of kings!
I will not hence till with my talk and tears,
Both full of truth, I make King Louis behold

160 Thy sly conveyance° and thy lord's false love,   *deceit*
For both of you are birds of selfsame feather.

      POST,° *blowing a horn within.*   *Messenger*

LOUIS   Warwick, this is some post to us or thee.

      Enter the POST.

POST (*speak[ing] to* WARWICK)   My lord ambassador, these let-
    ters are for you,
Sent from your brother, Marquess Montague.

165 (*to* LOUIS) These from our King unto your majesty.
(*to* MARGARET) And, madam, these for you, from whom I know
    not.

      They all read their letters.

OXFORD [*aside to* PRINCE EDWARD]   I like it well that our fair
    Queen and mistress
Smiles at her news, while Warwick frowns at his.

PRINCE EDWARD [*aside to* OXFORD]   Nay, mark how Louis stamps°   *(his foot)*
    as he were nettled.°   *angry*

170 I hope all's for the best.

LOUIS   Warwick, what are thy news? And yours, fair Queen?

MARGARET   Mine, such as fill my heart with unhoped joys.

WARWICK   Mine, full of sorrow and heart's discontent.

LOUIS   What? Has your King married the Lady Grey

175 And now, to soothe° your forgery° and his,   *smooth over / deceit*
Sends me a paper to persuade me patience?
Is this th'alliance that he seeks with France?
Dare he presume to scorn us in this manner?

MARGARET   I told your majesty as much before:

180 This proveth Edward's love and Warwick's honesty.

WARWICK   King Louis, I here protest, in sight of heaven
And by the hope I have of heavenly bliss,
That I am clear from this misdeed of Edward's—
No more my King, for he dishonors me,

185   But most himself, if he could see his shame.
        Did I forget that by the house of York
        My father came untimely to his death?⁹
        Did I let pass th'abuse done to my niece?¹
        Did I impale him° with the regal crown?   encircle his head
190   Did I put Henry from his native right?
        And am I guerdoned° at the last with shame?   rewarded
        Shame on himself! For my desert is honor,
        And to repair my honor lost for him
        I here renounce him and return to Henry.
195   My noble Queen, let former grudges pass
        And henceforth I am thy true servitor.°   servant
        I will revenge his wrong to Lady Bona
        And replant Henry in his former state.
MARGARET   Warwick, these words have turned my hate to love,
200   And I forgive and quite forget old faults
        And joy that thou becom'st King Henry's friend.
WARWICK   So much his friend, ay, his unfeignèd friend,
        That if King Louis vouchsafe to furnish us
        With some few bands of chosen soldiers,
205   I'll undertake to land them on our coast
        And force the tyrant from his seat by war.
        'Tis not his new-made bride shall succor him;
        And as for Clarence, as my letters tell me,
        He's very likely now to fall from° him   desert
210   For matching° more for wanton lust than honor,   marrying
        Or than for strength and safety of our country.
BONA   Dear brother, how shall Bona be revenged
        But by thy help to this distressèd Queen?
MARGARET   Renownèd Prince, how shall poor Henry live
215   Unless thou rescue him from foul despair?
BONA   My quarrel and this English Queen's are one.
WARWICK   And mine, fair Lady Bona, joins with yours.
LOUIS   And mine with hers, and thine, and Margaret's.
        Therefore, at last, I firmly am resolved
220   You shall have aid.
MARGARET   Let me give humble thanks for all at once.
LOUIS   —Then, England's messenger, return in post°   haste
        And tell false Edward, thy supposèd king,
        That Louis of France is sending over masquers²
225   To revel it with him and his new bride.
        Thou seest what's passed; go fear° thy King withal.°   frighten / with it
BONA   Tell him, in hope he'll prove a widower shortly,
        I wear the willow garland³ for his sake.
MARGARET   Tell him my mourning weeds° are laid aside   clothes
230   And I am ready to put armor on.
WARWICK   Tell him from me that he hath done me wrong,
        And therefore I'll uncrown him ere't be long.
        There's thy reward; be gone.   *Exit* POST.

---

9. Actually, Warwick's father, the Earl of Salisbury of *2 Henry VI,* was executed by the Lancastrians. Perhaps Warwick means that his father would not have died in the Yorkist cause had the Yorkists never tried to seize the throne.
1. Holinshed's *Chronicles* reports that while visiting Warwick's house, Edward attempted to sexually assault his host's daughter or niece.
2. The actors in courtly revels and entertainments that were often staged to celebrate the marriages of members of the Elizabethan aristocracy.
3. Token of a forsaken lover.

LOUIS   But Warwick,
    Thou and Oxford with five thousand men
235   Shall cross the seas and bid false Edward battle,
    And, as occasion serves, this noble Queen
    And Prince shall follow with a fresh supply.
    Yet, ere thou go, but answer me one doubt:
    What pledge have we of thy firm loyalty?
240 WARWICK   This shall assure my constant loyalty,
    That, if our Queen and this young Prince agree,
    I'll join mine eldest daughter and my joy
    To him forthwith in holy wedlock bands.[4]
    MARGARET   Yes, I agree, and thank you for your motion.°   *proposal*
245   Son Edward, she is fair and virtuous;
    Therefore delay not: give thy hand to Warwick,
    And, with thy hand, thy faith irrevocable
    That only Warwick's daughter shall be thine.
    PRINCE EDWARD   Yes, I accept her, for she well deserves it;
250   And here, to pledge my vow, I give my hand.
             He gives his hand to WARWICK.
LOUIS   Why stay we now? These soldiers shall be levied,
    And thou, Lord Bourbon, our High Admiral,
    Shall waft° them over with our royal fleet.   *convey by water*
    I long till Edward fall by war's mischance
255   For mocking marriage with a dame of France.
                    Exeunt all but WARWICK.
WARWICK   I came from Edward as ambassador,
    But I return his sworn and mortal foe.
    Matter of marriage was the charge he gave me,
    But dreadful war shall answer his demand.
260   Had he none else to make a stale° but me?   *laughingstock*
    Then none but I shall turn his jest to sorrow.
    I was the chief that raised him to the crown,
    And I'll be chief to bring him down again;
    Not that I pity Henry's misery,
265   But seek revenge on Edward's mockery.   *Exit.*

4.1 (O Scene 14)

Enter RICHARD, GEORGE, [*the Duke of*] SOMERSET,
and MONTAGUE.

RICHARD   Now tell me, brother Clarence, what think you
    Of this new marriage with the Lady Grey?
    Hath not our brother made a worthy choice?
GEORGE   Alas, you know, 'tis far from hence to France;
5   How could he stay° till Warwick made return?   *wait*
SOMERSET   My lords, forbear this talk. Here comes the King.
    Flourish. Enter King EDWARD, *Queen* ELIZABETH,
    [*the Earl of*] *Pembroke,* [*Lord*] *Stafford,* [*and Lord*]
    HASTINGS. *Four stand on one side* [*of the King*] *and*
    four on the other.
RICHARD   And his well-chosen bride.
GEORGE   I mind° to tell him plainly what I think.   *intend*

---

4. The historical Prince Edward was betrothed (but
never married) to Warwick's second daughter, Anne.
She eventually married Richard Duke of York (later
Richard III). Warwick's eldest daughter married
George of Clarence.
4.1 Location: The palace, London.

EDWARD Now, brother of Clarence, how like you our choice
10   That you stand pensive, as half malcontent?°   *partly discontented*
GEORGE As well as Louis of France or the Earl of Warwick,
      Which° are so weak of courage and in judgment   *Who*
      That they'll take no offense at our abuse.°   *insult*
EDWARD Suppose they take offense without a cause,
15   They are but Louis and Warwick; I am Edward,
      Your King and Warwick's, and must have my will.°   *way; sexual desire*
RICHARD And shall have your will, because our King.
      Yet hasty marriage seldom proveth well.
EDWARD Yea, brother Richard, are you offended too?
20 RICHARD Not I, no.
      God forbid that I should wish them severed
      Whom God hath joined together. Ay, and 'twere pity
      To sunder them that yoke° so well together.   *who are coupled*
EDWARD Setting your scorns and your mislike° aside,   *displeasure*
25   Tell me some reason why the Lady Grey
      Should not become my wife and England's Queen?
      And you too, Somerset and Montague,
      Speak freely what you think.
GEORGE Then this is mine opinion: that King Louis
30   Becomes your enemy for mocking him
      About the marriage of the Lady Bona.
RICHARD And Warwick, doing what you gave in charge,
      Is now dishonorèd by this new marriage.
EDWARD What if both Louis and Warwick be appeased
35   By such invention° as I can devise?   *scheme*
MONTAGUE Yet to have joined with France in such alliance
      Would more have strengthened this our commonwealth
      'Gainst foreign storms than any home-bred marriage.
HASTINGS Why, knows not Montague that of itself
40   England is safe, if true within itself?
MONTAGUE But the safer when 'tis backed with France.
HASTINGS 'Tis better using France than trusting France.
      Let us be backed with God and with the seas,
      Which he hath given for fence impregnable,
45   And with their helps only° defend ourselves.   *alone*
      In them, and in ourselves, our safety lies.
GEORGE For this one speech Lord Hastings well deserves
      To have the heir of the Lord Hungerford.[1]
EDWARD Ay, what of that? It was my will and grant,
50   And for this once my will shall stand for law.
RICHARD And yet methinks your grace hath not done well
      To give the heir and daughter of Lord Scales
      Unto the brother[2] of your loving bride;
      She better would have fitted me, or Clarence—
55   But in° your bride you bury° brotherhood.   *because of / forget*
GEORGE Or else you would not have bestowed the heir
      Of the Lord Bonville on your new wife's son,°   *(Sir Thomas Grey)*
      And leave your brothers to go speed elsewhere.
EDWARD Alas, poor Clarence, is it for a wife

---

1. To marry a rich heiress. George is objecting to the   given wealthy marriage partners.
Queen's upstart relatives, such as Hastings, being   2. That is, Anthony Woodville, Lord Rivers.

60   That thou art malcontent? I will provide thee.

  GEORGE In choosing for yourself you showed your judgment,
   Which, being shallow, you shall give me leave
   To play the broker° in mine own behalf.   *marriage broker*
   And to that end I shortly mind to leave you.

65 EDWARD Leave me or tarry, Edward will be King
   And not be tied unto his brother's[3] will.

  ELIZABETH My lords, before it pleased his majesty
   To raise my state to title of a queen,
   Do me but right and you must all confess

70   That I was not ignoble of descent,
   And meaner° than myself have had like fortune.[4] *people of lower rank*
   But as this title honors me and mine,
   So your dislikes, to whom I would be pleasing,
   Doth cloud my joys with danger° and with sorrow.   *apprehension*

75 EDWARD My love, forbear to fawn upon° their frowns.   *be abject before*
   What danger or what sorrow can befall thee
   So long as Edward is thy constant friend
   And their true sovereign whom they must obey?
   Nay, whom they shall obey, and love thee too,

80   Unless they seek for hatred at my hands—
   Which, if they do, yet will I keep thee safe,
   And they shall feel the vengeance of my wrath.

  RICHARD [*aside*] I hear, yet say not much, but think the more.
     Enter a POST.

  EDWARD Now, messenger, what letters or what news from
   France?

85 POST My sovereign liege, no letters and few words,
   But such as I without your special pardon
   Dare not relate.

  EDWARD Go to; we pardon thee. Therefore, in brief
   Tell me their words as near as thou canst guess° them. *approximate*

90   What answer makes King Louis unto our letters?

  POST At my depart these were his very words:
   "Go tell false Edward, the supposèd king,
   That Louis of France is sending over masquers
   To revel it with him and his new bride."

95 EDWARD Is Louis so brave? Belike° he thinks me Henry. *Perhaps*
   But what said Lady Bona to my marriage?

  POST These were her words, uttered with mild disdain:
   "Tell him, in hope he'll prove a widower shortly
   I'll wear the willow garland for his sake."

100 EDWARD I blame not her; she could say little less;
   She had the wrong. But what said Henry's queen?
   For I have heard that she was there in place.

  POST "Tell him," quoth she, "my mourning weeds are done
   And I am ready to put armor on."

105 EDWARD Belike she minds to play the Amazon.[5]
   But what said Warwick to these injuries?

  POST He, more incensed against your majesty
   Than all the rest, discharged me with these words:

---

3. TEXTUAL COMMENT F reads "brothers," leaving editors to decide whether to treat it as a singular or plural possessive. See Digital Edition TC 8 (Folio edited text).
4. In fact, the historical Lady Grey was the first commoner to become queen of England.
5. Legendary warrior woman. See note to 1.4.114.

"Tell him from me that he hath done me wrong
110 And therefore I'll uncrown him ere't be long."
EDWARD   Ha? Durst the traitor breathe out so proud words?
Well, I will arm me, being thus forewarned.
They shall have wars and pay for their presumption.
But say, is Warwick friends with Margaret?
115 POST   Ay, gracious sovereign, they are so linked in friendship
That young Prince Edward marries Warwick's daughter.
GEORGE [aside]   Belike, the elder; Clarence will have the younger.
—Now, brother King, farewell, and sit you fast,
For I will hence to Warwick's other daughter,
120 That, though I want° a kingdom, yet in marriage   lack
I may not prove inferior to yourself.
You that love me and Warwick, follow me.
                    Exit GEORGE, and SOMERSET follows.
RICHARD [aside]   Not I. My thoughts aim at a further matter:
I stay not for the love of Edward, but the crown.
125 EDWARD   Clarence and Somerset both gone to Warwick?
Yet am I armed against the worst can happen,
And haste is needful in this desperate case.
Pembroke and Stafford, you in our behalf
Go levy men and make prepare° for war.   preparation
130 They are already, or quickly will be, landed.
Myself in person will straight follow you.
                    Exeunt Pembroke and Stafford.
But, ere I go, Hastings and Montague,
Resolve my doubt. You twain of all the rest
Are near to Warwick, by blood and by alliance.
135 Tell me if you love Warwick more than me.
If it be so, then both depart to him;
I rather wish you foes than hollow° friends.   false
But if you mind to hold your true obedience,
Give me assurance with some friendly vow
140 That I may never have you in suspect.°   under suspicion
MONTAGUE   So God help Montague as he proves true.
HASTINGS   And Hastings as he favors Edward's cause.
EDWARD   Now, brother Richard, will you stand by us?
RICHARD   Ay, in despite of all that shall withstand you.
145 EDWARD   Why, so, then am I sure of victory.
Now therefore let us hence, and lose no hour
Till we meet Warwick with his foreign power.°   Exeunt.   army

4.2 (O Scene 15)

Enter WARWICK *and* OXFORD *in England, with
French Soldiers.*
WARWICK   Trust me, my lord, all hitherto° goes well;   thus far
The common people by numbers swarm to us.
                    Enter GEORGE *and* SOMERSET.
But see where Somerset and Clarence comes.
Speak suddenly, my lords: are we all friends?
5 GEORGE   Fear not that, my lord.
WARWICK   Then, gentle Clarence, welcome unto Warwick,
And welcome, Somerset. I hold it cowardice

4.2 Location: Fields near Warwick.

To rest mistrustful where a noble heart
Hath pawned° an open hand in sign of love;   *pledged*
10   Else might I think that Clarence, Edward's brother,
Were but a feignèd friend to our proceedings.
But welcome, sweet Clarence: my daughter shall be thine.
And now what rests° but in night's coverture,°   *remains / shadow*
Thy brother being carelessly encamped,
15   His soldiers lurking° in the town about   *idling*
And but attended by a simple guard,
We may surprise and take him at our pleasure?
Our scouts have found the adventure very easy:
That, as Ulysses and stout Diomed
20   With sleight° and manhood° stole to Rhesus' tents   *stealth / bravery*
And brought from thence the Thracian fatal steeds,[1]
So we, well covered with the night's black mantle,
At unawares° may beat down Edward's guard   *Suddenly*
And seize himself. I say not "slaughter him,"
25   For I intend but only to surprise° him.   *capture*
You that will follow me to this attempt,
Applaud the name of Henry with your leader.
          They all cry, "Henry!"
Why, then, let's on our way in silent sort,°   *manner*
For Warwick and his friends, God and Saint George!
                                        Exeunt.

4.3 (O Scene 15)

Enter three WATCHMEN *to guard the King's tent.*

FIRST WATCHMAN   Come on, my masters, each man take his
     stand.°   *post*
The King by this is set him down° to sleep.   *settled (in a chair)*
SECOND WATCHMAN   What, will he not to bed?
FIRST WATCHMAN   Why, no, for he hath made a solemn vow
5   Never to lie and take his natural rest
Till Warwick or himself be quite suppressed.°   *vanquished*
SECOND WATCHMAN   Tomorrow, then, belike shall be the day,
     If Warwick be so near as men report.
THIRD WATCHMAN   But say, I pray, what nobleman is that
10   That with the King here resteth in his tent?
FIRST WATCHMAN   'Tis the Lord Hastings, the King's chiefest
     friend.
THIRD WATCHMAN   Oh, is it so? But why commands the King
     That his chief followers lodge in towns about him
     While he himself keeps° in the cold field?   *lodges*
15   SECOND WATCHMAN   'Tis the more honor, because more
     dangerous.
THIRD WATCHMAN   Ay, but give me worship° and quietness;   *dignity*
     I like it better than a dangerous honor.
     If Warwick knew in what estate° he° stands   *condition / (Edward)*
     'Tis to be doubted° if he would waken him.   *feared*
20   FIRST WATCHMAN   Unless our halberds[1] did shut up° his passage.   *bar*

---

1. The Greek warriors Ulysses and Diomedes captured the horses of the Thracian prince Rhesus in a
night raid, after an oracle predicted that Troy would
not fall to the Greeks as long as the horses of Rhesus

grazed on the plains of Troy (see *The Iliad*, book 10).
fatal: fateful.
4.3 Location: King Edward's camp near Warwick.
1. Long-handled weapons with axlike blades.

SECOND WATCHMAN Ay, wherefore else guard we his royal tent
　　But to defend his person from night-foes?
　　　　　Enter WARWICK, GEORGE, OXFORD, SOMERSET, *and*
　　　　　French Soldiers, silent all.
WARWICK This is his tent, and see where stand his guard.
　　Courage, my masters: honor now or never.
25　But follow me, and Edward shall be ours.
FIRST WATCHMAN Who goes there?
SECOND WATCHMAN Stay, or thou diest!
　　　　　WARWICK *and the rest cry all, "Warwick, Warwick!"*
　　　　　and set upon the guard, who fly, crying, "Arm, arm!,"
　　　　　WARWICK *and the rest following them.*[2]

　　　　　The drum playing, and trumpet sounding, enter
　　　　　WARWICK, SOMERSET, *and the rest, bringing the King*
　　　　　[EDWARD] *out in his gown, sitting in a chair.* RICHARD
　　　　　and HASTINGS *fly over the stage.*
SOMERSET What are they that fly there?
WARWICK　　　　　　　　　　　　Richard and Hastings.
　　Let them go. Here is the Duke.
EDWARD　　　　　　　　　　The Duke?
30　Why, Warwick, when we parted thou called'st me King.
WARWICK Ay, but the case is altered.[3]
　　When you disgraced me in my embassade,°　　　　*diplomatic mission*
　　Then I degraded you from being king
　　And come now to create you Duke of York.
35　Alas, how should you govern any kingdom,
　　That know not how to use ambassadors,
　　Nor how to be contented with one wife,
　　Nor how to use your brothers brotherly,
　　Nor how to study for the people's welfare,
40　Nor how to shroud° yourself from enemies?　　　　*conceal*
EDWARD Yea, brother of Clarence, art thou here too?
　　Nay, then I see that Edward needs must down.°　　*must fall*
　　Yet, Warwick, in despite of all mischance,
　　Of thee thyself and all thy complices,
45　Edward will always bear himself as King.
　　Though Fortune's malice overthrow my state,°　　*sovereignty*
　　My mind exceeds the compass of her wheel.[4]
WARWICK Then, for his° mind, be Edward England's King,　　*in his (Edward's)*
　　　　　[*He*] *takes off his crown.*
　　But Henry now shall wear the English crown
50　And be true King indeed, thou but the shadow.
　　My lord of Somerset, at my request,
　　See that, forthwith, Duke Edward be conveyed
　　Unto my brother, Archbishop of York.
　　When I have fought with Pembroke and his fellows,
55　I'll follow you and tell what answer
　　Louis and the Lady Bona send to him.

---

2. TEXTUAL COMMENT Some editors start a new scene
here, since the stage has been cleared of all actors, but
the dramatic impact of this moment in the play depends
upon the audience being able to imagine continuous,
rapid action taking place in one location. See Digital
Edition TC 9 (Folio edited text).

3. Proverbial for "things have changed."
4. My thoughts escape the control of fortune. The
goddess Fortune was often depicted turning a wheel
on which human destinies both rose and fell, sometimes coming full circle.

Now for a while farewell, good Duke of York.
    They lead him out forcibly.
EDWARD   What fates impose, that men must needs abide;°   *endure*
   It boots not to resist both wind and tide.[5]
              Exeunt [EDWARD, SOMERSET, *and Soldiers*].
60   OXFORD   What now remains, my lords, for us to do
   But march to London with our soldiers?
WARWICK   Ay, that's the first thing that we have to do,
   To free King Henry from imprisonment
   And see him seated in the regal throne.   *Exeunt.*

4.4 (O Scene 17)
Enter [*Lord*] RIVERS *and* [*Queen* ELIZABETH].
RIVERS   Madam, what makes you in this sudden change?[1]
ELIZABETH   Why, brother Rivers, are you yet to learn
   What late misfortune is befallen King Edward?
RIVERS   What, loss of some pitched battle against Warwick?
5   ELIZABETH   No, but the loss of his own royal person.
RIVERS   Then is my sovereign slain?
ELIZABETH   Ay, almost slain, for he is taken prisoner,
   Either betrayed by falsehood of his guard
   Or by his foe surprised at unawares,
10   And, as I further have to understand,
   Is new committed to the Bishop of York,
   Fell° Warwick's brother, and by that° our foe.   *Cruel / therefore*
RIVERS   These news I must confess are full of grief.
   Yet, gracious madam, bear it as you may;
15   Warwick may lose that now hath won the day.
ELIZABETH   Till then fair hope must hinder life's decay,
   And I the rather° wean me from despair   *I am the more obliged to*
   For love of Edward's offspring in my womb.
   This is it that makes me bridle° passion   *control*
20   And bear with mildness my misfortune's cross;
   Ay, ay, for this I draw in many a tear
   And stop the rising of blood-sucking[2] sighs,
   Lest with my sighs or tears I blast° or drown   *blight*
   King Edward's fruit, true heir to th'English crown.
25   RIVERS   But, madam, where is Warwick then become?°   *gone*
ELIZABETH   I am informèd that he comes towards London
   To set the crown once more on Henry's head.
   Guess thou the rest: King Edward's friends must down.
   But to prevent the tyrant's violence—
30   For trust not him that hath once broken faith—
   I'll hence forthwith unto the sanctuary[3]
   To save at least the heir of Edward's right;
   There shall I rest secure from force and fraud.
   Come, therefore, let us fly while we may fly;
35   If Warwick take us, we are sure to die.   *Exeunt.*

---

5. Compare with 3.3.48, where Margaret says that
Warwick "moves both wind and tide." *boots*: profits.
4.4 Location: The palace, London.
1. What is the reason for this sudden change of mind?

2. It was popularly believed that each sigh consumed
a drop of blood from the heart.
3. Place that by law conferred immunity from arrest.

4.5 (O Scene 16)

Enter RICHARD, *Lord* HASTINGS, *and Sir William*
Stanley [with Soldiers].

RICHARD   Now, my lord Hastings and Sir William Stanley,
    Leave off to wonder why I drew you hither
    Into this chiefest thicket of the park.°   *hunting grounds*
    Thus stands the case: you know our King, my brother,
5   Is prisoner to the Bishop here, at whose hands
    He hath good usage and great liberty,
    And, often but attended with weak guard,
    Comes hunting this way to disport° himself.   *amuse*
    I have advertised° him by secret means   *informed*
10   That, if about this hour he make this way
    Under the color° of his usual game,°   *pretext / hunting*
    He shall here find his friends with horse and men
    To set him free from his captivity.
        Enter King EDWARD *and a* HUNTSMAN *with him.*
HUNTSMAN   This way, my lord, for this way lies the game.
15 EDWARD   Nay, this way, man, see where the huntsmen stand.
    —Now, brother of Gloucester, Lord Hastings, and the rest,
    Stand you thus close° to steal the Bishop's deer?   *concealed*
RICHARD   Brother, the time and case requireth haste.
    Your horse stands ready at the park corner.
20 EDWARD   But whither shall we then?
HASTINGS   To Lynn,[1] my lord, and shipped from thence to
    Flanders.
RICHARD   Well guessed, believe me, for that was my meaning.
EDWARD   Stanley, I will requite thy forwardness.°   *reward your zeal*
RICHARD   But wherefore stay we? 'Tis no time to talk.
25 EDWARD   Huntsman, what say'st thou? Wilt thou go along?
HUNTSMAN   Better do so than tarry and be hanged.
RICHARD   Come then away; let's ha' no more ado.
EDWARD   Bishop, farewell; shield thee from Warwick's frown,
    And pray that I may repossess the crown.   *Exeunt.*

4.6 (O Scene 19)

Flourish. Enter King HENRY *the Sixth,* GEORGE,
WARWICK, SOMERSET, *young Henry [of Richmond],*
OXFORD, MONTAGUE, *and [the]* LIEUTENANT *[of*
the Tower].

HENRY   Master Lieutenant, now that God and friends
    Have shaken Edward from the regal seat
    And turned my captive state to liberty,
    My fear to hope, my sorrows unto joys
5   At our enlargement,° what are thy due fees?[1]   *release*
LIEUTENANT   Subjects may challenge° nothing of their   *demand*
    sovereigns,
    But if an humble prayer may prevail,
    I then crave pardon of your majesty.
HENRY   For what, Lieutenant? For well using me?
10   Nay, be thou sure, I'll well requite thy kindness

4.5 Location: The Archbishop of York's park or hunting ground, Yorkshire.
1. King's Lynn, a town on the Norfolk coast.

4.6 Location: The Tower, London.
1. Wealthy prisoners paid fees for special food and
services.

For that it made my imprisonment a pleasure,
Ay, such a pleasure as encagèd birds
Conceive when, after many moody thoughts,
At last by notes of household harmony
15 They quite forget their loss of liberty.
But, Warwick, after God thou sett'st me free,
And chiefly, therefore, I thank God and thee.
He was the author, thou the instrument.
Therefore, that I may conquer Fortune's spite
20 By living low° where Fortune cannot hurt me,   humbly
And that the people of this blessèd land
May not be punished with my thwarting stars,[2]
Warwick, although my head still wear the crown,
I here resign my government to thee,
25 For thou art fortunate in all thy deeds.
WARWICK Your grace hath still° been famed for virtuous   always
And now may seem as wise as virtuous
By spying and avoiding Fortune's malice,
For few men rightly temper with the stars.[3]
30 Yet, in this one thing let me blame your grace:
For choosing me when Clarence is in place.
GEORGE No, Warwick, thou art worthy of the sway,°   rule
To whom the heavens in thy nativity[4]
Adjudged an olive branch and laurel crown[5]
35 As likely to be blest in peace and war;
And therefore I yield thee my free consent.
WARWICK And I choose Clarence only° for Protector.[6]   alone
HENRY Warwick and Clarence, give me both your hands.
Now join your hands, and with your hands your hearts,
40 That no dissension hinder government.
I make you both Protectors of this land,
While I myself will lead a private life
And in devotion spend my latter days,
To sin's rebuke and my Creator's praise.
45 WARWICK What answers Clarence to his sovereign's will?
GEORGE That he consents if Warwick yield consent,
For on thy fortune I repose myself.
WARWICK Why, then, though loath, yet must I be content.
We'll yoke together, like a double shadow
50 To Henry's body, and supply° his place—   take
I mean in bearing weight of government—
While he enjoys the honor and his ease.
And, Clarence, now then it is more than needful
Forthwith that Edward be pronounced a traitor
55 And all his lands and goods confiscate.
GEORGE What else? And that succession be determinèd.
WARWICK Ay, therein Clarence shall not want his part.[7]
HENRY But with the first of all your chief affairs

---

2. My bad luck. Stars were believed to emit influences that might either favor or thwart the actions of individuals.
3. Because not many men correctly conform to or come to terms with their fate.
4. The precise position of the stars at one's birth was held to determine the course of one's life.

5. Symbols of peace and victory, respectively.
6. The title of an individual given charge of the kingdom while the monarch is absent, incapacitated, or a youth.
7. George of Clarence would be next in line to the throne if the Lancastrian claim were dismissed and Edward pronounced a traitor. *want*: lack.

Let me entreat, for I command no more,
60   That Margaret your Queen and my son Edward
Be sent for, to return from France with speed.
For till I see them here, by doubtful fear
My joy of liberty is half eclipsed.
GEORGE   It shall be done, my sovereign, with all speed.
65   HENRY   My lord of Somerset, what youth is that
Of whom you seem to have so tender care?
SOMERSET   My liege, it is young Henry, Earl of Richmond.[8]
HENRY   Come hither, England's hope.
            [*He*] *lays his hand on his head.*
                                                If secret powers
Suggest but truth to my divining° thoughts,   *prophesying*
70   This pretty lad will prove our country's bliss.
His looks are full of peaceful majesty,
His head by nature framed to wear a crown,
His hand to wield a scepter, and himself
Likely in time to bless a regal throne.
75   Make much of him, my lords, for this is he
Must help you more than you are hurt by me.
                Enter a POST.
WARWICK   What news, my friend?
POST   That Edward is escapèd from your brother°   (*the Archbishop of York*)
And fled, as he hears since, to Burgundy.
80   WARWICK   Unsavory news! But how made he escape?
POST   He was conveyed by Richard, Duke of Gloucester,
And the Lord Hastings, who attended him
In secret ambush on the forest side
And from the bishop's huntsmen rescued him,
85   For hunting was his daily exercise.
WARWICK   My brother was too careless of his charge.
But let us hence, my sovereign, to provide
A salve for any sore that may betide.°   *occur*
                Exeunt all but SOMERSET, *Richmond, and* OXFORD.
SOMERSET   My lord, I like not of this flight of Edward's,
90   For doubtless Burgundy will yield him help,
And we shall have more wars before't be long.
As Henry's late presaging prophecy
Did glad my heart with hope of this young Richmond,
So doth my heart misgive me in these conflicts
95   What may befall him to his harm and ours.
Therefore, Lord Oxford, to prevent the worst,
Forthwith we'll send him hence to Bretagne
Till storms be past of civil enmity.
OXFORD   Ay, for if Edward repossess the crown
100   'Tis like that Richmond with the rest shall down.°   *fall*
SOMERSET   It shall be so; he shall to Bretagne.
Come, therefore, let's about it speedily.   *Exeunt.*

---

8. Somerset's nephew was the future Henry VII, the founder of the Tudor dynasty. The Wars of the Roses, represented in this play and in 2 *Henry VI*, ended upon his accession to the throne, depicted at the end of *Richard III*.

4.7 (O Scene 18)

Flourish. Enter [King] EDWARD, RICHARD, HASTINGS,
and Soldiers.

EDWARD   Now, brother Richard, Lord Hastings, and the rest,
Yet thus far Fortune maketh us amends
And says that once more I shall interchange
My wanèd° state for Henry's regal crown.   *diminished*
5 Well have we passed, and now repassed, the seas
And brought desirèd help from Burgundy.
What then remains, we being thus arrived
From Ravenspurgh[1] haven before the gates of York,
But that we enter as into our dukedom?
   [HASTINGS *knocks at the gates of York.*]
10 RICHARD   The gates made fast? Brother, I like not this,
For many men that stumble at the threshold
Are well foretold that danger lurks within.
EDWARD   Tush, man, abodements° must not now affright us.   *omens*
By fair or foul means we must enter in,
15 For hither will our friends repair to us.
HASTINGS   My liege, I'll knock once more to summon them.
   Enter on the walls the MAYOR *of York and his brethren[,
   the Aldermen].*
MAYOR   My lords, we were forewarnèd of your coming
And shut the gates for safety of ourselves,
For now we owe allegiance unto Henry.
20 EDWARD   But, master Mayor, if Henry be your King
Yet Edward, at the least, is Duke of York.
MAYOR   True, my good lord; I know you for no less.
EDWARD   Why, and I challenge nothing but my dukedom,
As being well content with that alone.
25 RICHARD [*aside*]   But when the fox hath once got in his nose,
He'll soon find means to make the body follow.
HASTINGS   Why, master Mayor, why stand you in a doubt?
Open the gates; we are King Henry's friends.
MAYOR   Ay, say you so? The gates shall then be opened.
   He descends [with his brethren].
30 RICHARD   A wise stout° captain, and soon persuaded.   *valiant*
HASTINGS   The good old man would fain° that all were well,   *wish*
So 'twere not long of him;[2] but being entered
I doubt not, I, but we shall soon persuade
Both him and all his brothers unto reason.
   Enter the MAYOR *and two Aldermen.*
35 EDWARD   So, master Mayor, these gates must not be shut
But in the night or in the time of war.
What! Fear not, man, but yield me up the keys,
   [*He*] *takes his keys.*
For Edward will defend the town and thee
And all those friends that deign° to follow me.   *are willing*
   March. Enter [Sir John] MONTGOMERY *with drum°*   *drummer*
   and Soldiers.
40 RICHARD   Brother, this is Sir John Montgomery,
Our trusty friend unless I be deceived.

4.7 Location: Outside the walls of York.   2. So long as he is not held responsible.
1. Town on the coast of Yorkshire.

EDWARD Welcome, Sir John, but why come you in arms?

MONTGOMERY To help King Edward in his time of storm
As every loyal subject ought to do.

45 EDWARD Thanks, good Montgomery. But we now forget
Our title to the crown and only claim
Our dukedom, till God please to send the rest.

MONTGOMERY Then fare you well, for I will hence again.
I came to serve a king and not a duke.

50 Drummer, strike up, and let us march away.
The drum begins to march.

EDWARD Nay, stay, Sir John, awhile, and we'll debate
By what safe means the crown may be recovered.

MONTGOMERY What talk you of debating? In few words,
If you'll not here proclaim yourself our King

55 I'll leave you to your fortune and be gone
To keep them back that come to succor you.
Why shall we fight if you pretend° no title?   claim

RICHARD Why, brother, wherefore stand you on nice points?[3]

EDWARD When we grow stronger, then we'll make our claim.

60 Till then 'tis wisdom to conceal our meaning.

HASTINGS Away with scrupulous wit;° now arms must rule.   reasoning

RICHARD And fearless minds climb soonest unto crowns.
Brother, we will proclaim you out of hand,
The bruit° thereof will bring you many friends.   news

65 EDWARD Then be it as you will, for 'tis my right,
And Henry but usurps the diadem.

MONTGOMERY Ay, now my sovereign speaketh like himself,
And now will I be Edward's champion.[4]

HASTINGS Sound trumpet; Edward shall be here proclaimed.

70 Come, fellow soldier, make thou proclamation.
Flourish. Sound.

SOLDIER [*reading*] "Edward the Fourth, by the Grace of
God, King of England and France, and Lord of Ireland, etc."

MONTGOMERY And whosoe'er gainsays° King Edward's right,   denies
By this I challenge him to single fight.
[*He*] *throws down his gauntlet.*[5]

75 ALL Long live Edward the Fourth!

EDWARD Thanks, brave Montgomery, and thanks unto you all.
If fortune serve me, I'll requite° this kindness.   repay
Now, for this night, let's harbor here in York,
And when the morning sun shall raise his car°   chariot

80 Above the border of this horizon
We'll forward towards Warwick and his mates,
For well I wot° that Henry is no soldier.   know
Ah, froward° Clarence, how evil it beseems thee   perverse
To flatter Henry and forsake thy brother!

85 Yet, as we may, we'll meet both thee and Warwick.
Come on, brave soldiers, doubt not of the day,
And that once gotten, doubt not of large pay.   *Exeunt.*

---

3. Why do you dwell on such overly precise distinctions?
4. TEXTUAL COMMENT O assigns lines 67–75, with the
exception of line 70, which does not appear there, to
Montgomery, but there is nothing wrong with the

Folio's assignment of these lines, so they are retained
here. See Digital Edition TC 10 (Folio edited text).
5. Throwing down a gauntlet, or glove, was a medieval rite of chivalry. To pick it up was to accept a challenge to duel.

4.8 (O Scene 19)

Flourish. Enter the King [HENRY], WARWICK,
MONTAGUE, GEORGE, OXFORD, *and* SOMERSET.

WARWICK What counsel, lords? Edward from Belgia,°   *the Low Countries*
 With hasty° Germans and blunt° Hollanders,   *rash / unfeeling*
 Hath passed in safety through the narrow seas
 And with his troops doth march amain° to London,   *at full speed*
5 And many giddy people flock to him.
GEORGE A little fire is quickly trodden out,
 Which, being suffered, rivers cannot quench.
WARWICK In Warwickshire I have true-hearted friends,
10 Not mutinous in peace, yet bold in war.
 Those will I muster up, and thou, son° Clarence,   *son-in-law*
 Shalt stir up in Suffolk, Norfolk, and in Kent,
 The knights and gentlemen to come with thee.
 Thou, brother Montague, in Buckingham,
15 Northampton, and in Leicestershire shalt find
 Men well inclined to hear what thou command'st.
 And thou, brave Oxford, wondrous well beloved
 In Oxfordshire, shalt muster up thy friends.
 My sovereign with the loving citizens,
20 Like to his island girt in with the ocean,
 Or modest Dian[1] circled with her nymphs,
 Shall rest in London till we come to him.
 Fair lords, take leave, and stand not to reply.
 Farewell, my sovereign.
25 HENRY Farewell, my Hector[2] and my Troy's true hope.
GEORGE In sign of truth, I kiss your highness' hand.
HENRY Well-minded Clarence, be thou fortunate.
MONTAGUE Comfort, my lord, and so I take my leave.
OXFORD And thus I seal my truth° and bid adieu.   *affirm my loyalty*
30 HENRY Sweet Oxford and my loving Montague,
 And all at once,° once more a happy farewell.   *together*
WARWICK Farewell, sweet lords; let's meet at Coventry.
        Exeunt.

4.9 (O Scene 20)

[*Enter* HENRY *and* EXETER.]

HENRY Here at the palace will I rest awhile.
 Cousin of Exeter, what thinks your lordship?
 Methinks the power that Edward hath in field
 Should not be able to encounter mine.
5 EXETER The doubt° is that he will seduce the rest.   *fear*
HENRY That's not my fear. My meed° hath got° me fame.   *merit / won*
 I have not stopped mine ears to their demands
 Nor posted off° their suits with slow delays.   *postponed*
 My pity hath been balm to heal their wounds;
10 My mildness hath allayed their swelling griefs;

4.8 Location: The Bishop of London's palace.
1. The goddess of the moon, of hunting, and of chastity, often depicted presiding over a circle of virginal
nymphs in the forest. Queen Elizabeth I was sometimes represented as Diana.
2. The greatest warrior of Troy, killed when the Greeks

conquered the city (see note to 2.1.51). By one legendary account, London was founded as a second Troy by
Brutus (or Brute), a Trojan who conquered Albion and
renamed it Britain.
4.9 Location: Scene continues.

My mercy dried their water-flowing tears.
I have not been desirous of their wealth
Nor much oppressed them with great subsidies,°   *taxes*
Nor forward of° revenge, though they much erred.   *eager for*
15 Then why should they love Edward more than me?
No, Exeter, these graces challenge grace,°   *claim favor*
And when the lion fawns upon the lamb,
The lamb will never cease to follow him.
      Shout within, "A Lancaster!° *A Lancaster!"*   *"To Lancaster"; a war cry.*
EXETER   Hark, hark, my lord. What shouts are these?
      Enter EDWARD [*with* RICHARD] *and his Soldiers.*
20 EDWARD   Seize on the shamefaced° Henry. Bear him hence,   *timid*
And once again proclaim us King of England.
You are the fount that makes small brooks to flow;
Now stops thy spring, my sea shall suck them dry
And swell so much the higher by their ebb.
25 Hence with him to the Tower. Let him not speak.
      Exeunt [*some Soldiers*] *with King* HENRY.
And lords, towards Coventry bend we our course,
Where peremptory° Warwick now remains.   *overbearing*
The sun shines hot and if we use delay,
Cold biting winter mars our hoped-for hay.°   *expected harvest*
30 RICHARD   Away betimes,° before his forces join,   *quickly*
And take the great-grown traitor unawares.
Brave warriors, march amain° towards Coventry.   *at full speed*
                       Exeunt.

5.1 (O Scene 21)

Enter WARWICK, *the Mayor of Coventry,*
two MESSENGERS, *and others upon the walls.*[1]
WARWICK   Where is the post that came from valiant Oxford?
  —How far hence is thy lord, mine honest fellow?
FIRST MESSENGER   By this° at Dunsmore,[2] marching   *By now*
   hitherward.
WARWICK   —How far off is our brother Montague?
5   Where is the post that came from Montague?
SECOND MESSENGER   By this at Daintry[3] with a puissant° troop.   *powerful*
                   [*Exeunt* MESSENGERS.]
      Enter SOMERVILLE.
WARWICK   Say, Somerville, what says my loving son?
   And by thy guess how nigh is Clarence now?
SOMERVILLE   At Southam[4] I did leave him with his forces
10   And do expect him here some two hours hence.
      [*Drum heard.*]
WARWICK   Then Clarence is at hand; I hear his drum.
SOMERVILLE   It is not his, my lord; here Southam lies.[5]
   The drum your honor hears marcheth from Warwick.

5.1 Location: Before and on the walls of Coventry.
1. This entire scene was probably played with Warwick's party in the gallery above the main stage and
King Edward and Richard of Gloucester below, looking upward in line 17 and throughout. In stage directions following lines 57, 66, and 71, first Oxford, then
the Marquess of Montague, and then the Duke of
Somerset enter. They may enter above to Warwick or,
more probably, enter below, cross the stage, and then
exit through a stage door as if "into the city" and thus
out of view. F gives each an entrance but no exit; O
marks both an entrance and an exit for each.
2. Dunsmore Heath, between Coventry and Daventry.
3. Daventry, a Northamptonshire town about 20 miles
southeast of Coventry.
4. A town about 10 miles southeast of Coventry.
5. Southam is in this direction.

WARWICK Who should that be? Belike° unlooked-for friends. *Perhaps*

15 SOMERVILLE They are at hand, and you shall quickly know.

[Exit.]

March. Flourish. Enter [King] EDWARD, RICHARD,
and Soldiers.

EDWARD Go, trumpet, to the walls and sound a parle.[6]

[Trumpet sounds.]

RICHARD See how the surly Warwick mans the wall.

WARWICK Oh, unbid° spite, is sportful° Edward come? *unwelcome / lecherous*

Where slept our scouts, or how are they seduced,

20 That we could hear no news of his repair?° *approach*

EDWARD Now, Warwick, wilt thou ope the city gates,

Speak gentle words, and humbly bend thy knee?

Call Edward king and at his hands beg mercy,

And he shall pardon thee these outrages.

25 WARWICK Nay, rather wilt thou draw thy forces hence,

Confess who set thee up and plucked thee down?

Call Warwick patron and be penitent,

And thou shalt still remain the Duke of York.

RICHARD I thought at least he would have said "the King,"

30 Or did he make the jest against his will?

WARWICK Is not a dukedom, sir, a goodly gift?

RICHARD Ay, by my faith, for a poor earl[7] to give.

I'll do thee service for so good a gift.

WARWICK 'Twas I that gave the kingdom to thy brother.

35 EDWARD Why, then, 'tis mine, if but by Warwick's gift.

WARWICK Thou art no Atlas[8] for so great a weight,

And, weakling, Warwick takes his gift again,

And Henry is my king, Warwick his subject.

EDWARD But Warwick's king is Edward's prisoner.

40 And, gallant Warwick, do but answer this:

What is the body when the head is off?

RICHARD Alas, that Warwick had no more forecast,° *anticipated*

But whiles he thought to steal the single ten,[9]

The king was slyly fingered° from the deck. *stolen*

45 You left poor Henry at the bishop's palace

And ten to one you'll meet him in the Tower.

EDWARD 'Tis even so, yet you are Warwick still.

RICHARD Come, Warwick, take the time;° kneel down, kneel *seize the moment*

down.

Nay, when? Strike now, or else the iron cools.[1]

50 WARWICK I had rather chop this hand off at a blow

And with the other fling it at thy face

Than bear so low a sail° to strike to thee. *be so humble as*

EDWARD Sail how thou canst, have wind and tide thy friend,

This hand, fast wound about thy coal-black hair,

55 Shall, whiles thy head is warm and new cut off,

Write in the dust this sentence with thy blood:

"Wind-changing° Warwick now can change no more." *Fickle*

Enter OXFORD *with drum and colors.*° *flags*

6. A trumpet signal requesting a conference between
warring troops.
7. Dukes are higher in rank than earls.
8. In Greek mythology, a giant who bore the weight
of the heavens on his shoulders.
9. Alluding to the conventions of card games in which
the ten is valuable, but less so than the king. *single:*
mere.
1. Referring to the proverb "Strike while the iron is
hot," with a pun on "strike" as meaning "to lower a sail"
or "to yield."

WARWICK   O cheerful colors! See where Oxford comes!

OXFORD   Oxford, Oxford, for Lancaster!

[OXFORD *and his Soldiers enter the city.*]

60   RICHARD   The gates are open; let us enter too.

EDWARD   So other foes may set upon our backs.

Stand we in good array, for they no doubt

Will issue out again and bid us battle.

If not, the city being but of small defense,

65   We'll quickly rouse[2] the traitors in the same.

[OXFORD *enters on the walls.*]

WARWICK   Oh, welcome, Oxford, for we want° thy help.   *need*

Enter MONTAGUE *with drum and colors.*

MONTAGUE   Montague, Montague, for Lancaster!

[MONTAGUE *and his Soldiers enter the city.*]

RICHARD   Thou and thy brother both shall buy° this treason   *atone for*

Even with the dearest blood your bodies bear.

70   EDWARD   The harder matched, the greater victory.

My mind presageth happy gain and conquest.

[*Enter* SOMERSET *with drum and colors.*]

SOMERSET   Somerset, Somerset, for Lancaster!

[SOMERSET *and his Soldiers enter the city.*]

RICHARD   Two of thy name, both Dukes of Somerset,

Have sold their lives unto the house of York,

75   And thou shalt be the third, if this sword hold.[3]

Enter GEORGE *with drum and colors.*

WARWICK   And lo, where George of Clarence sweeps along,

Of force enough to bid his brother battle,

With whom an upright zeal to right° prevails   *for justice*

More than the nature of a brother's love.

80   Come, Clarence, come; thou wilt, if Warwick call.

GEORGE   Father of Warwick, know you what this means?

[*He takes a red rose from his hat.*]

Look here, I throw my infamy at thee!

I will not ruinate my father's house,

Who gave his blood to lime° the stones together,   *cement*

85   And set up Lancaster. Why, trowest thou,° Warwick,   *do you believe*

That Clarence is so harsh, so blunt,° unnatural,   *uncivilized*

To bend the fatal instruments of war

Against his brother and his lawful King?

Perhaps thou wilt object° my holy oath;   *invoke*

90   To keep that oath were more impiety

Than Jephthah, when he sacrificed his daughter.[4]

I am so sorry for my trespass made

That, to deserve well at my brother's hands,

I here proclaim myself thy mortal foe,

95   With resolution, wheresoe'er I meet thee—

As I will meet thee, if thou stir abroad°—   *(outside Coventry)*

---

2. A hunting term meaning "to surprise creatures in their lair."
3. Richard addresses Edmund, the fourth Duke of Somerset. The defection of his older brother Henry, the third Duke, from Edward's cause is described in 4.1 and 4.2. Richard threw the head of their father, the second Duke, across the stage in the play's first scene.
4. Alluding to the biblical story in which Jephthah, an Israelite leader, kills his daughter in fulfillment of a vow. He swore that if he was victorious in battle, he would sacrifice to God whoever first met him from his house when he returned from the battlefield (see Judges 11).

To plague thee, for thy foul misleading me.
And so, proud-hearted Warwick, I defy thee
And to my brother turn my blushing cheeks.
100 Pardon me, Edward, I will make amends.
And, Richard, do not frown upon my faults,
For I will henceforth be no more unconstant.
EDWARD Now welcome, more, and ten times more, beloved
Than if thou never hadst deserved our hate.
105 RICHARD Welcome, good Clarence; this is brother-like.
WARWICK O passing° traitor, perjured and unjust.   *unsurpassed*
EDWARD What, Warwick, wilt thou leave the town and fight?
Or shall we beat the stones about thine ears?
WARWICK Alas, I am not cooped° here for defense.   *shut up*
110 I will away towards Barnet⁵ presently
And bid thee battle, Edward, if thou dar'st.
EDWARD Yes, Warwick, Edward dares, and leads the way.
Lords, to the field. Saint George and victory!
    Exeunt. March. WARWICK *and his company follows.*

5.2 (O Scene 22)
Alarum and excursions. Enter [King] EDWARD,
bringing forth WARWICK, *wounded.*
EDWARD So, lie thou there. Die thou and die our fear,
For Warwick was a bug° that feared° us all.   *goblin / frightened*
Now, Montague, sit fast:° I seek for thee   *be on guard*
That Warwick's bones may keep thine company. *Exit.*
5 WARWICK Ah, who is nigh? Come to me, friend or foe,
And tell me who is victor, York or Warwick?
Why ask I that? My mangled body shows,
My blood, my want of strength, my sick heart shows,
That I must yield my body to the earth
10 And, by my fall, the conquest to my foe.
Thus yields the cedar¹ to the ax's edge,
Whose arms gave shelter to the princely eagle²
Under whose shade the ramping lion³ slept,
Whose top branch overpeered° Jove's spreading tree⁴   *rose above*
15 And kept low shrubs from winter's powerful wind.
These eyes, that now are dimmed with death's black veil,
Have been as piercing as the midday sun
To search the secret treasons of the world.
The wrinkles in my brows, now filled with blood,
20 Were likened oft to kingly sepulchers,
For who lived king but I could dig his grave?
And who durst smile when Warwick bent his brow?
Lo, now my glory smeared in dust and blood,
My parks,° my walks, my manors that I had,   *hunting grounds*
25 Even now forsake me, and of all my lands

---

5. Shakespeare treats this town, which is about 10 miles north of London and 75 miles southeast of Coventry, as though it were near Coventry.
5.2 Location: Near Barnet.
1. Often regarded as the king of evergreens and thus a symbol of sovereignty.
2. Probably referring to Richard, Duke of York. In 2.1.91, his son Richard refers to the Duke of York as a

"princely eagle." The eagle was often described as the king of birds.
3. Under whose protection Henry VI rested. A reference both to the lion as king of the animal world and to the Lancastrian coat of arms, which showed three lions rampant, or reared on their hind legs.
4. Jove's tree, according to Virgil, was the oak, the king of deciduous trees.

Is nothing left me but my body's length.
Why, what is pomp, rule, reign but earth and dust?
And live we how we can, yet die we must.

   Enter OXFORD *and* SOMERSET.

SOMERSET Ah, Warwick, Warwick, wert thou as we are,
30   We might recover all our loss again.
The Queen from France hath brought a puissant power;°   *powerful army*
Even now we heard the news. Ah, couldst thou fly.

WARWICK Why, then, I would not fly. —Ah, Montague,
If thou be there, sweet brother, take my hand
35   And with thy lips keep in my soul awhile.[5]
Thou lov'st me not, for, brother, if thou didst,
Thy tears would wash this cold congealèd blood
That glues my lips and will not let me speak.
Come quickly, Montague, or I am dead.

40 SOMERSET Ah, Warwick, Montague hath breathed his last,
And to the latest gasp cried out for Warwick
And said, "Commend me to my valiant brother."
And more he would have said, and more he spoke,
Which sounded like a cannon in a vault
45   That might not be distinguished, but at last
I well might hear, delivered with a groan,
"Oh, farewell, Warwick."

WARWICK Sweet rest his soul. Fly, lords, and save yourselves,
For Warwick bids you all farewell, to meet in heaven.
    [*He dies.*]

50 OXFORD Away, away, to meet the Queen's great power!

    Here they bear away his body. Exeunt.

5.3 (O Scene 23)

Flourish. Enter [King] EDWARD *in triumph, with*
RICHARD, GEORGE, *and the rest.*

EDWARD Thus far our fortune keeps an upward course
And we are graced with wreaths of victory,
But in the midst of this bright-shining day
I spy a black, suspicious, threat'ning cloud
5   That will encounter with our glorious sun
Ere he attain his easeful western bed.
I mean, my lords, those powers that the Queen
Hath raised in Gallia° have arrived our coast   *France*
And, as we hear, march on to fight with us.

10 GEORGE A little gale will soon disperse that cloud
And blow it to the source from whence it came.
Thy very beams will dry those vapors up,
For every cloud engenders not a storm.

RICHARD The Queen is valued° thirty thousand strong,   *estimated to be*
15   And Somerset with Oxford fled to her:
If she have time to breathe,° be well assured   *gather her strength*
Her faction will be full as strong as ours.

EDWARD We are advertised° by our loving friends   *informed*
That they do hold their course toward Tewkesbury.[1]

---

5. Kiss me. Many Elizabethans believed the soul
escaped through the mouth at death.

5.3 Location: Scene continues.
1. A town in Gloucestershire.

20 We, having now the best at Barnet Field,
Will thither straight, for willingness rids way,[2]
And as we march our strength will be augmented
In every county as we go along.
Strike up the drum. Cry "Courage!," and away!   *Exeunt.*

5.4 (O Scene 24)
Flourish. March. Enter the Queen [MARGARET], *young*
[PRINCE] EDWARD, SOMERSET, OXFORD, *and Soldiers.*

MARGARET   Great lords, wise men ne'er sit and wail their loss,
But cheerly° seek how to redress their harms.   *cheerfully*
What though the mast be now blown overboard,
The cable broke, the holding-anchor[1] lost,
5 And half our sailors swallowed in the flood?
Yet lives our pilot° still. Is't meet that he   *(Henry)*
Should leave the helm and, like a fearful lad,
With tearful eyes add water to the sea
And give more strength to that which hath too much,
10 Whiles in his moan° the ship splits on the rock,   *state of grief*
Which industry and courage might have saved?
Ah, what a shame; ah, what a fault were this.
Say Warwick was our anchor: what of that?
And Montague our topmast: what of him?
15 Our slaughtered friends the tackles:[2] what of these?
Why, is not Oxford here another anchor?
And Somerset another goodly mast?
The friends of France our shrouds[3] and tacklings?
And, though unskillful, why not Ned° and I   *(her son Edward)*
20 For once allowed the skillful pilot's charge?°   *responsibility*
We will not from the helm to sit and weep,
But keep our course, though the rough wind say no,
From shelves° and rocks that threaten us with wreck.   *sandbanks*
As good to chide the waves as speak them fair.
25 And what is Edward but a ruthless sea?
What Clarence but a quicksand of deceit?
And Richard but a ragged° fatal rock?   *jagged*
All these the enemies to our poor bark.°   *ship*
Say you can swim: alas, 'tis but awhile;
30 Tread on the sand: why, there you quickly sink;
Bestride the rock: the tide will wash you off
Or else you famish—that's a threefold death.
This speak I, lords, to let you understand,
If° case some one of you would fly from us,   *In*
35 That there's no hoped-for mercy with the brothers
More than with ruthless waves, with sands and rocks.
Why, courage, then! What cannot be avoided
'Twere childish weakness to lament or fear.
PRINCE EDWARD   Methinks a woman of this valiant spirit
40 Should, if a coward heard her speak these words,
Infuse his breast with magnanimity°   *great courage*

___

2. For eagerness to travel makes the journey seem
shorter.
5.4 Location: Fields near Tewkesbury.
1. The anchor meant to stabilize the ship by taking
hold of the sea bottom.
2. Ropes and pulleys used for raising and lowering
sails.
3. Ropes that brace and support the mast.

And make him, naked,° foil° a man-at-arms.   unarmed / defeat
I speak not this as doubting any here
For, did I but suspect a fearful man,
45   He should have leave to go away betimes,°   at once
Lest in our need he might infect another
And make him of like spirit to himself.
If any such be here, as God forbid,
Let him depart before we need his help.
50   OXFORD   Women and children of so high a courage,
And warriors faint?° Why, 'twere perpetual shame!   fainthearted
O brave young Prince, thy famous grandfather°   (Henry V)
Doth live again in thee. Long mayst thou live
To bear his image and renew his glories.
55   SOMERSET   And he that will not fight for such a hope,
Go home to bed and, like the owl by day,
If he arise, be mocked and wondered at.
MARGARET   Thanks, gentle Somerset; sweet Oxford, thanks.
PRINCE EDWARD   And take his thanks that yet° hath nothing   who as yet
else.
        Enter a MESSENGER.
60   MESSENGER   Prepare you, lords, for Edward is at hand,
Ready to fight. Therefore be resolute.   [*Exit.*]
OXFORD   I thought no less; it is his policy
To haste thus fast to find us unprovided.°   unprepared
SOMERSET   But he's deceived; we are in readiness.
65   MARGARET   This cheers my heart, to see your forwardness.
OXFORD   Here pitch our battle;° hence we will not budge.   deploy our army
        Flourish and march. Enter [King] EDWARD, RICHARD,
            GEORGE, *and Soldiers.*
EDWARD   Brave followers, yonder stands the thorny wood
Which by the heavens' assistance and your strength
Must by the roots be hewn up yet ere night.
70   I need not add more fuel to your fire,
For well I wot° ye blaze to burn them out.   know
Give signal to the fight, and to it, lords!
MARGARET   Lords, knights, and gentlemen, what I should say
My tears gainsay,° for every word I speak   hinder
75   Ye see I drink the water of my eye.
Therefore, no more but this: Henry, your sovereign,
Is prisoner to the foe, his state usurped,
His realm a slaughterhouse, his subjects slain,
His statutes canceled, and his treasure spent,
80   And yonder is the wolf that makes this spoil.
You fight in justice. Then in God's name, lords,
Be valiant and give signal to the fight!
            Alarum. Retreat. Excursions. Exeunt.

5.5 (O Scene 25)

Flourish. Enter [King] EDWARD, RICHARD, GEORGE,
[and Soldiers,] [with] Queen [MARGARET], OXFORD,
[and] SOMERSET[, *prisoners*].
EDWARD   Now here a period of° tumultuous broils.   an end to
Away with Oxford to Hammes Castle¹ straight.

5.5 Location: Scene continues.   1. Near Calais.

For Somerset, off with his guilty head.
Go bear them hence; I will not hear them speak.

5 OXFORD For my part, I'll not trouble thee with words.

SOMERSET Nor I, but stoop with patience to my fortune.

Exeunt [OXFORD *and* SOMERSET, *guarded*].

MARGARET So part we sadly in this troublous world
To meet with joy in sweet Jerusalem.[2]

EDWARD Is proclamation made that who finds Edward
10 Shall have a high reward, and he his life?

RICHARD It is, and lo where youthful Edward comes.

Enter the PRINCE [EDWARD, *guarded*].

EDWARD Bring forth the gallant, let us hear him speak.
What! Can so young a thorn begin to prick?
Edward, what satisfaction° canst thou make   amends
15 For bearing arms, for stirring up my subjects,
And all the trouble thou hast turned me to?

PRINCE EDWARD Speak like a subject, proud ambitious York.
Suppose that I am now my father's mouth:
Resign thy chair, and where I stand, kneel thou
20 Whilst I propose the selfsame words to thee
Which, traitor, thou wouldst have me answer to.

MARGARET Ah, that thy father had been so resolved!

RICHARD That you might still have worn the petticoat
And ne'er have stol'n the breech° from Lancaster.   trousers
25 PRINCE EDWARD Let Aesop[3] fable° in a winter's night;   tell tales
His currish riddles sorts not with this place.[4]

RICHARD By heaven, brat, I'll plague ye for that word.

MARGARET Ay, thou wast born to be a plague to men.

RICHARD For God's sake, take away this captive scold!
30 PRINCE EDWARD Nay, take away this scolding crookback,° rather!   hunchback

EDWARD Peace, willful boy, or I will charm° your tongue.   silence with a spell

GEORGE Untutored lad, thou art too malapert.°   saucy

PRINCE EDWARD I know my duty: you are all undutiful.
Lascivous Edward, and thou perjured George,
35 And thou misshapen Dick, I tell ye all
I am your better, traitors as ye are,
And thou usurp'st my father's right and mine.

EDWARD Take that, the likeness of this railer° here!   scold (Margaret)
[*He*] *stabs him*.

RICHARD Sprawl'st thou?[5] Take that to end thy agony!
RICHARD *stabs him*.
40 GEORGE And there's for twitting me with perjury!
GEORGE *stabs him*.

MARGARET Oh, kill me too!

RICHARD Marry,[6] and shall.
[*He*] *offers to kill her*.

EDWARD Hold, Richard, hold, for we have done too much.

RICHARD Why should she live to fill the world with words?
45 EDWARD What, doth she swoon? Use means for her recovery.

---

2. Referring to heaven, which is described as the new Jerusalem in Revelation 21:2.
3. An ancient storyteller famous for his fables about animals. Like Richard, he reputedly was physically deformed.
4. His mean and cynical comments are not welcome here.
5. Do you convulse in the agonies of death?
6. A mild oath invoking the name of the Virgin Mary.

RICHARD   Clarence, excuse me to the King my brother.
I'll hence to London on a serious matter.
Ere ye come there, be sure° to hear some news.   *expect*
GEORGE   What? What?
50   RICHARD   Tower. The Tower!   *Exit.*
MARGARET   O Ned, sweet Ned, speak to thy mother, boy.
Canst thou not speak? O traitors, murderers!
They that stabbed Caesar shed no blood at all,
Did not offend, nor were not worthy blame,
55   If this foul deed were by to equal it.°   *to compare with it*
He was a man; this, in respect,° a child,   *in comparison*
And men ne'er spend their fury on a child.
What's worse than murderer, that I may name it?
No, no, my heart will burst an if I speak,
60   And I will speak, that so my heart may burst.
Butchers and villains, bloody cannibals,
How sweet a plant have you untimely cropped!
You have no children, butchers; if you had,
The thought of them would have stirred up remorse.
65   But if you ever chance to have a child,
Look in his youth to have him so cut off
As, deathsmen, you have rid° this sweet young Prince.   *killed*
EDWARD   Away with her! Go bear her hence perforce.
MARGARET   Nay, never bear me hence. Dispatch° me here.   *Kill*
70   Here sheathe thy sword;⁷ I'll pardon thee my death.
What, wilt thou not? Then, Clarence, do it thou.
GEORGE   By heaven, I will not do thee so much ease.
MARGARET   Good Clarence, do; sweet Clarence, do thou do it.
GEORGE   Didst thou not hear me swear I would not do it?
75   MARGARET   Ay, but thou usest° to forswear thyself.   *are accustomed*
'Twas sin before, but now 'tis charity.
What, wilt thou not? Where is that devil's butcher, Richard?
Hard-favored° Richard? Richard, where art thou?   *Ugly*
Thou art not here. Murder is thy alms-deed;°   *act of charity*
80   Petitioners for blood thou ne'er putt'st back.°   *you never turn away*
EDWARD   Away, I say! I charge ye bear her hence.
MARGARET   So come to you and yours as to this Prince!
          Exit MARGARET[, *guarded. Soldiers carry out the body*
                              of PRINCE EDWARD].
EDWARD   Where's Richard gone?
GEORGE   To London all in post° and, as I guess,   *haste*
85   To make a bloody supper in the Tower.
EDWARD   He's sudden if a thing comes in his head.
Now march we hence. Discharge the common sort°   *ordinary soldiers*
With pay and thanks, and let's away to London
And see our gentle Queen how well she fares.
90   By this,° I hope, she hath a son for me.   *Exeunt.*   *By now*

---

7. Bring your sword to rest (sheathe it) in my body.

5.6 (O Scene 26)

Enter [King] HENRY *the Sixth and* RICHARD, *with the*
LIEUTENANT, *on the [Tower] walls.*[1]

RICHARD Good day, my lord. What, at your book so hard?

HENRY Ay, my good lord—"my lord" I should say, rather.

'Tis sin to flatter. "Good" was little better;°　　　　　　*(than flattery)*

"Good Gloucester" and "good devil" were alike,

5　And both preposterous;° therefore not "good lord."　　　*unnatural*

RICHARD —Sirrah,° leave us to ourselves, we must confer.　*Fellow*

[*Exit* LIEUTENANT.]

HENRY So flies the reckless° shepherd from the wolf,　　*careless*

So first the harmless sheep doth yield his fleece

And next his throat unto the butcher's knife.

10　What scene of death hath Roscius[2] now to act?

RICHARD Suspicion always haunts the guilty mind;

The thief doth fear each bush an officer.

HENRY The bird that hath been limèd[3] in a bush

With trembling wings misdoubteth° every bush,　　　　*fears*

15　And I, the hapless male° to one sweet bird,°　　　*father / child*

Have now the fatal object in my eye

Where my poor young was limed, was caught and killed.

RICHARD Why, what a peevish° fool was that of Crete　　*silly*

That taught his son the office of a fowl,

20　And yet for all his wings the fool was drowned.[4]

HENRY I Daedalus, my poor boy Icarus,

Thy father Minos,[5] that denied our course,

The sun that seared the wings of my sweet boy

Thy brother Edward,[6] and thyself the sea

25　Whose envious gulf did swallow up his life.

Ah, kill me with thy weapon, not with words!

My breast can better brook° thy dagger's point　　　*tolerate*

Than can my ears that tragic history.

But wherefore dost thou come? Is't for my life?

30　RICHARD Think'st thou I am an executioner?

HENRY A persecutor I am sure thou art.

If murdering innocents be executing,

Why, then, thou art an executioner.

RICHARD Thy son I killed for his presumption.

35　HENRY Hadst thou been killed when first thou didst presume

Thou hadst not lived to kill a son of mine.

And thus I prophesy: that many a thousand

Which now mistrust no parcel of my fear,[7]

And many an old man's sigh and many a widow's,

40　And many an orphan's water-standing° eye,　　*flooded with tears*

Men for their sons, wives for their husbands,

5.6 Location: The Tower, London.

1. The precise setting is ambiguous. F's stage directions indicate that the scene takes place *"on the Walls,"* O's that it occurs *"in the Tower."* Richard's first line makes clear that Henry is reading, which may mean he is in an inner chamber. His murder could be staged in a small alcove at the back of the main stage, on the walls (up in the gallery), or in full view on the main stage.

2. An ancient Roman actor (actually best known as a comedian) whom many Elizabethans cited as the archetype of a great tragedian.

3. Caught with birdlime, a sticky substance smeared on twigs.

4. Alluding to the myth of Daedalus, who, in order to escape imprisonment in Crete, designed wings made of wax and feathers for himself and his son, Icarus. When Icarus flew too near the sun, the wax melted, and he fell to his death in the sea.

5. The king of Crete who imprisoned Daedalus and Icarus.

6. Referring to the sun insignia associated with Edward.

7. Who do not share any of my fears.

Orphans for their parents' timeless° death,   *untimely*
Shall rue the hour that ever thou wast born.
The owl shrieked at thy birth, an evil sign;
45 The night-crow[8] cried, aboding° luckless time;   *foretelling*
Dogs howled and hideous tempest shook down trees;
The raven rooked her° on the chimney's top;   *crouched*
And chatt'ring pies° in dismal discords sung.   *magpies*
Thy mother felt more than a mother's pain,
50 And yet brought forth less than a mother's hope—
To wit, an undigested° and deformèd lump,   *a shapeless*
Not like the fruit of such a goodly tree.
Teeth hadst thou in thy head when thou wast born[9]
To signify thou cam'st to bite the world.
55 And if the rest be true which I have heard,
Thou cam'st—
RICHARD I'll hear no more! Die, prophet, in thy speech.
          [*He*] *stabs him.*
For this amongst the rest was I ordained.
HENRY Ay, and for much more slaughter after this.
60 O God, forgive my sins and pardon thee.
          [*He*] *dies.*
RICHARD What, will the aspiring blood of Lancaster
Sink in the ground? I thought it would have mounted.
See how my sword weeps for the poor King's death.
Oh, may such purple° tears be alway shed   *blood-red*
65 From those that wish the downfall of our house.
If any spark of life be yet remaining,
Down, down to hell, and say I sent thee thither,
          [*He*] *stabs him again.*
I that have neither pity, love, nor fear.
Indeed, 'tis true that Henry told me of,
70 For I have often heard my mother say
I came into the world with my legs forward—
Had I not reason, think ye, to make haste
And seek their ruin that usurped our right?
The midwife wondered, and the women cried,
75 "O Jesus bless us, he is born with teeth!"
And so I was, which plainly signified
That I should snarl and bite and play the dog.
Then, since the heavens have shaped my body so,
Let hell make crooked my mind to answer° it.   *match*
80 I have no brother, I am like no brother;
And this word "love," which greybeards° call divine,   *elderly (experienced) men*
Be resident° in men like one another   *Reside*
And not in me. I am myself alone.
Clarence, beware: thou keep'st me from the light,
85 But I will sort° a pitchy° day for thee,   *arrange / dark*
For I will buzz° abroad such prophecies   *whisper*
That Edward shall be fearful of his life,
And then, to purge his fear, I'll be thy death.
King Henry and the Prince his son are gone;
90 Clarence, thy turn is next; and then the rest,

8. A mythical bird supposed to be an evil omen.
9. Richard III was popularly believed to have been
born with teeth, a physical sign of his monstrous character.

Counting myself but bad till I be best.
I'll throw thy body in another room,
And triumph, Henry, in thy day of doom!   *Exit.*

5.7 (O Scene 27)

Flourish. Enter King [EDWARD], Queen [ELIZABETH],
GEORGE, RICHARD, HASTINGS, *[a] Nurse [carrying*
infant Prince Edward,] and Attendants.

EDWARD   Once more we sit in England's royal throne,
Repurchased with the blood of enemies.
What valiant foemen, like to autumn's corn,
Have we mowed down in tops° of all their pride!   *at the peak*
5   Three Dukes of Somerset, threefold renowned
For hardy and undoubted° champions;   *fearless*
Two Cliffords, as the father and the son;
And two Northumberlands: two braver men
Ne'er spurred their coursers° at the trumpet's sound.   *warhorses*
10   With them the two brave bears, Warwick and Montague,[1]
That in their chains fettered the kingly lion
And made the forest tremble when they roared.
Thus have we swept suspicion° from our seat°   *worry / throne*
And made our footstool of security.
15   Come hither, Bess, and let me kiss my boy.
Young[2] Ned, for thee, thine uncles, and myself
Have in our armors watched° the winter's night,   *stayed awake during*
Went all afoot in summer's scalding heat,
That thou mightst repossess the crown in peace,
20   And of our labors thou shalt reap the gain.
RICHARD *[aside]*   I'll blast° his harvest, if your head were laid,[3]   *wither*
For yet I am not looked on° in the world.   *noticed*
This shoulder was ordained so thick to heave,
And heave it shall some weight or break my back.
25   Work thou the way, and that shalt execute.[4]
EDWARD   Clarence and Gloucester, love my lovely queen,
And kiss your princely nephew, brothers both.
GEORGE   The duty that I owe unto your majesty
I seal upon the lips of this sweet babe.
30   ELIZABETH   Thanks, noble Clarence; worthy brother, thanks.
RICHARD   And that I love the tree° from whence thou sprang'st,   *(family of York)*
Witness the loving kiss I give the fruit.
[aside] To say the truth, so Judas kissed his master
And cried, "All hail!" whenas he meant all harm.[5]
35   EDWARD   Now am I seated as my soul delights,
Having my country's peace and brothers' loves.
GEORGE   What will your grace have done with Margaret?
René, her father, to the King of France
Hath pawned the Sicils° and Jerusalem,   *Naples and Sicily*

5.7 Location: The palace, London.
1. The coat of arms of these brothers included the image of a bear chained to a staff.
2. TEXTUAL COMMENT Some copies of F have "Kong" here, while others have "Yong." Elizabethan printers frequently corrected typographical mistakes while a book was being printed, which means that some extant copies might have a corrected reading while others do not. See Digital Edition TC 11 (Folio edited text).
3. Once your head is laid in the grave.
4. Devise a way, (my head), and you, (shoulder and hand), shall carry it out.
5. Judas, identifying Jesus to the officers eager to arrest him, greeted him with a kiss and the salutation "All hail." *whenas:* when.

40   And hither have they sent it° for her ransom.   *(the money raised)*

    EDWARD   Away with her and waft her° hence to France.   *convey her by water*

    And now what rests° but that we spend the time   *remains*

    With stately triumphs,° mirthful comic shows,   *festivals*

    Such as befits the pleasure of the court.

45   Sound drums and trumpets! Farewell, sour annoy!°   *bitter troubles*

    For here I hope begins our lasting joy.   *Exeunt.*

The Taming of the Shrew

One of Shakespeare's first comedies—probably written in 1592 or earlier—*The Taming of the Shrew* is also one of his most controversial, focusing as it does on the battle between the sexes and on the process by which a strong-willed woman is made to submit to the control of her husband. When the play is read, and especially when it is experienced in performance, it is, however, much more interesting and complex than its title might suggest. An early example of Shakespeare's extraordinary theatrical craftsmanship, it consists of two interwoven plots and a frame tale. This complex structure allows for contrasts and parallels in the development of the play's main themes, complicating how the audience thinks about the drama's examination of the relationship between the sexes and the possibility that people can change their social identities as a result of either choice or coercion. Not surprisingly, *The Taming of the Shrew* has elicited wildly varying reactions from generations of readers, audiences, actors, and directors, easily speaking to present-day debates about gender equality and the persistence of attitudes and practices that make such equality often seem a chimera.

In the frame story, a poor tinker, Christopher Sly, who in the speech prefixes in the First Folio is simply called "Beggar," is made to believe that he is a nobleman with servants, a wife, fine food, and even erotic artwork at his command. This hoax, shown in the play's first two scenes (called "Inductions"), is engineered by a real lord who has found Sly drunk and asleep outside a tavern. The Lord's trick leads to many jokes at Sly's expense. While the tinker likes playing the part of a nobleman, he doesn't do it very well. His language, especially, betrays him. For example, Sly doesn't know how to address a lady, anxiously inquiring of his servants what to call his elegant spouse and settling on the absurd title "Madam wife" (Induction 2.108). The comedy of this scene is compounded by the fact that Sly's "wife" is really the Lord's page, Bartholomew, dressed up to impersonate a woman. Sly thus mistakes the sex of the person he would take to bed. He is also ignorant of the tastes and customs of the nobility, asking for cheap ale when he should call for sack, the sweet wine favored by gentlemen.

While these blunders make Sly an object of humor, he is also the figure for whose viewing pleasure the main play's two central plots unroll. As a temporary lord, Sly has a troupe of actors to entertain him. At least until he falls asleep, Sly watches them enact a comedy about courtship and marriage in which the primary plot involves a strong-willed woman, Katherina Minola, who is "tamed" by a fortune-seeking suitor named Petruccio. In the other plot, Katherina's seemingly demure sister, Bianca, is pursued by three adoring suitors and eventually elopes with one of them without her father's knowledge or consent. All three actions are united by themes of disguise and transformation. Snatched from the mud and given the clothes and the privileges of a lord, Sly is temporarily translated from one social class and identity to another, even though his behavior and the snickers of his "attendants" repeatedly remind the audience that he is not *really* a nobleman. In their pursuit of Bianca, several of her suitors also don disguises. One, Hortensio, poses as a teacher of music and mathematics; another, Lucentio, pretends to be Cambio, a language instructor; meanwhile, Lucentio's servant Tranio assumes his master's identity and in that disguise poses as yet another of Bianca's many admirers. Love makes men willing to transform themselves, although in this plot these changes are reversible. When the disguised gentlemen tire

343

of acting as scholars-for-hire, they simply reclaim their houses, fortunes, and social positions and demote their servants.

In the main plot, more subtle questions of disguise arise. Petruccio, to teach Katherina that she must obey him, acts the part of "shrew tamer," a role in which he appears at his own wedding in outlandish and ragged clothes and, during a sojourn at his country house, turns the world on its head by denying Katherina sleep, food, and any exercise of her own will. But if his servant Grumio is to be believed, this may not simply be a one-time disguise. Hearing of his master's plan to wed the rich and shrewish Katherina, Grumio says:

> O' my word, an she knew him as well as I do, she would think scolding would do little good upon him. She may perhaps call him half a score knaves or so. Why, that's nothing; an he begin once, he'll rail in his rope tricks. I'll tell you what, sir, an she stand him but a little, he will throw a figure in her face and so disfigure her with it that she shall have no more eyes to see withal than a cat. You know him not, sir.   (1.2.106–13)

Grumio's words raise doubts about Petruccio's "real" nature. Is he temporarily adopting the role of a shrew tamer and verbal bully, or is that his customary mode of being or a role that he has previously adopted in dealing with servants and other social inferiors? And as Petruccio attempts to transform Katherina from shrew to obedient spouse, new questions arise. Is he forcing her to deform her nature or helping her experiment with a role that might bring out untapped aspects of her personality or lead to greater control of her social environment? Is there, in fact, anything like a "real self," or is personhood a succession of social roles adopted because of coercion, social expectations, material circumstances, or the drive for social mastery?

The multiple instances of disguise and transformation in the three plots raise questions about how malleable people's identities really are and how much they are determined or constrained by social circumstance. The play invites us to see, for example, that lords and gentlemen can play with their social roles more successfully and with less risk than can tinkers. Sly's transformation is thrust upon him; but his lack of wealth and education makes it impossible for him to "pass" as nobility without the complicity of the lord who found him asleep outside the tavern. His transformation is precarious, a mere dream from which he will have to awaken, no matter how much he might want to continue as a lord. By contrast, Lucentio has more cultural capital and more ability to play with his identity. His role as a Latin master is nothing *but* a temporary stratagem, a part that his education enables him to play to perfection but that his social rank permits him to cast aside when he has won his bride.

Similarly, the social fact of gender sets different limits on possible presentations and transformations of self. Petruccio's outrageous behavior—striking his servants and starving his wife—makes him admired by other men. Hortensio, for example, one of Bianca's suitors who eventually marries a wealthy widow, decides to model himself after Petruccio and to take lessons from him on how to tame a wife. But what is deemed to be Katherina's outrageous behavior—striking a sister and defying a father and would-be husband—elicits only scorn and condemnation. Like class, gender limits one's permissible or possible range of action and the transformations of self one can effect. Unless she is willing to endure severe privation and penalties, Katherina can only undergo one kind of transformation—toward greater docility and subservience to her husband. In such circumstances, it is difficult to determine—as many critics wish to do—whether Katherina finds her "real" self through her encounters with Petruccio. Like many characters in the play, she can only improvise a self in relation to the social constraints and possibilities available to her, and the constraints operating upon a tinker or a woman are very different from those affecting a university-educated gentleman or a lord.

The social hierarchies that shape the possibilities for personal transformations are, in the Sly frame tale, given a peculiarly English inflection. The Sly episodes refer repeatedly to the Warwickshire countryside that was Shakespeare's own birthplace. Sly mentions Greet, an actual village near Stratford, and Barton Heath (probably Barton-on-the-Heath, another village close to Stratford), and the men enumerated as his tavern companions—Stephen Sly, John Naps, Peter Turf, and Henry Pimpernel—for the most part have homely English names. Moreover, the contrast between Sly and the lord who carries him to his house evokes the gap in sixteenth-century rural England between poor laborers, barely making a living at a succession of marginal jobs, and wealthy landowners. As arable and common land was fenced in or enclosed to increase the opportunities for grazing sheep, many landowners made huge profits, wool being one of England's most important exports. But enclosures, a number of which occurred in the Stratford region, also caused hardship for small tenant farmers forced off the enclosed land and, in some cases, driven into vagrancy.

Sly's appellation as "Beggar" suggests a fixed social identity. A poor man with a checkered employment history, he describes himself as "old Sly's son of Barton Heath, by birth a peddler, by education a cardmaker, by transmutation a bear-herd, and now by present profession a tinker" (Induction 2.17–19). A cardmaker makes the metal combs used to prepare wool for spinning; thus, Sly has had some tangential involvement with the wool industry, although he seems primarily to have led an itinerant life mending pots, selling cheap goods from a peddler's pack, and running up whatever tab he could at the local tavern. The Induction reveals the enormous gap in wealth and education separating this man from the leisured aristocrats who pick him up on the way home from hunting and use him for their evening's sport. The trick they play upon him is a fantastic one, but the details of the lord's privilege and Sly's drunken poverty are evoked with vivid realism. For such a man as Sly, what hope is there of becoming a lord?

By contrast, Bianca and her suitors exist in an Italian setting at many removes from Sly's English-countryside milieu. The events in this story line are drawn directly from George Gascoigne's *Supposes* (1566), itself an adaption of a work by Ariosto, *I Suppositi,* which employs the disguised identities, clever servants, and gullible fathers found in classical comedy. Wealth is also a crucial factor in this plot, for despite his speeches about the necessity for suitors to gain his daughters' love, Baptista is willing to give them to their wealthiest wooers. The suitors' money comes mostly

Woodcut of a "jovial" tinker, a person who mends pots, as Christopher Sly was said to do. From the Magdalene College Pepys Ballad Collection (1616).

from trade. Bianca's suitors testify to the number of ships they have at sea and to the luxury goods and property they have acquired through their ventures. In this world of prosperous urban merchants, Baptista can indulge his daughters with some training in the arts and languages, but he still expects to control their marriage choices. Katherina he delivers to the frankly fortune-hunting Petruccio, but his supposedly compliant daughter, Bianca—whose name, meaning "white," implies her virtue and purity—slips from his grasp. She not only elopes, but in the play's final banquet scene she refuses to come when her new husband summons her, suggesting that her earlier docility may have been a calculated pose. If her sister is gradually tamed, Bianca ultimately reveals her own considerable capacity for willfulness, her education and social position having given her the wherewithal to manipulate the courtship process to her own advantage.

It is against this backdrop that the particular features of the main plot become apparent. The relationship between Katherina and Petruccio has long been regarded as the play's most riveting story line. In fact, in the eighteenth century the famous actor David Garrick produced a shortened version of the play simply called *Catharine and Petruchio,* which cut the Bianca plot and held the stage for nearly one hundred years. The interest in Katherina and Petruccio is understandable, for Shakespeare created for them a story of taming at once enjoyable and deeply troubling. Though set in Italy, this plot line feels English, connected in subterranean ways to the world of Christopher Sly. For one thing, Petruccio is not just a creature of the city; he has a farmhouse that serves as this play's "green world," or place of transformations. Moreover, Petruccio is distinguished in many ways from the other Italian suitors. He has, for example, a sullen and quarrelsome servant, Grumio, in every respect the antithesis of the clever attendants, Tranio and Biondello, who help Lucentio win Bianca and, in fact, seem to do most of their master's thinking and plotting for him. This may be a kind of affectionate joke made at the expense of English domestic servants, who, despite their crude ways, at least aren't shown as mastering their masters. Moreover, while Hortensio, Gremio, and Lucentio woo Bianca with song and poetry, Petruccio woos Katherina by contradicting her every word and taming her, like a hawk, by making her go hungry and sleepless. The language of blood sport permeates both the Induction and the Petruccio scenes. The lord who picks up Sly has just returned from hunting and speaks knowledgeably about the abilities of each of his hounds; Petruccio repeatedly compares the taming of a wife to the transformation of a wild hawk into a docile hunting falcon, aligning wife taming with other manly English sports.

Finally, of course, the source for the Petruccio-Katherina plot is not an Italian comedy, as in the Bianca-Lucentio plot, but a folk story about taming a difficult wife. Variants of this type of story circulated throughout northern Europe in Shakespeare's day, including the vicious English ballad entitled "A Merry Jest of a Shrewd and Curst Wife Lapped in Morel's Skin for Her Good Behavior." In this ballad, a strong-willed wife is beaten bloody by her husband and then wrapped inside the salted skin of a dead horse named Morel. This mode of taming is more physically brutal than that employed by Petruccio, but both the play and the ballad assume that a husband can use extreme means to curb the will of a froward wife. Despite his Italian name, then, Petruccio is in many ways an Englishman; and the play implicitly suggests that unlike his Italian counterpart, the true Englishman defines his manhood through the firm and, if necessary, cruel mastery of wife and servant. By contrast, the less assertive Lucentio takes direction from his servant, supplicates his betrothed on bended knee, and ends up with a wife he cannot master.

Shakespeare's subtle Englishing of Katherina and Petruccio may have heightened the original audience's interest in and even identification with them, but the men and women in that audience may not have been equally drawn to what they witnessed. In the wake of the modern women's movement, certainly, the very idea of "taming" a woman and curbing her tongue has seemed offensive to many readers and viewers.

Cucking stool used to discipline scolds, shrews, and witches.

In *The Taming of the Shrew,* language is a vehicle for domination. Sly cannot effectively play a lord because he has not mastered the language of the elite. Katherina can be eloquent, but because of her gender her verbal independence is read by her father and suitors as a sign of shrewishness. In part, Petruccio tames Katherina's tart tongue by aggressive use of his own. A clear sign that he has succeeded occurs in 4.6, when, at her husband's behest, Katherina calls the sun the moon and an old man a budding virgin. Her words at this point no longer express her own perceptions but her husband's blatantly willful reading of reality. In the play's last scene, she makes a lengthy speech about a wife's duty to obey her husband that conforms to the patriarchal ideology of the day and her husband's wishes but is disturbingly far from her earlier expression of women's right to independent speech and thought.

Some directors have found this curbing of the female tongue and will so intolerable that they have made production choices that downplay the extent of Katherina's submission to Petruccio or that mitigate the linguistic coercion and physical cruelty that are part of his taming methods. For example, in many productions Katherina delivers her last speech about wifely duty while signaling, by winks and gestures, that she does not really believe it, or the director omits the lines in which Katherina offers to put her hand beneath her husband's foot as a token of submission. Such choices signal a desire to "save" Shakespeare from accusations that his play celebrates a crude form of male dominance.

Even in Shakespeare's own day, not everyone, including not all men, would have found Petruccio's behavior laudable. In 1611 John Fletcher, a young playwright in Shakespeare's company, the King's Men, wrote *The Woman's Prize, or the Tamer Tamed,* which answered Shakespeare's play by having Petruccio tamed by his second wife, Maria. The existence of this play suggests that some people took pleasure in seeing an aggressive husband brought to heel. In fact, the proper relationship between husband and wife was a matter of widespread discussion and debate in the early modern period, with many people suggesting limits to men's dominance within marriage. Some Protestant preachers enjoined husbands to use no violence against their wives and to treat them as spiritual equals and domestic helpmeets. They lauded marriage not merely as an economic arrangement but as a union demanding mutual affection and respect

Husband dominator. From a German playing card by Peter Flötner (1520).

from both parties. In practice, many women exercised considerable authority in their households: managing servants, helping to arrange their children's marriages, and overseeing many local market negotiations. At the same time, few women disputed that in the last analysis husbands were masters of their wives and that the household was "a little commonwealth," a realm in which the husband's supremacy over wife and children mirrored the supremacy of the monarch over his subjects. Disorder in the domestic realm was treated as a serious matter, intimating the possibility of a breakdown of order and hierarchy in the culture at large.

Strong-willed women were particularly apt to be labeled as disorderly in early modern towns and villages, even if their "crimes" involved nothing more than talkativeness. A shrew, in fact, was commonly defined as a woman with a wagging tongue who, partly because of her garrulousness, was not properly submissive to her husband. The ideal wife, by contrast, was imagined in the prescriptive literature as chaste, silent, and obedient. The talkativeness that could mark a woman as a shrew could also be interpreted as a sign of her sexual promiscuity, on the theory that one kind of looseness leads to another. Women deemed unruly were subject to various kinds of punishment. These could include being "cucked"—ducked into water on a "cucking stool"—or being fitted with a scold's bridle, a torturous harness that fitted around a woman's head with a metal bit that went into her mouth and prevented her from speaking and sometimes caused her to gag and her mouth to bleed or her teeth to be knocked loose. The husbands of disorderly and aggressive women could also be punished for failure to control their wives. Charivaris, or "rough ridings," were shaming rituals in which neighbors came to the house of a disorderly woman and made her or her husband ride backward through the town on a horse while bystanders shouted and played cacophonous music. This signaled that the world had been turned upside down and rendered inharmonious by her disorderliness and his inability to control his wife.

In *The Taming of the Shrew,* no man is submitted to a "rough riding" even though at the end of the play both Lucentio and Hortensio seem to have lost control of their wives. Instead, all the attention focuses on the taming of Katherina and on the strategies employed by Petruccio to make her compliant with his will. On the eighteenth- and nineteenth-century stage, Petruccio often carried a whip, symbol of his power to control his wife and servants with physical force. Whether or not he *literally* carries a whip, Petruccio employs coercion—verbal, psychological, and physical—to control his wife, subjecting her to public humiliation and private deprivation in order to teach her proper submissiveness to the authority of her husband. In so doing, he reinforces the hierarchical principle upon which the entire Elizabethan social order was premised, warning not only unruly men but also servants and beggars that, except in jest, they cannot usurp the places of their masters. But is this account of *The Taming of the Shrew* adequate? Is the play as fiercely repressive as some critics assume? It is precisely on this point that readers, critics, and actors differ.

Some critics, for example, emphasize how Shakespeare mitigates the violence of many versions of the folktale on which the main plot is modeled. Katherina is not, for example, beaten and wrapped in a salted horsehide, nor does Petruccio force her to sleep with him before their return to Padua. In his farmhouse, he keeps her awake by disordering the bed and talking at her, but only after their return to the relative safety and familiarity of her father's house does he speak of his intention to "bed" her. In short, sexual conquest does not seem to be part of his taming practices. Perhaps more important, many actors, audiences, and critics have seen in Katherina and Petruccio's relationship an attractive mutuality and vitality they find difficult to reconcile with the idea that the play is simply a lesson in how to subordinate a woman. For example, when Petruccio first woos Katherina in 2.1, the two of them engage in a verbal sparring match that is dazzling in its complexity and speed. Puns and insults fly back and forth, with Katherina giving as good as she gets. The following exchange is typical:

> PETRUCCIO Come, come, you wasp, i'faith you are too angry.
> KATHERINA If I be waspish, best beware my sting.
> PETRUCCIO My remedy is then to pluck it out.
> KATHERINA Ay, if the fool could find it where it lies.
> PETRUCCIO Who knows not where a wasp does wear his sting?
>   In his tail.
> KATHERINA In his tongue.
> PETRUCCIO   Whose tongue?
> KATHERINA Yours, if you talk of tales, and so farewell.
> PETRUCCIO What, with my tongue in your tail?
>   Nay, come again, good Kate, I am a gentleman—
> KATHERINA That I'll try.
>   *She strikes him.*
> PETRUCCIO I swear I'll cuff you if you strike again.
>
>   (2.1.209–19)

This is a beautifully orchestrated encounter, with Katherina and Petruccio trading rapid-fire, one-line insults and deftly topping one another's puns. Their exchange has erotic intensity. These two are taking one another's measure, listening intently, struggling for advantage. Petruccio is not above talking dirty, and Katherina is not above making physical contact, albeit with a blow and not a caress. This is light-years away from the vapid wooing of Lucentio and Bianca, hiding behind the screen of school Latin.

On the stage, something vital and alive goes on between Katherina and Petruccio, and they have often been compared with Shakespeare's other witty couples, such as Benedict and Beatrice in *Much Ado About Nothing,* iconoclasts who seem more real and finally better and more equally matched than the more conventional couples with whom they are contrasted. Many critics, in fact, have argued that the real love story of the play belongs to Katherina and Petruccio, and that his taming of her is merely a way of showing her the advantages of outwardly conforming to society's expectations so that she can have the husband, the home, and the social approval she surely must crave. Many critics argue that it is Katherina's spirit that attracts Petruccio and that her spirit is never broken, just redirected, as in the final scene when Katherina takes out her aggressions not against her husband but against the other wives, whom she lectures on their marriage duties. In fact, some critics have argued that in watching Petruccio discipline and abuse his servants and the tailor who makes a dress for Katherina, Katherina learns how to direct her aggression against social inferiors, or against other women, rather than against her husband—an outcome that would grant her some social power at the expense of making her, like Petruccio, a bully.

The debate about how to interpret *The Taming of the Shrew* will surely continue. In performance, directors and actors sometimes emphasize the drama's playful and farcical elements, sometimes its dark, violent, and repressive potential. For example, how should one stage the final lines of Katherina's lecture to Bianca and the widow about the marital duties of a good wife? In these lines Katherina offers to put her hand beneath her husband's foot, a reference to an ancient and out-of-date marriage custom. But does she, and how does Petruccio respond? One could stage this moment as Petruccio's final triumph over a beaten spouse: she kneels; he puts his foot on her extended hand; he smiles out at the audience and she remains expressionless, dazed and broken before being abruptly dragged to her feet and commanded to kiss her victorious husband, a kiss that feels likes a violation. Or at the other extreme, when Katherina kneels with hand extended, Petruccio could kneel also and take her hand in his, eyes fixed on hers, oblivious to the onlookers both onstage and in the audience. Completely enveloped in one another's gaze, the tableau could suggest they have moved beyond the exaggerated postures of shrew and shrew tamer into something that feels like mutual love. In this case, the words "Come on and kiss me, Kate" might be uttered as an entreaty, and not a command, to which Katherina willingly responds. Neither interpretive choice is "right," but the contrast suggests the diametrically different ways in which key moments in this text can be realized in performance.

Critics and readers remain similarly divided as to what they see in this tale of woman tamed. Most agree, however, that *The Taming of the Shrew* deals with issues that deserve the thoughtful and sometimes heated critical debate the play has engendered. For example, while Katherina's taming does not involve the kinds of physical brutality in the "Merry Jest" ballad, it is nonetheless true that in Petruccio's farmhouse Katherina is deprived of sleep, food, and the protection of family and female companionship—techniques akin to modern methods of torture and brainwashing. As Katherina says, she is "starved for meat, giddy for lack of sleep, / With oaths kept waking and with brawling fed" (4.3.9–10). This is horrifying, even if the horror is mitigated by the laughter-inducing techniques of knockabout farce. Grumio makes the audience laugh as he tantalizes Katherina with one kind of food and then another, while ultimately withholding them all, but this does not erase the fact that Katherina is hungry and that her hunger is used to starve her into complying with Petruccio's wishes. There is similar cruelty lurking behind the trick played on Sly in the Induction. The beggar is tantalized with the prospect of riches he can never retain. *The Taming of the Shrew* makes a joke out of the enormous gap between the poverty of a tinker and the privilege of a lord, comedy from the physical and psychic trials that lie in wait for a strong-willed woman.

It is perhaps appropriate to conclude by focusing again on the role of Sly. As he watches the play the actors perform for him, he at first makes comments on the action, but these stop after the first act, and he presumably falls asleep onstage. In another contemporary play, however, called *The Taming of a Shrew,* Sly makes interjections throughout, including a brief speech in which he vows to go home and tame his own wife, having learned from Petruccio how it is done. Scholars disagree about the relationship of *The Taming of the Shrew* and *The Taming of a Shrew*: they dispute which came first and whether Shakespeare had a hand in both (for a fuller discussion, see the Textual Introduction). Among the many differences between the two texts, however, is Sly's continuing stage prominence right to the end of *The Taming of a Shrew* and his final assertion that

> I'll to my
> Wife presently and tame her too,
> An if she anger me.

No one knows for certain if Shakespeare wrote these lines or why they don't appear in *The Taming of the Shrew*. Like almost everything else connected to this play, they are subject to various interpretations. Perhaps because they are put in Sly's mouth they are discredited, taken as another example of the reductiveness of his responses to the pastimes of the cultural elite—in this case, to the play staged in the Lord's house by the traveling players. Maybe *only* a tinker would take this as the "message" of the play. However, perhaps Sly's response to what he has just watched indicates why this vital and attractive play seems to many readers to traffic in dangerous matters and to be easily used to justify the crudest kinds of male tyranny. It is a little disconcerting that *even* a downtrodden tinker can find comfort in the thought that while he is neither a lord nor a gentleman, he shares with them the same right to tame his wife "an if she anger me." Impoverished and ridiculed, Sly nonetheless feels entitled by virtue of his gender to dominate his spouse, perhaps thereby compensating for his powerlessness in other areas. In short, there is always something lower than a beggar—a beggar's wife. The play published in the First Folio does not contain Sly's speech, but in our day *The Taming of the Shrew* nonetheless remains, along with *The Merchant of Venice,* one of Shakespeare's most controversial plays: a spur to thought and to debate, a reminder of the serious matters that often lie at the heart of Shakespeare's "festive" comedies.

JEAN E. HOWARD

SELECTED BIBLIOGRAPHY

Aspinall, Dana E., ed. *The Taming of the Shrew: Critical Essays.* New York: Routledge, 2002. A broad selection of twentieth-century critical essays about the play, plus reviews of notable film, television, and stage versions.

Bailey, Amanda. "Livery and Its Discontents in *The Taming of the Shrew.*" *Flaunting: Style and the Subversive Male Body in Renaissance England.* Toronto: U of Toronto P, 2007. 51–76. Examines how the excesses of male fashion could destabilize the early modern social order, including the disorder produced by servants who dress above their stations.

Boose, Lynda. "Scolding Brides and Bridling Scolds: Taming the Woman's Unruly Member." *Shakespeare Quarterly* 42 (1991): 179–213. Draws on the research of nineteenth-century scholars to recover the early modern punishments, including iron gags and cucking stools, used against women accused of being shrews or scolds.

Dolan, Frances E. "Household Chastisements: Gender, Authority and 'Domestic Violence.'" *Renaissance Culture and the Everyday.* Ed. Patricia Fumerton and Simon Hunt. Philadelphia: U of Pennsylvania P, 1999. 204–25. Scrutinizes forms of nearly invisible early modern domestic violence in which superiors discipline social subordinates, and argues that in *The Taming of the Shrew* Katherina is schooled by Petruccio to learn more socially acceptable targets for her anger, including the besting of servants.

Evett, David. "'Surprising Confrontations': Discourses of Service in *The Taming of the Shrew.*" *Discourses of Service in Shakespeare's England.* New York: Palgrave Macmillan, 2005. 35–54. Explores the many different representations of servants and service in *The Taming of the Shrew,* and argues that the play posits "willing service" as the best alternative to coercion or rebellion within the master-servant relationship.

Haring-Smith, Tori. *From Farce to Metadrama: A Stage History of "The Taming of the Shrew," 1594–1983.* Westport, CT: Greenwood, 1985. A comprehensive stage history of the play and of some major adaptations from the late 1590s to the early 1980s.

Henderson, Diana E. "The Return of the Shrew: New Media, Old Stories, and Shakespearean Comedy." *Collaborations with the Past: Reshaping Shakespeare across Time and Media.* Ithaca, NY: Cornell UP, 2006. 155–201. Presents an excellent analysis of twentieth-century film versions of *The Taming of the Shrew* from the

Mary Pickford/Douglas Fairbanks Jr. version of 1929 to *10 Things I Hate About You* in 1999.

Marcus, Leah. "The Shakespearean Editor as Shrew-Tamer." *English Literary Renaissance* 22 (1992): 177–200. Examines and queries the historical process by which *The Taming of a Shrew* came to be regarded not as a source for Shakespeare's *The Taming of the Shrew*, but as a debased derivative of it.

Newman, Karen. "Renaissance Family Politics and Shakespeare's *Taming of the Shrew.*" *Fashioning Femininity and English Renaissance Drama.* Chicago: U of Chicago P, 1991. 33–50. Argues that Katherina's linguistic freedom constitutes her main threat to male authority and that that freedom is never completely curtailed.

Smith, Amy L. "Performing Marriage with a Difference: Wooing, Wedding, and Bedding in *The Taming of the Shrew.*" *Comparative Drama* 36 (2002): 289–320. Uses Judith Butler's theories of performativity to argue that within Katherina and Petruccio's self-conscious performance of courtship and marriage lies the potential for a critical reworking of gender norms, rather than outright submission to or resistance of them.

FILMS

The Taming of the Shrew. 1929. Dir. Samuel Taylor. USA. 63 min. One of the first "talkies," this black-and-white film, starring Douglas Fairbanks as Petruccio and Mary Pickford as Katherina, ends with Pickford's famous "wink" at the conclusion of her speech of submission.

Kiss Me Kate. 1953. Dir. George Sidney. USA. 109 min. Film version of the Cole Porter musical starring Howard Keel and Kathryn Grayson in which a group of actors is shown performing Shakespeare's play, the events of which mirror their own circumstances. Songs include "Brush Up Your Shakespeare" and "Where Is the Life That Late I Led?"

The Taming of the Shrew. 1967. Dir. Franco Zeffirelli. USA. 122 min. Broad-comedy performance starring the real-life couple of Elizabeth Taylor and Richard Burton as Katherina and Petruccio.

The Taming of the Shrew. 1980. Dir. Jonathan Miller. UK. 127 min. Intelligent BBC/Time-Life version starring John Cleese as Petruccio and Sarah Badel as Katherina with sets modeled on Vermeer interiors.

10 Things I Hate About You. 1999. Dir. Gil Junger. USA. 97 min. Loose adaptation of Shakespeare's plot in which Julia Stiles plays a headstrong character, Kat Stratford, who comes to an accommodation with bad boy Heath Ledger as Patrick Verona.

TEXTUAL INTRODUCTION

The Taming of the Shrew was published for the first time in the 1623 First Folio, and it is that text that forms the basis for this edition. However, another play that seems to be closely related also circulated during the period: *The Taming of a Shrew. A Shrew* was first published as a quarto in 1594 and was reprinted in 1596 and 1607. The play shares many features with *The Shrew* beyond the similarity of their titles, including the plot of a woman who is "tamed" by her husband and a subplot of her sister and her various suitors. *A Shrew* is, however, dissimilar enough—the location and character names differ, the shrew has two sisters, the frame story is completed, the play is significantly shorter—that *A Shrew* and *The Shrew* cannot be understood as different names for one play. But there is no consensus about the relationship between these two plays. Various theories have been proposed to account for the similarities and differences between the two. Some scholars have suggested that *A Shrew* is an anonymous play that served as a source for Shakespeare's *The Shrew.* Others argue that *A*

Shrew derives from *The Shrew*, either as an imperfect copy of Shakespeare's play or as a memorial reconstruction of it. It has also been proposed that both *The Shrew* and *A Shrew* are imperfect derivatives of an even earlier *Shrew* play. While the Oxford editors believed that *The Shrew* was a source for *A Shrew*, the most recent editor (2010) for the Arden Shakespeare argues that *A Shrew* likely came before *The Shrew*.

Dating *The Shrew* is complicated first of all by its uncertain relationship to *A Shrew*. *A Shrew* was entered into the Stationers' Register on May 2, 1594 (the year it was first published), and its title page describes the play as having been performed by Pembroke's Men; if that is the case, the play must have been written before 1593, when that company went bankrupt. Consequently, if *The Shrew* predates *A Shrew*, it must have been written by 1592. Yet linguistic analysis shows similarities between *The Shrew* and *The Comedy of Errors* and *Love's Labor's Lost*, both written around 1594–95. Francis Meres's 1598 *Palladis Tamia: Wit's Treasury* mentions neither *A Shrew* nor *The Shrew* among Shakespeare's comedies—perhaps an omission, or perhaps evidence that *The Shrew* had not yet been written and that *A Shrew* is not Shakespeare's play.

Internal evidence for dating is not much more helpful. *The Shrew* includes the use of "*Sincklo*" as the speech prefix for one of the players in the Induction. Scholars agree that Sincklo is John Sincler, a hired man who was active as a player during the 1590s and early 1600s. More perplexing is the connection between Sincler and a character named "Soto," since the only Soto in an extant play is found in John Fletcher's *Women Pleased*, written sometime around 1619–23, well after Shakespeare's death. But these lines could have been inserted later. Finally, it has been argued that *A Shrew*'s gender politics are consistent with official Elizabethan gender views, while *The Shrew*'s are more akin to Jacobean visions of a companionate marriage. In summary, as with the relationship between *A Shrew* and *The Shrew*, there has been no consensus on the date of *The Shrew*, but it seems most likely to have been written in the early part of the decade, probably in 1591–92.

Questions about the play's date of composition and its relationship to *A Shrew*, however, have little bearing on editing *The Shrew*. The two are separate plays, and the decisions made in editing *The Shrew* are based on its text in the Folio and not on *A Shrew*'s text. A few notable issues arise in editing *The Shrew*, particularly concerning the play's irregular act divisions. The Folio starts the play with "*Actus primus. Scoena Prima.*" It was Alexander Pope who first labeled the two opening scenes as part of the Induction, a move that all subsequent editors have followed. There are also irregularities in subsequent act divisions. The Folio marks no act 2 and no scene divisions; the act and scenes inserted have been fairly consistent across the editorial tradition, and they are detailed here in the Textual Variants.

The character of Hortensio is more complicated to handle: he is not part of the "bidding" for Bianca in 2.1, despite being one of her wooers, and partway through the play Tranio seems to take over what has been Hortensio's role as Petruccio's old friend. These changes suggest that there might have been a revision to his character, but it is not possible to recover the earlier version of the play if there was one. There are also a number of clearly incorrect speech prefixes for his character, as indicated in the Textual Variants.

The stage directions in the Folio are often more detailed than is typical for early modern plays, describing actions, demeanor, and order of entry in some cases: for example, at the equivalent of 2.1.38, the Folio reads, "*Enter Gremio, Lucentio, in the habit of a meane man, Petruchio with Tranio, his boy bearing a Lute and Bookes.*" As is usual in early modern play texts, there are missing entrances and exits, and other directions appear incomplete: the Haberdasher, for instance, is given an entrance but is never provided with an exit. The placement and wording of stage directions can affect the way readers and audiences respond to the play; for some examples, see the Textual Comments.

SARAH WERNER

PERFORMANCE NOTE

To moderate anticipated moral opposition to a comedy that hinges on female subjection, directors of *The Taming of the Shrew* often endeavor not to engage audiences emotionally, but in fact to distance them from the action. In this they may follow Shakespeare, who stresses the plot's artificiality via framing scenes wherein characters deceive a drunkard, even regarding his own identity, then mount a performance full of role playing and disguise. Directors can complement the play's ostentatious theatricality by keeping Sly onstage throughout the *Taming* play, or conspicuously doubling him and others in the main plot, for example, with Sly and the Hostess renewing their feud as Petruccio and Katherina. Productions also routinely employ *commedia*-inflected or blatantly cartoonish characterizations and settings (such as the "wild west") to explain the play's violence and antifeminism as routine elements of farce. On the other hand, some directors unapologetically showcase the play's brutality, cutting the Induction scenes and trimming the Bianca subplot so that the violence leveled at Katherina appears more disturbing for the comparative simplicity of its representation.

In the further interests of rendering the taming plot more palatable, some productions shift the play's genre toward romantic comedy, softening objections to Katherina's gradual submission by presenting her interactions with Petruccio as mutually complicit banter or foreplay. Some productions depict Baptista as Katherina's main oppressor and offer Petruccio as a handsome alternative and a means of escape. Others make a feminist heroine of Katherina, implying that her incongruous behavior in the finale is a deliberate ploy to win Petruccio's bet, suggestive even of the power she holds in their present or future relationship. Still others, conversely, make her a tragic figure, brainwashed and/or beaten into submission. Petruccio, meanwhile, can be a cunning sadist or a dull brute, a dashing hero or a zany (clown), depending on whether the production casts Katherina more as victim or virago. The portrayal of Bianca inevitably influences Katherina's reception, since her sweetness can be sincere or yet another of the play's disguises—often revealed by productions' having her flout her sister behind their father's back, thus partly excusing the shrewishness for which Katherina is notorious.

BRETT GAMBOA

The Taming of the Shrew

[THE PERSONS OF THE PLAY

In the Induction:
Christopher Sly, a BEGGAR
HOSTESS
LORD
Bartholomew, PAGE to the Lord
HUNTSMEN attending the Lord
SERVANTS attending the Lord
PLAYERS

In the play-within-a-play:
BAPTISTA Minola, a gentleman of Padua
KATHERINA, elder daughter to Baptista
BIANCA, younger daughter to Baptista

PETRUCCIO, a gentleman of Verona, suitor to Katherina
GRUMIO ⎫
CURTIS ⎪
NATHANIEL ⎬ servants to Petruccio
PHILIP ⎪
JOSEPH ⎪
PETER ⎭
GREMIO, a rich old man of Padua, suitor to Bianca
HORTENSIO, suitor to Bianca, later disguised as Licio
LUCENTIO, a gentleman of Pisa, suitor to Bianca, later disguised as Cambio
TRANIO ⎫ servants to Lucentio
BIONDELLO ⎭

VINCENTIO, father to Lucentio
PEDANT, later disguised as Vincentio

WIDOW
TAILOR
HABERDASHER
OFFICER
SERVANTS
Attendants]

Induction 1
Enter [a] BEGGAR *[called] Christopher Sly and [a]* HOSTESS.[1]
BEGGAR   I'll feeze° you, in faith.   *fix; beat*
HOSTESS   A pair of stocks,[2] you rogue.

Induction 1 Location: In front of a country tavern.
1. TEXTUAL COMMENT To emphasize his societal role, the Folio (F) consistently uses "Beggar" for the character that editors usually refer to as "Sly." This edition follows F's use of roles rather than proper names to refer to the Induction's characters. See

Digital Edition TC 1.
2. A threat to have him put in the stocks (an instrument of public punishment consisting of two wooden planks with semicircles carved into them; the criminal sat with his or her feet clamped between the planks).

BEGGAR   You're a baggage;° the Slys are no rogues. Look in   *whore*
   the chronicles;[3] we came in with Richard Conqueror.[4]
5   Therefore *paucas palabras*:[5] let the world slide.° Sessa![6]   *go by*
HOSTESS   You will not pay for the glasses you have burst?°   *broken*
BEGGAR   No, not a denier.[7] Go by, Saint Jeronimy![8] Go to thy
   cold bed, and warm thee.
HOSTESS   I know my remedy: I must go fetch the headborough.°   *constable*
10 BEGGAR   Third, or fourth, or fifth borough, I'll answer him by
   law. I'll not budge an inch, boy.[9] Let him come, and kindly.°   *and welcome! (ironic)*
   Falls asleep.

               [*Exit* HOSTESS.][1]
   Wind horns.° Enter a LORD *from hunting, with his train*   *Horns sound*
   [*of* HUNTSMEN *and* SERVANTS].

LORD   Huntsman, I charge thee, tender well° my hounds.   *care well for*
   Breathe Meriman[2]—the poor cur is embossed°—   *exhausted*
   And couple Clowder with the deep-mouthed brach.[3]
15   Saw'st thou not, boy, how Silver made it good
   At the hedge corner, in the coldest fault?[4]
   I would not lose the dog for twenty pound.
FIRST HUNTSMAN   Why, Belman is as good as he, my lord.
   He cried upon it at the merest loss,[5]
20   And twice today picked out the dullest scent.
   Trust me, I take him for the better dog.
LORD   Thou art a fool. If Echo were as fleet,°   *fast*
   I would esteem him worth a dozen such.
   But sup° them well and look unto them all.   *feed*
25   Tomorrow I intend to hunt again.
FIRST HUNTSMAN   I will, my lord.
LORD [*seeing* BEGGAR]   What's here? One dead or drunk? See,
   doth he breathe?
SECOND HUNTSMAN   He breathes, my lord. Were he not warmed
   with ale,
   This were a bed but cold to sleep so soundly.
30 LORD   Oh, monstrous beast! How like a swine he lies.
   Grim death, how foul and loathsome is thine image.[6]
   Sirs, I will practice on° this drunken man.   *play a trick on*
   What think you if he were conveyed to bed,
   Wrapped in sweet° clothes, rings put upon his fingers,   *scented*
35   A most delicious banquet by his bed,
   And brave° attendants near him when he wakes—   *finely dressed*
   Would not the beggar then forget himself?
FIRST HUNTSMAN   Believe me, lord, I think he cannot choose.°   *do otherwise*
SECOND HUNTSMAN   It would seem strange unto him when he
   waked.

---

3. Histories, especially histories of England such as
Raphael Holinshed's *Chronicles of England, Scotland, and Ireland* (2nd ed., 1587).
4. A blunder for "William the Conqueror," who took
the English throne in 1066.
5. Misquoting *pocas palabras*, Spanish for "few words,"
a phrase from Thomas Kyd's *Spanish Tragedy* (ca. 1587).
6. Probably equivalent to "Be quiet."
7. *denier*: French coin of little value.
8. Misquoting a popular line—"Hieronimo, beware!
go by, go by!"—from Kyd's *Spanish Tragedy* and confusing Hieronimo, Kyd's hero, with Saint Jerome.
9. Term of abuse applicable to either sex.

1. TEXTUAL COMMENT The Folio does not provide a
stage direction for the Hostess's exit, which must occur
before the Lord arrives. This edition has her remain
onstage while the Beggar taunts her as "boy" and
refuses to pay, thus heightening their antagonism.
See Digital Edition TC 2.
2. Give Meriman time to recover his breath.
3. And put Clowder on a leash with the female
hound ("brach") who bays deeply.
4. When the scent was faintest.
5. When the scent had been completely lost.
6. Your likeness (invoking the common comparison
between sleep and death).

40	LORD Even as a flatt'ring° dream or worthless fancy.	*pleasing*
	Then take him up and manage well the jest.	
	Carry him gently to my fairest chamber,	
	And hang it round with all my wanton pictures.°	*erotic artworks*
	Balm° his foul head in warm distillèd waters,	*Anoint*
45	And burn sweet wood to make the lodging sweet.[7]	
	Procure me music ready when he wakes	
	To make a dulcet° and a heavenly sound.	*melodious*
	And, if he chance to speak, be ready straight°	*at once*
	And with a low, submissive reverence°	*deep bow*
50	Say, "What is it your honor will command?"	
	Let one attend him with a silver basin	
	Full of rosewater and bestrewed with flowers;	
	Another bear the ewer,° the third a diaper,°	*water jug / towel*
	And say, "Will't please your lordship cool your hands?"	
55	Someone be ready with a costly suit,	
	And ask him what apparel he will wear;	
	Another tell him of his hounds and horse	
	And that his lady mourns at his disease.	
	Persuade him that he hath been lunatic	
60	And, when he says he is,° say that he dreams,	*is indeed mad*
	For he is nothing but a mighty lord.	
	This do, and do it kindly,° gentle sirs:	*naturally; fittingly*
	It will be pastime passing° excellent	*exceedingly*
	If it be husbanded with modesty.°	*prudently managed*
65	FIRST HUNTSMAN My lord, I warrant you we will play our part	
	As° he shall think by our true diligence	*So*
	He is no less than what we say he is.	
	LORD Take him up gently and to bed with him,	
	And each one to his office° when he wakes.	*assigned role*
	[*The* BEGGAR *is carried out.*]	
	Sound trumpets.	
70	Sirrah,[8] go see what trumpet 'tis that sounds.	
	[*Exit a* SERVANT.]	
	Belike° some noble gentleman that means,	*Perhaps*
	Traveling some journey, to repose° him here.	*rest*
	Enter [SERVANT].	
	How now? Who is it?	
	SERVANT An't° please your honor, players	*If it*
	That offer service to your lordship.	
	Enter PLAYERS.	
75	LORD Bid them come near.	
	—Now, fellows, you are welcome.	
	PLAYERS We thank your honor.	
	LORD Do you intend to stay with me tonight?	
	FIRST PLAYER So please your lordship to accept our duty.°	*services; respect*
	LORD With all my heart. This fellow I remember	
80	Since once he played a farmer's eldest son.	
	—'Twas where you wooed the gentlewoman so well.	
	I have forgot your name, but sure that part	
	Was aptly fitted° and naturally performed.	*well suited (to you)*

7. Aromatic woods like juniper were often burned to make a room smell fragrant.   8. A form of address to social inferiors.

SECOND PLAYER   I think 'twas Soto[9] that your honor means.

85 LORD   'Tis very true. Thou didst it excellent.
    —Well, you are come to me in happy time,°   *at the right time*
    The rather for° I have some sport in hand   *Especially since*
    Wherein your cunning° can assist me much.   *skill*
    There is a lord will hear you play tonight.
90 But I am doubtful of your modesties,°   *self-control*
    Lest over-eying of° his odd behavior—   *noticing; staring at*
    For yet his honor never heard a play—
    You break into some merry passion°   *fit of laughter*
    And so offend him. For I tell you, sirs,
95 If you should smile, he grows impatient.

FIRST PLAYER   Fear not, my lord, we can contain ourselves,
    Were he the veriest antic° in the world.   *most eccentric fellow*

LORD [*to a* SERVANT]   Go, sirrah, take them to the buttery,[1]
    And give them friendly welcome, every one.
100 Let them want° nothing that my house affords.   *lack*

                Exit one [SERVANT] *with the players.*

    [*to another* SERVANT] Sirrah, go you to Bartholomew, my page,
    And see him dressed in all suits° like a lady.   *in every detail*
    That done, conduct him to the drunkard's chamber
    And call him "Madam," do him obeisance.°   *pay him respects*
105 Tell him° from me, as he will win my love,   *(Bartholomew, the page)*
    He bear himself with honorable° action   *becoming*
    Such as he hath observed in noble ladies
    Unto their lords by them accomplishèd.°   *performed*
    Such duty to the drunkard let him do
110 With soft low tongue° and lowly courtesy,   *voice*
    And say, "What is't your honor will command
    Wherein your lady and your humble wife
    May show her duty and make known her love?"
    And then with kind embracements, tempting kisses,
115 And with declining head into his bosom,[2]
    Bid him shed tears, as being overjoyed
    To see her noble lord restored to health,
    Who for this seven years hath esteemed him°   *thought himself to be*
    No better than a poor and loathsome beggar.
120 And if the boy have not a woman's gift
    To rain a shower of commanded° tears,   *produced on demand*
    An onion will do well for such a shift,°   *purpose*
    Which in a napkin being close conveyed°   *secretly carried*
    Shall in despite[3] enforce a watery eye.
125 See this dispatched with all the haste thou canst;
    Anon° I'll give thee more instructions.   *Soon*

                        Exit a [SERVANT].

    I know the boy will well usurp° the grace,   *assume*
    Voice, gait, and action of a gentlewoman.
    I long to hear him call the drunkard "husband,"

---

9. Possibly a reference to a character of this name in John Fletcher's *Women Pleased*. Since that play was first acted around 1620, the reference must either be a late addition to Shakespeare's text or else refer to a character in an earlier play, now lost.
1. Pantry, often used to store liquor as well as food.
2. And with his head bowing down onto his chest.
3. In spite of an inability to cry.

130 And how my men will stay° themselves from laughter   *restrain*
When they do homage to this simple peasant.
I'll in to counsel them. Haply° my presence   *Perhaps*
May well abate the over-merry spleen[4]
Which otherwise would grow into extremes.   [*Exeunt.*]

Induction 2

Enter aloft[1] the drunkard [BEGGAR] *with* [SERVANTS]—
some with apparel, basin and ewer, and other
appurtenances—and LORD.

BEGGAR   For God's sake, a pot of small ale!°   *weak, cheap ale*

FIRST SERVANT   Will't please your lordship drink a cup of
sack?°   *costly imported wine*

SECOND SERVANT   Will't please your honor taste of these
conserves?°   *candied fruits*

THIRD SERVANT   What raiment° will your honor wear today?   *clothing*

5 BEGGAR   I am Christophero Sly. Call not me "honor" nor
"lordship." I ne'er drank sack in my life—and if you give me
any conserves, give me conserves of beef.° Ne'er ask me what   *salted beef*
raiment I'll wear, for I have no more doublets° than backs,   *jackets*
no more stockings than legs, nor no more shoes than feet—
10 nay, sometime more feet than shoes, or such shoes as my
toes look through the over-leather.

LORD   Heaven cease this idle humor[2] in your honor.
Oh, that a mighty man of such descent,
Of such possessions and so high esteem,
15 Should be infusèd with so foul a spirit.

BEGGAR   What, would you make me mad? Am not I Christopher Sly, old Sly's son of Barton Heath,[3] by birth a peddler,
by education a cardmaker,[4] by transmutation a bear-herd,°   *keeper of a tame bear*
and now by present profession a tinker?° Ask Marian Hackett,   *pot mender*
20 the fat alewife[5] of Wincot, if she know me not. If she say I
am not fourteen pence on the score[6] for sheer° ale, score   *for nothing but*
me up for the lying'st knave in Christendom. What, I am not
bestraught.° Here's—   *crazy*

THIRD SERVANT   Oh, this it is that makes your lady mourn.

25 SECOND SERVANT   Oh, this is it that makes your servants
droop.

LORD   Hence comes it that your kindred shuns your house,
As beaten hence by your strange lunacy.
O noble lord, bethink thee of thy birth.
Call home thy ancient° thoughts from banishment   *former*
30 And banish hence these abject lowly dreams.
Look how thy servants do attend on thee,

---

4. May lessen the impulse to laugh. Emotional out-
bursts, including laughter, were thought to originate
in the spleen.
Induction 2 Location: A bedroom in the Lord's house.
1. Upon the gallery above the stage. Whether this
long and complex scene was in fact performed "aloft"
is open to question. At a later point (1.1.244–49),
F has the Beggar commenting from above on the play
presented by the traveling actors who arrive in Induction 1. If Induction 2 is played on the main stage, the
Beggar must at some point ascend to the gallery, or
he must observe the entire play from the side of the
main stage.

2. Heaven put an end to this foolish fantasy. According to Renaissance medical theory, humors, or bodily
fluids, determined one's disposition.
3. Possibly Barton-on-the-Heath, a village not far from
Stratford-upon-Avon.
4. Maker of metal combs used to prepare wool for
spinning.
5. Female proprietor of a tavern. Wincot is a small
village near Stratford; individuals named Hacket
were living there in 1591.
6. In debt. Accounts were originally kept by notch-
ing, or "scoring," a stick, later by making marks on a
wall or a door.

Each in his office ready at thy beck.°   *command*
Wilt thou have music? (*Music.*) Hark, Apollo[7] plays,
And twenty cagèd nightingales do sing.
35   Or wilt thou sleep? We'll have thee to a couch
Softer and sweeter than the lustful bed
On purpose trimmed up for Semiramis.[8]
Say thou wilt walk: we will bestrew the ground.
Or wilt thou ride? Thy horses shall be trapped,°   *fitted with adornments*
40   Their harness studded all with gold and pearl.
Dost thou love hawking? Thou hast hawks will soar
Above the morning lark. Or wilt thou hunt?
Thy hounds shall make the welkin° answer them   *sky*
And fetch shrill echoes from the hollow earth.
45   FIRST SERVANT   Say thou wilt course,° thy greyhounds are   *hunt hares*
     as swift
As breathèd° stags—ay, fleeter than the roe.[9]   *well-exercised*
SECOND SERVANT   Dost thou love pictures?[1] We will fetch thee
     straight
Adonis[2] painted by a running brook
And Cytherea all in sedges° hid,   *water rushes*
50   Which seem to move and wanton° with her breath,   *play amorously*
Even as the waving sedges play wi'th' wind.
LORD   We'll show thee Io[3] as she was a maid,
And how she was beguilèd and surprised,
As lively° painted as the deed was done.   *realistically*
55   THIRD SERVANT   Or Daphne[4] roaming through a thorny wood,
Scratching her legs that one shall swear she bleeds,
And at that sight shall sad Apollo weep,
So workmanly° the blood and tears are drawn.   *skillfully*
LORD   Thou art a lord and nothing but a lord.
60   Thou hast a lady far more beautiful
Than any woman in this waning age.[5]
FIRST SERVANT   And till the tears that she hath shed for thee,
Like envious° floods o'errun her lovely face,   *spiteful*
She was the fairest creature in the world—
65   And yet° she is inferior to none.   *still*
BEGGAR   Am I a lord? And have I such a lady?
Or do I dream? Or have I dreamed till now?
I do not sleep. I see, I hear, I speak.
I smell sweet savors° and I feel soft things.   *odors*
70   Upon my life, I am a lord indeed,
And not a tinker, nor Christopher Sly.
Well, bring our lady hither to our sight—
And once again, a pot o'th' smallest° ale!   *weakest*

---

7. Greek god of music, who played the lyre.
8. Legendary Queen of Assyria, known for her great beauty and many sexual adventures.
9. Small deer proverbial for its swiftness.
1. Probably the "wanton pictures" referred to earlier (Induction 1.43). As described in the following lines, they are conventional erotic scenes, mostly derived from Ovid's *Metamorphoses*.
2. In classical mythology, a beautiful boy whom Aphrodite (Cytherea) loved. This scene shows Aphro-

dite spying on Adonis while he bathes in the brook.
3. Raped by Zeus, who concealed himself in a cloud or thick mist, she was then turned into a cow by Hera, Geek goddess of marriage.
4. A nymph who was turned into a laurel tree as she fled from Apollo.
5. Alluding to the popular belief that the world had steadily degenerated from the perfection of paradise or the classical Golden Age.

SECOND SERVANT Will't please your mightiness to wash your
    hands?
75   Oh, how we joy to see your wit restored!
    Oh, that once more you knew but what you are!
    These fifteen years you have been in a dream
    Or, when you waked, so waked as if you slept.
BEGGAR   These fifteen years? By my fay,° a goodly nap.   *faith*
80   But did I never speak of° all that time?   *during*
FIRST SERVANT   Oh, yes, my lord, but very idle words.
    For though you lay here in this goodly chamber,
    Yet would you say ye were beaten out of door
    And rail upon the hostess of the house°   *tavern*
85   And say you would present° her at the leet°   *accuse / local court*
    Because she brought stone jugs and no sealed quarts.[6]
    Sometimes you would call out for Cicely Hackett.
BEGGAR   Ay, the woman's maid of the house.
THIRD SERVANT   Why, sir, you know no house nor no such maid,
90   Nor no such men as you have reckoned up,
    As Stephen Sly and old John Naps of Greet[7]
    And Peter Turf and Henry Pimpernel
    And twenty more such names and men as these,
    Which never were nor no man ever saw.
95 BEGGAR   Now Lord be thankèd for my good amends.°   *recovery*
ALL   Amen.
BEGGAR   I thank thee; thou shalt not lose by it.
      Enter [Bartholomew the PAGE,[8] *disguised as a] lady,*
      with Attendants.
PAGE   How fares my noble lord?
BEGGAR   Marry,[9] I fare° well, for here is cheer° enough.   *get on; feed / food*
    Where is my wife?
100 PAGE   Here, noble lord. What is thy will with her?
BEGGAR   Are you my wife and will not call me "husband"?
    My men should call me "lord"; I am your goodman.[1]
PAGE   My husband and my lord, my lord and husband:
    I am your wife in all obedience.
105 BEGGAR   I know it well. —What must I call her?
LORD   "Madam."
BEGGAR   "Alice Madam" or "Joan Madam"?[2]
LORD   "Madam" and nothing else: so lords call ladies.
BEGGAR   Madam wife, they say that I have dreamed
    And slept above some fifteen year or more.
110 PAGE   Ay, and the time seems thirty unto me,
    Being all this time abandoned° from your bed.   *banned*
BEGGAR   'Tis much. Servants, leave me and her alone.
      [Exeunt LORD *and* SERVANTS.][3]

---

6. She served from unmarked stone jugs rather than
from the officially measured and stamped ("sealed")
quarts.
7. Greet is a small village not far from Stratford. The
names may be those of Stratford citizens.
8. TEXTUAL COMMENT Editors have often referred to
the page as Bartholomew, the name by which the
Lord addresses him, but as it does with the Beggar,
this edition uses *"Page"* to emphasize the character's
societal role rather than his individuality. See Digital
Edition TC 3.
9. Mild oath, derived from the Virgin Mary's name.

1. Husband: a term normally not used by lords.
2. Misusing the usual title for a noblewoman. "Alice"
and "Joan" are names rarely associated with the
upper classes in Elizabethan texts.
3. TEXTUAL COMMENT The Folio has no stage direction
here that would indicate how the Induction scenes
are distinguished from the Petruccio and Katherina
play or whether the Lord exits with his men, but those
attending on the Beggar probably obey his command
and leave the stage along with the Lord here. See
Digital Edition TC 4.

Madam, undress you and come now to bed.
PAGE   Thrice noble lord, let me entreat of you
115   To pardon me yet for a night or two,
Or if not so, until the sun be set.
For your physicians have expressly charged,
In peril to incur[4] your former malady,
That I should yet absent me from your bed.
120   I hope this reason stands for my excuse.
BEGGAR   Ay, it stands[5] so that I may hardly tarry° so long. But   *delay*
I would be loath to fall into my dreams again. I will there-
fore tarry in despite of the flesh and the blood.
          Enter a MESSENGER.
MESSENGER   Your honor's players, hearing your amendment,
125   Are come to play a pleasant comedy.
For so your doctors hold it very meet,°   *suitable*
Seeing too much sadness hath congealed your blood
And melancholy is the nurse of frenzy,[6]
Therefore they thought it good you hear a play
130   And frame your mind to mirth and merriment,
Which bars° a thousand harms and lengthens life.   *prevents*
BEGGAR   Marry, I will let them play it. Is not a comonty° a   *(for "comedy")*
Christmas gambol° or a tumbling trick?   *frolic; game*
PAGE   No, my good lord, it is more pleasing stuff.
135   BEGGAR   What, household stuff?°   *furnishings; events*
PAGE   It is a kind of history.°   *story*
BEGGAR   Well, we'll see't.   [*Exit* MESSENGER.]
Come, madam wife, sit by my side,
And let the world slip. We shall ne'er be younger.[7]
          [BEGGAR *and* PAGE *sit and watch the play.*]

1.1

          Flourish.° Enter LUCENTIO *and his man* TRANIO.   *Fanfare of trumpets*
LUCENTIO   Tranio, since for° the great desire I had   *because of*
To see fair Padua, nursery of arts,[1]
I am arrived for° fruitful Lombardy,   *before*
The pleasant garden of great Italy,
5   And by my father's love and leave am armed
With his good will and thy good company—
My trusty servant well approved° in all—   *reliable*
Here let us breathe° and haply institute   *pause; rest*
A course of learning and ingenious° studies.   *liberal; intellectual*
10   Pisa, renownèd for grave citizens,
Gave me my being and my father first,°   *before me*
A merchant of great traffic° through the world,   *business*
Vincentio, come of the Bentivolii.[2]
Vincentio's son, brought up in Florence,
15   It shall become° to serve° all hopes conceived,[3]   *befit / fulfill*

4. *In peril to incur:* Because of the risk of bringing on.
5. Punning on "stand" as meaning "to have an erection."
6. According to Renaissance humoral theory, excessive sadness could cause thickening of the blood and thus delirium, or "frenzy." *nurse:* nourisher.
7. PERFORMANCE COMMENT As the Induction scenes are among the very few that Shakespeare set in Elizabethan England, some modern directors have chosen to establish that historical context, while others seek

to update it by presenting Sly as a contemporary of the audience's. See Digital Edition PC 1.
1.1 Location: A street in Padua.
1. A center for learning ("arts"). Padua's famous university attracted some English students in Shakespeare's time and was renowned for the study of law and medicine.
2. Descended from the Bentivolii (perhaps a reference to the famous Bentivoglio family of Bologna).
3. That is, by relatives and friends.

To deck° his fortune with his virtuous deeds.   *adorn*
And therefore, Tranio, for the time I study
Virtue, and that part of philosophy
Will I apply° that treats of happiness   *pursue; study*
20   By virtue specially to be achieved.
Tell me thy mind, for I have Pisa left
And am to Padua come as he that leaves
A shallow plash° to plunge him in the deep,   *pool*
And with satiety seeks to quench his thirst.
25   TRANIO   *Mi pardonato*,° gentle master mine,   *Pardon me*
I am in all affected° as yourself;   *inclined*
Glad that you thus continue your resolve
To suck the sweets of sweet philosophy.
Only, good master, while we do admire
30   This virtue and this moral discipline,
Let's be no stoics nor no stocks,[4] I pray,
Or so devote to Aristotle's checks[5]
As Ovid be an outcast quite abjured.[6]
Balk logic° with acquaintance that you have,   *Bandy words*
35   And practice rhetoric in your common talk.
Music and poesy use to quicken° you.   *revive; animate*
The mathematics and the metaphysics,
Fall to them as you find your stomach° serves you.   *appetite*
No profit grows where is no pleasure ta'en:
40   In brief, sir, study what you most affect.°   *like*
LUCENTIO   Gramercies,° Tranio, well dost thou advise.   *Thank you*
If, Biondello, thou wert come ashore,[7]
We could at once put us in readiness
And take a lodging fit to entertain
45   Such friends as time in Padua shall beget.
But stay a while, what company is this?
TRANIO   Master, some show to welcome us to town.
    Enter BAPTISTA *with his two daughters,* KATHERINA
    and BIANCA; GREMIO, *a pantaloon,*[8] [*and*] HORTENSIO,
    [*suitor*] *to Bianca.* LUCENTIO [*and*] TRANIO *stand by.*
BAPTISTA   Gentlemen, importune° me no farther,   *pester*
For how I firmly am resolved you know:
50   That is, not to bestow° my youngest daughter   *give in marriage*
Before I have a husband for the elder.
If either of you both love Katherina,
Because I know you well and love you well,
Leave shall you have to court her at your pleasure.
55   GREMIO   To cart her[9] rather. She's too rough for me.
There, there, Hortensio, will you° any wife?   *do you want*
KATHERINA[1] [*to* BAPTISTA]   I pray you, sir, is it your will

---

4. Wooden posts devoid of feeling. Punning on "stoics," the Greek philosophers who advocated both indifference to pleasure or pain and patient endurance.
5. Restraints. Aristotle defined virtue as a mean, the avoiding of excess (or deficiency).
6. As . . . *abjured*: That Ovid be renounced. Ovid was a Roman poet whose erotic writings were popular in the Renaissance. His *Ars Amatoria* (*The Art of Love*) is mentioned by Lucentio at 4.2.8.
7. Padua, an inland city, did not have a port. Shakespeare's knowledge of Italian geography seems to have been shaky.

8. Foolish old man: a stock character from the Italian *commedia dell'arte* whose usual role was to hinder young lovers.
9. To carry her through the street in, or tied to, a cart. This was a common punishment for disorderly women.
1. TEXTUAL COMMENT Although F uses "*Kate*" or "*Kat*" as the speech prefix and "*Katerina*" or "*Katherina*" in the stage directions for this character, this edition consistently uses "*Katherina*" (pronounced with a "t" rather than a "th" sound). Petruccio's shortening of her name to "Kate" is one of the ways by which he attempts to assert his authority over her. See Digital Edition TC 5.

To make a stale of me[2] amongst these mates?°   *fellows; husbands*
HORTENSIO   "Mates," maid? How mean you that? No mates
   for you,
60   Unless you were of gentler, milder mold.°   *nature*
KATHERINA   I'faith, sir, you shall never need to fear;
   Iwis it is not halfway to her heart.[3]
   But if it were, doubt not, her care should be
   To comb your noddle° with a three-legged stool   *hit your head*
65   And paint° your face and use you like a fool.   *(with blood)*
HORTENSIO   From all such devils, good Lord deliver us.
GREMIO   And me too, good Lord.
TRANIO   Hush, master, here's some good pastime toward;°   *in view*
   That wench is stark mad or wonderful froward.°   *incredibly willful*
70   LUCENTIO   But in the other's silence do I see
   Maid's mild behavior and sobriety.
   Peace, Tranio.
TRANIO   Well said, master; mum and gaze your fill.
BAPTISTA   Gentlemen, that I may soon make good
75   What I have said —Bianca, get you in,
   And let it not displease thee, good Bianca,
   For I will love thee ne'er the less, my girl.
KATHERINA   A pretty peat.° It is best put finger in the eye,[4] an°   *pet; spoiled child / if*
   she knew why.
80   BIANCA   Sister, content you° in my discontent.   *satisfy yourself*
   [*to* BAPTISTA] Sir, to your pleasure° humbly I subscribe:°   *will / submit*
   My books and instruments shall be my company,
   On them to look and practice by myself.
LUCENTIO   Hark, Tranio, thou mayst hear Minerva[5] speak.
85   HORTENSIO   Signor Baptista, will you be so strange?°   *unnatural; cruel*
   Sorry am I that our good will effects°   *causes*
   Bianca's grief.
GREMIO   Why, will you mew° her up,   *confine (like a falcon)*
   Signor Baptista, for° this fiend of hell,   *because of*
   And make her bear the penance° of her tongue?   *punishment*
90   BAPTISTA   Gentlemen, content ye; I am resolved.
   Go in, Bianca.   [*Exit* BIANCA.]
   And for I know she taketh most delight
   In music, instruments, and poetry,
   Schoolmasters will I keep within my house,
95   Fit to instruct her youth. If you, Hortensio,
   Or Signor Gremio, you, know any such,
   Prefer° them hither; for to cunning° men   *Recommend / skillful*
   I will be very kind and liberal
   To mine own children in good bringing up.
100 And so farewell. Katherina, you may stay,
   For I have more to commune with Bianca.   *Exit.*
KATHERINA   Why, and I trust I may go too, may I not? What,
   shall I be appointed hours, as though, belike, I knew not
   what to take and what to leave? Ha.   *Exit.*

2. To make me a laughingstock or a prostitute or a   here.)
decoy (for Bianca).   4. *put finger in the eye*: to weep.
3. Certainly, marriage does not even half interest   5. Roman goddess of wisdom.
her. (Katherina speaks of herself in the third person

105 GREMIO You may go to the devil's dam!⁶ Your gifts are so
good here's none will hold° you. Their love⁷ is not so great, *tolerate*
Hortensio, but we may blow our nails° together and fast it *wait patiently*
fairly out.⁸ Our cake's dough on both sides.⁹ Farewell. Yet
for the love I bear my sweet Bianca, if I can by any means
110 light on a fit man to teach her that wherein she delights, I
will wish° him to her father. *recommend*

HORTENSIO So will I, Signor Gremio. But a word, I pray.
Though the nature of our quarrel yet never brooked parle,¹
know now upon advice° it toucheth° us both—that we may *reflection / concerns*
115 yet again have access to our fair mistress and be happy rivals
in Bianca's love—to labor and effect one thing specially.

GREMIO What's that, I pray?

HORTENSIO Marry, sir, to get a husband for her sister.

GREMIO A husband? A devil!

120 HORTENSIO I say a husband.

GREMIO I say a devil. Think'st thou, Hortensio, though her
father be very rich, any man is so very° a fool to be married *completely*
to hell?

HORTENSIO Tush, Gremio. Though it pass° your patience and *exceeds*
125 mine to endure her loud alarums,° why, man, there be good *calls to arms; scoldings*
fellows in the world, an° a man could light on them, would *if*
take her with all faults, and money enough.

GREMIO I cannot tell, but I had as lief° take her dowry with *would as willingly*
this condition: to be whipped at the high cross² every
130 morning.

HORTENSIO Faith, as you say, there's small choice in rotten
apples. But come, since this bar in law° makes us friends, it *legal obstacle*
shall be so far forth friendly maintained³ till by helping Baptista's eldest daughter to a husband, we set his youngest free
135 for a husband, and then have to't° afresh. Sweet Bianca! *begin the fight*
Happy man be his dole;⁴ he that runs fastest, gets the ring.⁵
How say you, Signor Gremio?

GREMIO I am agreed, and would I had given him the best
horse in Padua to begin his wooing that would thoroughly
140 woo her, wed her, and bed her, and rid the house of her.
Come on.

Exeunt GREMIO *and* HORTENSIO. TRANIO *and*
LUCENTIO *remain.*

TRANIO I pray, sir, tell me, is it possible
That love should of a sudden take such hold?

LUCENTIO O Tranio, till I found it to be true,
145 I never thought it possible or likely.
But see, while idly I stood looking on,
I found the effect of love-in-idleness⁶
And now in plainness do confess to thee,
That art to me as secret° and as dear *intimate*

6. The devil's mother, imagined as the stereotypical
shrew and said to be worse than the devil himself.
7. Love of them (that is, of women).
8. And abstain as best we can.
9. Proverbial expression of failure.
1. *brooked parle:* permitted discussion.
2. Cross set on a pedestal in the town center, the
normal site for punishment in an English village.
3. *it . . . maintained:* we'll pursue the matter as friends.

4. May the winner's fate be that of a happy man.
5. A proverb alluding to the ring that riders in a
jousting match try to catch on their lances. Also punning on "ring" as referring to both "wedding ring"
and female genitalia.
6. Punning on a flower known as "love-in-idleness,"
whose juice was thought to induce love. (See *A Midsummer Night's Dream* 2.1.166–68.)

150	As Anna[7] to the Queen of Carthage was:	
	Tranio, I burn, I pine, I perish, Tranio,	
	If I achieve not this young modest girl.	
	Counsel me, Tranio, for I know thou canst;	
	Assist me, Tranio, for I know thou wilt.	
155	TRANIO Master, it is no time to chide you now;	
	Affection is not rated° from the heart.	*driven out by scolding*
	If love have touched you, naught remains but so,	
	Redime te captum quam queas minimo.[8]	
	LUCENTIO Gramercies,° lad! Go forward, this contents;	*Thanks*
160	The rest will comfort, for thy counsel's sound.	
	TRANIO Master, you looked so longly° on the maid	*persistently*
	Perhaps you marked not what's the pith° of all.	*main point*
	LUCENTIO Oh, yes, I saw sweet beauty in her face,	
	Such as the daughter of Agenor[9] had	
165	That made great Jove to humble him to her hand	
	When with his knees he kissed the Cretan strand.	
	TRANIO Saw you no more? Marked you not how her sister	
	Began to scold and raise up such a storm	
	That mortal ears might hardly endure the din?	
170	LUCENTIO Tranio, I saw her coral lips to move	
	And with her breath she did perfume the air;	
	Sacred and sweet was all I saw in her.	
	TRANIO Nay, then 'tis time to stir him from his trance.	
	—I pray, awake, sir! If you love the maid,	
175	Bend thoughts and wits to achieve her. Thus it stands:	
	Her elder sister is so curst° and shrewd°	*quarrelsome / shrewish*
	That till the father rid his hands of her,	
	Master, your love must live a maid at home,	
	And therefore has he closely mewed her up	
180	Because° she will not be annoyed with° suitors.	*So that / troubled with*
	LUCENTIO Ah, Tranio, what a cruel father's he.	
	But art thou not advised,° he took some care	*aware*
	To get her cunning schoolmasters to instruct her?	
	TRANIO Ay, marry am I, sir, and now 'tis plotted.	
	LUCENTIO I have it, Tranio.	
185	TRANIO Master, for° my hand,	*by*
	Both our inventions° meet and jump° in one.	*schemes / agree*
	LUCENTIO Tell me thine first.	
	TRANIO You will be schoolmaster	
	And undertake the teaching of the maid:	
	That's your device.°	*plan*
	LUCENTIO It is. May it be done?	
190	TRANIO Not possible: for who shall bear your part	
	And be in Padua here Vincentio's son,	
	Keep house and ply his book,° welcome his friends,	*study*
	Visit his countrymen and banquet them?	
	LUCENTIO *Basta,*° content thee, for I have it full.°	*Enough / fully planned*

7. Sister to Dido, Queen of Carthage. In both Virgil's *Aeneid* and Christopher Marlowe's *Dido, Queen of Carthage* (1594), Dido tells Anna of her secret love for Aeneas.

8. Latin: Ransom yourself from captivity at the lowest possible price. A phrase from Terence, quoted as it appears in William Lily's *A Short Introduction of Grammar*, a standard Elizabethan school text.

9. Europa. Jove transformed himself into a bull and carried her across the sea to Crete to rape her.

195 We have not yet been seen in any house,
  Nor can we be distinguished by our faces
  For man or master. Then it follows thus:
  Thou shalt be master, Tranio, in my stead,
  Keep house and port° and servants, as I should; *social position*
200 I will some other be, some Florentine,
  Some Neapolitan, or meaner° man of Pisa. *poorer*
  'Tis hatched and shall be so. Tranio, at once
  Uncase° thee: take my colored hat and cloak.[1] *Undress*
   [TRANIO *and* LUCENTIO *exchange clothes.*][2]
  When Biondello comes, he waits on thee,
205 But I will charm° him first to keep his tongue. *persuade; use magic on*
 TRANIO So had you need.
  In brief, sir, since it your pleasure is
  And I am tied to be obedient—
  For so your father charged me at our parting:
210 "Be serviceable° to my son," quoth he, *diligent in service*
  Although I think 'twas in another sense—
  I am content to be Lucentio,
  Because so well I love Lucentio.
 LUCENTIO Tranio, be so, because Lucentio loves,
215 And let me be a slave t'achieve that maid
  Whose sudden sight hath thralled° my wounded[3] eye. *enslaved*
   Enter BIONDELLO.
  Here comes the rogue. Sirrah, where have you been?
 BIONDELLO Where have I been? Nay, how now, where are
  you? Master, has my fellow Tranio stolen your clothes, or
220 you stolen his, or both? Pray, what's the news?
 LUCENTIO Sirrah, come hither; 'tis no time to jest,
  And therefore frame your manners to the time.
  Your fellow Tranio here, to save my life,
  Puts my apparel and my countenance on,
225 And I for my escape have put on his:
  For in a quarrel since I came ashore
  I killed a man and fear I was descried.° *observed*
  Wait you on him, I charge you, as becomes,° *is fitting*
  While I make way from hence to save my life.
  You understand me?
230 BIONDELLO   Ay, sir; ne'er a whit.° *not at all*
 LUCENTIO And not a jot of "Tranio" in your mouth;
  Tranio is changed into Lucentio.
 BIONDELLO The better for him; would I were so, too.
 TRANIO So could I, faith, boy, to have the next wish after,
235 That Lucentio indeed had Baptista's youngest daughter.
  But, sirrah, not for my sake, but your master's, I advise
  You use your manners discreetly in all kind of companies.
  When I am alone, why, then I am Tranio,
  But in all places else, your master Lucentio.

---

1. The outfit of an Elizabethan gentleman. Servants usually wore uniforms, like the "blue coats" of Petruccio's servants (4.1.76–77).
2. F does not indicate at what point in this exchange Lucentio and Tranio trade clothes; perhaps they begin during Lucentio's previous speech. This exchange of clothes, emphasizing the ease with which social identity is shifted, is an important visual enactment of one of the play's main preoccupations.
3. Wounded by Cupid's arrow.

240 LUCENTIO Tranio, let's go.
　　One thing more rests° that thyself execute:°　　　　　　　　*remains / must do*
　　To make one among these wooers. If thou ask me why,
　　Sufficeth my reasons are both good and weighty.　　*Exeunt.*
　　　　The Presenters[4] above speak.
　　SERVANT My lord, you nod; you do not mind° the play.　　　　*pay attention to*
245 BEGGAR Yes, by Saint Anne,[5] do I, a good matter surely. Comes
　　there any more of it?
　　PAGE My lord, 'tis but begun.
　　BEGGAR 'Tis a very excellent piece of work, madam lady. Would
　　'twere done.
　　　　They sit and mark.°　　　　　　　　　　　　　　　　*observe*

1.2

　　　　Enter PETRUCCIO *and his man* GRUMIO.
　　PETRUCCIO Verona, for a while I take my leave
　　To see my friends in Padua, but of all
　　My best belovèd and approvèd friend,
　　Hortensio. And I trow° this is his house.　　　　　　　　　*believe*
5　　Here, sirrah Grumio, knock, I say.
　　GRUMIO Knock, sir? Whom should I knock? Is there any man
　　has rebused[1] your worship?
　　PETRUCCIO Villain, I say, knock me here[2] soundly.
　　GRUMIO Knock you here, sir? Why, sir, what am I, sir, that I
10　　should knock you here, sir?
　　PETRUCCIO Villain, I say, knock me at this gate,
　　And rap me well or I'll knock your knave's pate.°　　　　　*head*
　　GRUMIO My master is grown quarrelsome. I should knock
　　　　you first,
　　And then I know after who comes by the worst.[3]
15　PETRUCCIO Will it not be?
　　Faith, sirrah, an° you'll not knock, I'll ring it.[4]　　　　　*if*
　　I'll try how you can *sol-fa*° and sing it.　　　　　　　*sing a scale*
　　　　He wrings him by the ears.
　　GRUMIO Help, masters, help! My master is mad.
　　PETRUCCIO Now knock when I bid you, sirrah villain.
　　　　Enter HORTENSIO.
20　HORTENSIO How now, what's the matter? My old friend
　　Grumio and my good friend Petruccio? How do you all at
　　Verona?
　　PETRUCCIO Signor Hortensio, come you to part the fray?
　　Con tutto il cuore ben trovato,[5] may I say.
25　HORTENSIO *Alla nostra casa ben venuto,*
　　Molto honorato signor mio Petruccio.[6]
　　Rise, Grumio, rise, we will compound° this quarrel.　　　　*settle*
　　GRUMIO Nay, 'tis no matter, sir, what he 'lleges° in Latin. If　　*alleges*
　　this be not a lawful cause for me to leave his service— Look

---

4. Figures who introduce and comment on the action of a play for the audience.
5. A common oath. Saint Anne was the mother of the Virgin Mary and the patron saint of married women.
1.2 Location: In front of Hortensio's house in Padua.
1. Grumio regularly blunders and puns. Here he means "abused" or "rebuked," or perhaps both.
2. Knock here for me: a conventional usage that Gru-

mio misunderstands or pretends to understand as "strike me." *Villain:* low-born man (often a contemptuous term of address).
3. *I should . . . worst:* You want me to give the first blow, but then I know I'd have the worst of it.
4. I'll ring the bell; with a pun on "wring."
5. With all my heart, welcome (Italian).
6. Welcome to our house, my most honored Signor Petruccio.

30 you, sir: he bid me knock him and rap him soundly, sir.
Well, was it fit for a servant to use his master so, being per-
haps, for aught I see, two-and-thirty, a pip out?⁷
Whom would to God I had well knocked at first,
Then had not Grumio come by the worst.

35 PETRUCCIO A senseless villain. Good Hortensio,
I bade the rascal knock upon your gate
And could not get him for my heart to do it.

GRUMIO Knock at the gate? O heavens, spoke you not these
words plain? "Sirrah, knock me here, rap me here, knock me
40 well, and knock me soundly"? And come you now with
knocking at the gate?

PETRUCCIO Sirrah, be gone, or talk not, I advise you.

HORTENSIO Petruccio, patience; I am Grumio's pledge.°   *guarantor*
Why this' a heavy chance⁸ twixt him and you,
45 Your ancient,° trusty, pleasant servant Grumio.   *long-standing*
And tell me now, sweet friend, what happy gale
Blows you to Padua here from old Verona?

PETRUCCIO Such wind as scatters young men through the
world
To seek their fortunes farther than at home,
50 Where small experience grows. But in a few,°   *in short*
Signor Hortensio, thus it stands with me:
Antonio, my father, is deceased,
And I have thrust myself into this maze,⁹
Haply to wive and thrive as best I may.
55 Crowns° in my purse I have, and goods at home,   *Five-shilling coins*
And so am come abroad to see the world.

HORTENSIO Petruccio, shall I then come roundly° to thee   *speak plainly*
And wish thee to a shrewd, ill-favored wife?
Thou'dst thank me but a little for my counsel;
60 And yet I'll promise thee she shall be rich
And very rich. But thou'rt too much my friend,
And I'll not wish thee to her.

PETRUCCIO Signor Hortensio, twixt such friends as we,
Few words suffice; and therefore if thou know
65 One rich enough to be Petruccio's wife—
As wealth is burden° of my wooing dance—   *refrain; chief theme*
Be she as foul° as was Florentius' love,¹   *ugly*
As old as Sibyl,² and as curst and shrewd
As Socrates' Xanthippe,³ or a worse,
70 She moves° me not, or not° removes, at least,°   *annoys / nor / at all*
Affection's edge° in me, were she as rough   *intensity*
As are the swelling Adriatic seas.
I come to wive it wealthily in Padua;
If wealthily, then happily in Padua.

7. Drunk; a bit crazy. Probably alluding to the card game one-and-thirty, in which the aim is to accumulate exactly thirty-one points. To collect thirty-two means the player has overshot or been excessive. A "pip" is a spot on a card; hence, "a pip out" means "off by one."
8. *Why . . . chance*: This is a sad occurrence.
9. This uncertain world; this unpredictable business of "wiving and thriving."
1. Florent, the knight in John Gower's *Confessio*

Amantis, who had to marry the ugly old woman who had saved his life by answering a riddle he had been commanded to solve. On their wedding night, as a reward for his compliance, she became young and beautiful. A version of this story also appears in Chaucer's *Wife of Bath's Tale*.
2. The Cumaean Sibyl, a prophetess in classical mythology, had immortality without eternal youth.
3. The philosopher's notoriously shrewish wife.

75 GRUMIO [*to* HORTENSIO]   Nay, look you, sir, he tells you flatly
  what his mind is. Why, give him gold enough and marry him
  to a puppet or an aglet-baby,[4] or an old trot° with ne'er a   *hag*
  tooth in her head, though she have as many diseases as two
  and fifty horses. Why, nothing comes amiss, so money comes
80 withal.°   *with it*
  HORTENSIO Petruccio, since we are stepped thus far in,
   I will continue that° I broached in jest.   *what*
   I can, Petruccio, help thee to a wife
   With wealth enough, and young and beauteous,
85   Brought up as best becomes a gentlewoman.
   Her only fault, and that is faults enough,
   Is that she is intolerable curst°   *shrewish*
   And shrewd and froward,° so beyond all measure *willful*
   That were my state° far worser than it is,   *fortune*
90   I would not wed her for a mine of gold.
  PETRUCCIO Hortensio, peace; thou know'st not gold's effect.
   Tell me her father's name and 'tis enough,
   For I will board[5] her, though she chide as loud
   As thunder when the clouds in autumn crack.
95 HORTENSIO Her father is Baptista Minola,
   An affable° and courteous gentleman;   *pleasant*
   Her name is Katherina Minola,
   Renowned in Padua for her scolding tongue.
  PETRUCCIO I know her father, though I know not her,
100 And he knew my deceasèd father well.
   I will not sleep, Hortensio, till I see her,
   And therefore let me be thus bold with you
   To give you over° at this first encounter—   *leave you*
   Unless you will accompany me thither.
105 GRUMIO [*to* HORTENSIO]   I pray you, sir, let him go while the
  humor° lasts. O' my word, an she knew him as well as I do, *mood*
  she would think scolding would do little good upon him.
  She may perhaps call him half a score knaves or so. Why,
  that's nothing; an he begin once, he'll rail in his rope tricks.[6]
110 I'll tell you what, sir, an she stand° him but a little, he will *withstand; arouse*
  throw a figure[7] in her face and so disfigure her with it that
  she shall have no more eyes to see withal than a cat. You
  know him not, sir.
  HORTENSIO Tarry, Petruccio, I must go with thee,
115 For in Baptista's keep° my treasure is.   *custody; stronghold*
   He hath the jewel of my life in hold,
   His youngest daughter, beautiful Bianca,
   And her withholds from me and other more,° *others besides*
   Suitors to her and rivals in my love,
120 Supposing it a thing impossible,
   For those defects I have before rehearsed,
   That ever Katherina will be wooed.
   Therefore this order hath Baptista ta'en:

---

4. Small figure used as a tag or an ornament on dresses, laces, and other goods.
5. Woo aggressively; go aboard, as in a sea battle; have sexual intercourse with.
6. An obscure phrase: "rope tricks" may refer to rhe-torical or sexual feats. Grumio's point seems to be that when Petruccio "rails," he will be more aggressive than Katherina.
7. A figure of speech.

That none shall have access unto Bianca
125 Till Katherine the Curst have got a husband.
GRUMIO   "Katherine the Curst,"
A title for a maid of all titles the worst.
HORTENSIO   Now shall my friend Petruccio do me grace°   *a favor*
And offer me disguised in sober robes
130 To old Baptista as a schoolmaster
Well seen° in music to instruct Bianca,   *skilled*
That so I may by this device at least
Have leave and leisure to make love to her
And unsuspected court her by herself.
      Enter GREMIO [*with a paper*][8] *and* LUCENTIO *disguised*
      [*as Cambio, a schoolmaster*].
135 GRUMIO   Here's no knavery![9] See, to beguile the old folks,
how the young folks lay their heads together. —Master,
master, look about you. Who goes there, ha?
HORTENSIO   Peace, Grumio, it is the rival of my love.
Petruccio, stand by a while.
140 GRUMIO   A proper stripling° and an amorous.   *handsome youth (ironic)*
      [HORTENSIO, PETRUCCIO, *and* GRUMIO *stand aside*.]
GREMIO   Oh, very well, I have perused the note.°   *listing of books*
Hark you, sir, I'll have them° very fairly bound—   *(the books)*
All books of love, see that at any hand°—   *in any case*
And see you read no other lectures to her;
145 You understand me. Over and beside
Signor Baptista's liberality
I'll mend° it with a largesse.° Take your paper, too,   *increase / gift*
And let me have them very well perfumed,
For she is sweeter than perfume itself
150 To whom they go to. What will you read to her?
LUCENTIO   Whate'er I read to her, I'll plead for you
As for my patron, stand you so assured,
As firmly as yourself were still in place;°   *always present*
Yea, and perhaps with more successful words
155 Than you, unless you were a scholar, sir.
GREMIO   Oh, this learning, what a thing it is!
GRUMIO   Oh, this woodcock,[1] what an ass it is!
PETRUCCIO [*to* GRUMIO]   Peace, sirrah.
HORTENSIO   Grumio, mum. —God save you, Signor Gremio.
160 GREMIO   And you are well met, Signor Hortensio.
Trow° you whither I am going? To Baptista Minola.   *Know*
I promised to enquire carefully
About a schoolmaster for the fair Bianca,
And by good fortune I have lighted well
165 On this young man, for learning and behavior
Fit for her turn,° well-read in poetry   *use*
And other books, good ones, I warrant ye.
HORTENSIO   'Tis well. And I have met a gentleman
Hath promised me to help one to another,

---

8. Presumably Lucentio's list of books for Bianca's studies.
9. Spoken sarcastically; perhaps referring to the plotting of Petruccio and Hortensio rather than to

that of Gremio and Lucentio, whom Grumio may not yet have seen.
1. Wild bird easily caught and so thought to be stupid.

170	A fine musician to instruct our mistress;	
	So shall I no whit be behind in duty	
	To fair Bianca, so beloved of me.	
	GREMIO Beloved of me, and that my deeds shall prove.	
	GRUMIO And that his bags° shall prove.	*money bags*
175	HORTENSIO Gremio, 'tis now no time to vent° our love.	*express*
	Listen to me and if you speak me fair,°	*courteously*
	I'll tell you news indifferent° good for either.	*equally*
	Here is a gentleman, whom by chance I met,	
	Upon agreement from us to his liking°	*If we accept his terms*
180	Will undertake to woo curst Katherine,	
	Yea, and to marry her, if her dowry please.	
	GREMIO So said, so done, is well.	
	Hortensio, have you told him all her faults?	
	PETRUCCIO I know she is an irksome brawling scold.	
185	If that be all, masters, I hear no harm.	
	GREMIO No, say'st me so, friend? What countryman?	
	PETRUCCIO Born in Verona, old Antonio's son.	
	My father dead, my fortune lives for me,°	*is mine*
	And I do hope good days and long to see.	
190	GREMIO O sir, such a life with such a wife were strange.°	*unknown; rare*
	But if you have a stomach, to't o'God's name;	
	You shall have me assisting you in all.	
	But will you woo this wildcat?	
	PETRUCCIO Will I live?	
	GRUMIO Will he woo her? Ay, or I'll hang her.	
195	PETRUCCIO Why came I hither but to that intent?	
	Think you a little din can daunt mine ears?	
	Have I not in my time heard lions roar?	
	Have I not heard the sea, puffed up with winds,	
	Rage like an angry boar chafed with sweat?	
200	Have I not heard great ordnance° in the field,	*cannon*
	And heaven's artillery thunder in the skies?	
	Have I not in a pitched battle heard	
	Loud larums,° neighing steeds, and trumpets clang?	*calls to arms*
	And do you tell me of a woman's tongue	
205	That gives not half so great a blow° to hear	*loud noise*
	As will a chestnut in a farmer's fire?	
	Tush, tush, fear° boys with bugs.°	*frighten / bogeymen*
	GRUMIO For he fears none.	
	GREMIO Hortensio, hark:	
	This gentleman is happily° arrived,	*fortunately*
210	My mind presumes, for his own good and yours.	
	HORTENSIO I promised we would be contributors	
	And bear his charge° of wooing whatsoe'er.	*expense*
	GREMIO And so we will, provided that he win her.	
	GRUMIO I would I were as sure of a good dinner.	
	Enter TRANIO, *brave*°[, *as Lucentio*]*, and* BIONDELLO.	*richly dressed*
215	TRANIO Gentlemen, God save you. If I may be bold,	
	Tell me, I beseech you, which is the readiest way	
	To the house of Signor Baptista Minola?	
	BIONDELLO He that has the two fair daughters: is't he you	
	mean?	
220	TRANIO Even he, Biondello.	
	GREMIO Hark you, sir, you mean not her to—	

TRANIO   Perhaps him and her, sir; what have you to do?[2]

PETRUCCIO   Not her that chides, sir, at any hand, I pray.

TRANIO   I love no chiders, sir. Biondello, let's away.

LUCENTIO [aside]   Well begun, Tranio.

225   HORTENSIO   Sir, a word ere you go:
    Are you a suitor to the maid you talk of, yea or no?

TRANIO   An if I be, sir, is it any offense?

GREMIO   No, if without more words you will get you hence.

TRANIO   Why, sir, I pray, are not the streets as free
    For me as for you?

230   GREMIO   But so is not she.

TRANIO   For what reason, I beseech you.

GREMIO   For this reason, if you'll know:
    That she's the choice° love of Signor Gremio.   chosen; excellent

HORTENSIO   That she's the chosen of Signor Hortensio.

235   TRANIO   Softly, my masters. If you be gentlemen
    Do me this right:° hear me with patience.   justice
    Baptista is a noble gentleman
    To whom my father is not all unknown,
    And were his daughter fairer than she is,
240   She may more suitors have, and me for one.
    Fair Leda's daughter[3] had a thousand wooers;
    Then well one more may fair Bianca have.
    And so she shall: Lucentio shall make one,
    Though Paris came[4] in hope to speed° alone.   succeed

245   GREMIO   What, this gentleman will out-talk us all.

LUCENTIO   Sir, give him head; I know he'll prove a jade.°   worn-out horse

PETRUCCIO   Hortensio, to what end are all these words?

HORTENSIO   Sir, let me be so bold as ask you:
    Did you yet ever see Baptista's daughter?

250   TRANIO   No, sir, but hear I do that he hath two:
    The one as famous for a scolding tongue
    As is the other for beauteous modesty.

PETRUCCIO   Sir, sir, the first's for me, let her go by.

GREMIO   Yea, leave that labor to great Hercules,
255   And let it be more than Alcides' twelve.[5]

PETRUCCIO   Sir, understand you this of me, in sooth:°   truth
    The youngest daughter, whom you hearken° for,   lie in wait; yearn
    Her father keeps from all access of suitors
    And will not promise her to any man
260   Until the elder sister first be wed.
    The younger then is free and not before.

TRANIO   If it be so, sir, that you are the man
    Must stead° us all, and me amongst the rest,   help
    An if you break the ice, and do this feat—
265   Achieve° the elder, set the younger free   Win
    For our access—whose hap shall be° to have her   he who is lucky enough
    Will not so graceless be, to be ingrate.°   ungrateful

HORTENSIO   Sir, you say well, and well you do conceive.°   understand
    And since you do profess to be a suitor,

270 You must as we do, gratify° this gentleman,   *reward*
To whom we all rest generally beholden.
TRANIO   Sir, I shall not be slack. In sign whereof,
Please ye we may contrive° this afternoon   *pass, spend (time)*
And quaff carouses° to our mistress' health,   *toasts*
275 And do as adversaries do in law:
Strive mightily, but eat and drink as friends.
GRUMIO, BIONDELLO   Oh, excellent motion!° Fellows, let's be   *proposal*
gone.
HORTENSIO   The motion's good indeed, and be it so.
Petruccio, I shall be your *ben venuto.*°   *Exeunt.*   *welcome (your host)*

2.1

Enter KATHERINA *and* BIANCA [*with her hands tied*].
BIANCA   Good sister, wrong me not, nor wrong yourself
To make a bondmaid° and a slave of me—   *female servant*
That I disdain. But for these other goods,°   *possessions*
Unbind my hands. I'll pull them off myself,
5 Yea, all my raiment to my petticoat,
Or what you will command me will I do,
So well I know my duty to my elders.
KATHERINA   Of all thy suitors here I charge° tell   *command you*
Whom thou lov'st best. See thou dissemble° not.   *deceive*
10 BIANCA   Believe me, sister, of all the men alive,
I never yet beheld that special face
Which I could fancy more than any other.
KATHERINA   Minion,° thou liest. Is't not Hortensio?   *Hussy*
BIANCA   If you affect° him, sister, here I swear   *love*
15 I'll plead for you myself, but you shall have him.
KATHERINA   Oh, then belike you fancy riches more:
You will have Gremio to keep you fair.
BIANCA   Is it for him you do envy me so?
Nay, then, you jest, and now I well perceive
20 You have but jested with me all this while.
I prithee, sister Kate, untie my hands.
     [KATHERINA] *strikes her.*
KATHERINA   If that be jest, then all the rest was so.
     Enter BAPTISTA.
BAPTISTA   Why, how now, dame, whence grows this insolence?
Bianca, stand aside; poor girl, she weeps.
25 Go ply thy needle, meddle not with her.
[*to* KATHERINA] For shame, thou hilding° of a devilish spirit,   *worthless creature*
Why dost thou wrong her, that did ne'er wrong thee?
When did she cross thee with a bitter word?
KATHERINA   Her silence flouts° me, and I'll be revenged.   *mocks*
     [*She*] *flies after* BIANCA.
30 BAPTISTA   What, in my sight? —Bianca, get thee in.
     Exit [BIANCA].
KATHERINA   What, will you not suffer me?° Nay, now I see   *let me have my way*
She is your treasure: she must have a husband,
I must dance barefoot on her wedding day[1]
And, for your love to her, lead apes in hell.[2]

2.1 Location: Baptista's house in Padua.   2. *lead apes in hell:* the proverbial destiny of unmar-
1. Proverbially expected of older unmarried sisters.   ried women.

35 Talk not to me. I will go sit and weep
  Till I can find occasion of revenge.   [*Exit* KATHERINA.]
 BAPTISTA Was ever gentleman thus grieved as I?
  But who comes here?

    Enter GREMIO; LUCENTIO [*disguised as Cambio*] *in the*
    habit of a mean man;° PETRUCCIO *with* [HORTENSIO *man of low social rank*
    disguised as Licio; and] TRANIO [*disguised as Lucentio*]
    with his boy [BIONDELLO] *bearing a lute and books.*

 GREMIO Good morrow, neighbor Baptista.
40 BAPTISTA Good morrow, neighbor Gremio. —God save you,
  gentlemen.
 PETRUCCIO And you, good sir. Pray, have you not a daughter
  Called Katherina, fair and virtuous?
 BAPTISTA I have a daughter, sir, called Katherina.
45 GREMIO [*to* PETRUCCIO] You are too blunt; go to it orderly.° *properly*
 PETRUCCIO You wrong me, Signor Gremio; give me leave.
  —I am a gentleman of Verona, sir,
  That, hearing of her beauty and her wit,
  Her affability and bashful modesty,
50 Her wondrous qualities and mild behavior,
  Am bold to show myself a forward° guest *eager*
  Within your house to make mine eye the witness
  Of that report, which I so oft have heard.
  And for an entrance to my entertainment[3]
55 I do present you with a man of mine,
  Cunning in music and the mathematics,
  To instruct her fully in those sciences,
  Whereof I know she is not ignorant.
  Accept of him, or else you do me wrong.
60 His name is Licio, born in Mantua.
 BAPTISTA You're welcome, sir, and he for your good sake.
  But for my daughter Katherine, this I know:
  She is not for your turn,° the more my grief. *She will not suit you*
 PETRUCCIO I see you do not mean to part with her,
65 Or else you like not of my company.
 BAPTISTA Mistake me not, I speak but as I find.° *as the facts stand*
  Whence are you, sir? What may I call your name?
 PETRUCCIO Petruccio is my name, Antonio's son,
  A man well known throughout all Italy.
70 BAPTISTA I know him well;[4] you are welcome for his sake.
 GREMIO Saving° your tale, Petruccio, I pray let us that are *With all respect to*
  poor petitioners speak too. *Baccare,*° you are marvelous *Stand back (mock Latin)*
  forward.
 PETRUCCIO Oh, pardon me, Signor Gremio; I would fain be
75 doing.[5]
 GREMIO I doubt it not, sir. But you will curse your wooing
  neighbors. [*to* BAPTISTA] This is a gift[6] very grateful,° I am *pleasing*
  sure of it. To express the like kindness, myself, that have
  been more kindly beholden to you than any, freely give unto
80 you this young scholar, that hath been long studying at
  Rheims,[7] as cunning in Greek, Latin, and other languages

---

3. And as an entrance fee for my reception ("entertainment") as a suitor.
4. Baptista probably means he knows him by reputation.
5. I am eager to get on with it (with a pun on "doing" as meaning "have sexual intercourse").
6. That is, Petruccio's gift of Hortensio/Licio.
7. French city famous for its university.

as the other in music and mathematics. His name is Cambio;[8] pray accept his service.

BAPTISTA A thousand thanks, Signor Gremio. Welcome, good
85   Cambio. [*to* TRANIO] But, gentle sir, methinks you walk like
a stranger. May I be so bold to know the cause of your
coming?

TRANIO   Pardon me, sir, the boldness is mine own,
That, being a stranger in this city here,
90   Do make myself a suitor to your daughter,
Unto Bianca, fair and virtuous.
Nor is your firm resolve unknown to me,
In the preferment of the eldest sister.
This liberty is all that I request:
95   That upon knowledge of my parentage,
I may have welcome 'mongst the rest that woo
And free access and favor as the rest.
And toward the education of your daughters,
I here bestow a simple instrument
100   And this small packet of Greek and Latin books.
If you accept them, then their worth is great.

BAPTISTA   Lucentio is your name;[9] of whence, I pray?

TRANIO   Of Pisa, sir, son to Vincentio.

BAPTISTA   A mighty man of Pisa; by report
105   I know him well. You are very welcome, sir.
[*to* HORTENSIO] Take you the lute [*to* LUCENTIO] and you the
    set of books;
You shall go see your pupils presently.°   *immediately*
Holla, within!
      Enter a SERVANT.
          Sirrah, lead these gentlemen
To my daughters, and tell them both
110   These are their tutors; bid them use them well.
      [*Exit* SERVANT *with* HORTENSIO *and* LUCENTIO.]
We will go walk a little in the orchard°   *garden*
And then to dinner. You are passing° welcome,   *extremely*
And so I pray you all to think yourselves.

PETRUCCIO   Signor Baptista, my business asketh haste,
115   And every day I cannot come to woo.
You knew my father well and in him me,
Left solely heir to all his lands and goods,
Which I have bettered rather than decreased.
Then tell me, if I get your daughter's love,
120   What dowry shall I have with her to wife?

BAPTISTA   After my death, the one half of my lands,
And in possession° twenty thousand crowns.   *upon the marriage*

PETRUCCIO   And for that dowry I'll assure her of
Her widowhood,[1] be it that she survive me,
125   In all my lands and leases whatsoever.
Let specialties° be therefore drawn between us,   *explicit contracts*
That covenants may be kept on either hand.

BAPTISTA   Ay, when the special thing is well obtained—
That is her love, for that is all in all.

---

8. Italian for "exchange."   the name in one of the schoolbooks.
9. How Baptista knows this is unclear. He may read   1. Widow's share of the estate.

130   PETRUCCIO   Why, that is nothing. For I tell you, father,
        I am as peremptory° as she proud minded,   *stubborn*
        And where two raging fires meet together
        They do consume the thing that feeds their fury.
        Though little fire grows great with little wind,
135   Yet extreme gusts will blow out fire and all.[2]
        So I to her and so she yields to me,
        For I am rough and woo not like a babe.
        BAPTISTA   Well mayst thou woo, and happy be thy speed;°   *fortune*
        But be thou armed for some unhappy words.
140   PETRUCCIO   Ay, to the proof,[3] as mountains are for winds,
        That shakes not though they blow perpetually.
                Enter HORTENSIO [*disguised as Licio*] *with his
                head broke.*
        BAPTISTA   How now, my friend, why dost thou look so pale?
        HORTENSIO   For fear, I promise you, if I look pale.
        BAPTISTA   What, will my daughter prove a good musician?
145   HORTENSIO   I think she'll sooner prove a soldier.
        Iron may hold with° her, but never lutes.   *withstand*
        BAPTISTA   Why, then, thou canst not break° her to the lute?   *train*
        HORTENSIO   Why, no, for she hath broke the lute to me.
        I did but tell her she mistook her frets[4]
150   And bowed° her hand to teach her fingering,   *bent*
        When, with a most impatient devilish spirit,
        "Frets,[5] call you these?" quoth she. "I'll fume° with them."   *be in a rage*
        And with that word she struck me on the head,
        And through the instrument my pate made way,
155   And there I stood amazèd for a while,
        As on a pillory,[6] looking through the lute,
        While she did call me rascal, fiddler,
        And twangling Jack,° with twenty such vile terms,   *knave*
        As° had she studied to misuse me so.   *As if*
160   PETRUCCIO   Now by the world, it is a lusty° wench.   *lively*
        I love her ten times more than e'er I did.
        Oh, how I long to have some chat with her.
        BAPTISTA [*to* HORTENSIO]   Well, go with me and be not so
                discomfited.
        Proceed in practice° with my younger daughter;   *Continue your lessons*
165   She's apt to learn and thankful for good turns.
        Signor Petruccio, will you go with us,
        Or shall I send my daughter Kate to you?
        PETRUCCIO   I pray you do.   *Exeunt all but* PETRUCCIO.
                                I'll attend° her here   *await*
        And woo her with some spirit when she comes.
170   Say that she rail, why, then I'll tell her plain
        She sings as sweetly as a nightingale.
        Say that she frown, I'll say she looks as clear
        As morning roses newly washed with dew.
        Say she be mute and will not speak a word,

2. Implying that those who have opposed Katherina so far have been too weak ("little wind") and that he will subdue her with his "extreme gusts."
3. In impenetrable armor. Proof armor was tested for its strength.
4. Placed her fingers upon the wrong bars ("frets")

on the lute's fingerboard.
5. Katherina plays on "frets" as also meaning "annoyances" or "vexations."
6. An instrument of public punishment in which the offender's head and hands were fastened in wooden clamps.

175 Then I'll commend her volubility
And say she uttereth piercing° eloquence.   *moving*
If she do bid me pack,° I'll give her thanks,   *go away*
As though she bid me stay by her a week.
If she deny to wed, I'll crave° the day   *beg to know*
180 When I shall ask the banns⁷ and when be married.
But here she comes, and now, Petruccio, speak.

    Enter KATHERINA.

Good morrow, Kate, for that's your name, I hear.
KATHERINA Well have you heard, but something° hard of   *somewhat*
    hearing:
They call me Katherine that do talk of me.
185 PETRUCCIO You lie, in faith, for you are called plain Kate,
And bonny° Kate, and sometimes Kate the curst.   *comely*
But Kate, the prettiest Kate in Christendom,
Kate of Kate Hall,⁸ my super dainty Kate—
For dainties are all cates⁹—and therefore, Kate,
190 Take this of me, Kate of my consolation:
Hearing thy mildness praised in every town,
Thy virtues spoke of and thy beauty sounded,¹
Yet not so deeply as to thee belongs,
Myself am moved to woo thee for my wife.
195 KATHERINA Moved, in good time.° Let him that moved you   *indeed*
    hither
Remove you hence. I knew you at the first
You were a movable.²
PETRUCCIO   Why, what's a movable?
KATHERINA A joint-stool.³
PETRUCCIO   Thou hast hit it: come, sit on me.
KATHERINA Asses are made to bear⁴ and so are you.
200 PETRUCCIO Women are made to bear and so are you.
KATHERINA No such jade° as you, if me you mean.   *worn-out horse*
PETRUCCIO Alas, good Kate, I will not burden⁵ thee,
For knowing° thee to be but young and light.⁶   *Because I know*
KATHERINA Too light° for such a swain° as you to catch,   *quick / bumpkin*
205 And yet as heavy as my weight should be.⁷
PETRUCCIO "Should be"? Should—buzz.⁸
KATHERINA   Well ta'en, and like a buzzard.⁹
PETRUCCIO O slow-winged turtle,° shall a buzzard take thee?   *turtledove*
KATHERINA Ay, for a turtle, as he takes a buzzard.¹
PETRUCCIO Come, come, you wasp, i'faith you are too angry.
210 KATHERINA If I be waspish, best beware my sting.

---

7. Have the banns read. Banns were required announcements in church of a forthcoming wedding.
8. Either an obscure allusion or an ironic reference to Katherina's home as a place that is famous because she lives there.
9. For delicacies ("dainties") are called "cates."
1. Proclaimed; tested for depth.
2. Piece of furniture; changeable person.
3. Wooden stool made by a joiner.
4. Carry loads; bear children; bear the weight of a lover.
5. Lie on you in sexual intercourse; make you pregnant; make accusations against you; accompany you with a musical refrain, or "burden."
6. Not heavy; wanton; lacking a musical accompa-

niment.
7. She is claiming social prominence ("weight") and refusing the implication that she is wanton ("light") or like a coin that has been clipped so that it is lighter than it should be.
8. Punning on "be" and "bee," Petruccio suggests Katherina should make a buzzing sound.
9. A hawk that cannot be trained to "take," or capture, prey; a fool.
1. Obscure line probably meaning that if a fool ("buzzard") mistakes me for a faithful love ("turtledove"), he'll be making as big a mistake as the turtledove makes when it captures a buzzing insect (another meaning of "buzzard").

PETRUCCIO   My remedy is then to pluck it out.

KATHERINA   Ay, if the fool could find it where it lies.

PETRUCCIO   Who knows not where a wasp does wear his sting?
   In his tail.

KATHERINA   In his tongue.

PETRUCCIO   Whose tongue?

215   KATHERINA   Yours, if you talk of tales,° and so farewell.   *gossip; genitals*

PETRUCCIO   What, with my tongue in your tail?
   Nay, come again, good Kate, I am a gentleman—

KATHERINA   That I'll try.°   *test*
       She strikes him.

PETRUCCIO   I swear I'll cuff you if you strike again.

220   KATHERINA   So may you lose your arms.[2]
   If you strike me, you are no gentleman,
   And if no gentleman, why, then, no arms.

PETRUCCIO   A herald,° Kate? Oh, put me in thy books.[3]   *An authority on heraldry*

KATHERINA   What is your crest,[4] a coxcomb?[5]

225   PETRUCCIO   A combless cock,[6] so Kate will be my hen.

KATHERINA   No cock of mine; you crow too like a craven.°   *cock that won't fight*

PETRUCCIO   Nay, come, Kate, come. You must not look so sour.

KATHERINA   It is my fashion when I see a crab.°   *crab apple; sour person*

PETRUCCIO   Why, here's no crab, and therefore look not sour.

230   KATHERINA   There is, there is.

PETRUCCIO   Then show it me.

KATHERINA   Had I a glass,° I would.   *mirror*

PETRUCCIO   What, you mean my face?

KATHERINA   Well aimed° of such a young one.   *A good guess*

235   PETRUCCIO   Now, by Saint George,° I am too young for you.   *England's patron saint*

KATHERINA   Yet you are withered.

PETRUCCIO   'Tis with cares.

KATHERINA   I care not.

PETRUCCIO   Nay, hear you, Kate. In sooth you scape° not so.   *escape*

KATHERINA   I chafe° you if I tarry. Let me go.   *annoy; inflame*

PETRUCCIO   No, not a whit; I find you passing gentle.

240   'Twas told me you were rough and coy° and sullen,   *disdainful*
   And now I find report a very liar,
   For thou art pleasant, gamesome,° passing° courteous,   *playful / very*
   But slow in speech, yet sweet as springtime flowers.
   Thou canst not frown, thou canst not look askance,°   *scornfully*

245   Nor bite the lip, as angry wenches will,
   Nor hast thou pleasure to be cross in talk;
   But thou with mildness entertain'st thy wooers
   With gentle conference,° soft and affable.   *conversation*
   Why does the world report that Kate doth limp?

250   Oh, sland'rous world! Kate, like the hazel twig,
   Is straight and slender and as brown in hue
   As hazelnuts, and sweeter than the kernels.
   Oh, let me see thee walk: thou dost not halt.°   *limp*

KATHERINA   Go, fool, and whom thou keep'st command.[7]

---

2. Lose your claim to a coat of arms (sign of noble status); loosen your grip on me.
3. Heralds kept books listing gentlemen and their coats of arms.
4. Image on a coat of arms; a fleshy ridge or comb on a rooster's head.

5. Court fool's cap (resembling a cock's comb or crest).
6. A cock with its comb cut down (and thought, therefore, to be gentle), with a pun on "cock" as "penis."
7. And command your servants (not me).

255 PETRUCCIO Did ever Dian[8] so become a grove
As Kate this chamber with her princely gait?
Oh, be thou Dian, and let her be Kate,
And then let Kate be chaste and Dian sportful.°　　　　　　　*playful; amorous*
KATHERINA Where did you study all this goodly speech?
260 PETRUCCIO It is *extempore*, from my mother wit.°　　　　　*native intelligence*
KATHERINA A witty mother, witless else° her son.　　　　　　　　*otherwise*
PETRUCCIO Am I not wise?
KATHERINA Yes, keep you warm.[9]
PETRUCCIO Marry, so I mean, sweet Katherine, in thy bed.
265 And therefore setting all this chat aside,
Thus in plain terms: your father hath consented
That you shall be my wife, your dowry 'greed on,
And will you, nill you,° I will marry you.　　　　　　*if you will or not*
Now, Kate, I am a husband for your turn,°　　　　　　　　　*needs*
270 For by this light, whereby I see thy beauty—
Thy beauty that doth make me like thee well—
Thou must be married to no man but me,

　　　　Enter BAPTISTA, GREMIO, [*and*] TRANIO [*disguised
　　　　as Lucentio*].

For I am he am born to tame you, Kate,
And bring you from a wild Kate° to a Kate　　　*(punning on "wildcat")*
275 Conformable° as other household Kates.　　　　　　　　　*Submissive*
Here comes your father. Never make denial;
I must and will have Katherine to my wife.
BAPTISTA Now, Signor Petruccio, how speed you with my
daughter?
280 PETRUCCIO How but well, sir, how but well?
It were impossible I should speed amiss.
BAPTISTA Why, how now, daughter Katherine, in your dumps?°　　*dejected*
KATHERINA Call you me daughter? Now I promise you
You have showed a tender fatherly regard,
285 To wish me wed to one half-lunatic,
A madcap ruffian and a swearing Jack,
That thinks with oaths to face the matter out.°　　*get his way brazenly*
PETRUCCIO Father, 'tis thus: yourself and all the world
That talked of her have talked amiss of her.
290 If she be curst, it is for policy,°　　　　　　　　*part of a scheme*
For she's not froward,° but modest as the dove.　　　　　　　*willful*
She is not hot, but temperate as the morn.
For patience she will prove a second Grissel,[1]
And Roman Lucrece[2] for her chastity.
295 And to conclude, we have 'greed so well together
That upon Sunday is the wedding day.
KATHERINA I'll see thee hanged on Sunday first.
GREMIO Hark, Petruccio, she says she'll see thee hanged first.
TRANIO Is this your speeding?° Nay, then, goodnight our part.[3]　　*progress*
300 PETRUCCIO Be patient, gentlemen. I choose her for myself.

---

8. Goddess of the hunt and of chastity.
9. Alluding to the proverbial phrase "enough wit to keep oneself warm," implying that the person has few brains.
1. Griselda, proverbial for "wifely patience." Chau-

cer's *Clerk's Tale* offers one version of her story.
2. In Roman legend, a married woman who killed herself after being raped by Tarquin. Shakespeare's *Rape of Lucrece* recounts the story.
3. Good-bye to our chances (of gaining Bianca).

If she and I be pleased, what's that to you?
'Tis bargained twixt us twain, being alone,
That she shall still be curst in company.
I tell you, 'tis incredible to believe
305   How much she loves me. Oh, the kindest Kate!
She hung about my neck, and kiss on kiss
She vied° so fast, protesting oath on oath,   *went me one better*
That in a twink° she won me to her love.   *instant*
Oh, you are novices. 'Tis a world° to see   *worth a world*
310   How tame, when men and women are alone,
A meacock° wretch can make the curstest shrew.   *timid*
—Give me thy hand, Kate. I will unto Venice
To buy apparel 'gainst° the wedding day.   *in preparation for*
—Provide the feast, father, and bid the guests;
315   I will be sure my Katherine shall be fine.°   *richly dressed*
BAPTISTA   I know not what to say, but give me your hands.
God send you joy, Petruccio, 'tis a match.
GREMIO *and* TRANIO   Amen, say we; we will be witnesses.
PETRUCCIO   Father and wife and gentlemen, adieu.
320   I will to Venice; Sunday comes apace.
We will have rings and things and fine array,
And kiss me, Kate. "We will be married o'Sunday."
                      Exeunt PETRUCCIO *and* KATHERINA.
GREMIO   Was ever match clapped up° so suddenly?   *settled*
BAPTISTA   Faith, gentlemen, now I play a merchant's part
325   And venture madly on a desperate mart.°   *risky bargain*
TRANIO   'Twas a commodity lay fretting by you;[4]
'Twill bring you gain or perish on the seas.
BAPTISTA   The gain I seek is quiet in the match.
GREMIO   No doubt but he hath got a quiet catch.
330   But now, Baptista, to your younger daughter.
Now is the day we long have looked for;
I am your neighbor and was suitor first.
TRANIO   And I am one that love Bianca more
Than words can witness or your thoughts can guess.
335 GREMIO   Youngling, thou canst not love so dear° as I.   *deeply; expensively*
TRANIO   Graybeard, thy love doth freeze.
GREMIO   But thine doth fry.
Skipper,° stand back; 'tis age that nourisheth.   *Irresponsible youth*
TRANIO   But youth in ladies' eyes that flourisheth.
BAPTISTA   Content you, gentlemen, I will compound° this   *settle*
    strife.
340   'Tis deeds must win the prize, and he of both°   *whichever of you*
That can assure my daughter greatest dower
Shall have my Bianca's love.
Say, Signor Gremio, what can you assure her?
GREMIO   First, as you know, my house within the city
345   Is richly furnishèd with plate and gold,
Basins and ewers to lave° her dainty hands,   *wash*
My hangings all of Tyrian[5] tapestry.

---

4. It (that is, Katherina) was a piece of merchandise deteriorating in value or a sexually available woman fretting with irritation while in your possession.

5. Crimson or purple. (The Mediterranean city of Tyre was famous for dye of this color.)

	In ivory coffers I have stuffed my crowns;°	*coins*
	In cypress chests my arras counterpoints,°	*tapestry bedcovers*
350	Costly apparel, tents,° and canopies,	*bed curtains*
	Fine linen, Turkey cushions bossed° with pearl,	*embossed*
	Valance° of Venice gold in needlework,	*Fringe on bed drapery*
	Pewter and brass, and all things that belongs	
	To house or housekeeping. Then at my farm	
355	I have a hundred milch kine° to the pail,	*dairy cows*
	Sixscore fat oxen standing in my stalls,	
	And all things answerable to° this portion.	*on the same scale as*
	Myself am struck° in years, I must confess,	*advanced*
	And if I die tomorrow this is hers,	
360	If whilst I live she will be only mine.	

GREMIO [*aside*]   Two thousand ducats by the year of land?

(lines continue)

TRANIO   That only came well in. Sir, list to me:
I am my father's heir and only son.
If I may have your daughter to my wife,
I'll leave her houses three or four as good
365   Within rich Pisa walls as any one
Old Signor Gremio has in Padua,
Besides two thousand ducats by the year
Of fruitful land,[6] all which shall be her jointure.°   *marriage settlement*
—What, have I pinched° you, Signor Gremio?   *distressed*
370 GREMIO [*aside*]   Two thousand ducats by the year of land?
My land amounts not to so much in all.
—That she shall have, besides an argosy°   *a merchant ship*
That now is lying in Marseilles' road.°   *harbor*
—What, have I choked you with an argosy?
375 TRANIO   Gremio, 'tis known my father hath no less
Than three great argosies, besides two galliasses°   *large cargo ships*
And twelve tight° galleys: these I will assure her   *watertight*
And twice as much, whate'er thou offer'st next.
GREMIO   Nay, I have offered all; I have no more,
380   And she can have no more than all I have.
[*to* BAPTISTA] If you like me, she shall have me and mine.
TRANIO   Why, then the maid is mine from all the world
By your firm promise: Gremio is outvied.°   *outbid*
BAPTISTA   I must confess your offer is the best,
385   And let° your father make her the assurance,   *provided*
She is your own. Else, you must pardon me,
If you should die before him, where's her dower?
TRANIO   That's but a cavil:° he is old, I young.   *frivolous objection*
GREMIO   And may not young men die as well as old?
390 BAPTISTA   Well, gentlemen, I am thus resolved:
On Sunday next you know
My daughter Katherine is to be married.
[*to* TRANIO] Now on the Sunday following shall Bianca
Be bride to you, if you make this assurance;
395   If not, to Signor Gremio.
And so I take my leave and thank you both.   *Exit.*
GREMIO   Adieu, good neighbor. —Now I fear thee not.
Sirrah, young gamester, your father were a fool

---

6. *Besides . . . land:* As well as fertile land that brings in an income of 2,000 ducats (Venetian gold coins) each year.

To give thee all and in his waning age
400 Set foot under thy table.[7] Tut, a toy!°   *nonsense*
An old Italian fox is not so kind, my boy.   *Exit.*
TRANIO   A vengeance on your crafty withered hide!
Yet I have faced it with a card of ten.[8]
'Tis in my head to do my master good:
405 I see no reason° but supposed Lucentio   *possible action*
Must get° a father called supposed Vincentio.   *beget; obtain*
And that's a wonder: fathers commonly
Do get their children, but in this case of wooing,
A child shall get a sire, if I fail not of my cunning.   *Exit.*

3.1

Enter LUCENTIO [*disguised as Cambio*], HORTENSIO
[*disguised as Licio*], *and* BIANCA.

LUCENTIO   Fiddler, forbear.° You grow too forward, sir.   *desist*
Have you so soon forgot the entertainment
Her sister Katherine welcomed you withal?°   *with*
HORTENSIO   But, wrangling pedant, this is
5 The patroness of heavenly harmony.
Then give me leave to have prerogative,°   *precedence*
And when in music we have spent an hour,
Your lecture° shall have leisure for as much.   *lesson*
LUCENTIO   Preposterous[1] ass, that never read so far
10 To know the cause why music was ordained!°   *ordered; appointed*
Was it not to refresh the mind of man
After his studies or his usual pain?°   *labor*
Then give me leave to read philosophy
And while I pause, serve in° your harmony.   *serve up (contemptuous)*
15 HORTENSIO   Sirrah, I will not bear these braves° of thine.   *insults*
BIANCA   Why, gentlemen, you do me double wrong
To strive for that which resteth in my choice.
I am no breeching[2] scholar in the schools:
I'll not be tied to hours nor 'pointed times,
20 But learn my lessons as I please myself.
And to cut off all strife: here sit we down,
[*to* HORTENSIO] Take you your instrument, play you the
        whiles;°   *in the meantime*
His lecture will be done ere you have tuned.
HORTENSIO   You'll leave his lecture when I am in tune?[3]
25 LUCENTIO   That will be never; tune your instrument.
BIANCA   Where left we last?
LUCENTIO   Here, madam:
[*He reads.*]   "Hic ibat Simois, hic est Sigeia tellus,
        Hic steterat Priami regia celsa senis."[4]
30 BIANCA   Construe them.°   *Translate the lines*

---

7. Become your dependent.
8. I have bluffed and won with a card of little value
(a ten spot).
3.1 Location: Baptista's house in Padua.
1. Literally, putting last what should come first;
reversing the natural order of things.
2. Youthful (in breeches); liable to be whipped
(breeched).

3. When my lute is in the proper pitch. Lucentio
responds with a pun on "in tune" as meaning "in harmony" with Bianca.
4. Latin lines from Penelope's letter to her husband,
Ulysses, in Ovid's *Heroides:* "Here flowed the Simois;
here is the Sigeian land; here stood old Priam's lofty
palace."

LUCENTIO *Hic ibat*, as I told you before; *Simois*, I am Lucentio; *hic est*, son unto Vincentio of Pisa; *Sigeia tellus*, disguised thus to get your love; *hic steterat*, and that Lucentio
that comes a-wooing; *Priami*, is my man Tranio; *regia*, bear-
35 ing my port;° *celsa senis*, that we might beguile the old   *taking my social place*
pantaloon.°   *foolish old man*
HORTENSIO Madam, my instrument's in tune.
BIANCA Let's hear. Oh, fie, the treble jars.°   *is discordant*
LUCENTIO Spit in the hole,[5] man, and tune again.
40 BIANCA [*to* LUCENTIO] Now let me see if I can construe it. *Hic
ibat Simois*, I know you not; *hic est Sigeia tellus*, I trust you
not; *hic staterat Priami*, take heed he hear us not; *regia*, presume not; *celsa senis*, despair not.
HORTENSIO Madam, 'tis now in tune.
LUCENTIO   All but the base.
45 HORTENSIO The base is right; 'tis the base knave that jars.
[*aside*] How fiery and forward our pedant is.
Now for my life, the knave doth court my love.
Pedascule,° I'll watch you better yet.   *Little pedant*
BIANCA [*to* LUCENTIO] In time I may believe, yet I mistrust.
50 LUCENTIO Mistrust it not, for sure Aeacides[6]
Was Ajax, called so from his grandfather.
BIANCA I must believe my master, else I promise you
I should be arguing still upon that doubt.
But let it rest. —Now, Licio, to you:
55 Good master, take it not unkindly, pray,
That I have been thus pleasant with you both.
HORTENSIO [*to* LUCENTIO] You may go walk and give me leave°   *allow me leisure*
a while.
My lessons make no music in three parts.°   *for three voices*
LUCENTIO Are you so formal,° sir? Well, I must wait.   *precise*
60 [*aside*] And watch withal, for, but° I be deceived,   *unless*
Our fine musician groweth amorous.
HORTENSIO Madam, before you touch the instrument,
To learn the order of my fingering,
I must begin with rudiments of art,
65 To teach you gamut[7] in a briefer sort,°   *quicker way*
More pleasant, pithy, and effectual
Than hath been taught by any of my trade;
And there it is in writing, fairly drawn.
BIANCA Why, I am past my gamut long ago.
70 HORTENSIO Yet read the gamut of Hortensio.
BIANCA [*reading*] "*Gamut* I am, the ground° of all accord: *lowest note; basis*
  A re, to plead Hortensio's passion;
  B mi, Bianca, take him for thy lord;
  C fa, ut, that loves with all affection;
75 *D sol, re*, one clef, two notes[8] have I;
  E la, mi, show pity or I die."

---

5. Moisten the lute's peg hole (to aid tuning). Lucentio speaks contemptuously and may not be giving
serious advice.
6. Aeacides, or Ajax, was named after his grandfather Aeacus. Lucentio pretends to continue the
lesson.
7. A musical scale, named after its lowest note,
"gamma-ut."
8. Referring perhaps to his one love and two identities.

Call you this gamut? Tut, I like it not.
Old fashions please me best; I am not so nice°   *capricious*
To change true rules for old inventions.
    Enter a MESSENGER.

80 MESSENGER   Mistress, your father prays you leave your books
And help to dress your sister's chamber up.
You know tomorrow is the wedding day.
BIANCA   Farewell, sweet masters both, I must be gone.
        [*Exeunt* BIANCA *and* MESSENGER.]
LUCENTIO   Faith, mistress, then I have no cause to stay.
                        [*Exit.*]

85 HORTENSIO   But I have cause to pry into this pedant:
Methinks he looks as though he were in love.
Yet if thy thoughts, Bianca, be so humble°   *low*
To cast thy wandering eyes on every stale,°   *bait; lure*
Seize thee that list.[9] If once I find thee ranging,°   *unfaithful*
90 Hortensio will be quit with thee by changing.[1]   *Exit.*

3.2

    Enter BAPTISTA, GREMIO, TRANIO [*disguised as*
    Lucentio], [LUCENTIO *disguised as Cambio*],[1]
    KATHERINA, BIANCA, *and others, Attendants.*
BAPTISTA   Signor Lucentio, this is the 'pointed day
That Katherine and Petruccio should be married,
And yet we hear not of our son-in-law.
What will be said, what mockery will it be,
5   To want° the bridegroom when the priest attends   *lack*
To speak the ceremonial rites of marriage?
What says Lucentio to this shame of ours?
KATHERINA   No shame but mine. I must forsooth° be forced   *truly*
To give my hand opposed against my heart
10   Unto a mad-brain rudesby° full of spleen,[2]   *unmannerly fellow*
Who wooed in haste and means to wed at leisure.
I told you, I, he was a frantic° fool,   *mad*
Hiding his bitter jests in blunt behavior,
And to be noted for a merry man,
15   He'll woo a thousand, 'point the day of marriage,
Make friends, invite, and proclaim the banns,
Yet never means to wed where he hath wooed.
Now must the world point at poor Katherine
And say, "Lo, there is mad Petruccio's wife,
20   If it would please him come and marry her."
TRANIO   Patience, good Katherine, and Baptista, too.
Upon my life Petruccio means but well,
Whatever fortune stays° him from his word.   *incident keeps*
Though he be blunt, I know him passing wise;
25   Though he be merry, yet withal he's honest.[3]

9. Let anyone who wants you take you.
1. Will get even with you or get rid of you by finding another love.
3.2 Location: In front of Baptista's house.
1. Although Lucentio speaks no lines in the events leading up to and including Petruccio's arrival for his wedding, this edition, like many others, includes him, disguised as Cambio, among the characters who enter at this point.
2. Caprice; impulsiveness. Contemporary medical theorists claimed that high and low spirits originated in the spleen.
3. Some critics find Tranio's familiarity with Petruccio improbable. Possibly these lines were originally meant to be spoken by Hortensio.

KATHERINA   Would Katherine had never seen him, though.
                    Exit weeping [with BIANCA *following*].[4]
BAPTISTA   Go, girl, I cannot blame thee now to weep,
   For such an injury would vex a very saint,
   Much more a shrew of impatient humor.
            Enter BIONDELLO.
30 BIONDELLO   Master, master, news! Old news and such news
   as you never heard of!
BAPTISTA   Is it new and old too? How may that be?
BIONDELLO   Why, is it not news to hear of Petruccio's coming?
BAPTISTA   Is he come?
35 BIONDELLO   Why, no, sir.
BAPTISTA   What, then?
BIONDELLO   He is coming.
BAPTISTA   When will he be here?
BIONDELLO   When he stands where I am and sees you there.
40 TRANIO   But say, what to thine old news?
BIONDELLO   Why, Petruccio is coming in a new hat and an old
   jerkin;° a pair of old breeches thrice turned;[5] a pair of boots   *jacket*
   that have been candlecases,[6] one buckled, another laced; an
   old rusty sword ta'en out of the town armory, with a broken
45 hilt and chapelesse,[7] with two broken points;[8] his horse
   hipped,° with an old mothy saddle and stirrups of no kin-   *lame in the hips*
   dred,° besides possessed with the glanders[9] and like to mose   *unmatched*
   in the chine;[1] troubled with the lampass,[2] infected with the
   fashions,° full of windgalls,[3] sped with spavins,[4] rayed with   *farcins (small tumors)*
50 the yellows,° past cure of the fives,[5] stark spoiled with the   *disfigured by jaundice*
   staggers,[6] begnawn with the bots,[7] weighed in the back° and   *swaybacked*
   shoulder-shotten,[8] near-legged before[9] and with a half-
   cheeked[1] bit and a headstall[2] of sheep's leather which, being
   restrained° to keep him from stumbling, hath been often   *tightened*
55 burst and now repaired with knots, one girth° six times   *saddle strap*
   pieced,° and a woman's crupper of velour[3] which hath two   *mended*
   letters for her name fairly set down in studs and here and
   there pieced with packthread.°   *twine*
BAPTISTA   Who comes with him?
60 BIONDELLO   O sir, his lackey, for all the world caparisoned°   *outfitted*
   like the horse, with a linen stock° on one leg and a kersey   *stocking*
   boot-hose[4] on the other, gartered with a red and blue list,°   *strip of cloth*

---

4. TEXTUAL COMMENT The Folio does not provide an exit for Bianca in this scene before her re-entry at line 177. This edition has her leave with Katherina to emphasize the way the marriage transaction is a competition between men. See Digital Edition TC 6.
5. Turned inside out three times (to make them last longer).
6. In other words, discarded and used to store old candle ends.
7. Without the metal tip that protects the sword's point.
8. With two laces that don't hold up his hose; with two points (instead of one) on his broken sword.
9. The first in a catalog of horse diseases, most of which are described in Gervase Markham's *Discourse of Horsemanship* (1593). The glanders caused swellings and nasal discharge.
1. Obscure phrase, probably meaning the horse was

apt to suffer discharge from the nostrils, indicating the last stage of glanders.
2. A disease characterized by swellings in the mouth.
3. Soft tumors usually appearing on the fetlock, so called because they were thought to contain air.
4. Rendered useless by swelling of the leg joints.
5. Swelling of glands below the ears.
6. A disease causing loss of balance.
7. Eaten by intestinal worms.
8. With sprained shoulders.
9. With knock-kneed forelegs.
1. *half-cheeked*: improperly attached.
2. The part of the bridle that fits around the horse's head. Sheepskin would be inferior to the animal skins normally used.
3. *crupper*: strap that passes under a horse's tail to keep the saddle straight; *velour*: velvet.
4. A coarse wool stocking.

an old hat, and the humor of forty fancies pricked in't for a
feather[5]—a monster, a very monster in apparel, and not like
65   a Christian footboy or a gentleman's lackey.
TRANIO   'Tis some odd humor pricks° him to this fashion,   *incites, urges*
  Yet oftentimes he goes but mean appareled.
BAPTISTA   I am glad he's come, howsoe'er he comes.
BIONDELLO   Why, sir, he comes not.
70   BAPTISTA   Didst thou not say he comes?
BIONDELLO   Who, that Petruccio came?
BAPTISTA   Ay, that Petruccio came.
BIONDELLO   No, sir, I say his horse comes with him on his back.
BAPTISTA   Why, that's all one.
75   BIONDELLO   Nay by Saint Jamy,
        I hold you a penny,
        A horse and a man
        Is more than one,
        And yet not many.
        Enter PETRUCCIO *and* GRUMIO.
80   PETRUCCIO   Come, where be these gallants? Who's at home?
BAPTISTA   You are welcome, sir.
PETRUCCIO   And yet I come not well.
BAPTISTA   And yet you halt° not.   *limp*
TRANIO   Not so well appareled as I wish you were.
85   PETRUCCIO   Were it better I should rush in thus?
  But where is Kate? Where is my lovely bride?
  How does my father? Gentles,[6] methinks you frown,
  And wherefore gaze this goodly company
  As if they saw some wondrous monument,
90   Some comet or unusual prodigy?°   *extraordinary thing*
BAPTISTA   Why, sir, you know this is your wedding day.
  First were we sad, fearing you would not come,
  Now sadder that you come so unprovided.°   *unprepared*
  Fie, doff this habit,° shame to your estate,°   *outfit / social place*
95   An eyesore to our solemn festival.
TRANIO   And tell us what occasion of import
  Hath all so long detained you from your wife
  And sent you hither so unlike yourself?
PETRUCCIO   Tedious it were to tell and harsh to hear.
100   Sufficeth I am come to keep my word,
  Though in some part enforcèd to digress,°   *deviate from my plan*
  Which at more leisure I will so excuse
  As you shall well be satisfied with all.
  But where is Kate? I stay too long from her;
105   The morning wears, 'tis time we were at church.
TRANIO   See not your bride in these unreverent° robes.   *disrespectful*
  Go to my chamber, put on clothes of mine.
PETRUCCIO   Not I, believe me; thus I'll visit her.
BAPTISTA   But thus, I trust, you will not marry her.
110   PETRUCCIO   Good sooth,° even thus. Therefore ha' done with   *Yes indeed*
    words:

---

5. Possibly an absurdly fanciful decoration attached
to the hat instead of a feather.

6. The polite term of address to men and women of
the gentry.

    To me she's married, not unto my clothes.
    Could I repair what she will wear° in me   *wear out (in sex)*
    As I can change these poor accoutrements,
    'Twere well for Kate and better for myself.
115   But what a fool am I to chat with you,
    When I should bid good morrow to my bride
    And seal the title with a lovely° kiss!   *loving*

                           Exit [with GRUMIO].

TRANIO   He hath some meaning in his mad attire.
    We will persuade him, be it possible,
120   To put on better ere he go to church.

BAPTISTA   I'll after him and see the event° of this.   *outcome*

           Exit [with GREMIO, BIONDELLO, *and Attendants].*

TRANIO [*to* LUCENTIO]   But, sir, to love concerneth us to add[7]
    Her father's liking, which to bring to pass,
    As before imparted to your worship,
125   I am to get a man—whate'er he be,
    It skills° not much, we'll fit him to our turn—   *matters*
    And he shall be Vincentio of Pisa
    And make assurance here in Padua
    Of greater sums than I have promisèd.
130   So shall you quietly enjoy your hope°   *what you hope for*
    And marry sweet Bianca with consent.

LUCENTIO   Were it not that my fellow schoolmaster
    Doth watch Bianca's steps so narrowly,
    'Twere good, methinks, to steal our marriage,°   *elope*
135   Which once performed, let all the world say no,
    I'll keep mine own, despite of all the world.

TRANIO   That by degrees we mean to look into,
    And watch our vantage° in this business.   *opportunity*
    We'll overreach the graybeard Gremio,
140   The narrow-prying° father Minola,   *overly suspicious*
    The quaint° musician, amorous Licio,   *skillful; crafty*
    All for my master's sake, Lucentio.

       Enter GREMIO.

    Signor Gremio, came you from the church?

GREMIO   As willingly as e'er I came from school.
145 TRANIO   And is the bride and bridegroom coming home?

GREMIO   A bridegroom, say you? 'Tis a groom° indeed—   *crude, lower-class man*
    A grumbling groom, and that the girl shall find.

TRANIO   Curster° than she? Why, 'tis impossible.   *More cantankerous*

GREMIO   Why, he's a devil, a devil, a very fiend.
150 TRANIO   Why, she's a devil, a devil, the devil's dam.°   *mother*

GREMIO   Tut, she's a lamb, a dove, a fool to him.[8]
    I'll tell you, Sir Lucentio, when the priest
    Should ask if Katherine should be his wife,
    "Ay, by gog's wounds,"[9] quoth he and swore so loud
155   That all amazed the priest let fall the book,
    And, as he stooped again to take it up,
    This mad-brained bridegroom took° him such a cuff   *gave*
    That down fell priest and book, and book and priest.
    "Now take them up," quoth he, "if any list."°   *choose*

7. To the love between Bianca and Lucentio it is   8. A good-natured innocent compared with him.
necessary for us to add.   9. By God's (Christ's) wounds (a common oath).

160   TRANIO   What said the wench when he rose again?

         GREMIO   Trembled and shook: for why,° he° stamped and swore,   *because / (Petruccio)*
         As if the vicar meant to cozen[1] him.
         But after many ceremonies done,
         He calls for wine—"a health," quoth he, as if
165   He had been aboard° carousing to his mates   *(a ship)*
         After a storm—quaffed off the muscatel[2]
         And threw the sops all in the sexton's face,
         Having no other reason
         But that his beard grew thin and hungerly°   *sparsely; as if hungry*
170   And seemed to ask him° sops as he was drinking.   *ask him for*
         This done, he took the bride about the neck
         And kissed her lips with such a clamorous smack
         That at the parting all the church did echo.
         And I, seeing this, came thence for very shame,
175   And after me I know the rout° is coming.   *crowd*
         Such a mad marriage never was before.

           Music plays.

         Hark, hark, I hear the minstrels play.

           Enter PETRUCCIO, KATHERINA, BIANCA, HORTENSIO
           [*as Licio*], BAPTISTA[, *and* GRUMIO].

         PETRUCCIO   Gentlemen and friends, I thank you for your pains.
         I know you think to dine with me today
180   And have prepared great store of wedding cheer,°   *food and drink*
         But so it is my haste doth call me hence,
         And therefore here I mean to take my leave.
         BAPTISTA   Is't possible you will away tonight?
         PETRUCCIO   I must away today before night come.
185   Make° it no wonder: if you knew my business,   *Consider*
         You would entreat me rather go than stay.
         And, honest° company, I thank you all   *worthy*
         That have beheld me give away myself
         To this most patient, sweet, and virtuous wife.
190   Dine with my father, drink a health to me,
         For I must hence, and farewell to you all.
         TRANIO   Let us entreat you stay till after dinner.
         PETRUCCIO   It may not be.
         GREMIO   Let me entreat you.
         PETRUCCIO   It cannot be.
         KATHERINA   Let me entreat you.
         PETRUCCIO   I am content.
195   KATHERINA   Are you content to stay?
         PETRUCCIO   I am content you shall entreat me stay;
         But yet not stay, entreat me how you can.
         KATHERINA   Now, if you love me, stay.
         PETRUCCIO   Grumio, my horse.
         GRUMIO   Ay, sir, they be ready, the oats have eaten the horses.[3]
200   KATHERINA   Nay, then,
         Do what thou canst, I will not go today,
         No, nor tomorrow, not till I please myself.

---

1. Cheat (by not performing a legally binding ceremony).
2. Wine with small cakes, or "sops," soaked in it, traditionally drunk by the newly married couple and their guests.
3. Either Grumio gets it the wrong way around, or he is joking about the great quantity of oats the horses have eaten.

The door is open, sir, there lies your way.
You may be jogging whiles your boots are green.[4]
205 For me, I'll not be gone till I please myself.
'Tis like you'll prove a jolly° surly groom,   *an arrogant*
That take it on you at the first so roundly.[5]
PETRUCCIO O Kate, content thee; prithee, be not angry.
KATHERINA I will be angry; what hast thou to do?[6]
210 —Father, be quiet; he shall stay° my leisure.   *await*
GREMIO Ay, marry, sir, now it begins to work.
KATHERINA Gentlemen, forward to the bridal dinner.
I see a woman may be made a fool
If she had not a spirit to resist.
215 PETRUCCIO They shall go forward, Kate, at thy command.
—Obey the bride, you that attend on her.
Go to the feast, revel and domineer,°   *feast sumptuously*
Carouse full measure to her maidenhead,
Be mad and merry or go hang yourselves.
220 But for my bonny Kate, she must with me.
Nay, look not big,° nor stamp, nor stare, nor fret.   *defiant*
I will be master of what is mine own.
She is my goods, my chattels; she is my house,
My household stuff, my field, my barn,
225 My horse, my ox, my ass, my anything,
And here she stands, touch her whoever dare.[7]
I'll bring mine action on° the proudest he   *attack; sue (in court)*
That stops my way in Padua. —Grumio,
Draw forth thy weapon; we are beset with thieves,
230 Rescue thy mistress if thou be a man.
—Fear not, sweet wench, they shall not touch thee, Kate;
I'll buckler° thee against a million.   *shield*
      Exeunt PETRUCCIO, KATHERINA[, *and* GRUMIO].
BAPTISTA Nay, let them go, a couple of quiet ones.
GREMIO Went they not quickly, I should die with laughing.
235 TRANIO Of all mad matches never was the like.
LUCENTIO Mistress, what's your opinion of your sister?
BIANCA That being mad herself, she's madly mated.
GREMIO I warrant him, Petruccio is Kated.[8]
BAPTISTA Neighbors and friends, though bride and
    bridegroom wants°   *are missing*
240 For to supply° the places at the table,   *to fill*
You know there wants no junkets° at the feast.   *sweetmeats*
Lucentio, you shall supply the bridegroom's place,
And let Bianca take her sister's room.
TRANIO Shall sweet Bianca practice how to bride it?
245 BAPTISTA She shall, Lucentio. Come, gentlemen, let's go.
                      Exeunt.

---

4. You can be off now while your boots are new
("green"). Proverbial expression for getting an early
start or getting rid of an unwelcome guest.
5. That takes charge at the outset so outspokenly.
6. What business is it of yours?
7. Petruccio warns others to leave Katherina alone.

In cataloging the ways she is one of his possessions,
he alludes to the Tenth Commandment, which forbids coveting a neighbor's wife or property.
8. Mated with a "Kate"; afflicted with Katherina
(imagined as a disease).

4.1

Enter GRUMIO.

GRUMIO Fie, fie on all tired jades,° on all mad masters, and
all foul° ways. Was ever man so beaten? Was ever man so
rayed?° Was ever man so weary? I am sent before to make a
fire, and they are coming after to warm them. Now were not
5 I a little pot and soon hot,[1] my very lips might freeze to my
teeth, my tongue to the roof of my mouth, my heart in my
belly, ere I should come by a fire to thaw me; but I with blowing the fire shall warm myself, for considering the weather,
a taller[2] man than I will take cold. Holla, ho, Curtis!

Enter CURTIS.

10 CURTIS Who is that calls so coldly?
GRUMIO A piece of ice. If thou doubt it, thou mayst slide from
my shoulder to my heel with no greater a run but my head
and my neck. A fire, good Curtis.
CURTIS Is my master and his wife coming, Grumio?
15 GRUMIO Oh, ay, Curtis, ay, and therefore fire, fire, cast on no
water.[3]
CURTIS Is she so hot a shrew as she's reported?
GRUMIO She was, good Curtis, before this frost; but thou
know'st winter tames man, woman, and beast, for it hath
20 tamed my old master and my new mistress and myself, fellow Curtis.
CURTIS Away, you three-inch° fool, I am no beast.
GRUMIO Am I but three inches? Why, thy horn[4] is a foot, and
so long am I at the least. But wilt thou make a fire, or shall I
25 complain on thee to our mistress, whose hand—she being
now at hand—thou shalt soon feel, to thy cold comfort, for
being slow in thy hot office?°
CURTIS I prithee, good Grumio, tell me, how goes the world?
GRUMIO A cold world, Curtis, in every office but thine, and
30 therefore, fire. Do thy duty and have thy duty,° for my master and mistress are almost frozen to death.
CURTIS There's fire ready, and therefore, good Grumio, the
news.
GRUMIO Why, "Jack boy, ho boy"[5] and as much news as wilt
35 thou.
CURTIS Come, you are so full of coney-catching.[6]
GRUMIO Why, therefore fire, for I have caught extreme cold.
Where's the cook? Is supper ready, the house trimmed,
rushes strewed,[7] cobwebs swept, the servingmen in their
40 new fustian,° their white stockings, and every officer° his
wedding garment on? Be the Jacks fair within, the Jills fair
without,[8] the carpets° laid, and everything in order?
CURTIS All ready, and therefore, I pray thee, news.

Right margin glosses:
worn-out horses
muddy
dirtied

short

fire-making duties

take your reward

coarse cloth / servant

table coverings

4.1 Location: Petruccio's country house.
1. Proverbial for a small person who quickly becomes
angry.
2. Punning on "taller" as meaning "sturdier."
3. Alluding to the popular song "Scotland's Burning," in which the words "Fire, fire" are followed by
"Cast on water, cast on water."
4. The proverbial sign of a cuckold; an erect penis.
Grumio implies that he is "long" enough to cuckold

Curtis.
5. A line from another popular song.
6. Trickery, with a play on the "catches," or songs, of
which Grumio is fond. A coney is a rabbit.
7. Scattered on the floor.
8. Jacks and Jills were manservants and maidser-
vants; also leather drinking vessels and metal drinking vessels.

GRUMIO   First, know my horse is tired, my master and mis-
45   tress fallen out.

CURTIS   How?

GRUMIO   Out of their saddles into the dirt, and thereby hangs
a tale.

CURTIS   Let's ha't, good Grumio.

50   GRUMIO   Lend thine ear.

CURTIS   Here.

GRUMIO [cuffing him]   There.

CURTIS   This 'tis to feel a tale, not to hear a tale.

GRUMIO   And therefore 'tis called a sensible tale,[9] and this
55   cuff was but to knock at your ear and beseech listening.
Now I begin: Inprimis,° we came down a foul° hill, my mas-   *First / muddy*
ter riding behind my mistress.

CURTIS   Both of° one horse?   *on*

GRUMIO   What's that to thee?

60   CURTIS   Why, a horse.

GRUMIO   Tell thou the tale: but hadst thou not crossed° me,   *interrupted*
thou shouldst have heard how her horse fell, and she under
her horse. Thou shouldst have heard in how mirey a place,
how she was bemoiled,° how he left her with the horse upon   *covered with mud*
65   her, how he beat me because her horse stumbled, how she
waded through the dirt to pluck him off me, how he swore,
how she prayed that never prayed before, how I cried, how
the horses ran away, how her bridle was burst, how I lost my
crupper, with many things of worthy memory which now
70   shall die in oblivion, and thou return unexperienced° to thy   *ignorant; unknowing*
grave.

CURTIS   By this reckoning he is more shrew than she.

GRUMIO   Ay, and that thou and the proudest of you all shall
find when he comes home. But what° talk I of this? Call   *why*
75   forth Nathaniel, Joseph, Nicholas, Philip, Walter, Sugarsop,
and the rest. Let their heads be slickly combed, their blue
coats[1] brushed, and their garters of an indifferent° knit; let   *ordinary; a matching*
them curtsy with their left legs and not presume to touch a
hair of my master's horsetail till they kiss their hands.[2] Are
80   they all ready?

CURTIS   They are.

GRUMIO   Call them forth.

CURTIS [calling]   Do you hear, ho? You must meet my master
to countenance[3] my mistress.

85   GRUMIO   Why, she hath a face of her own.

CURTIS   Who knows not that?

GRUMIO   Thou, it seems, that calls for company to countenance
her.

CURTIS   I call them forth to credit[4] her.
      Enter four or five [SERVANTS].

90   GRUMIO   Why, she comes to borrow nothing of them.

NATHANIEL   Welcome home, Grumio.

PHILIP   How now, Grumio.

---

9. Reasonable; capable of being felt.
1. The usual servant uniform.
2. A greeting signifying inordinate submissiveness.
3. Greet, pay respects to; with a pun in the next line

on "countenance" as meaning "face."
4. Honor, with pun in next line on "credit" as meaning "offer financial assistance."

JOSEPH What, Grumio.

NICHOLAS Fellow Grumio.

95 NATHANIEL How now, old lad.

GRUMIO Welcome, you; how now, you; what, you; fellow, you.
And thus much for greeting. Now, my spruce° companions,   *smartly dressed*
is all ready and all things neat?

NATHANIEL All things is ready. How near is our master?

100 GRUMIO E'en at hand, alighted by this, and therefore be not—
Cock's° passion, silence; I hear my master.   *God's (a common oath)*
        Enter PETRUCCIO *and* KATHERINA.[5]

PETRUCCIO Where be these knaves? What, no man at door
To hold my stirrup nor to take my horse?
Where is Nathaniel, Gregory, Philip?

105 ALL SERVANTS Here, here, sir; here, sir.

PETRUCCIO "Here, sir; here, sir; here, sir; here, sir."
You logger-headed° and unpolished grooms!   *stupid*
What, no attendance? No regard? No duty?
Where is the foolish knave I sent before?

110 GRUMIO Here, sir, as foolish as I was before.

PETRUCCIO You peasant swain,° you whoreson,° malt-horse   *farm laborer / bastard*
drudge,[6]
Did I not bid thee meet me in the park[7]
And bring along these rascal knaves with thee?

GRUMIO Nathaniel's coat, sir, was not fully made,

115 And Gabriel's pumps° were all unpinked° i'th' heel;   *shoes / not ornamented*
There was no link[8] to color Peter's hat,
And Walter's dagger was not come from sheathing.°   *having a sheath fixed*
There were none fine but Adam, Rafe, and Gregory;
The rest were ragged, old, and beggarly.

120 Yet as they are, here are they come to meet you.

PETRUCCIO Go rascals, go, and fetch my supper in.
        Exeunt SERVANTS.
[*Sings.*] "Where is the life that late I led?
        Where are those—"[9]
Sit down, Kate, and welcome. Soud, soud, soud, soud.[1]
        Enter SERVANTS *with supper.*

125 Why, when, I say? —Nay, good, sweet Kate, be merry.
—Off with my boots, you rogues; you villains, when?
[*Sings.*] "It was the Friar of orders gray,
        As he forth walkèd on his way."[2]
Out, you rogue, you pluck my foot awry!

130 Take that, and mend the plucking of the other.
—Be merry, Kate. —Some water here, what, ho!
        Enter one with water.
Where's my spaniel Troilus? Sirrah, get you hence
And bid my cousin Ferdinand come hither.
—One, Kate, that you must kiss and be acquainted with.

---

5. TEXTUAL COMMENT The interactions between Petruccio and his servants that begin here could be staged in a number of different ways. For instance, the servants may or may not be in on Petruccio's plan to scare Katherina. See Digital Edition TC 7.
6. Stupid, menial worker. The slow, heavy malt horse was used to grind malt by turning a treadmill.
7. A piece of ground comprising woodland and pasture

attached to a country house and used for recreation.
8. Torch, the smoke of which was used to blacken shoes.
9. Probably a fragment of a ballad, now lost, lamenting a newlywed's loss of freedom.
1. An expression of impatience.
2. Another fragment of a lost song, perhaps one of the many songs about a friar's seduction of a nun.

135   —Where are my slippers? Shall I have some water?
    —Come, Kate, and wash, and welcome heartily.
    —You whoreson villain, will you let it fall?
KATHERINA   Patience, I pray you, 'twas a fault unwilling.
PETRUCCIO   A whoreson, beetle-headed,° flap-eared knave!   *thick-headed*
140   —Come, Kate, sit down, I know you have a stomach.°   *an appetite; temper*
    Will you give thanks, sweet Kate, or else shall I?
    —What's this, mutton?
FIRST SERVANT   Ay.
PETRUCCIO   Who brought it?
PETER   I.
PETRUCCIO   'Tis burnt, and so is all the meat.
    What dogs are these? Where is the rascal cook?
145   How durst you villains bring it from the dresser°   *cook; sideboard*
    And serve it thus to me that love it not?
    There, take it to you, trenchers,° cups, and all,   *plates*
    You heedless jolt-heads° and unmannered slaves.   *careless blockheads*
    What, do you grumble? I'll be with you straight.
                        [*Exeunt* SERVANTS.]
150 KATHERINA   I pray you, husband, be not so disquiet;
    The meat was well, if you were so contented.
PETRUCCIO   I tell thee, Kate, 'twas burnt and dried away,
    And I expressly am forbid to touch it,
    For it engenders choler,[3] planteth anger,
155   And better 'twere that both of us did fast,
    Since of ourselves,° ourselves are choleric,   *by our natures*
    Than feed it with such over-roasted flesh.
    Be patient, tomorrow't shall be mended,
    And for this night we'll fast for company.°   *together*
160   Come, I will bring thee to thy bridal chamber.
             Exeunt [PETRUCCIO *and* KATHERINA;
                 GRUMIO *remains*].
      Enter SERVANTS *severally.*
NATHANIEL   Peter, didst ever see the like?
PETER   He kills her in her own humor.[4]
      Enter CURTIS, *a servant.*
GRUMIO   Where is he?
CURTIS   In her chamber, making a sermon of continency° to   *on self-control*
165   her, and rails and swears and rates° that she, poor soul,   *scolds*
  knows not which way to stand, to look, to speak, and sits as
  one new risen from a dream. Away, away, for he is coming
  hither.
                 [*Exeunt* SERVANTS *and* GRUMIO.]
      Enter PETRUCCIO.
PETRUCCIO   Thus have I politicly° begun my reign,   *cunningly*
170   And 'tis my hope to end successfully.
    My falcon[5] now is sharp° and passing° empty,   *hungry / extremely*
    And till she stoop[6] she must not be full gorged,°   *fully fed*
    For then she never looks upon her lure.°   *falconer's bait*
    Another way I have to man my haggard,°   *tame my female hawk*

---

3. It causes anger. An excess of the choleric humor
was believed to provoke anger.
4. He subdues her choleric humor by outdoing her in
bad temper.

5. In what follows, Petruccio likens his methods of
disciplining Katherina to the training of a wild hawk.
6. Fly to the bait; submit to my authority.

175 To make her come and know her keeper's call,
That is, to watch her° as we watch these kites°   *keep her awake / hawks*
That bait and beat[7] and will not be obedient.
She ate no meat today, nor none shall eat;
Last night she slept not, nor tonight she shall not.
180 As with the meat, some undeservèd fault
I'll find about the making of the bed,
And here I'll fling the pillow, there the bolster,[8]
This way the coverlet, another way the sheets.
Ay, and amid this hurly I intend°   *will pretend*
185 That all is done in reverend care of her.
And in conclusion, she shall watch° all night,   *stay awake*
And if she chance to nod, I'll rail and brawl
And with the clamor keep her still awake.
This is a way to kill a wife with kindness,
190 And thus I'll curb her mad and headstrong humor.
He that knows better how to tame a shrew,
Now let him speak; 'tis charity to show.°   *Exit.*   *(his methods)*

4.2

Enter TRANIO *[disguised as Lucentio] and* HORTENSIO
[disguised as Licio].

TRANIO   Is't possible, friend Licio, that Mistress Bianca
Doth fancy any other but Lucentio?
I tell you, sir, she bears me fair in hand.°   *leads me on*
HORTENSIO   Sir, to satisfy you in what I have said,
5   Stand by and mark the manner of his teaching.
      [They stand aside.]
      Enter BIANCA *[and* LUCENTIO *disguised as Cambio].*
LUCENTIO   Now, mistress, profit you in what you read?
BIANCA   What, master, read you? First resolve° me that.   *answer*
LUCENTIO   I read that I profess,° *The Art to Love.*[1]   *what I practice*
BIANCA   And may you prove, sir, master of your art.
10 LUCENTIO   While you, sweet dear, prove mistress of my heart.
      [They stand aside.]
HORTENSIO   Quick proceeders,[2] marry! Now tell me, I pray,
You that durst swear that your mistress Bianca
Loved none in the world so well as Lucentio—
TRANIO   O despiteful° love, unconstant womankind!   *cruel*
15   I tell thee, Licio, this is wonderful.°   *astonishing*
HORTENSIO   Mistake no more: I am not Licio,
Nor a musician, as I seem to be,
But one that scorn to live in this disguise
For such a one° as leaves a gentleman   *(Bianca)*
20   And makes a god of such a cullion.°   *base fellow*
Know, sir, that I am called Hortensio.
TRANIO   Signor Hortensio, I have often heard
Of your entire° affection to Bianca,   *sincere*

---

7. That flutter and flap their wings (instead of settling on the falconer's fist).
8. *bolster:* a long, firm pillow used to support the
sleeper's head.
4.2 Location: Padua, in front of Baptista's house.
1. Ovid's *Ars Amatoria,* in which the poet calls him-

self the "Professor of Love" and treats erotic love as a
skill or an art.
2. Taking up the allusion to a university degree
implicit in Bianca's "master of your art," Hortensio
puns on "proceeding" from a bachelor's to a master's
degree.

And since mine eyes are witness of her lightness°   *sexual infidelity*
25   I will with you, if you be so contented,
Forswear Bianca and her love forever.
HORTENSIO   See how they kiss and court! Signor Lucentio,
Here is my hand, and here I firmly vow
Never to woo her more, but do forswear her
30   As one unworthy all the former favors
That I have fondly° flattered them withal.   *foolishly*
TRANIO [*shaking hands*]   And here I take the like unfeignèd
          oath,
Never to marry with her, though she would entreat.
Fie on her, see how beastly° she doth court him.   *lewdly*
35   HORTENSIO   Would all the world but he had quite forsworn.[3]
For me, that I may surely keep mine oath,
I will be married to a wealthy widow,
Ere three days pass, which hath as long loved me
As I have loved this proud disdainful haggard.°   *intractable woman; hawk*
40   And so farewell, Signor Lucentio.
Kindness in women, not their beauteous looks,
Shall win my love; and so I take my leave
In resolution, as I swore before.   [*Exit.*]
TRANIO   Mistress Bianca, bless you with such grace
45   As 'longeth° to a lover's blessèd case.°   *belongs / state*
Nay, I have ta'en you napping, gentle love,
And have forsworn you with Hortensio.
BIANCA   Tranio, you jest—but have you both forsworn me?
TRANIO   Mistress, we have.
LUCENTIO   Then we are rid of Licio.
50   TRANIO   I'faith he'll have a lusty° widow now   *lively; lustful*
That shall be wooed and wedded in a day.
BIANCA   God give him joy.
TRANIO   Ay, and he'll tame her.
BIANCA   He says so, Tranio?
55   TRANIO   Faith, he is gone unto the taming school.
BIANCA   The taming school? What, is there such a place?
TRANIO   Ay, mistress, and Petruccio is the master
That teacheth tricks eleven-and-twenty long[4]
To tame a shrew and charm her chattering tongue.[5]
          Enter BIONDELLO.
60   BIONDELLO   O master, master, I have watched so long
That I am dog-weary, but at last I spied
An ancient angel[6] coming down the hill
Will serve the turn.
TRANIO   What is he, Biondello?
BIONDELLO   Master, a marcantant[7] or a pedant,°   *schoolmaster*
65   I know not what, but formal in apparel,
In gait and countenance surely like a father.

3. I wish that everyone but Cambio had given her over (so that she will be left an old maid as she deserves; Hortensio apparently assumes that Bianca would never marry a poor musician).
4. Who teaches tricks that are exactly appropriate or of just the right number. An allusion to the card game one-and-thirty, in which the object is to accumulate exactly thirty-one points. See note to 1.2.32.
5. Tranio's apparent knowledge of Hortensio's plans is puzzling and may be an indication that some text has been lost.
6. Worthy old man. Punning on "angel" as meaning both "valuable gold coin" and "divine messenger." The coin had a picture of the archangel Michael on it.
7. Biondello's version of *mercatante*, an older Italian word for "merchant."

LUCENTIO   And what of him, Tranio?

TRANIO   If he be credulous and trust my tale,
I'll make him glad to seem° Vincentio   *pretend to be*

70   And give assurance to Baptista Minola
As if he were the right Vincentio.
Take in your love and then let me alone.

[*Exeunt* LUCENTIO *and* BIANCA.]

Enter a PEDANT.[8]

PEDANT   God save you, sir.

TRANIO   And you, sir. You are welcome.
Travel you far on, or are you at the farthest?

75   PEDANT   Sir, at the farthest for a week or two,
But then up farther, and as far as Rome,
And so to Tripoli,[9] if God lend me life.

TRANIO   What countryman, I pray?

PEDANT   Of Mantua.

TRANIO   Of Mantua, sir? Marry, God forbid!

80   And come to Padua careless of your life?

PEDANT   My life, sir? How, I pray? For that goes hard.[1]

TRANIO   'Tis death for anyone in Mantua
To come to Padua. Know you not the cause?
Your ships are stayed° at Venice, and the Duke,   *detained*

85   For private quarrel twixt your Duke and him,
Hath published and proclaimed it openly.
'Tis marvel, but that you are but newly come,
You might have heard it else proclaimed about.[2]

PEDANT   Alas, sir, it is worse for me than so,°   *my plight is even worse*

90   For I have bills for money by exchange[3]
From Florence and must here deliver them.

TRANIO   Well, sir, to do you courtesy
This will I do, and this I will advise you.
First tell me, have you ever been at Pisa?

95   PEDANT   Ay, sir, in Pisa have I often been,
Pisa renowned for grave citizens.

TRANIO   Among them know you one Vincentio?

PEDANT   I know him not, but I have heard of him:
A merchant of incomparable wealth.

100   TRANIO   He is my father, sir, and sooth to say,
In count'nance somewhat doth resemble you.

BIONDELLO   As much as an apple doth an oyster, and all one.°   *but no matter*

TRANIO   To save your life in this extremity,
This favor will I do you for his sake—

105   And think it not the worst of all your fortunes
That you are like to Sir Vincentio.
His name and credit° shall you undertake,°   *social status / assume*
And in my house you shall be friendly lodged.
Look that you take upon you° as you should—   *act your part*

---

8. TEXTUAL COMMENT Although F is consistent in labeling this character as a Pedant (a stock comic type), because he is said at line 90 to have "bills for money," some editors have designated him a "merchant" like the corresponding character in George Gascoigne's comedy *Supposes* (1566). See Digital Edition TC 8.

9. The north African trading center or the city in Syria.
1. *goes hard:* is difficult to deal with.
2. *but that . . . about:* if you hadn't just arrived, you would have heard it announced everywhere.
3. Promissory notes that the bearer could exchange for cash.

110   You understand me, sir? So shall you stay
       Till you have done your business in the city.
       If this be court'sy, sir, accept of it.
    PEDANT   O sir, I do and will repute° you ever   *consider*
       The patron of my life and liberty.
115   TRANIO   Then go with me to make the matter good.
       This, by the way, I let you understand:
       My father is here looked for every day
       To pass assurance° of a dowry in marriage   *convey legal guarantee*
       Twixt me and one Baptista's daughter here;
120   In all these circumstances I'll instruct you.
       Go with me to clothe you as becomes you.   *Exeunt.*

4.3

Enter KATHERINA *and* GRUMIO.
GRUMIO   No, no, forsooth, I dare not for my life.
KATHERINA   The more my wrong, the more his spite appears.[1]
    What, did he marry me to famish me?
    Beggars that come unto my father's door
5   Upon entreaty have a present° alms;   *immediate*
    If not, elsewhere they meet with charity.
    But I, who never knew how to entreat,
    Nor never needed that I should entreat,
    Am starved for meat, giddy for lack of sleep,
10   With oaths kept waking and with brawling fed,
    And that which spites° me more than all these wants,   *vexes*
    He does it under name of perfect love,
    As who should say,° if I should sleep or eat   *As if to say*
    'Twere deadly sickness or else present° death.   *instant*
15   I prithee, go and get me some repast;
    I care not what, so it be wholesome food.
GRUMIO   What say you to a neat's foot?°   *ox foot or calf's foot*
KATHERINA   'Tis passing good; I prithee, let me have it.
GRUMIO   I fear it is too choleric° a meat.   *conducive to anger*
20   How say you to a fat tripe finely broiled?
KATHERINA   I like it well; good Grumio, fetch it me.
GRUMIO   I cannot tell, I fear 'tis choleric.
    What say you to a piece of beef and mustard?
KATHERINA   A dish that I do love to feed upon.
25   GRUMIO   Ay, but the mustard is too hot a little.
KATHERINA   Why, then the beef and let the mustard rest.
GRUMIO   Nay, then I will not. You shall have the mustard
    Or else you get no beef of Grumio.
KATHERINA   Then both or one or anything thou wilt.
30   GRUMIO   Why, then the mustard without the beef.
KATHERINA   Go, get thee gone, thou false deluding slave,
       [*She*] *beats him.*
    That feed'st me with the very name° of meat.   *only the name*
    Sorrow on thee and all the pack of you
    That triumph thus upon my misery.
35   Go, get thee gone, I say.
       Enter PETRUCCIO *and* HORTENSIO *with meat.*

4.3 Location: Petruccio's country house.
1. The more injustice I suffer, the more he seems to want me to suffer.

PETRUCCIO	How fares my Kate? What, sweeting,° all amort?°	*sweetheart / dejected*
HORTENSIO	Mistress, what cheer?	
KATHERINA	Faith, as cold as can be.	
PETRUCCIO	Pluck up thy spirits, look cheerfully upon me.	

    Here, love, thou seest how diligent I am

40   To dress° thy meat myself and bring it thee.   *prepare*

    I am sure, sweet Kate, this kindness merits thanks.

    What, not a word? Nay, then, thou lov'st it not,

    And all my pains is sorted to no proof.°   *are to no purpose*

    —Here, take away this dish.

45 KATHERINA	I pray you, let it stand.	
PETRUCCIO	The poorest service is repaid with thanks,	

    And so shall mine before you touch the meat.

KATHERINA	I thank you, sir.
HORTENSIO	Signor Petruccio, fie, you are to blame.

50   —Come, Mistress Kate, I'll bear you company.

PETRUCCIO [*aside*] Eat it up all, Hortensio, if thou lovest me.

    —Much good do it unto thy gentle heart.

    Kate, eat apace. And now, my honey love,

    Will we return unto thy father's house

55   And revel it as bravely as the best,

    With silken coats and caps, and golden rings,

    With ruffs and cuffs and farthingales[2] and things,

    With scarves and fans and double change of brav'ry,°   *finery*

    With amber bracelets, beads, and all this knav'ry.°   *tricks of dress*

60   What, hast thou dined? The tailor stays thy leisure

    To deck thy body with his ruffling° treasure.   *ornate (with ruffles)*

        Enter TAILOR.

    Come, tailor, let us see these ornaments;

    Lay forth the gown.

        Enter HABERDASHER.

        What news with you, sir?

HABERDASHER	Here is the cap your worship did bespeak.
65 PETRUCCIO	Why, this was molded on a porringer°—

    A velvet dish.[3] Fie, fie, 'tis lewd and filthy.   *porridge bowl*

    Why, 'tis a cockle° or a walnut shell,   *mollusk shell*

    A knack,° a toy, a trick,° a baby's cap.   *knickknack / trifle*

    Away with it! Come, let me have a bigger.

70 KATHERINA   I'll have no bigger; this doth fit the time,°   *suit current fashion*

    And gentlewomen wear such caps as these.

PETRUCCIO   When you are gentle, you shall have one too,

    And not till then.

HORTENSIO	That will not be in haste.
KATHERINA	Why, sir, I trust I may have leave to speak,

75   And speak I will. I am no child, no babe.

    Your betters have endured me say my mind,

    And if you cannot, best you stop your ears.

    My tongue will tell the anger of my heart,

    Or else my heart, concealing it, will break,

80   And rather than it shall, I will be free,

---

2. *ruffs:* fashionable high collars made of starched linen or lace. *cuffs:* bands, often made of lace, sewn onto sleeves for ornament. *farthingales:* hooped petticoats.
3. It's merely a dish made of velvet. Velvet caps were often associated with prostitutes.

Even to the uttermost as I please in words.

PETRUCCIO Why, thou say'st true; it is paltry cap,
    A custard-coffin,[4] a bauble, a silken pie.
    I love thee well in that thou lik'st it not.

85 KATHERINA Love me or love me not, I like the cap,
    And it I will have, or I will have none.

PETRUCCIO Thy gown? Why, ay: come, tailor, let us see't.
    O mercy, God, what masquing stuff[5] is here?
    What's this? A sleeve? 'Tis like a demi-cannon.°   *large cannon*
90   What, up and down, carved like an apple tart?[6]
    Here's snip and nip and cut and slish and slash,
    Like to a cithern in a barber's shop.
    Why, what a devil's name, tailor, call'st thou this?

HORTENSIO I see she's like° to have neither cap nor gown.   *likely*
95 TAILOR You bid me make it orderly and well,
    According to the fashion and the time.

PETRUCCIO Marry, and did,° but if you be remembered,   *Indeed I did*
    I did not bid you mar it to the time.
    Go, hop me[7] over every kennel° home,   *gutter*
100   For you shall hop without my custom,° sir.   *patronage; business*
    I'll none of it. Hence, make your best of it.

KATHERINA I never saw a better fashioned gown,
    More quaint,° more pleasing, nor more commendable.   *elegant*
    Belike° you mean to make a puppet of me.   *It seems*
105 PETRUCCIO Why true, he means to make a puppet of thee.

TAILOR She says your worship means to make a puppet of her.

PETRUCCIO Oh, monstrous arrogance! Thou liest, thou thread,
    thou thimble,
    Thou yard, three-quarters, half-yard, quarter, nail,[8]
    Thou flea, thou nit,° thou winter cricket, thou!   *egg of a louse*
110   Braved° in mine own house with° a skein of thread?   *Defied; adorned / by*
    Away, thou rag, thou quantity,° thou remnant,   *fragment*
    Or I shall so bemete° thee with thy yard°   *measure; beat / ruler*
    As thou shalt think on prating[9] whilst thou liv'st.
    I tell thee, I, that thou hast marred her gown.

115 TAILOR Your worship is deceived. The gown is made
    Just as my master had direction;
    Grumio gave order how it should be done.

GRUMIO I gave him no order; I gave him the stuff.°   *material*

TAILOR But how did you desire it should be made?

120 GRUMIO Marry, sir, with needle and thread.

TAILOR But did you not request to have it cut?

GRUMIO Thou hast faced° many things.   *trimmed; defied*

TAILOR I have.

GRUMIO Face not me. Thou hast braved° many men; brave°   *dressed finely / defy*
125   not me. I will neither be faced nor braved. I say unto thee, I

---

4. Pastry crust around a custard or an open pie (perhaps with a pun on "costard," slang for "head").
5. Extravagant clothing suitable for theatrical masques.
6. With slits like the top of an apple pie. The gown's sleeves may have been designed so as to reveal fabric of another color underneath.

7. You can go hopping.
8. Measure of cloth, a sixteenth of a yard; Petruccio is literally belittling the tailor. "Yard" is slang for "penis."
9. You will think twice before you talk idly, with a pun on "prat" as slang for "beat on the buttocks."

bid thy master cut out the gown, but I did not bid him cut it
to pieces. Ergo,° thou liest.   *Therefore*

TAILOR   Why, here is the note of the fashion to testify.

PETRUCCIO   Read it.

130 GRUMIO   The note lies in 's throat if he° say I said so.   *it*

TAILOR [*reading*]   "Inprimis,° a loose-bodied gown."[1]   *First*

GRUMIO   Master, if ever I said "loose-bodied gown," sew me in
the skirts of it, and beat me to death with a bottom° of   *spool*
brown thread. I said "a gown."

135 PETRUCCIO   Proceed.

TAILOR   "With a small compassed° cape."   *flared*

GRUMIO   I confess the cape.

TAILOR   "With a trunk° sleeve."   *wide*

GRUMIO   I confess two sleeves.

140 TAILOR   "The sleeves curiously° cut."   *carefully; elaborately*

PETRUCCIO   Ay, there's the villainy.

GRUMIO   Error i'th' bill,° sir, error i'th' bill! I commanded the   *order (for the dress)*
sleeves should be cut out and sewed up again, and that I'll
prove upon thee, though thy little finger be armed in a

145 thimble.

TAILOR   This is true that I say; an° I had thee in place where,°   *if / in a suitable place*
thou shouldst know it.

GRUMIO   I am for thee straight. Take thou the bill,[2] give me
thy mete-yard,° and spare not me.   *yardstick*

150 HORTENSIO   God-a-mercy, Grumio, then he shall have no
odds.°   *advantage*

PETRUCCIO   Well, sir, in brief, the gown is not for me.

GRUMIO   You are i'th' right, sir, 'tis for my mistress.

PETRUCCIO [*to* TAILOR]   Go take it up unto° thy master's use.[3]   *take it away for*

155 GRUMIO   Villain, not for thy life. Take up my mistress' gown
for thy master's use?

PETRUCCIO   Why, sir, what's your conceit° in that?   *meaning*

GRUMIO   O sir, the conceit is deeper than you think for. "Take
up my mistress' gown to his master's use." Oh, fie, fie, fie.

160 PETRUCCIO [*aside to* HORTENSIO]   Hortensio, say thou wilt see
the tailor paid.
—Go take it hence, be gone, and say no more.

HORTENSIO   Tailor, I'll pay thee for thy gown tomorrow,
Take no unkindness of his hasty words.
Away, I say. Commend me to thy master.

                           Exeunt TAILOR [*and* HABERDASHER].

165 PETRUCCIO   Well, come, my Kate, we will unto your father's
Even in these honest mean habiliments.
Our purses shall be proud, our garments poor,
For 'tis the mind that makes the body rich.
And as the sun breaks through the darkest clouds,

170 So honor 'peareth° in the meanest habit.   *can be seen*
What, is the jay more precious than the lark
Because his feathers are more beautiful?
Or is the adder better than the eel,

---

1. A loose-fitting dress. In the next line, Grumio
takes this to mean a dress suitable for a wanton, or
loose, woman.

2. Grumio puns on "bill" as also meaning a "weapon"
or "halberd," a staff with a blade attached.
3. *use*: sexual purposes.

Because his painted skin contents the eye?
175 Oh, no, good Kate; neither art thou the worse
For this poor furniture° and mean array.   *clothing; attire*
If thou account'st it shame, lay it on me,°   *blame me*
And therefore frolic: we will hence forthwith
To feast and sport us° at thy father's house.   *amuse ourselves*
180 [*to* GRUMIO] Go, call my men, and let us straight to him,
And bring our horses unto Long-lane end.
There will we mount and thither walk on foot.
Let's see, I think 'tis now some seven o'clock,
And well we may come there by dinner time.°   *about noon*
185 KATHERINA   I dare assure you, sir, 'tis almost two,
And 'twill be supper time° ere you come there.   *about 6 p.m.*
PETRUCCIO   It shall be seven ere I go to horse.
Look what I speak, or do, or think to do,
You are still crossing° it. —Sirs, let't alone.   *contradicting*
190 I will not go today, and ere I do,
It shall be what o'clock I say it is.
HORTENSIO   Why, so this gallant will command the sun.
                                                        [*Exeunt.*]

4.4

Enter TRANIO [*disguised as Lucentio*] *and the* PEDANT
dressed like Vincentio, booted and bareheaded.[1]
TRANIO   Sir, this is the house. Please it you that I call?
PEDANT   Ay, what else? And but[2] I be deceived,
Signor Baptista may remember me
Near twenty years ago in Genoa—
5 TRANIO   Where we were lodgers at the Pegasus.[3]
'Tis well, and hold your own° in any case   *keep to your role*
With such austerity as 'longeth° to a father.   *belongs*
       Enter BIONDELLO.
PEDANT   I warrant you. But, sir, here comes your boy;
'Twere good he were schooled.
10 TRANIO   Fear you not him. —Sirrah Biondello,
Now do your duty thoroughly, I advise you.
Imagine 'twere the right Vincentio.
BIONDELLO   Tut, fear not me.
TRANIO   But hast thou done thy errand to Baptista?
15 BIONDELLO   I told him that your father was at Venice
And that you looked for him this day in Padua.
TRANIO   Thou'rt a tall° fellow; hold thee° that to drink.   *worthy / take*
Here comes Baptista. Set your countenance, sir.
       Enter BAPTISTA *and* LUCENTIO [*disguised as Cambio*].
TRANIO   Signor Baptista, you are happily met.
20 [*to* PEDANT] Sir, this is the gentleman I told you of.
I pray you, stand good father to me now;
Give me Bianca for my patrimony.

4.4 Location: Padua, in front of Baptista's house.
1. In F, the Pedant is mistakenly given a second entry at line 18, where he is described as "booted and bare-headed," indicating that he is dressed for travel but has taken off his hat, perhaps in deference to Baptista, whom he is about to meet. The present stage direction conflates F's two stage directions regarding the Pedant's entrance.
2. Unless (the Pedant is rehearsing his speech to Baptista).
3. Common name for an inn (marked by a sign of the flying horse of classical mythology).

PEDANT Soft,° son. —Sir, by your leave, having come to   *Just a moment*
    Padua
    To gather in some debts, my son Lucentio
25   Made me acquainted with a weighty cause
    Of love between your daughter and himself.
    And for the good report I hear of you,
    And for the love he beareth to your daughter
    And she to him, to stay him° not too long   *keep him waiting*
30   I am content, in a good father's care,[4]
    To have him matched. And if you please to like
    No worse than I, upon some agreement
    Me shall you find ready and willing
    With one consent to have her so bestowed;
35   For curious° I cannot be with you,   *overly particular*
    Signor Baptista, of whom I hear so well.
BAPTISTA Sir, pardon me in what I have to say;
    Your plainness and your shortness please me well.
    Right true it is your son Lucentio here
40   Doth love my daughter, and she loveth him,
    Or both dissemble deeply their affections.
    And therefore if you say no more than this,
    That like a father you will deal with him
    And pass° my daughter a sufficient dower,   *grant*
45   The match is made and all is done:
    Your son shall have my daughter with consent.
TRANIO I thank you, sir. Where, then, do you know best
    We be affied° and such assurance ta'en   *betrothed*
    As shall with either part's agreement stand?[5]
50 BAPTISTA Not in my house, Lucentio, for you know
    Pitchers have ears,[6] and I have many servants.
    Besides, old Gremio is harkening still,°   *always listening*
    And haply° we might be interrupted.   *perhaps*
TRANIO Then at my lodging, an it like you.°   *if it please you*
55   There doth my father lie,° and there this night   *lodge*
    We'll pass° the business privately and well.   *settle*
    Send for your daughter by your servant here;
    My boy shall fetch the scrivener° presently.   *scribe; notary*
    The worst is this: that at so slender warning
60   You are like to have a thin and slender pittance.°   *scanty meal*
BAPTISTA It likes me well. —Cambio, hie° you home,   *hurry*
    And bid Bianca make her ready straight.
    And if you will, tell what hath happened:
    Lucentio's father is arrived in Padua,
65   And how she's like to be Lucentio's wife. [*Exit* LUCENTIO.][7]
BIONDELLO I pray the gods she may with all my heart.

---

4. Content with the care that should be shown by a good father.
5. As shall confirm the agreements of both parties.
6. Proverbial for "Someone may be eavesdropping." The handles of a pitcher are its "ears."
7. F does not mark an exit for Lucentio/Cambio here, but it makes sense that he would follow Baptista's order. If Lucentio exits here and Biondello at line 66 as in F, or at line 67 as in this text, then their *re*-entry a few lines later can mark a new scene. Some editors assume that Biondello and perhaps Lucentio never leave the stage since Biondello says (at 4.5.5–6) that he has been left behind by Tranio to explain things to Lucentio. In that case, no scene break would be introduced after Baptista exits.

TRANIO   Dally not with the gods, but get thee gone.

Exit [BIONDELLO.]⁸

Signor Baptista, shall I lead the way?

Welcome: one mess° is like to be your cheer.°   *dish / entertainment*

70   Come, sir, we will better it in Pisa.

BAPTISTA   I follow you.   *Exeunt.*

4.5

Enter LUCENTIO [*disguised as Cambio*] *and* BIONDELLO.

BIONDELLO   Cambio.

LUCENTIO   What say'st thou, Biondello?

BIONDELLO   You saw my master wink and laugh upon you?

LUCENTIO   Biondello, what of that?

5   BIONDELLO   Faith, nothing, but he's left me here behind to
expound the meaning or moral of his signs and tokens.

LUCENTIO   I pray thee, moralize° them.   *interpret*

BIONDELLO   Then thus: Baptista is safe, talking with the
deceiving father of a deceitful son.

10   LUCENTIO   And what of him?

BIONDELLO   His daughter is to be brought by you to the supper.

LUCENTIO   And then?

BIONDELLO   The old priest at Saint Luke's church is at your
command at all hours.

15   LUCENTIO   And what of all this?

BIONDELLO   I cannot tell, except they are busied about a
counterfeit assurance.° Take you assurance¹ of her, *cum*   *betrothal agreement*
*privilegio ad imprimendum solum;*² to th' church take the
priest, clerk, and some sufficient honest witnesses.

20   If this be not that you look for, I have no more to say,
But bid Bianca farewell forever and a day.

LUCENTIO   Hear'st thou, Biondello?

BIONDELLO   I cannot tarry. I knew a wench married in an
afternoon as she went to the garden for parsley to stuff a

25   rabbit, and so may you, sir. And so adieu, sir, my master
hath appointed me to go to Saint Luke's to bid the priest be
ready to come against° you come with your appendix.³   *by the time*

Exit.

LUCENTIO   I may and will, if she be so contented.
She will be pleased, then wherefore should I doubt?

30   Hap what hap may, I'll roundly go about her.⁴
It shall go hard° if Cambio go without her.   *Exit.*⁵   *be unfortunate*

8. F here has a mysterious stage direction: "*Enter Peter.*" Some editors have argued that this is the name of an actor inadvertently introduced into the stage directions. Others assume it is the name of one of Lucentio's servants, who enters to tell the disguised Tranio and Baptista that their meal is ready; this possibility is not entirely satisfactory, especially since Baptista and Tranio still have to *proceed* to Lucentio's house for their meal. Perhaps something has been lost or garbled in this portion of the scene.
4.5 Location: Scene continues.

1. Make yourself sure.
2. With the exclusive right to print (a Latin phrase used by printers on the title pages of their books). Biondello urges Lucentio to confirm his "exclusive right" to Bianca and may be punning on "print" as meaning "to father a child."
3. Appendage (the bride).
4. Come what may, I'll pursue her eagerly.
5. At the corresponding point in *A Shrew,* Sly, still onstage, comments on the action.

4.6

Enter PETRUCCIO, KATHERINA, [*and*] HORTENSIO.[1]

PETRUCCIO   Come on, i'God's name, once more toward our
    father's.
    Good lord, how bright and goodly shines the moon.
KATHERINA   The moon? The sun. It is not moonlight now.
PETRUCCIO   I say it is the moon that shines so bright.
5 KATHERINA   I know it is the sun that shines so bright.
PETRUCCIO   Now by my mother's son, and that's myself,
    It shall be moon, or star, or what I list,°   please
    Or e'er° I journey to your father's house.   Before
    —Go on, and fetch our horses back again.
10   Evermore crossed° and crossed, nothing but crossed.   contradicted
HORTENSIO [*to* KATHERINA]   Say as he says, or we shall never go.
KATHERINA   Forward, I pray, since we have come so far,
    And be it moon, or sun, or what you please.
    And if you please to call it a rush candle,[2]
15   Henceforth I vow it shall be so for me.
PETRUCCIO   I say it is the moon.
KATHERINA   I know it is the moon.
PETRUCCIO   Nay, then, you lie: it is the blessèd sun.
KATHERINA   Then God be blessed, it is the blessèd sun;
20   But sun it is not when you say it is not,
    And the moon changes even as your mind.[3]
    What you will have it named, even that it is,
    And so it shall be so for Katherine.
HORTENSIO   Petruccio, go thy ways;° the field is won.   do as you wish
25 PETRUCCIO   Well, forward, forward, thus the bowl should run
    And not unluckily against the bias.[4]
    But soft, company is coming here.

        Enter VINCENTIO.

    Good morrow, gentle mistress, where away?
    —Tell me, sweet Kate, and tell me truly, too,
30   Hast thou beheld a fresher gentlewoman?
    Such war of white and red within her cheeks!
    What stars do spangle heaven with such beauty
    As those two eyes become that heavenly face?
    —Fair lovely maid, once more good day to thee.
35   —Sweet Kate, embrace her for her beauty's sake.
HORTENSIO   'A° will make the man mad to make the woman of   He
    him.°   call him a woman
KATHERINA   Young budding virgin, fair, and fresh, and sweet,
    Whither away, or whither is thy abode?
40   Happy the parents of so fair a child;
    Happier the man whom° favorable stars   to whom
    Allots thee for his lovely bedfellow.

4.6 Location: A road somewhere between Petruccio's house and Padua.
1. TEXTUAL COMMENT Only Petruccio, Katherina,
and Hortensio are named in this entrance, but stage
tradition often includes Grumio in the scene, as
someone needs to perform the duties of a servant.
See Digital Edition TC 9.
2. Candle made from rush dripped in grease, thus giv-

ing poor light.
3. Implying that Petruccio is mad as well as fickle.
Lunatics and women were imagined to be governed
by the moon.
4. A metaphor from the game of bowls in which the
ball, or bowl, was weighted so that it ran along a "bias,"
or curving path.

PETRUCCIO   Why, how now, Kate, I hope thou art not mad;
  This is a man, old, wrinkled, faded, withered,
45 And not a maiden, as thou say'st he is.
KATHERINA   Pardon, old father, my mistaking eyes,
  That have been so bedazzled with the sun
  That everything I look on seemeth green.°   *youthful*
  Now I perceive thou art a reverend father.
50 Pardon, I pray thee, for my mad mistaking.
PETRUCCIO   Do, good old grandsire, and withal° make known   *in addition*
  Which way thou travelest; if along with us,
  We shall be joyful of thy company.
VINCENTIO   Fair sir, and you, my merry mistress,
55 That with your strange encounter° much amazed me,   *greeting*
  My name is called Vincentio, my dwelling Pisa,
  And bound I am to Padua, there to visit
  A son of mine, which long I have not seen.
PETRUCCIO   What is his name?
VINCENTIO   Lucentio, gentle sir.
60 PETRUCCIO   Happily met, the happier for thy son.
  And now by law, as well as reverend age,
  I may entitle thee my loving father:
  The sister to my wife, this gentlewoman,
  Thy son by this hath married.[5] Wonder not,
65 Nor be not grieved; she is of good esteem,
  Her dowry wealthy, and of worthy birth,
  Beside, so qualified° as may beseem   *with such qualities*
  The spouse of any noble gentleman.
  Let me embrace with old Vincentio,
70 And wander we to see thy honest son,
  Who will of thy arrival be full joyous.
VINCENTIO   But is this true, or is it else your pleasure
  Like pleasant travelers to break a jest°   *crack a joke*
  Upon the company you overtake?
75 HORTENSIO   I do assure thee, father, so it is.
PETRUCCIO   Come, go along and see the truth hereof,
  For our first merriment hath made thee jealous.°   *suspicious*
        Exeunt [PETRUCCIO, KATHERINA, *and* VINCENTIO].
HORTENSIO   Well, Petruccio, this has put me in heart;
  Have to my widow, and if she be froward,°   *difficult*
80 Then hast thou taught Hortensio to be untoward.°   *Exit.*   *unmannerly*

5.1

Enter [GREMIO *first, followed separately by*]
  BIONDELLO, LUCENTIO [*as himself*], *and* BIANCA.
BIONDELLO [*to* LUCENTIO]   Softly and swiftly, sir, for the priest
  is ready.
LUCENTIO   I fly, Biondello; but they may chance to need thee at
  home, therefore leave us.   *Exeunt* [LUCENTIO *and* BIANCA].

---

5. By now has married. It is unclear how Petruccio
and Hortensio know this, especially since Hortensio
has heard "Lucentio" (Tranio) forswear Bianca (in

4.2). The inconsistency may suggest textual alteration in the role of Hortensio.
5.1 Location: Padua, in front of Lucentio's house.

5   BIONDELLO   Nay, faith, I'll see the church o'your back,[1] and
       then come back to my mistress as soon as I can.   [*Exit.*][2]

    GREMIO   I marvel Cambio comes not all this while.

       Enter PETRUCCIO, KATHERINA, VINCENTIO, GRUMIO
       with Attendants.

    PETRUCCIO   Sir, here's the door; this is Lucentio's house.
       My father's bears° more toward the marketplace;   *lies*

10   Thither must I, and here I leave you, sir.

    VINCENTIO   You shall not choose but drink before you go.
       I think I shall command your welcome here,
       And by all likelihood some cheer is toward.°   *food is being prepared*
       [*He*] *knocks.*

    GREMIO   They're busy within; you were best knock louder.

       PEDANT [*disguised as Vincentio, above,*] *looks out of*
       the window.

15   PEDANT   What's he that knocks as he would beat down the
       gate?

    VINCENTIO   Is Signor Lucentio within, sir?

    PEDANT   He's within, sir, but not to be spoken withal.

    VINCENTIO   What if a man bring him a hundred pound or two

20   to make merry withal?

    PEDANT   Keep your hundred pounds to yourself; he shall need
       none so long as I live.

    PETRUCCIO [*to* VINCENTIO]   Nay, I told you your son was well
       beloved in Padua. —Do you hear, sir? To leave frivolous cir-
       cumstances,° I pray you tell Signor Lucentio that his father   *matters*
       is come from Pisa and is here at the door to speak with him.

    PEDANT   Thou liest: his father is come from Padua and here
       looking out at the window.

    VINCENTIO   Art thou his father?

30   PEDANT   Ay, sir, so his mother says, if I may believe her.

    PETRUCCIO   Why, how now, gentleman? Why, this is flat knav-
       ery, to take upon you another man's name.

    PEDANT   Lay hands on the villain! I believe 'a° means to   *he*
       cozen° somebody in this city under my countenance.°   *cheat / name; person*

       Enter BIONDELLO.

35   BIONDELLO   I have seen them in the church together, God
       send 'em good shipping.° But who is here? Mine old master   *fair sailing*
       Vincentio! Now we are undone and brought to nothing.

    VINCENTIO   Come hither, crackhemp.[3]

    BIONDELLO   I hope I may choose, sir.

40   VINCENTIO   Come hither, you rogue. What, have you forgot me?

    BIONDELLO   Forgot you? No, sir, I could not forget you, for I
       never saw you before in all my life.

    VINCENTIO   What, you notorious villain, didst thou never see
       thy master's father, Vincentio?

45   BIONDELLO   What, my old worshipful old master? Yes, marry,
       sir, see where he looks out of the window.

---

1. At your back. Probably, I'll see the church as you
leave it after the wedding.
2. In F, Lucentio and Bianca exit first (after line 4)
and Biondello presumably follows after line 6, though
no exit is explicitly marked for him. Gremio, onstage

before this trio, apparently does not see them stealing away to the church.
3. Rogue (deserving to stretch the hangman's hemp
rope).

VINCENTIO   Is't so indeed?
       He beats BIONDELLO.
BIONDELLO   Help, help, help! Here's a madman will murder me!
                                    [Exit.]
PEDANT   Help, son! Help, Signor Baptista!   *[Exit above.]*
50 PETRUCCIO   Prithee, Kate, let's stand aside and see the end of
     this controversy.
        Enter PEDANT *[below] with* SERVANTS, BAPTISTA,
        TRANIO *[disguised as Lucentio].*
TRANIO *[to* VINCENTIO*]*   Sir, what are you that offer° to beat   *presume*
     my servant?
VINCENTIO   What am I, sir? Nay, what are you, sir? O immor-
55   tal gods! O fine villain! A silken doublet, a velvet hose, a
     scarlet cloak, and a copatain° hat! Oh, I am undone, I am   *high-crowned*
     undone. While I play the good husband at home, my son and
     my servant spend all at the university.
TRANIO   How now, what's the matter?
60 BAPTISTA   What, is the man lunatic?
TRANIO   Sir, you seem a sober ancient gentleman by your
     habit, but your words show you a madman. Why, sir, what
     'cerns° it you if I wear pearl and gold? I thank my good   *concerns*
     father, I am able to maintain it.
65 VINCENTIO   Thy father? O villain, he is a sailmaker in
     Bergamo.⁴
BAPTISTA   You mistake, sir; you mistake, sir. Pray, what do
     you think is his name?
VINCENTIO   His name? As if I knew not his name: I have
70   brought him up ever since he was three years old, and his
     name is Tranio.
PEDANT   Away, away, mad ass. His name is Lucentio, and he is
     mine only son and heir to the lands of me, Signor Vincentio.
VINCENTIO   Lucentio? Oh, he hath murdered his master! Lay
75   hold on him, I charge you in the Duke's name. O my son, my
     son! Tell me, thou villain, where is my son Lucentio?
TRANIO   Call forth an officer.
       [Enter an Officer.]
     Carry this mad knave to the jail. Father Baptista, I charge
     you see that he be forthcoming.°   *available when needed*
80 VINCENTIO   Carry me to the jail?
GREMIO   Stay, officer, he shall not go to prison.
BAPTISTA   Talk not, Signor Gremio: I say he shall go to prison.
GREMIO   Take heed, Signor Baptista, lest you be coney-
     catched° in this business. I dare swear this is the right   *duped*
85   Vincentio.
PEDANT   Swear if thou dar'st.
GREMIO   Nay, I dare not swear it.
TRANIO   Then thou wert best say that I am not Lucentio.
GREMIO   Yes, I know thee to be Signor Lucentio.
90 BAPTISTA   Away with the dotard, to the jail with him.
       Enter BIONDELLO, LUCENTIO, *and* BIANCA.

---

4. An Italian town associated with Harlequin, the witty, resourceful servant of the Italian *commedia dell'arte.*

VINCENTIO Thus strangers may be haled° and abused. Oh,
monstrous villain!   *dragged about*

BIONDELLO Oh, we are spoiled, and yonder he is! Deny him,
forswear him, or else we are all undone.

    Exeunt BIONDELLO, TRANIO, *and* PEDANT *as fast as
may be.*

95 LUCENTIO Pardon, sweet father.

    [*He*] *kneels.*

VINCENTIO Lives my sweet son?

BIANCA Pardon, dear father.

BAPTISTA How hast thou offended? Where is Lucentio?

LUCENTIO Here's Lucentio, right son to the right Vincentio,

100 That have by marriage made thy daughter mine
While counterfeit supposes[5] bleared thine eyne.°   *deceived your eyes*

GREMIO Here's packing° with a witness,[6] to deceive us all.   *plotting*

VINCENTIO Where is that damned villain Tranio,
That faced and braved° me in this matter so?   *defied*

105 BAPTISTA Why, tell me, is not this my Cambio?

BIANCA Cambio is changed into Lucentio.

LUCENTIO Love wrought these miracles. Bianca's love
Made me exchange my state° with Tranio,   *social position*
While he did bear my countenance in the town;

110 And happily I have arrived at the last
Unto the wishèd haven of my bliss.
What Tranio did, myself enforced him to;
Then pardon him, sweet father, for my sake.

VINCENTIO I'll slit the villain's nose that would have sent me

115 to the jail.

BAPTISTA But do you hear, sir? Have you married my daughter
without asking my good will?

VINCENTIO Fear not, Baptista, we will content you, go to. But
I will in to be revenged for this villainy.   *Exit.*

120 BAPTISTA And I to sound the depth° of this knavery. *Exit.* *discover the extent*

LUCENTIO Look not pale, Bianca, thy father will not frown.

    Exeunt [LUCENTIO *and* BIANCA].

GREMIO My cake is dough,[7] but I'll in among the rest,
Out of hope of all° but my share of the feast. [*Exit.*] *With hope of nothing*

KATHERINA Husband, let's follow to see the end of this ado.

125 PETRUCCIO First kiss me, Kate, and we will.

KATHERINA What, in the midst of the street?

PETRUCCIO What, art thou ashamed of me?

KATHERINA No, sir, God forbid, but ashamed to kiss.

PETRUCCIO Why, then, let's home again. —Come, sirrah, let's

130 away.

KATHERINA Nay, I will give thee a kiss. Now, pray thee, love,
stay.

PETRUCCIO Is not this well? Come, my sweet Kate.
Better once than never, for never too late.[8]

    Exeunt.

---

5. False ideas. Possibly an allusion to Gascoigne's
Supposes (1566), which was Shakespeare's main
source for the Bianca and Lucentio plot.
6. With clear evidence; without any doubt.

7. Proverbial expression for a failed project.
8. Two proverbs combined: "Better late than never"
and "It is never too late to mend."

5.2

Enter BAPTISTA, VINCENTIO, GREMIO, *the* PEDANT,
LUCENTIO, BIANCA, [PETRUCCIO, KATHERINA,
HORTENSIO, *and the*] WIDOW, [*followed by*]
BIONDELLO, GRUMIO, *and* TRANIO *with the* [SERVANTS]
bringing in a banquet.[1]

LUCENTIO At last, though long,° our jarring notes agree,   *after a long time*
   And time it is when raging war is done
   To smile at scapes° and perils overblown.   *escapes*
   My fair Bianca, bid my father welcome,
5 While I with selfsame° kindness welcome thine.   *identical*
   Brother Petruccio, sister Katherina,
   And thou, Hortensio, with thy loving widow,
   Feast with the best, and welcome to my house.
   My banquet is to close our stomachs up
10 After our great good cheer.° Pray you, sit down,   *feast; happiness*
   For now we sit to chat as well as eat.
PETRUCCIO Nothing but sit and sit, and eat and eat.
BAPTISTA Padua affords this kindness, son Petruccio.
PETRUCCIO Padua affords nothing but what is kind.
15 HORTENSIO For both our sakes I would that word were true.
PETRUCCIO Now, for my life, Hortensio fears[2] his widow.
WIDOW Then never trust me if I be afeard.°   *afraid*
PETRUCCIO You are very sensible, and yet you miss my sense:
   I mean Hortensio is afeard of you.
20 WIDOW He that is giddy thinks the world turns round.[3]
PETRUCCIO Roundly° replied.   *Boldly*
KATHERINA   Mistress, how mean you that?
WIDOW Thus I conceive by him.[4]
PETRUCCIO Conceives° by me! How likes Hortensio that?   *Becomes pregnant*
HORTENSIO My widow says thus she conceives her tale.[5]
25 PETRUCCIO Very well mended. Kiss him for that, good widow.
KATHERINA "He that is giddy thinks the world turns round."
   I pray you tell me what you meant by that.
WIDOW Your husband, being troubled with a shrew,
   Measures my husband's sorrow by his woe:
30 And now you know my meaning.
KATHERINA A very mean meaning.
WIDOW   Right, I mean you.
KATHERINA And I am mean indeed, respecting you.[6]
PETRUCCIO To her, Kate!
HORTENSIO To her, Widow!
35 PETRUCCIO A hundred marks,[7] my Kate does put her down.°   *defeat her*
HORTENSIO That's my office.[8]
PETRUCCIO Spoke like an officer.[9] Ha' to thee,° lad.   *Here's to you*
   [*He*] *drinks to* HORTENSIO.

5.2 Location: Lucentio's house in Padua.
1. Light meal of fruit, sweetmeats, and wine following the main meal.
2. Is afraid of. The widow takes it to mean "frightens."
3. That is, people judge everything by their own experience, implying that Petruccio is afraid of his wife.
4. Thus I understand him.
5. Thus she understands or intends her remark, with a pun on "tail" as meaning "genitalia."

6. I am moderate (like the mathematical "mean") compared with you; I demean myself in dealing with you.
7. A substantial wager, since 1 mark was equivalent to 13 shillings and 4 pence, or two-thirds of a pound. An unskilled laborer might earn 6 to 8 pounds in a year.
8. That's my job, with a pun on "put her down" as meaning "force or lay her down in sexual intercourse."
9. Like one who knows his duty.

BAPTISTA   How likes Gremio these quick-witted folks?

GREMIO   Believe me, sir, they butt together¹ well.

40 BIANCA   Head and butt? An hasty-witted body
Would say your head and butt were head and horn.²

VINCENTIO   Ay, mistress bride, hath that awakened you?

BIANCA   Ay, but not frighted me; therefore I'll sleep again.

PETRUCCIO   Nay, that you shall not, since you have begun:

45   Have at° you for a better jest or two.   *I shall come at*

BIANCA   Am I your bird? I mean to shift my bush,³
And then pursue me as you draw your bow.
You are welcome all.

                    Exeunt BIANCA[, KATHERINA, *and* WIDOW].

PETRUCCIO   She hath prevented° me. Here, Signor Tranio,   *stopped; anticipated*

50   This bird you aimed at, though you hit her not—
Therefore a health to all that shot and missed.

TRANIO   O sir, Lucentio slipped° me like his greyhound,   *unleashed*
Which runs himself and catches for his master.

PETRUCCIO   A good swift° simile, but something currish.°   *witty / base; doglike*

55 TRANIO   'Tis well, sir, that you hunted for yourself:
'Tis thought your deer does hold you at a bay.⁴

BAPTISTA   Oh, oh, Petruccio, Tranio hits you now.

LUCENTIO   I thank thee for that gird,° good Tranio.   *taunt*

HORTENSIO   Confess, confess: hath he not hit you here?

60 PETRUCCIO   'A° has a little galled° me, I confess.   *He / wounded*
And as the jest did glance away from me,
'Tis ten to one it maimed you two outright.

BAPTISTA   Now in good sadness,° son Petruccio,   *in all seriousness*
I think thou hast the veriest shrew of all.

65 PETRUCCIO   Well, I say no, and therefore, sir, assurance:
Let's each one send unto° his wife,   *summon*
And he whose wife is most obedient
To come at first when he doth send for her
Shall win the wager which we will propose.

HORTENSIO   Content;° what's the wager?   *Agreed*

70 LUCENTIO   Twenty crowns.°   *coins worth five shillings*

PETRUCCIO   Twenty crowns?
I'll venture so much of° my hawk or hound,   *on*
But twenty times so much upon my wife.

LUCENTIO   A hundred, then.

HORTENSIO   Content.

PETRUCCIO   A match.° 'Tis done.   *Agreed*

HORTENSIO   Who shall begin?

75 LUCENTIO   That will I.
Go, Biondello, bid your mistress come to me.

BIONDELLO   I go.   *Exit.*

BAPTISTA   Son, I'll be your half Bianca comes.⁵

LUCENTIO   I'll have no halves; I'll bear it all myself.

                    Enter BIONDELLO.

How now, what news?

---

1. They thrust their heads or horns together, with a
pun on "butt" as meaning "buttocks."
2. Would say your butting head was a cuckold's
horned head.
3. Alluding to the Elizabethan sport of shooting sitting birds with a bow and arrow. There may also be a
bawdy pun on "bush" as meaning "pubic area" and

the target of Petruccio's (phallic) arrow.
4. Your deer turns on you and holds you at a distance. Punning on "deer" and "dear."
5. I'll put up half the stake (and therefore collect
half of any winnings) in wagering that Bianca will
come first.

80 BIONDELLO   Sir, my mistress sends you word
        That she is busy and she cannot come.
    PETRUCCIO   How? "She's busy and she cannot come."
        Is that an answer?
    GREMIO   Ay, and a kind one, too.
        Pray God, sir, your wife send you not a worse.
85 PETRUCCIO   I hope better.
    HORTENSIO   Sirrah Biondello, go and entreat my wife to come
        to me forthwith.
                                              Exit BIONDELLO.
    PETRUCCIO   Oh, ho, "entreat" her. Nay, then she must needs
        come.
    HORTENSIO   I am afraid, sir, do what you can,
        Yours will not be entreated.
              Enter BIONDELLO.
90   Now, where's my wife?
    BIONDELLO   She says you have some goodly jest in hand.
        She will not come; she bids you come to her.
    PETRUCCIO   Worse and worse. "She will not come." Oh, vile,
        Intolerable, not to be endured!
95   Sirrah Grumio, go to your mistress,
        Say I command her come to me.   *Exit* [GRUMIO].
    HORTENSIO   I know her answer.
    PETRUCCIO   What?
    HORTENSIO   She will not.
    PETRUCCIO   The fouler fortune mine, and there an end.[6]
              Enter KATHERINA.
    BAPTISTA   Now, by my halidom,° here comes Katherina.   *by all I hold sacred*
100 KATHERINA   What is your will, sir, that you send for me?
    PETRUCCIO   Where is your sister and Hortensio's wife?
    KATHERINA   They sit conferring by the parlor fire.
    PETRUCCIO   Go fetch them hither. If they deny° to come,   *refuse*
        Swinge me them soundly forth[7] unto their husbands.
105   Away, I say, and bring them hither straight.
                              [*Exit* KATHERINA.]
    LUCENTIO   Here is a wonder, if you talk of a wonder.
    HORTENSIO   And so it is. I wonder what it bodes.
    PETRUCCIO   Marry, peace it bodes, and love, and quiet life,
        An awful° rule and right supremacy   *awe-inspiring*
110   And, to be short, what not° that's sweet and happy.   *everything*
    BAPTISTA   Now fair befall thee, good Petruccio.
        The wager thou hast won, and I will add
        Unto their losses twenty thousand crowns,
        Another dowry to another daughter,
115   For she is changed as she had never been.[8]
    PETRUCCIO   Nay, I will win my wager better yet
        And show more sign of her obedience,
        Her new-built virtue and obedience.
              Enter KATHERINA, BIANCA, *and* WIDOW.
        See where she comes and brings your froward° wives   *willful*

---

6. Worse luck for me (if you're right), and that's that.
7. Beat them soundly for me, and bring them out.
8. As if she had never existed before; as if she had never been what she was before (a shrew).

120 As prisoners to her womanly persuasion.
Katherine, that cap of yours becomes you not.
Off with that bauble; throw it underfoot.
WIDOW   Lord, let me never have a cause to sigh
Till I be brought to such a silly pass.
125 BIANCA   Fie, what a foolish duty call you this?
LUCENTIO   I would your duty were as foolish too.
The wisdom of your duty, fair Bianca,
Hath cost me five hundred crowns since supper time.
BIANCA   The more fool you for laying° on my duty.   *gambling*
130 PETRUCCIO   Katherine, I charge thee tell these headstrong
women
What duty they do owe their lords and husbands.
WIDOW   Come, come, you're mocking; we will have no telling.
PETRUCCIO   Come on, I say, and first begin with her.
WIDOW   She shall not.
135 PETRUCCIO   I say she shall, and first begin with her.
KATHERINA   Fie, fie, unknit that threatening unkind brow,
And dart not scornful glances from those eyes
To wound thy lord, thy king, thy governor.
It blots° thy beauty as frosts do bite the meads,°   *disfigures / meadows*
140 Confounds thy fame° as whirlwinds shake fair buds   *Ruins your reputation*
And in no sense is meet° or amiable.   *fitting*
A woman moved° is like a fountain troubled,   *angry*
Muddy, ill-seeming,° thick, bereft of beauty,   *ugly*
And while it is so none so dry or thirsty
145 Will deign to sip or touch one drop of it.
Thy husband is thy lord, thy life, thy keeper,
Thy head, thy sovereign, one that cares for thee,
And for thy maintenance commits his body
To painful labor both by sea and land,
150 To watch the night in storms, the day in cold,
Whilst thou liest warm at home, secure and safe,
And craves no other tribute at thy hands
But love, fair looks, and true obedience—
Too little payment for so great a debt.
155 Such duty as the subject owes the prince,
Even such a woman oweth to her husband.
And when she is froward, peevish,° sullen, sour,   *obstinate*
And not obedient to his honest will,
What is she but a foul contending rebel
160 And graceless traitor to her loving lord?
I am ashamed that women are so simple°   *foolish*
To offer war where they should kneel for peace,
Or seek for rule, supremacy, and sway
When they are bound to serve, love, and obey.
165 Why are our bodies soft and weak and smooth,
Unapt to° toil and trouble in the world,   *Unfitted for*
But that our soft conditions° and our hearts   *dispositions*
Should well agree with our external parts?
Come, come, you froward and unable worms.°   *weak creatures*
170 My mind hath been as big° as one of yours,   *proud*
My heart° as great, my reason haply more   *spirit*
To bandy word for word and frown for frown.
But now I see our lances are but straws,

Our strength as weak,° our weakness past compare,   *(as straws)*
175 That seeming to be most which we indeed least are.
     Then vail your stomachs, for it is no boot,[9]
     And place your hands below your husband's foot—
     In token of which duty, if he please,
     My hand is ready, may it do him ease.°[1]   *give him comfort*
180 PETRUCCIO   Why, there's a wench. Come on and kiss me, Kate.
     LUCENTIO   Well, go thy ways, old lad, for thou shalt ha't.[2]
     VINCENTIO   'Tis a good hearing° when children are toward.[3]   *thing to hear*
     LUCENTIO   But a harsh hearing when women are froward.
     PETRUCCIO   Come, Kate, we'll to bed.
185 —We three are married, but you two are sped.°   *defeated*
     'Twas I won the wager, though you hit the white,[4]
     And being a winner,° God give you good night.   *since I am a winner*

                              Exit PETRUCCIO.[5]
     HORTENSIO   Now go thy ways, thou hast tamed a curst shrew.
     LUCENTIO   'Tis a wonder, by your leave, she will be tamed so.
                              [*Exeunt.*][6]

---

9. Then lower your pride, for it is of no profit.
1. PERFORMANCE COMMENT   Though Katherina's final speech may suggest she has been tamed, many actors have delivered it in ways that undercut or ironize its meaning. See Digital Edition PC 2.
2. You shall have the prize.
3. Obedient (as opposed to "froward," line 119).
4. Hit the target (with a pun on "Bianca," which means "white" in Italian).

5. TEXTUAL COMMENT   The sense of the play's resolution will be affected by editorial and performance choices about how Petruccio and Katherina exit the stage. F lists an exit only for Petruccio here, although many editors have Katherina leave the stage with him. See Digital Edition TC 10.
6. In *A Shrew,* the Christopher Sly story concludes the play.

The First Part of Henry the Sixth

A play filled with battles and political intrigue, *1 Henry VI* depicts England's attempts to retain a military and political foothold in France even as rivalries among the English nobility hamstring these efforts. The English claimed parts of France both by treaty and by inheritance. In 1360, the English king, Edward III, was granted sovereignty over Calais and Bordeaux by the Treaty of Bretigny, which concluded part of what came to be known as the Hundred Years' War. This same Edward, from whom Henry VI was descended, also claimed the French crown itself through his mother, Isabella, the daughter of Philip IV of France. Philip's three sons died without producing male heirs, but Isabella, married to Edward II of England, gave birth to Edward III, who vigorously pursued both the crown and the territory of France. In the fifteenth century, his great-grandson, Henry V, renewed these efforts and achieved remarkable military successes at Harfleur and Agincourt (see Shakespeare's *Henry V* for an account of his reign). His son, Henry VI, struggled to retain what his father had won, and it is his efforts that *1 Henry VI* depicts.

In this struggle, everything depends on England's one incomparable hero, the valiant Lord Talbot, who fights with such ferocity that the French flee the very sound of his name. In 1592, probably just a few months after the play was first performed, Thomas Nashe, Shakespeare's contemporary, and himself a playwright, wrote, "How would it have joyed brave Talbot (the terror of the French) to think that after he had lain two hundred years in his tomb, he should triumph again on the stage, and have his bones new embalmed with the tears of ten thousand spectators at least (at several times), who, in the Tragedian that represents his person, imagine they behold him fresh bleeding?" This comment—which imagines the long-dead Talbot cheered by the thought of having his mighty victories and lamentable death played again and again—forms part of Nashe's extended defense of stage plays. While many Elizabethan writers attacked the theater as a place of idleness where lies and lewd stories were circulated, Nashe used plays like *1 Henry VI* to argue for the value of the stage, partly because of its role in preserving the memory of England's glorious heroes. As Nashe says, "For the subject of them (for the most part) it is borrowed out of our English Chronicles, wherein our forefathers' valiant acts (that have lain long buried in rusty brass and worm-eaten books) are revived, and they themselves raised from the grave of oblivion, and brought to plead their aged honors in open presence." For Nashe, Talbot is one of those worthy forefathers, pleased to be resurrected in the person of an English actor.

Shakespeare was among those instrumental in creating the vogue in the 1590s for stage plays based on events from the reigns of England's former monarchs. It is now generally agreed that in writing his earliest history plays Shakespeare often worked collaboratively. In the case of *1 Henry VI*, textual scholars now assign act 1 of the play to the same Thomas Nashe, mentioned above, who praised the effect of Talbot on the stage; Shakespeare himself is presumed to be the primary author of the Temple Garden scene (2.4) (discussed below) and the moving sequence leading to Talbot's death (4.2–4.5). The rest of the play likely involved other collaborators whose identities are not certain (see Textual Introduction). By the time the First Folio was printed in 1623, the early histories were simply assigned to Shakespeare, regardless of their likely collaborative origins; and the division of the 1623 First Folio into histories, comedies, and tragedies indicates that the plays dealing with English history were perceived as a distinct and important group of works. From the beginning of his career until 1599, when *Henry V* was first acted, Shakespeare contributed to the writing of at least eight plays based loosely on the reigns of English kings from Richard II, who was deposed in 1399, to Henry VII, who assumed the English throne in 1485 after the Battle of Bosworth Field; in addition, there was one play on the reign of King John (1199–1216) and another on the reign of Edward III (1327–77), which scholars now attribute at least partly to Shakespeare. Some of these plays chronicle the English wars in France. And some depict the lengthy struggle, known as the Wars of the Roses, between two branches of England's royal family for possession of the English throne: on one side of this struggle were the Lancastrians, who wore the red rose as their badge; on the other side were the Yorkists, who wore the white. Both groups claimed descent from King Edward III. (Charts showing the genealogies of the Lancastrians and the Yorkists appear on the endpapers at the back of the print edition and are also included in the Digital Edition.) The Battle of Bosworth Field ended this civil strife when Henry Tudor, a descendant of John of Gaunt, Duke of Lancaster, defeated Richard III, the last of the Yorkist kings, and then married Elizabeth of York, the daughter of an earlier Yorkist king, Edward IV. Henry Tudor thus united the red rose and the white, and the Tudors ruled England until 1603, when Elizabeth I, granddaughter of Henry VII, died without issue. It was during the final years of Elizabeth's reign that Shakespeare was engaged in writing most of his English history plays.

Many scholars have speculated about why these plays about England's past became so popular. Nashe gives us a clue when he emphasizes their role in celebrating martial heroes and in creating for the common people a collective memory of their national past. In the sixteenth century, many chronicle histories of England were written, such as Edward Hall's *Union of the Two Noble and Illustrious Families of Lancaster and York* (1548) and Raphael Holinshed's *Chronicles of England, Scotland, and Ireland;* the second edition of Holinshed, published in 1587, was used extensively by Shakespeare in composing his history plays. These prose chronicles, in fact, may have been some of the "worm-eaten" books from which Nashe imagined Talbot being revived for a more pleasurable life on the stage. The theater, unlike obscure and musty texts, made a version of English history accessible even to those who could not read. For a penny, a common person could go to the theater, stand in the pit, and thrill to the exploits of Talbot and the treachery of the French. Dramatized history thus contributed to an emerging sense of national identity that depended not only on allegiance to a monarch but also on pride in a shared English culture, language, and identity. The theater played a role in constructing this shared identity, providing ordinary people with riveting representations of a common national past.

In the early 1590s, there were good reasons why arousing patriotic sentiment for an English military hero like Talbot might have been popular. In 1588, England had, with the help of bad weather, repulsed an attack by the Spanish Armada, an invasion fleet sent by Europe's most powerful Catholic power, Spain. This victory had encouraged many English people to feel that their country should play a more active role in supporting the Protestant powers of Europe against their Catholic enemies. In 1591–92, with some reluctance Elizabeth sent her charismatic nobleman the Earl of Essex into France to aid Henry IV of Navarre and the French Protestant faction. In this campaign, Essex participated in a struggle for control of the city of Rouen. We can date *1 Henry VI* to sometime in 1592 both because Nashe's comments on Talbot were published during that year and because the play seems to refer to this French campaign. It depicts fifteenth-century Englishmen invading French soil—and attacking Rouen—at the very moment an English army was once again before the city's walls. Many people in England might thus have seen in Talbot an image of their contemporary champion, the dashing Earl of Essex.

Shakespeare was involved in writing two more plays on the reign of Henry VI; in the First Folio, these were entitled, respectively, *The Second Part of Henry the Sixth* and *The Third Part of Henry the Sixth.* These two plays, however, were also published in earlier octavo or quarto versions, where they bore the titles *The First Part of the*

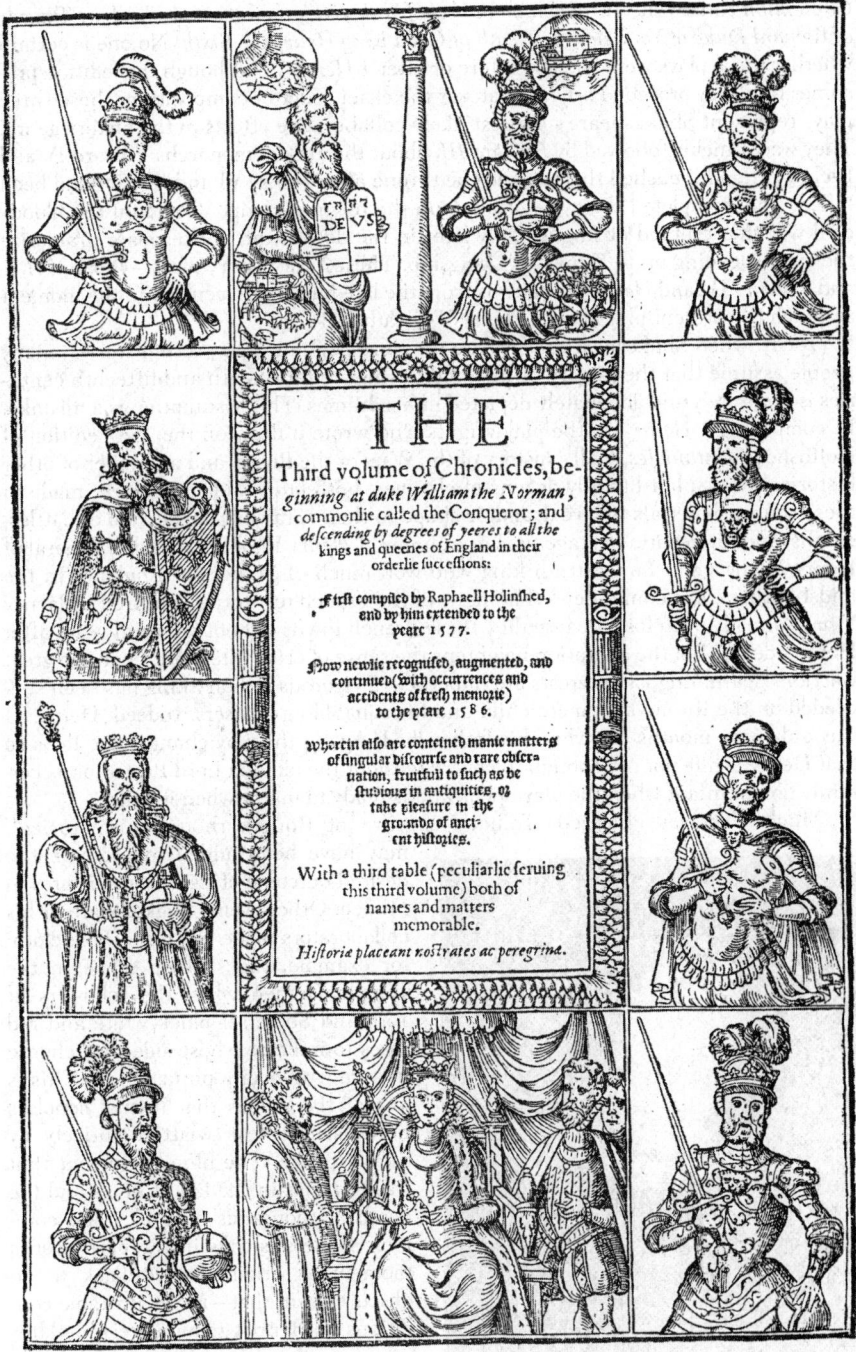

THE

Third volume of Chronicles, beginning at duke *William the Norman*,
commonlie called the Conqueror; and
descending by degrees of yeeres to all the
kings and queenes of England in their
orderlie successions:

First compiled by Raphaell Holinshed,
and by him extended to the
yeare 1577.

Now newlie recognised, augmented, and
continued (with occurrences and
accidents of fresh memorie)
to the yeare 1586.

Wherein also are conteined manie matters
of singular discourse and rare obseruation, fruitfull to such as be
studious in antiquities, or
take pleasure in the
groundo of anci-
ent histories.

With a third table (peculiarlie seruing
this third volume) both of
names and matters
memorable.

Historia placeant nostrates ac peregrina.

The title page of the third volume of Raphael Holinshed's *Chronicles* (1587 edition).

Contention betwixt the Two Famous Houses of York and Lancaster and *The True Tragedy of Richard Duke of York and the Death of Good King Henry the Sixth.* No one is certain whether these plays were written before or after *1 Henry VI,* although this edition presumes that they precede *Part 1.* Whatever the exact order of composition, these three plays represent Shakespeare's earliest likely collaborative efforts in the history genre. They were quickly followed by *Richard III,* about the Yorkist monarchs Edward IV and Richard III, who pushed their way to the throne after Henry VI and his son had been killed. This completed the cycle of plays on the reign of Henry VI and on the bloody civil war that erupted during it. Only later in the decade did Shakespeare dramatize the events leading up to Henry VI's kingship. These later history plays—*Richard II, 1* and *2 Henry IV,* and *Henry V*—take us from the late fourteenth century to the moment at which the present play begins: Henry V's death in 1422.

Today, when Shakespeare's plays are far more popular than prose histories, many people assume that the history of England in the late fourteenth and fifteenth centuries is accurately and adequately depicted in his dramas. This assumption is a mistake. In composing *1 Henry VI,* the playwrights who wrote it drew on the 1587 edition of Holinshed's *Chronicles,* Hall's history of the Wars of the Roses, and a number of other historical works; but literally dozens of changes, both large and small, were made in these source materials to give dramatic shape to their sprawling succession of battles, deaths, and diplomatic stratagems. For example, *1 Henry VI* opens with the funeral of Henry V, the great Lancastrian king who won much of France for England. In the midst of this scene comes news that many of the French territories captured by Henry V have already been lost. In actuality, these French towns did not fall until years after Henry's death. But the alteration heightens the sense of crisis attendant upon the great warrior's death: English interests are imperiled; a vigorous military king has been succeeded on the throne by a mere child and his squabbling advisers. Indeed, Henry VI was only nine months old when his father died. Again, the play changes the facts so that Henry, while not old enough to govern without the aid of a Lord Protector, is certainly not an infant when the play opens and is ready to marry when it ends.

Much else was changed. Talbot's capture of Rouen, though unhistorical,

King Henry VI. Artist and date unknown.

may have been added to indicate the desired outcome of Essex's adventures in France. Other events Shakespeare or his collaborators made up from whole cloth: for example, the striking scene in the Temple Garden when the followers of York and Somerset pluck white and red roses to indicate whose side they choose in a quarrel over a point in law. This is one of the scenes that textual scholars now assume was written entirely by Shakespeare. The bloody conflict that was to result in the fall of kings and the death of thousands of nobles and common soldiers is thus in the play given a moment of origin, traced back to an obscure event that—in the unstable conditions of Henry's tenuous reign—flares into a conflagration of blood and death. In some cases, the dramatists who wrote *1 Henry VI* simply repeat the historical confusion of their sources. In this play, for example, the Edmund Mortimer who had a claim to the throne is conflated with his cousin John Mortimer, who was imprisoned in the Tower for many years for supporting his kinsman's royal ambitions. Sir John Falstaff is treated as a cowardly knight, when in actuality he was a distinguished officer of Henry's forces in the French wars. Both of these inaccuracies were probably repetitions of what Shakespeare or his possible collaborators would have found in texts available to them. (Later, a cowardly character named Falstaff appears in Shakespeare's *1* and *2 Henry IV* and in *The Merry Wives of Windsor.*)

Indisputably, the play depicts events neither exactly as they were presented in the chronicles nor as a modern historian might present them. In turning historical materials into effective drama, Shakespeare or his collaborators gave one of many possible shapes to the welter of events recorded in the various sources. Many scholars have tried to discern what Shakespeare's "philosophy of history" could have been. Did he, for example, subscribe to the view expressed in Edward Hall's history that the turmoil of the fifteenth century was God's punishment for Henry IV's crime in deposing a rightful king, Richard II—a crime for which England paid in blood for over a hundred years? Or did he take a more secular view of history, in which events unfold as they do because of human choices and actions rather than because of God's intervention? One must read the plays to decide about these questions, and the answers may differ from play to play. An early and collaborative work, *1 Henry VI* does not necessarily adopt a single point of view toward why historical events unfold as they do. Unlike a history play such as *Richard III*, this one contains very little language suggesting that an angry God is punishing England for Henry IV's earlier deposition of Richard II. Rather, events seem to unfold as a direct consequence of human decisions and human rivalries. That demons actually appear to Joan of Arc in act 5, however, complicates matters. Their presence suggests the existence of a supernatural realm that has some influence, however ambiguous, on the course of human affairs.

In dramatic terms, *1 Henry VI* is structured by juxtaposing two conflicts. In the foreground is the struggle between the French and English forces in France. The English, led by Talbot, clash repeatedly with the army of Charles, the French Dauphin. He, in turn, is given aid throughout much of the play by a remarkable figure: the martial maid Joan of Arc. But a counterpoint to the struggle between French and English emerges by way of the feuding the play depicts among the English nobility. These two lines of action impinge on each other, as the internal squabbling among the English leaders keeps them from giving proper support to their soldiers in the field, eventually enabling Joan and Charles to kill Talbot before the walls of Bordeaux.

If the play has a message to deliver to the English, it would seem to be that petty rivalries and divisions among the English nobility can destroy England from within. As the boy King says to his quarreling nobles, Gloucester and Winchester,

> Believe me, lords, my tender years can tell,
> Civil dissension is a viperous worm
> That gnaws the bowels of the commonwealth.
> (3.1.71–73)

The play seldom lets the audience forget about this worm. As early as the first scene, Winchester, whose status as bishop and then later as cardinal connects him to the Church of Rome, quarrels with Gloucester, who has been appointed Protector of the Realm—that is, the one who effectively holds royal power while the King is still a child. Secular and religious authority clash, and the rent that this causes in the fabric of the commonwealth finds visual embodiment in the several arguments and stage fights that break out between Winchester's tawny-clothed followers and Gloucester's blue-coated servingmen. This striking visual juxtaposition of the two factions vividly reveals the cankerworm of civil dissension at work. The red and white roses worn by the followers, respectively, of Somerset and York serve the same purpose, splitting England into two parties just when a united front is needed to sustain the French wars. Young Henry, although aware of the danger of civil dissension, can do little to stop it. On the one hand, he empowers Richard of York by returning to him the lands and titles taken from his father, the Earl of Cambridge, who had been accused of treason; on the other hand, he decides to wear the red rose of the House of Lancaster. Striving, perhaps, for evenhandedness, he inadvertently encourages the dissension he would suppress.

Yet to modern readers, perhaps the most interesting part of the play is not its demonstration of the dangers of civil dissension but its handling of the opposition between Talbot, terror of the French, and Joan, scourge of the English. In contrast to the rivalrous and selfish nobles who surround the young Henry, Talbot is the epitome of the unselfish heroism that Nashe found so compelling. Like a good feudal lord, he lives to serve his king in battle, an arena in which he repeatedly confirms his noble lineage and demonstrates his masculinity. Captured by the French when stabbed in the back by "a base Walloon" (an inhabitant of a French-speaking province now in Belgium), he nonetheless so terrifies his captors that they keep a guard of armed bowmen around him even when he sleeps. Talbot embodies the play's nostalgia for an idealized feudal world in which the values of valor and loyalty are shared by a community of men and passed on by them to their sons. In this regard, the play quite possibly spoke to a longing on the part of some of Elizabeth's subjects to be ruled once more by a king, not by an aging female monarch. When 1 Henry VI was written, Elizabeth, no longer young and with no heir, was entering the fourth decade of her long reign. The play seems to tap into a yearning for a return to masculine rule and martial values.

In France, Talbot is surrounded by other great English warriors—most notably Salisbury, who dies at the siege of Orléans, and Bedford, who, though sick and dying, insists on being carried in a chair to the battlefield at Rouen in order to give courage to his men. Perhaps most touching, at Bordeaux, where the warring English nobles refuse to send him aid, Talbot is joined on the battlefield by his son John, a fledgling warrior come to learn from his father the skills and the values of the warrior class he aspires to join. Urged to flee, he refuses, certain that flight would prove him both effeminate and baseborn. Instead, he is initiated into the rites of manhood by shedding blood and sustaining wounds in what can only be described as an erotics of battle. Having rescued him from the Bastard of Orléans, his father says:

> When from the Dauphin's crest thy sword struck fire,
> It warmed thy father's heart with proud desire
> Of bold-faced victory. Then leaden age,
> Quickened with youthful spleen and warlike rage,
> Beat down Alençon, Orléans, Burgundy,
> And from the pride of Gallia rescued thee.
> The ireful bastard Orléans, that drew blood
> From thee, my boy, and had the maidenhood
> Of thy first fight, I soon encounterèd,
> And, interchanging blows, I quickly shed
> Some of his bastard blood. . . .
>
> (4.6.10–20)

Young Talbot, shedding blood in his first battle, is compared to a young girl who bleeds during her first experience of intercourse. The cut and thrust of battle is thus portrayed as a sexual encounter in which the goal is to penetrate the body and shed the blood of one's enemy. Young Talbot's willingness to participate in such struggles, no matter how inevitable his ultimate defeat, signifies the purity of his lineage and blood. Bound together by a code of chivalric values and by the rites of blood, Talbot, his son, and Bedford, Salisbury, and those who fight with them upon the fields of

France embody the heroism that Nashe suggested would stir the hearts of English theatergoers. By the play's end, however, all these warriors are dead. With young Talbot's premature slaughter on the plains of Bordeaux, the bright flame of English chivalry flickers out. England passes into the hands of mere politicians and rivalrous churchmen who, if they fight, fight not for king and country but for their own selfish interests.

The English in this play are defeated in part because of their failure to live up to and support their own best ideals as embodied in the figure of Talbot. Their defeat, however, also owes much to Talbot's chief antagonist, the charismatic and mysterious Joan of Arc. Depending on the vantage point from which she is viewed, Joan is a holy maid sent by God to aid her country, a servant of the devil, or a deceitful whore. When the Bastard of Orléans first introduces her to the Dauphin, he calls Joan a holy maid and a prophet, and after she both sees through the Dauphin's trick to substitute René for himself and defeats the Dauphin in single combat, he proclaims her an Amazon (one of the legendary race of women warriors) and a Deborah (an Old Testament prophet and judge who accompanied an Israelite army against their Canaanite oppressors). These comparisons suggest how highly the French at first value their female champion. For a time, Joan seems possessed of uncanny powers. Not only does she recognize the Dauphin without ever having seen him before, but, perhaps more remarkable, she seems to suck away the great Talbot's strength, leaving him confused and ashamed before the walls of Orléans.

The English respond to this powerful but disarmingly down-to-earth peasant girl by calling her a witch and a whore. Much of their language concerning Joan is filled with bawdy double meanings, beginning with their play on the word *pucelle,* meaning "maid" or "virgin" in French, but sounding like "puzzel," English slang for "whore." From the first time he meets her in battle, Talbot assumes that Joan's powers can come only from witchcraft, rather than from a heavenly or merely human source. Joan's circumstances invite this kind of denigration. She is an unmarried woman who has turned soldier and assumed the garments of a man. In the early modern period, to dress like a man was often read as a violation of woman's assigned place in the gender hierarchy and an indication of the cross-dresser's uncontrolled will and appetites. Such women were easily assumed to be sexually transgressive, as well as vulnerable to the temptations of the devil.

Even Elizabeth, the unmarried queen, was subject to endless rumors concerning her sexuality. Some whispered that she had had bastard children with the Earl of Leicester, some that her hymen was so thick that no man could penetrate her. The virgin and the whore, the heaven-sent exception and the unnatural monster—the one could easily be turned into the other. While it seems implausible that Joan was constructed explicitly to remind spectators of the English queen, nonetheless the shepherd girl serves as a lightning rod to capture some of the ambivalent emotions attached to the Queen and to the idea of powerful public women more generally. Occasionally, Joan is portrayed in language echoing that used of Elizabeth. Charles, for example, calls her

Fifteenth-century Franco-Flemish portrait of Joan of Arc.

Astraea's daughter—that is, daughter of the goddess of justice—a title often applied
to Elizabeth. Several critics have argued that Joan's battlefield exploits recall the stories circulated about Elizabeth in 1588, when she was said to have appeared in armor
before her troops at Tilbury as they prepared to go into battle against the Spanish.
Having the body of a woman but the role and the clothing of a man, each of these
women could incite reverence but also demonization. Anomalies, they could be read
as criminals or fiends rather than as miraculous exceptions to their cultures' expectations concerning virtuous women.

The play's Joan is built of contradictions. At first, she seems a miracle worker who
speaks confidently of her role as servant of "God's mother" (1.2.78) and savior of
France. At times, she demonstrates Amazonian strength and shrewd military leadership. At other times, she speaks with the sharp tongue and pragmatic realism of a
shepherd girl. When, for example, the English herald delivers an extended eulogy
over the body of Talbot on the plains of Bordeaux, Joan interrupts him: "Him that
thou magnifi'st with all these titles / Stinking and flyblown lies here at our feet"
(4.7.75–76). Elsewhere, having persuaded Burgundy to leave his alliance with Talbot
and rejoin the French side, she remarks with irony: "[aside] Done like a Frenchman:
turn and turn again" (3.3.85). The greatest shift in the presentation of Joan, however, occurs in act 5, when she unexpectedly dwindles into a frightened and ineffectual practitioner of witchcraft. Summoning demons, she offers to let them suck
her blood in return for doing her bidding. They refuse, leaving her vainly attempting
to save herself from burning by pleading pregnancy. This diminished Joan of the
last act—who, when directly depicted as a witch, is presented as an impotent one—
seems deployed in part to bring the play to a closure acceptable to English pride.
Talbot may have been defeated, but Joan is not allowed to win the war or even to live.
This ending also echoes historical fact. The English handed the actual Joan of Arc
over to the Inquisition, and, found guilty of heresy and witchcraft, she was burned in
May 1431.

Joan's connection with witchcraft also capitalizes on the widespread interest in
the phenomenon during the early 1590s. In 1591, accounts had reached England of
the Scottish king James's prosecution of witches; and some had dared to hint that
Elizabeth herself had used witchcraft to defeat the Spanish Armada. Several English
treatises had been published in the 1580s debating whether witches were indeed the
servants of the devil or were simply people, usually old women, scapegoated by their
communities or deluded into thinking they had powers that they actually lacked. The
play, of course, doesn't settle the matter, giving us a Joan whose success against the
English could have either a supernatural cause or a more mundane origin in her own
strength, cleverness, and ability to inspire others. And while she does summon demons
in the last act, they fail to aid her.

Joan is not the only woman in 1 Henry VI. There are two others: the Countess of
Auvergne and Margaret of Anjou, both French and both allied to Joan in the threat
they pose to English manhood. While the play certainly highlights the political and
military damage done to England by dissension among the English nobility, it also
constructs women, especially French women, as a source of danger to England and the
nation's male leaders. While no English women appear in 1 Henry VI, three French
women play important roles, and all threaten English interests. Joan almost ousts the
English from France. The Countess of Auvergne attempts to imprison Talbot in her
castle. Margaret conquers men's hearts by means of her great beauty, causing Henry
VI to accept the dowerless Margaret as his bride despite his promise to marry another
woman. Suffolk, the King's retainer, has already fallen prey to her charms, setting up
the possibility that, Joan gone, yet another French woman will cause rivalries and dissension in England.

In the warrior culture idealized in the person of Talbot, women would not seem to
figure very importantly, except perhaps as mothers who give birth to sons who will
continue the lineage and the values of the fathers. But 1 Henry VI depicts a more

complicated reality. It shows, for example, how a potential wife, like Margaret, can incite uncontrollable desires in men and so become much more than a vehicle for reproduction or a pawn in a dynastic settlement. It also shows that some men, like the French of this play, seem unable to be martial heroes without the extraordinary and exceptional help of a woman. And it acknowledges that sometimes fathers don't beget sons worthy of the paternal name, as seems to be the case with Henry VI. Sometimes women must fill the void left by masculine failings; occasionally, as with Elizabeth I, a woman must even become king. *1 Henry VI* puts all of these complex and contradictory knowledges in play. While it creates heroes for men weary of feminine rule, in the process it also acknowledges the potential weaknesses of men, the occasional failures of the patriarchal gender system to function as it should, and the sometimes surprising and terrifying powers of women. As it turns out, Nashe painted too simple a picture of the history plays. They are not only about the valiant acts of "our forefathers" but also about the failings of less admirable Englishmen and, indeed, about the actions of women, some of whom, though foreign, seem to have spoken to anxieties generated very close to home.

JEAN E. HOWARD

SELECTED BIBLIOGRAPHY

Hampton-Reeves, Stuart, and Carol Chillington Rutter. *The Henry VI Plays (Shakespeare in Performance)*. Manchester: Manchester UP, 2006. Discusses particularly notable modern British productions of the Henry VI plays, including those directed by Peter Hall, John Barton, Terry Hands, Adrian Noble, and others.

Harrawood, Michael. "Overreachers: Hyperbole, the 'circle in the water,' and Force in *1 Henry VI*." *English Literary Renaissance* 33.3 (2003): 309–27. Discusses the force of hyperbolic language and its exhaustion in *1 Henry VI* with comparisons to Marlowe's *Tamburlaine*.

Hodgdon, Barbara. "Enclosing Contention: 1, 2, and 3 Henry VI." *The End Crowns All: Closure and Contradiction in Shakespeare's History*. Princeton, NJ: Princeton UP, 1991. 44–99. Analyzes techniques for creating or disrupting dramatic closure in Shakespeare's early histories.

Jackson, Gabriele Bernhard. "Topical Ideology: Witches, Amazons, and Shakespeare's Joan of Arc." *English Literary Renaissance* 18 (1988): 40–65. Examines the contradictory aspects of the characterization of Joan of Arc, arguing that she is represented both as a positive force and analogue of Queen Elizabeth and also as a witch and a strumpet.

Lee, Patricia-Ann. "Reflections of Power: Margaret of Anjou and the Dark Side of Queenship." *Renaissance Quarterly* 39 (1986): 183–217. Analyzes how the historical Margaret was represented not only in Shakespeare's plays but also in the historical chronicles of the fifteenth and sixteenth centuries.

Levin, Carole. "'Murder not then the fruit within my womb': Shakespeare's Joan, Foxe's Guernsey Martyr, and Women Pleading Pregnancy in English History and Culture." *Shakespeare's Foreign Worlds: National and Transnational Identities in the Elizabethan Age*. Ed. Carole Levin and John Watkins. Ithaca, NY: Cornell UP, 2009. 25–50. Examines historical cases of early modern English and Scottish women pleading pregnancy to escape execution and their bearing on Joan of Arc's assertion of pregnancy in act 5 of *1 Henry VI*.

Rackin, Phyllis. *Stages of History: Shakespeare's English Chronicles*. Ithaca, NY: Cornell UP, 1990. 146–200. Discusses how women in Shakespeare's English history plays subvert and challenge the masculine writing of history.

Riggs, David. *Shakespeare's Heroical Histories: Henry VI and Its Literary Tradition.* Cambridge: Harvard UP, 1971. 93–139. Explores the deterioration of heroic ideals in Shakespeare's early English histories with special attention paid to the opposition of Talbot, the English hero, and Joan of Arc, his French antithesis.

Tricomi, Albert. "Joan la Pucelle and the Inverted Saints Play in *1 Henry VI.*" *Renaissance and Reformation* 25 (2001): 5–31. Reads *1 Henry VI* as a Reformation critique of Joan of Arc as a false prophet who incites men to idolatry and of *1 Henry VI* as an inversion of a Catholic saint's play.

Walsh, Brian. "'Unkind Division': The Double Absence of Performing History in *1 Henry VI.*" *Shakespeare Quarterly* 55 (2004): 119–47. Discusses the role of performance in evoking, but never fully capturing, the historical past to which *1 Henry VI* refers.

FILM

Henry VI, Part One. 1983. Dir. Jane Howell. UK. 112 min. Lavish costumes and some strong performances in a textually faithful version of the play from BBC-TV. With Trevor Peacock as Talbot, Peter Benson as Henry VI, and Brenda Blethyn as Joan.

TEXTUAL INTRODUCTION

Unlike *2 Henry VI* and *3 Henry VI*, which appeared during Shakespeare's lifetime in quarto or octavo editions, *1 Henry VI* was first printed in the 1623 Folio (F). Since all editions of *1 Henry VI* derive from the same text, editorial intervention is largely limited to modernization, standardization, and occasional correction. The F text shows some attempt at regularization; like most other Shakespeare plays printed during his lifetime, the quarto and octavo versions of *2 and 3 Henry VI* have no act and scene breaks, but *1 Henry VI* is broken into acts and, in some cases, scenes, and its stage directions tend to be more formal and less theatrical than those in the texts of *2 and 3 Henry VI.*

The stage directions represent one of the clearest points of necessary intervention in *1 Henry VI.* Vague or incomplete stage directions, using a catch-all phrase such as "and others," require editorial emendation to identify the other characters. For instance, at the opening of 2.4, F has "*Enter Richard Plantagenet, Warwick, Somerset, Poole, and others,*" but speech prefixes within the scene specify Vernon and a Lawyer as those "*others.*" Exits also are unreliable in F; in some scenes, an exit is neither specified for a given character nor obvious from the dialogue, and editors frequently differ over where to place the exit.

The history plays are full of battles, and these present particular difficulties for an editor, who needs to specify entrances, exits, and scene divisions to make the action comprehensible to a reader. Furthermore, battles do not follow the standard theatrical convention that a scene ends when the stage is cleared; instead, in these texts the stage is usually cleared with an "*Exit*" or "*Exeunt*" before a battle begins, even if one exiting character is going to re-enter immediately in the flow of battle, thus violating the so-called "law of re-entry," which maintains that a character cannot re-enter immediately after exiting.

Editing *1 Henry VI* is complicated by the fact that a long tradition exists, stretching back to the eighteenth century, of believing that the play is collaboratively written. An increasing amount of evidence supports the conclusion that Shakespeare was only one of a number of contributors to the play. Brian Vickers's survey of the history of attribution for *1 Henry VI*, together with Hugh Craig's recent tests using computational stylistics, appears to corroborate the theory that Thomas Nashe most likely wrote act 1, that Shakespeare was responsible for the Temple Garden scene

(2.4) and the scenes leading up to Talbot's death (4.2–4.5), and that one or more unknown authors assembled the rest of the play. At scene level attributions remain controversial—not least because statistical analysis requires a sample of more than a certain number of lines (usually a hundred). Craig suggests that Shakespeare may have written the scene containing Mortimer's death (2.5) as well as Talbot's scenes with his son (4.5–4.7.32), and that Marlowe may have been the author of at least some of the Joan scenes.

Multiple authorship may be one cause of the inconsistencies and apparent errors in the text. For example, aside from 1.3, where he is referred to as a cardinal, Winchester is represented as a bishop until 5.1, when he is officially installed as cardinal. The inconsistency at 1.3, possibly the result of hasty composition or limited opportunity for a collaborative final edit, may be confusing to readers. However, emending 1.3 to make Winchester a bishop there would create new problems, including altering the meter of some lines (including 19, 36, 49, 78, and 83), replacing references such as "broad cardinal's hat" (36) and "scarlet robes" (42), and affecting the characterization of Gloucester and Winchester and diminishing the play's foregrounding of the corruption of the Roman Catholic Church.

Other examples of stylistic difference that may be concealed by the editing process include lineation, punctuation, and repetitive diction. Editors have tended—sometimes unconsciously—to make all segments of a given play text sound like "Shakespeare," and this can affect the impulse to emend—to add, delete, or move words or phrases, for instance, in order to achieve a more regular iambic pentameter. However, the smoothing away of such idiosyncrasies inevitably takes place at the cost of obliterating part of the play's evidence of early modern collaboration.

One minor example occurs at the end of 1.1 and bears upon our perception of the character of Winchester. In the Folio, Winchester's final lines are: "The King from Eltham I intend to send / And sit at chiefest stern of public weal" (176–77). Most modern editions, including this one, emend "send" to "steal," thus creating a rhyming final couplet for the scene, a familiar element in many of Shakespeare's plays that appears erratically elsewhere in *1 Henry VI*—for example, in 1.3, 2.4, and every scene of the fourth act. Arguably, the compositor might have accidentally picked up the "-end" from "intend" earlier in the line and added it to the beginning of "steal." Even this small example, however, helps to create a particular vision of Winchester: if he *sends* the King, it is a power struggle; but if he *steals* the King, it is a greater indictment against him and of his motives.

While such occasions for editorial intervention abound in *1 Henry VI*, sometimes electing *not* to emend offers a more integral text, one that preserves valuable nuances that help to convey the story not only of the protagonists but also of the play's collaborative creation.

JENNIFER FORSYTH

TEXTUAL BIBLIOGRAPHY

Craig, Hugh. "The Three Parts of *Henry VI*." *Shakespeare, Computers, and the Mystery of Authorship*. Ed. Hugh Craig and Arthur F. Kinney. Cambridge: Cambridge UP, 2009. 40–77.

Vickers, Brian. "Incomplete Shakespeare: Or, Denying Authorship in *1 Henry VI*." *Shakespeare Quarterly* 58.3 (2007): 311–52.

PERFORMANCE NOTE

1 Henry VI tends to appear in repertory with parts 2 and 3, and companies some-times test their audiences' and their own endurance by performing the sequence on a single day. The plays are therefore routinely cut, adapted, or conflated in support of a broader narrative vision, with the result that Talbot and Joan can appear either central to productions concerned with English chivalry and imperialism or marginal to those focused on Henry and the political dissension surrounding him. Until the mid-twentieth century, productions of part 1 typically seemed nostalgic for England's martial glory, presenting Talbot, Salisbury, and Bedford as fading lights of a chival-rous age, while taking easy opportunities to mock the French for a lack of military and moral virtues. More recently, companies have introduced grimly realistic wars and nuanced portrayals of the French to critique the imperialist project and under-cut the sense of English romance and heroism. These productions often insinuate comparisons between Shakespeare's Tudor England and the time of Margaret Thatcher, some extending the play's potential topicality by citing religious or political divisions in, for example, Northern Ireland, Bosnia, or Israel as analogues to the fac-tions of Lancaster and York.

All companies face the challenges of preserving momentum and coherence of action while alternating between wars impending in England and ongoing in France. They must also decide whether to present Talbot as a valiant knight or chauvinistic marauder; Charles as a shallow fool or righteous patriot; and Joan as a seductress or holy prophetess, feminist heroine or witch. On the English side, Winchester, Suf-folk, and Somerset can appear as blatant intriguers or watchful guardians, accord-ingly increasing sympathy or suspicion for Humphrey and York. Henry's inability to reconcile the peers can indicate his weakness and naïveté or, alternately, his admi-rable sense of equity and restraint; his religion can either designate him as the play's moral touchstone or represent an escape from his responsibility to rule. Other dra-maturgical considerations include negotiating the striking incongruity of the rhym-ing dialogue in act 4 and clarifying the ontological status of the "fiends" Joan meets in 5.3.

BRETT GAMBOA

I HENRY VI

The First Part of Henry the Sixth

[THE PERSONS OF THE PLAY

The English:
Lancastrians and Wearers of the Red Rose:
KING HENRY the Sixth
Duke of BEDFORD, Regent of France, uncle to King Henry
Humphrey, Duke of GLOUCESTER, Lord Protector, uncle to King Henry
Thomas Beaufort, Duke of EXETER, great-uncle to King Henry
Henry Beaufort, Bishop of WINCHESTER (later, Cardinal), great-uncle to
   King Henry
Duke of SOMERSET
William de la Pole, Earl of SUFFOLK
BASSET

Yorkists and Wearers of the White Rose:
Richard Plantagenet, later Duke of YORK and Regent of France
Edmund MORTIMER
Earl of WARWICK
VERNON
LAWYER

English Military in France:
Duke of BURGUNDY, uncle to King Henry
Earl of SALISBURY
Lord TALBOT
JOHN TALBOT, son to Lord Talbot
Sir Thomas GARGRAVE
Sir William GLANSDALE
Sir John FALSTAFF
Sir William LUCY
CAPTAIN

Richard WOODVILLE, Lieutenant of the Tower of London
MAYOR of London
OFFICERS
MESSENGERS
SERVINGMEN
WARDERS
KEEPERS
SERVANT
SOLDIERS
Heralds, Trumpet, Drum, Guards, Attendants

The French:
CHARLES the Dauphin
Duke of ALENÇON
RENÉ, Duke of Anjou and Maine and titular King of Naples and Jerusalem; father
   to Margaret

BASTARD of Orléans
JOAN DE PUCELLE, also known as Joan of Arc
SHEPHERD, purported father to Joan
MASTER GUNNER of Orléans
BOY, son to Master Gunner
COUNTESS of Auvergne
PORTER
MARGARET, daughter to René
SERGEANT
SENTINELS
WATCHMAN
MESSENGERS
Governor of Paris
GENERAL
SCOUT
SOLDIERS
Drum, Ambassadors, Herald

Others:
PAPAL LEGATE
Fiends]

1.1

Dead march.° *Enter the funeral of King Henry the Fifth,*   *Funeral march*
attended on by the Duke of BEDFORD, *Regent of France; the*
Duke of GLOUCESTER, *Protector; the Duke of* EXETER;
[*the Earl of*] WARWICK; *the Bishop of* WINCHESTER; *and the*
Duke of SOMERSET[, *and Heralds*].[1]

BEDFORD   Hung be the heavens with black![2] Yield, day, to night;
   Comets, importing° change of times and states,   *foretelling*
   Brandish your crystal tresses[3] in the sky
   And with them scourge the bad revolting° stars   *rebellious*
5   That have consented unto Henry's death—
   King Henry the Fifth, too famous to live long![4]
   England ne'er lost a king of so much worth.
GLOUCESTER   England ne'er had a king until his time.
   Virtue° he had, deserving to command;   *Merit; power*
10   His brandished sword did blind men with his° beams;   *its*
   His arms spread wider than a dragon's wings;
   His sparkling eyes, replete with wrathful fire,
   More dazzled and drove back his enemies
   Than midday sun fierce bent against their faces.
15   What should I say? His deeds exceed all speech:
   He ne'er lift up his hand but conquerèd.[5]
EXETER   We mourn in black; why mourn we not in blood?°   *by shedding blood*
   Henry is dead and never shall revive.
   Upon a wooden coffin we attend,
20   And death's dishonorable victory

1.1 Location: Westminster Abbey, England.
1. TEXTUAL COMMENT The presence onstage of all of these characters, some of whom (Warwick and Somerset) do not speak during the scene, lends weight to the funeral procession and forms an important link to later parts of this play, as well as to 2 and 3 *Henry VI.* See Digital Edition TC 1.
2. Alluding to the theatrical practice, when a tragedy was performed, of hanging black draperies from the "heavens," or the roof projecting over the stage.

3. Flash your bright hair (the tails of the comets).
4. Henry V, the English conqueror of France who is the subject of a later play by Shakespeare, lived from 1387 until 1422. The assertion that he was too famous to live long may refer to the popular belief that jealous fate (the stars of line 4) prematurely cut down those whose fame became too great.
5. He never lifted up his hand (in battle) without conquering.

We with our stately presence glorify,
Like captives bound to a triumphant car.°   *chariot*
What, shall we curse the planets of mishap
That plotted thus our glory's overthrow?
25   Or shall we think the subtle-witted French
Conjurers and sorcerers that, afraid of him,
By magic verses have contrived his end?
WINCHESTER   He was a king blessed of the King of Kings.[6]
Unto the French, the dreadful Judgment Day
30   So dreadful will not be as was his sight.
The battles of the Lord of Hosts[7] he fought;
The church's prayers made him so prosperous.°   *successful*
GLOUCESTER   The church? Where is it? Had not churchmen
    prayed,[8]
His thread of life had not so soon decayed.°   *grown weak*
35   None do you like but an effeminate prince,
Whom like a schoolboy you may overawe.
WINCHESTER   Gloucester, whate'er we like, thou art Protector[9]
And lookest to command the prince and realm.
Thy wife[1] is proud; she holdeth thee in awe°   *overawes or rules you*
40   More than God or religious churchmen may.
GLOUCESTER   Name not religion, for thou lov'st the flesh,
And ne'er throughout the year to church thou go'st
Except it be to pray against thy foes.
BEDFORD   Cease, cease these jars,° and rest your minds in   *discords*
    peace.
45   Let's to the altar. Heralds, wait on us.°   *attend us*
Instead of gold, we'll offer up our arms,
Since arms avail not now that Henry's dead.
Posterity, await for° wretched years   *expect*
When at their mothers' moistened eyes babes shall suck,[2]
50   Our isle be made a nourish° of salt tears,   *wet nurse; foster mother*
And none but women left to wail the dead.
Henry the Fifth, thy ghost I invocate:
Prosper this realm, keep it from civil broils,°   *wars*
Combat with adverse planets in the heavens;
55   A far more glorious star thy soul will make
Than Julius Caesar[3] or bright—
      Enter a MESSENGER.
MESSENGER   My honorable lords, health to you all.
Sad tidings bring I to you out of France
Of loss, of slaughter, and discomfiture:°   *defeat*
60   Guyenne, Champagne, Reims, Rouen, Orléans,[4]
Paris, Gisors, Poitiers are all quite lost.
BEDFORD   What say'st thou, man, before dead Henry's corpse?
Speak softly, or the loss of those great towns
Will make him burst his lead° and rise from death.   *lead lining of coffin*

6. The name for God in biblical descriptions of the Last Judgment (see Revelation 19:16).
7. Another biblical name for God (see Psalms 24:10, Isaiah 13:13).
8. Punning on "preyed" and implying that Winchester conspired against the King.
9. Ruler of the kingdom during the King's youth. (Henry VI was an infant when his father died.)
1. Dame Eleanor Cobham. Accused of pride and overweening ambition, she is found guilty of witchcraft in 2 *Henry VI*.

2. When babies are fed only with their mothers' tears.
3. According to Roman tradition, Caesar's soul was turned into a shining star (Ovid's *Metamorphoses*) or a comet (Suetonius) after his murder.
4. TEXTUAL COMMENT The place currently known as Orléans is pronounced in 1 *Henry VI* as both a disyllable (Or-leens) and a trisyllable (Or-lay-ahn), depending on the line in which it appears. It is likely that the play's authors used whichever form fit best metrically. See Digital Edition TC 2.

65 GLOUCESTER Is Paris lost? Is Rouen yielded up?
     If Henry were recalled to life again,
     These news would cause him once more yield the ghost.°   to die
EXETER How were they lost? What treachery was used?
MESSENGER No treachery, but want° of men and money.   lack
70   Amongst the soldiers this is mutterèd:
     That here you maintain several factions,
     And whilst a field° should be dispatched and fought,   an army; a battle
     You are disputing of° your generals.   about
     One would have ling'ring wars with little cost;
75   Another would fly swift but wanteth wings;
     A third thinks, without expense at all,
     By guileful fair words peace may be obtained.
     Awake, awake, English nobility!
     Let not sloth dim your honors, new begot;
80   Cropped° are the flower-de-luces⁵ in your arms: Plucked
     Of England's coat,° one half is cut away.   [Exit.]   coat of arms
EXETER Were our tears wanting to this funeral,
     These tidings would call forth her° flowing tides.   (England's)
BEDFORD Me they concern; Regent⁶ I am of France.
85   Give me my steelèd coat; I'll fight for France.
     Away with these disgraceful wailing robes!
     Wounds will I lend the French instead of eyes
     To weep⁷ their intermissive° miseries.   temporarily interrupted
          Enter to them another MESSENGER.
SECOND MESSENGER Lords, view these letters, full of bad
          mischance.
90   France is revolted from the English quite,°   completely
     Except some petty towns of no import.
     The Dauphin⁸ Charles is crownèd king in Reims;
     The Bastard of Orléans⁹ with him is joined;
     René, Duke of Anjou, doth take his part;
95   The Duke of Alençon flyeth to his side.   Exit.
EXETER The Dauphin crownèd king? All fly to him?
     Oh, whither shall we fly from this reproach?
GLOUCESTER We will not fly but to our enemies' throats.
     Bedford, if thou be slack,° I'll fight it out.   negligent
100 BEDFORD Gloucester, why doubt'st thou of my forwardness?
     An army have I mustered in my thoughts
     Wherewith already France is overrun.
          Enter another MESSENGER.
THIRD MESSENGER My gracious lords, to add to your laments
     Wherewith you now bedew King Henry's hearse,
105 I must inform you of a dismal° fight   disastrous
     Betwixt the stout° Lord Talbot¹ and the French.   brave

5. English name for the French national emblem, the fleur-de-lis (lily flower), which appeared in the English coat of arms and signified the English claim to the French throne. By the Treaty of Troyes (1420), Henry V was named heir to the French king Charles VI, but Henry died shortly before Charles did; at Charles's death, the French throne passed to his son, the Dauphin, leading to the renewed struggles between the French and English depicted here.
6. Ruler in the King's absence.
7. Wounds . . . weep: Instead of weeping, I will give the French wounds, so that they will weep blood (from the wounds).
8. Charles VII (1403–1461) held the title of Dauphin (heir to the French throne) until he became King in 1422. Historically, his coronation at Reims did not occur until 1429.
9. Jean, Count of Dunois (1403–1468), illegitimate son of the Duke of Orléans and nephew of King Charles VI.
1. John Talbot, first Earl of Shrewsbury (1388–1453) and perhaps the most celebrated English military hero of his day, was captured by the French at the Battle of Patay, the "dismal fight" described here.

WINCHESTER   What? Wherein Talbot overcame, is't so?

THIRD MESSENGER   Oh, no: wherein Lord Talbot was o'erthrown.

The circumstance I'll tell you more at large.°   *in greater detail*

110 The tenth of August last, this dreadful° lord,   *fear-inspiring*

Retiring from the siege of Orléans,

Having full scarce° six thousand in his troop,   *barely*

By three-and-twenty thousand of the French

Was round encompassèd and set upon.

115 No leisure had he to enrank° his men.   *to set in battle lines*

He wanted pikes[2] to set before his archers,

Instead whereof, sharp stakes plucked out of hedges

They pitchèd in the ground confusedly

To keep the horsemen off from breaking in.

120 More than three hours the fight continuèd,

Where valiant Talbot, above human thought,

Enacted wonders with his sword and lance.

Hundreds he sent to hell, and none durst stand° him.   *face*

Here, there, and everywhere, enraged, he slew.

125 The French exclaimed the devil was in arms;

All the whole army stood agazed on° him.   *astonished at*

His soldiers spying his undaunted spirit,

"A° Talbot! A Talbot!" cried out amain°   *To / strongly*

And rushed into the bowels of the battle.

130 Here had the conquest fully been sealed up

If Sir John Falstaff[3] had not played the coward.

He, being in the vaward, placed behind[4]

With purpose to relieve and follow them,

Cowardly fled, not having struck one stroke.

135 Hence grew the general wrack° and massacre.   *destruction*

Enclosèd were they with° their enemies.   *by*

A base Walloon,[5] to win the Dauphin's grace,

Thrust Talbot with a spear into the back,

Whom all France with their chief assembled strength

140 Durst not presume to look once in the face.

BEDFORD   Is Talbot slain then? I will slay myself

For living idly here in pomp and ease

Whilst such a worthy leader, wanting aid,

Unto his dastard foemen° is betrayed.   *enemies*

145 THIRD MESSENGER   Oh, no, he lives but is took prisoner—

And Lord Scales with him and Lord Hungerford—

Most of the rest slaughtered or took likewise.

BEDFORD   His ransom there is none but I shall pay.

I'll hale° the Dauphin headlong from his throne;   *pull*

150 His crown shall be the ransom of my friend;

Four of their lords I'll change° for one of ours.   *exchange (kill)*

Farewell, my masters; to my task will I:

Bonfires in France forthwith I am to make

---

2. He lacked ironbound stakes (normally set in the ground in front of archers to protect them against attacking cavalry).

3. TEXTUAL COMMENT Some editors spell this character's surname as Fastolf, since the character is based on the historical figure Sir John Fastolf (1378?–1459). The play's authors follow a doubtful historical tradition here. Even though in some chronicles depicted as a coward, Sir John Fastolf was actu-

ally a distinguished soldier and officer of Henry V in the French wars. For this character's relationship with the cowardly knight Falstaff in (1 and 2) *Henry IV*, see the Introduction to *1 Henry IV*. See Digital Edition TC 3.

4. He being stationed in the rear of the vanguard ("vaward").

5. Inhabitant of a French-speaking province in what is now southern Belgium.

To keep our great Saint George's feast[6] withal.
155 Ten thousand soldiers with me I will take,
Whose bloody deeds shall make all Europe quake.
THIRD MESSENGER   So you had need, for Orléans is besieged.
The English army is grown weak and faint;
The Earl of Salisbury craveth supply°   *reinforcements*
160 And hardly keeps his men from mutiny
Since they, so few, watch such a multitude.   [*Exit.*]
EXETER   Remember, lords, your oaths to Henry sworn:
Either to quell the Dauphin utterly
Or bring him in obedience to your yoke.
165 BEDFORD   I do remember it and here take my leave
To go about my preparation.   *Exit.*
GLOUCESTER   I'll to the Tower[7] with all the haste I can
To view th'artillery and munition,
And then I will proclaim young Henry king.   *Exit.*
170 EXETER   To Eltham[8] will I, where the young King is,
Being ordained his special governor,
And for his safety there I'll best devise.
          Exit [EXETER *one way; exeunt* WARWICK, SOMERSET, *and the*
                    Heralds with the coffin of Henry V another way].
WINCHESTER   Each hath his place and function to attend;
I am left out: for me, nothing remains.
175 But long I will not be Jack-out-of-office:[9]
The King from Eltham I intend to steal
And sit at chiefest stern° of public weal.°   *Exit.* (as steersman) / the state

1.2

Sound a flourish.° *Enter* CHARLES [*the Dauphin, the*   fanfare of trumpets
Duke of] ALENÇON, *and* RENÉ[, *Duke of Anjou*],
marching with Drum and SOLDIERS.
CHARLES   Mars his true moving, even as in the heavens
So in the earth, to this day is not known.[1]
Late° did he shine upon the English side;   *Recently*
Now we are victors: upon us he smiles.
5 What towns of any moment° but we have?   *importance*
At pleasure here we lie, near Orléans;
Otherwhiles,° the famished English, like pale ghosts,   *Occasionally*
Faintly besiege us one hour in a month.
ALENÇON   They want their porridge and their fat bull-beeves.°   *beef*
10 Either they must be dieted° like mules   *fed*
And have their provender° tied to their mouths,   *food*
Or piteous they will look, like drownèd mice.
RENÉ   Let's raise the siege. Why live we idly here?
Talbot is taken, whom we wont° to fear;   *were accustomed*
15 Remaineth none but mad-brained Salisbury,
And he may well in fretting spend his gall:°   *exhaust his anger*
Nor° men nor money hath he to make war.   *Neither*
CHARLES   Sound, sound alarum!° We will rush on them.   (the call to arms)

---

6. The feast day of St. George, England's patron saint, April 23, was traditionally celebrated with bonfires. Bedford suggests that he will celebrate it every day with military victories over the French.
7. The Tower of London, which served as both a royal residence and an arsenal.
8. Another royal residence, located south of London.

9. Proverbial name for someone who has been dismissed from a job.
1.2 Location: Near Orléans, France.
1. The precise nature of the orbit of the planet Mars was a subject of debate until Johannes Kepler described it in 1609. Mars, the god of war, was known for his unpredictability.

Now for the honor of the forlorn[2] French:
20   Him I forgive my death that killeth me
When he sees me go back one foot or fly.   *Exeunt.*
    Here alarum. They are beaten back by the English with great
    loss. Enter CHARLES [*the Dauphin, the Duke of*] ALENÇON, *and*
    RENÉ[, *Duke of Anjou*].
CHARLES   Who ever saw the like? What men have I?
Dogs, cowards, dastards! I would ne'er have fled
But that they left me midst my enemies.
25 RENÉ   Salisbury is a desperate homicide;°   *murderer*
He fighteth as one weary of his life.
The other lords, like lions wanting food,
Do rush upon us as their hungry prey.°   *prey to their hunger*
ALENÇON   Froissart,[3] a countryman of ours, records
30 England all Olivers and Rolands[4] bred
During the time Edward the Third did reign.
More truly now may this be verified,
For none but Samsons and Goliases[5]
It sendeth forth to skirmish. One to ten?
35 Lean, raw-boned rascals!° Who would e'er suppose   *thin, inferior deer*
They had such courage and audacity?
CHARLES   Let's leave this town, for they are hare-brained slaves,
And hunger will enforce them to be more eager.°   *fierce*
Of old I know them; rather with their teeth
40 The walls they'll tear down than forsake the siege.
RENÉ   I think by some odd gimmers[6] or device
Their arms are set, like clocks, still to strike on,
Else ne'er could they hold out so as they do.
By my consent, we'll even let them alone.
45 ALENÇON   Be it so.
    Enter the BASTARD *of Orléans.*
BASTARD   Where's the Prince Dauphin? I have news for him.
CHARLES   Bastard of Orléans, thrice welcome to us.
BASTARD   Methinks your looks are sad, your cheer appalled.°   *countenance made pale*
Hath the late overthrow wrought this offense?
50 Be not dismayed, for succor is at hand:
A holy maid hither with me I bring,
Which, by a vision sent to her from heaven,
Ordainèd is to raise this tedious siege
And drive the English forth° the bounds of France.   *out of*
55 The spirit of deep prophecy she hath,
Exceeding the nine sibyls of old Rome;[7]
What's past and what's to come she can descry.°   *reveal*
Speak: shall I call her in? Believe my words,
For they are certain and unfallible.
CHARLES   Go call her in,   [*Exit* BASTARD.][8]
60   But first, to try her skill,

---

2. Performing their duty at the risk of death. The word "forlorn" also means "doomed," as well as "morally depraved."
3. Jean Froissart, author of a history of medieval France and England.
4. The most famous of Charlemagne's knights.
5. The biblical warriors Samson and Goliath were noted for their exceptional strength.
6. Gimmals, mechanical parts for transmitting motion

(as in clockwork).
7. Sibyls were women in antiquity who possessed the power of prophecy; perhaps "nine" here because of confusion with the nine prophetic books offered to Tarquin, the ruler of Rome, by the Cumaean Sibyl.
8. The Folio (F) does not indicate who brings in Joan, but it seems likely that it is the Bastard himself rather than a servant.

René, stand thou as Dauphin in my place.
Question her proudly; let thy looks be stern.
By this means shall we sound° what skill she hath.   test
    Enter JOAN [DE] PUCELLE[9] [*and the* BASTARD *of Orléans*].
RENÉ   Fair maid, is't thou wilt do these wondrous feats?
65   JOAN DE PUCELLE   René, is't thou that thinkest to beguile me?
Where is the Dauphin? [*to* CHARLES] Come, come from behind.
I know thee well, though never seen before.
Be not amazed; there's nothing hid from me.
In private will I talk with thee apart.
70   Stand back, you lords, and give us leave awhile.
    [ALENÇON, BASTARD, *and* RENÉ *stand apart*.]
RENÉ [*to* ALENÇON *and* BASTARD]   She takes upon her bravely
    at first dash.[1]
JOAN DE PUCELLE   Dauphin, I am by birth a shepherd's daughter,
My wit untrained in any kind of art.
Heaven and our Lady gracious° hath it pleased   (*the Virgin Mary*)
75   To shine on my contemptible estate.
Lo, whilst I waited on my tender lambs
And to sun's parching heat displayed my cheeks,
God's mother deignèd to appear to me,
And in a vision full of majesty
80   Willed me to leave my base vocation
And free my country from calamity.
Her aid she promised, and assured success.
In complete glory she revealed herself,
And whereas I was black[2] and swart° before,   *dark; swarthy*
85   With those clear rays which she infused° on me,   *shed*
That beauty am I blessed with which you may see.
Ask me what question thou canst possible,
And I will answer unpremeditated;
My courage try by combat, if thou dar'st,
90   And thou shalt find that I exceed my sex.
Resolve on° this: thou shalt be fortunate   *Be sure of*
If thou receive me for thy warlike mate.°   *co-worker; lover*
CHARLES   Thou hast astonished me with thy high terms.°   *lofty phrases*
Only this proof° I'll of thy valor make: *test*
95   In single combat thou shalt buckle° with me,   *contend; make love*
And if thou vanquishest, thy words are true;
Otherwise, I renounce all confidence.
JOAN DE PUCELLE   I am prepared: here is my keen-edged sword,
Decked with fine flower-de-luces on each side,
100   The which at Touraine in Saint Katherine's[3] churchyard
Out of a great deal of old iron I chose forth.
CHARLES   Then come, o'God's° name: I fear no woman.   *in God's*
JOAN DE PUCELLE   And while I live, I'll ne'er fly from a man.
    Here they fight, and JOAN DE PUCELLE *overcomes*.
CHARLES   Stay, stay thy hands! Thou art an Amazon[4]

---

9. TEXTUAL COMMENT French for "maid" or "virgin." Joan de Pucelle is the name the Folio uses most frequently for the figure we now commonly call Joan of Arc (1412–1431). She was celebrated by the French as the "Maid of Orléans" after she fought in the battle depicted here. A formidable warrior, she eventually became a prisoner of the English and was burned alive for heresy. See Digital Edition TC 4.
1. She plays her part well from the start.
2. Dark-skinned (probably from the sun).
3. Patroness of young maidens and female students; reputed to be the holiest of Christ's virgins.
4. One of the tribe of legendary female warriors claimed by Herodotus to live in Scythia.

105 And fightest with the sword of Deborah.[5]

JOAN DE PUCELLE   Christ's mother helps me; else I were too
weak.

CHARLES   Whoe'er helps thee, 'tis thou that must help me.
Impatiently I burn with thy desire;°   *with desire for you*
My heart and hands thou hast at once subdued.

110 Excellent Pucelle, if thy name be so,
Let me thy servant° and not sovereign be;   *lover*
'Tis the French Dauphin sueth to° thee thus.   *entreats*

JOAN DE PUCELLE   I must not yield to any rites of love,
For my profession's sacred from above.

115 When I have chasèd all thy foes from hence,
Then will I think upon a recompense.

CHARLES   Meantime, look gracious on thy prostrate thrall.°   *servant*

RENÉ [*apart to* ALENÇON *and* BASTARD]   My lord, methinks, is
very long in talk.

ALENÇON   Doubtless he shrives this woman to her smock,[6]

120 Else ne'er could he so long protract his speech.

RENÉ   Shall we disturb him since he keeps no mean?°   *moderation*

ALENÇON   He may mean more than we poor men do know:
These women are shrewd tempters with their tongues.

RENÉ [*to* CHARLES]   My lord, where are you? What devise°   *decide*
you on?

125 Shall we give o'er Orléans or no?

JOAN DE PUCELLE   Why, no, I say. Distrustful recreants,°   *cowards*
Fight till the last gasp; I'll be your guard.

CHARLES   What she says, I'll confirm: we'll fight it out.

JOAN DE PUCELLE   Assigned am I to be the English scourge.[7]

130 This night the siege assuredly I'll raise.
Expect Saint Martin's summer, halcyon days,[8]
Since I have entered into these wars.
Glory is like a circle in the water,
Which never ceaseth to enlarge itself

135 Till by broad spreading it disperse to naught.
With Henry's death, the English circle ends;
Dispersèd are the glories it included.
Now am I like that proud insulting° ship,   *exultant*
Which Caesar and his fortune bare at once.[9]

140 CHARLES   Was Mahomet inspired with a dove?[1]
Thou with an eagle[2] art inspired then.
Helen,[3] the mother of great Constantine,
Nor yet Saint Philip's daughters[4] were like thee.

---

5. An Old Testament prophet and judge who accompanied Barak as he led a victorious Israelite army against the Canaanites (see Judges 4–5).
6. Hears her confession completely; examines her intimately (to her "smock," or undergarments).
7. An individual sent by God to punish sin.
8. A period of unseasonable calm (the sea was thought to grow calm in December so that halcyons, or kingfishers, could build their nests upon it). *Saint Martin's summer:* Indian summer (St. Martin's Day falls on November 11).
9. According to Plutarch, an anxious sea captain was calmed when Caesar told him that his ship carried both Caesar and Caesar's natural good fortune.
1. Mohammed was the prophet and founder of Islam. Some Elizabethans claimed he was a fraud who fooled followers into thinking he was divinely inspired by training a dove to take seeds from his ear. Christians saw the dove as an incarnation of the Holy Spirit.
2. Attribute of the apostle St. John and hence a symbol of divine inspiration; also, an aggressive enemy of the dove.
3. St. Helena, the mother of the emperor who made Christianity the official religion of the Roman Empire, was said to have been led by a vision to discover Jesus's cross and sepulcher.
4. Four virgins noted in the New Testament (Acts 21:9) for their powers of prophecy.

Bright star of Venus,° fallen down on the earth,   *Roman goddess of love*
145   How may I reverently worship thee enough?
ALENÇON   Leave off delays, and let us raise the siege.
RENÉ   Woman, do what thou canst to save our honors.
Drive them from Orléans and be immortalized.
CHARLES   Presently° we'll try: come, let's away about it;   *Immediately*
150   No prophet will I trust if she prove false.   *Exeunt.*

1.3

*Enter [the Duke of] GLOUCESTER with his SERVINGMEN
[in blue coats.¹]*

GLOUCESTER   I am come to survey the Tower this day;
Since Henry's death I fear there is conveyance.°   *dishonesty*
Where be these warders° that they wait not here?   *guards*
[*A* SERVINGMAN *knocks on the gates.*]
Open the gates; 'tis Gloucester that calls.
5 FIRST WARDER [*within*]   Who's there that knocks so imperiously?
FIRST SERVINGMAN   It is the noble Duke of Gloucester.
SECOND WARDER [*within*]   Whoe'er he be, you may not be let in.
FIRST SERVINGMAN   Villains,° answer you so the Lord   *Scoundrels; peasants*
Protector?
FIRST WARDER [*within*]   The Lord protect him! —So we answer
him;
10 We do no otherwise than we are willed.°   *commanded*
GLOUCESTER   Who willèd you? Or whose will stands but mine?
There's none Protector of the Realm but I.
—Break up the gates; I'll be your warrantise.°   *surety; authorization*
Shall I be flouted thus by dunghill grooms?
*Gloucester's [*SERVINGMEN*] rush at the Tower gates, and
[Richard] WOODVILLE the Lieutenant speaks within.*
15 WOODVILLE² [*within*]³   What noise is this? What traitors have
we here?
GLOUCESTER   Lieutenant, is it you whose voice I hear?
Open the gates; here's Gloucester that would enter.
WOODVILLE [*within*]   Have patience, noble Duke; I may not open:
The Cardinal of Winchester forbids.⁴
20 From him I have express commandment
That thou nor none of thine shall be let in.
GLOUCESTER   Faint-hearted Woodville, prizest him fore° me—   *above*
Arrogant Winchester, that haughty prelate,
Whom Henry our late sovereign ne'er could brook?°   *tolerate*
25 Thou art no friend to God or to the King.
Open the gates, or I'll shut thee out shortly.
SERVINGMEN   Open the gates unto the Lord Protector,
Or we'll burst them open if that you come not quickly.

1.3 Location: The Tower of London.
1. The typical attire of Elizabethan servants.
2. Richard Woodville (died ca. 1441) was a loyal follower of the Lancastrian King Henry VI. His granddaughter Elizabeth married the Yorkist King Edward IV in 1464, a marriage Shakespeare depicts in *Richard III*.
3. The original stage direction at 1.3.14 reads: "*Gloster's men rush at the Tower Gates, and Wooduile the Lieutenant speakes within.*" The First and Second Warders most likely also speak here from within the

Tower, but it is unclear whether they speak from the upper stage or from behind some stage device suggesting a grate or window.
4. TEXTUAL COMMENT Although Winchester becomes a cardinal in 5.1 and should therefore only be a bishop here, there are numerous references in this scene to him as a cardinal. This might be either the result of authorial error or a deliberate choice that highlights Winchester's ambition. See Digital Edition TC 5.

Enter to the Protector at the Tower gates WINCHESTER
and his [SERVINGMEN] *in tawny coats.*[5]

WINCHESTER How now, ambitious Humphrey,[6] what means this?

30 GLOUCESTER Peeled° priest, dost thou command me to be   *Shaven; tonsured*
shut out?

WINCHESTER I do, thou most usurping proditor°   *traitor*
And not protector of the King or realm.

GLOUCESTER Stand back, thou manifest conspirator,
Thou that contrived'st to murder our dead lord,

35 Thou that giv'st whores indulgences to sin![7]
I'll canvas° thee in thy broad cardinal's hat   *shake*
If thou proceed in this thy insolence.

WINCHESTER Nay, stand thou back; I will not budge a foot.
This be Damascus;[8] be thou cursèd Cain

40 To slay thy brother Abel if thou wilt.

GLOUCESTER I will not slay thee, but I'll drive thee back.
Thy scarlet robes, as a child's bearing cloth,°   *christening gown*
I'll use to carry thee out of this place.

WINCHESTER Do what thou dar'st, I beard° thee to thy face.   *defy*

45 GLOUCESTER What? Am I dared and bearded to my face?
Draw, men, for all this privilegèd place,[9]
Blue coats to tawny coats!

[*Gloucester's* SERVINGMEN *draw their swords.*]
Priest, beware your beard:
I mean to tug it and to cuff you soundly.
Under my feet I stamp thy cardinal's hat;

50 In spite of Pope or dignities of Church,
Here by the cheeks I'll drag thee up and down.

WINCHESTER Gloucester, thou wilt answer this before the
Pope.

GLOUCESTER Winchester goose, I cry, a rope, a rope![1]
[*to his* SERVINGMEN] Now beat them hence; why do you let
them stay?

55 —Thee I'll chase hence, thou wolf in sheep's array.
Out, tawny coats; out, scarlet hypocrite!

Here Gloucester's SERVINGMEN *beat out the Cardinal's*
SERVINGMEN, *and enter in the hurly-burly the* MAYOR *of*
London and his OFFICERS.

MAYOR Fie, lords, that you, being supreme magistrates,
Thus contumeliously° should break the peace!   *contemptuously*

GLOUCESTER Peace, Mayor: thou know'st little of my wrongs.

60 Here's Beaufort, that regards nor° God nor king,   *neither*
Hath here distrained° the Tower to his use.   *seized*

WINCHESTER Here's Gloucester, a foe to citizens,

---

5. Typically worn by attendants of important church men.

6. TEXTUAL COMMENT F reads "*Vmpheir*," which has been emended in some editions to "umpire" or to "vizier" (a high state official in the Turkish Empire, which Elizabethans frequently denounced as barbaric). Because "*Vmpheir*" is capitalized and italicized in F, which indicates that it is a proper name, and because the initial "H" was often left off of words in the period, it is emended here to "Humphrey." See Digital Edition TC 6.

7. In 1426, Gloucester charged Winchester with attempting to have King Henry V ("our dead lord") killed. He here also accuses Winchester of encourag-

ing prostitution, referring to the revenues that the Bishop of Winchester collected from the brothels on the south bank of the Thames (where, in Shakespeare's time, many theaters were also located).

8. Damascus, in Syria, was believed to have been built on the spot where Adam and Eve's son Cain murdered his brother Abel (see Genesis 4).

9. It was illegal to draw swords near "privileged" sites, including royal residences. *for all this:* though this is a.

1. A call for a hangman's noose. Gloucester could also be asking for a rope with which to beat Winchester's servingmen. *Winchester goose:* slang expression for a swelling in the groin caused by venereal disease; a prostitute or a victim of venereal disease.

One that still motions° war and never peace,   *who always advocates*

O'ercharging your free purses[2] with large fines;°   *taxes*

65   That seeks to overthrow religion

Because he is Protector of the Realm;

And would have armor here out of the Tower

To crown himself king and suppress the Prince.

GLOUCESTER   I will not answer thee with words but blows.

Here they skirmish again.

70   MAYOR   Naught rests° for me in this tumultuous strife   *is left*

But to make open proclamation.

Come, officer. [*He gives the* OFFICER *a paper.*] As loud as e'er thou canst.

OFFICER (*cries*) "All manner of men assembled here in arms

this day, against God's peace and the King's, we charge and

75   command you in his highness' name to repair to your several

dwelling places and not to wear, handle, or use any sword,

weapon, or dagger henceforward, upon pain of death."

GLOUCESTER   Cardinal, I'll be no breaker of the law,

But we shall meet and break our minds° at large.   *express our views*

80   WINCHESTER   Gloucester, we'll meet to thy cost, be sure:

Thy heart-blood I will have for this day's work.

MAYOR   I'll call for clubs[3] if you will not away.

[*aside*] This Cardinal's more haughty than the devil.

GLOUCESTER   Mayor, farewell; thou dost but what thou

mayst.

85   WINCHESTER   Abominable Gloucester, guard thy head,

For I intend to have it ere long.

Exeunt [*severally*° WINCHESTER *and* GLOUCESTER   *separately*

with their SERVINGMEN].

MAYOR [*to his* OFFICERS] See the coast cleared and then we

will depart.

[*aside*] Good God, these nobles should such stomachs° bear!   *angry tempers*

I myself fight not once in forty year.   *Exeunt.*

1.4

Enter the MASTER GUNNER *of Orléans and his* BOY.

MASTER GUNNER   Sirrah,[1] thou know'st how Orléans is

besieged

And how the English have the suburbs won.

BOY   Father, I know, and oft have shot at them;

Howe'er, unfortunate, I missed my aim.

5   MASTER GUNNER   But now thou shalt not. Be thou ruled by me.

Chief Master Gunner am I of this town;

Something I must do to procure me grace.°   *honor*

The Prince' espials° have informèd me   *spies*

How the English, in the suburbs close entrenched,

10   Went through a secret grate of iron bars

In yonder tower, to overpeer the city

And thence discover how with most advantage

They may vex us with shot or with assault.

To intercept this inconvenience,°   *harm*

15   A piece of ordnance 'gainst° it I have placed,   *directed toward*

---

2. Overburdening your generous purses.

3. I'll shout for London apprentices to bring their clubs and quell this riot. "Prentices and clubs" was a common rallying cry.

1.4 Location: Orléans.

1. A term normally used to address social inferiors, but here used to address the Master Gunner's young son.

And even these three days have I watched
If I could see them. Now do thou watch,
For I can stay no longer.
If thou spy'st any, run and bring me word,
20 And thou shalt find me at the Governor's.   *Exit.*
    BOY   Father, I warrant you, take you no care;°   *don't worry*
       I'll never trouble you if° I may spy them.   *Exit.*   *unless*

1.5

Enter [the Earl of] SALISBURY and [Lord] TALBOT on the
turrets, with [Sir Thomas GARGRAVE, Sir William GLANSDALE,
and] others.

SALISBURY   Talbot, my life, my joy, again returned?
   How wert thou handled, being prisoner?
   Or by what means gott'st thou to be released?
   Discourse, I prithee, on this turret's top.
5 TALBOT   The Duke of Bedford had a prisoner
   Called the brave Lord Poton de Xaintrailles;
   For him was I exchanged and ransomèd;
   But with a baser man of arms° by far   *soldier of lower rank*
   Once, in contempt, they would have bartered me,
10 Which I, disdaining, scorned, and cravèd death
   Rather than I would be so pilled esteemed.°   *so cheaply valued*
   In fine,° redeemed I was as I desired.   *In short*
   But oh, the treacherous Falstaff wounds my heart,
   Whom with my bare fists I would execute
15 If I now had him brought into my power.
   SALISBURY   Yet tell'st thou not how thou wert entertained.°   *treated*
   TALBOT   With scoffs and scorns and contumelious taunts
      In open marketplace produced they me
      To be a public spectacle to all.
20   "Here," said they, "is the terror of the French,
      The scarecrow that affrights our children so."
      Then broke I from the officers that led me
      And with my nails digged stones out of the ground
      To hurl at the beholders of my shame.
25   My grisly countenance made others fly;
      None durst come near for fear of sudden death.
      In iron walls they deemed me not secure—
      So great fear of my name 'mongst them were spread
      That they supposed I could rend bars of steel
30   And spurn° in pieces posts of adamant[1]—   *kick*
      Wherefore a guard of chosen shot° I had   *selected marksmen*
      That walked about me every minute while,°   *constantly*
      And if I did but stir out of my bed,
      Ready they were to shoot me to the heart.
         Enter the BOY[, who passes over the stage] with a linstock.[2]
35 SALISBURY   I grieve to hear what torments you endured,
      But we will be revenged sufficiently.
      Now it is supper time in Orléans.

1.5 Location: Tower before the walls of Orléans.
1. A legendary stony substance said to be
impenetrable.
2. The Folio's stage direction reads: "*Enter the Boy*
with a Linstock." He probably does not stay onstage,

however, but passes from one side to the other on his
way to light the charge that will strike down Salisbury and Gargrave. *linstock:* a stick used to hold a
lighted match or torch for firing cannon.

Here, through this grate, I count each one
And view the Frenchmen how they fortify.
40 Let us look in; the sight will much delight thee.
Sir Thomas Gargrave and Sir William Glansdale,
Let me have your express° opinions: precise
Where is best place to make our batt'ry next?
       [They look through the grate.]

GARGRAVE I think at the North Gate, for there stands lords.³

45 GLANSDALE And I here, at the bulwark of the bridge.

TALBOT For aught I see, this city must be famishèd°   starved out
Or with light skirmishes enfeeblèd.
      Here they° [shoot from within], and SALISBURY   (the French)
      [and GARGRAVE *fall] down.*⁴

SALISBURY O Lord, have mercy on us wretched sinners!

GARGRAVE O Lord, have mercy on me, woeful man!

50 TALBOT What chance is this that suddenly hath crossed us?
Speak, Salisbury—at least if thou canst, speak.
How far'st thou, mirror° of all martial men?   best example
One of thy eyes and thy cheek's side struck off?
Accursèd tower, accursèd fatal hand
55 That hath contrived this woeful tragedy!
In thirteen battles Salisbury o'ercame;
Henry the Fifth he first trained to the wars.
Whilst any trump did sound or drum struck up,
His sword did ne'er leave striking in the field.
60 Yet liv'st thou, Salisbury? Though thy speech doth fail,
One eye thou hast to look to heaven for grace:
The sun with one eye vieweth all the world.
Heaven, be thou gracious to none alive
If Salisbury wants° mercy at thy hands!   lacks
65 —Sir Thomas Gargrave, hast thou any life?
Speak unto Talbot—nay, look up to him.
      *[*GARGRAVE *dies.]*
Bear hence his body; I will help to bury it.
      [Exit one with Gargrave's body.]
—Salisbury, cheer thy spirit with this comfort:
Thou shalt not die whiles°—   until
70 He beckons with his hand and smiles on me
As who should say, "When I am dead and gone,
Remember to avenge me on the French."
Plantagenet, I will, and Nero-like,⁵ will
Play on the lute, beholding the towns burn:
75 Wretched shall France be only in° my name.   at the mere sound of
      Here an alarum, and it thunders and lightens.
What stir is this? What tumult's in the heavens?
Whence cometh this alarum and the noise?
      Enter a MESSENGER.

MESSENGER My lord, my lord, the French have gathered head!°   assembled an army

---

3. TEXTUAL COMMENT The Folio has Gargrave say "lords" here, but some editors have emended to "Loire" (the river upon which Hall's chronicle history says the city of Orléans stands), or to "Lou" (for the Bastille of Saint Lou destroyed in the battle over Orléans), or to "Toures" (towers), which makes sense with the verb "stand." See Digital Edition TC 7.
4. TEXTUAL COMMENT The order of the events that follow the cannon attack is slightly confusing, as the stage directions in the Folio do not clearly describe the action: they tell us only that Salisbury falls in the assault, but as becomes evident, Gargrave does as well. See Digital Edition TC 8.
5. Talbot here compares himself with Nero, the emperor who played music while he watched Rome burn. Salisbury was a descendant of the Plantagenet dynasty, which ruled England from 1154 to 1485.

The Dauphin, with one Joan de Pucelle joined,
80 A holy prophetess new risen up,
    Is come with a great power° to raise the siege.   army
        Here SALISBURY *lifteth himself up and groans.*
TALBOT Hear, hear, how dying Salisbury doth groan!
    It irks his heart he cannot be revenged.
    Frenchmen, I'll be a Salisbury to you.
85 Puzzel or *pucelle*,[6] Dauphin or dogfish,[7]
    Your hearts I'll stamp out with my horse's heels
    And make a quagmire of your mingled brains.
    Convey me° Salisbury into his tent,   for me
    And then we'll try what these dastard Frenchmen dare.
        Alarum. Exeunt[*, carrying* SALISBURY].

1.6

Here an alarum again, and [Lord] TALBOT *pursueth* [CHARLES] *the Dauphin and driveth him; then enter* JOAN DE PUCELLE, *driving Englishmen before her* [*and exeunt*]. *Then enter* [Lord] TALBOT.

TALBOT Where is my strength, my valor, and my force?
    Our English troops retire; I cannot stay° them: stop
    A woman clad in armor chaseth them.
        Enter [JOAN DE] PUCELLE.
    Here, here she comes. —I'll have a bout[1] with thee.
5   Devil or devil's dam,° I'll conjure thee.   mother
    Blood will I draw on thee—thou art a witch[2]—
    And straightway give thy soul to him thou serv'st.
JOAN DE PUCELLE Come, come, 'tis only I that must disgrace thee.
        Here they fight.
TALBOT Heavens, can you suffer hell so to prevail?
10 My breast I'll burst with straining of my courage°   vital energy
    And from my shoulders crack my arms asunder
    But I will° chastise this high-minded° strumpet.   If I do not / arrogant
        They fight again.
JOAN DE PUCELLE Talbot, farewell; thy hour is not yet come.
    I must go victual° Orléans forthwith.   supply with provisions
        A short alarum; then [CHARLES *the Dauphin,* RENÉ,
        Duke of Anjou, and the Duke of ALENÇON] *enter the
        town with* SOLDIERS.
15 O'ertake me if thou canst; I scorn thy strength.
    Go, go, cheer up thy hunger-starvèd° men;   starving to death
    Help Salisbury to make his testament;
    This day is ours, as many more shall be.   *Exit.*
TALBOT My thoughts are whirlèd like a potter's wheel.
20 I know not where I am nor what I do.
    A witch by fear, not force, like Hannibal,[3]
    Drives back our troops and conquers as she lists;
    So bees with smoke and doves with noisome° stench   noxious
    Are from their hives and houses driven away.

---

6. Talbot puns on the similarity between the English slang for "slut" ("puzzel") and the French word for "virgin" (*pucelle*).
7. Punning on the Elizabethan spelling of "dauphin" as "dolphin"; hence, the taunt that the Dauphin is a "dogfish."
1.6 Location: In and before Orléans.

1. Fight; sexual encounter. Much of the speech to and about Joan has sexual overtones.
2. Whoever drew blood from a witch was supposed to be protected from her magic.
3. The Carthaginian military leader who once put to flight his Roman enemies by tying firebrands to the horns of two thousand oxen.

25   They called us, for our fierceness, English dogs;
      Now, like to whelps,° we crying run away.   *nursing puppies*
          A short alarum[; enter English SOLDIERS].
      Hark, countrymen! Either renew the fight
      Or tear the lions out of England's coat;°   *coat of arms*
      Renounce your soil; give sheep in lions' stead.[4]
30   Sheep run not half so treacherous° from the wolf   *cowardly*
      Or horse or oxen from the leopard
      As you fly from your oft-subduèd slaves.
          *Alarum. Here another skirmish [where the English
              unsuccessfully attempt to enter the town].*
      It will not be; retire into your trenches.
      You all consented unto Salisbury's death,
35   For none would strike a stroke in his revenge.°   *to avenge his death*
      Pucelle is entered into Orléans
      In spite of us or aught that we could do. [*Exeunt* SOLDIERS.]
      Oh, would I were to die with Salisbury!
      The shame hereof will make me hide my head.
                              Exit. Alarum. Retreat.[5]

                              1.7
          *Flourish. Enter on the walls [*JOAN DE* PUCELLE,
          [*CHARLES the] Dauphin,* RENÉ[*, Duke of Anjou,
          the Duke of]* ALENÇON, *and* SOLDIERS.
      JOAN DE PUCELLE   Advance° our waving colors on the walls;   *Raise*
          Rescued is Orléans from the English.
          Thus Joan de Pucelle hath performed her word.
      CHARLES   Divinest creature, Astraea's[1] daughter,
5   How shall I honor thee for this success?
          Thy promises are like Adonis' garden,[2]
          That one day bloomed and fruitful were the next.
          France, triumph in thy glorious prophetess.
          Recovered is the town of Orléans;
10   More blessèd hap° did ne'er befall our state.   *event*
      RENÉ   Why ring not out the bells aloud throughout the town?
          Dauphin, command the citizens make bonfires
          And feast and banquet in the open streets
          To celebrate the joy that God hath given us.
15   ALENÇON   All France will be replete with mirth and joy
          When they shall hear how we have played the men.°   *acted like men*
      CHARLES   'Tis Joan, not we, by whom the day is won,
          For which I will divide my crown with her,
          And all the priests and friars in my realm
20   Shall in procession sing her endless praise.
          A statelier pyramid to her I'll rear
          Than Rhodope's[3] or Memphis' ever was.
          In memory of her, when she is dead,
          Her ashes, in an urn more precious

4. Display (on your coat of arms) sheep instead of lions.
5. A trumpet call to signal a retreat.
1.7 Location: Scene continues.
1. Greek goddess of justice; she lived on earth during the Golden Age but fled to the heavens during the corruption of the Iron Age. Queen Elizabeth I was

often compared to Astraea.
2. A mythical garden noted for its fertility and described by Spenser in *The Faerie Queene.*
3. A Greek courtesan who married the king of Memphis (city in Egypt) and reputedly built the third pyramid.

25   Than the rich-jeweled coffer of Darius,[4]
      Transported shall be at high festivals
      Before the kings and queens of France.
      No longer on Saint Denis° will we cry,   *patron saint of France*
      But Joan de Pucelle shall be France's saint.
30   Come in and let us banquet royally
      After this golden day of victory.   *Flourish. Exeunt.*

2.1

Enter a [French] SERGEANT *of a band with two* SENTINELS
[on the walls].

SERGEANT   Sirs, take your places and be vigilant.
    If any noise or soldier you perceive
    Near to the walls, by some apparent° sign   *obvious*
    Let us have knowledge at the court of guard.°   *guardroom*
SENTINEL   Sergeant, you shall.   *[Exit* SERGEANT.*]*
5   Thus are poor servitors,
    When others sleep upon their quiet beds,
    Constrained to watch in darkness, rain, and cold.

Enter [Lord] TALBOT, *[the Duke of]* BEDFORD, *and
[the Duke of]* BURGUNDY *with scaling ladders [and*
SOLDIERS*], their drums beating a dead march.*[1]

TALBOT   Lord Regent and redoubted° Burgundy,   *distinguished*
    By whose approach the regions of Artois,
10   Wallon, and Picardy are friends to us,[2]
    This happy night the Frenchmen are secure,°   *overconfident*
    Having all day caroused and banqueted.
    Embrace we then this opportunity
    As fitting best to quittance° their deceit,   *repay*
15   Contrived by art° and baleful sorcery.   *craftiness*
BEDFORD   Coward of France![3] How much he wrongs his fame,°   *reputation*
    Despairing of his own arm's fortitude,
    To join with witches and the help of hell.
BURGUNDY   Traitors have never other company.
20   But what's that Pucelle whom they term so pure?
TALBOT   A maid, they say.
BEDFORD   A maid? And be so martial?
BURGUNDY   Pray God she prove not masculine ere long[4]
    If underneath the standard of the French[5]
    She carry armor,[6] as she hath begun.
25 TALBOT   Well, let them practice and converse[7] with spirits.
    God is our fortress, in whose conquering name
    Let us resolve to scale their flinty bulwarks.
BEDFORD   Ascend, brave Talbot; we will follow thee.
TALBOT   Not all together. Better far, I guess,
30   That we do make our entrance several ways,
    That if it chance the one of us do fail,

---

4. A jeweled treasure chest that Alexander allegedly
won from the Persian king Darius III and used to
store the works of Homer.
2.1 Location: In and before Orléans.
1. Either a funeral march for Salisbury or the muffled march that signifies a secret attack.
2. *By . . . us:* during Henry V's reign, the Duke of
Burgundy became an English ally and won support
for the English from the French and Netherlandish

regions to which Talbot refers.
3. The Dauphin.
4. She does not turn out to be a man; she does not
turn out to be carrying a male child. The following
lines are full of sexual innuendoes.
5. French ensign; French penis.
6. Wear armor; bear the weight of an armed man (in
intercourse).
7. Scheme and talk; have sex and be intimate.

The other yet may rise against their force.[8]

BEDFORD   Agreed. I'll to yond corner.

BURGUNDY   And I to this.

TALBOT   And here will Talbot mount or make his grave.

35   Now, Salisbury, for thee and for the right
      Of English Henry shall this night appear
      How much in duty I am bound to both.
      [*The English scale the walls.*]

SENTINEL   Arm, arm! The enemy doth make assault!

ENGLISH SOLDIERS (*cry*)   Saint George! A Talbot![9]
                            [*Exeunt the English aloft.*]

*The French leap o'er the walls in their shirts. Enter
several ways [the] BASTARD [of Orléans, the Duke of]
ALENÇON, [and] RENÉ[, Duke of Anjou],
half ready and half unready.*[1]

40   ALENÇON   How now, my lords? What, all unready so?

BASTARD   Unready? Ay, and glad we scaped° so well.   escaped

RENÉ   'Twas time, I trow,° to wake and leave our beds,   believe
        Hearing alarums at our chamber doors.

ALENÇON   Of all exploits since first I followed arms,

45   Ne'er heard I of a warlike enterprise
      More venturous° or desperate than this.   risky; bold

BASTARD   I think this Talbot be a fiend of hell.

RENÉ   If not of hell, the heavens sure favor him.

ALENÇON   Here cometh Charles; I marvel how he sped.°   fared
          Enter CHARLES [*the Dauphin*] *and* JOAN [DE PUCELLE].[2]

50   BASTARD   Tut, holy Joan[3] was his defensive guard.

CHARLES   Is this thy cunning,° thou deceitful dame?   skill; sorcery
          Didst thou at first, to flatter us withal,
          Make us partakers of a little gain,
          That now our loss might be ten times so much?

55   JOAN DE PUCELLE   Wherefore is Charles impatient with his friend?
                        At all times will you have my power alike?
                        Sleeping or waking, must I still prevail,
                        Or will you blame and lay the fault on me?
                        Improvident° soldiers, had your watch been good,   Negligent

60   This sudden mischief never could have fallen.

CHARLES   Duke of Alençon, this was your default,
          That, being captain of the watch tonight,
          Did look no better to that weighty charge.

ALENÇON   Had all your quarters been as safely kept

65   As that whereof I had the government,
      We had not been thus shamefully surprised.

BASTARD   Mine was secure.

RENÉ   And so was mine, my lord.

CHARLES   And for myself, most part of all this night
          Within her° quarter and mine own precinct   (Joan's)

---

8. May scale the walls despite French resistance.

9. To Talbot. This cry is included in the actual stage directions in F, but here it is assigned to nameless "English soldiers" (see also the stage directions preceding 2.1.79).

1. In this complicated piece of stage business, Talbot's men ascend ladders to the upper stage, which represents the walls of Orléans. They there surprise French soldiers, some of whom leap down from the upper to the lower stage as if fleeing from Orléans.

On the lower stage, the fleeing and defeated French nobles debate their plight. *half ready and half unready:* half dressed and half undressed.

2. PERFORMANCE COMMENT Directors sometimes have Joan and Charles enter here as if they had been interrupted in a sexual encounter; in other productions, they enter simply as allies. See Digital Edition PC.

3. A reference to her sexual availability; "hole" was slang for "vagina."

70   I was employed in passing to and fro
      About relieving of the sentinels.
      Then how, or which way, should they first break in?
   JOAN DE PUCELLE   Question, my lords, no further of the case,
      How or which way; 'tis sure they found some place
75   But weakly guarded where the breach was made.
      And now there rests° no other shift° but this: *remains / device*
      To gather our soldiers, scattered and dispersed,
      And lay new platforms° to endamage them.   *plots; schemes*
        Alarum. Enter [an English] SOLDIER, *crying, "A Talbot!*
        A Talbot!": [the French] fly, leaving their clothes behind.
   SOLDIER   I'll be so bold to take what they have left.
80   The cry of Talbot serves me for a sword,
      For I have loaden me with many spoils
      Using no other weapon but his name.   *Exit.*

2.2

      Enter [Lord] TALBOT, *[the Duke of]* BEDFORD,
      [the Duke of] BURGUNDY[, *a* CAPTAIN, *and* SOLDIERS].
   BEDFORD   The day begins to break, and night is fled,
      Whose pitchy mantle overveiled the earth.
      Here sound retreat and cease our hot pursuit.
        [A SOLDIER *sounds a] retreat.*
   TALBOT   Bring forth the body of old Salisbury
5   And here advance it° in the marketplace,   *raise it up (on a bier)*
      The middle center of this cursèd town.
        [Enter SOLDIERS *with the body of* SALISBURY,
        their drums beating a dead march.]
      Now have I paid my vow unto his soul:
      For every drop of blood was° drawn from him,   *that was*
      There hath at least five Frenchmen died tonight.
10   And that hereafter ages may behold
      What ruin happened in revenge of him,
      Within their chiefest temple I'll erect
      A tomb, wherein his corpse shall be interred,
      Upon the which, that everyone may read,
15   Shall be engraved the sack of Orléans,
      The treacherous manner of his mournful death,
      And what a terror he had been to France.
      But, lords, in all our bloody massacre,
      I muse° we met not with the Dauphin's grace,   *wonder*
20   His new-come champion, virtuous¹ Joan of Aire,
      Nor any of his false confederates.
   BEDFORD   'Tis thought, Lord Talbot, when the fight began,
      Roused on the sudden from their drowsy beds,
      They did amongst the troops of armèd men
25   Leap o'er the walls for refuge in the field.
   BURGUNDY   Myself, as far as I could well discern
      For smoke and dusky vapors of the night,
      Am sure I scared the Dauphin and his trull°   *whore*
      When arm in arm they both came swiftly running,
30   Like to a pair of loving turtledoves
      That could not live asunder day or night.

2.2 Location: Within Orléans.
1. Full of virtue or manly courage; chaste (said ironically).

After that things are set in order here,
We'll follow them with all the power we have.
        Enter a MESSENGER.
MESSENGER   All hail, my lords. Which of this princely train
35 Call ye the warlike Talbot, for his acts
    So much applauded through the realm of France?
TALBOT   Here is the Talbot; who would speak with him?
MESSENGER   The virtuous lady, Countess of Auvergne,
    With modesty admiring thy renown,
40 By me entreats, great lord, thou wouldst vouchsafe
    To visit her poor castle where she lies,°   dwells
    That she may boast she hath beheld the man
    Whose glory fills the world with loud report.°   acclaim; din of war
BURGUNDY   Is it even so? Nay, then I see our wars
45 Will turn unto a peaceful comic sport,
    When ladies crave to be encountered with.
    You may not, my lord, despise her gentle suit.°   well-bred request
TALBOT   Ne'er trust me then: for when a world of men
    Could not prevail with all their oratory,
50 Yet hath a woman's kindness overruled.
    —And therefore tell her I return great thanks
    And in submission will attend on her.   [*Exit* MESSENGER.]
    —Will not your honors bear me company?
BEDFORD   No, truly, 'tis more than manners will,°   etiquette allows
55 And I have heard it said unbidden guests
    Are often welcomest when they are gone.
TALBOT   Well then, alone, since there's no remedy,
    I mean to prove° this lady's courtesy.   test
    Come hither, captain. ([*He*] *whispers.*) You perceive my mind.
60 CAPTAIN   I do, my lord, and mean° accordingly.   *Exeunt.*   intend to act

2.3

        Enter COUNTESS [*of Auvergne and* PORTER].
COUNTESS   Porter, remember what I gave in charge,°   commanded
    And when you have done so, bring the keys to me.
PORTER   Madam, I will.   *Exit.*
COUNTESS   The plot is laid. If all things fall out right,
5   I shall as famous be by this exploit
    As Scythian Tomyris¹ by Cyrus' death.
    Great is the rumor° of this dreadful° knight,   fame / fear-inspiring
    And his achievements of no less account;
    Fain° would mine eyes be witness with mine ears   Gladly
10 To give their censure° of these rare° reports.   opinion / remarkable
        Enter MESSENGER *and* [*Lord*] TALBOT.
MESSENGER   Madam, according as your ladyship desired,
    By message craved, so is Lord Talbot come.
COUNTESS   And he is welcome. What? Is this the man?
MESSENGER   Madam, it is.
COUNTESS   Is this the scourge² of France?
15 Is this the Talbot so much feared abroad

2.3 Location: The Countess's castle, Auvergne.   wineskin filled with human blood.
1. Asian queen who, in revenge for her son's death,   2. Individual sent by God to punish sin. Joan
killed the Persian king Cyrus and kept his head in a   describes herself as "the English scourge" at 1.2.129.

That with his name the mothers still° their babes? *quiet*
I see report is fabulous and false.
I thought I should have seen some Hercules,[3]
A second Hector[4] for his grim aspect° *appearance*
20   And large proportion of his strong-knit limbs.
Alas, this is a child, a silly° dwarf. *feeble*
It cannot be this weak and writhled° shrimp *wrinkled*
Should strike such terror to his enemies.
TALBOT   Madam, I have been bold to trouble you,
25   But since your ladyship is not at leisure,
I'll sort some other time to visit you.
COUNTESS   What means he now? Go ask him whither he
        goes.
MESSENGER   Stay, my lord Talbot, for my lady craves
To know the cause of your abrupt departure.
30   TALBOT   Marry,[5] for that° she's in a wrong belief, *because*
I go to certify her Talbot's here.
                Enter PORTER *with keys.*
COUNTESS   If thou be he, then art thou prisoner.
TALBOT   Prisoner? To whom?
COUNTESS   To me, bloodthirsty lord,
And for that cause I trained° thee to my house. *enticed*
35   Long time thy shadow° hath been thrall° to me, *image / slave*
For in my gallery thy picture hangs,
But now the substance shall endure the like,
And I will chain these legs and arms of thine,
That hast by tyranny these many years
40   Wasted our country, slain our citizens,
And sent our sons and husbands captivate.° *into captivity*
TALBOT   Ha, ha, ha!
COUNTESS   Laughest thou, wretch? Thy mirth shall turn to moan.
TALBOT   I laugh to see your ladyship so fond° *foolish*
45   To think that you have aught but Talbot's shadow
Whereon to practice your severity.
COUNTESS   Why? Art not thou the man?
TALBOT   I am indeed.
COUNTESS   Then have I substance, too.
TALBOT   No, no, I am but shadow of myself.
50   You are deceived; my substance is not here,
For what you see is but the smallest part
And least proportion of humanity.[6]
I tell you, madam, were the whole frame[7] here,
It is of such a spacious lofty pitch° *height*
55   Your roof were not sufficient to contain't.
COUNTESS   This is a riddling merchant for the nonce.[8]
He will be here, and yet he is not here:
How can these contrarieties agree?
TALBOT   That will I show you presently.° *immediately*

---

3. Mythical hero famous for his immense strength.
4. Greatest of the Trojan warriors, celebrated in Homer's *Iliad.*
5. By the Virgin Mary, a mild oath.
6. Smallest part of the whole man (and, by implica-

tion, of the whole army that constitutes Talbot's military presence).
7. The entire structure of my body (and of my army).
8. This is a dealer in riddles as occasion requires.

[He] winds° his horn; drums strike up; a peal of ordnance.   *blows*
    Enter SOLDIERS.

60   How say you, madam? Are you now persuaded
    That Talbot is but shadow of himself?
    These are his substance, sinews, arms, and strength,
    With which he yoketh your rebellious necks,
    Razeth your cities, and subverts° your towns,   *overthrows*
65   And in a moment makes them desolate.
    COUNTESS   Victorious Talbot, pardon my abuse.°   *error; deception*
    I find thou art no less than fame hath bruited°   *proclaimed*
    And more than may be gathered by thy shape.
    Let my presumption not provoke thy wrath,
70   For I am sorry that with reverence
    I did not entertain° thee as thou art.   *receive*
    TALBOT   Be not dismayed, fair lady, nor misconster
    The mind of Talbot as you did mistake
    The outward composition of his body.
75   What you have done hath not offended me,
    Nor other satisfaction do I crave
    But only, with your patience,° that we may   *permission*
    Taste of your wine and see what cates° you have,   *delicacies*
    For soldiers' stomachs always serve them well.
80   COUNTESS   With all my heart, and think me honorèd
    To feast so great a warrior in my house.   *Exeunt.*

2.4

Enter Richard Plantagenet [of YORK, *the Earl of]* WARWICK,
[the Duke of] SOMERSET, *[William de la]* Pole *[the Earl of*
SUFFOLK, VERNON, *and a* LAWYER].

    YORK   Great lords and gentlemen, what means this silence?
    Dare no man answer in a case of truth?
    SUFFOLK   Within the Temple Hall we were° too loud;   *would have been*
    The garden here is more convenient.
5   YORK   Then say at once if I maintained the truth,
    Or else was wrangling° Somerset in th'error?   *quarrelsome*
    SUFFOLK   Faith, I have been a truant° in the law   *neglectful of study*
    And never yet could frame° my will to it,   *adapt*
    And therefore frame the law unto my will.
10   SOMERSET   Judge you, my lord of Warwick, then between us.
    WARWICK   Between two hawks, which flies the higher pitch,°   *height*
    Between two dogs, which hath the deeper mouth,°   *voice*
    Between two blades, which bears the better temper,[1]
    Between two horses, which doth bear him best,
15   Between two girls, which hath the merriest eye,
    I have perhaps some shallow spirit of judgment;
    But in these nice° sharp quillets° of the law,   *precise / distinctions*
    Good faith, I am no wiser than a daw.[2]
    YORK   Tut, tut, here is a mannerly forbearance!
20   The truth appears so naked on my side
    That any purblind° eye may find it out.   *half-blind*

2.4 Location: The Temple Garden, near the Middle
and Inner Temple, two buildings that housed the
London law schools known as the Inns of Court.
1. *the better temper:* this refers to the degree of hard-

ness attained by a steel sword blade when it is tempered (i.e., heated to a required temperature and
then plunged into cold liquid).
2. Jackdaw (a proverbially stupid bird).

SOMERSET   And on my side it is so well appareled,
   So clear, so shining, and so evident
   That it will glimmer through a blind man's eye.
25 YORK   Since you are tongue-tied and so loath to speak,
   In dumb significants° proclaim your thoughts: *silent gestures*
   Let him that is a true-born gentleman
   And stands upon the honor of his birth,
   If he suppose that I have pleaded truth,³
30 From off this brier pluck a white rose⁴ with me.
      [*He plucks a white rose.*]
SOMERSET   Let him that is no coward nor no flatterer
   But dare maintain the party° of the truth   *side*
   Pluck a red rose⁵ from off this thorn with me.
      [*He plucks a red rose.*]
WARWICK   I love no colors,° and without all color   *hues; pretenses*
35 Of base insinuating flattery,
   I pluck this white rose with Plantagenet.
SUFFOLK   I pluck this red rose with young Somerset
   And say withal° I think he held the right.   *besides*
VERNON   Stay, lords and gentlemen, and pluck no more
40 Till you conclude that he upon whose side
   The fewest roses are cropped from the tree
   Shall yield° the other in the right opinion.   *concede*
SOMERSET   Good Master Vernon, it is well objected;°   *urged*
   If I have fewest, I subscribe° in silence.   *submit*
45 YORK   And I.
VERNON   Then for the truth and plainness of the case,
   I pluck this pale and maiden blossom here,
   Giving my verdict on the white rose side.
SOMERSET   Prick not your finger as you pluck it off
50 Lest, bleeding, you do paint the white rose red
   And fall on my side so, against your will.
VERNON   If I, my lord, for my opinion° bleed,   *conviction*
   Opinion° shall be surgeon to my hurt   *Reputation*
   And keep me on the side where still I am.
55 SOMERSET   Well, well, come on, who else?
LAWYER   Unless my study and my books be false,
   The argument you held was wrong in you,
   In sign whereof I pluck a white rose too.
YORK   Now, Somerset, where is your argument?
60 SOMERSET   Here in my scabbard, meditating that°   *thinking of what*
   Shall dye your white rose in a bloody red.
YORK   Meantime your cheeks do counterfeit° our roses,   *imitate*
   For pale they look with fear, as witnessing
   The truth on our side.
SOMERSET   No, Plantagenet,
65 'Tis not for fear but anger that thy cheeks
   Blush for pure shame, to counterfeit our roses,
   And yet thy tongue will not confess thy error.

---

3. Presented the case for truth according to proper procedures. (This scene contains many legal terms.)
4. Badge of the House of York. In the mid-fifteenth century, two branches of the Plantagenet dynasty, the Yorkists and the Lancastrians, fought what was termed the Wars of the Roses over who would hold the English throne. This invented scene provides a point of origin for the quarrel that grew into the civil wars depicted in later plays on the reigns of Henry VI, Edward IV, and Richard III.
5. Badge of the House of Lancaster.

YORK   Hath not thy rose a canker,° Somerset?   *cankerworm; grub*
SOMERSET   Hath not thy rose a thorn, Plantagenet?
70 YORK   Ay, sharp and piercing to maintain his° truth   *its*
      Whiles thy consuming canker eats his falsehood.
SOMERSET   Well, I'll find friends to wear my bleeding roses,
      That shall maintain what I have said is true,
      Where false Plantagenet dare not be seen.
75 YORK   Now, by this maiden blossom in my hand,
      I scorn thee and thy fashion,° peevish boy.   *sort*
SUFFOLK   Turn not thy scorns this way, Plantagenet.
YORK   Proud Pole,[6] I will, and scorn both him and thee.
SUFFOLK   I'll turn my part thereof into thy throat.[7]
80 SOMERSET   Away, away, good William de la Pole;
      We grace° the yeoman[8] by conversing with him.   *do honor to*
WARWICK   Now, by God's will, thou wrong'st him, Somerset:
      His grandfather was Lionel, Duke of Clarence,
      Third son to the third Edward, King of England.[9]
85 Spring crestless° yeomen from so deep a root?   *without a coat of arms*
YORK   He bears him on the place's privilege[1]
      Or durst not for his craven° heart say thus.   *cowardly*
SOMERSET   By him that made me, I'll maintain my words
      On any plot of ground in Christendom.
90 Was not thy father, Richard, Earl of Cambridge,
      For treason executed in our late King's days?
      And by his treason stand'st not thou attainted,[2]
      Corrupted, and exempt° from ancient gentry?   *excluded*
      His trespass yet lives guilty in thy blood,
95 And till thou be restored,[3] thou art a yeoman.
YORK   My father was attachèd, not attainted;[4]
      Condemned to die for treason, but no traitor;
      And that I'll prove on better men than Somerset,
      Were growing time once ripened to my will.[5]
100 For your partaker° Pole, and you yourself,   *As for your ally*
      I'll note you in my book of memory,[6]
      To scourge you for this apprehension.°   *opinion*
      Look to it well and say you are well warned.
SOMERSET   Ah, thou shalt find us ready for thee still
105 And know us by these colors for thy foes—
      For these my friends in spite of° thee shall wear.   *in contempt of*
YORK   And by my soul, this pale and angry rose,
      As cognizance° of my blood-drinking hate,   *an emblem*
      Will I forever and my faction wear
110 Until it wither with me to my grave

---

6. The Duke of Suffolk's family name.
7. I'll throw the slanders back into your throat.
8. A man, below the rank of gentleman, holding a small estate. (Richard Plantagenet lost his lands and titles when Henry V executed his father, Richard, Earl of Cambridge, for treason.)
9. Clarence was actually Richard's great-great-grandfather on his mother's side. Edmund, Duke of York, fifth son of Edward III, was his paternal grandfather; thus, Richard could trace his descent from Edward III through both his mother and his father.
1. He takes advantage of the safety provided by a privileged place. Quarreling with drawn weapons was prohibited in some precincts, but the Temple,

though originally founded as a religious house, was not one of them.
2. Condemned for treason. One so convicted lost his estate and property. His blood was declared "corrupted" (see line 93), so he could neither inherit nor transmit property and titles.
3. Until you are given back your lands and titles.
4. Was arrested, not convicted. Plantagenet implies that his father's execution was illegal because there was no parliamentary bill of attainder.
5. If the unfolding of time brings me my desire.
6. *book of memory*: a writing tablet or the memory, which was imagined as being like a book or tablet upon which something is written.

Or flourish to the height of my degree.° _noble rank_
SUFFOLK Go forward and be choked with thy ambition,
And so farewell until I meet thee next.   _Exit._
SOMERSET Have with thee,° Pole; farewell, ambitious Richard. _Let us go_
                                               Exit.
115 YORK How I am braved° and must perforce endure it! _insulted_
WARWICK This blot that they object° against your house _allege_
Shall be wiped out in the next parliament,
Called for the truce of° Winchester and Gloucester; _to make peace between_
And if thou be not then created York,
120 I will not live to be accounted Warwick.
Meantime, in signal of my love to thee,
Against proud Somerset and William Pole
Will I upon thy party wear this rose;
And here I prophesy: this brawl today,
125 Grown to this faction° in the Temple Garden, _conflict_
Shall send between the red rose and the white
A thousand souls to death and deadly night.
YORK Good Master Vernon, I am bound to you,
That you on my behalf would pluck a flower.
130 VERNON In your behalf still will I wear the same.
LAWYER And so will I.
YORK Thanks, gentle sir.
Come, let us four to dinner. I dare say
This quarrel will drink blood another day.   _Exeunt._

2.5

Enter [Edmund] MORTIMER, brought in a chair, and
[KEEPERS].[1]
MORTIMER Kind keepers of my weak decaying age,
Let dying Mortimer here rest himself.
Even like a man new halèd° from the rack,[2] _newly dragged_
So fare my limbs with long imprisonment;
5 And these gray locks, the pursuivants° of death, _heralds_
Nestor-like[3] agèd in an age of care,
Argue the end of Edmund Mortimer.[4]
These eyes, like lamps whose wasting oil is spent,
Wax dim, as drawing to their exigent;° _end_
10 Weak shoulders, overborne with burdening grief;
And pithless° arms, like to a withered vine _strengthless_
That droops his° sapless branches to the ground. _its_
Yet are these feet, whose strengthless stay° is numb, _support_
Unable to support this lump of clay,
15 Swift-wingèd with desire to get a grave,
As witting° I no other comfort have. _knowing_
But tell me, Keeper, will my nephew come?
KEEPER Richard Plantagenet, my lord, will come.

2.5 Location: A cell in the Tower of London.
1. F's stage direction reads: "_Enter Mortimer, brought in a Chayre, and laylors._"
2. Instrument of torture on which the victim's body was stretched.
3. Like Nestor, the aged Homeric hero and adviser famous for his wisdom.
4. As in the sources the playwrights probably used, several historical Mortimers are conflated here. In

1385, Richard II declared Roger Mortimer, fourth Earl of March, his heir. When Roger died in battle in 1398, his claim passed to Edmund Mortimer, fifth Earl of March and uncle of Richard Plantagenet, who in turn inherited the Mortimer claim to the throne. It was Edmund's cousin Sir John Mortimer, however, who lay imprisoned in the Tower until 1424, when he was executed for advocating Edmund's claim to the throne.

We sent unto the Temple unto his chamber,
20   And answer was returned that he will come.
     MORTIMER   Enough: my soul shall then be satisfied.
     Poor gentleman, his wrong° doth equal mine.   *(wrong done to him)*
     Since Henry Monmouth° first began to reign,   *(Henry V)*
     Before whose glory I was great in arms,
25   This loathsome sequestration° have I had;   *imprisonment*
     And even since then hath Richard been obscured,°   *overshadowed; hidden*
     Deprived of honor and inheritance.
     But now the arbitrator of despairs,
     Just Death, kind umpire of men's miseries,
30   With sweet enlargement° doth dismiss me hence—   *release*
     I would his° troubles likewise were expired   *(Richard's)*
     That so he might recover what was lost.
              Enter Richard [Plantagenet of YORK].
     KEEPER   My lord, your loving nephew now is come.
     MORTIMER   Richard Plantagenet, my friend, is he come?
35   YORK   Ay, noble uncle, thus ignobly used,
     Your nephew, late° despisèd Richard, comes.   *recently*
     MORTIMER   Direct mine arms I may embrace his neck
     And in his bosom spend my latter° gasp.   *final*
     Oh, tell me when my lips do touch his cheeks
40   That I may kindly give one fainting kiss!
     And now declare, sweet stem from York's great stock,°   *trunk; lineage*
     Why didst thou say of late thou wert despised?
     YORK   First, lean thine agèd back against mine arm,
     And in that ease I'll tell thee my disease.°   *trouble*
45   This day, in argument upon a case,
     Some words there grew twixt Somerset and me,
     Among which terms he used his lavish tongue
     And did upbraid me with my father's death,
     Which obloquy° set bars before° my tongue,   *disgrace / blocked*
50   Else with the like I had requited him.
     Therefore, good uncle, for my father's sake,
     In honor of a true Plantagenet,
     And for alliance'° sake, declare the cause   *kinship's*
     My father, Earl of Cambridge, lost his head.
55   MORTIMER   That cause, fair nephew, that imprisoned me
     And hath detained me all my flow'ring youth
     Within a loathsome dungeon there to pine,
     Was cursèd instrument of his decease.
     YORK   Discover° more at large what cause that was,   *Explain*
60   For I am ignorant and cannot guess.
     MORTIMER   I will, if that my fading breath permit
     And death approach not ere my tale be done.
     Henry the Fourth, grandfather to this King,
     Deposed his nephew° Richard, Edward's son—   *kinsman (here, cousin)*
65   The first begotten and the lawful heir
     Of Edward King, the third of that descent—
     During whose° reign the Percies of the North,   *(Henry IV's)*
     Finding his usurpation most unjust,
     Endeavored my advancement to the throne.
70   The reason moved° these warlike lords to this   *that moved*
     Was for that°—young Richard thus removed,   *Was because*
     Leaving no heir begotten of his body—

I was the next° by birth and parentage,　　　　　　　　(*in line for the throne*)
For by my mother I derivèd° am　　　　　　　　　　　*descended*
75　From Lionel, Duke of Clarence, third son
To King Edward the Third; whereas he
From John of Gaunt doth bring his pedigree,
Being but fourth of that heroic line.
But mark: as in this haughty° great attempt　　　　　　*lofty*
80　They laborèd to plant the rightful heir,
I lost my liberty and they their lives.
Long after this, when Henry the Fifth,
Succeeding his father, Bolingbroke, did reign,
Thy father, Earl of Cambridge, then—derived
85　From famous Edmund Langley, Duke of York—
Marrying my sister, that thy mother was,
Again, in pity of my hard distress,
Levied an army, weening° to redeem　　　　　　　　*intending*
And have installed me in the diadem.°　　　　　　　　*crown*
90　But as the rest, so fell that noble Earl
And was beheaded. Thus the Mortimers,
In whom the title rested, were suppressed.
YORK　Of which, my lord, your honor is the last.
MORTIMER　True; and thou seest that I no issue have
95　And that my fainting words do warrant° death.　　　　*promise*
Thou art my heir; the rest, I wish thee gather;°　　　　*infer*
But yet be wary in thy studious° care.　　　　　　　*diligent*
YORK　Thy grave admonishments prevail with me,
But yet methinks my father's execution
100　Was nothing less than bloody tyranny.
MORTIMER　With silence, nephew, be thou politic.°　　　　*prudent*
Strong fixèd is the House of Lancaster
And, like a mountain, not to be removed.
But now thy uncle is removing° hence,　　　　　　　*departing*
105　As princes do their courts when they are cloyed°　　　*sickened*
With long continuance in a settled place.
YORK　O uncle, would some part of my young years
Might but redeem the passage of your age!
MORTIMER　Thou dost then wrong me, as the slaughterer doth
110　Which giveth many wounds when one will kill.
Mourn not except° thou sorrow for my good;　　　　　*unless*
Only give order for my funeral.
And so farewell, and fair be all thy hopes,
And prosperous be thy life in peace and war.
　　　　　　　[MORTIMER] *dies.*
115　YORK　And peace, no war, befall thy parting soul.
In prison hast thou spent a pilgrimage
And like a hermit overpassed° thy days.　　　　　　*spent*
Well, I will lock his counsel in my breast,
And what I do imagine, let that rest.
120　Keepers, convey him hence, and I myself
Will see his burial better than his life.⁵
　　　　　　　Exeunt [KEEPERS *with Mortimer's body*].
Here dies the dusky torch of Mortimer,

5. *better than his life:* more sumptuous than the life he led (in prison).

Choked with° ambition of the meaner sort.[6]   *by*
And for° those wrongs, those bitter injuries   *And as for*
125 Which Somerset hath offered to my house,
I doubt not but with honor to redress,
And therefore haste I to the Parliament,
Either to be restorèd to my blood°   *inherited rights*
Or make my will th'advantage of my good.[7]   *Exit.*

3.1

Flourish. Enter KING [HENRY],[1] [*the Duke of*] EXETER, [*the Duke of*] GLOUCESTER, [*and the Bishop of*] WINCHESTER; [*the Duke of*] SOMERSET [*and the Earl of*] SUFFOLK [*wearing red roses*]; [*and*] *Richard Plantagenet* [*of* YORK *and the Earl of*] WARWICK [*wearing white roses*[2]]. GLOUCESTER *offers to put up a bill;*° WINCHESTER *snatches it, tears it.*   *written statement*

WINCHESTER   Com'st thou with deep premeditated lines?
With written pamphlets, studiously devised?
Humphrey of Gloucester, if thou canst accuse
Or aught intend'st to lay unto my charge,
5 Do it without invention,° suddenly,   *premeditated design*
As I with sudden and extemporal speech
Purpose to answer what thou canst object.°   *lay to my charge*
GLOUCESTER   Presumptuous priest, this place° commands   *(Parliament)*
    my patience,
Or thou shouldst find thou hast dishonored me.
10 Think not, although in writing I preferred°   *set out*
The manner of thy vile outrageous crimes,
That therefore I have forged or am not able
Verbatim° to rehearse the method of my pen.[3]   *Orally*
No, prelate; such is thy audacious wickedness,
15 Thy lewd,° pestiferous,° and dissentious pranks,   *base / deadly*
As very° infants prattle of thy pride.   *That even*
Thou art a most pernicious usurer,[4]
Froward° by nature, enemy to peace,   *Perverse*
Lascivious, wanton more than well beseems
20 A man of thy profession and degree.°   *rank*
And for° thy treachery, what's more manifest,   *And as for*
In that thou laid'st a trap to take my life
As well at London Bridge as at the Tower?
Beside, I fear me if thy thoughts were sifted,°   *closely examined*
25 The King, thy sovereign, is not quite exempt
From envious malice of thy swelling heart.
WINCHESTER   Gloucester, I do defy thee. Lords, vouchsafe

---

6. *meaner sort:* people of lower rank (referring to Bolingbroke and his line).
7. Or turn the injuries I have suffered to my advantage.
3.1 Location: The Parliament House, London.
1. The historical Henry VI was five years old at the time of this Parliament in 1327. In this scene, Shakespeare refers to the King's "tender years" but does not specify his age.
2. F does not mention that roses are worn in this scene, but in 2.4 the rival factions promised to wear

them forever. This edition indicates their presence throughout the ensuing action.
3. To recount the order of the argument I wrote.
4. Alluding to the fact that Winchester's wealth was partly derived from his use of a papal bull and partly from the Southwark brothels (see 1.3.35 and note). In *Measure for Measure*, Shakespeare refers to prostitution as one of the "two usuries" (3.1.262). Money-lending bred interest; prostitution bred both illicit offspring and financial profit.

To give me hearing what I shall reply.
If I were covetous, ambitious, or perverse,
30 As he will have me, how am I so poor?
Or how haps it I seek not to advance
Or raise myself but keep my wonted° calling?   *customary*
And for dissension, who preferreth peace
More than I do—except I be provoked?
35 No, my good lords, it is not that offends;
It is not that that hath incensed the Duke.
It is because no one should sway° but he;   *rule*
No one but he should be about the King;
And that engenders thunder in his breast
40 And makes him roar these accusations forth.
But he shall know I am as good—
GLOUCESTER   As good?
Thou bastard of my grandfather![5]
WINCHESTER   Ay, lordly sir. For what are you, I pray,
But one imperious° in another's throne?   *ruling*
45 GLOUCESTER   Am I not Protector, saucy priest?
WINCHESTER   And am not I a prelate of the church?
GLOUCESTER   Yes, as an outlaw in a castle keeps,°   *dwells*
And useth it to patronage° his theft.   *protect*
WINCHESTER   Unreverent Gloucester!
GLOUCESTER   Thou art reverend
50 Touching° thy spiritual function, not thy life.   *With regard to*
WINCHESTER   Rome shall remedy this.
WARWICK   Roam thither then.
[*to* GLOUCESTER] My lord, it were your duty to forbear.°   *endure; submit*
SOMERSET   Ay, see the Bishop be not overborne.°   *overruled*
Methinks my lord° should be religious°   *(Gloucester) / (pious*
55 And know the office° that belongs to such.°   *duty / (prelates)*
WARWICK   Methinks his lordship° should be humbler;   *(Winchester)*
It fitteth not a prelate so to plead.°   *wrangle*
SOMERSET   Yes, when his holy state is touched so near.°   *affected so directly*
WARWICK   State holy or unhallowed, what of that?
60 Is not his grace Protector to the King?
YORK [*aside*]   Plantagenet, I see, must hold his tongue,
Lest it be said, "Speak, sirrah,[6] when you should.
Must your bold verdict enter talk° with lords?"—   *hold opinion; converse*
Else would I have a fling at° Winchester.   *argue with*
65 KING HENRY   Uncles of Gloucester and of Winchester,
The special watchmen of our English weal,°   *well-being; state*
I would prevail, if prayers might prevail,
To join your hearts in love and amity.
Oh, what a scandal is it to our crown
70 That two such noble peers as ye should jar!°   *quarrel*
Believe me, lords, my tender years can tell,
Civil dissension is a viperous worm
That gnaws the bowels of the commonwealth.
      A noise within.

---

5. Winchester was born an illegitimate son of Gloucester's grandfather, John of Gaunt, though later he was
made legitimate by an act of Parliament.
6. Term used to address social inferiors.

SERVINGMEN *to* GLOUCESTER [*within*]   Down with the tawny
    coats![7]

KING HENRY   What tumult's this?

75 WARWICK   An uproar, I dare warrant,
    Begun through malice of the Bishop's men.
        A noise again.

SERVINGMEN *to* GLOUCESTER *and* WINCHESTER [*within*]   Stones,
    stones!
        Enter MAYOR [*of London*].

MAYOR   O my good lords and virtuous Henry,
    Pity the city of London, pity us!
80 The Bishop and the Duke of Gloucester's men,   *lately*
    Forbidden late° to carry any weapon,
    Have filled their pockets full of pebble stones
    And, banding themselves in contrary parts,°   *opposing parties*
    Do pelt so fast at one another's pate
85 That many have their giddy brains knocked out.
    Our windows are broke down in every street,
    And we for fear compelled to shut our shops.
        Enter [SERVINGMEN *to* GLOUCESTER *and* WINCHESTER]
        in skirmish with bloody pates.

KING HENRY   We charge you, on allegiance to ourself,
    To hold your slaughtering hands and keep the peace.
90 Pray, Uncle Gloucester, mitigate this strife.

FIRST SERVINGMAN   Nay, if we be forbidden stones, we'll fall
    to it with our teeth.

SECOND SERVINGMAN   Do what ye dare, we are as resolute.
        [*The* SERVINGMEN] *skirmish again.*

GLOUCESTER   You of my household, leave this peevish broil°   *foolish fight*
95 And set this unaccustomed° fight aside.   *unusual; disorderly*

THIRD SERVINGMAN   My lord, we know your grace to be a man
    Just and upright, and, for your royal birth,
    Inferior to none but to his majesty;
    And ere that° we will suffer such a prince,   *And before*
100 So kind a father of the commonweal,
    To be disgracèd° by an inkhorn mate,°   *insulted / scribbler*
    We and our wives and children all will fight
    And have our bodies slaughtered by thy foes.

FIRST SERVINGMAN   Ay, and the very parings of our nails
    Shall pitch a field[8] when we are dead.
        [*The* SERVINGMEN] *begin* [*to skirmish*] *again.*

105 GLOUCESTER   Stay, stay, I say,
    And if you love me, as you say you do,
    Let me persuade you to forbear awhile.

KING HENRY   Oh, how this discord doth afflict my soul!
    Can you, my lord of Winchester, behold
110 My sighs and tears and will not once relent?
    Who should be pitiful° if you be not?   *merciful*
    Or who should study to prefer° a peace   *propose*
    If holy churchmen take delight in broils?

---

7. Again, this line is included as part of the stage
directions in F and is here plausibly assigned to
"*Servingmen.*" The same is true at line 77, where F's
stage direction reads: "*A noyse within, Stones, Stones.*"
8. Shall fortify a battlefield (usually with defensive
wood or iron stakes).

WARWICK Yield, my Lord Protector; yield, Winchester,
115 Except you mean with obstinate repulse°   *refusal*
  To slay your sovereign and destroy the realm.
  You see what mischief and what murder, too,
  Hath been enacted through your enmity.
  Then be at peace, except° ye thirst for blood.   *unless*
120 WINCHESTER He shall submit or I will never yield.
GLOUCESTER Compassion on the King commands me stoop,
  Or I would see his heart out ere the priest
  Should ever get that privilege of° me.   *advantage over*
WARWICK Behold, my lord of Winchester: the Duke
125 Hath banished moody° discontented fury,   *sullen*
  As by his smoothèd brows it doth appear;
  Why look you still so stern and tragical?
GLOUCESTER Here, Winchester; I offer thee my hand.
    [WINCHESTER *refuses it*.]
KING HENRY Fie, Uncle Beaufort! I have heard you preach
130 That malice was a great and grievous sin,
  And will not you maintain the thing you teach
  But prove a chief offender in the same?
WARWICK Sweet King! The Bishop hath a kindly gird.°   *a gentle rebuke*
  —For shame, my lord of Winchester, relent.
135 What, shall a child instruct you what to do?
WINCHESTER Well, Duke of Gloucester, I will yield to thee
  Love for thy love, and hand for hand I give.
GLOUCESTER [*aside*] Ay, but I fear me with a hollow° heart.   *an insincere*
  —See here, my friends and loving countrymen:
140 This token serveth for a flag of truce
  Betwixt ourselves and all our followers;
  So help me God, as I dissemble not.
WINCHESTER So help me God [*aside*] as I intend it not.
KING HENRY O loving uncle, kind Duke of Gloucester,
145 How joyful am I made by this contract!
  [*to* SERVINGMEN] Away, my masters; trouble us no more
  But join in friendship as your lords have done.
FIRST SERVINGMAN Content. I'll to the surgeons.
SECOND SERVINGMAN   And so will I.
THIRD SERVINGMAN And I will see what physic° the tavern affords.   *medicine*
    Exeunt [SERVINGMEN *and* MAYOR].
150 WARWICK Accept this scroll, most gracious sovereign,
  Which in the right of Richard Plantagenet
  We do exhibit to your majesty.
GLOUCESTER Well urged, my lord of Warwick. —For, sweet
    prince,
  An if your grace mark every circumstance,
155 You have great reason to do Richard right,
  Especially for those occasions°   *reasons*
  At Eltham Place I told your majesty.
KING HENRY And those occasions, uncle, were of force;
  Therefore, my loving lords, our pleasure is
160 That Richard be restorèd to his blood.
WARWICK Let Richard be restorèd to his blood;
  So shall his father's wrongs be recompensed.
WINCHESTER As will the rest, so willeth Winchester.
KING HENRY If Richard will be true,° not that alone   *loyal*

165 But all the whole inheritance I give
That doth belong unto the house of York,
From whence you spring by lineal descent.⁹
YORK   Thy humble servant vows obedience
And humble service till the point of death.
170 KING HENRY   Stoop, then, and set your knee against my foot,
And in reguerdon° of that duty done,   *reward*
I girt thee with the valiant sword of York.
Rise, Richard, like a true Plantagenet,
And rise created princely Duke of York.
175 YORK   And so thrive Richard as thy foes may fall;
And as my duty springs, so perish they
That grudge one thought° against your majesty.   *hold any grudges*
ALL *but* RICHARD *and* SOMERSET   Welcome, high prince, the
mighty Duke of York!
SOMERSET [*aside*]   Perish, base prince, ignoble Duke of York.
180 GLOUCESTER   Now will it best avail your majesty
To cross the seas and to be crowned in France.
The presence of a king engenders love
Amongst his subjects and his loyal friends,
As it disanimates° his enemies.   *discourages*
185 KING HENRY   When Gloucester says the word, King Henry goes,
For friendly counsel cuts off many foes.
GLOUCESTER   Your ships already are in readiness.
            Sennet.¹ Flourish. Exeunt all but EXETER.
EXETER   Ay, we may march in England or in France,
Not seeing what is likely to ensue.
190 This late° dissension grown betwixt the peers   *recent*
Burns under feigned ashes of forged love
And will at last break out into a flame;
As festered members° rot but by degree   *parts of the body*
Till bones and flesh and sinews fall away,
195 So will this base and envious discord breed.
And now I fear that fatal prophecy
Which in the time of Henry named the Fifth
Was in the mouth of every sucking babe:
That Henry born at Monmouth° should win all,   *(Henry V)*
200 And Henry born at Windsor° lose all,   *(Henry VI)*
Which is so plain that Exeter doth wish
His days may finish ere that hapless time.   *Exit.*

3.2

*Enter [*JOAN DE*] PUCELLE disguised [*as a peasant*],
with four* SOLDIERS *with sacks upon their backs.*

JOAN DE PUCELLE   These are the city gates, the gates of Rouen,
Through which our policy° must make a breach.   *trickery*
Take heed: be wary how you place your words;
Talk like the vulgar° sort of market men   *common*
5 That come to gather money for their corn.°   *grain*
If we have entrance, as I hope we shall,
And that° we find the slothful watch but weak,   *if*
I'll by a sign give notice to our friends

9. *But . . . descent*: The King restores Richard not
only to the earldom of Cambridge (inherited from his
father) but also to the dukedom of York (inherited
from his uncle).
1. Trumpet notes that accompany a procession.
3.2 Location: In and around Rouen, France.

That Charles the Dauphin may encounter them.

10 SOLDIER Our sacks shall be a mean° to sack the city   *means*
And we be lords and rulers over Rouen;
Therefore, we'll knock.
    [SOLDIER] *knock[s]*.

WATCHMAN [*within*] *Qui là?*°   *Who is there?*

JOAN DE PUCELLE   *Paysans, les pauvres gens de France*[1]—
Poor market folks that come to sell their corn.

15 WATCHMAN [*opening the gate*] Enter, go in; the market bell is rung.

JOAN DE PUCELLE Now, Rouen, I'll shake thy bulwarks to the
  ground.   *Exeunt.*
      Enter CHARLES [*the Dauphin, the*] BASTARD [*of Orléans, the*
      Duke of] ALENÇON[*, and* RENÉ, *Duke of Anjou*].

CHARLES Saint Denis bless this happy stratagem,
And once again we'll sleep secure in Rouen.

BASTARD Here entered Pucelle and her practisants.°   *conspirators*
20 Now she is there, how will she specify
"Here is the best and safest passage in"?

RENÉ By thrusting out a torch from yonder tower,
Which once discerned, shows that her meaning is
No way to that (for weakness) which she entered.[2]
      Enter [JOAN DE] PUCELLE *on the top, thrusting out*
      a torch burning.

25 JOAN DE PUCELLE Behold! This is the happy wedding torch
That joineth Rouen unto her countrymen,
But burning fatal to the Talbonites.°   *followers of Talbot*

BASTARD See, noble Charles, the beacon of our friend:
The burning torch in yonder turret stands.

30 CHARLES Now shine it° like a comet of revenge,   *may it shine*
A prophet to the fall of all our foes.

RENÉ Defer no time: delays have dangerous ends.
Enter and cry, "The Dauphin!" presently,°   *at once*
And then do execution on the watch.°   *Alarum.* [*Exeunt.*]   *then kill the guards*
      An alarum. [*Enter*] TALBOT *in an excursion.*°   *a skirmish*

35 TALBOT France, thou shalt rue° this treason with thy tears   *regret*
If Talbot but survive thy treachery.
Pucelle, that witch, that damnèd sorceress,
Hath wrought this hellish mischief unawares,°   *unexpectedly*
That hardly we escaped the pride of France.[3]   *Exit.*
      An alarum; excursions. [*The Duke of*] BEDFORD *brought in*
      sick in a chair [*by two Attendants*]. *Enter* [*Lord*] TALBOT *and*
      [*the Duke of*] BURGUNDY *without; within,*[4] [JOAN DE] PUCELLE,
      CHARLES [*the Dauphin, the*] BASTARD [*of Orléans*], *and* RENÉ[*,*
      Duke of Anjou] *on the walls.*

40 JOAN DE PUCELLE Good morrow, gallants. Want ye corn for bread?
I think the Duke of Burgundy will fast
Before he'll buy again at such a rate.
'Twas full of darnel;° do you like the taste?   *weeds*

BURGUNDY Scoff on, vile fiend and shameless courtesan!
45 I trust ere long to choke thee with thine own°   *your own bread*

---

1. Peasants, the poor folk of France.
2. No entrance is as weakly guarded as the one she entered.
3. That only with difficulty we escaped the princely power of France.
4. The stage directions suggest that Talbot's party is on the main stage; Joan's party may appear on the upper-stage gallery.

And make thee curse the harvest of that corn.

CHARLES   Your grace may starve, perhaps, before that time.

BEDFORD   Oh, let no words but deeds revenge this treason!

JOAN DE PUCELLE   What will you do, good graybeard? Break
    a lance

50   And run a-tilt at° Death within a chair?   *joust with*

TALBOT   Foul fiend of France and hag of all despite,°   *most despicable*
    Encompassed with thy lustful paramours,°   *lovers*
    Becomes it thee to taunt his valiant age
    And twit° with cowardice a man half dead?   *reproach; taunt*

55   Damsel, I'll have a bout° with you again,   *fight; sexual struggle*
    Or else let Talbot perish with this shame.

JOAN DE PUCELLE   Are ye so hot,° sir? Yet, Pucelle, hold thy   *angry; lustful*
    peace:
    If Talbot do but thunder, rain will follow.
        [*The English*] *whisper together in counsel.*
    God speed the parliament! Who shall be the Speaker?

60   TALBOT   Dare ye come forth and meet us in the field?

JOAN DE PUCELLE   Belike your lordship takes us then for fools,
    To try if that our own be ours or no.

TALBOT   I speak not to that railing Hecate[5]
    But unto thee, Alençon, and the rest.

65   Will ye, like soldiers, come and fight it out?

ALENÇON   *Seigneur,* no.

TALBOT   *Seigneur,* hang! Base muleteers° of France!   *Lowborn mule drivers*
    Like peasant footboys do they keep° the walls   *stay near*
    And dare not take up arms like gentlemen.

70   JOAN DE PUCELLE   Away, captains, let's get us from the walls,
    For Talbot means no goodness by his looks.
    Goodbye, my lord; we came but to tell you
    That we are here.   *Exeunt* [*the French*] *from the walls.*

TALBOT   And there will we be too ere it be long,

75   Or else reproach be Talbot's greatest fame.
    Vow, Burgundy, by honor of thy house,
    Pricked on° by public wrongs sustained in France,   *Urged on*
    Either to get the town again or die;
    And I, as sure as English Henry lives,

80   And as his father here was conqueror;[6]
    As sure as in this late° betrayèd town   *recently*
    Great Coeur-de-Lion's heart was buried,[7]
    So sure I swear to get the town or die.

BURGUNDY   My vows are equal partners with thy vows.

85   TALBOT   But ere we go, regard this dying prince,
    The valiant Duke of Bedford. —Come, my lord,
    We will bestow you in some better place,
    Fitter for sickness and for crazy° age.   *feeble*

BEDFORD   Lord Talbot, do not so dishonor me.

90   Here will I sit before the walls of Rouen
    And will be partner of your weal° or woe.   *happiness*

BURGUNDY   Courageous Bedford, let us now persuade you.

BEDFORD   Not to be gone from hence, for once I read

5. In classical mythology, the goddess of night and
the underworld and the patron of witchcraft.
6. Henry V had captured Rouen in 1419.
7. According to Holinshed's *Chronicles,* Richard

Coeur-de-Lion (the Lion-Hearted), who ruled
England from 1189 to 1199, willed that his heart be
buried in Rouen as a sign of his love for the city.

That stout Pendragon,[8] in his litter sick,
95 Came to the field and vanquishèd his foes.
Methinks I should revive the soldiers' hearts
Because I ever found them as myself.
TALBOT   Undaunted spirit in a dying breast!
Then be it so; heavens keep old Bedford safe.
100 And now no more ado, brave Burgundy,
But gather we our forces out of hand°   at once
And set upon our boasting enemy.
         Exeunt [all but BEDFORD *and his two Attendants].*
         An alarum; excursions. Enter Sir John FALSTAFF *and*
         a CAPTAIN.
CAPTAIN   Whither away, Sir John Falstaff, in such haste?
FALSTAFF   Whither away? To save myself by flight;
105 We are like to have the overthrow° again.   to be defeated
CAPTAIN   What? Will you fly and leave Lord Talbot?
FALSTAFF   Ay, all the Talbots in the world, to save my life.
                                                                              Exit.
CAPTAIN   Cowardly knight, ill fortune follow thee!
                                                                              Exit.
         Retreat. Excursions. [JOAN DE] PUCELLE, [*the Duke of*]
         ALENÇON, *and* CHARLES [*the Dauphin*] *fly.*
BEDFORD   Now, quiet soul, depart when heaven please,
110 For I have seen our enemies' overthrow.
What is the trust or strength of foolish man?
They that of late were daring with their scoffs
Are glad and fain° by flight to save themselves.   eager
         BEDFORD *dies and is carried [offstage] by [his] two*
         [*Attendants*] *in his chair.*
         An alarum. Enter [Lord] TALBOT, [*the Duke of*]
         BURGUNDY, *and the rest [of the English* SOLDIERS].
TALBOT   Lost and recovered in a day again!
115 This is a double honor, Burgundy,
Yet heavens have glory for this victory.
BURGUNDY   Warlike and martial Talbot, Burgundy
Enshrines thee in his heart and there erects
Thy noble deeds as valor's monuments.
120 TALBOT   Thanks, gentle° Duke, but where is Pucelle now?   noble
I think her old familiar° is asleep.   attendant demon
Now where's the Bastard's braves° and Charles his gleeks?°   boasts / Charles's jests
What, all amort?° Rouen hangs her head for grief   dispirited
That such a valiant company are fled.
125 Now will we take some order° in the town,   establish order
Placing therein some expert officers,
And then depart to Paris to the King,
For there young Henry with his nobles lie.°   is encamped
BURGUNDY   What wills Lord Talbot pleaseth Burgundy.
130 TALBOT   But yet, before we go, let's not forget
The noble Duke of Bedford, late deceased,
But see his exequies° fulfilled in Rouen.   funeral rites
A braver soldier never couchèd° lance;   leveled (for attack)

---

8. Uther Pendragon, the father of King Arthur. This story is told in Geoffrey of Monmouth's history of Britain (*Historia Regum Britanniae*). **stout:** brave.

A gentler heart did never sway in court—
135　But kings and mightiest potentates must die,
For that's the end of human misery.　　　　　　*Exeunt.*

3.3

Enter CHARLES [*the Dauphin, the*] BASTARD [*of Orléans,
the Duke of*] ALENÇON, [*and* JOAN DE] PUCELLE.

JOAN DE PUCELLE　Dismay not, princes, at this accident,
Nor grieve that Rouen is so recoverèd.
Care° is no cure, but rather corrosive,°　　　　　　　　　　*Sorrow / destructive*
For things that are not to be remedied.
5　Let frantic° Talbot triumph for a while　　　　　　　　　　*mad*
And like a peacock sweep along his tail;
We'll pull his plumes and take away his train°　　　*peacock's tail; army*
If Dauphin and the rest will be but ruled.
CHARLES　We have been guided by thee hitherto
10　And of thy cunning had no diffidence;°　　　　　　　　　　*doubt*
One sudden foil° shall never breed distrust.　　　　　　　　*defeat*
BASTARD　Search out thy wit for secret policies,°　　　　　*stratagems*
And we will make thee famous through the world.
ALENÇON　We'll set thy statue in some holy place
15　And have thee reverenced like a blessed saint;
Employ thee, then, sweet virgin, for our good.
JOAN DE PUCELLE　Then thus it must be; this doth Joan devise:
By fair persuasions mixed with sugared words,
We will entice the Duke of Burgundy
20　To leave the Talbot and to follow us.
CHARLES　Ay, marry, sweeting,° if we could do that,　　　*(a lover's nickname)*
France were no place for Henry's warriors,
Nor should that nation boast it so with us
But be extirpèd° from our provinces.　　　　　　　　　　*rooted out*
25　ALENÇON　For ever should they be expulsed from France
And not have title of an earldom here.
JOAN DE PUCELLE　Your honors shall perceive how I will work
To bring this matter to the wishèd end.
　　　　　Drum sounds afar off.
Hark! By the sound of drum you may perceive
30　Their powers are marching unto Parisward.°　　　　　　　*toward Paris*
　　　　　Here sound an English march.
There goes the Talbot with his colors spread°　　　　　　*flags unfurled*
And all the troops of English after him.
　　　　　[*Here sound a*] *French march.*
Now in the rearward comes the Duke and his;
Fortune in favor° makes him lag behind.　　　　　　　　　*as a favor to us*
35　Summon a parley;[1] we will talk with him.
　　　　　Trumpets sound a parley.
CHARLES　A parley with the Duke of Burgundy!
　　　　　[*Enter the Duke of* BURGUNDY.]
BURGUNDY　Who craves a parley with the Burgundy?
JOAN DE PUCELLE　The princely Charles of France, thy
　　countryman.

3.3 Location: Plains near Rouen.　　　　　1. Sound a trumpet to request a conference.

BURGUNDY   What say'st thou, Charles? For I am marching
    hence.

40 CHARLES   Speak, Pucelle, and enchant him with thy words.

JOAN DE PUCELLE   Brave Burgundy, undoubted° hope of France,   *certain*
    Stay, let thy humble handmaid speak to thee.

BURGUNDY   Speak on, but be not over-tedious.

JOAN DE PUCELLE   Look on thy country, look on fertile France,
45   And see the cities and the towns defaced
    By wasting ruin of the cruel foe,
    As looks the mother on her lowly babe
    When death doth close his tender-dying° eyes.   *young-dying*
    See, see the pining malady of France;
50   Behold the wounds, the most unnatural wounds
    Which thou thyself hast given her woeful breast.
    Oh, turn thy edgèd sword another way!
    Strike those that hurt, and hurt not those that help;
    One drop of blood drawn from thy country's bosom
55   Should grieve thee more than streams of foreign gore.
    Return thee, therefore, with a flood of tears
    And wash away thy country's stainèd spots.[2]

BURGUNDY [*aside*]   Either she hath bewitched me with her words,
    Or nature makes me suddenly relent.

60 JOAN DE PUCELLE   Besides, all French and France exclaims
      on° thee,   *denounces*
    Doubting thy birth and lawful progeny.°   *ancestry*
    Who join'st thou with but with a lordly nation
    That will not trust thee but for profit's sake?
    When Talbot hath set footing once in France
65   And fashioned thee that instrument of ill,
    Who then but English Henry will be lord,
    And thou be thrust out like a fugitive?
    Call we to mind and mark but this for proof:
    Was not the Duke of Orléans thy foe?
70   And was he not in England prisoner?
    But when they heard he was thine enemy,
    They set him free without his ransom paid,
    In spite of Burgundy and all his friends.[3]
    See, then, thou fight'st against thy countrymen
75   And join'st with them will be thy slaughtermen.
    Come, come, return; return, thou wandering lord;
    Charles and the rest will take thee in their arms.

BURGUNDY [*aside*]   I am vanquished:[4] these haughty° words of hers   *lofty*
    Have battered me like roaring cannon-shot
80   And made me almost yield upon my knees.
    —Forgive me, country and sweet countrymen;
    And lords, accept this hearty kind embrace.
    My forces and my power of men are yours.
    So farewell, Talbot; I'll no longer trust thee.

85 JOAN DE PUCELLE [*aside*]   Done like a Frenchman: turn and
    turn again.

---

2. And wash away the spots of blood that defile your
country.
3. The historical Orléans was not released by the
English until five years after Burgundy abandoned
the English alliance.
4. The historical Burgundy did not return to the
French side until four years after Joan's death.

CHARLES Welcome, brave Duke; thy friendship makes us fresh.
BASTARD And doth beget new courage in our breasts.
ALENÇON Pucelle hath bravely played her part in this
 And doth deserve a coronet of gold.
90 CHARLES Now let us on, my lords, and join our powers,
 And seek how we may prejudice° the foe. *Exeunt.*   *hurt*

3.4

[Flourish.] Enter KING *[*HENRY, *the Duke of]* GLOUCESTER,
[the Bishop of] WINCHESTER, *[Richard, Duke of]* YORK,
[the Earl of] SUFFOLK, *[the Duke of]* SOMERSET, *[the Earl of]*
WARWICK, *[the Duke of]* EXETER[, VERNON, *and* BASSET].
To them, with his SOLDIERS, *[enter Lord]* TALBOT.

TALBOT My gracious prince and honorable peers,
 Hearing of your arrival in this realm,
 I have a while given truce unto my wars
 To do my duty° to my sovereign.   *give homage*
5 In sign whereof this arm, that hath reclaimed
 To your obedience fifty fortresses,
 Twelve cities, and seven walled towns of strength,
 Beside five hundred prisoners of esteem,°   *noble rank*
 Lets fall his sword before your highness' feet,
10 And with submissive loyalty of heart
 Ascribes the glory of his conquest got
 First to my God and next unto your grace.
  [He kneels.][1]
KING HENRY Is this the Lord Talbot, Uncle Gloucester,
 That hath so long been resident in France?
15 GLOUCESTER Yes, if it please your majesty, my liege.
KING HENRY Welcome, brave captain and victorious lord.
 When I was young—as yet I am not old—
 I do remember how my father said
 A stouter champion never handled sword.
20 Long since we were resolvèd° of your truth,° *convinced / loyalty*
 Your faithful service, and your toil in war,
 Yet never have you tasted our reward
 Or been reguerdoned° with so much as thanks,   *rewarded*
 Because till now we never saw your face.
25 Therefore, stand up, and for these good deserts
 We here create you Earl of Shrewsbury,
 And in our coronation take your place.[2]
  Sennet. Flourish. Exeunt all but VERNON *and* BASSET.
VERNON Now, sir, to you that were so hot° at sea,   *angry*
 Disgracing of these colors° that I wear *this badge (the rose)*
30 In honor of my noble lord of York,
 Dar'st thou maintain the former words thou spak'st?
BASSET Yes, sir, as well as you dare patronage°   *defend*
 The envious barking of your saucy tongue
 Against my lord the Duke of Somerset.
35 VERNON Sirrah, thy lord I honor as he is.
BASSET Why, what is he? As good a man as York.

3.4 Location: The palace, Paris.
1. F does not indicate when Talbot kneels, but he must do so: at line 25, he is urged to "stand up."

2. The historical Talbot was created Earl of Shrews-bury in 1442, more than ten years after Henry's coronation.

VERNON   Hark ye, not so! In witness take ye that.
          [*He*] *strikes him.*
BASSET   Villain, thou knowest the law of arms³ is such
          That whoso draws a sword, 'tis present° death,   *immediate*
40   Or else this blow should broach° thy dearest blood.   *tap (as a wine vat)*
          But I'll unto his majesty and crave
          I may have liberty° to venge this wrong,   *permission*
          When thou shalt see I'll meet thee to thy cost.
VERNON   Well, miscreant,° I'll be there as soon as you,   *villain*
45   And after meet you sooner than you would.°   *Exeunt.*   *would wish*

4.1

          [*Flourish.*] *Enter* KING [HENRY], [*the Duke of*] GLOUCESTER,
          [*the Bishop of*] WINCHESTER, [*Richard, Duke of*] YORK,
          [*the Earl of*] SUFFOLK, [*the Duke of*] SOMERSET,
          [*the Earl of*] WARWICK, [*Lord*] TALBOT, [*the Duke of*] EXETER,
          [*and the*] *Governor* [*of Paris*].
GLOUCESTER   Lord Bishop, set the crown upon his head.
WINCHESTER [*crowning* KING HENRY]   God save King Henry,
          of that name the sixth!
GLOUCESTER   Now, Governor of Paris, take your oath:
          That you elect° no other king but him,   *acknowledge*
5   Esteem none friends but such as are his friends,
          And none your foes but such as shall pretend°   *propose*
          Malicious practices against his state—
          This shall ye do, so help you righteous God.
          [*Governor of Paris swears.*] *Enter* [*Sir John*] FALSTAFF.
FALSTAFF   My gracious sovereign, as I rode from Calais
10   To haste unto your coronation,
          A letter was delivered to my hands,
          Writ to your grace from th' Duke of Burgundy.
          [*He presents the letter.*]
TALBOT   Shame to the Duke of Burgundy and thee!
          [*He tears off Falstaff's garter.*]
          I vowed, base knight, when I did meet thee next,
15   To tear the garter¹ from thy craven's° leg,   *coward's*
          Which I have done because, unworthily,
          Thou wast installèd in that high degree.
          —Pardon me, princely Henry, and the rest:
          This dastard,° at the battle of Patay—   *coward*
20   When but in all° I was six thousand strong   *When all told*
          And that the French were almost ten to one—
          Before we met or that a stroke was given,
          Like to a trusty° squire did run away,   *faithful (here, ironic)*
          In which assault we lost twelve hundred men.
25   Myself and divers° gentlemen beside   *various*
          Were there surprised and taken prisoners.
          Then judge, great lords, if I have done amiss
          Or whether that such cowards ought to wear
          This ornament of knighthood—yea or no?
30   GLOUCESTER   To say the truth, this fact° was infamous   *deed*

---

3. The law that forbade fighting near a royal residence (see also 1.3.46 and 2.4.86).
4.1 Location: The palace, Paris.

1. A ribbon, worn below the left knee, signifying
membership in the Order of the Garter, the highest
rank of English knighthood.

And ill beseeming any common man,
Much more a knight, a captain, and a leader.
TALBOT   When first this order was ordained, my lords,
Knights of the Garter were of noble birth,
35   Valiant and virtuous, full of haughty° courage,   lofty
Such as were grown to credit° by the wars—   fame
Not fearing death, nor shrinking for distress,
But always resolute in most extremes.°   in greatest extremities
He, then, that is not furnished in this sort°   not endowed like this
40   Doth but usurp the sacred name of knight,
Profaning this most honorable order,
And should—if I were worthy to be judge—
Be quite degraded,° like a hedge-born swain²   reduced in rank
That doth presume to boast of gentle° blood.   noble
45   KING HENRY [to FALSTAFF]   Stain to thy countrymen, thou
hear'st thy doom!°   sentence
Be packing, therefore, thou that wast a knight.
Henceforth we banish thee on pain of death. [Exit FALSTAFF.]
And now, my Lord Protector, view the letter
Sent from our uncle, Duke of Burgundy.³
50   GLOUCESTER   What means his grace that he hath changed
his style?°   form of address
No more but plain and bluntly, "To the King"?
Hath he forgot he is his sovereign?
Or doth this churlish superscription°   rude address
Pretend° some alteration in goodwill?   Indicate
55   What's here? "I have upon especial cause,
Moved with compassion of my country's wrack,°   destruction
Together with the pitiful complaints
Of such as your oppression feeds upon,
Forsaken your pernicious faction
60   And joined with Charles, the rightful king of France."
Oh, monstrous treachery! Can this be so?
That in alliance, amity, and oaths
There should be found such false dissembling guile?
KING HENRY   What? Doth my uncle Burgundy revolt?
65   GLOUCESTER   He doth, my lord, and is become your foe.
KING HENRY   Is that the worst this letter doth contain?
GLOUCESTER   It is the worst, and all, my lord, he writes.
KING HENRY   Why, then, Lord Talbot there shall talk with him
And give him chastisement for this abuse.
70   —How say you, my lord? Are you not content?
TALBOT   Content, my liege? Yes. But that I am prevented,°   anticipated
I should have begged I might have been employed.
KING HENRY   Then gather strength and march unto him straight.°   at once
Let him perceive how ill we brook° his treason   tolerate
75   And what offense it is to flout his friends.
TALBOT   I go, my lord, in heart desiring still°   always
You may behold confusion of your foes.   [Exit.]
          Enter VERNON [wearing a white rose] and
          BASSET [wearing a red rose].

2. A lowly or illegitimate country person.
3. Henry VI's uncle, the Duke of Bedford, married Burgundy's sister Anne.

	VERNON Grant me the combat,° gracious sovereign.	*permission to duel*
	BASSET And me, my lord—grant me the combat too.	
80	YORK [*indicating* VERNON] This is my servant.° Hear him,	*follower*
	noble prince.	
	SOMERSET [*indicating* BASSET] And this is mine, sweet	
	Henry; favor him.	
	KING HENRY Be patient, lords, and give them leave to speak.	
	—Say, gentlemen, what makes you thus exclaim,	
	And wherefore crave you combat, or with whom?	
85	VERNON With him, my lord, for he hath done me wrong.	
	BASSET And I with him, for he hath done me wrong.	
	KING HENRY What is that wrong whereof you both complain	
	First let me know, and then I'll answer you.	
	BASSET Crossing the sea from England into France,	
90	This fellow here with envious carping° tongue	*fault-finding*
	Upbraided me about the rose I wear,	
	Saying the sanguine° color of the leaves°	*blood-red / petals*
	Did represent my master's blushing cheeks	
	When stubbornly he did repugn° the truth	*reject*
95	About a certain question[4] in the law	
	Argued betwixt the Duke of York and him,	
	With other vile and ignominious terms.	
	In confutation° of which rude reproach,	*disproof*
	And in defense of my lord's worthiness,	
100	I crave the benefit of law of arms.[5]	
	VERNON And that is my petition, noble lord.	
	For though he seem with forgèd quaint conceit°	*false cunning words*
	To set a gloss° upon his bold intent,	*good appearance*
	Yet know, my lord, I was provoked by him,	
105	And he first took exceptions at this badge,	
	Pronouncing that the paleness of this flower	
	Bewrayed° the faintness of my master's heart.	*Revealed*
	YORK Will not this malice, Somerset, be left?°	*put aside*
	SOMERSET Your private grudge, my lord of York, will out,	
110	Though ne'er so cunningly you smother it.	
	KING HENRY Good lord! What madness rules in brainsick men	
	When for so slight and frivolous a cause	
	Such factious emulations° shall arise?	*divisive jealousies*
	Good cousins both, of York and Somerset,	
115	Quiet yourselves, I pray, and be at peace.	
	YORK Let this dissension first be tried by fight,	
	And then your highness shall command a peace.	
	SOMERSET The quarrel toucheth none but us alone;	
	Betwixt ourselves let us decide it then.	
120	YORK [*throwing down a gage[6]*] There is my pledge; accept it,	
	Somerset.	
	VERNON Nay, let it rest where it began at first.[7]	
	BASSET Confirm it so, mine honorable lord.	
	GLOUCESTER Confirm it so? Confounded be your strife,	
	And perish ye with your audacious prate!°	*prattling*

---

4. The "certain question" apparently concerns the question of York's succession to the throne and the attainder of his father. See 2.4 and 2.5.45–129.
5. The right to decide the matter in a duel.

6. A glove or gauntlet thrown down in a duel.
7. Let the quarrel remain with me and Basset, who began it.

125 Presumptuous vassals, are you not ashamed
With this immodest clamorous outrage
To trouble and disturb the King and us?
[*to* YORK *and* SOMERSET] And you, my lords, methinks you
do not well
To bear with their perverse objections,°   *accusations*
130 Much less to take occasion° from their mouths   *the opportunity*
To raise a mutiny betwixt yourselves.
Let me persuade you take a better course.
EXETER   It grieves his highness. Good my lords, be friends.
KING HENRY [*to* VERNON *and* BASSET] Come hither, you that
would be combatants.
135 Henceforth I charge you, as you love our favor,
Quite to forget this quarrel and the cause.
[*to* YORK *and* SOMERSET] And you, my lords, remember where
we are:
In France, amongst a fickle wavering nation.
If they perceive dissension in our looks
140 And that within ourselves we disagree,
How will their grudging stomachs° be provoked   *resentful tempers*
To willful disobedience and rebel.
Beside, what infamy will there arise
When foreign princes shall be certified°   *informed*
145 That for a toy,° a thing of no regard,   *trifle*
King Henry's peers and chief nobility
Destroyed themselves and lost the realm of France!
Oh, think upon the conquest of my father,
My tender years, and let us not forgo
150 That for a trifle that was bought with blood.[8]
Let me be umpire in this doubtful° strife: *uncertain*
[*He takes a red rose and puts it on.*]
I see no reason if I wear this rose
That anyone should therefore be suspicious
I more incline to Somerset than York:
155 Both are my kinsmen, and I love them both.
As well they may upbraid me with my crown
Because, forsooth, the King of Scots is crowned.
But your discretions better can persuade
Than I am able to instruct or teach,
160 And therefore, as we hither came in peace,
So let us still continue peace and love.
Cousin of York, we institute° your grace   *appoint*
To be our Regent in these parts of France;
And good my lord of Somerset, unite
165 Your troops of horsemen with his bands of foot,°   *infantry*
And like true subjects, sons of your progenitors,
Go cheerfully together and digest°   *dissipate*
Your angry choler on your enemies.[9]
Ourself, my Lord Protector, and the rest,
170 After some respite will return to Calais;

8. *let . . . blood:* let us not lose for a trifle what was bought with blood (i.e., let us not lose France).
9. *angry choler on your enemies:* in the humoral model of the body, an excess of choler (yellow bile) was believed to cause anger. This line echoes the metaphorical comparisons made elsewhere in this scene between the diseased body and the disordered state.

From thence to England, where I hope ere long
To be presented by your victories,
With Charles, Alençon, and that traitorous rout.°   *rabble*

        [Flourish.] Exeunt all but YORK, WARWICK,
                  EXETER, *[and]* VERNON.

WARWICK   My lord of York, I promise you the King
175   Prettily, methought, did play the orator.
YORK   And so he did, but yet I like it not
    In that he wears the badge of Somerset.
WARWICK   Tush, that was but his fancy; blame him not.
    I dare presume, sweet prince, he thought no harm.
180   YORK   An if I wist° he did! But let it rest.   *If I knew for certain*
    Other affairs must now be managèd. *Exeunt all but* EXETER.
EXETER   Well didst thou, Richard, to suppress thy voice,
    For had the passions of thy heart burst out,
    I fear we should have seen deciphered° there   *revealed*
185   More rancorous spite, more furious raging broils,
    Than yet can be imagined or supposed.
    But howsoe'er, no simple man that sees
    This jarring discord of nobility,
    This shouldering of each other in the court,
190   This factious bandying° of their favorites,°   *quarreling / followers*
    But that° it doth presage some ill event.°   *But sees that / outcome*
    'Tis much when scepters are in children's hands,
    But more when envy breeds unkind° division: *unnatural*
    There comes the ruin; there begins confusion.   *Exit.*

4.2

    Enter [Lord] TALBOT *with Trump and Drum [and* SOLDIERS*]*
    before Bordeaux.
TALBOT   Go to the gates of Bordeaux, trumpeter;
    Summon their general unto the wall.
    [Trumpet] sounds [a parley]. Enter [French] GENERAL *aloft.*
    —English John Talbot, captains, calls you forth,
    Servant in arms to Harry, King of England,
5   And thus he would:° open your city gates,   *desires*
    Be humble to us, call my sovereign yours,
    And do him homage as obedient subjects,
    And I'll withdraw me and my bloody power.
    But if you frown upon this proffered peace,
10   You tempt the fury of my three attendants—
    Lean Famine, quartering° Steel, and climbing Fire—   *dismembering*
    Who in a moment, even° with the earth   *level*
    Shall lay your stately and air-braving° towers   *air-defying; lofty*
    If you forsake the offer of their love.
15   GENERAL   Thou ominous and fearful owl[1] of death,
    Our nation's terror and their bloody scourge,
    The period° of thy tyranny approacheth.   *end*
    On us thou canst not enter but by death,
    For I protest we are well fortified
20   And strong enough to issue out and fight.
    If thou retire, the Dauphin, well appointed,°   *equipped*

4.2 Location: Before Bordeaux.   (see Ovid's *Metamorphoses* 10.521–52 and *Macbeth*
1. The owl's cry was thought to portend evil or death   2.2.3).

Stands with the snares of war to tangle thee.
On either hand thee° there are squadrons pitched[2]   *On both sides of you*
To wall thee from the liberty of flight;
25   And no way canst thou turn thee for redress
But death doth front thee with apparent spoil,[3]
And pale destruction meets thee in the face.
Ten thousand French have ta'en the sacrament[4]
To rive° their dangerous artillery   *discharge*
30   Upon no Christian soul but English Talbot.
Lo, there thou stand'st, a breathing valiant man
Of an invincible unconquered spirit.
This is the latest° glory of thy praise   *final*
That I, thy enemy, due° thee withal,   *endow*
35   For ere the glass° that now begins to run   *hourglass*
Finish the process of his° sandy hour,   *progress of its*
These eyes that see thee now well colorèd°   *in good health*
Shall see thee withered, bloody, pale, and dead.
        Drum afar off.
Hark, hark, the Dauphin's drum, a warning bell,
40   Sings heavy music to thy timorous soul,
And mine shall ring thy dire departure out.[5]   *Exit.*
TALBOT   He fables not; I hear the enemy.
—Out, some light horsemen, and peruse their wings.°   *survey their flanks*
        [*Exeunt some* SOLDIERS.]
Oh, negligent and heedless° discipline!   *careless*
45   How are we parked° and bounded in a pale,°   *enclosed / fenced area*
A little herd of England's timorous deer,
Mazed with[6] a yelping kennel of French curs.
If we be English deer, be then in blood,°   *vigorous*
Not rascal-like[7] to fall down with a pinch°   *nip (from hounds)*
50   But rather moody-mad;° and, desperate stags,   *enraged*
Turn on the bloody hounds with heads of steel
And make the cowards stand aloof at bay.
Sell every man his life as dear as mine,
And they shall find dear° deer of us, my friends.   *costly*
55   God and Saint George,° Talbot and England's right,   *England's patron saint*
Prosper our colors in this dangerous fight!   [*Exeunt.*]

4.3

Enter a MESSENGER *that meets* [*Richard, Duke of*] YORK.
Enter YORK *with Trumpet and many* SOLDIERS.
YORK   Are not the speedy scouts returned again
That dogged° the mighty army of the Dauphin?   *tracked*
MESSENGER   They are returned, my lord, and give it out
That he is marched to Bordeaux with his power
5   To fight with Talbot. As he marched along,
By your espials° were discoverèd   *spies*
Two mightier troops than that the Dauphin led,

---

2. Arranged on the field for battle.
3. But death confronts you with obvious destruction.
4. Have received the Christian sacrament of Holy Communion (as a way of confirming their oaths).
5. And my drum—the alarm signal given when the

general's army is to "issue out and fight" (line 20) against Talbot—shall signal your death.
6. Bewildered by; trapped in a maze with.
7. Not like lean, worthless deer.
4.3 Location: An unspecified field in France.

Which joined with him and made their march for Bordeaux.
YORK   A plague upon that villain Somerset
10　That thus delays my promisèd supply
　　Of horsemen that were levied for this siege!
　　Renownèd Talbot doth expect my aid,
　　And I am louted° by a traitor villain　　　　　　　　　　　*made a fool of*
　　And cannot help the noble chevalier.
15　God comfort him in this necessity!
　　If he miscarry,° farewell wars in France.　　　　　　　　*comes to harm*
　　　　Enter another messenger[, Sir William LUCY].
LUCY[1]   Thou princely leader of our English strength,
　　Never so needful on the earth of France,
　　Spur to the rescue of the noble Talbot,
20　Who now is girdled with a waist° of iron　　　　　　　*vast expanse; belt*
　　And hemmed about with grim destruction.
　　To Bordeaux, warlike Duke; to Bordeaux, York!
　　Else farewell Talbot, France, and England's honor.
YORK   O God, that Somerset, who in proud heart
25　Doth stop my cornets,° were in Talbot's place!　　　*troops of cavalry*
　　So should we save a valiant gentleman
　　By forfeiting a traitor and a coward.
　　Mad ire and wrathful fury makes me weep
　　That thus we die while remiss° traitors sleep.　　　　*idle; negligent*
30　LUCY   Oh, send some succor to the distressed lord!
YORK   He dies, we lose; I break my warlike word;
　　We mourn, France smiles; we lose, they daily get—
　　All long° of this vile traitor Somerset.　　　　　　　　*because*
LUCY   Then God take mercy on brave Talbot's soul
35　And on his son young John, who two hours since
　　I met in travel toward his warlike father.
　　This seven years did not Talbot see his son,
　　And now they meet where both their lives are done.
YORK   Alas, what joy shall noble Talbot have
40　To bid his young son welcome to his grave?
　　Away! Vexation almost stops my breath,
　　That sundered friends greet in the hour of death.
　　Lucy, farewell; no more my fortune can°　　　　　　　　*can do*
　　But curse the cause I cannot aid the man.
45　Maine, Blois, Poitiers, and Tours are won away,
　　Long all° of Somerset and his delay.　*Exeunt [all but* LUCY].　　*All because*
LUCY   Thus while the vulture of sedition
　　Feeds in the bosom of such great commanders,
　　Sleeping neglection° doth betray to loss　　　　　　　*Careless disregard*
50　The conquest of our scarce-cold conqueror,[2]
　　That ever-living man of memory,[3]
　　Henry the Fifth. Whiles they each other cross,
　　Lives, honors, lands, and all hurry to loss.　　　　　*[Exit.]*[4]

1. In F, this and the subsequent three speeches assigned to Lucy are spoken by "Second Messenger" and "Messenger." However, at line 43, York addresses the speaker as "Lucy."
2. The conquest made by our recently dead conqueror. (The events of this scene actually took place thirty-one years after the death of the historical Henry V.)
3. That man who will live forever in memory.
4. F does not mark Lucy's exit at this point. Conceivably, he stays onstage as Somerset enters to him.

4.4

Enter [the Duke of] SOMERSET *with his army*
[and a CAPTAIN*].*

SOMERSET   It is too late; I cannot send them now.
   This expedition was by York and Talbot
   Too rashly plotted. All our general force
   Might with a sally of the very town
5   Be buckled with;[1] the over-daring Talbot
   Hath sullied all his gloss° of former honor   *luster*
   By this unheedful, desperate, wild adventure.
   York set him on to fight and die in shame,
   That, Talbot dead, great York might bear the name.°   *claim preeminence*
   [*Enter Sir William* LUCY.]
10 CAPTAIN   Here is Sir William Lucy, who with me
   Set from our o'ermatched forces forth for aid.
SOMERSET   How now, Sir William? Whither were you sent?
LUCY   Whither, my lord? From bought and sold[2] Lord Talbot,
   Who, ringed about with bold adversity,
15   Cries out for noble York and Somerset
   To beat assailing death from his weak regions.
   And whiles the honorable captain there
   Drops bloody sweat from his war-wearied limbs
   And, in advantage° ling'ring, looks for rescue,   *in a superior position*
20   You, his false hopes, the trust of England's honor,
   Keep off aloof with worthless emulation.°   *rivalry*
   Let not your private discord keep away
   The levied succors° that should lend him aid   *reinforcements*
   While he, renownèd noble gentleman,
25   Yield up his life unto a world of° odds.   *immense*
   Orléans the Bastard, Charles, Burgundy,
   Alençon, René compass him about,
   And Talbot perisheth by your default.
SOMERSET   York set him on; York should have sent him aid.
30 LUCY   And York as fast upon your grace exclaims,
   Swearing that you withhold his levied host,
   Collected for this expedition.
SOMERSET   York lies. He might have sent° and had the horse;   *sent for*
   I owe him little duty and less love,
35   And take foul scorn° to fawn on him by sending.   *find it disgraceful*
LUCY   The fraud of England, not the force of France,
   Hath now entrapped the noble-minded Talbot.
   Never to England shall he bear his life
   But dies betrayed to fortune by your strife.
40 SOMERSET   Come, go; I will dispatch the horsemen straight;°   *immediately*
   Within six hours they will be at his aid.
LUCY   Too late comes rescue! He is ta'en or slain,
   For fly he could not if he would have fled;
   And fly would Talbot never, though he might.
45 SOMERSET   If he be dead, brave Talbot then adieu.
LUCY   His fame lives in the world, his shame in you. *Exeunt.*

4.4 Location: Scene continues.
1. *All . . . with:* Our entire army might be engaged by
an attack simply from the French garrison in the
town (without taking into account the other French
forces coming as reinforcements).

2. *bought and sold:* a proverbial expression meaning
"betrayed," perhaps alluding to the biblical account
of Christ's betrayal by his disciple Judas for thirty
pieces of silver.

4.5

Enter [Lord] TALBOT *and his son[,* JOHN TALBOT].

TALBOT   O young John Talbot, I did send for thee
    To tutor thee in stratagems of war,
    That Talbot's name might be in thee revived
    When sapless° age and weak unable limbs   *withered*
5   Should bring thy father to his drooping chair.[1]
    But—O malignant and ill-boding stars!—
    Now thou art come unto a feast of death,
    A terrible and unavoided° danger.   *unavoidable*
    Therefore, dear boy, mount on my swiftest horse,
10 And I'll direct thee how thou shalt escape
    By sudden flight. Come, dally not, be gone!
JOHN TALBOT   Is my name Talbot? And am I your son?
    And shall I fly? Oh, if you love my mother,
    Dishonor not her honorable name
15 To make a bastard and a slave of me.
    The world will say, "He is not Talbot's blood
    That basely fled when noble Talbot stood."
TALBOT   Fly, to revenge my death if I be slain.
JOHN TALBOT   He that flies so will ne'er return again.
20 TALBOT   If we both stay, we both are sure to die.
JOHN TALBOT   Then let me stay, and, Father, do you fly.
    Your loss is great, so your regard° should be;   *concern for yourself*
    My worth unknown, no loss is known in me.
    Upon my death the French can little boast;
25 In yours they will; in you all hopes are lost.
    Flight cannot stain the honor you have won,
    But mine it will, that no exploit have done.
    You fled for vantage,° every one will swear,   *military advantage*
    But if I bow, they'll say it was for fear.
30 There is no hope that ever I will stay
    If the first hour I shrink and run away.
    Here on my knee I beg mortality°   *death*
    Rather than life preserved with infamy.
TALBOT   Shall all thy mother's hopes lie in one tomb?
35 JOHN TALBOT   Ay, rather than I'll shame my mother's womb.
TALBOT   Upon my blessing, I command thee go.
JOHN TALBOT   To fight I will, but not to fly the foe.
TALBOT   Part of thy father may be saved in thee.
JOHN TALBOT   No part of him but will be shame in me.
40 TALBOT   Thou never hadst renown nor canst not lose it.
JOHN TALBOT   Yes, your renownèd name; shall flight abuse it?
TALBOT   Thy father's charge° shall clear thee from that stain.   *order*
JOHN TALBOT   You cannot witness for me, being slain.°   *if you are slain*
    If death be so apparent,° then both fly.   *appear so likely*
45 TALBOT   And leave my followers here to fight and die?
    My age° was never tainted with such shame.   *life*
JOHN TALBOT   And shall my youth be guilty of such blame?
    No more can I be severed from your side
    Than can yourself yourself in twain divide.

4.5 Location: Battlefield near Bordeaux.
1. Chair where he sits wearily, as his strength and life decline.

50   Stay, go, do what you will; the like do I,
      For live I will not if my father die.
   TALBOT   Then here I take my leave of thee, fair son,
      Born to eclipse° thy life this afternoon.   *extinguish*
      Come, side by side, together live and die,
55   And soul with soul from France to heaven fly.   *Exeunt.*

4.6

    Alarum; excursions wherein Talbot's son [JOHN TALBOT]
    is hemmed about and [Lord] TALBOT [enters and]
    rescues him.

   TALBOT   Saint George° and victory! Fight, soldiers, fight!   *patron saint of England*
      The Regent[1] hath with Talbot broke his word
      And left us to the rage of France his° sword.   *(France's)*
      Where is John Talbot? Pause and take thy breath.
5   I gave thee life and rescued thee from death.
   JOHN TALBOT   O twice my father, twice am I thy son:
      The life thou gav'st me first was lost and done
      Till with thy warlike sword, despite of fate,
      To my determined° time thou gav'st new date.°   *exactly defined / limit*
10   TALBOT   When from the Dauphin's crest thy sword struck fire,
      It warmed thy father's heart with proud desire
      Of bold-faced victory. Then leaden age,
      Quickened with youthful spleen° and warlike rage,   *courage*
      Beat down Alençon, Orléans, Burgundy,
15   And from the pride of Gallia° rescued thee.   *France*
      The ireful bastard Orléans, that drew blood
      From thee, my boy, and had the maidenhood
      Of thy first fight,[2] I soon encounterèd,
      And, interchanging blows, I quickly shed
20   Some of his bastard blood and in disgrace°   *disdain*
      Bespoke him thus: "Contaminated, base,
      And misbegotten blood I spill of thine,
      Mean° and right poor, for that pure blood of mine   *Base*
      Which thou didst force from Talbot, my brave boy."
25   Here, purposing° the Bastard to destroy,   *as I was intending*
      Came in strong rescue. Speak, thy father's care:
      Art thou not weary, John? How dost thou fare?
      Wilt thou yet leave the battle, boy, and fly,
      Now thou art sealed° the son of chivalry?   *confirmed*
30   Fly, to revenge my death when I am dead;
      The help of one stands me in little stead.°   *does me little good*
      Oh, too much folly is it, well I wot,°   *knew*
      To hazard all our lives in one small boat.
      If I today die not with Frenchmen's rage,
35   Tomorrow I shall die with mickle° age.   *great*
      By me they nothing gain an if° I stay;   *an if = if*
      'Tis but the short'ning of my life one day.
      In thee thy mother dies, our household's name,
      My death's revenge, thy youth, and England's fame—
40   All these and more we hazard by thy stay;
      All these are saved if thou wilt fly away.

4.6 Location: Scene continues.
1. York, who was appointed Regent at 4.1.162–63.
2. *that drew . . . fight:* an allusion to the notion that a woman bleeds during her first experience of heterosexual intercourse. So young Talbot has bled during his first battle.

JOHN TALBOT   The sword of Orléans hath not made me smart;°   *suffer*
 These words of yours draw lifeblood from my heart.
 On that advantage,[3] bought with such a shame,
45 To save a paltry life and slay bright fame,
 Before young Talbot from old Talbot fly,
 The coward horse that bears me fall° and die;   *may it fall*
 And like me° to the peasant boys of France   *compare me*
 To be shame's scorn and subject of mischance![4]
50 Surely, by all the glory you have won,
 An if I fly, I am not Talbot's son.
 Then talk no more of flight; it is no boot:°   *use; profit*
 If son to Talbot, die at Talbot's foot.
TALBOT   Then follow thou thy desperate sire of Crete,
55 Thou Icarus;[5] thy life to me is sweet.
 If thou wilt fight, fight by thy father's side,
 And, commendable proved, let's die in pride.   *Exeunt.*

4.7

Alarum. Excursions. Enter old [Lord] TALBOT,
led [by a SERVANT].

TALBOT   Where is my other life? Mine own is gone.
 Oh, where's young Talbot? Where is valiant John?
 Triumphant Death, smeared with captivity,°   *the blood of captives*
 Young Talbot's valor makes me smile at thee.
5 When he perceived me shrink° and on my knee,   *weaken*
 His bloody sword he brandished over me
 And like a hungry lion did commence
 Rough deeds of rage and stern impatience;
 But when my angry guardant° stood alone,   *protector*
10 Tendering° my ruin and assailed of none,   *Concerned for*
 Dizzy-eyed fury and great rage of heart
 Suddenly made him from my side to start
 Into the clustering battle° of the French,   *crowded ranks*
 And in that sea of blood my boy did drench°   *drown*
15 His overmounting spirit and there died—
 My Icarus, my blossom—in his pride.
  *Enter [*SOLDIERS*] with* JOHN TALBOT, *borne.*
SERVANT   O my dear lord, lo where your son is borne.
TALBOT   Thou antic° Death, which laugh'st us here to scorn,   *grotesquely grinning*
 Anon° from thy insulting tyranny,   *Soon*
20 Coupled in bonds of perpetuity,
 Two Talbots, wingèd, through the lither° sky   *yielding*
 In thy despite° shall scape° mortality.   *spite of you / escape*
 O thou whose wounds become hard-favored Death,[1]
 Speak to thy father ere thou yield thy breath;
25 Brave° Death by speaking, whether he will or no: *Defy*
 Imagine him a Frenchman and thy foe.
 Poor boy, he smiles, methinks, as who° should say,   *as one who*
 "Had Death been French, then Death had died today."
 —Come, come, and lay him in his father's arms;

3. For the sake of that advantage (of safety).
4. To be an ashamed object of scorn and a victim of misfortune.
5. According to classical mythology, Icarus and his father, Daedalus, tried to escape imprisonment in Crete by using artificial wings of feathers and wax. Daedalus succeeded, but Icarus flew too close to the sun and died.
4.7 Location: Scene continues.
1. Whose wounds make ugly death attractive.

30 My spirit can no longer bear these harms.
   Soldiers, adieu: I have what I would have
   Now my old arms are young John Talbot's grave.
        [*He*] *dies.*
        [*Exeunt* SERVANT *and* SOLDIERS, *leaving the bodies.*]
        Enter CHARLES [*the Dauphin, the Duke of*] ALENÇON,
        [*the Duke of*] BURGUNDY, [*the*] BASTARD [*of Orléans*],
        and [JOAN DE] PUCELLE.
   CHARLES   Had York and Somerset brought rescue in,
   We should have found a bloody day of this.
35 BASTARD   How the young whelp of Talbot's,² raging wood,°   *mad*
   Did flesh his puny sword³ in Frenchmen's blood!
   JOAN DE PUCELLE   Once I encountered⁴ him, and thus I said:
   "Thou maiden⁵ youth, be vanquished by a maid."
   But with a proud, majestical, high scorn
40 He answered thus: "Young Talbot was not born
   To be the pillage of a giglot° wench"—   *plunder of a wanton*
   So rushing in the bowels° of the French,   *center*
   He left me proudly, as unworthy fight.
   BURGUNDY   Doubtless he would have made a noble knight.
45 See where he lies inhearsèd° in the arms   *(as in a coffin)*
   Of the most bloody nurser of his harms.⁶
   BASTARD   Hew them to pieces; hack their bones asunder,
   Whose life was England's glory, Gallia's° wonder!   *France's*
   CHARLES   Oh, no, forbear: for that which we have fled
50 During the life, let us not wrong it dead.
        Enter [*Sir William*] LUCY [*with a French Herald*].
   LUCY   Herald, conduct me to the Dauphin's tent
   To know who hath obtained the glory of the day.
   CHARLES   On what submissive message art thou sent?
   LUCY   Submission, Dauphin? 'Tis a mere° French word;   *pure*
55 We English warriors wot° not what it means.   *know*
   I come to know what prisoners thou hast ta'en
   And to survey the bodies of the dead.
   CHARLES   For prisoners ask'st thou? Hell our prison is.⁷
   But tell me whom thou seek'st.
60 LUCY   But where's the great Alcides⁸ of the field,
   Valiant Lord Talbot, Earl of Shrewsbury,
   Created for his rare success in arms
   Great Earl of Wexford, Waterford, and Valence;
   Lord Talbot of Goodrich and Archenfield;
65 Lord Strange of Blackmere; Lord Verdun of Alton;
   Lord Cromwell of Wingfield; Lord Furnival of Sheffield;
   The thrice-victorious Lord of Falconbridge;
   Knight of the Noble Order of Saint George—
   Worthy Saint Michael⁹ and the Golden Fleece—

2. The young puppy of Talbot's (John Talbot). The Bastard is punning on "talbot" as the name for a kind of hunting dog.
3. Plunged in his inexperienced sword for the first time, with a sexual wordplay: plunged in his inexperienced or diminutive penis for the first time.
4. Another bawdy pun: "encounter" may mean "to meet sexually."
5. Virginal; inexperienced in battle.
6. Person who taught him to harm his enemies; person who caused his injuries.

7. Charles implies that the French have killed their enemies (sent them to hell) rather than taking prisoners.
8. Hercules (a descendant of Alcaeus), the hero of classical mythology, famous for performing difficult feats of strength and bravery.
9. Worthy of; equal in value to. The Order of St. Michael was a French chivalric order established in 1469, after the events of the play occurred. The Order of the Golden Fleece was formed in Burgundy in 1430.

70	Great Marshall° to Henry the Sixth	*commander in chief*
	Of all his wars within the realm of France?	
	JOAN DE PUCELLE Here's a silly stately style° indeed!	*list of titles*
	The Turk° that two-and-fifty kingdoms hath	*Sultan of Turkey*
	Writes not so tedious a style as this.	
75	Him that thou magnifi'st with all these titles	
	Stinking and flyblown° lies here at our feet.	*putrefied*
	LUCY Is Talbot slain, the Frenchmen's only scourge,	
	Your kingdom's terror and black Nemesis?[1]	
	Oh, were mine eyeballs into bullets turned	
80	That I in rage might shoot them at your faces!	
	Oh, that I could but call these dead to life,	
	It were enough to fright the realm of France!	
	Were but his picture left amongst you here,	
	It would amaze° the proudest of you all.	*terrify*
85	Give me their bodies that I may bear them hence	
	And give them burial as beseems° their worth.	*as is appropriate to*
	JOAN DE PUCELLE I think this upstart is old Talbot's ghost,	
	He speaks with such a proud commanding spirit.	
	For God's sake, let him have him; to keep them here,	
90	They would but stink and putrefy the air.	
	CHARLES Go, take their bodies hence.	
	LUCY I'll bear them hence,	
	But from their ashes shall be reared	
	A phoenix[2] that shall make all France affeared.°	*afraid*
	CHARLES So we be rid of them, do with him what thou wilt.	
	[*Exeunt* LUCY *and Herald with the bodies.*]	
95	And now to Paris in this conquering vein;	
	All will be ours now bloody Talbot's slain. *Exeunt.*	

5.1[1]

Sennet. Enter KING [HENRY, *the Duke of*] GLOUCESTER,
and [*the Duke of*] EXETER.

	KING HENRY Have you perused° the letters from the Pope,	*read*
	The Emperor, and the Earl of Armagnac?	
	GLOUCESTER I have, my lord, and their intent is this:	
	They humbly sue unto your excellence	
5	To have a godly peace concluded of	
	Between the realms of England and of France.	
	KING HENRY How doth your grace affect their motion?°	*like their proposal*
	GLOUCESTER Well, my good lord, and as the only means	
	To stop effusion° of our Christian blood	*spilling*
10	And stablish quietness on every side.	
	KING HENRY Ay, marry, uncle, for I always thought	
	It was both impious and unnatural	
	That such immanity° and bloody strife	*barbarity*
	Should reign among professors of one faith.	
15	GLOUCESTER Beside, my lord, the sooner to effect	
	And surer bind this knot of amity,	

1. The Greek goddess of avenging justice.
2. A legendary bird that was said to live five hundred years, burn itself to ashes, and then be reborn from the ashes.
5.1 Location: The palace, London.
1. TEXTUAL COMMENT The act and scene divisions are incomplete in acts 4 and 5 of the F text of *1 Henry VI*.

Editors often begin act 5 with the conversation between King Henry and his men, as in this edition. Other editions, including F2, put the scene in which the French taunt Lucy with Talbot's death at the beginning of act 5 rather than at the end of act 4. See Digital Edition TC 9.

The Earl of Armagnac, near knit° to Charles,   *closely related*
A man of great authority in France,
Proffers his only daughter to your grace
20   In marriage with a large and sumptuous dowry.
KING HENRY Marriage, uncle? Alas, my years are young,
And fitter is my study and my books
Than wanton dalliance with a paramour.
Yet call th'ambassadors, and as you please,
25   So let them have their answers every one;
I shall be well content with any choice
Tends° to God's glory and my country's weal.°   *That tends / welfare*

      Enter WINCHESTER [*in cardinal's habit*] *and three*
      Ambassadors[, *one a* PAPAL LEGATE, *and one from*
      the Earl of Armagnac].

EXETER What, is my lord of Winchester installed
And called unto a cardinal's degree?
30   Then, I perceive, that will be verified
Henry the Fifth did sometime° prophesy: *at one time*
If once he come to be a cardinal,
He'll make his cap° coequal with the crown.   *(a cardinal's red hat)*
KING HENRY My lords ambassadors, your several suits
35   Have been considered and debated on.
Your purpose is both good and reasonable,
And therefore are we certainly resolved
To draw° conditions of a friendly peace,   *draft*
Which by my lord of Winchester we mean
40   Shall be transported presently to France.
GLOUCESTER [*to the Ambassador from Armagnac*] And for the
    proffer of my lord your master,
I have informed his highness so at large°   *in full*
As,° liking of the lady's virtuous gifts,   *That*
Her beauty, and the value of her dower,
45   He doth intend she shall be England's queen.
KING HENRY In argument° and proof of which contract,   *As evidence*
Bear her this jewel, pledge of my affection.
—And so, my Lord Protector, see them guarded
And safely brought to Dover, wherein shipped,°   *where once embarked*
50   Commit them to the fortune of the sea.

      Exeunt [*all except* WINCHESTER *and the* PAPAL LEGATE].

WINCHESTER Stay, my lord Legate; you shall first receive
The sum of money which I promisèd
Should be delivered to his holiness
For clothing me in these grave ornaments.°   *solemn robes of office*
55 PAPAL LEGATE I will attend upon your lordship's leisure.

      [*Exit.*][2]

WINCHESTER Now Winchester will not submit, I trow,°   *trust*
Or be inferior to the proudest peer.
Humphrey of Gloucester, thou shalt well perceive
That neither in birth or for authority
60   The bishop will be overborne° by thee: *overruled*
I'll either make thee stoop and bend thy knee
Or sack this country with a mutiny.°   *Exit.*   *an open revolt*

---

2. The Legate may leave at this point, but there is no exit marked in F. He may simply step to the side while Winchester makes his final speech and then exit with the prelate.

5.2

Enter CHARLES [*the Dauphin, the Duke of*] BURGUNDY,
[*the Duke of*] ALENÇON, [*the*] BASTARD [*of Orléans*], RENÉ[,
Duke of Anjou], *and* JOAN [DE PUCELLE].

CHARLES   These news, my lords, may cheer our drooping
    spirits:
    'Tis said the stout° Parisians do revolt   *valiant*
    And turn again unto the warlike French.
ALENÇON   Then march to Paris, royal Charles of France,
5   And keep not back your powers in dalliance.°   *idleness*
JOAN DE PUCELLE   Peace be amongst them if they turn to us,
    Else ruin combat with their palaces.[1]
       Enter SCOUT.
SCOUT   Success unto our valiant general
    And happiness to his accomplices!°   *allies*
10 CHARLES   What tidings send our scouts? I prithee speak.
SCOUT   The English army, that divided was
    Into two parties, is now conjoined in one[2]
    And means to give you battle presently.°   *immediately*
CHARLES   Somewhat too sudden, sirs, the warning is,
15   But we will presently provide for them.
BURGUNDY   I trust the ghost of Talbot is not there;
    Now he is gone, my lord, you need not fear.
JOAN DE PUCELLE   Of all base passions, fear is most accursed.
    Command the conquest, Charles; it shall be thine;
20   Let Henry fret and all the world repine.°   *complain*
CHARLES   Then on, my lords, and France be fortunate.
                       Exeunt.

5.3

Alarum. Excursions. Enter JOAN DE PUCELLE.

JOAN DE PUCELLE   The Regent° conquers and the Frenchmen   (*Richard, Duke of York*)
    fly.
    Now help, ye charming° spells and periapts,°   *magic / amulets*
    And ye choice spirits that admonish° me   *forewarn*
    And give me signs of future accidents.°   *events*
       Thunder.
5   You speedy helpers that are substitutes°   *deputies*
    Under the lordly monarch of the North,[1]
    Appear and aid me in this enterprise.
       Enter Fiends.
    This speedy and quick appearance argues° proof   *offers*
    Of your accustomed° diligence to me.   *customary*
10   Now, ye familiar spirits[2] that are culled
    Out of the powerful regions under earth,
    Help me this once, that France may get the field.°   *win the battle*
       They walk and speak not.
    Oh, hold me not with silence overlong!
    Where I was wont to feed you with my blood,[3]

5.2 Location: Plains in Anjou, France.
1. Otherwise, let ruin destroy their palaces.
2. In other words, York and Suffolk have joined
forces.
5.3 Location: Before Angiers (i.e., Angers), France.
1. The devil and his demons were frequently associated with the North.
2. Attendant spirits that could be summoned by a
witch; often, they inhabited the bodies of animals.
3. Witches were thought to have extra nipples with
which they fed their familiars, or attendant spirits.

15   I'll lop a member° off and give it you   *limb*
    In earnest° of a further benefit   *As an advance payment*
    So you do condescend to help me now.
        They hang their heads.
    No hope to have redress? My body shall
    Pay recompense if you will grant my suit!
        They shake their heads.
20   Cannot my body nor blood sacrifice
    Entreat you to your wonted furtherance?°   *usual assistance*
    Then take my soul—my body, soul, and all!—
    Before that England give the French the foil.° *They depart.*   *defeat*
    See, they forsake me. Now the time is come
25   That France must vale her lofty plumèd crest[4]
    And let her head fall into England's lap.
    My ancient° incantations are too weak   *former*
    And hell too strong for me to buckle° with.   *fight; do combat*
    Now, France, thy glory droopeth to the dust.   *Exit.*
        Excursions. [The Duke of] BURGUNDY *and [Richard,*
        Duke of] YORK *fight hand to hand. [The] French fly.*
        [YORK *captures* JOAN DE PUCELLE.]
30 YORK   Damsel of France, I think I have you fast.
    Unchain your spirits now with spelling° charms   *conjuring*
    And try if they can gain your liberty.
    A goodly prize, fit for the devil's grace![5]
    See how the ugly witch doth bend her brows°   *scowls*
35   As if, with Circe,[6] she would change my shape.
JOAN DE PUCELLE   Changed to a worser shape thou canst not be.
  YORK   Oh, Charles the Dauphin is a proper° man;   *handsome*
    No shape but his can please your dainty° eye.   *discerning*
JOAN DE PUCELLE   A plaguing mischief light on Charles and
    thee,
40   And may ye both be suddenly surprised
    By bloody hands, in° sleeping on your beds!   *while*
  YORK   Fell banning° hag, enchantress, hold thy tongue!   *Fierce cursing*
JOAN DE PUCELLE   I prithee, give me leave to curse awhile.
  YORK   Curse, miscreant,° when thou com'st to the stake.   *heretic*
                      Exeunt.

5.4

    Alarum. Enter [the Earl of] SUFFOLK *with* MARGARET
    in his hand.°   *led by the hand*
  SUFFOLK   Be what thou wilt, thou art my prisoner.
    [He] gazes on her.
    O fairest beauty, do not fear nor fly,
    For I will touch thee but with reverent hands.
    I kiss these fingers for eternal peace
5   And lay them gently on thy tender side.
    Who art thou, say, that I may honor thee.
  MARGARET   Margaret my name, and daughter to a king,
    The King of Naples,[1] whosoe'er thou art.

---

4. Must lower her high-feathered helmet.   (see Homer, *Odyssey* 10).
5. Fit for his grace, the devil (said sarcastically).   **5.4** Location: Scene continues.
6. According to Greek mythology, a witch who   1. That is, the René of earlier scenes, Duke of Anjou
seduced Odysseus and turned his men into swine   and also titular King of Naples and Sicily.

SUFFOLK An earl I am, and Suffolk am I called.

10 Be not offended, Nature's miracle,
Thou art allotted° to be ta'en by me; *destined*
So doth the swan her downy cygnets save,° *young swans protect*
Keeping them prisoner underneath his wings.
Yet, if this servile usage° once offend, *treatment as a slave*

15 Go, and be free again as Suffolk's friend.
      She is going.
Oh, stay! [*aside*] I have no power to let her pass.
My hand would free her, but my heart says no.
As plays the sun upon the glassy streams,
Twinkling another counterfeited° beam, *reflected*

20 So seems this gorgeous beauty to mine eyes.
Fain would I woo her, yet I dare not speak.
I'll call for pen and ink and write my mind.
Fie, de la Pole,² disable° not thyself: *disparage*
Hast not a tongue? Is she not here?

25 Wilt thou be daunted at a woman's sight?³
Ay: beauty's princely majesty is such,
Confounds° the tongue and makes the senses rough.° *That it confuses / dull*
MARGARET Say, Earl of Suffolk, if thy name be so,
What ransom must I pay before I pass?

30 For I perceive I am thy prisoner.
SUFFOLK [*aside*] How canst thou tell she will deny° thy suit *refuse*
Before thou make a trial of her love?
MARGARET Why speak'st thou not? What ransom must I pay?
SUFFOLK [*aside*] She's beautiful and therefore to be wooed;

35 She is a woman, therefore to be won.
MARGARET Wilt thou accept of ransom, yea or no?
SUFFOLK [*aside*] Fond° man, remember that thou hast a wife; *Foolish*
Then how can Margaret be thy paramour?° *mistress*
MARGARET I were best to leave him, for he will not hear.

40 SUFFOLK [*aside*] There° all is marred; there lies a cooling card.⁴ *By that fact*
MARGARET He talks at random; sure, the man is mad.
SUFFOLK [*aside*] And yet a dispensation⁵ may be had.
MARGARET And yet I would that you would answer me.
SUFFOLK [*aside*] I'll win this lady Margaret. For whom?

45 Why, for my King. Tush, that's a wooden⁶ thing!
MARGARET He talks of wood; it is some carpenter.
SUFFOLK [*aside*] Yet so my fancy° may be satisfied, *love*
And peace establishèd between these realms.
But there remains a scruple° in that, too: *an objection*

50 For though her father be the King of Naples,
Duke of Anjou and Maine, yet is he poor,
And our nobility will scorn the match.
MARGARET Hear ye, captain? Are you not at leisure?
SUFFOLK [*aside*] It shall be so, disdain they ne'er so much.

55 Henry is youthful and will quickly yield.
—Madam, I have a secret to reveal.

---

2. Suffolk's family name.
3. At the sight of a woman; at a woman's gaze.
4. An obstacle; literally, a card that, when played,
dashes the hopes of one's opponent.

5. Special permission from the Pope to dissolve a
marriage.
6. Stupid (referring either to King Henry or to his
own scheme to woo Margaret).

MARGARET [*pretending* SUFFOLK *cannot hear*][7] What though I
  be enthralled?° He seems a knight   *taken captive*
  And will not any way dishonor me.
SUFFOLK   Lady, vouchsafe to listen° what I say.   *listen to*
60 MARGARET [*pretending* SUFFOLK *cannot hear*]   Perhaps I shall
  be rescued by the French,
  And then I need not crave his courtesy.
SUFFOLK   Sweet madam, give me hearing in a cause.
MARGARET [*pretending* SUFFOLK *cannot hear*]   Tush, women
  have been captivate[8] ere now.
SUFFOLK   Lady, wherefore talk you so?
65 MARGARET   I cry you mercy; 'tis but *quid* for *quo.*°   *tit for tat*
SUFFOLK   Say, gentle princess, would you not suppose
  Your bondage happy, to be° made a queen?   *if you were to be*
MARGARET   To be a queen in bondage is more vile
  Than is a slave in base servility,°   *slavery*
  For princes should be free.
70 SUFFOLK   And so shall you,
  If happy England's royal King be free.
MARGARET   Why, what concerns his freedom unto me?
SUFFOLK   I'll undertake to make thee Henry's queen,
  To put a golden scepter in thy hand
75 And set a precious crown upon thy head
  If thou wilt condescend° to be my—   *agree*
MARGARET   What?
SUFFOLK   His love.
MARGARET   I am unworthy to be Henry's wife.
SUFFOLK   No, gentle madam, I unworthy am
80 To woo so fair a dame to be his wife—
  And have no portion° in the choice myself.   *share*
  How say you, madam? Are ye so content?
MARGARET   An if my father please, I am content.
SUFFOLK   Then call our captains and our colors forth,
85 And, madam, at your father's castle walls
  We'll crave a parley to confer with him.
      [*Trumpets*] *sound* [*a parley*]. *Enter* RENÉ[,
      Duke of Anjou,] *on the walls.*
  See, René, see thy daughter prisoner.
REIGNIER   To whom?
SUFFOLK   To me.
RENÉ   Suffolk, what remedy?
  I am a soldier and unapt° to weep   *unsuited*
90 Or to exclaim on° fortune's fickleness.   *complain of*
SUFFOLK   Yes, there is remedy enough, my lord.
  Consent, and for thy honor give consent
  Thy daughter shall be wedded to my King,
  Whom I with pain have wooed and won thereto,
95 And this, her easy-held° imprisonment,   *easily endured*
  Hath gained thy daughter princely liberty.
RENÉ   Speaks Suffolk as he thinks?
SUFFOLK   Fair Margaret knows

---

7. TEXTUAL COMMENT Margaret's lines here are usually marked as asides, but while asides are conventionally unheard by other characters onstage, it is
possible that Margaret is pretending that Suffolk
cannot hear her while knowing that he can. See Digital Edition TC 10.
8. Have been taken prisoner; have fallen in love
against their will.

That Suffolk doth not flatter, face,° or feign.   *deceive*
RENÉ   Upon thy princely warrant° I descend,   *guarantee*
100   To give thee answer of thy just demand.   [*Exit from the walls.*]
SUFFOLK   And here I will expect° thy coming.   *await*
        Trumpets sound. Enter RENÉ[, *Duke of Anjou, below*].
RENÉ   Welcome, brave earl, into our territories.
        Command in Anjou what your honor pleases.
SUFFOLK   Thanks, René, happy for° so sweet a child,   *fortunate in having*
105   Fit to be made companion with a king.
        What answer makes your grace unto my suit?
RENÉ   Since thou dost deign to woo her little worth
        To be the princely bride of such a lord,
        Upon condition I may quietly
110   Enjoy mine own, the country Maine and Anjou,
        Free from oppression or the stroke of war,
        My daughter shall be Henry's if he please.
SUFFOLK   That is her ransom; I deliver her,
        And those two counties° I will undertake   *domains of a count*
115   Your grace shall well and quietly enjoy.
RENÉ   And I again° in Henry's royal name,   *in return*
        As deputy unto that gracious King,
        Give thee her hand for sign of plighted faith.°   *a marriage pledge*
SUFFOLK   René of France, I give thee kingly thanks
120   Because this is in traffic° of a king.   *business*
        [*aside*] And yet methinks I could be well content
        To be mine own attorney in this case.[9]
        —I'll over then to England with this news
        And make this marriage to be solemnized.
125   So farewell, René; set this diamond safe
        In golden palaces, as it becomes.°   *as befits it*
RENÉ   I do embrace thee as I would embrace
        The Christian prince King Henry were he here.   [*Exit.*]
MARGARET   Farewell, my lord; good wishes, praise, and prayers
130   Shall Suffolk ever have of Margaret.
            She is going.
SUFFOLK   Farewell, sweet madam. But hark you, Margaret,
        No princely commendations° to my King?   *greetings*
MARGARET   Such commendations as becomes a maid,
        A virgin, and his servant, say to him.
135   SUFFOLK   Words sweetly placed and modestly directed.
        But madam, I must trouble you again:
        No loving token to his majesty?
MARGARET   Yes, my good lord: a pure unspotted heart,
        Never yet taint° with love, I send the King.   *tinged*
140   SUFFOLK   And this withal.°   *in addition*
            [*He*] kiss[*es*] *her.*
MARGARET   That for thyself; I will not so presume
        To send such peevish° tokens to a king.   [*Exit.*]   *trifling*
SUFFOLK   Oh, wert thou for myself! But, Suffolk, stay;
        Thou mayst not wander in that labyrinth:[1]
145   There minotaurs and ugly treasons lurk.

9. To act on my own behalf in this instance, with a   who kept in it the Minotaur (a monster born from
pun on "case" as slang for "vagina."   Queen Pasiphaë's sexual encounter with a bull).
1. A maze built by Daedalus for King Minos of Crete,

Solicit° Henry with her wondrous praise;   *Entice*
Bethink thee on her virtues that surmount—
Mad° natural graces that extinguish° art—   *Extravagant / eclipse*
Repeat their semblance² often on the seas,
150   That when thou com'st to kneel at Henry's feet,
Thou mayst bereave° him of his wits with wonder.   *Exit.*   *dispossess*

5.5

Enter [Richard Duke of] YORK, *[the Earl of]* WARWICK,
SHEPHERD, *[and* JOAN DE] PUCELLE[, *with Guards].*

YORK   Bring forth that sorceress condemned to burn.
SHEPHERD   Ah, Joan, this kills thy father's heart outright!
Have I sought° every country far and near,   *searched*
And, now it is my chance to find thee out,°   *discover you*
5   Must I behold thy timeless° cruel death?   *untimely*
Ah, Joan, sweet daughter Joan, I'll die with thee!
JOAN DE PUCELLE   Decrepit miser,° base ignoble wretch,   *Miserable person*
I am descended of a gentler° blood.   *more aristocratic*
Thou art no father nor no friend° of mine.   *kinsman*
10   SHEPHERD   Out, out! —My lords, an't please you, 'tis not so!
I did beget her, all the parish knows;
Her mother liveth yet, can testify
She was the first fruit of my bachelorship.¹
WARWICK   Graceless,° wilt thou deny thy parentage?   *Depraved person*
15   YORK   This argues° what her kind of life hath been: *testifies to*
Wicked and vile, and so her death concludes.°   *confirms; ends*
SHEPHERD   Fie, Joan, that thou wilt be so obstacle!²
God knows, thou art a collop° of my flesh,   *slice*
And for thy sake have I shed many a tear.
20   Deny me not, I prithee, gentle Joan.
JOAN DE PUCELLE   Peasant, avaunt!° —You have suborned³   *be off*
this man
Of purpose to obscure my noble birth.
SHEPHERD   'Tis true, I gave a noble⁴ to the priest
The morn that I was wedded to her mother.
25   Kneel down and take my blessing, good my girl.
Wilt thou not stoop? Now cursèd be the time
Of thy nativity! I would the milk
Thy mother gave thee when thou sucked'st her breast
Had been a little ratsbane° for thy sake,   *rat poison*
30   Or else when thou didst keep° my lambs afield,   *tend*
I wish some ravenous wolf had eaten thee.
Dost thou deny thy father, cursèd drab?°   *whore*
—Oh, burn her, burn her! Hanging is too good.   *Exit.*
YORK   Take her away, for she hath lived too long,
35   To fill the world with vicious qualities.
JOAN DE PUCELLE   First, let me tell you whom you have
condemned:
Not me begotten of a shepherd swain
But issued from the progeny of kings—

---

2. Recall the image or description of her virtues.
5.5 Location: Camp of the Duke of York, France.
1. The first child I had as an unmarried man.
2. Obstinate. This use of "obstacle" suggests the shep-

herd's country dialect.
3. Hired to give false evidence.
4. English gold coin worth about one-third of a
pound.

Virtuous and holy, chosen from above
40 By inspiration of celestial grace
To work exceeding° miracles on earth.   *exceptional*
I never had to do with wicked spirits.
But you that are polluted with your lusts,
Stained with the guiltless blood of innocents,
45 Corrupt and tainted with a thousand vices,
Because you want° the grace that others have,   *lack*
You judge it straight° a thing impossible   *immediately*
To compass° wonders but by help of devils.   *accomplish*
No, misconceivèd![5] Joan of Aire hath been
50 A virgin from her tender infancy,
Chaste and immaculate in very thought,
Whose maiden blood thus rigorously effused°   *cruelly shed*
Will cry for vengeance at the gates of heaven.
YORK Ay, ay. —Away with her to execution.
55 WARWICK And hark ye, sirs. Because she is a maid,
Spare for no faggots; let there be enough.
Place barrels of pitch upon the fatal stake
That so her torture may be shortenèd.[6]
JOAN DE PUCELLE   Will nothing turn° your unrelenting hearts?   *change*
60 Then, Joan, discover° thine infirmity,   *reveal*
That warranteth by law to be thy privilege:[7]
I am with child, ye bloody homicides.
Murder not then the fruit within my womb
Although ye hale° me to a violent death!   *drag*
65 YORK Now, heaven forfend! The holy maid with child?
WARWICK The greatest miracle that e'er ye wrought!
Is all your strict preciseness° come to this?   *propriety*
YORK She and the Dauphin have been juggling.°   *having sex*
I did imagine° what would be her refuge.°   *wonder / last defense*
70 WARWICK Well, go to; we'll have no bastards live,
Especially since Charles must father it.
JOAN DE PUCELLE You are deceived: my child is none of his;
It was Alençon[8] that enjoyed my love.
YORK Alençon, that notorious machiavel?[9]
75 It dies an if it had a thousand lives!
JOAN DE PUCELLE Oh, give me leave, I have deluded you:
'Twas neither Charles nor yet the Duke I named
But René, King of Naples, that prevailed.
WARWICK A married man! That's most intolerable.
80 YORK Why, here's a girl! I think she knows not well—
There were so many—whom she may accuse.
WARWICK It's sign she hath been liberal° and free.   *generous; promiscuous*
YORK And yet forsooth she is a virgin pure.
Strumpet, thy words condemn thy brat and thee.
85 Use no entreaty, for it is in vain.

---

5. Misunderstood, with a pun on "misconceived" as "miscreated in the womb."
6. The orders for wood and pitch are meant to ensure either that Joan will die quickly as a result of asphyxiation from the smoke, rather than from the flames themselves, or that she will die swiftly from the intensity of the fire.
7. The legal right of a pregnant woman to postpone her execution until after she has given birth.
8. Jean, second Duke of Alençon, was cousin to Charles, the Dauphin.
9. Scheming politician. Niccolò Machiavelli (1469–1527), author of *The Prince*, became associated with principles of cunning statecraft.

JOAN DE PUCELLE   Then lead me hence, with whom I leave
  my curse:
    May never glorious sun reflex° his beams   *throw*
    Upon the country where you make abode
    But darkness and the gloomy shade of death
90   Environ you till mischief° and despair   *misfortune*
    Drive you to break your necks or hang yourselves.
                            Exit [with Guards].
        Enter [the] Cardinal [of WINCHESTER].
YORK   Break thou in pieces and consume° to ashes,   *burn away*
    Thou foul accursèd minister of hell!
WINCHESTER   Lord Regent, I do greet your excellence
95   With letters of commission from the King.
    For know, my lords, the states of Christendom,
    Moved with remorse of° these outrageous broils,   *pity for*
    Have earnestly implored a general peace
    Betwixt our nation and the aspiring French,
100   And here at hand the Dauphin and his train
    Approacheth to confer about some matter.
YORK   Is all our travail° turned to this effect?   *labor*
    After the slaughter of so many peers,
    So many captains, gentlemen, and soldiers
105   That in this quarrel have been overthrown
    And sold their bodies for their country's benefit,
    Shall we at last conclude effeminate peace?
    Have we not lost most part of all the towns—
    By treason, falsehood, and by treachery—
110   Our great progenitors had conquerèd?
    O Warwick, Warwick, I foresee with grief
    The utter loss of all the realm of France.
WARWICK   Be patient, York. If we conclude a peace,
    It shall be with such strict and severe covenants
115   As° little shall the Frenchmen gain thereby.   *That*
        Enter CHARLES [*the Dauphin, the Duke of*] ALENÇON,
        [*the*] BASTARD [*of Orléans, and*] RENÉ[, *Duke of Anjou*].
CHARLES   Since, lords of England, it is thus agreed
    That peaceful truce shall be proclaimed in France,
    We come to be informèd by yourselves
    What the conditions of that league° must be.   *treaty*
120 YORK   Speak, Winchester, for boiling choler° chokes *anger*
    The hollow passage of my poisoned voice
    By sight of these our baleful° enemies.   *deadly*
WINCHESTER   Charles and the rest, it is enacted thus:
    That in regard° King Henry gives consent,   *since*
125   Of mere° compassion and of lenity,°   *Out of pure / mildness*
    To ease your country of distressful war
    And suffer° you to breathe in fruitful peace,   *allow*
    You shall become true liegemen[1] to his crown.
    And, Charles, upon condition thou wilt swear
130   To pay him tribute and submit thyself,
    Thou shalt be placed as viceroy under him
    And still enjoy thy regal dignity.

---

1. Those bound to serve a feudal lord; faithful subjects.

ALENÇON Must he be then as shadow of himself,
Adorn his temples with a coronet,[2]
135 And yet in substance and authority
Retain but privilege of a private man?
This proffer is absurd and reasonless.
CHARLES 'Tis known already that I am possessed
With more than half the Gallian° territories   *French*
140 And therein reverenced for their lawful king.
Shall I for lucre° of the rest° unvanquished   *gain / rest that are*
Detract so much from that prerogative
As to be called but° viceroy of the whole?   *merely*
No, lord ambassador, I'll rather keep
145 That which I have than, coveting for more,
Be cast° from possibility of all.   *excluded*
YORK Insulting Charles, hast thou by secret means
Used intercession to obtain a league
And, now the matter grows to compromise,°   *toward resolution*
150 Stand'st thou aloof upon comparison?[3]
Either accept the title thou usurp'st,
Of benefit° proceeding from our king   *As a benefaction*
And not of any challenge of desert,[4]
Or we will plague thee with incessant wars.
155 RENÉ [*aside to* CHARLES] My lord, you do not well in obstinacy
To cavil[5] in the course of this contract.
If once it be neglected,° ten to one   *disregarded*
We shall not find like opportunity.
ALENÇON [*aside to* CHARLES] To say the truth, it is your policy°   *astute course*
160 To save your subjects from such massacre
And ruthless slaughters as are daily seen
By our proceeding in hostility,
And therefore take this compact of a truce,
Although you break it when your pleasure serves.
165 WARWICK How say'st thou, Charles? Shall our condition stand?
CHARLES It shall, only reserved,° you claim no interest   *with the reservation*
In any of our towns of garrison.°   *fortified towns*
YORK Then swear allegiance to his majesty,
As thou art knight, never to disobey
170 Nor be rebellious to the crown of England,
Thou nor thy nobles, to the crown of England.
         [*The French swear allegiance.*]
So, now, dismiss your army when ye please;
Hang up your ensigns; let your drums be still;
For here we entertain a solemn peace.   *Exeunt.*

5.6

Enter [the Earl of] SUFFOLK *in conference with* KING [HENRY,
the Duke of] GLOUCESTER, *and [the Duke of]* EXETER.
KING HENRY Your wondrous rare description, noble earl,
Of beauteous Margaret hath astonished me.
Her virtues, gracèd with external gifts,

---

2. Small crown worn by nobles.   4. And not by any claim of inherent right.
3. Do you hold off in order to quibble about the   5. To raise frivolous objections.
terms?   5.6 Location: The palace, London.

Do breed love's settled° passions in my heart,   *unchanging*
5   And like as rigor° of tempestuous gusts   *violent force*
    Provokes° the mightiest hulk° against the tide,   *Drives / ship*
    So am I driven by breath of her renown°   *word of her fame*
    Either to suffer shipwreck or arrive
    Where I may have fruition° of her love.   *enjoyment; possession*
10 SUFFOLK Tush, my good lord; this superficial tale
    Is but a preface of her worthy praise;°   *the praise she deserves*
    The chief perfections of that lovely dame,
    Had I sufficient skill to utter them,
    Would make a volume of enticing lines
15   Able to ravish any dull conceit.°   *imagination*
    And, which is more, she is not so divine,
    So full° replete with choice of all delights,   *fully*
    But with as humble lowliness of mind
    She is content to be at your command—
20   Command, I mean, of virtuous chaste intents
    To love and honor Henry as her lord.
    KING HENRY And otherwise will Henry ne'er presume.
    —Therefore, my Lord Protector, give consent
    That Marg'ret may be England's royal queen.
25 GLOUCESTER So should I give consent to flatter sin.
    You know, my lord, your highness is betrothed
    Unto another lady of esteem;[1]
    How shall we then dispense with that contract
    And not deface your honor with reproach?
30 SUFFOLK As doth a ruler with unlawful oaths,
    Or one that, at a triumph,[2] having vowed
    To try his strength, forsaketh yet the lists[3]
    By reason of his adversary's odds.
    A poor earl's daughter is unequal odds
35   And therefore may be broke[4] without offense.
    GLOUCESTER Why, what, I pray, is Margaret more than that?
    Her father is no better than an earl,
    Although in glorious titles he excel.
    SUFFOLK Yes, my lord: her father is a king,
40   The King of Naples and Jerusalem,
    And of such great authority in France
    As his alliance will confirm our peace
    And keep the Frenchmen in allegiance.
    GLOUCESTER And so the Earl of Armagnac may do,
45   Because he is near kinsman unto Charles.
    EXETER Beside, his wealth doth warrant° a liberal dower,   *guarantee*
    Where René sooner will receive than give.
    SUFFOLK A dower, my lords? Disgrace not so your king,
    That he should be so abject, base, and poor
50   To choose for wealth and not for perfect love.
    Henry is able to enrich his queen
    And not to seek a queen to make him rich;
    So worthless peasants bargain for their wives

---

1. The daughter of the Earl of Armagnac (see 5.1.15–20).
2. Tournament or combat between two opponents on horseback and armed with lances.
3. *forsaketh yet the lists:* nevertheless leaves the tournament grounds.
4. That is, the marriage pledge may be broken.

As market men for oxen, sheep, or horse.
55 Marriage is a matter of more worth
Than to be dealt in by attorneyship;°   *proxy*
Not whom we will but whom his grace affects°   *desires*
Must be companion of his nuptial bed.
And therefore, lords, since he affects her most,
60 Most of all these reasons bindeth us
In our opinions she should be preferred.
For what is wedlock forcèd° but a hell,   *enforced marriage*
An age of discord and continual strife?
Whereas the contrary bringeth bliss
65 And is a pattern° of celestial peace.   *an example*
Whom should we match with Henry, being a king,
But Margaret, that is daughter to a king;
Her peerless feature,° joinèd with her birth,°   *form / high rank*
Approves her° fit for none but for a king.   *Confirms that she is*
70 Her valiant courage and undaunted spirit—
More than in women commonly is seen—
Will answer our hope in issue of a king.[5]
For Henry, son unto a conqueror,
Is likely to beget more conquerors
75 If with a lady of so high resolve°   *determination*
As is fair Margaret he be linked in love.
Then yield, my lords, and here conclude with me
That Margaret shall be queen, and none but she.
KING HENRY Whether it be through force of your report,
80 My noble lord of Suffolk, or for that°   *or because*
My tender youth was never yet attaint°   *infected*
With any passion of inflaming love,
I cannot tell, but this I am assured:
I feel such sharp dissension in my breast,
85 Such fierce alarums° both of hope and fear,   *alarms*
As I am sick with working of my thoughts.
Take, therefore, shipping; post,° my lord, to France;   *hasten*
Agree to any covenants and procure
That Lady Margaret do vouchsafe° to come   *promise*
90 To cross the seas to England and be crowned
King Henry's faithful and anointed queen.
For your expenses and sufficient charge,°   *money to spend*
Among the people gather up a tenth.[6]
Be gone, I say, for till you do return,
95 I rest perplexèd° with a thousand cares.   *I remain troubled*
—And you, good uncle, banish all offense.°   *hostility*
If you do censure me by what you were,[7]
Not what you are, I know it will excuse
This sudden execution of my will.
100 And so conduct me where from company°   *away from company, where*
I may revolve and ruminate my grief.[8] *Exit [with* EXETER].
GLOUCESTER Ay, grief, I fear me, both at first and last.
Exit GLOUCESTER.

---

5. Will satisfy our hopes by bringing forth a king.   were young.
6. A tax of 10 percent on income or property.   8. I may return again and again in my mind to my
7. If you judge me by how you behaved when you   grief.

SUFFOLK Thus Suffolk hath prevailed, and thus he goes
As did the youthful Paris[9] once to Greece,
105 With hope to find the like event° *the same outcome*
But prosper better than the Trojan did.
Margaret shall now be queen and rule the King,
But I will rule both her, the King, and realm. *Exit.*

---

9. According to Greek mythology, Paris went to Greece from Troy and abducted Helen, the wife of Menelaus. This act was said to have brought about the Trojan War, in which Paris was killed.

Titus Andronicus

Human sacrifice. Gang rape. Mutilation. Ritual butchery. Mother–son cannibalism. *Titus Andronicus* delighted audiences of the 1590s, and the memory of its enormous popular success was still alive more than twenty years later, when Shakespeare's contemporary, Ben Jonson, referred to it as a famous old crowd-pleaser in his comedy *Bartholomew Fair.* Several centuries of critics since then, however, have deplored the play's gratuitous violence. The late seventeenth-century playwright Edward Ravenscroft considered *Titus Andronicus* "a heap of rubbish"; the twentieth-century poet and critic T. S. Eliot called it "one of the stupidest and most uninspired plays ever written." Some have maintained that Shakespeare could not possibly have written *Titus Andronicus,* even though contemporaries testify to his authorship and the play inaugurates themes that will interest him again: he returns to the machiavellian villain in *Richard III,* to the urgency of revenge in *Hamlet,* to the old man unwisely relinquishing power in *Lear,* to questions of race and intermarriage in *Othello* and *The Tempest,* to important moments in Roman history in *The Rape of Lucrece, Julius Caesar, Coriolanus,* and *Antony and Cleopatra.*

Of course, Shakespeare himself, writing his first tragedy in 1592 (with, some scholars argue, the help of George Peele), could not have anticipated the reasons for which he would eventually be canonized. Moreover, the distinction between "high art" and "low entertainment" that often underlies complaints about *Titus Andronicus* would have been unfamiliar to Shakespeare and his audience: the contrast between popular and elite culture was drawn differently in early modern England than it has been in later centuries. Even by the standards of Shakespeare's contemporaries, however, *Titus Andronicus* is an extravagantly bloody play, often deliberately shocking or grotesque. It seems worth asking how it fits into an oeuvre in which many have been reluctant to grant it a place.

Generically speaking, *Titus Andronicus* is a tragedy of revenge, a very old form that originated in ancient Greece, flourished in ancient Rome, and was revived in the 1580s in England by Shakespeare's predecessor Thomas Kyd. English Renaissance revenge tragedies typically feature a man whose family members have been raped or murdered by a king, duke, or emperor. Because the administration of justice rests in the hands of the very person who has committed the outrage, no redress is obtainable through established institutions. As a result, the hero takes matters into his own hands. Ironically, as he struggles to impose a just order upon his world, he loses his own moral bearings and even his sanity: the commonsensical standards of "justice" upon which he has initially relied often come to seem either flawed or unreachable. In the final scenes, the revenger wreaks some appalling vengeance upon his enemies and then is killed or commits suicide himself. By staging the spectacle of a subject exterminating his "betters," Renaissance revenge tragedy taps into frustrations and ambivalences that must have accumulated in the hierarchical, deliberately inequitable social arrangements of early modern England. Spectators could experience a vicarious thrill of sympathy with the revenger and relish the atrocities represented onstage, even while, at the end of the play, acknowledging the moral unacceptability of revenge and the necessity for the revenger's death.

Titus Andronicus differs from roughly contemporary revenge tragedies in degree rather than in kind. Revengers typically begin as conscientious, law-abiding types:

otherwise their eventual descent into illegality would furnish little dramatic interest. In Titus's case, these traits are highly exaggerated: when offered the imperial diadem, his sense of propriety induces him to defer to Saturninus, the eldest son of the last emperor, even though in Rome the office of emperor was not necessarily an inherited one. Of course, the obligation that Saturninus thus incurs makes Titus's later suffering at the hands of the imperial family seem all the more galling. At the same time, Shakespeare complicates the action by giving Saturninus's wife, Tamora, an excellent reason for hating Titus: in the first scene, he has ignored her desperate pleas and sacrificed her eldest son. So, in fact, Titus's revenge is a response to Tamora's own vengeance. The doubling of reprisals in *Titus Andronicus* gives some pretext for the play's relentless bloodiness; but it is worth remembering too that bloodiness is an earmark of revenge tragedy then and now. One modern corollary to a play like *Titus Andronicus* is the movie thriller in which a rogue cop or ex-military officer brutally retaliates against those who have murdered his partners or loved ones: the kind of film, in other words, that is likely to attract a vast audience even while provoking condemnation of "media violence." *Titus* seems considerably less grotesque when it is compared with other plays of its kind rather than, say, *Romeo and Juliet*.

In its elaborately detailed antique setting, however, *Titus Andronicus* differs strikingly from most Renaissance revenge tragedies. The play is an early manifestation of Shakespeare's enduring interest in classical culture, a "Roman" play akin to *Julius Caesar, Coriolanus,* and *Antony and Cleopatra*. But in contrast to the later Roman plays, which are based on history and biography, the plot of *Titus Andronicus* is pure fiction. Unfettered by fact, Shakespeare is free to fabricate an extravagant nightmare universe that presses against the frontiers of plausibility. At the same time, he puts a great deal of emphasis on the play's "Roman-ness," making constant reference to classical myths, to legendary and historical figures, to imperial institutions, to the places and customs of ancient Rome.

Shakespeare creates what might be called a "Rome effect" by an eclectic process of extracting and combining motifs from a wide variety of classical stories. Titus as he appears in the opening scene, for instance—in his austere patriotism, his intolerance of dissent, his acute sense of personal and family honor, his traditional piety, and his ferocious commitment to patriarchal hierarchy—is a recurrent Roman personality type. Shakespeare could have found precedents for these traits in numerous figures from Roman history. After a victory in battle, Horatius killed his sister for lamenting her betrothed, a man of the enemy nation whom he himself had slain in combat; Gaius Mucius Scaevola deliberately burned off his right hand in the presence of an enemy king to demonstrate the resolution of the Romans; Titus Manlius Torquatus was a general so severe that he had his own son executed for eagerly anticipating an order to engage the enemy; Marcus Portius Cato's contempt for "softness" made him both an extraordinary military leader and an eloquent misogynist; Appius Claudius killed his daughter after her sexual honor was compromised. Most likely, Shakespeare had all these exemplary figures in mind, and probably more. Likewise, the career of Titus's son Lucius, a soldier who defends Rome bravely against external enemies but who finds himself persecuted by his own countrymen, recalls the experience of several historical figures: the brothers Publius Scipio Africanus and Lucius Scipio Asiaticus, who subdued much of North Africa and western Asia only to be falsely accused of embezzlement; or Caius Martius Coriolanus, who after his exile joined Rome's enemies and marched on his native city.

Similarly, Titus's daughter Lavinia has a number of classical precursors. The story of her rape and mutilation is loosely based on a story that, as retold in Ovid's *Metamorphoses*, was commonly assigned to Elizabethan boys in school. In this ancient legend, King Tereus rapes his sister-in-law Philomela and cuts out her tongue in order to prevent her from revealing his identity. Philomela, however, imparts the truth to her sister Procne, Tereus's wife, by weaving a tapestry that illustrates the crime. In revenge, Procne butchers her own son by Tereus and serves him to her husband as part of a

Procne serving Itys to Tereus. From Antonio Tempesta, *Ovid's "Metamorphoses"* (1606).

feast. The similarities between Lavinia's plight and Philomela's are often noted in *Titus Andronicus*, and Lavinia herself reveals the truth about the crime when she gets her stumps on a copy of the *Metamorphoses*.

But Philomela is not the only model for Lavinia. Shakespeare draws on the story of the rape of Lucretia, an ancient Roman matron violated by Tarquin, the king's son; she committed suicide after revealing the crime to her male relatives. Lucretia was revenged by a group of men who, like Lucius in *Titus Andronicus*, used the outrage as a pretext for overthrowing tyrannical power and setting up a new government. Shakespeare also incorporates into *Titus Andronicus* some features of the story of Appius and Virginia. Virginia was a young Roman woman who was sexually threatened by a powerful judge and killed by her father to prevent her rape; like Lucretia, she became the pretext for a revolutionary uprising. Lavinia's story, then, is an amalgam of classical rape narratives. Her terribly mutilated body condenses a long history of sporadic violence against women into a single, intensely imagined brutalization. Like Titus, Lavinia seems to sum up a whole tradition, one highly prestigious in an age that venerated the classics, and at the same time deeply disturbing.

This particular way of imagining "Rome," as an anthology of stories, reflects Shakespeare's education in sixteenth-century England. England had, of course, been a Roman territory, and marks of the Roman occupation persisted. Romans had built the road system still in use in Shakespeare's time; the remains of their fortifications were (and are) still visible in many locations. But England had been a remote outpost of the empire, not a place where the treasures of antiquity were commonly to be found. While Renaissance Italians could ground their knowledge of antiquity upon great architecture and statuary all around them, the English, few of whom traveled to Italy in the sixteenth century, imbibed the classical past through books, through a grammar school curriculum that emphasized a firm grounding in Latin literature and history. For Shakespeare and his compatriots, in other words, the Roman past had less to do with places or artifacts than with texts.

The influence of these texts echoes through *Titus Andronicus*: Ovid's *Metamorphoses*, a fantastic compilation of pagan myths; Virgil's *Aeneid*, which recounts the epic voyage of the Trojan prince Aeneas to Carthage and then Italy; the gory legends of vengeance dramatized by the tragedian Seneca; the histories of the Roman Republic and Empire, written by Livy, Plutarch, Tacitus, Sallust, and Suetonius. In *Titus Andronicus,* the sign of Rome's dominion often seems less a moral or political superiority than a kind of narrative ascendancy. Shakespeare's Goths and Africans apparently have no history, no myths, of their own: instead, they invoke and mimic examples provided by their conquerors, just as Renaissance Europeans revived the classical literary inheritance, testifying to its importance in the very acts of reading and imitating it.

All the characters in *Titus Andronicus* are acutely conscious of the glorious Roman past as it is enshrined in narrative. Their dependence on old stories means that their lives have a curiously derivative quality. The characters not only model their behavior on these stories, but consistently exceed the prototype. Whereas in the *Metamorphoses* one man rapes Philomela and cuts out her tongue afterward, in *Titus Andronicus* two men rape Lavinia and cut off not only her tongue but her hands as well. Whereas Procne cooks one child, Titus bakes two. "For worse than Philomel you used my daughter," Titus declares, "And worse than Procne I will be revenged" (5.2.193–94).* He both invokes and goes beyond his original example, intensifying the original crime in a way characteristic of revengers ancient and modern: "An act is not revenged," writes the ancient tragedian Seneca, "unless it is surpassed." Thus there is an interesting corollary between the spiraling ferocity typical of the revenge plot and the competitive way in which the characters in Shakespeare's revenge play fit themselves into a Roman tradition by exceeding its paradigms, enacting its stories "with a vengeance," as one says.

Of course, the oppressive weight of the past is a problem not merely for the characters of *Titus Andronicus* but also for its playwright. Like his characters, Shakespeare recycles the old stories with a difference, "surpassing" them just as the revenger surpasses the original crime. From our point of view, Shakespeare seems the world's preeminent dramatist, secure in the greatness that was already beginning to be accorded him at the time of his death. But in the early years of his career, Shakespeare might well have wondered whether and how it was possible to use, even while surpassing, the examples earlier writers had set for him. The notorious excesses of *Titus Andronicus* are one way of employing, even while going beyond, the examples he inherited.

If, in fact, Shakespeare worried about how he would measure up against his predecessors, and about whether the present and future would be able to compete with the past, it is interesting that he sets *Titus Andronicus* in the late fourth century C.E. At this point in history, Rome had dominated Europe, North Africa, and the Middle East for almost five hundred years. In both extent and duration, its empire was historically unprecedented and has never been achieved again. The Roman ritual that embodies and celebrates that rule is the "triumph" with which *Titus Andronicus* begins: a victory procession accorded to conquering Roman generals when they returned from the perimeters of the empire with barbarian chieftains in tow. By the fourth century, however, the long Roman dominion was drawing to a close. Shakespeare's sixteenth-century audience knows that although Titus may still be winning battles against the Goths, the time is near when the boundaries of the empire will crumble and invaders will sweep down from the north, annihilating Rome's power and bringing the era of classical civilization to an end.

In *Titus Andronicus,* then, Shakespeare portrays a society teetering on the verge of obsolescence: it has a long, long history but not much of a future. The signs of decadence, corruption, and loss of cultural confidence are everywhere. For instance, the difference between Roman and barbarian initially seems clearly, even absolutely, marked. Tamora and her sons are in chains, Titus and his sons conquering heroes. "Thou art a Roman; be not barbarous," Marcus advises Titus (1.1.381), as if the two

---

*All quotations are taken from the edited text of the Quarto, printed here. The Digital Edition includes edited texts of both the Quarto and the Folio.

Triumphal arch and its collapse. From Jan van der Noot, *A Theatre for Worldlings* (1569).

terms were necessarily incompatible. Even in the first scene, however, the Roman sense of superiority seems unwarranted. A quarrel over the imperial throne precedes Titus's victory celebration, suggesting the institutional instability that will ultimately subvert Rome from within even as uncouth armies threaten to overwhelm it from without. Moreover, the climax of Titus's victory celebration is his insistence on sacrificing Alarbus despite Tamora's maternal pleas: a case in which the traditional forms of piety that underlie Roman civilization seem to require the barbaric practice of human sacrifice. If Rome's conviction of racial and cultural supremacy—of *deserving* to rule the world—was once a workable notion, it is so no longer. The obsession with the past that pervades *Titus Andronicus* thus seems oddly empty. Even as inherited stories provide the only paradigms for action, they fail to nourish a fertile sense of tradition that might help Rome renew itself.

As traditional distinctions lose their prestige and plausibility, the social procedures that depend on such distinctions likewise begin to collapse. The play's first scene neatly exemplifies the problem. The brothers Saturninus and Bassianus quarrel first over the possession of the imperial throne and then over the possession of Lavinia, whom both wish to marry. In Shakespeare's England, the first dispute would have been settled according to the principle of "primogeniture," which gave priority in inheritance to the elder brother; the second would have been settled in favor of the younger brother, on the grounds of his preexisting betrothal to Lavinia. In Rome, however, it seems impossible to settle competing claims in an orderly way. In fact, Saturninus does eventually get the throne and Bassianus the woman, but not without a good deal of confusion and some lethal violence. The suggestion is that established methods of allocating property or privilege to one or another person may be quite arbitrary, but that the alternative to such methods is chaos.

In case the point is not sufficiently clear, Shakespeare immediately follows the quarrel between the two Roman brothers with another scene of sibling rivalry, this time between Tamora's sons, once again over sexual access to Lavinia. Unlike their Roman counterparts, these men are seeking not marriage but an adulterous relationship, and their villainous confidant Aaron has little difficulty massaging their illicit ambitions into plans for a rape. Adultery and rape seem the "opposites" of the marriage desired by the Roman men; and certainly the ferocity of the Gothic brothers' attack on Lavinia makes abundantly clear why such behavior is intolerable. At the same time, Shakespeare's juxtaposition of scenes suggests, subversively, the *similarities* between Roman marriage and rape. In neither case is Lavinia's consent at issue: she becomes the property of whoever happens to carry her off by force. Once again the distinction between legitimate and illegitimate behavior seems indispensable and at the same time remarkably indistinct.

The characters apparently best equipped to function in this world of collapsing distinctions are Aaron and Tamora, whose interracial adultery is perceived as particularly scandalous by both Romans and Goths. The classical account of racial difference, inherited by Shakespeare and his contemporaries, did not draw a binary distinction between "white" Europeans and "black" Africans; instead it contrasted the fair-skinned inhabitants of northern Europe on the one hand, and the dark-skinned inhabitants of Africa on the other, with the "temperate" natives of Mediterranean Europe (where, of course, this theory originated). Both Tamora and Aaron represent, in other words, outlandish extremes from a Roman point of view. Because Tamora and Aaron are outsiders, neither has much to gain by endorsing Rome's view of itself, which has relegated them to positions of servitude and powerlessness. They recognize from the outset the artificiality of the precepts by which Rome pretends to govern itself and the world, and understand that if they are ever to gain power, it must be by refusing to play by those rules. In a society in which women are treated as the sexual property of their male relatives, "good" women like Lavinia seem destined for passivity and victimization. In a few lines, then, Tamora—manipulative, ruthless, and cunning—transfers herself from the extreme of subjugation, as Titus's captive, to the apex of power as empress of Rome.

Aaron is a stage descendant of the "black men" of the medieval morality plays, which conflated traditional depictions of the devil with racist conceptions of "Moors" and "Africans." But at the same time that Shakespeare exploits to the full Aaron's capacity for gleeful villainy, he makes Aaron's point of view comprehensible, even at some points attractive, to the audience. Roman hierarchies would consign Aaron permanently to a subordinate position. Like Tamora, he sees no reason to accept the validity of that assignment. Why should he collaborate in his own oppression? It is no coincidence that Shakespeare's verse seems at its best in this play when Aaron is delivering a soliloquy. His view of the world is very close to what the play as a whole seems to endorse: that the assumptions upon which ethical behavior and social institutions depend represent fictions rather than facts.

For the dramatic technique of *Titus Andronicus,* like its villains, seems to insist that the "normal" or the "proper" is a mere construct, that apparently vivid distinctions are not as clear-cut as they seem, that moral opposites have a way of turning into one another. We have already seen Shakespeare setting the behavior of Bassianus and Saturninus beside the behavior of Chiron and Demetrius, as well as associating his white empress with his black slave. Such juxtapositions seem to be designed to induce a sort of evaluative vertigo, an effect that becomes most intense, perhaps, in the figure of the unnamed infant who results from Tamora's adultery with Aaron. In the view of most of the play's characters, this child physically embodies, and thus serves as both proof and symbol of, its parents' utter depravity. At the same time, Aaron's unexpectedly fierce solicitude for the child—which contrasts attractively with Titus's casual willingness to slaughter his own son—prevents the audience from taking at face value the rhetoric of disgust and fear discharged upon the little unfortunate from everyone else in the play. This is, after all, a baby. Every time it is brought onstage, the function it seems designed to serve in the play's symbolic economy powerfully conflicts with its intrinsic infant appeal.

In other cases, Shakespeare produces jarringly appropriate incongruities not by juxtaposing characters but by evoking apparently inappropriate dramatic genres. For instance, when Quintus and Martius find Bassianus's body, the audience knows they are being framed for murder, and one might expect a playwright to exploit the pathos of the situation, encouraging the audience to pity and sympathize with the innocent characters. Instead, the scene is played for laughs, as Titus's sons struggle farcically to pull one another out of a hole. Another jarring technique in *Titus Andronicus* is the deliberately awful play on words: "Mark, Marcus, mark" (3.1.143), cries Titus as they behold the ravished and mutilated Lavinia. In such cases, Shakespeare's humor shatters the norms of dramatic and moral suitability, implying the artificiality of what is conventionally considered "normal" or "proper."

Ethiopian soldier. From Cesare Vecellio, *De gli habiti antichi et moderni* (1590).

If the moral and social problem of *Titus* is that eventually nothing is taboo, the aesthetic problem of the play is that literary convention too comes to seem entirely artificial. Shakespeare's deliberate rule breaking in *Titus Andronicus* risks looking like, or simply being the equivalent of, tasteless incompetence. This is especially true when terrible suffering is at stake. Marcus's long, garishly metaphorical speech at the sight of his niece's bleeding body (2.4.13–57), for instance, seems grossly beside the point. Is Shakespeare merely being inept here—is he as out of control as Marcus seems to be? Or is he deliberately exploring the limits of his medium by unexpectedly violating its usual rules, in the manner of modern surrealists, absurdists, or postmodernists? The critical debate about *Titus Andronicus* has largely involved quarrels between those who claim the former and those who claim the latter.

Even if Shakespeare sometimes seems to share the heartlessness of Aaron and Tamora, he does not represent the Goth and the African as admirable characters. Rebelling against the principles of "civilization" puts them outside any moral community. At the end of the play, Lucius orders Aaron starved to death and Tamora's body thrown over the city walls, as if it were mere garbage. Their treatment indicates his conviction that their behavior has put themselves outside the classification of the human, so that when they are starving, no one has an obligation to relieve them, and when they are dead, no one need respect their remains. The final scene reasserts the difference between human society and what Titus calls "a wilderness of tigers," a difference that the revenge plot has come close to erasing. And despite the abundant evidence that Roman social organization is fundamentally flawed and soon to be toppled, it is not surprising that both Goths and Romans should greet Lucius's restoration of order at the end of the play with profound relief.

Titus Andronicus, then, suggests that the principles of Roman order are patently false and often arbitrarily oppressive; but it also suggests that acknowledging this arbitrariness or rebelling against this falsity and oppression will have disastrous consequences. What produces Roman "virtue" seems to be a delusion; but being undeluded, as Tamora and Aaron are and as Titus becomes, is even more terrible. In Shakespeare's later tragedies, the alternative to normality is often a visionary possibility that seems, if only it could be lived out, to improve upon the status quo: the loves of Romeo and Juliet, Antony and Cleopatra, Othello and Desdemona are examples of such "constructive rule breaking." In *Titus Andronicus,* however, traditional taboos, however cruel, brittle, or despotic they seem, are the sole guarantors of order. Once they are shattered, nothing can take their place, and sheer chaos ensues.

The pessimism, even nihilism, of this vision, combined with Shakespeare's almost playful emphasis on what most writers prefer to skirt or play down, is doubtless what has made *Titus* seem merely bad to so many readers since the late seventeenth century. From another point of view, however, *Titus Andronicus* is a daring experiment, one that Shakespeare did not repeat but that nonetheless provides fascinating insight into his development as a dramatist.

KATHARINE EISAMAN MAUS

SELECTED BIBLIOGRAPHY

Barker, Francis. "A Wilderness of Tigers: *Titus Andronicus,* Anthropology, and the Occlusion of Violence." *The Culture of Violence: Tragedy and History.* Chicago: U of Chicago P, 1993. 143–206. Shows how cultural anthropology and the history of criminal prosecution in early modern England illuminate *Titus Andronicus,* particularly the "Clown scene" (4.3).

Bartels, Emily. "Making More of the Moor: Aaron, Othello, and Renaissance Refashionings of Race." *Shakespeare Quarterly* 41 (1990): 433–54. Looks at Aaron in the context of other sixteenth-century English depictions of black Africans.

James, Heather. "Cultural Disintegration in *Titus Andronicus:* Mutilating Titus, Virgil, and Rome." *Violence in Drama.* Ed. James Redmond. New York: Cambridge UP, 1991. 123–40. Examines Shakespeare's debt to Virgil's *Aeneid.*

Kahn, Coppélia. "The Daughter's Seduction in *Titus Andronicus;* or, Writing Is the Best Revenge." *The Roman Shakespeare: Warriors, Wounds, and Women.* New York: Routledge, 1997. 46–76. Discusses Lavinia's role in the play.

Loomba, Ania. "Wilderness and Civilization in *Titus Andronicus.*" *Shakespeare, Race, and Colonialism.* New York: Oxford UP, 2002. 75–90. Focuses on the alliance between Aaron and Tamora.

Palmer, D. J. "The Unspeakable in Pursuit of the Uneatable: Language and Action in *Titus Andronicus.*" *Critical Quarterly* 14 (1972): 320–39. Analyzes the representation of suffering.

Rowe, Katherine. "Dismembering and Forgetting in *Titus Andronicus.*" *Shakespeare Quarterly* 45 (1994): 279–303. Examines amputated hands and frustrated agency in the play.

Royster, Francesca. "White-Limed Walls: Whiteness and Gothic Extremism in Shakespeare's *Titus Andronicus.*" *Shakespeare Quarterly* 51 (2000): 432–55. Looks at the play's presentation of racial difference in its Renaissance context.

Silverstone, Catherine. "'Honour the real thing': Gregory Doran's *Titus Andronicus* in South Africa." *Shakespeare, Trauma and Contemporary Performance.* New York: Routledge, 2011. 26–54. Discusses a 1995 production of *Titus* in South Africa as an exploration of violence, trauma, and national history.

Vickers, Brian. "*Titus Andronicus* with George Peele." *Shakespeare, Co-Author: A Historical Study of Five Collaborative Plays.* New York: Oxford UP, 2002. 148–243. Discusses the likelihood that Shakespeare and George Peele collaborated on *Titus Andronicus.*

FILMS

Titus Andronicus. 1985. Dir. Jane Howell. UK. 120 min. This production, stylized and self-consciously theatrical, is often considered one of the best of the BBC series and a major influence on Taymor's bigger-budget film (1999).

Titus. 1999. Dir. Julie Taymor. USA. 162 min. A visually stunning adaptation of Shakespeare's play, emphasizing its stomach-churning violence. The fine cast includes Anthony Hopkins as Titus and Jessica Lange as Tamora.

TEXTUAL INTRODUCTION

There are three quarto texts of *Titus Andronicus*: Q1 (1594), Q2 (1600), and Q3 (1611). There is only one surviving copy of Q1, *The Most Lamentable Roman Tragedy of Titus Andronicus*; it was purchased by Henry Clay Folger in 1905 following its discovery in Sweden in 1904. The Folger copy (Krafft) is necessarily the base text for any edition of Q1. Editors argue that there are several reasons to believe that Q1 was printed from a copy of Shakespeare's foul papers (working manuscript) or a scribal "fair copy," including variety in speech prefixes (e.g., "*Saturnine*," "*Emperour*," "*King*" are used variously for Saturninus), false starts (see Digital Edition TC 1), and the comparative lack of detail in stage directions in relation to the Folio text, *The Lamentable Tragedy of Titus Andronicus* (1623). Each of the quarto texts appears to have been printed from the preceding text.

F was printed from Q3 probably in conjunction with a theatrical prompt copy of Q1, Q2, or Q3, since F's stage directions are fuller; however, there is no conclusive evidence for the nature of the projected prompt copy. The compositor of Q2 made some corrections to Q1, including deleting the false start at 1.1.35–38; he is most likely the author of variant and new material, probably written in response to damage to the final (K) gathering of pages in the text from which he was working. Strikingly, he seems to have written new lines (5.3.163–67, 5.3.198–202) that were retained in Q3 and F, highlighting the role that compositors played in shaping the texts of Shakespeare's plays (see Digital Edition TC 9 and TC 10). The compositors of Q3 and F are generally regarded by editors as less experienced and less accurate than the compositors of Q1 and Q2. In particular, the compositor of Q3 omitted two lines (3.1.35, 4.4.102) and the compositor of F omitted five lines (2.1.102, 4.2.8, 4.2.76, 5.2.160, 5.3.51) and added two lines (1.1.398, 4.1.37); the *Norton Shakespeare* edition of F (available in the Digital Edition) has preserved these omissions and additions except where the deleted lines are judged necessary for sense (e.g., 2.1.102).

Most editors of *Titus Andronicus* use Q1 as the base text with the exception of 3.2 (the "fly-killing scene"), for which F is the earliest authority (see Digital Edition TC 4). Editors suggest that this scene was written after Q1 was printed, probably by Shakespeare for a revival of the play (it uses "*An.*" as the speech prefix for Titus, which is not used elsewhere in the text, suggesting a different date of composition). The scene was probably inserted into the prompt copy used by the compositor in preparing F. Editors also tend to replace and augment Q1's stage directions by way of those in F, which are generally taken to be closer to early modern theatrical practice.

The principles of single-text editing require that the *Norton Shakespeare* edition of Q1 does not contain scene 3.2. The phrasing and substance of Q1's stage directions are respected where possible. Nonetheless, some of Q1's stage directions have been augmented with information from F; others have been inserted from Q2, Q3, and F where this seems necessary to clarify the action. The false starts have been preserved in Q1 and F, and are marked by braces (curly brackets) to draw attention to the processes of authorship and printing. F retains the variant and new material introduced by the compositor of Q2 and reproduced in Q3 and F so as to draw further attention to the play's textual history and to the role of compositors in creating the text. Speech prefixes and variant spellings have been standardized between Q1 and F (e.g., "*Aaron*" for "*Moor*" in Q1 and F; "*Bassianus*" for "*Bascianus*" in Q1). F's "*Boy*" (named "*Young Lucius*" in stage directions) translates and replaces Q1's "*Puer*." Titus's sons in 1.1 have been given proper names in preference to generic descriptions (e.g., "2. *Sonne*") in preparation for their further development in 2.3; these decisions draw attention to a key editorial crux and to the ways in which editors influence characterization (see Digital Edition TC 3). Duplicated speech prefixes have been deleted (e.g., 2.2.11 in Q1 and F). Missing speech prefixes have been added (e.g., 1.1.18 in Q1 and F) where the speaker is given in the preceding stage direction, and in cases where the text suggests that there is a shift in speaker (e.g., 1.1.476 in Q1); the latter identifies how editorial practice can affect meaning and characterization (see Digital Edition TC 5 and TC 8). Punctuation has been standardized across the two texts where the words are identical. Act and scene divisions accord with the editorial tradition for the play, following the Folio's act divisions (the Quarto offers no such divisions) and Nicholas Rowe's scene divisions in his 1709 edition, further subdivided by subsequent editors, Alexander Pope, Edward Capell, and Alexander Dyce. Lineation has also been standardized as much as possible in order to aid the reader who wishes to compare the two texts; the main corollary of this is that a number of F's pairs of short lines have been set as single lines.

CATHERINE SILVERSTONE

PERFORMANCE NOTE

Featuring a protagonist who vies for the opportunity to chop off his hand, debates the respect due to a swatted housefly, and cooks his guests' offspring into their meat pies, *Titus Andronicus* is a tragedy constantly inclining toward farce. It thus challenges theater companies to maintain pathos amid episodes almost certain to prompt laughter, causing many directors to reduce the text's gratuitous violence through adaptation, or to dodge grotesquerie by stylizing the blocking, using symbolic sounds, and rendering blood abstractly, as ribbons or cloth. Directors also earn their productions some dignity and complement the play's high rhetorical style by amplifying the ceremony around the first scene, solemnizing the subsequent violence by having it echo Titus's ritual sacrifice of Alarbus. Some directors aim for visceral representations of violence, using gruesome stage blood and hyperrealistic stray heads and hands, while others mount full-blown farces, provoking audiences to laughter that potentially deepens the shock and suddenness of events such as Lavinia's execution.

Whatever the balance struck between tragedy and dark comedy, directors make critical choices about *Titus*'s characters, especially Titus and Aaron. Titus, whose early onstage acts include denying all mercy to Tamora's son and murdering his own, does not easily invite sympathy; the villainous Aaron, meanwhile, inevitably attracts support with his charisma and compelling paternal instinct. Titus can appear reactionary or simply confused, his offenses owing to ego and spite or to misguided attempts at fealty. Aaron can be a motiveless fiend or justified in revenging himself on clear oppressors. Tamora, too, can emerge as a revenger or a savage, depending on whether the portrayal emphasizes her maternal dimension or her sensuousness and duplicity. Lavinia can participate actively in Tamora's flouting and Titus's revenge or simply transition from innocence to catatonia; Lucius can offer promise as a clear-sighted ruler or seem destined to renew the cycle of violence. Directors must also manage the contradictory staging demands in 1.1 (see Digital Edition TC 2); Quintus and Martius's fall into a "pit" (2.2); and Marcus's infamously challenging speech (2.4). And they must decide the extent of Titus's madness, the fate of Aaron's child, and whether Lavinia is complicit in her death.

BRETT GAMBOA

The Most Lamentable Roman Tragedy of Titus Andronicus

[THE PERSONS OF THE PLAY

SATURNINUS, eldest son to the late Emperor of Rome; later Emperor
BASSIANUS, younger brother to Saturninus
MARCUS Andronicus, tribune
PUBLIUS, son to Marcus
TITUS Andronicus, general, brother to Marcus
LAVINIA, daughter to Titus, betrothed to Bassianus
LUCIUS ⎫
QUINTUS ⎬ sons to Titus
MARTIUS ⎪
MUTIUS ⎭
BOY, Young Lucius, son to Lucius
Sempronius ⎫
Caius ⎬ kinsmen to Titus
Valentine ⎭
TRIBUNES
AEMILIUS
ROMAN LORD
CAPTAIN
NURSE
CLOWN
MESSENGER
Other ROMANS, including Senators, Soldiers, Judges, and Attendants

TAMORA, Queen of the Goths, later wife to Saturninus and Empress of Rome
Alarbus ⎫
DEMETRIUS ⎬ sons to Tamora
CHIRON ⎭
AARON, a Moor, lover of Tamora
Baby, son to Aaron and Tamora
FIRST GOTH
SECOND GOTH
THIRD GOTH
Army of GOTHS]

1.1 (F 1.1)

Enter the TRIBUNES *and Senators*[1] *aloft. And then
enter [below]* SATURNINUS *and his followers [and
Soldiers] at one door and* BASSIANUS *and his followers
[and Soldiers at the other], with drums° and trumpets.*

    drummer

SATURNINUS *[to his followers]* Noble patricians, patrons° of
    my right,   *supporters*
Defend the justice of my cause with arms.
And countrymen, my loving followers,
Plead my successive title° with your swords.   *right to succeed*
5   I am his first-born son that was the last
That wore the imperial diadem of Rome:
Then let my father's honors live in me,
Nor wrong mine age° with this indignity.   *seniority*
BASSIANUS *[to his followers]* Romans, friends, followers,
    favorers of my right,
10   If ever Bassianus, Caesar's[2] son,
Were gracious° in the eyes of royal Rome,   *Found favor*
Keep° then this passage° to the Capitol,   *Defend / path*
And suffer not dishonor to approach
The imperial seat, to virtue consecrate,°   *consecrated*
15   To justice, continence, and nobility;
But let desert[3] in pure election[4] shine,
And, Romans, fight for freedom in your choice.
      [Enter] MARCUS *Andronicus, [aloft,] with the crown.*
MARCUS Princes that strive by factions and by friends
Ambitiously for rule and empery,°   *imperial rule*
20   Know that the people of Rome, for whom we stand
A special party,[5] have by common voice
In election for the Roman empery
Chosen Andronicus, surnamèd Pius,[6]
For many good and great deserts to Rome.
25   A nobler man, a braver warrior,
Lives not this day within the city walls.
He by the Senate is accited° home   *summoned*
From weary wars against the barbarous Goths,
That with his sons, a terror to our foes,
30   Hath yoked° a nation strong, trained up in arms.   *subdued*
Ten years are spent since first he undertook
This cause of Rome and chastised with arms
Our enemies' pride. Five times he hath returned
Bleeding to Rome, bearing his valiant sons
35   In coffins from the field; {and at this day[7]
To the monument of the Andronici
Done sacrifice of expiation,
And slain the noblest prisoner of the Goths.}

1.1 Location: Before the Roman Capitol, represented by the upper stage ("aloft"). The tomb of the Andronicus family, a stage structure or a trapdoor, is accessible onstage.
1. Respectively, the representatives of the common people (plebeians) and the upper classes (patricians).
2. The previous Emperor (Bassianus is Saturninus's younger brother).
3. Merit (as opposed to birth order).
4. Free choice of the citizens.

5. A representative elected for a particular purpose.
6. Titus has been given the honorary title of "Dutiful."
7. TEXTUAL COMMENT The lines in curly brackets appear in Q1 but not in Q2 or Q3; they describe, in the past tense, the death of Alarbus, which actually occurs later in the scene. To modern editors, this inconsistency suggests that the Quarto was set from Shakespeare's foul papers, or working manuscript; see Digital Edition TC 1 (Quarto edited text).

And now, at last, laden with honor's spoils,
40 Returns the good Andronicus to Rome,
Renownèd Titus, flourishing in arms.
Let us entreat, by honor of his° name   *(the late Emperor's)*
Whom worthily you would have now succeed,[8]
And in the Capitol and Senate's right,[9]
45 Whom you pretend° to honor and adore,   *claim*
That you withdraw you and abate your strength,
Dismiss your followers and, as suitors should,
Plead your deserts in peace and humbleness.
SATURNINUS How fair the tribune speaks to calm my thoughts.
50 BASSIANUS Marcus Andronicus, so I do affy°   *trust*
In thy uprightness and integrity,
And so I love and honor thee and thine,
Thy noble brother Titus and his sons
And her to whom my thoughts are humbled all,
55 Gracious Lavinia, Rome's rich ornament,
That I will here dismiss my loving friends
And to my fortunes and the people's favor
Commit my cause in balance to be weighed.
        Exeunt [his] Soldiers [and followers].
SATURNINUS Friends that have been thus forward in my right,
60 I thank you all and here dismiss you all,
And to the love and favor of my country
Commit myself, my person, and the cause.
      [Exeunt his Soldiers and followers.]
  [to the TRIBUNES *and Senators]* Rome, be as just and gracious
  unto me
As I am confident° and kind to thee.   *trusting*
65 Open the gates and let me in.
BASSIANUS Tribunes, and me, a poor competitor.°   *co-petitioner*
    *[*SATURNINUS *and* BASSIANUS*] go up into the Senate*
    House.
     [Exeunt aloft MARCUS, TRIBUNES, *and Senators.]*
    Enter a CAPTAIN.
CAPTAIN Romans, make way. The good Andronicus,
Patron° of virtue, Rome's best champion,   *Representative; pattern*
Successful in the battles that he fights,
70 With honor and with fortune is returned
From where he circumscribèd° with his sword   *restrained*
And brought to yoke the enemies of Rome.
    Sound drums and trumpets, and then enter two of
    *Titus' sons [*LUCIUS *and* MUTIUS*], and then men*
    bearing a coffin covered with black, then two other
    *sons [*MARTIUS *and* QUINTUS*], then* TITUS *Andronicus,*
    and then TAMORA *the Queen of Goths and her [sons,*
    Alarbus,] CHIRON, *and* DEMETRIUS, *with* AARON *the*
    Moor,[1] *and others, as many as can be. Then set down*
    the coffin, and TITUS *speaks.*

---

8. Whose place you want a worthy candidate to fill.
9. To choose a new emperor, traditionally an elected and not an inherited office.
1. "Moor" in classical times referred to an inhabitant of Mauretania, in northwest Africa; the term was later applied to Islamic Africans of Arab descent who conquered Spain in the Middle Ages. In Renaissance England, the word often was used of any black-skinned African.

TITUS   Hail Rome, victorious in thy mourning weeds!°   garments
Lo, as the bark° that hath discharged his fraught°   ship / its freight
75   Returns with precious lading° to the bay   cargo
From whence at first she weighed her anchorage,°   anchor
Cometh Andronicus, bound with laurel boughs,[2]
To re-salute his country with his tears,
Tears of true joy for his return to Rome.
80   Thou great defender[3] of this Capitol,
Stand gracious to the rites that we intend.
Romans, of five-and-twenty valiant sons,
Half of the number that King Priam[4] had,
Behold the poor remains, alive and dead:
85   These that survive, let Rome reward with love;
These that I bring unto their latest° home,   last
With burial amongst their ancestors.
Here Goths have given me leave[5] to sheathe my sword.
Titus, unkind[6] and careless of thine own,
90   Why suffer'st thou thy sons unburied yet
To hover on the dreadful shore of Styx?[7]
Make way to lay them by their brethren.
         They open the tomb.
There greet in silence, as the dead are wont,
And sleep in peace, slain in your country's wars.
95   O sacred receptacle of my joys,
Sweet cell of virtue and nobility,
How many sons hast thou of mine in store,
That thou wilt never render° to me more!°   return / again
LUCIUS   Give us the proudest prisoner of the Goths,
100   That we may hew his limbs and on a pile
Ad manes fratrum° sacrifice his flesh   To our brothers' shades (Latin)
Before this earthy prison of their bones,
That so the shadows° be not unappeased,   spirits
Nor we disturbed with prodigies° on earth.   evil happenings
105   TITUS   I give him you, the noblest that survives,
The eldest son of this distressèd Queen.
TAMORA [*kneeling*]   Stay, Roman brethren! Gracious conqueror,
Victorious Titus, rue° the tears I shed—   pity
A mother's tears in passion° for her son—   grief
110   And if thy sons were ever dear to thee,
Oh, think my son to be as dear to me!
Sufficeth not that we are brought to Rome
To beautify thy triumphs° and return   triumphal processions
Captive to thee and to thy Roman yoke?
115   But must my sons be slaughtered in the streets
For valiant doings in their country's cause?
Oh, if to fight for king and commonweal
Were piety in thine,° it is in these.°   (your sons) / (my sons)
Andronicus, stain not thy tomb with blood.
120   Wilt thou draw near the nature of the gods?

2. Laurel wreath, symbol of victory.
3. Jupiter Capitolinus, king of the Roman gods, to
whose shrine on the Capitol victorious generals
brought their spoils.
4. King of Troy during the Trojan War.

5. Allowed me (ironic, since the Goths were defeated
in battle).
6. Devoid of natural feeling; undutiful.
7. River surrounding the underworld; the dead could
not cross it until they had been properly buried.

Draw near them, then, in being merciful:
Sweet mercy is nobility's true badge.
Thrice-noble Titus, spare my first-born son.

TITUS   Patient° yourself, madam, and pardon me.   *Calm*
125   These are their brethren whom your Goths beheld
Alive and dead, and for their brethren slain
Religiously° they ask a sacrifice.   *On religious grounds*
To this your son is marked, and die he must
T'appease their groaning shadows that are gone.
130   LUCIUS   Away with him, and make a fire straight,°   *immediately*
And with our swords upon a pile of wood
Let's hew his limbs till they be clean consumed.
      Exeunt Titus' sons [LUCIUS, QUINTUS, MARTIUS, *and*
                                    MUTIUS] *with Alarbus.*

TAMORA [*rising*]   Oh, cruel irreligious piety!
CHIRON   Was never Scythia[8] half so barbarous!
135   DEMETRIUS   Oppose not Scythia to ambitious Rome.
Alarbus goes to rest and we survive
To tremble under Titus' threatening look.
Then, madam, stand resolved, but hope withal
The self-same gods that armed the Queen of Troy[9]
140   With opportunity of sharp revenge
Upon the Thracian tyrant in his tent
May favor Tamora the Queen of Goths—
When Goths were Goths and Tamora was Queen—
To quit° the bloody wrongs upon her foes.   *revenge*
      Enter the sons of Andronicus [LUCIUS, QUINTUS,
            MARTIUS, *and* MUTIUS] *again.*
145   LUCIUS   See, lord and father, how we have performed
Our Roman rites. Alarbus' limbs are lopped
And entrails feed the sacrificing fire,
Whose smoke like incense doth perfume the sky.
Remaineth naught but to inter our brethren
150   And with loud larums° welcome them to Rome.   *trumpet calls*
TITUS   Let it be so, and let Andronicus
Make this his latest° farewell to their souls.   *last*
      Sound trumpets and lay the coffin in the tomb.
In peace and honor rest you here, my sons;
Rome's readiest champions, repose you here in rest,
155   Secure from worldly chances and mishaps.
Here lurks no treason, here no envy° swells,   *malice*
Here grow no damnèd drugs,° here are no storms,   *poisons*
No noise, but silence and eternal sleep.
In peace and honor rest you here, my sons.
      Enter LAVINIA.
160   LAVINIA   In peace and honor live Lord Titus long;
My noble lord and father, live in fame.
Lo, at this tomb my tributary° tears   *tribute-bearing*
I render for my brethren's obsequies.°   *funeral rites*
[*She kneels.*] And at thy feet I kneel, with tears of joy
165   Shed on this earth, for thy return to Rome.

---

8. Uncivilized region north of the Black Sea.   her son Polydorus by killing the sons of his murderer,
9. In Ovid's *Metamorphoses* 13, Queen Hecuba,   Polymnestor, tyrant of Thrace.
enslaved by the Greeks after the defeat of Troy, avenged

Oh, bless me here with thy victorious hand,
Whose fortunes Rome's best citizens applaud.
TITUS   Kind Rome, that hast thus lovingly reserved
The cordial° of mine age to glad my heart!   comfort
170   Lavinia, live, outlive thy father's days
And fame's eternal date for virtue's praise.[1]
        [LAVINIA *rises. Enter aloft* TRIBUNES, *Senators,*
        SATURNINUS, BASSIANUS, *and* MARCUS, *with a white
        robe.*]
MARCUS   Long live Lord Titus, my belovèd brother,
Gracious triumpher in the eyes of Rome!
TITUS   Thanks, gentle tribune, noble brother Marcus.
175   MARCUS   And welcome, nephews, from successful wars,
You that survive and you that sleep in fame.
Fair lords, your fortunes are alike in all,
That in your country's service drew your swords.
But safer triumph is this funeral pomp
180   That hath aspired to Solon's happiness,[2]
And triumphs over chance in honor's bed.
Titus Andronicus, the people of Rome,
Whose friend in justice thou hast ever been,
Send thee by me, their tribune and their trust,
185   This palliament[3] of white and spotless hue,
And name thee in election for the empire
With these our late-deceasèd Emperor's sons.
Be *candidatus*,[4] then, and put it on,
And help to set a head on headless Rome.
190   TITUS   A better head her glorious body fits
Than his that shakes for age and feebleness.
What, should I don this robe and trouble you,
Be chosen with proclamations today,
Tomorrow yield up rule, resign my life,
195   And set abroad new business for you all?°   make you busy once again
Rome, I have been thy soldier forty years,
And led my country's strength successfully,
And buried one-and-twenty valiant sons,
Knighted in field, slain manfully in arms
200   In right° and service of their noble country.   the just cause
Give me a staff of honor for mine age,
But not a scepter to control the world.
Upright he held it, lords, that held it last.
MARCUS   Titus, thou shalt obtain and ask° the empery.   simply by asking
205   SATURNINUS   Proud and ambitious tribune, canst thou tell?°   how do you know
TITUS   Patience, Prince Saturninus.
SATURNINUS   Romans, do me right.
Patricians, draw your swords and sheathe them not
Till Saturninus be Rome's emperor.
Andronicus, would thou were shipped to hell,
210   Rather than rob me of the people's hearts!
LUCIUS   Proud Saturnine, interrupter of the good
That noble-minded Titus means to thee.

1. And may the praise of your virtue outlive eternity.   3. Ceremonial garment worn by aspirants to public
2. Solon, a Greek statesman, said, "Call no man happy   office.
until he is dead."   4. Candidate (literally, "one wearing the white toga").

TITUS Content thee, Prince. I will restore to thee
      The people's hearts and wean them from themselves.
215 BASSIANUS Andronicus, I do not flatter thee
      But honor thee and will do till I die.
      My faction if thou strengthen with thy friends
      I will most thankful be; and thanks to men
      Of noble minds is honorable meed.°   *reward*
220 TITUS People of Rome, and people's tribunes here,
      I ask your voices and your suffrages.°   *votes*
      Will ye bestow them friendly on Andronicus?
      TRIBUNES To gratify the good Andronicus
      And gratulate° his safe return to Rome,   *salute*
225   The people will accept whom he admits.°   *allows into office*
      TITUS Tribunes, I thank you, and this suit I make,
      That you create° our emperor's eldest son,   *elect*
      Lord Saturnine, whose virtues will, I hope,
      Reflect on Rome as Titan's° rays on earth,   *the sun god*
230   And ripen justice in this commonweal.°   *community*
      Then if you will elect by my advice,
      Crown him and say, "Long live our emperor!"
      MARCUS With voices and applause of every sort,
      Patricians and plebeians, we create
235   Lord Saturninus Rome's great emperor,
      And say, "Long live our emperor Saturnine!"
          [*A long flourish till* SATURNINUS, BASSIANUS, *and*
           MARCUS *come down.*][5]
      SATURNINUS Titus Andronicus, for thy favors done
      To us in our election this day
      I give thee thanks in part of thy deserts,[6]
240   And will with deeds requite thy gentleness.°   *pay back your kindness*
      And for an onset, Titus, to advance
      Thy name and honorable family,
      Lavinia will I make my empress,
      Rome's royal mistress, mistress of my heart,
245   And in the sacred Pantheon[7] her espouse.
      Tell me, Andronicus, doth this motion please thee?
      TITUS It doth, my worthy lord, and in this match
      I hold me highly honored of your grace.
      And here in sight of Rome to Saturnine,
250   King and commander of our commonweal,
      The wide world's emperor, do I consecrate
      My sword, my chariot, and my prisoners,
      Presents well worthy Rome's imperious° lord.   *imperial*
      Receive them, then, the tribute that I owe,
255   Mine honor's ensigns° humbled at thy feet.   *symbols*
      SATURNINUS Thanks, noble Titus, father of my life.
      How proud I am of thee and of thy gifts
      Rome shall record—and when I do forget
      The least of these unspeakable° deserts,   *inexpressible*

---

5. TEXTUAL COMMENT Most editors augment the Quarto base text of *Titus Andronicus* with the fuller stage directions from the Folio. *The Norton Shakespeare* follows this practice here, but the precise details of the staging nonetheless remain ambiguous; see Digital Edition TC 2 (Quarto edited text).
6. *in . . . deserts:* as part of what you deserve.
7. Roman temple dedicated to all the gods.

260 Romans, forget your fealty° to me.   *duty*
     TITUS [*to* TAMORA] Now, madam, are you prisoner to an emperor,
        To him that for your honor and your state°   *royal dignity*
        Will use you nobly, and your followers.
     SATURNINUS [*aside*] A goodly lady, trust me, of the hue°   *appearance; color*
265   That I would choose, were I to choose anew.
        —Clear up, fair Queen, that cloudy countenance.
        Though chance of war hath wrought this change of cheer,°   *expression*
        Thou com'st not to be made a scorn in Rome;
        Princely shall be thy usage every way.
270   Rest° on my word and let not discontent   *Rely*
        Daunt all your hopes. Madam, he comforts you
        Can° make you greater than the Queen of Goths.   *Who can*
        —Lavinia, you are not displeased with this?
     LAVINIA Not I, my lord, sith° true nobility   *since*
275   Warrants° these words in princely courtesy.   *Justifies*
     SATURNINUS Thanks, sweet Lavinia. —Romans, let us go.
        Ransomless here we set our prisoners free.
        Proclaim our honors, lords, with trump° and drum.   *trumpet*
           [*Flourish.* SATURNINUS, TAMORA, CHIRON, DEMETRIUS,
              and AARON *prepare to leave.*]
     BASSIANUS [*seizing* LAVINIA] Lord Titus, by your leave, this
        maid is mine.
280 TITUS How, sir? Are you in earnest, then, my lord?
     BASSIANUS Ay, noble Titus, and resolved withal
        To do myself this reason and this right.
     MARCUS *Suum cuique*° is our Roman justice.   *To each his own (Latin)*
        This prince in justice seizeth but his own.
285 LUCIUS And that he will and shall, if Lucius live.
     TITUS Traitors, avaunt!° Where is the Emperor's guard?   *be off*
        —Treason, my lord! Lavinia is surprised.
     SATURNINUS Surprised? By whom?
     BASSIANUS   By him that justly may
        Bear his betrothed from all the world away.
              [*Exeunt* BASSIANUS, LAVINIA, *and* MARCUS.]
290 MUTIUS Brothers, help to convey her hence away,
        And with my sword I'll keep this door safe.
              [*Exeunt* LUCIUS, QUINTUS, *and* MARTIUS.]
     TITUS Follow, my lord, and I'll soon bring her back.
     MUTIUS My lord, you pass not here.
     TITUS   What, villain boy,
        Barr'st me my way in Rome?
              [TITUS *attacks* MUTIUS.]
     MUTIUS   Help, Lucius, help!
              [TITUS *kills* MUTIUS.]
                 [*Exeunt* SATURNINUS, TAMORA, CHIRON,
                    DEMETRIUS, *and* AARON.]
              [*Enter* LUCIUS.]
295 LUCIUS My lord, you are unjust—and more than so:
        In wrongful quarrel you have slain your son.
     TITUS Nor thou, nor he, are any sons of mine.
        My sons would never so dishonor me.
        Traitor, restore Lavinia to the Emperor.
300 LUCIUS Dead, if you will, but not to be his wife
        That is another's lawful promised love.   [*Exit.*]

Enter aloft the Emperor [SATURNINUS] *with* TAMORA
and her two sons [CHIRON *and* DEMETRIUS], *and*
AARON *the Moor.*

SATURNINUS   No, Titus, no. The Emperor needs her not,
Nor° her, nor thee, nor any of thy stock.   *Neither*
I'll trust by leisure° him that mocks me once,   *I'm in no hurry to trust*
305   Thee never, nor thy traitorous haughty sons,
Confederates all thus to dishonor me.
Was none in Rome to make a stale°   *laughingstock*
But Saturnine? Full well, Andronicus,
Agree these deeds with that proud brag of thine
310   That said'st I begged the empire at thy hands.
TITUS   Oh, monstrous! What reproachful words are these?
SATURNINUS   But go thy ways. Go give that changing piece°   *fickle wench*
To him that flourished for her with his sword.[8]
A valiant son-in-law thou shalt enjoy,
315   One fit to bandy° with thy lawless sons,   *brawl*
To ruffle° in the commonwealth of Rome.   *swagger*
TITUS   These words are razors to my wounded heart.
SATURNINUS   And therefore, lovely Tamora, Queen of Goths,
That like the stately Phoebe° 'mongst her nymphs   *Diana (the moon)*
320   Dost overshine the gallant'st dames of Rome,
If thou be pleased with this my sudden choice,
Behold, I choose thee, Tamora, for my bride,
And will create thee Empress of Rome.
Speak, Queen of Goths, dost thou applaud my choice?
325   And here I swear by all the Roman gods,
Sith priest and holy water are so near,
And tapers burn so bright and everything
In readiness for Hymenaeus° stand,   *god of marriage*
I will not re-salute the streets of Rome,
330   Or climb° my palace, till from forth this place   *ascend to*
I lead espoused my bride along with me.
TAMORA   And here in sight of heaven to Rome I swear,
If Saturnine advance the Queen of Goths,
She will a handmaid be to his desires,
335   A loving nurse, a mother to his youth.°   *youthfulness*
SATURNINUS   Ascend, fair Queen, Pantheon. Lords, accompany
Your noble emperor and his lovely bride,
Sent by the heavens for Prince Saturnine,
Whose wisdom[9] hath her fortune conquerèd.
340   There shall we consummate our spousal rites.
                                        Exeunt [*all but* TITUS].
TITUS   I am not bid° to wait upon this bride.   *invited*
Titus, when wert thou wont to walk alone,
Dishonored thus and challengèd° of wrongs?   *accused*
           Enter MARCUS *and Titus' sons* [LUCIUS, QUINTUS,
           and MARTIUS].
MARCUS   O Titus, see! Oh, see what thou hast done—
345   In a bad quarrel slain a virtuous son.
TITUS   No, foolish tribune, no. No son of mine,
Nor thou, nor these, confederates in the deed

---

8. To him who brandished his sword to win her.   9. Wise consent to my proposal.

    That hath dishonored all our family.
    Unworthy brother and unworthy sons!
350 LUCIUS   But let us give him burial as becomes:°   *as is proper*
    Give Mutius burial with our brethren.
    TITUS   Traitors, away! He rests not in this tomb.
    This monument five hundred years hath stood,
    Which I have sumptuously re-edified.°   *rebuilt*
355 Here none but soldiers and Rome's servitors°   *defenders*
    Repose in fame, none basely slain in brawls.
    Bury him where you can; he comes not here.
    MARCUS   My lord, this is impiety in you.
    My nephew Mutius' deeds do plead for him.
360 He must be buried with his brethren.
    QUINTUS *and* MARTIUS   And shall, or him we will accompany.[1]
    TITUS   "And shall"? What villain was it spake that word?
    MARTIUS   He that would vouch it° in any place but here.   *back it up*
    TITUS   What, would you bury him in my despite?°   *in defiance of me*
365 MARCUS   No, noble Titus, but entreat of thee
    To pardon Mutius and to bury him.
    TITUS   Marcus, even thou hast struck upon my crest,
    And with these boys mine honor thou hast wounded.
    My foes I do repute° you every one,   *consider*
370 So trouble me no more but get you gone.
    QUINTUS   He is not with° himself; let us withdraw.   *is beside*
    MARTIUS   Not I, till Mutius' bones be buried.
        The brother [MARCUS] *and the sons* [LUCIUS, QUINTUS,
        and MARTIUS] *kneel.*
    MARCUS   Brother, for in that name doth nature plead—
    MARTIUS   Father, and in that name doth nature speak—
375 TITUS   Speak thou no more, if all the rest will speed.[2]
    MARCUS   Renownèd Titus, more than half my soul—
    LUCIUS   Dear father, soul, and substance of us all—
    MARCUS   Suffer thy brother Marcus to inter
    His noble nephew here in virtue's nest,
380 That died in honor and Lavinia's cause.
    Thou art a Roman; be not barbarous.
    The Greeks upon advice° did bury Ajax[3]   *deliberation*
    That slew himself; and wise Laertes' son
    Did graciously plead for his funerals.
385 Let not young Mutius, then, that was thy joy,
    Be barred his entrance here.
    TITUS   Rise, Marcus, rise.
    The dismal'st day is this that e'er I saw,
    To be dishonored by my sons in Rome.
    Well, bury him, and bury me the next.
        They put [*the body of* MUTIUS] *in the tomb.*
390 LUCIUS   There lie thy bones, sweet Mutius, with thy friends,
    Till we with trophies° do adorn thy tomb.   *memorial tributes*

---

1. TEXTUAL COMMENT In this exchange between Titus and his sons, neither Q nor F supplies the sons' proper names, leaving it unclear who says what. See Digital Edition TC 3 (Quarto edited text) for a discussion of the ambiguities and how *The Norton Shakespeare* resolves them.

2. If the rest of you wish to meet with good fortune (that is, escape my anger).

3. In the Trojan War, after the Greek hero Ajax committed suicide, Odysseus ("wise Laertes' son") convinced Agamemnon, leader of the Greeks, to grant him honorable burial.

MARCUS, LUCIUS, QUINTUS, *and* MARTIUS (*kneeling*)   No man
    shed tears for noble Mutius:
  He lives in fame that died in virtue's cause.
    [*They rise. Stand aside*] *all but* MARCUS *and* TITUS.

MARCUS   My lord, to step out of these dreary dumps,°   *melancholy*
395   How comes it that the subtle° Queen of Goths   *cunning*
  Is of a sudden thus advanced in Rome?

TITUS   I know not, Marcus, but I know it is—
  Whether by device° or no, the heavens can tell.   *scheming*
  Is she not then beholden to the man
400   That brought her for this high good turn⁴ so far?
    [*Flourish.*] *Enter the Emperor* [SATURNINUS], TAMORA
    and her two sons [CHIRON *and* DEMETRIUS], *with*
    [AARON] *the Moor at one door; enter at the other door*
    BASSIANUS *and* LAVINIA, *with others.*

SATURNINUS   So, Bassianus, you have played your prize.°   *won your bout*
  God give you joy, sir, of your gallant bride.

BASSIANUS   And you of yours, my lord. I say no more,
  Nor wish no less, and so I take my leave.

405 SATURNINUS   Traitor, if Rome have law, or we have power,
  Thou and thy faction shall repent this rape.°   *abduction*

BASSIANUS   "Rape" call you it, my lord, to seize my own,
  My true betrothèd love and now my wife?
  But let the laws of Rome determine all.
410   Meanwhile am I possessed of that° is mine.   *what*

SATURNINUS   'Tis good, sir; you are very short with us—
  But if we live we'll be as sharp with you.

BASSIANUS   My lord, what I have done as best I may
  Answer I must, and shall do with my life.
415   Only thus much I give your grace to know:
  By all the duties that I owe to Rome,
  This noble gentleman, Lord Titus here,
  Is in opinion° and in honor wronged   *reputation*
  That, in the rescue of Lavinia,
420   With his own hand did slay his youngest son
  In zeal to you, and highly moved to wrath
  To be controlled° in that he frankly gave.⁵   *opposed*
  Receive him then to favor, Saturnine,
  That hath expressed himself in all his deeds
425   A father and a friend to thee and Rome.

TITUS   Prince Bassianus, leave to plead° my deeds.   *stop defending*
  'Tis thou and those that have dishonored me.
  Rome and the righteous heavens be my judge
  How I have loved and honored Saturnine!
    [*He kneels.*]

430 TAMORA [*to* SATURNINUS]   My worthy lord, if ever Tamora
  Were gracious in those princely eyes of thine,
  Then hear me speak indifferently° for all;   *impartially*
  And at my suit, sweet, pardon what is past.

SATURNINUS   What, madam, be dishonored openly
435   And basely put it up° without revenge?   *ignobly submit*

---

4. Recompense; "turn" was also slang for the sexual   5. Freely bestowed (by Lavinia upon Saturninus).
act.

TAMORA Not so, my lord. The gods of Rome forfend°   *forbid*
      I should be author to dishonor[6] you.
      But on mine honor dare I undertake°   *vouch*
      For good Lord Titus' innocence in all,
440   Whose fury not dissembled speaks his griefs.
      Then at my suit look graciously on him.
      Lose not so noble a friend on vain suppose,°   *idle conjecture*
      Nor with sour looks afflict his gentle heart.
      [*aside to* SATURNINUS] My lord, be ruled by me; be won at last;
445   Dissemble all your griefs and discontents.
      You are but newly planted in your throne;
      Lest, then, the people, and patricians too,
      Upon a just survey° take Titus' part   *examination*
      And so supplant you for ingratitude,
450   Which Rome reputes to be a heinous sin.
      Yield at entreats°—and then let me alone.   *to entreaty*
      I'll find a day to massacre them all,
      And raze their faction and their family—
      The cruel father and his traitorous sons,
455   To whom I sued for my dear son's life—
      And make them know what 'tis to let a queen
      Kneel in the streets and beg for grace in vain.
      —Come, come, sweet Emperor. —Come, Andronicus.°   *(Marcus)*
      —Take up° this good old man and cheer the heart   *Raise to his feet*
460   That dies in tempest of thy angry frown.
SATURNINUS Rise, Titus, rise. My empress hath prevailed.
TITUS [*rising*] I thank your majesty and her, my lord.
      These words, these looks, infuse new life in me.
TAMORA Titus, I am incorporate in° Rome,   *made a part of*
465   A Roman now adopted happily,
      And must advise the Emperor for his good.
      This day all quarrels die, Andronicus.
      And let it be mine honor, good my lord,
      That I have reconciled your friends and you.
470   For you, Prince Bassianus, I have passed
      My word and promise to the Emperor
      That you will be more mild and tractable.
      And fear not, lords, and you, Lavinia;
      By my advice, all humbled on your knees,
475   You shall ask pardon of his majesty.
              [MARCUS, LAVINIA, LUCIUS, QUINTUS, *and* MARTIUS
              kneel.]
LUCIUS We do, and vow to heaven and to his highness
      That what we did was mildly as we might,°   *possible*
      Tend'ring° our sister's honor and our own.   *Having regard for*
MARCUS That on mine honor here do I protest.°   *solemnly declare*
480 SATURNINUS Away, and talk not; trouble us no more.
TAMORA Nay, nay, sweet Emperor, we must all be friends.
      The tribune and his nephews kneel for grace.
      I will not be denied. Sweetheart, look back.
SATURNINUS Marcus, for thy sake and thy brother's here,
485   And at my lovely Tamora's entreats,

---

6. I should be responsible for dishonoring.

I do remit° these young men's heinous faults.   *forgive*
Stand up!
    [*They rise.*]
            Lavinia, though you left me like a churl,°   *boorishly*
I found a friend, and sure as death I swore
I would not part° a bachelor from the priest.   *depart*

490   Come: if the Emperor's court can feast two brides,
You are my guest, Lavinia, and your friends.
This day shall be a love-day,[7] Tamora.
  TITUS   Tomorrow, an° it please your majesty   *if*
To hunt the panther and the hart with me,

495   With horn and hound we'll give your grace *bonjour.*°   *good day (French)*
  SATURNINUS   Be it so, Titus, and gramercy,° too.   *Exeunt.*   *thank you*
    Sound trumpets. [AARON *the*] *Moor remains.*

2.1 (F 2.1)

AARON   Now climbeth Tamora Olympus' top,[1]
Safe out of fortune's shot,° and sits aloft,   *range*
Secure of° thunder's crack or lightning flash,   *from*
Advanced above pale envy's° threat'ning reach.   *malice's*

5   As when the golden sun salutes the morn
And, having gilt the ocean with his beams,
Gallops° the zodiac in his glistering coach   *Gallops through*
And overlooks the highest-peering hills,
So.
So Tamora.

10   Upon her wit° doth earthly honor wait,°   *intelligence / attend*
And virtue stoops and trembles at her frown.
Then, Aaron, arm thy heart and fit thy thoughts
To mount aloft with thy imperial mistress,
And mount her pitch[2] whom thou in triumph long

15   Hast prisoner held, fettered in amorous chains
And faster bound to Aaron's charming eyes
Than is Prometheus tied to Caucasus.[3]
Away with slavish weeds° and servile thoughts!   *clothes*
I will be bright, and shine in pearl and gold

20   To wait upon this new-made empress.
To wait, said I? To wanton° with this queen,   *play amorously*
This goddess, this Semiramis,[4] this nymph,
This siren[5] that will charm Rome's Saturnine
And see his shipwreck and his commonweal's.
    Enter CHIRON *and* DEMETRIUS, *braving.*°   *defying each other*

25   Hello! What storm is this?
  DEMETRIUS   Chiron, thy years wants° wit, thy wits wants edge°   *lack / sharpness*
And manners to intrude where I am graced,°   *favored*
And may, for aught thou knowest, affected° be.   *loved*
  CHIRON   Demetrius, thou dost overween° in all,   *behave presumptuously*

30   And so in this, to bear me down with braves.°   *threats*

---

7. Day for love; day appointed to settle disputes amicably.
2.1 Scene continues, but the tomb is no longer needed.
1. Mountain home of the Greek gods.
2. Rise to her height; a hawking term (sexually suggestive).
3. In Greek mythology, Zeus punished Prometheus by chaining him to a rock in the Caucasus Mountains; a vulture fed on his liver daily.
4. In Mesopotamian mythology, the Assyrian queen who founded and ruled Babylon, and who also had attributes of Ishtar, goddess associated with sexual lust.
5. In Greek mythology, sirens were female creatures who lured sailors to destruction.

'Tis not the difference of a year or two
Makes me less gracious or thee more fortunate.
I am as able and as fit as thou
To serve and to deserve my mistress' grace,
35 And that my sword upon thee shall approve°   prove
And plead my passions for Lavinia's love.
AARON [aside]   Clubs, clubs![6] These lovers will not keep the peace.
DEMETRIUS   Why, boy, although our mother, unadvised,°   rashly
Gave you a dancing-rapier° by your side,   ornamental sword
40 Are you so desperate grown to threat° your friends?   threaten
Go to. Have your lath[7] glued within your sheath
Till you know better how to handle it.
CHIRON   Meanwhile, sir, with the little skill I have,
Full well shalt thou perceive how much I dare.
DEMETRIUS   Ay, boy, grow ye so brave?
            They draw.
45 AARON   Why, how now, lords?
So near the Emperor's palace dare ye draw
And maintain such a quarrel openly?[8]
Full well I wot° the ground of all this grudge.°   know / quarrel
I would not for a million of gold
50 The cause were known to them it most concerns,
Nor would your noble mother for much more
Be so dishonored in the court of Rome.
For shame, put up.°   sheathe your swords
DEMETRIUS   Not I, till I have sheathed
My rapier in his bosom and withal
55 Thrust those reproachful speeches down his throat
That he hath breathed in my dishonor here.
CHIRON   For that I am prepared and full resolved,
Foul-spoken coward, that thund'rest with thy tongue,
And with thy weapon nothing dar'st perform.
60 AARON   Away, I say!
Now, by the gods that warlike Goths adore,
This petty brabble° will undo us all.   quarrel
Why, lords, and think you not how dangerous
It is to jet° upon a prince's right?   encroach
65 What, is Lavinia, then, become so loose,
Or Bassianus so degenerate,
That for her love such quarrels may be broached°   begun
Without controlment,° justice, or revenge?   restraint
Young lords, beware! And should the Empress know
70 This discord's ground,[9] the music would not please.
CHIRON   I care not, I, knew she° and all the world.   if she knew
I love Lavinia more than all the world.
DEMETRIUS   Youngling, learn thou to make some meaner° choice;   lesser
Lavinia is thine elder brother's hope.
75 AARON   Why, are ye mad? Or know ye not in Rome
How furious and impatient they be
And cannot brook° competitors in love?   endure
I tell you, lords, you do but plot your deaths

6. Here's a brawl (a cry among London apprentices   8. In the Renaissance, it was illegal to draw a sword
to join or quell a fight).   in the presence of the sovereign or at court.
7. Wooden sword used in theatrical productions.   9. Basis; in music, the bass line.

By this device.

80 CHIRON   Aaron, a thousand deaths would I propose°   *face*
To achieve her whom I love.

AARON   To achieve her how?

DEMETRIUS   Why makes thou it so strange?
She is a woman, therefore may be wooed;
She is a woman, therefore may be won;

85 She is Lavinia, therefore must be loved.
What, man, more water glideth by the mill
Than wots the miller of, and easy it is
Of a cut loaf to steal a shive,° we know.   *slice*
Though Bassianus be the Emperor's brother,

90 Better than he have worn Vulcan's badge.[1]

AARON [*aside*]   Ay, and as good as Saturninus may.

DEMETRIUS   Then why should he despair that knows to court it°   *carry on a courtship*
With words, fair looks, and liberality?°   *generosity*
What, hast not thou full often struck° a doe   *struck dead*

95 And borne her cleanly° by the keeper's nose?   *deftly and unnoticed*

AARON   Why, then, it seems some certain snatch[2] or so
Would serve your turns.

CHIRON   Ay, so the turn were served.°   *(with sexual innuendo)*

DEMETRIUS   Aaron, thou hast hit it.

AARON   Would you had hit it,[3] too;
Then should not we be tired with this ado.°   *bothered with this fight*

100 Why, hark ye, hark ye, and are you such fools
To square° for this? Would it offend you, then,   *quarrel*
That both should speed?°   *succeed*

CHIRON   Faith, not me.

DEMETRIUS   Nor me, so° I were one.   *provided that*

AARON   For shame, be friends and join for that you jar.[4]

105 'Tis policy° and stratagem must do   *cunning*
That° you affect,° and so must you resolve   *What / desire*
That what you cannot as you would achieve
You must perforce accomplish as you may.
Take this of me: Lucrece[5] was not more chaste

110 Than this Lavinia, Bassianus' love.
A speedier course than lingering languishment°   *lovesickness*
Must we pursue, and I have found the path.
My lords, a solemn° hunting is in hand.   *ceremonial*
There will the lovely Roman ladies troop.°   *walk together*

115 The forest walks are wide and spacious,
And many unfrequented plots° there are,   *places*
Fitted by kind° for rape and villainy.   *nature*
Single° you thither, then, this dainty doe,   *Isolate*
And strike her home by force, if not by words.

120 This way, or not at all, stand you in hope.
Come, come: our empress, with her sacred wit
To villainy and vengeance consecrate,
Will we acquaint withal what we intend,

---

1. *worn Vulcan's badge*: been cuckolded, as the god
Vulcan was by Venus, the goddess of love.
2. Bite (with sexual innuendo).
3. Hit the nail on the head; "scored" sexually.
4. And join to get what you fight over.

5. Virtuous Roman matron raped by Tarquin, a member of the Roman royal family; after her suicide, her kin avenged her by overthrowing the king and establishing the Roman Republic. Shakespeare retells the story in *The Rape of Lucrece*.

	And she shall file our engines° with advice,	*sharpen our wits*
125	That will not suffer you to square yourselves,°	*be at odds*
	But to your wishes' height advance you both.	
	The Emperor's court is like the house of Fame,[6]	
	The palace full of tongues, of eyes and ears;	
	The woods are ruthless, dreadful, deaf, and dull.°	*insensible*
130	There speak and strike, brave boys, and take your turns.	
	There serve your lust, shadowed from heaven's eye,	
	And revel in Lavinia's treasury.	

CHIRON   Thy counsel, lad, smells of no cowardice.
DEMETRIUS   *Sit fas aut nefas,*° till I find the stream   *Be it right or wrong (Latin)*
135   To cool this heat, a charm to calm these fits,
         Per Stygia, per manes vehor.[7]   *Exeunt.*

2.2 (F 2.2)

Enter TITUS *Andronicus and his three sons* [LUCIUS,
QUINTUS, *and* MARTIUS], *making a noise with hounds
and horns*[, *and* MARCUS].

TITUS   The hunt is up, the moon is bright and gray,°   *(used of dawn light)*
         The fields are fragrant, and the woods are green.
         Uncouple[1] here, and let us make a bay°   *deep barking*
         And wake the Emperor and his lovely bride,
5   And rouse the Prince, and ring° a hunter's peal,   *sound*
         That all the court may echo with the noise.
         Sons, let it be your charge, as it is ours,
         To attend the Emperor's person carefully.
         I have been troubled in my sleep this night,
10   But dawning day new comfort hath inspired.
         Here a cry of hounds, and wind° horns in a peal.   *blow*
         Then enter SATURNINUS, TAMORA, BASSIANUS,
         LAVINIA, CHIRON, DEMETRIUS, *and their Attendants.*
         Many good morrows to your majesty;
         Madam, to you as many and as good.
         I promised your grace a hunter's peal.

SATURNINUS   And you have rung it lustily,° my lords,   *heartily*
15   Somewhat too early for new-married ladies.

BASSIANUS   Lavinia, how say you?

LAVINIA   I say no.
         I have been broad awake two hours and more.

SATURNINUS   Come on, then; horse and chariots let us have,
         And to our sport. [*to* TAMORA] Madam, now shall ye see
20   Our Roman hunting.

MARCUS   I have dogs, my lord,
         Will rouse the proudest panther in the chase°   *hunting ground*
         And climb the highest promontory top.

TITUS   And I have horse will follow where the game
         Makes way and runs like swallows o'er the plain.

25 DEMETRIUS [*aside*]   Chiron, we hunt not, we, with horse nor
            hound,
         But hope to pluck a dainty doe to ground.   *Exeunt.*

---

6. Rumor; the House of Fame is described by Ovid in *Metamorphoses* 12 and by Chaucer in *The House of Fame.*
7. I am carried through the underworld, through the spirits (that is, I am in hell). Adapted from Seneca's *Hippolytus.*
2.2 Location: A forest near the Emperor's palace.
1. Unleash the hounds.

2.3 (F 2.3)

Enter AARON *alone* [*with a bag of gold*].

AARON   He that had wit would think that I had none,
   To bury so much gold under a tree
   And never after to inherit° it.   *possess*
   Let him that thinks of me so abjectly
5 Know that this gold must coin a stratagem
   Which, cunningly effected, will beget
   A very excellent piece of villainy.
   And so repose, sweet gold, for their unrest
   That have their alms out of the Empress' chest.[1]
      [*He hides the gold.*]
   Enter TAMORA *alone to* [AARON] *the Moor.*

10 TAMORA   My lovely Aaron, wherefore lookest thou sad
   When everything doth make a gleeful boast?°   *display*
   The birds chant melody on every bush,
   The snake lies rolled in the cheerful sun,
   The green leaves quiver with the cooling wind
15 And make a checkered shadow on the ground.
   Under their sweet shade, Aaron, let us sit,
   And whilst the babbling echo mocks the hounds,
   Replying shrilly to the well-tuned horns,
   As if a double hunt were heard at once,
20 Let us sit down and mark their yellowing° noise.   *bellowing*
   And after conflict such as was supposed
   The wandering prince and Dido once enjoyed,[2]
   When with a happy storm they were surprised
   And curtained with a counsel-keeping° cave,   *secret-keeping*
25 We may, each wreathèd in the other's arms,
   Our pastimes done, possess a golden slumber,
   Whiles hounds and horns and sweet melodious birds
   Be unto us as is a nurse's song
   Of lullaby to bring her babe asleep.
30 AARON   Madam, though Venus govern your desires,
   Saturn is dominator over mine.[3]
   What signifies my deadly-standing° eye,   *murderously glaring*
   My silence, and my cloudy° melancholy,   *gloomy*
   My fleece of woolly hair that now uncurls
35 Even as an adder when she doth unroll
   To do some fatal execution?
   No, madam, these are no venereal[4] signs;
   Vengeance is in my heart, death in my hand,
   Blood and revenge are hammering in my head.
40 Hark, Tamora, the empress of my soul,
   Which never hopes more heaven than rests in thee,
   This is the day of doom for Bassianus.
   His Philomel[5] must lose her tongue today;

2.3 Location: The forest.
1. *That . . . chest*: Who get this gold, which comes from the Empress's treasury.
2. In Virgil's *Aeneid* 4, the Carthaginian queen Dido and Aeneas, later founder of Rome, make love in a cave where they have taken refuge. *conflict*: sexual intercourse.
3. Those born when the planet Venus was ascendant

were supposed to be amorous; Saturn produced a colder, gloomier temperament.
4. Sexual; derived from Venus.
5. In Greek mythology, an Athenian princess raped by her brother-in-law Tereus; he cut out her tongue, but she wove a tapestry incriminating him (see Introduction and Ovid, *Metamorphoses* 6).

Thy sons make pillage of her chastity
45 And wash their hands in Bassianus' blood.
Seest thou this letter? Take it up, I pray thee,
And give the King this fatal-plotted scroll.
Now question me no more.
      Enter BASSIANUS *and* LAVINIA.
                        We are espied.
Here comes a parcel° of our hopeful° booty,   *part / hoped-for*
50 Which dreads not yet their lives' destruction.
TAMORA   Ah, my sweet Moor, sweeter to me than life!
AARON   No more, great Empress; Bassianus comes.
  Be cross with him and I'll go fetch thy sons
  To back thy quarrels whatsoe'er they be.   [*Exit.*]
55 BASSIANUS   Who have we here? Rome's royal empress,
  Unfurnished of her well-beseeming troop?[6]
  Or is it Dian,[7] habited° like her,   *dressed*
  Who hath abandoned her holy groves
  To see the general hunting in this forest?
60 TAMORA   Saucy controller° of my private steps,   *Insolent observer*
  Had I the power that some say Dian had,
  Thy temples should be planted presently°   *immediately*
  With horns, as was Actaeon's, and the hounds
  Should drive° upon thy new-transformed limbs,   *rush*
65   Unmannerly intruder as thou art![8]
LAVINIA   Under your patience, gentle Empress,
  'Tis thought you have a goodly gift in horning,[9]
  And to be doubted° that your Moor and you   *suspected*
  Are singled forth° to try thy experiments.   *drawn apart*
70   Jove shield your husband from his hounds today!
  'Tis pity they should take him for a stag.
BASSIANUS   Believe me, Queen, your swarthy Cimmerian[1]
  Doth make your honor of his body's hue,
  Spotted, detested, and abominable.
75   Why are you sequestered from all your train,
  Dismounted from your snow-white goodly steed,
  And wandered hither to an obscure plot,
  Accompanied but with a barbarous Moor,
  If foul desire had not conducted you?
80 LAVINIA   And being intercepted in your sport,
  Great reason that my noble lord be rated°   *scolded*
  For sauciness. [*to* BASSIANUS] I pray you, let us hence,
  And let her joy° her raven-colored love.   *enjoy*
  This valley fits the purpose passing well.
85 BASSIANUS   The King, my brother, shall have notice of this.
LAVINIA   Ay, for these slips have made him noted° long.   *notorious*
  Good King, to be so mightily abused.°   *deceived*
TAMORA   Why, I have patience to endure all this.
      Enter CHIRON *and* DEMETRIUS.
DEMETRIUS   How now, dear sovereign and our gracious mother,

---

6. *Unfurnished . . . troop:* Not accompanied by an appropriate escort.
7. Diana, chaste goddess of the hunt (sarcastic).
8. In Greek mythology, the hunter Actaeon came upon Diana naked; she turned him into a stag and his own

hounds tore him apart (see Ovid, *Metamorphoses* 3).
9. The husbands of unfaithful women were supposed to grow staglike horns.
1. The Cimmerians were a legendary people upon whom the sun never shone.

90	Why doth your highness look so pale and wan?	
	TAMORA Have I not reason, think you, to look pale?	
	These two have 'ticed° me hither to this place.	*enticed*
	A barren detested vale you see it is:	
	The trees, though summer, yet forlorn and lean,	
95	Overcome° with moss and baleful² mistletoe;	*Overgrown*
	Here never shines the sun, here nothing breeds	
	Unless the nightly owl or fatal° raven;	*ominous*
	And when they showed me this abhorrèd pit,	
	They told me here at dead time of the night	
100	A thousand fiends, a thousand hissing snakes,	
	Ten thousand swelling toads, as many urchins,°	*goblins*
	Would make such fearful and confusèd cries	
	As any mortal body hearing it	
	Should straight fall mad, or else die suddenly.	
105	No sooner had they told this hellish tale	
	But straight they told me they would bind me here	
	Unto the body of a dismal yew,³	
	And leave me to this miserable death.	
	And then they called me foul adulteress,	
110	Lascivious Goth,⁴ and all the bitterest terms	
	That ever ear did hear to such effect.	
	And had you not by wondrous fortune come,	
	This vengeance on me had they executed.	
	Revenge it as you love your mother's life,	
115	Or be ye not henceforth called my children.	
	DEMETRIUS This is a witness that I am thy son.	
	[*He*] *stab*[*s* BASSIANUS].	
	CHIRON And this for me, struck home to show my strength.	
	[*He stabs* BASSIANUS, *who dies*.]	
	LAVINIA Ay, come, Semiramis⁵—nay, barbarous Tamora,	
	For no name fits thy nature but thy own.	
120	TAMORA Give me the poniard. You shall know, my boys,	
	Your mother's hand shall right your mother's wrong.	
	DEMETRIUS Stay, madam, here is more belongs to her.	
	First, thrash the corn, then after burn the straw.	
	This minion stood° upon her chastity,	*hussy prided herself*
125	Upon her nuptial vow, her loyalty,	
	And with that painted hope braves° your mightiness.	*defies*
	And shall she carry this unto her grave?	
	CHIRON An if° she do, I would I were an eunuch.	*An if = If*
	Drag hence her husband to some secret hole	
130	And make his dead trunk pillow to our lust.	
	TAMORA But when ye have the honey we desire,	
	Let not this wasp outlive us both to sting.	
	CHIRON I warrant you, madam, we will make that sure.	
	Come, mistress, now perforce we will enjoy	
135	That nice-preservèd honesty⁶ of yours.	
	LAVINIA O Tamora, thou bearest a woman's face—	

2. Harmful (mistletoe is parasitic).
3. The yew tree is associated with sadness.
4. Punning on "goat," a proverbially lustful animal.

5. See note to 2.1.22.
6. Fastidiously guarded chastity.

TAMORA   I will not hear her speak. Away with her!

LAVINIA   Sweet lords, entreat her hear me but a word.

DEMETRIUS [*to* TAMORA]   Listen, fair madam, let it be your glory

140 To see her tears, but be your heart to them
As unrelenting flint to drops of rain.

LAVINIA   When did the tiger's young ones teach the dam?°   *mother*
Oh, do not learn her wrath! She taught it thee.
The milk thou suck'st from her did turn to marble;

145 Even at thy teat thou hadst° thy tyranny.   *took in*
Yet every mother breeds not sons alike:
[*to* CHIRON] Do thou entreat her show a woman's pity.

CHIRON   What, wouldst thou have me prove myself a bastard?

LAVINIA   'Tis true the raven doth not hatch a lark.

150 Yet have I heard—oh, could I find it now—
The lion moved with pity did endure
To have his princely paws° pared all away.   *claws*
Some say that ravens foster forlorn children°   *abandoned baby birds*
The whilst their own birds famish in their nests.

155 Oh, be to me, though thy hard heart say no,
Nothing so kind but something pitiful.[7]

TAMORA   I know not what it means. Away with her!

LAVINIA   Oh, let me teach thee for my father's sake
That gave thee life when well he might have slain thee.

160 Be not obdurate; open thy deaf ears.

TAMORA   Hadst thou in person ne'er offended me,
Even for his sake am I pitiless.
Remember, boys, I poured forth tears in vain
To save your brother from the sacrifice,

165 But fierce Andronicus would not relent.
Therefore, away with her and use her as you will.
The worse to her, the better loved of me.

LAVINIA   O Tamora, be called a gentle queen,
And with thine own hands kill me in this place.

170 For 'tis not life that I have begged so long;
Poor I was slain when Bassianus died.

TAMORA   What begg'st thou, then, fond° woman? Let me go!   *foolish*

LAVINIA   'Tis present° death I beg, and one thing more   *immediate*
That womanhood denies° my tongue to tell:

175 Oh, keep me from their worse-than-killing lust,
And tumble me into some loathsome pit
Where never man's eye may behold my body.
Do this, and be a charitable murderer.

TAMORA   So should I rob my sweet sons of their fee.

180 No, let them satisfy their lust on thee.

DEMETRIUS   Away, for thou hast stayed us here too long.

LAVINIA   No grace? No womanhood? Ah, beastly creature,
The blot and enemy to our general name,°   *the reputation of women*
Confusion° fall—   *Destruction*

CHIRON   Nay, then I'll stop your mouth.

185 [*to* DEMETRIUS] Bring thou her husband;
This is the hole where Aaron bid us hide him.
          [DEMETRIUS *throws Bassianus' body into the pit.*]

---

7. Not so kind as the raven, but showing some pity.

[*Exeunt* CHIRON *and* DEMETRIUS, *dragging* LAVINIA.]

TAMORA   Farewell, my sons. See that you make her sure.[8]
　　Ne'er let my heart know merry cheer indeed
　　Till all the Andronici[9] be made away.°   *murdered*
190　Now will I hence to seek my lovely Moor,
　　And let my spleenful° sons this trull° deflower.   [*Exit.*]   *lustful / whore*
　　　　Enter AARON *with two of Titus' sons*[, QUINTUS *and*
　　　　MARTIUS].

AARON   Come on, my lords, the better foot before.
　　Straight will I bring you to the loathsome pit
　　Where I espied the panther fast asleep.
195　QUINTUS   My sight is very dull, whate'er it bodes.[1]
MARTIUS   And mine, I promise you. Were it not for shame,
　　Well could I leave our sport to sleep awhile.
　　　　[MARTIUS *falls into the pit.*]
QUINTUS   What, art thou fallen? What subtle° hole is this,   *treacherous*
　　Whose mouth is covered with rude-growing briars
200　Upon whose leaves are drops of new-shed blood
　　As fresh as morning dew distilled on flowers?
　　A very fatal° place it seems to me.   *ill-omened*
　　Speak, brother. Hast thou hurt thee with the fall?
MARTIUS   O brother, with the dismal'st object hurt
205　That ever eye with sight made heart lament.
AARON [*aside*]   Now will I fetch the King to find them here,
　　That he thereby may have a likely guess
　　How these were they that made away his brother.   [*Exit.*]
MARTIUS   Why dost not comfort me and help me out
210　From this unhallow and blood-stained hole?
QUINTUS   I am surprisèd with an uncouth° fear;   *uncanny*
　　A chilling sweat o'erruns my trembling joints.
　　My heart suspects more than mine eye can see.
MARTIUS   To prove thou hast a true-divining heart,
215　Aaron and thou look down into this den,
　　And see a fearful sight of blood and death.
QUINTUS   Aaron is gone, and my compassionate heart
　　Will not permit mine eyes once to behold
　　The thing whereat it trembles by surmise.°   *merely by imagining it*
220　Oh, tell me who it is, for ne'er till now
　　Was I a child to fear I know not what.
MARTIUS   Lord Bassianus lies berayed° in blood,   *defiled*
　　All on a heap, like to a slaughtered lamb,
　　In this detested, dark, blood-drinking pit.
225　QUINTUS   If it be dark, how dost thou know 'tis he?
MARTIUS   Upon his bloody finger he doth wear
　　A precious ring[2] that lightens all this hole,
　　Which like a taper° in some monument   *candle*
　　Doth shine upon the dead man's earthy° cheeks   *clay-colored*
230　And shows the ragged entrails° of this pit.   *rough interior*
　　So pale did shine the moon on Pyramus[3]

---

8. Make sure of her, keep her from doing harm; kill
her.
9. Family of Andronicus.
1. Sleepiness was a bad omen.
2. Perhaps a carbuncle, thought to emit light.

3. In Ovid's version of a classical legend (*Metamorphoses* 4), Pyramus thinks his beloved Thisbe dead
and kills himself; this is the subject of the mechanicals' play in *A Midsummer Night's Dream.*

When he by night lay bathed in maiden° blood.   *innocent*
O brother, help me with thy fainting hand—
If fear hath made thee faint, as me it hath—
235 Out of this fell° devouring receptacle,   *dreadful*
As hateful as Cocytus'° misty mouth.   *a river of hell*
QUINTUS Reach me thy hand that I may help thee out
Or, wanting° strength to do thee so much good,   *lacking*
I may be plucked into the swallowing womb
240 Of this deep pit, poor Bassianus' grave.
I have no strength to pluck thee to the brink—
MARTIUS Nor I no strength to climb without thy help.
QUINTUS Thy hand once more; I will not loose again
Till thou art here aloft or I below.
245 Thou canst not come to me—I come to thee.
        [QUINTUS *falls into the pit.*]
        Enter the Emperor [SATURNINUS], [*with Attendants,*]
        and AARON *the Moor.*
SATURNINUS Along with me; I'll see what hole is here
And what he is that now is leapt into it.
—Say, who art thou that lately didst descend
Into this gaping hollow of the earth?
250 MARTIUS The unhappy sons of old Andronicus,
Brought hither in a most unlucky hour
To find thy brother Bassianus dead.
SATURNINUS My brother dead? I know thou dost but jest.
He and his lady both are at the lodge
255 Upon the north side of this pleasant chase.°   *hunting ground*
'Tis not an hour since I left them there.
MARTIUS We know not where you left them all alive,
But, out° alas, here have we found him dead!   *(emphatic)*
        Enter TAMORA, [TITUS] *Andronicus, and* LUCIUS.
TAMORA Where is my lord the King?
260 SATURNINUS Here, Tamora, though grieved with killing grief.
TAMORA Where is thy brother Bassianus?
SATURNINUS Now to the bottom dost thou search° my wound.   *probe*
Poor Bassianus here lies murderèd.
TAMORA Then all too late I bring this fatal writ,°   *document*
265 The complot° of this timeless° tragedy,   *plot / untimely*
And wonder greatly that man's face can fold
In pleasing smiles such murderous tyranny.
        She giveth SATURNINUS *a letter.*
SATURNINUS (*read[ing] the letter*)
"An if we miss to meet him handsomely,°   *conveniently*
Sweet huntsman—Bassianus 'tis we mean—
270 Do thou so much as dig the grave for him.
Thou know'st our meaning. Look for thy reward
Among the nettles at the elder tree
Which overshades the mouth of that same pit
Where we decreed to bury Bassianus.
275 Do this and purchase us thy lasting friends."
O Tamora, was ever heard the like?
This is the pit, and this the elder tree.
—Look, sirs, if you can find the huntsman out
That should° have murdered Bassianus here.   *was to*
280 AARON My gracious lord, here is the bag of gold.

SATURNINUS [*to* TITUS]   Two of thy whelps,° fell curs of bloody *puppies; literally, sons*
  kind,°   *nature; breed*
  Have here bereft my brother of his life.
  —Sirs, drag them from the pit unto the prison.
  There let them bide until we have devised
285 Some never-heard-of torturing pain for them.
     [*Attendants drag* QUINTUS *and* MARTIUS *and*
     Bassianus' body from the pit.]
TAMORA What, are they in this pit? Oh, wondrous thing!
  How easily murder is discoverèd!°   *revealed*
TITUS [*kneeling*] High Emperor, upon my feeble knee
  I beg this boon with tears not lightly shed,
290 That this fell fault of my accursèd sons—
  Accursèd if the faults be proved in them—
SATURNINUS If it be proved? You see it is apparent.°   *obvious*
  Who found this letter? Tamora, was it you?
TAMORA Andronicus himself did take it up.
295 TITUS I did, my lord, yet let me be their bail.
  For by my father's reverent tomb I vow
  They shall be ready at your highness' will
  To answer their suspicion[4] with their lives.
SATURNINUS Thou shalt not bail them. See thou follow me.
300 Some bring the murdered body, some the murderers.
  Let them not speak a word; the guilt is plain.
  For by my soul, were there worse end than death,
  That end upon them should be executed.
TAMORA Andronicus, I will entreat the King.
305 Fear not° thy sons; they shall do well enough.   *Fear not for*
TITUS [*rising*] Come, Lucius, come. Stay not to talk with them.° *(Quintus and Martius)*
               [*Exeunt.*]

2.4 (F 2.4)

Enter the Empress' sons [CHIRON *and* DEMETRIUS],
with LAVINIA, *her hands cut off and her tongue cut*
out, and ravished.

DEMETRIUS So, now go tell, an if thy tongue can speak,
  Who 'twas that cut thy tongue and ravished thee.
CHIRON Write down thy mind, bewray° thy meaning so,   *reveal*
  An if thy stumps will let thee, play the scribe.
5 DEMETRIUS See how with signs and tokens she can scrawl.
CHIRON Go home; call for sweet° water; wash thy hands.   *perfumed*
DEMETRIUS She hath no tongue to call, nor hands to wash,
  And so let's leave her to her silent walks.
CHIRON An 'twere my cause,[1] I should go hang myself.
10 DEMETRIUS If thou hadst hands to help thee knit° the cord.   *knot*
       Exeunt [CHIRON *and* DEMETRIUS].
    Enter MARCUS *from hunting.*
MARCUS Who is this? My niece that flies away so fast?
  —Cousin,° a word. Where is your husband?   *Kinswoman*
     [LAVINIA *stops and turns.*]
  If I do dream, would all my wealth would wake me;[2]
  If I do wake, some planet strike me down

---

4. The suspicion they are under.   1. If I were in her position.
2.4 Location: Scene continues.   2. *would all . . . me:* I would give all I had to wake up.

15　That I may slumber an eternal sleep!
　　Speak, gentle niece. What stern ungentle hands
　　Hath lopped and hewed and made thy body bare
　　Of her two branches, those sweet ornaments
　　Whose circling shadows kings have sought to sleep in,
20　And might not gain so great a happiness
　　As half thy love? Why dost not speak to me?
　　Alas, a crimson river of warm blood,
　　Like to a bubbling fountain stirred with wind,
　　Doth rise and fall between thy rosèd lips,
25　Coming and going with thy honey breath.
　　But sure some Tereus³ hath deflowered thee
　　And, lest thou shouldst detect° him, cut thy tongue.　　　　*expose*
　　Ah, now thou turn'st away thy face for shame,
　　And notwithstanding all this loss of blood,
30　As from a conduit with three issuing spouts,
　　Yet do thy cheeks look red as Titan's face,°　　　　*(the sun)*
　　Blushing to be encountered with a cloud.
　　Shall I speak for thee? Shall I say 'tis so?⁴
　　Oh, that I knew thy heart,° and knew the beast　　　*what is in thy heart*
35　That I might rail at him to ease my mind!
　　Sorrow concealed, like an oven stopped,°　　　　*stopped up*
　　Doth burn the heart to cinders where it is.
　　Fair Philomela—why, she but lost her tongue,
　　And in a tedious sampler° sewed her mind;　　　*laborious tapestry*
40　But, lovely niece, that mean° is cut from thee.　　　　*method*
　　A craftier Tereus, cousin, hast thou met,
　　And he hath cut those pretty fingers off
　　That could have better sewed than Philomel.
　　Oh, had the monster seen those lily hands
45　Tremble like aspen leaves upon a lute
　　And make the silken strings delight to kiss them,
　　He would not then have touched them for his life.
　　Or, had he heard the heavenly harmony
　　Which that sweet tongue hath made,
50　He would have dropped his knife and fell asleep,
　　As Cerberus at the Thracian poet's feet.⁵
　　Come, let us go and make thy father blind,
　　For such a sight will blind a father's eye.
　　One hour's storm will drown the fragrant meads;°　　　*meadows*
55　What will whole months of tears thy father's eyes?
　　Do not draw back, for we will mourn with thee.
　　Oh, could our mourning ease thy misery!　　　　*Exeunt.*

3.1 (F 3.1)

Enter the Judges, [TRIBUNES,]¹ *and Senators with*
Titus' two sons [QUINTUS *and* MARTIUS] *bound, passing*
on the stage to the place of execution, and TITUS *going*
before, pleading.

TITUS　Hear me, grave fathers! Noble tribunes, stay!
　　For pity of mine age, whose youth was spent

---

3. See note to 2.3.43.
4. PERFORMANCE COMMENT Marcus's long, rhetorically elaborate speech presents difficulties in performance; for a discussion of the options, see Digital Edition PC 1.

5. The Thracian poet Orpheus, attempting to rescue his dead wife, Eurydice, used his music to lull to sleep Cerberus, the watchdog of the underworld.
3.1 Location: A Roman street.
1. Not including Marcus, who enters at line 58.

In dangerous wars whilst you securely slept;
For all my blood in Rome's great quarrel shed,
5   For all the frosty nights that I have watched,
And for these bitter tears which now you see
Filling the agèd wrinkles in my cheeks,
Be pitiful to my condemnèd sons,
Whose souls is not corrupted as 'tis thought.
10   For two-and-twenty sons I never wept,
Because they died in honor's lofty bed.
      [TITUS] *Andronicus lieth down, and the Judges [and others] pass by him.*
For these, tribunes, in the dust I write
My heart's deep languor° and my soul's sad tears.   grief
Let my tears staunch° the earth's dry appetite;   satisfy
15   My sons' sweet blood will make it shame° and blush.   feel shame
                  [*Exeunt* TRIBUNES *and others.*]
O earth, I will befriend thee more with rain
That shall distill from these two ancient ruins°   (his eyes)
Than youthful April shall with all his showers.
In summer's drought I'll drop upon thee still;
20   In winter with warm tears I'll melt the snow
And keep eternal springtime on thy face,
So° thou refuse to drink my dear sons' blood.   Provided that
            Enter LUCIUS *with his weapon drawn.*
O reverend tribunes! O gentle agèd men!
Unbind my sons, reverse the doom of death,
25   And let me say, that never wept before,
My tears are now prevailing° orators.   persuasive
LUCIUS   O noble father, you lament in vain.
The tribunes hear you not. No man is by,
And you recount your sorrows to a stone.
30   TITUS   Ah, Lucius, for thy brothers let me plead.
Grave tribunes, once more I entreat of you—
LUCIUS   My gracious lord, no tribune hears you speak.
TITUS   Why, 'tis no matter, man. If they did hear,
They would not mark° me; if they did mark,   attend to
35   They would not pity me; yet plead I must,
{And bootless° unto them.}   uselessly
Therefore, I tell my sorrows to the stones
Who, though they cannot answer my distress,
Yet in some sort they are better than the tribunes
40   For that they will not intercept° my tale.   interrupt
When I do weep, they humbly at my feet
Receive my tears and seem to weep with me;
And were they but attired in grave weeds,°   sober garments
Rome could afford° no tribunes like to these.   provide
45   A stone is soft as wax, tribunes more hard than stones;
A stone is silent and offendeth not,
And tribunes with their tongues doom men to death.
But wherefore stand'st thou with thy weapon drawn?
LUCIUS   To rescue my two brothers from their death,
50   For which attempt the judges have pronounced
My everlasting doom of banishment.
TITUS   O happy man! They have befriended thee.
Why, foolish Lucius, dost thou not perceive
That Rome is but a wilderness of tigers?

55   Tigers must prey, and Rome affords no prey
     But me and mine. How happy art thou, then,
     From these devourers to be banishèd!
     But who comes with our brother Marcus here?

           Enter MARCUS *with* LAVINIA.

     MARCUS   Titus, prepare thy agèd eyes to weep,
60   Or if not so, thy noble heart to break.
     I bring consuming sorrow to thine age.
     TITUS   Will it consume me? Let me see it, then.
     MARCUS   This was thy daughter.
     TITUS   Why, Marcus, so she is.
     LUCIUS [*falling to his knees*]   Ay me, this object° kills me.   *spectacle*
65   TITUS   Faint-hearted boy, arise and look upon her.

           [LUCIUS *rises.*]

     Speak, Lavinia, what accursèd hand
     Hath made thee handless in thy father's sight?
     What fool hath added water to the sea
     Or brought a faggot° to bright-burning Troy?[2]   *piece of firewood*
70   My grief was at the height before thou cam'st,
     And now, like Nilus, it disdaineth bounds.[3]
     Give me a sword! I'll chop off my hands too,
     For they have fought for Rome and all in vain;
     And they have nursed this woe in feeding life.[4]
75   In bootless° prayer have they been held up,   *useless*
     And they have served me to effectless° use.   *fruitless*
     Now all the service I require of them
     Is that the one will help to cut the other.
     'Tis well, Lavinia, that thou hast no hands,
80   For hands to do Rome service is but vain.
     LUCIUS   Speak, gentle sister, who hath martyred° thee?   *mutilated*
     MARCUS   Oh, that delightful engine° of her thoughts,   *instrument (her tongue)*
     That blabbed° them with such pleasing eloquence,   *uttered*
     Is torn from forth that pretty hollow cage
85   Where, like a sweet melodious bird, it sung
     Sweet varied notes, enchanting every ear.
     LUCIUS   Oh, say thou for her, who hath done this deed?
     MARCUS   Oh, thus I found her straying in the park,
     Seeking to hide herself, as doth the deer
90   That hath received some unrecuring° wound.   *incurable*
     TITUS   It was my dear, and he that wounded her
     Hath hurt me more than had he killed me dead.
     For now I stand as one upon a rock
     Environed° with a wilderness of sea,   *Surrounded*
95   Who marks the waxing tide grow wave by wave,
     Expecting° ever when some envious° surge   *Awaiting / malignant*
     Will in his° brinish bowels swallow him.   *its*
     This way to death my wretched sons are gone;
     Here stands my other son, a banished man;
100   And here my brother weeping at my woes;
     But that which gives my soul the greatest spurn°   *contemptuous blow*

2. Troy was torched by the Greeks after their victory.
3. Before it was dammed, the river Nile flooded annually.
4. And by defending Rome, they have induced this misery.

Is dear Lavinia, dearer than my soul.
—Had I but seen thy picture in this plight
It would have madded me.° What shall I do   *made me insane*
105   Now I behold thy lively° body so?   *living*
Thou hast no hands to wipe away thy tears,
Nor tongue to tell me who hath martyred thee;
Thy husband he is dead, and for his death
Thy brothers are condemned and dead by this.°   *this time*
110   —Look, Marcus! Ah, son Lucius, look on her!
When I did name her brothers, then fresh tears
Stood on her cheeks, as doth the honeydew
Upon a gathered lily almost withered.
MARCUS   Perchance she weeps because they killed her husband;
115   Perchance because she knows them innocent.
TITUS [*to* LAVINIA]   If they did kill thy husband, then be joyful,
Because the law hath ta'en revenge on them.
No, no, they would not do so foul a deed:
Witness the sorrow that their sister makes.
120   Gentle Lavinia, let me kiss thy lips,
Or make some sign how I may do thee ease.
Shall thy good uncle and thy brother Lucius
And thou and I sit round about some fountain,
Looking all downwards to behold our cheeks,
125   How they are stained like meadows yet not dry
With miry slime left on them by a flood?
And in the fountain shall we gaze so long
Till the fresh taste be taken from that clearness
And made a brine pit with our bitter tears?
130   Or shall we cut away our hands like thine?
Or shall we bite our tongues, and in dumb shows
Pass the remainder of our hateful days?
What shall we do? Let us that have our tongues
Plot some device° of further misery   *contrivance*
135   To make us wondered at in time to come.
LUCIUS   Sweet father, cease your tears, for at your grief
See how my wretched sister sobs and weeps.
MARCUS   Patience, dear niece. Good Titus, dry thine eyes.
TITUS   Ah, Marcus, Marcus, brother, well I wot°   *know*
140   Thy napkin° cannot drink a tear of mine,   *handkerchief*
For thou, poor man, hast drowned it with thine own.
LUCIUS   Ah, my Lavinia, I will wipe thy cheeks.
TITUS   Mark, Marcus, mark. I understand her signs.
Had she a tongue to speak, now would she say
145   That to her brother which I said to thee.
His napkin with her true tears all bewet
Can do no service on her sorrowful cheeks.
Oh, what a sympathy° of woe is this,   *consensus*
As far from help as limbo⁵ is from bliss!
        Enter AARON *the Moor alone.*
150   AARON   Titus Andronicus, my lord the Emperor
Sends thee this word: that if thou love thy sons,

---

5. Region in hell dedicated to those denied entrance to heaven ("bliss") through no fault of their own: for instance, unbaptized infants, or virtuous people who lived before the advent of Christianity.

Let Marcus, Lucius, or thyself, old Titus,
Or any one of you, chop off your hand
And send it to the King. He for the same
155 Will send thee hither both thy sons alive,
And that shall be the ransom for their fault.
TITUS O gracious Emperor! O gentle Aaron!
Did ever raven sing so like a lark
That gives sweet tidings of the sun's uprise?
160 With all my heart I'll send the Emperor my hand.
Good Aaron, wilt thou help to chop it off?
LUCIUS Stay, father, for that noble hand of thine,
That hath thrown down so many enemies,
Shall not be sent. My hand will serve the turn.
165 My youth can better spare my blood than you,
And therefore mine shall save my brothers' lives.
MARCUS Which of your hands hath not defended Rome
And reared aloft the bloody battleax,
Writing destruction on the enemy's castle?
170 Oh, none of both but are of high desert.
My hand hath been but idle; let it serve
To ransom my two nephews from their death;
Then have I kept it to a worthy end.
AARON Nay, come, agree whose hand shall go along,
175 For fear they die before their pardon come.
MARCUS My hand shall go.
LUCIUS   By heaven, it shall not go.
TITUS Sirs, strive no more. Such withered herbs as these
Are meet° for plucking up, and therefore mine.   *proper*
LUCIUS Sweet father, if I shall be thought thy son,
180 Let me redeem my brothers both from death.
MARCUS And for our father's sake and mother's care,
Now let me show a brother's love to thee.
TITUS Agree between you. I will spare my hand.
LUCIUS Then I'll go fetch an ax.
MARCUS   But I will use the ax.
                    Exeunt [LUCIUS *and* MARCUS].
185 TITUS Come hither, Aaron. I'll deceive them both.
Lend me thy hand and I will give thee mine.
AARON [*aside*] If that be called deceit, I will be honest
And never whilst I live deceive men so.
But I'll deceive you in another sort,°   *way*
190 And that you'll say ere half an hour pass.
                    He cuts off Titus' hand.
                    Enter LUCIUS *and* MARCUS *again.*
TITUS Now stay your strife. What shall be is dispatched.
Good Aaron, give his majesty my hand.
Tell him it was a hand that warded° him   *defended*
From thousand dangers; bid him bury it.
195 More hath it merited; that° let it have.   *(burial)*
As for my sons, say I account of them
As jewels purchased at an easy price—
And yet dear too, because I bought mine own.
AARON I go, Andronicus, and for thy hand
200 Look by and by to have thy sons with thee.
[*aside*] Their heads, I mean! Oh, how this villainy

Doth fat° me with the very thoughts of it!   *feast*
Let fools do good and fair men call for grace,
Aaron will have his soul black like his face.   *Exit.*
205 TITUS   Oh, here I lift this one hand up to heaven
[*kneeling*] And bow this feeble ruin to the earth.
If any power pities wretched tears,
To that I call. [*to* LAVINIA, *who kneels*] What, wouldst thou
    kneel with me?
Do, then, dear heart. For heaven shall hear our prayers,
210 Or with our sighs we'll breathe the welkin dim°   *make the heavens misty*
And stain the sun with fog, as sometime° clouds   *sometimes do*
When they do hug him in their melting° bosoms.   *(with rain)*
MARCUS   O brother, speak with possibility°   *what is possible*
And do not break into these deep extremes.
215 TITUS   Is not my sorrow deep, having no bottom?
Then be my passions° bottomless with them.   *expression of suffering*
MARCUS   But yet let reason govern thy lament.
TITUS   If there were reason for these miseries,
Then into limits could I bind my woes.
220 When heaven doth weep, doth not the earth o'erflow?
If the winds rage, doth not the sea wax mad,
Threatening the welkin with his big-swoll'n face?
And wilt thou have a reason for this coil?°   *turmoil*
I am the sea. Hark how her sighs doth flow!
225 She is the weeping welkin, I the earth.
Then must my sea be movèd with° her sighs;   *by*
Then must my earth with her continual tears
Become a deluge, overflowed and drowned,
For why° my bowels⁶ cannot hide her woes,   *Because*
230 But like a drunkard must I vomit them.
Then give me leave, for losers will have leave
To ease their stomachs⁷ with their bitter tongues.
        Enter a MESSENGER *with two heads and a hand.*
MESSENGER   Worthy Andronicus, ill art thou repaid
For that good hand thou sent'st the Emperor.
235 Here are the heads of thy two noble sons,
And here's thy hand in scorn to thee sent back—
        [*He sets down the heads and hand.*]
Thy grief their sports, thy resolution mocked,
That° woe is me to think upon thy woes,   *So that*
More than remembrance of my father's death.   [*Exit.*]
240 MARCUS   Now let hot Etna° cool in Sicily   *volcano in Sicily*
And be my heart an ever-burning hell!
These miseries are more than may be borne.
To weep with them that weep doth ease some deal,°   *somewhat*
But sorrow flouted° at is double death.   *mocked*
245 LUCIUS   Ah, that this sight should make so deep a wound,
And yet detested life not shrink thereat.
That ever death should let life bear his name,°   *be called life*
Where life hath no more interest but to breathe!⁸

---

6. The bowels were thought to be the seat of compas-   7. Resentments (with play on "vomit").
sion.   8. Where nothing is left of life but breathing.

[LAVINIA *kisses* TITUS.]

MARCUS   Alas, poor heart, that kiss is comfortless
250   As frozen water to a starvèd° snake.   *numb with cold*
TITUS   When will this fearful slumber° have an end?   *nightmare*
MARCUS   Now farewell, flattery.° Die, Andronicus.   *pleasing delusion*
        Thou dost not slumber. See thy two sons' heads,
        Thy warlike hand, thy mangled daughter here,
255   Thy other banished son with this dear sight
        Struck pale and bloodless, and thy brother, I,
        Even like a stony image, cold and numb.
        Ah, now no more will I control° thy griefs.   *try to restrain*
        Rent off thy silver hair, thy other hand
260   Gnawing with thy teeth, and be this dismal sight
        The closing up° of our most wretched eyes.   *(in death)*
        Now is a time to storm. Why art thou still?
TITUS   Ha, ha, ha!
MARCUS   Why dost thou laugh? It fits not with this hour.
265   TITUS   Why, I have not another tear to shed.
        Besides, this sorrow is an enemy
        And would usurp upon my watery eyes
        And make them blind with tributary[9] tears.
        Then which way shall I find Revenge's cave?
270   For these two heads do seem to speak to me
        And threat me I shall never come to bliss
        Till all these mischiefs° be returned° again   *calamities / turned back*
        Even in their throats that hath committed them.
        Come, let me see what task I have to do.
        [TITUS *and* LAVINIA *rise.*]
275   You heavy° people, circle me about,   *sad*
        That I may turn me to each one of you
        And swear unto my soul to right your wrongs.
                [LAVINIA, MARCUS, *and* LUCIUS *circle* TITUS. *He pledges*
                them.]
        The vow is made. Come, brother, take a head,
        And in this hand the other will I bear,
280   And, Lavinia, thou shalt be employèd in these arms.
        Bear thou my hand, sweet wench, between thy teeth.
        [*to* LUCIUS] As for thee, boy, go get thee from my sight.
        Thou art an exile and thou must not stay.
        Hie° to the Goths and raise an army there,   *Hurry*
285   And if ye love me, as I think you do,
        Let's kiss and part, for we have much to do.   *Exeunt.*
                [LUCIUS *remains.*]
LUCIUS   Farewell, Andronicus, my noble father,
        The woefull'st man that ever lived in Rome.
        Farewell, proud Rome, till Lucius come again;
290   He loves his pledges[1] dearer than his life.
        Farewell, Lavinia, my noble sister;
        Oh, would thou wert as thou tofore° hast been!   *formerly*
        But now nor° Lucius nor Lavinia lives   *neither*
        But in oblivion and hateful griefs.
295   If Lucius live, he will requite your wrongs

---

9. Paying tribute (to sorrow, the enemy).
1. Vows; hostages (family members left behind in Rome).

And make proud Saturnine and his empress
Beg at the gates like Tarquin and his queen.[2]
Now will I to the Goths and raise a power°   *army*
To be revenged on Rome and Saturnine.   *Exit.*[3]

4.1 (F 4.1)

Enter Lucius' son [the BOY] *and* LAVINIA *running after
him, and the* BOY *flies from her with his books under
his arm. Enter* TITUS *and* MARCUS.

BOY Help, grandsire, help! My aunt Lavinia
Follows me everywhere, I know not why.
Good uncle Marcus, see how swift she comes.
Alas, sweet aunt, I know not what you mean.
[*He drops his books.*]

5   MARCUS Stand by me, Lucius; do not fear thine aunt.
TITUS She loves thee, boy, too well to do thee harm.
BOY Ay, when my father was in Rome[1] she did.
MARCUS What means my niece Lavinia by these signs?
TITUS Fear her not, Lucius; somewhat° doth she mean.   *something*
10 See, Lucius, see how much she makes of thee.[2]
Somewhither° would she have thee go with her.   *Somewhere*
Ah, boy, Cornelia[3] never with more care
Read to her sons than she hath read to thee
Sweet poetry and Tully's[4] *Orator.*
15 Canst thou not guess wherefore she plies° thee thus?   *importunes*
BOY My lord, I know not, I, nor can I guess,
Unless some fit or frenzy do possess her;
For I have heard my grandsire say full oft
Extremity of griefs would make men mad,
20 And I have read that Hecuba of Troy[5]
Ran mad for sorrow: that made me to fear,
Although, my lord, I know my noble aunt
Loves me as dear as ever my mother did
And would not but in fury° fright my youth,   *except in madness*
25 Which made me down to throw my books and fly—
Causeless, perhaps. —But pardon me, sweet aunt;
And, madam, if my uncle Marcus go,°   *go with us*
I will most willingly attend your ladyship.
MARCUS Lucius, I will.
30 TITUS How now, Lavinia? Marcus, what means this?
Some book there is that she desires to see.
Which is it, girl, of these? Open them, boy.
[*to* LAVINIA] But thou art deeper read and better skilled;[6]
Come and take choice of all my library,

---

2. Tarquin and his family were banished from Rome
after the rape of Lucrece; see note to 2.1.109.
3. TEXTUAL COMMENT The Folio text contains an
additional scene here, the "fly-killing scene." While
most modern editors use the Quarto as their base text
and insert this one scene from F, the *Norton Shakespeare* text respects the integrity of the Quarto. Shakespeare probably wrote the fly-killing scene at a later
date for a revival of the play; see Digital Edition TC 4
(Quarto edited text).
4.1 Location: Titus's garden.
1. That is, here to protect me.

2. TEXTUAL COMMENT Some editors reassign part of
this speech to Marcus; for the rationale, see Digital
Edition TC 5 (Quarto edited text).
3. Mother of the two Gracchi, famous tribunes; Cornelia was viewed as the ideal Roman mother because
of her devotion to their education.
4. Cicero's; his *Orator* and *De oratore*, treatises on
rhetoric written ca. 50 B.C.E., were both standard texts
in Renaissance grammar schools.
5. See 1.1.139 and note.
6. Than to read schoolbooks.

35   And so beguile thy sorrow till the heavens
      Reveal the damned contriver of this deed.
      Why lifts she up her arms in sequence° thus?   *one after the other*
      MARCUS   I think she means that there were more than one
      Confederate in the fact.° Ay, more there was,   *crime*
40   Or else to heaven she heaves them for revenge.
      TITUS   Lucius, what book is that she tosseth[7] so?
      BOY   Grandsire, 'tis Ovid's *Metamorphoses*;
      My mother gave it me.
      MARCUS   For love of her that's gone,
      Perhaps, she culled° it from among the rest.   *picked*
45   TITUS   Soft,° so busily she turns the leaves.   *Wait*
      Help her. What would she find? Lavinia, shall I read?
      This is the tragic tale of Philomel,
      And treats of Tereus' treason and his rape[8]—
      And rape, I fear, was root of thy annoy.°   *injury*
50   MARCUS   See, brother, see. Note how she quotes° the leaves.   *examines*
      TITUS   Lavinia, wert thou thus surprised, sweet girl,
      Ravished and wronged as Philomela was,
      Forced in the ruthless, vast, and gloomy woods?
      See, see!
55   Ay, such a place there is where we did hunt—
      Oh, had we never, never hunted there!—
      Patterned by° that the poet here describes,   *On the pattern of*
      By nature made for murders and for rapes.
      MARCUS   Oh, why should nature build so foul a den,
60   Unless the gods delight in tragedies?
      TITUS   Give signs, sweet girl—for here are none but friends—
      What Roman lord it was durst do the deed,
      Or slunk not Saturnine,[9] as Tarquin erst,°   *once*
      That left the camp to sin in Lucrece' bed?[1]
65   MARCUS   Sit down, sweet niece. Brother, sit down by me.
      Apollo, Pallas, Jove, or Mercury,[2]
      Inspire me that I may this treason find.°   *discover the truth of*
      My lord, look here. Look here, Lavinia.
           He writes his name with his staff, and guides it with
           feet and mouth.
      This sandy plot is plain.° Guide, if thou canst,   *flat*
70   This after me. I have writ my name
      Without the help of any hand at all.
      Curst be that heart that forced us to this shift!°   *contrivance*
      Write thou, good niece, and here display at last
      What God will have discovered° for revenge.   *revealed*
75   Heaven guide thy pen to print thy sorrows plain
      That we may know the traitors and the truth.
           She takes the staff in her mouth, and guides it with
           her stumps, and writes.[3]
      Oh, do ye read, my lord, what she hath writ?

---

7. Clumsily turns the pages of.
8. See note to 2.3.43.
9. Was it Saturninus who slunk.
1. See note to 2.1.109.
2. Roman gods: Apollo was the god of prophecy, Pallas (Minerva) of wisdom, Mercury of hidden knowledge.

Jove (Jupiter), the king of the gods, was often imagined as all-knowing.
3. This action recalls Io in Ovid's *Metamorphoses* 1, who after her rape by Jove was turned into a heifer by Jove's jealous wife, Juno; she revealed her identity to her family by writing her story in the dust with her hoof.

	TITUS "*Stuprum*°—Chiron—Demetrius."	*Defilement*
	MARCUS What? What? The lustful sons of Tamora	
80	Performers of this heinous bloody deed?	
	TITUS *Magni dominator poli,*	
	Tam lentus audis scelera, tam lentus vides?[4]	
	MARCUS Oh, calm thee, gentle lord, although I know	
	There is enough written upon this earth	
85	To stir a mutiny in the mildest thoughts	
	And arm the minds of infants to exclaims.°	*exclamations*
	My lord, kneel down with me. Lavinia, kneel.	
	And kneel, sweet boy, the Roman Hector's[5] hope,	
	[*All kneel.*]	
	And swear with me—as, with the woeful fere°	*husband*
90	And father of that chaste dishonored dame,	
	Lord Junius Brutus[6] swore for Lucrece' rape—	
	That we will prosecute by good advice°	*after careful planning*
	Mortal revenge upon these traitorous Goths	
	And see their blood or die with this reproach.°	*dishonor*
	[*They rise.*]	
95	TITUS 'Tis sure enough, an° you knew how.	*if*
	But if you hunt these bear-whelps, then beware:	
	The dam° will wake, and if she wind° ye once,	*mother / scent*
	She's with the lion deeply still in league	
	And lulls him whilst she playeth on her back,	
100	And when he sleeps will she do what she list.°	*pleases*
	You are a young huntsman, Marcus: let alone	
	And come. I will go get a leaf° of brass	*sheet*
	And with a gad° of steel will write these words	*spike*
	And lay it by. The angry northern wind	
105	Will blow these sands like Sibyl's leaves abroad,[7]	
	And where's our lesson then? Boy, what say you?	
	BOY I say, my lord, that if I were a man	
	Their mother's bedchamber should not be safe	
	For these base bondmen to the yoke of Rome.	
110	MARCUS Ay, that's my boy! Thy father hath full oft	
	For his ungrateful country done the like.[8]	
	BOY And, uncle, so will I, an if I live.	
	TITUS Come, go with me into mine armory.	
	Lucius, I'll fit° thee, and withal° my boy	*equip / in addition*
115	Shall carry from me to the Empress' sons	
	Presents that I intend to send them both.	
	Come, come; thou'lt do my message, wilt thou not?	
	BOY Ay, with my dagger in their bosoms, grandsire.	
	TITUS No, boy, not so. I'll teach thee another course.	
120	Lavinia, come; Marcus, look to my house;	
	Lucius and I'll go brave it° at the court.	*cut a fine figure*
	Ay, marry, will we, sir, and we'll be waited on. *Exeunt.*	
	[MARCUS *remains.*]	

4. Ruler of the great heavens, are you so slow to hear and see crimes? (adapted from Seneca's *Hippolytus*).
5. Lucius the elder, champion of Rome as Hector was of Troy.
6. Leader of those who drove the Tarquins from Rome.

7. The Sybil of Cumae (in Italy) wrote prophecies on leaves and placed them outside her cave; they sometimes blew away before they could be read.
8. That is, fought against the Goths.

MARCUS   O heavens, can you hear a good man groan
 And not relent or not compassion° him?   *pity*
125 Marcus, attend him in his ecstasy°   *madness*
 That hath more scars of sorrow in his heart
 Than foemen's marks upon his battered shield,
 But yet so just that he will not revenge.
 Revenge the heavens[9] for old Andronicus!   *Exit.*

4.2 (F 4.2)

Enter AARON, CHIRON, *and* DEMETRIUS *at one door, and at
the other door Young Lucius [the* BOY*] and [an Attendant]
with a bundle of weapons and verses writ upon them.*

CHIRON   Demetrius, here's the son of Lucius.
 He hath some message to deliver us.
AARON   Ay, some mad message from his mad grandfather.
BOY   My lords, with all the humbleness I may,
5 I greet your honors from Andronicus
 [*aside*] And pray the Roman gods confound° you both.   *destroy*
DEMETRIUS   Gramercy,° lovely Lucius, what's the news?   *Thank you*
BOY [*aside*]   That you are both deciphered,° that's the news, *detected*
 For villains marked with rape. —May it please you,
10 My grandsire, well advised, hath sent by me
 The goodliest weapons of his armory
 To gratify° your honorable youth,   *grace*
 The hope of Rome, for so he bid me say,
 And so I do, and with his gifts present
15 Your lordships: whenever you have need,
 You may be armèd and appointed° well.   *equipped*
 And so I leave you both [*aside*] like bloody villains.
        Exeunt [BOY *and Attendant*].
DEMETRIUS   What's here? A scroll, and written round about?
 Let's see:
20 "*Integer vitae, scelerisque purus,*
   Non eget Mauri iaculis, nec arcu."[1]
CHIRON   Oh, 'tis a verse in Horace. I know it well:
 I read it in the grammar long ago.
AARON   Ay, just° a verse in Horace; right you have it.   *exactly*
25 [*aside*] Now what a thing it is to be an ass!
 Here's no sound° jest! The old man hath found their guilt *wholesome*
 And sends them weapons wrapped about with lines
 That wound beyond their feeling to the quick.[2]
 But were our witty° empress well afoot,°   *clever / up and about*
30 She would applaud Andronicus' conceit.°   *device*
 But let her rest in her unrest[3] a while.
 [*to* CHIRON *and* DEMETRIUS] And now, young lords, was't not
  a happy star
 Led us to Rome strangers—and more than so,
 Captives—to be advancèd to this height?
35 It did me good before the palace gate
 To brave[4] the tribune in his brother's hearing.

---

9. May the heavens take revenge.
4.2 Location: The imperial palace.
1. "The man upright in life and free from crime needs
neither the Moorish javelin nor the bow" (Horace,
Odes 1.22.1–2); quoted in William Lily's Latin grammar, standard in Elizabethan schools.
2. That pierce them deeply though they are too dull
to feel it.
3. Remain in her distress (Tamora is in childbirth).
4. To defy (not shown in the play).

DEMETRIUS   But me more good to see so great a lord
    Basely insinuate° and send us gifts.   *curry favor*
    AARON   Had he not reason, Lord Demetrius?
40   Did you not use his daughter very friendly?
    DEMETRIUS   I would we had a thousand Roman dames
    At such a bay,° by turn to serve our lust.   *Cornered like that*
    CHIRON   A charitable wish and full of love.
    AARON   Here lacks but your mother for to say amen.
45   CHIRON   And that would she for twenty thousand more.
    DEMETRIUS   Come, let us go and pray to all the gods
    For our beloved mother in her pains.°   *(labor pains)*
    AARON   Pray to the devils! The gods have given us over.
    Trumpets sound.
    DEMETRIUS   Why do the Emperor's trumpets flourish thus?
50   CHIRON   Belike° for joy the Emperor hath a son.   *Probably*
    DEMETRIUS   Soft, who comes here?
    Enter NURSE *with a blackamoor child.*
    NURSE   Good morrow, lords.
    Oh, tell me, did you see Aaron the Moor?
    AARON   Well, more° or less, or ne'er a whit at all.   *(punning on "Moor")*
    Here Aaron is, and what with Aaron now?
55   NURSE   O gentle Aaron, we are all undone.
    Now help or woe betide thee evermore!
    AARON   Why, what a caterwauling dost thou keep!
    What dost thou wrap and fumble° in thy arms?   *bundle up*
    NURSE   Oh, that which I would hide from heaven's eye:
60   Our Empress' shame and stately Rome's disgrace.
    She is delivered, lords, she is delivered!
    AARON   To whom?
    NURSE   I mean she is brought abed!°   *delivered of a child*
    AARON   Well, God give her good rest! What hath he sent her?
    NURSE   A devil.[5]
65   AARON   Why, then, she is the devil's dam; a joyful issue.°   *outcome; child*
    NURSE   A joyless, dismal, black, and sorrowful issue.
    Here is the babe, as loathsome as a toad
    Amongst the fair-faced breeders of our clime.
    The Empress sends it thee, thy stamp, thy seal,[6]
70   And bids thee christen it with thy dagger's point.
    AARON   Zounds,° ye whore! Is black so base a hue?   *God's wounds*
    [*to the baby*] Sweet blowse,° you are a beauteous blossom,   *red-cheeked wench*
    sure.
    DEMETRIUS   Villain, what hast thou done?
    AARON   That which thou canst not undo.
75   CHIRON   Thou hast undone our mother.
    AARON   Villain, I have done° thy mother.   *used sexually*
    DEMETRIUS   And therein, hellish dog, thou hast undone her.
    Woe to her chance and damned her loathèd choice,
    Accursed the offspring of so foul a fiend.
    CHIRON   It shall not live.
80   AARON   It shall not die.
    NURSE   Aaron, it must; the mother wills it so.

---

5. The devil was often imagined as black, and Africans as devils.   6. *thy stamp, thy seal:* bearing your imprint.

AARON   What, must it, Nurse? Then let no man but I
    Do execution on my flesh and blood.
DEMETRIUS   I'll broach° the tadpole on my rapier's point.   *impale*
85   Nurse, give it me; my sword shall soon dispatch it.
AARON   Sooner this sword shall plow thy bowels up.
    [AARON *draws his sword.*]
    Stay, murderous villains! Will you kill your brother?
    Now, by the burning tapers of the sky
    That shone so brightly when this boy was got,°   *conceived*
90   He dies upon my scimitar's sharp point
    That touches this, my first-born son and heir.
    I tell you, younglings, not Enceladus,[7]
    With all his threatening band of Typhon's° brood,   *father of the Titans*
    Nor great Alcides,[8] nor the god of war
95   Shall seize this prey out of his father's hands.
    What, what, ye sanguine[9] shallow-hearted boys!
    Ye white-limed° walls, ye alehouse painted signs![1]   *whitewashed*
    Coal-black is better than another hue
    In that it scorns to bear another hue;
100   For all the water in the ocean
    Can never turn the swan's black legs to white,
    Although she lave° them hourly in the flood.[2]   *bathe*
    Tell the Empress from me I am of age
    To keep mine own, excuse it how she can.
105 DEMETRIUS   Wilt thou betray thy noble mistress thus?
AARON   My mistress is my mistress, this myself,
    The vigor and the picture of my youth.
    This before all the world do I prefer;
    This maugre° all the world will I keep safe,   *in spite of*
110   Or some of you shall smoke° for it in Rome.   *suffer*
DEMETRIUS   By this our mother is forever shamed.
CHIRON   Rome will despise her for this foul escape.°   *escapade*
NURSE   The Emperor in his rage will doom° her death.   *decree*
CHIRON   I blush to think upon this ignomy.°   *ignominy*
115 AARON   Why, there's the privilege your beauty bears.
    Fie, treacherous hue, that will betray with blushing
    The close enacts° and counsels of thy heart.   *secret purposes*
    Here's a young lad framed of another leer.°   *complexion*
    Look how the black slave smiles upon the father,
120   As who should say, "Old lad, I am thine own."
    He is your brother, lords, sensibly° fed   *manifestly*
    Of that self° blood that first gave life to you,   *same*
    And from that womb where you imprisoned were
    He is enfranchisèd° and come to light.   *freed*
125   Nay, he is your brother by the surer side,°   *(the mother's)*
    Although my seal be stampèd in his face.
NURSE   Aaron, what shall I say unto the Empress?
DEMETRIUS   Advise thee,° Aaron, what is to be done,   *Consider*
    And we will all subscribe to° thy advice.   *follow*
130   Save thou the child, so° we may all be safe.   *provided that*

---

7. In Greek mythology, a Titan, or primeval deity, who warred against the gods of Mount Olympus.
8. Hercules (literally, descendant of Alcaeus).
9. Ruddy (as opposed to black).

1. Cheap, garish images of men.
2. Stream; alluding to the proverb "One cannot wash an Ethiop white."

AARON   Then sit we down and let us all consult.
    My son and I will have the wind of you.[3]
    Keep there. Now talk at pleasure of your safety.
DEMETRIUS [*to the* NURSE]   How many women saw this child of his?
135 AARON   Why, so, brave lords, when we join in league
    I am a lamb—but if you brave the Moor,
    The chafèd° boar, the mountain lioness,   *enraged*
    The ocean swells not so as Aaron storms.
    [*to the* NURSE] But say again: how many saw the child?
140 NURSE   Cornelia the midwife and myself,
    And no one else but the delivered Empress.
AARON   The Empress, the midwife, and yourself.
    Two may keep counsel when the third's away.
    Go to the Empress; tell her this I said—
        He kills her.
145   "Wheek, wheek!"[4] So cries a pig preparèd to the spit.
DEMETRIUS   What mean'st thou, Aaron? Wherefore didst thou this?
AARON   O Lord, sir, 'tis a deed of policy.°   *prudence*
    Shall she live to betray this guilt of ours—
    A long-tongued babbling gossip? No, lords, no.
150   And now be it known to you my full intent.
    Not far, one Muliteus, my countryman,
    His wife[5] but yesternight was brought to bed.
    His child is like to° her, fair as you are.   *resembles*
    Go pack° with him and give the mother gold,   *conspire*
155   And tell them both the circumstance of all,°   *the full details*
    And how by this their child shall be advanced
    And be receivèd for the Emperor's heir,
    And substituted in the place of mine,
    To calm this tempest whirling in the court;
160   And let the Emperor dandle him for his own.
    Hark ye, lords, you see I have given her physic,°   *medicine*
    And you must needs bestow her funeral;
    The fields are near and you are gallant grooms.°   *fellows*
    This done, see that you take no longer days,°   *waste no time*
165   But send the midwife presently to me.
    The midwife and the nurse well made away,
    Then let the ladies tattle what they please.
CHIRON   Aaron, I see thou wilt not trust the air with secrets.
DEMETRIUS   For this care of Tamora,
170   Herself and hers are highly bound to thee.
                   Exeunt [CHIRON *and* DEMETRIUS,
                     carrying the Nurse's body].
AARON   Now to the Goths, as swift as swallow flies,
    There to dispose° this treasure in mine arms   *bestow*
    And secretly to greet the Empress' friends.
    —Come on, you thick-lipped slave. I'll bear you hence,
175   For it is you that puts us to our shifts.°   *force us to scheme*
    I'll make you feed on berries and on roots,
    And feed on curds and whey, and suck the goat,
    And cabin in a cave, and bring you up
    To be a warrior and command a camp.°   *Exit.*   *an army*

---

3. Will keep downwind (as a wary hunter does when stalking game).
4. Aaron imitates her death cry.

5. *one . . . wife:* the wife of a certain Muliteus, my countryman.

4.3 (F 4.3)

Enter TITUS, *old* MARCUS, *Young Lucius [the* BOY], *and other*
gentlemen[, PUBLIUS, *Sempronius, and Caius,] with bows,*
and TITUS *bears the arrows with letters on the ends of them.*

TITUS   Come, Marcus, come; kinsmen, this is the way.
Sir boy, let me see your archery.
Look ye draw home° enough and 'tis there straight.°   fully / immediately
Terras Astraea reliquit.[1] Be you remembered,° Marcus,   Remember
5   She's gone, she's fled. Sirs, take you to your tools.
You, cousins, shall go sound the ocean
And cast your nets—
Happily° you may catch her in the sea,   Perhaps
Yet there's as little justice as at land.
10   No! Publius and Sempronius, you must do it;
'Tis you must dig with mattock and with spade
And pierce the inmost center of the earth.
Then, when you come to Pluto's region,[2]
I pray you deliver him this petition.
15   Tell him it is for justice and for aid,
And that it comes from old Andronicus,
Shaken with sorrows in ungrateful Rome.
Ah, Rome! Well, well, I made thee miserable
What time° I threw the people's suffrages°   When / votes
20   On him that thus doth tyrannize o'er me.
Go, get you gone, and pray be careful all,
And leave you not a man-of-war unsearched.
This wicked Emperor may have shipped her[3] hence,
And, kinsmen, then we may go pipe[4] for justice.
25 MARCUS   O Publius, is not this a heavy case°   sad situation
To see thy noble uncle thus distract?
PUBLIUS   Therefore, my lords, it highly us concerns
By day and night t'attend him carefully
And feed his humor° kindly as we may   humor him
30   Till time beget some careful° remedy.   solicitous; laborious
MARCUS   Kinsmen, his sorrows are past remedy.
But [   ][5]
Join with the Goths and with revengeful war
Take wreak on° Rome for this ingratitude,   Requite
35   And vengeance on the traitor Saturnine.
TITUS   Publius, how now? How now, my masters?
What, have you met with her?
PUBLIUS   No, my good lord, but Pluto sends you word.
If you will have Revenge from hell, you shall.
40   Marry, for° Justice, she is so employed,   as for
He thinks, with Jove in heaven or somewhere else,
So that perforce you must needs stay a time.[6]
TITUS   He doth me wrong to feed me with delays.
I'll dive into the burning lake[7] below

4.3 Location: Outside the Emperor's palace.
1. Astraea (goddess of justice) has abandoned the earth (Ovid, *Metamorphoses* 1.150).
2. The underworld, ruled by Pluto.
3. Astraea, whom the mad Titus imagines being smuggled out of Rome in a war boat.

4. Whistle (that is, seek in vain).
5. TEXTUAL COMMENT A line or lines may be missing here; see Digital Edition TC 6 (Quarto edited text).
6. So that by necessity ("perforce") you must wait a while.
7. Phlegethon, river of fire of the underworld.

45	And pull her out of Acheron° by the heels.	*river of the underworld*
	Marcus, we are but shrubs, no cedars we,	
	No big-boned men, framed of the Cyclops'[8] size,	
	But metal, Marcus, steel to the very back,	
	Yet wrung with wrongs more than our backs can bear.	
50	And sith° there's no justice in earth nor hell,	*since*
	We will solicit heaven and move the gods	
	To send down Justice for to wreak° our wrongs.	*revenge*
	Come, to this gear.° You are a good archer, Marcus.	*business*
	He gives them the arrows.	
	"*Ad Jovem,*" that's for you. Here, "*Ad Apollinem.*"	
55	"*Ad Martem,*"[9] that's for myself.	
	Here, boy, "To Pallas."° Here, "To Mercury."	*Minerva*
	"To Saturn,"° Caius, not to Saturnine!	*father of Jove*
	You were as good to° shoot against the wind.	*might as well*
	To it, boy! Marcus, loose° when I bid.	*(the arrows)*
60	Of° my word, I have written to effect;	*On*
	There's not a god left unsolicited.	

MARCUS   Kinsmen, shoot all your shafts into the court.
We will afflict the Emperor in his pride.

	TITUS Now, masters, draw. Oh, well said,° Lucius!	*done*
65	Good boy, in Virgo's[1] lap! Give it Pallas!	

MARCUS   My lord, I aim a mile beyond the moon.[2]
Your letter is with Jupiter by this.

TITUS   Ha, ha! Publius, Publius, what hast thou done?
See, see, thou hast shot off one of Taurus'[3] horns.

70	MARCUS This was the sport, my lord: when Publius shot,	
	The Bull, being galled,° gave Aries[4] such a knock	*angered*
	That down fell both the Ram's horns in the court,	
	And who should find them but the Empress' villain!°	*servant; scoundrel*
	She laughed and told the Moor he should not choose	
75	But give them[5] to his master for a present.	

TITUS   Why, there it goes. God give his lordship joy!

Enter the CLOWN° *with a basket and two pigeons in it.*	*(rustic)*

News! News from heaven! Marcus, the post is come.
—Sirrah, what tidings? Have you any letters?
Shall I have justice? What says Jupiter?[6]

CLOWN   Ho, the gibbet-maker?[7] He says that he hath taken
them down again, for the man must not be hanged till the
next week.

TITUS   But what says Jupiter, I ask thee?

CLOWN   Alas, sir, I know not Jubiter. I never drank with him
in all my life.

TITUS   Why, villain, art not thou the carrier?

CLOWN   Ay, of my pigeons, sir, nothing else.

TITUS   Why, didst thou not come from heaven?

---

8. One-eyed giants of Greek legend.
9. "To Jove," "To Apollo," "To Mars"; Mars was the god of war.
1. Constellation identified with Astraea after her flight from earth.
2. Marcus, humoring Titus, expects him to take the words literally; but they also mean "talk wildly, make extravagant claims."

3. Constellation of the bull.
4. Constellation of the ram.
5. The horns, as the sign of the cuckold.
6. TEXTUAL COMMENT The Quarto misspells "Jupiter" in both Titus's speech and the Clown's; see Digital Edition TC 7 (Quarto edited text) for the significance.
7. The Clown hears "Jupiter" as "gibbetter."

CLOWN From heaven? Alas, sir, I never came there. God for-
90   bid I should be so bold to press to heaven in my young days.
      Why, I am going with my pigeons to the tribunal plebs[8] to
      take up a matter of brawl betwixt my uncle and one of the
      Emperal's° men.   *(for "Emperor's")*
      {MARCUS [*to* TITUS] Why, sir, that is as fit as can be to serve for
95   your oration and let him deliver the pigeons to the Emperor
      from you.
      TITUS [*to the* CLOWN] Tell me, can you deliver an oration to
      the Emperor with a grace?
      CLOWN Nay, truly, sir, I could never say grace in all my life.}
100 TITUS Sirrah, come hither. Make no more ado
      But give your pigeons to the Emperor.
      By me thou shalt have justice at his hands.
      Hold, hold— [*He gives money.*] Meanwhile, here's money for
        thy charges.
      —Give me pen and ink.
105 —Sirrah, can you with a grace deliver up a supplication?
      CLOWN Ay, sir.
      TITUS Then here is a supplication for you. And when you
      come to him at the first approach, you must kneel, then kiss
      his foot, then deliver up your pigeons, and then look for your
110 reward. I'll be at hand, sir. See you do it bravely.°   *handsomely*
      CLOWN I warrant you, sir, let me alone.°   *leave it to me*
      TITUS Sirrah, hast thou a knife? Come, let me see it.
      —Here, Marcus, fold it in the oration.
      —For thou hast made it like an humble suppliant,
115 And when thou hast given it to the Emperor,
      Knock at my door and tell me what he says.
      CLOWN God be with you, sir; I will.   *Exit.*
      TITUS Come, Marcus, let us go. —Publius, follow me. *Exeunt.*

4.4 (F 4.4)

*Enter Emperor [SATURNINUS] and Empress [TAMORA]
and her two sons [CHIRON and DEMETRIUS, and
Attendants]. The Emperor brings the arrows in his
hand that TITUS shot at him.*

SATURNINUS Why, lords, what wrongs are these? Was ever seen
      An emperor in Rome thus overborne,°   *insolently treated*
      Troubled, confronted thus, and for the extent
      Of equal justice[1] used in such contempt?
5   My lords, you know the mightful gods,
      However these disturbers of our peace
      Buzz in the people's ears; there naught hath passed
      But even with° law against the willful sons   *according to*
      Of old Andronicus. And what an if
10   His sorrows have so overwhelmed his wits?
      Shall we be thus afflicted in his wreaks,°   *vindictive deeds*
      His fits, his frenzy, and his bitterness?
      And now he writes to heaven for his redress.
      See, here's "To Jove," and this "To Mercury,"

---

8. *Tribunus plebis*, tribune of the common people.   1. *for . . . justice*: in return for exercising impartial
4.4 Location: The Emperor's palace.   justice.

15 This "To Apollo," this "To the God of War"—
Sweet scrolls to fly about the streets of Rome!
What's this but libeling against the Senate
And blazoning° our unjustice everywhere?   proclaiming
A goodly humor,° is it not, my lords?   whim
20 As who would° say, in Rome no justice were.   As if one were to
But, if I live, his feignèd ecstasies°   pretended insanity
Shall be no shelter to these outrages,
But he and his shall know that justice lives
In Saturninus' health whom, if he sleep,
25 He'll so awake² as he in fury shall
Cut off the proud'st conspirator that lives.
TAMORA   My gracious lord, my lovely Saturnine,
Lord of my life, commander of my thoughts,
Calm thee and bear the faults of Titus' age,
30 Th'effects of sorrow for his valiant sons,
Whose loss hath pierced him deep and scarred his heart;
And rather comfort his distressèd plight
Than prosecute the meanest or the best³
For these contempts. [aside] Why, thus it shall become
35 High-witted° Tamora to gloze° with all.   Intelligent / delude
But, Titus, I have touched thee to the quick,
Thy life blood out. If Aaron now be wise,
Then is all safe; the anchor in the port.
          Enter CLOWN.
—How now, good fellow? Wouldst thou speak with us?
40 CLOWN   Yea, forsooth, an° your mistress-ship be emperial.   if
TAMORA   Empress I am, but yonder sits the Emperor.
CLOWN   'Tis he. God and Saint Stephen give you good e'en.°   good evening
I have brought you a letter and a couple of pigeons here.
          [SATURNINUS] reads the letter [and finds the knife
          within].
SATURNINUS   Go, take him away and hang him presently.°   instantly
45 CLOWN   How much money must I° have?   am I to
TAMORA   Come, sirrah, you must be hanged.
CLOWN   Hanged, by'r Lady?⁴ Then I have brought up a neck
to a fair end.   Exit [with Attendants].
SATURNINUS   Despiteful and intolerable wrongs!
50 Shall I endure this monstrous villainy?
I know from whence this same device proceeds.
May this be borne as if his traitorous sons,
That died by law for murder of our brother,
Have by my means been butchered wrongfully?
55 —Go, drag the villain hither by the hair.
Nor° age nor honor shall shape privilege.°   Neither / afford immunity
For this proud mock I'll be thy slaughterman,
Sly frantic wretch, that holp'st° to make me great   helped
In hope thyself should govern Rome and me.
          Enter a messenger, AEMILIUS.

---

2. whom . . . awake: A confusing passage. If the first
"he" (in line 24) refers to Titus, then the meaning is
"If Titus impairs Saturninus's health (tries to 'put him
to sleep'), then Saturninus will rouse himself angrily."
If the first "he" refers to Saturninus, then "Although

Saturninus seems not to respond now, he will awaken."
Some editors change the first and third (line 25) "he"s
to "she"s, making the phrase refer to justice.
3. Lowest- or highest-ranking.
4. By our Lady (the Virgin Mary).

60   SATURNINUS   What news with thee, Aemilius?
    AEMILIUS   Arm, my lords! Rome never had more cause.
    The Goths have gathered head° and with a power   *an army*
    Of high-resolvèd men bent to the spoil°   *eager to plunder*
    They hither march amain° under conduct°   *swiftly / command*
65   Of Lucius, son to old Andronicus,
    Who threats in course of this revenge to do
    As much as ever Coriolanus[5] did.
    SATURNINUS   Is warlike Lucius general of the Goths?
    These tidings nip me, and I hang the head
70   As flowers with frost or grass beat down with storms.
    Ay, now begins our sorrows to approach.
    'Tis he the common people love so much.
    Myself hath often heard them say,
    When I have walkèd like a private man,[6]
75   That Lucius' banishment was wrongfully,°   *wrongfully imposed*
    And they have wished that Lucius were their emperor.
    TAMORA   Why should you fear? Is not your city strong?
    SATURNINUS   Ay, but the citizens favor Lucius
    And will revolt from me to succor him.
80   TAMORA   King, be thy thoughts imperious like thy name.
    Is the sun dimmed, that° gnats do fly in it?   *because*
    The eagle suffers little birds to sing
    And is not careful° what they mean thereby,   *troubled*
    Knowing that with the shadow of his wings
85   He can at pleasure stint° their melody: *stop*
    Even so mayst thou the giddy° men of Rome.   *fickle*
    Then cheer thy spirit—for know thou, Emperor,
    I will enchant the old Andronicus
    With words more sweet and yet more dangerous
90   Than baits to fish or honey-stalks[7] to sheep,
    When as° the one is wounded with the bait,   *When*
    The other rotted[8] with delicious seed.
    SATURNINUS   But he will not entreat his son for us.
    TAMORA   If Tamora entreat him, then he will.
95   For I can smooth° and fill his agèd ears   *flatter*
    With golden promises that, were his heart
    Almost impregnable, his old ears deaf,
    Yet should both ear and heart obey my tongue.
    [*to* AEMILIUS] Go thou before to be our ambassador.
100 Say that the Emperor requests a parley
    Of warlike Lucius, and appoint the meeting
    Even at his father's house, the old Andronicus.
    SATURNINUS   Aemilius, do this message honorably,
    And if he stand in hostage[9] for his safety,
105 Bid him demand what pledge will please him best.
    AEMILIUS   Your bidding shall I do effectually.   *Exit.*
    TAMORA   Now will I to that old Andronicus
    And temper° him with all the art I have   *work on*
    To pluck proud Lucius from the warlike Goths.

---

5. Early Roman warrior who, after he was banished,
joined his former enemies and led an army against
Rome; the subject of Shakespeare's *Coriolanus*.
6. Disguised as an ordinary man.

7. Clover (large quantities make sheep ill).
8. Afflicted by the rot, a liver disease in sheep.
9. If he demand a hostage (to be killed if Titus is
threatened).

110 And now, sweet Emperor, be blithe again,
And bury all thy fear in my devices.
SATURNINUS Then go successantly° and plead to him. *Exeunt.*   right away

5.1 (F 5.1)

Enter LUCIUS *with an army of* GOTHS *with drums*°   drummers
and Soldiers.

LUCIUS Approvèd° warriors and my faithful friends,   Proven
I have received letters from great Rome
Which signifies what hate they bear their emperor
And how desirous of our sight they are.
5 Therefore, great lords, be, as your titles witness,
Imperious and impatient of your wrongs,
And wherein Rome hath done you any scathe°   harm
Let him make treble satisfaction.
FIRST GOTH Brave slip° sprung from the great Andronicus,   offspring
10 Whose name was once our terror, now our comfort,
Whose high exploits and honorable deeds
Ingrateful Rome requites with foul contempt,
Be bold° in us. We'll follow where thou lead'st,   confident
Like stinging bees in hottest summer's day
15 Led by their master[1] to the flowered fields,
And be avenged on cursèd Tamora.
ALL GOTHS And, as he saith, so say we all with him.
LUCIUS I humbly thank him, and I thank you all.
But who comes here, led by a lusty Goth?
Enter [SECOND] GOTH, *leading of* AARON *with his child*
in his arms.
20 SECOND GOTH Renownèd Lucius, from our troops I strayed
To gaze upon a ruinous monastery,
And as I earnestly did fix mine eye
Upon the wasted° building, suddenly   ruined
I heard a child cry underneath a wall.
25 I made unto the noise, when soon I heard
The crying babe controlled° with this discourse: calmed
"Peace, tawny slave,[2] half me and half thy dam.
Did not thy hue bewray° whose brat thou art,   show
Had nature lent thee but thy mother's look,
30 Villain, thou mightst have been an emperor.
But where the bull and cow are both milk-white,
They never do beget a coal-black calf.
Peace, villain, peace!"—even thus he rates° the babe—   scolds
"For I must bear thee to a trusty Goth
35 Who, when he knows thou art the Empress' babe,
Will hold thee dearly for thy mother's sake."
With this, my weapon drawn, I rushed upon him,
Surprised him suddenly, and brought him hither
To use as you think needful of° the man.   appropriate to
40 LUCIUS O worthy Goth, this is the incarnate devil
That robbed Andronicus of his good hand.
This is the pearl that pleased your Empress' eye,
And here's the base fruit of her burning lust.

5.1 Location: Outside Rome.   2. Used affectionately, like "brat" and "villain" below.
1. The queen bee was thought to be male.

[*to* AARON] Say, wall-eyed slave, whither wouldst thou convey
45   This growing image of thy fiend-like face?
Why dost not speak? What, deaf? Not a word?
A halter, soldiers! Hang him on this tree,
And by his side his fruit of bastardy.
AARON   Touch not the boy; he is of royal blood.
50 LUCIUS   Too like the sire for ever being° good.   *ever to be*
First, hang the child that he may see it sprawl:°   *twitch convulsively*
A sight to vex the father's soul withal.
Get me a ladder.
            [GOTHS *bring a ladder and force* AARON *to climb it.*]
AARON   Lucius, save the child
And bear it from me to the Empress.
55   If thou do this, I'll show thee wondrous things
That highly may advantage thee to hear.
If thou wilt not, befall what may befall,
I'll speak no more but "Vengeance rot you all!"
LUCIUS   Say on, an if it please me which thou speakest,
60   Thy child shall live and I will see it nourished.
AARON   An if it please thee? Why, assure thee, Lucius,
'Twill vex thy soul to hear what I shall speak.
For I must talk of murders, rapes, and massacres,
Acts of black night, abominable deeds,
65   Complots° of mischief, treason, villainies,   *Conspiracies*
Ruthful° to hear yet piteously[3] performed.   *Lamentable*
And this shall all be buried in my death
Unless thou swear to me my child shall live.
LUCIUS   Tell on thy mind. I say thy child shall live.
70 AARON   Swear that he shall and then I will begin.
LUCIUS   Who should I swear by? Thou believest no god.
That granted, how canst thou believe an oath?
AARON   What if I do not?—As indeed I do not—
Yet for I know thou art religious
75   And hast a thing within thee callèd conscience,
With twenty popish tricks and ceremonies
Which I have seen thee careful to observe,
Therefore I urge° thy oath; for that I know   *insist on*
An idiot holds his bauble° for a god,   *jester's stick*
80   And keeps the oath which by that god he swears,
To that I'll urge him. Therefore thou shalt vow
By that same god, what god so e'er it be
That thou adorest and hast in reverence,
To save my boy, to nourish and bring him up,
85   Or else I will discover naught to thee.
LUCIUS   Even by my god I swear to thee I will.
AARON   First know thou I begot him on the Empress.
LUCIUS   Oh, most insatiate and luxurious° woman!   *lascivious*
AARON   Tut, Lucius, this was but a deed of charity
90   To° that which thou shalt hear of me anon.   *Compared to*
'Twas her two sons that murdered Bassianus;
They cut thy sister's tongue, and ravished her,
And cut her hands, and trimmed her as thou sawest.
LUCIUS   O detestable villain! Call'st thou that "trimming"?

---

3. In a way that would excite pity.

95   AARON   Why, she was washed, and cut, and trimmed,
      And 'twas trim° sport for them which had the doing of it.   *fine*
    LUCIUS   Oh, barbarous beastly villains, like thyself!
    AARON   Indeed, I was their tutor to instruct them.
      That codding° spirit had they from their mother,   *lustful*
100   As sure a card as ever won the set.°   *game*
      That bloody mind I think they learned of me,
      As true a dog as ever fought at head.[4]
      Well, let my deeds be witness of my worth.
      I trained° thy brethren to that guileful hole   *lured*
105   Where the dead corpse of Bassianus lay.
      I wrote the letter that thy father found,
      And hid the gold within that letter mentioned,
      Confederate with the Queen and her two sons.
      And what not done that thou hast cause to rue
110   Wherein I had no stroke of mischief in it?
      I played the cheater[5] for thy father's hand,
      And when I had it drew myself apart°   *went off alone*
      And almost broke my heart° with extreme laughter;   *died*
      I pried me° through the crevice of a wall   *I peered*
115   When for his hand he had his two sons' heads,
      Beheld his tears, and laughed so heartily
      That both mine eyes were rainy like to his;
      And when I told the Empress of this sport,
      She swoonèd almost at my pleasing tale
120   And for my tidings gave me twenty kisses.
    FIRST GOTH   What, canst thou say all this and never blush?
    AARON   Ay, like a black dog, as the saying is.
    LUCIUS   Art thou not sorry for these heinous deeds?
    AARON   Ay, that I had not done a thousand more.
125   Even now I curse the day—and yet I think
      Few come within the compass of my curse—
      Wherein I did not some notorious ill,
      As kill a man or else devise his death,
      Ravish a maid or plot the way to do it,
130   Accuse some innocent and forswear myself,
      Set deadly enmity between two friends,
      Make poor men's cattle break their necks,
      Set fire on barns and haystacks in the night,
      And bid the owners quench them with their tears.
135   Oft have I digged up dead men from their graves
      And set them upright at their dear friends' door,
      Even when their sorrows almost was forgot,
      And on their skins, as on the bark of trees,
      Have with my knife carved in Roman letters,
140   "Let not your sorrow die though I am dead."
      But I have done a thousand dreadful things
      As willingly as one would kill a fly,
      And nothing grieves me heartily indeed
      But that I cannot do ten thousand more.
145   LUCIUS   Bring down the devil, for he must not die
      So sweet a death as hanging presently.°   *immediately*

---

4. As ever went for the bull's head (in the sport of bullbaiting).

5. Swindler; escheator, an officer appointed to look after property forfeited to the crown.

[AARON *is brought down from the ladder.*]

AARON   If there be devils, would I were a devil,
    To live and burn in everlasting fire,
    So I might have your company in hell,
150   But to torment you with my bitter tongue.

LUCIUS   Sirs, stop his mouth and let him speak no more.
    [AARON *is gagged.*]
    Enter AEMILIUS.

THIRD GOTH   My lord, there is a messenger from Rome
    Desires to be admitted to your presence.

LUCIUS   Let him come near.
155   —Welcome, Aemilius; what's the news from Rome?

AEMILIUS   Lord Lucius and you princes of the Goths,
    The Roman Emperor greets you all by me.
    And, for he understands you are in arms,
    He craves a parley at your father's house,
160   Willing you to demand your hostages,
    And they shall be immediately delivered.

FIRST GOTH   What says our general?

LUCIUS   Aemilius, let the Emperor give his pledges
    Unto my father and my uncle Marcus,
165   And we will come. —March away.   [*Flourish.*] [*Exeunt.*]

5.2 (F 5.2)

Enter TAMORA *and her two sons* [CHIRON *and*
DEMETRIUS], *disguised.*

TAMORA   Thus in this strange and sad habiliment°   *somber costume*
    I will encounter with Andronicus
    And say I am Revenge sent from below,
    To join with him and right his heinous wrongs.
5   Knock at his study where they say he keeps°   *stays*
    To ruminate strange plots of dire revenge.
    Tell him Revenge is come to join with him
    And work confusion on his enemies.
    They knock, and TITUS[, *aloft,*] *opens his study door.*

TITUS   Who doth molest my contemplation?
10   Is it your trick to make me ope the door,
    That so my sad decrees° may fly away   *solemn resolutions*
    And all my study be to no effect?
    You are deceived. For what I mean to do
    See here in bloody lines I have set down,
15   And what is written shall be executed.

TAMORA   Titus, I am come to talk with thee.

TITUS   No, not a word. How can I grace my talk,
    Wanting° a hand to give that accord?   *Lacking*
    Thou hast the odds° of me; therefore no more.   *advantage*

20 TAMORA   If thou didst know me, thou wouldst talk with me.

TITUS   I am not mad. I know thee well enough.
    Witness this wretched stump, witness these crimson lines,
    Witness these trenches° made by grief and care,   *wrinkles*
    Witness the tiring day and heavy night,
25   Witness all sorrow that I know thee well
    For our proud empress, mighty Tamora.

5.2 Location: Titus's courtyard.

Is not thy coming for my other hand?
TAMORA   Know thou, sad man, I am not Tamora.
        She is thy enemy and I thy friend.
30   I am Revenge, sent from th'infernal kingdom
        To ease the gnawing vulture[1] of thy mind
        By working wreakful° vengeance on thy foes.   *vindictive*
        Come down and welcome me to this world's light.
        Confer with me of murder and of death.
35   There's not a hollow cave or lurking place,
        No vast obscurity° or misty vale   *dark wasteland*
        Where bloody murder or detested rape
        Can couch° for fear, but I will find them out,   *hide*
        And in their ears tell them my dreadful name,
40   Revenge, which makes the foul offender quake.
TITUS   Art thou Revenge? And art thou sent to me
        To be a torment to mine enemies?
TAMORA   I am. Therefore come down and welcome me.
TITUS   Do me some service ere I come to thee.
45   Lo, by thy side where Rape and Murder stands.
        Now give some surance° that thou art Revenge: *proof*
        Stab them or tear them on thy chariot wheels,
        And then I'll come and be thy wagoner,
        And whirl along with thee about the globes;
50   Provide thee two proper palfreys,° black as jet,   *handsome horses*
        To hale° thy vengeful wagon swift away   *draw*
        And find out murder in their guilty caves;
        And when thy car is loaden with their heads,
        I will dismount and by thy wagon wheel
55   Trot like a servile footman all day long,
        Even from Hyperion's° rising in the East   *the sun god*
        Until his very downfall in the sea;
        And day by day I'll do this heavy task,
        So° thou destroy Rapine and Murder there.   *Provided that*
60 TAMORA   These are my ministers and come with me.
TITUS   Are they thy ministers? What are they called?
TAMORA   Rape and Murder, therefore callèd so
        'Cause they take vengeance of such kind of men.
TITUS   Good Lord, how like the Empress' sons they are,
65   And you the Empress! But we worldly° men   *mortal*
        Have miserable, mad, mistaking eyes.
        O sweet Revenge, now do I come to thee,
        And if one arm's embracement will content thee,
        I will embrace thee in it by and by.   [*Exit aloft.*]
70 TAMORA [*to* CHIRON *and* DEMETRIUS]   This closing° with him   *agreeing*
            fits his lunacy.
        Whate'er I forge° to feed his brain-sick humors   *invent*
        Do you uphold and maintain in your speeches.
        For now he firmly takes me for Revenge,
        And being credulous in this mad thought,
75   I'll make him send for Lucius, his son.
        And whilst I at a banquet hold him sure,
        I'll find some cunning practice out of hand[2]

1. Alluding to the story of Prometheus; see note to   2. I'll find some scheme on the spur of the moment.
2.1.17.

To scatter and disperse the giddy Goths,
Or at the least make them his enemies.
[*Enter* TITUS *below.*]
80 See, here he comes, and I must ply my theme.°   *keep up the act*
TITUS   Long have I been forlorn, and all for thee.
Welcome, dread Fury, to my woeful house;
Rapine and Murder, you are welcome too.
How like the Empress and her sons you are!
85 Well are you fitted, had you but a Moor;
Could not all hell afford you such a devil?
For well I wot° the Empress never wags°   *know / stirs*
But in her company there is a Moor,
And would you represent our queen aright
90 It were convenient° you had such a devil.   *fitting*
But welcome as you are. What shall we do?
TAMORA   What wouldst thou have us do, Andronicus?
DEMETRIUS   Show me a murderer; I'll deal with him.
CHIRON   Show me a villain that hath done a rape,
95 And I am sent to be revenged on him.
TAMORA   Show me a thousand that hath done thee wrong,
And I will be revenged on them all.
TITUS [*to* DEMETRIUS]   Look round about the wicked streets of
     Rome,
And when thou find'st a man that's like thyself,
100 Good Murder, stab him; he's a murderer.
[*to* CHIRON] Go thou with him, and when it is thy hap°   *chance*
To find another that is like to thee,
Good Rapine, stab him; he is a ravisher.
[*to* TAMORA] Go thou with them, and in the Emperor's court
105 There is a queen attended by a Moor—
Well shalt thou know her by thine own proportion,
For up and down° she doth resemble thee.   *top to toe*
I pray thee, do on them some violent death;
They have been violent to me and mine.
110 TAMORA   Well hast thou lessoned us; this shall we do.
But would it please thee, good Andronicus,
To send for Lucius, thy thrice-valiant son,
Who leads toward Rome a band of warlike Goths,
And bid him come and banquet at thy house?
115 When he is here, even at thy solemn° feast,   *ceremonious*
I will bring in the Empress and her sons,
The Emperor himself, and all thy foes,
And at thy mercy shall they stoop and kneel,
And on them shalt thou ease thy angry heart.
120 What says Andronicus to this device?
TITUS   —Marcus, my brother, 'tis sad Titus calls!
     Enter MARCUS.
Go, gentle Marcus, to thy nephew Lucius.
Thou shalt inquire him out among the Goths.
Bid him repair° to me and bring with him   *come*
125 Some of the chiefest princes of the Goths.
Bid him encamp his soldiers where they are.
Tell him the Emperor and the Empress too
Feast at my house and he shall feast with them.
This do thou for my love and so let him,

130 As he regards his agèd father's life.
    MARCUS This will I do and soon return again.   [*Exit.*]
    TAMORA Now will I hence about thy business
    And take my ministers along with me.
    TITUS Nay, nay, let Rape and Murder stay with me,
135 Or else I'll call my brother back again
    And cleave to no revenge but Lucius.[3]
    TAMORA [*aside to* CHIRON *and* DEMETRUS] What say you, boys?
      Will you abide with him
    Whiles I go tell my lord, the Emperor,
    How I have governed our determined jest?[4]
140 Yield to his humor, smooth, and speak him fair,°   *flatter and humor him*
    And tarry with him till I turn° again.   *return*
    TITUS [*aside*] I knew them all, though they supposed me mad,
    And will o'erreach them in their own devices—
    A pair of cursèd hellhounds and their dam.
145 DEMETRIUS Madam, depart at pleasure. Leave us here.
    TAMORA Farewell, Andronicus. Revenge now goes
    To lay a complot to betray thy foes.
    TITUS I know thou dost—and, sweet Revenge, farewell.
              [*Exit* TAMORA.]
    CHIRON Tell us, old man, how shall we be employed?
150 TITUS Tut, I have work enough for you to do.
    Publius, come hither! Caius and Valentine!
      [*Enter* PUBLIUS, *Valentine, and Caius.*]
    PUBLIUS What is your will?
    TITUS   Know you these two?
    PUBLIUS The Empress' sons I take them:° Chiron, Demetrius.   *take them to be*
    TITUS Fie, Publius, fie! Thou art too much deceived.
155 The one is Murder, and Rape is the other's name—
    And therefore bind them, gentle Publius;
    Caius and Valentine, lay hands on them.
    Oft have you heard me wish for such an hour,
    And now I find it. Therefore bind them sure,
160 And stop their mouths if they begin to cry.   [*Exit.*]
    CHIRON Villains, forbear! We are the Empress' sons.
    PUBLIUS And therefore do we what we are commanded.
    —Stop close their mouths. Let them not speak a word.
    Is he sure° bound? Look that you bind them fast.   *securely*
      Enter TITUS *Andronicus with a knife and* LAVINIA *with*
      a basin.
165 TITUS Come, come, Lavinia. Look: thy foes are bound.
    Sirs, stop their mouths. Let them not speak to me,
    But let them hear what fearful words I utter.
    O villains, Chiron and Demetrius!
    Here stands the spring whom you have stained with mud,
170 This goodly summer with your winter mixed.
    You killed her husband, and for that vile fault
    Two of her brothers were condemned to death,
    My hand cut off and made a merry jest,
    Both her sweet hands, her tongue, and that more dear
175 Than hands or tongue—her spotless chastity—

---

3. That is, depend on Lucius's invading army for   4. How have I managed the jest we planned.
revenge.

Inhuman traitors, you constrained and forced.
What would you say if I should let you speak?
Villains, for shame, you could not beg for grace.°   mercy
Hark, wretches, how I mean to martyr you.
180   This one hand yet is left to cut your throats,
Whiles that Lavinia 'tween her stumps doth hold
The basin that receives your guilty blood.
You know your mother means to feast with me,
And calls herself Revenge, and thinks me mad.
185   Hark, villains, I will grind your bones to dust,
And with your blood and it I'll make a paste,°   dough
And of the paste a coffin° I will rear,   piecrust (with wordplay)
And make two pasties of your shameful heads,
And bid that strumpet, your unhallowed dam,
190   Like to the earth swallow her own increase.°   progeny
This is the feast that I have bid her to,
And this the banquet she shall surfeit on.
For worse than Philomel you used my daughter,
And worse than Procne I will be revenged.[5]
195   And now prepare your throats. Lavinia, come,
Receive the blood, and when that they are dead,
Let me go grind their bones to powder small,
And with this hateful liquor temper° it,   mix
And in that paste let their vile heads be baked.
200   Come, come; be everyone officious°   busy
To make this banquet, which I wish may prove
More stern and bloody than the Centaurs' feast.[6]
He cuts their throats.
So, now bring them in, for I'll play the cook,
And see them ready against° their mother comes.   by the time
Exeunt [with the bodies].

5.3 (F 5.3)

Enter LUCIUS, MARCUS, *and the* GOTHS[, *with* AARON,
prisoner, and an Attendant with his child].
LUCIUS   Uncle Marcus, since 'tis my father's mind
That I repair to Rome, I am content.
FIRST GOTH   And ours with thine,[1] befall what fortune will.
LUCIUS   Good uncle, take you in this barbarous Moor,
5   This ravenous tiger, this accursèd devil.
Let him receive no sustenance; fetter him
Till he be brought unto the Empress' face
For testimony of her foul proceedings.
And see the ambush° of our friends be strong.   troops lying in wait
10   I fear the Emperor means no good to us.
AARON   Some devil whisper curses in my ear,
And prompt me that my tongue may utter forth
The venomous malice of my swelling heart.
LUCIUS   Away, inhuman dog, unhallowed slave!
15   —Sirs, help our uncle to convey him in.

5. Philomela's sister, Procne, revenged herself on her rapist husband, Tereus, by killing their son Itys and serving his flesh in a meal (see Introduction).
6. In Greek legend, the wedding feast of Hippodamia ended in a bloody battle when the Centaurs,

beings that were half human and half horse, tried to carry off the bride and other women (see Ovid, *Metamorphoses* 12).
5.3 Location: Titus's courtyard.
1. Our minds accord with yours.

[*Exeunt* GOTHS *with* AARON *and the Attendant with his child.*]
      Sound trumpets.
The trumpets show the Emperor is at hand.
      Enter Emperor [SATURNINUS] *and Empress* [TAMORA],
      with [AEMILIUS, ROMAN LORD,] TRIBUNES,
      [*Attendants,*] *and others.*

SATURNINUS What, hath the firmament more suns than one?
LUCIUS What boots° it thee to call thyself a sun?   *avails*
MARCUS Rome's emperor and nephew, break the parley:°   *stop the dispute*
20   These quarrels must be quietly debated.
    The feast is ready which the careful° Titus   *assiduous; troubled*
    Hath ordained to an honorable end,
    For peace, for love, for league, and good to Rome.
    Please you, therefore, draw nigh and take your places.
25 SATURNINUS Marcus, we will.
      Trumpets sounding. Enter TITUS [*dressed*] *like a cook,*
      placing the dishes, and LAVINIA *with a veil over her*
      face[, *and the* BOY].
TITUS Welcome, my lord; welcome, dread Queen;
    Welcome, ye warlike Goths; welcome, Lucius;
    And welcome, all. Although the cheer° be poor,   *refreshments*
    'Twill fill your stomachs. Please you, eat of it.
30 SATURNINUS Why art thou thus attired, Andronicus?
TITUS Because I would be sure to have all well
    To entertain your highness and your empress.
TAMORA We are beholden to you, good Andronicus.
TITUS An if your highness knew my heart, you were:
35   My lord the Emperor, resolve me this:
    Was it well done of rash Virginius[2]
    To slay his daughter with his own right hand
    Because she was enforced, stained, and deflowered?
SATURNINUS It was, Andronicus.
TITUS   Your reason, mighty lord?
40 SATURNINUS Because the girl should not survive her shame
    And by her presence still renew his sorrows.
TITUS A reason mighty, strong, and effectual.
    A pattern, precedent, and lively warrant
    For me, most wretched, to perform the like.
45   —Die, die, Lavinia, and thy shame with thee,
    And with thy shame thy father's sorrow die!
      [*He kills her.*]
SATURNINUS What hast thou done? Unnatural and unkind!
TITUS Killed her for whom my tears have made me blind.
    I am as woeful as Virginius was,
50   And have a thousand times more cause than he
    To do this outrage, and it now is done.
SATURNINUS What, was she ravished? Tell, who did the deed?
TITUS Will't please you eat? Will't please your highness feed?
TAMORA Why hast thou slain thine only daughter thus?
55 TITUS Not I; 'twas Chiron and Demetrius:
    They ravished her and cut away her tongue,
    And they, 'twas they, that did her all this wrong.
SATURNINUS Go, fetch them hither to us presently.°   *at once*

---

2. A Roman soldier who in some versions of the story killed his daughter to prevent her rape; in other versions, he killed her after the rape as Titus describes.

TITUS   Why, there they are, both bakèd in this pie,
60   Whereof their mother daintily hath fed,
    Eating the flesh that she herself hath bred.
    'Tis true, 'tis true; witness my knife's sharp point.
      He stabs the Empress [TAMORA].
SATURNINUS   Die, frantic° wretch, for this accursèd deed.   *deranged*
    [SATURNINUS *kills* TITUS.]
LUCIUS   Can the son's eye behold his father bleed?
65   There's meed for meed,° death for a deadly deed.   *measure for measure*
    [LUCIUS *kills* SATURNINUS. *Enter* GOTHS. LUCIUS,
      MARCUS, *and others go aloft.*]
MARCUS   You sad-faced men, people and sons of Rome,
    By uproars severed as a flight of fowl
    Scattered by winds and high tempestuous gusts,
    Oh, let me teach you how to knit again
70   This scattered corn° into one mutual° sheaf,   *grain / unified*
    These broken limbs again into one body.
ROMAN LORD   Let Rome herself be bane° unto herself,[3]   *destroyer*
    And she whom mighty kingdoms curtsy to,
    Like a forlorn and desperate castaway,
75   Do shameful execution on herself.
    But if my frosty signs and chaps° of age,   *white hair and wrinkles*
    Grave witnesses of true experience,
    Cannot induce you to attend my words,
    [*to* LUCIUS] Speak, Rome's dear friend, as erst° our ancestor,[4]   *once*
80   When with his solemn tongue he did discourse
    To lovesick Dido's sad-attending° ear   *seriously listening*
    The story of that baleful burning night
    When subtle Greeks surprised King Priam's Troy.
    Tell us what Sinon[5] hath bewitched our ears,
85   Or who hath brought the fatal engine[6] in
    That gives our Troy, our Rome, the civil° wound.   *incurred in civil war*
    My heart is not compact° of flint nor steel,   *composed*
    Nor can I utter all our bitter grief,
    But floods of tears will drown my oratory
90   And break° my utterance even in the time   *interrupt*
    When it should move ye to attend me most,
    And force you to commiseration.
    Here's Rome's young captain. Let him tell the tale,
    While I stand by and weep to hear him speak.
95 LUCIUS   Then, gracious auditory,° be it known to you   *audience*
    That Chiron and the damned Demetrius
    Were they that murderèd our emperor's brother,
    And they it were that ravishèd our sister.
    For their fell° faults our brothers were beheaded,   *cruel*
100   Our father's tears despised and basely cozened°   *cheated*
    Of that true hand that fought Rome's quarrel out°   *to the finish*
    And sent her enemies unto the grave;
    Lastly myself, unkindly° banishèd,   *unnaturally*
    The gates shut on me and turned, weeping, out

---

3. TEXTUAL COMMENT Q assigns this speech to an unnamed "*Romane Lord*"; F assigns it to a "*Goth*," although some phrases (e.g., "our Rome") suggest a Roman speaker. See Digital Edition TC 8 (Quarto edited text) for a fuller discussion of the editorial prob-

lem and the way modern editions have resolved it.
4. Aeneas, Trojan ancestor of the Roman people.
5. The Greek who persuaded the Trojans to admit the wooden horse full of soldiers.
6. Instrument (the wooden horse).

105 To beg relief among Rome's enemies,
Who drowned their enmity in my true tears
And oped their arms to embrace me as a friend.
I am the turned-forth, be it known to you,
That have preserved her° welfare in my blood,   (Rome's)
110 And from her bosom took the enemy's point,
Sheathing the steel in my advent'rous body.
Alas, you know, I am no vaunter,° I.   boaster
My scars can witness, dumb although they are,
That my report is just and full of truth.
115 But soft, methinks I do digress too much,
Citing my worthless praise. Oh, pardon me,
For when no friends are by, men praise themselves.

MARCUS   Now is my turn to speak. Behold the child.
        [*He points to Aaron's son.*]
Of this was Tamora deliverèd,
120 The issue of an irreligious Moor,
Chief architect and plotter of these woes.
The villain is alive in Titus' house,
And as he is to witness, this is true.
Now judge what cause had Titus to revenge
125 These wrongs, unspeakable past patience,°   endurance
Or more than any living man could bear.
Now have you heard the truth, what say you, Romans?
Have we done aught amiss? Show us wherein,
And from the place where you behold us pleading,
130 The poor remainder of Andronici
Will hand in hand all headlong hurl ourselves,[7]
And on the ragged stones beat forth our souls
And make a mutual closure° of our house.°   end / family
Speak, Romans, speak, and if you say we shall,
135 Lo, hand in hand, Lucius and I will fall.

AEMILIUS   Come, come, thou reverend man of Rome,
And bring our emperor gently in thy hand—
Lucius, our emperor, for well I know
The common voice do cry it shall be so.

140 MARCUS   Lucius, all hail! Rome's royal emperor!
        [*to Attendants*] Go, go into old Titus' sorrowful house
And hither hale that misbelieving Moor
To be adjudged some direful slaught'ring death
As punishment for his most wicked life.
                                        [*Exeunt Attendants.*]
        [LUCIUS *and* MARCUS *descend.*]
145 —Lucius, all hail, Rome's gracious governor!

LUCIUS   Thanks, gentle Romans. May I govern so
To heal Rome's harms and wipe away her woe.
But, gentle people, give me aim° awhile,   encourage me
For nature puts me to° a heavy task.   sets me
150 Stand all aloof, but, uncle, draw you near
To shed obsequious° tears upon this trunk.   mournful
Oh, take this warm kiss on thy pale cold lips,
        [*He kisses* TITUS.]

---

7. Traditionally, traitors were thrown from the Tarpeian Rock on the Capitoline Hill.

These sorrowful drops upon thy blood-stained face,
The last true duties of thy noble son.
155 MARCUS [*kissing* TITUS]   Tear for tear, and loving kiss for kiss,
Thy brother Marcus tenders on thy lips.
Oh, were the sum of these that I should pay
Countless and infinite, yet would I pay them.
LUCIUS [*to* BOY]   Come hither, boy; come, come, and learn of us
160 To melt in showers. Thy grandsire loved thee well.
Many a time he danced thee on his knee,
Sung thee asleep, his loving breast thy pillow.
Many a story hath he told to thee,[8]
And bid thee bear his pretty tales in mind,
165 And talk of them when he was dead and gone.
MARCUS   How many thousand times hath these poor lips,
When they were living, warmed themselves on thine!
Oh, now, sweet boy, give them their latest° kiss.   *last*
Bid him farewell. Commit him to the grave.
170 Do them° that kindness and take leave of them.   *(his lips)*
BOY   O grandsire, grandsire! Ev'n with all my heart
Would I were dead so° you did live again.   *provided that*
O Lord, I cannot speak to him for weeping.
My tears will choke me if I ope my mouth.
[*Enter Attendants with* AARON.]
175 ROMAN   You sad Andronici, have done with woes.
Give sentence on this execrable wretch
That hath been breeder of these dire events.
LUCIUS   Set him breast-deep in earth and famish him.
There let him stand, and rave, and cry for food.
180 If any one relieves or pities him,
For the offense he dies. This is our doom.°   *judgment*
Some stay to see him fastened in the earth.
AARON   Ah, why should wrath be mute and fury dumb?
I am no baby, I, that with base prayers
185 I should repent the evils I have done.
Ten thousand worse than ever yet I did
Would I perform if I might have my will.
If one good deed in all my life I did,
I do repent it from my very soul.
190 LUCIUS   Some loving friends convey the Emperor hence,
And give him burial in his father's grave.°   *ancestral tomb*
My father and Lavinia shall forthwith
Be closèd in our household's monument.
As for that ravenous tiger, Tamora,
195 No funeral rite, nor man in mourning weed,°   *garments*
No mournful bell shall ring her burial,
But throw her forth to beasts and birds to prey:°   *prey upon*
Her life was beastly and devoid of pity,
And, being dead, let birds on her take pity.[9]   *Exeunt.*

---

8. TEXTUAL COMMENT Variants between the Q and F texts at this point are likely due to a compositor (print house employee) of Q2 making up lines missing from his damaged copy of Q1. These lines were later incorporated into the Q3 and F texts. See Digital Edition TC 9 (Quarto edited text) for a fuller discussion.

9. TEXTUAL COMMENT The final lines of Q1 and F are different, probably because (as with lines 163–68) a compositor of Q2, likely working from a damaged copy of Q1, needed to "fill in the blanks": his changes were then reproduced in later texts of the play. See Digital Edition TC 10 (Quarto edited text).

Richard the Third

In 2013, the announcement that a skeleton unearthed six feet under a parking lot in the English Midlands city of Leicester was that of the fifteenth-century king Richard III excited a startling rush of media attention. One hundred and forty registered journalists and camera crews from seven countries crowded into a press conference at the University of Leicester and then were solemnly ushered into a room. There, laid out decorously on a black velvet cloth draped over four library tables pushed together, were the bones of the last Yorkist king, who reigned from 1483 until his death two years later at the Battle of Bosworth Field.

That battle ended the chaotic, violent dynastic struggle, known as the Wars of the Roses, between two noble houses, the Lancastrians and the Yorkists, and ushered in the first of the Tudors, Henry VII. The new king, who had a lineal claim to the throne far weaker than the man he had just murdered, did what victors in that situation always did: he encouraged his principal allies, such as John Morton (his Archbishop of Canterbury and Lord Chancellor), to besmirch the reputation of the vanquished.

Henry got a particularly impressive version of what he sought in *The History of King Richard III*, which was penned by an ambitious young man who had served as a page in Morton's household. The *History* weaves together every dark rumor about Richard's brief life (he died at age thirty-two) into a brilliant narrative that paints a portrait of a bold, gifted, but ineradicably evil man, a man whose evil was marked in his very body: "little of stature, ill-featured of limbs, crook-backed, his left shoulder much higher than his right, hard favored of visage." Even his birth had been a difficult one, and it was rumored as an ominous sign—though here the author of the *History* voices some reservation—that the newborn had teeth. In any case, he grew, the narrative reports, into a particularly nasty piece of work: arrogant beneath a fraudulent show of humility, friendly to those he inwardly hated, and prone "to kiss whom he thought to kill." His rise to power, achieved through such ruthless means as the murder of two young princes, only made him paranoid. According to the *History*, Richard ventured out with his eyes darting nervously in all directions and his hand always on his dagger, as if he never felt safe, while his nights were still worse: he "lay long waking and musing, sore wearied with care and watch, rather slumbered than slept, troubled with fearful dreams." Then he would "suddenly sometimes start up, leap out of his bed, and run about the chamber, so was his restless heart continually tossed and tumbled with the tedious impression and stormy remembrance of his abominable deeds." Such was the price of achieving the throne through villainy.

The author of this hatchet job was Thomas More, who would go on to write *Utopia* and to lose his head at the hands of the second Tudor monarch, Henry VIII. More's *History of King Richard III* was incorporated into the major sixteenth-century chronicles—most notably, Edward Hall in *The Union of the Noble and Illustrious Families of Lancaster and York* (1548) and Raphael Holinshed in *The Chronicles of England, Scotland, and Ireland* (1577, revised in 1587)—and thus in effect became the authorized depiction of the loser of the Battle of Bosworth Field. At the end of that battle, the chronicles report, the corpse of the vanquished ruler—the last English king to die in combat—was not given a royal funeral but stripped naked, strapped to a horse, and ignominiously hauled back to Leicester for a humiliatingly modest interment. The process of denigration had begun.

The bones that unexpectedly surfaced from beneath the parking lot bear eloquent witness to this grim end. The base of the skull was shattered by a violent blow, probably from a halberd (see the illustration on p. 266), that particularly gruesome two-handed pole weapon favored by late medieval soldiers. So the king was presumably killed from behind, and his bones bear marks of what are called "humiliation injuries," that is, stab wounds through the buttocks and elsewhere that enemies must have inflicted on his corpse in a frenzy of loathing. But the most interesting piece of evidence brought to light after more than five hundred years is the spine, curved in a startling S. The physical deformation seems vividly to conjure up the figure that actually accounted for the worldwide press coverage. That figure is not the relatively minor historical Richard III, but rather the unforgettable monster that Shakespeare created and unleashed onto the London stage.

Taking his cues from More's slanders, Shakespeare depicts a villain—"That bottled spider, that foul bunch-backed toad" (4.4.76)*—who was loathsome from birth. His own mother, the Duchess of York, recalls the earliest moments of her wicked son's miserable life—"A grievous burden was thy birth to me; / Tetchy and wayward was thy infancy" (4.4.160–61)—and she complains as well about her son's slow rate of growth: "He was the wretched'st thing when he was young, / So long a-growing and so leisurely" (2.4.18–19). Shakespeare even rehearses More's rumor about the neonatal teeth. "[T]hey say my uncle grew so fast," says the little Duke of York (whom Richard will contrive to murder, along with his brother), "[t]hat he could gnaw a crust at two hours old." "[W]ho told thee so?" asks the Duchess.

> YORK Grannam, his nurse.
> DUCHESS OF YORK His nurse? Why, she was dead ere thou wert born.
> YORK If 'twere not she, I cannot tell who told me.
>
> (2.4.27–34)

If, like More, Shakespeare airs some skepticism about the dental prodigy, he spares Richard little else in the way of both deformity and villainy: his king is a twisted, devious, ruthless murderer. And the playwright does something that More does not do, something that links the skeleton's spine to the deliberate, self-conscious choice of a life of crime. In More's *History*, Richard's physical deformity is an uncanny sign of his viciousness, a kind of preternatural portent or emblem. In Shakespeare it is the root condition of his psychopathology. There is nothing mechanical in this conditioning; certainly no suggestion that all people with twisted spines become cunning murderers. But Shakespeare does suggest that a child unloved by his mother, mocked by his peers, forced to regard himself as a monster will develop certain compensatory psychological strategies, some of them both destructive and self-destructive.

In the famous soliloquy he gives his villain at the beginning of *Richard III*—"Now is the winter of our discontent / Made glorious summer by this son of York"—Shakespeare opens a window into his character's sense of himself. England is at last at peace, but there is no peace for the twisted Duke of Gloucester. "Deformed, unfinished, sent before my time / Into this breathing world scarce half made up," Richard declares that he will not attempt to be a lover but will instead pursue power by any means necessary.

The strange and surprising thing in *Richard III* is that the hunchback does in fact—and almost immediately—prove to be a weirdly successful suitor. He seduces Lady Anne, a triumph all the more incredible since he has murdered her husband and father-in-law, and since she has just spat upon him in a visceral expression of loathing and disgust. Yet the success does not alter Richard's trajectory; on the contrary, it only furthers it by reinforcing his contempt for a world that despises and yet cannot resist him. And looking out at us from the stage, he invites us not only to share his gleeful

---

*All quotations are taken from the edited text of the Quarto, printed here. The Digital Edition includes edited texts of both the Quarto and the Folio.

contempt but also to experience for ourselves what it is to succumb to what we know is loathsome.

In his jaunty wickedness and perverse humor, Richard has seduced more than four centuries of audiences. As one of the rare anecdotes that survives from Shakespeare's own time suggests, that seduction began almost immediately. In 1602, a London law student, John Manningham, recorded a ribald story in his diary:

> Upon a time when Burbage played Richard III there was a citizen grew so far in liking with him, that before she went from the play she appointed him to come that night unto her by the name of Richard III. Shakespeare, overhearing their conclusion, went before, was entertained and at his game ere Burbage came. The message being brought that Richard III was at the door, Shakespeare caused return to be made that William the Conqueror was before Richard III.

Like most stories about celebrities, this one probably says more about those who circulated it than about those it describes. But it does at least suggest that Richard Burbage, the famous actor who first played Richard III (as well as such parts as Romeo and Hamlet), had not by virtue of his villainous role lost all of his glamour. Indeed, it is striking that Richard—the "elvish-marked, abortive, rooting hog" (1.3.224), the "poisonous bunch-backed toad" (1.3.242), the heartless cur sent, as he himself puts it, "[d]eformed" and "unfinished" (1.1.20) into the world—has seemed weirdly and compellingly attractive to generations of playgoers. From the start, the play seems to have aroused intense interest: first performed in 1592 or 1593, *Richard III* was published in quarto no fewer than five times during Shakespeare's lifetime.

What can account for this attraction? It is not an obvious feature in the chronicle histories upon which Shakespeare relied, nor does Richard seem to have a comparable allure in another play, of unknown authorship, that dates from the same period, *The True Tragedy of Richard III*. In these works, Richard simply figures as the pitiless, treacherous villain of what has been called the "Tudor Myth"—that is, the officially sanctioned account of the supposed monster whom the Tudors providentially supplanted. Modern historians emphasize Richard's solid administrative skills; Tudor apologists depict Richard not merely as a venal and unscrupulous politician but as the incarnation of evil, a creature whose moral viciousness was directly stamped on his twisted body.

Most sixteenth-century historians and chroniclers were, by our standards, far more interested in conveying moral meanings than in impartially recounting facts. Shakespeare allowed himself even greater latitude, freely reshaping and condensing his historical materials in order to heighten dramatic effect and to intensify the political, psychological, and metaphysical dimensions of his villainous antihero. The play compresses events that in reality occurred over a long period of time, so that, for example, Richard's murderous plot against his brother George, Duke of Clarence (1478), is cleverly twined around his cynical courtship of Lady Anne (1472), which is in turn depicted as occurring during the funeral procession of King Henry (1471). The historical Lady Anne had only been betrothed to King Henry's son Edward, but Shakespeare writes as if she had actually been married to him. Likewise, he folds the Earl of Richmond's unsuccessful attempt to invade England in 1483 into his successful invasion of 1485, and he has old Queen Margaret, who was not even in England during most of the events the play depicts, haunting the royal court like a bitter, half-crazed Greek tragic chorus.

Manipulating the insecurities, factional rivalries, and ambitions of everyone around him, Shakespeare's Richard is a consummate portrait of what sixteenth-century Englishmen termed a "machiavel": that is, a person who acts on the advice offered by the Florentine humanist Niccolò Machiavelli in *The Prince* (written in 1513). According to the period's lurid and grossly distorted account of this advice, Machiavelli had counseled princes to lie, cheat, and murder under the cover of hypocritical professions of virtue and piety. "I count Religion but a childish Toy," declares

Richard III. Portrait by unknown artist (ca. 1590).

the character called Machevil, who speaks the prologue to Marlowe's *Jew of Malta* (ca. 1590). Shakespeare's Richard, at first terrified by the apparition of the ghosts in act 5, rallies to express comparable sentiments: "Conscience is but a word that cowards use, / Devised at first to keep the strong in awe" (5.3.307–08). These are sentiments that, for the most part, Richard keeps to himself—or, rather, shares only with the audience in a succession of gleeful asides—for he is highly skilled at assuming the pose of religious faith. Aided by his fellow hypocrite Buckingham, Richard appears in a memorable scene, prayer book in hand, miming "devotion and right Christian zeal" (3.7.95) while cynically stage-managing the supposedly popular call for his coronation.

This vision of Richard as a consummate role player goes back to a brilliant sketch of the same character in one of three earlier plays Shakespeare had written on fifteenth-century English history. Taken together, these plays—*The First Part of Henry the Sixth, The First Part of the Contention betwixt the Two Famous Houses of York and Lancaster (2 Henry VI)*, and *The True Tragedy of Richard Duke of York and the Death of Good King Henry the Sixth (3 Henry VI)*—depict the struggle between the Lancastrians and the Yorkists as the death throes of feudal England. At the close of *3 Henry VI*, the Yorkist faction, led by the Duke of York's three surviving sons (Edward, George, and Richard), has triumphed. The last Lancastrian king, Henry VI, has been killed, and Richard's eldest brother has been crowned King Edward IV. But a shadow is cast across this decisive Yorkist victory by the ruthless and unsatisfied ambition of Richard.

Though it can easily stand (and is most often performed) entirely on its own, *Richard III* may be regarded as the fourth part of a tetralogy on the Wars of the Roses, for it picks up directly from the turbulent events depicted in *3 Henry VI* and, more particularly, from Richard's determination to seize the crown, a determination that is presented in effect as the pathological equivalent of a moral principle. Since nature, he declares, has cruelly seen fit

> To shrink mine arm up like a withered shrub,
> To make an envious mountain on my back,
> Where sits deformity to mock my body;
> To shape my legs of an unequal size,
> To disproportion me in every part
> (*3 Henry VI* 3.2.156–60)

he will abjure any hope of sexual success and will opt instead for the distinct but related pleasure it will bring him "to command, to check, to o'erbear such / As are of better person than myself" (3.2.166–67). And he possesses the skills needed to achieve his ends: "I can add colors to the chameleon," he boasts, "Change shapes with Proteus for advantages, / And set the murderous machiavel to school" (3.2.191–93). Here in this early play Shakespeare is already beginning to psychologize the machiavel, to provide inner motives for his violent ambition and his compulsive shape changing.

Richard III continues and intensifies this process: as his opening soliloquy suggests, Richard feels that nature has cheated him from birth. Deprived of the normal satisfactions of nurturing and kindness—it is as if his mother's womb itself had rejected him—he tries to find compensatory satisfaction through dissembling and cruelty. In doing so, he seeks not only vengeance against an unloving world but also the pleasure of cherishing himself. Yet at the end of the play, in a vigorous if crude moment of self-analysis, he discovers that even self-love eludes him: "I love myself. Wherefore? . . . Oh, no. Alas, I rather hate myself" (5.3.185–87).

Richard's self-hatred is psychologically revealing—evidently, he has internalized the loathing that he inspires in virtually everyone around him—but it is not simply generated from within: there is, the play's characters continually imply, a divinely sanctioned, objective moral order independent of both individuals and society, and by the fixed norms of this

Henry VII. Portrait by Michael Sittow (1505).

order Richard *is* hateful. It is possible for villains like Richard or the murderers of Clarence to close their ears to the admonitions of conscience, but all human actions are part of a larger design and will ultimately be judged by a heavenly power. From this perspective, the ghosts in act 5 are not merely psychological projections but metaphysical emissaries. The dead do not simply rot and disappear, nor do they survive only in the memories and dreams of the living: they are an ineradicable presence, a part of the structure of reality, an uncanny age group capable of blessing and cursing. Richard tries to shake off their condemnation, as earlier he had jauntily deflected Margaret's elaborate curse, but their words bring beads of sweat to his trembling flesh. For while he may tell himself that his victims' words are merely the impotent weapons of the powerless, he cannot escape the play's pervasive sense that there is something eerie and disturbing about curses, as if through incantatory verbal ritual they magically touch the hidden order of things.

Despite Richard's disruptive mockery and unceremonious violence, an atmosphere of ritual lingers over much of *Richard III*, tingeing the rhetorically elaborate expressions of grief and anger, solemnizing formal ceremonies, and shaping the perceptions of the guilt-ridden characters. Though the play gives us historical figures with psychological motivations and political stratagems, at moments we seem less in the secular world of disenchanted politics than in the world of classical tragedy or medieval rite. Thus, for example, Clarence's terrible nightmare just before his murder recalls the hell of the Roman playwright Seneca and, still more, the hell of fourteenth-century Christian painting, with its howling fiends and damned souls. Clarence is haunted by the sense of an unappeasable God preparing to punish him for his crimes, and his dream discloses what he does not yet consciously know: that the agent of divine retribution is his own brother, Richard.

This ritual process—the inexorable working out, through the agency of Richard, of retributive justice or (as ancient tragedians personified it) Nemesis—is best conveyed perhaps by the chorus of grief-crazed women, above all by old Queen Margaret, who identifies Richard as "hell's black intelligencer" (4.4.66), or secret agent. In a series of stiff antiphonal laments (4.4.32ff), Margaret (the widow of the slain Henry VI), Queen Elizabeth (the widow of Edward IV), and the Duchess of York (the widowed mother of Edward and his brothers, including Richard) tease out the strict eye-for-an-eye logic of the action. And at one startling moment, Richard himself comes close to acknowledging his role within this scheme: he likens himself to "the formal Vice, Iniquity" (3.1.82).

The character called the Vice is an inheritance of the medieval morality play: the busy enemy of mankind, the Vice was at once the agent of hell and the tool of divine providence, a master plotter and a puppet in a play that is not of his own making. Yet this fixed place in the divine plan did not preclude his acquiring an extraordinary theatrical power and resourcefulness, qualities that Shakespeare would later exploit in characters as different (and as magnificent) as Falstaff and Iago. Shakespeare constructs Richard out of many elements in the Vice tradition: a jaunty use of asides, a delight in sharing his schemes with the audience, a grotesque appearance, a penchant for disguise, a manic energy and humor, and a wickedly engaging ability to defer though not finally to escape well-deserved punishment. Richard's own allusion to the Vice calls attention to yet another element, a skill in playing with the doubleness of words and exploiting the slipperiness of language: "Thus like the formal Vice, Iniquity, / I moralize two meanings in one word" (3.1.82–83). Richard III puts the demonic master of this vicious skill on display and, in the end, stages his destruction: in a sense, the ritual that lingers over the play is an exorcism.

But, of course, Richard III is not in fact a ritual, and Shakespeare's subtle blending of psychological, metaphysical, and political perspectives carefully suspends any determination of their relative significance in the events he dramatizes. The psychological development of Richard is arrested by the intimation that psychology is itself the tool of a supernatural scheme; the supernatural is subverted (at least until the ghost scene) by the Machiavellian subordination of religion to power politics; but power politics is itself undermined by the suggestion that individuals act in the grip not of rational calculation but of psychological pressures and passions over which they have little or no control. The complex interplay of forces is reflected perhaps in an ambiguity about the play's genre: first appearing in print as The Tragedy of King Richard the Third, it was rechristened in the table of contents (the "catalogue") and grouped in the First Folio as one of Shakespeare's history plays, The Life and Death of Richard the Third.

That the multiple perspectives do not simply cancel each other out is the result of the extraordinary theatrical force of Richard himself. Only Hamlet, of all Shakespeare's plays, is comparably dominated by a single character, and only Macbeth is comparably structured around an evil hero. Without for a moment concealing from the audience Richard's monstrous evil, Shakespeare makes his villain immensely capti-

"For they account his head upon the bridge" (3.2.70). London Bridge adorned with the heads of traitors. From Claes Jansz Vischer, Londinum florentissima Britanniae urbs (1625).

vating. Appalling and appealing are braided together. Small wonder that the part has, for centuries, been beloved by ambitious actors. Much of his allure derives from what Keats called "gusto," the overwhelming liveliness in him as in so many of Shakespeare's characters. "Your eyes drop millstones when fools' eyes drop tears," says Richard to the murderers. "I like you, lads" (1.3.349–50). The startling frankness of this villainy has a comic charge, a charge renewed in the open wickedness of his plans for unsuspecting Hastings—"Chop off his head" (3.1.190)—or for the innocent young princes: "I wish the bastards dead" (4.2.17). There is gusto in Richard's slyness as well as in his frankness, a slyness that also is often comic: "So wise so young, they say, do never live long" (3.1.79).

The allure of such moments seems to be bound up with the allure of the theater itself, with its capacity for emotional intensification, surprise, deception, and heightened energy. The religious enemies of the theater in Shakespeare's age charged that this energy was essentially erotic—the playhouse, they complained, aroused sexual desire—and before dismissing their charges as preposterous, we might recall the comic anecdote from John Manningham's diary. Shakespeare himself in *Richard III* seems to play with the seductive power of theatrical performance in the scene in which Richard successfully courts Lady Anne. "Was ever woman in this humor wooed?" Richard exults. "Was ever woman in this humor won?" (1.2.214–15). Richard's wooing has nothing to do with tenderness, affection, sympathy, or even physical attraction; we witness an aggressive male assault upon Lady Anne's rooted, eloquently expressed, and eminently justified revulsion. Here, as elsewhere, Richard gets what he wants because he possesses greater power to control the scenario: more than Anne, more than anyone, he knows how to initiate action, conceal motives, threaten, intimidate, and hurt. He has killed Anne's husband as well as her father-in-law; he will, when she has served his purpose, kill Anne too. Anne knows this well enough—"Ill rest betide the chamber where thou liest" (1.2.110)—but she virtually invents uncertainties to mask the calculating murderousness she herself has perceived with cold clarity: "I would I knew thy heart," she muses, seconds after she has thoroughly inventoried Richard's villainous heart (1.2.179).

Anne is shallow, corruptible, naively ambitious, and, above all, frightened—all qualities that help to account for her spectacular surrender—but the scene's theatrical power rests less upon a depiction of her character than upon the spectacle of Richard's restless aggression transformed during the rapid-fire exchange of one-liners (called in rhetoric *stichomythia*) into a perverse form of sexual provocation and of Anne's verbal violence transformed, in spite of itself, into an erotic response. In light of this transformation, the misshapen Richard's celebration of his sexual attractiveness—

> I do mistake my person all this while!
> Upon my life, she finds, although I cannot,
> Myself to be a marvelous proper man.
> (1.2.238–40)

—is not wholly ironic, even if he himself thinks it is.

Eros has not been excluded from Richard's career; it has found a new and compelling form in his energetic, witty, and murderous chafing against the obstacles in his path. These obstacles are not simply set in opposition to his desire; rather they virtually constitute it, for it is the extent of his distance from power that generates Richard's craving for it. His politics, and hence the sexuality implied by that politics, is transgressive; it thrives on the violation of social and natural bonds. His is the psychology of the rapist, and the character in Shakespeare closest to Richard III is the rapist Tarquin (in *The Rape of Lucrece*), whose lust is excited precisely by the barriers he is forced to overcome. This chafing structure is why the violent verbal assaults upon Richard, most intense from the women in the play, seem only to intensify his aggressive energies. It is perhaps also why Richard seems to lose much of his erotic power as soon as he has established himself on the throne. When the obstacles in his path to the crown have been removed, when there is no legitimate authority to transgress, the erotic quality of his ambition immediately begins to wane.

The play has allowed Richard to be a perverse erotic champion—a role probably possible only in this highly theatrical vision of history—but the desire he embodies cannot be integrated into any viable social or natural order; nor does it constitute a coherent, stable inner life. By the play's end, he seems a hollow man, a set of theatrical masks that project grotesque shadows upon the world. Fittingly, when "shadows," in the form of those he has murdered, return to terrify him, he can only express his fear in histrionic terms, staging a miniature dialogue with himself and then imagining his conscience as the audience, with its thousand tongues condemning him for a villain.

Richard's manifest theatricality is only the extreme form of a theatricality diffused throughout the play. Virtually all of the speeches—lamentation, cursing, debate, persuasion—are cast as self-conscious performances: "What means this scene of rude impatience?" asks the Duchess of York. Queen Elizabeth replies, "To make an act of tragic violence" (2.2.37–38). Moreover, there is a pervasive sense that the characters exist as figures in someone else's play: through most of the performance, they are figures, without knowing it, in Richard's play, but Richard himself is a figure in another play, larger than himself. That larger play is at once the drama of history, scripted (as Tudor ideology claimed) by God, and the historical drama or tragedy, scripted by Shakespeare. If the script obliges all of the characters to display the power of divine providence, it obliges them at the same time to display the power of the theater. For if the stage pays homage to the state, it also makes a spectacle of the state. *Richard III* manages to imply that the whole vast enterprise of Tudor power exists to make this play, and the theater in which it is performed, possible.

STEPHEN GREENBLATT

SELECTED BIBLIOGRAPHY

Burnett, Mark Thornton. "'Monsters' and 'Molas': Body Politics in *Richard III*." *Constructing "Monsters" in Shakespearean Drama and Early Modern Culture*. New York: Palgrave Macmillan, 2002. 65–94. Argues that, fluctuating between images of monsters shaped and unfinished, Richard represented the anxieties of a barren Tudor line seeking new political form.

Garber, Marjorie. "Descanting on Deformity: Richard III and the Shape of History." *The Historical Renaissance: New Essays on Tudor and Stuart Literature and Culture*. Ed. Heather Dubrow and Richard Strier. Chicago: U of Chicago P, 1988. 79–103. Asserts that Richard theorizes his own deformity as his source of power and of the power of the deformed historical narrative that his misshapen form encodes.

Howard, Jean E., and Phyllis Rackin. "Weak Kings, Warrior Women, and the Assault on Dynastic Authority." *Engendering a Nation: A Feminist Account of Shakespeare's English Histories*. London: Routledge, 1997. 100–18. Examines how, shifting from history to tragedy, *Richard III* ennobles and disempowers women as passive emblems of pity, while Richard himself appropriates their seductive theatrical energy.

Hunter, Robert G. *Shakespeare and the Mystery of God's Judgments*. Athens: U of Georgia P, 1976. Shows how, poised between Augustinian and Calvinist conceptions of God's will, Richard's seemingly contradictory status as a tragic figure acting in a providential frame generates the complexity of Shakespeare's art.

Marche, Stephen. "Mocking Dead Bones: Historical Memory and the Theater of the Dead in *Richard III*." *Comparative Drama* 37.1 (2003): 37–57. Looks at how the play's ambivalent generic status—between tragedy and history—is reflected in Richard's tragic inability to overcome history by silencing the dead who challenge his shaping narrative.

Moulton, Ian Frederick. "'A Monster Great Deformed': The Unruly Masculinities of *Richard III.*" *Shakespeare Quarterly* 47.3 (1996): 251–68. Analyzes how Shakespeare both critiques and celebrates masculine aggression, revealing the incoherence of masculinity as an early modern cultural concept.

Rossiter, A. P. *Angel with Horns and Other Shakespeare Lectures.* New York: Theater Arts Books, 1961. Examines how Richard's demonic appeal as God's avenging angel makes the play less moral history than comic history built on paradoxical irony and inversion.

Sanders, Wilbur. "Providence and Policy in *Richard III.*" *The Dramatist and the Received Idea.* Cambridge: Cambridge UP, 1968. 72–109. Argues that below the surface of the play's superficial adherence to Tudor orthodoxy is a relentlessly skeptical questioning of divine providence and official moral values.

Targoff, Ramie. "'Dirty' Amens: Devotion, Applause, and Consent in *Richard III.*" *Renaissance Drama* 31 (2002): 61–84. Argues that Shakespeare tapped the resonance between audience and congregational response, spurring theatergoers to provide the affirmation of Richard's coronation that the play itself omits, even undermines.

Torrey, Michael. "'The Plain Devil and Dissembling Looks': Ambivalent Physiognomy and Shakespeare's *Richard III.*" *English Literary Renaissance* 30.2 (2000): 123–53. Investigates how Richard's ability to deceive his victims and manipulate his corporal image complicates the seeming intelligibility of his deformity.

Zamir, Tzachi. *Double Vision: Moral Philosophy and Shakespearean Drama.* Princeton, NJ: Princeton UP, 2007. 65–91. Asserts that, excluded from shared social life, Richard's deliberate choice of evil is a form of ethical skepticism, a challenge to morality itself.

FILMS

Richard III. 1912. Dir. André Calmettes and James Keane. France/USA. 55 min. Silent film version starring Robert Gemp and Frederick Warde.

Richard III. 1955. Dir. Laurence Olivier. UK. 161 min. A deformed and morally twisted yet seductively charismatic Richard.

Richard III. 1995. Dir. Richard Loncraine. USA. 104 min. Richard as a sly and ruthless fascist dictator in a stylishly corrupt 1930s Britain. Starring Ian McKellen and Robert Downey, Jr.

Looking for Richard. 1996. Dir. Al Pacino. USA. 111 min. Part adaptation, part behind-the-scenes documentary about bringing Shakespeare to modern audiences. With Al Pacino and Kevin Spacey.

TEXTUAL INTRODUCTION

Modern editions of Shakespeare's *Tragedy of King Richard the Third* are based either on the 1597 Quarto edition (Q) or on the longer 1623 First Folio edition (F). Seven additional Quarto editions appeared in 1598, 1602, 1605, 1612, 1622, 1629, and 1634 (Q2–Q8). Folio *Richard III* appears to have been set from copies of Q3 (1602) and Q6 (1622), but relies heavily on a now-lost independent manuscript (FMS) that differed in many particulars from the Q texts. Proponents of the authority of F base their argument on FMS's supposed priority as the fuller or "maximal" text, presumed to have been "allowed" by the Master of the Revels in 1597 but not edited or cut for purposes of performance. Such a text would be closely held by its acting company and not released for publication.

Determining which manuscript came first is the most vexed problem in debates about the texts of *Richard III*. Q was long held to be a "bad quarto" riddled with errors that had multiplied with successive reprintings. Because it shows evidence of streamlining and is the more performance-oriented of the two texts, Q was thought to have been assembled by means of memorial reconstruction by actors from the Lord Chamberlain's Men. Q would thus have been based on a second lost manuscript (QMS) that made deliberate cuts in and changes to material preserved in the longer Folio version, possibly for a touring production. However, many scholars have argued that the quality and relative completeness of Q, not to mention its inclusion of dramatically significant lines and passages not found in F, are inconsistent with the concept of the "bad" quarto. Some speculate that Q may be based on an earlier manuscript than FMS, which Shakespeare himself, or another author, might have revised into the form that lies behind F. Rather than "mistaken" or plainly inferior word- or line-readings, many of Q's flaws involve printer's errors; inconsistent verb tenses; pronouns of mismatched number and gender; and the spelling out of words that, metrically speaking, are better elided. Indeed, many of these mistakes—as recorded in Q3 and Q6—found their way into F, despite that text's reliance on the supposedly prior, hence more authoritative, FMS.

Folio *Richard III* contains over 200 lines of dialogue that do not appear in Q, which includes approximately 35 lines not in F. Examined side by side, Q and F reveal hundreds of additional variations in word choice, word order, verb tense, dialogue placement, and speech attribution, most of which have minimal effect on meaning. Apart from F's superior metrical regularity, its greater length—the product of considerable verbal elaboration, particularly in 4.4—and its failure to anticipate or reproduce Q's brilliant clock passage (see F 4.2.98–99 and Q 4.2.98–118), the main differences between Q and F are synonymic, that is, they involve the simple replacement of one word for another close in meaning, often for metrical regularity. F also excises from Q several words or phrases (e.g., "Zounds," an abbreviation for "God's wounds") that might have violated the 1606 statute prohibiting the inappropriate use "in any stage-play, interlude, or show, the name of the Holy Trinity, or any of the persons therein," despite that statute's restriction to performances as opposed to books. The excision of such words from what is said to be a text based on a "fair copy" manuscript composed well in advance of Q's 1597 publication date indicates that the compositors of F were working from an already annotated manuscript that likely recorded other changes over the course of the play's production history. Additional evidence suggests that more than a few synonymic variations between Q and F owe less to the faulty recall of would-be memorial reconstructors of 1597 than to the interventions of Folio compositors or FMS revisers seeking to "improve" the text of a play composed in the mid-1590s.

Such interventions might have been predicated on the aims of the Folio's sponsors to generate a publication event that had only one precedent in recent memory—the publication of Ben Jonson's *Works* in 1616—and to distinguish their publication of plays many of which had already appeared in quarto form. Some interventions might be attributable to Shakespeare himself, who may have made adjustments to the promptbook of one of his most frequently performed plays. Indeed, if we assume that F is based on a manuscript that *post*dates both the manuscript behind Q and Q itself, then we may be dealing with a revision, possibly drafted by Shakespeare. Given the length and literariness of many of F's revisions or elaborations, FMS might have been constructed as a text for *reading*. This might explain both the elaborations of 4.4 and some of the shorter, more felicitous additions and "corrections"; the frequent choice of formal over colloquial language; the expurgation of oaths; the fuller, more expressive stage directions; and even the elimination of the "clock passage," arguably a more theatrical than literary tour de force. Changes in F's appeal to its audience are even detectable on the play's title page, where instead of the 1597 text's lurid advertising of Richard's detestable deeds "and most deserved death," we find foregrounded "the Landing of Earle Richmond, and the / Battell at Bosworth Field," items of national interest not mentioned on Q's title page.

Since determining which of the two texts is more definitively "Shakespearean" is an impossible task, *The Norton Shakespeare* provides two single-text editions of Q and F, making the earlier, shorter, and arguably more theatrical Quarto version available in print, while offering both the Quarto and the later, longer, and arguably more literary Folio version in electronic format. This edition of Folio *Richard III* is not a conflation but occasionally draws on Q when a word, phrase, or passage appears to have been misprinted or accidentally omitted by the compositors of F, or when successive lines have been mistakenly transposed. Efforts have been made to avoid mixing and matching what may seem preferable words and phrases from the two texts in question, even when doing so may be traditional procedure.

THOMAS CARTELLI

PERFORMANCE NOTE

Like Lady Anne, spectators to *Richard III* are rendered powerless to resist a man they know to be a monster. Though their moral outrage over Richard's actions seldom mars—indeed, almost certainly enhances—the exceptional dramatic interest audiences take in him, productions still make critical choices about his motivations and the nature of the audience's support for him. Some present Richard as a brazenly theatrical type, his unabashed brutality, smiling deceits, and direct addresses showcasing the artifice and talent of the performer: paradoxically, this approach generally deepens engagement, making audiences willing accomplices in villainy. Others pursue a more sympathetic involvement for audiences by suggesting that Richard's antipathies arise from motherly neglect or from social isolation on account of his physical deformities. Still others define Richard by extremes of ambition almost indistinguishable from madness.

Whether Richard is vicious by nature or as a result of his upbringing, productions must decide if he preys on a cast of innocents or seems the most agile viper in the nest, and when, if ever, to reveal signs of his interior life. Anne, for example, can be a pawn in his quest for power or an object of sincere affection; Richard can fall out with Buckingham because of paranoia or merely because he has nobody else left to torment; the ghosts at Bosworth can inspire heroic displays of courage or expose the frightened everyman behind the façade. The best performances nimbly represent both mechanistic ruthlessness and vulnerability, comedic impulses and political cunning, and their Richards are convincing as both historic villain and tragic victim.

Though *Richard III* has often been presented as a star vehicle, directors in recent years have shown increasing interest in politics, either offering *Richard* alongside the three *Henry VI* plays or staging topical productions that suggest parallels between the Tudor tyrants and those of contemporary regimes. Whatever the approach, directors can decide whether Margaret acts as chorus, madwoman, or neglected voice of reason; whether Anne and Elizabeth are merely objects of manipulation or capable rivals for Richard; whether Buckingham's defection seems mercenary, traitorous, or wise; and whether Richmond is a welcome savior or another tyrant-in-waiting. They also must address the play's tendency toward anticlimax after Richard gains the throne; sustain interest through long and ostentatiously rhetorical set pieces (Clarence's dream, the pageant of the three queens); determine whether and how to stage the executions of Hastings and the Queen's kinsmen; fix the nature and representation of Richard's disfigurement; and decide on the ontological status and participation of the ghosts.

BRETT GAMBOA

The Tragedy of King Richard the Third

[THE PERSONS OF THE PLAY

Richard, Duke of GLOUCESTER, later KING RICHARD III
George, Duke of CLARENCE, his brother
KING Edward IV, their brother
DUCHESS OF YORK, their mother
QUEEN ELIZABETH, wife to King Edward
Anthony Woodville, Lord RIVERS, brother to Queen Elizabeth
Lord GREY
Marquess DORSET } sons to Queen Elizabeth by her first marriage
PRINCE EDWARD
Richard, Duke of YORK } sons to King Edward
BOY and GIRL, children to Clarence
Lady ANNE, later Duchess of Gloucester
QUEEN MARGARET, widow of King Henry VI
William, Lord HASTINGS, Lord Chamberlain
Duke of BUCKINGHAM
Lord STANLEY, Earl of Derby
Henry, Earl of RICHMOND, stepson to Stanley
Sir William CATESBY
Sir Richard RATCLIFFE
Sir Robert BRAKENBURY
GENTLEMEN attending corpse of Henry VI, including Tressel and Berkeley
Two EXECUTIONERS
CITIZENS
CARDINAL
LORD MAYOR of London
PURSUIVANT called Hastings
Priest
MESSENGERS

SCRIVENER
LIEUTENANT of the Tower

Sir Thomas VAUGHAN
BISHOP OF ELY
BOY, a page
James TYRREL
Sir CHRISTOPHER
LORDS, supporters of Richmond
Sir James BLUNT
John, Duke of NORFOLK
GHOSTS of Henry the Sixth, Edward, Prince of Wales (son to Henry the Sixth),
    Clarence, Rivers, Grey, Vaughan, Hastings, Prince Edward, York, Lady Anne,
    and Buckingham

Two Bishops, attendant on Richard
Carriers, Guards, Nobles, Soldiers]

1.1 (F 1.1)

Enter Richard, Duke of GLOUCESTER, *alone.*

GLOUCESTER[1] Now is the winter of our discontent
  Made glorious summer by this son of York,[2]
  And all the clouds that loured° upon our house°   *glowered / family*
  In the deep bosom of the ocean burièd.
5 Now are our brows bound with victorious wreaths;
  Our bruisèd arms° hung up for monuments;°   *armor / memorials*
  Our stern alarms° changed to merry meetings;   *call to arms*
  Our dreadful marches to delightful measures.°   *dances*
  Grim-visaged war hath smoothed his wrinkled front,°   *forehead*
10 And now, instead of mounting barbèd° steeds   *armored*
  To fright the souls of fearful adversaries,
  He capers[3] nimbly in a lady's chamber
  To the lascivious pleasing of a lute.
  But I, that am not shaped for sportive° tricks,   *amorous*
15 Nor made to court an amorous looking glass;
  I, that am rudely stamped[4] and want° love's majesty   *lack*
  To strut before a wanton ambling nymph;[5]
  I, that am curtailed of this fair proportion,°   *shape*
  Cheated of feature° by dissembling nature,   *good appearance*
20 Deformed, unfinished, sent before my time
  Into this breathing world scarce half made up,
  And that so lamely and unfashionable°   *badly formed*
  That dogs bark at me as I halt° by them;   *limp*
  Why, I, in this weak piping[6] time of peace,
25 Have no delight to pass away the time,
  Unless to spy my shadow in the sun
  And descant on[7] mine own deformity.[8]
  And therefore, since I cannot prove° a lover   *prove to be*
  To entertain these fair well-spoken days,
30 I am determinèd° to prove a villain   *resolved; fated*
  And hate the idle pleasures of these days.
  Plots have I laid, inductions[9] dangerous,
  By drunken prophecies, libels, and dreams,
  To set my brother Clarence[1] and the King
35 In deadly hate the one against the other.
  And if King Edward be as true and just
  As I am subtle, false, and treacherous,
  This day should Clarence closely be mewed up°   *caged (like a hawk)*
  About a prophecy, which says that "G"[2]
40 Of Edward's heirs the murderer shall be.
  Dive, thoughts, down to my soul: here Clarence comes.

1.1 Location: A street in London.
1. Until his crowning in 4.2, Richard, Duke of Gloucester, is identified in the speech prefixes as "Gloucester" (pronounced "Gloster").
2. *son of York*: Edward IV, son of the Duke of York and Richard's brother. "Son" plays on Edward's emblem, a sun in splendor.
3. In court dances, men often made "capers," or showy leaps; also suggests a sexual escapade.
4. Roughly, imperfectly shaped (alluding to the stamping of a coin with an image).
5. A woman who strolls lewdly, without constraint; suggests the ease and pace of a horse's "amble."
6. Music of a shepherd's flute; shrill-voiced, like

women or children.
7. *descant on*: comment upon; improvise (an improvised musical line, usually the highest part).
8. PERFORMANCE COMMENT How much to emphasize Gloucester's "deformity" is a key question in productions. See Digital Edition PC 1.
9. Initial moves; prologues.
1. George, Duke of Clarence, Richard, Duke of Gloucester, and King Edward IV were brothers. Clarence, being older than Richard, would be king if Edward and his heirs died.
2. Which Edward interprets as "George," but which could—and does—mean "Gloucester."

Enter CLARENCE, *with a guard of men*
[*and* BRAKENBURY].
Brother, good days. What means this armèd guard
That waits upon your grace?
CLARENCE   His majesty,
Tendering° my person's safety, hath appointed   *Caring about*
45   This conduct° to convey me to the Tower.[3]   *escort*
GLOUCESTER   Upon what cause?
CLARENCE   Because my name is George.
GLOUCESTER   Alack, my lord, that fault is none of yours;
He should for that commit° your godfathers.[4]   *arrest*
Oh, belike° his majesty hath some intent   *probably*
50   That you shall be new-christened in the Tower.
But what's the matter, Clarence, may I know?
CLARENCE   Yea, Richard, when I know; for I protest
As yet I do not. But as I can learn,
He hearkens after prophecies and dreams,
55   And from the cross-row° plucks the letter G,   *alphabet*
And says a wizard told him that by "G"
His issue° disinherited should be.   *children*
And for my name of George begins with G,
It follows in his thought that I am he.
60   These, as I learn, and suchlike toys° as these   *trifles*
Have moved his highness to commit me now.
GLOUCESTER   Why, this it is when men are ruled by women.
'Tis not the King that sends you to the Tower:
My lady Grey[5] his wife, Clarence, 'tis she
65   That tempers° him to this extremity.   *directs*
Was it not she and that good man of worship,[6]
Anthony Woodville, her brother there,
That made him send Lord Hastings to the Tower,
From whence this present day he is delivered?
70   We are not safe, Clarence, we are not safe.
CLARENCE   By heaven, I think there is no man is secured
But the Queen's kindred and night-walking heralds° *secret go-betweens*
That trudge betwixt the King and Mistress Shore.[7]
Heard ye not what an humble suppliant
75   Lord Hastings was to her for his delivery?
GLOUCESTER   Humbly complaining to her deity[8]
Got my Lord Chamberlain[9] his liberty.
I'll tell you what, I think it is our way,°   *best strategy*
If we will keep in favor with the King,
80   To be her men and wear her livery.[1]
The jealous o'erworn widow[2] and herself,°   *(Jane Shore)*

3. Tower of London, used to house noble prisoners as well as traitors and political agitators.
4. The godfather was responsible for the naming of a newborn child during baptism.
5. A sarcastic reference to the Queen, widow of Sir John Grey. Her maiden name was Elizabeth Woodville.
6. Honor. The term "goodman" referred to a male below the rank of gentleman, so the phrase "good man of worship" sarcastically aligns the Queen's brother, Anthony Woodville, with the middle class rather than with the titled nobility.
7. Jane Shore, wife of a London goldsmith. Her liaison with Edward was notorious. *Mistress*: here in both the polite and the abusive sense.
8. Jane Shore (ironically, by analogy with "her majesty").
9. Hastings's title (the senior official of the royal household). According to Shakespeare's sources, Jane Shore became his mistress after her affair with the King ended.
1. Servants ("men") in noble households wore the colors ("livery") of the family.
2. The Queen; she was a widow before she married Edward IV. *o'erworn*: faded.

Since that our brother dubbed them[3] gentlewomen,
Are mighty gossips° in this monarchy.   *busybodies*
BRAKENBURY   I beseech your graces both to pardon me;
85   His majesty hath straitly given in charge°   *has strictly ordered*
That no man shall have private conference,
Of what degree soever,[4] with his brother.
GLOUCESTER   Even so. An't° please your worship, Brakenbury,   *If it*
You may partake of anything we say.
90   We speak no treason, man. We say the King
Is wise and virtuous, and his noble queen
Well struck° in years, fair, and not jealous.   *advanced*
We say that Shore's wife hath a pretty foot,
A cherry lip, a bonny eye, a passing° pleasing tongue,   *an exceedingly*
95   And that the Queen's kindred are made gentlefolks.
How say you, sir? Can you deny all this?
BRAKENBURY   With this, my lord, myself have naught° to do.   *nothing*
GLOUCESTER   Naught[5] to do with Mistress Shore? I tell thee,
          fellow,
He that doth naught with her, excepting one,
100   Were best he do it secretly, alone.
BRAKENBURY   What one, my lord?[6]
GLOUCESTER   Her husband, knave. Wouldst thou betray me?
BRAKENBURY   I beseech your grace to pardon me, and withal°   *moreover*
Forbear your conference with the noble duke.
105   CLARENCE   We know thy charge, Brakenbury, and will obey.
GLOUCESTER   We are the Queen's abjects,° and must obey.   *base subjects*
Brother, farewell. I will unto the King.
And whatsoever you will employ me in,
Were it to call King Edward's widow° "sister,"   *(Queen Elizabeth)*
110   I will perform it to enfranchise° you.   *free*
Meantime, this deep disgrace in brotherhood
Touches me deeper[7] than you can imagine.
CLARENCE   I know it pleaseth neither of us well.
GLOUCESTER   Well, your imprisonment shall not be long.
115   I will deliver you or lie for you;[8]
Meantime, have patience.
CLARENCE   I must perforce.° Farewell.   *of necessity*
               Exit CLARENCE [*with* BRAKENBURY].
GLOUCESTER   Go tread the path that thou shalt ne'er return.
Simple, plain Clarence, I do love thee so
That I will shortly send thy soul to heaven,
120   If heaven will take the present at° our hands.   *from*
—But who comes here, the new-delivered° Hastings?   *newly released*
               Enter Lord HASTINGS.
HASTINGS   Good time of day unto my gracious lord.
GLOUCESTER   As much unto my good Lord Chamberlain.
Well are you welcome to the open air.

---

3. Invested them with the status of (usually used of knights). Gloucester grossly exaggerates the lowly status of the Queen's family before her marriage.
4. *no . . . soever:* That is, despite Richard's high rank ("degree"), he must not speak with the prisoner.
5. Wickedness; here, specifically, sexual intercourse.
6. TEXTUAL COMMENT We have retained two of the more sexually explicit lines of Brakenbury's and

Gloucester's charged banter that were omitted in the Quarto, apparently accidentally, and included in the revised Second Quarto and in the Folio. See Digital Edition TC 1 (Quarto edited text).
7. Wounds me more, but also (as a hidden meaning), implicates me more.
8. In prison, in place of Clarence (with a pun on "lie" as "tell falsehoods about").

125   How hath your lordship brooked° imprisonment?   *tolerated*
    HASTINGS   With patience, noble lord, as prisoners must.
      But I shall live, my lord, to give them thanks
      That were the cause of my imprisonment.
    GLOUCESTER   No doubt, no doubt, and so shall Clarence too,
130   For they that were your enemies are his,
      And have prevailed° as much on him as you.   *gained the advantage*
    HASTINGS   More pity that the eagle should be mewed
      While kites° and buzzards prey at liberty.   *scavenger birds*
    GLOUCESTER   What news abroad?°   *circulating*
135   HASTINGS   No news so bad abroad as this at home:
      The King is sickly, weak, and melancholy,
      And his physicians fear° him mightily.   *fear for*
    GLOUCESTER   Now, by Saint Paul,[9] this news is bad indeed.
      Oh, he hath kept an evil diet° long,   *way of life*
140   And overmuch consumed his royal person.[1]
      'Tis very grievous to be thought upon.
      What, is he in his bed?
    HASTINGS   He is.
    GLOUCESTER   Go you before, and I will follow you.

                          Exit HASTINGS.

      He cannot live, I hope, and must not die
145   Till George be packed with post-horse° up to heaven.   *by express means*
      I'll in to urge his hatred more to Clarence
      With lies well steeled° with weighty arguments.   *made strong*
      And if I fail not in my deep intent,
      Clarence hath not another day to live.
150   Which done, God take King Edward to His mercy,
      And leave the world for me to bustle in,
      For then I'll marry Warwick's youngest daughter.[2]
      What though I killed her husband and her father?[3]
      The readiest way to make the wench amends
155   Is to become her husband and her father.
      The which will I, not all so much for love
      As for another secret close intent°   *private purpose*
      By marrying her which I must reach unto.
      But yet I run before my horse to market:
160   Clarence still breathes; Edward still lives and reigns.
      When they are gone, then must I count my gains.   *Exit.*

1.2 (F 1.2)

Enter LADY ANNE *with the hearse of Harry the Sixth*[,
with GENTLEMEN *including Tressel and Berkeley,
Carriers, and Guards*].

    LADY ANNE   Set down, set down your honorable load,
      If honor may be shrouded in a hearse,°   *an open coffin*
      Whilst I awhile obsequiously° lament   *mournfully*
      The untimely fall of virtuous Lancaster.[1]

9. Throughout Q, Richard swears by St. Paul, a characteristic also occurring in Thomas More's *History of King Richard III.*
1. And has been weakened by extravagant living.
2. Lady Anne Neville, whose father, the powerful Earl of Warwick, was killed in battle in *3 Henry VI.* Anne had been betrothed (but not married) to Edward, Prince of Wales, the son of King Henry VI.

Shakespeare, however, writes of Anne as Edward's widow.
3. *her father*: Henry VI (father-in-law).
1.2 Location: Scene continues.
1. Henry VI, of the house of Lancaster, was deposed and murdered by the Yorkists. The dynastic quarrel dates from the deposition of Richard II and is dramatized in Shakespeare's three *Henry VI* plays.

5   Poor key-cold² figure of a holy king,
    Pale ashes of the house of Lancaster,
    Thou bloodless remnant of that royal blood,
    Be it lawful that I invocate thy ghost³
    To hear the lamentations of poor Anne,
10   Wife to thy Edward, to thy slaughtered son,
    Stabbed by the selfsame hands that made these holes.
    Lo, in those windows⁴ that let forth thy life
    I pour the helpless° balm of my poor eyes.   *useless*
    Cursed be the hand that made these fatal holes,
15   Cursed be the heart that had the heart to do it.
    More direful hap betide° that hated wretch   *fate befall*
    That makes us wretched by the death of thee
    Than I can wish to adders, spiders, toads,
    Or any creeping venomed thing that lives.
20   If ever he have child, abortive° be it,   *incompletely formed*
    Prodigious,° and untimely brought to light,   *Monstrous*
    Whose ugly and unnatural aspect°   *appearance*
    May fright the hopeful mother at the view.
    If ever he have wife, let her be made
25   As miserable by the death of him
    As I am made by my poor lord and thee.⁵
    —Come, now towards Chertsey° with your holy load,   *monastery near London*
    Taken from Paul's⁶ to be interrèd there;
    And still as° you are weary of the weight,   *Whenever*
30   Rest you whiles I lament King Henry's corpse.
            Enter GLOUCESTER.
    GLOUCESTER   Stay, you that bear the corpse, and set it down.
    LADY ANNE   What black magician conjures up this fiend
    To stop devoted charitable deeds?
    GLOUCESTER   Villains,° set down the corpse, or by Saint   *Scoundrels; peasants*
        Paul,
35   I'll make a corpse of him that disobeys.
    GENTLEMAN   My lord, stand back, and let the coffin pass.
    GLOUCESTER   Unmannered dog, stand thou when I
        command.
    Advance thy halberd⁷ higher than my breast,
    Or by Saint Paul, I'll strike thee to my foot
40   And spurn° upon thee, beggar, for thy boldness.   *tread*
    LADY ANNE   What, do you tremble? Are you all afraid?
    Alas, I blame you not, for you are mortal,
    And mortal eyes cannot endure the devil.
    Avaunt,° thou dreadful minister of hell!   *Begone*
45   Thou hadst but power over his mortal body;
    His soul thou canst not have. Therefore begone.
    GLOUCESTER   Sweet saint, for charity, be not so curst.°   *bad-tempered*
    LADY ANNE   Foul devil, for God's sake, hence, and trouble
        us not,
    For thou hast made the happy earth thy hell,
50   Filled it with cursing cries and deep exclaims.

---

2. Proverbial for "cold as death."
3. Conjuring of spirits was generally condemned.
invocate: invoke.
4. Stab wounds (possibly referring to the custom of opening the windows to let a dying soul pass).

5. By the deaths of Prince Edward and King Henry VI.
6. St. Paul's, cathedral of the City of London.
7. I.e., raise your halberd upright (rather than pointing it at me). *halberd*: a spearlike weapon with a blade as well as a point.

If thou delight to view thy heinous deeds,
Behold this pattern° of thy butcheries.   *example*
Oh, gentlemen, see, see dead Henry's wounds
Open their congealed mouths and bleed afresh!⁸
55 Blush, blush, thou lump of foul deformity,
For 'tis thy presence that exhales° this blood   *calls forth*
From cold and empty veins where no blood dwells.
Thy deed, inhuman and unnatural,
Provokes this deluge most unnatural.
60 O God, which this blood madest, revenge his death!
O earth, which this blood drink'st, revenge his death!
Either heaven with lightning strike the murderer dead,
Or earth gape open wide and eat him quick,°   *alive*
As thou dost swallow up this good king's blood,
65 Which his hell-governed arm hath butcherèd.
GLOUCESTER Lady, you know no rules of charity,
Which renders good for bad, blessings for curses.
LADY ANNE Villain, thou knowest no law of God nor man;
No beast so fierce but knows some touch of pity.
70 GLOUCESTER But I know none, and therefore am no beast.
LADY ANNE Oh, wonderful, when devils tell the truth!⁹
GLOUCESTER More wonderful when angels are so angry.
Vouchsafe,° divine perfection of a woman,   *Grant*
Of these supposed evils to give me leave,
75 By circumstance,° but to acquit myself.   *detailed argument*
LADY ANNE Vouchsafe, diffused¹ infection of a man,
For these known evils but to give me leave,
By circumstance, to curse thy cursèd self.
GLOUCESTER Fairer than tongue can name thee, let me have
80 Some patient leisure to excuse myself.
LADY ANNE Fouler than heart can think thee, thou canst
    make
No excuse current° but to hang thyself.   *valid*
GLOUCESTER By such despair I should accuse myself.
LADY ANNE And by despairing shouldst thou stand excused
85 For doing worthy vengeance on thyself,
Which didst unworthy slaughter upon others.
GLOUCESTER Say that I slew them not?
LADY ANNE   Why, then they are not dead.
But dead they are, and, devilish slave, by thee.
GLOUCESTER I did not kill your husband.
LADY ANNE   Why, then he is alive.
90 GLOUCESTER Nay, he is dead, and slain by Edward's hand.
LADY ANNE In thy foul throat thou liest. Queen Margaret
    saw
Thy bloody falchion° smoking in his blood,²   *curved sword*
The which thou once didst bend against° her breast,   *turn toward*
But that thy brothers beat aside the point.
95 GLOUCESTER I was provoked by her slanderous tongue,
Which laid their guilt upon my guiltless shoulders.

---

8. A murdered victim's wounds were supposed to
bleed again in the presence of the murderer.
9. That is, Gloucester is a devil, not man or beast.
1. *diffused:* misshapen; but also *diffused infection,* an

infection whose harmful effects are dispersed widely.
2. In *3 Henry VI* 5.5, King Edward stabbed the Prince
first, and Gloucester followed.

LADY ANNE Thou wast provoked by thy bloody mind,
Which never dreamt on aught° but butcheries.   *anything*
Didst thou not kill this king?
GLOUCESTER   I grant ye.
100 LADY ANNE Dost grant me, hedgehog?[3] Then God grant me
too
Thou mayst be damned for that wicked deed!
Oh, he was gentle, mild, and virtuous.
GLOUCESTER The fitter for the King of heaven that hath
him.
LADY ANNE He is in heaven, where thou shalt never come.
105 GLOUCESTER Let him thank me that holp° to send him   *helped*
thither,
For he was fitter for that place than earth.
LADY ANNE And thou unfit for any place but hell.
GLOUCESTER Yes, one place else, if you will hear me name it.
LADY ANNE Some dungeon.
GLOUCESTER   Your bedchamber.
110 LADY ANNE Ill rest betide° the chamber where thou liest.   *befall*
GLOUCESTER So will it, madam, till I lie with you.
LADY ANNE I hope so.
GLOUCESTER   I know so. But, gentle Lady Anne,
To leave this keen encounter of our wits,
And fall somewhat into a slower method:[4]
115 Is not the causer of the timeless° deaths   *untimely*
Of these Plantagenets,[5] Henry and Edward,
As blameful as the executioner?
LADY ANNE Thou art the cause and most accursed effect.
GLOUCESTER Your beauty was the cause of that effect,
120 Your beauty, which did haunt me in my sleep
To undertake the death of all the world,
So I might rest one hour in your sweet bosom.
LADY ANNE If I thought that, I tell thee, homicide,°   *murderer*
These nails should rend that beauty from my cheeks.
125 GLOUCESTER These eyes could never endure sweet beauty's
wrack;°   *destruction*
You should not blemish it if I stood by.
As all the world is cheerèd by the sun,
So I by that; it is my day, my life.
LADY ANNE Black night overshade thy day, and death thy
life!
130 GLOUCESTER Curse not thyself, fair creature, thou art both.
LADY ANNE I would I were, to be revenged on thee.[6]
GLOUCESTER It is a quarrel most unnatural
To be revenged on him that loveth you.
LADY ANNE It is a quarrel just and reasonable
135 To be revenged on him that slew my husband.
GLOUCESTER He that bereft thee, lady, of thy husband,
Did it to help thee to a better husband.

---

3. Term of abuse applied to someone who pays no
attention to others' feelings; alluding to Richard's
humped back and his heraldic badge, the boar.
4. And argue somewhat less hastily.
5. The royal house from which both Lancastrians,

including Henry and his son Edward, and Yorkists,
including Gloucester himself, descended.
6. That is, if Anne were Richard's day and his life,
she could end both and thus be revenged on him.

LADY ANNE His better doth not breathe upon the earth.
GLOUCESTER Go to: he lives that loves thee better than he°   *(Edward)*
   could.
LADY ANNE Name him.
GLOUCESTER   Plantagenet.
140 LADY ANNE   Why, that was he.
GLOUCESTER The selfsame name, but one of better nature.
LADY ANNE Where is he?
GLOUCESTER   Here.
    She spitteth at him.
                Why dost thou spit at me?
LADY ANNE Would it were mortal poison for thy sake.
GLOUCESTER Never came poison from so sweet a place.
145 LADY ANNE Never hung poison on a fouler toad.[7]
   Out of my sight! Thou dost infect my eyes.
GLOUCESTER Thine eyes, sweet lady, have infected mine.
LADY ANNE Would° they were basilisks[8] to strike thee dead!   *I wish that*
GLOUCESTER I would they were, that I might die at once,°   *once and for all*
150   For now they kill me with a living death.
   Those eyes of thine from mine have drawn salt tears,
   Shamed their aspect° with store of childish drops.   *appearance*
   I never sued° to friend nor enemy;   *petitioned*
   My tongue could never learn sweet smoothing° words.   *flattering*
155   But now thy beauty is proposed my fee,°   *recompense*
   My proud heart sues, and prompts my tongue to speak.
     [*She looks scornfully at him.*]
   Teach not thy lips such scorn, for they were made
   For kissing, lady, not for such contempt.
   If thy revengeful heart cannot forgive,
160   Lo, here, I lend thee this sharp-pointed sword,
   Which if thou please to hide in this true bosom
   And let the soul forth that adoreth thee,
   I lay it naked to the deadly stroke,
   And humbly beg the death upon my knee.
     [*He lays his breast open:° she offers° at it with*   *bare / thrusts*
     his sword.]
165   Nay, do not pause. 'Twas I that killed your husband,
   But 'twas thy beauty that provokèd me.
   Nay, now dispatch. 'Twas I that killed King Henry,
   But 'twas thy heavenly face that set me on.
     Here she lets fall the sword.
   Take up the sword again, or take up me.
170 LADY ANNE Arise, dissembler. Though I wish thy death,
   I will not be the executioner.
GLOUCESTER Then bid me kill myself, and I will do it.
LADY ANNE I have already.
GLOUCESTER Tush, that was in thy rage.
175   Speak it again, and even with the word,
   That hand, which for thy love did kill thy love,
   Shall for thy love kill a far truer love;
   To both their deaths shalt thou be accessory.
LADY ANNE I would I knew thy heart.

---

7. Toads were popularly regarded as "ugly and venomous" (*As You Like It* 2.1.13).

8. Legendary reptilian monsters also known as cockatrices, supposed to kill with a glance.

180	GLOUCESTER 'Tis figured in my tongue.	
	LADY ANNE I fear me both are false.	
	GLOUCESTER Then never was man true.	
	LADY ANNE Well, well, put up your sword.[9]	
	GLOUCESTER Say, then, my peace is made.	
185	LADY ANNE That shall you know hereafter.	
	GLOUCESTER But shall I live in hope?	
	LADY ANNE All men, I hope, live so.	
	GLOUCESTER Vouchsafe° to wear this ring.	*Consent*
	LADY ANNE To take is not to give.[1]	
190	GLOUCESTER Look how this ring encompasseth° thy finger;	*encircles*
	Even so thy breast encloseth my poor heart.	
	Wear both of them, for both of them are thine.	
	And if thy poor devoted suppliant° may	*petitioner*
	But beg one favor at thy gracious hand,	
195	Thou dost confirm his happiness forever.	
	LADY ANNE What is it?	
	GLOUCESTER That it would please thee leave these sad	
	designs°	*affairs*
	To him that hath more cause to be a mourner,	
	And presently° repair° to Crosby Place,[2]	*at once / return*
200	Where, after I have solemnly interred	
	At Chertsey monastery this noble king	
	And wet his grave with my repentant tears,	
	I will with all expedient° duty see you.	*prompt*
	For diverse unknown° reasons, I beseech you,	*various secret*
205	Grant me this boon.°	*favor*
	LADY ANNE With all my heart, and much it joys me too	
	To see you are become so penitent.	
	Tressel and Berkeley, go along with me.	
	GLOUCESTER Bid me farewell.	
	LADY ANNE 'Tis more than you deserve;[3]	
210	But since you teach me how to flatter you,	
	Imagine I have said farewell already. *Exit.*	
	GLOUCESTER Sirs, take up the corpse.	
	GENTLEMAN Towards Chertsey, noble lord?	
	GLOUCESTER No, to Whitefriars;[4] there attend° my coming.	*await*
	Exeunt all but GLOUCESTER.	
	Was ever woman in this humor° wooed?	*mood; manner*
215	Was ever woman in this humor won?	
	I'll have her, but I will not keep her long.	
	What? I, that killed her husband and his father,	
	To take her in her heart's extremest hate,	
	With curses in her mouth, tears in her eyes,	
220	The bleeding witness of her hatred by,	
	Having God, her conscience, and these bars° against me,	*obstacles*
	And I nothing to back my suit at all	
	But the plain devil and dissembling looks,	
	And yet to win her, all the world to nothing?° Ha!	*against such odds*

9. PERFORMANCE COMMENT Actors must decide how to stage Gloucester's motives in pursuing Anne, and likewise why Anne ultimately decides to accept Richard's suit. See Digital Edition PC 2.
1. To take your ring is not to give myself.

2. One of Richard's London residences.
3. That is, to fare well is more than you deserve.
4. A Carmelite monastery and zone of criminal immunity in London, noted for its disreputable frequenters.

225 Hath she forgot already that brave prince,
  Edward, her lord, whom I some three months since
  Stabbed in my angry mood at Tewkesbury?
  A sweeter and a lovelier gentleman,
  Framed in the prodigality of nature,[5]
230 Young, valiant, wise, and no doubt right royal,
  The spacious world cannot again afford.°   *provide*
  And will she yet debase° her eyes on me,   *lower; degrade*
  That cropped the golden prime[6] of this sweet prince,
  And made her widow to a woeful bed?
235 On me, whose all not equals Edward's moiety?°   *half*
  On me, that halt° and am unshapen thus?   *limp*
  My dukedom to a beggarly denier,[7]
  I do mistake my person all this while!
  Upon my life, she finds, although I cannot,
240 Myself to be a marvelous proper° man.   *handsome*
  I'll be at charges for° a looking glass,   *I'll buy*
  And entertain° some score or two of tailors   *hire*
  To study fashions to adorn my body.
  Since I am crept in° favor with myself,   *into*
245 I will maintain it with some little cost.
  But first I'll turn yon fellow in his grave
  And then return lamenting to my love.
  Shine out, fair sun, till I have bought a glass,°   *mirror*
  That I may see my shadow as I pass.   *Exit.*

1.3 (F 1.3)

Enter QUEEN [ELIZABETH], [*Marquess* DORSET,] *Lord*
RIVERS, *and* GREY.

RIVERS Have patience, madam. There's no doubt his majesty
  Will soon recover his accustomed health.
GREY In that you brook it ill,° it makes him worse; *take it badly*
  Therefore, for God's sake, entertain good comfort,
5 And cheer his grace with quick° and merry words. *lively*
QUEEN ELIZABETH If he were dead, what would betide
   of° me?   *become of*
RIVERS No other harm but loss of such a lord.
QUEEN ELIZABETH The loss of such a lord includes all harm.
GREY The heavens have blest you with a goodly son
10 To be your comforter when he is gone.
QUEEN ELIZABETH Oh, he is young, and his minority
  Is put unto the trust of Richard Gloucester,
  A man that loves not me nor none of you.
RIVERS Is it concluded° he shall be Protector?[1] *officially decreed*
15 QUEEN ELIZABETH It is determined,° not concluded yet; *decided*
  But so it must be if the King miscarry.°   *die*

  Enter BUCKINGHAM *and* [STANLEY, *Earl of*] *Derby.*

GREY Here come the lords of Buckingham and Derby.
BUCKINGHAM Good time of day unto your royal grace.
STANLEY God make your majesty joyful as you have been.

---

5. Created when nature was at its most lavish.
6. Springtime (Gloucester "cropped," or harvested, Edward's life prematurely).
7. *denier*: French coin, one-twelfth of a sou (extremely little).
1.3 Location: The royal palace of Westminster.
1. The title of the person selected to rule as head of state during a monarch's minority or absence.

20 QUEEN ELIZABETH   The Countess Richmond,[2] good my lord
          of Derby,
     To your good prayers will scarcely say "Amen."
     Yet Derby, notwithstanding she's your wife
     And loves not me, be you, good lord, assured
     I hate not you for her proud arrogance.
25 STANLEY   I do beseech you, either not believe
     The envious° slanders of her false accusers,   *malicious*
     Or, if she be accused in true report,
     Bear with her weakness, which I think proceeds
     From wayward° sickness and no grounded malice.   *not easily treated*
30 RIVERS   Saw you the King today, my lord of Derby?
     STANLEY   But° now the Duke of Buckingham and I   *Just*
     Came from visiting his majesty.
     QUEEN ELIZABETH   What likelihood of his amendment,°   *recovery*
          lords?
     BUCKINGHAM   Madam, good hope; his grace speaks
          cheerfully.
35 QUEEN ELIZABETH   God grant him health. Did you confer
          with him?
     BUCKINGHAM   Madam, we did. He desires to make
          atonement°   *reconciliation*
     Betwixt the Duke of Gloucester and your brothers,
     And betwixt them and my Lord Chamberlain,°   *(Hastings)*
     And sent to warn° them to his royal presence.   *summon*
40 QUEEN ELIZABETH   Would all were well, but that will
          never be.
     I fear our happiness is at the highest.[3]
          Enter GLOUCESTER [*and* HASTINGS].
     GLOUCESTER   They do me wrong, and I will not endure it.
     Who are they that complains unto the King
     That I, forsooth, am stern and love them not?
45 By holy Paul, they love his grace but lightly
     That fill his ears with such dissentious° rumors.   *quarrelsome*
     Because I cannot flatter and speak fair,
     Smile in men's faces, smooth,° deceive, and cog,°   *flatter / cheat*
     Duck with French nods[4] and apish° courtesy,   *imitative; clumsy*
50 I must be held a rancorous enemy.
     Cannot a plain man live and think no harm,
     But thus his simple truth must be abused
     By silken, sly, insinuating jacks?°   *nobodies*
     RIVERS   To whom in all this presence° speaks your grace?   *present company*
55 GLOUCESTER   To thee, that hast nor honesty nor grace.
     When have I injured thee? When done thee wrong?
     Or thee? Or thee? Or any of your faction?
     A plague upon you all! His royal person—
     Whom God preserve better than you would wish—
60 Cannot be quiet scarce a breathing while[5]
     But you must trouble him with lewd° complaints.   *ignorant*

2. Lady Margaret Beaufort, Lord Stanley's wife, was
(by an earlier marriage) the mother of Henry Tudor,
Earl of Richmond, who at play's end succeeds Richard
and becomes Henry VII. As a descendant of the house
of Lancaster, she was unlikely to have friendly feelings

toward the Yorkist King Edward IV or his family.
3. At its highest point on Fortune's proverbial wheel,
and thus about to decline.
4. *French nods*: elaborate bows.
5. Long enough to catch his breath.

QUEEN ELIZABETH   Brother of Gloucester, you mistake the
matter.
The King, of his own royal disposition°   *inclination*
And not provoked by any suitor else,
65   Aiming, belike,° at your interior hatred,   *Guessing, probably*
Which in your outward actions shows itself
Against my kindred, brother, and myself,
Makes him to send,[6] that thereby he may gather
The ground of your ill will[7] and remove it.
70   GLOUCESTER   I cannot tell: the world is grown so bad
That wrens make prey where eagles dare not perch.
Since every Jack[8] became a gentleman
There's many a gentle° person made a jack.[9]   *noble*
QUEEN ELIZABETH   Come, come, we know your meaning,
brother Gloucester:
75   You envy my advancement and my friends'.
God grant we never may have need of you.
GLOUCESTER   Meantime, God grants that we have need of
you.
Our brother° is imprisoned by your means,   *(Clarence)*
Myself disgraced, and the nobility
80   Held in contempt, whilst many fair promotions
Are daily given to ennoble those
That scarce some two days since were worth a noble.[1]
QUEEN ELIZABETH   By Him° that raised me to this careful   *(God)*
height
From that contented hap° which I enjoyed,   *fortune; lot*
85   I never did incense his majesty
Against the Duke of Clarence, but have been
An earnest advocate to plead for him.
My lord, you do me shameful injury
Falsely to draw me in these vile suspects.°   *suspicions*
90   GLOUCESTER   You may deny that you were not the cause
Of my Lord Hastings' late imprisonment.
RIVERS   She may, my lord.
GLOUCESTER   She may, Lord Rivers, why, who knows not so?
She may do more, sir, than denying that.
95   She may help you to many fair preferments,°   *lucrative positions*
And then deny her aiding hand therein,
And lay those honors on[2] your high deserts.
What may she not? She may, yea, marry[3] may she.
RIVERS   What, marry, may she?
100   GLOUCESTER   What, marry may she? Marry with a king,
A bachelor, a handsome stripling° too;   *young man*
Iwis your grandam had a worser match.[4]
QUEEN ELIZABETH   My lord of Gloucester, I have too long
borne
Your blunt upbraidings and your bitter scoffs.
105   By heaven, I will acquaint his majesty

---

6. I.e., causes the King himself to send for you
(because he suspects your hatred against my family).
7. *gather . . . will:* learn the basis of your ill will.
8. A common name, often used to refer to lowborn
individuals.
9. In this instance, in addition to serving as a sign of
contempt, "jack" refers to the small ball in the game

of bowls that is knocked about by the larger balls.
1. Gold coin, worth one-third of a pound sterling.
2. And attribute those honors to.
3. Indeed (originally, an oath on the Virgin Mary),
with pun in next line on "wed."
4. Your mother (and the Queen's) was born of a less
distinguished union. *Iwis:* Assuredly (already archaic).

With those gross taunts I often have endured.
I had rather be a country servant-maid
Than a great queen with this condition,
To be thus taunted, scorned, and baited at.°   *provoked*
110   Small joy have I in being England's queen.
       Enter QUEEN MARGARET.[5]
QUEEN MARGARET [*aside*]   And lessened be that small, God, I
    beseech thee.
Thy honor, state,° and seat° is due to me.   *rank / throne*
GLOUCESTER   What, threat you me with telling of the King?
Tell him, and spare not. Look what° I have said   *Whatever*
115   I will avouch in presence of the King.
'Tis time to speak; my pains[6] are quite forgot.
QUEEN MARGARET [*aside*]   Out, devil! I remember them too
    well:
Thou slewest my husband Henry in the Tower,
And Edward, my poor son, at Tewkesbury.
120 GLOUCESTER   Ere you were queen, yea, or your husband
    king,
I was a packhorse° in his great affairs,   *workhorse*
A weeder-out of his proud adversaries,
A liberal rewarder of his friends.
To royalize his blood I spilt mine own.
125 QUEEN MARGARET [*aside*]   Yea, and much better blood than
    his or thine.
GLOUCESTER   In all which time you and your husband Grey
Were factious° for the house of Lancaster,   *partisan*
And Rivers, so were you. Was not your husband
In Margaret's battle° at Saint Albans slain?[7]   *army*
130   Let me put in your minds, if yours forget,
What you have been ere now, and what you are;
Withal,° what I have been, and what I am.   *In addition; also*
QUEEN MARGARET [*aside*]   A murderous villain, and so still
    thou art.
GLOUCESTER   Poor Clarence did forsake his father[8] Warwick,
135   Yea, and forswore himself (which Jesu pardon)—
QUEEN MARGARET [*aside*]   Which God revenge!
GLOUCESTER   To fight on Edward's party° for the crown,   *side*
And for his meed,° poor lord, he is mewed up.   *reward*
I would to God my heart were flint, like Edward's,
140   Or Edward's soft and pitiful, like mine.
I am too childish-foolish for this world.
QUEEN MARGARET [*aside*]   Hie° thee to hell for shame, and   *Hurry*
    leave the world,
Thou cacodemon!° There thy kingdom is.   *evil spirit*
RIVERS   My lord of Gloucester, in those busy days
145   Which here you urge° to prove us enemies,   *recall*
We followed then our lord, our lawful king.

---

5. Historically, Margaret, widow of the Lancastrian King Henry VI, was held prisoner in England for five years after her husband's defeat at the Battle of Tewkesbury and then exiled to France. She does not present herself to the characters onstage until line 157.
6. Efforts, troubles (on the King's behalf).
7. Queen Elizabeth's first husband, Sir John Grey, died fighting for the Lancastrian faction.
8. Father-in-law. Clarence defied his brothers by supporting the Lancastrian faction alongside Warwick. He "forswore himself" (line 135) by returning to fight for the Yorkist faction, a moment dramatized in 5.1 of *3 Henry VI*.

So should we you, if you should be our king.
GLOUCESTER   If I should be? I had rather be a peddler.
Far be it from my heart, the thought of it.
150   QUEEN ELIZABETH   As little joy, my lord, as you suppose
You should enjoy were you this country's king,
As little joy may you suppose in me
That I enjoy being the queen thereof.
QUEEN MARGARET [aside]   A little joy enjoys the queen thereof,
155   For I am she and altogether joyless.
I can no longer hold me patient.
  [She moves forward.]
Hear me, you wrangling pirates, that fall out
In sharing that which you have pilled° from me.   pillaged
Which of you trembles not that looks on me?
160   If not, that I being queen, you bow like subjects,
Yet that, by you deposed, you quake like rebels.⁹
—O gentle villain,¹ do not turn away
GLOUCESTER   Foul wrinkled witch, what mak'st thou° in my   what are you doing
  sight?
QUEEN MARGARET   But repetition° of what thou hast marred;   simply recounting
165   That will I make before I let thee go.
A husband and a son thou owest to me,
  [to QUEEN ELIZABETH] And thou a kingdom—all of you
  allegiance.
The sorrow that I have by right is yours,
And all the pleasures you usurp are mine.
170   GLOUCESTER   The curse my noble father laid on thee
When thou didst crown his warlike brows with paper,
And with thy scorn° drew'st rivers from his eyes,   mocking speeches
And then, to dry them, gav'st the Duke a clout°   rag; handkerchief
Steeped in the faultless° blood of pretty Rutland²—   innocent
175   His curses then, from bitterness of soul
Denounced against thee, are all fallen upon thee;
And God, not we, hath plagued thy bloody deed.
QUEEN ELIZABETH   So just is God to right the innocent.
HASTINGS   Oh, 'twas the foulest deed to slay that babe,°   (Rutland)
180   And the most merciless that e'er was heard of.
RIVERS   Tyrants themselves wept when it was reported.
DORSET   No man but prophesied revenge for it.
BUCKINGHAM   Northumberland,³ then present, wept to see it.
QUEEN MARGARET   What, were you snarling all before I came,
185   Ready to catch each other by the throat,
And turn you all your hatred now on me?
Did York's dread curse prevail so much with heaven
That Henry's death, my lovely Edward's death,
Their kingdom's loss, my woeful banishment,
190   Could all but answer for° that peevish brat?   Could merely equal
Can curses pierce the clouds and enter heaven?
Why, then, give way, dull clouds, to my quick° curses.   lively

9. If . . . rebels: Even if you do not bow because I am queen, at least you tremble like rebels because you deposed me.
1. Well-born peasant; kindly scoundrel.
2. This is dramatized in 3 Henry VI 1.4, in which Margaret crowns the Duke of York with a paper crown

and waves a handkerchief dipped in his son Rutland's blood in front of his eyes.
3. An ally of King Henry VI. Though Northumberland helps capture York with Queen Margaret and Clifford, he notably pities York and cries as York is tormented and murdered. See 1.4 in 3 Henry VI.

If not by war, by surfeit° die your king,   *high living*
As ours by murder to make him a king.
195 [*to* QUEEN ELIZABETH] Edward thy son, which now is Prince
        of Wales,
     For Edward my son, which was Prince of Wales,
     Die in his youth by like° untimely violence.   *similarly*
     Thyself a queen, for me that was a queen,
     Outlive thy glory, like my wretched self.
200 Long mayst thou live to wail thy children's loss,
     And see another, as I see thee now,
     Decked° in thy rights, as thou art stalled° in mine.   *Dressed / installed*
     Long die thy happy days before thy death,
     And, after many lengthened hours of grief,
205 Die neither mother, wife, nor England's queen.
     Rivers and Dorset, you were standers by,
     And so wast thou, Lord Hastings,⁴ when my son
     Was stabbed with bloody daggers. God, I pray Him,
     That none of you may live your natural age
210 But by some unlooked° accident cut off.   *unlooked-for*
GLOUCESTER   Have done thy charm,° thou hateful withered   *spell; curse*
        hag.
QUEEN MARGARET   And leave out thee? Stay, dog, for thou
        shalt hear me.
     If heaven have any grievous plague in store
     Exceeding those that I can wish upon thee,
215 Oh, let them keep it till thy sins be ripe,
     And then hurl down their indignation
     On thee, the troubler of the poor world's peace.
     The worm of conscience still begnaw thy soul.
     Thy friends suspect for° traitors while thou livest,   *to be*
220 And take deep traitors for thy dearest friends.
     No sleep close up that deadly eye of thine,
     Unless it be whilst some tormenting dream
     Affrights thee with a hell of ugly devils.
     Thou elvish-marked, abortive, rooting hog,⁵
225 Thou that wast sealed° in thy nativity   *stamped*
     The slave of nature⁶ and the son of hell;
     Thou slander of thy mother's heavy° womb,   *pregnant; sorrowful*
     Thou loathèd issue of thy father's loins,
     Thou rag of honor, thou detested—
GLOUCESTER   Margaret.
QUEEN MARGARET   Richard.
GLOUCESTER   Ha?
230 QUEEN MARGARET   I call thee not.
GLOUCESTER   Then I cry thee mercy,° for I had thought   *I beg your pardon*
     That thou hadst called me all these bitter names.
QUEEN MARGARET   Why, so I did, but looked for no reply.
     Oh, let me make the period° to my curse.   *full stop; finish*
235 GLOUCESTER   'Tis done by me, and ends in "Margaret."
QUEEN ELIZABETH   Thus have you breathed your curse
        against yourself.

---

4. Rivers, Dorset, and Hastings were not present at
Prince Edward's murder at Tewkesbury as dramatized
in *3 Henry VI* 5.5, but they are in the chronicles that
served as Shakespeare's sources. The Prince, in fact,
was slain by unknown combatants during the battle.
5. Gloucester's emblem was the white boar. *elvish-
marked*: deformed by evil fairies. *abortive*: misshapen.
6. Because he was deformed from birth.

QUEEN MARGARET   Poor painted queen, vain flourish[7] of my
    fortune,
  Why strew'st thou sugar on that bottled° spider,   *bottle-shaped; swollen*
  Whose deadly web ensnareth thee about?
240 Fool, fool, thou whett'st a knife to kill thyself.
  The time will come that thou shalt wish for me
  To help thee curse that poisonous bunch-backed° toad.   *hunchbacked*
HASTINGS   False-boding° woman, end thy frantic curse,   *Falsely prophesying*
  Lest to thy harm thou move° our patience.   *try*
245 QUEEN MARGARET   Foul shame upon you! You have all moved
    mine.
RIVERS   Were you well served, you would be taught your duty.
QUEEN MARGARET   To serve me well, you all should do
    me duty,°   *show me deference*
  Teach me to be your queen, and you my subjects.
  Oh, serve me well, and teach yourselves that duty.
250 DORSET   Dispute not with her; she is lunatic.
QUEEN MARGARET   Peace, master Marquess, you are
    malapert:°   *impertinent*
  Your fire-new stamp of honor is scarce current.[8]
  Oh, that your young nobility could judge
  What 'twere to lose it and be miserable.
255 They that stand high have many blasts to shake them,
  And if they fall, they dash themselves to pieces.
GLOUCESTER   Good counsel, marry. Learn it, learn it,
    Marquess.
DORSET   It toucheth you, my lord, as much as me.
GLOUCESTER   Yea, and much more, but I was born so high.
260 Our aerie[9] buildeth in the cedar's top,
  And dallies with the wind and scorns the sun.
QUEEN MARGARET   And turns the sun to shade. Alas, alas,
  Witness my son, now in the shade of death,
  Whose bright outshining beams thy cloudy wrath
265 Hath in eternal darkness folded up.
  Your aerie buildeth in our aerie's nest.
  O God that seest it, do not suffer° it!   *tolerate*
  As it was won with blood, lost be it so!
BUCKINGHAM   Have done, for shame if not for charity.
270 QUEEN MARGARET   Urge neither charity nor shame to me.
  Uncharitably with me have you dealt,
  And shamefully by you my hopes are butchered.
  My charity is outrage, life my shame,°   *my life is one of shame*
  And in my shame still live my sorrow's rage.
275 BUCKINGHAM   Have done.
QUEEN MARGARET   O princely Buckingham, I will kiss
    thy hand
  In sign of league and amity with thee.
  Now fair befall° thee and thy princely house.   *good fortune to*
  Thy garments are not spotted with our blood,
280 Nor thou within the compass° of my curse.   *scope*
BUCKINGHAM   Nor no one here, for curses never pass

---

7. *painted*: counterfeit, with play on "use of cosmetics." *vain flourish*: empty, meaningless decoration.
8. Your recently acquired title is not yet secure (as

newly minted coins that have not yet achieved common currency).
9. Eagle's brood (the sons of York).

The lips of those that breathe them in the air.[1]
QUEEN MARGARET   I'll not believe but they ascend the sky
And there awake God's gentle-sleeping peace.

285   O Buckingham, beware of yonder dog.
Look when° he fawns, he bites; and when he bites,   *Whenever*
His venom tooth will rankle° thee to death.   *poison*
Have not to do with him, beware of him;
Sin, death, and hell have set their marks on him,

290   And all their ministers attend on him.
GLOUCESTER   What doth she say, my lord of Buckingham?
BUCKINGHAM   Nothing that I respect, my gracious lord.
QUEEN MARGARET   What, dost thou scorn me for my gentle
      counsel?
And soothe the devil that I warn thee from?

295   Oh, but remember this another day
When he shall split thy very heart with sorrow,
And say poor Margaret was a prophetess.
Live each of you the subjects of his hate,
And he to yours, and all of you to God's!   *Exit.*

300   HASTINGS   My hair doth stand on end to hear her curses.
RIVERS   And so doth mine. I wonder she's at liberty.
GLOUCESTER   I cannot blame her. By God's holy mother,
She hath had too much wrong, and I repent
My part thereof that I have done.

305   QUEEN ELIZABETH   I never did her any to my knowledge.
GLOUCESTER   But you have all the vantage of this wrong.[2]
I was too hot° to do somebody good   *eager*
That° is too cold° in thinking of it now.   *Who / ungrateful*
Marry, as for Clarence, he is well repaid;

310   He is franked up to fatting[3] for his pains.
God pardon them that are the cause of it.
RIVERS   A virtuous and a Christian-like conclusion,
To pray for them that have done scathe° to us.   *harm*
GLOUCESTER   So do I ever, being well advised,

315   [*He speaks to himself.*] For had I cursed now I had cursed
      myself.
         [*Enter* CATESBY.]
CATESBY   Madam, his majesty doth call for you,
And for your grace, and you, my noble lords.
QUEEN ELIZABETH   Catesby, we come. Lords, will you go
      with us?
RIVERS   Madam, we will attend your grace.
                    Exeunt all but GLOUCESTER.

320   GLOUCESTER   I do the wrong, and first begin to brawl.°   *complain; protest*
The secret mischiefs that I set abroach°   *set in motion*
I lay unto the grievous charge of[4] others.
Clarence, whom I indeed have laid in darkness,
I do beweep to many simple gulls,°   *credulous fools*

325   Namely to Hastings, Derby, Buckingham,
And say it is the Queen and her allies
That stir the King against the Duke my brother.

---

1. *curses . . . air*: it is as if curses were never spoken
or afflict only the curser.
2. All the benefits acquired as a result of the wrong

she has suffered.
3. He is penned up to fatten (for slaughter, like a pig).
4. I make into a serious accusation against.

Now they believe me, and withal whet me
To be revenged on Rivers, Vaughan, Grey.
330 But then I sigh, and with a piece of scripture
Tell them that God bids us do good for evil.
And thus I clothe my naked villainy
With old odd ends° stol'n out of holy writ,   *old bits and pieces*
And seem a saint when most I play the devil.
    Enter EXECUTIONERS.
335 But soft,° here come my executioners.   *wait; hush*
  —How now, my hardy, stout, resolvèd° mates,   *resolute*
Are you now going to dispatch this deed?
EXECUTIONER We are, my lord, and come to have the
    warrant
That we may be admitted where he is.
340 GLOUCESTER It was well thought upon. I have it here
    about me.
When you have done, repair to Crosby Place.
But, sirs, be sudden° in the execution—   *swift*
Withal obdurate. Do not hear him plead,
For Clarence is well-spoken, and perhaps
345 May move your hearts to pity if you mark° him.   *listen to*
EXECUTIONER Tush, fear not, my lord, we will not stand to
    prate.
Talkers are no good doers. Be assured
We come to use our hands and not our tongues.
GLOUCESTER Your eyes drop millstones when fools' eyes
    drop° tears.   *let fall*
350 I like you, lads. About your business.   *Exeunt.*

1.4 (F 1.4)
    Enter CLARENCE [*and*] BRAKENBURY.
BRAKENBURY Why looks your grace so heavily° today?   *melancholy*
CLARENCE Oh, I have passed a miserable night,
So full of ugly sights, of ghastly dreams,
That, as I am a Christian faithful man,
5 I would not spend another such a night,
Though 'twere to buy a world of happy days,
So full of dismal terror was the time.
BRAKENBURY What was your dream? I long to hear you
    tell it.
CLARENCE Methoughts I was embarked for Burgundy,
10 And in my company my brother Gloucester,
Who from my cabin tempted me to walk
Upon the hatches.[1] Thence we looked toward England,
And cited up° a thousand fearful times   *recalled*
During the wars of York and Lancaster
15 That had befallen us. As we paced along
Upon the giddy footing of the hatches,
Methought that Gloucester stumbled, and in stumbling
Struck me, that thought to stay° him, overboard   *who intended to steady*
Into the tumbling billows of the main.
20 Lord, Lord, methought what pain it was to drown;

1.4 Location: In the Tower of London.
1. Planks laid across the hold of a ship, forming a temporary deck.

What dreadful noise of waters in my ears;
What ugly sights of death within my eyes.
Methought I saw a thousand fearful wrecks,
Ten thousand men that fishes gnawed upon,
25   Wedges of gold, great anchors, heaps of pearl,
Inestimable° stones, unvalued° jewels.   *Countless / invaluable*
Some lay in dead men's skulls, and in those holes
Where eyes did once inhabit there were crept—
As 'twere in scorn of eyes—reflecting gems,
30   Which wooed the slimy bottom of the deep
And mocked the dead bones that lay scattered by.
BRAKENBURY   Had you such leisure in the time of death
To gaze upon the secrets of the deep?
CLARENCE   Methought I had, for still° the envious° flood[2]   *always / malicious*
35   Kept in my soul, and would not let it forth
To seek the empty, vast, and wandering air,
But smothered it within my panting bulk,°   *body*
Which almost burst to belch it in the sea.
BRAKENBURY   Awaked you not with this sore agony?
40   CLARENCE   Oh, no, my dream was lengthened after life.[3]
Oh, then began the tempest to my soul,
Who passed, methought, the melancholy flood,[4]
With that grim ferryman which poets write of,
Unto the kingdom of perpetual night.
45   The first that there did greet my stranger soul
Was my great father-in-law, renownèd Warwick,
Who cried aloud, "What scourge° for perjury   *punishment*
Can this dark monarchy afford false Clarence?"
And so he vanished. Then came wand'ring by
50   A shadow[5] like an angel in bright hair
Dabbled in blood, and he squeaked out aloud:
"Clarence is come, false, fleeting,° perjured Clarence,   *fickle*
That stabbed me in the field by Tewkesbury.
Seize on him, Furies,[6] take him to your torments!"
55   With that, methoughts a legion of foul fiends
Environed° me about, and howled in mine ears   *Surrounded*
Such hideous cries that with the very noise
I, trembling, waked, and for a season° after   *for a while*
Could not believe but that I was in hell,
60   Such terrible impression made the dream.
BRAKENBURY   No marvel, my lord, though° it affrighted you.   *that*
I promise you, I am afraid to hear you tell it.
CLARENCE   O Brakenbury, I have done those things
Which now bear evidence against my soul,
65   For Edward's sake, and see how he requites me.
I pray thee, gentle keeper, stay by me.
My soul is heavy, and I fain would° sleep.   *I desire to*

---

2. TEXTUAL COMMENT Differences in Clarence's response in the Folio, notably the added clause that dramatizes his struggle to "yield the ghost," suggest that the Folio is a revision of the Quarto rather than a revision of a shared manuscript. See Digital Edition TC 2 (Quarto edited text).
3. My dream also depicted my fate after death.
4. The river Styx, across which Charon (the "grim

ferryman" of the next line) ferried souls to Hades, the classical hell.
5. Shade, ghost (Edward, Prince of Wales—son of Henry VI, and Clarence's brother-in-law—whom Clarence helped to murder; see 3 *Henry VI* 5.5).
6. In Greek mythology, female spirits who enacted vengeance for blood crimes against relatives.

BRAKENBURY   I will, my lord. God give your grace good rest.
     [CLARENCE *sleeps.*]
Sorrow breaks seasons and reposing hours,[7]
70 Makes the night morning and the noontide night.
Princes have but° their titles for their glories,   *only*
An outward honor for an inward toil;
And for unfelt imagination,[8]
They often feel a world of restless cares,
75 So that betwixt their titles and low names
There's nothing differs but the outward fame.
     The Murderers [FIRST *and* SECOND EXECUTIONER]
     enter.
In God's name, what are you, and how came you hither?
FIRST EXECUTIONER   I would speak with Clarence, and I came
hither on my legs.
80 BRAKENBURY   Yea, are you so brief?
SECOND EXECUTIONER   O sir, it is better to be brief than tedious.
Show him our commission;° talk no more.   *authorization*
     [BRAKENBURY] *readeth it.*
BRAKENBURY   I am in this commanded to deliver
The noble Duke of Clarence to your hands.
85 I will not reason what is meant hereby,
Because I will be° guiltless of the meaning.   *wish to be*
Here are the keys, there sits the Duke asleep.
I'll to his majesty, and certify his grace
That thus I have resigned my charge° to you.   *responsibility*
90 FIRST EXECUTIONER   Do so; it is a point of wisdom.
              [*Exit* BRAKENBURY.]
SECOND EXECUTIONER   What, shall I stab him as he sleeps?
FIRST EXECUTIONER   No. Then he will say 'twas done cowardly
when he wakes.
SECOND EXECUTIONER   When he wakes? Why, fool, he shall
95 never wake till the Judgment Day.
FIRST EXECUTIONER   Why, then he will say we stabbed him
sleeping.
SECOND EXECUTIONER   The urging of that word "Judgment"
hath bred a kind of remorse in me.
100 FIRST EXECUTIONER   What, art thou afraid?
SECOND EXECUTIONER   Not to kill him, having a warrant for
it, but to be damned for killing him, from which no warrant
can defend us.
FIRST EXECUTIONER   Back to the Duke of Gloucester, tell
105 him so.
SECOND EXECUTIONER   I pray thee, stay a while. I hope my holy
humor° will change; 'twas wont to hold me but while one   *compassionate mood*
would tell° twenty.   *count*
FIRST EXECUTIONER   How dost thou feel thyself now?
110 SECOND EXECUTIONER   Faith,° some certain dregs of con-   *In truth*
science are yet within me.
FIRST EXECUTIONER   Remember our reward when the deed is
done.

---

7. Sorrow disrupts life's normal rhythms and disre-   8. *for unfelt imagination:* for imaginings not experi-
gards the hours appropriate to sleep.   enced.

SECOND EXECUTIONER   Zounds,° he dies. I had forgot the   *By God's wounds*
115   reward.
FIRST EXECUTIONER   Where is thy conscience now?
SECOND EXECUTIONER   In the Duke of Gloucester's purse.
FIRST EXECUTIONER   So when he opens his purse to give us
      our reward, thy conscience flies out.
120   SECOND EXECUTIONER   Let it go; there's few or none will
      entertain° it.   *host; employ*
FIRST EXECUTIONER   How if it come to thee again?
SECOND EXECUTIONER   I'll not meddle with it; it is a danger-
      ous thing. It makes a man a coward. A man cannot steal, but
125   it accuseth him; he cannot swear, but it checks him; he can-
      not lie with his neighbor's wife, but it detects him. It is a
      blushing shamefast° spirit that mutinies in a man's bosom; it   *shameful; bashful*
      fills one full of obstacles. It made me once restore a purse of
      gold that I found. It beggars any man that keeps it. It is
130   turned out of all towns and cities for a dangerous thing, and
      every man that means to live well endeavors to trust to him-
      self and to live without it.
FIRST EXECUTIONER   Zounds, it is even now at my elbow, per-
      suading me not to kill the Duke.
135   SECOND EXECUTIONER   Take the devil in thy mind, and believe
      him° not. He would insinuate with thee to make thee sigh.[9]   *(conscience)*
FIRST EXECUTIONER   Tut, I am strong in fraud; he cannot pre-
      vail with me, I warrant thee.
SECOND EXECUTIONER   Spoke like a tall° fellow that respects   *valiant*
140   his reputation. Come, shall we to this gear?°   *work*
FIRST EXECUTIONER   Take him over the costard with the hilts
      of thy sword, and then we will chop him in the malmsey
      butt[1] in the next room.
SECOND EXECUTIONER   Oh, excellent device: make a sop[2] of him!
145   FIRST EXECUTIONER   Hark, he stirs. Shall I strike?
SECOND EXECUTIONER   No, first let's reason with him.
      [CLARENCE *awakes*.]
CLARENCE   Where art thou, keeper? Give me a cup of wine.
FIRST EXECUTIONER   You shall have wine enough, my lord,
      anon.
CLARENCE   In God's name, what art thou?
SECOND EXECUTIONER   A man, as you are.
CLARENCE   But not as I am, royal.
150   SECOND EXECUTIONER   Nor you as we are, loyal.
CLARENCE   Thy voice is thunder, but thy looks are humble.
SECOND EXECUTIONER   My voice is now the King's,[3] my looks
      mine own.
CLARENCE   How darkly and how deadly dost thou speak.
      Tell me who are you. Wherefore come you hither?
BOTH   To, to, to—
CLARENCE   To murder me?
155   BOTH   Ay.
CLARENCE   You scarcely have the hearts to tell me so,

---

9. *He . . . sigh*: He (conscience) would ingratiate him-   *costard*: head (literally, a large apple).
self with you simply to cause you grief.   2. Piece of bread or wafer soaked in wine.
1. Wine barrel (malmsey is a strong, sweet wine).   3. I am now acting on the King's command.

And therefore cannot have the hearts to do it.
Wherein, my friends, have I offended you?
FIRST EXECUTIONER   Offended us you have not, but the King.
160   CLARENCE   I shall be reconciled to him again.
SECOND EXECUTIONER   Never, my lord; therefore prepare
        to die.
CLARENCE   Are you called forth from° out a world of men   *selected from*
To slay the innocent? What is my offense?
Where are the evidence that do accuse me?
165   What lawful quest° have given their verdict up   *jury*
Unto the frowning judge? Or who pronounced
The bitter sentence of poor Clarence' death
Before I be convict by course of law?
To threaten me with death is most unlawful.
170   I charge you, as you hope to have redemption
By Christ's dear blood shed for our grievous sins,
That you depart and lay no hands on me.
The deed you undertake is damnable.
FIRST EXECUTIONER   What we will do, we do upon command.
175   SECOND EXECUTIONER   And he that hath commanded is the
        King.
CLARENCE   Erroneous vassal!° The great King of kings   *Misguided subject*
Hath in the tables of His law° commanded   *the Ten Commandments*
That thou shalt do no murder. And wilt thou then
Spurn at His edict and fulfill a man's?
180   Take heed, for He holds vengeance in His hands
To hurl upon their heads that break His law.
SECOND EXECUTIONER   And that same vengeance doth He
        throw on thee
For false forswearing and for murder too.
Thou didst receive the holy sacrament[4]
185   To fight in quarrel of° the house of Lancaster.   *on the side of*
FIRST EXECUTIONER   And like a traitor to the name of God
Didst break that vow, and with thy treacherous blade
Unripped the bowels of thy sovereign's son.[5]
SECOND EXECUTIONER   Whom thou wert sworn to cherish
        and defend.
190   FIRST EXECUTIONER   How canst thou urge God's dreadful
        law to us
When thou hast broke it in so dear degree?
CLARENCE   Alas, for whose sake did I that ill deed?
For Edward, for my brother, for his sake.
Why, sirs, he sends ye not to murder me for this,
195   For in this sin he is as deep as I.
If God will be revengèd for this deed,
Take not the quarrel from His powerful arm.
He needs no indirect nor lawless course
To cut off those that have offended Him.
200   FIRST EXECUTIONER   Who made thee then a bloody minister°   *agent*
When gallant-springing,° brave Plantagenet,°   *sprightly / (Prince Edward)*
That princely novice,° was struck dead by thee?   *youth*

4. Take communion and, in doing so, swear by the   5. That is, Prince Edward, son of the then sovereign
body of God.   Henry VI.

CLARENCE   My brother's love,° the devil, and my rage.   *My love for my brother*
FIRST EXECUTIONER   Thy brother's love, the devil, and thy
     fault
205   Have brought us hither now to murder thee.
CLARENCE   Oh, if you love my brother, hate not me.
     I am his brother, and I love him well.
     If you be hired for meed,° go back again,   *reward*
     And I will send you to my brother Gloucester,
210   Who will reward you better for my life
     Than Edward will for tidings of my death.
SECOND EXECUTIONER   You are deceived; your brother
          Gloucester hates you.
CLARENCE   Oh, no, he loves me, and he holds me dear.
     Go you to him from me.
BOTH   Ay, so we will.
215   CLARENCE   Tell him, when that our princely father York
     Blessed his three sons with his victorious arm,
     And charged us from his soul to love each other,
     He little thought of this divided friendship.
     Bid Gloucester think of this, and he will weep.
220   BOTH   Ay, millstones, as he lessoned° us to weep.   *taught*
CLARENCE   Oh, do not slander him, for he is kind.⁶
FIRST EXECUTIONER   Right, as snow in harvest. Thou
          deceiv'st thyself.
     'Tis he hath sent us hither now to slaughter thee.
CLARENCE   It cannot be, for when I parted with him,
225   He hugged me in his arms and swore with sobs
     That he would labor° my delivery.   *work for*
SECOND EXECUTIONER   Why, so he doth, now he delivers thee
     From this world's thralldom to the joys of heaven.
FIRST EXECUTIONER   Make peace with God, for you must die,
          my lord.
230   CLARENCE   Hast thou that holy feeling in thy soul
     To counsel me to make my peace with God,
     And art thou yet to thy own soul so blind
     That thou wilt war with God by murd'ring me?
     Ah, sirs, consider, he that set you on
235   To do this deed will hate you for this deed.
SECOND EXECUTIONER   What shall we do?
CLARENCE   Relent, and save your souls.
FIRST EXECUTIONER   Relent? 'Tis cowardly and womanish.
CLARENCE   Not to relent is beastly, savage, devilish.
     [*to* SECOND EXECUTIONER] My friend, I spy some pity in thy
          looks.
240   Oh, if thy eye be not a flatterer,°   *deceiver (of Clarence)*
     Come thou on my side, and entreat for me.
     A begging prince what beggar pities not?
FIRST EXECUTIONER   Ay, thus, and thus.
          He stabs him.
                                     If this will not serve,
     I'll chop thee in the malmsey butt in the next room.
                         [*Exit with* CLARENCE.]

---

6. He is full of natural feelings (and hence a loving brother). The executioner's response, "as snow in harvest," suggests the opposite (that he is unnatural).

245 SECOND EXECUTIONER   A bloody deed, and desperately
　　　　performed.
　　　How fain,° like Pilate,[7] would I wash my hand　　　　　　　　*gladly*
　　　Of this most grievous guilty murder done.
　　　　[*Enter* FIRST EXECUTIONER.]
　　FIRST EXECUTIONER   Why dost thou not help me?
　　　By heavens, the Duke shall know how slack thou art.
250 SECOND EXECUTIONER   I would he knew that I had saved his
　　　　brother.
　　　Take thou the fee, and tell him what I say,
　　　For I repent me that the Duke is slain.　　　　　　　*Exit.*
　　FIRST EXECUTIONER   So do not I. Go, coward as thou art.
　　　Now must I hide his body in some hole
255 Until the Duke take order for his burial.
　　　And when I have my meed, I must away,
　　　For this will out,[8] and here I must not stay.　　　　　*Exit.*

2.1 (F 2.1)

Enter KING, QUEEN [ELIZABETH], HASTINGS, RIVERS,
DORSET, *and others* [*including* BUCKINGHAM].
　KING   So, now I have done a good day's work.
　　　You peers, continue this united league.
　　　I every day expect an embassage
　　　From my Redeemer to redeem me hence,
5 And now in peace my soul shall part to heaven
　　　Since I have set my friends at peace on earth.
　　　Rivers and Hastings, take each other's hand.
　　　Dissemble not[1] your hatred. Swear your love.
　　RIVERS   By heaven, my heart is purged from grudging hate,
10 And with my hand I seal my true heart's love.
　　HASTINGS   So thrive I° as I truly swear the like.　　　　*May I prosper*
　　KING   Take heed you dally° not before your king,　　　　　*trifle*
　　　Lest he that is the supreme King of kings
　　　Confound° your hidden falsehood and award°　　　*Defeat / cause*
15 Either of you to be the other's end.[2]
　　HASTINGS   So prosper I as I swear perfect love.
　　RIVERS   And I, as I love Hastings with my heart.
　　KING   Madam, yourself are not exempt in this,
　　　Nor your son Dorset —Buckingham, nor you.
20 You have been factious one against the other.
　　　Wife, love Lord Hastings, let him kiss your hand,
　　　And what you do, do it unfeignedly.
　　QUEEN ELIZABETH   Here, Hastings, I will never more
　　　　remember
　　　Our former hatred, so thrive I and mine.°　　　　　　*my family*
25 DORSET   This interchange of love, I here protest,°　　　　*affirm*
　　　Upon my part shall be unviolable.
　　HASTINGS   And so swear I, my lord.
　　　　[*They embrace.*]
　　KING   Now, princely Buckingham, seal thou this league
　　　With thy embracements to my wife's allies,

---

7. Pontius Pilate, the Roman judge who authorized
Jesus' crucifixion.
8. "Murder will out" was proverbial.

2.1 Location: The palace, London.
1. Do not merely disguise.
2. Each of you to cause the death of the other.

30   And make me happy in your unity.

BUCKINGHAM [*to* QUEEN ELIZABETH]   Whenever Buckingham
    doth turn his hate
    On you or yours, but with all duteous love
    Doth cherish you and yours, God punish me[3]
    With hate in those where I expect most love.
35   When I have most need to employ a friend,
    And most assurèd that he is a friend,
    Deep,° hollow, treacherous, and full of guile   *Crafty*
    Be he unto me. This do I beg of God
    When I am cold in zeal to you or yours.
40 KING   A pleasing cordial,° princely Buckingham,   *health-giving drink*
    Is this thy vow unto my sickly heart.
    There wanteth now our brother Gloucester here
    To make the perfect period° of this peace.   *conclusion*
    Enter GLOUCESTER.

BUCKINGHAM   And in good time here comes the noble Duke.
45 GLOUCESTER   Good morrow to my sovereign king and queen,
    And princely peers, a happy time of day.

KING   Happy, indeed, as we have spent the day.
    Brother, we have done deeds of charity,
    Made peace of enmity, fair love of hate,
50   Between these swelling, wrong-incensèd[4] peers.

GLOUCESTER   A blessèd labor, my most sovereign liege.
    Amongst this princely heap,° if any here   *company*
    By false intelligence° or wrong surmise   *information*
    Hold me a foe; if I unwittingly or in my rage
55   Have aught° committed that is hardly borne°   *anything / deeply resented*
    By any in this presence, I desire
    To reconcile me to his friendly peace.
    'Tis death to me to be at enmity:
    I hate it, and desire all good men's love.
60   First, madam, I entreat true peace of you,
    Which I will purchase with my duteous service;
    Of you, my noble cousin Buckingham,
    If ever any grudge were lodged between us;
    Of you, Lord Rivers, and Lord Grey, of you,
65   That all without desert° have frowned on me;   *entirely without cause*
    Dukes, earls, lords, gentlemen, indeed of all.
    I do not know that Englishman alive
    With whom my soul is any jot at odds
    More than the infant that is born tonight.
70   I thank my God for my humility.

QUEEN ELIZABETH   A holy day shall this be kept hereafter;
    I would to God all strifes were well compounded.°   *resolved*
    My sovereign liege, I do beseech your majesty
    To take our brother Clarence to your grace.
75 GLOUCESTER   Why, madam, have I offered love for this
    To be thus scorned° in this royal presence?   *mocked*
    Who knows not that the noble Duke is dead?
        [*They all start.*]

---

3. *Whenever . . . me:* If I neglect to love you and your
family, may God punish me.
4. *swelling:* inflated with anger and pride. *wrong-*

incensèd: mistakenly provoked; provoked by wrongs,
injuries.

You do him injury to scorn his corpse.[5]

RIVERS   Who knows not he is dead? Who knows he is?

80   QUEEN ELIZABETH   All-seeing heaven, what a world is this!

BUCKINGHAM   Look I so pale, Lord Dorset, as the rest?

DORSET   Ay, my good lord, and no one in this presence°   (of the King)
But his red color hath forsook his cheeks.

KING   Is Clarence dead? The order was reversed.

85   GLOUCESTER   But he, poor soul, by your first order died,
And that a wingèd Mercury[6] did bear.
Some tardy cripple bore the countermand,
That came too lag° to see him burièd.   late
God grant that some less noble and less loyal,

90   Nearer in bloody thoughts, but not in blood,[7]
Deserve not worse than wretched Clarence did,
And yet go current from suspicion.[8]

       Enter [STANLEY, *Earl of*] *Derby.*

STANLEY   A boon,° my sovereign, for my service done!   *favor*

KING   I pray thee, peace. My soul is full of sorrow.

95   STANLEY [*kneeling*]   I will not rise unless your highness
        grant.

KING   Then speak at once what is it thou demand'st?

STANLEY   The forfeit, sovereign, of my servant's life,[9]
Who slew today a riotous gentleman
Lately attendant on° the Duke of Norfolk.   *Recently employed by*

100   KING   Have I a tongue to doom° my brother's death,   *order*
And shall the same give pardon to a slave?
My brother slew no man. His fault was thought,
And yet his punishment was cruel death.
Who sued to me for him? Who, in my rage,

105   Kneeled at my feet and bade me be advised?°   *consider carefully*
Who spake of brotherhood? Who of love?
Who told me how the poor soul did forsake
The mighty Warwick and did fight for me?
Who told me, in the field by Tewkesbury

110   When Oxford had me down, he rescued me,
And said, "Dear brother, live, and be a king"?
Who told me, when we both lay in the field
Frozen almost to death, how he did lap° me   *wrap*
Even in his own garments, and gave himself

115   All thin° and naked to the numb-cold night?   *thinly clad*
All this from my remembrance brutish wrath
Sinfully plucked, and not a man of you
Had so much grace to put it in my mind.
But when your carters° or your waiting-vassals   *cart drivers*

120   Have done a drunken slaughter and defaced
The precious image[1] of our dear Redeemer,
You straight° are on your knees for "Pardon, pardon,"   *straightaway*
And I, unjustly too, must grant it you.
But for my brother not a man would speak,

5. *to scorn his corpse:* by (supposedly) speaking ironically of him.
6. The speedy messenger of the gods in classical
mythology.
7. That is, nearer to bloody plots than was the innocent Clarence, but not so near the King in blood

(another dig at the Queen's upstart relatives).
8. And yet are accepted at face value without suspicion.
9. That is, the release of his servant from a sentence
of death.
1. A man, thought to be created in God's image.

125 Nor I, ungracious, speak unto myself
For him, poor soul. The proudest of you all
Have been beholden° to him in his life,   *indebted*
Yet none of you would once plead for his life.
O God, I fear Thy justice will take hold
130 On me and you, and mine and yours for this.
—Come, Hastings, help me to my closet.°   *private (bed)room*
Oh, poor Clarence!
      [Exeunt some with KING *and* QUEEN ELIZABETH.]
GLOUCESTER This is the fruit of rashness. Marked you not
How that the guilty kindred of the Queen
135 Looked pale when they did hear of Clarence' death?
Oh, they did urge it still° unto the King.   *ceaselessly*
God will revenge it. But come, let's in
To comfort Edward with our company.   *Exeunt.*

2.2 (F 2.2)

Enter DUCHESS OF YORK, *with Clarence's children*[,
    a BOY *and a* GIRL].[1]

BOY Tell me, good grannam, is our father dead?
DUCHESS OF YORK No, boy.
BOY Why do you wring your hands, and beat your breast,
And cry, "O Clarence, my unhappy son"?
5 GIRL Why do you look on us, and shake your head,
And call us wretches, orphans, castaways,
If that our noble father be alive?
DUCHESS OF YORK My pretty cousins,° you mistake me much.   *kinsmen*
I do lament the sickness of the King,
10 As loath to lose him, not your father's death.
It were lost labor to weep for one that's lost.
BOY Then, grannam, you conclude that he is dead.
The King my uncle is to blame for this.
God will revenge it, whom I will importune°   *beg*
15 With daily prayers all to that effect.
DUCHESS OF YORK Peace, children, peace. The King doth
    love you well.
Incapable° and shallow innocents,   *Uncomprehending*
You cannot guess who caused your father's death.
BOY Grannam, we can, for my good uncle Gloucester
20 Told me the King, provoked by the Queen,
Devised impeachments° to imprison him.   *charges*
And when he told me so, he wept,
And hugged me in his arm, and kindly kissed my cheek,
And bade me rely on him as in my father,
25 And he would love me dearly as his child.
DUCHESS OF YORK Oh, that deceit should steal such gentle
    shapes,°   *appearances*
And with a virtuous vizard° hide foul guile.   *mask*
He is my son, yea, and therein my shame,
Yet from my dugs° he drew not this deceit.   *breasts*
30 BOY Think you my uncle did dissemble, grannam?

2.2 Location: Scene continues.
1. Edward and Margaret Plantagenet (not to be con-   fused with King Edward, Prince Edward, or Queen
Margaret).

DUCHESS OF YORK   Ay, boy.

BOY   I cannot think it. Hark, what noise is this?

    Enter the QUEEN [ELIZABETH].[2]

QUEEN ELIZABETH   Oh, who shall hinder me to wail and
    weep,

    To chide my fortune and torment myself?

35   I'll join with black despair against my soul,

    And to myself become an enemy.

DUCHESS OF YORK   What means this scene of rude°   *violent*
    impatience?

QUEEN ELIZABETH   To make an act of tragic violence.

    Edward, my lord, your son, our king, is dead.[3]

40   Why grow the branches, now the root is withered?

    Why wither not the leaves, the sap being gone?

    If you will live, lament; if die, be brief,

    That our swift-wingèd souls may catch the King's,

    Or like obedient subjects follow him

45   To his new kingdom of perpetual rest.

DUCHESS OF YORK   Ah, so much interest° have I in thy sorrow   *right to share*

    As I had title[4] in thy noble husband.

    I have bewept a worthy husband's[5] death,

    And lived by looking on his images.°   *likenesses (his sons)*

50   But now two mirrors° of his princely semblance   *(Clarence and Edward)*

    Are cracked in pieces by malignant death,

    And I for comfort have but one false glass,°   *(Richard)*

    Which grieves me when I see my shame in him.

    Thou art a widow, yet thou art a mother,

55   And hast the comfort of thy children left thee.

    But death hath snatched my children from mine arms,

    And plucked two crutches from my feeble limbs,

    Edward and Clarence. Oh, what cause have I,

    Thine being but a moiety° of my grief,   *half*

60   To overgo° thy plaints and drown thy cries!   *exceed*

BOY   Good aunt, you wept not for our father's death.

    How can we aid you with our kindred tears?°   *tears of relatives*

GIRL   Our fatherless distress was left unmoaned;

    Your widow's dolors° likewise be unwept.   *widow's grief*

65 QUEEN ELIZABETH   Give me no help in lamentation.

    I am not barren to bring forth laments.[6]

    All springs reduce[7] their currents to mine eyes,

    That I, being governed by the wat'ry moon,

    May send forth plenteous tears to drown the world.

70   Oh, for my husband, for my dear lord Edward!

CHILDREN   Oh, for our father, for our dear lord Clarence!

DUCHESS OF YORK   Alas, for both, both mine, Edward and
    Clarence!

QUEEN ELIZABETH   What stay° had I but Edward? And he is   *support*
    gone.

---

2. TEXTUAL COMMENT The Folio features more
detailed stage directions than the Quarto, which may
reflect the nature and uses of the Folio text. See
Digital Edition TC 3 (Quarto edited text).
3. Shakespeare is telescoping events. Edward actually died some five years after Clarence.
4. Legal right (as Edward's mother, the Duchess of

York has a right to mourn).
5. The Duke of York, whose death is dramatized in
3 Henry VI.
6. I can deliver my own lamentations.
7. Lead back (as to the sea, which is governed by the
moon).

CHILDREN   What stay had we but Clarence? And he is gone.

75   DUCHESS OF YORK   What stays had I but they? And they are
gone.

QUEEN ELIZABETH   Was never widow had so dear° a loss!   *grievous*

CHILDREN   Was never orphans had a dearer loss!

DUCHESS OF YORK   Was never mother had a dearer loss!

Alas, I am the mother of these moans.

80   Their woes are parceled;° mine are general.   *partial*

She for an Edward weeps, and so do I.

I for a Clarence weep, so doth not she.

These babes for Clarence weep, and so do I.

I for an Edward weep, so do not they.

85   Alas! You three, on me threefold distressed,

Pour all your tears. I am your sorrow's nurse,

And I will pamper° it with lamentations.   *(over)feed*

    Enter GLOUCESTER *with others* [*including*
    BUCKINGHAM].

GLOUCESTER   Sister, have comfort. All of us have cause

To wail the dimming of our shining star,

90   But none can cure their harms by wailing them.

Madam, my mother, I do cry you mercy;°   *I beg your pardon*

I did not see your grace. Humbly on my knee

I crave your blessing.

    [*He kneels.*]

DUCHESS OF YORK   God bless thee, and put meekness in thy
mind,

95   Love, charity, obedience, and true duty.

GLOUCESTER [*aside as he rises*]   Amen, and make me die
a good old man.

That's the butt-end° of a mother's blessing;   *conclusion*

I marvel why her grace did leave it out.

BUCKINGHAM   You cloudy° princes and heart-sorrowing peers   *sad; raining (tears)*

100   That bear this mutual heavy load of moan,°   *lamentation*

Now cheer each other in each other's love.

Though we have spent our harvest of this king,

We are to reap the harvest of his son.

The broken rancor[8] of your high-swollen hearts,

105   But lately° splinted, knit, and joined together,   *Only recently*

Must gently be preserved, cherished, and kept.

Me seemeth° good that with some little train°   *I think it / entourage*

Forthwith from Ludlow[9] the young prince be fetched

Hither to London, to be crowned our king.[1]

110   GLOUCESTER   Then be it so, and go we to determine

Who they shall be that straight shall post° to Ludlow.   *ride speedily*

Madam, and you, my mother, will you go

To give your censures° in this weighty business?   *opinions*

QUEEN ELIZABETH, DUCHESS OF YORK   With all our hearts.

    Exeunt all but BUCKINGHAM *and* GLOUCESTER.

115   BUCKINGHAM   My lord, whoever journeys to the Prince,

For God's sake, let not us two stay behind,

---

8. Bitterness that caused you to be divided (unnaturally, like a broken limb).

9. Royal castle in Shropshire, near the Welsh border, where Prince Edward, as Prince of Wales, was staying.

1. TEXTUAL COMMENT In the Folio, but not in the Quarto, Rivers briefly objects before acquiescing to Buckingham's and Gloucester's limitation of the Prince's train. See Digital Edition TC 4 (Quarto edited text).

For by the way I'll sort° occasion, *find*
As index° to the story we late° talked of, *prologue / lately*
To part the Queen's proud kindred from the Prince.[2]
120 GLOUCESTER My other self, my counsel's consistory,° *council chamber*
My oracle, my prophet, my dear cousin,
I, like a child, will go by thy direction.
Towards Ludlow then, for we will not stay behind.

[*Exeunt.*]

2.3 (F 2.3)

Enter two CITIZENS.
FIRST CITIZEN Neighbor, well met.[1] Whither away so fast?
SECOND CITIZEN I promise° you, I scarcely know myself. *assure*
FIRST CITIZEN Hear you the news abroad?° *circulating*
SECOND CITIZEN Ay, that the King is dead.
FIRST CITIZEN Bad news, by'r Lady;° seldom comes the better.[2] *by the Virgin Mary*
5 I fear, I fear, 'twill prove a troublous° world. *turbulent*
Enter another CITIZEN.
THIRD CITIZEN Good morrow, neighbors.
Doth this news hold of good King Edward's death?
FIRST CITIZEN It doth.
THIRD CITIZEN Then, masters,° look to see a troublous *sirs*
world.
10 FIRST CITIZEN No, no, by God's good grace, his son shall
reign.
THIRD CITIZEN Woe to that land that's governed by a child.
SECOND CITIZEN In him there is a hope of government,
That in his nonage, council under him,[3]
And in his full and ripened years himself,
15 No doubt shall then, and till then, govern well.
FIRST CITIZEN So stood the state when Harry the Sixth
Was crowned at Paris but at nine months old.
THIRD CITIZEN Stood the state so? No, good my friend,
not so,
For then this land was famously enriched
20 With politic° grave counsel;° then the King *astute / advisers*
Had virtuous uncles to protect his grace.
SECOND CITIZEN So hath this, both by the father and
mother.
THIRD CITIZEN Better it were they all came by the father,
Or by the father there were none at all,
25 For emulation° now who shall be nearest[4] *competition*
Will touch us all too near, if God prevent not.
Oh, full of danger is the Duke of Gloucester,
And the Queen's kindred haughty and proud.
And were they° to be ruled, and not to rule, *(both factions)*
30 This sickly land might solace° as before. *prosper*
SECOND CITIZEN Come, come, we fear the worst; all shall
be well.

---

2. TEXTUAL COMMENT Buckingham identifies Edward as the "King" in the Quarto rather than the technically correct "Prince" in the Folio, a substitution that suggests more than simply a compositor's error. See Digital Edition TC 5 (Quarto edited text).
2.3 Location: A street in London.

1. A standard greeting of a chance encounter.
2. Things rarely change for the better (proverbial).
3. The Privy Council governing in his name in the years of his minority ("his nonage").
4. Most influential with the King.

THIRD CITIZEN   When clouds appear, wise men put on their
   cloaks.
   When great leaves fall, the winter is at hand.
   When the sun sets, who doth not look for night?
35   Untimely storms make men expect a dearth.
   All may be well. But if God sort° it so,   *ordain*
   'Tis more than we deserve or I expect.
FIRST CITIZEN   Truly, the souls of men are full of dread.
   Ye cannot almost reason° with a man   *converse*
40   That looks not heavily and full of fear.
THIRD CITIZEN   Before the times of change still° is it so.   *always*
   By a divine instinct men's minds mistrust°   *suspect*
   Ensuing dangers, as by proof° we see   *experience*
   The waters swell before a boist'rous storm.
45   But leave it all to God. Whither away?
SECOND CITIZEN   We are sent for to the Justice.[5]
THIRD CITIZEN   And so was I. I'll bear you company.   *Exeunt.*

2.4 (F 2.4)

Enter CARDINAL,[1] DUCHESS OF YORK, QUEEN
[ELIZABETH], *young* YORK.

CARDINAL   Last night, I hear, they lay at Northampton.
   At Stony-Stratford[2] will they be tonight.
   Tomorrow, or next day, they will be here.
DUCHESS OF YORK   I long with all my heart to see the Prince.
5   I hope he is much grown since last I saw him.
QUEEN ELIZABETH   But I hear no; they say my son of York
   Hath almost overta'en him in his growth.
YORK   Ay, mother, but I would not have it so.
DUCHESS OF YORK   Why, my young cousin?° It is good to   *kinsman*
   grow.
10   YORK   Grandam, one night, as we did sit at supper,
   My uncle Rivers talked how I did grow
   More than my brother. "Ay," quoth my nuncle° Gloucester,   *uncle (colloquial)*
   "Small herbs have grace, great weeds grow apace."°   *rapidly*
   And since, methinks, I would not grow so fast
15   Because sweet flowers are slow, and weeds make haste.
DUCHESS OF YORK   Good faith, good faith, the saying did not
   hold°   *hold true*
   In him that did object° the same to thee.   *argue*
   He was the wretched'st thing when he was young,
   So long a-growing and so leisurely
20   That, if this were a true rule, he should be gracious.
CARDINAL   Why, madam, so no doubt he is.
DUCHESS OF YORK   I hope so too, but yet let mothers doubt.
YORK   Now by my troth, if I had been remembered,
   I could have given my uncle's grace a flout[3]

5. That is, the Justice of the Peace, or a magistrate.
2.4 Location: The palace, London.
1. TEXTUAL COMMENT In the Folio, the role of the
Quarto's Cardinal is split between the Archbishop
and Lord Cardinal, altering the perceived consistency of both characters. See Digital Edition TC 6

(Quarto edited text).
2. Town in Buckinghamshire (south of Northampton).
3. *if . . . flout:* if I had been told this, I could have
taunted my noble uncle.

25   That should have nearer touched° his growth than he did   *hit*
       mine.
    DUCHESS OF YORK   How, my pretty York? I pray thee, let me
       hear it.
    YORK   Marry, they say my uncle grew so fast
       That he could gnaw a crust at two hours old.
       'Twas full two years ere I could get a tooth.
30   Grannam, this would have been a biting jest.
    DUCHESS OF YORK   I pray thee, pretty York, who told thee so?
    YORK   Grannam, his nurse.
    DUCHESS OF YORK   His nurse? Why, she was dead ere thou
       wert born.
    YORK   If 'twere not she, I cannot tell who told me.
35   QUEEN ELIZABETH   A perilous[4] boy: go to,[5] you are too
       shrewd.°   *sharp*
    CARDINAL   Good madam, be not angry with the child.
    QUEEN ELIZABETH   Pitchers have ears.[6]
            Enter DORSET.
    CARDINAL   Here comes your son, Lord Marquess Dorset.
       —What news, Lord Marquess?
40   DORSET   Such news, my lord, as grieves me to unfold.
    QUEEN ELIZABETH   How fares the Prince?
    DORSET   Well, madam, and in health.
    DUCHESS OF YORK   What is thy news then?
    DORSET   Lord Rivers and Lord Grey are sent to Pomfret,[7]
45   With them Sir Thomas Vaughan, prisoners.
    DUCHESS OF YORK   Who hath committed them?
    DORSET   The mighty dukes, Gloucester and Buckingham.
    QUEEN ELIZABETH   For what offense?
    DORSET   The sum of all I can,° I have disclosed.   *know*
50   Why or for what these nobles were committed
       Is all unknown to me, my gracious lady.
    QUEEN ELIZABETH   Ay me! I see the downfall of our house.
       The tiger now hath seized the gentle hind.°   *doe*
       Insulting tyranny begins to jet°   *strut*
55   Upon the innocent and aweless[8] throne.
       Welcome, destruction, death, and massacre:
       I see, as in a map, the end of all.
    DUCHESS OF YORK   Accursèd and unquiet wrangling days,
       How many of you have mine eyes beheld?
60   My husband lost his life to get the crown,
       And often up and down my sons were tossed
       For me to joy and weep their gain and loss.
       And being seated,° and domestic broils°   *enthroned / disorders*
       Clean overblown,° themselves the conquerors   *Completely ended*
65   Make war upon themselves: blood against blood,
       Self against self. O preposterous
       And frantic outrage, end thy damnèd spleen,°   *malice*
       Or let me die, to look on death no more.

---

4. Dangerously clever; mischievous.   7. Modern Pontefract, in west Yorkshire, site of the
5. Expression of disapproval.   castle where Richard II was murdered.
6. Proverbially said of children who overhear remarks   8. Not able to command respect (because the King is
made by adults: "Little pitchers have big ears."   so young).

QUEEN ELIZABETH   Come, come, my boy, we will to
    sanctuary.[9]

70 DUCHESS OF YORK   I'll go along with you.

QUEEN ELIZABETH   You have no cause.

CARDINAL   My gracious lady, go,
    And thither bear your treasure and your goods.
    For my part, I'll resign° unto your grace   *hand over*
    The seal[1] I keep, and so betide° to me   *and so may it happen*
75   As well I tender° you and all of yours.   *care for*
    Come, I'll conduct you to the sanctuary.   *Exeunt.*

3.1[1] (F 3.1)

The trumpets sound. Enter young PRINCE [EDWARD],
the Dukes of GLOUCESTER *and* BUCKINGHAM,
   CARDINAL, *and others.*

BUCKINGHAM   Welcome, sweet Prince, to London, to your
    chamber.[2]

GLOUCESTER   Welcome, dear cousin, my thoughts'
    sovereign;°   *ruler of my thoughts*
    The weary way hath made you melancholy.

PRINCE EDWARD   No, uncle, but our crosses[3] on the way
5   Have made it tedious, wearisome, and heavy.
    I want° more uncles here to welcome me.   *lack; desire*

GLOUCESTER   Sweet Prince, the untainted virtue of your
    years
    Hath not yet dived into the world's deceit,
    Nor more can you distinguish of a man
10 Than of his outward show, which, God He knows,
    Seldom or never jumpeth° with the heart.   *coincides*
    Those uncles[4] which you want were dangerous.
    Your grace attended to their sugared words
    But looked not on the poison of their hearts.
15 God keep you from them, and from such false friends.

PRINCE EDWARD   God keep me from false friends, but they
    were none.

GLOUCESTER   My lord, the Mayor of London comes to greet
    you.
        Enter LORD MAYOR.

LORD MAYOR   God bless your grace with health and happy
    days.

PRINCE EDWARD   I thank you, good my lord, and thank
    you all.
20 I thought my mother and my brother York
    Would long ere this have met us on the way.

---

9. Anyone, including criminals, could claim the protection of the church ("sanctuary") and thus immunity from civil law, initially for forty days. The Queen sought sanctuary at Westminster Abbey.
1. An engraved stamp, signifying the authority of the bearer, used to authenticate legal documents; here, the Great Seal of England.
3.1 Location: A street in London.
1. Either because of defects in the original manuscript or because of blunders in the printing house, the text of this scene, up to line 148, is exceptionally

corrupt and has been editorially reconstructed.
2. Capital (London was known as *camera regis*, "the King's chamber").
3. Referring to the arrests of his uncle and half-brothers on the journey.
4. Of the two arrested, only Rivers, being Elizabeth's brother, was Prince Edward's real uncle; Grey, a son by Elizabeth's previous marriage, was therefore actually half-brother to the Prince (see similar confusion in 1.3.37).

Fie, what a slug° is Hastings that he comes not   *sluggard*
To tell us whether they will come or no.
      Enter Lord HASTINGS.

BUCKINGHAM   And in good time here comes the sweating
   lord.

25 PRINCE EDWARD   Welcome, my lord. What, will our mother
   come?

HASTINGS   On what occasion,° God He knows, not I,   *For what reason*
   The Queen your mother and your brother York
   Have taken sanctuary. The tender° prince   *young; affectionate*
   Would fain have° come with me to meet your grace,   *Would have liked to*

30   But by his mother was perforce° withheld.   *forcibly*

BUCKINGHAM   Fie, what an indirect and peevish° course   *perverse*
   Is this of hers! Lord Cardinal, will your grace
   Persuade the Queen to send the Duke of York
   Unto his princely brother presently?°   *immediately*

35   If she deny, Lord Hastings, go with him,
   And from her jealous° arms pluck him perforce.   *suspicious; mistrustful*

CARDINAL   My lord of Buckingham, if my weak oratory
   Can from his mother win the Duke of York,
   Anon° expect him here. But if she be obdurate   *Very soon*

40   To mild entreaties, God in heaven forbid
   We should infringe the holy privilege
   Of blessèd sanctuary. Not for all this land
   Would I be guilty of so deep a sin.

BUCKINGHAM   You are too senseless-obstinate,° my lord,   *irrationally stubborn*
45   Too ceremonious° and traditional.   *rule-bound*
   Weigh it but with the grossness° of this age;   *coarseness*
   You break not sanctuary in seizing him.
   The benefit thereof is always granted
   To those whose dealings have deserved the place,
50   And those who have the wit to claim the place.[5]
   This prince hath neither claimed it nor deserved it,
   And therefore, in mine opinion, cannot have it.
   Then taking him from thence that is not there,[6]
   You break no privilege nor charter there.
55   Oft have I heard of sanctuary men,[7]
   But sanctuary children never till now.

CARDINAL   My lord, you shall overrule my mind for once.
   Come on, Lord Hastings, will you go with me?

HASTINGS   I go, my lord.

60 PRINCE EDWARD   Good lords, make all the speedy haste you
   may.   [*Exeunt* CARDINAL *and* HASTINGS.]
   Say, uncle Gloucester, if our brother come,
   Where shall we sojourn° till our coronation?   *stay*

GLOUCESTER   Where it seems best unto your royal self.
   If I may counsel you, some day or two
65   Your highness shall repose you at the Tower,[8]
   Then where you please and shall be thought most fit

---

5. Buckingham argues that sanctuary is only for criminals or those mature enough to demand their own protection.
6. Taking the Prince from a place he has not claimed as sanctuary.
7. Criminals seeking to avoid prosecution.

8. It was customary for kings of England (before James II) to spend the night before their coronation in the Tower, it being a royal palace and one of the strongest fortresses in the country. But Edward fears its other aspect, as a prison.

For your best health and recreation.
PRINCE EDWARD   I do not like the Tower of any place.°   *of all places*
Did Julius Caesar build that place, my lord?[9]
70   BUCKINGHAM   He did, my gracious lord, begin that place,
Which since succeeding ages have re-edified.°   *built further*
PRINCE EDWARD   Is it upon record, or else reported[1]
Successively from age to age, he built it?
BUCKINGHAM   Upon record, my gracious lord.
75   PRINCE EDWARD   But say, my lord, it were not registered,°   *documented*
Methinks the truth should live from age to age,
As 'twere retailed° to all posterity,   *related orally*
Even to the general all-ending day.°   *Day of Judgment*
GLOUCESTER [*aside*]   So wise so young, they say, do never live
long.
80   PRINCE EDWARD   What say you, uncle?
GLOUCESTER   I say, "Without characters° fame lives long."   *writing*
[*aside*] Thus like the formal Vice, Iniquity,[2]
I moralize two meanings in one word.[3]
PRINCE EDWARD   That Julius Caesar was a famous man.
85   With what his valor did enrich his wit,
His wit set down to make his valor live.[4]
Death makes no conquest of this conqueror,
For now he lives in fame, though not in life.
I'll tell you what, my cousin Buckingham—
90   BUCKINGHAM   What, my gracious lord?
PRINCE EDWARD   An if° I live until I be a man,   *An if = If*
I'll win our ancient right[5] in France again,
Or die a soldier as I lived a king.
GLOUCESTER [*aside*]   Short summers lightly have a forward
spring.[6]
Enter young YORK, HASTINGS, CARDINAL.
95   BUCKINGHAM   Now in good time, here comes the Duke of
York.
PRINCE EDWARD   Richard of York, how fares our loving
brother?
YORK   Well, my dread[7] lord—so must I call you now.
PRINCE EDWARD   Ay, brother, to our grief, as it is yours.
Too late° he died that might have kept that title,   *recently*
100   Which by his death hath lost much majesty.
GLOUCESTER   How fares our cousin, noble lord of York?
YORK   I thank you, gentle uncle. O my lord,
You said that idle° weeds are fast in growth.   *useless*
The Prince my brother hath outgrown me far.
GLOUCESTER   He hath, my lord.
105   YORK   And therefore is he idle?

9. Elizabethans commonly attributed the building of
the White Tower of the Tower of London to Julius
Caesar, even though he lived almost a thousand years
before the Tower's eleventh-century construction.
1. Is it on written record or otherwise told orally.
2. The conventional ("formal") Vice figure, called
Iniquity, who in morality plays symbolized all of the
vices.
3. As the Vice often did, Gloucester makes the same
phrase have a double meaning.
4. *With . . . live:* The same valorous deeds that enliv-

ened Caesar's writing were themselves made immortal by the telling of them.
5. Right to the throne (claimed by Henry V and his
son Henry VI). See *Henry V* for a dramatization of
the conquest of the territory and *1* and *2 Henry VI* for
the loss of the territory.
6. Proverbial: Those who die young ("forward") are
often ("lightly") precocious.
7. Held in awe (a common formula for addressing a
king).

GLOUCESTER   O my fair cousin, I must not say so.
YORK   Then he is more beholden° to you than I.   *indebted*
GLOUCESTER   He may command me as my sovereign,
    But you have power in me as in a kinsman.
110 YORK   I pray you, uncle, give me this dagger.
GLOUCESTER   My dagger, little cousin? With all my heart.
PRINCE EDWARD   A beggar, brother?
YORK   Of my kind uncle that I know will give,
    And being but a toy,° which is no grief to give.   *trifle*
115 GLOUCESTER   A greater gift than that I'll give my cousin.
YORK   A greater gift? Oh, that's the sword to it.[8]
GLOUCESTER   Ay, gentle cousin, were it light enough.
YORK   Oh, then I see you will part but° with light° gifts;   *only / trivial*
    In weightier things you'll say a beggar nay.
120 GLOUCESTER   It is too heavy for your grace to wear.
YORK   I weigh it lightly were it heavier.[9]
GLOUCESTER   What, would you have my weapon, little lord?
YORK   I would, that I might thank you as you call me.
GLOUCESTER   How?
125 YORK   Little.
PRINCE EDWARD   My lord of York will still be cross° in talk.   *perverse; quarrelsome*
    Uncle, your grace knows how to bear with him.
YORK   You mean to bear me, not to bear with me.
    Uncle, my brother mocks both you and me.
130 Because that I am little, like an ape,
    He thinks that you should bear me on your shoulders.[1]
BUCKINGHAM   With what a sharp-provided° wit he reasons![2]   *pointed; apt*
    To mitigate the scorn he gives his uncle,
    He prettily and aptly taunts himself.
135 So cunning and so young is wonderful.°   *a cause of wonder*
GLOUCESTER [*to* PRINCE EDWARD]   My lord, will't please you
      pass along?
    Myself and my good cousin Buckingham
    Will° to your mother, to entreat of her   *Will go*
    To meet you at the Tower and welcome you.
140 YORK   What, will you go unto the Tower, my lord?
PRINCE EDWARD   My Lord Protector needs will have it so.
YORK   I shall not sleep in quiet at the Tower.
GLOUCESTER   Why, what should you fear?
YORK   Marry, my uncle Clarence' angry ghost.
145 My grannam told me he was murdered there.
PRINCE EDWARD   I fear no uncles dead.
GLOUCESTER   Nor none that live, I hope.
PRINCE EDWARD   And if they[3] live, I hope I need not fear.
    But come, my lord. With a heavy heart
    Thinking on them, go I unto the Tower.
        Exeunt PRINCE, YORK, HASTINGS, DORSET[, LORD
     MAYOR, *and* CARDINAL]. GLOUCESTER, BUCKINGHAM[,
             and CATESBY] *remain.*

---

8. *to it*: that is, to the dagger (the sword is to the dagger as the greater gift is to the lesser).
9. I'd consider it of little value, even if it were heavier.
1. Alluding to Richard's hunched back, which is
compared to the saddle worn by jesters who carried
monkeys about at carnivals and fairs.
2. TEXTUAL COMMENT Buckingham's comments on

the Duke of York are not marked as asides in either the
Quarto or Folio texts. We have chosen to keep them
unmarked in the light of their dramatic differences
from Gloucester's threats, which are explicitly denoted
as asides. See Digital Edition TC 7 (Quarto edited text).
3. Gloucester means himself; Edward refers to Rivers and Grey.

150 BUCKINGHAM Think you, my lord, this little prating° York   *chattering*
    Was not incensèd° by his subtle mother   *incited*
    To taunt and scorn you thus opprobriously?
GLOUCESTER No doubt, no doubt. Oh, 'tis a perilous° boy: *dangerously clever; shrewd*
    Bold, quick, ingenious, forward, capable.
155   He is all the mother's, from the top to toe.
BUCKINGHAM Well, let them rest. Come hither, Catesby.
    Thou art sworn as deeply to effect what we intend
    As closely° to conceal what we impart.   *secretly*
    Thou knowest our reasons urged upon the way.[4]
160   What thinkest thou? Is it not an easy matter
    To make William, Lord Hastings of our mind[5]
    For the installment° of this noble Duke   *enthroning*
    In the seat royal of this famous isle?
CATESBY He for his father's sake so loves the Prince[6]
165   That he will not be won to aught against him.
BUCKINGHAM What thinkest thou then of Stanley?° What   *(Earl of Derby)*
    will he?
CATESBY He will do all in all as Hastings doth.
BUCKINGHAM Well, then, no more but this:
    Go, gentle Catesby, and as it were afar off,
170   Sound° thou Lord Hastings, how he stands affected   *Probe*
    Unto[7] our purpose. If he be willing,
    Encourage him, and show him all our reasons.
    If he be leaden, icy, cold, unwilling,
    Be thou so too, and so break off your talk,
175   And give us notice of his inclination,
    For we tomorrow hold divided councils[8]
    Wherein thyself shalt highly° be employed.   *importantly*
GLOUCESTER Commend me to Lord William.° Tell him,   *(Hastings)*
    Catesby,
    His ancient knot[9] of dangerous adversaries
180   Tomorrow are let blood° at Pomfret Castle,   *are executed*
    And bid my friend, for joy of this good news,
    Give Mistress Shore[1] one gentle kiss the more.
BUCKINGHAM Good Catesby, effect this business soundly.°   *thoroughly; well*
CATESBY My good lords both, with all the heed I may.
185 GLOUCESTER Shall we hear from you, Catesby, ere we sleep?
CATESBY You shall, my lord.
GLOUCESTER At Crosby Place,° there shall you find us both.   *(Richard's residence)*
                         [*Exit* CATESBY.]
BUCKINGHAM Now, my lord, what shall we do if we perceive
    William Lord Hastings will not yield to our complots?°   *plots*
190 GLOUCESTER Chop off his head, man—somewhat° we   *something (like this)*
    will do.
    And look when° I am king, claim thou of me   *And as soon as*
    The earldom of Hereford and the movables[2]

---

4. On the journey from London to Ludlow.
5. To have Hastings share in our opinion.
6. Hastings loves the Prince as the son of the beloved King Edward.
7. *stands affected unto*: regards; likes.
8. There will be two separate council meetings, one public to plan the Prince's coronation, the other private to plot Gloucester's seizing of the crown.
9. Conspiracy, with additional meaning of "tumor," picked up in the next lines in the image of bloodletting as medical treatment.
1. After Edward's death, Jane Shore (see note to 1.1.73) became Hastings's mistress.
2. Personal as opposed to real property: furnishings, rather than land.

Whereof the King my brother stood possessed.
BUCKINGHAM　I'll claim that promise at your grace's hands.
195　GLOUCESTER　And look° to have it yielded with all　　　　　　　*And expect*
　　willingness.
　　Come, let us sup betimes,° that afterwards　　　　　　　　　　*early*
　　We may digest our complots in some form.³　　　*Exeunt.*

3.2 (F 3.2)

Enter a MESSENGER *to Lord* HASTINGS.

MESSENGER [*knocking*]　What ho, my lord!
HASTINGS [*within*]　Who knocks at the door?
MESSENGER　A messenger from the Lord Stanley.

Enter Lord HASTINGS.

HASTINGS　What's o'clock?
MESSENGER　　　　　　　　　Upon the stroke of four.
5　HASTINGS　Cannot thy master sleep these tedious nights?
MESSENGER　So it should seem by that I have to say.
　　First, he commends him to your noble lordship.
HASTINGS　And then?
MESSENGER　　　　　　　And then he sends you word
　　He dreamt tonight the boar had razed his helm.¹
10　Besides, he says, there are two councils held,
　　And that may be determined at the one
　　Which may make you and him to rue at° the other.　　　　　　*regret*
　　Therefore he sends to know your lordship's pleasure,
　　If presently° you will take horse with him　　　　　　　　　*immediately*
15　And with all speed post into the North
　　To shun the danger that his soul divines.°　　　　　　　　　*prophesies*
HASTINGS　Go, fellow, go. Return unto thy lord.
　　Bid him not fear the separated councils.
　　His honor and myself are at the one,
20　And at the other is my servant Catesby,
　　Where nothing can proceed that toucheth° us　　　　*concerns; harms*
　　Whereof I shall not have intelligence.°　　　　　　*secret information*
　　Tell him his fears are shallow, wanting instance.°　　　*lacking evidence*
　　And for his dreams, I wonder he is so fond°　　　　　　　　*foolish*
25　To trust the mockery of unquiet slumbers.
　　To fly the boar before the boar pursues us
　　Were to incense the boar to follow us
　　And make pursuit where he did mean° no chase.　　　　　　　*intend*
　　Go, bid thy master rise and come to me,
30　And we will both together to the Tower,
　　Where he shall see the boar will use us kindly.²
MESSENGER　My gracious lord, I'll tell him what you say.
　　　　　　　　　　　　　　　　　　　　　　　　[*Exit.*]

Enter CATESBY.

CATESBY　Many good morrows to my noble lord.
HASTINGS　Good morrow, Catesby. You are early stirring.
35　What news, what news, in this our tottering state?
CATESBY　It is a reeling° world, indeed, my lord,　　　　　*an unstable*

---

3. We may break plans down into an orderly system (with pun on "digest").
3.2 Location: Outside Lord Hastings's house, in London.

1. He dreamed the boar (Gloucester's emblem) had sheared off his helmet (figuratively, cut off his head).
2. Gently (but also, with unintended irony, characteristically).

And I believe it will never stand upright
Till Richard wear the garland of the realm.
HASTINGS   How wear the garland? Dost thou mean the
    crown?
40 CATESBY   Ay, my good lord.
HASTINGS   I'll have this crown° of mine cut from my   *head*
    shoulders
Ere I will see the crown so foul misplaced.
But canst thou guess that he doth aim at it?
CATESBY   Upon my life, my lord, and hopes to find you
    forward°   *a strong supporter*
45 Upon his party° for the gain thereof.   *On his side*
And thereupon he sends you this good news:
That this same very day your enemies,
The kindred of the Queen, must die at Pomfret.
HASTINGS   Indeed, I am no mourner for that news
50 Because they have been still mine enemies.
But that I'll give my voice on Richard's side
To bar my master's heirs in true descent—
God knows I will not do it, to the death.[3]
CATESBY   God keep your lordship in that gracious mind.
55 HASTINGS   But I shall laugh at this a twelvemonth hence,
That they who brought me in my master's hate,[4]
I live to look upon their tragedy.
I tell thee, Catesby—
CATESBY   What, my lord?
60 HASTINGS   Ere a fortnight make me elder,
I'll send some packing that yet think not on it.
CATESBY   'Tis a vile thing to die, my gracious lord,
When men are unprepared and look not for it.
HASTINGS   Oh, monstrous, monstrous. And so falls it out
65 With Rivers, Vaughan, Grey; and so 'twill do
With some men else who think themselves as safe
As thou and I, who, as thou knowest, are dear
To princely Richard and to Buckingham.
CATESBY   The princes both make high account of° you,   *highly esteem*
70 [*aside*] For they account° his head upon the bridge.[5]   *expect*
HASTINGS   I know they do, and I have well deserved it.
        Enter Lord STANLEY.
What, my lord, where is your boar-spear,[6] man?
Fear you the boar and go so unprovided?[7]
STANLEY   My lord, good morrow. Good morrow, Catesby.
75 You may jest on, but by the holy rood,°   *cross*
I do not like these several° councils, I.   *separate*
HASTINGS   My lord, I hold my life as dear as you do yours,
And never in my life, I do protest,
Was it more precious to me than it is now.
80 Think you but° that I know our state secure,   *if it were not*
I would be so triumphant as I am?

---

3. Even at the risk of death.
4. That those (Rivers, Vaughan, and Grey) who turned King Edward against me.
5. London Bridge (where the heads of traitors were displayed high on poles).

6. Specialized hunting spear with a crossbar to prevent the impaled boar's tusks from wounding the hunter.
7. Do you fear the boar, and (yet) go unprepared?

STANLEY   The lords at Pomfret, when they rode from
        London,
    Were jocund° and supposed their states were sure,°   *merry / secure*
    And they indeed had no cause to mistrust,
85 But yet you see how soon the day overcast.°   *became overcast*
    This sudden scab[8] of rancor I misdoubt.[9]
    Pray God, I say, I prove a needless coward.
    But come, my lord, shall we to the Tower?
HASTINGS   I go. But stay: hear you not the news?
90 This day those men you talked of are beheaded.
STANLEY   They for their truth° might better wear their heads   *honesty*
    Than some that have accused them wear their hats.°   *retain their offices*
    But come, my lord, let us away.
        Enter Hastings,[1] a PURSUIVANT.
HASTINGS   Go you before; I'll follow presently.
            [*Exeunt* STANLEY *and* CATESBY.]
95 Well met, Hastings. How goes the world with thee?
PURSUIVANT   The better that it please your lordship to ask.
HASTINGS   I tell thee, fellow, 'tis better with me now
    Than when I met thee last where now we meet.
    Then was I going prisoner to the Tower
100 By the suggestion° of the Queen's allies.   *incitement*
    But now, I tell thee—keep it to thyself—
    This day those enemies are put to death,
    And I in better state than ever I was.
PURSUIVANT   God hold it[2] to your honor's good content.
105 HASTINGS   Gramercy,° Hastings. Hold, spend thou that.   *Many thanks*
        He gives him his purse.
PURSUIVANT   God save your lordship!   [*Exit* PURSUIVANT.]
        Enter a Priest.
HASTINGS   What, Sir[3] John, you are well met.
    I am beholden to you for your last day's exercise.°   *sermon*
    Come the next Sabbath and I will content you.[4]
        He whispers in his ear.
        Enter BUCKINGHAM.
110 BUCKINGHAM   How now, Lord Chamberlain, what, talking
        with a priest?
    Your friends at Pomfret, they do need the priest;
    Your honor hath no shriving work[5] in hand.
HASTINGS   Good faith, and when I met this holy man,
    Those men you talk of came into my mind.
115 What, go you to the Tower, my lord?
BUCKINGHAM   I do, but long I shall not stay.
    I shall return before your lordship thence.
HASTINGS   'Tis like enough, for I stay dinner[6] there.

---

8. TEXTUAL COMMENT The Quarto's "scab," often
emended to the Folio's "stab," is here retained. See
Digital Edition TC 8 (Quarto edited text).
9. I mistrust such attacks, as those sudden attacks
that befell Rivers, Vaughan, and Grey.
1. The name, taken from Holinshed's *Chronicles*, may
be important in calling attention to the significance of
Lord Hastings's own name: the word means either
"someone who hurries" (here, to his destruction) or "a
fruit that ripens before its time." *pursuivant*: state mes-

senger with authority to execute warrants (particularly
of treason). Figuratively, a pursuivant was any sum-
moner or messenger.
2. May God maintain your prosperity.
3. Courteous title of respect for clergyman.
4. I will pay your "debt" with a donation.
5. Confession and absolution (here, before
execution).
6. I stay for dinner (eaten at about 11:00 A.M.).

BUCKINGHAM [*aside*]   And supper° too, although thou[7]   *evening meal*
    knowest it not.
120   Come, shall we go along?   *Exeunt.*

3.3 (F 3.3)

Enter Sir Richard RATCLIFFE *with the Lords* RIVERS,
    GREY, *and* VAUGHAN, *prisoners.*

RATCLIFFE   Come, bring forth the prisoners.
RIVERS   Sir Richard Ratcliffe, let me tell thee this:
    Today shalt thou behold a subject die
    For truth, for duty, and for loyalty.
5   GREY   God keep the Prince from all the pack of you:
    A knot° you are of damnèd bloodsuckers.   *group*
RIVERS   O Pomfret, Pomfret! O thou bloody prison,
    Fatal and ominous to noble peers!
    Within the guilty closure° of thy walls   *enclosure*
10   Richard the Second here was hacked to death.
    And for more slander to thy dismal soul,[1]
    We give thee up our guiltless bloods to drink.
GREY   Now Margaret's curse is fallen upon our heads,
    For standing by when Richard stabbed her son.
15   RIVERS   Then cursed she Hastings, then cursed she
      Buckingham,
    Then cursed she Richard. O remember, God,
    To hear her prayers for them as now for us,
    And for° my sister and her princely sons,   *as for*
    Be satisfied, dear God, with our true bloods,
20   Which, as Thou knowest, unjustly must be spilt.
RATCLIFFE   Come, come, dispatch. The limit of your lives is
    out.
RIVERS   Come, Grey, come, Vaughan. Let us all embrace
    And take our leave, until we meet in heaven.   *Exeunt.*

3.4 (F 3.4)

Enter the Lords [HASTINGS, BUCKINGHAM, BISHOP OF
    ELY, *and* STANLEY] *to Council.*

HASTINGS   My lords, at once—the cause why we are met
    Is to determine of° the coronation.   *decide upon*
    In God's name say: when is this royal day?
BUCKINGHAM   Are all things fitting for that royal time?
5   STANLEY   It is, and wants but nomination.°   *naming the day*
BISHOP OF ELY   Tomorrow, then, I guess a happy° time.   *suitable*
BUCKINGHAM   Who knows the Lord Protector's mind herein?
    Who is most inward° with the noble Duke?   *intimate*
BISHOP OF ELY   Why you, my lord.
10   Methinks you should soonest know his mind.
BUCKINGHAM   Who, I, my lord? We know each other's faces;
    But for° our hearts, he knows no more of mine   *As for*
    Than I of yours,
    Nor I no more of his than you of mine.

---

7. Here used contemptuously, as opposed to the formal "you" in line 115.
3.3 Location: Pomfret Castle.

1. And in order to increase the notoriety of this sinister castle.
3.4 Location: The Tower of London.

15   Lord Hastings, you and he are near in love.

HASTINGS   I thank his grace, I know he loves me well.
    But for his purpose in the coronation,
    I have not sounded him,° nor he delivered   *sounded him out*
    His grace's pleasure any way therein.

20   But you, my noble lords, may name the time,
    And in the Duke's behalf I'll give my voice,°   *vote*
    Which I presume he will take in gentle part.°   *he'll graciously approve*
        Enter GLOUCESTER.

BISHOP OF ELY   Now in good time, here comes the Duke
    himself.

GLOUCESTER   My noble lords and cousins all, good morrow.

25   I have been long a sleeper, but I hope
    My absence doth neglect no great designs,[1]
    Which by my presence might have been concluded.

BUCKINGHAM   Had not you come upon your cue, my lord,
    William, Lord Hastings had now pronounced your part—

30   I mean, your voice—for crowning of the King.

GLOUCESTER   Than my Lord Hastings no man might be
    bolder;[2]
    His lordship knows me well and loves me well.

HASTINGS   I thank your grace.

GLOUCESTER   My lord of Ely—

35 BISHOP OF ELY   My lord?

GLOUCESTER   When I was last in Holborn,[3]
    I saw good strawberries in your garden there.
    I do beseech you, send for some of them.

BISHOP OF ELY   I go, my lord.   [*Exit* BISHOP OF ELY.]

40 GLOUCESTER   Cousin Buckingham, a word with you.
    [*aside*] Catesby hath sounded Hastings in° our business,   *in respect to*
    And finds the testy gentleman so hot
    As he will lose his head ere give consent
    His master's son, as worshipful° he terms it,   *reverentially*
45   Shall lose the royalty° of England's throne.   *sovereignty*

BUCKINGHAM   Withdraw you hence, my lord. I'll follow you.
        [*Exeunt* GLOUCESTER *and* BUCKINGHAM.]

STANLEY   We have not yet set down this day of triumph.
    Tomorrow, in mine opinion, is too sudden,
    For I myself am not so well provided°   *equipped*
50   As else I would be were the day prolonged.°   *further off*
        Enter BISHOP OF ELY.

BISHOP OF ELY   Where is my Lord Protector? I have sent
    For these strawberries.

HASTINGS   His grace looks cheerfully and smooth° today.   *untroubled*
    There's some conceit° or other likes° him well   *thought / pleases*
55   When he doth bid good morrow with such a spirit.
    I think there is never a man in Christendom
    That can lesser hide his love or hate than he,
    For by his face straight° shall you know his heart.   *immediately*

STANLEY   What of his heart perceive you in his face
60   By any likelihood° he showed today?   *appearance*

---

1. My absence delays no important business.   3. The Bishop of Ely's official London residence.
2. No one could more confidently speak for me than
Hastings; but no one could be more presumptuous.

HASTINGS   Marry, that with no man here he is offended,
       For if he were, he would have shown it in his looks.
STANLEY   I pray God he be not, I say.
               Enter GLOUCESTER[4] [*with* CATESBY].
GLOUCESTER   I pray you all, what do they deserve
65   That do conspire my death with devilish plots
       Of damnèd witchcraft, and that have prevailed
       Upon my body with their hellish charms?
HASTINGS   The tender love I bear your grace, my lord,
       Makes me most forward in this noble presence
70   To doom the offenders, whosoe'er they be.
       I say, my lord, they have deservèd death.
GLOUCESTER   Then be your eyes the witness of this ill:
       See how I am bewitched. Behold, mine arm
       Is like a blasted sapling withered up.
75   This is° that Edward's wife, that monstrous witch,   *This is the work of*
       Consorted with° that harlot, strumpet Shore,   *In league with*
       That by their witchcraft thus have markèd me.
HASTINGS   If they have done this thing, my gracious lord—
GLOUCESTER   "If"? Thou protector of this damnèd strumpet,
80   Tell'st thou me of "ifs"? Thou art a traitor:
       Off with his head! Now, by Saint Paul,
       I will not dine today, I swear,
       Until I see the same. Some see it done.
       The rest that love me, come, and follow me.
                       Exeunt all but CATESBY *with* HASTINGS.
85   HASTINGS   Woe, woe for England, not a whit for me,[5]
       For I, too fond, might have prevented this.
       Stanley did dream the boar did raze his helm,
       But I disdained it and did scorn to fly.
       Three times today my footcloth horse[6] did stumble,
90   And startled when he looked upon the Tower,
       As° loath to bear me to the slaughterhouse.   *As though*
       Oh, now I want the priest that spake to me.
       I now repent I told the pursuivant,
       As 'twere triumphing° at mine enemies,   *exulting*
95   How they at Pomfret bloodily were butchered,
       And I myself secure in grace and favor.
       O Margaret, Margaret, now thy heavy curse
       Is lighted on poor Hastings' wretched head.
CATESBY   Dispatch, my lord, the Duke would be at dinner.
100   Make a short shrift;° he longs to see your head.   *confession (to a priest)*
HASTINGS   O momentary state of worldly men,
       Which we more hunt for than the grace of heaven!
       Who builds his hopes in air of your fair looks[7]
       Lives like a drunken sailor on a mast,
105   Ready with every nod[8] to tumble down

---

4. According to Holinshed, Gloucester "returned into the chamber . . . with a wonderful sour, angry countenance, knitting the brows, frowning and fretting, and gnawing on his lips."
5. TEXTUAL COMMENT In the Quarto, Catesby, rather than the Folio's Lovell and Ratcliffe, delivers his erstwhile master Hastings to his execution, a move with dramatic implications. See Digital Edition TC 9

(Quarto edited text).
6. Horse draped with a richly ornamented covering reaching almost to the ground.
7. *Who . . . looks*: Anyone who puts his faith in your seemingly favorable glances.
8. Complex play on words: ready as he dozes off; as the ship rolls; as the monarch, whose "good looks" upheld him, condemns him with a silent nod.

Into the fatal bowels of the deep.
Come, lead me to the block; bear him my head.
They smile at me that shortly shall be dead.   *Exeunt.*

3.5 (F 3.5)

Enter Duke of GLOUCESTER *and* BUCKINGHAM,
in armor.

GLOUCESTER   Come, cousin, canst thou quake, and change
  thy color,
Murder thy breath in middle of a word,
And then begin again, and stop again,
As if thou wert distraught and mad with terror?
5 BUCKINGHAM   Tut, fear not me.
I can counterfeit the deep tragedian:
Speak, and look back, and pry° on every side,   *peer*
Intending° deep suspicion. Ghastly looks   *Suggesting*
Are at my service, like enforcèd smiles,
10 And both are ready in their offices[1]
To grace my stratagems.
                Enter [LORD] MAYOR.
GLOUCESTER   Here comes the Mayor.
BUCKINGHAM   Let me alone to entertain him. Lord Mayor—
GLOUCESTER   Look to the drawbridge there!
BUCKINGHAM   The reason we have sent for you—
GLOUCESTER   Catesby, overlook° the walls![2]   *look (out) over*
15 BUCKINGHAM   Hark, I hear a drum.
GLOUCESTER   Look back, defend thee! Here are enemies.
BUCKINGHAM   God and our innocence defend us!
                Enter CATESBY *with Hastings' head.*
GLOUCESTER   Oh, oh, be quiet; it is Catesby.
CATESBY   Here is the head of that ignoble traitor,
20 The dangerous and unsuspected Hastings.
GLOUCESTER   So dear I loved the man that I must weep.
I took him for the plainest-harmless° man   *most manifestly innocent*
That breathed upon this earth a Christian,
Look ye, my lord Mayor,
25 Made him my book,° wherein my soul recorded   *diary*
The history of all her secret thoughts.
So smooth he daubed his vice with show of virtue
That, his apparent open guilt omitted—
I mean his conversation[3] with Shore's wife—
30 He laid from all attainder of suspect.[4]
BUCKINGHAM   Well, well, he was the covert'st-sheltered°   *the most hidden*
  traitor
That ever lived. Would you have imagined,
Or almost believe, were't not by great preservation[5]
We live to tell it you, the subtle traitor
35 Had this day plotted in the council house
To murder me and my good lord of Gloucester?
LORD MAYOR   What, had he so?

3.5 Location: Scene continues.
1. Both are eager to perform their functions.
2. TEXTUAL COMMENT Though in the Folio Catesby enters with the Lord Mayor, in the Quarto he appears to be offstage, given his later entrance with Hastings's

head. See Digital Edition TC 10 (Quarto edited text).
3. Intercourse (in both senses).
4. He lived free from all taint of suspicion.
5. By the most fortunate preservation (of our lives).

GLOUCESTER   What? Think you we are Turks or infidels,
 Or that we would, against the form of law,
40 Proceed thus rashly to the villain's death,
 But that the extreme peril of the case,
 The peace of England, and our persons' safety,
 Enforced us to this execution?
LORD MAYOR   Now, fair befall you! He deserved his death,
45 And you, my good lords both, have well proceeded°   *acted*
 To warn false traitors from the like° attempts.   *similar*
BUCKINGHAM   I never looked for better at his hands
 After he once fell in with Mistress Shore.
 Yet had not we determined he should die[6]
50 Until your lordship came to see his death—
 Which now the longing haste of these our friends,
 Somewhat against our meaning,° have prevented—   *intentions*
 Because, my lord, we would have had you heard
 The traitor speak and timorously confess
55 The manner and the purpose of his treason,
 That you might well have signified the same
 Unto the citizens, who haply° may   *perhaps*
 Misconster us in him[7] and wail his death.
LORD MAYOR   But, my good lord, your graces' word shall
  serve
60 As well as° I had seen or heard him speak.   *As well as = As if*
 And doubt you not, right noble princes both,
 But° I'll acquaint our duteous citizens   *That*
 With all your just proceedings in this cause.°   *action*
GLOUCESTER   And to that end we wished your lordship here,
65 To avoid the carping° censures of the world.   *overcritical*
BUCKINGHAM   But since you come too late of our intents,° *for what we intended*
 Yet witness° what we did intend. And so,   *bear witness to*
 My lord, adieu.   *Exit* [LORD] MAYOR.
GLOUCESTER   After, after, cousin Buckingham!
70 The Mayor towards Guildhall[8] hies him in all post.°   *haste*
 There, at your meet'st advantage of the time,[9]
 Infer° the bastardy of Edward's children.   *Allege*
 Tell them how Edward put to death a citizen
 Only for saying he would make his son
75 Heir to "The Crown," meaning indeed his house,°   *tavern*
 Which by the sign thereof was termèd so.
 Moreover, urge his hateful luxury°   *lasciviousness*
 And bestial appetite in change of lust,[1]
 Which stretchèd to their servants, daughters, wives,
80 Even where° his lustful eye or savage heart,   *Wherever*
 Without control, listed° to make his prey.   *desired*
 Nay, for a need, thus far come near my person:[2]
 Tell them, when that my mother went with child
 Of that unsatiate Edward,[3] noble York,
85 My princely father, then had wars in France

6. We had not determined he should die.
7. Misunderstand our treatment of him.
8. Center of municipal government in London.
9. At your most appropriate and advantageous moment.
1. In continually shifting the object of his lust.

2. *for . . . person:* if necessary, impugn even to this extent my own honor (by implying his mother was unfaithful).
3. *went . . . Edward:* was pregnant with dissolute Edward. *unsatiate:* impossible to satisfy.

And, by just computation of the time,
Found that the issue° was not his begot,   *offspring*
Which well appearèd in his lineaments,°   *features*
Being nothing like the noble Duke my father.
90   But touch this sparingly, as it were far off,
Because you know, my lord, my mother lives.
BUCKINGHAM   Fear not, my lord. I'll play the orator
As if the golden fee[4] for which I plead
Were for myself.
95   GLOUCESTER   If you thrive well, bring them to Baynard's
     Castle,[5]
Where you shall find me well accompanied
With reverend fathers and well-learnèd bishops.
BUCKINGHAM   About three or four o'clock look to hear
What news Guildhall affordeth. And so, my lord, farewell.
                                                        Exit.
100 GLOUCESTER   Now will I in to take some privy order[6]
To draw the brats of Clarence[7] out of sight,
And to give notice that no manner of[8] person
At any° time have recourse unto the princes.   *Exit.*

3.6 (F 3.6)

Enter a SCRIVENER° *with a paper in his hand.*   *scribe*
SCRIVENER   This is the indictment of the good Lord
     Hastings,
Which in a set hand fairly is engrossed[1]
That it may be this day read over in Paul's.[2]
And mark how well the sequel° hangs together.   *sequence of events*
5   Eleven hours I spent to write it over,
For yesternight by Catesby was it brought me.
The precedent° was full as long a-doing,   *rough draft*
And yet within these five hours lived Lord Hastings:
Untainted,° unexamined, free, at liberty.   *Unaccused*
10   Here's a good world the while! Why, who's so gross°   *stupid*
That sees not this palpable device?°   *obvious stratagem*
Yet who's so bold but says he sees it not?
Bad is the world, and all will come to naught°   *wickedness; nothing*
When such bad dealing must be seen in thought.[3]   *Exit.*

3.7 (F 3.7)

Enter GLOUCESTER *at one door,* BUCKINGHAM
at another.
GLOUCESTER   How now, my lord? What say the citizens?
BUCKINGHAM   Now by the holy mother of our Lord,
The citizens are mum and speak not a word.
GLOUCESTER   Touched you° the bastardy of Edward's   *Did you touch on*
     children?
5   BUCKINGHAM   I did, with the insatiate greediness of his
     desires,

---

4. The crown (punning on "lawyer's fee").
5. Gloucester's stronghold, between Blackfriars and
London Bridge.
6. To make some secret arrangements.
7. The two children seen in 2.2.
8. No kind of (in other words, of whatever status or
importance).

3.6 Location: Somewhere in London.
1. Which is written in official script (as opposed to a
draft copy) and in the format of a legal document.
2. St. Paul's Cathedral, which served as a secular as
well as sacred gathering place.
3. Must be perceived but not spoken of.
3.7 Location: Baynard's Castle.

His tyranny for trifles, his own bastardy,
As being got° your father then in France. *conceived*
Withal, I did infer your lineaments,° *distinctive features*
Being the right idea° of your father, *true image*
10 Both in your form[1] and nobleness of mind;
Laid open all your victories in Scotland,[2]
Your discipline in war, wisdom in peace,
Your bounty, virtue, fair humility;
Indeed, left nothing fitting for the purpose
15 Untouched or slightly handled° in discourse. *lightly mentioned*
And when mine oratory grew to an end,
I bid them that did love their country's good
Cry, "God save Richard, England's royal king!"
GLOUCESTER Ah, and did they so?
BUCKINGHAM   No, so God help me,
20 But like dumb statues or breathing stones
Gazed each on other and looked deadly pale,
Which when I saw, I reprehended them,
And asked the Mayor what meant this willful silence.
His answer was, the people were not wont° *accustomed*
25 To be spoke to but by the Recorder.° *(a city official)*
Then he was urged to tell my tale again:
"Thus saith the Duke; thus hath the Duke inferred,"° *asserted*
But nothing spake in warrant from himself.° *on his own authority*
When he had done, some followers of mine own
30 At the lower end of the hall hurled up their caps,
And some ten voices cried, "God save King Richard!"
"Thanks, loving citizens and friends," quoth I.
"This general applause and loving shout
Argues your wisdoms and your love to Richard."
35 And so brake off and came away.
GLOUCESTER What, tongueless blocks were they? Would
    they not speak?
BUCKINGHAM No, by my troth, my lord.
GLOUCESTER Will not the Mayor, then, and his brethren
    come?
BUCKINGHAM The Mayor is here at hand. Intend° some fear. *Pretend*
40 Be not spoken withal but with mighty suit.[3]
And look you get a prayer book in your hand,
And stand betwixt two churchmen, good my lord,
For on that ground I'll build a holy descant.[4]
Be not easily won to our request.
45 Play the maid's part:[5] say no, but take it.
GLOUCESTER Fear not me. If thou canst plead as well for
    them
As I can say nay to thee for myself,
No doubt we'll bring it to a happy issue.[6]

---

1. Given Gloucester's prominent deformities, the claim that his and his father's forms are similar is surprising; in the chronicles, it is Richard's *face* that is compared with his father's.
2. In 1482, as leader of an English expeditionary force against the Scots, Gloucester had advanced all the way to Edinburgh.
3. Do not let them speak with you unless they beg you.
4. Comment; improvised musical line, usually the highest part. *ground:* basis; musical theme or air, often the bass line.
5. Keep refusing, but at the same time take whatever is offered (proverbial, with sexual innuendo).
6. Conclusion, with the additional meaning of "offspring" suggested from the preceding sexual innuendos.

BUCKINGHAM   You shall see what I can do. Get you up to the
     leads.⁷   *Exit* [GLOUCESTER].
      [*Enter the* LORD MAYOR *and* CITIZENS.]
50   Now, my Lord Mayor, I dance attendance° here.   *am kept waiting*
     I think the Duke will not be spoke withal.
      Enter CATESBY.
     Here comes his servant. How now, Catesby, what says he?
CATESBY   My lord, he doth entreat your grace
     To visit him tomorrow or next day.
55   He is within with two right reverend fathers,
     Divinely bent to meditation,
     And in no worldly suit° would he be moved   *civil petition*
     To draw him from his holy exercise.
BUCKINGHAM   Return, good Catesby, to thy lord again.
60   Tell him myself, the Mayor, and citizens,
     In deep designs and matters of great moment,
     No less importing than⁸ our general good,
     Are come to have some conference with his grace.
CATESBY   I'll tell him what you say, my lord.   *Exit.*
65 BUCKINGHAM   Ah ha, my lord, this prince is not an Edward.
     He is not lulling on a lewd daybed,
     But on his knees at meditation;
     Not dallying with a brace° of courtesans,   *pair*
     But meditating with two deep° divines;   *profoundly learned*
70   Not sleeping, to engross° his idle body,   *fatten*
     But praying, to enrich his watchful° soul.   *vigilant*
     Happy were England would this gracious prince
     Take on himself the sovereignty thereof,
     But sure I fear we shall never win him to it.
75 LORD MAYOR   Marry, God forbid his grace should say us nay.
BUCKINGHAM   I fear he will.
      Enter CATESBY.
     How now, Catesby, what says your lord?
CATESBY   My lord,
     He wonders to what end you have assembled
     Such troops of citizens to speak with him,
80   His grace not being warned thereof before.
     My lord, he fears you mean no good to him.
BUCKINGHAM   Sorry I am my noble cousin should
     Suspect me that I mean no good to him.
     By heaven, I come in perfect love to him,
85   And so once more return and tell his grace.   *Exit* CATESBY.
     When holy and devout religious men
     Are at their beads,° 'tis hard to draw them thence,   *prayers*
     So sweet is zealous contemplation.
      Enter Richard [GLOUCESTER] *with two Bishops aloft*
      [*and* CATESBY *below*].
LORD MAYOR   See where he stands between two clergymen.
90 BUCKINGHAM   Two props of virtue for a Christian prince
     To stay him from the fall of vanity.⁹
     Famous Plantagenet, most gracious prince,

---

7. Flat roof covered with lead.   9. To prevent him from falling into the sin of vanity.
8. Of no less significance than.

Lend favorable ears to our request,
And pardon us the interruption
95 Of thy devotion and right Christian zeal.
GLOUCESTER My lord, there needs no such apology.
I rather do beseech you pardon me
Who, earnest in the service of my God,
Neglect the visitation of my friends.
100 But leaving this, what is your grace's pleasure?
BUCKINGHAM Even that, I hope, which pleaseth God above,
And all good men of this ungoverned isle.
GLOUCESTER I do suspect I have done some offense
That seems disgracious° in the city's eyes,   *displeasing*
105 And that you come to reprehend my ignorance.
BUCKINGHAM You have, my lord. Would it please your grace
At our entreaties to amend that fault.
GLOUCESTER Else wherefore breathe I in a Christian land?[1]
BUCKINGHAM Then know, it is your fault that you resign
110 The supreme seat, the throne majestical,
The sceptered office of your ancestors,
The lineal glory of your royal house,
To the corruption of a blemished stock,[2]
Whilst in the mildness of your sleepy° thoughts—   *contemplative*
115 Which here we waken to our country's good—
This noble isle doth want her proper° limbs,   *lack her own*
Her face defaced with scars of infamy,
And almost shouldered in° the swallowing gulf   *shoved into*
Of blind forgetfulness and dark oblivion.
120 Which to recure,° we heartily solicit   *restore*
Your gracious self to take on you the sovereignty thereof,
Not as Protector, steward, substitute,
Or lowly factor° for another's gain,   *agent*
But as successively° from blood to blood,   *in order of succession*
125 Your right of birth, your empery,° your own.   *absolute dominion*
For this, consorted° with the citizens,   *together*
Your very worshipful° and loving friends,   *respectful*
And by their vehement instigation,
In this just suit come I to move your grace.
130 GLOUCESTER I know not whether to depart in silence
Or bitterly to speak in your reproof
Best fitteth my degree° or your condition.°   *eminence / social rank*
Your love deserves my thanks, but my desert
Unmeritable[3] shuns your high request.
135 First, if all obstacles were cut away,
And that my path were even° to the crown,   *smooth*
As my ripe revenue° and due by birth,   *(rightful inheritance)*
Yet so much is my poverty of spirit,
So mighty and so many my defects,
140 As I had rather hide me from my greatness,
Being a bark to brook° no mighty sea,   *a boat to endure*
Than in my greatness covet to be hid[4]
And in the vapor of my glory smothered.

---

1. Why else do I lead a Christian life?
2. Edward's "family tree" is degraded by bastardy and immorality.
3. *my desert / Unmeritable:* my merit (being) undeserving; my unworthiness.
4. Than desire to be enveloped by my greatness.

But God be thanked, there's no need of me,
145 And much I need° to help you if need were.   *lack (ability)*
The royal tree hath left us royal fruit,
Which, mellowed by the stealing hours of time,
Will well become the seat of majesty,
And make, no doubt, us happy by his reign.
150 On him I lay what you would lay on me:
The right and fortune of his happy° stars,   *auspicious*
Which God defend that I should wring from him.
    BUCKINGHAM   My lord, this argues conscience in your grace,
But the respects thereof are nice and trivial,[5]
155 All circumstances well considerèd.
You say that Edward is your brother's son;
So say we too, but not by Edward's wife.
For first he was contract° to Lady Lucy[6]—   *betrothed*
Your mother lives a witness to that vow[7]—
160 And afterward by substitute° betrothed   *proxy*
To Bona, sister to the King of France.[8]
These both put by, a poor petitioner,°   *(Elizabeth)*
A care-crazed mother of a-many children,
A beauty-waning and distressèd widow,
165 Even in the afternoon of her best days,
Made prize and purchase° of his lustful eye,   *booty*
Seduced the pitch and height of all his thoughts[9]
To base declension° and loathed bigamy.   *degradation*
By her in his unlawful bed he got
170 This Edward, whom our manners° term the Prince.   *we in politeness*
More bitterly could I expostulate,
Save that for reverence to some alive[1]
I give a sparing limit to my tongue.
Then, good my lord, take to your royal self
175 This proffered benefit° of dignity,   *bestowal*
If not to bless us and the land withal,
Yet to draw out° your royal stock   *to rescue*
From the corruption of abusing time
Unto a lineal, true-derivèd course.
180   LORD MAYOR   Do, good my lord, your citizens entreat you.
    CATESBY   Oh, make them joyful; grant their lawful suit.
    GLOUCESTER   Alas, why would you heap these cares on me?
I am unfit for state and dignity.
I do beseech you, take it not amiss;
185 I cannot, nor I will not, yield to you.
    BUCKINGHAM   If you refuse it, as in love and zeal
Loath to depose the child, your brother's son—
As well we know your tenderness of heart
And gentle, kind, effeminate remorse,[2]

---

5. But the reasons you advance are nitpicking (thus, overscrupulous).
6. Lady Elizabeth Lucy bore Edward a child. If, as Buckingham alleges, there had been a formal engagement between them, Edward's subsequent marriage to Elizabeth Grey would have been ruled invalid.
7. Buckingham draws attention to the Duchess of York's objection to her son Edward's marriage to Elizabeth Grey and Edward's supposed betrothals. These, along with the fact of Elizabeth's widowhood, are put forward as evidence that the marriage should be con-

sidered bigamous and hence the offspring illegitimate.
8. The Earl of Warwick, as deputy, had contracted with Louis XI of France for the marriage of Edward to Bona of Savoy, the French queen's sister (see 3 *Henry VI* 3.3).
9. Drew him down from his eminence. *pitch:* the highest point a falcon reaches before seizing its prey.
1. Referring to Gloucester's own mother, the Duchess of York.
2. And natural, tender pity (feelings thought of at that time as primarily feminine).

190 Which we have noted in you to your kin,
And equally indeed to all estates°—   *social classes*
Yet whether you accept our suit or no,
Your brother's son shall never reign our king,
But we will plant some other in the throne
195 To the disgrace and downfall of your house.
And in this resolution here we leave you.
—Come, citizens. Zounds!° I'll entreat no more.   *By God's wounds*
GLOUCESTER   Oh, do not swear, my lord of Buckingham.
           [*Exeunt* BUCKINGHAM *with some* CITIZENS.]
CATESBY   Call them again, my lord, and accept their suit.
200 ANOTHER CITIZEN   Do, good my lord, lest all the land do
     rue° it.   *suffer for*
GLOUCESTER   Would you enforce° me to a world of care?   *condemn*
Well, call them again.   [*Exit* CATESBY.]
           I am not made of stones,
But penetrable to your kind entreats,°   *entreaties*
Albeit against my conscience and my soul.
     [*Enter* BUCKINGHAM *and the rest.*]
205 Cousin of Buckingham, and you sage, grave men,
Since you will buckle fortune on my back
To° bear her burden, whether I will or no,   *To make me*
I must have patience to endure the load.
But if black scandal or foul-faced reproach
210 Attend the sequel of your imposition,°   *what you impose on me*
Your mere° enforcement shall acquittance° me   *outright / acquit*
From all the impure blots and stains thereof.
For God He knows, and you may partly see,
How far I am from the desire thereof.
215 LORD MAYOR   God bless your grace. We see it and will say it.
GLOUCESTER   In saying so, you shall but say the truth.
BUCKINGHAM   Then I salute you with this kingly title:
Long live Richard, England's royal king!
LORD MAYOR   Amen.
220 BUCKINGHAM   Tomorrow will it please you to be crowned?
GLOUCESTER   Even when you will, since you will have it so.
BUCKINGHAM   Tomorrow, then, we will attend your grace.
GLOUCESTER [*to Bishops*]   Come, let us to our holy task
     again.
     —Farewell, good cousin. —Farewell, gentle friends.[3]
                                         Exeunt.

4.1 (F 4.1)

Enter QUEEN *mother* [ELIZABETH], DUCHESS OF YORK,
Marquess DORSET *at one door,* [LADY ANNE,] *Duchess
of Gloucester at another door.*

DUCHESS OF YORK   Who meets us here? My niece°   *daughter-in-law*
     Plantagenet?
QUEEN ELIZABETH   Sister,° well met. Whither away so fast?   *Sister-in-law*
LADY ANNE   No farther than the Tower and, as I guess,

---

3. PERFORMANCE COMMENT Gloucester's performance
of piety can be played in a variety of different ways,
whether as a charade that everyone cynically understands or as a convincing (if momentary) deception.
See Digital Edition PC 3.
4.1 Location: Before the Tower.

| | Upon the like devotion° as yourselves, | *devout duty* |
| 5 | To gratulate° the tender princes there. | *greet* |

QUEEN ELIZABETH   Kind sister, thanks. We'll enter all
    together.
        Enter LIEUTENANT.
And in good time, here the Lieutenant comes.
Master Lieutenant, pray you, by your leave,
How fares the Prince?

10	LIEUTENANT Well, madam, and in health. But by your leave,	
	I may not suffer° you to visit him.	*permit*
	The King hath straitly° charged the contrary.	*strictly*
	QUEEN ELIZABETH The King? Why, who's that?	
	LIEUTENANT I cry you mercy;° I mean the Lord Protector.	*I beg your pardon*
15	QUEEN ELIZABETH The Lord protect him from that kingly	
	title![1]	
	Hath he set bounds° betwixt their love and me?	*barriers*
	I am their mother. Who should keep me from them?	
	DUCHESS OF YORK I am their father's mother. I will see them.	
	LADY ANNE Their aunt I am in law, in love their mother.	
20	Then fear not thou; I'll bear thy blame	
	And take thy office from thee on my peril.[2]	
	LIEUTENANT I do beseech your graces all to pardon me.	
	I am bound by oath; I may not do it. [*Exit* LIEUTENANT.]	
	Enter Lord STANLEY.	
	STANLEY Let me but meet you ladies an hour hence,	
25	And I'll salute your grace of York as mother	
	And reverend looker-on° of two fair queens.[3]	*beholder*
	[*to* LADY ANNE] Come, madam, you must go with me to	
	Westminster,[4]	
	There to be crownèd Richard's royal queen.	
	QUEEN ELIZABETH Oh, cut my lace in sunder[5] that my pent	
	heart	
30	May have some scope to beat, or else I swoon	
	With this dead-killing news.	
	DORSET Madam, have comfort. How fares your grace?	
	QUEEN ELIZABETH O Dorset, speak not to me. Get thee	
	hence.	
	Death and destruction dog thee at the heels.	
35	Thy mother's name is ominous to children.[6]	
	If thou wilt outstrip death, go, cross the seas	
	And live with Richmond, from[7] the reach of hell.	
	Go, hie thee, hie thee, from this slaughterhouse,	
	Lest thou increase the number of the dead	
40	And make me die the thrall° of Margaret's curse,	*slave*
	Nor mother, wife, nor England's counted° queen.	*acknowledged*
	STANLEY Full of wise care is this your counsel, madam.	
	[*to* DORSET] Take all the swift advantage of the time.	
	You shall have letters from me to my son°	*stepson (Richmond)*

---

1. May God prevent Gloucester from acquiring the
title of king.
2. And take on the responsibilities of your position at
my own risk.
3. Elizabeth, widow of Edward IV, and Anne, wife of
Richard III.
4. To Westminster Abbey, where English monarchs

are traditionally crowned.
5. Elizabethan women wore tightly laced bodices.
6. The fact that you are my son places you in danger.
7. Away from. Henry Tudor, Earl of Richmond, had
fled to Brittany in 1472, when Edward IV secured his
grasp on the throne.

45   To meet you on the way and welcome you.
      Be not ta'en tardy by unwise delay.
    DUCHESS OF YORK   O ill-dispersing° wind of misery!   *misfortune-scattering*
      O my accursèd womb, the bed° of death,   *birthplace*
      A cockatrice[8] hast thou hatched to the world,
50   Whose unavoided eye is murderous.
    STANLEY [*to* LADY ANNE]   Come, madam, I in all haste was
      sent.
    LADY ANNE   And I in all unwillingness will go.
      I would to God that the inclusive verge°   *enclosing rim*
      Of golden metal that must round° my brow   *encircle*
55   Were red-hot steel to sear me to the brain.
      Anointed let me be with deadly poison,[9]
      And die ere men can say, "God save the Queen."
    QUEEN ELIZABETH   Alas, poor soul, I envy not thy glory.
      To feed my humor,° wish thyself no harm.   *To humor me*
60   LADY ANNE   No? When he that is my husband now
      Came to me as I followed Henry's corpse—
      When scarce the blood was well washed from his hands
      Which issued from my other angel husband
      And that dead saint which then I weeping followed—
65   Oh, when, I say, I looked on Richard's face,
      This was my wish: "Be thou," quoth I, "accursed
      For making me, so young, so old a widow.[1]
      And when thou wedd'st, let sorrow haunt thy bed;
      And be thy wife—if any be so mad—
70   As miserable by the life of thee
      As thou hast made me by my dear lord's death."
      Lo, ere I can repeat this curse again,
      Even in so short a space, my woman's heart
      Grossly° grew captive to his honey words   *Stupidly*
75   And proved the subject of my own soul's curse,
      Which ever since hath kept my eyes from sleep.
      For never yet one hour in his bed
      Have I enjoyed the golden dew of sleep,
      But have been wakèd by his timorous° dreams.   *fearful*
80   Besides, he hates me for° my father Warwick   *because of*
      And will, no doubt, shortly be rid of me.
    QUEEN ELIZABETH   Alas, poor soul, I pity thy complaints.°   *laments*
    LADY ANNE   No more from my soul I mourn for yours.
    DORSET   Farewell, thou woeful welcomer of glory.
85   LADY ANNE   Adieu, poor soul, thou tak'st thy leave of it.
    DUCHESS OF YORK [*to* DORSET]   Go thou to Richmond, and
      good fortune guide thee.
      [*to* LADY ANNE] Go thou to Richard, and good angels guard
      thee.
      [*to* QUEEN ELIZABETH] Go thou to sanctuary; good thoughts
      possess thee.
      I to my grave, where peace and rest lie with me.
90   Eighty-odd years of sorrow have I seen,
      And each hour's joy wracked with a week of teen.° [*Exeunt.*]   *grief*

---

8. Basilisk (see note to 1.2.148).   coronation.
9. Instead of the holy oil used in the ceremony of   1. Doomed to a long life of widowhood.

4.2 (F 4.2)

*The trumpets sound. Enter [*KING*] RICHARD crowned,*
BUCKINGHAM, CATESBY, with other Nobles [and BOY].

KING RICHARD[1]   Stand all apart.° —Cousin of Buckingham,   *aside*
Give me thy hand.
        Here he ascendeth the throne.
                Thus high by thy advice
And thy assistance is King Richard seated.
But shall we wear these honors for a day,
5   Or shall they last and we rejoice in them?[2]
BUCKINGHAM   Still° live they, and forever may they last.   *Perpetually*
KING RICHARD   O Buckingham, now do I play the touch[3]
To try if thou be current° gold indeed.   *real, genuine*
Young Edward lives: think now what I would say.
10 BUCKINGHAM   Say on, my gracious sovereign.
KING RICHARD   Why, Buckingham, I say I would be king.
BUCKINGHAM   Why so you are, my thrice-renownèd liege.
KING RICHARD   Ha! Am I king? 'Tis so—but Edward lives.
BUCKINGHAM   True, noble prince.
KING RICHARD   Oh, bitter consequence,°   *conclusion; retort*
15 That Edward still should live. "True, noble prince!"[4]
Cousin, thou wert not wont° to be so dull.   *accustomed*
Shall I be plain? I wish the bastards dead,
And I would have it suddenly° performed.   *at once*
What say'st thou? Speak suddenly. Be brief.
20 BUCKINGHAM   Your grace may do your pleasure.
KING RICHARD   Tut, tut, thou art all ice; thy kindness
    freezeth.
Say, have I thy consent that they shall die?
BUCKINGHAM   Give me some breath, some little pause, my
    lord,
Before I positively speak herein.
25 I will resolve° your grace immediately.°   *Exit.*   *answer / shortly*
CATESBY [*aside*]   The King is angry. See, he bites the lip.
KING RICHARD [*aside*]   I will converse with iron-witted fools
And unrespective° boys. None are for me   *unobservant*
That look into me with considerate° eyes.   *critical*
30 High-reaching° Buckingham grows circumspect.   *Ambitious*
—Boy!
BOY   My lord?
KING RICHARD   Know'st thou not any whom corrupting gold
Would tempt unto a close° exploit of death?   *secret*
35 BOY   My lord, I know a discontented gentleman
Whose humble means match not his haughty mind.
Gold were as good as twenty orators
And will, no doubt, tempt him to anything.

4.2 Location: The palace, London.
1. For the remainder of the play, Richard is identified in the speech prefixes not as "Gloucester" but as "King Richard."
2. PERFORMANCE COMMENT At this key turning point, productions often make important interpretive choices in the portrayal of the triumphant Richard and his supporters, whether to emphasize festivity or foreboding. See Digital Edition PC 4.

3. Touchstone: a means of testing gold (in the line that follows, *try:* to test; separate out metal from dross).
4. TEXTUAL COMMENT We have chosen to emend the Quarto's and Folio's unpunctuated "true noble prince" with "True, noble prince," which is more in line with Richard's sarcastic parroting of Buckingham's words throughout. See Digital Edition TC 11 (Quarto edited text).

KING RICHARD   What is his name?

BOY   His name, my lord, is Tyrrel.

40 KING RICHARD   Go call him hither presently.   [*Exit* BOY.]
    [*aside*] The deep-revolving,° witty° Buckingham   *deeply scheming / clever*
    No more shall be the neighbor to my counsel.
    Hath he so long held out° with me untired,   *kept up*
    And stops he now for breath?
        Enter [STANLEY, *Earl of*] *Derby.*
              How now, what news with you?

45 STANLEY   My lord, I hear the Marquess Dorset is fled
    To Richmond, in those parts beyond the seas
    Where he abides.

KING RICHARD   Catesby!

CATESBY   My lord.

KING RICHARD   Rumor it abroad
    That Anne my wife is sick and like to die;
50 I will take order for her keeping close.[5]
    Inquire me out some mean-born gentleman,
    Whom I will marry straight to Clarence' daughter.
    The boy[6] is foolish,° and I fear not him.   *simpleminded*
    Look how thou dream'st! I say again, give out
55 That Anne my wife is sick and like to die.
    About it, for it stands me much upon°   *is very important to me*
    To stop all hopes whose growth may damage me.
              [*Exit* CATESBY.]
    [*aside*] I must be married to my brother's daughter,[7]
    Or else my kingdom stands on brittle glass.
60 Murder her brothers, and then marry her—
    Uncertain way of gain. But I am in
    So far in blood that sin will pluck on° sin.   *incite*
    Tear-falling pity dwells not in this eye.
        Enter TYRREL.
    Is thy name Tyrrel?

65 TYRREL   James Tyrrel, and your most obedient subject.

KING RICHARD   Art thou, indeed?

TYRREL   Prove° me, my gracious sovereign.   *Test*

KING RICHARD   Dar'st thou resolve to kill a friend of mine?

TYRREL   Ay, my lord, but I had rather kill two enemies.

KING RICHARD   Why, there thou hast it: two deep enemies,
70 Foes to my rest and my sweet sleep's disturbers,
    Are they that I would have thee deal upon.[8]   *set to work upon*
    Tyrrel, I mean those bastards in the Tower.

TYRREL   Let me have open means to come[7] to them,
    And soon I'll rid you from the fear of them.

75 KING RICHARD   Thou sing'st sweet music. Come hither,
      Tyrrel.
    Go by that token.° Rise, and lend thine ear.   *sign of authority*
      He whispers in his ear.
    'Tis no more but so.° Say it is done,   *That's all*
    And I will love thee and prefer° thee too.   *promote*

TYRREL   'Tis done, my gracious lord.

---

5. I will arrange to have her kept out of sight.
6. Clarence's eldest son, Edward, Earl of Warwick.
7. To Edward's daughter, Elizabeth of York, who was later to unite the two houses by becoming queen to the Lancastrian Henry VII, formerly the Earl of Richmond.
8. Let me have free access.

80   KING RICHARD   Shall we hear from thee, Tyrrel, ere we sleep?
            Enter BUCKINGHAM.
  TYRREL   Ye shall, my lord.   *[Exit.]*
  BUCKINGHAM   My lord, I have considered in my mind
    The late demand that you did sound me in.
  KING RICHARD   Well, let that pass. Dorset is fled to
    Richmond.
85   BUCKINGHAM   I hear that news, my lord.
  KING RICHARD   Stanley, he° is your wife's son. Well look to it.   *(Richmond)*
  BUCKINGHAM   My lord, I claim your gift, my due by promise,
    For which your honor and your faith is pawned:
    The earldom of Hereford and the movables
90   The which you promisèd I should possess.
  KING RICHARD   Stanley, look to your wife. If she convey
    Letters to Richmond, you shall answer it.°   *for it*
  BUCKINGHAM   What says your highness to my just demand?
  KING RICHARD   As I remember, Henry the Sixth
95   Did prophesy that Richmond should be king
    When Richmond was a little peevish boy.
    A king: perhaps, perhaps—
  BUCKINGHAM   My lord.
  KING RICHARD   How chance the prophet could not at that
    time
    Have told me, I being by, that I should kill him?
100   BUCKINGHAM   My lord, your promise for the earldom.
  KING RICHARD   Richmond! When last I was at Exeter,
    The mayor in courtesy showed me the castle
    And called it Rougemont,⁹ at which name I started,
    Because a bard of Ireland¹ told me once
105   I should not live long after I saw Richmond.
  BUCKINGHAM   My lord!
  KING RICHARD   Ay, what's o'clock?
  BUCKINGHAM   I am thus bold to put your grace in mind
    Of what you promised me.
110   KING RICHARD   Well, but what's o'clock?
  BUCKINGHAM   Upon the stroke of ten.
  KING RICHARD   Well, let it strike.
  BUCKINGHAM   Why let it strike?
  KING RICHARD   Because that like a Jack² thou keep'st the
    stroke
115   Betwixt thy begging and my meditation.
    I am not in the giving vein today.
  BUCKINGHAM   Why, then, resolve me° whether you will or no.   *answer me resolutely*
  KING RICHARD   Tut, tut, thou troublest me. I am not in the
    vein.°   *Exeunt [all but* BUCKINGHAM].   *mood*
  BUCKINGHAM   Is it even so? Reward'st he my true service
120   With such deep contempt? Made I him king for this?
    Oh, let me think on Hastings and be gone
    To Brecknock° while my fearful head is on!   *Exit.*   *(manor house in Wales)*

---

9. Redhill (but punning on "Richmond").
1. Celtic bards, or poets, were also considered prophets.
2. A Jack was the mechanical figure who appeared to strike the hours in early clocks. By clockwork reiterations of his suit, Richard suggests, Buckingham is behaving like an annoying beggar and interfering with Richard's "meditation."

4.3 (F 4.3)

Enter Sir [James] TYRREL.

TYRREL   The tyrannous and bloody deed is done:
The most arch° act of piteous massacre   *preeminent*
That ever yet this land was guilty of.
Dighton and Forrest,[1] whom I did suborn°   *induce*
5   To do this ruthless piece of butchery,
Although they were fleshed[2] villains, bloody dogs,
Melting with tenderness and kind compassion,
Wept like two children in their deaths' sad stories.[3]
"Lo, thus," quoth Dighton, "lay those tender babes."
10   "Thus, thus," quoth Forrest, "girdling° one another   *embracing*
Within their innocent alabaster° arms.   *marble-white*
Their lips were four red roses on a stalk,
Which in their summer beauty kissed each other.
A book of prayers on their pillow lay,
15   Which once," quoth Forrest, "almost changed my mind.
But oh, the devil"— There the villain stopped
Whilst Dighton thus told on: "We smothered
The most replenishèd° sweet work of nature   *complete*
That from the prime° creation ever she framed."   *first*
20   Thus both are gone° with conscience and remorse.   *overcome*
They could not speak, and so I left them both
To bring this tidings to the bloody king.
            Enter KING RICHARD.
And here he comes. All hail, my sovereign liege.
KING RICHARD   Kind Tyrrel, am I happy in thy news?
25   TYRREL   If to have done the thing you gave in charge
Beget your happiness,[4] be happy then,
For it is done, my lord.
KING RICHARD   But didst thou see them dead?
TYRREL   I did, my lord.
KING RICHARD   And buried, gentle Tyrrel?
TYRREL   The chaplain of the Tower hath buried them,
30   But how or in what place I do not know.
KING RICHARD   Come to me, Tyrrel, soon at after-supper,°   *dessert*
And thou shalt tell the process° of their death.   *story*
Meantime, but think how I may do thee good,
And be inheritor of thy desire.[5]
35   Farewell till soon.   *Exit* TYRREL.
The son of Clarence have I pent° up close.   *locked*
His daughter meanly have I matched in marriage.[6]
The sons of Edward sleep in Abraham's bosom,[7]
And Anne my wife hath bid the world goodnight.
40   Now, for° I know the Breton[8] Richmond aims   *because*
At young Elizabeth, my brother's daughter,

4.3 Location: Scene continues.
1. For the murder of the princes, Tyrrel recruited his servant John Dighton, along with Myles Forrest and two others.
2. Experienced in killing; applied to hounds that had been fed part of their first kill in order to give them a taste for blood.
3. Wept in telling the sad story of the princes' deaths.
4. *If . . . happiness:* If it pleases you to have accom-

plished what you ordered done.
5. *but . . . desire:* you have only to think what you want of me, and you will possess it.
6. I have married off to a poor man.
7. In heaven (Luke 16:22–23).
8. Person from Bretagne (Brittany); Richmond spent fourteen years in exile there before returning to England to face Richard III in 1485.

And by that knot° looks proudly o'er the crown,   *marriage; alliance*
To her I go a jolly thriving wooer.[9]
     Enter CATESBY.
CATESBY My lord!
45 KING RICHARD Good news or bad, that thou com'st in so
     bluntly?
CATESBY Bad news, my lord. Ely is fled to Richmond,
  And Buckingham, backed with the hardy Welshmen,
  Is in the field, and still his power increaseth.
KING RICHARD Ely with Richmond troubles me more near°   *deeply*
50 Than Buckingham and his rash-levied° army.   *hastily raised*
  Come, I have heard that fearful commenting
  Is leaden servitor[1] to dull delay.
  Delay leads impotent and snail-paced beggary.°   *ruin*
  Then fiery expedition° be my wing—   *speed*
55 Jove's Mercury[2] and herald for a king.
  Come, muster men. My counsel is my shield.[3]
  We must be brief when traitors brave the field.[4]   *Exeunt.*

4.4 (F 4.4)

     Enter QUEEN MARGARET, *alone.*
QUEEN MARGARET So now prosperity begins to mellow°   *ripen*
  And drop into the rotten mouth of death.
  Here in these confines slyly have I lurked
  To watch the waning of mine adversaries.
5 A dire induction° am I witness to,   *prologue (as to a play)*
  And will to France, hoping the consequence°   *conclusion (as of a play)*
  Will prove as bitter, black, and tragical.
  Withdraw thee, wretched Margaret. Who comes here?
     Enter the QUEEN [ELIZABETH] *and the* DUCHESS
     OF YORK.
QUEEN ELIZABETH Ah, my young princes! Ah, my tender
     babes!
10 My unblown° flowers, new-appearing sweets!°   *unopened / blooms*
  If yet your gentle souls fly in the air
  And be not fixed in doom perpetual,[1]
  Hover about me with your airy wings
  And hear your mother's lamentation.
15 QUEEN MARGARET [*aside*] Hover about her; say that right for
     right
  Hath dimmed your infant morn to agèd night.[2]
QUEEN ELIZABETH Wilt Thou, O God, fly from such gentle
     lambs,
  And throw them in the entrails of the wolf?
  When° didst Thou sleep when such a deed was done?   *Whenever (up until now)*
20 QUEEN MARGARET [*aside*] When holy Harry[3] died, and my
     sweet son.

---

9. It was widely rumored that Anne was poisoned in order to facilitate a plan by Richard to marry Elizabeth, sister to the missing princes; modern historians believe that these allegations are probably untrue. Richard's alleged actions regarding Clarence's son and daughter (lines 36–37) are certainly untrue.
1. *fearful . . . servitor:* frightened talk is the sluggish attendant.
2. The swift messenger of the gods.
3. *My . . . shield:* I do not talk, but arm myself to fight.

counsel: adviser.
4. When traitors defy (us on) the battlefield.
4.4 Location: Before the palace.
1. *fixed in doom perpetual:* assigned by an irrevocable sentence to your final place of punishment or reward.
2. *right for . . . night:* evenhanded justice has destroyed the bright hopes of your lives.
3. Henry VI (Margaret's husband); notably pious in Shakespeare's characterization.

DUCHESS OF YORK Blind sight, dead life, poor mortal living
    ghost,[4]
    Woe's scene, world's shame, grave's due by life usurped,[5]
    Rest thy unrest on England's lawful earth,
    Unlawfully made drunk with innocents' blood.

25 QUEEN ELIZABETH Oh, that thou[6] wouldst as well afford° a   *bestow*
    grave
    As thou canst yield a melancholy seat,
    Then would I hide my bones, not rest them here.
    Oh, who hath any cause to mourn but I?

DUCHESS OF YORK So many miseries have crazed° my voice   *cracked*
30   That my woe-wearied tongue is mute and dumb.
    Edward Plantaganet, why art thou dead?

QUEEN MARGARET [*coming forward*] If ancient sorrow be
    most reverend,
    Give mine the benefit of seniory,[7]
    And let my woes frown on the upper hand.[8]
35   If sorrow can admit society,
    Tell over° your woes again by viewing mine.   *Count; narrate*
    I had an Edward, till a Richard killed him.
    I had a Harry, till a Richard killed him.
    [*to* QUEEN ELIZABETH] Thou hadst an Edward, till a
    Richard killed him.
40   Thou hadst a Richard,[9] till a Richard killed him.

DUCHESS OF YORK I had a Richard too, and thou didst kill
    him.
    I had a Rutland too;[1] thou holp'st to kill him.

QUEEN MARGARET Thou hadst a Clarence too, and Richard
    killed him.
    From forth the kennel of thy womb hath crept
45   A hell-hound that doth hunt us all to death.
    That dog that had his teeth before his eyes,[2]
    To worry° lambs and lap their gentle blood,   *tear apart*
    That foul defacer of God's handiwork,
    Thy womb let loose to chase us to our graves.
50   O upright, just, and true-disposing God,
    How do I thank Thee that this carnal cur
    Preys on the issue° of his mother's body   *offspring*
    And makes her pew-fellow° with others' moan.   *companion at church*

DUCHESS OF YORK O Harry's wife, triumph not in my woes.
55   God witness with me, I have wept for thine.

QUEEN MARGARET Bear with me. I am hungry for revenge,
    And now I cloy me° with beholding it.   *gorge myself*
    Thy Edward he is dead that stabbed my Edward.
    Thy other Edward dead to quit° my Edward.   *requite*
60   Young York, he is but boot,[3] because both they

---

4. *mortal living ghost:* a dead person doomed to exist among the living.
5. *graves . . . usurped:* person who ought to be dead, unlawfully alive.
6. Here, Elizabeth is addressing the earth directly.
7. Seniority; Q1–5 have "signorie," F "signeurie," which suggests that Margaret may mean "sovereignty" or "lordship" ("seigniory").
8. *frown . . . hand:* have precedence in mourning.

9. Edward and Richard were Queen Elizabeth's two sons (smothered in the Tower).
1. Her husband (Richard, Duke of York) and youngest son; both deaths are dramatized in act 1 of *3 Henry VI.*
2. His enemies rumored that the savage Richard was born with teeth.
3. He is thrown in simply to make the bargain even.

Match not the high perfection of my loss.
Thy Clarence he is dead that killed my Edward,
And the beholders of this tragic play,
The adulterate° Hastings, Rivers, Vaughan, Grey,   *adulterous*
65   Untimely smothered° in their dusky graves.   *buried*
Richard yet lives, hell's black intelligencer,°   *spy*
Only reserved their factor[4] to buy souls
And send them thither. But at hand, at hand,
Ensues his piteous and unpitied end.
70   Earth gapes, hell burns, fiends roar, saints pray,
To have him suddenly conveyed away.
Cancel his bond of life, dear God I pray,
That I may live to say, "The dog is dead."
QUEEN ELIZABETH   Oh, thou didst prophesy the time would
        come
75   That I should wish for thee to help me curse
That bottled spider, that foul bunch-backed toad.
QUEEN MARGARET   I called thee then vain flourish of my
        fortune.
I called thee then poor shadow,° painted queen:[5]   *semblance*
The presentation° of but what I was;   *copy*
80   The flattering index° of a direful pageant;°   *prologue / play*
One heaved a-high to be hurled down below;
A mother only mocked with two sweet babes;
A dream of which thou wert a breath, a bubble,
A sign° of dignity, a garish flag   *mere symbol*
85   To be the aim of every dangerous shot;[6]
A queen in jest, only to fill the scene.
Where is thy husband now? Where be thy brothers?
Where are thy children? Wherein dost thou joy?
Who sues to thee and cries, "God save the Queen"?
90   Where be the bending° peers that flattered thee?   *bowing; yielding*
Where be the thronging troops that followed thee?
Decline[7] all this, and see what now thou art:
For happy wife, a most distressèd widow;
For joyful mother, one that wails the name;
95   For queen, a very caitiff° crowned with care;   *wretch*
For one being sued to, one that humbly sues;
For one commanding all, obeyed of none;
For one that scorned at me, now scorned of° me.   *by*
Thus hath the course of justice wheeled about
100   And left thee but a very prey to time,
Having no more but thought of what thou wert
To torture thee the more, being what thou art.
Thou didst usurp my place, and dost thou not
Usurp the just proportion of my sorrow?
105   Now thy proud neck bears half my burdened° yoke,   *burdensome*
From which even here I slip my weary neck
And leave the burden of it all on thee.
Farewell, York's wife and queen of sad mischance.

4. *Only . . . factor:* Retained (or preserved from death) only in order to serve as hell's agent. *their:* the demonic inhabitants of hell.
5. See 1.3.237.
6. *garish . . . shot:* bearer of a brightly colored standard who draws the enemy fire.
7. Recite in order with the proper endings (as a noun in Latin grammar).

These English woes will make me smile in France.
110 QUEEN ELIZABETH   O thou, well skilled in curses, stay awhile
And teach me how to curse mine enemies.
QUEEN MARGARET   Forbear to sleep the nights, and fast the
days.
Compare dead happiness with living woe.
Think that thy babes were fairer than they were,
115 And he that slew them fouler than he is.
Bett'ring° thy loss makes the bad causer worse.   *Magnifying*
Revolving° this will teach thee how to curse.   *Musing on*
QUEEN ELIZABETH   My words are dull. Oh, quicken° them   *enliven; sharpen*
with thine.
QUEEN MARGARET   Thy woes will make them sharp and
pierce like mine.   *Exit.*
120 DUCHESS OF YORK   Why should calamity be full of words?
QUEEN ELIZABETH   Windy attorneys to their client woes,[8]
Airy succeeders of intestate joys,[9]
Poor breathing° orators of miseries—   *speaking*
Let them have scope. Though what they do impart
125 Help not at all, yet do they ease the heart.
DUCHESS OF YORK   If so, then be not tongue-tied. Go with
me,
And in the breath of bitter words let's smother
My damnèd son which thy two sweet sons smothered.
I hear his drum. Be copious in exclaims.°   *exclamations*
      Enter KING RICHARD, marching, with drums and
      trumpets.
130 KING RICHARD   Who intercepts my expedition?°   *haste; march*
DUCHESS OF YORK   A she that might have intercepted thee,
By strangling thee in her accursèd womb,
From all the slaughters, wretch, that thou hast done.
QUEEN ELIZABETH   Hid'st thou that forehead with a golden
crown
135 Where should be graven, if that right were right,
The slaughter of the prince that owed° that crown   *possessed*
And the dire death of my two sons and brothers?
Tell me, thou villain slave, where are my children?
DUCHESS OF YORK   Thou toad, thou toad, where is thy brother
Clarence
140 And little Ned Plantagenet, his son?
QUEEN ELIZABETH   Where is kind Hastings, Rivers, Vaughan,
Grey?
KING RICHARD   A flourish,° trumpets! Strike alarum,°   *trumpet call / Call to arms*
drums!
Let not the heavens hear these telltale women
Rail on the Lord's anointed. Strike, I say!
      The trumpets [sound]. [Flourish. Alarums.]
145 Either be patient and entreat me fair,°   *treat me courteously*
Or with the clamorous report° of war   *noise*
Thus will I drown your exclamations.
DUCHESS OF YORK   Art thou my son?
KING RICHARD   Ay, I thank God, my father, and yourself.

8. Words are long-winded pleaders for the sufferings   9. Words record joys that have died without bequeath-
that have hired them.   ing anything (*intestate:* without a will).

150 DUCHESS OF YORK   Then patiently hear my impatience.
   KING RICHARD   Madam, I have a touch of your condition,°   *temperament*
   Which cannot brook the accent° of reproof.   *abide the language*
   DUCHESS OF YORK   I will be mild and gentle in my speech.
   KING RICHARD   And brief, good mother, for I am in haste.
155 DUCHESS OF YORK   Art thou so hasty? I have stayed° for thee,   *waited*
   God knows, in anguish, pain, and agony.
   KING RICHARD   And came I not at last to comfort you?
   DUCHESS OF YORK   No, by the holy rood,° thou know'st it   *cross*
      well,
   Thou cam'st on earth to make the earth my hell.
160 A grievous burden was thy birth to me;
   Tetchy° and wayward was thy infancy;   *Irritable*
   Thy school days frightful,° desperate, wild, and furious;   *frightening*
   Thy prime° of manhood daring, bold, and venturous;   *beginning*
   Thy age confirmed° proud, subtle, bloody, treacherous.   *settled maturity*
165 What comfortable hour canst thou name
   That ever graced me[1] in thy company?
   KING RICHARD   Faith, none but Humphrey Hower[2] that
      called your grace
   To breakfast once forth° of my company.   *out*
   If I be so disgracious° in your sight,   *unpleasing*
170 Let me march on and not offend your grace.
   DUCHESS OF YORK   Oh, hear me speak, for I shall never see
      thee more.
   KING RICHARD   Come, come, you are too bitter.
   DUCHESS OF YORK   Either thou wilt die by God's just
      ordinance°   *decree*
   Ere from this war thou turn° a conqueror,   *return*
175 Or I with grief and extreme age shall perish
   And never look upon thy face again.
   Therefore take with thee my most heavy curse,
   Which in the day of battle tire° thee more   *exhaust; attire*
   Than all the complete armor that thou wear'st.
180 My prayers on the adverse party° fight,   *opposite side*
   And there the little souls of Edward's children
   Whisper° the spirits of thine enemies   *Whisper to*
   And promise them success and victory.
   Bloody thou art; bloody will be thy end.
185 Shame serves° thy life and doth thy death attend.   *Exit.*   *accompanies*
   QUEEN ELIZABETH   Though far more cause, yet much less
      spirit to curse
   Abides in me. I say "Amen" to all.
   KING RICHARD   Stay, madam, I must speak a word with you.
   QUEEN ELIZABETH   I have no more sons of the royal blood
190 For thee to murder. For my daughters, Richard,
   They shall be praying nuns, not weeping queens,
   And therefore level not to hit their lives.[3]
   KING RICHARD   You have a daughter called Elizabeth,
   Virtuous and fair, royal and gracious.

1. Gave me pleasure; but Richard interprets as "called
me by the title 'your grace.'"
2. A proper name, based on "ewer" (a servant who
waits at table), but also suggesting "huer" (someone
who makes a hue or cry) and playing on "hour" (line
165). Proverbially, "to dine with Duke Humphrey"
was not to dine at all.
3. And therefore do not take aim to kill them.

195 QUEEN ELIZABETH   And must she die for this? Oh, let her
live,
And I'll corrupt her manners,° stain her beauty,   *morals*
Slander myself as false to Edward's bed,
Throw over her the veil of infamy.
So° she may live unscarred from bleeding slaughter,   *Provided that*
200 I will confess she was not Edward's daughter.
KING RICHARD   Wrong not her birth. She is of royal blood.
QUEEN ELIZABETH   To save her life, I'll say she is not so.
KING RICHARD   Her life is only safest in her birth.[4]
QUEEN ELIZABETH   And only in that safety died her brothers.
205 KING RICHARD   Lo, at their births good stars were opposite.°   *adverse*
QUEEN ELIZABETH   No, to their lives bad friends were
contrary.°   *opposed*
KING RICHARD   All unavoided° is the doom° of destiny.   *unavoidable / sentence*
QUEEN ELIZABETH   True, when avoided grace[5] makes destiny.
My babes were destined to a fairer death,
210 If grace had blessed thee with a fairer life.
KING RICHARD   Madam, so thrive I in my enterprise
As I intend more good to you and yours
Than ever you or yours were by me wronged.[6]
QUEEN ELIZABETH   What good is covered with the face of
heaven[7]
215 To be discovered that can do me good?
KING RICHARD   The advancement of your children, mighty
lady.
QUEEN ELIZABETH   Up to some scaffold, there to lose their
heads.
KING RICHARD   No, to the dignity and height of honor,
The high imperial type° of this earth's glory.   *symbol*
220 QUEEN ELIZABETH   Flatter my sorrows with report of it.
Tell me what state, what dignity, what honor,
Canst thou demise° to any child of mine?   *transmit*
KING RICHARD   Even all I have, yea, and myself and all,
Will I withal endow a child of thine,
225 So° in the Lethe[8] of thy angry soul   *If*
Thou drown the sad remembrance of those wrongs
Which thou supposest I have done to thee.
QUEEN ELIZABETH   Be brief, lest that the process° of thy   *story*
kindness
Last longer telling° than thy kindness do.   *in the telling*
230 KING RICHARD   Then know that from my soul[9] I love thy
daughter.
QUEEN ELIZABETH   My daughter's mother thinks it with her
soul.
KING RICHARD   What do you think?
QUEEN ELIZABETH   That thou dost love my daughter from thy
soul.
So from thy soul's love didst thou love her brothers,

4. Her life is safe only because of her high birth.
5. When a man who has rejected God's grace (that is,
Richard).
6. *Madam . . . wronged:* (I pray) that the success of
my upcoming enterprise be as certain as my intention to do to you more good in the future than I have
done you wrong in the past.
7. What good is there on earth.
8. A river in the underworld whose waters induced
forgetfulness.
9. With all my soul (but Queen Elizabeth takes it as
"separated from," "at variance with").

235　　And from my heart's love I do thank thee for it.

KING RICHARD　Be not so hasty to confound° my meaning.　　*deliberately misconstrue*
　　I mean that with my soul I love thy daughter
　　And mean to make her queen of England.

QUEEN ELIZABETH　Say then, who dost thou mean shall be
　　her king?

240　KING RICHARD　Even he that makes her queen. Who should
　　be else?

QUEEN ELIZABETH　What, thou?

KING RICHARD　Ay, even I. What think you of it, madam?

QUEEN ELIZABETH　How canst thou woo her?

KING RICHARD　　　　　　　　　　That would I learn of you,
　　As one that are best acquainted with her humor.°　　*temperament*

QUEEN ELIZABETH　And wilt thou learn of me?

245　KING RICHARD　　　　　　　　Madam, with all my heart.

QUEEN ELIZABETH　Send to her, by the man that slew her
　　brothers,
　　A pair of bleeding hearts; thereon engrave
　　"Edward" and "York." Then haply° she will weep.　　*perhaps*
　　Therefore present to her—as sometimes° Margaret　　*once*

250　Did to thy father—a handkerchief steeped in Rutland's
　　blood,[1]
　　And bid her dry her weeping eyes therewith.°　　*with it*
　　If this inducement force her not to love,
　　Send her a story of thy noble acts.
　　Tell her thou mad'st away her uncle Clarence,

255　Her uncle Rivers, yea, and for her sake
　　Mad'st quick conveyance with° her good aunt Anne.　　*Got rid of*

KING RICHARD　Come, come, you mock me; this is not
　　the way
　　To win your daughter.

QUEEN ELIZABETH　　　　　　There is no other way
　　Unless thou couldst put on some other shape

260　And not be Richard that hath done all this.

KING RICHARD　Infer° fair England's peace by this alliance.　　*Give as a reason*

QUEEN ELIZABETH　Which she shall purchase with still
　　lasting° war.　　*perpetual*

KING RICHARD　Say that the King, which may command,
　　entreats.

QUEEN ELIZABETH　That at her hands which the King's King°　　*(God)*
　　forbids.

265　KING RICHARD　Say she shall be a high and mighty queen.

QUEEN ELIZABETH　To wail the title,° as her mother doth.　　*(of queen)*

KING RICHARD　Say I will love her everlastingly.

QUEEN ELIZABETH　But how long shall that title "ever" last?

KING RICHARD　Sweetly in force unto her fair life's end.

270　QUEEN ELIZABETH　But how long fairly° shall her sweet life　　*without foul play*
　　last?

KING RICHARD　So long as heaven and nature lengthens it.

QUEEN ELIZABETH　So long as hell and Richard likes of it.

KING RICHARD　Say I, her sovereign, am her subject love.

QUEEN ELIZABETH　But she, your subject, loathes such
　　sovereignty.

---

1. Dramatized in *3 Henry VI* 1.4 (see note to 1.3.174).

275 KING RICHARD Be eloquent in my behalf to her.

QUEEN ELIZABETH An honest tale speeds° best being plainly *succeeds*
    told.

KING RICHARD Then in plain terms tell her my loving tale.

QUEEN ELIZABETH Plain and not honest is too harsh a style.[2]

KING RICHARD Madam, your reasons are too shallow and too
    quick.[3]

280 QUEEN ELIZABETH Oh, no, my reasons are too deep and
    dead,

    Too deep and dead, poor infants, in their grave.

KING RICHARD Harp not on that string, madam; that is past.

QUEEN ELIZABETH Harp on it still shall I till heartstrings
    break.

KING RICHARD Now by my George, my Garter,[4] and my
    crown—

285 QUEEN ELIZABETH Profaned, dishonored, and the third
    usurped.

KING RICHARD I swear—

QUEEN ELIZABETH   By nothing, for this is no oath.

    The George, profaned, hath lost his° holy honor; *its*

    The Garter, blemished, pawned his knightly virtue;

    The crown, usurped, disgraced his kingly dignity.

290   If something thou wilt swear to be believed,

    Swear then by something that thou hast not wronged.

KING RICHARD Now by the world—

QUEEN ELIZABETH   'Tis full of thy foul wrongs.

KING RICHARD My father's death—

QUEEN ELIZABETH   Thy life hath that dishonored.

KING RICHARD Then by myself—

QUEEN ELIZABETH   Thyself thyself misusest.

KING RICHARD Why then, by God—

295 QUEEN ELIZABETH   God's wrong is most of all.

    If thou hadst feared to break an oath by Him,

    The unity the King my husband made[5]

    Had not been broken, nor my brother slain.

    If thou hadst feared to break an oath by Him,

300   The imperial metal circling now thy brow

    Had graced the tender temples of my child,

    And both the princes had been breathing here,

    Which now, two tender playfellows for dust,

    Thy broken faith hath made a prey for worms.

    What canst thou swear by now?

305 KING RICHARD   By the time to come.

QUEEN ELIZABETH That thou hast wronged in time o'erpast,

    For I myself have many tears to wash

    Hereafter time,° for time past wronged by thee. *The future*

    The children live whose parents thou hast slaughtered—

310   Ungoverned youth,[6] to wail it in their age.° *when they grow older*

    The parents live whose children thou hast butchered—

---

2. The plain style (as in the proverb "Truth is plain"), unless it is truth telling, will be too harsh; lies need elaborate decoration.

3. Rash, ill considered; but Elizabeth's response plays on "quick" as "alive."

4. A garter and a jeweled pendant with the figure of

St. George were parts of the insignia of the Order of the Garter, the highest order of knighthood.

5. The "reconciliation" staged in 2.1 between Queen Elizabeth and her enemies.

6. Youth without a father's guidance.

Old withered plants, to wail it with° their age.	*along with*

Swear not by time to come, for that thou hast
Misused ere used, by time misused o'erpast.[7]

315 KING RICHARD   As I intend[8] to prosper and repent,
So thrive I in my dangerous attempt

Of hostile arms. Myself myself confound;°	*May I ruin myself*

Day, yield me not thy light, nor night thy rest;
Be opposite all planets of good luck[9]

320 To my proceedings if, with pure heart's love,
Immaculate devotion, holy thoughts,

I tender° not thy beauteous, princely daughter.	*love*

In her consists my happiness and thine.
Without her follows to this land and me,
325 To thee, herself, and many a Christian soul,
Sad desolation, ruin, and decay.
It cannot be avoided but by this;
It will not be avoided but by this.

Therefore, good mother°—I must call you so—	*mother-in-law*

330 Be the attorney of my love to her.
Plead what I will be, not what I have been;
Not my deserts, but what I will deserve.

Urge the necessity and state of times,°	*state of affairs*
And be not peevish-fond° in great designs.	*foolishly obstinate*

335 QUEEN ELIZABETH   Shall I be tempted of the devil thus?
KING RICHARD   Ay, if the devil tempt thee to do good.
QUEEN ELIZABETH   Shall I forget myself to be myself?[1]
KING RICHARD   Ay, if your self's remembrance wrong
        yourself.[2]
QUEEN ELIZABETH   But thou didst kill my children.
340 KING RICHARD   But in your daughter's womb I bury them
Where, in that nest of spicery,[3] they shall breed

Selves of themselves to your recomforture.°	*consolation*

QUEEN ELIZABETH   Shall I go win my daughter to thy will?
KING RICHARD   And be a happy mother by the deed.
345 QUEEN ELIZABETH   I go. Write to me very shortly.
KING RICHARD   Bear her my true love's kiss. Farewell.
                              Exit [QUEEN ELIZABETH].
Relenting fool, and shallow changing woman!
        Enter RATCLIFFE [*and* CATESBY].
RATCLIFFE   My gracious sovereign, on the western coast

Rideth a puissant° navy. To the shore	*mighty*

350 Throng many doubtful, hollow-hearted friends,
Unarmed and unresolved to beat them back.

'Tis thought that Richmond is their° admiral,	*(the navy's)*
And there they hull,° expecting but the aid	*drift; wait*

Of Buckingham to welcome them ashore.

355 KING RICHARD   Some light-foot° friend post° to the Duke of   *swift-footed / hasten*
    Norfolk:
    Ratcliffe, thyself, or Catesby. —Where is he?

CATESBY   Here, my lord.

KING RICHARD   Fly to the Duke. [*to* RATCLIFFE] Post thou to
    Salisbury.
    When thou com'st there— [*to* CATESBY] Dull, unmindful
    villain,

360   Why stand'st thou still and goest not to the Duke?

CATESBY   First, mighty sovereign, let me know your mind,
    What from your grace I shall deliver him.

KING RICHARD   Oh, true, good Catesby. Bid him levy straight
    The greatest strength and power he can make,°   *raise*

365   And meet me presently° at Salisbury.   [*Exit* CATESBY.]   *without delay*

RATCLIFFE   What is it your highness' pleasure I shall do at
    Salisbury?

KING RICHARD   Why, what wouldst thou do there before I go?

RATCLIFFE   Your highness told me I should post before.

KING RICHARD   My mind is changed, sir, my mind is
    changed.

          Enter [STANLEY, *Earl of*] *Derby.*

370   How now, what news with you?

STANLEY   None good, my lord, to please you with the
    hearing,
    Nor none so bad but it may well be told.

KING RICHARD   Hoyday,° a riddle! Neither good nor bad!   *(an exclamation)*
    Why dost thou run so many mile about

375   When thou mayst tell thy tale a nearer° way?   *more direct*
    Once more, what news?

STANLEY   Richmond is on the seas.

KING RICHARD   There let him sink, and be the seas on him,
    White-livered runagate.° —What doth he there?   *Cowardly deserter*

STANLEY   I know not, mighty sovereign, but by guess.

380 KING RICHARD   Well, sir, as you guess, as you guess?

STANLEY   Stirred up by Dorset, Buckingham, and Ely,
    He makes for England, there to claim the crown.

KING RICHARD   Is the chair° empty? Is the sword unswayed?   *throne*
    Is the King dead? The empire° unpossessed?   *state*

385   What heir of York is there alive but we?
    And who is England's king but great York's heir?
    Then tell me, what doth he upon the sea?

STANLEY   Unless for that, my liege, I cannot guess.

KING RICHARD   Unless for that° he comes to be your liege,   *because*

390   You cannot guess wherefore the Welshman⁴ comes.
    Thou wilt revolt and fly to him, I fear.

STANLEY   No, mighty liege; therefore mistrust me not.

KING RICHARD   Where is thy power, then, to beat him back?
    Where are thy tenants and thy followers?

395   Are they not now upon the western shore,
    Safe-conducting the rebels from their ships?

STANLEY   No, my good lord, my friends are in the North.

---

4. Richmond's grandfather, Owen Tudor, was Welsh.

KING RICHARD Cold friends to Richard. What do they in the
    North
When they should serve their sovereign in the West?
400 STANLEY They have not been commanded, mighty sovereign.
    Please it° your majesty to give me leave,   *If it please*
    I'll muster up my friends and meet your grace
    Where and what time your majesty shall please.
KING RICHARD Ay, ay, thou wouldst be gone to join with
    Richmond.
    I will not trust you, sir.
405 STANLEY   Most mighty sovereign,
    You have no cause to hold my friendship doubtful.
    I never was nor never will be false.
KING RICHARD Well, go muster men. But hear you, leave
    behind
    Your son George Stanley. Look your faith be firm,
410 Or else his head's assurance is but frail.
STANLEY So deal with him as I prove true to you.   [*Exit.*]
        Enter a MESSENGER.
FIRST MESSENGER My gracious sovereign, now in
    Devonshire,
    As I by friends am well advisèd,°   *well informed*
    Sir Edward Courtney and the haughty prelate,
415 Bishop of Exeter, his brother there,
    With many more confederates are in arms.
        Enter another MESSENGER.
SECOND MESSENGER My liege, in Kent the Guildfords are in
    arms,
    And every hour more competitors°   *associates*
    Flock to their aid, and still their power increaseth.
        Enter another MESSENGER.
420 THIRD MESSENGER My lord, the army of the Duke of
    Buckingham—
KING RICHARD Out on you, owls!⁵ Nothing but songs of
    death?
        He striketh him.
    Take that, until thou bring me better news.
THIRD MESSENGER Your grace mistakes; the news I bring is
    good.
    My news is that by sudden flood and fall of water°   *rain*
425 The Duke of Buckingham's army is dispersed and
    scattered,
    And he himself fled, no man knows whither.
KING RICHARD Oh, I cry you mercy,° I did mistake.   *I beg your pardon*
    Ratcliffe, reward him for the blow I gave him.
    Hath any well-advisèd° friend given out   *foresighted*
430 Reward for him that brings in Buckingham?
THIRD MESSENGER Such proclamation hath been made, my
    liege.
        Enter another MESSENGER.
FOURTH MESSENGER Sir Thomas Lovell and Lord Marquess
    Dorset,
    'Tis said, my liege, are up in arms.

---

5. The cry of the owl was thought to portend evil.

Yet this good comfort bring I to your grace:
435 The Breton navy is dispersed. Richmond in Dor'shire°   *Dorsetshine*
Sent out a boat to ask them on the shore
If they were his assistants,° yea or no,   *allies*
Who answered him, they came from Buckingham
Upon his party.° He, mistrusting them,   *faction*
440 Hoist sail and made away for Bretagne.°   *Brittany*
KING RICHARD   March on, march on, since we are up in
       arms,
If not to fight with foreign enemies,
Yet to beat down these rebels here at home.
       Enter CATESBY.
CATESBY   My liege, the Duke of Buckingham is taken.
445 That's the best news. That the Earl of Richmond
Is with a mighty power landed at Milford[6]
Is colder tidings, yet they must be told.
KING RICHARD   Away towards Salisbury! While we reason°   *talk*
       here,
A royal battle might be won and lost.
450 Someone take order Buckingham be brought
To Salisbury. The rest march on with me.   *Exeunt.*

4.5 (F 4.5)

       Enter [STANLEY, *Earl of*] *Derby* [*and*]
       Sir CHRISTOPHER.
STANLEY   Sir Christopher, tell Richmond this from me:
That in the sty of this most bloody boar
My son George Stanley is franked up in hold.[1]
If I revolt, off goes young George's head.
5 The fear of that withholds my present aid.
But tell me, where is princely Richmond now?
CHRISTOPHER   At Pembroke, or at Harford-west[2] in Wales.
STANLEY   What men of name° resort to him?   *rank*
CHRISTOPHER   Sir Walter Herbert, a renownèd soldier,
10 Sir Gilbert Talbot, Sir William Stanley,[3]
Oxford, redoubted° Pembroke,[4] Sir James Blunt,   *dreaded*
And Rhys ap Thomas with a valiant crew,
With many more of noble fame and worth.
And towards London they do bend their course,
15 If by the way they be not fought withal.
STANLEY   Return unto thy lord; commend me to him.
Tell him the Queen hath heartily consented
He shall espouse Elizabeth her daughter.
These letters will resolve him of my mind.[5]
20 Farewell.   *Exeunt.*

6. Milford Haven, a large, deep natural harbor on the Welsh coast, far enough from centers of population to be ideal for an invading army. The events of Richmond's successful invasion at Milford in 1485 are telescoped, in the mouths of four messengers, with those of his unsuccessful rebellion against Richard two years earlier.
4.5 Location: A private place, perhaps Derby's house.

1. Is shut up (in a sty) in custody.
2. Haverford West, town at the northern end of Milford Haven. Pembroke was the county town of Pembrokeshire, situated on Milford Haven.
3. Lord Stanley, the Earl of Derby's brother.
4. Jasper Tudor, Richmond's uncle.
5. Will make my intentions clear to him.

5.1 (F 5.1)

Enter BUCKINGHAM[*, with* RATCLIFFE *and others,*] *to execution.*

BUCKINGHAM   Will not King Richard let me speak with him?

RATCLIFFE   No, my good lord; therefore be patient.

BUCKINGHAM   Hastings, and Edward's children, Rivers, Grey,
  Holy King Henry, and thy° fair son Edward,   (Henry's)
5   Vaughan, and all that have miscarried°   died
  By underhand, corrupted, foul injustice,
  If that your moody discontented souls¹
  Do through the clouds behold this present hour,
  Even for revenge mock my destruction.
10   This is All Souls' Day,² fellows, is it not?

RATCLIFFE   It is, my lord.

BUCKINGHAM   Why, then All Souls' Day is my body's
  doomsday.
  This is the day that in King Edward's time
  I wished might fall on me³ when I was found
15   False to his children or his wife's allies.°   kinsmen
  This is the day wherein I wished to fall
  By the false faith of him I trusted most.
  This, this All Souls' Day to my fearful soul
  Is the determined respite of my wrongs.⁴
20   That high All-Seer that I dallied with
  Hath turned my feignèd prayer on my head,
  And given in earnest what I begged in jest.
  Thus doth He force the swords of wicked men
  To turn their own points on their master's bosom.
25   Now Margaret's curse is fallen upon my head.
  "When he," quoth she, "shall split thy heart with sorrow,
  Remember Margaret was a prophetess."⁵
  Come, sirs, convey me to the block of shame.
  Wrong hath but wrong, and blame the due of blame.
        [*Exeunt.*]

5.2 (F 5.2)

Enter RICHMOND [*and* LORDS] *with drums and trumpets.*

RICHMOND   Fellows in arms, and my most loving friends,
  Bruised underneath the yoke of tyranny,
  Thus far into the bowels° of the land   center
  Have we marched on without impediment;
5   And here receive we from our father¹ Stanley
  Lines of fair comfort and encouragement.
  The wretched, bloody, and usurping boar,
  That spoiled your summer fields and fruitful vines,

5.1 Location: Salisbury.
1. Because they are unable to rest in peace until their violent deaths have been avenged. *moody:* angry.
2. November 2, the day on which the Roman Catholic Church intercedes for all Christian souls and on which spirits were supposed to walk (as in the following scenes at Shrewsbury).
3. See Buckingham's prophetic speech in 2.1.31–39.
4. Is the preordained ending of my wrongdoing (but

alluding to the more usual significance of All Souls' Day, "preordained final rest from suffering"). *respite:* day to which something is postponed.
5. See 1.3.296–97.
5.2 Location: Near Tamworth in Staffordshire.
1. Stepfather (Richmond was the son of Edmund Tudor and Margaret Beaufort; Lord Stanley, Earl of Derby, was his mother's third husband). *our:* royal plural.

Swills your warm blood like wash,° and makes his trough   *pig fodder*

10   In your embowelèd° bosoms—this foul swine   *disemboweled*

Lies now even in the center of this isle,

Near to the town of Leicester, as we learn.

From Tamworth thither is but one day's march.

In God's name, cheerly° on, courageous friends,   *cheerfully*

15   To reap the harvest of perpetual peace

By this one bloody trial of sharp war.

FIRST LORD   Every man's conscience is a thousand swords

To fight against that bloody homicide.°   *murderer*

SECOND LORD   I doubt not but his friends will fly to us.

20   THIRD LORD   He hath no friends but who are friends for fear,

Which in his greatest need will shrink from him.

RICHMOND   All for our vantage.° Then, in God's name,   *advantage*
    march.

True hope is swift and flies with swallows' wings;

Kings it makes gods and meaner° creatures kings.   *Exeunt.*   *baser*

5.3 (F 5.3)

Enter KING RICHARD, NORFOLK, RATCLIFFE, CATESBY,
with others.

KING RICHARD   Here pitch our tents, even here in Bosworth
    field.

Why, how now, Catesby, why look'st thou so sad?

CATESBY   My heart is ten times lighter than my looks.

KING RICHARD   Norfolk, come hither.

5   Norfolk, we must have knocks,° ha, must we not?   *blows*

NORFOLK   We must both give and take, my gracious lord.

KING RICHARD   Up with my tent there. Here will I lie tonight.

But where tomorrow? Well, all is one for that.°   *it makes no difference*

Who hath descried° the number of the foe?   *discerned*

10   NORFOLK   Six or seven thousand is their utmost number.

KING RICHARD   Why, our battalion° trebles that account.°   *army / number*

Besides, the King's name is a tower of strength,

Which they upon the adverse party want.°   *lack*

—Up with my tent there! —Valiant gentlemen,

15   Let us survey the vantage of the field.[1]

Call for some men of sound direction.°   *military judgment*

Let's want no discipline, make no delay,

For lords, tomorrow is a busy day.   *Exeunt.*

    Enter RICHMOND *with the* LORDS *and others,*
    [*including* BLUNT].

RICHMOND   The weary sun hath made a golden set,

20   And by the bright track of his fiery car[2]

Gives signal of a goodly day tomorrow.

Where is Sir William Brandon? He shall bear my
    standard.°   *flag*

The Earl of Pembroke keeps° his regiment.   *stays with*

5.3 Location: The rest of the play takes place on Bosworth Field. This particular scene, depicting preparations on both sides of the ensuing struggle, stages simultaneously two distinct places on the battlefield. This is traditionally indicated in perfor-mance by two tents pitched on separate parts of the stage.

1. *vantage of the field:* military advantages offered by the spot chosen for battle.

2. Chariot (of the sun god Phoebus).

Good Captain Blunt, bear my goodnight to him,
25   And by the second hour in the morning
Desire the Earl to see me in my tent.
Yet one thing more, good Blunt, before thou goest:
Where is Lord Stanley quartered, dost thou know?
BLUNT   Unless I have mista'en his colors much,
30   Which well I am assured I have not done,
His regiment lies half a mile at least
South from the mighty power of the King.
RICHMOND   If without peril it be possible,
Good Captain Blunt, bear my goodnight to him,
35   And give him from me this most needful scroll.
BLUNT   Upon my life, my lord, I'll undertake it.
RICHMOND   Farewell, good Blunt.   [*Exit* BLUNT.]
Give me some ink and paper in my tent.
I'll draw the form and model° of our battle,   *plan*
40   Limit° each leader to his several charge,°   *Appoint / separate duty*
And part° in just proportion our small strength.   *divide*
Come, let us consult upon tomorrow's business.
Into our tent; the air is raw and cold.
            [*They withdraw into the tent.*]³
            Enter KING RICHARD, NORFOLK, RATCLIFFE, CATESBY,
            and others.
KING RICHARD   What is o'clock?
45   CATESBY   It is six of clock, full supper time.
KING RICHARD   I will not sup tonight. Give me some ink and
        paper.
What, is my beaver easier° than it was,   *my helmet visor looser*
And all my armor laid into my tent?
CATESBY   It is, my liege, and all things are in readiness.
50   KING RICHARD   Good Norfolk, hie° thee to thy charge;   *hasten*
Use careful watch, choose trusty sentinel.
NORFOLK   I go, my lord.
KING RICHARD   Stir with the lark tomorrow, gentle Norfolk.
NORFOLK   I warrant° you, my lord.   [*Exit.*]   *assure; guarantee*
55   KING RICHARD   Catesby.
CATESBY   My lord.
KING RICHARD   Send out a pursuivant-at-arms°   *one who attends a herald*
To Stanley's regiment. Bid him bring his power°   *forces*
Before sun-rising, lest his son George fall
60   Into the blind cave of eternal night.   [*Exit* CATESBY.]
Fill me a bowl of wine. Give me a watch.⁴
Saddle white Surrey⁵ for the field tomorrow.
Look that my staves° be sound and not too heavy.   *lance shafts*
—Ratcliffe!
65   RATCLIFFE   My lord?
KING RICHARD   Saw'st thou the melancholy Lord
        Northumberland?
RATCLIFFE   Thomas the Earl of Surrey and himself,
Much about cock-shut° time, from troop to troop   *twilight*

3. Richmond and his allies move into their open tent
onstage, where they may remain visible.
4. Probably a watch light (a slow-burning candle, to
write by); possibly a special guard (see line 74).

5. The chroniclers report that Richard was mounted
on a "great white courser," but the horse's name is
Shakespeare's.

Went through the army, cheering up the soldiers.

70 KING RICHARD   So, I am satisfied. Give me a bowl of wine.
I have not that alacrity of spirit
Nor cheer of mind that I was wont to have.
    [*Wine is brought.*]
Set it down. Is ink and paper ready?

RATCLIFFE   It is, my lord.

KING RICHARD   Bid my guard watch. Leave me.
75 Ratcliffe, about the mid of night come to my tent
And help to arm me. Leave me, I say.
                    Exit RATCLIFFE [*with others*].
                Enter [STANLEY, *Earl of*] *Derby to* RICHMOND *in
                his tent.*

STANLEY   Fortune and victory sit on thy helm.°   helmet

RICHMOND   All comfort that the dark night can afford
Be to thy person, noble father-in-law.°   stepfather
80 Tell me, how fares our loving mother?

STANLEY   I, by attorney,° bless thee from thy mother,   by proxy
Who prays continually for Richmond's good.
So much for that. The silent hours steal on,
And flaky° darkness breaks within the East.   streaked with light
85 In brief—for so the season° bids us be—   time of day
Prepare thy battle early in the morning,
And put thy fortune to the arbitrement°   determination; verdict
Of bloody strokes and mortal-staring[6] war.
I as I may—that which I would I cannot—
90 With best advantage will deceive the time[7]
And aid thee in this doubtful shock° of arms.   this uncertain clash
But on thy side I may not be too forward
Lest, being seen, thy brother,° tender° George,   stepbrother / young
Be executed in his father's sight.
95 Farewell. The leisure° and the fearful time   time available
Cuts off the ceremonious vows of love
And ample interchange of sweet discourse
Which so-long-sundered friends should dwell upon.
God give us leisure for these rites of love.
100 Once more, adieu. Be valiant and speed well.

RICHMOND   Good lords, conduct him to his regiment.
I'll strive with° troubled thoughts to take a nap,   despite
Lest leaden slumber peise° me down tomorrow   weigh
When I should mount with wings of victory.
105 Once more, good night, kind lords and gentlemen.
                    Exeunt [*all but* RICHMOND].
O Thou whose captain I account myself,
Look on my forces with a gracious eye.
Put in their hands Thy bruising irons° of wrath   swords
That they may crush down with a heavy fall
110 The usurping helmets of our adversaries.
Make us Thy ministers of chastisement
That we may praise Thee in the victory.
To Thee I do commend my watchful° soul   alert

---

6. Suggests the commonplace image of war as both evil-looking and able to cause damage with its glance (like a basilisk).

7. *as . . . time:* as best I can—for I cannot fight openly on your side—I will mislead Richard.

Ere I let fall the windows° of mine eyes.   *eyelids*
115   Sleeping and waking, oh, defend me still!
        [*He sleeps.*]
        Enter the GHOST OF *young* PRINCE EDWARD, *son* [*to*]
        Harry the Sixth, to RICHARD.[8]

GHOST OF PRINCE EDWARD (*to* RICHARD)   Let me sit heavy on
        thy soul tomorrow.
      Think how thou stabb'st me in my prime of youth
      At Tewkesbury. Despair, therefore, and die.
      (*to* RICHMOND) Be cheerful, Richmond, for the wrongèd
        souls
120   Of butchered princes fight in thy behalf.
      King Henry's issue,° Richmond, comforts thee.   [*Exit.*][9]   *offspring*
        Enter the GHOST OF HENRY THE SIXTH.

GHOST OF HENRY THE SIXTH (*to* RICHARD)   When I was
        mortal, my anointed° body   *(with sacred oil)*
      By thee was punchèd full of deadly holes.
      Think on the Tower[1] and me. Despair and die.
125   Harry the Sixth bids thee despair and die.
      (*to* RICHMOND) Virtuous and holy, be thou conqueror.
      Harry that prophesied[2] thou shouldst be king
      Doth comfort thee in thy sleep. Live and flourish.   [*Exit.*]
        Enter the GHOST OF CLARENCE.

GHOST OF CLARENCE [*to* RICHARD]   Let me sit heavy in thy
        soul tomorrow,
130   I that was washed to death with fulsome° wine,   *sickening*
      Poor Clarence, by thy guile betrayed to death.
      Tomorrow in the battle think on me,
      And fall° thy edgeless sword. Despair and die.   *drop*
      (*to* RICHMOND) Thou offspring of the house of Lancaster,
135   The wrongèd heirs of York do pray for thee.
      Good angels guard thy battle.° Live and flourish.   [*Exit.*]   *army*
        Enter the GHOSTS OF RIVERS, GREY, *and* VAUGHAN.

GHOST OF RIVERS [*to* RICHARD]   Let me sit heavy in thy soul
        tomorrow,
      Rivers that died at Pomfret. Despair and die.
GHOST OF GREY [*to* RICHARD]   Think upon Grey, and let thy
        soul despair.
140   GHOST OF VAUGHAN [*to* RICHARD]   Think upon Vaughan, and
        with guilty fear
      Let fall thy lance. Despair and die.
GHOSTS OF RIVERS, GREY, *and* VAUGHAN (*to* RICHMOND)   Awake,
        and think our wrongs in Richard's bosom
      Will conquer him. Awake, and win the day!   [*Exeunt.*]
        Enter the GHOSTS OF THE *two young* PRINCES.

GHOSTS OF THE PRINCES (*to* RICHARD)   Dream on thy cousins[3]
        smothered in the Tower.
145   Let us be lead within thy bosom, Richard,

---

8. Q and F do not specify how or where the ghosts
enter.
9. Exits not given in Q and F. The ghosts could exeunt together at the end.
1. Where Henry VI was supposedly murdered.
2. See *3 Henry VI* 4.6, in which King Henry (some-

times "Harry"), declaring the young Richmond
"England's hope," foresees Richmond's accession to
the throne and the beginning of what was to become
the Tudor dynasty.
3. Nephews ("cousins" was a term used for any
kinsmen).

And weigh thee down to ruin, shame, and death.
Thy nephews' souls bid thee despair and die.
(*to* RICHMOND) Sleep, Richmond, sleep in peace and wake
    in joy.
Good angels guard thee from the boar's annoy.
150   Live, and beget a happy race of kings.
Edward's unhappy sons do bid thee flourish.   [*Exeunt.*]
    Enter the GHOST OF HASTINGS.
GHOST OF HASTINGS [*to* RICHARD]   Bloody and guilty, guiltily
    awake,
And in a bloody battle end thy days.
Think on Lord Hastings. Despair and die.
155   (*to* RICHMOND) Quiet, untroubled soul, awake, awake.
Arm, fight, and conquer, for fair England's sake!   [*Exit.*]
    Enter the GHOST OF LADY ANNE, *his wife.*
GHOST OF LADY ANNE [*to* RICHARD]   Richard, thy wife, that
    wretched Anne thy wife,
That never slept a quiet hour with thee,
Now fills thy sleep with perturbations.
160   Tomorrow in the battle think on me,
And fall thy edgeless sword. Despair and die.
(*to* RICHMOND) Thou quiet soul, sleep thou a quiet sleep.
Dream of success and happy victory.
Thy adversary's wife doth pray for thee.   [*Exit.*]
    Enter the GHOST OF BUCKINGHAM.
165 GHOST OF BUCKINGHAM [*to* RICHARD]   The first was I that
    helped thee to the crown.
The last was I that felt thy tyranny.
Oh, in the battle think on Buckingham
And die in terror of thy guiltiness.
Dream on, dream on, of bloody deeds and death.
170   Fainting,° despair; despairing, yield thy breath.   *Losing heart*
(*to* RICHMOND) I died for hope[4] ere I could lend thee aid,
But cheer thy heart, and be thou not dismayed.
God and good angels fight on Richmond's side,
And Richard falls in height of all his pride.   [*Exit.*]
    RICHARD *starteth up out of a dream.*
175 KING RICHARD   Give me another horse! Bind up my wounds!
Have mercy, Jesu. —Soft, I did but dream.[5]
O coward conscience, how dost thou afflict me.
The lights burn blue.[6] It is now dead midnight.
Cold fearful drops stand on my trembling flesh.
180   What do I fear? Myself? There's none else by.
Richard loves Richard; that is I and I.[7]
Is there a murderer here? No. Yes, I am.
Then fly. What, from myself? Great reason why?
Lest I revenge. What, myself upon myself?
185   Alack, I love myself. Wherefore?° For any good   *Why*
That I myself have done unto myself?

---

4. I died hoping I could aid you.
5. PERFORMANCE COMMENT A production's choices
here depend in part on whether the "ghosts" that visit
Richard in his dreams are products of his diseased
mind or genuine metaphysical agents. See Digital

Edition PC 5.
6. Thought to indicate the presence of ghosts.
7. TEXTUAL COMMENT The Quarto's "I and I,"often
corrected to the Folio's "I am I," is here retained. See
Digital Edition TC 12 (Quarto edited text).

Oh, no. Alas, I rather hate myself
For hateful deeds committed by myself.
I am a villain. Yet I lie; I am not.
190 Fool, of thyself speak well. Fool, do not flatter.
My conscience hath a thousand several° tongues,   *separate*
And every tongue brings in a several tale,
And every tale condemns me for a villain.
Perjury, perjury, in the highest degree;
195 Murder, stern murder, in the direst degree.
All several sins, all used in each degree,[8]
Throng to the bar,° crying all, "Guilty, guilty!"   *(of the court)*
I shall despair.[9] There is no creature loves me,
And if I die, no soul will pity me.
200 And wherefore should they, since that I myself
Find in myself no pity to myself?
Methought the souls of all that I had murdered
Came to my tent, and every one did threat
Tomorrow's vengeance on the head of Richard.
        Enter RATCLIFFE.
205 RATCLIFFE   My lord.
KING RICHARD   Zounds! Who is there?
RATCLIFFE   Ratcliffe, my lord, 'tis I. The early village cock
Hath twice done salutation to the morn.
Your friends are up and buckle on their armor.
210 KING RICHARD   O Ratcliffe, I have dreamed a fearful dream.
What think'st thou, will our friends prove all true?
RATCLIFFE   No doubt, my lord.
KING RICHARD   O Ratcliffe, I fear, I fear.
RATCLIFFE   Nay, good my lord, be not afraid of shadows.°   *illusions; ghosts*
KING RICHARD   By the Apostle Paul, shadows tonight
215 Have struck more terror to the soul of Richard
Than can the substance of ten thousand soldiers
Armed in proof° and led by shallow Richmond.   *impenetrable armor*
'Tis not yet near day. Come, go with me.
Under our tents I'll play the eavesdropper,
220 To see if any mean to shrink from me.   *Exeunt.*
        Enter the LORDS *to* RICHMOND.
LORDS   Good morrow, Richmond.
RICHMOND   Cry mercy,° lords and watchful gentlemen,   *Beg your pardon*
That you have ta'en a tardy sluggard here.
LORDS   How have you slept, my lord?
225 RICHMOND   The sweetest sleep and fairest-boding° dreams   *most propitious*
That ever entered in a drowsy head
Have I since your departure had, my lords.
Methought their souls whose bodies Richard murdered
Came to my tent and cried on[1] victory.
230 I promise you, my soul is very jocund°   *joyful*
In the remembrance of so fair a dream.
How far into the morning is it, lords?
LORDS   Upon the stroke of four.

8. Every kind of sin, from least to most wicked.   1. And called out (a hunting term); here, urged me
9. Despair was considered the only unforgivable sin;   on to.
see 1.2.83–86.

RICHMOND   Why, then, 'tis time to arm and give direction.
    His oration to his soldiers.
235 More than I have said, loving countrymen,
  The leisure° and enforcement of the time   *time available*
  Forbids to dwell upon. Yet remember this:
  God and our good cause fight upon our side.
  The prayers of holy saints and wrongèd souls,
240 Like high-reared bulwarks, stand before our faces.
  Richard except,° those whom we fight against   *excepted*
  Had rather have us win than him they follow.
  For what is he they follow? Truly, gentlemen,
  A bloody tyrant and a homicide;
245 One raised in blood, and one in blood established;[2]
  One that made means° to come by what he hath,   *that contrived*
  And slaughtered those that were the means to help him;
  A base foul stone, made precious by the foil[3]
  Of England's chair where he is falsely set;[4]
250 One that hath ever been God's enemy.
  Then if you fight against God's enemy,
  God will, in justice, ward° you as His soldiers.   *guard*
  If you do sweat to put a tyrant down,
  You sleep in peace, the tyrant being slain.
255 If you do fight against your country's foes,
  Your country's fat° shall pay your pains the hire.   *abundance*
  If you do fight in safeguard of your wives,
  Your wives shall welcome home the conquerors.
  If you do free your children from the sword,
260 Your children's children quits° it in your age.   *repays*
  Then in the name of God and all these rights,
  Advance° your standards, draw your willing swords.   *Raise*
  For me, the ransom of my bold attempt
  Shall be this cold corpse on the earth's cold face.[5]
265 But if I thrive,° the gain of my attempt   *succeed*
  The least of you shall share his part thereof.
  Sound drums and trumpets boldly and cheerfully.
  God and Saint George!° Richmond and victory! [*Exeunt.*] *patron saint of England*
    Enter KING RICHARD, RATCLIFFE, *and others.*
KING RICHARD   What said Northumberland as touching°   *regarding*
  Richmond?
270 RATCLIFFE   That he was never trainèd up in arms.
KING RICHARD   He said the truth. And what said Surrey
  then?
RATCLIFFE   He smiled and said, "The better for our purpose."
KING RICHARD   He was in the right, and so indeed it is.
    The clock striketh.
  Tell the clock there.[6] Give me a calendar.°   *an almanac*
  Who saw the sun today?
275 RATCLIFFE   Not I, my lord.
KING RICHARD   Then he disdains to shine, for by the book° *(the almanac)*

---

2. *One raised . . . established:* One who has come to the throne by bloodshed and has held it through further bloodshed.
3. Metal leaf ("foil") was often placed under a jewel as part of its setting, in order to increase its radiance.

4. Of the throne of England, on which he is wrongly placed; with a pun on "being set like a jewel."
5. *the ransom . . . face:* the only ransom I will give them is my dead body.
6. Count the clock's strokes.

He should have braved° the East an hour ago.   *made resplendent*
A black day will it be to somebody.
Ratcliffe!

RATCLIFFE   My lord?

280   KING RICHARD   The sun will not be seen today.
The sky doth frown and lour° upon our army.   *glower*
I would these dewy tears were from° the ground.   *gone from*
Not shine today? Why, what is that to me
More than to Richmond? For the selfsame heaven

285   That frowns on me looks sadly upon him.

Enter NORFOLK.

NORFOLK   Arm, arm, my lord! The foe vaunts° in the field.   *flaunts his strength*

KING RICHARD   Come, bustle, bustle! Caparison° my horse.   *Put the trappings on*
Call up Lord Stanley; bid him bring his power.°   *forces*
I will lead forth my soldiers to the plain,

290   And thus my battle° shall be orderèd: *army*
My foreward° shall be drawn out all in length,°   *front rank / in a line*
Consisting equally of horse and foot;
Our archers shall be placèd in the midst.
John, Duke of Norfolk, Thomas, Earl of Surrey,

295   Shall have the leading of this foot and horse.
They thus directed,° we will follow   *positioned*
In the main battle, whose puissance° on either side   *power*
Shall be well wingèd° with our chiefest horse.°   *flanked / best cavalry*
This, and Saint George to boot!⁷ What think'st thou,
Norfolk?

300   NORFOLK   A good direction, warlike sovereign.
This found I on my tent this morning.

He sheweth him a paper.

"Jockey of Norfolk, be not so bold,
For Dickon thy master is bought and sold."⁸

KING RICHARD   A thing devisèd by the enemy.

305   Go, gentlemen, every man unto his charge.
Let not our babbling dreams affright our souls:
Conscience is but a word that cowards use,
Devised at first to keep the strong in awe.
Our strong arms be our conscience, swords our law.

310   March on, join° bravely. Let us to it pell-mell: *join battle*
If not to heaven, then hand in hand to hell!

His oration to his army.

What shall I say more than I have inferred?°   *put forward*
Remember whom you are to cope withal:°   *with*
A sort° of vagabonds, rascals, and runaways,   *gang*

315   A scum of Bretons and base lackey° peasants   *lowly*
Whom their o'ercloyèd° country vomits forth   *nauseously overfull*
To desperate adventures and assured destruction.
You sleeping safe, they bring to you unrest.
You having lands and blest with beauteous wives,

320   They would restrain° the one, distain° the other.   *confiscate / dishonor*
And who doth lead them but a paltry fellow,

---

7. *and . . . boot*: with the aid of our patron saint as a   8. Is betrayed. *Jockey of Norfolk*: John, Duke of Nor-
bonus.   folk. *Dickon*: Dick (that is, Richard).

Long kept in Bretagne at our mother's⁹ cost?
A milksop, one that never in his life
Felt so much cold as over shoes in snow.¹
325 Let's whip² these stragglers o'er the seas again,
Lash hence these overweening rags of France,
These famished beggars, weary of their lives,
Who, but for° dreaming on this fond° exploit,   *were it not for / foolish*
For want of means,° poor rats, had hanged themselves.   *livelihood*
330 If we be conquered, let men conquer us,
And not these bastard Bretons, whom our fathers
Have in their own land beaten, bobbed,° and thumped,   *pounded*
And in record left them the heirs of shame.³
Shall these enjoy our lands, lie with our wives,
Ravish our daughters?
        [*Drum afar off.*]
335   Hark, I hear their drum.
Fight, gentlemen of England! Fight, bold yeomen!
Draw, archers, draw your arrows to the head!
Spur your proud horses hard, and ride in blood!
Amaze the welkin° with your broken staves!   *sky*
        [*Enter a* MESSENGER.]
340 What says Lord Stanley? Will he bring his power?
MESSENGER My lord, he doth deny° to come.   *refuse*
KING RICHARD Off with his son George's head!
NORFOLK My lord, the enemy is past the marsh.
After the battle let George Stanley die.
345 KING RICHARD A thousand hearts are great within my
        bosom.
Advance our standards, set upon our foes!
Our ancient word° of courage, fair Saint George,   *battle cry*
Inspire us with the spleen° of fiery dragons!   *anger*
Upon them! Victory sits on our helms.°   *Exeunt.*   *helmets*

5.4 (F 5.4)

Alarum, excursions.° Enter CATESBY.   *military sallies*
CATESBY Rescue, my lord of Norfolk. Rescue, rescue!
The King enacts more wonders than a man,¹
Daring an opposite° to every danger.   *to oppose himself*
His horse is slain, and all on foot he fights,
5 Seeking for Richmond in the throat of death.
Rescue, fair lord, or else the day is lost!
        Enter [KING] RICHARD.
KING RICHARD A horse, a horse, my kingdom for a horse!
CATESBY Withdraw, my lord. I'll help you to a horse.
KING RICHARD Slave, I have set my life upon a cast,²
10 And I will stand the hazard of the die.
I think there be six Richmonds³ in the field;

9. Apparently from a misprint in Holinshed, which should have read "brother's" (that is, Richard's brother-in-law, Charles, Duke of Burgundy, who supported Richmond in exile). Possibly: to the detriment of England, the mother country.
1. *as . . . snow:* as one does who walks in snow that covers the tops of his shoes.
2. English vagabonds were whipped out of the parish by a local official.
3. And gave them a shameful record in history.
5.4
1. More wonders than seems possible for a man.
2. A throw of the die (one of a pair of dice) in line 10.
3. In addition to Richmond, five other men dressed and armed to resemble him (as decoys).

Five have I slain today instead of him.
A horse, a horse, my kingdom for a horse!   [*Exeunt.*]

5.5

Alarum. Enter [KING] RICHARD *and* RICHMOND. *They*
fight. RICHARD *is slain.*   [*Exit* RICHMOND.]
Then retreat[1] *being sounded, enter* RICHMOND,
[STANLEY,] *bearing the crown, with other* LORDS [*and*
Soldiers].

RICHMOND   God and your arms be praised, victorious
   friends.
The day is ours; the bloody dog is dead.

STANLEY   Courageous Richmond, well hast thou acquit°   *acquitted; conducted*
   thee.
[*He presents the crown.*] Lo, here, this long-usurpèd
   royalty[2]
5   From the dead temples of this bloody wretch
Have I plucked off to grace thy brows withal.°   *with*
Wear it, enjoy it, and make much of it.

RICHMOND   Great God of heaven, say "Amen" to all.
But tell me, is young George Stanley living?

10 STANLEY   He is, my lord, and safe in Leicester town,
Whither, if it please you, we may now withdraw us.

RICHMOND   What men of name° are slain on either side?   *rank*

STANLEY   John, Duke of Norfolk, Walter Lord Ferrers,
Sir Robert Brakenbury, and Sir William Brandon.

15 RICHMOND   Inter their bodies as become their births.°   *befits their rank*
Proclaim a pardon to the soldiers fled
That in submission will return to us,
And then, as we have ta'en the sacrament,[3]
We will unite the white rose and the red.[4]
20   Smile heaven upon this fair conjunction,°   *union*
That long have frowned upon their enmity.
What traitor hears me and says not "Amen"?
England hath long been mad and scarred herself:
The brother blindly shed the brother's blood;
25   The father rashly slaughtered his own son;
The son, compelled, been butcher to the sire.
All this divided York and Lancaster,
Divided in their dire division.[5]
Oh, now let Richmond and Elizabeth,
30   The true succeeders of each royal house,
By God's fair ordinance° conjoin together;   *decree*
And let their heirs, God, if Thy will be so,
Enrich the time to come with smooth-faced peace,
With smiling plenty, and fair prosperous days.
35   Abate° the edge of traitors, gracious Lord,   *Blunt*

5.5
1. A trumpet signal for (Richard's) men to retire.
2. Emblem of sovereignty; here, the crown.
3. Referring to the oath, taken by Richmond in the cathedral at Rheims, that he would marry Princess Elizabeth as soon as he was crowned.
4. The badges of the Yorkist (white) and Lancastrian

(red) factions. The marriage of Richmond (Lancastrian) and Princess Elizabeth (Yorkist) brought to an end the so-called Wars of the Roses, dramatized in the three *Henry VI* plays.
5. Joined by hatred, having nothing in common but mutual antagonism.

That would reduce° these bloody days again   *bring back*
And make poor England weep in streams of blood.
Let them not live to taste this land's increase°   *prosperity*
That would with treason wound this fair land's peace.
40   Now civil wounds are stopped, peace lives again.
That she may long live here, God say "Amen."   [*Exeunt.*]

Edward the Third

Did Shakespeare write *The Reign of King Edward the Third?* The jury is out, but scholars have generally come to believe that he wrote at least part of it, finding in this chronicle history traces of the issues that frequently preoccupied him in his early years as a writer of English history plays, namely, the legitimacy of competing claims to the throne, the effects of sexual passion on kingly self-mastery, and the qualities of a successful monarch. Scholars have also identified a number of lines and scenes that recall other plays and poems Shakespeare wrote in the early 1590s, including *The Rape of Lucrece* and the sonnets, and anticipate plays written later in his career, including *Henry V* and *Measure for Measure. Edward III,* written entirely in verse, was first printed in 1596, with a second edition appearing in 1599. Neither title page, however, gave any indication of authorship, stating only that "it hath bin sundrie times plaied about the Citie of London." Many scholars believe that the play was first performed by Pembroke's Men, a company that staged several of Shakespeare's early plays before he joined the Lord Chamberlain's Men in 1594. In 1656, two printers attributed *Edward III* to Shakespeare in a list of printed plays, but the list has many errors. In 1760, Shakespearean editor and scholar Edward Capell seconded the idea, but admitted that there was little external evidence to support it. He, however, provided the first modern version of the text, leaving it to readers to decide the authorship question on their own. Seldom acted, until recent years the play has not been included in collected editions of Shakespeare's works.

The tide, however, has begun to turn. *Edward III* has been given several recent stage productions, mostly notably by the Royal Shakespeare Company in 2002; it is printed in several collected editions of Shakespeare's works; and it is now included in the Digital Edition of *The Norton Shakespeare.* What caused this new willingness to entertain the possibility that the play is in part or in its entirety by Shakespeare? First, scholars have increasingly realized that a number of early modern plays were collaboratively written, including some traditionally assigned to Shakespeare such as *Pericles, The Two Noble Kinsmen,* and a number of his early history plays. Why, then, exclude *Edward III,* which, on stylistic and thematic grounds, seems to many scholars to contain at least several scenes indicating Shakespeare's authorship? While only a few critics believe the play to be entirely his, a number find it likely that he had a hand in those parts involving the Countess of Salisbury and possibly some involving Prince Edward, especially 1.2, 2.1, 2.2, 4.4, and possibly 4.5. Second, the play, which most scholars believe was written between 1590 and 1594, takes up and extends Shakespeare's early interest in dramatizing England's late medieval monarchs. Its central characters are the great Plantagenet king Edward III and his oldest son, Edward the Black Prince; its central action their heroic conquest of France. Throughout the 1590s, Shakespeare wrote about the aftermath of this king's reign as, after the Black Prince's early death, the Yorkist and Lancastrian branches of the Plantagenet family began a bitter fight over the crown, in the process losing effective control of England's French territories. In most of Shakespeare's other history plays, Edward III and his eldest son are revered as exemplars of English chivalry and military prowess. It is plausible, then, to think that Shakespeare would have been drawn to the direct dramatization of the king so often alluded to in his other histories.

Setting aside the issue of who wrote it, *Edward III* is an interesting and highly patriotic example of dramatized English history, a genre popular throughout the

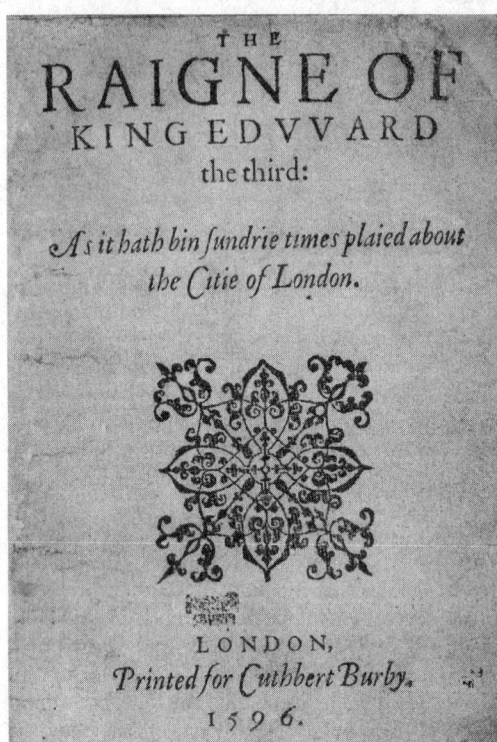

THE
RAIGNE OF
KING EDVVARD
the third:

As it hath bin sundrie times plaied about the Citie of London.

LONDON,
Printed for Cuthbert Burby.
1596.

The title page for *The Raigne of King Edward the third* (1596) gives no indication of who wrote the play.

1590s. Written in the wake of the destruction of the Spanish Armada in 1588, an event to which the play several times alludes, *Edward III* presents England as a nearly invincible military force. As the action opens, Scottish forces have invaded England's northern borders, and Edward III has been insultingly summoned to France to pay tribute to its king. By play's end, Edward has captured both David, King of Scotland, and Jean of Valois, King of France (named King John II in the play), and he has triumphed in a great naval battle (historically known as the battle of Sluys) as well as in land battles at Crécy, Poitiers, and Calais, a series of events that historically took place over a number of years but are here conveniently collapsed into one continuous arc of action.

The play focuses particular attention on the exploits of Prince Edward, who, a little like Prince Hal of the *Henry IV* plays, is shown growing into his role as military hero and prospective monarch. Before the all-important Battle of Crécy, to mark the significance of the Prince's participation in it, his father ritualistically invests his son with the accoutrements of knighthood:

> And, Ned, because this battle is the first
> That ever yet thou foughtest in pitchèd field,
> As ancient custom is of martialists,
> To dub thee with the type of chivalry,
> In solemn manner we will give thee arms.
> Come, therefore, heralds, orderly bring forth
> A strong attirement for the Prince, my son.
> (3.3.172–78)

The Prince is then ceremoniously given a coat of armor, and then a helmet, a lance, a shield, and finally the honor of leading the vanguard in the coming battle. In the midst of that battle, when the Prince is surrounded by an overwhelming number of foes, the English nobles plead with King Edward to rescue him. Edward refuses. Demonstrating a species of "tough love," he says that the Prince's courage and skill are being tested and that he must fight this battle by himself, whatever the outcome.

Critics have divided over Edward's behavior here and elsewhere. Is he being unnaturally harsh and unfeeling toward his eldest son? Later, when he demands that six of the most prosperous and prominent citizens of Calais abase themselves before him and submit to death before he will raise the siege of the town, is he showing an unchivalric lack of generosity? Or in both cases is he demonstrating wisdom, foresight, and kingly strength? In English national mythology, Edward III came to stand for the good king, a powerful military leader and governor, as well as the father of seven sons. In this play, his representation seems designed in part to publically demonstrate his virtues. Though Edward allows his son to take enormous risks, the Prince twice miraculously returns to his father in triumph. At Crécy he enters *"bearing in his hand his shivered lance; and the [dead]* KING OF BOHEMIA *borne before, wrapped in the colors"* (stage direction after 3.5.60). At Poitiers, after defeating a vast host of Frenchmen, the Prince enters with King John as his prisoner. In both cases, Edward's faith in his son pays enormous dividends, both in terms of the Black Prince's reputation and in terms of the success of England's French campaign and Edward's own reputation for invincibility and wisdom. Likewise, at the siege of Calais, Edward III's stern ultimatum both produces results (the town surrenders and renders up the six required prosperous citizens) and also gives Edward the opportunity publicly to show mercy to those whom he has brought to heel. At the Queen's request, Edward releases all six citizens unharmed.

The play's representation of a young man's induction into the ways of chivalry recalls *1 Henry VI* and the exploits of the English hero, Talbot, and his son John. Although in that play these mighty English warriors are slain by the French, this occurs only after they have made a remarkable account of themselves against great odds. Moreover, King Edward's successful management of his public persona looks ahead to Shakespeare's second tetralogy and the riotous Prince Hal's public conversion into a hugely successful monarch, one whose miraculous victory over the French at Agincourt self-consciously recalls the French exploits of Edward III and the Black Prince. Not mentioned in *Edward III,* but probably known to many in the audience, was the fact that Edward III established the Order of the Garter, a chivalric institution that honored England's most distinguished warrior nobles. In the play, King Edward,

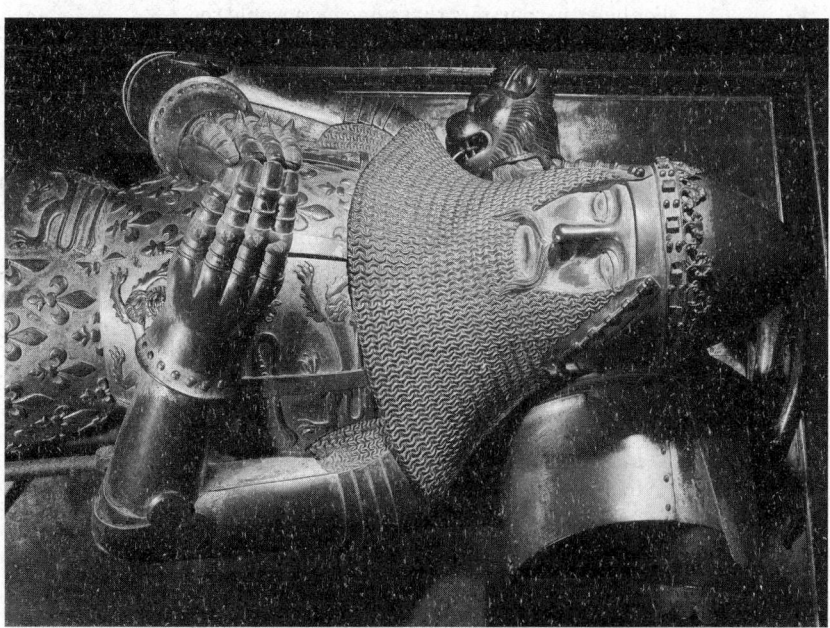

This funeral monument to Edward the Black Prince, emphasizing his military power, was erected in Canterbury Cathedral during the reign of Richard II (1377–99).

his son, and his chief officers all come to embody Garter values of honor, courage, and military prowess.

The stage deeds of Edward and his son must have been memorable. They were explicitly recalled by Thomas Heywood in *An Apology for Actors* (1612), when he exclaimed:

> What English Prince should hee behold the true portrature of that famous King *Edward* the third, foraging France, taking so great a King captive in his owne country, quartering the English Lyons with the French Flower-delyce, . . . would not bee suddenly Inflam'd with so royall a spectacle, being made apt and fit for the like atchievement. So of *Henry* the fift.

The play clearly could make an impression on spectators, and its consistent emphasis on the overconfidence and pride of the French allowed for easy identification with the courageous and ultimately victorious English forces, just as in *Henry V*.

Edward III's opening scenes, however, deal with other issues, and those scenes are the ones most often attributed to Shakespeare. Edward III does not start the play as a paragon of virtue, even though he is a mighty warrior. Moving north to repel the Scots, who have besieged the castle where the Countess of Salisbury is ensconced, Edward falls swiftly and irrevocably in love with her, despite the fact that both he and she have spouses and children. On first seeing her, the King immediately begins to speak in the mannered imagery of contemporary love poetry. Of her "conspiring eye," he says that it

> shoots infected poison in my heart,
> Beyond repulse of wit or cure of art.
> Now in the sun alone it doth not lie
> With light to take light from a mortal eye:
> For here two daystars that mine eyes would see
> More than the sun steals mine own light from me.
> (1.2.129–34)

Like the Italian love poet Petrarch, the King is fixated by his beloved's eyes, here imagined to have the power both to infect him with love poison and to strike him blind. Casting himself as a helpless servant powerless before her eyebeams, the King sees the Countess as a force more potent than the sun. And yet, the scenes between them suggest a more complex relationship, that of the hunter and his prey. Edward relentlessly pursues the Countess, and she parries his advances with all her skill. In several remarkable exchanges in which Edward pursues and the Countess resists, the playwright dramatizes a powerful struggle between two equally matched antagonists. In the end, the Countess prevails, after threatening to kill herself should Edward insist on making her violate her marriage vows. As if waking from a dream, he says:

> I never mean to part my lips again
> In any words that tends to such a suit.
> Arise, true English lady, whom our isle
> May better boast of than ever Roman might
> Of her whose ransacked treasury hath tasked
> The vain endeavor of so many pens.
> Arise, and be my fault thy honor's fame,
> Which after-ages shall enrich thee with.
> I am awakèd from this idle dream.
> (2.2.190–98)

A homegrown Lucrece, the Countess is Edward's ideal of an English lady, her chastity the guarantor of the purity of English bloodlines and, finally, the spur to Edward's own sense of honor. Prior to this moment, however, the play has vividly depicted the psychological torment of a man caught in the throes of a passion he can't control, a passion that draws him from affairs of state and very nearly makes him willing to murder his own wife and the Countess's husband. It is only after Edward overcomes this passion, with the Countess's help, that he is able to lead his army to France. Self-conquest seems the prerequisite for military conquest.

This representation of the education of a king and his eventual mastery of passion recalls a number of comic histories written in the late 1580s and early 1590s such as Robert Greene's *Friar Bacon and Friar Bungay* and *The Scottish History of James IV* and the anonymous *Fair Em*. In each, a king or a prince experiences an ill-considered infatuation that must be overcome before he and his realm can prosper. In each case, the monarch's sexual desire gets redirected toward a proper dynastic mate. In *Friar Bacon and Friar Bungay*, for example, King Henry III's son, Prince Edward, is supposed to marry Eleanor of Castile, an appropriately noble wife. However, while hunting in the English countryside, Edward falls suddenly in love with Margaret, the Fair Maid of Fressingfield. She, in turn, falls in love with Lacy, the Earl of Lincoln and Edward's friend. Only in the middle of the play does Edward undergo a sudden transformation as he listens to Margaret and Lacy both plead for death so that the other can be spared. Reproving himself for succumbing to "fancy's passion," Edward returns his affections to Eleanor of Castile. In the richly fecund atmosphere of early-1590s theater culture, such striking theatrical scenarios circulated from one playwright to another, one theatrical company to another. Whoever wrote the first two acts of *Edward III* undoubtedly had a working knowledge of the other 1590s plays in which a king or prince dramatically gives over an inappropriate sexual dalliance and turns to a proper dynastic mate.

Interestingly, the first half of the play contains its only memorably comic character, the hapless Lodowick, secretary to King Edward, who is commanded by the King to pen a letter to the Countess expressing Edward's passion. Lodowick is not much of a love poet and seems completely flummoxed by the task. After he ekes out a few lines, the King critiques them roundly, especially for commending the Countess's chastity—for, as he says, "I had rather have her chased than chaste" (2.1.153)—and for likening her to the moon when Edward would have her likened to the sun. The scene is both a sly comment on the frustrations of writing poetry at somebody else's command and also a lovely example of the ironic tonal juxtapositions so often found in early modern drama, especially drama by Shakespeare. The King is wrapped up in his own passion, forgetful of all the world, and both the grandeur and the dangerous self-absorption of his passion are highlighted through the contrast provided by the commonsensical, nonlyrical voice of his secretary just trying to do a job. Edward is in raptures over his beloved; Lodowick needs the facts: "To whom, my lord, shall I direct my style?" (2.1.80); "Write I to a woman?" (2.1.95); "Of what condition or estate she is, / 'Twere requisite that I should know, my lord" (2.1.99–100). Eventually, in frustration, the King grabs Lodowick's pen and paper, and vows to write the letter himself. Whoever wrote this scene, and it may well have been Shakespeare, was sending up the conventions of the sugary love poetry so popular in the sonnets and love lyrics of the 1580s and 1590s.

As the Countess of Salisbury scenes predict, throughout *Edward III* English women are given unusually powerful roles. The Countess may be the English Lucrece, but the play's most striking embodiment of female power is Queen Philippe, Edward's wife, who, though pregnant, actively takes part in the suppression of the Scots while her husband is in France. As one lord describes her, she, "big with child, was every day in arms" (4.2.45). At the end of the play, she appears in France, still pregnant, for the moment when the Scottish and French kings both surrender to Edward. In *Edward III*, women can be warriors without causing scandal. While the central battles in France make war seem an affair between men, the edges of the text suggest that this is not so, that women, too, can be warriors, and important ones.

Women's key role in dynastic continuity is equally acknowledged. Edward's claim to France rests on his mother's status as the only direct heir of the French monarch, King Philip. As the Count of Artois says, she

> Was all the daughters that this Philip had,
> Whom afterward your father took to wife.
> And from the fragrant garden of her womb
> Your gracious self, the flower of Europe's hope,
> Derivèd is inheritor to France.
>
> (1.1.12–16)

The womb as a fragrant garden is a striking image, suggesting the beauty of his mother's fecundity, which in this instance has brought forth "the flower of Europe's hope" and secured that son a kingdom. Edward's wife, in turn, has brought forth heirs, in this play exemplified by the Black Prince, upon whose face his mother's image is vividly stamped. Looking at his young son while adulterously pursuing the Countess of Salisbury, Edward exclaims:

> Oh, how his mother's face,
> Modeled in his, corrects my strayed desire,
> And rates my heart, and chides my thievish eye,
> Who, being rich enough in seeing her,
> Yet seek elsewhere.
>
> (2.2.75–79)

Rather than passive matter molded by the active father's impress, the mother in this instance has shaped the features of her son. Bearing his father's name, he bears his mother's face. It is women like the Countess whose sexual fidelity assures the legitimacy of the husband's children, and women like Edward's mother and wife who make dynastic lineage possible. The pregnant Philippe's appearance onstage at the end of the play brings together in one body the powerful martial and procreative roles that women in this play exemplify.

Prior to the enmity depicted between them in *Edward III*, King David of Scotland and Edward III of England had signed the Treaty of Berwick (1357), an event represented here. That treaty mandated the release of David from English custody in exchange for a yearly ransom payment to the English, an obligation that was not met.

If *Edward III* is primarily concerned with establishing English claims to French territory, its treatment of the Scots may be one factor in its seeming disappearance from print and stage at the end of the sixteenth century. The Scots are depicted as craven opportunists who besiege Roxburgh Castle, the Countess of Salisbury's home, and invade the northern shires of England once Edward's attention turns toward France. The Countess fears their "rough insulting barbarism" and the "vile uncivil skipping jigs" in which they will "bray forth" their imagined conquest of her castle (1.2.9, 12, 13). Despite their boasting, however, the Scots run away when Edward unexpectedly appears to lift the siege of the castle. Later, these same Scots are defeated by English forces led by Queen Philippe, and the dramatist invents an unhistorical scene in which David, their king, is brought to France to be part of Edward's spectacle of conquest. It might not be surprising if, under a Scottish king like James I, who ascended the English throne in 1603, canny theater companies who wished to avoid his displeasure might have ceased to make *Edward III* an active part of their repertory. Whatever the cause, the play fell from sight for most of the four hundred years following its first appearance in the 1590s. Now, however, it is available for all to judge what hand Shakespeare may have had—if any—in its composition, but also simply as another interesting example of how early modern playwrights told the story of their nation's past.

JEAN E. HOWARD

SELECTED BIBLIOGRAPHY

Cahill, Patricia. "Biopower in the English Pale: Generation and Genocide in *King Edward III*." *Unto the Breach: Martial Formations, Historical Trauma, and the Early Modern Stage*. London: Oxford UP, 2008. Argues that the play is indirectly concerned with the conquest of Ireland and shows how military action and the control of sexual reproduction together guarantee English ascendancy and the purity of English identity.

Caldwell, Ellen. "War in Shakespeare's *Edward III*." *Shakespeare and War*. Ed. Ros King and Paul J. C. M. Franssen. New York: Palgrave Macmillan, 2008. 30–42. Argues that the play links Edward's aggressive sexual assault on the Countess of Salisbury to his bloody invasion of France, where he employs weapons and tactics that reflect the destructiveness of post-chivalric warfare.

Champion, Larry S. "'Answere to This Perillous Time': Ideological Ambivalence in *The Reigne of King Edward III* and the English Chronicle Plays." *English Studies* 69 (1988): 117–29. Views *Edward III* as a play marked by ideological ambivalence. It can be read as praise of the monarch and also as a critique of his indifference to the suffering of ordinary subjects and his playing fast and loose with his word.

Melchiori, Giorgio. *Shakespeare's Garter Plays: "Edward III" to "Merry Wives of Windsor."* Newark: U of Delaware P, 1994. Argues that because the historical Edward III founded the Order of the Garter and because *Edward III* deals with the theme of honor and the education of princes, it should be grouped with five other Shakespeare plays preoccupied with the Order and its values.

Melchiori, Giorgio, ed. *King Edward III*. Cambridge: Cambridge UP, 1998. The introduction to this edition discusses the play's date of composition, the authorship question, and matters of style, theme, and dramatic structure.

Metz, G. Harold, ed. *Sources of Four Plays Ascribed to Shakespeare: "The Reign of King Edward III," "Sir Thomas More," "The History of Cardenio," "The Two Noble Kinsmen."* Columbia: U of Missouri P, 1989. Summarizes scholarship on the play and provides primary source material from Jean Froissart, Raphael Holinshed, and William Painter.

Proudfoot, Richard. "*The Reign of Edward III* (1596) and Shakespeare." *Proceedings of the British Academy* 71 (1985): 159–85. Discusses many aspects of the play, including arguing that it has a three-part structure and was first performed by Pembroke's Men.

Rackin, Phyllis. "Women's Roles in the Elizabethan History Plays." *The Cambridge Companion to Shakespeare's History Plays*. Ed. Michael Hattaway. Cambridge: Cambridge UP, 2002. 71–85. Questioning Shakespeare's authorship of *Edward III*,

Rackin argues that, unlike most of Shakespeare's history plays, it shows women who are both virtuous and powerful in the persons of the Countess of Salisbury and Queen Philippe.

Sams, Eric, ed. *Shakespeare's "Edward III."* New Haven, CT: Yale UP, 1996. Argues that Shakespeare was the author of *Edward III* because of parallels to other Shakespeare plays and poems and on the basis of diction, versification, and imagery.

Thompson, Leslie. "The Theatrical Rhetoric of *Edward III.*" *Medieval and Renaissance Drama in England* 15 (2003): 43–56. Argues that as a theater piece *Edward III* makes effective use of performance elements such as sound, props, and significant actions such as kneeling to guide and involve the audience.

TEXTUAL INTRODUCTION

Edward III was first published in a 1596 quarto, *The Raigne of King Edward the third* (Q1), printed by Thomas Scarlet for Cuthbert Burby, who had entered the play into the Stationers' Register on December 1, 1595. A second quarto appeared in 1599 (Q2), printed by Simon Stafford. The rights to the text were transferred multiple times between a number of stationers from 1609 to 1639, but no further printings survive.

This edition is based on Q1, the only text with evident independent authority. However, Q2 was set from a carefully proofread and emended copy of Q1 and deserves an editor's attention. Many of the small changes made for this second printing have been taken into account here, even though there is no evidence that they derive from authorial copy or have any independent authority. They are probably the best guesses of a sixteenth-century editor.

On the whole, the 1596 text is relatively well produced and does not pose too many challenges to the modern editor. However, it omits a substantial number of speech prefixes, likely because these had not been inserted consistently into the manuscript underlying the text. (Some dramatists and many scribes wrote entire scenes marking only breaks between speeches, but not adding speech prefixes until later in the process; sometimes, not all speech prefixes were supplied.) Q2 adds most of the missing prefixes, and this edition adopts most of these emendations.

Modernizing a play such as *Edward III* means confronting significant differences between early modern and contemporary English habits of spelling names and words from foreign languages, here largely French. This edition uses French place-names instead of English approximations; thus the original text's "Bullen" becomes "Boulogne"; "Calice" becomes "Calais"; "Cressey" becomes "Crécy"; and so forth. It also opts for "Bretagne" instead of the modern English "Brittany," in an effort to approximate the metrical value of the original text's "Brittayne"—a disyllabic word that could be voiced as three syllables. Other French expressions are also rendered as in the original language, not in the anglicized versions of Q1 or Q2 (thus Q1's "fluerdeluce," which Q2 changes to "Flower de Luce," is "fleur-de-lis" [3.2.43] in this edition).

The question of Shakespeare's authorship of the play remains in dispute. Neither Quarto named an author, and the play was not included in any of the seventeenth-century folios of Shakespeare's works. Since the eighteenth century, however, the idea that at least part of *Edward III* was written by Shakespeare has gathered increasing support. In particular, there is strong textual, linguistic, and stylistic evidence that scenes 1.2, 2.1, 2.2, 4.4, and possibly 4.5 are Shakespeare's, although the rest of the play may have been written by one or more collaborators (as is the case with other early Shakespeare plays); it may also have been written by him at an earlier date, while the four or five scenes that have been identified as "Shakespearean" may represent his later revision or rewriting. Of all the "apocryphal" plays proposed as wholly or partly Shakespearean, *Edward III* is generally considered the strongest and most likely candidate, but in the absence of positive evidence, this has to remain a matter of interpretation.

HOLGER SCHOTT SYME

PERFORMANCE NOTE

Edward III has so limited a stage history that meaningful traditions are still developing. With little recourse to precedent, most directors forgo conceits, instead focusing their energy on smoothing the play's abrupt transitions, managing its extensive use of rhetoric and exposition, and deepening otherwise wooden characterizations. They must also sustain interest in repetitive battle sequences without the benefit of a significant subplot or comic interlude. The play's greatest challenge, though, lies in resolving the incongruity between the two acts focused on Edward's pursuit of the Countess of Salisbury and the three acts dedicated to young Edward's victories in France. Productions often attempt to unify the disparate halves by asserting a relationship between young Edward's military trials in France and his father's (self-imposed) moral trials in England. Such productions thus present parallel stage pictures and moments of reflection, demonstrating that the two halves combine the military and moral education necessary for England's king.

Productions can unify the action further by having King John's effort to convince Charles to break his promise to Salisbury recall Edward's like effort with Warwick (the Countess's father), and by revealing how Villiers's and then Charles's offers to give over their lives and titles before their honor recall the Countess's promise to stab herself before yielding her body to Edward. Casting, too, can help establish coherence, if, for example, the actors playing the Countess and Warwick reappear as Queen Philippe and Salisbury. Whatever approach is taken to the episodic composition of the plot, each production must decide whether Edward is tempted by real passion or merely a desire to possess, and whether he refuses to rescue his son out of extreme faith in him or flippancy, the decisions inevitably affecting the audience's ability to engage with him. Meanwhile, the Countess can be a true innocent or a capable deceiver; young Edward can seem bloodthirsty and reckless or divinely inspired; the French can be chauvinist stereotypes or tragic victims. Other considerations include whether to show or merely describe the battles and how to stage the spectacles of chivalry, particularly the one in which armor designating Edward the "black prince" is presented to him.

Venus and Adonis

When Shakespeare wrote the narrative poem *Venus and Adonis,* he was already an up-and-coming playwright; but he called his poem "the first heir of my invention" because, in 1593, it was his earliest work to see print. While plays were considered the property of the theater company and found their way to the printing house errati-cally if at all, an author could publish nondramatic works like *Venus and Adonis* and *The Rape of Lucrece* without impediment. It was customary to dedicate such pub-lished poems to aristocrats who might provide financial support or other forms of patronage. Shakespeare dedicated *Venus and Adonis* to Henry Wriothesley, Earl of Southampton, a handsome nineteen-year-old aristocrat with sophisticated literary tastes, who was soon to come into a substantial fortune. But despite the convention-ally flattering language of the dedication, Shakespeare intended to appeal to a larger audience than merely the patron to whom the poem was nominally addressed. Indeed, *Venus and Adonis* was exceedingly popular in Shakespeare's lifetime, appar-ently the most popular poem of the period. It went through at least nine editions during his lifetime—sixteen before 1640—and Shakespeare's contemporaries quote passages from it more often than they quote from any other Shakespearean play or poem.

Part of the attraction of the poem for Shakespeare's contemporaries was its appar-ently effortless deployment of an elaborate poetic form. The poem's *ababcc* stanza, a quatrain followed by a couplet, was popular among many Elizabethan poets—George Gascoigne, Thomas Lodge, Edmund Spenser, and Philip Sidney, among others—but Shakespeare's virtuosity was so widely recognized that it has henceforth been known in English not by its Italian name, *sesta rima,* but as the "Venus and Adonis stanza." A sort of abbreviated sonnet, this stanza, in Shakespeare's hands, tends often to proffer a snatch of narrative in the quatrain, followed by a summarizing or reflective couplet, thus alternating between advancing the plot and commenting, pithily and wittily, upon the action.

Yet the key to the extraordinary success of *Venus and Adonis* was probably not merely its formal beauty but its witty, profound, and, by the standards of its time, explicit treatment of a sexual encounter. *Venus and Adonis* is an "erotic epyllion," a narrative poem of a type that had become popular in the 1580s and grew even more so in the 1590s, partly because of the success of Shakespeare's poem and of Christo-pher Marlowe's roughly contemporaneous *Hero and Leander.* Like Marlowe and most of the other writers of epyllia, Shakespeare found his story in Ovid's *Metamorphoses,* a poem in fifteen books that retells, in beautiful Latin, more than two hundred pagan myths of transformation. Since Elizabethan schoolboys were required to memorize long passages from the *Metamorphoses,* many of Shakespeare's readers knew Ovid in the original; others read him in a popular 1567 English translation by Arthur Golding. Shakespeare would have been aware that the cult of Adonis was widespread in antiq-uity, a cult that involved rites of fertility and seasonal renewal and was associated with the adoration of a mother goddess variously identified as Venus, Aphrodite, Astoreth, Isis, or Cybele. In the Old Testament, the Israelites are periodically chas-tised for abandoning their male divinity for the worship of this heathen goddess; her cult thus seems, at least for the Jews of antiquity, to have constituted an alluring alternative to patriarchal monotheism. For Christian interpreters, the myth of the muti-lated, transformed Adonis resembles the story of Christ closely enough to be read, on the one hand, as a pagan analogue to Christ's death and resurrection and, on the

Cupid taking aim. From George Wither, *A Collection of Emblems* (1635). The motto reads: "Be wary, whosoe're thou be, / For from Love's arrows, none are free."

other hand, as a demonstration of the superior power of the Judeo-Christian God, who, unlike Venus, can confer true immortality.

While Shakespeare acquired his plot from a classical source, he learned how to treat that plot from a medieval and Renaissance tradition of erotic poetry, deriving from the Italian poet Petrarch and developed in English by such poets as Thomas Wyatt, Philip Sidney, and Edmund Spenser. In *Venus and Adonis*, Shakespeare reconceives his mythological protagonists so that his poem might in some respects more closely approximate a Petrarchan norm. When Ovid's Venus is dazzled by Adonis, she resolves to appeal to him by feigning an interest in his favorite sport. By donning hunting gear and resolutely chasing rabbits, she successfully captures the gorgeous huntsman, her true quarry. Shakespeare's Venus declares herself in a much more forthright fashion, but his Adonis, unlike Ovid's, remains unresponsive to her charms. Thus *Venus and Adonis* reproduces a dynamic that Petrarch and his followers had made familiar by the late sixteenth century, in which a yearning lover pleads endlessly with a chilly love object.

The enduring fascination of this scenario for Renaissance poets lay in their recognition that "An oven that is stopped, or river stayed, / Burneth more hotly, swelleth with more rage" (lines 331–32). In Petrarchan poetry, little of consequence seems to happen, but the apparent lack of momentum is actually a prime stimulus to creativity. Frustration hones techniques of erotic persuasion; it energizes lament and interestingly complicates the poet-lover's state of mind. The sophisticated pleasure of intense self-awareness replaces the straightforward, even mindless pleasure of the sex act itself. In *Venus and Adonis*, Shakespeare's concentration on psychological detail produces an extraordinary slowing down and drawing out of the action. Ovid spends about eighty-five lines on Adonis, beginning with a brisk description of his birth and ending with an equally succinct account of his metamorphosis into an anemone flower. Shakespeare manages to devote almost twelve hundred lines to the last twenty-four hours of Adonis's life.

In some important respects, however, the story of Venus and Adonis encourages Shakespeare to play with the tradition he has inherited from Ovid and Petrarch. Most of the classical stories in the *Metamorphoses* involve male gods—Jupiter, Neptune,

Apollo, or Pluto—courting or raping beautiful young women or boys. In Petrarchan poetry, although the pleading lover is no rapist, he does take the rhetorical intiative: his beloved is generally passive and silent. In the case of Venus and Adonis, though, the powerful deity is female and the vulnerable beloved is male.

Shakespeare's revisions of the story exaggerate the effects of this gender switch. He attributes some conventionally "masculine" traits to his heroine and some conventionally "feminine" ones to his hero. His Venus is experienced, immensely strong, and apparently quite a bit larger than the Adonis whom she effortlessly tucks under one arm. Shakespeare's Adonis is dimpled, tender, coy, and virginal. At the same time, a female, even one as formidable as Venus, is imagined to be incapable of rape, so Venus cannot simply overpower her beloved as Apollo or Jove might do. Anatomical constraints force her to play a quite different but also conventionally masculine part: the pleading, unsatisfied role conventionally assigned to the male lover in Petrarchan poetry.

Since in Renaissance erotic poetry the positions of actively desiring, verbally fluent male and passive, unwilling female are ordinarily strictly demarcated, the sexual transpositions in the Venus and Adonis story have immediate consequences for Shakespeare's use of poetic conventions. Obviously they give those conventions a fresh twist. In Shakespeare's hands, such novelty is often comic: the aggressive, rhetorically hyperbolic Venus and the fastidious Adonis are funny, because now as then they violate conventional notions of appropriate gender-specific behavior. Some of these reversals are obvious to a modern reader, since our courtship rituals retain vestiges of the assumption that males are naturally dominant and inclined to take the sexual initiative. Other reversals are more specific to the poetic tradition in which Shakespeare wrote. In traditional love poetry, for instance, the enamored man "blazons," or elaborately describes, the features of the woman he desires, dwelling on the incomparable beauty of her eyes, hair, lips, hands, voice, gestures, and so forth. But in *Venus and Adonis,* Venus is compelled to blazon her own charms, because Adonis will not do it for her.

> "Mine eyes are gray and bright and quick in turning.
> My beauty as the spring doth yearly grow;
> My flesh is soft and plump, my marrow burning;
> . . . .
> Bid me discourse, I will enchant thine ear,
> Or like a fairy trip upon the green,
> Or like a nymph, with long disheveled hair,
> Dance on the sands, and yet no footing seen."
> (lines 140–48)

While in the conventional love situation the blazon is a man's cry of yearning for an exquisite object, here it becomes a woman's calculated, but unsuccessful, advertising campaign.

Shakespeare also dwells on the comic quality of Venus's divine attributes, such as the miraculous weightlessness of her robust body. At one point, Venus describes herself as a kind of giant balloon: "Witness this primrose bank whereon I lie: / These forceless flowers like sturdy trees support me" (lines 151–52). Her physical strength contrasts vividly with her quintessentially feminine body: when Venus "locks her lily fingers one in one" (line 228), she turns out to have a grip of steel. Shakespeare's interest in such apparent incongruities foreshadowed his much more elaborate exploration of the effects of transvestism and sexual reversal in such plays as *As You Like It, Twelfth Night, All's Well That Ends Well, Macbeth,* and *Antony and Cleopatra.* The humor of *Venus and Adonis* is two-edged, however, for it implicitly mocks not merely the aberrant protagonists but the standards from which they deviate. In what sense are particular traits or behaviors "naturally" masculine or feminine if actual males and females do not possess them?

Two horses mating. From Antonio Tempesta, *Horses of Different Lands.*

The upending of gender stereotypes in *Venus and Adonis* is only one of the strategies of reversal that structure the imagery of the poem. Again and again, its metaphors and similes insist on the similarity of what seems different, the difference in what seems the same. Hunting is and is not like sexual pursuit; killing is and is not like loving; female sexual desire is and is not like maternal nurture; the boar, savagely rooting in Adonis's groin, is and is not like Venus; Adonis is and is not like the sun god or the flower into which he eventually transforms. Many of these comparisons or implied comparisons are traditional ones; Shakespeare's virtuosity is evident not as much in the originality of his individual conceits as in their extraordinary profusion and in the surprising way in which apparently incompatible images are tellingly juxtaposed.

The handling of imagery corresponds with the poem's abrupt reversals of mood and with the unpredictable, accidental quality of the story. The frank comedy of the beginning swerves into tragedy, or at least pathos, at the close, as the immortal goddess confronts the death of her reluctant beloved. Over the course of the poem, our estimation of both characters undergoes dizzying shifts. Venus—goddess, whore, cradle robber, and queen—is funny, scary, eloquent, and pitiable by turns. Adonis's sexual diffidence at first seems as ridiculous to the reader as it does to Venus; but he suddenly seems less absurd when he replies, gravely even if rather too sanctimoniously, to Venus's importunities.

Venus's frank joy in the pleasures of sex suggests an uninhibited pagan universe, in which gods, animals, and human beings all are ruled by the same laws of generation and sensual enjoyment. Shakespeare's lavish attention to the forest setting in which the poem takes place suggests his keen appreciation of the sensuous possibilities of a purely natural world. The bodies of animals—Adonis's splendid courser, inflamed by lust; the ferocious boar, bursting through the thorniest thickets; the zigzagging hunted hare—all are accorded blazons of their own, as if they, not merely the human lovers, were full participants in the story of love and death. At such moments, the poem seems enthusiastically to endorse the original religious significance of the Venus and Adonis story, which linked human lives with the rhythms of a natural environment.

But Shakespeare's poem hardly evokes a sexual utopia. Even though the pagan setting of the poem presumably frees the characters from the sexually abstemious culture of Christianity, the heroine and hero still disagree vehemently about the value of sexual indulgence. Chastity has its attractions even apart from whatever supernatural reinforcement Christian faith might lend to it—especially, as Adonis notes, for

The boar attacking Adonis. From Henry Peacham, *Minerva Britanna* (1612).

those who are not yet fully adult. The immortal Venus thinks of experience as an endless series of pleasurable present-tense moments; the mortal Adonis wants to conceive of his life in terms of narrative development, building slowly and coherently to a future maturity. His untimely death suggests the risks of thinking of one's life in this fashion; he seems unwisely to have forgone present satisfaction in the hope of a reward that will never materialize.

On the other hand, why should Adonis, the victim of a sexual attack, enjoy caresses he has neither invited nor encouraged? Just as Shakespeare's reversal of gender stereotypes calls into question the adequacy of those stereotypes, so Adonis's recoil from Venus calls into question the naturalness of reproductive sexuality. Venus, the goddess of love, is supposed to be the apex of heterosexual desirability, both source and goal of every man's desire. Adonis, however, does not desire her even when she presses herself upon him. The congress of male and female thus seems simultaneously natural— what Adonis's palfrey, or riding horse, and a passing mare know without tutelage—and optional, a possibility that some males, at any rate, may be willing to do without.

Shakespeare writes almost entirely from Venus's perspective: the boy, not the woman, is the sex object in *Venus and Adonis*. In an age lacking our comparatively rigid conception of sexual orientation, lovely androgynous boys were assumed to be attractive to adult men and women alike. Shakespeare returned to the subject of the adolescent boy's ambiguous, half-conscious sexiness in his transvestite comedies, and to the adult man's reluctance to commit himself to exclusively heterosexual alliances in those plays as well as in *The Merchant of Venice*. *Venus and Adonis* can thus be read both as a narrative of frustrated heterosexual desire and, perhaps, as a parable of desire for a beautiful boy by a male poet—a scenario also sketched in many of Shakespeare's sonnets.

What is the meaning of sexuality? *Venus and Adonis* suggests a wide variety of possibilities: it is both a joke and a cosmic principle, a function of stern reproductive necessity and of sheer animal exuberance, a link with the animal world and an escape from it, a necessity and an option, a reminder of mortality and an intimation of immortality, a celebration of personal uniqueness and a threat to the formation of an individual identity. The shifting perspectives of the poem exploit the ambivalence with which Shakespeare's culture, as well as our own, treats sexual matters as simultaneously comical and deeply serious. The language of *Venus and Adonis* is especially good at capturing the confusing, contradictory array of sensations produced by another person's unfamiliar body close to one's own, a sensation at once grand, comic, oppressive, arousing, and repellant. The sweating, reeking, melting, and liquefying that at first seem specific to Venus's courtship of Adonis appear, by the end of the poem, to represent a principle of mortal existence and moral evaluation, as one thing merges unsteadily, unexpectedly, into another.

Biographical critics have found in *Venus and Adonis* ample grounds for speculation.

Does the sexual dynamic of this poem reflect Shakespeare's experience with the older Anne Hathaway, hauling him into some bosky nook outside Stratford? Or, alternatively, does it register an infatuation with the poem's dedicatee, Henry Wriothesley, the gorgeous youth to whom, some speculate, the early sonnets are devoted in both senses of the word? Given the scanty biographical data that have come down to us, it is impossible to know. What is clear is that *Venus and Adonis* inaugurates many of the distinctive features of Shakespeare's later work: a fascination, and capacity to sympathize, with sexually assertive women and self-contained, immature young men; an erotic energy that is both exuberant and hard to pin down; a complex moral sensibility capable of apprehending contradictory ethical imperatives at the same time; and an uncanny ability to combine comic, tragic, pathetic, and sensuous effects in a single work, even in a single poetic moment.

KATHARINE EISAMAN MAUS

SELECTED BIBLIOGRAPHY

Bate, Jonathan. "Sexual Poetry." *Shakespeare and Ovid*. Oxford: Oxford UP, 1993. 48–65. Examines Shakespeare's adaptation of Ovid's story of transgressive desire.

Belsey, Catherine. "Love as Trompe l'Oeil: Taxonomies of Desire in *Venus and Adonis*." *Shakespeare Quarterly* 46 (1995): 257–76. Argues that the poem reflects cultural changes in the understanding of love and lust, and the relationship between them.

Erne, Lukas, and Tamsin Badcoe. "Shakespeare and the Popularity of Poetry Books in Print, 1583–1622." *Review of English Studies* 65 (2014): 33–57. Presents a comprehensive statistical comparison of printed editions of Shakespeare's poetry with his contemporaries', demonstrating the remarkable and unparalleled popularity of *Venus and Adonis*.

Hughes, Ted. "Conception and Gestation of the Equation's Tragic Myth." *Shakespeare and the Goddess of Complete Being*. London: Faber and Faber, 1992. 49–92. Sees *Venus and Adonis* as Shakespeare's version of an ancient myth, filtered through Roman Catholicism, of goddess and sacrificed consort.

Hulse, Clark. *Metamorphic Verse: The Elizabethan Minor Epic*. Princeton, NJ: Princeton UP, 1981. 141–75. Looks at *Venus and Adonis* in relation to its sources and immediate predecessors.

Kahn, Coppélia. "Self as Eros in *Venus and Adonis*." *Man's Estate: Masculine Identity in Shakespeare*. Berkeley: U of California P, 1981. 21–46. Analyzes Adonis as a narcissist.

Keach, William. "Venus and Adonis." *Elizabethan Erotic Narratives: Irony and Pathos in the Ovidian Poetry of Shakespeare, Marlowe, and Their Contemporaries*. New Brunswick, NJ: Rutgers UP, 1977. 52–84. Considers the poem among others of its genre.

Kolin, Philip C. *Venus and Adonis: Critical Essays*. New York: Garland, 1997. A collection of articles.

Menon, Madhavi. "Spurning Teleology in *Venus and Adonis*." *GLQ: A Journal of Lesbian and Gay Studies* 11 (2005): 491–519. Looks at the failure of end-directed activity in sexuality and narrative.

Rambuss, Richard. "What It Feels Like for a Boy: Shakespeare's *Venus and Adonis*." *A Companion to Shakespeare's Works*, vol. 4: *Poems, Problem Comedies, Late Plays*. Ed. Richard Dutton and Jean Howard. Malden, MA: Blackwell, 2003. Examines *Venus and Adonis* as a "proto-gay" poem.

TEXTUAL INTRODUCTION

Venus and Adonis was entered in the Stationers' Register on April 18, 1593. This entry records the first reference to a printed work by William Shakespeare, but it does not mention the author by name. Instead, it enters the work to the printer, Richard Field. Since Field was from Stratford-upon-Avon, he was a likely choice for Shakespeare to turn to for his first publication. Yet Field had established a reputation for producing well-set books with literary cachet—most notably, Sir John Harington's elaborately printed translation of Ariosto's *Orlando Furioso* in 1591.

Venus and Adonis was published later in 1593 as a quarto and includes prefatory material designed to advertise it as an important literary work. In addition to a floral border at the top, the title page includes a Latin epigraph from Ovid, Shakespeare's favorite poet (*Amores*, Elegy 1.15.35–36), while the next page adds a prose dedicatory epistle, addressed to Henry Wriothesley, Earl of Southampton, and signed "William Shakespeare." *Venus* is thus the first work to be publicly signed by this author, and one of only two works extant to do so (the other is the dedicatory epistle to *The Rape of Lucrece*, also addressed to Southampton). *Venus* shows Shakespeare in the process of trying to secure patronage from a wealthy young aristocrat.

Accordingly, the handsome book of twenty-eight leaves is carefully printed throughout. Unfortunately, it survives in only a single copy, held in the Bodleian Library, Oxford. This copy is missing the final or H leaf, which likely was left blank anyway. Since no other copies of the 1593 edition exist, there are no known press variants. We also do not know whether the book was printed from Shakespeare's autograph copy or from a copy prepared by a scribe; attempts to base a judgment on spelling have proved inconclusive. In any case, Shakespeare may have read copy in Field's shop, as the book includes very few typographical errors. However, the compositor occasionally misplaced a letter, as in "Bnt" at line 393 (for 'But") or in "aud" at line 301 (for "and"). He especially had difficulty preserving the layout of Shakespeare's six-line stanza (a sixain, rhyming *ababcc*), which indented the concluding couplet: on more than half the pages, he tried to save space by varying the indentation, sometimes within the couplet itself. He also resorted to two other devices that could save space: the use of a tilde (a mark printed above a letter to indicate omission of another letter) and an ampersand (&).

Because of the careful printing of the text, editors have had to make very few interventions. As recorded in the list of variants, some subsequently printed quartos (nine editions were published in Shakespeare's lifetime) began silently correcting a few errors, while over the centuries editors have made a few changes of their own. Yet no substantial textual cruxes exist; this is unusual for a work of Shakespeare.

PATRICK CHENEY

TEXTUAL BIBLIOGRAPHY

Burrow, Colin, ed. *The Complete Sonnets and Poems.* The Oxford Shakespeare. Oxford World's Classics. Oxford: Oxford UP, 2002.

Duncan-Jones, Katherine, and H. R. Woudhuysen, eds. *Shakespeare's Poems.* The Arden Shakespeare. London: Thomson Learning, 2007.

Roe, John, ed. *The Poems: Venus and Adonis, The Rape of Lucrece, The Phoenix and the Turtle, The Passionate Pilgrim, A Lover's Complaint.* The New Cambridge Shakespeare. Updated Edition. Cambridge: Cambridge UP, 2006.

Venus and Adonis

Vilia miretur vulgus: mihi flauus Apollo
Pocula Castalia plena ministret aqua.[1]

To the Right Honorable, Henry Wriothesley,
Earl of Southampton and Baron of Titchfield[2]

Right Honorable,
I know not how I shall offend in dedicating my unpolished lines
to your lordship, nor how the world will censure° me for choos-   *judge*
ing so strong a prop to support so weak a burden. Only if your
honor seem but pleased, I account myself highly praised, and
vow to take advantage of all idle hours, till I have honored you
with some graver labor. But if the first heir[3] of my invention
prove deformed, I shall be sorry it had so noble a godfather;
and never after ear° so barren a land, for fear it yield me still°   *cultivate / always*
so bad a harvest. I leave it to your honorable survey, and your
honor to your heart's content, which I wish may always answer
your own wish and the world's hopeful expectation.

Your honor's in all duty,
William Shakespeare

Even as the sun with purple-colored face
Had ta'en his last leave of the weeping morn,[1]
Rose-cheeked Adonis hied him° to the chase: *hurried*
Hunting he loved, but love he laughed to scorn.
5   Sick-thoughted° Venus makes amain° unto him,   *Lovesick / speedily*
       And like a bold-faced suitor gins to woo him.

"Thrice fairer than myself," thus she began,
"The field's chief flower, sweet above compare,
Stain to all nymphs,° more lovely than a man,   *Eclipsing all women*
10 More white and red than doves or roses are:
       Nature that made thee with herself at strife
       Saith that the world hath ending with thy life.[2]

"Vouchsafe, thou wonder, to alight thy steed,
And rein his proud head to the saddle bow.

Dedication
1. "Let vile people admire vile things; may fair-haired
Apollo serve me goblets filled with Castalian water"
(Ovid, *Amores*, Elegy 1.15.35–36). Apollo is the god of
poetry; the Castalian spring is sacred to the Muses.
2. Prominent courtier, nineteen years old at the time
of *Venus and Adonis*'s publication. Shakespeare also
dedicated *The Rape of Lucrece* to him.

3. *Venus and Adonis* was Shakespeare's first published work.
Poem
1. Aurora, goddess of the dawn, weeps tears of dew
when forsaken each morning by her lover, the sun.
2. *Nature . . . life*: Nature, who strove to surpass herself in making you, says that if you die, the world will
end.

15 If thou wilt deign this favor, for thy meed°   *reward*
 A thousand honey secrets shalt thou know.
   Here come and sit, where never serpent hisses,
   And being set, I'll smother thee with kisses;

 "And yet not cloy thy lips with loathed satiety,
20 But rather famish them amid their plenty,
 Making them red and pale with fresh variety:
 Ten kisses short as one, one long as twenty.
   A summer's day will seem an hour but short,
   Being wasted° in such time-beguiling sport."   *spent*

25 With this she seizeth on his sweating palm,
 The precedent of pith and livelihood,[3]
 And trembling in her passion, calls it balm,
 Earth's sovereign° salve, to do a goddess good.   *potent*
   Being so enraged, desire doth lend her force
30   Courageously to pluck him from his horse.

 Over one arm the lusty courser's rein;
 Under her other was the tender boy,
 Who blushed and pouted in a dull disdain,
 With leaden appetite, unapt to toy:[4]
35   She red and hot, as coals of glowing fire;
   He red for shame, but frosty in desire.

 The studded bridle on a ragged bough
 Nimbly she fastens (oh, how quick is love!);
 The steed is stallèd° up, and even now   *fastened*
40 To tie the rider she begins to prove.°   *try*
   Backward she pushed him, as she would be thrust,
   And governed him in strength, though not in lust.

 So soon was she along° as he was down,   *alongside him*
 Each leaning on their elbows and their hips.
45 Now doth she stroke his cheek, now doth he frown,
 And gins to chide, but soon she stops his lips,
   And kissing speaks, with lustful language broken,°   *interrupted*
   "If thou wilt chide, thy lips shall never open."

 He burns with bashful shame; she with her tears
50 Doth quench the maiden burning of his cheeks.
 Then with her windy sighs and golden hairs
 To fan and blow them dry again she seeks.
   He saith she is immodest, blames her miss;°   *misbehavior*
   What follows more, she murders with a kiss.

55 Even as an empty eagle, sharp by fast,°   *hungry from fasting*
 Tires° with her beak on feathers, flesh, and bone,   *Tears*
 Shaking her wings, devouring all in haste,
 Till either gorge° be stuffed, or prey be gone: *stomach*
   Even so she kissed his brow, his cheek, his chin,
60   And where she ends she doth anew begin.

---

3. The evidence of strength and liveliness.   4. Uninterested in sex play.

Forced to content,° but never to obey,°　　　　　　　　　　*acquiesce / respond*
Panting he lies, and breatheth in her face.
She feedeth on the steam, as on a prey,
And calls it heavenly moisture, air of grace,
65　　　Wishing her cheeks were gardens full of flowers,
　　　So they were dewed with such distilling° showers.　　*gently dropping*

Look how a bird lies tangled in a net,
So fastened in her arms Adonis lies.
Pure shame and awed° resistance made him fret,　　　　　*overpowered*
70　Which bred more beauty in his angry eyes:
　　　Rain added to a river that is rank°　　　　　　　　*full*
　　　Perforce will force it overflow the bank.

Still she entreats, and prettily entreats,
For to a pretty ear she tunes her tale.
75　Still is he sullen, still he lours° and frets,　　　　　*frowns*
Twixt crimson shame and anger ashy pale.
　　　Being red, she loves him best, and being white,
　　　Her best is bettered with a more delight.

Look how he can, she cannot choose but love,
80　And by her fair immortal hand she swears
From his soft bosom never to remove
Till he take truce° with her contending tears,　　　　　*come to terms*
　　　Which long have rained, making her cheeks all wet:
　　　And one sweet kiss shall pay this countless debt.

85　Upon this promise did he raise his chin,
Like a dive-dapper⁵ peering through a wave,
Who, being looked on, ducks as quickly in:
So offers he to give what she did crave;
　　　But when her lips were ready for his pay,
90　He winks,° and turns his lips another way.　　　　　　*shuts his eyes*

Never did passenger° in summer's heat　　　　　　　　　*traveler*
More thirst for drink than she for this good turn.
Her help she sees, but help she cannot get;
She bathes in water, yet her fire must burn.
95　　　"Oh, pity," gan she cry, "flint-hearted boy,
　　　'Tis but a kiss I beg; why art thou coy?

"I have been wooed as I entreat thee now,
Even by the stern and direful god of war,°　　　　　　　*Mars*
Whose sinewy neck in battle ne'er did bow,
100　Who conquers where he comes in every jar;°　　　　　*conflict*
　　　Yet hath he been my captive and my slave,
　　　And begged for that which thou unasked shalt have.

"Over my altars hath he hung his lance,
His battered shield, his uncontrollèd° crest,　　　　　　*unvanquished*
105　And for my sake hath learned to sport and dance,

5. Grebe (small English waterbird).

To toy, to wanton, dally, smile, and jest,
     Scorning his churlish drum and ensign red,
     Making my arms° his field, his tent my bed.   *(a pun)*

"Thus he that overruled I over-swayed,
110 Leading him prisoner in a red-rose chain.
Strong-tempered steel his stronger strength obeyed;
Yet was he servile to my coy disdain.
     Oh, be not proud, nor brag not of thy might,
     For mast'ring her that foiled° the god of fight.   *conquered*

115 "Touch but my lips with those fair lips of thine—
Though mine be not so fair, yet are they red—
The kiss shall be thine own as well as mine.
What see'st thou in the ground? Hold up thy head.
     Look in mine eyeballs; there thy beauty lies.°   *lies reflected*
120   Then why not lips on lips, since eyes in eyes?

"Art thou ashamed to kiss? Then wink again,
And I will wink; so shall the day seem night.
Love keeps his revels where there are but twain;
Be bold to play; our sport is not in sight.°   *unobserved*
125   These blue-veined violets whereon we lean
     Never can blab, nor know not[6] what we mean.

"The tender spring° upon thy tempting lip   *growth of new beard*
Shows thee unripe; yet mayst thou well be tasted.
Make use of time, let not advantage slip;
130 Beauty within itself should not be wasted:
     Fair flowers that are not gathered in their prime
     Rot and consume themselves in little time.

"Were I hard-favored,° foul, or wrinkled old,   *ugly*
Ill-nurtured, crooked, churlish, harsh in voice,
135 O'er-worn,° despisèd, rheumatic, and cold,   *Worn out*
Thick-sighted,° barren, lean, and lacking juice,   *Partly blind*
     Then mightst thou pause, for then I were not for thee;
     But having no defects, why dost abhor me?

"Thou canst not see one wrinkle in my brow;
140 Mine eyes are gray[7] and bright and quick in turning.
My beauty as the spring doth yearly grow;°   *rejuvenate*
My flesh is soft and plump, my marrow° burning;   *vital spirits*
     My smooth moist hand, were it with thy hand felt,
     Would in thy palm dissolve, or seem to melt.

145 "Bid me discourse, I will enchant thine ear,
Or like a fairy trip upon the green,
Or like a nymph, with long disheveled hair,
Dance on the sands, and yet no footing° seen.   *footprint*
     Love is a spirit all compact° of fire,   *made up*
150   Not gross° to sink, but light, and will aspire.°   *heavy / rise*

---

6. The double negative ("nor . . . not") was accept-able in Elizabethan English.

7. Considered the best eye color by medieval and Renaissance love poets.

"Witness this primrose bank whereon I lie:
These forceless flowers like sturdy trees support me.
Two strengthless doves[8] will draw me through the sky
From morn till night, even where I list° to sport me.   *wherever I wish*
155   Is love so light, sweet boy, and may it be
        That thou should think it heavy unto thee?

"Is thine own heart to thine own face affected?°   *attracted*
Can thy right hand seize love upon thy left?°   *by clasping the left*
Then woo thyself, be of thyself rejected,
160 Steal thine own freedom,° and complain on theft.   *Capture your affections*
        Narcissus[9] so himself himself forsook,
        And died to kiss his shadow in the brook.

"Torches are made to light, jewels to wear,
Dainties to taste, fresh beauty for the use,
165 Herbs for their smell, and sappy plants to bear.
Things growing to themselves° are growth's abuse;   *only for themselves*
        Seeds spring from seeds, and beauty breedeth beauty:
        Thou wast begot; to get° it is thy duty.   *beget*

"Upon the earth's increase why shouldst thou feed,
170 Unless the earth with thy increase be fed?
By law of nature thou art bound to breed,
That thine° may live when thou thyself art dead: *(your children)*
        And so in spite of death thou dost survive,
        In that thy likeness still is left alive."

175 By this° the lovesick queen began to sweat,   *By this time*
For where they lay the shadow had forsook them,
And Titan,° tired in the midday heat,   *sun god*
With burning eye did hotly overlook them,
        Wishing Adonis had his team° to guide,   *(of sun horses)*
180   So he° were like him° and by Venus' side.   *(Titan) / (Adonis)*

And now Adonis with a lazy sprite°   *dull spirit*
And with a heavy, dark, disliking eye,
His louring brows o'erwhelming° his fair sight,   *overhanging*
Like misty vapors when they blot the sky,
185   Souring his cheeks,° cries, "Fie, no more of love!   *Frowning*
        The sun doth burn my face; I must remove."°   *leave*

"Ay me," quoth Venus, "young, and so unkind,°   *unnatural*
What bare° excuses mak'st thou to be gone?   *poor*
I'll sigh celestial breath, whose gentle wind
190 Shall cool the heat of this descending sun.
        I'll make a shadow for thee of my hairs;
        If they burn too, I'll quench them with my tears.

"The sun that shines from heaven shines but warm,°   *merely warms me*
And, lo, I lie between that sun and thee;

---

8. Traditionally, Venus's chariot was drawn by swans
or doves; see lines 1190–92.
9. In classical mythology, a young man who fell in
love with his own image reflected in the water; after
he pined to death, he was turned into a flower.

195 The heat I have from thence doth little harm;
Thine eye darts forth the fire that burneth me.
And were I not immortal, life were done,°   *destroyed*
Between this heavenly and earthly sun.

"Art thou obdurate, flinty, hard as steel?
200 Nay, more than flint, for stone at rain relenteth.°   *wears away*
Art thou a woman's son, and canst not feel
What 'tis to love, how want of love° tormenteth?   *being denied love*
Oh, had thy mother borne so hard a mind,
She had not brought forth thee, but died unkind.¹

205 "What am I, that thou shouldst contemn° me this?   *deny; scorn*
Or what great danger dwells upon my suit?
What were thy lips the worse for one poor kiss?
Speak, fair, but speak fair words, or else be mute.
Give me one kiss, I'll give it thee again,
210 And one for int'rest, if thou wilt have twain.

"Fie, lifeless picture, cold and senseless° stone,   *insensible*
Well-painted idol, image dull and dead,
Statue contenting but the eye alone,
Thing like a man, but of no woman bred:
215 Thou art no man, though of a man's complexion,°   *appearance*
For men will kiss even by their own direction."°   *inclination*

This said, impatience chokes her pleading tongue
And swelling passion doth provoke a pause;
Red cheeks and fiery eyes blaze forth° her wrong: *display; flame out*
220 Being judge in love, she cannot right her cause.²
And now she weeps, and now she fain° would speak,   *gladly*
And now her sobs do her intendments° break.   *intended words*

Sometime she shakes her head, and then his hand;
Now gazeth she on him, now on the ground;
225 Sometime her arms enfold him like a band:°   *fetter*
She would, he will not in her arms be bound.
And when from thence he struggles to be gone,
She locks her lily fingers one in one.

"Fondling,"° she saith, "since I have hemmed thee here   *Foolish one; beloved*
230 Within the circuit of this ivory pale,°   *fence*
I'll be a park, and thou shalt be my deer:
Feed where thou wilt, on mountain or in dale;
Graze on my lips, and if those hills be dry,
Stray lower, where the pleasant fountains lie.

235 "Within this limit is relief³ enough,
Sweet bottom-grass⁴ and high delightful plain,
Round rising hillocks, brakes obscure and rough,°   *dark, shaggy thickets*
To shelter thee from tempest and from rain:

---

1. Without fulfilling her nature.
2. *Being . . . cause*: Although (or because) she is love's arbiter, she cannot win her own case.
3. Pasture; variety of landscape; sexual gratification.
4. Valley grass (pubic hair); Venus's body-landscape is intentionally suggestive throughout.

Then be my deer, since I am such a park;
240 No dog shall rouse thee,° though a thousand bark."   *drive you from cover*

At this Adonis smiles as in disdain,
That in each cheek appears a pretty dimple.
Love made those hollows; if° himself were slain,   *so that if*
He might be buried in a tomb so simple,
245   Foreknowing well, if there he came to lie,
    Why, there love lived, and there he could not die.

These lovely caves, these round enchanting pits,
Opened their mouths to swallow Venus' liking;°   *to engulf her desire*
Being mad before, how doth she now for wits?[5]
250 Struck dead at first, what needs a second striking?
    Poor Queen of Love, in thine own law forlorn,°   *condemned to suffer*
    To love a cheek that smiles at thee in scorn.

Now which way shall she turn? What shall she say?
Her words are done, her woes the more increasing;
255 The time is spent, her object will away,
And from her twining arms doth urge releasing.
    "Pity," she cries, "some favor, some remorse."°   *compassion*
    Away he springs, and hasteth to his horse.

But lo, from forth a copse° that neighbors by,   *thicket*
260 A breeding jennet,° lusty, young, and proud,   *mare in heat*
Adonis' trampling courser doth espy;
And forth she rushes, snorts, and neighs aloud.
    The strong-necked steed, being tied unto a tree,
    Breaketh his rein, and to her straight goes he.

265 Imperiously he leaps, he neighs, he bounds,
And now his woven girths he breaks asunder.
The bearing[6] earth with his hard hoof he wounds,
Whose hollow womb resounds like heaven's thunder.
    The iron bit he crusheth tween his teeth,
270   Controlling what he was controllèd with.

His ears up pricked, his braided hanging mane
Upon his compassed crest° now stand on end;   *arched neck*
His nostrils drink the air, and forth again,
As from a furnace, vapors doth he send.
275   His eye, which scornfully glisters like fire,
    Shows his hot courage° and his high desire.   *lust*

Sometime he trots, as if he told° the steps,   *counted*
With gentle majesty and modest pride.
Anon he rears upright, curvets[7] and leaps,
280 As who° should say, "Lo, thus my strength is tried.°   *one who / tested*
    And this I do to captivate the eye
    Of the fair breeder that is standing by."

---

5. *how . . . wits:* how does she keep her sanity now?   7. Bounds on his hind legs with raised forelegs.
6. Supporting; suffering; generative.

What recketh he° his rider's angry stir,°   *cares he about / noise*
His flattering° "Holla" or his "Stand, I say"?   *cajoling*
285 What cares he now for curb° or pricking spur,   *bit*
For rich caparisons,° or trappings gay?   *saddle blankets*
      He sees his love, and nothing else he sees,
      For nothing else with his proud sight agrees.

Look when° a painter would surpass the life   *Just as*
290 In limning out° a well-proportioned steed,   *depicting*
His art with nature's workmanship at strife,
As if the dead the living should exceed:
      So did this horse excel a common one
      In shape, in courage, color, pace, and bone.°   *frame*

295 Round-hoofed, short-jointed, fetlocks shag and long,[8]
Broad breast, full eye, small head, and nostril wide,
High crest, short ears, straight legs, and passing° strong,   *extremely*
Thin mane, thick tail, broad buttock, tender hide:
      Look what° a horse should have, he did not lack,   *Whatever*
300   Save a proud rider on so proud a back.

Sometime he scuds° far off and there he stares;   *darts*
Anon he starts at stirring of a feather.
To bid the wind a base[9] he now prepares,
And where° he run or fly they know not whether:°   *whether / which*
305   For through his mane and tail the high wind sings,
      Fanning the hairs, who wave like feathered wings.

He looks upon his love and neighs unto her;
She answers him, as if she knew his mind.
Being proud, as females are, to see him woo her,
310 She puts on outward strangeness,° seems unkind,   *reserve*
      Spurns at° his love, and scorns the heat he feels,   *Repels; kicks*
      Beating his kind° embracements with her heels.   *amorous; natural*

Then like a melancholy malcontent
He vails° his tail that, like a falling plume,   *lowers*
315 Cool shadow to his melting buttock lent;
He stamps, and bites the poor flies in his fume.°   *anger*
      His love, perceiving how he was enraged,
      Grew kinder, and his fury was assuaged.

His testy° master goeth about° to take him,   *angry / tries*
320 When lo, the unbacked breeder,[1] full of fear,
Jealous of catching,° swiftly doth forsake him—   *Fearful of being caught*
With her the horse, and left Adonis there.
      As they were mad, unto the wood they hie them,
      Outstripping crows that strive to overfly them.

325 All swoll'n with chafing,° down Adonis sits,   *anger*
Banning° his boist'rous and unruly beast.   *Cursing*

---

8. *short-jointed . . . long:* with short pasterns (the bone just above the horse's hoof) and shaggy joints above the hooves.

9. To dare the wind to run (from a children's game, prisoner's base).

1. Mare without mount (rider or stallion).

And now the happy season once more fits°   *is suited*
That lovesick Love by pleading may be blest:
  For lovers say the heart hath treble wrong
330 When it is barred the aidance of the tongue.

An oven that is stopped, or river stayed,°   *dammed*
Burneth more hotly, swelleth with more rage:
So of concealèd sorrow may be said,
Free vent of words love's fire doth assuage.
335 But when the heart's attorney° once is mute, *pleader (the tongue)*
  The client breaks,[2] as desperate in his suit.

He sees her coming and begins to glow,
Even as a dying coal revives with wind;
And with his bonnet° hides his angry brow,   *hat*
340 Looks on the dull earth with disturbèd mind,
  Taking no notice that she is so nigh,
  For all askance he holds her in his eye.

Oh, what a sight it was wistly° to view   *intently*
How she came stealing to the wayward boy,
345 To note the fighting conflict of her hue:
How white and red each other did destroy.
  But now her cheek was pale, and by and by
  It flashed forth fire, as lightning from the sky.

Now was she just before him as he sat,
350 And like a lowly lover down she kneels;
With one fair hand she heaveth up his hat,
Her other tender hand his fair cheek feels.
  His tend'rer cheek receives her soft hand's print,
  As apt as new-fall'n snow takes any dint.°   *dent*

355 Oh, what a war of looks was then between them,
Her eyes petitioners to his eyes suing.
His eyes saw her eyes as they had not seen them;
Her eyes wooed still, his eyes disdained the wooing.
  And all this dumb play had his° acts made plain   *its*
360 With tears, which chorus-like her eyes did rain.[3]

Full gently now she takes him by the hand,
A lily prisoned in a jail of snow,
Or ivory in an alabaster band:
So white a friend engirts° so white a foe.   *encircles*
365 This beauteous combat, willful and unwilling,
  Showed° like two silver doves that sit a-billing. *Looked*

Once more the engine of her thoughts began:
"O fairest mover on this mortal round,°   *earth*
Would thou wert as I am, and I a man.
370 My heart all whole as thine, thy heart my wound,° *suffering my wound*

---

2. Breaks apart; goes bankrupt.
3. Venus's tears interpret her mute gestures as the chorus in a play explains a dumb show.

For one sweet look thy help I would assure thee,
Though nothing but my body's bane° would cure thee."   *destruction*

"Give me my hand," saith he, "why dost thou feel it?"
"Give me my heart," saith she, "and thou shalt have it.
375 Oh, give it me, lest thy hard heart do steel it,[4]
And being steeled, soft sighs can never grave° it.   *engrave*
    Then love's deep groans I never shall regard,
    Because Adonis' heart hath made mine hard."

"For shame," he cries, "let go, and let me go;
380 My day's delight is past, my horse is gone,
And 'tis your fault I am bereft him so.
I pray you, hence, and leave me here alone,
    For all my mind, my thought, my busy care,
    Is how to get my palfrey° from the mare."   *riding horse*

385 Thus she replies: "Thy palfrey, as he should,
Welcomes the warm approach of sweet desire.
Affection° is a coal that must be cooled,   *Passion*
Else, suffered,° it will set the heart on fire.   *allowed to persist*
    The sea hath bounds, but deep desire hath none.
390   Therefore, no marvel though thy horse be gone.

"How like a jade° he stood, tied to the tree,   *nag*
Servilely mastered with a leathern rein.
But when he saw his love, his youth's fair fee,°   *reward*
He held such petty bondage in disdain,
395   Throwing the base thong from his bending crest,
    Enfranchising° his mouth, his back, his breast.   *Setting free*

"Who sees his true-love in her naked bed,
Teaching the sheets a whiter hue than white,
But when his glutton eye so full hath fed,
400 His other agents° aim at like delight?   *faculties*
    Who is so faint that dares not be so bold
    To touch the fire, the weather being cold?

"Let me excuse thy courser, gentle boy,
And learn of him, I heartily beseech thee,
405 To take advantage on° presented joy.   *of*
Though I were dumb, yet his proceedings teach thee.
    Oh, learn to love; the lesson is but plain,
    And once made perfect,° never lost again."   *learned by heart*

"I know not love," quoth he, "nor will not know it,
410 Unless it be a boar, and then I chase it.
'Tis much to borrow, and I will not owe it.
My love to love is love but to disgrace it,[5]
    For I have heard it is a life in death,
    That laughs and weeps, and all but with a breath.

---

4. *steel it*: turn my heart to steel; steal my heart.
5. *My . . . it*: My only interest in love is in discrediting it.

415 "Who wears a garment shapeless and unfinished?
Who plucks the bud before one leaf put forth?
If springing° things be any jot diminished,   *immature*
They wither in their prime, prove nothing worth.
    The colt that's backed° and burdened being young   *ridden*
420   Loseth his pride, and never waxeth strong.

"You hurt my hand with wringing; let us part,
And leave this idle° theme, this bootless° chat.   *useless / pointless*
Remove your siege from my unyielding heart;
To love's alarms° it will not ope the gate.   *assaults*
425   Dismiss your vows, your feignèd tears, your flatt'ry,
    For where a heart is hard they make no batt'ry."°   *breach*

"What, canst thou talk," quoth she, "hast thou a tongue?
Oh, would thou hadst not, or I had no hearing.
Thy mermaid's voice[6] hath done me double wrong;
430 I had my load before, now pressed° with bearing: *oppressed*
    Melodious discord, heavenly tune harsh sounding,
    Ears' deep sweet music, and heart's deep sore wounding.

"Had I no eyes but ears, my ears would love
That inward beauty and invisible;
435 Or were I deaf, thy outward parts would move
Each part in me that were but sensible.°   *perceiving*
    Though neither eyes nor ears, to hear nor see,
    Yet should I be in love by touching thee.

"Say that the sense of feeling were bereft me,
440 And that I could not see, nor hear, nor touch,
And nothing but the very smell were left me,
Yet would my love to thee be still as much;
    For from the stillatory[7] of thy face excelling°   *incomparable*
    Comes breath perfumed, that breedeth love by smelling.

445 "But oh, what banquet wert thou to the taste,
Being nurse and feeder of the other four.°   *(senses)*
Would they not wish the feast might ever last,
And bid Suspicion° double-lock the door,   *Wariness*
    Lest Jealousy, that sour unwelcome guest,
450   Should by his stealing in disturb the feast?"

Once more the ruby-colored portal° opened,   *threshold (mouth)*
Which to his speech did honey passage yield,
Like a red morn that ever yet betokened
Wrack° to the seaman, tempest to the field,   *Shipwreck*
455   Sorrow to shepherds, woe unto the birds,
    Gusts and foul flaws° to herdmen and to herds.   *winds*

This ill presage advisedly she marketh,[8]
Even as the wind is hushed before it raineth,

6. Which, irresistible in song, was supposed to lure sailors onto rocks.
7. Apparatus used to distill perfume.

8. *This . . . marketh*: She notices this bad omen carefully.

Or as the wolf doth grin° before he barketh,   *show his teeth*
460 Or as the berry breaks before it staineth,
    Or like the deadly bullet of a gun,
    His meaning struck her ere his words begun.

And at his look she flatly falleth down,
For looks kill love, and love by looks reviveth.
465 A smile recures° the wounding of a frown,   *cures*
But blessed bankrupt that by loss so thriveth.⁹
    The silly° boy, believing she is dead,   *naive*
    Claps her pale cheek, till clapping makes it red.

And all amazed,° brake° off his late intent,   *perplexed / broke*
470 For sharply he did think to reprehend her,
Which cunning love did wittily prevent.
Fair fall¹ the wit that can so well defend her,
    For on the grass she lies as she were slain,
    Till his breath breatheth life in her again.

475 He wrings her nose, he strikes her on the cheeks,
He bends her fingers, holds her pulses hard,°   *takes her pulse*
He chafes her lips: a thousand ways he seeks
To mend the hurt that his unkindness marred.°   *caused to injure her*
    He kisses her, and she by her good will°   *consent*
480   Will never rise, so he will kiss her still.°   *keep kissing her*

The night of sorrow now is turned to day.
Her two blue windows° faintly she upheaveth,   *(her eyes)*
Like the fair sun when in his fresh array
He cheers the morn and all the earth relieveth.
485   And as the bright sun glorifies the sky,
    So is her face illumined with her eye,

Whose beams upon his hairless face are fixed,
As if from thence they borrowed all their shine.
Were never four such lamps together mixed,
490 Had not his clouded with his brows' repine.°   *discontent*
    But hers, which through the crystal tears gave light,
    Shone like the moon in water seen by night.

"Oh, where am I," quoth she, "in earth or heaven,
Or in the ocean drenched,° or in the fire?   *submerged*
495 What hour is this? Or° morn or weary even?°   *Either / evening*
Do I delight to die or life desire?
    But° now I lived, and life was death's annoy;°   *Just / deathly pain*
    But now I died, and death was lively° joy.   *living*

"Oh, thou didst kill me; kill me once again.
500 Thy eyes' shrewd° tutor, that hard heart of thine,   *stern*
Hath taught them scornful tricks and such disdain
That they have murdered this poor heart of mine;

---

9. TEXTUAL COMMENT "Loss" is "love" in the First Quarto. For the rationale behind the emendation to "loss," see Digital Edition TC 1.

1. Good luck befall (with wordplay on "fall down").

And these mine eyes, true leaders° to their queen,   *guides*
But for thy piteous° lips no more had seen.   *pitying*

505 "Long may they kiss each other for this cure.
Oh, never let their crimson liveries wear;°   *wear out*
And as they last, their verdure² still endure,
To drive infection from the dangerous year,
        That the stargazers, having writ on death,°   *predicted plague*
510   May say the plague is banished by thy breath.

"Pure lips, sweet seals in my soft lips imprinted,
What bargains may I make, still to be sealing?°   *kissing; making deals*
To sell myself I can be well contented,
So° thou wilt buy, and pay, and use good dealing,   *If*
515   Which purchase if thou make, for fear of slips,°   *fraud*
        Set thy seal manual° on my wax-red lips.   *identifying stamp*

"A thousand kisses buys my heart from me,
And pay them at thy leisure, one by one.
What is ten hundred touches° unto thee?   *(of the lips)*
520 Are they not quickly told,° and quickly gone?   *counted*
        Say for non-payment that the debt should double,
        Is twenty hundred kisses such a trouble?"

"Fair queen," quoth he, "if any love you owe me,
Measure my strangeness° with my unripe years.   *Explain my coldness*
525 Before I know myself, seek not to know me;
No fisher but the ungrown fry forbears.³
        The mellow plum doth fall, the green sticks fast,
        Or being early plucked, is sour to taste.

"Look, the world's comforter° with weary gait   *(the sun)*
530 His day's hot task hath ended in the West.
The owl (night's herald) shrieks: 'tis very late.
The sheep are gone to fold, birds to their nest,
        And coal-black clouds, that shadow heaven's light,
        Do summon us to part, and bid good night.

535 "Now let me say good night, and so say you;
If you will say so, you shall have a kiss."
"Good night," quoth she, and ere he says adieu
The honey° fee of parting tendered° is.   *sweet / given*
        Her arms do lend his neck a sweet embrace,
540   Incorporate° then they seem: face grows to face.   *United in one body*

Till breathless he disjoined, and backward drew
The heavenly moisture, that sweet coral mouth,
Whose precious taste her thirsty lips well knew,
Whereon they surfeit, yet complain on drouth.
545   He with her plenty pressed, she faint with dearth,
        Their lips together glued, fall to the earth.

---

2. Literally, greenness; here, freshness. The lips   3. *No . . . forbears*: Every fisherman spares the young
ward off disease as fresh parsley was believed to do.   fish.

Now quick desire hath caught the yielding prey,
And glutton-like she feeds, yet never filleth.
Her lips are conquerors, his lips obey,
550 Paying what ransom the insulter° willeth: *conqueror*
    Whose vulture° thought doth pitch the price so high   *ravenous*
    That she will draw his lips' rich treasure dry.

And having felt the sweetness of the spoil,
With blindfold fury she begins to forage.
555 Her face doth reek° and smoke; her blood doth boil;   *steam*
And careless° lust stirs up a desperate courage,   *reckless*
    Planting° oblivion, beating reason back,   *Implanting*
    Forgetting shame's pure blush and honor's wrack.°   *ruin*

Hot, faint, and weary, with her hard embracing,
560 Like a wild bird being tamed with too much handling,
Or as the fleet-foot roe that's tired with chasing,
Or like the froward° infant stilled with dandling,   *fretful*
    He now obeys, and now no more resisteth,
    While she takes all she can, not all she listeth.°   *desires*

565 What wax so frozen but dissolves with temp'ring,°   *fingering*
And yields at last to every light impression?
Things out of° hope are compassed° oft with vent'ring,   *beyond / accomplished*
Chiefly in love, whose leave exceeds commission.[4]
    Affection faints° not like a pale-faced coward,   *Passion relents*
570   But then woos best when most his choice is froward.

When he did frown, oh, had she then gave over,
Such nectar from his lips she had not sucked.
Foul° words and frowns must not repel a lover.   *Harsh*
What though the rose have prickles? Yet 'tis plucked.
575   Were beauty under twenty locks kept fast,
    Yet love breaks through, and picks them all at last.

For pity now she can no more detain him;
The poor fool° prays her that he may depart.   *(term of affection)*
She is resolved no longer to restrain him,
580 Bids him farewell, and look well to° her heart,   *take good care of*
    The which by Cupid's bow she doth protest
    He carries thence encagèd in his breast.

"Sweet boy," she says, "this night I'll waste in sorrow,
For my sick heart commands mine eyes to watch.
585 Tell me, love's master, shall we meet tomorrow?
Say, shall we, shall we, wilt thou make the match?"
    He tells her no; tomorrow he intends
    To hunt the boar with certain of his friends.

"The boar," quoth she, whereat a sudden pale,
590 Like lawn° being spread upon the blushing rose,   *fine linen*
Usurps her cheek; she trembles at his tale,

4. *whose . . . commission*: which is permitted to do extraordinary things.

And on his neck her yoking arms she throws.
      She sinketh down, still hanging by his neck;
      He on her belly falls, she on her back.

595 Now is she in the very lists[5] of love,
Her champion mounted for the hot encounter.
All is imaginary she doth prove:[6]
He will not manage her,° although he mount her,   *ride her (like a horse)*
      That worse than Tantalus is her annoy,[7]
600   To clip Elysium[8] and to lack her joy.

Even so poor birds, deceived with painted grapes,
Do surfeit by the eye and pine the maw.[9]
Even so she languisheth in her mishaps,
As° those poor birds that helpless° berries saw.   *Like / unusable*
605   The warm effects° which she in him finds missing   *outward signs*
      She seeks to kindle with continual kissing.

But all in vain, good queen, it will not be;
She hath assayed° as much as may be proved.°   *attempted / tried*
Her pleading hath deserved a greater fee:[1]
610 She's Love, she loves, and yet she is not loved.
      "Fie, fie," he says, "you crush me; let me go;
      You have no reason to withhold me so."

"Thou hadst been gone," quoth she, "sweet boy, ere this,
But that thou told'st me thou wouldst hunt the boar.
615 Oh, be advised, thou know'st not what it is,
With javelin's point a churlish swine to gore,
      Whose tushes° never sheathed he whetteth still,°   *tusks / continually*
      Like to a mortal° butcher bent° to kill.   *deadly / intending*

"On his bow-back° he hath a battle[2] set   *arched back*
620 Of bristly pikes that ever threat his foes;
His eyes like glowworms shine when he doth fret;
His snout digs sepulchers where'er he goes.
      Being moved,° he strikes whate'er is in his way,   *angered*
      And whom he strikes his crooked tushes slay.

625 "His brawny sides with hairy bristles armed
Are better proof° than thy spear's point can enter.   *armor*
His short thick neck cannot be easily harmed:
Being ireful,° on the lion he will venture.   *angry*
      The thorny brambles and embracing bushes,
630   As° fearful of him, part, through whom° he rushes.   *As if / which*

"Alas, he naught esteems that face of thine,
To which love's eyes pays tributary gazes;

---

5. Enclosed tournament arena.
6. *All . . . prove*: The hot encounter is only imaginary, she finds.
7. Torment. In classical mythology, Tantalus was
punished by eternal hunger and thirst; food and
water were always visible but receded at his approach.
8. In classical mythology, the abode of the blessed

dead. *clip*: embrace.
9. Starve the stomach. The ancient Greek artist Zeuxis
painted grapes so realistic that birds pecked at them.
1. *Her . . . fee*: A legal metaphor: Venus, acting as an
attorney, deserves a better payment.
2. Row of armed soldiers.

Nor thy soft hands, sweet lips, and crystal eyne,°   *eyes (archaic)*
Whose full perfection all the world amazes.
635   But having thee at vantage°—wondrous dread!—   *his mercy*
      Would root° these beauties as he roots the mead.°   *root up / meadow*

"Oh, let him keep° his loathsome cabin° still;   *stay in / lair*
Beauty hath naught to do with such foul fiends.
Come not within his danger by thy will;
640   They that thrive well take counsel of their friends.
      When thou didst name the boar, not to dissemble,[3]
      I feared thy fortune, and my joints did tremble.

"Didst thou not mark my face? Was it not white?
Sawest thou not signs of fear lurk in mine eye?
645   Grew I not faint, and fell I not downright?
Within my bosom, whereon thou dost lie,
      My boding heart pants, beats, and takes no rest,
      But like an earthquake shakes thee on my breast.

"For where Love reigns, disturbing Jealousy°   *Apprehension*
650   Doth call himself Affection's sentinel;
Gives false alarms, suggesteth mutiny,°   *incites rebellion*
And in a peaceful hour doth cry, 'Kill, kill!'°   *(a battle cry)*
      Distemp'ring° gentle Love in his desire,   *Quenching*
      As air and water do abate the fire.

655   "This sour informer, this bate-breeding° spy,   *conflict-breeding*
This canker° that eats up love's tender spring,°   *cankerworm / sprout*
This carry-tale,° dissentious° Jealousy,   *tale-bearer / quarrelsome*
That sometime true news, sometime false doth bring,
      Knocks at my heart and whispers in mine ear,
660   That if I love thee, I thy death should fear.

"And more than so, presenteth to mine eye
The picture of an angry chafing boar,
Under whose sharp fangs on his back doth lie
An image like thyself, all stained with gore,
665   Whose blood upon the fresh flowers being shed
      Doth make them droop with grief, and hang the head.

"What should I do, seeing thee so indeed,
That tremble at th'imagination?
The thought of it doth make my faint heart bleed,
670   And fear doth teach it divination:
      I prophesy thy death, my living sorrow,
      If thou encounter with the boar tomorrow.

"But if thou needs wilt° hunt, be ruled by me: *must*
Uncouple° at the timorous flying° hare,   *Unleash the dogs / fleeing*
675   Or at the fox, which lives by subtlety,
Or at the roe, which no encounter dare.
      Pursue these fearful° creatures o'er the downs,   *timid*
      And on thy well-breathed horse keep with thy hounds.

---

3. *not to dissemble*: to tell the truth.

"And when thou hast on foot the purblind° hare,   *dim-sighted*
680 Mark the poor wretch, to overshoot° his troubles,   *run past*
How he outruns the wind, and with what care
He cranks and crosses° with a thousand doubles.   *twists and turns*
   The many musits° through the which he goes   *hedge gaps*
   Are like a labyrinth to amaze° his foes.   *confuse*

685 "Sometime he runs among a flock of sheep
To make the cunning hounds mistake their smell;
And sometime where earth-delving conies° keep,   *rabbits*
To stop the loud pursuers in their yell;
   And sometime sorteth° with a herd of deer: *consorts*
690   Danger deviseth shifts;° wit waits on fear.   *tricks*

"For there his smell with others being mingled,
The hot scent-snuffing hounds are driven to doubt,
Ceasing their clamorous cry till they have singled
With much ado the cold fault° cleanly out.   *lost scent*
695   Then do they spend their mouths;° Echo replies, *give tongue*
   As if another chase were in the skies.

"By this poor Wat,° far off upon a hill,   *(name for a hare)*
Stands on his hinder legs with list'ning ear,
To hearken if his foes pursue him still.
700 Anon their loud alarums° he doth hear,   *calls to battle*
   And now his grief may be comparèd well
   To one sore sick that hears the passing bell.[4]

"Then shalt thou see the dew-bedabbled wretch
Turn, and return, indenting° with the way.   *zigzagging*
705 Each envious° briar his weary legs do scratch;   *malicious*
Each shadow makes him stop, each murmur stay,
   For misery is trodden on by many,
   And being low, never relieved by any.

"Lie quietly, and hear a little more;
710 Nay, do not struggle, for thou shalt not rise.
To make thee hate the hunting of the boar,
Unlike myself thou hear'st me moralize,[5]
   Applying° this to that, and so to so,   *Showing the pertinence of*
   For love can comment upon every woe.

715 "Where did I leave?"° "No matter where," quoth he.   *leave off*
"Leave me, and then the story aptly ends.
The night is spent." "Why, what of that?" quoth she.
"I am," quoth he, "expected of° my friends;   *by*
   And now 'tis dark, and going I shall fall."
720   "In night," quoth she, "desire sees best of all.

"But if thou fall, oh, then imagine this,
The earth, in love with thee, thy footing trips,
And all is but to rob thee of a kiss.

---

4. Bell tolled for one who has just died.
5. *Unlike . . . moralize:* Although I (the goddess of love) do not usually make moral points, I do so now.

Rich preys° make true° men thieves: so do thy lips   *spoils / honest*
725 Make modest Dian[6] cloudy and forlorn,
   Lest she should steal a kiss and die forsworn.[7]

"Now of this dark night I perceive the reason:
Cynthia for shame obscures her silver shine,
Till forging° Nature be condemned of treason,   *counterfeiting*
730 For stealing molds from heaven that were divine,
   Wherein she framed thee in high heaven's despite,°   *defiance*
   To shame the sun by day, and her by night.

"And therefore hath she bribed the Destinies
To cross the curious° workmanship of Nature,   *elaborate*
735 To mingle beauty with infirmities,
And pure perfection with impure defeature,°   *disfigurement*
   Making it subject to the tyranny
   Of mad mischances, and much misery.

"As burning fevers, agues pale and faint,
740 Life-poisoning pestilence, and frenzies wood,°   *insane fits*
The marrow-eating sickness,[8] whose attaint°   *infection*
Disorder breeds by heating of the blood,
   Surfeits, impostumes,° grief, and damned despair   *abscesses*
   Swear Nature's death for framing° thee so fair.   *making*

745 "And not the least of all these maladies
But in one minute's fight brings beauty under.
Both favor, savor,° hue, and qualities,   *beauty; smell*
Whereat th'impartial gazer late did wonder,
   Are on the sudden wasted,° thawed, and done,   *wasted away*
750   As mountain snow melts with the midday sun.

"Therefore, despite of fruitless° chastity,   *defying barren*
Love-lacking vestals° and self-loving nuns,   *virgins*
That on the earth would breed a scarcity
And barren dearth of daughters and of sons,
755   Be prodigal: the lamp that burns by night
   Dries up his oil to lend the world his light.

"What is thy body but a swallowing grave,
Seeming to bury that posterity
Which by the rights of time thou needs must have,
760 If thou destroy them not in dark obscurity?
   If so, the world will hold thee in disdain,
   Sith° in thy pride so fair a hope is slain.   *Since*

"So in thyself thyself art made away,°   *destroyed*
A mischief° worse than civil homebred strife,   *An evil*
765 Or theirs whose desperate hands themselves do slay,
Or butcher-sire, that reaves° his son of life.   *robs*
   Foul cank'ring rust the hidden treasure frets,°   *eats away*
   But gold that's put to use more gold begets."

---

6. Goddess of the moon, hunting, and virginity, also of Adonis.
called "Cynthia" (line 728); "cloudy" because covered 7. Die having violated her oath of chastity.
with clouds and because made sorrowful by her love 8. Syphilis, which attacks the bones.

"Nay, then," quoth Adon, "you will fall again
770 Into your idle° over-handled theme.   *unprofitable*
The kiss I gave you is bestowed in vain,
And all in vain you strive against the stream.
        For by this black-faced night, desire's foul nurse,
        Your treatise° makes me like you worse and worse.   *discussion; plea*

775 "If love have lent you twenty thousand tongues,
And every tongue more moving than your own,
Bewitching like the wanton mermaid's songs,
Yet from mine ear the tempting tune is blown.
        For know my heart stands armèd in mine ear,
780   And will not let a false sound enter there,

"Lest the deceiving harmony should run
Into the quiet closure° of my breast;   *enclosure*
And then my little heart were quite undone,
In his bedchamber to be barred of rest.
785   No, lady, no; my heart longs not to groan,
        But soundly sleeps, while now it sleeps alone.

"What have you urged that I cannot reprove?
The path is smooth that leadeth on to danger.
I hate not love, but your device° in love,   *tactics*
790 That lends embracements unto every stranger.
        You do it for increase.° Oh, strange excuse,   *procreation; reproduction*
        When reason is the bawd° to lust's abuse!   *pimp*

"Call it not love, for Love to heaven is fled,
Since sweating Lust on earth usurped his name,
795 Under whose simple° semblance he hath fed   *innocent*
Upon fresh beauty, blotting it with blame,
        Which the hot tyrant stains and soon bereaves,
        As caterpillars do the tender leaves.

"Love comforteth like sunshine after rain;
800 But Lust's effect is tempest after sun;
Love's gentle spring doth always fresh remain;
Lust's winter comes ere summer half be done.
        Love surfeits not; Lust like a glutton dies;
        Love is all truth; Lust full of forgèd lies.

805 "More I could tell, but more I dare not say:
The text is old, the orator too green.
Therefore, in sadness° now I will away.   *truly*
My face is full of shame, my heart of teen;°   *grief*
        Mine ears that to your wanton talk attended
810   Do burn themselves for having so offended."

With this he breaketh from the sweet embrace
Of those fair arms, which bound him to her breast,
And homeward through the dark laund° runs apace;   *glade*
Leaves Love upon her back, deeply distressed.
815   Look how a bright star shooteth from the sky:
        So glides he in the night from Venus' eye,

Which after him she darts, as one on shore
Gazing upon a late embarkèd friend,
Till the wild waves will have him seen no more,
820   Whose ridges with the meeting clouds contend:
        So did the merciless and pitchy night
        Fold in the object that did feed her sight.

Whereat amazed,° as one that unaware   *shocked*
Hath dropped a precious jewel in the flood,
825   Or 'stonished,° as night wand'rers often are,   *confused*
Their light blown out in some mistrustful° wood: *anxiety-producing*
        Even so, confounded in the dark she lay,
        Having lost the fair discovery of her way.[9]

And now she beats her heart, whereat it groans,
830   That all the neighbor caves, as seeming troubled,
Make verbal repetition of her moans:
Passion° on passion deeply is redoubled.   *Lamentation*
        "Ay me," she cries, and twenty times, "woe, woe,"
        And twenty echoes twenty times cry so.

835   She, marking them, begins a wailing note,
And sings extemporally a woeful ditty,
How love makes young men thrall° and old men dote, *enslaved*
How love is wise in folly, foolish witty.
        Her heavy° anthem still concludes in woe,   *sorrowful*
840   And still the choir of echoes answer so.

Her song was tedious and outwore the night,
For lovers' hours are long, though seeming short.
If pleased themselves, others, they think, delight
In suchlike circumstance, with suchlike sport:
845   Their copious stories, oftentimes begun,
        End without audience, and are never done.

For who hath she to spend the night withal,°   *with*
But idle sounds resembling parasites?° *flattering hangers-on*
Like shrill-tongued tapsters° answering every call, *tavern keepers*
850   Soothing the humor of fantastic wits.[1]
        She says "'tis so"; they answer all "'tis so,"
        And would say after her, if she said "no."

Lo, here the gentle lark, weary of rest,
From his moist cabinet° mounts up on high,   *nest*
855   And wakes the morning,° from whose silver breast *(Aurora)*
The sun ariseth in his majesty,
        Who doth the world so gloriously behold,
        That cedar tops and hills seem burnished gold.

Venus salutes him with this fair good morrow:
860   "O thou clear° god and patron of all light,   *bright*
From whom each lamp and shining star doth borrow

---

9. *the fair . . . way:* a clear view of her path; a beauti-   1. *Soothing . . . wits:* Catering to the moods of erratic
ful guide.   people.

The beauteous influence[2] that makes him bright,
    There lives a son° that sucked an earthly mother   *(Adonis)*
    May° lend thee light, as thou dost lend to other."   *Who may*

865 This said, she hasteth to a myrtle grove,
    Musing° the morning is so much o'erworn,°   *Wondering / spent*
    And yet she hears no tidings of her love.
    She hearkens for his hounds and for his horn.
        Anon° she hears them chant it lustily,°   *Soon / sing out heartily*
870   And all in haste she coasteth° to the cry.   *rushes*

And as she runs, the bushes in the way,
    Some catch her by the neck, some kiss her face,
    Some twined about her thigh to make her stay.
    She wildly breaketh from their strict° embrace,   *restricting*
875   Like a milch° doe, whose swelling dugs° do ache,   *milk / udders*
        Hasting to feed her fawn, hid in some brake.°   *thicket*

By this° she hears the hounds are at a bay,[3]   *By now*
    Whereat she starts, like one that spies an adder
    Wreathed up in fatal folds just in his way,
880 The fear whereof doth make him shake and shudder.
        Even so the timorous yelping of the hounds
        Appalls her senses and her spirit confounds.

For now she knows it is no gentle chase,
    But the blunt° boar, rough bear, or lion proud,   *rude*
885 Because the cry remaineth in one place,
    Where fearfully the dogs exclaim aloud.
        Finding their enemy to be so cursed,°   *vicious*
        They all strain court'sy[4] who shall cope° him first.   *contend with*

This dismal cry rings sadly in her ear,
890 Through which it enters to surprise° her heart,   *assault*
    Who, overcome by doubt and bloodless fear,
    With cold-pale weakness numbs each feeling part:°   *sense organ*
        Like soldiers when their captain once doth yield,
        They basely fly and dare not stay° the field.   *remain in*

895 Thus stands she in a trembling ecstasy,°   *stupor*
    Till, cheering up her senses all dismayed,
    She tells them 'tis a causeless fantasy
    And childish error that they are afraid;
        Bids them leave quaking; bids them fear no more.
900   And with that word she spied the hunted boar,

Whose frothy mouth bepainted all with red,
    Like milk and blood being mingled both together,
    A second fear through all her sinews spread,
    Which madly hurries her she knows not whither.
905   This way she runs, and now she will no further,
        But back retires, to rate° the boar for murther.°   *berate / murder*

---

2. The ethereal stream that in Renaissance astrology was supposed to flow from stars and planets.
3. Stopped by the quarry, which is making a stand.
4. Politely defer to one another.

A thousand spleens° bear her a thousand ways;   *impulses*
She treads the path that she untreads again.
Her more than haste is mated° with delays,   *counteracted*
910 Like the proceedings of a drunken brain:
      Full of respects,° yet naught at all respecting,   *considerations*
      In hand with all things, naught at all effecting.[5]

Here kenneled in a brake, she finds a hound,
And asks the weary caitiff° for his master;   *wretch*
915 And there another licking of his wound,
'Gainst venomed sores the only sovereign plaster;°   *effective remedy*
      And here she meets another sadly scowling,
      To whom she speaks, and he replies with howling.

When he hath ceased his ill-resounding noise,
920 Another flap-mouthed mourner, black and grim,
Against the welkin° volleys out his voice.   *sky*
Another and another answer him,
      Clapping their proud tails to the ground below,
      Shaking their scratched ears, bleeding as they go.

925 Look how the world's poor people are amazed
At apparitions, signs, and prodigies,°   *strange occurrences*
Whereon with fearful eyes they long have gazed,
Infusing them with° dreadful prophecies.   *Reading into them*
      So she at these sad signs draws up her breath,
930   And sighing it again, exclaims on° Death: *berates*

"Hard-favored tyrant, ugly, meager, lean,
Hateful divorce of love," thus chides she Death,
"Grim-grinning° ghost, earth's worm, what dost thou mean   *(like a skull)*
To stifle beauty and to steal his breath,
935   Who, when he lived, his breath and beauty set
      Gloss on the rose, smell to the violet?

"If he be dead—oh, no, it cannot be,
Seeing his beauty, thou shouldst strike at it—
Oh, yes, it may: thou hast no eyes to see,[6]
940 But hatefully at random dost thou hit.
      Thy mark° is feeble age, but thy false dart   *target*
      Mistakes that aim and cleaves an infant's heart.

"Hadst thou but bid beware, then he° had spoke,   *(Adonis)*
And hearing him, thy power had lost his° power.   *its*
945 The Destinies will curse thee for this stroke:
They bid thee crop a weed; thou pluck'st a flower.
      Love's golden arrow at him should have fled,°   *flown*
      And not Death's ebon° dart to strike him dead.   *black*

"Dost thou drink tears, that thou provok'st such weeping?
950 What may a heavy groan advantage° thee?   *benefit*
Why hast thou cast into eternal sleeping

---

5. *In . . . effecting*: Full of notions, yet actually   6. Death's eye sockets are empty, like a skull's.
attending to nothing.

Those eyes that taught all other eyes to see?
　　　　Now Nature cares not for thy mortal vigor,[7]
　　　　Since her best work is ruined with thy rigor."

955 Here overcome as one full of despair
　　She veiled° her eyelids, who, like sluices, stopped　　　　　　　　*lowered*
　　The crystal tide that from her two cheeks fair
　　In the sweet channel of her bosom dropped;
　　　　But through the floodgates breaks the silver rain
960 　　　　And with his strong course opens them again.

Oh, how her eyes and tears did lend and borrow.°　　　　　　*(by reflection)*
Her eye seen in the tears, tears in her eye:
Both crystals, where they viewed each other's sorrow—
Sorrow that friendly° sighs sought still to dry;　　　　*consoling; like-minded*
965 　　But like a stormy day, now wind, now rain,
　　　　Sighs dry her cheeks, tears make them wet again.

Variable passions throng her constant woe,
As striving who should best become° her grief.　　　　　　　　*fit*
All entertained,° each passion labors so　　　　　　*permitted to enter*
970 That every present sorrow seemeth chief;
　　　　But none is best. Then join they all together,
　　　　Like many clouds consulting° for foul weather.　　　　*gathering*

By this far off she hears some huntsman hallow;°　　　　　*(hunting call)*
A nurse's song ne'er pleased her babe so well.
975 The dire imagination° she did follow　　　　　　*train of thought*
This sound of hope doth labor to expel.
　　　　For now reviving joy bids her rejoice,
　　　　And flatters her it is Adonis' voice.

Whereat her tears began to turn their tide,°　　　　　　　*to ebb*
980 Being prisoned in her eye, like pearls in glass;
Yet sometimes falls an orient° drop beside,　　　　　　*a glistening*
Which her cheek melts, as° scorning it should pass　　　　　　*as if*
　　　　To wash the foul° face of the sluttish ground,　　　　*dirty*
　　　　Who is but drunken when she seemeth drowned.

985 O hard-believing love, how strange it seems
Not to believe, and yet too credulous!
Thy weal° and woe are both of them extremes;　　　　　　*prosperity*
Despair and hope makes thee ridiculous:
　　　　The one doth flatter thee in thoughts unlikely;
990 　　　　In likely thoughts the other kills thee quickly.

Now she unweaves the web that she hath wrought:
Adonis lives, and Death is not to blame;
It was not she that called him all to naught.[8]
Now she adds honors to his hateful name:
995 　　She clepes° him king of graves, and grave for kings,　　　*calls (archaic)*
　　　　Imperious supreme° of all mortal things.　　　　　　*Imperial ruler*

---

7. *Nature . . . vigor:* Nature does not heed your lethal　　8. *She . . . naught:* she who called Death everything
power.　　　　　　　　　　　　　　　　　　　　　　　bad.

"No, no," quoth she, "sweet Death, I did but jest.
Yet pardon me: I felt a kind of fear
Whenas I met the boar, that bloody beast,
1000   Which knows no pity but is still severe.
        Then, gentle shadow—truth I must confess—
        I railed on thee, fearing my love's decease.

"'Tis not my fault; the boar provoked my tongue.
Be wreaked° on him, invisible commander.   *revenged*
1005   'Tis he, foul creature, that hath done thee wrong.
I did but act;° he's author of thy slander.   *(as an agent)*
        Grief hath two tongues,° and never woman yet   *is doubly loud*
        Could rule them both without ten women's wit."

Thus, hoping that Adonis is alive,
1010   Her rash suspect° she doth extenuate,   *suspicion*
And that his beauty may the better thrive,
With Death she humbly doth insinuate:°   *curry favor*
        Tells him of trophies, statues, tombs; and stories[9]
        His victories, his triumphs, and his glories.

1015   "O Jove," quoth she, "how much a fool was I
To be of such a weak and silly mind
To wail his death who lives and must not die
Till mutual° overthrow of mortal kind?   *universal*
        For he being dead, with him is beauty slain,
1020   And beauty dead, black chaos comes again.

"Fie, fie, fond° love, thou art as full of fear   *foolish; affectionate*
As one with treasure laden, hemmed with thieves.
Trifles unwitnessed with eye or ear
Thy coward heart with false bethinking° grieves."   *imagination*
1025   Even at this word she hears a merry horn,
        Whereat she leaps° that was but late° forlorn.   *(for joy) / lately*

As falcons to the lure, away she flies.
The grass stoops not, she treads on it so light,
And in her haste unfortunately spies
1030   The foul boar's conquest on her fair delight,
        Which seen, her eyes, as murdered with the view,[1]
        Like stars ashamed of° day, themselves withdrew.°   *put to shame by / shut*

Or as the snail, whose tender horns being hit,
Shrinks backward in his shelly cave with pain,
1035   And there, all smothered up, in shade doth sit,
Long after fearing to creep forth again:
        So at his bloody view her eyes are fled
        Into the deep-dark cabins of her head,

---

9. TEXTUAL COMMENT Although the First Quarto prints a comma after "stories," editors consider it a verb meaning "to tell about." In this edition, a semicolon after "tombs" clarifies the grammar of the sentence. For a fuller explanation, see Digital Edition TC 2.
1. TEXTUAL COMMENT The First Quarto prints "are murdered," not "as murdered." This edition, though not all modern editions, accepts an emendation from the Third Quarto that clarifies the simile-within-the-simile. For a longer discussion of the textual crux, see Digital Edition TC 3.

Where they resign their office and their light
1040 To the disposing of her troubled brain,
Who bids them still consort with° ugly night,   always accompany
And never wound the heart with looks again;
    Who,° like a king perplexèd° in his throne,   (the heart) / troubled
    By their suggestion° gives a deadly groan,   (the eyes') incitement

1045 Whereat each tributary subject² quakes,
As when the wind imprisoned in the ground,
Struggling for passage, earth's foundation shakes,³
Which with cold terror doth men's minds confound.
    This mutiny each part doth so surprise°   assail
1050   That from their dark beds once more leap her eyes;

And, being opened, threw unwilling light
Upon the wide wound that the boar had trenched
In his soft flank, whose wonted° lily white   usual
With purple tears, that his wound wept, was drenched.
1055   No flower was nigh, no grass, herb, leaf, or weed
    But stole his blood and seemed with him to bleed.

This solemn sympathy poor Venus noteth;
Over one shoulder doth she hang her head.
Dumbly° she passions,° frantically she doteth: Mutely / suffers
1060 She thinks he could not die; he is not dead.
    Her voice is stopped, her joints forget to bow;°   cannot bend
    Her eyes are mad that they have wept till° now.   before

Upon his hurt she looks so steadfastly
That her sight, dazzling,° makes the wound seem three;   blurring
1065 And then she reprehends her mangling eye
That makes more gashes where no breach should be:
    His face seems twain; each several limb is doubled;
    For oft the eye mistakes, the brain being troubled.

"My tongue cannot express my grief for one,
1070 And yet," quoth she, "behold two Adons dead.
My sighs are blown away, my salt tears gone;
Mine eyes are turned to fire, my heart to lead.
    Heavy heart's lead, melt at mine eyes' red fire:
    So shall I die by drops of hot desire.

1075 "Alas, poor world, what treasure hast thou lost?
What face remains alive that's worth the viewing?
Whose tongue is music now? What canst thou boast
Of things long since, or anything ensuing?
    The flowers are sweet, their colors fresh and trim,
1080   But true sweet beauty lived and died with him.

"Bonnet nor veil henceforth no creature wear,°   (to preserve complexion)
Nor sun nor wind will ever strive to kiss you.
Having no fair° to lose, you need not fear.   beauty
The sun doth scorn you, and the wind doth hiss you.

---

2. Each inferior organ of Venus's body.   3. Sixteenth-century explanation of earthquakes.

1085   But when Adonis lived, sun and sharp air
    Lurked like two thieves to rob him of his fair.

    "And therefore would he put his bonnet on,
    Under whose brim the gaudy sun would peep.
    The wind would blow it off, and, being gone,
1090   Play with his locks. Then would Adonis weep,
      And straight° in pity of his tender years   *immediately*
      They both would strive who first should dry his tears.

    "To see his face, the lion walked along
    Behind some hedge, because he would not fear° him;   *frighten*
1095   To recreate° himself° when he hath sung,   *entertain / (Adonis)*
    The tiger would be tame and gently hear him.
      If he had spoke, the wolf would leave his prey
      And never fright the silly° lamb that day.   *innocent*

    "When he beheld his shadow in the brook,
1100   The fishes spread on it their golden gills.
    When he was by, the birds such pleasure took
    That some would sing, some other in their bills
      Would bring him mulberries and ripe-red cherries:
      He fed them with his sight, they him with berries.

1105   "But this foul, grim, and urchin-snouted° boar,   *hedgehog-snouted*
    Whose downward eye still looketh for a grave,
    Ne'er saw the beauteous livery[4] that he wore.
    Witness the entertainment° that he gave.   *reception*
      If he did see his face, why then I know
1110   He thought to kiss him, and hath killed him so.

    "'Tis true, 'tis true, thus was Adonis slain.
    He ran upon the boar with his sharp spear,
    Who did not whet his teeth at him again,°   *in return*
    But by a kiss thought to persuade him° there.   *win him over*
1115   And, nuzzling in his flank, the loving swine
      Sheathed unaware the tusk in his soft groin.

    "Had I been toothed like him, I must confess,
    With kissing him I should have killed him first.
    But he is dead, and never did he bless
1120   My youth with his: the more am I accursed."
      With this, she falleth in the place she stood
      And stains her face with his congealèd blood.

    She looks upon his lips, and they are pale;
    She takes him by the hand, and that is cold;
1125   She whispers in his ears a heavy tale,
    As if they heard the woeful words she told.
      She lifts the coffer-lids° that close his eyes,   *treasure-chest lids*
      Where, lo, two lamps burned out in darkness lies:

4. His appearance (literally, garment).

Two glasses where herself herself beheld
1130 A thousand times, and now no more reflect,
Their virtue° lost wherein they late excelled,   *power*
And every beauty robbed of his° effect.   *its*
  "Wonder of time," quoth she, "this is my spite,° *torment*
  That, thou being dead, the day should yet be light.

1135 "Since thou art dead, lo, here I prophesy:
Sorrow on love hereafter shall attend;
It° shall be waited on with jealousy,   *(Love)*
Find sweet beginning but unsavory end;
  Ne'er settled equally, but high or low,⁵
1140   That all love's pleasure shall not match his woe.

"It shall be fickle, false, and full of fraud,
Bud, and be blasted,° in a breathing while;° *blighted / moment*
The bottom poison, and the top o'er-strawed° *strewn over*
With sweets that shall the truest sight beguile.
1145   The strongest body shall it make most weak,
  Strike the wise dumb,° and teach the fool to speak. *mute*

"It shall be sparing° and too full of riot,° *miserly / excess*
Teaching decrepit age to tread the measures;⁶
The staring° ruffian shall it keep in quiet,   *glaring*
1150 Pluck down the rich, enrich the poor with treasures;
  It shall be raging mad and silly mild,
  Make the young old, the old become a child.

"It shall suspect where is no cause of fear;
It shall not fear where it should most mistrust;
1155 It shall be merciful and too severe,
And most deceiving when it seems most just;° *honest*
  Perverse it shall be where it shows most toward,⁷
  Put fear to valor, courage to the coward.

"It shall be cause of war and dire events,
1160 And set dissension twixt the son and sire;
Subject and servile to all discontents,⁸
As dry combustious matter is to fire.
  Sith° in his prime death doth my love destroy, *Since*
  They that love best their loves shall not enjoy."

1165 By this the boy that by her side lay killed
Was melted like a vapor from her sight;
And in his blood that on the ground lay spilled
A purple flower sprung up, checkered with white,° *(the anemone)*
  Resembling well his pale cheeks and the blood
1170   Which in round drops upon their whiteness stood.

She bows her head the new-sprung flower to smell,
Comparing it to her Adonis' breath,

---

5. *Ne'er . . . low:* Love shall involve extremes of happiness and grief rather than equanimity; lovers shall come from different social stations.
6. To dance (inappropriately).

7. *Perverse . . . toward:* It shall be stubborn where it seems most compliant.
8. *Subject . . . discontents:* Cause and slave of all discontentedness.

And says within her bosom it shall dwell,
Since he himself is reft° from her by death.   *torn*
1175   She crops the stalk, and in the breach appears
        Green-dropping sap, which she compares to tears.

"Poor flower," quoth she, "this was thy father's guise,°   *habit*
Sweet issue° of a more sweet-smelling sire,   *offspring; emission*
For every little grief to wet his eyes.
1180 To grow unto himself° was his desire,   *mature independently*
        And so 'tis thine; but know it is as good
        To wither in my breast as in his blood.

"Here was thy father's bed, here in my breast.
Thou art the next of blood,° and 'tis thy right.   *heir (with wordplay)*
1185 Lo, in this hollow cradle take thy rest;
My throbbing heart shall rock thee day and night.
        There shall not be one minute in an hour
        Wherein I will not kiss my sweet love's flower."

Thus weary of the world, away she hies,
1190 And yokes her silver doves, by whose swift aid
Their mistress, mounted through the empty skies
In her light chariot, quickly is conveyed,
        Holding their course to Paphos,[9] where their queen
        Means to immure° herself and not be seen.   *confine*

9. Venus's abode in Cyprus.

The Rape of Lucrece

In the dedication to *Venus and Adonis* in 1593, Shakespeare promised his patron the Earl of Southampton a "graver labor"; a year later, *The Rape of Lucrece* delivered on his pledge. Like most nondramatic poems of the period, in other words, this one was dedicated to a wealthy individual whom Shakespeare hoped would reward his efforts, and may reflect Shakespeare's awareness of that person's tastes. Perhaps not surprisingly, then, the two poems have much in common: their classical inspiration; their lush, highly rhetorical narrative verse; their interest in the dynamic of a one-sided sexual passion. Yet whereas *Venus and Adonis*, despite its sad end, remains playful even in its pathos, *The Rape of Lucrece* retells a politically and psychologically complex story of rape and revolution. It is written in rhyme royal, a seven-line iambic-pentameter stanza with the rhyme scheme *ababbcc*, a verse form reserved since the time of Chaucer for elevated, tragic subjects. Shakespeare's contemporary Gabriel Harvey captures the difference between the two poems when he comments that *Venus and Adonis* appeals to "the younger sort," while *The Rape of Lucrece*, like *Hamlet*, pleases "the wiser sort." Certainly both poems were remarkably popular: *The Rape of Lucrece* was reprinted at least six times during Shakespeare's lifetime.

Slightly different versions of the tale of Tarquin and Lucretia were available in Livy's history of Rome and in Ovid's *Fasti*, both commonly read in Elizabethan grammar schools. In 509 B.C.E., Rome's king was Tarquin the Proud, a good military leader but an oppressive ruler over his own subjects. Sextus Tarquinius, the king's son, raped Lucretia, the wife of Collatinus, one of his aristocratic retainers. Lucretia committed suicide after revealing the crime to her male relatives and exhorting them to revenge her. After her corpse was exhibited in the Roman Forum, a wholesale revolt against the Tarquins erupted, led by the king's nephew Lucius Junius Brutus. The royal family was defeated and exiled, and Rome became a republic, ruled by a Senate and administered by one or more elected "consuls," of which Lucius Junius Brutus was the first.

For a Renaissance as well as for its original Roman audience, the story of Tarquin and Lucretia displayed vividly the complicated relationship between civic and domestic order, between public and private realms, between sexual and political violence. In the patriarchal society of ancient Rome, political or public agency was vested exclusively in men, especially elite men, while women resided in households governed by their male kin. A man like Collatinus, then, was simultaneously subject to his ruler, in the civic sphere, and the lord over his own family, in the domestic sphere. This conception would have been familiar to Shakespeare and his readers, for while ancient Roman and sixteenth-century English society differed in many respects, some of the same assumptions still prevailed about politics, gender, and the relationship between monarchical and husbandly authority. When he rapes Lucretia, then, Tarquin is not merely perpetrating an act of brutal violence against her; he is refusing to respect her husband Collatinus's exclusive rights over her body. This double sense of rape, both as a crime against the victim of sexual assault and, just as important, as an outrage against the property rights of her male relatives, pervades the poem and helps explain the conduct of the principal characters.

As a political fable, the story of Tarquin suggested the limits of sovereign authority and the circumstances in which subjects were permitted, even obliged, to challenge the authority of their sovereign. In the late sixteenth century, when monarchies in

Lucretia. Raphael.

western Europe were strengthening their power at the expense of parliaments and the higher aristocracy, the story could be cited as a precedent for resisting tyranny. Purely as a sexual melodrama, too, the story had wide appeal. Again and again, Renaissance painters portrayed Tarquin stealing into Lucretia's bed, Lucretia stabbing herself, and Lucius Junius Brutus exhorting over her body in the marketplace, often incorporating all three scenes into the same picture. Lucretia became a focus of especially fierce debate. On the one hand, she seemed a model of wifely duty, a woman to whom marital fidelity was not merely a matter of social respectability but a fundamental life principle. On the other hand, suicide by the sword—the traditional last, defiant gesture of heroic Roman men—could seem improperly self-assertive in a woman. Moreover, some Christian writers considered Lucretia's suicide not merely indecorous but sinful. In *The City of God*, Augustine argued that since virtues are properties of the will and not the body, Lucretia was innocent of unchastity. But ironically, her sexual blamelessness rendered her suicide completely inexcusable; Augustine considered her a murderess who had taken her own life out of misplaced pride. By Shakespeare's time, therefore, Lucretia could be held up, variously, as a model of female propriety and as an example of pagan willfulness, as a woman who breaks from the usual constraints upon her sex even while she seems most strenuously to endorse them.

Adapting the story to his own purposes, Shakespeare makes interesting changes of detail and emphasis. As Ovid and Livy recount it, the story of violation, suicide, and revolution is full of turbulent physical action and unexpected revelations—and in Livy especially, the political consequences of the rape receive much more attention than the sexual assault itself. Shakespeare's version downplays—though it does not eliminate—the political aspects of the story, and it contains most of the feverish momentum of the original story in the prefatory "Argument": "The same night he treacherously stealeth into her chamber, violently ravished her, and early in the morning speedeth away. Lucrece, in this lamentable plight, hastily dispatcheth messengers. . . ." The poem itself, by contrast, concentrates not upon moments of violence or haste but upon what precedes and follows those moments: what Tarquin thinks as he stealthily makes his way to Lucrece's bedchamber, how Lucrece occupies herself between the time she sends off her messenger and Collatine's return.

Like *Venus and Adonis, The Rape of Lucrece* eschews eventfulness for elaborate psychological analysis, attempting to capture in verse the uneven surge and flow of troubled, self-divided consciousnesses. In Shakespeare's hands, the story of Tarquin and Lucrece becomes a story about how first the perpetrator of a crime, and then its victim, make choices that lead to violence. Everything in the poem is the consequence of a decision, not an accident of fate, and nothing seems inevitable. The poem teases the reader with alternative possibilities. What if Collatine had kept his marital happiness to himself? What if Tarquin's conscience had overcome his lust? What if Lucrece's beauty had blinded Tarquin permanently instead of temporarily? What if Collatine had arrived to save Lucrece at the last moment? What if Lucrece had resolved to kill Tarquin rather than herself? The poem is constantly suggesting that the characters would be better off doing something else; and, interestingly, the characters themselves at times seem lucidly aware of that fact. Tarquin tells himself that his assault will desecrate the very virtue he admires in Lucrece, destroy his own self-respect, and bring dishonor upon himself and his family. Then he rapes Lucrece. Lucrece argues to herself what her husband and father will tell her later: that she cannot incur guilt by a sexual act to which she has not consented, and that therefore she need not take her own life. Then she commits suicide.

In both cases, the characters' stubborn refusal to acknowledge the obvious seems to follow from their tendency to conceive of themselves in terms of a few crucial metaphors. In Tarquin's case, the metaphors are military: "Affection is my captain, and he leadeth; / . . . My heart shall never countermand mine eye" (lines 271, 276). Such images attract Tarquin because they portray a rash, grossly disorderly act in terms of strict discipline. Even as he overturns the proper subordination of passion to reason, he elaborates a clear, if perverse, hierarchy of priorities. Moreover, by casting himself as a warrior and Lucrece as an enemy territory, Tarquin minimizes the blame that attaches to rape, an act conventionally associated with (and often excused in) soldiers pillaging an enemy town.

Of course, as Lucrece reminds him, she is not his foe, and Tarquin's actions violate not only her bodily integrity but her husband's trust in a friend and superior. Her pleas show how tendentious are Tarquin's interpretations of the metaphors he attaches to himself. Eventually, the rape that Tarquin tries to think of as an orderly military maneuver leads not only to his psychological fragmentation and self-torment but to literal exile, an exile Lucrece describes as already having occurred metaphorically.

After the rape and Tarquin's departure, the narrative focus shifts to Lucrece. Although she knows that she is not intentionally guilty of breaking her marital vows, she nonetheless construes herself as culpable. Like her violator, Lucrece thinks of herself and her body in symbolic terms, although in her case the governing metaphors are fortress, house, mansion, temple, tree. By emphasizing the protective function of the body, these metaphors make it easy for Lucrece to think of herself as irreparably damaged once her body has been assaulted by Tarquin's lust:

> Ay me, the bark pilled from the lofty pine,
> His leaves will wither and his sap decay;
> So must my soul, her bark being pilled away.
> (lines 1167–69)

Once Tarquin sacks and batters Lucrece's fortress, she suffers regardless of her innocence, like the inhabitant of a plundered town. While she is able to distinguish between her body and her soul, she desperately attempts to resolve the inconsistency between them by declaring herself irredeemably contaminated. In doing so, she endorses—indeed, almost celebrates—a literally fatal ambivalence in the definition of female chastity. For despite Augustine's objections, female chastity ordinarily refers to a physical condition as well as to a mental attitude in cultures that value female bodily "purity." This ambivalence still haunts many rape survivors today: they often blame themselves for their own victimization, and in some societies they are shamed and punished as if they, as well as their rapists, had committed a crime.

Comprehensible though Lucrece's suicide may be, however, it is ironically fraught with the very contradictions she seeks to avoid. She "revenges" herself upon Tarquin by completing the assault he began, plunging the phallic blade into what Shakespeare calls the "sheath" of her breast (the Latin word for sheath is *vagina*). She insists that she is acting in Collatine's interests even while she ignores his clearly stated wishes. She proves her innocence by demanding of herself that she pay the penalty for guilt. She validates her version of the rape story by silencing herself more effectively than Tarquin had with the bedclothes.

Tarquin and Lucretia. Titian.

Although the ways Tarquin and Lucrece think about their respective situations may be highly problematic, their trains of thought are definitely not arbitrary. Both protagonists derive their figures of speech from the same medieval and Renaissance poetic tradition Shakespeare had already drawn upon in *Venus and Adonis.* The configuration of characters—the warrior-lover desperately pursuing his passion, the beautiful woman whose chastity makes her irresistibly desirable—is likewise conventional. Shakespeare suggests the importance of this poetic mentality for *The Rape of Lucrece* by anachronistically importing the language of chivalry into a poem about ancient Rome: Tarquin agonizes about the consequences of his transgression for his family's coat of arms, and Lucrece accuses him of breaking "knighthood, gentry, and sweet friendship's oath" (line 569). This is closer to the world of Thomas Malory's Arthurian romances, Thomas Wyatt's sonnets, Philip Sidney's *Arcadia,* or Edmund Spenser's *Faerie Queene* than it is to the world of Livy or Ovid.

In fact, it is possible to see *The Rape of Lucrece*, like *Venus and Adonis*, as attempting to renovate a rhetoric of sexual passion that had begun to seem trite by Shakespeare's time. But the two poems employ almost exactly opposite strategies of renewal. *Venus and Adonis* surprises the reader by turning conventional expectations of gendered behavior upside down, assigning the aggressive, desiring role to the woman and casting the male as an uncorrupted fortress of virtue. *The Rape of Lucrece*, on the other hand, pushes the conventional language of love poetry in a relentlessly literal direction, making it disturbingly interesting by unleashing the latent ferocity and misogyny of a courtly love aesthetic. Lovers in the poetry of Spenser and Sidney, Petrarch and Wyatt, think of themselves as soldiers of desire, but they are so awed by their mistresses that aggressive thoughts are quenched by a mere glance from their imperious beloveds. Shakespeare's Tarquin, in contrast, more consistent and less exquisitely sensitive, uses the implicitly coercive rhetoric of love poetry as a pretext for violence.

Given the poem's intense interest in the use and misuse of language, it is not surprising that *The Rape of Lucrece* is also attentive to the relationship of rhetoric to other forms of representation. This persistent concern culminates in a long passage in which Lucrece contemplates a tapestry of Troy. In multiple ways, the tapestry is relevant to her own case, for the Trojan War was the consequence of a rape, and after the city's destruction, Trojan refugees were supposed to have founded Rome. After Lucrece's suicide, the account of her rape will provide the pretext for another founding, that of the Roman Republic. Eventually, her story will be displayed by artists in the same way that the legend of Troy is illustrated here—a series of chronologically distinct episodes represented simultaneously on the same panel. As Lucrece gazes at the painter's vast panorama of violation and suffering, the poet emphasizes both the vivid realism of the depiction and the artificial means by which that realism is produced: "Here one man's hand leaned on another's head, / His nose being shadowed by his neighbor's ear" (lines 1415–16). Portraying people according to the laws of perspective makes them look "natural," but it also reduces them to a collection of

From Jost Amman, *Icones Livianae* (1572). This picture shows both the rape of Lucretia, in the left background, and her suicide, in the right foreground.

grotesquely amputated shapes. Like *Venus and Adonis*, *The Rape of Lucrece* invokes nature as a category of value and then subverts it; but whereas the earlier poem undermines "nature" by suggesting that its supposed precepts are inadequate, the later poem undermines "nature" by suggesting that its effect is achieved only by extraordinary artifice. Shakespeare will consider the issue again in such plays as *A Midsummer Night's Dream*, *The Winter's Tale*, *The Tempest*, and, of course, *Hamlet*.

KATHARINE EISAMAN MAUS

SELECTED BIBLIOGRAPHY

Arkin, Samuel. "'That map which deep impression bears': Lucrece and the Anatomy of Shakespeare's Sympathy." *Shakespeare Quarterly* 64 (2013): 349–71. Looks at sympathy, witnessing, and consent within the poem and in the experience of reading it.

Belsey, Catherine. "Tarquin Dispossessed: Expropriation and Consent in *The Rape of Lucrece*." *Shakespeare Quarterly* 52 (2001): 45–70. Examines Lucrece as property and as person.

Donaldson, Ian. *The Rapes of Lucretia: A Myth and Its Transformations*. Oxford: Oxford UP, 1982. Discusses Shakespeare's poem alongside other literary and artistic treatments of the story.

Fineman, Joel. "Shakespeare's Will: The Temporality of Rape." *Representations* 20 (Fall 1987): 25–76. Features an ingenious discussion of the "let" as both hindering Tarquin and spurring him to action.

Hadfield, Andrew. "Tarquin's Everlasting Banishment: Republicanism and Constitutionalism in *The Rape of Lucrece* and *Titus Andronicus*." *Parergon: Journal of the Australian and New Zealand Association for Medieval and Renaissance Studies* 19 (2002): 77–104. Discusses the political issues in the poem.

Hehmeyer, Jeffrey Paxton. "Heralding the Commonplace: Authorship, Voice, and the Commonplace in Shakespeare's *Rape of Lucrece*." *Shakespeare Quarterly* 64 (2013): 139–64. Looks at aphorism and originality in the voices of the poet and of the raped woman.

Kahn, Coppélia. "The Rape in Shakespeare's *Lucrece*." *Shakespeare Studies* 9 (1976): 45–72. Presents a feminist account of rape and patriarchy in the poem.

Maus, Katharine Eisaman. "Taking Tropes Seriously: Language and Violence in Shakespeare's *Rape of Lucrece*." *Shakespeare Quarterly* 37 (1986): 66–82. Analyzes *The Rape of Lucrece* as a literalization of Petrarchan metaphors.

Vickers, Nancy. "The Blazon of Sweet Beauty's Best: Shakespeare's *Lucrece*." *Shakespeare and the Question of Theory*. Ed. Patricia Parker and Geoffrey Hartman. New York: Methuen, 1985. 95–115. Explores the sexual politics of the blazon, or detailed description of Lucrece's body.

TEXTUAL INTRODUCTION

The Rape of Lucrece was entered in the Stationers' Register on May 9, 1594, to John Harrison, Senior, and was printed by Shakespeare's fellow Stratfordian Richard Field.

Lucrece was published as a quarto probably in summer 1594. Like *Venus and Adonis*, the book includes prefatory material designed to advertise it as an important literary work. The title page prints the title simply as *Lucrece*, with the longer version reserved for the running heads: *The Rape of Lucrece*. The title page includes a floral border at the top and a printer's device (an anchor) in the middle, both used in *Venus and Adonis*, although Field's device is larger in *Lucrece* because, unlike *Venus*, the title page does not require room for a Latin tag. Like *Venus*, nonetheless, the next page adds a prose dedicatory epistle, again addressed to Henry Wriothesley, Earl of Southampton, and signed "William Shakespeare." New to the design of the book is a prose "Argument," which details the historical background leading up to the poem's action. Like *Venus*, then, *Lucrece* presents Shakespeare as securing patronage from a wealthy young aristocrat in an attempt to make a significant contribution to English poetry.

The book is thus another handsome one under Shakespeare's name. It is carefully printed and includes forty-eight leaves, collated as A2 B-M4 N2. The book survives in ten copies and a fragment, none of which includes the final leaf (sig. N2), which most likely would have been blank. The extant copies exist in two states: uncorrected (Qu) and corrected (Qc). The press corrections were made to the inner forme of signatures B and H and the outer formes of C, D, I, K, and M, affecting readings in the following lines: 24, 31, 50, 125, 126, 162, 396, 1118, 1182, 1335, 1350, and 1832 (see the list of Textual Variants for details). Outer I is unique in that it survives in two corrected states. Nothing in any of the corrections confirms that Shakespeare made them himself. In two cases (lines 31 and 1350), some modern editors have chosen to retain the uncorrected reading because it seems to make more sense. The corrected copy of Q1 found in the Folger Shakespeare Library is the base text for this edition.

Three textual cruxes exist. First, at lines 129–30 the syntax is extremely complex and the punctuation evidently in error, as the compositor was perhaps thrown off by Shakespeare's unusual use of a stanza with five feminine rhyme-endings: "revolving . . . obtaining . . . resolving . . . abstaining . . . gaining" (cf. lines 428–34 for seven feminine rhyme-endings, as well as *VA* 409–12). The confusing punctuation exists in both states of the Quarto, but it prompted correction in later quartos. The question becomes just how to group the various clauses. Q1 includes a period at the end of line 129, and no punctuation at the end of line 130, so that the first five lines of the stanza read (in modern spelling):

As one of which doth Tarquin lie revolving
The sundry dangers of his will's obtaining;
Yet ever to obtain his will resolving.
130 Though weak-built hopes persuade him to abstaining
Despair to gain doth traffic oft for gaining . . .

Most modern editors agree that the lines contain at least one error in punctuation, but they do not always parse the lines identically. They agree on missing punctuation at the end of line 130 after "abstaining," but disagree about what the punctuation should be, and about the punctuation after "resolving" in line 129. Retaining a period after "resolving," but inserting a comma after "abstaining," adopted in this edition, ensures that line 129 completes the thought of the first two lines, and gives the next two lines their own thought: although Tarquin's weak hopes persuade him to abstain from raping Lucrece, his strong despair overtakes that hope.

In the second crux, at line 639, the text prints the phrase "rash relier," apparently meaning a headstrong dependent. This has prompted editorial speculation—for instance, Q6 first prints "rash reply"—but the OED lists Shakespeare's usage of "relier" as its only example, and it has accordingly been retained here.

A third crux occurs at line 1544, where the compositor printed "beguild" in the difficult phrase "armèd to beguild," which could mean either "beguiled" or "be-gilded," suggesting that Tarquin comes to Lucrece either armed to beguile or armed to gloss over his true intent. The spelling "beguild" has been adopted for the present text to retain this double meaning.

A final feature of the 1594 Quarto is worth mentioning: a number of lines or sets of lines begin with double opening inverted commas (") to mark off "sentences" or sententiae, pithy moral maxims (lines 87–88, 460, 528, 530, 560, 831–32, 853, 867–68, 1109–18, 1125, 1127, 1216, 1687). The present edition does not retain these markings, in part because the original Quarto does not identify the sententiae in a clear and consistent manner and in part because of a design feature for The Norton Shakespeare as a whole (Venus and Adonis, for instance, does not print the markings, even though it, too, includes sententiae).

As with Venus, editors have been unable to determine whether the book was printed from Shakespeare's autograph copy or from a copy prepared by a scribe. Nevertheless, editors have found more spellings in Lucrece than in Venus that appear to be characteristically Shakespearean, especially "bedred" for "bedrid" (line 975) and "on" for "one" (line 1680).

As with Venus, the compositor confronted a layout problem, made more challenging because of Lucrece's seven-line rhyme royal stanza (rhyming ababbcc), for which the last two lines of each stanza were indented. To remain within his margins, he resorted to various devices: running the lines over, relying on tildes (a mark printed above a letter to indicate omission of another letter), and using ampersands (&).

Because of the generally careful printing of the text, editors have made only a few interventions. As recorded in the list of variants, some subsequently printed editions (six were published in Shakespeare's lifetime) began silently correcting a few errors. For a work of William Shakespeare, Lucrece is in a relatively pristine state.

PATRICK CHENEY

The Rape of Lucrece

To the Right Honorable Henry Wriothesley,
Earl of Southampton and Baron of Titchfield[1]

The love I dedicate to your lordship is without end, whereof this pamphlet° without beginning[2] is but a superfluous moiety.° The warrant° I have of your honorable disposition, not the worth of my untutored lines, makes it assured of acceptance. What I have done is yours; what I have to do is yours; being part in all I have, devoted yours. Were my worth greater, my duty would show greater; meantime, as it is, it is bound to your Lordship, to whom I wish long life still° lengthened with all happiness.

> Your lordship's in all duty,
> William Shakespeare

short work / part
assurance

continually

THE ARGUMENT°

Lucius Tarquinius, for his excessive pride surnamed Super-bus,° after he had caused his own father-in-law Servius Tullius to be cruelly murdered and, contrary to the Roman laws and customs, not requiring[3] or staying for the people's suffrages,° had possessed himself of the kingdom, went, accompanied with his sons and other noblemen of Rome, to besiege Ardea.[4] During which siege, the principal men of the army meeting one evening at the tent of Sextus Tarquinius, the King's son, in their discourses after supper everyone commended the virtues of his own wife, among whom Collatinus extolled the incomparable chastity of his wife Lucretia. In that pleasant humor° they all posted° to Rome, and intending by their secret and sudden arrival to make trial of that which every one had before avouched, only Collatinus finds his wife (though it were late in the night) spinning amongst her maids; the other ladies were all found dancing and reveling, or in several disports.° Whereupon the noblemen yielded Collatinus the victory, and his wife the fame. At that time Sextus Tarquinius, being enflamed with Lucrece' beauty, yet smothering his passions for the present, departed with the rest back to the camp. From whence he shortly after privily° withdrew himself, and was (according to his estate°) royally entertained and lodged by Lucrece at Collatium.[5] The same night he treacherously stealeth into her chamber, violently ravished her, and early in the morning speedeth away. Lucrece, in

plot

"the Proud"

approval

merry mood / hurried

diversions

secretly
rank

Dedication and **Argument**
1. Prominent courtier, twenty years old at the time of the publication of *The Rape of Lucrece*. Shakespeare also dedicated *Venus and Adonis* to him.
2. *The Rape of Lucrece* begins *in medias res* (in the middle of the story), as the Latin poet Horace recommends in *The Art of Poetry*.
3. Not asking for.
4. City twenty-five miles south of Rome.
5. Town ten miles east of Rome; the ancestral home of Collatinus's family.

this lamentable plight, hastily dispatcheth messengers, one to
Rome for her father, another to the camp for Collatine. They
came, the one accompanied with Junius Brutus, the other with
Publius Valerius; and finding Lucrece attired in mourning habit,
demanded the cause of her sorrow. She, first taking an oath of
them for her revenge, revealed the actor° and whole manner of   *doer*
his dealing, and withal° suddenly stabbed herself. Which done,   *moreover*
with one consent they all vowed to root out the whole hated family of the Tarquins; and bearing the dead body to Rome, Brutus
acquainted the people with the doer and manner of the vile
deed, with a bitter invective against the tyranny of the King.
Wherewith the people were so moved that, with one consent and
a general acclamation, the Tarquins were all exiled, and the state
government changed from kings to consuls.[6]

From the besiegèd Ardea all in post,°   *haste*
Borne by the trustless wings of false desire,
Lust-breathèd° Tarquin leaves the Roman host,   *Lust-inspired*
And to Collatium bears the lightless° fire,   *smoldering*
5 Which, in pale embers hid, lurks to aspire°   *rise up*
     And girdle with embracing flames the waist
     Of Collatine's fair love, Lucrece the chaste.

Haply° that name of "chaste" unhapp'ly° set   *Perhaps / unfortunately*
This bateless° edge on his keen appetite,   *unbluntable*
10 When Collatine unwisely did not let°   *forbear*
To praise the clear unmatchèd red and white,
Which triumphed in that sky of his delight,°   *(Lucrece's face)*
     Where mortal stars° as bright as heaven's beauties   *(her eyes)*
     With pure aspects[1] did him peculiar° duties.   *exclusive*

15 For he, the night before in Tarquin's tent,
Unlocked the treasure of his happy state:
What priceless wealth the heavens had him lent
In the possession of his beauteous mate,
Reck'ning his fortune at such high proud rate
20   That kings might be espousèd to more fame,
     But° king nor peer to such a peerless dame.[2]   *But neither*

Oh, happiness enjoyed but of° a few,   *only by*
And if possessed as soon decayed and done
As is the morning's silver melting dew[3]
25 Against the golden splendor of the sun,
An expired date° canceled ere well begun.   *time limit*
     Honor and beauty in the owner's arms
     Are weakly fortressed from a world of harms.

---

6. Chief magistrates, elected for one-year terms.
Poem
1. Looks; astral influences.
2. TEXTUAL COMMENT In line 21, the Second Quarto
substitutes "prince" for "peer," but this is probably a
mistake and the First Quarto reading is retained here.

For a fuller discussion, see Digital Edition TC 1.
3. TEXTUAL COMMENT Some copies of the First
Quarto have "morning silver dew," corrected to "mornings" (i.e., "morning's," turning the word into a possessive). This edition chooses "morning's" for reasons
explained in Digital Edition TC 2.

Beauty itself doth of° itself persuade   *by*
30 The eyes of men without an orator.
What needeth then apology be made[4]
To set forth that which is so singular?°   *unique*
Or why is Collatine the publisher°   *publicizer*
Of that rich jewel he should keep unknown
35   From thievish ears, because it is his own?

Perchance his boast of Lucrece' sov'reignty°   *superiority*
Suggested° this proud issue° of a king;   *Tempted / offspring*
For by our ears our hearts oft tainted be.
Perchance that envy of so rich a thing,
40 Braving compare,° disdainfully did sting   *Defying comparison*
His high-pitched thoughts that meaner° men should   *inferior*
vaunt°   *boast*
That golden hap° which their superiors want.°   *luck / lack*

But some untimely thought did instigate
His all-too-timeless° speed, if none of those.   *untimely; rapid*
45 His honor, his affairs, his friends, his state,°   *rank*
Neglected all, with swift intent he goes
To quench the coal which in his liver° glows.   *(seat of lust)*
O rash false heat, wrapped in repentant cold,
Thy hasty spring still blasts° and ne'er grows old.   *is always frostbitten*

50 When at Collatium this false lord arrived,
Well was he welcomed by the Roman dame,
Within whose face Beauty and Virtue strived
Which of them both should underprop her fame.
When Virtue bragged, Beauty would blush for shame;
55   When Beauty boasted blushes, in despite°   *defiance*
Virtue would stain° that o'er with silver white.   *dye*

But Beauty, in that white entitlèd°   *claiming title*
From Venus' doves, doth challenge that fair field.[5]
Then Virtue claims from Beauty Beauty's red,
60 Which Virtue gave the golden age to gild[6]
Their silver cheeks, and called it then their shield,
Teaching them thus to use it in the fight:
When shame assailed, the red should fence° the white.   *defend*

This heraldry in Lucrece' face was seen,
65 Argued° by Beauty's red and Virtue's white.   *Demonstrated; disputed*
Of either's color was the other queen,
Proving from world's minority° their right.   *earliest age*
Yet their ambition makes them still to fight,
The sovereignty of either being so great
70   That oft they interchange each other's seat.

---

4. TEXTUAL COMMENT Here is another press variant:
the word "apology" was corrected to "apologies." But
the Norton editor believes the correction was made
in error and retains the original reading; for reasoning, see Digital Edition TC 3.

5. Territory; battlefield; surface on which a coat of
arms is displayed. *Venus' doves:* white turtledoves draw
the chariot of Venus, the love goddess.
6. Coat with gold; cover with red (as in a blush). *the
golden age:* a mythical, ideal era of innocence and plenty.

This silent war of lilies and of roses,
Which Tarquin viewed in her fair face's field,
In their pure ranks his traitor eye encloses,
Where, lest between them both it should be killed,
75 The coward-captive vanquishèd doth yield
    To those two armies that would let him go,
    Rather than triumph in° so false a foe.   *over*

Now thinks he that her husband's shallow tongue,
The niggard prodigal that praised her so,
80 In that high task hath done her beauty wrong,
Which far exceeds his barren skill to show.°   *describe*
Therefore that praise which Collatine doth owe°   *fail to render*
    Enchanted Tarquin answers° with surmise,   *compensates for*
    In silent wonder of still-gazing eyes.

85 This earthly saint adorèd by this devil
Little suspecteth the false worshipper:
For unstained thoughts do seldom dream on evil;
Birds never limed° no secret bushes fear.   *trapped*
So, guiltless, she securely° gives good cheer[7]   *unsuspectingly*
90   And reverent welcome to her princely guest,
    Whose inward ill no outward harm expressed.

For that he colored° with his high estate,   *disguised*
Hiding base sin in pleats° of majesty,   *folds*
That° nothing in him seemed inordinate,°   *So that / out of order*
95 Save sometime too much wonder of his eye,
Which, having all, all could not satisfy.
    But, poorly rich, so wanteth in his store°   *plenty*
    That, cloyed with much, he pineth still for more.

But she that never coped with stranger° eyes   *strangers'*
100 Could pick no meaning from their parling° looks,   *persuasive*
Nor read the subtle shining secrecies
Writ in the glassy margins[8] of such books.
She touched no unknown baits, nor feared no hooks,
    Nor could she moralize° his wanton sight°   *interpret / looking*
105   More than his eyes were opened to the light.[9]

He stories to her ears her husband's fame,
Won in the fields of fruitful Italy,
And decks with praises Collatine's high name,
Made glorious by his manly chivalry,
110 With bruisèd arms° and wreaths of victory.   *dented weapons*
    Her joy with heaved-up hand she doth express,
    And wordless so greets heaven for his success.

Far from the purpose of his coming thither,
He makes excuses for his being there.

7. Hospitable entertainment.
8. Where summaries and interpretive remarks were often placed. *glassy:* shiny.
9. *opened to the light:* made obvious.

115 No cloudy show of stormy blust'ring weather
     Doth yet in his fair welkin° once appear,   *sky (face)*
     Till sable° night, mother of dread and fear,   *black*
          Upon the world dim darkness doth display,
          And in her vaulty prison stows the day.

120 For then is Tarquin brought unto his bed,
     Intending° weariness with heavy sprite.°   *Pretending / spirit*
     For after supper long he questionèd°   *conversed*
     With modest Lucrece and wore out the night.
     Now leaden slumber with life's strength doth fight,
125   And everyone to rest themselves betake,[1]
          Save thieves, and cares, and troubled minds that wake.

     As one of which doth Tarquin lie revolving°   *considering*
     The sundry dangers of his will's obtaining;°   *gratifying his desire*
     Yet ever to obtain his will resolving.[2]
130 Though weak-built hopes[3] persuade him to abstaining,
     Despair to gain doth traffic oft for gaining,[4]
          And when great treasure is the meed° proposed,   *prize*
          Though death be adjunct,[5] there's no death supposed.° *thought of*

     Those that much covet are with gain so fond°   *infatuated*
135 That what° they have not—that which they possess—   *That for what*
     They scatter and unloose it from their bond,°   *ownership*
     And so by hoping more they have but less;
     Or gaining more, the profit° of excess   *advantage*
          Is but to surfeit, and such griefs[6] sustain
140   That they° prove bankrupt in this poor-rich gain.   *(the covetous)*

     The aim of all is but to nurse the life
     With honor, wealth, and ease in waning age;
     And in this aim there is such thwarting strife
     That one for all or all for one we gage°—   *risk*
145 As° life for honor, in fell° battle's rage,   *For instance / cruel*
          Honor for wealth, and oft that wealth doth cost
          The death of all, and altogether lost.

     So that, in vent'ring ill,[7] we leave to be
     The things we are for that which we expect;
150 And this ambitious foul infirmity,
     In having° much, torments us with defect   *While we have*
     Of that we have; so then we do neglect
          The thing we have, and all for want of wit°   *lack of sense*
          Make something nothing by augmenting it.

1. Textual Comment Lines 125–26 exist in two slightly different states, and editors disagree on which one to choose; *The Norton Shakespeare* prints the version that is closer to modern usage. For a discussion of the options, see Digital Edition TC 4.
2. Textual Comment In the Quarto the punctuation of lines 129–30 seems to be erroneous, but modern editors disagree about what the proper punctuation ought to be. For a discussion of the problem and its possible solutions, see Digital Edition TC 5.
3. The fact that his hopes are flimsy.
4. *Despair . . . gaining:* Despair of gaining her (rightfully) often encourages him to gain her (by any means possible).
5. Be joined with it.
6. That is, the ills that accompany excess.
7. In taking serious risks; in undertaking evil deeds.

155 Such hazard now must doting Tarquin make,
  Pawning his honor to obtain his lust,
  And for himself himself he must forsake.
  Then where is truth if there be no self-trust?°   truth to oneself
  When shall he think to find a stranger just,
160   When he himself himself confounds, betrays
       To sland'rous tongues and wretched hateful days?

  Now stole upon the time the dead of night,
  When heavy sleep had closed up mortal eyes.
  No comfortable star did lend his° light,   its
165 No noise but owls' and wolves' death-boding cries.
  Now serves the season that they may surprise
       The silly° lambs. Pure thoughts are dead and still,   innocent
       While lust and murder wakes to stain° and kill.   defile

  And now this lustful lord leaped from his bed,
170 Throwing his mantle rudely o'er his arm,
  Is madly tossed between desire and dread:
  Th'one sweetly flatters, th'other feareth harm;
  But honest fear, bewitched with lust's foul charm,
       Doth too too oft betake him to retire,°   retreat
175   Beaten away by brainsick rude desire.

  His falchion° on a flint he softly smiteth,   curved sword
  That from the cold stone sparks of fire do fly,
  Whereat a waxen torch forthwith he lighteth,
  Which must be lodestar° to his lustful eye,   guiding light
180 And to the flame thus speaks advisedly:°   deliberately
       "As from this cold flint I enforced this fire,
       So Lucrece must I force to my desire."

  Here, pale with fear, he doth premeditate
  The dangers of his loathsome enterprise,
185 And in his inward mind he doth debate
  What following sorrow may on this arise.
  Then, looking scornfully, he doth despise
       His naked armor of still-slaughtered lust,[8]
       And justly thus controls° his thoughts unjust.   rebukes; restrains

190 "Fair torch, burn out thy light, and lend it not
  To darken her whose light excelleth thine;
  And die, unhallowed thoughts, before you blot
  With your uncleanness that which is divine.
  Offer pure incense to so pure a shrine.
195   Let fair humanity abhor the deed
       That spots and stains love's modest snow-white weed.° attire (chastity)

  "Oh, shame to knighthood and to shining arms!
  Oh, foul dishonor to my household's grave!°   ancestral tomb
  Oh, impious act including° all foul harms—   encompassing

---

8. *His . . . lust:* His ineffective defense against his lust, always quenched in the moment of fulfillment; his not-yet-erect penis.

200   A martial man to be soft fancy's° slave!   *love's*
           True valor still a true respect[9] should have;
                 Then my digression° is so vile, so base,   *error*
                 That it will live engraven in my face.

           "Yea, though I die the scandal will survive
205   And be an eyesore in my golden coat.°   *(of arms)*
           Some loathsome dash[1] the herald will contrive
           To cipher me how fondly° I did dote,   *To show how foolishly*
           That my posterity, shamed with the note,°   *stigma*
                 Shall curse my bones and hold it for no sin
210   To wish that I their father had not been.

           "What win I if I gain the thing I seek?
           A dream, a breath, a froth of fleeting joy.
           Who buys a minute's mirth to wail a week,
           Or sells eternity to get a toy?°   *trifle*
215   For one sweet grape who will the vine destroy?
                 Or what fond beggar, but to touch the crown,
                 Would with the scepter straight be strucken down?

           "If Collatinus dream of my intent,
           Will he not wake, and in a desp'rate rage
220   Post hither this vile purpose to prevent?
           This siege that hath engirt° his marriage,   *surrounded*
           This blur° to youth, this sorrow to the sage,   *blot*
                 This dying virtue, this surviving shame,
                 Whose crime will bear an ever-during° blame.   *everlasting*

225   "Oh, what excuse can my invention° make   *ingenuity*
           When thou shalt charge me with so black a deed?
           Will not my tongue be mute, my frail joints shake,
           Mine eyes forgo their light,° my false heart bleed?   *power of vision*
           The guilt being great, the fear doth still exceed,
230   And extreme fear can neither fight nor fly,
                 But coward-like with trembling terror die.

           "Had Collatinus killed my son or sire,
           Or lain in ambush to betray my life,
           Or were he not my dear friend, this desire
235   Might have excuse to work upon his wife,
           As in revenge or quittal° of such strife.   *requital*
                 But as he is my kinsman,° my dear friend,   *(Collatine was a cousin.)*
                 The shame and fault finds no excuse nor end.

           "Shameful it is—ay, if the fact° be known,   *deed*
240   Hateful it is. There is no hate in loving.
           I'll beg her love, but she is not her own.
           The worst is but denial and reproving.
           My will is strong, past reason's weak removing.

---

9. A suitable awareness of virtue.
1. Bar in a coat of arms, indicating a dishonorable action by an ancestor.

Who fears a sentence° or an old man's saw°   *maxim / proverb*
245   Shall by a painted cloth be kept in awe."[2]

Thus graceless holds he disputation
Tween frozen conscience and hot-burning will,
And with good thoughts makes dispensation,°   *dispenses*
Urging the worser sense for vantage still,
250   Which in a moment doth confound and kill
        All pure effects,° and doth so far proceed   *tendencies*
        That what is vile shows like a virtuous deed.

Quoth he, "She took me kindly by the hand,
And gazed for tidings in my eager eyes,
255   Fearing some hard news from the warlike band
Where her belovèd Collatinus lies.
Oh, how her fear did make her color rise!
        First red as roses that on lawn° we lay,   *fine linen*
        Then white as lawn, the roses took away.

260   "And how her hand, in my hand being locked,
Forced it to tremble with her loyal fear,
Which struck her sad, and then it faster rocked,
Until her husband's welfare she did hear,
Whereat she smilèd with so sweet a cheer°   *an expression*
265   That had Narcissus[2] seen her as she stood
        Self-love had never drowned him in the flood.

"Why hunt I then for color° or excuses?   *pretext*
All orators are dumb when beauty pleadeth.
Poor wretches have remorse in poor abuses.°   *regret minor lapses*
270   Love thrives not in the heart that shadows° dreadeth;   *illusory scruples*
Affection° is my captain, and he leadeth;   *Passion*
        And when his gaudy banner is displayed,
        The coward fights and will not be dismayed.

"Then childish fear avaunt,° debating die,   *be gone*
275   Respect° and reason wait on° wrinkled age!   *Circumspection / attend*
My heart shall never countermand mine eye.
Sad° pause and deep regard beseems the sage;   *Serious*
My part is youth and beats these from the stage.[4]
        Desire my pilot is, beauty my prize.°   *pirate's booty*
280   Then who fears sinking where such treasure lies?"

As corn° o'ergrown by weeds, so heedful fear   *grain*
Is almost choked by unresisted lust.
Away he steals with open list'ning ear,
Full of foul hope and full of fond° mistrust,   *foolish; passionate*
285   Both which, as servitors° to the unjust,   *servants*
        So cross him with their opposite persuasion
        That now he vows a league, and now invasion.

---

2. *Shall . . . awe:* Will be awed by a tapestry (often depicting morally significant narratives, as in lines 1366ff).
3. In classical mythology, a youth who fell in love with his reflection in a pool; in some versions of the tale, he drowned attempting to kiss the image.
4. Like the Vice character in medieval morality plays.

Within his thought her heavenly image sits,
And in the selfsame seat sits Collatine.
290 That eye which looks on her confounds his wits,
That eye which him beholds, as° more divine,   *because it is*
Unto a view so false will not incline,
     But with a pure appeal seeks° to the heart,   *applies*
     Which once corrupted takes the worser part;

295 And therein heartens up his servile powers,[5]
Who, flattered by their leader's jocund show,
Stuff up his lust as minutes fill up hours;
And as their captain, so their pride doth grow,
Paying more slavish tribute than they owe.[6]
300   By reprobate desire thus madly led,
     The Roman lord marcheth to Lucrece' bed.

The locks between her chamber and his will,
Each one by him enforced, retires his ward;°   *withdraws its bolt*
But as they open they all rate° his ill,   *berate (by squeaking)*
305 Which drives the creeping thief to some regard.°   *caution*
The threshold grates the door to have him heard;
     Night-wand'ring weasels[7] shriek to see him there:
     They fright him, yet he still pursues his fear.°   *that which makes him fear*

As each unwilling portal yields him way,
310 Through little vents and crannies of the place
The wind wars with his torch to make him stay,
And blows the smoke of it into his face,
Extinguishing his conduct° in this case.   *guide; behavior*
     But his hot heart, which fond desire doth scorch,
315   Puffs forth another wind that fires the torch.

And being lighted, by the light he spies
Lucretia's glove wherein her needle sticks.
He takes it from the rushes where it lies
And, gripping it, the needle his finger pricks,
320 As who should say, "This glove to wanton tricks
     Is not inured. Return again in haste.
     Thou seest our mistress' ornaments are chaste."

But all these poor forbiddings could not stay him;
He in the worst sense consters° their denial.   *construes*
325 The doors, the wind, the glove that did delay him
He takes for accidental things of trial;°   *tests of resolve*
Or as those bars which stop the hourly dial,[8]
     Who with a ling'ring stay his course doth let°   *hinder; permit*
     Till every minute pays the hour his debt.

330 "So, so," quoth he, "these lets attend the time,
Like little frosts that sometime threat the spring

---

5. Appetites or passions, imagined as servants of the heart, the seat of conscience.
6. That is, debasing themselves by collaborating and encouraging the corrupted heart.

7. Weasels were kept to catch vermin.
8. The marks on a clock face, where the hands pause before jerking forward.

To add a more rejoicing to the prime,°   *spring*
And give the sneapèd° birds more cause to sing.   *pinched with cold*
Pain pays the income° of each precious thing.   *is the price*
335   Huge rocks, high winds, strong pirates, shelves,° and sands   *reefs*
          The merchant fears, ere rich at home he lands."

Now is he come unto the chamber door
That shuts him from the heaven of his thought,
Which with a yielding latch, and with no more,
340 Hath barred him from the blessèd thing he sought.
So from° himself impiety hath wrought°   *unlike / made him*
          That for his prey to pray he doth begin,
          As if the heavens should countenance his sin.

But in the midst of his unfruitful prayer,
345 Having solicited th'eternal power
That his foul thoughts might compass° his fair fair,⁹   *obtain; embrace*
And they would stand auspicious to the hour,
Even there he starts.° Quoth he, "I must deflower;   *is startled*
          The powers to whom I pray abhor this fact.°   *deed*
350   How can they then assist me in the act?

"Then love and fortune be my gods, my guide.
My will is backed with resolution.
Thoughts are but dreams till their effects be tried.
The blackest sin is cleared with absolution.
355 Against love's fire, fear's frost hath dissolution.
          The eye of heaven is out,° and misty night   *extinguished*
          Covers the shame that follows sweet delight."

This said, his guilty hand plucked up the latch,
And with his knee the door he opens wide.
360 The dove sleeps fast that this night-owl will catch.
Thus treason works ere traitors be espied.
Who sees the lurking serpent steps aside,
          But she, sound sleeping, fearing no such thing,
          Lies at the mercy of his mortal° sting.   *lethal*

365 Into the chamber wickedly he stalks,°   *steals*
And gazeth on her yet unstainèd bed.
The curtains being close,° about he walks,   *shut*
Rolling his greedy eyeballs in his head.
By their high treason is his heart misled,
370   Which gives the watchword to his hand full soon
          To draw the cloud° that hides the silver moon.   *(the bed curtain)*

Look as° the fair and fiery-pointed sun,   *See how*
Rushing from forth a cloud, bereaves our sight;
Even so, the curtain drawn, his eyes begun
375 To wink,° being blinded with a greater light.   *close*
Whether it is that she reflects so bright
          That dazzleth them, or else some shame supposed,
          But blind they are and keep themselves enclosed.

9. *his fair fair:* his virtuous and beautiful one.

Oh, had they in that darksome prison died,
380 Then had they seen the period° of their ill.   *end*
Then Collatine again by Lucrece' side
In his clear° bed might have reposèd still.   *undefiled*
But they must ope, this blessèd league° to kill,   *marriage*
  And holy-thoughted Lucrece to their sight
385   Must sell her joy, her life, her world's delight.

Her lily hand her rosy cheek lies under,
Coz'ning° the pillow of a lawful kiss,   *Cheating*
Who, therefore angry, seems to part in sunder,°   *in two*
Swelling on either side to want his bliss;[1]
390 Between whose hills her head entombèd is,
  Where like a virtuous monument she lies
  To be admired of lewd unhallowed eyes.

Without the bed her other fair hand was
On the green coverlet, whose perfect white
395 Showed like an April daisy on the grass,
With pearly sweat resembling dew of night.
Her eyes like marigolds[2] had sheathed their light,
  And canopied in darkness sweetly lay
  Till they might open to adorn the day.

400 Her hair like golden threads played with her breath—
Oh, modest wantons, wanton modesty!—
Showing life's triumph in the map° of death,   *image*
And death's dim look in life's mortality.
Each° in her sleep themselves so beautify,   *(life and death)*
405   As if between them twain there were no strife,
  But that life lived in death, and death in life.

Her breasts like ivory globes circled with blue,
A pair of maiden[3] worlds unconquerèd,
Save of their lord no bearing yoke they knew,
410 And him by oath they truly honorèd.
These worlds in Tarquin new ambition bred,
  Who like a foul usurper went about
  From this fair throne to heave the owner out.

What could he see but mightily he noted?
415 What did he note but strongly he desired?
What he beheld, on that he firmly doted,
And in his will° his willful eye he tired.[4]   *lust*
With more than admiration he admired
  Her azure veins, her alabaster skin,
420   Her coral lips, her snow-white dimpled chin.

As the grim lion fawneth° o'er his prey,   *shows delight*
Sharp hunger by the conquest satisfied,

---

1. Because it is denied its pleasure (of her lips touching its surface).
2. The pot marigold folds up its flowers at day's end.

3. Used of an unconquered citadel.
4. Wearied; fed greedily (as a hawk tears flesh with its beak).

So o'er this sleeping soul doth Tarquin stay,
His rage of lust by gazing qualified,°   *mollified*
425   Slaked, not suppressed, for standing by her side.
      His eye, which late this mutiny restrains,
      Unto a greater uproar tempts his veins;

And they, like straggling slaves° for pillage fighting,   *lowborn soldiers*
Obdurate vassals fell° exploits effecting,   *fierce*
430   In bloody death and ravishment delighting,
Nor° children's tears nor mothers' groans respecting,   *Neither*
Swell in their pride, the onset still° expecting.   *at any moment*
      Anon his beating heart, alarum° striking,   *signal to attack*
      Gives the hot charge, and bids them do their liking.

435   His drumming heart cheers up his burning eye;
His eye commends° the leading to his hand.   *entrusts*
His hand, as proud of such a dignity,
Smoking with pride, marched on to make his stand
On her bare breast, the heart of all her land,
440   Whose ranks of blue veins, as his hand did scale,°   *climb*
      Left their round turrets destitute and pale.

They must'ring° to the quiet cabinet°   *gathering / room (heart)*
Where their dear governess° and lady lies,   *ruler*
Do tell her she is dreadfully beset,
445   And fright her with confusion of their cries.
She much amazed breaks ope her locked-up eyes,
      Who, peeping forth this tumult to behold,
      Are by his flaming torch dimmed and controlled.°   *overwhelmed*

Imagine her as one in dead of night
450   From forth dull sleep by dreadful fancy waking,
That thinks she hath beheld some ghastly sprite,
Whose grim aspect sets every joint a-shaking.
What terror 'tis! But she in worser taking,°   *plight*
      From sleep disturbèd, heedfully doth view
455   The sight which makes supposèd terror true.

Wrapped and confounded in a thousand fears,
Like to a new-killed bird she trembling lies.
She dares not look, yet winking° there appears   *shutting her eyes*
Quick-shifting antics,° ugly in her eyes.   *grotesque shapes*
460   Such shadows are the weak brain's forgeries,
      Who, angry that the eyes fly from their lights,
      In darkness daunts them with more dreadful sights.

His hand that yet remains upon her breast—
Rude ram° to batter such an ivory wall—   *battering ram*
465   May feel her heart, poor citizen, distressed,
Wounding itself to death, rise up and fall,
Beating her bulk,° that his hand shakes withal.°   *chest / as well*
      This moves in him more rage and lesser pity,
      To make the breach and enter this sweet city.

470   First like a trumpet doth his tongue begin
       To sound a parley[5] to his heartless° foe,   *terrified*
       Who o'er the white sheet peers her whiter chin,
       The reason of this rash alarm to know,
       Which he by dumb demeanor° seeks to show.   *mute gesture*
475   But she with vehement prayers urgeth still
           Under what color° he commits this ill.   *pretext*

       Thus he replies: "The color in thy face,
       That even for anger makes the lily pale
       And the red rose blush at her own disgrace,
480   Shall plead for me and tell my loving tale.
       Under that color° am I come to scale   *pretext; hue; flag*
           Thy never-conquered fort. The fault is thine,
           For those thine eyes betray thee unto mine.

       "Thus I forestall thee, if thou mean to chide:
485   Thy beauty hath ensnared thee to this night,
       Where thou with patience must my will abide,
       My will that marks thee for my earth's° delight,   *earthly; bodily*
       Which I to conquer sought with all my might.
           But as reproof and reason beat it° dead,   *(my lust)*
490   By thy bright beauty was it newly bred.

       "I see what crosses° my attempt will bring;   *misfortunes*
       I know what thorns the growing rose defends;
       I think° the honey guarded with a sting: *know*
       All this beforehand counsel° comprehends.   *wisdom*
495   But Will is deaf, and hears no heedful friends.
           Only he hath an eye to gaze on beauty,
           And dotes on what he looks, 'gainst law or duty.

       "I have debated even in my soul,
       What wrong, what shame, what sorrow I shall breed;
500   But nothing can affection's° course control,   *passion's*
       Or stop the headlong fury of his speed.
       I know repentant tears ensue° the deed,   *follow*
           Reproach, disdain, and deadly enmity,
           Yet strive I to embrace mine infamy."

505   This said, he shakes aloft his Roman blade,
       Which like a falcon tow'ring in the skies
       Coucheth the fowl° below with his wings' shade, *Makes the prey crouch*
       Whose crookèd beak threats, if he° mount he dies.   *(the fowl)*
       So under his insulting° falchion lies   *triumphantly exulting*
510   Harmless Lucretia, marking what he tells
           With trembling fear, as fowl hear falcons' bells.[6]

       "Lucrece," quoth he, "this night I must enjoy thee.
       If thou deny, then force must work my way,
       For in thy bed I purpose to destroy thee.
515   That done, some worthless slave of thine I'll slay

---

5. A call to a negotiation.   6. Hunting falcons had bells attached to their legs.

To kill thine honor with thy life's decay;[7]
　　　And in thy dead arms do I mean to place him,
　　　Swearing I slew him, seeing thee embrace him.

"So thy surviving husband shall remain
520　The scornful mark of every open eye;°　　　　　　　　　　　　　　*observer*
　　Thy kinsmen hang their heads at this disdain;
　　Thy issue blurred with nameless bastardy;[8]
　　And thou, the author of their obloquy,
　　　　Shalt have thy trespass cited up in rhymes°　　　*described in ballads*
525　　　And sung by children in succeeding times.

"But if thou yield, I rest thy secret friend:
　　The fault unknown is as a thought unacted.
　　A little harm done to a great good end
　　For lawful policy remains enacted.[9]
530　The poisonous simple° sometime is compacted°　　　*ingredient / mixed*
　　　　In a pure° compound; being so applied,　　　　　　　　*benign*
　　　　His venom in effect is purified.

"Then for thy husband and thy children's sake
　　Tender my suit;° bequeath not to their lot　　　　　　*Regard my plea*
535　The shame that from them no device[1] can take,
　　The blemish that will never be forgot,
　　Worse than a slavish wipe or birth-hour's blot.[2]
　　　　For marks descried in men's nativity
　　　　Are nature's faults, not their own infamy."

540　Here with a cockatrice'[3] dead-killing eye,
　　He rouseth up himself, and makes a pause,
　　While she, the picture of pure piety,
　　Like a white hind° under the gripe's° sharp claws,　　　*doe / griffin's*
　　Pleads in a wilderness where are no laws
545　　　To the rough beast that knows no gentle right,°　*law of gentility*
　　　　Nor aught° obeys but his foul appetite.　　　　　　　　*anything*

But when a black-faced cloud the world doth threat,
　　In his dim mist th'aspiring mountains hiding,
　　From earth's dark womb some gentle gust doth get,
550　Which blow these pitchy vapors from their biding,°　　*place*
　　Hind'ring their present° fall by this dividing,　　　　*immediate*
　　　　So his unhallowed haste her words delays,
　　　　And moody Pluto winks while Orpheus plays.[4]

Yet, foul night-waking cat, he doth but dally
555　While in his holdfast foot the weak mouse panteth;
　　Her sad behavior feeds his vulture folly,°　　　　　*ravenous insanity*
　　A swallowing gulf° that even in plenty wanteth.　　*whirlpool; belly*

7. *To kill . . . decay:* To destroy your reputation along with your life.
8. *Thy . . . bastardy:* Your children suspected of being bastards whose father's name is unknown.
9. *For . . . enacted:* Is allowed as proper statesmanship.
1. Ingenuity; heraldic emblem.
2. A slave's brand or birthmark.
3. Legendary monster whose glance was deadly.
4. When Orpheus, a legendary musician and poet, attempted to regain his dead wife from the underworld, he charmed Pluto, god of the underworld, by playing on the lyre.

His ear her prayers admits, but his heart granteth
    No penetrable entrance to her plaining:°   *lament*
560   Tears harden lust, though marble wear with raining.

Her pity-pleading eyes are sadly fixed
In the remorseless wrinkles of his face.
Her modest eloquence with sighs is mixed,
Which to her oratory adds more grace.
565 She puts the period often from his° place,   *its*
    And midst the sentence so her accent breaks,
    That twice she doth begin ere once she speaks.

She conjures him by high almighty Jove,
By knighthood, gentry,° and sweet friendship's oath,   *noble birth*
570 By her untimely tears, her husband's love,
By holy human law, and common troth,[5]
By heaven and earth and all the power of both,
    That to his borrowed° bed he make retire,   *(guest)*
    And stoop[6] to honor, not to foul desire.

575 Quoth she, "Reward not hospitality
With such black payment as thou hast pretended;°   *offered*
Mud not the fountain that gave drink to thee;
Mar not the thing that cannot be amended;
End thy ill aim before thy shoot be ended.
580   He is no woodman° that doth bend his bow   *sportsman*
    To strike a poor unseasonable° doe.   *out-of-season*

"My husband is thy friend; for his sake spare me.
Thyself art mighty; for thine own sake leave me.
Myself a weakling; do not then ensnare me.
585 Thou look'st not like deceit; do not deceive me.
My sighs like whirlwinds labor hence to heave thee.
    If ever man were moved with woman's moans,
    Be movèd with my tears, my sighs, my groans.

"All which together, like a troubled ocean,
590 Beat at thy rocky and wreck-threat'ning heart
To soften it with their continual motion,
For stones dissolved to water do convert.
Oh, if no harder than a stone thou art,
    Melt at my tears and be compassionate:
595   Soft pity enters at an iron gate.

"In Tarquin's likeness I did entertain thee.
Hast thou put on his shape to do him shame?
To all the host of heaven I complain me.
Thou wrong'st his honor, wound'st his princely name.
600 Thou art not what thou seem'st, and if the same,
    Thou seem'st not what thou art, a god, a king:
    For kings like gods should govern everything.

---

5. *common troth:* the good faith that binds commu-   6. Swoop down to a lure (in falconry); lie down; sub-
nities together.   ject himself.

"How will thy shame be seeded° in thine age   *ripened*
When thus thy vices bud before thy spring?
605 If in thy hope° thou dar'st do such outrage,   *If not yet in power*
What dar'st thou not when once thou art a king?
Oh, be remembered, no outrageous thing
     From vassal actors° can be wiped away: *lowborn criminals*
     Then kings' misdeeds cannot be hid in clay.°   *(even after death)*

610 "This deed will make thee only loved for° fear;   *obeyed out of*
But happy monarchs still° are feared for love.   *always*
With foul offenders thou perforce must bear,
When they in thee the like offenses prove;
If but for fear of this, thy will remove.
615   For princes are the glass,° the school, the book,   *mirror*
     Where subjects' eyes do learn, do read, do look.

"And wilt thou be the school where lust shall learn?
Must he in thee read lectures of such shame?
Wilt thou be glass wherein it shall discern
620 Authority for sin, warrant for blame,
To privilege° dishonor in thy name?   *justify*
     Thou back'st° reproach against long-living laud,°   *support / praise*
     And mak'st fair reputation but a bawd.

"Hast thou command?° By him° that gave it thee,   *authority / (God)*
625 From a pure heart command thy rebel will.
Draw not thy sword to guard iniquity,
For it was lent thee all that brood° to kill.   *kind of thing*
Thy princely office how canst thou fulfill
     When, patterned° by thy fault, foul Sin may say *given a precedent*
630   He learned to sin, and thou didst teach the way?

"Think but how vile a spectacle it were
To view thy present trespass in another.
Men's faults do seldom to themselves appear;
Their own transgressions partially they smother.° *hide (from themselves)*
635 This guilt would seem death-worthy in thy brother.
     Oh, how are they wrapped in with infamies,
     That from their own misdeeds askance° their eyes!   *turn away*

"To thee, to thee, my heaved-up hands appeal,
Not to seducing lust, thy rash relier.[7]
640 I sue for exiled majesty's repeal;°   *recall from exile*
Let him return, and flatt'ring thoughts retire.
His true respect° will prison false desire,   *judgment*
     And wipe the dim mist from thy doting eyne,°   *eyes (archaic)*
     That thou shalt see thy state, and pity mine."

645 "Have done," quoth he; "my uncontrollèd tide
Turns not, but swells the higher by this let.°   *restraint*
Small lights are soon blown out; huge fires abide,

---

7. *thy rash relier:* on which you rashly rely. TEXTUAL COMMENT Since the word "relier" had never been used before and Shakespeare did not use it again, some people have believed that there is a misprint here; but most modern editors retain the First Quarto reading. For a fuller discussion of the textual problem, see Digital Edition TC 6.

And with the wind in greater fury fret.
The petty streams, that pay a daily debt
650   To their salt sovereign,° with their fresh falls' haste   *(the sea)*
    Add to his flow, but alter not his taste."

"Thou art," quoth she, "a sea, a sovereign king,
And lo, there falls into thy boundless flood
Black lust, dishonor, shame, misgoverning,
655 Who seek to stain the ocean of thy blood.°   *disposition; birthright*
If all these petty ills shall change thy good,
    Thy sea within a puddle's womb is hearsed,°   *enclosed*
    And not the puddle in thy sea dispersed.

"So shall these slaves° be king, and thou their slave;   *(lust, dishonor, etc.)*
660 Thou nobly base, they basely dignified;
Thou their fair life, and they thy fouler grave;
Thou loathèd in their shame, they in thy pride.
The lesser thing should not the greater hide:
    The cedar stoops not to the base shrub's foot,
665   But low shrubs wither at the cedar's root.

"So let thy thoughts, low vassals to thy state—"
"No more," quoth he. "By heaven, I will not hear thee.
Yield to my love. If not, enforcèd hate
Instead of love's coy° touch shall rudely tear thee.   *gentle*
670 That done, despitefully° I mean to bear thee   *maliciously*
    Unto the base bed of some rascal groom°   *servant*
    To be thy partner in this shameful doom."

This said, he sets his foot upon the light,
For light and lust are deadly enemies.
675 Shame folded up in blind concealing night,
When most unseen, then most doth tyrannize.
The wolf hath seized his prey, the poor lamb cries,
    Till with her own white fleece° her voice controlled,°   *(bedclothes) / overpowered*
    Entombs her outcry in her lips' sweet fold.°   *crevice; sheep pen*

680 For with the nightly linen that she wears
He pens her piteous clamors in her head,
Cooling his hot face in the chastest tears
That ever modest eyes with sorrow shed.
Oh, that prone° lust should stain so pure a bed![8]   *eager; face-down*
685   The spots whereof could weeping purify,°   *if weeping could purify*
    Her tears should drop on them perpetually.

But she hath lost a dearer thing than life,
And he hath won what he would lose again.
This forcèd league° doth force a further strife;   *joining together*
690 This momentary joy breeds months of pain;
This hot desire converts to cold disdain:

---

8. **Textual Comment** The Fourth Quarto (1600) emended "prone" to "proud," and the Sixth (1616) emended it to "fowle," but modern editors accept the original reading. For discussion of these choices, see Digital Edition TC 7.

Pure chastity is rifled of her store,
And lust, the thief, far poorer than before.

Look° as the full-fed hound or gorgèd hawk,   *Just*
695 Unapt for tender° smell or speedy flight,   *delicate*
Make slow pursuit, or altogether balk°   *turn from*
The prey wherein by nature they delight,
So surfeit-taking Tarquin fares° this night: *behaves; feeds*
        His taste delicious, in digestion souring,
700   Devours his will that lived by foul devouring.

Oh, deeper sin than bottomless conceit°   *unlimited fantasy*
Can comprehend in still imagination!
Drunken desire must vomit his receipt°   *what he swallowed*
Ere he can see his own abomination.
705 While lust is in his pride, no exclamation
        Can curb his heat or rein his rash desire,
        Till like a jade° self-will himself doth tire.   *recalcitrant horse*

And then with lank and lean discolored cheek,
With heavy eye, knit brow, and strengthless pace,
710 Feeble desire all recreant,[9] poor, and meek,
Like to a bankrupt beggar wails his case.
The flesh being proud, desire doth fight with grace,
        For there it revels, and when that decays,°   *subsides*
        The guilty rebel for remission° prays.   *pardon*

715 So fares it with this faultful lord of Rome,
Who this accomplishment so hotly chased,
For now against himself he sounds° this doom,°   *pronounces / sentence*
That through the length of times he stands disgraced.
Besides, his soul's fair temple is defaced,
720   To whose weak ruins muster troops of cares,
        To ask the spotted princess° how she fares.   *(the defiled soul)*

She says her subjects with foul insurrection
Have battered down her consecrated wall,
And by their mortal° fault brought in subjection   *deadly*
725 Her immortality, and made her thrall
To living death and pain perpetual,
        Which° in her prescience she controllèd still,   *(the soul's subjects)*
        But her foresight could not forestall their will.

E'en in this thought through the dark night he stealeth,
730 A captive victor that hath lost in gain;
Bearing away the wound that nothing healeth,
The scar that will, despite of cure, remain,
Leaving his spoil° perplexed in greater pain.   *prey*
        She bears the load of lust he left behind,
735   And he the burden of a guilty mind.

He like a thievish dog creeps sadly thence;
She like a wearied lamb lies panting there.

9. Cowardly; faithless; exhausted.

He scowls and hates himself for his offense;
She, desperate, with her nails her flesh doth tear.
740 He faintly flies, sweating with guilty fear;
   She stays, exclaiming on° the direful night.   *denouncing*
   He runs and chides his vanished loathed delight.

He thence departs, a heavy convertite;°   *sad penitent*
She there remains, a hopeless castaway.
745 He in his speed looks for the morning light;
She prays she never may behold the day.
"For day," quoth she, "night's scapes° doth open lay,   *sins*
   And my true eyes have never practiced how
   To cloak offenses with a cunning brow.

750 "They think not but that° every eye can see   *only think*
The same disgrace which they themselves behold;
And therefore would they still in darkness be,
To have their unseen sin remain untold.
For they their guilt with weeping will unfold
755   And grave,° like water that doth eat in steel,[1]   *engrave*
   Upon my cheeks what helpless shame I feel."

Here she exclaims against repose and rest,
And bids her eyes hereafter still° be blind.   *always*
She wakes her heart by beating on her breast,
760 And bids it leap from thence where it may find
Some purer chest to close° so pure a mind.   *enclose*
   Frantic with grief, thus breathes she forth her spite°   *reproach*
   Against the unseen secrecy of night:

"O comfort-killing Night, image of hell,
765 Dim register° and notary of shame,   *recorder*
Black stage for tragedies and murders fell,
Vast sin-concealing chaos, nurse of blame!
Blind muffled bawd, dark harbor for defame,°   *infamy*
   Grim cave of death, whisp'ring conspirator,
770   With close-tongued treason and the ravisher!

"O hateful, vaporous, and foggy Night!
Since thou art guilty of my cureless crime,
Muster thy mists to meet the eastern light;
Make war against proportioned° course of time;   *orderly*
775 Or if thou wilt permit the sun to climb
   His wonted height, yet ere he go to bed,
   Knit poisonous clouds about his golden head.

"With rotten damps° ravish the morning air;   *vapors*
Let their exhaled unwholesome breaths make sick
780 The life of purity, the supreme fair,°   *(the sun)*
Ere he arrive his weary noontide prick;°   *mark on a clock*
And let thy musty vapors march so thick

---

1. *water . . . steel:* aqua fortis (literally, "strong water"), nitric acid.

That in their smoky ranks his smothered light
May set at noon and make perpetual night.

785 "Were Tarquin Night, as he is but Night's child,
The silver-shining queen[2] he would distain;°   *stain*
Her twinkling handmaids° too—by him defiled—   *(the stars)*
Through Night's black bosom should not peep again.
So should I have copartners in my pain,
790   And fellowship in woe doth woe assuage,
      As palmers'° chat makes short their pilgrimage.   *pilgrims'*

"Where now I have no one to blush with me,
To cross their arms[3] and hang their heads with mine,
To mask their brows and hide their infamy;
795 But I alone, alone must sit and pine,
Seasoning the earth with showers of silver brine,
      Mingling my talk with tears, my grief with groans,
      Poor wasting monuments° of lasting moans.   *short-lived tokens*

"O Night, thou furnace of foul-reeking smoke!
800 Let not the jealous° day behold that face,   *suspicious*
Which underneath thy black all-hiding cloak
Immodestly lies martyred with disgrace.
Keep still possession of thy gloomy place,
      That all the faults which in thy reign are made
805   May likewise be sepulchered° in thy shade.   *entombed*

"Make me not object° to the telltale day;   *manifest*
The light will show charactered° in my brow   *written*
The story of sweet chastity's decay,
The impious breach of holy wedlock vow.
810 Yea, the illiterate, that know not how
      To cipher° what is writ in learnèd books,   *decipher*
      Will quote° my loathsome trespass in my looks.   *note*

"The nurse to still her child will tell my story,
And fright her crying babe with Tarquin's name.
815 The orator to deck his oratory
Will couple my reproach to Tarquin's shame.
Feast-finding minstrels,[4] tuning my defame,
      Will tie the hearers to attend° each line,   *listen to*
      How Tarquin wrongèd me, I Collatine.

820 "Let my good name, that senseless° reputation,   *intangible*
For Collatine's dear love be kept unspotted.
If that be made a theme for disputation,
The branches of another root are rotted,[5]
And undeserved reproach to him allotted,
825   That is as clear from this attaint° of mine   *stain*
      As I ere this was pure to Collatine.

---

2. The moon, symbol of chastity.   4. Minstrels were paid to perform at banquets.
3. This is a conventional gesture of melancholy.   5. That is, Collatine's reputation is also destroyed.

"Oh, unseen shame, invisible disgrace!
Oh, unfelt sore, crest-wounding[6] private scar!
Reproach° is stamped in Collatinus' face,   *Reproof; dishonor*
830   And Tarquin's eye may read the mot° afar,   *motto*
How he in peace is wounded, not in war.
          Alas, how many bear such shameful blows,
          Which not themselves but he that gives them knows.

"If, Collatine, thine honor lay in me,
835   From me by strong assault it is bereft;
My honey lost, and I, a drone-like bee,
Have no perfection of my summer left,[7]
But robbed and ransacked by injurious theft.
          In thy weak hive a wandering wasp hath crept,
840   And sucked the honey which thy chaste bee kept.

"Yet am I guilty of thy honor's wrack;°   *ruin*
Yet for thy honor did I entertain him.
Coming from thee I could not put him back,
For it had been dishonor to disdain him.
845   Besides, of weariness he did complain him,
          And talked of virtue—oh, unlooked-for evil,
          When virtue is profaned in such a devil!

"Why should the worm intrude the maiden bud,
Or hateful cuckoos hatch in sparrows' nests,
850   Or toads infect fair founts with venom° mud,   *venomous*
Or tyrant folly° lurk in gentle breasts,   *cruel lewdness*
Or kings be breakers of their own behests?°   *commands*
          But no perfection is so absolute
          That some impurity doth not pollute.

855   "The agèd man that coffers up his gold
Is plagued with cramps and gouts and painful fits,
And scarce hath eyes his treasure to behold;
But like still-pining Tantalus[8] he sits,
And useless barns° the harvest of his wits,   *hoards*
860   Having no other pleasure of his gain,
          But torment that it cannot cure his pain.

"So then he hath it when he cannot use it,
And leaves it to be mastered° by his young,°   *possessed / children*
Who in their pride do presently° abuse it.   *immediately*
865   Their father was too weak and they too strong
To hold their cursèd-blessèd fortune long.
          The sweets we wish for turn to loathèd sours,
          Even in the moment that we call them ours.

"Unruly blasts wait on the tender spring;
870   Unwholesome weeds take root with precious flowers;

---

6. Damaging the coat of arms, hence family honor (cf. lines 204–10).
7. *Have . . . left:* Have nothing left of what I made in the summer; have none of the purity of my prime

remaining.
8. A mythological figure who was punished in Hades by eternal hunger and thirst; food and water were always visible but receded at his approach.

The adder hisses where the sweet birds sing:
What virtue breeds, iniquity devours.
We have no good that we can say is ours,
      But ill-annexèd Opportunity[9]
875   Or° kills his life or else his quality.   *Either*

"O Opportunity, thy guilt is great!
'Tis thou that execut'st the traitor's treason;
Thou sets the wolf where he the lamb may get;
Whoever plots the sin, thou point'st° the season.   *appoint*
880 'Tis thou that spurn'st at° right, at law, at reason;   *rejects*
      And in thy shady cell, where none may spy him,
      Sits Sin to seize the souls that wander by him.

"Thou makest the vestal[1] violate her oath;
Thou blowest the fire when temperance is thawed;
885 Thou smotherest honesty, thou murd'rest troth,
Thou foul abettor, thou notorious bawd;°   *pimp*
Thou plantest scandal and displacest laud.°   *praise*
      Thou ravisher, thou traitor, thou false thief,
      Thy honey turns to gall, thy joy to grief.

890 "Thy secret pleasure turns to open shame;
Thy private feasting to a public fast,
Thy smoothing° titles to a ragged name,   *flattering*
Thy sugared tongue to bitter wormwood taste;
Thy violent vanities can never last.
895   How comes it then, vile Opportunity,
      Being so bad, such numbers seek for thee?

"When wilt thou be the humble suppliant's friend,
And bring him where his suit may be obtained?
When wilt thou sort° an hour great strifes to end,   *select*
900 Or free that soul which wretchedness hath chained?
Give physic° to the sick, ease to the pained?   *medicine*
      The poor, lame, blind, halt,° creep, cry out for thee,   *limp*
      But they ne'er meet with Opportunity.

"The patient dies while the physician sleeps;
905 The orphan pines while the oppressor feeds;
Justice is feasting while the widow weeps;
Advice° is sporting while infection breeds.   *(medical advice)*
Thou grant'st no time for charitable deeds:
      Wrath, envy, treason, rape, and murder's rages,
910   Thy heinous hours wait on them as their pages.

"When Truth and Virtue have to do with thee,
A thousand crosses° keep them from thy aid.   *impediments*
They buy° thy help, but Sin ne'er gives a fee;   *(must pay for)*
He gratis comes, and thou art well apaid°   *satisfied*
915 As well to hear as grant what he hath said.

9. *ill-annexèd Opportunity:* bad circumstances joined to or following from the good.
1. The priestess of Vesta, Roman goddess of the hearth and household; vestals were sworn to lifelong virginity.

My Collatine would else have come to me
When Tarquin did, but he was stayed by thee.

"Guilty thou art of murder and of theft,
Guilty of perjury and subornation,[2]
920 Guilty of treason, forgery, and shift,°   *fraud*
Guilty of incest, that abomination:
An accessory by thine inclination°   *nature*
      To all sins past and all that are to come,
      From the creation to the general doom.°   *Judgment Day*

925 "Misshapen Time, copesmate° of ugly Night,   *comrade*
Swift subtle post,° carrier of grisly care,   *messenger*
Eater of youth, false slave to false delight,
Base watch° of woes, sin's packhorse, virtue's snare,   *town crier; announcer*
Thou nursest all, and murd'rest all that are.
930   Oh, hear me then, injurious shifting° Time: *changing; traitorous*
      Be guilty of my death, since° of my crime.   *as you are*

"Why hath thy servant Opportunity
Betrayed the hours thou gav'st me to repose,
Canceled my fortunes, and enchainèd me
935 To endless date° of never-ending woes?   *duration*
Time's office is to fine° the hate of foes,   *end; punish*
      To eat up errors by opinion° bred,   *rumor*
      Not spend the dowry of a lawful bed.

"Time's glory is to calm contending kings,
940 To unmask falsehood and bring truth to light,
To stamp the seal of time in agèd things,
To wake the morn and sentinel° the night,   *guard*
To wrong the wronger till he render right,
      To ruinate proud buildings with thy hours,
945   And smear with dust their glitt'ring golden towers;

"To fill with wormholes stately monuments,
To feed oblivion with decay of things,
To blot old books and alter their contents,
To pluck the quills from ancient ravens' wings,
950 To dry the old oak's sap and cherish springs,[3]
      To spoil antiquities of hammered steel,
      And turn the giddy round of Fortune's wheel;

"To show the beldam° daughters of her daughter,   *old woman*
To make the child a man, the man a child,
955 To slay the tiger that doth live by slaughter,
To tame the unicorn and lion wild,
To mock the subtle in themselves beguiled,[4]
      To cheer the plowman with increaseful crops,
      And waste huge stones with little water drops.

2. Bribing others to give false testimony.
3. Textual Comment The phrase "cherish springs," meaning "nourish the shoots of trees," has sometimes been emended, but the contrast with "dry the old oak's sap" is consistent with the double focus, in the following lines, on Time as both a destroyer and a nurturer. For a fuller discussion, see Digital Edition TC 8.
4. *the subtle . . . beguiled:* the cunning, taken in by their own schemes.

960   "Why work'st thou mischief in thy pilgrimage,
     Unless thou couldst return to make amends?
     One poor retiring⁵ minute in an age
     Would purchase thee a thousand thousand friends,
     Lending him wit that to bad debtors lends.
965   Oh, this dread night, wouldst thou one hour come back,
         I could prevent this storm, and shun thy wrack!

     "Thou ceaseless lackey° to eternity,   *eternal servant*
     With some mischance cross Tarquin in his flight.
     Devise extremes beyond extremity
970   To make him curse this cursèd crimeful night.
     Let ghastly shadows his lewd eyes affright,
         And the dire thought of his committed evil
         Shape every bush a hideous shapeless devil.

     "Disturb his hours of rest with restless trances;°   *dreams; seizures*
975   Afflict him in his bed with bedrid° groans;   *bedridden*
     Let there bechance him pitiful mischances
     To make him moan, but pity not his moans.
     Stone him with hardened hearts harder than stones,
         And let mild women to him lose their mildness,
980   Wilder to him than tigers in their wildness.

     "Let him have time to tear his curlèd hair,
     Let him have time against himself to rave,
     Let him have time of Time's help to despair,
     Let him have time to live a loathèd slave,
985   Let him have time a beggar's orts° to crave,   *scraps*
         And time to see one that by alms doth live
         Disdain to him disdainèd scraps to give.

     "Let him have time to see his friends his foes,
     And merry fools to mock at him resort;°   *gather*
990   Let him have time to mark how slow time goes
     In time of sorrow, and how swift and short
     His time of folly and his time of sport;
         And ever let his unrecalling crime⁶
         Have time to wail th'abusing of his time.

995   "O Time, thou tutor both to good and bad,
     Teach me to curse him that thou taught'st this ill;
     At his own shadow let the thief run mad,
     Himself himself seek every hour to kill;
     Such wretched hands such wretched blood should spill.
1000   For who so base would such an office have
         As sland'rous deathsman° to so base a slave?   *detested executioner*

     "The baser is he, coming from a king,
     To shame his hope with deeds degenerate.
     The mightier man, the mightier is the thing
1005 That makes him honored or begets him hate,

5. Returning (thus permitting people to do things   6. Crime that cannot be undone.
differently).

For greatest scandal waits on greatest state.[7]
      The moon being clouded presently° is missed,   *immediately*
      But little stars may hide them when they list.°   *wish*

     "The crow may bathe his coal-black wings in mire,
1010 And unperceived fly with the filth away;
     But if the like the snow-white swan desire,
     The stain upon his silver down will stay.
     Poor grooms° are sightless° night, kings glorious day;   *servants / dark*
        Gnats are unnoted wheresoe'er they fly,
1015   But eagles gazed upon with every eye.

     "Out, idle words, servants to shallow fools,
     Unprofitable sounds, weak arbitrators!
     Busy your selves in skill-contending schools;°   *(of rhetoric)*
     Debate where leisure serves with dull debaters;
1020 To trembling clients be you mediators.
        For me, I force° not argument a straw,   *value*
        Since that my case is past the help of law.

     "In vain I rail at Opportunity,
     At Time, at Tarquin, and uncheerful Night;
1025 In vain I cavil with° mine infamy;   *object to*
     In vain I spurn at my confirmed despite.°   *irreparable injury*
     This helpless° smoke of words doth me no right.   *unhelpful; weak*
        The remedy indeed to do me good
        Is to let forth my foul defilèd blood.

1030 "Poor hand, why quiver'st thou at this decree?
     Honor thyself to rid me of this shame.
     For if I die, my honor lives in thee;
     But if I live, thou liv'st in my defame.°   *infamy*
     Since thou couldst not defend thy loyal dame,
1035   And wast afeard to scratch her wicked foe,
        Kill both thyself and her for yielding so."

     This said, from her betumbled couch she starteth,
     To find some desp'rate instrument of death.
     But this, no slaughterhouse, no tool imparteth°   *furnishes*
1040 To make more vent° for passage of her breath,   *a bigger hole*
     Which thronging through her lips so vanisheth
        As smoke from Etna° that in air consumes,   *(a volcanic mountain)*
        Or that which from dischargèd cannon fumes.

     "In vain," quoth she, "I live, and seek in vain
1045 Some happy mean to end a hapless life.
     I feared by Tarquin's falchion to be slain,
     Yet for the selfsame purpose seek a knife.
     But when I feared, I was a loyal wife;
        So am I now—oh, no, that cannot be:
1050   Of that true type° hath Tarquin rifled me.   *pattern of virtue*

---

7. *waits on greatest state:* attends those of highest rank.

"Oh, that is gone for which I sought to live,
And therefore now I need not fear to die.
To clear this spot by death, at least I give
A badge of fame to slander's livery,°   *servant's uniform*
1055   A dying life to living infamy.
      Poor helpless help, the treasure stol'n away,
      To burn the guiltless casket where it lay.

"Well, well, dear Collatine, thou shalt not know
The stainèd taste of violated troth.
1060   I will not wrong thy true affection so,
To flatter thee with an infringèd oath.
This bastard graft[8] shall never come to growth:
      He shall not boast who did thy stock pollute
      That thou art doting father of his fruit.

1065   "Nor shall he smile at thee in secret thought,
Nor laugh with his companions at thy state.
But thou shalt know thy int'rest° was not bought   *property*
Basely with gold, but stol'n from forth thy gate.
For me, I am the mistress of my fate,
1070   And with my trespass never will dispense°   *dispense with = excuse*
      Till life to death acquit° my forced offense.   *atone for*

"I will not poison thee with my attaint,°   *contamination*
Nor fold° my fault in cleanly coined excuses.   *envelop*
My sable ground[9] of sin I will not paint
1075   To hide the truth of this false night's abuses.
My tongue shall utter all; mine eyes, like sluices,
      As from a mountain spring that feeds a dale,
      Shall gush pure streams to purge my impure tale."

By this, lamenting Philomel[1] had ended
1080   The well-tuned warble of her nightly sorrow,
And solemn night with slow sad gait descended
To ugly hell, when lo, the blushing morrow
Lends light to all fair eyes that light will borrow.
      But cloudy° Lucrece shames° herself to see,   *melancholy / is ashamed*
1085   And therefore still in night would cloistered be.

Revealing day through every cranny spies,
And seems to point her out where she sits weeping,
To whom she sobbing speaks, "O eye of eyes,
Why pry'st thou through my window? Leave thy peeping;
1090   Mock with thy tickling beams eyes that are sleeping;
      Brand not my forehead with thy piercing light,
      For day hath naught to do° what's done by night."   *nothing to do with*

Thus cavils she with everything she sees:
True grief is fond° and testy as a child   *foolish*

---

8. Lucrece assumes that Tarquin has made her pregnant. Her image is from the grafting of plants, in which two different kinds of plants are artificially forced to grow as one; a "bastard slip" is an unwanted shoot.

9. Black background (a heraldic term).
1. The nightingale. In classical mythology, Philomel was raped by King Tereus, her sister's husband, and with her sister took vengeance on him. All three were changed into birds (see Ovid, *Metamorphoses* 6).

1095 Who, wayward once,° his mood with naught agrees.   *once out of sorts*
Old woes, not infant sorrows, bear them mild:°   *bear themselves mildly*
Continuance tames the one; the other wild,
    Like an unpracticed swimmer plunging still°   *constantly*
    With too much labor drowns for want of skill.

1100 So she, deep drenchèd in a sea of care,
Holds disputation with each thing she views,
And to herself all sorrow doth compare.
No object but her passion's strength renews,
And as one shifts,° another straight° ensues.   *moves / immediately*
1105   Sometime her grief is dumb° and hath no words;   *mute*
    Sometime 'tis mad and too much talk affords.

The little birds that tune their morning's joy
Make her moans mad with their sweet melody,
For mirth doth search° the bottom of annoy;°   *probe / vexation*
1110 Sad souls are slain° in merry company;   *overcome with distress*
Grief best is pleased with grief's society:
    True sorrow then is feelingly sufficed°   *properly contented*
    When with like semblance it is sympathized.°   *matched*

'Tis double death to drown in ken° of shore;   *sight*
1115 He ten times pines° that pines beholding food;   *starves*
To see the salve doth make the wound ache more;
Great grief grieves most at that would do it good;
Deep woes roll forward like a gentle flood
    Who, being stopped, the bounding° banks o'erflows: *confining*
1120   Grief dallied° with nor° law nor limit knows.   *trifled / neither*

"You mocking birds," quoth she, "your tunes entomb
Within your hollow-swelling feathered breasts,
And in my hearing be you mute and dumb:
My restless discord loves no stops nor rests;
1125 A woeful hostess brooks° not merry guests.   *tolerates*
    Relish° your nimble notes to pleasing ears;   *Warble; make pleasing*
    Distress likes dumps° when time is kept with tears.   *sad songs*

"Come, Philomel, that sing'st of ravishment:
Make thy sad grove in my disheveled hair.
1130 As the dank earth weeps at thy languishment,°   *lamentation*
So I at each sad strain will strain a tear,
And with deep groans the diapason° bear: *harmony*
    For burden-wise,[2] I'll hum on Tarquin still,
    While thou on Tereus descants better skill.[3]

1135 "And whiles against a thorn[4] thou bear'st thy part,
To keep thy sharp woes waking, wretched I,
To imitate thee well, against my heart
Will fix a sharp knife to affright mine eye,
Who° if it wink° shall thereon fall and die.   *(I) / (my eye) close*

---

2. Like a bass line; playing on "burden" as sorrow, weight.
3. Sing the treble part more skillfully.
4. The nightingale was imagined to press against a thorn to keep itself awake during the night.

1140   These means, as frets° upon an instrument,   *(punning on "vexation")*
        Shall tune our heartstrings to true languishment.

        "And for,° poor bird, thou sing'st not in the day,   *because*
        As shaming any eye should thee behold,
        Some dark deep desert seated from the way,[5]
1145   That knows not parching heat nor freezing cold,
        Will we find out, and there we will unfold
            To creatures stern sad tunes to change their kinds:°   *natures*
            Since men prove beasts, let beasts bear gentle minds."

        As the poor frighted deer that stands at gaze,
1150   Wildly determining which way to fly,
        Or one encompassed with a winding maze
        That cannot tread the way out readily,
        So with herself is she in mutiny,
            To live or die which of the twain were better
1155   When life is shamed and death reproach's debtor.°   *will incur reproach*

        "To kill myself," quoth she, "alack, what were it,
        But with my body my poor soul's pollution?[6]
        They that lose half with greater patience bear it
        Than they whose whole is swallowed in confusion.°   *ruin*
1160   That mother tries a merciless conclusion°   *experiment*
            Who, having two sweet babes, when death takes one
            Will slay the other, and be nurse to none.

        "My body or my soul, which was the dearer
        When the one pure, the other made divine?
1165   Whose love of either to myself was nearer
        When both were kept for heaven and Collatine?   *peeled*
        Ay me, the bark pilled° from the lofty pine,
            His leaves will wither and his sap decay:
            So must my soul, her bark being pilled away.

1170   "Her house is sacked, her quiet interrupted,
        Her mansion battered by the enemy,
        Her sacred temple spotted, spoiled, corrupted,
        Grossly engirt with daring° infamy.   *unrestrained*
        Then let it not be called impiety,
1175   If in this blemished fort° I make some hole,   *(my body)*
            Through which I may convey° this troubled soul.   *steal away*

        "Yet die I will not till my Collatine
        Have heard the cause of my untimely death,
        That he may vow in that sad hour of mine
1180   Revenge on him that made me stop my breath.
        My stainèd blood to Tarquin I'll bequeath,
            Which by him tainted shall for him be spent,
            And as his due writ° in my testament.°   *written / last will*

---

5. *Some . . . way:* Some uninhabited place located far from the road.

6. *with . . . pollution:* to pollute my poor soul, as my body has already been polluted.

"My honor I'll bequeath unto the knife
1185 That wounds my body so dishonorèd.
'Tis honor to deprive° dishonored life;   *take away*
The one° will live, the other° being dead.   *(honor) / (life)*
So of shame's ashes shall my fame be bred,[7]
          For in my death I murder shameful scorn;
1190   My shame so dead, mine honor is new born.

"Dear lord of that dear jewel° I have lost,   *(chastity)*
What legacy shall I bequeath to thee?
My resolution, love, shall be thy boast,
By whose example thou revenged mayst be.
1195 How Tarquin must be used, read it in me:
          Myself, thy friend, will kill myself, thy foe,
          And for my sake serve° thou false Tarquin so.   *treat*

"This brief abridgement of my will I make:
My soul and body to the skies and ground.
1200 My resolution, husband, do thou take;
Mine honor be the knife's that makes my wound;
My shame be his that did my fame confound,
          And all my fame that lives disbursèd be°   *that remains be paid out*
          To those that live and think no shame of me.

1205 "Thou, Collatine, shalt oversee° this will.   *execute*
How was I overseen° that thou shalt see it?   *deluded*
My blood shall wash the slander of mine ill;
My life's foul deed my life's fair end shall free it.
Faint not, faint heart, but stoutly say, 'So be it.'
1210   Yield to my hand; my hand shall conquer thee:
          Thou dead, both die, and both shall victors be."

This plot of death when sadly she had laid
And wiped the brinish° pearl from her bright eyes,   *salty*
With untuned° tongue she hoarsely calls her maid,   *inharmonious*
1215 Whose swift obedience to her mistress hies,°   *hastens*
For fleet-winged duty with thought's feathers flies.
          Poor Lucrece' cheeks unto her maid seem so
          As winter meads° when sun doth melt their snow.   *meadows*

Her mistress she doth give demure good-morrow,
1220 With soft slow tongue, true mark of modesty,
And sorts° a sad look to her lady's sorrow,   *suits*
For why° her face wore sorrow's livery,°   *Because / attire*
But durst not ask of her audaciously
          Why her two suns° were cloud-eclipsèd so,   *(her eyes)*
1225   Nor why her fair cheeks over-washed with woe.

But as the earth doth weep, the sun being set,
Each flower moistened like a melting eye:
Even so the maid with swelling drops gan° wet   *began to*

7. *So . . . bred:* My honor will be like the mythological phoenix, consumed in fire only to be reborn from the ashes.

Her circled° eyne, enforced° by sympathy   *rounded / compelled*
1230 Of those fair suns set in her mistress' sky,
    Who in a salt-waved ocean quench their light,
    Which makes the maid weep like the dewy night.

A pretty while° these pretty creatures stand,   *fair amount of time*
Like ivory conduits coral cisterns filling:
1235 One justly weeps, the other takes in hand°   *acknowledges*
No cause but company of her drops spilling.
Their gentle sex to weep are often willing,
    Grieving themselves to guess at° others' smarts,° *conjecture / pains*
    And then they drown their eyes or break their hearts.

1240 For men have marble, women waxen minds,
And therefore are they formed as marble will.
The weak oppressed, th'impression of strange kinds°   *alien natures*
Is formed in them by force, by fraud, or skill.
Then call them not the authors of their ill,
1245   No more than wax shall be accounted evil
    Wherein is stamped the semblance of a devil.

Their smoothness, like a goodly champaign plain,°   *open field*
Lays open° all the little worms that creep;   *Reveals*
In men, as in a rough-grown grove, remain
1250 Cave-keeping° evils that obscurely° sleep.   *Concealed / unseen*
Through crystal walls each little mote° will peep.   *speck*
    Though men can cover crimes with bold stern looks,
    Poor women's faces are their own faults' books.

No man° inveigh against the withered flower,   *Let no man*
1255 But chide rough winter that the flower hath killed;
Not that devoured, but that which doth devour,
Is worthy blame. Oh, let it not be held
Poor women's faults that they are so fulfilled
    With men's abuses: those proud lords, to blame,
1260   Make weak-made women tenants to their shame.

The precedent° whereof in Lucrece view,   *proof*
Assailed by night with circumstances strong
Of present° death, and shame that might ensue   *immediate*
By that her death, to do her husband wrong.
1265 Such danger to resistance did belong
    That dying fear through all her body spread;
    And who cannot abuse a body dead?

By this,° mild patience bid fair Lucrece speak   *this time*
To the poor counterfeit of her complaining.°   *(the weeping maid)*
1270 "My girl," quoth she, "on what occasion break
Those tears from thee that down thy cheeks are raining?
If thou dost weep for grief of my sustaining,°   *borne by me*
    Know, gentle wench, it small avails° my mood: *little helps*
    If tears could help, mine own would do me good.

1275 "But tell me, girl, when went"—and there she stayed
Till after a deep groan—"Tarquin from hence?"

"Madam, ere I was up," replied the maid,
"The more to blame my sluggard negligence.
Yet with the fault I thus far can dispense:°   *excuse*
1280   Myself was stirring ere the break of day,
          And ere I rose was Tarquin gone away.

"But, lady, if your maid may be so bold,
She would request to know your heaviness."°   *sorrow*
"Oh, peace," quoth Lucrece, "if it should be told,
1285   The repetition cannot make it less,
For more it is than I can well express,
          And that deep torture may be called a hell
          When more is felt than one hath power to tell.

"Go get me hither paper, ink, and pen;
1290   Yet save that labor, for I have them here.
What should I say? One of my husband's men
Bid thou be ready by and by to bear
A letter to my lord, my love, my dear.
          Bid him with speed prepare to carry it;
1295   The cause craves° haste, and it will soon be writ."   *requires*

Her maid is gone, and she prepares to write,
First hovering o'er the paper with her quill.
Conceit° and grief an eager combat fight: *Imagination*
What wit° sets down is blotted straight with will.°   *thought / passion*
1300 This is too curious-good,° this blunt and ill: *elaborate*
          Much like a press° of people at a door   *crowd*
          Throng her inventions, which shall go before.°   *first*

At last she thus begins: "Thou worthy lord
Of that unworthy wife that greeteth thee,
1305 Health to thy person! Next, vouchsafe t'afford
(If ever, love, thy Lucrece thou wilt see)
Some present° speed to come and visit me.   *immediate*
          So I commend me,° from our house in grief;   *ask to be remembered*
          My woes are tedious, though my words are brief."

1310 Here folds she up the tenor° of her woe,   *gist*
Her certain sorrow writ uncertainly.
By this short schedule° Collatine may know   *summary*
Her grief, but not her grief's true quality.
She dares not thereof make discovery,°   *revelation*
1315   Lest he should hold it her own gross abuse,°   *trespass*
          Ere she with blood had stained her stained excuse.

Besides, the life and feeling of her passion
She hoards, to spend when he is by to hear her,
When sighs and groans and tears may grace the fashion°   *appearance; fashioning*
1320 Of her disgrace, the better so to clear her
From that suspicion which the world might bear her.
          To shun this blot, she would not blot the letter
          With words, till action might become° them better.   *suit*

To see sad sights moves more than hear them told,
1325 For then the eye interprets to the ear

The heavy motion° that it doth behold,   *sad action*
When every part a part of woe doth bear.
'Tis but a part of sorrow that we hear:
      Deep sounds make lesser noise than shallow fords,
1330   And sorrow ebbs, being blown with wind of words.

Her letter now is sealed, and on it writ
"At Ardea to my lord with more than haste."
The post attends,° and she delivers it,   *messenger waits*
Charging the sour-faced groom to hie as fast
1335 As lagging fowls before the northern blast.
      Speed more than speed° but dull and slow she deems: *Even unusual speed*
      Extremity still urgeth such extremes.

The homely villain° curtsies to her low,   *unpolished menial*
And blushing on her with a steadfast eye
1340 Receives the scroll without or° yea or no,   *either*
And forth with bashful innocence doth hie.
But they whose guilt within their bosoms lie
      Imagine every eye beholds their blame:
      For Lucrece thought he blushed to see her shame,

1345 When, silly groom,° God wot,° it was defect   *simple servant / knows*
Of spirit, life, and bold audacity.
Such harmless creatures have a true respect
To talk in deeds,[8] while others saucily
Promise more speed, but do it leisurely.
1350   Even so, this pattern of the worn-out age°   *old-fashioned model*
      Pawned° honest looks, but laid no words to gage.°   *Offered / as a pledge*

His kindled duty[9] kindled her mistrust,
That two red fires in both their faces blazed.
She thought he blushed as knowing Tarquin's lust,
1355 And blushing with him, wistly° on him gazed.   *attentively*
Her earnest eye did make him more amazed:°   *bewildered*
      The more she saw the blood his cheeks replenish,
      The more she thought he spied in her some blemish.

But long she thinks° till he return again,   *she thinks it long*
1360 And yet the duteous vassal scarce is gone.
The weary time she cannot entertain,°   *while away*
For now 'tis stale to sigh, to weep, and groan.
So woe hath wearied woe, moan tired moan,
      That she her plaints a little while doth stay,
1365   Pausing for means to mourn some newer way.

At last she calls to mind where hangs a piece
Of skillful painting made for° Priam's Troy,   *representing*
Before the which is drawn the power° of Greece,   *army*
For Helen's rape the city to destroy,
1370 Threat'ning cloud-kissing Ilion° with annoy,°   *high-built Troy / injury*

---

8. *have . . . deeds:* rightly express their deference by   9. His blushing bow; his ardent loyalty.
their actions (rather than merely by their words).

Which the conceited° painter drew so proud .... *ingenious*
As heaven (it seemed) to kiss the turrets bowed.

A thousand lamentable objects there,
In scorn of° nature, art gave lifeless life; .... *Defying*
1375 Many a dry drop seemed a weeping tear,
Shed for the slaughtered husband by the wife.
The red blood reeked° to show the painter's strife,[1] .... *smoked*
   And dying eyes gleamed forth their ashy lights,
   Like dying coals burnt out in tedious nights.

1380 There might you see the laboring pioneer° .... *trench digger*
Begrimed with sweat and smearèd all with dust;
And from the tow'rs of Troy there would appear
The very eyes of men through loopholes thrust,
Gazing upon the Greeks with little lust.° .... *pleasure*
1385   Such sweet observance° in this work was had .... *verisimilitude*
   That one might see those far-off eyes look sad.

In great commanders grace and majesty
You might behold, triumphing in their faces;
In youth, quick°-bearing and dexterity; .... *lively*
1390 And here and there the painter interlaces
Pale cowards marching on with trembling paces,
   Which heartless° peasants did so well resemble .... *dejected*
   That one would swear he saw them quake and tremble.

In Ajax and Ulysses, oh, what art
1395 Of physiognomy might one behold!
The face of either ciphered° either's heart; .... *represented*
Their face their manners most expressly told.
In Ajax' eyes blunt° rage and rigor rolled, ... *rude*
   But the mild glance that sly Ulysses lent
1400   Showed deep regard° and smiling government.° ... *judgment / self-control*

There pleading° might you see grave Nestor stand, ... *persuading*
As 'twere encouraging the Greeks to fight,
Making such sober action with his hand
That it beguiled attention, charmed the sight.
1405 In speech it seemed his beard, all silver-white,
   Wagged up and down, and from his lips did fly
   Thin winding breath, which purled° up to the sky. .... *curled*

About him were a press of gaping faces,
Which seemed to swallow up his sound advice,
1410 All jointly list'ning, but with several graces,° .... *various attitudes*
As if some mermaid did their ears entice:
Some high, some low, the painter was so nice.° .... *skillful; subtle*
   The scalps of many, almost hid behind,
   To jump up higher seemed to mock the mind.° .... *(by artistic illusion)*

1415 Here one man's hand leaned on another's head,
His nose being shadowed by his neighbor's ear;

---

1. Conflict between Trojans and Greeks; conflict between nature and art.

Here one being thronged bears° back, all boll'n° and red;   *crowded pushes / swollen*
Another, smothered, seems to pelt° and swear;   *scold*
And in their rage such signs of rage they bear
1420   As, but for loss of° Nestor's golden words,   *That except they might miss*
     It seemed they would debate with angry swords.

For much imaginary° work was there: *creative*
Conceit deceitful, so compact,° so kind,°   *efficient / natural*
That for Achilles' image stood his spear,
1425 Gripped in an armèd hand; himself behind
Was left unseen, save to the eye of mind:
     A hand, a foot, a face, a leg, a head
     Stood for the whole to be imaginèd.

And from the walls of strong-besiegèd Troy,
1430 When their brave hope, bold Hector, marched to field,
Stood many Trojan mothers, sharing joy
To see their youthful sons bright weapons wield;
And to their hope they such odd action° yield   *contrary gestures*
     That through their light joy seemèd to appear,
1435   Like bright things stained, a kind of heavy fear.

And from the strand° of Dardan where they fought,   *shore*
To Simois'° reedy banks the red blood ran,   *Trojan river*
Whose waves to imitate the battle sought
With swelling ridges; and their ranks began
1440 To break upon the gallèd° shore, and then   *eroded; injured*
     Retire again, till meeting greater ranks
     They join, and shoot their foam at Simois' banks.

To this well-painted piece is Lucrece come,
To find a face where all distress is stelled.°   *engraved*
1445 Many she sees where cares have carvèd some,
But none where all distress and dolor dwelled,
Till she despairing Hecuba° beheld,   *Queen of Troy*
     Staring on Priam's° wounds with her old eyes,   *King of Troy*
     Which bleeding under Pyrrhus' proud foot lies.

1450 In her the painter had anatomized°   *laid open*
Time's ruin, beauty's wrack, and grim care's reign.
Her cheeks with chops° and wrinkles were disguised:°   *cracks / disfigured*
Of what she was no semblance did remain.
Her blue blood changed to black in every vein,
1455   Wanting° the spring that those shrunk pipes had fed,   *Lacking*
     Showed life imprisoned in a body dead.

On this sad shadow Lucrece spends her eyes,
And shapes her sorrow to the beldam's° woes,   *old woman's*
Who nothing wants to answer her² but cries
1460 And bitter words to ban° her cruel foes.   *curse*
The painter was no god to lend her those,
     And therefore Lucrece swears he did her wrong
     To give her so much grief, and not a tongue.

---

2. *Who . . . her:* Who lacks nothing to resemble her.

"Poor instrument," quoth she, "without a sound,
1465 I'll tune° thy woes with my lamenting tongue,   *sing*
And drop sweet balm in Priam's painted wound,
And rail on Pyrrhus that hath done him wrong,
And with my tears quench Troy that burns so long,
     And with my knife scratch out the angry eyes
1470   Of all the Greeks that are thine enemies.

"Show me the strumpet° that began this stir,°   *(Helen) / dispute*
That with my nails her beauty I may tear.
Thy heat of lust, fond Paris, did incur
This load of wrath that burning Troy doth bear:
1475 Thy eye kindled the fire that burneth here,
     And here in Troy, for trespass of thine eye,
     The sire, the son, the dame, and daughter die.

"Why should the private pleasure of someone
Become the public plague of many moe?°   *more*
1480 Let sin, alone° committed, light alone   *by one person*
Upon his head that hath transgressèd so;
Let guiltless souls be freed from guilty woe.
     For one's offense why should so many fall,
     To plague a private sin in general?°   *collectively*

1485 "Lo, here weeps Hecuba, here Priam dies,
Here manly Hector faints, here Troilus sounds,°   *swoons*
Here friend by friend in bloody channel° lies,   *gutter*
And friend to friend gives unadvisèd° wounds,   *unintended*
And one man's lust these many lives confounds.
1490   Had doting Priam checked his son's desire,
     Troy had been bright with fame, and not with fire."

Here feelingly she weeps Troy's painted woes;
For sorrow, like a heavy hanging bell,
Once set on ringing, with his° own weight goes;   *its*
1495 Then little strength rings out the doleful knell.
So Lucrece set a-work, sad tales doth tell
     To penciled pensiveness and colored sorrow;
     She lends them words, and she their looks doth borrow.

She throws her eyes about the painting round,
1500 And who she finds forlorn she doth lament.
At last she sees a wretched image bound,
That piteous looks to Phrygian shepherds lent.[3]
His face, though full of cares, yet showed content.
     Onward to Troy with the blunt swains° he goes,   *rough rustics*
1505   So mild that patience° seemed to scorn his woes.   *his patience*

In him the painter labored with his skill
To hide deceit and give the harmless show°   *appearance*
An humble gait, calm looks, eyes wailing still,°   *weeping continually*
A brow unbent that seemed to welcome woe,
1510 Cheeks neither red nor pale, but mingled so

---

3. *That . . . lent:* That made Phrygian shepherds look on in pity (Phrygia was the area around Troy).

That blushing red no guilty instance° gave,   *sign*
Nor ashy pale the fear that false hearts have.

But like a constant and confirmèd devil
He entertained° a show so seeming just,   *maintained*
1515 And therein so ensconced° his secret evil   *concealed*
That jealousy° itself could not mistrust°   *suspicion / suspect*
False creeping craft and perjury should thrust
    Into so bright a day such black-faced storms,
    Or blot with hell-born sin such saintlike forms.

1520 The well-skilled workman this mild image drew
For perjured Sinon,[4] whose enchanting° story   *deluding*
The credulous old Priam after slew;
Whose words like wildfire[5] burnt the shining glory
Of rich-built Ilion, that the skies were sorry,
1525   And little stars shot from their fixed places
    When their glass° fell, wherein they viewed their faces.   *mirror (Troy)*

This picture she advisedly° perused,   *carefully*
And chid° the painter for his wondrous skill,   *scolded*
Saying, some shape° in Sinon's was abused: *(other person's shape)*
1530 So fair a form lodged not a mind so ill.
And still on him she gazed, and gazing still,
    Such signs of truth in his plain° face she spied   *open*
    That she concludes the picture was belied.°   *shown to be false*

"It cannot be," quoth she, "that so much guile"—
1535 She would have said "can lurk in such a look."
But Tarquin's shape came in her mind the while,
And from her tongue "can lurk" from "cannot" took.
"It cannot be" she in that sense forsook,
    And turned it thus: "It cannot be, I find,
1540   But such a face should bear a wicked mind.

"For even as subtle Sinon here is painted,
So sober sad, so weary, and so mild,
As if with grief or travail° he had fainted,   *effort*
To me came Tarquin armèd to beguild[6]
1545 With outward honesty, but yet defiled
    With inward vice. As Priam him did cherish,
    So did I Tarquin, so my Troy did perish.

"Look, look, how list'ning Priam wets his eyes
To see those borrowed° tears that Sinon sheds.   *inauthentic*
1550 Priam, why art thou old and yet not wise?
For every tear he falls° a Trojan bleeds: *(Sinon) lets fall*
His eye drops fire, no water thence proceeds.

---

4. Sinon was a Greek who pretended to have fled from his own people; once "rescued" and brought to Troy, he persuaded the Trojans to receive the wooden horse into their city.
5. A mixture of sulfur, tar, and other combustible substances, used to set fires during battle.

6. Textual Comment "Beguild" means "trick," but also "cover with gold" (that is, Tarquin's magnificence is all on the surface). The difficulty of the line led some eighteenth- and nineteenth-century editors to emend it, but most modern editors retain the original wording. For a fuller discussion, see Digital Edition TC 9.

Those round clear pearls of his that move thy pity
Are balls of quenchless fire to burn thy city.

1555 "Such devils steal effects° from lightless hell,   *illusions*
For Sinon in his fire doth quake with cold,
And in that cold hot-burning fire doth dwell.
These contraries such unity do hold
Only to flatter° fools and make them bold;   *encourage*
1560 So Priam's trust false Sinon's tears doth flatter
  That he finds means to burn his Troy with water."

Here, all enraged, such passion her assails
That patience is quite beaten from her breast.
She tears the senseless° Sinon with her nails,   *unfeeling*
1565 Comparing him to that unhappy° guest   *misfortune-bringing*
Whose deed hath made herself herself detest.
  At last she smilingly with this gives o'er:
  "Fool, fool," quoth she, "his wounds will not be sore."

Thus ebbs and flows the current of her sorrow,
1570 And time doth weary time with her complaining.
She looks for night, and then she longs for morrow,
And both she thinks too long with her remaining.
Short time seems long in sorrow's sharp sustaining:° *painful enduring*
  Though woe be heavy, yet it seldom sleeps,
1575 And they that watch° see time how slow it creeps. *remain awake*

Which all this time hath overslipped her thought
That she with painted images hath spent,
Being from the feeling of her own grief brought
By deep surmise° of others' detriment,° *contemplation / suffering*
1580 Losing her woes in shows of discontent.°   *pictures of sorrow*
  It easeth some, though none it ever cured,
  To think their dolor others have endured.

But now the mindful° messenger come back   *dutiful*
Brings home his lord and other company,
1585 Who finds his Lucrece clad in mourning black,
And round about her tear-distainèd° eye   *tear-stained*
Blue circles streamed, like rainbows in the sky:
  These water-galls° in her dim element° *rainbow fragments / sky*
  Foretell new storms to° those already spent. *in addition to*

1590 Which when her sad-beholding husband saw,
Amazedly in her sad face he stares:
Her eyes, though sod° in tears, looked red and raw,   *sodden*
Her lively color killed with deadly cares.
He hath no power to ask her how she fares.
1595 Both stood like old acquaintance in a trance,
  Met far from home, wond'ring each other's chance.° *fortune*

At last he takes her by the bloodless hand,
And thus begins: "What uncouth° ill event   *strange*
Hath thee befall'n, that thou dost trembling stand?
1600 Sweet love, what spite° hath thy fair color spent?   *harm*

Why art thou thus attired in discontent?[7]
        Unmask,° dear dear, this moody heaviness,   *Disclose*
        And tell thy grief, that we may give redress."

Three times with sighs she gives her sorrow fire,[8]
1605 Ere once she can discharge one word of woe.
At length addressed° to answer his desire,   *ready*
She modestly prepares to let them know
Her honor is ta'en prisoner by the foe,
        While Collatine and his consorted° lords   *accompanying*
1610   With sad attention long to hear her words.

And now this pale swan in her wat'ry nest
Begins the sad dirge of her certain ending:[9]
"Few words," quoth she, "shall fit the trespass best,
Where no excuse can give the fault amending.
1615 In me more woes than words are now depending,°   *weighing; belonging*
        And my laments would be drawn out too long
        To tell them all with one poor tired tongue.

"Then be this all the task it hath to say:
Dear husband, in the interest° of thy bed   *claiming possession*
1620 A stranger came, and on that pillow lay
Where thou wast wont to rest thy weary head;
And what wrong else may be imaginèd
        By foul enforcement might be done to me,
        From that, alas, thy Lucrece is not free.

1625 "For in the dreadful dead of dark midnight,
With shining falchion in my chamber came
A creeping creature with a flaming light,
And softly cried, 'Awake, thou Roman dame,
And entertain° my love, else lasting shame   *receive*
1630   On thee and thine this night I will inflict,
        If thou my love's desire do contradict.

"'For some hard-favored° groom of thine,' quoth he,   *ugly*
'Unless thou yoke thy liking to my will,
I'll murder straight,° and then I'll slaughter thee,   *immediately*
1635 And swear I found you where you did fulfill
The loathsome act of lust, and so did kill
        The lechers in their deed: this act will be
        My fame, and thy perpetual infamy.'

"With this I did begin to start and cry,
1640 And then against my heart he set his sword,
Swearing, unless I took all patiently,
I should not live to speak another word.
So should my shame still rest upon record,
        And never be forgot in mighty Rome
1645   Th'adulterate° death of Lucrece and her groom.   *adulterous*

---

7. In black; see line 1585.
8. As sixteenth-century gunners lighted firearms with matches.

9. Swans were supposed to sing only when they were on the point of death.

"Mine enemy was strong, my poor self weak,
And far the weaker with so strong a fear.
My bloody judge forbade my tongue to speak;
No rightful plea might plead for justice there.
His scarlet lust came° evidence to swear   gave
    That my poor beauty had purloined his eyes,
    And when the judge is robbed, the prisoner dies.

"Oh, teach me how to make mine own excuse,
Or at the least this refuge let me find:
Though my gross blood be stained with this abuse,
Immaculate and spotless is my mind.
That was not forced, that never was inclined
    To accessory yieldings,[1] but still pure
    Doth in her poisoned closet yet endure."

Lo, here the hopeless merchant° of this loss,   owner (Collatine)
With head declined° and voice dammed up with woe,   bent
With sad-set eyes and wreathèd arms across,[2]
From lips new waxen° pale begins to blow   newly grown
The grief away that stops his answer so.
    But, wretched as he is, he strives in vain:
    What he breathes out, his breath drinks up again.

As through an arch° the violent roaring tide   (under a bridge)
Outruns the eye that doth behold his° haste,   its (the tide's)
Yet in the eddy boundeth in his pride
Back to the strait that forced him on so fast,
In rage sent out, recalled in rage being past:
    Even so his° sighs; his sorrows make a saw,[3]   (Collatine's)
    To push grief on, and back the same grief draw.

Which speechless woe of his poor she attendeth,°   poor Lucrece notes
And his untimely frenzy° thus awaketh: delirium
"Dear lord, thy sorrow to my sorrow lendeth
Another power;° no flood by raining slaketh.   Greater strength
My woe too sensible° thy passion maketh   acutely felt
    More feeling painful. Let it then suffice
    To drown one woe, one pair of weeping eyes.

"And for my sake, when I might charm thee so,[4]
For she that was thy Lucrece, now attend me:
Be suddenly revengèd on my foe—
Thine, mine, his own. Suppose thou dost defend me
From what is past; the help that thou shalt lend me
    Comes all too late, yet let the traitor die:
    For sparing° justice feeds° iniquity.   lenient / encourages

"But ere I name him, you fair lords," quoth she,
Speaking to those that came with Collatine,

---

1. To yielding that would make me an accessory to the crime.
2. See line 793 and note.
3. Go back and forth (inhaling and exhaling), like a saw cutting wood.
4. *when . . . so:* as I used to be when I charmed you (before the rape).

1690 "Shall plight° your honorable faiths to me,   *pledge*
       With swift pursuit to venge this wrong of mine.
       For 'tis a meritorious fair design°   *intention*
              To chase injustice with revengeful arms:
              Knights, by their oaths, should right poor ladies' harms."

1695 At this request, with noble disposition°   *purpose*
       Each present lord began to promise aid,
       As bound in knighthood to her imposition,°   *imposed task*
       Longing to hear the hateful foe bewrayed.°   *revealed*
       But she that yet her sad task hath not said,°   *completed*
1700   The protestation stops. "Oh, speak," quoth she,
              "How may this forcèd stain be wiped from me?

       "What is the quality of my offense,
       Being constrained with dreadful circumstance?
       May my pure mind with the foul act dispense,
1705 My low-declinèd honor to advance?°   *raise*
       May any terms acquit me from this chance?°   *mishap*
              The poisoned fountain clears itself again,
              And why not I from this compellèd stain?"

       With this they all at once began to say
1710 Her body's stain her mind untainted clears,
       While with a joyless smile she turns away
       The face, that map which deep impression bears
       Of hard misfortune, carved in it with tears.
              "No, no," quoth she, "no dame hereafter living
1715   By my excuse shall claim excuses giving."

       Here with a sigh as if her heart would break,
       She throws forth Tarquin's name. "He, he," she says,
       But more than "he" her poor tongue could not speak,
       Till after many accents° and delays,   *sighs*
1720 Untimely breathings, sick and short assays,°   *attempts*
              She utters this: "He, he, fair lords, 'tis he
              That guides this hand to give this wound to me."

       Even here she sheathèd in her harmless° breast   *innocent*
       A harmful knife, that thence her soul unsheathed.
1725 That blow did bail° it from the deep unrest   *liberate*
       Of that polluted prison where it breathed.
       Her contrite sighs unto the clouds bequeathed
              Her wingèd sprite,° and through her wounds doth fly   *spirit*
              Life's lasting date[5] from canceled destiny.

1730 Stone-still, astonished° with this deadly deed,   *stunned*
       Stood Collatine and all his lordly crew,
       Till Lucrece' father that beholds her bleed
       Himself on her self-slaughtered body threw;

---

5. *lasting date*: eternal duration. The line is difficult, and could mean that Lucrece's immortal soul separates from her earthly life and body (canceled destiny), or that Lucrece, by taking her fate into her own hands (canceling her destiny), makes her fame eternal.

And from the purple fountain Brutus[6] drew
1735   The murd'rous knife, and as it left the place,
         Her blood in poor revenge held it in chase;

And bubbling from her breast, it doth divide
In two slow rivers, that the crimson blood
Circles her body in on every side,
1740   Who like a late-sacked° island vastly° stood   *just-looted / devastated*
         Bare and unpeopled in this fearful° flood.   *fearsome*
             Some of her blood still pure and red remained,
             And some looked black, and that false Tarquin stained.

About the mourning and congealèd face
1745   Of that black blood, a wat'ry rigol° goes,   *circle*
         Which seems to weep upon the tainted place;
         And ever since, as pitying Lucrece' woes,
         Corrupted blood some watery token shows,
             And blood untainted still doth red abide,
1750   Blushing at that which is so putrefied.

"Daughter, dear daughter," old Lucretius cries,
"That life was mine which thou hast here deprived.
If in the child the father's image lies,
Where shall I live now Lucrece is unlived?°   *slain*
1755   Thou wast not to this end from me derived.
             If children predecease progenitors,
             We are their offspring, and they none of ours.

"Poor broken glass,° I often did behold   *mirror*
In thy sweet semblance my old age new born;
1760   But now that fair fresh mirror, dim and old,
         Shows me a bare-boned death° by time outworn.   *skull*
         Oh, from thy cheeks my image thou hast torn,
             And shivered all the beauty of my glass,
             That I no more can see what once I was.

1765   "O Time, cease thou thy course and last no longer,
         If they surcease° to be that should survive.   *cease*
         Shall rotten death make conquest of the stronger,
         And leave the falt'ring feeble souls alive?
             The old bees die, the young possess their hive.
1770   Then live, sweet Lucrece, live again and see
             Thy father die, and not thy father thee."

By this starts Collatine as from a dream,
And bids Lucretius give his sorrow place;°   *precedence*
And then in key-cold° Lucrece' bleeding stream   *cold as metal*
1775   He falls, and bathes the pale fear in his face,
         And counterfeits to die with her a space,
             Till manly shame bids him possess his breath,
             And live to be revengèd on her death.

6. Lucius Junius Brutus. Tarquin the Proud, the rapist's father, had killed Brutus's brother, but Brutus,
whose name means "stupid," escaped royal suspicion
by pretending to be mentally retarded. After Lucrece's
rape, he led the coup that overthrew the Tarquins and
established republican government in Rome.

The deep vexation of his inward soul
1780   Hath served a dumb arrest° upon his tongue,   *silent injunction*
Who, mad that sorrow should his use control,°   *prevent*
Or keep him from heart-easing words so long,
Begins to talk; but through his lips do throng
      Weak words, so thick come in his poor heart's aid
1785   That no man could distinguish what he said.

Yet sometime "Tarquin" was pronouncèd plain,
But through his teeth, as if the name he tore.
This windy tempest, till it blow up rain,
Held back his sorrow's tide to make it more.
1790   At last it rains, and busy winds give o'er.
      Then son° and father weep with equal strife   *son-in-law*
      Who should weep most, for daughter or for wife.

The one doth call her his, the other his,
Yet neither may possess the claim they lay.
1795   The father says, "She's mine"; "Oh, mine she is,"
Replies her husband: "do not take away
My sorrow's interest.° Let no mourner say   *title of possession*
      He weeps for her, for she was only mine,
      And only must be wailed by Collatine."

1800   "Oh," quoth Lucretius, "I did give that life
Which she too early and too late hath spilled."
"Woe, woe," quoth Collatine, "she was my wife.
I owed° her, and 'tis mine that she hath killed."   *owned*
"My daughter" and "my wife" with clamors filled
1805   The dispersèd air, who, holding Lucrece' life,[7]
      Answered° their cries, "my daughter" and "my wife."   *Echoed*

Brutus, who plucked the knife from Lucrece' side,
Seeing such emulation° in their woe,   *competition*
Began to clothe his wit in state° and pride,   *dignity*
1810   Burying in Lucrece' wound his folly's show.°   *pretended stupidity*
He with the Romans was esteemèd so
      As silly jeering idiots° are with kings,   *court jesters*
      For sportive words and utt'ring foolish things.

But now he throws that shallow habit° by,   *foolish appearance*
1815   Wherein deep policy° did him disguise,   *shrewdness*
And armed his long-hid wits advisedly,°   *prudently*
To check the tears in Collatinus' eyes.
"Thou wrongèd lord of Rome," quoth he, "arise.
      Let my unsounded° self, supposed a fool,   *of unknown depth*
1820   Now set thy long-experienced wit to school.

"Why, Collatine, is woe the cure for woe?
Do wounds help wounds, or grief help grievous deeds?
Is it revenge to give thyself a blow
For his foul act by whom thy fair wife bleeds?
1825   Such childish humor° from weak minds proceeds.   *silly behavior*

7. See lines 1727ff.

Thy wretched wife mistook the matter so
To slay herself, that should have slain her foe.

"Courageous Roman, do not steep thy heart
In such relenting dew of lamentations,
1830   But kneel with me and help to bear thy part
To rouse our Roman gods with invocations,
That they will suffer° these abominations,   *allow*
      Since Rome herself in them doth stand disgraced,
      By our strong arms from forth her fair streets chased.°   *to be chased*

1835   "Now by the Capitol⁸ that we adore,
And by this chaste blood so unjustly stained,
By heaven's fair sun that breeds the fat° earth's store,°   *fertile / plenty*
By all our country° rights in Rome maintained,   *civic*
And by chaste Lucrece' soul that late complained
1840   Her wrongs to us, and by this bloody knife,
      We will revenge the death of this true wife."

This said, he struck his hand upon his breast,
And kissed the fatal knife to end his vow,
And to his protestation urged the rest,
1845   Who, wond'ring at him, did his words allow.°   *approve*
Then jointly to the ground their knees they bow,
      And that deep vow which Brutus made before
      He doth again repeat, and that they swore.

When they had sworn to this advisèd doom,°   *considered judgment*
1850   They did conclude to bear dead Lucrece thence,
To show her bleeding body thorough° Rome,   *throughout*
And so to publish° Tarquin's foul offense,   *publicize*
Which, being done with speedy diligence,
      The Romans plausibly° did give consent   *with applause*
1855   To Tarquins' everlasting banishment.

---

8. The Capitol was the religious and political center of ancient Rome.

The Comedy of Errors

In his essay "On Cripples," Shakespeare's great contemporary Michel de Montaigne alludes to a strange case of impersonation in a small rural community in southwestern France. There, a cunning imposter succeeded in assuming the identity of Martin Guerre, a man who had disappeared some years earlier. The imposter lived in the community for three years, sleeping with Guerre's wife and farming his land, until the real Martin Guerre unexpectedly returned. Convicted of fraud, the imposter confessed and was hanged.

Montaigne was dismayed by the execution, for he felt that the evidence was too murky, the imposture too convincing, and human identity too elusive a possession to justify capital punishment. The court, he writes, should have emulated the ancient Greek tribunal that, confronted by a similarly baffling case, ordered the parties to come back in a hundred years. Montaigne was not only advising judicial caution; he was urging his readers to take everyday life less automatically, to acknowledge the inevitability of ignorance and error, and to respond to their own existence with wonder. "I have seen no more evident monstrosity and miracle in the world than myself," he writes in the same essay in which he talks about Martin Guerre. "We become habituated to anything strange by use and time; but the more I frequent myself and know myself, the more my deformity astonishes me, and the less I understand myself."

Montaigne's reflections on Martin Guerre have no direct bearing on *The Comedy of Errors*, but they alert us to the play's wholesale unsettling of the familiar. The comfortable assumptions that condition a normal life—I know who I am; these things belong to me and not to someone else; these are the people I love, command, work for, do business with, or avoid—are undermined by the tangled interactions of two sets of identical twins. Antipholus of Syracuse and Antipholus of Ephesus, along with their servants, Dromio of Syracuse and Dromio of Ephesus, have been raised apart from one another in separate cities and are unaware that their paths are now unexpectedly crossing. Through a breathless succession of zany doublings and confusions, Shakespeare's comedy discloses the hidden strangeness of ordinary existence. An invitation to dinner, a simple transaction with a goldsmith, the operation of commercial and civil laws, the relationship between master and servant, the bond between husband and wife (or mistress or sister-in-law)—all become unhinged, as if by sorcery. "There's not a man I meet but doth salute me," says Antipholus of Syracuse, "As if I were their well-acquainted friend, / And everyone doth call me by my name" (4.3.1–3). These are the familiar practices of everyday life, but to this stranger who is, unbeknownst to him, being mistaken for his identical (and identically named) twin, they confirm the unsavory reputation of Ephesus as a place of "nimble jugglers," "Dark-working sorcerers," "Soul-killing witches," and "Disguisèd cheaters" (1.2.98–101).

The audience knows, of course, that Antipholus's uncanny experiences have been caused neither by witchcraft nor by deliberate identity theft. The wonder that seems to suffuse everything is the result of nothing more magical or malicious than twinship and a shared name; hence, we could say, such wonder is spurious or misplaced, the result of misunderstandings. "This is the fairy land" (2.2.190), exclaims one of the Dromios, mystified by the succession of inexplicable events, and his similarly disoriented master invokes the notorious wiles of far-off Lapland. But in *The Comedy of Errors*, there is in reality only daylight and the familiar city street of Roman comedy, a street reassuringly adapted to the commercial world of Shakespeare's

An Italian merchant pictured on a Florentine playing card.

London. Disorientation and danger lurk, to be sure, in this conventional urban landscape—Antipholus of Syracuse suspects he is the victim of sorcery, Antipholus of Ephesus is treated as a madman, Adriana fears the loss of her husband's love, Luciana is convinced that her brother-in-law is trying to seduce her, the servants are constantly beaten for faults they have not in fact committed, and poor Egeon is condemned to die at day's end. Yet though the pressure of time weighs heavily on virtually all of the characters, enmeshed as they are in humiliating, menacing, and apparently insoluble difficulties, the confusions that bedevil their lives are all neatly resolved by the appointed hour of 5:00 P.M.

This comic resolution, however, does not quite make weirdness or wonder altogether evaporate from the play. Montaigne urged his readers to abandon their confident belief in the ordered rationality of life and to find the marvelous in the everyday. Identical twins are fairly commonplace and the fact that two people can bear the same name even more so, but Shakespeare's play calls attention to all that is potentially disorienting in such familiar circumstances. The end of *The Comedy of Errors* seems to restore order and reason—to make the ordinary world ordinary again—but the closing gestures lightly unsettle this restoration. The Abbess, who turns out to be Egeon's long-lost wife and the mother of the twin Antipholuses, finds a strange image, at once touching and grotesque, to describe her experiences: she declares that she has been pregnant for thirty-three years and has only now given birth. Though officially everything has been sorted out, in fact everything is just beginning. A family that has had virtually no shared experience has been suddenly reconstituted and will need to rework all the relationships among its members. The Antipholus brothers, physically indistinguishable, have almost nothing else in common. Adriana is formally reconciled with her estranged husband but has no assurance that things will improve. And the twin Dromios, unable to determine which of them is the elder and should therefore go first through the door, decide that they will draw lots for seniority; meanwhile, they will dispense with hierarchy and go through the door hand in hand.

More telling, perhaps, the questions raised by the strange case of Martin Guerre linger unresolved at the end of Shakespeare's comedy: What is the self? What are the guarantees of identity? Who possesses a name, and by what right? How is individuality secured? How can one person represent another? The drama is the perfect medium for an exploration of these questions, for the form of the drama itself invites reflection on the extent to which it is possible for one person to assume the identity of another.

From this perspective, *The Comedy of Errors* is not, as it is sometimes said to be, a simple and even simpleminded farce, the crude work of a novice playwright, but a remarkably subtle and acute deployment of the very conditions of the theater to engage with problems that haunted Shakespeare throughout his career.

While it is a mistake to view it as mere apprentice work, *The Comedy of Errors* is nonetheless one of the earliest of Shakespeare's plays (and it is also, perhaps not coincidentally, the shortest). Its exact date of composition and first performance are unknown; there was a performance at Gray's Inn, one of London's law schools, on December 28, 1594, but the play's thematic and stylistic resemblances to Shakespeare's other early comedies, *The Two Gentlemen of Verona*, *Love's Labor's Lost*, and *The Taming of the Shrew*, have led many scholars to conclude that he wrote it some years earlier. It was not printed until 1623, as part of the First Folio.

The anonymous recorder of the Gray's Inn performance—apparently something of a debacle because of the pushing and shoving of unexpectedly large crowds—noted the play's resemblance to an ancient comedy, the *Menaechmi*, written by the Roman playwright Plautus. Shakespeare probably read this much-admired play in Latin, since an English translation, by William Warner, was not printed until 1595. The *Menaechmi* is a brilliant, energetic farce, fast-paced, funny, and, as farces often are, cold at heart. A prologue carefully explains the premise: a Syracusan merchant took one of his twin sons, seven years old, on a business trip abroad. During a festival, he accidentally became separated from the son. The boy was found by a childless trader, who took him off to Epidamnum; the father, crazed with grief, died a few days later. When news of the catastrophe reached Syracuse, the remaining son was given the name of his missing brother.

The action of Plautus's play is set some years later, when Menaechmus of Syracuse, searching for his twin, finds himself in Epidamnum. Greeted warmly by perfect strangers, Menaechmus realizes that some mistake is being made, but he is not filled with dread. "I can lose nothing," he cheerfully tells his slave, as he accepts food, gifts, and sexual favors from a woman who, evidently confusing him with someone else, imagines that she is his mistress. What most strikes him is that it is all free of charge. His twin, a prosperous citizen who is normally comfortable in an entourage that includes wife, household slaves, mistress, and an obnoxious hanger-on nicknamed the Sponge, is frustrated by the fact that everyone seems to have gone mad, and in fact, he becomes enraged when he himself is treated as a madman. The dizzying confusions steadily mount until the brothers find themselves face-to-face and, with delicious slowness, figure out that they are the long-separated identical twins. The brothers plan to return together to Syracuse, and the play ends with the announcement of the forthcoming auction of Menaechmus's property: "slaves, household effects, house, land, etcetera—and a wife, should there be any purchaser."

Though he took over much of Plautus's farce, Shakespeare made highly revealing changes and additions. For a start, he shifted the setting from Epidamnum to Ephesus, a city associated with sorcery, exorcism, mystery cults, and early Christianity. As if to multiply the comic confusion generated by one set of identical twins, he added a second set—the servants, who, for reasons that are not really explained, bear like their masters a single name. (The device of the identical slaves is borrowed from another play by Plautus, the *Amphitruo*.) Shakespeare also chose to double the plot by framing the main action with the anguished figure of the Syracusan merchant Egeon, caught up in his city's murderous commercial struggle with rival city Ephesus. The melancholy personal history that Egeon relates is adapted not from the ancient comedy but from a medieval romance, the tale of Apollonius of Tyre as told by the fourteenth-century poet John Gower in his *Confessio Amantis* (a tale to which Shakespeare again turned many years later for the plot of *Pericles*). Egeon's fate quickly recedes from the audience's attention, but the threat to his life provides a somber context for the play's hilarity, and his return to the stage at the close, on the way to the place of execution, suddenly raises the stakes of the resolution. The closing scene

A scene in the street/the street as scene.
Woodcut from a German edition of Terence's
Eunuchus (1486).

highlights the romance elements that Shakespeare introduced into his frenetic scheme of mistaken identity: the reuniting of parents and children who had been tragically separated, the miraculous recovery of a beloved spouse long presumed dead, and a sense of wonder that does not entirely evaporate with the solving of the puzzle. Plautus's Epidamnum is a city full of rogues, parasites, and courtesans, a place where you can lose your cloak, your chain, and your money; Shakespeare's Ephesus is a place where you can lose—or regain—your identity, your marriage, and your life.

Egeon's story in *The Comedy of Errors* has a shape that merits attention: he is condemned to death through the operation of an inflexible law that even the sympathetic Duke cannot mitigate, and then, through a wondrous turn of events, his life is spared, and he recovers the loved ones he thought he had lost forever. Even though the play is set in pagan antiquity, in this shape we may sense the psychic and moral rhythm of Christianity: the mortal penalty of the harsh law is wiped out, altogether unexpectedly and gratuitously, by a miraculous, loving dispensation. The farcical core of the play is at a considerable remove from this portentous rhythm, but Christianity's influence is not restricted to the frame. Since Shakespeare and his age were relatively indifferent to anachronism, Antipholus of Syracuse can say to his servant, "Now, as I am a Christian, answer me" (1.2.77), and the servant can cross himself and call for his rosary beads (2.2.189). The fear of demonic possession takes a specifically Christian form when Satan himself is exorcised by Doctor Pinch. And although pagan antiquity had shrines such as the Temple of Diana at Ephesus (where the tale of Apollonius of Tyre reaches its climax), the priory and its abbess seem to belong in a Christian community, a community invoked by the very name of Ephesus, where St. Paul preached and to which he wrote an influential epistle.

A central concern of the Epistle to the Ephesians is marriage, where, in the words of Genesis, "two shall be one flesh." Paul spells out what is required: "Wives, submit yourselves unto your own husbands, as unto the Lord. . . . Husbands, love your wives, even as Christ also loved the church." These strikingly asymmetrical admonitions make themselves felt throughout *The Comedy of Errors*. Where Plautus's Menaechmus cheerfully cheats on his wife, Shakespeare's married twin seems to have some traces of moral restraint. Antipholus turns to the courtesan only when his wife, Adriana, seems to lock him out of his own house—and even then, protesting to his friends that his wife's suspicions are unfounded, he seems mainly interested in dinner and pleasant conversation. Where the nameless wife in Plautus is above all outraged that her husband has stolen from her a gown and a bracelet to bestow as presents on his mistress, Shakespeare's Adriana is obsessed with the possibility that her husband no

"I'll to the mart" (3.2.187). London's Royal Exchange, founded by Sir Thomas Gresham, 1565. Etching by Wenceslaus Hollar (1644).

longer loves her. It is this tormenting fear of marital estrangement that has driven her to a querulousness that only confirms her overwhelming craving for perfect union:

> Ah, do not tear away thyself from me;
> For know, my love, as easy mayst thou fall
> A drop of water in the breaking gulf
> And take unmingled thence that drop again
> Without addition or diminishing,
> As take from me thyself, and not me too.
>   (2.2.125–30)

The oneness that is envisioned here, the poignant longing for wholeness, and the fear of pollution and self-loss have no place in the emotional register of the *Menaechmi*. Where Plautus's farce ends with a joke about offering the wife for sale, *The Comedy of Errors* ends with the characters, reconciled and reunited, entering the abbey for a feast.

Near the close of Shakespeare's play, the Abbess seems to reflect the spirit of St. Paul's admonition to wives when she observes that by robbing her husband of the "sweet recreation" that he should find at home, Adriana's "jealous fits" have driven him mad (5.1.76, 85). This criticism echoes both Antipholus's own complaint that his wife is "shrewish" (3.1.2) and the distinctly Pauline opinions voiced by Adriana's sister, Luciana. Luciana—a character for whom there is no precedent in Plautus— argues that males of every species are "masters to their females, and their lords" (2.1.24) and therefore that Adriana should patiently submit to her husband. Such views, similar to those expressed by the "reformed" Katherina in *The Taming of the Shrew*, are given considerable prominence in *The Comedy of Errors*, and yet they are neither unchallenged nor unequivocally endorsed. Adriana observes wryly that her sister is single and hence that her views on marriage are untested by experience. And the Abbess's moralizing diagnosis—that Antipholus would not have mistreated Adriana or gone mad if she had reined in her tongue—turns out to be merely another of the mistaken conjectures that all of the characters incessantly advance in their attempts to account for the day's weird events.

There is a kind of laughter that functions as social regulation: comedy, writes Sir Philip Sidney in his *Defense of Poesy* (ca. 1583), "is an imitation of the common errors of our life," which the dramatist represents "in the most ridiculous and scornful sort that may be, so as it is impossible that any beholder can be content to be such a one." By such means shrewish wives, philandering husbands, and negligent servants are disciplined and put back in their proper places. But in *The Comedy of Errors*, though the errors are ridiculous enough, they are hardly common, and the audience's laughter seems something other than scornful or regulative. None of the explanatory accounts—not even the moral values and providential rhythm of Christianity with which Shakespeare has infused his pagan plot—seems entirely adequate as a response to the chain of mad mistakings. The characters are subject not to a divine plan or to the social order but to fortune. And if this fortune turns out to have the happy air of providence—epitomized by the reuniting of the divided and dispersed family—there seems to be no particularly uplifting lesson to be learned.

Shakespeare's play is cannily alert to the arbitrariness of human relations. An innocent merchant is condemned to death: no one thinks he is a malefactor, but he will be executed for being in the wrong place at the wrong time. One set of twins is destined through poverty to be the servants, casually beaten and abused, of the other set. The servants, called "knaves" and "villains," are in no way less intelligent or able than their masters; their fate is the consequence of the accident of birth. A man, "master of his liberty" (2.1.7), gads about the city, bestowing gifts on a courtesan. His neglected wife, fuming at home, must "practice to obey" (2.1.29). The wife protests the double standard—"Why should their liberty than ours be more?" (2.1.10)—and in doing so gives voice to a question that haunts virtually the entire social nexus of the play. At stake are not only the weird, unintended consequences of the day's zany misrecognitions; rather, those misrecognitions cast a sharp, satirical light on the gender and class distinctions that make up the structure of everyday life. "I have served him from the hour of my nativity to this instant," Dromio of Ephesus bitterly remarks, "and have nothing at his hands for my service but blows" (4.4.30–32).

Yet if *The Comedy of Errors* casts doubt on the supposed naturalness and justice of the ways things are, it does not imagine the possibility of a radical transformation. In the midst of the farcical confusions, characters repeatedly long for greater justice, equality, and emotional fulfillment, but Shakespeare does not encourage us to believe that such an existence can be realized. There may be a happy resolution, but there is no escape from the pervasive, fundamentally inequitable social order and from the mercantile world based on credit, trade, exchange, bonds, and debt.

Several of Shakespeare's best-loved comedies are structured around alternative worlds: the familiar, daylit realm of the court or city is set against the magical realm of the woods and the enchanted night. But in *The Comedy of Errors*, there is only the single urban setting, a setting that would have reminded contemporary audiences of the bustling city that stretched out beyond the walls of the playhouse. In the sixteenth century, London had become the center of a commercial culture that Shakespeare deftly sketches with quick strokes. We learn that Antipholus keeps a purse of ducats locked "in the desk / That's covered o'er with Turkish tapestry" (4.1.103–04), that the courtesan considers a ring worth forty ducats "too much to lose" (4.3.92), and that the goldsmith plans to discharge his overdue debt to a merchant with the money that Antipholus has promised to pay him for the gold chain. That gold chain functions as a convenient symbol of the interlinked network of obligations and exchanges in which the twins—who seem as like one another as two coins of equal value—are caught and which their uncontrolled interchangeability temporarily disrupts.

A closer look reveals that Antipholus of Ephesus and Antipholus of Syracuse are not in fact interchangeable. The former is confident, well connected, and somewhat irascible; the latter is anxious, insecure, and driven by restless longing:

> I to the world am like a drop of water
> That in the ocean seeks another drop,
> Who, falling there to find his fellow forth,
> Unseen, inquisitive, confounds himself.
> (1.2.35–38)

This poignant sense of self-loss, which anticipates the alienation and existential anxiety of the tragedies, is intensified by the mad confusions that follow: the events of *The Comedy of Errors* may be deliciously amusing to the audience, but to the characters they are mystifying and even nightmarish. Antonin Artaud, a modern writer who championed what he called the "Theater of Cruelty," praises the Marx Brothers' movies in terms that seem at least as relevant to Shakespeare's comedy: "In order to understand the powerful, total, definitive, absolute originality . . . of films like *Animal Crackers*," Artaud writes, "you would have to add to humor the notion of something disquieting and tragic, a fatality (neither happy nor unhappy, difficult to formulate) which would hover over it like the cast of an appalling malady upon an exquisitely beautiful profile." And yet it is not the nightmare that triumphs but laughter—laughter at what another sixteenth-century writer, George Gascoigne, called "supposes." Gascoigne defined a suppose as "a mistaking or imagination of one thing for another," and it is with a frantic succession of these supposes, all equally wide of the mark, that the baffled characters of *The Comedy of Errors* occupy themselves.

The "imagination of one thing for another" could serve as a definition of the theater. The spectators of Shakespeare's comedy have paid for the pleasure of watching identity slip away from the characters' grasp, as if in the home or the marketplace who you are is no more secure than it is onstage. They have paid, too, for the pleasure of watching identity serendipitously return, as if Shakespeare's theater had the magic power to restore the human family, however broken and scattered, and to restore stability to the battered self. If neither the loss nor the recovery is altogether plausible, the delicious intertwining of the two seems designed to provoke what Montaigne urged upon his readers: a skeptical wonder.

STEPHEN GREENBLATT

SELECTED BIBLIOGRAPHY

Christensen, Ann C. "'Because their business still lies out a' door': Resisting the Separation of the Spheres in Shakespeare's *The Comedy of Errors*." *Literature and History* 5 (1996): 19–37. Examines how *The Comedy of Errors* charts the growing divide both between public and private and between the commercial and domestic spheres.

Finkelstein, Richard. "*The Comedy of Errors* and the Theology of Things." *Studies in English Literature, 1500–1900* 52 (2012): 325–44. Argues that by exploring the connection between spiritual and commercial capital, *The Comedy of Errors* places increased emphasis on the possibility of redemption not through religious means but through the marketplace.

Frye, Northrop. "The Argument of Comedy." *English Institute Essays*. New York: AMS Press, 1948. 58–73. Argues that Shakespeare's comic form is a synthesis of Aristophanes' Old Comedy and the New Comedy of Plautus and Terence.

Hunt, Maurice. "Slavery, English Servitude and *The Comedy of Errors*." *English Literary Renaissance* 27 (1997): 31–56. Looks at how the rough treatment of the Dromio twins and their ambiguous status—somewhere between servants and slaves—reflect similar features of Elizabethan servitude.

Miola, Robert S., ed. *"The Comedy of Errors": Critical Essays*. New York: Routledge, 2001. See esp. Laurie Maguire, "The Girls from Ephesus," 355–91. A collection of essays on *The Comedy of Errors* spanning a range of topics, including stage history, performance studies, genre conventions, and gender studies. In her essay, Maguire argues that Shakespeare's comedy explores contrasting models for female conduct, one independent and the other submissive.

Parker, Patricia. "The Bible and the Marketplace: *The Comedy of Errors*." *Shakespeare from the Margins: Language, Culture, Context*. Chicago: U of Chicago P, 1996. 56–82. Asserts that while displaying a wealth of biblical allusions, Shakespeare's comedy attempts at the same time to undermine the Bible as a cultural authority.

Perry, Curtis. "Commerce, Community, and Nostalgia in *The Comedy of Errors*." *Money and the Age of Shakespeare: Essays in New Economic Criticism*. Ed. Linda Woodbridge. New York: Palgrave Macmillan, 2003. 39–51. Looks at how the longing for family in *The Comedy of Errors* reveals the alienating forces of the market economy.

Sohrawardy, Ameer. "Twin Obligations in Soloman Plaatje's *Diphosho-phosho*." *Native Shakespeares: Indigenous Appropriations on a Global Stage*. Ed. Craig Dionne and Parmita Kapadia. Burlington, VT: Ashgate, 2008. 187–200. Argues that South African writer Solomon Plaatje's controversial translation of *The Comedy of Errors* into Setswana constitutes an intertextual challenge to Shakespeare's play.

van Elk, Martine. " 'This sympathized one day's error': Genre, Representation, and Subjectivity in *The Comedy of Errors*." *Shakespeare Quarterly* 60 (2009): 47–72. Dissects how the play's foundations in both romance and farce reveal not only a clash of genres but also competing modes of self-representation.

Witmore, Michael. "The Avoidance of Ends in *The Comedy of Errors*." *Culture of Accidents: Unexpected Knowledges in Early Modern England*. Stanford, CA: Stanford UP, 2001. 62–81. Asserts that rather than constituting a series of haphazard accidents, *The Comedy of Errors* is a self-conscious exploration of the problems inherent in representing accidents within the context of larger narratives.

FILM

The Comedy of Errors. 1983. Dir. James Cellan Jones. UK. 109 min. A BBC-TV production, with Roger Daltrey (lead singer of The Who) as the Dromios.

TEXTUAL INTRODUCTION

The base text for *The Comedy of Errors* is the First Folio of 1623, the earliest and only authoritative text of the play. With some notable exceptions, the Folio text is a good one, and most textual scholars agree that some form of the author's own manuscript was used as the copy text. Certain features of the text support this conclusion, including a particularly high degree of variation and uncertainty in speech prefixes and unnecessary or unnecessarily specific information in the stage directions.

Three different characters—Egeon, the First Merchant, and the Second Merchant—are identified with the same speech prefix, "*Mer*." We learn from the stage direction opening the second act that Adriana is "*wife to Antipholis Sereptus*," a description that is not used in the dialogue but that does derive from Shakespeare's source, Plautus's *Menaechmi*. The corresponding twin, Antipholus of Syracuse, is identified as "*Antipholis Erotes*" in the stage direction at 1.2.0, presumably resulting in the speech prefix "*E. Ant.*" (for Antipholus of Syracuse) in act 2. Confusingly, the same prefix is later used for Antipholus of Ephesus in act 5. A reference to Pinch's vocation as "*a Schoole-master*" in the stage direction marking his entrance at 4.4.38 provides information that is dramatically irrelevant. Another example of inconsistency is the identification of Adriana's kitchen maid as *"Luce"* throughout 3.1 and *"Nell"* in the dialogue at 3.2.110. Though the later reference is clearly to the character from 3.1, *"Luce"* cannot be a compositor's error, as the name appears consistently in the stage directions, speech prefixes, and dialogue of 3.1. Another example of such confusion occurs in 3.2, where Luciana is identified as *"Iuliana"* in the opening stage direction and *"Iulia"* in the first speech prefix.

References to locations in the stage directions, *"from the Bay"* (4.1.84) and *"from the Courtizans"* (4.1.13), may suggest an authorial desire to guide the theatrical staging, though they are not consistently included. It is also possible that location directions could have been added to the playing company manuscript while preparing the play for production. In the *Norton Shakespeare* text, references to characters in stage directions and speech prefixes have been regularized, though elsewhere the goal has been to stay as close as possible to the Folio text, retaining inconsistencies such as the name Luce/Nell for the same character.

The Folio's act divisions have been retained, and scene divisions have been added following the editorial tradition.

JAMES A. KNAPP

PERFORMANCE NOTE

The Comedy of Errors requires theater companies to present two pairs of twins that are mistaken for one another by the Ephesians, yet easily distinguished by the audience. Most pursue an illusion of likeness by casting actors of similar height and complexion and dressing them to match, though there exists a strong countertradition of doubling the roles, using one actor for the Antipholuses and another for the Dromios. The latter choice asks actors to differentiate the twins by slight changes in costume, voice, or personality (e.g., playing an urbane against a more rustic brother), and it also requires body doubles, curtain tricks, or textual revision so that the twins can meet each other in the final scene. Other productions cast "twins" starkly different in appearance, testing the audience's credulity and even the value of credibility in the theater. Given the play's farcical atmosphere and interest in exchanges—for example, of marks, blows, rope's ends, and rings—matching (for instance) a slim white Dromio to a portly black one, as Hudson Valley Shakespeare's 2002 production did, can prove an emphatic thematic complement to the action.

In light of its strong farcical elements, *The Comedy of Errors* tends to inspire highly stylized productions, often influenced by clowning and other traditional comic forms. The population of Ephesus—full of "courtesans," "witches," and "sorcerers"—is naturally conducive to *commedia*-inflected productions, which can help explain and excuse the play's wanton violence. Productions can also present the violence more naturalistically, complicating the genre and underscoring the play's presentation of master–servant relationships. In the same vein, productions face crucial choices in portraying Adriana, who even in highly farcical productions can stand out as the lone realistic figure in a sea of types. Presenting Adriana as a sensible, emotionally accessible woman can distinguish her as a sympathetic center, complicating the comic resolution with aspects of romance, while playing her as an archetypically jealous wife can help assure that the audience's focus remains with the Antipholi as they move through an unqualified farce.

BRETT GAMBOA

The Comedy of Errors

[THE PERSONS OF THE PLAY

Solinus, DUKE of Ephesus
EGEON, a merchant of Syracuse, father of the Antipholus twins
ANTIPHOLUS OF EPHESUS ⎱ twin brothers, sons of Egeon
ANTIPHOLUS OF SYRACUSE ⎰
DROMIO OF EPHESUS ⎱ twin brothers, bondmen of the Antipholuses
DROMIO OF SYRACUSE ⎰
ADRIANA, wife of Antipholus of Ephesus
LUCIANA, her sister
LUCE, Adriana's kitchen maid, also known as Nell
BALTHASAR, a merchant
ANGELO, a goldsmith
Doctor PINCH, a schoolmaster
FIRST MERCHANT, friend to Antipholus of Ephesus
SECOND MERCHANT, to whom Angelo owes a debt
Emilia, an ABBESS at Ephesus
COURTESAN
JAILER
MESSENGER
OFFICERS
Headsman, Attendants]

1.1

Enter [Solinus,] the DUKE *of Ephesus, with [*EGEON*] the*
Merchant of Syracuse, JAILER, *and other Attendants.*

EGEON[1] Proceed, Solinus, to procure my fall,
  And by the doom° of death end woes and all.   *sentence*
DUKE Merchant of Syracusa,[2] plead no more.
  I am not partial° to infringe our laws.   *inclined*
5 The enmity and discord which of late
  Sprung from the rancorous outrage of your Duke
  To merchants, our well-dealing[3] countrymen,
  Who, wanting° guilders[4] to redeem° their lives,   *lacking / ransom*
  Have sealed° his rigorous statutes with their bloods,   *ratified*
10 Excludes all pity from our threat'ning looks.
  For since the mortal° and intestine jars°   *deadly / internal strife*
  Twixt thy seditious countrymen and us,

1.1 Location: The play is set in Ephesus (modern Turkish *Efes*), a wealthy and important ancient Greek city-
state in Asia Minor. Much of the action takes place, as
in this opening scene, in a public space, a street or
"mart" (i.e., marketplace). There are also three distinct
houses, signified, as in the stage setting of ancient
Roman comedy, by three doors, each possibly bearing
a different sign. The house of Antipholus of Ephesus,
identified as the Phoenix, is flanked by that of the
courtesan, identified as the Porcupine. The priory in
the last act may have borne anachronistically the sign
of the cross.
1. TEXTUAL COMMENT The first speech prefix given to

this character in the Folio (F) is "*Marchant*," and it is
not until the end of the scene that we learn his proper
name: Egeon. Never identified in the Folio speech
prefixes as Egeon, he is also called "*Mer.*," "*Merch.*,"
"*Mar. Fat.*," "*Fa.*," "*Fath.*," and "*Father.*" See Digital
Edition TC 1.
2. Syracusa or Syracuse (modern Italian *Siracusa*, on
the southeast coast of Sicily) was a powerful ancient
city-state founded by Greek settlers.
3. Honest-trading; more generally, civil or well-
behaved; fair in their business transactions.
4. Money, not specifically referring to Dutch or German coins.

	It hath in solemn synods° been decreed,	*assemblies*
	Both by the Syracusians and ourselves,	
15	To admit no traffic to⁵ our adverse° towns.	*hostile*
	Nay more, if any born at Ephesus	
	Be seen at any Syracusian marts° and fairs;	*markets*
	Again, if any Syracusian born	
	Come to the bay of Ephesus, he dies,	
20	His goods confiscate to the Duke's dispose,°	*disposal*
	Unless a thousand marks⁶ be levièd°	*raised*
	To quit° the penalty and to ransom him.	*pay*
	Thy substance,° valued at the highest rate,	*goods*
	Cannot amount unto a hundred marks;	
25	Therefore by law thou art condemned to die.	

EGEON   Yet this my comfort: when your words are done,
My woes end likewise with the evening sun.

DUKE   Well, Syracusian, say in brief the cause
Why thou departed'st from thy native home,

30   And for what cause thou cam'st to Ephesus.

EGEON A heavier task could not have been imposed,	
Than I° to speak my griefs unspeakable.	*Than for me*
Yet that the world may witness that my end	
Was wrought by nature,⁷ not by vile offense,	
35 I'll utter what my sorrow gives me leave.	
In Syracusa was I born, and wed	
Unto a woman happy but for me,⁸	
And by me,° had not our hap° been bad.	*by me made happy / luck*
With her I lived in joy; our wealth increased	
40 By prosperous voyages I often made	
To Epidamnum,⁹ till my factor's° death,	*agent's*
And the great care of goods at random° left,	*untended*
Drew me from kind embracements of my spouse,	
From whom my absence was not six months old	
45 Before her self—almost at fainting under	
The pleasing punishment that women bear°—	*pregnancy*
Had made provision for her following me,	
And soon and safe arrivèd where I was.	
There had she not been long, but she became	
50 A joyful mother of two goodly sons;	
And, which was strange, the one so like the other	
As° could not be distinguished but by names.	*That they*
That very hour, and in the selfsame inn,	
A mean woman° was deliverèd	*woman of low birth*
55 Of such a burden male, twins both alike.	
Those, for° their parents were exceeding poor,	*because*
I bought and brought up to attend my sons.	
My wife, not meanly° proud of two such boys,	*in no small degree*
Made daily motions° for our home return.	*requests*
60 Unwilling, I agreed. Alas, too soon	
We came aboard.	
A league from Epidamnum had we sailed	
Before the always wind-obeying deep	

5. To allow no trade between.
6. A mark was two-thirds of a pound in English money, although there was no coin of this amount.
7. Was brought about by natural feeling: a father's love.

8. Fortunate except in her association with me.
9. Plautus's setting for the *Menaechmi*, now Durrës in Albania; Shakespeare's play, however, seems to treat it as if it were in Greece.

Gave any tragic instance° of our harm.   *sign*
65 But longer did we not retain much hope,
For what obscurèd light the heavens did grant
Did but convey unto our fearful minds
A doubtful warrant° of immediate death,   *A fearsome confirmation*
Which though my self would gladly have embraced,
70 Yet the incessant weepings of my wife—
Weeping before° for what she saw must come—   *in advance*
And piteous plainings° of the pretty babes   *cries*
That mourned for fashion, ignorant what to fear,[1]
Forced me to seek delays° for them and me.   *reprieves*
75 And this it was—for other means was none—
The sailors sought for safety by our boat,°   *lifeboat*
And left the ship then sinking ripe[2] to us.
My wife, more careful° for the latter-born,°   *anxious / younger*
Had fastened him unto a small spare mast,
80 Such as seafaring men provide for storms.
To him one of the other twins was bound,
Whilst I had been like heedful of° the other.   *equally attentive to*
The children thus disposed,° my wife and I,   *placed*
Fixing our eyes on whom our care was fixed,
85 Fastened ourselves at either end the mast,
And floating straight,° obedient to the stream,   *immediately*
Was carried towards Corinth, as we thought.
At length the sun, gazing upon the earth,
Dispersed those vapors° that offended° us,   *clouds / harmed*
90 And by the benefit of his wishèd light
The seas waxed calm, and we discoverèd
Two ships from far, making amain° to us: *speeding*
Of Corinth that, of Epidaurus[3] this.
But ere they came—oh, let me say no more!
95 Gather the sequel by that went before.[4]
DUKE   Nay, forward, old man. Do not break off so,
For we may pity, though not pardon thee.
EGEON   Oh, had the gods done so, I had not now
Worthily° termed them merciless to us.   *Justly*
100 For ere the ships could meet by° twice five leagues   *come within*
We were encountered by a mighty rock,
Which being violently borne upon,
Our helpful ship° was splitted in the midst;   *(the mast)*
So that in this unjust divorce of us,
105 Fortune had left to both of us alike°   *equally*
What° to delight in, what to sorrow for.   *Something*
Her° part, poor soul, seeming as burdenèd   *(My wife's)*
With lesser weight,[5] but not with lesser woe,
Was carried with more speed before the wind,
110 And in our sight they three were taken up
By fishermen of Corinth, as we thought.
At length another ship had seized on us,°   *hauled us up*
And knowing whom it was their hap° to save,   *luck*

---

1. That imitated the adults' lamentation without understanding it.
2. At the point of sinking; softened and ready to drop.
3. Either modern Dubrovnik, on the Adriatic and north of Durrës (Epidamnum), or the Greek city actu-ally called Epidaurus, near Corinth.
4. Deduce what followed from that which I have already recounted.
5. Lighter than her husband and the other child.

Gave healthful welcome to their shipwrecked guests,
115　And would have reft° the fishers of their prey,[6]　　　　　　　*deprived*
Had not their bark° been very slow of sail;　　　　　　　　　*vessel*
And therefore homeward did they bend their course.
Thus have you heard me severed from my bliss,
That by misfortunes was my life prolonged
120　To tell sad stories of my own mishaps.
　　DUKE　And for the sake of them thou sorrowest for,
Do me the favor to dilate at° full　　　　　　　　　　　　*relate in*
What have befall'n of them and thee till now.
　　EGEON　My youngest boy,[7] and yet my eldest care,
125　At eighteen years became inquisitive
After his brother, and importuned me
That his attendant—so his case was like,[8]
Reft of his brother but retained his name[9]—
Might bear him company in the quest of him;
130　Whom whilst I labored of a love to see,[1]
I hazarded the loss of whom I loved.
Five summers have I spent in farthest Greece,
Roaming clean through the bounds of Asia,
And coasting° homeward came to Ephesus,　　　　　　　　*sailing*
135　Hopeless to find,° yet loath to leave unsought　　　　　*find them*
Or° that or any place that harbors men.　　　　　　　　　*Either*
But here must end the story of my life,
And happy were I in my timely death
Could all my travels[2] warrant° me they live.　　　　　　*assure*
140　DUKE　Hapless° Egeon, whom the fates have marked　　*Unlucky*
To bear the extremity of dire mishap!
Now, trust me, were it not against our laws,
Against my crown, my oath, my dignity—
Which princes, would they, may not disannul[3]—
145　My soul should sue as advocate for thee.
But though thou art adjudgèd° to the death,　　　　　　*sentenced*
And passèd sentence may not be recalled
But° to our honor's great disparagement,°　　　　*Except / disgrace*
Yet will I favor thee in what I can.[4]
150　Therefore, merchant, I'll limit° thee this day　　　　　*allot*
To seek thy health° by beneficial help.　　　　　　　　　*deliverance*
Try all the friends thou hast in Ephesus;
Beg thou, or borrow, to make up the sum,
And live. If no, then thou art doomed to die.
155　　—Jailer, take him to thy custody.
　　JAILER　I will, my lord.
　　EGEON　Hopeless and helpless doth Egeon wend,°　　　　　*go*
But to procrastinate° his lifeless end.　　*Exeunt.*　　*postpone*

---

6. Those whom they have fished out of the sea.
7. An inconsistency of detail (see line 78).
8. *so . . . like:* in this way his situation was similar.
9. Bore the name of the brother from whom he was separated.

1. *Whom . . . see:* Since I longed to see my lost son.
2. Journeys; "travails," efforts.
3. *would . . . disannul:* even if they wished to, cannot cancel or overrule.
4. Yet I will bend the law's strictness as much as I can.

1.2

Enter ANTIPHOLUS [OF SYRACUSE], [FIRST] MERCHANT,
and DROMIO [OF SYRACUSE].

FIRST MERCHANT   Therefore give out° you are of Epidamnum,   *say*
    Lest that your goods too soon be confiscate.
    This very day a Syracusian merchant
    Is apprehended for arrival here,
5   And, not being able to buy out° his life,   *ransom*
    According to the statute of the town
    Dies ere the weary sun set in the west.
    There is your money that I had to keep.°   *in my keeping*
ANTIPHOLUS OF SYRACUSE [*to* DROMIO OF SYRACUSE]   Go bear
    it to the Centaur,[1] where we host,°   *lodge*
10   And stay there, Dromio, till I come to thee.
    Within this hour it will be dinnertime.[2]
    Till that,° I'll view the manners of the town,   *then*
    Peruse° the traders, gaze upon the buildings,   *Observe*
    And then return and sleep within mine inn;
15   For with long travel I am stiff and weary.
    Get thee away.
DROMIO OF SYRACUSE   Many a man would take you at your
    word,
    And go indeed, having so good a mean.[3]   *Exit.*
ANTIPHOLUS OF SYRACUSE   A trusty villain,[4] sir, that very oft,
20   When I am dull° with care and melancholy,   *gloomy*
    Lightens my humor[5] with his merry jests.
    What,° will you walk with me about the town   *Now then*
    And then go to my inn and dine with me?
FIRST MERCHANT   I am invited, sir, to certain merchants,
25   Of whom I hope to make much benefit.
    I crave your pardon; soon° at five o'clock,   *promptly*
    Please° you, I'll meet with you upon the mart,   *If it please*
    And afterward consort° you till bedtime.   *accompany*
    My present business calls me from you now.
30 ANTIPHOLUS OF SYRACUSE   Farewell till then. I will go lose
    myself
    And wander up and down to view the city.
FIRST MERCHANT   Sir, I commend you to your own content.°   *pleasures; peace*
                                             Exit.
ANTIPHOLUS OF SYRACUSE   He that commends me to mine
    own content
    Commends me to the thing I cannot get.
35   I to the world am like a drop of water
    That in the ocean seeks another drop,
    Who, falling there to find his fellow forth,[6]
    Unseen, inquisitive, confounds° himself.   *mingles; destroys*
    So I, to find a mother and a brother,
40   In quest of them, unhappy, lose myself.
        Enter DROMIO OF EPHESUS.

1.2 Location: A street in Ephesus.
1. The name of an inn; taverns, inns, and shops were frequently identified by a pictorial sign.
2. Noon, time for the midday meal.
3. Opportunity, but punning on "means" ("wealth").
4. Servant or slave ("villein"); also, rogue or scoun-drel (often used affectionately).
5. Mood, determined by the humors, bodily fluids that formed the basis of Elizabethan medical psychology.
6. To locate a matching drop.

Here comes the almanac of my true date.[7]
—What now? How chance° thou art returned so soon?　　　*What happened that*
DROMIO OF EPHESUS　Returned so soon? Rather approached
　　too late.
The capon burns, the pig falls from the spit,
45　The clock hath strucken twelve upon the bell;
My mistress made it one[8] upon my cheek.
She is so hot° because the meat is cold;　　　　　　　　　*angry*
The meat is cold because you come not home;
You come not home because you have no stomach;°　　　*appetite*
50　You have no stomach, having broke your fast.°　　　　　*eaten*
But we that know what 'tis to fast and pray
Are penitent[9] for your default° today.　　　　　　　　　　*fault*
ANTIPHOLUS OF SYRACUSE　Stop in your wind,° sir. Tell me　　*Shut your mouth*
　　this, I pray:
Where have you left the money that I gave you?
55　DROMIO OF EPHESUS　Oh, sixpence that I had o'Wednesday
　　last,
To pay the saddler for my mistress' crupper?[1]
The saddler had it, sir, I kept it not.
ANTIPHOLUS OF SYRACUSE　I am not in a sportive humor now.
Tell me, and dally not, where is the money?
60　We being strangers here, how dar'st thou trust
So great a charge from° thine own custody?　　　　*responsibility out of*
DROMIO OF EPHESUS　I pray you, jest, sir, as° you sit at dinner.　　*when*
I from my mistress come to you in post.°　　　　　　　　　*haste*
If I return I shall be post[2] indeed,
65　For she will scour° your fault upon my pate.°　　*score; flog / head*
Methinks your maw,° like mine, should be your clock　　*stomach*
And strike[3] you home without a messenger.
ANTIPHOLUS OF SYRACUSE　Come, Dromio, come, these jests
　　are out of season;
Reserve them till a merrier hour than this.
70　Where is the gold I gave in charge to thee?
DROMIO OF EPHESUS　To me, sir? Why, you gave no gold to me.
ANTIPHOLUS OF SYRACUSE　Come on, sir knave,[4] have done
　　your foolishness,
And tell me how thou hast disposed° thy charge.　　　*dealt with*
DROMIO OF EPHESUS　My charge was but to fetch you from
　　the mart
75　Home to your house, the Phoenix,[5] sir, to dinner;
My mistress and her sister stays° for you.　　　　　　　　*wait*
ANTIPHOLUS OF SYRACUSE　Now, as I am a Christian,[6] answer me
In what safe place you have bestowed my money,
Or I shall break that merry sconce° of yours　　　　　　*head*
80　That stands° on tricks when I am undisposed.°　　*insists / not in the mood*

---

7. The measure of my exact age (because born on the same date).
8. *made it one:* struck one o'clock.
9. Are doing penance in the ordinary way by praying and fasting (since the meal is delayed), and also through being beaten.
1. A strap passed under a horse's tail to prevent the saddle from slipping forward.
2. Beaten, like a wooden doorpost on which tavern charges were tallied (scored).

3. Beat; ring time like a clock.
4. Ironic: "knave," like "villain," means both "servant" and "rogue."
5. Antipholus of Ephesus's house is, like the inn (line 9), identified by a sign, this one depicting the mythological bird that symbolized resurrection. Many Londoners lived above their places of business.
6. A common oath, though anachronistic in classical Greece.

Where is the thousand marks thou hadst of me?

DROMIO OF EPHESUS   I have some marks of yours upon my
pate,
Some of my mistress' marks upon my shoulders,
But not a thousand marks between you both.
85 If I should pay your worship those again,°   back
Perchance you will not bear them patiently.

ANTIPHOLUS OF SYRACUSE   Thy mistress' marks? What
mistress, slave, hast thou?

DROMIO OF EPHESUS   Your worship's wife, my mistress, at the
Phoenix—
She that doth fast till you come home to dinner,
90 And prays that you will hie° you home to dinner.   hasten

ANTIPHOLUS OF SYRACUSE   What, wilt thou flout° me thus   mock; disobey
unto my face,
Being forbid? There, take you that, sir knave!
[He strikes him.]

DROMIO OF EPHESUS   What mean you, sir? For God sake,
hold° your hands!   stop
Nay, an° you will not, sir, I'll take my heels.°   Exit.   if / run away
95 ANTIPHOLUS OF SYRACUSE   Upon my life, by some device° or   trick
other
The villain is o'er-raught° of all my money.   cheated
They say this town is full of cozenage:°   deception
As° nimble jugglers⁷ that deceive the eye,   Such as
Dark-working⁸ sorcerers that change the mind,
100 Soul-killing witches that deform⁹ the body,
Disguisèd cheaters, prating mountebanks,°   fast-talking quacks
And many suchlike liberties¹ of sin.
If it prove so, I will be gone the sooner.
I'll to the Centaur to go seek this slave.
105 I greatly fear my money is not safe.   Exit.

2.1

Enter ADRIANA, *wife to* ANTIPHOLUS [OF EPHESUS], *with*
LUCIANA, *her sister.*

ADRIANA   Neither my husband nor the slave returned
That in such haste I sent to seek his master?
Sure,° Luciana, it is two o'clock.   Surely

LUCIANA   Perhaps some merchant hath invited him,
5   And from the mart he's somewhere gone to dinner.
Good sister, let us dine and never fret.
A man is master of his liberty.
Time is their master, and when they see time
They'll go or come. If so, be patient, sister.
10 ADRIANA   Why should their liberty than ours be more?

LUCIANA   Because their business still° lies out o'door.   always

ADRIANA   Look, when I serve him so, he takes it ill.¹

---

7. Performers skilled in manipulating appearances;
the term "juggler" could mean either an actual sor-
cerer or a mere illusionist.
8. Operating secretly or producing darkness.
9. Injure, disfigure; change the shape of (like the
enchantress Circe of Homer's *Odyssey*, who transformed Odysseus's men into swine).

1. "Liberties" possibly refers to the district that
housed many of London's theaters (including Shakespeare's company), which were situated just outside
the City's legal jurisdictions.
2.1 Location: Before the house of Antipholus of
Ephesus.
1. Whenever I treat him so, he takes it badly.

LUCIANA   Oh, know he is the bridle of your will.[2]

ADRIANA   There's none but° asses will be bridled so.   *Only*

15   LUCIANA   Why, headstrong liberty is lashed° with woe.   *beaten; tied down*
     There's nothing situate under heaven's eye
     But hath his bound° in earth, in sea, in sky.   *its limits*
     The beasts, the fishes, and the wingèd fowls
     Are their males' subjects and at their controls.°   *under their control*
20   Man, more divine,[3] the master of all these,
     Lord of the wide world and wild wat'ry seas,
     Indued° with intellectual sense and souls,   *Endowed*
     Of more preeminence than fish and fowls,
     Are masters to their females, and their lords:[4]
25   Then let your will attend on their accords.[5]

ADRIANA   This servitude makes you to keep unwed.

LUCIANA   Not this, but troubles of the marriage bed.[6]

ADRIANA   But were you wedded, you would bear some sway.°   *wield some power*

LUCIANA   Ere I learn love, I'll practice to obey.

30   ADRIANA   How if your husband start° some other where?°   *strays; wanders / elsewhere*

LUCIANA   Till he come home again, I would forbear.°   *be patient*

ADRIANA   Patience unmoved! No marvel though she pause.[7]
     They can be meek that have no other cause.°   *reason not to be*
     A wretched soul, bruised with adversity,
35   We bid be quiet when we hear it cry;
     But were we burdened with like° weight of pain,   *equal*
     As much or more we should ourselves complain.
     So thou, that hast no unkind mate to grieve thee,
     With urging helpless° patience would relieve° me;   *futile / comfort*
40   But if thou live to see like right bereft,[8]
     This fool-begged[9] patience in thee will be left.°   *abandoned*

LUCIANA   Well, I will marry one day, but to try.°   *test*
     Here comes your man.° Now is your husband nigh.°   *servant / near*
     Enter DROMIO OF EPHESUS.

ADRIANA   Say, is your tardy master now at hand?

45   DROMIO OF EPHESUS   Nay, he's at two hands with me, and that
     my two ears can witness.[1]

ADRIANA   Say, didst thou speak with him? Know'st thou his mind?

DROMIO OF EPHESUS   I? Ay, he told[2] his mind upon mine ear.
     Beshrew° his hand, I scarce could understand it.   *Curse*

50   LUCIANA   Spake he so doubtfully° thou couldst not feel his   *ambiguously*
     meaning?

DROMIO OF EPHESUS   Nay, he struck so plainly I could too well
     feel his blows, and withal so doubtfully° that I could scarce   *dreadfully; stoutly*
     understand° them.   *stand under*

55   ADRIANA   But say, I prithee,° is he coming home?   *pray thee*

---

2. He is meant to restrain your desires.
3. Nearer to God (in the great hierarchy of all beings).
4. *Man . . . lords:* Man's dominion over the creatures of earth and water derives from Genesis 1:28–29; his rule over woman is expressed in Paul's epistles, especially 1 Corinthians 11:3ff and Ephesians 5:22ff ("Wives, submit yourselves unto your husbands, as unto the Lord").
5. *attend . . . accords:* serve their wishes.
6. Compare 1 Corinthians 7:28: "And if a virgin

marry, she sinneth not: nevertheless such shall have trouble in the flesh."
7. That she hesitates (to marry).
8. *like . . . bereft:* yourself similarly deprived of rights.
9. Declaredly foolish; to "beg a person for a fool" was to petition the Court of Wards for custody of a lunatic (and thus custody of all his or her possessions).
1. *he's . . . witness:* he boxed my ears with both of his hands.
2. Communicated, but playing on "struck" ("tolled").

It seems he hath great care to please his wife.[3]

DROMIO OF EPHESUS   Why, mistress, sure my master is
    horn-mad.[4]

ADRIANA   Horn-mad, thou villain?

DROMIO OF EPHESUS   I mean not cuckold mad,
    But sure he is stark mad.

60   When I desired him to come home to dinner,
    He asked me for a thousand marks in gold.
    "'Tis dinner time," quoth I. "My gold!" quoth he.
    "Your meat doth burn," quoth I. "My gold!" quoth he.
    "Will you come?" quoth I. "My gold!" quoth he;

65   "Where is the thousand marks I gave thee, villain?"
    "The pig," quoth I, "is burned." "My gold!" quoth he.
    "My mistress, sir—" quoth I. "Hang up° thy mistress!   *Enough of*
    I know not thy mistress. Out° on thy mistress!"   *A curse*

LUCIANA   Quoth who?

70   DROMIO OF EPHESUS   Quoth my master.
    "I know," quoth he, "no house, no wife, no mistress."
    So that my errand,° due unto my tongue,[5]   *delivery; message*
    I thank him, I bare° home upon my shoulders;   *bore*
    For in conclusion he did beat me there.

75   ADRIANA   Go back again, thou slave, and fetch him home.

DROMIO OF EPHESUS   Go back again and be new° beaten home?   *again*
    For God's sake, send some other messenger.

ADRIANA   Back, slave, or I will break thy pate across.

DROMIO OF EPHESUS   An he will bless that cross with other
    beating,[6]

80   Between you I shall have a holy[7] head.

ADRIANA   Hence, prating peasant,° fetch thy master home.   *babbling fellow*

DROMIO OF EPHESUS   Am I so round[8] with you, as you with me,
    That like a football you do spurn° me thus?   *maltreat; kick*
    You spurn me hence, and he will spurn me hither;

85   If I last in this service you must case me in leather.[9]   [*Exit.*]

LUCIANA   Fie, how impatience loureth° in your face!   *frowns*

ADRIANA   His company must do his minions grace,[1]
    Whilst I at home starve for a merry look.
    Hath homely age th'alluring beauty took

90   From my poor cheek? Then he hath wasted it.[2]
    Are my discourses dull? Barren my wit?
    If voluble and sharp° discourse be marred,   *witty*
    Unkindness blunts it more than marble hard.[3]
    Do their° gay vestments° his affections bait?[4]   *(the minions')* / *clothing*

---

3. Ironic: compare 1 Corinthians 7:32–33: "The unmarried careth for the things of the Lord, how he may please the Lord: But he that is married careth for the things that are of the world, how he may please his wife."

4. Uncontrolled and wild as a horned beast (a common expression, as intended by Dromio); enraged at being made a cuckold, who by popular repute grew horns (as Adriana takes it).

5. *due . . . tongue:* which I should have carried back in words.

6. If he will give me another beating (playing on "across," a cross made by blows on my head, and "bless," the French *blesser,* "to injure").

7. Blessed (because marked with the sign of the cross); also, full of holes.

8. Blunt, disrespectful (with a play on "spherical," like a football).

9. If I survive as your servant, you must cover me with leather, like a football; with a play on "last," a wooden model of a foot used in making leather shoes.

1. Must grace his paramours.

2. Caused it to waste away; squandered it.

3. More than hard marble would blunt a sharp tool.

4. Lure away (bait); lessen (abate) toward Adriana.

95 That's not my fault; he's master of my state.[5]
What ruins are in me that can be found
By him not ruined?[6] Then is he the ground°   *cause*
Of my defeatures.° My decayèd fair,°   *disfigurement / beauty*
A sunny look of his would soon repair.
100 But, too unruly deer, he breaks the pale[7]
And feeds from° home. Poor I am but his stale.[8]   *away from*
LUCIANA Self-harming jealousy! Fie, beat it hence!
ADRIANA Unfeeling fools can with such wrongs dispense.
I know his eye doth homage otherwhere,
105 Or else what lets° it but he would be here?   *prevents*
Sister, you know he promised me a chain.
Would that alone o'love he would detain,[9]
So° he would keep fair quarter° with his bed.[1]   *If then / faith*
I see the jewel best enamelèd
110 Will lose his beauty. Yet the gold bides° still   *remains*
That others touch,[2] and often touching will
Wear gold, and no man that hath a name°   *reputation*
By falsehood and corruption doth it shame.[3]
Since that my beauty cannot please his eye,
115 I'll weep what's left away, and weeping die.
LUCIANA How many fond° fools serve mad jealousy!   *infatuated*

Exeunt.

2.2
Enter ANTIPHOLUS [OF SYRACUSE].

ANTIPHOLUS OF SYRACUSE The gold I gave to Dromio is laid up
Safe at the Centaur, and the heedful° slave   *careful*
Is wandered forth in care to seek me out.
By computation and mine host's report,[1]
5 I could not speak° with Dromio since at first   *could not have spoken*
I sent him from the mart. See, here he comes.
Enter DROMIO [OF] SYRACUSE.
How now, sir, is your merry humor altered?
As you love strokes,° so jest with me again.   *blows*
You know no Centaur? You received no gold?
10 Your mistress sent to have me home to dinner?
My house was at the Phoenix?—Wast thou mad,
That thus so madly thou didst answer me?
DROMIO OF SYRACUSE What answer, sir? When spake I such
a word?
ANTIPHOLUS OF SYRACUSE Even now, even here, not half an
hour since.
15 DROMIO OF SYRACUSE I did not see you since you sent me
hence

---

5. Estate or general condition, including clothes; also, metaphorically, kingdom.
6. *What . . . ruined:* What deterioration can be found in me that he is not responsible for?
7. He goes beyond the park boundary ("pale").
8. Lover held up to the ridicule of her rivals; prostitute.
9. *Would . . . detain:* I wish he would withhold that one manifestation of love.
1. TEXTUAL COMMENT The following five lines (109–13) as printed in the Folio appear to be corrupt and have been emended since the eighteenth century. For the passage as it originally appears, see Digital

Edition TC 2.
2. *touch:* test (the fineness of gold was tested by rubbing it on a touchstone); caress, referring to her husband's infidelities.
3. *I see . . . shame:* a difficult passage, possibly owing to omitted lines. The general idea is that reputation, like gold, withstands corruption and yet may be worn away. Her husband's infidelities have not tarnished his name, but they may diminish her substance.
2.2 Location: A street in Ephesus.
1. Based on a calculation of the time elapsed and the innkeeper's account of Dromio's doings.

Home to the Centaur with the gold you gave me.

ANTIPHOLUS OF SYRACUSE　Villain, thou didst deny the gold's
　　receipt,°　　　　　　　　　　　　　　　　　　　　　　　　*receiving the gold*
And told'st me of a mistress and a dinner,
For which I hope thou felt'st[2] I was displeased.

20　DROMIO OF SYRACUSE　I am glad to see you in this merry vein.°　　*disposition*
What means this jest? I pray you, master, tell me?

ANTIPHOLUS OF SYRACUSE　Yea, dost thou jeer and flout me in
　　the teeth?°　　　　　　　　　　　　　　　　　　　　　　　　*to my face*
Think'st thou I jest? Hold,° take thou that, and that!　　*Stop*
　　[*He*] *beats* DROMIO.

DROMIO OF SYRACUSE　Hold, sir, for God's sake! Now your
　　jest is earnest.[3]

25　Upon what bargain[4] do you give it me?

ANTIPHOLUS OF SYRACUSE　Because that I familiarly
　　sometimes
Do use you for my fool° and chat with you,　　*jester*
Your sauciness will jest upon my love[5]
And make a common[6] of my serious hours.

30　When the sun shines let foolish gnats make sport,°　　*play*
But creep in crannies when he hides his beams.
If you will jest with me, know my aspect,[7]
And fashion your demeanor to° my looks,　　*to match*
Or I will beat this method° in your sconce.°　　*rule / head*

35　DROMIO OF SYRACUSE　"Sconce,"° call you it? So° you would　　*Small fort / If*
leave battering,[8] I had rather have it a head. An° you use　　*If*
these blows long, I must get a sconce° for my head, and　　*protective screen*
ensconce° it too, or else I shall seek my wit° in my shoulders.　　*shelter / brains*
But I pray, sir, why am I beaten?

40　ANTIPHOLUS OF SYRACUSE　Dost thou not know?

DROMIO OF SYRACUSE　Nothing, sir, but that I am beaten.

ANTIPHOLUS OF SYRACUSE　Shall I tell you why?

DROMIO OF SYRACUSE　Ay, sir, and wherefore;° for, they say,　　*for what reason*
every why hath a wherefore.

45　ANTIPHOLUS OF SYRACUSE　Why first—for flouting me; and then
wherefore—for urging° it the second time to me.　　*repeating*

DROMIO OF SYRACUSE　Was there ever any man thus beaten
　　out of season,°　　　　　　　　　　　　　　　　　　　　　　*unjustly*
When in the why and the wherefore is neither rhyme nor
　　reason?
Well, sir, I thank you.

50　ANTIPHOLUS OF SYRACUSE　Thank me, sir, for what?

DROMIO OF SYRACUSE　Marry,[9] sir, for this something that you
gave me for nothing.

ANTIPHOLUS OF SYRACUSE　I'll make you amends next: to give°　　*by giving*
you nothing for something. But say, sir, is it dinnertime?

55　DROMIO OF SYRACUSE　No, sir, I think the meat wants that° I　　*lacks what*
have.

---

2. Perceived, with an allusion to the beating.
3. Serious, with a play on "earnest" as a deposit to secure a business transaction.
4. Transaction (playing on the financial sense of "earnest"); in this context, contention or quarrel.
5. *Your . . . love:* You impertinently assume the right to joke because of my benevolence.
6. Land belonging to the whole community (Dromio

maintains an egalitarian spirit at inappropriate times).
7. Countenance, expression; in astrology, the position of a heavenly body, as the sun (lines 30–31).
8. Beating; here, with a play on "sconce," attacking with a battering ram.
9. By the Virgin Mary, a mild oath.

ANTIPHOLUS OF SYRACUSE In good time,[1] sir, what's that?

DROMIO OF SYRACUSE Basting.[2]

ANTIPHOLUS OF SYRACUSE Well, sir, then 'twill be dry.

60   DROMIO OF SYRACUSE If it be, sir, I pray you eat none of it.

ANTIPHOLUS OF SYRACUSE Your reason?

DROMIO OF SYRACUSE Lest it make you choleric,[3] and pur-
chase me another dry basting.°   *severe beating*

ANTIPHOLUS OF SYRACUSE Well, sir, learn to jest in good
65   time;[4] there's a time for all things.

DROMIO OF SYRACUSE I durst° have denied that before you   *dared*
were so choleric.

ANTIPHOLUS OF SYRACUSE By what rule,° sir?   *principle*

DROMIO OF SYRACUSE   Marry, sir, by a rule as plain as the
70   plain bald pate of Father Time himself.[5]

ANTIPHOLUS OF SYRACUSE Let's hear it.

DROMIO OF SYRACUSE There's no time for a man to recover his
hair that grows bald by nature.

ANTIPHOLUS OF SYRACUSE May he not do it by fine and
75   recovery?[6]

DROMIO OF SYRACUSE Yes, to pay a fine° for a periwig, and   *fee*
recover the lost hair of another man.[7]

ANTIPHOLUS OF SYRACUSE Why is Time such a niggard of
hair, being, as it is, so plentiful an excrement?°   *outward growth*

80   DROMIO OF SYRACUSE Because it is a blessing that he bestows
on beasts, and what he hath scanted° men in hair, he hath   *given less to*
given them in wit.°   *intellect*

ANTIPHOLUS OF SYRACUSE Why, but there's many a man hath
more hair than wit.

85   DROMIO OF SYRACUSE Not a man of those but he hath the wit
to lose his hair.[8]

ANTIPHOLUS OF SYRACUSE Why, thou didst conclude hairy
men plain dealers without wit.[9]

DROMIO OF SYRACUSE The plainer dealer,[1] the sooner lost; yet
90   he loseth it in a kind of jollity.°   *sexual pleasure*

ANTIPHOLUS OF SYRACUSE For what reason?

DROMIO OF SYRACUSE For two, and sound° ones too.   *strong*

ANTIPHOLUS OF SYRACUSE Nay, not sound,° I pray you.   *healthy*

DROMIO OF SYRACUSE Sure° ones, then.   *Certain*

95   ANTIPHOLUS OF SYRACUSE Nay, not sure° in a thing falsing.[2]   *trustworthy*

DROMIO OF SYRACUSE Certain ones, then.

ANTIPHOLUS OF SYRACUSE Name them.

DROMIO OF SYRACUSE The one, to save the money that he
spends in tiring;° the other, that at dinner they should not   *hairstyling*
100   drop in his porridge.

ANTIPHOLUS OF SYRACUSE You would all this time have proved
there is no time for all things.

---

1. Indeed! (an expression of ironical acquiescence).
2. Punning on a second meaning, "beating."
3. Angry. Choler was the hot, dry humor (see note to 1.2.21); both climate and diet were thought to affect the humors. Thus, for example, the consumption of overly dry meat was thought to be linked to a choleric disposition.
4. Opportunely; in a merry or good-humored time.
5. Time was commonly depicted as a bald old man.
6. *fine and recovery:* the legal method of transferring the ownership of property that could not normally be

sold, especially to break an entail.
7. *to pay . . . man:* to buy a wig made from someone else's hair (as wigs usually were).
8. *wit . . . hair:* ironic—clever enough to catch syphilis (which may cause hair loss).
9. *conclude . . . wit:* argue that hairy men are simple, lacking in cunning and therefore being honest (plain dealers).
1. With a pun on "deal," meaning "have sex."
2. In a deceptive matter; perhaps punning on "thing" as "sexual organ."

DROMIO OF SYRACUSE Marry, and did, sir: namely, e'en° no
　　time to recover hair lost by nature.

　　　　　　　　　　　　　　　　　　　　　　even; precisely

105 ANTIPHOLUS OF SYRACUSE But your reason was not substan-
　　tial,° why there is no time to recover.

　　　　　　　　　　　　　　　　　　　　　　firmly based

DROMIO OF SYRACUSE Thus I mend° it: Time himself is bald,
　　and therefore to the world's end will have bald followers.

　　　　　　　　　　　　　　　　　　　　　　improve

ANTIPHOLUS OF SYRACUSE I knew 'twould be a bald° conclu-
110 sion. But soft, who wafts° us yonder?

　　　　　　　　　　　　　　　　　　　　　　an inane
　　　　　　　　　　　　　　　　　　　　　　beckons

　　　　　Enter ADRIANA *and* LUCIANA.

ADRIANA Ay, ay, Antipholus, look strange[3] and frown;
　　Some other mistress hath thy sweet aspects.°

　　　　　　　　　　　　　　　　　　　　　　loving looks

　　I am not Adriana, nor thy wife.
　　The time was once when thou unurged wouldst vow
115 That never words were music to thine ear,
　　That never object pleasing in thine eye,
　　That never touch well welcome to thy hand,
　　That never meat sweet-savored in thy taste,
　　Unless I spake, or looked, or touched, or carved to° thee.

　　　　　　　　　　　　　　　　　　　　　　for

120 How comes it now, my husband, oh, how comes it,
　　That thou art then estrangèd from thyself?
　　Thy "self" I call it, being strange to me
　　That, undividable, incorporate,°

　　　　　　　　　　　　　　　　　　　　　　united in one body

　　Am better than thy dear self's better part.[4]
125 Ah, do not tear away thyself from me;
　　For know, my love, as easy mayst thou fall°

　　　　　　　　　　　　　　　　　　　　　　let fall

　　A drop of water in the breaking gulf
　　And take unmingled thence that drop again
　　Without addition or diminishing,
130 As take from me thyself and not me too.[5]
　　How dearly° would it touch thee to the quick,

　　　　　　　　　　　　　　　　　　　　　　deeply

　　Shouldst thou but° hear I were licentious,

　　　　　　　　　　　　　　　　　　　　　　only

　　And that this body, consecrate to thee,
　　By ruffian lust should be contaminate?
135 Wouldst thou not spit at me, and spurn° at me,

　　　　　　　　　　　　　　　　　　　　　　strike

　　And hurl the name of husband in my face,[6]
　　And tear the stained skin[7] of my harlot brow,
　　And from my false hand cut the wedding ring,
　　And break it with a deep-divorcing vow?
140 I know thou canst, and therefore see° thou do it!

　　　　　　　　　　　　　　　　　　　　　　make sure

　　I am possessed with° an adulterate blot;[8]

　　　　　　　　　　　　　　　　　　　　　　in possession of

　　My blood is mingled with the crime of lust:
　　For if we two be one, and thou play false,
　　I do digest the poison of thy flesh,
145 Being strumpeted° by thy contagion.

　　　　　　　　　　　　　　　　　　　　　　made a whore

　　Keep then fair league[9] and truce with thy true bed,
　　I live dis-stained, thou undishonorèd.[1]

---

3. Look distant, but suggesting "without recognition," as if a foreigner—which he is.
4. Either his better qualities or his soul (which is better than his body). Adriana's plea depends on the doctrine of marriage as "one flesh" articulated in Genesis
2:23–24 and echoed in Paul's mystical view of the
church as wedded to God. Compare Ephesians
5:28–33.
5. *not me too:* not take me away from myself as
well.
6. And bitterly confront me with my degraded mar-

riage vow.
7. Mark of impure character, as if she had been
legally branded as a harlot.
8. The stain, or disgrace, of adultery.
9. *Keep . . . league:* If you keep faithful alliance.
1. TEXTUAL COMMENT The Folio's "distain'd," often
changed by editors to "unstained," is here emended
to the archaic word "dis-stained," referring to the
removal of color during the dying process. See Digital Edition TC 3.

ANTIPHOLUS OF SYRACUSE   Plead you to me, fair dame? I know
  you not.
  In Ephesus I am but two hours old,
150   As strange unto your town as to your talk,
  Who, every word by all my wit being scanned,°   *analyzed*
  Wants° wit in all, one word to understand.   *Lacks*
LUCIANA   Fie, brother,° how the world is changed with you!   *brother-in-law*
  When were you wont to use° my sister thus?   *treat*
155   She sent for you by Dromio home to dinner.
ANTIPHOLUS OF SYRACUSE   By Dromio?
DROMIO OF SYRACUSE   By me?
ADRIANA   By thee; and this thou didst return° from him: *bring back*
  That he did buffet thee and, in his blows,
160   Denied my house for° his, me for his wife.   *to be*
ANTIPHOLUS OF SYRACUSE   Did you converse, sir, with this
  gentlewoman?
  What is the course and drift of your compact?[2]
DROMIO OF SYRACUSE   I, sir? I never saw her till this time.
ANTIPHOLUS OF SYRACUSE   Villain, thou liest; for even her
  very° words   *exact*
165   Didst thou deliver to me on the mart.
DROMIO OF SYRACUSE   I never spake with her in all my life.
ANTIPHOLUS OF SYRACUSE   How can she thus then call us by
  our names?—
  Unless it be by inspiration.°   *divine revelation*
ADRIANA   How ill agrees it with° your gravity°   *does it suit / dignity*
170   To counterfeit° thus grossly° with your slave,   *dissemble / blatantly*
  Abetting him to thwart me in my mood!
  Be it my wrong you are from me exempt,[3]
  But wrong not that wrong with a more contempt.[4]
  Come, I will fasten on this sleeve of thine:
175   Thou art an elm, my husband; I, a vine,[5]
  Whose weakness married to thy stronger state°   *condition*
  Makes me with thy strength to communicate.°   *share*
  If aught possess thee from me,[6] it is dross,°   *worthless*
  Usurping ivy, brier, or idle moss,
180   Who, all° for want of pruning, with intrusion,°   *entirely / invasively*
  Infect thy sap and live on thy confusion.[7]
ANTIPHOLUS OF SYRACUSE   [aside]   To me she speaks; she moves°   *uses*
  me for her theme.°   *topic*
  What, was I married to her in my dream?
  Or sleep I now and think I hear all this?
185   What error drives our eyes and ears amiss?
  Until I know this sure uncertainty,
  I'll entertain° the offered fallacy.°   *accept / delusion*
LUCIANA   Dromio, go bid the servants spread° for dinner.   *lay the table*
DROMIO OF SYRACUSE   [aside]   Oh, for my beads!° I cross me[8]   *rosary beads*
  for° a sinner.   *as*
190   This is the fairy land. Oh, spite of spites!

---

2. What is the purpose and meaning of your conspiracy?
3. Be . . . exempt: Grant that it is my fault that you are alienated from me.
4. But do not add to that injury with mockery.
5. This image occurs both in Ovid's *Metamorphoses*

14.665–66 and in Psalm 128:3, included in the Elizabethan homily on marriage.
6. If anything takes possession of you away from (or apart from) me.
7. live . . . confusion: take life from your destruction.
8. Make the sign of the cross (to ward off evil).

We talk with goblins, owls,[9] and sprites.°   *spirits*
If we obey them not, this will ensue:
They'll suck our breath or pinch us black and blue.[1]

LUCIANA   Why prat'st° thou to thyself and answer'st not?   *babble*

195   Dromio, thou drone,° thou snail, thou slug, thou sot!°   *idler / blockhead*

DROMIO OF SYRACUSE   I am transformèd, master, am I not?

ANTIPHOLUS OF SYRACUSE   I think thou art in mind, and so
    am I.

DROMIO OF SYRACUSE   Nay, master, both in mind and in my
    shape.

ANTIPHOLUS OF SYRACUSE   Thou hast thine own form.

DROMIO OF SYRACUSE   No, I am an ape.[2]

200   LUCIANA   If thou art changed to aught,° 'tis to an ass.   *anything*

DROMIO OF SYRACUSE   'Tis true: she rides° me, and I long for   *tyrannizes*
    grass.[3]
  'Tis so, I am an ass; else it could never be,
  But I should know her as well as she knows me.

ADRIANA   Come, come, no longer will I be a fool

205   To put the finger in the eye and weep
Whilst man and master laughs my woes to scorn.[4]
Come, sir, to dinner. —Dromio, keep the gate.
—Husband, I'll dine above with you today,
And shrive you of[5] a thousand idle pranks.

210   —Sirrah,[6] if any ask you for your master,
Say he dines forth,° and let no creature enter.   *out*
Come, sister. —Dromio, play the porter well.

ANTIPHOLUS OF SYRACUSE   Am I in earth, in heaven, or in hell?
Sleeping or waking? Mad or well advised?°   *sane*

215   Known unto these, and to myself disguised?
I'll say as they say, and persever so,
And in this mist at all adventures° go.   *whatever occurs*

DROMIO OF SYRACUSE   Master, shall I be porter at the gate?

ADRIANA   Ay, and let none enter, lest I break your pate.°   *head*

220   LUCIANA   Come, come, Antipholus, we dine too late.

                                [Exeunt.]

3.1

Enter ANTIPHOLUS OF EPHESUS, *his man* DROMIO
[OF EPHESUS], ANGELO *the goldsmith, and* BALTHASAR
the merchant.

ANTIPHOLUS OF EPHESUS   Good Signor Angelo, you must
    excuse us all.
My wife is shrewish° when I keep not hours.°   *ill tempered / am late*
Say that I lingered with you at your shop
To see the making of her carcanet,°   *jeweled necklace*

5   And that tomorrow you will bring it home.
But here's a villain that would face me down[1]—
He met me on the mart, and that I beat him,
And charged him with[2] a thousand marks in gold,

---

9. A possible reference to witchcraft.
1. Traditional recreations for fairies.
2. An imitation (of myself); a fool.
3. Freedom, as when a horse is put out to pasture.
4. *laughs . . . scorn:* make a mockery of my pain.
5. And act as your confessor to hear and pardon.

6. Standard term for addressing inferiors.
3.1 Location: Before the house of Antipholus of
Ephesus.
1. That would insist despite my denial that.
2. And accused him of possessing.

And that I did deny my wife and house!

10 —Thou drunkard, thou, what didst thou mean by this?

DROMIO OF EPHESUS   Say what you will, sir, but I know what
I know.

That you beat me at the mart I have your hand[3] to show.

If the skin were parchment, and the blows you gave were ink,

Your own handwriting would tell you what I think.

ANTIPHOLUS OF EPHESUS   I think thou art an ass.

15 DROMIO OF EPHESUS   Marry, so it doth appear

By the wrongs I suffer and the blows I bear.

I should kick, being kicked, and being at that pass,°   in that predicament

You would keep from my heels and beware of an ass.

ANTIPHOLUS OF EPHESUS   You're sad,° Signor Balthasar. Pray   serious

God our cheer°   fare

20 May answer° my good will and your good welcome here.   equal

BALTHASAR   I hold your dainties cheap, sir, and your welcome dear.[4]

ANTIPHOLUS OF EPHESUS   O Signor Balthasar, either at flesh
or fish,

A table full of welcome makes scarce° one dainty dish.   scarcely makes

BALTHASAR   Good meat, sir, is common; that every churl°   peasant
affords.

25 ANTIPHOLUS OF EPHESUS   And welcome more common, for
that's nothing but words.

BALTHASAR   Small cheer° and great welcome makes a merry   Little food
feast.

ANTIPHOLUS OF EPHESUS   Ay, to a niggardly host and more
sparing° guest.   temperate

But though my cates° be mean,° take them in good part.   provisions / poor

Better cheer may you have, but not with better heart.

30 But soft,[5] my door is locked. [to DROMIO OF EPHESUS] Go, bid
them let us in.

DROMIO OF EPHESUS [calling]   Maud, Bridget, Marian, Cicely,
Gillian, Ginn!

[Enter DROMIO OF SYRACUSE within.]

DROMIO OF SYRACUSE [within]   Mome, Malt-horse, Capon,
Coxcomb, Idiot, Patch![6]

Either get thee from the door, or sit down at the hatch.[7]

Dost thou conjure for° wenches, that thou call'st for such   summon by spells
store°   plenty

35 When one is one too many? Go, get thee from the door.

DROMIO OF EPHESUS   What patch is made our porter? My
master stays° in the street.   waits

DROMIO OF SYRACUSE [within]   Let him walk from whence he
came, lest he catch cold on 's° feet.   on his

ANTIPHOLUS OF EPHESUS   Who talks within there? Ho, open
the door!

DROMIO OF SYRACUSE [within]   Right, sir, I'll tell you when,
an° you'll tell me wherefore.   if

40 ANTIPHOLUS OF EPHESUS   Wherefore? For my dinner: I have
not dined today.

---

3. The mark of Antipholus's hand.
4. I value your welcome more highly than the delicacies of your table.
5. An exclamation of surprise.

6. Dolt, plodding oaf, eunuch, fool, idiot, clown.
7. Literally, sit down at the gate or half door, but
playing on the proverbial phrase "set a hatch (gate)
before the door" of the tongue: keep silent.

DROMIO OF SYRACUSE [*within*]   Nor today here you must not.
    Come again when you may.
ANTIPHOLUS OF EPHESUS   What art thou that keep'st me out
    from the house I owe?°   own
DROMIO OF SYRACUSE [*within*]   The porter for this time,° sir,   for now
    and my name is Dromio.
DROMIO OF EPHESUS   O villain, thou hast stol'n both mine
    office° and my name: function
45   The one ne'er got me credit, the other mickle blame.[8]
    If thou hadst been Dromio today in my place,
    Thou wouldst have changed thy face[9] for a name or thy
        name for an ass.
        Enter LUCE [*within*].[1]
LUCE [*within*]   What a coil° is there, Dromio? Who are those   disturbance
    at the gate?
DROMIO OF EPHESUS   Let my master in, Luce.
LUCE [*within*]   Faith, no, he comes too late,
    And so tell your master.
50 DROMIO OF EPHESUS   O Lord, I must laugh,
    Have at you[2] with a proverb: "Shall I set in my staff?"[3]
LUCE [*within*]   Have at you with another, that's —"When?
    Can you tell?"[4]
DROMIO OF SYRACUSE [*within*]   If thy name be called Luce,
    Luce, thou hast answered him well.
ANTIPHOLUS OF EPHESUS   Do you hear, you minion?° You'll   subordinate
    let us in, I trow?[5]
LUCE [*within*]   I thought to have asked you.
55 DROMIO OF SYRACUSE [*within*]   And you said no.°   (already)
DROMIO OF EPHESUS   So come help.
    [DROMIO OF EPHESUS *and* ANTIPHOLUS OF EPHESUS
    knock at the door.]
        Well struck! There was blow for blow.[6]
ANTIPHOLUS OF EPHESUS   Thou baggage,° let me in.   good-for-nothing
LUCE [*within*]   Can you tell for whose sake?
DROMIO OF EPHESUS   Master, knock the door hard.
LUCE [*within*]   Let him knock till it ache.
ANTIPHOLUS OF EPHESUS   You'll cry for this, minion, if I beat
    the door down.
60 LUCE [*within*]   What needs all that, and a pair of stocks in
    the town?[7]
        Enter ADRIANA [*within*].
ADRIANA [*within*]   Who is that at the door that keeps° all this   keeps up
    noise?
DROMIO OF SYRACUSE [*within*]   By my troth, your town is
    troubled with unruly boys.

---

8. My reputation ("name") has never brought me credit, but in the course of my duties I have received much reproof ("mickle blame").
9. I.e., tried to change your identity (?). F's reading is obscure, and most editors emend the line: for example, "Thou wouldst have changed thy face for an aim" (i.e., you would have exchanged your face for a target).
1. TEXTUAL COMMENT The Folio refers to Adriana's kitchen maid as both "Luce" and "Nell," signaling perhaps a change in Shakespeare's mind while writing the play. We have chosen to retain both names. See Digital Edition TC 4.
2. A challenge or warning in a fight (as with a quar-

ter staff): Now I attack you.
3. "Shall I take up residence?" (proverbial).
4. Proverbial response of defiance.
5. TEXTUAL COMMENT In order to preserve the rhyme scheme, the Folio's "hope" has been emended to "trow" ("believe"). See Digital Edition TC 5.
6. Blows to the door in response to verbal blows from within.
7. Why should I worry when there is a legal punishment for such behavior? *stocks*: instrument of punishment in which a person was seated with his or her legs locked in a wooden frame.

ANTIPHOLUS OF EPHESUS   Are you there, wife? You might
    have come before.
ADRIANA [*within*]   Your wife, sir knave? Go, get you from the
    door.
65 DROMIO OF EPHESUS   If you went in pain, master, this knave
    would go sore.[8]
ANGELO   Here is neither cheer, sir, nor welcome; we would
    fain° have either.   *gladly*
BALTHASAR   In° debating which was best, we shall part° with   *After / depart*
    neither.
DROMIO OF EPHESUS   They stand at the door, master; bid
    them welcome hither.
ANTIPHOLUS OF EPHESUS   There is something in the wind°   *afoot*
    that we cannot get in.
70 DROMIO OF EPHESUS   You would say so, master, if your
    garments were thin.°   *(taking "wind" literally)*
    Your cake[9] here is warm within; you stand here in the cold.
    It would make a man mad as a buck[1] to be so bought and sold.°   *betrayed*
ANTIPHOLUS OF EPHESUS   Go fetch me something. I'll break
    ope° the gate.   *open*
DROMIO OF SYRACUSE [*within*]   Break° any breaking here, and   *Do*
    I'll break your knave's pate.
75 DROMIO OF EPHESUS   A man may break° a word with you, sir,   *speak*
    and words are but wind;
    Ay, and break it in your face, so he break it° not behind.   *break wind*
DROMIO OF SYRACUSE [*within*]   It seems thou want'st break-
    ing.[2] Out upon thee, hind!°   *slave; fellow*
DROMIO OF EPHESUS   Here's too much "out upon thee"! I pray
    thee, let me in.
DROMIO OF SYRACUSE [*within*]   Ay, when fowls have no
    feathers and fish have no fin.
80 ANTIPHOLUS OF EPHESUS   Well, I'll break in! —Go borrow me
    a crow.°   *crowbar*
DROMIO OF EPHESUS   A crow without feather? Master, mean
    you so?
    For a fish without a fin, there's a fowl without a feather.
    [*to* DROMIO OF SYRACUSE] If a crow help us in, sirrah, we'll
    pluck a crow° together.   *settle accounts*
ANTIPHOLUS OF EPHESUS   Go, get thee gone; fetch me an iron
    crow.
85 BALTHASAR   Have patience, sir. Oh, let it not be so.
    Herein you war against your reputation,
    And draw within the compass of suspect°   *scope of suspicion*
    Th'unviolated honor of your wife.
    Once this:° your long experience of her wisdom,   *In brief*
90   Her sober virtue, years,° and modesty,   *maturity*
    Plead on her part some cause° to you unknown;   *explanation; excuse*
    And doubt not, sir, but she will well excuse°   *explain*
    Why at this time the doors are made° against you.   *barred*
    Be ruled by me: depart in patience,
95   And let us to the Tiger[3] all to dinner,

8. If you, the master, get punished as a knave, so will
I, the actual servant ("knave").
9. Referring either to Adriana or to the meal.
1. Angry, with an allusion to cuckoldry (see 2.1.57

and note).
2. Need a beating; need to be "broken in," or tamed
like a horse.
3. The name of an inn; see 1.2.9.

And about evening come yourself alone
To know the reason of this strange restraint.° — exclusion
If by strong hand you offer° to break in — attempt
Now in the stirring passage° of the day, — traffic
100 A vulgar° comment will be made of it, — public; lewd
And that supposèd° by the common rout° — assumed / mob
Against your yet ungallèd estimation,[4]
That may with foul intrusion enter in
And dwell upon your grave when you are dead.
105 For slander lives upon succession,° — perpetuates itself
Forever housèd where it gets possession.
ANTIPHOLUS OF EPHESUS   You have prevailed. I will depart in
    quiet,
And in despite of mirth° mean to be merry. — ridicule
I know a wench of excellent discourse,
110 Pretty and witty; wild, and yet, too, gentle.
There will we dine. This woman that I mean
My wife—but I protest without desert°— — my deserving
Hath oftentimes upbraided me withal.° — scolded me about
To her will we to dinner. [to ANGELO] Get you home
115 And fetch the chain. By this° I know 'tis made. — this time
Bring it, I pray you, to the Porcupine,
For there's the house.° That chain will I bestow— — That is where she lives
Be it for nothing but to spite my wife—
Upon mine hostess there. Good sir, make haste:
120 Since mine own doors refuse to entertain° me, — welcome
I'll knock elsewhere to see if they'll disdain me.
ANGELO   I'll meet you at that place some hour hence.
ANTIPHOLUS OF EPHESUS   Do so. This jest shall cost me some
    expense.   Exeunt.

3.2

Enter [LUCIANA] with ANTIPHOLUS OF SYRACUSE.
LUCIANA   And may it be that you have quite forgot
A husband's office?° Shall, Antipholus, — duty
Even in the spring of love, thy love-springs° rot? — young shoots of love
Shall love in building grow so ruinous?[1]
5 If you did wed my sister for her wealth,
Then for her wealth's sake use° her with more kindness; — treat
Or if you like elsewhere, do it by stealth:
Muffle° your false love with some show of blindness.[2] — Hide
Let not my sister read it in your eye.
10 Be not thy tongue thy own shame's orator.
Look sweet, speak fair, become disloyalty;[3]
Apparel vice like virtue's harbinger.° — herald
Bear a fair presence,° though your heart be tainted: — Present a pleasant front
Teach sin the carriage° of a holy saint. — bearing
15 Be secret false: what° need she be acquainted? — why
What simple thief brags of his own attaint?° — crime
'Tis double wrong to truant with° your bed — be unfaithful to

4. yet . . . estimation: as yet uninjured reputation.
3.2 Location: Scene continues.
1. Shall love become a ruin at the time of its building?
2. Seem to blindfold yourself so that your glances do

not reveal your faithlessness.
3. become disloyalty: put an attractive face on your
unfaithfulness.

And let her read it in thy looks at board.°   *table*
Shame hath a bastard fame, well managèd;°   *if properly handled*
20 Ill deeds is° doubled with an evil word.   *are*
Alas, poor women, make us but believe,
Being compact of credit,[4] that you love us.
Though others have the arm, show us the sleeve.[5]
We in your motion turn,[6] and you may move° us.   *control; touch*
25 Then, gentle brother, get you in again.
Comfort my sister, cheer her, call her wife.
'Tis holy sport to be a little vain°   *false*
When the sweet breath of flattery conquers strife.

ANTIPHOLUS OF SYRACUSE   Sweet mistress, what your name is
    else I know not,
30 Nor by what wonder you do hit of° mine.   *on*
Less in your knowledge and your grace you show not
Than our earth's wonder,[7] more than earth° divine.   *mortal flesh*
Teach me, dear creature, how to think and speak.
Lay open to my earthy gross conceit,[8]
35 Smothered in errors, feeble, shallow, weak,
The folded° meaning of your words' deceit.   *hidden*
Against my soul's pure truth why labor you
To make it wander in an unknown field?
Are you a god? Would you create me new?°   *anew*
40 Transform me then, and to your power I'll yield.
But if that I am I, then well I know
Your weeping sister is no wife of mine,
Nor to her bed no homage° do I owe.   *duty*
Far more, far more, to you do I decline.°   *incline; submit*
45 Oh, train° me not, sweet mermaid,[9] with thy note   *entice*
To drown me in thy sister's flood of tears.
Sing, siren, for thyself, and I will dote.
Spread o'er the silver waves thy golden hairs,
And as a bed I'll take thee, and there lie,
50 And in that glorious supposition° think: *(that the hair is a bed)*
He gains by death that° hath such means to die.[1]   *who*
Let love, being light,[2] be drownèd if she sink.

LUCIANA   What, are you mad, that you do reason so?
ANTIPHOLUS OF SYRACUSE   Not mad, but mated[3]—how, I do
    not know.
55 LUCIANA   It is a fault that springeth from your eye.°   *from looking lustfully*
ANTIPHOLUS OF SYRACUSE   For gazing on your beams,° fair   *eyes*
    sun, being by.
LUCIANA   Gaze where you should, and that will clear your sight.
ANTIPHOLUS OF SYRACUSE   As good to wink,° sweet love, as   *shut one's eyes*
    look on° night.   *at*

---

4. Being made of credulity; gullible.
5. Although others have the reality of your love, present us the appearance.
6. We are subject to your influence (as heavenly bodies were believed to follow the rotations of concentric celestial spheres).
7. *Less . . . wonder:* You seem as wise and as gracious as the wonder of the world (probably an allusion to Queen Elizabeth, before whom the play might have been performed).

8. *earthy gross conceit:* clumsy mortal understanding.
9. Siren; in Greek legend, mermaids' singing lured sailors to their death (see line 47).
1. Perhaps with a pun on "to die" as the Elizabethan expression for "to have an orgasm."
2. The line has two implications: only false love could sink, because true love is too light and buoyant; and love deserves drowning because it is giddy and wanton.
3. Amazed, confounded; in love; married.

LUCIANA   Why call you me love? Call my sister so.

ANTIPHOLUS OF SYRACUSE   Thy sister's sister.

LUCIANA   That's my sister.

60   ANTIPHOLUS OF SYRACUSE   No,
It is thyself, mine own self's better part,
Mine eye's clear eye, my dear heart's dearer heart,
My food, my fortune, and my sweet hope's aim,
My sole earth's heaven, and my heaven's claim.[4]

65   LUCIANA   All this my sister is, or else should be.

ANTIPHOLUS OF SYRACUSE   Call thyself sister, sweet, for I am
thee.°   thine
Thee will I love, and with thee lead my life.
Thou hast no husband yet, nor I no wife.
Give me thy hand.

LUCIANA   Oh, soft, sir, hold you still;
70   I'll fetch my sister to get her good will.   Exit.
          Enter DROMIO [OF SYRACUSE].

ANTIPHOLUS OF SYRACUSE   Why, how now, Dromio, where
runn'st thou so fast?

DROMIO OF SYRACUSE   Do you know me, sir? Am I Dromio?
Am I your man? Am I myself?

75   ANTIPHOLUS OF SYRACUSE   Thou art Dromio, thou art my
man, thou art thyself.

DROMIO OF SYRACUSE   I am an ass, I am a woman's man, and
besides° myself.   in addition

ANTIPHOLUS OF SYRACUSE   What woman's man? And how
80   besides thyself?

DROMIO OF SYRACUSE   Marry, sir, besides myself, I am due to
a woman: one that claims me, one that haunts me, one that
will have me.

ANTIPHOLUS OF SYRACUSE   What claim lays she to thee?

85   DROMIO OF SYRACUSE   Marry, sir, such claim as you would lay
to your horse, and she would have me as a beast—not that I,
being a beast, she would have me, but that she, being a very
beastly creature, lays claim to me.

ANTIPHOLUS OF SYRACUSE   What is she?

90   DROMIO OF SYRACUSE   A very reverend° body; ay, such a one as   worthy
a man may not speak of without he say, "sir reverence."[5] I
have but lean luck in the match, and yet is she a wondrous
fat marriage.

ANTIPHOLUS OF SYRACUSE   How dost thou mean, a fat
95   marriage?

DROMIO OF SYRACUSE   Marry, sir, she's the kitchen wench,°   servant
and all grease; and I know not what use to put her to, but to
make a lamp of her and run from her by her own light. I
warrant° her rags and the tallow in them will burn a Poland   guarantee
100   winter.[6] If she lives till doomsday, she'll burn a week longer
than the whole world.[7]

ANTIPHOLOUS OF SYRACUSE   What complexion is she of?

---

4. My only heaven on earth and only claim on heaven.
5. "Saving your reverence," an apology for a potentially offensive remark.
6. The length of a winter in Poland—a long time.
7. Than the rest of the world (the popular Christian belief being that the earth would end in fire).

DROMIO OF SYRACUSE   Swart° like my shoe, but her face noth-   *Dark*
    ing like so clean kept. For why?° She sweats a man may go   *How so?*
105   over shoes[8] in the grime of it.
ANTIPHOLUS OF SYRACUSE   That's a fault that water will mend.
DROMIO OF SYRACUSE   No, sir, 'tis in grain.° Noah's flood   *ingrained*
    could not do it.
ANTIPOHOLUS OF SYRACUSE   What's her name?
110 DROMIO OF SYRACUSE   Nell, sir. But her name and three
    quarters—that's an ell° and three quarters—will not mea-   *more than a yard*
    sure her from hip to hip.
ANTIPHOLUS OF SYRACUSE   Then she bears some breadth?
DROMIO OF SYRACUSE   No longer from head to foot than from
115   hip to hip. She is spherical, like a globe. I could find out°   *discover*
    countries in her.
ANTIPHOLUS OF SYRACUSE   In what part of her body stands
    Ireland?
DROMIO OF SYRACUSE   Marry, sir, in her buttocks. I found it
120   out by the bogs.°   *peat marsh; sponginess*
ANTIPHOLUS OF SYRACUSE   Where Scotland?
DROMIO OF SYRACUSE   I found it by the barrenness, hard in
    the palm of the hand.[9]
ANTIPHOLUS OF SYRACUSE   Where France?
125 DROMIO OF SYRACUSE   In her forehead, armed and reverted,[1]
    making war against her hair.[2]
ANTIPHOLUS OF SYRACUSE   Where England?
DROMIO OF SYRACUSE   I looked for the chalky cliffs,[3] but I could
    find no whiteness in them. But I guess it stood in her chin,
130   by° the salt rheum° that ran between France and it.   *judging by / mucus*
ANTIPHOLUS OF SYRACUSE   Where Spain?
DROMIO OF SYRACUSE   Faith, I saw it not, but I felt it hot in her
    breath.[4]
ANTIPHOLUS OF SYRACUSE   Where America, the Indies?
135 DROMIO OF SYRACUSE   O sir, upon her nose, all o'er embel-
    lished with rubies, carbuncles, sapphires,[5] declining their rich
    aspect[6] to the hot breath of Spain, who sent whole armadas
    of carracks to be ballast[7] at her nose.
ANTIPHOLUS OF SYRACUSE   Where stood Belgium, the
140   Netherlands?
DROMIO OF SYRACUSE   O, sir, I did not look so low.[8] To con-
    clude, this drudge or diviner° laid claim to me, called me   *witch*
    Dromio, swore I was assured° to her, told me what privy°   *betrothed / private; secret*
    marks I had about me—as the mark of my shoulder, the
145   mole in my neck, the great wart on my left arm—that I,
    amazed, ran from her as a witch.

8. She sweats so much that a man may be up to his ankles.
9. Hard with calluses and dry (a moist hand prover-bially indicated fertility; hence a dry hand could connote barrenness).
1. In rebellion (perhaps referring to syphilitic sores).
2. TEXTUAL COMMENT In the Folio's "heire," there is a pun on "hair" and "heir" that is no longer possible in standard English orthography. See Digital Edition TC 6.

3. Teeth; an allusion to the white chalk cliffs of Dover.
4. As if she had been eating pungent food.
5. Glistening skin blemishes (as well as precious stones).
6. Casting their gaze down; paying tribute to.
7. *armadas . . . ballast:* fleets of galleons to be loaded.
8. The Netherlands and Belgium were also known as the Low Countries; the words offer a sexual double-entendre.

And I think, if my breast had not been made of faith and my
    heart of steel,[9]
She had transformed me to a curtal° dog and made me turn   *tailless*
    i'th' wheel.°   *turn a roasting spit*
ANTIPHOLUS OF SYRACUSE Go, hie thee presently.° Post° to   *now / Hasten*
    the road,°   *harbor*
150   An if° the wind blow any way from shore,°   *An if=If / out to sea*
    I will not harbor in this town tonight.
    If any bark put forth, come to the mart,
    Where I will walk till thou return to me.
    If everyone knows us, and we know none,
155   'Tis time, I think, to trudge,° pack, and be gone.   *depart*
DROMIO OF SYRACUSE As from a bear a man would run for life,
    So fly I from her that would be my wife.   *Exit.*
ANTIPHOLUS OF SYRACUSE There's none but witches do
    inhabit here,
    And therefore 'tis high time that I were hence.
160   She that doth call me husband, even my° soul   *my very*
    Doth for a wife abhor. But her fair sister,
    Possessed with such a gentle sovereign° grace,   *excellent*
    Of such enchanting presence and discourse,
    Hath almost made me traitor to myself.
165   But lest myself be guilty to° self-wrong,   *of*
    I'll stop mine ears against the mermaid's song.
        Enter ANGELO *with the chain.*
ANGELO Master Antipholus.
ANTIPHOLUS OF SYRACUSE Ay, that's my name.
ANGELO I know it well, sir. Lo, here's the chain
170   I thought to have ta'en° you at the Porcupine.   *overtaken*
    The chain unfinished made me stay° thus long.   *delay*
ANTIPHOLUS OF SYRACUSE What is your will that I shall do
    with this?
ANGELO What please° yourself, sir. I have made it for you.   *pleases*
ANTIPHOLUS OF SYRACUSE Made it for me, sir? I bespoke° it not.   *ordered*
175 ANGELO Not once, nor twice, but twenty times you have.
    Go home with it, and please your wife withal,°   *with it*
    And soon at suppertime I'll visit you,
    And then receive my money for the chain.
ANTIPHOLUS OF SYRACUSE I pray you, sir, receive the money
    now,
180   For fear you ne'er see chain nor money more.
ANGELO You are a merry man, sir; fare you well.   *Exit.*
ANTIPHOLUS OF SYRACUSE What I should think of this, I
    cannot tell.
    But this I think: there's no man is so vain°   *foolish*
    That would refuse so fair an offered chain.
185   I see a man here needs not live by shifts,°   *his own efforts*
    When in the streets he meets such golden gifts.
    I'll to the mart, and there for Dromio stay.
    If any ship put out, then straight° away.   *Exit.*   *immediately*

---

9. Compare Ephesians 6:11ff: "Put on the whole armor of God, that ye may be able to stand against the assaults of the devil. . . . having on the breast plate of righteousness. . . . Above all, take the shield of faith."

4.1

Enter a [SECOND] MERCHANT, [ANGELO *the*] *goldsmith,*
and an OFFICER.

SECOND MERCHANT   You know since Pentecost[1] the sum is due,
And since I have not much importuned you;
Nor now I had not,° but° that I am bound   *I would not have / except*
To Persia and want° guilders for my voyage.   *lack*
5   Therefore make present satisfaction,°   *immediate payment*
Or I'll attach° you by this officer.   *arrest*
ANGELO   Even just the sum that I do owe to you
Is growing° to me by Antipholus,   *owing*
And in the instant that I met with you,
10   He had of me a chain. At five o'clock
I shall receive the money for the same.
Pleaseth you° walk with me down to his house;   *If it please you to*
I will discharge my bond, and thank you too.

Enter ANTIPHOLUS [OF] EPHESUS, [*and*] DROMIO
[OF EPHESUS] *from the Courtesan's* [*house*].

OFFICER   That labor may you save; see where he comes.
15   ANTIPHOLUS OF EPHESUS [*to* DROMIO OF EPHESUS]   While I go
to the goldsmith's house, go thou
And buy a rope's end;° that will I bestow°   *piece of rope / employ (as a whip)*
Among my wife and her confederates
For locking me out of my doors by day.
But soft,° I see the goldsmith. Get thee gone.   *wait*
20   Buy thou a rope, and bring it home to me.
DROMIO OF EPHESUS   I buy a thousand pound a year, I buy a
rope![2]   *Exit.*
ANTIPHOLUS OF EPHESUS [*to* ANGELO]   A man is well holp up°   *helped*
that trusts to you!
I promisèd your presence and the chain,
But neither chain nor goldsmith came to me.
25   Belike° you thought our love° would last too long   *Perhaps / friendship*
If it were chained together, and therefore came not.
ANGELO   Saving° your merry humor, here's the note   *Without offense to*
How much your chain weighs to the utmost carat,
The fineness of the gold, and chargeful fashion,°   *costly craftsmanship*
30   Which doth amount to three odd ducats° more   *gold coins*
Than I stand debted° to this gentleman.   *indebted*
I pray you see him presently discharged,°   *paid off now*
For he is bound to sea and stays but° for it.   *waits only*
ANTIPOHOLUS OF EPHESUS   I am not furnished with the
present° money.   *ready*
35   Besides, I have some business in the town.
Good signor, take the stranger to my house,
And with you take the chain, and bid my wife
Disburse the sum on the receipt thereof.
Perchance° I will be there as soon as you.   *Perhaps*
40   ANGELO   Then you will bring the chain to her yourself?
ANTIPHOLUS OF EPHESUS   No, bear it with you, lest I come not
time° enough.   *soon*

4.1 Location: A street in Ephesus.
1. Christian festival observed on the seventh Sunday
after Easter, in commemoration of the descent of the
Holy Ghost on the disciples on the day of the Jewish

harvest holiday of Shavuoth.
2. Perhaps in exasperated contrast with Antipholus
of Syracuse's earlier demand for a thousand marks
(1.2.81).

ANGELO   Well, sir, I will. Have you the chain about you?

ANTIPHOLUS OF EPHESUS   An if I have not, sir, I hope you have,
Or else you may return without your money.

45 ANGELO   Nay, come, I pray you, sir, give me the chain.
Both wind and tide stays° for this gentleman,   *wait*
And I, to blame, have held him here too long.

ANTIPHOLUS OF EPHESUS   Good lord! You use this dalliance°   *trifling delay*
to excuse
Your breach of promise to° the Porcupine.   *to go to*
50 I should have chid you for not bringing it,
But like a shrew° you first begin to brawl.   *sour person*

SECOND MERCHANT [*to* ANGELO]   The hour steals on. I pray
you, sir, dispatch.°   *hurry*

ANGELO   You hear how he importunes me. The chain!

ANTIPHOLUS OF EPHESUS   Why, give it to my wife and fetch
your money.

55 ANGELO   Come, come, you know I gave it you even° now.   *just*
Either send the chain, or send me by some token.³

ANTIPHOLUS OF EPHESUS   Fie, now you run this humor out of
breath.°   *exhaust this joke*
Come, where's the chain? I pray you, let me see it.

SECOND MERCHANT   My business cannot brook° this dalliance.   *tolerate*
60 Good sir, say whe'er° you'll answer° me or no.   *whether / repay*
If not, I'll leave him to the officer.

ANTIPHOLUS OF EPHESUS   I answer you? What should I answer
you?

ANGELO   The money that you owe me for the chain.

ANTIPHOLUS OF EPHESUS   I owe you none till I receive the
chain.

65 ANGELO   You know I gave it you half an hour since.

ANTIPHOLUS OF EPHESUS   You gave me none. You wrong me
much to say so.

ANGELO   You wrong me more, sir, in denying it.
Consider how it stands upon° my credit.⁴   *affects*

SECOND MERCHANT   Well, officer, arrest him at my suit.

70 OFFICER [*to* ANGELO]   I do, and charge you in the Duke's name
to obey me.

ANGELO [*to* ANTIPHOLUS OF EPHESUS]   This touches° me in   *injures*
reputation.
Either consent to pay this sum for me,
Or I attach° you by this officer.   *arrest*

ANTIPHOLUS OF EPHESUS   Consent to pay thee that° I never   *for what*
had?
75 Arrest me, foolish fellow, if thou dar'st.

ANGELO   Here is thy fee:⁵ arrest him, officer.
I would not spare my brother in this case,
If he should scorn me so apparently.°   *openly*

OFFICER [*to* ANTIPHOLUS OF EPHESUS]   I do arrest you, sir. You
hear the suit.

80 ANTIPHOLUS OF EPHESUS   I do obey thee, till I give thee bail.
[*to* ANGELO] But sirrah, you shall buy this sport as dear⁶

---

3. With some sign of yours (so that Adriana will
know to pay me).
4. Financial standing; more generally, reputation.

5. Public officers were entitled to private payment.
6. You shall pay as dearly for this amusement.

As all the metal in your shop will answer.°   *amount to*

ANGELO   Sir, sir, I shall have law° in Ephesus—   *my legal rights*
    To your notorious shame, I doubt it not.

          Enter DROMIO [OF] SYRACUSE *from the bay.*

85   DROMIO OF SYRACUSE   Master, there's a bark of Epidamnum
    That stays but till her owner comes aboard,
    And then, sir, she bears away. Our freightage,° sir,   *luggage; goods*
    I have conveyed aboard, and I have bought
    The oil, the balsamum,[7] and aqua vitae.°   *alcohol*
90   The ship is in her trim,° the merry wind   *ready to sail*
    Blows fair from land; they stay for naught° at all   *nothing*
    But for their owner, master, and yourself.

ANTIPHOLUS OF EPHESUS   How now? A madman? Why, thou
     peevish° sheep,[8]   *bleating*
    What ship of Epidamnum stays for me?

95   DROMIO OF SYRACUSE   A ship you sent me to, to hire waftage.°   *buy our passage*

ANTIPHOLUS OF EPHESUS   Thou drunken slave! I sent thee for
     a rope,
    And told thee to what purpose and what end.

DROMIO OF SYRACUSE   You sent me for a rope's end° as soon!   *a beating*
    You sent me to the bay, sir, for a bark.

100   ANTIPHOLUS OF EPHESUS   I will debate this matter at more leisure
    And teach your ears to list° me with more heed.   *listen to*
    To Adriana, villain, hie thee straight.°   *go immediately*
    Give her this key, and tell her in the desk
    That's covered o'er with Turkish tapestry
105   There is a purse of ducats. Let her send it.
    Tell her I am arrested in the street,
    And that shall bail me.° Hie thee, slave, be gone!   *pay my bail*
    —On, officer, to prison, till it come.

          Exeunt [all but DROMIO OF SYRACUSE].

DROMIO OF SYRACUSE   To Adriana. That is where we dined,
110   Where Dowsabel[9] did claim me for her husband.
    She is too big, I hope, for me to compass.[1]
    Thither I must, although against my will;
    For servants must their masters' minds° fulfill.   *Exit.*   *wishes*

4.2

          Enter ADRIANA *and* LUCIANA.

ADRIANA   Ah, Luciana, did he tempt thee so?
    Mightst thou perceive austerely in his eye[1]
    That he did plead in earnest, yea or no?
    Looked he or° red or pale, or sad or merrily?   *either*
5   What observation mad'st thou in this case
    Of his heart's meteors tilting[2] in his face?

LUCIANA   First he denied you had in him no° right.   *any*

ADRIANA   He meant he did me none, the more my spite.°   *grief*

LUCIANA   Then swore he that he was a stranger here.

---

7. A healing resin.
8. Idiot, punning on "ship" in the next line (the words were similarly pronounced).
9. English form of "Dulcibella," a generic name for a sweetheart.
1. Encompass; a pun on the cartographic description

of Nell's body (see 3.2.110–41).
4.2 Location: Before the house of Antipholus of Ephesus.
1. By the seriousness of his expression.
2. Conflicting emotions, as if heavenly bodies were engaged in combat ("tilting").

10   ADRIANA   And true he swore, though yet forsworn[3] he were.
     LUCIANA   Then pleaded I for you.
     ADRIANA   And what said he?
     LUCIANA   That love I begged for you, he begged of me.
     ADRIANA   With what persuasion did he tempt thy love?
     LUCIANA   With words that in an honest suit° might move.   *courtship*
15   First he did praise my beauty, then my speech.
     ADRIANA   Didst speak him fair?°   *encourage him*
     LUCIANA   Have patience, I beseech.
     ADRIANA   I cannot, nor I will not hold me still.°   *silent*
     My tongue, though not my heart, shall have his° will.   *its*
     He is deformèd, crooked, old, and sere,°   *withered*
20   Ill-faced, worse-bodied, shapeless° everywhere,   *ill shaped*
     Vicious, ungentle, foolish, blunt, unkind,
     Stigmatical in making,[4] worse in mind.
     LUCIANA   Who would be jealous, then, of such a one?
     No evil lost is wailed when it is gone.
25   ADRIANA   Ah, but I think him better than I say,
     And yet would herein others' eyes were worse.[5]
     Far from her nest the lapwing[6] cries away;
     My heart prays for him, though my tongue do curse.
                    Enter DROMIO [OF] SYRACUSE.
     DROMIO OF SYRACUSE   Here go—the desk, the purse! Sweet
          now, make haste![7]
     LUCIANA   How hast thou lost thy breath?
30   DROMIO OF SYRACUSE   By running fast.
     ADRIANA   Where is thy master, Dromio? Is he well?
     DROMIO OF SYRACUSE   No, he's in Tartar limbo,[8] worse than hell.
     A devil in an everlasting[9] garment hath him,
     One whose hard heart is buttoned up with steel;
35   A fiend, a fairy,[1] pitiless and rough;
     A wolf, nay worse, a fellow all in buff;[2]
     A back friend,[3] a shoulder-clapper,° one that   *arresting officer*
          countermands°   *prohibits*
     The passages of allies, creeks, and narrow lands;[4]
     A hound that runs counter[5] and yet draws dryfoot well;[6]
40   One that before the judgment[7] carries poor souls to hell.
     ADRIANA   Why, man, what is the matter?
     DROMIO OF SYRACUSE   I do not know the matter,° he is   *dispute*
          'rested ° on the case.[8]   *arrested*

---

3. *true . . . forsworn:* he is behaving like a stranger to
me, but he is lying and is being false to his marriage
vows if he claims to be one.
4. Deformed in his physical makeup.
5. And nevertheless wish others' eyes to be deceived
(and so think him ugly).
6. A bird (the peewit) that diverts attention away
from her nest to protect her young; Adriana wishes to
turn other women's attention away from Antipholus's
attractions.
7. Dromio is possibly speaking to himself as he
rushes in.
8. Hellish prison. "Tartar" is short for "Tartarus,"
the classical hell, but it also suggests the Tartars, a
central Asian people reputed by Elizabethans to be
particularly savage. "Limbo" was common slang for
"prison."
9. Term for the durable material used in the Elizabethan period for the uniform of prison officers; eter-

nal, like hell's punishments.
1. Malevolent fairy, like the goblins in 2.2.191–93.
2. Stout leather used in uniforms.
3. False friend; also referring to the officer's hand on
the culprit's back during an arrest.
4. The traffic through alleys, small passageways, and
narrow pathways. *lands:* launds; glades or clearings,
pathways through woods.
5. Runs in the opposite direction to the prey; also
perhaps alluding to the Counter, as several debtors'
prisons in London were known.
6. *draws . . . well:* tracks game by the scent of its
foot.
7. *before the judgment:* in a court of law, with an
allusion to the Day of Judgment.
8. *on the case:* in a legal action in which the injury
was not specifically addressed by precedent; by means
of the officer's hand on his outer clothing ("case").

ADRIANA   What, is he arrested? Tell me at whose suit?

DROMIO OF SYRACUSE   I know not at whose suit he is arrested
    well,

45   But is in a suit of buff which 'rested him, that can I tell.
    Will you send him, mistress, redemption, the money in his
        desk?

ADRIANA   Go fetch it, sister.   *Exit* LUCIANA.
                        This I wonder at,
    That he unknown to me should be in debt.
    Tell me, was he arrested on° a band?°   *for breaking / (i.e., bond)*

50 DROMIO OF SYRACUSE   Not on a band, but on a stronger thing:
    A chain, a chain! Do you not hear it ring?

ADRIANA   What, the chain?

DROMIO OF SYRACUSE   No, no, the bell. 'Tis time that I were gone.
    It was two ere I left him, and now the clock strikes one.[9]

ADRIANA   The hours come back! That did I never hear.

55 DROMIO OF SYRACUSE   Oh, yes, if any hour[1] meet a sergeant,
    'a° turns back for very fear.   *he*

ADRIANA   As if Time were in debt. How fondly° dost thou   *foolishly*
    reason!

DROMIO OF SYRACUSE   Time is a very bankrupt and owes
    more than he's worth to season.[2]
    Nay, he's a thief too: have you not heard men say
    That time comes stealing on by night and day?

60 If 'a be in debt and theft, and a sergeant in° the way,   *stands in*
    Hath he not reason to turn back an hour in a day?
                    Enter LUCIANA.

ADRIANA   Go, Dromio, there's the money. Bear it straight,°   *quickly*
    And bring thy master home immediately.
                        [*Exit* DROMIO OF SYRACUSE.]
    Come, sister, I am pressed° down with conceit:°   *depressed / imaginings*

65 Conceit, my comfort and my injury.   *Exeunt.*

4.3

Enter ANTIPHOLUS [OF] SYRACUSE.

ANTIPHOLUS OF SYRACUSE   There's not a man I meet but doth
    salute° me   *greet*
    As if I were their well-acquainted friend,
    And everyone doth call me by my name.
    Some tender° money to me, some invite me,   *offer*

5   Some other give me thanks for kindnesses.
    Some offer me commodities to buy.
    Even now a tailor called me in his shop,
    And showed me silks that he had bought for me,
    And therewithal° took measure of my body.   *with that*

10 Sure, these are but imaginary wiles,°   *delusions*
    And Lapland sorcerers[1] inhabit here.
                Enter DROMIO [OF] SYRACUSE.

---

9. "On" and "one" were pronounced similarly.
1. Perhaps a pun on "ower" ("debtor") or "whore."
2. "Seisin," a legal term for "possession"; opportunity; thus, there is too little time to make good the
promises of the occasion.
4.3 Location: A street in Ephesus.
1. Lapland was known for having witches.

DROMIO OF SYRACUSE Master, here's the gold you sent me
for. What, have you got the picture of old Adam new
appareled?[2]

15   ANTIPHOLUS OF SYRACUSE What gold is this? What Adam dost
thou mean?

DROMIO OF SYRACUSE Not that Adam that kept the Paradise,
but that Adam that keeps the prison; he that goes in the
calf's-skin[3] that was killed for the Prodigal;[4] he that came
behind you, sir, like an evil angel, and bid you forsake your
20   liberty.[5]

ANTIPHOLUS OF SYRACUSE I understand thee not.

DROMIO OF SYRACUSE No? Why, 'tis a plain case: he that went
like a bass viol[6] in a case of leather; the man, sir, that when
gentlemen are tired gives them a sob[7] and 'rests them; he,
25   sir, that takes pity on decayed° men and gives them suits of   *ruined*
durance;[8] he that sets up his rest[9] to do more exploits with
his mace° than a morris-pike.[1]   *staff of office*

ANTIPHOLUS OF SYRACUSE What, thou mean'st an officer?

DROMIO OF SYRACUSE Ay, sir, the sergeant of the band; he that
30   brings any man to answer it° that breaks his band;° one that   *for it / bond*
thinks a man always going to bed, and says, "God give you
good rest."°   *arrest*

ANTIPHOLUS OF SYRACUSE Well, sir, there rest in° your foolery.   *cease*
Is there any ships puts forth tonight? May we be gone?

35   DROMIO OF SYRACUSE Why, sir, I brought you word an hour
since that the bark *Expedition* put forth tonight, and then
were you hindered by the sergeant to tarry for the hoy[2] *Delay.*
Here are the angels[3] that you sent for to deliver you.

ANTIPHOLUS OF SYRACUSE The fellow is distract,° and so am I,   *distracted; mad*
40   And here we wander in illusions.
Some blessèd power deliver us from hence.

        Enter a COURTESAN.

COURTESAN Well met, well met, Master Antipholus.
I see, sir, you have found the goldsmith now.
Is that the chain you promised me today?

45   ANTIPHOLUS OF SYRACUSE Satan, avoid![4] I charge thee, tempt
me not!

DROMIO OF SYRACUSE Master, is this Mistress Satan?

ANTIPHOLUS OF SYRACUSE It is the devil.

DROMIO OF SYRACUSE Nay, she is worse: she is the devil's dam°—   *mother*
and here she comes in the habit° of a light° wench, and   *clothing / wanton*
50   thereof comes that the wenches say, "God damn me." That's

---

2. *have . . . appareled:* i.e., "is the sergeant who was
taking you into custody still with you?" Sergeants
wore leather uniforms, and Dromio's punning words
refer to the skins in which Adam was dressed after
the Fall (Genesis 3:21). There is also a possible reference to Ephesians 4:22: "put off . . . the old man,
which is corrupt . . . put on the new man, which after
God is created in righteousness."
3. The buff of the officer's garments.
4. The prodigal son of Luke 15:11–32; his father
killed a calf for a feast on his return home.
5. *bid . . . liberty:* arrested you.
6. Large stringed instrument, like a cello (continuing the jokes about the officer's leather uniform).

7. A rest (for tired horses) as well as a lament, picked
up in the following puns of "rests" and "pity."
8. *suits of durance:* lawsuits or prosecutions ending
in imprisonment; clothes made of hard-wearing
material.
9. *sets up his rest:* gambles all (punning on "arrest").
1. *morris-pike:* another word for "Moorish pike," a
lance of North African origin or design.
2. A small, slow vessel used in coastal waters. The
names of the ships are Dromio's improvisations.
3. Gold coins bearing a figure of the archangel
Michael.
4. Away! An echo of Jesus' words to Satan in Matthew 4:10: "Avoid Satan."

as much to say, "God make me a light wench." It is written,
they appear to men like angels of light.[5] Light is an effect of
fire, and fire will burn. Ergo,° light wenches will burn.[6] Come   *Therefore*
not near her.

55 COURTESAN Your man and you are marvelous merry, sir.
Will you go with me? We'll mend° our dinner here?   *complete*
DROMIO OF SYRACUSE Master, if you do, expect spoon-meat,[7]
or bespeak° a long spoon.   *request*
ANTIPHOLUS OF SYRACUSE Why, Dromio?
60 DROMIO OF SYRACUSE Marry, he must have a long spoon that
must eat with the devil.
ANTIPHOLUS OF SYRACUSE [*to* COURTESAN] Avoid, then, fiend!
What tell'st thou me of supping?
Thou art, as you are all, a sorceress.
I conjure° thee to leave me and be gone.   *order; charge*
65 COURTESAN Give me the ring of mine you had at dinner,
Or for my diamond the chain you promised,
And I'll be gone, sir, and not trouble you.
DROMIO OF SYRACUSE Some devils ask but° the parings of   *only*
one's nail, a rush,° a hair, a drop of blood, a pin, a nut, a   *straw*
70 cherry-stone; but she, more covetous, would have a chain.
Master, be wise. An if° you give it her, the devil will shake   *If*
her chain[8] and fright us with it.
COURTESAN I pray you, sir, my ring, or else the chain.
I hope you do not mean to cheat me so?
75 ANTIPHOLUS OF SYRACUSE Avaunt,° thou witch! —Come,   *Go away*
Dromio, let us go.
DROMIO OF SYRACUSE "Fly pride," says the peacock.[9] Mistress,
that you know.
               Exeunt [ANTIPHOLUS OF SYRACUSE *and* DROMIO OF
                                                      SYRACUSE].
COURTESAN Now out of doubt Antipholus is mad,
Else would he never so demean° himself.   *conduct; debase*
A ring he hath of mine worth forty ducats,
80 And for the same he promised me a chain.
Both one and other he denies me now.
The reason that I gather he is mad,
Besides this present instance of his rage,
Is a mad tale he told today at dinner
85 Of his own doors being shut against his entrance.
Belike° his wife, acquainted with his fits,   *Probably*
On purpose shut the doors against his way.°   *entrance*
My way is now to hie° home to his house   *hasten*
And tell his wife that, being lunatic,
90 He rushed into my house and took perforce°   *forcibly*
My ring away. This course I fittest choose,
For forty ducats is too much to lose.   [*Exit.*]

5. From 2 Corinthians 11:14: "Satan himself is
transformed into an angel of light."
6. Will transmit venereal disease; will suffer in hell.
7. Soft food for babies or invalids, mentioned for the
sake of the proverb in lines 60–61.

8. Alluding to the binding of the devil in a chain in
Revelation 20:1.
9. For the conniving courtesan to complain about
cheating is, in Dromio's view, analogous to a proud
peacock decrying pride.

4.4

Enter ANTIPHOLUS [OF] EPHESUS *with [an* OFFICER].

ANTIPHOLUS OF EPHESUS   Fear me not, man. I will not break
    away.
  I'll give thee ere I leave thee so much money
  To warrant thee° as I am 'rested for.   *As surety*
  My wife is in a wayward mood today
5 And will not lightly° trust the messenger   *readily*
  That I should be attached° in Ephesus.   *arrested*
  I tell you, 'twill sound harshly in her ears.

Enter DROMIO [OF] EPHESUS *with a rope's end.*

  Here comes my man. I think he brings the money.
  How now, sir? Have you that I sent you for?
10 DROMIO OF EPHESUS   Here's that I warrant you will pay[1] them
  all.
ANTIPHOLUS OF EPHESUS   But where's the money?
DROMIO OF EPHESUS   Why, sir, I gave the money for the rope.
ANTIPHOLUS OF EPHESUS   Five hundred ducats, villain, for a
  rope?
DROMIO OF EPHESUS   I'll serve° you, sir, five hundred at the   *provide*
  rate.°   *for that price*
15 ANTIPHOLUS OF EPHESUS   To what end did I bid thee hie thee
  home?
DROMIO OF EPHESUS   To° a rope's end, sir, and to that end am   *For*
  I returned.
ANTIPHOLUS OF EPHESUS   And to that end, sir, I will welcome
  you.[2]

    [*He beats* DROMIO.]

OFFICER   Good sir, be patient.
DROMIO OF EPHESUS   Nay, 'tis for me to be patient: I am in
20 adversity.[3]
OFFICER   Good now,° hold thy tongue.   *Please*
DROMIO OF EPHESUS   Nay, rather persuade him to hold° his   *hold off*
  hands.
ANTIPHOLUS OF EPHESUS   Thou whoreson,[4] senseless villain!
25 DROMIO OF EPHESUS   I would I were senseless, sir, that I might
  not feel your blows.
ANTIPHOLUS OF EPHESUS   Thou art sensible in° nothing but   *responsive to*
  blows, and so is an ass.
DROMIO OF EPHESUS   I am an ass indeed. You may prove it by
30 my long ears.[5] I have served him from the hour of my nativity
  to this instant and have nothing at his hands for my service
  but blows. When I am cold, he heats me with beating; when
  I am warm, he cools me with beating. I am waked with it
  when I sleep, raised with it when I sit, driven out of doors
35 with it when I go from home, welcomed home with it when I
  return. Nay, I bear it on my shoulders, as a beggar wont her
  brat,[6] and I think when he hath lamed me, I shall beg with it[7]
  from door to door.

4.4 Location: Scene continues.
1. With a beating (see 4.1.15–21).
2. I will treat you to a rope's end (a beating).
3. In painful circumstances; alluding to Psalm 94:13.
4. Literally, son of a whore; more generally, a term of
contemptuous familiarity.

5. Playing on "ears"/"years," which were pronounced
in the same way.
6. *wont her brat*: is accustomed to carrying her child.
7. I shall receive a beating (a frequent punishment
for begging).

Enter ADRIANA, LUCIANA, COURTESAN, *and a*
   schoolmaster, called PINCH.

ANTIPHOLUS OF EPHESUS Come, go along. My wife is coming
   yonder.

40 DROMIO OF EPHESUS [*to* ADRIANA] Mistress, *respice finem,*[8]
   respect your end; or rather, to prophesy like the parrot,[9]
   "Beware the rope's end."

ANTIPHOLUS OF EPHESUS Wilt thou still talk?
   [*He*] *beats* DROMIO.

COURTESAN [*to* ADRIANA] How say you now? Is not your
   husband mad?

45 ADRIANA His incivility confirms no less.
   —Good Doctor Pinch, you are a conjurer.[1]
   Establish him in his true sense[2] again,
   And I will please you° what you will demand.   *repay you with*

LUCIANA Alas, how fiery and how sharp° he looks!   *fierce*

50 COURTESAN Mark how he trembles in his ecstasy!°   *frenzy*

PINCH [*to* ANTIPHOLUS OF EPHESUS] Give me your hand, and
   let me feel your pulse.

ANTIPHOLUS OF EPHESUS There is my hand, and let it feel
   your ear.
   [*He strikes* PINCH.]

PINCH I charge thee, Satan, housed within this man,
   To yield possession to my holy prayers,
55   And to thy state of darkness hie thee straight.
   I conjure thee by all the saints in heaven.

ANTIPHOLUS OF EPHESUS Peace, doting wizard, peace! I am
   not mad.

ADRIANA Oh, that thou wert not, poor distressèd soul.

ANTIPHOLUS OF EPHESUS You minion,° you, are these your   *hussy*
   customers?

60 Did this companion° with the saffron° face   *rascal / yellow*
   Revel and feast it at my house today,
   Whilst upon me the guilty doors were shut,
   And I denied to enter in my house?

ADRIANA O husband, God doth know you dined at home,
65   Where would you had remained until this time,
   Free from these slanders° and this open shame.   *scandals*

ANTIPHOLUS OF EPHESUS Dined at home? [*to* DROMIO OF
   EPHESUS] Thou villain, what sayest thou?

DROMIO OF EPHESUS Sir, sooth to say,° you did not dine at   *to speak truly*
   home.

ANTIPHOLUS OF EPHESUS Were not my doors locked up, and I
   shut out?

70 DROMIO OF EPHESUS Perdie,° your doors were locked, and   *By God (pardieu)*
   you shut out.

ANTIPHOLUS OF EPHESUS And did not she herself revile me
   there?

DROMIO OF EPHESUS Sans° fable, she herself reviled you there.   *Without*

---

8. A religious injunction to "think on your end," but
punning on *respice funem,* "think on the rope" (on
hanging).
9. Parrots were often taught to cry "rope," an exclamation or curse; the "prophecy" is that the hearer
deserves to be hanged.
1. Capable of exorcising devils; exorcism required a

"doctor"—a learned man—since it was thought that
devils needed to be addressed in Latin.
2. In his right mind. Possession and lunacy were not
necessarily medically distinct, since both involved
the displacement of reason (by passion, sickness, or
demons).

ANTIPHOLUS OF EPHESUS   Did not her kitchen maid rail, taunt, and scorn me?

DROMIO OF EPHESUS   Certes° she did. The kitchen vestal³ scorned you.   *Certainly*

75 ANTIPHOLUS OF EPHESUS   And did not I in rage depart from thence?

DROMIO OF EPHESUS   In verity you did. My bones bears witness,
That since have felt the vigor of his rage.

ADRIANA [*aside to* PINCH]   Is't good to soothe° him in these contraries?   *humor*

PINCH [*aside to* ADRIANA]   It is no shame.° The fellow finds his vein,   *harm*

80 And, yielding to him, humors well his frenzy.

ANTIPHOLUS OF EPHESUS   Thou hast suborned° the goldsmith to arrest me.   *induced*

ADRIANA   Alas, I sent you money to redeem you,
By Dromio here, who came in haste for it.

DROMIO OF EPHESUS   Money by me? Heart and good will you might,

85 But surely, master, not a rag° of money.   *farthing*

ANTIPHOLUS OF EPHESUS   Went'st not thou to her for a purse of ducats?

ADRIANA   He came to me, and I delivered it.

LUCIANA   And I am witness with her that she did.

DROMIO OF EPHESUS   God and the rope-maker bear me witness

90 That I was sent for nothing but a rope.

PINCH [*aside to* ADRIANA]   Mistress, both man and master is possessed;
I know it by their pale and deadly° looks.   *deathlike*
They must be bound and laid in some dark room.⁴

ANTIPHOLUS OF EPHESUS [*to* ADRIANA]   Say wherefore didst thou lock me forth° today,   *out*

95 [*to* DROMIO OF EPHESUS] And why dost thou deny the bag of gold?

ADRIANA   I did not, gentle husband, lock thee forth.

DROMIO OF EPHESUS   And, gentle master, I received no gold.
But I confess, sir, that we were locked out.

ADRIANA   Dissembling villain, thou speak'st false in both.

100 ANTIPHOLUS OF EPHESUS   Dissembling harlot, thou art false in all,
And art confederate with a damnèd pack°   *conspiracy; posse*
To make a loathsome abject scorn of me.
But with these nails I'll pluck out these false eyes,
That would behold in me this shameful sport.

Enter three or four, and offer to bind him; he strives.

105 ADRIANA   Oh, bind him, bind him! Let him not come near me.

PINCH   More company!° The fiend is strong within him.   *Get help*

LUCIANA   Ay me, poor man, how pale and wan he looks.

ANTIPHOLUS OF EPHESUS   What, will you murder me? —Thou, jailer, thou,

---

3. Ironic: a virgin priestess of the household goddess Vesta's temple, responsible for keeping the fire burning.

4. An ordinary sixteenth-century treatment for insanity.

I am thy prisoner. Wilt thou suffer them
To make a rescue?[5]

110 OFFICER   Masters, let him go.
He is my prisoner, and you shall not have him.
PINCH   Go bind this man, for he is frantic too.
       [*They bind* DROMIO OF EPHESUS.]
ADRIANA   What wilt thou do, thou peevish° officer?   *stupid*
Hast thou delight to see a wretched man
115 Do outrage and displeasure° to himself?   *harm*
OFFICER   He is my prisoner. If I let him go,
The debt he owes will be required of me.
ADRIANA   I will discharge° thee ere I go from thee.   *repay*
Bear me forthwith unto his creditor,
120 And knowing how the debt grows,[6] I will pay it.
Good Master Doctor, see him safe conveyed
Home to my house. Oh, most unhappy day!
ANTIPHOLUS OF EPHESUS   Oh, most unhappy strumpet!
DROMIO OF EPHESUS   Master, I am here entered in bond for
    you.
125 ANTIPHOLUS OF EPHESUS   Out on thee, villain. Wherefore
    dost thou mad° me?   *goad*
DROMIO OF EPHESUS   Will you be bound for nothing? Be mad,
    good master. Cry, "The devil!"[7]
LUCIANA   God help poor souls, how idly do they talk.
ADRIANA   Go bear him hence. Sister, go you with me.
          Exeunt [PINCH *and his assistants, carrying off*
      ANTIPHOLUS OF EPHESUS *and* DROMIO OF EPHESUS].
      OFFICER, ADRIANA, LUCIANA, *and* COURTESAN *remain.*
130 [*to* OFFICER] Say now, whose suit is he arrested at?
OFFICER   One Angelo, a goldsmith. Do you know him?
ADRIANA   I know the man. What is the sum he owes?
OFFICER   Two hundred ducats.
ADRIANA   Say, how grows it due?
OFFICER   Due for a chain your husband had of him.
135 ADRIANA   He did bespeak° a chain for me, but had it not.   *order*
COURTESAN   Whenas your husband, all in rage today,
Came to my house, and took away my ring—
The ring I saw upon his finger now—
Straight after did I meet him with a chain.
140 ADRIANA   It may be so, but I did never see it.
Come, jailer, bring me where the goldsmith is.
I long to know the truth hereof at large.°   *in full*
      Enter ANTIPHOLUS [OF] SYRACUSE *and* DROMIO [OF]
      SYRACUSE, *with* [*their rapiers*] *drawn.*
LUCIANA   God, for thy mercy, they are loose again!
ADRIANA   And come with naked° swords; let's call more help   *drawn*
To have them bound again. [ADRIANA *and* LUCIANA] *run out.*
145 OFFICER   Away, they'll kill us.
     Exeunt all, as fast as may be, frighted. [ANTIPHOLUS OF
      SYRACUSE *and* DROMIO OF SYRACUSE *remain.*]

---

5. To release by force from legal custody.
6. *knowing . . . grows:* when I know how the debt
came about.

7. A cry of exasperation; a direct address to the devil,
which would lend support to the view that he is
possessed.

ANTIPHOLUS OF SYRACUSE I see these witches are afraid of
swords.

DROMIO OF SYRACUSE She that would be your wife, now ran
from you.

ANTIPHOLUS OF SYRACUSE Come to the Centaur. Fetch our
stuff from thence.
I long that we were safe and sound aboard.

150 DROMIO OF SYRACUSE Faith, stay here this night. They will
surely do us no harm: you saw they speak us fair, give us gold.
Methinks they are such a gentle nation, that but for the
mountain of mad flesh that claims marriage of me, I could
find in my heart to stay here still,° and turn witch.   *always*

155 ANTIPHOLUS OF SYRACUSE I will not stay tonight for all the
town.
Therefore away, to get our stuff aboard.   *Exeunt.*

5.1

Enter [SECOND] MERCHANT *and* [ANGELO] *the goldsmith.*

ANGELO I am sorry, sir, that I have hindered you,
But I protest he had the chain of me,
Though most dishonestly he doth deny it.

SECOND MERCHANT How is the man esteemed here in the city?

5 ANGELO Of very reverend reputation, sir,
Of credit infinite, highly beloved,
Second to none that lives here in the city.
His word might bear my wealth at any time.[1]

SECOND MERCHANT Speak softly. Yonder, as I think, he walks.

Enter ANTIPHOLUS [OF SYRACUSE] *and* DROMIO
[OF SYRACUSE] *again.*

10 ANGELO 'Tis so, and that self° chain about his neck,   *same*
Which he forswore° most monstrously to have.   *denied on oath*
Good sir, draw near to me, I'll speak to him.
—Signor Antipholus, I wonder much
That you would put me to this shame and trouble,

15 And not without some scandal to yourself,
With circumstance° and oaths so to deny   *detailed argument*
This chain which now you wear so openly.
Beside the charge,° the shame, imprisonment,   *cost*
You have done wrong to this my honest friend,

20 Who, but for staying on° our controversy,   *as a result of*
Had hoisted sail and put to sea today.
This chain you had of me. Can you deny it?

ANTIPHOLUS OF SYRACUSE I think I had. I never did deny it.

SECOND MERCHANT Yes, that you did, sir, and forswore it too.

25 ANTIPHOLUS OF SYRACUSE Who heard me to deny it or
forswear it?

SECOND MERCHANT These ears of mine thou know'st did hear
thee.
Fie on thee, wretch! 'Tis pity that thou liv'st
To walk where any honest men resort.

ANTIPHOLUS OF SYRACUSE Thou art a villain to impeach° me   *accuse*
thus.

5.1 Location: Before a priory.
1. His word alone would be enough security to borrow all I have.

30   I'll prove mine honor and mine honesty
        Against thee presently,° if thou dar'st stand.°   *now / defend yourself*
SECOND MERCHANT   I dare, and do defy thee for a villain.
        They draw. Enter ADRIANA, LUCIANA, COURTESAN, *and*
        others.
ADRIANA   Hold, hurt him not, for God sake! He is mad.
        Some get within him;[2] take his sword away.
35   Bind Dromio too, and bear them to my house.
DROMIO OF SYRACUSE   Run, master, run! For God's sake,
        take° a house.   *take cover in*
        This is some priory—in, or we are spoiled.°   *ruined*
        Exeunt [ANTIPHOLUS OF SYRACUSE *and*
        DROMIO OF SYRACUSE] *to the priory.*
    Enter Lady ABBESS [*from the priory*].
ABBESS   Be quiet, people. Wherefore throng you hither?
ADRIANA   To fetch my poor distracted husband hence.
40   Let us come in that we may bind him fast
        And bear him home for his recovery.
ANGELO   I knew he was not in his perfect wits.
SECOND MERCHANT   I am sorry now that I did draw on him.
ABBESS   How long hath this possession held the man?
45 ADRIANA   This week he hath been heavy, sour, sad,
        And much different from the man he was;
        But till this afternoon his passion°   *insanity*
        Ne'er brake° into extremity of rage.   *broke*
ABBESS   Hath he not lost much wealth by wreck of sea?
50   Buried some dear friend? Hath not else his eye
        Strayed° his affection in unlawful love—   *Led astray*
        A sin prevailing much in youthful men,
        Who give their eyes the liberty of gazing?
        Which of these sorrows is he subject to?
55 ADRIANA   To none of these, except it be the last,
        Namely, some love that drew him oft from home.
ABBESS   You should for that have reprehended him.
ADRIANA   Why, so I did.
ABBESS   Ay, but not rough enough.
ADRIANA   As roughly as my modesty would let me.
ABBESS   Haply° in private.   *Perhaps*
60 ADRIANA   And in assemblies too.
ABBESS   Ay, but not enough.
ADRIANA   It was the copy of our conference.[3]
        In bed he slept not for my urging it;
        At board° he fed not for my urging it;   *table*
65   Alone, it was the subject of my theme;
        In company I often glanced° it;   *alluded to*
        Still° did I tell him it was vile and bad.   *Continually*
ABBESS   And thereof came it that the man was mad.
        The venom° clamors of a jealous woman   *venomous*
70   Poisons more deadly than a mad dog's tooth.
        It seems his sleeps were hindered by thy railing,
        And thereof comes it that his head is light.

---

2. *get within him*: stand within his guard; Adriana is
requesting to have someone stand between the two
dueling men.

3. *copy of our conference*: exact topic of our
conversation.

Thou say'st his meat was sauced with thy upbraidings;
Unquiet meals make ill digestions.
75　Thereof the raging fire of fever bred,
And what's a fever, but a fit of madness?[4]
Thou sayest his sports were hindered by thy brawls.
Sweet recreation barred, what doth ensue
But moody and dull melancholy,
80　Kinsman to grim and comfortless despair,
And at her heels a huge infectious troop
Of pale distemperatures° and foes to life?　　　　　　　*illnesses; imbalances*
In food, in sport, and life-preserving rest
To be disturbed would mad or° man or beast.　　　　　　*would make mad either*
85　The consequence is, then, thy jealous fits
Hath scared thy husband from the use of wits.
LUCIANA　She never reprehended him but mildly
When he demeaned himself rough, rude, and wildly.
[*to* ADRIANA] Why bear you these rebukes and answer not?
90　ADRIANA　She did betray me to my own reproof.
—Good people, enter, and lay hold on him.
ABBESS　No, not a creature enters in my house.
ADRIANA　Then let your servants bring my husband forth.
ABBESS　Neither. He took this place for sanctuary,[5]
95　And it shall privilege him from your hands
Till I have brought him to his wits again,
Or lose my labor in assaying it.
ADRIANA　I will attend my husband, be his nurse,
Diet° his sickness, for it is my office,°　　　　　　　　*Treat / duty*
100　And will have no attorney° but myself,　　　　　　　　*proxy*
And therefore let me have him home with me.
ABBESS　Be patient, for I will not let him stir
Till I have used the approvèd° means I have,　　　　　　*tested*
With wholesome syrups, drugs, and holy prayers
105　To make of him a formal° man again.　　　　　　　　*complete; sane*
It is a branch and parcel° of mine oath,　　　　　　　　*part*
A charitable duty of my order.
Therefore depart, and leave him here with me.
ADRIANA　I will not hence and leave my husband here,
110　And ill it doth beseem your holiness
To separate the husband and the wife.[6]
ABBESS　Be quiet and depart. Thou shalt not have him.
　　　　　　　　　　　　　　　　　　　　　　　　[*Exit.*]
LUCIANA [*to* ADRIANA]　Complain unto the Duke of this
　　indignity.
ADRIANA　Come, go. I will fall prostrate at his feet,
115　And never rise until my tears and prayers
Have won his grace to come in person hither
And take perforce my husband from the Abbess.
SECOND MERCHANT　By this I think the dial point's at five.
Anon° I'm sure the Duke himself in person　　　　　　　*Soon*
120　Comes this way to the melancholy vale,

---

4. Both are imbalances in the body's humors; see
note to 4.4.47.
5. Churches and other sacred buildings provided refuge from legal prosecution until the seventeenth
century.

6. Against the Abbess's defense of sanctuary, Adriana cites the competing biblical injunction against
separating individuals united in holy matrimony. See
Matthew 19 and Mark 10.

The place of death and sorry execution,
Behind the ditches of the abbey here.

ANGELO Upon what cause?

SECOND MERCHANT To see a reverend Syracusian merchant,
125 Who put unluckily into this bay
Against the laws and statutes of this town,
Beheaded publicly for his offense.

ANGELO See where they come. We will behold his death.

LUCIANA Kneel to the Duke before he pass the abbey.

Enter the DUKE *of Ephesus, and* [EGEON] *the Merchant of Syracuse, barehead, with the Headsman,° and other*   executioner
OFFICERS.

130 DUKE Yet once again proclaim it publicly:
If any friend will pay the sum for him,
He shall not die; so much we tender[7] him.

ADRIANA Justice, most sacred Duke, against the Abbess!

DUKE She is a virtuous and a reverend lady.
135 It cannot be that she hath done thee wrong.

ADRIANA May it please your grace, Antipholus my husband,
Who I made lord of me and all I had
At your important° letters,[8] this ill day   urgent
A most outrageous fit of madness took him,
140 That desp'rately he hurried through the street—
With him his bondman, all as mad as he—
Doing displeasure to the citizens
By rushing in their houses, bearing thence
Rings, jewels, anything his rage° did like.   he in his madness
145 Once did I get him bound and sent him home,
Whilst to take order for° the wrongs I went,   settle up
That here and there his fury had committed.
Anon, I wot° not by what strong° escape,   know / forcible
He broke from those that had the guard of him,
150 And with his mad attendant and himself,
Each one with ireful passion, with drawn swords,
Met us again, and madly bent on us
Chased us away, till raising of more aid
We came again to bind them. Then they fled
155 Into this abbey, whither we pursued them,
And here the Abbess shuts the gates on us
And will not suffer us to fetch him out,
Nor send him forth, that we may bear him hence.
Therefore, most gracious Duke, with thy command,
160 Let him be brought forth and borne hence for help.

DUKE Long since, thy husband served me in my wars,
And I to thee engaged a prince's word—
When thou didst make him master of thy bed—
To do him all the grace° and good I could.   favor; patronage
165 Go, some of you, knock at the abbey gate,
And bid the lady Abbess come to me.
I will determine this before I stir.

Enter a MESSENGER.

MESSENGER O mistress, mistress, shift° and save yourself!   do what you can

---

7. Offer; feel tender regard for.
8. Formal instructions. Adriana may have been the Duke's ward.

My master and his man are both broke loose,
170 Beaten the maids a-row,° and bound the Doctor,   *one after another*
Whose beard they have singed off with brands° of fire,   *torches*
And ever as it blazed, they threw on him
Great pails of puddled° mire to quench the hair.   *foul*
My master preaches patience to him, and the while
175 His man with scissors nicks him like a fool,[9]
And sure—unless you send some present help—
Between them they will kill the conjurer.

ADRIANA Peace, fool, thy master and his man are here,
And that is false thou dost report to us.

180 MESSENGER Mistress, upon my life I tell you true.
I have not breathed almost since I did see it.
He cries for you, and vows, if he can take you,
To scorch your face and to disfigure you.
        Cry within.
Hark, hark, I hear him, mistress. Fly, be gone!

185 DUKE [*to* ADRIANA] Come stand by me. Fear nothing. Guard
    with halberds!°   *spears with blades*

ADRIANA Ay me, it is my husband! Witness you
That he is borne about invisible.
Even now we housed him in° the abbey here,   *chased him into*
And now he's there, past thought of human reason.
        Enter ANTIPHOLUS [OF EPHESUS] *and* DROMIO OF
        EPHESUS.

190 ANTIPHOLUS OF EPHESUS Justice, most gracious Duke, oh,
    grant me justice!
Even for the service that long since I did thee,
When I bestrid thee[1] in the wars and took
Deep scars to save thy life; even for the blood
That then I lost for thee, now grant me justice.

195 EGEON [*aside*] Unless the fear of death doth make me dote,°   *grow senile*
I see my son Antipholus and Dromio.

ANTIPHOLUS OF EPHESUS Justice, sweet prince, against that
    woman there,
She whom thou gav'st to me to be my wife,
That hath abused and dishonored me,
200 Even in the strength and height of injury.
Beyond imagination is the wrong
That she this day hath shameless thrown on me.

DUKE Discover° how, and thou shalt find me just.   *Reveal*

ANTIPHOLUS OF EPHESUS This day, great Duke, she shut the
    doors upon me
205 While she with harlots° feasted in my house.   *scoundrels*

DUKE A grievous fault. Say, woman, didst thou so?

ADRIANA No, my good lord. Myself, he, and my sister
Today did dine together. So befall my soul
As this is false he burdens me withal.[2]

210 LUCIANA Ne'er may I look on day, nor sleep on night,
But° she tells to your highness simple truth.   *Unless*

ANGELO [*aside*] O perjured woman! They are both forsworn.

---

9. Cuts his hair in a foolish or fantastical fashion.
1. Stood over you (to defend you when you were down).
2. So . . . withal: Let the fate of my soul depend on whether what he charges me with is false.

In this the madman justly chargeth them.

ANTIPHOLUS OF EPHESUS My liege, I am advisèd° what I say,   *fully aware*
215 Neither disturbed with the effect of wine,
Nor heady-rash provoked with raging ire,
Albeit my wrongs might make one wiser mad.
This woman locked me out this day from dinner.
That goldsmith there, were he not packed° with her,   *conspiring*
220 Could witness it, for he was with me then,
Who parted with me to go fetch a chain,
Promising to bring it to the Porcupine,
Where Balthasar and I did dine together.
Our dinner done, and he not coming thither,
225 I went to seek him. In the street I met him,
And in his company that gentleman.
      [*He indicates the* SECOND MERCHANT.]
There did this perjured goldsmith swear me down°   *contradict me in swearing*
That I this day of him received the chain,
Which, God he knows, I saw not. For the which,
230 He did arrest me with an officer.
I did obey, and sent my peasant° home   *servant*
For certain ducats; he with none returned.
Then, fairly,° I bespoke° the officer   *courteously / asked*
To go in person with me to my house.
235 By th' way, we met my wife, her sister, and a rabble more
Of vile confederates. Along with them
They brought one Pinch, a hungry, lean-faced villain;
A mere anatomy,° a mountebank,°   *skeleton / quack*
A threadbare juggler,° and a fortune-teller,   *illusionist*
240 A needy, hollow-eyed, sharp-looking° wretch,   *emaciated*
A living dead man. This pernicious slave
Forsooth took on him as° a conjurer,   *posed as*
And gazing in mine eyes, feeling my pulse,
And with no face, as 'twere, outfacing me,[3]
245 Cries out I was possessed. Then altogether
They fell upon me, bound me, bore me thence,
And in a dark and dankish vault at home
There left me and my man, both bound together,
Till, gnawing with my teeth my bonds in sunder,°   *apart*
250 I gained my freedom, and immediately
Ran hither to your grace, whom I beseech
To give me ample satisfaction
For these deep shames and great indignities.

ANGELO My lord, in truth, thus far I witness with him:
255 That he dined not at home but was locked out.

DUKE But had he such a chain of thee, or no?

ANGELO He had, my lord, and when he ran in here
These people saw the chain about his neck.

SECOND MERCHANT Besides, I will be sworn these ears of mine
260 Heard you confess you had the chain of him,
After you first forswore it on the mart,
And thereupon I drew my sword on you,
And then you fled into this abbey here,
From whence I think you are come by miracle.

---

3. And with his thin face staring me down.

265 ANTIPHOLUS OF EPHESUS   I never came within these abbey
      walls,
      Nor ever didst thou draw thy sword on me.
      I never saw the chain, so help me heaven,
      And this is false you burden me withal.°   *with*
DUKE   Why, what an intricate impeach° is this!   *complex charge*
270   I think you all have drunk of Circe's cup.[4]
      If here you housed° him, here he would have been.   *enclosed*
      If he were mad, he would not plead so coldly.°   *rationally*
      [to ADRIANA] You say he dined at home; the goldsmith here
      Denies that saying. [to DROMIO OF EPHESUS] Sirrah, what say
      you?
275 DROMIO OF EPHESUS [indicating the COURTESAN]   Sir, he dined
      with her, there, at the Porcupine.
COURTESAN   He did, and from my finger snatched that ring.
ANTIPHOLUS OF EPHESUS   'Tis true, my liege, this ring I had of her.
DUKE [to the COURTESAN]   Saw'st thou him enter at the abbey
      here?
COURTESAN   As sure, my liege, as I do see your grace.
280 DUKE   Why, this is strange. Go call the Abbess hither.
      I think you are all mated° or stark mad.   *bewildered*
                              Exit one to the ABBESS.
EGEON   Most mighty Duke, vouchsafe me speak a word.
      Haply° I see a friend will save my life   *Maybe*
      And pay the sum that may deliver me.
285 DUKE   Speak freely, Syracusian, what thou wilt.
EGEON [to ANTIPHOLUS OF EPHESUS]   Is not your name, sir,
      called Antipholus?
      And is not that your bondman Dromio?
DROMIO OF EPHESUS   Within this hour I was his bondman,[5] sir,
      But he, I thank him, gnawed in two my cords.
290   Now am I Dromio, and his man, unbound.
EGEON   I am sure you both of you remember me.
DROMIO OF EPHESUS   Ourselves we do remember, sir, by you:
      For lately we were bound as you are now.[6]
      You are not Pinch's patient, are you, sir?
295 EGEON   Why look you strange° on me? You know me well.   *unknowingly*
ANTIPHOLUS OF EPHESUS   I never saw you in my life till now.
EGEON   Oh, grief hath changed me since you saw me last,
      And careful° hours with Time's deformèd° hand   *sorrowful / deforming*
      Have written strange defeatures° in my face.   *disfigurements*
300   But tell me yet, dost thou not know my voice?
ANTIPHOLUS OF EPHESUS   Neither.
EGEON   Dromio, nor thou?
DROMIO OF EPHESUS   No, trust° me, sir, nor I.   *believe*
EGEON   I am sure thou dost.
305 DROMIO OF EPHESUS   Ay, sir, but I am sure I do not, and
      whatsoever a man denies, you are now bound to believe
      him.
EGEON   Not know my voice! O time's extremity,
      Hast thou so cracked and splitted my poor tongue

4. The drink by means of which the enchantress   pun continues in line 290.)
Circe turned men into swine.   6. By looking at you, we remember how we were
5. His indentured servant; tied up with him. (The   (bound).

310 In seven short years that here my only son
Knows not my feeble key of untuned cares?[7]
Though now this grainèd° face of mine be hid   lined
In sap-consuming winter's drizzled snow,
And all the conduits of my blood froze up,
315 Yet hath my night of life some memory;
My wasting lamps° some fading glimmer left;   failing eyes
My dull deaf ears a little use to hear.
All these old witnesses, I cannot err,
Tell me thou art my son Antipholus.

ANTIPHOLUS OF EPHESUS   I never saw my father in my life.

320 EGEON   But° seven years since,° in Syracusa, boy,   Only / ago
Thou know'st we parted, but perhaps, my son,
Thou sham'st to acknowledge me in misery.

ANTIPHOLUS OF EPHESUS   The Duke, and all that know me in
the city,
325 Can witness with me that it is not so.
I ne'er saw Syracusa in my life.

DUKE   I tell thee, Syracusian, twenty years
Have I been patron to Antipholus,
During which time he ne'er saw Syracusa.
330 I see thy age and dangers make thee dote.

Enter the ABBESS *with* ANTIPHOLUS [OF] SYRACUSE *and*
DROMIO [OF] SYRACUSE.

ABBESS   Most mighty Duke, behold a man much wronged.

All gather to see them.

ADRIANA   I see two husbands, or mine eyes deceive me.

DUKE   One of these men is genius[8] to the other,
And so, of these, which is the natural° man,   human; mortal
335 And which the spirit? Who deciphers them?

DROMIO OF SYRACUSE   I, sir, am Dromio. Command him away.

DROMIO OF EPHESUS   I, sir, am Dromio. Pray let me stay.

ANTIPHOLUS OF SYRACUSE   Egeon, art thou not? Or else his
ghost.

DROMIO OF SYRACUSE   O my old master! Who hath bound
him here?

340 ABBESS   Who ever bound him, I will loose his bonds
And gain a husband by his liberty.
Speak, old Egeon, if thou beest the man
That hadst a wife once called Emilia,
That bore thee at a burden° two fair sons.   in one birth
345 Oh, if thou beest the same Egeon, speak,
And speak unto the same Emilia.

DUKE   Why, here begins his morning story right:
These two Antipholus', these two so like,
And these two Dromios, one in semblance—
350 Besides her urging° of her wreck at sea—   claim
These are the parents to these children,
Which accidentally are met together.

EGEON   If I dream not, thou art Emilia.
If thou art she, tell me, where is that son

---

7. My weak voice born of harsh sorrows.
8. Attendant spirit. It was a classical belief that each

person had such a spirit, identical in appearance,
allotted to him or her at birth.

355   That floated with thee on the fatal° raft?   *ill-fated*
    ABBESS   By men of Epidamnum, he, and I,
    And the twin Dromio, all were taken up.
    But, by and by, rude° fishermen of Corinth   *harsh; boorish*
    By force took Dromio and my son from them,
360   And me they left with those of Epidamnum.
    What then became of them, I cannot tell;
    I, to this fortune that you see me in.
    DUKE   Antipholus, thou cam'st from Corinth first.°   *originally*
    ANTIPHOLUS OF SYRACUSE   No, sir, not I. I came from
        Syracuse.
365   DUKE   Stay, stand apart. I know not which is which.
    ANTIPHOLUS OF EPHESUS   I came from Corinth, my most
        gracious lord.
    DROMIO OF EPHESUS   And I with him.
    ANTIPHOLUS OF EPHESUS   Brought to this town by that most
        famous warrior,
    Duke Menaphon, your most renownèd uncle.
370   ADRIANA   Which of you two did dine with me today?
    ANTIPHOLUS OF SYRACUSE   I, gentle mistress.
    ADRIANA   And are not you my husband?
    ANTIPHOLUS OF EPHESUS   No, I say nay to that.
    ANTIPHOLUS OF SYRACUSE   And so do I. Yet did she call me so,
375   And this fair gentlewoman her sister here
    Did call me brother. [*to* LUCIANA] What I told you then,
    I hope I shall have leisure° to make good,   *opportunity*
    If this be not a dream I see and hear.
    ANGELO   That is the chain, sir, which you had of me.
380   ANTIPHOLUS OF SYRACUSE   I think it be, sir. I deny it not.
    ANTIPHOLUS OF EPHESUS   And you, sir, for this chain arrested
        me.
    ANGELO   I think I did, sir. I deny it not.
    ADRIANA   I sent you money, sir, to be your bail
    By Dromio, but I think he brought it not.
385   DROMIO OF EPHESUS   No, none by me.
    ANTIPHOLUS OF SYRACUSE   This purse of ducats I received
        from you,
    And Dromio my man did bring them me.
    I see we still° did meet each other's man,   *constantly*
    And I was ta'en for him, and he for me,
390   And thereupon these errors are arose.
    ANTIPHOLUS OF EPHESUS   These ducats pawn I for my father
        here.
    DUKE   It shall not need. Thy father hath his life.
    COURTESAN   Sir, I must have that diamond from you.
    ANTIPHOLUS OF EPHESUS   There, take it, and much thanks for
        my good cheer.
395   ABBESS   Renownèd Duke, vouchsafe to take the pains
    To go with us into the abbey here,
    And hear at large discoursèd° all our fortunes.   *recounted in full*
    And all that are assembled in this place,
    That by this sympathizèd° one day's error   *shared*
400   Have suffered wrong, go, keep us company,
    And we shall make full satisfaction.
    Thirty-three years have I but gone in travail°   *labor*

Of you, my sons, and till this present hour
My heavy burden ne'er deliverèd.
405 The Duke, my husband, and my children both,
And you the calendars of their nativity,[9]
Go to a gossips' feast,[1] and go with me—
After so long grief such nativity![2]
DUKE With all my heart, I'll gossip at° this feast.   *join in*
        Exeunt all. The two DROMIOS *and two*
        [ANTIPHOLUS] *Brothers remain.*
410 DROMIO OF SYRACUSE Master, shall I fetch your stuff from
    shipboard?
ANTIPHOLUS OF EPHESUS Dromio, what stuff of mine hast
    thou embarked?°   *placed on board*
DROMIO OF SYRACUSE Your goods that lay at host, sir, in the
    Centaur.
ANTIPHOLUS OF SYRACUSE He speaks to me. I am your
    master, Dromio.
Come, go with us, we'll look to that anon.
415 Embrace thy brother there; rejoice with him.
        Exeunt [ANTIPHOLUS OF SYRACUSE *and* ANTIPHOLUS
        OF EPHESUS. DROMIO OF SYRACUSE *and* DROMIO OF
        EPHESUS *remain*].
DROMIO OF SYRACUSE There is a fat friend at your master's
    house
That kitchened me for you[3] today at dinner.
She now shall be my sister, not my wife.
DROMIO OF EPHESUS Methinks you are my glass° and not my   *mirror*
    brother:
420 I see, by you,° I am a sweet-faced youth.   *by means of you*
Will you walk in to see their gossiping?°   *merrymaking*
DROMIO OF SYRACUSE Not I, sir; you are my elder.[4]
DROMIO OF EPHESUS That's a question. How shall we try° it?   *test*
DROMIO OF SYRACUSE We'll draw cuts° for the senior. Till   *straws*
    then, lead thou first.
425 DROMIO OF EPHESUS Nay, then, thus:
We came into the world like brother and brother,
And now let's go hand in hand, not one before another.
        Exeunt.

---

9. (Addressed to the Dromios): the two servants are a record of their masters' age, having been born at the same time.
1. A feast attended by the godparents ("gossips") to celebrate the christening of a child.
2. TEXTUAL COMMENT The repetition of "nativity" and "go" in lines 406–08 has struck many editors as

unpoetic and has led to many suggested emendations. See Digital Edition TC 7.
3. Who entertained me in the kitchen while mistaking me for you.
4. The elder customarily takes precedence and enters first.

Love's Labor's Lost

Love's Labor's Lost (1594–96) is an experimental play disguised as a conventional one. Its most striking feature—its language of sexualized verbal wit—goes well with its aristocratic love plot. Yet the work is complicated by an unexpected concluding twist; challenges to hierarchies of gender, class, nation, and race; a scatological and homoerotic view of bodily function; and partly buried political and religious references. Without jettisoning the spirit of romantic comedy, then, Love's Labor's Lost offers a complex view of wooing and wedding with broad social implications.

Initially, Shakespeare telegraphs what is coming next. King Ferdinand of Navarre and his three courtiers—Biron, Dumaine, and Longueville—swear to shun women for three years to pursue the studious life of an ancient Greek or Renaissance Italian philosophical academy. Yet the arrival of a diplomatic embassy led by the Princess of France and including three ladies-in-waiting—Rosaline, Katherine, and Maria—induces the men to fall in love. They are ridiculed for their about-face. In a multiple eavesdropping scene, they overhear one another confessing this change of heart and hypocritically denounce such oath breaking. In a court masque (a dramatic form in which costumed aristocrats are the performers), they disguise themselves as Russians to advance their claims, but the ladies' own disguises lead each man to woo the wrong woman. Then, roughly two hundred lines from the end, a messenger reports that the Princess's father, the King of France, has died. The world of romantic comedy—Navarre's rural retreat from the ordinary affairs of life—is invaded by death. When the men obliviously continue their wooing, the women, who all along have mistrusted their forsworn suitors (arguably with even more justification in the Quarto than in the Folio version of the play), insist on a year's separation, which returns the plot to the opening rejection of heterosexual life.

From Two Gentlemen of Verona (1591–92) to Twelfth Night (1600–1601), Shakespeare's young lovers marry off. Love's Labor's Lost's open-ended conclusion thus sets it apart from the other romantic comedies, pointing instead to the problem plays, Troilus and Cressida (1601–02), Measure for Measure (1604), and All's Well That Ends Well (1606–07). Here, as Biron remarks with the work's typical self-consciousness, "Our wooing doth not end like an old play: / Jack hath not Jill" (5.2.860–61).* Both the romantic plot and the deflating outcome are suggested by the final poetic dialogue—between Spring, associated with fertility and love, and Winter, linked to coldness and suffering. Yet Spring also brings "unpleasing" cuckoldry and Winter "a merry note" (5.2.895, 912).

Before then, the aristocrats' verbal ingenuity dominates Love's Labor's Lost. No other Shakespearean play so emphasizes its own brilliance, so centrally concerns language itself, so heavily draws on bookishness, so revels in courtly style. Love's Labor's Lost possesses the highest ratio of rhyme to blank verse among the dramatic works—rivaled only by A Midsummer Night's Dream (1594–96). Shakespeare's most heavily rhymed tragedy, Romeo and Juliet (1594–96), and history, Richard II (1595), also date from these years, sometimes thought of as Shakespeare's lyrical period. Rhyming calls attention to the medium of language itself. By contrast, when Shakespeare seeks to render speech naturalistically, to make his language a more neutral expression of thought, he resorts to blank verse or prose.

*All quotations are taken from the edited text of the Folio, printed here. The Digital Edition includes edited texts of both the Folio and the Quarto.

In *Love's Labor's Lost*, Shakespeare generally employs blank verse for serious moments in long speeches, while reserving rhyme for the witty repartee of love that is a microcosm of the play's larger debate structure. In the opening scene, each male courtier discusses, in blank verse, the vow of abstinence from women before capping his speech with a concluding couplet (lines 1–48, couplets at 22–23, 26–27, 31–32, 47–48). But when the men then debate the plan, they produce more studied and playful effects by switching to rhyme—usually rhymed pentameter couplets, sometimes known as heroic couplets. At times, Shakespeare shifts to quatrains rhymed *abab*. If such a passage is followed by a couplet (see, for example, 1.1.61–66), the result is the six-line stanza of Shakespeare's amatory narrative poem *Venus and Adonis* (1592–93), a work that meditates comically on gender reversal, though of a different sort from what the play offers.

If three quatrains are followed by a couplet, a sonnet is born (for instance, 1.1.80–93). There are at least eight sonnets or sonnet-like structures in the play (also 1.1.160–74; 4.2.98–111; 4.3.22–37 and 55–68; 5.2.275–90, 344–57, and 403–16). In the subplot, the braggart Armado, in love with the peasant Jaquenetta, remarks, "I am sure I shall turn sonnet" (that is, sonneteer; 1.2.164). The boom of the English love sonnet begins in 1591 with the publication of Sidney's *Astrophil and Stella,* and Shakespeare is thought to have started his own sequence around 1592–93. Three of the lords' poems to the ladies were lifted from the 1598 Quarto of the play for *The Passionate Pilgrim,* an unauthorized 1599 collection attributed to Shakespeare on the title page but actually containing poetry by various writers. Within the play, the sonnets do not promote the men's romantic goals. The ladies coolly receive their suitors' poetic protestations, and the two sonnets in dialogue belittle the men. The sonnet form turns upon itself when Biron, having embraced plain speaking, avows his love to Rosaline—"Oh, never will I . . . woo in rhyme" (5.2.403–06)—in what proves to be the opening of a sonnet.

Wooing rhetoric is also associated with male bonding. The lords begin by misogynistically excluding any woman from their company "[o]n pain of losing her tongue" (1.1.123). Once in love, they switch to a Renaissance courtier's style, derived from two influential Italian writers—the fourteenth-century lyric poet Petrarch, founder of the European sonnet craze, and the fifteenth-century Neoplatonic philosopher Ficino. In the eavesdropping scene, they express their feelings not to the ladies but inadvertently to one another, through overheard soliloquies. Biron, the King, Longueville, and Dumaine successively confess their love, whereupon Dumaine's oath breaking is denounced by Longueville, Longueville's by the King, and the King's by Biron. The scene thus enacts the rhetorical figure of chiasmus—common to many passages in the play—in which the second of two parallel structures inverts the order of the first.

Like the play's linguistic fireworks, the obtrusive patterning here underscores the artificiality of the men's behavior. Biron, who like Armado's page Mote speaks directly to the audience, is the only courtier whose initial confession is not overheard, and he alone denounces himself, albeit under compulsion. Thereafter, the courtiers imagine their wooing as collective sexual attack: "Advance your standards, and upon them, lords! / Pell-mell, down with them!" (4.3.362–63). Fittingly, the play's jaundiced view of the sexual style of men in groups results in a year of isolation that separates the courtiers not only from women—as their initial academy stipulated—but also from one another. As in *The Merchant of Venice* (1596–97), another play that punishes male lovers who break their vows, the dissolution of male bonds precedes durable heterosexual attachment. Holofernes, a character from the subplot, is the play's only professional teacher ("Pedant"), and he is often ridiculous. But education shapes the main plot as well, partly in the lords' proposed intellectual retreat but especially in the ladies' schooling of the lords, a turn of events that reverses the gendered hierarchy of Renaissance pedagogy.

The language of *Love's Labor's Lost* is also marked by sexualized punning. Here, the men are no match for the women. The following exchange occurs during the Russian masque:

KATHERINE [*as* MARIA]   What, was your visor made without a
    tongue?
LONGUEVILLE   I know the reason, lady, why you ask.
KATHERINE   Oh, for your reason! Quickly, sir, I long.
LONGUEVILLE   You have a double tongue within your mask,
    And would afford my speechless visor half.
KATHERINE   "Veal!" quoth the Dutchman. Is not veal a calf?
LONGUEVILLE   A calf, fair lady?
KATHERINE   No, a fair lord-calf.
LONGUEVILLE   Let's part the word.
KATHERINE   No, I'll not be your half.
    Take all and wean it: it may prove an ox.
LONGUEVILLE   Look how you butt yourself in these sharp mocks.
    Will you give horns, chaste lady? Do not so.
KATHERINE   Then die a calf before your horns do grow.
LONGUEVILLE   One word in private with you ere I die.
KATHERINE   Bleat softly, then: the butcher hears you cry.
                               (5.2.243–56)

Referring to the mouthpiece keeping the mask in place, Katherine notes Longueville's silence ("without a tongue"). Longueville's second reply ("double tongue") accuses Katherine of punning, concealing her identity, being deceptive, and speaking enough for two, and then urges her to relinquish one tongue so he can speak and she will reveal her identity. Katherine's "Veal" combines Dutch for "well," German for "much," and a pun on "veil." And when the word is combined with the end of her second comment ("long"), we get "long-veal," a veiled assertion of her interlocutor's identity—Longueville. "Veal" also anticipates "calf" at the line's end—source of the passage's remaining jokes. Katherine reverses Longueville's question—his "lady" becomes her "lord"—thus branding him "a fair lord-calf," a dolt. Longueville's offer of compromise ("part the word") inspires Katherine's construal of "part" as "divide"; hence, her refusal to "be your half" (better half, or wife) and covert acknowledgment that the first half of the word ("ca") suggests her name. Longueville should raise the calf into an "ox," a castrated dolt with "horns," the symbol of cuckoldry. This argument sullies her reputation, he warns, but Katherine tells him that to avoid cuckoldry he should drop dead. Longueville asks for a tête-à-tête "ere I die" (have an orgasm), to which Katherine agrees, while warning him of his impending doom.

    The ladies also best the lords by critique of male verbal excess (*sans* is French for "without"):

BIRON   My love to thee is sound, *sans* crack or flaw.
ROSALINE   *Sans* "*sans*," I pray you!
                         (5.2.416–17)

The men, Biron realizes, must drop their bookish language to approximate the women's norm: "Honest plain words best pierce the ears of grief" (5.2.739). Rosaline sentences him to a year of jesting among "the speechless sick and . . . groaning wretches" (5.2.837–38), where he will learn the value—or valuelessness—of wit. And the Princess usually exercises a dignified stylistic restraint that eludes the men. Yet the women's actual practice often repudiates their theory. Early on, Rosaline praises Biron's wit. The ladies then embrace the game of verbal one-upmanship and obscene punning, as the Katherine-Longueville exchange demonstrates. Thus, they violate the principle that Rosaline claims Biron has ignored:

    A jest's prosperity lies in the ear
    Of him that hears it, never in the tongue
    Of him that makes it.
                    (5.2.847–49)

The women's self-contradictory avowal of wit and sobriety alike renders them romantically desirable in a fashion alien to the stereotypes of love poetry. Their possibly cynical economic mission may depend, as Boyet, their attending lord, suggests, on the Princess's ability to win the King's love. There are repeated jibes at their appearance as well as accusations of unchastity leveled at Rosaline by Biron, Boyet, and Katherine. The sexual innuendos in Katherine and Rosaline's exchange turn on "light" (bright, frivolous, or wanton), contrasted with both "heavy" (serious, overweight, pregnant) and "dark" (black, obscure, wanton; 5.2.14–46; see also 4.3.223–73). While not erasing the ladies' moral superiority, these countertendencies justify modern productions that have treated them without idealism or sentimentality.

The subplot, in which Armado and Costard, the clown, compete for Jaquenetta's affections, provides a different critique. More a series of set pieces than a continuous story, it offers both parallels and contrasts to the main plot. The first eight scenes (in modern editions) alternate between main plot and subplot; the concluding, ninth scene unites the two sets of characters. In each plot, the characters are divided into two groups, one of which intrudes from the outside—the ladies in the main plot, Armado and his page in the subplot. Such symmetries, which reinforce the work's formalized, dancelike structure and give it an aristocratic feel, recall the comedies that John Lyly wrote in the 1580s for boy actors. But this formalism acquires special force from the subplot's rootedness in popular culture, a culture reinvoked in the concluding speeches of Spring and Winter. Costard and Jaquenetta are from the rural lower classes; Dull, the constable, who anticipates Dogberry in *Much Ado About Nothing* (1598), barely stands above them. Mote is a page; Nathaniel, Holofernes, and Armado, although of higher rank, derive from the stock characters (minister, schoolmaster, braggart) of Italian commedia dell'arte, an originally popular, improvisational theater.

The juxtaposition of the two plots exalts and deflates the aristocrats. The subplot's fractured prose and doggerel verse set off Biron's polished poetry to advantage. Holofernes is the leading practitioner of the popular characters' penchant for synonyms. An apple hangs in the "*caelo,* the sky, the welkin, the heaven, and . . . falleth . . . on . . . terra,* the soil, the land, the earth" (4.2.5–6). Armado's forte is schematic syntax: "The time when? . . . Now for the ground which. . . . Then, for the place where" (1.1.227–32). But if Armado's language is excessive, Biron's is only slightly less so. Similarly, Costard's violation of the edict against being "taken with a wench" (1.1.271–72) anticipates the failure of the aristocrats. This leveling continues when Armado's love letter to Jaquenetta is echoed by those of the lords. Armado and Biron both have their epistles delivered by Costard, whose confusion of the two exposes each writer to ridicule. The courtiers' Muscovite masque is paralleled by the popular pageant of the Nine Worthies, a scene resembling the humble theatricals of *A Midsummer Night's Dream.* Moreover, both masque and pageant anticipate the larger plot of *Love's Labor's Lost* in their failure to end as their performers wish.

Costard's verbal sparring with the King and Princess, in which he holds his own, also reduces the sense of social superiority. His pointed response to dismissal by the forsworn courtiers—"Walk aside, the true folk, and let the traitors stay" (4.3.207)—recalls his, but not their, honesty. The lords' ridicule of the Nine Worthies prompts Holofernes' telling reply: "This is not generous, not gentle, not humble" (5.2.623). Although the aristocrats learn nothing from Marcadé's announcement of the death of the Princess's father, Armado, whom Costard has just accused of getting Jaquenetta pregnant, sees the need to reform. The lords accept their one-year sentences reluctantly, whereas Armado's voluntary longer commitment echoes and reverses their opening oaths: "I am a votary: I have vowed to Jaquenetta / To hold the plough for her sweet love three years" (5.2.868–69). The oddity here is Biron. More than any other aristocratic character, he internalizes popular culture, moving from refined verse to colloquial and proverbial expression in what is one of Shakespeare's most proverb-rich plays. For instance, he is the only figure from the main plot with an extended prose speech (4.3.1–17). In Shakespeare, this sort of linguistic range is

Garden scene. From Thomas Hill, *The Gardener's Labyrinth* (1577).

often integral to a character's unique ability to negotiate life's complexities. Yet Biron proves almost as hapless as his fellow suitors.

The subplot also reflects on the main plot through scatological or homoerotic bodily imagery, which includes terms for constipation—"immured," "restrained," "bound," "purgation," "loose" (3.1.114–17)—as well as Armado's boast of intimacy with the King, who has a tendency "with his royal finger thus [to] dally with my excrement" (5.1.90). In the play of the Nine Worthies, Holofernes as Judas Maccabeus is reduced to Judas (Iscariot), betrayer of Jesus:

> BOYET   Therefore, as he is an ass, let him go.
>   And so, adieu, sweet Jude. Nay, why dost thou stay?
> DUMAINE   For the latter end of his name.
> BIRON   For the "ass" to the "Jude"? Give it him: Jud-as, away!
>   (5.2.619–22)

Here, emphasis on "ass" activates the synonymous connotation of "end," the end of his body as well as "of his name." This material suggests that the main courtship plot is not the whole story. Aristocratic romantic language is balanced by a more excremental and homoerotic view of the body. Such passages exploit the possibilities of a transvestite theater, in which boys played the women's parts. The hints of homosexuality in the subplot answer the normative heterosexuality of the main plot. This verbal patterning expands the play's notions of the body and sexuality beyond what events themselves offer.

Such imagery also promotes religious, national, and racial xenophobia. Costard calls Armado's page "my incony [fine-quality] jew" (3.1.125), where "incony" inspires "inkle" (tape; 3.1.128), which suggests "ingle" (catamite, a boy kept by a pederast; see also 1.2.7). When Judas Maccabeus is "clipped" of his surname (5.2.593), Jewish circumcision is evoked. Holofernes' expulsion as "Jud-as" suggests the age's association of Jews with excrement and sodomy. Coming from "tawny Spain," "Dun"-colored Armado, "in all the world's new fashion planted" and hence perhaps associated with New World plantations, is also an alien figure (1.1.171, 4.3.194, 1.1.162). Yet he is less

Queen Elizabeth hunting. From George Gascoigne, *The Noble Art of Venerie or Hunting* (1575).

foreign than the Russians, much less their accompanying blackamoors, whose presence glances at racial subjugation. They could be based on a report of an earlier Tudor masque or on a contemporary amateur entertainment at one of London's law schools. The play and these two performances may draw on the period's link of Russia with dark skin. Although *Love's Labor's Lost* dramatizes a practice of scapegoating foreigners, it does not ratify this practice. Holofernes as Judas issues a pointed rebuke to the aristocrats; Armado reveals a depth of commitment unknown to them; the Russian masque backfires. Just as the play undermines convention in the central love plot, here, too, it questions—without openly attacking—cultural norms.

But the aristocrats themselves, unlike many of the popular characters, are also foreign. Behind the play lie contemporary political events that assume importance, given the plot's lack of literary sources. The comedy's King of Navarre draws on King Henri of Navarre, who established a philosophical academy and was accused of withdrawing from public life. His three courtiers are named for the historical king's aristocratic contemporaries, two of whom (the play's Biron and Dumaine) served him. The Princess may derive from Princess Marguerite de Valois, daughter of King Henri II of France. Marguerite was already Henri of Navarre's estranged wife when she led an embassy of reconciliation to him in 1578, accompanied by her ladies-in-waiting. As in *Love's Labor's Lost*, one topic of discussion was "Aquitaine—a dowry for a queen" (2.1.8).

Negotiations proceeded amid rampant adultery that undermined the vows of reconciliation and, contemporaries believed, caused renewal of France's Wars of Religion (1562–98), the bloody conflict between Protestant and Catholic aristocrats arguably noticed in the play's "civil war of wits" (2.1.225). Boyet, Marcadé, and perhaps Armado's page, Mote, also have prominent namesakes from these wars. To end the conflict and secure his claim on the French throne, Henri of Navarre converted to Catholicism in 1593, a further oath breaking that provoked criticism in Protestant England. The sympathy and judgment directed toward the play's lords, the serious treatment of their repudiated vows, the current of threatening sexuality, the emphasis on conflict, the invasion of death into the festive aristocratic world—all match this background. In short, the apparently anomalous intrusion of religious and political violence lends a surprising depth to what might otherwise be a lightweight romantic tale.

Foreignness and sexuality converge in the debate about the aristocrats' own colors. A 1984 production of the play cast a black actress as Rosaline. Although only Rosaline's hair and eyes are black, the play goes farther metaphorically. Unwillingly in love with Rosaline, Biron initially complains of her color (3.1.182–85, 4.3.2–3). But echoing Shakespeare's sonnets to the "dark lady," he later takes blackness as beauty's standard:

> KING By heaven, thy love is black as ebony!
> . . . .
> BIRON No face is fair that is not full so black.
> KING Oh, paradox! Black is the badge of hell . . . .
>   (4.3.241, 247–48)

If black is beautiful, even "Ethiops," who presumably share the King's distaste for their own appearance, "of their sweet complexion crack [boast]" (4.3.262). But it is not only the women whose faces suggest darkness. "Biron they call him," Rosaline remarks, "but a merrier man . . . I never spent an hour's talk withal" (2.1.66–68). The contrast is between "merrier" and "Biron," punning on a brown study, or seriousness. Before "the heavenly Rosaline," Biron imagines himself "a rude and savage man of Ind" (4.3.215–16), a claim he repeats to her: "Vouchsafe to show the sunshine of your face, / That we, like savages, may worship it" (5.2.202–03). The inclusion of the blackamoors thus accords with the play's association of its central couple with blackness.

Love's Labor's Lost went unperformed from 1642 to 1839, remaining unpopular until the mid-twentieth century. But modern enthusiasm for wordplay and demonstrations of the comedy's theatrical potential have changed things. Perhaps today its significance lies in linguistic artifice that is and is not rejected, an upper class that learns its manners from the lower, a capacious sense of bodily and sexual experience, a sympathetic evocation of blackness, a plot that takes a clear-eyed but not dismissive view of romantic love, and a company of women who ride off into the sunset without their men.

WALTER COHEN

SELECTED BIBLIOGRAPHY

Archer, John Michael. "*Love's Labour's Lost.*" *A Companion to Shakespeare's Works.* Vol. 3: *The Comedies.* Ed. Richard Dutton and Jean E. Howard. Malden, MA: Blackwell, 2003. 320–37. Treats issues of race and nation in relation to language, gender, and sexuality.

Flanigan, Tom. "On Fashionable Education and the Art of Rhetoric: Reflections of a Not-Indifferent Student in *Love's Labour's Lost.*" *Journal of the Wooden O Symposium* 5 (2005): 13–33. Offers a historical context for the play's treatment of education.

Hudson, Judith. "Punishing Perjury in *Love's Labour's Lost.*" *Early Modern Drama and the Bible: Contexts and Readings, 1570–1625.* Ed. Adrian Streete. London: Palgrave Macmillan, 2012. 118–36. Discusses perjury in the play as both religious and secular crime.

Lewis, Cynthia. "'We Know What We Know': Reckoning in *Love's Labor's Lost.*" *Studies in Philology* 105 (2008): 245–64. Examines the play's meditation on negotiations and calculations that go into formations of worth.

Londré, Felicia Hardison, ed. *"Love's Labour's Lost": Critical Essays*. New York: Routledge, 2001. Presents critical perspectives from 1598 to 2000 on theme, structure, gender, rhetoric, race, and performance history.

Maus, Katharine Eisaman. "Transfer of Title in *Love's Labour's Lost*: Language, Individualism, Gender." *Shakespeare Left and Right*. Ed. Ivo Kamps. New York: Routledge, 1991. 206–23. Explores the play's interrelated questioning of gender and linguistic norms.

Mazzio, Carla. "The Melancholy of Print: *Love's Labour's Lost*." *Historicism, Psychoanalysis, and Early Modern Culture*. Ed. Carla Mazzio and Douglas Trevor. New York: Routledge, 2000. 186–227. Analyzes the intersection of the speech(lessness) of love and early modern print culture.

Moncrief, Kathryn M. "'Teach Us, Sweet Madam': Masculinity, Femininity, and Gendered Instruction in *Love's Labor's Lost*." *Performing Pedagogy in Early Modern England: Gender, Instruction, and Performance*. Ed. Kathryn M. Moncrief and Kathryn R. McPherson. Surrey: Ashgate, 2011. 113–27. Discusses pedagogy as the inversion of traditional gendered hierarchy.

Parker, Patricia. "Preposterous Reversals: *Love's Labour's Lost*." *Modern Language Quarterly* 54 (1993): 435–82. Examines the play's obscene bodily punning as a challenge to class, gender, and sexual hierarchy.

Woods, Gillian. "Catholicism and Conversion in *Love's Labour's Lost*." *How to Do Things with Shakespeare: New Approaches, New Essays*. Ed. Laurie Maguire. Malden, MA: Blackwell, 2008. 101–30. Explores the tension between comic plot in Shakespeare and contemporary French wars of religion.

Films

Love's Labour's Lost. 1985. Dir. Elijah Moshinsky. UK. 120 min. Inspired by eighteenth-century European painting and music.

Love's Labour's Lost. 2000. Dir. Kenneth Branagh. UK. 93 min. Musical comedy, 1930s songs and settings, half of Shakespeare's lines retained, in the shadow of World War II, with Branagh, Alicia Silverstone, and Nathan Lane.

TEXTUAL INTRODUCTION

Despite its claim on the title page to be "Newly corrected and augmented," the 1598 Quarto of *Love's Labor's Lost* (Q) is urgently in need of editorial attention. Confusion over which character is speaking; inconsistency about which woman Biron is courting; vague stage directions; and a final line attributed to no one: all imply that the newly formed Lord Chamberlain's Men, when they first acted the play in 1594, must have relied upon a significantly different text. The kinds of errors that Q presents, such as its wide variation in names and speech prefixes, and the presence of "ghost" characters, suggest that the base text was authorial manuscript. However, evidence derived from the spelling conventions used by the printer, William White, points to the compositors working from a printed text—which would seem to endorse the title page's claim of a lost quarto, based on foul papers, reprinted by Q. For all its frustrations, the surviving Quarto remains a fascinating glimpse of Shakespeare at work, suggesting not only his process of revision but also his confidence that errors and inconsistencies would be worked out in the playhouse.

The Folio *Love's Labor's Lost* is clearly reprinted from the 1598 Quarto, yet its revisions suggest familiarity with the play in performance. It makes a concerted (if still incomplete) effort to smooth out the course of true love between Biron and Rosaline by altering speech prefixes in 2.1. It also redistributes some of the lines spoken by the Princess's "three lords," whose silent presence may have seemed indulgent, given how little scope for doubling the play affords. In F, at the beginning of

Berowne. Did not I dance with you in *Brabant* once?	*Berow.* Did not I dance with you in *Brabant* once?
Kather. Did not I dance with you in *Brabant* once?	*Rosa.* Did not I dance with you in *Brabant* once?
Ber. I know you did.	*Ber.* I know you did.
Kath. How needles was it then to aske the question?	*Rosa.* How needlesse was it then to ask the question?
Ber. You must not be so quicke.	*Ber.* You must not be so quicke.
Kath. Tis long of you that spur me with such questions,	*Rosa.* 'Tis long of you ȳ spur me with such questions.
Ber. Your wit's too hot,it speedes too fast, t'will tire.	*Ber.* Your wit's too hot,it speeds too fast, 'twill tire.
Kath. Not till it leaue the rider in the mire,	*Rosa.* Not till it leaue the Rider in the mire.
Ber. What time a day?	*Ber.* What time a day?
Kath. The houre that fooles should aske.	*Rosa.* The howre that fooles should aske.
Ber. Now faire befall your maske.	*Ber.* Now faire befall your maske.
Kath. Faire fall the face it couers.	*Rosa.* Faire fall the face it couers.
Ber. And send you manie louers,	*Ber.* And send you many louers,
Kath. Amen,so you be none.	*Rosa.* Amen,so you be none.
Ber. Nay then will I be gon.	*Ber.* Nay then will I be gone.

Biron's first flirtatious exchange with Katherine in Q (2.1.114–27) (left); revised to Rosaline in F (2.1.114–27) (right).

3.1, we find a stage direction, "*Song*," which is not required until Mote sings "Concolinel" at line 3 but possibly recalls the "plot" held backstage to jog the memory of the players or musicians. The play's final lines, "The words of Mercury are harsh, / After the songs of Apollo," which were printed in a larger typeface in Q, with no speech prefix, and so look like a bibliographical comment, are spoken by Armado in F. His additional instruction (which does not appear in Q), "You that way; we this way," might be directed at the players or the audience. Finally, the text is divided into five acts, which may be editorial but could also reflect theater practice after 1607.

Unfortunately, the Folio reproduces many of the errors that make the Quarto unactable. Most egregiously, the wrongful distribution of speeches between Nathaniel and Holofernes in 4.2 remains, though the bookkeeper would have needed to correct this in order to draw up the players' parts. In 5.2, when the disguised ladies torment their suitors, "*Mar.*" has a dialogue with first Dumaine and then Longueville, when the latter should clearly encounter Katherine (lines 239–56). Furthermore, draft passages in Q, where Shakespeare has written a speech and then immediately reused the material, have been reprinted in F alongside the revised versions (4.3.290–312, 5.2.130–33). More generally, we would expect a performance manuscript to improve upon the extremely vague stage directions provided by Q, but examples in act 5 such as "*Enter Ladies*" and "*Enter the King and the rest*" remain untouched, while exit cues are missing for the King in 1.1, Dumaine in 2.1, Biron in 3.1, and Armado in 5.2.

If F's changes reflect consultation with a theatrical manuscript, this must have been severely limited—perhaps only a few pages from 2.1 and 5.2—or it may be that the annotator of Q drew upon his memory of the play in performance. This would explain one of the Folio's oddest emendations, where the line "Climb o'er the house to unlock the little gate" is rendered "That were to climb o'er the house to unlock the gate" (1.1.109). However, it is also possible that the annotator had access to a further authorial manuscript or scribal copy that was still some way from promptbook material. Ultimately, the most systematic correction of Q was done in the printing house, for the vast majority of the Folio's changes are corrections of typographical errors and attempts to standardize spelling. For example, in 1.1 "sedule" becomes "schedule," "pome" is corrected to "pompe," though the nonsense of being expressly forbidden to "fast" rather than "feast" remains (line 62). For all the infelicities that stand in 4.2, the Folio has corrected a host of small details: "indiscreet" replaces "indistreell," "scurrilitie" "squirilitie," and "forgive" "forgine," though proofreading has failed to pick up the missing "of" in "we taste and feeling," or the use of "cald" instead of "call I" (lines 25, 47). In the process of correction, F has also added a number of errors: in 1.1, "hanted" replaces Q's "haunted;" in 2.1, F prints "repaie" where Q has "repaide," and "point out" where Q has "point you." There are also omissions that look like compositorial eye-skip rather than deliberate revision—for example, nine lines introducing the verse "The fox, the ape, and the humble-bee" are missing (3.1.75–82); Holofernes' Mantuan eulogy excludes the phrase "loves thee not" (4.2.90), and 5.2 omits Armado's assertion about Hector: "When he breathed he was a man" (lines 654–55).

Without ignoring the errors added by F or the uncertain origin of its changes, some of which may have been made without Shakespeare's consent or after his death, it is undeniable that many of the corrections to Q required by modern editors have already been made in F, and that this text appears more closely to reflect the play as it was originally performed.

JANE KINGSLEY-SMITH

TEXTUAL BIBLIOGRAPHY

Kerrigan, John. "*Love's Labor's Lost* and Shakespearean Revision." *Shakespeare Quarterly* 33 (Autumn 1982): 337–39.
———. "Shakespeare at Work: The Katherine-Rosaline Tangle in *Love's Labor's Lost*." RES 33 (May 1982): 129–36.
Wells, Stanley. "The Copy for the Folio Text of *Love's Labour's Lost*." RES 33 (May 1982): 137–47.

PERFORMANCE NOTE

Love's Labor's Lost, conspicuously among Shakespeare's plays, taxes companies with the fundamental challenge of making the play intelligible. As its meager production history perhaps demonstrates, the comedy's copious servings of abstruse puns, defunct satire, and (in Biron's terms) "taffeta phrases" and "figures pedantical" threaten the accessibility of a quite straightforward plot. Onstage, though, the play's preoccupation with the written word makes way for rich theatricality. So while productions can facilitate comprehension by implying that obfuscation is a comic character trait or by cutting the script, they often engage audiences most when they emphasize the artificiality of characters and action, complementing a play that uses nearly every character as an actor or spectator in several self-consciously theatrical set pieces.

Few plays make directors think so much about style. The premise of the plot is so thin, and the secondary characters so ripe for caricature, that the whole often plays as farce: an elegant comedy of manners wherein perfectly matched lords and ladies proceed toward inevitable unions. But modern directors increasingly probe beneath the play's surfaces, satirizing the principals or building improbable sympathies for lesser characters. Some seek to frustrate generic expectations (as does the play's conclusion) by magnifying the divide between the lords' immaturity and the ladies' sophistication, or by playing the women's indifference as earnest, not affected. Thus the lords' initial vow can seem attractively naïve or foolish, and the dispute over Navarre's debt a mere pretext for romance or a source of lasting suspicion.

The choices made often reflect two overarching directorial decisions: first, whether to inflect the production with the melancholy and estrangement that characterize the comedy's eventual irresolution, or to play unadulterated comedy straight into an ending that confounds it; second, whether the mood around the couples' leave-taking is dubious or optimistic about their futures together. Along the way, productions must strike a balance between Armado's boasting and his evident loyalty and courage; Holofernes' pedantry and his potentially endearing sensitivity; Boyet's acute perception and his priggishness. Meanwhile, Costard can appear a bumpkin of accidental wit or a self-assured ally of the audience, and Jaquenetta an innocent dairymaid or a lewd social climber. Productions must also work out the mood and suddenness of Marcadé's entrance and the complex blocking required for the eavesdropping scene (4.3) and the pageant of "Nine Worthies."

BRETT GAMBOA

Love's Labor's Lost

[THE PERSONS OF THE PLAY

Ferdinand, KING of Navarre
BIRON
LONGUEVILLE } lords attending on the King
DUMAINE
Blackamoors

PRINCESS of France, later QUEEN
MARIA
KATHERINE } ladies attending on the Princess
ROSALINE
BOYET
Two other lords } lords attending on the Princess
FORESTER
MARCADÉ, a messenger from France

Don Adriano de ARMADO, a Spanish braggart
Mote, PAGE to Armado
COSTARD, a clown
JAQUENETTA, a country wench
Anthony DULL, a constable

HOLOFERNES, a schoolmaster
NATHANIEL, a curate]

1.1 (Q 1.1)

Enter Ferdinand, KING *of Navarre [holding a paper],*
BIRON, LONGUEVILLE, *and* DUMAINE.[1]

KING Let Fame, that all hunt after in their lives,
 Live registered upon our brazen° tombs,   *brass; long-lasting*
 And then grace° us in the disgrace° of death   *honor / disfigurement*
 When, spite of cormorant° devouring Time,[2]   *despite ravenous*
5 Th'endeavor of this present breath° may buy   *speech; life*
 That honor which shall bate° his scythe's keen edge   *blunt*
 And make us heirs of all eternity.°   *eternally renowned*
 Therefore, brave conquerors—for so you are,
 That war against your own affections°   *passions*
10 And the huge army of the world's desires—
 Our late° edict shall strongly stand in force.   *recent*

1.1 Location: The whole play takes place in the King
of Navarre's park.
1. TEXTUAL COMMENT Until Henri of Navarre's
accession to the French throne in 1589, Navarre was
an independent kingdom in southwestern France.
For the historical background to these figures, and
the spelling and pronunciation of their names, see
the Introduction and especially Digital Edition
TC 1 (Folio edited text).
2. Proverbial; one of the play's many proverbs, used
by aristocrats and commoners alike.

Navarre shall be the wonder of the world;
Our court shall be a little academe,
Still° and contemplative in living art.[3]   *Peaceful*
15   You three, Biron, Dumaine, and Longueville,
Have sworn for three years' term to live with me,
My fellow-scholars, and to keep those statutes
That are recorded in this schedule° here.   *document*
Your oaths are passed,° and now subscribe° your names,   *pledged / sign*
20   That his own hand may strike his honor down
That violates the smallest branch° herein.   *clause*
If you are armed to do as sworn to do,
Subscribe to your deep oaths, and keep it too.[4]
LONGUEVILLE   I am resolved; 'tis but a three years' fast.
25   The mind shall banquet, though the body pine.
Fat paunches have lean pates,° and dainty bits°   *heads / bites*
Make rich the ribs but bankrupt quite the wits.
        [*He signs.*]
DUMAINE   My loving lord, Dumaine is mortified.°   *dead to worldliness*
The grosser manner of these world's delights
30   He throws upon the gross world's baser slaves.
To love, to wealth, to pomp, I pine and die,
With all these[5] living in philosophy.
        [*He signs.*]
BIRON   I can but say their protestation over.°   *again*
So much, dear liege,° I have already sworn: *lord*
35   That is, to live and study here three years.
But there are other strict observances,
As not to see a woman in that term,
Which I hope well is not enrollèd° there;   *listed*
And one day in a week to touch no food,
40   And but one meal on every day beside,
The which I hope is not enrollèd there;
And then to sleep but three hours in the night,
And not be seen to wink of° all the day—   *close my eyes during*
When I was wont to think no harm all night,[6]
45   And make a dark night too of half the day—
Which I hope well is not enrollèd there.
Oh, these are barren tasks, too hard to keep:
Not to see ladies, study, fast, not sleep.
KING   Your oath is passed to pass away from these.
50   BIRON   Let me say no, my liege, an if° you please.   *an if = if*
I only swore to study with your grace,
And stay here in your court for three years' space.
LONGUEVILLE   You swore to that, Biron, and to the rest.
BIRON   By yea and nay,[7] sir, then I swore in jest.
55   What is the end of study? Let me know.
KING   Why, that to know which else we should not know.
BIRON   Things hid and barred, you mean, from common sense?°   *ordinary perception*

---

3. The art of living (this meaning goes back to ancient Stoic thought); learning invigorated by life. *academe* (line 13): a philosophical academy like Plato's, revived during the Renaissance.
4. The first couplet to cap a blank-verse speech. For more on rhyme, see the Introduction. *armed*: equipped.
5. His three companions; the conditions prescribed

in the document; or the suggestion that philosophy is a source or substitute for the worldly attractions of line 31.
6. Proverbial. *no harm*: it harmless (to sleep).
7. Earnestly (a solemn oath based on Matthew 5:37); ambiguously.

KING   Ay, that is study's godlike recompense.

BIRON   Come on,[8] then. I will swear to study so,

60   To know the thing I am forbid[9] to know,
     As thus: to study where I well may dine,
     When I to feast expressly am forbid;
     Or study where to meet some mistress fine,
     When mistresses from common sense are hid;

65   Or, having sworn too hard-a-keeping° oath,   *a too-demanding*
     Study to break it and not break my troth.°   *pledged faith*
     If study's gain be thus, and this be so,
     Study knows that which yet it doth not know.[1]
     Swear me to this and I will ne'er say no.°   *(first rhyming triplet)*

70 KING   These be the stops° that hinder study quite,   *obstacles*
     And train° our intellects to vain delight.   *allure*

BIRON   Why, all delights are vain, and that most vain
     Which with pain° purchased doth inherit pain;°   *labor / suffering*
     As,° painfully to pore upon a book   *Such as*

75   To seek the light of truth, while truth the while
     Doth falsely° blind the eyesight of his look.°   *deceitfully / its vision*
     Light seeking light doth light of light beguile;[2]
     So, ere you find where light in darkness lies,
     Your light grows dark by losing of your eyes.

80   Study me[3] how to please the eye indeed
     By fixing it upon a fairer° eye,   *woman's*
     Who, dazzling so,[4] that eye shall be his heed,°   *what he heeds*
     And give him light that it° was blinded by.   *(his eye)*
     Study is like the heavens' glorious sun

85   That will not be deep searched with saucy° looks.   *presumptuous; insolent*
     Small° have continual plodders ever won,   *Little*
     Save base° authority from others' books.   *Except commonplace*
     These earthly godfathers of heaven's lights,°   *astronomers*
     That give a name to every fixèd star,

90   Have no more profit of their shining nights
     Than those that walk and wot° not what they are.   *know*
     Too much to know is to know naught but fame,°   *hearsay; reputation*
     And every godfather can give a name.°   *(as astronomers do)*

KING   How well he's read to reason against reading!

95 DUMAINE   Proceeded° well to stop all good proceeding.[5]   *Argued*

LONGUEVILLE   He weeds° the corn° and still lets grow the   *pulls up / wheat*
     weeding.°   *weeds*

BIRON   The spring is near when green geese are a-breeding.[6]

DUMAINE   How follows that?

BIRON   Fit in his° place and time.   *its*

DUMAINE   In reason nothing.

BIRON   Something, then, in rhyme.[7]

---

8. Q has "Com'on," possibly punning on "common" (line 57).
9. Deliberately misinterpreting "should" (line 56) as "ought" rather than "would."
1. *If . . . know:* If study means experiencing the forbidden (line 60), study does indeed enable one to know what isn't yet known (line 56). *and:* and if.
2. The eye, from too much study (reading), is blinded (as if from looking at a bright light).
3. Study, I say: the beginning of the first sonnet (lines 80–93). This is Biron's initial claim that a man's spiritual enlightenment depends not on read-

ing books but on gazing into a beautiful woman's eyes—derived from Petrarch and Ficino. For these writers and for sonnets, see the Introduction.
4. The man (who does this) being thus bedazzled.
5. Toward a university degree.
6. When young geese are mating (as will the young lords, Biron implies). A goose is also a prostitute.
7. "In reason," it follows "nothing" (not at all); but in rhyme, "something" (somewhat)—an allusion to the proverbial phrase "neither rhyme nor reason" and perhaps to their own rhyming repartee.

100	KING Biron is like an envious, sneaping° frost	*a malicious, biting*
	That bites the firstborn infants° of the spring.	*buds*
	BIRON Well, say I am; why should proud° summer boast	*splendid*
	Before the birds have any cause to sing?	
	Why should I joy in any abortive° birth?	*premature*
105	At Christmas I no more desire a rose	
	Than wish a snow in May's newfangled shows,°	*displays of flowers*
	But like of° each thing that in season grows.	*But enjoy*
	So you to study now it is too late:	
	That were to climb o'er the house to unlock the gate.[8]	
110	KING Well, sit you out.° Go home, Biron; adieu.	*don't take part*
	BIRON No, my good lord, I have sworn to stay with you.	
	And though I have for barbarism° spoke more	*on behalf of ignorance*
	Than° for that angel, Knowledge, you can say,	*Than what*
	Yet confident I'll keep what I have sworn,	
115	And bide the penance of each three years' day.°	*day of the three years*
	Give me the paper. Let me read the same,	
	And to the strictest decrees I'll write my name.	
	KING [*handing him the paper*] How well this yielding rescues	
	thee from shame!	
	BIRON [*reads*] "Item: That no woman shall come within a mile	
120	of my court."	
	Hath this been proclaimed?	
	LONGUEVILLE Four days ago.	
	BIRON Let's see the penalty: "On pain of losing her tongue."	
	Who devised this penalty?	
	LONGUEVILLE Marry,[9] that did I.	
125	BIRON Sweet lord, and why?	
	LONGUEVILLE To fright them hence with that dread penalty.	
	BIRON A dangerous law against gentility!°	*courtesy*
	"Item: If any man be seen to talk with a woman within the	
	term of three years, he shall endure such public shame as	
130	the rest of the court shall possibly devise."	
	This article, my liege, yourself must break.	
	For well you know, here comes in embassy	
	The French King's daughter with yourself to speak—	
	A maid of grace and complete majesty—	
135	About surrender up of Aquitaine[1]	
	To her decrepit, sick, and bedrid father.	
	Therefore, this article is made in vain,	
	Or vainly comes th'admired Princess hither.	
	KING What say you, lords? Why, this was quite forgot!	
140	BIRON So study evermore is overshot.°	*wide of the mark*
	While it doth study to have what it would,	
	It doth forget to do the thing it should;	
	And when it hath the thing it hunteth most,	
	'Tis won as towns with fire:[2] so won, so lost.	
145	KING We must of force° dispense with this decree.	*necessity*
	She must lie° here, on mere° necessity.	*lodge / absolute*
	BIRON Necessity will make us all forsworn	

8. Set about things in a senseless, backward way—
rather than climbing over the gate to unlock the house.
9. Indeed (invocation of the Virgin Mary).

1. A large area in southern France.
2. That is, destroyed in being captured.

Three thousand times within this three years' space.
For every man with his affects° is born,   *passions*
150 Not by° might mastered, but by special grace.°   *by his own / (of God)*
If I break faith, this word° shall speak for me: *motto*
I am forsworn "on mere necessity."
So to the laws at large° I write my name,   *in general*
    [*He signs.*]
And he that breaks them in the least degree
155 Stands in attainder of° eternal shame.   *condemned to*
Suggestions° are to others as to me,   *Temptations*
But I believe, although I seem so loath,
I am the last that will last° keep his oath.   *longest; least likely*
But is there no quick° recreation granted?   *lively*
160 KING Ay, that there is. Our court, you know, is haunted[3]
With° a refinèd traveler of° Spain,   *By / from*
A man in all the world's new fashion planted,[4]
That hath a mint of phrases in his brain;
One who° the music of his own vain tongue   *whom*
165 Doth ravish like enchanting harmony;
A man of compliments,° whom right and wrong   *fashion; attainments?*
Have chose as umpire of their mutiny.°   *discord*
This child of Fancy,° that Armado hight,°   *fantastic being / is called*
For interim° to our studies shall relate   *interlude*
170 In high-born words the worth of many a knight
From tawny° Spain, lost in the world's debate.°   *sunburned / warfare*
How you delight, my lords, I know not, I,
But I protest I love to hear him lie,
And I will use him for my minstrelsy.°   *entertainment*
175 BIRON Armado is a most illustrious wight,°   *person*
A man of fire-new° words, fashion's own knight.   *newly coined*
LONGUEVILLE Costard the swain[5] and he shall be our sport,
And so to study three years is but short.
    Enter [DULL,] *a constable*[,] *with* COSTARD *with*
    a letter.
DULL Which is the Duke's° own person?   *King's*
180 BIRON This, fellow. What wouldst?
DULL I myself reprehend° his own person, for I am his grace's   *(blunder for "represent")*
farborough.[6] But I would see his own person in flesh and
blood.
BIRON This is he.
185 DULL [*to the* KING] Señor Arm—Arm—commends° you. There's   *greets*
villainy abroad. This letter will tell you more.
COSTARD Sir, the contempts[7] thereof are as touching me.
KING [*reads*] A letter from the magnificent Armado![8]
BIRON How low soever the matter, I hope in God for high words.
190 LONGUEVILLE A high hope for a low heaven.° God grant us   *a small blessing*
patience!
BIRON To hear, or forbear hearing?
LONGUEVILLE To hear meekly, sir, and to laugh moderately,
or to forbear both.

---

3. *haunted*: frequented; beginning of a sonnet of fifteen lines (lines 160–74).
4. Established; see Introduction.
5. The costard is a large apple; also, comically, the head. *swain*: country lad.

6. Blunder for "thirdborough," a petty constable.
7. Blunder for "contents"; but also, inadvertently, "contempt."
8. Phrase used of the Spanish Armada (1588).

195   BIRON   Well, sir, be it as the style shall give us cause to climb in merriness.[9]

  COSTARD   The matter° is to me, sir, as concerning Jaquenetta. The manner of it is, I was taken with the manner.°   *(perhaps sexual)* / *caught red-handed*

  BIRON   In what manner?

200   COSTARD   In manner and form[1] following, sir—all those three. I was seen with her in the manor house, sitting with her upon the form,° and taken following her into the park, which put   *bench* together is "in manner and form following." Now, sir, for the "manner"—it is the manner of a man to speak to a woman; for

205   the "form"—in some form.

  BIRON   For the "following," sir?

  COSTARD   As it shall follow in my correction,° and God defend   *punishment* the right!°   *(prayer before combat)*

  KING   Will you hear this letter with attention?

210   BIRON   As we would hear an oracle.

  COSTARD   Such is the simplicity[2] of man to hearken after the flesh.

  KING [*reads*]   "Great deputy, the welkin's vicegerent,° and sole   *heaven's deputy* dominator of Navarre, my soul's earth's° god, and body's   *earthly*

215   fostering patron—"

  COSTARD   Not a word of Costard yet.

  KING   "So it is—"

  COSTARD   It may be so; but if he say it is so, he is, in telling true, but so.°   *truly only so-so*

220   KING   Peace!

  COSTARD   Be to me and every man that dares not fight.

  KING   No words!

  COSTARD   Of other men's secrets, I beseech you.

  KING   "So it is, besieged with sable-colored° melancholy, I did   *black*

225   commend the black oppressing humor° to the most wholesome   *melancholy* physic° of thy health-giving air, and, as I am a gentleman,   *medicine* betook myself to walk. The time when? About the sixth hour, when beasts most graze, birds best peck, and men sit down to that nourishment which is called supper; so much for the

230   time when. Now for the ground which—which, I mean, I walked upon—it is ycleped° thy park. Then, for the place   *called (archaic)* where—where, I mean, I did encounter that obscene° and   *disgusting; wanton* most preposterous[3] event that draweth from my snow-white pen° the ebon-colored° ink, which here thou viewest, behold-   *goose quill / black*

235   est, surveyest, or seest. But to the place where: it standeth north-north-east and by east from the west corner of thy curious-knotted° garden. There did I see that low-   *intricately patterned* spirited° swain, that base minnow° of thy mirth—"   *base / shrimp*

  COSTARD [*aside*]   Me?

240   KING   "That unlettered,° small-knowing soul—"   *illiterate*

  COSTARD [*aside*]   Me.

  KING   "That shallow vassal°—"   *base wretch; vessel*

  COSTARD [*aside*]   Still me.

---

9. *style . . . merriness:* stile=fence; the humble subject of "merriness" does not ordinarily lead one "to climb" to a high prose "style." A "style" is also a pen and, hence, perhaps a penis that will "climb" (swell) in "merriness" (pleasure).

1. Legal, then proverbial, phrase.
2. Simplicity (folly); perhaps a pun on "sin" as well.
3. Unnatural; in reversed position—with "obscene" (line 232) anatomically suggesting placement of the rear, or posterior, in front. See 5.1.77, 79, 104.

KING   "Which, as I remember, hight Costard—"

245   COSTARD   Oh, me!

KING   "Sorted° and consorted, contrary to thy established,   *Associated*
proclaimed edict and continent canon,° which with—oh,   *restraining law*
with—but with this—I passion° to say wherewith!"   *grieve*

COSTARD   With a wench.

250   KING   "With a child of our grandmother Eve, a female, or—for
thy more sweet understanding—a woman. Him I—as my ever-
esteemed duty pricks[4] me on—have sent to thee, to receive
the meed° of punishment, by thy sweet grace's officer,   *reward*
Anthony Dull: a man of good repute, carriage, bearing, and

255   estimation."

DULL   Me, an't° shall please you. I am Anthony Dull.   *if it*

KING   "For Jaquenetta—so is the weaker vessel° called which I   *woman (1 Peter 3:7)*
apprehended with the aforesaid swain—I keep her as a vessel
of thy law's fury, and shall, at the least of thy sweet notice,°   *as soon as you order*

260   bring her to trial.° Thine in all compliments of devoted and   *(legally; sexually)*
heart-burning heat of duty,

                      Don Adriano de Armado."

BIRON   This is not so well as I looked for, but the best that
ever I heard.

265   KING   Ay, the best for° the worst. [*to* COSTARD] But, sirrah,[5]   *best example of*
what say you to this?

COSTARD   Sir, I confess the wench.

KING   Did you hear the proclamation?

COSTARD   I do confess much of the hearing it, but little of the

270   marking of° it.   *paying attention to*

KING   It was proclaimed a year's imprisonment to be taken
with a wench.

COSTARD   I was taken with none, sir. I was taken with a damosell.

275   KING   Well, it was proclaimed "damosell."

COSTARD   This was no damosell neither, sir: she was a virgin.

KING   It is so varied° too, for it was proclaimed "virgin."   *covers that variation*

COSTARD   If it were, I deny her virginity. I was taken with a maid.

KING   This "maid" will not serve your turn, sir.

280   COSTARD   This maid will serve my turn,° sir.   *(sexually)*

KING   Sir, I will pronounce your sentence:
You shall fast a week with bran and water—

COSTARD   I had rather pray a month with mutton and
porridge.[6]

285   KING   And Don Armado shall be your keeper.
My lord Biron, see him delivered o'er,
And go we, lords, to put in practice that
Which each to other hath so strongly sworn.

          [*Exeunt the* KING, LONGUEVILLE, *and* DUMAINE.]

BIRON   I'll lay° my head to any goodman's hat,   *bet*

290   These oaths and laws will prove an idle scorn.
—Sirrah, come on.

COSTARD   I suffer for the truth, sir. For true it is, I was taken
with Jaquenetta, and Jaquenetta is a true° girl, and therefore   *an honest*

---

4. Spurs (sexual). See also 2.1.188; 4.1.131, 137;   5. Standard term for addressing social inferiors.
4.2.11, 18, 44, 47, 51, 54.   6. Mutton soup; "mutton" is also slang for "prostitute."

welcome the sour cup of prosperity! Affliction[7] may one day
295 smile again, and until then, sit thee down,° Sorrow! *Exeunt.*   *stay with me*

1.2 (Q 1.2)

Enter ARMADO *and Mote, his* PAGE.[1]

ARMADO Boy, what sign is it° when a man of great spirit grows   *what does it mean*
melancholy?

PAGE A great sign, sir, that he will look sad.

ARMADO Why, sadness is one and the selfsame thing,° dear imp.°   *(as melancholy) / child*

5 PAGE No, no, O Lord, sir, no.

ARMADO How canst thou part° sadness and melancholy, my   *distinguish between*
tender juvenal?[2]

PAGE By a familiar° demonstration of the working,° my tough   *plain / their operation*
señor.[3]

10 ARMADO Why "tough señor"? Why "tough señor"?

PAGE Why "tender juvenal"? Why "tender juvenal"?

ARMADO I spoke it, tender juvenal, as a congruent epitheton
appertaining to° thy young days, which we may nominate°   *suitable term for / call*
"tender."

15 PAGE And I, tough señor, as an appertinent° title to your old   *appropriate*
time, which we may name "tough."

ARMADO Pretty and apt!

PAGE How mean you, sir? I pretty and my saying apt, or I apt
and my saying pretty?

20 ARMADO Thou pretty because little.°   *(proverbial)*

PAGE Little pretty because little. Wherefore apt?

ARMADO And therefore apt because quick.°   *quick-witted*

PAGE Speak you this in my praise, master?

ARMADO In thy condign° praise.   *well-deserved*

25 PAGE I will praise an eel with the same praise.

ARMADO What, that an eel is ingenious?

PAGE That an eel is quick.°   *alive*

ARMADO I do say thou art quick in answers. Thou heat'st my
blood.°   *You make me angry*

30 PAGE I am answered, sir.

ARMADO I love not to be crossed.

PAGE [*aside*] He speaks the mere° contrary: crosses[4] love not   *absolute*
him.

ARMADO I have promised to study three years with the Duke.

35 PAGE You may do it in an hour, sir.

ARMADO Impossible!

PAGE How many is one thrice told?°   *counted*

ARMADO I am ill at reckoning; it fits the spirit of a tapster.°   *bartender*

PAGE You are a gentleman and a gamester,° sir.   *gambler*

40 ARMADO I confess both; they are both the varnish of a complete man.

PAGE Then I am sure you know how much the gross sum of
deuce-ace° amounts to.   *a two and a one (dice)*

ARMADO It doth amount to one more than two.

---

7. Blunder for reverse order: "affliction! Prosperity."
1.2 Location: The King's park.
1. TEXTUAL COMMENT The Folio has "Moth," meaning "moth" or "mote" (speck). It is pronounced like
the latter word, and that sense may be primary. Hence,

it is spelled "Mote" in both F and Q in this edition. See
Digital Edition TC 2 (Folio edited text).
2. Youth; Juvenal, ancient Roman satirist.
3. Sir; senior.
4. Coins (often imprinted with crosses).

45	PAGE Which the base vulgar° call three?	*common people*
	ARMADO True.	
	PAGE Why, sir, is this such a piece of study?° Now, here's three	*hard work*
	studied ere you'll thrice wink, and how easy it is to put "years"	
	to the word "three" and study three years in two words the	
50	dancing horse⁵ will tell you.	
	ARMADO A most fine figure!°	*verbal turn; number*
	PAGE [aside] To prove you a cipher.°	*zero*
	ARMADO I will hereupon confess I am in love, and as it is base°	*ignoble*
	for a soldier to love, so am I in love with a base° wench. If draw-	*lowborn*
55	ing my sword against the humor of affection° would deliver	*inclination to love*
	me from the reprobate thought of it, I would take Desire pris-	
	oner and ransom him to any French courtier for a new-	
	devised curtsy.° I think scorn° to sigh. Methinks I should	*bowing fashion / disdain*
	outswear° Cupid. Comfort me, boy—what great men have	*renounce*
60	been in love?	
	PAGE Hercules, master.	
	ARMADO Most sweet Hercules! More authority, dear boy,	
	name more; and, sweet my child, let them be men of good	
	repute and carriage.°	*behavior*
65	PAGE Samson, master. He was a man of good carriage, great	
	carriage, for he carried the town gates on his back⁶ like a	
	porter, and he was in love.	
	ARMADO O well-knit Samson, strong-jointed Samson, I do excel	
	thee in my rapier as much as thou didst me in carrying gates.	
70	I am in love too. Who was Samson's love, my dear Mote?	
	PAGE A woman, master.	
	ARMADO Of what complexion?⁷	
	PAGE Of all the four, or the three, or the two, or one of the four.	
	ARMADO Tell me precisely of what complexion.	
75	PAGE Of the sea-water green,⁸ sir.	
	ARMADO Is that one of the four complexions?	
	PAGE As I have read, sir, and the best of them too.	
	ARMADO Green, indeed, is the color of lovers, but to have a	
	love of that color? Methinks Samson had small reason for it.	
80	He surely affected° her for her wit.°	*loved / intelligence*
	PAGE It was so, sir, for she had a green wit.⁹	
	ARMADO My love is most immaculate white and red.	
	PAGE Most maculate° thoughts, master, are masked under	*impure*
	such colors.°	*hues; pretexts*
85	ARMADO Define,° define, well-educated infant.	*Explain your meaning*
	PAGE My father's wit and my mother's tongue assist me!	
	ARMADO Sweet invocation of a child—most pretty and	
	pathetical!°	*touching*
	PAGE If she be made° of white and red,	*(also "maid")*
90	Her faults will ne'er be known,	
	For blushing cheeks by faults are bred,	
	And fears by pale white shown.	

---

5. Morocco, a performing horse trained to "count" with its hooves, was a London sensation in 1591. The Page jokingly takes the phrase "three years" as the object of "study" (line 34).
6. For the gates, see Judges 16:3. Love proved disastrous for both Hercules and Samson.
7. Temperament (Armado's meaning), as determined by the balance of bodily humors: blood, phlegm, melancholy (from black bile), choler; skin coloring (the Page's meaning).
8. Ill colored; evidence of chlorosis, an anemic condition affecting young women.
9. Immature understanding (proverbial).

Then if she fear or be to blame,
By this you shall not know,
95   For still her cheeks possess the same
    Which native° she doth owe.°   *naturally / own*
A dangerous rhyme, master, against the reason of white and
red.

ARMADO   Is there not a ballad, boy, of the King and the Beggar?[1]
100 PAGE   The world was very guilty of such a ballad some three
    ages since, but I think now 'tis not to be found, or if it were
    it would neither serve° for the writing nor the tune.   *be acceptable*
ARMADO   I will have that subject newly writ o'er, that I may
    example my digression° by some mighty precedent. Boy, I do   *justify my lapse*
105   love that country girl that I took in the park with the ratio-
    nal hind,[2] Costard. She deserves well—
PAGE [*aside*]   To be whipped,° and yet a better love than my   *(as a prostitute)*
    master.
ARMADO   Sing, boy. My spirit grows heavy in love.
110 PAGE [*aside*]   And that's great marvel, loving a light° wench.   *wanton*
ARMADO   I say, sing.
PAGE   Forbear till this company be passed.
        Enter [COSTARD, *the*] *clown,* [DULL, *the*] *constable,*
        and [JAQUENETTA, *a*] *wench.*
DULL   Sir, the Duke's pleasure is that you keep Costard safe,
    and you must let him take no delight nor no penance,° but   *(for "pleasance"?)*
115   he must fast three days a week. For this damsel, I must keep
    her at the park. She is allowed for the dey-woman.° Fare you   *approved as dairymaid*
    well.   *Exit.*
ARMADO [*aside*]   I do betray myself with blushing. [*to* JAQUEN-
    ETTA] Maid—
120 JAQUENETTA   Man.
ARMADO   I will visit thee at the lodge.
JAQUENETTA   That's hereby.[3]
ARMADO   I know where it is situate.
JAQUENETTA   Lord, how wise you are!
125 ARMADO   I will tell thee wonders.
JAQUENETTA   With that face?°   *Really?*
ARMADO   I love thee.
JAQUENETTA   So I heard you say.°   *You don't say so*
ARMADO   And so, farewell.
130 JAQUENETTA   Fair weather after you.°   *(proverbial)*
COSTARD   Come, Jaquenetta. Away!
                  Exeunt [DULL *and* JAQUENETTA].
ARMADO   Villain,° thou shalt fast for thy offenses ere thou be   *Peasant; rascal*
    pardoned.
COSTARD   Well, sir, I hope when I do it, I shall do it on a full
135   stomach.°   *well fed; bravely*
ARMADO   Thou shalt be heavily punished.
COSTARD   I am more bound to you than your fellows,° for they   *servants*
    are but lightly rewarded.
ARMADO   Take away this villain! Shut him up.
140 PAGE   Come, you transgressing slave. Away!

---

1. The ballad concerns the love of King Cophetua for
the beggar maid Zenelophon. See also 4.1.65–67.
2. Peasant (or deer?) capable of reason.
3. Nearby; neither here nor there (?).

COSTARD   Let me not be pent up,° sir. I will fast, being loose.[4]   *jailed; constipated*
PAGE   No, sir, that were fast and loose.° Thou shalt to prison.   *a cheating trick*
COSTARD   Well, if ever I do see the merry days of desolation°   *(for "elation"?)*
that I have seen, some shall see—
145   PAGE   What shall some see?
COSTARD   Nay, nothing, Master Mote, but what they look upon.
It is not for prisoners to be silent in their words, and therefore
I will say nothing. I thank God I have as little patience as
another man, and therefore I can be quiet.

Exeunt [PAGE *and* COSTARD].

150   ARMADO   I do affect° the very ground—which is base—where   *love*
her shoe—which is baser—guided by her foot—which is
basest—doth tread. I shall be forsworn—which is a great
argument° of falsehood—if I love. And how can that be true   *proof*
love which is falsely attempted? Love is a familiar;° Love is a   *an attendant evil spirit*
155   devil. There is no evil angel but Love. Yet Samson was so
tempted, and he had an excellent strength. Yet was Solomon
so seduced, and he had a very good wit. Cupid's butt-shaft° is   *unbarbed arrow*
too hard for Hercules' club, and therefore too much odds for a
Spaniard's rapier. The first and second cause° will not serve   *(in the dueling code)*
160   my turn. The *passado*[5] he respects not; the *duello*° he regards   *dueling code*
not. His disgrace is to be called "Boy," but his glory is to sub-
due men. Adieu, valor; rust, rapier; be still, drum: for your
manager° is in love. Yea, he loveth. Assist me, some extempo-   *wielder*
ral° god of rhyme, for I am sure I shall turn sonnet.° Devise,   *impromptu / sonneteer*
165   wit; write, pen: for I am for whole volumes in folio.°   *Exit.*   *largest book size*

2.1 (Q 2.1)

Enter the PRINCESS *of France, with three attending*
ladies [MARIA, KATHERINE, *and* ROSALINE], *and three*
lords [*including* BOYET].[1]

BOYET   Now, madam, summon up your dearest spirits.°   *utmost energies*
Consider who the King your father sends,
To whom he sends, and what's his embassy:
Yourself, held precious in the world's esteem,
5   To parley with the sole inheritor°   *owner*
Of all perfections that a man may owe,
Matchless Navarre; the plea° of no less weight   *that which is claimed*
Than Aquitaine—a dowry for a queen.
Be now as prodigal of° all, dear grace,   *generous with*
10   As Nature was in making graces dear,[2]
When she did starve the general world beside°   *except (you)*
And prodigally gave them all to you.
PRINCESS   Good Lord Boyet, my beauty, though but mean,°   *average*
Needs not the painted flourish° of your praise.   *embellishment*
15   Beauty is bought by judgment of the eye,
Not uttered[3] by base sale of chapmen's° tongues.   *salesmen's*
I am less proud to hear you tell° my worth   *speak of; reckon up*

---

4. Being free; being loose in the bowels.
5. Fencing thrust.
2.1 Location: Outside the gates of the King's court.
1. Pronounced "Boy-ett." TEXTUAL COMMENT For
this character and the "three lords," see Digital Edition TC 3 (Folio edited text).

2. *dear grace . . . graces dear:* chiasmus, an *abba* rhetorical structure common to the aristocrats' speech
and the larger movement of the play. See 4.3 and the
Introduction. The second "dear" means costly (because
rare).
3. Not spoken; not offered for sale.

Than you much willing to be counted wise
In spending your wit in the praise of mine.

20   But now to task the tasker:[4] good Boyet,
You are not ignorant, all-telling Fame°   *rumor*
Doth noise abroad° Navarre hath made a vow, *spread the rumor that*
Till painful° study shall outwear three years   *taxing*
No woman may approach his silent court.

25   Therefore, to 's° seemeth it a needful course,   *to us*
Before we enter his forbidden gates,
To know his pleasure; and in that behalf,
Bold° of your worthiness, we single you   *Confident*
As our best-moving, fair° solicitor.   *most eloquent, just*

30   Tell him the daughter of the King of France,
On serious business, craving quick dispatch,
Importunes personal conference with his grace.
Haste, signify so much, while we attend,°   *wait upon*
Like humble-visaged suitors, his high will.

35 BOYET   Proud of° employment, willingly I go.   *Exit.*   *Honored with*
PRINCESS [*aside*]   All pride is willing pride,° and yours is so. *vanity*
  —Who are the votaries,° my loving lords,   *vow takers*
That are vow-fellows with this virtuous duke?
LORD   Longueville is one.
PRINCESS   Know you the man?
40 MARIA   I know him, madam. At a marriage feast,
Between Lord Périgort[5] and the beauteous heir
Of Jacques Falconbridge, solemnized
In Normandy, saw I this Longueville.
A man of sovereign parts° he is esteemed: *outstanding qualities*
45   Well fitted in arts, glorious in arms,
Nothing becomes him ill that he would° well.   *wishes to do*
The only soil of° his fair virtue's gloss—   *stain on*
If virtue's gloss will stain with any soil—
Is a sharp wit matched with too blunt° a will, *rough; unfeeling*
50   Whose edge hath power to cut, whose will still° wills *always*
It should none spare that come within his° power.   *its*
PRINCESS   Some merry, mocking lord, belike°—is't so?   *probably*
MARIA   They say so most that most his humors know.
PRINCESS   Such short-lived wits do wither as they grow.
55   Who are the rest?
KATHERINE   The young Dumaine—a well-accomplished youth,
Of° all that virtue love, for virtue loved;   *By*
Most power to do most harm, least knowing ill,[6]
For he hath wit to make an ill shape good,
60   And shape to win grace though he had no wit.[7]
I saw him at the Duke Alençon's once,
And much too little° of that good I saw   *short*
Is my report to° his great worthiness.   *my report compared with*

---

4. Impose a task on you who have given me one; chastise the task setter.
5. Not otherwise mentioned; Périgord is in Aquitaine.
6. Potentially dangerous by virtue of his very innocence; although he theoretically could do harm, he is free of all misdeeds.
7. *For . . . wit:* He is intelligent enough to make up for a displeasing appearance, if he had one (or perhaps to make something evil seem virtuous) and good-looking enough to win favor (from people or perhaps from God), even if he lacked intelligence.

ROSALINE[8]   Another of these students at that time
65   Was there with him, as I have heard a truth.
Biron[9] they call him, but a merrier man,
Within the limit of becoming° mirth,   *decorous*
I never spent an hour's talk withal.°   *with*
His eye begets occasion° for his wit,   *finds opportunities*
70   For every object that the one doth catch
The other turns to a mirth-moving jest,
Which his fair tongue—conceit's expositor°—   *thought's expounder*
Delivers in such apt and gracious words
That agèd ears play truant at° his tales   *neglect work to hear*
75   And younger hearings are quite ravishèd,
So sweet and voluble° is his discourse.   *fluent*
PRINCESS   God bless my ladies! Are they all in love,
That every one her own hath garnishèd
With such bedecking ornaments of praise?
80   MARIA   Here comes Boyet.
           Enter BOYET.
PRINCESS   Now, what admittance,° lord?   *reception*
BOYET   Navarre had notice of your fair approach,
And he and his competitors° in oath   *partners*
Were all addressed° to meet you, gentle lady,   *ready*
85   Before I came. Marry,° thus much I have learnt: *Indeed*
He rather means to lodge you in the field,
Like one that comes here to besiege his court,
Than seek a dispensation for his oath
To let you enter his unpeopled° house.   *servantless*
           Enter [the KING *of]* Navarre, LONGUEVILLE, DUMAINE,
           and BIRON.
90   Here comes Navarre.
KING   Fair Princess, welcome to the court of Navarre.
PRINCESS   "Fair" I give you back again, and "welcome" I have
not yet. The roof of this court° is too high to be yours, and   *sky*
welcome to the wide fields too base to be mine.
95   KING   You shall be welcome, madam, to my court.
PRINCESS   I will be welcome, then. Conduct me thither.
KING   Hear me, dear lady; I have sworn an oath.
PRINCESS   Our Lady help my lord! He'll be forsworn.
KING   Not for the world, fair madam, by my will.°   *willingly (mild oath)*
100   PRINCESS   Why, will° shall break it—will, and nothing else.   *(sexual) desire*
KING   Your ladyship is ignorant what it° is.   *(the oath)*
PRINCESS   Were my lord so, his ignorance were wise,
Where now his knowledge must prove ignorance.[1]
I hear your grace hath sworn out housekeeping.°   *repudiated hospitality*
105   'Tis deadly sin to keep that oath, my lord,
And sin to break it.
But pardon me, I am too sudden° bold;   *rashly*
To teach a teacher ill beseemeth me.

---

8. TEXTUAL COMMENT For F's partial revision of
Q's uncertain treatment of whom Biron courts—
Katherine or Rosaline—see Digital Edition TC 4 (Folio
edited text).
9. Probable pun on "Biron/brown." "Brown" was associated with somberness or melancholy (as in a "brown

study") and is contrasted in this line with "merrier" by
means of "but."
1. Perhaps: ignorance of your sexual desire would make
you wise, but your knowledge of it will make you a fool.
Or: ignorance would be wise, but the pursuit of knowledge is not.

Vouchsafe to read the purpose of my coming,
110   And suddenly resolve° me in my suit.   *immediately answer*
          [*She hands him a letter.*]
    KING   Madam, I will, if suddenly I may.
    PRINCESS   You will the sooner that I were away,°   *so that I'll go*
    For you'll prove perjured if you make me stay.
          [*The* KING *reads apart.*]
    BIRON   Did not I dance with you in Brabant once?
115   ROSALINE   Did not I dance with you in Brabant once?
    BIRON   I know you did.
    ROSALINE   How needless was it, then,
    To ask the question!
    BIRON   You must not be so quick.°   *sharp; hasty; witty*
    ROSALINE   'Tis 'long of° you that spur° me with such questions.   *due to / prod*
    BIRON   Your wit's too hot. It speeds too fast; 'twill tire.
120   ROSALINE   Not till it leave the rider in the mire.
    BIRON   What time o'day?
    ROSALINE   The hour that fools should ask.
    BIRON   Now fair befall° your mask!   *good luck to*
    ROSALINE   Fair fall° the face it covers.   *befall*
125   BIRON   And send you many lovers.
    ROSALINE   Amen, so you be none.
    BIRON   Nay, then, will I be gone.
          [*The* KING *steps forward.*]
    KING   Madam, your father here doth intimate
    The payment of² a hundred thousand crowns,
130   Being but th'one half of an entire sum
    Disbursèd by my father in his° wars.   *(the King of France's)*
    But say that he° or we—as neither have—   *(Navarre's father)*
    Received that sum, yet there remains unpaid
    A hundred thousand more, in surety of the which
135   One part of Aquitaine is bound to us,
    Although not valued° to the money's worth.   *equal in value*
    If, then, the King your father will restore
    But that one half which is unsatisfied,
    We will give up our right in Aquitaine,
140   And hold fair friendship with his majesty.
    But that, it seems, he little purposeth.
    For here he doth demand to have repaid
    An hundred thousand crowns, and not demands°   *rather than offering*
    On payment of a hundred thousand crowns
145   To have his title live in Aquitaine,
    Which we much rather had depart withal,°   *would surrender*
    And have the money by our father lent,
    Than Aquitaine, so gelded as it is.³
    Dear Princess, were not his requests so far
150   From reason's yielding,° your fair self should make   *what reason might concede*
    A yielding—'gainst some reason—in my breast,
    And go well satisfied to France again.
    PRINCESS   You do the King my father too much wrong,

2. *intimate . . . of:* suggest he paid.
3. Navarre says that of the 200,000 crowns he's owed, the King of France falsely claims to have paid back half and has given him Aquitaine as collateral for the other half, even though it isn't worth that much.

Navarre is willing to return Aquitaine and forget the entire debt in return for 100,000 crowns, but France wants Navarre to pay that sum and keep Aquitaine. *gelded:* reduced; castrated.

And wrong the reputation of your name,
155 In so unseeming° to confess receipt · · · · · · · · · · · · · · · · · · · *seeming unwilling*
Of that° which hath so faithfully been paid. · · · · · · · · · · · *(200,000 crowns)*
  KING I do protest I never heard of it,
And if you prove it I'll repay it back,
Or yield up Aquitaine.
  PRINCESS   We arrest° your word. · · · · · · · · · · *seize as security*
160 Boyet, you can produce acquittances° · *receipts*
For such a sum from special officers
Of Charles his° father. · *(Navarre's)*
  KING   Satisfy me so.
  BOYET So please your grace, the packet is not come
Where that and other specialties° are bound. · · · · · · · · · · · *legal contracts*
165 Tomorrow you shall have a sight of them.
  KING It shall suffice me; at which interview
All liberal° reason will I yield unto. · *civilized*
Meantime, receive such welcome at my hand
As honor, without breach of honor, may
170 Make tender of to thy true worthiness.
You may not come, fair Princess, in my gates,
But here without° you shall be so received · *outside*
As you shall deem yourself lodged in my heart,
Though so denied further harbor in my house.
175 Your own good thoughts excuse me, and farewell.
Tomorrow we shall visit you again.
  PRINCESS Sweet health and fair desires consort° your grace. · · · *accompany*
  KING Thy own wish wish I thee in every place.

                   Exeunt [the KING, LONGUEVILLE,
                         DUMAINE, *and* BIRON].

  BOYET Lady, I will commend you to my own heart.
180 ROSALINE Pray you, do my commendations.
I would be glad to see it.[4]
  BOYET I would you heard it groan.
  ROSALINE Is the fool° sick? · *poor thing*
  BOYET Sick at the heart.
185 ROSALINE Alack, let it blood.° · *bleed it (medically)*
  BOYET Would that do it good?
  ROSALINE My physic° says "Ay." · *medical knowledge*
  BOYET Will you prick't with your eye?[5]
  ROSALINE *Non point,°* with my knife. · · · · · · · · · · · · · *Not at all; it's blunt*
190 BOYET Now God save thy life!
  ROSALINE And yours from long living.
  BOYET I cannot stay thanksgiving.[6]
      [*He starts to withdraw.*]
      Enter DUMAINE.
  DUMAINE Sir, I pray you, a word. What lady is that same?
  BOYET The heir of Alençon; Katherine her name.
195 DUMAINE A gallant lady! Monsieur, fare you well.   [*Exit.*]
      [*Enter* LONGUEVILLE.]
  LONGUEVILLE I beseech you, a word. What is she in the white?
      [*He indicates* MARIA.]

---

4. Know your real feelings; literally, behold your heart
and, hence, see you dead.
5. "Eye" puns on "Ay" (line 187), suggesting a needle

but also a vagina, impossibly serving as a penis.
6. Stay long enough to thank you (for that rude
remark).

BOYET A woman sometime, if you saw her in the light.

LONGUEVILLE Perchance light in the light°—I desire her   *wanton if seen clearly*
name.

BOYET She hath but one for herself; to desire that were a
shame.

200 LONGUEVILLE Pray you, sir, whose daughter?

BOYET Her mother's, I have heard.

LONGUEVILLE [*preparing to leave*] God's blessing o'your beard!°   *(insult)*

BOYET Good sir, be not offended.
She is an heir of Falconbridge—

205 LONGUEVILLE Nay, my choler° is ended.   *anger*
She is a most sweet lady.

BOYET Not unlike,° sir; that may be.   *Exit* LONGUEVILLE.   *unlikely*
Enter BIRON.

BIRON What's her name in the cap?

BOYET Rosaline, by good hap.

210 BIRON Is she wedded or no?

BOYET To her will, sir, or so.°   *or something like that*

BIRON You are welcome, sir. Adieu.

BOYET Farewell to me, sir, and welcome to you.° *Exit* [BIRON].   *you're welcome to go*

MARIA That last is Biron, the merry madcap lord;
Not a word with him but a jest—

215 BOYET   And every jest but a word.

PRINCESS It was well done of you to take him at his word.°   *(literally; punningly)*

BOYET I was as willing to grapple as he was to board.[7]

MARIA Two hot sheeps,° marry.   *(pronounced like "ships")*

BOYET   And wherefore not ships?
No sheep, sweet lamb, unless we feed on your lips.

220 MARIA You sheep and I pasture.° Shall that finish the jest? *pun on "pastor" (shepherd)*

BOYET So° you grant pasture for me—   *So long as*
[*He attempts to kiss her.*]

MARIA   Not so, gentle beast.
My lips are no common, though several they be.[8]

BOYET Belonging to whom?

MARIA   To my fortunes and me.

PRINCESS Good wits will be jangling,° but, gentles,° agree!   *quarreling / gentlefolk*

225 This civil war of wits were much better used
On Navarre and his bookmen,° for here 'tis abused.°   *scholars / misapplied*

BOYET If my observation—which very seldom lies,
By the heart's still rhetoric,° disclosed with eyes—   *silent eloquence*
Deceive me not now, Navarre is infected.

230 PRINCESS With what?

BOYET With that which we lovers entitle "affected."°   *being in love*

PRINCESS Your reason?

BOYET Why, all his behaviors did make their retire°   *withdrawal*
To the court of his eye, peeping through desire.

235 His heart, like an agate with your print impressed,[9]
Proud with his form,° in his eye pride expressed.   *the Princess's image*
His tongue, all impatient to speak[1] and not see,
Did stumble with haste in his eyesight to be.

7. Join ships ("grapple") for hand-to-hand combat ("board"): metaphor for competitive wordplay, with sexual overtones.
8. My lips are not commonly owned grazing land, though they are pasture—they are privately owned,
enclosed land. *several:* more than one; separate; parted.
9. Engraved with your image. Agates were engraved and set in rings.
1. Impatient at being able only to speak.

All senses to that sense did make their repair,°   *resort*
240   To feel° only looking° on fairest of fair.   *experience / by looking*
Methought all his senses were locked in his eye,
As jewels in crystal for some prince to buy,
Who, tend'ring° their own worth from whence they were   *displaying*
     glassed,°   *encased in crystal*
Did point° you to buy them along as you passed.   *direct*
245   His face's own margin[2] did quote° such amazes,   *indicate*
That all eyes saw his eyes enchanted with gazes.
I'll give you° Aquitaine and all that is his,   *bet you get*
An° you give him, for my sake, but one loving kiss.   *If*
PRINCESS   Come! To our pavilion! Boyet is disposed.°   *(to be merry)*
250   BOYET   But to speak that in words which his eye hath disclosed.

               [*Exeunt the* PRINCESS *and lords.*]

I only have made a mouth of his eye
By adding a tongue, which I know will not lie.
ROSALINE[3]   Thou art an old love-monger and speakest skilfully.
MARIA   He is Cupid's grandfather and learns news of him.
255   KATHERINE   Then was Venus° like her mother, for her father   *Cupid's mother*
     is but grim.°   *not handsome*
BOYET   Do you hear, my mad° wenches?   *high-spirited*
MARIA   No.
BOYET   What, then, do you see?
KATHERINE   Ay, our way to be gone.
BOYET   You are too hard for me.

                         Exeunt.

3.1 (Q 3.1)

Enter [ARMADO, *the*] braggart,[1] *and* [PAGE, *his*] *boy.*

ARMADO   Warble, child! Make passionate° my sense of   *responsive*
hearing.
PAGE [*sings*]   Concolinel.[2]
ARMADO   Sweet air!° Go, tenderness of years. Take this   *tune*
5   key, give enlargement° to the swain, bring him festinately°   *freedom / in a hurry*
hither. I must employ him in a letter to my love.
PAGE   Will you win your love with a French brawl?°   *dance*
ARMADO   How meanest thou? Brawling in French?[3]
PAGE   No, my complete master, but to jig off a tune° at the   *sing a jiglike tune*
10   tongue's end, canary° to it with the feet, humor° it with   *dance / adapt to*
turning up your eyes, sigh a note and sing a note, sometime
through the throat—as if you swallowed love with singing
love—sometime through the nose—as if you snuffed up
love by smelling love—with your hat penthouse-like° o'er the   *like an awning*
15   shop of your eyes, with your arms crossed° on your thin-   *(from love melancholy)*
belly[4] doublet like a rabbit on a spit, or your hands in your
pocket like a man after° the old painting; and keep not too   *in the style of*
long in one tune, but a snip° and away. These are compli-   *snatch*

2. The part of a book in which comments were printed.
3. It is uncertain which of the ladies should speak these lines.
3.1 Location: The King's park.
1. The braggart soldier was a stock figure in the contemporary Italian commedia dell'arte, a theatrical form with popular roots. His theatrical ancestry can be traced back to ancient Roman comedy.

2. *Concolinel:* song title or opening. TEXTUAL COMMENT On the song and the stage direction for it, see Digital Edition TC 5 (Folio edited text).
3. "Brawling" means "quarreling," but the phrase may also refer to popular rioting against immigrant French merchants and artisans.
4. Unpadded belly or lower part; also suggesting that Armado is wasting away for love.

ments;[5] these are humors;° these betray nice° wenches that   *caprices / seduce wanton*
20   would be betrayed without these, and make them men of
note—do you note, men?—that most are affected° to these.   *given*
ARMADO   How hast thou purchased this experience?
PAGE   By my penny of observation.
ARMADO   "But oh, but oh—"
25   PAGE   "The hobbyhorse is forgot."[6]
ARMADO   Call'st thou my love "hobbyhorse"?
PAGE   No, master. The hobbyhorse is but a colt,° and your love   *young horse; wanton*
perhaps a hackney.° But have you forgot your love?   *riding horse; whore*
ARMADO   Almost I had.
30   PAGE   Negligent student! Learn her by heart.
ARMADO   By heart and in heart, boy.
PAGE   And out of heart,° master. All those three I will prove.   *disheartened*
ARMADO   What wilt thou prove?
PAGE   A man, if I live, and this "by," "in," and "without" upon
35   the instant. "By" heart you love her, because your heart cannot come by her; "in" heart you love her, because your heart
is in love with her; and "out" of heart you love her, being out
of heart that you cannot enjoy her.
ARMADO   I am all these three.
40   PAGE   [*aside*]   And three times as much more, and yet nothing
at all.
ARMADO   Fetch hither the swain. He must carry me° a letter.   *for me*
PAGE   [*aside*]   A message well sympathized°—a horse to be   *matched*
ambassador for an ass!
45   ARMADO   Ha, ha! What sayest thou?
PAGE   Marry, sir, you must send the ass upon the horse, for he
is very slow-gaited. But I go.
ARMADO   The way is but short. Away!
PAGE   As swift as lead, sir.
50   ARMADO   Thy meaning, pretty ingenious?
Is not lead a metal heavy, dull, and slow?
PAGE   *Minime*,° honest master; or rather, master, no.   *By no means*
ARMADO   I say lead is slow.
PAGE   You are too swift, sir, to say so.
Is that lead slow which is fired from a gun?
55   ARMADO   Sweet smoke of rhetoric!
He reputes me a cannon, and the bullet—that's he.
I shoot thee at the swain—
PAGE   Thump,° then, and I flee. [*Exit*.]   *Bang*
ARMADO   A most acute juvenal—voluble° and free of grace.   *quick-witted*
By thy favor, sweet welkin,° I must sigh in thy face.   *sky*
60   Most rude melancholy, valor gives thee place.°   *gives way to you*
     Enter PAGE *and* [COSTARD, *the*] *clown*[, *limping*].
My herald is returned.
PAGE   A wonder, master! Here's a costard broken in a shin.[7]
ARMADO   Some enigma, some riddle—come, thy l'envoy:° begin!   *explanation*

---

5. Refined behaviors.
6. A lament for the passing of the good old days; perhaps the refrain of a song. A hobbyhorse—a person costumed as a horse—was used in popular dancing; the word also meant "whore," perhaps suggested by the association between "oh" (line 24), in its suggestion of "O" and "vagina."
7. A head with a cut shin (an anatomical impossibility that provokes the Page's amusement); disappointed in love or sex (alluding to Armado's triumph over Costard); taking a loan.

COSTARD No egma, no riddle, no l'envoy, no salve in the
65   mail,[8] sir! O sir, plantain,° a plain plantain! No l'envoy, no   *healing herb*
     l'envoy, no salve, sir, but a plantain.
ARMADO By virtue, thou enforcest laughter; thy silly thought,
     my spleen.[9] The heaving of my lungs provokes me to ridicu-
     lous° smiling. O pardon me, my stars! Doth the inconsider-   *mocking; absurd*
70   ate° take *salve* for l'envoy, and the word "l'envoy" for a salve?   *thoughtless person*
PAGE Do the wise think them other? Is not l'envoy a *salve?*
ARMADO No, page, it is an epilogue or discourse to make plain
     Some obscure precedence that hath tofore been sain.[1]
     I will example° it: *give an example of*
75   The fox, the ape, and the humble-bee,°   *bumblebee*
              Were still at odds,[2] being but three.
     There's the moral.° Now the l'envoy—   *lesson*
PAGE I will add the l'envoy. Say the moral again.
ARMADO   The fox, the ape, and the humble-bee,
80   Were still at odds, being but three.
PAGE   Until the goose came out of door,
               And stayed° the odds by adding four.°   *stopped / a fourth*
     Now will I begin your moral, and do you follow with my
     l'envoy.
85   The fox, the ape, and the humble-bee,
              Were still at odds, being but three.
ARMADO   Until the goose came out of door,
              Staying the odds by adding four.
PAGE A good l'envoy, ending in the goose.[3] Would you desire
90   more?
COSTARD [*aside*] The boy hath sold him a bargain: a goose,°   *made him a fool*
     that's flat.°   *certain*
     [*to* ARMADO] Sir, your pennyworth° is good an° your   *bargain / if*
     goose be fat.
     To sell a bargain well is as cunning as fast and loose.°   *cheating; (of bowels)*
     Let me see: a fat l'envoy? Ay, that's a fat goose.
95   ARMADO Come hither, come hither. How did this argument°   *topic*
     begin?
PAGE By saying that a costard was broken in a shin.
     Then called you for the l'envoy.
COSTARD True, and I for a plantain—thus came your argu-
     ment° in. Then the boy's fat l'envoy—the goose that you   *(enema?)*
100 bought—and he ended the market.°   *bargaining*
ARMADO But tell me, how was there a costard broken in a
     shin?
PAGE I will tell you sensibly.°   *clearly; with feeling*
COSTARD Thou hast no feeling of it, Mote. I will speak that
105 l'envoy.

---

8. Costard takes Armado to be proposing remedies
for his shin. "Egma" for "enigma" may be an error for
an "egg" solution or "enema." "L'envoy" (French
l'envoi) refers to a salve or an ointment, perhaps by
confusion with "lenify" (to soothe or purge). There is
also a pun on the Latin *salve* ("greetings"), the opposite of *"l'envoy"'s* sense of "farewell." *mail:* traveling
bag. In addition, a salve inserted in or an anal salvo
discharged from the male.

9. Amusement: the spleen was regarded as the organ
controlling laughter.
1. *Some . . . sain:* What was obscurely said before.
2. Were always quarreling; were always an odd
number.
3. Punning on the French *oie* ("goose"), the final
sound in *envoy*, "ending in the goose" also because it
is inserted in the end of the goose (prostitute, victim
of venereal disease).

  I, Costard, running out, that was safely within,[4]
  Fell over the threshold and broke my shin.
ARMADO We will talk no more of this matter—
COSTARD Till there be more matter° in the shin.   *pus; semen*
110 ARMADO Sirrah Costard, I will enfranchise° thee.   *free*
  COSTARD Oh, marry me to one Frances?[5] I smell some l'envoy,
   some goose in this!
  ARMADO By my sweet soul, I mean setting thee at liberty,
   enfreedoming thy person; thou wert immured,° restrained,   *shut in*
115 captivated, bound.°   *(of bowels)*
  COSTARD True, true, and now you will be my purgation° and *liberator; enema*
   let me loose.°   *(my bowels)*
  ARMADO I give thee thy liberty, set° thee from durance,° and, *free / imprisonment*
   in lieu thereof, impose on thee nothing but this: bear this
120 significant° to the country maid Jaquenetta [*giving him a* *token*
   letter]. There is remuneration [*giving him a coin*], for the best
   ward° of mine honors is rewarding my dependants. Mote,   *guard*
   follow.
  PAGE Like the sequel, I. Seigneur Costard, adieu.
           Exeunt [ARMADO *and* PAGE].
125 COSTARD My sweet ounce of man's flesh, my incony jew![6]
   Now will I look to his remuneration. "Remuneration"? Oh,
   that's the Latin word for three farthings.° Three farthings: *a coin worth 3/4 pence*
   remuneration. "What's the price of this inkle?"[7] "One
   penny." "No, I'll give you a remuneration." Why, it carries
130 it!° "Remuneration"? Why, it is a fairer name than "French *carries the day*
   crown."[8] I will never buy and sell out of° this word.   *without using*
     Enter BIRON.
  BIRON[9] My good knave, Costard, exceedingly well met.
  COSTARD Pray you, sir, how much carnation° ribbon may a *flesh-colored*
   man buy for a remuneration?
135 BIRON What is a remuneration?
  COSTARD Marry, sir, halfpenny-farthing.°   *three farthings*
  BIRON Why, then, three farthings' worth of silk.
  COSTARD I thank your worship. God be wi'you.
  BIRON Stay, slave, I must employ thee.
140 As thou wilt win my favor, good my knave,
   Do one thing for me that I shall entreat.
  COSTARD When would you have it done, sir?
  BIRON This afternoon.
  COSTARD Well, I will do it, sir. Fare you well.
145 BIRON Thou knowest not what it is!
  COSTARD I shall know, sir, when I have done it.
  BIRON Why, villain, thou must know first.
  COSTARD I will come to your worship tomorrow morning.

---

4. *running out . . . within:* possible reference to bodily emissions.
5. Punning on "enfranchise" (line 110); "Frances" was probably a common name for a prostitute.
6. Religious reference from the mishearing of "adieu" (line 124); playful diminutive of "jewel" or "juvenal." *incony:* fine, quality.
7. Linen tape, suggested by "incony" (line 125); near

homonym of "ingle," a catamite (boy kept by a pederast), and perhaps thereby evoking the period's association of the "jew" (line 125) with sodomy.
8. A coin; syphilis (the "French disease") results in a bald head ("crown").
9. TEXTUAL COMMENT For the problems with Biron's speech prefixes here and elsewhere, see Digital Edition TC 6 (Folio edited text).

150   BIRON   It must be done this afternoon. Hark, slave, it is but
       this:
       The Princess comes to hunt here in the park,
       And in her train there is a gentle lady.
       When tongues speak sweetly, then they name her name,
       And Rosaline they call her. Ask for her,
155   And to her white hand see thou do commend
       This sealed-up counsel.° [*He gives him a letter.*] There's thy   *message*
          guerdon.° Go!   *reward*
           [*He gives him money.*]
     COSTARD   "Gardon"? O sweet gardon! Better than remunera-
       tion: elevenpence-farthing better.[1] Most sweet gardon! I will
       do it, sir, in print.° Gardon! Remuneration!   *Exit.*   *to the letter*
160   BIRON   And I, forsooth, in love? I that have been love's whip,
       A very beadle[2] to a humorous° sigh,   *moody*
       A critic, nay, a night-watch constable,
       A domineering pedant° o'er the boy°—   *schoolmaster / Cupid*
       Than whom no mortal so magnificent.
165   This wimpled,° whining, purblind,° wayward boy,   *blindfolded / all-blind*
       This Seigneur° Junior, giant dwarf, Dan° Cupid,   *Sir; senior / Master*
       Regent of love-rhymes, lord of folded arms,
       Th'anointed sovereign of sighs and groans,
       Liege of all loiterers and malcontents,
170   Dread prince of plackets, king of codpieces,[3]
       Sole imperator° and great general   *Absolute ruler*
       Of trotting paritors[4]—O my little heart!
       And I to be a corporal of his field,°   *field officer*
       And wear his colors like a tumbler's hoop!°   *(adorned with ribbons)*
175   What, I love, I sue, I seek a wife?
       A woman that is like a German clock:
       Still° a-repairing, ever out of frame,°   *Always / order*
       And never going aright, being° a watch,   *though*
       But being° watched that it may still go right.   *Except when*
180   Nay, to be perjured, which is worst of all,
       And among three to love the worst of all:
       A whitely° wanton with a velvet° brow,   *pale / smooth*
       With two pitch° balls stuck in her face for eyes;   *tar black*
       Ay, and by heaven, one that will do the deed°   *sexual act*
185   Though Argus[5] were her eunuch° and her guard.   *harem warden*
       And I to sigh for her, to watch° for her,   *stay awake at night*
       To pray for her? Go to!° It is a plague   *Come now!*
       That Cupid will impose for my neglect
       Of his almighty, dreadful, little might.
190   Well, I will love, write, sigh, pray, sue, and groan;
       Some men must love my lady, and some Joan.°   [*Exit.*]   *lower-class woman*

1. Biron has given Costard a "guerdon" of one shilling, or twelve pence, which is "elevenpence-farthing"
(eleven pence and one farthing) "better than remuneration," defined earlier by Costard as "three-
farthings" (where four farthings equal one pence;
lines 127–28).
2. Minor parish official who punished lesser offenses
(for instance, by whipping).
3. The parts of clothes covering the male sexual
organ (hence, penises, or men). *plackets:* slits in petticoats (hence, female genitalia, or women).
4. Officers who summoned sexual offenders to
ecclesiastical courts.
5. Mythical watchman with a hundred eyes.

4.1 (Q 4.1)

Enter the PRINCESS, *a* FORESTER, *her ladies* [MARIA,
KATHERINE, *and* ROSALINE], *and her lords* [*including*
BOYET].

PRINCESS Was that the King that spurred his horse so hard,
  Against the steep uprising of the hill?

BOYET I know not, but I think it was not he.

PRINCESS Whoe'er 'a° was, 'a showed a mounting mind.   *he*
5 Well, lords, today we shall have our dispatch.
  On Saturday we will return to France.
  Then Forester, my friend, where is the bush
  That we must stand and play the murderer in?

FORESTER Hereby, upon the edge of yonder coppice°—   *thicket*
10 A stand° where you may make the fairest° shoot.   *hunter's station / best*

PRINCESS I thank my beauty, I am fair° that shoot,   *beautiful*
  And thereupon thou speak'st "the fairest shoot."

FORESTER Pardon me, madam, for I meant not so.

PRINCESS What, what? First praise me, and then again say no?
15 Oh, short-lived pride! Not fair? Alack for woe!

FORESTER Yes, madam, fair—

PRINCESS   Nay, never paint° me now!   *flatter*
  Where fair° is not, praise cannot mend the brow.   *beauty*
  Here, good my glass,° take this for telling true.   *my good mirror*
    [*She gives him money.*]
  Fair payment for foul words is more than due.

20 FORESTER Nothing but fair is that which you inherit.°   *own*

PRINCESS See, see, my beauty will be saved by merit![1]
  Oh, heresy in fair, fit for these days;[2]
  A giving hand, though foul, shall have fair praise.
  But come: the bow. Now mercy° goes to kill,   *the merciful Princess*
25 And shooting well is then accounted ill.°   *unmerciful*
  Thus will I save my credit in the shoot:
  Not wounding, pity would not let me do't;[3]
  If wounding, then it was to show my skill,
  That more for praise than purpose meant to kill.
30 And out of question° so it is sometimes: *beyond doubt*
  Glory° grows guilty of detested crimes,   *The desire for glory*
  When, for fame's sake, for praise, an outward part,
  We bend to that the working of the heart;
  As I for praise alone now seek to spill
35 The poor deer's blood, that my heart° means no ill.   *pun on "hart" (male deer)*

BOYET Do not curst° wives hold that self-sovereignty[4]   *shrewish*
  Only for praise' sake, when they strive to be
  Lords o'er their lords?

PRINCESS Only for praise, and praise we may afford
40 To any lady that subdues a lord.

    Enter [COSTARD, *the*] *clown.*

BOYET Here comes a member of the commonwealth.°   *common people*

COSTARD God dig-you-den° all. Pray you, which is the head lady? *give you good evening*

4.1 Location: A hunter's station in the King's park.
1. Desert; good works (her "payment").
2. Believing in salvation by faith, Protestants considered it a common "heresy" "these days" to think, as
Catholics did, that one could be "saved by merit." *in
fair*: in regard to beauty.

3. *Thus . . . do't*: I will save my reputation as a hunter
by saying, if I miss, that pity for the deer caused me
to miss deliberately.
4. *hold that self-sovereignty*: exercise that same power
over themselves (and their husbands).

PRINCESS   Thou shalt know her, fellow, by the rest that have
45   no heads.⁵
COSTARD   Which is the greatest lady? The highest?
PRINCESS   The thickest and the tallest.
COSTARD   The thickest and the tallest? It is so; truth is truth.
An your waist, mistress, were as slender as my wit
50   One o'these maids' girdles for your waist should be fit.
Are not you the chief woman? You are the thickest here.
PRINCESS   What's your will, sir? What's your will?
COSTARD   I have a letter from Monsieur Biron
To one Lady Rosaline.
55   PRINCESS   Oh, thy letter, thy letter! He's a good friend of mine.
            [*She seizes the letter.*]
Stand aside, good bearer. —Boyet, you can carve;°   *cut meat; act affected*
Break up° this capon.⁶   *Cut up; open*
BOYET   I am bound to serve.
            [*He reads the superscription.*]
This letter is mistook; it importeth° none here.   *matters to*
It is writ to Jaquenetta.
PRINCESS   We will read it, I swear.
60   Break the neck of the wax,° and everyone give ear.   *seal; (capon)*
BOYET (*reads*) "By heaven, that thou art fair is most infallible,° true that thou art beauteous, truth itself that thou art   *certain*
lovely. More fairer than fair, beautiful than beauteous, truer
than truth itself, have commiseration on thy heroical vassal.
65   The magnanimous and most illustrate° King Cophetua set°   *illustrious / set his*
eye upon the pernicious and indubitate° beggar Zenelo-   *undoubted*
phon,° and he it was that might rightly say, '*Veni, vidi, vici*,'⁷   *(see 1.2.99)*
which to annothanize° in the vulgar—O base and obscure   *anatomize; annotate*
vulgar!°—*videlicet*,° 'He came, see, and overcame.' He   *vernacular / namely*
70   came, one; see, two; overcame, three. Who came? The King.
Why did he come? To see. Why did he see? To overcome. To
whom came he? To the beggar. What saw he? The beggar.
Who overcame he? The beggar. The conclusion is victory.
On whose side? The King's. The captive is enriched. On
75   whose side? The beggar's. The catastrophe° is a nuptial. On   *outcome*
whose side? The King's? No, on both in one, or one in both.
I am the King, for so stands the comparison; thou the beggar, for so witnesseth thy lowliness. Shall I command thy
love? I may. Shall I enforce thy love? I could. Shall I entreat
80   thy love? I will. What shalt thou exchange for rags? Robes.
For tittles?° Titles. For thyself? Me. Thus expecting thy   *jots; specks*
reply, I profane my lips on thy foot, my eyes on thy picture,
and my heart on thy every part.
            Thine in the dearest design of industry,°   *(gallantry?); diligence*
85   Don Adriano de Armado.
Thus dost thou hear the Nemean lion⁸ roar
'Gainst thee, thou lamb, that standest as his prey.
Submissive fall his princely feet before,
And he from forage° will incline to play.   *raging*

---

5. Part of the body, literalizing metaphorical use of   7. Originally said by Julius Caesar.
"head" as "leader" (line 42); maidenhead.   8. Killed by Hercules as the first of his labors.
6. Love letter; castrated male chicken.

90   But if thou strive, poor soul, what art thou then?
      Food for his rage, repasture° for his den."   *food*
PRINCESS   What plume of feathers° is he that indited° this   *silly bird / wrote*
      letter?
      What vane?[9] What weathercock?° Did you ever hear better?   *(example of showiness)*
BOYET   I am much deceived, but I remember the style.
95 PRINCESS   Else your memory is bad, going o'er[1] it erewhile.
BOYET   This Armado is a Spaniard that keeps° here in court: *dwells*
      A phantasime,° a Monarcho,[2] and one that makes sport   *fantastic being*
      To° the Prince and his bookmates.   *For*
PRINCESS   Thou, fellow, a word.
      Who gave thee this letter?
COSTARD   I told you: my lord.
100 PRINCESS   To whom shouldst thou give it?
COSTARD   From my lord to my lady.
PRINCESS   From which lord to which lady?
COSTARD   From my lord Biron, a good master of mine,
      To a lady of France that he called Rosaline.
105 PRINCESS   Thou hast mistaken his letter. Come, lords, away!
      —Here, sweet, put up this.   [*She gives* ROSALINE *the letter.*]
                              'Twill be thine another day.°   *Your turn will come*
                  Exeunt [*the* PRINCESS, *the* FORESTER, *and lords*].
BOYET   Who is the shooter? Who is the shooter?
ROSALINE   Shall I teach you to know?
BOYET   Ay, my continent° of beauty.   *container of all*
ROSALINE   Why, she that bears the bow.
      Finely put off!°   *evaded*
110 BOYET   My lady goes to kill horns, but if thou marry,
      Hang me by the neck if horns that year miscarry.[3]
      Finely put on!°   *applied*
ROSALINE   Well, then, I am the shooter.
BOYET   And who is your deer?°   *prey; dear*
ROSALINE   If we choose by the horns, yourself come not near.[4]
115   Finely put on, indeed!
MARIA   You still wrangle with her, Boyet, and she strikes at the
      brow.[5]
BOYET   But she herself is hit lower[6]—have I hit her° now?   *found her out*
ROSALINE   Shall I come upon thee with an old saying, that
      was a man when King Pépin of France was a little boy,[7] as
120   touching the hit-it?[8]
BOYET   So I may answer thee with one as old, that was a woman
      when Queen Guinevere of Britain[9] was a little wench, as
      touching the hit-it.

9. Weathervane, often in the form of a heraldic banner; vanity.
1. Having read; having climbed (taking "style" in line
94 as "stile," "fence").
2. Pretentious person—from the nickname of an
eccentric Italian of Shakespeare's time who claimed
to be a monarch of the world.
3. If you do not soon cuckold your husband; possibly,
if penises fail or lead to a miscarriage. From here
through line 138, there are almost continuous sexual
references.

4. Probably: If you want to be safe, don't come close,
because you have cuckold's horns.
5. Aims well; taunts you about your cuckold's horns.
6. In the heart; in the genitals.
7. Was already old when Charlemagne's father (d.
768) was a little boy.
8. *the hit-it:* bawdy popular round and the dance
done to it.
9. Notoriously unfaithful wife of the legendary King
Arthur.

ROSALINE   Thou canst not hit it, hit it, hit it,
125 Thou canst not hit it, my good man.
BOYET   An I cannot, cannot, cannot,
    An I cannot, another can.   *Exit* [ROSALINE].
COSTARD   By my troth, most pleasant. How both did fit it!°   *sing well; (bawdy)*
MARIA   A mark° marvelous well shot, for they both did hit it.   *target*
130 BOYET   A mark? Oh, mark but that mark! "A mark," says my
    lady.
    Let the mark have a prick° in't to mete° at, if it may be.   *bull's-eye; penis / aim*
MARIA   Wide o'the bow hand.[1] I'faith, your hand is out.°   *out of practice*
COSTARD [*aside*]   Indeed, 'a° must shoot nearer, or he'll ne'er   *he*
    hit the clout.°   *bull's-eye; (bawdy)*
BOYET   An if my hand be out, then belike your hand is in.[2]
135 COSTARD [*aside*]   Then will she get the upshoot[3] by cleaving
    the pin.°   *center*
MARIA   Come, come, you talk greasily.° Your lips grow foul.   *indecently*
COSTARD   She's too hard for you at pricks,° sir. Challenge her   *archery; sex*
    to bowl.
BOYET   I fear too much rubbing.[4] Goodnight, my good owl.[5]
           [*Exeunt* BOYET, KATHERINE, *and* MARIA.]
COSTARD   By my soul, a swain, a most simple clown!
140 Lord, lord, how the ladies and I have put him down.
    O'my troth, most sweet jests, most incony° vulgar wit,   *fine-quality*
    When it comes so smoothly off, so obscenely,[6] as it were,
    so fit.
    Armado o'th' other side°—Oh, a most dainty° man!   *by contrast / elegant*
    To see him walk before a lady and to bear her fan;
145 To see him kiss his hand, and how most sweetly° 'a will   *stylishly*
    swear!
    And his page o' t'other side, that handful of wit.
    Ah heavens, it is a most pathetical nit!°   *affecting little fellow*
        Shout° *within.*   *Loud voice; shooting*
    Sola, sola!°   *Exit.*   *(hunting cry)*

4.2 (Q 4.2)

Enter DULL, HOLOFERNES, *the pedant*[,][1] *and*
    NATHANIEL[, *the curate*].

NATHANIEL   Very reverent° sport, truly, and done in the testi-   *respectable*
    mony° of a good conscience.   *with the warrant*
HOLOFERNES   The deer was, as you know, *sanguis*,[2] in blood,°   *robust*
    ripe as a pomewater° who now hangeth like a jewel in the ear   *kind of apple*
5 of *caelo*, the sky, the welkin, the heaven, and anon° falleth   *soon after*
    like a crab° on the face of *terra*, the soil, the land, the earth.   *crab apple*

---

1. Too far to the left side (a cry in archery).
2. If I'm out of practice (at archery, at sex), you're not.
3. Winning shot; ejaculation.
4. In the game of bowls, touching obstacles; sexual friction.
5. "Owl," a bird of night, is suggested by "Goodnight"; to "take owl" is to take offense; rhyming with "bowl," "owl" suggests "ole" (hole) in the sexual sense.
6. Inadvertently accurate; perhaps a blunder for "seemly."
4.2 Location: The King's park.
1. Holofernes—a character based on a warrior whose decapitation by the heroine of the apocryphal Book of Judith saves Jerusalem—was a familiar tyrant in medieval religious plays; also a doctor of theology and tutor to Gargantua in Rabelais's *Gargantua and Pantagruel*. Like the braggart soldier, the pedant or schoolmaster was a stock character in commedia dell'arte (see Introduction); his prominence is due to the humanist-inspired, early Tudor educational reforms that presumably shaped Shakespeare's own formal education.
2. The Latin in this scene, some of it inaccurate, is translated only when the characters themselves fail to do so. It is often unclear whether an error is the character's or the printer's.

NATHANIEL   Truly, Master Holofernes, the epithets are sweetly
varied, like a scholar at the least; but, sir, I assure ye, it was a
buck of the first head.[3]

10   HOLOFERNES   Sir[4] Nathaniel, *haud credo.*°   *I hardly think so*

DULL   'Twas not a "auld grey doe," 'twas a pricket.[5]

HOLOFERNES   Most barbarous intimation!° Yet a kind of insinu-   *intrusion*
ation, as it were, *in via,* in way of explication, *facere,*° as it   *to make*
were, replication,° or rather *ostentare,* to show, as it were, his   *explanation*
15   inclination, after his undressed, unpolished, uneducated,
unpruned, untrained, or rather unlettered, or ratherest uncon-
firmed° fashion, to insert again° my "*haud credo*" for a deer.   *inexperienced / interpret*

DULL   I said the deer was not a "auld grey doe," 'twas a pricket.

HOLOFERNES   Twice-sod simplicity, *bis coctus!*[6]
20   O thou monster, Ignorance, how deformed dost thou look!

NATHANIEL   Sir, he hath never fed of the dainties that are
        bred in a book.
He hath not eat paper, as it were; he hath not drunk ink.
His intellect is not replenished; he is only an animal—only
        sensible° in the duller parts.   *capable of feeling*
And such barren plants are set before us that we thankful
        should be—
25   Which we of taste and feeling are—for those parts that do
        fructify° in us more than he.   *bear fruit*
For as it would ill become me to be vain, indiscreet, or a
        fool,
So were there a patch set on learning[7] to see him in a school.
But *omne bene,*° say I, being of an old father's° mind: *all is well / sage's*
Many can brook the weather that love not the wind.[8]

30   DULL   You two are bookmen. Can you tell, by your wit,
What was a month old at Cain's birth that's not five weeks
        old as yet?

HOLOFERNES   Dictynna, goodman° Dull. Dictynna, goodman   *yeoman*
Dull.

DULL   What is "Dictima"?

35   HOLOFERNES[9]   A title to° Phoebe, to *luna,* to the moon.   *name for*

NATHANIEL   The moon was a month old when Adam was no
        more,
And raught° not to five weeks when he came to fivescore.   *reached*
Th'allusion holds in the exchange.[1]

DULL   'Tis true, indeed: the collusion° holds in the exchange.   *(for "allusion")*

40   NATHANIEL   God comfort° thy capacity! I say th'allusion holds   *pity*
in the exchange.

DULL   And I say the pollution[2] holds in the exchange, for the
moon is never but a month old—and I say beside, that 'twas
a pricket that the Princess killed.

---

3. With his first head of antlers; in his fifth year.
4. Used generally of graduates, including priests
(like "Reverend").
5. Buck in its second year, with a sexual hint.
6. *Twice . . . coctus:* Twice-boiled folly, twice-cooked;
"*coctus*" also continues the sexual innuendo of "pricket"
(line 18) with the suggestion of "cock."
7. It would mean that a fool ("patch") had been put to
his studies; there would be a black mark on learning.
8. Many can endure the weather while disliking
some of its features (?); one must live with what one
cannot change (proverbial).

9. TEXTUAL COMMENT For the confusion of Holofernes' and Nathaniel's speech prefixes here, and the
grounds for their correction, see Digital Edition TC
7 (Folio edited text).
1. The riddle works as well with Adam as with Cain.
2. Dull's blunder for "allusion" again, but in each
case a commentary on his interlocutors. "Collusion"
can refer to a verbal trick designed to promote collusion in the sense of conspiracy; linguistic pollution
occurs when one favors difficult foreign words over
straightforward English.

45 HOLOFERNES Sir Nathaniel, will you hear an extemporal epitaph on the death of the deer?—and, to humor the ignorant,
call I the deer the Princess killed a pricket.

NATHANIEL *Perge*,° good Master Holofernes, *perge*,   *Proceed*
So it shall please you to abrogate scurrility.³

50 HOLOFERNES I will something affect the letter,⁴ for it
argues° facility: *shows*
The preyful° Princess pierced and pricked a pretty pleasing   *desirous of prey*
pricket;
Some say a sore,⁵ but not a sore till now made sore with
shooting.
The dogs did yell; put "l" to sore, then "sorrel"° jumps from   *buck in its third year*
thicket.
Or° pricket, sore or else sorrel, the people fall a-hooting.   *Either*

55 If sore be sore, then "l"° to sore makes fifty sores o'sorrel. *Roman numeral for 50*
Of one sore I an hundred make by adding but one more "l."°   *50 more; one moral*

NATHANIEL A rare talent!°   *talon; ability*

DULL [*aside*] If a talent be a claw, look how he claws° him   *scratches; flatters*
with a talent!

60 HOLOFERNES This is a gift that I have simple,° simple: a fool-   *naturally*
ish, extravagant° spirit, full of forms, figures, shapes,   *wandering*
objects, ideas, apprehensions, motions,° revolutions.° These *impulses/ reflections*
are begot in the ventricle° of memory, nourished in the   *part of the brain*
womb of *pia mater*,⁶ and delivered upon the mellowing of

65 occasion.° But the gift is good in those in whom it is acute, *when the time is ripe*
and I am thankful for it.

NATHANIEL Sir, I praise the Lord for you, and so may my
parishioners, for their sons are well tutored by you, and their
daughters profit very greatly under you.⁷ You are a good

70 member of the commonwealth.

HOLOFERNES *Mehercle*,° if their sons be ingenious, they shall   *By Hercules*
want° no instruction. If their daughters be capable, I will put   *lack*
it to them.

Enter JAQUENETTA *and* [COSTARD,] *the clown.*

But *vir sapit qui pauca loquitur*⁸—a soul feminine saluteth us.

75 JAQUENETTA God give you good morrow, Master Person.

HOLOFERNES Master Person? *Quasi*° Pierce-one!⁹ An if one   *As if*
should be pierced, which is the one?

COSTARD Marry, Master Schoolmaster, he that is likest to° a   *most like*
hogshead.¹

80 HOLOFERNES "Of piercing a hogshead"°—a good luster of   *(getting drunk?)*
conceit° in a turf of earth, fire enough for a flint, pearl   *spark of imagination*
enough for a swine.² 'Tis pretty; it is well.

JAQUENETTA Good Master Parson, be so good as read me this
letter. It was given me by Costard, and sent me from Don

85 Armado. [*She gives* NATHANIEL *the letter.*] I beseech you,
read it.

---

3. *abrogate scurrility*: avoid indecency. Nathaniel is
probably worrying about "pricket"—justifiably, given
line 51, below. *"Perge"* may suggest "purging."
4. I will to some extent aspire to alliteration.
5. Deer in its fourth year.
6. Membrane surrounding the brain.
7. In conjunction with "member" (line 70), "capable"
(line 72), and "put it to them" (lines 72–73), probably

bawdy.
8. "That man is wise that speaketh few things or
words" (William Lily's early sixteenth-century Latin
grammar, translating a common proverb).
9. Pronounced like "parson" or "person"; bawdy.
1. Large cask used for beer or wine; fool.
2. To "cast pearls before swine," a biblical phrase,
was already proverbial.

HOLOFERNES   "*Fauste precor, gelida quando pecus omne sub umbra Ruminat*"[3]—and so forth. Ah, good old Mantuan! I may speak of thee as the traveler doth of Venice: "*Venetia,*

90   *Venetia, Chi non ti vede, non ti pretia.*"[4] Old Mantuan, old Mantuan, who understandeth thee not, loves thee not. [*He sings.*] *Ut, re, sol, la, mi, fa.*[5] [*to* NATHANIEL] Under pardon, sir, what are the contents? Or rather, as Horace° says in   *ancient Roman poet* his—What, my soul, verses?[6]

95 NATHANIEL   Ay, sir, and very learned.

HOLOFERNES   Let me hear a staff, a stanza, a verse.[7] *Lege, domine.*°   *Read, sir*

NATHANIEL [*reads*]   "If love make me forsworn, how shall I swear to love?[8]

  Ah, never faith could hold, if not to beauty vowed.

100   Though to myself forsworn, to thee I'll faithful prove;

  Those thoughts to me were oaks,[9] to thee like osiers°   *willows*
    bowed.

  Study his bias leaves° and makes his book thine eyes,   *goes off course*

  Where all those pleasures live that art would
    comprehend.

  If knowledge be the mark,° to know thee shall   *aim*
    suffice.

105   Well learnèd is that tongue that well can thee
    commend;

  All ignorant that soul that sees thee without wonder,

  Which is to me some praise, that I thy parts° admire.   *qualities*

  Thy eye Jove's lightning bears, thy voice his dreadful
    thunder,

  Which, not to anger bent, is music and sweet fire.

110   Celestial as thou art, O pardon, love, this wrong,

  That sings heaven's praise with such an earthly tongue."

HOLOFERNES   You find not the *apostrophus*° and so miss the   *elision mark* accent. Let me supervise° the canzonet.° [*He takes the let-*   *look over / little poem* *ter.*] Here are only numbers ratified,° but for the elegancy,   *correct meters*

115 facility, and golden cadence of poesy, *caret.*° Ovidius Naso[1]   *it is lacking* was the man; and why, indeed, "Naso," but for smelling out the odoriferous flowers of fancy, the jerks of invention?° *Imi-*   *strokes of imagination* *tari*° is nothing: so doth the hound his master, the ape his   *To imitate* keeper, the tired° horse his rider. —But, *domicella*—virgin—   *attired*

120 was this directed to you?

JAQUENETTA   Ay, sir, from one Monsieur Biron, one of the strange queen's lords.[2]

---

3. The first line of a Latin poem by the Italian poet Mantuan (1448–1516), a poem well known even to schoolboys in Shakespeare's time: "Faustus, while all the cattle are chewing the cud in the cool shade, I pray you" (let us talk a little about our old love affairs).
4. Italian proverb, translated by John Florio as "Venice, who seeth thee not, praiseth thee not" (*First Fruits*, 1578).
5. Notes of the scale ("ut" is the modern "do"). If Holofernes sings them as a scale, he gets them in the wrong order; but they may represent a tune.
6. TEXTUAL COMMENT For the attribution of the misquotation of Latin and Italian in this speech to the printer rather than to Holofernes or Shakespeare, see Digital Edition TC 8 (Folio edited text).
7. A *staff, a stanza, a verse*: three ways of saying

"stanza."
8. The beginning of a sonnet (lines 97–111), with six stresses per line. Like the poems of Longueville (4.3.55–68) and Dumaine (4.3.96–115), it was reprinted in *The Passionate Pilgrim* (1599). See the Introduction.
9. Those resolutions that seemed to me to be as strong as oaks.
1. The full name of the ancient Roman poet Ovid was Publius Ovidius Naso; *nasus* is Latin for "nose."
2. Jaquenetta has just said (lines 84–85) that Armado wrote and Costard gave her the letter, and she can't know that Biron, who is not a "strange" (foreign) courtier attending upon the Princess, actually composed it. Probably the errors are Shakespeare's.

HOLOFERNES   I will over-glance the superscript.° [*He reads.*]   *address*
    "To the snow-white hand of the most beauteous Lady Rosa-
125 line." I will look again on the intellect° of the letter for the   *meaning; contents*
    nomination of the party writing to the person written unto:
    "Your ladyship's, in all desired employment, Biron."

NATHANIEL   Master Holofernes, this Biron is one of the vota-
    ries with the King, and here he hath framed a letter to a
130 sequent° of the stranger queen's, which accidentally, or by   *follower*
    the way of progression,° hath miscarried. [*to* JAQUENETTA]   *in transit*
    Trip and go,[3] my sweet. Deliver this paper into the hand of
    the King; it may concern much. Stay not thy compliment. I
    forgive thy duty.[4] Adieu.

135 JAQUENETTA   Good Costard, go with me. [*to* NATHANIEL] Sir,
    God save your life!

COSTARD   Have with thee,° my girl.   *I'll come with you*

            Exeunt [COSTARD *and* JAQUENETTA].

NATHANIEL   Sir, you have done this in the fear of God, very
    religiously, and, as a certain father° sayeth—   *church father*
140 HOLOFERNES   Sir, tell not me of the father; I do fear colorable
    colors.[5] But to return to the verses: did they please you, Sir
    Nathaniel?

NATHANIEL   Marvelous well, for the pen.°   *penmanship*

HOLOFERNES   I do dine today at the father's of a certain pupil
145 of mine where, if before repast it shall please you to gratify°   *grace; please*
    the table with a grace, I will, on my privilege I have with the
    parents of the foresaid child or pupil, undertake your *ben*
    venuto,[6] where I will prove those verses to be very unlearned,
    neither savoring of poetry, wit, nor invention. I beseech your
150 society.

NATHANIEL   And thank you too, for society, sayeth the text,[7] is
    the happiness of life.

HOLOFERNES   And, certes,° the text most infallibly concludes   *certainly*
    it. [*to* DULL] Sir, I do invite you too. You shall not say me nay.
155 *Pauca verba*.° Away! The gentles are at their game,[8] and we   *Few words*
    will to our recreation.   *Exeunt.*

4.3 (Q 4.3)

Enter BIRON *with a paper in his hand, alone.*

BIRON   The King he is hunting the deer; I am coursing°   *pursuing*
    myself. They have pitched a toil;° I am toiling in a pitch[1]—   *set a snare*
    pitch that defiles. "Defile"? A foul word. Well, sit thee down,° *stay with me*
    Sorrow; for so they say the fool said, and so say I, and I the
5   fool. Well proved, wit! By the Lord, this love is as mad as
    Ajax. It kills sheep;[2] it kills me: I, a sheep. Well proved again
    o'my side! I will not love. If I do, hang me. I'faith, I will not.
    Oh, but her eye! By this light, but for her eye, I would not
    love her; yes, for her two eyes. Well, I do nothing in the world
10 but lie, and lie in my throat.° By heaven, I do love, and it   *scandalously*

---

3. A common expression, the title of a popular song
and dance.
4. Do not delay in order to take leave politely. I
excuse you from making a curtsy.
5. I do mistrust plausible—but specious—arguments
(a rejection of popishness?).
6. Undertake your welcome (Italian).
7. No convincing source has been identified.

8. The gentlefolk are at their sport (hunting).
4.3. Location: Scene continues.
1. In tar; in Rosaline's eyes (?).
2. At the Greek siege of Troy, when Agamemnon
awards Achilles' armor to Odysseus, Ajax goes mad
with rage and kills a flock of sheep, believing them to
be the Greek army.

hath taught me to rhyme and to be melancholy, and here is
part of my rhyme [*indicating the paper*], and here my melancholy [*indicating his breast*]. Well, she hath one o'my sonnets
already. The clown bore it, the fool sent it, and the lady hath
15   it. Sweet clown, sweeter fool, sweetest lady! By the world, I
would not care a pin if the other three were in.°   *similarly involved*
    Enter the KING.
Here comes one with a paper. God give him grace to groan!°   *(out of love)*
    [BIRON] *stands aside.*³
KING Ay me!
BIRON [*aside*] Shot, by heaven! Proceed, sweet Cupid. Thou
20   hast thumped him with thy bird-bolt under the left pap.°   *your arrow in the heart*
    [*The* KING *unfolds a paper.*]
In faith, secrets!
KING [*reads*] "So sweet a kiss the golden sun gives not⁴
    To those fresh morning drops upon the rose,
    As thy eyebeams when their fresh rays have smote
25   The night of dew° that on my cheeks down flows.   *nightly tears*
    Nor shines the silver moon one half so bright
    Through the transparent bosom of the deep,
    As doth thy face through tears of mine give light.
    Thou shin'st in every tear that I do weep;
30   No drop but as a coach doth carry thee;
    So ridest thou, triumphing in my woe.
    Do but behold the tears that swell in me,
    And they thy glory through my grief will show.
    But do not love thyself: then thou wilt keep
35   My tears for glasses,° and still make me weep.   *mirrors*
    O Queen of queens, how far dost thou excel,
    No thought can think, nor tongue of mortal tell."
How shall she know my griefs? I'll drop the paper.
Sweet leaves° shade° folly.   *(of trees; paper) / hide*
    Enter LONGUEVILLE [*with a paper*].
               Who is he comes here?
40   What, Longueville? And reading? Listen, ear.
    The KING *steps aside.*
BIRON [*aside*] Now, in thy° likeness, one more fool appear!   *(the King's)*
LONGUEVILLE Ay me, I am forsworn.
BIRON [*aside*] Why, he comes in like a perjure,° wearing papers.⁵ *perjurer*
KING [*aside*] In love, I hope. Sweet fellowship in shame!
45   BIRON [*aside*] One drunkard loves another of the name.°   *another drunkard*
LONGUEVILLE Am I the first that have been perjured so?
BIRON [*aside*] I could put thee in comfort: not by two that I know.
    Thou makest the triumviry,⁶ the corner cap° of society,   *three-cornered cap*
    The shape of love's Tyburn⁷ that hangs up simplicity.°   *folly*
50   LONGUEVILLE I fear these stubborn° lines lack power to move.   *rough*
    O sweet Maria, empress of my love!
    These numbers° will I tear and write in prose.   *verses*
BIRON [*aside*] Oh, rhymes are guards° on wanton Cupid's hose;   *decorative bands*

---

3. At line 74, Biron says, "here sit I in the sky." At some
point before then—perhaps here—he mounts to a
higher level.
4. The beginning of a sonnet that actually extends to
sixteen lines (lines 22–37).
5. Wearing a poem (lines 55–68). Convicted perjurers

were exposed by having to wear papers that explained
their guilt.
6. You complete the triumvirate (group of three
rulers).
7. The common place of execution in London, here
metaphorically for gallows, which were triangular.

Disfigure not his slop.°   *breeches*
LONGUEVILLE   This same shall go.[8]
        He reads the sonnet.
55   "Did not the heavenly rhetoric of thine eye,
            'Gainst whom the world cannot hold argument,
            Persuade my heart to this false perjury?
            Vows for thee broke deserve not punishment.
            A woman I forswore, but I will prove,
60   Thou being a goddess, I forswore not thee.
            My vow was earthly, thou a heavenly love;
            Thy grace° being gained cures all disgrace in me.   *favor*
            Vows are but breath, and breath a vapor is.
            Then thou, fair sun which on my earth dost shine,
65   Exhalest° this vapor-vow; in thee it is.   *Draw up*
            If broken then, it is no fault of mine.
            If by me broke, what fool is not so wise
            To lose an oath to win a paradise?"
    BIRON [*aside*]   This is the liver vein[9] which makes flesh a deity.
70   A green goose° a goddess? Pure, pure idolatry!   *silly girl; whore*
            God amend us, God amend! We are much out o'th' way.°   *badly astray*
            Enter DUMAINE.
LONGUEVILLE   By whom shall I send this? —Company? Stay.
            [LONGUEVILLE *stands aside.*]
    BIRON [*aside*]   All hid, all hid, an old infant play![1]
            Like a demigod here sit I in the sky,
75   And wretched fools' secrets heedfully o'er-eye.
            More sacks to the mill.° O heavens, I have my wish: *More to come!*
            Dumaine transformed! Four woodcocks° in a dish!   *fools*
DUMAINE   O most divine Kate!
    BIRON [*aside*]   O most profane coxcomb!°   *fool*
80 DUMAINE   By heaven, the wonder of a mortal eye!
    BIRON [*aside*]   By earth, she is not. Corporal,[2] there you lie.
DUMAINE   Her amber hairs for foul hath amber quoted.[3]
    BIRON [*aside*]   An amber-colored raven was well noted.[4]
DUMAINE   As upright as the cedar!
    BIRON [*aside*]   Stoop,[5] I say.
            Her shoulder is with child.°   *bulging; bowed down*
85 DUMAINE   As fair as day!
    BIRON [*aside*]   Ay, as some days, but then no sun must shine.
DUMAINE   Oh, that I had my wish!
LONGUEVILLE [*aside*]   And I had mine!
    KING [*aside*]   And I mine too, good Lord!
    BIRON [*aside*]   Amen, so I had mine. Is not that a good word?[6]
90 DUMAINE   I would forget her, but a fever she
            Reigns in my blood, and will remembered be.
    BIRON [*aside*]   A fever in your blood? Why, then, incision°   *bloodletting*

---

8. Either he has hesitated before tearing the paper or he pieces it together, as if in response to Biron's aside.
9. Style of the lover (the liver was thought of as the seat of love).
1. Hide-and-seek ("play" means "game"); perhaps also a medieval religious play in which God views the actions from above, like Biron does (line 74).
2. Officer in Cupid's army; perhaps: (she is merely) corporeal, or human. The possible application to

both Dumaine and Katherine, but in different ways, is characteristic of Biron's asides here.
3. Her amber-colored hairs have caused amber itself to be regarded as foul by comparison.
4. Dumaine is an acute observer, Biron remarks ironically, in describing Katherine's hair as amber. (Katherine more resembles the raven, a black fowl, punning on "foul," line 82.)
5. She's stooped; come down to earth.
6. Isn't that a kind wish; isn't "Amen" a "good word"?

Would let her out in saucers.[7] Sweet misprision!°   *misinterpretation*
DUMAINE   Once more I'll read the ode that I have writ.
95   BIRON [*aside*]   Once more I'll mark how love can vary° wit.   *inspire; impair*
DUMAINE *reads his sonnet.*
DUMAINE   "On a day—alack the day!—
       Love, whose month is ever May,
       Spied a blossom, passing° fair,   *surpassingly*
       Playing in the wanton° air.   *playful*
100   Through the velvet leaves the wind
       All unseen can° passage find,   *did*
       That° the lover, sick to death,   *So that*
       Wish himself the heaven's breath.
       'Air,' quoth he, 'thy cheeks may blow;
105   Air, would I might triumph so!
       But, alack, my hand is sworn
       Ne'er to pluck thee from thy thorn.
       Vow, alack, for youth unmeet;°   *inappropriate*
       Youth so apt to pluck a sweet.
110   Do not call it sin in me
       That I am forsworn for thee,
       Thou, for whom Jove would swear
       Juno but an Ethiop[8] were,
       And deny himself for° Jove,   *to be*
115   Turning mortal for thy love.'"
   This will I send, and something else more plain
   That shall express my true love's fasting pain.
   Oh, would the King, Biron, and Longueville
   Were lovers too! Ill to example° ill   *be a precedent for*
120   Would from my forehead wipe a perjured note;[9]
   For none offend where all alike do dote.
LONGUEVILLE [*stepping forward*]   Dumaine, thy love is far from
     charity,°   *Christian love*
   That in love's grief desir'st society.°   *company*
   You may look pale, but I should blush, I know,
125   To be o'erheard and taken napping so.
KING [*stepping forward*]   Come, sir, you blush. As his, your case
     is such.
   You chide at him, offending twice as much.
   You do not love Maria? Longueville
   Did never sonnet for her sake compile,
130   Nor never lay his wreathèd arms athwart[1]
   His loving bosom, to keep down his heart?
   I have been closely° shrouded in this bush   *secretly*
   And marked you both, and for you both did blush.
   I heard your guilty rhymes, observed your fashion,
135   Saw sighs reek° from you, noted well your passion.   *rise*
   "Ay me!" says one. "O Jove!" the other cries.
   One her hairs were gold, crystal the other's eyes.
   [*to* LONGUEVILLE] You would for paradise break faith and troth,
   [*to* DUMAINE] And Jove for your love would infringe an oath.

---

7. Into basins used to catch the blood; by the basinful.
8. Black African (used here in racist fashion to signify ugliness).

9. Inscription (and see Biron's description of Longueville, line 43).
1. Folded arms across. (Folded arms were a sign of love melancholy.)

140   What will Biron say when that he shall hear
    Faith infringèd, which such zeal did swear?
    How will he scorn! How will he spend his wit!
    How will he triumph, leap, and laugh at it!
    For all the wealth that ever I did see,
145   I would not have him know so much by° me.   *about*
    BIRON [*stepping forward*]   Now step I forth to whip hypocrisy.
    Ah, good my liege, I pray thee, pardon me.
    Good heart, what grace hast thou thus to reprove
    These worms for loving, that art most in love?
150   Your eyes do make no coaches° in your tears;   *(ironic: see lines 29–31)*
    There is no certain princess that appears.
    You'll not be perjured; 'tis a hateful thing!
    Tush, none but minstrels like of sonneting!
    But are you not ashamed? Nay, are you not,
155   All three of you, to be thus much o'ershot?°   *wide of the mark*
    [*to* LONGUEVILLE] You found his° mote; the King your mote   *(Dumaine's)*
       did see;
    But I a beam² do find in each of three.
    Oh, what a scene of fool'ry have I seen—
    Of sighs, of groans, of sorrow, and of teen!°   *grief*
160   O me, with what strict patience have I sat
    To see a king transformèd to a gnat,
    To see great Hercules whipping a gig,°   *spinning a top*
    And profound Solomon tuning° a jig,   *playing*
    And Nestor³ play at push-pin° with the boys,   *child's game*
165   And critic Timon⁴ laugh at idle toys.°   *foolish fancies*
    Where lies thy grief? Oh, tell me, good Dumaine!
    And gentle Longueville, where lies thy pain?
    And where my liege's? All about the breast.
    A caudle,° ho!   *warm, healing drink*
    KING   Too bitter is thy jest.
170   Are we betrayed thus to thy overview?
    BIRON   Not you by me, but I betrayed to you.
    I that am honest, I that hold it sin
    To break the vow I am engagèd in.
    I am betrayed by keeping company
175   With men like you, men of inconstancy.
    When shall you see me write a thing in rhyme,
    Or groan for Joan, or spend a minute's time
    In pruning me?° When shall you hear that I   *preening myself*
    Will praise a hand, a foot, a face, an eye,
180   A gait, a state,° a brow, a breast, a waist,   *an attitude; bearing*
    A leg, a limb—
        Enter JAQUENETTA [*with a paper*] *and* [COSTARD, *the*]
        clown. [BIRON *catches sight of them and prepares to*
        exit.]
    KING   Soft! Whither away so fast?
    A true° man or a thief that gallops so.   *An honest*
    BIRON   I post° from love. Good lover, let me go.   *hasten*

---

2. Larger defect: "And why beholdest thou the mote that is in thy brother's eye, but considerest [or "perceivest"] not the beam that is in thine own eye?" (Matthew 7:3–5; Luke 6:41–42).

3. Homeric hero, a type figure of wise old age; later portrayed in Shakespeare's *Troilus and Cressida*.

4. Cynical Greek misanthrope; later, the central character of Shakespeare's *Timon of Athens*.

JAQUENETTA   God bless the King!
KING   What present° hast thou there?   *writing; gift*
COSTARD   Some certain treason.
185   KING   What makes treason° here?   *is treason doing*
COSTARD   Nay, it makes nothing, sir.
KING   If it mar nothing neither,
The treason and you go in peace away together.
JAQUENETTA   I beseech your grace, let this letter be read.
Our Person misdoubts° it; it was treason, he said.   *suspects*
190   KING   Biron, read it over.
                    [BIRON] *reads the letter.*
Where hadst thou it?
JAQUENETTA   Of Costard.
KING   Where hadst thou it?
COSTARD   Of Dun Adramadio,[5] Dun Adramadio.
                    [BIRON *tears up the letter.*]
195   KING   How now? What is in you? Why dost thou tear it?
BIRON   A toy, my liege, a toy. Your grace needs not fear it.
LONGUEVILLE   It did move him to passion, and therefore let's
    hear it.
DUMAINE [*picking up the pieces*]   It is Biron's writing, and here
    is his name.
BIRON [*to* COSTARD]   Ah, you whoreson loggerhead!° You were   *foolish blockhead*
    born to do me shame.
200   [*to the* KING]   Guilty, my lord, guilty! I confess, I confess!
KING   What?
BIRON   That you three fools lacked me, fool, to make up
    the mess.°   *group of four at table*
He, he, and you, and you, my liege, and I,
Are pickpurses° in love, and we deserve to die.   *cheaters*
Oh, dismiss this audience, and I shall tell you more.
DUMAINE   Now the number is even.
205   BIRON   True, true, we are four.
Will these turtles° be gone?   *turtledoves; lovers*
KING   Hence, sirs, away!
COSTARD   Walk aside, the true folk, and let the traitors stay.
                    [*Exeunt* COSTARD *and* JAQUENETTA.]
BIRON   Sweet lords, sweet lovers—oh, let us embrace!
As true we are as flesh and blood can be.
210   The sea will ebb and flow; heaven will show his face;
Young blood doth not obey an old decree.
We cannot cross° the cause why we are born;   *oppose*
Therefore of all hands° must we be forsworn.   *in any case*
KING   What? Did these rent° lines show some love of thine?   *torn*
215   BIRON   "Did they?" quoth you. Who sees the heavenly
    Rosaline
That, like a rude° and savage man of Ind°   *an ignorant / India*
At the first opening of the gorgeous East,
Bows not his vassal head and, stricken blind,
Kisses the base ground with obedient breast?
220   What peremptory,° eagle-sighted eye[6]   *determined*

---

5. *Dun*: error for Don meaning "gray-brown," referring to skin color and recalling "tawny Spain"
(1.1.171). *Adramadio*: error for Adriano that encom-

passes "drama," "mad," "amado" ("loved").
6. The eagle, king of birds, was thought to be the
only one able to look directly at the sun.

Dares look upon the heaven of her brow
That is not blinded by her majesty?
KING What zeal, what fury, hath inspired thee now?
My love, her mistress, is a gracious moon;
225 She an attending star, scarce seen alight.°   *hardly visible*
BIRON My eyes are then no eyes, nor I Biron.
Oh, but for my love, day would turn to night.
Of all complexions the culled sovereignty°   *those chosen as best*
Do meet as at a fair in her fair cheek,
230 Where several Worthies make one dignity,[7]
Where nothing wants° that want° itself doth seek.   *lacks / desire*
Lend me the flourish of all gentle tongues—
Fie, painted rhetoric! Oh, she needs it not!
To things of sale a seller's praise belongs.
235 She passes praise—then praise too short doth blot.[8]
A withered hermit, fivescore winters worn,
Might shake off fifty looking in her eye.
Beauty doth varnish age, as if new born,
And gives the crutch the cradle's infancy.
240 Oh, 'tis the sun that maketh all things shine!
KING By heaven, thy love is black as ebony!
BIRON Is ebony like her? Oh, word divine!
A wife of such wood were felicity.
Oh, who can give an oath? Where is a book?°   *a Bible*
245 That I may swear Beauty doth beauty lack
If that she learn not of her eye to look:[9]
No face is fair that is not full so° black.   *just as*
KING Oh, paradox! Black is the badge of hell,
The hue of dungeons, and the school of night;[1]
250 And beauty's crest becomes the heavens well.[2]
BIRON Devils soonest tempt, resembling spirits of light.[3]
Oh, if in black my lady's brows be decked,
It mourns that painting and usurping hair°   *makeup and false hair*
Should ravish doters with a false aspect,
255 And therefore is she born to make black fair.
Her favor° turns the fashion of the days,   *appearance*
For native blood° is counted painting now;   *natural red coloring*
And therefore red, that would avoid dispraise,
Paints itself black to imitate her brow.
260 DUMAINE To look like her are chimney sweepers black.
LONGUEVILLE And since her time are colliers counted bright.
KING And Ethiops of their sweet complexion crack.°   *boast*
DUMAINE Dark needs no candles now, for dark is light.
BIRON Your mistresses dare never come in rain,
265 For fear their colors should be washed away.
KING 'Twere good yours did; for, sir, to tell you plain,
I'll find a fairer face not° washed today.   *that has not been*
BIRON I'll prove her fair, or talk till doomsday here.

7. Various kinds of excellence together produce a single preeminent beauty.
8. Hence praise inevitably falls short and mars her reputation.
9. If beauty doesn't learn from Rosaline's eye how she (beauty) could look.
1. *school*: title. The phrase "school of night" has been supposed to refer to a secret society of Shakespeare's time; alternatively, it may mean that night learns to be black in black's school.
2. (And yet, you say,) the badge of your dark beauty is heavenly (said incredulously).
3. Fair beauties are not to be trusted, "for Satan himself is transformed into an angel of light" (2 Corinthians 11:14).

KING   No devil will fright thee, then,° so much as she.   (at doomsday)
270   DUMAINE   I never knew man hold vile stuff so dear.
LONGUEVILLE [*indicating his shoe*]   Look, here's thy love: my
    foot and her face see.[4]
BIRON   Oh, if the streets were pavèd with thine eyes,
    Her feet were much too dainty for such tread.
DUMAINE   Oh, vile! Then as she goes what upward° lies   *up her dress (bawdy)*
275   The street should see as she walked overhead.
KING   But what of this? Are we not all in love?
BIRON   Nothing so sure—and thereby all forsworn.
KING   Then leave this chat; and, good Biron, now prove
    Our loving lawful and our faith not torn.
280   DUMAINE   Ay, marry, there: some flattery° for this evil.   *excuse*
LONGUEVILLE   Oh, some authority how to proceed,
    Some tricks, some quillets° how to cheat the devil.   *verbal tricks*
DUMAINE   Some salve for perjury.°   *oath breaking; purging*
BIRON   'Tis more than need!°   *really essential*
    Have at you,° then, Affection's° men-at-arms!   *Here goes / Love's*
285   Consider what you first did swear unto:
    To fast, to study, and to see no woman—
    Flat treason against the kingly state of youth!
    Say, can you fast? Your stomachs are too young,
    And abstinence engenders maladies.
290   And where that you have vowed to study, lords,[5]
    In that[6] each of you have forsworn his book,
    Can you still dream and pore and thereon look?
    For when would you, my lord, or you, or you,
    Have found the ground of study's excellence
295   Without the beauty of a woman's face?
    From women's eyes this doctrine I derive:
    They are the ground, the books, the academes
    From whence doth spring the true Promethean fire.[7]
    Why, universal plodding poisons up
300   The nimble° spirits in the arteries,   *life-giving*
    As motion and long-during° action tires   *long-lasting*
    The sinewy vigor of the traveler.
    Now, for not looking on a woman's face,
    You have in that forsworn the use of eyes,
305   And study, too, the causer of your vow.
    For where is any author in the world
    Teaches such beauty as a woman's eye?
    Learning is but an adjunct to our self,
    And where we are, our learning likewise is.
310   Then when ourselves we see in ladies' eyes,
    With ourselves—
    Do we not likewise see our learning there?
    Oh, we have made a vow to study, lords,
    And in that vow we have forsworn our books.[8]
315   For when would you, my liege, or you, or you,
    In leaden contemplation have found out

---

4. You may see her face in my (black) shoes.
5. TEXTUAL COMMENT For the presence of both a first draft and a revised version of Biron's speech in the following lines, a practice found elsewhere in the play, see Digital Edition TC 9 (Folio edited text).

And where that: And whereas.
6. Inasmuch as; in that vow.
7. Divine fire. In Greek mythology, Prometheus stole fire from heaven and gave it to humanity.
8. Our true books, women's eyes.

Such fiery numbers° as the prompting eyes   *passionate verses*
Of Beauty's tutors have enriched you with?
Other slow arts° entirely keep° the brain,   *disciplines / fill up*
320   And therefore, finding barren practicers,°   *practitioners of the "arts"*
Scarce show a harvest of their° heavy toil.   *(the practicers')*
But love, first learned in a lady's eyes,
Lives not alone immurèd° in the brain,   *only shut up*
But with the motion of all elements[9]
325   Courses° as swift as thought in every power,°   *Flows / faculty*
And gives to every power a double power,
Above° their functions and their offices.°   *Beyond / normal duties*
It adds a precious seeing to the eye:
A lover's eyes will gaze an eagle blind.[1]
330   A lover's ear will hear the lowest sound,
When the suspicious head of theft is stopped.[2]
Love's feeling is more soft and sensible°   *sensitive*
Than are the tender horns of cockled snails.°   *snails with shells*
Love's tongue proves dainty Bacchus° gross in taste.   *Greek god of wine*
335   For valor, is not love a Hercules,
Still° climbing trees in the Hesperides?[3]   *Constantly*
Subtle as Sphinx,[4] as sweet and musical
As bright Apollo's° lute, strung with his hair?   *Greek god of music*
And when love speaks, the voice of all the gods
340   Make heaven drowsy with the harmony.
Never durst poet touch a pen to write,
Until his ink were tempered with love's sighs.
Oh, then his lines would ravish savage ears
And plant in tyrants mild humility.
345   From women's eyes this doctrine I derive:
They sparkle still the right Promethean fire.
They are the books, the arts, the academes,
That show, contain, and nourish all the world,
Else none° at all in aught proves excellent.   *Without them no one*
350   Then fools you were these women to forswear,
Or keeping what is sworn you will prove fools.
For wisdom's sake—a word that all men love—
Or for love's sake—a word that loves[5] all men—
Or for men's sake—the author of these women—
355   Or women's sake—by whom we men are men—
Let us once lose our oaths to find ourselves,[6]
Or else we lose ourselves to keep our oaths.
It is religion to be thus forsworn;
For charity itself fulfills the law,[7]
360   And who can sever love from charity?
KING   Saint Cupid, then! And, soldiers, to the field!
BIRON   Advance your standards,° and upon them, lords!   *(with a sexual sense)*
Pell-mell, down with them! But be first advised

---

9. Earth, air, fire, and water.
1. Can stare at the sun (here, the beloved woman) without injury longer than even an eagle can.
2. When even an alert thief (or someone listening for a thief) hears nothing.
3. Garden of golden apples that Hercules had to pick as his eleventh labor.
4. Monster in Greek mythology that killed travelers who failed to solve her riddle.

5. Meaning is uncertain: is a friend to; values; pleases; inspires with love; is lovable to.
6. "For whosoever will save his life shall lose it: and whosoever will lose his life for my sake shall find it" (Matthew 16:25).
7. "He that loveth another hath fulfilled the law" (Romans 13:8). "Love worketh no ill to his neighbor: therefore is love the fulfilling of the law" (Romans 13:10).

In conflict that you get the sun of them.[8]

365 LONGUEVILLE Now to plain dealing—lay these glozes° by.   *verbal sophistries*
    Shall we resolve to woo these girls of France?
KING And win them, too. Therefore let us devise
    Some entertainment for them in their tents.
BIRON First, from the park let us conduct them thither.
370 Then, homeward, every man attach° the hand   *seize*
    Of his fair mistress. In the afternoon
    We will with some strange° pastime solace them,   *novel*
    Such as the shortness of the time can shape;
    For revels, dances, masques, and merry hours
375 Forerun° fair Love, strewing her way with flowers.   *Run before*
KING Away, away! No time shall be omitted,
    That will by time and may by us be fitted.°   *used well*
BIRON *Allons, allons!°* Sowed cockle reaps no corn,[9]   *Come on, come on*
    And justice always whirls in equal measure.°   *acts impartially*
380 Light° wenches may prove plagues to men forsworn;   *Frivolous*
    If so, our copper buys° no better treasure.   *Exeunt.*   *base coin deserves*

5.1 (Q 5.1)

Enter [HOLOFERNES,] *the pedant,* [NATHANIEL, *the*]
curate, and DULL.

HOLOFERNES *Satis quid sufficit.*[1]
NATHANIEL I praise God for you, sir. Your reasons° at dinner   *discourses*
have been sharp and sententious, pleasant without scurril-
ity, witty without affectation, audacious without impudency,
5 learned without opinion,° and strange° without heresy. I did   *arrogance / original*
converse this *quondam* day° with a companion of the King's   *the other day*
who is intituled, nominated, or called Don Adriano de
Armado.
HOLOFERNES *Novi hominem tanquam te.*[2] His humor° is   *temperament*
10 lofty, his discourse peremptory,° his tongue filed,° his eye   *overbearing / polished*
ambitious, his gait majestical, and his general behavior vain,
ridiculous, and thrasonical.[3] He is too picked,° too spruce,   *fastidious*
too affected, too odd, as it were, too peregrinate,° as I may   *exotic*
call it.
15 NATHANIEL A most singular and choice epithet!
    [*He*] *draw*[*s*] *out his table-book*° [*and writes in it*].   *notebook*
HOLOFERNES He draweth out the thread of his verbosity finer
than the staple of his argument.[4] I abhor such fanatical
phantasimes,[5] such insociable and point-device° compan-   *extremely precise*
ions, such rackers of orthography:[6] as to speak "dout" *sine*° "b,"   *without*
20 when he should say "doubt"; "det" when he should pronounce
"debt"—d, e, b, t, not d, e, t. He clepeth° a "calf," "cauf," "half,"   *calls*

---

8. Get the sun in their eyes (get the advantage); also, probably bawdy, playing on "beget the son."
9. Wheat ("corn") was never reaped where weeds ("cockle") were sown (proverbial): in other words, we won't get something for nothing; we must make an effort.
5.1 Location: The King's park.
1. Should be *Satis est quod sufficit:* "Enough is enough," but recalling the English proverb "Enough is as good as a feast." The Latin in this scene, some of it inaccurate, again is translated only when the characters themselves fail to do so. Here, too, it is often unclear whether the error is the character's, the

printer's, or Shakespeare's.
2. I know the man as well as I know you.
3. Boastful, bragging. From "Thraso," the braggart soldier in *Eunuchus,* by the Roman dramatist Terence.
4. He's wordy. (Unintentionally ironic, coming from Holofernes; "staple" means "fiber," "argument" means "subject matter.")
5. Extravagant, fantastic beings.
6. Tormentors of spelling. Holofernes speaks for those educational theorists who urged, unsuccessfully, that English words be spelled and pronounced like their Latin roots.

"hauf," "neighbor" *vocatur*° "nebor"—"neigh" abbreviated "ne."   *is called*
This is "abhominable," which he would call "abominable." It
insinuateth me of *insanire*[7]—*ne intelligis, domine?*[8]—to make
25   frantic, lunatic.
NATHANIEL   *Laus Deo, bone intelligo.*[9]
HOLOFERNES   *"Bone"? "Bone"* for *"bene"*! Priscian a little
   scratched;[1] 'twill serve.
        Enter [ARMADO, *the*] *braggart,* [*and* PAGE, *his*] *boy*[,
        with COSTARD].
NATHANIEL   *Videsne quis venit?*°   *Do you see who's coming?*
30   HOLOFERNES   *Video, et gaudio.*°   *I see, and rejoice.*
ARMADO   Chirrah![2]
HOLOFERNES   *Quare*° "Chirrah," not "Sirrah"?   *Why*
ARMADO   Men of peace, well encountered!
HOLOFERNES   Most military sir, salutation!
35   PAGE [*to* COSTARD]   They have been at a great feast of lan-
   guages and stolen the scraps.
COSTARD [*to* PAGE]   Oh, they have lived long on the alms-
   basket[3] of words. I marvel thy master hath not eaten thee for
   a word, for thou art not so long by the head as "*honorific-*
40   *abilitudinitatibus.*"[4] Thou art easier swallowed than a
   flap-dragon.[5]
PAGE [*to* COSTARD]   Peace! The peal° begins.   *jangling; babble*
ARMADO [*to* HOLOFERNES]   Monsieur, are you not lettered?°   *learned; literate*
PAGE   Yes, yes, he teaches boys the hornbook.° What is "a, b"   *alphabet book*
45   spelled backward with the horn on his head?°   *as a cuckold*
HOLOFERNES   "Ba," *pueritia,*° with a horn added.   *child(ishness)*
PAGE   Ba, most silly sheep with a horn. You hear his learning?
HOLOFERNES   *Quis, quis,* thou consonant?[6]
PAGE   The last of the five vowels,° if you° repeat them, or the   *"u" / ewe*
50   fifth° if I.   *you*
HOLOFERNES   I will repeat them: a, e, i—
PAGE   The sheep.[7] The other two concludes it: o, u.[8]
ARMADO   Now, by the salt° wave of the *Mediterraneum,* a sweet   *salty; witty*
   touch,° a quick venue° of wit! Snip-snap, quick and home![9] It   *hit / thrust*
55   rejoiceth my intellect. True wit—
PAGE   Offered by a child to an old man, which is wit-old.[1]
HOLOFERNES   What is the figure?° What is the figure?   *figure of speech*
PAGE   Horns.
HOLOFERNES   Thou disputes like an infant. Go, whip thy gig!°   *spin your top*
60   PAGE   Lend me your horn to make one, and I will whip about
   your infamy *manu cita.*[2] A gig of° a cuckold's horn!   *made of*
COSTARD   An° I had but one penny in the world, thou shouldst   *If*

---

7. Puts me in mind of madness; perhaps, drives me mad.
8. Don't you understand, master?
9. Praise God, I understand well.
1. *Priscian a little scratched:* imperfect Latin (Priscian was a sixth-century Latin grammarian). Holofernes is ridiculing Nathaniel's mistake of using *bone* for *bene.*
2. Pseudo-Spanish or dialectal pronunciation of "Sirrah"; or garbled Greek for "Hail."
3. Basket in which the leftovers of a feast were collected for the poor.
4. Dative and ablative plural of a Latin word meaning "honorableness," renowned for its length. *word:* "mote" equals the French *mot,* which means "word."
5. A raisin floated on flaming brandy, which had to

be snapped up with the mouth and eaten in the game of snapdragon.
6. Nonentity (because a consonant alone is soundless). *Quis:* Latin for "who;" also, pronounced "kiss" and hence referring back to "ba" (lines 46–47), a sheep's bleat but also meaning "kiss."
7. The Spanish for "sheep"—*oveja,* often spelled *oueia*—seems to have been used as a device for memorizing the vowels.
8. Proves what I say (or completes the list): oh, you (ewe).
9. And to the target.
1. Mentally feeble; "wittol," a contented cuckold.
2. With a swift hand.

have it to buy gingerbread. [*He searches his pockets.*] Hold!
There is the very remuneration I had of thy master, thou
65   halfpenny° purse of wit, thou pigeon egg of discretion. Oh, — *tiny*
an the heavens were so pleased that thou wert but my bastard! What a joyful father wouldst thou make me! Go to,
thou hast it *ad dunghill*, at the fingers' ends,° as they say. — *exactly; (scatological)*
    [*He gives him the coin.*]
HOLOFERNES   Oh, I smell false Latin: "*dunghill*" for "*unguem.*"° — *fingernail*
70   ARMADO   Arts-man, *preambulate*.[3] We will be singled° from — *separated*
    the barbarous. [*They withdraw.*] Do you not educate youth
    at the charge-house° on the top of the mountain? — *endowed school*
HOLOFERNES   Or *mons*, the hill.
ARMADO   At your sweet pleasure, for the mountain.
75   HOLOFERNES   I do, *sans*° question. — *without*
ARMADO   Sir, it is the King's most sweet pleasure and affection° — *wish*
    to congratulate° the Princess at her pavilion, in the *posteriors*[4] — *greet*
    of this day, which the rude multitude call the afternoon.
HOLOFERNES   The "*posterior*" of the day, most generous° sir, is — *noble*
80   liable,° congruent, and measurable° for the afternoon. The — *fitting / suitable*
    word is well culled,[5] choice, sweet, and apt,° I do assure you, — *(synonyms)*
    sir, I do assure you.
ARMADO   Sir, the King is a noble gentleman and my familiar,° — *close friend*
    I do assure ye, very good friend. For what is inward° between — *confidential; (sexual?)*
85   us, let it pass—I do beseech thee, remember thy courtesy; I
    beseech thee, apparel thy head[6]—and among other impor-
    tunate° and most serious designs, and of great import indeed, — *pressing*
    too—but let that pass.[7] For I must tell thee, it will please his
    grace, by the world, sometime to lean upon my poor shoulder,
90   and with his royal finger thus dally with my excrement°— — *growth of hair; feces*
    with my mustachio. But, sweetheart, let that pass. By the
    world, I recount no fable. Some certain special honors it
    pleaseth his greatness to impart to Armado: a soldier, a man
    of travel that hath seen the world. But let that pass. The very
95   all of all° is—but, sweetheart, I do implore secrecy—that — *sum of everything*
    the King would have me present the Princess—sweet
    chuck!°—with some delightful ostentation,° or show, or pag- — *chick / show*
    eant, or antic,° or firework. Now, understanding that the — *grotesque pageant*
    curate and your sweet self are good at such eruptions° and — *(scatological)*
100   sudden breaking-out° of mirth, as it were, I have acquainted — *(scatological)*
    you withal° to the end to crave your assistance. — *with it*
HOLOFERNES   Sir, you shall present before her the Nine Wor-
    thies.[8] —Sir Nathaniel, as concerning some entertainment
    of° time, some show in the *posterior* of this day, to be ren- — *way of spending*
105   dered by our assistance the King's command, and this most
    gallant, illustrate,° and learned gentleman, before the Prin- — *illustrious*
    cess, I say none so fit as to present the Nine Worthies!

3. Scholar, walk ahead, with a play on "arse"
(behind, rather than "pre-," or ahead).
4. End (temporal and anatomical).
5. With a play on "cul," French for "backside."
6. *remember . . . head:* remember that you removed
your hat in courtesy (perhaps at line 34). I beseech
you, put it back on.
7. Suggestion of sodomy and excrement, developed
in the repeated phrase "but [butt] let that pass" (lines

85, 88, 91, 94).
8. Famous conquerors often represented in folk
plays and pageants. Usually three pagans—Hector,
Alexander, Julius Caesar; three Jews—Joshua, David,
Judas Maccabeus; and three Christians—Arthur,
Charlemagne, and Godfrey of Bouillon or Guy of
Warwick. Of these, only Alexander, Judas Maccabeus, and Hector appear in the next scene; Shakespeare adds Pompey and Hercules.

NATHANIEL   Where will you find men worthy enough to present them?

110 HOLOFERNES   Joshua, yourself;[9] myself—; and this gallant
gentleman, Judas Maccabeus. This swain, because of his
great limb or joint, shall pass Pompey the Great;[1] the page,
Hercules—[2]

ARMADO   Pardon, sir, error! He is not quantity enough for
115 that Worthy's thumb. He is not so big as the end of his club.

HOLOFERNES   Shall I have audience?° He shall present Her-   attention
cules in minority.° His *Enter*° and *Exit* shall be strangling a   childhood / entrance
snake,[3] and I will have an Apology° for that purpose.   explanatory speech

PAGE   An excellent device! So if any of the audience hiss, you
120 may cry, "Well done, Hercules! Now thou crushest the
snake!" That is the way to make an offense gracious, though
few have the grace to do it.

ARMADO   For the rest of the Worthies?

HOLOFERNES   I will play three myself.

125 PAGE   Thrice-worthy gentleman!

ARMADO   Shall I tell you a thing?

HOLOFERNES   We attend.°   listen

ARMADO   We will have, if this fadge° not, an antic. I beseech   succeed
you, follow.

130 HOLOFERNES   *Via,*° goodman Dull. Thou hast spoken no word   Come on
all this while.

DULL   Nor understood none neither, sir.

HOLOFERNES   *Allons!*° We will employ thee.   Come on!

DULL   I'll make one° in a dance or so, or I will play on the   join
135 tabor° to the Worthies and let them dance the hay.°   small drum / reel

HOLOFERNES   Most Dull, honest Dull! To our sport. Away!

Exeunt.

5.2 (Q 5.2)

Enter ladies [the PRINCESS, MARIA, KATHERINE, *and*
ROSALINE].

PRINCESS   Sweethearts, we shall be rich ere we depart
If fairings° come thus plentifully in.   gifts
A lady walled about with diamonds:[1]
Look you what I have from the loving King!
[*She shows them a pendant.*]

5 ROSALINE   Madam, came nothing else along with that?

PRINCESS   Nothing but this? Yes, as much love in rhyme
As would be crammed up in a sheet of paper,
Writ on both sides the leaf, margin and all,
That he was fain to seal on Cupid's name.[2]

10 ROSALINE   That was the way to make his godhead wax,°   grow; sealing wax
For he hath been five thousand years° a boy.   (age of the world)

KATHERINE   Ay, and a shrewd unhappy gallows,[3] too.

---

9. In the event, Nathaniel plays Alexander.
1. *great . . . Great:* Costard's considerable size
enables him to "pass" for Pompey the Great, suggesting "penis" through "limb" or "joint," and, through
the jingle with "pump" in "Pompey," both "penis" and
"pudendum."
2. TEXTUAL COMMENT For the textual uncertainty
here over the casting of the Nine Worthies, see Digital Edition TC 10 (Folio edited text).

3. Hercules strangled two snakes sent by Juno to kill
him in his cradle.
5.2 Location: The ladies' lodgings in the King's park.
1. This describes the gift.
2. So that he was obliged to obliterate Cupid's name
with his seal.
3. Ill-natured, pernicious gallows bird, deserving to
be hanged.

ROSALINE You'll ne'er be friends with him: 'a° killed your sister.　　　　　　*he*
KATHERINE He made her melancholy, sad, and heavy,
15 And so she died. Had she been light like you,
Of such a merry, nimble, stirring spirit,
She might ha' been a grandam ere she died;
And so may you, for a light heart lives long.
ROSALINE What's your dark° meaning, mouse, of this light°　　　*covert / careless*
word?
20 KATHERINE A light° condition in a beauty dark.　　　　　　　*frivolous; wanton*
ROSALINE We need more light to find your meaning out.
KATHERINE You'll mar the light by taking it in snuff;[4]
Therefore, I'll darkly end the argument.
ROSALINE Look what° you do, you do it still i'th' dark.°　　　*whatever / (bawdy)*
25 KATHERINE So do not you, for you are a light wench.
ROSALINE Indeed, I weigh not° you, and therefore light.　　　*weigh less than*
KATHERINE You weigh me not? Oh, that's you care not for me!
ROSALINE Great reason, for past care is still past cure.[5]
PRINCESS Well bandied both! A set of wit well played.
30 But Rosaline, you have a favor° too.　　　　　　　　　*love token*
Who sent it, and what is it?
ROSALINE　　　　　　　　　　　I would you knew.
An if my face were but as fair as yours,
My favor were as great; be witness this.
[*She shows them a brooch.*]
Nay, I have verses too, I thank Biron:
35 The numbers° true, and were the numb'ring° too　　*meter / evaluation*
I were the fairest goddess on the ground.
I am compared to twenty thousand fairs°—　　　　　　*beauties*
Oh, he hath drawn my picture in his letter!
PRINCESS Anything like?
40 ROSALINE Much in the letters,° nothing in the praise.　　　*black ink*
PRINCESS Beauteous as ink°—a good conclusion.　　　　　　*(that is, black)*
KATHERINE Fair as a text° "B" in a copybook.　　　　*formally written black*
ROSALINE 'Ware pencils,[6] ho! Let me not die your debtor,°　*I'll pay you back*
My red dominical,[7] my golden letter.[8]
45 Oh, that your face were not so full of Os!°　　　*pockmarks; pudenda*
PRINCESS A pox of that jest! And I beshrew° all shrews.　*wish mischief upon*
But, Katherine, what was sent to you from fair Dumaine?
KATHERINE Madame, this glove.
[*She shows them a glove.*]
PRINCESS　　　　　　　　　　　Did he not send you twain?
KATHERINE Yes, madam, and, moreover,
50 Some thousand verses of a faithful lover:
A huge translation° of hypocrisy,　　　　　　　　*expression*
Vilely compiled, profound simplicity!°　　　　　　　*folly*
MARIA This, and these pearls, to me sent Longueville.
[*She shows them a letter and a chain of pearls.*]
The letter is too long by half a mile.
55 PRINCESS I think no less. Dost thou not wish in heart
The chain were longer, and the letter short?

4. Taking it amiss; snuffing a candle.
5. Reversing the proverb's normal order: past cure is past care.
6. Beware of introducing the subject of brushes (used for cosmetic purposes as well as for drawing

portraits).
7. Red letter marking Sundays and feast days in an almanac; reference to Katherine's ruddy complexion.
8. Also used to mark Sunday; reference to Katherine's fair hair.

MARIA   Ay, or I would these hands might never part.[9]

PRINCESS   We are wise girls to mock our lovers so.

ROSALINE   They are worse fools to purchase mocking so.

60   That same Biron I'll torture ere I go.
       Oh, that I knew he were but in by th' week,°   *permanently caught*
       How I would make him fawn and beg and seek,
       And wait the season and observe the times,°   *servilely attend on me*
       And spend his prodigal wits in bootless° rhymes,   *fruitless*
65   And shape his service wholly to my device,
       And make him proud to make me proud that jests.[1]
       So, pursuivant°-like, would I o'ersway his state,   *arresting officer*
       That he should be my fool and I his fate.

PRINCESS   None are so surely caught, when they are catched,

70   As wit turned fool. Folly in wisdom hatched
       Hath wisdom's warrant and the help of school
       And wit's own grace to grace a learnèd fool.

ROSALINE   The blood of youth burns not with such excess
       As gravity's° revolt to wantonness.   *a wise person's*

75   MARIA   Folly in fools bears not so strong a note°   *stigma*
       As fool'ry in the wise when wit doth dote,°   *act foolishly*
       Since all the power thereof it doth apply
       To prove, by wit, worth in simplicity.°   *folly*
            Enter BOYET.

PRINCESS   Here comes Boyet, and mirth is in his face.

80   BOYET   Oh, I am stabbed with laughter! Where's her grace?

PRINCESS   Thy news, Boyet?

BOYET   Prepare, madam, prepare!
       Arm, wenches, arm! Encounters mounted are°   *An attack is prepared*
       Against your peace. Love doth approach disguised,
       Armed in arguments—you'll be surprised!°   *taken by surprise attack*
85   Muster your wits; stand in your own defense;
       Or hide your heads like cowards and fly hence.

PRINCESS   Saint Denis to Saint Cupid![2] What are they
       That charge° their breath against us? Say, scout, say.   *level (a weapon)*

BOYET   Under the cool shade of a sycamore
90   I thought to close mine eyes some half an hour,
       When, lo, to interrupt my purposed rest,
       Toward that shade I might behold addressed°   *I could see approaching*
       The King and his companions. Warily,
       I stole into a neighbor thicket by
95   And overheard what you shall overhear:°   *hear over again*
       That, by and by, disguised they will be here!
       Their herald is a pretty knavish page,
       That well by heart hath conned his embassage.°   *learned his message*
       Action and accent° did they teach him there: *Gesture and intonation*
100   "Thus must thou speak, and thus thy body bear,"
       And ever and anon they made a doubt,°   *expressed fear*
       Presence majestical would put him out.°   *make him forget his lines*
       "For," quoth the King, "an angel shalt thou see.
       Yet fear not thou, but speak audaciously."

---

9. Perhaps she has twisted the chain around them; or, she'd never separate her hands to give one hand in marriage to so ungenerous a man.
1. And be pleased to praise the one who mocks him; and be glad to be ridiculed.
2. St. Denis (the patron saint of France) against St. Cupid.

105   The boy replied: "An angel is not evil.
    I should have feared her had she been a devil."
    With that, all laughed and clapped him on the shoulder,
    Making the bold wag by their praises bolder.
    One rubbed his elbow[3] thus, and fleered,° and swore   *grinned*
110   A better speech was never spoke before.
    Another with his finger and his thumb°   *(snapping his fingers)*
    Cried "*Via!*° We will do't, come what will come!"   *Come on!*
    The third he capered and cried, "All goes well!"
    The fourth turned on the toe° and down he fell.   *did a pirouette*
115   With that, they all did tumble on the ground,
    With such a zealous laughter, so profound,
    That in this spleen ridiculous° appears,   *absurd fit (of laughter)*
    To check their folly, passion's solemn tears.
    PRINCESS   But what, but what? Come they to visit us?
120   BOYET   They do, they do, and are appareled thus,[4]
    Like Muscovites or Russians, as I guess.
    Their purpose is to parley, to court, and dance,
    And every one his love-suit will advance
    Unto his several° mistress, which they'll know   *particular*
125   By favors several which they did bestow.
    PRINCESS   And will they so? The gallants shall be tasked;°   *put to the test*
    For, ladies, we will everyone be masked;
    And not a man of them shall have the grace,°   *luck*
    Despite of suit,° to see a lady's face.   *pleading; costume*
130   Hold, Rosaline! This favor thou shalt wear,
    And then the King will court thee for his dear.
    Hold, take thou this, my sweet, and give me thine.
        [*They exchange favors.*]
    So shall Biron take me for Rosaline.
    [*to* MARIA *and* KATHERINE] And change your favors too. So
      shall your loves
135   Woo contrary, deceived by these removes.°   *exchanges*
        [*They exchange favors.*]
    ROSALINE   Come on, then. Wear the favors most in sight.°   *conspicuously*
    KATHERINE   But in this changing what is your intent?
    PRINCESS   The effect of my intent is to cross theirs.
    They do it but in mocking merriment,°   *satirical mirth*
140   And mock for mock is only my intent.
    Their several counsels° they unbosom shall   *confidences*
    To loves mistook, and so be mocked withal
    Upon the next occasion that we meet,
    With visages displayed, to talk and greet.
145   ROSALINE   But shall we dance if they desire us to't?
    PRINCESS   No, to the death we will not move a foot;
    Nor to their penned speech render we no grace,
    But while 'tis spoke each turn away her face.
    BOYET   Why, that contempt will kill the speaker's heart,
150   And quite divorce his memory from his part!
    PRINCESS   Therefore I do it; and I make no doubt,
    The rest will ne'er come in if he be out.[5]

---

3. Sign of satisfaction.
4. Absence of a rhyme for "guess" and a referent for "thus" suggests that a line describing the lords' costumes has been lost.
5. The rest of his prepared speech will be forgotten if he's confused ("out" of his part).

There's no such sport as sport by sport o'erthrown,
To make theirs ours and ours none but our own.
155 So shall we stay, mocking intended game,
And they, well mocked, depart away with shame.
　　　　Sound [trumpet].
BOYET　The trumpet sounds. Be masked! The maskers come!
　　　　[The ladies put on their masks.]
　　　　Enter Black[a]moors with music,[6] *the boy* [PAGE] *with*
　　　　a speech, and the rest of the lords [LONGUEVILLE,
　　　　DUMAINE, BIRON, *and the* KING] *disguised.*
PAGE　"All hail, the richest beauties on the earth!"
BIRON *[aside]*　Beauties no richer than rich taffeta.°　　　　*(masks of taffeta)*
160 PAGE　"A holy parcel° of the fairest dames　　　　　　　*party*
　　　　That ever turned—
　　　　　　The ladies turn their backs to him.
　　　　　　　　　　their backs to mortal views."
BIRON　Their "eyes," villain, their "eyes"!
PAGE　"That ever turned their eyes to mortal views.
　　　　Out—"
165 BOYET　True: "out,"° indeed!　　　　　　　　　　*(of his part)*
PAGE　"Out of your favors, heavenly spirits,
　　　　Vouchsafe° not to behold—"　　　　　　　　*Be willing*
BIRON　"Once to behold," rogue!
PAGE　"Once to behold, with your sun-beamed eyes—
170 　　　　With your sun-beamed eyes—"
BOYET　They will not answer to that epithet.
　　　　You were best call it "daughter-beamed eyes."
PAGE *[to* BIRON]　They do not mark° me, and that brings me out!　　*listen to*
BIRON　Is this your perfectness?° Begone, you rogue!　　*(in saying your lines)*
　　　　　　　　　　　　　[Exit PAGE.]
　　　　[The ladies turn to face the maskers.]
175 ROSALINE *[as the* PRINCESS][7]　What would these strangers?°　　*foreigners*
　　　　Know their minds, Boyet.
　　　　If they do speak our language, 'tis our will
　　　　That some plain° man recount their purposes.　　　*plainspoken*
　　　　Know what they would.
BOYET　What would you with the Princess?
180 BIRON　Nothing but peace and gentle visitation.°　　　　*visiting*
ROSALINE　What would they, say they?
BOYET　Nothing but peace and gentle visitation.
ROSALINE　Why, that they have, and bid them so be gone.
BOYET　She says you have it, and you may be gone.
185 KING　Say to her, we have measured° many miles　　　　*paced*
　　　　To tread a measure° with you on this grass.　　　　*dance*
BOYET　They say that they have measured many a mile
　　　　To tread a measure with you on this grass.
ROSALINE　It is not so. Ask them how many inches
190 　　　　Is in one mile. If they have measured many,
　　　　The measure, then, of one is eas'ly told.°　　　　*counted*
BOYET　If to come hither you have measured miles,
　　　　And many miles, the Princess bids you tell

---

6. Presumably non-speaking musicians dressed as
black Africans to provide an exotic accompaniment
(see Introduction).

7. From here to line 230, Rosaline speaks as the
Princess.

How many inches doth fill up one mile.
195 BIRON Tell her we measure them by weary steps.
BOYET She hears herself.
ROSALINE [*to* BIRON] How many weary steps,
  Of many weary miles you have o'ergone,
  Are numbered in the travel of one mile?
BIRON We number nothing that we spend for you.
200 Our duty is so rich, so infinite,
  That we may do it still° without account.°   *always / reckoning*
  Vouchsafe to show the sunshine of your face,
  That we, like savages, may worship it.
ROSALINE My face is but a moon,⁸ and clouded° too.   *masked; dark*
205 KING Blessèd are clouds, to do as such clouds do!
  Vouchsafe, bright moon—and these thy stars°—to shine,   *companions*
  Those clouds removed, upon our watery eyne.°   *eyes*
ROSALINE O vain petitioner, beg a greater matter:
  Thou now requests but moonshine in the water.°   *nothing*
210 KING Then in our measure vouchsafe but one change.⁹
  Thou bidd'st me beg; this begging is not strange.°   *odd; foreign*
ROSALINE Play music, then! Nay, you must do it soon.
  Not yet? No dance! Thus change I like the moon.
    [*Music plays.*]
KING Will you not dance? How come you thus estranged?
215 ROSALINE You took the moon at full, but now she's changed.
KING Yet still she is the moon, and I the man.¹
  The music plays. Vouchsafe some motion° to it.   *movement; response*
ROSALINE Our ears vouchsafe it—
KING   But your legs should do it.
ROSALINE Since you are strangers, and come here by chance,
  We'll not be nice.° Take hands.   *coy*
    [*The ladies take the men by the hand.*]
220   We will not dance.
KING Why take you hands, then?
ROSALINE   Only to part friends.
  —Curtsy, sweethearts, and so the measure ends.
    [*The ladies curtsy and disengage their hands. The
    music ceases.*]
KING More measure° of this measure! Be not nice.   *A larger amount*
ROSALINE We can afford no more at such a price.
225 KING Price you yourselves. What buys your company?
ROSALINE Your absence only.
KING   That can never be.
ROSALINE Then cannot we be bought; and so, adieu—
  Twice to your visor, and half once to you.²
KING If you deny to dance, let's hold more chat.
ROSALINE In private, then.
230 KING   I am best pleased with that.
    [*They converse apart.*]
BIRON White-handed mistress, one sweet word with thee.

---

8. Because it shines with a borrowed light.
9. Of the moon; of the figure in the dance; *measure:*
dance.
1. *the man:* (in the moon). A line rhyming with

"man" seems to have dropped out.
2. Perhaps: your masked ("visor") (double) face
deserves two farewells, but yourself less than one (for
behaving so foolishly).

PRINCESS [*as* ROSALINE]   "Honey" and "milk" and "sugar":
    there is three.
BIRON   Nay, then, two treys,° an if you grow so nice:°   *threes (dice) / subtle*
    "Metheglin," "wort," and "malmsey"°—well run, dice!   *(three sweet drinks)*
    There's half-a-dozen sweets.
235 PRINCESS   Seventh sweet, adieu.
    Since you can cog,° I'll play no more with you.   *cheat (at dice)*
BIRON   One word in secret.
PRINCESS   Let it not be sweet.
BIRON   Thou griev'st my gall.°   *chafe my sore place*
PRINCESS   Gall?° Bitter.   *Liver bile*
BIRON   Therefore meet.°   *fitting; (let's meet?)*
    [*They converse apart.*]
DUMAINE   Will you vouchsafe with me to change a word?°   *exchange words*
MARIA [*as* KATHERINE]   Name it.
DUMAINE   Fair lady—
240 MARIA   Say you so? Fair lord!
    Take you that for° your "Fair lady."   *in exchange for*
DUMAINE   Please it you
    As much in private, and I'll bid adieu.
    [*They converse apart.*]
KATHERINE [*as* MARIA]   What, was your visor made without a
    tongue?³
LONGUEVILLE   I know the reason, lady, why you ask.
245 KATHERINE   Oh, for your reason! Quickly, sir, I long.
LONGUEVILLE   You have a double tongue within your mask,
    And would afford my speechless visor half.⁴
KATHERINE   "Veal!" quoth the Dutchman. Is not veal a calf?⁵
LONGUEVILLE   A calf, fair lady?
KATHERINE   No, a fair lord-calf.°   *dolt*
LONGUEVILLE   Let's part the word.°   *compromise*
250 KATHERINE   No, I'll not be your half.⁶
    Take all and wean° it: it may prove an ox.⁷   *raise*
LONGUEVILLE   Look how you butt° yourself in these sharp mocks.   *attack*
    Will you give horns,⁸ chaste lady? Do not so.
KATHERINE   Then die a calf before your horns do grow.
255 LONGUEVILLE   One word in private with you ere I die.°   *have an orgasm*
KATHERINE   Bleat softly, then: the butcher hears you cry.
    [*They converse apart.*]
BOYET [*aside*]   The tongues of mocking wenches are as keen
    As is the razor's edge—invisible,
    Cutting a smaller hair than may be seen.
260   Above the sense of sense, so sensible⁹

---

3. A projection within a mask permitting it to be held in place with the mouth. Katherine is also alluding to Longueville's silence.
4. *You . . . half:* You are double-tongued (masked; punning; deceptive; speaking enough for two) and ask about my silence because you wish to give up half your speech by giving me one of the tongues (the one that keeps her mask on; this would reveal her identity).
5. *"Veal":* Well (ironic: Dutch pronunciation of "well" or German *viel,* meaning "much"; "Dutch" could mean "German"); veil (mask). Combined with Katherine's previous word, "long" (line 245), the result is "Longueville"—thus demonstrating that she knows the identity of her disguised suitor and had anticipated his "half" (line 247) by uttering half his name. *Veau,* French for "veal," does also mean "calf" (a dunce in Renaissance English).
6. Taking "part" as "divide": half of what you are the other half of; your better half (your wife); half of "calf" ("ca," for "Katherine").
7. Dolt; castrated male.
8. Butt with horns; equip with horns; cuckold.
9. *Above . . . sense:* Above the power of the senses to apprehend (perhaps with the ironic meaning of "non-sense"); *so sensible:* so acutely felt by the hearer.

Seemeth their conference.° Their conceits° have wings   *conversation / fancies*
Fleeter than arrows, bullets, wind, thought—swifter things.
ROSALINE [*coming forward*]   Not one word more, my maids.
   Break off! Break off!
      [*The* PRINCESS, MARIA, *and* KATHERINE
      join ROSALINE.]
BIRON   By heaven, all dry-beaten with pure scoff!¹
265 KING   Farewell, mad wenches. You have simple wits!
                  Exeunt [*the* KING, LONGUEVILLE, DUMAINE,
                        and BIRON *with the Blackamoors*].
      [*The ladies unmask.*]
PRINCESS   Twenty adieus, my frozen Muscovites.
   Are these the breed of wits so wondered at?°   *admired*
BOYET   Tapers they are, with° your sweet breaths puffed out.°   *by / extinguished*
ROSALINE   Well-liking° wits they have—gross, gross, fat, fat!   *Plump*
270 PRINCESS   Oh, poverty in wit! Kingly-poor flout!²
   Will they not, think you, hang themselves tonight,
   Or ever but in visors show their faces?
   This pert Biron was out of count'nance° quite.   *disconcerted; masked*
ROSALINE   They were all in lamentable cases.°   *states; outfits*
275 The King was weeping-ripe for a good word.³
PRINCESS   Biron did swear himself out of all suit.⁴
MARIA   Dumaine was at my service, and his sword.
   "*Non point*,"° quoth I—my servant straight was mute.   *Not at all; it's blunt*
KATHERINE   Lord Longueville said I came o'er his heart,
   And trow you° what he called me?   *can you believe*
280 PRINCESS   "Qualm,"⁵ perhaps?
KATHERINE   Yes, in good faith.
PRINCESS   Go, sickness as thou art!
ROSALINE   Well, better wits have worn plain statute-caps.⁶
   But will you hear? The King is my love sworn.
PRINCESS   And quick Biron hath plighted faith to me.
285 KATHERINE   And Longueville was for my service born.
MARIA   Dumaine is mine as sure as bark on tree.
BOYET   Madam, and pretty mistresses, give ear:
   Immediately they will again be here
   In their own shapes,° for it can never be   *Undisguised*
290 They will digest° this harsh indignity.   *accept*
PRINCESS   Will they return?
BOYET   They will, they will, God knows;
   And leap for joy, though they are lame with blows.
   Therefore, change favors, and, when they repair,°   *return*
   Blow° like sweet roses in this summer air.   *Bloom*
295 PRINCESS   How "blow"? How "blow"? Speak to be understood!
BOYET   Fair ladies masked are roses in their bud;
   Dismasked—their damask sweet commixture⁷ shown—
   Are angels vailing° clouds, or roses blown.°   *letting fall / blooming*

---

1. Soundly beaten without bloodshed; battered by mocking words.
2. Reversed wordplay ("kingly-poor") on "well-li-king" (or like-king," line 269), possibly criticizing Rosaline's "flout" (gibe) but probably the King's (line 265).
3. The beginning of a sixteen-line dialogue sonnet. *weeping-ripe for*: near tears for lack of.
4. Avowed his passion—beyond all reason; out of character for his Russian "suit" (costume); in a mis-

taken "suit" at love (to the wrong woman).
5. Heartburn: perhaps punning on "came" (line 279) and picked up in "Go" (line 281).
6. Cleverer people have been ordinary apprentices (whose headwear was regulated by statute); perhaps an allusion to fancy caps forming part of the lords' disguise.
7. Sweet red and white complexion.

PRINCESS   Avaunt, perplexity!° What shall we do   *Be off, riddler!*
300   If they return in their own shapes to woo?
ROSALINE   Good madam, if by me you'll be advised,
    Let's mock them still, as well known[8] as disguised.
    Let us complain to them what fools were here,
    Disguised like Muscovites in shapeless gear,°   *ill-cut clothes*
305   And wonder what they were, and to what end
    Their shallow shows, and prologue vilely penned,
    And their rough carriage° so ridiculous   *awkward manner*
    Should be presented at our tent to us.
BOYET   Ladies, withdraw: the gallants are at hand.
310   PRINCESS   Whip to our tents, as roes° run o'er land.   *deer*

>   *Exeunt [the* PRINCESS, ROSALINE,
>   MARIA, *and* KATHERINE].
>   *Enter the* KING *and the rest [*LONGUEVILLE, DUMAINE,
>   *and* BIRON, *as themselves*].

KING   Fair sir, God save you! Where's the Princess?
BOYET   Gone to her tent. Please it your majesty,
    Command me any service to her?
KING   That she vouchsafe me audience for one word.
315   BOYET   I will, and so will she, I know, my lord.   *Exit.*
BIRON   This fellow picks up wit as pigeons peas,
    And utters° it again when Jove doth please.   *speaks; sells*
    He is wit's peddler, and retails his wares
    At wakes and wassails,° meetings, markets, fairs;   *festivals and revels*
320   And we that sell by gross,° the Lord doth know,   *wholesale*
    Have not the grace to grace it with such show.
    This gallant pins the wenches on his sleeve;°   *attracts all the girls*
    Had he been Adam, he had° tempted Eve!   *would have*
    He can carve,[9] too, and lisp.° Why, this is he   *speak affectedly*
325   That kissed away his hand in courtesy.
    This is the ape of form,° Monsieur the Nice,°   *good form / fastidious*
    That when he plays at tables° chides the dice   *backgammon*
    In honorable° terms. Nay, he can sing   *polite*
    A mean most meanly,[1] and in ushering°   *as a gentleman usher*
330   Mend° him who can. The ladies call him "Sweet";   *Improve on*
    The stairs as he treads on them kiss his feet.
    This is the flower that smiles on everyone
    To show his teeth as white as whale's bone,°   *walrus ivory*
    And consciences that will not die in debt
335   Pay him the duty of "Honey-tongued Boyet."
KING   A blister on his sweet tongue, with my heart,
    That put Armado's page out of his part!

>   *Enter [*BOYET *with] the ladies [*MARIA, KATHERINE,
>   *and* ROSALINE, *and the* PRINCESS].

BIRON   See where it° comes! Behavior,° what wert thou   *(Boyet) / Fine manners*
    Till this madman° showed thee, and what art thou now?   *madcap*
340   KING   All hail, sweet madam, and fair time of day!
PRINCESS   "Fair" in "All hail"° is foul, as I conceive.   *(as in "hailstorm")*
KING   Construe my speeches better, if you may.
PRINCESS   Then wish me better—I will give you leave.

---

8. Let's mock them just as much now that they are known for themselves.
9. He can act with social grace, flirt.

1. *he . . . meanly:* he can sing an in-between vocal part (tenor or alto) in the appropriate way (make himself generally useful).

KING　We came to visit you, and purpose now[2]
345　　To lead you to our court. Vouchsafe it, then.
PRINCESS　This field shall hold me, and so hold your vow.
　　Nor° God nor I delights in perjured men.　　　　　　　　　　*Neither*
KING　Rebuke me not for that which you provoke:
　　The virtue° of your eye must break my oath.　　　　　　　　*power*
350　PRINCESS　You nickname virtue;° "vice" you should have spoke,　*misname goodness*
　　For virtue's office° never breaks men's troth.　　　　　　　　*action*
　　Now, by my maiden honor—yet as pure
　　As the unsullied lily—I protest,
　　A world of torments though I should endure,
355　　I would not yield to be your house's guest.
　　So much I hate a breaking cause° to be　　　　　　　　　*cause of breaking*
　　Of heavenly oaths, vowed with integrity.
KING　Oh, you have lived in desolation here,
　　Unseen, unvisited, much to our shame.
360　PRINCESS　Not so, my lord; it is not so, I swear.
　　We have had pastimes here, and pleasant game.
　　A mess of° Russians left us but of late.　　　　　　　　　　*group of four*
KING　How, madam? Russians?
PRINCESS　　　　　　　　　　Ay, in truth, my lord:
　　Trim° gallants, full of courtship and of state.°　　　　*Elegant / dignity*
365　ROSALINE　Madam, speak true! —It is not so, my lord.
　　My lady, to the manner of the days,°　　　　　　　*in the present fashion*
　　In courtesy gives undeserving praise.
　　We four, indeed, confronted were with four
　　In Russian habit. Here they stayed an hour
370　　And talked apace; and in that hour, my lord,
　　They did not bless us with one happy° word!　　　　　　　*well-chosen*
　　I dare not call them fools, but this I think:
　　When they are thirsty, fools would fain have drink.°　　*They are fools*
BIRON [*aside*]　This jest is dry° to me. —Gentle sweet,　*barren (punning)*
375　　Your wits makes wise things foolish. When we greet,
　　With eyes' best seeing, heaven's fiery eye,
　　By light we lose light.[3] Your capacity
　　Is of that nature, that, to° your huge store,　　　　　　　*compared to*
　　Wise things seem foolish and rich things but poor.
380　ROSALINE　This proves you wise and rich, for in my eye—
BIRON　I am a fool and full of poverty.
ROSALINE　But that you take what doth to you belong,
　　It were a fault to snatch words from my tongue.
BIRON　Oh, I am yours, and all that I possess.
ROSALINE　All the fool mine?
385　BIRON　　　　　　　　　I cannot give you less.
ROSALINE　Which of the visors was it that you wore?
BIRON　Where? When? What visor? Why demand° you this?　　　　*ask*
ROSALINE　There, then, that visor: that superfluous case°　　　　*mask*
　　That hid the worse and showed the better face.
390　KING [*aside*]　We are descried!° They'll mock us now downright.　*uncovered*
DUMAINE [*aside*]　Let us confess and turn it to a jest.
PRINCESS　Amazed, my lord? Why looks your highness sad?

---

2. The beginning of another dialogue sonnet (lines　3. When we gaze intently at the sun, we go blind.
344–57).

ROSALINE Help! Hold his° brows! He'll swoon. Why look you   *(Biron's)*
    pale?
    Seasick, I think, coming from Muscovy!

395 BIRON Thus pour the stars down plagues for perjury.
    Can any face of brass° hold longer out?   *brazen shamelessness*
    Here stand I, lady. Dart thy skill at me;
    Bruise me with scorn; confound me with a flout;°   *put-down*
    Thrust thy sharp wit quite through my ignorance;
400   Cut me to pieces with thy keen conceit;°   *intelligence*
    And I will wish° thee never more to dance,   *invite*
    Nor never more in Russian habit wait.°   *attend on you*
    Oh, never will I trust to speeches penned,[4]
    Nor to the motion of a schoolboy's tongue,
405   Nor never come in visor to my friend,°   *sweetheart*
    Nor woo in rhyme, like a blind harper's song.
    Taffeta phrases, silken terms precise,
    Three-piled° hyperboles, spruce affectation,   *Rich velvet; elaborate*
    Figures° pedantical—these summer flies   *(of speech)*
410   Have blown me full of maggot ostentation.°   *laid maggot eggs in me*
    I do forswear them, and I here protest
    By this white glove—how white the hand, God knows!—
    Henceforth my wooing mind shall be expressed
    In russet° "yeas" and honest kersey° "noes."   *homely / plain*
415   And to begin: wench, so God help me, law!°   *indeed (humble oath)*
    My love to thee is sound, *sans*° crack or flaw.   *without*
ROSALINE *Sans "sans,"* I pray you!
BIRON   Yet° I have a trick°   *Still / touch*
    Of the old rage.° Bear with me: I am sick.   *fever*
    I'll leave it by degrees. Soft, let us see:
420   Write "Lord, have mercy on us"[5] on those three.°   *(his companions)*
    They are infected; in their hearts it lies.
    They have the plague and caught it of your eyes.
    These lords are visited;° you are not free,   *afflicted by plague*
    For the lords' tokens° on you do I see.   *favors; plague spots*
425 PRINCESS No, they are free[6] that gave these tokens to us.
BIRON Our states are forfeit.[7] Seek not to undo us![8]
ROSALINE It is not so; for how can this be true
    That you stand forfeit, being those that sue?°   *sue at law; beg; woo*
BIRON Peace! For I will not have to do° with you.   *deal; copulate*
430 ROSALINE Nor shall not, if I do as I intend.
BIRON [*to the* KING, DUMAINE, *and* LONGUEVILLE] Speak for
    yourselves. My wit is at an end.
KING Teach us, sweet madam, for our rude transgression
    Some fair excuse.
PRINCESS   The fairest is confession.
    Were you not here, but even now, disguised?
KING Madam, I was.
435 PRINCESS   And were you well advised?°   *in your right mind*

4. The beginning of a sonnet (lines 403–16)—ironic, considering Biron's renunciation of literary effects.
5. A common inscription on the doors of plague-visited houses.
6. Generous; at liberty; free of love; free of obligation.
7. (Denying the Princess's claim in line 425 that the men are "free"): Our estates are subject to confisca-tion; our condition as bachelors is ended; because we're in love, we've lost power over ourselves; as would-be husbands, we owe you our estates; we've acted dishonorably.
8. Don't undo our forfeiture (don't ruin us) by calling us "free" (by rejecting our love).

KING I was, fair madam.

PRINCESS   When you then were here,
 What did you whisper in your lady's ear?

KING That more than all the world I did respect° her.   *value*

PRINCESS When she shall challenge° this you will reject her.   *assert her claim to*

KING Upon mine honor, no.

440 PRINCESS   Peace, peace! Forbear!
 Your oath once broke, you force not° to forswear.   *find it easy*

KING Despise me when I break this oath of mine!

PRINCESS I will, and therefore keep it. —Rosaline,
 What did the Russian whisper in your ear?

445 ROSALINE Madam, he swore that he did hold me dear
 As precious eyesight, and did value me
 Above this world, adding thereto, moreover,
 That he would wed me or else die my lover.

PRINCESS God give thee joy of him! The noble lord

450 Most honorably doth uphold his word.
       [*She joins their hands together.*]

KING What mean you, madam? By my life, my troth,
 I never swore this lady such an oath.

ROSALINE By heaven, you did; and to confirm it plain,
 You gave me this [*indicating a love token*], but take it, sir,
  again.

455 KING My faith, and this, the Princess I did give.
 I knew her by this jewel on her sleeve.

PRINCESS Pardon me, sir, this jewel did she wear;
 And lord Biron, I thank him, is my dear.
       [*to* BIRON] What, will you have me or your pearl again?

460 BIRON Neither of either;° I remit° both twain.   *the two / surrender*
 I see the trick on't.° Here was a consent,°   *of it / plot*
 Knowing aforehand of our merriment,
 To dash it like a Christmas comedy.
 Some carry-tale, some please-man, some slight zany,

465 Some mumble-news, some trencher-knight, some Dick,[9]
 That smiles his cheek in years° and knows the trick   *into wrinkles*
 To make my lady laugh when she's disposed,
 Told our intents before, which, once disclosed,
 The ladies did change favors, and then we,

470 Following the signs, wooed but the sign of she.°   *each mistress*
 Now to our perjury to add more terror,
 We are again forsworn in will° and error!°   *willfully / mistakenly*
 Much upon this 'tis.[1] [*He seizes* BOYET.] And might not you
 Forestall° our sport, to make us thus untrue?   *Have undermined*

475 Do not you know my lady's foot by th' square,[2]
 And laugh upon the apple[3] of her eye,
 And stand between her back, sir, and the fire,°   *keep the heat from her*
 Holding a trencher,° jesting merrily?   *serving plate*
 You put our page out—

---

9. *carry-tale*: talebearer; *please-man*: toady; *zany*: clownish, rustic servant in commedia dell'arte; *mumble-news*: gossip; *trencher-knight*: parasite, who dines from his lord's dish ("trencher") or who has a lordly appetite; *Dick*: low fellow.
1. It happened very much like this.

2. Know how to please your mistress. *square*: a carpenter's rule (Boyet "has her measure"); possible pun on "squire" (an "apple-squire" was a pimp; see "apple," line 476 and note).
3. Pupil. Boyet can wittily catch the Princess's eye; he is on intimate terms with her.

[*At a sign from the* PRINCESS, *he releases* BOYET.]
           Go, you are allowed.°   *privileged (as a fool)*

480   Die when you will, a smock[4] shall be your shroud.
     You leer upon° me, do you? There's an eye   *look malevolently at*
     Wounds like a leaden sword.°   *harmless stage sword*
BOYET   Full merrily
     Hath this brave manège, this career, been run.
BIRON   Lo, he is tilting straight.[5] Peace! I have done.
     Enter [COSTARD, *the*] *clown.*
485   Welcome, Pure Wit. Thou part'st a fair fray.
COSTARD   O Lord, sir, they would know
     Whether the three Worthies shall come in, or no?
BIRON   What, are there but three?
COSTARD   No, sir, but it is vara° fine,   *very*
     For every one pursents° three.   *(re)presents*
BIRON   And three times thrice is nine.
490 COSTARD   Not so, sir—under° correction, sir, I hope it is not so.   *subject to*
     You cannot beg us,° sir. I can assure you, sir, we know what   *show we're fools*
       we know.
     I hope, sir, three times thrice, sir—
BIRON   Is not nine?
COSTARD   Under correction, sir, we know whereuntil° it doth   *to what*
     amount.
495 BIRON   By Jove, I always took three threes for nine.
COSTARD   O Lord, sir, it were pity you should get your living
     by reckoning,[6] sir.
BIRON   How much is it?
COSTARD   O Lord, sir, the parties themselves—the actors,
500   sir—will show whereuntil it doth amount. For mine own
     part, I am, as they say, but to perfect° one man in one poor   *present*
     man: Pompion[7] the Great, sir.
BIRON   Art thou one of the Worthies?
COSTARD   It pleased them to think me worthy of Pompey the
505   Great. For mine own part, I know not the degree° of the   *rank*
     Worthy, but I am to stand for him.
BIRON   Go! Bid them prepare.
COSTARD   We will turn it finely off,° sir. We will take some care.   *perform it*
                      Exit.
KING   Biron, they will shame us. Let them not approach.
510 BIRON   We are shame-proof, my lord; and 'tis some policy°   *clever strategy*
     To have one show worse than the King's and his company.
KING   I say they shall not come.
PRINCESS   Nay, my good lord, let me o'errule you now:
     That sport best pleases that doth least know how.
515   Where zeal strives to content, and the contents
     Dies in the zeal of that which it presents,[8]
     Their form confounded makes most form in mirth,[9]
     When great things laboring° perish in their birth.   *(to be born)*

---

4. Woman's garment (either a charge of effeminacy or equivalent to "women will be the death of you").
5. Jousting (linguistically) at once; *manège* (line 483): feat of horsemanship; *career:* short gallop at full speed.
6. It would be a shame if you had to earn your living by arithmetic.
7. Pumpkin (blunder for "Pompey").
8. *and . . . presents:* and the enthusiasm of those who present the play is fatal to the substance.
9. Artistry defeated produces the greatest comic effect.

BIRON   A right description of our sport,° my lord.   *(the Russian masque)*
     Enter [ARMADO, *the*] *braggart*[, *with a paper*].
520 ARMADO [*to the* KING]   Anointed,° I implore so much expense   *Anointed one*
     of thy royal sweet breath as will utter a brace° of words.   *pair*
          [ARMADO *and the* KING *talk apart*.]
     PRINCESS   Doth this man serve God?
     BIRON   Why ask you?
     PRINCESS   He speaks not like a man of God's making.
525 ARMADO [*to the* KING]   That's all one, my fair, sweet, honey
     monarch; for, I protest, the schoolmaster is exceeding
     fantastical—too, too vain, too, too vain. But we will put it, as
     they say, to *fortuna de la guerre*.° [*He gives him a paper*.] I wish   *the fortune of war*
     you the peace of mind, most royal couplement.   [*Exit*.]
530 KING [*reading*]   Here is like to be a good presence of Worthies.
     He presents Hector of Troy; the swain, Pompey the Great;
     the parish curate, Alexander; Armado's page, Hercules; the
     pedant, Judas Maccabeus.
          An if these four Worthies in their first show thrive,
535 These four will change habits° and present the other five!   *costumes*
     BIRON   There is five in the first show.
     KING   You are deceived; 'tis not so.
     BIRON   The pedant, the braggart, the hedge-priest,° the fool,   *illiterate priest*
     and the boy.
540 Abate throw at novum¹ and the whole world again
     Cannot prick out five such, take each one in 's vein.°   *characteristic manner*
     KING   The ship is under sail and here she comes amain.°   *at full speed*
          Enter [COSTARD *as*] *Pompey*.
     COSTARD   "I Pompey am—"
     BIRON   You lie: you are not he.
     COSTARD   "I Pompey am—"
     BOYET   With leopard's head on knee.²
545 BIRON   Well said, old mocker! I must needs be friends with
          thee.
     COSTARD   "I Pompey am, Pompey surnamed 'the Big'°—"   *(sexual)*
     DUMAINE   "The Great."
     COSTARD [*to* DUMAINE]   It is "Great," sir.
          "—Pompey surnamed 'the Great,'
550 That oft in field, with targe and shield, did make my foe to
          sweat;³
     And traveling along this coast, I here am come by chance,
     And lay my arms before the legs° of this sweet lass of France."   *(bawdy)*
          [*He sets down his sword and shield*.]
          [*to the* PRINCESS]   If your ladyship would say, "Thanks,
     Pompey," I had done.
555 PRINCESS   Great thanks, great Pompey.
     COSTARD   'Tis not so much worth, but I hope I was perfect.° I   *I recited correctly*
     made a little fault in "Great."
     BIRON   My hat to a halfpenny,° Pompey proves the best Worthy!   *I'll bet anything*
          [COSTARD *stands aside*.]
          Enter [NATHANIEL, *the*] *curate, for Alexander*.

---

1. Barring a lucky chance in the dice game of novum
(in which the main throws were five and nine—like
the five actors playing the Nine Worthies).
2. Embossed either on the knee piece of his armor or
on his shield, which he might then be holding upside
down; or Biron's "You lie" (line 543) may indicate that

Costard has fallen down.
3. The first of three lines in fourteeners (fourteen-
syllable lines)—an archaic meter by the 1590s, like
most of those used by the non-aristocratic characters.
targe: shield.

NATHANIEL   "When in the world I lived, I was the world's
        commander.
560   By east, west, north, and south, I spread my conquering
        might.
     My scutcheon° plain° declares that I am Alisander."   *coat of arms / clearly*
BOYET   Your nose says no, you are not, for it stands too right.⁴
BIRON [*to* BOYET]   Your nose smells "no"⁵ in this, most tender-
        smelling° knight.   *sensitive-to-smell*
PRINCESS   The conqueror is dismayed. Proceed, good Alexander.
565   NATHANIEL   "When in the world I lived, I was the world's
        commander—"
BOYET   Most true, 'tis right. You were so, Alisander.
BIRON   Pompey the Great!
COSTARD [*comes forward*]   Your servant—and Costard!
BIRON   Take away the conqueror! Take away Alisander!
570   COSTARD   O sir, you have overthrown Alisander the Con-
        queror. [*to* NATHANIEL] You will be scraped out of the painted
        cloth⁶ for this. Your lion, that holds his pole-axe, sitting on a
        close stool, will be given to Ajax.⁷ He will be the ninth Wor-
        thy. A conqueror and afraid to speak? Run away, for shame,
575   Alisander!   [*Exit* NATHANIEL.]
     There, an't° shall please you: a foolish mild man—an honest   *if it*
        man, look you, and soon dashed. He is a marvelous good
        neighbor, in sooth, and a very good bowler, but for Alisander?
     Alas, you see how 'tis: a little o'er-parted.° But there are Wor-   *given too hard a role*
580   thies a-coming will speak their mind in some other sort.
PRINCESS   Stand aside, good Pompey.
            [COSTARD *withdraws.*]
            Enter [HOLOFERNES, *the*] *pedant, for Judas, and*
            [PAGE,] *the boy, for Hercules.*
HOLOFERNES   "Great Hercules is presented by this imp,°   *child*
     Whose club killed Cerberus, that three-headed *canus*;⁸
     And when he was a babe, a child, a shrimp,
585   Thus did he strangle serpents in his *manus*.⁹
     Quoniam,° he seemeth in minority,°   *Since / a child*
     Ergo,° I come with this Apology."   *Therefore*
     [*to* PAGE] Keep some state° in thy exit and vanish.   *dignity*
                          Exit [PAGE, *the*] *boy.*
     "Judas I am—"
590   DUMAINE   A Judas?
HOLOFERNES [*to* DUMAINE]   Not Iscariot, sir.
     "Judas I am, ycleped° 'Maccabeus'—"   *named*
DUMAINE   "Judas Maccabeus" clipped° is plain "Judas."   *shortened; circumcised*
BIRON   A kissing traitor!¹ How° art thou proud, Judas?   *Why*
595   HOLOFERNES   "Judas I am—"
DUMAINE   The more shame for you, Judas!

---

4. Straight (alluding to Alexander's reputed crooked
neck).
5. Implying that Nathaniel smells bad; according to
the Greek biographer Plutarch, Alexander was
reputed to have "a marvelous good savor" (Thomas
North's translation).
6. Referring to the practice of representing the Worthies on wall hangings.
7. Alexander's arms, which showed a lion holding a
battle-ax (or penis) and seated (a "close-stool" is a
toilet), will be given to another warrior, Ajax (punning

on "a jakes," a toilet), a Greek hero from the Trojan
War who coveted the armor of Achilles. See 4.3.6 and
note.
8. In classical mythology, the three-headed watchdog ("canis") of Hades.
9. Hands; pronounced "máy-ness," hence punning on
"anus."
1. Alluding to the kiss with which Judas Iscariot
betrayed Jesus, with a pun on "clipped" (embraced,
kissed), itself punning on "ycleped" (lines 592–93).

HOLOFERNES What mean you, sir?

BOYET To make Judas hang himself.

HOLOFERNES Begin,° sir; you are my elder.   *Hang yourself first*

600 BIRON Well followed: Judas was hanged on an elder.°   *(tree)*

HOLOFERNES I will not be put out of countenance.°   *be upset*

BIRON Because thou hast no face.°   *countenance*

HOLOFERNES What is this?[2]

BOYET A cittern head.°   *guitar*

605 DUMAINE The head of a bodkin.°   *hairpin; small dagger*

BIRON A death's-face° in a ring.   *death's head*

LONGUEVILLE The face of an old Roman coin, scarce seen.°   *worn down*

BOYET The pommel° of Caesar's falchion.°   *handle / sword*

DUMAINE The carved-bone face on a flask.°   *gunpowder horn*

610 BIRON Saint George's half-cheek° in a brooch.   *profile*

DUMAINE Ay, and in a brooch of lead.°   *(indicating low rank)*

BIRON Ay, and worn in the cap of a tooth-drawer.[3] [*to* HOLOFERNES] And now forward, for we have put thee in countenance.°   *depicted you*

615 HOLOFERNES You have put me out of countenance.

BIRON False! We have given thee faces.

HOLOFERNES But you have outfaced° them all.   *mocked*

BIRON An thou wert a lion, we would do so.

BOYET Therefore, as he is an ass,[4] let him go.

620 And so, adieu, sweet Jude. Nay, why dost thou stay?

DUMAINE For the latter end of his name.

BIRON For the "ass" to the "Jude"? Give it him: Jud-as, away![5]

HOLOFERNES This is not generous,° not gentle,° not humble.[6]   *noble / courteous*

[*Exit.*]

BOYET [*calling after him*] A light for Monsieur Judas! It grows dark; he may stumble.

625 PRINCESS Alas, poor Maccabeus! How hath he been baited!

Enter [ARMADO, *the*] *braggart*[, *as Hector*].

BIRON Hide thy head, Achilles![7] Here comes Hector in arms.

DUMAINE Though my mocks come home by° me, I will now be merry.   *later rebound on*

KING Hector was but a Trojan[8] in respect of° this.   *in comparison with*

BOYET But is this Hector?

630 KING I think Hector was not so clean-timbered.°   *well built*

LONGUEVILLE His leg is too big for Hector.

DUMAINE More calf,° certain.   *part of the leg; fool*

BOYET No, he is best endued° in the small.°   *endowed / (below the calf)*

BIRON This cannot be Hector.

635 DUMAINE He's a god or a painter, for he makes faces.°   *grimaces; creates life*

ARMADO "The armipotent° Mars, of lances the almighty, Gave Hector a gift—"   *powerful in arms*

DUMAINE A gilt nutmeg.[9]

---

2. Indicating his face. The replies refer to ornamental faces on objects.

3. Worn by a lowly dentist as a sign of his trade.

4. An ass disguises himself as a lion in one of Aesop's fables—only to have his own nature undo him. "Ass" in the sense of "backside" is punningly evoked by "end" (line 621).

5. *As*, in "Jud-as," is "the latter end of his name" (line 621), but "end" also means "ass."

6. PERFORMANCE COMMENT For more on this line, see Digital Edition PC 1.

7. Leading Greek hero in the Trojan War; Hector's chief opponent and slayer in Homer, but his inferior and a coward in *Troilus and Cressida*.

8. An ordinary guy (slang).

9. A nutmeg glazed with egg yolk, used, like "lemon" and "cloves" (lines 639, 640), to flavor drinks. A common lover's gift, the "gilt nutmeg" may also allude to Armado's makeup. "Lemon" perhaps puns on "leman" (lover, sweetheart), in which case "cloven" (line 641) would have a sexual innuendo.

BIRON   A lemon.
640   LONGUEVILLE   Stuck with cloves.
DUMAINE   No, cloven.
ARMADO   "The armipotent Mars, of lances the almighty,
Gave Hector a gift, the heir of Ilion;°   *Troy*
A man so breathed,° that certain he would fight—yea,   *fit*
645   From morn till night, out of his pavilion.°   *jousting tent*
I am that flower—"
DUMAINE   That mint.
LONGUEVILLE   That columbine.
ARMADO   Sweet Lord Longueville, rein thy tongue!
LONGUEVILLE   I must rather give it the rein, for it runs° against   *jousts; races; speaks*
Hector.
650   DUMAINE   Ay, and Hector's a greyhound.[1]
ARMADO   The sweet war-man is dead and rotten. Sweet chucks,
beat not the bones of the buried! When he breathed he was a
man—but I will forward with my device.° [*to the* PRINCESS]   *performance*
Sweet royalty, bestow on me the sense of hearing.
        BIRON *steps forth*[, *but the* PRINCESS *ignores him*].
655   PRINCESS   Speak, brave Hector. We are much delighted.
ARMADO [*bowing*]   I do adore thy sweet grace's slipper.
BOYET   Loves her by the foot.
DUMAINE   He may not by the yard.°   *penis (slang)*
ARMADO   "This Hector far surmounted Hannibal.[2]
660   The party is gone°—"   *Hector is dead*
COSTARD [*coming forward*]   Fellow Hector, she is gone! She
is two months on her way.[3]
ARMADO   What meanest thou?
COSTARD   Faith, unless you play the honest Trojan, the poor
665   wench is cast away. She's quick!° The child brags in her belly   *pregnant*
already: 'tis yours.°   *(because it brags)*
ARMADO   Dost thou infamonize° me among potentates? Thou   *defame (a coinage)*
shalt die.
COSTARD   Then° shall Hector be whipped for Jaquenetta that   *In that case*
670   is quick by him, and hanged for Pompey that is dead by him.[4]
DUMAINE   Most rare Pompey!
BOYET   Renowned Pompey!
BIRON   Greater than great, great, great, great Pompey! Pom-
pey the Huge!°   *(bawdy)*
675   DUMAINE   Hector trembles.
BIRON   Pompey is moved. More, Ates,° more, Ates! Stir them   *goddess of discord*
on! Stir them on!
DUMAINE   Hector will challenge him.
BIRON   Ay, if 'a° have no more man's blood in 's belly than will   *he*
680   sup° a flea.   *feed*
ARMADO   By the North Pole, I do challenge thee.
COSTARD   I will not fight with a pole, like a northern° man. I'll   *an uncivilized (Scot)*
slash; I'll do it by the sword. I pray you, let me borrow my
arms° again.   *(from the Princess)*

1. Famous as a runner; "Hector" was a common name for a greyhound.
2. Surpassed Hannibal, leader of Carthage against Rome (with the unintentional homosexual innuendo of "surmounted").
3. Jaquenetta is two months pregnant. Since at most only a few days seem to have passed in the aristocratic plot, it is possible to infer that Costard is the actual father; but this may be an example of Shakespearean double time.
4. Whom Armado has killed; whose hopes of Jaquenetta Armado has killed.

685 DUMAINE   Room for the incensed Worthies!

COSTARD   I'll do it in my shirt.

DUMAINE   Most resolute Pompey!

PAGE [*to* ARMADO]   Master, let me take you a buttonhole
lower.[5] Do you not see? Pompey is uncasing° for the combat.   *undressing*
690 [ARMADO *backs away*.] What mean you? You will lose your
reputation.

ARMADO   Gentlemen and soldiers, pardon me. I will not combat in my shirt.

DUMAINE   You may not deny it. Pompey hath made the
695 challenge.

ARMADO   Sweet bloods,° I both may and will.   *men of fiery spirit*

BIRON   What reason have you for't?

ARMADO   The naked truth of it is, I have no shirt. I go wool-
ward for penance.[6]

700 PAGE   True, and it was enjoined him in Rome° for want of linen.   *center of Catholicism*
Since when, I'll be sworn, he wore none but a dishclout° of   *dishcloth*
Jaquenetta's, and that he wears next his heart for a favor.

            Enter a messenger, Monsieur MARCADÉ.[7]

MARCADÉ   God save you, madam.

PRINCESS   Welcome, Marcadé—
But that thou interruptest our merriment.

705 MARCADÉ   I am sorry, madam, for the news I bring
Is heavy in my tongue. The King your father—

PRINCESS   Dead, for° my life!   *upon*

MARCADÉ   Even so. My tale is told.

BIRON   Worthies, away! The scene begins to cloud.

ARMADO   For mine own part, I breathe free breath. I have
710 seen the day of wrong through the little hole of discretion,
and I will right myself like a soldier.[8]

            Exeunt Worthies [ARMADO, COSTARD, *and the* PAGE].

KING   How fares your majesty?°   *(her new title)*

QUEEN   Boyet, prepare! I will away tonight.

KING   Madam, not so. I do beseech you: stay.

715 QUEEN   Prepare, I say! —I thank you, gracious lords,
For all your fair endeavors, and entreat,
Out of a new-sad soul, that you vouchsafe
In your rich wisdom to excuse or hide°   *overlook*
The liberal° opposition of our spirits.   *unrestrained*
720 If over-boldly we have borne ourselves
In the converse of breath,° your gentleness°   *conversation / courtesy*
Was guilty of it.° [*to the* KING] Farewell, worthy lord.   *Gave us license*
A heavy heart bears not a humble tongue.
Excuse me so, coming so short of thanks
725 For my great suit, so easily obtained.[9]

KING   The extreme parts of time extremely forms
All causes to the purpose of his speed,[1]
And often at his very loose° decides   *the last moment*

5. Help you to take off your doublet; take you down a
peg or two (both proverbial).
6. He has no linen between his wool outer garments
and his skin—a form of Catholic self-punishment.
7. Associated with the *danse macabre*, the dance of
death; possibly Mercury, the classical messenger of
the gods and guide of souls to the underworld; perhaps also Mar-Arcadia, a reminder that death enters

even the pastoral, Arcadian world of Navarre's park.
8. I have enough sense to acknowledge my wrongdoing and will honorably put myself in the right.
9. Even though there is no mention of the suit after
2.1, we must assume that it was settled.
1. *The extreme . . . speed*: Final moments enforce
rapid decisions.

That which long process could not arbitrate;
730 And though the mourning brow of progeny
Forbid the smiling courtesy of love
The holy suit° which fain it would convince,°   *marriage / give proof of*
Yet since love's argument was first° on foot,   *already*
Let not the cloud of sorrow jostle it
735 From what it purposed, since to wail friends lost
Is not by much so wholesome-profitable
As to rejoice at friends but newly found.
QUEEN I understand you not; my griefs are double.[2]
BIRON Honest plain words best pierce the ears of grief,
740 And by these badges° understand the King.   *signs; words*
For your fair sakes have we neglected time,
Played foul-play with our oaths. Your beauty, ladies,
Hath much deformed us, fashioning our humors
Even to the opposèd end of our intents;[3]
745 And what in us hath seemed ridiculous—
As love is full of unbefitting strains,°   *impulses*
All wanton° as a child, skipping and vain,   *careless*
Formed by the eye, and therefore, like the eye,
Full of straying shapes, of habits, and of forms,
750 Varying in subjects as the eye doth roll
To every varied object in his glance—
Which parti-coated° presence of loose° love   *foolish / unrestrained*
Put on by us, if in your heavenly eyes
Have misbecomed° our oaths and gravities,   *been unbecoming to*
755 Those heavenly eyes that look into these faults
Suggested° us to make. Therefore, ladies,   *Tempted*
Our love being yours, the error that love makes
Is likewise yours. We to ourselves prove false
By being once false, forever to be true
760 To those that make us both—fair ladies, you;
And even that falsehood, in itself a sin,
Thus purifies itself and turns to grace.
QUEEN We have received your letters full of love,
Your favors, the ambassadors of love,
765 And in our maiden counsel rated them
At° courtship, pleasant jest, and courtesy,   *As*
As bombast[4] and as lining to the time;
But more devout° than this in our respects°   *serious / consideration*
Have we not been, and therefore met your loves
770 In their own fashion, like a merriment.
DUMAINE Our letters, madam, showed much more than jest.
LONGUEVILLE So did our looks.
ROSALINE   We did not quote° them so.   *interpret*
KING Now, at the latest minute of the hour,
Grant us your loves.
QUEEN   A time, methinks, too short
775 To make a world-without-end° bargain in.   *an everlasting (biblical)*
No, no, my lord, your grace is perjured much,
Full of dear° guiltiness, and therefore this: *grievous; precious*
If for my love—as there is no such cause[5]—

---

2. Doubled because I cannot understand you.
3. *fashioning . . . intents:* distorting our behavior into the opposite of what we intended.
4. Wool stuffing for clothes; inflated rhetoric.
5. No reason why you should feel obliged to do so.

You will do aught,° this shall you do for me: *anything*
780   Your oath I will not trust, but go with speed
To some forlorn and naked hermitage,
Remote from all the pleasures of the world.
There stay until the twelve celestial signs°   *(of the zodiac)*
Have brought about their annual reckoning.
785   If this austere insociable life
Change not your offer, made in heat of blood—
If frosts and fasts, hard lodging and thin weeds°   *clothes*
Nip not the gaudy blossoms of your love,
But that it bear this trial and last° love—   *remain*
790   Then, at the expiration of the year,
Come challenge° me, challenge me by these deserts;   *claim*
        [*She takes his hand.*]
And by this virgin palm, now kissing thine,
I will be thine; and till that instant shut
My woeful self up in a mourning-house,
795   Raining the tears of lamentation
For the remembrance of my father's death.
If this thou do deny, let our hands part;
Neither entitled in the other's heart.
KING   If this, or more than this, I would deny,
800   To flatter up° these powers of mine with rest,   *So as to pamper*
The sudden hand of death close up mine eye.
Hence hermit,° then! My heart is in thy breast.   *I'm off to be a hermit*
        [*They converse apart.*]
BIRON   And what to me, my love, and what to me?
ROSALINE   You must be purged too. Your sins are racked;
805   You are attaint° with faults and perjury.   *dishonored; infected*
Therefore, if you my favor mean to get,
A twelvemonth shall you spend and never rest,
But seek the weary beds of people sick.
DUMAINE   But what to me, my love, but what to me?
810   KATHERINE   A wife? A beard,[6] fair health, and honesty,
With threefold love: I wish you all these three.
DUMAINE   Oh, shall I say, "I thank you, gentle wife"?
KATHERINE   Not so, my lord. A twelvemonth and a day
I'll mark no words that smooth-faced wooers say.
815   Come when the King doth to my lady come.
Then if I have much love, I'll give you some.
DUMAINE   I'll serve thee true and faithfully till then.
KATHERINE   Yet swear not, lest ye be forsworn again.
LONGUEVILLE   What says Maria?
MARIA   At the twelvemonth's end,
820   I'll change my black gown for a faithful friend.°   *lover*
LONGUEVILLE   I'll stay° with patience, but the time is long.   *wait*
MARIA   The liker you: few taller are so young.[7]
BIRON   Studies my lady?° Mistress, look on me.   *Are you preoccupied*
Behold the window of my heart, mine eye.
825   What humble suit attends° thy answer there?   *waits for*
Impose some service on me for thy love.
ROSALINE   Oft have I heard of you, my lord Biron,

---

6. Implying that he looks immature; perhaps also   7. The more like you—although tall ("long"), you are
that as a hermit he'll grow a beard.   still young.

Before I saw you, and the world's large tongue
Proclaims you for a man replete with mocks,
830   Full of comparisons° and wounding flouts,   *satirical similes*
Which you on all estates° will execute   *classes of people*
That lie within the mercy of your wit.
To weed this wormwood° from your fruitful brain,   *bitterness*
And therewithal to win me, if you please—
835   Without the which I am not to be won—
You shall this twelvemonth term, from day to day,
Visit the speechless sick and still converse°   *always associate*
With groaning wretches; and your task shall be,
With all the fierce° endeavor of your wit,   *forceful*
840   To enforce the painèd impotent° to smile.   *the sick*
   BIRON   To move wild laughter in the throat of death?
It cannot be; it is impossible.
Mirth cannot move a soul in agony.
   ROSALINE   Why, that's the way to choke a gibing spirit,
845   Whose influence is begot of that loose grace°   *uncritical acceptance*
Which shallow laughing hearers give to fools.
A jest's prosperity lies in the ear
Of him that hears it, never in the tongue
Of him that makes it. Then, if sickly ears,
850   Deafed with the clamors of their own dear groans,
Will hear your idle scorns, continue then,
And I will have you and that fault withal;°   *as well*
But if they will not, throw away that spirit,
And I shall find you empty of that fault,
855   Right joyful of your reformation.
   BIRON   A twelvemonth? Well, befall what will befall,
I'll jest a twelvemonth in an hospital.
           [*The* KING *and* QUEEN *come forward.*]
   QUEEN   Ay, sweet my lord, and so I take my leave.
   KING   No, madam, we will bring° you on your way.   *escort*
860   BIRON   Our wooing doth not end like an old play:
Jack hath not Jill. These ladies' courtesy
Might well have made our sport a comedy.
   KING   Come, sir, it wants° a twelvemonth and a day,   *lacks*
And then 'twill end.
   BIRON   That's too long for a play.
           Enter [ARMADO, *the*] *braggart.*
865   ARMADO   Sweet majesty, vouchsafe me—
           [*He approaches the* KING.]
   QUEEN   Was not that Hector?
   DUMAINE   The worthy knight of Troy.
   ARMADO   I will kiss thy royal finger and take leave.
I am a votary: I have vowed to Jaquenetta
To hold the plough° for her sweet love three years.   *To farm (bawdy)*
870   But, most esteemed greatness, will you hear the dialogue°   *debate*
that the two learned men[8] have compiled in praise of the owl
and the cuckoo? It should have followed in the end of our
show.
   KING   Call them forth quickly. We will do so.

---

8. Holofernes and Nathaniel (?).

875 ARMADO Holla! Approach!
          Enter all [HOLOFERNES, NATHANIEL, COSTARD, *the*
          PAGE, DULL, *and* JAQUENETTA].
     This side is Hiems, winter; this Ver, the spring: the one main-
     tained° by the owl, t'other by the cuckoo. Ver, begin!   *supported*
                    The Song.
     SPRING [*sings*] When daisies pied and violets blue⁹
                And cuckoo-buds° of yellow hue   *(buttercups?)*
880   And lady-smocks,° all silver-white,   *cuckoo flowers*
                Do paint the meadows with delight,
                The cuckoo, then, on every tree,
                Mocks married men, for thus sings he:
                "Cuckoo!
885   Cuckoo! Cuckoo!" Oh, word of fear,¹
                Unpleasing to a married ear.

                When shepherds pipe on oaten straws,
                And merry larks are ploughmen's clocks,
                When turtles tread,° and rooks and daws,   *turtledoves mate*
890   And maidens bleach their summer smocks,
                The cuckoo, then, on every tree,
                Mocks married men, for thus sings he:
                "Cuckoo!
                Cuckoo! Cuckoo!" Oh, word of fear,
895   Unpleasing to a married ear.

     WINTER [*sings*]   When icicles hang by the wall,
                And Dick the shepherd blows his nail,²
                And Tom bears logs into the hall,
                And milk comes frozen home in pail,
900   When blood is nipped° and ways° be foul,   *chilled / pathways*
                Then nightly sings the staring owl:
                "Tu-whit, tu-whoo!"³
                A merry note,
                While greasy Joan doth keel° the pot.   *stir to cool*

905   When all aloud the wind doth blow,
                And coughing drowns the parson's saw,°   *moralizing*
                And birds sit brooding in the snow,
                And Marian's nose looks red and raw,
                When roasted crabs° hiss in the bowl,°   *crab apples / (of ale)*
910   Then nightly sings the staring owl:
                "Tu-whit, tu-whoo!"
                A merry note,
                While greasy Joan doth keel the pot.

     ARMADO The words of Mercury are harsh
915   After the songs of Apollo.⁴
        You that way; we this way.⁵   *Exeunt.*

9. The dialogue is in iambic tetrameter, a song meter.
pied: multicolored.
1. Because it sounds like "cuckold."
2. Blows on his hands to keep warm; is idle.
3. Perhaps: to it (a hunting cry, with possible sexual
overtones), to woo; or: to wit, to woo (two central
themes of the play).
4. Presumably the love poetry of the King and court-

iers. *words of Mercury*: probably referring to Marcadé's somber message. (See note to the stage direction
following line 702.)
5. This line may distinguish the audience ("you")
from the actors ("we"), the aristocratic from the
humbler characters, the French ladies from the
inhabitants of Navarre, or even the actor playing
Spring from the one playing Winter.

The Passionate Pilgrim

The Passionate Pilgrim, a collection of love poetry, appeared under Shakespeare's name in 1599, apparently without his approval and to his dismay. Of its twenty poems, five are lifted from Shakespeare's other works—*Love's Labor's Lost* and the sonnets—and hence also appear elsewhere in this volume; four can clearly be assigned to other writers; and eleven remain unattributed. Numbers 4, 6, and 9—all sonnets—are noteworthy for their focus on the theme of *Venus and Adonis*, to which they may be a response. By 1599, Shakespeare's name had considerable cachet. *The Passionate Pilgrim* very possibly seeks to exploit that cachet, interweaving a few pieces by Shakespeare with other poems so as to produce a thematically resonant sequence that obscures the homoeroticism of some of the sonnets and in effect becomes a testament to poetic artifice. In the present volume, this collection is placed chronologically not by year of publication but according to the date by which Shakespeare is likely to have composed the five poems in it that are his. (See the Textual Introductions to *Love's Labor's Lost* and the sonnets.)

Walter Cohen

SELECTED BIBLIOGRAPHY

Bednarz, James P. "*The Passionate Pilgrim* and 'The Phoenix and Turtle.'" *The Cambridge Companion to Shakespeare's Poetry*. Ed. Patrick Cheney. New York: Cambridge UP, 2007. 108–24. Locates these works in the context of late Elizabethan poetic publication and literary and theatrical competition.

Roberts, Sasha. *Reading Shakespeare's Poems in Early Modern England*. Houndmills, Basingstoke: Palgrave Macmillan, 2003. 154–58, 177–90. Emphasizes the various interpretive contexts generated by different collections, seeing *The Passionate Pilgrim* as suppressing the homoeroticism of Shakespeare's sonnets, contributing to misogynistic literature, and celebrating erotic poetry.

Schoenfeldt, Michael. *The Cambridge Introduction to Shakespeare's Poetry*. Cambridge: Cambridge UP, 2010. 122–43. Focuses on the simple but elusive language of "The Phoenix and Turtle" and the "fantasies of Shakespearean authorship" in the various poems.

TEXTUAL INTRODUCTION

The Passionate Pilgrim survives in three early modern editions, all octavos: O1 (undated and without title page, but probably printed in 1599, though possibly in 1598); O2 (1599); and O3 (1612). Scholars believed that the current O2 was the first edition until 1939, when Joseph Quincy Adams determined that a fragment in the Folger Library was in fact the first edition: not simply does the 1612 edition call itself "The Third Edition," suggesting that an edition before O2 existed, but the Folger copy includes substantial textual variants from O2. In other words, the earliest surviving text for *The Passionate Pilgrim* is drastically abbreviated, presenting textual editors with a rare conundrum in Shakespeare studies, especially for those basing a modern text on a single extant copy. Consequently, the present text follows O2 and records variants to it from O1 and other editions and copies of individual poems available.

The O1 fragment consists of eleven leaves, none of which includes a signature or page number. Since the title page is not among the extant leaves, we lack bibliographical information such as the title of the work, its date, its printer, and its publisher. Scholars believe that the original text consisted of twenty-eight leaves, with the collation formula A=C8, D4 (meaning that the first three gatherings of pages, labeled A, B, and C, each have eight leaves of paper, and the fourth gathering, D, four leaves). Only signatures A3–A7 and C2–C7 remain extant, printing eight of the twenty poems that survive in O2, numbered by modern editions Poems 1, 2, 3, 4, 5, 16, 17, 18. Scholars speculate that O1 was printed by T. Judson for William Jaggard.

The title page to O2 supplies the bibliographical information missing in O1:

THE | PASSIONATE | PILGRIME. | *By W. Shakespeare.* | [Ornament] | *AT LON-DON* | Printed for W. Iaggard, and are | to be sold by W. Leake, at the Grey- | hound in Paules Churchyard. | 1599.

Since Leake owned copyright to *Venus and Adonis*, Jaggard was almost certainly trying to capitalize on the enormous success of Shakespeare's narrative poem, along with that of *The Rape of Lucrece*, and thus on Shakespeare's standing as an important Elizabethan poet. Even so, as a book *The Passionate Pilgrim* is rare among Elizabethan examples because it prints individual poems on rectos alone, as if Jaggard lacked material to make a complete book; toward the end, however, he abandoned this plan when space suddenly became constricted, so he printed poems on both rectos and versos (i.e., on both sides of each leaf). O2 consists of thirty-two leaves, collates A–D8, and is extant in only two copies: in the collections of Trinity College, Cambridge, and the Huntington Library, San Marino, California.

A second title page appears on signature C3r, reading "SONNETS | To sundry notes of Musicke," effectively dividing the book into two parts, Poems 1–14 and Poems 15–20. Some scholars speculate that Jaggard inserted the second title page to appease Shakespeare's wrath at being identified as the author of the entire book, while others think that the second title page was inserted simply to pad out the volume.

Modern scholarship has determined that only five of the twenty poems were written by Shakespeare. Poems 1 and 2 are variations on Sonnets 138 and 144. Poems 3, 5, and 16 are songs and sonnets from *Love's Labor's Lost*, first published in 1598. Poems 8 and 20 are now assigned to Richard Barnfield, and Poem 11 to Bartholomew Griffin. Poem 19 combines two poems: part of Marlowe's "The Passionate Shepherd to His Love" and a stanza of Sir Walter Ralegh's "The Nymph's Reply," here set off with a subtitle, "Love's Answer." (The full texts of both poems appeared the next year, 1600, in *England's Helicon*.) The final eleven poems remain anonymous; cases have sometimes been made for Shakespeare's authorship of some of them, but modern editors reject the attributions. Curiously, then, Jaggard's attempt to present "W. Shakespeare" as "The Passionate Pilgrim"—an allusion to Romeo and Juliet's use of the pilgrim metaphor in their love-sonnet—falsifies the record and caused immediate (and long-lasting) indignation, including by Shakespeare.

A third edition of *The Passionate Pilgrim* was published in 1612. O3 is important especially because it exists with two different title pages: one with Shakespeare's name on it, and one without. The one with Shakespeare's name on it reads,

THE | PASSIONATE | PILGRIME. | OR | *Certaine Amorous Sonnets,* | *betweene* Venus *and* Adonis, | *newly corrected and aug-* | *mented.* | *By W. Shakespere.* | The third Edition. | Where-unto is newly ad- | ded two Loue-Epistles, the first | from *Paris* to *Hellen,* and | *Hellens* answere backe | againe to *Paris.* | Printed by W. Iaggard. | 1612.

The reference to the sonnets about Venus and Adonis singles out a group of four poems on this topic (Poems 4, 6, 9, 11), likely trying to draw in readers of Shakespeare's narrative poem, while the two new "Loue-Epistles" were two of nine written by Thomas Heywood. We know this because Heywood in a postscript to his 1612 *Apology for Actors* accused Jaggard of printing his own poems dishonestly, and added that he knew Shakespeare to be "much offended with M. Jaggard (that altogether unknowne to him) presumed to make so bold with his name." Scholars speculate that Heywood's accusation led Jaggard to produce a new title page to the 1612 octavo, deleting Shakespeare's name.

The text of *The Passionate Pilgrim* presents few editorial problems. In a few cases, O1 provides a preferred reading (see Textual Variants), while occasionally later emendations are adopted. The major change between O1 and O2 occurs in Poem 18, where O2 prints O1's lines 13–24 after the current line 36. The present edition adopts O1 as preferable.

While *The Passionate Pilgrim* is a poorly designed book, it consolidates Shakespeare's standing, at the midpoint of his career, as a major English poet. Jaggard has been accused of many things, including bad judgment and dishonesty, but because he was the first to publish Shakespeare's collected plays (the First Folio), he qualifies as the first publisher of collected editions of Shakespeare's poems and plays.

PATRICK CHENEY

The Passionate Pilgrim

1[1]

When my love swears that she is made of truth,
I do believe her (though I know she lies),
That° she might think me some untutored youth,   *So that*
Unskillful in the world's false forgeries.
5   Thus vainly° thinking that she thinks me young,   *in vain; with vanity*
Although I know my years be past the best,
I, smiling, credit° her false-speaking tongue,   *(pretend to) believe*
Outfacing faults in love with love's ill rest.
But wherefore says my love that she is young?
10 And wherefore say not I that I am old?
Oh, love's best habit is° a soothing tongue,   *love is best dressed in*
And age, in love, loves not to have years told.°   *counted*
     Therefore I'll lie° with love, and love with me,   *tell lies; lie down*
     Since that our faults in love thus smothered be.

2[1]

Two loves I have, of comfort and despair,
That like two spirits do suggest° me still: *entice*
My better angel is a man (right fair)
My worser spirit a woman (colored ill).°   *darkly*
5   To win me soon to hell, my female evil
Tempteth my better angel from my side,
And would corrupt my saint to be a devil,
Wooing his purity with her fair pride.
And whether that my angel be turned fiend,
10 Suspect I may, yet not directly tell:
For being both to me, both to each, friend,[2]
I guess one angel in another's hell.[3]
     The truth I shall not know, but live in doubt,
     Till my bad angel fire my good one out.[4]

3[1]

Did not the heavenly rhetoric of thine eye,
'Gainst whom the world could not hold argument,
Persuade my heart to this false perjury?
Vows for thee broke deserve not punishment.
5   A woman I forswore; but I will prove,
Thou being a goddess, I forswore not thee:
My vow was earthly, thou a heavenly love;

1
1. Textual Comment This is another version of Sonnet 138. For the differences, see Digital Edition TC 1 and appendix of comparative scenes.
2
1. Textual Comment This is another version of Sonnet 144. For the differences, see Digital Edition TC 2 and appendix of comparative scenes.
2. The two are both my lovers, and both are lovers to each other.
3. Each torments the other; they are in the "hell," or middle den, of a (sexual) game called barley-break; the man occupies the sex organ ("hell") of the woman.
4. Until my bad angel expels my good one, who has become an animal to be smoked out of a burrow; until my bad angel infects my good one with venereal disease; until bad money ("angel" = gold coin) drives out good.
3
1. Textual Comment This is another version of a sonnet that appears in *Love's Labor's Lost* at 4.3.55–68. For the differences, see Digital Edition TC 3.

Thy grace° being gained cures all disgrace in me. *favor*
My vow was breath, and breath a vapor is;
10   Then thou, fair sun, that on this earth doth shine,
Exhale° this vapor vow; in thee it is. *Draw up*
If broken, then it is no fault of mine.
        If by me broke, what fool is not so wise
        To break an oath to win a paradise?

4

Sweet Cytherea,¹ sitting by a brook
With young Adonis, lovely, fresh, and green,° *young; inexperienced*
Did court the lad with many a lovely° look— *amorous*
Such looks as none could look but beauty's queen.
5   She told him stories to delight his ear;
She showed him favors to allure his eye.
To win his heart, she touched him here and there:
Touches so soft still° conquer chastity. *always*
But whether unripe years did want conceit,° *lack understanding*
10   Or he refused to take her figured° proffer, *implied*
The tender nibbler would not touch the bait,
But smile and jest at every gentle offer.
        Then fell she on her back, fair queen, and toward;° *ready*
        He rose and ran away, ah, fool too froward.° *obstinate*

5¹

If love make me forsworn, how shall I swear to love?
Oh, never faith could hold, if not to beauty vowed.
Though to myself forsworn, to thee I'll constant prove;
Those thoughts to me like oaks,² to thee like osiers° bowed. *willows*
5   Study his bias leaves,° and make his book thine eyes, *goes off course*
Where all those pleasures live that art can comprehend.
If knowledge be the mark,° to know thee shall suffice: *aim*
Well-learnèd is that tongue that well can thee commend;
All ignorant that soul that sees thee without wonder,
10   Which is to me some praise, that I thy parts° admire. *qualities*
Thine eye Jove's lightning seems, thy voice his dreadful thunder,
Which (not to anger bent) is music and sweet fire.
        Celestial as thou art, oh, do not love that wrong
        To sing heaven's praise with such an earthly tongue.³

6

Scarce had the sun dried up the dewy morn,
And scarce the herd gone to the hedge for shade,
When Cytherea (all in love forlorn)
A longing tarriance° for Adonis made *waiting*
5   Under an osier growing by a brook,

4
1. Sonnets 4, 6, 9, and 11 all treat the unsuccessful wooing of the beautiful but unresponsive young man Adonis by Venus ("Cytherea"), the goddess of love.
5
1. TEXTUAL COMMENT This is another version of a sonnet—composed, however, in hexameters—that appears in *Love's Labor's Lost* at 4.2.98–111. For the differences, see Digital Edition TC 4.

2. Those resolutions that seemed to me to be as strong as oaks.
3. *do . . . tongue:* possibly a misprint of the *Love's Labor's Lost* version. As printed, the lines might be stretched to mean: do not love those that do wrong by singing (or: do not love [me] if it is "wrong / To sing") "heaven's praise with such an earthly tongue." But since it is not wrong, *do* love me.

A brook where Adon used to cool his spleen.° *hot temper*
Hot was the day; she hotter, that did look
For his approach that often there had been.
Anon he comes and throws his mantle by,
10   And stood stark naked on the brook's green brim.
The sun looked on the world with glorious eye,
Yet not so wistly° as this queen on him. *eagerly; longingly*
        He, spying her, bounced in whereas he stood.[1]
        "O Jove," quoth she, "why was not I a flood?"° *body of water*

7

Fair is my love, but not so fair as fickle;
Mild as a dove, but neither true nor trusty;° *trustworthy*
Brighter than glass, and yet as glass is, brittle;
Softer than wax, and yet as iron rusty:° *corrupt (morally)*
5   A lily pale, with damask° dye to grace her, *red*
        None fairer, nor none falser to deface her.[1]

Her lips to mine how often hath she joined,
Between each kiss her oaths of true love swearing.
How many tales to please me hath she coined,° *invented*
10   Dreading my love, the loss whereof still fearing.[2]
        Yet in the midst of all her pure protestings
        Her faith, her oaths, her tears, and all were jestings.

She burned with love as straw with fire flameth;
She burned out love as soon as straw out burneth;
15   She framed° the love, and yet she foiled° the framing; *built / ruined*
She bade love last, and yet she fell a-turning.° *(to another lover)*
        Was this a lover, or a lecher, whether?° *which of the two*
        Bad in the best, though excellent in neither.[3]

8[1]

If music and sweet poetry agree,
As they must needs (the sister and the brother),
Then must the love be great twixt thee and me,
Because thou lov'st the one,° and I the other.° *(music) / (poetry)*
5   Dowland[2] to thee is dear, whose heavenly touch
Upon the lute doth ravish human sense;
Spenser[3] to me, whose deep conceit° is such *understanding*
As passing all conceit° needs no defense. *esteem*
Thou lov'st to hear the sweet melodious sound
10   That Phoebus'[4] lute (the queen of music) makes;
And I in deep delight am chiefly drowned,
When as° himself to singing he betakes. *When*
        One god is god of both (as poets feign),
        One knight° loves both, and both in thee remain. *(the reference is unknown)*

6
1. Jumped in from where he stood.
7
1. Nor is anyone more false, to her discredit; with a possible reference to cosmetics in "falser" and "deface."
2. Continually being anxious about losing my love, and upset at that prospect.
3. Bad in romance, but not outstanding merely as a sexual partner either.

8
1. From *Poems in Diverse Humors,* an appendix that Richard Barnfield added to his *Encomion of Lady Pecunia* (1598).
2. John Dowland (1563?–1626), composer, singer, instrumentalist.
3. Poet Edmund Spenser (1552–1599), author of *The Faerie Queene* (1590, 1596).
4. Apollo's. Here, Apollo is god of music, in line 12 ("singing") god of poetry, and in line 13 "god of both."

9

Fair was the morn, when the fair queen of love,°   *(Venus)*
. . . . .¹
Paler for sorrow than her milk-white dove,
For Adon's sake, a youngster proud and wild,
5 Her stand she takes upon a steep-up hill.
Anon° Adonis comes with horn and hounds;   *Soon*
She, silly° queen, with more than love's good will,   *foolish*
Forbade the boy he should not pass those grounds.°   *cross those valleys*
"Once," quoth she, "did I see a fair sweet youth
10 Here in these brakes,° deep wounded with° a boar,   *thickets / by*
Deep in the thigh, a spectacle of ruth.°   *pity*
See in my thigh," quoth she, "here was the sore."
      She showèd hers; he saw more wounds than one,°   *(sexual)*
      And blushing fled, and left her all alone.

10

Sweet rose, fair flower, untimely plucked, soon vaded,°   *faded; departed*
Plucked in the bud, and vaded in the spring;
Bright orient pearl, alack too timely shaded,¹
Fair creature killed too soon by death's sharp sting,
5   Like a green plum that hangs upon a tree,
      And falls (through wind) before the fall should be.

I weep for thee, and yet no cause I have;
For why° thou left'st me nothing in thy will.   *Because*
And yet thou left'st me more than I did crave;
10 For why I cravèd nothing of thee still.²
      Oh, yes, dear friend, I pardon crave of thee:³
      Thy discontent° thou didst bequeath to me.   *sadness*

11¹

Venus with Adonis sitting by her
Under a myrtle shade began to woo him.
She told the youngling how god Mars did try her,
And as he fell to her, she fell to him.
5 "Even thus," quoth she, "the warlike god embraced me."
And then she clipped° Adonis in her arms;   *embraced*
"Even thus," quoth she, "the warlike god unlaced me,"
As if the boy should use like° loving charms.   *similar*
"Even thus," quoth she, "he seizèd on my lips,"
10 And with her lips on his did act the seizure.
And as she fetchèd breath, away he skips,
And would not take her meaning nor her pleasure.²
      Ah, that I had my lady at this bay,°   *cornered in this way*
      To kiss and clip me till I run away.

9
1. A line is missing here in the original edition.
10
1. Darkened too soon. "Orient" pearls were valued as more lustrous than their European counterparts, with overtones of the sun rising in the East and setting in the West.
2. "Nothing" (lines 8, 10) evokes the tangibility of absence caused by death. But "nothing" also may denote female sexual organs. In line 8, it would go with "will" (testament; lust) to suggest that the dead wom-

an's desire (formerly) made her sexually available to the speaker. In line 10, the speaker would be saying that he always ("still") desired her.
3. This line seems to contradict the previous one by claiming that the speaker did, after all, "crave" something—"pardon."
11
1. From *Fidessa*, a sonnet sequence by Bartholomew Griffin (published 1596).
2. *take . . . pleasure:* understand "her meaning" or agree to (accept) the "pleasure" she wanted and offered.

12

Crabbèd° age and youth cannot live together: *Ill-tempered*
Youth is full of pleasance, age is full of care;
Youth like summer morn, age like winter weather;
Youth like summer brave,° age like winter bare.   *well dressed*
5   Youth is full of sport, age's breath is short;
Youth is nimble, age is lame;
Youth is hot and bold, age is weak and cold;
Youth is wild, and age is tame.
      Age, I do abhor thee; youth, I do adore thee.
10   Oh, my love, my love is young.
      Age, I do defy thee. O sweet shepherd, hie thee,°   *hurry up*
        For methinks thou stays° too long.   *delays*

13

Beauty is but a vain and doubtful good,
A shining gloss that vadeth° suddenly,   *fades*
A flower that dies when first it gins° to bud,   *begins*
A brittle glass that's broken presently,°   *immediately*
5   A doubtful good, a gloss, a glass, a flower,
    Lost, vaded, broken, dead within an hour.

And as goods lost are seld° or never found,   *seldom*
As vaded gloss no rubbing will refresh,
As flowers dead lie withered on the ground,
10   As broken glass no cement can redress,°   *repair*
    So beauty blemished once, for ever lost,°   *is forever lost*
    In spite of physic,° painting,° pain,° and cost.   *medicine / make-up / labor*

14

Good night, good rest, ah, neither be my share.
She bade good night that kept my rest away,
And daffed° me to a cabin hanged° with care,   *dismissed / room adorned*
To descant on the doubts° of my decay.   *expand upon the fears*
5   "Farewell," quoth she, "and come again tomorrow."
    Fare° well I could not, for I supped with sorrow.   *Do; eat*

Yet at my parting sweetly did she smile,
In scorn or friendship, nil I conster whether:[1]
'T may be she joyed to jest at my exile;
10   'T may be again to make me wander thither.
    Wander—a word for shadows like myself,
    As take the pain but cannot pluck the pelf.°   *reward*

Lord, how mine eyes throw gazes to the East!
My heart doth charge the watch;[2] the morning rise°   *break of day*
15   Doth cite° each moving° sense from idle rest,   *summon / living*
Not daring trust the office of mine eyes.[3]
    While Philomela° sits and sings, I sit and mark,°   *the nightingale / listen*
    And wish her lays were tunèd like the lark.[4]

14
1. I will not guess which of the two.
2. Perhaps: My heart orders those on night watch to watch for morning.
3. Since daybreak doesn't trust my eyes to be alert, it rouses all my senses.
4. And wish her (nighttime) songs were the songs of the (morning) lark.

For she doth welcome daylight with her ditty,°   *song*
20   And drives away dark dreaming night:
The night so packed,° I post° unto my pretty.   *sent off / hurry*
Heart hath his hope, and eyes their wishèd sight;
        Sorrow changed to solace, and solace mixed with sorrow;
        For why° she sighed and bade me come tomorrow.   *Because*

25   Were I with her, the night would post too soon,
But now are minutes added to the hours.
To spite me now, each minute seems a moon;°   *night; month*
Yet not for me, shine sun[5] to succor flowers.
        Pack night, peep day; good day, of night now borrow;
30   Short night tonight, and length thyself tomorrow.[6]

Sonnets
to Sundry Notes of Music

15

It was a lording's° daughter, the fairest one of three,   *lord's*
That likèd of her master,° as well as well might be,   *tutor*
Till looking on an Englishman, the fairest that eye could see,
        Her fancy fell a-turning.°   *(to another lover)*
5   Long was the combat doubtful,° that love with love did fight   *uncertain*
To leave the master loveless, or kill the gallant knight;
To put in practice either, alas it was a spite°   *would be a vexation*
        Unto the silly° damsel.   *helpless*
But one must be refused; more mickle° was the pain,   *great*
10   That nothing could be used° to turn them both to gain,   *done*
For of the two the trusty knight was wounded with disdain,
        Alas, she could not help it.
Thus art° with arms contending was victor of the day,   *learning*
Which by a gift of learning did bear the maid away.
15   Then, lullaby, the learnèd man hath got the lady gay,
        For now my song is ended.

16[1]

On a day (alack the day)
Love, whose month was ever May,
Spied a blossom passing° fair,   *surpassingly*
Playing in the wanton° air.   *playful*
5   Through the velvet leaves the wind
All unseen gan passage find,°   *began to find passage*
That° the lover, sick to death,   *So that*
Wished himself the heaven's breath.
"Air," quoth he, "thy cheeks may blow;
10   Air, would I might triumph so.
But (alas) my hand hath sworn
Ne'er to pluck thee from thy thorn;[2]

---

5. Let the sun shine, not for my sake, but.
6. The speaker is asking night to shorten now and to lengthen tomorrow, when he's with his mistress.
16
1. TEXTUAL COMMENT This poem is another version

of lines that appear in *Love's Labor's Lost* at 4.3.96–115. For the differences, see Digital Edition TC 5.
2. TEXTUAL COMMENT For the editorial emendation of the printed version both here and in *Love's Labor's Lost*, see Digital Edition TC 6.

Vow (alack) for youth unmeet,° inappropriate
Youth, so apt to pluck a sweet.
15 Thou for whom Jove would swear
Juno but an Ethiop³ were,
And deny himself for° Jove, to be
Turning mortal for thy love.

17

My flocks feed not, my ewes breed not,
My rams speed° not, all is amiss. thrive
Love is dying, faith's defying,¹
Heart's denying, causer of this.
5 All my merry jigs° are quite forgot; dances; sports
All my lady's love is lost (God wot°). knows
Where her faith was firmly fixed in love,
There a "nay" is placed without remove.° immovably
    One silly cross° wrought all my loss. foolish mishap
10 O frowning Fortune, cursèd fickle dame,
    For now I see inconstancy
    More in women than in men remain.

In black mourn I, all fears scorn I;
Love hath forlorn me, living in thrall.° enslaved (to love)
15 Heart is bleeding, all help needing.
Oh, cruel speeding,° fraughted° with gall.° fortune / laden / rancor
My shepherd's pipe can sound no deal;° not at all
My wether's² bell rings doleful knell;
My curtal dog³ that wont to° have played, formerly liked to
20 Plays not at all, but seems afraid.
    With sighs so deep, procures° to weep, is able
    In howling wise,° to see my doleful plight. fashion
    How sighs resound through heartless ground,
    Like a thousand vanquished men in bloody fight.

25 Clear wells spring not, sweet birds sing not,
Green plants bring not forth their dye,
Herds stand weeping, flocks all sleeping,
Nymphs back° peeping fearfully. back up
All our pleasure known to us poor swains,° shepherds
30 All our merry meetings on the plains,
All our evening sport from us is fled,
All our love is lost, for love is dead.
    Farewell, sweet love, thy like ne'er was
    For a sweet content, the cause all my woe.
35 Poor Corydon⁴ must live alone:
    Other help for him I see that there is none.

---

3. Black African (used here in racist fashion to signify ugliness).
17
1. Faith's rejection; "de-fying" means de-faithing.
2. A male sheep castrated while still immature. The

"bellwether" is the lead sheep of the flock.
3. Dog with a cut tail.
4. Conventional name for a shepherd (from one of
Virgil's *Eclogues*, ca. 39–38 B.C.E., a collection of pastoral poems).

18

Whenas° thine eye hath chose the dame,   *When*
And stalled° the deer° that thou shouldst strike,   *trapped / (pun on "dear")*
Let reason rule things worthy blame,
As well as fancy, partial might.[1]
5   Take counsel of some wiser head,
     Neither too young, nor yet unwed.

And when thou com'st thy tale to tell,
Smooth not thy tongue with filèd° talk,   *rehearsed; scheming*
Lest she some subtle practice° smell—   *deception*
10 A cripple soon can find a halt[2]—
     But plainly say thou lov'st her well,
     And set her person forth to sale.[3]

And to her will° frame all thy ways;°   *desire / habits*
Spare not to spend, and chiefly there
15 Where thy desert may merit praise
By ringing in thy lady's ear.[4]
     The strongest castle, tower, and town,
     The golden bullet° beats it down.   *words; money*

Serve always with assurèd trust,°   *reliability*
20 And in thy suit be humble true;
Unless thy lady prove unjust,°   *unfaithful*
Press never thou to choose a new.[5]
     When time° shall serve, be thou not slack   *occasion*
     To proffer, though she put thee back.[6]

25 What though° her frowning brows be bent,   *Although*
Her cloudy looks will calm ere night,
And then too late she will repent
That thus dissembled her delight,[7]
     And twice desire,° ere it be day,   *(sexual gratification)*
30   That which with scorn she put away.°   *rejected*

What though she strive to try her strength
And ban° and brawl,° and say thee "nay,"   *curse / shout*
Her feeble force will yield at length,
When craft° hath taught her thus to say,   *craftiness*
35   "Had women been so strong as men,
     In faith, you had not had it then."

The wiles and guiles that women work,°   *employ*
Dissembled with an outward show;
The tricks and toys° that in them lurk,   *whims*

18

1. Let reason as well as desire ("fancy"), which is biased and by itself inadequate, govern your potentially blameworthy love affairs.
2. Those practiced in deceit can easily sense deception. *find a halt*: detect a limp.
3. Like a salesman, start praising her qualities. One of the manuscript versions of this poem has "& set thy body forth to sell."
4. Don't be stingy about spending your money in ways that will draw your lady's attention to your merit.
5. Don't make attempts to choose someone else (?).
6. Even if she resists you. The "proffer," at first an offer, becomes outright rape here and in the following stanzas.
7. She who in this way concealed her desire.

40   The cock that treads them[8] shall not know.
                    Have you not heard it said full oft,
                    "A woman's 'nay' doth stand for naught"?[9]

        Think women still to strive with men
        To sin, and never for to saint.[1]
45   There is no heaven: be holy then
        When time with age shall them attaint.[2]
                    Were kisses all the joys in bed,
                    One woman would another wed.

        But soft, enough; too much I fear,
50   Lest that my mistress hear my song.
        She will not stick to round me on the ear,[3]
        To teach my tongue to be so long.
                    Yet will she blush, here be it said,
                    To hear her secrets so bewrayed.°   *revealed*

                    ### 19[1]
        Live with me and be my love,
        And we will all the pleasures prove°   *try*
        That hills and valleys, dales and fields,
        And all the craggy mountains yield.

5   There will we sit upon the rocks,
        And see the shepherds feed their flocks,
        By shallow rivers, by whose falls
        Melodious birds sing madrigals.

        There will I make thee a bed of roses,
10   With a thousand fragrant posies,°   *flower bunches*
        A cap of flowers and a kirtle°   *gown or skirt*
        Embroidered all with leaves of myrtle.

        A belt of straw and ivy buds,
        With coral clasps and amber studs,
15   And if these pleasures may thee move,
        Then live with me, and be my love.

                    ### Love's Answer
        If that the world and love were young,
        And truth in every shepherd's tongue,
        These pretty pleasures might me move
        To live with thee and be thy love.

---

8. The man who copulates with them.
9. Nothing; (sexual) naughtiness; female sexual organ.
1. Expect women always to engage (compete) with men in sin but not in saintliness, or chastity.
2. There is no thought of heaven (purity) in women seeking sexual pleasure. Let them be holy when they're old and unattractive.

3. She won't refrain from scolding me (boxing me) on the ear.

19
1. Part of a poem by Christopher Marlowe (1564–1593), with a reply by Walter Ralegh (1552–1618). See the Textual Introduction.

20

As it fell upon a day,
In the merry month of May,
Sitting in a pleasant shade,
Which a grove of myrtles made,
5   Beasts did leap, and birds did sing,
Trees did grow, and plants did spring.
Every thing did banish moan,
Save the nightingale alone.
She (poor bird) as all forlorn,
10   Leaned her breast up-till a thorn,
And there sung the dolful'st ditty,
That to hear it was great pity.
"Fie, fie, fie," now would she cry;
"Tereu, Tereu,"[1] by and by:
15   That to hear her so complain
Scarce I could from tears refrain,
For her griefs so lively shown
Made me think upon mine own.
Ah, thought I, thou mourn'st in vain,
20   None takes pity on thy pain:
Senseless trees, they cannot hear thee;
Ruthless bears, they will not cheer thee.
King Pandion,[2] he is dead;
All thy friends are lapped° in lead.   *wrapped up*
25   All thy fellow birds do sing,
Careless of thy sorrowing.
Whilst as fickle Fortune smiled,
Thou and I were both beguiled.
Everyone that flatters thee
30   Is no friend in misery.
Words are easy, like the wind;
Faithful friends are hard to find.
Every man will be thy friend,
Whilst thou hast wherewith to spend;
35   But if store of crowns be scant,
No man will supply thy want.
If that one be prodigal,
"Bountiful" they will him call,
And with suchlike flattering:
40   "Pity but he were° a king."   *It's a pity he's not*
If he be addict to vice,
Quickly him they will entice;
If to women he be bent,°   *inclined*
They have° at commandment;°   *(women) / on demand*
45   But if Fortune once do frown,
Then farewell his great renown:
They that fawned on him before
Use his company no more.

20
1 The nightingale's sound, from Tereus, who, in Ovid's *Metamorphoses* (by 8 C.E.), rapes Philomela (hence, a name for a nightingale) and cuts out her tongue.
2. Father of Philomela and legendary king of Athens.

He that is thy friend indeed,
50 He will help thee in thy need.
If thou sorrow, he will weep;
If thou wake, he cannot sleep.
Thus of every grief in heart
He with thee doth bear a part.
55 These are certain signs to know
Faithful friend from flatt'ring foe.

Richard the Second

In the first scene of *Richard II,* two armed noblemen face each other before the royal throne. They hurl insults at one another, their deadly antagonism barely held in check by the formality of the occasion. This is an "appeal for treason," a kind of trial already archaic in Shakespeare's time, in which plaintiff and defendant present their cases in their own persons before the king, who instantly dispenses justice. The structure of the situation suggests what the men themselves insist upon: that one lies and one tells the truth, that one is a traitor and one a true subject. But even while we are implicitly asked to judge between rival claims, we have no way of knowing what has happened or whom to trust.

In the ensuing scenes, we learn that Bolingbroke and Mowbray are fighting about the murder of Thomas of Woodstock, the uncle of King Richard II. Apparently Bolingbroke knows that Richard secretly ordered Woodstock's death. Since he cannot say so, he picks Richard's agent Mowbray as his target, for Woodstock had been in Mowbray's safekeeping. Meanwhile, Mowbray, likewise unable to blame the true culprit openly, is outraged at being called a traitor when it was his allegiance to Richard that led him to acquiesce in the killing.

This is a far more tangled situation than the simple yes-or-no structure of the appeal for treason or, several scenes later, the "trial by combat" could allow anyone to acknowledge. Moreover, the King's participation in the crime upon which he is supposed to be passing judgment obviously compromises his impartiality. The institution of the appeal for treason is premised on the assumptions that, as Richard himself states emphatically, the king has no part in his subjects' quarrels, and that it is in his best interests to have the truth revealed. Here, neither assumption is correct. The ceremonies of royal authority so colorfully staged in the first few scenes turn out to be inconclusive, avoiding rather than confronting real sources of discord.

As the play continues, we come to realize that the confusion of the first few scenes, a confusion Shakespeare forces his audience momentarily to share, results from an intractable problem in a system of monarchical government. Since the king's subjects are obliged to obey him, it is not clear how, short of direct divine intervention, his follies or vices may be checked. To admit that subjects have a right to judge or even to remove their king threatens the stability of the realm, since any subject, discontented for any reason, might incite a revolt. But to allow the king to have his own way no matter what opens the way to tyranny.

The proper extent of a monarch's power was a crucial, and unresolved, political issue in sixteenth- and early seventeenth-century England, when first the Tudors and then the Stuarts struggled to extend their traditional prerogatives. A few decades after Shakespeare's death, disagreement about the nature of royal authority would provoke the English Civil War. In the 1590s, when Shakespeare was writing his history plays, the lines of stress upon which the country would eventually fracture were already apparent, even though the disasters to come would not have seemed inevitable.

When Shakespeare wrote about the medieval reign of Richard II, in other words, he saw the conflicts of that reign through the lens of the late sixteenth century. His meticulous re-creation of antiquated judicial processes did not conceal from audiences in his own time the contemporary relevance of the play. In all sixteenth-century texts and perhaps in performance, 4.1.149–311,* the lines in which Richard gives up his crown, were omitted: many scholars theorize that this episode was considered too inflammatory to print or stage. When the Earl of Essex rebelled against Elizabeth I in 1601, some of his supporters cited Richard's reign as providing a historical precedent for the deposition of a monarch. They paid Shakespeare's company to perform a play about Richard's reign—almost certainly Shakespeare's play—in an attempt to rally supporters to their cause. "I am Richard II," snapped the furious Queen; "know ye not that?"

Twenty-first-century readers and audiences of *Richard II*, of course, see the play's political concerns at yet a further remove: monarchs no longer govern most of us, and we no longer believe in the divine right of kings. And yet the general issues with which *Richard II* deals are perennial ones. How much power should a ruler have, and how ought that power to be controlled and tempered? How much should the institutions of government be respected, and when does disruption or outright revolt become acceptable? Like Richard and Bolingbroke, like Shakespeare and Elizabeth, we, too, struggle to understand and manage the blend of ceremony and violence that together constitute the power of the state.

To acknowledge the relevance of Richard's reign to Shakespeare's time is not, however, to claim that Shakespeare wrote his play purely as a means of commenting obliquely on the policies of Elizabeth I. Rather, the urgent task of defining a nation-state in the late sixteenth century led Shakespeare to an extended historical inquiry into the institution of the English monarchy, an inquiry of which *Richard II* is a part. By looking at points at which the normal order of royal succession is challenged, Shakespeare illuminates interesting inconsistencies in Renaissance theories of kingship and political authority. Several years earlier, he had written the three *Henry VI* plays and *Richard III*, which while not originally conceived as a series eventually constituted what critics call the "first tetralogy": a group of plays that together present a continuous chronicle of the long Wars of the Roses in the fifteenth century. Soon after finishing *Richard III*, Shakespeare began writing another group of history plays, the "second tetralogy," which backtrack in time to treat the origins of the conflicts he had already brought to the stage.

As he had for his earlier history plays, Shakespeare turned to Raphael Holinshed's *Chronicles of England, Scotland, and Ireland* (1587). There he found in the reign of Richard II a remote cause of the war to be waged many years hence. Richard II was a grandson of Edward III, whose formidable precedent haunts all the plays of the second tetralogy. King Edward had five sons who survived to adulthood, but his eldest, Edward the Black Prince, predeceased him. The Black Prince left a son of his own, however, the future Richard II, to whom the throne descended after Edward III's death. At the time of his accession, Richard was ten years old, and during his adolescence his powerful uncles, the younger brothers of the Black Prince, administered his kingdom on his behalf. After Richard reached young adulthood and began to rule in his own name, he found it difficult to gain the respect of his uncles, experienced middle-aged men who had become accustomed to command. His own rashness and ineffectuality only compounded his troubles. Shakespeare's play opens upon the young Richard, already complicit in the murder of one of his uncles; the remaining uncles, who scorn Richard's maladroit rule but realize they owe allegiance to him; and Richard's cousin Bolingbroke who is more willing than his elders to act on the recognition of the ruler's weakness.

Early in the play, Richard reacts to Bolingbroke's veiled challenge by exiling him; shortly thereafter, he confiscates Bolingbroke's estate. When, exasperated, Bolingbroke invades England and successfully seizes the crown from his cousin, his action neatly ruptures two traditional sources of royal authority. Unquestionably, Bolingbroke is the more astute tactician, the more effective leader. Richard, however, is equally undoubtedly the rightful heir of Edward III, and as such has been anointed

---

*All quotations are taken from the edited text of the Folio, printed here. The Digital Edition includes edited texts of both the Folio and the Quarto.

king in a sacred coronation ceremony. Thus one character has all the advantages when considered from a material and practical point of view, while the other derives his claim to authority from the more abstract principle of divinely sanctioned hereditary right.

Shakespeare imagines the division between the two men not merely as a political issue but as a question of character. A vivid sense of Bolingbroke's personality emerges in his confrontation with Mowbray. Mowbray harps on Bolingbroke's lies, laments the damage Bolingbroke's accusation has done to his reputation, and experiences Bolingbroke's verbal accusation as a physical attack: he is "[p]ierced to the soul with slander's venomed spear" (1.1.171). Bolingbroke, by contrast, trusts not words but physical strength: "What my tongue speaks, my right-drawn sword may prove," he stoutly declares (1.1.46). Tellingly, his

Richardus ii. From John Rastell, *The Pastime of People* (1529).

word "right" conflates his proficiency as a warrior with the uprightness of his cause, suggesting that he does not care to recognize the potential difference. Likewise, Bolingbroke repeatedly speaks of making his words *good,* by which he means backing them up by force. As a corollary, he is suspicious or dismissive of anything that seems merely imaginary, verbal, or abstract. When his father, Gaunt, encourages him to reconcile himself to his exile by renaming it an educational tour or a pleasure junket, Bolingbroke replies:

> Oh, who can hold a fire in his hand
> By thinking on the frosty Caucasus?
> Or cloy the hungry edge of appetite
> By bare imagination of a feast?
> (1.3.258–61)

As the play proceeds, this insistence on material facts rather than words or imagination comes to seem entirely characteristic of a man who has no legal claim on the throne, but who takes it because he is able to do so.

Unlike Bolingbroke, Richard is an inept manager of practical affairs. In the first act, most of his powerful kinfolk let him literally get away with murder; but in the second act, it becomes clear that they will not tolerate his infringement of property rights. Medieval kings were expected to cover most of the expenses of government from their own large estates, but to raise additional funds Richard "farms out" the realm—that is, grants the power to tax to private individuals who can confiscate subjects' property virtually as they please, provided the King gets a share of the spoils. Not surprisingly, such legalized theft produces widespread resentment. For the upper aristocracy, the last straw is Richard's seizure of the Duchy of Lancaster upon John of Gaunt's death: the encroachment seems to them worse than homicide, because it directly threatens the social structure upon which their status depends. Inherited land distinguishes noblemen from "men of no name": in fact, noble names are derived from the land: Lancaster, Gloucester, York, Northumberland, and so forth.

In *Richard II*, both social disruptions and identity crises are marked by a struggle over such titles and the power they signify. Bolingbroke, returning to England, insists on being called "Lancaster," not "Hereford"; Northumberland presumptuously forgets to call Richard "King"; Richard himself laments, upon his deposition, that "I must nothing be . . . I have no name, no title" (4.1.194, 248).

Technically, medieval aristocrats did not own their land outright but were conditionally granted it by a feudal superior—in a duke's case, that superior would be the king himself. By Richard's time, however, Magna Carta protected the right of property holders to pass their lands to their heirs. Only a conviction for treason could forfeit the family claim. Ironically, at the moment Richard commandeers the Lancastrian estates, the exiled Bolingbroke is apparently on the verge of invading England with an armed force, so he is actually a traitor and Richard could eventually have appropriated his property in a perfectly legal manner. But Richard's characteristic neglect of proper procedure makes Bolingbroke's return seem a response to the dispossession and thus turns the nobility toward the rebel cause.

Why does Richard behave so heedlessly? He does not imagine that he must earn the respect of the people he governs, or balance his budget, or follow laws. He does not believe that his royal authority depends on the consent of the governed or on the effective manipulation of material resources. Whereas Bolingbroke thinks of power as emanating from "below"—from the king's subjects, from the deployment of material resources—Richard thinks of it as descending from "above," from the God whose representative on earth he was born to be. His assertion in 3.2.49–52 is entirely characteristic:

> Not all the water in the rough rude sea
> Can wash the balm from an anointed king.
> The breath of worldly men cannot depose
> The deputy elected by the Lord.

Later in the same scene, deserted by all but a few supporters, he exclaims: "Is not the king's name forty thousand names? / Arm, arm, my name!" (3.2.80–81). What Richard needs now, of course, is not names but soldiers, but he deliberately refuses to acknowledge the difference.

Richard's drastic impracticalities derive from his conviction that the God who put him on the throne is immanent in the created universe and vigilant in defense of His deputy. Richard is not unique in this conviction: the assumption that God intervenes continuously in human affairs in order to guarantee just outcomes underlies the ritual of the trial by combat as it is staged in 1.3. The way spirit informs and controls the material world can render "dead matter" sympathetic to human beings. "This earth shall have a feeling," Richard claims (3.2.24). Thus he is confident that the earth will put toads in the way of traitors, and that angels will rush to save a king in trouble. Medieval histories are full of such narratives: the ground opens up and swallows an atheist; lightning strikes a perjurer dead.

By Shakespeare's time, the trial by combat had been discredited and the conception of the world to which Richard adheres was beginning to seem obsolete. Some thinkers were increasingly discarding anthropocentric ways of thinking and conceiving of the material world as something alien to human consciousness, ruled by purely physical laws of cause and effect. This change in mentality affected historians, who were subjecting long-accepted myths to critical scrutiny; scientists, who began to place a new value on empirical experimentation; and theologians, who were becoming more skeptical of the continuation of miracles in postbiblical times. Political theorists such as Machiavelli insisted on describing political power as it really was exercised, and not as God or moral scruples might dictate that it ought to be exercised. The pragmatic Bolingbroke, then, is associated with a new, effective, but not necessarily moral or satisfying way of thinking about the manipulation of men and matter.

Richard's assumptions about the world and his place in it turn out to be wrong. His naïveté about the relationship of language and power, spirit and matter, leaves him vulnerable to Bolingbroke's assault. Bolingbroke's supplanting of Richard, then, might be seen not merely as a personal or even a political victory, but as the uprooting of one worldview by another. Whether this displacement represents an advance or a deterioration is, however, another question. The second part of the play, in which Bolingbroke emerges victorious, reexamines the nature of the conflict between the two men and the principles they represent.

In a pivotal scene in act 3, Bolingbroke, Northumberland, and York approach the castle in which Richard has sequestered himself. When Richard finally emerges on the battlements, Bolingbroke exclaims:

> See, see, King Richard doth himself appear,
> As doth the blushing discontented sun
> From out the fiery portal of the East,
> When he perceives the envious clouds are bent
> To dim his glory and to stain the tract
> Of his bright passage to the Occident.
>
> (3.3.62–67)

Bolingbroke is untypically eloquent here but, interestingly, his extended simile works against his own interests. The comparison between king and sun, a traditional figure of speech, implies that the king is both unique and indispensable. Rebels are not rival suns; they are transient clouds that the mighty king will eventually burn away. Even while he mutinies against Richard's misgovernment, Bolingbroke seems unable to escape a conservative conception of monarchy in which rebellion is a form of envy doomed to failure.

Bolingbroke's linguistic slip suggests that it may be easier to amass an army and seize the throne than to put aside one's inherited convictions about the nature of

Death of Phaëthon. From Antonio Tempesta, Ovid's "Metamorphoses" (1606). Richard compares himself to Phaëthon in 3.3.178.

royal authority. Bolingbroke does not have an alternative vocabulary in which to justify his own behavior. Thus, throughout the play, it is hard to be sure whether he is cunningly concealing his true motives or simply incapable of articulating them even to himself. In the opening scenes, although Richard recognizes Bolingbroke's challenge to his authority, Bolingbroke himself seems a bit obtuse about his own purposes, as if his accusation of Mowbray were merely an effect of his sturdy loyalty to Richard. Likewise, it is unclear whether he initially realizes that his return from exile commits him not merely to regaining the Lancastrian estates but to a more thorough attack on Richard's sovereignty. Bolingbroke never appears before us, alone or in company, to ponder his own conduct and motives. In this regard, he differs not only from the obsessively self-reflective Richard but from other Shakespearean usurpers: Richard III, Macbeth, *Hamlet*'s Claudius.

In act 4, however unable he may be to justify the grounds of his own authority, Bolingbroke—now King Henry IV—astutely recognizes that he must convince his subjects that he is legitimately entitled to the crown. Henry needs, somehow, to transfer to himself that mysterious sense of royal sanctity in which Richard had initially placed so much confidence, and to which Henry has no plausible claim. Henry and his followers thus attempt to paper over his gross procedural breach with procedural punctiliousness. Richard cannot be summarily imprisoned or executed; rather, he must seem voluntarily and publicly to resign his sovereignty to Henry.

Unfortunately for Henry, he is not good at managing such rituals, while Richard is in his element. In 4.1, Richard masterfully seizes the symbolic initiative from the apparent victors. "Now mark me how I will undo myself," he announces:

> I give this heavy weight from off my head,
> And this unwieldy scepter from my hand,
> The pride of kingly sway from out my heart.
> With mine own tears I wash away my balm,
> With mine own hands I give away my crown,
> With mine own tongue deny my sacred state,
> With mine own breath release all duteous oaths.
> All pomp and majesty I do forswear;
> My manors, rents, revenues I forgo;
> My acts, decrees, and statutes I deny.
>
> (4.1.196–206)

Richard's actions and words here are meant to recall a coronation ceremony, in which the king is invested with the crown and scepter as his insignia of office, anointed with balm as a sign that he is God's chosen, promised the allegiance of his subjects, and given formal title to the royal domains. One of the main points of this ceremony is its permanence: it cannot be undone. By referring to this ritual at the moment of his deposition, Richard implies that giving up the crown is an impossible act, a kind of absurdity. Moreover, reversing the ceremonies—taking off the crown rather than putting it on, relinquishing rather than accepting the scepter—suggests a special scandal. In medieval and early modern Europe, as among some fundamentalist religious groups today, reversing beneficent ceremonies supposedly evoked their diabolical opposites. One called up devils by reciting Scripture passages backward, or bound oneself to Satan by performing an inversion of baptismal rites. Not surprisingly, Richard's enthusiastic self-dramatization of his plight does not quell doubts about the legitimacy of the usurpation, but encourages those doubts. Immediately after Richard departs, his friends begin to conspire on his behalf; and although their plot is eventually crushed, Henry's reign will never be quiet thereafter.

As the play proceeds, the view of politics associated with Bolingbroke, a view that initially seems hardheaded and realistic, begins to seem not very practical after all.

An acceptable social order requires more than the brute force Henry deploys so expertly. It requires a common set of ideas and practices, a common language and attitude, a set of rituals—all the immaterial abstractions Henry had originally been inclined to disregard.

Just as Shakespeare, over the course of the play, alters our view of the political dilemma represented by the rebellion, so he manipulates our outlook on its main characters. As soon as Richard has lost his throne, we need no longer evaluate him in terms of his effectiveness as a ruler. Immediately his talents seem more obvious, his faults less reprehensible. Richard's extraordinary poetic and introspective gifts allow him to analyze his own situation with a delicacy and insight of which Bolingbroke is entirely incapable. He is acutely aware of the figure he cuts to the only audience that matters to him, himself; in fact, his self-destructive behavior might be seen as an unconscious quest for the expressive opportunities provided only by misery. Always preoccupied with analogies between kingship and godhead, Richard identifies more and more, as the play continues, with the suffering Christ, consoling himself with the comparison and deriving from it a certain sad grandeur. Obviously Richard's self-dramatizing talents are intrinsically connected to his weaknesses, but that does not mean that those strengths are negligible. They are especially hard to ignore in a *play*, in which poetic language, symbolic thought, and the effective deployment of spectacle are central concerns.

Our shifting view of Richard has produced, in both Shakespeare's time and our own, a certain ambiguity as to the play's genre. When Shakespeare's friends and fellow actors compiled his works in the First Folio, they grouped *Richard II* with the history plays—understandably, since it concerns itself with problems of rule and the legitimacy of rulers, is based on historical materials, and inaugurates a series of plays that deals with the reigns of three successive kings. Yet in its earliest printed version the play was called *The Tragedie of King Richard the Second*, a title that suggests a focus not on the fate of a nation but on the disastrous career of a fascinating, flawed individual.

Richard's case encourages us to reflect on the way the politics and the values of political life—the dominant concerns of history plays—constrain our evaluation of him. In *Richard II*, Shakespeare uses female characters to suggest the possibility of an alternative perspective on the events he depicts. In the second scene, the Duchess of Gloucester urges Gaunt to revenge Thomas of Woodstock, her husband and his brother. Gaunt refuses: in his view, the subject's duty to his monarch must outweigh his obligation to his kin. Their conversation reminds us that England's political crisis is also a familial disaster, and that construing it as one rather than the other has important consequences.

Throughout the play, the men, like Gaunt, tend to subordinate domestic concerns to political ones, family bonds to the all-important relationship between king and subject. The women, like the Duchess of Gloucester, do the opposite. Although the historical Richard's queen was only ten years old at the time of Bolingbroke's invasion, Shakespeare makes Isabella a mature young woman and invents touching, wholly nonfactual scenes in which she intuitively senses her husband's trouble, then learns of the usurpation in a garden, and later suffers through an imposed parting from her husband. The pathos of these scenes derives from the Queen's utter helplessness. She is imagined as Richard's wife, a domestic function, not England's Queen, a public one. All her responses are thus founded on her singleminded loyalty to the marital tie, as sharply distinguished from the bonds of politics. "Banish us both, and send the King with me," she begs Northumberland when he informs them that she will be exiled and her husband kept in England. "That were some love, but little policy," Northumberland replies (5.1.83–84). The last thing Bolingbroke needs is a legitimate child of Richard's to confuse his claims to the throne even more. But the Queen fails to grasp Northumberland's meaning, because she does not understand "policy"—that is, politics. It is not her sphere.

"Like perspectives which, rightly gazed upon, / Show nothing but confusion; eyed awry, / Distinguish form" (*Richard II* 2.2.18–20). The most famous Renaissance example of such a "perspective" or anamorphic picture is Hans Holbein's *The Ambassadors* (1533); when the painting is viewed from the side ("awry"), the elongated object in the foreground reveals itself to be a skull.

The difference between civic and domestic domains also appears in the scenes immediately following, which stage a dispute between the Duke and Duchess of York over their son, Aumerle. Here again Shakespeare altered his sources, unhistorically making Aumerle an only child and the Duchess his natural mother. Having discovered that Aumerle is involved in a plot to kill the new Henry IV and reinstate Richard, York feels bound to inform Henry of the treason. He puts what he sees as his sworn duty to his sovereign above the ties of blood. The Duchess is outraged. "Wilt thou not hide the trespass of thine own?" she asks. "Have we more sons? Or are we like to have?" (5.2.89–90). For her, the familial relationship takes precedence over the public one. In the dispute between York and his Duchess in 5.2 and 5.3, the incongruity of their perspectives is registered in a shift of tone and genre. Despite the desperate stakes, their disagreement devolves into an elderly couple's ridiculous marital squabble. And this ridiculousness plays into the Duchess's hands: as the Duchess convinces Henry to view her son's transgression in an indulgent light, domestic comedy briefly interrupts political tragedy, facilitating royal mercy.

This dividing of the "public" male role from the "private" female role is hardly a Shakespearean invention. But Shakespeare puts that division of perspective to thematic use in *Richard II*. In 2.2, when Isabella has a presentiment of ruin, Bushy tries to console her in an elaborate speech about perspective glasses and "anamorphic" paintings. These two Renaissance inventions encourage speculation about the difference between the "right" or "centered" way of seeing and an oblique outlook from which shapes look very different. Of course, Isabella's inexplicable presentiment of disaster turns out to be more apt than her male companions' optimism. Perhaps the women's different perspective implies that the history play's focus on traditionally masculine political concerns may exclude whole realms of human experience.

In the fifth act, Richard—weeping, enclosed, suffering, and excluded from authority—finds himself in the position the play has defined as a feminine one. Politically marginalized, he nonetheless dominates the closing moments of the play, first by his powerful soliloquizing and later by his courageous defiance of his murderers. In some respects, the final scenes of *Richard II* recall its opening. What seems to be a simple opposition turns out to be far more complex, as categories of expedience and impracticality, power and weakness, right and wrong mutate and change places. Once again, however, the apparent conclusion of a conflict merely postpones its resolution. The *Henry IV* plays will stage the aftermath.

KATHARINE EISAMAN MAUS

SELECTED BIBLIOGRAPHY

Calderwood, James L. "*Richard II* and the Fall of Speech." *Shakespearean Metadrama: The Argument of the Play in "Titus Andronicus," "Love's Labour's Lost," "Romeo and Juliet," and "Richard II."* Minneapolis: U of Minnesota P, 1971. 149–86. Looks at the transfer of power from Richard to Bolingbroke as a version of Shakespeare's move from lyric stylization to a sparer dramatic language.

Hamilton, Donna. "The State of Law in *Richard II*." *Shakespeare Quarterly* 34 (1983): 5–17. Analyzes the relation between monarchy and law in *Richard II* and in early modern political theory.

Kantorowicz, Ernst H. Chapter 2. *The King's Two Bodies: A Study in Mediaeval Political Theology*. Princeton, NJ: Princeton UP, 1957. 24–41. Examines the theory of kingship in *Richard II*.

Lopez, Jeremy, ed. *Richard II: New Critical Essays*. New York: Routledge, 2012. Essays on historical, literary, and performance issues.

Maus, Katharine. "Being and Having in *Richard II*" and "Prodigal Princes." *Being and Having in Shakespeare*. Oxford: Oxford UP, 2013. 1–57. Explores the issues of landed property, prodigality, and selfhood in the play.

McMillin, Scott. "*Richard II*: Eyes of Sorrow, Eyes of Desire." *Shakespeare Quarterly* 35 (1984): 40–52. Argues that an impulse to self-expressiveness is at odds with the exercise of political power in *Richard II*.

Moore, Jeanie Grant. "Queen of Sorrow, King of Grief: Reflections and Perspectives in *Richard II*." *In Another Country: Feminist Perspectives on Renaissance Drama*. Ed. Dorothea Kehler and Susan Baker. Metuchen, NJ: Scarecrow, 1991. 19–35. Explores the imagery of mirrors and anamorphic pictures in *Richard II*.

Norbrook, David. "'A Liberal Tongue': Language and Rebellion in *Richard II*." *Shakespeare's Universe: Renaissance Ideas and Conventions*. Ed. John M. Mucciolo. Aldershot, Hampshire: Scolar, 1996. 37–51. Presents a critique of monarchy in *Richard II*.

Saccio, Peter. *Shakespeare's English Kings: History, Chronicle, and Drama*. 2nd ed. New York: Oxford UP, 2000. 17–35. Offers a succinct account of the historical background to Shakespeare's play.

Zitner, Sheldon. "Aumerle's Conspiracy." *Studies in English Literature* 14 (1974): 238–57. Argues for the importance of the Aumerle scenes for the end of *Richard II*.

FILMS

King Richard the Second. 1978. Dir. David Giles. UK. 158 mins. In this BBC-TV production, Derek Jacobi as an effeminate Richard II confronts Jon Finch as the calculating Bolingbroke. John Gielgud is a notable John of Gaunt.

Richard II. 2012. Dir. Rupert Goold. A slightly abridged, star-studded version in the BBC series *The Hollow Crown*, beautifully filmed on location. With Ben Whishaw as Richard, Rory Kinnear as Bolingbroke, and Lindsay Duncan as a memorable Dutchess of York.

TEXTUAL INTRODUCTION

Richard II was one of the most published of Shakespeare's plays during his lifetime, with five quarto editions (Q1 through Q5) appearing by 1615. The First Quarto edition, entitled *The Tragedie of King Richard the Second*, was published anonymously in 1597, printed by Valentine Simmes for publisher Andrew Wise. Q1 is a relatively clean text, although it has limited stage directions; editors have posited that it might derive from Shakespeare's own working manuscript. Q1 formed the basis for two more quartos in 1598, Q2 and Q3, also printed by Simmes for Wise, both of which were among the earliest play texts to credit Shakespeare on the title page. These three early editions, however, lack a crucial sequence, the so-called deposition scene (in 4.1) in which Richard II hands over his crown to Henry Bolingbroke. A Fourth Quarto, Q4, was printed by William White for Matthew Law in 1608 and included extra material, advertised as "new additions of the Parliament scene, and the deposing of King Richard." Q5, based on Q4, was printed in 1615, again by White for Law. Seven years after Shakespeare's death, the 1623 First Folio (F) included *The Life and Death of King Richard the Second* as the second of its ten "Histories." The Folio includes a version of the deposition (or abdication) scene (4.1.149–311) that is different from and superior to that contained in Q4 and Q5.

The existence of these different versions of *Richard II* raises the question of whether the deposition scene formed part of the original play but was deleted in Q1, Q2, and Q3, or whether it was added to the play sometime before the printing of Q4 in 1608. Several factors suggest strongly that such a scene was part of the play as originally written and acted onstage, but was omitted from the published version because it was too politically sensitive to be printed. It is notable, for example, that the first printed editions containing the deposition scene date from the Jacobean period, after the death of Queen Elizabeth I in 1603. Elizabeth was known to fear the threat of deposition and to identify with this play's subject, on one occasion allegedly telling the antiquarian William Lambarde, "I am Richard II; know ye not that?" Another printed book dealing with Richard's deposition, by John Haywarde in 1599, was subject to a formal inquiry, and its publisher was imprisoned in the Tower of London. Andrew Wise, the publisher of Q1, Q2, and Q3, may have deemed it more prudent to avoid such a possibility by cutting the depiction of the moment of deposition. But the scene is perhaps not gone altogether. At the end of 4.1 in these quartos, the Abbot of Westminster exclaims, "A woeful pageant have we here beheld" (Q 4.1.158). In the Quarto version, we have beheld no "pageant"—but that is an apt description for the highly visual scene of Richard's handling of the crown and scepter and breaking of a mirror included in the Folio version. We might therefore see the Abbot's line as the telltale trace of a "pageant" that did indeed form part of the play, but which was cut from its earliest printed editions.

While the Quarto text lacks this important scene, the Folio in turn lacks certain lines that exist in the Quarto text (1.3.129–33, 1.3.238–41, 1.3.267–92, 2.2.77, 3.2.29–32, 4.1.53–60). These omissions may suggest that Shakespeare or another hand revised the text between 1597 and 1623, probably for theatrical performance; the presence of more elaborate stage directions has led some editors to believe the

Folio is based on a promptbook. The revisions here include some minor cuts that streamline the playing of certain scenes; but they also notably present Gaunt, the Duke of Lancaster, as a less pragmatic, more sympathetic character. The Quarto and Folio also differ in their treatment of the speech prefixes used to designate the characters of King Richard and Bolingbroke, later King Henry. While the Quarto attempts to show the differing fortunes of the two men by giving the title of *"King"* first to Richard and later to Bolingbroke, F largely refers to the men as *"Richard"* and *"Bolingbroke."* Taken as a whole, the revisions evident in the Folio and the decision to change the speech prefixes work to produce a subtly different play.

In order to include "all" the possible lines, modern editions have tended to use Q1 as a base text, but to add the deposition scene from F. *The Norton Shakespeare* presents the Folio text in the print edition, and both the Folio and the Quarto texts in the Digital Edition. In the Digital Edition, readers will be able to appreciate how, without an extended deposition scene, Q1 offers a decidedly less dramatic, less heightened version of events.

ALAN STEWART

PERFORMANCE NOTE

Richard II, the weak, overindulged ruler who unexpectedly turns dignified sufferer and visionary, ranks among Shakespeare's most coveted roles. As with *Hamlet* and *Antony and Cleopatra*, productions of this play are often built around virtuosic performances by the lead actor, who must balance petulance and piety, jesting and introspection, and who must help determine whether Richard's theatricality is self-conscious or natural, whether he resigns the crown as a result of fear or insight, and whether his dying scene is marked by regret, resignation, or transcendence. These choices inevitably implicate representations of Henry Bolingbroke, who can be portrayed as a populist hero or a cunning rival, his coronation a sign of purification and promise, or of sustained corruption and loss.

Bolingbroke has often been presented as Richard's antithesis: a plain-dealing soldier opposite an effete, lyrically indulgent king. This contrast suggests that the character's cool efficiency and confidence are either disappointing alternatives to Richard's theatrical passions or the very qualities that justify the deposition. Exaggerating Bolingbroke's insensitivity can secure Richard's tragic position, while focusing on Richard's vanity and vindictiveness can deepen an audience's investment in Bolingbroke and his humbler, more ambivalent relationship to power. On the other hand, topical productions increasingly choose to present the two kings as parallel figures, attracting interest and scrutiny for Henry by making clear that his ethical compromises and plots to maintain control are reminiscent of Richard's own. Such productions tend to focus not so much on personal triumph and tragedy as on the corrupting influence of power, and the disappointment that follows once a political challenger begins his period of rule.

Depending on the approach to the kings, Richard's courtiers can appear as victims of Bolingbroke's ambition or as justly punished sycophants and schemers, while the nobles can act chiefly for England's interests or for their own. Meanwhile, York can change sides deliberately or in seeming ignorance, either adding to political tensions or disrupting them with comedy. Additional dramaturgical considerations include whether to give contemporary political relevance to the deposition scene; Richard's sexuality and relationship to the Queen (several productions have implied or established an intimate relationship between Richard and Aumerle); managing the play's many instances of medieval pageantry; and integrating the potentially slapstick comedy of the Aumerle episodes (4.1, 5.3).

BRETT GAMBOA

The Life and Death of
King Richard the Second

[THE PERSONS OF THE PLAY

King RICHARD II
QUEEN, wife to King Richard
John of GAUNT, Duke of Lancaster, uncle to Richard
Henry BOLINGBROKE, Duke of Hereford, son to John of Gaunt, later Duke of
    Lancaster and King Henry IV
DUCHESS OF GLOUCESTER, widow to the Duke of Gloucester, Gaunt's and
    York's brother
Duke of YORK, uncle to Richard and Bolingbroke, brother to Gaunt
DUCHESS OF YORK
Duke of AUMERLE, later Rutland, son to York and Duchess of York
Thomas MOWBRAY, Duke of Norfolk
GREENE ⎫
BAGOT ⎬ followers of King Richard
BUSHY ⎭
Henry Percy, Earl of NORTHUMBERLAND ⎫
Harry PERCY, his son   ⎬ supporters of Bolingbroke
Lord ROSS   ⎭
Lord WILLOUGHBY
Earl of SALISBURY ⎫
Bishop of CARLISLE ⎬ supporters of King Richard
Sir Stephen SCROPE ⎭
Lord BERKELEY
Lord FITZWATER
Duke of SURREY
ABBOT of Westminster
Sir Piers EXTON
Lord MARSHAL
MOWBRAY'S HERALD
BOLINGBROKE'S HERALD
Welsh CAPTAIN
Two LADIES attending on the Queen
GARDENER
Two SERVANTS working with the Gardener
SERVANT to York
KEEPER of the prison at Pomfret Castle
GROOM
Nobles, Soldiers, Attendants, Officers, Servants, Guard]

1.1 (Q 1.1)

Enter King RICHARD, *John of* GAUNT, [*Lord* MARSHAL,]
with other Nobles and Attendants.[1]

RICHARD   Old John of Gaunt,[2] time-honored Lancaster,
    Hast thou, according to thy oath and band,°   *bond*
    Brought hither Henry Hereford, thy bold son,
    Here to make good the boist'rous late appeal,°   *violent recent accusation*
5   Which then our leisure[3] would not let us hear,
    Against the Duke of Norfolk, Thomas Mowbray?
GAUNT   I have, my liege.
RICHARD   Tell me, moreover, hast thou sounded° him   *inquired of*
    If he appeal the Duke on ancient malice,[4]
10   Or worthily, as a good subject should,
    On some known ground of treachery in him?
GAUNT   As near as I could sift° him on that argument,°   *discover from / topic*
    On some apparent° danger seen in him   *manifest*
    Aimed at your highness, no inveterate malice.
15 RICHARD   Then call them to our presence. Face to face,
    And frowning brow to brow, ourselves will hear
    Th'accuser and the accusèd freely speak.
    High-stomached° are they both and full of ire,   *Haughty*
    In rage, deaf as the sea, hasty as fire.

Enter BOLINGBROKE *and* MOWBRAY.

20 BOLINGBROKE   Many years of happy days befall
    My gracious sovereign, my most loving liege.
MOWBRAY   Each day still better others' happiness[5]
    Until the heavens, envying earth's good hap,°   *fortune*
    Add an immortal title to your crown.
25 RICHARD   We thank you both—yet one but flatters us,
    As well appeareth by the cause you come,
    Namely, to appeal each other of high treason.
    Cousin of Hereford, what dost thou object°   *charge*
    Against the Duke of Norfolk, Thomas Mowbray?
30 BOLINGBROKE   First, heaven be the record to my speech.
    In the devotion of a subject's love,
    Tendering° the precious safety of my prince,   *Having care for*
    And free from other misbegotten hate,
    Come I appellant° to this princely presence.   *as accuser*
35   Now, Thomas Mowbray, do I turn to thee,
    And mark my greeting° well: for what I speak   *address*
    My body shall make good upon this earth,
    Or my divine° soul answer it in heaven.   *immortal*
    Thou art a traitor and a miscreant,
40   Too good° to be so, and too bad to live,   *wellborn*
    Since the more fair and crystal is the sky,
    The uglier seem the clouds that in it fly.
    Once more, the more to aggravate the note,°   *emphasize the reproach*
    With a foul traitor's name stuff I thy throat,
45   And wish, so please my sovereign, ere I move,

1.1 Location: Windsor Castle, near London.
1. TEXTUAL COMMENT The Folio text designates the
principal characters as "Richard" and "Bolingbroke"
in speech prefixes for most of the play. The Quarto
texts, by contrast, call Richard "King" until his deposition, and call Bolingbroke "King Henry" after the
deposition and simply "King" after Richard's death.

See Digital Edition TC 1 (Folio edited text) for a discussion of the implications.
2. Named after his birthplace, Ghent (in Flanders); his
title was Duke of Lancaster. He was fifty-eight years old.
3. That is, lack of leisure. Richard uses the royal "we."
4. Out of long-standing enmity.
5. May each day be better than the last.

What my tongue speaks, my right-drawn sword may prove.
MOWBRAY Let not my cold words here accuse my zeal.°   *cast doubt on my loyalty*
  'Tis not the trial of a woman's war,
  The bitter clamor of two eager° tongues,   *sharp*
50 Can arbitrate[6] this cause betwixt us twain.
  The blood is hot that must be cooled for this.
  Yet can I not of such tame patience boast
  As to be hushed and naught at all to say.
  First, the fair reverence of your highness curbs me
55 From giving reins and spurs to my free speech,
  Which else would post° until it had returned   *ride fast*
  These terms of treason doubly down his throat.
  Setting aside his high blood's royalty,[7]
  And let him be° no kinsman to my liege,   *And as if he were*
60 I do defy him, and I spit at him,
  Call him a slanderous coward and a villain;
  Which to maintain, I would allow him odds
  And meet him, were I tied° to run afoot   *obliged*
  Even to the frozen ridges of the Alps,
65 Or any other ground inhabitable
  Wherever Englishman durst set his foot.
  Meantime, let this defend my loyalty:
  By all my hopes, most falsely doth he lie.
BOLINGBROKE [*throwing down his gage*] Pale trembling coward,
    there I throw my gage,[8]
70 Disclaiming here the kindred of[9] a king,
  And lay aside my high blood's royalty,
  Which fear, not reverence, makes thee to except.°   *set aside*
  If guilty dread hath left thee so much strength
  As to take up mine honor's pawn,° then stoop.   *(the gage)*
75 By that, and all the rites of knighthood else,
  Will I make good against thee, arm to arm,
  What I have spoken or thou canst devise.
MOWBRAY [*picking up the gage*] I take it up,[1] and by that sword
    I swear
  Which gently laid my knighthood on my shoulder,
80 I'll answer thee in any fair degree°   *honorable manner*
  Or chivalrous design of knightly trial.
  And when I mount, alive may I not light°   *dismount*
  If I be traitor or unjustly fight.
RICHARD [*to* BOLINGBROKE] What doth our cousin lay to
    Mowbray's charge?
85 It must be great that can inherit us°   *make us have*
  So much as of a thought of ill in him.
BOLINGBROKE Look what I said, my life shall prove it true:
  That Mowbray hath received eight thousand nobles°   *gold coins*
  In name of lendings° for your highness' soldiers,   *As advances on pay*
90 The which he hath detained for lewd employments,°   *improper uses*
  Like a false traitor and injurious villain.
  Besides I say, and will in battle prove,
  Or° here or elsewhere to the furthest verge°   *Either / horizon*
  That ever was surveyed by English eye,

---

6. Judge (without implying compromise).
7. Bolingbroke, like Richard, was a grandson of
Edward III.
8. Pledge to combat—probably a glove.
9. The privilege of kinship with.
1. Thereby accepting the challenge.

95   That all the treasons for these eighteen years[2]
        Complotted° and contrivèd in this land   *Plotted*
        Fetched° from false Mowbray their first head° and spring.   *Derive / source*
        Further I say, and further will maintain
        Upon his bad life, to make all this good,
100   That he did plot the Duke of Gloucester's death,[3]
        Suggest° his soon-believing° adversaries,   *Incite / credulous*
        And consequently,° like a traitor coward,   *subsequently*
        Sluiced° out his innocent soul through streams of blood—   *Let flow*
        Which blood, like sacrificing Abel's,[4] cries
105   Even from the tongueless caverns of the earth
        To me for justice and rough chastisement;
        And by the glorious worth of my descent,
        This arm shall do it, or this life be spent.
    RICHARD   How high a pitch[5] his resolution soars!
110   Thomas of Norfolk, what sayest thou to this?
    MOWBRAY   Oh, let my sovereign turn away his face
        And bid his ears a little while be deaf
        Till I have told this slander of his blood,°   *disgrace to his ancestry*
        How God and good men hate so foul a liar.
115 RICHARD   Mowbray, impartial are our eyes and ears.
        Were he my brother, nay, our kingdom's heir,
        As he is but my father's brother's son,
        Now, by my scepter's awe, I make a vow
        Such neighbor-nearness to our sacred blood
120   Should nothing privilege him nor partialize°   *bias*
        The unstooping firmness of my upright soul.
        He is our subject, Mowbray; so art thou.
        Free speech and fearless I to thee allow.
    MOWBRAY   Then, Bolingbroke, as low as to thy heart
125   Through the false passage of thy throat, thou liest.
        Three parts of that receipt° I had for Calais   *money received*
        Disbursed I to his highness' soldiers;
        The other part reserved I by consent,
        For that my sovereign liege was in my debt
130   Upon remainder of a dear account[6]
        Since last I went to France to fetch his Queen.
        Now swallow down that lie. For° Gloucester's death,   *As for*
        I slew him not, but to mine own disgrace
        Neglected my sworn duty in that case.[7]
135   [*to* GAUNT] For you, my noble lord of Lancaster,
        The honorable father to my foe,
        Once I did lay an ambush for your life,
        A trespass that doth vex my grievèd soul;
        But ere I last received the sacrament
140   I did confess it, and exactly° begged   *expressly*
        Your grace's pardon, and I hope I had it.
        This is my fault. As for the rest appealed,°   *accused*

2. Since the Peasants' Revolt of 1381.
3. Thomas of Woodstock, Duke of Gloucester, was mysteriously murdered while in the custody of Mowbray. Richard had reason to hate him; earlier Woodstock had attempted to curtail the young King's power by placing authority in the hands of a royal council, of which Woodstock was the head.
4. In Genesis 4, Cain murders his brother Abel because God prefers Abel's offering of sheep to Cain's fruits of the ground.
5. Highest point of a falcon's flight.
6. For the balance of a large sum.
7. Mowbray is circumspect here; in the next scene, Gaunt and the Duchess assert less ambiguously that Richard ordered him to kill Woodstock.

It issues from the rancor of a villain,
A recreant° and most degenerate° traitor, *faithless / cowardly*
145 Which in myself° I boldly will defend, *my own person*
And interchangeably° hurl down my gage *reciprocally*
Upon this overweening traitor's foot,
To prove myself a loyal gentleman,
Even in the best blood chambered° in his bosom. *enclosed*
 [*He throws down his gage.* BOLINGBROKE *picks it up.*]
150 In haste whereof,° most heartily I pray *To hasten which*
Your highness to assign our trial day.
 RICHARD   Wrath-kindled gentlemen, be ruled by me.
Let's purge this choler without letting blood.[8]
This we prescribe, though no physician;
155 Deep malice[9] makes too deep incision.
Forget, forgive, conclude,° and be agreed; *come to terms*
Our doctors say this is no time to bleed.
 [*to* GAUNT] Good uncle, let this end where it begun;
We'll calm the Duke of Norfolk, you your son.
160 GAUNT   To be a make-peace shall become° my age. *befit*
Throw down, my son, the Duke of Norfolk's gage.[1]
 RICHARD   And Norfolk, throw down his.
 GAUNT   When, Harry, when?
Obedience bids I should not bid again.
 RICHARD   Norfolk, throw down, we bid; there is no boot.° *help for it*
165 MOWBRAY [*kneeling*]   Myself I throw, dread sovereign, at thy
     foot.
My life thou shalt command, but not my shame.
The one my duty owes; but my fair name,
Despite of death, that lives upon my grave,
To dark dishonor's use thou shalt not have.
170 I am disgraced, impeached, and baffled[2] here,
Pierced to the soul with slander's venomed spear,
The which no balm can cure but his heart-blood
Which breathed° this poison. *uttered*
 RICHARD   Rage must be withstood.
Give me his gage. Lions make leopards tame.[3]
175 MOWBRAY   Yea, but not change his spots.[4] Take but my shame,
And I resign my gage. My dear, dear lord,
The purest treasure mortal times° afford *earthly lives*
Is spotless reputation; that away,
Men are but gilded loam or painted clay.
180 A jewel in a ten-times-barred-up chest
Is a bold spirit in a loyal breast.
Mine honor is my life, both grow in one;° *united*
Take honor from me and my life is done.
Then, dear my liege, mine honor let me try;° *put to the test*
185 In that I live, and for that will I die.
 RICHARD [*to* BOLINGBROKE]   Cousin, throw down your gage.
     Do you begin.
 BOLINGBROKE   O heaven, defend my soul from such foul sin!

---

8. Let's expel the bile (thought to be the physiological cause of anger) without bloodletting (in combat; as a medical remedy).
9. Enmity; virulence (of a disease).
1. As a gesture of reconciliation.

2. Publicly stripped of knighthood (a chivalric term).
3. Lions were the King's emblem; leopards were Mowbray's. Heraldic banners are likely to be displayed onstage in this scene.
4. Leopard spots; stains of reproach.

Shall I seem crestfall'n in my father's sight?
Or with pale beggar-fear impeach my height°   *disgrace my rank*
190   Before this out-dared dastard?° Ere my tongue   *coward*
Shall wound mine honor with such feeble wrong
Or sound so base a parle,° my teeth shall tear   *trumpet call for a truce*
The slavish motive° of recanting fear   *instrument (the tongue)*
And spit it bleeding in his° high disgrace,   *its*
195   Where shame doth harbor, even in Mowbray's face.

                                       Exit GAUNT.

RICHARD   We were not born to sue but to command;
Which since we cannot do to make you friends,
Be ready as your lives shall answer it
At Coventry upon Saint Lambert's Day.°   *September 17*
200   There shall your swords and lances arbitrate
The swelling difference of your settled hate.
Since we cannot atone° you, you shall see   *reconcile*
Justice design the victor's chivalry.[5]
Lord Marshal, command our officers at arms
205   Be ready to direct these home alarms.°   *Exeunt.*   *domestic disturbances*

1.2 (Q 1.2)

Enter [John of] GAUNT *and [the]* DUCHESS
OF GLOUCESTER.

GAUNT   Alas, the part I had in Gloucester's blood[1]
Doth more solicit me than your exclaims°   *exclamations*
To stir against the butchers of his life.
But since correction lieth in[2] those hands
5   Which made the fault that we cannot correct,
Put we our quarrel to the will of heaven,
Who, when they see the hours ripe on earth,
Will rain hot vengeance on offenders' heads.

DUCHESS OF GLOUCESTER   Finds brotherhood in thee no sharper
     spur?
10   Hath love in thy old blood no living fire?
Edward's° seven sons, whereof thyself art one,   *(Edward III's)*
Were as seven vials of his sacred blood,
Or seven fair branches springing from one root.
Some of those seven are dried by nature's course,
15   Some of those branches by the destinies cut;
But Thomas, my dear lord, my life, my Gloucester,
One vial full of Edward's sacred blood,
One flourishing branch of his most royal root,
Is cracked, and all the precious liquor spilt;
20   Is hacked down, and his summer leaves all faded,
By envy's° hand and murder's bloody ax.   *hatred's*
Ah, Gaunt, his blood was thine; that bed, that womb,
That mettle,° that self° mold that fashioned thee   *substance / same*
Made him a man; and though thou liv'st and breath'st,
25   Yet art thou slain in him. Thou dost consent
In some large measure to thy father's death,
In that thou seest thy wretched brother die,
Who was the model of thy father's life.

5. Indicate the victor in knightly combat.   Gaunt's younger brother.
1.2 Location: John of Gaunt's house.   2. Since punishment depends on (Gaunt blames
1. Thomas of Woodstock, Duke of Gloucester, was   Richard for Woodstock's death).

Call it not patience, Gaunt; it is despair.
30 In suff'ring thus thy brother to be slaughtered,
Thou show'st the naked° pathway to thy life,   defenseless; obvious
Teaching stern murder how to butcher thee.
That which in mean° men we entitle patience   common
Is pale cold cowardice in noble breasts.
35 What shall I say? To safeguard thine own life,
The best way is to venge° my Gloucester's death.   avenge
GAUNT   Heaven's is the quarrel, for heaven's substitute,
His deputy anointed in His sight,
Hath caused his death, the which, if wrongfully,
40 Let heaven revenge, for I may never lift
An angry arm against His minister.°   agent
DUCHESS OF GLOUCESTER   Where, then, alas, may I complain
myself?
GAUNT   To heaven, the widow's champion to defense.
DUCHESS OF GLOUCESTER   Why, then, I will. Farewell, old
Gaunt.
45 Thou go'st to Coventry, there to behold
Our cousin° Hereford and fell° Mowbray fight.   kinsman / ruthless
Oh, sit my husband's wrongs on Hereford's spear,
That it may enter butcher Mowbray's breast;
Or if misfortune miss the first career,³
50 Be Mowbray's sins so heavy in his bosom
That they may break his foaming courser's° back   horse's
And throw the rider headlong in the lists,°   jousting arena
A caitiff° recreant° to my cousin Hereford.   wretch / yielding
Farewell, old Gaunt. Thy sometimes° brother's wife   former
55 With her companion, grief, must end her life.
[She starts to leave.]
GAUNT   Sister, farewell. I must to Coventry.
As much good stay with thee as go with me.
[He starts to leave.]
DUCHESS OF GLOUCESTER   Yet one word more. Grief boundeth⁴
where it falls,
Not with the empty hollowness, but weight.⁵
60 I take my leave before I have begun,
For sorrow ends not when it seemeth done.
Commend me to my brother, Edmund York.
Lo, this is all—nay, yet depart not so.
Though this be all, do not so quickly go.
65 I shall remember more. Bid him—oh, what?—
With all good speed at Plashy⁶ visit me.
Alack, and what shall good old York there see
But empty lodgings° and unfurnished walls,   rooms
Unpeopled offices,° untrodden stones?   servants' quarters
70 And what hear there for welcome but my groans?
Therefore commend me; let him not come there
To seek out sorrow that dwells everywhere.
Desolate, desolate, will I hence and die;
The last leave of thee takes my weeping eye.   Exeunt.

3. If (Mowbray's) downfall fails to occur at the first
encounter.
4. Rebounds (causing further sound; the Duchess
apologizes for continuing to speak).

5. Not because it is hollow, like a bouncing ball, but
because it is heavy.
6. Gloucester's house in Essex.

1.3 (Q 1.3)

Enter [Lord] MARSHAL *and* AUMERLE.

MARSHAL My lord Aumerle, is Harry Hereford armed?

AUMERLE Yea, at all points,° and longs to enter in.   *completely*

MARSHAL The Duke of Norfolk, sprightfully° and bold,   *spiritedly*

  Stays but° the summons of the appellant's° trumpet.   *Awaits only / accuser's*

5 AUMERLE Why, then, the champions are prepared and stay

  For nothing but his majesty's approach.

     Flourish.

     Enter King [RICHARD], GAUNT, BUSHY, BAGOT, GREENE,

     [*Attendant,*] *and others; then* MOWBRAY *in armor, and*

     [MOWBRAY'S] HERALD.

RICHARD Marshal, demand of yonder champion

  The cause of his arrival here in arms.

  Ask him his name, and orderly° proceed   *according to the rules*

10   To swear him in the justice of his cause.

MARSHAL [*to* MOWBRAY] In God's name and the King's, say

    who thou art

  And why thou com'st thus knightly clad in arms,

  Against what man thou com'st, and what's thy quarrel.

  Speak truly, on thy knighthood and thine oath,

15   As so defend thee heaven and thy valor.

MOWBRAY My name is Thomas Mowbray, Duke of Norfolk,

  Who hither comes engagèd by my oath,

  Which heaven defend° a knight should violate,   *forbid*

  Both to defend my loyalty and truth

20   To God, my King, and his succeeding issue

  Against the Duke of Hereford that appeals me;

  And, by the grace of God and this mine arm,

  To prove him, in defending of myself,

  A traitor to my God, my King, and me;

25   And as I truly fight, defend me heaven.

     Tucket.° Enter [BOLINGBROKE, *Duke of*] *Hereford, and*   *Trumpet flourish*

     [BOLINGBROKE'S] HERALD.

RICHARD Marshal, ask yonder knight in arms

  Both who he is and why he cometh hither

  Thus placed in habiliments of war.[1]

  And formally, according to our law,

30   Depose° him in the justice of his cause.   *Take testimony from*

MARSHAL [*to* BOLINGBROKE] What is thy name? And wherefore

    com'st thou hither

  Before King Richard in his royal lists?

  Against whom com'st thou, and what's thy quarrel?

  Speak like a true knight, so defend thee heaven.

35 BOLINGBROKE Harry of Hereford, Lancaster, and Derby

  Am I, who ready here do stand in arms

  To prove, by heaven's grace and my body's valor,

  In lists, on Thomas Mowbray, Duke of Norfolk,

  That he's a traitor foul and dangerous

40   To God of heaven, King Richard, and to me;

  And as I truly fight, defend me heaven.

MARSHAL On pain of death, no person be so bold

1.3 Location: The lists (tournament arena) at   1. Wearing plated battle armor.
Coventry.

Or daring-hardy as to touch the lists
Except the Marshal and such officers

45   Appointed to direct these fair designs.°   *procedures*
BOLINGBROKE   Lord Marshal, let me kiss my sovereign's hand
And bow my knee before his majesty.
For Mowbray and myself are like two men
That vow a long and weary pilgrimage;

50   Then let us take a ceremonious leave
And loving farewell of our several° friends.   *respective*
MARSHAL [*to* RICHARD]   The appellant in all duty greets your
    highness
And craves to kiss your hand and take his leave.
RICHARD   We will descend and fold him in our arms.

55   [*to* BOLINGBROKE] Cousin of Hereford, as° thy cause is just,   *insofar as*
So be thy fortune in this royal fight.
Farewell, my blood, which if today thou shed,
Lament we may, but not revenge thee dead.[2]
BOLINGBROKE   Oh, let no noble eye profane° a tear   *misuse*

60   For me if I be gored with Mowbray's spear.
As confident as is the falcon's flight
Against a bird do I with Mowbray fight.
[*to* MARSHAL] My loving lord, I take my leave of you;
[*to* AUMERLE] Of you, my noble cousin, Lord Aumerle,

65   Not sick, although I have to do with death,
But lusty,° young, and cheerily drawing breath.   *vigorous*
[*to* GAUNT] Lo, as at English feasts, so I regreet°   *greet*
The daintiest[3] last, to make the end most sweet.
O thou, the earthy author of my blood,

70   Whose youthful spirit in me regenerate°   *reborn*
Doth with a twofold rigor lift me up
To reach at victory above my head,
Add proof° unto mine armor with thy prayers,   *invulnerability*
And with thy blessings steel° my lance's point   *harden*

75   That it may enter Mowbray's waxen° coat   *(that is, soft)*
And furnish new the name of John o'Gaunt,
Even in the lusty 'havior° of his son.   *conduct*
GAUNT   Heaven in thy good cause make thee prosp'rous.
Be swift like lightning in the execution

80   And let thy blows, doubly redoubled,
Fall like amazing° thunder on the casque°   *stupefying / helmet*
Of thy amazed pernicious enemy.
Rouse up thy youthful blood, be valiant, and live.
BOLINGBROKE   Mine innocence and Saint George° to thrive!   *(England's patron saint)*

85   MOWBRAY   However heaven or fortune cast my lot,
There lives or dies, true to King Richard's throne,
A loyal, just, and upright gentleman.
Never did captive with a freer heart
Cast off his chains of bondage and embrace

90   His golden uncontrolled enfranchisement°   *unrestrained liberation*
More than my dancing soul doth celebrate
This feast of battle with mine adversary.
Most mighty liege and my companion peers,

---

2. TEXTUAL COMMENT The Folio has "thee dead," while the Quarto has "the dead." This might be merely a spelling variant, or it might suggest a change in meaning; instead of promising to refrain from general vengeance as in Q, Richard specifically renounces any retaliation if Bolingbroke is killed. See Digital Edition TC 2 (Folio edited text).
3. Finest thing, like a dessert.

Take from my mouth the wish of happy years.
95 As gentle and as jocund as to jest°   *take part in revels*
Go I to fight; truth hath a quiet breast.
RICHARD   Farewell, my lord. Securely° I espy   *Confidently*
Virtue with valor couchèd[4] in thine eye.
Order the trial, Marshal, and begin.
100 MARSHAL   Harry of Hereford, Lancaster, and Derby,
Receive thy lance; and heaven defend thy right.
[Attendant gives lance to BOLINGBROKE.]
BOLINGBROKE   Strong as a tower in hope, I cry "Amen!"°   *(from Psalm 61:3)*
MARSHAL *[to Attendant]*   Go bear this lance to Thomas,
Duke of Norfolk.
[Attendant takes lance to MOWBRAY.]
BOLINGBROKE'S HERALD   Harry of Hereford, Lancaster, and Derby
105 Stands here for God, his sovereign, and himself,
On pain to be found false and recreant,
To prove the Duke of Norfolk, Thomas Mowbray,
A traitor to his God, his King, and him,
And dares him to set forwards to the fight.
110 MOWBRAY'S HERALD   Here standeth Thomas Mowbray, Duke
of Norfolk,
On pain to be found false and recreant,
Both to defend himself and to approve°   *prove*
Henry of Hereford, Lancaster, and Derby
To God, his sovereign, and to him disloyal,
115 Courageously and with a free desire
Attending but the signal to begin.
MARSHAL   Sound trumpets and set forward combatants.
*A charge sounded. [*RICHARD *throws down his warder.°]*   *staff*
Stay! The King hath thrown his warder down.[5]
RICHARD   Let them lay by their helmets and their spears
120 And both return back to their chairs again.
[to Nobles] Withdraw with us, and let the trumpets sound
While we return° these dukes what we decree.   *Until we deliver to*
*A long flourish.° [*RICHARD *and Nobles confer.]*   *An extended trumpet call*
[to BOLINGBROKE *and* MOWBRAY] Draw near,
And list what with our counsel we have done.[6]
125 For that° our kingdom's earth should not be soiled   *Because*
With that dear blood which it hath fosterèd;
And for° our eyes do hate the dire aspect°   *because / spectacle*
Of civil wounds plowed up with neighbors' swords,
Which so roused up with boist'rous untuned drums,
130 With harsh resounding trumpets' dreadful bray,
And grating shock of wrathful iron arms,
Might from our quiet confines fright fair peace
And make us wade even in our kindred's blood;
Therefore we banish you our territories.
135 You, cousin Hereford, upon pain° of death,   *penalty*
Till twice five summers have enriched our fields,

4. Lodged; aimed in readiness (like a lance).
5. PERFORMANCE COMMENT The decision to halt the trial by combat can be staged in a way that suggests Richard's political savvy, or alternatively makes him seem weak and indecisive. The reactions of Mowbray and Bolingbroke to their sentences of exile can also be inflected in different ways in performance that reflect the two characters' ambition and guilt. See Digital Edition PC 1.
6. TEXTUAL COMMENT The Folio has "councell," a word that can refer either to a group of advisors (modern "council") or to the advice they give ("counsel"). A modernized text must choose one spelling or the other. See Digital Edition TC 3 (Folio edited text).

Shall not regreet° our fair dominions, · greet again
But tread the stranger° paths of banishment. · foreign
BOLINGBROKE   Your will be done. This must my comfort be:
140   That sun that warms you here shall shine on me,
And those his golden beams to you here lent
Shall point on me and gild my banishment.
RICHARD   Norfolk, for thee remains a heavier doom,° · sentence
Which I with some unwillingness pronounce:
145   The sly° slow hours shall not determinate° · stealthy / bring to an end
The dateless limit° of thy dear° exile. · limitless period / grievous
The hopeless word of "Never to return"
Breathe I against thee, upon pain of life.
MOWBRAY   A heavy sentence, my most sovereign liege,
150   And all unlooked for from your highness' mouth.
A dearer merit,° not so deep a maim° · better reward / an injury
As to be cast forth in the common air,
Have I deservèd at your highness' hands.
The language I have learned these forty years,
155   My native English, now I must forgo,
And now my tongue's use is to me no more
Than an unstringèd viol° or a harp, · six-stringed instrument
Or like a cunning° instrument cased up, · skillfully made
Or, being open, put into his hands
160   That knows no touch to tune the harmony.
Within my mouth you have enjailed my tongue,
Doubly portcullised° with my teeth and lips, · shut in by an iron gate
And dull, unfeeling, barren Ignorance
Is made my jailer to attend on me.
165   I am too old to fawn upon a nurse,
Too far in years to be a pupil now.
What is thy sentence, then, but speechless death
Which robs my tongue from breathing native breath?
RICHARD   It boots° thee not to be compassionate;° · helps / sorrowful
170   After our sentence, plaining° comes too late. · lamenting
MOWBRAY   Then thus I turn me from my country's light
To dwell in solemn shades of endless night.
       [He starts to leave.]
RICHARD   Return again, and take an oath with thee.
       [to MOWBRAY and BOLINGBROKE] Lay on our royal sword your
          banished hands.
       [They place their hands on his sword.]
175   Swear by the duty that you owe to heaven—
Our part therein⁷ we banish with yourselves—
To keep the oath that we administer:
You never shall, so help you truth and heaven,
Embrace each other's love in banishment;
180   Nor ever look upon each other's face;
Nor ever write, regreet, or reconcile
This louring° tempest of your homebred hate; · frowning
Nor ever by advisèd° purpose meet · deliberated
To plot, contrive, or complot any ill
185   'Gainst us, our state, our subjects, or our land.

_____

7. Your allegiance to me as God's deputy.

BOLINGBROKE   I swear.

MOWBRAY   And I, to keep all this.

BOLINGBROKE   Norfolk, so far as to mine enemy:
By this time, had the King permitted us,
One of our souls had wandered in the air,
190   Banished this frail sepulcher of our flesh,
As now our flesh is banished from this land.
Confess thy treasons ere thou fly this realm.
Since thou hast far to go, bear not along
The clogging° burden of a guilty soul.   *encumbering*

195   MOWBRAY   No, Bolingbroke. If ever I were traitor,
My name be blotted from the book of life,°   *eternal life*
And I from heaven banished as from hence.
But what thou art, heaven, thou, and I do know,
And all too soon, I fear, the King shall rue.
200   [*to* RICHARD] Farewell, my liege. Now no way can I stray;°   *lose my way*
Save back to England, all the world's my way.   *Exit.*

RICHARD [*to* GAUNT]   Uncle, even in the glasses° of thine eyes   *windows*
I see thy grievèd heart. Thy sad aspect°   *appearance*
Hath from the number of his banished years
205   Plucked four away. [*to* BOLINGBROKE] Six frozen winters spent,
Return with welcome home from banishment.

BOLINGBROKE   How long a time lies in one little word!
Four lagging winters and four wanton° springs   *luxuriant*
End in a word; such is the breath of kings.

210   GAUNT   I thank my liege that in regard of me
He shortens four years of my son's exile.
But little vantage° shall I reap thereby;   *profit*
For ere the six years that he hath to spend
Can change their moons and bring their times about,
215   My oil-dried lamp and time-bewasted° light   *extinguished by time*
Shall be extinct with age and endless night.
My inch of taper will be burnt and done,
And blindfold death[8] not let me see my son.

RICHARD   Why, uncle, thou hast many years to live.

220   GAUNT   But not a minute, King, that thou canst give.
Shorten my days thou canst with sudden sorrow,
And pluck nights from me, but not lend a morrow.
Thou canst help time to furrow me with age,
But stop no wrinkle in his pilgrimage.
225   Thy word is current° with him for my death,   *valid*
But dead, thy kingdom cannot buy my breath.

RICHARD   Thy son is banished upon good advice,
Whereto thy tongue a party-verdict[9] gave.
Why at our justice seem'st thou then to lour?

230   GAUNT   Things sweet to taste prove in digestion sour.
You urged me as a judge, but I had rather
You would have bid me argue like a father.
Alas, I looked when° some of you should say   *I expected that*
I was too strict to make mine own away;
235   But you gave leave to my unwilling tongue

---

8. Because death's emblem is a hooded figure or an   9. A share in the joint verdict.
eyeless skull, and because the dead cannot see.

Against my will to do myself this wrong.
RICHARD [*to* BOLINGBROKE]   Cousin, farewell; [*to* GAUNT] and
    uncle, bid him so.
Six years we banish him, and he shall go.
                  Exit [RICHARD *with* BUSHY, BAGOT,
                    GREENE, HERALDS, *and Attendant*].
    Flourish.
AUMERLE [*to* BOLINGBROKE]   Cousin, farewell. What presence
    must not know,[1]
240   From where you do remain° let paper show.   [*Exit.*]   *stay*
MARSHAL [*to* BOLINGBROKE]   My lord, no leave take I, for I
    will ride
As far as land will let me by your side.
    [*He stands apart.*]
GAUNT [*to* BOLINGBROKE]   Oh, to what purpose dost thou hoard
    thy words
That thou return'st no greeting to thy friends?
245 BOLINGBROKE   I have too few to take my leave of you,
    When the tongue's office° should be prodigal   *function*
    To breathe th'abundant dolor of the heart.
GAUNT   Thy grief is but thy absence for a time.
BOLINGBROKE   Joy absent, grief is present for that time.
250 GAUNT   What is six winters? They are quickly gone.
BOLINGBROKE   To men in joy; but grief makes one hour ten.
GAUNT   Call it a travel that thou tak'st for pleasure.[2]
BOLINGBROKE   My heart will sigh when I miscall it so,
    Which finds it an enforcèd pilgrimage.
255 GAUNT   The sullen passage of thy weary steps
    Esteem a foil[3] wherein thou art to set
    The precious jewel of thy home return.[4]
BOLINGBROKE   Oh, who can hold a fire in his hand
    By thinking on the frosty Caucasus?[5]
260   Or cloy the hungry edge of appetite
    By bare imagination of a feast?
    Or wallow naked in December snow
    By thinking on fantastic° summer's heat?   *imagined*
    Oh, no, the apprehension of the good
265   Gives but the greater feeling to the worse;
    Fell Sorrow's tooth doth never rankle° more   *irritate*
    Than when it bites but lanceth[6] not the sore.
GAUNT   Come, come, my son, I'll bring thee on thy way.
    Had I thy youth and cause, I would not stay.°   *linger*
270 BOLINGBROKE   Then England's ground, farewell; sweet soil,
    adieu—
My mother and my nurse which bears me yet.
Where'er I wander, boast of this I can:
Though banished, yet a true-born Englishman.   [*Exeunt.*]

---

1. What you cannot tell me personally because of your absence.
2. TEXTUAL COMMENT "Travel" and "travail" (labor, hardship) were the same word in early modern English; a modern editor must choose between the two modern spellings, obscuring Gaunt's play on the two meanings. See Digital Edition TC 4 (Folio edited text).
3. Thin metal against which jewels were set to enhance their luster.

4. TEXTUAL COMMENT The Folio omits an extended, 26-line exchange between Gaunt and Bolingbroke in which Gaunt elaborates on the possible advantages of exile; see Digital Edition TC 5 (Folio edited text) for the implications of this revision.
5. Mountain range between the Black and Caspian Seas.
6. Probes (to release the pus from an abscess).

1.4 (Q 1.4)

Enter King [RICHARD], AUMERLE, GREENE, *and* BAGOT.

RICHARD We did observe.[1] Cousin Aumerle,
How far brought you high Hereford on his way?

AUMERLE I brought high Hereford—if you call him so—
But to the next highway, and there I left him.

5   RICHARD And say, what store of parting tears were shed?

AUMERLE Faith, none for me,° except the northeast wind,   *my part*
Which then grew bitterly against our faces,
Awaked the sleepy rheum,° and so by chance   *tears*
Did grace our hollow parting with a tear.

10 RICHARD What said our cousin when you parted with him?

AUMERLE "Farewell"—
And for° my heart disdainèd that my tongue   *because*
Should so profane the word, that[2] taught me craft
To counterfeit oppression of such grief,

15 That word seemed buried in my sorrow's grave.
Marry,° would the word "Farewell" have lengthened hours   *Indeed*
And added years to his short banishment,
He should have had a volume of farewells;
But since it would not, he had none of me.

20 RICHARD He is our cousin, cousin,[3] but 'tis doubt,
When time shall call him home from banishment,
Whether our kinsman come to see his friends.°   *relatives*
Ourself and Bushy here, Bagot, and Greene
Observed his courtship to the common people:

25 How he did seem to dive into their hearts
With humble and familiar courtesy;
What reverence he did throw away on slaves,
Wooing poor craftsmen with the craft of souls
And patient underbearing° of his fortune,   *enduring*

30 As 'twere to banish their affects with him.[4]
Off goes his bonnet° to an oyster-wench;   *cap*
A brace of draymen° bid God speed him well,   *couple of cart drivers*
And had the tribute of his supple knee
With "Thanks, my countrymen, my loving friends,"

35 As were our England in reversion[5] his,
And he our subjects' next degree in hope.

GREENE Well, he is gone, and with him go these thoughts.
Now for the rebels which stand out in Ireland,
Expedient manage° must be made, my liege,   *Hasty arrangements*

40 Ere further leisure yield them further means
For their advantage and your highness' loss.

RICHARD We will ourself in person to this war,
And for° our coffers with too great a court   *because*
And liberal largesse are grown somewhat light,

45 We are enforced to farm our royal realm,[6]

1.4 Location: The court.
1. The scene begins in midconversation; the King is replying to a remark by Bagot or Greene.
2. His heart. Unwilling to give Hereford good wishes insincerely, Aumerle pretends to be overwhelmed with grief.
3. Richard, Bolingbroke, and Aumerle were sons of three brothers.
4. As if taking their affections with him into exile.

5. A legal term for property that reverts to the original owner on the expiring of a contract.
6. To lease the King's right to tax. A medieval king did not have a taxation bureaucracy. Instead, he sold the power to collect taxes to a leaseholder who collected taxes from the king's subjects, compensating himself with a percentage of the proceeds. "Farming" could also refer to the leasing of land for money rents, another way to raise funds.

The revenue whereof shall furnish us
For our affairs in hand. If that come short,
Our substitutes° at home shall have blank charters⁷   *deputies*
Whereto, when they shall know what men are rich,
50   They shall subscribe them° for large sums of gold,   *put them down for*
And send them after to supply our wants;
For we will make for Ireland presently.°   *at once*
       Enter BUSHY.
    Bushy, what news?
BUSHY   Old John of Gaunt is very sick, my lord,
55   Suddenly taken, and hath sent posthaste
To entreat your majesty to visit him.
RICHARD   Where lies he?
BUSHY   At Ely House.
RICHARD   Now put it, heaven, in his physician's mind
To help him to his grave immediately!
60   The lining⁸ of his coffers shall make coats
To deck our soldiers for these Irish wars.
Come, gentlemen, let's all go visit him.
Pray heaven we may make haste, and come too late.
                              Exeunt.

2.1 (Q 2.1)

Enter GAUNT, *sick, [carried in a chair,] with* YORK.
GAUNT   Will the King come, that I may breathe my last
In wholesome counsel to his unstaid° youth?   *unruly*
YORK   Vex not yourself, nor strive not with your breath,
For all in vain comes counsel to his ear.
5   GAUNT   Oh, but they say the tongues of dying men
Enforce attention like deep harmony.
Where words are scarce, they are seldom spent in vain,
For they breathe truth that breathe their words in pain.
He that no more must say is listened more
10   Than they whom youth and ease have taught to glose.°   *talk speciously*
More are men's ends marked than their lives before.
The setting sun and music at the close,
As the last taste of sweets, is sweetest last,
Writ in remembrance more than things long past.
15   Though Richard my life's counsel would not hear,
My death's sad tale may yet undeaf his ear.
YORK   No, it is stopped with other, flatt'ring sounds,
As praises of his state. Then there are found
Lascivious meters, to whose venom sound
20   The open ear of youth doth always listen;
Report of fashions in proud Italy,
Whose manners still° our tardy apish¹ nation   *always*
Limps after in base imitation.
Where doth the world thrust forth a vanity—
25   So° it be new, there's no respect° how vile—   *Provided / regard for*
That is not quickly buzzed into his ears?

7. Documents enabling the King to raise money by
forced loans; the deputies can fill in the blanks with
any amount they see fit.
8. Contents (playing on "fabric used to line

garments").
2.1 Location: Ely House.
1. Imitative but outmoded.

Then all too late comes counsel to be heard
Where will doth mutiny with wit's regard.[2]
Direct not him whose way himself will choose;
30 'Tis breath thou lack'st, and that breath wilt thou lose.
GAUNT   Methinks I am a prophet new inspired,
And thus expiring do foretell of him:
His rash fierce blaze of riot° cannot last,   *wastefulness*
For violent fires soon burn out themselves;
35 Small showers last long but sudden storms are short;
He tires betimes° that spurs too fast betimes;   *soon*
With eager feeding food doth choke the feeder.
Light vanity, insatiate cormorant,[3]
Consuming means, soon preys upon itself.
40 This royal throne of kings, this sceptered isle,
This earth of majesty, this seat of Mars,°   *war god's dwelling*
This other Eden, demi-paradise,
This fortress built by Nature for herself
Against infection° and the hand of war,   *disease; depravity*
45 This happy breed of men, this little world,
This precious stone set in the silver sea,
Which serves it in the office° of a wall   *function*
Or as a moat defensive to a house
Against the envy° of less happier lands—   *malice*
50 This blessèd plot, this earth, this realm, this England,
This nurse, this teeming womb of royal kings,
Feared by their breed[4] and famous for their birth,
Renownèd for their deeds as far from home—
For Christian service and true chivalry[5]—
55 As is the sepulcher in stubborn Jewry[6]
Of the world's ransom, blessèd Mary's son;
This land of such dear souls, this dear, dear land,
Dear for her reputation through the world,
Is now leased out—I die pronouncing it—
60 Like to a tenement° or pelting° farm.   *rental property / worthless*
England, bound in with the triumphant sea,
Whose rocky shore beats back the envious siege
Of watery Neptune, is now bound in with shame,
With inky blots and rotten parchment bonds.[7]
65 That England that was wont to conquer others
Hath made a shameful conquest of itself.
Ah, would the scandal vanish with my life,
How happy then were my ensuing death!
    Enter King [RICHARD], QUEEN, AUMERLE, BUSHY,
        GREENE, BAGOT, ROSS, *and* WILLOUGHBY.
YORK   The King is come. Deal mildly with his youth,
70 For young hot colts being raged do rage the more.
QUEEN [*to* GAUNT]   How fares our noble uncle Lancaster?
RICHARD [*to* GAUNT]   What comfort, man? How is't with agèd
    Gaunt?

---

2. Where willfulness overthrows sound judgment.
3. Glutton (a cormorant is a bird that swallows fish
whole).
4. For their inherited valor.

5. Alluding to the English kings' accomplishments in
the Crusades.
6. Judaea, stubborn in its resistance to Christianity.
7. Richard's "blank charters" (1.4.48).

GAUNT   Oh, how that name befits my composition!°   *constitution*
    Old Gaunt indeed, and gaunt in being old.
75   Within me grief hath kept a tedious fast,
    And who abstains from meat° that is not gaunt?   *food*
    For sleeping England long time have I watched;°   *stayed awake*
    Watching breeds leanness, leanness is all gaunt.
    The pleasure that some fathers feed upon
80   Is my strict fast—I mean my children's looks[8]—
    And therein, fasting, hast thou made me gaunt.
    Gaunt am I for the grave, gaunt as a grave
    Whose hollow womb inherits naught but bones.
RICHARD   Can sick men play so nicely° with their names?   *subtly*
85 GAUNT   No, misery makes sport to mock itself.
    Since thou dost seek to kill my name in me,[9]
    I mock my name, great King, to flatter thee.
RICHARD   Should dying men flatter those that live?
GAUNT   No, no, men living flatter those that die.
90 RICHARD   Thou, now a-dying, say'st thou flatter'st me?
GAUNT   Oh, no, thou diest, though I the sicker be.
RICHARD   I am in health, I breathe, I see thee ill.
GAUNT   Now He that made me knows I see thee ill:
    Ill in myself to see, and in thee seeing ill.[1]
95   Thy deathbed is no lesser than the land
    Wherein thou liest in reputation sick;
    And thou, too careless patient as thou art,
    Committ'st thy anointed body to the cure
    Of those physicians[2] that first wounded thee.
100   A thousand flatterers sit within thy crown,
    Whose compass° is no bigger than thy head;   *circumference*
    And yet, encagèd in so small a verge,[3]
    The waste[4] is no whit lesser than thy land.
    Oh, had thy grandsire with a prophet's eye
105   Seen how his son's son should destroy his sons,
    From forth° thy reach he would have laid thy shame,   *out of*
    Deposing thee before thou wert possessed,[5]
    Which art possessed° now to depose thyself.   *in a diabolical frenzy*
    Why, cousin,° were thou regent° of the world,   *kinsman / ruler*
110   It were a shame to let his land by lease;
    But for thy world enjoying but this land,[6]
    Is it not more than shame to shame it so?
    Landlord of England art thou, and not king:
    Thy state of law[7] is bondslave to the law,
    And—
115 RICHARD   And thou, a lunatic lean-witted fool,
    Presuming on an ague's privilege,°   *the privilege of the sick*
    Dar'st with thy frozen° admonition   *rigid; caused by a chill*
    Make pale our cheek, chasing the royal blood
    With fury from his native residence?°   *its natural place*

---

8. Since Bolingbroke is exiled.
9. Destroy my family (by exiling Bolingbroke).
1. Too ill to see well, and seeing evil in you.
2. Richard's favorites, or his own bad impulses.
3. Area; distance of twelve miles around the court, to which special rules applied.

4. Destruction (specifically, injury done to a property by a tenant); waist, narrowest part.
5. In possession of the crown.
6. Since this realm alone constitutes your world.
7. Legal status (as landlord, not king).

120	Now, by my seat's° right royal majesty,	*throne's*
	Wert thou not brother to great Edward's son,[8]	
	This tongue that runs so roundly° in thy head	*freely*
	Should run thy head from thy unreverent shoulders.	
	GAUNT Oh, spare me not, my brother Edward's son,	
125	For that I was his father Edward's son.	
	That blood already, like the pelican,[9]	
	Thou hast tapped out[1] and drunkenly caroused.	
	My brother Gloucester, plain, well-meaning soul—	
	Whom fair befall in heaven 'mongst happy souls—	
130	May be a precedent and witness good	
	That thou respect'st not spilling° Edward's blood.	*don't hesitate to spill*
	Join with the present sickness that I have,	
	And thy unkindness be like crooked age,	
	To crop° at once a too-long-withered flower.	*cut*
135	Live in thy shame, but die not shame with thee;[2]	
	These words hereafter thy tormentors be.	
	Convey me to my bed, then to my grave;	
	Love they to live that love and honor have.	

Exit[, carried off].

	RICHARD And let them die that age and sullens° have,	*sulks*
140	For both hast thou, and both become the grave.	
	YORK I do beseech your majesty, impute his words	
	To wayward sickliness and age in him.	
	He loves you, on my life, and holds you dear	
	As Harry, Duke of Hereford, were he here.	
145	RICHARD Right, you say true. As Hereford's love, so his;[3]	
	As theirs, so mine; and all be as it is.	

Enter NORTHUMBERLAND.

	NORTHUMBERLAND My liege, old Gaunt commends him to	
	your majesty.	
	RICHARD What says he?	
	NORTHUMBERLAND Nay, nothing; all is said.	
	His tongue is now a stringless instrument;	
150	Words, life, and all old Lancaster hath spent.	
	YORK Be York the next that must be bankrupt so;	
	Though death be poor, it ends a mortal woe.	
	RICHARD The ripest fruit first falls, and so doth he;	
	His time is spent, our pilgrimage must be.°	*continue*
155	So much for that. Now for our Irish wars.	
	We must supplant those rough, rug-headed kerns,[4]	
	Which live like venom where no venom else	
	But only they have privilege to live.[5]	
	And, for° these great affairs do ask some charge,[6]	*because*
160	Towards our assistance we do seize to us	
	The plate, coin, revenues, and movables°	*personal property*
	Whereof our uncle Gaunt did stand possessed.	

---

8. Edward the Black Prince, Edward III's son and Richard's father.
9. A mother pelican was thought to wound her breast so her ungrateful young could feed on her blood.
1. Let run as from a barrel tap.
2. May your shame outlive you.
3. York claims that Gaunt loves Richard as much as he loves his own son; Richard deliberately miscon- strues York to mean that Gaunt loves Richard as much as Hereford does.
4. Shag-haired Irish foot soldiers.
5. Alluding to the legend that St. Patrick drove snakes out of Ireland.
6. Do demand some expenditure.

YORK How long shall I be patient? Oh, how long
        Shall tender° duty make me suffer wrong?   *scrupulous*
165   Not Gloucester's death, nor Hereford's banishment,
        Nor Gaunt's rebukes, nor England's private wrongs,[7]
        Nor the prevention of poor Bolingbroke
        About his marriage,[8] nor my own disgrace
        Have ever made me sour my patient cheek
170   Or bend one wrinkle° on my sovereign's face.   *frown*
        I am the last of noble Edward's sons,
        Of whom thy father, Prince of Wales, was first.
        In war was never lion raged more fierce,
        In peace was never gentle lamb more mild
175   Than was that young and princely gentleman.
        His face thou hast, for even so looked he
        Accomplished with the number of thy hours.°   *When he was your age*
        But when he frowned, it was against the French
        And not against his friends; his noble hand
180   Did win what he did spend, and spent not that
        Which his triumphant father's hand had won;
        His hands were guilty of no kindred's blood,
        But bloody with the enemies of his kin.
        O Richard! York is too far gone with grief,
185   Or else he never would compare between—
RICHARD   Why, uncle, what's the matter?
YORK   O my liege,
        Pardon me if you please; if not, I, pleased
        Not to be pardoned, am content withal.°   *nevertheless*
        Seek you to seize and gripe° into your hands   *grasp*
190   The royalties[9] and rights of banished Hereford?
        Is not Gaunt dead? And doth not Hereford live?
        Was not Gaunt just? And is not Harry true?
        Did not the one deserve to have an heir?
        Is not his heir a well-deserving son?
195   Take Hereford's rights away, and take from Time
        His° charters and his customary rights;   *Its*
        Let not tomorrow then ensue° today;   *follow*
        Be not thyself, for how art thou a king
        But by fair sequence and succession?
200   Now, afore God—God forbid I say true—
        If you do wrongfully seize Hereford's right,
        Call in° his letters patents that he hath   *Revoke*
        By his attorneys general to sue
        His livery, and deny his offered homage,[1]
205   You pluck° a thousand dangers on your head;   *pull*
        You lose a thousand well-disposèd hearts,
        And prick my tender patience to those thoughts
        Which honor and allegiance cannot think.
RICHARD   Think what you will, we seize into our hands
210   His plate, his goods, his money, and his lands.

---

7. Wrongs committed against private individuals.
8. Richard intervened against Bolingbroke's proposed marriage to the King of France's cousin.
9. Privileges granted by a king through "letters patents" (line 202).

1. The letters patents allow Hereford, through his
legal representatives ("attorneys general"), to make a
legal claim for the inheritance of his land ("sue" his
livery), provided he swears allegiance ("offers homage") to the King.

YORK I'll not be by the while.[2] My liege, farewell.
 What will ensue hereof there's none can tell,
 But by bad courses may be understood
 That their events° can never fall out good.   *Exit.*   outcomes
215 RICHARD Go, Bushy, to the Earl of Wiltshire straight.
 Bid him repair° to us to Ely House   go
 To see° this business. Tomorrow next   attend to
 We will for Ireland, and 'tis time, I trow.°   think
 And we create, in absence of ourself,
220 Our uncle York Lord Governor of England,
 For he is just and always loved us well.
 Come on, our Queen. Tomorrow must we part;
 Be merry, for our time of stay is short.
       Flourish.

       [*Exeunt all except*] NORTHUMBERLAND,
                WILLOUGHBY, *and* ROSS.

NORTHUMBERLAND Well, lords, the Duke of Lancaster is dead.
225 ROSS And living, too, for now his son is Duke.
WILLOUGHBY Barely in title, not in revenue.
NORTHUMBERLAND Richly in both, if Justice had her right.
ROSS My heart is great,° but it must break with silence   full of emotion
 Ere't be disburdened with a liberal° tongue.   unrestrained
230 NORTHUMBERLAND Nay, speak thy mind, and let him ne'er
    speak more
 That speaks thy words again to do thee harm.
WILLOUGHBY Tends that thou'dst speak to[3] th' Duke of
    Hereford?
 If it be so, out with it boldly, man.
 Quick is mine ear to hear of good towards him.
235 ROSS No good at all that I can do for him,
 Unless you call it good to pity him,
 Bereft and gelded of his patrimony.
NORTHUMBERLAND Now, afore heaven, 'tis shame such wrongs
    are borne
 In him, a royal prince, and many more
240 Of noble blood in this declining land.
 The King is not himself, but basely led
 By flatterers; and what they will inform
 Merely in° hate 'gainst any of us all,   Purely out of
 That will the King severely prosecute
245 'Gainst us, our lives, our children, and our heirs.
ROSS The commons° hath he pilled° with grievous taxes,   common people / stripped
 And quite lost their hearts. The nobles hath he fined
 For ancient quarrels, and quite lost their hearts.
WILLOUGHBY And daily new exactions are devised,
250 As blanks, benevolences,° and I wot° not what.   forced loans / know
 But what, i'God's name, doth become of this?°   this money
NORTHUMBERLAND Wars hath not wasted it, for warred he
    hath not,
 But basely yielded upon compromise
 That which his ancestors achieved with blows.[4]
255 More hath he spent in peace than they in wars.

---

2. Present during the seizure.
3. Does what you would say concern.

4. Referring to the ceding of Brest, a city in western
France, to the Duke of Bretagne.

ROSS   The Earl of Wiltshire hath the realm in farm.[5]
WILLOUGHBY   The King's grown bankrupt like a broken man.
NORTHUMBERLAND   Reproach and dissolution hangeth over
　　him.
ROSS   He hath not money for these Irish wars,
260　His burdenous taxations notwithstanding,
　　But by the robbing of the banished Duke.
NORTHUMBERLAND   His noble kinsman—most degenerate King!
　　But lords, we hear this fearful tempest sing
　　Yet seek no shelter to avoid the storm.
265　We see the wind sit sore° upon our sails　　　　　　　　　blow hard
　　And yet we strike[6] not, but securely° perish.　　　　　　heedlessly
ROSS   We see the very wrack that we must suffer,
　　And unavoided° is the danger now　　　　　　　　　　unavoidable
　　For suffering° so the causes of our wrack.　　　　　　　enduring
270　NORTHUMBERLAND   Not so. Even through the hollow eyes° of　　eye sockets
　　death
　　I spy life peering, but I dare not say
　　How near the tidings of our comfort is.
WILLOUGHBY   Nay, let us share thy thoughts, as thou dost ours.
ROSS   Be confident to speak, Northumberland.
275　We three are but thyself, and speaking so
　　Thy words are but as thoughts. Therefore be bold.
NORTHUMBERLAND   Then thus: I have from Port le Blanc,
　　A bay in Bretagne,[7] received intelligence
　　That Harry, Duke of Hereford, Rainold, Lord Cobham,
280　Thomas, son and heir to th'Earl of Arundel,[8]
　　That late broke from the Duke of Exeter,
　　His[9] brother, Archbishop late° of Canterbury,　　　　　until recently
　　Sir Thomas Erpingham, Sir John Ramston,
　　Sir John Norberry, Sir Robert Waterton, and Francis Coint,
285　All these well furnished by the Duke of Bretagne
　　With eight tall ships, three thousand men of war,°　　　　soldiers
　　Are making hither with all due expedience
　　And shortly mean to touch our northern shore.
　　Perhaps they had ere this, but that they stay
290　The first departing of the King[1] for Ireland.
　　If then we shall shake off our slavish yoke,
　　Imp out[2] our drooping country's broken wing,
　　Redeem from broking pawn° the blemished crown,　　　　pawnbrokers
　　Wipe off the dust that hides our scepter's gilt,
295　And make high majesty look like itself,
　　Away with me in post° to Ravenspurgh.[3]　　　　　　　speedily
　　But if you faint,° as fearing to do so,　　　　　　　　are fainthearted
　　Stay and be secret, and myself will go.
ROSS   To horse, to horse! Urge doubts to them that fear.
300　WILLOUGHBY   Hold out my horse° and I will first be there.　　If my horse holds up
　　　　　　　　　　　　　　　　　Exeunt.

---

5. *in farm:* on lease (as in 1.4.45–47).
6. Lower sails; deliver blows.
7. In northwest France.
8. TEXTUAL COMMENT An editorial approximation of a line apparently accidentally omitted from early texts. Shakespeare's source states that Arundel's son and heir, Thomas, escaped from Exeter's custody.

See Digital Edition TC 6 (Folio edited text).
9. The Earl of Arundel's.
1. *they stay . . . King:* they wait for the King to depart first.
2. Engraft new feathers on (from falconry).
3. Then a port on the river Humber, in Yorkshire.

2.2 (Q 2.2)

Enter QUEEN, BUSHY, *and* BAGOT.

BUSHY Madam, your majesty is too much sad.[1]
   You promised, when you parted with the King,
   To lay aside self-harming heaviness°   *melancholy*
   And entertain° a cheerful disposition.   *assume*
5 QUEEN To please the King I did; to please myself
   I cannot do it. Yet I know no cause
   Why I should welcome such a guest as grief,
   Save bidding farewell to so sweet a guest
   As my sweet Richard. Yet again, methinks
10 Some unborn sorrow, ripe in Fortune's womb,
   Is coming towards me, and my inward soul
   With nothing trembles. At something it grieves
   More than with parting from my lord the King.
BUSHY Each substance of a grief hath twenty shadows
15 Which shows like grief itself, but is not so;
   For sorrow's eye, glazed with blinding tears,
   Divides one thing entire to many objects,
   Like perspectives which, rightly gazed upon,
   Show nothing but confusion; eyed awry,
20 Distinguish form.[2] So your sweet majesty,
   Looking awry upon your lord's departure,
   Find shapes° of grief more than himself to wail°   *images / bewail*
   Which, looked on as it is, is naught but shadows
   Of what it is not. Then, thrice-gracious Queen,
25 More than your lord's departure weep not. More's not seen,
   Or if it be, 'tis with false sorrow's eye,
   Which for things true weeps things imaginary.
QUEEN It may be so, but yet my inward soul
   Persuades me it is otherwise. Howe'er it be,
30 I cannot but be sad; so heavy sad
   As though on thinking on no thought I think,[3]
   Makes me with heavy nothing faint and shrink.
BUSHY 'Tis nothing but conceit,° my gracious lady.   *imagination*
QUEEN 'Tis nothing less;[4] conceit is still° derived   *always*
35 From some forefather grief. Mine is not so,
   For nothing hath begot my something° grief,   *substantial*
   Or something hath the nothing that I grieve;[5]
   'Tis in reversion that I do possess,[6]
   But what it is that is not yet known what,
40 I cannot name. 'Tis nameless woe, I wot.
      Enter GREENE.
GREENE Heaven save your majesty, and well met, gentlemen.

2.2 Location: Windsor Castle.
1. Shakespeare makes Richard's Queen a mature young woman; the historical Isabella was married to Richard at age seven and was ten at the time of Bolingbroke's invasion.
2. *For sorrow's . . . form:* Bushy first compares the Queen's view of the world, through tear-glazed eyes, to a perspective glass that multiplies one image into many. He then goes on to compare her way of looking to the way one must look at a perspective picture, one that seems distorted unless viewed at an angle ("awry"). See the Introduction to this play.
3. *As though . . . think:* a difficult line. The Queen is playing with the paradox that her premonition, a thought of nothing, or "no thought," is nonetheless almost physically oppressive.
4. Anything but conceit.
5. Or the grief that I feel apparently over nothing actually has some cause.
6. It will come at a later date (that is, her grief anticipates its occasion).

I hope the King is not yet shipped for Ireland.
QUEEN   Why hop'st thou so? 'Tis better hope he is,
For his designs crave° haste, his haste good hope.   *demand*
45   Then wherefore dost thou hope he is not shipped?
GREENE   That he, our hope, might have retired his power°   *brought back his forces*
And driven into despair an enemy's hope,
Who strongly hath set footing in this land.
The banished Bolingbroke repeals° himself,   *recalls from exile*
50   And with uplifted arms° is safe arrived   *weapons*
At Ravenspurgh.
QUEEN   Now God in heaven forbid!
GREENE   O madam, 'tis too true; and, that is worse,
The Lord Northumberland, his young son Henry Percy,
The lords of Ross, Beaumont, and Willoughby,
55   With all their powerful friends are fled to him.
BUSHY   Why have you not proclaimed Northumberland
And the rest of the revolted faction, traitors?°   *treasonous conspirators*
GREENE   We have—whereupon the Earl of Worcester
Hath broke his staff,[7] resigned his stewardship,
60   And all the household servants fled with him
To Bolingbroke.
QUEEN   So, Greene, thou art the midwife of my woe,
And Bolingbroke my sorrow's dismal heir.
Now hath my soul brought forth her prodigy,°   *monstrous birth; portent*
65   And I, a gasping new-delivered mother,
Have woe to woe, sorrow to sorrow joined.
BUSHY   Despair not, madam.
QUEEN   Who shall hinder me?
I will despair and be at enmity
With cozening° hope. He° is a flatterer,   *cheating / (Hope)*
70   A parasite, a keeper-back of death,
Who° gently would dissolve° the bands of life   *(Death) / loosen*
Which false hope lingers in extremity.
          Enter YORK.
GREENE   Here comes the Duke of York.
QUEEN   With signs of war about his agèd neck.
75   Oh, full of careful business° are his looks!   *anxious preoccupation*
[*to* YORK] Uncle, for heaven's sake speak comfortable° words.   *comforting*
YORK   Comfort's in heaven, and we are on the earth,
Where nothing lives but crosses,° care, and grief.   *misfortunes*
Your husband, he is gone to save far off,
80   Whilst others come to make him lose at home.
Here am I left to underprop his land
Who, weak with age, cannot support myself.
Now comes the sick hour that his surfeit made;
Now shall he try° his friends that flattered him.   *test*
          Enter a SERVANT.
85   SERVANT [*to* YORK]   My lord, your son was gone before I came.
YORK   He was? Why, so; go all which way it will.
The nobles they are fled; the commons° they are cold   *common people*
And will, I fear, revolt on Hereford's side.

---

7. Symbolically resigning his office as Lord Steward of the King's household. Worcester is Northumberland's brother.

Sirrah, get thee to Plashy to my sister° Gloucester;   *sister-in-law*

90   Bid her send me presently° a thousand pound—   *immediately*

    Hold, take my ring.[8]

SERVANT   My lord, I had forgot to tell your lordship:

    Today I came by and callèd there—

    But I shall grieve you to report the rest.

95   YORK   What is't, knave?°   *fellow*

SERVANT   An hour before I came, the Duchess died.

YORK   Heav'n for His mercy, what a tide of woes

    Come rushing on this woeful land at once!

    I know not what to do. I would to heaven—

100   So my untruth° had not provoked him to it—   *disloyalty*

    The King had cut off my head with my brother's.

    What, are there posts° dispatched for Ireland?   *fast messengers*

    How shall we do for money for these wars?

    [*to* QUEEN] Come, sister—cousin, I would say—pray,

       pardon me.[9]

105   [*to* SERVANT] Go, fellow, get thee home; provide some carts

    And bring away the armor that is there.   [*Exit* SERVANT.]

    [*to* BUSHY, BAGOT, *and* GREENE] Gentlemen, will you muster

       men?

    If I know how or which way to order these affairs

    Thus disorderly thrust into my hands,

110   Never believe me. Both are my kinsmen:

    Th'one is my sovereign, whom both my oath

    And duty bids defend; th'other again

    Is my kinsman whom the King hath wronged,

    Whom conscience and my kindred bids to right.

115   Well, somewhat we must do.

    [*to* QUEEN] Come, cousin, I'll dispose of° you.   *make arrangements for*

    [*to* BUSHY, BAGOT, *and* GREENE] Gentlemen, go muster up

       your men,

    And meet me presently at Berkeley Castle.[1]

    I should to Plashy too, but time will not permit.

120   All is uneven, and everything is left at six and seven.°   *in confusion*

               Exeunt [YORK *and* QUEEN].

BUSHY   The wind sits fair[2] for news to go to Ireland,

    But none returns. For us to levy power

    Proportionable to th'enemy is all impossible.

GREENE   Besides, our nearness to the King in love

125   Is near° the hate of those love not the King.   *Implies*

BAGOT   And that's the wavering commons, for their love

    Lies in their purses, and whoso empties them,

    By so much fills their hearts with deadly hate.

BUSHY   Wherein the King stands generally condemned.

130   BAGOT   If judgment lie in them,° then so do we,   *is in the people's hands*

    Because we have been ever near the King.

GREENE   Well, I will for refuge straight to Bristol Castle;

    The Earl of Wiltshire is already there.

BUSHY   Thither will I with you, for little office°   *service*

135   Will the hateful commons perform for us

---

8. As proof that he comes with York's authorization.   1. In Gloucestershire, in western England.
9. The Duchess's death is uppermost in York's mind.   2. The wind blows from a favorable direction.

Except like curs to tear us all in pieces.
[*to* BAGOT] Will you go along with us?
BAGOT   No, I will to Ireland to his majesty.
Farewell. If heart's presages be not vain,
140   We three here part that ne'er shall meet again.
BUSHY   That's as York thrives³ to beat back Bolingbroke.
GREENE   Alas, poor Duke. The task he undertakes
Is numb'ring sands and drinking oceans dry;
Where one on his side fights, thousands will fly.
145   BAGOT   Farewell at once, for once, for all, and ever.
BUSHY   Well, we may meet again.
BAGOT   I fear me never.   *Exeunt.*

2.3 (Q 2.3)
Enter [BOLINGBROKE,] *the Duke of Hereford, and*
NORTHUMBERLAND.

BOLINGBROKE   How far is it, my lord, to Berkeley now?
NORTHUMBERLAND   Believe me, noble lord,
I am a stranger here in Gloucestershire.
These high wild hills and rough uneven ways
5   Draws out our miles and makes them wearisome,
And yet our fair discourse hath been as sugar,
Making the hard way sweet and delectable.
But I bethink me what a weary way
From Ravenspurgh to Cottshold¹ will be found
10   In° Ross and Willoughby, wanting° your company,   *By / lacking*
Which I protest hath very much beguiled
The tediousness and process° of my travel.   *tedious course*
But theirs is sweetened with the hope to have
The present benefit that I possess;
15   And hope to joy is little less in joy
Than hope enjoyed. By this° the weary lords   *this expectation*
Shall make their way seem short as mine hath done
By sight of what I have, your noble company.
BOLINGBROKE   Of much less value is my company
Than your good words.
          Enter H[arry] PERCY.
20   But who comes here?
NORTHUMBERLAND   It is my son, young Harry Percy,²
Sent from my brother Worcester whencesoever.°   *wherever he may be*
Harry, how fares your uncle?°   *(Worcester)*
PERCY   I had thought, my lord, to have learned his health
          of you.
25   NORTHUMBERLAND   Why, is he not with the Queen?
PERCY   No, my good lord. He hath forsook the court,
Broken his staff of office, and dispersed
The household of the King.
NORTHUMBERLAND   What was his reason?
He was not so resolved when we last spake together.

---

3. That depends on York's success.
2.3 Location: Gloucestershire.
1. Hilly part of Gloucestershire.

2. Shakespeare makes Harry Percy, the Hotspur of
1 Henry IV, a boy here; the historical Percy was two
years older than Bolingbroke.

30 PERCY Because your lordship was proclaimèd traitor.
But he, my lord, is gone to Ravenspurgh
To offer service to the Duke of Hereford,
And sent me over by Berkeley to discover
What power the Duke of York had levied there,
35 Then with direction to repair to Ravenspurgh.
NORTHUMBERLAND Have you forgot the Duke of Hereford,
    boy?[3]
PERCY No, my good lord, for that is not forgot
Which ne'er I did remember; to my knowledge
I never in my life did look on him.
40 NORTHUMBERLAND Then learn to know him now: this is the
    Duke.
PERCY [to BOLINGBROKE] My gracious lord, I tender you my
    service,
Such as it is, being tender, raw, and young,
Which elder days shall ripen and confirm
To more approvèd° service and desert.   fully demonstrated
45 BOLINGBROKE I thank thee, gentle Percy, and be sure
I count myself in nothing else so happy
As in a° soul rememb'ring my good friends;   my
And as my fortune ripens with thy love,
It shall be still thy true love's recompense.
50 My heart this covenant makes; my hand thus seals it.
    [He clasps Percy's hand.]
NORTHUMBERLAND [to PERCY] How far is it to Berkeley? And
    what stir°   activity
Keeps good old York there with his men of war?
PERCY There stands the castle by yond tuft of trees,
Manned with three hundred men, as I have heard,
55 And in it are the lords of York, Berkeley, and Seymour;
None else of name° and noble estimate.°   title / reputation
    Enter ROSS and WILLOUGHBY.
NORTHUMBERLAND Here come the lords of Ross and
    Willoughby,
Bloody with spurring, fiery red with haste.
BOLINGBROKE Welcome, my lords. I wot° your love pursues   know
60 A banished traitor. All my treasury
Is yet but unfelt° thanks which, more enriched,   immaterial
Shall be your love and labor's recompense.
ROSS Your presence makes us rich, most noble lord.
WILLOUGHBY And far surmounts our labor to attain it.
65 BOLINGBROKE Evermore thanks, th'exchequer[4] of the poor,
Which till my infant fortune comes to years°   of age
Stands for° my bounty.   in place of
    Enter BERKELEY.
                    But who comes here?
NORTHUMBERLAND It is my lord of Berkeley, as I guess.
BERKELEY My lord of Hereford, my message is to you—
70 BOLINGBROKE My lord, my answer is to "Lancaster,"[5]

---

3. Northumberland scolds his son for not greeting
Bolingbroke respectfully.
4. Gratitude is always the treasury.

5. I only reply to the title of Lancaster (which Richard has refused to allow Bolingbroke to inherit).

And I am come to seek that name in England;
And I must find that title in your tongue
Before I make reply to aught you say.

BERKELEY   Mistake me not, my lord, 'tis not my meaning
75   To raze one title of your honor out.
To you, my lord, I come, what lord you will,
From the most glorious of this land,
The Duke of York, to know what pricks you on°   incites you
To take advantage of the absent time°   time of absence
80   And fright our native peace with self-borne⁶ arms.
        Enter YORK.

BOLINGBROKE   I shall not need transport my words by you.
Here comes his grace in person. [*He kneels to* YORK.] My
    noble uncle.

YORK   Show me thy humble heart and not thy knee,
Whose duty is deceivable° and false.   deceptive

85   BOLINGBROKE [*rising*]   My gracious uncle—

YORK   Tut, tut! Grace me no "grace," nor "uncle" me.
I am no traitor's uncle, and that word "grace"
In an ungracious mouth is but profane.
Why have these banished and forbidden legs
90   Dared once to touch a dust° of England's ground?   speck
But more than why—why have they dared to march
So many miles upon her peaceful bosom,
Frighting her pale-faced villages with war
And ostentation° of despisèd arms?   display
95   Com'st thou because th'anointed King is hence?
Why, foolish boy! The King is left behind,
And in my loyal bosom lies his power.
Were I but now the lord of such hot youth
As when brave Gaunt, thy father, and myself
100   Rescued the Black Prince, that young Mars of men,
From forth the ranks of many thousand French,
Oh, then how quickly should this arm of mine,
Now prisoner to the palsy, chastise thee
And minister correction° to thy fault.   administer punishment

105   BOLINGBROKE   My gracious uncle, let me know my fault:
On what condition stands it, and wherein?⁷

YORK   Even in condition of the worst degree:
In gross rebellion and detested treason.
Thou art a banished man, and here art come
110   Before th'expiration of thy time,
In braving° arms against thy sovereign.   defiant

BOLINGBROKE   As I was banished, I was banished Hereford;
But as I come, I come for Lancaster.
And noble uncle, I beseech your grace,
115   Look on my wrongs with an indifferent° eye.   impartial
You are my father, for methinks in you
I see old Gaunt alive. O then, my father,
Will you permit that I shall stand condemned

6. Borne for oneself, not for the King; borne against   7. What is its nature, and in what does it consist?
fellow countrymen.

A wand'ring vagabond, my rights and royalties
120 Plucked from my arms perforce and given away
To upstart unthrifts?° Wherefore was I born?   *spendthrifts*
If that my cousin King be King of England,
It must be granted I am Duke of Lancaster.
You have a son, Aumerle, my noble kinsman.
125 Had you first died and he been thus trod down,
He should have found his uncle Gaunt a father
To rouse his wrongs and chase them to the bay.[8]
I am denied to sue my livery[9] here,
And yet my letters patents give me leave.
130 My father's goods are all distrained° and sold,   *confiscated*
And these, and all, are all amiss employed.
What would you have me do? I am a subject,
And challenge law.° Attorneys are denied me,   *demand my rights*
And therefore personally I lay my claim
135 To my inheritance of free descent.°   *legal succession*
NORTHUMBERLAND The noble Duke hath been too much
       abused.
ROSS It stands your grace upon[1] to do him right.
WILLOUGHBY Base men by his endowments° are made great.   *property*
YORK My lords of England, let me tell you this:
140 I have had feeling of my cousin's wrongs
And labored all I could to do him right.
But in this kind° to come, in braving arms—   *manner*
Be his own carver[2] and cut out his way—
To find out right with wrongs,[3] it may not be;
145 And you that do abet him in this kind
Cherish rebellion and are rebels all.
NORTHUMBERLAND The noble Duke hath sworn his coming is
But for his own; and for the right of that
We all have strongly sworn to give him aid—
150 And let him ne'er see joy that breaks that oath.
YORK Well, well, I see the issue° of these arms.   *consequence*
I cannot mend it, I must needs confess,
Because my power° is weak and all ill-left;   *army*
But if I could, by Him that gave me life,
155 I would attach° you all and make you stoop   *arrest*
Unto the sovereign mercy of the King.
But since I cannot, be it known to you
I do remain as neuter.° So fare you well—   *neutral*
Unless you please to enter in the castle
160 And there repose you for this night.
BOLINGBROKE An offer, uncle, that we will accept;
But we must win° your grace to go with us   *persuade*
To Bristol Castle, which they say is held
By Bushy, Bagot, and their complices,°   *accomplices*
165 The caterpillars° of the commonwealth,   *devourers*
Which I have sworn to weed and pluck away.

---

8. *rouse:* startle an animal from its cover. *bay:* point   2. Help himself to meat (instead of waiting to be
where the animal turns on its pursuers.   served).
9. See note to 2.1.204.   3. To illegally obtain what he deserves.
1. It is incumbent on your grace.

YORK　It may be I will go with you—but yet I'll pause,
　　For I am loath to break our country's laws.
　　Nor° friends nor foes to me, welcome you are;　　　　　　*Neither*
170　Things past redress are now with me past care.　　*Exeunt.*

2.4 (Q 2.4)

Enter SALISBURY *and a* CAPTAIN.

CAPTAIN　My lord of Salisbury, we have stayed° ten days　　　　*waited*
　　And hardly° kept our countrymen together,　　　　　*with difficulty*
　　And yet we hear no tidings from the King.
　　Therefore we will disperse ourselves. Farewell.
5　SALISBURY　Stay yet another day, thou trusty Welshman.
　　The King reposeth all his confidence in thee.
　　CAPTAIN　'Tis thought the King is dead. We will not stay.
　　The bay trees in our country all are withered,
　　And meteors fright the fixèd stars of heaven;
10　The pale-faced moon looks bloody on the earth,[1]
　　And lean-looked prophets whisper fearful change;
　　Rich men look sad and ruffians dance and leap,
　　The one in fear to lose what they enjoy,
　　The other to enjoy° by rage and war.　　　　　　*hoping to profit*
15　These signs forerun the death of kings.
　　Farewell. Our countrymen are gone and fled,
　　As well assured Richard their King is dead.　　　　*Exit.*
SALISBURY　Ah, Richard! With eyes of heavy mind
　　I see thy glory like a shooting star
20　Fall to the base earth from the firmament.
　　Thy sun sets weeping in the lowly West,
　　Witnessing° storms to come, woe, and unrest.　　　　*Testifying to*
　　Thy friends are fled to wait upon thy foes,
　　And crossly° to thy good all fortune goes.　　　　*Exit.*　　*adversely*

3.1 (Q 3.1)

Enter BOLINGBROKE, YORK, NORTHUMBERLAND, ROSS,
PERCY, WILLOUGHBY, *with* BUSHY *and* GREENE
prisoners.

BOLINGBROKE　Bring forth these men.
　　[BUSHY *and* GREENE *are brought forward.*]
　　Bushy and Greene, I will not vex° your souls—　　　　*afflict*
　　Since presently° your souls must part your bodies—　　*immediately*
　　With too much urging° your pernicious lives,　　　　*emphasizing*
5　For 'twere no charity; yet to wash your blood
　　From off my hands, here in the view of men
　　I will unfold some causes of your deaths.
　　You have misled a prince, a royal king,
　　A happy° gentleman in blood and lineaments[1]　　　　*fortunate*
10　By you unhappied and disfigured clean.°　　　　　　*utterly*
　　You have in manner° with your sinful hours　　　　*so to speak*
　　Made a divorce betwixt his queen and him,
　　Broke the possession of a royal bed,
　　And stained the beauty of a fair queen's cheeks

2.4 Location: A camp in Wales.
1. Holinshed records the first of these omens (line
8); the others are poetic commonplaces.

3.1 Location: Before Bristol Castle.
1. In descent and qualities.

15 With tears drawn from her eyes with your foul wrongs.[2]
    Myself a prince by fortune of my birth,
    Near to the King in blood, and near in love
    Till you did make him misinterpret me,
    Have stooped my neck under your injuries
20 And sighed my English breath in foreign clouds,°   air
    Eating the bitter bread of banishment,
    While you have fed upon my signories,°   estates
    Disparked my parks[3] and felled my forest woods,
    From mine own windows torn my household coat,[4]
25 Razed° out my impress,° leaving me no sign,   Scraped / heraldic emblem
    Save men's opinions and my living blood,
    To show the world I am a gentleman.
    This and much more, much more than twice all this,
    Condemns you to the death. See them delivered over
30 To execution and the hand of death.
BUSHY   More welcome is the stroke of death to me
    Than Bolingbroke to England.
GREENE   My comfort is that heaven will take our souls
    And plague injustice with the pains of hell.
35 BOLINGBROKE   My lord Northumberland, see them dispatched.
        [*Exit* NORTHUMBERLAND, *with* BUSHY *and* GREENE.]
    [*to* YORK] Uncle, you say the Queen is at your house.
    For heaven's sake fairly° let her be entreated.°   courteously / treated
    Tell her I send to her my kind commends;°   greetings
    Take special care my greetings be delivered.
40 YORK   A gentleman of mine I have dispatched
    With letters of your love to her at large.°   fully described
BOLINGBROKE   Thanks, gentle uncle. Come, lords, away,
    To fight with Glendower[5] and his complices.
    A while to work, and after holiday.   *Exeunt.*

3.2 (Q 3.2)

    Drums, flourish, and colors.°   flags
    Enter RICHARD, AUMERLE, [*Bishop of*] CARLISLE,
    and Soldiers.
RICHARD   Barkloughly Castle call you this at hand?
AUMERLE   Yea, my lord. How brooks° your grace the air   enjoys
    After your late° tossing on the breaking seas?   recent
RICHARD   Needs must° I like it well. I weep for joy   Necessarily
5 To stand upon my kingdom once again.
    Dear earth, I do salute thee with my hand,
    Though rebels wound thee with their horses' hooves.
    As a long-parted mother with her child
    Plays fondly with her tears and smiles in meeting,
10 So weeping, smiling, greet I thee, my earth,
    And do thee favor with my royal hands.
    Feed not thy sovereign's foe, my gentle earth,
    Nor with thy sweets° comfort his ravenous sense;[1]   bounty

---

2. Bolingbroke implies that Bushy and Greene had homosexual relations with Richard; Holinshed claims that they procured female paramours for him.
3. Put my hunting lands to other use.
4. Removed the stained glass bearing my coat of arms.

5. This character appears in *1 Henry IV* and is perhaps to be identified with the Welsh Captain of 2.4.
3.2 Location: Near Harlech Castle, on the coast of Gwynedd, Wales.
1. Appetite; intention.

But let thy spiders that suck up thy venom[2]
15 And heavy-gaited toads[3] lie in their way,
Doing annoyance to the treacherous feet
Which with usurping steps do trample thee.
Yield stinging nettles to mine enemies,
And when they from thy bosom pluck a flower,
20 Guard it, I prithee, with a lurking adder
Whose double° tongue may with a mortal touch   *forked*
Throw death upon thy sovereign's enemies.
Mock not my senseless conjuration,[4] lords.
This earth shall have a feeling and these stones
25 Prove armèd soldiers ere her native king°   *king entitled by birth*
Shall falter under foul rebellious arms.
CARLISLE Fear not, my lord. That power that made you king
Hath power to keep you king in spite of all.
AUMERLE He means, my lord, that we are too remiss,
30 Whilst Bolingbroke, through our security,°   *overconfidence*
Grows strong and great in substance and in friends.
RICHARD Discomfortable° cousin, knowest thou not   *Disheartening*
That when the searching eye of heaven is hid
Behind the globe that lights the lower world,
35 Then thieves and robbers range abroad unseen
In murders and in outrage bloody here.
But when from under this terrestrial ball
He fires° the proud tops of the eastern pines   *lights up*
And darts his lightning through ev'ry guilty hole,
40 Then murders, treasons, and detested sins,
The cloak of night being plucked from off their backs,
Stand bare and naked, trembling at themselves?
So when this thief, this traitor Bolingbroke,
Who all this while hath reveled in the night,
45 Shall see us rising in our throne, the East,[5]
His treasons will sit blushing in his face
Not able to endure the sight of day,
But, self-affrighted, tremble at his sin.
Not all the water in the rough rude sea
50 Can wash the balm° from an anointed king.   *oil of consecration*
The breath of worldly men cannot depose
The deputy elected by the Lord.
For every man that Bolingbroke hath pressed°   *drafted*
To lift shrewd° steel against our golden crown,   *wicked; sharp*
55 Heaven for His Richard hath in heavenly pay
A glorious angel. Then, if angels fight,
Weak men must fall, for heaven still° guards the right.   *always*
        Enter SALISBURY.
Welcome, my lord. How far off lies your power?
SALISBURY Nor near° nor farther off, my gracious lord,   *Neither nearer*
60 Than this weak arm. Discomfort guides my tongue
And bids me speak of nothing but despair.
One day too late, I fear, my noble lord,
Hath clouded all thy happy days on earth.

2. It was thought that spiders drew their venom from   earth).
the earth.   5. *So when . . . East:* Richard compares his return
3. Also thought to be poisonous.   from visiting Ireland to the sun rising.
4. Injunction addressed to an insentient being (the

Oh, call back yesterday, bid time return,
65 And thou shalt have twelve thousand fighting men.
Today, today, unhappy day too late,
O'erthrows thy joys, friends, fortune, and thy state;°   *prosperity; nation*
For all the Welshmen, hearing thou wert dead,
Are gone to Bolingbroke, dispersed, and fled.
70 AUMERLE   Comfort, my liege. Why looks your grace so pale?
RICHARD   But now° the blood of twenty thousand men   *A moment ago*
Did triumph° in my face, and they are fled;   *shine*
And till so much blood thither come again,
Have I not reason to look pale and dead?
75 All souls that will be safe, fly from my side,
For time hath set a blot upon my pride.
AUMERLE   Comfort, my liege, remember who you are.
RICHARD   I had forgot myself. Am I not king?
Awake, thou sluggard majesty, thou sleepest.
80 Is not the king's name forty thousand names?
Arm, arm, my name! A puny subject strikes
At thy great glory. Look not to the ground,
Ye favorites of a king. Are we not high?
High be our thoughts. I know my uncle York
Hath power enough to serve our turn.
        Enter SCROPE.
85   But who comes here?
SCROPE   More health and happiness betide my liege
Than can my care-tuned[6] tongue deliver° him.   *offer*
RICHARD   Mine ear is open and my heart prepared.
The worst is worldly loss thou canst unfold.
90 Say, is my kingdom lost? Why, 'twas my care,°   *trouble*
And what loss is it to be rid of care?
Strives Bolingbroke to be as great as we?
Greater he shall not be. If he serve God,
We'll serve Him too, and be his fellow so.[7]
95 Revolt our subjects? That we cannot mend.
They break their faith to God as well as us.
Cry° woe, destruction, ruin, loss, decay;   *Though you may cry*
The worst is death, and death will have his° day.   *its*
SCROPE   Glad am I that your highness is so armed
100 To bear the tidings of calamity.
Like an unseasonable stormy day,
Which make the silver rivers drown their shores
As if the world were all dissolved to tears,
So high above his limits° swells the rage   *bounds; banks*
105 Of Bolingbroke, covering your fearful° land   *alarmed*
With hard bright steel and hearts harder than steel.
Whitebeards have armed their thin and hairless scalps
Against thy majesty, and boys with women's voices
Strive to speak big and clap their female° joints   *weak*
110 In stiff unwieldy arms° against thy crown.   *armor*
Thy very beadsmen[8] learn to bend their bows
Of double-fatal[9] yew against thy state.

---

6. Tuned to the key of sorrow.
7. Be Bolingbroke's equal in that regard.
8. Poor elderly men who received charity in return

for praying for their benefactors' souls.
9. Because yew is poisonous, and its wood was used to make bows.

Yea, distaff-women° manage rusty bills[1]   *spinners*
Against thy seat.° Both young and old rebel,   *throne*
115   And all goes worse than I have power to tell.
RICHARD   Too well, too well, thou tell'st a tale so ill.
Where is the Earl of Wiltshire? Where is Bagot?[2]
What is become of Bushy? Where is Greene,
That they have let the dangerous enemy
120   Measure our confines[3] with such peaceful° steps?   *unopposed*
If we prevail, their heads shall pay for it.
I warrant they have made peace with Bolingbroke.
SCROPE   Peace have they made with him indeed, my lord.
RICHARD   Oh, villains, vipers, damned without redemption!
125   Dogs easily won to fawn on any man;
Snakes, in my heart-blood warmed, that sting my heart;
Three Judases, each one thrice worse than Judas[4]—
Would they make peace? Terrible hell make war
Upon their spotted° souls for this offense!   *blemished*
130   SCROPE   Sweet love, I see, changing his property,°   *its quality*
Turns to the sourest and most deadly hate.
Again uncurse their souls. Their peace is made
With heads and not with hands. Those whom you curse
Have felt the worst of Death's destroying hand
135   And lie full low, graved in the hollow ground.
AUMERLE   Is Bushy, Greene, and the Earl of Wiltshire dead?
SCROPE   Yea, all of them at Bristol lost their heads.
AUMERLE   Where is the Duke my father with his power?
RICHARD   No matter where. Of comfort no man speak.
140   Let's talk of graves, of worms, and epitaphs,
Make dust our paper, and with rainy eyes
Write sorrow on the bosom of the earth.
Let's choose executors and talk of wills—
And yet not so, for what can we bequeath
145   Save our deposèd° bodies to the ground?   *dethroned; prostrate*
Our lands, our lives, and all are Bolingbroke's,
And nothing can we call our own but death
And that small model[5] of the barren earth
Which serves as paste[6] and cover to our bones.
150   For heaven's sake let us sit upon the ground
And tell sad stories of the death of kings:
How some have been deposed, some slain in war,
Some haunted by the ghosts they have deposed,
Some poisoned by their wives, some sleeping killed—
155   All murdered. For within the hollow crown
That rounds° the mortal temples of a king   *encircles*
Keeps Death his court, and there the antic° sits,   *jester*
Scoffing his state[7] and grinning at his pomp,
Allowing him a breath, a little scene
160   To monarchize,° be feared, and kill with looks,[8]   *play the monarch*

---

1. Spiked axes on long shafts.
2. Bagot is not one of the "Judases" (line 127) actually executed by Bolingbroke; he reappears in 4.1. Bolingbroke executes Bushy, Greene, and the Earl of Wiltshire.
3. Travel over our territories.

4. Disciple who betrayed Jesus.
5. Microcosm (the body); enveloping shape (the grave).
6. Pastry shell (also known as "coffin").
7. Mocking the king's regality (as "antic Death," a court jester, would be expected to do).
8. Order executions with a glance.

Infusing him with self and vain conceit,[9]
As if this flesh which walls about our life
Were brass impregnable; and humored thus,[1]
Comes at the last and with a little pin
165 Bores through his castle walls—and farewell, king.
Cover your heads,[2] and mock not flesh and blood
With solemn reverence. Throw away respect,
Tradition, form, and ceremonious duty,
For you have but mistook me all this while.
170 I live with bread like you, feel want,
Taste grief, need friends. Subjected thus,[3]
How can you say to me I am a king?
CARLISLE   My lord, wise men ne'er wail their present woes,
But presently prevent the ways to wail.[4]
175 To fear the foe, since fear oppresseth° strength,   *suppresses*
Gives in your weakness strength unto your foe.
Fear and be slain—no worse can come to fight;°   *in fighting*
And fight and die is death destroying death,[5]
Where fearing dying pays death servile breath.
180 AUMERLE   My father hath a power.° Inquire of him,   *an army*
And learn to make a body of a limb.
RICHARD   Thou chid'st me well. Proud Bolingbroke, I come
To change blows with thee for our day of doom.[6]
This ague° fit of fear is overblown.°   *chill / blown over*
185 An easy task it is to win our own.
Say, Scrope, where lies our uncle with his power?
Speak sweetly, man, although thy looks be sour.
SCROPE   Men judge by the complexion° of the sky   *appearance*
The state and inclination of the day;
190 So may you by my dull and heavy eye.
My tongue hath but a heavier tale to say.
I play the torturer, by small and small°   *little by little*
To lengthen out the worst that must be spoken:
Your uncle York is joined with Bolingbroke,
195 And all your northern castles yielded up,
And all your southern gentlemen° in arms   *men of rank*
Upon his faction—
RICHARD   Thou hast said enough.
[*to* AUMERLE] Beshrew° thee, cousin, which didst lead me   *Woe to*
forth
Of that sweet way I was in to despair.
200 What say you now? What comfort have we now?
By heaven, I'll hate him everlastingly
That bids me be of comfort any more.
Go to Flint Castle.° There I'll pine away.   (*Welsh castle near Chester*)
A king, woe's slave, shall kingly woe obey.
205 That power I have, discharge, and let 'em go
To ear° the land that hath some hope to grow,   *till*
For I have none. Let no man speak again
To alter this, for counsel is but vain.

9. Instilling in him vain ideas about himself.
1. And Death having thus amused himself.
2. Replace your hats (do not respectfully remain bareheaded).
3. Made a subject to such needs (with pun).

4. But immediately vanquish the causes of grief.
5. To die fighting is to destroy death's power by dying.
6. To exchange blows with you in order to determine our fates.

AUMERLE   My liege, one word.
RICHARD   He does me double wrong
210 That wounds me with the flatteries of his tongue.
Discharge my followers. Let them hence away
From Richard's night to Bolingbroke's fair day.   *Exeunt.*

3.3 (Q 3.3)

Enter, with drum and colors, BOLINGBROKE, YORK,
NORTHUMBERLAND, [*and*] *Attendants.*
BOLINGBROKE   So that by this intelligence° we learn   *information*
The Welshmen are dispersed, and Salisbury
Is gone to meet the King, who lately landed
With some few private friends upon this coast.
5 NORTHUMBERLAND   The news is very fair and good, my lord.
Richard not far from hence hath hid his head.
YORK   It would beseem the Lord Northumberland
To say "King Richard." Alack the heavy day,
When such a sacred king should hide his head.
10 NORTHUMBERLAND   Your grace mistakes; only to be brief
Left I his title out.
YORK   The time hath been,
Would you have been so brief with him, he would
Have been so brief with you to shorten you,
For taking so the head,[1] your whole head's length.
15 BOLINGBROKE   Mistake not, uncle, farther than you should.
YORK   Take not, good cousin, farther than you should.
Lest you mistake° the heavens are o'er your head.   *forget*
BOLINGBROKE   I know it, uncle, and oppose not myself
Against their will.
        Enter PERCY.
                               But who comes here?
20 [*to* PERCY] Welcome, Harry. What, will not this castle yield?
PERCY   The castle royally is manned, my lord,
Against thy entrance.
BOLINGBROKE   Royally? Why, it contains no king.
PERCY   Yes, my good lord,
25 It doth contain a king. King Richard lies
Within the limits of yond lime and stone,
And with him the Lord Aumerle, Lord Salisbury,
Sir Stephen Scrope, besides a clergyman
Of holy reverence—who, I cannot learn.
30 NORTHUMBERLAND   Oh, belike° it is the Bishop of Carlisle.   *probably*
BOLINGBROKE [*to* NORTHUMBERLAND]   Noble lord,
Go to the rude ribs° of that ancient castle;   *rough walls*
Through brazen trumpet send the breath of parle
Into his ruined ears,° and thus deliver: *its battered loopholes*
35 Henry Bolingbroke
Upon his knees doth kiss King Richard's hand
And sends allegiance and true faith of heart
To his royal person, hither come
Even at his feet to lay my arms and power,
40 Provided that my banishment repealed°   *revoked*

3.3 Location: Before Flint Castle, in North Wales.
1. For omitting the title thus; for acting without restraint.

And lands restored again be freely granted.
If not, I'll use th'advantage of my power
And lay° the summer's dust with showers of blood   *settle*
Rained from the wounds of slaughtered Englishmen—
45 The which, how far off from the mind of Bolingbroke
It is such crimson tempest should bedrench
The fresh green lap of fair King Richard's land,
My stooping duty° tenderly shall show.   *submissive kneeling*
Go signify as much, while here we march
50 Upon the grassy carpet of this plain.
        [NORTHUMBERLAND *goes to the walls*.]
Let's march without the noise of threat'ning drum,
That from this castle's tattered° battlements   *dilapidated*
Our fair appointments° may be well perused.   *equipment*
Methinks King Richard and myself should meet
55 With no less terror than the elements
Of fire and water,° when their thund'ring smoke   *lightning and rain*
At meeting tears the cloudy cheeks of heaven.
Be he the fire, I'll be the yielding water;
The rage be his, while on the earth I rain°   *(punning on "reign"?)*
60 My waters—on the earth and not on him.
March on, and mark King Richard how he looks.
        Parle° without and answer within; then a flourish.   Trumpet call
        Enter on the walls[2] [*above*] RICHARD, [*Bishop of*]
        CARLISLE, AUMERLE, SCROPE, [*and*] SALISBURY.
See, see, King Richard doth himself appear,
As doth the blushing[3] discontented sun
From out the fiery portal of the East,
65 When he perceives the envious° clouds are bent   *malicious*
To dim his glory and to stain the tract
Of his bright passage to the Occident.
YORK   Yet looks he like a king. Behold his eye,
As bright as is the eagle's, lightens forth[4]
70 Controlling majesty. Alack, alack for woe,
That any harm should stain so fair a show!
RICHARD [*to* NORTHUMBERLAND *below*]   We are amazed, and
        thus long have we stood
To watch° the fearful bending of thy knee,   *wait for*
Because we thought ourself thy lawful king;
75 And if we be, how dare thy joints forget
To pay their awful° duty to our presence?   *reverential*
If we be not, show us the hand of God
That hath dismissed us from our stewardship;
For well we know no hand of blood and bone
80 Can gripe the sacred handle of our scepter,
Unless he do profane, steal, or usurp.
And though you think that all, as you have done,
Have torn° their souls by turning them from us,   *ruined (by disloyalty)*
And we are barren and bereft of friends,
85 Yet know: my master, God omnipotent,
Is must'ring in His clouds on our behalf

---

2. That is, on the balcony of the tiring-house, a two-   bad weather).
story structure at the back of the stage.   4. Flashes out (the eagle is a traditional royal symbol).
3. Red (proverbially, a red morning sky anticipates

Armies of pestilence, and they shall strike
Your children yet unborn and unbegot
That lift your vassal hands against my head
90   And threat° the glory of my precious crown.   *threaten*
Tell Bolingbroke, for yond methinks he is,
That every stride he makes upon my land
Is dangerous treason. He is come to ope
The purple testament° of bleeding war;   *blood-red document*
95   But ere the crown he looks for live in peace,
Ten thousand bloody crowns° of mothers' sons   *heads*
Shall ill become the flower of England's face,[5]
Change the complexion of her maid-pale° peace   *innocent white*
To scarlet indignation, and bedew
100   Her pastor's° grass with faithful English blood.   *shepherd's*
NORTHUMBERLAND   The King of heaven forbid our lord the King
Should so with civil and uncivil[6] arms
Be rushed upon. Thy thrice-noble cousin,
Harry Bolingbroke, doth humbly kiss thy hand;
105   And by the honorable tomb he swears
That stands upon your royal grandsire's° bones,   *(Edward III's)*
And by the royalties of both your bloods,
Currents that spring from one most gracious head,°   *source*
And by the buried hand of warlike Gaunt,
110   And by the worth and honor of himself,
Comprising all that may be sworn or said—
His coming hither hath no further scope°   *aim*
Than for his lineal royalties,° and to beg   *hereditary rights*
Enfranchisement° immediate on his knees;   *Recall from exile*
115   Which on thy royal party° granted once,   *part*
His glittering arms he will commend° to rust,   *commit*
His barbèd° steeds to stables, and his heart   *armed*
To faithful service of your majesty.
This swears he, as he is a prince and just,
120   And, as I am a gentleman, I credit° him.   *believe*
RICHARD   Northumberland, say thus the King returns:°   *replies*
His noble cousin is right welcome hither,
And all the number of his fair demands
Shall be accomplished without contradiction.
125   With all the gracious utterance thou hast,
Speak to his gentle hearing kind commends.°   *regards*
      [NORTHUMBERLAND *returns to* BOLINGBROKE.]
[*to* AUMERLE] We do debase ourself, cousin, do we not,
To look so poorly° and to speak so fair?   *abjectly*
Shall we call back Northumberland, and send
130   Defiance to the traitor, and so die?
AUMERLE   No, good my lord. Let's fight with gentle words
Till time lend friends, and friends their helpful swords.
RICHARD   O God, O God, that e'er this tongue of mine
That laid the sentence of dread banishment
135   On yond proud man, should take it off again
With words of sooth!° Oh, that I were as great   *soothing words*
As is my grief, or lesser than my name,

---

5. Blooming surface of England; faces of England's
choicest youth.

6. Of the same country and violent; playing on
"civil" as "peaceful" and "uncivil" as "alien."

Or that I could forget what I have been,
Or not remember what I must be now.
140 Swell'st thou, proud heart? I'll give thee scope to beat,
Since foes have scope to beat both thee and me.
　　　　[NORTHUMBERLAND *returns to the walls.*]
AUMERLE　Northumberland comes back from Bolingbroke.
RICHARD　What must the King do now? Must he submit?
The King shall do it. Must he be deposed?
145 The King shall be contented. Must he lose
The name of King? I'°God's name, let it go.　　　　　　　*In*
I'll give my jewels for a set of beads,°　　　　　　　　　*rosary*
My gorgeous palace for a hermitage,
My gay apparel for an almsman's° gown,　　　　　　　*a beggar's*
150 My figured° goblets for a dish of wood,　　　　　　　*engraved*
My scepter for a palmer's° walking staff,　　　　　　　*pilgrim's*
My subjects for a pair of carvèd saints,
And my large kingdom for a little grave,
A little, little grave, an obscure grave;
155 Or I'll be buried in the king's highway,[7]
Some way of common trade,° where subjects' feet　　　*passage*
May hourly trample on their sovereign's head;
For on my heart they tread now whilst I live,
And, buried once, why not upon my head?
160 Aumerle, thou weep'st, my tender-hearted cousin.
We'll make foul weather with despisèd tears;
Our sighs and they shall lodge° the summer corn　　　*beat down*
And make a dearth° in this revolting° land.　　*famine / rebellious*
Or shall we play the wantons° with our woes　　　　　　*frolic*
165 And make some pretty match° with shedding tears,　*clever game*
As thus, to drop them still° upon one place　　　　　*continually*
Till they have fretted° us a pair of graves　　　　　*eroded for*
Within the earth; and therein laid, there lies
Two kinsmen digged their graves with weeping eyes?
170 Would not this ill do well? Well, well, I see
I talk but idly,° and you mock at me.　　　　　　　　*foolishly*
　　　[*to* NORTHUMBERLAND] Most mighty prince, my lord
　　　　　　Northumberland,
What says King Bolingbroke? Will his majesty
Give Richard leave to live till Richard die?
175 You make a leg,° and Bolingbroke says "Ay."　　*an obeisance*
NORTHUMBERLAND　My lord, in the base court° he doth attend　*outer courtyard*
To speak with you. May it please you to come down.
RICHARD　Down, down I come, like glist'ring Phaëthon,[8]
Wanting the manage° of unruly jades.[9]　　　　　*Lacking control*
180 In the base court? Base court, where kings grow base,
To come at traitors' calls and do them grace.°　　　*submit to them*
In the base court? Come down; down court, down king—
For night-owls shriek where mounting larks should sing.[1]
　　　　　[*Exeunt* RICHARD *and his retinue above.*]

---

7. A public road, open to all passengers; suicides were often buried there.
8. In Greek mythology, the son of the sun god. He attempted to drive his father's sun chariot but was too weak to control the horses; Zeus, king of the gods, struck him down with a thunderbolt to prevent him from destroying the earth.
9. Horses (contemptuous).
1. PERFORMANCE COMMENT Although Shakespeare's stage was not equipped with a staircase visible to spectators, modern productions often highlight Richard's literal and symbolic "descent from the heights." For the interpretive options, see Digital Edition PC 2.

[NORTHUMBERLAND *returns to* BOLINGBROKE.]

BOLINGBROKE   What says his majesty?

NORTHUMBERLAND   Sorrow and grief of heart
185   Makes him speak fondly,° like a frantic° man.   *foolishly / an insane*
         [*Enter below* RICHARD *and his retinue.*]
         Yet he is come.

BOLINGBROKE   Stand all apart,
         And show fair duty to his majesty.
         [*He kneels.*] My gracious lord—

RICHARD   Fair cousin, you debase your princely knee
190   To make the base earth proud with kissing it.
         Me rather had° my heart might feel your love   *I had rather*
         Than my unpleased eye see your courtesy.
         Up, cousin, up; [*raising* BOLINGBROKE] your heart is up, I know—
         Thus high at least [*indicating his crown*], although your
              knee be low.

195 BOLINGBROKE   My gracious lord, I come but for mine own.

RICHARD   Your own is yours, and I am yours, and all.

BOLINGBROKE   So far be mine, my most redoubted° lord,   *dreaded*
         As my true service shall deserve your love.

RICHARD   Well you deserved. They well deserve to have
200   That know the strong'st and surest way to get.
         [*to* YORK] Uncle, give me your hand—nay, dry your eyes.
         Tears show their love but want their remedies.°   *do no good*
         [*to* BOLINGBROKE] Cousin, I am too young to be your father,
         Though you are old enough to be my heir.
205   What you will have, I'll give, and willing, too;
         For do we must what force will have us do.
         Set on towards London, cousin, is it so?

BOLINGBROKE   Yea, my good lord.

RICHARD   Then I must not say no.
         Flourish.

                                                   Exeunt.

3.4 (Q 3.4)

Enter the QUEEN *and two* LADIES.

QUEEN   What sport shall we devise here in this garden
         To drive away the heavy thought of care?

FIRST LADY   Madame, we'll play at bowls.°   *lawn bowling*

QUEEN   'Twill make me think the world is full of rubs,[1]
5   And that my fortune runs against the bias.[2]

SECOND LADY   Madame, we'll dance.

QUEEN   My legs can keep no measure° in delight   *dance step*
         When my poor heart no measure° keeps in grief.   *moderation*
         Therefore, no dancing, girl; some other sport.

10 FIRST LADY   Madame, we'll tell tales.

QUEEN   Of sorrow, or of grief?

FIRST LADY   Of either, madame.

QUEEN   Of neither, girl.
         For if of joy, being altogether wanting,
         It doth remember° me the more of sorrow;   *remind*

3.4 Location: The Duke of York's garden.   2. Runs askew. *bias:* literally, a lead weight in the
1. Impediments (a term from the game of bowls).   bowl that makes it run smoothly.

15 Or if of grief, being altogether had,°   *possessed*
It adds more sorrow to my want of joy.
For what I have, I need not to repeat,
And what I want, it boots° not to complain.   *helps*

SECOND LADY   Madame, I'll sing.

QUEEN   'Tis well that thou hast cause,

20 But thou shouldst please me better wouldst thou weep.

SECOND LADY   I could weep, madame, would it do you good.

QUEEN   And I could sing, would weeping do me good,
And never borrow any tear of thee.

      Enter a GARDENER *and two* SERVANTS.

But stay, here comes the gardeners.

25 Let's step into the shadow of these trees.
My wretchedness unto a row of pins[3]
They'll talk of state, for everyone doth so
Against° a change; woe is forerun with woe.   *In anticipation of*

    [QUEEN *and* LADIES *stand apart.*]

GARDENER [*to* FIRST SERVANT]   Go bind thou up yond dangling
    apricots,

30 Which like unruly children make their sire
Stoop with oppression of their prodigal° weight.   *excessive*
Give some supportance to the bending twigs.
[*to* SECOND SERVANT] Go thou, and like an executioner
Cut off the heads of too-fast-growing sprays

35 That look too lofty in our commonwealth.
All must be even° in our government.   *equal*
You thus employed, I will go root away
The noisome° weeds that without profit suck   *harmful*
The soil's fertility from wholesome flowers.

40 FIRST SERVANT   Why should we in the compass of a pale[4]
Keep law and form and due proportion,
Showing, as in a model, our firm estate,°   *stable government*
When our sea-walled garden, the whole land,
Is full of weeds, her fairest flowers choked up,

45 Her fruit trees all unpruned, her hedges ruined,
Her knots[5] disordered, and her wholesome herbs
Swarming with caterpillars?

GARDENER   Hold thy peace.
He that hath suffered° this disordered spring   *permitted*
Hath now himself met with the fall of leaf.

50 The weeds that his broad-spreading leaves did shelter,
That seemed in eating him to hold him up,
Are pulled up, root and all, by Bolingbroke—
I mean the Earl of Wiltshire, Bushy, Greene.

SECOND SERVANT   What, are they dead?

GARDENER   They are. And Bolingbroke

55 Hath seized the wasteful King. Oh, what pity is it
That he had not so trimmed and dressed° his land   *cultivated*
As we this garden. We at time of year°   *in season*
Do wound the bark, the skin of our fruit trees,[6]
Lest being over-proud° with sap and blood   *excessively swollen*

---

3. I'll bet my great wretchedness against a trivial row of pins.
4. In the limits of a fenced enclosure.

5. Intricate flower beds; social bonds.
6. *Do . . . trees:* This restricts the tree's food supply, encouraging fruit buds to form.

60 With too much riches it confound° itself.   *ruin*
    Had he done so to great and growing men,
    They might have lived to bear and he to taste
    Their fruits of duty. Superfluous branches
    We lop away that bearing boughs may live.
65 Had he done so, himself had borne° the crown[7]   *retained*
    Which waste and idle hours hath quite thrown down.
FIRST SERVANT   What, think you the King shall be deposed?
GARDENER   Depressed° he is already, and deposed   *Brought low*
    'Tis doubted° he will be. Letters came last night   *feared*
70 To a dear friend of the Duke of York's
    That tell black tidings—
QUEEN   Oh, I am pressed to death
    Through want of speaking![8]
        [QUEEN *and* LADIES *come forward.*]
                               Thou, old Adam's[9] likeness,
    Set to dress° this garden, how dares   *cultivate*
    Thy harsh rude° tongue sound this unpleasing news?   *ignorant*
75 What Eve, what serpent hath suggested° thee   *tempted*
    To make a second fall of cursèd man?
    Why dost thou say King Richard is deposed?
    Dar'st thou, thou little better thing than earth,
    Divine° his downfall? Say where, when, and how   *Prophesy*
80 Cam'st thou by this ill tidings? Speak, thou wretch!
GARDENER   Pardon me, madam. Little joy have I
    To breathe these news. Yet what I say is true:
    King Richard, he is in the mighty hold
    Of Bolingbroke. Their fortunes both are weighed:
85 In your lord's scale is nothing but himself
    And some few vanities that make him light;
    But in the balance of great Bolingbroke,
    Besides himself, are all the English peers,
    And with that odds he weighs King Richard down.
90 Post° you to London and you'll find it so;   *Hasten*
    I speak no more than everyone doth know.
QUEEN   Nimble Mischance, that art so light of foot,
    Doth not thy embassage° belong to me,   *message*
    And am I last that knows it? Oh, thou think'st
95 To serve me last that I may longest keep
    Thy sorrow in my breast. Come, ladies, go
    To meet at London London's King in woe.
    What, was I born to this, that my sad look
    Should grace the triumph° of great Bolingbroke?   *triumphal procession*
100 Gard'ner, for telling me this news of woe,
    I would the plants thou graft'st may never grow.
                               Exeunt [QUEEN *and* LADIES].
GARDENER   Poor Queen, so that° thy state might be no worse,   *if as a result*
    I would my skill were subject to thy curse.
    Here did she drop a tear; here in this place
105 I'll set a bank of rue,[1] sour herb of grace.

---

7. Playing on the "crown" of a tree.   killed with weights laid on the stomach.
8. In medieval and Renaissance England, indicted   9. Adam was the first gardener.
persons who refused to plead guilty or not guilty were   1. Herb associated with compassion and repentance.

Rue e'en for ruth° here shortly shall be seen   *pity*
In the remembrance of a weeping queen.   *Exeunt.*

4.1 (Q 4.1)

Enter, as to the Parliament, BOLINGBROKE, AUMERLE,
NORTHUMBERLAND, PERCY, FITZWATER, SURREY,
[*Bishop of*] CARLISLE, ABBOT *of Westminster,* HERALD,
Officers, and BAGOT.

BOLINGBROKE   Call forth Bagot.
       [BAGOT *comes forward.*]
Now, Bagot, freely speak thy mind
What thou dost know of noble Gloucester's death,
Who wrought it with[1] the King, and who performed
5   The bloody office° of his timeless° end.   *deed / untimely*
BAGOT   Then set before my face the Lord Aumerle.
BOLINGBROKE [*to* AUMERLE]   Cousin, stand forth and look
     upon that man.
       [AUMERLE *comes forward.*]
BAGOT   My lord Aumerle, I know your daring tongue
Scorns to unsay° what it hath once delivered.   *deny*
10   In that dead° time when Gloucester's death was plotted,   *fatal; dark*
I heard you say, "Is not my arm of length,°   *long enough*
That reacheth from the restful English court
As far as Calais to my uncle's head?"
Amongst much other talk that very time,[2]
15   I heard you say that you had rather refuse
The offer of an hundred thousand crowns
Than° Bolingbroke's return to England,   *Than accept*
Adding withal° how blessed this land would be   *besides*
In this your cousin's death.
20   AUMERLE   Princes and noble lords,
What answer shall I make to this base man?
Shall I so much dishonor my fair stars°   *honorable birth*
On equal terms to give him chastisement?[3]
Either I must, or have mine honor soiled
25   With th'attainder° of his sland'rous lips.   *accusation*
       [*He throws down his gage.*]
There is my gage, the manual seal of death
That marks thee out for hell. I say thou liest,
And will maintain° what thou hast said is false   *uphold in combat*
In thy heart-blood, though being all too base
30   To stain the temper[4] of my knightly sword.
BOLINGBROKE   Bagot, forbear; thou shalt not take it up.
AUMERLE   Excepting one,° I would he° were the best   *(Bolingbroke) / (Bagot)*
In all this presence that hath moved° me so.   *angered*
FITZWATER [*to* AUMERLE]   If that thy valor stand on sympathy,[5]
35   There is my gage, Aumerle, in gage to thine.
       [*He throws down his gage.*]
By that fair sun that shows me where thou stand'st,
I heard thee say, and vauntingly° thou spak'st it,   *boastfully*

4.1 Location: Westminster Hall.
1. Who persuaded; who collaborated with.
2. *that very time:* inconsistent, since Gloucester was
killed long before Bolingbroke's exile.

3. Punishment (a lord could refuse to fight a lowborn
man in the trial by combat).
4. Quality (literally, "hardness").
5. Insists on equality of rank.

That thou wert cause of noble Gloucester's death.
If° thou deniest it twenty times, thou liest,   *Even if*
40   And I will turn thy falsehood to thy heart,
Where it was forged, with my rapier's point.
AUMERLE   Thou dar'st not, coward, live to see the day.
        [*He takes up Fitzwater's gage.*]
FITZWATER   Now, by my soul, I would it were this hour.
AUMERLE   Fitzwater, thou art damned to hell for this.
45   PERCY   Aumerle, thou liest. His honor is as true
In this appeal° as thou art all unjust.   *accusation*
And that thou art so, there I throw my gage
        [*throwing down his gage*]
To prove it on thee, to th'extremest point
Of mortal breathing. Seize it if thou dar'st.
50   AUMERLE   And if I do not, may my hands rot off
And never brandish more° revengeful steel   *again*
Over the glittering helmet of my foe.
        [*He takes up Percy's gage.*]
SURREY   My lord Fitzwater, I do remember well
The very time Aumerle and you did talk.
55   FITZWATER   My lord,
'Tis very true. You were in presence° then,   *present*
And you can witness with me this is true.
SURREY   As false, by heaven, as heaven itself is true.
FITZWATER   Surrey, thou liest.
SURREY   Dishonorable boy,
60   That lie shall lie so heavy on my sword
That it shall render vengeance and revenge
Till thou the lie-giver and that lie do lie
In earth as quiet as thy father's skull,
In proof whereof there is mine honor's pawn.
        [*He throws down his gage.*]
65   Engage it to the trial if thou dar'st.
FITZWATER   How fondly dost thou spur a forward horse!
        [*He takes up Surrey's gage.*]
If I dare eat or drink or breathe or live,
I dare meet Surrey in a wilderness
And spit upon him, whilst I say he lies
70   And lies and lies. [*He throws down another gage.*] There is
   my bond of faith
To tie thee to my strong correction.
As I intend to thrive in this new world,
Aumerle is guilty of my true appeal.°   *accusation*
Besides, I heard the banished Norfolk° say   *(Mowbray)*
75   That thou, Aumerle, didst send two of thy men
To execute the noble Duke at Calais.
AUMERLE   Some honest Christian trust me with° a gage—   *lend me*
        [*He borrows a gage.*]
That Norfolk lies, here do I throw down this,
        [*throwing down another gage*]
If he may be repealed° to try his honor.   *recalled from exile*
80   BOLINGBROKE   These differences shall all rest under gage[6]
Till Norfolk be repealed. Repealed he shall be,

---

6. Shall remain as standing challenges.

And, though mine enemy, restored again
To all his lands and signories.° When he's returned,   *estates*
Against Aumerle we will enforce his trial.
85   CARLISLE   That honorable day shall ne'er be seen.
Many a time hath banished Norfolk fought
For Jesu Christ in glorious Christian field,[7]
Streaming the ensign of the Christian cross
Against black pagans, Turks, and Saracens;
90   And, toiled° with works of war, retired himself   *exhausted*
To Italy, and there at Venice gave
His body to that pleasant country's earth,
And his pure soul unto his captain, Christ,
Under whose colors he had fought so long.
95   BOLINGBROKE   Why, Bishop, is Norfolk dead?
CARLISLE   As sure as I live, my lord.
BOLINGBROKE   Sweet peace conduct his sweet soul
To the bosom of good old Abraham.[8] Lords appellants,°   *Noble complainants*
Your differences° shall all rest under gage   *disputes*
100   Till we assign you to your days of trial.
             Enter YORK.
YORK   Great Duke of Lancaster, I come to thee
From plume-plucked° Richard, who with willing soul   *humbled*
Adopts thee heir, and his high scepter yields
To the possession of thy royal hand.
105   Ascend his throne, descending now from him,
And long live Henry, of that name the fourth!
BOLINGBROKE   In God's name I'll ascend the regal throne.
CARLISLE   Marry, heaven forbid!
Worst° in this royal presence may I speak,   *Least worthy*
110   Yet best beseeming° me to speak the truth.   *fitting (as a clergyman)*
Would God that any in this noble presence
Were enough noble to be upright judge
Of noble Richard; then true nobleness° would   *nobility*
Learn° him forbearance from so foul a wrong.   *Teach*
115   What subject can give sentence on his king?
And who sits here that is not Richard's subject?
Thieves are not judged but° they are by° to hear,   *except when / present*
Although apparent° guilt be seen in them;   *obvious*
And shall the figure° of God's majesty,   *image*
120   His captain, steward, deputy elect,°   *chosen*
Anointed, crowned, planted many years,
Be judged by subject and inferior breath,
And he himself not present? O forbid° it, God,   *prohibit*
That in a Christian climate souls refined[9]
125   Should show so heinous, black, obscene° a deed.   *odious*
I speak to subjects, and a subject speaks,
Stirred up by heaven, thus boldly for his king.
My lord of Hereford here, whom you call king,
Is a foul traitor to proud Hereford's king;
130   And if you crown him, let me prophesy
The blood of English shall manure the ground,
And future ages groan for his foul act.

---

7. In battle for the Christian cause.
8. *the bosom . . . Abraham:* that is, heavenly rest; see
Luke 16:22.
9. Spiritually improved; aristocratic.

Peace shall go sleep with Turks and infidels,
And in this seat° of peace tumultuous wars   *region; throne*
135 Shall kin with kin, and kind with kind, confound.[1]
Disorder, horror, fear, and mutiny
Shall here inhabit, and this land be called
The field of Golgotha[2] and dead men's skulls.
Oh, if you rear this house against this house,°   *(Lancaster against York)*
140 It will the woefullest division prove
That ever fell upon this cursèd earth.
Prevent it, resist it, and let it not be so,
Lest child, child's children, cry against you "Woe!"
NORTHUMBERLAND Well have you argued, sir; and for your pains
145 Of capital treason we arrest you here.
My lord of Westminster, be it your charge
To keep him safely till his day of trial.[3]
May it please you, lords, to grant the commons' suit?[4]
BOLINGBROKE Fetch hither Richard, that in common° view   *public*
150 He may surrender;[5] so we shall proceed
Without suspicion.
YORK   I will be his conduct.°   *Exit.*   *escort*
BOLINGBROKE Lords, you that here are under our arrest,
Procure your sureties for your days of answer.[6]
Little are we beholden to your love,
155 And little looked for° at your helping hands.   *expected*
    Enter RICHARD *and* YORK.
RICHARD Alack, why am I sent for to a king,
Before I have shook off the regal thoughts
Wherewith I reigned? I hardly yet have learned
To insinuate, flatter, bow, and bend my knee.
160 Give sorrow leave a while to tutor me
To this submission. Yet I well remember
The favors° of these men: were they not mine?   *faces; benefits*
Did they not sometime cry, "All hail!" to me?
So Judas did to Christ, but He in twelve
165 Found truth in all but one; I, in twelve thousand, none.
God save the King! Will no man say "Amen"?
Am I both priest and clerk?[7] Well, then, "Amen."
God save the King, although I be not he;
And yet Amen, if heaven do think him me.
170 To do what service am I sent for hither?
YORK To do that office° of thine own goodwill   *task; ceremony*
Which tired majesty did make thee offer:
The resignation of thy state and crown
To Henry Bolingbroke.
RICHARD   Give me the crown.
175 [*to* BOLINGBROKE] Here, cousin, seize the crown. Here, cousin,
On this side my hand, on that side thine.
Now is this golden crown like a deep well

---

1. Shall destroy kinsman by fellow kinsman and countryman by fellow countryman.
2. Place of Christ's crucifixion, the name of which means "place of dead men's skulls."
3. TEXTUAL COMMENT Richard's deposition (4.1.149–311), the most famous and politically explosive scene in the play, was not included in the earliest Quarto editions (until 1608). Evidence suggests that it was cut from the original, not added later on. See Digital Edition TC 7 (Folio edited text).
4. The House of Commons' request that Richard should have judgment passed on him.
5. Abdicate (the legitimacy of the commons' suit depended on Richard's having given up the crown and thus his royal immunity from prosecution).
6. Procure persons guaranteeing your appearance on the day of trial.
7. Priest's assistant who utters the responses to prayers.

That owes° two buckets, filling one another,[8]   *has*
The emptier ever dancing in the air,
180   The other down, unseen, and full of water.
That bucket down and full of tears am I,
Drinking my griefs whilst you mount up on high.
BOLINGBROKE   I thought you had been willing to resign.
RICHARD   My crown I am, but still my griefs are mine:
185   You may my glories and my state° depose,   *royal status*
But not my griefs; still° am I king of those.   *permanently*
BOLINGBROKE   Part of your cares you give me with your crown.
RICHARD   Your cares set up do not pluck my cares down.
My care is loss of care, by old care done;
190   Your care is gain of care, by new care won.[9]
The cares I give, I have, though given away;
They 'tend° the crown, yet still with me they stay.   *attend; accompany*
BOLINGBROKE   Are you contented to resign the crown?
RICHARD   Ay, no; no, ay—for I must nothing be.[1]
195   Therefore no "no," for I resign to thee.[2]
Now mark me how I will undo° myself: *ruin; strip*
I give this heavy weight from off my head,
And this unwieldy scepter from my hand,
The pride of kingly sway from out my heart.
200   With mine own tears I wash away my balm,
With mine own hands I give away my crown,
With mine own tongue deny my sacred state,°   *divine right to be king*
With mine own breath release all duteous oaths.°   *oaths of allegiance*
All pomp and majesty I do forswear;
205   My manors, rents, revenues I forgo;
My acts, decrees, and statutes I deny.°   *repudiate*
God pardon all oaths that are broke to me;
God keep all vows unbroke are made to thee.
Make me, that nothing have, with nothing grieved,[3]
210   And thou with all pleased that hast all achieved.
Long mayst thou live in Richard's seat to sit,
And soon lie Richard in an earthy pit.
"God save King Henry," unkinged Richard says,
"And send him many years of sunshine° days."   *sunny*
What more remains?
215   NORTHUMBERLAND [*presenting a paper*]   No more, but that
you read°   *read aloud*
These accusations and these grievous crimes
Committed by your person and your followers
Against the state and profit° of this land,   *established prosperity*
That, by confessing them, the souls of men
220   May deem that you are worthily deposed.
RICHARD   Must I do so? And must I ravel out
My weaved-up follies? Gentle Northumberland,
If thy offenses were upon record,
Would it not shame thee in so fair a troop°   *company*

8. That is, the raising of one causing the other to descend and fill.
9. *Your cares . . . won*: an extended wordplay on "care": Your assuming cares of state does not relieve me of grief. I mourn the loss of responsibility, by lack of diligence in the past; you concern yourself with gaining responsibility, won by effort.
1. Playing on "ay" (yes) and "I": since I am no thing, then "I"—that is, "ay"—is "no."
2. PERFORMANCE COMMENT Directors and actors have creatively staged the moment at which Richard relinquishes the crown, in order to complicate our view of both Richard and Bolingbroke. For a discussion of some possibilities, see Digital Edition PC 3.
3. Grieved at nothing; grieved at having nothing.

225   To read a lecture° of them? If thou wouldst,   *give a public reading*
        There shouldst thou find one heinous article
        Containing the deposing of a king
        And cracking the strong warrant of an oath,
        Marked with a blot, damned in the book of heaven.
230   Nay, all of you that stand and look upon me,
        Whilst that my wretchedness doth bait⁴ myself,
        Though some of you, with Pilate, wash your hands,⁵
        Showing an outward pity, yet you Pilates
        Have here delivered me to my sour° cross,   *bitter*
235   And water cannot wash away your sin.
    NORTHUMBERLAND   My lord, dispatch.° Read o'er these articles.   *hurry up*
    RICHARD   Mine eyes are full of tears; I cannot see.
        And yet salt water blinds them not so much
        But they can see a sort° of traitors here.   *pack*
240   Nay, if I turn mine eyes upon myself,
        I find myself a traitor with the rest;
        For I have given here my soul's consent
        T'undeck the pompous° body of a king,   *splendidly dressed*
        Made glory base, a sovereignty a slave,
245   Proud majesty a subject, state° a peasant.   *royalty*
    NORTHUMBERLAND   My lord—
    RICHARD   No lord of thine, thou haught° insulting man—   *haughty*
        No, nor no man's lord. I have no name, no title—
        No, not that name was given me at the font—
250   But 'tis usurped. Alack the heavy day,
        That I have worn so many winters out
        And know not now what name to call myself.
        Oh, that I were a mockery king of snow,
        Standing before the sun of Bolingbroke,
255   To melt myself away in water-drops.
        Good King, great King, and yet not greatly good,
        An if my word be sterling° yet in England,   *valid (like currency)*
        Let it command a mirror hither straight,°   *immediately*
        That it may show me what a face I have,
260   Since it is bankrupt of his° majesty.   *its*
    BOLINGBROKE   Go, some of you, and fetch a looking glass.
                              [Exit Officer.]
    NORTHUMBERLAND *[to* RICHARD*]*   Read o'er this paper, while
        the glass° doth come.   *until the mirror*
    RICHARD   Fiend, thou torments me ere I come to hell.
    BOLINGBROKE   Urge it no more, my lord Northumberland.
265   NORTHUMBERLAND   The commons will not then be satisfied.
    RICHARD   They shall be satisfied. I'll read enough
        When I do see the very book indeed
        Where all my sins are writ, and that's myself.
              Enter [Officer] with a glass.
        Give me that glass, and therein will I read.
            [Officer gives glass to RICHARD*.]*
270   No deeper wrinkles yet? Hath sorrow struck
        So many blows upon this face of mine
        And made no deeper wounds? O flatt'ring glass,

---

4. Torment (as in bearbaiting).
5. Pilate, Jesus' judge, washed his hands to signify   his disclaiming of responsibility for the death sentence that he imposed at the request of the Jews.

Like to my followers in prosperity,
Thou dost beguile me. Was this face the face
275 That every day under his household roof
Did keep ten thousand men? Was this the face
That like the sun did make beholders wink?° *shut their eyes*
Is this the face which faced[6] so many follies,
That was at last outfaced° by Bolingbroke? *stared down*
280 A brittle glory shineth in this face,
As brittle as the glory is the face—
        [*He breaks the glass.*]
For there it is, cracked in an hundred shivers.
Mark, silent King, the moral of this sport:
How soon my sorrow hath destroyed my face.
285 BOLINGBROKE   The shadow[7] of your sorrow hath destroyed
The shadow° of your face. *image*
RICHARD   Say that again.
The shadow of my sorrow? Ha, let's see.
'Tis very true, my grief lies all within;
And these external manner of laments
290 Are merely shadows to the unseen grief
That swells with silence in the tortured soul.
There lies the substance. And I thank thee, King,
For thy great bounty that not only giv'st
Me cause to wail, but teachest me the way
295 How to lament the cause. I'll beg one boon,° *favor*
And then be gone and trouble you no more.
Shall I obtain it?
BOLINGBROKE   Name it, fair cousin.
RICHARD   Fair cousin? I am greater than a king,
For when I was a king, my flatterers
300 Were then but subjects. Being now a subject,
I have a king here to my flatterer.
Being so great, I have no need to beg.
BOLINGBROKE   Yet ask.
RICHARD   And shall I have?
305 BOLINGBROKE   You shall.
RICHARD   Then give me leave to go.
BOLINGBROKE   Whither?
RICHARD   Whither you will, so° I were from your sights. *provided that*
BOLINGBROKE   Go, some of you, convey° him to the Tower. *conduct*
310 RICHARD   Oh, good—"Convey."° Conveyers are you all *Steal*
That rise thus nimbly by a true king's fall.
                        [*Exit* RICHARD, *guarded.*]
BOLINGBROKE   On Wednesday next, we solemnly set down
Our coronation. Lords, prepare yourselves.
                Exeunt [*all except* ABBOT *of Westminster, Bishop of*
                                CARLISLE, *and* AUMERLE].
ABBOT   A woeful pageant have we here beheld.
315 CARLISLE   The woe's to come: the children yet unborn
Shall feel this day as sharp to them as thorn.
AUMERLE   You holy clergymen, is there no plot

---

6. Countenanced; adorned (as a garment trimmed with "facings").
7. Bolingbroke uses "shadow" to mean "outward dis-

play," but Richard plays on the word's other meanings—darkness; image, reflection; unhappiness—in the following passage.

To rid the realm of this pernicious blot?
ABBOT   Before I freely speak my mind herein,
320   You shall not only take the sacrament[8]
To bury mine intents,[9] but also to effect
Whatever I shall happen to devise.
I see your brows are full of discontent,
Your heart of sorrow, and your eyes of tears.
325   Come home with me to supper. I'll lay a plot
Shall show us all a merry day.   *Exeunt.*

5.1 (Q 5.1)

Enter QUEEN *and* LADIES.
QUEEN   This way the King will come. This is the way
To Julius Caesar's ill-erected Tower,[1]
To whose flint bosom my condemnèd lord
Is doomed a prisoner by proud Bolingbroke.
5   Here let us rest, if this rebellious earth
Have any resting for her true King's Queen.
Enter RICHARD *and Guard.*
But soft°—but see, or rather do not see   *wait*
My fair rose wither. Yet look up, behold,
That you in pity may dissolve to dew
10   And wash him fresh again with true-love tears.
Ah, thou, the model where old Troy did stand,[2]
Thou map° of honor, thou King Richard's tomb,   *epitome*
And not King Richard. Thou most beauteous inn,
Why should hard-favored° grief be lodged in thee,   *ugly; unfortunate*
15   When triumph is become an alehouse[3] guest?
RICHARD   Join not with grief, fair woman, do not so,
To make my end too sudden. Learn, good soul,
To think our former state a happy dream,
From which awaked, the truth of what we are
20   Shows us but this. I am sworn brother, sweet,
To grim Necessity, and he and I
Will keep a league till death. Hie° thee to France   *Hasten*
And cloister thee in some religious house.°   *convent*
Our holy lives must win a new world's° crown,   *(heaven's)*
25   Which our profane hours here have stricken down.
QUEEN   What, is my Richard both in shape and mind
Transformed and weakened? Hath Bolingbroke
Deposed thine intellect? Hath he been in thy heart?
The lion, dying, thrusteth forth his paw
30   And wounds the earth, if nothing else, with rage
To be° o'erpowered; and wilt thou, pupil-like,   *At being*
Take thy correction mildly, kiss the rod,
And fawn on rage with base humility,
Which art a lion and a king of beasts?
35   RICHARD   A king of beasts indeed[4]—if aught but beasts,
I had been still a happy king of men.

---

8. A solemn oath, accompanied by the rite of Communion.
9. To keep my intentions secret.
5.1 Location: A street near the Tower of London.
1. The Tower of London (popularly thought to have been built by Caesar). *ill-erected:* poorly built;
erected for evil ends.
2. The pattern of fallen greatness, like Troy.
3. Poorer class of lodging (referring to Bolingbroke) than an "inn."
4. Lion (Richard's emblem); ruler of beastly men.

Good sometime° Queen, prepare thee hence for France.   *former*
Think I am dead, and that even here thou tak'st,
As from my deathbed, my last living leave.
40   In winter's tedious nights sit by the fire
With good old folks, and let them tell thee tales
Of woeful ages long ago betide;[5]
And ere thou bid good night, to quit their grief,°   *repay their sad tales*
Tell thou the lamentable fall of me
45   And send the hearers weeping to their beds.
For why the senseless brands will sympathize[6]
The heavy accent of thy moving[7] tongue
And in compassion weep the fire out;
And some° will mourn in ashes, some coal-black,   *(firebrands)*
50   For the deposing of a rightful king.
        Enter NORTHUMBERLAND.
NORTHUMBERLAND   My lord, the mind of Bolingbroke is changed.
You must to Pomfret,° not unto the Tower.   *(castle in Yorkshire)*
And, madam, there is order ta'en[8] for you:
With all swift speed you must away to France.
55   RICHARD   Northumberland, thou ladder wherewithal
The mounting Bolingbroke ascends my throne,
The time shall not be many hours of age
More than it is ere foul sin, gathering head,
Shall break into corruption.[9] Thou shalt think
60   Though he divide the realm and give thee half
It is too little, helping[1] him to all.
He shall think that thou which know'st the way
To plant unrightful kings, wilt know again,
Being ne'er so little urged, another way
65   To pluck him headlong from the usurpèd throne.
The love of wicked friends converts to fear,
That fear to hate, and hate turns one or both
To worthy° danger and deservèd death.   *severe*
NORTHUMBERLAND   My guilt be on my head, and there an end.[2]
70   Take leave and part,° for you must part° forthwith.   *separate / depart*
RICHARD   Doubly divorced! Bad men, ye violate
A twofold marriage: twixt my crown and me,
And then betwixt me and my married wife.
[*to* QUEEN] Let me unkiss the oath twixt thee and me—
75   And yet not so, for with a kiss 'twas made.
[*to* NORTHUMBERLAND] Part us, Northumberland: I towards
        the North,
Where shivering cold and sickness pines the clime;°   *afflicts the region*
My Queen to France, from whence, set forth in pomp,
She came adornèd hither like sweet May,
80   Sent back like Hallowmas° or short'st of day.[3]   *November 1*
QUEEN   And must we be divided? Must we part?
RICHARD   Ay, hand from hand, my love, and heart from heart.

---

5. Woe that happened long ago.
6. Because even the insentient firewood will respond empathetically.
7. Physically and emotionally.
8. Arrangements have been made.
9. Pus (the image is of a swelling abscess). *1* and *2 Henry IV*, the sequels to *Richard II*, dramatize North-

umberland's rebellion against "the mounting Bolingbroke."
1. *helping*: since you helped.
2. Recalling the cry of the Jews at Jesus' trial: "His death be upon our heads, and the heads of our children" (Matthew 27:25).
3. Winter solstice.

QUEEN [*to* NORTHUMBERLAND]   Banish us both, and send the
　　King with me.
NORTHUMBERLAND   That were some love, but little policy.°　　*but politically naive*
85　QUEEN   Then whither he goes, thither let me go.
RICHARD [*to* QUEEN]   So two together weeping make one woe.
　　Weep thou for me in France, I for thee here;
　　Better far off than near, be ne'er the near.[4]
　　Go count thy way with sighs, I mine with groans.
90　QUEEN   So longest way shall have the longest moans.
RICHARD   Twice for one step I'll groan, the way being short,
　　And piece the way out° with a heavy heart.　　*lengthen the way*
　　Come, come, in wooing sorrow let's be brief,
　　Since, wedding it, there is such length in grief.
95　　One kiss shall stop our mouths, and dumbly° part;　　*silently*
　　Thus give I mine, and thus take I thy heart.
　　　　　[*They kiss.*]
QUEEN   Give me mine own again; 'twere no good part[5]
　　To take on me to keep and kill thy heart.
　　　　　[*They kiss again.*]
　　So now I have mine own again, be gone,
100　　That I may strive to kill it with a groan.
RICHARD   We make woe wanton[6] with this fond delay.
　　Once more, adieu; the rest let sorrow say.　　*Exeunt.*

5.2 (Q 5.2)

Enter YORK *and his* DUCHESS [OF YORK].
DUCHESS OF YORK   My lord, you told me you would tell the rest,
　　When weeping made you break the story off,
　　Of our two cousins'° coming into London.　　*kinsmen's*
YORK   Where did I leave?
DUCHESS OF YORK　　　　　At that sad stop, my lord,
5　　Where rude misgoverned° hands from windows' tops°　　*unruly / upper windows*
　　Threw dust and rubbish on King Richard's head.
YORK   Then, as I said, the Duke, great Bolingbroke,
　　Mounted upon a hot and fiery steed,
　　Which his aspiring rider[1] seemed to know,
10　　With slow but stately pace kept on his course,
　　While all tongues cried, "God save thee, Bolingbroke!"
　　You would have thought the very windows spake,
　　So many greedy looks of young and old
　　Through casements darted their desiring eyes
15　　Upon his visage, and that all the walls
　　With painted imagery[2] had said at once,
　　"Jesu preserve thee! Welcome, Bolingbroke!"
　　Whilst he, from one side to the other turning,
　　Bareheaded, lower than his proud steed's neck,
20　　Bespake° them thus: "I thank you, countrymen";　　*Addressed*
　　And thus still doing, thus he passed along.
DUCHESS OF YORK   Alas, poor Richard, where rides he the whilst?

---

4. Better to be far away than to be near but never
nearer to our happiness.
5. It would not be good of me.
6. We make our woe unrestrained; we make a sport
of our grief.

5.2 Location: The Duke of York's house.
1. Object of "seemed to know."
2. Painted cloths that were hung on walls in pageants; figures in these sometimes had "speech bubbles."

YORK   As in a theater the eyes of men,
After a well-graced actor leaves the stage,
25   Are idly bent on him that enters next,
Thinking his prattle to be tedious;
Even so, or with much more contempt, men's eyes
Did scowl on Richard. No man cried, "God save him,"
No joyful tongue gave him his welcome home,
30   But dust was thrown upon his sacred head,
Which with such gentle sorrow he shook off,
His face still combating° with tears and smiles,   *continually struggling*
The badges° of his grief and patience,   *emblems*
That had not God for some strong purpose steeled
35   The hearts of men, they must perforce have melted
And barbarism itself have pitied him.
But heaven hath a hand in these events,
To whose high will we bound our calm contents.[3]
To Bolingbroke are we sworn subjects now,
40   Whose state and honor I for aye allow.°   *forever acknowledge*
            Enter AUMERLE.
DUCHESS OF YORK   Here comes my son, Aumerle.
YORK   Aumerle that was,[4]
But that is lost for being Richard's friend.
And, madam, you must call him Rutland now.
I am in Parliament pledge for his truth°   *guarantor of his loyalty*
45   And lasting fealty° to the new-made king.   *fidelity*
DUCHESS OF YORK [*to* AUMERLE]   Welcome, my son. Who are
        the violets now
That strew the green lap of the new-come spring?
AUMERLE   Madam, I know not, nor I greatly care not.
God knows I had as lief° be none as one.   *had rather*
50   YORK   Well, bear you well in this new spring of time,
Lest you be cropped° before you come to prime.   *cut*
What news from Oxford? Hold those jousts and triumphs?°   *processions*
AUMERLE   For aught I know, my lord, they do.
YORK   You will be there, I know.
55   AUMERLE   If God prevent not, I purpose so.
YORK   What seal is that that hangs without thy bosom?[5]
Yea, look'st thou pale? Let me see the writing.
AUMERLE   My lord, 'tis nothing.
YORK   No matter then who sees it.
I will be satisfied. Let me see the writing.
60   AUMERLE   I do beseech your grace to pardon me.
It is a matter of small consequence,
Which for some reasons I would not have seen.
YORK   Which for some reasons, sir, I mean to see.
I fear, I fear—
DUCHESS OF YORK   What should you fear?
65   'Tis nothing but some bond that he is entered into
For gay apparel against° the triumph.   *in time for*
YORK   Bound to himself?[6] What doth he with a bond

3. Bind ourselves to be calmly contented.
4. Aumerle has been deprived of his dukedom; he remains Earl of Rutland.
5. The document is in Aumerle's doublet, with the

seal on a visibly dangling slip of attached paper.
6. If Aumerle had signed a bond to borrow money, the creditor would have the bond.

That he is bound to? Wife, thou art a fool.
Boy, let me see the writing.
70 AUMERLE   I do beseech you pardon me; I may not show it.
YORK   I will be satisfied. Let me see it, I say.
　　　　[*He*] *snatches it* [*from* AUMERLE, *and reads it*].
Treason, foul treason, villain, traitor, slave!
DUCHESS OF YORK   What's the matter, my lord?
YORK [*calling offstage*]   Ho, who's within there?
　　　　[*Enter* SERVANT.]
　　　　　　　　　　　　　　　　　　　Saddle my horse.
75 Heaven for His mercy, what treachery is here?
DUCHESS OF YORK   Why, what is't, my lord?
YORK   Give me my boots, I say. Saddle my horse.
　　　　　　　　　　　　　　[*Exit* SERVANT.]
Now by my honor, my life, my troth,
I will appeach° the villain.   accuse
DUCHESS OF YORK   What is the matter?
80 YORK   Peace, foolish woman.
DUCHESS OF YORK   I will not peace. What is the matter, son?
AUMERLE   Good mother, be content; it is no more
Than my poor life must answer.
DUCHESS OF YORK   Thy life answer?
　　　　Enter SERVANT *with boots.*
YORK   Bring me my boots. I will unto the King.
85 DUCHESS OF YORK   Strike him,° Aumerle! Poor boy, thou art   (*the servant*)
　　　amazed.°   *distraught*
　　　　[*to* SERVANT] Hence, villain! Never more come in my sight.
YORK   Give me my boots, I say.
　　　　　　　　[SERVANT *gives boots to* YORK, *and exit.*]
DUCHESS OF YORK   Why, York, what wilt thou do?
Wilt thou not hide the trespass of thine own?
90 Have we more sons?[7] Or are we like to have?
Is not my teeming date° drunk up with time?   *period of childbearing*
And wilt thou pluck my fair son from mine age
And rob me of a happy mother's name?
Is he not like thee? Is he not thine own?
95 YORK   Thou fond° mad woman,   *foolish*
Wilt thou conceal this dark conspiracy?
A dozen of them here have ta'en the sacrament
And interchangeably set down their hands[8]
To kill the King at Oxford.
DUCHESS OF YORK   He shall be none.°   *not be one of them*
100 We'll keep him here. Then what is that to him?
YORK   Away, fond woman! Were he twenty times my son,
I would appeach him.
DUCHESS OF YORK   Hadst thou groaned° for him   *suffered labor pains*
As I have done, thou wouldst be more pitiful.
But now I know thy mind: thou dost suspect
105 That I have been disloyal to thy bed,
And that he is a bastard, not thy son.
Sweet York, sweet husband, be not of that mind.
He is as like thee as a man may be,

---

7. Historically, Aumerle had a brother and a sister,
and the Duchess of York, the Duke's second wife, was

Aumerle's stepmother.
8. And mutually committed themselves in writing.

Not like to me nor any of my kin,
And yet I love him.

110 YORK   Make way, unruly woman.   *Exit.*

DUCHESS OF YORK   After, Aumerle! Mount thee upon his horse,
Spur post,° and get before him to the King,   *Ride fast*
And beg thy pardon ere he do accuse thee.
I'll not be long behind. Though I be old,

115 I doubt not but to ride as fast as York,
And never will I rise up from the ground
Till Bolingbroke have pardoned thee. Away, be gone.   *Exeunt.*

5.3 (Q 5.3)

Enter BOLINGBROKE, PERCY, *and other Lords.*

BOLINGBROKE   Can no man tell of my unthrifty son?[1]
'Tis full three months since I did see him last.
If any plague hang over us, 'tis he.
I would to heaven, my lords, he might be found.

5 Inquire at London 'mongst the taverns there,
For there, they say, he daily doth frequent
With unrestrainèd loose companions—
Even such, they say, as stand in narrow lanes,
And rob our watch,° and beat our passengers,°   *watchmen / wayfarers*

10 Which he, young wanton and effeminate° boy,   *pleasure-seeking and unmanly*
Takes on° the point of honor to support   *Makes it*
So dissolute a crew.

PERCY   My lord, some two days since° I saw the Prince,   *ago*
And told him of these triumphs held at Oxford.

15 BOLINGBROKE   And what said the gallant?

PERCY   His answer was, he would unto the stews°   *brothels*
And from the common'st creature pluck a glove
And wear it as a favor,[2] and with that
He would unhorse the lustiest° challenger.   *most vigorous*

20 BOLINGBROKE   As dissolute as desp'rate;° yet through both   *reckless*
I see some sparks of better hope, which elder days
May happily[3] bring forth.

Enter AUMERLE.

                   But who comes here?

AUMERLE   Where is the King?

BOLINGBROKE   What means our cousin, that he stares

25 And looks so wildly?

AUMERLE   God save your grace. I do beseech your majesty
To have some conference with your grace alone.

BOLINGBROKE [*to Lords*]   Withdraw yourselves and leave us
     here alone.

         [*Exeunt all but* BOLINGBROKE *and* AUMERLE.]

What is the matter with our cousin now?

30 AUMERLE [*kneeling*]   Forever may my knees grow° to the earth,   *be fixed*
My tongue cleave to my roof within my mouth,
Unless a pardon ere I rise or speak.

BOLINGBROKE   Intended or committed was this fault?
If on the first,° how heinous e'er it be,   *only intended*

5.3 Location: Windsor Castle.
1. Henry's eldest son is Prince Hal of *1* and *2 Henry
IV,* later King Henry V. *unthrifty:* dissolute.

2. Lady's gift to a knight that is worn in combat.
3. Perhaps; with good fortune.

35   To win thy after-love I pardon thee.
AUMERLE Then give me leave that I may turn the key,
  That no man enter till my tale be done.
BOLINGBROKE Have thy desire.
    [AUMERLE *locks the door.*]
YORK (*within*) My liege, beware, look to thyself!
40 Thou hast a traitor in thy presence there.
BOLINGBROKE [*to* AUMERLE] Villain, I'll make thee safe.°   *harmless*
    [*He goes to draw his sword.*]
AUMERLE Stay° thy revengeful hand, thou hast no cause to fear.   *Restrain*
YORK [*within*] Open the door, secure° foolhardy King!   *overconfident*
  Shall I for° love speak treason[4] to thy face?   *out of*
45 Open the door or I will break it open.
    [BOLINGBROKE *unlocks the door.*] *Enter* YORK.
BOLINGBROKE What is the matter, uncle? Speak.
  Recover breath. Tell us how near is danger
  That we may arm us to encounter it.
YORK [*presenting paper*] Peruse this writing here, and thou
   shalt know
50 The reason that my haste forbids me show.°   *to explain*
AUMERLE [*to* BOLINGBROKE] Remember, as thou read'st, thy
   promise passed.°   *given*
  I do repent me. Read not my name there;
  My heart is not confederate with my hand.°   *signature*
YORK [*to* AUMERLE] It was, villain, ere thy hand did set it down.
55 I tore it° from the traitor's bosom, King.   *(the bond)*
  Fear, and not love, begets his penitence.
  Forget to pity him, lest thy pity prove
  A serpent that will sting thee to the heart.
BOLINGBROKE Oh, heinous, strong, and bold conspiracy!
60 O loyal father of a treacherous son,
  Thou sheer,° immaculate, and silver fountain,   *clear*
  From whence this stream, through muddy passages,
  Hath had his current and defiled himself!
  Thy overflow of good converts to bad,
65 And thy abundant goodness shall excuse
  This deadly° blot in thy digressing[5] son.   *damnable; death-dealing*
YORK So shall my virtue be his vices' bawd,°   *pimp*
  And he shall spend mine honor with his shame,
  As thriftless sons their scraping fathers' gold.
70 Mine honor lives when his dishonor dies,
  Or my shamed life in his dishonor lies.
  Thou kill'st me in his life, giving him breath;
  The traitor lives, the true man's put to death.
DUCHESS OF YORK (*within*) What ho, my liege! For heaven's
   sake, let me in.
75 BOLINGBROKE What shrill-voiced suppliant makes this
   eager cry?
DUCHESS [*within*] A woman, and thine aunt, great King: 'tis I.
  Speak with me, pity me, open the door;
  A beggar begs that never begged before.

---

4. Disrespectfully criticize (as "secure" and "foolhardy").
5. Diverging from course (as of a stream); transgressing.

BOLINGBROKE   Our scene is altered from a serious thing,
80   And now changed to "The Beggar and the King."°   *(the name of a ballad)*
    [*to* AUMERLE] My dangerous cousin, let your mother in.
    I know she's come to pray for your foul sin.
YORK [*to* BOLINGBROKE]   If thou do pardon whosoever pray,
    More sins for this forgiveness prosper may.
85   This festered joint° cut off, the rest rests sound;   *infected limb*
    This let alone will all the rest confound.°   *destroy*
        [AUMERLE *opens the door.*] *Enter* DUCHESS [OF YORK].
DUCHESS OF YORK   O King, believe not this hardhearted man;
    Love loving not itself none other can.[6]
YORK   Thou frantic woman, what dost thou make° here?   *do*
90   Shall thy old dugs° once more a traitor rear?   *breasts*
DUCHESS OF YORK   Sweet York, be patient. [*She kneels.*] Hear
    me, gentle liege.
BOLINGBROKE   Rise up, good aunt.
DUCHESS OF YORK   Not yet, I thee beseech.
    Forever will I kneel upon my knees
    And never see day that the happy sees
95   Till thou give joy, until thou bid me joy,
    By pardoning Rutland, my transgressing boy.
AUMERLE [*kneeling*]   Unto° my mother's prayers I bend my   *In support of*
    knee.
YORK [*kneeling*]   Against them both my true joints bended be.
DUCHESS OF YORK   Pleads he in earnest? Look upon his face.
100   His eyes do drop no tears; his prayers are in jest;
    His words come from his mouth, ours from our breast.
    He prays but faintly and would be denied;
    We pray with heart and soul and all beside.
    His weary joints would gladly rise, I know;
105   Our knees shall kneel till to the ground they grow.
    His prayers are full of false hypocrisy,
    Ours of true zeal and deep integrity.
    Our prayers do out-pray his; then let them have
    That mercy which true prayers ought to have.
BOLINGBROKE   Good aunt, stand up.
110   DUCHESS OF YORK   Nay, do not say, "Stand up,"
    But "Pardon" first, and afterwards "Stand up."
    An if° I were thy nurse, thy tongue to teach,   *An if = If*
    "Pardon" should be the first word of thy speech.
    I never longed to hear a word till now.
115   Say "Pardon," King, let pity teach thee how.
    The word is short, but not so short as sweet;
    No word like "Pardon" for kings' mouths so meet.°   *fit*
YORK   Speak it in French, King, say, "*Pardonnez-moi.*"[7]
DUCHESS OF YORK   Dost thou teach pardon pardon to destroy?[8]
120   Ah, my sour° husband, my hardhearted lord,   *harsh*
    That sets the word itself against the word.
    [*to* BOLINGBROKE] Speak "Pardon" as 'tis current in our land;
    The chopping[9] French we do not understand.

---

6. If one does not love one's own flesh and blood, one
can love no one else (not even the King).
7. "Excuse me," a polite refusal.

8. Rhymes with "moi" in anglicized pronunciation.
9. Logic-chopping, changing the meaning.

Thine eye begins to speak, set thy tongue there;
125   Or in thy piteous heart plant thou thine ear
That, hearing how our plaints and prayers do pierce,
Pity may move thee "Pardon" to rehearse.°   recite
BOLINGBROKE   Good aunt, stand up.
DUCHESS OF YORK   I do not sue to stand.
Pardon is all the suit I have in hand.
130   BOLINGBROKE   I pardon him, as heaven shall pardon me.
DUCHESS OF YORK   Oh, happy vantage° of a kneeling knee!   gain; position
Yet am I sick for fear. Speak it again;
Twice saying "Pardon" doth not pardon twain,°   divide
But makes one pardon strong.
135   BOLINGBROKE   I pardon him with all my heart.
DUCHESS OF YORK   A god on earth thou art.
[YORK, *the* DUCHESS OF YORK, *and* AUMERLE *rise.*]
BOLINGBROKE   But for our trusty brother-in-law[1] and the Abbot,°   (*of Westminster*)
With all the rest of that consorted° crew,   confederated
Destruction straight shall dog them at the heels.
140   [*to* YORK] Good uncle, help to order several powers°   forces
To Oxford, or where'er these traitors are.
They shall not live within this world, I swear,
But I will have them if I once know where.
Uncle, farewell, and cousin, adieu;
145   Your mother well hath prayed, and prove you true.°   loyal
DUCHESS OF YORK [*to* AUMERLE]   Come, my old[2] son. I pray
heaven make thee new.   *Exeunt.*

5.4 (Q 5.4)

Enter [Sir Piers] EXTON *and* SERVANTS.
EXTON   Didst thou not mark the King what words he spake?
"Have I no friend will rid me of this living fear?"
Was it not so?
SERVANT   Those were his very words.
EXTON   "Have I no friend?" quoth he. He spake it twice,
5   And urged it twice together, did he not?
SERVANT   He did.
EXTON   And speaking it, he wistly° looked on me,   intently
As who° should say, "I would thou wert the man   As if he
That would divorce this terror from my heart,"
10   Meaning the King at Pomfret. Come, let's go.
I am the King's friend and will rid° his foe.   *Exeunt.*   get rid of

5.5 (Q 5.5)

Enter RICHARD.
RICHARD   I have been studying how to compare
This prison where I live unto the world;
And, for because the world is populous
And here is not a creature but myself,
5   I cannot do it. Yet I'll hammer't° out.   work it
My brain I'll prove the female° to my soul,   (*that is, receptive*)

---

1. The Duke of Exeter and Earl of Huntingdon, husband of Bolingbroke's sister; like Aumerle, he had been deprived of his dukedom.
2. Unregenerate (recalling the baptism service: "O merciful God, grant that the old Adam in this child

may be so buried that the new man may be raised up in him").
5.4 Scene continues.
5.5 Location: Pomfret Castle.

My soul the father, and these two beget
A generation of still-breeding° thoughts;   *ever-breeding*
And these same thoughts people this little world
10 In humors[1] like the people of this world,°   *(the real world)*
For no thought is contented. The better sort,
As thoughts of things divine, are intermixed
With scruples° and do set the faith itself   *doubts*
Against the faith,[2] as thus: "Come, little ones";[3]
15 And then again,
"It is as hard to come as for a camel
To thread the postern of a needle's eye."[4]
Thoughts° tending to ambition, they do plot   *Other thoughts*
Unlikely wonders:° how these vain weak nails   *miracles*
20 May tear a passage through the flinty ribs
Of this hard world, my raggèd° prison walls;   *rugged*
And, for they cannot, die in their own pride.°   *prime of life; arrogance*
Thoughts tending to content° flatter themselves   *contentment*
That they are not the first of Fortune's slaves,
25 Nor shall not be the last, like silly° beggars   *simpleminded*
Who sitting in the stocks refuge[5] their shame
That many have and others must sit there;
And in this thought they find a kind of ease,
Bearing their own misfortune on the back
30 Of such as have before endured the like.
Thus play I in one prison many people,
And none contented. Sometimes am I king,
Then treason makes me wish myself a beggar,
And so I am; then crushing penury
35 Persuades me I was better when a king;
Then am I kinged again, and by and by
Think that I am unkinged by Bolingbroke,
And straight° am nothing. But whate'er I am,   *at once*
Nor I nor any man that but° man is   *merely*
40 With nothing shall be pleased, till he be eased
With being nothing. (*Music.*) Music do I hear?
Ha, ha, keep time. How sour sweet music is
When time is broke and no proportion kept.
So is it in the music of men's lives;
45 And here have I the daintiness of ear
To hear time broke in a disordered string,°   *string instrument*
But for the concord° of my state and time   *harmony*
Had not an ear to hear my true time broke.
I wasted time, and now doth Time waste me;
50 For now hath Time made me his numb'ring clock:[6]
My thoughts are minutes, and with sighs they jar
Their watches° on unto mine eyes, the outward watch,[7]   *periods of vigil*
Whereto my finger, like a dial's point,°   *clock's hand*
Is pointing still,° in cleansing them from tears.[8]   *always*

---

1. Temperaments; caprices.
2. *the faith . . . faith*: scriptural passage against scriptural passage.
3. From Matthew 19:14, Mark 10:14, and Luke 18:25, implying the ease of obtaining salvation.
4. Adapting Matthew 19:24, Mark 10:25, or Luke 18:25, which describe the unlikeliness of the rich reaching heaven.
5. Find refuge for; rationalize.
6. Clock that counts hours and minutes, not an hourglass.
7. Clockface; mind's external watcher.
8. Wiping tears from my eyes.

55 Now, sir, the sound that tells what hour it is
Are clamorous groans that strike upon my heart,
Which is the bell. So sighs and tears and groans
Show minutes, hours, and times; but my time
Runs posting° on in Bolingbroke's proud joy,   *speeding*
60 While I stand fooling here, his jack o'th' clock.⁹
This music mads° me; let it sound no more,   *maddens*
    [*Music stops.*]
For though it have holp° madmen to their wits,   *helped*
In me it seems it will make wise men mad.
Yet blessing on his heart that gives it me,
65 For 'tis a sign of love, and love to Richard
Is a strange brooch° in this all-hating world.   *rare ornament*
    Enter GROOM.
GROOM   Hail, royal prince.
RICHARD   Thanks, noble peer.
The cheapest of us is ten groats too dear.¹
What art thou, and how com'st thou hither
70 Where no man ever comes but that sad dog
That brings me food to make misfortune live?
GROOM   I was a poor groom of thy stable, King,
When thou wert king, who, traveling towards York,
With much ado at length have gotten leave
75 To look upon my sometimes° royal master's face.   *former*
Oh, how it yearned° my heart when I beheld   *grieved*
In London streets that coronation day,
When Bolingbroke rode on roan Barbary,
That horse that thou so often hast bestrid,
80 That horse that I so carefully have dressed.°   *groomed*
RICHARD   Rode he on Barbary? Tell me, gentle friend,
How went he under him?
GROOM   So proudly as if he had disdained the ground.
RICHARD   So proud that Bolingbroke was on his back.
85 That jade° hath ate bread from my royal hand;   *nag*
This hand hath made him proud with clapping° him.   *patting*
Would he not stumble, would he not fall down,
Since pride must have a fall, and break the neck
Of that proud man that did usurp his back?
90 Forgiveness, horse! Why do I rail on thee,
Since thou, created to be awed by man,
Wast born to bear? I was not made a horse,
And yet I bear a burden like an ass,
Spur-galled² and tired by jauncing° Bolingbroke.   *rough-riding*
    Enter KEEPER *with a dish.*
95 KEEPER [*to* GROOM]   Fellow, give place,° here is no longer stay.   *leave*
RICHARD [*to* GROOM]   If thou love me, 'tis time thou wert
    away.
GROOM   What my tongue dares not, that my heart shall say.
                                  Exit.
KEEPER   My lord, wilt please you to fall to?°   *begin eating*

---

9. Manikin that strikes the clock's bell.
1. You have overpriced the cheaper of us (me, a prisoner) in calling me "royal." The difference between
the coins "royal" (10 shillings) and "noble" (6 shillings 8 pence) is "ten groats" (40 pence). In other
words, we are equal in worth.
2. Made sore by spurring.

RICHARD Taste of it first,[3] as thou wert wont to do.
100 KEEPER My lord, I dare not. Sir Piers of Exton,
   Who lately came from th' King, commands the contrary.
RICHARD The devil take Henry of Lancaster and thee!
   Patience is stale, and I am weary of it.
      [*He attacks* KEEPER.][4]
KEEPER Help, help, help!
      Enter EXTON *and* SERVANTS.
105 RICHARD How now? What means death in this rude assault?
   [*to a* SERVANT] Villain, thine own hand yields thy death's
      instrument—
      [*He grabs the weapon from him and kills him.*]
   [*to another* SERVANT] Go thou and fill another room in hell.
      [*He kills him.*]
      EXTON *strikes him down.*
   That hand shall burn in never-quenching fire
   That staggers thus my person.° Exton, thy fierce hand   *thus makes me stagger*
110 Hath with the King's blood stained the King's own land.
   Mount, mount, my soul! Thy seat° is up on high,   *residence*
   Whilst my gross flesh sinks downward here to die.
      [*He dies.*]
EXTON As full of valor as of royal blood;
   Both have I spilled. Oh, would the deed were good!
115 For now the devil that told me I did well
   Says that this deed is chronicled in hell.
   This dead King to the living King I'll bear.
   [*to* KEEPER *and* SERVANTS] Take hence the rest, and give
      them burial here.   *Exeunt* [*with the bodies*].

5.6 (Q 5.6)

Flourish. Enter BOLINGBROKE, YORK, *with other Lords
and Attendants.*

BOLINGBROKE Kind uncle York, the latest news we hear
   Is that the rebels have consumed with fire
   Our town of Ci'cester° in Gloucestershire,   *Cirencester*
   But whether they be ta'en or slain we hear not.
      Enter NORTHUMBERLAND.
5 Welcome, my lord. What is the news?
NORTHUMBERLAND First, to thy sacred state wish I all
      happiness.
   The next news is, I have to London sent
   The heads of Salisbury, Spencer, Blunt, and Kent.°   *(Aumerle's co-conspirators)*
   The manner of their taking may appear
10 At large discoursèd° in this paper here.   *Narrated in full*
      [*He presents a paper.*]
BOLINGBROKE We thank thee, gentle Percy, for thy pains,
   And to thy worth will add right worthy° gains.   *valuable; well-deserved*
      Enter FITZWATER.
FITZWATER My lord, I have from Oxford sent to London
   The heads of Broccas and Sir Benet Seely,°   *(more co-conspirators)*

---

3. To make sure it is not poisoned.
4. TEXTUAL COMMENT In both the Folio and the
Quarto texts, the stage directions for Richard's murder are very scanty. The modern editor must infer
them from clues provided by the text and by Shakespeare's source, Holinshed's *Chronicles*. See Digital
Edition TC 8 (Folio edited text).
5.6 Location: Windsor Castle.

15 Two of the dangerous consorted° traitors   confederated
    That sought at Oxford thy dire overthrow.
    BOLINGBROKE   Thy pains, Fitzwater, shall not be forgot;
        Right noble is thy merit, well I wot.°   know
            Enter PERCY *and* [*Bishop of*] CARLISLE [*as prisoner*].
    PERCY   The grand conspirator, Abbot of Westminster,
20   With clog° of conscience and sour melancholy,   burden
        Hath yielded up his body to the grave.
        But here is Carlisle living, to abide
        Thy kingly doom° and sentence of his pride.   judgment
    BOLINGBROKE   Carlisle, this is your doom:
25   Choose out some secret place, some reverend room
        More than thou hast,¹ and with it joy° thy life.   enjoy
        So as thou liv'st in peace, die free from strife;
        For though mine enemy thou hast ever been,
        High sparks of honor in thee have I seen.
            Enter EXTON *with* [SERVANTS *bearing*] *a coffin.*
30 EXTON   Great King, within this coffin I present
        Thy buried fear. Herein all breathless lies
        The mightiest of thy greatest enemies,
        Richard of Bordeaux, by me hither brought.
    BOLINGBROKE   Exton, I thank thee not, for thou hast wrought
35   A deed of slaughter with thy fatal hand
        Upon my head and all this famous land.
    EXTON   From your own mouth, my lord, did I this deed.
    BOLINGBROKE   They love not poison that do poison need,
        Nor do I thee. Though I did wish him dead,
40   I hate the murderer, love him murdered.
        The guilt of conscience take thou for thy labor,
        But neither my good word nor princely favor.
        With Cain² go wander through the shade of night
        And never show thy head by day nor light.   [*Exit* EXTON.]
45   Lords, I protest my soul is full of woe
        That blood should sprinkle me to make me grow.
        Come, mourn with me for that I do lament
        And put on sullen black incontinent.°   immediately
        I'll make a voyage to the Holy Land
50   To wash this blood off from my guilty hand.
        March sadly after; grace my mourning here
        In weeping after this untimely bier.   *Exeunt.*

---

1. More suitable for prayer than the prison cell you inhabit now.

2. After Cain murdered his brother, Abel, he was condemned to be a vagabond (Genesis 4:14).

Romeo and Juliet

Plato's dialogue *The Symposium* recounts a dinner party where the guests spent a long night in impassioned philosophical conversation about love. By daybreak, most of the guests had fallen asleep, but Socrates, who had spoken with particularly luminous intelligence, was still awake, trying to prove that a single playwright should be capable of writing both comedy and tragedy. As he clinched his case, his weary interlocutors nodded off. Thus we never learn Socrates' argument, and neither the ancient Greek nor the Roman world has left us an instance of that versatility. But we have its supreme embodiment in Shakespeare. The achievement is particularly striking in two plays probably written around 1595. Scholars have been unable to determine whether *Romeo and Juliet* was written before or after *A Midsummer Night's Dream;* one of Shakespeare's most delightful comedies and one of his most beloved tragedies appear to have been written at virtually the same time, using very similar materials.

In the entertainment performed for the newlyweds at the close of *A Midsummer Night's Dream,* the young lovers, Pyramus and Thisbe, are separated by a "vile wall." They attempt to elope together, but Pyramus, mistakenly thinking that Thisbe has been killed, rashly commits suicide, whereupon Thisbe in despair stabs herself. A strange way, it would seem, to celebrate festive nuptials, but Shakespeare's comedy continually triumphs over fears of rashness, mutability, and death by staging and laughing at them. The inept amateur actors call attention so crudely to the tragedy's artificiality and contrivance that it provokes derisive laughter: "This is the silliest stuff that ever I heard" (5.1.207).

In *Romeo and Juliet,* whose climax closely resembles that of Pyramus and Thisbe, Shakespeare does not shy away from artifice and contrivance. His tragedy is unusually dependent on coincidence, mischance, and accident to produce what the Chorus, in the sonnet that serves as the prologue, calls the lovers' "misadventured piteous overthrows."* Nor does he forswear the note of witty, wicked parody that transformed the woes of Pyramus and Thisbe into an occasion for mirth. Romeo's friend Mercutio gives voice to an irrepressible spirit of mockery, a spirit that seems to challenge the very possibility of romantic love or tragic destiny. But Shakespeare manages to make the story of his reckless, star-crossed lovers immensely moving, resistant at once to corrosive irony and to moralizing disapproval. He does so principally through his mastery of what the bumbling performers in *A Midsummer Night's Dream* conspicuously lack: the power of language to make and unmake the world.

It is this poetic power—"poetic" derives from the Greek word for "making"—that enables Shakespeare to transform his rather shopworn source materials into something rich and strange. The story of the ill-fated lovers from bitterly feuding families had been told many times in the sixteenth century by Italian and French writers and had already appeared more than once in English. Shakespeare's direct source is Arthur Brooke's *Tragical History of Romeus and Juliet* (1562), a long, leaden English poem based on a French prose version by Pierre Boiastuau (1559), who was in turn adapting an Italian version by Matteo Bandello (1554), who in turn based his narrative on Luigi da Porto's version (1525) of a tale by Masuccio Salernitano (1476).

---

*All quotations are taken from the edited text of the Second Quarto, printed here. The Digital Edition includes edited texts of both the Second Quarto and the First Quarto.

Though he follows the main outline of Brooke's narrative poem, Shakespeare makes many changes in the interests of theatrical compression and intensification. He telescopes the events that in Brooke take nine months into a few days. He brilliantly expands the figure of the vulgar, meddling, earthy Nurse and almost too brilliantly develops the character of Mercutio. (There is a seventeenth-century report—it doesn't date from the playwright's own lifetime—that Shakespeare remarked that he was forced to kill Mercutio in the third act to prevent being killed by him.) He depicts Juliet, eighteen years old in Bandello's version and sixteen in Brooke's, as only thirteen, a young girl suddenly awakening to passionate desires that set her against the will of her family. And at the end he deftly removes the consoling fantasies, conspicuous in the sources, that the dead lovers will be reunited in a happier afterlife. "Here, here will I remain," says Shakespeare's Romeo, in the tomb of his beloved, "With worms that are thy chambermaids" (5.3.108–109).

But it is principally by means of the incandescent brilliance of its language that *Romeo and Juliet* has earned its place as one of the greatest love stories in world literature. Shakespeare makes linguistic power figure thematically in the play by insisting on the crucial importance of naming and, more generally, by repeatedly calling attention to the force of verbal actions. This was by no means the playwright's private obsession. His play is the product of a rhetorical culture, a culture steeped in an awareness—in the philosopher J. L. Austin's phrase—of "how to do things with words." What are some of the things that characters do with words? For a start, they insult each other, a dangerous pastime of both servants and masters. They also invite one another (Capulet's favorite pastime); they confess (formally, to a priest; informally, to friends); they conjure; they curse; they make contracts; they vow; and, if they have the power of the prince, they banish. And through all of these verbal actions, no matter how serious or even deadly they may be, they constantly play with language.

Romeo and Juliet is saturated with language games: paradoxes, oxymorons, double entendres, rhyming tricks, verbal echoings, multiple puns. The obvious question is, why? One possible answer, proposed as early as the eighteenth century, is that Shakespeare could not resist: verbal wit was an addiction, an obsession, the object of an irrational passion. He could indulge this passion because a display of wit would appeal to those segments of the audience most attuned to rhetorical acrobatics. Another answer is that puns are a clarifying challenge, an assault on sentiments to test whether they are genuine or merely forced and empty. Hence Mercutio attempts to mock Romeo's passion with a set of ribald jests, jests that are reiterated unconsciously by the Nurse in such exclamations as "Stand up, stand up! Stand an you be a man!" (3.3.89). To survive the corrosive effect of such mockery is a measure of true love and a sign of authenticity: "He jests at scars that never felt a wound" (2.1.43).

But this explanation for the tragedy's pervasive wordplay is not wholly adequate, since at the height of both their love and their despair, Romeo and Juliet also pun. Romeo on the verge of suicide plays with the word "engrossing" (death as wholesaler; monopolist; lawyer); Juliet plays with the word "restorative" (the kiss as medicine; poison; death; resurrection); and both play with the Elizabethan "to die" as a term for "to have an orgasm." Here wordplay functions not to deflate but to cram into brief utterances more meanings than language would ordinarily hold and to force us to confront both unresolvable contradictions and hidden connections. That is, puns work to juxtapose or hold open possibilities that normally are viewed as mutually exclusive. Thus they may be said to reach both a psychological and a thematic level at which oppositions—pain and joy, loss and restoration, love and death, comedy and tragedy—are canceled.

Wordplay would be impossible in a language in which words were strictly bound to things in a perfect correspondence between naming and nature. Punning is possible only if there is some slippage in sound and meaning, so that one sign can refer to two or more objects or, as Mercutio wittily demonstrates in his Queen Mab speech, to nothing at all. Yet wordplay can also suggest surprising linkages and secret realities.

Two gallants fight a duel in the street.
From George Wither, *A Collection of Emblems* (1635).

Hence, for example, the punning in Romeo and Juliet's initial exchange at the Capulet ball derives its power from the lovers' conviction that there really is an essential relation between the touching of their hands and lips and a religious experience. This relation, invisible to the ordinary social world around them, is disclosed in the language game they spontaneously play, a game that takes the form of a shared sonnet.

Even to speak of this first exchange as a game, which it certainly is, is to risk diminishing its intense seriousness. For in the intertwining of these fourteen complexly rhymed lines, Romeo and Juliet, who do not yet so much as know each other's names, disclose a mutual longing in language whose formal elegance confers on physical desire a spiritual exaltation. The sonnet's blend of order and energy lends words the power of prayer. For Mercutio, by contrast, words are fantastic trifles in a world fit only for satire, sexual teasing, and make-believe. He is a young man in love with masks; indeed, as he readies himself for the masked ball, he seems to regard his own face as a mask: "Give me a case to put my visage in— / A visor for a visor" (1.4.27–28). The moment Romeo and Juliet meet, all masks seem to fall away, all prior emotions fade into nothingness, and all games become earnest. "Did my heart love till now?" asks Romeo (1.4.163), and Juliet, sending the Nurse to find out Romeo's name, declares, "If he be marrièd, / My grave is like to be my wedding-bed" (1.4.245–46).

At some moments in *Romeo and Juliet,* then, wordplay reveals the arbitrariness of language; at other moments, it seems to reveal a hidden reality, even a sacred truth. These contradictory revelations are explored in the famous balcony scene in act 2. Mercutio's mockery gives way, after Romeo's abrupt, one-line dismissal, to incantatory language so intense as to create a new heaven and a new earth. A bare, daylit stage (as it would have been in the Elizabethan playhouse) becomes a dark garden above which Juliet appears like the sun. Visibility is canceled and then restored, by means of metaphor, to the "white upturnèd wond'ring eyes / Of mortals" (2.1.71–72).

Romeo's ecstatic words are the poetic record of a revelation, a vision of a creature unique, perfect, and infinitely beautiful.

The visionary moment turns into a moment of auditory revelation as well, as Romeo, in an intense, eroticized version of what audiences routinely do, overhears Juliet's soliloquy. He has entered into her most intimate thoughts and longings and has an overpowering proof of their authenticity, since she speaks with no awareness of his presence. The inner world his lyrical utterance has conjured up is miraculously united with her own. But her words at once offer a complete fulfillment of this union and a shattering of fulfillment: "O Romeo, Romeo, wherefore art thou Romeo?" (2.1.75). Only if Romeo's name is an arbitrary sign, to be stripped away, discarded, and replaced, can her love be realized. But in a world in which words are divorced from reality, what would be the status of a love made by language? In a world in which names are mere empty signs, how could language create a new reality?

If words are arbitrary, then Romeo and Juliet's love, woven of words, is wedded to nothingness. If they are not arbitrary, if they cannot float free of the body and society, then their love will be destroyed by the rage of feuding parents—the parents who have bestowed proper names on their offspring—and by the whole daylight world of social exchange that gives ordinary language its normal meanings. Against the magical, passionate, transformative language of Romeo and Juliet is set not only Mercutio's mockery but the Nurse's garrulous evocation of the inescapable life cycle: birth, weaning, sexual maturity, and death.

"Then I deny you, stars" (5.1.24). *Imagines Constellationum.*
From Ptolemy, *Almagest* (1541 ed.), after Dürer.

In the Nurse's view, all lives have a certain interchangeability. Juliet's value can be measured in gold coins—"I tell you, he that can lay hold of her / Shall have the chinks" (1.4.227–28)—and an exiled husband can be replaced: Paris is "a lovely gentleman!" she tells the grieving Juliet, "Romeo's a dishclout to him" (3.5.219–20). Romeo and Juliet insist by contrast on the absolute singularity of their love, on the stilling of cyclical time, and on the cancellation of the social network of form and compliment. For a moment on her balcony, Juliet regrets that Romeo has heard her declare her "true-love passion," but then she bids farewell to conventional restraint and boldly steps forward into the magical realm of reciprocal desire. This realm is not without its own solemn order: their love must be formally confirmed in honorable vows of holy matrimony spoken before the friar. But first in the garden, away from church and family and friends, the fullness of the lovers' matched longings finds expression in words that seem to possess mythic power, power to transform darkness into intense light and at the same time to block out the harsh, unforgiving light of the everyday.

The everyday has its own powerful resources, however, and forces its way back into the world that love has transformed. It does so through the ability of names like "Capulet" and "Montague" to conjure up bitter social rivalries. For, as *Romeo and Juliet* repeatedly discloses, words as we ordinarily use them are rarely wholly arbitrary or wholly mythic. They are social constructions, communal creations that are neither complete unto themselves nor empty and hence malleable by individuals. Both language as arbitrary and language as mythic are radical attempts to challenge this notion of words as shared creations carrying with them the tensions and resolutions present in communities, but the community in effect kills off the challenge— whether it comes from Mercutio, who tries to turn social hatred and love alike into a game about "nothing," or from Romeo and Juliet, who try to escape through darkness, subterfuge, and the language of love into a realm apart.

How does the communitarian spirit of language, and with it a sense of the inescapability of the social, manifest itself in *Romeo and Juliet*? It does so, first of all, through a series of characters such as those we glimpse in the opening moments of the play, when the Capulet servants, Samson and Gregory, provoke the absurd quarrel with the Montague servants, Abraham and Balthasar. The point is not only the foolishness of the social codes—"Do you bite your thumb at us, sir?" "I do bite my thumb, sir" (1.1.40–41)—but also their pervasiveness. In a tragedy memorable for its dreams of the most intense privacy—Juliet longs for Romeo to leap to her arms "untalked of and unseen" (3.2.7)—the bustling world makes its presence felt as insistently as the Nurse's voice calling again and again to Juliet as she stands at her window. Shakespeare is wonderfully resourceful in conveying this presence. There is, for example, the nameless servant whose inability to read the list of those invited to the Capulets' ball leads him to turn for assistance to Romeo and Benvolio, who chance at that moment to be walking by. The list itself deftly conjures up the social elite of Verona, with its network of kinship bonds:

> Signor Placentio and his lovely nieces;
> Mercutio and his brother Valentine;
> Mine uncle Capulet, his wife and daughters . . .

and so on through the whole "fair assembly" (1.2.68ff). At the ball itself, Shakespeare is careful to include a glimpse of the servants, hurrying to clear the dishes but finding time to put aside a piece of marzipan for themselves or arranging for a private party with Susan Grindstone and Nell. And, in the midst of the horror and lamenting, when Juliet's cold and stiff body is discovered on the morning she was to be married to Paris, Shakespeare turns our attention to the musicians who had been hired to entertain the wedding guests and who now stand around cracking lame jokes and hoping for a bit of dinner (as if—to invert a celebrated line from *Hamlet*—the marriage baked meats will coldly furnish forth the funeral table).

The city of Verona. From John Speed, *Prospect of the Most Famous Parts of the World* (1646).

There are, besides the servants, other social units that carry the glacial weight of the collective norms and ordinary interests against which Romeo and Juliet struggle. The exclusiveness and intensity of their love are clearly in tension with the bond that links Romeo to his friends, a bond affirmed in displays of masculine aggression and homosocial affection. An infatuation with this or that woman may on occasion seem to threaten the tight circle of friendship—as Romeo, mooning for Rosaline at the beginning of the play, has withdrawn by himself—but the threat is not a very serious one. No one in this world expects that love will seriously reconstitute personal identity or the social order. "Now art thou sociable," says Mercutio with evident relief, when Romeo briefly resumes the old mocking repartee; "now art thou Romeo" (2.3.81).

But from the moment they have encountered one another, neither Romeo nor Juliet is any longer the same person, and the passionate love that divides Romeo from his friends sets both lovers still more decisively against the values of their powerful families. Those values involve a complex intertwining of honor, dignity, love, will, and property, a blend that can manifest itself as gracious hospitality or as murderous feuding, as gentle nostalgia or as cold calculation, as a father's indulgent affection for his daughter or as blind rage when she attempts to thwart his will. Romeo and Juliet's love and clandestine marriage can find no place in this familial order of things, just as its absoluteness is incompatible with the familial sense of cyclical time.

Beyond the structure of the family in the society of Verona, though linked to that structure by ties of kinship, lies the state, embodied in the figure of Prince Escalus. Formally, *Romeo and Juliet* is built around the well-meaning ruler's attempt to stop the "civil brawls" (1.1.84) at the play's beginning, his banishment of Romeo at its midpoint, and his final inquiry, to "clear these ambiguities" (5.3.217), at its close. But this necessary principle of civic order, though it has important consequences, seems almost beside the point, as inadequate and irrelevant as the statues in pure gold that the grieving fathers propose to erect.

A much deeper social principle is figured in Friar Laurence, who embodies the collective wisdom and sanctity of the community. Though set apart, the friar is not a hermit or a recluse; he is an active agent in the community's affairs. His attempt to use Romeo and Juliet's love as a means to resolve the feud between the Montagues and the Capulets disastrously backfires, and with his sleeping potions, his elaborate plots, and, at the close, his fatal cowardice, he has some of the qualities of the stereotypical meddling friar of anticlerical satire. But Friar Laurence is a more complex figure, with a subtle grasp of the doubleness—both poison and medicine—of the natural world and a thoughtful advocacy of moderation. This advocacy draws on an ancient and powerful critique of extremes in passion, which the play's tragic outcome would seem to endorse.

Yet few readers or spectators come away from *Romeo and Juliet* with the conviction that it would be better to love moderately. The intensity of the lovers' passion seems to have its own compelling, self-justifying force, which quietly brushes away all social obstacles and moralizing warnings: "Think true love acted simple modesty" (3.2.16). And the play's incantatory language of love—braiding together the wildly fanciful and the exquisitely simple—has after four hundred years an unforgettable freshness:

> Come, gentle night; come, loving, black-browed night,
> Give me my Romeo; and, when I shall die,
> Take him and cut him out in little stars,
> And he will make the face of heaven so fine
> That all the world will be in love with night
> And pay no worship to the garish sun.
>
> (3.2.20–25)

If the society of the play will not tolerate such ecstatic desire, if the contingencies of the ordinary world manage to destroy it, *Romeo and Juliet* offers us the consoling realization that the lovers themselves have all along been in love with night.

STEPHEN GREENBLATT

SELECTED BIBLIOGRAPHY

Belsey, Catherine. "The Name of the Rose in *Romeo and Juliet*." *Yearbook of English Studies* 23 (1993): 126–42. Argues that *Romeo and Juliet* dramatizes both the desire to transcend the realm of signifiers into a metaphysical ideal and the impossibility of attaining it.

Callaghan, Dympna. "The Ideology of Romantic Love: The Case of *Romeo and Juliet*." *"Romeo and Juliet": Contemporary Critical Essays*. Ed. R. S. White. New York: Palgrave, 2001. 85–115. Proposes that rather than representing a timeless and universal love story, the play valorizes a particular construction of desire that emerged with the centralization of political power, the rise of bourgeois capitalism, and an assumption of patriarchal authority.

Kottman, Paul A. "Defying the Stars: Tragic Love as the Struggle for Freedom in *Romeo and Juliet*." *Shakespeare Quarterly* 63 (2012): 1–38. Asserts that the most important struggle in the play is not the one between lovers and a society hostile to their desires, but the struggle of Romeo and Juliet to realize their own distinct individuality.

Kristeva, Julia. "*Romeo and Juliet*: Love-Hatred in the Couple." *Shakespearean Tragedy*. Ed. John Drakakis. Harlow, Essex: Longman, 1992. 296–315. Offers a closer look, informed by Freud and Lacan, at the symptomatic (unconscious) response to transgressive and fantastic love as manifested in the characters, the playwright, and ourselves.

Nevo, Ruth. "Tragic Form in *Romeo and Juliet*." *Studies in English Literature* 9 (1969): 241–58. Argues that Shakespeare develops a distinctive style of tragedy, predicated on the heroic embodiment of opposing forces, the subversion of appearances, the presence of the uncanny, and the complex ideal of sexual love.

Porter, Joseph A. *Shakespeare's Mercutio: His History and Drama*. Chapel Hill: U of North Carolina P, 1988. Analyzes how, from a patchwork of sources, classical and contemporary, Shakespeare breathed life into the complex. subversive, homosexual Mercutio.

Snow, Edward. "Language and Sexual Difference in *Romeo and Juliet.*" *Shakespeare's "Rough Magic": Essays in Honor of C. L. Barber.* Ed. Peter Erickson and Coppélia Kahn. Newark: U of Delaware P, 1985. 168–92. Argues that, if the language of Juliet and Romeo articulates their profound interconnectedness, it also discloses ominous differences between them and suggests that gender difference is the tragedy's deepest dichotomy.

Snyder, Susan. "*Romeo and Juliet*: Comedy into Tragedy." *Essays in Criticism* 20 (1970): 391–402. Proposes that, at first possessing all the markings of a comedy, *Romeo and Juliet* morphs from one genre to another: the descent into tragedy becomes ineluctable upon the death of Mercutio.

Targoff, Ramie. "Mortal Love: Shakespeare's *Romeo and Juliet* and the Practice of Joint Burial." *Representations* 120 (2012): 17–38. Argues that whereas Shakespeare's sources imagine the lovers posthumously united in heaven, his own play rejects this consolation and gains its tragic power by insisting that love is mortal.

Watson, Robert N., and Stephen Dickey. "Wherefore Art Thou Tereu? Juliet and the Legacy of Rape." *Renaissance Quarterly* 58 (2005): 127–56. Proposes that *Romeo and Juliet*'s allusions to mythical perpetrators of rape make us aware of the specter of possible predatory sexuality that haunts the play, as well as Juliet's ultimate act of claiming her own erotic desire for herself.

FILMS

Romeo and Juliet. 1936. Dir. George Cukor. USA. 125 mins. A lavish, big-studio release, Cukor's film starred Leslie Howard, then forty-two, and Norma Shearer in the lead roles. John Barrymore played Mercutio.

West Side Story. 1961. Dir. Jerome Robbins and Robert Wise. USA. 152 mins. A musical, modernized adaptation of the play set in New York with rival ethnic gangs. Leonard Bernstein wrote the celebrated score.

Romeo and Juliet. 1968. Dir. Franco Zeffirelli. Italy. 138 mins. A flower-power, 1960s youth-culture interpretation of the play, featuring teenaged actors Leonard Whiting and Olivia Hussey in the title roles.

William Shakespeare's Romeo + Juliet. 1996. Dir. Baz Luhrmann. USA. 120 mins. Starring Leonardo DiCaprio and Claire Danes, Luhrmann's frenetic update, set in modern-day "Verona Beach," explains the family feud in terms of a gang conflict.

Qing ren jie (*A Time to Love*). 2005. Dir. Jianqi Huo. China. 113 mins. In this film, in Mandarin, set during the Cultural Revolution, two lovers read and watch versions of Shakespeare's play together, and enact the balcony scene.

TEXTUAL INTRODUCTION

The two earliest substantive versions of *Romeo and Juliet* are both quartos; they appeared in print two years apart, the first of them only two years or so after the play's first performance. The title page of the earlier quarto, of which five copies survive, reads: "AN EXCELLENT conceited Tragedie of Romeo and Iuliet, As it hath been often (with great applause) plaid publiquely, by the right Honourable the L. of *Hunsdon* his Seruants. LONDON, Printed by Iohn Danter. 1597." (A second printer, Edward Allde, was in fact responsible for printing slightly over half of the text.) This is now known as Q1, and has been, from the outset, both a revelation and a puzzle. It was not entered in the Stationers' Register, as was required of printed texts at this time. A second, lengthier quarto appeared two years later; its title page reads: "THE MOST EXcellent and lamentable Tragedie, of Romeo and Iuliet. *Newly corrected, augmented, and amended:* As it hath bene sundry times publiquely acted, by the right Honourable the Lord Chamberlaine his Seruants. LONDON Printed by Thomas Creede, for Cuthbert Burby, and are to be sold at his shop neare the Exchange. 1599." This, now known as Q2, is the source for all seventeenth-century editions of the play, including Q3, Q4, and the First Folio (which is why *The Norton Shakespeare* does not include an edition of the F version), and is the version familiar to modern readers and audiences.

Q2 may represent the *Romeo and Juliet* we know best, then, but Q1 has always interested editors and scholars, not only because of its intriguing differences from Q2 but also because, at times, its readings have seemed preferable to those of its better-known cousin. Furthermore, a section of Q2 (1.2.53–1.3.36) is in effect identical to that in Q1 (2.44–3.36) and appears to have been set not from Q2's primary manuscript source but from Q1 itself, perhaps because a page or two of the copy manuscript had been mislaid. A good instance of a generally preferred Q1 reading is Juliet's line about the prospect of marriage to Paris, "It is an honor that I dream not of" (Q1 3.59), which in Q2 reads, "It is an hour that I dream not of" (Q2 1.3.68). Editors have tended to choose the Q1 reading, presuming the "n" in "honour" (the original, also the modern British English, spelling) to have been accidentally omitted in Q2; thus one of the play's best-known lines derives from Q1, not Q2.

By and large, though, Q1 has been denigrated as one of the group of early Shakespeare quartos for which, at the beginning of the twentieth century, A. W. Pollard coined the term "Bad Quarto" and which have since come to be known more prosaically as "short" quartos so as to avoid the inappropriate moral associations of "good" and "bad." Various theories have been put forward to account for the features of the short quartos — that they are Shakespeare's "first drafts"; that they are unofficial, "pirated" texts memorially reconstructed by actors who had played in them (certainly, there are strong indications of garbled recall at times in Q1); or that Shakespeare wrote two distinct versions of several of his plays, a "literary" version for publication and a shorter "acting" version. The latter theory has particular appeal in the case of *Romeo and Juliet*, given that the Prologue in both Q1 and Q2 claims that the play will last only two hours when performed.

The central issues in the complex textual history of *Romeo and Juliet* derive from the differences between Q1 and Q2, for which editors have consistently sought explanations. Q2 is a fuller, more authoritative text in most ways ("augmented, and amended"): it is a quarter or so (739 lines in this edition) longer than Q1; certain well-known passages in Q2 have no equivalent in Q1; lines attributed to one character in Q1 are spoken by another in Q2; lineation diverges frequently; and there are many differences at the level of the individual word. Certain features of Q2—e.g., words or lines that appear to have been added in the wrong place, or have been retained despite an attempt at deletion—strongly suggest that it was set from Shakespeare's "foul papers"—that is, from a draft of the play in the playwright's own hand, one that contains evidence of the creative process—as opposed to a "fair copy," a finished manuscript without insertions, deletions, or other afterthoughts.

The Norton Shakespeare provides editions of both Q1 and Q2 in the Digital Edition, with Q2 representing the play in the print edition. The differences make a fine starting point for critical reflection on the play. As is noted in the Textual Comments, Q1's prologue differs from that in Q2 in instructive ways: for Q2 the mutual hatred of the Montagues and Capulets is "ancient," habitual, a feud lasting generations; Q1, by contrast, suggests that the two familes were close ("household friends") until they fell out. Key speeches, such as Mercutio's "Queen Mab" narrative, vary in intriguing ways, suggesting that the two quartos represent different stages of the composition process. Characterization differs at times, too: the Nurse is more proactive, and more sympathetically engaged with Juliet's situation, in Q1 than in Q2; Friar Laurence's tendency to vacillate and fawn is more apparent in Q2. Both texts offer evidence of the practicalities of early staging, from movements between the upper and lower stage to possible doublings of minor roles.

Through the two texts of *Romeo and Juliet*, we gain access to the processes through which theatrical texts became printed texts, and we can develop a good, if by no means fully explained, sense of the variety of forms through which Shakespeare's plays, in their irresolvable multiplicity, came into being.

GORDON MCMULLAN

PERFORMANCE NOTE

Productions of *Romeo and Juliet*—an archetypical story whose iconic leading characters dependably retain the capacity to disquiet and disarm—are dogged by expectations. The play is so familiar that directors often feel unusual pressure to reinvent it, with the result that casting the feuding households into contemporary analogues (Mafia families, old wealth vs. new money, Christians vs. Muslims), or activating subtextual sources of drama by playing characters against type (a sinister Friar Laurence, flamboyant Mercutio, or adulterous Lady Capulet) constitute minor performance traditions in themselves. Simultaneously, though, audiences tend to anticipate a simpler, more sympathetic pair of lovers than Shakespeare provides. Directors aiming to refresh a familiar plot must therefore take heed of the play's innate potential to alienate spectators expecting an idealized romance. Crucially in this respect, they must decide whether to stress or smooth over Romeo's rough edges: his fickleness in love; his attempt to bribe Rosaline to "ope her lap" (1.1.209) for him; his threat to strew the churchyard with Balthasar's limbs; his indiscriminate slaughter of Paris.

Casting the eponymous characters presents unique challenges, in line with the adage that actors experienced and versatile enough to play them are no longer young enough to do so. Romeo combines youthful impulsivity and Hamlet-like deliberation, equal parts melancholy versifier and man of action. Juliet is still more complex, tempering frankness with guile, trepidation with fierce resolve, innocence with raw sexuality. Actors can emphasize one set of characteristics over another, though the best performances seem to preserve paradoxes. Capulet, Friar Laurence, and Juliet's Nurse—respectively, a doting tyrant, faithful fraud, and loose-lipped confidante— likewise thrive by actors who can be convincingly inconsistent. Meanwhile, productions must decide whether Paris is innocuous or threatening, and whether Mercutio is primarily a tragic or comic figure, the answers helping to determine whether the play proceeds ominously toward its tragic end, or as a comedy spoiled at the last gasp. Other considerations include assigning the Prologue; managing passages of ostentatiously poetic dialogue; resolving difficult staging at the Capulets' ball (1.4) and tomb (5.3); and handling the famously challenging mourning scene that follows Juliet's death (4.4).

BRETT GAMBOA

The Most Lamentable Tragedy
of Romeo and Juliet

[THE PERSONS OF THE PLAY

CHORUS

PRINCE Escalus
MERCUTIO, kinsman to the Prince
County PARIS, kinsman to the Prince
Page to Mercutio
PAGE to Paris

CAPULET
CAPULET'S WIFE
JULIET, daughter to Capulet
TYBALT, nephew to Capulet's wife
CAPULET'S COUSIN
NURSE
PETER, servant to Nurse
PETRUCCIO, companion to Tybalt
Page to Tybalt
SAMSON, a Capulet retainer
GREGORY, a Capulet retainer
HEAD SERVINGMAN in the Capulet household
Three SERVINGMEN in the Capulet household

MONTAGUE
MONTAGUE'S WIFE
ROMEO, son to Montague
BENVOLIO, nephew to Montague
BALTHASAR, servant to Romeo
ABRAHAM, a Montague retainer
Servingmen

FRIAR LAURENCE
FRIAR JOHN

CHIEF WATCHMAN
WATCHMEN
OFFICER
CITIZENS of Verona
APOTHECARY
Three MUSICIANS
Masquers, Guests, Gentlewomen, Musicians, Attendants]

The Prologue[1]

[*Enter* CHORUS.]

CHORUS   Two households, both alike in dignity,°   *status*
   In fair Verona, where we lay our scene,
   From ancient grudge break to new mutiny,°   *wrangling*
   Where civil blood makes civil hands unclean.[2]
5   From forth the fatal° loins of these two foes,   *ill-fated*
   A pair of star-crossed[3] lovers take their life,
   Whose misadventured° piteous overthrows   *unfortunate*
   Doth with their death bury their parents' strife.
   The fearful passage of their death-marked love
10 And the continuance of their parents' rage—
   Which, but their children's end, naught could remove—
   Is now the two hours' traffic° of our stage;   *business; movement*
   The which, if you with patient ears attend,
   What here shall miss, our toil shall strive to mend.[4]   [*Exit.*]

1.1 (Q1 Scene 1)

Enter SAMSON *and* GREGORY *of the house of Capulet,*
   with swords and bucklers.°   *small round shields*

SAMSON   Gregory, on my word, we'll not carry coals.[1]
GREGORY   No, for then we should be colliers.[2]
SAMSON   I mean, an° we be in choler,° we'll draw.°   *if / anger / draw swords*
GREGORY   Ay. While you live, draw your neck out of collar.°   *a noose*
5 SAMSON   I strike quickly,° being moved.[3]   *vigorously*
GREGORY   But thou art not quickly° moved to strike.   *speedily*
SAMSON   A dog of the house of Montague moves me.
GREGORY   To move is to stir, and to be valiant is to stand;[4]
   therefore, if thou art moved, thou runn'st away.
10 SAMSON   A dog of that house shall move me to stand. I will
   take the wall of[5] any man or maid of Montague's.
GREGORY   That shows thee a weak slave, for the weakest goes
   to the wall.[6]
SAMSON   'Tis true—and therefore women, being the weaker
15 vessels,[7] are ever thrust to the wall;° therefore I will push Mon-   *(sexually) assaulted*
   tague's men from the wall, and thrust his maids to the wall.
GREGORY   The quarrel is between our masters and us their
   men.
SAMSON   'Tis all one.° I will show myself a tyrant: when I have   *the same*
20 fought with the men, I will be civil with the maids—I will
   cut off their heads.
GREGORY   The heads of the maids?
SAMSON   Ay, the heads of the maids—or their maidenheads;
   take it in what sense thou wilt.
25 GREGORY   They must take it in sense° that feel it.   *through sensation*

The Prologue
1. TEXTUAL COMMENT On the different versions of the Prologue in Q2 and Q1, see Digital Edition TC 1 (Second Quarto edited text). PERFORMANCE COMMENT On the directorial possibilities for representing the Chorus onstage, see Digital Edition PC 1.
2. Where citizens' hands are stained with the blood of their fellow citizens.
3. Thwarted by the adverse influence of the stars appearing at the time of their birth, which controlled their destinies.
4. *What . . . mend*: The actors will try to rectify

whatever is missing or ill told in the Prologue.
1.1 Location: A street or public place in Verona.
1. We'll not suffer humiliation.
2. Professional coal porters, proverbially sneaky.
3. Being roused to anger.
4. Stand firm against assault. Playing, as with "strike" and "stir," on sexual arousal.
5. I will assert superiority over. The sidewalk nearest the wall was cleaner than that nearer the street.
6. Proverbial: The weakest are always pushed aside.
7. Paul's description of women in 1 Peter 3:7.

SAMSON   Me they shall feel while I am able to stand, and 'tis
known I am a pretty piece of flesh.[8]

GREGORY   'Tis well thou art not fish; if thou hadst, thou hadst
been Poor John.[9]

Enter [ABRAHAM *and another Servingman*
of the Montagues].

30   Draw thy tool;[1] here comes of the house of Montagues.

SAMSON   My naked weapon is out. Quarrel; I will back thee.

GREGORY   How, turn thy back and run?

SAMSON   Fear me not.[2]

GREGORY   No, marry,[3] I fear thee!

35   SAMSON   Let us take the law of our sides; let them begin.

GREGORY   I will frown as I pass by, and let them take it as they
list.°   like

SAMSON   Nay, as they dare. I will bite my thumb at them,[4]
which is disgrace to them if they bear it.

[*He bites his thumb.*]

40   ABRAHAM   Do you bite your thumb at us, sir?

SAMSON   I do bite my thumb, sir.

ABRAHAM   Do you bite your thumb at us, sir?

SAMSON [*aside to* GREGORY]   Is the law of our side if I say "Ay"?

GREGORY [*aside to* SAMSON]   No.

45   SAMSON   —No, sir, I do not bite my thumb at you, sir; but I
bite my thumb, sir.

GREGORY   Do you quarrel, sir?

ABRAHAM   Quarrel, sir? No, sir.

SAMSON   But if you do, sir, I am for you;[5] I serve as good a man

50   as you.

ABRAHAM   No better.

SAMSON   Well, sir.

Enter BENVOLIO.

GREGORY [*aside to* SAMSON]   Say "better." Here comes one of
my master's kinsmen.

55   SAMSON [*to* ABRAHAM]   Yes, better, sir.

ABRAHAM   You lie.

SAMSON   Draw, if you be men. —Gregory, remember thy wash-
ing° blow.   slashing; violent

They fight.

BENVOLIO [*drawing*]   Part, fools!

60   Put up your swords. You know not what you do.

Enter TYBALT.

TYBALT   What, art thou drawn among these heartless hinds?[6]

[*He draws.*] Turn thee, Benvolio; look upon thy death.

BENVOLIO   I do but keep the peace. Put up thy sword,

Or manage° it to part these men with me.   wield

65   TYBALT   What? Drawn, and talk of peace? I hate the word
As I hate hell, all Montagues, and thee.
Have at thee, coward.

[*They fight.*]

---

8. An attractive fellow possessed of an impressive
member.
9. Dried salted hake, appropriate as a taunt because
shriveled and cheap. "Neither fish nor flesh" was proverbial for an uncategorizable oddity.
1. Weapon (and continuing the bawdy wordplay).
2. Do not doubt my fortitude; in the next line, Gregory takes it in the modern sense of "Do not be afraid

of me."
3. By the Virgin Mary, a mild oath with a meaning
similar to "indeed."
4. Flick the thumbnail from behind the upper teeth,
an insulting gesture.
5. I accept your invitation to fight.
6. These cowardly servants, punning on female deer
("hinds") unprotected by a stag ("hart/heart").

Enter three or four CITIZENS[, *including an* OFFICER,]
    with clubs or partisans.°   *broad-tipped spears*
OFFICER   Clubs, bills,° and partisans! Strike! Beat them down!   *ax-bladed spears*
   Down with the Capulets! Down with the Montagues!
     Enter old CAPULET, *in his gown, and* [CAPULET'S] WIFE.
70 CAPULET   What noise is this? Give me my long sword, ho!
   CAPULET'S WIFE   A crutch, a crutch! Why call you for a sword?
   CAPULET   My sword, I say!
     Enter old MONTAGUE *and* [MONTAGUE'S] WIFE.
                  Old Montague is come,
   And flourishes his blade in spite° of me.   *defiance*
   MONTAGUE   Thou villain Capulet!
   [*to* MONTAGUE'S WIFE]   Hold me not: let me go!
75 MONTAGUE'S WIFE   Thou shalt not stir one foot to seek a foe.
     Enter PRINCE *Escalus, with his train.*
   PRINCE   Rebellious subjects, enemies to peace,
   Profaners of this neighbor-stainèd steel[7]—
   Will they not hear? —What ho, you men, you beasts
   That quench the fire of your pernicious rage
80 With purple° fountains issuing from your veins!   *crimson*
   On pain of torture, from those bloody hands
   Throw your mistempered[8] weapons to the ground,
   And hear the sentence of your movèd° prince.   *furious*
   Three civil brawls, bred of an airy° word   *unsubstantial*
85 By thee, old Capulet, and Montague,
   Have thrice disturbed the quiet of our streets
   And made Verona's ancient° citizens   *elderly*
   Cast by° their grave-beseeming ornaments[9]   *Cast away*
   To wield old partisans in hands as old,
90 Cankered° with peace, to part your cankered° hate.   *Rusty / malignant*
   If ever you disturb our streets again,
   Your lives shall pay the forfeit° of the peace.   *ransom*
   For this time, all the rest depart away!
   —You, Capulet, shall go along with me;
95 —And Montague, come you this afternoon,
   To know our farther pleasure in this case,
   To old Freetown,[1] our common judgment-place.
   Once more, on pain of death, all men depart!
     Exeunt [*all but* MONTAGUE, MONTAGUE'S WIFE,
             and BENVOLIO].
   MONTAGUE   Who set this ancient quarrel new abroach?°   *open*
100 Speak, nephew. Were you by when it began?
   BENVOLIO   Here were the servants of your adversary
   And yours, close fighting ere I did approach.
   I drew to part them. In the instant came
   The fiery Tybalt, with his sword prepared,
105 Which, as he breathed° defiance to my ears,   *uttered*
   He swung about his head and cut the winds
   Who, nothing hurt withal,° hissed him in scorn.   *by that*
   While we were interchanging thrusts and blows
   Came more and more, and fought on part and part[2]

---

7. You who defile weapons with the stains of your
neighbors' blood.
8. Badly shaped and hardened, as well as unnecessarily wrathful by disposition.
9. Attire and symbolic staffs appropriate to grave old

age. Possibly playing on the old men's proximity to
the grave.
1. In the Italian source, the Capulet house is called
Villa Franca, which Brooke translates as "Freetown."
2. Fought for one side and the other.

110	Till the Prince came, who parted either part.	
	MONTAGUE'S WIFE Oh, where is Romeo? Saw you him today?	
	Right glad I am he was not at this fray.	
	BENVOLIO Madam, an hour before the worshipped sun	
	Peered forth° the golden window of the East,	*out from*
115	A troubled mind drive° me to walk abroad	*drove*
	Where, underneath the grove of sycamore³	
	That westward rooteth° from this city side,	*grows out*
	So early walking did I see your son.	
	Towards him I made, but he was ware° of me	*wary*
120	And stole into the covert° of the wood.	*covering*
	I, measuring his affections° by my own,	*inclination*
	Which then most sought where most might not be found,⁴	
	Being one too many by my weary self,	
	Pursued my humor,° not pursuing his,	*mood*
125	And gladly shunned who gladly fled from me.⁵	
	MONTAGUE Many a morning hath he there been seen,	
	With tears augmenting the fresh morning's dew,	
	Adding to clouds more clouds with his deep sighs;	
	But all so soon as the all-cheering sun	
130	Should in the farthest East begin to draw	
	The shady curtains from Aurora's⁶ bed,	
	Away from light steals home my heavy° son	*melancholy*
	And private in his chamber pens himself,	
	Shuts up his windows, locks fair daylight out,	
135	And makes himself an artificial night.	
	Black and portentous° must this humor⁷ prove,	*ominous (of illness)*
	Unless good counsel may the cause remove.	
	BENVOLIO My noble uncle, do you know the cause?	
	MONTAGUE I neither know it nor can learn of him.	
140	BENVOLIO Have you importuned him by any° means?	*all*
	MONTAGUE Both by myself and many other friends;	
	But he his own affection's counselor°	*confidant*
	Is to himself—I will not say how true⁸—	
	But to himself so secret and so close,°	*discreet*
145	So far from sounding and discovery,°	*fathoming and revelation*
	As is the bud bit with an envious worm°	*a spiteful grub (larva)*
	Ere he can spread his sweet leaves° to the air	*petals*
	Or dedicate his beauty to the same.	
	Could we but learn from whence his sorrows grow,	
150	We would as willingly give cure as know.	
	Enter ROMEO.	
	BENVOLIO See where he comes. So please you,° step aside;	*please you = please*
	I'll know his grievance or be much denied.	
	MONTAGUE I would° thou wert so happy° by thy stay	*wish / fortunate*
	To hear true shrift.° —Come, madam, let's away.	*confession*
	Exeunt [MONTAGUE *and* MONTAGUE'S WIFE].	
	BENVOLIO Good morrow, cousin.	

---

3. Associated with melancholy lovers, who are "sick-amour."

4. *where . . . found:* in a place where I was unlikely to have company.

5. TEXTUAL COMMENT Q1's briefer version of the following exchange (lines 126–50) entails a direct juxtaposition between Romeo and Benvolio, whose melancholy here takes on darker connotations in light of Q1's version of the final scene. See Digital Edition

TC 2 (Second Quarto edited text).

6. Goddess of the dawn in classical legend.

7. "Humors," essential bodily fluids, were considered the basis of human beings' physical and psychological constitution. Too much black bile caused melancholy and a host of illnesses and derangements.

8. Loyal, but also invoking the proverbial wisdom that only one who is "true to him- or herself" can be upstanding in dealing with others.

155 ROMEO   Is the day so young?
BENVOLIO   But new° struck nine.   *Only just*
ROMEO   Ay me. Sad hours seem long.
  Was that my father that went hence so fast?
BENVOLIO   It was. What sadness lengthens Romeo's hours?
ROMEO   Not having that which, having, makes them short.
160 BENVOLIO   In love?
ROMEO   Out.
BENVOLIO   Of love?
ROMEO   Out of her favor where I am in love.
BENVOLIO   Alas that Love, so gentle in his view,°   *appearance*
165   Should be so tyrannous and rough in proof.°   *experience*
ROMEO   Alas that Love, whose view is muffled still,⁹
  Should without eyes see pathways to his will.°   *intention; lust*
  Where shall we dine?
    [*He sees signs of the brawl.*]
                                    Oh, me! What fray was here?
  Yet tell me not, for I have heard it all;
170   Here's much to do with hate, but more with love.
  Why, then, O brawling love, O loving hate,
  O anything of nothing first created,¹
  O heavy lightness, serious vanity,
  Misshapen chaos of well-seeming forms,
175   Feather of lead, bright smoke, cold fire, sick health,
  Still-waking° sleep that is not what it is—   *Always awake*
  This love feel I, that feel no love in this.
  Dost thou not laugh?
BENVOLIO   No, coz,° I rather weep.   *cousin*
ROMEO   Good heart, at what?
BENVOLIO   At thy good heart's oppression.°   *affliction*
180 ROMEO   Why, such is love's transgression.
  Griefs of mine own lie heavy in my breast,
  Which thou wilt propagate° to have it pressed²   *multiply*
  With more of thine: this love that thou hast shown
  Doth add more grief to too much of mine own.
185   Love is a smoke made with the fume of sighs;
  Being purged,° a fire sparkling in lovers' eyes;   *clarified*
  Being vexed,° a sea nourished with loving tears.   *stirred up*
  What is it else? A madness most discreet,°   *wise*
  A choking gall, and a preserving sweet.
  Farewell, my coz.
190 BENVOLIO   Soft;° I will go along.   *Wait*
  An if° you leave me so, you do me wrong.   *An if = if*
ROMEO   Tut, I have lost myself; I am not here.
  This is not Romeo: he's some other where.
BENVOLIO   Tell me, in sadness,³ who is that you love?
195 ROMEO   What, shall I groan and tell thee?
BENVOLIO   Groan? Why, no. But sadly tell me who.
ROMEO   A sick man in sadness makes his will:
  A word ill urged to one that is so ill.
  In sadness, cousin, I do love a woman—

9. Who cannot see. Cupid was often depicted as
blind or blindfolded.
1. Inverting the proverb "Nothing can come of nothing" and also recalling the doctrine that God made
the world out of nothing. Romeo catalogues the

"miraculous" paradoxes of love.
2. Burdened; embraced.
3. Seriousness, although Romeo plays on the sense
"melancholy."

200 BENVOLIO   I aimed so near when I supposed you loved.
ROMEO   A right good mark,° man!—and she's fair I love.   *target; vulva*
BENVOLIO   A right fair mark, fair coz, is soonest hit.
ROMEO   Well, in that hit you miss; she'll not be hit
With Cupid's arrow. She hath Dian's wit,[4]
205 And, in strong proof° of chastity well-armed,°   *tested armor / covered*
From Love's weak childish bow she lives uncharmed.
She will not stay° the siege of loving terms,   *undergo*
Nor bide th'encounter of assailing eyes,[5]
Nor ope her lap to saint-seducing gold.[6]
210 Oh, she is rich in beauty; only poor
That, when she dies, with beauty dies her store.°   *wealth*
BENVOLIO   Then she hath sworn that she will still° live chaste?   *always*
ROMEO   She hath, and in that sparing° make huge waste: *refraining; thrift*
For beauty starved with her severity
215 Cuts beauty off from all posterity.[7]
She is too fair, too wise, wisely too fair,°   *just*
To merit bliss° by making me despair.[8]   *heaven's blessing*
She hath forsworn to love, and in that vow
Do I live dead that live to tell it now.
220 BENVOLIO   Be ruled by me: forget to think of her.
ROMEO   Oh, teach me how I should forget to think!
BENVOLIO   By giving liberty unto thine eyes.
Examine other beauties.
ROMEO   'Tis the way
To call hers, exquisite, in question more.[9]
225 These happy masks that kiss fair ladies' brows,
Being black, puts us in mind they hide the fair.
He that is strucken blind cannot forget
The precious treasure of his eyesight lost.
Show me a mistress that is passing° fair: *surpassingly*
230 What doth her beauty serve but as a note
Where I may read who passed that passing fair?
Farewell. Thou canst not teach me to forget.
BENVOLIO   I'll pay° that doctrine, or else die in debt.[1]   *Exeunt.*   *impart*

1.2 (Q1 Scene 2)

Enter CAPULET, *County*° PARIS, *and* [*a* SERVINGMAN].   *Count*
CAPULET   But Montague is bound° as well as I,   *under oath*
In penalty alike, and 'tis not hard, I think,
For men so old as we to keep the peace.
PARIS   Of honorable reckoning[1] are you both,
5 And pity 'tis you lived at odds so long.
But now, my lord, what say you to my suit?
CAPULET   But saying o'er what I have said before:
My child is yet a stranger in the world;
She hath not seen the change of fourteen years.
10 Let two more summers wither in their pride
Ere we may think her ripe to be a bride.

---

4. The scruples and cleverness of Diana, the classical goddess of hunting and chastity.
5. *th'encounter of assailing eyes*: military metaphors for courtship conventionally used in Petrarchan love poetry.
6. To golden gifts that are irresistibly persuasive. Also, in classical legend, Jupiter descended upon Danaë as a shower of gold.

7. *For . . . posterity*: Since she will not have children, her beauty will die with her. *starved*: killed.
8. Despair of salvation, a grave sin.
9. *in question more*: more intensely to mind.
1. Die whatever the cost to me; die still owing you the doctrine of forgetfulness.
1.2 Location: A street or plaza in Verona.
1. Repute, with a play on "accounting."

PARIS   Younger than she are happy mothers made.
CAPULET   And too soon marred are those so early made.
    Earth hath swallowed all my hopes but she;[2]
15   She's the hopeful lady of my earth.°   body
    But woo her, gentle Paris; get her heart—
    My will to her consent is but a part—
    And, she agreed, within her scope of choice
    Lies my consent and fair-according voice.
20   This night I hold an old-accustomed feast
    Whereto I have invited many a guest,
    Such as I love; and you among the store
    One more, most welcome, makes my number more.
    At my poor house look to behold this night
25   Earth-treading stars that make dark heaven light.
    Such comfort as do lusty young men feel
    When well-appareled April on the heel
    Of limping winter treads, even such delight,
    Among fresh fennel[3] buds, shall you this night
30   Inherit° at my house. Hear all, all see,   Enjoy
    And like her most whose merit most shall be;
    Which one more view, of many, mine being one,
    May stand in number, though in reck'ning none.[4]
    Come, go with me. [to SERVINGMAN] Go, sirrah;° trudge about   (address to an inferior)
35   Through fair Verona; find those persons out
    Whose names are written there [giving him a paper], and to
        them say
    My house and welcome on their pleasure stay.°   wait
                    Exeunt [CAPULET and PARIS].
SERVINGMAN   "Find them out whose names are written."
    Here[5] it is written that the shoemaker should meddle with
40   his yard° and the tailor with his last,° the fisher with his   yardstick / shoe form
    pencil° and the painter with his nets. But I am sent to find   paintbrush
    those persons whose names are here writ, and can never
    find° what names the writing person hath here writ. I must   figure out
    to the learned.
                    Enter BENVOLIO and ROMEO.
45   In good time—
BENVOLIO   Tut, man, one fire burns out another's burning;
    One pain is lessened by another's anguish;
    Turn giddy,° and be holp° by backward turning;   Turn until dizzy / helped
    One desperate grief cures with another's languish.[6]
50   Take thou some new infection[7] to thy eye,
    And the rank poison of the old will die.
ROMEO   Your plantain leaf[8] is excellent for that.[9]
BENVOLIO   For what, I pray thee?

---

2. Many editors have felt that this and the following line, which are not present in Q1, were deleted by Shakespeare in the process of writing the scene.
3. A plant associated with weddings and brides.
4. Which . . . none: Upon another inspection of the many young women, my daughter may make a part of the gorgeous display, but be of no account by herself. "One" was proverbially "no number."
5. Editors sometimes change Q2's punctuation and move "Here" to the end of the previous sentence. In either case, the illiterate Servingman is exasperated.

6. Cures . . . languish: is displaced by the languishing pain of a new grief.
7. New object of passion, which causes a distortion of sight in the lover.
8. The ordinary plantain leaf, used to dress wounds or bruises and thought to have curative powers.
9. TEXTUAL COMMENT Lines 1.2.53–1.3.36 in Q2 are almost identical to those found in Q1, suggesting that Q2's printers relied not on a manuscript copy but on Q1 itself for this passage. See Digital Edition TC 3 (Second Quarto edited text).

ROMEO   For your broken° shin.   *gashed*

BENVOLIO   Why, Romeo, art thou mad?

55   ROMEO   Not mad, but bound more than a madman is:
Shut up in prison, kept without my food,
Whipped and tormented, and—
[*to* SERVINGMAN]   Good e'en,° good fellow.   *evening (afternoon)*

SERVINGMAN   God gi'° good e'en. I pray, sir, can you read?   *give you*

ROMEO   Ay—mine own fortune in my misery.[1]

60   SERVINGMAN   Perhaps you have learned it without book.[2] But,
I pray, can you read anything you see?

ROMEO   Ay, if I know the letters and the language.

SERVINGMAN   Ye say honestly. Rest you merry.[3]

ROMEO   Stay, fellow. I can read.

         He reads the letter.

65   "Signor Martino and his wife and daughters;
County Anselm and his beauteous sisters;
The lady widow of Vitruvio;
Signor Placentio and his lovely nieces;
Mercutio and his brother Valentine;

70   Mine uncle Capulet, his wife and daughters;
My fair niece Rosaline; Livia;
Signor Valentio and his cousin Tybalt;
Lucio and the lively Helena."
A fair assembly! Whither should they come?

75   SERVINGMAN   Up.[4]

ROMEO   Whither to supper?

SERVINGMAN   To our house.

ROMEO   Whose house?

SERVINGMAN   My master's.

80   ROMEO   Indeed, I should have asked you that before.

SERVINGMAN   Now I'll tell you without asking. My master is
the great rich Capulet, and—if you be not of the house of
Montagues—I pray come and crush° a cup of wine. Rest you   *drink*
merry.   [*Exit.*]

85   BENVOLIO   At this same ancient° feast of Capulet's   *traditional*
Sups the fair Rosaline, whom thou so loves,
With all the admired beauties of Verona.
Go thither, and with unattainted° eye   *unbiased*
Compare her face with some that I shall show,

90   And I will make thee think thy swan a crow.

ROMEO   When the devout religion° of mine eye   *pious belief*
Maintains such falsehood, then turn tears to fire;
And these° who, often drowned, could never die,   *these eyes*
Transparent° heretics, be burnt for liars.   *Obvious; self-evident*

95   One fairer than my love? The all-seeing sun
Ne'er saw her match since first the world begun.

BENVOLIO   Tut, you saw her fair, none else being by,
Herself poised with° herself in either eye;   *balanced against*
But in that crystal scales let there be weighed

100   Your lady's love against some other maid

---

1. Romeo takes "read" to mean "understand" or "perceive," as in "to read one's fortune."
2. *without book*: from memory or by ear, as well as through experience rather than education.
3. A farewell. The Servingman takes Romeo to mean "if only I knew the letters and the language."
4. "Come up" is an expression of scorn.

That I will show you shining at this feast,
And she shall scant show well that now seems best.
ROMEO   I'll go along no such sight to be shown,
But to rejoice in splendor of mine own.   [*Exeunt.*]

1.3 (Q1 Scene 3)

Enter CAPULET'S WIFE[1] *and* NURSE.

CAPULET'S WIFE   Nurse, where's my daughter? Call her forth
to me.
NURSE   Now, by my maidenhead at twelve year old,[2]
I bade her come. —What,[3] lamb! What, ladybird!
God forbid[4]—where's this girl? What, Juliet!

Enter JULIET.

5   JULIET   How now? Who calls?
NURSE   Your mother.
JULIET   Madam, I am here. What is your will?
CAPULET'S WIFE   This is the matter. —Nurse, give leave° a while;   excuse us
We must talk in secret.—Nurse, come back again;
10   I have remembered me. Thou's° hear our counsel.°   You shall / secrets
Thou knowest my daughter's of a pretty age.
NURSE   Faith, I can tell her age unto an hour.
CAPULET'S WIFE   She's not fourteen.
NURSE   I'll lay fourteen of my teeth—and yet, to my teen° be   sorrow
15   it spoken, I have but four—she's not fourteen. How long is
it now to Lammastide?[5]
CAPULET'S WIFE   A fortnight and odd days.
NURSE   Even or odd, of all days in the year,
Come Lammas Eve at night shall she be fourteen.
20   Susan[6] and she—God rest all Christian souls—
Were of an age. Well, Susan is with God;
She was too good for me. But, as I said,
On Lammas Eve at night shall she be fourteen—
That shall she, marry! I remember it well.
25   'Tis since the earthquake now eleven years,
And she was weaned—I never shall forget it—
Of all the days of the year upon that day;
For I had then laid wormwood[7] to my dug,°   on my nipple
Sitting in the sun under the dovehouse wall—
30   My lord and you were then at Mantua—
Nay, I do bear a brain°—but, as I said,   memory
When it did taste the wormwood on the nipple
Of my dug and felt it bitter, pretty fool°—   (an endearment)
To see it tetchy,° and fall out with the dug!   peevish
35   "Shake," quoth the dovehouse;[8] 'twas no need, I trow,
To bid me trudge.°   remove myself
And since that time it is eleven years,
For then she could stand high-lone°—nay, by th' rood,°   upright alone / cross

---

1.3 Location: Capulet's house.
1. TEXTUAL COMMENT On Lady Capulet's changing speech prefixes in Q2 and Q1, see Digital Edition TC 4 (Second Quarto edited text).
2. Presumably the latest date that the Nurse could swear by her virginity.
3. An expression of impatience.
4. Either an apology for the promiscuous connota-

tion of "ladybird" or fearing something amiss in Juliet's absence.
5. August 1, originally celebrated by the church as a harvest festival.
6. The Nurse evidently suckled Juliet after her own daughter died.
7. A proverbially bitter plant extract.
8. The dovehouse shook with the earthquake.

She could have run and waddled all about,
40 For, even the day before, she broke her brow,°   *cut her forehead*
And then my husband—God be with his soul;
'A° was a merry man—took up the child.   *He*
"Yea?" quoth he. "Dost thou fall upon thy face?
Thou wilt fall backward when thou hast more wit,°   *knowledge*
45 Wilt thou not, Jule?" And, by my holidam,°   *Holy Lady*
The pretty wretch left° crying, and said "Ay!"   *stopped*
To see now how a jest shall come about!°   *come true*
I warrant, an° I should live a thousand years,   *if*
I never should forget it. "Wilt thou not, Jule?" quoth he,
50 And, pretty fool, it stinted° and said "Ay!"   *she ceased*
CAPULET'S WIFE   Enough of this. I pray thee, hold thy peace.
NURSE   Yes, madam—yet I cannot choose but laugh
To think it should leave crying and say "Ay!"
And yet I warrant° it had upon it° brow   *assure you / its*
55 A bump as big as a young cock'rel's stone°—   *rooster's testicle*
A perilous knock—and it cried bitterly.
"Yea?" quoth my husband. "Fall'st upon thy face?
Thou wilt fall backward when thou comest to age,
Wilt thou not, Jule?" It stinted and said "Ay!"
60 JULIET   And stint thou too, I pray thee, Nurse, say I.
NURSE   Peace, I have done. God mark° thee to his grace,   *elect*
Thou wast the prettiest babe that e'er I nursed;
An° I might live to see thee married once,°   *If / one day*
I have my wish.
65 CAPULET'S WIFE   Marry,° that "marry" is the very theme   *Truly*
I came to talk of. —Tell me, daughter Juliet,
How stands your dispositions to be married?
JULIET   It is an hour that I dream not of.
NURSE   "An hour"! Were not I thine only nurse,
70 I would say thou hadst sucked wisdom from thy teat.[9]
CAPULET'S WIFE   Well, think of marriage now. Younger
       than you
Here in Verona, ladies of esteem,
Are made already mothers; by my count,
I was your mother much upon these years
75 That you are now a maid. Thus, then, in brief:
The valiant Paris seeks you for his love.
NURSE   A man, young lady! Lady, such a man
As all the world— Why, he's a man of wax![1]
CAPULET'S WIFE   Verona's summer hath not such a flower.
80 NURSE   Nay, he's a flower, in faith, a very flower!
CAPULET'S WIFE   What say you? Can you love the gentleman?
This night you shall behold him at our feast;
Read o'er the volume of young Paris' face,
And find delight writ there with beauty's pen;
85 Examine every married lineament,[2]
And see how one° another lends content;[3]   *one to*
And what obscured in this fair volume lies
Find written in the margin[4] of his eyes.

9. From the teat that nourished you.
1. Model of perfection, as if sculpted rather than born.
2. Harmoniously composed feature; a joined line of
flowing handwriting.

3. Meaning; happiness.
4. Glosses to difficult passages of text were set in the
margin.

This precious book of love, this unbound° lover,   *single; unrestrained*
90   To beautify him only lacks a cover.
The fish lives in the sea, and 'tis much pride
For fair without the fair within to hide;[5]
That book in many's eyes doth share the glory
That in gold clasps locks in the golden story.[6]
95   So shall you share all that he doth possess
By having him, making yourself no less.
NURSE   No less? Nay, bigger—women grow° by men!   *swell with child*
CAPULET'S WIFE   Speak briefly: can you like of Paris' love?
JULIET   I'll look° to like, if looking liking move;[7]   *expect; examine*
100   But no more deep will I endart mine eye[8]
Than your consent gives strength to make it fly.
          Enter a SERVINGMAN.[9]
SERVINGMAN   Madam, the guests are come; supper served up;
you called; my young lady asked for; the Nurse cursed in the
pantry; and everything in extremity.° I must hence to wait;°   *a terrible state / serve*
105   I beseech you follow straight.°   *immediately*
CAPULET'S WIFE   We follow thee.   [*Exit* SERVINGMAN.]
                    —Juliet, the County stays.°   *the Count awaits*
NURSE   Go, girl! Seek happy nights to° happy days.   *Exeunt.*   *at the end of*

1.4 (Q1 Scene 4)

Enter ROMEO, MERCUTIO, [*and*] BENVOLIO, *with five or*
six other Masquers,[1] *torchbearers.*
ROMEO   What, shall this speech° be spoke for our excuse,   *prologue*
Or shall we on without apology?
BENVOLIO   The date is out of° such prolixity.   *past for*
We'll have no Cupid, hoodwinked[2] with a scarf,
5   Bearing a Tartar's painted bow of lath,[3]
Scaring the ladies like a crowkeeper.°   *scarecrow*
But let them measure° us by what they will,   *judge*
We'll measure° them a measure° and be gone.   *apportion / dance*
ROMEO   Give me a torch. I am not for this ambling;°   *dancing*
10   Being but heavy,° I will bear the light.   *melancholy*
MERCUTIO   Nay, gentle° Romeo, we must have you dance.   *noble; softhearted*
ROMEO   Not I, believe me. You have dancing shoes
With nimble soles; I have a soul of lead
So stakes me to the ground I cannot move.
15   MERCUTIO   You are a lover; borrow Cupid's wings,
And soar with them above a common bound.[4]
ROMEO   I am too sore° empiercèd with his shaft   *deeply*
To soar with his light° feathers, and, so bound,   *cheery; agile; wanton*
I cannot bound a pitch[5] above dull woe;

---

5. *For fair . . . hide:* For a lovely setting (Juliet) to
frame and enrich the fair Paris.
6. *That book . . . story:* Many esteem a book's golden
binding as highly as the story it contains. The speech
thoroughly confuses who is covering whom.
7. If looking can motivate liking.
8. Sink my eye like an arrow into its target; shoot
glances that, like Cupid's arrows, inflame his passions.
9. TEXTUAL COMMENT On the roles of the Capulets'
servingmen throughout the play, see Digital Edition
TC 5 (Second Quarto edited text).
1.4 Location: Before Capulet's house.

1. Performers or participants in an aristocratic
masked entertainment, consisting of dances and
sometimes dumb shows and set speeches.
2. Blindfolded and foolish Cupid, a typical costume
for the presenter of the masque's theme.
3. Short bow shaped like the upper lip, made of the
thin wood used for theatrical properties. Tartars, a
dark-skinned, supposedly savage people in Asia
Minor, were famed for their archery.
4. A normal limit; an average dancer's leap.
5. Height from which a hawk stoops to kill.

20   Under love's heavy burden do I sink.

MERCUTIO   And to sink in it should you burden love:
    Too great oppression for a tender thing.[6]

ROMEO   Is love a tender thing? It is too rough,
    Too rude, too boist'rous, and it pricks like thorn.

25 MERCUTIO   If love be rough with you, be rough with love;
    Prick° love for pricking, and you beat love down.[7]   *Stab; sexually penetrate*
    Give me a case[8] to put my visage in—
    A visor for a visor[9]—what care I
    What curious eye doth quote° deformities?   *notice*

30   Here are the beetle brows° shall blush for me.   *protruding eyebrows*

BENVOLIO   Come, knock and enter—and, no sooner in,
    But every man betake him to his legs.°   *to dancing; to flight*

ROMEO   A torch for me. Let wantons light of heart
    Tickle the senseless rushes° with their heels,   *floor matting*

35   For I am proverbed with a grandsire° phrase: *an ancient*
    I'll be a candleholder and look on.[1]
    The game was ne'er so fair, and I am done.[2]

MERCUTIO   Tut, dun's the mouse[3]—the constable's own word.°   *phrase*
    If thou art dun, we'll draw thee from the mire[4]

40   Or—save your reverence[5]—love wherein thou stickest
    Up to the ears. Come; we burn daylight.° Ho!   *waste time*

ROMEO   Nay, that's not so.

MERCUTIO   I mean, sir, in delay
    We waste our lights in vain, light lights by day.
    Take our good meaning, for our judgment sits

45   Five times in that ere once in our fine wits.[6]

ROMEO   And we mean° well in going to this masque;   *intend*
    But 'tis no wit° to go.   *intelligence*

MERCUTIO   Why, may one ask?

ROMEO   I dreamed a dream tonight.°   *last night*

MERCUTIO   And so did I.

ROMEO   Well, what was yours?

MERCUTIO   That dreamers often lie.

50 ROMEO   In bed asleep while they do dream things true.

MERCUTIO   Oh, then, I see Queen Mab[7] hath been with you.[8]
    She is the fairies' midwife, and she comes
    In shape no bigger than an agate stone[9]
    On the forefinger of an alderman,

55   Drawn with a team of little atomi°   *atoms*
    Over men's noses as they lie asleep,

---

6. Suggesting a pudendum.
7. *Prick . . . down:* Playing on the sense "satiate desire by fulfilling it."
8. Literally, "mask," but also slang for the vagina.
9. Mask for an ugly face. Proverbial: "A well-favored visor to hide an ill-favored face."
1. Proverbial: "A good candleholder proves a good gamester. A spectator loses nothing."
2. Proverbial: "When play is best, it is time to leave."
3. Proverbial: "Keep silent and unseen, like a mouse."
4. In the Christmas game "Dun Is in the Mire," players pantomimed drawing a log representing a horse out of a boggy road. Mercutio is suggesting that Romeo is a stick-in-the-mud.
5. An apology for crude language, here used mockingly.

6. *Take . . . wits:* Understand my intended good meaning using common sense ("judgment"), which is five times as trustworthy as witty ingenuity ("fine wits").
7. Possibly Celtic, but probably Shakespeare's invention. "Queen" suggested "quean," which meant "whore," and "Mab" was a stereotypical name for prostitutes.
8. PERFORMANCE COMMENT Mercutio's speech on Queen Mab can accommodate a range of styles and tones. For more about actors' varying interpretations of Mercutio and his relationship to Romeo, see Digital Edition PC 2. TEXTUAL COMMENT On the different versions of this speech in Q2 and Q1, see Digital Edition TC 6 (Second Quarto edited text).
9. A small human figure was often carved on agate stones set in seal rings.

Her wagon-spokes made of long spinners'° legs,   *spiders'*
The cover of the wings of grasshoppers,
Her traces of the smallest spider web,
60   Her collars of the moonshine's wat'ry beams,
Her whip of cricket's bone, the lash of film,°   *spider's-web thread*
Her wagoner° a small gray-coated gnat   *driver*
Not half so big as a round little worm
Pricked from the lazy finger of a maid.[1]
65   Her chariot is an empty hazelnut
Made by the joiner° squirrel or old grub[2]—   *carpenter*
Time out o'mind the fairies' coach-makers—
And in this state° she gallops night by night   *regal finery*
Through lovers' brains, and then they dream of love;
70   On courtiers' knees, that dream on curtsies straight;[3]
O'er lawyers' fingers, who straight dream on fees;
O'er ladies' lips, who straight on kisses dream,
Which oft the angry Mab with blisters plagues
Because their breath with sweetmeats° tainted are.   *candies*
75   Sometime she gallops o'er a courtier's nose,
And then dreams he of smelling out a suit;[4]
And sometime comes she with a tithe-pig's[5] tail,
Tickling a parson's nose as 'a° lies asleep—   *he*
Then he dreams of another benefice;[6]
80   Sometime she driveth o'er a soldier's neck,
And then dreams he of cutting foreign throats,
Of breaches, ambuscadoes, Spanish blades,[7]
Of healths five fathom deep[8]—and then anon°   *soon*
Drums in his ear, at which he starts and wakes
85   And, being thus frighted, swears a prayer or two
And sleeps again. This is that very Mab
That plaits° the manes of horses in the night,   *entangles*
And bakes the elflocks[9] in foul sluttish° hairs   *dirty*
Which, once untangled, much misfortune bodes.
90   This is the hag, when maids lie on their backs,
That presses them,[1] and learns° them first to bear, *teaches*
Making them women of good carriage.[2]
This is she—
ROMEO   Peace, peace, Mercutio, peace!
Thou talk'st of nothing.°   *imaginings; a vagina*
MERCUTIO   True, I talk of dreams,
95   Which are the children of an idle brain,
Begot of nothing but vain fantasy,°   *empty imagination*
Which is as thin of substance as the air
And more inconstant than the wind, who woos

1. According to popular belief, worms generated in idle girls' fingers.
2. Grubs bore holes.
3. Dream of respectful bows immediately.
4. A petition at court, which the courtier could facilitate for a fee.
5. Pig paid as a tithe to the parish for the support of the priest.
6. Pluralism (holding multiple benefices simultaneously) was a common source of corruption in the early modern church.

7. *breaches:* burst fortifications. *ambuscadoes:* ambushes. *Spanish blades:* swords made in Toledo were famous for their quality.
8. Fantastically deep cups of liquor.
9. And hardens the tangles. According to folk legend, unknotting them would anger the malicious elves.
1. Evil spirits were supposed to be responsible for erotic dreams, taking the form of an illusory sexual partner.
2. Excellent deportment; the capacity for carrying the weight of a lover; childbearing.

Even now the frozen bosom of the North
100 And, being angered, puffs away from thence,
Turning his side to the dew-dropping South.
BENVOLIO   This wind you talk of blows us from ourselves;
Supper is done, and we shall come too late.
ROMEO   I fear too early, for my mind misgives°   *fears*
105 Some consequence yet hanging in the stars
Shall bitterly begin his fearful date°   *period*
With this night's revels and expire° the term   *finish*
Of a despisèd life closed in my breast
By some vile forfeit of untimely death.[3]
110 But He that hath the steerage of my course
Direct my suit. —On, lusty gentlemen!
BENVOLIO   Strike, drum!
        They march about the stage, and SERVINGMEN *come*
        forth with napkins. Enter [HEAD SERVINGMAN].
HEAD SERVINGMAN   Where's Potpan, that he helps not to take
away? He shift a trencher!° He scrape a trencher!   *wooden plate*
115 FIRST SERVINGMAN   When good manners shall lie all in one
or two men's hands—and they unwashed too—'tis a foul°   *bad; dirty*
thing.
HEAD SERVINGMAN   Away with the joint-stools![4] Remove the
court-cupboard!° Look to the plate!° —Good thou, save me   *sideboard / silverware*
120 a piece of marzipan, and, as thou loves me, let the porter let
in Susan Grindstone and Nell, Anthony, and Potpan.
SECOND SERVINGMAN   Ay, boy, ready.
HEAD SERVINGMAN   You are looked for and called for, asked
for and sought for, in the great chamber.
125 THIRD SERVINGMAN   We cannot be here and there too.
—Cheerly, boys! Be brisk a while, and the longer liver take
all.[5]   *Exeunt* [SERVINGMEN].
        Enter [CAPULET, CAPULET'S WIFE, JULIET, CAPULET'S
        COUSIN, PARIS,[6] TYBALT, NURSE, *a* SERVINGMAN,
        Attendants, Tybalt's Page, Musicians, and] *all the*
        Guests and Gentlewomen to the Masquers.
CAPULET   Welcome, gentlemen![7] Ladies that have their toes
Unplagued with corns will walk a bout° with you.   *dance a turn*
130 —Ah, my mistresses, which of you all
Will now deny to dance? She that makes dainty,°   *coyly demurs*
She I'll swear hath corns. Am I come near ye now?[8]
—Welcome, gentlemen! I have seen the day
That I have worn a visor, and could tell
135 A whispering tale in a fair lady's ear,
Such as would please: 'tis gone, 'tis gone, 'tis gone!
You are welcome, gentlemen! —Come, musicians, play.
        Music plays, and they dance.

---

3. As fate prematurely foreclosing on a mortgaged
life.
4. Stools made by a furniture maker, commonly used
for seating at large banquets.
5. Proverbial, meaning "Life is short."
6. PERFORMANCE COMMENT Although neither Paris
nor Rosaline speaks in this scene, directors have
sometimes used the ball as an opportunity to develop
their presence in the play. See Digital Edition PC 3.
7. TEXTUAL COMMENT On Capulet's rapid change of
addressees, see Digital Edition TC 7 (Second Quarto
edited text).
8. Does that strike home?

A hall,[9] a hall! Give room! —And foot it, girls!
[*to Attendants*] More light, you knaves! And turn the tables
   up,[1]
140 And quench the fire; the room is grown too hot.
—Ah, sirrah,[2] this unlooked-for° sport comes well!   *unexpected*
—Nay, sit, nay, sit, good cousin° Capulet,   *kinsman*
For you and I are past our dancing days.
How long is't now since last yourself and I
Were in a masque?
145 CAPULET'S COUSIN   By'r Lady, thirty years.
CAPULET   What, man? 'Tis not so much, 'tis not so much;
'Tis since the nuptial of Lucentio—
Come Pentecost[3] as quickly as it will,
Some five-and-twenty years—and then we masqued.
150 CAPULET'S COUSIN   'Tis more, 'tis more! His son is elder, sir;
His son is thirty.
CAPULET   Will you tell me that?
His son was but a ward[4] two years ago.
ROMEO [*apart to a* SERVINGMAN]   What lady's that which doth
   enrich the hand
Of yonder knight?
SERVINGMAN   I know not, sir.
155 ROMEO   Oh, she doth teach the torches to burn bright!
It seems she hangs upon the cheek of night
As a rich jewel in an Ethiop's ear:[5]
Beauty too rich for use, for earth too dear.[6]
So shows a snowy dove trooping° with crows   *flocking*
160 As yonder lady o'er her fellows shows.
The measure° done, I'll watch her place of stand[7]   *dance*
And, touching hers, make blessèd my rude hand.
Did my heart love till now? Forswear it, sight,
For I ne'er saw true beauty till this night.
165 TYBALT   This, by his voice, should be a Montague.
[*to his Page*] Fetch me my rapier, boy.   [*Exit Tybalt's Page.*]
                          What? Dares the slave
Come hither, covered with an antic face,[8]
To fleer° and scorn at our solemnity?°   *sneer / festivity*
Now, by the stock and honor of my kin,
170 To strike him dead I hold it not a sin.
CAPULET   Why, how now, kinsman? Wherefore storm you so?
TYBALT   Uncle, this is a Montague, our foe,
A villain° that is hither come in spite   *An ill-doer; a slave*
To scorn at our solemnity this night.
CAPULET   Young Romeo, is it?
175 TYBALT   'Tis he, that villain Romeo.
CAPULET   Content° thee, gentle coz. Let him alone.   *Calm*
'A bears him like a portly° gentleman,   *dignified*
And, to say truth, Verona brags of him

---

9. Make space in the hall.
1. Dismantle and stack the trestle tables.
2. TEXTUAL COMMENT For the implications of "sirrah" here, see Digital Edition TC 7 (Second Quarto edited text).
3. The seventh Sunday after Easter, a standard reference point in the medieval and Renaissance calendar.
4. Subject to a guardian; a minor.
5. In Romeo's image, a jewel shines brighter against an Ethiopian's proverbially dark skin.
6. Too precious for this world; too valuable to die and be buried in earth.
7. Where Juliet waits between dances.
8. A grotesque mask; a playful mask.

To be a virtuous and well-governed° youth;   *sensible*
180   I would not for the wealth of all this town
Here in my house do him disparagement.
Therefore, be patient; take no note of him.
It is my will, the which if thou respect,
Show a fair presence,° and put off these frowns,   *demeanor*
185   An ill-beseeming semblance° for a feast.   *expression*
TYBALT   It fits when such a villain is a guest;
I'll not endure him.
CAPULET   He shall be endured!
What, goodman[9] boy? I say he shall. Go to![1]
Am I the master here or you? Go to!
190   You'll "not endure him"? God shall mend my soul,
You'll make a mutiny° among my guests!   *brawl*
You will set cock-a-hoop![2] You'll be the man!
TYBALT   Why, uncle, 'tis a shame—
CAPULET   Go to, go to;
You are a saucy boy. Is't so, indeed?
195   This trick° may chance to scathe° you. I know what:[3]   *stupidity / harm*
You must contrary me—marry, 'tis time[4]—
        [*A dance ends, and* JULIET *moves to her place of*
        stand, where ROMEO *awaits.*]
[*to Masquers*] Well said,° my hearts! [*to* TYBALT] You are a   *done*
princock.° Go.   *cheeky boy*
Be quiet, or— [*to Attendants*] More light! More light, for
shame!
—I'll make you quiet. [*to Masquers*] What, cheerly, my hearts!
200   TYBALT [*aside*]   Patience perforce° with willful choler° meeting   *enforced / rash anger*
Makes my flesh tremble in their different° greeting.   *hostile*
I will withdraw, but this intrusion shall,
Now seeming sweet, convert to bitt'rest gall.   *Exit.*
ROMEO   If I profane with my unworthiest hand[5]
205   This holy shrine, the gentle sin is this:
My lips, two blushing pilgrims,[6] did ready stand
To smooth that rough touch with a tender kiss.
JULIET   Good pilgrim, you do wrong your hand too much,
Which mannerly° devotion shows in this;   *seemly*
210   For saints[7] have hands that pilgrims' hands do touch,
And palm to palm is holy palmers'° kiss.   *pilgrims'*
ROMEO   Have not saints lips, and holy palmers too?
JULIET   Ay, pilgrim, lips that they must use in prayer.
ROMEO   Oh, then, dear saint, let lips do what hands do:
215   They pray; grant thou, lest faith turn to despair.
JULIET   Saints do not move, though grant for prayer's sake.[8]

---

9. Courtesy title applied to a commoner (and thus an insult to the noble Tybalt).
1. An expression of impatience.
2. You will abandon restraint, like a drinker who removes the tap ("cock") from the barrel or like a boastfully crowing rooster.
3. I mean what I say.
4. Time to teach you a lesson; time that you became obedient.
5. Romeo and Juliet's first conversation takes the form of a shared sonnet.

6. John Florio's *World of Words* (1598) translates the Italian word *romeo* as "roamer," "wanderer," or "palmer" (pilgrim to the Holy Land).
7. Statues or pictures of saints, which attracted Catholic pilgrims. The Elizabethan Anglican Church held that the worship of such images was blasphemy; to an English audience, therefore, Romeo's description of his love could sound like idolatry.
8. Again identifying the saint with her image. As a statue she does not move, but as a saint in heaven she can intercede with God on behalf of the worshipper.

ROMEO   Then move not while my prayer's effect I take.
        [*He kisses her.*]
   Thus from my lips, by thine, my sin is purged.
JULIET   Then have my lips the sin that they have took.
220 ROMEO   Sin from my lips? Oh, trespass sweetly urged!⁹
        Give me my sin again.°   back
        [*He kisses her.*]
JULIET   You kiss by th' book.¹
NURSE   Madam, your mother craves a word with you.
        [JULIET *goes to speak with* CAPULET'S WIFE.]
ROMEO [*to* NURSE]   What is her mother?
NURSE   Marry, bachelor,°   young man
        Her mother is the lady of the house,
225   And a good lady, and a wise and virtuous.
        I nursed her daughter that you talked withal.°   with
        I tell you, he that can lay hold of her
        Shall have the chinks.°   plenty of coins
ROMEO [*aside*]   Is she a Capulet?
        Oh, dear account!° My life is my foe's debt.²   costly reckoning
230 BENVOLIO   Away! Begone! The sport is at the best.
ROMEO   Ay, so I fear; the more is my unrest.
        [*The Masquers prepare to depart.*]
CAPULET   Nay, gentlemen, prepare not to be gone!
        We have a trifling foolish banquet towards.³
        [*They whisper in his ear.*]
        Is it e'en so? Why, then I thank you all;
235   I thank you, honest gentlemen. Good night!
        —More torches here! —Come on, then: let's to bed.
        —Ah, sirrah, by my fay,° it waxes late!   faith
        I'll to my rest.
        [*Exeunt* CAPULET, CAPULET'S WIFE, *and* CAPULET'S
        COUSIN, *and* SERVINGMAN; *all others move toward
        the doors, and exeunt;* JULIET *and* NURSE *remain.*]
JULIET   Come hither, Nurse. What is yond gentleman?
240 NURSE   The son and heir of old Tiberio.
JULIET   What's he that now is going out of door?
NURSE   Marry, that, I think, be young Petruccio.
JULIET   What's he that follows here that would not dance?
NURSE   I know not.
JULIET   Go ask his name.   [*Exit* NURSE.]
245   If he be marrièd,
        My grave is like° to be my wedding-bed.   likely
        [*Enter* NURSE.]
NURSE   His name is Romeo, and a Montague,
        The only son of your great enemy.
JULIET   My only love sprung from my only hate!
250   Too early seen unknown, and known too late!
        Prodigious° birth of love it is to me   Monstrous; ominous
        That I must love a loathèd enemy.
NURSE   What's 'tis?° What's 'tis?   this (dialect pronunciation)

---

9. Sweetly argued that the first kiss was a transgression, and sweetly advocated that the transgression of a second kiss is needed to take away the sin of the first.

1. According to the rules; implies "proficiently," "politely," or "with poetic flatteries."
2. A debt owing to my foe; in the power of my foe.
3. A paltry dessert coming.

JULIET   A rhyme I learned even now
    Of one I danced withal.
       One calls within, "Juliet!"
NURSE   Anon,° anon!   *Right away*
255   Come, let's away; the strangers all are gone.   *Exeunt.*

2.0
    [*Enter* CHORUS.]
CHORUS   Now old° desire doth in his deathbed lie,   *Romeo's former*
    And young affection gapes° to be his heir;   *longs*
    That fair for which love groaned for and would die,
    With tender Juliet matched,° is now not fair.   *compared*
5   Now Romeo is beloved and loves again,°   *in return; once more*
    Alike bewitchèd by the charm of looks;[1]
    But to his foe supposed° he must complain,[2]   *presumed*
    And she steal love's sweet bait from fearful° hooks.   *fearsome*
    Being held a foe, he may not have access
10 To breathe such vows as lovers use° to swear,   *are accustomed*
    And she as much in love, her means much less
    To meet her new belovèd anywhere.
    But passion lends them power, time means, to meet,
    Temp'ring extremities° with extreme sweet.   [*Exit.*]   *Mitigating dangers*

2.1 (Q1 Scene 5)
    Enter ROMEO *alone.*[1]
ROMEO   Can I go forward when my heart is here?
    Turn back, dull earth,[2] and find thy center[3] out.
    [*He withdraws.*]
    Enter BENVOLIO *with* MERCUTIO.
BENVOLIO   Romeo! My cousin Romeo! Romeo!
MERCUTIO   He is wise and, on my life, hath stol'n him° home   *himself*
    to bed.
5   BENVOLIO   He ran this way, and leapt this orchard wall.
    Call, good Mercutio.
MERCUTIO   Nay, I'll conjure,° too.   *summon as a spirit*
    Romeo! Humors![4] Madman! Passion! Lover!
    Appear thou in the likeness of a sigh;
    Speak but one rhyme, and I am satisfied;
10 Cry but "Ay me!"; pronounce but "love" and "dove";
    Speak to my gossip° Venus one fair word,   *crony*
    One nickname for her purblind° son and heir,   *dim-sighted; blind*
    Young Abraham Cupid,[5] he that shot so true
    When King Cophetua loved the beggar maid.[6]
15 —He heareth not, he stirreth not, he moveth not:

2.0
1. Appearances; desirous glances.
2. Conventionally, make lovesick speeches.
2.1 Location: Outside Capulet's house.
1. The main stage represents the area outside the wall of Capulet's orchard and then the inside of the orchard below the window of Juliet's room. Romeo is imagined to leap over the garden wall when he withdraws at line 2.
2. Romeo's flesh, drawing on two traditional views of the human body: animated dust or clay, and a "microcosm," or little world, which mirrors the order of the

universe. Earth was the most sluggish and immobile element.
3. The point in the earth toward which everything falls; or Romeo's heart (metaphorically, Juliet).
4. Pure moods, not mixed together to form an even "temper."
5. Cupid, as Mercutio's nickname suggests, is at once a young boy and a patriarch, the oldest of the gods.
6. The story of a king who falls in love with a beggar and makes her his queen was the subject of a popular ballad.

The ape[7] is dead, and I must conjure him.
—I conjure thee by Rosaline's bright eyes,
By her high forehead and her scarlet lip,
By her fine foot, straight leg, and quivering thigh,
20   And the demesnes° that there adjacent lie,   *estates*
That in thy likeness thou appear to us!
BENVOLIO   An if he hear thee, thou wilt anger him.
MERCUTIO   This cannot anger him. 'Twould anger him
To raise a spirit[8] in his mistress' circle
25   Of some strange° nature, letting it there stand   *other person's*
Till she had laid it and conjured it down:
That were some spite. My invocation
Is fair and honest in his mistress' name;
I conjure only but to raise up him.
30   BENVOLIO   Come, he hath hid himself among these trees
To be consorted° with the humorous[9] night.   *in company*
Blind is his love, and best befits the dark.
MERCUTIO   If love be blind, love cannot hit the mark.°   *target; vulva*
Now will he sit under a medlar[1] tree
35   And wish his mistress were that kind of fruit
As maids call medlars when they laugh alone.
—O Romeo, that she were—oh, that she were—
An open-arse,° thou a popp'rin' pear![2]   *medlar*
Romeo, good night! —I'll to my truckle bed;[3]
40   This field bed[4] is too cold for me to sleep.
Come: shall we go?
BENVOLIO   Go, then; for 'tis in vain
To seek him here that means not to be found.
                              Exeunt [BENVOLIO *and* MERCUTIO].
               [ROMEO *comes forward.*]
ROMEO   He jests at scars that never felt a wound[5]—
But soft,° what light through yonder window breaks?   *wait; hush*
45   It is the East, and Juliet is the sun.
Arise, fair sun, and kill the envious moon,[6]
Who is already sick and pale with grief
That thou, her maid, art far more fair than she.
Be not her maid, since she is envious;
50   Her vestal° livery is but sick and green,[7]   *virginal*
And none but fools do wear it. Cast it off.
               [Enter JULIET *above.*]
It is my lady—oh, it is my love—
Oh, that she knew she were!
She speaks, yet she says nothing. What of that?
55   Her eye discourses; I will answer it.
I am too bold; 'tis not to me she speaks.

---

7. Foolish creature (a disrespectful endearment), or alluding to a magician's trick of "reviving" an ape that had been trained to play dead.
8. A word for "semen"; the entire speech is filled with obscene wordplay.
9. Damp; melancholy.
1. A fruit thought to resemble the female sex organs or the anus, with a play on "meddle" in the sense "have sexual intercourse with."
2. A pear from Poperinghe in Flanders, punning on "popper-in" or "pop her in."
3. Small bed, often for a child, that was stored under

a larger one.
4. A lying place in the open, and a soldier's portable bed.
5. Rhymes with "found." This line precedes a scene change in most editions, although the location remains the same if both the inside and the outside of the orchard are supposed to be visible onstage.
6. Emblem of Diana, goddess of chastity.
7. Unfulfilled sexual desire was thought to cause green sickness (anemia) in adolescent girls; also alluding to the moon's pallor.

Two of the fairest stars in all the heaven,
Having some business, do entreat her eyes
To twinkle in their spheres[8] till they return.
60   What if her eyes were there, they in her head?
The brightness of her cheek would shame those stars
As daylight doth a lamp; her eye in heaven
Would through the airy region° stream so bright   *ethereal sky*
That birds would sing and think it were not night.
65   See how she leans her cheek upon her hand—
Oh, that I were a glove upon that hand,
That I might touch that cheek!
JULIET   Ay me!
ROMEO [*aside*]   She speaks.
Oh, speak again, bright angel, for thou art
As glorious to this night, being o'er my head,
70   As is a wingèd messenger° of heaven   *angel*
Unto the white upturnèd[9] wond'ring eyes
Of mortals that fall back to gaze[1] on him
When he bestrides the lazy puffing clouds
And sails upon the bosom of the air.
75   JULIET   O Romeo, Romeo, wherefore° art thou Romeo?   *why*
Deny thy father and refuse thy name;
Or, if thou wilt not, be but sworn my love,
And I'll no longer be a Capulet.
ROMEO [*aside*]   Shall I hear more, or shall I speak at this?
80   JULIET   'Tis but thy name that is my enemy;
Thou art thyself, though° not a Montague.   *even if*
What's "Montague"? It is nor hand, nor foot,
Nor arm, nor face, nor any other part
Belonging to a man. Oh, be some other name!
85   What's in a name? That which we call a rose
By any other word would smell as sweet;
So Romeo would, were he not Romeo called,
Retain that dear perfection which he owes°   *owns*
Without that title. Romeo, doff° thy name,   *shed*
90   And, for thy name, which is no part of thee,
Take all myself.
ROMEO   I take thee at thy word.[2]
Call me but "love," and I'll be new baptized:[3]
Henceforth I never will be Romeo.
JULIET   What man art thou that, thus bescreened in night,
So stumblest on my counsel?°   *private thoughts*
95   ROMEO   By a name
I know not how to tell thee who I am.
My name, dear saint, is hateful to myself
Because it is an enemy to thee;
Had I it written, I would tear the word.
100   JULIET   My ears have yet not drunk a hundred words
Of thy tongue's uttering, yet I know the sound.
Art thou not Romeo, and a Montague?

---

8. In Ptolemaic astrology, crystalline spheres around
the earth that carried the heavenly bodies in their
rotations.
9. Turned up, revealing the whites at the bottoms.

1. Fall backward in gazing.
2. At face value; as you have asked me to.
3. Given a new name; born into a new persona.

ROMEO   Neither, fair maid, if either thee dislike.° — *displeases you*

JULIET   How camest thou hither, tell me—and wherefore?

105 The orchard walls are high and hard to climb,
And the place death, considering who thou art,
If any of my kinsmen find thee here.

ROMEO   With love's light wings did I o'erperch° these walls, — *fly over*
For stony limits cannot hold love out,

110 And what love can do, that dares love attempt;
Therefore thy kinsmen are no stop° to me. — *obstacle*

JULIET   If they do see thee, they will murder thee.

ROMEO   Alack, there lies more peril in thine eye
Than twenty of their swords. Look thou but sweet,

115 And I am proof against° their enmity. — *impervious to*

JULIET   I would not for the world they saw thee here.

ROMEO   I have night's cloak to hide me from their eyes,
And, but° thou love me, let them find me here: — *unless*
My life were better ended by their hate

120 Than death proroguèd,° wanting of° thy love. — *deferred / lacking*

JULIET   By whose direction found'st thou out this place?

ROMEO   By love, that first did prompt me to inquire.
He lent me counsel, and I lent him eyes.
I am no pilot, yet wert thou as far

125 As that vast shore washed with the farthest sea,
I should adventure° for such merchandise. — *voyage*

JULIET   Thou knowest the mask of night is on my face,
Else would a maiden blush bepaint my cheek
For that which thou hast heard me speak tonight.

130 Fain° would I dwell on form°—fain, fain deny — *Gladly / propriety*
What I have spoke—but farewell, compliment.° — *polite convention*
Dost thou love me? I know thou wilt say "Ay,"
And I will take thy word; yet, if thou swear'st,
Thou mayst prove false. At lovers' perjuries

135 They say Jove laughs. O gentle Romeo,
If thou dost love, pronounce° it faithfully, — *utter*
Or if thou thinkest I am too quickly won,
I'll frown and be perverse° and say thee nay — *contrary*
So thou wilt woo—but else° not for the world. — *otherwise*

140 In truth, fair Montague, I am too fond,° — *infatuated*
And therefore thou mayst think my behavior light.° — *loose*
But trust me, gentleman, I'll prove more true
Than those that have the coying° to be strange.° — *coyness / distant*
I should have been more strange, I must confess,

145 But that thou overheard'st, ere I was ware,° — *aware*
My true-love passion. Therefore pardon me,
And not° impute this yielding to light love, — *do not*
Which the dark night hath so discoverèd.° — *revealed*

ROMEO   Lady, by yonder blessèd moon I vow,

150 That tips with silver all these fruit-tree tops—

JULIET   Oh, swear not by the moon, th'inconstant moon
That monthly changes in her circled orb,° — *orbital sphere*
Lest that thy love prove likewise variable.

ROMEO   What shall I swear by?

JULIET   Do not swear at all,

155 Or, if thou wilt, swear by thy gracious self,

Which is the god of my idolatry,[4]
And I'll believe thee.
ROMEO   If my heart's dear love—
JULIET   Well, do not swear. Although I joy in thee,
I have no joy of this contract° tonight;   *exchange of vows*
160   It is too rash, too unadvised,° too sudden,   *undeliberated*
Too like the lightning which doth cease to be
Ere one can say, "It lightens." Sweet, good night.
This bud of love by summer's ripening breath
May prove a beauteous flower when next we meet.
165   Good night, good night; as sweet repose and rest
Come to thy heart as that within my breast.
ROMEO   Oh, wilt thou leave me so unsatisfied?
JULIET   What satisfaction canst thou have tonight?
ROMEO   Th'exchange of thy love's faithful vow for mine.
170   JULIET   I gave thee mine before thou didst request it,
And yet I would it were° to give again.   *were available*
ROMEO   Wouldst thou withdraw it? For what purpose, love?
JULIET   But to be frank° and give it thee again;   *generous; honest*
And yet I wish but for the thing I have.
175   My bounty is as boundless as the sea,
My love as deep; the more I give to thee,
The more I have, for both are infinite.
              [NURSE *calls within.*]
I hear some noise within! Dear love, adieu.
—Anon,° good Nurse! —Sweet Montague, be true.   *One moment*
180   Stay but a little. I will come again.   [*Exit* JULIET.]
ROMEO   O blessèd, blessèd night! I am afeared,
Being in night, all this is but a dream,
Too flattering-sweet to be substantial.
              [*Enter* JULIET *above.*]
JULIET   Three words, dear Romeo, and good night indeed.
185   If that thy bent of love be honorable,
Thy purpose marriage, send me word tomorrow,
By one that I'll procure to come to thee,
Where and what time thou wilt perform the rite,
And all my fortunes at thy foot I'll lay,
190   And follow thee, my lord, throughout the world.
NURSE [*within*]   Madam!
JULIET   I come; anon! —But if thou meanest not well,
I do beseech thee—
NURSE [*within*]   Madam!
JULIET   By and by! I come!
—To cease thy strife,° and leave me to my grief.   *striving*
Tomorrow will I send.
195   ROMEO   So thrive my soul.[5]
JULIET   A thousand times good night.   [*Exit.*]
ROMEO   A thousand times the worse to want° thy light.   *lack*
Love goes toward love as schoolboys from their books,
But love from love toward school with heavy looks.
              Enter JULIET *again.*

4. Not only was loving a man more than God idolatrous, but so was swearing oaths by anything other
than God.
5. On peril of damnation.

200 JULIET Hist,° Romeo, hist! —Oh, for a falconer's voice   *(falconer's call)*
    To lure this tercel-gentle[6] back again.
    Bondage[7] is hoarse and may not speak aloud,
    Else would I tear° the cave where Echo[8] lies   *split with cries*
    And make her airy tongue more hoarse than mine
205   With repetition of my "Romeo."
    ROMEO It is my soul that calls upon my name.
    How silver-sweet sound lovers' tongues by night,
    Like softest music to attending ears.
    JULIET Romeo!
    ROMEO   Mine eyas?°   *young hawk*
    JULIET   What o'clock tomorrow
    Shall I send to thee?
210   ROMEO   By the hour of nine.
    JULIET I will not fail. 'Tis twenty year till then.
    I have forgot why I did call thee back.
    ROMEO Let me stand here till thou remember it.
    JULIET I shall forget to have thee still° stand there,   *always*
215   Rememb'ring how I love thy company.
    ROMEO And I'll still stay to have thee still forget,
    Forgetting any other home but this.
    JULIET 'Tis almost morning. I would have thee gone,
    And yet no farther than a wanton's° bird,   *spoiled child's*
220   That lets it hop a little from his hand,
    Like a poor prisoner in his twisted gyves,°   *fetters*
    And with a silken thread plucks it back again,
    So loving-jealous of his liberty.
    ROMEO I would° I were thy bird.   *wish*
    JULIET   Sweet, so would I—
225   Yet I should kill thee with much cherishing.
    Good night, good night. Parting is such sweet sorrow
    That I shall say "good night" till it be morrow.
    ROMEO Sleep dwell upon thine eyes, peace in thy breast;
    Would I were sleep and peace, so sweet to rest.
                         [Exit JULIET.*]*
230   Hence will I to my ghostly° friar's close° cell   *spiritual / small; private*
    His help to crave and my dear hap° to tell.   *Exit.*   *fortune*

2.2 (Q1 Scene 6)

Enter FRIAR LAURENCE *alone, with a basket.*

    FRIAR LAURENCE The gray°-eyed morn smiles on the   *pale blue*
      frowning night,
    Check'ring the eastern clouds with streaks of light,
    And fleckled° darkness like a drunkard reels   *dappled*
    From forth° day's path and Titan's[1] burning wheels.[2]   *Out of*
5   Now ere the sun advance° his burning eye   *brings up*

---

6. A male peregrine falcon. Literally, a noble ("gentle") hawk.
7. Confinement within her family's home; duty owed her family.
8. In classical legend, a woman who, scorned by Narcissus, wasted away with grief until only a voice remained to haunt empty caves.
2.2 Location: A street in Verona.

1. Helios, a classical sun god, was descended from the Titans. He traveled across the sky in a chariot.
2. TEXTUAL COMMENT In Q2, these four lines (2.2.1–4) appear twice, once spoken by Romeo at the end of the previous scene and again by Friar Laurence here, a textual redundancy that requires editorial intervention. See Digital Edition TC 8 (Second Quarto edited text).

The day to cheer and night's dank dew to dry,
I must upfill this osier cage° of ours   *willow basket*
With baleful weeds and precious-juicèd flowers.
The earth that's nature's mother is her tomb;
10 What is her burying grave, that is her womb,
And from her womb children of divers° kind   *several; varied*
We sucking on her natural bosom find:
Many for many virtues° excellent,   *healthful properties*
None but for some,³ and yet all different.
15 Oh, mickle° is the powerful grace° that lies   *great / divine beneficence*
In plants, herbs, stones, and their true qualities;
For naught° so vile that on the earth doth live   *nothing is*
But to the earth some special good doth give;
Nor aught so good but, strained° from that fair use,   *twisted*
20 Revolts from true birth, stumbling on abuse.⁴
Virtue itself turns vice, being misapplied,
And vice sometime by action dignified.
        Enter ROMEO.
Within the infant rind of this weak flower
Poison hath residence and medicine power:
25 For this, being smelled, with that part° cheers each part;°   *act / bodily member*
Being tasted, stays all senses with the heart.⁵
Two such opposèd kings encamp them still°   *always*
In man as well as herbs—grace and rude will—
And, where the worser is predominant,
30 Full soon the canker° death eats up that plant.   *grub; cancer*
ROMEO   Good morrow, Father.
FRIAR LAURENCE   *Benedicite.*°   *God bless you (Latin)*
What early tongue so sweet saluteth me?
Young son, it argues a distempered° head   *disturbed*
So soon to bid good morrow to thy bed.
35 Care keeps his watch in every old man's eye,
And, where care lodges, sleep will never lie;
But where unbruisèd° youth with unstuffed° brain   *fresh / unanxious*
Doth couch his limbs, there golden sleep doth reign.
Therefore thy earliness doth me assure
40 Thou art uproused with some distemp'rature—
Or, if not so, then here I hit it right:
Our Romeo hath not been in bed tonight.
ROMEO   That last is true; the sweeter rest was mine.
FRIAR LAURENCE   God pardon sin! Wast thou with Rosaline?
45 ROMEO   With Rosaline, my ghostly Father? No,
I have forgot that name and that name's woe.
FRIAR LAURENCE   That's my good son. But where hast thou
        been, then?
ROMEO   I'll tell thee ere thou ask it me again.
I have been feasting with mine enemy,
50 Where on a sudden one hath wounded me
That's by me wounded; both our remedies
Within thy help and holy physic° lies.   *medicine*
I bear no hatred, blessèd man, for, lo,

---

3. None that is not excellent for some use.
4. Turns from its intended benefits if it happens to be misused.
5. *stays . . . heart:* paralyzes the heart, along with all the senses.

My intercession° likewise steads° my foe. *request / benefits*

55   FRIAR LAURENCE   Be plain, good son, and homely° in thy drift; *direct*
    Riddling confession finds but riddling shrift.° *absolution*
  ROMEO   Then plainly know my heart's dear love is set
    On the fair daughter of rich Capulet.
    As mine on hers, so hers is set on mine,
60   And all combined, save what thou must combine
    By holy marriage. When, and where, and how
    We met, we wooed, and made exchange of vow,
    I'll tell thee as we pass; but this I pray,
    That thou consent to marry us today.
65   FRIAR LAURENCE   Holy Saint Francis, what a change is here!
    Is Rosaline, that thou didst love so dear,
    So soon forsaken? Young men's love, then, lies
    Not truly in their hearts but in their eyes.
    Jesu Maria, what a deal of brine
70   Hath washed thy sallow° cheeks for Rosaline! *yellowed*
    How much salt water thrown away in waste
    To season° love that of it doth not taste! *preserve; flavor*
    The sun not yet thy sighs[6] from heaven clears,
    Thy old° groans yet ringing in mine ancient ears; *former*
75   Lo, here upon thy cheek the stain doth sit
    Of an old tear that is not washed off yet.
    If ere thou wast thyself and these woes thine,
    Thou and these woes were all for Rosaline—
    And art thou changed? Pronounce this sentence,° then: *maxim; verdict*
80   Women may fall when there's no strength in men.
  ROMEO   Thou chid'st me oft for loving Rosaline—
  FRIAR LAURENCE   For doting, not for loving, pupil mine.
  ROMEO   And bad'st me bury love.
  FRIAR LAURENCE   Not in a grave
    To lay one in, another out to have.
85   ROMEO   I pray thee, chide me not. Her I love now
    Doth grace for grace and love for love allow;
    The other did not so.
  FRIAR LAURENCE   Oh, she knew well
    Thy love did read by rote, that could not spell.[7]
    But come, young waverer, come, go with me.
90   In one respect I'll thy assistant be,
    For this alliance may so happy prove
    To turn your households' rancor to pure love.
  ROMEO   Oh, let us hence; I stand° on sudden haste. *depend; insist*
  FRIAR LAURENCE   Wisely and slow; they stumble that run fast.
                                  Exeunt.

2.3 (Q1 Scene 7)
Enter BENVOLIO *and* MERCUTIO.
MERCUTIO   Where the devil should this Romeo be? Came he
  not home tonight?° *last night*

---

6. The mist Romeo's exhalations produced.
7. *did read . . . spell*: did recite the memorized phrases of love poetry, without understanding or meaning them.
2.3 Location: Scene continues.

BENVOLIO   Not to his father's; I spoke with his man.

MERCUTIO   Why, that same pale,° hard-hearted wench, that   *fair-skinned; frigid*
Rosaline,

5   Torments him so that he will sure run mad.

BENVOLIO   Tybalt, the kinsman to old Capulet,
Hath sent a letter to his father's house.

MERCUTIO   A challenge, on my life.

BENVOLIO   Romeo will answer° it.   *accept*

10   MERCUTIO   Any man that can write may answer a letter.

BENVOLIO   Nay, he will answer the letter's master how he
dares, being dared.

MERCUTIO   Alas, poor Romeo, he is already dead—stabbed with
a white wench's black eye, run through the ear with a love

15   song, the very pin[1] of his heart cleft with the blind bow-boy's
butt-shaft[2]—and is he a man to encounter Tybalt?

BENVOLIO   Why, what is Tybalt?

MERCUTIO   More than Prince of Cats.[3] Oh, he's the coura-
geous captain of compliments!° He fights as you sing prick-   *formalities of dueling*

20   song;[4] keeps time, distance,[5] and proportion;° he rests his   *harmony; form*
minim rests,[6] one, two—and the third in your bosom; the
very butcher of a silk button;[7] a duelist, a duelist; a gentleman of the very first house, of the first and second cause[8]—
ah, the immortal *passata*, the *punta riversa*, the *hai*![9]

25   BENVOLIO   The what?

MERCUTIO   The pox of° such antic,° lisping, affecting° fanta-   *on / grotesque / affected*
sies,° these new tuners of accent.[1] "By Jesu, a very good   *bizarrely mannered men*
blade, a very tall° man, a very good whore!" Why,° is not   *valiant / Why, now*
this a lamentable thing, grandsire, that we should be thus

30   afflicted with these strange[2] flies, these fashionmongers,
these "pardon-me's,"[3] who stand so much on the new form
that they cannot sit at ease on the old bench?[4] Oh, their
bones, their bones![5]

         Enter ROMEO.

BENVOLIO   Here comes Romeo! Here comes Romeo!

35   MERCUTIO   Without his roe, like a dried herring.[6] O flesh,
flesh, how art thou fishified![7] Now is he for the numbers°   *verses*

---

1. Peg in the center of an archery target.
2. Blunt practice arrow, fit for children and hence for Cupid.
3. Called Tybalt or Tibert in medieval stories of Reynard the fox. "Catso," from the Italian word for "penis," was also a slang term for a rogue.
4. Sung from sheet music and thus more precise and invariable than extempore or remembered music.
5. Musical intervals between notes; also, a set space to be kept between combatants.
6. Short musical rests, referring to the brief strategic pauses in a duel.
7. Alluding to the boast of an Italian fencing master in London that he could "hit any Englishman with a thrust upon any button."
8. *gentleman . . . cause*: superior practitioner of taking up quarrels as duels. *first house*: the best fencing school. *cause*: a reason that according to the etiquette of fencing would require an honorable gentleman to seek a duel.
9. Italian fencing terms for, respectively, a lunging

sword thrust, backhanded thrust, and thrust that reaches through.
1. These faddishly novel speakers, such as those importing foreign phrases. A typical Renaissance English satire, here seemingly unaffected by the fact that Italian is the native tongue of Verona.
2. Newfangled; foreign.
3. *pardon-me's*: the fastidiously mannered, affecting the French *pardonnez-moi*.
4. *who . . . bench*: as if both Mercutio and Benvolio were elderly ("grandsire"), viewing the decline of the young. *stand*: insist. *form*: etiquette; fashion; bench.
5. *Oh . . . bones*: Aching on the austere furniture of their predecessors; infected with the "bone disease," syphilis.
6. Emaciated, since the roe is removed in curing. This leaves Romeo's name a mournful wail, "Me, O." He is also missing his roe deer (female, named Rosaline).
7. Gone pale and limp, turned into a herring. Fish, thought weak and relatively unnourishing, was the substitute for "flesh" (meat) during fasts.

that Petrarch[8] flowed in; Laura to° his lady was a kitchen   *compared to*
wench—marry, she had a better love to berhyme her—Dido[9]
a dowdy, Cleopatra a gypsy,[1] Helen and Hero[2] hildings° and   *hussies*
40   harlots, Thisbe[3] a gray-eye° or so. But not to the purpose.[4]   *blue-eyed*
Signor Romeo, *bonjour*: there's a French salutation to your
French slop.° You gave us the counterfeit fairly last night.   *loose breeches*

ROMEO   Good morrow to you both. What counterfeit did I
give you?

45 MERCUTIO   The slip,[5] sir, the slip—can you not conceive?°   *understand*

ROMEO   Pardon, good Mercutio. My business was great, and
in such a case as mine, a man may strain° courtesy.   *nearly abandon*

MERCUTIO   That's as much as to say such a case as yours con-
strains a man to bow in the hams.[6]

50 ROMEO   Meaning to curtsy?[7]

MERCUTIO   Thou hast most kindly hit it.[8]

ROMEO   A most courteous exposition.

MERCUTIO   Nay, I am the very pink° of courtesy.   *nonpareil; carnation*

ROMEO   Pink for flower?°   *dianthus; vulva*

55 MERCUTIO   Right.

ROMEO   Why, then, is my pump° well flowered.[9]   *shoe; penis*

MERCUTIO   Sure wit! Follow me° this jest now till thou hast   *Chase; respond to*
worn out thy pump, that when the single° sole of it is worn,   *thin*
the jest may remain after the wearing, solely singular.°   *utterly unique*

60 ROMEO   Oh, single-soled° jest, solely° singular for the   *shoddy / only*
singleness!°   *foolishness*

MERCUTIO   Come between us, good Benvolio; my wits faints.[1]

ROMEO   Switch and spurs,[2] switch and spurs, or I'll cry a
match!°   *claim a victory*

65 MERCUTIO   Nay, if our wits run the wild goose chase,[3] I am
done; for thou hast more of the wild goose° in one of thy   *folly*
wits than I am sure I have in my whole five.° Was I with° you   *(five senses) / even with*
there for the goose?

ROMEO   Thou wast never with me for anything when thou
70   wast not there for the goose.[4]

MERCUTIO   I will bite thee by the ear[5] for that jest.

ROMEO   Nay, good goose, bite not![6]

MERCUTIO   Thy wit is very bitter sweeting;° it is a most sharp   *apple*
sauce.°   *mockery*

75 ROMEO   And is it not, then, well served in to a sweet goose?

MERCUTIO   Oh, here's a wit of cheverel° that stretches from   *kid leather*
an inch narrow to an ell broad![7]

---

8. Petrarch's sonnets addressed to Laura were the model for an English love-sonnet craze.
9. The beautiful queen of Carthage who fell in love with Aeneas but was deserted by him in Virgil's *Aeneid*.
1. A term of abuse. Gypsies were supposed to have come from Egypt, where Cleopatra was queen and lover of Julius Caesar and Mark Antony.
2. Helen's abduction by Paris initiated the Trojan War. Hero was Leander's lover in a tragic legend.
3. Beloved of Pyramus in a classical legend that parallels *Romeo and Juliet*. The young lovers, coming from hostile families, die as a result of a missed meeting and misinterpreted evidence.
4. *to the purpose*: of consequence.
5. Counterfeit coin. To "give the slip" is to steal off.

6. Playing on "business" as "sexual intercourse" and "case" as "vagina." Mercutio suggests that Romeo is sexually exhausted and cannot stand up straight.
7. Pronounced the same as "courtesy."
8. Most truly guessed it; most truly sexually penetrated it.
9. Pinked, or decoratively perforated.
1. Treating the exchange of wit as a duel.
2. Flog your wits to a full gallop; continue.
3. A cross-country horse race in which the leader chose the course and the rest had to follow.
4. Silliness; whore's company.
5. Usually suggesting affectionate nibbling.
6. A proverbial cry for mercy, here used ironically.
7. That spreads itself very thin (an ell was 45 inches).

ROMEO   I stretch it out for that word "broad," which, added to
the goose, proves thee far and wide a broad goose.[8]

80 MERCUTIO   Why, is not this better now than groaning for love?
Now art thou sociable; now art thou Romeo; now art thou
what thou art by art° as well as by nature, for this driveling   *learning*
love is like a great natural° that runs lolling up and down to   *idiot*
hide his bauble[9] in a hole.

85 BENVOLIO   Stop there! Stop there!

MERCUTIO   Thou desirest me to stop in[1] my tale° against the hair.[2]   *story; penis ("tail")*

BENVOLIO   Thou wouldst else have made thy tale large.

MERCUTIO   Oh, thou art deceived! I would have made it short,
for I was come to the whole depth of my tale, and meant
90 indeed to occupy the argument° no longer.   *topic*

                Enter NURSE *and her man*[, PETER].

ROMEO   Here's goodly gear![3] A sail! A sail![4]

MERCUTIO   Two, two: a shirt° and a smock.°   *man / woman*

NURSE   Peter.

PETER   Anon.°   *At your service*

95 NURSE   My fan, Peter.

MERCUTIO   Good Peter, to hide her face, for her fan's the
fairer face.

NURSE   God ye° good morrow,° gentlemen.   *give you / morning*

MERCUTIO   God ye good e'en,° fair gentlewoman.   *afternoon*

100 NURSE   Is it good e'en?

MERCUTIO   'Tis no less, I tell ye, for the bawdy hand of the
dial is now upon the prick° of noon.   *mark; penis*

NURSE   Out upon you![5] What° a man are you?   *What sort of*

ROMEO   One, gentlewoman, that God hath made himself to
105 mar.[6]

NURSE   By my troth, it is well said. "For himself to mar,"
quoth 'a?° —Gentlemen, can any of you tell me where I   *he*
may find the young Romeo?

ROMEO   I can tell you, but young Romeo will be older when
110 you have found him than he was when you sought him. I am
the youngest of that name, for fault° of a worse.   *lack*

NURSE   You say well.

MERCUTIO   Yea, is the worst well? Very well took, i'faith; wisely,
wisely.

115 NURSE   [*to* ROMEO]   If you be he, sir, I desire some confidence
with you.

BENVOLIO   She will indite[7] him to some supper.

MERCUTIO   A bawd, a bawd, a bawd! So, ho![8]

ROMEO   What hast thou found?°   *spotted; figured out*

120 MERCUTIO   No hare,° sir, unless a hare, sir, in a lenten pie[9] that   *prostitute*

---

8. A gross idiot; a licentious fellow; a goose fattened
for the table.
9. *that . . . bauble:* who runs to cover up a jester's
wand, grotesquely carved at one end; "bauble" also
suggests penis.
1. Cease; stuff in.
2. Against the grain; against the pubic hair.
3. Spoken ironically of Mercutio's witticisms or the
Nurse's voluminous appearance.
4. A sailor's cry upon sighting another ship.
5. An expression of indignation.
6. *One . . . mar:* combines two proverbial expres-

sions. "It is his to make or mar" suggests that Mercutio has the free will to determine his own character.
"He is a man of God's making" places the blame for
Mercutio's character on God.
7. Deliberately substituted for "invite," to mock the
Nurse's erroneous use of "confidence" for "conference" in the line above.
8. The cry of a hunter who has spotted his quarry.
9. Meat illicitly eaten during Lent by disguising it in
a pie, just as the Nurse's unattractiveness hides whatever promiscuity she may practice.

is something stale and hoar ere it be spent.[1]
    [*He walks by them and sings.*]
          An old hare hoar,
          And an old hare hoar
          Is very good meat in Lent;
125   But a hare that is hoar
          Is too much for a score[2]
          When it hoars° ere it be spent.   *turns moldy; whores*
Romeo, will you come to your father's? We'll to dinner thither.
  ROMEO   I will follow you.
130 MERCUTIO   Farewell, ancient lady, farewell.
    [*Sings.*]   Lady, lady, lady![3]
                 Exeunt [MERCUTIO *and* BENVOLIO].
  NURSE   I pray you, sir, what saucy merchant° was this that   *commoner*
    was so full of his ropery?°   *knavery*
  ROMEO   A gentleman, Nurse, that loves to hear himself talk,
135   and will speak more in a minute than he will stand to° in a   *perform*
    month.
  NURSE   An 'a° speak anything against me, I'll take him down°   *If he / humble him*
    an 'a were lustier[4] than he is, and twenty such jacks;° and, if   *scoundrels*
    I cannot, I'll find those that shall. Scurvy knave! I am none
140   of his flirt-gills;° I am none of his skains mates.[5] [*She turns*   *loose women*
    to PETER, *her man.*] And thou must stand by, too, and suffer
    every knave to use me at his pleasure!
  PETER   I saw no man use you at his pleasure; if I had, my
    weapon should quickly have been out. I warrant you, I dare
145   draw as soon as another man if I see occasion in a good quar-
    rel, and the law on my side.
  NURSE   Now, afore God, I am so vexed that every part about
    me quivers. Scurvy knave! [*to* ROMEO] Pray you, sir, a word;
    and, as I told you, my young lady bid me inquire you out.
150   What she bid me say I will keep to myself; but first let me
    tell ye, if ye should lead her in a fool's paradise, as they say,
    it were a very gross° kind of behavior, as they say, for the   *outrageous*
    gentlewoman is young, and therefore if you should deal
    double° with her, truly it were an ill thing to be offered to   *falsely; forcefully*
155   any gentlewoman, and very weak° dealing.   *poor*
  ROMEO   Nurse, commend me to thy lady and mistress. I pro-
    test° unto thee—   *swear*
  NURSE   Good heart—and i'faith I will tell her as much. Lord,
    Lord, she will be a joyful woman!
160 ROMEO   What wilt thou tell her, Nurse? Thou dost not mark°   *pay attention to*
    me.
  NURSE   I will tell her, sir, that you do protest[6]—which, as I take
    it, is a gentlemanlike offer.
  ROMEO   Bid her devise some means to come to shrift this
    afternoon,
165   And there she shall, at Friar Laurence' cell,

---

1. Somewhat stale and moldy by the time the last of the rationed luxury is consumed.
2. Is too much to pay for.
3. Refrain to a ballad about a perfectly chaste woman, intended derisively.

4. Stronger; hornier.
5. Knife-wielding rogues.
6. The Nurse takes this as a marriage offer, probably confusing "protest" with "propose."

Be shrived° and married. [*He offers money.*] Here is for   *absolved after confession*
    thy pains.
NURSE   No, truly, sir, not a penny.
ROMEO   Go to—I say you shall.
NURSE   This afternoon, sir? Well, she shall be there.
170 ROMEO   And stay, good Nurse, behind the abbey wall.
    Within this hour my man shall be with thee
    And bring thee cords made like a tackled stair,°   *a knotted ladder*
    Which to the high topgallant[7] of my joy
    Must be my convoy° in the secret night.   *means of conveyance*
175   Farewell. Be trusty, and I'll quit° thy pains.   *repay*
    Farewell. Commend me to thy mistress.
NURSE   Now God in heaven bless thee! Hark you, sir.
ROMEO   What say'st thou, my dear Nurse?
NURSE   Is your man secret?° Did you ne'er hear say,   *discreet*
180 "Two may keep counsel, putting one away"?
ROMEO   Warrant thee, my man's as true as steel.
NURSE   Well, sir, my mistress is the sweetest lady. Lord, Lord,
    when 'twas a little prating thing— Oh, there is a nobleman
    in town, one Paris, that would fain lay knife aboard;[8] but she,
185 good soul, had as lief° see a toad, a very toad, as see him. I   *gladly*
    anger her sometimes, and tell her that Paris is the properer°   *more handsome*
    man; but, I'll warrant you, when I say so she looks as pale as
    any clout° in the versal° world. Doth not "rosemary"[9] and   *sheet / entire*
    "Romeo" begin both with a° letter?   *the same*
190 ROMEO   Ay, Nurse. What of that? Both with an "R."
NURSE   Ah, mocker, that's the dog's name![1] "R" is for the—no,
    I know it begins with some other letter; and she hath the
    prettiest sententious[2] of it—of you and rosemary—that it
    would do you good to hear it.
195 ROMEO   Commend me to thy lady.
NURSE   Ay, a thousand times. Peter!
PETER   Anon!
NURSE   Before,° and apace.°   ***Exeunt.***   *Lead / quickly*

2.4 (Q1 Scene 8)

Enter JULIET.
JULIET   The clock struck nine when I did send the Nurse;
    In half an hour she promised to return.
    Perchance she cannot meet him— That's not so.
    Oh, she is lame! Love's heralds should be thoughts
5   Which ten times faster glides than the sun's beams,
    Driving back shadows over louring° hills.   *dark; threatening*
    Therefore do nimble-pinioned° doves draw Love;°   *winged / Venus*
    And therefore hath the wind-swift Cupid wings.
    Now is the sun upon the highmost hill°   *zenith*
10   Of this day's journey, and from nine till twelve
    Is three long hours, yet she is not come.
    Had she affections° and warm youthful blood,   *passions*

---

7. The highest platform on a mast, from which the
topgallant sail was handled.
8. One claimed a place at dinner by laying one's personal knife on the table ("board").
9. A token of remembrance, between lovers and also

of the dead.
1. "R"—the sound "arr"—was thought to resemble a
dog's snarl.
2. Blunder for "sentences"; sayings.
2.4 Location: Capulet's orchard.

She would be as swift in motion as a ball;
My words would bandy° her to my sweet love,   *volley (as in tennis)*
15   And his to me.
But old folks: many feign° as they were dead,   *act*
Unwieldy, slow, heavy, and pale as lead.
            Enter NURSE [*and* PETER].
O God, she comes! O honey Nurse, what news?
Hast thou met with him? Send thy man away.
20 NURSE   Peter, stay° at the gate.   [*Exit* PETER.]   *wait*
     JULIET   Now, good sweet Nurse— O Lord, why lookest thou
         sad?
Though news be sad, yet tell them merrily;
If good, thou shamest the music of sweet news
By playing it to me with so sour a face.
25 NURSE   I am a-weary; give me leave° a while.   *let me alone*
Fie, how my bones ache! What a jaunce° have I!   *trotting about*
     JULIET   I would thou hadst my bones and I thy news.
Nay, come; I pray thee, speak. Good, good Nurse, speak.
     NURSE   Jesu, what haste! Can you not stay a while?
30 Do you not see that I am out of breath?
     JULIET   How art thou out of breath when thou hast breath
To say to me that thou art out of breath?
The excuse that thou dost make in this delay
Is longer than the tale thou dost excuse!
35 Is thy news good or bad? Answer to that—
Say either, and I'll stay° the circumstance.°   *wait for / full details*
Let me be satisfied: is't good or bad?
     NURSE   Well, you have made a simple° choice. You know not   *foolish*
how to choose a man. Romeo? No, not he. Though his face
40 be better than any man's, yet his leg excels all men's; and for
a hand, and a foot, and a body, though they be not to be
talked on,° yet they are past compare. He is not the flower of   *worth mentioning*
courtesy, but I'll warrant him as gentle as a lamb. Go thy
ways,[1] wench; serve God. What, have you dined at home?
45 JULIET   No, no. But all this did I know before.
What says he of our marriage? What of that?
     NURSE   Lord, how my head aches! What a head have I!
It beats as it would fall in twenty pieces.
My back!—O't' other side—ah, my back, my back![2]
50 Beshrew° your heart for sending me about   *Curse (mild oath)*
To catch my death with jauncing up and down.
     JULIET   I'faith, I am sorry that thou art not well.
Sweet, sweet, sweet Nurse, tell me: what says my love?
     NURSE   Your love says, like an honest gentleman,
55 And a courteous, and a kind, and a handsome,
And I warrant a virtuous— Where is your mother?
     JULIET   Where is my mother? Why, she is within.
Where should she be? How oddly thou repliest:
"Your love says, like an honest° gentleman,   *honorable*
'Where is your mother?'"
60 NURSE   O God's Lady,° dear,   *Mary, Mother of God*

---

1. Off you go; do as you will do.
2. Perhaps the Nurse is giving Juliet directions to rub her back.

Are you so hot?° Marry, come up, I trow!³   *impatient; aroused*
Is this the poultice for my aching bones?
Henceforward do your messages yourself.

JULIET   Here's such a coil!° Come, what says Romeo?   *to-do*

65   NURSE   Have you got leave to go to shrift today?

JULIET   I have.

NURSE   Then hie° you hence to Friar Laurence' cell;   *hurry*
There stays a husband to make you a wife.
Now comes the wanton° blood up in your cheeks;   *fickle; lustful*

70   They'll be in scarlet straight° at any news.   *immediately*
Hie you to church. I must another way
To fetch a ladder by the which your love
Must climb a bird's nest soon when it is dark.
I am the drudge and toil in your delight,

75   But you shall bear the burden⁴ soon at night.
Go! I'll to dinner; hie you to the cell.

JULIET   Hie to high fortune! Honest Nurse, farewell.   *Exeunt.*

2.5 (Q1 Scene 9)

Enter FRIAR [LAURENCE] *and* ROMEO.

FRIAR LAURENCE   So smile the heavens upon this holy act
That after-hours with sorrow chide us not.

ROMEO   Amen, amen. But come what sorrow can,
It cannot countervail the exchange of joy

5   That one short minute gives me in her sight.
Do thou but close° our hands with holy words,   *join*
Then love-devouring death do what he dare—
It is enough I may but call her mine.

FRIAR LAURENCE   These violent° delights have violent ends   *sudden; intense*

10   And in their triumph die, like fire and powder¹
Which, as they kiss, consume. The sweetest honey
Is loathsome in his own deliciousness,
And in the taste confounds the appetite.²
Therefore love moderately: long love doth so;

15   Too swift arrives as tardy as too slow.

Enter JULIET.

Here comes the lady. Oh, so light³ a foot
Will ne'er wear out the everlasting flint;⁴
A lover may bestride the gossamers°   *spiders' threads*
That idles in the wanton° summer air   *playful*

20   And yet not fall, so light is vanity.⁵

JULIET   Good even° to my ghostly° confessor.   *evening / spiritual*

FRIAR LAURENCE   Romeo shall thank thee, daughter, for us
both.

[ROMEO *kisses her.*]

JULIET   As much⁶ to him, else is his thanks too much.

[JULIET *returns his kiss.*]

ROMEO   Ah, Juliet, if the measure° of thy joy   *measuring vessel*

---

3. *Marry . . . trow:* an expression of indignant or amused surprise and reproof.
4. Do the work; carry a lover; sing the theme of a duet, alluding to the sounds of lovemaking.
2.5 Location: Friar Laurence's cell.
1. Gunpowder. *triumph:* victory; celebration.
2. *The sweetest . . . appetite:* from the proverb "Too

much honey cloys the stomach." *his:* its. *confounds:* overwhelms.
3. Swift; dainty; free of care; sexually open.
4. Will never endure or subdue the hard road of life.
5. Temporary worldly pleasure.
6. An equal amount.

25 Be heaped like mine, and that thy skill be more
   To blazon° it, then sweeten with thy breath°   *describe; trumpet / speech*
   This neighbor air, and let rich music tongue
   Unfold the imagined° happiness that both   *unexpressed ideas of*
   Receive in either by this dear encounter.
30 JULIET   Conceit,° more rich in matter than in words,   *Imagination*
   Brags of his substance,[7] not of ornament.°   *rhetoric; form*
   They are but beggars that can count their worth,
   But my true love is grown to such excess,
   I cannot sum up sum of half my wealth.[8]
35 FRIAR LAURENCE   Come; come with me, and we will make short
        work.
   For, by your leaves, you shall not stay alone
   Till holy church incorporate two in one.[9]   [*Exeunt.*]

3.1 (Q1 Scene 10)

Enter MERCUTIO, BENVOLIO, [*Mercutio's Page,*] *and*
[*Montague's*] *Men.*

BENVOLIO   I pray thee, good Mercutio, let's retire.
   The day is hot, the Capels abroad,°   *about*
   And if we meet we shall not scape a brawl—
   For now, these hot days, is the mad blood stirring.
5 MERCUTIO   Thou art like one of these fellows that, when he
   enters the confines of a tavern, claps me° his sword upon the   *claps me = claps*
   table and says, "God send me no need of thee"—and, by
   the operation° of the second cup, draws him on the drawer[1]   *effect*
   when indeed there is no need.
10 BENVOLIO   Am I like such a fellow?
   MERCUTIO   Come, come, thou art as hot a jack° in thy mood   *rogue*
   as any in Italy, and as soon moved° to be moody,° and as   *provoked / angry*
   soon moody to be° moved.   *at being*
   BENVOLIO   And what to?
15 MERCUTIO   Nay, an there were two such, we should have none
   shortly, for one would kill the other. Thou—why, thou wilt
   quarrel with a man that hath a hair more or a hair less in his
   beard than thou hast. Thou wilt quarrel with a man for cracking nuts, having no other reason but because thou hast hazel
20 eyes. What eye but such an eye would spy out such a quarrel?
   Thy head is as full of quarrels as an egg is full of meat,° and   *foodstuff*
   yet thy head hath been beaten as addle° as an egg for quar-   *rotten; confused*
   reling. Thou hast quarreled with a man for coughing in the
   street, because he hath wakened thy dog that hath lain
25 asleep in the sun. Didst thou not fall out with a tailor for
   wearing his new doublet before Easter?[2] With another for
   tying his new shoes with old ribbon? And yet thou wilt tutor
   me from quarreling!
   BENVOLIO   An I were so apt to quarrel as thou art, any man
30 should buy the fee-simple[3] of my life for an hour and a
   quarter.

---

7. Wealth; content.
8. *I . . . wealth:* The amount is too large to be understood precisely.
9. Literally, put two into one body. Marriage mystically united man and woman in "one flesh" (Genesis 2:2).

3.1 Location: A street in Verona.
1. Draws his sword on the server.
2. New fashions came out at Easter, after the austere penitence of Lent.
3. Outright possession of land, usually an inherited right; here, the whole value of Benvolio's life.

MERCUTIO   The fee-simple? Oh, simple!°   *foolish*
   Enter TYBALT, PETRUCCIO, *and others*
   [*of Capulet's Men*].
BENVOLIO   By my head, here comes the Capulets.
MERCUTIO   By my heel, I care not.
35 TYBALT [*to* PETRUCCIO *and Capulets*]   Follow me close, for I will
   speak to them.
   [*to the Montagues*] Gentlemen, good e'en. A word with one
   of you.
MERCUTIO   And but one word with one of us? Couple it with
   something; make it a word and a blow.
TYBALT   You shall find me apt enough to that, sir, an you will
40 give me occasion.
MERCUTIO   Could you not take some occasion without giving?
TYBALT   Mercutio, thou consortest° with Romeo.   *associate*
MERCUTIO   "Consort"?° What, dost thou make us minstrels?   *Play in a band*
   An thou make minstrels of us, look to hear nothing but dis-
45 cords. Here's my fiddlestick;° here's that shall make you dance.   *(rapier)*
   Zounds!° "Consort"!   *By God's wounds*
BENVOLIO   We talk here in the public haunt° of men.   *gathering place*
   Either withdraw unto some private place,
   Or reason coldly° of your grievances,   *dispassionately*
50 Or else depart.° Here all eyes gaze on us.   *separate*
MERCUTIO   Men's eyes were made to look, and let them gaze.
   I will not budge for no man's pleasure, I.
      Enter ROMEO.
TYBALT   Well, peace be with you, sir; here comes my man.
MERCUTIO   But I'll be hanged, sir, if he wear your livery.[4]
55 Marry, go before to field, he'll be your follower;°   *servant; pursuer*
   Your worship in that sense may call him "man."
TYBALT   Romeo, the love I bear thee can afford
   No better term than this: thou art a villain.°   *base commoner; rogue*
ROMEO   Tybalt, the reason that I have to love thee
60 Doth much excuse the appertaining rage
   To[5] such a greeting. Villain am I none.
   Therefore, farewell. I see thou knowest me not.
TYBALT   Boy, this shall not excuse the injuries
   That thou hast done me; therefore turn and draw.
65 ROMEO   I do protest I never injuried thee,
   But love thee better than thou canst devise
   Till thou shalt know the reason of my love.
   And so, good Capulet—which name I tender°   *regard; love*
   As dearly as mine own—be satisfied.
70 MERCUTIO   Oh, calm, dishonorable, vile submission!
   Alla stoccata carries it away![6]
      [*He draws.*]
   Tybalt, you ratcatcher, will you walk?°   *withdraw to fight*
TYBALT   What wouldst thou have with me?
MERCUTIO   Good King of Cats, nothing but one of your nine
75 lives. That I mean to make bold withal° and, as you shall use   *be so bold as to take*
   me hereafter,[7] dry-beat° the rest of the eight. Will you pluck   *soundly thrash*

---

4. Mercutio obnoxiously mistakes Tybalt's "my man"
for "personal servant."
5. *Doth . . . To:* Permits me to put aside my otherwise
appropriate anger at.
6. The rapier thrust wins the day.
7. And, according to how you subsequently treat me.

your sword out of his pilcher° by the ears? Make haste, lest   *leather scabbard*
mine be about your ears ere it be out.
TYBALT [*drawing*] I am for you.
      [*They fight.*]
80 ROMEO   Gentle Mercutio, put thy rapier up!
MERCUTIO [*to* TYBALT] Come, sir, your *passata!*°   *forward thrust*
ROMEO   Draw, Benvolio! Beat down their weapons.
  Gentlemen, for shame, forbear this outrage.°   *criminal violence*
  Tybalt! Mercutio! The Prince expressly hath
85 Forbid this bandying° in Verona streets.   *strife*
  Hold, Tybalt! Good Mercutio—
     [TYBALT *under Romeo's arm thrusts* MERCUTIO *in.*]
PETRUCCIO Away, Tybalt!
      [*Exeunt* TYBALT, PETRUCCIO, *and Capulet's Men.*]
MERCUTIO I am hurt.
  A plague o'both houses! I am sped.°   *finished*
  Is he gone and hath nothing?
90 BENVOLIO   What, art thou hurt?
MERCUTIO Ay, ay, a scratch, a scratch. Marry, 'tis enough.
  Where is my page? —Go, villain: fetch a surgeon.
                          [*Exit Page.*]
ROMEO   Courage, man; the hurt cannot be much.
MERCUTIO No? 'Tis not so deep as a well, nor so wide as a
95 church door, but 'tis enough; 'twill serve. Ask for me tomor-
row, and you shall find me a grave man: I am peppered,° I   *done for*
warrant, for this world. A plague o'both your houses! Zounds!
A dog, a rat, a mouse, a cat, to scratch a man to death—a
braggart, a rogue, a villain that fights by the book of arith-
100 metic.[8] Why the devil came you between us? I was hurt
under your arm.
ROMEO   I thought all for the best.
MERCUTIO Help me into some house, Benvolio,
  Or I shall faint. A plague o'both your houses!
105 They have made worms' meat of me;
  I have it, and soundly, too. Your houses—
                  Exeunt[9] [*all but* ROMEO].
ROMEO   This gentleman, the Prince's near ally,°   *relative*
  My very° friend, hath got this mortal hurt   *true*
  In my behalf, my reputation stained
110 With Tybalt's slander—Tybalt, that an hour
  Hath been my cousin. O sweet Juliet,
  Thy beauty hath made me effeminate,
  And in my temper[1] softened valor's steel.
     Enter BENVOLIO.
BENVOLIO O Romeo, Romeo, brave Mercutio is dead.
115 That gallant spirit hath aspired° the clouds,   *ascended to*
  Which too untimely here did scorn the earth.
ROMEO   This day's black fate on more days doth depend;°   *hang over*
  This but begins the woe others must end.
     [*Enter* TYBALT.]

---

8. By the numbers; according to a fencing manual.
9. PERFORMANCE COMMENT Directors have found widely differing ways to stage the duel scene and the death of Mercutio, with varying implications for the rest of the play. For more, see Digital Edition PC 4.

1. Emotional makeup, here suggesting the hardened character of a fighting man (*temper:* to harden steel). It was believed that too much time with or passion for women would cause a man to become effeminate.

BENVOLIO   Here comes the furious Tybalt back again.

120 ROMEO   He gan° in triumph, and Mercutio slain? *going*
Away to heaven, respective lenity,° *respectful lenience*
And fire and fury be my conduct° now! *guide*
—Now, Tybalt, take the "villain" back again
That late thou gavest me, for Mercutio's soul

125 Is but a little way above our heads,
Staying for thine to keep him company;
Either thou, or I, or both, must go with him.

TYBALT   Thou, wretched boy, that didst consort° him here, *accompany*
Shalt with him hence.

ROMEO   This shall determine that.

They fight; TYBALT *falls [and dies].*

130 BENVOLIO   Romeo, away; be gone!
The citizens are up,° and Tybalt slain. *up in arms*
Stand not amazed;° the Prince will doom thee° death *stupefied / sentence you to*
If thou art taken. Hence! Be gone! Away!

ROMEO   Oh, I am fortune's fool.° *dupe*

BENVOLIO   Why dost thou stay?

Exit ROMEO.

Enter CITIZENS.

135 CITIZEN   Which way ran he that killed Mercutio?
Tybalt, that murderer—which way ran he?

BENVOLIO   There lies that Tybalt.

CITIZEN   Up, sir; go with me.
I charge thee in the Prince's name obey.

Enter PRINCE, *old* MONTAGUE, CAPULET[, MONTAGUE'S
WIFE, CAPULET'S WIFE, *and Attendants].*

PRINCE   Where are the vile beginners of this fray?

140 BENVOLIO   O noble Prince, I can discover° all *reveal*
The unlucky manage° of this fatal brawl. *handling*
There lies the man, slain by young Romeo,
That slew thy kinsman, brave Mercutio.

CAPULET'S WIFE   Tybalt, my cousin! O my brother's child!

145 O Prince, O cousin, husband! Oh, the blood is spilled
Of my dear kinsman! Prince, as thou art true,
For blood of ours shed blood of Montague.
O cousin, cousin!

PRINCE   Benvolio, who began this bloody fray?

150 BENVOLIO   Tybalt here slain, whom Romeo's hand did slay—
Romeo that spoke him° fair,° bid him bethink *to him / courteously*
How nice° the quarrel was, and urged withal° *trivial / also*
Your high displeasure. All this, utterèd
With gentle breath, calm look, knees humbly bowed,

155 Could not take° truce with the unruly spleen° *arrange / bitter mood*
Of Tybalt, deaf to peace, but that he tilts
With piercing steel at bold Mercutio's breast,
Who, all as hot, turns deadly point to point,
And, with a martial scorn, with one hand beats

160 Cold death aside,[2] and with the other sends
It back to Tybalt, whose dexterity

---

2. *with . . . aside:* The two would have been fighting either with daggers in or cloaks rolled about their second hand to ward off the other's weapon.

	Retorts° it. Romeo he cries aloud,	*Returns*
	"Hold, friends! Friends, part!" and, swifter than his tongue,	
	His agile arm beats down their fatal points,	
165	And twixt them rushes—underneath whose arm	
	An envious° thrust from Tybalt hit the life	*A malicious*
	Of stout° Mercutio. And then Tybalt fled—	*courageous*
	But by and by comes back to Romeo,	
	Who had but newly entertained° revenge,	*considered*
170	And to't they go like lightning, for ere I	
	Could draw to part them was stout Tybalt slain	
	And, as he fell, did Romeo turn and fly.	
	This is the truth, or let Benvolio die.	

CAPULET'S WIFE   He is a kinsman to the Montague:
175   Affection makes him false; he speaks not true.
        Some twenty of them fought in this black strife,
        And all those twenty could but kill one life.
        I beg for justice—which thou, Prince, must give.
        Romeo slew Tybalt; Romeo must not live.

180 PRINCE   Romeo slew him; he slew Mercutio;
        Who now the price of his° dear blood doth owe?   *(Mercutio's)*

MONTAGUE   Not Romeo, Prince; he was Mercutio's friend.
        His fault° concludes but what the law should end—   *offense*
        The life of Tybalt.

PRINCE   And for that offense
185   Immediately we do exile him hence.
        I have an interest in your hearts' proceeding;
        My blood° for your rude brawls doth lie a-bleeding.   *kinsman*
        But I'll amerce° you with so strong a fine   *penalize*
        That you shall all repent the loss of mine:
190   It will be deaf to pleading and excuses.
        Nor tears nor prayers shall purchase out° abuses;   *compensate for*
        Therefore use none. Let Romeo hence in haste;
        Else, when he is found, that hour is his last.
        Bear hence this body, and attend our will.
195   Mercy but murders, pardoning those that kill.   *Exeunt.*

3.2 (Q1 Scene 11)

Enter JULIET *alone.*

	JULIET Gallop apace,° you fiery-footed steeds,	*quickly*
	Towards Phoebus' lodging;[1] such a wagoner°	*charioteer*
	As Phaëton[2] would whip you to the west,	
	And bring in cloudy night immediately.	
5	Spread thy close° curtain, love-performing night,	*covering*
	That runaways'[3] eyes may wink,° and Romeo	*close*
	Leap to these arms, untalked of and unseen.	
	Lovers can see to do their amorous rites,	
	And by their own beauties; or, if love be blind,	
10	It best agrees with night. Come, civil° night,	*solemn*
	Thou sober-suited matron all in black,	

3.2 Location: Capulet's house.
1. Under the world to the west, where the sun god
Phoebus Apollo was imagined to rest with his fiery
chariot at night.
2. The son of Apollo, who rashly attempted to steer

his father's chariot across the sky. To save the earth
from scorching, Jupiter struck him down with a lightning bolt.
3. Either the runaway horses of the sun or roving
and curious vagabonds.

And learn me how to lose a winning match,[4]
Played for a pair of stainless maidenhoods.
Hood my unmanned° blood, bating[5] in my cheeks,   *untamed; virgin*
15   With thy black mantle, till strange° love grow bold;   *shy*
Think true love acted simple° modesty.   *mere; innocent*
Come, night; come, Romeo; come, thou day in night,
For thou wilt lie upon the wings of night
Whiter than new snow upon a raven's back.
20   Come, gentle night; come, loving, black-browed night,
Give me my Romeo; and, when I shall die,
Take him and cut him out in little stars,[6]
And he will make the face of heaven so fine
That all the world will be in love with night
25   And pay no worship to the garish sun.
Oh, I have bought the mansion of a love,
But not possessed it; and though I am sold,[7]
Not yet enjoyed. So tedious is this day
As is the night before some festival
30   To an impatient child that hath new robes
And may not wear them.

        Enter NURSE *with cords.*

                      Oh, here comes my nurse,
And she brings news, and every tongue that speaks
But Romeo's name speaks heavenly eloquence.
Now, Nurse, what news? What, hast thou there
The cords that Romeo bid thee fetch?
35 NURSE   Ay, ay, the cords.
JULIET   Ay me, what news? Why dost thou wring thy hands?
NURSE   Ah, welladay,° he's dead, he's dead, he's dead!   *alas*
We are undone, lady; we are undone.
Alack the day—he's gone, he's killed, he's dead!
JULIET   Can heaven be so envious?°   *spiteful; jealous*
40 NURSE   Romeo can,
Though heaven cannot. O Romeo, Romeo!
Whoever would have thought it? Romeo!
JULIET   What devil art thou that dost torment me thus?
This torture should be roared in dismal hell.
45   Hath Romeo slain himself? Say thou but "Ay,"
And that bare vowel "I" shall poison more
Than the death-darting eye of cockatrice;[8]
I am not I if there be such an "Ay,"
Or those eyes shut that makes thee answer "Ay."
50   If he be slain, say "Ay," or, if not, "No."
Brief sounds determine my weal° or woe.   *welfare*
NURSE   I saw the wound—I saw it with mine eyes,
God save the mark[9]—here on his manly breast.
A piteous corpse, a bloody, piteous corpse,
55   Pale, pale as ashes, all bedaubed in blood,

---

4. *match:* competition. A husband and a marriage ("match") are won by surrendering.
5. Fluttering like a restless falcon before its eyes are covered with a "hood" to calm it.
6. *Take . . . stars:* an imagined transformation, based on those in Ovid's *Metamorphoses*, whereby Romeo also dies and is immortalized. Also, "die" could mean

"have an orgasm."
7. *Oh . . . sold:* The image is inverted: first Juliet buys the mansion, and then she becomes the "sold" house.
8. A mythical serpent that kills by merely looking.
9. An apology for mentioning something unpleasant, but also emphasizing the fatal "mark" of the rapier.

All in gore° blood; I swoonèd at the sight. — *clotted*

JULIET   O break, my heart; poor bankrupt, break at once!
To prison,[1] eyes; ne'er look on liberty.
Vile earth,[2] to earth resign; end motion° here; — *movement; emotion*
60   And thou and Romeo press[3] one heavy° bier. — *weighty; sad*

NURSE   O Tybalt, Tybalt, the best friend I had!
O courteous Tybalt, honest° gentleman, — *honorable*
That ever I should live to see thee dead!

JULIET   What storm is this that blows so contrary?
65   Is Romeo slaughtered, and is Tybalt dead,
My dearest cousin and my dearer lord?
Then, dreadful trumpet, sound the general doom,[4]
For who is living if those two are gone?

NURSE   Tybalt is gone, and Romeo banishèd;
70   Romeo, that killed him, he is banishèd.

JULIET   O God, did Romeo's hand shed Tybalt's blood?

NURSE   It did, it did, alas the day, it did!

JULIET   O serpent heart, hid with° a flow'ring° face! — *by / lovely; benign*
Did ever dragon keep° so fair a cave? — *guard*
75   Beautiful tyrant, fiend angelical,
Dove-feathered raven, wolvish-ravening lamb,
Despisèd substance of divinest show,° — *appearance*
Just opposite to what thou justly° seem'st, — *precisely; rightfully*
A damnèd saint, an honorable villain.
80   O nature, what hadst thou to do[5] in hell
When thou didst bower[6] the spirit of a fiend
In mortal paradise of such sweet flesh?
Was ever book containing such vile matter
So fairly bound? Oh, that deceit should dwell
In such a gorgeous palace.

85   NURSE   There's no trust,
No faith, no honesty in men: all perjured,
All forsworn, all naught,° all dissemblers. — *wicked*
Ah, where's my man? Give me some aqua vitae.° — *brandy*
These griefs, these woes, these sorrows, make me old.
Shame come to Romeo.

90   JULIET   Blistered be thy tongue
For such a wish! He was not born to shame;
Upon his brow shame is ashamed to sit,
For 'tis a throne where honor may be crowned
Sole monarch of the universal earth.
95   Oh, what a beast was I to chide at him!

NURSE   Will you speak well of him that killed your cousin?

JULIET   Shall I speak ill of him that is my husband?
Ah, poor my° lord, what tongue shall smooth° thy name — *my poor / praise*
When I, thy three hours' wife, have mangled it?
100   But wherefore, villain, didst thou kill my cousin?
That villain cousin would have killed my husband.
Back, foolish tears, back to your native spring;
Your tributary[7] drops belong to woe,

---

1. Bankruptcy—to "break" financially—was punishable by imprisonment.
2. The despised body, echoing Ecclesiastes 12:7: "Then shall the dust return to the earth as it was."
3. Burden; embrace.
4. The Last Judgment announced with angels' trumpets.
5. What were you doing.
6. Lodge or enclose, suggesting a surrounding garden.
7. Tribute-paying; in-flowing.

Which you, mistaking, offer up to joy.[8]
105 My husband lives that Tybalt would have slain,
And Tybalt's dead that would have slain my husband:
All this is comfort. Wherefore° weep I, then?   *Why*
Some word there was, worser than Tybalt's death,
That murdered me; I would forget it fain,°   *gladly*
110 But, oh, it presses to my memory
Like damnèd guilty deeds to sinners' minds:
Tybalt is dead and Romeo banishèd.
That "banishèd"—that one word, "banishèd"—
Hath slain ten thousand Tybalts. Tybalt's death
115 Was woe enough if it had ended there;
Or, if sour woe delights in fellowship,
And needly° will be ranked with[9] other griefs,   *necessarily*
Why followed not, when she said, "Tybalt's dead,"
"Thy father" or "Thy mother"—nay, or both—
120 Which modern° lamentation might have moved?°   *ordinary / produced*
But with a rearward[1] following "Tybalt's death,"
"Romeo is banishèd"—to speak that word
Is father, mother, Tybalt, Romeo, Juliet,
All slain, all dead. "Romeo is banishèd"—
125 There is no end, no limit, measure, bound,
In that word's death; no words can that woe sound.°   *utter; fathom*
—Where is my father and my mother, Nurse?
NURSE   Weeping and wailing over Tybalt's corpse.
Will you go to them? I will bring you thither.
130 JULIET   Wash they his wounds with tears? Mine shall be spent,
When theirs are dry, for Romeo's banishment.
Take up those cords. Poor ropes, you are beguiled°—   *cheated*
Both you and I—for Romeo is exiled;
He made you for a highway to my bed,
135 But I, a maid, die maiden-widowèd.
Come, cords; come, Nurse; I'll to my wedding bed,
And death, not Romeo, take my maidenhead.
NURSE   Hie to your chamber. I'll find Romeo
To comfort you; I wot° well where he is.   *know*
140 Hark ye, your Romeo will be here at night.
I'll to him; he is hid at Laurence' cell.
JULIET   Oh, find him! Give this ring to my true knight,
And bid him come to take his last farewell.   *Exeunt.*

3.3 (Q1 Scene 12)

Enter FRIAR [LAURENCE].
FRIAR LAURENCE   Romeo, come forth, come forth, thou fear-
    ful man.
Affliction is enamored of thy parts,°   *qualities*
And thou art wedded to calamity.
    [*Enter* ROMEO.]
ROMEO   Father, what news? What is the Prince's doom?°   *sentence*
5 What sorrow craves acquaintance at my hand

---

8. Offer up to a joyful (and thus inappropriate) occasion.
9. Will be accompanied by.
1. *rearward*: rearguard action, with a pun on "afterword."
3.3 Location: Friar Laurence's cell.

That I yet know not?
FRIAR LAURENCE   Too familiar
Is my dear son with such sour company.
I bring thee tidings of the Prince's doom.
ROMEO   What less than doomsday is the Prince's doom?
10   FRIAR LAURENCE   A gentler judgment vanished° from his lips: escaped
Not body's death, but body's banishment.
ROMEO   Ha? Banishment? Be merciful; say "death,"
For exile hath more terror in his look,
Much more than death. Do not say "banishment."
15   FRIAR LAURENCE   Here from Verona art thou banishèd.
Be patient,° for the world is broad and wide.   able to endure
ROMEO   There is no world without° Verona walls   outside
But purgatory, torture, hell itself;
Hence banishèd is banished from the world,
20   And world's exile is death. Then "banishèd"
Is death mis-termed: calling death "banishèd,"
Thou cutt'st my head off with a golden ax,
And smilest upon the stroke that murders me.
FRIAR LAURENCE   Oh, deadly° sin! Oh, rude unthankfulness!   damnable
25   Thy fault our law calls death,° but the kind Prince,   a capital offense
Taking thy part, hath rushed° aside the law,   forced
And turned that black word "death" to "banishment."
This is dear mercy, and thou seest it not.
ROMEO   'Tis torture and not mercy! Heaven is here
30   Where Juliet lives—and every cat and dog
And little mouse, every unworthy thing,
Live here in heaven and may look on her,
But Romeo may not. More validity,°   health
More honorable state, more courtship,° lives   courtly state; wooing
35   In carrion flies than Romeo. They may seize
On the white wonder of dear Juliet's hand,
And steal immortal blessing from her lips,
Who even in pure and vestal° modesty   virginal
Still° blush, as thinking their own kisses¹ sin.   Always
40   This may flies do, when I from this must fly—
And sayest thou yet that exile is not death?
But Romeo may not; he is banishèd.
Flies may do this, but I from this must fly;
They are free men, but I am banishèd.
45   Hadst thou no poison mixed, no sharp-ground knife,
No sudden mean° of death—though ne'er so mean°—   method / ignoble
But "banishèd" to kill me? "Banishèd"?
O Friar, the damnèd use that word in hell;²
Howling attends it. How hast thou the heart,
50   Being a divine, a ghostly confessor,
A sin-absolver, and my friend professed,
To mangle me with that word "banishèd"?
FRIAR LAURENCE   Then, fond° madman, hear me a little speak.   foolish; infatuated
ROMEO   Oh, thou wilt speak again of banishment.
55   FRIAR LAURENCE   I'll give thee armor to keep off that word:
Adversity's sweet milk, philosophy,

---

1. Their touching each other in closing.   2. Because they are banished from heaven.

To comfort thee, though thou art banishèd.

ROMEO   Yet "banishèd"? Hang up° philosophy!   *Hang up = Hang*
Unless philosophy can make a Juliet,
60   Displant° a town, reverse a prince's doom,   *Uproot*
It helps not, it prevails not. Talk no more.

FRIAR LAURENCE   Oh, then I see that madmen have no ears.

ROMEO   How should they, when that wise men have no eyes?

FRIAR LAURENCE   Let me dispute° with thee of thy estate.°   *discuss / position*

65   ROMEO   Thou canst not speak of that thou dost not feel.
Wert thou as young as I, Juliet thy love,
An hour but° married, Tybalt murderèd,   *Only an hour*
Doting like me, and like me banishèd,
Then mightst thou speak; then mightst thou tear thy hair
70   And fall upon the ground, as I do now,
Taking the measure of an unmade grave.

           NURSE *knocks* [*within*].

FRIAR LAURENCE   Arise! One knocks. Good Romeo, hide
thyself.

ROMEO   Not I, unless the breath of heartsick groans
Mistlike enfold me from the search of eyes.

           Knock [*within*].

75   FRIAR LAURENCE   Hark, how they knock! —Who's there?
—Romeo, arise;
Thou wilt be taken! —Stay a while! —Stand up!
           [*Loud*] *knock* [*within*].
Run to my study. —By and by! —God's will,°   *By providence*
What simpleness° is this? —I come, I come!   *stupidity*
           Knock [*within*].
Who knocks so hard? Whence come you? What's your will?

80   NURSE [*within*]³   Let me come in, and you shall know my
errand.
I come from Lady Juliet.

           Enter NURSE.

FRIAR LAURENCE   Welcome, then.

NURSE   O holy Friar! Oh, tell me, holy Friar,
Where's my lady's lord? Where's Romeo?

FRIAR LAURENCE   There on the ground, with his own tears
made drunk.

85   NURSE   Oh, he is even° in my mistress' case,°   *exactly / condition; vagina*
Just in her case. Oh, woeful sympathy,
Piteous predicament! Even so lies she,
Blubb'ring and weeping, weeping and blubb'ring.
—Stand up, stand up! Stand an° you be a man!   *if*
90   For Juliet's sake, for her sake, rise and stand.
Why should you fall into so deep an O?°   *a groaning; a vagina*

ROMEO   Nurse—

NURSE   Ah, sir; ah, sir; death's the end of all.⁴

ROMEO   Spakest thou of Juliet? How is it with her?
Doth not she think me an old° murderer   *a practiced*
95   Now I have stained the childhood of our joy
With blood removed but little from her own?
Where is she? And how doth she? And what says

---

3. Behind one of the doors at the back of the stage,   4. A proverbial consolation.
representing the door of the cell.

My concealed lady° to our canceled° love?   secret wife / invalidated

NURSE Oh, she says nothing, sir, but weeps and weeps,
100 And now falls on her bed, and then starts up,
And Tybalt calls, and then on Romeo cries,
And then down falls again.
ROMEO   As if that name,
Shot from the deadly level° of a gun,   aim
Did murder her, as that name's cursèd hand
105 Murdered her kinsman. Oh, tell me, Friar, tell me,
In what vile part of this anatomy
Doth my name lodge? Tell me, that I may sack
The hateful mansion.
           [*He offers to stab himself.*][5]
FRIAR LAURENCE   Hold° thy desperate hand!   Restrain
Art thou a man? Thy form cries out thou art.
110 Thy tears are womanish; thy wild acts denote
The unreasonable° fury of a beast: incapable of reason
Unseemly° woman in a seeming man,   Inappropriate; immodest
And ill-beseeming beast in seeming both[6]—
Thou hast amazed me. By my holy order,
115 I thought thy disposition better tempered.
Hast thou slain Tybalt? Wilt thou slay thyself?
And slay thy lady, that in thy life lives,
By doing damnèd° hate upon thyself?   sinful
Why railest thou on thy birth, the heaven, and earth,
120 Since birth,° and heaven,° and earth,° all three, do meet   nobility / soul / body
In thee at once, which thou at once wouldst lose?
Fie, fie! Thou shamest thy shape, thy love, thy wit,
Which like a usurer abound'st in all,
And usest none in that true use indeed
125 Which should bedeck thy shape, thy love, thy wit.[7]
Thy noble shape is but a form° of wax,   figure
Digressing° from the valor of a man;   If it deviates
Thy dear love sworn but hollow perjury,
Killing that love which thou hast vowed to cherish;
130 Thy wit, that ornament° to shape and love,   necessary accessory
Misshapen° in the conduct° of them both,   Inept / management
Like powder in a skill-less soldier's flask,
Is set afire by thine own ignorance,
And thou dismembered with thine own defense.°   weapon
135 What, rouse thee, man! Thy Juliet is alive,
For whose dear sake thou wast but lately dead;
There art thou happy. Tybalt would kill thee,
But thou slewest Tybalt; there art thou happy.
The law that threatened death becomes thy friend
140 And turns it to exile; there art thou happy.
A pack of blessings light upon thy back;
Happiness courts thee in her best array;
But, like a mishavèd° and sullen wench,   misbehaved
Thou pouts upon thy fortune and thy love.

5. TEXTUAL COMMENT In Q1's version of this scene, a stage direction indicates that the Nurse *"snatches the dagger away"* from Romeo. See Digital Edition TC 9 (Second Quarto edited text).
6. An unnatural beast in seeming both man and unreasoning animal, or both man and woman.
7. *Thou shamest . . . wit:* You abound in looks, love, and intelligence ("wit"), but you do not use them judiciously and are therefore like a usurer who acquires money for its own sake, without putting it to good use.

145 Take heed, take heed, for such die miserable.
Go; get thee to thy love as was decreed;
Ascend her chamber; hence and comfort her.
But look thou stay not till the watch be set,[8]
For then thou canst not pass to Mantua,
150 Where thou shalt live till we can find a time
To blaze° your marriage, reconcile your friends,°   *make public / kin*
Beg pardon of the Prince, and call thee back
With twenty hundred thousand times more joy
Than thou went'st forth in lamentation.
155 —Go before, Nurse. Commend me to thy lady,
And bid her hasten all the house to bed,
Which heavy sorrow makes them apt unto.
Romeo is coming.
NURSE   O Lord, I could have stayed here all the night
160 To hear good counsel. Oh, what learning is!
My lord, I'll tell my lady you will come.
ROMEO   Do so, and bid my sweet prepare to chide.
NURSE   Here, sir: a ring she bid me give you, sir.
Hie you,° make haste, for it grows very late.   [*Exit.*]   *Hurry*
165 ROMEO   How well my comfort° is revived by this.   *happiness*
FRIAR LAURENCE   Go hence. Good night—and here stands°   *and on this depends*
all your state:
Either be gone before the watch be set,
Or, by the break of day, disguised from hence.
Sojourn in Mantua. I'll find out your man,
170 And he shall signify from time to time
Every good hap° to you that chances here.   *event*
Give me thy hand. 'Tis late. Farewell. Goodnight.
ROMEO   But that a joy past joy calls out on me,
It were a grief so brief° to part with thee.   *hastily*
175 Farewell.   *Exeunt.*

3.4 (Q1 Scene 13)

Enter old CAPULET, [CAPULET'S] WIFE, *and* PARIS.

CAPULET   Things have fall'n out, sir, so unluckily
That we have had no time to move° our daughter.   *persuade*
Look you, she loved her kinsman Tybalt dearly,
And so did I. Well, we were born to die.
5 'Tis very late; she'll not come down tonight.
I promise you, but for your company
I would have been abed an hour ago.
PARIS   These times of woe afford no times to woo.
—Madam, good night; commend me to your daughter.
10 CAPULET'S WIFE   I will, and know her mind early tomorrow.
Tonight she's mewed up to[1] her heaviness.°   *sadness*
CAPULET   Sir Paris, I will make a desperate tender°   *reckless offer*
Of my child's love. I think she will be ruled
In all respects by me; nay, more, I doubt it not.
15 —Wife, go you to her ere you go to bed,
Acquaint her here of my son Paris' love,
And bid her—mark you me?—on Wednesday next —

---

8. Until the guards take up their positions (at the city gates).

3.4 Location: Capulet's house.
1. Shut in with. The "mews" are hawks' housing.

But soft, what day is this?

PARIS   Monday, my lord.

CAPULET   Monday? Ha, ha! Well, Wednesday is too soon;

20   O'Thursday let it be; o'Thursday, tell her,
She shall be married to this noble earl.
—Will you be ready? Do you like this haste?
We'll keep° no great ado—a friend or two—   celebrate with
For, hark you, Tybalt being slain so late,°   recently

25   It may be thought we held° him carelessly,°   regarded / indifferently
Being our kinsman, if we revel much.
Therefore we'll have some half a dozen friends,
And there an end. But what say you to Thursday?

PARIS   My lord, I would° that Thursday were tomorrow.   wish

30   CAPULET   Well, get you gone; o'Thursday be it, then.
[to CAPULET'S WIFE] Go you to Juliet ere you go to bed.
Prepare her, wife, against° this wedding day.   for
—Farewell, my lord. —Light to my chamber, ho!
—Afore me,² it is so very late

35   That we may call it early by and by!
Goodnight.   Exeunt.

3.5 (Q1 Scene 14)

Enter ROMEO *and* JULIET *aloft.*

JULIET   Wilt thou be gone? It is not yet near day.
It was the nightingale, and not the lark,
That pierced the fearful hollow of thine ear.
Nightly she sings on yond pom'granate tree.

5   Believe me, love: it was the nightingale.

ROMEO   It was the lark, the herald of the morn,
No nightingale. Look, love, what envious° streaks   spiteful
Do lace the severing° clouds in yonder East.   parting
Night's candles are burnt out, and jocund day

10   Stands tiptoe on the misty mountain tops.
I must be gone and live, or stay and die.

JULIET   Yond light is not daylight—I know it, I—
It is some meteor that the sun exhales¹
To be to thee this night a torchbearer

15   And light thee on thy way to Mantua.
Therefore stay yet; thou need'st not to be gone.

ROMEO   Let me be ta'en, let me be put to death;
I am content, so° thou wilt have it so.   as long as
I'll say yon gray is not the morning's eye—

20   'Tis but the pale reflex° of Cynthia's° brow—   reflection / the moon's
Nor that is not the lark whose notes do beat
The vaulty heaven so high above our heads.
I have more care° to stay than will to go.   desire
Come, death, and welcome: Juliet wills it so.

25   How is't, my soul? Let's talk; it is not day.

JULIET   It is, it is! Hie hence; be gone. Away!
It is the lark that sings so out of tune,

---

2. *Afore me:* A mild oath.
3.5 Location: The upper acting area represents
Juliet's window or balcony. The main stage represents
Capulet's orchard until line 59, then Juliet's bedroom

from line 64.
1. Breathes. Meteors were thought to be impure
vapors that the sun had drawn up from the earth and
ignited and were usually considered bad omens.

Straining° harsh discords and unpleasing sharps.[2]   *Distorting; tuning up*
Some say the lark makes sweet division;°   *variations on a melody*
30 This doth not so, for she divideth us.
Some say the lark and loathèd toad change eyes;[3]
Oh, now I would they had changed voices too,
Since arm from arm that voice doth us affray,°   *frighten*
Hunting thee hence with hunt's-up[4] to the day.
35 Oh, now be gone! More light and light it grows.

ROMEO   More light and light, more dark and dark our woes.

    Enter NURSE.

NURSE   Madam!

JULIET   Nurse?

NURSE   Your lady mother is coming to your chamber.
40 The day is broke; be wary; look about.   [*Exit.*]

JULIET   Then, window, let day in and let life out.

ROMEO   Farewell, farewell. One kiss, and I'll descend.
    [*He goeth down.*][5]

JULIET   Art thou gone so, love, lord—ay, husband, friend?°   *lover*
I must hear from thee every day in the hour,
45 For in a minute there are many days—
Oh, by this count I shall be much in years
Ere I again behold my Romeo!

ROMEO   Farewell.
I will omit no opportunity
50 That may convey my greetings, love, to thee.

JULIET   Oh, think'st thou we shall ever meet again?

ROMEO   I doubt it not, and all these woes shall serve
For sweet discourses° in our times to come.   *conversations*

JULIET   O God, I have an ill-divining° soul!   *a misfortune-predicting*
55 Methinks I see thee, now thou art so low,
As one dead in the bottom of a tomb;
Either my eyesight fails, or thou lookest pale.

ROMEO   And trust me, love, in my eye so do you;
Dry sorrow drinks our blood.[6] Adieu, adieu.   *Exit.*

60 JULIET   O Fortune, Fortune, all men call thee fickle;
If thou art fickle, what dost thou with him
That is renowned for faith?° Be fickle, Fortune,   *fidelity*
For then I hope thou wilt not keep him long,
But send him back.

    Enter [CAPULET'S WIFE *below*].

CAPULET'S WIFE   Ho, daughter, are you up?

65 JULIET   Who is't that calls? —It is my lady mother.
Is she not down° so late or up so early?   *in bed*
What unaccustomed cause procures° her hither?   *brings*
    [JULIET *goeth down and enters below.*][7]

CAPULET'S WIFE   Why, how now, Juliet?

JULIET   Madam, I am not well.

CAPULET'S WIFE   Evermore weeping for your cousin's death?

---

2. Harsh sounds, too-high tones.
3. A folk explanation for the supposed ugliness of the lark's eyes and the beauty of the toad's. *change:* exchange.
4. Morning song used to wake the bride after the wedding night.
5. Romeo descends using the ladder of cords men-

tioned earlier.
6. *Dry . . . blood:* Each sigh supposedly cost the heart a drop of blood. Thus, the lovers are pale. *Dry:* Thirsty.
7. TEXTUAL COMMENT On the representation of this scene's location changes in Q2 and Q1, see Digital Edition TC 10 (Second Quarto edited text).

70 What, wilt thou wash him from his grave with tears?
An if thou couldst, thou couldst not make him live;
Therefore have done. Some grief shows much of love,
But much of grief shows still° some want° of wit.   *always / lack*
JULIET Yet let me weep for such a feeling° loss.   *profound*
75 CAPULET'S WIFE So shall you feel° the loss, but not the friend° *experience; touch / kin*
Which you weep for.
JULIET   Feeling so the loss,
I cannot choose but ever weep the friend.°   *lover*
CAPULET'S WIFE Well, girl, thou weep'st not so much for his
death
As that the villain lives which slaughtered him.
JULIET What villain, madam?
80 CAPULET'S WIFE   That same villain Romeo.
JULIET [aside] Villain and he be many miles asunder.
—God pardon; I do with all my heart,
And yet no man like° he doth grieve my heart.   *so much as; resembling*
CAPULET'S WIFE That is because the traitor murderer lives.
85 JULIET Ay, madam, from the reach of these my hands.
Would none but I might venge my cousin's death.
CAPULET'S WIFE We will have vengeance for it, fear thou not.
Then weep no more. I'll send to one in Mantua,
Where that same banished renegade doth live,
90 Shall give him such an unaccustomed dram
That he shall soon keep Tybalt company;
And then I hope thou wilt be satisfied.°   *sufficiently avenged*
JULIET Indeed, I never shall be satisfied
With Romeo till I behold him—dead—
95 Is my poor heart[8] so for a kinsman vexed.
Madam, if you could find out but a man
To bear a poison, I would temper° it   *mix; dilute*
That Romeo should, upon receipt thereof,
Soon sleep in quiet. Oh, how my heart abhors
100 To hear him named, and cannot come to him—
To wreak the love I bore my cousin
Upon his body that hath slaughtered him.
CAPULET'S WIFE Find thou the means, and I'll find such a man.
But now I'll tell thee joyful tidings, girl.
105 JULIET And joy comes well in such a needy time.
What are they, beseech your ladyship?
CAPULET'S WIFE Well, well, thou hast a careful° father, child;   *solicitous*
One who, to put thee from thy heaviness,
Hath sorted out a sudden° day of joy   *chosen an immediate*
110 That thou expects not, nor I looked not for.
JULIET Madam, in happy° time. What day is that?   *at a fortunate*
CAPULET'S WIFE Marry, my child, early next Thursday morn,
The gallant, young, and noble gentleman,
The County Paris, at Saint Peter's Church
115 Shall happily make thee there a joyful bride!
JULIET Now, by Saint Peter's Church—and Peter, too—
He shall not make me there a joyful bride!
I wonder° at this haste, that I must wed   *am astonished*

---

8. *till . . . heart:* Juliet allows her mother to understand that she will not be satisfied "till I behold him dead,"
while privately meaning that until she beholds him, "dead is my poor heart."

Ere he that should be husband comes to woo.
120 I pray you tell my lord and father, madam,
I will not marry yet—and when I do, I swear
It shall be Romeo, whom you know I hate,
Rather than Paris. These are news indeed!

CAPULET'S WIFE   Here comes your father; tell him so
yourself,
125 And see how he will take it at your hands.

Enter CAPULET *and* NURSE.

CAPULET   When the sun sets, the earth doth drizzle° dew; *weep out*
But for the sunset of my brother's son
It rains downright.
How now? A conduit,° girl? What, still in tears? *fountain*
130 Evermore show'ring? In one little body
Thou counterfeits a bark,° a sea, a wind— *represent a ship*
For still thy eyes, which I may call the sea,
Do ebb and flow with tears; the bark thy body is,
Sailing in this salt flood, the winds thy sighs,
135 Who,° raging with thy tears and they with them, *Which*
Without a sudden calm will overset
Thy tempest-tossèd body. —How now, wife,
Have you delivered to her our decree?

CAPULET'S WIFE   Ay, sir, but she will none,° she gives you *not agree*
thanks.
140 I would the fool° were married to her grave. *peevish child*

CAPULET   Soft! Take me with you;[9] take me with you, wife.
How? Will she none? Doth she not give us thanks?
Is she not proud?° Doth she not count her blessed, *gratified*
Unworthy as she is, that we have wrought° *contrived for*
145 So worthy a gentleman to be her bride?° *bridegroom*

JULIET   Not proud you have, but thankful that you have.
Proud can I never be of what I hate,
But thankful even for hate° that is meant love.° *a hateful thing / as love*

CAPULET   How, how, how, how? Chopped logic?° What is this? *Mere sophistry*
150 "Proud," and "I thank you," and "I thank you not,"
And yet "not proud," mistress minion,° you? *spoiled child*
Thank me no thankings, nor proud me no prouds,
But fettle° your fine joints 'gainst° Thursday next *prepare / for*
To go with Paris to Saint Peter's Church,
155 Or I will drag thee on a hurdle[1] thither.
Out,[2] you green-sickness carrion! Out, you baggage,
You tallow face!

CAPULET'S WIFE   Fie, fie! What, are you mad?

JULIET   Good father, I beseech you on my knees,
Hear me with patience but to speak a word.

160 CAPULET   Hang thee, young baggage, disobedient wretch!
I tell thee what: get thee to church o'Thursday,
Or never after look me in the face.
Speak not; reply not; do not answer me.
My fingers itch. —Wife, we scarce thought us blessed
165 That God had lent us but this only child,
But now I see this one is one too much,

---

9. Not so fast, let me understand you. to execution.
1. A sledge used to draw traitors through the streets 2. An expression of disgust and impatience.

And that we have a curse in having her.
Out on her, hilding!°   *hussy*
NURSE   God in heaven bless her!
You are to blame, my lord, to rate° her so.   *berate*
170 CAPULET And why, my Lady Wisdom? Hold your tongue,
Good Prudence. Smatter° with your gossips.° Go!   *Chatter / cronies*
NURSE I speak no treason.
CAPULET   Oh, God gi' good e'en!°   *(for God's sake)*
NURSE May not one speak?
CAPULET   Peace, you mumbling fool!
Utter your gravity° o'er a gossip's bowl,°   *wisdom / drinking bowl*
For here we need it not.
175 CAPULET'S WIFE   You are too hot.°   *irascible; rash*
CAPULET God's bread,° it makes me mad!   *By the communion bread*
Day, night, hour, tide, time, work, play,
Alone, in company—still my care° hath been   *business*
To have her matched; and, having now provided
180 A gentleman of noble parentage,
Of fair demesnes,° youthful, and nobly lined,°   *estates / descended*
Stuffed, as they say, with honorable parts,°   *qualities*
Proportioned as one's thought would wish a man,[3]
And then to have a wretched, puling fool,
185 A whining mammet° in her fortune's tender,[4]   *puppet*
To answer, "I'll not wed; I cannot love;
I am too young; I pray you, pardon me."
—But, an you will not wed, I'll pardon you:°   *excuse you (to leave)*
Graze where you will, you shall not house with me!
190 Look to't; think on't; I do not use° to jest.   *make it customary*
Thursday is near. Lay hand on heart;[5] advise.°   *consider*
An you be mine, I'll give you to my friend;
An you be not, hang, beg, starve, die in the streets—
For, by my soul, I'll ne'er acknowledge thee,
195 Nor what is mine shall never do thee good,
Trust to't. Bethink you; I'll not be forsworn.   *Exit.*
JULIET Is there no pity sitting in the clouds
That sees into the bottom of my grief?
O sweet my° mother, cast me not away!   *my sweet*
200 Delay this marriage for a month, a week—
Or, if you do not, make the bridal bed
In that dim monument° where Tybalt lies.   *sepulcher*
CAPULET'S WIFE Talk not to me, for I'll not speak a word.
Do as thou wilt, for I have done with thee.   *Exit.*
205 JULIET O God! O Nurse, how shall this be prevented?
My husband is on earth, my faith° in heaven.   *marriage vows*
How shall that faith return again to earth
Unless that husband send it me from heaven
By leaving earth?[6] Comfort me; counsel me!
210 Alack, alack, that heaven should practice stratagems
Upon so soft a subject as myself!
What say'st thou? Hast thou not a word of joy?

---

3. Shaped as handsomely as you can imagine.
4. When good fortune is offered her.
5. Ascertain your feelings.

6. *How . . . earth:* How can I swear marriage vows
again unless Romeo dies first, thus releasing me from
my vows to him?

Some comfort, Nurse!

NURSE   Faith, here it is.
Romeo is banished, and all the world to nothing[7]
215   That he dares ne'er come back to challenge° you;   *claim*
Or, if he do, it needs must be by stealth.
Then, since the case so stands as now it doth,
I think it best you married with the County.
Oh, he's a lovely gentleman!
220   Romeo's a dishclout° to him. An eagle, madam,   *dishcloth*
Hath not so green, so quick, so fair an eye
As Paris hath. Beshrew° my very heart,   *Curse*
I think you are happy° in this second match,   *lucky*
For it excels your first—or, if it did not,
225   Your first is dead, or 'twere as good he were
As living here and you no use of him.

JULIET   Speak'st thou from thy heart?

NURSE   And from my soul, too; else beshrew them both.

JULIET   Amen.

230 NURSE   What?

JULIET   Well, thou hast comforted me marvelous much.
Go in and tell my lady I am gone,
Having displeased my father, to Laurence' cell
To make confession and to be absolved.

235 NURSE   Marry, I will, and this is wisely done.   [*Exit.*]

JULIET   Ancient damnation![8] O most wicked fiend!
Is it more sin to wish me thus forsworn,
Or to dispraise my lord with that same tongue
Which she hath praised him with, above compare,
240   So many thousand times? Go, counselor;
Thou and my bosom° henceforth shall be twain.°   *heart's contents / divided*
I'll to the Friar to know his remedy.
If all else fail, myself have power to die.   *Exit.*

4.1 (Q1 Scene 15)
Enter FRIAR [LAURENCE] *and County* PARIS.

FRIAR LAURENCE   On Thursday, sir? The time is very short.

PARIS   My father Capulet will have it so,
And I am nothing slow[1] to slack his haste.

FRIAR LAURENCE   You say you do not know the lady's mind?
5   Uneven is the course;[2] I like it not.

PARIS   Immoderately she weeps for Tybalt's death,
And therefore have I little talk of love,
For Venus smiles not in a house of tears.
Now, sir, her father counts it dangerous
10   That she do give her sorrow so much sway,
And in his wisdom hastes our marriage
To stop the inundation of her tears,
Which, too much minded° by herself alone,   *brooded over*
May be put from her by society.°   *company*
15   Now do you know the reason of this haste.

---

7. *all . . . nothing*: it's a sure bet.
8. Damnable old woman (with a hint of "original sin").
4.1 Location: Friar Laurence's cell.

1. Not reluctant; not trying to drag behind him.
2. The plan is irregular; this is a tricky road to follow.

FRIAR LAURENCE [*aside*]   I would I knew not why it should be
   slowed.
       Enter JULIET.
  —Look, sir, here comes the lady toward my cell.
PARIS   Happily met, my lady and my wife.
JULIET   That may be, sir, when I may be a wife.

20 PARIS   That "may be" must be, love, on Thursday next.
JULIET   What must be shall be.
FRIAR LAURENCE   That's a certain text.
PARIS   Come you to make confession to this father?
JULIET   To answer that, I should confess to you.
PARIS   Do not deny to him that you love me.

25 JULIET   I will confess to you that I love him.
PARIS   So will ye, I am sure, that you love me.
JULIET   If I do so, it will be of more price°   *value*
   Being spoke behind your back than to your face.
PARIS   Poor soul, thy face is much abused with tears.

30 JULIET   The tears have got small victory by that,
   For it was bad enough before their spite.°   *injury*
PARIS   Thou wrong'st it more than tears with that report.
JULIET   That is no slander, sir, which is a truth;
   And what I spake, I spake it to my face.

35 PARIS   Thy face is mine, and thou hast slandered it.
JULIET   It may be so, for it is not mine own.[3]
  —Are you at leisure, holy Father, now,
   Or shall I come to you at evening mass?
FRIAR LAURENCE   My leisure serves me, pensive° daughter,   *sorrowful*
   now.

40 —My lord, we must entreat the time alone.
PARIS   God shield° I should disturb devotion.   *forbid*
  —Juliet, on Thursday early will I rouse ye;
   Till then, adieu, and keep this holy kiss.   *Exit.*
JULIET   Oh, shut the door, and, when thou hast done so,

45 Come weep with me—past hope, past care, past help.
FRIAR LAURENCE   O Juliet, I already know thy grief;°   *grievous situation*
   It strains me past the compass° of my wits.   *limit*
   I hear thou must—and nothing may prorogue° it—   *postpone*
   On Thursday next be married to this County.

50 JULIET   Tell me not, Friar, that thou hearest of this
   Unless thou tell me how I may prevent it.
   If in thy wisdom thou canst give no help,
   Do thou but call my resolution wise,
   And with this knife I'll help it presently.°   *immediately*

55 God joined my heart and Romeo's, thou our hands,
   And ere this hand, by thee to Romeo's sealed,
   Shall be the label[4] to another deed,
   Or my true heart with treacherous revolt
   Turn to another, this shall slay them both.

60 Therefore, out of thy long-experienced time,
   Give me some present counsel, or behold,
      [*She draws a knife.*]

---

3. Because it belongs to Romeo; also because Juliet, in her ambiguous replies, is not showing Paris her true face.

4. Ribbon attaching a seal to a legal document (deed), and so a pledge confirming another marriage.

Twixt my extremes° and me, this bloody knife | *extreme difficulties*
Shall play the umpire, arbitrating that
Which the commission° of thy years and art° | *authority / learning*
65 Could to no issue of true honor bring.
Be not so long to speak; I long to die
If what thou speak'st speak not of remedy.

FRIAR LAURENCE   Hold, daughter! I do spy a kind of hope,
Which craves as desperate° an execution[5] | *reckless*
70 As that is desperate° which we would prevent. | *hopeless*
If, rather than to marry County Paris,
Thou hast the strength of will to slay thyself,
Then is it likely thou wilt undertake
A thing like death to chide away this shame,
75 That cop'st° with death himself to scape from it.° | *Who wrestles / (shame)*
An if thou darest, I'll give thee remedy.

JULIET   Oh, bid me leap, rather than marry Paris,
From off the battlements of any tower,
Or walk in thievish° ways, or bid me lurk | *thief-infested*
80 Where serpents are; chain me with roaring bears;
Or hide me nightly in a charnel house,° | *burial vault*
O'ercovered quite with dead men's rattling bones,
With reeky° shanks and yellow chapless[6] skulls; | *foully damp*
Or bid me go into a new-made grave,
85 And hide me with a dead man in his shroud—
Things that, to hear them told, have made me tremble—
And I will do it without fear or doubt° | *dread; hesitation*
To live an unstained wife to my sweet love.

FRIAR LAURENCE   Hold, then. Go home; be merry; give consent
90 To marry Paris. Wednesday is tomorrow.
Tomorrow night look° that thou lie alone; | *be sure*
Let not the Nurse lie with thee in thy chamber.
Take thou this vial, being then in bed,
And this distilling° liquor drink thou off, | *permeating*
95 When presently through all thy veins shall run
A cold and drowsy humor°—for no pulse | *bodily fluid*
Shall keep his° native progress but surcease;° | *its / cease*
No warmth, no breath shall testify thou livest;
The roses in thy lips and cheeks shall fade
100 To wanny° ashes; thy eyes' windows° fall | *pale / lids*
Like death when he shuts up the day of life;
Each part, deprived of supple government,° | *control of movement*
Shall stiff and stark and cold appear, like death—
And in this borrowed likeness of shrunk death
105 Thou shalt continue two-and-forty hours,
And then awake as from a pleasant sleep.
Now, when the bridegroom in the morning comes
To rouse thee from thy bed, there art thou dead.
Then, as the manner of our country is,
110 In thy best robes, uncovered on the bier,
Be borne to burial in thy kindred's grave—
Thou shalt be borne to that same ancient vault
Where all the kindred of the Capulets lie.
In the meantime, against° thou shalt awake, | *in preparation for when*

---

5. A performance; a killing.   6. Without lower jaws.

115 Shall Romeo by my letters know our drift;°   *scheme*
    And hither shall he come, and he and I
    Will watch° thy waking, and that very night   *keep vigil for*
    Shall Romeo bear thee hence to Mantua,
    And this shall free thee from this present shame,
120 If no inconstant toy° nor womanish fear   *fickle whim*
    Abate thy valor in the acting it.
JULIET   Give me, give me—oh, tell not me of fear!
FRIAR LAURENCE   Hold! Get you gone; be strong and
    prosperous
    In this resolve. I'll send a friar with speed
125 To Mantua, with my letters° to thy lord.   *letter*
JULIET   Love give me strength, and strength shall help afford.
    Farewell, dear Father.   *Exeunt.*

4.2 (Q1 Scene 16)

Enter Father CAPULET, [CAPULET'S WIFE,] NURSE,
and two or three SERVINGMEN.

CAPULET [*to* FIRST SERVINGMAN, *giving him a paper*]   So many
    guests invite as here are writ.   [*Exit* FIRST SERVINGMAN.]
    [*to* SECOND SERVINGMAN] Sirrah, go hire me twenty cun-
    ning° cooks.   *skillful*
SECOND SERVINGMAN   You shall have none ill, sir, for I'll try°   *test*
    if they can lick their fingers.
5 CAPULET   How, canst thou try them so?
SECOND SERVINGMAN   Marry, sir, 'tis an ill cook that cannot
    lick his own fingers; therefore he that cannot lick his fingers
    goes not with me.
CAPULET   Go! Be gone.
10 We shall be much unfurnished° for this time.   *unprepared*
                 [*Exit* SECOND SERVINGMAN.]
    —What, is my daughter gone to Friar Laurence?
NURSE   Ay, forsooth.
CAPULET   Well, he may chance to do some good on her.
    A peevish, self-willed harlotry it is.[1]
    Enter JULIET.
15 NURSE   See where she comes from shrift° with merry look.   *absolution*
CAPULET   How now, my headstrong, where have you been
    gadding?
JULIET   Where I have learnt me to repent the sin
    Of disobedient opposition
    To you and your behests, and am enjoined
20 By holy Laurence to fall prostrate here
    To beg your pardon.
          [*She kneels down.*]
                 Pardon, I beseech you.
    Henceforward I am ever ruled by you.
CAPULET   —Send for the County! Go tell him of this.
    I'll have this knot knit up tomorrow morning.
25 JULIET   I met the youthful lord at Laurence' cell,
    And gave him what becomèd° love I might,   *becoming; suitable*
    Not stepping o'er the bounds of modesty.
CAPULET   Why, I am glad on't!° This is well. Stand up!   *of it*

4.2 Location: Capulet's house.   1. An obstinate, self-willed brat she is.

This is as't should be. —Let me see the County;
30 Ay, marry, go, I say, and fetch him hither.
Now, afore God, this reverend holy friar—
All our whole city is much bound to him.
JULIET   Nurse, will you go with me into my closet°   *chamber*
To help me sort such needful ornaments
35 As you think fit to furnish me tomorrow?
CAPULET'S WIFE   No, not till Thursday; there is time enough.
CAPULET   Go, Nurse; go with her. We'll to church tomorrow.
                         Exeunt [JULIET *and* NURSE].
CAPULET'S WIFE   We shall be short in our provision:
'Tis now near night.
CAPULET   Tush, I will stir about,
40 And all things shall be well, I warrant thee, wife.
Go thou to Juliet; help to deck up her.
I'll not to bed tonight. Let me alone;
I'll play the housewife for this once. —What ho!
—They are all forth. Well, I will walk myself
45 To County Paris to prepare up him
Against tomorrow. My heart is wondrous light
Since this same wayward girl is so reclaimed.[2]   *Exeunt.*

4.3 (Q1 Scene 17)
Enter JULIET *and* NURSE.
JULIET   Ay, those attires are best. But, gentle Nurse,
I pray thee leave me to myself tonight,
For I have need of many orisons°   *prayers*
To move the heavens to smile upon my state,
5 Which, well thou knowest, is cross° and full of sin.   *adverse*
                         Enter [CAPULET'S WIFE].
CAPULET'S WIFE   What, are you busy, ho? Need you my help?
JULIET   No, madam. We have culled such necessaries
As are behooveful° for our state° tomorrow.   *needful / ceremony*
So please° you, let me now be left alone,   *If it pleases*
10 And let the Nurse this night sit up with you,
For I am sure you have your hands full all
In this so sudden business.
CAPULET'S WIFE   Good night.
Get thee to bed and rest, for thou hast need.
JULIET   Farewell.   *Exeunt* [CAPULET'S WIFE *and* NURSE].
                         God knows when we shall meet again.
15 I have a faint cold fear thrills° through my veins,   *pierces*
That almost freezes up the heat of life.
I'll call them back again to comfort me.
—Nurse! —What should she do here?
My dismal° scene I needs must act alone.   *calamitous*
20 Come, vial.
What if this mixture do not work at all?
Shall I be married, then, tomorrow morning?
No, no, this shall forbid it. [*She places a knife beside her.*] Lie
    thou there.
What if it be a poison which the Friar

---

2. Reformed; claimed in marriage.   4.3 Location: Scene continues.

25 Subtly hath ministered to have me dead,
Lest in this marriage he should be dishonored
Because he married me before to Romeo?
I fear it is—and yet methinks it should not,°   *not be*
For he hath still° been tried° a holy man.   *always / proved*
30 How, if when I am laid into the tomb,
I wake before the time that Romeo
Come to redeem me? There's a fearful point!
Shall I not then be stifled in the vault,
To whose foul mouth no healthsome air breathes in,
35 And there die, strangled,° ere my Romeo comes?   *suffocated*
Or, if I live, is it not very like°   *likely*
The horrible conceit of death and night,
Together with the terror of the place,
As° in a vault, an ancient receptacle   *As it is*
40 Where, for this many hundred years, the bones
Of all my buried ancestors are packed—
Where bloody Tybalt, yet but green° in earth,   *newly*
Lies fest'ring in his shroud—where, as they say,
At some hours in the night spirits resort—
45 Alack, alack! Is it not like that I,
So early waking, what with loathsome smells
And shrieks like mandrakes[1] torn out of the earth
That living mortals, hearing them, run mad—
Oh, if I wake, shall I not be distraught,
50 Environèd with all these hideous fears,
And madly play with my forefathers' joints,
And pluck the mangled Tybalt from his shroud,
And, in this rage,° with some great kinsman's bone,   *insanity*
As with a club, dash out my desp'rate brains?
55 Oh, look! Methinks I see my cousin's ghost,
Seeking out Romeo that did spit his body
Upon a rapier's point. —Stay, Tybalt, stay!
—Romeo, Romeo, Romeo! Here's drink. I drink to thee.
    [*She drinks from the vial and falls upon her bed*
    within the curtains.]

4.4 (Q1 Scene 17 [continued])
Enter [CAPULET'S WIFE] *and* NURSE.
CAPULET'S WIFE   Hold! Take these keys and fetch more spices,
    Nurse.
NURSE   They call for dates and quinces in the pastry.°   *pastry kitchen*
    Enter old CAPULET.
CAPULET   Come, stir, stir, stir! The second cock hath crowed;
    The curfew bell[1] hath rung; 'tis three o'clock!
5   Look to the baked meats, good Angelica;[2]
    Spare not for cost.
NURSE   Go, you cotquean,° go!   *old housewife*
    Get you to bed. Faith, you'll be sick tomorrow
    For this night's watching.°   *wakefulness*

---

1. Plants with forked roots thought to resemble a man. Popular belief held that they uttered a death- or madness-producing shriek upon being pulled up.
4.4 Location: Scene continues.

1. Also rung at daybreak.
2. It is unclear whether Capulet refers to his wife or the Nurse.

CAPULET   No, not a whit. What, I have watched ere now

10   All night for lesser cause, and ne'er been sick!

CAPULET'S WIFE   Ay, you have been a mouse-hunt° in your time,   *skirt chaser*

But I will watch° you from such watching now.   *guard*

Exeunt [CAPULET'S WIFE] *and* NURSE.

CAPULET   A jealous-hood,³ a jealous-hood!

Enter three or four [SERVINGMEN] *with spits and logs
and baskets.*

—Now, fellow, what is there?

FIRST SERVINGMAN   Things for the cook, sir, but I know not
what.

CAPULET   Make haste, make haste!   [*Exit* FIRST SERVINGMAN.]

15   —Sirrah, fetch drier logs.

Call Peter; he will show thee where they are.

SECOND SERVINGMAN   I have a head, sir, that will find out logs,⁴

And never trouble Peter for the matter.

[*Exit* SECOND SERVINGMAN.]

CAPULET   Mass,° and well said! A merry whoreson,° ha!   *By the mass / rogue*

20   Thou shalt be loggerhead.° Good Father, 'tis day!   *wooden-headed*

The County will be here with music straight,

For so he said he would.

Play music [*within*].

I hear him near!

Nurse! Wife! What ho! What, Nurse, I say!

Enter NURSE.

Go waken Juliet; go and trim her up.

25   I'll go and chat with Paris. Hie, make haste,

Make haste! The bridegroom, he is come already!

Make haste, I say!

NURSE   Mistress! What, Mistress Juliet! —Fast,° I warrant   *Asleep*

her, she—

Why, lamb! Why, lady! Fie, you slug-a-bed!

30   Why, love, I say! Madam! Sweetheart! Why, bride!

What, not a word? You take your pennyworth's° now;   *bits (of sleep)*

Sleep for a week—for the next night, I warrant,

The County Paris hath set up his rest⁵

That you shall rest but little, God forgive me.

35   Marry, and amen! —How sound is she asleep!

I needs must wake her. —Madam, madam, madam!

Ay, let the County take° you in your bed: *catch; sexually possess*

He'll fright you up, i'faith. Will it not be?

[*She draws back the curtains.*]

What, dressed and in your clothes, and down again?

40   I must needs wake you. Lady, lady, lady!

Alas, alas! —Help, help! My lady's dead!

Oh, welladay,° that ever I was born!   *alas*

Some aqua vitae, ho! My lord! My lady!

[*Enter* CAPULET'S WIFE.]

CAPULET'S WIFE   What noise is here?

NURSE   Oh, lamentable day!

CAPULET'S WIFE   What is the matter?

45   NURSE   Look! Look! Oh, heavy day!

---

3. Jealousy; jealous woman.

4. I have a good head for finding things, so I can
certainly find the logs; my head knows all about logs

(I am a blockhead).

5. *hath ... rest:* has resolved (from staking everything in the card game primero), with bawdy pun.

CAPULET'S WIFE   O me, O me! —My child, my only life!
Revive, look up, or I will die with thee!
—Help, help! Call help!

Enter [CAPULET].

CAPULET   For shame, bring Juliet forth! Her lord is come.
50 NURSE   She's dead, deceased; she's dead, alack the day!
CAPULET'S WIFE   Alack the day! She's dead, she's dead, she's
dead!
CAPULET   Ha! Let me see her. Out,° alas, she's cold!   *Woe*
Her blood is settled,° and her joints are stiff;   *motionless*
Life and these lips have long been separated.
55   Death lies on her like an untimely frost
Upon the sweetest flower of all the field.
NURSE   Oh, lamentable day!
CAPULET'S WIFE   Oh, woeful time!
CAPULET   Death, that hath ta'en her hence to make me wail,
Ties up my tongue and will not let me speak.

Enter FRIAR [LAURENCE] *and the County* [PARIS].

60   FRIAR LAURENCE   Come, is the bride ready to go to church?
CAPULET   Ready to go, but never to return.
—O son, the night before thy wedding day
Hath Death lain with thy wife. There she lies,
Flower as she was, deflowered by him.
65   Death is my son-in-law; Death is my heir;
My daughter he hath wedded. I will die
And leave him all. Life, living,° all is Death's.   *property*
PARIS [*as to* JULIET]   Have I thought,° love, to see this   *expected*
morning's face,
And doth it give me such a sight as this?
70   CAPULET'S WIFE   Accursed, unhappy, wretched, hateful day!
Most miserable hour that e'er time saw
In lasting labor of his pilgrimage!
But one, poor one, one poor and loving child,
But one thing to rejoice and solace in—
75   And cruel death hath catched it from my sight.
NURSE   Oh, woe! Oh, woeful, woeful, woeful day!
Most lamentable day! Most woeful day
That ever, ever I did yet behold!
Oh, day! Oh, day! Oh, day! Oh, hateful day!
80   Never was seen so black a day as this.
Oh, woeful day! Oh, woeful day!
PARIS   Beguiled,° divorcèd, wrongèd, spited,° slain!   *Cheated / injured*
Most detestable death, by thee beguiled,
By cruel, cruel thee quite overthrown.
85   O love, O life—not life, but love in death.
CAPULET   Despised, distressed, hated, martyred, killed!
Uncomfortable° time, why cam'st thou now   *Comfortless*
To murder, murder our solemnity?°   *festivity*
O child, O child, my soul and not my child,[6]
90   Dead art thou. Alack, my child is dead,
And with my child my joys are burièd.
FRIAR LAURENCE   Peace, ho, for shame! Confusion's° care   *Destruction's*
lives not

---

6. *not my child:* because dead and only a corpse.

In these confusions.° Heaven and yourself   *commotions*
Had part in this fair maid; now heaven hath all,
95   And all the better is it for the maid.
Your part in her you could not keep from death,
But heaven keeps his part in eternal life.
The most you sought was her promotion,°   *social advancement*
For 'twas your heaven° she should be advanced;   *highest ambition*
100 And weep ye now, seeing she is advanced
Above the clouds, as high as heaven itself?
Oh, in this love you love your child so ill
That you run mad, seeing that she is well.
She's not well married that lives married long,
105 But she's best married that dies married young.
Dry up your tears, and stick your rosemary[7]
On this fair corpse; and, as the custom is,
And in her best array, bear her to church.
For, though some nature° bids us all lament,   *affection*
110 Yet nature's tears are reason's merriment.°   *laughable idiocy*
CAPULET   All things that we ordainèd festival
Turn from their office° to black funeral: *due function*
Our instruments to melancholy bells,
Our wedding cheer° to a sad burial feast,   *fare*
115 Our solemn° hymns to sullen° dirges change;   *ceremonial / mournful*
Our bridal flowers serve for a buried corpse,
And all things change them to the contrary.
FRIAR LAURENCE Sir, go you in; and, madam, go with him;
And go, Sir Paris. Everyone prepare
120 To follow this fair corpse unto her grave.
The heavens do lour° upon you for some ill;°   *hang threatening / offense*
Move° them no more by crossing their high will.   *Anger*

Exeunt [all but the NURSE].

[*Enter three* MUSICIANS.]
FIRST MUSICIAN Faith, we may put° up our pipes and be gone.   *pack*
NURSE Honest good fellows—ah, put up, put up!
125 For well you know this is a pitiful case.
FIRST MUSICIAN Ay, by my troth, the case may be amended.[8]

*Exit [*NURSE].

*Enter [*PETER].
PETER Musicians! O musicians! "Heart's Ease"!° "Heart's   *(popular song)*
Ease"! Oh, an you will have me live, play "Heart's Ease"!
FIRST MUSICIAN Why "Heart's Ease"?
130 PETER O musicians, because my heart itself plays "My heart
is full." Oh, play me some merry dump° to comfort me.   *sad tune*
MUSICIANS Not a dump, we! 'Tis no time to play now.
PETER You will not, then?
FIRST MUSICIAN No.
135 PETER I will, then, give it you soundly.°   *thoroughly; in sound*
FIRST MUSICIAN What will you give us?
PETER No money, on my faith, but the gleek.[9] I will give you
the minstrel.[1]

---

7. Traditionally, a symbol of remembrance.
8. Things could be better; the instrument case can be repaired.
9. To "give the gleek" was to make a fool of or play a trick on.
1. I will insultingly call you a minstrel.

FIRST MUSICIAN   Then will I give you the serving-creature.

140   PETER   Then will I lay the serving-creature's dagger on your
pate. I will carry° no crotchets;[2] I'll re you, I'll fa you, do you   *bear; sing*
note° me?   *heed*

FIRST MUSICIAN   An you re us and fa us, you note° us.   *give notes to*

SECOND MUSICIAN   Pray you, put up your dagger, and put out°   *show; quench*
145   your wit.

PETER   Then have at you with my wit! I will dry-beat° you with   *thrash*
an iron° wit, and put up my iron dagger. Answer[3] me like men.   *a merciless*
[*Sings.*]   When griping griefs the heart doth wound,
Then music with her silver sound[4]—

150   Why "silver sound"? Why "music with her silver sound"?
What say you, Simon Catling?[5]

FIRST MUSICIAN   Marry, sir, because silver hath a sweet sound.

PETER   Prates!° What say you, Hugh Rebeck?[6]   *Chatter*

SECOND MUSICIAN   I say "silver sound," because musicians
155   sound for silver.

PETER   Prates, too! What say you, James Soundpost?[7]

THIRD MUSICIAN   Faith, I know not what to say.

PETER   Oh, I cry you mercy!° You are the singer; I will say for   *beg your pardon*
you. It is "music with her silver sound," because musicians
160   have no gold for sounding.[8]
[*Sings.*]   Then music with her silver sound
With speedy help doth lend redress.   *Exit.*

FIRST MUSICIAN   What a pestilent knave is this same!

SECOND MUSICIAN   Hang him, jack! Come, we'll in here, tarry
165   for the mourners, and stay° dinner.   *Exeunt.*   *await*

5.1 (Q1 Scene 18)

Enter ROMEO.

ROMEO   If I may trust the flattering° truth of sleep,   *encouraging*
My dreams presage some joyful news at hand.
My bosom's lord sits lightly in his throne,[1]
And all this day an unaccustomed spirit
5   Lifts me above the ground with cheerful thoughts.
I dreamt my lady came and found me dead—
Strange dream that gives a dead man leave to think—
And breathed such life with kisses in° my lips   *into*
That I revived and was an emperor.
10   Ah me, how sweet is love itself possessed°   *enjoyed in reality*
When but love's shadows° are so rich in joy!   *dreams; images*
Enter [BALTHASAR,] *Romeo's man.*[2]
News from Verona! How now, Balthasar?
Dost thou not bring me letters from the Friar?
How doth my lady? Is my father well?
15   How doth my lady Juliet? That I ask again,
For nothing can be ill if she be well.

BALTHASAR   Then she is well, and nothing can be ill.

---

2. Whimsy; quarter notes.
3. Defy; respond to.
4. Lines from the song "In Commendation of
Music," by Richard Edwardes, printed in *The Paradise of Dainty Devices* (1576).
5. *Catling*: catgut used for stringed instruments.
6. *Rebeck*: three-stringed instrument.
7. *Soundpost*: supporting peg fixed between the

sounding board and back of a stringed instrument.
8. Musicians are given no gold for playing; they are
poor and have no gold to jingle.
5.1 Location: A street in Mantua.
1. Love rules in the heart; the heart is at ease in the
chest.
2. In Q1, the stage direction indicates that Romeo's
man is "*booted*," as if he has just dismounted.

Her body sleeps in Capels' monument,
And her immortal part with angels lives.
20 I saw her laid low in her kindred's vault,
And presently° took post³ to tell it you.   *immediately*
Oh, pardon me for bringing these ill news,
Since you did leave it for my office,° sir.   *duty*
ROMEO   Is it e'en so? Then I deny° you, stars!   *repudiate*
25 —Thou knowest my lodging. Get me ink and paper,
And hire post-horses; I will hence tonight.
BALTHASAR   I do beseech you, sir, have patience:
Your looks are pale and wild, and do import°   *signify*
Some misadventure.
ROMEO   Tush, thou art deceived.
30 Leave me, and do the thing I bid thee do.
Hast thou no letters to me from the Friar?
BALTHASAR   No, my good lord.
ROMEO   No matter. Get thee gone,
And hire those horses. I'll be with thee straight.
                                    Exit [BALTHASAR].
Well, Juliet, I will lie with thee tonight.
35 Let's see for means. O mischief, thou art swift
To enter in the thoughts of desperate men.
I do remember an apothecary,
And hereabouts 'a dwells, which late I noted,
In tattered weeds,° with overwhelming° brows,   *clothes / overhanging*
40 Culling of simples.° Meager were his looks;   *herbs*
Sharp misery had worn him to the bones;
And in his needy° shop a tortoise hung,   *poor*
An alligator stuffed, and other skins
Of ill-shaped fishes; and, about his shelves,
45 A beggarly account° of empty boxes,   *sparse collection*
Green earthen pots, bladders, and musty seeds,
Remnants of packthread,° and old cakes of roses⁴   *twine*
Were thinly scattered to make up a show.
Noting this penury, to myself I said,
50 "An if a man did need a poison now,
Whose sale is present death⁵ in Mantua,
Here lives a caitiff° wretch would sell it him."   *pitiful*
Oh, this same thought did but forerun my need,
And this same needy man must sell it me.
55 As I remember, this should be the house.
Being holiday, the beggar's shop is shut.
—What ho, Apothecary!
          [*Enter* APOTHECARY.]
APOTHECARY   Who calls so loud?
ROMEO   Come hither, man. I see that thou art poor.
Hold, there is forty ducats.⁶ Let me have
60 A dram of poison, such soon-speeding gear⁷
As will disperse itself through all the veins
That the life-weary taker may fall dead,
And that the trunk° may be discharged of breath   *body*

3. Set out on post-horses.
4. Rose petals pressed into cake form and used as a
sachet.
5. Punishable by immediate death.

6. Various gold coins used at times in much of Europe,
and Shakespeare's usual currency for plays not set in
England.
7. Quick-working stuff; quick-killing stuff.

As violently as hasty powder fired

65 Doth hurry from the fatal cannon's womb.

APOTHECARY Such mortal drugs I have, but Mantua's law

Is death to any he° that utters° them.   *man / offers to sell*

ROMEO Art thou so bare° and full of wretchedness,   *destitute*

And fearest to die? Famine is in thy cheeks;

70 Need and oppression starveth in thy eyes;

Contempt and beggary hangs upon thy back.

The world is not thy friend, nor the world's law;

The world affords° no law to make thee rich;   *provides*

Then be not poor, but break it, and take this.

75 APOTHECARY My poverty, but not my will, consents.

ROMEO I pay thy poverty and not thy will.

APOTHECARY Put this in any liquid thing you will,

And drink it off; and if you had the strength

Of twenty men, it would dispatch you straight.°   *immediately*

80 ROMEO There is thy gold—worse poison to men's souls,

Doing more murder in this loathsome world

Than these poor compounds that thou mayst not sell.

I sell thee poison; thou hast sold me none.

Farewell. Buy food, and get thyself in flesh.°   *grow fatter*

[*Exit* APOTHECARY.]

85 Come, cordial° and not poison, go with me   *restorative*

To Juliet's grave, for there must I use thee.   *Exit.*

5.2 (Q1 Scene 19)

Enter FRIAR JOHN.

FRIAR JOHN Holy Franciscan Friar! Brother, ho!

Enter FRIAR LAURENCE.

FRIAR LAURENCE This same should be the voice of Friar John.

—Welcome from Mantua! What says Romeo?

Or, if his mind° be writ, give me his letter.   *thoughts*

5 FRIAR JOHN Going to find a barefoot brother out,

One of our order, to associate me,[1]

Here in this city visiting the sick,

And finding him, the searchers[2] of the town,

Suspecting that we both were in a house

10 Where the infectious pestilence did reign,

Sealed up the doors and would not let us forth,

So that my speed to Mantua there was stayed.°   *stopped*

FRIAR LAURENCE Who bare my letter, then, to Romeo?

FRIAR JOHN I could not send it—here it is again—

15 Nor get a messenger to bring it thee,

So fearful were they of infection.°   *contagion*

FRIAR LAURENCE Unhappy fortune! By my brotherhood,

The letter was not nice° but full of charge,°   *trivial / importance*

Of dear import,° and the neglecting it   *serious consequence*

20 May do much danger. Friar John, go hence,

Get me an iron crow,° and bring it straight   *crowbar*

Unto my cell.

FRIAR JOHN   Brother, I'll go and bring it thee.   *Exit.*

FRIAR LAURENCE Now must I to the monument alone.

5.2 Location: Friar Laurence's cell.   accompany.
1. Franciscan friars (barefoot because the order is   2. Health officers appointed to examine corpses and
sworn to poverty) traveled only in pairs. *associate:*   identify houses infected with the plague.

Within this three hours will fair Juliet wake;
25 She will beshrew° me much that Romeo   *curse*
Hath had no notice of these accidents,°   *events*
But I will write again to Mantua
And keep her at my cell till Romeo come.
Poor living corpse, closed in a dead man's tomb!   *Exit.*

5.3 (Q1 Scene 20)

Enter PARIS *and his* PAGE.

PARIS   Give me thy torch, boy—hence, and stand aloof°—   *stay apart*
Yet put it out, for I would not be seen.
Under yond young trees lay thee all along,°   *stretched out*
Holding thy ear close to the hollow ground;
5 So shall no foot upon the churchyard tread,
Being° loose, unfirm with digging up of graves,   *The ground being*
But thou shalt hear it. Whistle then to me
As signal that thou hearest something approach.
Give me those flowers. Do as I bid thee. Go.
10 PAGE [*aside*]   I am almost afraid to stand alone
Here in the churchyard, yet I will adventure.°   *risk it*
      [*He retires.*]
PARIS [*as to* JULIET]   Sweet flower, with flowers thy bridal bed
      I strew—
Oh, woe, thy canopy° is dust and stones—   *covering; bed hangings*
Which with sweet° water nightly I will dew,   *perfumed*
15 Or, wanting that, with tears distilled by moans.
The obsequies° that I for thee will keep°   *funeral rites / perform*
Nightly shall be to strew thy grave and weep.
      [PAGE *whistles.*]
The boy gives warning something doth approach.
What cursèd foot wanders this way tonight
20 To cross° my obsequies and true love's rite?   *thwart*
      Enter ROMEO *and* [BALTHASAR].
What? With a torch? Muffle me, night, a while.
      [*He retires.*]
ROMEO   Give me that mattock° and the wrenching iron.   *pickax*
Hold; take this letter; early in the morning
See thou deliver it to my lord and father.
25 Give me the light. Upon thy life, I charge thee,
Whate'er thou hearest or seest, stand all aloof,
And do not interrupt me in my course.
Why I descend into this bed of death
Is partly to behold my lady's face,
30 But chiefly to take thence from her dead finger
A precious ring, a ring that I must use
In dear° employment. Therefore, hence; be gone.   *important; tender*
But if thou, jealous,° dost return to pry   *suspicious*
In what I farther shall intend to do,
35 By heaven, I will tear thee joint by joint
And strew this hungry churchyard with thy limbs!
The time and my intents are savage-wild,
More fierce and more inexorable far
Than empty° tigers or the roaring sea.   *hungry*

5.3 Location: The Capulet mausoleum.

40 BALTHASAR I will be gone, sir, and not trouble ye.
   ROMEO So shalt thou show me friendship. Take thou that.
      [*He gives* BALTHASAR *money.*]
   Live, and be prosperous; and farewell, good fellow.
   BALTHASAR [*aside*] For all this same, I'll hide me here about.
   His looks I fear, and his intents I doubt.°   *suspect*
      [*He retires.*]
      [ROMEO *opens the tomb.*]
45 ROMEO Thou detestable maw, thou womb¹ of death,
   Gorged with the dearest morsel of the earth,
   Thus I enforce thy rotten jaws to open,
   And, in despite,° I'll cram thee with more food.   *defiant ill will*
   PARIS [*apart*] This is that banished haughty Montague
50 That murdered my love's cousin, with which grief
   It is supposèd the fair creature died,
   And here is come to do some villainous shame
   To the dead bodies. I will apprehend him.
      [*He steps forward.*]
   —Stop thy unhallowed° toil, vile Montague!   *unholy*
55 Can vengeance be pursued further than death?
   Condemnèd villain, I do apprehend thee.
   Obey and go with me, for thou must die.
   ROMEO I must indeed, and therefore came I hither.
   Good gentle youth, tempt not a desp'rate° man;   *despairing; violent*
60 Fly hence and leave me. Think upon these gone;
   Let them affright thee. I beseech thee, youth,
   Put not another sin upon my head
   By urging me to fury. Oh, be gone!
   By heaven, I love thee better than myself,
65 For I come hither armed against myself.
   Stay not; be gone. Live, and hereafter say
   A madman's mercy bid thee run away.
   PARIS I do defy thy conjuration,°   *entreaty*
   And apprehend thee for a felon here.
70 ROMEO Wilt thou provoke me? Then have at thee, boy!
      [*They fight.*]
   PAGE O Lord, they fight! I will go call the watch.   [*Exit.*]
   PARIS Oh, I am slain! If thou be merciful,
   Open the tomb; lay me with Juliet.
      [*He dies.*]
   ROMEO In faith, I will. —Let me peruse this face.
75 Mercutio's kinsman, noble County Paris!
   What said my man when my betossèd° soul   *storm-tossed*
   Did not attend° him as we rode? I think   *listen to*
   He told me Paris should have married Juliet.
   Said he not so? Or did I dream it so?
80 Or am I mad, hearing him talk of Juliet,
   To think it was so? —Oh, give me thy hand,
   One writ with me in sour misfortune's book.
   I'll bury thee in a triumphant° grave,   *magnificent*
   A grave—oh, no, a lantern,° slaughtered youth,   *lighthouse*
85 For here lies Juliet, and her beauty makes

---

1. Belly; also playing on the birthplace of Romeo's death.

This vault a feasting presence[2] full of light.
Death, lie thou there, by a dead man interred.
How oft when men are at the point of death
Have they been merry, which their keepers° call   *sick nurses; jailers*
90   A light'ning before death? Oh, how may I
Call this a light'ning? —O my love, my wife,
Death that hath sucked the honey of thy breath
Hath had no power yet upon thy beauty.
Thou art not conquered:° beauty's ensign° yet   *overpowered; seduced / flag*
95   Is crimson in thy lips and in thy cheeks,
And death's pale flag is not advancèd there.
—Tybalt, liest thou there in thy bloody sheet?
Oh, what more favor can I do to thee
Than with that hand that cut thy youth in twain
100   To sunder his° that was thine enemy?   *the youth of him*
Forgive me, cousin. —Ah, dear Juliet,
Why art thou yet so fair? Shall I believe
That unsubstantial° death is amorous,   *immaterial*
And that the lean abhorrèd monster keeps
105   Thee here in dark to be his paramour?
For fear of that I still will stay with thee,
And never from this pallet of dim night
Depart again. Here, here will I remain
With worms that are thy chambermaids; oh, here
110   Will I set up my everlasting rest,[3]
And shake the yoke of inauspicious stars
From this world-wearied flesh. Eyes, look your last;
Arms, take your last embrace; and lips—O you,
The doors of breath—seal with a righteous kiss
115   A dateless bargain° to engrossing[4] death.   *An eternal contract*
Come, bitter conduct;° come, unsavory guide,   *conductor; leader*
Thou desperate pilot, now at once run on
The dashing rocks thy seasick, weary bark!
Here's to my love. [*He drinks.*] O true apothecary,
120   Thy drugs are quick.° Thus, with a kiss, I die.[5]   *fast; vigorous*
        [*He falls and dies.*]
        Enter FRIAR [LAURENCE] *with lantern, crow,*
        and spade.
FRIAR LAURENCE   Saint Francis be my speed!° How oft tonight   *help*
Have my old feet stumbled at graves! —Who's there?
        [BALTHASAR *steps forward.*]
BALTHASAR   Here's one, a friend, and one that knows you
    well.
FRIAR   Bliss be upon you! Tell me, good my friend,
125   What torch is yond that vainly lends his light
To grubs and eyeless skulls? As I discern,
It burneth in the Capels' monument.
BALTHASAR   It doth so, holy sir, and there's my master,
One that you love.
FRIAR LAURENCE   Who is it?
BALTHASAR   Romeo.

2. Festive royal chamber for receiving guests.
3. Make my final determination.
4. Buying up in large quantities to monopolize; writing a legal document.

5. PERFORMANCE COMMENT On the different directorial possibilities for staging Romeo's death, see Digital Edition PC 5.

FRIAR LAURENCE   How long hath he been there?

130 BALTHASAR   Full half an hour.

FRIAR LAURENCE   Go with me to the vault.

BALTHASAR   I dare not, sir.
My master knows not but I am gone hence,
And fearfully° did menace me with death   *fearsomely*
If I did stay to look on his intents.

135 FRIAR LAURENCE   Stay, then. I'll go alone. Fear comes upon
    me.
Oh, much I fear some ill unthrifty° thing.   *unfortunate*

BALTHASAR   As I did sleep under this young tree here,
I dreamt my master and another fought,
And that my master slew him.
            [FRIAR LAURENCE *moves toward the vault.*]

FRIAR LAURENCE   Romeo!

140 Alack, alack, what blood is this which stains
The stony entrance of this sepulcher?
What mean these masterless and gory swords
To lie discolored by this place of peace?
Romeo! Oh, pale! Who else? What, Paris too?

145 And steeped in blood? Ah, what an unkind° hour   *an unnatural; a cruel*
Is guilty of this lamentable chance!°   *event*
            [JULIET *rises.*]
The lady stirs!

JULIET   O comfortable° Friar, where is my lord?   *solace-giving*
I do remember well where I should be,

150 And there I am. Where is my Romeo?

FRIAR LAURENCE   I hear some noise. —Lady, come from that
    nest
Of death, contagion, and unnatural sleep.
A greater power than we can contradict
Hath thwarted our intents. Come. Come away!

155 Thy husband in thy bosom there lies dead,
And Paris, too. Come—I'll dispose of thee
Among a sisterhood of holy nuns.
Stay not to question, for the watch is coming.
Come! Go, good Juliet! I dare no longer stay.

160 JULIET   Go, get thee hence, for I will not away.
                                 Exit [FRIAR LAURENCE].
What's here? A cup closed in my true love's hand?
Poison I see hath been his timeless° end.   *untimely; lasting*
O churl,° drunk all, and left no friendly drop   *miser*
To help me after? I will kiss thy lips:

165 Haply° some poison yet doth hang on them   *Perhaps*
To make me die with a restorative.[6]
Thy lips are warm!
            Enter [PAGE *and* WATCHMEN].

CHIEF WATCHMAN   Lead, boy. Which way?

JULIET   Yea, noise? Then I'll be brief.
            [*She takes Romeo's dagger.*]
                        O happy° dagger,   *fortunate*

170 This is thy sheath; there rust and let me die.
            [*She stabs herself and falls.*]

6. Both the kiss, which is healing, and the poison, which restores them to each other.

PAGE   This is the place—there, where the torch doth burn.
CHIEF WATCHMAN   The ground is bloody. Search about the
   churchyard.
   Go, some of you; whoe'er you find, attach.°   arrest
                        [*Exeunt some of the watch.*]
   Pitiful sight! Here lies the County, slain,
175   And Juliet, bleeding, warm, and newly dead,
   Who here hath lain this two days burièd.
   Go tell the Prince! Run to the Capulets;
   Raise up the Montagues! Some others, search.
                        [*Exeunt others of the watch.*]
   We see the ground° whereon these woes do lie,   earth
180   But the true ground° of all these piteous woes   cause
   We cannot without circumstance° descry.   a fuller account
            Enter [SECOND WATCHMAN *with*] *Romeo's man*
            [BALTHASAR].
SECOND WATCHMAN   Here's Romeo's man; we found him in
   the churchyard.
CHIEF WATCHMAN   Hold him in safety° till the Prince come   securely
   hither.
            Enter [THIRD WATCHMAN *with* FRIAR LAURENCE].
THIRD WATCHMAN   Here is a friar that trembles, sighs, and
   weeps.
185   We took this mattock and this spade from him
   As he was coming from this churchyard's side.[7]
CHIEF WATCHMAN   A great suspicion! Stay° the Friar, too.   Hold
            Enter the PRINCE [*with Attendants*].
PRINCE   What misadventure is so early up
   That calls our person from our morning rest?
            Enter [CAPULET *and* CAPULET'S WIFE].
190   CAPULET   What should it be that is so shrieked abroad?
CAPULET'S WIFE   Oh, the people in the street cry "Romeo,"
   Some "Juliet," and some "Paris," and all run
   With open° outcry toward our monument!   public; open-mouthed
PRINCE   What fear is this which startles° in your ears?   bursts out
195   CHIEF WATCHMAN   Sovereign, here lies the County Paris slain,
   And Romeo dead, and Juliet—dead before—
   Warm, and new killed.
PRINCE   Search, seek, and know how this foul murder comes.
CHIEF WATCHMAN   Here is a friar, and slaughtered Romeo's
   man,
200   With instruments upon them fit to open
   These dead men's tombs.
CAPULET   O Heavens! O wife, look how our daughter bleeds!
   This dagger hath mista'en, for lo, his house°   scabbard
   Is empty on the back of Montague,
205   And it mis-sheathèd in my daughter's bosom.
CAPULET'S WIFE   O me, this sight of death is as a bell
   That warns° my old age to a sepulcher.   summons
            Enter MONTAGUE [*with Attendants*].
PRINCE   Come, Montague, for thou art early up
   To see thy son and heir now early down.
210   MONTAGUE   Alas, my liege, my wife is dead tonight;

---

7. This side of the churchyard.

Grief of my son's exile hath stopped her breath.
What further woe conspires against mine age?

PRINCE   Look, and thou shalt see.

MONTAGUE [*as to* ROMEO]   O thou untaught! What manners is
in this,

215   To press before° thy father to a grave?   *To shove ahead of*

PRINCE   Seal up the mouth of outrage[8] for a while,
Till we can clear these ambiguities
And know their spring, their head, their true descent;
And then will I be general of your woes

220   And lead you even to death. Meantime, forbear,
And let mischance be slave to° patience.   *overruled by*
Bring forth the parties of suspicion.

FRIAR LAURENCE   I am the greatest,° able to do least,   *most suspect*
Yet most suspected as the time and place

225   Doth make against me of this direful murder.
And here I stand both to impeach and purge,
Myself condemnèd and myself excused.[9]

PRINCE   Then say at once what thou dost know in this.

FRIAR   I will be brief, for my short date° of breath   *duration*

230   Is not so long as is a tedious tale.
Romeo, there dead, was husband to that Juliet,
And she, there dead—that's Romeo's faithful wife.
I married them, and their stol'n marriage day
Was Tybalt's doomsday, whose untimely death

235   Banished the new-made bridegroom from this city—
For whom, and not for Tybalt, Juliet pined.
—You, to remove that siege of grief from her,
Betrothed and would have married her perforce°   *forcibly*
To County Paris. Then comes she to me,

240   And, with wild looks, bid me devise some mean°   *method*
To rid her from this second marriage,
Or in my cell there would she kill herself.
Then gave I her—so tutored by my art[1]—
A sleeping potion, which so took effect

245   As I intended, for it wrought on her
The form° of death. Meantime I writ to Romeo   *appearance*
That he should hither come as this° dire night   *as this = this*
To help to take her from her borrowed grave,
Being the time the potion's force should cease.

250   But he which bore my letter, Friar John,
Was stayed by accident, and yesternight
Returned my letter back. Then, all alone,
At the prefixèd° hour of her waking,   *prearranged*
Came I to take her from her kindred's vault,

255   Meaning to keep her closely° at my cell   *secretly*
Till I conveniently° could send to Romeo.   *befittingly*
But when I came, some minute ere the time
Of her awakening, here untimely lay
The noble Paris and true Romeo, dead.

260   She wakes, and I entreated her come forth
And bear this work of heaven with patience;

---

8. Of impassioned exclamation.
9. *to impeach . . . excused:* to accuse myself of what I   am guilty of and clear myself of what I am not.
1. As I knew through my medical study to do.

But then a noise did scare me from the tomb,
And she, too desperate, would not go with me,
But, as it seems, did violence on herself.
265 All this I know—and to the marriage
Her Nurse is privy; and, if aught in this
Miscarried by my fault, let my old life
Be sacrificed some hour before his° time   *its*
Unto the rigor of severest law.
270 PRINCE   We still° have known thee for a holy man.   *always*
  —Where's Romeo's man? What can he say to this?
BALTHASAR   I brought my master news of Juliet's death,
And then in post° he came from Mantua   *haste*
To this same place, to this same monument.
275 This letter he early bid me give his father,
And threatened me with death, going in the vault,
If I departed not and left him there.
PRINCE   Give me the letter; I will look on it.
  Where is the County's page that raised the watch?
280   —Sirrah, what made° your master in this place?   *did*
PAGE   He came with flowers to strew his lady's grave,
And bid me stand aloof, and so I did.
Anon° comes one with light to ope the tomb,   *Soon*
And by and by my master drew on him,
285 And then I ran away to call the watch.
PRINCE   This letter doth make good the Friar's words—
Their course of love, the tidings of her death.
And here he writes that he did buy a poison
Of a poor 'pothecary, and therewithal
290 Came to this vault to die and lie with Juliet.
Where be these enemies? —Capulet, Montague:
See what a scourge is laid upon your hate,
That heaven finds means to kill your joys° with love,   *happiness; children*
And I, for winking at° your discords, too   *closing my eyes to*
295 Have lost a brace of kinsmen. All are punished.
CAPULET   O brother Montague, give me thy hand.
This is my daughter's jointure,° for no more   *marriage portion*
Can I demand.
MONTAGUE   But I can give thee more;
For I will ray° her statue in pure gold,   *array (i.e., gild)*
300 That whiles Verona by that name is known
There shall no figure at such rate be set[2]
As that of true and faithful Juliet.
CAPULET   As rich shall Romeo's by his lady's lie,
Poor sacrifices of our enmity.
305 PRINCE   A glooming° peace this morning with it brings;   *frowning; dark*
The sun for sorrow will not show his head.
Go hence to have more talk of these sad things—
Some shall be pardoned, and some punishèd—
For never was a story of more woe
310 Than this of Juliet and her Romeo.   [*Exeunt.*]

---

2. No figure shall be so valued; no figure shall be erected at such a price.

A Midsummer Night's Dream

How secure is the borderline, the seventeenth-century French philosopher Blaise Pascal wondered, that divides daylight reality from the illusions of dreams? Since dreams generally have very little continuity from night to night and even from moment to moment, their effect upon us, compared to the stability of the waking world, is relatively slight. But, he observed, given their vivid intensity, all it would take would be consistency in dreaming to blur the boundaries: "If an artisan were sure to dream every night for twelve hours' duration that he was a king, I believe he would be almost as happy as a king, who should dream every night for twelve hours on end that he was an artisan." The most one can say, Pascal concluded, is that "life is a dream a little less inconstant."

Weaving its way along the borderline between reality and dream, *A Midsummer Night's Dream* eschews even so modest a conclusion. The characters, to be sure, draw many sharp distinctions—between waking and sleep, men and women, aristocrats and commoners, humans and animals, mortals and fairies. But though none of these distinctions disappears in the course of the play—on the contrary, they are constantly insisted upon—the comedy deftly and subtly calls them into question. How do you know whether you are sleeping or awake? What makes you certain that the boundaries of your identity are secure? Perhaps such questioning particularly befits a play written by an actor, part of a small all-male troupe accustomed to doubling and shifting roles rapidly across the whole spectrum of real and imagined existence.

Some scholars have speculated that the comedy's original occasion was an aristocratic wedding in an English country house, perhaps with the Queen herself in attendance, so that when, at the end of the play-within-the-play, the stage brides and grooms exit to consummate their marriage, the real newlyweds, amid the blessings and sly jokes of their guests, would also have retired to bed. But though a hall-of-mirrors event of this kind is plausible, there is no historical evidence that *A Midsummer Night's Dream* was ever performed at, let alone written expressly for, such a wedding. What we do know is that it was repeatedly performed on the London stage: the title page of the First Quarto says that it "hath been sundry times publikely acted" by the Lord Chamberlain's Men and that it was written by William Shakespeare.

The precise date that *A Midsummer Night's Dream* was written and first performed is unknown; the Elizabethan writer Francis Meres mentions it admiringly in 1598, and certain of its stylistic features have led many scholars to place it around 1594–96, the probable period of the comparably lyrical *Romeo and Juliet* and *Richard II*. Attempts to find more precise coordinates by locating an allusion to a particular royal progress in Oberon's lines about the "fair vestal thronèd by the west" (2.1.158)* or to a particular wet season in Titania's lines about the miserable weather (2.1.88ff) have been defeated by the frequency of both Queen Elizabeth's travels and English rainstorms.

Shakespeare's comedy has been beloved for more than four centuries. To be sure, there have been a few dissenters: the diarist Samuel Pepys wrote after seeing a production in 1662 that "it is the most insipid ridiculous play that ever I saw in my life," though he took note of "some good dancing and some handsome women." Most audiences have been vastly more enthusiastic. The play has inspired musical compositions,

---

*All quotations are taken from the edited text of the Quarto, printed here. The Digital Edition includes edited texts of both the Quarto and the Folio.

Cupid and his victims. From Gilles Corrozet,
Hecatomgraphie (1540).

of which Felix Mendelssohn's Overture in E Major is the most celebrated, along with famously lavish productions. By the nineteenth century, it was routinely staged on gorgeous sets, with twinkling lights, fairies rising on midnight mushrooms, the moon shining over the Acropolis, and live rabbits hopping across carpets of flowers. But *A Midsummer Night's Dream* has proved equally at home in the simplest of settings. Generations of schoolchildren have romped through cardboard forests, while in Peter Brook's influential 1970 production for the Royal Shakespeare Company the actors performed (often on trapeze) in a three-sided, brightly lit, bare white box.

Shakespeare's visionary poetic drama appeals to an unusually broad spectrum of spectators. Though the play depicts the private pleasures of the elite, it does so with the resources of the public stage. Its humor crosses all boundaries. If it mocks working-class artisans (skilled craftsmen who are simply called "the rabble" in one Quarto stage direction), it also laughs at well-born young lovers. If it ridicules the folly of mortals, it also takes pleasure in the blunders of fairies. If it poses cunning philosophical riddles, it also delights in farce.

The language of *A Midsummer Night's Dream* reflects an unusually high incidence of the tropes familiar to those who had received advanced rhetorical and literary training, but you do not have to know the Greek names for these tropes—*anaphora, isocolon, anadiplosis,* and the like—to enjoy their effects. The Elizabethan rhetorician George Puttenham characterized the mere repetition of words—*epizeuxis*—as "a very foolish impertinency of speech," but familiarity with rhetorical handbooks is not required to know that Bottom's attempt at grand passion—

> O grim-looked night, O night with hue so black,
> O night, which ever art when day is not,
> O night, O night, alack, alack, alack . . .
>
> (5.1.168–70)

—sounds asinine. Nor do you need to have read Puttenham's subtle advice for creating musical effects in language to savor the ravishing harmonies of Oberon's words:

> once I sat upon a promontory
> And heard a mermaid on a dolphin's back
> Uttering such dulcet and harmonious breath
> That the rude sea grew civil at her song
> And certain stars shot madly from their spheres
> To hear the sea-maid's music.
>
> (2.1.149–54)

All you need to do is read the words aloud for yourself.

Let us consider, as one further example of Shakespeare's ability to make sophisticated rhetorical schemes accessible, the exchange between Lysander and Hermia in the wake of Egeus's attempt to block their betrothal:

> LYSANDER   The course of true love never did run smooth,
>   But either it was different in blood—
> HERMIA   Oh, cross! Too high to be enthralled to low.
> LYSANDER   Or else misgraffèd in respect of years—

> HERMIA   Oh, spite! Too old to be engaged to young.
> LYSANDER   Or else it stood upon the choice of friends—
> HERMIA   Oh, hell! To choose love by another's eyes.
>   (1.1.134–40)

The alternation of carefully calibrated single lines, or *stichomythia,* is a scheme that Shakespeare borrowed from the Roman playwright Seneca and used in different ways in many of his plays. The effect here is to convey the lovers' mutual anguish, tingeing it slightly perhaps with a gently ironic distance that evaporates in the poignant lament that follows (lines 141–49).

These rhetorical devices, along with the subtle modulations from blank verse to rhymed couplets to boisterous comic prose, are so deftly handled that their pleasures are accessible to the learned and unlearned alike. This breadth also reflects the very wide range of cultural materials that the playwright has cunningly woven together— from the classical heritage of the educated elite to popular ballads, from court culture to folklore, from refined and sophisticated entertainments to the coarser delights of burlesque.

There is no single literary source for *A Midsummer Night's Dream,* but Shakespeare is indebted for the legendary Theseus and Hippolyta to Thomas North's translation (1579) of Plutarch's *Lives of the Noble Grecians and Romans,* and still more to Chaucer's *Knight's Tale.* The play repeatedly echoes Chaucer's references to observing "the rite of May," a folk custom still current in Elizabethan England and quite possibly known to Shakespeare personally. To the dismay of Puritans, who regarded the celebration as a lascivious remnant of paganism, young men and women of all classes would go out into the woods and fields to welcome the May with singing and dancing. Shakespeare's title associates this custom with another occasion for festive release: Midsummer Eve (June 23), when the solstice was marked by holiday license and by tales of fairy spells and temporary madness.

Some Elizabethan aristocrats kept theatrical troupes as liveried servants, along with young pages who could sing and perform; and powerful magnates, both secular and religious, often had plays, masquerades, and elaborate shows staged in their houses. From this milieu Shakespeare derives a vision of what we can call the revels of power—performances designed to entertain, gratify, and reflect the values of those at the top of society. From this milieu, too, Shakespeare absorbs a sense of social hierarchy: a distinction between Duke Theseus, at once imperious and genteel, and Egeus, wealthy but distinctly lower in rank and harping on what is his by law, along with a more marked distinction between these characters and the artisans, members of the lower orders, regarded by their social superiors with condescending indulgence.

The artisans—or "rude mechanicals," as they are called—enable Shakespeare to introduce wonderful swoops into earthy prose, snatches of jigs, a comical taste for the grotesque, a glimpse of a world that usually resides beyond the horizon of courtly vision. The lovers at the pinnacle of the play's society do not know the names and trades of the "[h]ard-handed men that work in Athens here" (5.1.72) who have come to offer them entertainment, but we the audience do, and we even know something of their hopes, fears, and dreams. We know that young Francis Flute the bellows-mender has (or thinks he has) a beard coming; that Snug the joiner worries that he is a slow learner; that Bottom the weaver wants to play all the parts. As with the Pageant of the Nine Worthies in *Love's Labor's Lost,* we are invited at once to join in the mockery of the inept performers and to distance ourselves from the mockers' lame, somewhat disagreeable attempts at wisecracks. That is, the audience of *A Midsummer Night's Dream* is not simply mirrored in the play's upper classes; the real audience is given a broader perspective, a more capacious understanding, than anyone onstage.

This understanding is signaled not only in our ability to take in both the courtly and popular dimensions of the play, but also in our ability to see what escapes both aristocrats and artisans: the world of the fairies. But what are the fairies? From what social milieu do they spring? It is tempting to reply that they are denizens of the country—that is, characters drawn from the semipagan folklore of a rural England that was at least partially intact and that Shakespeare himself could easily have encountered. Reginald Scot, who wrote a brilliant attack on witchcraft persecutions (*The Discovery of Witchcraft*, 1584), suggests that Robin Goodfellow, the mischievous spirit also called a "puck," was once feared by villagers, though most recognize him now to be a figure of mere "illusion and knaverie." Yet intensive scholarly research over several generations has suggested that Shakespeare's fairies are quite unlike those his audience might have credited, half-credited, or—as Scot hoped—discredited.

The fairies of Elizabethan popular belief were often threatening and dangerous, while those of *A Midsummer Night's Dream* are generally benevolent. The former steal human infants, perhaps to sacrifice them to the devil, while the latter, even when they quarrel over the possession of a young boy, do so to bestow love and favor upon him; the former leave deformed, emaciated children in place of those they have stolen, while the latter trip nimbly through the palace blessing the bride-beds and warding off deformities. Shakespeare's fairies have some of the menacing associations of "real" fairies—Robin speaks of shrouds and gaping graves, while the quarrel between Oberon and Titania has disrupted the seasons and damaged the crops, as wicked spirits were said to do. But the fairies we see are, as Oberon says, "spirits of another sort." Though they have very little goodwill toward each other, Oberon and Titania (whose names Shakespeare took from the French romance *Huon of Bordeaux* and from Ovid, respectively) repeatedly demonstrate their goodwill toward mortals. The fairy king and queen are distressed at the unintended consequences of their quarrel, and each is involved, with romantic generosity, in the happiness of Theseus and Hippolyta. This generosity extends beyond the immediate range of their interests: in the midst of plotting to humiliate Titania, Oberon attempts to intervene on behalf of the spurned Helena, and though this intervention proves, through Robin's mistake, to lead to hopeless confusion, the fairies make amends.

Indeed, if Robin takes mischievous delight in the discord he has helped to sow among the four young lovers—"Lord, what fools these mortals be!" (3.2.115)—he is not the originator of that discord, and he is the indispensable agent for setting things right. In his role as both mischief maker and matchmaker, Robin resembles the crafty slave in comedies by the Latin playwrights Plautus and Terence, a stock character who sometimes seems to enjoy and contribute to the plot's tangles but who manages in the end to remove the obstacles that stand in the way of the young lovers.

This resemblance brings us to yet another of the cultural elements that Shakespeare cunningly interweaves in the plot of *A Midsummer Night's Dream*. From the classical literary tradition he must have first encountered in grammar school, Shakespeare derives the ancient Greek setting, the story of Pyramus and Thisbe as told in Ovid's *Metamorphoses*, the transformation of a man into an ass as told in Apuleius's *Golden Ass*, and, above all, the basic plot convention of young lovers contriving to escape the rigid will of a stern father. This literary convention, rooted in the ancient comedies of Menander, Plautus, and Terence, corresponds to certain aspects of actual life in Shakespeare's England, where lawsuits provide records of parents trying to compel children to marry against their will. But the historical problem of marital consent has a complex relation to its artistic representation. Not only does the play exaggerate the actual punitive power of the father—Egeus threatens his disobedient daughter with death (to which Theseus offers, as a grim alternative, the nunnery)—but it also exaggerates the release from this power by staging the giddy possibility of a marriage based entirely on love and desire rather than parental will.

In *A Midsummer Night's Dream*, this triumph of youth, a highly implausible dream for any Elizabethan member of the propertied classes, is brought about by yet another plot convention: the escape from the court or city to the "green world" of the forest. This theatrical structure is not characteristic of ancient Roman comedies, but

Pyramus and Thisbe. From George Wither, *A Collection of Emblems* (1635).

the festive release from the discipline and sobriety of everyday life somewhat resembles the Saturnalian rhythms found in the Greek playwright Aristophanes; still more perhaps, it reflects certain English folk customs, such as Maying. When Theseus comes upon the four exhausted lovers asleep in the woods, he thinks that "they rose up early to observe / The rite of May" (4.1.130–31).

But, of course, Theseus is wrong. The lovers were not out a-Maying. They had spent the night stumbling through the woods in a confused state of fear, anger, and desire. When it enters the charmed, moonlit space of *A Midsummer Night's Dream*, "the rite of May," along with the other rituals and representations Shakespeare stitched together in creating his play, is transformed; to use Peter Quince's term for the metamorphosed Bottom, the rites and rituals are "translated." Folk customs, the revels of power, the classical tradition as taught in schools—all are displaced from their points of origin, their enabling institutions and assumptions, and brought into a new space, the space of the Shakespearean stage.

This "translation" has, in every case, the odd effect of simultaneous elevation and enervation, celebration and parody. Just when you are ready to write something off as a joke, it becomes moving; just when you start to take something seriously, it is comically undermined. Thus, the minor Ovidian tale of Pyramus and Thisbe is greatly elaborated but also travestied; the mechanicals are at once sympathetically represented and mercilessly ridiculed; the revels of power are lovingly reproduced but also ironically distanced.

Some of the play's most wonderful moments spring from the zany conjunction of distinct and even opposed theatrical modes (a conjunction characteristically parodied in the oxymoronic title of the artisans' play, "A tedious brief scene of young Pyramus / And his love Thisbe; very tragical mirth" [5.1.56–57]). Thus, for example, exquisite love poetry and low comedy meet in the wonderful moment in which the Queen of the Fairies awakens to become enraptured at the sight of the most flatulently absurd of the mechanicals, Bottom. Bottom has been transformed with perfect appropriateness into an ass, yet it is he who is granted the play's most exquisite vision of delight and who articulates, in a comically confused burlesque of St. Paul (1 Corinthians 2:9), the deepest sense of wonder: "The eye of man hath not heard, the ear of man hath not seen, man's hand is not able to taste, his tongue to conceive, nor his heart to report what my dream was" (4.1.207–10).

It would be asinine, the play suggests, to try to expound this dream, but we can at least suggest that whatever its meaning, its existence is closely linked to the nature of the theater itself. Robin suggests as much when he proposes in his epilogue that the audience imagine that it has all along been slumbering: the play it has seen has been a collective hallucination. The play, then, is a dream about watching a play about dreams. Fittingly, the comedy devotes much of its last act to a parody of a theatrical performance, as if its most enduring concern were not the fate of the lovers but the possibility of performing plays. The entire last act of *A Midsummer Night's Dream* is unnecessary in terms of the plot: by Oberon's intervention and Theseus's fiat, the plot complications have all been resolved at the end of act 4. Knots that had seemed almost impossible to untangle—Theseus had declared in act 1 that he was powerless to overturn the ancient privilege of Athens invoked by Egeus—suddenly dissolve. The absurdly easy resolution of an apparently hopeless dilemma characterizes not only the lovers' legal but also their emotional condition, a blend of mad confusion and geometric logic that is settled, apparently permanently, with the aid of the fairies' magical love juice.

But this diagrammatic settling of affairs sits uncomfortably with all that the lovers have experienced in the woods. Both critics and directors have given different weight to this experience. Some treat the lovers as mindless comic puppets, jerked by the playwright's invisible strings, while others take more seriously the darkness that shadows their words and actions. This darkness includes emotional violence and masochism, the betrayal of friendship, the radical fickleness of desire. It extends to the play's sexual politics. Under the strain of the night's adventures, the friendship between Hermia and Helena begins to crack apart, while Lysander and Demetrius become bitter rivals. Though they are eventually reconciled, it is as if the heterosexual couplings can only be formed by painfully sundering the intimate same-sex bonds that preceded them. Shakespeare had begun to reflect on this problem as early as *The Two Gentlemen of Verona*, possibly his first play, and throughout his career he returned to it repeatedly, including in what is possibly his last play, *The Two Noble Kinsmen*. For the most part, the broken friendships are repaired, but, as with Anto-

A fairy hill. From Olaus Magnus, *Historia de Gentibus Septentrionalibus* (1558).

nio and Sebastian in *Twelfth Night* and Leontes and Polixenes in *The Winter's Tale,* there is usually a lingering sense of loss, from which even the sunnier *Midsummer Night's Dream* is not completely exempt.

In another very early play, *The Taming of the Shrew,* Shakespeare had also begun his lifelong reflection on the struggle between men and women, a struggle frequently focused on the male desire to dominate and subdue the female. In *A Midsummer Night's Dream,* tension flares in the case of the fairies into open conflict over the Indian boy, the locus of Oberon's assertion of patriarchal power and Titania's claim to independence. In the human world of the play, this tension is less immediately apparent; but in the first scene Theseus alludes to his military conquest of the Amazon queen Hippolyta, and there are other brief glimpses of cruelty, indifference, and rage. We never completely forget that the reconciliation of the quarreling fairies is brought about by the nasty demeaning of Titania or that the human lovers are sorted out by a trick.

Those who see *A Midsummer Night's Dream* as lighthearted entertainment must somehow laugh off this darkness; those who wish to emphasize the play's more troubling and discordant notes must somehow neutralize the comic register in which such notes are sounded. For example, the brutal insults hurled at Hermia by the young man who had loved her and with whom she has eloped might well seem extremely painful, but the fantastic language in which these insults are expressed—

> Get you gone, you dwarf,
> You minimus of hind'ring knot-grass made,
> You bead, you acorn.
>
> (3.2.328–30)

—distances audiences from the pain and generates laughter.

Audiences for most productions tend to oscillate between engagement and detachment. In the young lovers' choices and sufferings, we encounter a situation in which the final outcome doesn't matter greatly to us but matters greatly to them. And while we see the characters from a distance—though Hermia and Helena are distinct enough, even attentive readers occasionally find it difficult to remember which is Lysander and which Demetrius—we also experience at least glancingly *their* sense of how important the difference is, how unbearable to be matched against one's consent, how painfully difficult to make a match that corresponds to one's desires.

Desires in *A Midsummer Night's Dream* are intense, irrational, and alarmingly mobile. This mobility, the speed with which desire can be detached from one object and attached to a different object, does not diminish the exigency of the passion, for the lovers are convinced at every moment that their choices are irrefutably rational and irresistibly compelling. But there is no security in these choices, and the play is repeatedly haunted by a fear of abandonment and by the disquieting erasure of the boundary between human and animal.

The emblem, as well as the agent, of a dangerously mobile desire is the fairies' love juice. No human being in the play experiences a purely abstract, objectless desire; when you desire, you desire *someone.* But the love juice is the distilled essence of erotic mobility itself, and it is appropriately in the power of the fairies. For the fairies seem to embody the principle of what we might call polytropic desire—that is, desire that can instantaneously alight on any object, including an ass-headed man, and that can with equal instantaneousness swerve away from that object and onto another. Oberon and Titania have, we learn, long histories of amorous adventures; they are aware of each other's wayward passions; and, endowed with an extraordinary, eroticizing rhetoric, they move endlessly through the spiced, moonlit night.

If there is a link between the fairies and the erotic, there is a still more powerful link between the fairies and the imagination. Theseus makes the connection explicit when he rejects the stories that the lovers have told him: "I never may believe / These antique fables, nor these fairy toys." In a famous speech (5.1.2–22), he accounts for such fables and toys as products of the imagination. The speech reflects Theseus's misplaced confidence in his own sense of waking reality, a reality that does not include fairies. Yet paradoxically, in dismissively categorizing the lunatic, the lover, and the poet as "of imagination all compact," he manages to articulate insights that the play seems to uphold. Those in the grip of a powerful imagination may be loosed from the moorings of reason and nature, and they may inhabit a world of wish fulfillment and its converse, nightmare. But the poet whose imagination "bodies forth / The forms of things unknown" (5.1.14–15) has created *A Midsummer Night's Dream,* giving his fantasies—including the fantasy called "Theseus"—"[a] local habitation and a name." Finally, it is the imagination that enables giddy, restless, changeable mortals to attach their desires to a particular person.

For Theseus, the imagination is the agent of delusion—and there is much in the play that would seem to support this conclusion. But his account is not complete without Hippolyta's insistence that the story the four young lovers tell seems to have something that goes beyond delusion. Their minds, she observes, have been "transfigured" together, and this shared transfiguration bears witness to "something of great constancy; / But, howsoever, strange and admirable" (5.1.26–27). It is as if we were all to wake up one morning and discover we had had the same dream.

And, of course, *we* in the audience have had, as Robin's epilogue suggests, just this experience: the experience of the theater. In the theater, we confront a living representation of the complex relation between transfiguration and delusion, a relation explored with fantastic, anxious literalness in the artisans' performance of *Pyramus and Thisbe.* In reassuring the ladies that the lion is only Snug the joiner, that nothing is what it claims to be, the players simultaneously burlesque the stage and call attention to the basic elements from which any performance is made: rudimentary scenery, artisans, language, imagination, desire.

There is precious little evidence, to be sure, of either imagination or desire in the *Pyramus and Thisbe* staged at the close of *A Midsummer Night's Dream.* Their absence is part of the comical awfulness of the play-within-the-play—the reason, in effect, that it does not become the Shakespearean tragedy it so strikingly resembles, *Romeo and Juliet.* And yet, as Theseus says, "The best in this kind are but shadows, and the worst are no worse if imagination amend them." "It must be your imagination, then," Hippolyta points out, "and not theirs" (5.1.208–10). But that is true of performances far greater than that of which the artisans are capable.

In the theater, we are always aware of a gap between what we see and what is represented. In heightening our awareness of this gap, the play-within-the-play at once intensifies the illusion of reality elsewhere in the comedy (including the illusion that the actors playing their parts actually are bumbling mechanicals) and calls attention to what is required in order to bring any of the interconnected worlds of this play to life. If we are to see fairies onstage in *A Midsummer Night's Dream,* and not simply flesh-and-blood actors (probably boy actors in Shakespeare's theater), it must be our imagination that makes amends. So, too, if we are to believe in the lovers' desire and sympathize with their predicament, it must be *our* desire that animates their words.

Such, at least, is the vision of the theater suggested by the play that Bottom and company offer to the newlyweds. There is nothing really out there, their performance implies, except what the audience graciously consents to dream is there. Yet in the closing moments of the play, when the fairies emerge from the woods and venture into Theseus's mansion to bless the bride-beds, a quite different vision of theater is suggested—one in which the dreams and desires that we have are determined by forces over which we have no control, forces that only a playwright's love juice can make visible under an imaginary moon.

STEPHEN GREENBLATT

SELECTED BIBLIOGRAPHY

Barber, C. L. "May Games and Metamorphoses on a Midsummer's Night." *Shakespeare's Festive Comedy*. Princeton, NJ: Princeton UP, 2012. 135–84. Explains how *A Midsummer Night's Dream* combines folk customs, Ovidian fancy, and Elizabethan pageantry to produce a clarifying release of imagination.

Bate, Jonathan. *Shakespeare and Ovid*. New York: Oxford UP, 1993. Argues that *A Midsummer Night's Dream* indirectly dramatizes Ovid, gathering themes of myth, metamorphosis, and love into a mixed mode typical of sixteenth-century mythography.

Boehrer, Bruce. "Economies of Desire in *A Midsummer Night's Dream*." *Shakespeare Studies* 32 (2004): 99–117. Explores the competing impulses in the play to embrace and repudiate otherness in same-sex and cross-species attachments.

Briggs, K. M. *The Anatomy of Puck*. London: Routledge & Kegan Paul, 1959. Offers a survey of early modern notions about fairies, especially in English literary tradition, describing also the influence of Shakespeare's innovations.

Dash, Irene. *Women's Worlds in Shakespeare's Plays*. London: Associated UP, 1997. Looks at *A Midsummer Night's Dream* in performance, arguing that traditional staging practices have tended reductively to simplify Shakespeare's women.

Loomba, Ania. "The Great Indian Vanishing Trick—Colonialism, Property and the Family in *A Midsummer Night's Dream*." *A Feminist Companion to Shakespeare*. Ed. Dympna Callaghan. Malden, MA: Blackwell, 2000. 163–87. Argues that the Indian boy represents the shaping dialectic between non-European practices and Western domestic ideology.

Montrose, Louis. *The Purpose of Playing: Shakespeare and the Cultural Politics of the Elizabethan Theatre*. Chicago: U of Chicago P, 1996. Examines the play's relation to Elizabethan ideology through discourses of gender, physiology, social rank, and royal iconography.

Traub, Valerie. *The Renaissance of Lesbianism in Early Modern England*. Cambridge: Cambridge UP, 2002. Observes how renovated classical idioms and new scientific knowledge made female-female desire intelligible during the Renaissance.

Williams, Gary Jay. *Our Moonlight Revels: "A Midsummer Night's Dream" in the Theatre*. Iowa City: U of Iowa P, 1997. Explores the major stage, film, and opera adaptations, understood in relation to the cultures that produced them.

Young, David P. *Something of Great Constancy: The Art of "A Midsummer Night's Dream."* New Haven, CT: Yale UP, 1966. Presents an extensive, variegated study covering sources, structure, performance, and contexts.

FILMS

A Midsummer Night's Dream. 1935. Dir. William Dieterle and Max Reinhardt. USA. 133 min. Sumptuous production, with balletic fairies, a serpentine Hippolyta, an elaborate Mendelssohn score, and Mickey Rooney as Robin Goodfellow.

A Midsummer Night's Dream. 1968. Dir. Peter Hall. UK. 124 min. Noted for its miniskirted sensuality, body paint, and extremely gnarled and muddy forest. With Diana Rigg and Helen Mirren.

A Midsummer Night's Dream. 1996. Dir. Adrian Noble. UK. 105 min. Theseus and Hippolyta double as Oberon and Titania, with a frame device of a boy dreaming the play. Starring Lindsay Duncan and Alex Jennings.

A Midsummer Night's Dream. 1999. Dir. Michael Hoffman. USA. 116 min. In Victorian costume against the Tuscan backdrop, this dreamy and erotic version amplifies Bottom's role. With Kevin Kline and Michelle Pfeiffer.

The Children's Midsummer Night's Dream. 2001. Dir. Christine Edzard. UK. 115 min. Performed entirely by child actors, between eight and twelve years old.

Were the World Mine. 2008. Dir. Tom Gustafson. USA. 95 min. In this musical, a bullied gay teenager cast as Puck (Robin) in a high school production of *A Midsummer Night's Dream* discovers the secret of love juice and uses it to turn some of the students in his all-boys' school gay.

TEXTUAL INTRODUCTION

A Midsummer Night's Dream was entered in the Stationers' Register to Thomas Fisher on October 8, 1600, and was published by him in the same year in quarto format (Q1) in a text printed by Richard Bradock. The title page states that the play has been "sundry times publickely acted, by the Right Honourable, the Lord Chamberlaine his seruants," and was "Written by William Shakespeare." The play was reprinted in 1619 (Q2) by William Jaggard for the publisher Thomas Pavier in an edition misdated "1600." In 1623, it was included in the First Folio (F) edition of Shakespeare's *Comedies, Histories, and Tragedies*. Reprints of F were included in the subsequent Folio editions of 1632 (F2), 1664–65 (F3), and 1685 (F4).

Q1 is believed to have been set up from Shakespeare's manuscript or a faithful transcript thereof. It has been chosen as the primary text in the present edition on the grounds that it provides the best witness to how Shakespeare originally conceived the play. Q2 has no independent authority but simply reprints Q1 by correcting a few printing errors while adding others. F was chiefly set up from Q2 but contains a number of important differences that may reflect performance practice by Shakespeare's company. The theatrical manuscript from which they are believed to originate may date from after Shakespeare's death: an F-only stage direction asks for "*Tawyer with a Trumpet*" (5.1.125), a reference to William Tawyer, a musician of the King's Men according to a document of 1624, who is referred to as "Mr Heminges man" the year after. No extant reference to Tawyer is earlier than 1623.

Although they are significant, the differences between Q1 and F *Midsummer Night's Dream* are local and subtle rather than pervasive. The most consequential difference is that in the last act, F reassigns Philostrate's Q1 speeches to Egeus, who thus occupies the role of Theseus's "usual manager of mirth" (5.1.35), responsible for the wedding entertainment. As a result, the conclusion to the two texts is rather different. In Q1's act 4, scene 1, Egeus vociferously opposes his daughter's love for Lysander. Overruled by Theseus, who allows the lovers to get married, Egeus leaves the stage defeated and does not reappear. In the final scene, when the lovers and the royal couple are celebrating, Hermia's father is thus conspicuously absent, excluded from the comic ending, not unlike Malvolio in *Twelfth Night* and Shylock in *The Merchant of Venice*. F, by contrast, has Egeus reappear in act 5, which means he is onstage at the same time as Hermia, the daughter who did not obey him, and Lysander, the son-in-law he did not want—which can create interesting tensions in performance.

Other significant differences include a passage early in 5.1: a lengthy speech by Theseus in Q1 is broken up in F into eight short speeches alternatingly assigned to Lysander and Theseus (5.1.44–60). F adds numerous stage directions, signaling music (4.1.28, 4.1.81, 5.1.384) and Lion's roaring (5.1.253), pointing out that characters lie down (3.2.417), sleep (2.2.24, 2.2.65, 3.2.462, 4.1.100), and awake (3.2.137, 4.1.196); and providing entrance (3.2.437, 5.1.302) and exit stage directions (2.1.244, 2.2.87, 3.1.93, 3.1.182, 3.2.101, 3.2.338, 4.1.184, 4.1.196, 4.1.212, 4.2.39, 5.1.203). At one point, F has Robin enter earlier than Q1 does (F 3.1.46, Q 3.1.64), and on two occasions F's Bottom exits and re-enters, whereas Q1 keeps him onstage (3.1.93–99, 5.1.150–66). F also alters or expands some of Q1's stage directions (for example, 3.2.419). The dialogue text is often but not always identical. Three lines are present in Q1 but absent from F (3.2.344, 4.1.190–91, 5.1.308–09), and the two texts differ in many individual words. Some of the changes may have occurred during typesetting, including "filly" to "silly" (2.1.46), "interchainèd" to "interchangèd" (2.2.49), and "favors" to "savors" (4.1.47), or such minor substitutions as "off from" to "from off" (2.1.183) and "my" to "mine" (3.2.243). Yet other F changes may well be intentional—for instance, "merit" where Q1 has "friends" (1.1.139). F also omits some words present in Q1—"Ay me!" (1.1.132), "round" (2.1.175), "Helen" (3.2.173), "right" (4.2.28), and "trusty" (5.1.144)—and adds a few others, notably "here" (2.2.104), "now" (2.2.113), "passionate" (3.2.220), and "thou" (4.1.69).

Q1 and Q2 provide neither act nor scene divisions, while F divides the play into acts only. In keeping with editorial tradition and thus for the convenience of readers consulting criticism about the play, the present edition adheres to the Folio act division and inserts scene breaks when the stage is cleared and the action is discontinuous.

LUKAS ERNE

PERFORMANCE NOTE

Few plays draw attention to their artificiality like *A Midsummer Night's Dream*. In *Midsummer*, even "rude mechanicals" debate issues of theatrical representation and reception, in the course of a plot that features sudden reversals of affection, fairies visible and invisible, a man turned into an ass, and the casting, rehearsal, and performance of a play. Each production's approach to stage realism, casting, and mise-en-scène may therefore prove pivotal. Whether a production chooses to stylize the lovers' abrupt changes in affection or to mark these out as psychologically revealing, to isolate Bottom in his desire to play all the parts or to have its own actors double roles, or to cast wispy children or grown men as fairies can accentuate or hedge against the play's many advertisements of artifice.

Companies must also determine how to depict the green world and how far to complicate the play's mood and genre in their representations thereof. Benign fairy kingdoms full of flower-strewing nymphs have given way on modern stages to shadier places and menacing creatures. Is Robin Goodfellow a mischievous prankster or a predator? Should Oberon be dismayed at finding Titania matched (and mated) with an ass, or should he exult in sadistic satisfaction? Does Lysander brush Hermia aside out of adoration for Helena, or does he linger over the chance to eviscerate his former lover? Productions face a challenge in exploring the play's darker aspects, particularly the dissension and sexual aggression underlying its principal relationships, without destroying the comedy. At the return to Athens, directors must also decide whether to include Egeus in 5.1 (the Quarto text doesn't), thereby suggesting his reconciliation or continuing umbrage; whether the nobles' harsh criticism of the mechanicals' performance is superficial banter or a further means to cloud the comedy; and whether the tone of Robin's epilogue is friendly or frightening.

BRETT GAMBOA

A Midsummer Night's Dream

[THE PERSONS OF THE PLAY

THESEUS, Duke of Athens
HIPPOLYTA, Queen of the Amazons, betrothed to Theseus
EGEUS, father to Hermia
HERMIA, daughter to Egeus, in love with Lysander
LYSANDER, in love with Hermia
DEMETRIUS, in love with Hermia
HELENA, in love with Demetrius
PHILOSTRATE, Master of the Revels at the court of Theseus
Lords and Attendants on Theseus and Hippolyta

OBERON, King of the Fairies
TITANIA, Queen of the Fairies
ROBIN Goodfellow, a puck°   *an imp or a mischievous sprite*
PEASEBLOSSOM ⎫
COBWEB   ⎬ fairies in Titania's service
MOTH   ⎪
MUSTARDSEED ⎭
Other FAIRIES

Peter QUINCE, a carpenter, Prologue in the Interlude
Nick BOTTOM, a weaver, Pyramus in the Interlude
Francis FLUTE, a bellows-mender, Thisbe in the Interlude
Tom SNOUT, a tinker, Wall in the Interlude
SNUG, a joiner, Lion in the Interlude
Robin STARVELING, a tailor, Moonshine in the Interlude]

1.1 (F 1.1)

Enter THESEUS, HIPPOLYTA, [*and* PHILOSTRATE,]
with others.

THESEUS   Now, fair Hippolyta, our nuptial hour
Draws on apace. Four happy days bring in
Another moon; but, oh, methinks, how slow
This old moon wanes! She lingers° my desires   *delays fulfillment of*
5   Like to a stepdame° or a dowager   *stepmother*
Long withering out a young man's revenue.[1]
HIPPOLYTA   Four days will quickly steep° themselves in night;   *plunge*
Four nights will quickly dream away the time;
And then the moon—like to a silver bow
10   Now bent in heaven—shall behold the night
Of our solemnities.
THESEUS   Go, Philostrate,
Stir up the Athenian youth to merriments,
Awake the pert and nimble spirit of mirth,
Turn melancholy forth to funerals;

1.1 Location: Theseus's palace in Athens.   inheritance that will go to her husband's (young) heir
1. *a dowager . . . revenue*: a widow using up the   on her death.

15 The pale companion is not for our pomp.

[Exit PHILOSTRATE.]

Hippolyta, I wooed thee with my sword
And won thy love doing thee injuries;[2]
But I will wed thee in another key,
With pomp, with triumph,° and with reveling.   *public festivity*

Enter EGEUS and his daughter HERMIA, and LYSANDER
and DEMETRIUS.

20 EGEUS   Happy be Theseus, our renownèd duke!

THESEUS   Thanks, good Egeus. What's the news with thee?

EGEUS   Full of vexation come I, with complaint
Against my child, my daughter Hermia.
—Stand forth, Demetrius. —My noble lord,
25 This man hath my consent to marry her.
—Stand forth, Lysander. —And, my gracious duke,
This man hath bewitched the bosom of my child.
—Thou, thou, Lysander, thou hast given her rhymes,
And interchanged love tokens with my child.
30 Thou hast by moonlight at her window sung
With feigning[3] voice verses of feigning love,
And stolen the impression of her fantasy[4]
With bracelets of thy hair, rings, gauds,° conceits,°   *trinkets / clever gifts*
Knacks,° trifles, nosegays,° sweetmeats—messengers   *Knickknacks / bouquets*
35 Of strong prevailment° in unhardened youth.   *persuasiveness*
With cunning hast thou filched my daughter's heart,
Turned her obedience, which is due to me,
To stubborn harshness. —And, my gracious duke,
Be it so° she will not here before your grace   *If*
40 Consent to marry with Demetrius,
I beg the ancient privilege of Athens:
As she is mine, I may dispose of her,
Which shall be either to this gentleman
Or to her death, according to our law
45 Immediately° provided in that case.   *Expressly*

THESEUS   What say you, Hermia? Be advised, fair maid:
To you your father should be as a god,
One that composed° your beauties, yea, and one   *fashioned*
To whom you are but as a form in wax
50 By him imprinted,[5] and within his power
To leave° the figure or disfigure° it.   *maintain / destroy*
Demetrius is a worthy gentleman.

HERMIA   So is Lysander.

THESEUS   In himself he is,
But in this kind,° wanting your father's voice,[6]   *respect*
55 The other must be held the worthier.

HERMIA   I would my father looked but with my eyes.

THESEUS   Rather your eyes must with his judgment look.

HERMIA   I do entreat your grace to pardon me.
I know not by what power I am made bold,

---

2. Theseus captured Hippolyta in his military conquest of the Amazons.
3. A pun: deceitful; desiring ("faining"); soft (in music).
4. *stolen . . . fantasy:* by craftily impressing your image on her imagination, like a seal in wax, (you have) stolen her love.
5. *you are . . . imprinted:* you are merely a wax impression of his seal.
6. Lacking your father's consent or vote.

60	Nor how it may concern° my modesty	*befit*

60 Nor how it may concern° my modesty   *befit*
In such a presence here to plead my thoughts,
But I beseech your grace that I may know
The worst that may befall me in this case
If I refuse to wed Demetrius.

65 THESEUS Either to die the death° or to abjure   *be executed*
For ever the society of men.
Therefore, fair Hermia, question your desires,
Know° of your youth, examine well your blood,°   *Inquire / passions*
Whether, if you yield not to your father's choice,

70 You can endure the livery° of a nun,[7]   *habit*
For aye° to be in shady cloister mewed,°   *ever / caged*
To live a barren sister all your life,
Chanting faint hymns to the cold fruitless moon.[8]
Thrice blessèd they that master so their blood

75 To undergo such maiden pilgrimage;°   *life as a virgin*
But earthlier happy is the rose distilled[9]
Than that which, withering on the virgin thorn,
Grows, lives, and dies in single blessedness.°   *in celibacy*

HERMIA So will I grow, so live, so die, my lord,
80 Ere I will yield my virgin patent[1] up
Unto his lordship whose unwishèd yoke
My soul consents not to give sovereignty.

THESEUS Take time to pause, and by the next new moon—
The sealing day betwixt my love and me
85 For everlasting bond of fellowship—
Upon that day either prepare to die
For disobedience to your father's will,
Or else to wed Demetrius, as he would,
Or on Diana's altar to protest°   *vow*
90 For aye° austerity and single life.   *Forever*

DEMETRIUS Relent, sweet Hermia, and, Lysander, yield
Thy crazèd title° to my certain right.   *flawed claim*

LYSANDER You have her father's love, Demetrius;
Let me have Hermia's. Do you marry him.

95 EGEUS Scornful Lysander! True, he hath my love,
And what is mine my love shall render him;
And she is mine, and all my right of her
I do estate° unto Demetrius.   *settle; bestow*

LYSANDER [*to* THESEUS] I am, my lord, as well derived° as he,   *descended*
100 As well possessed,° my love is more than his,   *endowed with wealth*
My fortunes every way as fairly ranked,
If not with vantage,° as Demetrius'.   *superiority*
And, which is more than all these boasts can be,
I am beloved of beauteous Hermia.

105 Why should not I then prosecute° my right?   *pursue*
Demetrius, I'll avouch it to his head,°   *face*
Made love to° Nedar's daughter, Helena,   *Wooed*
And won her soul, and she, sweet lady, dotes,
Devoutly dotes, dotes in idolatry

7. Christian orders of nuns were established in the Middle Ages, but Elizabethans used the term as well for women devoted to a religious life in classical antiquity.
8. The emblem of Diana, goddess of chastity.
9. Preserved in a perfume (figuratively, preserved in her children). *earthlier happy:* happier on earth.
1. My right to remain a virgin.

110 Upon this spotted and inconstant[2] man.
THESEUS   I must confess that I have heard so much
And with Demetrius thought to have spoke thereof,
But, being overfull of self-affairs,°   *my own concerns*
My mind did lose it. —But, Demetrius, come,
115 —And come, Egeus; you shall go with me.
I have some private schooling° for you both.   *advice*
—For you, fair Hermia, look you arm° yourself   *prepare*
To fit your fancies° to your father's will,   *desires*
Or else the law of Athens yields you up,
120 Which by no means we may extenuate,°   *mitigate*
To death or to a vow of single life.
—Come, my Hippolyta. What cheer, my love?
—Demetrius and Egeus, go along.
I must employ you in some business
125 Against° our nuptial and confer with you   *In preparation for*
Of something nearly that[3] concerns yourselves.
EGEUS   With duty and desire we follow you.
               Exeunt [all but LYSANDER *and* HERMIA].
LYSANDER   How now, my love, why is your cheek so pale?
How chance the roses there do fade so fast?
130 HERMIA   Belike° for want of rain, which I could well   *Probably*
Beteem° them from the tempest of my eyes.   *Afford; grant*
LYSANDER   Ay me! For aught that I could ever read,
Could ever hear by tale or history,
The course of true love never did run smooth,
135 But either it was different in blood°—   *hereditary rank*
HERMIA   Oh, cross!° Too high to be enthralled to low.   *vexation*
LYSANDER   Or else misgraffèd[4] in respect of years—
HERMIA   Oh, spite! Too old to be engaged to young.
LYSANDER   Or else it stood° upon the choice of friends°—   *rested / kin*
140 HERMIA   Oh, hell! To choose love by another's eyes.
LYSANDER   Or if there were a sympathy° in choice,   *an agreement*
War, death, or sickness did lay siege to it,
Making it momentany° as a sound,   *momentary*
Swift as a shadow, short as any dream,
145 Brief as the lightning in the collied° night   *coal-black*
That in a spleen° unfolds° both heaven and earth   *swift impulse / reveals*
And ere a man hath power to say "Behold!"
The jaws of darkness do devour it up.
So quick bright things come to confusion.
150 HERMIA   If then true lovers have been ever° crossed,   *always*
It stands as an edict in destiny.
Then let us teach our trial patience[5]
Because it is a customary cross,
As due to love as thoughts and dreams and sighs,
155 Wishes and tears, poor fancy's° followers.   *love's*
LYSANDER   A good persuasion.° Therefore hear me, Hermia: *argument; principle*
I have a widow aunt, a dowager
Of great revenue, and she hath no child.
From Athens is her house remote seven leagues,

2. *spotted and inconstant:* fickle.
3. *nearly that:* that closely.
4. Badly matched; improperly grafted.
5. Let us teach ourselves to be patient in this trial.

160	And she respects° me as her only son.	*regards*
	There, gentle Hermia, may I marry thee,	
	And to that place the sharp Athenian law	
	Cannot pursue us. If thou lovest me then	
	Steal forth thy father's house tomorrow night,	
165	And in the wood, a league without° the town,	*outside*
	Where I did meet thee once with Helena	
	To do observance to a morn of May,°	*celebrate May Day*
	There will I stay for thee.	

HERMIA   My good Lysander,
I swear to thee by Cupid's strongest bow,

170	By his best arrow with the golden head,[6]	
	By the simplicity° of Venus' doves,[7]	*innocence*
	By that which knitteth souls and prospers loves,	
	And by that fire which burned the Carthage Queen	
	When the false Trojan under sail was seen,[8]	
175	By all the vows that ever men have broke,	
	In number more than ever women spoke,	
	In that same place thou hast appointed me	
	Tomorrow truly will I meet with thee.	

LYSANDER   Keep promise, love. Look, here comes Helena.

           Enter HELENA.

180	HERMIA God speed, fair[9] Helena! Whither away?	
	HELENA Call you me fair? That "fair" again unsay.	
	Demetrius loves your fair; oh, happy fair!°	*fortunate beauty*
	Your eyes are lodestars,° and your tongue's sweet air°	*guiding stars / melody*
	More tunable° than lark to shepherd's ear	*tuneful*
185	When wheat is green, when hawthorn buds appear.	
	Sickness is catching; oh, were favor° so,	*looks; charms*
	Your words I catch, fair Hermia, ere I go;	
	My ear should catch your voice, my eye your eye,	
	My tongue should catch your tongue's sweet melody.	
190	Were the world mine, Demetrius being bated,°	*excepted*
	The rest I'd give to be to you translated.	
	Oh, teach me how you look, and with what art	
	You sway the motion of Demetrius' heart.	
	HERMIA I frown upon him, yet he loves me still.	
195	HELENA Oh, that your frowns would teach my smiles such skill!	
	HERMIA I give him curses, yet he gives me love.	
	HELENA Oh, that my prayers could such affection move!	
	HERMIA The more I hate, the more he follows me.	
	HELENA The more I love, the more he hateth me.	
200	HERMIA His folly, Helena, is no fault of mine.	
	HELENA None but your beauty; would that fault were mine!	
	HERMIA Take comfort: he no more shall see my face.	
	Lysander and myself will fly this place.	
	Before the time I did Lysander see	

---

6. Cupid's sharp golden arrow was said to create love; his blunt lead arrow caused dislike.
7. Said to draw Venus's chariot.
8. *fire . . . seen:* Dido, Queen of Carthage, burned herself on a funeral pyre when her lover, Aeneas, sailed away.
9. The dialogue plays on the meanings "blonde," "beautiful," "beauty." Helena is presumably fair-haired and Hermia (called a "raven" at 2.2.114) a brunette.

205 Seemed Athens as a paradise to me.
     Oh, then, what graces in my love do dwell
     That he hath turned a heaven unto a hell?
LYSANDER Helen, to you our minds we will unfold:
     Tomorrow night, when Phoebe° doth behold   Diana (the moon)
210 Her silver visage in the watery glass,
     Decking with liquid pearl the bladed grass,
     A time that lovers' flights doth still° conceal,   always
     Through Athens' gates have we devised to steal.
HERMIA And in the wood where often you and I
215 Upon faint° primrose beds were wont° to lie,   pale / accustomed
     Emptying our bosoms of their counsel sweet,
     There my Lysander and myself shall meet,
     And thence from Athens turn away our eyes
     To seek new friends and stranger companies.°   the company of strangers
220 Farewell, sweet playfellow; pray thou for us,
     And good luck grant thee thy Demetrius.
     —Keep word, Lysander; we must starve our sight
     From lovers' food till morrow deep midnight.   *Exit.*
LYSANDER I will, my Hermia. —Helena, adieu.
225 As you on him, Demetrius dote on you.   *Exit.*
HELENA How happy some o'er other some[1] can be!
     Through Athens I am thought as fair as she.
     But what of that? Demetrius thinks not so.
     He will not know what all but he do know.
230 And as he errs, doting on Hermia's eyes,
     So I, admiring of his qualities.
     Things base and vile, holding no quantity,°   shape; proportion
     Love can transpose to form and dignity.
     Love looks not with the eyes but with the mind,[2]
235 And therefore is winged Cupid painted blind.
     Nor hath love's mind of any judgment taste,°   any trace of judgment
     Wings and no eyes figure° unheedy haste.   symbolize
     And therefore is love said to be a child
     Because in choice he is so oft beguiled.
240 As waggish° boys in game° themselves forswear,   playful / sport; play
     So the boy Love is perjured everywhere.
     For ere Demetrius looked on Hermia's eyne,°   eyes
     He hailed down oaths that he was only mine.
     And when this hail some heat from Hermia felt,
245 So he dissolved,° and showers of oaths did melt.   broke faith; melted
     I will go tell him of fair Hermia's flight:
     Then to the wood will he tomorrow night
     Pursue her; and for this intelligence°   information
     If I have thanks, it is a dear[3] expense.
250 But herein mean I to enrich my pain,
     To have his sight thither and back again.   *Exit.*

---

1. *o'er other some:* in comparison with others.
2. Love is promoted not by the evidence of the senses, but by the fancies of the mind.
3. Costly (because of the betrayal of secrecy and because it leads Demetrius to Hermia); or welcome (because the potential return is Demetrius's love regained).

1.2 (F 1.2)

Enter QUINCE *the carpenter, and* SNUG *the joiner, and*
BOTTOM *the weaver, and* FLUTE *the bellows-mender,*
and SNOUT *the tinker, and* STARVELING *the tailor.*[1]

QUINCE   Is all our company here?

BOTTOM   You were best to call them generally,[2] man by man,
according to the scrip.°   *script; list*

QUINCE   Here is the scroll of every man's name which is
5   thought fit through all Athens to play in our interlude° before   *brief play*
the Duke and the Duchess on his wedding day at night.

BOTTOM   First, good Peter Quince, say what the play treats on;
then read the names of the actors; and so grow to a point.[3]

QUINCE   Marry,° our play is *The Most Lamentable Comedy*   *By the Virgin Mary*
10   *and Most Cruel Death of Pyramus and Thisbe.*[4]

BOTTOM   A very good piece of work, I assure you, and a merry.
Now, good Peter Quince, call forth your actors by the scroll.
Masters, spread yourselves.

QUINCE   Answer as I call you. —Nick Bottom, the weaver?

15   BOTTOM   Ready. Name what part I am for, and proceed.

QUINCE   You, Nick Bottom, are set down for Pyramus.

BOTTOM   What is Pyramus? A lover or a tyrant?

QUINCE   A lover that kills himself, most gallant, for love.

BOTTOM   That will ask some tears in the true performing of
20   it. If I do it, let the audience look to their eyes. I will move
storms. I will condole° in some measure. To the rest. —Yet   *lament; arouse pity*
my chief humor° is for a tyrant. I could play Ercles[5] rarely,°   *inclination / excellently*
or a part to tear a cat° in, to make all split.°   *rant / go to pieces*
The raging rocks
25   And shivering shocks°   *shattering blows*
Shall break the locks
Of prison gates,
And Phibbus' car[6]
Shall shine from far
30   And make and mar
The foolish Fates.
This was lofty. Now name the rest of the players. This is
Ercles' vein, a tyrant's vein. A lover is more condoling.

QUINCE   Francis Flute, the bellows-mender?

35   FLUTE   Here, Peter Quince.

QUINCE   Flute, you must take Thisbe on you.

FLUTE   What is Thisbe, a wandering knight?°   *knight-errant*

QUINCE   It is the lady that Pyramus must love.

FLUTE   Nay, faith, let not me play a woman:[7] I have a beard
40   coming.

1.2 Location: Somewhere in the city of Athens.
1. The artisans' names recall their occupations.
Quince's name is probably derived from "quoins,"
wooden wedges used by carpenters who made buildings such as houses and theaters. The name "Snug"
evokes well-finished wooden furniture made by join-
ers. A bottom was the piece of wood on which thread
was wound; Bottom's name also connotes "ass" and
"lowest point." As Flute's name suggests, domestic
bellows whistle through holes when needing repair.
Snout's name may refer either to the spouts of the
kettles he repairs or to his nose. Tailors, as Starveling's name recalls, were proverbially thin.
2. Bottom's error for "individually" (he frequently
misuses words in this manner).
3. *grow to a point*: draw to a conclusion.
4. Parodying titles such as that of Thomas Preston's
*Cambyses: A Lamentable Tragedy Mixed Full of Pleas-
ant Mirth* . . . (ca. 1570).
5. Hercules (a stock ranting role in early plays).
6. The chariot of Phoebus Apollo, the sun god (the
odd spelling may represent Bottom's pronunciation).
7. On the Elizabethan stage, women's parts were
played by boys and young men.

QUINCE   That's all one.° You shall play it in a mask,[8] and you   *irrelevant*
  may speak as small° as you will.   *high-pitched; shrill*
BOTTOM   An° I may hide my face, let me play Thisbe too. I'll   *If*
  speak in a monstrous little voice, "Thisne, Thisne!"[9] —"Ah,
45 Pyramus, my lover dear, thy Thisbe dear and lady dear."
QUINCE   No, no, you must play Pyramus; and Flute, you Thisbe.
BOTTOM   Well, proceed.
QUINCE   Robin Starveling, the tailor?
STARVELING   Here, Peter Quince.
50 QUINCE   Robin Starveling, you must play Thisbe's mother.
  —Tom Snout, the tinker?
SNOUT   Here, Peter Quince.
QUINCE   You, Pyramus' father; myself, Thisbe's father; Snug the
  joiner, you, the lion's part; and I hope here is a play fitted.°   *(well) cast*
55 SNUG   Have you the lion's part written? Pray you, if it be, give
  it me, for I am slow of study.
QUINCE   You may do it extempore, for it is nothing but roaring.
BOTTOM   Let me play the lion too. I will roar that I will do any
  man's heart good to hear me. I will roar that I will make the
60 Duke say, "Let him roar again! Let him roar again!"
QUINCE   An you should do it too terribly, you would fright the
  Duchess and the ladies that they would shriek, and that
  were enough to hang us all.
ALL   That would hang us, every mother's son.
65 BOTTOM   I grant you, friends, if you should fright the ladies
  out of their wits, they would have no more discretion but to
  hang us. But I will aggravate° my voice so that I will roar you   *(for "moderate")*
  as gently as any sucking dove.[1] I will roar you an 'twere° any   *as though it were*
  nightingale.
70 QUINCE   You can play no part but Pyramus; for Pyramus is a
  sweet-faced man, a proper° man as one shall see in a sum-   *handsome*
  mer's day, a most lovely, gentlemanlike man. Therefore you
  must needs play Pyramus.
BOTTOM   Well, I will undertake it. What beard were I best to
75 play it in?
QUINCE   Why, what you will.
BOTTOM   I will discharge° it in either your straw-color beard,   *perform*
  your orange-tawny[2] beard, your purple-in-grain° beard, or   *very deep red*
  your French-crown-color° beard, your perfect yellow.   *gold-coin-colored*
80 QUINCE   Some of your French crowns have no hair at all,[3] and
  then you will play bare-faced.° —But, masters, here are your   *beardless; undisguised*
  parts,[4] and I am to entreat you, request you, and desire you
  to con° them by tomorrow night, and meet me in the palace   *memorize*
  wood, a mile without the town, by moonlight. There will we
85 rehearse; for if we meet in the city, we shall be dogged with
  company, and our devices° known. In the meantime, I will   *plans*
  draw a bill° of properties such as our play wants. I pray you,   *list*
  fail me not.

8. Elizabethan ladies regularly wore masks to remain
anonymous and to protect their complexions.
9. Probably intended as a pet name for Thisbe; or it
may mean "in this manner" ("thissen").
1. Bottom confuses "sitting dove" and "sucking lamb."
2. Dark yellow, a recognized name for the dye. (Bot-

tom the weaver shows his professional knowledge.)
3. Referring to the baldness caused by venereal disease (called "the French disease").
4. Literally; an Elizabethan actor was generally given
only his own lines and cues.

BOTTOM We will meet, and there we may rehearse most
90   obscenely⁵ and courageously. Take pains; be perfect.⁶ Adieu.
QUINCE At the Duke's oak we meet.
BOTTOM Enough! Hold, or cut bowstrings.⁷   *Exeunt.*

2.1 (F 2.1)

Enter a FAIRY *at one door and* ROBIN *Goodfellow*[, *a
puck,*]¹ *at another.*

ROBIN How now, spirit, whither wander you?²
FAIRY Over hill, over dale,
    Thorough° bush, thorough briar,   *Through*
    Over park, over pale,°   *enclosure; fence*
5   Thorough flood, thorough fire,
    I do wander everywhere
    Swifter than the moon's sphere;³
    And I serve the Fairy Queen
    To dew her orbs⁴ upon the green.
10   The cowslips tall her pensioners° be;   *royal bodyguards*
    In their gold coats spots you see.
    Those be rubies, fairy favors,°   *gifts*
    In those freckles live their savors.°   *scent*
    I must go seek some dewdrops here
15   And hang a pearl in every cowslip's ear.
    Farewell, thou lob° of spirits, I'll be gone.   *country bumpkin*
    Our queen and all her elves come here anon.
ROBIN The King doth keep his revels here tonight.
    Take heed the Queen come not within his sight,
20   For Oberon is passing fell and wrath⁵
    Because that she as her attendant hath
    A lovely boy stolen from an Indian king—
    She never had so sweet a changeling⁶—
    And jealous Oberon would have the child
25   Knight of his train, to trace° the forests wild.   *range*
    But she perforce° withholds the lovèd boy,   *forcibly*
    Crowns him with flowers, and makes him all her joy.
    And now they never meet in grove or green,
    By fountain° clear or spangled starlight sheen,°   *spring / shining starlight*
30   But they do square,° that all their elves for fear   *quarrel*
    Creep into acorn cups and hide them there.
FAIRY Either I mistake your shape and making° quite,   *form*
    Or else you are that shrewd° and knavish sprite   *mischievous*
    Called Robin Goodfellow. Are not you he

5. A comic blunder, possibly for "out of sight" ("from the scene" or "from being seen").
6. Be letter perfect in learning your parts.
7. *Hold, or cut bowstrings* (from military archery): Be present at the rehearsal, or else quit the troupe (?).
2.1 Location: A wood near Athens.
1. TEXTUAL COMMENT A puck is an imp or a mischievous sprite; in Elizabethan folklore, Robin Goodfellow was a puck who would do housework if well treated. In the speech prefixes of the First Quarto (Q1) and the Folio (F), this character is variously identified as "Robin" and "Puck"; this edition regularizes based on his proper name Robin Goodfellow. For more on the issue of speech prefixes and names, see Digital Edition TC 1 (Quarto edited text).

2. PERFORMANCE COMMENT While productions of *A Midsummer Night's Dream* have traditionally depicted the play's fairy forest as a place of beauty and benevolence, directors in the second half of the twentieth century began to explore the darker possibilities beneath its surface. For more, see Digital Edition PC 1.
3. Each planet, including the moon, was thought to be fixed in a transparent hollow globe revolving around the earth.
4. To sprinkle her fairy rings (circles of dark grass).
5. *passing fell and wrath:* exceedingly fierce and angry.
6. Usually a child left by fairies in exchange for one stolen, but here the stolen child.

35   That frights the maidens of the villagery,°   *villages*
    Skim milk, and sometimes labor in the quern,°   *hand mill*
    And bootless° make the breathless housewife churn,   *in vain*
    And sometime° make the drink to bear no barm,°   *at times / froth on ale*
    Mislead night-wanderers, laughing at their harm?
40   Those that "hobgoblin" call you, and "sweet puck,"
    You do their work, and they shall have good luck.
    Are not you he?
    ROBIN   Thou speakest aright;
    I am that merry wanderer of the night.
    I jest to Oberon and make him smile
45   When I a fat and bean-fed horse beguile,°   *trick*
    Neighing in likeness of a filly foal.
    And sometime lurk I in a gossip's° bowl   *an old woman's*
    In very likeness of a roasted crab,[7]
    And when she drinks, against her lips I bob,
50   And on her withered dewlap° pour the ale.   *loose skin on neck*
    The wisest aunt° telling the saddest° tale   *old woman / most serious*
    Sometime for three-foot stool mistaketh me.
    Then slip I from her bum, down topples she,
    And "tailor" cries,[8] and falls into a cough;
55   And then the whole choir° hold their hips and laugh,   *company*
    And waxen° in their mirth, and neeze,° and swear   *increase / sneeze*
    A merrier hour was never wasted there.
    But room, fairy: here comes Oberon.
    FAIRY   And here my mistress. Would that he were gone.
           Enter [OBERON,] *the King of Fairies, at one door, with*
           his train, and [TITANIA,] *the Queen, at another, with*
           hers.[9]
60   OBERON   Ill met by moonlight, proud Titania.
    TITANIA   What, jealous Oberon? —Fairy, skip hence.
    I have forsworn his bed and company.
    OBERON   Tarry, rash wanton!° Am not I thy lord?   *impetuous creature*
    TITANIA   Then I must be thy lady; but I know
65   When thou hast stolen away from fairyland
    And in the shape of Corin[1] sat all day
    Playing on pipes of corn and versing love[2]
    To amorous Phillida. Why art thou here
    Come from the farthest step° of India   *limit*
70   But that, forsooth, the bouncing° Amazon,   *vigorous*
    Your buskined° mistress and your warrior love,   *wearing hunting boots*
    To Theseus must be wedded, and you come
    To give their bed joy and prosperity?
    OBERON   How canst thou thus, for shame, Titania,
75   Glance at my credit° with Hippolyta,   *Question my good name*
    Knowing I know thy love to Theseus?
    Didst not thou lead him through the glimmering night

---

7. Crab apple ("lamb's wool," a winter drink, was made with roasted apples and warm ale).
8. Possibly the old woman cries this because she ends up cross-legged on the floor, as tailors sat to do their work, or because she falls on her "tail."
9. PERFORMANCE COMMENT Many productions of the play have opted to cast actors and actresses in more than one role, such as having the same actor perform

as both Theseus and Oberon. For more on doubling and its interpretive implications for the play, see Digital Edition PC 2.
1. "Corin" and "Phillida" are typical names for a shepherd and shepherdess in pastoral poetry.
2. Making or reciting love poetry. *pipes of corn:* musical instruments made of oat stalks.

From Perigenia, whom he ravishèd,
And make him with fair Aegles[3] break his faith,
80 With Ariadne, and Antiopa?[4]
TITANIA These are the forgeries of jealousy;
And never since the middle summer's spring°   *beginning of midsummer*
Met we on hill, in dale, forest, or mead,
By pavèd fountain or by rushy[5] brook,
85 Or in° the beachèd margin° of the sea   *on / shore*
To dance our ringlets° to the whistling wind,   *circle dances*
But with thy brawls thou hast disturbed our sport.
Therefore the winds, piping to us in vain,
As in revenge have sucked up from the sea
90 Contagious fogs which, falling in the land,
Hath every pelting° river made so proud   *paltry*
That they have overborne their continents.°   *banks*
The ox hath therefore stretched his yoke in vain,
The plowman lost his sweat, and the green corn°   *grain*
95 Hath rotted ere his youth attained a beard.
The fold stands empty in the drownèd field,
And crows are fatted with the murrain° flock;   *dead of disease*
The nine-men's morris[6] is filled up with mud,
And the quaint mazes in the wanton green[7]
100 For lack of tread are undistinguishable.
The human mortals want° their winter cheer;[8]   *lack*
No night is now with hymn or carol blessed.
Therefore[9] the moon, the governess of floods,
Pale in her anger, washes° all the air,   *moistens; wets*
105 That rheumatic[1] diseases do abound.
And thorough this distemperature° we see   *bad weather; disturbance*
The seasons alter; hoary-headed frosts
Fall in the fresh lap of the crimson rose,
And on old Hiems'° chin and icy crown   *winter's*
110 An odorous chaplet° of sweet summer buds   *wreath*
Is, as in mockery, set. The spring, the summer,
The childing° autumn, angry winter, change   *fruitful*
Their wonted liveries,[2] and the mazèd° world   *bewildered*
By their increase° now knows not which is which.   *crop yield*
115 And this same progeny of evils comes
From our debate,° from our dissension;   *quarrel*
We are their parents and original.°   *origin*
OBERON Do you amend it then; it lies in you.
Why should Titania cross her Oberon?
120 I do but beg a little changeling boy
To be my henchman.°   *page of honor*
TITANIA   Set your heart at rest.[3]

---

3. In Plutarch's *Lives*, Theseus previously had mistresses named Perigouna and Aegles. "Perigenia" may be Shakespeare's alteration.
4. Taken from Plutarch; some writers used "Antiopa" as an alternative name for the Amazonian queen whom Theseus married, although here it seems to refer to a different woman. Ariadne helped Theseus to kill the Minotaur and escape from his labyrinth on Crete; she fled with Theseus, but he deserted her on Naxos.
5. Fringed with reeds. *pavèd:* pebbled.
6. The playing area for this outdoor game (tradition-

ally, a board game played with nine pebbles or pegs) was cut in turf.
7. Luxuriant grass. *quaint mazes:* intricate arrangements of paths (kept visible by frequent use).
8. Winter cheer would include the hymns and carols of the Yuletide. But Q1 and F read "here."
9. As in lines 88 and 93 above, referring to the consequences of their quarrel.
1. Characterized by rheum: colds, coughs, and the like.
2. Customary clothing.
3. Proverbial expression for "Abandon that idea."

The fairyland buys not the child of me.
His mother was a votress[4] of my order,
And in the spicèd Indian air by night
125 Full often hath she gossiped by my side
And sat with me on Neptune's yellow sands,
Marking the embarkèd traders° on the flood,°   merchant ships / tide
When we have laughed to see the sails conceive
And grow big-bellied with the wanton° wind,   playful; amorous
130 Which she, with pretty and with swimming[5] gait
Following°—her womb then rich with my young squire—   Copying
Would imitate, and sail upon the land
To fetch me trifles and return again,
As from a voyage, rich with merchandise.
135 But she, being mortal, of that boy did die,
And for her sake do I rear up her boy,
And for her sake I will not part with him.
OBERON   How long within this wood intend you stay?
TITANIA   Perchance till after Theseus' wedding day.
140 If you will patiently dance in our round
And see our moonlight revels, go with us.
If not, shun me, and I will spare° your haunts.   avoid
OBERON   Give me that boy, and I will go with thee.
TITANIA   Not for thy fairy kingdom. —Fairies, away!
145 We shall chide° downright if I longer stay.   quarrel
                    Exeunt [TITANIA *and her train*].
OBERON   Well, go thy way. Thou shalt not from° this grove   go from
Till I torment thee for this injury.
—My gentle puck, come hither. Thou rememberest
Since° once I sat upon a promontory   When
150 And heard a mermaid on a dolphin's back
Uttering such dulcet° and harmonious breath°   sweet / voice; song
That the rude° sea grew civil at her song   rough
And certain stars shot madly from their spheres°   orbits
To hear the sea-maid's music?
ROBIN   I remember.
155 OBERON   That very time I saw—but thou couldst not—
Flying between the cold moon and the earth,
Cupid, all armed. A certain aim he took
At a fair vestal thronèd by the west,[6]
And loosed his love-shaft° smartly from his bow   golden arrow
160 As° it should pierce a hundred thousand hearts.   As though
But I might° see young Cupid's fiery shaft   could
Quenched in the chaste beams of the watery moon;
And the imperial votress passèd on
In maiden meditation, fancy-free.°   free of love thoughts
165 Yet marked I where the bolt° of Cupid fell.   arrow
It fell upon a little western flower,
Before milk-white, now purple with love's wound,
And maidens call it "love-in-idleness."[7]

---

4. A woman who has taken a vow to serve (often, religious).
5. As though gliding through the waves.
6. To the west of India; in England. *vestal:* virgin (a compliment to Queen Elizabeth, the Virgin Queen, and possibly an allusion to a specific entertainment in her honor, such as the water pageant at Elvetham in 1591).
7. Pansy. (Classical legend describes how the mulberry turned purple with Pyramus's blood and the hyacinth with Hyacinthus's, but it does not mention the pansy.)

Fetch me that flower. The herb I showed thee once:
170   The juice of it on sleeping eyelids laid
  Will make or° man or woman madly dote   *either*
  Upon the next live creature that it sees.
  Fetch me this herb, and be thou here again
  Ere the leviathan[8] can swim a league.
175 ROBIN   I'll put a girdle° round about the earth   *circle*
  In forty minutes.
    OBERON   Having once this juice,
  I'll watch Titania when she is asleep
  And drop the liquor° of it in her eyes.   *juice*
  The next thing then she waking looks upon—
180   Be it on lion, bear, or wolf, or bull,
  On meddling monkey or on busy ape—
  She shall pursue it with the soul of love.
  And ere I take this charm from off her sight—
  As I can take it with another herb—
185   I'll make her render up her page to me.
  But who comes here? I am invisible,
  And I will overhear their conference.
         Enter DEMETRIUS, HELENA *following him.*
  DEMETRIUS   I love thee not, therefore pursue me not.
  Where is Lysander and fair Hermia?
190   The one I'll stay, the other stayeth me.[9]
  Thou told'st me they were stolen unto this wood,
  And here am I, and wood° within this wood   *insane*
  Because I cannot meet my Hermia.
  Hence, get thee gone, and follow me no more.
195 HELENA   You draw me, you hard-hearted adamant,[1]
  But yet you draw not iron, for my heart
  Is true as steel.[2] Leave you° your power to draw,   *Relinquish*
  And I shall have no power to follow you.
  DEMETRIUS   Do I entice you? Do I speak you fair?[3]
200   Or rather do I not in plainest truth
  Tell you I do not nor I cannot love you?
  HELENA   And even for that do I love you the more.
  I am your spaniel, and, Demetrius,
  The more you beat me I will fawn on you.
205   Use me but as your spaniel: spurn me, strike me,
  Neglect me, lose me—only give me leave,
  Unworthy as I am, to follow you.
  What worser place can I beg in your love—
  And yet a place of high respect with me—
210   Than to be usèd as you use your dog?
  DEMETRIUS   Tempt not too much the hatred of my spirit,
  For I am sick when I do look on thee.
  HELENA   And I am sick when I look not on you.
  DEMETRIUS   You do impeach° your modesty too much   *call into question*
215   To leave the city and commit yourself

---

8. Biblical sea monster, identified with the whale.
9. The one (Lysander) I'll bring to a halt, the other (Hermia) stops me in my tracks.
1. Very hard stone supposed to have magnetic properties. *draw me:* that is, with the magnetic power of attraction.
2. Hermia contrasts the base metal iron with steel, which holds its temper.
3. Do I speak kindly to you?

Into the hands of one that loves you not,
To trust the opportunity of night
And the ill counsel of a desert° place   *deserted*
With the rich worth of your virginity.
220   HELENA   Your virtue is my privilege.° For that°   *protection / Because*
It is not night when I do see your face.
Therefore I think I am not in the night,
Nor doth this wood lack worlds of company,
For you in my respect° are all the world.   *as far as I am concerned*
225   Then how can it be said I am alone
When all the world is here to look on me?
DEMETRIUS   I'll run from thee and hide me in the brakes,°   *thickets*
And leave thee to the mercy of wild beasts.
HELENA   The wildest hath not such a heart as you.
230   Run when you will. The story shall be changed:
Apollo flies, and Daphne holds the chase;[4]
The dove pursues the griffin;[5] the mild hind°   *doe*
Makes speed to catch the tiger: bootless° speed   *useless*
When cowardice pursues and valor flies.
235   DEMETRIUS   I will not stay thy questions.[6] Let me go!
Or if thou follow me, do not believe
But I shall do thee mischief in the wood.   [*Exit.*][7]
HELENA   Ay, in the temple, in the town, the field,
You do me mischief. Fie, Demetrius,
240   Your wrongs do set a scandal on my sex.[8]
We cannot fight for love as men may do;
We should be wooed and were not made to woo.
I'll follow thee and make a heaven of hell
To die upon the hand I love so well.   [*Exit.*]
245   OBERON   Fare thee well, nymph. Ere he do leave this grove
Thou shalt fly him, and he shall seek thy love.
          Enter [ROBIN *Goodfellow, the*] *puck.*
Hast thou the flower there? Welcome, wanderer.
ROBIN   Ay, there it is.
OBERON   I pray thee give it me.
I know a bank where the wild thyme blows,
250   Where oxlips[9] and the nodding violet grows,
Quite over-canopied with luscious woodbine,°   *honeysuckle*
With sweet musk-roses,[1] and with eglantine.°   *sweetbrier (a type of rose)*
There sleeps Titania sometime of the night,
Lulled in these flowers with dances and delight;
255   And there the snake throws° her enameled skin,   *throws off; casts away*
Weed° wide enough to wrap a fairy in.   *Garment*
And with the juice of this I'll streak° her eyes,   *anoint*
And make her full of hateful fantasies.
Take thou some of it, and seek through this grove.
260   A sweet Athenian lady is in love

---

4. A reversal of the traditional myth in which the nymph Daphne, flying from Apollo, was transformed into a laurel tree to escape him.
5. A fabulous monster with a lion's body and an eagle's head and wings.
6. I will not wait here any longer to hear you talk.
7. TEXTUAL COMMENT Neither Q1 nor F provides an exit for Demetrius in this scene; however, when exactly

he leaves has important implications for the tone of Helena's speech. See Digital Edition TC 2 (Quarto edited text).
8. Your injustices to me cause me to behave in a way that disgraces my sex (by wooing him rather than being wooed).
9. Hybrid between primrose and cowslip.
1. Large rambling white roses.

With a disdainful youth. Anoint his eyes,
But do it when the next thing he espies
May be the lady. Thou shalt know the man
By the Athenian garments he hath on.
265   Effect it with some care, that he may prove
More fond° on her than she upon her love.   doting
And look thou meet me ere the first cock crow.[2]
ROBIN   Fear not, my lord; your servant shall do so.   *Exeunt.*

2.2 (F 2.2)

Enter TITANIA, *Queen of Fairies, with her train.*
TITANIA   Come, now a roundel° and a fairy song;   circle dance
Then, for the third part of a minute,[1] hence,
Some to kill cankers° in the musk-rose buds,   caterpillars
Some war with reremice° for their leathern wings   bats
5   To make my small elves coats, and some keep back
The clamorous owl that nightly hoots and wonders
At our quaint° spirits. Sing me now asleep;   dainty
Then to your offices, and let me rest.
        [*She lies down.*] FAIRIES *sing* [*and dance*].
FIRST FAIRY   You spotted snakes with double° tongue,   forked
10   Thorny hedgehogs, be not seen;
              Newts and blindworms,[2] do no wrong,
              Come not near our Fairy Queen.
CHORUS   Philomel,[3] with melody
              Sing in our sweet lullaby;
15   Lulla, lulla, lullaby, lulla, lulla, lullaby.
              Never harm,
              Nor spell, nor charm
              Come our lovely lady nigh.
              So good night, with lullaby.
20   FIRST FAIRY   Weaving spiders, come not here;
              Hence, you long-legged spinners, hence!
              Beetles black, approach not near;
              Worm nor snail, do no offense.
CHORUS   Philomel, with melody, etc.
        [TITANIA *sleeps.*]
25   SECOND FAIRY   Hence, away! Now all is well.
One aloof° stand sentinel.   at a distance
        [*Exeunt* FAIRIES, *leaving one sentinel.*]
        Enter OBERON. [*He squeezes the juice on Titania's eyes.*]
OBERON   What thou seest when thou dost wake,
Do it for thy true love take;
Love and languish for his sake.
30   Be it ounce° or cat or bear,   lynx
Pard,° or boar with bristled hair,   Leopard
In thy eye that shall appear
When thou wak'st, it is thy dear.
Wake when some vile thing is near.   [*Exit.*]
        Enter LYSANDER *and* HERMIA.

---

2. Some spirits were thought unable to bear daylight
(compare *Hamlet* 1.1.138–56).
2.2 Location: The wood.
1. The fairies are quick enough to do their tasks in
twenty seconds.

2. Newts (water lizards) and blindworms were thought
to be poisonous, as were spiders (line 20).
3. Philomel, the nightingale (in classical mythology,
a woman who, having been raped by her sister's husband, was transformed into a bird).

35 LYSANDER Fair love, you faint with wandering in the wood,
  And to speak truth, I have forgot our way.
  We'll rest us, Hermia, if you think it good,
  And tarry for the comfort of the day.
  HERMIA Be it so, Lysander. Find you out a bed,
40 For I upon this bank will rest my head.
  LYSANDER One turf shall serve as pillow for us both;
  One heart, one bed, two bosoms, and one troth.°   *pledged faith*
  HERMIA Nay, good Lysander: for my sake, my dear,
  Lie further off yet; do not lie so near.
45 LYSANDER Oh, take the sense,° sweet, of my innocence!   *true meaning*
  Love takes the meaning in love's conference.[4]
  I mean that my heart unto yours is knit,
  So that but one heart we can make of it.
  Two bosoms interchainèd with an oath;
50 So, then, two bosoms and a single troth.
  Then by your side no bed-room me deny,
  For lying so, Hermia, I do not lie.[5]
  HERMIA Lysander riddles very prettily.
  Now much beshrew[6] my manners and my pride
55 If Hermia meant to say Lysander lied.
  But, gentle friend, for love and courtesy
  Lie further off in human° modesty.   *courteous*
  Such separation as may well be said
  Becomes a virtuous bachelor and a maid,
60 So far be distant. And good night, sweet friend;
  Thy love ne'er alter till thy sweet life end.
  LYSANDER Amen, amen, to that fair prayer say I,
  And then end life when I end loyalty.
  Here is my bed. Sleep give thee all his rest.
65 HERMIA With half that wish the wisher's eyes be pressed.[7]
  [*They sleep separately.*]
  Enter [ROBIN *Goodfellow, the*] *puck.*
  ROBIN Through the forest have I gone,
  But Athenian found I none
  On whose eyes I might approve°   *test*
  This flower's force in stirring love.
70 Night and silence. Who is here?
  Weeds of Athens he doth wear.
  This is he my master said
  Despisèd the Athenian maid;
  And here the maiden, sleeping sound
75 On the dank and dirty ground.
  Pretty soul, she durst not lie
  Near this lack-love, this kill-courtesy.
  Churl,° upon thy eyes I throw   *Rude fellow*
  All the power this charm doth owe.°   *own*
  [*He squeezes the juice on Lysander's eyes.*]
80 When thou wak'st, let love forbid
  Sleep his seat on thy eyelid.[8]

---

4. Love should enable lovers truly to understand each other.
5. Deceive; punning on "lie down."
6. Curse (used in a mild sense).

7. May sleep's rest be shared between us. *pressed:* closed in sleep.
8. *forbid . . . eyelid:* prevent you from sleeping.

So awake when I am gone,
For I must now to Oberon.   *Exit.*
    Enter DEMETRIUS *and* HELENA, *running.*
  HELENA   Stay, though thou kill me, sweet Demetrius.
85 DEMETRIUS   I charge thee: hence, and do not haunt me thus.
  HELENA   Oh, wilt thou darkling° leave me? Do not so.   *in darkness*
  DEMETRIUS   Stay, on thy peril;⁹ I alone will go.   [*Exit.*]
  HELENA   Oh, I am out of breath in this fond° chase.   *foolish*
The more my prayer, the lesser is my grace.°   *reward*
90 Happy is Hermia, wheresoe'er she lies,
For she hath blessèd and attractive° eyes.   *magnetic*
How came her eyes so bright? Not with salt tears;
If so, my eyes are oftener washed than hers.
No, no; I am as ugly as a bear,
95 For beasts that meet me run away for fear.
Therefore no marvel though Demetrius
Do, as° a monster, fly my presence thus.   *as if I were*
What wicked and dissembling glass of mine
Made me compare° with Hermia's sphery eyne?°   *compete / starry eyes*
100 But who is here? Lysander, on the ground?
Dead or asleep? I see no blood, no wound.
Lysander, if you live, good sir, awake.
  LYSANDER [*awaking*]   And run through fire I will for thy
      sweet sake.
Transparent¹ Helena, nature shows art°   *skill; magic power*
105 That through thy bosom makes me see thy heart.
Where is Demetrius? Oh, how fit a word
Is that vile name to perish on my sword!
  HELENA   Do not say so, Lysander; say not so.
What though he love your Hermia? Lord, what though?
110 Yet Hermia still loves you; then be content.
  LYSANDER   Content with Hermia? No, I do repent
The tedious minutes I with her have spent.
Not Hermia but Helena I love.
Who will not change a raven for a dove?
115 The will of man is by his reason swayed,²
And reason says you are the worthier maid.
Things growing are not ripe until their season,
So I, being young, till now ripe not to reason.
And, touching now the point of human skill,³
120 Reason becomes the marshal⁴ to my will
And leads me to your eyes, where I o'erlook°   *look over; read*
Love's stories written in love's richest book.
  HELENA   Wherefore was I to this keen° mockery born?   *sharp*
When at your hands did I deserve this scorn?
125 Is't not enough, is't not enough, young man,
That I did never—no, nor never can—
Deserve a sweet look from Demetrius' eye,
But you must flout my insufficiency?⁵

---

9. Stay here, or risk peril (if you follow me).
1. Radiant; capable of being seen through.
2. Renaissance psychology considered the will (that is, the passions) to be in constant conflict with, and ideally subject to, the faculty of reason.

3. Reaching (only) now the highest point of human judgment.
4. An officer who led guests to their appointed places.
5. *flout my insufficiency:* mock my shortcomings by pretending they are wonderful qualities.

Good troth,° you do me wrong—good sooth,° you do—   *Truly / indeed*
130 In such disdainful manner me to woo.
But fare you well. Perforce I must confess
I thought you lord of more true gentleness.°   *courtesy; breeding*
Oh, that a lady of one man refused
Should of° another therefore be abused!   *Exit.*   *by*
135 LYSANDER   She sees not Hermia. —Hermia, sleep thou there,
And never mayst thou come Lysander near;
For as a surfeit of the sweetest things
The deepest loathing to the stomach brings,
Or as the heresies that men do leave
140 Are hated most of those they did deceive,[6]
So thou, my surfeit and my heresy,
Of all be hated, but the most of me!
And, all my powers, address° your love and might   *direct; apply*
To honor Helen and to be her knight.   *Exit.*
145 HERMIA [*awaking*]   Help me, Lysander, help me! Do thy best
To pluck this crawling serpent from my breast!
Ay me, for pity! What a dream was here!
Lysander, look how I do quake with fear.
Methought a serpent ate my heart away,
150 And you sat smiling at his cruel prey.°   *act of preying*
Lysander? What, removed? Lysander! Lord!
What, out of hearing, gone? No sound, no word?
Alack, where are you? Speak an if° you hear,   *an if = if*
Speak, of° all loves! I swoon almost with fear.   *for the sake of*
155 No? Then I well perceive you are not nigh.
Either death or you I'll find immediately.
                    Exit. [TITANIA *remains lying asleep.*]

3.1 (F 3.1)

Enter the clowns°[, BOTTOM, QUINCE, SNOUT,   *rustics*
    STARVELING, FLUTE, *and* SNUG].

BOTTOM   Are we all met?
QUINCE   Pat,° pat; and here's a marvelous convenient place for   *On the dot*
    our rehearsal. This green plot shall be our stage, this haw-
    thorn brake° our tiring-house,° and we will do it in action as   *thicket / dressing room*
5   we will do it before the Duke.
BOTTOM   Peter Quince?
QUINCE   What sayest thou, bully° Bottom?   *good fellow; jolly*
BOTTOM   There are things in this comedy of Pyramus and
    Thisbe that will never please. First, Pyramus must draw a
10   sword to kill himself, which the ladies cannot abide. How
    answer you that?
SNOUT   By'r lakin,[1] a parlous° fear.   *perilous*
STARVELING   I believe we must leave the killing out, when all
    is done.[2]
15 BOTTOM   Not a whit. I have a device to make all well. Write me
    a prologue, and let the prologue seem to say we will do no
    harm with our swords, and that Pyramus is not killed indeed.
    And for the more better assurance, tell them that I, Pyramus,

---

6. *as the heresies . . . deceive:* as men most hate the
false opinions they once held.
3.1 Location: Remains the same, although F introduces an act break.
1. By our ladykin (Virgin Mary): a mild oath.
2. When all is said and done.

am not Pyramus but Bottom the weaver. This will put them
out of fear.

20

QUINCE Well, we will have such a prologue, and it shall be
written in eight and six.[3]

BOTTOM No, make it two more: let it be written in eight and
eight.

25 SNOUT Will not the ladies be afeard of the lion?

STARVELING I fear it, I promise you.

BOTTOM Masters, you ought to consider with yourself, to bring
in—God shield us!—a lion among ladies is a most dreadful
thing.[4] For there is not a more fearful° wildfowl than your lion   *frightening*

30 living. And we ought to look to't.

SNOUT Therefore another prologue must tell he is not a lion.

BOTTOM Nay, you must name his name, and half his face
must be seen through the lion's neck, and he himself must
speak through, saying thus or to the same defect:° "Ladies,"   *(for "effect")*

35 or "Fair Ladies, I would wish you," or "I would request you,"
or "I would entreat you not to fear, not to tremble. My life
for yours.[5] If you think I come hither as a lion, it were pity
of° my life. No, I am no such thing. I am a man as other men   *a threat to*
are"—and there indeed let him name his name, and tell

40 them plainly he is Snug the joiner.

QUINCE Well, it shall be so. But there is two hard things: that
is, to bring the moonlight into a chamber—for you know
Pyramus and Thisbe meet by moonlight.

SNOUT[6] Doth the moon shine that night we play our play?

45 BOTTOM A calendar, a calendar! Look in the almanac; find
out moonshine, find out moonshine!

QUINCE Yes, it doth shine that night.

BOTTOM Why, then may you leave a casement of the great
chamber window where we play open, and the moon may

50 shine in at the casement.

QUINCE Ay, or else one must come in with a bush of thorns
and a lantern and say he comes to disfigure,[7] or to present,°   *represent*
the person of Moonshine. Then there is another thing: we
must have a wall in the great chamber; for Pyramus and

55 Thisbe, says the story, did talk through the chink of a wall.

SNOUT You can never bring in a wall. What say you, Bottom?

BOTTOM Some man or other must present Wall; and let him
have some plaster, or some loam, or some roughcast[8] about
him to signify "wall"; or let him hold his fingers thus, and

60 through that cranny shall Pyramus and Thisbe whisper.

QUINCE If that may be, then all is well. Come, sit down, every
mother's son, and rehearse your parts. Pyramus, you begin.
When you have spoken your speech, enter into that brake,
and so everyone according to his cue.

Enter ROBIN[*, invisible*].[9]

---

3. Alternate lines of eight and six syllables (a common ballad measure).
4. In 1594, at a feast in honor of the christening of King James's son, a tame lion that was supposed to draw a chariot was replaced by a black African man in order to avoid frightening the audience.
5. I pledge my life to defend yours.
6. Or Snug: Q1 and F abbreviate as "*Sn.*"
7. Blunder for "figure," represent. *bush of thorns:*

bundle of thornbush kindling (like the lantern, a traditional accessory of the man in the moon).
8. Mixture of lime and gravel used to plaster exterior walls.
9. TEXTUAL COMMENT Throughout the scene, the various entrances of Robin and Bottom differ between Q1 and F, with significant implications for staging possibilities. See Digital Edition TC 3 (Quarto edited text).

65 ROBIN [*aside*]   What hempen homespuns[1] have we swaggering
  here
  So near the cradle of the Fairy Queen?
  What, a play toward?° I'll be an auditor—   *in preparation*
  An actor too perhaps, if I see cause.
QUINCE Speak, Pyramus. —Thisbe, stand forth.
70 BOTTOM [*as Pyramus*]   "Thisbe, the flowers of odious° savors *(for "odorous")*
  sweet—"
QUINCE Odors—"odorous"!
BOTTOM [*as Pyramus*]   "—Odors savors sweet.
  So hath thy breath, my dearest Thisbe dear.
  But hark, a voice! Stay thou but here a while,
75   And by and by I will to thee appear."   *Exit.*
QUINCE A stranger Pyramus than e'er played here. [*Exit.*]
FLUTE Must I speak now?
QUINCE Ay, marry, must you. For you must understand he
  goes but to see a noise that he heard and is to come again.
80 FLUTE [*as Thisbe*]   "Most radiant Pyramus, most lily-white
  of hue,
  Of color like the red rose on triumphant briar,
  Most brisky juvenal° and eke° most lovely Jew,[2] *lively youth (juvenile) / also*
  As true as truest horse that yet would never tire,
  I'll meet thee, Pyramus, at Ninny's tomb—"
85 QUINCE "Ninus'[3] tomb," man! Why, you must not speak that
  yet; that you answer to Pyramus. You speak all your part at
  once, cues and all. —Pyramus, enter! Your cue is past; it is
  "never tire."
FLUTE Oh,
90   [*as Thisbe*] "As true as truest horse that yet would never tire."
    [*Enter* ROBIN, *invisible, and* BOTTOM *with the
    ass head on.*]
BOTTOM [*as Pyramus*]   "If I were fair,° Thisbe, I were° only *handsome / would be*
  thine."
QUINCE Oh, monstrous! Oh, strange! We are haunted! Pray,
  masters! Fly, masters! Help!
     [*Exeunt* QUINCE, SNOUT, STARVELING,
       FLUTE, *and* SNUG.]
ROBIN I'll follow you, I'll lead you about a round,° *in circles*
95   Through bog, through bush, through brake, through briar.
  Sometime a horse I'll be, sometime a hound,
  A hog, a headless bear, sometime a fire,° *will-o'-the-wisp*
  And neigh and bark and grunt and roar and burn,
  Like horse, hound, hog, bear, fire, at every turn. *Exit.*
100 BOTTOM Why do they run away? This is a knavery of them to
  make me afeard.
    Enter SNOUT.
SNOUT O Bottom, thou art changed! What do I see on thee?

---

1. Peasants, or country bumpkins, dressed in coarse
homespun fabric made from hemp.
2. Not often considered "lovely" by Elizabethan Christians; usually, a term of abuse (here, echoing the first
syllable of "juvenal").

3. Mythical founder of Nineveh, whose wife, Semiramis, was believed to have founded Babylon, the setting for the story of Pyramus and Thisbe. Flute's
mistake, "Ninny," means "fool."

BOTTOM   What do you see? You see an ass head of your own,[4]
do you?   [*Exit* SNOUT.]
     Enter QUINCE.

105   QUINCE   Bless thee, Bottom, bless thee! Thou art translated.°   transformed
                                                                         Exit.

BOTTOM   I see their knavery. This is to make an ass of me, to
fright me, if they could. But I will not stir from this place,
do what they can. I will walk up and down here, and I will
sing, that they shall hear I am not afraid.

110   [*Sings.*]   The ouzel cock,° so black of hue,   male blackbird
               With orange-tawny bill,
               The throstle° with his note so true,   song thrush
               The wren with little quill°—   feathers

TITANIA [*awaking*]   What angel wakes me from my flowery
       bed?

115   BOTTOM [*sings*]   The finch, the sparrow, and the lark,
               The plainsong[5] cuckoo gray,
               Whose note full many a man doth mark
               And dares not answer "Nay"[6]—
for indeed, who would set his wit to° so foolish a bird? Who   pay heed to

120   would give a bird the lie,[7] though he cry "cuckoo" never so?°   ever so much

TITANIA   I pray thee, gentle mortal, sing again.
Mine ear is much enamored of thy note;
So is mine eye enthrallèd to thy shape,
And thy fair virtue's force[8] perforce doth move me

125   On the first view to say, to swear, I love thee.

BOTTOM   Methinks, mistress, you should have little reason
for that. And yet, to say the truth, reason and love keep little
company together nowadays—the more the pity that some
honest neighbors will not make them friends. Nay, I can

130   gleek° upon occasion.   make jokes

TITANIA   Thou art as wise as thou art beautiful.

BOTTOM   Not so neither; but if I had wit enough to get out of
this wood, I have enough to serve mine own turn.°   purpose

TITANIA   Out of this wood do not desire to go.

135   Thou shalt remain here, whether thou wilt or no.
I am a spirit of no common rate°—   rank
The summer still° doth tend upon my state[9]—   always; continually
And I do love thee. Therefore go with me.
I'll give thee fairies to attend on thee,

140   And they shall fetch thee jewels from the deep
And sing while thou on pressèd flowers dost sleep.
And I will purge thy mortal grossness° so   fleshly being
That thou shalt like an airy spirit go.
Peaseblossom, Cobweb, Moth, and Mustardseed!
     Enter four FAIRIES[: PEASEBLOSSOM, COBWEB, MOTH,[1]
     and MUSTARDSEED].

PEASEBLOSSOM   Ready.

COBWEB   And I.

---

4. You see a figment of your own asinine imagination.
5. A melody sung without adornment (that is, the cuckoo's call).
6. Deny. (The cuckoo's call was associated with cuckoldry.)

7. Who would call a bird a liar?
8. The power of your good or beauteous qualities.
9. Serves me, as part of my royal retinue.
1. As it is spelled in Q1 and F, or "Mote": speck. Both words were spelled and pronounced alike.

MOTH	And I.
MUSTARDSEED	And I.

145   ALL   Where shall we go?

TITANIA   Be kind and courteous to this gentleman.
      Hop in his walks and gambol in his eyes;
      Feed him with apricots and dewberries,
      With purple grapes, green figs, and mulberries;
150   The honey bags steal from the humble-bees,°   *bumblebees*
      And for night-tapers crop their waxen thighs,
      And light them at the fiery glowworms' eyes
      To have° my love to bed and to arise;   *lead*
      And pluck the wings from painted butterflies
155   To fan the moonbeams from his sleeping eyes.
      Nod to him, elves, and do him courtesies.
PEASEBLOSSOM   Hail, mortal!
COBWEB   Hail!
MOTH   Hail!
160   MUSTARDSEED   Hail!
BOTTOM   I cry your worships mercy,[2] heartily. —I beseech
      your worship's name.
COBWEB   Cobweb.
BOTTOM   I shall desire you of more acquaintance, good Mas-
165   ter Cobweb. If I cut my finger,[3] I shall make bold with you.
      —Your name, honest gentleman?
PEASEBLOSSOM   Peaseblossom.
BOTTOM   I pray you commend me to Mistress Squash, your
      mother, and to Master Peascod,[4] your father. Good Master
170   Peaseblossom, I shall desire you of more acquaintance too.
      —Your name, I beseech you, sir?
MUSTARDSEED   Mustardseed.
BOTTOM   Good Master Mustardseed, I know your patience[5]
      well. That same cowardly, giant-like ox-beef[6] hath devoured
175   many a gentleman of your house. I promise you, your kin-
      dred hath made my eyes water ere now. I desire you of more
      acquaintance, good Master Mustardseed.
TITANIA [*to the* FAIRIES]   Come, wait upon him. Lead him to
      my bower.
      The moon methinks looks with a watery eye,
180   And when she weeps, weeps every little flower,[7]
      Lamenting some enforcèd° chastity.   *violated; involuntary*
      Tie up my lover's tongue;[8] bring him silently.   [*Exeunt.*]

3.2 (F 3.2)

Enter [OBERON,] *King of Fairies.*

OBERON   I wonder if Titania be awaked;
      Then what it was that next came in her eye,
      Which she must dote on in extremity.

      Enter ROBIN *Goodfellow.*

      Here comes my messenger. How now, mad spirit?

---

2. I beg pardon of your honors.
3. Cobwebs were used to stop bleeding.
4. Ripe pea pod (called "your father" because it suggests "codpiece"). *Squash:* Unripe pea pod.
5. What you have suffered with fortitude.
6. Because beef is often eaten with mustard, or

because oxen munch on mustard plants.
7. Dew was thought to originate on the moon.
8. Bottom is perhaps making involuntary asinine
noises.
3.2 Location: The wood.

5   What night-rule° now about this haunted grove?   *night revels; sports*
ROBIN   My mistress with a monster is in love.
    Near to her close° and consecrated bower,   *private*
    While she was in her dull° and sleeping hour,   *drowsy*
    A crew of patches,° rude mechanicals°   *fools / rough workmen*
10   That work for bread upon Athenian stalls,°   *market stands*
    Were met together to rehearse a play
    Intended for great Theseus' nuptial day.
    The shallowest thick-skin of that barren sort,°   *witless lot*
    Who Pyramus presented° in their sport,   *acted*
15   Forsook his scene° and entered in a brake.   *stage*
    When I did him at this advantage take,
    An ass's nole° I fixèd on his head.   *head*
    Anon his Thisbe must be answerèd,
    And forth my mimic° comes. When they him spy—   *burlesque actor*
20   As wild geese that the creeping fowler° eye,   *hunter of birds*
    Or russet-pated choughs, many in sort,[1]
    Rising and cawing at the gun's report,
    Sever° themselves and madly sweep the sky—   *Scatter*
    So at his sight away his fellows fly,
25   And at our stamp[2] here o'er and o'er one falls.
    He° "Murder!" cries and help from Athens calls.   *One (workman)*
    Their sense thus weak, lost with their fears thus strong,
    Made senseless things begin to do them wrong.
    For briars and thorns at their apparel snatch,
30   Some sleeves, some hats: from yielders all things catch.[3]
    I led them on in this distracted fear
    And left sweet Pyramus translated there,
    When in that moment, so it came to pass,
    Titania waked and straightway loved an ass.
35 OBERON   This falls out better than I could devise.
    But hast thou yet latched° the Athenian's eyes   *anointed*
    With the love juice, as I did bid thee do?
ROBIN   I took him sleeping—that is finished, too—
    And the Athenian woman by his side,
40   That° when he waked, of force° she must be eyed.   *So that / necessity*
             Enter DEMETRIUS *and* HERMIA.
OBERON   Stand close. This is the same Athenian.
ROBIN   This is the woman, but not this the man.
         [OBERON *and* ROBIN *stand apart.*]
DEMETRIUS   Oh, why rebuke you him that loves you so?
    Lay breath so bitter on your bitter foe.
45 HERMIA   Now I but chide, but I should use thee worse,
    For thou, I fear, hast given me cause to curse.
    If thou hast slain Lysander in his sleep,
    Being o'er shoes° in blood, plunge in the deep,   *Having waded so far*
    And kill me too.
50   The sun was not so true unto the day
    As he to me. Would he have stolen away
    From sleeping Hermia? I'll believe as soon
    This whole° earth may be bored, and that the moon   *solid*

---

1. Together, in a flock. *russet-pated choughs:* gray-headed jackdaws.
2. Editors have wondered how a fairy's presumably tiny foot could cause the human to fall.
3. Everything robs the timid.

May through the center creep and so displease
55 Her brother's noontide with the Antipodes.[4]
It cannot be but thou hast murdered him.
So should a murderer look: so dead,° so grim.   *deathly pale*
DEMETRIUS So should the murdered look, and so should I,
Pierced through the heart with your stern cruelty.
60 Yet you, the murderer, look as bright, as clear,
As yonder Venus in her glimmering sphere.°   *orbit*
HERMIA What's this to my Lysander? Where is he?
Ah, good Demetrius, wilt thou give him me?
DEMETRIUS I had rather give his carcass to my hounds.
65 HERMIA Out, dog! Out, cur! Thou driv'st me past the bounds
Of maiden's patience. Hast thou slain him, then?
Henceforth be never numbered among men.
Oh, once tell true; tell true, even for my sake:
Durst thou have looked upon him being awake,
70 And hast thou killed him sleeping? Oh, brave touch!°   *noble stroke*
Could not a worm,° an adder do so much?   *serpent*
An adder did it; for with doubler[5] tongue
Than thine, thou serpent, never adder stung.
DEMETRIUS You spend your passion on a misprised mood.°   *in misconceived anger*
75 I am not guilty of Lysander's blood,
Nor is he dead, for aught that I can tell.
HERMIA I pray thee, tell me then that he is well.
DEMETRIUS And if I could, what should I get therefore?°   *for that*
HERMIA A privilege, never to see me more;
80 And from thy hated presence part I so.
See me no more, whether he be dead or no.   *Exit.*
DEMETRIUS There is no following her in this fierce vein.
Here therefore for a while I will remain.
So sorrow's heaviness[6] doth heavier grow
85 For debt that bankrupt sleep doth sorrow owe,[7]
Which now in some slight measure it will pay,
If for his tender here I make some stay.[8]
          [*He*] *lies down* [*and sleeps*].
OBERON [*to* ROBIN] What hast thou done? Thou hast
          mistaken quite
And laid the love juice on some true love's sight.
90 Of thy misprision° must perforce ensue   *mistake*
Some true love turned, and not a false turned true.
ROBIN Then fate o'errules, that, one man holding troth,°   *faith*
A million fail, confounding oath on oath.[9]
OBERON About the wood go swifter than the wind,
95 And Helena of Athens look° thou find.   *be sure*
All fancy-sick° she is and pale of cheer°   *lovesick / face*
With sighs of love that costs the fresh blood dear.[1]
By some illusion see thou bring her here;

---

4. *that . . . Antipodes:* that the moon could creep
through a hole bored through the earth's center and
emerge on the other side, the Antipodes, displacing
the inhabitants by displacing the noontime sun with
the darkness of night. (Apollo, the sun god, was the
brother of Diana, the moon goddess.)
5. More forked (of the adder); more duplicitous (of
Demetrius).

6. Sadness (punning on "heavy": drowsy).
7. *For . . . owe:* Because sorrow worsens without sleep.
8. *Which . . . stay:* I will rest here awhile, giving
sleep capital ("tender") to pay off some of its debt to
sorrow.
9. Among the millions of faithless men, the one true
man's oath has been subverted by fate.
1. Sighs were thought to cause a loss of blood.

I'll charm his eyes against° she do appear.   *in readiness for when*

100 ROBIN   I go, I go; look how I go,
Swifter than arrow from the Tartar's bow.[2]   [*Exit.*]
OBERON [*squeezing the juice on Demetrius' eyes*]   Flower of
        this purple dye,
Hit with Cupid's archery,
Sink in apple° of his eye.   *pupil*
105 When his love he doth espy,
Let her shine as gloriously
As the Venus of the sky.
When thou wak'st, if she be by,
Beg of her for remedy.
                    Enter [ROBIN *Goodfellow, the*] *puck.*
110 ROBIN   Captain of our fairy band,
Helena is here at hand,
And the youth mistook by me,
Pleading for a lover's fee.°   *reward*
Shall we their fond° pageant see?   *foolish*
115 Lord, what fools these mortals be!
OBERON   Stand aside. The noise they make
Will cause Demetrius to awake.
ROBIN   Then will two at once woo one;
That must needs be sport alone.°   *in itself*
120 And those things do best please me
That befall preposterously.°   *ass backward*
                    [*They stand apart.*]
                    Enter LYSANDER *and* HELENA.
LYSANDER   Why should you think that I should woo in scorn?
Scorn and derision never come in tears.
Look when I vow, I weep, and vows so born,
125 In their nativity all truth appears.[3]
How can these things in me seem scorn to you,
Bearing the badge of faith[4] to prove them true?
HELENA   You do advance° your cunning more and more.   *increase; display*
When truth kills truth[5]—oh, devilish-holy fray!
130 These vows are Hermia's. Will you give her o'er?
Weigh oath with oath, and you will nothing weigh.[6]
Your vows to her and me put in two scales
Will even weigh, and both as light as tales.°   *lies; fiction*
LYSANDER   I had no judgment when to her I swore.
135 HELENA   Nor none, in my mind, now you give her o'er.
LYSANDER   Demetrius loves her, and he loves not you.
DEMETRIUS [*awaking*]   O Helen, goddess, nymph, perfect,
        divine!
To what, my love, shall I compare thine eyne?
Crystal is muddy. Oh, how ripe in show°   *appearance*
140 Thy lips, those kissing cherries, tempting grow!
That pure congealèd white, high Taurus'[7] snow,

---

2. Tartars, a dark-skinned, supposedly savage people in Asia Minor, were famed for their skills in archery.
3. *Look . . . appears:* The fact that I am weeping authenticates my vow's sincerity.
4. Insignia, such as that worn on a servant's livery (here, his tears).

5. When one vow nullifies another.
6. *you . . . weigh:* you will find that neither oath has any substance; you, Lysander, will be found to have no substance.
7. Range of high mountains in Asia Minor.

Fanned with the eastern wind, turns to a crow[8]
When thou hold'st up thy hand. Oh, let me kiss
This princess of pure white, this seal° of bliss!   *pledge*

145 HELENA   Oh, spite! Oh, hell! I see you all are bent
To set against me for your merriment.
If you were civil and knew courtesy,
You would not do me thus much injury.
Can you not hate me, as I know you do,
150 But you must join in souls to mock me too?
If you were men, as men you are in show,
You would not use a gentle° lady so,   *well-born; mild*
To vow and swear and superpraise my parts,°   *overpraise my qualities*
When I am sure you hate me with your hearts.
155 You both are rivals and love Hermia,
And now both rivals to mock Helena.
A trim° exploit, a manly enterprise,   *fine*
To conjure tears up in a poor maid's eyes
With your derision. None of noble sort°   *rank; nature*
160 Would so offend a virgin and extort°   *torture*
A poor soul's patience, all to make you sport.

LYSANDER   You are unkind, Demetrius; be not so.
For you love Hermia; this you know I know.
And here, with all good will, with all my heart,
165 In Hermia's love I yield you up my part;
And yours of Helena to me bequeath,
Whom I do love and will do till my death.

HELENA   Never did mockers waste more idle breath.

DEMETRIUS   Lysander, keep thy Hermia. I will none.[9]
170 If e'er I loved her, all that love is gone.
My heart to her but as guest-wise° sojourned,   *as a guest*
And now to Helen is it home returned,
There to remain.

LYSANDER   Helen, it is not so.

DEMETRIUS   Disparage not the faith thou dost not know,
175 Lest to thy peril thou aby it dear.°   *pay for it dearly*
Look where thy love comes; yonder is thy dear.

     Enter HERMIA.

HERMIA   Dark night, that from the eye his° function takes,   *its*
The ear more quick of apprehension makes.
Wherein it doth impair the seeing sense,
180 It pays the hearing double recompense.
Thou art not by mine eye, Lysander, found;
Mine ear, I thank it, brought me to thy sound.
But why unkindly didst thou leave me so?

LYSANDER   Why should he stay whom love doth press to go?

185 HERMIA   What love could press Lysander from my side?

LYSANDER   Lysander's love, that would not let him bide:
Fair Helena, who more engilds the night
Than all yon fiery oes and eyes of light.[1]
[*to* HERMIA] Why seek'st thou me? Could not this make
    thee know

---

8. *turns to a crow*: appears black by contrast.
9. I will have nothing to do with her.

1. Stars (punning on the vowels and on lovers' exclamatory "oh"s and "ay"s). An "o" was a spangle.

190   The hate I bare thee made me leave thee so?

HERMIA   You speak not as you think; it cannot be.

HELENA   Lo, she is one of this confederacy.

    Now I perceive they have conjoined all three

    To fashion this false sport in spite of° me.   *to spite*

195   Injurious Hermia, most ungrateful maid,

    Have you conspired, have you with these contrived

    To bait² me with this foul derision?

    Is all the counsel° that we two have shared,   *intimacy*

    The sisters' vows, the hours that we have spent

200   When we have chid the hasty-footed time

    For parting us—oh, is all forgot,

    All schooldays' friendship, childhood innocence?

    We, Hermia, like two artificial° gods   *artfully skilled*

    Have with our needles created both one flower,

205   Both on one sampler, sitting on one cushion,

    Both warbling of one song, both in one key,

    As if our hands, our sides, voices, and minds

    Had been incorporate.° So we grew together   *of one body*

    Like to a double cherry, seeming parted,

210   But yet an union in partition,

    Two lovely berries molded on one stem;

    So with two seeming bodies but one heart,

    Two of the first,³ like coats in heraldry,

    Due but to one and crownèd with one crest.

215   And will you rent our ancient love asunder,

    To join with men in scorning your poor friend?

    It is not friendly, 'tis not maidenly.

    Our sex as well as I may chide you for it,

    Though I alone do feel the injury.

220 HERMIA   I am amazèd at your words.

    I scorn you not; it seems that you scorn me.

HELENA   Have you not set Lysander, as in scorn,

    To follow me and praise my eyes and face?

    And made your other love, Demetrius—

225   Who even but now° did spurn me with his foot—   *just now*

    To call me goddess, nymph, divine, and rare,

    Precious, celestial? Wherefore speaks he this

    To her he hates? And wherefore doth Lysander

    Deny your love—so rich within his soul—

230   And tender° me, forsooth, affection,   *offer*

    But by your setting on, by your consent?

    What though I be not so in grace° as you,   *favor*

    So hung upon with love, so fortunate,

    But miserable most, to love unloved?

235   This you should pity rather than despise.

HERMIA   I understand not what you mean by this.

HELENA   I do. Persever, counterfeit sad° looks,⁴   *serious*

    Make mouths upon° me when I turn my back,   *Make faces at*

---

2. To torment (as Elizabethans set dogs to bait a bear).
3. A technical phrase in heraldry, referring to the first quartering in a coat of arms, which may be repeated. The friends then have two bodies but a single, overarching identity.

4. TEXTUAL COMMENT Owing to the ambiguous nature of early modern spelling, Helena's response to Hermia could mean two quite different things, one of which is supported by Q1's punctuation, the other by F's. See Digital Edition TC 4 (Quarto edited text).

Wink each at other, hold the sweet jest up.°   *keep up the joke*
240   This sport well carried shall be chronicled.
       If you have any pity, grace, or manners,
       You would not make me such an argument.°   *a subject of merriment*
       But fare ye well. 'Tis partly my own fault,
       Which death or absence soon shall remedy.
245 LYSANDER   Stay, gentle Helena, hear my excuse,
       My love, my life, my soul, fair Helena!
     HELENA   Oh, excellent!
     HERMIA [*to* LYSANDER]   Sweet, do not scorn her so.
     DEMETRIUS   If she cannot entreat, I can compel.[5]
     LYSANDER   Thou canst compel no more than she entreat.
250   Thy threats have no more strength than her weak prayers.
       —Helen, I love thee, by my life, I do!
       I swear by that which I will lose for thee
       To prove him false that says I love thee not.
     DEMETRIUS [*to* HELENA]   I say I love thee more than he can do.
255 LYSANDER   If thou say so, withdraw,[6] and prove it too.
     DEMETRIUS   Quick, come!
     HERMIA   Lysander, whereto tends all this?
     LYSANDER   Away, you Ethiope![7]
       [*He tries to break away from* HERMIA.]
     DEMETRIUS [*to* HERMIA]   No, no, he'll
       Seem to break loose.[8] [*to* LYSANDER] Take on as° you would   *Pretend*
         follow,
       But yet come not. You are a tame man, go!
260 LYSANDER [*to* HERMIA]   Hang off,° thou cat, thou burr! Vile   *Let go*
         thing, let loose,
       Or I will shake thee from me like a serpent.
     HERMIA   Why are you grown so rude? What change is this,
       Sweet love?
     LYSANDER   Thy love? Out, tawny Tartar, out!
       Out, loathèd medicine![9] O hated potion, hence!
     HERMIA   Do you not jest?
265 HELENA   Yes, sooth,° and so do you.   *truly*
     LYSANDER   Demetrius, I will keep my word with thee.
     DEMETRIUS   I would I had your bond, for I perceive
       A weak bond[1] holds you. I'll not trust your word.
     LYSANDER   What? Should I hurt her, strike her, kill her dead?
270   Although I hate her, I'll not harm her so.
     HERMIA   What? Can you do me greater harm than hate?
       Hate me? Wherefore? Oh, me, what news,° my love?   *what has happened*
       Am not I Hermia? Are not you Lysander?
       I am as fair now as I was erewhile.°   *a while ago*
275   Since night you loved me, yet since night you left me.
       Why then, you left me—oh, the gods forbid—
       In earnest, shall I say?
     LYSANDER   Ay, by my life,
       And never did desire to see thee more.

---

5. If Hermia cannot entreat you to stop, I can make
you do it.
6. Come with me ("step outside").
7. Allusion to Hermia's dark hair and complexion.
Elizabethans generally regarded light complexions as
more beautiful than dark and often stigmatized dark-
skinned peoples (such as Ethiopians or Tartars) as ugly.
8. Lysander will only pretend to break free from
Hermia.
9. Any drug (including poison).
1. Hermia's weak grasp (with a pun on "bond": signed
oath, the meaning in the previous line).

Therefore be out of hope, of question, of doubt;
280 Be certain, nothing truer. 'Tis no jest
That I do hate thee and love Helena.
HERMIA [*to* HELENA]   Oh, me, you juggler,° you   *trickster*
      canker-blossom,[2]
You thief of love! What, have you come by night
And stolen my love's heart from him?
HELENA   Fine, i'faith.
285 Have you no modesty, no maiden shame,
No touch of bashfulness? What, will you tear
Impatient answers from my gentle tongue?
Fie, fie, you counterfeit, you puppet,[3] you!
HERMIA   "Puppet"? Why so? —Ay, that way goes the game.
290 Now I perceive that she hath made compare
Between our statures; she hath urged her height,
And with her personage, her tall personage,
Her height, forsooth, she hath prevailed with him.
—And are you grown so high in his esteem
295 Because I am so dwarfish and so low?
How low am I, thou painted maypole?[4] Speak!
How low am I? I am not yet so low
But that my nails can reach unto thine eyes.
HELENA   I pray you, though you mock me, gentlemen,
300 Let her not hurt me. I was never curst;°   *quarrelsome*
I have no gift at all in shrewishness.
I am a right° maid for my cowardice.   *proper*
Let her not strike me. You perhaps may think
Because she is something° lower than myself   *somewhat*
That I can match her.
305 HERMIA   "Lower"? Hark, again!
HELENA   Good Hermia, do not be so bitter with me.
I evermore did love you, Hermia,
Did ever keep your counsels, never wronged you,
Save that, in love unto Demetrius,
310 I told him of your stealth° unto this wood.   *stealing away*
He followed you; for love I followed him.
But he hath chid me hence and threatened me
To strike me, spurn me, nay, to kill me too.
And now, so° you will let me quiet go,   *if only*
315 To Athens will I bear my folly back
And follow you no further. Let me go.
You see how simple and how fond° I am.   *foolish*
HERMIA   Why, get you gone. Who is't that hinders you?
HELENA   A foolish heart that I leave here behind.
HERMIA   What, with Lysander?
320 HELENA   With Demetrius.
LYSANDER   Be not afraid; she shall not harm thee, Helena.
DEMETRIUS   No, sir, she shall not, though you take her part.
HELENA   Oh, when she is angry she is keen° and shrewd.°   *sharp / shrewish*
She was a vixen when she went to school,
325 And though she be but little, she is fierce.

2. A worm that devours blossoms (of love).
3. Fraudulent imitation; but Hermia interprets "puppet" as a reference to her height.

4. Proverbial epithet for someone tall and skinny.
painted: insulting allusion to the use of cosmetics.

HERMIA "Little" again? Nothing but "low" and "little"?
  Why will you suffer her to flout me thus?
  Let me come to her.
LYSANDER   Get you gone, you dwarf,
  You minimus of hind'ring knot-grass⁵ made,
  You bead, you acorn.
330 DEMETRIUS   You are too officious
  In her behalf that scorns your services.
  Let her alone: speak not of Helena;
  Take not her part. For if thou dost intend
  Never so little° show of love to her,   *Even the smallest*
  Thou shalt aby° it.   *pay for*
335 LYSANDER   Now she holds me not;
  Now follow, if thou dar'st, to try whose right,
  Of thine or mine, is most in Helena.
DEMETRIUS Follow? Nay, I'll go with thee, cheek by jowl.⁶
           [*Exeunt* LYSANDER *and* DEMETRIUS.]
HERMIA You, mistress, all this coil° is long° of you.   *turmoil / because*
  Nay, go not back.
340 HELENA   I will not trust you, I,
  Nor longer stay in your curst company.
  Your hands than mine are quicker for a fray;°   *fight*
  My legs are longer, though, to run away.   [*Exit.*]
HERMIA I am amazed and know not what to say.   [*Exit.*]
      [OBERON *and* ROBIN *come forward.*]
345 OBERON This is thy negligence. Still° thou mistak'st   *Always*
  Or else committ'st thy knaveries willfully.
ROBIN Believe me, king of shadows,° I mistook.   *fairy spirits*
  Did not you tell me I should know the man
  By the Athenian garments he had on?
350 And so far° blameless proves my enterprise   *to this extent*
  That I have 'nointed an Athenian's eyes;
  And so far am I glad it so did sort,°   *turn out*
  As° this their jangling° I esteem a sport.   *Since / bickering*
OBERON Thou seest these lovers seek a place to fight.
355 Hie° therefore, Robin, overcast the night;   *Hurry*
  The starry welkin° cover thou anon   *sky*
  With drooping fog as black as Acheron,°   *(river of hell)*
  And lead these testy rivals so astray
  As° one come not within another's way.   *So that*
360 Like to Lysander sometime frame thy tongue,
  Then stir Demetrius up with bitter wrong;°   *insults*
  And sometime rail thou like Demetrius,
  And from each other look thou lead them thus
  Till o'er their brows death-counterfeiting sleep
365 With leaden legs and batty° wings doth creep.   *batlike*
  Then crush this herb into Lysander's eye,
  Whose liquor hath this virtuous° property: *potent*
  To take from thence all error with his might
  And make his eyeballs roll with wonted° sight.   *normal*
370 When they next wake, all this derision

---

5. Creeping binding weed (its sap was thought to stunt human growth). *minimus:* diminutive thing (Latin).   6. Proverbial saying for "side by side."

Shall seem a dream and fruitless° vision,   *inconsequential*
And back to Athens shall the lovers wend°   *go*
With league° whose date° till death shall never end.   *covenant / duration*
Whiles I in this affair do thee employ,
375   I'll to my queen and beg her Indian boy;
And then I will her charmèd° eye release   *enchanted*
From monster's view, and all things shall be peace.
ROBIN   My fairy lord, this must be done with haste,
For night's swift dragons[7] cut the clouds full fast,
380   And yonder shines Aurora's harbinger,[8]
At whose approach ghosts wandering here and there
Troop home to churchyards; damnèd spirits all,
That in crossways and floods[9] have burial,
Already to their wormy beds are gone,
385   For fear lest day should look their shames upon:
They willfully themselves exile from light
And must for aye° consort with black-browed night.   *forever*
OBERON   But we are spirits of another sort.
I with the morning's love[1] have oft made sport,
390   And like a forester[2] the groves may tread
Even till the eastern gate, all fiery red,
Opening on Neptune° with fair blessèd beams   *(the sea)*
Turns into yellow gold his salt° green streams.   *salty*
But notwithstanding, haste, make no delay;
395   We may effect this business yet ere day.   [*Exit.*]
ROBIN   Up and down, up and down,
I will lead them up and down.
I am feared in field and town.
Goblin,° lead them up and down.   *(Robin himself)*
400   Here comes one.
     Enter LYSANDER.
LYSANDER   Where art thou, proud Demetrius? Speak
    thou now.
ROBIN[3]   Here, villain, drawn° and ready. Where art thou?   *with sword drawn*
LYSANDER   I will be with thee straight.°   *immediately*
ROBIN   Follow me then
To plainer° ground.   [*Exit* LYSANDER.][4]   *clearer*
     Enter DEMETRIUS.
DEMETRIUS   Lysander, speak again.
405   Thou runaway, thou coward, art thou fled?
Speak! In some bush? Where dost thou hide thy head?
ROBIN   Thou coward, art thou bragging to the stars,
Telling the bushes that thou look'st for wars,
And wilt not come? Come, recreant;° come, thou child.   *coward; wretch*
410   I'll whip thee with a rod. He is defiled

---

7. Imagined as drawing the chariots of the goddess of night.
8. Herald of the goddess of dawn; the morning star.
9. In which the drowned were "buried," without Christian sacrament. *crossways:* crossroads (where suicides were buried, also without Christian sacrament). Robin is differentiating here between two types of spirits: those who wandered from their churchyard graves and those who have no proper resting place.

These two types, both ghosts of former humans, are differentiated in turn from the fairy spirits by Oberon in the ensuing lines.
1. The love of Aurora, goddess of dawn (or Cephalus, a brave hunter, Aurora's lover).
2. Keeper of a royal forest or private park.
3. In what follows, Robin presumably mimics the voices of Demetrius and Lysander.
4. He might instead wander about the stage.

That draws a sword on thee.[5]

DEMETRIUS   Yea, art thou there?

ROBIN   Follow my voice; we'll try° no manhood here.   *test*

Exeunt.

[*Enter* LYSANDER.]

LYSANDER   He goes before me and still dares me on.
When I come where he calls, then he is gone.

415   The villain is much lighter-heeled than I.
I followed fast, but faster he did fly,
That° fallen am I in dark uneven way,   *With the result that*
And here will rest me.

[*He lies down.*]

                    Come, thou gentle day.
For if but once thou show me thy gray light,

420   I'll find Demetrius and revenge this spite.

[*He sleeps.*]

[*Enter*] ROBIN *and* DEMETRIUS.

ROBIN   Ho, ho, ho! Coward, why com'st thou not?

DEMETRIUS   Abide° me, if thou dar'st; for well I wot°   *Wait for / know*
Thou runn'st before me, shifting every place,
And dar'st not stand nor look me in the face.
Where art thou now?

425   ROBIN   Come hither; I am here.

DEMETRIUS   Nay, then, thou mock'st me. Thou shalt buy°   *pay for*
this dear°   *dearly*
If ever I thy face by daylight see.
Now, go thy way. Faintness constraineth me
To measure out my length on this cold bed.

[*He lies down.*]

430   By day's approach look to be visited.

[*He sleeps.*]

Enter HELENA.

HELENA   O weary night, O long and tedious night,
Abate° thy hours; shine comforts from the east,   *Shorten*
That I may back to Athens by daylight
From these that my poor company detest;

435   And sleep, that sometimes shuts up sorrow's eye,
Steal me a while from mine own company.

[*She lies down and*] *sleep*[*s*].

ROBIN   Yet but three? Come one more;
Two of both kinds makes up four.

[*Enter* HERMIA.]

Here she comes, curst° and sad.   *angry*

440   Cupid is a knavish lad
Thus to make poor females mad.

HERMIA   Never so weary, never so in woe,
Bedabbled with the dew and torn with briars,
I can no further crawl, no further go;

445   My legs can keep no pace with my desires.
Here will I rest me till the break of day.

[*She lies down.*]

Heavens shield Lysander, if they mean a fray.

[*She sleeps.*]

5. That is, it would be a disgrace to treat you as an honorable opponent.

ROBIN   On the ground,
    Sleep sound.
450 I'll apply
    To your eye,
    Gentle lover, remedy.
      [*He squeezes the juice on Lysander's eyes.*]
    When thou wak'st,
    Thou tak'st
455 True delight
    In the sight
    Of thy former lady's eye;
    And the country proverb known,
    That every man should take his own,
460 In your waking shall be shown.
    Jack shall have Jill,
    Naught shall go ill,
    The man shall have his mare again, and all shall be well.
      [*Exit. The lovers remain onstage, asleep.*]

4.1 (F 4.1)

Enter [TITANIA,] *Queen of Fairies, and* [BOTTOM, *the*]
clown [*with the ass head*], *and* FAIRIES[, PEASEBLOSSOM,
COBWEB, MOTH, *and* MUSTARDSEED], *and* [OBERON,]
the King, behind them.

TITANIA [*to* BOTTOM]   Come, sit thee down upon this flowery
    bed
  While I thy amiable° cheeks do coy,°   lovable / caress
  And stick musk-roses in thy sleek smooth head,
  And kiss thy fair large ears, my gentle joy.
5 BOTTOM   Where's Peaseblossom?
PEASEBLOSSOM   Ready.
BOTTOM   Scratch my head, Peaseblossom. —Where's Monsieur
  Cobweb?
COBWEB   Ready.
10 BOTTOM   Monsieur Cobweb, good monsieur, get you your
  weapons in your hand and kill me a red-hipped humble-bee
  on the top of a thistle; and, good monsieur, bring me the
  honey-bag. Do not fret yourself too much in the action,
  monsieur; and, good monsieur, have a care the honey-bag
15 break not. I would be loath to have you overflown with° a   submerged by
  honey-bag, signor.   [*Exit* COBWEB.]
  —Where's Monsieur Mustardseed?
MUSTARDSEED   Ready.
BOTTOM   Give me your neaf,° Monsieur Mustardseed. Pray   fist
20 you leave your courtesy,[1] good monsieur.
MUSTARDSEED   What's your will?
BOTTOM   Nothing, good monsieur, but to help Cavaliery[2]
  Cobweb to scratch. I must to the barber's, monsieur, for
  methinks I am marvelous hairy about the face. And I am
25 such a tender ass, if my hair do but tickle me, I must scratch.
TITANIA   What, wilt thou hear some music, my sweet love?

4.1 Location: The wood. Q1 has no act break here. F
has the four lovers sleep through the action onstage.
1. *leave your courtesy:* stop bowing, or do not stand

bareheaded.
2. Blunder for "Cavalier," perhaps influenced by the
Italian term *cavaliere.*

115   Seemed all one mutual cry. I never heard
    So musical a discord, such sweet thunder.
    THESEUS My hounds are bred out of the Spartan kind,
    So flewed,[3] so sanded;° and their heads are hung   *sandy-colored*
    With ears that sweep away the morning dew;
120   Crook-kneed, and dewlapped[4] like Thessalian bulls;
    Slow in pursuit, but matched in mouth like bells,
    Each under each.[5] A cry more tunable[6]
    Was never holla'd to nor cheered with horn
    In Crete, in Sparta, nor in Thessaly.
125   Judge when you hear. But soft,° what nymphs are these?   *stop; look*
    EGEUS My lord, this is my daughter here asleep,
    And this Lysander, this Demetrius is,
    This Helena, old Nedar's Helena.
    I wonder of their being here together.
130   THESEUS No doubt they rose up early to observe
    The rite of May and, hearing our intent,
    Came here in grace of our solemnity.°   *ceremony*
    But speak, Egeus: is not this the day
    That Hermia should give answer of her choice?
135   EGEUS It is, my lord.
    THESEUS Go bid the huntsmen wake them with their horns.
                                [*Exit an Attendant.*]
          Shout within; wind horns; [the lovers] all start up.
    Good morrow, friends. Saint Valentine[7] is past.
    Begin these woodbirds but to couple now?
    LYSANDER Pardon, my lord.
          [*The lovers kneel.*]
    THESEUS   I pray you all, stand up.
          [*The lovers stand.*]
140   [*to* DEMETRIUS *and* LYSANDER] I know you two are rival
      enemies.
    How comes this gentle concord in the world,
    That hatred is so far from jealousy°   *suspicion*
    To sleep by hate and fear no enmity?
    LYSANDER My lord, I shall reply amazèdly,°   *confusedly*
145   Half sleep, half waking. But as yet, I swear,
    I cannot truly say how I came here.
    But as I think—for truly would I speak,
    And now I do bethink me, so it is—
    I came with Hermia hither. Our intent
150   Was to be gone from Athens where we might
    Without° the peril of the Athenian law—   *Outside*
    EGEUS [*to* THESEUS] Enough, enough, my lord; you have
      enough.
    I beg the law, the law upon his head!
    —They would have stolen away, they would, Demetrius,
155   Thereby to have defeated° you and me,   *defrauded*
    You of your wife and me of my consent,
    Of my consent that she should be your wife.

---

3. Flews were large hanging, fleshy chaps.
4. With hanging folds of skin under the neck (compare 2.1.50).
5. *matched . . . each:* harmoniously matched in the

pitch of their barking, like a set of bells.
6. A pack of hounds more well tuned.
7. Birds were said to choose their mates on Valentine's Day.

DEMETRIUS [*to* THESEUS]   My lord, fair Helen told me of their
    stealth,
    Of this their purpose hither to this wood,
160   And I in fury hither followed them,
    Fair Helena in fancy° following me.   *love*
    But, my good lord, I wot not by what power—
    But by some power it is—my love to Hermia,
    Melted as the snow, seems to me now
165   As the remembrance of an idle gaud°   *a worthless trinket*
    Which in my childhood I did dote upon;
    And all the faith, the virtue of my heart,
    The object and the pleasure of mine eye,
    Is only Helena. To her, my lord,
170   Was I betrothed ere I saw Hermia,
    But like a sickness[8] did I loathe this food;
    But, as in health come to my natural taste,
    Now I do wish it, love it, long for it,
    And will for evermore be true to it.
175 THESEUS   Fair lovers, you are fortunately met.
    Of this discourse we more will hear anon.
    —Egeus, I will overbear your will;
    For in the temple, by and by, with us
    These couples shall eternally be knit.
180   And, for° the morning now is something° worn,   *since / somewhat*
    Our purposed hunting shall be set aside.
    Away with us to Athens. Three and three,
    We'll hold a feast in great solemnity.
    —Come, Hippolyta.
         [*Exit* THESEUS *with* HIPPOLYTA, EGEUS, *and his train.*]
185 DEMETRIUS   These things seem small and undistinguishable,
    Like far-off mountains turnèd into clouds.
  HERMIA   Methinks I see these things with parted eye,°   *(double vision)*
    When everything seems double.
  HELENA   So methinks;
    And I have found Demetrius like a jewel,
    Mine own and not mine own.
190 DEMETRIUS   Are you sure
    That we are awake? It seems to me
    That yet we sleep, we dream. Do not you think
    The Duke was here and bid us follow him?
  HERMIA   Yea, and my father.
  HELENA   And Hippolyta.
195 LYSANDER   And he did bid us follow to the temple.
  DEMETRIUS   Why, then, we are awake. Let's follow him,
    And by the way let's recount our dreams.
                       [*Exeunt lovers.*]
  BOTTOM [*awaking*]   When my cue comes, call me, and I will
    answer. My next is "Most fair Pyramus." Heigh-ho,° *(a call; perhaps a yawn)*
200   Quince? Flute the bellows-mender? Snout the tinker?
    Starveling? God's my life!° Stolen hence and left me asleep! *Good Lord*
    I have had a most rare vision. I have had a dream past the
    wit of man to say what dream it was. Man is but an ass if he

---

8. Only as a person does when ill or nauseated.

205 go about° to expound this dream. Methought I was—there   *try*
is no man can tell what. Methought I was—and methought
I had—but man is but patched a fool[9] if he will offer° to say   *venture*
what methought I had. The eye of man hath not heard, the
ear of man hath not seen, man's hand is not able to taste, his
tongue to conceive, nor his heart to report[1] what my dream
210 was. I will get Peter Quince to write a ballad of this dream.
It shall be called "Bottom's Dream," because it hath no bottom;[2] and I will sing it in the latter end of a play, before the
Duke. Peradventure,° to make it the more gracious, I shall   *Perhaps*
sing it at her° death.   [*Exit.*]   *(Thisbe's?)*

4.2 (F 4.2)

Enter QUINCE, FLUTE[, SNOUT, *and* STARVELING].

QUINCE   Have you sent to Bottom's house? Is he come home
yet?

STARVELING   He cannot be heard of. Out of doubt° he is trans-   *Doubtless*
ported.[1]

5 FLUTE   If he come not, then the play is marred. It goes not
forward, doth it?

QUINCE   It is not possible. You have not a man in all Athens
able to discharge° Pyramus but he.   *perform*

FLUTE   No, he hath simply the best wit° of any handicraft   *intellect*
10 man in Athens.

QUINCE   Yea, and the best person° too; and he is a very par-   *looks*
amour for a sweet voice.

FLUTE   You must say "paragon." A paramour is—God bless
us—a thing of naught.°   *something wicked*

Enter SNUG *the joiner.*

15 SNUG   Masters, the Duke is coming from the temple, and
there is two or three lords and ladies more married. If our
sport° had gone forward, we had all been made men.[2]   *entertainment*

FLUTE   Oh, sweet bully Bottom! Thus hath he lost sixpence a
day[3] during his life; he could not have 'scaped sixpence a day.
20 An° the Duke had not given him sixpence a day for playing   *If*
Pyramus, I'll be hanged. He would have deserved it. Sixpence a day in Pyramus, or nothing.

Enter BOTTOM.

BOTTOM   Where are these lads? Where are these hearts?°   *mates*

QUINCE   Bottom! Oh, most courageous[4] day! Oh, most happy
25 hour!

BOTTOM   Masters, I am to discourse wonders; but ask me not
what; for if I tell you, I am not true Athenian. I will tell you
everything right as it fell out.

QUINCE   Let us hear, sweet Bottom.

30 BOTTOM   Not a word of° me. All that I will tell you is that the   *out of*
Duke hath dined. Get your apparel together, good strings°   *(to attach the beards)*

---

9. Patchwork or motley costumes were worn by jesters.
1. *The eye . . . report:* Burlesque of scripture: "The eye hath not seen, and the ear hath not heard, neither have entered into the heart of man" those things that God has prepared (1 Corinthians 2:9–10 [Bishops' Bible]).
2. Because it is unfathomable, or has no substance

(foundation).
4.2 Location: Athens.
1. Carried away (by the fairies); transformed.
2. *we . . . men:* our fortunes would have been made.
3. As a royal pension, considerably more than the average daily wage of an Elizabethan workman.
4. Blunder for "brave," meaning "splendid."

to your beards, new ribbons to your pumps. Meet presently° *immediately*
at the palace; every man look o'er his part. For the short and
the long is, our play is preferred.° In any case, let Thisbe have *recommended*
35 clean linen; and let not him that plays the lion pare his nails,
for they shall hang out for the lion's claws. And, most dear
actors, eat no onions nor garlic, for we are to utter sweet
breath; and I do not doubt but to hear them say it is a sweet
comedy. No more words. Away! Go, away!   [*Exeunt.*]

5.1 (F 5.1)

Enter THESEUS, HIPPOLYTA, PHILOSTRATE[, *Lords, and
Attendants*].

HIPPOLYTA   'Tis strange, my Theseus, that° these lovers *that which*
   speak of.
THESEUS[1]   More strange than true. I never may believe
   These antique[2] fables, nor these fairy toys.° *trifles*
   Lovers and madmen have such seething brains,
5   Such shaping fantasies,° that apprehend° more *imaginations / conceive*
   Than cool reason ever comprehends.
   The lunatic, the lover, and the poet
   Are of imagination all compact.° *composed*
   One sees more devils than vast hell can hold;
10   That is the madman. The lover, all as frantic,
   Sees Helen's beauty in a brow of Egypt.[3]
   The poet's eye, in a fine frenzy rolling,
   Doth glance from heaven to earth, from earth to heaven.
   And as imagination bodies forth
15   The forms of things unknown, the poet's pen
   Turns them to shapes and gives to airy nothing
   A local habitation and a name.
   Such tricks hath strong imagination
   That if it would but apprehend some joy,
20   It comprehends some bringer° of that joy; *source*
   Or in the night, imagining some fear,° *object to be feared*
   How easy is a bush supposed a bear!
HIPPOLYTA   But all the story of the night told over,
   And all their minds transfigured so together,
25   More witnesseth than fancy's images[4]
   And grows to something of great constancy;° *consistency*
   But, howsoever,° strange and admirable.° *in any case / wondrous*

   Enter [the] lovers, LYSANDER, DEMETRIUS, HERMIA,
   and HELENA.

THESEUS   Here come the lovers, full of joy and mirth.
   Joy, gentle friends, joy and fresh days of love
   Accompany your hearts.
30 LYSANDER   More than to us
   Wait in your royal walks, your board, your bed.[5]
THESEUS   Come now, what masques, what dances shall we have

5.1 Location: Athens. Theseus's palace.
1. TEXTUAL COMMENT Substantial portions of this
famous speech by Theseus are mislined in Q1 and F,
perhaps because Shakespeare added the lines on the
poet's imagination as an afterthought. For more
details and speculations on the original versions, see
Digital Edition TC 5 (Quarto edited text).

2. Ancient; strange, grotesque (as in "antic").
3. In a gypsy's face. *Helen:* Helen of Troy.
4. *More . . . images:* Testifies to something more than
mere figments of the imagination.
5. *More . . . bed:* May even more joy and love attend
your daily lives.

To wear away this long age of three hours
Between our after-supper and bedtime?
35   Where is our usual manager of mirth?
What revels are in hand? Is there no play
To ease the anguish of a torturing hour?
Call Philostrate.
PHILOSTRATE[6]   Here, mighty Theseus.
THESEUS   Say, what abridgement[7] have you for this evening,
40   What masque, what music? How shall we beguile
The lazy time if not with some delight?
PHILOSTRATE [*giving* THESEUS *a paper*]   There is a brief° how   *short list*
many sports are ripe.
Make choice of which your highness will see first.
THESEUS [*reads*][8]   "The battle with the Centaurs,[9] to be sung
45   By an Athenian eunuch to the harp."
We'll none of that. That have I told my love
In glory of my kinsman Hercules.[1]
[*Reads.*] "The riot of the tipsy Bacchanals
Tearing the Thracian singer in their rage."[2]
50   That is an old device,° and it was played   *show*
When I from Thebes came last a conqueror.
[*Reads.*] "The thrice-three muses mourning for the death
Of learning, late deceased in beggary."[3]
That is some satire, keen and critical,
55   Not sorting with° a nuptial ceremony.   *befitting*
[*Reads.*] "A tedious brief scene of young Pyramus
And his love Thisbe; very tragical mirth."
Merry and tragical? Tedious and brief?
That is hot ice and wondrous strange snow!
60   How shall we find the concord of this discord?
PHILOSTRATE   A play there is, my lord, some ten words long,
Which is as brief as I have known a play,
But by ten words, my lord, it is too long,
Which makes it tedious. For in all the play
65   There is not one word apt, one player fitted.°   *appropriately cast*
And tragical, my noble lord, it is,
For Pyramus therein doth kill himself,
Which, when I saw rehearsed, I must confess,
Made mine eyes water; but more merry tears
70   The passion of loud laughter never shed.
THESEUS   What are they that do play it?
PHILOSTRATE   Hard-handed men that work in Athens here,
Which never labored in their minds till now,

---

6. TEXTUAL COMMENT The speeches by Philostrate throughout 5.1 in Q1 are assigned to Egeus in F; this change significantly affects the nature of the scene and allows for a wide variety of interpretations in performance. See Digital Edition TC 6 (Quarto edited text).
7. Pastime, something to make the evening seem shorter.
8. TEXTUAL COMMENT In F's version of this speech, Lysander reads out the descriptions of the entertainments on offer, while Theseus comments. For further details on possibilities for staging this arrangement, see Digital Edition TC 7 (Quarto edited text).
9. Probably the battle that occurred when the Cen-

taurs tried to carry off the bride of Theseus's friend Pirithous.
1. According to Plutarch, Hercules and Theseus were cousins.
2. The murder of the poet Orpheus by drunken women, devotees of Dionysus.
3. Possibly a topical reference: Robert Greene, Christopher Marlowe, and Thomas Kyd, university wits who began writing for the stage in the 1580s, all died in desperate circumstances in 1592–94. But satiric laments on the poverty of scholars and poets were commonplace.

And now have toiled° their unbreathed° memories   *taxed / unexercised*
75   With this same play against° your nuptial.   *in preparation for*
THESEUS   And we will hear it.
PHILOSTRATE   No, my noble lord,
   It is not for you. I have heard it over,
   And it is nothing, nothing in the world;
   Unless you can find sport in their intents,
80   Extremely stretched° and conned° with cruel pain,   *strained / memorized*
   To do you service.
THESEUS   I will hear that play.
   For never anything can be amiss
   When simpleness and duty tender it.
   Go, bring them in; and take your places, ladies.
                          [*Exit* PHILOSTRATE.]
85 HIPPOLYTA   I love not to see wretchedness o'ercharged,[4]
   And duty in his service° perishing.   *its attempt to serve*
THESEUS   Why, gentle sweet, you shall see no such thing.
HIPPOLYTA   He says they can do nothing in this kind.°   *kind of thing*
THESEUS   The kinder we, to give them thanks for nothing.
90   Our sport shall be to take what they mistake.
   And what poor duty cannot do, noble respect°   *consideration*
   Takes it in might, not merit.[5]
   Where I have come, great clerks° have purposèd   *scholars*
   To greet me with premeditated welcomes,
95   Where I have seen them shiver and look pale,
   Make periods in the midst of sentences,
   Throttle their practiced accent[6] in their fears,
   And in conclusion dumbly have broke off,
   Not paying me a welcome. Trust me, sweet,
100   Out of this silence yet I picked a welcome;
   And in the modesty of fearful° duty   *frightened*
   I read as much as from the rattling tongue
   Of saucy and audacious eloquence.
   Love, therefore, and tongue-tied simplicity
105   In least speak most, to my capacity.°   *in my judgment*
           [*Enter* PHILOSTRATE.]
PHILOSTRATE   So please your grace, the Prologue is
   addressed.[7]
THESEUS   Let him approach.
        Enter [QUINCE *as*] *the Prologue.*
QUINCE [*as Prologue*]   If we offend, it is with our good will.
   That you should think, we come not to offend
110   But with good will. To show our simple skill,
   That is the true beginning of our end.
   Consider, then, we come but in despite.
   We do not come as minding° to content you,   *intending*
   Our true intent is. All for your delight
115   We are not here. That you should here repent you
   The actors are at hand; and by their show
   You shall know all that you are like to know.[8]

---

4. Overburdened. *wretchedness:* incompetence or weakness; poor people.
5. *in . . . merit:* with respect to the giver's capacity, not the merit of the performance.
6. Rehearsed eloquence; usual manner of speaking.

7. The speaker of the Prologue is ready.
8. The humor of Quince's speech rests in its mispunctuation; repunctuated, it becomes a typical courteous address.

THESEUS   This fellow doth not stand upon points.[9]

LYSANDER   He hath rid his prologue like a rough° colt: he   *an unbroken*
120   knows not the stop.[1] A good moral, my lord: it is not enough
to speak, but to speak true.

HIPPOLYTA   Indeed he hath played on this prologue like a child
on a recorder: a sound, but not in government.°   *control*

THESEUS   His speech was like a tangled chain: nothing°   *not at all*
125   impaired, but all disordered.[2] Who is next?

Enter [BOTTOM *as*] *Pyramus, and* [FLUTE *as*] *Thisbe,*
and [SNOUT *as*] *Wall, and* [STARVELING *as*] *Moonshine,*
and [SNUG *as*] *Lion.*

QUINCE [*as Prologue*]   Gentles, perchance you wonder at this
show,
But wonder on till truth make all things plain.
This man is Pyramus, if you would know;
This beauteous lady Thisbe is, certain.
130   This man with lime and roughcast doth present
Wall, that vile wall which did these lovers sunder;
And through Wall's chink, poor souls, they are content
To whisper—at the which let no man wonder.
This man with lantern, dog, and bush of thorn
135   Presenteth Moonshine. For, if you will know,
By moonshine did these lovers think no scorn°   *(it) no disgrace*
To meet at Ninus' tomb, there, there to woo.
This grisly beast, which "Lion" hight° by name,   *is called*
The trusty Thisbe, coming first by night,
140   Did scare away, or rather did affright;
And as she fled, her mantle she did fall,°   *drop*
Which Lion vile with bloody mouth did stain.
Anon comes Pyramus, sweet youth and tall,°   *handsome*
And finds his trusty Thisbe's mantle slain;
145   Whereat with blade, with bloody, blameful blade,
He bravely broached° his boiling bloody breast;   *stabbed*
And Thisbe, tarrying in mulberry shade,
His dagger drew and died. For all the rest
Let Lion, Moonshine, Wall, and lovers twain
150   At large° discourse, while here they do remain.   *length*

Exeunt [QUINCE *as Prologue,* SNUG *as*] *Lion,* [FLUTE
as] *Thisbe, and* [STARVELING *as*] *Moonshine.*[3]

THESEUS   I wonder if the lion be to speak.

DEMETRIUS   No wonder, my lord; one lion may when many
asses do.

SNOUT [*as Wall*]   In this same interlude° it doth befall   *play*
155   That I, one Snout by name, present a wall;
And such a wall as I would have you think
That had in it a crannied hole or chink
Through which the lovers, Pyramus and Thisbe,
Did whisper often very secretly.
160   This loam, this roughcast, and this stone doth show

---

9. Bother about niceties; heed punctuation marks.
1. How to rein the colt to a stop; punctuation mark.
2. PERFORMANCE COMMENT In performance, the tone of the Athenian nobles' criticisms of the Interlude can range from innocuous banter to cruel intimidation, thus changing the overall effect of the scene.

For more, see Digital Edition PC 3.
3. TEXTUAL COMMENT The exits and entrances for the Interlude's players differ subtly between Q1 and F, but with poignant implications. See Digital Edition TC 8 (Quarto edited text).

That I am that same wall; the truth is so.
And this the cranny is, right and sinister,[4]
Through which the fearful lovers are to whisper.

THESEUS   Would you desire lime and hair to speak better?

165 DEMETRIUS   It is the wittiest partition[5] that ever I heard discourse, my lord.

THESEUS   Pyramus draws near the wall: silence!

BOTTOM [as Pyramus]   O grim-looked° night, O night with   grim-looking
hue so black,

O night, which ever art when day is not,

170 O night, O night, alack, alack, alack,
I fear my Thisbe's promise is forgot.
And thou, O wall, O sweet, O lovely wall,
That stand'st between her father's ground and mine,
Thou wall, O wall, O sweet and lovely wall,

175 Show me thy chink, to blink through with mine eyne.
        [SNOUT, as Wall, shows his chink.]
Thanks, courteous wall; Jove shield thee well for this.
But what see I? No Thisbe do I see.
O wicked wall, through whom I see no bliss,
Cursed be thy stones[6] for thus deceiving me!

180 THESEUS   The wall, methinks, being sensible,° should curse   capable of feeling
again.°   back

BOTTOM [to THESEUS]   No, in truth, sir, he should not. "Deceiving me" is Thisbe's cue. She is to enter now, and I am to spy
her through the wall. You shall see it will fall pat° as I told   precisely

185 you. Yonder she comes.
            Enter [FLUTE as] Thisbe.

FLUTE [as Thisbe]   O wall, full often hast thou heard my
    moans
For parting my fair Pyramus and me.
My cherry lips have often kissed thy stones,
Thy stones with lime and hair knit up in thee.

190 BOTTOM [as Pyramus]   I see a voice; now will I to the chink
To spy an° I can hear my Thisbe's face.   if
Thisbe?

FLUTE [as Thisbe]   My love! Thou art my love, I think.

BOTTOM [as Pyramus]   Think what thou wilt, I am thy lover's
    grace,°   gracious lover
And like Limander[7] am I trusty still.

195 FLUTE [as Thisbe]   And I like Helen,[8] till the fates me kill.

BOTTOM [as Pyramus]   Not Shafalus to Procrus[9] was so true.

FLUTE [as Thisbe]   As Shafalus to Procrus, I to you.

BOTTOM [as Pyramus]   Oh, kiss me through the hole of this
    vile wall.

FLUTE [as Thisbe]   I kiss the wall's hole, not your lips at all.

200 BOTTOM [as Pyramus]   Wilt thou at Ninny's tomb meet me
    straightway?

---

4. Left; running horizontally. Or on the one side
(Pyramus's) and the other (Thisbe's).
5. Wall; formal term for part of an oration.
6. Punning, unintentionally, on "testicles."
7. Blunder for "Leander," who drowned while swimming across the Hellespont to meet his lover, Hero.

8. Helen of Troy was notoriously untrustworthy; a
blunder for "Hero."
9. Blunder for "Cephalus" and "Procris." Procris was
in fact seduced by her husband in disguise as another
man; he later accidentally killed her.

FLUTE [*as Thisbe*] Tide° life, tide death, I come without delay.   *Betide; come*
                    [*Exeunt* BOTTOM *and* FLUTE.]
SNOUT [*as Wall*] Thus have I, Wall, my part dischargèd so;
    And, being done, thus Wall away doth go.   [*Exit.*]
THESEUS Now is the mural° down between the two neighbors.   *wall*
205   DEMETRIUS No remedy, my lord, when walls are so willful to°   *as to*
    hear without warning.¹
HIPPOLYTA This is the silliest stuff that ever I heard.
THESEUS The best in this kind are but shadows,² and the
    worst are no worse if imagination amend them.
210   HIPPOLYTA It must be your imagination, then, and not theirs.
THESEUS If we imagine no worse of them than they of them-
    selves, they may pass for excellent men. Here come two
    noble beasts in, a man and a lion.
          Enter [SNUG *as*] *Lion and* [STARVELING *as*] *Moonshine*
          [*with a lantern, thornbush, and dog*].
SNUG [*as Lion*] You ladies, you whose gentle hearts do fear
215   The smallest monstrous mouse that creeps on floor,
    May now, perchance, both quake and tremble here
    When lion rough in wildest rage doth roar.
    Then know that I as Snug the joiner am
    A lion fell,³ nor else no lion's dam.
220   For if I should as lion come in strife
    Into this place, 'twere pity on my life.
THESEUS A very gentle beast, and of a good conscience.
DEMETRIUS The very best at a beast, my lord, that e'er I saw.
LYSANDER This lion is a very fox⁴ for his valor.
225   THESEUS True; and a goose⁵ for his discretion.
DEMETRIUS Not so, my lord. For his valor cannot carry his
    discretion, and the fox carries the goose.
THESEUS His discretion, I am sure, cannot carry his valor; for
    the goose carries not the fox. It is well. Leave it to his discre-
230   tion, and let us listen to the moon.
STARVELING [*as Moonshine*] This lantern doth the hornèd°   *crescent*
    moon present.
DEMETRIUS He should have worn the horns on his head.⁶
THESEUS He is no crescent,⁷ and his horns are invisible
    within the circumference.
235   STARVELING [*as Moonshine*] This lantern doth the hornèd
    moon present;
    Myself the man i'th' moon do seem to be.
THESEUS This is the greatest error of all the rest: the man
    should be put into the lantern; how is it else the man i'th'
    moon?
240   DEMETRIUS He dares not come there for° the candle. For you   *for fear of*
    see it is already in snuff.⁸
HIPPOLYTA I am aweary of this moon; would he would change!
THESEUS It appears by his small light of discretion that he is

---

1. Informing the parents. *hear:* proverbially, "walls have ears."
2. Mere likenesses without substance. *kind:* profession (that is, actors).
3. Fierce; or skin (punning on the costume to which Snug reassuringly calls attention).
4. Symbolic of low cunning, rather than courage.
5. Symbolic of foolishness.
6. The symbol of a cuckold.
7. Waxing moon. Perhaps a joke about Starveling's thinness.
8. In need of snuffing; angry.

in the wane; but yet in courtesy, in all reason, we must stay
245   the time.

LYSANDER   Proceed, Moon.

STARVELING   All that I have to say is to tell you that the lantern is the moon, I the man i'th' moon, this thornbush my
thornbush, and this dog my dog.

250   DEMETRIUS   Why, all these should be in the lantern, for all
these are in the moon. But silence; here comes Thisbe.

            Enter [FLUTE as] Thisbe.

FLUTE [*as Thisbe*]   This is old Ninny's tomb. Where is my love?

SNUG [*as Lion*]   Oh!

            [*Lion roars.*]

            [*Thisbe runs off, dropping her mantle.*]

DEMETRIUS   Well roared, Lion!

255   THESEUS   Well run, Thisbe!

HIPPOLYTA   Well shone, Moon! Truly, the moon shines with a
good grace.

            [*Lion worries° Thisbe's mantle.*]   gnaws on

THESEUS   Well moused,⁹ Lion!

            Enter [BOTTOM as] Pyramus.

DEMETRIUS   And then came Pyramus.   [*Exit SNUG as Lion.*]

260   LYSANDER   And so the lion vanished.

BOTTOM [*as Pyramus*]   Sweet moon, I thank thee for thy
            sunny beams;
    I thank thee, moon, for shining now so bright.
    For by thy gracious, golden, glittering gleams
    I trust to take of truest Thisbe sight.
265   But stay, oh, spite!
    But mark, poor knight,
    What dreadful dole° is here?   grief
    Eyes, do you see?
    How can it be?
270   O dainty duck! O dear!
    Thy mantle good,
    What, stained with blood?
    Approach, ye Furies fell!
    O Fates,¹ come, come,
275   Cut thread and thrum,²
    Quail,° crush, conclude, and quell!°   Overpower / kill

THESEUS   This passion, and³ the death of a dear friend, would
go near to make a man look sad.

HIPPOLYTA   Beshrew my heart, but I pity the man.

280   BOTTOM [*as Pyramus*]   Oh, wherefore, Nature, didst thou
            lions frame,
    Since lion vile hath here deflowered⁴ my dear?
    Which is—no, no, which was—the fairest dame
    That lived, that loved, that liked, that looked with cheer.
    Come, tears, confound!
285   Out, sword, and wound

---

9. The mantle is like a mouse in the mouth of a cat.
1. The three Fates in Greek mythology spun and cut
the thread of a person's life.
2. A technical term from Bottom's occupation: the
tufted end of a weaver's warp, or set of yarns placed
lengthwise in a loom when the woven fabric is cut.
3. Only if combined with. *passion:* suffering; extravagant speech.
4. Ruined (but commonly suggesting "deprived of
her virginity"); his error for "devoured."

The pap° of Pyramus,   *breast*
Ay, that left pap,
Where heart doth hop.
          [*He stabs himself.*]
Thus die I, thus, thus, thus.
290   Now am I dead;
Now am I fled.
My soul is in the sky.
Tongue, lose thy light;
Moon, take thy flight.   [*Exit* STARVELING *as Moonshine.*]
295   Now die, die, die, die, die.
          [*Pyramus dies.*]
DEMETRIUS   No die, but an ace for him; for he is but one.[5]
LYSANDER   Less than an ace, man; for he is dead, he is
nothing.
THESEUS   With the help of a surgeon he might yet recover,
300   and yet prove an ass.
HIPPOLYTA   How chance Moonshine is gone before Thisbe
comes back and finds her lover?
THESEUS   She will find him by starlight.
          [*Enter* FLUTE *as Thisbe.*]
Here she comes, and her passion° ends the play.   *passionate speech*
305   HIPPOLYTA   Methinks she should not use a long one for such a
Pyramus; I hope she will be brief.
DEMETRIUS   A mote° will turn the balance which Pyramus,   *speck*
which[6] Thisbe, is the better: he for a man, God warrant us;
she for a woman, God bless us.
310   LYSANDER   She hath spied him already with those sweet eyes.
DEMETRIUS   And thus she means, *videlicet:*[7]
FLUTE [*as Thisbe*]   Asleep, my love?
What, dead, my dove?
O Pyramus, arise!
315   Speak, speak! Quite dumb?
Dead, dead? A tomb
Must cover thy sweet eyes.
These lily lips,
This cherry nose,
320   These yellow cowslip cheeks
Are gone, are gone.
Lovers, make moan.
His eyes were green as leeks.
O sisters three,°   *(the Fates)*
325   Come, come to me
With hands as pale as milk;
Lay them in gore,
Since you have shore°   *shorn*
With shears his thread of silk.
330   Tongue, not a word!
Come, trusty sword,
Come, blade, my breast imbrue.°   *stain with blood*
          [*She stabs herself.*]
And farewell, friends,

5. Pun on "die" as one of a pair of dice. *one:* the ace,   7. As follows. *means:* moans; lodges a formal legal
or lowest throw.   complaint.
6. *which . . . which:* whether . . . or.

Thus Thisbe ends.

335 Adieu, adieu, adieu.

    [*Thisbe dies.*]

THESEUS Moonshine and Lion are left to bury the dead.

DEMETRIUS Ay, and Wall too.

BOTTOM [*starting up*] No, I assure you, the wall is down that
parted their fathers. [FLUTE *rises.*] Will it please you to see

340 the epilogue or to hear a Bergomask dance[8] between two of
our company?

THESEUS No epilogue, I pray you; for your play needs no
excuse. Never excuse; for when the players are all dead, there
need none to be blamed. Marry, if he that writ it had played

345 Pyramus and hanged himself in Thisbe's garter, it would
have been a fine tragedy; and so it is, truly, and very notably
discharged. But come, your Bergomask; let your epilogue
alone.   [BOTTOM *and* FLUTE[9] *dance; then exeunt.*]

The iron tongue of midnight hath told° twelve.   *counted; tolled*

350 Lovers, to bed; 'tis almost fairy time.

I fear we shall outsleep the coming morn

As much as we this night have overwatched.°   *stayed awake too late*

This palpable-gross° play hath well beguiled   *palpably crude*

The heavy° gait of night. Sweet friends, to bed.   *drowsy; slow*

355 A fortnight hold we this solemnity

In nightly revels and new jollity.   *Exeunt.*

    Enter [ROBIN *Goodfellow, the*] *puck*[, *with a broom*].

ROBIN Now the hungry lion roars,

And the wolf behowls the moon,

Whilst the heavy° plowman snores,   *weary*

360 All with weary task fordone.°   *"done in"; exhausted*

Now the wasted brands° do glow,   *burned-out logs*

Whilst the screech-owl, screeching loud,

Puts the wretch that lies in woe

In remembrance of a shroud.

365 Now it is the time of night

That the graves, all gaping wide,

Every one lets forth his sprite[1]

In the churchway paths to glide;

And we fairies that do run

370 By the triple Hecate's[2] team

From the presence of the sun,

Following darkness like a dream,

Now are frolic.° Not a mouse   *merry*

Shall disturb this hallowed house.

375 I am sent with broom[3] before

To sweep the dust behind° the door.   *from behind*

    Enter [OBERON *and* TITANIA,] *King and Queen of*
    Fairies, with all their train.

---

8. A dance named after Bergamo, in Italy (commonly
ridiculed for its rusticity).

9. The only "two of our company" onstage at the end
of the interlude. The role of Bottom may have been
first performed by the actor Will Kemp, who was
famous for his dancing.

1. Each grave lets forth its ghost.

2. Hecate was goddess of the moon and night, and
she had three realms: heaven (as Cynthia), earth (as
Diana), and hell (as Proserpine).

3. One of his traditional emblems; he helped good
housekeepers and punished lazy ones.

OBERON   Through the house give glimmering light
　　　By the dead and drowsy fire;
　　　Every elf and fairy sprite
380　　Hop as light as bird from briar;
　　　And this ditty after me
　　　Sing, and dance it trippingly.
TITANIA   First rehearse your song by rote,
　　　To each word a warbling note.
385　　Hand in hand with fairy grace
　　　Will we sing and bless this place.
　　　　　[*The* FAIRIES *dance to a song.*]⁴
OBERON   Now until the break of day
　　　Through this house each fairy stray.
　　　To the best bride-bed will we,⁵
390　　Which by us shall blessèd be;
　　　And the issue there create°　　　　　　　　　　　　　*created; conceived*
　　　Ever shall be fortunate.
　　　So shall all the couples three
　　　Ever true in loving be.
395　　And the blots of nature's hand
　　　Shall not in their issue stand;
　　　Never mole, harelip, nor scar,
　　　Nor mark prodigious,° such as are　　　　　　　*ominous birthmark*
　　　Despisèd in nativity,
400　　Shall upon their children be.
　　　With this field-dew consecrate⁶
　　　Every fairy take his gait,°　　　　　　　　　　　　　　　*way*
　　　And each several° chamber bless　　　　　　　　　　*separate*
　　　Through this palace with sweet peace;
405　　And the owner of it blessed
　　　Ever shall in safety rest.
　　　Trip away, make no stay;
　　　Meet me all by break of day.　　　*Exeunt* [*all but* ROBIN].
ROBIN [*to the audience*]   If we shadows have offended,
410　　Think but this, and all is mended,
　　　That you have but slumbered here
　　　While these visions did appear.
　　　And this weak and idle theme,
　　　No more yielding but° a dream,　　　　　　　　　　　*than*
415　　Gentles, do not reprehend;
　　　If you pardon, we will mend.
　　　And as I am an honest puck,
　　　If we have unearnèd luck
　　　Now to 'scape the serpent's tongue,⁷
420　　We will make amends ere long;
　　　Else the puck a liar call.
　　　So, good night unto you all.
　　　Give me your hands,° if we be friends,　　　　　　*applause*
　　　And Robin shall restore amends.　　　　　　　[*Exit.*]

---

4. TEXTUAL COMMENT In F, the words of Oberon's speech constitute the text of the fairies' song, perhaps due to a misunderstanding in the printing house. See Digital Edition TC 9 (Quarto edited text).
5. Oberon and Titania will bless the bed of Theseus and Hippolyta.
6. Consecrated, blessed. Playfully alludes to the traditional Catholic custom of blessing the marriage bed with holy water.
7. Hissing from the audience.

King John

What if history is just one damned thing after another? What if the concatenation of events takes no meaningful direction, reveals no pattern, discloses no moral meaning? Although *The Life and Death of King John* (1595–96) focuses on how human actions fit together over time, it suggests the larger significance of John's reign (1199–1216) only in disorienting fashion. The plot promises more coherence than it delivers; the apparent trajectory of events repeatedly proves illusory; seemingly decisive moments turn out to be mere episodes in the open-ended, ironic, unpredictable movement of history. The play thus breaks with the providential conclusion to Shakespeare's first tetralogy (four related plays on English history) provided by *Richard III* (1592) and, more generally, with the moralizing strategy of Renaissance humanist historians. A transitional work, it moves Shakespeare closer to the pragmatic, secular political thinking of Niccolò Machiavelli (1469–1527) and to the concerns with the problematic relationship between hereditary legitimacy and fitness to rule characteristic of his second tetralogy, from *Richard II* to *Henry V* (1595–99).

The logic of the plot is to undermine logic, to reveal the uncertain relationship between intention and outcome in a world that offers only fragments of consolation for the futility of human endeavor. The basic antagonisms arise from John's efforts to retain the English crown and its overseas French territories. John faces challenges from the French, ostensibly acting on behalf of his young nephew Arthur, whose hereditary claim to the throne is stronger, and from the Catholic Church, with which John is also at odds. These conflicts repeatedly take unanticipated turns. The first-act struggle over inheritance between the Bastard, the play's central character, and his younger half brother Robert Falconbridge leads to the unexpected conclusion that illegitimate birth does not bar legitimate inheritance. Even more surprisingly, the Bastard quickly renounces that inheritance. Similarly, after the English and French battle each other to a stalemate in seeking mastery over the town of Angers, they join forces with the intent of leveling it as punishment for its autonomy and then instead resolve to end their quarrel—thus sparing the town—through a cynical political marriage. But this resolution proves as transitory as the previous ones when Pandulph, the Pope's ambassador, excommunicates John, and France, as a result, repudiates the deal.

Although John now seems in trouble, his ensuing military triumph shifts his fortunes. Yet by ordering Arthur's murder, he undermines his position. John appears poised to escape the consequences of his crime when Hubert, the executioner, spares Arthur. But Arthur dies attempting to escape, an accident the English lords interpret as murder. Their defection to the French invaders apparently seals John's fate. Although John's submission to the Pope eliminates the invasion's ostensible rationale, this tactic characteristically fails. But when the lords learn that the Dauphin, son of the French King, plans to kill them after securing the English throne, they return to John.

The war itself turns less on climactic battles than on both sides' careless habit of losing their armies at sea. But even these accidents, which render the antagonists incapable of continuing the war, do not save John. Hated by the English clergy for his extortions from the monasteries, he is poisoned by a vengeful monk. This outcome lacks dramatic logic: the looting of the monasteries is undramatized and given little weight; John has been reconciled with Rome; and he is apparently dying of a fever

Philip II Augustus strikes an alliance with John "Lackland" (1167–1216), King of England.
Early thirteenth century.

even before his poisoning. Finally, Prince Henry, the King's young son, conveniently
materializes just as peace breaks out. Accordingly, the orthodox conclusion, with
the legitimate heir succeeding his father, feels contingent—a feeling reinforced by
the characters' repudiation of their oaths, and by the numerous unexplained acts of
uncertain significance.

This view of history, in which the meaning of events proves problematic, is of a
piece with Shakespeare's treatment of his sources, his characters, his themes, and
his possible allusions to contemporary Elizabethan politics, as well as with the play's
later theatrical fortunes. *King John*'s closest analogue is the anonymous play *The
Troublesome Reign of John, King of England* (published 1591). If *The Troublesome
Reign* is the earlier work and Shakespeare's primary source, as is assumed here (see
the Textual Introduction), it partly relies on Raphael Holinshed's *Chronicles of
England, Scotland, and Ireland* (second edition, 1587), the narrative of English history
that Shakespeare himself drew on during the 1590s for his national history plays.
The Troublesome Reign's author reshapes chronology and invents episodes, alterations that *King John* generally adopts, and promotes Protestant and national chauvinism, which *King John* mutes. During the English Reformation, John was seen as a
proto-Protestant martyr who challenged Roman Catholicism by rejecting the Pope's
choice for Archbishop of Canterbury and by heavily taxing the church. Hence he was

thought to have anticipated Queen Elizabeth's father, Henry VIII, whose break with Rome and expropriation of the monasteries initiated the Reformation.

But Shakespeare weakens the connection to Henry, toning down the rhetoric of *The Troublesome Reign* by more closely following Holinshed, who combines the Protestant view with a centuries-old Catholic hostility to John. Whereas the anonymous play portrays monks committing sexual outrages, Shakespeare omits the scene and calls John's taxes pillaging. Similarly, although John's submission to Rome is lamented in *King John*, the decision is hardly catastrophic. Although Shakespeare retains some of *The Troublesome Reign*'s anti-Catholicism—for instance, in John's defense of an English church—overall, *King John* offers scant comfort to Catholics and Protestants alike. This outlook may reflect Shakespeare's dislike of religious controversy and perhaps his partly Catholic family background and education.

Shakespeare also softens *The Troublesome Reign*'s nationalism, despite concluding with the Bastard's patriotic credo:

> This England never did, nor never shall,
> Lie at the proud foot of a conqueror
> But when it first did help to wound itself.
> Now these her princes are come home again,
> Come the three corners of the world in arms
> And we shall shock them. Naught shall make us rue
> If England to itself do rest but true!
>
> (5.7.112–18)

These lines are more ambiguous than at first appears. Although they oppose foreign conquest of England, the play considers the possibility that such domination is preferable to rule by a murderous English monarch. Moreover, the use of "but when" in the first sentence and the "if" in the third temper optimism, especially given the prior conduct of the aristocracy.

This skeptical view of traditional authority shapes the characterization of *King John*. Most striking is the relative inattention to John himself, the figure whose "life and death" the play ostensibly dramatizes. The resulting vacuum is filled by women and a bastard, personages usually peripheral to dynastic history. Nowhere in Shakespeare's two historical tetralogies do women play so active a role. In act 1, John's mother, Queen Eleanor, challenges the French ambassador even before her son has a chance to do so. She then recognizes the Bastard as the illegitimate offspring of her dead son, King Richard I, the Lionheart, John's oldest brother and predecessor on the throne, and recruits her newly found grandson into royal service.

In acts 2 and 3, the dispute between John and Arthur (represented by the King of France) is partly carried out by proxy. Eleanor and especially Arthur's mother, Constance, whose role Shakespeare expanded from his sources, are more active than their children and (with the Bastard) rhetorically dominate the stage—particularly in their confrontation in act 2, scene 1 and in Constance's subsequent lamentations. More than any other character, Constance expresses herself through verbal repetition and word play. For instance, when Salisbury tells her that Louis and Blanche are to be married, thus dashing her hopes that Arthur will gain the throne, she retorts: "I trust I may not trust thee . . . / Believe me, I do not believe thee" (2.2.7–9). Going beyond the common female role—victim of history—she and Eleanor attempt to direct the action. Notably, they question each other's sexual honor—an issue broached earlier when the Bastard's mother acknowledges her adulterous affair with King Richard. This recurrent concern underscores the uncertainty of biologically legitimate patriarchal succession. Hereditary descent from father to son accords a central role to women, whose sexual fidelity is considered necessary but unreliable. Still, though *King John* emphasizes women's dubious fidelity, it denies any consequence for hereditary succession. The mothers' attacks on each other weaken claims of male legitimacy but change no one's mind. Crucially, midway through the play both Constance and Eleanor disappear from the plot; their offstage deaths are reported shortly thereafter.

King John's tomb in Worcester Cathedral. From Francis Sandford,
A *Genealogical History of the Kings and Queens of England* (1707).

With them go the challenges they pose but not all they represent. Rather than executing Arthur, Hubert protects the boy, assuming an arguably maternal role; the Bastard's relationship to John late in the play is similar. Prince Henry sheds tears over his dying father; Pandulph calls the church "our holy mother" (3.1.67); and the Bastard attacks the treasonous lords for "ripping up the womb / Of your dear mother England" (5.2.152–53). But it is unclear how effective these surrogates prove. The sons become increasingly inept, memorable less in themselves than for the way the often-personified physical imagery running through *King John* is reliteralized in the accounts of their suffering. Arthur leaps to his accidental death when the "Good ground" of England, which he hopes does "not break my limbs," proves inhospitable "stones" (4.3.2, 6, 9). In like manner, a "tyrant fever burns [John] up" (5.3.14). More generally, John's stunned response to his mother's death helps explain his transformation from an active to a passive role. Late in the play, he is neither tragic nor even entirely villainous but simply irrelevant, his fall coinciding with the Bastard's ascent.

The rise of this almost entirely invented figure in the least historically accurate of Shakespeare's history plays enables a defense of illegitimacy. Although critics have traced the development of the Bastard's character, he is arguably less a coherent fictional figure than a series of discontinuous theatrical functions, his changes dictated more by plot twists than by psychological transformation. The Bastard initially embodies a mischievous popular culture. Theatrically, he descends from the devilish Vice figure, a character in the earlier English morality plays. The Vice combined commitment to evil, intimacy with the audience, and a penchant for fun. Similarly, the Bastard speaks to and for the audience in playful asides and soliloquies, denouncing the moral failings of the powerful while conceding that he is no better. When John speaks of "Twice fifteen thousand hearts of England's breed," the Bastard comments, "Bastards and else" (others). And when King Philip replies that his French forces contain "As many and as well-born bloods as those," the Bastard remarks, in a further deflationary observation, "Some bastards too" (2.1.275–79). Earlier, soon after John knights him, he imagines himself a member of the upper class in a soliloquy that is partly revelation of character, partly satire on social elites (1.1.182–216). In *King John*, as in most of Shakespeare's English and Roman history plays, blank verse is dominant—presumably because it imparts dignity to the primarily upper-class characters. But the Bastard turns his iambic pentameter lines to distinctive ends, resorting to popular speech—"'a pops me out" (1.1.68; he deprives me of)—and proverbs—"In at the window or else o'er the hatch" (1.1.171; born out of wedlock).

In diabolical fashion, the Bastard appears immune to bodily harm; he also takes pleasure in promoting discord, as when he proposes that the two kings, rivals for the allegiance of Angers, temporarily combine forces and level the obstinate town. Similarly, but with more motivation, he taunts the Duke of Austria—in this play, but not historically, slayer of his biological father, Richard the Lionheart. When Constance realizes that Arthur's claims to the crown have been abandoned by his supposed protectors, she denounces Austria.

> CONSTANCE Thou wear a lion's hide! Doff it for shame,
>   And hang a calf's-skin on those recreant limbs.
> AUSTRIA Oh, that a man should speak those words to me!
> BASTARD And hang a calf's-skin on those recreant limbs.
> AUSTRIA Thou dar'st not say so, villain, for thy life.
> BASTARD And hang a calf's-skin on those recreant limbs.
>
> (3.1.54–59)

The Bastard repeats this taunt through the remainder of the scene and next appears, in the ensuing battle, with the head of his foe.

But as that deed suggests, the Bastard is a positive character, unlike an earlier Shakespearean Vice figure such as Richard III. This other side to the character only gradually becomes dominant. After John deems him legitimate and the Bastard nonetheless rejects his patrimony in favor of knighthood and recognition as King Richard's illegitimate son, his simultaneous financial fall and social rise allow the identification of royalty with illegitimacy. His loyalty contrasts with the self-serving deal between John and the King of France, a deal the Bastard denounces as "commodity," or self-interest (2.1.561–98). Later, that loyalty casts a harsh light on the English aristocrats' treasonous alliance with the French. The Bastard thus becomes more responsible, if less entertaining—a transformation managed by keeping him offstage for five hundred lines. Horrified by the death of Arthur, whom he now seems to view as the legitimate monarch, but persuaded that the death was accidental, he defends crown and realm alike. He thereby proves the ethical center of a world almost devoid of positive value.

The Bastard owes this authority to his social and theatrical range. The reembodiment of his biological father, he reflects both badly and well on the King. He, rather than John, exacts family vengeance by killing Austria. He offers the appropriate response to the death of Arthur, for which the King bears partial—arguably full—responsibility. By comparison, John looks at best mediocre, at worst evil. Yet the Bastard's presence also suggests that Richard's spirit guards the throne and, hence, that John is the man for the job. As the Bastard insists in referring to John, "his royalty doth speak in me" (5.2.129).

Thus a man of illegitimate birth validates the fitness to rule of a man with disputed claim to the crown. Shakespeare goes beyond *The Troublesome Reign* in weakening John's legal position, which is based on King Richard's will naming him successor. When Constance asserts Arthur's right, Eleanor retorts, "I can produce / A will that bars the title of thy son" (2.1.191–92). But a will is trumped by the rule of succession: the crown goes to the firstborn male or his oldest male descendant. That person is Arthur, son of Geoffrey, deceased younger brother of Richard but older brother of John. Hence, when John explains why he will defeat the French and Arthur—"Our strong possession and our right for us" (1.1.39)—his mother cautions, "Your strong possession much more than your right" (line 40). And John unwittingly concedes the decisiveness of order of birth by awarding the Falconbridge inheritance to the illegitimate Bastard rather than to the Bastard's younger, legitimate brother, whose claim depends on his father's will.

But though Arthur has a legitimate claim to the throne and John does not, hereditary legitimacy is not synonymous with fitness to rule. Shakespeare departs from his sources by making Arthur a helpless child heavily dependent on his mother, the King of France, and the Duke of Austria. Arthur also has no interest in monarchy: John's "strong possession" accordingly matters. But by ordering Arthur's murder, John squanders his authority, thereby weakening the conflict between hereditary legitimacy and fitness to rule. *King John*'s skepticism about the meaningfulness of history thus undermines this central theme. A similar fate awaits even the Bastard, despite his crucial role in recognizing John's heir and articulating a vision of national unity. In Holinshed, John "lost a great part of his army" to drowning; in *The Troublesome Reign*, the Bastard reports that the sea has "swallowed up the most of all our men." *King John's* Bastard narrates this event twice, both times making himself more responsible for the debacle—"half my power," "the best part of my power" (5.6.39, 5.7.61). Ineptitude is soon replaced by irrelevance: the Bastard opts for war after others have negotiated peace. Although the Bastard is not shunted aside by the unpredictable concatenation of events, the resolution turns less on human acts than on the collapse of both contending parties.

Where does this leave England? *King John* differs from Shakespeare's other history plays of the 1590s in treating the early thirteenth rather than the late fourteenth and fifteenth centuries. Independent of any tetralogy, it does not develop a dynastic sense of "England" by depicting the sequence of reigns. Sociologically, the play is also atypical. John's reign is remembered for the Magna Carta and, ahistorically, Robin Hood. Both concern resistance to royal tyranny—by the aristocracy and the lower class, respectively. Although both stories circulated in the 1590s, neither appears in the play. The lords rebel, but relations between King and nobility remain secondary. And despite brief reference to popular unrest, *King John* accords the English people an even more marginal role in constituting the nation. This treatment of aristocracy and populace contrasts with Shakespeare's approach soon after in his second tetralogy.

King John points elsewhere. Richard the Lionheart's legacy is dispersed among three of his blood relatives—John, Arthur, and the Bastard—none of whom is a fully adequate successor. Like the Bastard, Constance and Eleanor are part of the royal family. But these three relatively peripheral characters suggest an expanded outlook, a shift from dynasty to nation and, hence, a repudiation of absolutist rule. That expansion is implied by the importance in act 2 of the citizens of Angers, who must decide which claimant is their legitimate king, and arguably by the valorization of humane feeling and personal loyalty late in the play. Yet the Bastard's rise from obscurity to protector of England suggests a partial analogue to the sixteenth-century emergence of a nonhereditary elite to fill positions in the new state bureaucracy. On this reading, the play ends not with a less authoritarian view but with a redeployed ruling apparatus. If so, this political reorganization remains tentative in *King John*. So, too, does a national sense of England. Perhaps no such perspective was available without dynastic legitimacy. Devoid of climactic battle or concluding marriage, *King John* is more effective at undermining than reconstituting authority. Its distinctiveness lies here.

As such, the play may have provided its initial audiences with a projection into the thirteenth century of Queen Elizabeth's questionable legitimacy and the competing claims of Mary, Queen of Scots. John's monarchical right depends on Richard's will; the will of Henry VIII named Elizabeth heir. But the legitimacy of appointing one's successors by will had been challenged even in Henry's lifetime. Again, Shakespeare's John is accused of being a bastard and excommunicated by the Pope; Elizabeth was declared a bastard by her father and excommunicated by the Pope. Arthur is the son of John's older brother; Mary, Queen of Scots, was the granddaughter of Henry's older sister. Arguably, then, Elizabeth's legal claim to the crown was weaker than Mary's.

Furthermore, Arthur's cause is championed by King Philip of France; Mary, too, was supported by foreign Catholic monarchs, including King Philip II of Spain. After ordering Arthur's death, John tries to absolve himself of the crime he commissioned but did not commit; in 1587, Elizabeth ordered Mary's execution and then distanced herself from the deed. Arthur's death provokes an invasion from France to impose foreign Catholic rule. The invaders are led by the Dauphin, whose claim to the English crown rests on his marriage to John's niece, Blanche. Philip II, widowed husband of Mary Tudor—older sister of Elizabeth and her predecessor as queen—launched the Spanish Armada the year after the death of Mary, Queen of Scots. Finally, in *King John* a providential storm destroys much of the French navy. Similarly, a storm wrecked the Armada, a catastrophe interpreted by the victors as God's deliverance of Protestant England from its Catholic enemies.

Although these summaries oversimplify theater and history alike, they suggest the explosive issues Shakespeare dramatized—struggle with the papacy, threat of invasion, and especially the problem of legitimate rule. There were risks to questioning Elizabeth's royal legitimacy or accusing her of murdering the rightful queen—even by historical analogy. Yet King John raises these matters not to resolve them but to meditate on their complexity. John both is and is not Arthur's murderer; he both is and is not the legitimate king.

Finally, the enigmatic logic of King John has affected its theatrical fortunes. Since the eighteenth century, the play has been cut to render its uncertain nationalism unambiguous. In the nineteenth century, its discontinuities and confrontations between characters encouraged productions that sacrificed narrative sweep to pageantry and individual scenes, especially involving Constance. King John has also proven useful for political allegory in times of crisis. It was marshaled to support loyalist opposition to the Catholic invasion of England in 1745. It served similar ends in the French and Indian War fifteen years later, during the Napoleonic Wars at the beginning of the nineteenth century, as a justification for British imperialism during the Boer War in South Africa in 1899, and as a rallying cry before and during World War II. A 1961 production took the contested city of Angers as an image of Berlin, recently divided by a wall between East and West. Although King John was the first of Shakespeare's plays to be filmed (1899; see Selected Bibliography below), the work's theatrical standing declined in the twentieth century. There may be promise, however, in the contemporary rebellion against politically orthodox interpretations in criticism and performance alike. Recent productions are noteworthy for their often satiric view of male authority in an unstable world. Perhaps a revival of interest depends less on the play's pageantry or jingoism than on its disabused view of power, its refusal to find reassurance in the interconnected, yet uncertain, sequence of historical events.

WALTER COHEN

SELECTED BIBLIOGRAPHY

Anderson, Thomas. "'Legitimation, name, and all is gone': Bastardy and Bureaucracy in Shakespeare's King John." Journal for Early Modern Cultural Studies 4.2 (Fall/Winter 2004): 35–61. Sees the Bastard's rise as indicative less of monarchical power than of the emergence of a new model of impersonal bureaucratic efficiency.

Bloom, Harold. Shakespeare: The Invention of the Human. New York: Riverhead, 1998. 51–63. Sees the Bastard as the first Shakespearean character with intense interiority: the Bastard "inaugurates Shakespeare's invention of the human."

Cousin, Geraldine. King John. Manchester: Manchester UP, 1994. Offers performance history, including discussion of the 1984 BBC film (see below).

Gieskes, Edward. "'He is but a Bastard to the Time': Status and Service in The Troublesome Raigne of John and Shakespeare's King John." ELH 65 (1998): 779–98. Focuses on the Bastard, contrasting his social elevation based on blood in The Troublesome Reign with his more modern conscious choice of the vocation of nobility in Shakespeare's play.

Howard, Jean E., and Phyllis Rackin. Engendering a Nation: A Feminist Account of Shakespeare's English Histories. London: Routledge, 1997. 119–33. Sees King John as a challenge to patriarchal, dynastic orthodoxy through skeptical women's voices.

Knapp, Jeffrey. Shakespeare's Tribe: Church, Nation, and Theater in Renaissance England. Chicago: U of Chicago P, 2002. 95–106. Examines King John as a quasi-allegorical account of the dangers of focusing on intra-Christian conflict rather than confronting the Turks.

Piesse, A. J. "King John: Changing Perspectives." The Cambridge Companion to Shakespeare's History Plays. Ed. Michael Hattaway. Cambridge: Cambridge UP, 2002. 126–40. Presents the theatrical and critical heritage, with stress on the play's experimental quality, especially in dramatizing the tension between history and historiography—between events as they happen and as they are interpreted.

Roe, John. *Shakespeare and Machiavelli*. Woodbridge, Suffolk: D. S. Brewer, 2002. 94–132. Analyzes *King John* as a Machiavellian play in its handling of calculating behavior as well as of both risk-taking and conscience.

Vaughan, Virginia Mason. *"King John." A Companion to Shakespeare's Works*. Vol. 2: *The Histories*. Ed. Richard Dutton and Jean E. Howard. Malden, MA: Blackwell, 2003. 379–94. Offers an overview of the play, looking especially at how it advocates limits on absolute secular or religious power.

Weimann, Robert, and Douglas Bruster. *Shakespeare and the Power of Performance: Stage and Page in the Elizabethan Theatre*. Cambridge: Cambridge UP, 2008. 57–76. Analyzes the Bastard, who combines the popular role of speaking to the audience with the realistic portrayal of a character.

FILMS

King John. 1899. Dir. Walter Pfeffer Dando and William K. L. Dickson. UK. 2 min. The first Shakespeare film, an extremely brief black-and-white silent consisting of three scenes—Constance's lamentation, John's temptation of Hubert, and John's death scene.

The Life and Death of King John. 1984. Dir. David Giles. UK. 155 min. A relatively conservative BBC production notable for Claire Bloom's innovative, coolly rational Constance.

TEXTUAL INTRODUCTION

The only text of *The Life and Death of King John* was printed in the First Folio of 1623. No indisputable evidence exists as to the date when Shakespeare composed the play, and this question has provoked controversy. A minority of editors and scholars have suggested that *King John* was written early in Shakespeare's career, perhaps around 1590, and that it may even precede the anonymous history play usually deemed to be its principal source, *The Troublesome Reign of John, King of England*, published in 1591. However, this view has not displaced a consensus based largely on detailed verbal and prosodic comparisons that would date the play significantly later, to 1595–96.

The Folio text of *King John* contains a number of peculiarities and problems. The two most significant of these have led to extensive consideration of what kind of text the compositors of the Folio were working from in the printing house and how this was prepared. First, there are frequent inconsistencies in the speech prefixes that identify each speaker, and there are further irregularities with names within the dialogue. For example, Philip, the King of France, is addressed as "King Lewis" by Austria (a slip corrected in this edition at 2.1.149) and later a speech prefix attributes to King Philip a statement that unquestionably belongs to the Citizen of Angers (2.1.368–72). Many editors have suggested that such variations can be attributed to the dramatist's own hand. On this view, the Folio *King John* is thought to preserve traces of the compositional process, and these discrepancies in naming derive from the papers of an author who may have written rapidly at times or who was, at least, untroubled by irregularities that could be dealt with later or in the playhouse. This theory has seemed more convincing than the use of a promptbook copy of the play by the compositors. That kind of manuscript would have belonged to Shakespeare's theatrical company and been prepared by them for use in performance, which, it has often been assumed, would have necessitated the clarification of such obvious inconsistencies. Yet there is no certainty as to the kind of manuscript the compositors were working from. For example, scholars have shown that theatrical companies tolerated a good deal of irregularity in the promptbook copies that they used, and this included variations in speech prefixes. Furthermore, even if the text used by the printers most likely derived from its author, this does not mean that it was written in Shakespeare's own hand. Indeed, substantive grounds exist to suggest that the author's manuscript was transcribed and prepared for the printing house by at least two scribes.

The key piece of evidence for this is a striking change in spelling: the exclamation "O," which is used widely in the play, appears consistently as "Oh" after 4.2.260, and this strongly suggests that a second scribe took responsibility for the transcription at this juncture. (This shift is unlikely to be attributable to the two compositors, known as B and C, as there is no such distinctive pattern in their deployment of these forms elsewhere in the Folio.) In addition, both scribes attempted to make the text conform to the 1606 "Act to Restrain Abuses of Players" by replacing the profane use of "God" in the dialogue with the more decorous "heaven." However, this process was not carried out consistently, and in this edition these milder terms have not been amended or restored to a hypothetical condition that is deemed to accord with a lost original manuscript of the play.

The second most glaring problem presented by the Folio text concerns the puzzling division of the action into acts and scenes. It should be noted immediately, however, that in performance this "problem" vanishes, as the action simply flows sequentially; the early quarto editions of Shakespeare's plays, which do not mark acts and scenes, show that he had little interest in neoclassical act divisions, which were the printer's or editor's responsibility. However, in the Folio what are usually distinguished in modern editions as *King John*'s first two acts are instead defined as its first two scenes: *Actus Primus, Scaena Prima* is followed by a lengthy *Scaena Secunda*. Even more bizarrely, when *Actus Secundus* does appear it is severely truncated and consists of only seventy-four lines. How this occurred is unclear. Perhaps the compositor misread Shakespeare's own notation of act and scene divisions. Or he may have followed erroneous divisions made by one of the two scribes in his transcription of this part of the manuscript. This edition follows the simplest, but not the only, solution to this problem by designating the Folio's *Scaena Secunda* as the first scene of act 2 and its *Actus Secundus* as the second scene of act 2.

DERMOT CAVANAGH

PERFORMANCE NOTE

Because *King John* consists of several loosely related episodes that progress largely through declamation, it can prove difficult for theater companies to define a coherent action and render it satisfactorily dramatic in performance. Add an underwhelming hero, fuzzy dramatic logic, and a series of anticlimaxes, and *King John* ranks among Shakespeare's most challenging plays to produce. Directors sometimes address its challenges by making John more central than the text does, exploiting his potential for Oedipal dependence on his mother, while diminishing the size and importance of comparatively appealing characters like the Bastard and Arthur. Other directors resign themselves to John's dramatic shortcomings and rely on the energy and soliloquies of the Bastard to carry the play, sometimes moderating his extreme irreverence and cartoonish loyalty to make him a more viable protagonist. Still others work to secure sympathy for Arthur, thereby making his interactions with Hubert and subsequent death the play's emotional center.

The characterizations of Eleanor and Constance almost inevitably manipulate the balance between the other three: a dominant Eleanor, for instance, may attract sympathy for John as he crumbles under the pressures of leadership after her death, while Constance can undermine support for her son's otherwise righteous cause by indulging her lengthy and repetitive complaints. Other considerations in performance include determining how sincere characters are in their religious and national loyalties, since many reject (and return to) them for political or personal advantage: Pandulph may be a scheming or a pious politician; John may tremble on hearing Peter of Pomfret's prophecy or laugh at it. Productions also must resolve such questions as how Arthur falls from the tower walls, and how to costume and situate a play that presents a medieval king amid a version of Shakespeare's England before a contemporary audience.

BRETT GAMBOA

The Life and Death of King John

1.1

Enter KING JOHN, QUEEN ELEANOR,[1] [*the Earls of*]
  PEMBROKE, ESSEX, *and* SALISBURY, *with* [*them*]
  CHATILLON[, *Ambassador*] *of France.*
KING JOHN   Now say, Chatillon, what would France with us?[2]
CHATILLON   Thus, after greeting, speaks the King of France
  In my behavior° to the majesty—   *person*
  The borrowed° majesty—of England here.   *usurped*

1.1 Location: John's court in London.
1. This scene, which occupies the first act, is unhistorical. The youngest son of Henry II and "Queen Eleanor" (Eleanor of Aquitaine), John (1167–1216) succeeded his brother, the famed crusader Richard I (the Lionheart), in 1199 and ruled until his death. Eleanor of Aquitaine (ca. 1122–1204) was Queen first of France and then of England.
2. What does (the King of) France want with us?

5   QUEEN ELEANOR A strange beginning: "borrowed majesty"?

KING JOHN Silence, good mother: hear the embassy.°   *message*

CHATILLON Philip of France, in right and true behalf
    Of thy deceasèd brother Geoffrey's³ son,
    Arthur Plantagenet,⁴ lays most lawful claim
10   To this fair island and the territories—
    To Ireland, Poitou, Anjou, Touraine, Maine⁵—
    Desiring thee to lay aside the sword
    Which sways° usurpingly these several titles°   *rules / separate lands*
    And put the same into young Arthur's hand,
15   Thy nephew and right royal sovereign.

KING JOHN What follows if we disallow of this?

CHATILLON The proud control° of fierce and bloody war,   *compulsion*
    To enforce these rights so forcibly withheld.

KING JOHN Here have we war for war and blood for blood,
20   Controlment for controlment. So answer France.

CHATILLON Then take my King's defiance from my mouth,
    The farthest limit° of my embassy.   *harshest stance*

KING JOHN Bear mine° to him, and so depart in peace.   *(my defiance)*
    Be thou as lightning in the eyes of France,
25   For ere thou canst report,⁶ I will be there;
    The thunder of my cannon° shall be heard.   *(not used in John's reign)*
    So hence. Be thou the trumpet of our wrath
    And sullen presage° of your own decay.°   *gloomy omen / downfall*
    An honorable conduct° let him have.   *escort*
30   Pembroke, look to't. —Farewell, Chatillon.

               Exeunt CHATILLON *and* PEMBROKE.

QUEEN ELEANOR What now, my son? Have I not ever° said   *always*
    How that ambitious Constance⁷ would not cease
    Till she had kindled France and all the world
    Upon° the right and party of her son?   *On behalf of*
35   This might have been prevented and made whole°   *settled*
    With very easy arguments of love,°   *friendly discussions*
    Which now the manage° of two kingdoms must   *government*
    With fearful bloody issue° arbitrate.   *outcome*

KING JOHN Our strong possession and our right for us.°   *on our side*

40   QUEEN ELEANOR Your strong possession much more than
       your right,
    Or else it must go wrong with you and me.
    So much my conscience whispers in your ear,
    Which none but heaven and you and I shall hear.

            Enter a Sheriff. [He whispers to ESSEX.]

ESSEX My liege,° here is the strangest controversy   *lord*
45   Come from the country to be judged by you
    That e'er I heard. Shall I produce the men?

---

3. Geoffrey was older than John and younger than Richard I; he died before Henry II. Because of changes in the laws of inheritance, John's claims to the throne would have been weaker in Shakespeare's lifetime—and are so represented—than they were in his own day, the early thirteenth century.
4. "Plantagenet" was the family name of most English monarchs from the accession of Henry II in 1154 to the deposition of Richard III in 1485. The historical Arthur was in his late teens; Shakespeare makes him much younger.

5. Except for Ireland, English territories in western and central France. Historically, it was these French territories, rather than the English crown itself, that Arthur claimed.
6. But even before you can deliver your message (pun on "report," meaning the noise of thunder or cannon).
7. Arthur's mother, Geoffrey's widow in Shakespeare and in his main source, *The Troublesome Reign of King John.* Historically, Constance remarried twice after Geoffrey's death.

KING JOHN   Let them approach.
—Our abbeys and our priories shall pay[8]
This expeditious charge.°   *sudden cost (of war)*
          Enter Robert FALCONBRIDGE *and Philip [the* BASTARD[9]*].*
                    What men are you?
50   BASTARD   Your faithful subject I, a gentleman
     Born in Northamptonshire and eldest son,
     As I suppose, to Robert Falconbridge,
     A soldier, by the honor-giving hand
     Of Coeur-de-lion° knighted in the field.   *Richard the Lionheart*
55   KING JOHN *[to* FALCONBRIDGE*]*   What art thou?
     FALCONBRIDGE   The son and heir to that same Falconbridge.
     KING JOHN   Is that the elder, and art thou the heir?
     You came not of one mother then, it seems.
     BASTARD   Most certain of one mother, mighty King—
60   That is well known—and, as I think, one father.
     But for the certain knowledge of that truth
     I put you o'er to° heaven and to my mother: *refer you to*
     Of that° I doubt as all men's children may.   *(my true paternity)*
     QUEEN ELEANOR   Out on thee,° rude man! Thou dost shame   *Away with you*
          thy mother
65   And wound her honor with this diffidence.°   *distrust*
     BASTARD   I, madam? No, I have no reason for it.
     That is my brother's plea and none of mine,
     The which if he can prove, 'a pops me out°   *he deprives me of*
     At least from fair° five hundred pound a year.[1]   *a full*
70   Heaven guard my mother's honor and my land!
     KING JOHN   A good blunt fellow. —Why, being younger born,
     Doth he lay claim to thine inheritance?
     BASTARD   I know not why, except to get the land,
     But once he slandered me with bastardy.
75   But whe'er° I be as true° begot or no,   *whether / legitimately*
     That still I lay upon my mother's head;°   *I let my mother answer*
     But that I am as well begot, my liege—
     Fair fall the bones that took the pains for me[2]—
     Compare our faces and be judge yourself.
80   If old Sir Robert did beget us both
     And were our father, and this son like him—
     O old sir Robert, father, on my knee
     I give heaven thanks I was not like to thee.
     KING JOHN   Why, what a madcap hath heaven lent us here!
85   QUEEN ELEANOR[3]   He hath a trick° of Coeur-de-lion's face;   *distinguishing trait*
     The accent of his tongue affecteth° him.   *resembles*
     Do you not read some tokens of my son
     In the large composition° of this man?   *openness; build*

---

8. Alluding to John's much-resented taxation of the monastic orders.
9. Drawing upon a passing reference in Holinshed's *Chronicles, The Troublesome Reign* invents a major role for this character, a role that Shakespeare further expands.
1. It is difficult to provide even approximate modern equivalents of financial data from 800 years ago. The purchasing power today of 500 pounds per year would be on the order of $600,000—a large amount. But its economic power, its relative share of national income, would be more like $180 million—a staggering figure. See also note to 2.1.530.
2. May good fortune befall the bones (of the dead man) who went to the trouble of begetting me.
3. The Queen may speak the following lines privately to John.

KING JOHN Mine eye hath well examinèd his parts°   *attributes*
  And finds them perfect Richard.
90 [*to* FALCONBRIDGE]   Sirrah,° speak: *(used to inferiors)*
  What doth move you to claim your brother's land?
BASTARD Because he hath a half-face° like my father! *profile; thin face*
  With half that face[4] would he have all my land—
  A half-faced groat[5] five hundred pound a year!
95 FALCONBRIDGE My gracious liege, when that my father lived,
  Your brother° did employ my father much—   *(Richard)*
BASTARD Well, sir, by this you cannot get my land.
  Your tale must be how he employed my mother.
FALCONBRIDGE And once dispatched him in an embassy
100 To Germany, there with the Emperor
  To treat of high affairs touching that time.
  Th'advantage of his absence took the King
  And in the meantime sojourned at my father's,
  Where how he did prevail I shame to speak.
105 But truth is truth: large lengths of seas and shores
  Between my father and my mother lay,
  As I have heard my father speak himself,
  When this same lusty° gentleman was got.° *vigorous / conceived*
  Upon his deathbed he by will bequeathed
110 His lands to me, and took it on his death°   *solemnly swore*
  That this, my mother's son, was none of his;
  And, if he were, he came into the world
  Full fourteen weeks before the course of time.
  Then, good my liege, let me have what is mine:
115 My father's land, as was my father's will.
KING JOHN Sirrah, your brother is legitimate.°   *legally correct*
  Your father's wife did after wedlock bear him,
  And if she did play false the fault° was hers, *flaw; (vaginal?) crack*
  Which fault lies on the hazards of° all husbands *is a risk for*
120 That marry wives. Tell me, how if° my brother, *what if*
  Who, as you say, took pains to get this son,
  Had of your father claimed this son for his?
  In sooth, good friend, your father might have kept
  This calf, bred from his cow, from all the world;
125 In sooth he might. Then if he were my brother's,
  My brother might not claim him, nor your father,
  Being none of his, refuse him.[6] This concludes:
  My mother's son did get your father's heir;
  Your father's heir must have your father's land.
130 FALCONBRIDGE Shall then my father's will be of no force
  To dispossess that child which is not his?
BASTARD Of no more force to dispossess me, sir,
  Than was his will° to get me, as I think. *legal instrument; lust*
QUEEN ELEANOR Whether hadst° thou rather be: a Falconbridge, *Which would*
135 And like thy brother to enjoy thy land,
  Or the reputed son of Coeur-de-lion,
  Lord of thy presence° and no land beside?   *yourself*

---

4. Half of his father's face, since Falconbridge inherits maternal features as well; "face" is also "impudence."
5. A coin showing the monarch's head in profile; also Falconbridge, who as a person is worth only as much

as a groat (four pence), despite his inheritance.
6. *nor . . . him:* nor could your father, though not the biological father to the Bastard, disown him.

BASTARD Madam, an if° my brother had my shape, *an if = if*
And I had his, Sir Robert's his° like him, *(Sir Robert's)*
140 And if my legs were two such riding-rods,° *riding switches*
My arms such eel-skins stuffed, my face so thin
That in mine ear I durst not stick a rose
Lest men should say, "Look where three-farthings goes!"[7]
And to° his shape were heir to all this land, *in addition to*
145 Would I might never stir from off this place.[8]
I would give it, every foot,° to have this face; *every foot of it*
It would not be Sir Nob in any case.[9]
QUEEN ELEANOR I like thee well. Wilt thou forsake thy fortune,
Bequeath thy land to him, and follow me?
150 I am a soldier and now bound to France.
BASTARD Brother, take you my land; I'll take my chance.
Your face hath got five hundred pound a year,
Yet sell your face for fivepence and 'tis dear.° *expensive*
Madam, I'll follow you unto the death.
155 QUEEN ELEANOR Nay, I would have you go before me thither.
BASTARD Our country manners give our betters way.[1]
KING JOHN What is thy name?
BASTARD Philip, my liege, so is my name begun;
Philip, good old Sir Robert's wife's eldest son.
160 KING JOHN From henceforth bear his name whose form thou bearest.
Kneel thou down Philip, but rise more great:
    [*He knights the* BASTARD.]
Arise Sir Richard and Plantagenet.[2]
BASTARD Brother by th' mother's side, give me your hand.
My father gave me honor, yours gave land.
165 Now blessèd be the hour,° by night or day, *(with pun on "whore")*
When I was got, Sir Robert was away.
QUEEN ELEANOR The very spirit of Plantagenet!
I am thy grandam, Richard: call me so.
BASTARD Madam, by chance but not by truth;° what though?° *chastely / but so what?*
170 Something about,° a little from the right,° *a bit off / unlawful*
In at the window or else o'er the hatch;[3]
Who dares not stir by day must walk° by night, *go; rob (sexually)*
And have is have, however men do catch.[4]
Near or far off, well won is still well shot,[5]
175 And I am I, howe'er I was begot.
KING JOHN Go, Falconbridge, now hast thou thy desire:
A landless knight° makes thee a landed squire. *(the Bastard)*
Come, madam, and come, Richard: we must speed
For France, for France, for it is more than need.

---

7. A rose appeared behind the Queen's head on a three farthing coin, which was thin and of small value (less than a penny).
8. May I be struck dead here and now.
9. My appearance would not be that of Sir Robert under any circumstances. The speech is full of sexual innuendo. "Riding-rods" (line 140) and "eel-skins" (line 141) hint at sexual inadequacy associated with a thin penis. "Nob" (line 147) is also slang for "penis." "Rose" (line 142), "shape" (line 144), and "case" (line 147) may refer to the vagina; "riding" (line 140), "stuffed" (line 141), "stick a rose" (line 142), and "foot" (line 146) suggest copulation; and "stir" (line 145) can

mean "sexually arouse."
1. The Bastard jokes that it's proper to let social superiors go first.
2. Perhaps the shift from blank verse to rhyme (lines 142–81), though not fully systematic, reinforces the Bastard's social elevation here.
3. Both phrases are proverbial for birth out of wedlock. *hatch:* the lower half of a divided door.
4. That is, possession is nine-tenths of the law.
5. Archery metaphor, with sexual innuendo, as with "stir" (line 172). The entire passage is also marked by mock-proverbial expressions.

180 BASTARD   Brother, adieu: good fortune come to thee,
     For thou wast got i'th' way of honesty.

                      Exeunt all but [the] BASTARD.

     A foot of honor[6] better than I was,
     But many a many foot of land the worse.
     Well, now can I make any Joan° a lady.   *lower-class woman*

185   "Good den, Sir Richard" —"Godamercy,[7] fellow,"
     An if his name be George I'll call him Peter,
     For new-made honor doth forget men's names:
     'Tis too respective and too sociable
     For your conversion.[8] Now your traveler,

190   He and his toothpick at my worship's mess;
     And when my knightly stomach is sufficed,
     Why, then I suck my teeth[9] and catechize
     My pickèd° man of countries. "My dear sir"—   *affected; tooth-picked*
     Thus leaning on mine elbow I begin—

195   "I shall beseech you." That is Question now,
     And then comes Answer like an Absey book:°   *school (ABC) primer*
     "O sir," says Answer, "at your best command,
     At your employment, at your service, sir."
     "No, sir," says Question, "I, sweet sir, at yours."

200   And so ere Answer knows what Question would,°   *wishes*
     Saving in dialogue of compliment,°   *Except empty flattery*
     And talking of the Alps and Apennines,
     The Pyrenean and the river Po,
     It draws toward supper° in conclusion so.   *(another meal)*

205   But this is worshipful society
     And fits the mounting spirit° like myself;   *ambitious character*
     For he is but a bastard to° the time   *no true child of*
     That doth not smack of observation,°   *courtly obsequiousness*
     And so am I,° whether I smack or no.   *so I intend*

210   And not alone in habit° and device,°   *clothes / heraldic emblem*
     Exterior form, outward accoutrement,
     But from the inward motion° to deliver   *impulse*
     Sweet, sweet, sweet poison° for the age's tooth,° *flattery / appetite*
     Which,° though I will not practice° to deceive, *(flattery) / make a habit*

215   Yet to avoid deceit° I mean to learn,   *being deceived*
     For it shall strew the footsteps of my rising.[1]
     But who comes in such haste in riding-robes?
     What woman-post° is this? Hath she no husband   *female post-rider*
     That will take pains to blow a horn[2] before her?

          Enter LADY FALCONBRIDGE *and James* GURNEY.

220   Oh, me, 'tis my mother. How now, good lady?
     What brings you here to court so hastily?

---

6. A degree of status. The Bastard contrasts his newly acquired aristocratic "honor" with Falconbridge's middle-class "honesty" (line 181).
7. God reward you: the patronizing reply of a social superior. The Bastard imagines himself encountering a social inferior who says, "Good evening." His soliloquy continues in this vein, parodying the affectation of courtiers and foreign travelers, in part through the ironic use of religious rhetoric—"conversion" (line 189, referring to his new rank), "my worship's mess" (line 190; "my worship" means both "a lord" and "the Lord"; "mess" points to both "a dinner table" and "the Mass," the commemoration of Christ's Last Supper),

"catechize" (line 192; orally question, usually about religious principles), and "worshipful" (line 205, where the secular sense is primary but perhaps with the same double meaning as in line 190).
8. *'Tis . . . conversion:* Remembering names is beneath the dignity of a newly created knight.
9. The Bastard defiantly cleans his teeth in the vulgar English fashion, rather than resorting to the traveler's and courtier's affectation of a toothpick.
1. For flattery will ease my ascent; awareness of deceptive flattery will do so.
2. Post horn announcing the rider's approach; also, the symbol of a cuckold.

LADY FALCONBRIDGE   Where is that slave thy brother? Where is he
  That holds in chase° mine honor up and down?   *Who hunts*
BASTARD   My brother Robert, old Sir Robert's son?
225   Colbrand the Giant,[3] that same mighty man?
  Is it Sir Robert's son that you seek so?
LADY FALCONBRIDGE   Sir Robert's son, ay, thou unreverend° boy.   *irreverent*
  "Sir Robert's son"? Why scorn'st thou at Sir Robert?
  He is Sir Robert's son, and so art thou.
230   BASTARD   James Gurney, wilt thou give us leave° a while?   *leave us*
GURNEY   Good leave, good Philip.
BASTARD   Philip Sparrow,[4] James!
  There's toys abroad;[5] anon I'll tell thee more.
                                   Exit James [GURNEY].
  Madam, I was not old Sir Robert's son:
235   Sir Robert might have ate his part in me
  Upon Good Friday and ne'er broke his fast.
  Sir Robert could do° well, marry,° to confess.   *(perform sexually) / indeed*
  Could get° me? Sir Robert could not do it: *Could he have begotten*
  We know his handiwork.° Therefore, good mother,   *(Falconbridge)*
  To whom am I beholden for these limbs?
240   Sir Robert never holp° to make this leg.   *helped*
LADY FALCONBRIDGE   Hast thou conspired with thy brother too,
  That for thine own gain shouldst defend mine honor?
  What means this scorn, thou most untoward° knave?   *unmannerly*
BASTARD   Knight, knight, good mother, Basilisco-like.[6]
245   What, I am dubbed! I have it° on my shoulder.   *(a sword tap)*
  But, mother, I am not Sir Robert's son;
  I have disclaimed Sir Robert and my land:
  Legitimation, name, and all is gone.
  Then, good my mother, let me know my father—
250   Some proper man, I hope. Who was it, mother?
LADY FALCONBRIDGE   Hast thou denied thyself a Falconbridge?
BASTARD   As faithfully as I deny the devil.
LADY FALCONBRIDGE   King Richard Coeur-de-lion was thy father.
  By long and vehement suit I was seduced
255   To make room for him in my husband's bed.
  Heaven lay not my transgression to my charge!
  Thou art the issue° of my dear° offense,   *result / costly; loving*
  Which was so strongly urged past my defense.
BASTARD   Now, by this light, were I to get° again,   *be conceived*
260   Madam, I would not wish a better father.
  Some sins do bear their privilege° on earth,   *are pardonable*
  And so doth yours. Your fault was not your folly;°   *Your sin wasn't foolish*
  Needs must you lay your heart at his dispose,°   *disposal*
  Subjected tribute to commanding love,
265   Against whose fury and unmatchèd force
  The aweless° lion could not wage the fight   *fearless*
  Nor keep his princely heart from Richard's hand.

---

3. Danish giant killed by Guy in the popular romance *Guy of Warwick*.
4. Recalling the popularity of Philip as a name for a mere bird, the Bastard considers the name beneath him.

5. There's trivial news (ironic), or rumors.
6. The cowardly braggart Basilisco in an anonymous play *Solyman and Perseda*, probably from the early 1590s, calls himself a knight while his servant calls him a knave.

He that perforce° robs lions of their hearts[7]   *by his strength*

May easily win a woman's. Ay, my mother,

270   With all my heart I thank thee for my father.

Who lives and dares but say thou didst not well

When I was got, I'll send his soul to hell.

Come, lady, I will show thee to my kin,

And they shall say, when Richard me begot,

275   If thou hadst said him nay, it had been sin.

Who says it was, he lies; I say 'twas not.[8]   *Exeunt.*

2.1

Enter before Angers [on one side], KING PHILIP *of France,* LOUIS [THE] DAUPHIN, CONSTANCE, [*and*] ARTHUR [*and, on the other side,*] AUSTRIA [*with Soldiers*].[1]*

KING PHILIP[2]   Before Angers well met, brave Austria.

Arthur, that great forerunner of thy blood,

Richard,° that robbed the lion of his heart   *(Arthur's uncle)*

And fought the holy wars in Palestine,°   *(Third Crusade, 1189–92)*

5   By this brave duke came early to his grave;[3]

And for amends to his posterity

At our importance° hither is he come   *urgent request*

To spread his colors,° boy, in thy behalf,   *battle flags*

And to rebuke the usurpation

10   Of thy unnatural uncle, English John.

Embrace him, love him, give him welcome hither.

ARTHUR [*to* AUSTRIA]   God shall forgive you Coeur-de-lion's death,

The rather that° you give his offspring life,   *All the more because*

Shadowing° their right under your wings of war.   *Protecting*

15   I give you welcome with a powerless hand

But with a heart full of unstainèd love.

Welcome before the gates of Angers, Duke.

KING PHILIP   A noble boy. Who would not do thee right?

AUSTRIA [*to* ARTHUR]   Upon thy cheek lay I this zealous kiss

20   As seal to this indenture° of my love: *contract*

That to my home I will no more return

Till Angers and the right thou hast in France,

Together with that pale, that white-faced shore,°   *chalk cliffs of Dover*

Whose foot° spurns back the ocean's roaring tides   *(of the cliffs)*

25   And coops° from other lands her islanders,   *protects*

Even till that England, hedged in with the main,°   *ocean*

That water-wallèd bulwark, still° secure   *always*

---

7. Alluding to Richard I's legendary feat of killing a lion by putting his hand down its throat and pulling out its heart (hence the epithet Coeur-de-lion, Lionheart).

8. Not a sin; naught (nothing); but also, perhaps, punningly, naughty, and hence something, a sin.

2.1 Location: Before the town wall of Angers.

1. This is *"Scaena Secunda"* in F (see the Textual Introduction). The back of the stage represents the town wall, with the town notionally behind it. The Citizen's entry *"upon the walls"* (SD after line 200) is onto the upper stage. Below the upper stage, central tiring-house doors would probably represent the gates of Angers, the capital of John's French holdings. These

remain closed; the French and English armies appear from side entrances.

2. TEXTUAL COMMENT The Folio assigns this speech, the comment at line 18, and the remarks beginning at line 150 to the Dauphin, rather than the French King. This probably, though not certainly, represents a mix-up of the names of the King and his son on Shakespeare's part. See Digital Edition TC 1.

3. Austria, the "brave duke," imprisoned Richard, but Richard was actually killed while besieging the castle of the Viscount of Limoges in France. Shakespeare follows his main source in combining the two historical figures in the character of Austria.

     And confident from foreign purposes,
     Even till that utmost corner of the West
30   Salute thee for her king. Till then, fair boy,
     Will I not think of home, but follow arms.
     CONSTANCE   Oh, take his mother's thanks, a widow's thanks,
     Till your strong hand shall help to give him strength
     To make a more° requital to your love.   greater
35   AUSTRIA   The peace of heaven is theirs that lift their swords
     In such a just and charitable war.
     KING PHILIP   Well, then, to work. Our cannon shall be bent°   aimed
     Against the brows° of this resisting town.   walls
     Call for our chiefest men of discipline,°   military skill
40   To cull the plots of best advantages.[4]
     We'll lay before this town our royal bones,
     Wade to the marketplace in Frenchmen's blood,
     But we will° make it subject to this boy.   In order to; unless we
     CONSTANCE   Stay for an answer to your embassy,
45   Lest unadvised° you stain your swords with blood.   rashly
     My lord Chatillon may from England bring
     That right in peace which here we urge° in war,   seek
     And then we shall repent each drop of blood
     That hot rash haste so indirectly° shed.   wrongfully
          Enter CHATILLON.
50   KING PHILIP   A wonder, lady! Lo, upon thy wish
     Our messenger Chatillon is arrived.
     —What England° says, say briefly, gentle lord,   the King of England
     We coldly° pause for thee. Chatillon, speak.   calmly
     CHATILLON   Then turn your forces from this paltry siege
55   And stir them up against a mightier task:
     England, impatient of your just demands,
     Hath put himself in arms. The adverse winds,
     Whose leisure I have stayed,° have given him time Which I had to wait out
     To land his legions all as soon as I.
60   His marches are expedient° to this town,   coming quickly
     His forces strong, his soldiers confident.
     With him along is come the mother-queen,
     An Ate,° stirring him to blood and strife.   goddess of discord
     With her her niece,[5] the Lady Blanche of Spain;
65   With them a bastard of the King's deceased,°   of Richard's
     And all th'unsettled humors[6] of the land,
     Rash, inconsiderate,° fiery voluntaries,°   imprudent / volunteers
     With ladies'° faces and fierce dragons' spleens,°   beardless / tempers
     Have sold their fortunes at their native homes,
70   Bearing their birthrights proudly on their backs,[7]
     To make a hazard of° new fortunes here.   take a chance on
     In brief, a braver choice of dauntless spirits
     Than now the English bottoms° have waft o'er   ships
     Did never float upon the swelling tide,

---

4. To pick the positions of greatest advantage (for the
cannons).
5. Actually, Eleanor's granddaughter: "niece" is used
in a broad sense.
6. Men of discontented spirits; masterless men of no
fixed abode. The soldiers are seen as "humors" (phys-

ical elements of the body, which affect temperament)
discharged from the body of England.
7. In the form of armor bought by selling their land
("fortunes" and "birthrights," lines 69–70). "All his
clothes are on his back" is proverbial.

75	To do offense and scathe° in Christendom.	*damage*
	Drum beats.	
	The interruption of their churlish drums	
	Cuts off more circumstance.° They are at hand	*detail*
	To parley or to fight; therefore prepare!	
	KING PHILIP How much unlooked for is this expedition!°	*military force; speed*
80	AUSTRIA By how much unexpected, by so much	
	We must awake endeavor for defense,	
	For courage mounteth with occasion.°	*necessity*
	Let them be welcome, then; we are prepared.	
	Enter KING [JOHN] *of England,* [*the*] BASTARD,	
	Queen [ELEANOR], BLANCHE, [*the Earl of*] PEMBROKE,	
	and others.	
	KING JOHN Peace be to France, if France in peace permit	
85	Our just and lineal° entrance to our own;°	*hereditary / (Angers)*
	If not, bleed France,° and peace ascend to heaven,	*let France bleed*
	Whiles we, God's wrathful agent, do correct°	*punish*
	Their proud contempt that beats his peace to heaven.	
	KING PHILIP Peace be to England, if that war° return	*if the English forces*
90	From France to England, there to live in peace.	
	England we love, and for that England's° sake	*that land's; Arthur's*
	With burden of our armor here we sweat.	
	This toil of ours should be a work of thine;	
	But thou from loving England art so far	
95	That thou hast underwrought° his lawful king,	*undermined*
	Cut off the sequence of posterity,°	*succession*
	Outfacèd infant state° and done a rape	*Defied Arthur's right*
	Upon the maiden virtue of the crown.	
	Look here upon thy brother Geoffrey's face.	
100	These eyes, these brows were moulded out of his;	
	This little abstract° doth contain that large°	*précis / full version*
	Which died in Geoffrey, and the hand of time	
	Shall draw this brief° into as huge a volume.	*summary*
	That Geoffrey was thy elder brother born,	
105	And this his son. England was Geoffrey's right,	
	And this is Geoffrey's.° In the name of God,	*(son and heir)*
	How comes it then that thou art called a king,	
	When living blood doth in these temples beat	
	Which owe° the crown that thou o'ermasterest?	*own*
110	KING JOHN From whom hast thou this great commission, France,	
	To draw my answer from thy articles?°	*charges*
	KING PHILIP From that supernal° judge that stirs good thoughts	*heavenly*
	In any breast of strong authority,°	*powerful ruler*
	To look into the blots and stains of right.	
115	That judge hath made me guardian to this boy,	
	Under whose warrant I impeach° thy wrong,	*challenge*
	And by whose help I mean to chastise it.	
	KING JOHN Alack, thou dost usurp authority.	
	KING PHILIP Excuse it is to beat usurping down.[8]	
120	QUEEN ELEANOR Who is it thou dost call usurper, France?	
	CONSTANCE Let me make answer: thy usurping son.	

---

8. My (so-called) usurpation is excusable because I am using it to put down (real) usurpation.

QUEEN ELEANOR　Out,° insolent! Thy bastard shall be king　　　　　*Begone*
　　That thou mayst be a queen and check° the world.　　　　　　*master*
CONSTANCE　My bed was ever° to thy son as true　　　　　　　　*always*
125　As thine was to thy husband, and this boy
　　Liker in feature to his father Geoffrey
　　Than thou and John in manners, being as like
　　As rain to water or devil to his dam.°　　　　　　　　　　　*mother*
　　My boy a bastard? By my soul, I think
130　His father never was so true begot.
　　It cannot be an if° thou wert his mother.　　　　　　　　*an if = if*
QUEEN ELEANOR　[*to* ARTHUR]　There's a good mother, boy, that
　　blots° thy father.　　　　　　　　　　　　　　　　　　*slanders*
CONSTANCE　[*to* ARTHUR]　There's a good grandam, boy, that
　　would blot thee.
AUSTRIA　Peace.
BASTARD　　　　　Hear the crier!⁹
AUSTRIA　　　　　　　　　What the devil art thou?
135　BASTARD　One that will play the devil, sir, with you,
　　An 'a° may catch your hide¹ and you alone.　　　　　　　*If he (I)*
　　You are the hare° of whom the proverb goes,　　　　　　　*coward*
　　Whose valor plucks dead lions by the beard.°　　　　　　*(an insult)*
　　I'll smoke your skin-coat° an I catch you right.　　　*thrash your hide*
140　Sirrah,° look to't; i'faith I will, i'faith.　　　　*Boy (an insult)*
BLANCHE　Oh, well did he° become that lion's robe　　　　　*(Richard)*
　　That did disrobe the lion of that robe.
BASTARD　It lies as sightly° on the back of him　　　　　　*fitly*
　　As great Alcides' shoes upon an ass.²
145　But ass, I'll take that burden from your back,
　　Or lay on that° shall make your shoulders crack.　*that burden which*
AUSTRIA　What cracker° is this same that deafs our ears　　*boaster*
　　With this abundance of superfluous breath?
　　King Philip, determine what we shall do straight.°　　*immediately*
150　KING PHILIP　Women and fools,° break off your conference.　*children*
KING JOHN, this is the very sum of all:
　　England and Ireland, Anjou,³ Touraine, Maine,
　　In right of Arthur do I claim of thee.
　　Wilt thou resign them and lay down thy arms?
155　KING JOHN　My life as soon! I do defy thee, France!
　　Arthur of Bretagne,⁴ yield thee to my hand,
　　And out of my dear love I'll give thee more
　　Than e'er the coward hand of France can win.
　　Submit thee, boy.
QUEEN ELEANOR　　　Come to thy grandam, child.

---

9. The Bastard mockingly compares Austria to an officer in a law court who calls for order.
1. The lion skin Austria wears, which antagonizes the Bastard, since it is a memento of his father's death.
2. The lion skin of King Richard looks as absurd on Austria as would an article belonging to the classical hero Hercules ("Alcides") upon an ass. The Bastard has earlier used proverbs to insult Austria (lines 137–38) and here conflates two sayings: "An ass in a lion's skin" and "A great [Hercules'] shoe will not fit a little [child's] foot." Some editors emend "shoes" to

"shows" (distinctive clothing). This also makes sense: both meanings may be present.
3. Here and at line 487, Shakespeare appears to confuse the province (Anjou) with the besieged town (Angers; French: *Angiers*). Elsewhere he maintains a distinction, as do his sources.
4. TEXTUAL COMMENT The Folio has "Arthur of Britaine," an archaic spelling of Brittany. Since using "Brittany" to avoid the now confusing use of "Britaine" would mean adding a syllable to its pronunciation, the modern French spelling has been preferred. See Digital Edition TC 2.

160	CONSTANCE Do, child, go to it° grandam, child.	*its*
	Give grandam kingdom and it grandam will	
	Give it a plum, a cherry, and a fig.°	*(obscene gesture)*
	There's a good grandam.°	*(sarcastic baby talk)*
	ARTHUR Good my mother, peace.	
	I would that I were low laid in my grave:	
165	I am not worth this coil° that's made for me.	*commotion*
	QUEEN ELEANOR[5] His mother shames him so, poor boy, he weeps.	
	CONSTANCE Now shame upon you, whe'er° she does or no.	*whether*
	His grandam's wrongs and not his mother's shames	
	Draws those heaven-moving pearls from his poor eyes,	
170	Which heaven shall take in nature° of a fee.	*as a kind*
	Ay, with these crystal beads° heaven shall be bribed	*tears*
	To do him justice and revenge on you.	
	QUEEN ELEANOR Thou monstrous slanderer of heaven and earth!	
	CONSTANCE Thou monstrous injurer of heaven and earth!	
175	Call not me slanderer: thou and thine usurp	
	The dominations, royalties,° and rights	*domains, royal powers*
	Of this oppressèd boy. This is thy eldest son's son,[6]	
	Infortunate in nothing but in thee.	
	Thy sins are visited° in this poor child:	*punished*
180	The canon of the law° is laid on him,	*biblical decree*
	Being but the second generation	
	Removèd from thy sin-conceiving womb.[7]	
	KING JOHN Bedlam,° have done.	*Lunatic*
	CONSTANCE I have but this to say:	
	That he° is not only plaguèd for her sin,°	*(Arthur) / (adultery)*
185	But God hath made her sin° and her the plague	*(John; with pun on "son"?)*
	On this removèd issue,° plagued for her,	*(Arthur)*
	And with her plague,[8] her sin his injury,	
	Her injury, the beadle to her sin,	
	All punished in the person of this child,	
190	And all for her.[9] A plague upon her!	
	QUEEN ELEANOR Thou unadvisèd° scold, I can produce	*rash*
	A will that bars the title of thy son.	
	CONSTANCE Ay, who doubts that? A will, a wicked will,	
	A woman's will,[1] a cankered grandam's will.	
195	KING PHILIP Peace, lady; pause, or be more temperate.	
	It ill beseems this presence° to cry aim	*royal assembly*
	To[2] these ill-tunèd repetitions.	
	Some trumpet summon hither to the walls	

---

5. TEXTUAL COMMENT The speech prefix for Eleanor in the Folio is *"Queen"* when she defies King Philip earlier in this scene (2.1.120). Here it is *"Qu. Mo."* (Queen Mother)—perhaps a sign that Shakespeare intends to suggest her sympathy for her grandson. The prefix becomes *"Old Qu."* later in the scene (2.1.468), when she provides her son with cynical, worldly advice that implicitly comes with age. See Digital Edition TC 3.

6. Oldest grandson; but perhaps deliberately meant to produce the false inference that Arthur is really the "eldest son's [Richard's] son."

7. Implying sexual infidelity in the conception of John. These lines (especially 179) echo the Second Commandment (Exodus 20:5, "the law" of line 180):

"visiting the iniquity of the fathers upon the children unto the third and fourth generation."

8. *plagued . . . plague:* punished because of and by her.

9. *her sin his injury . . . her:* her wrongful action is like a parish constable (a "beadle," who whipped petty criminals) urging on her son to afflict Arthur; all (Eleanor's sin, John as its embodiment) are punished in Arthur, and all because of Eleanor.

1. Testament influenced by a woman (Eleanor; ironically, it was illegal for women to make wills themselves, for fear their husbands would influence them); a woman's desire (as in the proverbial "A woman will have her will").

2. *to cry aim / To:* to encourage.

These men of Angers. Let us hear them speak,
200 Whose title they admit: Arthur's or John's.
       Trumpet sounds. Enter a CITIZEN[3] *upon the walls.*
CITIZEN   Who is it that hath warned° us to the walls?   *summoned*
KING PHILIP   'Tis France, for England.
KING JOHN   England for itself.
   You men of Angers and my loving subjects—
KING PHILIP   You loving men of Angers, Arthur's subjects,
205 Our trumpet called you to this gentle parle°—   *parley*
KING JOHN   For our° advantage; therefore hear us first.   *(England's; John's)*
   These flags of France that are advancèd here
   Before the eye and prospect of your town,
   Have hither marched to your endamagement.
210 The cannons have their bowels full of wrath,
   And ready mounted are they to spit forth
   Their iron indignation 'gainst your walls.
   All preparation for a bloody siege
   And merciless proceeding by these French
215 Confronts your city's eyes, your winking° gates,   *closed (in sleep)*
   And, but for our approach, those sleeping stones,
   That as a waist° doth girdle you about,   *girdle*
   By the compulsion of their ordnance°   *artillery*
   By this time from their fixèd beds of lime°   *their foundations*
220 Had been dishabited,[4] and wide havoc made
   For bloody power to rush upon your peace.
   But, on the sight of us, your lawful King,
   Who painfully° with much expedient° march   *laboriously / hurried*
   Have brought a countercheck before your gates,
225 To save unscratched your city's threatened cheeks,
   Behold, the French, amazed,° vouchsafe° a parle;   *terrified / grant*
   And now, instead of bullets wrapped in fire
   To make a shaking fever in your walls,
   They shoot but calm words folded up in smoke,°   *deceit*
230 To make a faithless error° in your ears;   *lie*
   Which trust accordingly, kind citizens,
   And let us in, your King, whose labored° spirits,   *worn out*
   Forewearied in this action of swift speed,
   Craves harborage within your city walls.
235 KING PHILIP   When I have said, make answer to us both.
       [He takes ARTHUR *by the hand.]*
   Lo, in this° right hand, whose protection   *(Philip's)*
   Is most divinely vowed upon the right
   Of him° it holds, stands young Plantagenet,   *(Arthur)*
   Son to the elder brother of this man,°   *(John)*
240 And king o'er him and all that he enjoys.
   For this downtrodden equity° we tread   *right*
   In warlike march these greens before your town,
   Being no further enemy to you

---

3. Some editors believe that Shakespeare may have taken some steps toward conflating this character with Hubert (see Textual Comment at line 325), who appears later in the play as a follower of King John. But there are compelling reasons for keeping these roles distinct and preserving the part of the Citizen. For example, no early text survives in which such an identification of characters has been fully effected.
4. Dislodged, unclothed ("habit" picking up "waist" and "girdle" in line 217). Angers continues to be personified here ("cheeks," line 225; "fever," line 228) and later in the scene.

	Than the constraint° of hospitable zeal	*necessity*
245	In the relief of this oppressèd child	
	Religiously° provokes. Be pleasèd then	*Solemnly*
	To pay that duty which you truly owe	
	To him that owes° it, namely this young prince,	*has a right to*
	And then our arms, like to a muzzled bear,	
250	Save in aspect,° hath all offense° sealed up.	*appearance / aggression*
	Our cannons' malice vainly shall be spent	
	Against th'invulnerable clouds of heaven,	
	And with a blessèd and unvexed retire,°	*unmolested retreat*
	With unhacked swords and helmets all unbruised,	
255	We will bear home that lusty blood again	
	Which here we came to spout against your town,	
	And leave your children, wives, and you in peace.	
	But if you fondly pass° our proffered offer,	*foolishly disregard*
	'Tis not the roundure° of your old-faced walls	*roundness; circumference*
260	Can hide you from our messengers of war,°	*cannonballs*
	Though all these English and their discipline°	*military skill*
	Were harbored in their rude° circumference.	*rugged*
	Then tell us: shall your city call us lord,	
	In that behalf which° we have challenged it?	*in which; for whom*
265	Or shall we give the signal to our rage	
	And stalk in blood to our possession?	
	CITIZEN In brief, we are the King of England's subjects:	
	For him, and in his right, we hold this town.	
	KING JOHN Acknowledge then the King and let me in.	
270	CITIZEN That can we not. But he that proves° the king,	*proves to be*
	To him will we prove loyal. Till that time	
	Have we rammed up our gates against the world.	
	KING JOHN Doth not the crown of England prove the king?	
	And if not that, I bring you witnesses:	
275	Twice fifteen thousand hearts of England's breed—	
	BASTARD Bastards and else.°	*others*
	KING JOHN To verify our title with their lives.	
	KING PHILIP As many and as well-born bloods as those—	
	BASTARD Some bastards too.	
280	KING PHILIP Stand in his face° to contradict his claim.	*against him*
	CITIZEN Till you compound° whose right is worthiest,	*settle*
	We for the worthiest hold° the right from both.	*withhold*
	KING JOHN Then God forgive the sin of all those souls	
	That to their everlasting residence,	
285	Before the dew of evening fall, shall fleet°	*leave their bodies*
	In dreadful trial of° our kingdom's king.	*contest to determine*
	KING PHILIP Amen, amen. Mount, chevaliers,° to arms!	*horsemen*
	BASTARD Saint George that swinged° the dragon and e'er since	*thrashed*
	Sits on on 's horseback at mine hostess' door,[5]	
290	Teach us some fence!° [*to* AUSTRIA] Sirrah, were I at home	*swordsmanship*
	At your den, sirrah, with your lioness,°	*whore; wife*
	I would set an ox-head° to your lion's hide	*add cuckold's horns*
	And make a monster of you.	
	AUSTRIA Peace, no more.	

---

5. The idea that St. George, England's patron saint, is ever on horseback yet never rides was proverbial. *at mine hostess' door:* on an inn sign.

BASTARD Oh, tremble, for you hear the lion roar.
295 KING JOHN Up higher to the plain, where we'll set forth
In best appointment° all our regiments.   *readiness*
BASTARD Speed then to take advantage of the field.°   *best battle positions*
KING PHILIP It shall be so, and at the other hill
Command the rest to stand.[6] God and our right!°   *(English royal motto)*
                              Exeunt [all but CITIZEN].
                    Here, after excursions,° enter [on one side] the   *onstage skirmishes*
                    HERALD *of France with Trumpet[er]s to the gates.*
300 FRENCH HERALD You men of Angers, open wide your gates,
And let young Arthur, Duke of Bretagne, in,
Who by the hand of France this day hath made
Much work for tears in many an English mother,
Whose sons lie scattered on the bleeding ground.
305 Many a widow's husband groveling lies,
Coldly embracing the discolored earth,
And victory with little loss doth play
Upon the dancing banners of the French,
Who are at hand, triumphantly displayed,°   *drawn up*
310 To enter conquerors and to proclaim
Arthur of Bretagne, England's King and yours.
                    Enter [on another side] ENGLISH HERALD *with [a]*
                    Trumpet[er].
ENGLISH HERALD Rejoice, you men of Angers, ring your bells:
King John, your King and England's, doth approach,
Commander of this hot malicious day.
315 Their armors that marched hence so silver-bright,
Hither return all gilt° with Frenchmen's blood.   *smeared; golden*
There stuck no plume in any English crest°   *(on a helmet)*
That is removèd by a staff° of France.   *spear*
Our colors° do return in those same hands   *banners*
320 That did display them when we first marched forth,
And like a jolly troop of huntsmen come
Our lusty English, all with purpled hands,
Dyed in the dying slaughter of their foes.
Open your gates and give the victors way.
325 CITIZEN[7] Heralds, from off our towers we might° behold   *could*
From first to last the onset and retire
Of both your armies, whose equality
By our best eyes cannot be censurèd.°   *differentiated*
Blood hath bought blood, and blows have answered blows;
330 Strength matched with strength, and power confronted power;
Both are alike, and both alike we like.
One must prove greatest. While they weigh so even,
We hold our town for neither, yet for both.
                    Enter the two Kings with their powers,° at several doors.   *armies*
                    [*On one side,* KING JOHN, QUEEN ELEANOR, BLANCHE,
                    the BASTARD, *the Earl of* SALISBURY; *on the other,* KING
                    PHILIP, LOUIS THE DAUPHIN, *and* AUSTRIA.][8]

---

6. Command the reserves to be in readiness. (This concludes an unheard conversation in parallel with John's.)
7. TEXTUAL COMMENT This and subsequent speeches of the Citizen are attributed to Hubert in the earliest Folio text. But this looks like a printing-house error—an error, moreover, that obscures the conflict in the play between an ideal of citizenship and a dynastic view of government. See note to line 200 SD and especially Digital Edition TC 4.
8. F calls for "the two Kings with their powers"; this seems to exclude Constance and Arthur.

KING JOHN France, hast thou yet more blood to cast away?
335 Say, shall the current of our right roam° on,   *make its way*
Whose passage, vexed with thy impediment,
Shall leave his native channel° and o'erswell°   *normal course / flood*
With course disturbed even thy confining shores,
Unless thou let his silver water keep
340 A peaceful progress to the ocean?
KING PHILIP England, thou hast not saved one drop of blood
In this hot trial more than we of France—
Rather lost more. And by this hand I swear,
That sways the earth this climate° overlooks,   *part of the sky*
345 Before we will lay down our just-borne arms,
We'll put thee down 'gainst whom these arms we bear,
Or add a royal number° to the dead,   *(Philip)*
Gracing the scroll that tells of this war's loss
With slaughter coupled to the name of kings.
350 BASTARD Ha, majesty! How high thy glory towers
When the rich blood of kings is set on fire.
Oh, now doth Death line his dead chaps° with steel;   *deadly jaws*
The swords of soldiers are his teeth, his fangs;
And now he feasts, mousing° the flesh of men   *tearing; biting*
355 In undetermined differences° of kings.   *unresolved disputes*
Why stand these royal fronts° amazèd thus?   *faces*
Cry havoc,[9] Kings! Back to the stainèd field
You equal potents,° fiery-kindled spirits.   *equally strong rulers*
Then let confusion° of one part° confirm   *let overthrow / side*
360 The other's peace. Till then, blows, blood, and death!
KING JOHN Whose party do the townsmen yet admit?
KING PHILIP Speak, citizens, for England. Who's your king?
CITIZEN The King of England, when we know the king.
KING PHILIP Know him in us,° that here hold up his right.   *me*
365 KING JOHN In us, that are our own great deputy°   *representative*
And bear possession of our person° here,   *represent my own claim*
Lord of our presence,° Angers, and of you.   *myself*
CITIZEN A greater power than we denies all this,
And till it be undoubted, we do lock
370 Our former scruple in our strong-barred gates,
Kings of our fear, until our fears resolved
Be by some certain king purged and deposed.[1]
BASTARD By heaven, these scroyles° of Angers flout you, Kings,   *scoundrels*
And stand securely on their battlements
375 As in a theater, whence they gape and point
At your industrious scenes and acts of death.
Your royal presences° be ruled by me.   *persons*
Do like the mutines of Jerusalem:[2]
Be friends awhile and both conjointly° bend   *together*
380 Your sharpest deeds of malice on this town.
By east and west let France and England mount
Their battering cannon chargèd to° the mouths,   *loaded to*

---

9. Order given to troops for pillaging and merciless slaughter.
1. The citizens will remain their own rulers, and hence both rulers of and ruled by their fears, until the unambiguous determination of who the rightful king is has "purged" their fears, which in this way will be "deposed" from their current ruling position.
2. Warring factions of Jerusalem who temporarily united against besieging Roman forces in 70 C.E.

Till their soul-fearing° clamors have brawled° down   *terrifying / broken*
The flinty ribs° of this contemptuous city.   *walls*
385   I'd play incessantly upon these jades,³
Even till unfencèd° desolation   *unwalled*
Leave them as naked as the vulgar° air.   *common*
That done, dissever your united strengths,
And part your mingled colors once again,
390   Turn face to face and bloody point to point.
Then in a moment Fortune shall cull° forth   *choose*
Out of one side her happy minion,°   *darling*
To whom in favor she shall give the day°   *triumph*
And kiss him with a glorious victory.
395   How like you this wild counsel, mighty states?°   *rulers*
Smacks it not something of the policy?°   *political cunning*
KING JOHN   Now by the sky that hangs above our heads,
I like it well. —France, shall we knit° our powers   *join*
And lay this Angers even with the ground,
400   Then after fight who shall be king of it?
BASTARD [*to* KING PHILIP]   An if thou hast the mettle of a king,
Being wronged as we are by this peevish° town,   *obstinate*
Turn thou the mouth of thy artillery,
As we will ours, against these saucy° walls;   *presumptuous*
405   And when that we have dashed them to the ground,
Why, then defy each other, and pell-mell,°   *quickly*
Make work upon ourselves, for⁴ heaven or hell.
KING PHILIP   Let it be so. —Say, where will you assault?
KING JOHN   We from the west will send destruction
410   Into this city's bosom.
AUSTRIA   I from the north.
KING PHILIP   Our thunder° from the south   *cannon*
Shall rain their drift of bullets° on this town.   *shower of cannonballs*
BASTARD [*aside*]   Oh, prudent discipline!° From north to south: *tactics*
Austria and France shoot in each other's mouth.
415   I'll stir them to it. —Come, away, away!
CITIZEN   Hear us, great Kings. Vouchsafe awhile to stay,
And I shall show you peace and fair-faced league,
Win you this city without stroke or wound,
Rescue those breathing lives to die in beds
420   That here come sacrifices for the field.
Persever not, but hear me, mighty Kings!
KING JOHN   Speak on with favor;° we are bent° to hear.   *permission / willing*
CITIZEN   That daughter there of Spain, the Lady Blanche,
Is near to England. Look upon the years°   *ages*
425   Of Louis the Dauphin and that lovely maid.
If lusty love should go in quest of beauty,
Where should he find it fairer than in Blanche?
If zealous° love should go in search of virtue,   *pious*
Where should he find it purer than in Blanche?
430   If love ambitious sought a match of birth,
Whose veins bound° richer blood than Lady Blanche?   *contain*

---

3. I'd unceasingly fire at (or torment) these wretches.   to a man.)
(A "jade" was a decrepit horse or an insulting term   4. On behalf of; for the destination of.
for a woman—and hence a double insult when applied

Such as she is, in beauty, virtue, birth,
Is the young Dauphin every way complete.°   *perfect*
If not complete of, say he is not she,
435   And she again wants nothing, to name want,
If want it be not that she is not he.[5]
He is the half part of a blessèd man,
Left to be finishèd by such as she;
And she a fair divided excellence,
440   Whose fullness of perfection lies in him.
Oh, two such silver currents when they join
Do glorify the banks that bound them in;
And two such shores, to two such streams made one,
Two such controlling bounds shall you be, Kings,
445   To these two princes, if you marry them.
This union shall do more than battery can
To our fast-closèd gates: for at this match,[6]
With swifter spleen° than powder can enforce,   *passion*
The mouth of passage shall we fling wide ope
450   And give you entrance. But without this match,
The sea enragèd is not half so deaf,
Lions more confident, mountains and rocks
More free from motion, no, not Death himself
In mortal fury half so peremptory,°   *resolved*
As we to keep this city.
455   BASTARD [*aside*]   Here's a stay°   *obstacle; cease-fire*
That shakes the rotten carcass of old Death
Out of his rags.[7] Here's a large mouth° indeed,   *(of a cannon or human)*
That spits forth death and mountains, rocks and seas,
Talks as familiarly of roaring lions
460   As maids of thirteen do of puppy dogs.
What cannoneer begot this lusty blood?
He speaks plain cannon-fire and smoke and bounce;°   *bang*
He gives the bastinado° with his tongue.   *a cudgeling*
Our ears are cudgeled; not a word of his
465   But buffets better than a fist of France.
Zounds!° I was never so bethumped with words   *God's wounds (common oath)*
Since I first called my brother's father dad.
QUEEN ELEANOR [*to* KING JOHN]   Son, list° to this conjunction,° *listen / proposition*
make this match.
Give with our niece a dowry large enough;
470   For by this knot thou shalt so surely tie
Thy now unsured assurance to the crown,
That yon green° boy shall have no sun to ripe   *unripe; young*
The bloom that promiseth a mighty fruit.
I see a yielding in the looks of France;
475   Mark how they whisper. Urge them while their souls
Are capable of° this ambition,   *susceptible to*
Lest zeal,° now melted by the windy breath   *(on Arthur's behalf)*
Of soft petitions, pity, and remorse,
Cool and congeal° again to what it was.   *freeze*

---

5. *If not . . . he:* The Dauphin is perfect insofar as he lacks Blanche, and vice versa. *wants:* lacks.
to name: if I must name.

6. Marriage; device for lighting gun "powder" (line
448).

7. *That . . . rags:* That steals what belongs to death.

480 CITIZEN Why answer not the double majesties
This friendly treaty° of our threatened town?   *entreaty; proposal*
KING PHILIP Speak England first, that hath been forward first
To speak unto this city: what say you?
KING JOHN If that the Dauphin there, thy princely son,
485 Can in this book of beauty° read "I love,"   *(Blanche)*
Her dowry shall weigh equal with a queen:
For Anjou and fair Touraine, Maine, Poitou,[8]
And all that we upon this side the sea—
Except this city now by us besieged—
490 Find liable° to our crown and dignity,   *subject*
Shall gild her bridal bed and make her rich
In titles, honors, and promotions,°   *elevations in rank*
As she in beauty, education, blood,
Holds hand with° any princess of the world.   *Is equal to*
495 KING PHILIP What say'st thou, boy? Look in the lady's face.
LOUIS THE DAUPHIN I do, my lord, and in her eye I find
A wonder or a wondrous miracle;
The shadow of myself formed in her eye,
Which being but the shadow of your son,
500 Becomes a sun and makes your son a shadow.[9]
I do protest I never loved myself
Till now, infixèd° I beheld myself,   *imprinted*
Drawn in the flattering table° of her eye.   *surface*
     [LOUIS THE DAUPHIN] *whispers with* BLANCHE.
BASTARD [*aside*] Drawn in the flattering table of her eye,
505 Hanged in the frowning wrinkle of her brow,
And quartered in her heart![1] He doth espy
Himself love's traitor. This is pity now,
That hanged and drawn and quartered there should be
In such a love so vile a lout as he.
510 BLANCHE [*to* LOUIS THE DAUPHIN] My uncle's will in this
     respect is mine.
If he see aught° in you that makes him like,   *anything*
That anything he sees which moves his liking,
I can with ease translate it to my will,
Or if you will, to speak more properly,°   *precisely*
515 I will enforce it easily to my love.
Further I will not flatter you, my lord,
That all I see in you is worthy° love,   *deserving of*
Than this:[2] that nothing do I see in you,
Though churlish° thoughts themselves should be your judge,   *grudging*
520 That I can find should merit any hate.
KING JOHN What say these young ones? What say you, my niece?
BLANCHE That she is bound in honor still° to do   *always*
What you in wisdom still vouchsafe° to say.   *deign*

---

8. The French territories claimed by both John and Arthur will go to the Dauphin.
9. *The shadow of myself . . . a shadow:* The Dauphin speaks in elaborate clichés of courtly love poetry: the conceit is common, as is the "sun/son" wordplay. He claims that his "shadow," from being a mere reflection or pale imitation of the King's son (or a shadow of the sun) in Blanche's eyes, becomes a "sun" because her eyes are so bright, with the result that

the actual "son" becomes a mere "shadow" of his own reflection.
1. *Drawn . . . heart:* The Bastard alludes to the punishment of being hanged, drawn (disemboweled; but also painted, as in line 503), and quartered (cut in pieces; but also lodged) for treason. The rhyme scheme of lines 504–09 mimics the last six lines of a Shakespearean sonnet.
2. Taking up "Further," line 516.

KING JOHN   Speak then, Prince Dauphin. Can you love this lady?

525 LOUIS THE DAUPHIN   Nay, ask me if I can refrain from love,
For I do love her most unfeignedly.

KING JOHN   Then I do give Volquessen,[3] Touraine, Maine,
Poitou, and Anjou, these five provinces,
With her to thee, and this addition more:
530 Full thirty thousand marks[4] of English coin.
Philip of France, if thou be pleased withal,°   with this
Command thy son and daughter to join hands.

KING PHILIP   It likes° us well. Young princes, close your hands.   pleases

AUSTRIA   And your lips too, for I am well assured
535 That I did so when I was first assured.°   betrothed

KING PHILIP   Now citizens of Angers, ope your gates.
Let in that amity which you have made,
For at Saint Mary's chapel presently°   immediately
The rites of marriage shall be solemnized.
540 —Is not the Lady Constance in this troop?
I know she is not, for this match made up
Her presence would have interrupted much.
Where is she and her son? Tell me who knows.

LOUIS THE DAUPHIN   She is sad and passionate° at your highness' tent.   sorrowful

545 KING PHILIP   And, by my faith, this league that we have made
Will give her sadness very little cure.
—Brother of England, how may we content
This widow lady? In her right we came,
Which we, God knows, have turned another way,
To our own vantage.°   advantage

550 KING JOHN   We will heal up all,
For we'll create young Arthur Duke of Bretagne[5]
And Earl of Richmond, and this rich fair town
We make him lord of. Call the Lady Constance;
Some speedy messenger bid her repair°   come
555 To our solemnity.° I trust we shall,   (marriage) ceremony
If not fill up the measure of her will,
Yet in some measure satisfy her so
That we shall stop her exclamation.°   loud reproaches
Go we as well as haste will suffer° us   allow
560 To this unlooked-for, unprepared pomp.°   ceremony

                    Exeunt [all but the BASTARD].

BASTARD   Mad world, mad kings, mad composition!°   treaty
John, to stop Arthur's title in the whole,
Hath willingly departed° with a part,   parted
And France, whose armor conscience buckled on,
565 Whom zeal and charity brought to the field
As God's own soldier, rounded° in the ear   whispered
With° that same purpose-changer,[6] that sly devil,   By
That broker that still breaks the pate[7] of faith,

---

3. Modern Vexin, northwest of Paris.
4. Perhaps $25 million in purchasing power, but over $70 billion in economic power. See note to 1.1.69.
5. An inconsistency: Arthur already holds this title, as John himself acknowledges (line 156).
6. "Purpose-changer," as well as the subsequent noun phrases in lines 567–69, is in apposition to those in

line 573, in particular "commodity" (self-interest, profit-seeking: that which translates everything into its market value to the exclusion of noneconomic considerations).
7. Cracks the skull (giving colloquial vigor to "breaks faith"). *broker*: go-between, sexual procurer (leading to wordplay in "breaks" and "break-vow," lines 568–69).

That daily break-vow, he that wins of° all,	gets the best of
570 Of kings, of beggars, old men, young men, maids—	
Who° having no external° thing to lose	(maids) / material
But the word "maid,"° cheats° the poor maid of that—	(their virginity) / he cheats
That smooth-faced° gentleman, tickling° commodity!	plausible / cajoling
Commodity, the bias⁸ of the world,	
575 The world, who of itself is peisèd° well,	balanced
Made to run even upon even ground,	
Till this advantage, this vile-drawing° bias,	drawing to evil
This sway° of motion, this commodity,	swayer; swerver
Makes it take head° from all indifferency,°	flee / impartiality
580 From all direction, purpose, course, intent.	
And this same bias, this commodity,	
This bawd,° this broker, this all-changing word,	procurer
Clapped on the outward eye⁹ of fickle France,	
Hath drawn him from his own determined aid,	
585 From a resolved and honorable war,	
To a most base and vile-concluded peace.	
And why rail I on this commodity?	
But for° because he hath not wooed me yet.	Only
Not that I have the power to clutch° my hand	clench (in refusal)
590 When his fair angels would salute¹ my palm,	
But for° my hand, as unattempted° yet,	Because / untempted
Like a poor beggar raileth on the rich.	
Well, whiles I am a beggar, I will rail	
And say there is no sin but to be rich,	
595 And being rich, my virtue then shall be	
To say there is no vice but beggary.	
Since kings break faith upon° commodity,	on account of
Gain be my lord, for I will worship thee. *Exit.*	

2.2¹

Enter CONSTANCE, ARTHUR, *and* [*the Earl of*]
     SALISBURY.

CONSTANCE [*to* SALISBURY] Gone to be married? Gone to	
swear a peace?	
False blood to false blood joined! Gone to be friends?	
Shall Louis have Blanche and Blanche those provinces?	
It is not so; thou hast misspoke, misheard.	
5 Be well advised,° tell o'er thy tale again.	Consider carefully
It cannot be; thou dost but say 'tis so.	
I trust I may not trust thee, for thy word	
Is but the vain breath of a common° man.	(as opposed to royal)
Believe me, I do not believe thee, man;	
10 I have a king's oath to the contrary.	
Thou shalt be punished for thus frighting me,	
For I am sick and capable of° fears,	susceptible to

---

8. Literally, in the game of bowls, the off-center weight of a bowl that causes it to veer from a straight course.
9. Fixed its hold on the outer edge of a bowl so as to make it swerve from a true course; suddenly caught the "outward eye" of self-interest as opposed to the inward eye of conscience. Both meanings are applicable to King Philip.

1. *angels would salute:* ten-shilling coins (with the archangel Michael on them) would kiss (greet); alluding to the Annunciation and Michael's "salute" to the Virgin Mary.
2.2 Location: The French camp by Angers.
1. This is "*Actus Secundus*" in F. (See Textual Introduction.)

Oppressed with wrongs and therefore full of fears,
A widow, husbandless, subject to fears,
15   A woman naturally born to fears;
And though° thou now confess thou didst but jest   *even if*
With my vexed spirits, I cannot take a truce,°   *make peace*
But they will quake and tremble all this day.
What dost thou mean by shaking of thy head?
20   Why dost thou look so sadly on my son?
What means that hand upon that breast of thine?
Why holds thine eye that lamentable rheum,°   *tears*
Like a proud° river peering o'er his bounds?°   *swollen / banks*
Be these sad signs confirmers of thy words?
25   Then speak again; not all thy former tale,
But this one word: whether thy tale be true.
SALISBURY   As true as I believe you think them° false   *(the French and English)*
That give you cause to prove my saying true.
CONSTANCE   Oh, if thou teach me to believe this sorrow,
30   Teach thou this sorrow how to make me die,
And let belief and life encounter so
As doth the fury of two desperate men,
Which in the very meeting fall and die.[2]
Louis marry Blanche! —O boy, then where art thou?
35   France friend with England! What becomes of me?
[*to* SALISBURY] Fellow,° be gone: I cannot brook° thy sight.   *(an insult) / endure*
This news hath made thee a most ugly man.
SALISBURY   What other harm have I, good lady, done,
But spoke the harm that is by others done?
40   CONSTANCE   Which harm within itself so heinous is,
As it makes harmful all that speak of it.
ARTHUR   I do beseech you, madam, be content.°   *calm*
CONSTANCE   If thou that bidd'st me be content wert grim,
Ugly, and sland'rous to thy mother's womb,[3]
45   Full of unpleasing blots and sightless° stains,   *unsightly*
Lame, foolish, crooked, swart,° prodigious,[4]   *dark*
Patched° with foul moles and eye-offending marks,   *Blotched*
I would not care, I then would be content,
For then I should not love thee, no, nor thou
50   Become thy great birth, nor deserve a crown.
But thou art fair, and at thy birth, dear boy,
Nature and Fortune joined to make thee great.
Of Nature's gifts, thou mayst with lilies boast,
And with the half-blown° rose. But Fortune, oh,   *half-blossomed; young*
55   She is corrupted, changed, and won from thee.
She adulterates° hourly with thine uncle John,   *prostitutes herself*
And with her golden hand hath plucked on° France   *enticed*
To tread down fair respect of sovereignty,°   *(Arthur's rights)*
And made his majesty the bawd to theirs.[5]
60   France is a bawd to Fortune and King John,
That strumpet Fortune, that usurping John.

---

2. *Oh . . . die:* In this image, drawn from emblem-book representations of Fury, sorrow (or belief) dies at the same time that Constance does.
3. Malformed babies were seen as a divine punish-ment for wickedness.
4. Monstrous (and thereby foretelling evil).
5. And made Philip the go-between for John and Fortune.

—Tell me, thou fellow, is not France forsworn?°   *an oath breaker*
Envenom° him with words, or get thee gone   *Poison*
And leave those woes alone which I alone
Am bound to underbear.°   *suffer under*
65 SALISBURY   Pardon me, madam,
I may not go without you to the Kings.
CONSTANCE   Thou mayst, thou shalt; I will not go with thee.
I will instruct my sorrows to be proud,
For grief is proud and makes his owner stoop.
70 To me and to the state° of my great grief   *throne (ironic)*
Let kings assemble. For my grief's so great
That no supporter but the huge firm earth
Can hold it up. [*She sits.*] Here I and sorrows sit.
Here is my throne, bid kings come bow to it.
            [*Exeunt* SALISBURY *and* ARTHUR.]

3.1

Enter KING JOHN, [KING PHILIP *of*] *France,* [LOUIS
THE] DAUPHIN, BLANCHE, [QUEEN] ELEANOR, *Philip*
[*the* BASTARD], AUSTRIA.[1]
KING PHILIP [*to* BLANCHE]   'Tis true,[2] fair daughter, and this
    blessèd day
Ever in France shall be kept festival.
To solemnize this day the glorious sun
Stays in his course° and plays the alchemist,[3]   *Stands still*
5 Turning with splendor of his precious eye
The meager cloddy earth to glittering gold.
The yearly course that brings this day about
Shall never see it but a holy day.
CONSTANCE [*rises*]   A wicked day and not a holy day!
10 What hath this day deserved? What hath it done
That it in golden letters should be set
Among the high tides° in the calendar?   *great festivals*
Nay, rather turn this day out of° the week,   *expel this day from*
This day of shame, oppression, perjury.
15 Or, if it must stand still,° let wives with child   *remain*
Pray that their burdens may not fall° this day,   *they not give birth*
Lest that their hopes prodigiously be crossed.[4]
But° on this day let seamen fear no wreck,   *Except*
No bargains break that are not this day made:
20 This day all things begun come to ill end,
Yea, faith itself to hollow falsehood change.
KING PHILIP   By heaven, lady, you shall have no cause
To curse the fair proceedings of this day.
Have I not pawned° to you my majesty?°   *pledged / royal word*
25 CONSTANCE   You have beguiled me with a counterfeit°   *false coin or portrait*
Resembling majesty, which, being touched and tried,°   *tested for gold*
Proves valueless. You are forsworn, forsworn!

3.1 Location: The French camp by Angers.
1. Shakespeare may have intended no break in the action here, though the division between acts appears in F. Constance's words at 2.2.67–74 seem to require her to remain onstage.

2. King Philip enters in midconversation.
3. Alchemists sought to turn base metals such as lead into gold.
4. By an ominously monstrous child.

You came in arms to spill mine enemy's blood,
But now in arms° you strengthen it with yours.   *arm in arm; militarily*
30   The grappling vigor and rough frown of war
Is cold in amity and painted° peace,   *counterfeit*
And our oppression° hath made up° this league.   *affliction / possible*
Arm, arm, you heavens, against these perjured kings!
A widow cries: be husband to me, heavens!
35   Let not the hours of this ungodly day
Wear out° the days in peace, but, ere sunset,   *Finish*
Set armèd discord twixt these perjured kings.
Hear me, O hear me!
AUSTRIA   Lady Constance, peace.
CONSTANCE   War, war, no peace! Peace is to me a war.
40   O Limoges, O Austria,[5] thou dost shame
That bloody spoil.° Thou slave, thou wretch, thou coward!   *(the lion skin)*
Thou little valiant, great in villainy;
Thou ever strong upon the stronger side;
Thou Fortune's champion that dost never fight
45   But when her humorous ladyship° is by   *changeable Fortune*
To teach thee safety—thou art perjured too,
And sooth'st up greatness.° What a fool art thou,   *flatter the powerful*
A ramping° fool, to brag and stamp and swear   *showily threatening*
Upon my party.° Thou cold-blooded slave: *cause*
50   Hast thou not spoke like thunder on my side?°   *behalf*
Been sworn my soldier, bidding me depend
Upon thy stars, thy fortune, and thy strength,
And dost thou now fall over° to my foes?   *defect*
Thou wear a lion's hide! Doff it for shame,
55   And hang a calf's-skin[6] on those recreant° limbs.   *cowardly; traitorous*
AUSTRIA   Oh, that a man should speak those words to me!
BASTARD   And hang a calf's-skin on those recreant limbs.
AUSTRIA   Thou dar'st not say so, villain, for thy life.
BASTARD   And hang a calf's-skin on those recreant limbs.
60   KING JOHN [*to the* BASTARD]   We like not this: thou dost forget
     thyself.°   *your rank; protocol*
           Enter [Cardinal] PANDULPH.
KING PHILIP   Here comes the holy legate of the Pope.[7]
PANDULPH   Hail, you anointed deputies of heaven!°   *kings*
    —To thee, King John, my holy errand is.
I Pandulph, of fair Milan Cardinal,
65   And from Pope Innocent the legate here,
Do in his name religiously demand
Why thou against the church, our holy mother,
So willfully dost spurn,° and force perforce°   *kick / forcibly*
Keep Stephen Langton, chosen° Archbishop   *(by the Pope)*
70   Of Canterbury, from that holy see?
This in our foresaid holy father's name,
Pope Innocent, I do demand of thee.
KING JOHN   What earthy name to interrogatories

---

5. See note to 2.1.5.
6. Symbolizing cowardice or folly.
7. Shakespeare follows his main source in combin-

ing two papal legates in one, as he does in the use of
Austria to represent two of Richard I's adversaries.

Can task the free breath of a sacred king?[8]
75 Thou canst not, Cardinal, devise a name
So slight, unworthy, and ridiculous
To charge me to an° answer as the Pope. °to make an
Tell him this tale, and from the mouth of England
Add thus much more: that no Italian priest° °(the Pope)
80 Shall tithe or toll° in our dominions, °collect church revenue
But as we, under heaven, are supreme head,[9]
So under him that great supremacy° °sovereignty
Where we do reign, we will alone uphold
Without th'assistance of a mortal hand.
85 So tell the Pope, all reverence set apart° °rejected
To him and his usurped authority.
KING PHILIP Brother of England, you blaspheme in this.
KING JOHN Though you and all the kings of Christendom
Are led so grossly by this meddling priest,
90 Dreading the curse that money may buy out,[1]
And by the merit of vile gold, dross, dust,
Purchase corrupted pardon of a man,[2]
Who in that sale sells pardon from himself;[3]
Though you and all the rest, so grossly led,
95 This juggling° witchcraft with revenue cherish, °deceiving
Yet I alone, alone do me oppose
Against the Pope and count his friends my foes.
PANDULPH Then by the lawful power that I have,
Thou shalt stand cursed and excommunicate,° °excommunicated
100 And blessèd shall he be that doth revolt
From his allegiance to an heretic,
And meritorious shall that hand be called,
Canonized and worshipped as a saint,
That takes away by any secret course
Thy hateful life.
105 CONSTANCE   Oh, lawful let it be
That I have room° with Rome to curse awhile! °opportunity
Good Father Cardinal, cry thou "Amen"
To my keen curses; for without my wrong° °the wrongs done to me
There is no tongue hath power to curse him right.° °properly
110 PANDULPH There's law and warrant, lady, for my curse.
CONSTANCE And for mine too. When law can do no right,
Let it be lawful that law bar no wrong.° °cursing
Law cannot give my child his kingdom here,
For he that holds his kingdom, holds the law.
115 Therefore, since law° itself is perfect wrong, °(secular)
How can the law° forbid my tongue to curse? °(ecclesiastical)

---

8. *What . . . king?*: What person holding an earthly title (the Pope or his deputy) can demand answers from a king who governs by divine right? John attributes to himself the divine authority he has just denied the Pope.
9. "Supreme head" of the English Church is the title adopted in 1534 by Henry VIII, Elizabeth's father, in defiance of the papacy. This passage is perhaps the most openly and anachronistically Protestant, anti-Catholic moment in the play.

1. Excommunication is the "curse" that a bribe can buy off, or reverse.
2. An allusion to the sale of indulgences, or papal dispensations for sin, by a member of the Catholic clergy ("a man").
3. The clergyman "sells" (gives up) hope of God's forgiveness for himself and is hence damned by his selling. The pardon he sells lacks efficacy because it comes "from himself," rather than from God.

PANDULPH   Philip of France, on peril of a curse,°   *excommunication*
   Let go the hand of that arch-heretic,
   And raise the power of France upon his head,
120   Unless he do submit himself to Rome.
QUEEN ELEANOR   Look'st thou pale, France? Do not let go thy hand.
CONSTANCE [*to* KING JOHN]   Look to that, devil, lest that France repent,
   And by disjoining hands, hell lose a soul.
AUSTRIA   King Philip, listen to the Cardinal.
125 BASTARD   And hang a calf's-skin on his recreant limbs.
AUSTRIA   Well, ruffian, I must pocket up° these wrongs,   *put up with*
   Because—
BASTARD   Your breeches best may carry them.[4]
KING JOHN   Philip, what say'st thou to the Cardinal?
CONSTANCE   What should he say, but as° the Cardinal?   *the same as*
130 LOUIS THE DAUPHIN   Bethink you, father, for the difference
   Is purchase of a heavy curse from Rome
   Or the light loss of England for a friend.
   Forgo the easier.
BLANCHE   That's the curse of Rome.
CONSTANCE   O Louis, stand fast: the devil tempts thee here
135 In likeness of a new untrimmèd° bride.   *virginal*
BLANCHE   The Lady Constance speaks not from her faith,
   But from her need.
CONSTANCE [*to* KING PHILIP]   Oh, if thou grant my need,
   Which only lives but by the death of faith,[5]
   That need must needs infer this principle:[6]
140 That faith would live again by death of need.°   *by the end of my woes*
   Oh, then, tread down my need and faith mounts up;
   Keep my need up and faith is trodden down.
KING JOHN   The King is moved and answers not to this.
CONSTANCE [*to* KING PHILIP]   Oh, be removed from him and answer well.
145 AUSTRIA   Do so, King Philip; hang no more in doubt.
BASTARD   Hang nothing but a calf's-skin, most sweet lout.
KING PHILIP   I am perplexed and know not what to say.
PANDULPH   What canst thou say but will perplex° thee more   *trouble*
   If thou stand excommunicate and cursed?
150 KING PHILIP   Good reverend father, make my person yours,°   *put yourself in my place*
   And tell me how you would bestow yourself.°   *what you would do*
   This royal hand and mine are newly knit,°   *joined*
   And the conjunction of our inward souls
   Married in league, coupled, and linked together
155 With all religious strength of sacred vows.
   The latest breath that gave the sound of words
   Was deep-sworn faith, peace, amity, true love
   Between our kingdoms and our royal selves.
   And even° before this truce, but new° before,   *just / only just*
160 No longer than we well could wash our hands°   *(of blood)*

---

4. Probably, you may best carry them (the "wrongs" of line 126, or kicks) in the pocket of your breeches; possibly implying that Austria will be kicked in the breeches.
5. Which (my need) exists only because of your bro-ken faith (the pledge to support Arthur) or my loss of faith in you; perhaps, which will live only if you break your faith (to the church).
6. That need necessarily implies this truth.

To clap this royal bargain up of peace,[7]
Heaven knows, they were besmeared and overstained
With slaughter's pencil,° where revenge did paint   paintbrush
The fearful difference° of incensèd kings.   dispute
165 And shall these hands so lately purged of blood,
So newly joined in love, so strong in both,°   (blood and love)
Unyoke this seizure[8] and this kind regreet?°   return of salutation
Play fast and loose with faith? So jest with heaven,
Make such unconstant children of ourselves,
170 As now again to snatch our palm from palm,
Unswear faith sworn, and on the marriage bed
Of smiling peace to march a bloody host
And make a riot on the gentle brow
Of true sincerity? O holy sir,
175 My reverend father, let it not be so!
Out of your grace, devise, ordain, impose
Some gentle order, and then we shall be blessed
To do your pleasure and continue friends.
PANDULPH   All form is formless, order orderless,
180 Save what is opposite to England's love.
Therefore, to arms! Be champion of our church,
Or let the church our mother breathe her curse,
A mother's curse, on her revolting son.
France, thou mayst hold° a serpent by the tongue,   may more easily hold
185 A casèd lion by the mortal° paw,   deadly
A fasting tiger safer by the tooth,
Than keep in peace that hand which thou dost hold.
KING PHILIP   I may disjoin my hand, but not my faith.
PANDULPH   So mak'st thou faith an enemy to faith,[9]
190 And like a civil war sett'st oath to oath,
Thy tongue against thy tongue. Oh, let thy vow
First made to heaven, first be to heaven performed,
That is, to be the champion of our church.
What since thou swor'st[1] is sworn against thyself
195 And may not be performèd by thyself,
For that which thou hast sworn to do amiss
Is not amiss when it is truly done;[2]
And being not done, where doing tends to ill,
The truth is then most done not doing it.
200 The better act of purposes mistook,[3]
Is to mistake again; though indirect,°   circuitous; wrong
Yet indirection thereby grows direct,
And falsehood falsehood cures, as fire cools fire
Within the scorchèd veins of one new burned.[4]
205 It is religion that doth make vows kept,°   make us honor our vows
But thou hast sworn against religion:

---

7. To seal this royal peace treaty by shaking hands.
8. Of hands joined together.
9. You set your faith to John against your faith to the church. The confusing rhetoric of this speech exemplifies the elaborate and sometimes equivocal reasoning known as casuistry that was practiced by sixteenth-century Catholics and hated by English Protestants.

1. What you've subsequently sworn (amity with John).
2. For . . . done: For it's not immoral to break an immoral vow. *truly done*: an immoral act that is not performed is (paradoxically) an act that is "truly done."
3. The better act when you've done wrong.
4. *as fire . . . burned*: The theory that one fire cools another was proverbial but false.

By what thou swear'st, against the thing thou swear'st,[5]
And mak'st an oath the surety for thy truth
Against an oath.[6] The truth, thou art unsure
210 To swear, swears only not to be forsworn,[7]
Else what a mockery should it be to swear!
But thou dost swear only to be forsworn,
And most forsworn to keep what thou dost swear.[8]
Therefore thy later vows, against thy first,
215 Is in thyself rebellion to° thyself,   against
And better conquest never canst thou make
Than arm thy constant and thy nobler parts
Against these giddy loose suggestions.°   dissolute temptations
Upon° which better part° our prayers come in,   On behalf of / side
220 If thou vouchsafe° them. But if not, then know   accept
The peril of our curses light on thee
So heavy as thou shalt not shake them off
But in despair° die under their black weight.   (because damned)
AUSTRIA   Rebellion, flat rebellion.
BASTARD   Will't not be?[9]
225 Will not a calf's-skin stop that mouth of thine?
LOUIS THE DAUPHIN   Father, to arms!
BLANCHE   Upon thy wedding day?
Against the blood that thou hast married?
What, shall our feast be kept with° slaughtered men?   attended by
Shall braying trumpets and loud churlish drums,
230 Clamors of hell, be measures° to our pomp?°   music / celebration
O husband, hear me! Ay, alack, how new
Is "husband" in my mouth! Even for that name
Which till this time my tongue did ne'er pronounce,
Upon my knee I beg, go not to arms
235 Against mine uncle.
CONSTANCE   Oh, upon my knee
Made hard with kneeling, I do pray to thee,
Thou virtuous Dauphin, alter not the doom°   fate
Forethought by heaven.[1]
BLANCHE [to LOUIS THE DAUPHIN]   Now shall I see thy love.
What motive may
240 Be stronger with thee than the name of wife?
CONSTANCE   That which upholdeth him that thee upholds:°   who supports you
His honor. O thine honor, Louis, thine honor!
LOUIS THE DAUPHIN [to KING PHILIP]   I muse your majesty
doth seem so cold,
When such profound respects° do pull you on.   weighty considerations
245 PANDULPH   I will denounce a curse upon his head.
KING PHILIP   Thou shalt not need. —England, I will fall from° thee.   desert

---

5. By your oath to John, which opposes your more
fundamental oath to your religion.
6. *And mak'st . . . Against an oath:* You make an oath
the guarantee of your "truth" (with pun on "troth,"
agreement with John); but this offends against a
higher oath (your commitment to the church).
7. *The truth . . . forsworn:* Religious truth, which you
waver over swearing to, is something you must swear
to so as not to break your foundational faith.
8. *But thou . . . dost swear:* But your (secular) oath-

taking leads only to (religious) oath-breaking, especially in maintaining your oath to John.
9. Is it all in vain; won't you be quiet?
1. Constance self-interestedly treats as a single issue
John's two separate matters—Arthur's right to the
throne and Pandulph's insistence on papal right. The
belief that people are preordained for either salvation
or damnation ("doom / Forethought by heaven") is
more Protestant than Catholic.

CONSTANCE   Oh, fair return of banished majesty!

QUEEN ELEANOR   Oh, foul revolt of French inconstancy!

KING JOHN   France, thou shalt rue this hour within this hour.

250 BASTARD   Old Time the clock-setter, that bald sexton Time,
     Is it as he will? Well, then, France shall rue.[2]

BLANCHE   The sun's o'ercast with blood. Fair day, adieu!
     Which is the side that I must go withal?°   *with*
     I am with both. Each army hath a hand,

255 And in their rage, I having hold of both,
     They whirl asunder° and dismember me.   *dash apart*
     Husband, I cannot pray that thou mayst win;
     Uncle, I needs must pray that thou mayst lose;
     Father,° I may not wish the fortune thine;   *Father-in-law (Philip)*

260 Grandam, I will not wish thy wishes thrive.
     Whoever wins, on that side shall I lose;
     Assurèd loss, before the match be played.

LOUIS THE DAUPHIN   Lady, with me, with me thy fortune° lies.   *prosperity*

BLANCHE   There where my fortune° lives, there° my life dies.   *fate / (with Louis)*

265 KING JOHN   Cousin, go draw our puissance° together.   *army*

                          [*Exit the* BASTARD.]

     France, I am burned up with inflaming wrath,
     A rage whose heat hath this condition
     That nothing can allay,° nothing but blood,   *cure*
     The blood and dearest-valued blood of France.

270 KING PHILIP   Thy rage shall burn thee up, and thou shalt turn
     To ashes ere our blood shall quench that fire.
     Look to thyself; thou art in jeopardy.

KING JOHN   No more than he that threats. —To arms let's hie!°   *hasten*

                                             Exeunt.

                          3.2

          Alarums,° excursions.° Enter [the] BASTARD *with*   *Call to arms / battles*
          Austria's head.

BASTARD   Now, by my life, this day grows wondrous hot;
     Some airy devil[1] hovers in the sky
     And pours down mischief. Austria's head lie there
     While Philip breathes.

          *Enter [*KING*]* JOHN, ARTHUR, *[and]* HUBERT.

5 KING JOHN   Hubert, keep this boy. —Philip,° make up:°   *(the Bastard) / press on*
     My mother is assailèd in our tent,
     And ta'en,° I fear.   *captured*

BASTARD   My lord, I rescued her:
     Her highness is in safety, fear you not;
     But on, my liege, for very little pains

10 Will bring this labor to an happy end.   *Exeunt.*

---

2. *Old . . . rue:* The sexton set the church clock and
dug graves. Hence, the "hour" (line 249), or time,
which was usually portrayed as bald, will indeed be
fatal. "Time" and "rue" recall the punning proverb
about herbs, "Thyme and rue grow both in one garden," in which the pleasant taste of thyme is contrasted with the bitterness of rue: the passage of time
is accompanied by regret. Together the two lines
mean something like "If things proceed according to
the fatal effects of time, France will indeed be sorry,
because time (thyme) and rue go together."
3.2 Location: Plains near Angers.
1. Aerial devils or spirits held to cause thunder-
storms and subsequent death.

3.3

Alarums, excursions, retreat.° Enter [KING] JOHN,   *signal for retreat*
    [QUEEN] ELEANOR, ARTHUR, [*the*] BASTARD, HUBERT,
    Lords.[1]

KING JOHN [*to* QUEEN ELEANOR]   So shall it be; your grace
    shall stay behind[2]
    So° strongly guarded. [*to* ARTHUR] Cousin,° look not sad: *Thus / Kinsman*
    Thy grandam loves thee, and thy uncle will
    As dear be to thee as thy father was.
5   ARTHUR   Oh, this will make my mother die with grief.
    KING JOHN [*to the* BASTARD]   Cousin, away for England. Haste before,°   *Go ahead*
    And, ere our coming, see thou shake the bags
    Of hoarding abbots;[3] imprisoned angels°   *gold coins; spirits*
    Set at liberty. The fat ribs of peace
10   Must by the hungry now be fed upon.
    Use our commission° in his° utmost force.   *(to tax) / its*
    BASTARD   Bell, book, and candle[4] shall not drive me back,
    When gold and silver becks° me to come on.   *beckons*
    I leave your highness. —Grandam, I will pray—
15   If ever I remember to be holy—
    For your fair safety. So, I kiss your hand.
    QUEEN ELEANOR   Farewell, gentle cousin.
    KING JOHN   Coz, farewell.
                      [*Exit the* BASTARD.]
    QUEEN ELEANOR [*to* ARTHUR]   Come hither, little kinsman.
    Hark, a word.
            [*She takes* ARTHUR *aside.*]
    KING JOHN   Come hither, Hubert. O my gentle Hubert,
20   We owe thee much. Within this wall of flesh°   *(John's body)*
    There is a soul counts thee her creditor
    And with advantage° means to pay thy love,   *interest*
    And, my good friend, thy voluntary oath°   *oath of allegiance*
    Lives in this bosom, dearly cherishèd.
25   Give me thy hand. I had a thing to say,
    But I will fit it with some better tune.°   *words; reward*
    By heaven, Hubert, I am almost ashamed
    To say what good respect° I have of thee.   *opinion*
    HUBERT   I am much bounden° to your majesty.   *indebted*
30   KING JOHN   Good friend, thou hast no cause to say so yet,
    But thou shalt have, and creep time ne'er so slow,
    Yet it shall come for me to do thee good.
    I had a thing to say, but let it go.
    The sun is in the heaven, and the proud day,
35   Attended with the pleasures of the world,
    Is all too wanton° and too full of gauds°   *merry / playthings*
    To give me audience.° If the midnight bell   *For you to listen*
    Did with his iron tongue and brazen mouth
    Sound on into the drowsy race° of night;   *course*

3.3 Location: Scene continues.
1. F does not begin a new scene here, but it does
empty the stage—hence the scene division adopted
here and in most modern editions.
2. In France, to control the French possessions
while John returns to England.

3. *shake . . . abbots:* pillage the monasteries, which
have hoarded wealth. When Henry VIII made himself head of the English Church, he confiscated
monastic treasure.
4. Articles used in the rite of excommunication.

40 If this same were a churchyard° where we stand,   *graveyard*
    And thou possessèd° with a thousand wrongs;   *obsessed*
    Or if that surly spirit, melancholy,
    Had baked° thy blood and made it heavy, thick,   *congealed*
    Which else° runs tickling up and down the veins,   *otherwise*
45 Making that idiot,° laughter, keep° men's eyes   *jester / stay in*
    And strain their cheeks to idle merriment—
    A passion° hateful to my purposes—   *mood*
    Or if that thou couldst see me without eyes,
    Hear me without thine ears, and make reply
50 Without a tongue, using conceit° alone,   *understanding*
    Without eyes, ears, and harmful sound of words,
    Then, in despite° of broad-eyed watchful day,   *defiance*
    I would into thy bosom pour my thoughts.
    But, ah, I will not. Yet I love thee well,
55 And, by my troth,° I think thou lov'st me well.   *faith*
    HUBERT   So well that what you bid me undertake,
    Though that° my death were adjunct to my act,   *Even if*
    By heaven, I would do it.
    KING JOHN   Do not I know thou wouldst?
    Good Hubert, Hubert, Hubert, throw thine eye
60 On yon young boy. I'll tell thee what, my friend:
    He is a very serpent in my way,
    And wheresoe'er this foot of mine doth tread
    He lies before me. Dost thou understand me?
    Thou art his keeper.
    HUBERT   And I'll keep him so
65 That he shall not offend your majesty.
    KING JOHN   Death.
    HUBERT   My lord.
    KING JOHN   A grave.
    HUBERT   He shall not live.
    KING JOHN   Enough.
    I could be merry now. Hubert, I love thee.
    Well, I'll not say what I intend for thee.
    Remember. —Madam, fare you well;
70 I'll send those powers° o'er to your majesty.   *troops*
    QUEEN ELEANOR   My blessing go with thee.
    KING JOHN [*to* ARTHUR]   For England, cousin, go.
    Hubert shall be your man, attend on you
    With all true duty. —On toward Calais, ho.   *Exeunt.*

3.4
Enter [KING PHILIP *of*] *France,* [LOUIS THE] DAUPHIN,
[*Cardinal*] PANDULPH, [*and*] *Attendants.*

KING PHILIP   So by a roaring tempest on the flood,
    A whole armada of convicted sail
    Is scattered and disjoined from fellowship.[1]
PANDULPH   Courage and comfort: all shall yet go well.
5 KING PHILIP   What can go well when we have run° so ill?   *performed; run away*
    Are we not beaten? Is not Angers lost?

3.4 Location: The French camp by Angers.   the Spanish Armada of 1588 (see the Introduction).
1. *So . . . fellowship:* This French naval defeat is not   *convicted sail:* doomed ships.
in Shakespeare's sources. It is probably a reference to

Arthur ta'en prisoner? Divers° dear friends slain?   *Various*
And bloody England° into England gone,   *John*
O'erbearing interruption, spite of France?[2]

10   LOUIS THE DAUPHIN   What he hath won, that hath he fortified.
So hot a speed, with such advice disposed,°   *judgment regulated*
Such temperate° order in so fierce a cause,   *calm*
Doth want example.° Who hath read or heard   *lack precedent*
Of any kindred action like to this?

15   KING PHILIP   Well could I bear that England had this praise,
So° we could find some pattern° of our shame.   *If / precedent*
      Enter CONSTANCE [*with her hair down*].
Look who comes here: a grave° unto a soul,   *(Constance's body)*
Holding th'eternal spirit against her will[3]
In the vile prison of afflicted breath.°   *life*

20   —I prithee, lady, go away with me.
CONSTANCE   Lo now! Now see the issue° of your peace.   *outcome*
KING PHILIP   Patience, good lady. Comfort, gentle Constance.
CONSTANCE   No, I defy all counsel, all redress,°   *comfort*
But that which ends all counsel: true redress.

25   Death, Death, O amiable, lovely Death!
Thou odoriferous° stench, sound rottenness,   *fragrant*
Arise forth from the couch of lasting° night,   *bed of everlasting*
Thou hate and terror to prosperity,
And I will kiss thy detestable bones,

30   And put my eyeballs in thy vaulty brows,[4]
And ring these fingers with thy household worms,[5]
And stop this gap of breath with fulsome dust,[6]
And be a carrion° monster like thyself.   *corpse-eating*
Come, grin on me, and I will think thou smil'st

35   And buss° thee as thy wife. Misery's love,   *kiss*
O come to me!
KING PHILIP   O fair affliction,° peace!   *afflicted one*
CONSTANCE   No, no, I will not, having breath to cry.
Oh, that my tongue were in the thunder's mouth!
Then with a passion° would I shake the world   *emotional outcry*

40   And rouse from sleep that fell anatomy°   *fierce skeleton*
Which cannot hear a lady's feeble voice,
Which scorns a modern invocation.°   *ordinary plea*
PANDULPH   Lady, you utter madness and not sorrow.
CONSTANCE   Thou art holy to belie me so!

45   I am not mad; this hair I tear is mine;
My name is Constance; I was Geoffrey's wife;
Young Arthur is my son and he is lost!
I am not mad. I would to heaven I were,
For then 'tis like° I should forget myself.   *likely*

50   Oh, if I could, what grief should I forget!
Preach some philosophy to make me mad,
And thou shalt be canonized, Cardinal.
For, being not mad but sensible° of grief,   *subject to feelings*

---

2. Overcoming hindrances, in spite of France.
3. *Holding . . . will:* that is, she wants to die.
4. Hollow forehead; the eye sockets of the imagined skull of Death's corpse.

5. And wear the worms that serve you and live inside you as rings around my fingers.
6. And kiss this mouth with nauseous dust.

My reasonable part produces reason
55 How I may be delivered of° these woes,   *freed from*
And teaches me to kill or hang myself.
If I were mad, I should forget my son,
Or madly think a babe of clouts° were he.   *cloth doll*
I am not mad: too well, too well I feel
60 The different plague° of each calamity.   *distinct affliction*
KING PHILIP   Bind up those tresses. Oh, what love I note
In the fair multitude of those her hairs.
Where but by chance a silver drop° hath fall'n,   *tear*
Even to that drop ten thousand wiry friends°   *hairs*
65 Do glue themselves° in sociable grief,   *mat together*
Like true, inseparable, faithful loves,
Sticking together in calamity.
CONSTANCE   To England, if you will.[7]
KING PHILIP   Bind up your hairs.
CONSTANCE   Yes, that I will; and wherefore will I do it?
70 I tore them from their bonds and cried aloud,
"Oh, that these hands could so redeem my son
As they have given these hairs their liberty!"
But now I envy at their liberty
And will again commit them to their bonds,
75 Because my poor child is a prisoner.
      [*She binds up her hair.*]
And, Father Cardinal, I have heard you say
That we shall see and know our friends in heaven.
If that be true, I shall see my boy again;
For since the birth of Cain, the first male child,
80 To him that did but yesterday suspire,°   *take his first breath*
There was not such a gracious creature born.
But now will canker-sorrow eat my bud[8]
And chase the native beauty from his cheek,
And he will look as hollow as a ghost,
85 As dim and meager° as an ague's° fit;   *pale and thin / fever's*
And so he'll die, and rising so again,
When I shall meet him in the court of heaven
I shall not know him. Therefore never, never
Must I behold my pretty Arthur more.
90 PANDULPH   You hold too heinous a respect° of grief.   *view*
CONSTANCE   He talks to me that never had a son.
KING PHILIP   You are as fond of grief as of your child.
CONSTANCE   Grief fills the room up of my absent child,
Lies in his bed, walks up and down with me,
95 Puts on his pretty looks, repeats his words,
Remembers° me of all his gracious parts,   *Reminds*
Stuffs out his vacant garments with his form:
Then have I reason to be fond of grief?
Fare you well; had you such a loss as I,
100 I could give better comfort than you do.
I will not keep this form upon my head,
When there is such disorder in my wit.

7. Apparently a reply to line 20, delayed because of
Constance's distraction. Or perhaps the intervening
passage is a revision interpolated after the original

composition.
8. But now sorrow, like a cankerworm, will eat my
flower (Arthur); this is proverbial.

[*She loosens her hair.*]
O Lord! My boy, my Arthur, my fair son!
My life, my joy, my food, my all the world!
105   My widow-comfort and my sorrows' cure!   *Exit.*
KING PHILIP   I fear some outrage° and I'll follow her.   *Exit.*   *(perhaps suicide)*
LOUIS THE DAUPHIN   There's nothing in this world can make me joy.
Life is as tedious as a twice-told tale
Vexing the dull ear of a drowsy man,
110   And bitter shame hath spoiled the sweet word's taste,
That° it yields naught but shame and bitterness.   *So that*
PANDULPH   Before the curing of a strong disease,
Even in the instant of repair and health,
The fit° is strongest. Evils that take leave   *symptom*
115   On their departure most of all show evil.
What have you lost by losing of this day?
LOUIS THE DAUPHIN   All days of glory, joy, and happiness.
PANDULPH   If you had won it, certainly you had.
No, no, when Fortune means° to men most good,   *intends*
120   She looks upon them with a threatening eye.
'Tis strange to think how much King John hath lost
In this which he accounts so clearly won.
Are not you grieved that Arthur is his prisoner?
LOUIS THE DAUPHIN   As heartily as he is glad he hath him.
125   PANDULPH   Your mind is all as youthful as your blood.
Now hear me speak with a prophetic spirit,
For even the breath of what I mean to speak
Shall blow each dust,° each straw, each little rub°   *speck / obstacle*
Out of the path which shall directly lead
130   Thy foot to England's throne. And therefore mark:
John hath seized Arthur, and it cannot be
That whiles warm life plays in that infant's veins
The misplaced° John should entertain an hour,   *usurping*
One minute, nay, one quiet breath of rest.
135   A scepter snatched with an unruly hand
Must be as boisterously° maintained as gained.   *violently*
And he that stands upon a slipp'ry place
Makes nice of no vile hold to stay[9] him up.
That John may stand, then Arthur needs must fall;
140   So be it, for it cannot be but so.
LOUIS THE DAUPHIN   But what shall I gain by young Arthur's fall?
PANDULPH   You, in the right of Lady Blanche your wife,
May then make all the claim that Arthur did.[1]
LOUIS THE DAUPHIN   And lose it, life and all, as Arthur did.
145   PANDULPH   How green you are and fresh in this old world!
John lays you plots;° the times conspire with you;   *plots to your benefit*
For he that steeps his safety in true blood
Shall find but bloody safety and untrue.[2]
This act, so evilly borne, shall cool the hearts
150   Of all his people and freeze up their zeal,°   *enthusiastic loyalty*
That none so small advantage shall step forth

---

9. Is not fussy about the vileness of any hold to keep.   blood, by man shall his blood be shed." *true*: legitimate.
1. In Shakespeare's sources, but not historical.   *untrue*: untrustworthy.
2. Compare Genesis 9:6: "Whoso sheddeth man's

To check his reign but they will cherish it.[3]
No natural exhalation° in the sky,   *meteor*
No scope° of nature, no distempered° day,   *effect / stormy*
155 No common wind, no customèd° event,   *everyday*
But they will pluck away his° natural cause   *its*
And call them meteors,° prodigies, and signs,   *portents*
Abortives,[4] presages, and tongues of° heaven,   *signs from*
Plainly denouncing vengeance upon John.
160 LOUIS THE DAUPHIN Maybe he will not touch young Arthur's life,
But hold° himself safe in his prisonment.   *consider*
PANDULPH O sir, when he shall hear of your approach,
If that young Arthur be not gone already,
Even at that news he dies; and then the hearts
165 Of all his people shall revolt from him,
And kiss the lips of unacquainted° change,   *unfamiliar*
And pick strong matter of° revolt and wrath   *reasons for*
Out of the bloody fingers' ends of John.
Methinks I see this hurly all on foot;°   *commotion all under way*
170 And oh, what better matter breeds for you,
Than I have named! The bastard Falconbridge
Is now in England ransacking the church,
Offending charity. If but a dozen French
Were there in arms, they would be as a call°   *decoy; call to arms*
175 To train° ten thousand English to their side,   *draw*
Or, as a little snow, tumbled about,
Anon becomes a mountain. O noble Dauphin,
Go with me to the King. 'Tis wonderful
What may be wrought out of their discontent,
180 Now that their souls are topful of offense.°   *grievances*
For England, go! I will whet on° the King.   *provoke*
LOUIS THE DAUPHIN Strong reasons makes strange actions. Let us go.
If you say ay, the King will not say no.   *Exeunt.*

4.1

Enter HUBERT *and* EXECUTIONERS [*with rope and irons*].
HUBERT Heat me these irons hot, and look thou stand
Within the arras.[1] When I strike my foot
Upon the bosom of the ground, rush forth
And bind the boy which you shall find with me
5 Fast to the chair. Be heedful. Hence, and watch.
EXECUTIONER I hope your warrant will bear out° the deed.   *authorize*
HUBERT Uncleanly° scruples fear not you; look to't.°   *Improper / do it*
[*The* EXECUTIONERS *withdraw behind the arras.*]
Young lad, come forth. I have to say° with you.   *something to discuss*
Enter ARTHUR.
ARTHUR Good morrow, Hubert.
HUBERT   Good morrow, little prince.
10 ARTHUR As little prince, having so great a title
To be more prince, as may be.[2] You are sad.

---

3. *none . . . it*: they will seize the smallest opportunity to dethrone him.
4. Untimely or monstrous births (seen as portents).
4.1 Location: A castle prison in England.

1. Behind the tapestry hangings.
2. *As . . . be*: Although I have title to be a great prince (king), I am as little a prince as is possible.

HUBERT Indeed, I have been merrier.

ARTHUR   Mercy on me!
Methinks nobody should be sad but I.
Yet I remember, when I was in France,

15   Young gentlemen would be as sad as night
Only for wantonness.° By my Christendom,°   *affectation / faith*
So° I were out of prison and kept sheep   *If*
I should be as merry as the day is long;
And so I would be here but that I doubt°   *fear*

20   My uncle practices° more harm to me.   *plots*
He is afraid of me and I of him.
Is it my fault that I was Geoffrey's son?
No, indeed is't not. And I would to heaven
I were your son, so you would love me, Hubert.

25   HUBERT [*aside*] If I talk to him with his innocent prate°   *prattle*
He will awake my mercy which lies dead:
Therefore I will be sudden and dispatch.

ARTHUR Are you sick, Hubert? You look pale today.
In sooth, I would° you were a little sick,   *Truly, I wish*

30   That I might sit all night and watch with you.
I warrant I love you more than you do me.

HUBERT [*aside*] His words do take possession of my bosom.
[*He shows a paper.*] Read here, young Arthur. [*aside*] How
     now, foolish rheum?°   *tears*
Turning dispiteous° torture out of door?   *pitiless*

35   I must be brief, lest resolution drop
Out at mine eyes in tender womanish tears.
—Can you not read it? Is it not fair writ?°   *legible; legal*

ARTHUR Too fairly, Hubert, for so foul effect.
Must you with hot irons burn out both mine eyes?³

HUBERT Young boy, I must.

ARTHUR   And will you?

40   HUBERT   And I will.

ARTHUR Have you the heart? When your head did but ache,
I knit my handkerchief about your brows—
The best I had; a princess wrought it° me—   *made it for*
And I did never ask it you° again,   *back from you*

45   And with my hand at midnight held your head,
And like the watchful minutes to the hour,
Still and anon cheered up the heavy time,⁴
Saying, "What lack you?" and "Where lies your grief?"°   *pain*
Or "What good love° may I perform for you?"   *loving deed*

50   Many a poor man's son would have lain still
And ne'er have spoke a loving word to you,
But you, at your sick service, had a prince.
Nay, you may think my love was crafty love
And call it cunning. Do, an if you will.

55   If heaven be pleased that you must use me ill,
Why, then, you must. Will you put out mine eyes?
These eyes, that never did nor never shall
So much as frown on you.

---

3. The order to blind Arthur here is at odds with the death sentence of 3.3.66, as well as with Hubert's decision later in this scene (line 128) falsely to report Arthur's death, a decision he makes good on in 4.2.
4. The minutes are seen as breaking up the time to make it pass easily. *Still and anon:* Continually.

HUBERT   I have sworn to do it,
And with hot irons must I burn them out.
60 ARTHUR   Ah, none but in this iron age⁵ would do it.
The iron of itself, though heat° red-hot,   *heated*
Approaching near these eyes would drink my tears
And quench this fiery indignation
Even in the matter° of mine innocence.   *substance; tears*
65 Nay, after that, consume° away in rust,   *dissolve*
But° for containing fire to harm mine eye.   *Merely*
Are you more stubborn-hard than hammered iron?
An if an angel should have come to me
And told me Hubert should put out mine eyes,
70 I would not have believed him; no tongue but Hubert's.
HUBERT [*stamping*]   Come forth.
         [*The* EXECUTIONERS *come forth.*]
                              Do as I bid you do.
ARTHUR   O save me, Hubert, save me! My eyes are out
Even with the fierce looks of these bloody men.
HUBERT   Give me the iron, I say, and bind him here.
75 ARTHUR   Alas, what need you be so boist'rous-rough?
I will not struggle, I will stand stone-still.
For heaven's sake, Hubert, let me not be bound!
Nay, hear me, Hubert, drive these men away,
And I will sit as quiet as a lamb.
80 I will not stir, nor wince, nor speak a word,
Nor look upon the iron angerly.°   *angrily*
Thrust but these men away and I'll forgive you
Whatever torment you do put me to.
HUBERT [*to* EXECUTIONERS]   Go stand within. Let me alone
         with him.
85 EXECUTIONER   I am best pleased to be from° such a deed.   *away from*
                              [*Exeunt* EXECUTIONERS.]
ARTHUR   Alas, I then have chid° away my friend.   *scolded*
He hath a stern look but a gentle heart.
Let him come back that his compassion may
Give life to yours.
HUBERT   Come, boy, prepare yourself.
ARTHUR   Is there no remedy?
90 HUBERT   None but to lose your eyes.
ARTHUR   O heaven, that there were but a mote° in yours,   *speck of dust*
A grain, a dust, a gnat, a wandering hair,
Any annoyance in that precious sense°—   *sight*
Then feeling what small things are boisterous° there,   *painful*
95 Your vile intent must needs seem horrible.
HUBERT   Is this your promise? Go to,° hold your tongue.   *Stop it (rebuke)*
ARTHUR   Hubert, the utterance of a brace of tongues
Must needs want pleading for a pair of eyes.⁶
Let° me not hold my tongue, let me not, Hubert;   *Make*
100 Or Hubert, if you will, cut out my tongue,
So° I may keep mine eyes. Oh, spare mine eyes,   *If*
Though to no use but still to look on you.

---

5. Cruel, degenerate world, in contrast to the legend-   6. *the utterance . . . eyes*: not even a pair of tongues
ary "golden" and "silver" ages; with a play on the hot   would be enough to plead for a pair of eyes.
irons.

Lo, by my troth,° the instrument is cold   *faith*
And would not harm me.

HUBERT   I can heat it, boy.

105 ARTHUR   No, in good sooth,° the fire is dead with grief,   *truly*
Being create° for comfort, to be° used   *created / at being*
In undeserved extremes.° See else° yourself: *extreme suffering / for*
There is no malice in this burning coal,
The breath of heaven hath blown his spirit° out   *(dead person's) soul*
110 And strewed repentant ashes° on his head.   *(of a penitent sinner)*

HUBERT   But with my breath I can revive it, boy.

ARTHUR   An if you do, you will but make it blush
And glow with shame of your proceedings, Hubert.
Nay, it perchance will sparkle° in your eyes;   *cast sparks*
115 And, like a dog that is compelled to fight,
Snatch at his master that doth tarre° him on.   *set*
All things that you should° use to do me wrong   *would*
Deny their office.° Only you do lack   *Disobey*
That mercy which fierce fire and iron extends,
120 Creatures of note° for mercy-lacking uses.   *Things noteworthy*

HUBERT   Well, see to live;[7] I will not touch thine eye
For all the treasure that thine uncle owes.°   *owns*
Yet am I sworn, and I did purpose, boy,
With this same very iron to burn them out.

125 ARTHUR   Oh, now you look like Hubert. All this while
You were disguisèd.

HUBERT   Peace, no more. Adieu.
Your uncle must not know but° you are dead.   *otherwise than that*
I'll fill these doggèd° spies with false reports,   *unfeeling*
And, pretty child, sleep doubtless° and secure   *without fear*
130 That Hubert for the wealth of all the world
Will not offend° thee.   *harm*

ARTHUR   O heaven! I thank you, Hubert.

HUBERT   Silence, no more; go closely° in with me.   *secretly*
Much danger do I undergo for thee.   *Exeunt.*

4.2

Enter [KING] JOHN, [*the Earls of*] PEMBROKE [*and*]
SALISBURY, *and other Lords.* [KING JOHN *sits on the*
throne.]

KING JOHN   Here once again we sit, once again crowned,[1]
And looked upon, I hope, with cheerful eyes.

PEMBROKE   This "once again," but that your highness pleased,
Was once superfluous.[2] You were crowned before,
5 And that high royalty was ne'er plucked off,
The faiths of men ne'er stainèd with revolt.
Fresh expectation° troubled not the land   *Hope of a new king*
With any longed-for change or better state.[3]

SALISBURY   Therefore, to be possessed with double pomp,
10 To guard° a title that was rich before,   *adorn*

To gild refinèd gold, to paint the lily,
To throw a perfume on the violet,
To smooth the ice or add another hue
Unto the rainbow, or with taper-light°   *candlelight*
15   To seek the beauteous eye of heaven to garnish°   *to adorn the sun*
Is wasteful and ridiculous excess.
PEMBROKE   But that your royal pleasure must be done,
This act is as an ancient tale new told
And, in the last repeating, troublesome,
20   Being urged at a time unseasonable.°   *inappropriate*
SALISBURY   In this the antique and well-noted° face   *familiar*
Of plain old form° is much disfigurèd,   *custom*
And like a shifted wind unto a sail,
It makes the course of thoughts to fetch about,°   *change directions*
25   Startles and frights consideration,[4]
Makes sound opinion sick and truth suspected,
For putting on so new a fashioned robe.[5]
PEMBROKE   When workmen strive to do better than well,
They do confound° their skill in covetousness,[6]   *destroy*
30   And oftentimes excusing of a fault
Doth make the fault the worse by th'excuse—
As patches set upon a little breach°   *tear*
Discredit more in hiding of the fault
Than did the fault before it was so patched.
35   SALISBURY   To this effect, before you were new crowned
We breathed our counsel,° but it pleased your highness   *spoke our advice*
To overbear° it; and we are all well pleased,   *overrule*
Since all and every part of what we would°   *wish*
Doth make a stand° at what your highness will.°   *stop; resist / desires*
40   KING JOHN   Some reasons of this double coronation
I have possessed you with° and think them strong.   *instructed you in*
And more, more strong, than lesser is my fear[7]
I shall endue° you with. Meantime, but ask   *supply*
What you would have reformed that is not well,
45   And well shall you perceive how willingly
I will both hear and grant you your requests.[8]
PEMBROKE   Then I, as one that am the tongue° of these   *spokesman*
To sound° the purposes of all their hearts,   *express*
Both for myself and them, but chief of all
50   Your safety, for the which, myself and them
Bend° their best studies,° heartily request   *Direct / efforts*
Th'enfranchisement° of Arthur, whose restraint   *release*
Doth move the murmuring lips of discontent
To break into this dangerous argument:
55   If what in rest° you have, in right you hold,   *in peace*
Why then your fears, which, as they say, attend
The steps of wrong, should move you to mew up°   *confine*
Your tender kinsman and to choke his days

---

4. Encourages questions about John's claim to the throne.
5. For behaving so uncustomarily; for donning a coronation robe.
6. By greedily trying to do even better.
7. *more, more . . . fear:* more reasons, and stronger ones, than the amount by which my fear is (consequently) diminished.
8. Lines 43–46 may allude to the historical King John's submission to the baronial demands spelled out in the Magna Carta. See also line 168 and 5.2.20–23.

With barbarous ignorance and deny his youth
60 The rich advantage of good exercise?°   *education*
That the time's enemies may not have this
To grace occasions,° let it be our suit—   *justify opposition*
That you have bid us ask—his liberty;
Which for our goods we do no further ask,
65 Than whereupon our weal, on you depending,
Counts it your weal he have his liberty.⁹
        Enter HUBERT.
KING JOHN Let it be so: I do commit his youth
To your direction. —Hubert, what news with you?
        [*He takes* HUBERT *aside.*]
PEMBROKE This is the man should° do the bloody deed;   *who is supposed to*
70 He showed his warrant to a friend of mine.
The image of a wicked heinous fault°   *crime*
Lives in his eye. That close aspect° of his   *furtive appearance*
Does show the mood of a much troubled breast,
And I do fearfully believe 'tis done
75 What we so feared he had a charge to do.
SALISBURY The color of the King doth come and go
Between his purpose and his conscience,
Like heralds twixt two dreadful battles set.°   *armies set for battle*
His passion is so ripe it needs must break.°   *burst (like a boil)*
80 PEMBROKE And when it breaks, I fear will issue thence
The foul corruption° of a sweet child's death.   *pus*
KING JOHN We cannot hold° mortality's strong hand.   *hold back*
Good lords, although my will to give is living,
The suit which you demand is gone and dead.
85 He tells us Arthur is deceased tonight.°   *last night*
SALISBURY Indeed, we feared his sickness was past cure.
PEMBROKE Indeed, we heard how near his death he was,
Before the child himself felt he was sick.
This must be answered° either here or hence.°   *answered for / in heaven*
90 KING JOHN Why do you bend such solemn brows on me?
Think you I bear the shears of destiny?¹
Have I commandment on the pulse of life?
SALISBURY It is apparent° foul play, and 'tis shame   *blatant*
That greatness should so grossly offer° it.   *brazenly flaunt*
95 So thrive it in your game,² and so farewell.
PEMBROKE Stay yet, Lord Salisbury, I'll go with thee
And find th'inheritance of this poor child,
His little kingdom of a forcèd° grave.   *violently imposed*
That blood which owed° the breadth of all this isle,   *owned (by right)*
100 Three foot of it doth hold. Bad world the while!°   *while such deeds occur*
This must not be thus borne; this will break out°   *break out in conflict*
To all our sorrows, and ere long I doubt.°   *fear*
        Exeunt [*the Earls of* PEMBROKE, SALISBURY, *and other Lords*].
KING JOHN They burn in indignation. I repent.
There is no sure foundation set on blood,
105 No certain life achieved by others' death.

---

9. *Which . . . liberty:* Which we ask for ourselves only
insofar as our well-being depends on you, and your
welfare on Arthur's demands.

1. The shears with which, in Greek mythology, the
Fates cut the thread of life.
2. May you suffer a similar fate.

Enter [a] MESSENGER.

A fearful eye thou hast. Where is that blood
That I have seen inhabit in those cheeks?
So foul a sky° clears not without a storm.   *(his face)*
Pour down thy weather: how goes all° in France?   *everything; everyone*

110 MESSENGER From France to England, never such a power
For any foreign preparation°   *military expedition*
Was levied in the body of a land.
The copy° of your speed is learned by them,   *example*
For when you should be told they do prepare,
115 The tidings comes that they are all arrived.
KING JOHN Oh, where hath our intelligence° been drunk?   *spy network*
Where hath it slept? Where is my mother's care,
That such an army could be drawn in France,
And she not hear of it?
MESSENGER   My liege, her ear
120 Is stopped with dust. The first of April died
Your noble mother, and, as I hear, my lord,
The Lady Constance in a frenzy died
Three days before. But this from Rumor's tongue
I idly heard: if true or false I know not.
125 KING JOHN *[aside]* Withhold thy speed,° dreadful Occasion.°   *Slow down / events*
O make a league with me till I have pleased
My discontented peers. What? Mother dead!
How wildly then walks my estate° in France!   *fare my possessions*
—Under whose conduct came those powers of France
130 That thou for truth giv'st out° are landed here?   *claim*
MESSENGER Under the Dauphin.
Enter [the] BASTARD *and* PETER *of Pomfret.*[3]
KING JOHN   Thou hast made me giddy
With these ill tidings. —Now, what says the world
To your proceedings?° Do not seek to stuff   *(monastic pillaging)*
My head with more ill news, for it is full.
135 BASTARD But if you be afeard to hear the worst,
Then let the worst unheard fall on your head.
KING JOHN Bear with me, cousin,[4] for I was amazed°   *confused; stunned*
Under the tide,° but now I breathe again   *sea (of bad tidings)*
Aloft the flood and can give audience
140 To any tongue, speak it of what it will.
BASTARD How I have sped° among the clergymen,   *fared*
The sums I have collected shall express.
But as I traveled hither through the land,
I find the people strangely fantasied;°   *full of peculiar ideas*
145 Possessed with rumors, full of idle° dreams,   *foolish*
Not knowing what they fear, but full of fear.
And here's a prophet that I brought with me
From forth the streets of Pomfret, whom I found
With many hundreds treading on his heels,
150 To whom he sung in rude,° harsh-sounding rhymes   *unpolished*
That ere the next Ascension Day[5] at noon,
Your highness should deliver up° your crown.   *give up*

---

3. Modern Pontefract, west Yorkshire.
4. TEXTUAL COMMENT The changing names by which the Bastard is called reflect his growing sobri-

ety and stature. See Digital Edition TC 5.
5. The Thursday, forty days after Easter, on which Christ is supposed to have ascended to heaven.

KING JOHN Thou idle dreamer, wherefore didst thou so?
PETER Foreknowing that the truth will fall out so.
155 KING JOHN Hubert, away with him. Imprison him,
And on that day at noon whereon he says
I shall yield up my crown, let him be hanged.
Deliver him to safety° and return,   *custody*
For I must use thee.
              [Exeunt HUBERT *and* PETER *of Pomfret.]*
              O my gentle cousin,
160 Hear'st thou the news abroad? Who are arrived?
BASTARD The French, my lord; men's mouths are full of it.
Besides, I met Lord Bigot and Lord Salisbury
With eyes as red° as new-enkindled fire,   *(in rage)*
And others more, going to seek the grave
165 Of Arthur, whom they say is killed tonight°   *last night*
On your suggestion.
KING JOHN   Gentle kinsman, go
And thrust thyself into their companies.
I have a way to win their loves again.
Bring them before me.
BASTARD   I will seek them out.
170 KING JOHN Nay, but make haste, the better foot before.°   *go quickly*
Oh, let me have no subject° enemies   *subjects who are my*
When adverse foreigners affright my towns
With dreadful pomp of stout invasion.
Be Mercury, set feathers to thy heels,[6]
175 And fly like thought° from them to me again.   *(proverbially swift)*
BASTARD The spirit of the time° shall teach me speed.   *Exit.*   *present occasion*
KING JOHN Spoke like a sprightful° noble gentleman.   *spirited*
—Go after him: for he perhaps shall need
Some messenger betwixt me and the peers,
And be thou he.
180 MESSENGER   With all my heart, my liege.   *[Exit.]*
KING JOHN My mother dead!
         Enter HUBERT.
HUBERT My lord, they say five moons° were seen tonight: *(an ominous portent)*
Four fixèd, and the fifth did whirl about
The other four in wondrous motion.
KING JOHN Five moons?
185 HUBERT   Old men and beldams° in the streets   *hags*
Do prophesy upon it dangerously.
Young Arthur's death is common in their mouths,
And when they talk of him, they shake their heads
And whisper one another in the ear.
190 And he that speaks doth grip the hearer's wrist,
Whilst he that hears makes fearful action°   *shows fear*
With wrinkled brows, with nods, with rolling eyes.
I saw a smith stand with his hammer, thus,
The whilst his iron did on the anvil cool,
195 With open mouth swallowing a tailor's news,
Who, with his shears and measure in his hand,
Standing on slippers, which his nimble haste

---

6. Mercury, swift messenger of the Roman gods, wore winged sandals.

Had falsely thrust upon contrary° feet,   *the wrong*
Told of a many thousand warlike French
200 That were embattailèd° and ranked in Kent.   *in battle order*
Another lean unwashed artificer°   *artisan*
Cuts off his° tale and talks of Arthur's death.   *(the tailor's)*
KING JOHN   Why seek'st thou to possess me with these fears?
Why urgest thou so oft young Arthur's death?
205 Thy hand hath murdered him. I had a mighty cause
To wish him dead, but thou hadst none to kill him.
HUBERT   No had,° my lord? Why, did you not provoke me?   *Hadn't I*
KING JOHN   It is the curse of kings to be attended
By slaves that take their humors° for a warrant   *whims*
210 To break within the bloody house of life,[7]
And on the winking° of authority   *hint; lapse*
To understand a law,° to know the meaning   *To infer a command*
Of dangerous majesty, when perchance it frowns
More upon humor than advised respect.°   *considered opinion*
215 HUBERT [*showing a paper*] Here is your hand° and seal for   *signature*
    what I did.
KING JOHN   Oh, when the last account twixt heaven and earth
Is to be made,[8] then shall this hand and seal
Witness against us to damnation.
How oft the sight of means to do ill deeds
220 Make deeds ill done! Hadst not thou been by,°   *on hand*
A fellow by the hand of nature marked,°   *(by ugliness)*
Quoted,° and signed° to do a deed of shame,   *Noted / assigned*
This murder had not come into my mind.
But taking note of thy abhorred aspect,°   *appearance*
225 Finding thee fit for bloody villainy,
Apt, liable° to be employed in danger,°   *suitable / doing harm*
I faintly broke° with thee of Arthur's death,   *vaguely spoke*
And thou, to be endearèd to a king,
Made it no conscience° to destroy a prince.   *no matter of conscience*
230 HUBERT   My lord—
KING JOHN   Hadst thou but shook thy head or made a pause
When I spake darkly° what I purposèd;   *insinuated*
Or turned an eye of doubt upon my face,
As° bid me tell my tale in express° words;   *As if to / plain*
235 Deep shame had struck me dumb, made me break off,
And those thy fears might have wrought fears in me.
But thou didst understand me by my signs,
And didst in signs again parley° with sin;   *negotiate*
Yea, without stop didst let thy heart consent,
240 And consequently thy rude° hand to act   *rough*
The deed, which both our tongues held vile° to name.   *refused*
Out of my sight and never see me more!
My nobles leave me, and my state is braved°   *challenged*
Even at my gates with ranks of foreign powers.
245 Nay, in the body of this fleshly land,°   *(John's body)*
This kingdom, this confine° of blood and breath,   *territory*
Hostility and civil tumult reigns

---

7. The human body, which contains blood and which   8. *when . . . made:* when Judgment Day arrives.
murder makes bloody.

Between my conscience and my cousin's death.

HUBERT   Arm you against your other enemies;
250   I'll make a peace between your soul and you.
Young Arthur is alive. This hand of mine
Is yet a maiden° and an innocent hand,   *virgin*
Not painted with the crimson spots of blood.
Within this bosom never entered yet
255   The dreadful motion° of a murderous thought,   *impulse*
And you have slandered nature° in my form,°   *my nature / appearance*
Which howsoever rude exteriorly,
Is yet the cover of a fairer mind
Than to be butcher of an innocent child.
260   KING JOHN   Doth Arthur live? Oh, haste thee to the peers,
Throw this report° on their incensèd° rage,   *(like water) / burning*
And make them tame to their obedience.°   *(to John)*
Forgive the comment that my passion made
Upon thy feature,° for my rage was blind,   *features*
265   And foul imaginary eyes of blood[9]
Presented thee more hideous than thou art.
Oh, answer not, but to my closet° bring   *private room*
The angry lords with all expedient° haste.   *necessary*
I conjure° thee but slowly. Run more fast!   *Exeunt.*   *urge*

4.3

Enter ARTHUR *on the walls [disguised as a ship-boy].*

ARTHUR   The wall is high and yet will I leap down.
Good ground, be pitiful and hurt me not.
There's few or none do know me. If they did,
This ship-boy's semblance° hath disguised me quite.°   *disguise / completely*
5   I am afraid, and yet I'll venture it.
If I get down and do not break my limbs,
I'll find a thousand shifts° to get away: *stratagems*
As good to die and go, as die and stay.
     [He leaps down.]
O me! My uncle's spirit is in these stones.
10   Heaven take my soul, and England keep my bones!
     [He] dies.
     Enter [the Earls of] PEMBROKE *[and]* SALISBURY, *and*
     [Lord] BIGOT.

SALISBURY   Lords, I will meet him° at Saint Edmundsbury.[1]   *(the Dauphin)*
It is our safety,° and we must embrace   *means of safety*
This gentle offer of the perilous time.

PEMBROKE   Who brought that letter from the Cardinal?°   *Pandulph*
15   SALISBURY   The Count Melun, a noble lord of France,
Whose private° with me of the Dauphin's love   *communication*
Is much more general° than these lines import.   *greater*

BIGOT   Tomorrow morning let us meet him then.

SALISBURY   Or rather, then set forward, for 'twill be
20   Two long days' journey, lords, or ere° we meet.   *before*
     Enter [the] BASTARD.

---

9. John's, bloody from rage; Hubert's, bloody from guilt; Arthur's, bloody from murder.

4.3 Location: Outside the castle.
1. Bury St. Edmunds, Suffolk (a place of pilgrimage).

BASTARD   Once more today well met, distempered° lords.   *ill-humored*
The King by me requests your presence straight.°   *immediately*
SALISBURY   The King hath dispossessed himself of us.
We will not line his thin bestainèd cloak
25   With our pure honors, nor attend the foot
That leaves the print of blood where'er it walks.
Return and tell him so. We know the worst.
BASTARD   Whate'er you think, good words, I think, were best.
SALISBURY   Our griefs and not our manners reason now.
30   BASTARD   But there is little reason in your grief;
Therefore 'twere reason° you had manners now.   *reasonable*
PEMBROKE   Sir, sir, impatience hath his privilege.°   *its particular right*
BASTARD   'Tis true: to hurt his master, no man else.[2]
SALISBURY   This is the prison. What is he lies here?
35   PEMBROKE   O death, made proud with pure and princely beauty!
The earth had not a hole° to hide this deed.   *grave*
SALISBURY   Murder, as° hating what himself hath done,   *as though*
Doth lay it open° to urge on revenge.   *on public display*
BIGOT   Or when he° doomed this beauty to a grave,   *(Murder)*
40   Found it too precious-princely for a grave.
SALISBURY [*to the* BASTARD]   Sir Richard, what think you? You
    have beheld.
Or have you° read, or heard, or could you think,   *Have you either*
Or do you almost think, although you see,
That you do see? Could thought, without this object,
45   Form such another?[3] This is the very top,
The height, the crest,° or crest unto the crest   *(atop a coat of arms)*
Of murder's arms. This is the bloodiest shame,
The wildest savagery, the vilest stroke
That ever wall-eyed° wrath or staring rage   *glaring*
50   Presented to the tears of soft remorse.°   *pity*
PEMBROKE   All murders past do stand excused in° this.   *in comparison with*
And this, so sole° and so unmatchable,   *unique*
Shall give a holiness, a purity,
To the yet unbegotten sin of times,°   *the future*
55   And prove a deadly bloodshed but a jest,
Exampled by° this heinous spectacle.   *Given the precedent of*
BASTARD   It is a damnèd and a bloody work,
The graceless° action of a heavy° hand,   *impious / oppressive*
If that it be the work of any hand.
60   SALISBURY   If that it be the work of any hand!
We had a kind of light° what would ensue.   *premonition*
It is the shameful work of Hubert's hand,
The practice° and the purpose of the King,   *plot*
From whose obedience I forbid my soul,
65   Kneeling before this ruin of sweet life,
And breathing to his breathless excellence
The incense of a vow, a holy vow:
Never to taste the pleasures of the world,
Never to be infected with delight,

2. Angry words hurt no one but the speaker
(proverbial).
3. *Or do . . . another?*: Could you even approach the

thought of what you actually see here? Without seeing Arthur's body, would it be possible to imagine
such a sight?

70 Nor conversant with ease and idleness,
Till I have set a glory to this hand°   *(his own; Arthur's)*
By giving it the worship° of revenge.   *honor*
PEMBROKE *and* BIGOT   Our souls religiously confirm thy words.
         Enter HUBERT.
HUBERT   Lords, I am hot with haste in seeking you.
75 Arthur doth live; the King hath sent for you.
SALISBURY   Oh, he is bold and blushes not at death.
—Avaunt,° thou hateful villain, get thee gone!   *Begone*
HUBERT   I am no villain.
SALISBURY   Must I rob the law?[4]
        [*He draws his sword.*]
BASTARD   Your sword is bright,° sir; put it up° again.   *unused / sheathe it*
80 SALISBURY   Not till I sheathe it in a murderer's skin.
HUBERT [*drawing his sword*]   Stand back, Lord Salisbury,
     stand back, I say!
By heaven, I think my sword's as sharp as yours.
I would not have you, lord, forget yourself,[5]
Nor tempt° the danger of my true° defense,   *test / honest; able*
85 Lest I, by marking of° your rage, forget   *responding to*
Your worth, your greatness and nobility.
BIGOT   Out, dunghill! Dar'st thou brave° a nobleman?   *defy*
HUBERT   Not for my life; but yet I dare defend
My innocent life against an emperor.
SALISBURY   Thou art a murderer.
90 HUBERT   Do not prove me so;°   *(by making me kill)*
Yet° I am none. Whose tongue soe'er speaks false,   *Up to now*
Not truly speaks; who speaks not truly, lies.
PEMBROKE   Cut him to pieces!
BASTARD   Keep the peace, I say.
SALISBURY   Stand by,° or I shall gall° you, Falconbridge.   *aside / wound*
95 BASTARD   Thou wert better gall the devil, Salisbury.
If thou but frown on me, or stir thy foot,
Or teach thy hasty spleen° to do me shame,   *temper*
I'll strike thee dead. Put up thy sword betime,°   *immediately*
Or I'll so maul you and your toasting-iron°   *sword (belittling)*
100 That you shall think the devil is come from hell.
BIGOT   What wilt thou do, renownèd Falconbridge?
Second° a villain and a murderer?   *Back up*
HUBERT   Lord Bigot, I am none.
BIGOT   Who killed this prince?
HUBERT   'Tis not an hour since I left him well.
105 I honored him, I loved him, and will weep
My date° of life out for his sweet life's loss.   *term*
SALISBURY   Trust not those cunning waters of his eyes,
For villainy is not without such rheum;
And he, long traded° in it, makes it seem   *experienced*
110 Like rivers of remorse and innocency.
Away with me, all you whose souls abhor
Th'uncleanly savors° of a slaughterhouse,   *odors*
For I am stifled with this smell of sin.

---

4. Deprive the law of its due (by killing Hubert).
5. Lose self-control; forget your rank (it not being honorable for a lord to challenge a commoner, or vice versa, as lines 85–86 suggest).

BIGOT Away, toward Bury,° to the Dauphin there.   *Saint Edmundsbury (Bury St Edmunds)*
115 PEMBROKE   There tell the King he may inquire° us out.   *seek*

     Exeunt Lords [the Earls of PEMBROKE *and*
       SALISBURY, *and Lord* BIGOT].

BASTARD   Here's a good world! Knew you of this fair work?
 Beyond the infinite and boundless reach
 Of mercy, if thou didst this deed of death,
 Art thou damned, Hubert.
HUBERT   Do but hear me, sir—
120 BASTARD   Ha! I'll tell thee what:
 Thou'rt damned as black—nay, nothing is so black—
 Thou art more deep damned than Prince Lucifer—
 There is not yet so ugly a fiend of hell
 As thou shalt be, if thou didst kill this child.
HUBERT   Upon my soul—
125 BASTARD   If thou didst but consent
 To this most cruel act, do but despair;⁶
 And if thou want'st° a cord, the smallest thread   *lack*
 That ever spider twisted from her womb
 Will serve to strangle thee; a rush° will be a beam   *reed*
130 To hang thee on. Or wouldst thou° drown thyself,   *if you wish to*
 Put but a little water in a spoon,
 And it shall be as all the ocean,
 Enough to stifle such a villain up.
 I do suspect thee very grievously.
135 HUBERT   If I in act, consent, or sin of thought,
 Be guilty of the stealing that sweet breath
 Which was embounded° in this beauteous clay,°   *enclosed / (Arthur's body)*
 Let hell want pains enough to torture me.
 I left him well.
BASTARD   Go, bear him in thine arms:
   [HUBERT *lifts up* ARTHUR.]
140 I am amazed,° methinks, and lose my way   *bewildered*
 Among the thorns and dangers of this world.
 How easy dost thou take all England up,
 From forth° this morsel of dead royalty!   *Out of*
 The life, the right, and truth of all this realm
145 Is fled to heaven, and England now is left
 To tug and scamble and to part by th' teeth
 The unowed interest⁷ of proud swelling state.
 Now for the bare-picked bone of majesty
 Doth doggèd° war bristle his angry crest⁸   *cruel*
150 And snarleth in the gentle eyes of peace;
 Now powers from home° and discontents at home   *foreign armies*
 Meet in one line;° and vast confusion waits,°   *rank / chaos awaits*
 As doth a raven on a sick-fall'n beast,
 The imminent decay of wrested pomp.°   *usurped power*
155 Now happy he whose cloak and ceinture° can   *belt*
 Hold out this tempest. Bear away that child,
 And follow me with speed. I'll to the King.

---

6. Lose all hope of salvation and hence commit suicide.
7. Contested or unowned possession; obedience ("interest") that is not due ("unowed"), because John lacks legitimacy.
8. Dog's hackles (hairs on neck and back); crest on a coat of arms.

A thousand businesses are brief in hand,°   *need urgent action*
And heaven itself doth frown upon the land.   *Exeunt.*

5.1

Enter KING JOHN *and* [*Cardinal*] PANDULPH, [*and*]
Attendants.

KING JOHN [*giving the crown to* PANDULPH]   Thus have I
  yielded up into your hand
  The circle of my glory.
PANDULPH [*returning the crown*]   Take again
  From this my hand, as holding of° the Pope,   *as land rented from*
  Your sovereign greatness and authority.
5 KING JOHN   Now keep your holy word: go meet the French,
  And from his Holiness° use all your power   *the Pope*
  To stop their marches fore we are inflamed.
  Our discontented counties° do revolt.   *shires; nobles*
  Our people quarrel with obedience,
10 Swearing allegiance and the love of soul
  To stranger° blood, to foreign royalty.   *foreign*
  This inundation of mistempered humor
  Rests by you only to be qualified.[1]
  Then pause not, for the present time's so sick
15 That present° medicine must be ministered,   *immediate*
  Or overthrow incurable ensues.
PANDULPH   It was my breath° that blew this tempest up,   *words*
  Upon your stubborn usage of the Pope;
  But since you are a gentle convertite,°   *convert*
20 My tongue shall hush again this storm of war
  And make fair weather in your blustering land.
  On this Ascension Day, remember well,
  Upon your oath of service to the Pope,
  Go I to make the French lay down their arms.
          Exeunt [*all but* KING JOHN].[2]
25 KING JOHN   Is this Ascension Day? Did not the prophet
  Say that before Ascension Day at noon,
  My crown I should give off?[3] Even so I have.
  I did suppose it should be on constraint,
  But, heaven be thanked, it is but voluntary.
          Enter [*the*] BASTARD.
30 BASTARD   All Kent hath yielded; nothing there holds out
  But Dover Castle. London hath received,
  Like a kind host, the Dauphin and his powers.°   *army*
  Your nobles will not hear you, but are gone
  To offer service to your enemy,
35 And wild amazement hurries° up and down   *confusion drives*
  The little number of your doubtful° friends.   *untrustworthy; fearful*
KING JOHN   Would not my lords return to me again
  After they heard young Arthur was alive?
BASTARD   They found him dead and cast into the streets,
40 An empty casket, where the jewel of life
  By some damned hand was robbed and ta'en away.

5.1 Location: John's court.
1. *This . . . qualified:* Only you can cure this surge of
diseased behavior.

2. F leaves the attendants onstage with John. But even
in that case, this speech could easily be a soliloquy.
3. See 4.2.147–52.

KING JOHN   That villain Hubert told me he did live.
BASTARD   So on my soul he did, for aught he knew.
  But wherefore do you droop? Why look you sad?
45 Be great in act, as you have been in thought.
  Let not the world see fear and sad distrust
  Govern the motion of a kingly eye.
  Be stirring as the time,[4] be fire with° fire,   against
  Threaten the threatener and outface the brow
50 Of bragging horror. So shall inferior eyes,
  That borrow their behaviors from the great,
  Grow great by your example and put on
  The dauntless spirit of resolution.
  Away, and glister like the god of war
55 When he intendeth to become the field.°   adorn the battlefield
  Show boldness and aspiring confidence!
  What, shall they seek the lion in his den,
  And fright him there and make him tremble there?
  Oh, let it not be said! Forage° and run   Range (for prey)
60 To meet displeasure farther from the doors,
  And grapple with him ere he come so nigh.
KING JOHN   The legate of the Pope hath been with me,
  And I have made a happy peace with him,
  And he hath promised to dismiss the powers
  Led by the Dauphin.
65 BASTARD   Oh, inglorious league!
  Shall we, upon the footing of our land,°   standing on our own soil
  Send fair-play orders° and make compromise,   equitable conditions
  Insinuation,° parley, and base truce   Ingratiating proposals
  To arms invasive?° Shall a beardless boy,   invading
70 A cockered silken wanton,° brave our fields,   spoiled dandyish child
  And flesh his spirit in a warlike soil,[5]
  Mocking the air with colors idly° spread,   carelessly
  And find no check? Let us, my liege, to arms!
  Perchance the Cardinal cannot make your peace;
75 Or if he do, let it at least be said
  They saw we had a purpose of defense.
KING JOHN   Have thou the ordering of this present time.
BASTARD   Away then, with good courage! [*aside*] Yet I know
  Our party may well meet a prouder foe.[6]   *Exeunt.*

5.2

Enter, in arms, LOUIS THE DAUPHIN, [the Earls of]
  SALISBURY [*and*] PEMBROKE, [*Count*] MELUN, [*Lord*]
  BIGOT, [*and*] *Soldiers.*
LOUIS THE DAUPHIN [*extending a paper*]   My lord Melun, let
    this[1] be copied out,
  And keep it safe for our remembrance.

---

4. Be as vigorous as the times demand.
5. Initiate himself in bloodshed (in the "soil," as a sword is "fleshed" in a body).
6. TEXTUAL COMMENT May be up against an enemy more powerful than we are; perhaps, is well able to handle an even stronger enemy than the French. The passage is marked in this edition as an aside, spoken only to the audience. But in this case, the Bastard

might actually be addressing the King. The choice of one of the antithetical meanings given here could influence how this brief passage is performed or interpreted. See Digital Edition TC 6.
5.2 Location: St. Edmundsbury (Bury St. Edmunds) in Suffolk.
1. This agreement with the English lords.

Return the precedent° to these lords again;   *original copy*
That having our fair order° written down,   *arrangements*
5   Both they and we, perusing o'er these notes,
May know wherefore we took the sacrament[2]
And keep our faiths firm and inviolable.
SALISBURY   Upon our sides it never shall be broken.
And, noble Dauphin, albeit we swear
10   A voluntary zeal° and an unurged° faith   *commitment / unforced*
To your proceedings; yet believe me, prince,
I am not glad that such a sore of time
Should seek a plaster° by contemnèd° revolt,   *bandage / despised*
And heal the inveterate canker° of one wound   *infection*
15   By making many. Oh, it grieves my soul
That I must draw this metal° from my side   *(his sword)*
To be a widow-maker. Oh, and there
Where honorable rescue and defense
Cries out upon[3] the name of Salisbury!
20   But such is the infection of the time
That for the health and physic° of our right,   *cure*
We cannot deal but with the very hand
Of stern injustice and confusèd wrong.[4]
And is't not pity, O my grievèd friends,
25   That we, the sons and children of this isle,
Was born to see so sad an hour as this,
Wherein we step after a stranger,° march   *foreigner*
Upon her gentle bosom, and fill up
Her enemies' ranks? I must withdraw and weep
30   Upon the spot° of this enforcèd cause,   *place; stain*
To grace the gentry of a land remote
And follow unacquainted colors° here.   *unfamiliar banners*
What, here? O nation, that thou couldst remove;°   *move elsewhere*
That Neptune's arms,° who clippeth thee about,°   *the sea / embraces you*
35   Would bear thee from the knowledge of thyself
And grapple° thee unto a pagan shore,   *join*
Where these two Christian armies might combine
The blood of malice in a vein of league,°   *(against a pagan foe)*
And not to spend° it so unneighborly.   *shed*
40   LOUIS THE DAUPHIN   A noble temper° dost thou show in this,   *disposition*
And great affections° wrestling in thy bosom   *emotions; loyalties*
Doth make an earthquake of nobility.°   *out of a noble nature*
Oh, what a noble combat hast thou fought
Between compulsion° and a brave respect!°   *necessity / patriotism*
45   Let me wipe off this honorable dew,
That silverly doth progress on thy cheeks.
My heart hath melted at a lady's tears,
Being an ordinary inundation;
But this effusion of such manly drops,
50   This shower blown up by tempest of the soul,
Startles mine eyes and makes me more amazed
Than had I seen the vaulty° top of heaven   *arched*

---

2. The mass, taken as a solemn dedication to the task.
3. Exclaims against; appeals to.

4. *We . . . wrong:* we cannot act except with unjust means; or, possibly, we cannot act except against the unjust hand of John.

Figured quite o'er° with burning meteors.⁵   *Adorned thoroughly*
Lift up thy brow, renownèd Salisbury,
55 And with a great heart heave away this storm.
Commend° these waters to those baby eyes   *Leave*
That never saw the giant° world enraged,   *grown-up*
Nor met with Fortune other than at feasts,
Full warm of° blood, of mirth, of gossiping.   *with*
60 Come, come: for thou shalt thrust thy hand as deep
Into the purse of rich prosperity
As Louis himself. So, nobles, shall you all,
That knit your sinews° to the strength of mine.   *join your powers*
      Enter [Cardinal] PANDULPH.
And even there, methinks, an angel⁶ spake:
65 Look where the holy legate comes apace,
To give us warrant from the hand of heaven°   *the Pope; God*
And on our actions set the name of right
With holy breath.
PANDULPH   Hail, noble prince of France!
The next° is this: King John hath reconciled   *next thing I have to say*
70 Himself to Rome; his spirit is come in,°   *has submitted*
That so stood out against the holy church,
The great metropolis and see of Rome.
Therefore thy threatening colors° now wind up,°   *banners / put away*
And tame the savage spirit of wild war,
75 That, like a lion fostered up at hand,°   *by human hand*
It may lie gently at the foot of peace
And be no further harmful than in show.
LOUIS THE DAUPHIN   Your grace shall pardon me, I will not back:°   *go back*
I am too high-born to be propertied°   *manipulated*
80 To be a secondary° at control,   *subordinate*
Or useful serving-man and instrument
To any sovereign state° throughout the world.   *(the papacy)*
Your breath first kindled the dead coal of wars
Between this chastised kingdom and myself,
85 And brought in matter° that should feed this fire.   *fuel*
And now 'tis far too huge to be blown out
With that same weak wind which enkindled it.
You taught me how to know the face of right,°   *my rightful claim*
Acquainted me with interest° to this land,   *my claim*
90 Yea, thrust this enterprise into my heart;
And come ye now to tell me John hath made
His peace with Rome? What is that peace to me?
I, by the honor of my marriage bed,
After young Arthur claim this land for mine;
95 And now it is half-conquered must I back
Because that John hath made his peace with Rome?
Am I Rome's slave? What penny hath Rome borne,°   *contributed*
What men provided, what munition sent
To underprop° this action? Is't not I   *support*

5. Meteors were seen as portents of disaster.
6. Some editions add a stage direction requiring a trumpet to sound at Pandulph's entrance. But "angel" also means "gold coin," thus developing the money imagery of lines 61–63—"purse of rich prosperity,"
"nobles" (also a coin), and perhaps "sinews" (where "sinews of war" connotes money). The Dauphin's point, perhaps made in an aside, would be that money talks in persuading the English peers to join his cause.

100	That undergo this charge? Who else but I,	
	And such as to my claim are liable,°	*are liable to me*
	Sweat in this business and maintain° this war?	*pay for*
	Have I not heard these islanders shout out,	
	"*Vive le roi*," as I have banked their towns?	
105	Have I not here the best cards for the game	
	To win this easy match, played for a crown?	
	And shall I now give o'er the yielded set?⁷	
	No, no, on my soul, it never shall be said.	
	PANDULPH You look but on the outside of this work.	
110	LOUIS THE DAUPHIN Outside or inside, I will not return	
	Till my attempt° so much be glorifièd,	*warlike enterprise*
	As to my ample hope was promisèd	
	Before I drew° this gallant head of war,°	*gathered / army*
	And culled° these fiery spirits from the world	*picked out*
115	To outlook conquest° and to win renown	*To defy defeat*
	Even in the jaws of danger and of death.	
	[*A trumpet sounds.*]	
	What lusty° trumpet thus doth summon us?	*vigorous*
	Enter [*the*] BASTARD.	
	BASTARD According to the fair play° of the world,	*code of chivalry*
	Let me have audience: I am sent to speak.	
120	My holy lord of Milan, from the King	
	I come to learn how you have dealt for him;	
	And, as° you answer, I do know the scope	*according to how*
	And warrant limited unto my tongue.	
	PANDULPH The Dauphin is too willful-opposite°	*stubbornly hostile*
125	And will not temporize with° my entreaties.	*heed*
	He flatly says he'll not lay down his arms.	
	BASTARD By all the blood that ever fury breathed,	
	The youth says well. Now hear our English King,	
	For thus his royalty doth speak in me:	
130	He is prepared, and reason too he should.°	*as he should be*
	This apish and unmannerly approach,	
	This harnessed masque and unadvisèd revel,⁸	
	This unheard° sauciness and boyish troops,	*unheard of*
	The King doth smile at and is well prepared	
135	To whip this dwarfish war, these pigmy arms,	
	From out the circle° of his territories.	*confines*
	That hand which had the strength, even at your door,	
	To cudgel you and make you take the hatch,°	*beat a hasty retreat*
	To dive like buckets in concealèd wells,	
140	To crouch in litter° of your stable planks,	*animal's bedding*
	To lie like pawns° locked up in chests and trunks,	*pawned goods*
	To hug° with swine, to seek sweet safety out	*bed down*
	In vaults and prisons, and to thrill° and shake,	*shiver*
	Even at the crying of your nation's crow,°	*the cock*
145	Thinking this voice an armèd Englishman—	
	Shall that victorious hand be feebled here,	

---

7. "*Vive*" . . . *set*: The Dauphin uses an extended card-playing metaphor, including "Vive le Roi" ("Long live the King"), "banked" (put in the bank, won; but also, sailed by the banks of, or perhaps besieged), "cards," "game," "match, played," "crown" (the coin as a stake in a card game; John's crown), and "yielded set" (the hand already won).

8. This courtly entertainment in armor and rashly undertaken revelry.

That in your chambers° gave you chastisement?   *your own home*
No! Know the gallant monarch is in arms,
And like an eagle over his aerie towers,°   *soaring over his nest*
150 To souse° annoyance that comes near his nest.   *swoop down on*
And you degenerate, you ingrate revolts,°   *ungrateful rebels*
You bloody Neroes, ripping up the womb
Of your dear mother England,[9] blush for shame!
For your own ladies and pale-visaged maids,
155 Like Amazons[1] come tripping after drums,
Their thimbles into armèd gauntlets° change,   *steel-plated gloves*
Their needles to lances, and their gentle hearts
To fierce and bloody inclination.°   *disposition*
LOUIS THE DAUPHIN There end thy brave° and turn thy face° *defiance / return*
 in peace.
160 We grant thou canst outscold us. Fare thee well;
We hold our time too precious to be spent
With such a brabbler.°   *quarreler*
PANDULPH   Give me leave to speak.
BASTARD No, I will speak.
LOUIS THE DAUPHIN   We will attend° to neither.   *listen*
Strike up the drums and let the tongue of war
165 Plead for our interest and our being here.
BASTARD Indeed, your drums, being beaten, will cry out,
And so shall you, being beaten. Do but start
An echo with the clamor of thy drum,
And, even at hand, a drum is ready braced°   *ready to be struck*
170 That shall reverberate all as loud as thine.
Sound but another and another shall,
As loud as thine, rattle the welkin's° ear   *sky's*
And mock° the deep-mouthed thunder. For at hand— *outrival*
Not trusting to this halting° legate here,   *wavering*
175 Whom he hath used rather for sport than need—
Is warlike John; and in his forehead sits
A bare-ribbed Death, whose office° is this day   *task*
To feast upon whole thousands of the French.
LOUIS THE DAUPHIN Strike up our drums to find this danger out.
180 BASTARD And thou shalt find it, Dauphin, do not doubt.
             Exeunt.

5.3

Alarums. Enter [KING] JOHN *and* HUBERT.
KING JOHN How goes the day with us? Oh, tell me, Hubert.
HUBERT Badly, I fear. How fares your majesty?
KING JOHN This fever that hath troubled me so long
Lies heavy on me. Oh, my heart is sick.
   Enter a MESSENGER.
5 MESSENGER My lord, your valiant kinsman Falconbridge
Desires your majesty to leave the field
And send him word by me which way you go.
KING JOHN Tell him toward Swinsted,° to the abbey there. *Swineshead in Lincolnshire*
MESSENGER Be of good comfort; for the great supply°   *reinforcements*

---

9. The Roman emperor Nero was supposed to have murdered his mother by ripping open her womb.

1. Female warriors of classical legend.
5.3 Location: The battlefield.

10 That was expected by the Dauphin here
Are wrecked three nights ago on Goodwin Sands.°　　　　*shoals off Kent*
This news was brought to Richard° but even now.　　　　*(the Bastard)*
The French fight coldly and retire themselves.°　　　　*retreat*
KING JOHN　Ay me, this tyrant fever burns me up
15 And will not let me welcome this good news.
Set on toward Swinsted: to my litter straight.°　　　　*portable bed at once*
Weakness possesseth me and I am faint.　　　　*Exeunt.*

5.4

Enter [the Earls of] SALISBURY *and* PEMBROKE, *and*
[Lord] BIGOT.

SALISBURY　I did not think the King so stored° with friends.　　　　*well provided*
PEMBROKE　Up once again; put spirit in the French.
If they miscarry,° we miscarry too.　　　　*fail*
SALISBURY　That misbegotten devil Falconbridge,
5 In spite of spite,° alone upholds the day.°　　　　*everything / battle*
PEMBROKE　They say King John, sore° sick, hath left the field.　　　　*grievously*
　　　Enter [Count] MELUN, *wounded [led by Soldiers].*
MELUN　Lead me to the revolts° of England here.　　　　*rebels*
SALISBURY　When we were happy, we had other names.
PEMBROKE　It is the Count Melun.
SALISBURY　　　　　　　　　　Wounded to death.
10 MELUN　Fly, noble English, you are bought and sold.°　　　　*betrayed*
Unthread the rude eye of rebellion,[1]
And welcome home again discarded faith.
Seek out King John and fall before his feet,
For if the French be lords of° this loud° day,　　　　*win / hectic*
15 He° means to recompense the pains you take　　　　*(Louis)*
By cutting off your heads. Thus hath he sworn,
And I with him, and many more with me,
Upon the altar at Saint Edmundsbury—
Even on that altar where we swore to you
20 Dear amity and everlasting love.
SALISBURY　May this be possible? May this be true?
MELUN　Have I not hideous death within my view,
Retaining but a quantity of life
Which bleeds away, even as a form of wax
25 Resolveth from his figure° 'gainst the fire?　　　　*Melts out of shape*
What in the world should make me now deceive,
Since I must lose the use of all deceit?
Why should I then be false, since it is true
That I must die here, and live hence° by truth?　　　　*in the next world*
30 I say again, if Louis do win the day,
He is forsworn° if e'er those eyes of yours　　　　*perjured*
Behold another day break in the East.
But even this night, whose black contagious breath
Already smokes about the burning crest
35 Of the old, feeble, and day-wearied sun—
Even this ill night, your breathing shall expire,

5.4 Location: Scene continues.
1. Turn back from the barbarous path of rebellion
down which you've been led (like a thread that has
been inserted into the needle's eye and must be
pulled out).

Paying the fine of rated° treachery,   *assessed (as penalty)*
Even with a treacherous fine° of all your lives,   *payment; end*
If Louis by your assistance win the day.
40   Commend me to one Hubert, with your King.
The love of him, and this respect° besides,   *consideration*
For that° my grandsire was an Englishman,   *Because*
Awakes my conscience to confess all this.
In lieu° whereof, I pray you, bear me hence   *recompense*
45   From forth the noise and rumor° of the field,   *tumult*
Where I may think the remnant of my thoughts
In peace, and part this body and my soul
With contemplation and devout desires.
SALISBURY   We do believe thee, and beshrew° my soul,   *woe to*
50   But° I do love the favor° and the form   *Unless / look*
Of this most fair occasion, by the which
We will untread° the steps of damnèd flight,°   *retrace / desertion*
And, like a bated° and retired flood,   *abated*
Leaving our rankness° and irregular course,   *flooding*
55   Stoop low within those bounds we have o'erlooked,°   *overflowed; ignored*
And calmly run on in obedience
Even to our ocean, to our great King John.
My arm shall give thee help to bear thee hence,
For I do see the cruel pangs of death
60   Right in thine eye. —Away, my friends! New flight,°   *change of allegiance*
And happy newness, that intends old right!²   *Exeunt.*

5.5

Enter [LOUIS THE] DAUPHIN, *and his train.*
LOUIS THE DAUPHIN   The sun of heaven, methought, was loath
       to set,
But stayed and made the western welkin blush,
When English measured° backward their own ground   *crossed*
In faint retire.° Oh, bravely came we off,¹   *weak retreat*
5   When with a volley of our needless° shot,   *unnecessary*
After such bloody toil, we bid good night
And wound our tott'ring colors clearly up,²
Last in the field and almost lords of it.
       Enter a MESSENGER.
MESSENGER   Where is my prince, the Dauphin?
LOUIS THE DAUPHIN   Here. What news?
10   MESSENGER   The Count Melun is slain, the English lords
By his persuasion are again fall'n off,°   *changed in allegiance*
And your supply,° which you have wished so long,   *supplies*
Are cast away and sunk on Goodwin Sands.
LOUIS THE DAUPHIN   Ah, foul shrewd° news! Beshrew° thy very   *harmful / Curse*
       heart!
15   I did not think to be so sad tonight
As this hath made me. Who was he that said
King John did fly an hour or two before
The stumbling night³ did part our weary powers?
MESSENGER   Whoever spoke it, it is true, my lord.

---

2. That intends to restore the ancient right—John's
claim to rule and our just conduct.
5.5 Location: Scene continues.
1. We acquitted ourselves valiantly.

2. We rolled our tattered (waving) banners up without obstruction from the English.
3. That is, night that causes stumbling.

20 LOUIS THE DAUPHIN   Well, keep good quarter° and good care   *guard*
    tonight.
    The day shall not be up so soon as I,
    To try the fair adventure° of tomorrow.   *Exeunt.*   *chance*

5.6

Enter [the] BASTARD *and* HUBERT, *severally.*

HUBERT   Who's there? Speak, ho! Speak quickly, or I shoot.
BASTARD   A friend. What art thou?
HUBERT   Of the part° of England.   *side*
BASTARD   Whither dost thou go?
HUBERT   What's that to thee?
    Why may not I demand of thine affairs,
    As well as thou of mine?
5 BASTARD   Hubert, I think.
HUBERT   Thou hast a perfect° thought.[1]   *correct*
    I will upon all hazards° well believe   *against all odds*
    Thou art my friend, that know'st my tongue so well.
    Who art thou?
BASTARD   Who thou wilt: an if thou please,
10   Thou mayst befriend me so much as to think
    I come one way° of the Plantagenets.   *by one parent*
HUBERT   Unkind remembrance![2] Thou and endless night
    Have done me shame. Brave soldier, pardon me,
    That any accent° breaking from thy tongue   *sound*
15   Should scape the true acquaintance of mine ear.
BASTARD   Come, come; sans compliment.° What news abroad?   *no formalities*
HUBERT   Why, here walk I in the black brow of night
    To find you out.
BASTARD   Brief, then. And what's the news?
HUBERT   O my sweet sir, news fitting to the night:
20   Black, fearful, comfortless, and horrible.
BASTARD   Show me the very wound of this ill news:
    I am no woman; I'll not swoon at it.
HUBERT   The King, I fear, is poisoned by a monk.
    I left him almost speechless, and broke out°   *hurried away*
25   To acquaint you with this evil, that you might
    The better arm you to the sudden time°   *for this emergency*
    Than if you had at leisure° known of this.   *later*
BASTARD   How did he take it?° Who did taste to° him?   *(poison) / taste (the food) for*
HUBERT   A monk, I tell you, a resolvèd villain,[3]
30   Whose bowels suddenly burst out. The King
    Yet° speaks, and peradventure may recover.   *Still*
BASTARD   Who didst thou leave to tend his majesty?
HUBERT   Why, know you not? The lords are all come back
    And brought Prince Henry[4] in their company,
35   At whose request the King hath pardoned them,
    And they are all about his majesty.

5.6 Location: Near Swinsted (Swineshead) Abbey.
1. TEXTUAL COMMENT For the allocation of speeches in lines 1–6, in particular the Bastard-like, feisty response of Hubert in line 3, see Digital Edition TC 7.
2. Bad memory (criticizing himself for not recognizing the Bastard).

3. A "resolvèd villain" since, as the person whose job it was to protect the King by tasting his food, he knowingly took poison himself just so that he could succeed in poisoning the King.
4. John's son; later, King Henry III.

BASTARD Withhold thine indignation, mighty heaven,
And tempt us not to bear above our power.[5]
I'll tell thee, Hubert, half my power this night,
40   Passing these flats, are taken° by the tide—   *drowned*
These Lincoln Washes[6] have devoured them.
Myself, well mounted, hardly° have escaped.   *barely; with trouble*
Away before:° conduct me to the King.   *Go on ahead*
I doubt° he will be dead or ere° I come.   *Exeunt.*   *fear / before*

5.7

Enter PRINCE HENRY, [*the Earl of*] SALISBURY, *and*
[*Lord*] BIGOT.

PRINCE HENRY It is too late. The life of all his blood
Is touched° corruptibly, and his pure° brain,   *infected / (once) lucid*
Which some suppose the soul's frail dwelling-house,
Doth by the idle° comments that it makes   *foolish*
5   Foretell the ending of mortality.°   *mortal life*
Enter [*the Earl of*] PEMBROKE.

PEMBROKE His highness yet doth speak and holds belief
That, being brought into the open air,
It would allay the burning quality
Of that fell° poison which assaileth him.   *savage*
10   PRINCE HENRY Let him be brought into the orchard here.
                                   [*Exit Lord* BIGOT.][1]
Doth he still rage?
PEMBROKE   He is more patient
Than when you left him; even° now he sung.   *just*
PRINCE HENRY Oh, vanity° of sickness! Fierce extremes°   *delusion / (of pain)*
In their continuance will not feel themselves.[2]
15   Death, having preyed upon the outward parts,°   *the body*
Leaves them invisible,[3] and his siege is now
Against the mind, the which he pricks and wounds
With many legions of strange fantasies,
Which in their throng and press to that last hold°   *stronghold (the mind)*
20   Confound° themselves. 'Tis strange that Death should sing.   *Destroy*
I am the cygnet° to this pale faint swan,   *young swan*
Who chants a doleful hymn to his own death,[4]
And from the organ-pipe° of frailty sings   *voice box*
His soul and body to their lasting rest.
25   SALISBURY Be of good comfort, Prince, for you are born
To set a form upon that indigest°   *chaos*
Which he hath left so shapeless and so rude.°   *unfinished*
                     [KING] JOHN [*is*] *brought in* [*by Lord* BIGOT].
KING JOHN Ay, marry, now° my soul hath elbow room;   *(now being outdoors)*
It would not out at° windows nor at doors.   *go out through*
30   There is so hot a summer in my bosom

---

5. And don't push us (or me) past our power to endure.
"Bear above our power" may also hint at the Bastard's
previous thoughts, here put aside, of assuming the
throne himself.
6. The tides of the Wash (tidal flatlands south of
Lincolnshire).
5.7 Location: The orchard of Swinsted (Swineshead)
Abbey.
1. F has no stage direction. Someone must fetch

John: either Bigot here or Pembroke after line 12.
2. By continuing for a long time will cease to be felt.
3. TEXTUAL COMMENT For the grounds for retaining
F's somewhat obscure reading "invisible" to describe
the workings of death, rather than adopting either of
the two frequently proposed emendations, "invincible" or "insensible," see Digital Edition TC 8.
4. John's swan song; swans were thought to sing only
as they died.

That all my bowels crumble up to dust.
I am a scribbled form drawn with a pen
Upon a parchment, and against° this fire°   *before / (of poison)*
Do I shrink up.

PRINCE HENRY   How fares your majesty?

35 KING JOHN   Poisoned, ill fare!° Dead, forsook, cast off;   *food; state of things*
And none of you will bid the winter come
To thrust his icy fingers in my maw,°   *stomach; mouth; throat*
Nor let my kingdom's rivers take their course
Through my burned bosom, nor entreat the North

40 To make his bleak winds kiss my parchèd lips
And comfort me with cold. I do not ask you much;
I beg cold° comfort, and you are so strait°   *slight; cooling / mean*
And so ingrateful you deny me that.

PRINCE HENRY   Oh, that there were some virtue° in my tears   *remedial power*
That might relieve you!

45 KING JOHN   The salt in them is hot.
Within me is a hell, and there the poison
Is, as a fiend, confined to tyrannize
On unreprievable condemnèd blood.

        Enter [the] BASTARD.

BASTARD   Oh, I am scalded with my violent motion°   *haste*
50 And spleen° of speed to see your majesty.   *impetuosity*

KING JOHN   O cousin, thou art come to set° mine eye.   *close*
The tackle° of my heart is cracked and burnt,   *rigging (heartstrings)*
And all the shrouds° wherewith my life should sail   *sail ropes*
Are turned to one thread, one little hair.

55 My heart hath one poor string to stay° it by,   *support*
Which holds but till thy news be utterèd,
And then all this thou seest is but a clod
And module° of confounded° royalty.   *counterfeit / destroyed*

BASTARD   The Dauphin is preparing° hitherward,   *coming*
60 Where heaven he knows how we shall answer him.
For in a° night the best part of my power,   *a single*
As I upon° advantage did remove,   *to gain*
Were in the Washes all unwarily
Devourèd by the unexpected flood.

        [KING JOHN *dies.*]

65 SALISBURY   You breathe these dead° news in as dead an ear.   *fatal*
[*to* KING JOHN] My liege, my lord! —But° now a king, now thus.   *Just*

PRINCE HENRY   Even so must I run on, and even so stop.
What surety of the world, what hope, what stay,°   *support; continuation*
When this was now a king and now is clay?

70 BASTARD [*to* KING JOHN]   Art thou gone so? I do but stay behind
To do the office° for thee of revenge,   *duty*
And then my soul shall wait on° thee to heaven,   *follow*
As it on earth hath been thy servant still.°   *always*
—Now, now, you stars,° that move in your right spheres,[5]   *(the nobles)*
75 Where be your powers?° Show now your mended faiths,°   *armies / loyalties*
And instantly return with me again
To push destruction and perpetual shame

---

5. Proper orbits, around the King, as the stars were thought to orbit the earth.

Out of the weak door of our fainting° land.   *dispirited*
Straight° let us seek, or straight we shall be sought;   *Immediately*
80   The Dauphin rages at our very heels.
      SALISBURY   It seems you know not then so much as we:
      The Cardinal Pandulph is within at rest,
      Who half an hour since came from the Dauphin,
      And brings from him such offers of our peace
85   As we with honor and respect may take,
      With purpose presently° to leave this war.   *immediately*
      BASTARD   He will the rather do it when he sees
      Ourselves well sinewed° to our defense.   *strongly armed*
      SALISBURY   Nay, 'tis in a manner done already,
90   For many carriages° he hath dispatched   *vehicles*
      To the seaside, and put his cause and quarrel
      To the disposing of the Cardinal,
      With° whom yourself, myself, and other lords,   *To*
      If you think meet,° this afternoon will post°   *fit / hurry*
95   To consummate° this business happily.   *conclude*
      BASTARD   Let it be so. —And you, my noble prince,
      With other princes° that may best be spared,   *nobles*
      Shall wait upon° your father's funeral.   *attend*
      PRINCE HENRY   At Worcester must his body be interred,
      For so he willed it.
100   BASTARD   Thither shall it then,
      And happily° may your sweet self put on   *with good fortune*
      The lineal state° and glory of the land,   *inherited kingship*
      To whom, with all submission, on my knee,
      I do bequeath° my faithful services   *give*
105   And true subjection everlastingly.
                [*He kneels.*]
      SALISBURY   And the like tender° of our love we make,   *offer*
      To rest° without a spot° for evermore.   *remain / blemish*
                [*The Earls of* SALISBURY *and* PEMBROKE *and Lord*
                BIGOT *kneel.*]
      PRINCE HENRY   I have a kind soul that would give thanks,
      And knows not how to do it but with tears.
110   BASTARD [*rises*]   Oh, let us pay the time but needful° woe,   *only the necessary*
      Since it hath been beforehand with our griefs.[6]
      This England never did, nor never shall,
      Lie at the proud foot of a conqueror
      But° when it first did help to wound itself.   *Except*
115   Now these her princes are come home again,
      Come the three corners of the world[7] in arms
      And we shall shock° them. Naught shall make us rue   *resist; repel*
      If England to itself do rest but true!   *Exeunt.*

6. Since we have already suffered and grieved—   fering is now over.
perhaps with the additional implication that the suf-   7. England itself is seen as the fourth corner.

The First Part of Henry the Fourth

A roadside inn that fails to provide chamber pots for its customers, a castle in Wales where a magician summons spirits to be his musicians, the royal palace in London from which the King of England launches a campaign against rebel forces—these are but a few of the disparate venues where the action of *1 Henry IV* occurs. With this drama, the Shakespearean history play broadens out to encompass a rich diversity of languages, characters, and locales. Nothing in Shakespeare's earlier English histories quite anticipates this one. The great prose chronicles of the sixteenth century, such as Raphael Holinshed's *Chronicles of England, Scotland, and Ireland* (2nd ed., 1587), which Shakespeare consulted and whose materials he freely adapted and supplemented, stand behind all his history plays. The earlier plays, however, like the chronicles, focus primarily on the world of court and battlefield in which the monarch and his nobles appear as history's significant players, their rivalries and their achievements the focal point of the action. Common people such as Jack Cade have roles in these works, but their stories are typically subordinated to the monarchical plot. In *1 Henry IV*, something different happens. Several lines of action unfold at once, each connected to particular geographical locales, and each commenting upon, without simply displacing, the others. Henry IV, who had seized the throne from Richard II, is the play's title character, but from the start he is a beleaguered figure kept from his dream of making a crusade to the Holy Land by discontent and rebellion among his nobles, especially the Percy family, and burdened with an oldest son, Prince Hal, who acts more like a prodigal child than the heir to the throne. The King appears in some key scenes, but for long stretches the action focuses on other characters and on places, like a common London tavern, that the King would never deign to visit.

Some events take place in the north of England, in the Northumberland stronghold of the Percy family. The play is set in the early fifteenth century, but even in the late sixteenth century the north of England was popularly regarded as lawless, wild, and linked to marginalized Catholic practices and beliefs, its nobility not fully incorporated into the increasingly centralized state being constructed by the Tudor monarchs. In 1569, members of the Percy family had been prominent in the Northern Rebellion, an attempt to overthrow Queen Elizabeth and put Mary Queen of Scots, a Catholic, on the throne. In drawing his portrait of the Percys, Shakespeare makes their champion, Hotspur, an impassioned embodiment of medieval chivalry, eager above all for honor and for the glory to be won in battle. While the historical Hotspur was actually much older than the King's son, Prince Hal, Shakespeare follows Samuel Daniel's poem *The Civil Wars Between the Two Houses of Lancaster and York* (1595) in making him Hal's coequal in years and his rival for preeminence in the kingdom. He is joined in rebellion by other figures from the threatening territories on the perimeter of England: by the Earl of Douglas, a formidable Scottish warrior, and by the Welshman Owain Glyndŵr, a self-proclaimed magician with a fiery temper, a lyrical sensibility, and a daughter who marries Edmund Mortimer, the man presented in this play as Richard II's designated heir to the throne. Wales thus harbors both rebellion and the man who was arguably the legitimate King of England.

Another of the play's crucial locales is a tavern in Eastcheap, a commercial district in the east of London. This tavern is Prince Hal's second home, where he comes to drink and amuse himself—and particularly to carouse with Falstaff, the dissipated knight who is the young Prince's tutor in folly, his intimate friend, and surrogate father. In Eastcheap, Hal rubs elbows with commoners such as Mistress Quickly, the Hostess of the tavern, and with Francis, the inarticulate apprentice tapster. Shakespeare took his cue about Hal's presence amid this crew from the many popular accounts of the Prince's dissolute youth, especially from a play printed in 1598 called *The Famous Victories of Henry the Fifth,* some version of which seems to have been staged in the late 1580s. It depicts not only episodes from Hal's madcap youth but also his eventual reformation and assumption of the throne. Shakespeare elaborated extensively on this story of youthful prodigality. Mistress Quickly, for example, is entirely his invention, and the character of Falstaff, while loosely modeled on a figure in *The Famous Victories,* is utterly transformed by Shakespeare into what has remained one of the great comic creations of the English theater. Witty, opportunistic, and utterly indifferent to the decorum expected of a knight of advanced years, Falstaff makes the tavern a place of perpetual play and the antithesis of the duty-driven world of the court. That the Prince seems irresistibly drawn to Eastcheap makes others, especially his father, question his fitness to rule, but the high-spirited playfulness of Falstaff's world suggests why the Prince might take refuge there from the demands of his public role and the exacting expectations of the King, his father.

From one perspective, *1 Henry IV* is a story about a young man growing up and deciding if he will follow in his father's footsteps or choose another path; if he wants his friends to be lively disreputable types or the respectable companions his father would choose. This is a common dilemma made uncommon by the fact that Hal is a prince, and on his choice depends the welfare of a kingdom. By making the tavern a place of high-spirited fun and Falstaff such a seductive figure, Shakespeare forces Hal's choice to be a difficult one. The Prince is the only character in the play who moves between the worlds of court, tavern, and battlefield. Something of a chameleon, he at times can seem at home in each, but at some point he must choose which will have his most lasting and decisive allegiance. On the way to that choice, however, Hal mixes with an extraordinary range of social types and classes.

One of the objections to English popular theater voiced by a contemporary poet, Sir Philip Sidney, was that it mingled clowns with kings in a way that violated codes of aesthetic and social decorum; these codes insisted on the strict separation of high and low subject matter, language, and people. In contrast to Sidney's dicta, *1 Henry IV* is thoroughly hybrid in its mingling of the high matter of rebellion and affairs of state with the low matter of drinking, jokes, and highway robbery. The play is also a temporal hybrid in that the tavern scenes seem to take place not in the early fifteenth century, when Henry IV was struggling to secure his rule, but in the late sixteenth century, when Shakespeare was actually writing his play. In the tavern scenes, for example, characters make fun of plays and modes of writing popular in the 1570s and 1580s, such as Thomas Preston's ranting tyrant play *Cambyses* (1569) and the baroquely ornate rhetoric popularized by John Lyly in his *Euphues* (1578). The tavern world is also filled with references to the commodities that passed through London's markets in the late sixteenth century. The characters there drink sack, Madeira, and bastard—popular alcoholic beverages, some (such as Madeira) imported from as far away as an island off the northwestern coast of Africa; and they refer to articles of clothing, such as the Spanish-leather wallets and leather jerkins with crystal buttons, worn by London's aspiring mercantile classes. Eastcheap itself, where the tavern is located, was a major market street in Shakespeare's London, and the tavern scenes are steeped in references to the commercial culture, including the theatrical culture, of early modern England.

There is every indication, however, that if a Sidney would have found the hybridity of the play a problem, ordinary consumers did not. Judging by its publication history, in its own time *1 Henry IV* was one of Shakespeare's most popular plays. It appeared in two quarto versions in 1598 and then in five more before the First Folio was printed in 1623. Even after that, individual quarto editions of the play continued to appear. The play's popularity probably stemmed from several factors: the comic appeal of

The historical Owain Glyndŵr claimed the title of Prince of Wales. His great seal, both sides of which are shown here, bears the inscription "Owain, by the grace of God, prince of Wales" and depicts four upreared (rampant) lions, the coat of arms of the Gwynedd dynasty, to which Glyndŵr belonged.

Falstaff; the poignancy of Prince Hal's dilemma, caught between duty and desire; and the variety of character types and settings the play affords. Structurally, *1 Henry IV* is not only modeled on chronicle history, which focuses on monarchs, nobles, and affairs of state, but also on chorography: a mode of writing popular in the late sixteenth century that described and surveyed the land of England focusing on the products, the terrain, and the customs of England's various regions. *1 Henry IV* is a chorography in the sense that the play's distinct lines of action are each defined in relation to specific places, customs, and social groups. The commercial, bawdy world of the tavern, with its cast of lowlife characters and its rituals of drinking and play, differs from the more formal milieu of Westminster, where the King and his nobles are immersed in the tasks of statecraft, and differs again from the world of passion and magic centered in Glyndŵr's Welsh castle. Through the multiple plots, the spectator watching the play experiences the illusion of complex temporal simultaneity and social and geographic heterogeneity. Thus, in successive scenes, the rebels, in Wales, plot the dismemberment of England and listen to a song sung in Welsh (3.1); King Henry, in Westminster, berates his wayward son (3.2); Falstaff, in Eastcheap, tries to cheat Mistress Quickly by claiming that his ring was stolen in her tavern (3.3). All these actions go on at the same time but in widely disparate locales, creating a theatrical illusion of the diversity encompassed by the ongoing life of the nation and its bordering regions.

But the play's complex elaboration of difference also makes evident its monarch's central problem: how to maintain control over and enforce unity upon the territories over which he claims dominion but which threaten to break away or assert a worrisome autonomy. As in *Henry V,* Shakespeare here dramatizes the tension between efforts at nation building and the cultural, religious, and political differences that promote fragmentation. The problem of furthering national unity is especially pressing for Henry IV because he did not lineally inherit the throne; he seized it from Richard II. He is on shaky ground, then, should he attempt to unify England under the banner of his own legitimacy. In fact, for much of the play Henry is a king in search of a strategy of rule. He had hoped to unify his people and quiet his conscience for his part in Richard's deposition and death by undertaking a crusade to recover Jerusalem for European Christianity. But trouble at home keeps him from enacting his plan as rebellion bubbles up on the Scottish border, on the Welsh border, in the northern counties, and even in the church, in the person of the Archbishop of York. The land seethes with the murmurings of rebels.

In the England of the 1590s, the monarch's most pressing problem of control was posed by Ireland; there, after 1595, the Earl of Tyrone led the challenge to English rule. Like Glyndŵr, Tyrone was educated in England and in some accounts was even Glyndŵr's descendant. While Ireland is not directly depicted in 1 Henry IV, Hotspur verbally links Wales and Ireland. Urged to listen to a song sung in Welsh, he says that he would rather hear his hunting dog "howl in Irish" (3.1.231), thereby confirming the common English view that Welsh and Irish were equally barbarous languages. More important, Wales stands in the play as a displaced image of the contemporary Irish situation. In the popular imagination, Wales often seemed a foreign place of mystery and danger, even though it had been officially incorporated into England in the 1530s and the Welsh language banned. In 1 Henry IV, Wales represents the threat not only of rebellion but also of effeminization and seduction. Mortimer, the supposed heir to the English throne, falls in love with Glyndŵr's daughter, promises to learn her language, and never appears on the battlefield against Henry's forces. In essence, he "goes native," a persistent fear voiced by the English concerning their soldiers and settlers in Ireland. The English had long worried that through prolonged contact with the Irish, English men and women might adopt their uncivilized ways and forfeit their English identity. They even feared that their children, in drinking the milk of Irish wet nurses, could be transformed into people more Irish than English.

In 1 Henry IV, the threat posed by the dangerous Welsh borderlands and by the northern Percy faction directly challenges the King's authority. Hampered by the questionable means by which he came to the throne, Henry invites his subjects to forget the shaky lineal legitimacy of his rule and to focus on his successes as a sitting king. Force and guile prove his most effective instruments for maintaining power. Henry can win battles, and he is willing to use deception to improve his position. At Shrewsbury, his major battle against the rebels, a number of Henry's nobles dress like the King, frustrating the enemy's ability to identify the true monarch and encouraging Henry's own forces by the seeming ubiquity of their leader. Perpetual battle, however, is a costly way to rule, and having many nobles dress like him runs counter to Henry's stated belief that the King should be seldom seen in order to be the more wondered at when he does appear. To have many men marching in the King's clothing and answering to the King's name might, in fact, subversively suggest that "King" is a part any man could play, given the right accoutrements.

Prince Hal faces the pressing task of finding better strategies for ruling the changed world his father brought into being by his deposition of King Richard. Hal cannot assume that his kingship will be uncontested simply because he is Henry's son. A usurper's offspring has more legitimacy than a usurper, but not much. Rather, Hal must *make* himself King by a convincing performance of the part, and he must beat out those who would be his rivals, such as Harry Hotspur. Viewed one way, 1 Henry IV is a study in the political and theatrical skills necessary for rule in a world where the inevitability and assumed legitimacy of inherited kingship has been called into question. In 1532, Niccolò Machiavelli's The Prince, a manual of practical statecraft, was published and quickly became notorious throughout Europe. Machiavelli taught rulers how to maintain their power through a mixture of guile, alliance, warfare, and personal force of character. Popularly viewed as irreligious and amoral, Machiavelli nonetheless was a byword for political pragmatism.

In his sophisticated manipulation of power, Hal shows himself a good student of Machiavelli, and the Machiavellian strand of his characterization has caused a split in critical assessments of him. To many scholars, Hal personifies the ideal English king, the perfect mean between the self-indulgence of a Falstaff and the impassioned inflexibility of a Hotspur. He is thus an object of desire and emulation. Other critics focus on what they perceive as a lack of humanity at the heart of this consummate politician and recoil from his calculated use of other people to serve his own ends. For example, at the end of the first scene in which he appears, Hal in soliloquy speaks about his tavern mates:

> I know you all, and will a while uphold
> The unyoked humor of your idleness.
> Yet herein will I imitate the sun,
> Who doth permit the base contagious clouds
> To smother up his beauty from the world,
> That, when he please again to be himself,
> Being wanted he may be more wondered at
> By breaking through the foul and ugly mists
> Of vapors that did seem to strangle him.
> (1.2.170–78)

These lines reveal the calculation that is one part of this character's representation. Comparing himself to the royal symbol, the sun, Hal casts his companions as the contaminating clouds and ugly mists that temporarily obscure his own radiance. Hal is chillingly disdainful of those he elsewhere treats as boon companions, but he also finds their baseness *useful*, since it will set in high relief his own glory, once he has cast them off.

Hal is an interesting dramatic character and not merely a personification of political expediency, however, precisely because his calculated use of his companions does not necessarily preclude his being attracted to them and to the world of play and good fellowship that they represent. In *1 Henry IV*, Hal is not yet king, and the moment of repudiation is not yet upon him. In this play, he can both enjoy his time in Eastcheap and also acquire skills there that he will need when he ascends his father's troubled throne. In the tavern, for example, he and Falstaff take turns playing King and Prince in a theatrical staging of the prodigal Hal's encounter with his reproving father. Hal rehearses the cadences and the sentiments of royal speech, trying out a part, learning to inhabit it convincingly. But it is not just his own part he masters. Unlike his father, Hal does not hold himself aloof from his would-be subjects. His ventures into Eastcheap are in part a mapping of one corner of England, a survey of the customs and strange languages of this locale. To Ned Poins he boasts that having been instructed by three tapsters in the terminology of drinking, "I can drink with any tinker in his own language during my life" (2.4.16–17).

In the tavern, Hal also meditates on the strange tongue of his great rival, Hotspur, whose impatient but impassioned speech Hal parodies:

> I am not yet of Percy's mind, the Hotspur of the North, he that kills me some six or seven dozen of Scots at a breakfast, washes his hands, and says to his wife, "Fie upon this quiet life! I want work." "O my sweet Harry," says she, "how many hast thou killed today?" "Give my roan horse a drench," says he, and answers, "Some fourteen," an hour after, "A trifle, a trifle." I prithee call in Falstaff. I'll play Percy, and that damned brawn shall play Dame Mortimer his wife. (2.4.93–101)

Learning the language of others and rehearsing their tongues is, for Hal, one of the arts of power. He can—and later he will—repudiate some of those whose language and customs he has imbibed, making the repudiation a justification for his own rule. Knowing disorderliness, the King will use his office to punish it. He can also appropriate the language of others, as at Shrewsbury he appropriates the chivalric accents of Hotspur; or he can co-opt others to serve his own purposes by speaking to them in a tongue they can comprehend. By his own account, Hal is beloved of the tapsters who have taught him their language, and they have promised that when he is king, he "shall command all the good lads in Eastcheap" (2.4.12–13). Many of them he will eventually command in his wars in France. It can be argued, therefore, that there is a profound instrumentality to Hal's sojourn outside the court. He is acquiring theatrical skills, listening skills, linguistic skills, and above all a knowledge of the diverse corners of an England he must rule by a mixture of charm, guile, and strategic

This knight suggests Shakespeare's portrait of the chivalric heroes Prince Hal and Hotspur at the battle of Shrewsbury. From Henry Peacham's *Minerva Britanna* (1612).

severity—demonizing some subjects to win the loyalty of others, outstripping rivals by outdoing them at their own particular strengths. While all this may be true, it does not erase the countervailing perception of many readers and audiences that Hal is also genuinely attracted to the tavern world and its inhabitants and that abandoning them will cost him dearly. Nor does awareness of Hal's calculating side erase the exquisite courtesy with which he treats the corpse of Hotspur at Shrewsbury. With nobody watching and so nobody to impress or persuade, the Prince articulates a moving tribute to his dead foe and covers his "mangled face" (5.4.95). What to make of Hal is a question the play both solicits and makes difficult to answer, partly because Hal can never be separated, in his mind or ours, from his role as heir apparent to the throne of England. This makes him an object of scrutiny, certainly, but makes it hard to discern whether he ever acts without a calculated awareness of a political imperative.

1 Henry IV puts the question of values at the heart of its action. How valuable and important is the life of public duty for which Hal seems destined? What is won and lost by its pursuit? The play's defining structural principle—the repeated juxtaposition of one locale and one set of characters against another—keeps these questions to the fore. Consider, for example, 3.1 and 3.2, the play's central scenes, which take the audience first to Glyndŵr's castle in Wales, where he, Hotspur, Mortimer, and Worcester are plotting their rebellion, and then to the King's palace at Westminster to which Henry has summoned his son. The first scene graphically establishes the kingdom-cleaving threat posed by the rebels. They have a map and are planning how they will divide the territory of England into three parts. But the scene also establishes the danger, mystery, and beauty of this borderland. Glyndŵr is a man trained in occult arts who boasts that the earth shook at his birth and that he can summon spirits to do his bidding. Hotspur scoffs, but when Glyndŵr's daughter promises to sing in Welsh, Glyndŵr says:

> Do so, and those musicians that shall play to you
> Hang in the air a thousand leagues from hence,
> And straight they shall be here. Sit and attend.
> (3.1.219–21)

Three lines later, music plays, its origins a mystery. When Glyndŵr speaks, Wales seems a land of enchantment, haunted by spirits.

Wales is also a place where women are integral to the action as they seldom are elsewhere in the play. Except for Mistress Quickly, Kate Percy and Glyndŵr's daughter are the play's only two female characters; and 3.1, the play's only scene in which two women are onstage at the same time, is set in Wales and is largely Shakespeare's invention. In the chronicles, Glyndŵr, Mortimer, and Hotspur's proposed division of conquered territory is negotiated by representatives in the Archbishop of Bangor's house. By contrast, in *1 Henry IV* it occurs at Glyndŵr's home with the women present. In short, Shakespeare went to some trouble to link the rebels with women—more specifically, with wives and daughters. The question is why. In part, the choice portrays the rebels, unlike the Lancastrians, as having private as well as public lives.

Glyndŵr is fond of his daughter and worries about her happiness. Mortimer dotes on this daughter and seems to have married her for love as much as for political alliance. Hotspur's affection for his wife is displayed through the teasing banter with which he persistently addresses her. Scornful of mooning lovers, he nonetheless is careful to take his wife with him when he journeys to Wales.

The passions so nakedly on display in 3.1 clearly signal the rebels' vulnerabilities. In the patriarchal thought of the period, men were presented as superior to women because they were supposedly more rational and less subject to their passions. If men loved women too much, they risked becoming effeminate—that is, *like* a woman in placing desire above reason, especially if that desire kept a man from performing his public duties, such as going to war. Hotspur prizes his masculinity and the public honor to be won in battle. He is contemptuous of the affected courtier who appeared at Holmedon after the fighting, demanding Hotspur's prisoners (1.3.29–69). In his dealings with his wife, Hotspur seems to use banter and jokes to maintain, with difficulty, control of his affection for her. He would not, for a woman, forgo the man-to-man erotics of battle when, "hot horse to horse" (4.1.121), he clashes against the bosom of Prince Hal. Mortimer, by contrast, simply succumbs to the charms of the Welsh woman. He never appears in battle: Wales and a wife swallow him up.

This Welsh world of danger, mystery, and passion sits strangely against the world of calculation that unfolds immediately thereafter, when in 3.2 King Henry castigates Prince Hal for his dissolute life and together they discuss strategies of monarchical self-presentation. The throne room is a place not of enchantment but of business. No women are shown at court, and passion manifests itself most strongly as the desire to rule. Father and son are both preoccupied with the tactics and strategies by which they can most effectively command the loyalty of subjects. While Henry fears that his son misunderstands the task before him, Hal shows that he is every bit as astute as his father. But after the high emotions and alluring lyricism of the Welsh scene, the throne room at Westminster can seem a pragmatic and claustrophobic space. In concentrating their energies on rule, Henry and Hal here are divorced from many things that give the rebel world its charm.

Falstaff and the tavern pose a different challenge to the values of Westminster. As critics have shown, the fat man's tutoring of Hal in riotous living mimics the pedagogical relationship of master to student that was sometimes eroticized in the early modern period. Much of the poignancy of the play's depiction of the friendship between the two comes from the tension between their apparent intimacy and the Prince's stated intention to repudiate his companion. Falstaff's threat to monarchical values is obvious. Against the future-oriented calculations of Hal and his father, he insists on living in the present. As his huge body testifies, he demands the immediate gratification of physical desires. To eat, drink, and jest—these are pleasures that for Falstaff brook no delay. Hal can discipline himself. He is thin, as Falstaff points out, and he can plot a personal reformation sometime far in the future and work toward that end. Falstaff cannot or will not; and yet, while a figure of disorder, he has for many readers been the play's most interesting and memorable character. Aside from Hamlet, no other Shakespearean figure has attracted as much critical attention as the fat knight.

When Shakespeare first wrote the play, he called this character "Sir John Oldcastle." The choice was unfortunate, for the Cobham family, descendants of the historical Oldcastle, protested. William Brooke, the tenth Baron Cobham, had been Lord Chamberlain from August 1596 to March 1597, the very months when most scholars believe Shakespeare completed *1 Henry IV*. Since the Lord Chamberlain oversaw the licensing of plays through the office of the Master of the Revels, Cobham was in an especially favorable position to object to this comic rendition of his ancestor. Shakespeare apparently changed the character's name in response to this act of censorship, though traces of his original intentions can be discerned, including the fact that in 1.2.37 Falstaff is still referred to as "my old lad of the castle." In addition, in the first complete quarto of *1 Henry IV*, there are a few traces of the fact that Peto once bore the name "Harvey," and Bardolph the name "Russell." Again, the objections of powerful figures may have forced changes. "Russell" was the family name of the prominent earls of Bedford, and "Harvey" the name of the stepfather of the Earl of Southampton.

Shakespeare may originally have chosen to name his fat knight "Oldcastle" because of that figure's place in the religious controversies of the time. The historical Oldcastle was a knight who served Henry IV in battle in both France and Wales, but who was also a Lollard; that is, he was connected with the religious group often seen as a forerunner of English Protestantism for its critiques of the Catholic Church and its advocacy of a vernacular Bible to be made available to laypeople. At first, Henry IV treated Oldcastle's religious views leniently, but eventually he was sent to the Tower of London and condemned as a heretic by the Archbishop of Canterbury. He escaped, and Henry was warned that Oldcastle was leading an armed force against him. Oldcastle was captured in 1417 and eventually hung in chains and then burned on the gallows.

In the sixteenth century, how one viewed Oldcastle depended largely on one's religious perspective. To many zealous Protestants, such as John Foxe, Oldcastle was a Protestant hero, a victim of Catholic oppression rather than a traitor; Foxe included Oldcastle in his *Book of Martyrs*. But by the 1590s, Lollards were also sometimes linked with "extremist" Protestant groups pushing for radical reforms in the Church of England. Making a well-known Lollard martyr a fat figure of disorder could therefore be a way of suggesting the hypocrisy of zealous reformers. In other plays, especially in his portrait of Malvolio in *Twelfth Night*, Shakespeare makes fun of "puritans" who claimed a greater righteousness and strictness of life than their more moderate contemporaries. In *1 Henry IV*, Falstaff is a glutton and lover of sack whose language is liberally studded with biblical quotations, most of which he misapplies or contradicts by his behavior. Thus, he tells Hal that one must labor in one's vocation (1.2.91–92), an injunction found in 1 Corinthians 7:20 and in Ephesians 4:1. But the vocation in which *he* would labor is that of thief—not exactly what Protestant divines meant when discussing the virtues of a vocation.

The name Shakespeare fastened upon to replace Oldcastle had its own history. The historical Fastolf (1378?–1459) was a courageous officer in Henry VI's war in France, though in some chronicles he appears erroneously to have been called a coward, a detail that Shakespeare repeats in *1 Henry VI*. Having once used the name without repercussion in the former play, Shakespeare might have felt it was safe to employ it as a replacement for "Oldcastle" and to play upon the figure's reputation for cowardice.

It reduces the complexity of Falstaff as a comic creation, however, to tie him too closely to any historical counterpart. In his fat person a rich amalgam of popular and literary traditions converge. In part, he resembles the irreverent Vice figure from the medieval morality plays. Traditionally, the Vice, a comic and clever character, tempted the hero to sin while voices of virtue or duty tried to steer him along a more reputable path. In *1 Henry IV*, Hal is torn between his allegiances to Falstaff and his father, to vice and virtue, to the tavern and the court. Falstaff also conjures up the topsy-turvy world of Carnival in which rulers were temporarily displaced and the body's pleasures (eating, drinking, breaking wind, having sex) were celebrated before the arrival of abstemious Lent. The unending jokes about Falstaff's fat paunch highlight his symbolic connection to bodily excess, and his contempt for the law and for military duty make him the antithesis of the King and a perpetual emblem of disorder. In creating Falstaff, Shakespeare also drew on the figure from classical tradition of the braggart warrior who is really a coward. At Shrewsbury, Falstaff plays the coward, and yet he falsely claims credit for having killed Hotspur. The gap between his words and his deeds is enormous, though in this instance, as in many others, the Prince graciously does not reveal this lie for what it is.

Above all, however, Falstaff embodies traditions of popular critique associated with the stage clown. In early productions, Will Kemp, the famous clown in Shakespeare's company, probably played the part. Sometimes speaking from a downstage position near the audience, the clown traditionally poked fun at upstage authority figures. Falstaff does so in spades, whether mocking the elevated speech of King Henry or twitting Hal for being so skinny. But Falstaff is more than a gadfly or a parasite swollen fat on others' folly. He also embodies a mode of being in the world that serves as a powerful alternative both to the calculations of Hal and to Hotspur's headlong, death-courting pursuit of honor. For example, before the Battle of Shrewsbury Falstaff meditates witheringly on just what honor means and on its value:

Falstaff and Prince Hal. Pen and watercolor drawing on paper by William Blake (ca. 1780).

> Can honor set to a leg? No. Or an arm? No. Or take away the grief of a wound? No. Honor hath no skill in surgery, then? No. What is honor? A word. What is in that word "honor"? What is that "honor"? Air. A trim reckoning! Who hath it? He that died o'Wednesday. Doth he feel it? No. Doth he hear it? No. 'Tis insensible, then? Yea, to the dead. But will it not live with the living? No. Why? Detraction will not suffer it. Therefore I'll none of it. Honor is a mere scutcheon. And so ends my catechism. (5.1.130–39)

Others, like Hotspur, find honor worth dying for, and generations of soldiers have gone into battle believing the same thing. But for Falstaff, honor is worth the loss of neither a leg nor a life. During the ensuing battle, Falstaff carries a bottle of sack in his pistol case and ingloriously feigns death when attacked by Douglas. But though Hotspur and others are slain, Falstaff rises up. He embraces neither honor nor death, but life, and many readers and theatergoers have cheered his choice while others have been repulsed by his opportunism and cowardice.

The events before, during, and after the Battle of Shrewsbury occupy much of the play's final act. Shrewsbury is the one locale where many of the play's otherwise widely dispersed characters come together as the King, Prince Hal, Hotspur, the other rebels, and even Falstaff assemble in one spot. Shrewsbury is a kind of testing ground where the audience is invited to judge the relative worth of the values embraced by these different characters. Perhaps the character set off to best advantage is Prince Hal. Shrewsbury is his happiest hour. During the battle, he finds a way to redeem his reputation and distinguish himself from Falstaff without repudiating his friend, even when Falstaff brazenly lies about his role in the battle. And while Hal defeats Hotspur, he also pays moving homage to his rival's courage and chivalric accomplishments. But the equipoise of this battle's conclusion is precarious. Hal is not yet king, and the demands of that role still lie before him. Falstaff has not reformed and probably never will. And the rebels have not been destroyed. Hotspur is dead, but the Archbishop of York, Glyndŵr, and Mortimer are still in arms. In other words, it is an illusion that Hal has carried all before him. In the corners and crevices of the realm, dissension and difference remain. In such conditions, the work of rule is a performance with no end.

JEAN E. HOWARD

SELECTED BIBLIOGRAPHY

Baldo, Jonathan. "All Is Truancy: Rebellious Uses of the Past in *1 Henry IV.*" Chapter 2 of *Memory in Shakespeare's Histories: Stages of Forgetting in Early Modern England*. New York: Routledge, 2012. 51–72. Explores how Falstaff, Hotspur, and Hal, in particular, manipulate remembering and forgetting in the construction of the nation or in challenges to it.

Barber, C. L. "Rule and Misrule in *Henry IV.*" *Shakespeare's Festive Comedy: A Study of Dramatic Form and Its Relation to Social Custom*. Princeton, NJ Princeton UP, 1959. 192–221. Explores the ritual subtext of *Henry IV, Parts 1* and *2*, arguing that Falstaff becomes a scapegoat whose banishment rids the community of bad luck.

Barker, Roberta. "Tragical-Comical-Historical Hotspur." *Shakespeare Quarterly* 54 (2003): 288–307. Examines how Hotspur has been interpreted through the centuries and argues that the role is central to the play's examination of masculine heroism.

Botelho, Keith. "Bruits and Britons: Rumor, Counsel, and the Henriad." Chapter 2 of *Renaissance Earwitnesses: Rumor and Early Modern Masculinity*. New York: Palgrave Macmillan, 2009. 49–73. Discusses the role of discerning listening in successful kingship with special attention to Prince Hal's acquisition of listening skills and to his ability both to perceive rumor and to use it.

Grady, Hugh. "The Resistance to Power in *1 Henry IV*: Subjectivity in the World." Chapter 4 of *Shakespeare, Machiavelli, and Montaigne: Power and Subjectivity from Richard II to Hamlet*. Oxford: Oxford UP, 2002. 126–79. Argues that in *1 Henry IV* Prince Hal is divided between a commitment to Machiavellian power politics and the world of play and aesthetic freedom that Grady sees embodied in Falstaff.

Greenblatt, Stephen. "Invisible Bullets." *Shakespearean Negotiations: The Circulation of Social Energy in Renaissance England*. Berkeley: U of California P, 1988. 21–65. Discusses how Renaissance texts such as Thomas Hariot's *A Brief and True Report of the New Found Land of Virginia* and Shakespeare's *1 Henry IV* subvert their culture's dominant values regarding religious belief and political authority and yet contain or mitigate the doubts they raise.

Highley, Christopher. "Wales, Ireland, and *1 Henry IV.*" *Renaissance Drama*, n.s., 21 (1990): 91–114. Discusses England's Elizabethan wars in Ireland as a subtext for *1 Henry IV* and Glyndŵr as a displaced image of the Irish leader Hugh O'Neill, Earl of Tyrone.

Howard, Jean E., and Phyllis Rackin. "Gender and Nation: Anticipations of Modernity in the Second Tetralogy." *Engendering a Nation: A Feminist Account of Shakespeare's English Histories*. London: Routledge, 1997. 137–215. Focuses on the disruptive role of women in the play—both the Welsh women, including Glyndŵr's daughter, and the women of the Eastcheap tavern.

Kastan, David Scott. "'The King Hath Many Marching in His Coats'; or, What Did You Do during the War, Daddy?" *Shakespeare Left and Right*. Ed. Ivo Kamps. New York: Routledge, 1991. 241–58. Argues that the theater does not just reproduce the political ideologies of the powerful but instead makes space for unauthorized and heterogeneous views, including, in *Henry IV*, the view that kingship itself is just a role.

McMillin, Scott. *Henry IV, Part One*. Shakespeare in Performance series. Manchester: Manchester UP, 1991. Analyzes theatrical, film, and television performances of *1 Henry IV* in the second half of the twentieth century, arguing that this is the period when Hal, rather than Falstaff or Hotspur, became the focus of critical and theatrical attention.

FILMS

Chimes at Midnight. 1965. Dir. Orson Welles. 115 min. Spain. In black and white, the film combines scenes from several plays to focus on Falstaff and his relationship with Prince Hal. An imaginative and moving adaptation, it boasts memorable performances by Welles as Falstaff, John Gielgud as Henry IV, and Keith Baxter as the Prince.

Henry IV, Part 1. 1979. Dir. David Giles. 155 min. UK. This BBC-TV production features strong performances by Anthony Quayle as Falstaff and Tim Pigott-Smith as Hotspur in an otherwise dutifully faithful version of the play.

My Own Private Idaho. 1991. Dir. Gus Van Sant. 102 min. USA. Set in modern-day Portland, Oregon, and loosely based on the *Henry IV* plays, the film stars River Phoenix and Keanu Reeves as two young men who for a time join William Richert, the Falstaff figure, in a life of dissipation.

Henry IV, Part 1. 2012. Dir. Richard Eyre. This second part of *The Hollow Crown* is a top-flight PBS-TV Great Performances production with Simon Russell Beale as a wonderfully smart and ingratiating Falstaff, a stern and forceful Jeremy Irons as Henry IV, and a sensitive and intelligent Tom Hiddleston as Prince Hal. Set in winter, the Shrewsbury scenes depict the unglamorous side of war.

TEXTUAL INTRODUCTION

This edition is based on the earliest extant printing of the entire play: the First Quarto (Q1). Published in 1598 by Andrew Wise and printed by Peter Short, Q1 was in fact preceded by an earlier quarto, known as Q0. Unfortunately, all that remains of Q0, also printed by Peter Short in 1598, is a four-leaf fragment (C1–C4) that was discovered in the binding of a copy of William Thomas's *Rules of the Italian Grammar* (1567) in the mid-nineteenth century and is now in the Folger Shakespeare Library. Comparison of these two earliest printings indicates that Q1 was set from Q0. The priority of Q0 would normally mean that it, rather than its successor, would have greater authority and thus serve as the basis of a modern edition produced according to the principles of single-text editing. However, since Q0 cannot perform this function because it provides only a small fraction of the entire text, Q1 is the obvious choice as base text for *The Norton Shakespeare*. Fortunately, there are very few substantive differences between Q1 and Q0 (see Digital Edition TC 8).

Q1 was followed by a series of quartos each printed from its predecessor: Q2 (1599), Q3 (1604), Q4 (1608), Q5 (1613). Though the title page of Q2 advertises it as "Newly corrected by *W. Shakespeare*," there is little evidence that the changes, which include the correction of misprints in Q1, are actually authorial. Indeed, the various changes made in Q2 are all well within the capacity of a compositor or corrector working directly from Q1. The quality of these changes, along with the failure to correct some obvious errors, does not support the title-page claim that they are authorial corrections. Though subsequent quartos continue to introduce minor changes, there is no reason to grant any of them independent authority.

The status of the Folio (F) text printed in 1623 has occasioned greater controversy. Scholars generally agree that F was based on a corrected copy of Q5. However, the source and authority of these alterations have been variously characterized. One possibility is that the editors of F, Heminges and Condell, drew on a theatrical prompt-book (either directly or in the form of a literary transcript) to make changes to Q5. Many of the changes in F are worthy of consideration, but the case for a prompt-book source is not compelling, nor is it necessary. As with the changes visible in the quarto line of transmission, the changes in F do not exceed the capacity of an intelligent editor. As such, they only merit consideration in cases where Q1 is evidently deficient. For this reason, *The Norton Shakespeare* does not treat *1 Henry IV* as a two-text play, and so does not include a Folio-based text.

Though the play as presented in Q1 is remarkably clear, there are indications that it underwent a process of revision. The major evidence in support of this theory is the renaming of several characters as well as some uncertainty in the depiction of minor figures. Though traces of this revision remain, they do not present an intractable problem. Q1, after all, represents a slightly revised version of the play first written by Shakespeare, and a modern edition prepared according to the principles of single-text editing will aim to present a clear version of this revised state of the text and will remove accidental remnants of the earlier version in order to ensure internal consistency.

JESSE M. LANDER

PERFORMANCE NOTE

Few plays gain so much in the transition from page to stage as *1 Henry IV*. The prime beneficiary of performance is Falstaff, whose vivacity and inventiveness are accessible to readers, but who generates extraordinary pathos onstage when insecurities about his diminishing importance to Hal seem to underlie his large persona. In performance, Falstaff's charm and jollity are often interspersed with moments of tenderness and introspection, embarrassment or envy, which can make him as much a source of dramatic tension as of laughter. In addition to striking a balance between Falstaff's comedy and pathos, productions make critical decisions about his analogic relationship to King Henry and his rapport with Hal. A patient, pious Henry can help portray Falstaff as a depraved Vice figure that Hal must overcome, while a disgruntled or domineering king can render Falstaff an appealing alternative, a surrogate father who offers the compassion and charm that Henry lacks. In either case, Falstaff can be mercenary or sincere in his affection, while Hal can treat his friend with warmth or condescension, his jokes amounting to good-natured ribbing or biting sarcasm.

Productions must also address Hal's poor treatment of Poins and Francis, as well as explain his decision to exploit the degeneracy of his friends so as to appear noble by comparison (see Digital Edition PC 2), behavior that can cause audiences to resist allying themselves to the protagonist. Some productions excuse Hal's practical jokes and condescension by presenting the tavern as debauched and full of caricatures; others moderate his abusive language by underplaying it or exaggerating the festive atmosphere of Eastcheap, sometimes suggesting that Hal takes refuge there from an austere and joyless court. The contrast in settings applies to the rebel camp in Wales too: a production that emphasizes its infighting can argue the nobility and order at Henry's court, while one that lingers over the intimate exchanges between Hotspur and his wife, along with Glyndŵr's fatherly tenderness, can illuminate dysfunction and the dearth of feminine voices on the English side. Hotspur's portrayal is pivotal, since he can appear as the macho ranter that Hal imagines or the princely son that Henry envies, in either case affecting the audience's alliances at Shrewsbury and its appreciation of Hal's triumph.

BRETT GAMBOA

The History of Henry the Fourth

[THE PERSONS OF THE PLAY

KING Henry IV
PRINCE Harry (also Hal), Prince of Wales ⎫
Lord John of LANCASTER   ⎬ sons to King Henry
Earl of WESTMORLAND   ⎭
Sir Walter BLOUNT

Henry Percy, Earl of NORTHUMBERLAND
Thomas Percy, Earl of WORCESTER, younger brother to Northumberland
Sir Henry Percy, known as HOTSPUR, son to Northumberland
Kate, LADY PERCY, wife to Hotspur
Lord Edward MORTIMER, brother to Lady Percy
LADY MORTIMER, daughter to Glyndŵr and wife to Mortimer
Owain GLYNDWR, a Welsh nobleman

Earl of DOUGLAS
Sir Richard VERNON
Richard Scrope, ARCHBISHOP of York
SIR MICHAEL, a member of the Archbishop's household

Sir John FALSTAFF
Edward (Ned) POINS
BARDOLPH
PETO
GADSHILL
CHAMBERLAIN
FRANCIS, a drawer
VINTNER
HOSTESS, Mistress Quickly

SHERIFF
FIRST CARRIER
SECOND CARRIER
FIRST TRAVELER
SECOND TRAVELER
OSTLER
MESSENGERS
SERVANT
Attendants, Soldiers]

1.1

Enter the KING, *Lord John of* LANCASTER,
Earl of WESTMORLAND, *with others.*

KING   So shaken as we are, so wan° with care,   *pale*
    Find we° a time for frighted peace to pant   *Let us find*

1.1 Location: The palace, London.

And breathe short-winded accents° of new broils   *words*
To be commenced in strands afar remote.[1]
5   No more the thirsty entrance° of this soil   *parched mouth*
Shall daub her lips with her own children's blood;
No more shall trenching° war channel° her fields,   *cutting / furrow*
Nor bruise her flow'rets with the armèd hoofs
Of hostile paces.° Those opposèd eyes—   *horses' footsteps*
10   Which, like the meteors of a troubled heaven,[2]
All of one nature, of one substance bred,
Did lately meet in the intestine° shock   *internal*
And furious close° of civil butchery—   *hand-to-hand combat*
Shall now, in mutual well-beseeming° ranks,   *orderly*
15   March all one way and be no more opposed
Against acquaintance, kindred, and allies.
The edge of war, like an ill-sheathèd knife,
No more shall cut his master. Therefore, friends,
As far as to the sepulcher of Christ—
20   Whose soldier now, under whose blessèd cross
We are impressèd° and engaged to fight—   *conscripted*
Forthwith a power of English shall we levy,°   *raise*
Whose arms were molded in their mothers' womb
To chase these pagans in those holy fields
25   Over whose acres walked those blessèd feet
Which fourteen hundred years ago were nailed
For our advantage on the bitter cross.
But this our purpose now is twelve month old,
And bootless° 'tis to tell you we will go.   *useless*
30   Therefor° we meet not now. Then let me hear   *On that account*
Of you, my gentle cousin° Westmorland,   *noble kinsman*
What yesternight our Council did decree
In forwarding this dear expedience.°   *urgent undertaking*
WESTMORLAND   My liege, this haste was hot in question,°   *under urgent debate*
35   And many limits of the charge[3] set down
But yesternight, when all athwart° there came   *at cross-purposes*
A post° from Wales, loaden with heavy news,   *messenger*
Whose worst was that the noble Mortimer,
Leading the men of Herefordshire to fight
40   Against the irregular[4] and wild Glyndŵr,[5]
Was by the rude hands of that Welshman taken,
A thousand of his people butcherèd,
Upon whose dead corpse° there was such misuse,   *corpses*
Such beastly shameless transformation,[6]
45   By those Welshwomen done, as may not be
Without much shame retold or spoken of.

1. On distant shores. King Henry is alluding to the Holy Land, to which he vowed to lead a crusade at the close of *Richard II*.
2. Unusual events in the sky, such as comets or shooting stars, were thought to portend strife and disaster.
3. Many particulars concerning responsibilities and expenses.
4. Glyndŵr is probably "irregular" in the sense of using guerrilla tactics in his warfare; possibly, the word alludes to his alleged sorcery.
5. TEXTUAL COMMENT The first full quarto and the 1623 Folio (F) versions of *1 Henry IV* use the angli-

cized name, Owen Glendower, for the Welsh lord. This edition modernizes the name to the contemporary Welsh form Owain Glyndŵr. See Digital Edition TC 1.
6. Mutilation. Holinshed's 1587 *Chronicles*, one of Shakespeare's sources, says the Welsh women's acts on this occasion were too shameful to relate; but contemporary editor Abraham Fleming, in the same edition of the *Chronicles*, includes an account of another battle in which Welsh women cut off the sexual organs and the noses of conquered enemies and put them, respectively, in the mouths and anuses of those enemies.

KING It seems then that the tidings of this broil
 Brake° off our business for the Holy Land.   *Broke*
WESTMORLAND This matched with other did, my gracious lord,
50 For more uneven° and unwelcome news   *disturbing*
 Came from the North, and thus it did import:
 On Holy Rood Day,[7] the gallant Hotspur there—
 Young Harry Percy—and brave Archibald,
 That ever valiant and approvèd° Scot,   *worthy*
55 At Humbleton[8] met, where they did spend
 A sad and bloody hour,
 As by° discharge of their artillery   *As judging by*
 And shape of likelihood° the news was told;   *And probable outcome*
 For he that brought them° in the very heat   *(the news)*
60 And pride° of their contention did take horse,   *height*
 Uncertain of the issue° any way.   *outcome*
KING Here is a dear, a true industrious friend,
 Sir Walter Blount,[9] new lighted from his horse,
 Stained with the variation of each soil
65 Betwixt that Humbleton and this seat° of ours;   *dwelling*
 And he hath brought us smooth° and welcome news.   *agreeable*
 The Earl of Douglas is discomfited.°   *defeated*
 Ten thousand bold Scots, two-and-twenty knights
 Balked° in their own blood, did Sir Walter see   *Heaped up; thwarted*
70 On Humbleton's plains. Of prisoners Hotspur took
 Murdoch Earl of Fife and eldest son
 To beaten Douglas,[1] and the Earl of Atholl,
 Of Moray, Angus, and Menteith.
 And is not this an honorable spoil?
 A gallant prize? Ha, cousin, is it not?
75 WESTMORLAND   In faith,
 It is a conquest for a prince to boast of.
KING Yea, there thou mak'st me sad, and mak'st me sin
 In envy that my lord Northumberland
 Should be the father to so blest a son,
80 A son who is the theme of honor's tongue,
 Amongst a grove the very straightest plant,
 Who is sweet Fortune's minion° and her pride;   *favorite*
 Whilst I, by looking on the praise of him,
 See riot and dishonor stain the brow
85 Of my young Harry. Oh, that it could be proved
 That some night-tripping fairy had exchanged
 In cradle clothes our children where they lay[2]
 And called mine "Percy," his "Plantagenet";[3]
 Then would I have his Harry, and he mine.
90 But let him° from my thoughts. What think you, coz,°   *let him go / kinsman*
 Of this young Percy's pride? The prisoners
 Which he in this adventure hath surprised°   *captured*

---

7. Holy Cross Day, September 14.
8. Humbleton in Northumberland was the site in 1402 of a Scottish invasion of England.
9. It is not clear whether Blount comes onstage now. He could have entered at the beginning of the scene; alternatively, as in this edition, he may not come onstage at all. Blount has no lines in the scene, and Henry could at this point receive a letter containing Blount's news or could be reporting news he has already learned. "Here" would thus refer in a general way to Blount's being at court.
1. Murdoch was not actually Douglas's son, but an understandable misreading of Holinshed led Shakespeare to believe he was.
2. It was popularly believed that fairies stole beautiful children and left bad or malformed ones in their place.
3. Henry was descended from the Plantagenet dynasty; the Percys were a distinguished family from the north of England to which Hotspur belonged.

To his own use[4] he keeps, and sends me word
I shall have none but Murdoch, Earl of Fife.

95 WESTMORLAND   This is his uncle's teaching. This is Worcester,
Malevolent to you in all aspects,[5]
Which makes him prune[6] himself and bristle up
The crest of youth against your dignity.

KING   But I have sent for him to answer this;
100   And for this cause awhile we must neglect
Our holy purpose to Jerusalem.
Cousin, on Wednesday next our Council we
Will hold at Windsor. So inform the lords,
But come yourself with speed to us again,
105   For more is to be said and to be done
Than out of anger can be utterèd.

WESTMORLAND   I will, my liege.   *Exeunt.*

1.2

Enter PRINCE *of Wales and Sir John* FALSTAFF.[1]

FALSTAFF   Now, Hal, what time of day is it, lad?[2]

PRINCE   Thou art so fat-witted° with drinking of old sack,[3] and   *thick-witted*
unbuttoning thee after supper, and sleeping upon benches
after noon, that thou hast forgotten to demand that truly which
5   thou wouldst truly know. What a devil hast thou to do with
the time of the day? Unless hours were cups of sack, and min-
utes capons,[4] and clocks the tongues of bawds, and dials° the   *clock faces*
signs of leaping houses,° and the blessed sun himself a fair   *brothels*
hot wench in flame-colored taffeta,[5] I see no reason why thou
10   shouldst be so superfluous° to demand the time of the day.   *needlessly curious*

FALSTAFF   Indeed you come near me° now, Hal, for we that   *are near the mark*
take purses go by the moon and the seven stars,[6] and not by
Phoebus, he, "that wand'ring knight so fair."[7] And I prithee,
sweet wag,° when thou art a king, as God save thy grace—   *mischievous boy*
15   "majesty," I should say, for grace[8] thou wilt have none—

PRINCE   What, none?

FALSTAFF   No, by my troth, not so much as will serve to be
prologue to an egg and butter.[9]

PRINCE   Well, how, then? Come, roundly,° roundly.   *to the point*

20 FALSTAFF   Marry,° then, sweet wag, when thou art king, let not   *By Mary (a mild oath)*
us that are squires of the night's body[1] be called thieves of the

---

4. Prisoners were routinely used as a source of revenue.
5. Habitually hostile to you. The line suggests that Worcester is a planet whose influence is always harmful, regardless of his position, or "aspect," in the sky.
6. A term from falconry suggesting the hawk's trimming of its feathers as preparation for action.
1.2 Location: A room in the Prince's apartments, London.
1. See Introduction and Digital Edition TC 3 for a discussion of Falstaff's name.
2. PERFORMANCE COMMENT This scene frequently begins with stage business suggesting one or both characters waking up from a night of hard drinking. Their ensuing banter can be hostile or lighthearted depending on how the production stages their relationship. See Digital Edition PC 1.
3. Spanish white wine.
4. Castrated male chickens (an Elizabethan delicacy).

5. Silk cloth, which in some contexts was associated with prostitutes.
6. *go by the moon:* go about at moonlight; tell time by the light of the moon. *seven stars:* the constellation known as the Pleiades.
7. TEXTUAL COMMENT Quotation marks were irregularly used to set off direct quotations in the early modern period. They have been added here to indicate that this line is probably drawn from a contemporary ballad or romance about Phoebus, the sun god of classical mythology. See Digital Edition TC 2.
8. Virtue; with a pun also on "grace" as meaning "God's favor" and "a prayer before meals." Falstaff asserts that Hal has none of these and so must be called "your majesty" rather than "your grace," which was also a title of honor.
9. *egg and butter:* a mere snack needing only the shortest grace.
1. Let not we who steal by night. Falstaff alludes to the attendants of knights known as "squires of the body."

day's beauty. Let us be Diana's foresters,[2] gentlemen of the
shade, minions of the moon; and let men say we be men of
good government,° being governed, as the sea is, by our noble   conduct
25   and chaste mistress the moon, under whose countenance° we   face; protection
steal.
PRINCE   Thou sayest well, and it holds well,° too, for the for-   the comparison is apt
tune of us that are the moon's men doth ebb and flow like
the sea, being governed, as the sea is, by the moon. As for
30   proof now: a purse of gold most resolutely snatched on Monday night and most dissolutely spent on Tuesday morning,
got with swearing "Lay by!"[3] and spent with crying "Bring
in!";[4] now in as low an ebb as the foot of the ladder, and by
and by in as high a flow as the ridge° of the gallows.[5]   crossbar
35   FALSTAFF   By the Lord, thou say'st true, lad—and is not my
hostess of the tavern a most sweet wench?
PRINCE   As the honey of Hybla,[6] my old lad of the castle;[7] and
is not a buff jerkin[8] a most sweet robe of durance?°   durability; imprisonment
FALSTAFF   How now, how now, mad wag? What, in thy quips and
40   thy quiddities?° What a plague have I to do with a buff jerkin?   quibbles (wordplay)
PRINCE   Why, what a pox[9] have I to do with my hostess of the
tavern?
FALSTAFF   Well, thou hast called her to a reckoning[1] many a
time and oft.
45   PRINCE   Did I ever call for thee to pay thy part?[2]
FALSTAFF   No, I'll give thee thy due; thou hast paid all there.
PRINCE   Yea, and elsewhere, so far as my coin would stretch,[3]
and where it would not I have used my credit.
FALSTAFF   Yea, and so used it that were it not here apparent
50   that thou art heir apparent—but I prithee, sweet wag, shall
there be gallows standing in England when thou art king?
And resolution thus fubbed[4] as it is with the rusty curb of
old Father Antic° the law? Do not thou, when thou art king,   buffoon
hang a thief.
55   PRINCE   No, thou shalt.
FALSTAFF   Shall I? Oh, rare! By the Lord, I'll be a brave° judge.   fine; well-dressed
PRINCE   Thou judgest false already. I mean thou shalt have
the hanging of the thieves and so become a rare hangman.
FALSTAFF   Well, Hal, well; and in some sort it jumps° with my   agrees
60   humor° as well as waiting in the court,[5] I can tell you.   temperament
PRINCE   For obtaining of suits?[6]

2. Hunters by moonlight; thieves. In classical mythology, Diana was goddess of the moon.
3. A thief's cry similar to "Hands up!"
4. A tavern customer's call for more food or wine.
5. The Prince's speech is riddled with sexual slang, including "purse" (line 30) as meaning "vagina" or "scrotum"; "snatched" (line 30) as "forcibly had sexual relations with"; "spent" (line 31) as "exhausted by sexual activity"; "Lay by" (line 32) as "Lie back"; "spent with" (line 32) as "reached orgasm with"; and "low" (line 33) and "high" (line 34) as referring to a penis, first limp and then erect.
6. Region of Sicily renowned for its honey.
7. TEXTUAL COMMENT Slang for "roisterer" (a boisterous reveler or carouser); also a play on the name "Oldcastle," which Shakespeare originally used to

designate this character until a powerful descendant of Oldcastle objected and the name was changed to "Falstaff." See Digital Edition TC 3.
8. Leather jacket often worn by jailers.
9. The equivalent of "what the devil." The pox literally was plague or syphilis.
1. You have asked that she present the bill; asked that she show her value sexually.
2. To pay your bill; to use your penis.
3. So far as my money would go; so far as my ability to engender, or "coin," a child would take me.
4. And valor (of thieves) thus thwarted.
5. Being in attendance at the royal court or at the court of justices.
6. Petitions; clothing. The hangman was entitled to claim the victims' clothing.

FALSTAFF Yea, for obtaining of suits, whereof the hangman
hath no lean wardrobe. 'Sblood,[7] I am as melancholy as a gib
cat,° or a lugged bear.[8]   *tomcat*

65 PRINCE Or an old lion, or a lover's lute.

FALSTAFF Yea, or the drone of a Lincolnshire bagpipe.

PRINCE What sayest thou to a hare,[9] or the melancholy of
Moorditch?[1]

FALSTAFF Thou hast the most unsavory similes, and art indeed

70 the most comparative,° rascalliest, sweet young prince. But   *quickest at comparisons*
Hal, I prithee trouble me no more with vanity.° I would to   *worthless things*
God thou and I knew where a commodity° of good names°   *supply / reputations*
were to be bought. An old lord of the Council rated° me the   *berated*
other day in the street about you, sir, but I marked him not;

75 and yet he talked very wisely, but I regarded him not; and
yet he talked wisely, and in the street, too.

PRINCE Thou didst well, for wisdom cries out in the streets,
and no man regards it.[2]

FALSTAFF Oh, thou hast damnable iteration[3] and art indeed

80 able to corrupt a saint. Thou hast done much harm upon me,
Hal; God forgive thee for it. Before I knew thee, Hal, I knew
nothing, and now am I, if a man should speak truly, little
better than one of the wicked. I must give over this life, and
I will give it over. By the Lord, an° I do not, I am a villain. I'll   *if*

85 be damned for never a° king's son in Christendom.   *for no*

PRINCE Where shall we take a purse tomorrow, Jack?

FALSTAFF Zounds,[4] where thou wilt, lad; I'll make one;° an I   *I'll take part*
do not, call me villain and baffle me.[5]

PRINCE I see a good amendment of life in thee, from praying

90 to purse-taking.

FALSTAFF Why, Hal, 'tis my vocation,° Hal. 'Tis no sin for a   *calling*
man to labor in his vocation.[6]

    Enter POINS.

Poins! Now shall we know if Gadshill[7] have set a match.° Oh,   *planned a theft*
if men were to be saved by merit,[8] what hole in hell were hot

95 enough for him? This is the most omnipotent villain that
ever cried "Stand!" to a true° man.   *an honest*

PRINCE Good morrow, Ned.

POINS Good morrow, sweet Hal. What says Monsieur Remorse?
What says Sir John, Sack-and-Sugar Jack?[9] How agrees the

100 devil and thee about thy soul, that thou soldest him on Good
Friday[1] last for a cup of Madeira[2] and a cold capon's leg?

---

7. By His blood (an oath alluding to Christ's
crucifixion).
8. A baited bear. In a popular form of entertainment,
bears were chained to a stake and set upon by dogs.
9. The hare's sadness was proverbial. Its flesh, when
eaten, was supposed to generate melancholy.
1. An open sewer outside the walls of London.
2. A biblical allusion to Proverbs 1:20–24.
3. You have a soul-endangering way of reading Scripture. This is one of several speeches in which Falstaff uses language associated with puritans.
4. By Christ's wounds (a strong oath).
5. And subject me to public disgrace. Falstaff alludes
to the practice of "baffling," in which perjured knights
or effigies of them were hung upside down in public
places.

6. Allusion to 1 Corinthians 7:20 and Ephesians 4:1.
Falstaff is misusing the biblical injunction to work at
one's vocation to justify robbery.
7. A thief named after Gad's Hill, the place where he
practices his robberies. This hill, near Rochester on
the road from Canterbury to London, was notorious
for highway robberies.
8. By good works (as opposed to salvation by God's
grace).
9. "Jack" is a nickname for "John," but the word also
means "a drinking vessel" or "a knave." Falstaff likes
sugar in his sack, or sweet white wine.
1. The strictest of fast days in the Christian calendar.
2. A white wine exported from Madeira, an island
off the coast of western Africa.

PRINCE   Sir John stands to° his word—the devil shall have his   *keeps*
bargain—for he was never yet a breaker of proverbs: he will
give the devil his due.

105   POINS   Then art thou damned for keeping thy word with the
devil.

PRINCE   Else he had been damned for cozening° the devil.   *cheating*

POINS   But my lads, my lads, tomorrow morning, by four o'clock
early at Gad's Hill, there are pilgrims going to Canterbury

110   with rich offerings and traders riding to London with fat
purses. I have vizards° for you all; you have horses for your-   *masks*
selves; Gadshill lies° tonight in Rochester. I have bespoke°   *lodges / ordered*
supper tomorrow night in Eastcheap.[3] We may do it as
secure° as sleep. If you will go, I will stuff your purses full of   *safely*

115   crowns; if you will not, tarry at home and be hanged.

FALSTAFF   Hear ye, Yedward,[4] if I tarry at home and go not,
I'll hang you for going.

POINS   You will, chops?°   *fat cheeks*

FALSTAFF   Hal, wilt thou make one?

120   PRINCE   Who, I? Rob? I, a thief? Not I, by my faith.

FALSTAFF   There's neither honesty,° manhood, nor good fel-   *honor*
lowship in thee, nor thou cam'st not of the blood royal, if
thou darest not stand for° ten shillings.[5]   *fight for; be worth*

PRINCE   Well, then, once in my days I'll be a madcap.

125   FALSTAFF   Why, that's well said.

PRINCE   Well, come what will, I'll tarry at home.

FALSTAFF   By the Lord, I'll be a traitor then, when thou art king.

PRINCE   I care not.

POINS   Sir John, I prithee leave the Prince and me alone. I

130   will lay him down such reasons for this adventure that he
shall go.

FALSTAFF   Well, God give thee the spirit of persuasion and
him the ears of profiting, that what thou speakest may move
and what he hears may be believed, that the true prince

135   may, for recreation sake, prove a false thief, for the poor
abuses of the time want countenance.[6] Farewell, you shall
find me in Eastcheap.

PRINCE   Farewell, the latter spring; farewell, All-hallow
summer.[7]   [*Exit* FALSTAFF.]

140   POINS   Now, my good sweet honey lord, ride with us tomorrow. I have a jest to execute that I cannot manage alone.
Falstaff, Peto, Bardolph, and Gadshill[8] shall rob those men
that we have already waylaid—yourself and I will not be
there—and when they have the booty, if you and I do not

145   rob them, cut this head off from my shoulders.

PRINCE   How shall we part with them in setting forth?

---

3. A street and market district in London, evidently
the location of the play's tavern.
4. *Yedward*: dialectical form of Edward.
5. A 10-shilling coin was called a "royal," thus punning on the Prince's "blood royal."
6. Lack encouragement (from those of high rank).
7. Addressing Falstaff as youth in age (a second
spring) and likening him to a period of unusually
mild weather (a second summer) occurring around

All Hallows' Day, November 1.
8. TEXTUAL COMMENT Names of characters are often
unstable and vary between texts (and even within one
text): in Q1 and F, the characters listed here as Peto
and Bardolph are "Haruey" and "Rossill," but editors
have concluded that these are probably the same
characters that are known in the rest of the play as
"Peto" and "Bardoll." See Digital Edition TC 4.

POINS   Why, we will set forth before or after them and appoint
them a place of meeting, wherein it is at our pleasure to fail;
and then will they adventure upon the exploit themselves,
150   which they shall have no sooner achieved but we'll set upon
them.

PRINCE   Yea, but 'tis like that they will know us by our horses, by
our habits,° and by every other appointment° to be ourselves.   *clothing / item*

POINS   Tut, our horses they shall not see: I'll tie them in the
155   wood; our vizards we will change after we leave them; and,
sirrah,[9] I have cases of buckram for the nonce,[1] to immask°   *hide*
our noted° outward garments.   *known*

PRINCE   Yea, but I doubt they will be too hard for us.[2]

POINS   Well, for two of them, I know them to be as true-bred
160   cowards as ever turned back, and for the third, if he fight
longer than he sees reason, I'll forswear arms. The virtue of
this jest will be the incomprehensible° lies that this same fat   *boundless*
rogue will tell us when we meet at supper: how thirty at
least he fought with, what wards,° what blows, what extrem-   *parries*
165   ities he endured; and in the reproof° of this lives the jest.   *disproof*

PRINCE   Well, I'll go with thee. Provide us all things necessary
and meet me tomorrow night in Eastcheap. There I'll sup.
Farewell.

POINS   Farewell, my lord.   *Exit* POINS.

170   PRINCE   I know you all,[3] and will awhile uphold
The unyoked humor° of your idleness.   *unbridled whims*
Yet herein will I imitate the sun,
Who doth permit the base contagious° clouds   *disease-carrying*
To smother up his beauty from the world,
175   That,° when he please again to be himself,   *So that*
Being wanted° he may be more wondered at   *Having been missed*
By breaking through the foul and ugly mists
Of vapors that did seem to strangle him.
If all the year were playing holidays,
180   To sport would be as tedious as to work;
But when they seldom come, they wished-for come,
And nothing pleaseth but rare accidents.°   *exceptional events*
So when this loose behavior I throw off
And pay the debt I never promisèd,
185   By how much better than my word I am,
By so much shall I falsify men's hopes;°   *expectations*
And, like bright metal on a sullen ground,°   *dull background*
My reformation, glittering o'er my fault,
Shall show more goodly and attract more eyes
190   Than that which hath no foil to set it off.
I'll so offend to° make offense a skill,°   *as to / an art*
Redeeming[4] time when men think least I will.   *Exit.*

---

9. A familiar form of address, conventionally used
with social inferiors.
1. I have suits of coarse cloth for the purpose.
2. But I fear they will be more than we can manage.
3. PERFORMANCE COMMENT This speech has often
made the Prince seem cold and calculating. It can,

however, be played as a hastily composed self-
justification for Hal's continued presence in the tavern. See Digital Edition PC 2.
4. Making amends for misspent time. Injunctions to
redeem time were both proverbial and biblical: see
Ephesians 5:16 or Colossians 4:5.

1.3

Enter the KING, NORTHUMBERLAND, WORCESTER,
HOTSPUR, *Sir Walter* BLOUNT, *with others.*

KING My blood hath been too cold and temperate,
    Unapt° to stir at these indignities,   *Slow*
    And you have found me,° for accordingly   *discovered this fact*
    You tread upon my patience. But be sure
5   I will from henceforth rather be myself,°   *(i.e., my royal self)*
    Mighty and to be feared, than my condition,[1]
    Which hath been smooth as oil, soft as young down,
    And therefore lost that title of° respect   *claim to*
    Which the proud soul ne'er pays but to the proud.
10 WORCESTER Our house,[2] my sovereign liege, little deserves
    The scourge of greatness to be used on it,
    And that same greatness, too, which our own hands
    Have holp° to make so portly.°   *helped / majestic*
NORTHUMBERLAND My lord—
15 KING Worcester, get thee gone, for I do see
    Danger and disobedience in thine eye.
    O sir, your presence is too bold and peremptory,°   *proud*
    And majesty might never yet endure
    The moody frontier[3] of a servant brow.
20   You have good leave° to leave us. When we need   *full permission*
    Your use and counsel we shall send for you.   *Exit* WORCESTER.
    [*to* NORTHUMBERLAND] You were about to speak.
NORTHUMBERLAND   Yea, my good lord.
    Those prisoners in your highness' name demanded,
    Which Harry Percy here at Humbleton took,
25   Were, as he says, not with such strength denied
    As is delivered° to your majesty.   *reported*
    Either envy,° therefore, or misprision°   *malice / error*
    Is guilty of this fault and not my son.
HOTSPUR My liege, I did deny no prisoners.
30   But I remember when the fight was done,
    When I was dry° with rage and extreme toil,   *thirsty*
    Breathless and faint, leaning upon my sword,
    Came there a certain lord, neat and trimly dressed,
    Fresh as a bridegroom, and his chin, new reaped,[4]
35   Showed° like a stubble-land at harvest-home.[5]   *Looked*
    He was perfumèd like a milliner,[6]
    And twixt his finger and his thumb he held
    A pouncet-box,[7] which ever and anon
    He gave his nose and took't away again—
40   Who° therewith angry, when it next came there,   *(the nose)*
    Took it in snuff[8]—and still he smiled and talked;

1.3 Location: A royal residence, probably Windsor Castle.
1. My natural (mild) temperament.
2. The Percy family, which had supported Henry against Richard II.
3. The angry expression (punning on "frontier" as meaning both "forehead" and "military fortifications").
4. Newly trimmed. London in the 1590s witnessed a fashion for close-shaved beards.
5. At the end of harvest (when the fields are cut back to stubble).
6. Seller of finely scented apparel such as bonnets, ribbons, and gloves. The name derives from the fact that these goods were often imports from Milan.
7. Perfume box with a perforated lid.
8. Took offense at it; inhaled it.

And, as the soldiers bore dead bodies by,
He called them "untaught knaves," "unmannerly,"
To bring a slovenly° unhandsome corpse   *base; nasty*
45 Betwixt the wind and his nobility.
With many holiday and lady° terms   *dainty and effeminate*
He questioned me; amongst the rest demanded
My prisoners in your majesty's behalf.
I then, all smarting with my wounds being cold,
50 To be so pestered with a popinjay,°   *parrot; vain dandy*
Out of my grief° and my impatience   *pain*
Answered neglectingly,° I know not what—   *negligently*
He should, or he should not—for he made me mad
To see him shine so brisk, and smell so sweet,
55 And talk so like a waiting-gentlewoman
Of guns, and drums, and wounds—God save the mark!⁹—
And telling me the sovereignest° thing on earth   *best*
Was parmacety¹ for an inward bruise,
And that it was great pity, so it was,
60 This villainous saltpeter² should be digged
Out of the bowels of the harmless earth,
Which many a good tall° fellow had destroyed   *brave*
So cowardly, and but for these vile guns
He would himself have been a soldier.
65 This bald unjointed° chat of his, my lord,   *This trivial incoherent*
I answered indirectly, as I said,
And I beseech you, let not his report
Come current° for an accusation   *Be taken as valid*
Betwixt my love and your high majesty.
70 BLOUNT   The circumstance considered, good my lord,
Whate'er Lord Harry Percy then had said
To such a person and in such a place,
At such a time, with all the rest retold,
May reasonably die, and never rise
75 To do him wrong, or any way impeach
What then he said, so° he unsay it now.   *if*
KING   Why, yet he doth deny° his prisoners,   *refuse to hand over*
But with proviso and exception
That we at our own charge shall ransom straight°   *immediately*
80 His brother-in-law, the foolish Mortimer,³
Who, on my soul, hath willfully betrayed
The lives of those that he did lead to fight
Against that great magician, damned Glyndŵr,
Whose daughter, as we hear, that Earl of March
85 Hath lately married. Shall our coffers then
Be emptied to redeem a traitor home?
Shall we buy treason and indent with fears⁴

9. God keep evil away (an expression of indignation).
1. Spermaceti, an oily substance from the sperm
whale that was used in various medicines and potions.
The spelling "parmacety" probably derives from the
ointment's association with the Italian city of Parma.
2. The main ingredient of gunpowder.
3. Shakespeare follows Holinshed's *Chronicles* in
confusing or conflating two Edmund Mortimers. One
was captured by Glyndŵr and later became Glyndŵr's

son-in-law and Hotspur's brother-in-law. The other,
the fifth Earl of March, was his nephew and claimed
the English throne as a descendant of Lionel, Duke
of Clarence, third son of Edward III. This Mortimer
was the one named by Richard II as his presumptive
heir.
4. And bargain with those whom we have reason to
fear.

When they have lost and forfeited themselves?
No, on the barren mountains let him starve;
90 For I shall never hold that man my friend
Whose tongue shall ask me for one penny cost
To ransom home revolted° Mortimer.   *rebellious*
HOTSPUR "Revolted Mortimer"?[5]
He never did fall off,° my sovereign liege,   *change allegiance*
95 But by the chance of war. To prove that true
Needs no more but one tongue for all those wounds,
Those mouthèd° wounds, which valiantly he took   *gaping; eloquent*
When on the gentle Severn's[6] sedgy° bank,   *marshy*
In single opposition, hand to hand,
100 He did confound° the best part of an hour   *consume*
In changing hardiment° with great Glyndŵr.   *matching valor*
Three times they breathed,° and three times did they drink,   *rested*
Upon agreement, of swift Severn's flood,
Who, then affrighted with their bloody looks,
105 Ran fearfully among the trembling reeds
And hid his crisp° head in the hollow bank   *rippled*
Bloodstainèd with these valiant combatants.
Never did bare and rotten policy°   *cunning*
Color° her working with such deadly wounds,   *Disguise*
110 Nor never could the noble Mortimer
Receive so many, and all willingly.
Then let not him be slandered with revolt.[7]
KING Thou dost belie° him, Percy; thou dost belie him.   *misrepresent*
He never did encounter with Glyndŵr.
115 I tell thee, he durst as well have met the devil alone
As Owain Glyndŵr for an enemy.
Art thou not ashamed? But, sirrah, henceforth
Let me not hear you speak of Mortimer.
Send me your prisoners with the speediest means,
120 Or you shall hear in such a kind from me
As will displease you. —My lord Northumberland,
We license your departure with your son.
Send us your prisoners, or you will hear of it.
        Exit KING [*with* BLOUNT *and Attendants*].
HOTSPUR An if° the devil come and roar for them   *An if = If*
125 I will not send them. I will after straight°   *go after him at once*
And tell him so, for I will ease my heart,
Albeit I make a hazard of my head.
NORTHUMBERLAND What, drunk with choler?° Stay and pause   *anger*
        awhile.
        Enter WORCESTER.
Here comes your uncle.
HOTSPUR   "Speak of Mortimer"?
130 Zounds, I will speak of him, and let my soul
Want mercy° if I do not join with him.   *Be damned*
Yea, on his part, I'll empty all these veins

---

5. TEXTUAL COMMENT The question mark F prints here could also make sense as an exclamation mark, since early modern printers did not reliably distinguish between the two. When editors modernize punctuation, they often make interpretative decisions—a question mark suggests that Hotspur responds with sarcasm; an exclamation mark indicates vengeance. See Digital Edition TC 5.
6. The Severn River flows from Wales into Bristol Channel in England.
7. With the accusation of having revolted.

And shed my dear blood drop by drop in the dust,
But I will lift the downtrod Mortimer
135 As high in the air as this unthankful King,
As this ingrate and cankered° Bolingbroke.[8]   *corrupted*
NORTHUMBERLAND Brother, the King hath made your nephew mad.
WORCESTER Who struck this heat up after I was gone?
HOTSPUR He will forsooth have all my prisoners;
140 And when I urged the ransom, once again,
Of my wife's brother, then his cheek looked pale,
And on my face he turned an eye of death,°   *a menacing look*
Trembling even at the name of Mortimer.
WORCESTER I cannot blame him. Was not he proclaimed
145 By Richard, that dead is, the next of blood?°   *heir to the throne*
NORTHUMBERLAND He was; I heard the proclamation.
And then it was when the unhappy° King—   *unfortunate*
Whose wrongs in us° God pardon!—did set forth   *done by us*
Upon his Irish expedition;[9]
150 From whence he, intercepted,° did return   *interrupted*
To be deposed and shortly murderèd.
WORCESTER And for whose death we in the world's wide mouth
Live scandalized° and foully spoken of.   *disgraced*
HOTSPUR But soft,° I pray you, did King Richard then   *wait*
155 Proclaim my brother° Edmund Mortimer   *brother-in-law*
Heir to the crown?
NORTHUMBERLAND He did; myself did hear it.
HOTSPUR Nay, then I cannot blame his cousin[1] King,
That wished him on the barren mountains starve.
But shall it be that you that set the crown
160 Upon the head of this forgetful man
And for his sake wear the detested blot
Of murderous subornation[2]—shall it be
That you a world of curses undergo,
Being the agents or base second means,
165 The cords, the ladder, or the hangman rather?
Oh, pardon me that I descend so low
To show the line and the predicament
Wherein you range[3] under this subtle° King!   *cunning*
Shall it for shame be spoken in these days,
170 Or fill up chronicles in time to come,
That men of your nobility and power
Did gage° them both in an unjust behalf,°   *pledge / cause*
As both of you—God pardon it!—have done:
To put down Richard, that sweet lovely rose,
175 And plant this thorn, this canker,[4] Bolingbroke?
And shall it in more shame be further spoken
That you are fooled, discarded, and shook off
By him for whom these shames ye underwent?
No! Yet time serves° wherein you may redeem   *is available*

---

8. Henry's family name. Hotspur's use of it suggests
his unwillingness to acknowledge Henry as King.
9. As Shakespeare dramatizes in *Richard II*, Bolingbroke returned to England from exile in France while
Richard was at war in Ireland.
1. Punning on "cozen" (cheat).
2. Of assisting with a murder.

3. *To . . . range:* To show the degree and category
into which you might be classified (with puns on
"line" as meaning "hangman's rope" and on "predicament" as meaning "an unpleasant situation").
4. Wild and inferior kind of rose; also, cankerworm
(which destroys plants), or ulcerated sore.

180 Your banished honors and restore yourselves
     Into the good thoughts of the world again;
     Revenge the jeering and disdained° contempt   *disdainful*
     Of this proud King, who studies day and night
     To answer° all the debt he owes to you   *satisfy*
185 Even with the bloody payment of your deaths.
     Therefore, I say—
     WORCESTER   Peace, cousin, say no more.
     And now I will unclasp a secret book,
     And to your quick-conceiving discontents
     I'll read you matter deep and dangerous,
190 As full of peril and adventurous spirit
     As to o'erwalk° a current roaring loud   *walk across*
     On the unsteadfast footing of a spear.
     HOTSPUR   If he fall in, good night. Or sink or swim,⁵
     Send danger from the east unto the west,
195 So° honor cross it from the north to south,   *Provided*
     And let them grapple. Oh, the blood more stirs
     To rouse a lion than to start a hare!
     NORTHUMBERLAND [*to* WORCESTER]   Imagination of some
        great exploit
     Drives him beyond the bounds of patience.
200 HOTSPUR   By heaven, methinks it were an easy leap
     To pluck bright honor from the pale-faced moon,
     Or dive into the bottom of the deep,
     Where fathom-line⁶ could never touch the ground,
     And pluck up drownèd honor by the locks,
205 So he that doth redeem her thence might wear
     Without corrival° all her dignities.   *competitor*
     But out upon this half-faced fellowship!°   *paltry sharing of honors*
     WORCESTER   He apprehends a world of figures⁷ here,
     But not the form of what he should attend.°   *pay attention to*
210 —Good cousin, give me audience for a while.
     HOTSPUR   I cry you mercy.°   *I beg your pardon*
     WORCESTER   Those same noble Scots⁸
     That are your prisoners—
     HOTSPUR   I'll keep them all.
     By God, he shall not have a Scot of them;
     No, if a scot would save his soul, he shall not.
     I'll keep them, by this hand.
215 WORCESTER   You start away,
     And lend no ear unto my purposes.
     Those prisoners you shall keep.
     HOTSPUR   Nay, I will; that's flat.
     He said he would not ransom Mortimer,
     Forbade my tongue to speak of Mortimer,
220 But I will find him when he lies asleep,
     And in his ear I'll holler "Mortimer!"
     Nay, I'll have a starling shall be taught to speak
     Nothing but "Mortimer" and give it him
     To keep his anger still° in motion.   *constantly*

---

5. Whether he sinks or swims (loses or wins).
6. A weighted line used in testing the depth of the sea.

7. Figures of speech; fantasies.
8. Inhabitants of Scotland (with a pun in the following lines on "scot" as meaning "a small sum").

225 WORCESTER Hear you, cousin, a word.
HOTSPUR All studies here I solemnly defy,°   renounce
Save how to gall and pinch° this Bolingbroke   torment
And that same sword-and-buckler[9] Prince of Wales.
But that I think his father loves him not
230 And would be glad he met with some mischance,
I would have him poisoned with a pot of ale.[1]
WORCESTER Farewell, kinsman. I'll talk to you
When you are better tempered to attend.
NORTHUMBERLAND [to HOTSPUR] Why, what a wasp-stung and
impatient fool
235 Art thou to break into this woman's mood,[2]
Tying thine ear to no tongue but thine own?
HOTSPUR Why, look you, I am whipped and scourged with rods,
Nettled and stung with pismires,° when I hear   ants
Of this vile politician° Bolingbroke.   schemer
240 In Richard's time—what do you call the place?
A plague upon it, it is in Gloucestershire;
'Twas where the madcap Duke his uncle kept,
His uncle York, where I first bowed my knee
Unto this king of smiles, this Bolingbroke.[3]
245 'Sblood, when you and he came back from Ravenspur.[4]
NORTHUMBERLAND At Berkeley Castle.
HOTSPUR You say true.
Why, what a candy deal of° courtesy   quantity of sweet
This fawning greyhound then did proffer me!
250 "Look when° his infant fortune came to age,"   Whenever; as soon as
And "gentle Harry Percy," and "kind cousin."
Oh, the devil take such cozeners!° God forgive me;   cheaters
—Good uncle, tell your tale; I have done.
WORCESTER Nay, if you have not, to it again;
We will stay° your leisure.   await
255 HOTSPUR   I have done, i'faith.
WORCESTER Then once more to your Scottish prisoners.
Deliver them up° without their ransom straight,   Release them
And make the Douglas'[5] son your only mean°   agent; means
For powers° in Scotland, which, for diverse reasons   raising an army
260 Which I shall send you written, be assured
Will easily be granted. [to NORTHUMBERLAND] You, my lord,
Your son in Scotland being thus employed,
Shall secretly into the bosom creep
Of that same noble prelate well beloved,
265 The Archbishop.
HOTSPUR Of York, is it not?
WORCESTER True, who bears hard°   resents
His brother's death at Bristol, the Lord Scrope.[6]

---

9. In Elizabethan England, the sword and buckler, or small shield, were associated with ordinary fighting men. A prince should use rapier and dagger.
1. A drink associated with the common people.
2. Alluding to the commonplace that women were, by nature, unable to hold their tongues.
3. This event is depicted in *Richard II* at 2.3.20–56.
4. Bolingbroke's landing place at the mouth of the Humber River in Yorkshire upon his return from exile.

5. The "the" before Douglas's name indicates that he is head of a Scottish clan or noble family.
6. Richard Scroop (or le Scrope), the Archbishop of York and an ally of the rebels in this play, was actually a distant cousin of William Scroop, Earl of Wiltshire, who was a favorite of Richard II and was executed by Henry IV in 1399. His death is mentioned in *Richard II* at 3.2.117–37.

I speak not this in estimation,°   *as a guess*
270 As what I think might be, but what I know
    Is ruminated, plotted, and set down,
    And only stays° but to behold the face   *waits*
    Of that occasion that shall bring it on.
HOTSPUR I smell it. Upon my life, it will do well.
275 NORTHUMBERLAND Before the game is afoot thou still lett'st slip.[7]
HOTSPUR Why, it cannot choose but be a noble plot.
    And then the power° of Scotland and of York   *army*
    To join with Mortimer, ha?
WORCESTER   And so they shall.
HOTSPUR In faith, it is exceedingly well aimed.
280 WORCESTER And 'tis no little reason bids us speed
    To save our heads by raising of a head;°   *an army*
    For, bear ourselves as even° as we can,   *carefully*
    The King will always think him in our debt,
    And think we think ourselves unsatisfied,
285 Till he hath found a time to pay us home.°   *repay us fully*
    And see already how he doth begin
    To make us strangers to his looks of love.
HOTSPUR He does; he does. We'll be revenged on him.
WORCESTER Cousin, farewell. No further go in this
290 Than I by letters shall direct your course.
    When time is ripe, which will be suddenly,°   *soon*
    I'll steal to Glyndŵr and Lord Mortimer,
    Where you and Douglas and our powers at once,
    As I will fashion it, shall happily meet
295 To bear our fortunes in our own strong arms,
    Which now we hold at° much uncertainty.   *with*
NORTHUMBERLAND Farewell, good brother. We shall thrive,
    I trust.
HOTSPUR Uncle, adieu. Oh, let the hours be short
    Till fields° and blows and groans applaud our sport! *Exeunt.*   *battlefields*

2.1

Enter a CARRIER[1] *with a lantern in his hand.*
FIRST CARRIER Heigh-ho! An it° be not four by the day,° I'll   *If it / in the morning*
    be hanged. Charles's Wain[2] is over the new chimney, and yet
    our horse° not packed. —What, ostler![3]   *horses*
OSTLER [*within*] Anon°, anon!   *Right away*
5 FIRST CARRIER I prithee, Tom, beat Cut's saddle;[4] put a few
    flocks in the point.[5] Poor jade is wrung in the withers,[6] out of
    all cess.°   *measure*
    Enter another CARRIER.

7. Before the quarry is even in the field, you always let loose the dogs. This image from hunting implies that Hotspur habitually jumps the gun.
2.1 Location: An innyard in Rochester, Kent.
1. One who transports goods for hire.
2. The constellation now known as the Plow or the Great Bear.
3. One who attends to horses at an inn.

4. Soften the horse's saddle. "Cut" was a term for a horse with a docked tail or a gelding; here, it may be the horse's name.
5. Put a few tufts of wood in the saddle's pommel (to soften it).
6. The poor old horse is extremely sore in the ridge between its shoulder blades.

SECOND CARRIER   Peas and beans° are as dank here as a dog,   (horse feed)
and that is the next way to give poor jades the bots.° This   intestinal worms
10   house is turned upside down since Robin Ostler died.
FIRST CARRIER   Poor fellow never joyed since the price of oats
rose; it was the death of him.
SECOND CARRIER   I think this be the most villainous house in
all London road for fleas. I am stung like a tench.⁷
15   FIRST CARRIER   Like a tench? By the mass, there is ne'er a king
christen° could be better bit than I have been since the first   Christian king
cock.°   midnight
SECOND CARRIER   Why, they will allow us ne'er a jordan,° and   chamber pot
then we leak° in your chimney, and your chamber-lye° breeds   urinate / urine
20   fleas like a loach.⁸
FIRST CARRIER   What, ostler! Come away, and be hanged! Come
away!
SECOND CARRIER   I have a gammon of bacon° and two races°   a ham / roots
of ginger to be delivered as far as Charing Cross.⁹
25   FIRST CARRIER   God's body, the turkeys in my pannier° are   basket
quite starved. What, ostler! A plague on thee, hast thou never
an eye in thy head? Canst not hear? An° 'twere not as good   If
deed as drink to break the pate° on thee, I am a very villain.   skull
Come, and be hanged! Hast no faith° in thee?   responsibility
Enter GADSHILL.
30   GADSHILL   Good morrow, carriers. What's o'clock?
FIRST CARRIER   I think it be two o'clock.
GADSHILL   I prithee, lend me thy lantern to see my gelding in
the stable.
FIRST CARRIER   Nay, by God, soft.° I know a trick worth two   wait
35   of that, i'faith.
GADSHILL [to SECOND CARRIER]   I pray thee, lend me thine.
SECOND CARRIER   Ay, when, canst tell?¹ "Lend me thy lan-
tern," quoth he. Marry, I'll see thee hanged first.
GADSHILL   Sirrah carrier, what time do you mean to come to
40   London?
SECOND CARRIER   Time enough to go to bed with a candle, I
warrant° thee. Come, neighbor Mugs, we'll call up the gen-   assure
tlemen. They will along° with company, for they have great   travel
charge.°   Exeunt [CARRIERS].   have valuable cargo
Enter CHAMBERLAIN.
45   GADSHILL   What ho, chamberlain!²
CHAMBERLAIN   "At hand," quoth pickpurse.³
GADSHILL   That's even as fair° as "'at hand,' quoth the chamber-   good
lain," for thou variest no more from picking of purses than
giving direction doth from laboring:⁴ thou layest the plot° how.   plan
50   CHAMBERLAIN   Good morrow, Master Gadshill. It holds current that° I told you yesternight. There's a franklin in the   holds true what

---

7. A spotted fish whose markings may have looked like flea bites.
8. A fish. The comparison means that urine breeds fleas either as a loach breeds loaches or as a loach breeds fleas. There was a popular belief that some fish spawned flies or fleas.
9. A marketplace between London and Westminster.
1. A retort similar to "Never."

2. Bedroom attendant. In popular discourse, chamberlains were notorious for their complicity with thieves.
3. "I am at your disposal," as the thief said (evidently a popular tag).
4. For you are not more different from a pickpocket than an overseer is from a laborer.

Weald[5] of Kent hath brought three hundred marks[6] with him in gold. I heard him tell it to one of his company last night at supper—a kind of auditor, one that hath abundance of charge too, God knows what. They are up already and call for eggs and butter. They will away presently.

GADSHILL Sirrah, if they meet not with Saint Nicholas' clerks,[7] I'll give thee this neck.

CHAMBERLAIN No, I'll none of it; I pray thee keep that for the hangman, for I know thou worshippest Saint Nicholas as truly as a man of falsehood may.

GADSHILL What talkest thou to me of the hangman? If I hang, I'll make a fat pair of gallows; for if I hang, old Sir John hangs with me, and thou knowest he is no starveling. Tut, there are other Trojans[8] that thou dream'st not of, the which° for sport sake are content to do the profession° some grace; that would, if matters should be looked into, for their own credit sake make all whole.° I am joined with no foot-landrakers,[9] no long-staff sixpenny strikers,[1] none of these mad mustachio purple-hued maltworms,[2] but with nobility and tranquility, burgomasters and great oneyers,[3] such as can hold in,° such as will strike sooner than speak, and speak sooner than drink, and drink sooner than pray. And yet, zounds, I lie, for they pray continually to their saint, the commonwealth, or rather not pray to her but prey on her, for they ride up and down[4] on her and make her their boots.°

CHAMBERLAIN What, the commonwealth their boots? Will she hold out water in foul way?[5]

GADSHILL She will, she will; justice hath liquored her.[6] We steal as in a castle,° cocksure. We have the receipt of fern seed;[7] we walk invisible.

CHAMBERLAIN Nay, by my faith, I think you are more beholding to the night than to fern seed for your walking invisible.

GADSHILL Give me thy hand; thou shalt have a share in our purchase,° as I am a true man.

CHAMBERLAIN Nay, rather let me have it as you are a false thief.

GADSHILL Go to. *Homo*° is a common name to all men. Bid the ostler bring my gelding out of the stable. Farewell, you muddy° knave. [*Exeunt.*]

Glosses (right margin):
- (l. 66) who / (of robbery)
- (l. 67) set things right
- (l. 72) can keep a secret
- (l. 76) booty; footwear
- (l. 80) in complete safety
- (l. 85) plunder
- (l. 87) (Latin for "man")
- (l. 89) stupid

5. There's a small landowner in the wooded region.
6. Coins worth two-thirds of a pound each.
7. Slang for "highway robbers." St. Nicholas was variously regarded as the patron saint of travelers and of thieves.
8. Slang for "lusty fellows."
9. Highwaymen who travel on foot (rather than on horse).
1. Thieves who carry crude weapons and rob for small sums.
2. These drunkards with wild mustaches and purple faces.

3. Officers of the Exchequer, who collect taxes and revenues. TEXTUAL COMMENT The meaning of this word is uncertain and has provoked a wide range of editorial emendations. See Digital Edition TC 6.
4. They travel (with a pun on "ride" as meaning "to mount sexually").
5. Will she keep water out (off your feet) on a muddy road; will she protect you in difficulty?
6. Greased her (as one waterproofs leather); bribed her.
7. Popularly supposed to make those who wore it invisible.

2.2

Enter PRINCE, POINS, PETO[, *and* BARDOLPH].

POINS   Come, shelter, shelter! I have removed Falstaff's horse,
and he frets° like a gummed velvet.[1]   *worries; frays*

PRINCE   Stand close!°   *concealed*

[*They retire.*]

Enter FALSTAFF.

FALSTAFF   Poins! Poins, and be hanged! Poins!

5   PRINCE [*coming forward*]   Peace, ye fat-kidneyed rascal! What
a brawling dost thou keep!

FALSTAFF   Where's Poins, Hal?

PRINCE   He is walked up to the top of the hill. I'll go seek him.

[PRINCE *retires with the others.*]

FALSTAFF   I am accursed to rob in that thief's company. The
10   rascal hath removed my horse and tied him I know not
where. If I travel but four foot by the square° further afoot, I   *(a measuring tool)*
shall break my wind.[2] Well, I doubt not but to die a fair death
for[3] all this, if I scape hanging for killing that rogue. I have
forsworn his company hourly any time this two-and-twenty
15   years, and yet I am bewitched with the rogue's company. If the
rascal have not given me medicines° to make me love him,   *love potions*
I'll be hanged. It could not be else: I have drunk medicines.
Poins! Hal! A plague upon you both! Bardolph! Peto! I'll
starve ere I'll rob a foot further. An 'twere not as good a
20   deed as drink to turn true man° and to leave these rogues, I   *repent; turn informer*
am the veriest varlet° that ever chewed with a tooth. Eight   *rascal; servant*
yards of uneven ground is threescore and ten miles afoot
with me, and the stony-hearted villains know it well enough.
A plague upon it when thieves cannot be true one to another.
25   (*They whistle.*)[4] Whew! A plague upon you all! Give me my
horse, you rogues; give me my horse and be hanged.

PRINCE [*coming forward*]   Peace, ye fat-guts. Lie down, lay
thine ear close to the ground, and list if thou canst hear the
tread of travelers.

30   FALSTAFF   Have you any levers to lift me up again, being down?
'Sblood, I'll not bear mine own flesh so far afoot again for all
the coin in thy father's exchequer. What a plague mean ye to
colt° me thus?   *trick*

PRINCE   Thou liest. Thou art not colted; thou art uncolted.°   *unhorsed*

35   FALSTAFF   I prithee, good Prince Hal, help me to my horse,
good king's son.

PRINCE   Out, ye rogue; shall I be your ostler?

FALSTAFF   Hang thyself in thine own heir-apparent garters![5]
If I be ta'en, I'll peach° for this. An I have not ballads made   *inform against you*
40   on you all and sung to filthy tunes,[6] let a cup of sack be my

---

2.2 Location: The highway, Gad's Hill.
1. Like cheap velvet treated with gum. Gummed velvet was shiny but wore out quickly.
2. Become breathless; fart.
3. Die a natural death, despite.
4. TEXTUAL COMMENT It is not clear exactly when the
Prince and his companions show themselves to the
frustrated Falstaff. Editors have several choices:
the men can all enter here, or the Prince and Poins
could enter at line 27 and Bardolph and Peto at the
same time as Gadshill at line 42. Why Poins asks

Bardolph for news at lines 44–45 if Bardolph enters
at the beginning of the scene has especially puzzled
editors. See Digital Edition TC 7.
5. Falstaff's version of the proverb "He may hang
himself in his own garters." As the heir to the throne,
the Prince was a member of the Order of the Garter,
the highest order of English knighthood.
6. Ballads on topical themes were sung by ballad
singers and sold cheaply as broadsides in streets, theaters, and other public places.

poison. When a jest is so forward, and afoot too![7] I hate it.

Enter GADSHILL.

GADSHILL Stand!

FALSTAFF So I do, against my will.

POINS Oh, 'tis our setter;° I know his voice. —Bardolph, what   *one who sets up a crime*
45   news?

BARDOLPH Case ye,° case ye; on with your vizards! There's   *Disguise yourselves*
money of the King's coming down the hill; 'tis going to the
King's exchequer.

FALSTAFF You lie, ye rogue; 'tis going to the King's tavern.

50 GADSHILL There's enough to make° us all—   *make fortunes for*

FALSTAFF To be hanged.

PRINCE Sirs, you four shall front° them in the narrow lane;   *confront*
Ned Poins and I will walk lower. If they scape° from your   *escape*
encounter, then they light on us.

55 PETO How many be there of them?

GADSHILL Some eight or ten.

FALSTAFF Zounds, will they not rob us?

PRINCE What, a coward, Sir John Paunch?

FALSTAFF Indeed, I am not John of Gaunt,[8] your grandfather,
60   but yet no coward, Hal.

PRINCE Well, we leave that to the proof.°   *test*

POINS Sirrah Jack, thy horse stands behind the hedge. When
thou needest him, there thou shalt find him. Farewell, and
stand fast.

65 FALSTAFF Now cannot I strike him, if I should be hanged.

PRINCE [*aside to* POINS] Ned, where are our disguises?

POINS [*aside to* PRINCE] Here, hard by. Stand close.

[*Exeunt* PRINCE *and* POINS.]

FALSTAFF Now, my masters, happy man be his dole,[9] say I.
Every man to his business.

Enter the TRAVELERS.

70 FIRST TRAVELER Come, neighbor, the boy shall lead our horses
down the hill. We'll walk afoot awhile and ease our legs.

THIEVES Stand!

SECOND TRAVELER Jesus bless us!

FALSTAFF Strike! Down with them! Cut the villains' throats!
75   Ah, whoreson caterpillars,[1] bacon-fed knaves! They hate us
youth. Down with them, fleece them!

FIRST TRAVELER Oh, we are undone, both we and ours for ever.

FALSTAFF Hang ye, gorbellied° knaves, are ye undone? No, ye   *potbellied*
fat chuffs;[2] I would your store° were here. On, bacons,° on!   *all you own / fat men*
80   What, ye knaves? Young men must live. You are grand-jurors,[3]
are ye? We'll jure ye, faith.

Here they rob them and bind them.   *Exeunt.*

Enter the PRINCE *and* POINS.

PRINCE The thieves have bound the true° men; now could thou   *honest*
and I rob the thieves and go merrily to London, it would be
argument° for a week, laughter for a month, and a good jest for   *topic for discussion*
85   ever.

---

7. When a plot (to rob) is so advanced and goes so
well; when a joke (on me) goes so far and makes me
go on foot.
8. Henry IV's father. Falstaff puns on "Gaunt" as
meaning "lean"; in fact, his name is derived from
"Ghent," his birthplace.
9. Proverbial expression meaning "Good luck to

everyone."
1. Parasites. *whoreson:* an insult derived from
"whore's son."
2. Rude, churlish fellows; misers.
3. Referring to the fact that only prosperous citizens
served on grand juries.

POINS   Stand close. I hear them coming.
       [*They retire.*]
       Enter the THIEVES *again.*
FALSTAFF   Come, my masters, let us share and then to horse
    before day. An° the Prince and Poins be not two arrant cow-   If
    ards, there's no equity stirring.° There's no more valor in   justice to be found
90 that Poins than in a wild duck.
               As they are sharing, the PRINCE *and* POINS *set*
               upon them.
PRINCE   Your money!
POINS   Villains!
               They all run away, and FALSTAFF, *after a blow or two,*
               runs away too, leaving the booty behind them.
PRINCE   Got with much ease. Now merrily to horse.
    The thieves are all scattered and possessed with fear
95 So strongly that they dare not meet each other;
    Each takes his fellow for an officer.
    Away, good Ned. Falstaff sweats to death
    And lards° the lean earth as he walks along.   drips fat on
    Were't not for laughing I should pity him.
100 POINS   How the rogue⁴ roared!   *Exeunt.*

2.3

Enter HOTSPUR *alone, reading a letter.*
HOTSPUR   "But, for mine own part, my lord, I could be well
    contented to be there, in respect of° the love I bear your   because of
    house."° He could be contented; why is he not, then? In the   family
    respect of the love he bears our house! He shows in this he
5   loves his own barn better than he loves our house. Let me
    see some more. "The purpose you undertake is dangerous"—
    Why, that's certain. 'Tis dangerous to take a cold, to sleep, to
    drink; but I tell you, my lord fool, out of this nettle, danger,
    we pluck this flower, safety. "The purpose you undertake is
10 dangerous, the friends you have named uncertain, the time
    itself unsorted,° and your whole plot too light for the counter-   unsuitable
    poise of° so great an opposition." Say you so, say you so? I say   to counterbalance
    unto you again you are a shallow cowardly hind,° and you lie.   peasant
    What a lack-brain is this! By the Lord, our plot is a good plot
15 as ever was laid, our friends true and constant; a good plot,
    good friends, and full of expectation; an excellent plot, very
    good friends. What a frosty-spirited rogue is this! Why, my
    lord of York° commends the plot and the general course of   (Archbishop Scrope)
    the action. Zounds, an° I were now by this rascal, I could   if
20 brain him with his lady's fan. Is there not my father, my
    uncle, and myself; Lord Edmund Mortimer, my lord of York,
    and Owain Glyndŵr? Is there not, besides, the Douglas?
    Have I not all their letters to meet me in arms by the ninth of
    the next month, and are they not some of them set forward
25 already? What a pagan rascal is this! An infidel! Ha, you

---

4. TEXTUAL COMMENT Q0 has "fat rogue" here,   serves all readings from its base text (in this case,
which echoes what Poins calls Falstaff at 1.2.162–63   Q1) that are not deficient. See Digital Edition TC 8.
and what the Prince calls him at 2.4.495; but this   2.3 Location: The Percys' home, Warkworth Castle,
edition, in distinction to traditional editing, con-   in Northumberland.

shall see now in very sincerity of fear and cold heart will he
to the King and lay open all our proceedings! Oh, I could
divide myself and go to buffets[1] for moving° such a dish of   *urging*
skim milk with so honorable an action. Hang him! Let him
30   tell the King. We are prepared; I will set forward tonight.

        Enter his lady[, LADY PERCY].

  How now, Kate? I must leave you within these two hours.
LADY PERCY   O my good lord, why are you thus alone?
  For what offense have I this fortnight been
  A banished woman from my Harry's bed?
35   Tell me, sweet lord, what is't that takes from thee
  Thy stomach,° pleasure, and thy golden sleep?   *appetite*
  Why dost thou bend thine eyes upon the earth
  And start so often when thou sitt'st alone?
  Why hast thou lost the fresh blood in thy cheeks
40   And given my treasures and my rights[2] of thee
  To thick-eyed° musing and cursed melancholy?   *vacantly staring*
  In thy faint° slumbers I by thee have watched   *restless*
  And heard thee murmur tales of iron wars,
  Speak terms of manage° to thy bounding steed,   *horsemanship*
45   Cry, "Courage! To the field!" And thou hast talked
  Of sallies and retires,° of trenches, tents,   *advances and retreats*
  Of palisadoes,[3] frontiers,° parapets,   *ramparts*
  Of basilisks, of cannon, culverin,[4]
  Of prisoners' ransom, and of soldiers slain,
50   And all the currents of a heady° fight.   *headlong*
  Thy spirit within thee hath been so at war,
  And thus hath so bestirred thee in thy sleep,
  That beads of sweat have stood upon thy brow
  Like bubbles in a late-disturbèd° stream,   *recently disturbed*
55   And in thy face strange motions have appeared
  Such as we see when men restrain their breath
  On some great sudden hest.° Oh, what portents° are these?   *command / omens*
  Some heavy° business hath my lord in hand,   *serious; sad*
  And I must know it, else he loves me not.
HOTSPUR   —What ho!

      [*Enter* SERVANT.]

60   Is Gilliams with the packet gone?
SERVANT   He is, my lord, an hour ago.
HOTSPUR   Hath Butler brought those horses from the Sheriff?
SERVANT   One horse, my lord, he brought even now.
HOTSPUR   What horse? Roan, a crop-ear, is it not?
SERVANT   It is, my lord.
65 HOTSPUR   That roan shall be my throne.
  Well, I will back him straight. O Esperance![5]
  Bid Butler lead him forth into the park.   [*Exit* SERVANT.]

---

1. I could split myself into two and fall to blows with
myself.
2. Marriage rights. Alluding to the belief that husbands and wives owe a mutual marriage debt that
obliges them regularly to engage in sexual relations
with each other.
3. Pointed stakes driven into the ground as defensive

barriers.
4. *basilisks:* large cannons, named after a deadly
mythological reptile. *culverin:* a name for both a kind
of long cannon and a firearm noted for its long range.
5. Referring to the Percy motto *Esperance ma com-
forte,* or "Hope is my reliance."

LADY PERCY   But hear you, my lord.

HOTSPUR   What say'st thou, my lady?

LADY PERCY   What is it carries you away?

70 HOTSPUR   Why, my horse, my love, my horse.

LADY PERCY   Out, you mad-headed ape!
A weasel[6] hath not such a deal of spleen°   *impulsiveness; anger*
As you are tossed with. In faith,
I'll know your business, Harry, that I will.

75 I fear my brother Mortimer doth stir
About his title and hath sent for you
To line° his enterprise; but if you go—   *strengthen*

HOTSPUR   So far afoot I shall be weary, love.

LADY PERCY   Come, come, you paraquito,° answer me   *little parrot*

80 Directly unto this question that I ask.
In faith, I'll break thy little finger, Harry,
An if thou wilt not tell me all things true.

HOTSPUR   Away, away, you trifler! Love? I love thee not;
I care not for thee, Kate. This is no world

85 To play with mammets[7] and to tilt° with lips.   *duel*
We must have bloody noses and cracked crowns,[8]
And pass them current,[9] too. God's me,° my horse!   *God save me*
What say'st thou, Kate? What wouldst thou have with me?

LADY PERCY   Do you not love me? Do you not indeed?

90 Well, do not, then, for since you love me not
I will not love myself. Do you not love me?
Nay, tell me if you speak in jest or no?

HOTSPUR   Come, wilt thou see me ride?
And when I am a-horseback,[1] I will swear

95 I love thee infinitely. But hark you, Kate,
I must not have you henceforth question me
Whither I go, nor reason whereabout.°   *discuss about what*
Whither I must, I must, and to conclude,
This evening must I leave you, gentle Kate.

100 I know you wise but yet no farther wise
Than Harry Percy's wife. Constant you are
But yet a woman;[2] and for secrecy
No lady closer,° for I well believe   *more secretive*
Thou wilt not utter what thou dost not know,

105 And so far will I trust thee, gentle Kate.

LADY PERCY   How, so far?

HOTSPUR   Not an inch further. But hark you, Kate,
Whither I go, thither shall you go too.
Today will I set forth, tomorrow you.
Will this content you, Kate?

110 LADY PERCY   It must, of force.°   *Exeunt.*   *of necessity*

---

6. Weasels were proverbially quarrelsome.
7. Breasts; dolls; false gods. The term derived from "Mahomet," whom European Christians viewed as a false god worshipped by heathen peoples.
8. Punning on "cracked crowns" as meaning "broken heads" and "counterfeit currency." Hotspur may be alluding to the acts of rape associated with warfare:

"nose" is slang for "penis," and a "cracked crown" can mean a "whore" or a "deflowered woman."
9. Establish them as the norm; let them circulate.
1. On my horse; having sexual intercourse.
2. Women were assumed to be great talkers who could keep no secrets.

2.4

Enter PRINCE *and* POINS.

PRINCE   Ned, prithee come out of that fat° room and lend me   *stuffy*
   thy hand to laugh a little.

POINS   Where hast been, Hal?

PRINCE   With three or four loggerheads,° amongst three or   *blockheads*
5   fourscore hogsheads.° I have sounded the very bass string of   *casks for liquor*
   humility. Sirrah, I am sworn brother to a leash of drawers°   *group of three tapsters*
   and can call them all by their Christian names, as Tom, Dick,
   and Francis. They take it already, upon their salvation, that
   though I be but Prince of Wales, yet I am the king of cour-
10   tesy, and tell me flatly I am no proud jack,° like Falstaff, but a   *fellow*
   Corinthian,[1] a lad of mettle, a "good boy"—by the Lord, so
   they call me—and, when I am King of England, I shall command all the good lads in Eastcheap. They call drinking
   deep "dyeing scarlet,"[2] and when you breathe in your water-
15   ing,[3] they cry "Hem!" and bid you "Play it off!"°   *Drink up*   To conclude,
   I am so good a proficient in one quarter of an hour that I can
   drink with any tinker° in his own language during my life. I tell   *itinerant pot mender*
   thee, Ned, thou hast lost much honor that thou wert not with
   me in this action. But, sweet Ned—to sweeten which name of
20   Ned, I give thee this pennyworth of sugar,[4] clapped even now
   into my hand by an underskinker,° one that never spake other   *assistant tapster*
   English in his life than "Eight shillings and six pence," and
   "You are welcome," with this shrill addition, "Anon,° anon,   *At once*
   sir! Score° a pint of bastard[5] in the Half Moon,"[6] or so. But,   *Chalk up*
25   Ned, to drive away the time till Falstaff come, I prithee, do
   thou stand in some by-room, while I question my puny° drawer   *inexperienced*
   to what end he gave me the sugar, and do thou never leave calling "Francis!" that his tale to me may be nothing but "Anon."
   Step aside and I'll show thee a precedent.°   [*Exit* POINS.]   *give you a foretaste*

30   POINS [*within*]   Francis!

PRINCE   Thou art perfect.

POINS [*within*]   Francis!

         Enter drawer [FRANCIS].

FRANCIS   Anon, anon, sir! —Look down into the Pomegranate,[7]
   Ralph!

35   PRINCE   Come hither, Francis.

FRANCIS   My lord?

PRINCE   How long hast thou to serve,[8] Francis?

FRANCIS   Forsooth, five years, and as much as to—

POINS [*within*]   Francis!

40   FRANCIS   Anon, anon, sir!

2.4 Location: An inn in Eastcheap, London.
1. A rich, licentious man. In contemporary texts, ancient Corinth was famous for wealth and sensuality.
2. Referring to the ruddy complexion associated with drunkards or to the fact that urine, a product of drink, was used to dye wool.
3. When you pause to breathe in your drink.
4. Tapsters sold sugar to sweeten wine.

5. A Spanish wine, so named because it was mixed or adulterated with honey.
6. Name of the inn room to which the wine is to be charged.
7. Name of another room in the inn.
8. Serve as apprentice. Apprenticeship typically began at age twelve or fourteen and lasted seven years.

PRINCE   Five year! By'r Lady,[9] a long lease for the clinking of
pewter. But Francis, darest thou be so valiant as to play the
coward with thy indenture,° and show it a fair pair of heels,   contract
and run from it?

45 FRANCIS   O Lord, sir, I'll be sworn upon all the books° in   (Bibles)
England, I could find in my heart—

POINS [*within*]   Francis!

FRANCIS   Anon, sir!

PRINCE   How old art thou, Francis?

50 FRANCIS   Let me see; about Michaelmas[1] next I shall be—

POINS [*within*]   Francis!

FRANCIS   Anon, sir! Pray stay a little, my lord.

PRINCE   Nay, but hark you, Francis. For the sugar thou gavest
me, 'twas a pennyworth, was't not?

55 FRANCIS   O Lord, I would it had been two!

PRINCE   I will give thee for it a thousand pound. Ask me when
thou wilt, and thou shalt have it.

POINS [*within*]   Francis!

FRANCIS   Anon, anon!

60 PRINCE   "Anon," Francis? No, Francis, but tomorrow, Francis;
or, Francis, o'Thursday; or, indeed, Francis, when thou wilt.
But Francis—

FRANCIS   My lord?

PRINCE   Wilt thou rob this leathern-jerkin, crystal-button,
65   knot-pated, agate-ring, puke-stocking, caddis-garter, smooth-
tongue, Spanish-pouch?[2]

FRANCIS   O Lord, sir, who do you mean?

PRINCE   Why, then, your brown bastard is your only drink![3]
For look you, Francis, your white canvas doublet will sully.°   get dirty
70 In Barbary,[4] sir, it cannot come to° so much.   be worth

FRANCIS   What, sir?

POINS [*within*]   Francis!

PRINCE   Away, you rogue! Dost thou not hear them call?
Here they both call him; the drawer [FRANCIS] *stands
amazed, not knowing which way to go.*
Enter VINTNER.°   Innkeeper

VINTNER   What, stand'st thou still and hear'st such a calling?
75 Look to the guests within.   [*Exit* FRANCIS.]
My lord, old Sir John with half a dozen more are at the door.
Shall I let them in?

PRINCE   Let them alone awhile and then open the door.
[*Exit* VINTNER.]

9. By our Lady (an oath invoking the Virgin Mary).
1. September 29, a holy day honoring the archangel
Michael and signifying to tradespeople the close of
an accounting period.
2. Referring (satirically) to Francis's employer, who
would be robbed of Francis's labor if the apprentice
were to run away. This employer is imagined as dressing in the manner of an upwardly mobile Londoner,
wearing a leather jacket ("jerkin") with crystal buttons and keeping his hair close-cropped ("knot-
pated"). He also wears a signet ring with a carved

agate, dark ("puke") stockings, and garters made from
caddis ribbon (a cheap alternative to silk). He has a
simpering style of speech and carries a vintner's
pouch made of Spanish leather.
3. The best of all drinks; the only drink you'll get
(if you stay in the tavern). This entire speech seems
meant to mystify Francis while obliquely warning
him that he will get dirty and be poor if he fulfills his
apprenticeship.
4. North African region from which England
acquired sugar.

Poins!
   Enter POINS.
80 POINS Anon, anon, sir!
PRINCE Sirrah, Falstaff and the rest of the thieves are at the
  door. Shall we be merry?
POINS As merry as crickets, my lad. But hark ye, what cun-   *game*
  ning match° have you made with this jest of the drawer?   *outcome*
85 Come, what's the issue?°
PRINCE I am now of all humors that have showed themselves
  humors[5] since the old days of Goodman[6] Adam to the pupil°   *youthful*
  age of this present twelve o'clock at midnight.
    [*Enter* FRANCIS.]
  What's o'clock, Francis?
90 FRANCIS Anon, anon, sir!   [*Exit.*]
PRINCE That ever this fellow should have fewer words than a
  parrot, and yet the son of a woman! His industry is upstairs
  and downstairs, his eloquence the parcel of a reckoning.° I   *items of a bill*
  am not yet of Percy's mind, the Hotspur of the North, he
95 that kills me° some six or seven dozen of Scots at a break-   *he that slays*
  fast, washes his hands, and says to his wife, "Fie upon this
  quiet life! I want work." "O my sweet Harry," says she, "how
  many hast thou killed today?" "Give my roan horse a drench,"° *dose of medicine*
  says he, and answers, "Some fourteen," an hour after, "A trifle,
100 a trifle." I prithee call in Falstaff. I'll play Percy, and that
  damned brawn° shall play Dame Mortimer his wife. "Rivo!"[7]   *fat boar*
  says the drunkard. Call in Ribs; call in Tallow.°   *Fat drippings*
    Enter FALSTAFF[, BARDOLPH, PETO, *and* GADSHILL,
    followed by FRANCIS *with wine*].
POINS Welcome, Jack. Where hast thou been?
FALSTAFF A plague of all cowards, I say, and a vengeance too!
105 Marry and amen! —Give me a cup of sack, boy. —Ere I lead
  this life long, I'll sew netherstocks,° and mend them and foot[8]   *stockings*
  them, too. A plague of all cowards. —Give me a cup of sack,
  rogue. —Is there no virtue extant?
    He drinketh.
PRINCE Didst thou never see Titan° kiss a dish of butter—   *the sun*
110 pitiful-hearted Titan—that melted at the sweet tale of the
  sun's? If thou didst, then behold that compound.[9]
FALSTAFF [*to* FRANCIS] You rogue, here's lime[1] in this sack
  too.—There is nothing but roguery to be found in villainous
  man, yet a coward is worse than a cup of sack with lime in it.
115 A villainous coward! Go thy ways, old Jack, die when thou
  wilt; if manhood, good manhood, be not forgot upon the face
  of the earth, then am I a shotten herring.[2] There lives not
  three good men unhanged in England, and one of them is fat
  and grows old, God help the while!° A bad world, I say. I   *these times*

---

5. That is, I am in the mood for anything. Renaissance medical theory held that four body fluids, or
humors, determined by their relative proportions the
health, temperament, and moods of an individual.
6. A title for a farmer.
7. An exclamation associated with boisterous
drinking.

8. Make a new foot for.
9. Combination; that is, the melted butter (referring
to Falstaff).
1. Often added to bad wine to make it dry and
sparkling.
2. A herring that has spawned its roe and is thus very
thin.

120 would I were a weaver.[3] I could sing psalms or anything. A
plague of all cowards, I say still.

PRINCE   How now, woolsack, what mutter you?

FALSTAFF   A king's son! If I do not beat thee out of thy kingdom
with a dagger of lath[4] and drive all thy subjects afore thee like
125 a flock of wild geese, I'll never wear hair on my face more.
You, Prince of Wales!

PRINCE   Why, you whoreson round man, what's the matter?

FALSTAFF   Are not you a coward? Answer me to that. And
Poins there?

130 POINS   Zounds, ye fat paunch, an ye call me coward, by the
Lord, I'll stab thee.

FALSTAFF   I call thee coward? I'll see thee damned ere I call
thee coward, but I would give a thousand pound I could run
as fast as thou canst. You are straight enough in the shoul-
135 ders; you care not who sees your back. Call you that backing
of your friends? A plague upon such backing! Give me them
that will face me. Give me a cup of sack. I am a rogue if I
drunk today.

PRINCE   O villain, thy lips are scarce wiped since thou drunk'st
140 last.

FALSTAFF   All is one for that.°   *It doesn't matter*
He drinketh.
A plague of all cowards, still say I.

PRINCE   What's the matter?

FALSTAFF   What's the matter? There be four of us here have
145 ta'en a thousand pound this day morning.°   *this morning*

PRINCE   Where is it, Jack? Where is it?

FALSTAFF   Where is it? Taken from us it is. A hundred upon
poor four of us.

PRINCE   What, a hundred, man?

150 FALSTAFF   I am a rogue if I were not at half-sword° with a   *dueling closely*
dozen of them two hours together. I have scaped by miracle.
I am eight times thrust through the doublet, four through
the hose, my buckler[5] cut through and through, my sword
hacked like a handsaw. *Ecce signum!*[6] I never dealt better
155 since I was a man. All would not do.[7] A plague of all cowards!
Let them speak. If they speak more or less than truth, they
are villains and the sons of darkness.

PRINCE[8]   Speak, sirs, how was it?

BARDOLPH   We four set upon some dozen—

160 FALSTAFF   Sixteen at least, my lord.

BARDOLPH   —and bound them.

PETO   No, no, they were not bound.

FALSTAFF   You rogue, they were bound every man of them, or
I am a Jew else, an Hebrew Jew.

---

3. Weavers were reputed to sing the Psalms of the
Bible at work. Many were puritans, and some had emi-
grated from the zealously Protestant Low Countries.
4. A wooden dagger, which was the weapon associated with the Vice figure in medieval morality plays
(see note to line 412).
5. *doublet*: short jacket. *hose*: breeches. *buckler*: shield.
6. Behold the evidence (Latin).
7. All I did was not enough; the whole group was

insufficient opposition.
8. TEXTUAL COMMENT In Q1, this line is assigned to
Gadshill and the following line to Russell (whose
name was changed to "Bardolph"; see Digital Edition
TC 4 at 1.2.142). In F, this line is assigned to the
Prince and the following line to Gadshill. This edition follows F's attribution of the line to the Prince
because he is the character interrogating Falstaff
and his companions. See Digital Edition TC 9.

165   BARDOLPH   As we were sharing, some six or seven fresh men
     set upon us.
     FALSTAFF   And unbound the rest, and then come in the other.
     PRINCE   What, fought you with them all?
     FALSTAFF   All? I know not what you call all, but if I fought not
170   with fifty of them, I am a bunch of radish. If there were not
     two- or three-and-fifty upon poor old Jack, then am I no
     two-legged creature.
     PRINCE   Pray God you have not murdered some of them.
     FALSTAFF   Nay, that's past praying for. I have peppered° two   *made it hot for*
175   of them. Two I am sure I have paid,° two rogues in buckram°   *killed / fine cotton*
     suits. I tell thee what, Hal, if I tell thee a lie, spit in my face,
     call me horse. Thou knowest my old ward.[9] Here I lay,° and   *stood*
     thus I bore my point.° Four rogues in buckram let drive at me—   *sword point*
     PRINCE   What, four? Thou said'st but two even now.
180   FALSTAFF   Four, Hal, I told thee four.
     POINS   Ay, ay, he said four.
     FALSTAFF   These four came all afront° and mainly° thrust at me.   *abreast / mightily*
     I made me no more ado, but took all their seven points in my
     target,° thus.   *shield*
185   PRINCE   Seven? Why, there were but four even now.
     FALSTAFF   In buckram?
     POINS   Ay, four in buckram suits.
     FALSTAFF   Seven, by these hilts,° or I am a villain else.   *sword handles*
     PRINCE   [*to* POINS]   Prithee, let him alone. We shall have more
190   anon.
     FALSTAFF   Dost thou hear me, Hal?
     PRINCE   Ay, and mark° thee too, Jack.   *pay attention to; count*
     FALSTAFF   Do so, for it is worth the listening to. These nine in
     buckram that I told thee of—
195   PRINCE   So, two more already.
     FALSTAFF   —their points[1] being broken—
     POINS   Down fell their hose.
     FALSTAFF   —began to give me ground, but I followed me° close,   *I followed*
     came in, foot and hand, and, with a thought,° seven of the   *swift as thought*
200   eleven I paid.
     PRINCE   Oh, monstrous! Eleven buckram men grown out of
     two!
     FALSTAFF   But as the devil would have it, three misbegotten
     knaves in Kendal green[2] came at my back and let drive at me,
205   for it was so dark, Hal, that thou couldst not see thy hand.
     PRINCE   These lies are like their father that begets them,
     gross as a mountain, open, palpable. Why, thou clay-brained
     guts, thou knotty-pated° fool, thou whoreson obscene greasy   *blockheaded*
     tallow-catch[3]—
210   FALSTAFF   What, art thou mad? Art thou mad? Is not the truth
     the truth?
     PRINCE   Why, how couldst thou know these men in Kendal
     green when it was so dark thou couldst not see thy hand?
     Come, tell us your reason. What sayest thou to this?

---

9. Posture of defense.
1. Sword points, but Poins takes it as meaning "fastenings for hose."
2. A coarse green cloth made in Kendal, Cumbria. It was associated with poor country people, especially forest dwellers, as well as outlaws.
3. Greasy lump of fat (gathered by butchers for candle making).

215 POINS   Come, your reason, Jack, your reason.

FALSTAFF   What, upon compulsion? Zounds, an I were at the
strappado,[4] or all the racks[5] in the world, I would not tell you
on compulsion. Give you a reason on compulsion? If reasons
were as plentiful as blackberries, I would give no man a rea-
220   son upon compulsion, I.

PRINCE   I'll be no longer guilty of this sin. This sanguine°   *red-faced*
coward, this bed-presser,° this horse-back-breaker, this huge   *licentious man*
hill of flesh—

FALSTAFF   'Sblood, you starveling, you eel-skin, you dried neat's°   *ox's*
225   tongue, you bull's pizzle, you stock-fish![6] Oh, for breath to
utter what is like thee, you tailor's yard,[7] you sheath, you bow-
case, you vile standing tuck[8]—

PRINCE   Well, breathe a while and then to it again, and when
thou hast tired thyself in base comparisons, hear me speak
230   but this.

POINS   Mark, Jack.

PRINCE   We two saw you four set on four, and bound them, and
were masters of their wealth. Mark now how a plain tale shall
put you down. Then did we two set on you four, and, with a
235   word, outfaced you from your prize, and have it, yea, and can
show it you here in the house. And, Falstaff, you carried your
guts away as nimbly, with as quick dexterity, and roared for
mercy, and still run and roared, as ever I heard bull-calf.
What a slave art thou to hack thy sword as thou hast done
240   and then say it was in fight! What trick, what device, what
starting-hole° canst thou now find out to hide thee from this   *refuge*
open and apparent shame?

POINS   Come, let's hear, Jack. What trick hast thou now?

FALSTAFF   By the Lord, I knew ye as well as he that made ye.
245   Why, hear you, my masters, was it for me to kill the heir apparent? Should I turn upon the true prince? Why, thou knowest
I am as valiant as Hercules,[9] but beware instinct. The lion will
not touch the true prince.[1] Instinct is a great matter. I was
now a coward on instinct. I shall think the better of myself,
250   and thee, during my life—I for a valiant lion and thou for
a true prince. But by the Lord, lads, I am glad you have the
money. Hostess, clap to the doors. Watch tonight, pray tomorrow.[2] Gallants, lads, boys, hearts of gold, all the titles of good
fellowship come to you! What, shall we be merry? Shall we
255   have a play extempore?°   *spontaneously*

PRINCE   Content, and the argument° shall be thy running away.   *subject*

FALSTAFF   Ah, no more of that, Hal, an thou lovest me.

          Enter HOSTESS.

HOSTESS   O Jesu, my lord the Prince!

---

4. A torture device in which victims were lifted off
the ground by ropes attached to their hands, which
were tied behind their backs, and then let fall.
5. A torture device in which victims' limbs were
pulled apart.
6. *bull's pizzle:* a bull's penis that when dried and
stretched was used as a whip. *stock-fish:* dried cod.
7. Tailors were popularly imagined to lack virility.
Falstaff puns on "yard" as referring both to a tailor's
measuring stick and to his penis.
8. *sheath:* empty case (punning on "sheath" as mean-

ing "foreskin"). *bow-case:* a long, thin case for
unstrung bows. *standing tuck:* a stiff rapier (with a
pun on "standing" as meaning "sexually erect").
9. In classical mythology, a hero who performed prodigious acts of strength and courage.
1. A popular belief derived from classical texts.
2. Falstaff alludes here to Matthew 26:41: "Watch
and pray, that ye enter not into temptation." He puns
on "watch" as meaning "keep vigil" and "carouse"
and on "pray" as meaning "prey."

PRINCE   How now, my lady the hostess, what say'st thou to me?

260   HOSTESS   Marry, my lord, there is a nobleman of the court
at door would speak with you. He says he comes from your
father.

PRINCE   Give him as much as will make him a royal man[3] and
send him back again to my mother.

265   FALSTAFF   What manner of man is he?

HOSTESS   An old man.

FALSTAFF   What doth gravity out of his bed at midnight? Shall
I give him his answer?

PRINCE   Prithee, do, Jack.

270   FALSTAFF   Faith, and I'll send him packing.   *Exit.*

PRINCE   Now, sirs, by'r Lady, you fought fair; so did you, Peto;
so did you, Bardolph; you are lions too; you ran away upon
instinct. You will not touch the true prince, no, fie!

BARDOLPH   Faith, I ran when I saw others run.

275   PRINCE   Faith, tell me now in earnest, how came Falstaff's
sword so hacked?

PETO   Why, he hacked it with his dagger, and said he would
swear truth out of England[4] but he would make you believe
it was done in fight, and persuaded us to do the like.

280   BARDOLPH   Yea, and to tickle our noses with spear-grass[5] to
make them bleed, and then to beslubber our garments with
it and swear it was the blood of true men. I did that° I did   *what*
not this seven year before: I blushed to hear his monstrous
devices.

285   PRINCE   O villain, thou stolest a cup of sack eighteen years
ago, and wert taken with the manner,° and ever since thou   *caught in the act*
hast blushed extempore. Thou hadst fire[6] and sword on thy
side, and yet thou rann'st away; what instinct hadst thou for it?

BARDOLPH   My lord, do you see these meteors? Do you behold
290   these exhalations?[7]

PRINCE   I do.

BARDOLPH   What think you they portend?°   *signify*

PRINCE   Hot livers[8] and cold° purses.   *empty*

BARDOLPH   Choler,[9] my lord, if rightly taken.°   *understood*

Enter FALSTAFF.

295   PRINCE   No, if rightly taken, halter.[1] Here comes lean Jack;
here comes bare-bone. How now, my sweet creature of bombast?[2] How long is't ago, Jack, since thou sawest thine own
knee?

FALSTAFF   My own knee? When I was about thy years, Hal, I
300   was not an eagle's talon in the waist; I could have crept into
any alderman's° thumb-ring. A plague of sighing and grief,   *civil officer's*
it blows a man up like a bladder. There's villainous news
abroad. Here was Sir John Bracy from your father; you must

3. Punning on "nobles" and "royals" as names of coins, the latter being more valuable.
4. Swear so excessively that Truth, imagined as an allegorical figure, would run out of England to escape him.
5. A plant with sharply pointed leaves.
6. A reference to Bardolph's red face, the focus of the jests that follow.
7. "Meteors" and "exhalations" refer to the red blotches on Bardolph's face, here compared to disturbances in the heavens.
8. Short tempers; livers inflamed by drink.
9. The humor associated with an angry disposition.
1. No, if rightly arrested, a noose. The Prince forces a legal reading on the previous line, playing on "choler" as "collar," or "noose," and taking "taken" to mean "arrested."
2. Cotton padding; pompous speech.

305 to the court in the morning. That same mad fellow of the
North, Percy, and he of Wales that gave Amaimon° the bas-
tinado° and made Lucifer cuckold³ and swore the devil his
true liegeman° upon the cross of a Welsh hook⁴—what a
plague call you him?

POINS   Oh, Glyndŵr.

310 FALSTAFF   Owain, Owain, the same; and his son-in-law
Mortimer, and old Northumberland, and that sprightly
Scot of Scots, Douglas, that runs a-horseback up a hill
perpendicular—

PRINCE   He that rides at high speed and with his pistol kills a
315 sparrow flying.

FALSTAFF   You have hit it.

PRINCE   So did he never the sparrow.

FALSTAFF   Well, that rascal hath good metal in him; he will
not run.

320 PRINCE   Why, what a rascal art thou, then, to praise him so
for running?

FALSTAFF   A-horseback, ye cuckoo, but afoot he will not budge
a foot.

PRINCE   Yes, Jack, upon instinct.

325 FALSTAFF   I grant ye, upon instinct. Well, he is there too, and
one Murdoch, and a thousand blue-caps° more. Worcester
is stolen away tonight. Thy father's beard is turned white
with the news. You may buy land now as cheap as stinking
mackerel.

330 PRINCE   Why, then, it is like if there come a hot June and this
civil buffeting hold,° we shall buy maidenheads as they buy
hobnails, by the hundreds.⁵

FALSTAFF   By the mass, lad, thou say'st true; it is like we shall
have good trading that way. But tell me, Hal, art not thou
335 horrible afeard? Thou being heir apparent, could the world
pick thee out three such enemies again as that fiend Douglas, that spirit Percy, and that devil Glyndŵr? Art thou not
horribly afraid? Doth not thy blood thrill° at it?

PRINCE   Not a whit, i'faith. I lack some of thy instinct.

340 FALSTAFF   Well, thou wilt be horribly chid tomorrow when
thou comest to thy father. If thou love me, practice an answer.

PRINCE   Do thou stand for° my father and examine me upon
the particulars of my life.

FALSTAFF   Shall I? Content. This chair shall be my state,° this
345 dagger my scepter, and this cushion my crown.

PRINCE   Thy state is taken for a joint-stool,⁶ thy golden scepter for a leaden dagger, and thy precious rich crown for a
pitiful bald crown.

FALSTAFF   Well, an° the fire of grace be not quite out of thee,
350 now shalt thou be moved. Give me a cup of sack to make my

(a devil)
a beating
subject

Scottish soldiers

continue

shudder

impersonate

throne

if

---

3. Slept with the devil's own wife; gave the devil his
horns (the proverbial sign of a cuckold).
4. A heavy weapon with a crooked end, lacking the
cross shape on which oaths were usually made.
5. Alluding to rape as a practice of war or to the

notion that women would be likely to relinquish their
virginity cheaply during wartime.
6. A stool made of wooden pieces fitted or joined
together.

eyes look red, that it may be thought I have wept, for I must
speak in passion, and I will do it in King Cambyses' vein.[7]

PRINCE   Well, here is my leg.°   *bow*

FALSTAFF   And here is my speech. Stand aside, nobility.

355   HOSTESS   O Jesu, this is excellent sport, i'faith.

FALSTAFF   Weep not, sweet Queen,[8] for trickling tears are vain.

HOSTESS   O the Father, how he holds his countenance!°   *keeps a straight face*

FALSTAFF   For God's sake, lords, convey° my trustful[9] Queen,   *lead away*
For tears do stop° the floodgates of her eyes.   *fill*

360   HOSTESS   O Jesu, he doth it as like one of these harlotry° play-   *vagabond; scurvy*
ers as ever I see!

FALSTAFF   Peace, good pint-pot; peace, good tickle-brain.[1]
—Harry, I do not only marvel where thou spendest thy time,
but also how thou art accompanied. For though the chamo-
365   mile,° the more it is trodden on, the faster it grows, so youth,   *(an herb)*
the more it is wasted, the sooner it wears.[2] That thou art my
son, I have partly thy mother's word, partly my own opinion,
but chiefly a villainous trick° of thine eye and a foolish hang-   *trait*
ing of thy nether° lip that doth warrant° me. If, then, thou   *lower / assure*
370   be son to me, here lies the point: why, being son to me, art
thou so pointed at?° Shall the blessed sun of heaven prove a   *criticized*
micher° and eat blackberries? A question not to be asked.   *truant*
Shall the son of England prove a thief and take purses? A
question to be asked. There is a thing, Harry, which thou
375   hast often heard of, and it is known to many in our land by
the name of pitch.° This pitch, as ancient writers do report,   *sticky, black tar*
doth defile;[3] so doth the company thou keepest. For, Harry,
now I do not speak to thee in drink but in tears; not in pleasure but in passion; not in words only but in woes also. And
380   yet there is a virtuous man whom I have often noted in thy
company, but I know not his name.

PRINCE   What manner of man, an it like your majesty?

FALSTAFF   A goodly, portly man, i'faith, and a corpulent; of a
cheerful look, a pleasing eye, and a most noble carriage;°   *bearing*
385   and, as I think, his age some fifty, or, by'r Lady, inclining to
threescore. And now I remember me: his name is Falstaff.
If that man should be lewdly given,° he deceiveth me; for,   *be lustful*
Harry, I see virtue in his looks. If, then, the tree may be
known by the fruit, as the fruit by the tree,[4] then perempto-
390   rily I speak it: there is virtue in that Falstaff. Him keep with;
the rest banish. And tell me now, thou naughty varlet, tell
me, where hast thou been this month?

PRINCE   Dost thou speak like a king? Do thou stand for me,
and I'll play my father.

---

7. In the exaggerated rhetorical style associated with
such early Elizabethan plays as *Cambyses,* a tragedy
about a despotic Persian king.

8. Possibly addressed to the Hostess, with a pun on
"quean" as slang for "whore."

9. TEXTUAL COMMENT Loyal. Most editors emend to
"tristful," which emphasizes the sad, tearful aspect
of the queen, but this edition, following the early
quartos and folios, retains "trustful." See Digital Edition TC 10.

1. Slang term for a strong alcoholic drink, and hence
for the drinker.

2. Falstaff's entire speech is a parody of the previously fashionable ornate rhetoric exemplified by John
Lyly's *Euphues* (1578).

3. See Ecclesiasticus 13:1 (also cited in Lyly's
Euphues).

4. An allusion to Matthew 12:33 (which also appears
in Lyly's *Euphues*).

395   FALSTAFF   Depose me? If thou dost it half so gravely, so majes-
tically both in word and matter, hang me up by the heels for
a rabbit-sucker° or a poulter's hare.[5]   *an unweaned rabbit*
    PRINCE   Well, here I am set.°   *seated*
    FALSTAFF   And here I stand. Judge, my masters.
400   PRINCE   Now, Harry, whence come you?
    FALSTAFF   My noble lord, from Eastcheap.
    PRINCE   The complaints I hear of thee are grievous.
    FALSTAFF   'Sblood, my lord, they are false! —Nay, I'll tickle ye
for° a young prince, i'faith.   *amuse you as*
405   PRINCE   Swearest thou, ungracious boy? Henceforth ne'er look
on me. Thou art violently carried away from grace. There is
a devil haunts thee in the likeness of an old fat man; a tun°   *large barrel*
of man is thy companion. Why dost thou converse° with that   *associate*
trunk of humors,[6] that bolting-hutch[7] of beastliness, that
410   swollen parcel of dropsies,[8] that huge bombard° of sack,   *leather wine vessel*
that stuffed cloak-bag° of guts, that roasted Manningtree[9] ox   *suitcase*
with the pudding° in his belly, that reverend Vice,[1] that grey   *stuffing*
Iniquity, that father Ruffian, that Vanity in years? Wherein
is he good,° but to taste sack and drink it? Wherein neat   *virtuous; proficient*
415   and cleanly,° but to carve a capon and eat it? Wherein   *deft*
cunning, but in craft? Wherein crafty, but in villainy?
Wherein villainous, but in all things? Wherein worthy, but
in nothing?
    FALSTAFF   I would your grace would take me with you.° Whom   *explain what you mean*
420   means your grace?
    PRINCE   That villainous abominable misleader of youth, Fal-
staff, that old white-bearded Satan.
    FALSTAFF   My lord, the man I know.
    PRINCE   I know thou dost.
425   FALSTAFF   But to say I know more harm in him than in myself
were to say more than I know. That he is old, the more the
pity; his white hairs do witness it. But that he is, saving your
reverence,[2] a whoremaster, that I utterly deny. If sack and
sugar be a fault, God help the wicked. If to be old and merry
430   be a sin, then many an old host° that I know is damned. If   *innkeeper*
to be fat be to be hated, then Pharaoh's lean kine[3] are to be
loved. No, my good lord, banish Peto, banish Bardolph, banish Poins, but for sweet Jack Falstaff, kind Jack Falstaff,
true Jack Falstaff, valiant Jack Falstaff, and therefore more
435   valiant being, as he is, old Jack Falstaff, banish not him thy
Harry's company, banish not him thy Harry's company.
Banish plump Jack and banish all the world.
              [*Knocking within. Exeunt* BARDOLPH *and* HOSTESS.][4]
    PRINCE   I do; I will.

---

5. A hare sold in a poultry shop.
6. A chest full of body fluids, whose excess, according to Renaissance medical theory, was extremely
unhealthy.
7. *bolting-hutch:* bin for coarse meal.
8. Diseases characterized by retention of water.
9. Market town in Essex noted for the Manningtree
Fair, where a roasted ox may have been part of the
festivities.
1. An irreverent, comic, and (usually) youthful character representing evil and sin in the medieval morality plays. Sometimes named "Iniquity."
2. If you will excuse the expression.
3. In a biblical story in Genesis 41:18–21, Pharaoh
dreams of seven lean cows ("kine") that portend seven
years of famine.
4. Neither F nor Q1 marks an exit for the Hostess,
but both indicate her re-entry at line 442. It makes
sense for her to exit here to see about the commotion
at her door.

Enter BARDOLPH *running.*

BARDOLPH   O my lord, my lord, the Sheriff with a most mon-
440   strous watch° is at the door.   *group of constables*

FALSTAFF   Out, ye rogue! Play out the play. I have much to say
in the behalf of that Falstaff.

Enter the HOSTESS.

HOSTESS   O Jesu, my lord, my lord!

PRINCE   Hey, hey, the devil rides upon a fiddlestick.[5] What's
445   the matter?

HOSTESS   The Sheriff and all the watch are at the door. They
are come to search the house. Shall I let them in?

FALSTAFF   Dost thou hear, Hal? Never call a true piece of gold
a counterfeit. Thou art essentially made without seeming so.[6]

450   PRINCE   And thou a natural coward without instinct.

FALSTAFF   I deny your major.° If you will deny[7] the Sheriff, so;   *main premise*
if not, let him enter. If I become° not a cart° as well as   *adorn / hangman's cart*
another man, a plague on my bringing up. I hope I shall as
soon be strangled with a halter as another.

455   PRINCE   Go hide thee behind the arras.° The rest walk up above.   *tapestry wall hanging*
Now, my masters, for a true face and good conscience.

FALSTAFF   Both which I have had, but their date is out;° and   *has expired*
therefore I'll hide me.

[*He hides behind the arras.*]

[*Exeunt all except the* PRINCE *and* PETO.]

PRINCE   Call in the Sheriff.

Enter SHERIFF *and the* CARRIER.

460   PRINCE   Now, master Sheriff, what is your will with me?

SHERIFF   First, pardon me, my lord. A hue and cry[8]
Hath followed certain men unto this house.

PRINCE   What men?

SHERIFF   One of them is well known, my gracious lord,
A gross, fat man.

465   CARRIER   As fat as butter.

PRINCE   The man, I do assure you, is not here,
For I myself at this time have employed him.
And, Sheriff, I will engage° my word to thee   *pledge*
That I will by tomorrow dinnertime
470   Send him to answer thee or any man
For anything he shall be charged withal;
And so let me entreat you leave the house.

SHERIFF   I will, my lord. There are two gentlemen
Have in this robbery lost three hundred marks.

475   PRINCE   It may be so. If he have robbed these men,
He shall be answerable. And so, farewell.

SHERIFF   Good night, my noble lord.

PRINCE   I think it is good morrow, is it not?

SHERIFF   Indeed, my lord, I think it be two o'clock.

Exit [*with* CARRIER].

---

5. That is, what a row about nothing.
6. A famously difficult passage. Falstaff may be
insisting he is true gold, not a counterfeit (and
so should not be turned over to the watch), just as

Hal is a true Prince ("essentially made") despite
appearances.
7. If you will refuse to let in.
8. A group of citizens who pursue a criminal.

480   PRINCE   This oily rascal is known as well as Paul's.° Go call   *St. Paul's Cathedral*
       him forth.

       PETO   Falstaff! —Fast asleep behind the arras and snorting
       like a horse.

       PRINCE   Hark how hard he fetches breath. Search his pockets.
       [PETO] *searcheth his pocket and findeth certain*
       papers.
       What hast thou found?

485   PETO   Nothing but papers, my lord.

       PRINCE   Let's see what they be. Read them.

       PETO   "*Item*: a capon, 2 shillings, two pence. *Item*: sauce, four
       pence. *Item*: sack, two gallons, 5 shillings, eight pence. *Item*:
       anchovies and sack after supper, two shillings, six pence.

490   *Item*: bread, *ob.*"°   *obolus (halfpenny)*

       PRINCE   Oh, monstrous! But one halfpennyworth of bread to
       this intolerable deal° of sack? What there is else keep close;   *quantity*
       we'll read it at more advantage.° There let him sleep till day.   *a better opportunity*
       I'll to the court in the morning. We must all to the wars, and

495   thy place shall be honorable. I'll procure this fat rogue a
       charge of foot,[9] and I know his death will be a march of
       twelve score.[1] The money shall be paid back again with
       advantage.° Be with me betimes° in the morning, and so good   *interest / early*
       morrow, Peto.

500   PETO   Good morrow, good my lord.   *Exeunt.*

3.1

Enter HOTSPUR, WORCESTER, Lord MORTIMER, [*and*]
Owain GLYNDŴR.[1]

       MORTIMER   These promises are fair, the parties sure,
       And our induction° full of prosperous hope.[2]   *beginning*

       HOTSPUR   Lord Mortimer and cousin Glyndŵr, will you sit
       down? And uncle Worcester—a plague upon it, I have forgot
5   the map!

       GLYNDŴR   No, here it is. Sit, cousin Percy.
       Sit, good cousin Hotspur, for by that name,
       As oft as Lancaster[3] doth speak of you,
       His cheek looks pale, and with a rising sigh
       He wisheth you in heaven.

10   HOTSPUR   And you in hell
       As oft as he hears Owain Glyndŵr spoke of.

       GLYNDŴR   I cannot blame him. At my nativity
       The front° of heaven was full of fiery shapes,   *forehead*
       Of burning cressets;[4] and at my birth
15   The frame and huge foundation of the earth
       Shaked like a coward.

       HOTSPUR   Why, so it would have done at the same season if
       your mother's cat had but kittened, though yourself had
       never been born.

---

9. Command of an infantry company.
1. I know it will kill him to march twelve times
twenty yards or paces.
3.1 Location: Glyndŵr's castle, Wales.
1. According to Holinshed's *Chronicles*, the events of
this scene take place in the house of the Archdeacon
of Bangor, but he is not present in Shakespeare's

scene, and Glyndŵr acts as host throughout.
2. Full of the hope of prospering.
3. Referring to Henry's title as Duke and hence
implying a denial of the legitimacy of his kingship.
4. Metal baskets of fire suspended from long poles;
meteors.

20	GLYNDWR I say the earth did shake when I was born.	
	HOTSPUR And I say the earth was not of my mind,	
	If you suppose as fearing you it shook.	
	GLYNDWR The heavens were all on fire; the earth did tremble.	
	HOTSPUR Oh, then the earth shook to see the heavens on fire	
25	And not in fear of your nativity.	
	Diseasèd nature oftentimes breaks forth	
	In strange eruptions. Oft the teeming° earth	*fertile*
	Is with a kind of colic pinched and vexed	
	By the imprisoning of unruly wind	
30	Within her womb, which for enlargement° striving	*release*
	Shakes the old beldam° earth and topples down	*grandmother*
	Steeples and moss-grown towers. At your birth	
	Our grandam earth, having this distemperature,°	*disorder*
	In passion shook.	
	GLYNDWR Cousin, of many men	
35	I do not bear these crossings.° Give me leave	*contradictions*
	To tell you once again that at my birth	
	The front of heaven was full of fiery shapes,	
	The goats ran from the mountains, and the herds	
	Were strangely clamorous to the frighted fields.	
40	These signs have marked me extraordinary,	
	And all the courses of my life do show	
	I am not in the roll of common men.	
	Where is he living clipped in with° the sea	*encircled by*
	That chides the banks° of England, Scotland, Wales,	*shores*
45	Which° calls me pupil or hath read to° me?	*Who / tutored*
	And bring him out° that is but woman's son	*show me any man*
	Can trace° me in the tedious ways of art[5]	*follow*
	And hold me pace° in deep experiments.	*keep up with me*
	HOTSPUR I think there's no man speaks better Welsh.[6]	
50	I'll to dinner.	
	MORTIMER Peace, cousin Percy; you will make him mad.	
	GLYNDWR I can call spirits from the vasty deep.°	*lower world*
	HOTSPUR Why, so can I, or so can any man,	
	But will they come when you do call for them?	
55	GLYNDWR Why, I can teach you, cousin, to command the devil.	
	HOTSPUR And I can teach thee, coz, to shame the devil	
	By telling truth. Tell truth and shame the devil.	
	If thou have power to raise him, bring him hither,	
	And I'll be sworn I have power to shame him hence.	
60	Oh, while you live, tell truth and shame the devil.	
	MORTIMER Come, come, no more of this unprofitable chat.	
	GLYNDWR Three times hath Henry Bolingbroke made head°	*raised an army*
	Against my power;° thrice from the banks of Wye	*army*
	And sandy-bottomed Severn have I sent him	
65	Bootless° home and weather-beaten back.[7]	*Unsuccessful*
	HOTSPUR Home without boots, and in foul weather too!	
	How scapes he agues,° in the devil's name?	*fevers*
	GLYNDWR Come, here is the map. Shall we divide our right°	*what we are entitled to*

---

5. The long, laborious ways of magic.
6. The Welsh language was often described by English writers as a barbaric one, and "to speak Welsh" commonly meant to use a strange, unintelli-

gible language. Hotspur implies that Glyndŵr speaks nonsense.
7. According to Holinshed, Glyndŵr used magic to raise storms that frustrated Henry's attacks.

According to our threefold order ta'en?[8]

70 MORTIMER   The Archdeacon hath divided it
Into three limits° very equally;   regions
England, from Trent and Severn hitherto,°   to here
By south and east is to my part assigned;
All westward, Wales beyond the Severn shore
75 And all the fertile land within that bound,
To Owain Glyndŵr; and, dear coz, to you
The remnant northward lying off from Trent;
And our indentures tripartite° are drawn,   in triplicate
Which being sealed interchangeably[9]—
80 A business that this night may execute°—   may be done tonight
Tomorrow, cousin Percy, you and I
And my good lord of Worcester will set forth
To meet your father and the Scottish power,
As is appointed us, at Shrewsbury.
85 My father° Glyndŵr is not ready yet,   father-in-law
Nor shall we need his help these fourteen days.
[to GLYNDWR]   Within that space you may have drawn together
Your tenants, friends, and neighboring gentlemen.
GLYNDWR   A shorter time shall send me to you, lords;
90 And in my conduct° shall your ladies come,   escort
From whom you now must steal and take no leave,
For there will be a world of water shed
Upon the parting of your wives and you.
HOTSPUR   Methinks my moiety,° north from Burton here,   portion
95 In quantity equals not one° of yours.   either
See how this river comes me cranking in[1]
And cuts me from the best of all my land
A huge half-moon, a monstrous scantle,° out.   piece
I'll have the current in this place dammed up,
100 And here the smug° and silver Trent shall run   smooth
In a new channel fair and evenly.
It shall not wind with such a deep indent
To rob me of so rich a bottom° here.   lowland plain
GLYNDWR   Not wind? It shall; it must. You see it doth.
105 MORTIMER   Yea, but mark how he bears his course and runs me up°   turns upward
With like advantage on the other side,
Gelding the opposèd continent[2] as much
As on the other side it takes from you.
WORCESTER   Yea, but a little charge° will trench° him here,   expense / rechannel
110 And on this north side win this cape of land,
And then he runs straight and even.
HOTSPUR   I'll have it so; a little charge will do it.
GLYNDWR   I'll not have it altered.
HOTSPUR   Will not you?
GLYNDWR   No, nor you shall not.
HOTSPUR   Who shall say me nay?
115 GLYNDWR   Why, that will I.
HOTSPUR   Let me not understand you, then; speak it in Welsh.

---

8. *threefold:* either an agreement made in triplicate
(see line 78) or an agreement having three parts (see
the rebels' plan to divide the island into three pieces
at lines 70–78). *order ta'en:* agreement made.

9. Bearing the seals of all three nobles.
1. Comes bending in on my shores.
2. Cutting a vital piece from ("gelding") the opposite
bank.

GLYNDWR   I can speak English, lord, as well as you,
   For I was trained up in the English court,
   Where, being but young, I framèd to the harp
120   Many an English ditty lovely well
   And gave the tongue a helpful ornament[3]—
   A virtue that was never seen in you.
HOTSPUR   Marry, and I am glad of it, with all my heart.
   I had rather be a kitten and cry mew
125   Than one of these same meter ballad-mongers.[4]
   I had rather hear a brazen can'stick turned[5]
   Or a dry wheel grate on the axletree,°   *axle*
   And that would set my teeth nothing on edge,
   Nothing so much as mincing° poetry.   *affected*
130   'Tis like the forced gait of a shuffling nag.
GLYNDWR   Come, you shall have Trent turned.
HOTSPUR   I do not care. I'll give thrice so much land
   To any well-deserving friend;
   But, in the way of bargain, mark ye me,
135   I'll cavil on° the ninth part of a hair.   *quibble about*
   Are the indentures drawn? Shall we be gone?
GLYNDWR   The moon shines fair, you may away by night.
   I'll haste the writer, and withal°   *simultaneously*
   Break with° your wives of your departure hence.   *Inform*
140   I am afraid my daughter will run mad,
   So much she doteth on her Mortimer.   *Exit.*
MORTIMER   Fie, cousin Percy, how you cross my father!
HOTSPUR   I cannot choose. Sometime he angers me
   With telling me of the moldwarp[6] and the ant,
145   Of the dreamer Merlin[7] and his prophecies,
   And of a dragon and a finless fish,
   A clip-winged griffin[8] and a molten° raven,   *moulted*
   A couching lion and a ramping cat,[9]
   And such a deal of skimble-skamble° stuff   *stupid*
150   As puts me from my faith.[1] I tell you what:
   He held me last night at least nine hours
   In reckoning up the several devils' names
   That were his lackeys.° I cried "Hum," and "Well, go to,"   *footmen*
   But marked him not a word. Oh, he is as tedious
155   As a tired horse, a railing wife,
   Worse than a smoky house. I had rather live
   With cheese and garlic in a windmill, far,
   Than feed on cates° and have him talk to me   *delicacies*
   In any summer-house° in Christendom.   *luxurious residence*
160 MORTIMER   In faith, he is a worthy gentleman,
   Exceedingly well read and profited°   *proficient*
   In strange concealments,° valiant as a lion,   *In occult arts*

---

3. And gave the English language the ornament of a musical setting; and supplemented the English lyrics with pleasing music.
4. Sellers or writers of ballads.
5. A brass candlestick scraped and polished on a lathe after casting. John Stow's *Survey of London* (1598) records contemporary complaints about the noise of candlestick making.
6. Mole. Holinshed records a prophecy whereby Henry, figured as a mole, would be overthrown by a dragon, a lion, and a wolf, representing Glyndŵr, Percy, and Mortimer, respectively.
7. Legendary Welsh prophet, wizard, and bard at King Arthur's court.
8. A fabulous beast, part lion and part eagle.
9. Alluding to the heraldic terms "couchant" and "rampant," which mean "crouching" and "rearing fiercely." Hotspur is making fun of Glyndŵr's heraldic preoccupations.
1. As makes me a skeptic, even of religion.

And wondrous affable, and as bountiful
As mines of India. Shall I tell you, cousin?
165 He holds your temper in a high respect
And curbs himself even of his natural scope°   *freedom of speech*
When you come cross° his humor. Faith, he does.   *contradict*
I warrant you that man is not alive
Might so have tempted° him as you have done   *provoked*
170 Without the taste of danger and reproof.
But do not use it oft, let me entreat you.
WORCESTER   In faith, my lord, you are too willful-blame,°   *stubborn*
And since your coming hither have done enough
To put him quite besides° his patience.   *out of*
175 You must needs learn, lord, to amend this fault.
Though sometimes it show greatness, courage, blood°—   *spirit; noble birth*
And that's the dearest grace° it renders you—   *best distinction*
Yet oftentimes it doth present° harsh rage,   *show*
Defect of manners, want of government,
180 Pride, haughtiness, opinion,° and disdain,   *self-conceit*
The least of which haunting a nobleman
Loseth men's hearts and leaves behind a stain
Upon the beauty of all parts besides,°   *all other qualities*
Beguiling° them of commendation.   *Depriving*
185 HOTSPUR   Well, I am schooled. Good manners be your speed.°   *give you success*
    Enter GLYNDWR *with the* LADIES [PERCY *and*
    MORTIMER].
Here come our wives, and let us take our leave.
MORTIMER   This is the deadly spite° that angers me: *vexation*
My wife can speak no English, I no Welsh.
GLYNDWR   My daughter weeps; she'll not part with you.
190 She'll be a soldier too; she'll to the wars.
MORTIMER   Good father, tell her that she and my aunt Percy²
Shall follow in your conduct speedily.
    GLYNDWR *speaks to her in Welsh, and she answers him*
    *in the same.*³
GLYNDWR   She is desperate here;° a peevish, self-willed harlotry,°   *on this point / hussy*
One that no persuasion can do good upon.
    The Lady speaks in Welsh.
195 MORTIMER   I understand thy looks. That pretty Welsh,°   *(i.e., her tears)*
Which thou pourest down from these swelling heavens,°   *overflowing eyes*
I am too perfect° in, and but for shame   *proficient*
In such a parley° should I answer thee.   *In a similar language*
    The Lady [speaks] again in Welsh.
I understand thy kisses and thou mine,
200 And that's a feeling disputation;⁴
But I will never be a truant, love,
Till I have learned thy language, for thy tongue
Makes Welsh as sweet as ditties highly° penned,   *eloquently*
Sung by a fair queen in a summer's bower,
205 With ravishing division° to her lute.   *embellishments*
GLYNDWR   Nay, if you melt,° then will she run mad.   *weep*
    The Lady speaks again in Welsh.

---

2. Kate, Lady Percy. Her historical counterpart was the sister, not the aunt, of Glyndŵr's son-in-law.
3. Here and elsewhere in this scene (lines 194, 198, 206, 239), stage directions call for the speaking of Welsh but do not specify what should be said. This suggests that the Chamberlain's Men had at least two Welsh speakers in their company (see Digital Edition TC 1).
4. A conversation rooted in emotions or in touch.

MORTIMER   Oh, I am ignorance itself in this!

GLYNDWR   She bids you on the wanton° rushes[5] lay you down   *luxurious*

   And rest your gentle head upon her lap,[6]

210   And she will sing the song that pleaseth you,

   And on your eyelids crown the god of sleep,

   Charming your blood with pleasing heaviness,°   *sleepiness*

   Making such difference twixt wake and sleep

   As is the difference betwixt day and night

215   The hour before the heavenly harnessed team[7]

   Begins his golden progress in the east.

MORTIMER   With all my heart, I'll sit and hear her sing.

   By that time will our book,° I think, be drawn.   *document*

GLYNDWR   Do so, and those musicians that shall play to you

220   Hang in the air a thousand leagues from hence,

   And straight they shall be here. Sit and attend.

HOTSPUR   Come, Kate, thou art perfect in lying down;°   *expert at lovemaking*

   Come, quick, quick, that I may lay my head in thy lap.[8]

LADY PERCY   Go, ye giddy goose!

      The music plays.[9]

225 HOTSPUR   Now I perceive the devil understands Welsh,

   And 'tis no marvel he is so humorous.°   *eccentric; whimsical*

   By'r Lady, he is a good musician.

LADY PERCY   Then should you be nothing but musical,

   For you are altogether governed by humors.°   *whims*

230   Lie still, ye thief, and hear the lady sing in Welsh.

HOTSPUR   I had rather hear Lady, my brach,° howl in Irish.   *female hunting dog*

LADY PERCY   Wouldst thou have thy head broken?

HOTSPUR   No.

LADY PERCY   Then be still.

235 HOTSPUR   Neither; 'tis a woman's fault.[1]

LADY PERCY   Now God help thee!

HOTSPUR   To the Welsh lady's bed.

LADY PERCY   What's that?

HOTSPUR   Peace; she sings.

      Here the Lady sings a Welsh song.

240 HOTSPUR   Come, Kate, I'll have your song too.

LADY PERCY   Not mine, in good sooth.°   *truth*

HOTSPUR   Not yours, in good sooth!

   Heart,° you swear like a comfit-maker's[2] wife,   *By God's heart*

   "Not you, in good sooth," and "As true as I live,"

245   And "As God shall mend me," and "As sure as day,"

   And givest such sarcenet[3] surety for thy oaths,

   As if thou never walkest further than Finsbury.[4]

   Swear me, Kate, like a lady as thou art,

   A good mouth-filling oath, and leave "In sooth,"

250   And such protest of pepper gingerbread[5]

---

5. Used as a floor covering, both in houses and on the theater stage.

6. Often, a euphemism for the genitals.

7. The sun was supposedly carried in a chariot drawn by horses.

8. "Head" was slang for "penis" and "lap" for "vagina."

9. Instrumental music would probably be played in a so-called music house behind the upper stage in the Elizabethan theater and so might well seem to "hang in the air" (see lines 219–20).

1. No, I won't be still—it is a woman's trait (and I am a man).

2. Confectioner's.

3. Flimsy (from the name of a fine silk).

4. Finsbury Fields, north of London, was a popular resort for London's middling classes. Hotspur implies that Kate's mild oaths make her sound like a burgher's wife.

5. Watered-down oaths. Gingerbread was cheaply available at fairs and markets, and sometimes pepper was used as an inexpensive substitute for ginger.

To velvet-guards and Sunday citizens.[6]
Come, sing.

LADY PERCY I will not sing.

HOTSPUR 'Tis the next° way to turn tailor[7] or be redbreast   *quickest*
255   teacher.° An the indentures be drawn, I'll away within these   *or teach birds to sing*
two hours; and so come in when ye will.   *Exit.*

GLYNDWR Come, come, Lord Mortimer. You are as slow
As hot Lord Percy is on fire to go.
By this° our book is drawn. We'll but seal   *now*
260   And then to horse immediately.

MORTIMER With all my heart.   *Exeunt.*

3.2

Enter the KING, PRINCE *of Wales, and [Lords].*

KING Lords, give us leave; the Prince of Wales and I
Must have some private conference, but be near at hand,
For we shall presently have need of you.   *Exeunt Lords.*
—I know not whether God will have it so
5   For some displeasing service I have done,
That, in His secret doom,° out of my blood°   *judgment / lineage*
He'll breed revengement and a scourge for me;
But thou dost in thy passages° of life   *course*
Make me believe that thou art only marked
10   For° the hot vengeance and the rod of heaven   *To be*
To punish my mistreadings. Tell me else,
Could such inordinate° and low desires,   *unsuitable*
Such poor, such bare, such lewd, such mean attempts,°   *base undertakings*
Such barren pleasures,[1] rude society
15   As thou art matched withal° and grafted to,   *with*
Accompany the greatness of thy blood
And hold their level° with thy princely heart?   *claim equality*

PRINCE So please your majesty, I would I could
Quit° all offenses with as clear excuse   *Clear myself of*
20   As well as I am doubtless° I can purge   *certain*
Myself of many I am charged withal.
Yet such extenuation let me beg
As, in reproof° of many tales devised—   *upon disproof*
Which oft the ear of greatness needs must hear—
25   By smiling pickthanks° and base newsmongers,°   *flatterers / gossips*
I may for some things true, wherein my youth
Hath faulty wandered and irregular,
Find pardon on my true submission.°   *admission of guilt*

KING God pardon thee! Yet let me wonder, Harry,
30   At thy affections,° which do hold a wing   *inclinations*
Quite from[2] the flight of all thy ancestors.
Thy place in Council thou hast rudely[3] lost,
Which by thy younger brother is supplied,

---

6. *To velvet-guards:* To those, like citizens' wives,
whose clothes are trimmed ("guarded") with velvet.
Sunday citizens: citizens who doff their work clothes
and dress up only on Sundays.
7. Tailors were noted for singing.
3.2 Location: The palace, London.
1. Unprofitable   habits;   nonreproductive   erotic

pursuits.
2. *which . . . from:* which do fly a course contrary to.
3. By violence. Perhaps alluding to the story, dramatized in *The Famous Victories of Henry the Fifth,* that
Prince Hal boxed the Lord Chief Justice on the ear
and was subsequently punished.

And art almost an alien to the hearts
35 Of all the court and princes of my blood.
The hope and expectation of thy time°   *time of life; youth*
Is ruined, and the soul of every man
Prophetically do forethink thy fall.
Had I so lavish of my presence been,
40 So common-hackneyed⁴ in the eyes of men,
So stale and cheap to vulgar company,
Opinion,° that did help me to the crown,   *Public opinion*
Had still kept loyal to possession⁵
And left me in reputeless° banishment,   *inglorious*
45 A fellow of no mark nor likelihood.°   *promise of success*
By being seldom seen, I could not stir
But like a comet I was wondered at,
That men would tell their children, "This is he!"
Others would say, "Where? Which is Bolingbroke?"
50 And then I stole all courtesy from heaven⁶
And dressed myself in such humility
That I did pluck allegiance from men's hearts,
Loud shouts and salutations from their mouths,
Even in the presence of the crownèd King.
55 Thus did I keep my person fresh and new,
My presence, like a robe pontifical,°   *churchman's rich dress*
Ne'er seen but wondered at; and so my state,°   *magnificence; royalty*
Seldom but sumptuous, showed like a feast
And won by rareness such solemnity.
60 The skipping King, he ambled up and down
With shallow jesters and rash bavin° wits,   *brushwood*
Soon kindled and soon burnt; carded his state,⁷
Mingled his royalty with cap'ring fools,
Had his great name profanèd with their scorns,°   *by their scornful manners*
65 And gave his countenance,° against his name,⁸   *approval*
To laugh at gibing boys and stand the push°   *tolerate the impudence*
Of every beardless vain comparative;°   *wit*
Grew a companion to the common streets,
Enfeoffed° himself to popularity,   *Surrendered*
70 That, being daily swallowed by men's eyes,
They surfeited with honey and began
To loathe the taste of sweetness, whereof a little
More than a little is by much too much.
So, when he had occasion to be seen,
75 He was but as the cuckoo is in June,⁹
Heard, not regarded; seen, but with such eyes
As, sick and blunted with community,°   *familiarity*
Afford no extraordinary gaze,
Such as is bent on sun-like majesty
80 When it shines seldom in admiring eyes,
But rather drowsed and hung their eyelids down,
Slept in his face,° and rendered such aspect°   *before his eyes / looks*

---

4. Cheapened. A hackney was a horse available for common hire.
5. The possessor of the throne (Richard II).
6. That is, surpassed heaven itself for graciousness.
7. Adulterated his royal dignity. The term refers to a process ("carding") whereby wool or liquids were mixed with inferior substances.
8. To the detriment of his reputation.
9. Referring to a proverbial saying, "No one regards the June cuckoo's song."

As cloudy° men use to their adversaries,   *sullen*
Being with his presence glutted, gorged, and full.
85 And in that very line,° Harry, standest thou;   *category*
For thou hast lost thy princely privilege
With vile participation.° Not an eye   *base companionship*
But is a-weary of thy common sight,
Save mine, which hath desired to see thee more;
90 Which now doth that° I would not have it do,   *what*
Make blind itself with foolish tenderness.

PRINCE   I shall hereafter, my thrice-gracious lord,
Be more myself.

KING   For all the world,
As thou art to this hour was Richard then
95 When I from France set foot at Ravenspur,
And even as I was then is Percy now.
Now, by my scepter, and my soul to boot,
He hath more worthy interest° to the state   *more claim by worth*
Than thou the shadow° of succession.   *mere image*
100 For of° no right, nor color° like to right,   *having / pretext*
He doth fill fields with harness° in the realm,   *armor*
Turns head° against the lion's° armèd jaws,   *Leads a revolt / king's*
And, being no more in debt to years than thou,
Leads ancient lords and reverend bishops on
105 To bloody battles and to bruising arms.
What never-dying honor hath he got
Against renownèd Douglas, whose high deeds,
Whose hot incursions, and great name in arms,
Holds from all soldiers chief majority°   *preeminence*
110 And military title capital[1]
Through all the kingdoms that acknowledge Christ.
Thrice hath this Hotspur, Mars° in swaddling clothes,   *god of war*
This infant warrior, in his enterprises
Discomfited° great Douglas; ta'en him once,   *Defeated*
115 Enlargèd° him, and made a friend of him,   *Released*
To fill the mouth of deep defiance up[2]
And shake the peace and safety of our throne.
And what say you to this? Percy, Northumberland,
The Archbishop's grace of York, Douglas, Mortimer,
120 Capitulate° against us and are up.°   *Combine / up in arms*
But wherefore do I tell these news to thee?
Why, Harry, do I tell thee of my foes,
Which° art my nearest and dearest enemy?   *Who*
Thou that art like enough, through vassal° fear,   *servile*
125 Base inclination, and the start of spleen,°   *fit of temper*
To fight against me under Percy's pay,
To dog his heels and curtsy at his frowns,
To show how much thou art degenerate.

PRINCE   Do not think so. You shall not find it so.
130 And God forgive them that so much have swayed
Your majesty's good thoughts away from me.
I will redeem all this on Percy's head
And in the closing of some glorious day

---

1. And claim to the title of principal (capital) warrior.
2. To add volume to the voice of deep defiance; to fill up the appetite of deep defiance.

Be bold to tell you that I am your son,
135 When I will wear a garment all of blood
And stain my favors° in a bloody mask,   *features*
Which, washed away, shall scour my shame with it—
And that shall be the day, whene'er it lights,°   *comes*
That this same child of honor and renown,
140 This gallant Hotspur, this all-praisèd knight,
And your unthought-of Harry chance to meet.
For every honor sitting on his helm,
Would they were multitudes, and on my head
My shames redoubled, for the time will come
145 That I shall make this northern youth exchange
His glorious deeds for my indignities.
Percy is but my factor,° good my lord,   *agent*
To engross up° glorious deeds on my behalf;   *amass*
And I will call him to so strict account
150 That he shall render every glory up,
Yea, even the slightest worship of his time,°   *honor of his life*
Or I will tear the reckoning from his heart.
This, in the name of God, I promise here,
The which if He be pleased I shall perform,
155 I do beseech your majesty may salve°   *heal*
The long-grown wounds of my intemperance.°   *disorder*
If not, the end of life cancels all bonds,
And I will die a hundred thousand deaths
Ere break the smallest parcel of this vow.
160 KING   A hundred thousand rebels die in this.
Thou shalt have charge° and sovereign trust herein.   *military command*
        Enter BLOUNT.
How now, good Blount? Thy looks are full of speed.
BLOUNT   So hath the business that I come to speak of.
Lord Mortimer of Scotland[3] hath sent word
165 That Douglas and the English rebels met
The eleventh of this month at Shrewsbury.
A mighty and a fearful head° they are—   *army*
If promises be kept on every hand—
As ever offered foul play in a state.
170 KING   The Earl of Westmorland set forth today,
With him my son, Lord John of Lancaster,
For this advertisement° is five days old.   *news*
On Wednesday next, Harry, you shall set forward.
On Thursday we ourselves will march. Our meeting
175 Is Bridgnorth.[4] And, Harry, you shall march
Through Gloucestershire, by which account,°   *calculation*
Our business valuèd,° some twelve days hence   *taken into account*
Our general forces at Bridgnorth shall meet.
Our hands are full of business. Let's away.
180 Advantage feeds him fat[5] while men delay.   *Exeunt.*

---

3. A Scottish lord who is unrelated to Glyndŵr's son-in-law.
4. A town about twenty miles southeast of Shrewsbury.
5. Opportunities (for rebellion) flourish; the superior position (of the rebels) improves.

3.3

Enter FALSTAFF *and* BARDOLPH.

FALSTAFF   Bardolph, am I not fallen away° vilely since this   *shrunk*
last action?[1] Do I not bate?° Do I not dwindle? Why, my skin   *grow thin*
hangs about me like an old lady's loose gown. I am withered
like an old apple-john.[2] Well, I'll repent, and that suddenly,
5   while I am in some liking.° I shall be out of heart[3] shortly,   *in the mood*
and then I shall have no strength to repent. An I have not
forgotten what the inside of a church is made of, I am a pep-
percorn, a brewer's horse.° The inside of a church! Company,   *an old workhorse*
villainous company, hath been the spoil of me.

10 BARDOLPH   Sir John, you are so fretful you cannot live long.

FALSTAFF   Why, there is it. Come, sing me a bawdy song; make
me merry. I was as virtuously given° as a gentleman need   *inclined*
to be. Virtuous enough: swore little, diced not above seven
times—a week, went to a bawdy house not above once in a
15   quarter—of an hour, paid money that I borrowed—three or
four times, lived well and in good compass.° And now I live   *limits*
out of all order, out of all compass.

BARDOLPH   Why, you are so fat, Sir John, that you must needs
be out of all compass,° out of all reasonable compass, Sir John.   *circumference; girth*

20 FALSTAFF   Do thou amend thy face, and I'll amend my life.
Thou art our admiral,° thou bearest the lantern in the poop,[4]   *flagship*
but 'tis in the nose of thee. Thou art the Knight of the Burning Lamp.[5]

BARDOLPH   Why, Sir John, my face does you no harm.

25 FALSTAFF   No, I'll be sworn, I make as good use of it as many
a man doth of a death's head[6] or a *memento mori.*[7] I never
see thy face but I think upon hellfire and Dives that lived
in purple: for there he is in his robes, burning, burning.[8] If
thou wert any way given to virtue, I would swear by thy face;
30   my oath should be, "By this fire, that's God's angel." But
thou art altogether given over° and wert indeed, but for the   *dedicated to vice*
light in thy face, the son of utter darkness. When thou
rann'st up Gad's Hill in the night to catch my horse, if I did
not think thou hadst been an *ignis fatuus,* or a ball of wild-
35   fire,[9] there's no purchase in money. Oh, thou art a perpetual
triumph,° an everlasting bonfire-light! Thou hast saved me   *torchlight procession*
a thousand marks[1] in links° and torches walking with thee   *small torches*
in the night betwixt tavern and tavern. But the sack that
thou hast drunk me° would have bought me lights as good   *drunk (at my cost)*
40   cheap° at the dearest chandler's[2] in Europe. I have maintained   *as cheaply*

3.3 Location: The inn in Eastcheap, London.
1. This last military engagement (referring to the
Gad's Hill episode).
2. A kind of apple often eaten long after picking,
when its skin was shriveled.
3. Disinclined; weary.
4. The ship's main deck.
5. Parodying figures from popular romance such as
Amadis, the Knight of the Burning Sword.
6. A skull, or representation of a skull, such as was
engraved as an emblem of mortality on seal rings.
7. An object serving as a reminder of mortality
(Latin for "remember you must die").
8. Referring to a biblical parable about a rich man
named Dives "clothed in purple and fine linen" who

regularly refused to feed the beggar Lazarus and was
ultimately forced to suffer in hell for his sin (Luke
16:19–23); also referring to Bardolph's body as bearing the signs of venereal disease. "Burning" implies
"on fire with lust" as well as "infected with syphilitic
sores."
9. A flaming explosive used in warfare or in fireworks; skin marked by erysipelas, an inflammatory
disease. *ignis fatuus* (Latin for "foolish fire"): a phenomenon in which phosphorescent light appears on
marshy ground; a false hope.
1. Considerable money (each mark was worth two-
thirds of a pound).
2. The most expensive candle maker's.

that salamander[3] of yours with fire any time this two-and-
thirty years, God reward me for it.

BARDOLPH 'Sblood, I would my face were in your belly![4]

FALSTAFF God-a-mercy! So should I be sure to be heartburned.

Enter HOSTESS.

45 How now, Dame Partlet[5] the hen? Have you inquired yet
who picked my pocket?

HOSTESS Why, Sir John? What do you think, Sir John? Do you
think I keep thieves in my house? I have searched, I have
inquired, so has my husband, man by man, boy by boy, servant
50 by servant. The tithe° of a hair was never lost in my house   *tenth part*
before.

FALSTAFF Ye lie, hostess. Bardolph was shaved and lost many
a hair;[6] and I'll be sworn my pocket was picked. Go to, you
are a woman, go.

55 HOSTESS Who, I? No, I defy thee. God's light, I was never
called so in mine own house before.

FALSTAFF Go to. I know you well enough.

HOSTESS No, Sir John, you do not know me,[7] Sir John. I know
you, Sir John. You owe me money, Sir John, and now you
60 pick a quarrel to beguile me of it. I bought you a dozen of
shirts to your back.

FALSTAFF Dowlas,° filthy dowlas. I have given them away to   *Coarse linen*
bakers' wives; they have made bolters° of them.   *sieves*

HOSTESS Now, as I am a true woman, holland° of eight shil-   *fine linen*
65 lings an ell.° You owe money here besides, Sir John, for your   *a measure of 45 inches*
diet, and by-drinkings,° and money lent you: four-and-twenty   *drinks between meals*
pound.

FALSTAFF He had his part of it. Let him pay.

HOSTESS He? Alas, he is poor; he hath nothing.

70 FALSTAFF How, poor? Look upon his face. What call you rich?
Let them coin his nose; let them coin his cheeks. I'll not pay
a denier.[8] What, will you make a younker° of me? Shall I not   *novice; gull*
take mine ease in mine inn, but I shall have my pocket picked?
I have lost a seal ring of my grandfather's worth forty mark.

75 HOSTESS O Jesu, I have heard the Prince tell him, I know not
how oft, that that ring was copper!

FALSTAFF How? The Prince is a jack,° a sneak-up.° 'Sblood, an   *rascal / sly villain*
he were here, I would cudgel him like a dog if he would say so.

Enter the PRINCE [*with* PETO,] *marching, and*
FALSTAFF *meets him, playing upon his truncheon*°   *officer's club*
like a fife.

FALSTAFF How now, lad, is the wind in that door,° i'faith?   *quarter*
80 Must we all march?

BARDOLPH Yea, two and two, Newgate fashion.[9]

HOSTESS My lord, I pray you hear me.

PRINCE What say'st thou, Mistress Quickly? How doth thy
husband? I love him well; he is an honest man.

---

3. A fabled lizard capable of living in fire. The implication is that Falstaff has maintained the salamander Bardolph with the "fires" of sack or lust.
4. Equivalent to "Stick it down your throat" (a proverbial retort to an insult).
5. A traditional name for hens and for women who
supposedly talked too much.

6. Had his beard cut; was cheated or robbed of his
money; lost his hair because of syphilis.
7. That is, you don't know how honest I am; you don't
have sexual knowledge of me.
8. French copper coin of little value.
9. Bound like convicts taken to and from London's
Newgate prison.

85   HOSTESS   Good my lord, hear me.

    FALSTAFF   Prithee, let her alone and list to me.

    PRINCE   What say'st thou, Jack?

    FALSTAFF   The other night I fell asleep here, behind the arras, and had my pocket picked. This house is turned bawdy
90   house; they pick pockets.

    PRINCE   What didst thou lose, Jack?

    FALSTAFF   Wilt thou believe me, Hal? Three or four bonds of forty pound apiece and a seal ring of my grandfather's.

    PRINCE   A trifle, some eightpenny matter.

95   HOSTESS   So I told him, my lord, and I said I heard your grace say so; and, my lord, he speaks most vilely of you, like a foul-mouthed man as he is, and said he would cudgel you.

    PRINCE   What? He did not.

    HOSTESS   There's neither faith, truth, nor womanhood in me
100   else.

    FALSTAFF   There's no more faith in thee than in a stewed prune,[1] nor no more truth in thee than in a drawn fox,[2] and, for womanhood, Maid Marian[3] may be the deputy's wife of the ward to° thee. Go, you thing,[4] go!   *compared to*

105   HOSTESS   Say, what thing, what thing?

    FALSTAFF   What thing? Why, a thing to thank God on.

    HOSTESS   I am no thing to thank God on. I would thou shouldst know it. I am an honest man's wife, and, setting thy knighthood aside, thou art a knave to call me so.

110   FALSTAFF   Setting thy womanhood aside, thou art a beast to say otherwise.

    HOSTESS   Say, what beast, thou knave thou?

    FALSTAFF   What beast? Why, an otter.

    PRINCE   An otter, Sir John? Why an otter?

115   FALSTAFF   Why? She's neither fish nor flesh;[5] a man knows not where to have her.[6]

    HOSTESS   Thou art an unjust man in saying so. Thou or any man knows where to have me, thou knave thou!

    PRINCE   Thou say'st true, hostess, and he slanders thee most
120   grossly.

    HOSTESS   So he doth you, my lord, and said this other day you owed him a thousand pound.

    PRINCE   Sirrah, do I owe you a thousand pound?

    FALSTAFF   A thousand pound, Hal? A million. Thy love is
125   worth a million; thou owest me thy love.

    HOSTESS   Nay, my lord, he called you "jack" and said he would cudgel you.

    FALSTAFF   Did I, Bardolph?

    BARDOLPH   Indeed, Sir John, you said so.

130   FALSTAFF   Yea, if he said my ring was copper.

    PRINCE   I say 'tis copper. Darest thou be as good as thy word now?

---

1. Symbol of a bawd. Brothels often displayed a dish of stewed prunes in the window.
2. A hunted fox drawn out from its hiding spot; a dead fox dragged to lay a false trail.
3. A disreputable character, usually played by a cross-dressed man, in the boisterous May games and morris dances denounced by puritan preachers. The figure is here juxtaposed to the respectable wife of the deputy of the ward.
4. A euphemism for "female genitalia."
5. The otter's unusual appearance led to debates about whether it was a fish or an animal.
6. How to understand her; how to have sexual relations with her.

FALSTAFF Why, Hal, thou knowest, as thou art but man, I
dare, but as thou art prince, I fear thee as I fear the roaring
135 of the lion's whelp.°   cub
PRINCE And why not as the lion?
FALSTAFF The King himself is to be feared as the lion. Dost
thou think I'll fear thee as I fear thy father? Nay, an I do, I
pray God my girdle break.
140 PRINCE Oh, if it should, how would thy guts fall about thy
knees? But sirrah, there's no room for faith, truth, nor honesty in this bosom of thine; it is all filled up with guts and
midriff. Charge an honest woman with picking thy pocket?
Why, thou whoreson, impudent, embossed rascal,[7] if there
145 were anything in thy pocket but tavern reckonings, memo-
randums° of bawdy houses, and one poor pennyworth of   bills
sugar candy to make thee long-winded,° if thy pocket were   to give you energy
enriched with any other injuries[8] but these, I am a villain.
And yet you will stand to it;° you will not pocket up° wrong.   persist / suppress
150 Art thou not ashamed?
FALSTAFF Dost thou hear, Hal? Thou knowest in the state of
innocency Adam fell, and what should poor Jack Falstaff
do in the days of villainy? Thou seest I have more flesh than
another man and therefore more frailty. You confess, then,
155 you picked my pocket?
PRINCE It appears so by the story.
FALSTAFF Hostess, I forgive thee. Go make ready breakfast,
love thy husband, look to thy servants, cherish thy guests.
Thou shalt find me tractable to any honest reason; thou seest
160 I am pacified still.° Nay, prithee, be gone.   Exit HOSTESS.   always
Now, Hal, to the news at court: for the robbery, lad, how is
that answered?°   settled
PRINCE O my sweet beef, I must still be good angel to thee.
The money is paid back again.
165 FALSTAFF Oh, I do not like that paying back; 'tis a double labor.
PRINCE I am good friends with my father and may do anything.
FALSTAFF Rob me the exchequer the first thing thou dost,
and do it with unwashed hands° too.   do it at once
BARDOLPH Do, my lord.
170 PRINCE I have procured thee, Jack, a charge of foot.°   an infantry command
FALSTAFF I would it had been of horse. Where shall I find
one° that can steal well? Oh, for a fine thief of the age of   someone
two-and-twenty or thereabouts. I am heinously unprovided.°   ill equipped
Well, God be thanked for these rebels; they offend none but
175 the virtuous. I laud them; I praise them.
PRINCE Bardolph.
BARDOLPH My lord.
PRINCE Go, bear this letter to Lord John of Lancaster,
To my brother John; this to my lord of Westmorland.
[*Exit* BARDOLPH.]
180 Go, Peto, to horse, to horse, for thou and I
Have thirty miles to ride yet ere dinner time.   [*Exit* PETO.]
Jack, meet me tomorrow in the Temple hall[9]

---

7. *embossed rascal:* bloated rogue; hunted deer,   8. Any other things whose loss causes you injury.
exhausted and foaming at the mouth.   9. One of the Inns of Court, London's law schools.

At two o'clock in the afternoon.
There shalt thou know thy charge and there receive
185 Money and order for their furniture.°   *equipment*
The land is burning, Percy stands on high,
And either we or they must lower lie.
FALSTAFF   Rare words! Brave world! Hostess, my breakfast,
    come!
Oh, I could wish this tavern were my drum!¹   [*Exeunt.*]

4.1
[*Enter* HOTSPUR, WORCESTER, *and* DOUGLAS.]
HOTSPUR   Well said, my noble Scot. If speaking truth
In this fine age were not thought flattery,
Such attribution° should the Douglas have   *praise*
As not a soldier of this season's stamp°   *coinage*
5 Should go so general current° through the world.   *be so widely accepted*
By God, I cannot flatter—I do defy
The tongues of soothers°—but a braver place   *flatterers*
In my heart's love hath no man than yourself.
Nay, task° me to my word; approve° me, lord.   *hold / test*
10 DOUGLAS   Thou art the king of honor.
No man so potent breathes upon the ground
But I will beard° him.   *defy*
HOTSPUR   Do so, and 'tis well.
    Enter [MESSENGER] *with letters.*
—What letters hast thou there? —I can but thank you.
MESSENGER   These letters come from your father.
15 HOTSPUR   Letters from him? Why comes he not himself?
MESSENGER   He cannot come, my lord. He is grievous sick.
HOTSPUR   Zounds, how has he the leisure to be sick
In such a jostling° time? Who leads his power?   *turbulent*
Under whose government° come they along?   *command*
20 MESSENGER   His letters bears his mind, not I, my lord.
WORCESTER   I prithee, tell me: doth he keep his bed?
MESSENGER   He did, my lord, four days ere I set forth,
And at the time of my departure thence
He was much feared° by his physicians.   *feared for*
25 WORCESTER   I would the state of time° had first been whole°   *of the times / healthy*
Ere he by sickness had been visited.
His health was never better worth° than now.   *of more value*
HOTSPUR   Sick now? Droop now? This sickness doth infect
The very life blood of our enterprise.
30 'Tis catching° hither, even to our camp.   *infectious*
He writes me here that inward sickness—
And that his friends by deputation°   *through deputies*
Could not so soon be drawn,° nor did he think it meet°   *assembled / suitable*
To lay so dangerous and dear a trust
35 On any soul removed° but on his own.   *not directly involved*
Yet doth he give us bold advertisement°   *counsel*
That with our small conjunction° we should on   *joint force*

---

1. A disputed passage. Perhaps Falstaff means he
wishes that he could stay at the tavern rather than go
to war or that he could make the tavern ring with the
noise of his departure. He puns on "taborn" (tabor), a
kind of drum used to call soldiers to battle.
4.1 Location: The rebel camp near Shrewsbury.

To see how fortune is disposed to us;
For, as he writes, there is no quailing now,
40 Because the King is certainly possessed°   *informed*
Of all our purposes. What say you to it?
WORCESTER Your father's sickness is a maim to us.
HOTSPUR A perilous gash, a very limb lopped off—
And yet, in faith, it is not. His present want°   *absence*
45 Seems more than we shall find it. Were it good
To set° the exact wealth of all our states°   *stake / resources*
All at one cast?° To set so rich a main¹   *throw of the dice*
On the nice hazard° of one doubtful hour?   *precarious chance*
It were not good, for therein should we read
50 The very bottom and the soul² of hope,
The very list,° the very utmost bound   *limit*
Of all our fortunes.
DOUGLAS   Faith, and so we should.
Where now remains a sweet reversion,°   *future inheritance*
We may boldly spend upon the hope of what is to come in.
55 A comfort of retirement³ lives in this.
HOTSPUR A rendezvous, a home to fly unto,
If that the devil and mischance look big°   *threateningly*
Upon the maidenhead° of our affairs.   *virgin state; start*
WORCESTER But yet I would your father had been here.
60 The quality and hair° of our attempt   *character*
Brooks° no division. It will be thought   *Tolerates*
By some that know not why he is away
That wisdom, loyalty, and mere° dislike   *absolute*
Of our proceedings kept the Earl from hence.
65 And think how such an apprehension
May turn the tide of fearful faction°   *timid support*
And breed a kind of question in our cause.
For, well you know, we of the off'ring° side   *challenging*
Must keep aloof from strict arbitrament°   *rigorous judgment*
70 And stop all sight-holes, every loop° from whence   *loophole*
The eye of reason may pry in upon us.
This absence of your father's draws° a curtain   *opens*
That shows the ignorant a kind of fear
Before not dreamt of.
HOTSPUR   You strain too far.
75 I rather of his absence make this use:
It lends a luster and more great opinion,°   *prestige*
A larger dare° to our great enterprise,   *daring*
Than if the Earl were here; for men must think
If we without his help can make a head°   *raise an army*
80 To push against a kingdom, with his help
We shall o'erturn it topsy-turvy down.
Yet° all goes well; yet all our joints° are whole.   *So far / limbs*
DOUGLAS As heart can think. There is not such a word
Spoke of in Scotland as this term of fear.
        Enter Sir Richard VERNON.

---

1. A stake in gambling; an army.   a shoe).
2. Essence, with a pun on "sole" (the undersurface of   3. Refuge to which one can retreat.

85 HOTSPUR My cousin Vernon, welcome, by my soul.

VERNON Pray God my news be worth a welcome, lord.
The Earl of Westmorland, seven thousand strong,
Is marching hitherwards; with him Prince John.

HOTSPUR No harm. What more?

VERNON   And further I have learned

90 The King himself in person is set forth,
Or hitherwards intended speedily
With strong and mighty preparation.

HOTSPUR He shall be welcome too. Where is his son,
The nimble-footed madcap Prince of Wales,

95 And his comrades that daffed° the world aside   *tossed*
And bid it pass?

VERNON   All furnished,° all in arms,   *equipped*
All plumed like ostriches that with the wind
Bated,° like eagles having lately bathed,   *Fluttered their wings*
Glittering in golden coats like images,°   *gilded statues*

100 As full of spirit as the month of May
And gorgeous as the sun at midsummer,
Wanton° as youthful goats, wild as young bulls.   *Frisky*
I saw young Harry with his beaver° on,   *visor; helmet*
His cuisses° on his thighs, gallantly armed,   *armor for the thighs*

105 Rise from the ground like feathered Mercury,[4]
And vaulted with such ease into his seat
As if an angel dropped down from the clouds
To turn and wind° a fiery Pegasus[5]   *wheel about*
And witch° the world with noble horsemanship.   *bewitch*

110 HOTSPUR No more, no more. Worse than the sun in March
This praise doth nourish agues.[6] Let them come.
They come like sacrifices in their trim,°   *fine trappings*
And to the fire-eyed maid of smoky war°   *Bellona, goddess of war*
All hot and bleeding will we offer them.

115 The mailèd° Mars shall on his altars sit   *dressed in armor*
Up to the ears in blood. I am on fire
To hear this rich reprisal° is so nigh   *prize*
And yet not ours! Come, let me taste° my horse,   *test; try*
Who is to bear me like a thunderbolt

120 Against the bosom of the Prince of Wales.
Harry to Harry shall, hot horse to horse,
Meet and ne'er part till one drop down a corpse.
Oh, that Glyndŵr were come.

VERNON   There is more news:
I learned in Worcester, as I rode along,

125 He cannot draw° his power this fourteen days.   *assemble*

DOUGLAS That's the worst tidings that I hear of yet.

WORCESTER Ay, by my faith, that bears a frosty sound.

HOTSPUR What may the King's whole battle° reach unto?   *army*

VERNON To thirty thousand.

HOTSPUR   Forty let it be,

---

4. The Roman messenger of the gods, often represented as a young man with winged sandals or a
winged hat.
5. A winged horse of classical mythology.

6. The March sun was popularly imagined as warm
enough to kindle feverish diseases ("agues") without
being strong enough to dispel them.

130 My father and Glyndŵr being both away,
The powers° of us may serve so great a day.   *armies*
Come, let us take a muster speedily.
Doomsday is near. Die all; die merrily.
DOUGLAS Talk not of dying; I am out of° fear   *free from*
135 Of death or death's hand for this one half year.   *Exeunt.*

4.2

Enter FALSTAFF [*and*] BARDOLPH.

FALSTAFF Bardolph, get thee before to Coventry. Fill me a
bottle of sack. Our soldiers shall march through. We'll to
Sutton Coldfield[1] tonight.
BARDOLPH Will you give me money, captain?
5 FALSTAFF Lay out,° lay out.   *Use your own*
BARDOLPH This bottle makes an angel.[2]
FALSTAFF An if it do, take it for thy labor; an if it make twenty,
take them all. I'll answer the coinage.[3] Bid my lieutenant
Peto meet me at town's end.
10 BARDOLPH I will, captain. Farewell.   *Exit.*
FALSTAFF If I be not ashamed of my soldiers, I am a soused
gurnard.° I have misused the King's press[4] damnably. I have *a pickled fish*
got in exchange of a hundred and fifty soldiers, three hundred
and odd pounds. I press me° none but good householders, yeo-   *I draft*
15 man's sons; inquire me out contracted° bachelors, such as had *engaged to be wed*
been asked twice on the banns,[5] such a commodity° of warm   *quantity*
slaves[6] as had as lief° hear the devil as a drum, such as fear the *willingly*
report of a caliver° worse than a struck° fowl or a hurt wild   *musket / wounded*
duck. I pressed me none but such toasts-and-butter,° with   *such weaklings*
20 hearts in their bellies no bigger than pins' heads, and they
have bought out their services;[7] and now my whole charge
consists of ensigns, corporals, lieutenants, gentlemen of com-
panies[8]—slaves as ragged as Lazarus[9] in the painted cloth,°   *cheap wall hangings*
where the glutton's dogs licked his sores—and such as indeed
25 were never soldiers, but discarded unjust° servingmen,   *dishonest*
younger sons to younger brothers, revolted° tapsters and   *runaway*
ostlers trade-fallen,° the cankers[1] of a calm world and a long *out of work*
peace, ten times more dishonorable-ragged than an old feazed
ensign.° And such have I to fill up the rooms of them as[2]   *tattered flag*
30 have bought out their services that you would think that I
had a hundred and fifty tattered prodigals lately come from
swine-keeping, from eating draff and husks.[3] A mad fellow
met me on the way and told me I had unloaded all the gib-
bets° and pressed the dead bodies. No eye hath seen such   *gallows*
35 scarecrows. I'll not march through Coventry with them,

4.2 Location: The road approaching Coventry.
1. Town about twenty miles northwest of Coventry in Warwickshire.
2. Brings my outlay to several shillings (an "angel"). Falstaff retorts by punning on "makes" as meaning "earns a profit of."
3. I'll be responsible for the money coined.
4. Commission for conscripting soldiers.
5. Proclamations made on three consecutive Sundays affirming one's intent to marry.
6. Well-off or comfort-loving cowards.

7. They have paid me to excuse them from military service.
8. Gentlemen volunteers who were not officers.
9. For the story of Lazarus and the rich man, see the note to 3.3.28.
1. Cankerworms; parasites.
2. Places of those who.
3. Alluding to the biblical parable of the prodigal son, who longs to eat swill ("draff") and corn husks meant for pigs after he has squandered his inheritance in debauchery (see Luke 15:11–16).

that's flat. Nay, and the villains march wide betwixt the legs
as if they had gyves° on, for indeed I had the most of them   *fetters*
out of prison. There's not a shirt and a half in all my company, and the half-shirt is two napkins tacked together and
40   thrown over the shoulders like a herald's coat without sleeves;
and the shirt, to say the truth, stolen from my host° at Saint   *innkeeper*
Albans, or the red-nose innkeeper of Daventry.[4] But that's
all one; they'll find linen enough on every hedge.[5]

    Enter the PRINCE [*and the*] *Lord of* WESTMORLAND.

PRINCE   How now, blown Jack?[6] How now, quilt?
45   FALSTAFF   What, Hal? How now, mad wag? What a devil dost
thou in Warwickshire? —My good lord of Westmorland, I
cry you mercy.° I thought your honor had already been at   *I beg your pardon*
Shrewsbury.
WESTMORLAND   Faith, Sir John, 'tis more than time that I were
50   there, and you, too; but my powers are there already. The
King, I can tell you, looks for us all. We must away° all night.   *must march*
FALSTAFF   Tut, never fear° me. I am as vigilant as a cat to steal   *worry about*
cream.
PRINCE   I think to steal cream indeed, for thy theft hath
55   already made thee butter.[7] But tell me, Jack, whose fellows
are these that come after?
FALSTAFF   Mine, Hal, mine.
PRINCE   I did never see such pitiful rascals.
FALSTAFF   Tut, tut, good enough to toss;[8] food for powder,° food   *cannon fodder*
60   for powder. They'll fill a pit as well as better. Tush, man: mortal men, mortal men.
WESTMORLAND   Ay, but Sir John, methinks they are exceeding
poor and bare,° too beggarly.   *threadbare*
FALSTAFF   Faith, for their poverty, I know not where they had
65   that, and for their bareness, I am sure they never learned that
of me.
PRINCE   No, I'll be sworn, unless you call three fingers in the
ribs[9] bare. But, sirrah, make haste. Percy is already in the field.
                                    Exit.
FALSTAFF   What, is the King encamped?
70   WESTMORLAND   He is, Sir John. I fear we shall stay too long.
                                    [*Exit.*]
FALSTAFF   Well, to the latter end of a fray and the beginning of
    a feast
Fits a dull fighter and a keen guest.   *Exit.*

4.3

    Enter HOTSPUR, WORCESTER, DOUGLAS, [*and*] VERNON.

HOTSPUR   We'll fight with him tonight.
WORCESTER   It may not be.
DOUGLAS   You give him then advantage.
VERNON   Not a whit.

---

4. Saint Albans is a town north of London, Daventry
a town southeast of Coventry.
5. Where laundresses set it out to dry.
6. Punning on "jack" as referring to what many Elizabethan soldiers wore: a quilted jacket covered with
leather or cloth and worn over iron plates. *blown:*
swollen; short-winded.

7. The riches ("cream") you have stolen have made
you rich, or turned you into fat.
8. Good enough to be tossed on pikes.
9. Three fingers of fat over the ribs. A finger was a
measure of three-quarters of an inch.
4.3 Location: The rebels' camp, Shrewsbury.

	HOTSPUR Why say you so? Looks he not for supply?°	*reinforcements*
	VERNON So do we.	
	HOTSPUR His is certain; ours is doubtful.	
5	WORCESTER Good cousin, be advised. Stir not tonight.	
	VERNON Do not, my lord.	
	DOUGLAS You do not counsel well;	
	You speak it out of fear and cold heart.	
	VERNON Do me no slander, Douglas. By my life,	
	And I dare well maintain it with my life,	
10	If well-respected° honor bid me on,	*well-considered*
	I hold as little counsel with weak fear,	
	As you, my lord, or any Scot that this day lives.	
	Let it be seen tomorrow in the battle	
	Which of us fears.	
	DOUGLAS Yea, or tonight.	
	VERNON Content.	
15	HOTSPUR Tonight, say I.	
	VERNON Come, come, it may not be. I wonder much,	
	Being men of such great leading° as you are,	*leadership*
	That you foresee not what impediments	
	Drag back our expedition.° Certain horse°	*rapid progress / cavalry*
20	Of my cousin Vernon's are not yet come up.	
	Your uncle Worcester's horse came but today,	
	And now their pride° and mettle is asleep,	*spirit*
	Their courage with hard labor tame and dull,	
	That not a horse is half the half of himself.	
25	HOTSPUR So are the horses of the enemy	
	In general journey-bated° and brought low.	*weary from travel*
	The better part of ours are full of rest.	
	WORCESTER The number of the King exceedeth ours.	
	For God's sake, cousin, stay° till all come in.	*wait*
	The trumpet sounds a parley.[1]	
	Enter Sir Walter BLOUNT.	
30	BLOUNT I come with gracious offers from the King,	
	If you vouchsafe me hearing and respect.	
	HOTSPUR Welcome, Sir Walter Blount; and would to God	
	You were of our determination.°	*on our side*
	Some of us love you well, and even those some°	*those same persons*
35	Envy your great deservings and good name	
	Because you are not of our quality°	*party*
	But stand against us like an enemy.	
	BLOUNT And God defend° but still I should stand so,	*forbid*
	So long as out of limit° and true rule	*bounds of allegiance*
40	You stand against anointed majesty.	
	But to my charge: the King hath sent to know	
	The nature of your griefs° and whereupon	*grievances*
	You conjure from the breast of civil peace	
	Such bold hostility, teaching his duteous land	
45	Audacious cruelty. If that the King	
	Have any way your good deserts forgot,	
	Which he confesseth to be manifold,	
	He bids you name your griefs, and with all speed	

---

1. Summons to a conference with the enemy.

You shall have your desires with interest
50 And pardon absolute for yourself and these
Herein misled by your suggestion.°   *instigation*
  HOTSPUR   The King is kind, and well we know the King
Knows at what time to promise, when to pay.
My father and my uncle and myself
55 Did give him that same royalty he wears;
And when he was not six-and-twenty strong,
Sick in the world's regard, wretched and low,
A poor unminded° outlaw sneaking home,   *insignificant*
My father gave him welcome to the shore;
60 And when he heard him swear and vow to God
He came but to be Duke of Lancaster,
To sue his livery² and beg his peace
With tears of innocency and terms of zeal,
My father, in kind heart and pity moved,
65 Swore him assistance and performed it too.
Now when the lords and barons of the realm
Perceived Northumberland did lean to him,
The more and less came in with cap and knee,³
Met him in boroughs, cities, villages,
70 Attended him on bridges, stood in lanes,⁴
Laid gifts before him, proffered him their oaths,
Gave him their heirs as pages, followed him
Even at the heels in golden° multitudes.   *resplendent*
He presently, as greatness knows itself,°   *recognizes its power*
75 Steps me° a little higher than his vow   *Steps*
Made to my father while his blood° was poor   *spirit*
Upon the naked shore at Ravenspur,
And now, forsooth, takes on him to reform
Some certain edicts and some strait° decrees   *strict*
80 That lie too heavy on the commonwealth,
Cries out upon abuses, seems to weep
Over his country's wrongs; and, by this face,°   *outward show*
This seeming brow of justice, did he win
The hearts of all that he did angle for;
85 Proceeded further: cut me off° the heads   *cut off*
Of all the favorites that the absent King
In deputation° left behind him here   *As deputies*
When he was personal° in the Irish war.   *engaged in person*
  BLOUNT   Tut, I came not to hear this.
  HOTSPUR   Then to the point.
90 In short time after he deposed the King,
Soon after that deprived him of his life,
And in the neck of that tasked° the whole state. *And immediately taxed*
To make that worse, suffered his kinsman March⁵—
Who is, if every owner were well placed,⁶
95 Indeed his king—to be engaged° in Wales,   *held hostage*

---

2. To plead for the restitution of his lands (which Richard II had seized when John of Gaunt, Bolingbroke's father, died).
3. Those of both high and low social status deferentially presented themselves (with cap in hand and bended knee).
4. Stood in rows along the roadways.
5. The Earl of March. For his claim to the throne, see the note to 1.3.80.
6. If everyone had possessions according to his entitlement.

There without ransom to lie forfeited;°   *unredeemed*
Disgraced me in my happy victories,
Sought to entrap me by intelligence,°   *spying*
Rated° mine uncle from the Council board,   *Drove away*
100 In rage dismissed my father from the court,
Broke oath on oath, committed wrong on wrong,
And, in conclusion, drove us to seek out
This head of safety[7] and withal° to pry   *also*
Into his title, the which we find
105 Too indirect° for long continuance.   *irregular*
BLOUNT   Shall I return this answer to the King?
HOTSPUR   Not so, Sir Walter. We'll withdraw awhile.
Go to the King, and let there be impawned°   *pledged*
Some surety for a safe return again,
110 And in the morning early shall mine uncle
Bring him our purposes. And so farewell.
BLOUNT   I would you would accept of grace and love.
HOTSPUR   And maybe so we shall.
BLOUNT   Pray God you do. [*Exeunt.*]

4.4

Enter [the] ARCHBISHOP *of York [and]* SIR MICHAEL.
ARCHBISHOP   Hie, good Sir Michael, bear this sealèd brief°   *dispatch*
With wingèd haste to the Lord Marshal,
This to my cousin Scrope, and all the rest
To whom they are directed. If you knew
5 How much they do import, you would make haste.
SIR MICHAEL   My good lord, I guess their tenor.
ARCHBISHOP   Like enough you do.
Tomorrow, good Sir Michael, is a day
Wherein the fortune of ten thousand men
Must bide the touch;° for, sir, at Shrewsbury,   *stand the test*
10 As I am truly given to understand,
The King with mighty and quick-raisèd power
Meets with Lord Harry. And I fear, Sir Michael,
What with the sickness of Northumberland,
Whose power was in the first proportion,°   *magnitude*
15 And what with Owain Glyndŵr's absence thence,
Who with them was a rated sinew[1] too
And comes not in, overruled by prophecies,
I fear the power of Percy is too weak
To wage an instant° trial with the King.   *immediate*
20 SIR MICHAEL   Why, my good lord, you need not fear;
There is Douglas and Lord Mortimer.
ARCHBISHOP   No, Mortimer is not there.
SIR MICHAEL   But there is Murdoch, Vernon, Lord Harry Percy.
And there is my lord of Worcester, and a head°   *troop*
25 Of gallant warriors, noble gentlemen.
ARCHBISHOP   And so there is; but yet the King hath drawn
The special head of all the land together:
The Prince of Wales, Lord John of Lancaster,

7. That is, safety in these gathered forces.   1. A much-valued source of strength.
4.4 Location: The Archbishop's palace, York.

The noble Westmorland and warlike Blount,
30   And many more corrivals° and dear° men   associates / noble
      Of estimation° and command in arms.   reputation
SIR MICHAEL   Doubt not, my lord, they shall be well opposed.
ARCHBISHOP   I hope no less, yet needful 'tis to fear;
      And to prevent the worst, Sir Michael, speed.
35   For if Lord Percy thrive not, ere the King
      Dismiss his power he means to visit us,
      For he hath heard of our confederacy,
      And 'tis but wisdom to make strong against him.
      Therefore make haste. I must go write again
40   To other friends. And so, farewell, Sir Michael.   *Exeunt.*

                              5.1
         Enter KING, PRINCE *of Wales, Lord John of* LANCASTER,
         Sir Walter BLOUNT, [*and*] FALSTAFF.
KING   How bloodily the sun begins to peer
      Above yon bulky hill. The day looks pale
      At his distemperature.°   sick appearance
PRINCE   The southern wind
      Doth play the trumpet to his° purposes,   (the sun's)
5   And by his hollow whistling in the leaves
      Foretells a tempest and a blustering day.
KING   Then with the losers let it sympathize,°   accord
      For nothing can seem foul to those that win.
         The trumpet sounds.
         Enter WORCESTER [*and* VERNON].¹
KING   How now, my lord of Worcester? 'Tis not well
10   That you and I should meet upon such terms
      As now we meet. You have deceived our trust
      And made us doff our easy robes of peace
      To crush our old limbs in ungentle steel.
      This is not well, my lord; this is not well.
15   What say you to it? Will you again unknit
      This churlish knot of all-abhorrèd war
      And move in that obedient orb² again
      Where you did give a fair and natural light,
      And be no more an exhaled meteor,³
20   A prodigy of fear,° and a portent   A fearful omen
      Of broachèd mischief° to the unborn times?   Of evil set flowing
WORCESTER   Hear me, my liege:
      For mine own part I could be well content
      To entertain the lag-end° of my life   latter end
25   With quiet hours. For I protest
      I have not sought the day of this dislike.°   discord
KING   You have not sought it? How comes it, then?
FALSTAFF   Rebellion lay in his way, and he found it.

5.1 Location: King Henry's camp at Shrewsbury.
1. Neither Q1 nor F indicates that Vernon accompanies Worcester in this scene, but it seems lacking in
ceremony for Worcester to go to King Henry's camp
alone. Also, in the next scene, Worcester discusses
with Vernon what the King has said and whether to
inform Hotspur, making it appear that Vernon was
present at this meeting.

2. Orbit. Henry, drawing on a conventional analogy
between social and cosmological order, compares
Worcester to a star or a planet that, in Ptolemaic cos-
mology, should move properly in its sphere (orbit)
around the earth.
3. Meteors were thought to be made of gas exhaled
by the sun and were considered bad omens.

PRINCE   Peace, chewet,° peace.   *jackdaw; chatterer*

30 WORCESTER   It pleased your majesty to turn your looks
      Of favor from myself and all our house;
      And yet I must remember° you, my lord,   *remind*
      We were the first and dearest of your friends.
      For you my staff of office did I break
35   In Richard's time, and posted° day and night   *rode swiftly*
      To meet you on the way and kiss your hand
      When yet you were in place° and in account°   *social status / esteem*
      Nothing so strong and fortunate as I.
      It was myself, my brother, and his son
40   That brought you home and boldly did outdare
      The dangers of the time. You swore to us,
      And you did swear that oath at Doncaster,
      That you did nothing purpose° 'gainst the state,   *intend*
      Nor claim no further than your new-fallen right,[4]
45   The seat° of Gaunt, dukedom of Lancaster.   *estate*
      To this we swore our aid, but in short space
      It rained down fortune show'ring on your head,
      And such a flood of greatness fell on you—
      What with our help, what with the absent King,
50   What with the injuries° of a wanton° time,   *evils / lawless*
      The seeming sufferances° that you had borne,   *wrongs*
      And the contrarious° winds that held the King   *adverse*
      So long in his unlucky Irish wars
      That all in England did repute him dead—
55   And from this swarm of fair advantages
      You took occasion to be quickly wooed
      To grip the general sway into your hand,
      Forgot your oath to us at Doncaster
      And, being fed by us, you used us so
60   As that ungentle gull,° the cuckoo's bird,   *rude young bird*
      Useth the sparrow:[5] did oppress our nest,
      Grew by our feeding to so great a bulk
      That even our love° durst not come near your sight   *we who loved you*
      For fear of swallowing.° But with nimble wing   *being swallowed*
65   We were enforced for safety sake to fly
      Out of your sight and raise this present head
      Whereby we stand opposèd° by such means   *in opposition to you*
      As you yourself have forged against yourself
      By unkind usage, dangerous° countenance,   *threatening*
70   And violation of all faith and troth
      Sworn to us in your younger enterprise.
    KING   These things indeed you have articulate,°   *expressed*
      Proclaimed at market crosses,[6] read in churches,
      To face° the garment of rebellion   *adorn*
75   With some fine color° that may please the eye   *hue; pretext*
      Of fickle changelings° and poor discontents,   *turncoats*
      Which gape and rub the elbow[7] at the news

---

4. The right newly descended to you (upon the death of your father).
5. The female cuckoo lays its eggs in the nests of smaller birds such as the sparrow, which raises the cuckoo's young until they grow so large that they threaten the sparrow and its nest.
6. Crosses set up in marketplaces, often atop polygonal structures with open archways on each of the sides and vaulted within.
7. And hug themselves with crossed arms (a conventional expression of delight).

Of hurly-burly innovation;°   *rebellion*
And never yet did insurrection want°   *lack*
80   Such watercolors to impaint his cause,
Nor moody beggars starving for a time
Of pell-mell° havoc and confusion.   *chaotic*
   PRINCE   In both your armies there is many a soul
Shall pay full dearly for this encounter
85   If once they join in trial.° Tell your nephew   *combat*
The Prince of Wales doth join with all the world
In praise of Henry Percy. By my hopes,
This present enterprise set off his head,°   *not counted against him*
I do not think a braver gentleman,
90   More active-valiant or more valiant-young,
More daring or more bold, is now alive
To grace this latter age with noble deeds.
For my part, I may speak it to my shame,
I have a truant been to chivalry,
95   And so I hear he doth account me too.
Yet this before my father's majesty:
I am content that he shall take the odds°   *have the advantage*
Of his great name and estimation,°   *reputation*
And will, to save the blood on either side,
100   Try fortune with him in a single fight.
   KING   And, Prince of Wales, so dare we venture thee,
Albeit° considerations infinite   *Were it not that*
Do make against it. —No, good Worcester, no.
We love our people well, even those we love
105   That are misled upon your cousin's° part,   *kinsman's*
And will they take the offer of our grace,°   *mercy*
Both he and they and you, yea, every man
Shall be my friend again, and I'll be his.
So tell your cousin, and bring me word
110   What he will do. But if he will not yield,
Rebuke and dread correction wait on° us,   *serve*
And they shall do their office. So, be gone.
We will not now be troubled with reply.
We offer fair; take it advisedly.
                              Exeunt WORCESTER [*and* VERNON].
115   PRINCE   It will not be accepted, on my life.
The Douglas and the Hotspur both together
Are confident against the world in arms.
   KING   Hence, therefore, every leader to his charge,
For on their answer will we set on them,
120   And God befriend us as our cause is just.
                         Exeunt all but PRINCE [*and*] FALSTAFF.
  FALSTAFF   Hal, if thou see me down in the battle and bestride
    me,° so;° 'tis a point of friendship.   *stand over me / good*
  PRINCE   Nothing but a Colossus[8] can do thee that friendship.
    Say thy prayers, and farewell.
125   FALSTAFF   I would 'twere bedtime, Hal, and all well.
  PRINCE   Why, thou owest God a death.   [*Exit.*]

---

8. Referring to a massive statue of Apollo that purportedly stood over the entrance to the harbor in ancient Rhodes and was referred to as the Colossus of Rhodes.

FALSTAFF 'Tis not due yet. I would be loath to pay him before his day. What need I be so forward with him that calls not on me? Well, 'tis no matter; honor pricks° me on. Yea, but
130 how if honor prick me off⁹ when I come on? How, then? Can honor set to° a leg? No. Or an arm? No. Or take away the grief of a wound? No. Honor hath no skill in surgery, then? No. What is honor? A word. What is in that word "honor"? What is that "honor"? Air. A trim reckoning!° Who hath it?
135 He that died o'Wednesday. Doth he feel it? No. Doth he hear it? No. 'Tis insensible,¹ then? Yea, to the dead. But will it not live with the living? No. Why? Detraction° will not suffer° it. Therefore I'll none of it. Honor is a mere scutcheon.² And so ends my catechism.   *Exit.*

spurs

mend

A nice summing up

Slander
allow

5.2
Enter WORCESTER [*and*] *Sir Richard* VERNON.
WORCESTER   Oh, no, my nephew must not know, Sir Richard,
The liberal and kind offer of the King.
VERNON   'Twere best he did.
WORCESTER   Then are we all undone.
It is not possible, it cannot be
5 The King should keep his word in loving us.
He will suspect us still,° and find a time
To punish this offense in other faults.
Supposition all our lives shall be stuck full of eyes,¹
For treason is but trusted like the fox,
10 Who, never so° tame, so cherished and locked up,
Will have a wild trick of his ancestors.
Look how we can—or° sad or merrily—
Interpretation will misquote our looks,
And we shall feed like oxen at a stall,
15 The better cherished still the nearer death.
My nephew's trespass may be well forgot;
It hath the excuse of youth and heat of blood,
And an adopted name of privilege,²
A hare-brained Hotspur governed by a spleen.°
20 All his offenses live upon my head
And on his father's. We did train° him on
And, his corruption being ta'en from us,
We as the spring° of all shall pay for all.
Therefore, good cousin, let not Harry know
25 In any case the offer of the King.
        Enter HOTSPUR [*and* DOUGLAS].
VERNON   Deliver what you will; I'll say 'tis so.
Here comes your cousin.
HOTSPUR   My uncle is returned.
Deliver up³ my lord of Westmorland.
Uncle, what news?

always

no matter how

whether

hot temper

lead

source

9. Selects me to die; marks me off the list.
1. Imperceptible to the senses.
2. Heraldic shield exhibited at funerals displaying the deceased person's coat of arms.
5.2 Location: The rebels' camp.
1. The King's suspicion will cause him constantly to spy on us. Worcester is referring to an allegorical

representation of Suspicion dressed in a coat of eyes or to secret agents similar to those whom Elizabeth's government maintained.
2. A nickname, "Hotspur," which may excuse his rashness.
3. Release (as the hostage for the safe return of Worcester and Vernon).

30 WORCESTER   The King will bid you battle presently.
DOUGLAS   Defy him by the Lord of Westmorland.
HOTSPUR   Lord Douglas, go you and tell him so.
DOUGLAS   Marry, and shall, and very willingly.

Exit DOUGLAS.

WORCESTER   There is no seeming° mercy in the King.   *semblance of*
35 HOTSPUR   Did you beg any? God forbid!
WORCESTER   I told him gently of our grievances,
   Of his oath-breaking, which he mended thus:
   By now forswearing that he is forsworn.
   He calls us rebels, traitors, and will scourge
40   With haughty arms this hateful name in us.

Enter DOUGLAS.

DOUGLAS   Arm, gentlemen, to arms; for I have thrown
   A brave° defiance in King Henry's teeth,   *proud*
   And Westmorland, that was engaged,° did bear it,   *held as hostage*
   Which cannot choose but bring him quickly on.
45 WORCESTER   The Prince of Wales stepped forth before the King
   And, nephew, challenged you to single fight.
HOTSPUR   Oh, would the quarrel lay upon our heads
   And that no man might draw short breath today
   But I and Harry Monmouth!⁴ Tell me, tell me,
50   How showed his tasking?° Seemed it in contempt?   *challenge*
VERNON   No, by my soul. I never in my life
   Did hear a challenge urged more modestly,
   Unless a brother should a brother dare
   To gentle° exercise and proof of arms.⁵   *noble*
55   He gave you all the duties of° a man,   *respect due to*
   Trimmed up your praises⁶ with a princely tongue,
   Spoke your deservings like a chronicle,
   Making you ever better than his praise
   By still° dispraising praise valued with you;⁷   *constantly*
60   And, which became him like a prince indeed,
   He made a blushing cital° of himself   *mention*
   And chid his truant youth with such a grace
   As if he mastered there a double spirit
   Of teaching and of learning instantly.°   *simultaneously*
65   There did he pause. But let me tell the world,
   If he outlive the envy° of this day,   *malice*
   England did never owe° so sweet a hope   *own*
   So much misconstrued in his wantonness.°   *self-indulgence*
HOTSPUR   Cousin, I think thou art enamorèd
70   On° his follies. Never did I hear   *Of*
   Of any prince so wild a liberty.°   *such unrestrained license*
   But be he as he will, yet once ere night
   I will embrace him with a soldier's arm
   That he shall shrink under my courtesy.
75   Arm, arm with speed! And fellows, soldiers, friends,
   Better consider what you have to do
   Than I, that have not well the gift of tongue,
   Can lift your blood⁸ up with persuasion.

---

4. Harry of Monmouth, the town in Wales where the Prince was born.
5. Trial of skill at weapons.
6. Embellished his praises of you.

7. As measured against you (because your merit exceeds all praise).
8. Rebelliousness; self-indulgence.

Enter a MESSENGER.

FIRST MESSENGER   My lord, here are letters for you.

80   HOTSPUR   I cannot read them now.
O gentlemen, the time of life is short;
To spend that shortness basely were too long
If life did ride upon a dial's point,
Still ending at the arrival of an hour.[9]

85   An if we live, we live to tread on kings;
If die, brave death when princes die with us!
Now, for our consciences, the arms are fair
When the intent of bearing them is just.

Enter another [MESSENGER].

SECOND MESSENGER   My lord, prepare. The King comes on apace.

90   HOTSPUR   I thank him that he cuts me from my tale,
For I profess not° talking. Only this: am not skilled at
Let each man do his best. And here draw I
A sword whose temper° I intend to stain   tempered steel
With the best blood that I can meet withal

95   In the adventure of this perilous day.
Now, Esperance![1] Percy! And set on!
Sound all the lofty instruments of war,
And by that music let us all embrace,
For, heaven to earth,[2] some of us never shall

100   A second time do such a courtesy.

Here they embrace. The trumpets sound.   [*Exeunt.*]

5.3

The KING *enters with his power. Alarum*[1] *to the battle.*
Then enter DOUGLAS *and Sir Walter* BLOUNT
[*disguised as the King*].

BLOUNT   What is thy name that in battle thus thou crossest me?
What honor dost thou seek upon my head?

DOUGLAS   Know then my name is Douglas,
And I do haunt thee in the battle thus

5   Because some tell me that thou art a king.

BLOUNT   They tell thee true.

DOUGLAS   The Lord of Stafford dear today hath bought
Thy likeness,[2] for instead of thee, King Harry,
This sword hath ended him. So shall it thee

10   Unless thou yield thee as my prisoner.

BLOUNT   I was not born a yielder, thou proud Scot,
And thou shalt find a king that will revenge
Lord Stafford's death.

They fight. DOUGLAS *kills* BLOUNT.
Then enter HOTSPUR.

HOTSPUR   O Douglas, hadst thou fought at Humbleton thus,

---

9. *To spend . . . hour:* If life only lasted an hour (*dial's point:* hand of a clock), it would still be too long if it were basely spent.
1. Hope (the Percy motto; see the note to 2.3.66).
2. The odds are as great as the distance from heaven to earth.

5.3 Location: The remaining scenes take place on the battlefield at Shrewsbury.
1. A call to arms, usually sounded on drum or trumpets.
2. *hath . . . likeness:* has paid for impersonating you; has paid for his resemblance to you.

15   I never had triumphed upon a Scot.
        DOUGLAS   All's done; all's won. Here breathless lies the King.
        HOTSPUR   Where?
        DOUGLAS   Here.
        HOTSPUR   This, Douglas? No. I know this face full well.
20   A gallant knight he was; his name was Blount,
        Semblably furnished° like the King himself.   *Similarly equipped*
        DOUGLAS [*to* BLOUNT]   A fool go with thy soul³ whither it goes!
        A borrowed title hast thou bought too dear.
        Why didst thou tell me that thou wert a king?
25   HOTSPUR   The King hath many marching in his coats.⁴
        DOUGLAS   Now, by my sword, I will kill all his coats.
        I'll murder all his wardrobe, piece by piece,
        Until I meet the King.
        HOTSPUR   Up and away!
        Our soldiers stand full fairly for the day.⁵   [*Exeunt.*]
                Alarum. Enter FALSTAFF, *alone.*
30   FALSTAFF   Though I could scape shot-free⁶ at London, I fear the
        shot here. Here's no scoring⁷ but upon the pate. —Soft, who
        are you? Sir Walter Blount. There's honor for you. Here's no
        vanity. I am as hot as molten lead and as heavy too. God keep
        lead out of me; I need no more weight than mine own bowels.
35   I have led my ragamuffins where they are peppered; there's
        not three of my hundred and fifty left alive, and they are for
        the town's end⁸ to beg during life. But who comes here?
                Enter the PRINCE.
        PRINCE   What, stands thou idle here? Lend me thy sword.
        Many a nobleman lies stark and stiff
40   Under the hoofs of vaunting enemies,
        Whose deaths are yet unrevenged. I prithee
        Lend me thy sword.
        FALSTAFF   O Hal, I prithee give me leave to breathe awhile.
        Turk Gregory⁹ never did such deeds in arms as I have done
45   this day. I have paid° Percy; I have made him sure.¹   *settled with (killed)*
        PRINCE   He is, indeed, and living to kill thee.
        I prithee, lend me thy sword.
        FALSTAFF   Nay, before God, Hal, if Percy be alive thou gets
        not my sword. But take my pistol if thou wilt.
50   PRINCE   Give it me. What, is it in the case?
        FALSTAFF   Ay, Hal, 'tis hot, 'tis hot. There's that will sack a city.
                The PRINCE *draws it out, and finds it to be a bottle
                of sack.*
        PRINCE   What, is it a time to jest and dally now?
                He throws the bottle at him.   *Exit.*
        FALSTAFF   Well, if Percy be alive, I'll pierce him; if he do

---

3. May the title of "fool" go with your soul (for impersonating the King).
4. In his surcoat, or loose robes of rich material, embroidered with the royal coat of arms and worn over armor.
5. Our soldiers look as though they will win the day.
6. Escape without paying the tavern bill ("shot"), with a pun in the following line on "shot" as ammunition (projectiles, cannon shot, etc.).
7. Recording of debts by means of "scores," or notches

on a board (customary in taverns); wounding or cutting.
8. By the town gates, where people often begged.
9. A conflation of the idea of the Turk, taken to be a cruel and fierce fighter and an enemy of Protestant England, and either Pope Gregory VII or Pope Gregory XIII, both regarded as violent and cruel by Protestant writers.
1. I have killed him; but the Prince takes "sure" to mean "secure."

come in my way, so; if he do not, if I come in his willingly,
55 let him make a carbonado[2] of me. I like not such grinning[3]
honor as Sir Walter hath. Give me life, which if I can save,
so; if not, honor comes unlooked for, and there's an end.
[Exit.]

5.4

Alarum. Excursions. Enter the KING, *the* PRINCE, *Lord*
John of LANCASTER, [*and the*] *Earl of* WESTMORLAND.

KING   I prithee, Harry, withdraw thyself; thou bleedest too
much. Lord John of Lancaster, go you with him.

LANCASTER   Not I, my lord, unless I did bleed too.

PRINCE   I beseech your majesty, make up,°   go forward
5 Lest your retirement do amaze° your friends.   alarm

KING   I will do so.
My lord of Westmorland, lead him to his tent.

WESTMORLAND   Come, my lord, I'll lead you to your tent.

PRINCE   Lead me, my lord? I do not need your help,
10 And God forbid a shallow scratch should drive
The Prince of Wales from such a field as this,
Where stained[1] nobility lies trodden on
And rebels' arms triumph in massacres!

LANCASTER   We breathe° too long. Come, cousin Westmorland;   rest
15 Our duty this way lies. For God's sake, come.
[*Exeunt* LANCASTER *and* WESTMORLAND.]

PRINCE   By God, thou hast deceived me, Lancaster;
I did not think thee lord of such a spirit.
Before I loved thee as a brother, John,
But now I do respect thee as my soul.

20 KING   I saw him hold Lord Percy at the point°   sword point
With lustier maintenance° than I did look for   more valiant bearing
Of such an ungrown warrior.

PRINCE   Oh, this boy lends mettle to us all!   Exit.
[*Enter* DOUGLAS.]

DOUGLAS   Another king! They grow like Hydra's heads.[2]
25 I am the Douglas, fatal to all those
That wear those colors on them. What art thou
That counterfeit'st the person of a king?

KING   The King himself, who, Douglas, grieves at heart
So many of his shadows° thou hast met   likenesses
30 And not the very King. I have two boys
Seek° Percy and thyself about the field,   Who seek
But seeing thou fall'st on me so luckily,
I will assay° thee; and defend thyself.   challenge

DOUGLAS   I fear thou art another counterfeit,
35 And yet, in faith, thou bearest thee like a king.
But mine° I am sure thou art, whoe'er thou be,   (my prize of war)
And thus I win thee.
They fight. The KING *being in danger, enter* PRINCE
of Wales.

---

2. Meat slashed to grill.
3. *grinning*: menacing; displaying teeth, as in a skeleton. Falstaff finds the honor of those who die in
battle frightening because it is won by death.

5.4
1. Bloodstained; disgraced by defeat.
2. A monster in classical mythology that grew two
heads whenever one was cut off. The hydra was a
common image of political disorder.

PRINCE   Hold up thy head, vile Scot, or thou art like
Never to hold it up again. The spirits
40   Of valiant Shirley, Stafford, Blount are in my arms.
It is the Prince of Wales that threatens thee,
Who never promiseth but he means to pay.
     They fight.   DOUGLAS *flieth.*
Cheerly, my lord. How fares your grace?
Sir Nicholas Gawsey hath for succor sent,
45   And so hath Clifton. I'll to Clifton straight.
KING   Stay and breathe awhile.
Thou hast redeemed thy lost opinion°   *reputation*
And showed thou mak'st some tender of° my life   *have some regard for*
In this fair rescue thou hast brought to me.
50   PRINCE   O God, they did me too much injury
That ever said I hearkened for° your death.   *desired*
If it were so, I might have let alone
The insulting° hand of Douglas over you,   *scornful*
Which would have been as speedy in your end
55   As all the poisonous potions in the world
And saved the treacherous labor of your son.
KING   Make up° to Clifton; I'll to Sir Nicholas Gawsey. *Exit.*   *Go forward*
     Enter HOTSPUR.
HOTSPUR   If I mistake not, thou art Harry Monmouth.
PRINCE   Thou speak'st as if I would deny my name.
HOTSPUR   My name is Harry Percy.
60   PRINCE   Why, then, I see
A very valiant rebel of the name.
I am the Prince of Wales; and think not, Percy,
To share with me in glory any more.
Two stars keep not their motion in one sphere,[3]
65   Nor can one England brook° a double reign   *endure*
Of Harry Percy and the Prince of Wales.
HOTSPUR   Nor shall it, Harry, for the hour is come
To end the one of us, and would to God
Thy name in arms were now as great as mine.
70   PRINCE   I'll make it greater ere I part from thee,
And all the budding honors on thy crest°   *helmet; coat of arms*
I'll crop° to make a garland for my head.   *cut*
HOTSPUR   I can no longer brook thy vanities.°   *empty boasts*
     They fight.
     Enter FALSTAFF.
FALSTAFF   Well said, Hal! To it, Hal! Nay, you shall find no
75   boy's play here, I can tell you.
     Enter DOUGLAS. *He fighteth with* FALSTAFF, *who falls*
     down as if he were dead.[4]
                         [*Exit* DOUGLAS.]
     The PRINCE *killeth* HOTSPUR.
HOTSPUR   O Harry, thou hast robbed me of my youth.
I better brook the loss of brittle life
Than those proud titles thou hast won of me.

---

3. Alluding to the theory that stars moved in concentric spheres around a center. Only one star could occupy a single sphere.
4. PERFORMANCE COMMENT Falstaff's falling down is often played comically. He either faints from fear or deliberately pretends to be dead. However, sometimes he actually appears to the audience to *be* dead, giving the play a tragic feel before the truth is revealed. Either staging affects how the audience perceives Prince Hal. See Digital Edition PC 3.

They wound my thoughts worse than thy sword my flesh.
80　But thoughts, the slaves of life, and life, time's fool,
And time, that takes survey of all the world,
Must have a stop.° Oh, I could prophesy,　　　　　　　　　*an end*
But that the earthy and cold hand of death
Lies on my tongue. No, Percy, thou art dust
85　And food for—
　　　　　　[*He dies.*]
PRINCE　For worms, brave Percy. Fare thee well, great heart.
Ill-weaved ambition, how much art thou shrunk!
When that this body did contain a spirit
A kingdom for it was too small a bound,
90　But now two paces of the vilest earth
Is room enough. This earth that bears thee dead
Bears not alive so stout° a gentleman.　　　　　　　　　*valiant*
If thou wert sensible° of courtesy　　　　　　　　　　　*conscious*
I should not make so dear° a show of zeal.°　　*heartfelt / emotion*
95　But let my favors⁵ hide thy mangled face,
And even in thy behalf I'll thank myself
For doing these fair rites of tenderness.
Adieu, and take thy praise with thee to heaven.
Thy ignominy sleep with thee in the grave
100　But not remembered in thy epitaph.
　　　　　He spies FALSTAFF *on the ground.*
What, old acquaintance, could not all this flesh
Keep in a little life? Poor Jack, farewell.
I could have better spared a better man.
Oh, I should have a heavy° miss of thee　　　　　　　*sad; weighty*
105　If I were much in love with vanity.
Death hath not struck so fat a deer today,
Though many dearer in this bloody fray.
Emboweled⁶ will I see thee by and by;
Till then, in blood by noble Percy lie.　　　　　　　*Exit.*
　　　　　FALSTAFF *rises up.*
110　FALSTAFF　Emboweled? If thou embowel me today, I'll give
you leave to powder° me, and eat me too, tomorrow. 'Sblood,　　*pickle in salt*
'twas time to counterfeit, or that hot termagant⁷ Scot had
paid me, scot and lot° too. Counterfeit? I lie; I am no coun-　　*in full*
terfeit. To die is to be a counterfeit, for he is but the counter-
115　feit of a man who hath not the life of a man. But to counterfeit
dying when a man thereby liveth is to be no counterfeit but
the true and perfect image of life indeed. The better part of
valor is discretion, in the which better part° I have saved my　　*role*
life. Zounds, I am afraid of this gunpowder Percy, though
120　he be dead. How if he should counterfeit too and rise? By
my faith, I am afraid he would prove the better counterfeit.
Therefore I'll make him sure, yea, and I'll swear I killed him.
Why may not he rise as well as I? Nothing confutes me but
eyes,⁸ and nobody sees me. Therefore, sirrah [*stabbing him*],
125　with a new wound in your thigh, come you along with me.
　　　　　He takes up HOTSPUR *on his back.*

---

5. Ornaments such as plumes or gloves worn into
battle.
6. Prepared for embalming and burial as noblemen
were; disemboweled in the manner of a hunted deer.

7. A quarrelsome or shrewish person; the name of an
imaginary deity who, according to medieval morality
plays, was worshipped by Muslims.
8. No one could confute my story but an eyewitness.

Enter PRINCE *[and] John of* LANCASTER.

PRINCE   Come, brother John. Full bravely hast thou fleshed
Thy maiden sword.[9]

LANCASTER   But soft, whom have we here?
Did you not tell me this fat man was dead?

PRINCE   I did; I saw him dead,

130   Breathless and bleeding on the ground. —Art thou alive?
Or is it fantasy° that plays upon our eyesight?   *hallucination*
I prithee, speak; we will not trust our eyes
Without our ears. Thou art not what thou seem'st.

FALSTAFF   No, that's certain, I am not a double man;° but if   *ghost; two men*

135   I be not Jack Falstaff, then am I a jack.° There is Percy. If   *knave*
your father will do me any honor, so; if not, let him kill the
next Percy himself. I look to be either earl or duke, I can
assure you.

PRINCE   Why, Percy I killed myself, and saw thee dead.

140   FALSTAFF   Didst thou? Lord, Lord, how this world is given to
lying! I grant you I was down and out of breath, and so was
he; but we rose both at an instant° and fought a long hour by   *simultaneously*
Shrewsbury clock. If I may be believed, so; if not, let them
that should reward valor bear the sin upon their own heads.

145   I'll take it upon my death° I gave him this wound in the   *swear on my deathbed*
thigh. If the man were alive and would deny it, zounds, I
would make him eat a piece of my sword.

LANCASTER   This is the strangest tale that ever I heard.

PRINCE   This is the strangest fellow, brother John.

150   —Come, bring your luggage nobly on your back.
For my part, if a lie may do thee grace°   *get you favor*
I'll gild it with the happiest° terms I have.   *most favorable*

A retreat is sounded.

PRINCE   The trumpet sounds retreat; the day is ours.
Come, brother, let us to the highest° of the field,   *highest ground*

155   To see what friends are living, who are dead.

Exeunt [PRINCE *and* LANCASTER].

FALSTAFF   I'll follow, as they say, for reward. He that rewards me,
God reward him. If I do grow great, I'll grow less, for I'll purge[1]
and leave sack and live cleanly, as a nobleman should do.

Exit.

5.5

The trumpets sound. Enter the KING, *the* PRINCE
of Wales, Lord John of LANCASTER, *Earl of*
WESTMORLAND, *with* WORCESTER *and* VERNON
prisoners[, and Soldiers].

KING   Thus ever did rebellion find rebuke.
Ill-spirited Worcester, did not we send grace,
Pardon, and terms of love to all of you?
And wouldst thou turn our offers contrary,

5   Misuse the tenor° of thy kinsman's trust?   *Abuse the substance*

---

9. *Full . . . sword:* How courageously or splendidly
have you initiated in bloodshed your untried weapon
(fought your first battle). The phrase alludes to hunting practices in which hawks or hounds were "fleshed,"
or made eager for prey by the taste of blood. Also

alluding, by way of the slang meaning of "sword" as
"penis," to a man's first sexual encounters with the
flesh of others.
1. I'll take laxatives (to reduce my weight); I'll repent.

Three knights upon our party slain today,
A noble earl, and many a creature else
Had been alive this hour
If like a Christian thou hadst truly borne
10 Betwixt our armies true intelligence.°   *information*
WORCESTER What I have done my safety urged me to;
And I embrace this fortune patiently,
Since not to be avoided it falls on me.
KING Bear Worcester to the death, and Vernon too.
15 Other offenders we will pause upon.°   *reflect upon*
            [*Exeunt* WORCESTER *and* VERNON, *under guard.*]
How goes the field?
PRINCE The noble Scot, Lord Douglas, when he saw
The fortune of the day quite turned from him,
The noble Percy slain, and all his men
20 Upon the foot of fear,° fled with the rest;   *Fleeing in fear*
And, falling from a hill, he was so bruised
That the pursuers took him. At my tent
The Douglas is, and I beseech your grace
I may dispose of him.
KING   With all my heart.
25 PRINCE Then, brother John of Lancaster,
To you this honorable bounty° shall belong.   *act of generosity*
Go to the Douglas and deliver him
Up to his pleasure, ransomless and free.
His valors shown upon our crests° today   *helmets*
30 Have taught us how to cherish such high deeds
Even in the bosom of our adversaries.
LANCASTER I thank your grace for this high courtesy,
Which I shall give away immediately.
KING Then this remains, that we divide our power.
35 You, son John, and my cousin Westmorland,
Towards York shall bend you° with your dearest speed   *direct your course*
To meet Northumberland and the prelate Scrope,
Who, as we hear, are busily in arms.
Myself and you, son Harry, will toward Wales
40 To fight with Glyndŵr and the Earl of March.
Rebellion in this land shall lose his sway
Meeting the check of such another day;
And since this business so fair is done,
Let us not leave° till all our own be won.   *Exeunt.*   *leave off*

The Second Part of
Henry the Fourth

The title page of the 1600 Quarto of *2 Henry IV* highlights the delicate moment of succession when one king dies and another is crowned: *The Second Part of Henry the Fourth, Continuing to His Death, and Coronation of Henry the Fifth. With the Humors of Sir John Falstaff, and Swaggering Pistol.* Shakespeare's audience was facing such a delicate moment at the end of the 1590s. Elizabeth I was old, having been on the English throne since 1558; she had never married, and she had no heirs. The uncertainties of the coming succession may, by contrast, have heightened the pleasure of watching a male heir, Henry V, seamlessly succeed his father as king. Whatever his father's sins in seizing the crown from Richard II, by 1600 Henry V had become in the popular imagination a symbol of kingly perfection and English masculinity—a figure, in short, who might seem an attractive alternative to an aging queen. With his customary subtlety, Shakespeare complicates and somewhat darkens the popular image of the wayward prince who undergoes a miraculous transformation, but Hal's coronation nonetheless is the end point toward which the play inexorably moves.

Besides its royal plot, the play also deals in some decidedly "low" and mostly unhistorical matter, suggested on the title page by mention of the "humours" of Falstaff and the presence of swaggering Pistol. These characters hold pride of place alongside Henry IV and Henry V, indicating the popularity of the antic parts of the play— Falstaff's jokes and his flouting of authority, or Pistol's madly bombastic language. Some of the matter for the play's comic scenes probably derives from *The Famous Victories of Henry the Fifth*, a popular play about the life of Henry V first published in 1598 but believed to have been performed well before that date, while the main plot is derived from the second edition of Raphael Holinshed's *Chronicles of England, Scotland, and Ireland* (1587) and Samuel Daniel's *First Four Books of the Civil Wars Between the Two Houses of Lancaster and York* (1595). In *2 Henry IV*, Prince Hal does not mingle with the comic figures as freely as he did in *1 Henry IV*; in fact, he appears only once—in 2.4, in the Eastcheap tavern where Falstaff holds court. Nonetheless, the total number of low, unhistorical characters expands considerably in this play. Pistol is a new character, and Mistress Quickly is joined in her Eastcheap tavern by Doll Tearsheet, a prostitute whose name graphically suggests one consequence of unrestrained fornication. Further, a number of country characters are introduced: the Gloucestershire justices of the peace, Shallow and Silence; Shallow's servant, Davy; and the five rural recruits (Mouldy, Bullcalf, Wart, Feeble, and Shadow) whom Falstaff considers for conscription into the army. *2 Henry IV* is the only history play of which more than half is written in prose, and much of that richly varied prose occurs in the numerous scenes involving these humble figures that Shakespeare added to the historical narrative of one king's death and another's coronation.

2 Henry IV was probably written soon after the very popular *1 Henry IV*, published in 1598 but believed to have been written and staged in 1596–97. The Quarto of *2 Henry IV* saw print in 1600, but there is a reference to the character of Justice Silence in Ben Jonson's *Every Man out of His Humor* (1599). *2 Henry IV* was therefore probably performed sometime between February 1598, when *1 Henry IV* was entered in the Stationers' Register with no indication that it was the first part of a two-part play, and early in 1599. Censorship of Shakespeare's original naming of Falstaff as

THE
Second part of Henrie

the fourth, continuing to his death,
and coronation of Henrie
the fift.

With the humours of sir Iohn Fal-
staffe, and swaggering
Pistoll.

As it hath been sundrie times publikely
acted by the right honourable, the Lord
Chamberlaine his seruants.

Written by William Shakespeare.

LONDON
Printed by V.S.for Andrew Wise, and
William Aspley.
1600.

Title page of the 1600 Quarto of *The Second Part of Henry the Fourth* . . . , promising to combine royal history and the comic events involving Falstaff and his tavern companions.

"Oldcastle," Bardolph as "Russell," and Peto as "Harvey" (see Introduction to *1 Henry IV*) probably had occurred before Shakespeare completed *2 Henry IV*, although a few traces of the original names appear in the speech prefixes and stage directions in the first two acts of the Quarto text.

Narrowing down the play's date of composition, however, does not answer the question of why Shakespeare wrote two plays dealing with the reign of Henry IV. Some critics believe that the playwright once intended to encompass all the material of both plays in one, but in writing *1 Henry IV* he found that he had room to depict only the events up to the Battle of Shrewsbury and Hal's emergence as a chivalric hero through his defeat of Hotspur. Therefore, what was "left over" was, in effect, put into *2 Henry IV* with the patchwork addition of enough comic material to scrape together a play. It is also possible that Shakespeare intended to dramatize only the events now in *1 Henry IV*, but that having done so, he was encouraged by his success to add another chapter to the story of Hal's reformation and gradual progression toward the throne. Alternatively, Shakespeare may have planned two plays from the beginning, intending to undertake two quite different explorations of the prodigal narrative by which the wild Prince becomes first a chivalric hero and eventually the King of England.

Whatever the original impetus for writing it, the finished play now called *2 Henry IV* has an integrity of its own and a set of preoccupations that sharply distinguish it from *1 Henry IV*. The rebels, for example, are a less flamboyant crew than in the earlier play, and they are not vanquished in combat as at Shrewsbury; rather, at Galtres Prince John tricks them into laying down their weapons. Policy, not chivalry, wins the day. Hal's challenge, moreover, is no longer to prove himself the prince of chivalry, with the rebel Henry Percy (Hotspur) as his main antagonist. Rather, he must show himself fit for civil rule. Hence, the importance in *2 Henry IV* of the Lord Chief Justice, a figure who in popular accounts of Hal's life had had the Prince imprisoned for impudently giving him a box on the ear. This event is not dramatized in either of Shakespeare's *Henry IV* plays, as it had been in *The Famous Victories*, but it is alluded to several times. In *2 Henry IV*, the Chief Justice emerges as the main foil to the disorderly Falstaff. Upon hearing that Henry IV is dead and Hal is King, the fat knight exclaims, "the laws of England are at my commandment" (5.3.124).* It seems quite possible that under Henry V, law will give way before the appetites and desires of individual subjects. Hal and the Chief Justice do not share the stage until 5.2, but their encounter is a pivotal moment in the text, revealing whether Hal will recognize and honor the authority of the Chief Justice or follow Falstaff in disregarding the law.

Also unique is this play's pervasive concern with the passing of time. As Hastings says at the end of act 1, "We are Time's subjects" (1.3.63); arguably, he sounds the play's central theme. Even the King, to whom so many are subject, is himself subject to time. Shakespeare portrays him as old and sick, though the historical Henry successfully ruled England for ten years after the Battle of Shrewsbury. His sickness and the urgency of the rebel threat pressure the Prince, forcing him to realize that his idle days in the tavern are numbered and that if he lingers longer, he will "profane the precious time" (2.4.329)—time he should spend coming to terms with his father and defending a kingdom still threatened by rebels. Even the irrepressible Falstaff now feels time's hand. He enters the play in 1.2 asking what the doctor has said about the urine he has sent for examination, and to Quickly and Tearsheet he confesses, "I am old, I am old" (2.4.243). If *1 Henry IV* is an expansive work, infused with a feeling of infinite play and infinite possibility, *2 Henry IV* has a melancholy, autumnal aura. It is a play of limits and constrictions. Shallow intones, "Death . . . is certain to all; all shall die" (3.2.33–34). Through its many images of sickness, disease, and old age, the play is permeated with intimations of mortality.

---

*All quotations are taken from the edited text of the Quarto, printed here. The Digital Edition includes edited texts of both the Quarto and the Folio.

The play's portrayal of Prince Hal shares in the somber mood that suffuses all of
2 *Henry IV*. When the audience first sees him, he is with Poins (2.2), brooding on the
impasse to which his own actions have brought him. Rather than remaining distant
from his tavern companion, Hal ruefully acknowledges what he shares with common
men. Tired, he desires nothing more exalted than small beer, the common drink of
every London apprentice. He admits that he should not, because of his rank, be intimate with Poins; and yet he confesses that he is, revealing how thoroughly he knows
his companion's wardrobe and using Poins as a sounding board for his misgivings
about his own behavior and its consequences. While the scene's mood changes when
Bardolph enters with an absurdly pompous letter from Falstaff, its fretful beginning
indicates a new strain in Shakespeare's depiction of Hal's progress toward the throne.
In *1 Henry IV*, everything seemed easy for the Prince. He announced a course of
reform and enacted it with little apparent cost to himself. In *2 Henry IV*, Shakespeare
constructs a more sober Prince who articulates anxiety about the gap between his plebeian taste for small beer and the grandeur of the office he will assume, a Prince who
knows that to have acted the wastrel in order to make a dazzling reform may have cost
him his father's affection and made it impossible to express his love for the King without appearing to be a hypocrite. In the opening acts of *2 Henry IV*, Hal's capacity for
self-critique and for uncertainty makes him more vulnerable, and perhaps more lik-
able, than the shiny and assured paragon of *1 Henry IV*.

Shakespeare also shows changes in Hal's father, King Henry IV, who in Part 2
reveals a new capacity for introspection. In 3.1, speaking about the burdens of office, he
acknowledges the costs of his success and admits that at the start of his reign he could
little foresee the changes time would effect in him and in his plans and alliances. Yet like
his son, in the end Henry finds his office worth the cost. Power may bring burdens, but
for both characters it is irresistible. Each one sentimentally envies common men (whose
poverty and powerlessness they do not share), but neither one renounces the office of
king. And neither ever gives up the attempt to control his destiny. Having contem-
plated the many unforeseen changes of his reign, Henry IV finally breaks off his rev-
erie to plan a campaign against the rebels:

> Are these things, then, necessities?
> Then let us meet them like necessities;
> And that same word even now cries out on us.
> They say the Bishop and Northumberland
> Are fifty thousand strong.
>
> (3.1.92–96)

This is the pragmatic voice of rule, the blunt determination that Shakespeare attributes both to Prince Hal and to his father.

Yet despite (and perhaps because of) their similarities, Shakespeare makes the
relationship between Henry and Hal a troubled one. Part of the complexity of *2 Henry
IV* is that while it tellingly anatomizes how these kings, father and then son, acquire
and maintain power, it simultaneously creates the impression of a psychodrama
between the two of them that, though inseparable from their political roles, is never
fully understood by either. Hal, despite telling Poins he loves his father, does not
appear in the King's presence until the end of act 4, when Henry is on his deathbed.
Then, with what has seemed to many observers to be unseemly haste, Hal, believing
his father dead, takes the crown from the sleeping King's pillow and sets it on his own
head. Is this, as the King fears, Hal's acting out of a fantasy of parricide, that is, a fantasy of father killing? Or, as Hal protests, is it his attempt to come to terms with the
burdens of office that have hastened his father's death and that will now fall to him?

In part, the relationship between Hal and Henry is complicated by the guilt each
one feels about the politically useful and carefully managed "wildness" that each has
employed. Hal, of course, has cultivated wildness as a prelude to reform. It is the foil
by which he aims to set off his achievement of perfect chivalry and justice. But to come

by his throne, Henry himself had to enact the wildness of usurpation, seizing the crown from a lawfully anointed king, an act Shakespeare depicted in *Richard II*. Once in the seat of rule, Henry repudiated such wildness and embraced the law, justifying his own reign in part by presenting himself as the bulwark against disorder. There is no doubt that Hal displays prodigal behavior, but his father dwells on and exaggerates his son's lawlessness, picturing England's distress when ruled by a man who "from curbed license plucks / The muzzle of restraint" (4.3.260–61). This preoccupation with Hal's lawlessness may signal Henry's guilt about his own act of usurpation, for which he has long planned a penitential crusade to the Holy Land (a crusade that would *also* have the effect of distracting his nobles from thoughts of rebellion at home). But Henry does not seem to perceive the ways in which his son's tactics resemble his own. Truly his father's child, Hal angles for power with an unerring sense of when to embrace wildness and when to repudiate it. Just as Henry's act of seizing the crown raises the specter of parricide, Henry's obsession with curbing Hal's wildness hints at castration. Without seeming fully to realize the consequences of his actions, the King would cut off one source of Hal's power, even though he himself once embraced disorder and still needs it to justify his rule.

In Henry's last conversation with Hal and at his death, father and son switch positions in the discourse of "wildness" that runs through the play. The King has been the principle of order, the Prince the ungovernable prodigal. On his deathbed, however, the King acknowledges to Hal:

> God knows, my son,
> By what bypaths and indirect crooked ways
> I met this crown; and I myself know well
> How troublesome it sat upon my head.
> To thee it shall descend with better quiet,
> Better opinion, better confirmation,
> For all the soil of the achievement goes
> With me into the earth.
> (4.3.312–19)

Hal picks up the theme when he announces after his father's death, "My father is gone wild into his grave" (5.2.122), as if Henry himself embodied the principle of disorder, now buried. Yet Hal continues, suddenly making problematic whose wildness the grave holds:

> For in his tomb lie my affections,
> And with his spirits sadly I survive
> To mock the expectation of the world. . . .
> (5.2.123–25)

Now it is *Hal's* wildness that the grave holds, his father's sober spirits that live on in the son. The wild Prince has become the order-loving King. It will now be his turn to repudiate those who live outside the compass of the law, beginning with Falstaff. In doing so, he shows an unerring instinct for the improvisations that allow him to acquire and retain power.

But though Hal publicly repudiates wildness, the play does not. Wildness surges up unpredictably, not only in the actions of the rebels but also in the actions and particularly in the unruly language of those many "minor" characters who are Shakespeare's additions to his historical sources and whose existence is signaled on the title page by reference to the humors of Falstaff and swaggering Pistol. In the late sixteenth century, the English language was undergoing expansion and entering a period of vibrant linguistic experimentation. Many writers were interested in making English a fit language in which to write verse that would rival the achievements of classical literature. They experimented with imitating the verse forms used by Latin writers in particular; they also coined new words, and they attempted to purge English of uncouth or infelicitous elements. But it was not just poets who affected the language. Trade brought new products to England, and those products had to have names. Foreign visitors, merchants, and workers were a common sight in the London landscape, and they, of course, brought their own languages with them. Foreign terms were regularly absorbed into the English vernacular. Meanwhile, the theater offered auditors the high-sounding rhetoric of kings and tyrants, while London preachers made their reputations with dazzling displays of oratorical power.

This atmosphere generated an infectious excitement about language, and not all of this excitement was easy to control. Rhetorical handbooks proliferated, each sketching out the styles and figures of speech appropriate to different occasions, and each also listing rhetorical "vices," examples of indecorous or ungrammatical or infelicitous speech. 2 Henry IV could be considered a casebook of linguistic vices. The minor characters speak a hodgepodge of tongues that defy the desire for linguistic order. Swaggering Pistol is a case in point. Much of his speech is composed of scraps of rhetoric that he has picked up from going to the London theater—especially, perhaps, to the Rose, where Edward Alleyn, chief actor for the Admiral's Men, specialized in a highly rhetorical and hyperbolic acting style that Pistol seems both to channel and to parody. Pistol, for example, imagines himself as Tamburlaine, the overreaching hero of Marlowe's two-part play about a Scythian shepherd who became one of the great military conquerors of all time. Alleyn was famous for this role, and Pistol's swaggering style aspires to Alleyn's (and Tamburlaine's) rhetorical pyrotechnics. Pistol, however, mangles his references to Marlowe's hero, intermingling what he can remember of Tamburlaine's speeches with a mishmash of fine-sounding names and lines from drinking songs, as when he proclaims:

> Shall packhorses,
> And hollow pampered jades of Asia,
> Which cannot go but thirty mile a day,
> Compare with Caesars and with cannibals,
> And Trojan Greeks?
> Nay, rather damn them with King Cerberus,
> And let the welkin roar. —Shall we fall foul for toys?
> (2.4.142–48)

Pistol's "mistakes" are pervasive. First he imitates what he can remember of the moment when Tamburlaine taunts the conquered kings whom he has put in harness to draw his chariot. But then he veers into nonsense, mistaking "cannibal" for "Hannibal," the heroic leader of Carthage; describing Greeks as Trojans, while in The Iliad the Greeks and Trojans were two peoples at war with one another; then attributing a crown to Cerberus, the three-headed dog that guarded the gates of hell; and ending with a tag from a drinking song: "And let the welkin roar." The sheer exuberance of the speech is partly what makes it pleasurable—Pistol's delight in the sound of big words, whatever those words may mean—along with the lawless incongruity with which one bit of remembered rhetoric is stitched onto the next. Self-mockingly, but also self-importantly, the passage points to the power of the theater to intoxicate spectators with fine rhetoric. Choleric, explosive, overflowing with the excesses of stage rhetoric, Pistol is a wild card in the play's quest for order and the rule of law.

He is not alone. The play opens with a prologue spoken by Rumor, whose business is telling lies, substituting the untrue for the true. That Shakespeare opens the play with this figure indicates the play's preoccupation with the vagaries of language and how often it can obscure simple truth. For example, powerful figures like Prince John at Galtres take advantage of language's ambiguities to trick the opposing army into laying down its arms and then promptly execute its leaders. By contrast, one of the play's most remarkable rhetoricians, Mistress Quickly, did not make it to the title page of the Quarto, but her verbal blunders are legion and more benign than John's deliberate obfuscations. Quickly is not the same person she was in *1 Henry IV*. For one thing, she seems to have lost the husband who was mentioned often, though never glimpsed, in the previous play; and she has acquired a new companion in the person of the prostitute Doll Tearsheet. Unmarried, economically independent, and associated with the criminality of prostitution and perhaps of murder (in 5.4, the women are accused with Pistol of having beaten a man to death), Quickly emerges as a figure of disorder who must be purged from a reformed commonwealth. In part, she represents linguistic anarchy. Her signature utterance is the malapropism, the verbal blunder by which one word is mistaken for another. For example, telling the Chief Justice of Falstaff's whereabouts, she says he was "indited," meaning "invited," to dinner (2.1.22). The malapropism is interesting because it is a kind of lawless speech in which the speaker is guided by the sound of words, or by a private logic, rather than by the usual rules of sense. Quickly, for

The Rumor of Shakespeare's Induction is derived from the classical figure of Fame, here depicted as covered with ears (to gather reports from all quarters) and blowing a horn (to broadcast news abroad). From Vicenzo Cartari, *Imagines deorum* (1581).

example, in mistaking "indicted" for "invited" has blundered into her own kind of sense, since she would indeed like to see Falstaff indicted, or brought to legal judgment, for the debts he owes her. Malapropisms, to those who know better, make the speaker appear foolish. Yet they also can disrupt the institutions that depend on clear and predictable communication. Not even the Chief Justice knows quite what to make of Quickly, so persistently does her speech elude the net of common sense, enveloping her in a tangle of meanings—some obscene, some suggestively significant—that she may or may not intend. Sir Francis Bacon called revenge "wild justice"; the malapropism might be called "wild speech," so thoroughly does it defy semantic predictability.

The distinctiveness of the prose assigned to the comic figures in *2 Henry IV* is one of the play's most striking features. Shallow's mindless repetition of simple words, Falstaff's puns, Quickly's malapropisms, and Pistol's bombast are all ways of individuating these figures. They also suggest the fecundity of speech in Henry's England and register, at the linguistic level, a wild disorder that no principle of decorum or law can entirely contain. By means of the double entendre, much of what characters speak in the tavern world alludes to the body and its pleasures, even while they intend or appear to talk of something else. For example, Quickly, complaining of Falstaff to the Chief Justice, says, "he stabbed me in mine own house, most beastly, in good faith. 'A cares not what mischief he does; if his weapon be out, he will foin like any devil; he will spare neither man, woman, nor child" (2.1.11–14). "Foin" means "thrust" or "strike." Overtly, Quickly describes a Falstaff who takes out his sword or dagger and indiscriminately stabs whoever happens to be handy. Indirectly, and perhaps inadvertently, she describes a Falstaff who, when his sexual "weapon," or penis, is out, will indiscriminately engage

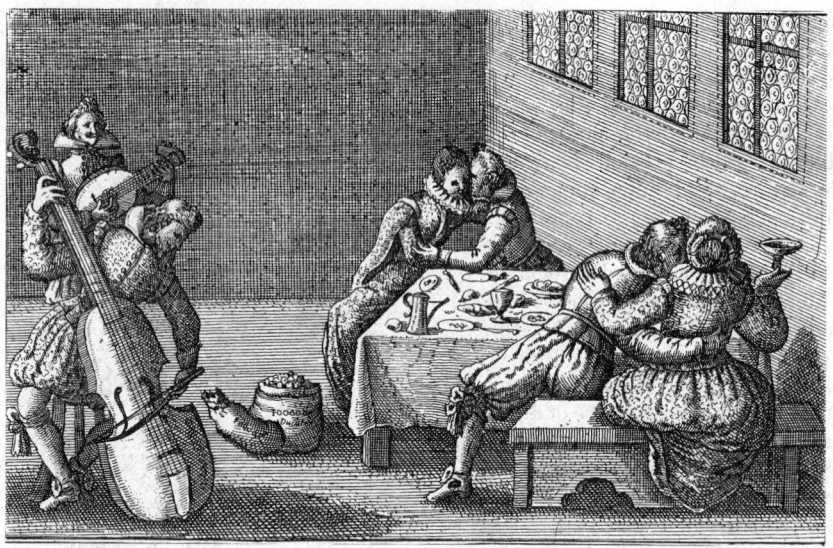

A seventeenth-century tavern scene recalling Mistress Quickly's Eastcheap tavern. From Peter Rollos, *Le Centre de l'amour* (1630?).

in sex with whoever happens to be near. The tavern scenes teem with similar instances of sexualized speech or, more accurately, speech that tells two stories at the same time, one of them a story of sex: its pleasures and diseases and persistence.

In *2 Henry IV*, the authority of the law is one of the chief bulwarks against the linguistic, sexual, and political disorder of the King's subjects. Law is comically embodied in the countryside in the person of Justice Shallow and in the court in the more imposing figure of the Lord Chief Justice. It is easy to make fun of Shallow, a man who repeatedly confuses the trivial and the serious; is bossed about by his servant, Davy; is exploited by Falstaff; and is given to boasting about a wild youth that he may never have experienced. Yet the Gloucestershire scenes where he appears also affectionately depict a rural way of life rooted in intimate knowledge of one's neighbors and in certain customary activities like going to Stamford Fair or managing the local muster for the Crown's wars. Shallow is a comic justice of the peace, but in his person the laws of England are associated with the customary life of rural England and the stability that that life promises.

The Lord Chief Justice, by contrast, shows the law in all its majesty. He is a constant force throughout the play: addressing Quickly's grievances against Falstaff, scolding the fat knight into assuming his military duties, and, somewhere in the distant past, committing Prince Hal to prison for dishonoring his person by giving him a box to the ear. At Henry V's ascension to the throne, however, the Chief Justice assumes a position of special importance as the King's chief counselor and his symbolic father. At Henry IV's death, many feared that England would fall into chaos, that Falstaff would flout the law unchecked, and that Hal would indulge in sensual excesses that would make him resemble the Eastern despots made famous on the English stage by figures like Marlowe's Tamburlaine or Thomas Preston's Cambyses. When Hal first appears after his father's death, he at once moves to dispel these fears, assuring his brothers that he is not an "Amurath" (that is, a Turkish tyrant) but a "Harry," a true English king. Above all else, the play suggests that that means a monarch who sees himself and his own heirs as subject to the laws of England and as ruling in concert with "the high court of Parliament" and with the advice of the Lord Chief Justice. The good governance of England depends, then, not only on the personal "reform" of a charismatic leader but also on the confirmation and continuance of the laws and customs of the nation.

What must follow, as a test of Hal's sincerity, is his public repudiation of Falstaff. In *2 Henry IV*, Falstaff is kept separate from the Prince except for the one scene (2.4) in which the Prince disguises himself as a tavern barman and overhears Falstaff talking with Doll and Quickly. Moreover, the exploitative side of Falstaff is more fully displayed here than in the earlier play. He leeches off Quickly; he takes bribes to release able-bodied men from service in the army; he worms a thousand pounds from Shallow. Yet he is still able, as in the stunning speech in which he indicts Prince John for cold-bloodedness (4.2.79–113), to offer a telling critique of his betters and to embody a frank physicality that they eschew. Given Falstaff's wit and his centrality to the pleasure afforded by both *1* and *2 Henry IV*, the new king's repudiation of him—"I know thee not, old man. Fall to thy prayers" (5.5.45)—continues to trouble critics and audiences. Certainly, how the moment is staged can mitigate or harshen its implications. In Terry Hands's 1975 Royal Shakespeare Company production, for example, the newly crowned King came onstage in glittering gold and masked, the epitome of detached and heartless power. In other productions, he rejects his former friend with a sob, emphasizing his own sense of loss and his continuing affection for Falstaff. But however it is staged, the moment suggests that whatever his "personal" feelings, Hal has severed himself in the public eye from lawlessness and excess to embrace his role as a true English king. When he leaves the stage, the Chief Justice orders Falstaff to be taken to the Fleet, a London prison.

The final scene, however, is not the play's last word: it is followed by an Epilogue. It is likely that this Epilogue was spoken by the company's clown—in this case probably Will Kemp, a famed comic actor who in this play is believed to have played Falstaff. It is especially likely that Kemp spoke the Epilogue because of the several references in it to the actor's willingness to use his legs, or to dance, should his words not prove agreeable. Kemp was a skilled dancer, and when he left Shakespeare's company in 1599 he undertook a famous morris dance from London to Norwich. The Epilogue gives the common actor who had played Falstaff the play's last word and its final display of physical skill. At Shrewsbury, Hal had thought Falstaff dead; but, faking death, the fat man had arisen. In *2 Henry IV*, the old knight is banished from the King's presence in the play's final scene; but in the Epilogue, the actor who had played him reappears—soliciting the audience's applause, denying that Falstaff is a representation of the Lollard martyr Sir John Oldcastle (see the Introduction to *1 Henry IV*), and kicking up his heels in a virtuoso display of dancing skill. If in the play proper the forces of order have attempted to demonize the energies associated with popular culture and the low life of the tavern, in the Epilogue those energies have free rein. The body of the common actor holds center stage as Kemp, throwing aside the character Falstaff's mantle of age, delights the audience with a jig.

The Epilogue has another effect as well. It pluralizes the "authorities" to which the theater is beholden. With its references to the Oldcastle controversy and its final allusion to praying for Queen Elizabeth, the Epilogue acknowledges the power embodied in the person of the monarch and in the state's censorship apparatus. But it also refers to pleasing both the gentlewomen and the gentlemen of the audience—in other words, the paying customers who came to the theater for all sorts of pleasures. If the title page of the Quarto is to be believed, readers, and probably audiences, were as much delighted by the irrepressible and irresponsible antics of Falstaff and swaggering Pistol as by the sober reformation of Hal and the suffering of his father, just as they were undoubtedly as delighted by the mangling of the King's English as by its decorous deployment. In short, while in this play the rule of law officially triumphs over the forces of disorder, the comic actor has the last dance, and theater finds a way to offer pleasures in excess of the regime of sobriety to which the new king has publically committed himself.

JEAN E. HOWARD

SELECTED BIBLIOGRAPHY

Baldo, Jonathan. "'Washed in Lethe': Laundering the Past in 2 *Henry IV*." Chapter 3 of *Memory in Shakespeare's Histories: Stages of Forgetting in Early Modern England*. London: Routledge, 2012. 73–101. Explores the dispersion and heterogeneity of memory in 2 *Henry IV* and the new king's obliteration of the memory of Falstaff as preparation for his creation of a unified national memory in *Henry V*.

Crewe, Jonathan. "Reforming Prince Hal: The Sovereign Inheritor in 2 *Henry IV*." *Renaissance Drama* n.s. 21 (1990): 225–42. Discusses the play's obsession with Hal's reform and the role of the father's death in effecting that reform.

Evans, Meredith. "Rumor, the Breath of Kings, and the Body of Law in 2 *Henry IV*." *Shakespeare Quarterly* 60 (2009): 1–24. Argues that the important transfer of power in 2 *Henry IV* is between Rumor and the Lord Chief Justice as kingship built on charisma and lies is restrained and legitimized by law.

Goldberg, Jonathan. "Hal's Desire, Shakespeare's Idaho." *Shakespeare's Hand*. Minneapolis: U Minnesota P, 2003. 222–52. Uses Gus Van Sant's film *My Own Private Idaho* to explore sex and gender relations in 1 and 2 *Henry IV,* including Hal's potentially sodomitical relations with Falstaff.

Harris, Jonathan Gil. "Performing History: East-West Palimpsests in William Shakespeare's Second Henriad." Chapter 2 of *Untimely Matter in the Time of Shakespeare*. Philadephia: U of Pennsylvania P, 2009. 66–87. Discusses references in 1 and 2 *Henry IV* to Eastern tyrants and to the bombastic acting styles in which the early modern stage presented such tyrants; argues that these references create a temporal layering that intimates the triumph of West over East and of new acting styles over old.

Hodgdon, Barbara. "'Let the End Try the Man': 1 and 2 *Henry IV*." *The End Crowns All: Closure and Contradiction in Shakespeare's History*. Princeton, NJ: Princeton UP, 1991. 151–84. Discusses the endings of both *Part I* and *Part II* and the different ways in which they have been staged.

Levine, Nina. "Extending Credit in the *Henry IV* Plays." *Shakespeare Quarterly* 51 (2000): 403–31. Discusses the pervasiveness and ideological complexity of the language of credit in both *Henry IV* plays.

MacDonald, Ronald R. "Uses of Diversity: Bakhtin's Theory of Utterance and Shakespeare's Second Tetralogy." *Henry IV, Parts One* and *Two*. Ed. Nigel Wood. Theory in Practice series. Buckingham: Open UP, 1995. 65–91. Uses Bakhtin's theories of language to discuss the heteroglossia, or profusion of disparate voices, in the plays containing Prince Hal and Henry V.

Rackin, Phyllis. "Historical Kings/Theatrical Clowns." *Stages of History: Shakespeare's English Chronicles*. Ithaca, NY: Cornell UP, 1990. 201–47. Explores in all the histories the threat to authority embodied in the disorderly conduct and subversive speech of common men and of Falstaff.

Wiles, David. *Shakespeare's Clown: Actor and Text in the Elizabethan Playhouse*. New York: Cambridge UP, 1987. Esp. "Kemp's Jigs" (43–60) and "Falstaff" (116–35). Argues that Falstaff's role is the clown's part and that it was originally played by Will Kemp, a notable clown in Shakespeare's company who was also famous for his dancing of jigs.

FILMS

Henry IV, Part II. 1979. Dir. David Giles. UK. 155 min. Judicious cuts and a strong performance by Anthony Quayle as Falstaff strengthen this sober BBC-TV version of the play.

Henry IV, Part II. 2012. Dir. Richard Eyre. UK. The third part of *The Hollow Crown.* A dark and grimly realistic production with both Falstaff and Henry IV as sick old men. Wonderfully acted with Jeremy Irons as Henry, Tom Hiddleston as Prince Hal, and Simon Russell Beale as Falstaff.

TEXTUAL INTRODUCTION

2 Henry IV exists in both Quarto (Q) and Folio (F) versions. Editors typically use Q as their base text, granting it a higher degree of authority than F: *The Norton Shakespeare* makes it the base text for the print edition and in the Digital Edition also offers the first modern version to be thoroughly based on the Folio.

The Quarto was entered in the Stationers' Register on August 23, 1600, along with *Much Ado About Nothing,* noting that both were "Wrytten by master Shakespere." The play was printed in the same year, as indicated by the title page:

> THE Second part of Henrie the fourth, continuing to his death, *and coronation of Henrie* the fift. With the humours of sir Iohn Fal-*staffe, and swaggering* Pistoll. *As it hath been sundrie times publikely* acted by the right honourable, the Lord Chamberlaine his seruants. *Written by William Shakespeare.* LONDON Printed by V[alentine]. S[immes]. for Andrew Wise, and William Aspley. 1600.

The Quarto went through two issues: Qa (eleven copies extant) and Qb (twelve copies extant). Scene 1 of act 3, in which Henry IV meditates on the passing of time, was omitted from Qa but reintroduced in the second issue (Qb), where four pages of Qa (two leaves, signed E3 and E4) were canceled and replaced by eight pages (four leaves, signed E3, E4, E5, [E6]) to make room for the omitted scene. This also entailed resetting a portion of the text, in 2.4, from line 348 to the end of the scene, and in 3.2, lines 1–93. Qb includes seven minor variants to these passages also present in Qa, indicated in the Textual Variants only when they are significant. Moreover, Qa and Qb exist in two different states, corrected (Qc) and uncorrected (Qu). Qc is usually more reliable than Qu, but omits two lines only present in uncorrected copies (4.1.68 and 70). There are fourteen passages present in Q but not in F, mainly single lines, except for four longer passages: 1.1.195–200, 2.2.20–24, 3.1.53–56, 3.2.280–85. *The Norton Shakespeare* uses Qa as base text, except for 3.1, where Qb is the sole authority. The rest of the play follows Qc when it differs from the other quartos, except for the two canceled lines, which are reintroduced into our text.

The Folio version includes eight substantial passages (168 lines in total) absent from Q. It also differs from Q in a number of significant ways:

- oaths have been suppressed following the 1606 statute against profanity on the stage;
- punctuation, syntax, line distribution, and style have been regularized and most colloquialisms removed;
- stage directions have been clarified and regularized (eliminating "ghost characters"); in several scenes, characters have been grouped for a "massed entry" even when only some of them are required;
- new part-lines have been inserted;
- a list of "The Actors' Names," including all speaking parts, has been added.

When setting the text, the F compositor found that too little space had been allocated to the play; he added four extra sheets, omitting words and compressing the text and then, when he found he had space left, adding words, expanding the text, and printing the Epilogue in large type. "The Actors' Names" may have been added to fill the verso of the spare leaf.

Critical debate has focused on the relationship between F and Q. There is consensus that Q probably derives from an authorial draft (or "foul papers") not marked up for performance. Q shows variations in the forms of speech prefixes, imprecision in entry directions, occasional "ghost characters," and the kind of descriptive details in stage directions normally considered typical of an authorial first draft. The absence of 3.1 from Qa suggests that the scene was marked for excision in the foul papers, either to abridge the play or because of the politically sensitive nature of the passage, in which Henry IV justifies his deposition of Richard II; in the year of the Earl of Essex's failed rising, this might have been construed as an apology for rebellion. Some critics, though, believe that the scene might have been copied on a separate leaf that became loose and was overlooked by the compositor; others suggest the scene might have been added as an afterthought but missed by the compositor.

The text of F was fairly carefully prepared by a professional scribe. The nature of the manuscript he used is unclear, although it seems obvious that it was not a prompt book. This has led some critics to dismiss the Folio as derivative in comparison with Q, but it may also represent a more polished state of the text than Q, carefully edited by a contemporary of the author, if not by Shakespeare himself. As it stands, it constitutes a clean, coherent text that requires relatively few editorial interventions.

Critics disagree about the reason for the eight fairly substantial passages found in F but not in Q. Most modern editors argue that the passages in question were originally present in the manuscript used for setting Q but probably marked for excision. Four of the eight additional Folio passages, dealing with the issue of rebellion, may have been cut for political reasons: they involve figures from the rebels' party: 1.1.188–208, 1.3.85–108, 4.1.55–79, 4.1.101–37. The other four passages are amplifications and may have been cut to streamline the action or to make better connections with the rest of the tetralogy: 1.1.165–78, 1.3.21–24, 1.3.36–55, 2.3.23–45. This last passage, part of Lady Percy's moving homage to Hotspur, was perhaps excised because it might have been read as an homage to Essex. The Folio compositor may have used a prompt book that included authorial revisions of the Q text, but he seems also to have had access to the Quarto for consultation. Some revisions to the Folio text—regularization of style, syntax, or punctuation—may reflect the habits of a particular scribe. The Folio is fairly thorough as regards act and scene divisions: both Norton editions follow these divisions, although in Q the Induction has been included as a separate section rather than as part of the first scene as in F; a scene break has also been added at 4.2.

LINE COTTEGNIES

PERFORMANCE NOTE

As *2 Henry IV* is typically produced in repertory with the first, or as part of a conflation, audiences often begin with preconceptions about its prominent characterizations and style. Directors can honor or frustrate those expectations, depending on whether they broadly conceive *2 Henry IV* as a history of Hal's coming of age or as a tragedy centered on Falstaff. In some productions, Falstaff seems a necessary casualty in a great national epic: his age and mounting inefficacy can argue strongly against his place in Hal's life, the cyclical pattern of the two plays serving chiefly to illustrate Hal's progress and moral education. In other productions, the optimism surrounding Hal's succession creates pity for a Falstaff fast slipping into obsolescence. Hal's coolness and barely suggested interiority in *2 Henry IV* may intensify the sympathetic portrait of Falstaff that emerges with his dawning awareness of the fragility and irrelevance—and inescapability—of his braggart persona.

Three scenes can prove pivotal in influencing the audience's sympathies. Productions that have Prince John revel in his trickery at Galtres before a sympathetic Archbishop (4.1), Henry's officers violently seize Doll Tearsheet and Mistress Quickly and march them toward what seems an ominous end (5.4), and Henry appear callous and hypocritical while publicly rebuking Falstaff (5.5) garner sympathy for those in East-cheap and complicate the reception of the royals. Yet productions can also exaggerate the Archbishop's villainy or the commoners' comic traits, implying that Henry's shows of authority disguise compassionate aims to protect the realm and to save its people from vice. To similar ends, Hal can condescend to Poins in jest or in earnest; he can appear impatient to get the crown, or reluctant to wear it even after becoming king; and Henry IV can be a hot-tempered bully or, like Falstaff, increasingly introspective and humble before death. Meanwhile, Shallow's nostalgia can be foolish or endearing; Pistol's flamboyant persona can define him utterly or be a mask for Falstaff's last loyal friend; Doll can be sweet or mercenary; Quickly can exhibit a mother's pride in Doll or a rival's jealousy. Other considerations include how to represent the King's illness and the staging of the Prologue and Epilogue, especially Rumor.

BRETT GAMBOA

The Second Part of Henry the Fourth, Continuing to His Death, and Coronation of Henry the Fifth

[THE PERSONS OF THE PLAY

RUMOR
EPILOGUE

KING Henry the Fourth
PRINCE Henry, afterwards crowned KING Henry the Fifth
PRINCE JOHN of Lancaster
Humphrey, Duke of GLOUCESTER } sons to Henry the Fourth and brethren
Thomas, Duke of CLARENCE } to Henry the Fifth

Opposites against King Henry the Fourth:
Earl of NORTHUMBERLAND
WIFE to Northumberland
KATE, Lady Percy, widow to Hotspur
TRAVERS, servant to Northumberland
MORTON, a messenger
ARCHBISHOP of York
LORD BARDOLPH
Lord MOWBRAY, Earl Marshal
Lord HASTINGS
Sir John COLEVILLE

Of the King's party:
LORD CHIEF JUSTICE
SERVANT to Lord Chief Justice
Earl of WARWICK
Earl of WESTMORLAND
Earl of Surrey
HARCOURT
GOWER
Sir John Blunt
Kent
Page to the King

Robert SHALLOW, a country justice
SILENCE, a country justice
DAVY, servant to Shallow

Country soldiers:
Ralph MOLDY
Simon SHADOW
Thomas WART

Francis FEEBLE
Peter BULLCALF

Irregular humorists:
Sir John FALSTAFF
POINS
BARDOLPH
PISTOL
PETO
PAGE to Falstaff

HOSTESS Quickly
DOLL TEARSHEET
FANG and SNARE, two sergeants

Three DRAWERS, including FRANCIS and WILL
Three STREWERS of rushes
SINCKLO
PORTER
MESSENGER
Captain
Lords, Musicians, Officers, Soldiers, Attendants]

Induction[1] (F Induction)
Enter RUMOR,[2] *painted full of tongues.*

RUMOR Open your ears; for which of you will stop°		*plug up*
The vent of hearing° when loud Rumor speaks?		*The ear*
I, from the Orient° to the drooping West,		*East*
Making the wind my post-horse,° still° unfold		*hired-horse / continually*

5   The acts commencèd on this ball of earth.
Upon my tongues continual slanders ride,
The which in every language I pronounce,
Stuffing the ears of men with false reports.
I speak of peace, while covert° enmity,   *concealed*
10 Under the smile of safety, wounds the world;
And who but Rumor, who but only I,
Make fearful musters and prepared defense,[3]
Whiles the big° year, swoll'n with some other grief,   *pregnant*
Is thought with child by the stern tyrant War,
15 And no such matter? Rumor is a pipe
Blown by surmises, jealousies, conjectures,
And of so easy and so plain a stop[4]

Induction Location: Outside Northumberland's castle at Warkworth.
1. TEXTUAL COMMENT Reflecting the fluidity with which Shakespeare has his characters enter and exit the stage, the Quarto is not divided into acts and scenes, unlike the Folio. This edition, like most modern editions, follows F's division of the play, with two primary changes: printing the Induction as a separate prologue before act 1, thus renumbering F's scenes; and breaking up F's two long scenes in act 4 into three scenes. See Digital Edition TC 1 (Quarto edited text).
2. A personification, possibly based on Virgil's "Fama," depicted as a female monster with many eyes, ears, and tongues who circulated both true and false accounts of

events. See *Aeneid* 4.179–90.
3. Cause soldiers, prompted by fear, to assemble and defenses to be made ready. These lines may be topical: fear of imminent Spanish invasion led the Privy Council to mobilize militia forces frequently throughout the latter years of Elizabeth's reign.
4. And whose "stops," or openings, are so easy to play upon. The ease with which Rumor's pipe can be played means that even the common people can do it. In the next lines, Rumor refers to these commoners as a many-headed monster—a common derogatory image of the people, especially when they aspire to participation in governance.

That the blunt° monster with uncounted° heads,   *stupid / innumerable*
The still discordant, wav'ring multitude,
20 Can play upon it. But what° need I thus   *why*
My well-known body to anatomize°   *dissect; lay open*
Among my household?° Why is Rumor here?   *(the theater audience)*
I run before King Harry's victory,
Who in a bloody field by Shrewsbury⁵
25 Hath beaten down young Hotspur and his troops,
Quenching the flame of bold rebellion
Even with the rebels' blood. But what mean I
To speak so true at first? My office is
To noise abroad that Harry Monmouth⁶ fell
30 Under the wrath of noble Hotspur's sword,
And that the King before the Douglas' rage
Stooped his anointed head as low as death.
This have I rumored through the peasant° towns   *rural*
Between that royal field of Shrewsbury
35 And this worm-eaten hold° of raggèd stone,   *stronghold*
When Hotspur's father, old Northumberland,
Lies crafty-sick.° The posts come tiring on,⁷   *pretending to be ill*
And not a man of them brings other news
Than they have learned of me. From Rumor's tongues
40 They bring smooth comforts false, worse than true wrongs.
                                            Exit.

1.1 (F 1.1)

Enter the LORD BARDOLPH¹ *at one door[, and the*
    PORTER *at another].*
LORD BARDOLPH Who keeps the gate here, ho? Where is the
    Earl?
PORTER What shall I say you are?
LORD BARDOLPH   Tell thou the Earl
That the Lord Bardolph doth attend° him here.   *await*
PORTER His lordship is walked forth into the orchard.
5 Please it your honor knock but at the gate,
And he himself will answer.
      Enter the Earl NORTHUMBERLAND.
LORD BARDOLPH   Here comes the Earl.
                            [Exit PORTER.]
NORTHUMBERLAND What news, Lord Bardolph? Every
    minute now
Should be the father of some stratagem.°   *military artifice; trick*
The times are wild; contention, like a horse
10 Full of high feeding,° madly hath broke loose   *overly rich food*
And bears down all before him.
LORD BARDOLPH   Noble Earl,
I bring you certain news from Shrewsbury.
NORTHUMBERLAND Good, an° God will.   *if*
LORD BARDOLPH   As good as heart can wish.

---

5. In Shakespeare's rendition of the Battle of Shrewsbury, staged in *1 Henry IV*, Prince Hal kills Henry
Percy (Hotspur), and his forces capture the Scottish
Earl of Douglas, two of the principal leaders of
rebellion.
6. Prince Hal was called "Harry Monmouth" in honor

of his birthplace, Monmouth, in Wales.
7. The messengers, exhausting themselves, gallop on.
1.1 Location: Scene continues.
1. A nobleman associated with the rebel Percy faction; Falstaff's companion with the same name is
unrelated.

The King is almost wounded to the death,
15 And in the fortune° of my lord your son,   *good luck*
Prince Harry slain outright, and both the Blunts[2]
Killed by the hand of Douglas. Young Prince John
And Westmorland and Stafford fled the field,
And Harry Monmouth's brawn,° the hulk Sir John,   *fattened pig*
20 Is prisoner to your son. Oh, such a day,
So fought, so followed,° and so fairly won,   *carried through*
Came not till now to dignify the times
Since Caesar's fortunes.°   *successes*
NORTHUMBERLAND   How is this derived?°   *obtained*
Saw you the field? Came you from Shrewsbury?
25 LORD BARDOLPH   I spake with one, my lord, that came from
      thence,
          Enter TRAVERS.
A gentleman well bred and of good name,
That freely rendered me these news for true.
NORTHUMBERLAND   Here comes my servant Travers, who I sent
On Tuesday last to listen after news.
30 LORD BARDOLPH   My lord, I overrode° him on the way,   *overtook*
And he is furnished with no certainties
More than he haply° may retail from me.   *perhaps*
NORTHUMBERLAND   Now, Travers, what good tidings comes
      with you?
34 TRAVERS   My lord, Sir John Umfrevile[3] turned me back
35 With joyful tidings and, being better horsed,
Outrode me. After him came spurring hard
A gentleman almost forspent° with speed,   *worn out*
That stopped by me to breathe° his bloodied horse.   *rest*
He asked the way to Chester,[4] and of him
40 I did demand what news from Shrewsbury.
He told me that rebellion had bad luck,
And that young Harry Percy's spur was cold.[5]
With that he gave his able horse the head
And, bending forward, struck his armèd heels
45 Against the panting sides of his poor jade°   *worn-out horse*
Up to the rowel-head[6] and, starting so,
He seemed in running to devour the way,
Staying° no longer question.   *Awaiting*
NORTHUMBERLAND   Ha? Again:
Said he young Harry Percy's spur was cold?
50 Of Hotspur, Coldspur? That rebellion
Had met ill luck?
LORD BARDOLPH   My lord, I'll tell you what:
If my young lord your son have not the day,
Upon mine honor, for a silken point°   *lace for tying a garment*
I'll give my barony; never talk of it.

---

2. In *1 Henry IV*, only one Blunt—Sir Walter—dies at Shrewsbury.
3. Although in both F and Q, Travers says that Sir John Umfrevile turns him back, since Lord Bardolph reports having met Travers on the road, most critics agree that Umfrevile and Lord Bardolph are the same character whose name got changed at some point. At 1.1.161, Q assigns one line to "*Umfr.*," another indication that a character with this name was once to figure in the play. This edition attributes the line, which does not appear in F, to Morton.
4. A town north of Shrewsbury.
5. The announcement of Henry Percy's death invokes considerable wordplay on his nickname, his "hot" spur being transformed into a "cold" spur by death.
6. The spiked wheel at the end of the spur.

55 NORTHUMBERLAND Why should that gentleman that rode
   by Travers
  Give, then, such instances of loss?
  LORD BARDOLPH   Who, he?
  He was some hilding° fellow that had stol'n   *worthless*
  The horse he rode on and, upon my life,
  Spoke at a venture.°   *speculatively*
   Enter MORTON.
      Look, here comes more news.
60 NORTHUMBERLAND Yea, this man's brow, like to a title-leaf,
  Foretells the nature of a tragic volume.[7]
  So looks the strand° whereon the imperious flood   *shore*
  Hath left a witnessed usurpation.[8]
  Say, Morton, didst thou come from Shrewsbury?
65 MORTON I ran from Shrewsbury, my noble lord,
  Where hateful death put on his ugliest mask
  To fright our party.
  NORTHUMBERLAND How doth my son and brother?[9]
  Thou tremblest, and the whiteness in thy cheek
  Is apter than thy tongue to tell thy errand.
70   Even such a man, so faint, so spiritless,
  So dull, so dead in look, so woebegone,
  Drew Priam's curtain[1] in the dead of night
  And would have told him half his Troy was burnt.
  But Priam found the fire ere he his tongue,
75   And I my Percy's death ere thou report'st it.
  This thou wouldst say: "Your son did thus and thus,
  Your brother thus; so fought the noble Douglas,"
  Stopping° my greedy ear with their bold deeds.   *Filling*
  But, in the end, to stop° my ear indeed,   *plug up; obstruct*
80   Thou hast a sigh to blow away this praise,
  Ending with "Brother, son, and all are dead."
  MORTON Douglas is living, and your brother yet;
  But for my lord your son—
  NORTHUMBERLAND   Why, he is dead?
  See what a ready tongue suspicion hath.
85   He that but fears the thing he would not know
  Hath by instinct knowledge from others' eyes
  That what he feared is chanced.° Yet speak, Morton, *has happened*
  Tell thou an earl his divination lies,[2]
  And I will take it as a sweet disgrace
90   And make thee rich for doing me such wrong.
  MORTON You are too great to be by me gainsaid;° *contradicted*
  Your spirit is too true, your fears too certain.
  NORTHUMBERLAND Yet, for all this, say not that Percy's dead.
  I see a strange confession in thine eye.

---

7. Alluding to the descriptive title pages of early modern printed books, which often indicated the principal actions of the work and sometimes characterized them as tragic or comic. For an example, see the descriptive title page of the Quarto version of this play, reprinted in the Introduction.

8. *whereon . . . usurpation:* where the sea has left evidence of its conquest (of the land). The comparison is between Morton's brow, wrinkled by sorrow, and sand furrowed by the sea's encroachment.

9. The Earl of Worcester, who helped lead the rebellion staged in *1 Henry IV*.

1. Opened Priam's bed curtain. Priam was King of Troy during the Trojan War. This may allude to a scene from Virgil's *Aeneid* in which Hector appears to Aeneas, not Priam, in a dream, warning him of danger. Aeneas wakes to find Troy in flames.

2. Tell me, who am an earl, that in my prophecy I lie. To say that a social superior lies would normally be a grave offense, but Northumberland would be happy to be proven wrong.

95	Thou shak'st thy head and hold'st it fear or sin	
	To speak a truth. If he be slain,	
	The tongue offends not that reports his death;	
	And he doth sin that doth belie° the dead,	*lie about*
	Not he which says the dead is not alive.	
100	Yet the first bringer of unwelcome news	
	Hath but a losing office,° and his tongue	*thankless duty*
	Sounds ever after as a sullen° bell	*mournful*
	Remembered, tolling a departing friend.	

LORD BARDOLPH   I cannot think, my lord, your son is dead.

105 MORTON   I am sorry I should force you to believe
That which I would to God I had not seen.
But these mine eyes saw him in bloody state,
Rend'ring faint quittance,[3] wearied and out-breathed,°   *out of breath*
To Harry Monmouth, whose swift wrath beat down
110 The never-daunted Percy to the earth,
From whence with life he never more sprung up.
In few,° his death whose spirit lent a fire   *In short*
Even to the dullest peasant in his camp,
Being bruited° once, took fire and heat away   *reported*
115 From the best-tempered courage[4] in his troops.
For from his metal° was his party steeled,   *courage*
Which once in him abated,° all the rest   *blunted*
Turned on themselves[5] like dull and heavy lead;
And as the thing that's heavy in itself
120 Upon enforcement° flies with greatest speed,   *When forced into motion*
So did our men, heavy in Hotspur's loss,
Lend to this weight such lightness with their fear
That arrows fled not swifter toward their aim
Than did our soldiers, aiming at their safety,
125 Fly from the field. Then was that noble Worcester
So soon ta'en prisoner, and that furious Scot,
The bloody Douglas, whose well-laboring sword
Had three times slain th'appearance of the King,[6]
Gan vail his stomach[7] and did grace° the shame   *sanction*
130 Of those that turned their backs and, in his flight,
Stumbling in fear, was took. The sum of all
Is that the King hath won and hath sent out
A speedy power° to encounter you, my lord,   *quickly moving army*
Under the conduct° of young Lancaster   *command*
135 And Westmorland. This is the news at full.

NORTHUMBERLAND   For this, I shall have time enough to mourn.
In poison there is physic,° and these news,   *medicine*
Having been° well, that would have made me sick,   *If I had been*
Being sick, have in some measure made me well;
140 And as the wretch whose fever-weakened joints,
Like strengthless hinges, buckle under life,[8]
Impatient of his fit, breaks like a fire
Out of his keeper's° arms, even so my limbs,   *nurse's*

---

3. Repayment (return of blows).
4. Courage of the finest quality. The implicit comparison is to steel that had been tempered, or made strong, by extreme heat.
5. Bent backward (like soft metal); fled.
6. In *1 Henry IV*, at the Battle of Shrewsbury, mem-

bers of the rebel faction slew several noblemen dressed in the King's coats whom they mistook for Henry himself. See *1 Henry IV*, 5.3.1–13 and 5.4.24–37.
7. Began to lose courage (stomach).
8. Collapse from the burden of living.

Weakened with grief, being now enraged with grief,
145 Are thrice themselves. Hence, therefore, thou nice° crutch!   *unmanly*
A scaly° gauntlet now with joints of steel   *mailed*
Must glove this hand. And hence, thou sickly coif!
Thou art a guard too wanton° for the head   *effeminate; luxurious*
Which princes fleshed with conquest⁹ aim to hit.
150 Now bind my brows with iron, and approach
The ragged'st° hour that time and spite dare bring   *roughest*
To frown upon th'enragèd Northumberland!
Let heaven kiss earth! Now let not Nature's hand
Keep the wild flood confined! Let order die,
155 And let this world no longer be a stage
To feed contention in a ling'ring act;¹
But let one spirit of the first-born Cain²
Reign in all bosoms that, each heart being set
On bloody courses, the rude scene may end,
160 And darkness be the burier of the dead.
MORTON   This strainèd passion doth you wrong, my lord.
LORD BARDOLPH   Sweet earl, divorce not wisdom from your
    honor.
MORTON   The lives of all your loving complices°   *associates*
Lean on your health, the which if you give o'er
165 To stormy passion, must perforce decay.³
LORD BARDOLPH   We all that are engagèd to° this loss   *involved in*
Knew that we ventured on such dangerous seas
That, if we wrought out life, 'twas ten to one;⁴
And yet we ventured for the gain proposed,
170 Choked the respect of° likely peril feared,   *Refused to consider*
And, since we are o'erset,° venture again.   *overthrown*
Come, we will all put forth, body and goods.
MORTON   'Tis more than time and, my most noble lord,
I hear for certain and dare speak the truth.
175 NORTHUMBERLAND   I knew of this before but, to speak truth,
This present grief had wiped it from my mind.
Go in with me, and counsel every man
The aptest way for safety and revenge.
Get posts° and letters, and make° friends with speed;   *messengers / gather*
180 Never so few, and never yet more need.   *Exeunt.*

1.2 (F 1.2)

*Enter Sir John [FALSTAFF] alone, with his PAGE
bearing his sword and buckler.°*   *shield*
FALSTAFF   Sirrah,¹ you giant,² what says the doctor to my water?°   *urine*
PAGE   He said, sir, the water itself was a good healthy water
    but, for the party that owed° it, he might have more diseases   *owned*
    than he knew for.°   *was aware of*
5 FALSTAFF   Men of all sorts take a pride to gird° at me. The   *mock*

---

9. Which princes made eager for bloody victories by
having tasted raw flesh (been victorious). Hounds
were "fleshed," or given a taste of raw meat, to prepare them for the hunt.
1. *And let . . . act:* And let the world stop being a stage
where strife is encouraged in a prolonged action.
2. In the Bible, the first human being to be born and
the murderer of his brother.
3. At this point, thirteen lines appear in F that are not

in Q. In all, eight substantial passages appear in F and
not in Q. For a list of them, and for possible explanations for their absence, see the Textual Introduction.
4. The odds were ten to one against our preserving
life.
1.2 Location: A street in London.
1. Form of address to a social inferior.
2. Ironic description of the page, who is small.

brain of this foolish compounded clay, man,[3] is not able to
invent anything that intends to laughter more than I invent
or is invented on me. I am not only witty in myself but the
cause that wit is in other men. I do here walk before thee
10 like a sow that hath overwhelmed° all her litter but one. If _crushed_
the Prince put thee into my service for any other reason
than to set me off,[4] why then I have no judgment. Thou
whoreson mandrake,[5] thou art fitter to be worn in my cap
than to wait at my heels. I was never manned with° an _attended by_
15 agate[6] till now, but I will inset you neither in gold nor silver,
but in vile apparel, and send you back again to your master
for a jewel—the juvenal,° the Prince your master, whose _youth_
chin is not yet fledge.° I will sooner have a beard grow in _covered with down_
the palm of my hand than he shall get one off his cheek,
20 and yet he will not stick° to say his face is a face-royal.[7] God _hesitate_
may finish it when He will; 'tis not a hair amiss yet. He may
keep it still at° a face-royal, for a barber shall never earn _at the value of_
sixpence out of it, and yet he'll be crowing as if he had writ
"man"° ever since his father was a bachelor. He may keep _called himself a man_
25 his own grace,° but he's almost out of mine, I can assure _title (Prince); favor_
him. What said Master Dommelton about the satin for my
short cloak and my slops?[8]
PAGE He said, sir, you should procure him better assurance
than Bardolph. He would not take his bond and yours; he
30 liked not the security.
FALSTAFF Let him be damned like the glutton;[9] pray God his
tongue be hotter! A whoreson Achitophel![1] A rascal yea-
forsooth knave,[2] to bear a gentleman in hand° and then stand _lead a gentleman on_
upon security! The whoreson smoothy-pates[3] do now wear
35 nothing but high shoes and bunches of keys at their girdles;[4]
an if a man is through with them in honest taking up,[5] then
they must stand upon security. I had as lief° they would put _gladly_
ratsbane° in my mouth as offer to stop it with security. I _rat poison_
looked 'a° should have sent me two-and-twenty yards of satin, _that he_
40 as I am a true knight,[6] and he sends me "security"! Well, he
may sleep in security, for he hath the horn of abundance,
and the lightness of his wife shines through it.[7] Where's

3. This witless man formed from various elements like clay (an image derived from the biblical account of the first human being as formed out of clay).
4. To make me stand out by contrast. (The page is tiny, and Falstaff is huge).
5. An herb with a forked root that was popularly supposed to resemble a miniature man. It was believed to shriek when pulled from the ground and to have aphrodisiacal powers. *whoreson*: an insult, derived from the phrase "whore's son."
6. A small jewel often carved with images of people and worn on caps.
7. The face of royalty (with a pun on "royal," a coin worth 10 shillings and stamped with the monarch's face).
8. Baggy knee breeches, fashionable in Elizabethan London.
9. Referring to the biblical parable of Dives, a rich glutton who ignored the pleas of the beggar Lazarus and at death was condemned to hell, where he implored Lazarus to dip his finger in water and lay it on his tongue to cool the flames (see Luke 16:19–31).
1. A biblical figure: King David's trusted counselor,

who betrayed him by supporting the treason of the king's son (2 Samuel 15).
2. A villainous knave who appears to be agreeable. A "yea-forsooth" knave makes promises with mild oaths (but then breaks them).
3. Alluding disparagingly to the fashion among tradesmen, especially puritans, for short hair.
4. Wear the most fashionable shoes and display a mass of keys (habits suggesting pride and conspicuous consumption).
5. If a man makes a deal with them for a purchase on credit.
6. Referring to Tudor sumptuary codes, which prescribed the fabrics that could be worn by people of different social ranks. As a knight, Falstaff can wear satin.
7. For he is rich and his wife's promiscuity is visible to all, with puns on "horn" as referring to the horn lanterns sold by merchants; to a symbol of overflowing plenty (a cornucopia); and to cuckoldry (deceived husbands were said to wear horns). "Lightness" can mean both illumination and sexual promiscuity.

Bardolph? —And yet cannot he see, though he have his own
lantern to light him.

45 PAGE   He's gone in Smithfield[8] to buy your worship a horse.

FALSTAFF   I bought him in Paul's,[9] and he'll buy me a horse in
Smithfield. An° I could get me but a wife in the stews,° I   *If / brothels*
were manned, horsed, and wived.

Enter LORD CHIEF JUSTICE [*and* SERVANT].

PAGE   Sir, here comes the nobleman that committed° the   *imprisoned*
50   Prince for striking him about Bardolph.[1]

FALSTAFF   Wait close;° I will not see him.[2]   *concealed*

LORD CHIEF JUSTICE   What's he that goes there?

SERVANT   Falstaff, an't please your lordship.

LORD CHIEF JUSTICE   He that was in question° for the robbery?[3]   *under investigation*

55 SERVANT   He, my lord, but he hath since done good service at
Shrewsbury and, as I hear, is now going with some charge°   *command of soldiers*
to the Lord John of Lancaster.

LORD CHIEF JUSTICE   What, to York? Call him back again.

SERVANT   Sir John Falstaff.

60 FALSTAFF   Boy, tell him I am deaf.

PAGE   —You must speak louder; my master is deaf.

LORD CHIEF JUSTICE   I am sure he is, to the hearing of anything good. —Go pluck him by the elbow; I must speak with
him.

SERVANT   Sir John!

65 FALSTAFF   What, a young knave and begging? Is there not
wars?[4] Is there not employment? Doth not the King lack
subjects? Do not the rebels need soldiers? Though it be a
shame to be on any side but one, it is worse shame to beg
than to be on the worst side, were it worse than the name of
70   rebellion can tell how to make° it.   *regard*

SERVANT   You mistake me, sir.

FALSTAFF   Why, sir, did I say you were an honest man? Setting
my knighthood and my soldiership aside, I had lied in my
throat° if I had said so.   *deliberately lied*

75 SERVANT   I pray you, sir, then set your knighthood and your
soldiership aside, and give me leave to tell you you lie in
your throat if you say I am any other than an honest man.

FALSTAFF   I give thee leave to tell me? So I lay aside that which
grows to me?° If thou gett'st any leave of me, hang me. If thou   *is part of me*
80   tak'st leave, thou wert better be hanged; you hunt counter.[5]
Hence, avaunt!°   *be gone*

SERVANT   Sir, my lord would speak with you.

LORD CHIEF JUSTICE   Sir John Falstaff, a word with you.

FALSTAFF   My good lord! God give your lordship good time of
85   day. I am glad to see your lordship abroad. I heard say your
lordship was sick; I hope your lordship goes abroad by advice.°   *by medical advice*
Your lordship, though not clean past your youth, have yet

8. A district northwest of London's city walls, used as a market for animals.
9. St. Paul's Cathedral in London, where masterless men presented themselves for employment.
1. Alluding to the apocryphal account of the youthful Prince's assault on the Lord Chief Justice, staged in *The Famous Victories of Henry V,* the anonymous play from which Shakespeare's is partly derived.
2. Falstaff's determination not to acknowledge the

Lord Chief Justice presumably causes him to turn his back on the magistrate or walk off in another direction.
3. The Gadshill robbery, in which Falstaff took part. See *1 Henry IV,* 2.2.
4. Alluding to the Elizabethan practice of mass conscription of impoverished men.
5. You pursue the scent of the game in the wrong direction.

some smack of an ague in you, some relish of the saltness of
time in you, and I most humbly beseech your lordship to have
90   a reverend care of your health.

LORD CHIEF JUSTICE   Sir John, I sent for you before your expedition to Shrewsbury.

FALSTAFF   An't please your lordship, I hear his majesty is
returned with some discomfort from Wales.[6]

95 LORD CHIEF JUSTICE   I talk not of his majesty. You would not
come when I sent for you.

FALSTAFF   And I hear moreover his highness is fallen into this
same whoreson apoplexy.°   *paralysis*

LORD CHIEF JUSTICE   Well, God mend him. I pray you, let me
100   speak with you.

FALSTAFF   This apoplexy, as I take it, is a kind of lethargy, an't
please your lordship, a kind of sleeping in the blood, a
whoreson tingling.

LORD CHIEF JUSTICE   What° tell you me of it? Be it as it is.   *Why*

105 FALSTAFF   It hath it original° from much grief, from study,   *its origin*
and perturbation of the brain. I have read the cause of his
effects in Galen;[7] it is a kind of deafness.

LORD CHIEF JUSTICE   I think you are fallen into the disease,
for you hear not what I say to you.

110 FALSTAFF[8]   Very well, my lord, very well. Rather, an't please you,
it is the disease of not listening, the malady of not marking,
that I am troubled withal.°   *with*

LORD CHIEF JUSTICE   To punish you by the heels[9] would amend
the attention of your ears, and I care not if I do become your
115   physician.

FALSTAFF   I am as poor as Job,[1] my lord, but not so patient.
Your lordship may minister the potion of imprisonment to
me in respect of° poverty, but how I should be your patient   *on account of*
to follow your prescriptions, the wise may make some dram
120   of a scruple, or indeed a scruple itself.[2]

LORD CHIEF JUSTICE   I sent for you, when there were matters
against you for your life,[3] to come speak with me.

FALSTAFF   As I was then advised by my learned counsel in the
laws of this land-service,° I did not come.   *military duty*

125 LORD CHIEF JUSTICE   Well, the truth is, Sir John, you live in
great infamy.

FALSTAFF   He that buckles himself in my belt cannot live in less.

LORD CHIEF JUSTICE   Your means are very slender and your
waste is great.

130 FALSTAFF   I would it were otherwise; I would my means were
greater and my waist slender.

LORD CHIEF JUSTICE   You have misled the youthful Prince.

---

6. Some discouragement from Wales (where the
King promised to fight Glyndŵr and Mortimer at the
end of *1 Henry IV*).
7. Ancient Greek physician whose anatomical texts
were widely translated and printed in early modern
Europe. Galen was commonly regarded as the chief
authority in human physiology.
8. TEXTUAL COMMENT Q's speech prefix mistakenly
lists "Old." here. Oldcastle was the name given to the
character of Falstaff when *1 Henry IV* was first performed, but, probably due to objections by a powerful

descendant of the historical Sir John Oldcastle, the
name was changed. See Digital Edition TC 2 (Quarto
edited text).
9. By putting your feet in the stocks or in shackles.
1. A biblical figure who, in the Book of Job, patiently
endured the many adversities with which God
afflicted him, including poverty.
2. The wise may feel a particle of doubt. Drams and
scruples were small weights used to measure medicines in apothecary shops.
3. For which your life was at stake.

FALSTAFF The young Prince hath misled me; I am the fellow
with the great belly and he my dog.[4]

135 LORD CHIEF JUSTICE Well, I am loath to gall° a new-healed   *to injure by rubbing*
wound: your day's service at Shrewsbury hath a little gilded
over your night's exploit on Gad's Hill. You may thank
th'unquiet time for your quiet o'er-posting° that action.   *passing swiftly over*

FALSTAFF My lord?

140 LORD CHIEF JUSTICE But since all is well, keep it so; wake not
a sleeping wolf.

FALSTAFF To wake a wolf is as bad as smell a fox.°   *as being suspicious*

LORD CHIEF JUSTICE What? You are as a candle, the better part
burnt out.

145 FALSTAFF A wassail candle,[5] my lord, all tallow°—if I did say   *animal fat*
of wax,[6] my growth would approve° the truth.   *attest to*

LORD CHIEF JUSTICE There is not a white hair in your face but
should have his effect° of gravity.   *manifestation*

FALSTAFF His effect of gravy, gravy, gravy.[7]

150 LORD CHIEF JUSTICE You follow the young Prince up and down
like his ill angel.°   *evil spirit*

FALSTAFF Not so, my lord; your ill angel is light,[8] but I hope he
that looks upon me will take me without weighing; and yet in
some respects I grant I cannot go.° I cannot tell: virtue is of   *walk; be circulated*

155 so little regard in these costermongers' times[9] that true valor
is turned bearherd.[1] Pregnancy° is made a tapster, and his   *Mental agility*
quick wit wasted in giving reckonings;° all the other gifts   *tavern bills*
appertinent° to man, as the malice of his age shapes the one,   *belonging*
not worth a gooseberry. You that are old consider not the

160 capacities of us that are young: you do measure the heat of
our livers with the bitterness of your galls;[2] and we that are
in the vanguard° of our youth, I must confess, are wags too.   *most advanced stage*

LORD CHIEF JUSTICE Do you set down your name in the scroll
of youth, that are written down old with all the characters° of   *letters; signs*

165 age? Have you not a moist eye, a dry hand, a yellow cheek, a
white beard, a decreasing leg, an increasing belly? Is not your
voice broken, your wind short, your chin double, your wit
single, and every part about you blasted with antiquity? And
will you yet call yourself young? Fie, fie, fie, Sir John!

170 FALSTAFF My lord, I was born about three of the clock in the
afternoon, with a white head and something a° round belly.   *a somewhat*
For my voice, I have lost it with hallooing[3] and singing of
anthems. To approve° my youth further, I will not. The truth   *prove*
is, I am only old in judgment and understanding; and he that

175 will caper° with me for a thousand marks,[4] let him lend me   *dance (in competition)*
the money—and have at him! For the box of the ear that the

---

4. An obscure allusion. It may refer to the man in the
moon, a mythical figure who supposedly carried a
bush and was accompanied by a dog.
5. A large fat candle used at holiday festivities.
6. Beeswax, with pun on "wax" as meaning "grow."
7. Grease; sweat. Falstaff implies that sweat should
drop from his face as fat (gravy) drops from hot meat.
8. Your bad coin weighs less. Falstaff puns on
"angel" as the name of a gold coin that could illegally
be clipped so that it weighed less than it should.
9. In these commercial times. A costermonger sold

trifling commodities such as fruits and vegetables.
1. Keeper of bears, such as those used for the popular entertainment of bearbaiting.
2. You measure the strength of our passions by the
bitterness of your melancholy. The liver was believed
to be the seat of youthful passions, and bile or gall
produced the melancholy and anger characteristic of
old age.
3. *hallooing:* shouting to hounds.
4. A unit of money; one mark was equal to two-thirds
of a pound.

Prince gave you, he gave it like a rude° prince, and you took it   *violent; uncivilized*
like a sensible lord.[5] I have checked him for it, and the young
lion repents—marry,° not in ashes and sackcloth, but in new   *by the Virgin Mary*
180   silk and old sack.[6]   *(oath)*
LORD CHIEF JUSTICE   Well, God send the Prince a better companion.
FALSTAFF   God send the companion a better prince; I cannot
rid my hands of him.
185   LORD CHIEF JUSTICE   Well, the King hath severed you; I hear
you are going with Lord John of Lancaster against the Archbishop and the Earl of Northumberland.
FALSTAFF   Yea, I thank your pretty sweet wit for it. But look°   *see that*
you pray, all you that kiss my lady Peace at home, that our
190   armies join not in a hot day; for, by the Lord, I take but two
shirts out with me, and I mean not to sweat extraordinarily.
If it be a hot day, and I brandish anything but a bottle, I
would I might never spit white again.[7] There is not a dangerous action° can peep out his head, but I am thrust upon it.   *military action*
195   Well, I cannot last ever,[8] but it was alway yet the trick° of   *habit*
our English nation, if they have a good thing, to make it too
common. If ye will needs say I am an old man, you should
give me rest. I would to God my name were not so terrible to
the enemy as it is; I were better to be eaten to death with a
200   rust than to be scoured to nothing with perpetual motion.
LORD CHIEF JUSTICE   Well, be honest, be honest, and God bless
your expedition.
FALSTAFF   Will your lordship lend me a thousand pound to furnish me forth?
205   LORD CHIEF JUSTICE   Not a penny, not a penny; you are too
impatient to bear crosses.[9] Fare you well. Commend me to my
cousin Westmorland.
            [*Exeunt* LORD CHIEF JUSTICE *and* SERVANT.]
FALSTAFF   If I do, fillip° me with a three-man beetle.[1] A man   *strike*
can no more separate age and covetousness than 'a° can part   *he*
210   young limbs and lechery; but the gout[2] galls the one and the
pox pinches° the other, and so both the degrees prevent my   *syphilis torments*
curses.[3] —Boy?
PAGE   Sir.
FALSTAFF   What money is in my purse?
215   PAGE   Seven groats° and two pence.   *coins worth fourpence*
FALSTAFF   I can get no remedy against this consumption of
the purse. Borrowing only lingers and lingers it out, but the
disease is incurable. Go bear this letter to my lord of Lancaster, this to the Prince, this to the Earl of Westmorland,

---

5. Like a reasonable lord; like a lord capable of feeling pain. For the story of Hal's striking the Lord Chief
Justice, see note to 1.2.50.
6. A Spanish white wine that improved with age.
7. A disputed passage. Perhaps: may I never drink
again (white spit was thought to be the result of
heavy drinking).
8. Lines 195 (from "but")–200 do not appear in F.
While there are many single lines and phrases that
appear only in Q, there are only four longer passages
only in Q, of which this is the first. (See Textual
Introduction.)
9. To endure afflictions like a good Christian; to

carry silver coins, which bear the sign of a cross.
1. A huge sledgehammer designed to be lifted by three
laborers at once.
2. A disease characterized by painful inflammation
of the joints, often of the toe joints in particular, and
associated with the excessive consumption of rich
food and alcohol. Gout may have been the reason
Falstaff sent his urine to be examined by the doctor
at the beginning of this scene.
3. So both conditions (age and youth) anticipate my
curses. Venereal disease torments young lecherous
men; gout afflicts old men.

220 and this to old Mistress Ursula,[4] whom I have weekly sworn
to marry since I perceived the first white hair of my chin.
About it; you know where to find me. A pox of this gout, or a
gout of this pox! For the one or the other plays the rogue
with my great toe. 'Tis no matter if I do halt;° I have the   *limp*
225 wars for my color,° and my pension shall seem the more rea-   *pretext*
sonable. A good wit will make use of anything; I will turn
diseases to commodity.°   [*Exeunt.*]   *profit*

1.3 (F 1.3)

Enter the ARCHBISHOP [*of York*], *Thomas* MOWBRAY
[*the*] *Earl Marshal,*[1] *the Lord* HASTINGS, *and* [LORD]
BARDOLPH.

ARCHBISHOP　Thus have you heard our cause and known our
　　means,
　　And, my most noble friends, I pray you all
　　Speak plainly your opinions of our hopes;
　　And first, Lord Marshal, what say you to it?
5 MOWBRAY　I well allow the occasion of our arms,[2]
　　But gladly would be better satisfied
　　How in our means° we should advance ourselves   *with our resources*
　　To look with forehead bold and big enough
　　Upon the power and puissance° of the King.   *strength*
10 HASTINGS　Our present musters grow upon the file°   *according to our list*
　　To five-and-twenty thousand men of choice,°   *choice men*
　　And our supplies° live largely in the hope   *reinforcements*
　　Of great Northumberland, whose bosom burns
　　With an incensèd fire of injuries.
15 LORD BARDOLPH　The question, then, Lord Hastings,
　　　　standeth thus:
　　Whether our present five-and-twenty thousand
　　May hold up head° without Northumberland.   *May succeed*
　　HASTINGS　With him we may.
　　LORD BARDOLPH　　　　　　　Yea, marry, there's the point;
　　But if without him we be thought too feeble,
20 　My judgment is we should not step too far.
　　ARCHBISHOP　'Tis very true, Lord Bardolph, for indeed
　　It was young Hotspur's cause at Shrewsbury.
　　LORD BARDOLPH　It was, my lord, who lined° himself with hope,   *strengthened*
　　Eating the air and promise of supply,[3]
25 　Flatt'ring himself in project of a power°   *expectation of an army*
　　Much smaller° than the smallest of his thoughts,   *smaller in actuality*
　　And so with great imagination,
　　Proper to madmen, led his powers to death
　　And, winking,° leaped into destruction.   *shutting his eyes*
30 HASTINGS　But, by your leave, it never yet did hurt
　　To lay down likelihoods and forms of hope.[4]
　　LORD BARDOLPH　We fortify in paper and in figures,
　　Using the names of men instead of men,
　　Like one that draws the model of an house

---

4. A name nowhere else mentioned in this play. It
could be the first name of Mistress Quickly. It could
also be an inadvertent reference to the Ursula of
Much Ado About Nothing, a play also printed in
1600.
1.3 Location: The Archbishop's palace in York.

1. The officer in charge of arranging royal ceremonies.
2. I grant the justice of our taking arms.
3. Sustaining himself on nothing but the promise of
aid; believing the empty words he had heard concerning promised aid.
4. And hopeful plans.

35   Beyond his power to build it; who, half through,
      Gives o'er, and leaves his part-created cost[5]
      A naked subject° to the weeping clouds,   *An exposed object*
      And waste for churlish winter's tyranny.
  HASTINGS   Grant that our hopes, yet° likely of fair birth,   *still*
40   Should be stillborn, and that we now possessed
      The utmost man of expectation:[6]
      I think we are a body strong enough,
      Even as we are, to equal with the King.
  LORD BARDOLPH   What, is the King but five-and-twenty
      thousand?
45   HASTINGS   To us, no more—nay, not so much, Lord Bardolph—
      For his divisions, as the times do brawl,°   *are full of conflict*
      And in three heads: one power against the French,
      And one against Glyndŵr;[7] perforce a third
      Must take up us.° So is the unfirm King   *oppose us*
50   In three divided, and his coffers sound
      With hollow poverty and emptiness.
  ARCHBISHOP   That he should draw his several° strengths   *separate*
      together
      And come against us in full puissance
      Need not to be dreaded.
  HASTINGS   If he should do so,
55   He leaves his back unarmed, the French and Welsh
      Baying him at the heels:[8] never fear that.
  LORD BARDOLPH   Who is it like° should lead his forces hither?   *likely*
  HASTINGS   The Duke of Lancaster and Westmorland;
      Against the Welsh, himself and Harry Monmouth;
60   But who is substituted° against the French   *delegated*
      I have no certain notice.
  ARCHBISHOP   Shall we go draw our numbers° and set on?   *gather our forces*
  HASTINGS   We are Time's subjects, and Time bids be gone.
                               Exeunt.

2.1 (F 2.1)

Enter HOSTESS *of the tavern and* [*two Officers,*
FANG *and* SNARE[1]].

  HOSTESS   Master Fang, have you entered the action?°   *begun the lawsuit*
  FANG   It is entered.
  HOSTESS   Where's your yeoman?° Is't a lusty[2] yeoman? Will 'a   *assistant*
      stand to't?[3]
5   FANG   —Sirrah! —Where's Snare?
  HOSTESS   O Lord, ay, good Master Snare.
  SNARE   Here, here.
  FANG   Snare, we must arrest Sir John Falstaff.
  HOSTESS   Yea, good Master Snare, I have entered him[4] and all.

---

5. And leaves his costly building half-completed.
6. The last man whom we can expect.
7. *Glyndŵr*: the leader of the Welsh forces fighting the King in *1 Henry IV.*
8. That is, following him like hunting dogs.
2.1 Location: Eastcheap, a street and market in London.
1. That Snare should linger behind Fang is suggested by the subsequent lines in which Fang cannot locate his fellow officer. Perhaps Snare is slow and lazy; or

perhaps he deliberately lags behind to sniff out trouble and "ensnare" villains.
2. Sturdy; lustful. The following lines are full of sexual puns.
3. Will he fight vigorously? Will he maintain an erect penis?
4. I have brought suit against him, with a pun on "entered him" as meaning "had sexual relations with him." The phrase usually denotes a man's sexual entry into a woman.

10 SNARE It may chance° cost some of us our lives, for he will stab.   *perhaps*

HOSTESS Alas the day, take heed of him: he stabbed[5] me in
mine own house, most beastly, in good faith. 'A cares not
what mischief he does; if his weapon° be out, he will foin°   *dagger; penis / thrust*
like any devil; he will spare neither man, woman, nor child.

15 FANG If I can close[6] with him, I care not for his thrust.

HOSTESS No, nor I neither. I'll be at your elbow.

FANG An I but fist° him once, an 'a come but within my view—   *seize; masturbate*

HOSTESS I am undone by his going, I warrant you; he's an
infinitive thing upon my score.[7] Good Master Fang, hold him

20 sure; good Master Snare, let him not scape. 'A comes continually to Pie Corner[8]—saving your manhoods—to buy a sad-
dle,[9] and he is indited° to dinner to the Lubber's[1] Head in   *(for "invited")*
Lumbert[2] Street to Master Smooth's, the silkman. I pray you,
since my exion is entered,[3] and my case° so openly known to   *lawsuit; vagina*

25 the world, let him be brought in to his answer. A hundred
mark is a long one° for a poor lone woman to bear, and I have   *huge account*
borne,[4] and borne, and borne, and have been fubbed off,° and   *put off*
fubbed off, and fubbed off, from this day to that day, that it is
a shame to be thought on. There is no honesty in such deal-

30 ing, unless a woman should be made an ass and a beast, to
bear every knave's wrong.

      Enter Sir John [FALSTAFF], *and* BARDOLPH, *and*
      the [PAGE].[5]

Yonder he comes, and that arrant° malmsey-nose[6] knave   *notorious*
Bardolph with him. Do your offices,° do your offices, Master   *duties*
Fang and Master Snare; do me,[7] do me, do me your offices!

35 FALSTAFF How now, whose mare's dead? What's the matter?

FANG I arrest you at the suit of Mistress Quickly.

FALSTAFF Away, varlets! —Draw, Bardolph! Cut me off the
villain's head; throw the quean° in the channel.°   *whore / street gutter*

HOSTESS Throw me in the channel? I'll throw thee in the

40 channel. Wilt thou, wilt thou, thou bastardly rogue? Murder, murder! Ah, thou honeysuckle[8] villain, wilt thou kill
God's officers and the King's? Ah, thou honeyseed° rogue;   *(for "homicidal")*
thou art a honeyseed, a man-queller, and a woman-queller.

FALSTAFF Keep them off, Bardolph.

45 FANG A rescue,[9] a rescue!

---

5. With a pun on "stabbed" as meaning "sexually penetrated."
6. Fight hand to hand; clinch.
7. "Infinitive" is Quickly's malapropism, or verbal
blunder, for "infinite." She implies that the board
("score") on which her accounts are tallied has innumerable markings corresponding to Falstaff's debts
to her.
8. Pie Corner was an area of Smithfield named for
its cooks' shops and known for its commerce in
horses and sex. *continually*: blunder for "continually" or "incontinently."
9. With a pun on "saddle" as also meaning "female
genitalia."
1. Blunder for "Libbard's," an Elizabethan form of
"Leopard's." The silk merchant's shop sign evidently
displayed the image of a leopard's head.
2. "Lumbert" is a blunder for "Lombard."
3. Since my legal action has begun, with a pun on

"entered" suggesting sexual penetration.
4. Endured, with a pun on "have borne" as meaning
"have supported the weight of a partner in sexual
relations."
5. As here, Q's stage directions sometimes refer to "*the
boy*" rather than "*the page*." These have been standardized to "Page" throughout.
6. Red-nosed from drinking alcohol. Malmsey was a
strong red wine named after its place of origin in
Greece and available from Spain, Portugal, and their
colonies as well as from Greece.
7. Do your jobs for me, with a pun on "do me" as slang
for "have sexual relations with me."
8. For "homicidal," with a pun on "honey" as slang for
"sexual pleasure."
9. A cry for help in resisting arrest. Fang fears Falstaff is being rescued, but Quickly in the next line
takes "rescue" to mean "reinforcements" and seems
to call for the rescue that Fang is trying to stop.

HOSTESS Good people, bring a rescue or two! Thou wot,° wot   *You will*
thou, thou wot, wot ta? Do, do, thou rogue; do, thou hemp-
seed!¹

PAGE Away, you scullion,° you rampallian,° you fustilarian!²   *kitchen wench / ruffian*
50   I'll tickle your catastrophe.³

Enter LORD CHIEF JUSTICE *and his men.*

LORD CHIEF JUSTICE What is the matter? Keep the peace
here, ho!

HOSTESS Good my lord, be good to me; I beseech you stand
to me.⁴

LORD CHIEF JUSTICE How now, Sir John? What, are you
brawling here?
55   Doth this become your place,° your time,° and business?   *social place / age*
You should have been well on your way to York.
—Stand from him, fellow; wherefore hang'st thou upon
him?

HOSTESS O my most worshipful lord, an't° please your grace, I   *if it*
am a poor widow of Eastcheap, and he is arrested at my suit.

60   LORD CHIEF JUSTICE For what sum?

HOSTESS It is more than for some, my lord; it is for all I have.
He hath eaten me out of house and home; he hath put all my
substance into that fat belly of his. [*to* FALSTAFF] But I will
have some of it out again, or I will ride thee a-nights like the
65   mare.⁵

FALSTAFF I think I am as like to ride the mare, if I have any
vantage of ground to get up.°   *mount*

LORD CHIEF JUSTICE How comes this, Sir John? What man of
good temper would endure this tempest of exclamation? Are
70   you not ashamed to enforce a poor widow to so rough a course
to come by her own?

FALSTAFF What is the gross sum that I owe thee?

HOSTESS Marry, if thou wert an honest man, thyself and the
money too. Thou didst swear to me upon a parcel-gilt° gob-   *partly gilded*
let, sitting in my Dolphin chamber° at the round table by a   *(an inn room)*
sea-coal fire,⁶ upon Wednesday in Wheeson week,⁷ when
the Prince broke thy head for liking° his father to a singing   *likening*
man of Windsor⁸—thou didst swear to me then, as I was
washing thy wound, to marry me, and make me my lady thy
80   wife. Canst thou deny it? Did not goodwife Keech⁹ the butcher's wife come in then and call me Gossip¹ Quickly, coming
in to borrow a mess of° vinegar, telling us she had a good dish   *some*
of prawns, whereby thou didst desire to eat some, whereby I
told thee they were ill for a green° wound? And didst thou   *fresh*
85   not, when she was gone downstairs, desire me to be no more
so familiarity° with such poor people, saying that ere long   *(for "familiar")*

---

1. Another version of "homicide," with an allusion to
the hangman's hempen rope.
2. Fat, unkempt woman.
3. Expression meaning "I'll whip your rear end."
4. Support me; be sexually erect for me.
5. Referring to a kind of goblin that supposedly produced nightmares by sitting on the chest of a sleeper,
with puns on "ride" as meaning "mount sexually" and
on "mare" as a disparaging term for "woman."
6. Fire generated from charcoal shipped by sea rather
than from the inferior, locally produced charcoal.

7. *Wheeson week:* the week after Whitsunday (Pentecost), observed on the seventh Sunday after Easter in
the Christian liturgical calendar.
8. One of the professional singers in the chapel at
Windsor, a royal residence west of London.
9. "Goodwife" was the title of a married woman.
"Keech" meant "a lump of animal fat."
1. Familiar form of address for a female friend, derived
from "godmother," the name for the female guardian
of a newly christened child.

they should call me "madam"?[2] And didst thou not kiss me, and bid me fetch thee thirty shillings? I put thee now to thy book-oath;° deny it if thou canst.

  oath on the Bible

90   FALSTAFF   My lord, this is a poor mad soul, and she says up and down the town that her eldest son is like you. She hath been in good case,° and the truth is poverty hath distracted her.° But for these foolish officers, I beseech you I may have redress against them.

  prosperous
  driven her mad

95   LORD CHIEF JUSTICE   Sir John, Sir John, I am well acquainted with your manner of wrenching the true cause the false way. It is not a confident brow,° nor the throng of words that come with such more than impudent sauciness from you, can thrust me from a level° consideration. You have, as it appears

  countenance

  just

100   to me, practiced upon the easy-yielding spirit of this woman, and made her serve your uses both in purse and in person.

HOSTESS   Yea, in truth, my lord.

LORD CHIEF JUSTICE   Pray thee, peace. —Pay her the debt you owe her, and unpay the villainy you have done with her: the

105   one you may do with sterling money, and the other with current° repentance.

  genuine
  reproof

FALSTAFF   My lord, I will not undergo this sneap° without reply. You call honorable boldness impudent sauciness; if a man will make curtsy and say nothing, he is virtuous. No, my

110   lord—my humble duty° remembered—I will not be your suitor. I say to you, I do desire deliverance from these officers, being upon hasty employment in the King's affairs.

  due respect to you

LORD CHIEF JUSTICE   You speak as having power to do wrong; but answer in the effect of your reputation,° and satisfy the

  as befits your status

115   poor woman.

FALSTAFF   Come hither, hostess.

     Enter [Master GOWER,] a Messenger.

LORD CHIEF JUSTICE   Now, Master Gower, what news?

GOWER   The King, my lord, and Harry, Prince of Wales,
  Are near at hand; the rest the paper tells.

    [GOWER *gives* LORD CHIEF JUSTICE *a letter; he reads it,*
    and they converse apart.]

120   FALSTAFF   As I am a gentleman!

HOSTESS   Faith, you said so before.

FALSTAFF   As I am a gentleman! Come, no more words of it.

HOSTESS   By this heavenly ground I tread on, I must be fain° to pawn both my plate and the tapestry of my dining chambers.

  content

125   FALSTAFF   Glasses, glasses, is the only drinking,[3] and for thy walls, a pretty slight drollery,° or the story of the prodigal,[4] or the German hunting in waterwork[5] is worth a thousand of these bed-hangers° and these fly-bitten tapestries. Let it be ten pound, if thou canst. Come, an 'twere not for thy humors,°

  comic painting

  bed curtains
  moods

130   there's not a better wench in England. Go, wash thy face, and draw° the action. Come, thou must not be in this humor with me. Dost not know me? Come, come, I know thou wast set on to this.

  withdraw

---

2. A form of address for a knight's wife; a whore.
3. Glass drinking vessels began to replace metal tankards in the late sixteenth century.
4. Alluding to a biblical parable about a profligate

son who repents, which was a frequent subject for cheap painted cloths. See Luke 15:11–32.
5. A hunting scene of German or Dutch origin painted on a wall in imitation of tapestry.

HOSTESS   Pray thee, Sir John, let it be but twenty nobles;[6]
135   i'faith, I am loath to pawn my plate, so God save me, la.
FALSTAFF   Let it alone; I'll make other shift.[7] You'll be a fool
    still.°   *always*
HOSTESS   Well, you shall have it, though I pawn my gown. I
    hope you'll come to supper; you'll pay me all together?
140   FALSTAFF   Will I live? [*to* BARDOLPH] Go with her, with her;
    hook on,° hook on.   *stick to her*
HOSTESS   Will you have Doll[8] Tearsheet meet you at supper?
FALSTAFF   No more words; let's have her.
                    Exeunt HOSTESS, *and* [*Sergeants* SNARE
                            and FANG, *and* BARDOLPH].
LORD CHIEF JUSTICE   I have heard better news.[9]
145   FALSTAFF   What's the news, my lord?
LORD CHIEF JUSTICE   Where lay the King tonight?°   *last night*
GOWER   At Basingstoke,[1] my lord.
FALSTAFF   I hope, my lord, all's well. What is the news, my
    lord?
150   LORD CHIEF JUSTICE   Come all his forces back?
GOWER   No, fifteen hundred foot, five hundred horse
    Are marched up to my lord of Lancaster
    Against Northumberland and the Archbishop.
FALSTAFF   Comes the King back from Wales, my noble lord?
155   LORD CHIEF JUSTICE   You shall have letters of me presently.°   *at once*
    Come, go along with me, good Master Gower.
FALSTAFF   My lord.
LORD CHIEF JUSTICE   —What's the matter?
FALSTAFF   Master Gower, shall I entreat you with me to
160   dinner?
GOWER   I must wait upon my good lord here, I thank you,
    good Sir John.
LORD CHIEF JUSTICE   Sir John, you loiter here too long, being
    you are to take soldiers up° in counties as you go.   *levy soldiers*
165   FALSTAFF   Will you sup with me, Master Gower?
LORD CHIEF JUSTICE   What foolish master taught you these
    manners, Sir John?
FALSTAFF   Master Gower, if they become me not, he was a
    fool that taught them me.[2] This is the right fencing grace,°   *style*
170   my lord: tap for tap, and so part fair.°   *on good terms*
LORD CHIEF JUSTICE   Now the Lord lighten° thee; thou art a   *enlighten; make thin*
    great fool.   [*Exeunt.*]

---

6. Gold coins. Twenty were worth about 6 pounds.
7. *I'll make other shift:* I'll manage otherwise.
8. A common name for a prostitute.
9. TEXTUAL COMMENT For Q's "better news," F has
"bitter news." In the context of the Lord Chief Justice's reaction to the news of the rebels' success, "better" is an antiphrasis, a form of understatement
indicating a sense of disbelief at the bad news. See
Digital Edition TC 3 (Quarto edited text).
1. TEXTUAL COMMENT This is a textual crux, as Basingstoke (a town about forty-five miles southwest of

London) is not mentioned in any of Shakespeare's
sources as a place where the King stayed, and Q's variant, "Billingsgate," a neighborhood in east London
famous for its wharf and fish market, is a most unlikely
place for the King to stay. This edition, like most modern editions, retains F's reading, as it makes more
sense. See Digital Edition TC 4 (Quarto edited text).
2. Falstaff suggests that the habit of ignoring others
is something he learned from a fool—namely, the
Chief Justice, who a few lines earlier would not answer
Falstaff's questions.

2.2 (F 2.2)

Enter PRINCE *[Henry] and* POINS.[1]

PRINCE   Before God, I am exceeding weary.

POINS   Is't come to that? I had thought weariness durst not
have attached° one of so high blood.   *laid hold of*

PRINCE   Faith, it does me, though it discolors the complexion
5   of my greatness[2] to acknowledge it. Doth it not show vilely
in me to desire small° beer?   *weak*

POINS   Why, a prince should not be so loosely studied° as to   *disposed*
remember so weak a composition.

PRINCE   Belike then my appetite was not princely got, for, by
10   my troth, I do now remember the poor creature small beer.
But indeed, these humble considerations make me out of
love with my greatness. What a disgrace is it to me to remember thy name![3] Or to know thy face tomorrow! Or to take
note how many pair of silk stockings thou hast with these,
15   and those that were thy peach-colored once, or to bear° the   *remember*
inventory of thy shirts, as: one for superfluity° and another   *as a spare*
for use. But that the tennis-court keeper knows better than
I, for it is a low ebb of linen with thee when thou keepest not
racket° there, as thou hast not done a great while, because   *do not play*
20   the rest of the low countries have ate up thy holland;[4] and
God knows whether those that bawl out the ruins of thy
linen[5] shall inherit His kingdom[6]—but the midwives say the
children are not in the fault, whereupon the world increases,
and kindreds are mightily strengthened.

25   POINS   How ill it follows, after you have labored so hard, you
should talk so idly! Tell me how many good young princes
would do so, their fathers being so sick as yours at this time is?

PRINCE   Shall I tell thee one thing, Poins?

POINS   Yes, faith, and let it be an excellent good thing.

30   PRINCE   It shall serve among wits of no higher breeding than
thine.

POINS   Go to. I stand the push of° your one thing that you will   *I can tolerate*
tell.

PRINCE   Marry, I tell thee it is not meet° that I should be sad   *appropriate*
35   now my father is sick, albeit I could tell to thee, as to one it
pleases me for fault° of a better to call my friend, I could be   *lack*
sad, and sad indeed, too.

POINS   Very hardly,° upon such a subject.   *With great difficulty*

PRINCE   By this hand, thou thinkest me as far in the devil's

---

2.2 Location: Prince Hal's dwelling.
1. Q's stage direction reads: "*Enter the Prince, Poynes,
Sir John Russel, with other.*" This is the only place in Q
where the name "Russel" is employed instead of "Bardolph," but it indicates that Shakespeare had been
working on some portion of this play before he was
forced to change "Oldcastle" to "Falstaff," "Russell" to
"Bardolph," and "Harvey" to "Peto" (see Introduction
to *1 Henry IV*).
2. It mars my noble countenance (by turning it pale
from weakness or red from shame).
3. Men of high rank should not be on familiar terms
with, or remember the names of, those below them in
status.
4. Because the brothels ("low countries") have contrived to eat up all the money you would have spent on
linen ("holland"). With puns on "low countries" as also

meaning "sexual organs" and "the Netherlands" as well
as "brothels"; and with a pun on "holland" as referring
to the country of Holland as well as to the fine linen
made there. Poins has spent his money either on
whores or on providing linen for the babies he has
prodigally fathered. His lack of shirts makes it impossible for him to play at the tennis courts, where players
sweat so much that they frequently have to change
their shirts. Lines 20 (after "holland")–24 are not in F.
5. The bastard children who are wrapped in your old
shirts.
6. Go to heaven. With allusions to Matthew 25:34
("Come, ye blessed of my Father, inherit the kingdom
prepared for you from the foundation of the world") and
19:14 ("Suffer little children, and forbid them not, to
come unto me: for of such is the kingdom of heaven").

40 book as thou and Falstaff for obduracy° and persistency. Let   *stubbornness*
the end try the man. But I tell thee, my heart bleeds inwardly
that my father is so sick; and keeping such vile company as
thou art hath in reason taken from me all ostentation° of   *signs; display*
sorrow.

45 POINS   The reason?

PRINCE   What wouldst thou think of me if I should weep?

POINS   I would think thee a most princely hypocrite.

PRINCE   It would be every man's thought, and thou art a
blessed fellow to think as every man thinks. Never a man's

50 thought in the world keeps the roadway[7] better than thine:
every man would think me an hypocrite indeed—and what
accites° your most worshipful thought to think so?   *induces*

POINS   Why, because you have been so lewd° and so much   *base*
engraft° to Falstaff.   *attached*

55 PRINCE   And to thee.

POINS   By this light, I am well spoke on;° I can hear it with   *of*
mine own ears. The worst that they can say of me is that I am
a second brother,[8] and that I am a proper fellow of my hands,°   *a good fighter*
and those two things, I confess, I cannot help.

Enter BARDOLPH *and* [PAGE].

60 By the mass,[9] here comes Bardolph.

PRINCE   And the boy that I gave Falstaff: 'a° had him from me   *he*
Christian, and look if the fat villain have not transformed
him ape.[1]

BARDOLPH   God save your grace.

65 PRINCE   And yours, most noble Bardolph.

POINS [*to* BARDOLPH]   Come, you virtuous ass,[2] you bashful
fool, must you be blushing?[3] Wherefore blush you now? What
a maidenly man-at-arms are you become? Is't such a matter°   *so difficult*
to get a pottle-pot's maidenhead?[4]

70 PAGE   'A calls me e'en now, my lord, through a red lattice,[5]
and I could discern no part of his face from the window. At
last I spied his eyes, and methought he had made two holes
in the alewife's petticoat, and so peeped through.

PRINCE [*to* POINS]   Has not the boy profited?°   *(from Falstaff)*

75 BARDOLPH [*to* PAGE]   Away, you whoreson upright rabble, away!

PAGE   Away, you rascally Althaea's dream,[6] away!

PRINCE   Instruct us, boy: what dream, boy?

7. Adheres to the popular viewpoint.
8. That is, a younger brother (and therefore without prospect of inheritance).
9. TEXTUAL COMMENT Profanities like "by the mass" enliven the tavern scenes in Q. The F text, which suppresses this oath as well as many others, reflects the expurgation that followed in the wake of the 1606 act against profanity. 2 *Henry IV* is one of the most systematically censored plays in F. See Digital Edition TC 5 (Quarto edited text).
1. Made him look ridiculous, like an ape or a monkey rather than a human being. Falstaff has perhaps dressed the Page in an outlandish livery, or uniform.
2. TEXTUAL COMMENT For Q's "virtuous ass," F has "pernicious ass." While F's "pernicious" reflects the ironic and duplicitous praise that Poins lavishes on Bardolph, Q's reading has been favored by modern editors, since it probably alludes to the contemporary

proverbial saying that "blushing is virtue's color"— that is, a visible sign of virtue. See Digital Edition TC 6 (Quarto edited text).
3. The jokes in this portion of the scene often refer to Bardolph's notoriously red face. The color may be due to drink, venereal disease, or some form of acne or rosacea.
4. To open and drain a two-quart tankard of ale (with implicit comparison to penetrating a virgin).
5. Sign of an alehouse window.
6. A conflation of two dreams from classical mythology. It was Hecuba, the Queen of Troy, who, pregnant with Paris, dreamed she gave birth to a firebrand that set fire to her city. Althaea was told that her newborn son, Meleager, would live only as long as a brand in the fire was not consumed, so she snatched it from the hearth.

PAGE   Marry, my lord, Althaea dreamt she was delivered of a
firebrand, and therefore I call him her dream.

80   PRINCE   A crown's-worth of good interpretation. [*He gives him*
money.] There 'tis, boy.

POINS   Oh, that this blossom could be kept from cankers!°   *cankerworms*
[*He gives him money.*] Well, there is sixpence to preserve thee.

BARDOLPH   An° you do not make him hanged among you, the   *If*
85   gallows shall have wrong.

PRINCE   And how doth thy master, Bardolph?

BARDOLPH   Well, my lord. He heard of your grace's coming to
town. There's a letter for you.
        [PRINCE *reads the letter.*]

POINS   Delivered with good respect°—and how doth the   *(said ironically)*
90   martlemas,[7] your master?

BARDOLPH   In bodily health, sir.

POINS   Marry, the immortal part° needs a physician, but that   *the soul*
moves not him; though that be sick, it dies not.

PRINCE   I do allow this wen° to be as familiar with me as my   *wart*
95   dog; and he holds his place,° for look you how he writes.   *maintains his position*

POINS   [*reading*]   "John Falstaff, knight." Every man must
know that,° as oft as he has occasion to name himself. Even   *(Falstaff's rank)*
like those that are kin to the King, for they never prick their
finger but they say, "There's some of the King's blood spilt."
100   "How comes that?" says he that takes upon him not to con-
ceive.° The answer is as ready as a borrowed cap:[8] "I am the   *understand*
King's poor cousin,° sir."   *relative*

PRINCE   Nay, they will be kin to us, or they will fetch it° from   *derive kinship*
Japhet.[9] But the letter: "Sir John Falstaff, knight, to the son of
105   the King nearest his father, Harry Prince of Wales, greeting."

POINS   Why, this is a certificate.°   *legal document*

PRINCE   Peace. "I will imitate the honorable Romans in brevity."

POINS   He sure means brevity in breath, short-winded. [*He*
reads.] "I commend me to thee, I commend thee, and I leave
110   thee. Be not too familiar with Poins, for he misuses thy favors
so much that he swears thou art to marry his sister Nell.
Repent at idle times as thou mayst, and so farewell. Thine by
yea and no,[1] which is as much as to say, as thou usest him:
Jack Falstaff with my family,° John with my brothers and sis-   *friends*
115   ters, and Sir John with all Europe." —My lord, I'll steep this
letter in sack and make him eat it.

PRINCE   That's to make him eat twenty of his words. But do
you use me thus, Ned? Must I marry your sister?

POINS   God send the wench no worse fortune, but I never
120   said so.

PRINCE   Well, thus we play the fools with the time, and the
spirits of the wise sit in the clouds and mock us. —Is your
master here in London?

BARDOLPH   Yea, my lord.

---

7. Fatted cattle or pigs that were slaughtered on
November 11, the feast day of St. Martin (Martlemas).
8. As readily produced as a cap borrowed from
another person (so the borrower does not care how

much it is used).
9. One of Noah's sons (Genesis 10:2–5), imagined to
be the common ancestor of all Europeans.
1. Parodying the mild oaths associated with puritans.

125 PRINCE Where sups he? Doth the old boar feed in the old frank?[2]

BARDOLPH At the old place, my lord, in Eastcheap.

PRINCE What company?

PAGE Ephesians, my lord, of the old church.[3]

PRINCE Sup any women with him?

130 PAGE None, my lord, but old Mistress Quickly and Mistress
 Doll Tearsheet.

PRINCE What pagan° may that be?   *heathen; prostitute*

PAGE A proper gentlewoman, sir, and a kinswoman of my
 master's.

135 PRINCE Even such kin as the parish heifers are to the town-
 bull. —Shall we steal upon them, Ned, at supper?

POINS I am your shadow, my lord; I'll follow you.

PRINCE —Sirrah, you boy, and Bardolph, no word to your
 master that I am yet come to town. There's for your silence.
 [*He gives them money.*]

140 BARDOLPH I have no tongue, sir.

PAGE And for mine, sir, I will govern it.

PRINCE Fare you well: go.   [*Exeunt* BARDOLPH *and* PAGE.]
 This Doll Tearsheet should be some road.[4]

POINS I warrant you, as common as the way between St Albans[5]

145 and London.

PRINCE How might we see Falstaff bestow° himself tonight   *behave*
 in his true colors, and not ourselves be seen?

POINS Put on two leathern jerkins° and aprons, and wait   *jackets*
 upon him at his table as drawers.°   *tavern servants*

150 PRINCE From a god to a bull: a heavy descension!° It was Jove's   *a sad degradation*
 case.[6] From a prince to a prentice: a low transformation—
 that shall be mine. For in everything the purpose must weigh
 with° the folly. Follow me, Ned.   *Exeunt.*   *match*

2.3 (F 2.3)

Enter NORTHUMBERLAND, *his* WIFE, *and* [KATE,] *the*
wife to Harry Percy.[1]

NORTHUMBERLAND I pray thee, loving wife and gentle
 daughter,°   *daughter-in-law*
 Give even way° unto my rough affairs;   *Allow free scope*
 Put not you on the visage° of the times,   *appearance*
 And be, like them, to Percy troublesome.

5 WIFE I have given over; I will speak no more.
 Do what you will: your wisdom be your guide.

NORTHUMBERLAND Alas, sweet wife, my honor is at pawn,

---

2. Pigsty. Possibly a reference to Eastcheap's famous
tavern, the Boar's Head.

3. Carousers of the usual kind. The Page alludes to
the biblical account of the Ephesians, whom St. Paul
admonished against lust and drunkenness before
their conversion, with a possible reference to Catholics (members of "the old church"), whom English
Protestants accused of moral laxity.

4. Some common prostitute. "Road" is slang for
"vagina."

5. Town on the heavily traveled road north from
London.

6. Referring to Jove's transformation into a bull before
his rape of Europa.

2.3 Location: Outside Northumberland's castle at
Warkworth.

1. TEXTUAL COMMENT Reflecting its tendency to designate characters by their functions, Q's stage direction
designates the women only as wives: "*Enter Northumberland, his wife, and the wife to Harry Percie.*" Q's
speech prefix refers to Lady Percy as Kate, emphasizing
the domesticity of this scene, in which the two women
convince Northumberland to distance himself from the
rebels. See Digital Edition TC 7 (Quarto edited text).

And, but° my going, nothing can redeem it.   *except by*
KATE   Oh, yet, for God's sake, go not to these wars!
10   The time was, father, that you broke your word,[2]
   When you were more endeared° to it than now,   *bound*
   When your own Percy, when my heart's dear Harry,
   Threw many a northward look to see his father
   Bring up his powers, but he did long in vain.
15   Who then persuaded you to stay at home?
   There were two honors lost: yours and your son's.
   For yours, the God of heaven brighten it;
   For his, it stuck upon him as the sun
   In the gray° vault of heaven, and by his light   *pale blue*
20   Did all the chivalry° of England move   *chivalrous warriors*
   To do brave acts. He was indeed the glass°   *mirror*
   Wherein the noble youth did dress themselves.
NORTHUMBERLAND   Beshrew your heart,°   *Curse your passion*
   Fair daughter, you do draw my spirits from me
25   With new lamenting ancient oversights.°   *old mistakes*
   But I must go and meet with danger there,
   Or it will seek me in another place,
   And find me worse provided.
WIFE   Oh, fly to Scotland,
   Till that the nobles and the armèd commons,
30   Have of their puissance° made a little taste.   *strength*
KATE   If they get ground and vantage° of the King,   *advantage*
   Then join you with them, like a rib of steel,
   To make strength stronger; but, for all our loves,
   First let them try themselves. So did your son;
35   He was so suffered.° So came I a widow,   *allowed to proceed*
   And never shall have length of life enough
   To rain upon remembrance with mine eyes,[3]
   That it may grow and sprout as high as heaven
   For recordation° to my noble husband.   *As a memorial*
40   NORTHUMBERLAND   Come, come; go in with me. 'Tis with my
      mind
   As with the tide swelled up unto his height
   That makes a still stand,° running neither way.   *standstill*
   Fain would I go to meet the Archbishop,
   But many thousand reasons hold me back.
45   I will resolve for Scotland: there am I
   Till time and vantage° crave my company.   *Exeunt.*   *opportunity*

2.4 (F 2.4)

[*Enter* FRANCIS *and another* DRAWER.°]   *servant in a tavern*
FRANCIS   What the devil hast thou brought there? Apple-
   johns?[1] Thou knowest Sir John cannot endure an apple-john.
DRAWER   Mass,[2] thou say'st true: the Prince once set a dish of
   apple-johns before him, and told him there were five more

---

2. Alluding to Northumberland's absence from the Battle of Shrewsbury. See *1 Henry IV.*
3. To rain tears upon his memory, here imagined as a plant—perhaps rosemary, the conventional symbol of remembrance.
2.4 Location: A tavern, perhaps the Boar's Head, in Eastcheap.
1. A kind of apple that could be kept for two years and was meant to be eaten when the skin was wrinkled and shriveled up.
2. An oath derived from the name of the Catholic church service.

5   Sir Johns and, putting off his hat, said, "I will now take my
       leave of these six dry, round, old, withered knights." It angered
       him to the heart, but he hath forgot that.

FRANCIS   Why, then, cover° and set them down, and see if   *spread the cloth*
       thou canst find out Sneak's noise:° Mistress Tearsheet would   *band of musicians*
10   fain hear some music.

DRAWER   Dispatch. The room where they supped is too hot;
       they'll come in straight.
              Enter WILL.

WILL   Sirrah, here will be the Prince and Master Poins anon,°   *soon*
       and they will put on two of our jerkins and aprons, and Sir
15   John must not know of it; Bardolph hath brought word.

DRAWER   By the mass, here will be old utis!° It will be an   *merrymaking; a din*
       excellent stratagem.

FRANCIS   I'll see if I can find out Sneak.   *Exeunt.*
              Enter Mistress Quickly [the HOSTESS] and
              DOLL TEARSHEET.

HOSTESS   I'faith, sweetheart, methinks now you are in an
20   excellent good temperality.° Your pulsidge³ beats as extraordi-   *(for "temper")*
       narily as heart would desire, and your color, I warrant you, is
       as red as any rose, in good truth, la; but i'faith you have drunk
       too much canaries,⁴ and that's a marvelous searching° wine,   *strong*
       and it perfumes the blood ere one can say "What's this?"
25   How do you now?

DOLL TEARSHEET   Better than I was—hem.°   *(clearing her throat)*

HOSTESS   Why, that's well said; a good heart's worth gold.
              Enter Sir John [FALSTAFF].
       Lo, here comes Sir John.

FALSTAFF [*singing*]   "When Arthur first in court"⁵ —Empty
30   the jordan!° —"and was a worthy king." —How now, Mis-   *chamber pot*
       tress Doll?

HOSTESS   Sick of a calm;⁶ yea, good faith.

FALSTAFF   So is all her sect;° an they be once in a calm,⁷ they   *kind; sex*
       are sick.

35 DOLL TEARSHEET   A pox damn you, you muddy rascal,⁸ is that
       all the comfort you give me?

FALSTAFF   You make fat rascals, Mistress Doll.

DOLL TEARSHEET   I make them? Gluttony and diseases make;
       I make them not.

40 FALSTAFF   If the cook help to make the gluttony, you help to
       make the diseases, Doll; we catch of you,° Doll, we catch of   *are infected by you*
       you. Grant that, my poor virtue, grant that.

DOLL TEARSHEET   Yea, joy, our chains and our jewels.⁹

FALSTAFF   "Your brooches, pearls, and ouches"¹—for to serve
45   bravely is to come halting off,² you know; to come off the

---

3. For "pulse."
4. Sweet wine from the Canary Islands.
5. Lines from the ballad "Sir Lancelot du Lake."
6. Blunder for "qualm," or fainting fit (perhaps the
result of pregnancy).
7. Quiet; not sexually active.
8. You dull knave. A "rascal" was a young, lean deer.
They were called "muddy" when sluggish and out of
season. In his next speech, Falstaff will accuse Doll

of making even lean deer fat, probably by tempting
them to gluttony and vice.
9. Yes, you steal ("catch") our valuables.
1. Perhaps a line from a ballad, with puns on the
three items of jewelry as slang for the carbuncles and
sores that result from venereal disease.
2. To fight bravely is to return limping; to engage in
vigorous sex is to be wounded in the process.

breach with his pike bent bravely,[3] and to surgery bravely; to
venture upon the charged chambers[4] bravely.

DOLL TEARSHEET Hang yourself, you muddy conger,° hang   *eel (term of abuse)*
yourself!

50 HOSTESS By my troth, this is the old fashion. You two never
meet but you fall to some discord. You are both, i'good truth,
as rheumatic° as two dry toasts; you cannot one bear with   *(for "choleric")*
another's confirmities.° What the goodyear? [*to* DOLL] One   *(for "infirmities")*
must bear,[5] and that must be you: you are the weaker vessel,
55 as they say, the emptier vessel.

DOLL TEARSHEET Can a weak empty vessel bear such a huge
full hogshead?° There's a whole merchant's venture° of Bor-   *cask / cargo*
deaux stuff° in him; you have not seen a hulk better stuffed   *wine*
in the hold. —Come, I'll be friends with thee, Jack: thou art
60 going to the wars, and whether I shall ever see thee again or
no, there is nobody cares.

       Enter DRAWER.

DRAWER Sir, Ensign[6] Pistol's below and would speak with you.

DOLL TEARSHEET Hang him, swaggering° rascal! Let him not   *blustering; quarreling*
come hither: it is the foul-mouth'dst rogue in England.

65 HOSTESS If he swagger, let him not come here. No, by my faith,
I must live among my neighbors; I'll no swaggerers; I am in
good name and fame with the very best. Shut the door! There
comes no swaggerers here. I have not lived all this while to
have swaggering now; shut the door, I pray you.

70 FALSTAFF Dost thou hear, Hostess?

HOSTESS Pray ye, pacify yourself, Sir John; there comes no
swaggerers here.

FALSTAFF Dost thou hear? It is mine ensign.

HOSTESS Tilly-fally,° Sir John, ne'er tell me; and your ancient[7]   *Nonsense*
75 swaggerer comes not in my doors. I was before Master Tis-
ick[8] the debuty° t'other day, and as he said to me—'twas no   *(for "deputy")*
longer ago than Wed'sday last, i'good faith—"Neighbor
Quickly," says he—Master Dumb our minister was by then—
"Neighbor Quickly," says he, "receive those that are civil, for,"
80 said he, "you are in an ill name." Now 'a said so; I can tell
whereupon.[9] "For," says he, "you are an honest woman, and
well thought on; therefore take heed what guests you receive.
Receive," says he, "no swaggering companions." There comes
none here. You would bless you° to hear what he said. No,   *feel fortunate*
85 I'll no swaggerers.

FALSTAFF He's no swaggerer, Hostess: a tame cheater,[1] i'faith;
you may stroke him as gently as a puppy greyhound. He'll
not swagger with a Barbary hen° if her feathers turn back in   *guinea hen; prostitute*
any show of resistance. —Call him up, drawer.

       [*Exit* DRAWER.]

90 HOSTESS Cheater,[2] call you him? I will bar no honest man my

---

3. To come away from the gap in the fortifications
(the breech) with one's weapon finely bent (with puns
on "breech" as slang for "female genitalia" and "pike"
as slang for "penis").
4. Interior of a mine loaded with munitions; the sexually aroused interior of a woman.
5. Endure; carry goods; support the weight of a sexual partner; give birth. *What the goodyear:* a phrase
probably meaning "What the devil."

6. A military title for the army's standard-bearer.
7. The Hostess mistakes "ensign" for "ancient."
8. The name signifies a hacking cough.
9. Now I can tell why he (" 'a") said so.
1. A decoy in a scheme to defraud people.
2. Quickly apparently understands the word as
"escheator," an officer responsible for returning to
the Crown any property whose title had lapsed.

house, nor no cheater, but I do not love swaggering, by my troth. I am the worse when one says "swagger." Feel, masters, how I shake, look you, I warrant you.

DOLL TEARSHEET So you do, Hostess.

95 HOSTESS Do I? Yea, in very truth do I, an 'twere° an aspen leaf: I cannot abide swaggerers.   *as if I were*

Enter Ensign PISTOL[, BARDOLPH, *and* PAGE].

PISTOL God save you, Sir John.

FALSTAFF Welcome, Ensign Pistol. Here, Pistol, I charge you[3] with a cup of sack; do you discharge[4] upon mine hostess.

100 PISTOL I will discharge upon her, Sir John, with two bullets.°   *(slang for "testicles")*

FALSTAFF She is pistol-proof, sir; you shall not hardly offend° her.   *injure*

HOSTESS Come, I'll drink no proofs, nor no bullets; I'll drink no more than will do me good for no man's pleasure, I.

105 PISTOL Then to you, Mistress Dorothy! I will charge° you.   *toast; arouse; order*

DOLL TEARSHEET Charge me? I scorn you, scurvy companion. What, you poor, base, rascally, cheating, lack-linen mate?°   *fellow who has no linen* Away, you moldy rogue, away; I am meat for your master.[5]

PISTOL I know you, Mistress Dorothy.

110 DOLL TEARSHEET Away, you cutpurse° rascal, you filthy bung,[6]   *thieving; castrated* away. By this wine, I'll thrust my knife in your moldy chaps°   *cheeks; buttocks* an you play the saucy cuttle with me.[7] Away, you bottle-ale rascal, you basket-hilt stale juggler,[8] you. Since when, I pray you, sir? God's light, with two points[9] on your shoulder? Much!

115 PISTOL God, let me not live, but I will murder your ruff° for   *starched collar* this.

FALSTAFF No more, Pistol; I would not have you go off here. Discharge yourself of our company, Pistol.

HOSTESS No, good Captain Pistol; not here, sweet Captain.

120 DOLL TEARSHEET "Captain"? Thou abominable damned cheater, art thou not ashamed to be called "captain"? An captains were of my mind, they would truncheon° you out for taking   *cudgel* their names upon you before you have earned them. You, a captain? You, slave? For what? For tearing a poor whore's

125 ruff in a bawdy house? —He a captain? Hang him, rogue; he lives upon moldy stewed prunes[1] and dried cakes. A captain? God's light, these villains will make the word as odious as the word "occupy,"[2] which was an excellent good word before it was ill sorted. Therefore captains had need

130 look to't.

BARDOLPH Pray thee, go down, good Ensign.

FALSTAFF Hark thee hither, Mistress Doll.

PISTOL Not I. I tell thee what, Corporal Bardolph: I could tear her. I'll be revenged of her.

135 PAGE Pray thee, go down.

---

3. Toast to you; load you with ammunition (punning on Pistol's name); arouse you sexually.
4. Return the toast; empty the cup; shoot; ejaculate.
5. That is, I am superior to you; with a pun on "meat" as meaning "a body available for sexual pleasure."
6. Thief; anus.
7. If you continue to abuse me (with a pun on "cuttle" as signifying both "knife" and "cuttlefish," which was supposed to vomit a black liquid to conceal itself from enemies).

8. You imposter with a cheap, outdated sword. Basketwork hilts were found on inexpensive weapons or those used only for practice.
9. Tags for fastening armor.
1. Available in brothels as a supposed preventative of venereal disease, with a pun on "stew" as meaning "brothel."
2. Playing on the double meaning of "occupy" as (1) "to take possession of" and (2) "to have sex with."

PISTOL I'll see her damned first! To Pluto's damned lake,° by   *(the lake of hell)*
    this hand,[3] to th'infernal deep, with Erebus° and tortures   *god of the underworld*
    vile also! Hold hook and line, say I! Down, down, dogs!
    Down, faitors!° "Have we not Hiren here?"[4]   *imposters; cheats*

140 HOSTESS Good Captain Pizzle,° be quiet—'tis very late,   *Penis*
    i'faith—I beseek you now, aggravate° your choler.   *(for "moderate")*

PISTOL These be good humors indeed! Shall packhorses,
    And hollow pampered jades of Asia,[5]
    Which cannot go but thirty mile a day,
145   Compare with Caesars, and with cannibals,[6]
    And Trojan Greeks?[7]
    Nay, rather damn them with King Cerberus,[8]
    And let the welkin° roar. Shall we fall foul for toys?[9]   *heavens*

HOSTESS By my troth, Captain, these are very bitter words.

150 BARDOLPH Be gone, good Ensign. This will grow to a brawl anon.

PISTOL Men like dogs give crowns like pins.[1]
    "Have we not Hiren here?"

HOSTESS O'my word, Captain, there's none such here. What
    the goodyear, do you think I would deny her? For God's sake,
155   be quiet.

PISTOL Then feed and be fat, my fair Calipolis.[2]
    Come, give some sack.
    Si fortuna me tormente, sperato me contento.[3]
    Fear we broadsides?[4] No, let the fiend give fire.°   *shoot*
160   Give me some sack; [*to his sword*] and, sweetheart, lie thou
    there.
    Come we to full points here, and are etceteras nothings?[5]

FALSTAFF Pistol, I would be quiet.

PISTOL Sweet knight, I kiss thy neaf.° What, we have seen the   *fist*
    seven stars![6]

165 DOLL TEARSHEET For God's sake, thrust him downstairs. I can-
    not endure such a fustian° rascal.   *worthless*

PISTOL Thrust him downstairs? Know we not Galloway nags?[7]

FALSTAFF Quoit° him down, Bardolph, like a shove-groat   *Throw*
    shilling.[8] Nay, an 'a do° nothing but speak nothing, 'a shall be   *if he does*
170   nothing here.

BARDOLPH Come, get you downstairs.

PISTOL What, shall we have incision? Shall we imbrue?°   *steep in blood*
    Then Death rock me asleep; abridge my doleful days!

3. In this and subsequent speeches, Pistol rants in an affected style that recalls and parodies the language of sensational plays from the 1590s and earlier, which were often set in non-European locales and involved military and erotic adventures.

4. Apparently a line from *The Turkish Mahomet and Hiren* [*Irene*] *the Fair Greek*, a lost play by George Peele. Pistol may be referring to his sword as "Hiren" with a pun on "iron."

5. A garbled allusion to Marlowe's *2 Tamburlaine* 4.3.1–2, in which Tamburlaine taunts the kings whom he has captured and whom he uses in lieu of horses to draw his chariot.

6. Pistol may mean "Hannibals." Hannibal was a famous general from Carthage.

7. In the Trojan War, the Greeks and Trojans fought on opposite sides. Pistol conflates the two.

8. In classical mythology, the three-headed dog guarding the underworld.

9. Quarrel over trifles.

1. Alluding to Tamburlaine's extravagance in distributing the crowns of conquered kings among his followers.

2. Echoing Peele's *Battle of Alcazar*, in which the Moorish king Muly Mahamet offers his starving wife the raw flesh of a lion he has just killed.

3. If fortune torments me, hope contents me (a motto that Pistol renders in a mixture of Italian, French, and Spanish).

4. Shots fired from the side of a ship.

5. That is, have we come to a stop? Is there no further satisfaction to be had in the rest (the "etceteras")? Pistol puns on "etceteras" and "nothings" as slang for "female genitalia."

6. We have caroused all night (with an allusion to the Ursa Major constellation).

7. Small Scottish horses; prostitutes.

8. Shilling coin used in a game like shuffleboard.

Why, then, let grievous, ghastly, gaping wounds
175 Untwine the Sisters three![9] Come, Atropos, I say!
HOSTESS Here's goodly stuff toward!°   *about to happen*
FALSTAFF Give me my rapier, boy.
DOLL TEARSHEET I pray thee, Jack, I pray thee, do not draw.
FALSTAFF [*taking his rapier*] —Get you downstairs.
          [*They brawl.*]
180 HOSTESS Here's a goodly tumult. I'll forswear keeping house
     afore I'll be in these tirrits° and frights. So, murder, I war-   *(for "terrors" or "fits")*
     rant now! Alas, alas! Put up your naked weapons, put up
     your naked weapons! [*Exit* PISTOL, *pursued by* BARDOLPH.]
DOLL TEARSHEET I pray thee, Jack, be quiet; the rascal's gone.
185 Ah, you whoreson little valiant villain, you!
HOSTESS Are you not hurt i'th' groin? Methought 'a made a
     shrewd° thrust at your belly.   *vicious*
          [*Enter* BARDOLPH.]
FALSTAFF Have you turned him out o'doors?
BARDOLPH Yea, sir. The rascal's drunk. You have hurt him,
190 sir, i'th' shoulder.
FALSTAFF A rascal, to brave° me!   *defy*
DOLL TEARSHEET Ah, you sweet little rogue, you! Alas, poor
     ape, how thou sweat'st! Come, let me wipe thy face: come on,
     you whoreson chops.° Ah, rogue, i'faith I love thee: thou art   *fat cheeks*
195 as valorous as Hector of Troy,[1] worth five of Agamemnon,[2]
     and ten times better than the nine Worthies.[3] —Ah, villain!
FALSTAFF A rascally slave! I will toss the rogue in a blanket.[4]
DOLL TEARSHEET Do, an thou dar'st for thy heart; an thou dost,
     I'll canvas° thee between a pair of sheets.   *toss*
          Enter [*Musicians*].
200 PAGE The music is come, sir.
FALSTAFF Let them play. —Play, sirs. —Sit on my knee, Doll. A
     rascal, bragging slave! The rogue fled from me like quicksilver.°   *mercury*
DOLL TEARSHEET I'faith, and thou followed'st him like a
     church.° Thou whoreson little tidy° Bartholomew boar-pig,[5]   *(i.e., sedately) / plump*
205 when wilt thou leave fighting o'days, and foining° o'nights,   *thrusting*
     and begin to patch up thine old body for heaven?
          Enter PRINCE and POINS[, *disguised*].
FALSTAFF Peace, good Doll, do not speak like a death's-head;[6]
     do not bid me remember mine end.
DOLL TEARSHEET Sirrah, what humor's° the Prince of?   *disposition is*
210 FALSTAFF A good shallow young fellow: 'a would have made a
     good pantler;° 'a would ha' chipped° bread well.   *pantry worker / cut*
DOLL TEARSHEET They say Poins has a good wit.
FALSTAFF He a good wit? Hang him, baboon; his wit's as thick
     as Tewkesbury[7] mustard: there's no more conceit° in him   *intellect*
215 than is in a mallet.

---

9. The three Fates of Greek mythology: Clotho, Lache-
sis, and Atropos. Atropos cut the thread of life.
1. The greatest Trojan warrior in Homer's *Iliad*.
2. Leader of the Greeks in the battle for Troy.
3. Nine legendary brave men: three Christians—
Arthur, Charlemagne, Godfrey of Boulogne; three
pagans—Hector, Alexander, Julius Caesar; and three
Jews—Joshua, David, Judas Maccabaeus.

4. A punishment for cowardice.
5. A roasted pig associated with an annual London
carnival held on August 24, St. Bartholomew's Day.
6. Skull or representation of a skull used as a reminder
of mortality.
7. Market town in Gloucestershire famed for its
mustard.

DOLL TEARSHEET   Why does the Prince love him so, then?

FALSTAFF   Because their legs are both of a bigness, and 'a° plays   *he*
at quoits[8] well, and eats conger and fennel,[9] and drinks off
candles' ends for flap-dragons,[1] and rides the wild mare[2] with
220   the boys, and jumps upon joint-stools, and swears with a good
grace, and wears his boots very smooth, like unto the sign of
the Leg,[3] and breeds no bate° with telling of discreet stories,   *discord*
and such other gambol° faculties 'a has that show a weak   *sportive*
mind and an able body, for the which the Prince admits him.
225   For the Prince himself is such another: the weight of a hair
will turn scales between their avoirdupois.°   *weight*

PRINCE [*apart*]   Would not this nave° of a wheel have his ears   *hub*
cut off?

POINS [*apart*]   Let's beat him before his whore.

230   PRINCE [*apart*]   Look where the withered elder[4] hath not his
poll° clawed like a parrot.[5]   *head*

POINS [*apart*]   Is it not strange that desire should so many years
outlive performance?

FALSTAFF   Kiss me, Doll.

235   PRINCE [*apart*]   Saturn and Venus[6] this year in conjunction?
What says th'almanac to that?

POINS [*apart*]   And look whether the fiery trigon,[7] his man, be
not lisping to his master old tables,° his notebook, his   *writing tablets*
counsel-keeper![8]

240   FALSTAFF   Thou dost give me flattering busses.°   *kisses*

DOLL TEARSHEET   By my troth, I kiss thee with a most constant heart.

FALSTAFF   I am old, I am old.

DOLL TEARSHEET   I love thee better than I love e'er a scurvy
245   young boy of them all.

FALSTAFF   What stuff° wilt have a kirtle° of? I shall receive   *material / skirt*
money a Thursday: shalt° have a cap tomorrow. —A merry   *you shall*
song, come! —It grows late; we'll to bed. Thou'lt forget me
when I am gone.

250   DOLL TEARSHEET   By my troth, thou'lt set me a-weeping, an
thou say'st so; prove° that ever I dress myself handsome till   *if you ever prove*
thy return. Well, hearken° a'th' end.   *judge*

FALSTAFF   Some sack, Francis!

PRINCE *and* POINS   Anon, anon, sir.

255   FALSTAFF   Ha? A bastard son of the King's? And art not thou
Poins, his brother?°   *the brother of Poins*

PRINCE   Why, thou globe of sinful continents,[9] what a life
dost thou lead?

FALSTAFF   A better than thou: I am a gentleman, thou art a
260   drawer.

---

8. A game involving the throwing of a heavy iron ring
toward a target on the ground.
9. Conger eel, a heavy, hard-to-digest food, was served
with fennel.
1. Referring to a tavern game in which one drank
liquor on which burning objects (flap-dragons) had
been set afloat.
2. Plays at a form of leapfrog; has sexual relations with
a woman.
3. As in the sign over the bootmaker's shop (depicting a well-booted leg).
4. Sapless elder tree; impotent old man.

5. Doll may here be running her hands through Falstaff's hair.
6. The planets governing old age and love.
7. The signs of the zodiac were divided into four sets
of three (trigons). Aries, Leo, and Sagittarius are the
"fiery trigon," being hot and dry. Poins alludes to
Bardolph's red face.
8. Apparently, Bardolph is wooing Quickly, here
referred to as Falstaff's confidante and the keeper of
his secrets.
9. World composed of sinful lands; a vast receptacle
of sin.

PRINCE   Very true, sir, and I come to draw you out by the ears.

HOSTESS   Oh, the Lord preserve thy grace! By my troth, welcome to London. Now the Lord bless that sweet face of
thine! O Jesu, are you come from Wales?

265 FALSTAFF   Thou whoreson mad compound of majesty, by this
light° flesh and corrupt blood [*indicating* DOLL TEARSHEET],   *unchaste*
thou art welcome.

DOLL TEARSHEET   How, you fat fool? I scorn you!

POINS   My lord, he will drive you out of your revenge and turn
270   all to a merriment if you take not the heat.°   *don't act at once*

PRINCE   You whoreson candlemine° you, how vilely did you   *storehouse of tallow*
speak of me now, before this honest,° virtuous, civil gentle-   *chaste*
woman?

HOSTESS   God's blessing of your good heart, and so she is, by
275   my troth.

FALSTAFF   Didst thou hear me?

PRINCE   Yea, and you knew me as you did when you ran away
by Gad's Hill;[1] you knew I was at your back, and spoke it on
purpose to try my patience.

280 FALSTAFF   No, no, no, not so; I did not think thou wast within
hearing.

PRINCE   I shall drive you, then, to confess the willful abuse,
and then I know how to handle you.

FALSTAFF   No abuse, Hal; o'mine honor, no abuse.

285 PRINCE   Not? To dispraise me, and call me pantler and bread-
chipper, and I know not what?

FALSTAFF   No abuse, Hal.

POINS   No abuse?

FALSTAFF   No abuse, Ned, i'th' world, honest Ned, none. I
290   dispraised him before the wicked, that the wicked might not
fall in love with thee. In which doing, I have done the part of
a careful° friend and a true subject, and thy father is to give   *caring*
me thanks for it. No abuse, Hal, none, Ned, none; no, faith,
boys, none.

295 PRINCE   See now whether pure fear and entire cowardice doth
not make thee wrong this virtuous gentlewoman to close
with° us. Is she of the wicked? Is thine hostess here of the   *in order to pacify*
wicked? Or is thy boy of the wicked? Or honest Bardolph,
whose zeal burns in his nose, of the wicked?

300 POINS   Answer, thou dead elm, answer.

FALSTAFF   The fiend hath pricked down Bardolph irrecover-
able,[2] and his face is Lucifer's privy° kitchen, where he doth   *private*
nothing but roast malt-worms.° For the boy, there is a good   *weevils; drunkards*
angel about him, but the devil blinds him° too.   *(the good angel)*

305 PRINCE   For the women?

FALSTAFF   For one of them, she's in hell already and burns°   *infects with syphilis*
poor souls; for th'other, I owe her money, and whether she be
damned for that, I know not.[3]

HOSTESS   No, I warrant you.

310 FALSTAFF   No, I think thou art not; I think thou art quit for°   *acquitted of*
that. Marry, there is another indictment upon thee, for suf-

---

1. Referring to events staged in act 2 of *1 Henry IV*.
2. Marked Bardolph as beyond redemption.

3. Referring to the view that usury (lending money at
interest) was a sin.

fering flesh to be eaten in thy house, contrary to the law,[4] for
the which I think thou wilt howl.

HOSTESS   All victualers° do so: what's a joint of mutton[5] or   *innkeepers; bawds*
315   two in a whole Lent?

PRINCE   You, gentlewoman—

DOLL TEARSHEET   What says your grace?

FALSTAFF   His grace says that which his flesh rebels against.[6]
        PETO *knocks at door.*

HOSTESS   Who knocks so loud at door? Look to th' door there,
320   Francis.
        [*Enter* PETO.]

PRINCE   Peto, how now? What news?

PETO   The King your father is at Westminster,
    And there are twenty weak and wearied posts°   *messengers*
    Come from the north; and, as I came along,
325   I met and overtook a dozen captains,
    Bare-headed, sweating, knocking at the taverns,
    And asking everyone for Sir John Falstaff.

PRINCE   By heaven, Poins, I feel me much to blame
    So idly to profane the precious time,
330   When tempest of commotion, like the south,°   *the south wind*
    Borne° with black vapor, doth begin to melt   *Laden*
    And drop upon our bare unarmèd heads.
    Give me my sword and cloak. Falstaff, good night.
            Exeunt PRINCE *and* POINS [*with* BARDOLPH].

FALSTAFF   Now comes in the sweetest morsel of the night,
335   and we must hence and leave it unpicked.
        [*Knocking within.*]
    More knocking at the door?
        [*Enter* BARDOLPH.]
    How now? What's the matter?

BARDOLPH   You must away to court, sir, presently;°   *at once*
    A dozen captains stay° at door for you.   *wait*

340   FALSTAFF   Pay the musicians, sirrah. Farewell, Hostess; fare-
    well, Doll. You see, my good wenches, how men of merit are
    sought after: the undeserver° may sleep when the man of   *unimportant officer*
    action is called on. Farewell, good wenches! If I be not sent
    away post,° I will see you again ere I go.   *hastily*

345   DOLL TEARSHEET   I cannot speak. If my heart be not ready to
    burst— Well, sweet Jack, have a care of thyself.

FALSTAFF   Farewell, farewell.
            Exit [*with* BARDOLPH, PETO, *and* PAGE].

HOSTESS   Well, fare thee well. I have known thee these
    twenty-nine years, come peascod time,[7] but an honester and
350   truer-hearted man— Well, fare thee well.
        [*Enter* BARDOLPH.]

BARDOLPH   Mistress Tearsheet.

HOSTESS   What's the matter?

---

4. Alluding to laws enacted against the eating of meat
during the Christian penitential days known as Lent
as well as to laws against the sex trade, with a pun on
"house" as "brothel."
5. *joint of mutton:* piece of lamb; whore.

6. Implying that the Prince's virtuous speech can't
hide a body filled with lust for Tearsheet.
7. The time of year when peas form in the pod (early
spring).

BARDOLPH Bid Mistress Tearsheet come to my master.
HOSTESS Oh, run, Doll, run; run, good Doll, come. —She comes
355 blubbered.° —Yea, will you come, Doll?   *Exeunt.*   *covered with tears*

3.1 (F 3.1)

Enter the KING *in his nightgown°[, with a Page].*   *dressing gown*
KING Go, call the earls of Surrey and of Warwick;
But, ere they come, bid them o'er-read these letters
And well consider of them. Make good speed.   *[Exit Page.]*
How many thousand of my poorest subjects
5 Are at this hour asleep? O Sleep, O gentle Sleep,
Nature's soft nurse, how have I frighted° thee,   *frightened*
That thou no more wilt weigh my eyelids down
And steep my senses in forgetfulness?
Why, rather, Sleep, liest thou in smoky cribs,°   *hovels*
10 Upon uneasy pallets° stretching thee   *hard straw beds*
And hushed with buzzing night-flies to thy slumber,
Than in the perfumed chambers of the great,
Under the canopies of costly state,°   *splendor*
And lulled with sound of sweetest melody?
15 O thou dull° god, why li'st thou with the vile°   *drowsy / lowly*
In loathsome beds and leavest the kingly couch
A watch-case,° or a common larum bell?   *sentry box*
Wilt thou upon the high and giddy mast
Seal up the ship-boy's eyes, and rock his brains
20 In cradle of the rude° imperious surge,   *rough*
And in the visitation of the winds,
Who take the ruffian billows by the top,
Curling their monstrous heads and hanging them
With deafing° clamor in the slippery clouds,   *deafening*
25 That, with the hurly,° death itself awakes?   *tumult*
Canst thou, O partial Sleep, give them repose
To the wet sea son[1] in an hour so rude,°   *wild*
And in the calmest and most stillest night,
With all appliances° and means to boot,°   *devices / as well*
30 Deny it to a king? Then, happy low,° lie down;   *happy humble people*
Uneasy lies the head that wears a crown.
Enter WARWICK, *Surrey, and Sir John Blunt.*[2]
WARWICK Many good morrows to your majesty.
KING Is it good morrow, lords?
WARWICK 'Tis one o'clock, and past.
35 KING Why, then, good morrow to you all, my lords.
Have you read o'er the letter that I sent you?
WARWICK We have, my liege.°   *sovereign*
KING Then you perceive the body of our kingdom,
How foul it is, what rank° diseases grow,   *loathsome*
40 And with what danger near the heart of it.
WARWICK It is but as a body yet distempered,°   *sick*
Which to his former strength may be restored

3.1 Location: The palace at Westminster.
1. Son of the sea, possibly referring to the ship-boy
mentioned in line 19.
2. TEXTUAL COMMENT This edition retains the pres-

ence of Sir John Blunt here, mentioned in Qb, since
he appears again in 4.2 and seems to be included in
the King's address to "you all" in line 35. See Digital
Edition TC 8 (Quarto edited text).

With good advice and little medicine.
My lord Northumberland will soon be cooled.
45 KING O God, that one might read the book of fate,
And see the revolution of the times[3]
Make mountains level, and the continent,°   *dry land*
Weary of solid firmness, melt itself
Into the sea, and other times to see
50 The beachy girdle° of the ocean   *sandy belt (shores)*
Too wide for Neptune's[4] hips; how chance's mocks
And changes fill the cup of alteration
With diverse° liquors![5] Oh, if this were seen,   *various*
The happiest youth, viewing his progress through°—   *through life*
55 What perils past, what crosses° to ensue—   *afflictions*
Would shut the book and sit him down and die.
'Tis not ten years gone
Since Richard and Northumberland, great friends,
Did feast together, and in two year after
60 Were they at wars. It is but eight years since
This Percy° was the man nearest my soul,   *(Northumberland)*
Who like a brother toiled in my affairs
And laid his love and life under my foot°—   *at my disposal*
Yea, for my sake, even to° the eyes of Richard   *before*
65 Gave him defiance. But which of you was by—
[*to* WARWICK] You, cousin Neville,[6] as I may remember—
When Richard, with his eye brimful of tears,
Then, checked and rated° by Northumberland,   *chided*
Did speak these words,[7] now proved a prophecy:
70 "Northumberland, thou ladder by the which
My cousin Bolingbroke ascends my throne"?
Though then, God knows, I had no such intent,
But that necessity so bowed the state
That I and greatness were compelled to kiss—
75 "The time shall come"—thus did he follow it—
"The time will come that foul sin, gathering head,[8]
Shall break into corruption." So went on,
Foretelling this same time's condition
And the division of our amity.°   *friendship*
80 WARWICK There is a history in all men's lives
Figuring° the natures of the times deceased;°   *Showing / past*
The which observed, a man may prophesy
With a near aim of the main chance° of things   *general probability*
As yet not come to life, who° in their seeds   *which*
85 And weak beginning lie intreasurèd.°   *stored*
Such things become the hatch and brood° of time;   *progeny and offspring*
And by the necessary form of this,[9]
King Richard might create a perfect guess

3. The changes that time will bring.
4. In classical mythology, the god of the sea. Here, the seashore is depicted as a girdle worn by Neptune. That the girdle is too wide or too large indicates that the sea is retreating from the land, in contrast to the prior image of land being absorbed into the ocean.
5. The following three and a half lines (53–56) do not appear in F.
6. An apparent error. The King is addressing the Earl of Warwick, whose surname was Beauchamp, not Neville. Shakespeare may be confusing him with Richard Neville, an important character in his plays on the life of Henry VI.
7. See *Richard II*, 5.1, in which similar lines are spoken, though neither Bolingbroke nor Warwick was present.
8. Coming to maturity; coming to a head, like pus on a sore.
9. And by this requisite pattern (of cause and effect).

That great Northumberland, then false to him,
90   Would of that seed grow to a greater falseness,
Which should not find a ground to root upon
Unless on you.

KING   Are these things, then, necessities?
Then let us meet them like necessities;
And that same word even now cries out on° us.   *denounces*
95   They say the Bishop and Northumberland
Are fifty thousand strong.

WARWICK   It cannot be, my lord.
Rumor doth double, like the voice and echo,
The numbers of the feared. Please it your grace
To go to bed; upon my soul, my lord,
100 The powers that you already have sent forth
Shall bring this prize in very easily.
To comfort you the more, I have received
A certain instance° that Glyndŵr is dead.   *proof*
Your majesty hath been this fortnight ill,
105 And these unseasoned° hours perforce must add   *irregular*
Unto your sickness.

KING   I will take your counsel,
And were these inward° wars once out of hand,   *civil*
We would, dear lords, unto the Holy Land.   *Exeunt.*

3.2 (F 3.2)

Enter Justice SHALLOW *and Justice* SILENCE.

SHALLOW   Come on, come on, come on, sir! Give me your hand,
sir, give me your hand, sir. An early stirrer, by the rood!° And   *cross*
how doth my good cousin° Silence?   *kinsman*

SILENCE   Good morrow, good cousin Shallow.

5   SHALLOW   And how doth my cousin, your bedfellow? And your
fairest daughter and mine, my goddaughter Ellen?

SILENCE   Alas, a black ousel,[1] cousin Shallow.

SHALLOW   By yea and no, sir. I dare say my cousin William is
become a good scholar: he is at Oxford still, is he not?

10   SILENCE   Indeed, sir, to my cost.

SHALLOW   'A° must then to the Inns o'Court[2] shortly. I was   *He*
once of Clement's Inn,[3] where I think they will talk of mad
Shallow yet.

SILENCE   You were called Lusty Shallow then, cousin.

15   SHALLOW   By the mass, I was called anything, and I would have
done anything indeed, too, and roundly° too. There was I, and   *thoroughly*
little John Doit of Staffordshire, and black George Barnes,
and Francis Pickbone, and Will Squeal, a Cotswold man—
you had not four such swinge-bucklers° in all the Inns o'Court   *swashbucklers*
20   again. And I may say to you we knew where the bona robas°   *well-dressed prostitutes*
were and had the best of them all at commandment. Then
was Jack Falstaff, now Sir John, a boy, and page to Thomas
Mowbray, Duke of Norfolk.

SILENCE   This Sir John, cousin, that comes hither anon° about   *soon*
25   soldiers?

3.2 Location: Outside Justice Shallow's house in
Gloucestershire.
1. Blackbird. Women with black hair and/or complexions were often viewed as "foul" rather than "fair."

2. Prestigious legal schools in London that admitted
men to the bar.
3. One of the Inns of Chancery, less prestigious legal
colleges.

SHALLOW   The same Sir John, the very same. I see him break
        Scoggin's[4] head at the Court Gate, when 'a was a crack,° not   *young fellow*
        thus high; and the very same day did I fight with one Samson
        Stockfish, a fruiterer, behind Gray's Inn.[5] Jesu, Jesu, the mad
30   days that I have spent! And to see how many of my old acquain-
        tance are dead.
SILENCE   We shall all follow, cousin.
SHALLOW   Certain, 'tis certain, very sure, very sure. Death, as
        the Psalmist saith, is certain to all; all shall die. How° a   *What's the price of*
35   good yoke of bullocks at Stamford Fair?
SILENCE   By my troth, I was not there.
SHALLOW   Death is certain. Is old Double of your town living
        yet?
SILENCE   Dead, sir.
40 SHALLOW   Jesu, Jesu, dead! 'A° drew a good bow—and dead? 'A   *He*
        shot a fine shoot. John o'Gaunt° loved him well and betted   *(Henry IV's father)*
        much money on his head. Dead? 'A would have clapped i'th'
        clout at twelve score,[6] and carried you a forehand shaft a four-
        teen and fourteen and a half,[7] that it would have done a man's
45   heart good to see. How a score of ewes now?
SILENCE   Thereafter as they be:[8] a score of good ewes may be
        worth ten pounds.
SHALLOW   And is old Double dead?
        Enter BARDOLPH *and one with him.*
SILENCE   Here come two of Sir John Falstaff's men, as I think.
50   Good morrow, honest gentlemen.
BARDOLPH   I beseech you, which is Justice Shallow?
SHALLOW   I am Robert Shallow, sir, a poor esquire of this
        county, and one of the King's justices of the peace. What is
        your good pleasure with me?
55 BARDOLPH   My captain, sir, commends him° to you, my cap-   *sends his respects*
        tain Sir John Falstaff, a tall° gentleman, by heaven, and a   *valiant*
        most gallant leader.
SHALLOW   He greets me well, sir; I knew him a good backsword
        man.° How doth the good knight? May I ask how my lady his   *fencer*
60   wife doth?
BARDOLPH   Sir, pardon, a soldier is better accommodated than
        with a wife.
SHALLOW   It is well said, in faith, sir, and it is well said indeed,
        too. "Better accommodated"—it is good; yea, indeed is it.
65   Good phrases are surely, and ever were, very commendable.
        "Accommodated": it comes of *accommodo*—very good, a
        good phrase.
BARDOLPH   Pardon, sir, I have heard the word—"phrase" call
        you it? By this day, I know not the phrase, but I will main-
70   tain the word with my sword to be a soldier-like word, and a
        word of exceeding good command,° by heaven. "Accommo-   *fit for many uses*
        dated": that is when a man is, as they say, accommodated; or
        when a man is being whereby 'a may be thought to be accom-
        modated, which is an excellent thing.

4. A buffoon (possibly referring to Edward IV's court
jester of that name and famous as the main character
of *Scogin's Jests*, a popular Elizabethan jestbook).
5. One of the Inns of Court.
6. Hit the target from 240 yards.

7. He could shoot an arrow straight, to 280 or 290
yards. A "forehand shaft" is an arrow shot in a straight
line rather than with the curved trajectory common
for long shots.
8. The price depends on their quality.

Enter FALSTAFF.

75 SHALLOW It is very just.° Look, here comes good Sir John. | *true*
—Give me your good hand, give me your worship's good
hand. By my troth, you like well,° and bear your years very | *you are thriving*
well. Welcome, good Sir John.

FALSTAFF I am glad to see you well, good Master Robert
80 Shallow. —Master Soccard, as I think.

SHALLOW No, Sir John, it is my cousin Silence, in commis-
sion⁹ with me.

FALSTAFF Good Master Silence, it well befits you should be
of the peace.

85 SILENCE Your good worship is welcome.

FALSTAFF Fie, this is hot weather, gentlemen! Have you pro-
vided me here half a dozen sufficient° men? | *able*

SHALLOW Marry, have we, sir. Will you sit?

FALSTAFF Let me see them, I beseech you.

90 SHALLOW Where's the roll,° where's the roll, where's the roll? | *list*
Let me see, let me see, let me see. So, so, so, so, so. So, so, yea,
marry, sir. —Rafe Moldy! —Let them appear as I call, let
them do so, let them do so. Let me see, where is Moldy?

[*Enter* MOLDY, SHADOW, WART, FEEBLE, *and* BULLCALF.]

MOLDY Here, an't please you.

95 SHALLOW What think you, Sir John? A good-limbed fellow:
young, strong, and of good friends.° | *well connected*

FALSTAFF Is thy name Moldy?

MOLDY Yea, an't please you.

FALSTAFF 'Tis the more time° thou wert used. | *well past time*

100 SHALLOW Ha, ha, ha, most excellent, i'faith! Things that are
moldy lack use—very singular good, in faith. Well said, Sir
John, very well said.

FALSTAFF Prick him.° | *Mark his name*

MOLDY I was pricked¹ well enough before, an you could have
105 let me alone. My old dame° will be undone now for one to do | *wife*
her husbandry² and her drudgery. You need not to have
pricked me; there are other men fitter to go out than I.

FALSTAFF Go to; peace, Moldy, you shall go. Moldy, it is time
you were spent.° | *used up*

110 MOLDY Spent?

SHALLOW Peace, fellow, peace; stand aside. Know you where
you are? For th'other, Sir John, let me see: Simon Shadow!

FALSTAFF Yea, marry, let me have him to sit under. He's like
to be a cold° soldier. | *dead; cowardly*

115 SHALLOW Where's Shadow?

SHADOW Here, sir.

FALSTAFF Shadow, whose son art thou?

SHADOW My mother's son, sir.

FALSTAFF Thy mother's son! Like enough, and thy father's
120 shadow.° So the son of the female is the shadow° of the male; | *likeness / faint copy*
it is often so indeed, but much of the father's substance.³

---

9. Having a position (as justice of the peace).
1. Vexed; provided with a penis.
2. Will be lacking someone to perform the sexual
duties of a husband; will be lacking someone to do
the work of the farm.

3. *but . . . substance*: though the son shares much of
his father's essence (from the sex act from which he
was conceived); though the son shares in the father's
wealth (as heir).

SHALLOW Do you like him, Sir John?

FALSTAFF Shadow will serve for summer. Prick him, for we
have a number of shadows[4] fill up the muster-book.

125 SHALLOW Thomas Wart!

FALSTAFF Where's he?

WART Here, sir.

FALSTAFF Is thy name Wart?

WART Yea, sir.

130 FALSTAFF Thou art a very ragged Wart.

SHALLOW Shall I prick him, Sir John?

FALSTAFF It were superfluous, for apparel is built° upon his   *pieced together*
back, and the whole frame stands upon pins:[5] prick him no
more.

135 SHALLOW Ha, ha, ha, you can do it, sir, you can do it! I commend you well. —Francis Feeble!

FEEBLE Here, sir.

SHALLOW What trade art thou, Feeble?

FEEBLE A woman's tailor,[6] sir.

140 SHALLOW Shall I prick him, sir?

FALSTAFF You may, but if he had been a man's tailor, he'd ha'
pricked[7] you. Wilt thou make as many holes in an enemy's
battle° as thou hast done in a woman's petticoat?   *army*

FEEBLE I will do my good will,° sir; you can have no more.   *do my best*

145 FALSTAFF Well said, good woman's tailor; well said, courageous Feeble! Thou wilt be as valiant as the wrathful dove
or most magnanimous° mouse. —Prick the woman's tailor   *brave*
well, Master Shallow, deep, Master Shallow.

FEEBLE I would Wart might have gone, sir.

150 FALSTAFF I would thou wert a man's tailor, that thou mightst
mend him and make him fit to go.° I cannot put him to a   *to serve; to have sex*
private soldier,[8] that is the leader of so many thousands.°   *(of lice)*
Let that suffice, most forcible Feeble.

FEEBLE It shall suffice, sir.

155 FALSTAFF I am bound to thee, reverend Feeble. —Who is next?

SHALLOW Peter Bullcalf o'th' Green.

FALSTAFF Yea, marry, let's see Bullcalf.

BULLCALF Here, sir.

FALSTAFF 'Fore God, a likely° fellow. Come, prick Bullcalf till   *promising*
160 he roar again.

BULLCALF O Lord, good my lord Captain—

FALSTAFF What, dost thou roar before thou art pricked?

BULLCALF O Lord, sir, I am a diseased man.

FALSTAFF What disease hast thou?

165 BULLCALF A whoreson cold, sir, a cough, sir, which I caught
with ringing in the King's affairs[9] upon his coronation day, sir.

FALSTAFF Come, thou shalt go to the wars in a gown:° we will   *dressing gown*
have away° thy cold, and I will take such order° that thy   *get rid of / measures*
friends shall ring for thee.[1] —Is here all?

---

4. Fictitious names that officers recorded in order to collect additional pay from the Crown.
5. The whole structure depends upon pegs ("pins"); stands upon legs ("pins").
6. "Women's tailors" were bywords for effeminacy and cowardice.

7. Dressed; stabbed; penetrated.
8. Make him a private soldier; offer him sexually to a private soldier.
9. Ringing the church bells in the King's honor.
1. In your place; at your death.

170   SHALLOW   Here is two more called than your number;[2] you
must have but four here, sir, and so I pray you go in with me
to dinner.

  FALSTAFF   Come, I will go drink with you, but I cannot tarry°   *stay for*
dinner. I am glad to see you, by my troth, Master Shallow.

175   SHALLOW   O Sir John, do you remember since we lay all night
in the Windmill in Saint George's Field?[3]

  FALSTAFF   No more of that, Master Shallow.

  SHALLOW   Ha, 'twas a merry night! And is Jane Nightwork
alive?

180   FALSTAFF   She lives, Master Shallow.

  SHALLOW   She never could away with° me.   *tolerate*

  FALSTAFF   Never, never; she would always say she could not
abide Master Shallow.

  SHALLOW   By the mass, I could anger her to th'heart. She was
185   then a bona roba. Doth she hold her own well?

  FALSTAFF   Old, old, Master Shallow.

  SHALLOW   Nay, she must be old, she cannot choose but be
old; certain she's old, and had Robin Nightwork by old
Nightwork before I came to Clement's Inn.

190   SILENCE   That's fifty-five year ago.

  SHALLOW   Ha, cousin Silence, that thou hadst seen that that
this knight and I have seen! Ha, Sir John, said I well?

  FALSTAFF   We have heard the chimes at midnight, Master
Shallow.

195   SHALLOW   That we have, that we have, that we have; in faith,
Sir John, we have. Our watchword was "Hem,° boys!" Come,   *Drink up*
let's to dinner; come, let's to dinner. Jesus, the days that we
have seen. Come, come.

              Exeunt [FALSTAFF, SHALLOW, *and* SILENCE].

  BULLCALF   Good Master Corporate° Bardolph, stand° my   *(for "Corporal") / act as*
200   friend, and here's four Harry ten shillings in French crowns
for you.[4] In very truth, sir, I had as lief° be hanged, sir, as go;   *willingly*
and yet, for mine own part, sir, I do not care, but rather
because I am unwilling and, for mine own part, have a
desire to stay with my friends. Else, sir, I did not care, for
205   mine own part, so much.

  BARDOLPH   Go to; stand aside.

  MOLDY   And good Master Corporal Captain, for my old dame's
sake, stand my friend: she has nobody to do anything about
her when I am gone; and she is old and cannot help herself.
210   You shall have forty,° sir.   *(shillings)*

  BARDOLPH   Go to; stand aside.

  FEEBLE   By my troth, I care not, a man can die but once: we
owe God a death. I'll ne'er bear a base mind: an't be my destiny, so; an't be not, so. No man's too good to serve's° prince;   *serve his*
215   and, let it go which way it will, he that dies this year is quit
for° the next.   *released from (dying)*

---

2. An inconsistency: there have been five, not six,
recruits called.
3. A region of London south of the Thames near
Southwark, known as a market for sex. "The Windmill" was the name of a brothel or an inn.
4. An elaborate way of offering a bribe. The refer-

ence to "Harry ten shillings" is anachronistic; shillings originated during Henry VII's reign and by the
1590s had been devalued to half their original worth.
Therefore, Bullcalf is offering about 1 pound to be
paid in French crowns (coins worth 4 shillings each).

BARDOLPH Well said; th'art a good fellow.

FEEBLE Faith, I'll bear no base mind.

Enter FALSTAFF[, SHALLOW, *and* SILENCE].

FALSTAFF Come, sir, which men shall I have?

220 SHALLOW Four of which you please.

BARDOLPH —Sir, a word with you. [*aside*] I have three pound to free Moldy and Bullcalf.

FALSTAFF Go to; well.

SHALLOW Come, Sir John, which four will you have?

225 FALSTAFF Do you choose for me.

SHALLOW Marry, then: Moldy, Bullcalf, Feeble, and Shadow.

FALSTAFF Moldy and Bullcalf: for you, Moldy, stay at home till you are past service,⁵ and for your part, Bullcalf, grow till you come unto it.⁶ I will none of you.

230 SHALLOW Sir John, Sir John, do not yourself wrong! They are your likeliest men, and I would have you served with the best.

FALSTAFF Will you tell me, Master Shallow, how to choose a man? Care I for the limb, the thews,° the stature, bulk, and   *strength* big assemblance° of a man? Give me the spirit, Master Shal-   *composition*

235 low. Here's Wart: you see what a ragged appearance it is: 'a shall charge you and discharge you° with the motion of a   *load and fire* pewterer's hammer,° come off and on swifter than he that   *with a steady motion* gibbets on the brewer's bucket.⁷ And this same half-faced°   *thin-faced* fellow Shadow: give me this man. He presents no mark° to   *target*

240 the enemy; the foeman may with as great aim level at° the   *fire against* edge of a penknife. And for a retreat, how swiftly will this Feeble, the woman's tailor, run off! Oh, give me the spare men, and spare me the great ones. —Put me a caliver° into   *musket* Wart's hand, Bardolph.

245 BARDOLPH Hold, Wart! Traverse!° Thas, thas, thas!   *March*

FALSTAFF Come, manage me your caliver. So, very well; go to, very good, exceeding good. Oh, give me always a little, lean, old, chopped, bald shot.° Well said, i'faith; Wart, th'art a   *marksman* good scab. Hold, there's a tester° for thee.   *sixpence*

250 SHALLOW He is not his craft's master; he doth not do it right. I remember at Mile-End Green,⁸ when I lay° at Clement's   *lodged* Inn—I was then Sir Dagonet in Arthur's show⁹—there was a little quiver° fellow, and 'a would manage you his piece thus,   *nimble* and 'a would about and about, and come you in,° and come   *thrust at you*

255 you in: "Rah, tah, tah," would 'a say; "Bounce,"° would 'a say;   *Bang* and away again would 'a go, and again would 'a come. I shall ne'er see such a fellow.

FALSTAFF These fellows will do well, Master Shallow. God keep you, Master Silence, I will not use many words with you;

260 fare you well, gentlemen both, I thank you. I must° a dozen   *must go* mile tonight. Bardolph, give the soldiers coats.

SHALLOW Sir John, the Lord bless you; God prosper your affairs! God send us peace. At your return, visit our house; let

---

5. Past the time of military duty; past the time of sexual potency.

6. That is, grow until you come into the time of military service; the time of sexual potency. Falstaff plays on the fact that Bullcalf is a *calf*, not a *bull*.

7. Retreat and advance, or raise and lower your gun, faster than he who hangs pails on each end of the wooden bar (gibbet) that a brewer carries on his shoulders.

8. Open land east of London used as a training ground for citizen militias and for fairs and shows.

9. Referring to his role as King Arthur's fool in an archery pageant in which each participant took the name of one of the knights of the Round Table.

our ol . acquaintance be renewed. Peradventure I will with
265 ye to the court.
FALSTAFF   'Fore God, would you would.
SHALLOW   Go to; I have spoke at a word.° God keep you.   spoken sincerely
FALSTAFF   Fare you well, gentle gentlemen.
                                    Exeunt [SHALLOW and SILENCE].
On, Bardolph, lead the men away.
                    [Exeunt BARDOLPH, WART, SHADOW, and FEEBLE.]
270 As I return, I will fetch off° these justices. I do see the bottom   defraud
of Justice Shallow. Lord, Lord, how subject we old men are to
this vice of lying! This same starved justice hath done nothing
but prate to me of the wildness of his youth and the feats he
hath done about Turnbull street,[1] and every third word a lie,
275 duer paid° to the hearer than the Turk's tribute.[2] I do remem-   sooner paid
ber him at Clement's Inn, like a man made after supper of a
cheese paring. When 'a was naked, he was for all the world like
a forked radish,[3] with a head fantastically carved upon it with
a knife. 'A was so forlorn° that his dimensions to any thick°   thin / imperfect
280 sight were invincible.° 'A was the very genius° of famine,[4] yet   (for "invisible") / spirit
lecherous as a monkey, and the whores called him mandrake.
'A came over in the rearward of the fashion, and sung those
tunes to the overscutched housewives that he heard the
carmen° whistle, and swear they were his fancies or his good-   wagoners
285 nights.° And now is this Vice's dagger[5] become a squire, and   his own love songs
talks as familiarly of John o'Gaunt as if he had been sworn
brother to him; and I'll be sworn 'a ne'er saw him but once in
the tiltyard,[6] and then he° burst his° head for crowding   (Gaunt) / (Shallow's)
among the marshal's men. I saw it, and told John o'Gaunt he
290 beat his own name,[7] for you might have thrust° him and all   packed
his apparel into an eel-skin: the case of a treble hautboy°   oboe
a mansion for him, a court. And now has he land and beefs.°   oxen
Well, I'll be acquainted with him, if I return; and't shall go
hard but I'll make him a philosopher's two stones to me.[8] If
295 the young dace° be a bait for the old pike, I see no reason in   small fish
the law of nature but I may snap at him, till time shape, and
there an end.   [Exit.]

4.1(F 4.1)

Enter the ARCHBISHOP, MOWBRAY, HASTINGS[, *with a*
Captain], *within the forest of Galtres.*[1]

ARCHBISHOP   What is this forest called?
HASTINGS   'Tis Galtres Forest, an't° shall please your grace.   if it
ARCHBISHOP   Here stand, my lords, and send discoverers° forth   scouts
To know the numbers of our enemies.
HASTINGS   We have sent forth already.

1. An area of Smithfield associated with criminal
activities, especially prostitution.
2. Money extracted from those the Turkish sultan conquered or who engaged in trade with him. The penalty
for failure to pay was death, so presumably money was
paid punctually. Shallow is even quicker to tell lies.
3. A mandrake root, said to resemble a man's body.
See note to 1.2.13.
4. Parts of the following lines (between "yet lecherous" and "mandrake" in lines 280–81, and between
"and sung" and "good-nights" in lines 282–85) do not
appear in F.

5. The wooden dagger used by the Vice, a comic
character in medieval morality plays.
6. *tiltyard*: tournament arena.
7. Attacked someone very gaunt or thin.
8. I'll make him twice as valuable to me as the philosopher's stone that was supposed to transmute base
metals into gold, with a pun on "stones" as meaning
"testicles."
4.1 Location: Galtres Forest in Yorkshire.
1. Galtres was a royal forest north and west of York.
In Holinshed's *Chronicles* and in Q and F, it is spelled
"Gaultree."

5   ARCHBISHOP   'Tis well done.
      My friends and brethren in these great affairs,
      I must acquaint you that I have received
      New-dated° letters from Northumberland,   *Recent*
      Their cold intent, tenor, and substance thus:
10   Here doth he wish his person, with such powers
      As might hold sortance° with his quality,°   *accord / rank*
      The which he could not levy, whereupon
      He is retired to ripe° his growing fortunes   *ripen*
      To Scotland, and concludes in hearty prayers
15   That your attempts may overlive the hazard
      And fearful meeting of their opposite.°   *enemy*
  MOWBRAY   Thus do the hopes we have in him touch ground
      And dash themselves to pieces.
              Enter MESSENGER.
  HASTINGS   Now, what news?
  MESSENGER   West of this forest, scarcely off a mile,
20   In goodly form° comes on the enemy,   *battle array*
      And by the ground they hide,° I judge their number   *cover*
      Upon or near the rate of thirty thousand.
  MOWBRAY   The just proportion° that we gave them out.°   *exact size / estimated*
      Let us sway on and face them in the field.
              Enter WESTMORLAND.
25   ARCHBISHOP   What well-appointed leader fronts° us here?   *confronts*
  MOWBRAY   I think it is my lord of Westmorland.
  WESTMORLAND   Health and fair greeting from our general,
      The Prince, Lord John and Duke of Lancaster.
  ARCHBISHOP   Say on, my lord of Westmorland, in peace,
      What doth concern your coming.
30   WESTMORLAND   Then, my lord,
      Unto your grace do I in chief address
      The substance of my speech. If that rebellion
      Came like itself, in base and abject routs,°   *lowborn disorderly bands*
      Led on by bloody youth, guarded° with rage,   *adorned*
35   And countenanced° by boys and beggary—   *approved*
      I say, if damned commotion so appear
      In his true, native, and most proper shape,
      You, reverend father, and these noble lords
      Had not been here to dress the ugly form
40   Of base and bloody insurrection
      With your fair honors. You, Lord Archbishop,
      Whose see° is by a civil peace maintained,   *diocese*
      Whose beard the silver hand of peace hath touched,
      Whose learning and good letters° peace hath tutored,   *scholarship*
45   Whose white investments figure° innocence,   *robes represent*
      The dove and very blessèd spirit of peace,
      Wherefore do you so ill translate° yourself   *transform*
      Out of the speech of peace that bears such grace
      Into the harsh and boist'rous tongue of war,
50   Turning your books to graves, your ink to blood,
      Your pens to lances, and your tongue divine
      To a loud trumpet and a point° of war?   *signal*
  ARCHBISHOP   Wherefore do I this? So the question stands.
      Briefly to this end: we are all diseased.
55   The dangers of the days but newly gone,

Whose memory is written on the earth
With yet°-appearing blood, and the examples | *still*
Of every minute's instance,° present now, | *Occurring every minute*
Hath put us in these ill-beseeming° arms, | *unsuitable*
60 Not to break peace or any branch of it,
But to establish here a peace indeed,
Concurring both in name and quality.

WESTMORLAND   Whenever yet was your appeal denied?
Wherein have you been gallèd° by the King? | *vexed; aggrieved*
65 What peer hath been suborned to grate on° you | *induced to annoy*
That you should seal° this lawless bloody book | *license*
Of forged rebellion with a seal divine²
And consecrate commotion's° bitter edge? | *insurrection's*

ARCHBISHOP   My brother general, the commonwealth,
70 To brother born an household cruelty,
I make my quarrel in particular.³

WESTMORLAND   There is no need of any such redress—
Or, if there were, it not belongs to you.

MOWBRAY   Why not to him in part, and to us all
75 That feel the bruises of the days before,
And suffer the condition of these times
To lay a heavy and unequal° hand | *unjust*
Upon our honors?° | *dignities; good names*

WESTMORLAND   But this is mere digression from my purpose.
80 Here come I from our princely general
To know your griefs, to tell you from his grace
That he will give you audience; and wherein
It shall appear that your demands are just,
You shall enjoy them, everything set off° | *forgotten*
85 That might so much as think you enemies.

MOWBRAY   But he hath forced us to compel° this offer, | *go ahead with*
And it proceeds from policy,° not love. | *political cunning*

WESTMORLAND   Mowbray, you overween° to take it so: | *presume too much*
This offer comes from mercy, not from fear;
90 For lo, within a ken° our army lies, | *the field of vision*
Upon mine honor all too confident
To give admittance to a thought of fear.
Our battle° is more full of names° than yours, | *army / titled men*
Our men more perfect in the use of arms,
95 Our armor all as strong, our cause the best;
Then reason will° our hearts should be as good. | *it follows that*
Say you not, then, our offer is compelled.

MOWBRAY   Well, by my will, we shall admit no parley.° | *discussion of terms*

WESTMORLAND   That argues but the shame of your offense:
100 A rotten case° abides no handling. | *cause*

HASTINGS   Hath the Prince John a full commission,
In very ample virtue° of his father, | *With full authority*
To hear and absolutely to determine
Of what° conditions we shall stand upon? | *whatever*

2. Alluding to bishops as official licensers of books with the ability to exercise censorship. Westmorland accuses the Archbishop of licensing rather than censoring the book of rebellion.
3. *My brother . . . particular*: these three lines are obscure. York seems to be saying that he is called to act by the commonwealth. The men of the commonwealth being his brothers, wrongs done to them ("household cruelty") are the reason he fights.

105	WESTMORLAND That is intended° in the general's name.	indicated
	I muse° you make so slight a question.	wonder
	ARCHBISHOP Then take, my lord of Westmorland, this	
	schedule,°	document
	For this contains our general grievances.	
	Each several° article herein redressed,	individual
110	All members of our cause, both here and hence,	
	That are ensinewed° to this action,	tightly bound (by sinews)
	Acquitted° by a true substantial form°	Pardoned / binding act
	And present execution of our wills,	
	To us and our purposes confined,⁴	
115	We come within our awful banks again,⁵	
	And knit our powers to the arm of peace.	
	WESTMORLAND This will I show the general. Please you, lords,	
	In sight of both our battles we may meet	
	At either end in peace—which God so frame°—	bring to pass
120	Or to the place of difference° call the swords	conflict
	Which must decide it.	
	ARCHBISHOP My lord, we will do so.	
	Exit WESTMORLAND.	
	MOWBRAY There is a thing within my bosom tells me	
	That no conditions of our peace can stand.	
	HASTINGS Fear you not that: if we can make our peace	
125	Upon such large° terms, and so absolute,	liberal
	As our conditions shall consist° upon,	insist
	Our peace shall stand as firm as rocky mountains.	
	MOWBRAY Yea, but our valuation° shall be such	his estimation of us
	That every slight and false-derivèd° cause—	wrongly attributed
130	Yea, every idle, nice,° and wanton° reason—	petty / frivolous
	Shall to the King taste of this action;°	(of rebellion)
	That, were our royal faiths martyrs in love,⁶	
	We shall be winnowed with so rough a wind	
	That even our corn shall seem as light as chaff,	
135	And good from bad find no partition.°	distinction
	ARCHBISHOP No, no, my lord, note this: the King is weary	
	Of dainty and such picking° grievances,	trivial
	For he hath found to end one doubt° by death	fear
	Revives two greater in the heirs of life,	
140	And therefore will he wipe his tables° clean	tablets
	And keep no telltale to his memory	
	That may repeat and history° his loss	retell
	To new remembrance. For full well he knows	
	He cannot so precisely weed this land	
145	As his misdoubts° present occasion:	suspicions
	His foes are so enrooted with his friends	
	That, plucking to unfix an enemy,	
	He doth unfasten so and shake a friend.	
	So that this land, like an offensive wife	
150	That hath enraged him on to offer strokes,°	attempt beatings
	As he is striking, holds his infant up	

4. _And . . . confined:_ And immediate ("present") fulfillment of our demands, which are limited to us and
to our ends (not those of other would-be rebels).
5. We come again within the bounds of respect (with

the suggestion of a flooded river returning to its banks).
6. So that even if our loyalty to the King made us loving martyrs.

And hangs resolved correction in the arm
That was upreared to execution.[7]

HASTINGS Besides, the King hath wasted all his rods°   *means of punishment*
155 On late° offenders, that he now doth lack   *recent*
The very instruments of chastisement,
So that his power, like to a fangless lion,
May offer,° but not hold.   *threaten*

ARCHBISHOP   'Tis very true,
And therefore be assured, my good lord Marshal,
160 If we do now make our atonement° well,   *reconciliation*
Our peace will, like a broken limb united,
Grow stronger for the breaking.

MOWBRAY   Be it so.

Enter WESTMORLAND.

Here is returned my lord of Westmorland.

WESTMORLAND The Prince is here at hand. Pleaseth your
lordship
165 To meet his grace just° distance 'tween our armies?   *equal*

MOWBRAY Your grace of York, in God's name, then, set forward.

ARCHBISHOP Before, and greet his grace. —My lord, we come.

Enter PRINCE JOHN *and his army.*

PRINCE JOHN You are well encountered here, my cousin
Mowbray;
Good day to you, gentle Lord Archbishop,
170 And so to you, Lord Hastings, and to all.
My lord of York, it better showed with you
When that your flock, assembled by the bell,
Encircled you to hear with reverence
Your exposition on the holy text
175 Than now to see you here, an iron° man, talking,   *armored; fierce*
Cheering a rout° of rebels with your drum,   *disorderly band*
Turning the word° to sword and life to death.   *(Scripture)*
That man that sits within a monarch's heart
And ripens in the sunshine of his favor,
180 Would he° abuse the countenance° of the King?   *Should he / favor*
Alack, what mischiefs might he set abroach°   *afoot*
In shadow° of such greatness! With you, Lord Bishop,   *Under cover*
It is even so. Who hath not heard it spoken
How deep you were within the books of God—
185 To us, the speaker in His° parliament;   *(God's)*
To us, th'imagined voice of God Himself,
The very opener° and intelligencer°   *interpreter / informer*
Between the grace, the sanctities of heaven,
And our dull workings?° Oh, who shall believe   *ignorant thoughts*
190 But you misuse the reverence of your place,
Imply° the countenance and grace of heav'n   *Entangle*
As a false favorite doth his prince's name
In deeds dishonorable? You have ta'en up,°   *enlisted*
Under the counterfeited zeal of God,[8]
195 The subjects of His substitute, my father,
And both against the peace of heaven and him,

---

7. *And . . . execution:* And so punishment that was
about to be executed is held in suspended action.

8. Under the pretense of zeal toward God; under the
pretense of God's approval.

Have here upswarmed them.[9]
ARCHBISHOP   Good my lord of Lancaster,
I am not here against your father's peace
But, as I told my lord of Westmorland,
200 The time misordered doth, in common sense,
Crowd us and crush us to this monstrous form
To hold our safety up. I sent your grace
The parcels° and particulars of our grief,   items; details
The which hath been with scorn shoved from the court,
205 Whereon this Hydra son[1] of war is born,
Whose dangerous eyes may well be charmed asleep[2]
With grant° of our most just and right desires,   the granting
And true obedience, of this madness cured,
Stoop tamely to the foot of majesty.
210 MOWBRAY   If not, we ready are to try our fortunes
To the last man.
HASTINGS   And, though we here fall down,
We have supplies° to second our attempt;   reinforcements
If they miscarry, theirs shall second them,
And so success of° mischief shall be born,   from
215 And heir from heir shall hold his quarrel up,
Whiles° England shall have generation.°   As long as / offspring
PRINCE JOHN   You are too shallow, Hastings, much too shallow,
To sound the bottom of the aftertimes.°   future
WESTMORLAND   Pleaseth your grace to answer them directly
220 How far forth you do like their articles.
PRINCE JOHN   I like them all, and do allow° them well,   grant
And swear here, by the honor of my blood,
My father's purposes have been mistook,
And some about him have too lavishly°   freely
225 Wrested his meaning and authority.
[to the ARCHBISHOP] My lord, these griefs shall be with speed
    redressed;
Upon my soul, they shall. If this may please you,
Discharge your powers unto their several counties,
As we will ours; and here between the armies
230 Let's drink together friendly and embrace,
That all their eyes may bear those tokens home
Of our restorèd love and amity.
ARCHBISHOP   I take your princely word for these redresses.
PRINCE JOHN   I give it you, and will maintain my word;
235 And thereupon I drink unto your grace.
        [He drinks.]
HASTINGS   Go, Captain, and deliver to the army
This news of peace. Let them have pay and part.
I know it will well please them. Hie thee,° Captain.   Get thee gone
                [Exit Captain.]
ARCHBISHOP [drinking]   To you, my noble lord of Westmorland.
240 WESTMORLAND [drinking]   I pledge your grace; an if you knew
        what pains

---

9. Have raised them up in angry swarms (like bees).
1. Hydra-like offspring. The Archbishop alludes to
the many-headed monster of classical mythology,
which was almost impossible to kill because its heads
grew again as fast as they were cut off.
2. Alluding to another monster of classical mythology, the hundred-eyed Argus, which Hermes overcame by charming it to sleep.

I have bestowed to breed this present peace,
You would drink freely; but my love to ye
Shall show itself more openly hereafter.
ARCHBISHOP   I do not doubt you.
WESTMORLAND   I am glad of it.
245 [*He drinks.*] Health to my lord and gentle cousin Mowbray.
MOWBRAY   You wish me health in very happy season,°   *at an apt moment*
For I am on the sudden something ill.
ARCHBISHOP   Against° ill chances men are ever merry,   *Before*
But heaviness° foreruns the good event.   *sorrow*
250 WESTMORLAND   Therefore be merry, coz,° since sudden sorrow   *kinsman*
Serves to say thus: "Some good thing comes tomorrow."
ARCHBISHOP   Believe me, I am passing° light in spirit.   *exceptionally*
MOWBRAY   So much the worse, if your own rule be true.
              Shout.
PRINCE JOHN   The word of peace is rendered: hark how they
      shout!
255 MOWBRAY   This had° been cheerful after victory.   *would have*
ARCHBISHOP   A peace is of the nature of a conquest,
For then both parties nobly are subdued,
And neither party loser.
PRINCE JOHN   Go, my lord,
And let our army be dischargèd, too.   [*Exit* WESTMORLAND.]
260 —And, good my lord, so please you, let our trains°   *troops*
March by us, that we may peruse the men
We should have coped withal.°   *fought against*
ARCHBISHOP   Go, good Lord Hastings,
And, ere they be dismissed, let them march by.
                              [*Exit* HASTINGS.]
              Enter WESTMORLAND.
PRINCE JOHN   I trust, lords, we shall lie° tonight together.   *lodge*
265 Now, cousin, wherefore stands our army still?
WESTMORLAND   The leaders, having charge from you to stand,
Will not go off until they hear you speak.
PRINCE JOHN   They know their duties.
              Enter HASTINGS.
HASTINGS   My lord, our army is dispersed already:
270 Like youthful steers unyoked they take their courses
East, west, north, south; or, like a school broke up,
Each hurries toward his home and sporting place.
WESTMORLAND   Good tidings, my lord Hastings—for the which
I do arrest thee, traitor, of high treason;
275 And you, Lord Archbishop, and you, Lord Mowbray,
Of capital treason I attach° you both.   *arrest*
MOWBRAY   Is this proceeding just and honorable?
WESTMORLAND   Is your assembly so?
ARCHBISHOP   Will you thus break your faith?
PRINCE JOHN   I pawned° thee none.   *pledged*
280 I promised you redress of these same grievances
Whereof you did complain; which, by mine honor,
I will perform with a most Christian care.
But for you, rebels, look to taste the due
Meet° for rebellion.   *Appropriate*
285 Most shallowly did you these arms° commence,   *military actions*
Fondly° brought here and foolishly sent hence.   *Foolishly*

—Strike up our drums; pursue the scattered stray:
God, and not we, hath safely fought today.
—Some guard this traitor to the block of death,
290 Treason's true bed and yielder-up of breath.   [*Exeunt.*]

4.2 (F 4.2)

Alarum;° excursions.° Enter [Sir John] FALSTAFF   *call to arms / attacks; sorties*
[*and* COLEVILLE].

FALSTAFF   What's your name, sir? Of what condition° are you,   *social status*
and of what place?

COLEVILLE   I am a knight, sir, and my name is Coleville of the
Dale.

5 FALSTAFF   Well, then, Coleville is your name, a knight is your
degree,° and your place the dale. Coleville shall be still your   *rank*
name, a traitor your degree, and the dungeon your place—a
place deep enough: so shall you be still Coleville of the Dale.

COLEVILLE   Are not you Sir John Falstaff?

10 FALSTAFF   As good a man as he, sir, whoe'er I am. Do ye yield,
sir, or shall I sweat for you? If I do sweat, they are the drops°   *tears*
of thy lovers,° and they weep for thy death; therefore rouse   *friends*
up fear and trembling, and do observance° to my mercy.   *pay homage (kneel)*

COLEVILLE   I think you are Sir John Falstaff, and in that
15 thought yield me.

FALSTAFF [*aside*]   I have a whole school of tongues in this belly
of mine, and not a tongue of them all speaks any other word
but my name; an I had but a belly of any indifferency,° I were   *of moderate size*
simply the most active fellow in Europe. My womb,° my   *belly*
20 womb, my womb undoes me. Here comes our general.

*Enter [*PRINCE*] JOHN, WESTMORLAND, [Sir John Blunt,]
and the rest. Retreat.*

PRINCE JOHN   The heat° is past; follow no further now.   *chase*
Call in the powers, good cousin Westmorland.

        [*Exit* WESTMORLAND.]

Now, Falstaff, where have you been all this while?
When everything is ended, then you come.
25 These tardy tricks of yours will, on my life,
One time or other break some gallows' back.[1]

FALSTAFF   I would be sorry, my lord, but it should be thus. I
never knew yet but rebuke and check° was the reward of   *censure*
valor. Do you think me a swallow, an arrow, or a bullet? Have
30 I in my poor and old motion the expedition° of thought? I   *speed*
have speeded hither with the very extremest° inch of possi-   *utmost*
bility; I have foundered° nine score and odd posts,° and here,   *made lame / horses*
travel-tainted as I am, have in my pure and immaculate valor
taken Sir John Coleville of the Dale, a most furious knight
35 and valorous enemy. But what of that? He saw me and
yielded, that I may justly say with the hook-nosed fellow of
Rome:[2] "There, cousin, I came, saw, and overcame."

PRINCE JOHN   It was more of his courtesy than your deserving.

FALSTAFF   I know not: here he is, and here I yield him, and I
40 beseech your grace, let it be booked with the rest of this

---

4.2 Location: Scene continues.
1. Cause you to be hanged, which will break the gallows.

2. Referring to Julius Caesar, whose portrait and imperial exploits would be familiar to Elizabethans through
Thomas North's translation of Plutarch.

day's deeds, or, by the Lord, I will have it in a particular ballad[3] else, with mine own picture on the top on't—Coleville
kissing my foot—to the which course, if I be enforced, if you
do not all show like gilt twopences to me,[4] and I in the clear
45   sky of fame o'ershine you as much as the full moon doth the
cinders of the element°—which show like pins' heads to   *the stars*
her—believe not the word of the noble. Therefore let me have
right, and let desert mount.°   *merit be rewarded*

PRINCE JOHN   Thine's too heavy to mount.
50 FALSTAFF   Let it shine, then.
PRINCE JOHN   Thine's too thick° to shine.   *opaque; dim*
FALSTAFF   Let it do something, my good lord, that may do me
    good, and call it what you will.
PRINCE JOHN   —Is thy name Coleville?
55 COLEVILLE   It is, my lord.
PRINCE JOHN   A famous rebel art thou, Coleville.
FALSTAFF   And a famous true subject took him.
COLEVILLE   I am, my lord, but as my betters are
    That led me hither. Had they been ruled by me,
60   You should have won them dearer° than you have.   *at greater cost*
FALSTAFF   I know not how they sold themselves, but thou, like
    a kind fellow, gavest thyself away gratis, and I thank thee for
    thee.

        Enter WESTMORLAND.

PRINCE JOHN   Now, have you left pursuit?
65 WESTMORLAND   Retreat is made, and execution stayed.°   *stopped*
PRINCE JOHN   Send Coleville with his confederates
    To York, to present° execution.   *immediate*
    Blunt, lead him hence, and see you guard him sure.

        [*Exit Blunt with* COLEVILLE.]

    And now dispatch we toward the court, my lords.
70   I hear the King my father is sore° sick.   *severely*
    Our news shall go before us to his majesty,
    Which, cousin, you shall bear to comfort him,
    And we with sober speed will follow you.
FALSTAFF   My lord, I beseech you give me leave to go through
75   Gloucestershire and, when you come to court, stand° my   *let me stand*
    good lord in your good report.
PRINCE JOHN   Fare you well, Falstaff. I, in my condition,°   *position*
    Shall better speak of you than you deserve.

        [*Exeunt all but* FALSTAFF.]

FALSTAFF   I would you had the wit: 'twere better than your
80   dukedom. Good faith, this same young sober-blooded boy
    doth not love me, nor a man cannot make him laugh—but
    that's no marvel: he drinks no wine. There's never none of
    these demure boys come to any proof,° for thin drink° doth   *turn out well / beer*
    so overcool their blood, and making many fish meals, that
85   they fall into a kind of male green-sickness,[5] and then, when
    they marry, they get wenches.° They are generally fools and   *beget females*

---

3. Ballad specifically about me. Ballads often reported
contemporary scandals and events.
4. If you do not all look like counterfeits when compared with me.
5. An anemic condition that affected young women
in puberty and that was supposed to be cured through
sexual activity. Throughout this speech, Falstaff
indicts John for lacking the heat necessary for masculine valor and the begetting of male children. Diet
was believed to affect the balance of the four humors,
or fluids, that determined temperament and the relative "heat" of the body.

cowards, which some of us should be too, but for inflamma-
tion.[6] A good sherry-sack° hath a twofold operation in it: it   *Spanish sherry*
ascends me into the brain, dries me there[7] all the foolish and
90   dull and cruddy° vapors which environ° it, makes it apprehen-   *coagulated / surround*
sive,° quick, forgetive,[8] full of nimble, fiery, and delectable   *witty*
shapes, which delivered o'er to the voice, the tongue, which is
the birth, becomes excellent wit. The second property of your
excellent sherry is the warming of the blood, which before,
95   cold and settled,° left the liver[9] white and pale, which is the   *stagnant*
badge of pusillanimity and cowardice. But the sherry warms it,
and makes it course from the inwards to the parts' extremes.°   *extremities*
It illumineth the face which, as a beacon, gives warning to all
the rest of this little kingdom, man, to arm; and then the vital
100   commoners and inland° petty spirits[1] muster me° all to their   *internal / assemble*
captain, the heart, who, great and puffed up with this reti-
nue,° doth any deed of courage. And this valor comes of   *train of followers*
sherry. So that skill in the weapon is nothing without sack,
for that sets it a-work, and learning a mere hoard of gold kept
105   by a devil,[2] till sack commences it and sets it in act and use.[3]
Hereof comes it that Prince Harry is valiant, for the cold
blood he did naturally inherit of his father he hath, like lean,°   *barren*
sterile, and bare land, manured, husbanded,° and tilled, with   *cultivated*
excellent endeavor of drinking good and good store of fertile
110   sherry, that he is become very hot and valiant. If I had a thousand sons, the first human principle I would teach them
should be to forswear thin potations, and to addict themselves to sack.

     Enter BARDOLPH.

How now, Bardolph?
115   BARDOLPH   The army is dischargèd all and gone.
FALSTAFF   Let them go. I'll through Gloucestershire, and
there will I visit Master Robert Shallow, esquire. I have him
already tempering[4] between my finger and my thumb, and
shortly will I seal with him.[5] Come, away!   [*Exeunt.*]

4.3 (F 4.3)

Enter the KING, WARWICK, *Kent, Thomas Duke of*
CLARENCE, [*and*] *Humphrey of* GLOUCESTER.

KING   Now, lords, if God doth give successful end
To this debate° that bleedeth at our doors,   *conflict*
We will our youth lead on to higher fields,[1]
And draw no swords but what are sanctified.
5   Our navy is addressed,° our power collected,   *prepared*
Our substitutes in absence well invested,°   *installed in office*
And everything lies level to° our wish;   *in accordance with*
Only we want a little personal strength,

---

6. The passions that alcohol inflames.
7. It ascends into the brain and to my benefit dries up.
8. Inventive.
9. The supposed seat of the passions.
1. Alluding to the medical doctrine of "vital spirits,"
or highly refined fluids, that were supposed to suffuse the blood.
2. Referring to the popular belief that hidden treasures were guarded by evil spirits.
3. Until sack sets learning free; confers a degree

upon learning (punning on "commencement" and
"act," two terms used for the granting of a university
degree).
4. Softening like warm sealing wax.
5. Mold him to my use; conclude with him.
4.3 Location: The Jerusalem Chamber, the palace at
Westminster. (This room was actually in the Abbot's
house beside Westminster Abbey.)
1. That is, those of Palestine, where the King proposes
to lead a crusade.

And pause us till these rebels, now afoot,
10 Come underneath the yoke of government.
WARWICK   Both which we doubt not but your majesty
    Shall soon enjoy.
KING   Humphrey, my son of Gloucester,
    Where is the Prince your brother?
GLOUCESTER   I think he's gone to hunt, my lord, at Windsor.
KING   And how accompanied?
15 GLOUCESTER   I do not know, my lord.
KING   Is not his brother Thomas of Clarence with him?
GLOUCESTER   No, my good lord, he is in presence here.
CLARENCE   What would my lord and father?
KING   Nothing but well to thee, Thomas of Clarence.
20 How chance thou art not with the Prince, thy brother?
    He loves thee, and thou dost neglect him, Thomas.
    Thou hast a better place in his affection
    Than all thy brothers; cherish it, my boy,
    And noble offices° thou mayst effect   duties
25 Of mediation, after I am dead,
    Between his greatness and thy other brethren.
    Therefore omit° him not, blunt not his love,   neglect
    Nor lose the good advantage of his grace
    By seeming cold or careless of his will;
30 For he is gracious if he be observed:°   shown respect
    He hath a tear for pity and a hand
    Open as day for meting° charity.   dealing out
    Yet, notwithstanding, being incensed, he is flint,
    As humorous° as winter, and as sudden   changeable
35 As flaws congealèd° in the spring° of day.   As snowflakes frozen / dawn
    His temper therefore must be well observed.
    Chide him for faults, and do it reverently,
    When you perceive his blood inclined to mirth;
    But, being moody, give him time and scope,°   free range
40 Till that his passions, like a whale on ground,
    Confound° themselves with working. Learn this, Thomas,   Exhaust
    And thou shalt prove a shelter to thy friends,
    A hoop of gold² to bind thy brothers in,
    That the united vessel of their blood,³
45 Mingled with venom of suggestion,°   malicious gossip
    As force perforce the age will pour it in,
    Shall never leak, though it do work as strong,
    As aconitum⁴ or rash gunpowder.
CLARENCE   I shall observe him with all care and love.
50 KING   Why art thou not at Windsor with him, Thomas?
CLARENCE   He is not there today; he dines in London.
KING   And how accompanied?
CLARENCE   With Poins and other his continual° followers.   constant
KING   Most subject is the fattest° soil to weeds,   richest
55 And he, the noble image of my youth,
    Is overspread with them; therefore my grief
    Stretches itself beyond the hour of death.
    The blood weeps from my heart when I do shape

---

2. A barrel with a golden hoop; a golden ring.   blood.
3. The vessel—a vial or chalice—that holds their   4. Monkshood, an especially virulent poison.

	In forms imaginary th'unguided days°	*days lacking a ruler*
60	And rotten times that you shall look upon	
	When I am sleeping with my ancestors.	
	For when his headstrong riot hath no curb,	
	When rage° and hot blood are his counselors,	*passion*
	When means° and lavish manners meet together,	*opportunity*
65	Oh, with what wings shall his affections° fly	*desires; inclinations*
	Towards fronting peril and opposed decay?[5]	
WARWICK	My gracious lord, you look beyond° him quite.	*misjudge*
	The Prince but studies his companions	
	Like a strange tongue,° wherein, to gain the language,	*foreign language*
70	'Tis needful that the most immodest word	
	Be looked upon and learnt; which once attained,	
	Your highness knows comes to no further use	
	But to be known and hated. So, like gross° terms,	*vulgar; common*
	The Prince will in the perfectness of time	
75	Cast off his followers, and their memory	
	Shall as a pattern or a measure live	
	By which his grace must mete° the lives of other,°	*appraise / others*
	Turning past evils to advantages.	
KING	'Tis seldom when the bee doth leave her comb	
	In the dead carrion.[6]	

Enter WESTMORLAND.

80	Who's here? Westmorland?	
WESTMORLAND	Health to my sovereign, and new happiness	
	Added to that that I am to deliver.	
	Prince John, your son, doth kiss your grace's hand:	
	Mowbray, the Bishop Scrope, Hastings, and all	
85	Are brought to the correction of your law.	
	There is not now a rebel's sword unsheathed,	
	But Peace puts forth her olive[7] everywhere.	
	The manner how this action hath been borne	
	Here at more leisure may your highness read,	
90	With every course° in his° particular.	*stage in the action / its*
KING	O Westmorland, thou art a summer bird,	
	Which ever in the haunch° of winter sings	*hind part*
	The lifting up of day.°	*dawn*

Enter HARCOURT.

	Look, here's more news.	
HARCOURT	From enemies heavens keep your majesty;	
95	And, when they stand against you, may they fall	
	As those that I am come to tell you of.	
	The Earl Northumberland and the Lord Bardolph,	
	With a great power of English and of Scots,	
	Are by the Shrieve° of Yorkshire overthrown.	*Sheriff*
100	The manner and true order of the fight	
	This packet, please it you, contains at large.	
KING	And wherefore should these good news make me sick?	
	Will Fortune never come with both hands full,	
	But whet° her fair words still in foulest terms?	*sharpen*
105	She either gives a stomach° and no food—	*an appetite*

---

5. Toward the peril and destruction that confront him.
6. 'Tis . . . *carrion:* It is rare that the bee who has placed her honeycomb in a carcass abandons it. (So the new King will be unlikely to abandon his old pleasures.)
7. Olive branches were traditional symbols of peace.

Such are the poor in health—or else a feast,
And takes away the stomach—such are the rich,
That have abundance and enjoy it not.
I should rejoice now at this happy news,
110   And now my sight fails, and my brain is giddy.
Oh, me! Come near me now; I am much ill.
GLOUCESTER   Comfort your majesty!
CLARENCE   O my royal father!
WESTMORLAND   My sovereign lord, cheer up yourself. Look up!°   *Take courage*
WARWICK   Be patient, princes; you do know these fits
115   Are with his highness very ordinary.
Stand from him; give him air; he'll straight be well.
CLARENCE   No, no, he cannot long hold out° these pangs.   *endure*
Th'incessant care and labor of his mind
Hath wrought the mure° that should confine it in   *made the wall*
120   So thin that life looks through.
GLOUCESTER   The people fear° me, for they do observe   *frighten*
Unfathered heirs and loathly births of nature.[8]
The seasons change their manners, as° the year   *as if*
Had found some months asleep and leaped them over.
125   CLARENCE   The river° hath thrice flowed, no ebb between,   *(the Thames)*
And the old folk, time's doting chronicles,
Say it did so a little time before
That our great-grandsire Edward° sicked and died.   *(Edward III)*
WARWICK   Speak lower, princes, for the King recovers.
130   GLOUCESTER   This apoplexy will certain be his end.
KING   I pray you take me up and bear me hence
Into some other chamber.
Let there be no noise made, my gentle friends,
Unless some dull° and favorable hand   *restful*
135   Will whisper music to my weary spirit.
WARWICK   —Call for the music in the other room.
KING   Set me the crown upon my pillow here.
CLARENCE [*apart*]   His eye is hollow, and he changes° much.   *(in complexion)*
WARWICK   Less noise, less noise.
        Enter [PRINCE] *Harry.*
140   PRINCE   Who saw the Duke of Clarence?
CLARENCE   I am here, brother, full of heaviness.°   *sadness*
PRINCE   How now, rain within doors, and none abroad?
How doth the King?
GLOUCESTER   Exceeding ill.
PRINCE   Heard he the good news yet? Tell it him.
145   GLOUCESTER   He altered much upon the hearing it.
PRINCE   If he be sick with joy, he'll recover without physic.
WARWICK   Not so much noise, my lords; sweet Prince,
        speak low:
The King your father is disposed to sleep.
CLARENCE   Let us withdraw into the other room.
150   WARWICK   Will't please your grace to go along with us?
PRINCE   No, I will sit and watch here by the King.
        [*Exeunt all but the* PRINCE *and the* KING.]
Why doth the crown lie there upon his pillow,

---

8. Children supernaturally begotten and malformed offspring resulting from normal conception.

Being so troublesome a bedfellow?
O polished perturbation,° golden care,   *source of unease*
155   That keep'st the ports° of slumber open wide   *gates (the eyes)*
To many a watchful° night! —Sleep with it° now;   *wakeful / (the crown)*
Yet not so sound and half so deeply sweet
As he whose brow, with homely biggen° bound,   *nightcap*
Snores out the watch of night.⁹ O majesty!
160   When thou dost pinch thy bearer, thou dost sit
Like a rich armor worn in heat of day,
That scald'st with safety; by his gates of breath°   *his lips*
There lies a downy feather which stirs not;
Did he suspire,° that light and weightless down   *If he breathed*
165   Perforce must move. —My gracious lord, my father!
This sleep is sound indeed; this is a sleep
That from this golden rigol° hath divorced   *ring*
So many English kings. Thy due from me
Is tears and heavy sorrows of the blood,
170   Which nature, love, and filial tenderness
Shall, O dear father, pay thee plenteously.
My due from thee is this imperial crown
Which, as immediate from° thy place and blood,   *as next in line to*
Derives itself° to me.   *Descends*
     [*He puts the crown on his head.*]
               Lo, where it sits,
175   Which God shall guard; and put the world's whole strength
Into one giant arm, it shall not force
This lineal° honor from me. This from thee   *hereditary*
Will I to mine leave, as 'tis left to me.   *Exit.*
KING [*awaking*] Warwick! Gloucester! Clarence!
    Enter WARWICK, GLOUCESTER, [*and*] CLARENCE.
CLARENCE   Doth the King call?
180   WARWICK What would your majesty?
KING Why did you leave me here alone, my lords?
CLARENCE We left the Prince my brother here, my liege,
Who undertook to sit and watch by you.
KING The Prince of Wales? Where is he? Let me see him.
185   He is not here.
WARWICK This door is open; he is gone this way.
GLOUCESTER He came not through the chamber where we
    stayed.
KING Where is the crown? Who took it from my pillow?
WARWICK When we withdrew, my liege, we left it here.
190   KING The Prince hath ta'en it hence. Go seek him out.
Is he so hasty that he doth suppose
My sleep my death?
Find him, my lord of Warwick; chide him hither.
                       [*Exit* WARWICK.]
This part° of his conjoins° with my disease,   *act / unites*
195   And helps to end me. See, sons, what things you are:
How quickly nature falls into revolt
When gold becomes her object!
For this the foolish overcareful fathers

---

9. Nighttime. "Watch" alludes to the periods of sentry duty into which the night was divided.

Have broke their sleep with thoughts,
200 Their brains with care, their bones with industry.
For this they have engrossèd° and piled up   *gathered*
The cankered° heaps of strange-achievèd gold;[1]   *diseased*
For this they have been thoughtful° to invest   *careful*
Their sons with arts and martial exercises,
205 When, like the bee, tolling° from every flower,   *taking payment*
Our thighs packed with wax, our mouths with honey,
We bring it to the hive and, like the bees,
Are murdered for our pains. This bitter taste
Yields his engrossments to the ending father.[2]
       Enter WARWICK.
210 —Now where is he that will not stay so long,
Till his friend Sickness' hands determined° me?   *put an end to*
WARWICK   My lord, I found the Prince in the next room,
Washing with kindly° tears his gentle° cheeks,   *filial / noble*
With such a deep demeanor,° in great sorrow,   *sad countenance*
215 That tyranny, which never quaffed° but blood,   *drank*
Would, by beholding him, have washed his knife
With gentle eye-drops.° He is coming hither.   *tears*
KING   But wherefore did he take away the crown?
       Enter [PRINCE] *Harry.*
Lo, where he comes. —Come hither to me, Harry.
220 —Depart the chamber; leave us here alone.
                           Exeunt [all but KING and PRINCE].
PRINCE   I never thought to hear you speak again.
KING   Thy wish was father, Harry, to that thought.
I stay too long by thee; I weary thee.
Dost thou so hunger for mine empty chair
225 That thou wilt needs invest thee with my honors
Before thy hour be ripe? O foolish youth!
Thou seek'st the greatness that will overwhelm thee.
Stay but a little, for my cloud of dignity°   *fragile greatness*
Is held from falling with so weak a wind°   *(his breath)*
230 That it will quickly drop. My day is dim.
Thou hast stol'n that which after some few hours
Were thine without offense, and at my death
Thou hast sealed up° my expectation.   *confirmed*
Thy life did manifest thou loved'st me not,
235 And thou wilt have me die assured of it.
Thou hid'st a thousand daggers in thy thoughts,
Whom° thou hast whetted on thy stony heart   *Which*
To stab at half an hour of my life.
What, canst thou not forbear me° half an hour?   *grant me but*
240 Then get thee gone and dig my grave thyself,
And bid the merry bells ring to thine ear
That thou art crownèd, not that I am dead.
Let all the tears that should bedew my hearse°   *coffin*
Be drops of balm[3] to sanctify thy head.
245 Only compound° me with forgotten dust: *mix*

---

1. Gold gained in foreign lands or by unnatural or unusual means.
2. *This . . . father:* This bitter taste is all the dying father's amassing of wealth amounts to.
3. The consecrated oils with which new monarchs were anointed during their coronation.

Give that which gave thee life unto the worms.
Pluck down my officers, break my decrees;
For now a time is come to mock at form.°   decorum
Harry the Fifth is crowned: up, vanity!
250   Down, royal state!° All you sage counselors, hence!   ceremony
And to the English court assemble now,
From every region, apes° of idleness!   fools
Now, neighbor confines,° purge you of your scum!   bordering regions
Have you a ruffian that will swear, drink, dance,
255   Revel the night? Rob, murder, and commit
The oldest sins the newest kind of ways?
Be happy: he will trouble you no more:
England shall double gild° his treble guilt;   paint over
England shall give him office, honor, might;
260   For the fifth Harry from curbed license[4] plucks
The muzzle of restraint, and the wild dog
Shall flesh his tooth on° every innocent.   taste the flesh of
O my poor kingdom, sick with civil blows,°   domestic conflicts
When that my care could not withhold° thy riots,°   control / strife
265   What wilt thou do when riot is thy care?[5]
Oh, thou wilt be a wilderness again,
Peopled with wolves, thy old inhabitants.
PRINCE   Oh, pardon me, my liege. But for my tears,
The moist impediments unto my speech,
270   I had forestalled this dear° and deep rebuke   grievous
Ere you with grief had spoke, and I had heard
The course of it so far. There is your crown,
And He° that wears the crown immortally   (God)
Long guard it yours. If I affect° it more   desire
275   Than as your honor and as your renown,
Let me no more from this obedience rise,
Which my most inward true and duteous spirit
Teacheth this prostrate and exterior° bending.   outward
God witness with me, when I here came in
280   And found no course of breath within your majesty,
How cold it struck my heart! If I do feign,
Oh, let me in my present wildness° die,   sinfulness
And never live to show th'incredulous world
The noble change that I have purposèd.°   intended
285   Coming to look on you, thinking you dead,
And dead almost, my liege, to think you were,
I spake unto this crown as having sense,°   as if it had senses
And thus upbraided it: "The care on thee depending[6]
Hath fed upon the body of my father;
290   Therefore, thou best of gold art worse than gold,
Other, less fine in carat, more precious,
Preserving life in med'cine potable;[7]
But thou, most fine, most honored, most renowned,
Hast ate thy bearer up." Thus, my most royal liege,

---

4. *license:* excessive freedom. The image is of a wild
dog that has been curbed, or kept under restraint,
until his muzzle is removed and chaos ensues.
5. When debauchery (in the person of Hal) is your
caretaker; when strife becomes your concern (rather

than mine after my death).
6. The trouble that comes along with the crown.
7. Gold in a drinkable solution ("potable") was widely
considered to be healthful.

295   Accusing it, I put it on my head,
        To try° with it as with an enemy   *struggle*
        That had before my face murdered my father,
        The quarrel of a true inheritor.°   *legitimate heir*
        But if it did infect my blood with joy,
300   Or swell my thoughts to any strain of pride,
        If any rebel or vain spirit of mine
        Did with the least affection of° a welcome   *inclination toward*
        Give entertainment to the might of it,
        Let God for ever keep it from my head,
305   And make me as the poorest vassal is
        That doth with awe and terror kneel to it.
    KING   God put in thy mind to take it hence
        That thou mightst win the more thy father's love,
        Pleading so wisely in excuse of it!
310   Come hither, Harry; sit thou by my bed
        And hear, I think, the very latest° counsel   *last*
        That ever I shall breathe. God knows, my son,
        By what bypaths and indirect crooked ways
        I met this crown; and I myself know well
315   How troublesome it sat upon my head.
        To thee it shall descend with better quiet,
        Better opinion,° better confirmation,   *public support*
        For all the soil° of the achievement goes   *stain*
        With me into the earth. It seemed in me
320   But as an honor snatched with boist'rous hand,
        And I had many living to upbraid
        My gain of it by their assistances,[8]
        Which daily grew to quarrel and to bloodshed,
        Wounding supposèd peace. All these bold fears°   *fearful acts*
325   Thou seest with peril I have answerèd;
        For all my reign hath been but as a scene
        Acting that argument.° And now my death   *theme*
        Changes the mood, for what in me was purchased[9]
        Falls upon thee in a more fairer sort,
330   So thou the garland wear'st successively.[1]
        Yet though thou stand'st more sure than I could do,
        Thou art not firm enough, since griefs are green,°   *grievances are fresh*
        And all thy friends, which thou must make thy friends,
        Have but their stings and teeth newly ta'en out,
335   By whose fell° working I was first advanced,   *cruel*
        And by whose power I well might lodge a fear
        To be again displaced; which to avoid,
        I cut them off, and had a purpose now
        To lead out many to the Holy Land,
340   Lest rest and lying still might make them look°   *examine*
        Too near° unto my state. Therefore, my Harry,   *Too closely*
        Be it thy course to busy giddy° minds   *restless*
        With foreign quarrels, that action° hence borne out *military exploits*
        May waste° the memory of the former days.   *obliterate*
345   More would I, but my lungs are wasted so

---

8. *And . . . assistances:* And many were living who
made demands on me and reproved me on the strength
of the fact that they had helped me to seize the throne.

9. Was acquired by acts, not by inheritance.
1. So that you wear the sign of victory (the crown) by
right of succession.

That strength of speech is utterly denied me.
How I came by the crown, O God forgive,
And grant it may with thee in true peace live.
PRINCE   You won it, wore it, kept it, gave it me;
350 Then plain and right must my possession be;
Which I with more than with a common pain°   *effort*
'Gainst all the world will rightfully maintain.
      Enter [PRINCE JOHN *of*] *Lancaster* [*and* WARWICK].
KING   Look, look! Here comes my John of Lancaster.
PRINCE JOHN   Health, peace, and happiness to my royal father.
355 KING   Thou bring'st me happiness and peace, son John,
But health, alack, with youthful wings is flown
From this bare withered trunk. Upon thy sight
My worldly business makes a period.°   *an end*
Where is my lord of Warwick?
PRINCE   My lord of Warwick.
360 KING   Doth any name particular belong
Unto the lodging° where I first did swoon?   *room*
WARWICK   'Tis called "Jerusalem," my noble lord.
KING   Laud be to God. Even there my life must end.
It hath been prophesied to me, many years,
365 I should not die but in Jerusalem,
Which vainly I supposed the Holy Land.
But bear me to that chamber; there I'll lie:
In that Jerusalem shall Harry die.   [*Exeunt.*]

5.1 (F 5.1)

  Enter SHALLOW, FALSTAFF, BARDOLPH[, *and* PAGE].
SHALLOW [*to* FALSTAFF]   By cock and pie,[1] sir, you shall not
away tonight. —What, Davy, I say!
FALSTAFF   You must excuse me, Master Robert Shallow.
SHALLOW   I will not excuse you; you shall not be excused;
5   excuses shall not be admitted; there is no excuse shall serve.
You shall not be excused. —Why, Davy!
    [*Enter* DAVY.]
DAVY   Here, sir.
SHALLOW   Davy, Davy, Davy, Davy, let me see, Davy, let me see,
Davy, let me see. Yea, marry,° William cook: bid him come   *indeed*
10   hither. —Sir John, you shall not be excused.
DAVY   Marry, sir, thus: those precepts° cannot be served; and   *warrants*
again,° sir, shall we sow the hade land[2] with wheat?   *moreover*
SHALLOW   With red wheat, Davy. But for William cook: are
there no young pigeons?
15   DAVY   Yes, sir. Here is now the smith's note° for shoeing and   *bill*
plough-irons.
SHALLOW   Let it be cast° and paid. —Sir John, you shall not be   *calculated*
excused.
DAVY   Now, sir, a new link° to the bucket must needs be had;   *chain*
20   and, sir, do you mean to stop any of William's wages about
the sack he lost at Hinckley[3] Fair?

5.1 Location: Shallow's house in Gloucestershire.   the church calendar.
1. A mild oath. "Cock" was a euphemism for "God,"   2. Unplowed strip of land between two plowed fields.
and "pie" was a colloquial word for the collection of   3. A market town near Coventry.
rules by which the pre-Reformation church ordered

SHALLOW 'A° shall answer° it. Some pigeons, Davy, a couple   *He / pay for*
  of short-legged hens, a joint of mutton, and any pretty little
  tiny kickshaws,° tell William cook.   *fancy dishes*

25 DAVY Doth the man of war stay all night, sir?

SHALLOW Yea, Davy. I will use him well. A friend i'th' court is
  better than a penny in purse. Use his men well, Davy, for
  they are arrant knaves and will backbite.°   *slander*

DAVY No worse than they are backbitten,° sir, for they have   *(by fleas)*
30   marvelous° foul linen.   *amazingly*

SHALLOW Well conceited,° Davy. About thy business, Davy.   *quipped*

DAVY I beseech you, sir, to countenance° William Visor of   *favor*
  Wo'ncot against Clement Perks o'th' Hill.[4]

SHALLOW There is many complaints, Davy, against that
35   Visor; that Visor is an arrant knave on my knowledge.

DAVY I grant your worship that he is a knave, sir. But yet God
  forbid, sir, but a knave should have some countenance at his
  friend's request. An honest man, sir, is able to speak for himself when a knave is not. I have served your worship truly, sir,
40   this eight years; an I cannot once or twice in a quarter bear
  out° a knave against an honest man, I have little credit with   *support*
  your worship. The knave is mine honest friend, sir; therefore
  I beseech you let him be countenanced.

SHALLOW Go to, I say he shall have no wrong. Look about,
45   Davy.   [*Exit* DAVY.]
  Where are you, Sir John? Come, come, come, off with your
  boots. Give me your hand, Master Bardolph.

BARDOLPH I am glad to see your worship.

SHALLOW I thank thee with my heart, kind Master Bardolph.
50   [*to* PAGE] And welcome, my tall° fellow. —Come, Sir John.   *valiant*

FALSTAFF I'll follow you, good Master Robert Shallow.
                                       [*Exit* SHALLOW.]
  Bardolph, look to our horses. [*Exeunt* BARDOLPH *and* PAGE.]
  If I were sawed into quantities,° I should make four dozen of   *pieces*
  such bearded hermits' staves as Master Shallow. It is a won-
55   derful thing to see the semblable coherence° of his men's   *close correspondence*
  spirits and his. They, by observing him, do bear themselves
  like foolish justices; he, by conversing° with them, is turned   *associating*
  into a justice-like servingman. Their spirits are so married in
  conjunction, with the participation of society,° that they flock   *by close association*
60   together in consent like so many wild geese. If I had a suit to
  Master Shallow, I would humor his men with the imputation
  of being near their master; if to his men, I would curry° with   *employ flattery*
  Master Shallow that no man could better command his ser-
  vants. It is certain that either wise bearing or ignorant car-
65   riage° is caught, as men take° diseases one of another.   *demeanor / catch*
  Therefore, let men take heed of their company. I will devise
  matter enough out of this Shallow to keep Prince Harry in
  continual laughter the wearing out of six fashions—which is
  four terms,[5] or two actions°—and 'a shall laugh without   *lawsuits*

---

4. Possibly Stinchcombe Hill, not far from "Wo'ncot"   Gloucestershire).
(the local pronunciation of Woodmancot in   5. Alluding to the four divisions of the judicial year.

70   intervallums.⁶ Oh, it is much that a lie with a slight oath, and
       a jest with a sad° brow, will do with a fellow that never had   *serious*
       the ache in his shoulders.⁷ Oh, you shall see him laugh till his
       face be like a wet cloak ill laid up!⁸
       SHALLOW [*within*]   Sir John!
75   FALSTAFF   I come, Master Shallow; I come, Master Shallow.
                                                                            [*Exit.*]

                                 5.2 (F 5.2)
                  [*Enter* WARWICK *and the* LORD CHIEF JUSTICE.]
       WARWICK   How now, my lord Chief Justice? Whither away?
       LORD CHIEF JUSTICE   How doth the King?
       WARWICK   Exceeding well: his cares are now all ended.
       LORD CHIEF JUSTICE   I hope not dead.
       WARWICK   He's walked the way of nature,
5   And to our purposes he lives no more.
       LORD CHIEF JUSTICE   I would his majesty had called me with
          him.
       The service that I truly did his life
       Hath left me open to all injuries.
       WARWICK   Indeed I think the young King loves you not.
10   LORD CHIEF JUSTICE   I know he doth not and do arm myself
       To welcome the condition° of the time,   *(new) circumstances*
       Which cannot look more hideously upon me
       Than I have drawn it in my fantasy.
                  Enter [PRINCE] JOHN, *Thomas* [*Duke of* CLARENCE],
                  and Humphrey [*Duke of* GLOUCESTER].
       WARWICK   Here come the heavy issue° of dead Harry.   *sad offspring*
15   Oh, that the living Harry had the temper
       Of he, the worst of these three gentlemen!
       How many nobles then should hold their places
       That must strike sail° to spirits of vile sort?°   *submit / low rank*
       LORD CHIEF JUSTICE   O God, I fear all will be overturned.
20   PRINCE JOHN   Good morrow, cousin Warwick, good morrow.
       GLOUCESTER *and* CLARENCE   Good morrow, cousin.
       PRINCE JOHN   We meet like men that had forgot to speak.
       WARWICK   We do remember, but our argument°   *subject matter*
       Is all too heavy to admit much talk.
25   PRINCE JOHN   Well, peace be with him that hath made us
          heavy.
       LORD CHIEF JUSTICE   Peace be with us, lest we be heavier.
       GLOUCESTER   O good my lord, you have lost a friend indeed;
       And I dare swear you borrow not that face
       Of seeming sorrow—it is sure your own.
30   PRINCE JOHN   Though no man be assured what grace to find,°   *favor he will find*
       You stand in coldest expectation.
       I am the sorrier; would 'twere otherwise.
       CLARENCE   Well, you must now speak Sir John Falstaff fair,
       Which swims against your stream of quality.°   *character; rank*
35   LORD CHIEF JUSTICE   Sweet princes, what I did, I did in honor,

---

6. Time between terms.   8. *ill laid up:* carelessly put away (so that it is wrin-
7. With someone who has not experienced old age or   kled).
troubles.   5.2 Location: The palace at Westminster.

Led by th'impartial conduct of my soul,
And never shall you see that I will beg
A raggèd° and forestalled remission.[1]   base
If truth and upright innocency fail me,
40   I'll to the King, my master that is dead,
And tell him who hath sent me after him.
          Enter PRINCE [*Henry*] *and* [*Sir John*] *Blunt.*
WARWICK Here comes the Prince.
LORD CHIEF JUSTICE Good morrow, and God save your majesty.
PRINCE This new and gorgeous garment, majesty,
45   Sits not so easy on me as you think.
Brothers, you mixed your sadness with some fear.
This is the English, not the Turkish, court:
Not Amurath[2] an Amurath succeeds,
But Harry Harry. Yet be sad, good brothers,
50   For, by my faith, it very well becomes you:
Sorrow so royally in you appears
That I will deeply° put the fashion on   solemnly
And wear it in my heart. Why, then, be sad,
But entertain no more of it, good brothers,
55   Than a joint burden laid upon us all.
For me, by heaven, I bid you be assured
I'll be your father and your brother too.
Let me but bear° your love; I'll bear your cares.   have; carry
Yet weep that Harry's dead, and so will I;
60   But Harry lives that shall convert those tears
By number° into hours of happiness.   One by one
PRINCE JOHN, GLOUCESTER, *and* CLARENCE We hope no
          otherwise from your majesty.
PRINCE You all look strangely on me, [*to* LORD CHIEF JUSTICE]
          and you most;
You are, I think, assured I love you not.
65   LORD CHIEF JUSTICE I am assured, if I be measured rightly,
Your majesty hath no just cause to hate me.
PRINCE No? How might a prince of my great hopes forget
So great indignities you laid upon me?
What? Rate,° rebuke, and roughly send to prison   Chide
70   Th'immediate heir of England? Was this easy?
May this be washed in Lethe[3] and forgotten?
LORD CHIEF JUSTICE I then did use the person° of your father: act as a deputy
The image of his power lay then in me;
And in th'administration of his law,
75   Whiles I was busy for the commonwealth,
Your highness pleasèd to forget my place,°   rank; position
The majesty and power of law and justice,
The image of the King whom I presented,
And struck me in my very seat of judgment,
80   Whereon, as° an offender to your father,   as you were
I gave bold way to my authority
And did commit° you. If the deed were ill,   imprison

---

1. Either a pardon sure to be denied or a pardon secured in advance (by an act of submission).
2. An English name for the Turkish sultan Murad III, who had his brothers executed upon his succession in 1574. Turks were bywords for cruelty and tyranny in early modern England.
3. The river in Hades that induced forgetfulness.

Be you contented, wearing now the garland,°   *crown*
To have a son set your decrees at naught?
85   To pluck down justice from your awful° bench?   *awe-inspiring*
To trip the course of law, and blunt the sword
That guards the peace and safety of your person?
Nay, more, to spurn at your most royal image,
And mock your workings in a second body?°   *representative*
90   Question your royal thoughts, make the case yours,
Be now the father and propose° a son;   *imagine*
Hear your own dignity so much profaned,
See your most dreadful laws so loosely slighted,
Behold yourself so by a son disdained—
95   And then imagine me taking your part,
And in your power soft° silencing your son.   *gently*
After this cold considerance, sentence me;
And, as you are a king, speak in your state°   *role as monarch*
What I have done that misbecame my place,
100   My person, or my liege's sovereignty.
PRINCE   You are right, Justice, and you weigh this well.
Therefore still bear the balance and the sword;[4]
And I do wish your honors may increase
Till you do live to see a son of mine
105   Offend you and obey you as I did.
So shall I live to speak my father's words:
"Happy am I that have a man so bold
That dares do justice on my proper° son,   *own*
And not less happy having such a son
110   That would deliver up his greatness so
Into the hands of justice." You did commit° me,   *imprison*
For which I do commit° into your hand   *place*
Th'unstainèd sword that you have used° to bear,   *were accustomed*
With this remembrance:° that you use the same   *reminder*
115   With the like bold, just, and impartial spirit
As you have done 'gainst me. There is my hand.
You shall be as a father to my youth;
My voice shall sound° as you do prompt mine ear,   *speak*
And I will stoop and humble my intents
120   To your well-practiced, wise directions.
—And, princes all, believe me, I beseech you:
My father is gone wild into his grave,
For in his tomb lie my affections,°   *wild passions*
And with his spirits sadly I survive
125   To mock° the expectation of the world,   *defy*
To frustrate prophecies, and to raze out
Rotten opinion, who hath writ me down
After my seeming.[5] The tide of blood° in me   *passion*
Hath proudly flowed in vanity till now;
130   Now doth it turn and ebb back to the sea,
Where it shall mingle with the state of floods,°   *majesty of the sea*
And flow henceforth in formal majesty.
Now call we our high court of Parliament,
And let us choose such limbs° of noble counsel   *members*
135   That the great body of our state may go

---

4. The traditional emblems of justice.   5. According to my (false) appearance.

In equal rank with the best-governed nation;
That war, or peace, or both at once, may be
As things acquainted and familiar to us;
[*to* LORD CHIEF JUSTICE] In which you, father, shall have
 foremost hand.
140 Our coronation done, we will accite,°   *summon*
As I before remembered, all our state;°   *nobility*
And, God consigning to° my good intents,   *endorsing*
No prince nor peer shall have just cause to say,
"God shorten Harry's happy life one day."   *Exeunt.*

5.3 (F 5.3)

Enter Sir John [FALSTAFF], SHALLOW, SILENCE, DAVY,
BARDOLPH, *and* PAGE.

SHALLOW Nay, you shall see my orchard, where, in an arbor,
we will eat a last year's pippin[1] of mine own graffing,° with a   *grafting*
dish of caraways,[2] and so forth—come, cousin Silence—and
then to bed.
5 FALSTAFF 'Fore God, you have here goodly dwelling and rich.
SHALLOW Barren, barren, barren; beggars all, beggars all, Sir
John. Marry, good air. —Spread, Davy; spread, Davy; well
said,° Davy.   *done*
FALSTAFF This Davy serves you for good uses: he is your serv-
10 ingman and your husband.°   *steward*
SHALLOW A good varlet,° a good varlet, a very good varlet, Sir   *servant*
John. By the mass, I have drunk too much sack at supper. A
good varlet. Now sit down, now sit down. —Come, cousin.
SILENCE Ah, sirrah, quoth 'a,° we shall   *said he*
15 [*Sings.*] Do nothing but eat, and make good cheer,
     And praise God for the merry year,
     When flesh is cheap, and females dear,
     And lusty lads roam here and there,
     So merrily,
20   And ever among so merrily.
FALSTAFF There's a merry heart, good Master Silence; I'll
give you a health° for that anon.   *drink a toast to you*
SHALLOW Give Master Bardolph some wine, Davy.
DAVY Sweet sir, sit; I'll be with you anon. Most sweet sir, sit.
25 Master Page, good Master Page, sit. Proface![3] What you
want° in meat, we'll have in drink; but you must bear.° The   *lack / be forbearing*
heart's all.   [*Exit.*]
SHALLOW Be merry, Master Bardolph —and, my little soldier
there, be merry.
30 SILENCE [*sings*] Be merry, be merry, my wife has all,
     For women are shrews, both short and tall,
     'Tis merry in hall, when beards wags all,
     And welcome merry Shrovetide;[4] be merry, be merry.
FALSTAFF I did not think Master Silence had been a man of
35 this mettle.°   *boldness*

5.3 Location: Shallow's garden in Gloucestershire.
1. A kind of apple traditionally kept for a year before
eating.
2. Caraway seeds or sweet biscuits containing these
seeds, often eaten with apples.

3. A greeting used as a welcome to a meal, from an
Italian phrase meaning "May it do you good."
4. The season of festivities preceding the Christian
penitential season, Lent.

SILENCE   Who, I? I have been merry twice and once ere now.
     Enter DAVY.
DAVY   There's a dish of leather-coats° for you.   *russet apples*
SHALLOW   Davy!
DAVY   Your worship, I'll be with you straight. —A cup of wine,
40   sir?
SILENCE [*sings*]   A cup of wine
          That's brisk and fine,
          And drink unto the leman° mine;   *sweetheart*
          And a merry heart lives long-a.
45 FALSTAFF   Well said, Master Silence.
SILENCE   An we shall be merry, now comes in the sweet o'th'
  night.
FALSTAFF   Health and long life to you, Master Silence.
SILENCE [*sings*]   Fill the cup, and let it come,
50   I'll pledge you a mile to th'bottom.[5]
SHALLOW   Honest Bardolph, welcome. If thou want'st anything and wilt not call, beshrew thy heart. —Welcome, my
  little tiny thief, and welcome indeed, too. I'll drink to Master Bardolph, and to all the cabilleros[6] about London.
55 DAVY   I hope to see London once ere I die.
BARDOLPH   An I might see you there, Davy!
SHALLOW   By the mass, you'll crack° a quart together, ha, will   *drink*
  you not, Master Bardolph?
BARDOLPH   Yea, sir, in a pottle pot.°   *two-quart glass*
60 SHALLOW   By God's liggens,[7] I thank thee. The knave will stick
  by thee, I can assure thee that. 'A will not out,° 'a; 'tis   *drop out*
  true-bred.
BARDOLPH   And I'll stick by him, sir.
SHALLOW   Why, there spoke a king: lack nothing, be merry.
     One knocks at door.
65   —Look who's at door there, ho! Who knocks?   [*Exit* DAVY.]
FALSTAFF   Why, now you have done me right.[8]
SILENCE [*sings*]   Do me right,
          And dub me knight,
          Samingo.[9]
70   Is't not so?
FALSTAFF   'Tis so.
SILENCE   Is't so? Why, then say an old man can do somewhat.
     [*Enter* DAVY.]
DAVY   An't please your worship, there's one Pistol come from
  the court with news.
75 FALSTAFF   From the court? Let him come in.
     Enter PISTOL.
  How now, Pistol?
PISTOL   Sir John, God save you.
FALSTAFF   What wind blew you hither, Pistol?
PISTOL   Not the ill wind which blows no man to good. Sweet
80   knight, thou art now one of the greatest men in this realm.

---

5. I'll drink to the bottom of the cup, even if it were a
mile.
6. *cabilleros*: blunder for *cavaliers*, meaning "gallants."
7. An obscure oath, possibly derived from "by God's
(eye)lid."

8. Done me justice (by drinking well).
9. Translated lines from a French drinking song,
"Monsieur Mingo." "Sa" may be a mispronunciation
of "Sir." "Mingo" means "I urinate."

SILENCE   By'r Lady, I think 'a be—but goodman° Puff of Barson.¹   *except for yeoman*
PISTOL   Puff?
    Puff i'thy teeth, most recreant coward base.
    Sir John, I am thy Pistol and thy friend,
85   And helter-skelter have I rode to thee,
    And tidings do I bring, and lucky joys,
    And golden times, and happy news of price.
FALSTAFF   I pray thee now, deliver them like a man of this
    world.
90 PISTOL   A foutre° for the world and worldlings base!   *fig*
    I speak of Africa and golden joys.
FALSTAFF   O base Assyrian knight,² what is thy news?
    Let King Cophetua³ know the truth thereof.
SILENCE [*sings*]   And Robin Hood, Scarlet, and John⁴—
95 PISTOL   Shall dunghill curs confront the Helicons?⁵
    And shall good news be baffled?°   *disgraced*
    Then, Pistol, lay thy head in Furies' lap.⁶
SHALLOW   Honest gentleman, I know not your breeding.
PISTOL   Why, then, lament therefor.
100 SHALLOW   Give me pardon, sir. If, sir, you come with news
    from the court, I take it there's but two ways; either to utter
    them or conceal them. I am, sir, under the King in some
    authority.
PISTOL   Under which king, bezonian?° Speak or die.   *beggarly fellow*
SHALLOW   Under King Harry.
105 PISTOL   Harry the Fourth, or Fifth?
SHALLOW   Harry the Fourth.
PISTOL   A foutre for thine office!
    Sir John, thy tender lambkin now is King.
    Harry the Fifth's the man. I speak the truth.
    When Pistol lies, do this, and fig me,⁷ like
    The bragging Spaniard.
110 FALSTAFF   What, is the old King dead?
PISTOL   As nail in door. The things I speak are just.°   *true*
FALSTAFF   Away, Bardolph! Saddle my horse! —Master Robert
    Shallow, choose what office thou wilt in the land, 'tis thine.
    —Pistol, I will double-charge thee⁸ with dignities.
115 BARDOLPH   Oh, joyful day! I would not take a knight for my
    fortune.
PISTOL   What, I do bring good news?
FALSTAFF   —Carry Master Silence to bed. —Master Shallow,
    my lord Shallow, be what thou wilt; I am Fortune's steward.
120   Get on thy boots, we'll ride all night. O sweet Pistol! —Away,
    Bardolph. —Come, Pistol, utter more to me, and withal° devise   *at the same time*
    something to do thyself good. —Boot, boot, Master Shallow!

1. Referring either to Barcheston, a town ten miles
south of Stratford, or Barston, a town between Coventry and Solihull.
2. Adopting Pistol's elevated rhetorical style, Falstaff calls him a knight of Assyria, an Asian empire
that the Elizabethans associated with pillage and
robbery.
3. Alluding to the African king who marries a beggar
in the popular ballad "A Beggar and a King."
4. A line from the ballad "Robin Hood and the Jolly
Pinder of Wakefield."
5. That is, "the true Muses." Pistol conflates the

Muses of classical mythology with Mt. Helicon, part
of the Parnassus mountain range on which they
dwelt.
6. Then let Pistol appeal to the goddesses of revenge.
7. An obscene gesture, known as "the Spanish fig," in
which the thumb is put between the fore and middle
fingers in a way meant to be suggestive of genitalia
and sex acts. In the next line, Pistol refers to a "bragging" (lying) Spaniard who was "figged."
8. Load you (with honors) twice over; load you like a
gun twice over, with a pun on Pistol's name.

I know the young King is sick for me. Let us take any man's
horses: the laws of England are at my commandment. Blessed
125   are they that have been my friends, and woe to my lord
Chief Justice.

PISTOL   Let vultures vile seize on his lungs also!
"Where is the life that late I led?"⁹ say they;
Why, here it is! Welcome these pleasant days.   *Exeunt.*

5.4 (F 5.4)

Enter SINCKLO *and three or four Officers[, with*
HOSTESS *and* DOLL TEARSHEET].¹

HOSTESS   No, thou arrant knave! I would to God that I might
die, that I might have thee hanged. Thou hast drawn my
shoulder out of joint.

SINCKLO   The constables have delivered her over to me, and
5   she shall have whipping-cheer,² I warrant her. There hath
been a man or two killed about her.³

DOLL TEARSHEET   Nut-hook,⁴ nut-hook, you lie! Come on, I'll
tell thee what, thou damned tripe-visaged° rascal: an° the   *flabby-faced / if*
child I go with do miscarry,⁵ thou wert better thou hadst
10   struck thy mother, thou paper-faced° villain.   *white-faced*

HOSTESS   Oh, the Lord, that Sir John were come! I would
make this a bloody day to somebody. But I pray God the
fruit of her womb miscarry!

SINCKLO   If it do, you shall have a dozen of cushions again:
15   you have but eleven now.⁶ Come, I charge you both go with
me, for the man is dead that you and Pistol beat amongst
you.

DOLL TEARSHEET   I'll tell you what, you thin man in a censer:⁷
I will have you as soundly swinged° for this, you bluebottle⁸   *beaten*
20   rogue, you filthy famished correctioner! If you be not swinged,
I'll forswear half-kirtles.°   *give up wearing skirts*

SINCKLO   Come, come, you she-knight-errant, come.

HOSTESS   O God, that right should thus overcome might!
Well, of sufferance° comes ease.   *from suffering*

25 DOLL TEARSHEET   Come, you rogue, come; bring me to a
justice.

HOSTESS   I come, you starved bloodhound!

DOLL TEARSHEET   Goodman death, goodman bones!

HOSTESS   Thou atomy,° thou!   *(for "anatomy"; skeleton)*

30 DOLL TEARSHEET   Come, you thin thing! Come, you rascal!°   *lean deer*
SINCKLO   Very well.   [*Exeunt.*]

---

9. A line from a lost poem or ballad.
5.4 Location: A street in London.
1. TEXTUAL COMMENT John Sincklo or Sinclair, who
also appears in *3 Henry VI* 3.1 and in the Induction of
Taming of the Shrew, was an actor with the Chamberlain's Men. Shakespeare may have had Sincklo in mind
when he wrote this part, for this scene contains a number of unflattering references to an officer's skinniness.
Q is consistent in calling this character Sincklo. See
Digital Edition TC 9 (Quarto edited text).
2. That is, a whipping for her entertainment or supper ("cheer"). Beadles (the parish officers responsible

for enforcing laws) commonly meted out this punishment for prostitution.
3. Because of her; in her company.
4. A hook for pulling nuts from trees; the arresting
constable.
5. Women who were pregnant might escape the full
force of the law until after they gave birth.
6. Implying that Tearsheet feigns pregnancy by
carrying one of Quickly's pillows under her gown.
7. You figure of a man embossed on the lid of a pot
for burning incense.
8. Alluding to the blue tunics worn by beadles.

5.5 (F 5.5)

Enter [three] STREWERS *of rushes.*[1]

FIRST STREWER   More rushes, more rushes!

SECOND STREWER   The trumpets have sounded twice.

THIRD STREWER   'Twill be two o'clock ere they come from the
coronation. Dispatch, dispatch.   [*Exeunt.*]

Trumpets sound, and the KING *and his train pass over
the stage. After them enter* FALSTAFF, SHALLOW,
PISTOL, BARDOLPH, *and the* [PAGE].[2]

5   FALSTAFF   Stand here by me, Master Shallow; I will make the
King do you grace.° I will leer upon him as 'a comes by, and   *honor*
do but mark the countenance that he will give me.

PISTOL   God bless thy lungs, good knight.

FALSTAFF   Come here, Pistol; stand behind me. [*to* SHALLOW]

10   Oh, if I had had time to have made new liveries,[3] I would
have bestowed° the thousand pound I borrowed of you. But   *spent*
'tis no matter: this poor show doth better; this doth infer°   *imply*
the zeal I had to see him.

PISTOL   It doth so.

15   FALSTAFF   It shows my earnestness of affection.

PISTOL   It doth so.

FALSTAFF   My devotion—

PISTOL   It doth, it doth, it doth.

FALSTAFF   —As it were, to ride day and night, and not to delib-

20   erate, not to remember, not to have patience to shift me.°   *change my clothes*

SHALLOW   It is best, certain.

FALSTAFF   But to stand, stained with travel and sweating with
desire to see him, thinking of nothing else, putting all affairs
else in oblivion, as if there were nothing else to be done but

25   to see him.

PISTOL   'Tis *semper idem,* for *obsque hoc nihil est.*[4] 'Tis in every
part.

SHALLOW   'Tis so indeed.

PISTOL   My knight, I will inflame thy noble liver,

30   And make thee rage:
Thy Doll and Helen[5] of thy noble thoughts
Is in base durance° and contagious° prison,   *imprisonment / noxious*
Haled° thither   *Dragged*
By most mechanical° and dirty hand.   *menial*

35   Rouse up revenge from ebon den° with fell Alecto's snake,[6]   *dark cave (hell)*
For Doll is in. Pistol speaks naught but truth.

FALSTAFF   I will deliver her.
[*Trumpets sound.*]

PISTOL   There roared the sea, and trumpet clangor sounds.

5.5 Location: A public place near Westminster Abbey.
1. TEXTUAL COMMENT Floor coverings, here strewn
on the ground before the King's entrance. This SD
exemplifies the functional nature of many of Q's character names. Although modern editions tend to specify the number of functional characters like these,
Q's lack of specificity suggests that the company
made decisions based on the availability of actors. See
Digital Edition TC 10 (Quarto edited text).
2. In Q, Falstaff and his friends enter after "Trumpets
sound, and the King, and his train pass over the
stage." There are thus two royal processions: one
before Falstaff enters and one later in the scene (after
line 38). F contains only the latter procession.
3. Uniforms such as those worn by the retainers in a
noble household.
4. The first Latin motto, "ever the same," was associated with Queen Elizabeth; the second means "apart
from this, there is nothing."
5. The famously beautiful woman whose abduction
by Paris is said to have started the Trojan War.
6. Alecto was one of the Furies of classical mythology; her head was covered with snakes.

Enter the KING *and his train[, including* LORD
CHIEF JUSTICE*]*.

FALSTAFF   God save thy grace, King Hal, my royal Hal!

40 PISTOL   The heavens thee guard and keep, most royal imp° of   offspring
fame!

FALSTAFF   God save thee, my sweet boy!

KING   My lord Chief Justice, speak to that vain° man.   foolish

LORD CHIEF JUSTICE [*to* FALSTAFF]   Have you your wits? Know
you what 'tis you speak?

FALSTAFF   My King, my Jove,[7] I speak to thee, my heart!

45 KING   I know thee not, old man. Fall to thy prayers.
How ill white hairs becomes a fool and jester!
I have long dreamt of such a kind of man,
So surfeit-swelled,° so old, and so profane;   bloated from excess
But, being awaked, I do despise my dream.

50 Make less thy body hence,° and more thy grace.   henceforth
Leave gourmandizing.° Know the grave doth gape   gluttony
For thee thrice wider than for other men.
Reply not to me with a fool-born jest;
Presume not that I am the thing I was,

55 For God doth know, so shall the world perceive,
That I have turned away my former self.
So will I those that kept me company.
When thou dost hear I am as I have been,
Approach me, and thou shalt be as thou wast,

60 The tutor and the feeder of my riots.
Till then, I banish thee, on pain of death,
As I have done the rest of my misleaders,
Not to come near our person by ten mile.
For competence of life[8] I will allow you,

65 That lack of means enforce you not to evils;
And as we hear you do reform yourselves,
We will, according to your strengths and qualities,°   attainments
Give you advancement. [*to* LORD CHIEF JUSTICE] Be it your
charge, my lord,
To see performed the tenor of my word.

70 —Set on.   [*Exeunt* KING *and train.*]

FALSTAFF   Master Shallow, I owe you a thousand pound.

SHALLOW   Yea, marry, Sir John, which I beseech you to let me
have home with me.

FALSTAFF   That can hardly be, Master Shallow. Do not you

75 grieve at this. I shall be sent for in private to him. Look you,
he must seem thus to the world. Fear not your advance-
ments. I will be the man yet that shall make you great.

SHALLOW   I cannot perceive how, unless you give me your
doublet and stuff me out with straw. I beseech you, good Sir

80 John, let me have five hundred of my thousand.

FALSTAFF   Sir, I will be as good as my word. This that you heard
was but a color.°   pretense

SHALLOW   A color[9] that I fear you will die in, Sir John.

FALSTAFF   Fear no colors; go with me to dinner. —Come,

---

7. In classical mythology, the ruler of the gods.   9. Punning on "collar" as meaning "hangman's noose."
8. An allowance sufficient to supply life's necessities.

85 Lieutenant Pistol; come, Bardolph; I shall be sent for soon
at night.
    Enter [LORD CHIEF] JUSTICE *and* PRINCE JOHN[,
    with Officers].
LORD CHIEF JUSTICE [*to Officers*] Go, carry Sir John Falstaff
to the Fleet;°   *(a London prison)*
Take all his company along with him.
FALSTAFF My lord, my lord—
90 LORD CHIEF JUSTICE I cannot now speak; I will hear you soon.
—Take them away.
PISTOL *Si fortuna me tormenta, spero contenta.*[1]
      Exeunt [*all except* PRINCE JOHN *and*
        LORD CHIEF JUSTICE].
PRINCE JOHN I like this fair proceeding of the King's.
He hath intent his wonted° followers   *customary*
95 Shall all be very well provided for,
But all are banished till their conversations°   *conduct*
Appear more wise and modest to the world.
LORD CHIEF JUSTICE And so they are.
PRINCE JOHN The King hath called his parliament, my lord.
100 LORD CHIEF JUSTICE He hath.
PRINCE JOHN I will lay odds that ere this year expire
We bear our civil swords and native fire[2]
As far as France. I heard a bird so sing,
Whose music, to my thinking, pleased the King.
105 Come, will you hence?   [*Exeunt.*]

Epilogue (F Epilogue)
[*Enter* EPILOGUE.]
EPILOGUE First, my fear; then my curtsy;° last, my speech. *bow*
My fear is your displeasure, my curtsy my duty, and my
speech to beg your pardons. If you look for a good speech
now, you undo° me; for what I have to say is of mine own *ruin*
5 making, and what, indeed, I should say will, I doubt,° prove *fear*
mine own marring. But to the purpose, and so to the venture:° be it known to you, as it is very well, I was lately here *hazard*
in the end of a displeasing play to pray your patience for it
and to promise you a better. I meant indeed to pay you with
10 this, which, if like an ill venture[1] it come unluckily home, I
break,° and you, my gentle creditors, lose. Here I promised *go bankrupt*
you I would be, and here I commit my body to your mercies:
bate° me some, and I will pay you some and, as most debtors *excuse*
15 do, promise you infinitely. And so I kneel down before you,
but indeed to pray for the Queen.[2]
  If my tongue cannot entreat you to acquit me, will you
command me to use my legs? And yet that were but light
payment, to dance out of your debt. But a good conscience
will make any possible satisfaction, and so would I. All the

---

1. See note to 2.4.158.
2. Our swords used up to now in civil war and our
native zeal.
Epilogue
1. An unlucky commercial speculation, especially in
a cargo at sea.
2. The lines "and so I kneele downe before you; but

indeed, to pray for the Queene," conclude the Epilogue
in F but are inserted into Q here. This is one of several
indications that the Epilogue was rewritten and
expanded at some point, but that in Q these lines, with
their reference to the Queen, were not moved to their
proper place at the end of the speech.

20   gentlewomen here have forgiven me; if the gentlemen will
not, then the gentlemen do not agree with the gentlewomen,
which was never seen in such an assembly.

      One word more, I beseech you. If you be not too much
cloyed with fat meat, our humble author will continue the
25   story, with Sir John in it,[3] and make you merry with fair Katherine of France, where, for anything I know, Falstaff shall die
of a sweat,[4] unless already 'a° be killed with your hard opin-   he
ions. For Oldcastle[5] died martyr, and this is not the man. My
tongue is weary. When my legs are too, I will bid you good
30   night.   [*Exit.*]

3. In fact, Sir John Falstaff does not appear in *Henry*   5. Alluding to the fact that Sir John was originally
V, the play here anticipated.   called "Oldcastle" in *1 Henry IV*. See the Introduc-
4. A sweating sickness; the plague; a venereal disease.   tion to that play.

The Merchant of Venice

Jew. Jew. Jew. The word echoes through *The Merchant of Venice.* The play has generated controversy for centuries. Is it anti-Semitic? Does it criticize anti-Semitism? Does it merely represent anti-Semitism without either endorsement or condemnation? Are the Christians right to call Shylock, the Jewish moneylender, a "devil," an "inexorable dog"; or is he merely the understandably resentful victim of their bigotry? Does Portia, Shylock's antagonist in the courtroom, exemplify the best in womanly virtue, or is she a manipulative virago? These questions about character suggest others that might be phrased more generally. What are the obligations of majority cultures to minorities in their midst? Do universally shared human characteristics outweigh racial and religious differences, or are such differences decisive?

Perhaps these issues seem more pressing for us than they did for Shakespeare. He hardly could have predicted Nazi genocide or other savagely efficient modern forms of "ethnic cleansing." Nor could he have foreseen the opportunities and problems faced by multiracial societies centuries after his death. Nevertheless, by Shakespeare's time, the legacy of Jew hating in western Europe was already long and bitter. Depictions of fiendish Jews were routine in medieval and Renaissance drama; the villainous protagonist of Christopher Marlowe's *Jew of Malta,* a popular success in the early 1590s, was only the latest precedent. In 1594, shortly before Shakespeare wrote *The Merchant of Venice,* an outpouring of anti-Semitic outrage was triggered by the case of Roderigo Lopez, a Portuguese Jewish convert to Christianity accused of attempting to murder Queen Elizabeth.

Of course, the existence of anti-Semitism in sixteenth-century England says little about Shakespeare's own attitudes. He could have written *The Merchant of Venice* either to capitalize on or to criticize the prejudices of his society. Interestingly, Shakespeare had probably never encountered practicing Jews, since they had been forcibly expelled from England in the Middle Ages. And England was not alone in its intolerance of religious difference. In 1492, Spain banished all non-Christians. During the sixteenth century, northern Europe saw decades of bloody conflict between Catholics and Protestants, while much of southern Europe was in the grip of the Inquisition. The impulse behind these persecutions was the conviction that a stable society required a shared belief system. A community based on consensus can indeed be impressively cohesive. Its homogeneity, however, makes it impatient of those who do not share its assumptions. Moreover, by the 1590s, when Shakespeare wrote *The Merchant of Venice,* wars of religion all over Europe were making such consensus seem increasingly elusive—something obtainable, if at all, only at appalling human cost.

Possibly Venice seemed to Shakespeare to offer an alternative social prototype. Although it had no natural resources to speak of, it was the richest city in Renaissance Europe, located where the products of Asia could most conveniently be exchanged with those of western Europe. As a town of traders, Venice was full of foreigners: Turks, Jews, Arabs, Africans, Christians of various nationalities and denominations. By sixteenth-century standards, the city was unusually tolerant of diversity. This relative toleration was intimately linked with the city's wealth: its legal guarantees of fair treatment for all were designed to keep its markets running smoothly. Antonio tells Solanio:

> The Duke cannot deny the course of law,
> For the commodity that strangers have

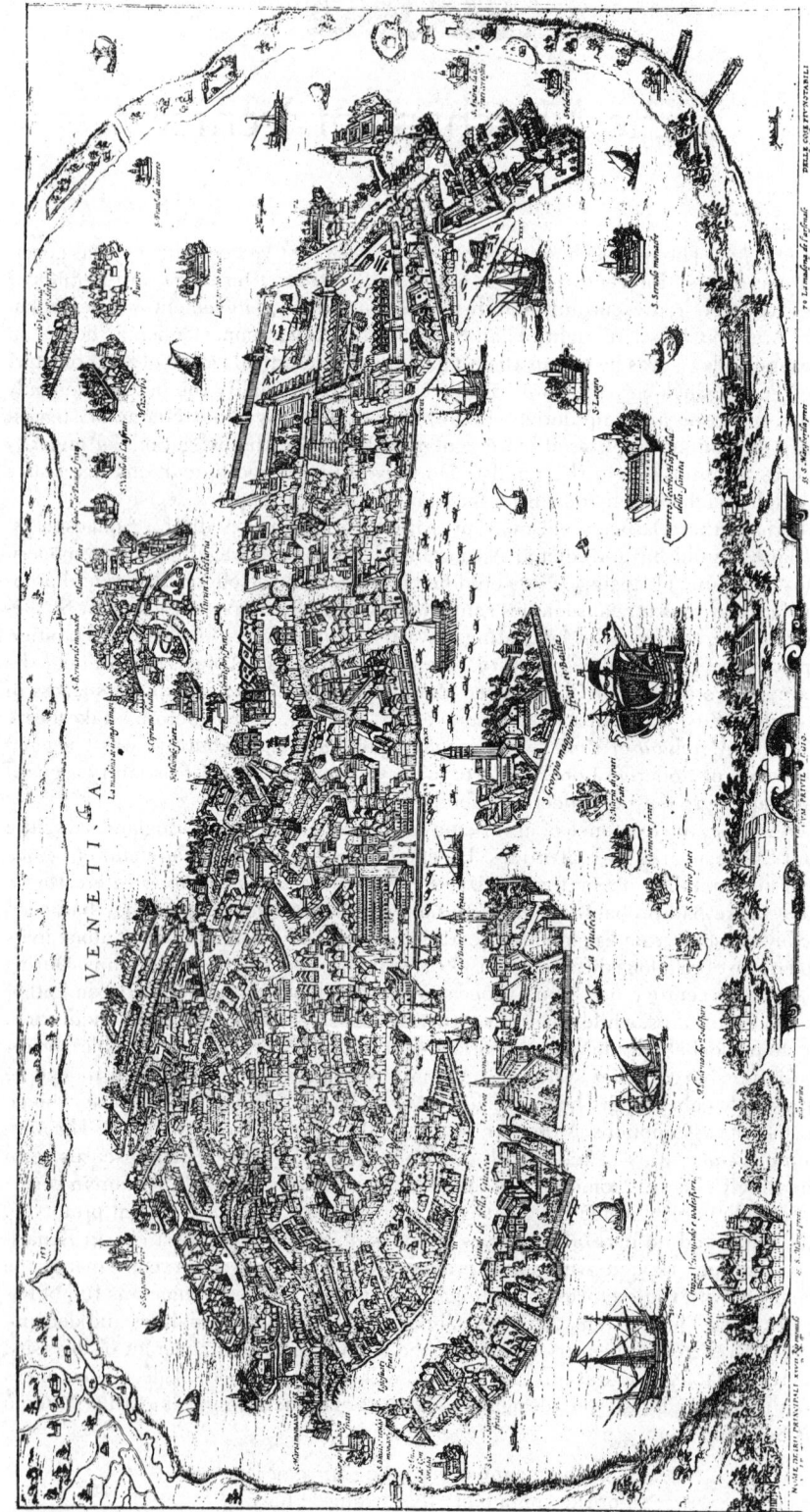

Prospect of Venice. From George Braun and Franz Hogenberg, *Civitates Orbis Terrarum* (1593).

> With us in Venice, if it be denied,
> Will much impeach the justice of the state,
> Since that the trade and profit of the city
> Consisteth of all nations.
>
> (3.3.26–31)

Shakespeare stresses, even exaggerates, this evenhanded cosmopolitanism. Historically, for instance, Venetian Jews were confined to a ghetto, gated and locked at night, but Shakespeare either did not know this fact or chose to ignore it. Venice thus provided Shakespeare with an example—perhaps the only example in sixteenth-century Europe—of a place where people with little in common culturally might coexist peacefully solely because it was materially expedient to do so. The laws of the marketplace seemed to have little to do with religion or nationality.

In *The Merchant of Venice,* the Christian gentlemen who populate the opening scenes associate friendship with generous, even reckless, expenditure. When Bassanio asks Antonio for a loan, Antonio rushes to supply him even though he does not have the money at hand. When Graziano asks a favor of Bassanio, Bassanio grants it before he even hears what it is. Later in the play, when Portia finds out that Antonio's life is forfeit because of 3,000 ducats, she instantly offers to pay twelve times that sum to redeem him. Not entirely surprisingly, Bassanio is an amiable spendthrift who does not fret too much about waste or loss:

> In my school days, when I had lost one shaft,
> I shot his fellow of the selfsame flight
> The selfsame way, with more advisèd wa'ch,
> To find the other forth; and by adventuring both,
> I oft found both.
>
> (1.1.140–44)

"Oft" is not "always." Sometimes, presumably, Bassanio lost both arrows. His temperamental similarity to his friend Antonio, the merchant-adventurer, is an optimism about gambling at long odds.

Such prodigal panache is undeniably attractive, especially in comedy, where generic conventions typically ensure that characters beat long odds. It generates, moreover, some of the most gorgeous poetry of the play, a language of risky munificence, in which phenomenal wealth is accumulated only to be splendidly dispersed. Salerio, for instance, describes a shipwreck as a beautiful squandering of luxury goods:

> dangerous rocks
> Which, touching but my gentle vessel's side,
> Would scatter all her spices on the stream,
> Enrobe the roaring waters with my silks.
>
> (1.1.31–34)

Likewise, Portia tells Bassanio:

> for myself alone
> I would not be ambitious in my wish
> To wish myself much better, yet for you
> I would be rebled twenty times myself—
> A thousand times more fair, ten thousand times
> More rich; that only to stand high in your account
> I might in virtues, beauties, livings, friends,
> Exceed account.
>
> (3.2.150–57)

Unfortunately, it soon becomes obvious that the Christians' generosity is not extended to everybody. The magnanimous, depressive Antonio proudly acknowledges kicking and spitting on Shylock. The charming Portia ridicules her foreign suitors and rejoices in the failure of her black suitor to choose the correct casket: "Let all of his complexion choose me so" (2.7.79). These people find it hard to deal with those different from themselves: their society is based as much on the exclusion of the alien as on the inclusion of the similar. The moral ambiguity of the Christians' outlook is captured in their fondness for the loaded word *kind,* which in Renaissance English meant not only "compassionate" but "similar," or "akin." People act benevolently toward those who are of the same *kind* as themselves.

Shylock's relation to the Venetian Christians exemplifies a different social mechanism. Unable to trust to love and generosity, Shylock relies instead on contractually enforceable promises and networks of mutual material need and self-interest. Shylock's emphasis on purely economic factors means that he does not think about money the way Antonio and Bassanio do. He tends not to spend but to conserve, not to expand but to defend, not to seek risk but to minimize it. When he imagines a disaster at sea, he envisions not a spectacular swirl of silk and spices, but a sordid scenario of thievery and nibbling rats.

Although Shylock identifies strongly with his "sacred nation," his "tribe," and although he relies on fellow Jews like Tubal, the play gives little sense of Jewish community. The play represents Shylock as an isolated figure, shunned by his daughter, abandoned by his servant. His calculating, loveless existence seems to result from the way he manages his property. Or perhaps isolation has made him cautious and selfish. Shylock has little motive to be generous with the Christians who despise him, and every reason to believe that he cannot depend on others to rescue him from misfortune.

The psychological and social contrasts between the Christians and Shylock reflect both class and religious differences. The Christians' magnificent improvidence is, in Shakespeare's time, a distinctively aristocratic trait. A true gentleman refuses to be too obviously concerned with monetary expenditure, especially where friends are concerned. He also feels socially obliged to display himself properly. Bassanio spends huge sums of borrowed money equipping himself for his trip to Belmont to woo Portia, even though all he technically need do is arrive alone and select the correct casket. Coming to Portia unattended or in shabby clothes is unthinkable even though (or perhaps because) "all the wealth I had," as Bassanio freely admits, "ran in my veins" (3.2.252–53). By contrast Shylock, despite his evident wealth, is obviously no gentleman. He locks up his possessions, regrets how much his servant eats, fumes over the money he spends searching for his missing daughter.

"Jews." From Jost Amman, *The Panoplia* (1568).

At the same time, the opposition between the Christians and Shylock seems rooted in religious disparities. Judaism in the play is presented not in its actual complexity but as a sixteenth-century Christian like Shakespeare would have construed it, as a set of dramatically vivid contrasts with Christian norms. The law of Moses, as set down in Deuteronomy and Leviticus, specifies numerous aspects of the observant Jew's life—what to eat and wear, how to worship, how to conduct business, how to punish crimes. The Mosaic code places a high value upon justice and emphasizes the importance of adhering to the letter of the law. Shylock's Judaism reveals itself not merely in his distinctive dress and his avoidance of pork, but in his trust of literal meanings, his respect for material possessions and observable facts, his expectation that contracts will be rigorously enforced.

The typical Christian outlook is different. Christians obtain divine approval not by wearing certain garments, avoiding particular foods, or circumcising their boys, but by believing in Christ's power to save them. The central virtues in this religious system are not justice and scrupulous compliance with the law but charity and mercy, and a willingness to believe what seems incredible. In the terms Shakespeare provides in *The Merchant of Venice*, the Christian demeanor is entrepreneurial, even reckless, the spiritual equivalent of what Antonio does with his ships or Bassanio does with the money he borrows from his friend. "Give up everything you have and follow me," Jesus tells his would-be follower, advice echoed in the inscription on the lead casket: "Who chooseth me must give and hazard all he hath" (2.7.16). Like the word *kind*, the similarly complex word *gentle* is used repeatedly in the play to describe this distinctive set of traits: the word simultaneously refers to considerate behavior, to aristocratic family background, and to "gentile," or Christian, religious convictions.

Young man in Venice. From Cesare Vecellio, *De gli habiti antichi et moderni* (1590).

As the play proceeds, it modifies somewhat these initially vivid contrasts between Christian and Jew by showing the sharp contrasts between what the characters claim to be and how they actually behave. For instance, Shylock pretends that he thinks of people in purely material, economic terms. Antonio may treat him badly, but when he applies for a loan, Shyock calls him "a good man." "[M]y meaning in saying he is a good man is to have you understand me that he is sufficient" (1.3.13–15): in other words, Antonio's wealth makes him a good credit risk. Within a few lines, however, Shylock informs us in an aside that he hates Antonio and wants revenge upon him. After Jessica's flight, Solanio claims that Shylock has been seen running through the streets crying, "O my ducats, O my daughter! . . . [M]y ducats, and my daughter!" (2.8.15ff). It is impossible to know how accurate this rumor might be: the equation of ducats and daughter is exactly what Christians expect of the moneygrubbing Shylock. But when Shylock finally appears onstage, he says nothing of the kind. When Tubal tells him that Jessica has exchanged a turquoise ring for a monkey, Shylock replies: "Out upon her; thou torturest me, Tubal! It was my turquoise; I had it of Leah when I was a bachelor. I would not have given it for a wilderness of monkeys" (3.1.100–102). He insists, in other words, upon the sentimental value of the turquoise ring, not upon its monetary value. His grief over his daughter's defection, and her insensitivity to his relation with her dead mother, much exceeds his financial loss. Likewise in the courtroom, Shylock is remarkable not for his businesslike prudence but for his refusal to be swayed by monetary appeals. There is something in the quality of his oppression that he refuses to convert into a payoff.

The Christians are also more complicated than they profess to be. Their faith teaches that all human beings are precious and demands that they love not only neighbors but even enemies. However, only some persons elicit a humane response, while others are disregarded or treated as nonhuman. When Salerio and Solanio ridicule Shylock, he protests: "Hath not a Jew eyes? Hath not a Jew hands, organs, dimensions, senses, affections, passions—fed with the same food, hurt with the same weapons, subject to the same diseases, healed by the same means, warmed and cooled by the same winter and summer as a Christian is?" (3.1.49–53). Shylock asserts that a common human experience of embodiment ought to override considerations of religious or racial difference. These lines are among the most memorable in the play, but the argument does not follow from the position Shylock has taken earlier. Rather, it is effective because it exposes Christian hypocrisy. Similarly, in the trial scene, Shylock points out that the Christian practice of slavery plainly treats some human beings as mere property. "You have among you many a purchased slave, / Wh   like your asses and your dogs and mules / You use in abject and in slavish parts Because you bought them" (4.1.90–93). The Christians' creed mandates universal love, but they fail to behave in accord with their precepts.

These inconsistencies haunt the play's friendships and marriages. Marriage is a hybrid social relation: obviously associated with love and procreation, it is simultaneously a property relation, involving the economic alliance of individuals and families. Bassanio's courtship of Portia is doubly motivated: he loves her, and he needs her money. The language of his attraction, even at its most generous and disinterested, is full of the metaphors of commerce and exchange. And although Antonio protests against thinking of friendship purely as an economic transaction, it is not difficult to construe his self-sacrificing generosity as an attempt to buy Bassanio's love. So although the Christians attempt to differentiate spiritual values from economic ones, those values continually turn out to be intimately intertwined.

The casket test directly confronts this problem. The failures of Morocco and Aragon demonstrate that it is possible to find a plausible reason for choosing any one of the three caskets. But when Bassanio makes his choice, we see how the test works: it can be solved only by one who views its puzzles from the correct point of view. Bassanio must abstract from his particular relation with Portia to a general distinction between "ornament" and "truth":

> Look on beauty,
> And you shall see 'tis purchased by the weight,
> Which therein works a miracle in nature,
> Making them lightest that wear most of it.
> (3.2.88–91)

Surely Bassanio does not believe that because Portia is lovely, she must be unchaste. Instead, his upbringing as a Christian gentleman has acquainted him with a particular frame of mind that prefers invisible over visible things, spirit over body, metaphor over literal meaning. The same cultural background makes him willing to take chances: to "hazard all he hath" on the unprepossessing lead casket. Because every suitor gets the same chance, the casket test seems to be fair; in fact, it is rather like those "objective" intelligence tests that, in subtle or not-so-subtle ways, reward the belief systems of dominant groups while stigmatizing outsiders. In this case, the person best fitted to be Portia's husband is one who, by Christian standards, knows the limitations and right use of wealth. This knowledge enables him to value characteristics in his wife—virtue, intelligence, and beauty—that make her precious in more than monetary ways.

One of the surprises of the casket test is that it takes place at all. Portia's obedience to her dead father's apparently irrational plans for her is remarkable in comedy, for comic heroines mo   often, like Jessica, defy their fathers than conscientiously follow their orders. Perhaps Portia could be seen as synthesizing the best of Jewish and Christian characteristics; obeying the letter of a wise father's law, even while cultivating the spiritual virtues of love and generosity. Perhaps, then, Jewish and Christian outlooks are not *necessarily* in conflict (any more than there is a necessary conflict in being, as Portia is, both rich and beautiful). Certainly Portia's respect for the letter of the law, combined with her willingness to go beyond that letter, makes her the only character who can effectively confront Shylock in the trial scene.

When she disguises herself as a young lawyer, Portia becomes one of many Shakespearean comic heroines to assume male attire. The power that she achieves by her transvestism signals an interesting development in Shakespeare's treatment of the relations between men and women. Earlier plays often differentiate sharply between the sexes: between the male political domain and the female domestic domain in *Richard II*, between the male streetcorner and the female bedchamber in *Romeo and Juliet*. In *The Merchant of Venice* and the come dies Shakespeare wrote immediately thereafter, women seem to possess a new liberty of action. Their freedom coincides with another new development in Shakespearean comedy, the presence of a scapegoat character—someone like Shylock, who cannot be assimilated into the comic society at the end of the play. Perhaps when the most serious social threats seem to be posed by outsiders, there is more freedom for women within the "in" group: the crucial bifurcation is no longer between male and female but between "us" and "them."

Portia's legal strategy is complex, and thus the trial has several stages. At first, she both offers and recommends generosity:

> Therefore, Jew,
> Though justice be thy plea, consider this—
> That in the course of justice none of us
> Should see salvation. We do pray for mercy,
> And that same prayer doth teach us all to render
> The deeds of mercy.
>
> (4.1.195–200)

Not surprisingly, Shylock is deaf to this eloquence. Portia's argument is based on the distinctively Christian premise that salvation is an undeserved gift. She derives her authority from the Lord's Prayer: "forgive us our trespasses as we forgive those who trespass against us." But Shylock doesn't accept, or even perhaps know the existence of, a prayer that supposedly "teaches us all." Portia's plea for tolerance and compassion might seem to rest on universal premises, but in fact Portia's "we" who "pray for mercy" neatly excludes the Jew.

The judgment upon Shylock at the end of the trial has disturbed many critics and audiences. After the Christians win the case—not only saving Antonio's life but also keeping the 3,000 ducats Shylock had lent Bassanio—Portia seems to take exactly the revenge she has up to now deplored. Her legal ground is provided by a previously unmentioned law against any alien who plots the death of a Venetian citizen. The law in which Shylock trusted, because it seemed to provide a refuge from prejudice, turns out to have prejudice inscribed within it from the start. In this respect, it resembles the casket test—everybody seems to get the same chance, but in fact the test blatantly favors the insider.

Portia and the Duke apparently regard the dismissal of Shylock as merciful; his *life* is preserved, although half or all of his mere money is taken away. Portia's sentence forces Shylock to behave as a Christian citizen and father should: to worship in a Christian church, to grant money to his daughter, to recognize the difference between spiritual and economic well-being. Eschewing lethal force, the Duke demands that Shylock acquiesce in his punishment: "I am content" (4.1.392), Shylock says at last. But what else can he say? The coercive inclusion of Shylock in the Christian community seems all the more violent because it pretends to renounce coercion. If designating people outcasts is bad, compelling them to participate in a society they find intolerable may be even worse.

The Merchant of Venice thus hovers on the edge of tragedy. Shylock's ferocious negativity is poised against, and arguably elicited by, the Christians' hypocritical refusal to admit the way their spiritual lives depend on material prosperity. The presence of the scapegoated Jew lays bare the mechanisms by which Venetian society works. Shylock can be reviled and dismissed, but the possibilities that he represents do not simply vanish when he flees the courtroom. Thus the moral disquiet the play raises among directors, readers, and audiences: Christian and Jewish perspectives seem mutually invalidating, and both finally inadequate.

Shakespeare suggests the stubbornness of the problems broached by the play in the way he structures the last act. Most Shakespeare comedies return to the city or the court at the end, or at least look forward to that return; but in The Merchant of Venice, the play ends at Belmont, the nostalgically depicted, magically copious "green world." It is as if the formal demand for comic closure conflicts with Shakespeare's awareness that no neat resolution of Venice's problems is forthcoming.

Indeed, some muted version of those problems pursues the Christians even to Portia's estate. The act begins with the banter between the newlyweds Jessica and Lorenzo, who have stayed behind at Belmont in Portia's absence. It is a bit ominous that all the love stories they recall are unhappy ones. Still, the couple's affectionate teasing makes the scene a welcome change from what has immediately preceded it. Showing Jessica and Lorenzo in witty conversation minutes after the brutal expulsion of Shylock seems an attempt to confine the punitive energies of the play to the usurer alone. The scene offers an alternative vision of interaction between racial groups, one that involves love rather than hatred. Of course, this is a vision not of mutual tolerance but of assimilation: Jessica's marriage to a Christian has exempted her from Shylock's fate. In 5.1 Lorenzo describes to his wife the "music of the spheres"—a perfect heavenly harmony made inaudible by the corruption of this life. Perhaps, analogously, the Christians' failure lies not in the nature of their ideals, but in the imperfect realization of those ideals in the everyday world. The inevitable dissonance between the mundane and the ideal world does not necessarily, however, simply drain the ideal of its meaning.

The moral dilemmas posed by high but perhaps unrealizable ideals come under scrutiny yet again in the ring trick with which the play ends. In The Merchant of Venice, as in many of Shakespeare's plays, courtship and marriage coexist with, and are potentially or actually in competition with, intense same-sex friendships. In the trial scene, just before, it seems, Shylock will kill Antonio, Bassanio makes a desperate declaration:

> Antonio, I am married to a wife
> Which is as dear to me as life itself;
> But life itself, my wife, and all the world
> Are not with me esteemed above thy life.
> I would lose all—ay, sacrifice them all
> Here to this devil—to deliver you.
>
> (4.1.280–85)

To which Portia, disguised as Balthazar, responds in an acid aside, "Your wife would give you little thanks for that / If she were by to hear you make the offer" (286–87). After the conclusion of the trial, Portia-as-Balthazar asks Bassanio for his wedding ring as payment for legal services. This request presents Bassanio with a harder problem than Shylock had. Bassanio can imagine breaking a written contract, but not denying the request of an ally to whom he's indebted. By giving the ring to

Balthazar, Bassanio demonstrates both that his loyalty to Antonio still outweighs his allegiance to Portia and that he has trouble governing his generous impulses. Portia's trick teaches Bassanio, and Antonio as well, that the marital relationship involves unique responsibilities and that those responsibilities impose a limit on reckless munificence. At play's end, Antonio is once again "standing surety" for Bassanio, this time to Portia rather than to Shylock, promising to help sustain rather than interfere with his friend's marriage vows.

In this moment, as happens again and again in *The Merchant of Venice,* oppositions between potentially tragic alternatives miraculously dissolve—between being rich and being virtuous, marrying for money and marrying for love, following paternal orders and making one's own choice, enforcing the letter of the law and enforcing its spirit, remaining faithful to one's wife and loving one's male friend. Balthazar turns out to have been Portia, Bassanio has given his ring to its original owner, and all seems to be well. But by setting the play's last act in a magical world of trust and abundance, Shakespeare stresses the artifice involved in his resolution. Even as this beautiful, troubling play comes to a close, it pointedly emphasizes the distance between the final act's charmed fictional world and the intransigent real one.

KATHARINE EISAMAN MAUS

SELECTED BIBLIOGRAPHY

Adelman, Janet. *Blood Relations: Christian and Jew in "The Merchant of Venice."* Chicago: U of Chicago P, 2008. Offers the most complete account of the significance of the religious conflicts in the play, focusing upon the different ways Jews and Christians understand the same biblical stories.

Bailey, Amanda. "Shylock and the Slaves: Owing and Owning in *The Merchant of Venice.*" *Shakespeare Quarterly* 62 (2011): 1–24. Considers the "pound of flesh" bargain in the context of actual procedures for punishing delinquent debtors in early modern England.

Barber, C. L. "The Merchants and the Jew of Venice: Wealth's Communion and an Intruder." *Shakespeare's Festive Comedy: A Study of Dramatic Form and Its Relation to Social Custom.* Princeton, NJ: Princeton UP, 1959. Looks at the Christians' opulent festivity as challenged by Shylock's fiercely reductive attitude toward money.

Burckhardt, Sigurd. "*The Merchant of Venice:* The Gentle Bond." *Shakespearean Meanings.* Princeton, NJ: Princeton UP, 1968. 206–89. Examines the importance of various kinds of bonds in *The Merchant of Venice.*

Cohen, Walter. "*The Merchant of Venice* and the Possibilities of Historical Criticism." *English Literary History* 49 (1982): 765–89. Explores the play's theatrical artifice as reflecting economic conflicts in early modern Europe.

Danson, Lawrence. *The Harmonies of "The Merchant of Venice."* New Haven, CT: Yale UP, 1978. Describes the play's conflicts in detail and argues for their satisfactory resolution.

Engle, Lars. "Money and Moral Luck in *The Merchant of Venice.*" *Shakespearean Pragmatism: Market of His Time.* Chicago: U of Chicago P, 1993. 77–106. Reads *The Merchant of Venice* through the lens of late twentieth-century ethical philosophy.

Gross, Kenneth. *Shylock Is Shakespeare.* Chicago: U of Chicago P, 2006. Analyzes Shakespeare's personal connection to Shylock.

Lewalski, Barbara. "Biblical Allusion and Allegory in *The Merchant of Venice.*" *Shakespeare Quarterly* 13 (1962): 327–43. Looks at Shakespeare's use of biblical typology.

Lupton, Julia Reinhard. "Merchants of Venice, Circles of Citizenship." *Citizen-Saints: Shakespeare and Political Theology.* Chicago: U of Chicago P, 2005. 75–101. Explores Judaism and citizenship in early modern Venice.

Maus, Katharine Eisaman. *Being and Having in Shakespeare*. Oxford: Oxford UP, 2013. Chapters 3 and 4. Traces the flow of wealth in the play's marriages, friendships, and business relationships.

Newman, Karen. "Portia's Ring: Unruly Women and the Structure of Exchange in *The Merchant of Venice*." *Shakespeare Quarterly* 38 (1987): 19–33. Looks at how Portia, as gift-giver, occupies a position of power usually coded as masculine.

Shapiro, James. *Shakespeare and the Jews*. New York: Columbia UP, 1996. Examines anti-Semitism in Shakespeare's time.

Shell, Marc. "'The Wether and the Ewe': Verbal Usury in *The Merchant of Venice*." *Kenyon Review* 1.4 (1979): 65–92. Analyzes exchange and redemption in *The Merchant of Venice*, focusing particularly on Shylock's story of Laban and Jacob.

Wilson, Luke. "Drama and Marine Insurance in Shakespeare's London." *The Law in Shakespeare*. Ed. Constance Jordan and Karen Cunningham. London: Palgrave Macmillan, 2007. 127–42. Looks at some of the legal complexities of the play in the context of Shakespeare's time.

FILMS

The Merchant of Venice. 1973. Dir. John Sichel. UK. 131 min. Laurence Olivier as Shylock.

The Merchant of Venice. 1980. Dir. Jack Gold. UK. 157 min. Textually faithful but stilted. Gemma Jones is a chilly, calculating Portia.

The Merchant of Venice. 2001. Dir. Trevor Nunn. UK. 141 min. The film version of an acclaimed Royal National Theatre production, set in Europe between the world wars. Vividly acted, with many interesting directorial choices. Henry Goodman's Shylock is especially memorable.

The Merchant of Venice. 2004. Dir. Michael Radford. UK. 131 min. Al Pacino as Shylock, Lynn Collins as Portia. Sumptuous period costumes and sets. This production emphasizes the disquieting aspects of the play, not only the Venetians' anti-Semitism but the struggle between Portia and Antonio over Bassanio's allegiance.

TEXTUAL INTRODUCTION

The first known edition of *The Merchant of Venice* was published in 1600 and called on its title page, rather flamboyantly, "The most excellent / Historie of the *Merchant* / *of Venice*. / With the extreame crueltie of *Shylocke* the Iewe / towards the sayd Merchant, in cutting a iust pound / of his flesh: and the obtayning of *Portia* / by the choyce of three / chests. / *As it hath beene diuers times acted by the Lord* / *Chamberlaine his Servants*." This edition, known as the First Quarto or Q1, is remarkably well printed by the standards of the time and is used as the textual basis of most modern editions of the play, including this one. The next quarto edition that we know of, Q2, appeared in 1619 as one of the so-called "Pavier quartos"—a collection of nine Shakespeare plays published for Thomas Pavier by William Jaggard, who would go on to publish the Shakespeare First Folio in 1623. The date on Q2's title page was, however, spurious: it claimed to have been produced in 1600—the same year as Q1. Perhaps Jaggard was trying to get around the Stationers' Company restrictions in publishing Q2 with its fictitious date; in any case, he published the play again in the Shakespeare First Folio (F) four years later. Q2 and F are not significantly better printed than Q1, though they do correct a few Q1 misprints and supply a few additional stage directions. As is common among Shakespeare quartos, neither Q1 nor Q2 contains act and scene divisions. F helpfully divides the play into acts; the scene divisions in this edition are derived from later editorial tradition, which assumed that a scene ended when the stage was cleared.

The most interesting textual issue in relation to *The Merchant of Venice* is the vexed matter of speech prefixes. In Shakespeare's time, quarto playtexts were typically printed without cast lists, and there was no convention requiring that a speech prefix remain constant through the course of the play. As a result we sometimes experience confusion about who is speaking. Take the vexed matter of Antonio and Bassanio's friends whose names begin with "S." How many are there and what are their names? "*Salerio*," "*Salanio*," "*Solanio*," "*Salarino*," "*Salaryno*," "*Salario*," "*Sal.*," "*Sol.*," "*Sola.*," "*Sala.*"—all of these forms occur in the First Quarto version, and they are by no means used consistently. At some points, one of these seemingly interchangeable characters is indicated in the stage directions as entering, but the actual speech prefixes that follow name another. A case can be made for three characters rather than two—Salerio, Solanio, and Salarino—but even then, they are not differentiated in the quarto with anything approaching consistency. This edition follows most previous editions in boiling all the "S" names down to two: Salerio and Solanio.

A slightly different problem exists for Lancelet the clown, whose name in most editions of the play has been Launcelot or Lancelot. In stage directions and speech prefixes to Q1, Q2, and F, he is variously called "*Lancelet*" or "*Clown*," but he is never called "Launcelot" or "Lancelot." *The Norton Shakespeare* restores what we believe is his original name, which can mean "little lance" or "little knife"—an interesting choice of name in a play that centers on Shylock's knife.

The name of Shylock the Jew is even more problematic. Sometimes in Q1 prefixes he is "*Shylock*" and sometimes he is "*Jew*." At one point in act 4, Portia addresses him, "Is your name Shylock?" and he answers, "Shylock is my name," but the speech prefix before this answer calls him "*Jew*." The speech prefix "*Jew*" is especially prevalent at points in the play in which the action resonates with traditional anti-Semitic stereotypes (see Digital Edition TC 3, 1.3.26). By looking in the Digital Edition at each textual variant associated with Shylock's name, users of *The Norton Shakespeare* will be able to trace the substitutions of "*Jew*" for "*Shylock*" over the course of the play. Q2 switches several of the "*Jew*" prefixes back to "*Shylock*" or "*Shy.*," but in F all of these follow Q1 and use "*Jew*." Like so many other textual variants in Shakespeare, this one remains mysterious in terms of its possible motivation: it could go back to Shakespeare's own manuscript, or have been introduced during the copying or printing of the play. Some bibliographers believe that the original speech prefix was "*Jew*" throughout, and that the speech prefix "*Shylock*" was only introduced because of type shortages in the printing house. But that hypothesis seems unlikely: the argument depends on assumptions about the way early texts were printed that are not supported by subsequent research on the way printing jobs were typically managed in a printing house. Here, as so often in Shakespeare, we view the lost "original" through so many veils of mediation that the author's intentions cannot reliably be recovered.

LEAH S. MARCUS

PERFORMANCE NOTE

With its controversial subjects, uncertain genre, and multiple subplots, *The Merchant of Venice* presents unique challenges to theater companies that undertake to perform it. Perhaps foremost among these challenges is deciding just how much of the play to perform. *Merchant* is stocked with robust roles, each with unsavory elements, so what is kept or cut can decisively influence which story is told and which character emerges at its center. One production may work to sanitize the Venetians and heighten Shylock's savagery, steering the play toward a less adulterated comic resolution; another may emphasize the Christians' cruelty in order to intensify Shylock's tragic situation, thus overshadowing the comic ending in Belmont. Both can work, and that neither choice wholly occludes aspects of the other is one of the play's strengths and a source of tension and engagement for audiences. In orchestrating the balance between comic and tragic elements, directors also must decide on issues such as the centrality of Antonio, whose sadness is never explicitly revisited, and whether to present Shylock as eager to assimilate, mirroring Antonio's bearing and behavior, or to emphasize his foreignness and isolation.

Each of the play's first six scenes initiates a new subplot featuring a new character. *Merchant* therefore requires an unusually strong and versatile ensemble, one that can maintain interest while plot threads and protagonists vie for primacy. Similar vying is apparent within the characters too. Shylock and Antonio are tender one moment and vicious the next. Portia must be charming even in condescension, as winning when seeking mercy as she is severe when showing none. These characters thrive on ambivalences, so a further challenge in production is to reconcile extremes credibly, yet without dulling their edges. The characterizations of lesser roles are relevant too. Lancelet can either sport with or torment Jessica about her conversion in 3.5; Morocco can invite mockery or move audiences to sympathize with the plights of foreigners. And Salerio and Solanio stand in for Venetians at large, so how they parody Shylock and respond to his complaints will affect the audience's judgment of its comic heroes, and investment in its tragic one.

BRETT GAMBOA

The Comical History of the Merchant of Venice

[THE PERSONS OF THE PLAY

At Venice:
DUKE of Venice
ANTONIO, a merchant of Venice
BASSANIO, friend to Antonio and suitor to Portia
LORENZO ⎫
GRAZIANO ⎪
SALERIO ⎬ friends to Antonio and Bassanio
SOLANIO ⎭
SERVINGMAN to Antonio
LEONARDO, servant to Bassanio
SHYLOCK, a Jewish moneylender
JESSICA, daughter to Shylock
TUBAL, another Jew
LANCELET, a clown, servant to Shylock and then to Bassanio
GOBBO, father to Lancelet
Magnificoes of Venice
Jailer

At Belmont:
PORTIA, an heiress
NERISSA, attending on Portia
BALTHAZAR ⎫
MESSENGER ⎪
MUSICIANS ⎬ servants to Portia
STEFANO ⎪
Servitor ⎭
Prince of MOROCCO ⎫
Prince of ARAGON ⎬ suitors to Portia]

1.1

Enter ANTONIO, SALERIO, *and* SOLANIO.[1]

ANTONIO In sooth° I know not why I am so sad.   *truth*
  It wearies me, you say it wearies you,
  But how I caught it, found it, or came by it,
  What stuff 'tis made of, whereof it is born,
5   I am to learn;°   *have yet to discover*
  And such a want-wit° sadness makes of me   *dullard*
  That I have much ado to know myself.
SALERIO Your mind is tossing on the ocean,
  There where your argosies° with portly° sail   *merchant ships / stately*
10   Like signors° and rich burghers on the flood   *lords*
  Or, as it were, the pageants[2] of the sea,

1.1 Location: Venice.
1. TEXTUAL COMMENT Stage directions and speech-prefix abbreviations in early editions of *Merchant* leave it unclear whether there are two or three nearly interchangeable friends whose names all begin with "S." See Digital Edition TC 1.
2. Movable stages used by itinerant actors or in parades.

Do over-peer° the petty traffickers   *tower over*
That curtsy³ to them, do them reverence,
As they fly by them with their woven wings.

15 SOLANIO Believe me, sir, had I such venture° forth, *a risky undertaking*
The better part of my affections would
Be with my hopes abroad. I should be still°   *always*
Plucking the grass to know where sits the wind,
Peering in maps for ports and piers and roads,°   *open harbors*
20 And every object that might make me fear
Misfortune to my ventures, out of doubt,
Would make me sad.

SALERIO   My wind cooling my broth
Would blow me to an ague° when I thought   *make me shiver*
What harm a wind too great might do at sea.
25 I should not see the sandy hourglass run
But I should think of shallows and of flats°   *shoals*
And see my wealthy Andrew⁴ dock in sand,
Vailing her high top° lower than her ribs *Lowering her topmast*
To kiss her burial.° Should I go to church   *burial place*
30 And see the holy edifice of stone
And not bethink me straight° of dangerous rocks *immediately think*
Which, touching but my gentle vessel's side,
Would scatter all her spices on the stream,
Enrobe the roaring waters with my silks,
35 And, in a word, but even now° worth this° *moments ago / so much*
And now worth nothing? Shall I have the thought
To think on this, and shall I lack the thought
That such a thing bechanced° would make me sad? *having occurred*
But tell not me; I know Antonio
40 Is sad to think upon his merchandise.

ANTONIO Believe me, no. I thank my fortune for it:
My ventures are not in one bottom° trusted,   *ship*
Nor to one place,° nor is my whole estate   *destination*
Upon the fortune of this present year;
45 Therefore my merchandise makes not sad.

SOLANIO Why, then, you are in love.

ANTONIO   Fie, fie!

SOLANIO Not in love neither? Then let us say you are sad
Because you are not merry; and 'twere as easy
For you to laugh and leap and say you are merry
50 Because you are not sad. Now, by two-headed Janus,⁵
Nature hath framed strange fellows in her time:
Some that will evermore peep through their eyes⁶
And laugh like parrots° at a bagpiper,⁷ *(screeching loudly)*
And other of such vinegar aspect°   *sour looks*
55 That they'll not show their teeth in way of smile
Though Nestor⁸ swear the jest be laughable.

    Enter BASSANIO, LORENZO, *and* GRAZIANO.

Here comes Bassanio, your most noble kinsman,
Graziano, and Lorenzo. Fare ye well!

---

3. By bobbing on the waves or by lowering their flags in salute.
4. Name of a Spanish galleon captured by the English at Cádiz in 1596.
5. Roman god with faces looking both forward and backward.
6. Eyes almost shut by violent laughter.
7. Whose music was considered woeful.
8. Sober, elderly Greek hero in *The Iliad*.

We leave you now with better company.[9]

60   SALERIO   I would have stayed till I had made you merry
    If worthier friends had not prevented me.
  ANTONIO   Your worth is very dear in my regard.
    I take it your own business calls on you,
    And you embrace th'occasion to depart.
65   SALERIO   Good morrow, my good lords.
  BASSANIO   Good signors both, when shall we laugh?°   *make merry together*
    Say, when?
    You grow exceeding strange!° Must it be so?   *reserved*
  SALERIO   We'll make our leisures to attend on° yours.   *suit*

                Exeunt SALERIO *and* SOLANIO.

  LORENZO   My lord Bassanio, since you have found Antonio,
70   We two will leave you; but at dinnertime
    I pray you have in mind where we must meet.
  BASSANIO   I will not fail you.
  GRAZIANO   You look not well, Signor Antonio.
    You have too much respect upon the world:°   *anxiety about business*
75   They lose it that do buy it with much care.
    Believe me, you are marvelously changed.
  ANTONIO   I hold the world but as the world, Graziano—
    A stage where every man must play a part
    And mine a sad one.
  GRAZIANO   Let me play the fool—
80   With mirth and laughter let old[1] wrinkles come,
    And let my liver[2] rather heat with wine
    Than my heart cool with mortifying[3] groans.
    Why should a man whose blood is warm within
    Sit like his grandsire cut in alabaster,[4]
85   Sleep when he wakes, and creep into the jaundice[5]
    By being peevish? I tell thee what, Antonio,
    I love thee, and 'tis my love that speaks:
    There are a sort of men whose visages
    Do cream and mantle[6] like a standing° pond,   *stagnant*
90   And do a willful stillness entertain
    With purpose to be dressed in an opinion°   *a reputation*
    Of wisdom, gravity, profound conceit—°   *judgment*
    As who should say, "I am Sir Oracle,
    And when I ope my lips let no dog bark."
95   O my Antonio, I do know of these
    That therefore only are reputed wise
    For saying nothing, when I am very sure
    If they should speak would almost damn those ears
    Which, hearing them, would call their brothers fools.[7]
100   I'll tell thee more of this another time.
    But fish not with this melancholy bait
    For this fool gudgeon,° this opinion.   *tiny, easily caught fish*

---

9. PERFORMANCE COMMENT The play never explicitly revisits the source of Antonio's sadness. In productions, directors often imply that it results from an unrequited romantic attachment to Bassanio. See Digital Edition PC 1.

1. Accompanying old age; abundant.

2. The liver was considered the seat of passion.

3. Deadly (groans were believed to drain blood from the heart).

4. Stone from which tomb effigies were carved.

5. Thought to result from too much yellow bile, a bodily substance associated with irritability.

6. *cream and mantle:* grow a scum; that is, assume a fixed countenance.

7. *would . . . fools:* alluding to Matthew 5:22: "And whosoever shall say to his brother . . . , fool, shall be in danger of hellfire."

Come, good Lorenzo. [to ANTONIO and BASSANIO] Fare ye well
    awhile.
I'll end my exhortation after dinner.
105 LORENZO Well, we will leave you then till dinnertime.
    I must be one of these same dumb° wise men,   *mute*
    For Graziano never lets me speak.
    GRAZIANO Well, keep me company but two years more—
    Thou shalt not know the sound of thine own tongue!
110 ANTONIO Fare you well! I'll grow a talker for this gear.[8]
    GRAZIANO Thanks i'faith, for silence is only commendable
    In a neat's° tongue dried and a maid not vendible.[9]   *an ox's*
               Exeunt [LORENZO *and* GRAZIANO].
    ANTONIO It is that—anything now.
    BASSANIO Graziano speaks an infinite deal of nothing, more
115   than any man in all Venice. His reasons° are as two grains of   *sensible remarks*
    wheat hid in two bushels of chaff: you shall seek all day ere
    you find them, and when you have them they are not worth
    the search.
    ANTONIO Well, tell me now—what lady is the same
120   To whom you swore a secret pilgrimage
    That you today promised to tell me of?
    BASSANIO 'Tis not unknown to you, Antonio,
    How much I have disabled mine estate
    By something showing a more swelling port°   *extravagant lifestyle*
125   Than my faint means would grant continuance.°   *allow to continue*
    Nor do I now make moan to be abridged°   *reduced*
    From such a noble rate;° but my chief care   *style*
    Is to come fairly off from the great debts
    Wherein my time, something too prodigal,
130   Hath left me gaged.° To you, Antonio,   *pledged*
    I owe the most in money and in love,
    And from your love I have a warranty°   *sanction*
    To unburden all my plots and purposes
    How to get clear of all the debts I owe.
135 ANTONIO I pray you, good Bassanio, let me know it,
    And if it stand, as you yourself still do,
    Within the eye of honor, be assured
    My purse, my person, my extremest means
    Lie all unlocked to your occasions.°   *requirements*
140 BASSANIO In my school days, when I had lost one shaft,
    I shot his° fellow of the selfsame flight°   *its / size and weight*
    The selfsame way, with more advisèd° watch,   *careful*
    To find the other forth; and by adventuring° both,   *hazarding*
    I oft found both. I urge this childhood proof
145   Because what follows is pure innocence.
    I owe you much, and like a willful youth
    That which I owe is lost; but if you please
    To shoot another arrow that self° way   *same*
    Which you did shoot the first, I do not doubt,
150   As I will watch the aim, or° to find both,   *either*
    Or bring your latter hazard° back again   *risk*
    And thankfully rest debtor for the first.

8. *for this gear:* as a result of your talk.   9. Sellable—that is, marriageable.

ANTONIO   You know me well, and herein spend but° time   *only lose*
    To wind about my love with circumstance;°   *circumlocution*
155 And out of doubt you do me now more wrong
    In making question of my uttermost[1]
    Than if you had made waste of all I have.
    Then do but say to me what I should do
    That, in your knowledge, may by me be done,
160 And I am pressed unto° it—therefore speak.   *obliged to do*
BASSANIO   In Belmont is a lady richly left,°   *left a fortune*
    And she is fair, and fairer than that word,
    Of wondrous virtues. Sometimes° from her eyes   *At times*
    I did receive fair speechless messages.
165 Her name is Portia, nothing undervalued
    To[2] Cato's daughter, Brutus' Portia.[3]
    Nor is the wide world ignorant of her worth,
    For the four winds blow in from every coast
    Renownèd suitors; and her sunny locks
170 Hang on her temples like a golden fleece,
    Which makes her seat of Belmont Colchis' strand,[4]
    And many Jasons come in quest of her.
    O my Antonio, had I but the means
    To hold a rival place with one of them,
175 I have a mind presages me such thrift°   *prosperity*
    That I should questionless be fortunate.
ANTONIO   Thou know'st that all my fortunes are at sea:
    Neither have I money nor commodity°   *goods*
    To raise a present sum. Therefore go forth—
180 Try what my credit can in Venice do;
    That shall be racked° even to the uttermost   *stretched*
    To furnish thee to Belmont to fair Portia.
    Go presently inquire, and so will I,
    Where money is; and I no question make
185 To have it of my trust or for my sake.[5]   *Exeunt.*

1.2

Enter PORTIA *with her waiting woman,* NERISSA.

PORTIA   By my troth,° Nerissa, my little body is a-weary of this   *faith*
  great world.
NERISSA   You would be,[1] sweet madam, if your miseries were
  in the same abundance as your good fortunes are. And yet,
5 for aught I see, they are as sick that surfeit with too much as
  they that starve with nothing. It is no mean° happiness, there-   *slight*
  fore, to be seated in the mean:° superfluity comes sooner   *middle / sooner gets*
  by° white hairs, but competency° lives longer.   *moderate estate*
PORTIA   Good sentences,° and well pronounced.   *aphorisms*
10 NERISSA   They would be better if well followed.
PORTIA   If to do were as easy as to know what were good to do,
  chapels had been churches and poor men's cottages princes'
  palaces. It is a good divine° that follows his own instruc-   *clergyman*
  tions. I can easier teach twenty what were good to be done

---

1. In doubting that I would do my utmost to help you.
2. *nothing . . . / To:* no less worthy than.
3. Roman matron famous for heroic fidelity to her husband; a character in *Julius Caesar.*
4. Coast of Colchis, where in classical mythology Jason won the Golden Fleece.
5. *of . . . sake:* because of my creditworthiness or as a personal favor.
1.2 Location: Belmont.
1. You would have reason to be weary.

15 than to be one of the twenty to follow mine own teaching.
The brain may devise laws for the blood,° but a hot temper[2]   passion
leaps o'er a cold decree: such a hare is madness, the youth,
to skip o'er the meshes° of good counsel, the cripple.[3] But   snares
this reasoning is not in the fashion° to choose me a husband.   of a kind
20 O me! The word "choose"! I may neither choose who I would
nor refuse who I dislike; so is the will° of a living daughter   wish
curbed by the will° of a dead father. Is it not hard, Nerissa,   testament
that I cannot choose one nor refuse none?

NERISSA   Your father was ever virtuous, and holy men at their
25 death have good inspirations; therefore the lottery that he
hath devised in these three chests of gold, silver, and lead,
whereof who chooses his meaning chooses you, will no doubt
never be chosen by any rightly but one who you shall rightly
love. But what warmth is there in your affection towards any
30 of these princely suitors that are already come?

PORTIA   I pray thee, over-name them, and as thou namest
them I will describe them and, according to my description,
level° at my affection.   guess

NERISSA   First, there is the Neapolitan prince.

35 PORTIA   Ay, that's a colt[4] indeed! For he doth nothing but talk
of his horse, and he makes it a great appropriation° to his   augmentation
own good parts° that he can shoe him himself. I am much   own abilities
afeared my lady, his mother, played false with a smith.

NERISSA   Then is there the County Palatine.[5]

40 PORTIA   He doth nothing but frown—as who should say,
"An° you will not have me, choose."° He hears merry tales   If / do as you wish
and smiles not. I fear he will prove the weeping philosopher[6]
when he grows old, being so full of unmannerly° sadness in   immoderate
his youth. I had rather be married to a death's head with a
45 bone in his mouth than to either of these. God defend me
from these two!

NERISSA   How say you by the French lord, Monsieur Le Bon?

PORTIA   God made him, and therefore let him pass for a man.
In truth I know it is a sin to be a mocker, but he—why he hath
50 a horse better than the Neapolitan's, a better bad habit of
frowning than the Count Palatine: he is every man in no man.
If a throstle° sing he falls straight° a-capering; he will fence   thrush / immediately
with his own shadow. If I should marry him, I should marry
twenty husbands. If he would despise me, I would forgive
55 him; for if he love me to madness, I shall never requite him.

NERISSA   What say you, then, to Falconbridge, the young baron
of England?

PORTIA   You know I say nothing to him, for he understands-
not me nor I him: he hath neither Latin, French, nor Italian,
60 and you will come into the court and swear that I have a
poor pennyworth in the English. He is a proper° man's pic-   handsome
ture, but alas! Who can converse with a dumb show?° How   pantomime
oddly he is suited! I think he bought his doublet° in Italy, his   upper garment
round hose[7] in France, his bonnet° in Germany, and his   hat
65 behavior everywhere.

2. An impetuous disposition.
3. Because wisdom is imagined as elderly.
4. Foolish young man. Neapolitans were excellent
horsemen.

5. Count possessing royal powers.
6. Heracleitus, a melancholy Greek philosopher.
7. Puffed breeches.

NERISSA   What think you of the Scottish lord, his neighbor?[8]

PORTIA   That he hath a neighborly charity in him, for he borrowed a box of the ear of the Englishman and swore he
would pay him again when he was able. I think the French-
70   man became his surety and sealed under for another.[9]

NERISSA   How like you the young German, the Duke of Sax-
ony's nephew?

PORTIA   Very vilely in the morning when he is sober, and most
vilely in the afternoon when he is drunk. When he is best,
75   he is a little worse than a man, and when he is worst, he
is little better than a beast. An the worst fall that ever fell,
I hope I shall make shift° to go without him.   *manage
                                                                                                                    *endeavor

NERISSA   If he should offer° to choose, and choose the right
casket, you should refuse to perform your father's will if you
80   should refuse to accept him.

PORTIA   Therefore, for fear of the worst, I pray thee set a deep
glass of Rhenish wine° on the contrary casket; for if the dev-   *white German wine*
il be within and that temptation without, I know he will
choose it. I will do anything, Nerissa, ere I will be married
85   to a sponge!

NERISSA   You need not fear, lady, the having any of these
lords. They have acquainted me with their determinations,
which is, indeed, to return to their home and to trouble you
with no more suit, unless you may be won by some other sort°   *way*
90   than your father's imposition,° depending on the caskets.   *conditions*

PORTIA   If I live to be as old as Sibylla,[1] I will die as chaste as
Diana unless I be obtained by the manner of my father's will.
I am glad this parcel of wooers are so reasonable, for there is
not one among them but I dote on his very absence, and I
95   pray God grant them a fair departure.

NERISSA   Do you not remember, lady, in your father's time, a
Venetian—a scholar and a soldier—that came hither in
company of the Marquess of Montferrat?

PORTIA   Yes, yes—it was Bassanio; as I think, so was he called.

100   NERISSA   True, madam. He of all the men that ever my foolish
eyes looked upon was the best deserving a fair lady.

PORTIA   I remember him well, and I remember him worthy of
thy praise.

Enter STEFANO.

How now? What news?

105   STEFANO   The four strangers seek for you, madam, to take
their leave; and there is a forerunner come from a fifth, the
Prince of Morocco, who brings word the Prince his master
will be here tonight.

PORTIA   If I could bid the fifth welcome with so good heart as
110   I can bid the other four farewell, I should be glad of his
approach. If he have the condition° of a saint and the com-   *character*
plexion of a devil,[2] I had rather he should shrive me° than   *absolve me of my sins*

---

8. TEXTUAL COMMENT "Scottish" in the 1601 Q was
changed to "other" in the 1624 F edition; after King
James of Scotland came to the English throne in
1603, playwrights who ridiculed Scotland could find
themselves in trouble. See Digital Edition TC 2.
9. The Frenchman vouched for the Scot's payment
(of a box on the ear) and promised to add another

himself (referring to France's frequent promises to
help the Scots against the English).
1. In classical mythology, the Cumaean Sibyl asked
Apollo for as many years of life as the grains of sand
she held in her hand; she forgot to ask for eternal
youth.
2. Devils were imagined as black.

wive me. Come, Nerissa. —Sirrah, go before. Whiles we shut
the gate upon one wooer, another knocks at the door.

Exeunt.

1.3

Enter BASSANIO *with* SHYLOCK *the Jew.*

SHYLOCK   Three thousand ducats[1]—well.

BASSANIO   Ay, sir—for three months.

SHYLOCK   For three months—well.

BASSANIO   For the which, as I told you, Antonio shall be bound.°   *contractually responsible*

5   SHYLOCK   Antonio shall become bound—well.

BASSANIO   May you stead° me? Will you pleasure me? Shall I   *accommodate*
know your answer?

SHYLOCK   Three thousand ducats for three months, and Antonio bound.

10   BASSANIO   Your answer to that?

SHYLOCK   Antonio is a good man.

BASSANIO   Have you heard any imputation to the contrary?

SHYLOCK   Ho, no, no, no, no: my meaning in saying he is a
good man is to have you understand me that he is suffi-
15   cient.[2] Yet his means are in supposition:° he hath an argosy   *doubt*
bound to Tripoli, another to the Indies. I understand, more-
over, upon the Rialto,[3] he hath a third at Mexico, a fourth
for England, and other ventures he hath squandered abroad.
But ships are but boards, sailors but men; there be land rats
20   and water rats, water thieves and land thieves—I mean
pirates. And then there is the peril of waters, winds, and
rocks. The man is, notwithstanding, sufficient. Three thousand ducats: I think I may take his bond.

BASSANIO   Be assured you may.

25   SHYLOCK   I will be assured[4] I may; and that I may be assured,
I will bethink me. May I speak with Antonio?[5]

BASSANIO   If it please you to dine with us.

SHYLOCK   Yes—to smell pork, to eat of the habitation which
your prophet the Nazarite[6] conjured the devil into? I will
30   buy with you, sell with you, talk with you, walk with you,
and so following. But I will not eat with you, drink with you,
nor pray with you.

Enter ANTONIO.

What news on the Rialto? Who is he comes here?

BASSANIO   This is Signor Antonio.

35   SHYLOCK   [*aside*]   How like a fawning publican[7] he looks!
I hate him for he is a Christian,
But more for that in low simplicity[8]
He lends out money gratis° and brings down   *free*
The rate of usance° here with us in Venice.   *interest*
40   If I can catch him once upon the hip,[9]
I will feed fat the ancient grudge I bear him.
He hates our sacred nation,° and he rails,   *(the Jews)*

1.3 Location: Street in Venice.
1. Gold coins. The sum is very large.
2. *sufficient:* of adequate wealth.
3. Merchants' exchange in Venice.
4. Sure (but Shylock uses the word to mean "given
financial guarantees").
5. TEXTUAL COMMENT In early printed texts the
speech prefix for Shylock varies over the course of
the play; sometimes he is "Shylock," and other times

he is "Jew." See Digital Edition TC 3.
6. Jesus, who cast devils into a herd of swine.
7. Tax collector; he robs me, but now, like the publican in Luke 18:10–14 who prays to Jesus for mercy,
tries to ingratiate himself because he wants a favor.
8. In meek honesty; in base folly.
9. *upon the hip:* at a disadvantage (wrestling
terminology).

Even there where merchants most do congregate,
On me, my bargains, and my well-won thrift,°   *profit*
45   Which he calls interest. Cursed be my tribe
If I forgive him.
BASSANIO   Shylock, do you hear?
SHYLOCK   I am debating of my present store°   *supply of money*
And, by the near guess of my memory,
I cannot instantly raise up the gross°   *total*
50   Of full three thousand ducats. What of that?
Tubal, a wealthy Hebrew of my tribe,
Will furnish me. But soft;° how many months   *wait*
Do you desire? —Rest you fair, good signor,
Your worship was the last man in our mouths.[1]
55 ANTONIO   Shylock, albeit I neither lend nor borrow
By taking nor by giving of excess,
Yet to supply the ripe° wants of my friend   *urgent*
I'll break a custom. —Is he yet possessed°   *informed*
How much ye would?
SHYLOCK   Ay, ay—three thousand ducats.
60 ANTONIO   And for three months.
SHYLOCK   I had forgot: three months. You told me so.
Well, then, your bond. And let me see, but hear you—
Methoughts you said you neither lend nor borrow
Upon advantage.°   *interest*
ANTONIO   I do never use it.
65 SHYLOCK   When Jacob grazed his uncle Laban's sheep,
This Jacob from our holy Abram was—
As his wise mother wrought in his behalf—
The third possessor; ay, he was the third[2]—
ANTONIO   And what of him? Did he take interest?
70 SHYLOCK   No, not take interest—not, as you would say,
Directly interest. Mark what Jacob did:
When Laban and himself were compromised°   *agreed*
That all the eanlings° which were streaked and pied°   *lambs / spotted*
Should fall as Jacob's hire, the ewes, being rank,°   *in heat*
75 In end of autumn turnèd to the rams;
And when the work of generation° was   *mating*
Between these woolly breeders in the act,
The skillful shepherd peeled me certain wands,[3]
And in the doing of the deed of kind°   *nature*
80 He stuck them up before the fulsome ewes,
Who then, conceiving, did in eaning° time   *lambing*
Fall° particolored lambs; and those were Jacob's.   *Deliver*
This was a way to thrive, and he was blest;
And thrift is blessing, if men steal it not.
85 ANTONIO   This was a venture, sir, that Jacob served for[4]—
A thing not in his power to bring to pass,
But swayed and fashioned by the hand of heaven.
Was this inserted to make interest good?[5]
Or is your gold and silver ewes and rams?
90 SHYLOCK   I cannot tell; I make it breed as fast.

---

1. We were just mentioning you.
2. After Abraham and Isaac; his mother, Rebecca, helped him cheat his brother Esau of his birthright. The story of Laban's sheep is told in Genesis 30:25–43.
3. Stripped part of the bark off some sticks ("me" is colloquial).
4. This was a speculative enterprise on which Jacob staked his wages as a servant.
5. Was this brought up to defend taking interest?

But note me, signor—

ANTONIO   —Mark you this, Bassanio:
  The devil can cite scripture for his purpose.
  An evil soul producing holy witness
  Is like a villain with a smiling cheek,
95   A goodly apple rotten at the heart.
  Oh, what a goodly outside falsehood hath!

SHYLOCK   Three thousand ducats—'tis a good round sum.
  Three months from twelve—then let me see the rate.

ANTONIO   Well, Shylock, shall we be beholden to you?

100 SHYLOCK   Signor Antonio, many a time and oft
  In the Rialto you have rated° me   *berated*
  About my moneys and my usances.
  Still° have I borne it with a patient shrug,   *Always*
  For suff'rance is the badge[6] of all our tribe.
105   You call me "misbeliever," "cut-throat dog,"
  And spit upon my Jewish gabardine,°   *long coat*
  And all for use of that which is mine own.
  Well, then, it now appears you need my help.
  Go to, then: you come to me and you say,
110   "Shylock, we would have moneys": you say so—
  You that did void your rheum° upon my beard   *spit*
  And foot me as you spurn° a stranger cur   *contemptuously kick*
  Over your threshold. Moneys is your suit.
  What should I say to you? Should I not say,
115   "Hath a dog money? Is it possible
  A cur can lend three thousand ducats?" Or
  Shall I bend low and in a bondman's° key,   *slave's*
  With bated breath and whispering humbleness,
  Say this: "Fair sir, you spit on me on Wednesday last;
120   You spurned me such a day; another time
  You called me dog, and for these courtesies
  I'll lend you thus much moneys"?

ANTONIO   I am as like to call thee so again—
  To spit on thee again, to spurn thee, too.
125   If thou wilt lend this money, lend it not
  As to thy friends, for when did friendship take
  A breed[7] for barren metal of his friend?
  But lend it rather to thine enemy,
  Who, if he break,° thou mayst with better face   *fail to repay*
  Exact the penalty.

130 SHYLOCK   Why, look you, how you storm!
  I would be friends with you and have your love,
  Forget the shames that you have stained me with,
  Supply your present wants and take no doit°   *small coin*
  Of usance for my moneys—and you'll not hear me.
  This is kind[8] I offer.

135 BASSANIO   This were° kindness.   *would be*

SHYLOCK   This kindness will I show:
  Go with me to a notary; seal me there
  Your single bond[9] and, in a merry sport,

---

6. For enduring insult is the characteristic.
7. Offspring (interest); alluding to an ancient argument that it was unnatural to use money to "breed," or make, more money.

8. Benevolent; natural (but perhaps with the covert suggestion "in kind").
9. Bond signed by the debtor alone (Antonio) without additional guarantors.

If you repay me not, on such a day
140 In such a place, such sum or sums as are
Expressed in the condition, let the forfeit°   *penalty*
Be nominated for an equal° pound   *Be stipulated as an exact*
Of your fair flesh, to be cut off and taken
In what part of your body pleaseth me.
145 ANTONIO   Content, in faith. I'll seal to such a bond
And say there is much kindness in the Jew.
BASSANIO   You shall not seal to such a bond for me;
I'll rather dwell in my necessity.°   *remain in need*
ANTONIO   Why, fear not, man: I will not forfeit it.
150 Within these two months—that's a month before
This bond expires—I do expect return
Of thrice three times the value of this bond.
SHYLOCK   O father Abram, what these Christians are,
Whose own hard dealings teaches them suspect
155 The thoughts of others! Pray you, tell me this:
If he should break his day, what should I gain
By the exaction of the forfeiture?
A pound of man's flesh taken from a man
Is not so estimable,° profitable neither,   *valuable*
160 As flesh of muttons, beefs, or goats. I say
To buy his favor I extend this friendship.
If he will take it, so; if not, adieu,
And for my love I pray you wrong me not.
ANTONIO   Yes, Shylock, I will seal unto this bond.
165 SHYLOCK   Then meet me forthwith at the notary's.
Give him direction for this merry bond,
And I will go and purse the ducats straight;
See to my house, left in the fearful° guard   *doubtful*
Of an unthrifty knave; and presently
I'll be with you.   *Exit.*
170 ANTONIO   Hie thee,° gentle Jew!   *Hurry*
The Hebrew will turn Christian—he grows kind.
BASSANIO   I like not fair terms and a villain's mind.
ANTONIO   Come on—in this there can be no dismay;
My ships come home a month before the day.   *Exeunt.*

2.1

Enter [the Prince of] MOROCCO, a tawny Moor all in
white, and three or four followers accordingly,[1] with
PORTIA, NERISSA, and their train.
MOROCCO   Mislike me not for my complexion,
The shadowed livery° of the burnished sun,   *servant's uniform*
To whom I am a neighbor and near bred.°   *close kin*
Bring me the fairest creature northward born,
5 Where Phoebus'° fire scarce thaws the icicles,   *the sun god's*
And let us make incision for your love
To prove whose blood is reddest[2]—his or mine.
I tell thee, lady, this aspect° of mine   *countenance*
Hath feared° the valiant; by my love I swear   *frightened*
10 The best regarded virgins of our clime

2.1 Location: Belmont.   2. Red blood was considered a sign of valor.
1. Of similar complexion and dress.

Have loved it too. I would not change this hue
Except to steal your thoughts, my gentle queen.

PORTIA   In terms of choice I am not solely led
By nice direction° of a maiden's eyes.   *fastidious guidance*

15   Besides, the lott'ry of my destiny
Bars me the right of voluntary choosing.
But if my father had not scanted° me,   *limited*
And hedged° me by his wit° to yield myself   *restricted / wisdom*
His wife who wins me by that means I told you,

20   Yourself, renownèd prince, then stood as fair³
As any comer I have looked on yet
For my affection.

MOROCCO   Even for that I thank you.
Therefore, I pray you, lead me to the caskets
To try my fortune. By this scimitar

25   That slew the Sophy° and a Persian prince,   *Shah of Persia*
That won three fields of Sultan Suleiman,°   *Turkish ruler*
I would o'er-stare the sternest eyes that look,
Outbrave the heart most daring on the earth,
Pluck the young sucking cubs from the she-bear;

30   Yea, mock the lion when 'a° roars for prey,   *he*
To win the lady. But alas the while,
If Hercules and Lychas° play at dice   *Hercules' servant*
Which is the better man, the greater throw
May turn by fortune from the weaker hand—

35   So is Alcides° beaten by his rage⁴   *Hercules*
And so may I, blind Fortune leading me,
Miss that which one unworthier may attain
And die with grieving.

PORTIA   You must take your chance
And either not attempt to choose at all,

40   Or swear before you choose, if you choose wrong
Never to speak to lady afterward
In way of marriage. Therefore be advised.°   *careful*

MOROCCO   Nor will not. Come, bring me unto my chance.

PORTIA   First forward to the temple; after dinner
Your hazard shall be made.

45   MOROCCO   Good fortune, then,
To make me blest or cursèd'st among men.   *Exeunt.*

2.2

*Enter [LANCELET,] the clown, alone.*¹

LANCELET   Certainly, my conscience will serve° me to run   *allow*
from this Jew, my master. The fiend is at mine elbow and
tempts me, saying to me, "Gobbo, Lancelet Gobbo, good
Lancelet" or "good Gobbo" or "good Lancelet Gobbo, use your

5   legs, take the start,° run away." My conscience says, "No,   *begone*
take heed, honest Lancelet; take heed, honest Gobbo," or,
as aforesaid, "honest Lancelet Gobbo, do not run, scorn
running with thy heels."° Well, the most courageous fiend   *indignantly (with pun)*

---

3. Seemed as attractive; stood as good a chance.
4. Often amended to "page."
2.2 Location: Venice.
1. TEXTUAL COMMENT In early editions, just as Shy-

lock is often called "*Jew*" in speech prefixes and stage
directions, Lancelet is often called "*Clown*." Both his
first and his last names vary somewhat in Q1, Q2, and
F. See Digital Edition TC 4 and TC 5.

bids me pack: "Fia!"° says the fiend. "Away!" says the fiend,   *Away*
10   "for the heavens rouse up a brave mind," says the fiend,
"and run!" Well, my conscience, hanging about the neck of
my heart, says very wisely to me, "My honest friend Lancelet, being an honest man's son," or rather, "an honest woman's son"—for indeed my father did something smack,
15   something grow to; he had a kind of taste.² Well, my conscience says, "Lancelet, budge not." "Budge," says the fiend.
"Budge not," says my conscience. "Conscience," say I, "you
counsel well." "Fiend," say I, "you counsel well." To be ruled
by my conscience I should stay with the Jew my master, who
20   —God bless the mark³—is a kind of devil. And to run away
from the Jew, I should be ruled by the fiend, who—saving
your reverence—is the devil himself. Certainly the Jew is
the very devil incarnation.° And in my conscience, my con-   *(for "incarnate")*
science is but a kind of hard conscience to offer to counsel
25   me to stay with the Jew. The fiend gives the more friendly
counsel: I will run. Fiend, my heels are at your commandment; I will run!

     Enter old GOBBO *with a basket.*

GOBBO Master young man—you, I pray you—which is the
way to Master Jew's?
30 GOBBO ~~GOBBO~~ LANCELET O heavens! This is my true-begotten father, who,
being more than sand-blind—high gravel-blind⁴—knows me
not. I will try confusions⁵ with him.
GOBBO Master young gentleman, I pray you, which is the way
to Master Jew's?
35 LANCELET Turn up on your right hand at the next turning,
but at the next turning of all on your left. Marry, at the very
next turning turn of no hand, but turn down indirectly to
the Jew's house.
GOBBO By God's sonties,° 'twill be a hard way to hit! Can you   *saints*
40   tell me whether one Lancelet that dwells with him dwell
with him or no?
LANCELET Talk you of young Master⁶ Lancelet? —Mark me
now; now will I raise the waters.⁷ —Talk you of young Master Lancelet?
45 GOBBO No "Master," sir, but a poor man's son. His father,
though I say't, is an honest, exceeding poor man and, God
be thanked, well to live.⁸
LANCELET Well, let his father be what 'a° will, we talk of   *he*
young Master Lancelet.
50 GOBBO Your worship's friend and Lancelet, sir.
LANCELET But, I pray you, ergo,° old man, ergo, I beseech   *therefore*
you, talk you of young Master Lancelet?
GOBBO Of Lancelet, an't° please your mastership.   *if it*
LANCELET Ergo, Master Lancelet! Talk not of Master Lance-
55   let, father,⁹ for the young gentleman, according to fates and
destinies and such odd sayings, the sisters three° and such   *the Fates*

---

2. *my father . . . taste:* that is, my father was licentious.
3. Conventional apology before a rude remark, like "saving your reverence."
4. Lancelet's coinage for a degree of blindness between sand-blind (partly blind) and stone-blind.

5. Lancelet's version of "try conclusions" (experiment).
6. "Master" was only applied to gentlemen's sons.
7. Start something; bring on tears.
8. Well-to-do (contradicts the previous line).
9. Customary address to an old man.

branches of learning, is indeed deceased, or as you would
say in plain terms, gone to heaven.

GOBBO   Marry, God forbid! The boy was the very staff of my
60   age, my very prop!

LANCELET   Do I look like a cudgel or a hovel post,° a staff or a   shed post
prop? Do you know me, father?

GOBBO   Alack the day! I know you not, young gentleman; but
I pray you tell me: is my boy, God rest his soul, alive or dead?

65   LANCELET   Do you not know me, father?

GOBBO   Alack, sir, I am sand-blind. I know you not.

LANCELET   Nay, indeed, if you had your eyes you might fail
of the knowing me: it is a wise father that knows his own
child.[1] Well, old man, I will tell you news of your son. Give

70   me your blessing. Truth will come to light; murder cannot
be hid long; a man's son may, but in the end truth will out.

GOBBO   Pray you, sir, stand up. I am sure you are not Lancelet, my boy.

LANCELET   Pray you, let's have no more fooling about it, but

75   give me your blessing. I am Lancelet—your boy that was,
your son that is, your child that shall be.

GOBBO   I cannot think you are my son.

LANCELET   I know not what I shall think of that, but I am
Lancelet, the Jew's man; and I am sure Margery, your wife,

80   is my mother.

GOBBO   Her name is Margery, indeed. I'll be sworn if thou be
Lancelet, thou art mine own flesh and blood. Lord, worshipped might He be, what a beard hast thou got![2] Thou
hast got more hair on thy chin than Dobbin my fill-horse°   cart horse

85   has on his tail.

LANCELET   It should seem then that Dobbin's tail grows backward.[3] I am sure he had more hair of his tail than I have of
my face when I last saw him.

GOBBO   Lord, how art thou changed! How dost thou and thy

90   master agree?° I have brought him a present; how 'gree you   get along
now?

LANCELET   Well, well. But for mine own part, as I have set up
my rest[4] to run away, so I will not rest till I have run some
ground. My master's a very Jew.[5] Give him a present?—give

95   him a halter!° I am famished in his service. You may tell°   noose / count
every finger I have with my ribs. Father, I am glad you are
come. Give me° your present to one Master Bassanio, who,   Give
indeed, gives rare new liveries.° If I serve not him, I will run   servants' uniforms
as far as God has any ground. Oh, rare fortune! Here comes

100   the man: to him, father, for I am a Jew if I serve the Jew any
longer.

        Enter BASSANIO with [LEONARDO and] a follower or two.

BASSANIO   You may do so, but let it be so hasted° that supper   hurried
be ready at the farthest° by five of the clock. See these let-   latest
ters delivered, put the liveries to making, and desire° Gra-   tell

105   ziano to come anon° to my lodging.   at once

---

1. Transposing the proverb "A wise child knows his
own father."
2. Gobbo mistakes Lancelet's hair for a beard.
3. Gets shorter; grows from the wrong end.

4. As I have definitely determined (phrase in the
card game primero meaning "risk everything").
5. Cruel, grasping person; Hebrew. *a very*: an absolute.

LANCELET To him, father!

GOBBO God bless your worship.

BASSANIO Gramercy.° Wouldst thou aught° with me?   *Many thanks / anything*

GOBBO Here's my son, sir, a poor boy.

110 LANCELET Not a poor boy, sir, but the rich Jew's man that
would, sir, as my father shall specify.

GOBBO He hath a great infection,° sir, as one would say, to   *(for "affection"; wish)*
serve.

LANCELET Indeed the short and the long is, I serve the Jew

115 and have a desire as my father shall specify.

GOBBO His master and he, saving your worship's reverence,
are scarce cater-cousins.°   *close friends*

LANCELET To be brief, the very truth is that the Jew, having
done me wrong, doth cause me, as my father, being I hope

120 an old man, shall fructify° unto you—   *(for "certify")*

GOBBO I have here a dish of doves that I would bestow upon
your worship, and my suit is—

LANCELET In very brief, the suit is impertinent° to myself, as   *(for "pertinent")*
your worship shall know by this honest old man and, though

125 I say it, though old man, yet poor man, my father—

BASSANIO One speak for both: what would you?

LANCELET Serve you, sir.

GOBBO That is the very defect° of the matter, sir.   *(for "effect")*

BASSANIO I know thee well; thou hast obtained thy suit.

130 Shylock thy master spoke with me this day
And hath preferred thee, if it be preferment[6]
To leave a rich Jew's service to become
The follower of so poor a gentleman.

LANCELET The old proverb[7] is very well parted between my

135 master Shylock and you, sir: you have the grace of God, sir,
and he hath enough.

BASSANIO Thou speak'st it well. —Go, father, with thy son.
—Take leave of thy old master and inquire
My lodging out. —Give him a livery

140 More guarded° than his fellows'. See it done.   *decorated*

LANCELET Father, in. I cannot get a service—no! I have ne'er
a tongue in my head. Well, if any man in Italy have a fairer
table[8] which doth offer to swear upon a book[9]—I shall have
good fortune. Go to—here's a simple° line of life; here's a   *unremarkable (ironic)*

145 small trifle of wives. Alas, fifteen wives is nothing! Eleven
widows and nine maids is a simple coming in[1] for one man,
and then to scape drowning thrice, and to be in peril of my
life with the edge of a featherbed.[2] Here are simple scapes!
Well, if Fortune be a woman, she's a good wench, for this

150 gear.° Father, come. I'll take my leave of the Jew in the twin-   *matter*
kling.   *Exit* [LANCELET *the*] *clown* [*with old* GOBBO].

BASSANIO I pray thee, good Leonardo, think on this.
These things being bought and orderly bestowed,°   *stowed on ship*
Return in haste, for I do feast tonight

155 My best esteemed acquaintance. Hie thee; go!

---

6. And has recommended you, if it be advancement.
7. "The grace of God is gear enough."
8. Palm (Lancelet reads the lines of his palm to predict the future).

9. To tell the truth (referring to the practice of taking an oath with the palm on the Bible).
1. A scanty income; an easy sexual entrance.
2. Alluding to a sexual adventure.

LEONARDO My best endeavors shall be done herein.
    Enter GRAZIANO.
GRAZIANO Where's your master?
LEONARDO   Yonder, sir, he walks.   *Exit.*
GRAZIANO Signor Bassanio!
BASSANIO   Graziano!
GRAZIANO I have suit to you.
BASSANIO   You have obtained it.
160 GRAZIANO You must not deny me. I must go with you to
    Belmont.
BASSANIO Why, then you must; but hear thee, Graziano:
    Thou art too wild, too rude and bold of voice—
    Parts° that become thee happily enough   *Attributes*
    And in such eyes as ours appear not faults.
165   But where thou art not known, why there they show
    Something too liberal.° Pray thee, take pain   *unrestrained*
    To allay with some cold drops of modesty
    Thy skipping spirit, lest through thy wild behavior
    I be misconstered° in the place I go to,   *misconstrued*
    And lose my hopes.
170 GRAZIANO   Signor Bassanio, hear me.
    If I do not put on a sober habit,°   *behavior; clothing*
    Talk with respect, and swear but now and then,
    Wear prayer books in my pocket, look demurely,
    Nay, more—while grace is saying, hood mine eyes
175   Thus with my hat,³ and sigh, and say "Amen"—
    Use all the observance of civility,
    Like one well studied in a sad ostent°   *solemn appearance*
    To please his grandam,° never trust me more.°   *grandmother / again*
BASSANIO Well, we shall see your bearing.
180 GRAZIANO Nay, but I bar tonight—you shall not gauge me
    By what we do tonight.
BASSANIO   No, that were pity!
    I would entreat you rather to put on
    Your boldest suit of mirth, for we have friends
    That purpose merriment. But fare you well;
185   I have some business.
GRAZIANO And I must to Lorenzo and the rest;
    But we will visit you at supper time.   *Exeunt.*

2.3
Enter JESSICA *and* [LANCELET] *the clown.*
JESSICA I am sorry thou wilt leave my father so;
    Our house is hell, and thou, a merry devil,
    Didst rob it of some taste of tediousness.
    But fare thee well; there is a ducat for thee.
5   And, Lancelet, soon at supper shalt thou see
    Lorenzo, who is thy new master's guest.
    Give him this letter; do it secretly,
    And so farewell. I would not have my father
    See me in talk with thee.
10 LANCELET Adieu! Tears exhibit° my tongue, most beautiful   *(for "inhibit")*
    pagan, most sweet Jew. If a Christian do not play the knave

---

3. Hats were worn at meals but taken off for grace.   **2.3** Location: Shylock's house in Venice.

and get thee, I am much deceived. But adieu! These foolish
drops do something drown my manly spirit. Adieu!   [*Exit.*]
JESSICA   Farewell, good Lancelet.

15 Alack, what heinous sin is it in me
To be ashamed to be my father's child!
But though I am a daughter to his blood
I am not to his manners.° O Lorenzo,   behavior
If thou keep promise, I shall end this strife—
20 Become a Christian and thy loving wife.   *Exit.*

2.4

Enter GRAZIANO, LORENZO, SALERIO, *and* SOLANIO.

LORENZO   Nay, we will slink away in° supper time,   during
Disguise us at my lodging, and return
All in an hour.
GRAZIANO   We have not made good preparation.
5 SALERIO   We have not spoke us yet of° torchbearers.   not yet arranged for
SOLANIO   'Tis vile unless it may be quaintly ordered,°   cleverly managed
And better in my mind not undertook.
LORENZO   'Tis now but four of clock; we have two hours
To furnish us.
Enter LANCELET [*with a letter*].
Friend Lancelet, what's the news?
10 LANCELET   An° it shall please you to break up° this, it shall   If / open
seem to signify.
LORENZO   I know the hand: in faith, 'tis a fair hand,
And whiter than the paper it writ on
Is the fair hand that writ.
GRAZIANO   Love news, in faith.
LANCELET   By your leave, sir—
15 LORENZO   Whither goest thou?
LANCELET   Marry, sir, to bid my old master the Jew to sup
tonight with my new master the Christian.
LORENZO   Hold°—here, take this. Tell gentle Jessica   Wait
I will not fail her; speak it privately. *Exit* [LANCELET *the*] *clown.*
20 Go, gentlemen.
Will you prepare you for this masque tonight?
I am provided of a torchbearer.
SALERIO   Ay, marry, I'll be gone about it straight.°   immediately
SOLANIO   And so will I.
LORENZO   Meet me and Graziano
25 At Graziano's lodging some hour hence.
SALERIO   'Tis good we do so.   *Exit* [*with* SOLANIO].
GRAZIANO   Was not that letter from fair Jessica?
LORENZO   I must needs tell thee all: she hath directed
How I shall take her from her father's house,
30 What gold and jewels she is furnished with,
What page's suit she hath in readiness.
If e'er the Jew her father come to heaven,
It will be for his gentle daughter's sake;
And never dare misfortune cross her foot
35 Unless she° do it under this excuse: (*misfortune*)
That she° is issue° to a faithless Jew.   (*Jessica*) / *offspring*

2.4 Location: Street in Venice.

Come, go with me; peruse this as thou goest.
Fair Jessica shall be my torchbearer.   *Exeunt.*

2.5

Enter [SHYLOCK *the*] *Jew and his man that*
was°[, LANCELET] *the clown.*   *former servant*

SHYLOCK   Well, thou shalt see, thy eyes shall be thy judge,
The difference of old Shylock and Bassanio.
—[*He calls.*] What, Jessica! —Thou shalt not gourmandize°   *overeat*
As thou hast done with me. —[*He calls.*] What, Jessica!
5   —And sleep, and snore, and rend apparel out.°   *wear out clothes*
—[*He calls.*] Why, Jessica, I say!
LANCELET   Why, Jessica!
SHYLOCK   Who bids thee call? I do not bid thee call.
LANCELET   Your worship was wont to tell me I could do noth-
ing without bidding.
        Enter JESSICA.
10   JESSICA   Call you? What is your will?
SHYLOCK   I am bid forth to supper, Jessica.
There are my keys. But wherefore° should I go?   *why*
I am not bid for love—they flatter me—
But yet I'll go in hate to feed upon
15   The prodigal Christian. Jessica, my girl,
Look to my house. I am right loath° to go;   *very unwilling*
There is some ill a-brewing towards my rest,
For I did dream of moneybags tonight.°   *last night*
LANCELET   I beseech you, sir, go. My young master doth expect
20   your reproach.°   *(for "approach")*
SHYLOCK   So do I his.
LANCELET   And they have conspired together. I will not say
you shall see a masque, but if you do, then it was not for
nothing that my nose fell a-bleeding on Black Monday° last   *Easter Monday*
25   at six o'clock i'th' morning, falling out that year on Ash
Wednesday was four year in th'afternoon.[1]
SHYLOCK   What, are there masques? Hear you me, Jessica:
Lock up my doors, and when you hear the drum
And the vile squealing of the wry-necked[2] fife,
30   Clamber not you up to the casements then,
Nor thrust your head into the public street
To gaze on Christian fools with varnished° faces;   *painted; masked*
But stop my house's ears—I mean my casements.
Let not the sound of shallow fopp'ry° enter   *frivolity*
35   My sober house. By Jacob's staff[3] I swear
I have no mind of feasting forth° tonight;   *away from home*
But I will go. —Go you before me, sirrah.
Say I will come.
LANCELET   I will go before, sir.
—Mistress, look out at window for all this[4]—
40   There will come a Christian by
Will be worth a Jewess' eye.   [*Exit.*]
SHYLOCK   What says that fool of Hagar's offspring?[5] Ha?

2.5 Location: Outside Shylock's house.
1. Lancelet mocks Shylock's superstition.
2. Fifes were played with the head turned sideways.
3. See Genesis 32:10 and Hebrews 11:21.
4. *for all this:* despite Shylock's instructions.

5. That despicable gentile. Hagar, Abraham's gentile
servant, bore him a son, Ishmael; she and her child
were cast out after the birth of Abraham's legitimate
son, Isaac.

JESSICA His words were "Farewell, mistress," nothing else.

SHYLOCK The patch° is kind enough, but a huge feeder,   *fool*

45   Snail-slow in profit,° and he sleeps by day   *proficiency*
        More than the wildcat. Drones hive not with me;
        Therefore I part with him, and part with him
        To one that I would have him help to waste
        His borrowed purse. Well, Jessica, go in.

50   Perhaps I will return immediately.
        Do as I bid you; shut doors after you.
        Fast bind, fast find:[6]
        A proverb never stale in thrifty mind.   *Exit.*

JESSICA Farewell, and if my fortune be not crossed,

55   I have a father, you a daughter, lost.   *Exit.*

2.6

Enter the Masquers GRAZIANO *and* SALERIO.

GRAZIANO This is the penthouse[1] under which Lorenzo
        Desired us to make stand.

SALERIO His hour is almost past.

GRAZIANO And it is marvel he outdwells his hour,

5   For lovers ever run before the clock.

SALERIO Oh, ten times faster Venus' pigeons[2] fly
        To seal love's bonds new made than they are wont
        To keep obligèd° faith unforfeited.°   *pledged / unbroken*

GRAZIANO That ever holds°: who riseth from a feast   *remains true*

10   With that keen appetite that he sits down?
        Where is the horse that doth untread° again   *retrace*
        His tedious measures with the unbated fire
        That he did pace them first? All things that are
        Are with more spirit chasèd than enjoyed.

15   How like a younker or a prodigal[3]
        The scarfèd bark° puts from her native bay,   *streamer-bedecked ship*
        Hugged and embracèd by the strumpet wind;
        How like the prodigal doth she return
        With over-weathered ribs° and ragged sails,   *weatherbeaten timbers*

20   Lean, rent,° and beggared by the strumpet wind!   *torn*
            Enter LORENZO.

SALERIO Here comes Lorenzo; more of this hereafter.

LORENZO Sweet friends, your patience for my long abode°;   *delay*
        Not I but my affairs have made you wait.
        When you shall please to play the thieves for wives,

25   I'll watch° as long for you then. Approach.   *wait*
        Here dwells my father° Jew. —How? Who's within?   *father-in-law*
            [*Enter*] JESSICA *above*[*, dressed like a boy*].

JESSICA Who are you? Tell me for more certainty,
        Albeit I'll swear that I do know your tongue.

LORENZO Lorenzo, and thy love.

30 JESSICA Lorenzo, certain, and my love indeed;
        For who love I so much? And now who knows
        But you, Lorenzo, whether I am yours?

LORENZO Heaven and thy thoughts are witness that thou art.

JESSICA Here—catch this casket. It is worth the pains.

---

6. Something firmly secured will remain fastened.
2.6 Location: Scene continues.
1. Projecting roof of an upper story.

2. Doves that drew the love goddess's chariot.
3. See Luke 15:11–31. *younker:* fashionable youth;
junior seaman.

35   I am glad 'tis night—you do not look on me—
    For I am much ashamed of my exchange.°   *change of clothes*
    But love is blind, and lovers cannot see
    The pretty° follies that themselves commit.   *ingenious*
    For if they could, Cupid himself would blush
40   To see me thus transformèd to a boy.
LORENZO   Descend, for you must be my torchbearer.
JESSICA   What? Must I hold a candle to my shames?
    They in themselves, good sooth,° are too, too light.°   *in truth / clear; wanton*
    Why, 'tis an office of discovery,[4] love,
    And I should be obscured.
45 LORENZO   So are you, sweet,
    Even in the lovely garnish° of a boy.   *dress*
    But come at once,
    For the close° night doth play the runaway,°   *secret / steals away*
    And we are stayed° for at Bassanio's feast.   *waited*
50 JESSICA   I will make fast the doors, and gild myself
    With some more ducats, and be with you straight. [*Exit above.*]
GRAZIANO   Now by my hood, a gentle° and no Jew.   *gentile; gentle person*
LORENZO   Beshrew° me, but I love her heartily;   *Evil befall*
    For she is wise, if I can judge of her;
55   And fair she is, if that mine eyes be true;
    And true she is, as she hath proved herself.
    And therefore like herself—wise, fair, and true—
    Shall she be placèd in my constant soul.
          Enter JESSICA [*below*].
    What, art thou come? On, gentlemen, away.
60   Our masquing mates by this time for us stay.
              Exeunt [LORENZO, JESSICA, *and* SALERIO].
        Enter ANTONIO.
ANTONIO   Who's there?
GRAZIANO   Signor Antonio?
ANTONIO   Fie, fie, Graziano—where are all the rest?
    'Tis nine o'clock; our friends all stay for you.
    No masque tonight; the wind is come about.
65   Bassanio presently° will go aboard.   *immediately*
    I have sent twenty out to seek for you.
GRAZIANO   I am glad on't. I desire no more delight
    Than to be under sail and gone tonight.   *Exeunt.*

2.7

    Enter PORTIA *with* [*the Prince of*] MOROCCO *and*
    both their trains.
PORTIA   Go, draw aside the curtains and discover°   *reveal*
    The several caskets to this noble prince.
    —Now make your choice.
MOROCCO   This first of gold, who° this inscription bears: *which*
5   "Who chooseth me shall gain what many men desire."
    The second, silver, which this promise carries:
    "Who chooseth me shall get as much as he deserves."
    This third, dull lead, with warning all as blunt:[1]
    "Who chooseth me must give and hazard all he hath."

---

4. (Torchbearing) is a task of disclosure.   1. Plainly spoken; not sharp (with play on "dull lead").
2.7 Location: Belmont.

10   How shall I know if I do choose the right?
    PORTIA   The one of them contains my picture, Prince.
    If you choose that, then I am yours withal.°   *with it*
    MOROCCO   Some god direct my judgment. Let me see.
    I will survey th'inscriptions back again.
15   What says this leaden casket?
    "Who chooseth me must give and hazard all he hath."
    Must give for what? For lead—hazard for lead?
    This casket threatens; men that hazard all
    Do it in hope of fair advantages.
20   A golden mind stoops not to shows of dross;°   *rubbish*
    I'll then nor° give nor hazard aught for lead.   *neither*
    What says the silver with her virgin hue?
    "Who chooseth me shall get as much as he deserves."
    As much as he deserves—pause there, Morocco,
25   And weigh thy value with an even° hand.   *impartial*
    If thou beest rated by thy estimation
    Thou dost deserve enough, and yet enough
    May not extend so far as to the lady.
    And yet to be afeared of my deserving
30   Were but a weak disabling° of myself.   *disparagement*
    As much as I deserve—why, that's the lady!
    I do in birth deserve her, and in fortunes,
    In graces, and in qualities of breeding;
    But more than these, in love I do deserve.
35   What if I strayed no farther but chose here?
    Let's see once more this saying graved in gold:
    "Who chooseth me shall gain what many men desire."
    Why, that's the lady! All the world desires her;
    From the four corners of the earth they come
40   To kiss this shrine, this mortal breathing saint.
    The Hyrcanian deserts[2] and the vasty° wilds   *vast*
    Of wide Arabia are as thoroughfares° now   *main roads*
    For princes to come view fair Portia.
    The watery kingdom, whose ambitious head°   *(of a storm)*
45   Spits in the face of heaven, is no bar
    To stop the foreign spirits, but they come,
    As o'er a brook, to see fair Portia.
    One of these three contains her heavenly picture.
    Is't like° that lead contains her? 'Twere damnation   *probable*
50   To think so base a thought. It° were too gross   *(lead)*
    To rib her cerecloth[3] in the obscure grave.
    Or shall I think in silver she's immured,°   *enclosed*
    Being ten times undervalued to tried° gold?   *purified*
    Oh, sinful thought! Never so rich a gem
55   Was set in worse than gold. They have in England
    A coin that bears the figure of an angel[4]
    Stamped in gold, but that's insculped° upon.   *engraved*
    But here an angel in a golden bed
    Lies all within. —Deliver me the key!
60   Here do I choose, and thrive I as I may.

---

2. Wild region south of the Caspian Sea.
3. To enclose her shroud (normally covered with a layer of lead).

4. The gold coin called angel had the figure of St. Michael on its face.

PORTIA There—take it, Prince, and if my form° lie there   *image*
  Then I am yours.
MOROCCO [*opening the golden casket*]
         O hell! What have we here?
  A carrion death,° within whose empty eye   *A skull*
  There is a written scroll. I'll read the writing:
65   "All that glisters is not gold.
       Often have you heard that told.
       Many a man his life hath sold
       But my outside⁵ to behold.
       Gilded timber do worms enfold.°   *enclose*
70   Had you been as wise as bold,
       Young in limbs, in judgment old,
       Your answer had not been inscrolled.
       Fare you well; your suit is cold."
  Cold indeed and labor lost.
75 Then farewell, heat, and welcome, frost.
  Portia, adieu; I have too grieved a heart
  To take a tedious leave. Thus losers part.   *Exit* [*with his train*].
PORTIA A gentle riddance! Draw the curtains; go.
  Let all of his complexion choose me so.⁶   *Exeunt.*

2.8

Enter SALERIO *and* SOLANIO.
SALERIO Why, man, I saw Bassanio under sail.
  With him is Graziano gone along,
  And in their ship I am sure Lorenzo is not.
SOLANIO The villain Jew with outcries raised° the Duke,   *roused*
5 Who went with him to search Bassanio's ship.
SALERIO He came too late; the ship was under sail.
  But there the Duke was given to understand
  That in a gondola were seen together
  Lorenzo and his amorous Jessica.
10 Besides, Antonio certified the Duke
  They were not with Bassanio in his ship.
SOLANIO I never heard a passion° so confused,   *an outburst*
  So strange, outrageous, and so variable
  As the dog Jew did utter in the streets:
15 "My daughter, O my ducats, O my daughter!
  Fled with a Christian! O my Christian ducats!
  Justice, the law, my ducats, and my daughter!
  A sealèd bag—two sealèd bags of ducats—
  Of double ducats stolen from me by my daughter;
20 And jewels—two stones, two rich and precious stones¹
  Stolen by my daughter! Justice! Find the girl.
  She hath the stones upon her, and the ducats."
SALERIO Why, all the boys in Venice follow him
  Crying, "His stones, his daughter, and his ducats."
25 SOLANIO Let good Antonio look he keep his day,°   *repay his debt on time*

---

5. Gold; face that once covered the skull.
6. PERFORMANCE COMMENT Portia's final line is often cut from productions so as not to compromise her standing with audiences. Rescuing the play from its objectionable speeches is common in *Merchant* and

can affect the story and its generic balance considerably. See Digital Edition PC 2.
2.8 Location: Venice.
1. With the suggestion "testicles," taken up by the mocking boys in line 24.

Or he shall pay for this.

SALERIO   Marry, well remembered.
I reasoned° with a Frenchman yesterday   *conversed*
Who told me in the narrow seas° that part   *(English Channel)*
The French and English there miscarrièd°   *wrecked*
30   A vessel of our country richly fraught.°   *laden*
I thought upon Antonio when he told me
And wished in silence that it were not his.
SOLANIO   You were best to tell Antonio what you hear.
Yet do not suddenly, for it may grieve him.
35   SALERIO   A kinder gentleman treads not the earth.
I saw Bassanio and Antonio part.
Bassanio told him he would make some speed
Of his return; he answered, "Do not so;
Slubber not° business for my sake, Bassanio;   *Do not hastily perform*
40   But stay the very riping of the time.
And for the Jew's bond which he hath of me,
Let it not enter in your mind° of love.   *interrupt your thoughts*
Be merry and employ your chiefest thoughts
To courtship and such fair ostents° of love   *displays*
45   As shall conveniently° become you there."   *properly*
And even there, his eye being big with tears,
Turning his face, he put his hand behind him
And with affection wondrous sensible°   *obvious; heartfelt*
He wrung Bassanio's hand; and so they parted.
50   SOLANIO   I think he only loves the world for him.
I pray thee, let us go and find him out
And quicken his embracèd heaviness[2]
With some delight or other.
SALERIO   Do we so.   *Exeunt.*

2.9

Enter NERISSA *and a Servitor.*

NERISSA   Quick, quick, I pray thee, draw the curtain straight;°   *immediately*
The Prince of Aragon hath ta'en his oath
And comes to his election presently.°   *his choice at once*
Enter [the Prince of] ARAGON, *his train, and* PORTIA.
PORTIA   Behold, there stand the caskets, noble Prince.
5   If you choose that wherein I am contained
Straight shall our nuptial rites be solemnized;
But if you fail, without more speech, my lord,
You must be gone from hence immediately.
ARAGON   I am enjoined by oath to observe three things:
10   First, never to unfold to anyone
Which casket 'twas I chose; next, if I fail
Of the right casket, never in my life
To woo a maid in way of marriage; lastly,
If I do fail in fortune of my choice,
15   Immediately to leave you and be gone.
PORTIA   To these injunctions everyone doth swear
That comes to hazard° for my worthless self.   *gamble*
ARAGON   And so have I addressed° me. Fortune now   *prepared*
To my heart's hope! Gold, silver, and base lead.

---

2. And lighten the grief he embraces.   **2.9 Location:** Belmont.

20   "Who chooseth me must give and hazard all he hath."
    You shall look fairer ere I give or hazard.
    What says the golden chest? Ha, let me see:
    "Who chooseth me shall gain what many men desire."
    What many men desire—that "many" may be meant
25   By° the fool multitude that choose by show,   *For*
    Not learning more than the fond° eye doth teach,   *foolish*
    Which pries not to th'interior but like the martlet°   *swallow*
    Builds in the weather° on the outward wall,   *open air*
    Even in the force and road of casualty.°   *mishap*
30   I will not choose what many men desire,
    Because I will not jump° with common spirits   *agree*
    And rank me with the barbarous multitudes.
    Why, then, to thee, thou silver treasure-house.
    Tell me once more what title thou dost bear:
35   "Who chooseth me shall get as much as he deserves."
    And well said, too, for who shall go about
    To cozen° fortune and be honorable   *cheat*
    Without the stamp° of merit? Let none presume   *official seal*
    To wear an undeservèd dignity.
40   Oh, that estates, degrees,° and offices   *social ranks*
    Were not derived° corruptly, and that clear honor   *gained*
    Were purchased° by the merit of the wearer!   *acquired*
    How many then should cover that stand bare;[1]
    How many be commanded that command;
45   How much low peasantry would then be gleaned°   *separated*
    From the true seed of honor; and how much honor
    Picked from the chaff and ruin of the times
    To be new varnished?° Well—but to my choice: *regain its luster*
    "Who chooseth me shall get as much as he deserves."
50   I will assume° desert: give me a key for this,   *claim*
    And instantly unlock my fortunes here.
            [*He opens the silver casket.*]
    PORTIA   Too long a pause for that which you find there.
    ARAGON What's here—the portrait of a blinking idiot
    Presenting me a schedule?° I will read it.   *document*
55   How much unlike art thou to Portia!
    How much unlike my hopes and my deservings!
    "Who chooseth me shall have as much as he deserves"?
    Did I deserve no more than a fool's head?
    Is that my prize? Are my deserts no better?
60   PORTIA   To offend and judge are distinct offices,[2]
    And of opposèd natures.
    ARAGON   What is here?
        "The fire seven times tried° this;   *purified*
        Seven times tried that judgment is
        That did never choose amiss.
65   Some there be that shadows kiss;[3]
        Such have but a shadow's bliss.
        There be fools alive, iwis,°   *in truth*
        Silvered[4] o'er, and so was this.

---

1. Should wear hats who now stand bareheaded (before their social superiors).
2. To err and to judge are different functions.
3. Like Narcissus in classical mythology, a youth who fell in love with his own reflection.
4. Silver-haired (thus apparently wise).

70	Take what wife you will to bed,	
	I° will ever be your head.	*(the blinking idiot)*
	So be gone; you are sped."°	*finished*
	Still more fool I shall appear	
	By the time I linger here.	
	With one fool's head I came to woo,	
75	But I go away with two.	
	Sweet, adieu; I'll keep my oath	
	Patiently to bear my wroth.°	*grief*

[*Exit the Prince of* ARAGON *with his train.*]

PORTIA Thus hath the candle singed the moth.
Oh, these deliberate° fools—when they do choose   *careful*
80   They have the wisdom by their wit to lose!
NERISSA The ancient saying is no heresy:
Hanging and wiving goes by destiny.
PORTIA Come, draw the curtain, Nerissa.
      Enter MESSENGER.
MESSENGER Where is my lady?
PORTIA   Here—what would my lord?
85   MESSENGER Madam, there is alighted at your gate
A young Venetian, one that comes before
To signify th'approaching of his lord,
From whom he bringeth sensible regreets:°   *tangible greetings*
To wit, besides commends and courteous breath,
90   Gifts of rich value. Yet° I have not seen   *Until now*
So likely° an ambassador of love.   *suitable*
A day in April never came so sweet
To show how costly° summer was at hand,   *lavish*
As this fore-spurrer comes before his lord.
95   PORTIA No more, I pray thee. I am half afeared
Thou wilt say anon° he is some kin to thee,   *soon*
Thou spend'st such high-day⁵ wit in praising him.
Come, come, Nerissa, for I long to see
Quick Cupid's post° that comes so mannerly.   *messenger*
100   NERISSA Bassanio, Lord Love,° if thy will it be.   *Exeunt.*   *Cupid*

3.1

[*Enter*] SOLANIO *and* SALERIO.

SOLANIO Now, what news on the Rialto?
SALERIO Why, yet it lives there unchecked¹ that Antonio hath
a ship of rich lading wrecked on the narrow seas—the Good-
wins² I think they call the place, a very dangerous flat, and
5   fatal, where the carcasses of many a tall ship lie buried, as they
say, if my gossip Report° be an honest woman of her word.   *Dame Rumor*
SOLANIO I would she were as lying a gossip in that as ever
knapped° ginger or made her neighbors believe she wept for   *nibbled*
the death of a third husband. But it is true, without any slips
10   of prolixity° or crossing the plain highway of talk, that the   *any wordy lies*
good Antonio, the honest Antonio—oh, that I had a title
good enough to keep his name company—
SALERIO Come, the full stop.°   *period*

---

5. Holiday (fit for special occasions).
3.1 Location: Venice.
1. It circulates there without denial.

2. Goodwin Sands, where the Thames joins the sea.
"Goodwin" means "friend."

SOLANIO   Ha, what sayest thou? Why the end is, he hath lost a
15   ship.
SALERIO   I would it might prove the end of his losses.
         Enter SHYLOCK.
SOLANIO   Let me say amen betimes lest the devil cross° my   *thwart*
         prayer, for here he comes in the likeness of a Jew.
         —How now, Shylock, what news among the merchants?
20   SHYLOCK   You knew, none so well, none so well as you, of my
         daughter's flight.
SALERIO   That's certain. I, for my part, knew the tailor that
         made the wings³ she flew withal.
SOLANIO   And Shylock, for his own part, knew the bird was
25   fledge,° and then it is the complexion° of them all to leave   *feathered / disposition*
         the dam.°   *mother (here, parent)*
SHYLOCK   She is damned for it.
SALERIO   That's certain, if the devil may be her judge.
SHYLOCK   My own flesh and blood to rebel!⁴
30   SOLANIO   Out upon it, old carrion! Rebels it at these years?
SHYLOCK   I say my daughter is my flesh and my blood.
SALERIO   There is more difference between thy flesh and hers
         than between jet° and ivory; more between your bloods than   *black mineral*
         there is between red wine and Rhenish.° But tell us: do you   *white wine*
35   hear whether Antonio have had any loss at sea, or no?
SHYLOCK   There I have another bad match:° a bankrupt, a   *bad deal*
         prodigal who dare scarce show his head on the Rialto, a beg-
         gar that was used to come so smug upon the mart! Let him
         look to his bond. He was wont to call me usurer; let him look
40   to his bond. He was wont to lend money for a° Christian   *out of*
         courtesy; let him look to his bond.
SALERIO   Why, I am sure if he forfeit thou wilt not take his
         flesh. What's that good for?
SHYLOCK   To bait fish withal.° If it will feed nothing else, it   *with*
45   will feed my revenge. He hath disgraced me and hindered me
         half a million, laughed at my losses, mocked at my gains,
         scorned my nation, thwarted my bargains, cooled my friends,
         heated mine enemies, and what's his reason? I am a Jew.
         Hath not a Jew eyes? Hath not a Jew hands, organs, dimen-
50   sions,° senses, affections, passions—fed with the same food,   *bodily form*
         hurt with the same weapons, subject to the same diseases,
         healed by the same means, warmed and cooled by the same
         winter and summer as a Christian is? If you prick us do we
         not bleed? If you tickle us do we not laugh? If you poison us
55   do we not die, and if you wrong us shall we not revenge? If we
         are like you in the rest, we will resemble you in that. If a Jew
         wrong a Christian, what is his° humility? Revenge! If a Chris-   *(the Christian's)*
         tian wrong a Jew, what should his sufferance° be by Christian   *patience*
         example? Why, revenge! The villainy you teach me I will exe-
60   cute, and it shall go hard but I will better the instruction.⁵
         Enter a SERVINGMAN *from* ANTONIO.

---

3. Playing on "wing," a decorative flap on the upper
sleeve.
4. Shylock means "my own offspring"; Solanio pretends he means "carnal appetite."
5. PERFORMANCE COMMENT Depending on the characterization of Shylock, the speech can be delivered
as a sympathetic plea for the Christians to recognize
the common humanity of all inhabitants of Venice or
as a justification for Shylock's imminent revenge on
Antonio. Actors often mingle aspects of both interpretations. See Digital Edition PC 3.

SERVINGMAN   Gentlemen, my master Antonio is at his house
and desires to speak with you both.

SALERIO   We have been up and down to seek him.

Enter TUBAL.

SOLANIO   Here comes another of the tribe; a third cannot be
65   matched° unless the devil himself turn Jew.   *found to match*

Exeunt Gentlemen [—SALERIO, *and* SOLANIO—
and SERVINGMAN].[6]

SHYLOCK   How now, Tubal! What news from Genoa? Hast
thou found my daughter?

TUBAL   I often came where I did hear of her, but cannot find her.

SHYLOCK   Why, there, there, there, there—a diamond gone
70   cost me two thousand ducats in Frankfurt![7] The curse never
fell upon our nation till now. I never felt it till now: two
thousand ducats in that and other precious, precious jewels!
I would my daughter were dead at my foot and the jewels in
her ear! Would she were hearsed° at my foot and the ducats   *coffined*
75   in her coffin! No news of them? Why so? And I know not
what's spent in the search. Why, thou: loss upon loss, the
thief gone with so much, and so much to find the thief, and
no satisfaction, no revenge, nor no ill luck stirring but what
lights o'my shoulders, no sighs but o'my breathing, no tears
80   but o'my shedding.

TUBAL   Yes, other men have ill luck too. Antonio, as I heard in
Genoa—

SHYLOCK   What, what, what? Ill luck, ill luck?

TUBAL   —hath an argosy cast away coming from Tripoli.

85   SHYLOCK   I thank God! I thank God! Is it true, is it true?

TUBAL   I spoke with some of the sailors that escaped the
wreck.

SHYLOCK   I thank thee, good Tubal. Good news, good news.
Ha, ha, heard in Genoa!

90   TUBAL   Your daughter spent in Genoa, as I heard, one night
fourscore ducats.

SHYLOCK   Thou stick'st a dagger in me; I shall never see my
gold again! Fourscore ducats at a sitting, fourscore ducats!

TUBAL   There came divers of Antonio's creditors in my com-
95   pany to Venice that swear he cannot choose but break.°   *go bankrupt*

SHYLOCK   I am very glad of it. I'll plague him; I'll torture him. I
am glad of it.

TUBAL   One of them showed me a ring that he had of your
daughter for a monkey.

100   SHYLOCK   Out upon her; thou torturest me, Tubal! It was my
turquoise; I had it of Leah when I was a bachelor. I would
not have given it for a wilderness of monkeys.

TUBAL   But Antonio is certainly undone.

SHYLOCK   Nay, that's true, that's very true. Go, Tubal, fee° me   *hire*
105   an officer; bespeak him a fortnight before. I will have the
heart of him if he forfeit, for were he out of Venice I can
make what merchandise° I will. Go, Tubal, and meet me at   *drive what bargains*
our synagogue. Go, good Tubal; at our synagogue, Tubal.

Exeunt.

---

6. TEXTUAL COMMENT The stage direction implies   considered "gentlemen." See Digital Edition TC 6.
that the Jewish characters, Shylock and Tubal, are not   7. Site of a jewel market.

3.2

Enter BASSANIO, PORTIA, [NERISSA,] GRAZIANO,
[MUSICIANS,] *and all their trains.*

PORTIA I pray you, tarry; pause a day or two
Before you hazard, for in choosing° wrong   *if you choose*
I lose your company.[1] Therefore forbear a while.
There's something tells me—but it is not love—
5   I would not lose you; and you know yourself
Hate counsels not in such a quality.°   *way*
But lest you should not understand me well—
And yet a maiden hath no tongue but thought—
I would detain you here some month or two
10   Before you venture for me. I could teach you
How to choose right, but then I am forsworn;
So° will I never be. So may you miss me,[2]   *(forsworn)*
But if you do, you'll make me wish a sin—
That I had been forsworn. Beshrew your eyes!
15   They have o'erlooked° me and divided me.   *bewitched*
One half of me is yours, the other half yours—
Mine own I would say—but if mine, then yours,
And so all yours. Oh, these naughty° times   *evil*
Puts bars between the owners and their rights—
20   And so, though yours, not yours. Prove it so,
Let fortune go to hell for it, not I.[3]
I speak too long, but 'tis to peise° the time,   *extend*
To eke° it and to draw it out in length   *augment*
To stay° you from election.°   *delay / choosing*
BASSANIO   Let me choose.
25   For as I am I live upon the rack.[4]
PORTIA Upon the rack, Bassanio? Then confess
What treason there is mingled with your love.
BASSANIO None but that ugly treason of mistrust,°   *uncertainty*
Which makes me fear° th'enjoying of my love.   *doubt*
30   There may as well be amity and life
'Tween snow and fire, as treason and my love.
PORTIA Ay, but I fear you speak upon the rack,
Where men, enforcèd, do speak anything.
BASSANIO Promise me life, and I'll confess the truth.
PORTIA Well, then, confess and live.
35 BASSANIO   Confess and love
Had been the very sum of my confession.
Oh, happy torment when my torturer
Doth teach me answers for deliverance!°   *release*
But let me to my fortune and the caskets.
40 PORTIA Away, then. I am locked in one of them;
If you do love me, you will find me out.
Nerissa and the rest, stand all aloof.
Let music sound while he doth make his choice.
Then if he lose, he makes a swanlike end,[5]

3.2 Location: Belmont.
1. PERFORMANCE COMMENT In productions the intermission often falls just before 3.2, and directors
sometimes use the entrance to suggest that Bassanio
has been in Belmont for some time before the action
resumes. Consequently, Bassanio's and Portia's
entrance may suggest a full-blown romance, raising
the stakes for the impending casket choice. See Digi-

tal Edition PC 4.
2. Fail to attain me.
3. *Prove . . . I:* If it turns out thus, let it be fortune's
fault, not mine (for breaking my oath).
4. Instrument of torture used on traitors.
5. The swan was thought to sing only once, just
before its death.

45   Fading in music. That the comparison
      May stand more proper, my eye shall be the stream
      And watery deathbed for him. He may win,
      And what is music then? Then music is
      Even as the flourish° when true subjects bow   *fanfare*
50   To a new-crowned monarch. Such it is
      As are those dulcet sounds in break of day
      That creep into the dreaming bridegroom's ear
      And summon him to marriage.[6] Now he goes,
      With no less presence° but with much more love   *dignity*
55   Than young Alcides when he did redeem
      The virgin tribute paid by howling Troy
      To the sea monster.[7] I stand for sacrifice;
      The rest aloof are the Dardanian° wives   *Trojan*
      With blearèd° visages come forth to view   *weepy*
60   The issue° of th'exploit. Go, Hercules!   *outcome*
      Live thou,° I live! With much, much more dismay   *If you live*
      I view the fight than thou that mak'st the fray.
           A song, the whilst BASSANIO *comments on the caskets to
           himself.*[8]
      FIRST MUSICIAN   Tell me where is fancy° bred: *love; infatuation*
                        Or° in the heart or in the head;   *Whether*
65   How begot, how nourishèd?
                        Reply, reply!
      SECOND MUSICIAN   It is engend'red in the eye,[9]
                        With gazing fed; and fancy dies
                        In the cradle[1] where it lies.
70   Let us all ring fancy's knell.
                        I'll begin it: Ding dong, bell.
      ALL   Ding, dong, bell.
      BASSANIO   So may the outward shows be least themselves.[2]
      The world is still° deceived with ornament.   *continually*
75   In law, what plea so tainted and corrupt
      But, being seasoned with a gracious voice,
      Obscures the show of evil? In religion,
      What damnèd error but some sober brow
      Will bless it and approve° it with a text,   *prove*
80   Hiding the grossness with fair ornament?
      There is no vice so simple° but assumes   *unalloyed; stupid*
      Some mark of virtue on his° outward parts.   *its*
      How many cowards, whose hearts are all as false
      As stairs of sand, wear yet upon their chins
85   The beards of Hercules and frowning Mars,
      Who, inward searched,° have livers white as milk;[3]   *examined*
      And these assume but valor's excrement[4]
      To render them redoubted.° Look on beauty,   *feared*
      And you shall see 'tis purchased by the weight,°   *(like cosmetics)*
90   Which therein works a miracle in nature,

---

6. It was customary to play music under a bride-groom's window on the morning of his wedding.
7. Alcides (Hercules) saved the Trojan princess Hesione when she was to be sacrificed to a sea monster, not because he loved her but to win two horses her father offered as a reward.
8. TEXTUAL COMMENT Early editions of the play do not indicate who sings the song or whether "All" in line 72 refers to all Portia's servants, or only to the musicians. See Digital Edition TC 7.

9. Love was imagined to enter through the eyes. TEXTUAL COMMENT The spelling "engendred" in early editions emphasizes the rhyme with "bred," "head," and "nourishèd" (the last pronounced as a three-syllable word). See Digital Edition TC 8.
1. In infancy, in the eyes (?).
2. Least express the truth.
3. Lily-livered (the liver was considered the seat of courage).
4. External attribute; hair (the beard).

Making them lightest° that wear most of it.   *most licentious*
So are those crispèd,° snaky golden locks,   *curled*
Which maketh such wanton gambols with the wind
Upon supposèd fairness,° often known   *beauty*
95   To be the dowry° of a second head—   *endowment (in a wig)*
The skull that bred them in the sepulcher.
Thus ornament is but the guilèd° shore   *beguiling*
To a most dangerous sea, the beauteous scarf
Veiling an Indian° beauty—in a word,   *a swarthy (pejorative)*
100   The seeming truth which cunning times put on
To entrap the wisest. Therefore, then, thou gaudy gold,
Hard food for Midas,[5] I will none of thee.
Nor none of thee, thou pale and common drudge°   *laborer (in coins)*
'Tween man and man. But thou! Thou meager lead,
105   Which rather threaten'st than dost promise aught,
Thy paleness moves me more than eloquence,
And here choose I—joy be the consequence!
PORTIA   How all the other passions fleet to air—
As° doubtful thoughts and rash-embraced despair   *Such as*
110   And shudd'ring fear and green-eyed jealousy!
O Love, be moderate, allay thy ecstasy,
In measure rein thy joy, scant° this excess.[6]   *lessen*
I feel too much thy blessing; make it less
For fear I surfeit!
BASSANIO [*opening the leaden casket*]
        What find I here?
115   Fair Portia's counterfeit!° What demigod[7]   *likeness*
Hath come so near creation? Move these eyes,
Or whether, riding on the balls of mine,°   *my eyes*
Seem they in motion? Here are severed lips,
Parted with sugar breath; so sweet a bar
120   Should sunder such sweet friends. Here in her hairs
The painter plays the spider and hath woven
A golden mesh t'entrap the hearts of men
Faster than gnats in cobwebs. But her eyes—
How could he see to do them? Having made one,
125   Methinks it should have power to steal both his
And leave itself unfurnished.° Yet look—how far   *unaccompanied*
The substance of my praise doth wrong this shadow°   *portrait*
In underprizing° it, so far this shadow   *understating*
Doth limp behind the substance.° Here's the scroll,   *real thing (Portia)*
130   The continent° and summary of my fortune: *container*
        "You that choose not by the view
        Chance as fair° and choose as true.   *Gamble as luckily*
        Since this fortune falls to you,
        Be content and seek no new.
135   If you be well pleased with this,
        And hold your fortune for your bliss,
        Turn you where your lady is
        And claim her with a loving kiss."
A gentle scroll! Fair lady, by your leave—
        [*He kisses her.*]

5. Everything King Midas touched, including his   6. Synonym for "interest" or "usury."
food, turned to gold.   7. Supernaturally gifted painter.

140　　　I come by note to give[8] and to receive.
　　　　Like one of two contending in a prize°　　　　　　　　　　*contest*
　　　　That thinks he hath done well in people's eyes—
　　　　Hearing applause and universal shout,
　　　　Giddy in spirit, still gazing in a doubt
145　　　Whether those peals of praise be his° or no—　　　　　　*for him*
　　　　So, thrice-fair lady, stand I even so,
　　　　As doubtful whether what I see be true
　　　　Until confirmed, signed, ratified by you.
　　　PORTIA　You see me, Lord Bassanio, where I stand,
150　　　Such as I am. Though for myself alone
　　　　I would not be ambitious in my wish
　　　　To wish myself much better, yet for you
　　　　I would be trebled twenty times myself—
　　　　A thousand times more fair, ten thousand times
155　　　More rich; that only to stand high in your account°　　　*estimation*
　　　　I might in virtues, beauties, livings,° friends　　　　　　*possessions*
　　　　Exceed account. But the full sum of me
　　　　Is sum of something, which to term in gross°　　　　*to describe fully*
　　　　Is an unlessoned girl, unschooled, unpracticed;
160　　　Happy° in this: she is not yet so old　　　　　　　　　　*Fortunate*
　　　　But she may learn; happier than this:
　　　　She is not bred so dull but she can learn;
　　　　Happiest of all is that her gentle spirit
　　　　Commits itself to yours to be directed
165　　　As from her lord, her governor, her king.
　　　　Myself and what is mine to you and yours
　　　　Is now converted.° But° now, I was the lord　　　*transferred / Just*
　　　　Of this fair mansion, master of my servants,
　　　　Queen o'er myself; and even now, but now,
170　　　This house, these servants, and this same myself
　　　　Are yours, my lord's. I give them with this ring,
　　　　Which when you part from, lose, or give away,
　　　　Let it presage the ruin of your love
　　　　And be my vantage to exclaim on you.[9]
175　　PORTIA BASSANIO　Madam, you have bereft me of all words.
　　　　Only my blood speaks to you in my veins;
　　　　And there is such confusion in my powers°　　　　　　*faculties*
　　　　As after some oration fairly spoke
　　　　By a beloved prince, there doth appear
180　　　Among the buzzing, pleasèd multitude—
　　　　Where every something, being blent° together,　　　　　*blended*
　　　　Turns to a wild° of nothing save of joy　　　　　　　　　*chaos*
　　　　Expressed and not expressed. But when this ring
　　　　Parts from this finger, then parts life from hence:
185　　　Oh, then be bold to say° Bassanio's dead.　　　　*say confidently*
　　　NERISSA　My lord and lady, it is now our time,
　　　　That have stood by and seen our wishes prosper,
　　　　To cry good joy, good joy, my lord and lady!
　　　GRAZIANO　My lord Bassanio and my gentle lady,
190　　　I wish you all the joy that you can wish,
　　　　For I am sure you can wish none from me.[1]

---

8. I come by written authorization to give a kiss; to
give myself.

9. And be my opportunity to reproach you.
1. You do not need my good wishes.

And when your honors mean to solemnize
The bargain of your faith, I do beseech you
Even at that time I may be married too.

195 BASSANIO   With all my heart, so° thou canst get a wife.   *if*

GRAZIANO   I thank your lordship, you have got me one.
My eyes, my lord, can look as swift as yours.
You saw the mistress; I beheld the maid.
You loved, I loved; for intermission°   *delay*

200 No more pertains to me, my lord, than you.
Your fortune stood upon the caskets there,
And so did mine, too, as the matter falls.
For wooing here until I sweat again,°   *repeatedly*
And swearing till my very roof° was dry   *(of his mouth)*

205 With oaths of love, at last, if promise² last,
I got a promise of this fair one here
To have her love, provided that your fortune
Achieved her mistress.

PORTIA   Is this true, Nerissa?

NERISSA   Madam, it is, so you stand pleased withal.

210 BASSANIO   And do you, Graziano, mean good faith?

GRAZIANO   Yes, faith, my lord.

BASSANIO   Our feast shall be much honored in your marriage.

GRAZIANO   We'll play° with them the first boy for a thousand ducats.   *wager*

NERISSA   What, and stake down?³

215 GRAZIANO   No, we shall ne'er win at that sport and stake down!

Enter LORENZO, JESSICA, *and* SALERIO [*as*] *a messenger
from Venice.*

But who comes here? Lorenzo and his infidel?
What, and my old Venetian friend Salerio?

BASSANIO   Lorenzo and Salerio, welcome hither,
If that the youth of my new interest° here   *position*

220 Have power° to bid you welcome. By your leave,   *Gives me the right*
I bid my very° friends and countrymen,   *true*
Sweet Portia, welcome.

PORTIA   So do I, my lord; they are entirely welcome.

LORENZO   I thank your honor. For my part, my lord,

225 My purpose was not to have seen you here,
But meeting with Salerio by the way
He did entreat me past all saying nay
To come with him along.

SALERIO   I did, my lord,
And I have reason for it. Signor Antonio
Commends him° to you.   *Sends greeting*

[*He gives* BASSANIO *a letter.*]

230 BASSANIO   Ere I ope his letter
I pray you tell me how my good friend doth.

SALERIO   Not sick, my lord, unless it be in mind;
Nor well, unless in mind: his letter there
Will show you his estate.°   *situation*

[BASSANIO *opens*] *the letter.*

235 GRAZIANO   Nerissa, cheer yond stranger; bid her welcome.
Your hand, Salerio; what's the news from Venice?

---

2. Nerissa's, to wed Graziano.
3. Put the money down now (Graziano follows with a bawdy joke on "flaccid penis").

How doth that royal° merchant, good Antonio?   *princely*
I know he will be glad of our success.
We are the Jasons: we have won the fleece.

240 SALERIO   I would you had won the fleece° that he hath lost.   *(punning on "fleets")*

PORTIA   There are some shrewd° contents in yond same paper   *evil*
That steals the color from Bassanio's cheek—
Some dear friend dead, else nothing in the world
Could turn° so much the constitution   *change*
245 Of any constant° man. What, worse and worse?   *resolute*
With leave, Bassanio—I am half yourself,
And I must freely have the half of anything
That this same paper brings you.

BASSANIO   O sweet Portia,
Here are a few of the unpleasant'st words
250 That ever blotted paper. Gentle lady,
When I did first impart my love to you,
I freely told you all the wealth I had
Ran in my veins—I was a gentleman—
And then I told you true. And yet, dear lady,
255 Rating myself at nothing, you shall see
How much I was a braggart. When I told you
My state° was nothing, I should then have told you   *wealth*
That I was worse than nothing; for indeed
I have engaged° myself to a dear friend,   *pledged*
260 Engaged my friend to his mere° enemy,   *utter*
To feed my means. Here is a letter, lady,
The paper° as the body of my friend,   ·   *(ripped open)*
And every word in it a gaping wound
Issuing lifeblood. But is it true, Salerio?
265 Hath all his ventures failed? What, not one hit,°   *success*
From Tripoli, from Mexico and England,
From Lisbon, Barbary, and India,
And not one vessel scape the dreadful touch
Of merchant-marring rocks?

SALERIO   Not one, my lord.
270 Besides, it should appear that if he had
The present° money to discharge° the Jew,   *ready / pay*
He° would not take it. Never did I know   *(Shylock)*
A creature that did bear the shape of man
So keen° and greedy to confound° a man.   *eager / destroy*
275 He plies the Duke at morning and at night,
And doth impeach the freedom of the state[4]
If they deny him justice. Twenty merchants,
The Duke himself, and the magnificoes°   *Venetian magnates*
Of greatest port° have all persuaded° with him,   *dignity / argued*
280 But none can drive him from the envious° plea   *malicious*
Of forfeiture, of justice, and his bond.

JESSICA   When I was with him I have heard him swear
To Tubal and to Chus, his countrymen,
That he would rather have Antonio's flesh
285 Than twenty times the value of the sum
That he did owe him; and I know, my lord,
If law, authority, and power deny not,

---

4. Accuse the state of not preserving commercial liberty.

It will go hard with poor Antonio.

PORTIA   Is it your dear friend that is thus in trouble?

290 BASSANIO   The dearest friend to me, the kindest man,
The best-conditioned° and unwearied spirit   *best-natured*
In doing courtesies, and one in whom
The ancient Roman honor more appears
Than any that draws breath in Italy.

295 PORTIA   What sum owes he the Jew?

BASSANIO   For me, three thousand ducats.

PORTIA   What, no more?
Pay him six thousand and deface° the bond;   *destroy*
Double six thousand and then treble that,
Before a friend of this description

300 Shall lose a hair through Bassanio's fault.
First go with me to church and call me wife,
And then away to Venice to your friend.
For never shall you lie by Portia's side
With an unquiet soul. You shall have gold

305 To pay the petty debt twenty times over.
When it is paid, bring your true friend along.
My maid Nerissa and myself meantime
Will live as maids and widows. Come, away,
For you shall hence upon your wedding day.

310 Bid your friends welcome; show a merry cheer;°   *countenance*
Since you are dear° bought, I will love you dear.°   *expensively / dearly*
But let me hear the letter of your friend.

BASSANIO [*reads*]   "Sweet Bassanio, my ships have all miscarried; my creditors grow cruel; my estate is very low; my bond

315 to the Jew is forfeit; and since in paying it, it is impossible I
should live, all debts are cleared between you and I if I might
but see you at my death. Notwithstanding, use your pleasure;°   *follow your wishes*
if your love do not persuade you to come, let not my letter."

PORTIA   O love, dispatch all business and be gone!

320 BASSANIO   Since I have your good leave to go away,
I will make haste; but till I come again
No bed shall e'er be guilty of my stay,
Nor rest be interposer twixt us twain.   *Exeunt.*

3.3

Enter [SHYLOCK] *the Jew and* [SOLANIO] *and* ANTONIO
and the Jailer.

SHYLOCK   Jailer, look to him; tell not me of mercy.
This is the fool that lent out money gratis.
Jailer, look to him.

ANTONIO   Hear me yet, good Shylock—

SHYLOCK   I'll have my bond; speak not against my bond.

5 I have sworn an oath that I will have my bond.
Thou called'st me dog before thou hadst a cause;
But since I am a dog, beware my fangs.
The Duke shall grant me justice. —I do wonder,
Thou naughty° jailer, that thou art so fond°   *wicked / foolish*

10 To come abroad° with him at his request.   *outside*

ANTONIO   I pray thee, hear me speak.

3.3 Location: Street in Venice.

SHYLOCK   I'll have my bond; I will not hear thee speak.
  I'll have my bond, and therefore speak no more.
  I'll not be made a soft and dull-eyed° fool,   *gullible*
15 To shake the head, relent and sigh, and yield
  To Christian intercessors. Follow not.
  I'll have no speaking; I will have my bond.
                              Exit [SHYLOCK *the*] *Jew.*
SOLANIO   It is the most impenetrable cur
  That ever kept° with men.   *lived*
ANTONIO   Let him alone.
20 I'll follow him no more with bootless° prayers.   *fruitless*
  He seeks my life; his reason well I know:
  I oft delivered° from his forfeitures   *saved*
  Many that have at times made moan to me;
  Therefore he hates me.
SOLANIO   I am sure the Duke
25 Will never grant this forfeiture to hold.
ANTONIO   The Duke cannot deny° the course of law,   *prevent*
  For the commodity that strangers¹ have
  With us in Venice, if it be denied,
  Will much impeach the justice of the state,
30 Since that the trade and profit of the city
  Consisteth of all nations. Therefore go.
  These griefs and losses have so bated° me   *diminished*
  That I shall hardly spare a pound of flesh
  Tomorrow to my bloody creditor.
35 Well, jailer, on! Pray God Bassanio come
  To see me pay his debt, and then I care not.   *Exeunt.*

3.4

Enter PORTIA, NERISSA, LORENZO, JESSICA, *and*
  [BALTHAZAR,] *a man of Portia's.*
LORENZO   Madam, although I speak it in your presence,
  You have a noble and a true conceit°   *conception*
  Of godlike amity, which appears most strongly
  In bearing thus the absence of your lord.
5 But if you knew to whom you show this honor,
  How true a gentleman you send relief,
  How dear a lover° of my lord your husband,   *friend*
  I know you would be prouder of the work
  Than customary bounty can enforce you.¹
10 PORTIA   I never did repent for doing good,
  Nor shall not now; for in companions
  That do converse and waste° the time together,   *spend (not pejorative)*
  Whose souls do bear an equal yoke of love,
  There must needs be a like proportion
15 Of lineaments, of manners, and of spirit;
  Which makes me think that this Antonio,
  Being the bosom lover of my lord,
  Must needs be like my lord. If it be so,
  How little is the cost I have bestowed
20 In purchasing the semblance of my soul²

---

1. For the trading privileges that foreigners have
(including Jews).
3.4 Location: Belmont.

1. Than ordinary generosity permits you.
2. In redeeming the likeness of my Bassanio
(Antonio).

From out the state of hellish cruelty!
This comes too near the praising of myself;
Therefore no more of it. Hear other things:
Lorenzo, I commit into your hands
25 The husbandry° and manage of my house   care
Until my lord's return. For mine own part,
I have toward heaven breathed a secret vow
To live in prayer and contemplation,
Only attended by Nerissa here,
30 Until her husband and my lord's return.
There is a monastery two miles off,
And there we will abide. I do desire you
Not to deny this imposition,°   decline this charge
The which my love and some necessity
35 Now lays upon you.
LORENZO   Madam, with all my heart
I shall obey you in all fair commands.
PORTIA   My people do already know my mind
And will acknowledge you and Jessica
In place of Lord Bassanio and myself.
40 So fare you well till we shall meet again.
LORENZO   Fair thoughts and happy hours attend on you!
JESSICA   I wish your ladyship all heart's content.
PORTIA   I thank you for your wish, and am well pleased
To wish it back on you. Fare you well, Jessica!
                    Exeunt [LORENZO *and* JESSICA].
45 Now, Balthazar,
As I have ever found thee honest true,
So let me find thee still: take this same letter
And use thou all th'endeavor of a man
In speed to Padua; see thou render this
50 Into my cousin's hands, Doctor Bellario,
And look what notes and garments he doth give thee.
Bring them, I pray thee, with imagined° speed   all imaginable
Unto the traject,° to the common° ferry   ferry / public
Which trades° to Venice. Waste no time in words,   goes back and forth
55 But get thee gone; I shall be there before thee.
BALTHAZAR   Madam, I go with all convenient° speed.   [*Exit.*]   due
PORTIA   Come on, Nerissa. I have work in hand
That you yet know not of. We'll see our husbands
Before they think of us!
NERISSA   Shall they see us?
60 PORTIA   They shall, Nerissa, but in such a habit°   garb
That they shall think we are accomplishèd°   equipped
With that we lack.° I'll hold thee any wager   (i.e., penises)
When we are both accoutred like young men
I'll prove the prettier fellow of the two,
65 And wear my dagger with the braver grace,
And speak between the change of man and boy
With a reed° voice, and turn two mincing steps   piping
Into a manly stride, and speak of frays
Like a fine bragging youth, and tell quaint° lies   elaborate
70 How honorable ladies sought my love,
Which I denying, they fell sick and died—
I could not do withal!° Then I'll repent   help it

And wish, for all that, that I had not killed them;
And twenty of these puny lies I'll tell,
75　That men shall swear I have discontinued° school　　　　*been out of*
　　Above° a twelve-month. I have within my mind　　　　*At least*
　　A thousand raw tricks of these bragging Jacks,°　　　　*fellows*
　　Which I will practice.
NERISSA　　　　　　　　Why, shall we turn to³ men?
PORTIA　Fie, what a question's that,
80　If thou wert near a lewd interpreter!
　　But come, I'll tell thee all my whole device°　　　　*plan*
　　When I am in my coach, which stays for us
　　At the park gate; and therefore haste away,
　　For we must measure twenty miles today.　　　　*Exeunt.*

3.5

Enter [LANCELET *the*] *clown and* JESSICA.

LANCELET　Yes, truly, for look you, the sins of the father are
　　to be laid upon the children; therefore, I promise you, I fear°　　　*fear for*
　　you. I was always plain with you, and so now I speak my agi-
　　tation° of the matter. Therefore be o'good cheer, for truly I　　　*(for "cogitation")*
5　think you are damned. There is but one hope in it that can
　　do you any good, and that is but a kind of bastard hope
　　neither.
JESSICA　And what hope is that, I pray thee?
LANCELET　Marry, you may partly hope that your father got
10　you not, that you are not the Jew's daughter.
JESSICA　That were a kind of bastard hope indeed—so the sins
　　of my mother should be visited upon me!
LANCELET　Truly, then, I fear you are damned both by father
　　and mother; thus when I shun Scylla, your father, I fall into
15　Charybdis, your mother.¹ Well, you are gone° both ways.　　　*doomed*
JESSICA　I shall be saved by my husband.² He hath made me a
　　Christian.
LANCELET　Truly, the more to blame he! We were Christians
　　enough before, e'en as many as could well live one by
20　another.³ This making of Christians will raise the price of
　　hogs; if we grow all to be pork eaters, we shall not shortly
　　have a rasher° on the coals for money.°　　　*bacon strip / any price*
　　　　　Enter LORENZO.
JESSICA　I'll tell my husband, Lancelet, what you say—here he
　　comes!
25　LORENZO　I shall grow jealous of you shortly, Lancelet, if you
　　thus get my wife into corners.
JESSICA　Nay, you need not fear us, Lorenzo. Lancelet and I
　　are out.° He tells me flatly there's no mercy for me in heaven　　　*quarreling*
　　because I am a Jew's daughter; and he says you are no good
30　member of the commonwealth, for in converting Jews to
　　Christians you raise the price of pork.
LORENZO　I shall answer° that better to the commonwealth　　　*explain*

---

3. Turn into (with bawdy suggestion).
3.5 Location: Portia's garden in Belmont.
1. Scylla was a mythological sea monster, Charybdis
a whirlpool in the Strait of Messina. Mariners had to
avoid both, a proverbially difficult task.

2. "The unbelieving wife is sanctified by the husband" (1 Corinthians 7:14).
3. *well . . . another:* reside next door to one another;
earn a living off one another.

than you can the getting up of the negro's belly: the Moor[4] is
with child by you, Lancelet!

35 LANCELET It is much that the Moor should be more than
reason,[5] but if she be less than an honest° woman she is   *a chaste*
indeed more than I took her for.

LORENZO How every fool can play upon the word! I think the
best grace of wit will shortly turn into silence, and discourse

40 grow commendable in none only but parrots. Go in, sirrah;
bid them prepare for dinner.

LANCELET That is done, sir; they have all stomachs.°   *appetites*

LORENZO Goodly Lord! What a wit snapper are you! Then bid
them prepare dinner!

45 LANCELET That is done too, sir; only "cover"[6] is the word.

LORENZO Will you cover then, sir?

LANCELET Not so, sir, neither; I know my duty.

LORENZO Yet more quarreling with occasion![7] Wilt thou show
the whole wealth of thy wit in an instant? I pray thee under-

50 stand a plain man in his plain meaning: go to thy fellows,
bid them cover the table, serve in the meat, and we will
come in to dinner.

LANCELET For the table,° sir, it shall be served in; for the   *meal*
meat, sir, it shall be covered;[8] for your coming in to dinner,

55 sir, why let it be as humors and conceits° shall govern.   *whims and notions*

Exit [LANCELET the] clown.

LORENZO O dear discretion, how his words are suited![9]
The fool hath planted in his memory
An army of good words, and I do know
A many fools that stand in better place,

60 Garnished° like him, that for a tricksy word   *Provided (with words)*
Defy the matter.° How cheer'st thou,[1] Jessica?   *Refuse to talk sense*
And now, good sweet, say thy opinion:
How dost thou like the Lord Bassanio's wife?

JESSICA Past all expressing. It is very meet°   *proper*
65 The Lord Bassanio live an upright life,
For, having such a blessing in his lady,
He finds the joys of heaven here on earth.
And if on earth he do not mean it, it
Is reason he should never come to heaven.

70 Why, if two gods should play some heavenly match
And on the wager lay two earthly women
And Portia one, there must be something else
Pawned° with the other, for the poor rude world   *Wagered*
Hath not her fellow.

LORENZO   Even such a husband
75 Hast thou of me as she is for wife.

JESSICA Nay, but ask my opinion, too, of that!

LORENZO I will anon;° first let us go to dinner.   *soon*

JESSICA Nay, let me praise you while I have a stomach.°   *an appetite; desire*

LORENZO No, pray thee, let it serve for table talk—

---

4. Apparently an African woman of Portia's household.
5. Should be bigger than is reasonable (punning on "more/Moor").
6. Set the table; but Lancelet puns on "cover" as meaning "put on the hat."

7. Playing on words whenever possible.
8. Served in covered dishes (playfully or unconsciously reversing Lorenzo's instructions).
9. Adapted to the occasion. *dear discretion*: precious discrimination (ironic).
1. How are you?

80 Then howsoe'er° thou speak'st, 'mong other things   *however*
I shall digest° it.   *ingest; analyze*

JESSICA   Well, I'll set you forth.[2]   *Exeunt.*

4.1

Enter the DUKE, *the Magnificoes,* ANTONIO, BASSANIO,
[SALERIO,] *and* GRAZIANO.

DUKE   What, is Antonio here?

ANTONIO   Ready, so please your grace.

DUKE   I am sorry for thee. Thou art come to answer
A stony adversary, an inhuman wretch,
5 Uncapable of pity, void and empty
From any dram° of mercy.   *trace*

ANTONIO   I have heard
Your grace hath ta'en great pains to qualify°   *alleviate*
His rigorous course; but since he stands obdurate,
And that no lawful means can carry me
10 Out of his envy's° reach, I do oppose   *malice's*
My patience to his fury and am armed°   *prepared*
To suffer with a quietness of spirit
The very tyranny° and rage of his.   *cruelty*

DUKE   Go one, and call the Jew into the court.

15 SALERIO   He is ready at the door; he comes, my lord.

Enter SHYLOCK.

DUKE   Make room and let him stand before our° face.   *(the royal "we")*
Shylock, the world thinks, and I think so too,
That thou but leadest this fashion° of thy malice   *sustain the pretense*
To the last hour of act;° and then, 'tis thought,   *brink of performance*
20 Thou'lt show thy mercy and remorse° more strange°   *compassion / extraordinary*
Than is thy strange apparent cruelty.
And where thou now exacts the penalty,
Which is a pound of this poor merchant's flesh,
Thou wilt not only lose° the forfeiture,   *waive*
25 But, touched with human gentleness and love,
Forgive a moiety° of the principal,   *part*
Glancing an eye of pity on his losses
That have of late so huddled° on his back—   *piled*
Enough to press a royal merchant down
30 And pluck commiseration of this state's,
From brassy° bosoms and rough hearts of flints,   *unfeeling*
From stubborn Turks and Tartars never trained
To offices° of tender courtesy.   *acts*
We all expect a gentle answer, Jew.

35 SHYLOCK   I have possessed° your grace of what I purpose,   *informed*
And by our holy Sabbath have I sworn
To have the due and forfeit of my bond.
If you deny it, let the danger° light   *damage*
Upon your charter and your city's freedom!
40 You'll ask me why I rather choose to have
A weight of carrion flesh than to receive
Three thousand ducats. I'll not answer that,
But say it is my humor.° Is it answered?   *caprice*

---

2. I'll serve you up (like a dinner); I'll extol you.   **4.1 Location:** The Venetian court

What if my house be troubled with a rat
45 And I be pleased to give ten thousand ducats
To have it baned?° What, are you answered yet?   poisoned
Some men there are love not a gaping pig;[1]
Some that are mad if they behold a cat;
And others, when the bagpipe sings i'th' nose,
50 Cannot contain their urine; for affection,°   impulse
Masters of passion, sways it to the mood
Of what it likes or loathes. Now for your answer:
As there is no firm reason to be rendered
Why he° cannot abide a gaping pig,   one man
55 Why he° a harmless necessary cat,   another
Why he° a woolen bagpipe, but of force°   yet another / necessarily
Must yield to such inevitable shame
As to offend, himself being offended;
So can I give no reason, nor I will not,
60 More than a lodged° hate and a certain loathing   settled
I bear Antonio, that I follow thus
A losing° suit against him. Are you answered?   An unprofitable
BASSANIO   This is no answer, thou unfeeling man,
To excuse the current of thy cruelty!
65 SHYLOCK   I am not bound to please thee with my answers.
BASSANIO   Do all men kill the things they do not love?
SHYLOCK   Hates any man the thing he would not kill?
BASSANIO   Every offense is not a hate at first.
SHYLOCK   What, wouldst thou have a serpent sting thee twice?
70 ANTONIO   I pray you, think you question° with the Jew.   dispute
You may as well go stand upon the beach
And bid the main flood bate his° usual height;   high tide reduce its
You may as well use question with the wolf
Why he hath made the ewe bleat for the lamb;
75 You may as well forbid the mountain of pines
To wag their high tops and to make no noise
When they are fretten° with the gusts of heaven;   fretted; agitated
You may as well do anything most hard
As seek to soften that than which what's harder—
80 His Jewish heart. Therefore, I do beseech you,
Make no more offers, use no farther means,
But with all brief and plain conveniency°   suitability
Let me have judgment and the Jew his will.
BASSANIO   For thy three thousand ducats here is six.
85 SHYLOCK   If every ducat in six thousand ducats
Were in six parts, and every part a ducat,
I would not draw° them. I would have my bond.   take
DUKE   How shalt thou hope for mercy, rend'ring none?
SHYLOCK   What judgment shall I dread, doing no wrong?
90 You have among you many a purchased slave,
Which like your asses and your dogs and mules
You use in abject and in slavish parts°   roles
Because you bought them. Shall I say to you,
"Let them be free; marry them to your heirs!
95 Why sweat they under burdens? Let their beds

---

1. Roasted pig with its mouth propped open.

Be made as soft as yours, and let their palates
Be seasoned with such viands"?° You will answer,   *food*
"The slaves are ours." So do I answer you:
The pound of flesh which I demand of him
100   Is dearly bought, 'tis mine, and I will have it.
If you deny me, fie upon your law:
There is no force in the decrees of Venice.
I stand for judgment. Answer! Shall I have it?

DUKE   Upon° my power I may dismiss this court   *In accordance with*
105   Unless Bellario, a learned doctor
Whom I have sent for to determine° this,   *resolve*
Come here today.

SALERIO   My lord, here stays without°   *waits outside*
A messenger with letters from the doctor,
New come from Padua.

110   DUKE   Bring us the letters. Call the messenger.

BASSANIO   Good cheer, Antonio! What, man, courage yet!
The Jew shall have my flesh, blood, bones and all,
Ere thou shalt lose for me one drop of blood!

ANTONIO   I am a tainted wether° of the flock,   *castrated ram*
115   Meetest for death.° The weakest kind of fruit   *Most fit for slaughter*
Drops earliest to the ground, and so let me.
You cannot better be employed, Bassanio,
Than to live still and write mine epitaph.

        Enter NERISSA [*disguised as Bellario's messenger*].

DUKE   Come you from Padua, from Bellario?
120   NERISSA   From both, my lord. Bellario greets your grace.
      [*She presents a letter.*]

BASSANIO   Why dost thou whet thy knife so earnestly?

SHYLOCK   To cut the forfeiture from that bankrupt there.

GRAZIANO   Not on thy sole, but on thy soul, harsh Jew,
Thou mak'st thy knife keen. But no metal can—
125   No, not the hangman's° ax—bear° half the keenness   *executioner's / have*
Of thy sharp envy.° Can no prayers pierce thee?   *malice*

SHYLOCK   No, none that thou hast wit enough to make.

GRAZIANO   Oh, be thou damned, inexecrable dog,
And for thy life° let justice be accused.   *for allowing you to live*
130   Thou almost mak'st me waver in my faith—
To hold opinion with Pythagoras[2]
That souls of animals infuse themselves
Into the trunks of men. Thy currish spirit
Governed a wolf who hanged for human slaughter;[3]
135   Even from the gallows did his fell soul fleet°   *his cruel soul flit*
And, whilst thou layest in thy unhallowed dam,
Infused itself in thee; for thy desires
Are wolvish, bloody, starved, and ravenous.

SHYLOCK   Till thou canst rail the seal from off my bond
140   Thou but offend'st° thy lungs to speak so loud.   *hurt*
Repair thy wit, good youth, or it will fall
To cureless° ruin. I stand here for law.   *incurable*

DUKE   This letter from Bellario doth commend

---

2. Greek philosopher who believed in the transmigration of souls.
3. In Elizabethan times, animals were tried and hanged for wrongdoing; possibly an allusion to the 1594 execution of the Jewish physician Lopez (Latin *lupus*, "wolf").

A young and learned doctor to our court.
Where is he?

145 NERISSA   He attendeth here hard by
To know your answer whether you'll admit him.

DUKE With all my heart. Some three or four of you
Go give him courteous conduct° to this place;   escort

[*Exeunt some Magnificoes.*]

Meantime the court shall hear Bellario's letter:

150 [*He reads.*] "Your grace shall understand that at the receipt
of your letter I am very sick, but in the instant that your
messenger came, in loving visitation was with me a young
doctor of Rome; his name is Balthazar. I acquainted him
with the cause in controversy between the Jew and Antonio

155 the merchant. We turned o'er many books together. He is
furnished with my opinion which, bettered with his own
learning—the greatness whereof I cannot enough commend—
comes with him at my importunity to fill up° your grace's   answer
request in my stead. I beseech you, let his lack of years be

160 no impediment to let him lack° a reverend estimation; for I   keep him from having
never knew so young a body with so old a head. I leave him
to your gracious acceptance, whose trial shall better publish his commendation."[4]

Enter PORTIA [*disguised as*] *Balthazar*[, *attended by
Magnificoes*].

You hear the learn'd Bellario, what he writes;

165 And here, I take it, is the doctor come.
Give me your hand; come you from old Bellario?

PORTIA I did, my lord.

DUKE You are welcome; take your place.
Are you acquainted with the difference°   dispute

170 That holds this present question[5] in the court?

PORTIA I am informed throughly° of the cause.°   thoroughly / case
Which is the merchant here and which the Jew?[6]

DUKE Antonio and old Shylock, both stand forth.

PORTIA Is your name Shylock?

SHYLOCK   Shylock is my name.

175 PORTIA Of a strange nature is the suit you follow,
Yet in such rule° that the Venetian law   order
Cannot impugn you as you do proceed.
—You stand within his danger,° do you not?   power to harm

ANTONIO Ay, so he says.

PORTIA   Do you confess the bond?

ANTONIO I do.

180 PORTIA   Then must the Jew be merciful.

SHYLOCK On what compulsion must I? Tell me that.

PORTIA The quality of mercy is not strained;°   compelled
It droppeth as the gentle rain from heaven
Upon the place beneath. It is twice blest:

185 It blesseth him that gives and him that takes.
'Tis mightiest in the mightiest; it becomes

---

4. Whose performance ("trial") shall better make
known his worth.
5. That is now being tried.
6. PERFORMANCE COMMENT Portia's inability to distinguish Antonio from Shylock is surprising given both
that Jews in other Renaissance plays appear to have

been marked by dress, hair color, or physiognomy and
that *Merchant* refers to Shylock's distinctive dress at
1.3.106–11. Stage traditions vary, with some Shylocks
eager to assimilate and others equally intent on not
fitting in. See Digital Edition PC 5.

The thronèd monarch better than his crown.
His scepter shows the force of temporal power,
The attribute to° awe and majesty   *of*
190 Wherein doth sit the dread and fear of kings.
But mercy is above this sceptered sway;
It is enthronèd in the hearts of kings;
It is an attribute to God himself,
And earthly power doth then show likest° God's   *most like*
195 When mercy seasons° justice. Therefore, Jew,   *moderates*
Though justice be thy plea, consider this—
That in the course of justice none of us
Should see salvation. We do pray for mercy,
And that same prayer° doth teach us all to render   *(the Lord's Prayer)*
200 The deeds of mercy. I have spoke thus much
To mitigate the justice of thy plea,°   *your demand for justice*
Which if thou follow, this strict court of Venice
Must needs give sentence 'gainst the merchant there.
SHYLOCK   My deeds upon my head![7] I crave the law,
205 The penalty and forfeit of my bond.
PORTIA   Is he not able to discharge the money?
BASSANIO   Yes, here I tender it for him in the court—
Yea, twice the sum; if that will not suffice,
I will be bound to pay it ten times o'er
210 On forfeit of my hands, my head, my heart.
If this will not suffice, it must appear
That malice bears down° truth. And I beseech you—   *overwhelms*
Wrest once° the law to your authority;   *For once twist*
To do a great right do a little wrong
215 And curb this cruel devil of his will.
PORTIA   It must not be. There is no power in Venice
Can alter a decree establishèd.
'Twill be recorded for a precedent,
And many an error by the same example
220 Will rush into the state. It cannot be.
SHYLOCK   A Daniel come to judgment! Yea, a Daniel![8]
O wise young judge, how I do honor thee!
PORTIA   I pray you, let me look upon the bond.
SHYLOCK   Here 'tis, most reverend doctor, here it is.
225 PORTIA   Shylock, there's thrice thy money offered thee.
SHYLOCK   An oath, an oath, I have an oath in heaven.
Shall I lay perjury upon my soul?
Not, not for Venice!
PORTIA   Why, this bond is forfeit,
And lawfully by this the Jew may claim
230 A pound of flesh to be by him cut off
Nearest the merchant's heart. Be merciful—
Take thrice thy money; bid me tear the bond!
SHYLOCK   When it is paid according to the tenor.°   *condition*
It doth appear you are a worthy judge;
235 You know the law; your exposition
Hath been most sound. I charge you by the law

---

7. The Jewish crowd at Jesus' trial cried, "His blood
be on us, and on our children" (Matthew 27:25).
8. In the Apocrypha, the youth Daniel judges the
case of Susanna, accused of inchastity by the Elders;
he rescues her and convicts them.

Whereof you are a well-deserving pillar,
Proceed to judgment. By my soul I swear
There is no power in the tongue of man
240   To alter me! I stay° here on my bond.   *insist*
ANTONIO   Most heartily I do beseech the court
To give the judgment.
PORTIA   Why, then, thus it is:
You must prepare your bosom for his knife.
SHYLOCK   O noble judge, O excellent young man!
245 PORTIA   For the intent and purpose of the law
Hath full relation to⁹ the penalty,
Which here appeareth due upon the bond.
SHYLOCK   'Tis very true. O wise and upright judge,
How much more elder art thou than thy looks!
PORTIA   Therefore lay bare your bosom.
250 SHYLOCK   Ay—his breast.
So says the bond, doth it not, noble judge?
"Nearest his heart"; those are the very words.
PORTIA   It is so. Are there balance° here   *scales*
To weigh the flesh?
SHYLOCK   I have them ready.
255 PORTIA   Have by some surgeon, Shylock, on your charge,°   *expense*
To stop his wounds lest he do bleed to death.
SHYLOCK   Is it so nominated in the bond?
PORTIA   It is not so expressed, but what of that?
'Twere good you do so much for charity.
260 SHYLOCK   I cannot find it; 'tis not in the bond.
PORTIA   You, merchant, have you anything to say?
ANTONIO   But little. I am armed and well prepared.
Give me your hand, Bassanio; fare you well.
Grieve not that I am fallen to this for you,
265 For herein Fortune shows herself more kind
Than is her custom: it is still her use°   *commonly her habit*
To let the wretched man outlive his wealth,
To view with hollow eye and wrinkled brow
An age of poverty; from which lingering penance
270 Of such misery doth she cut me off.
Commend me to your honorable wife:
Tell her the process° of Antonio's end;   *tale*
Say how I loved you; speak me fair° in death.   *well of me*
And when the tale is told, bid her be judge
275 Whether Bassanio had not once a love.
Repent but you° that you shall lose your friend   *Sorrow only*
And he repents not that he pays your debt;
For if the Jew do cut but deep enough,
I'll pay it instantly with all my heart.
280 BASSANIO   Antonio, I am married to a wife
Which is as dear to me as life itself;
But life itself, my wife, and all the world
Are not with me esteemed above thy life.
I would lose all—ay, sacrifice them all
285 Here to this devil—to deliver you.
PORTIA   Your wife would give you little thanks for that

---

9. Is entirely in agreement with.

If she were by to hear you make the offer.
GRAZIANO   I have a wife who I protest I love—
I would she were in heaven so she could
290   Entreat some power to change this currish Jew.
NERISSA   'Tis well you offer it behind her back;
The wish would make else an unquiet house.
SHYLOCK   These be the Christian husbands! I have a daughter—
Would any of the stock of Barabbas[1]
295   Had been her husband rather than a Christian!
We trifle° time; I pray thee, pursue° sentence.   *waste / proceed with*
PORTIA   A pound of that same merchant's flesh is thine:
The court awards it and the law doth give it.
SHYLOCK   Most rightful judge!
300   PORTIA   And you must cut this flesh from off his breast:
The law allows it and the court awards it.
SHYLOCK   Most learned judge, a sentence! —Come, prepare!
PORTIA   Tarry a little. There is something else:
This bond doth give thee here no jot of blood.
305   The words expressly are "A pound of flesh."
Take then thy bond, take thou thy pound of flesh;
But in the cutting it, if thou dost shed
One drop of Christian blood, thy lands and goods
Are by the laws of Venice confiscate
310   Unto the state of Venice.
GRAZIANO   O upright judge! Mark, Jew! O learned judge!
SHYLOCK   Is that the law?
PORTIA   Thyself shall see the act;
For as thou urgest justice, be assured
Thou shalt have justice more than thou desir'st.
315   GRAZIANO   O learned judge! Mark, Jew, a learned judge!
SHYLOCK   I take this offer then; pay the bond thrice
And let the Christian go.
BASSANIO   Here is the money.
PORTIA   Soft°—   *Not so fast*
The Jew shall have all justice! Soft, no haste—
320   He shall have nothing but the penalty.
GRAZIANO   O Jew, an upright judge, a learned judge!
PORTIA   Therefore prepare thee to cut off the flesh.
Shed thou no blood, nor cut thou less nor more
But just° a pound of flesh. If thou tak'st more   *exactly*
325   Or less than a just pound, be it but so much
As makes it light or heavy in the substance°   *weight*
Or the division° of the twentieth part   *fraction*
Of one poor scruple°—nay, if the scale do turn   *tiny weight*
But in the estimation° of a hair—   *amount*
330   Thou diest and all thy goods are confiscate.
GRAZIANO   A second Daniel, a Daniel, Jew!
Now, infidel, I have you on the hip![2]
PORTIA   Why doth the Jew pause? Take thy forfeiture!
SHYLOCK   Give me my principal and let me go.
335   BASSANIO   I have it ready for thee; here it is.
PORTIA   He hath refused it in the open court.

---

1. Thief whom the Jews asked Pilate to set free   2. At a disadvantage (see 1.3.40).
instead of Jesus (Mark 15:6–15).

He shall have merely justice and his bond.

GRAZIANO   A Daniel, still say I; a second Daniel!
I thank thee, Jew, for teaching me that word.

340 SHYLOCK   Shall I not have barely° my principal?   *even*

PORTIA   Thou shalt have nothing but the forfeiture
To be so taken at thy peril, Jew.

SHYLOCK   Why, then, the devil give him good of it!
I'll stay no longer question.[3]

PORTIA   Tarry, Jew—
345 The law hath yet another hold on you.
It is enacted in the laws of Venice
If it be proved against an alien
That by direct or indirect attempts
He seek the life of any citizen,

350 The party 'gainst the which he doth contrive°   *plot*
Shall seize one half his goods; the other half
Comes to the privy coffer° of the state;   *private treasury*
And the offender's life lies in° the mercy   *at*
Of the Duke only, 'gainst all other voice.

355 In which predicament I say thou stand'st:
For it appears by manifest proceeding
That indirectly, and directly too,
Thou hast contrived against the very life
Of the defendant; and thou hast incurred

360 The danger° formerly by me rehearsed.°   *penalty / described*
Down, therefore, and beg mercy of the Duke.

GRAZIANO   Beg that thou mayst have leave to hang thyself!
And yet, thy wealth being forfeit to the state,
Thou hast not left the value of a cord;

365 Therefore thou must be hanged at the state's charge.°   *expense*

DUKE   That thou shalt see the difference of our spirit,
I pardon thee thy life before thou ask it.
For half thy wealth, it is Antonio's;
The other half comes to the general state,

370 Which humbleness may drive° unto a fine.   *reduce*

PORTIA   Ay, for the state, not for Antonio.[4]

SHYLOCK   Nay, take my life and all, pardon not that.
You take my house when you do take the prop
That doth sustain my house; you take my life

375 When you do take the means whereby I live.[5]

PORTIA   What mercy can you render him, Antonio?

GRAZIANO   A halter° gratis—nothing else, for God's sake!   *hangman's noose*

ANTONIO   So please my lord the Duke, and all the court,
To quit the fine for one half of his goods

380 I am content, so he will let me have
The other half in use,[6] to render it
Upon his death unto the gentleman
That lately stole his daughter.

---

3. I'll press my case no further.
4. With respect to the state's half, not Antonio's.
5. "He that taketh away his neighbor's living, slayeth him" (Ecclesiastes 34:22).
6. Antonio's conditions are unclear, because "quit" in line 379 (requite) could mean "pardon" or "make him pay," and "in use" (line 381) could mean either

"in trust" or "for my own purposes." But the arrangements for Shylock's property later in the scene suggest that Antonio succeeds in getting Shylock's penalty reduced: Shylock retains half of his wealth, and Antonio holds the other half in trust for Jessica and Lorenzo until Shylock dies, at which point they inherit the whole estate.

Two things provided more: that for this favor
385 He presently° become a Christian;   *immediately*
The other, that he do record a gift
Here in the court of all he dies possessed
Unto his son Lorenzo and his daughter.
  DUKE He shall do this or else I do recant°   *withdraw*
390 The pardon that I late pronouncèd here.
  PORTIA Art thou contented, Jew? What dost thou say?
  SHYLOCK I am content.[7]
  PORTIA   Clerk, draw a deed of gift.
  SHYLOCK I pray you, give me leave to go from hence;
I am not well. Send the deed after me
And I will sign it.
395   DUKE   Get thee gone, but do it.
  GRAZIANO In christening shalt thou have two godfathers.
Had I been judge, thou shouldst have had ten more°   *(to constitute a jury)*
To bring thee to the gallows, not to the font.
                                Exit [SHYLOCK].
  DUKE —Sir, I entreat you home with me to dinner.
400   PORTIA I humbly do desire your grace of pardon.
I must away this night toward Padua,
And it is meet° I presently set forth.   *proper*
  DUKE I am sorry that your leisure serves you not.°   *you haven't the time*
Antonio, gratify° this gentleman,   *reward*
405 For in my mind you are much bound to him.
                         Exeunt DUKE *and his train.*
  BASSANIO Most worthy gentleman, I and my friend
Have by your wisdom been this day acquitted
Of grievous penalties, in lieu whereof
Three thousand ducats due unto the Jew
410 We freely cope° your courteous pains withal.   *repay*
  ANTONIO And stand indebted over and above
In love and service to you evermore.
  PORTIA He is well paid that is well satisfied;
And I, delivering you, am satisfied,
415 And therein do account myself well paid.
My mind was never yet more mercenary.
I pray you, know me when we meet again.
I wish you well, and so I take my leave.
  BASSANIO Dear sir, of force° I must attempt you further.   *necessity*
420 Take some remembrance of us as a tribute,
Not as fee. Grant me two things, I pray you:
Not to deny me, and to pardon me.°   *excuse my urging*
  PORTIA You press me far, and therefore I will yield.
Give me your gloves; I'll wear them for your sake.
425 And for your love I'll take this ring from you.
Do not draw back your hand; I'll take no more,
And you, in love, shall not deny me this!
  BASSANIO This ring, good sir, alas—it is a trifle;
I will not shame myself to give you this!

---

7. **PERFORMANCE COMMENT** An audience that welcomes Antonio's deliverance is often made uncomfortable by the exaction of these penalties against Shylock. How far the Venetians go, and who goes farthest, can undercut the joyful resolution to Antonio's trial and overshadow the fifth act. See Digital Edition PC 6.

430   PORTIA   I will have nothing else but only this,
And now, methinks, I have a mind to it!
   BASSANIO   There's more depends on this° than on the value.   *involved here*
The dearest ring in Venice will I give you,
And find it out by proclamation.
435   Only for this, I pray you, pardon me.
   PORTIA   I see, sir, you are liberal in offers.
You taught me first to beg, and now, methinks,
You teach me how a beggar should be answered.
   BASSANIO   Good sir, this ring was given me by my wife,
440   And when she put it on she made me vow
That I should neither sell nor give nor lose it.
   PORTIA   That 'scuse serves many men to save their gifts;
An if° your wife be not a madwoman,   *An if = If*
And know how well I have deserved this ring,
445   She would not hold out enemy forever
For giving it to me. Well, peace be with you.
                       Exeunt [PORTIA *and* NERISSA].
   ANTONIO   My lord Bassanio, let him have the ring.
Let his deservings and my love withal
Be valued 'gainst your wife's commandment.
450   BASSANIO   Go, Graziano, run and overtake him.
Give him the ring and bring him, if thou canst,
Unto Antonio's house. Away, make haste!   *Exit* GRAZIANO.
Come, you and I will thither presently,
And in the morning early will we both
455   Fly toward Belmont. Come, Antonio.   *Exeunt.*

4.2

Enter [PORTIA *and*] NERISSA [*still in disguise*].
   PORTIA   Inquire the Jew's house out; give him this deed,[1]
And let him sign it. We'll away tonight
And be a day before our husbands home.
This deed will be well welcome to Lorenzo!
       Enter GRAZIANO.
5   GRAZIANO   Fair sir, you are well o'erta'en:
My lord Bassanio, upon more advice,°   *further thought*
Hath sent you here this ring, and doth entreat
Your company at dinner.
   PORTIA   That cannot be.
His ring I do accept most thankfully,
10   And so I pray you tell him. Furthermore,
I pray you show my youth old Shylock's house.
   GRAZIANO   That will I do.
   NERISSA   Sir, I would speak with you.
   [*to* PORTIA] I'll see if I can get my husband's ring,
Which I did make him swear to keep forever.
15   PORTIA   Thou mayst, I warrant. We shall have old° swearing   *lots of*
That they did give the rings away to men;
But we'll outface them and outswear them too.
Away, make haste! Thou know'st where I will tarry.
   NERISSA   Come, good sir, will you show me to this house?
                              [*Exeunt.*]

4.2 Location: Street in Venice.   1. Mentioned in 4.1.392 and 394.

5.1

Enter LORENZO *and* JESSICA.

LORENZO   The moon shines bright. In such a night as this,
　When the sweet wind did gently kiss the trees
　And they did make no noise, in such a night
　Troilus methinks mounted the Trojan walls
5　And sighed his soul toward the Grecian tents
　Where Cressid lay that night.[1]

JESSICA　　　　　　　　　　　In such a night
　Did Thisbe fearfully o'ertrip the dew,
　And saw the lion's shadow ere himself,
　And ran dismayed away.[2]

LORENZO　　　　　　　　In such a night
10　Stood Dido with a willow in her hand
　Upon the wild sea banks and waft her love
　To come again to Carthage.[3]

JESSICA　　　　　　　　　　In such a night
　Medea gathered the enchanted herbs
　That did renew old Aeson.[4]

LORENZO　　　　　　　　In such a night
15　Did Jessica steal° from the wealthy Jew　　　　　　　　　　*escape; rob*
　And with an unthrift° love did run from Venice　　　　　　*a spendthrift*
　As far as Belmont.

JESSICA　　　　　　In such a night
　Did young Lorenzo swear he loved her well,
　Stealing her soul with many vows of faith,
　And ne'er a true one.

20　LORENZO　　　　　　In such a night
　Did pretty Jessica, like a little shrew,
　Slander her love, and he forgave it her.

JESSICA   I would out-night you did nobody come,
　But hark—I hear the footing° of a man.　　　　　　　　　*footsteps*

Enter [STEFANO,] *a messenger.*

25　LORENZO   Who comes so fast in silence of the night?

STEFANO   A friend.

LORENZO   A friend? What friend? Your name, I pray you, friend?

STEFANO   Stefano is my name, and I bring word
　My mistress will before the break of day
30　Be here at Belmont. She doth stray about
　By holy crosses° where she kneels and prays　　　　　*roadside shrines*
　For happy wedlock hours.

LORENZO　　　　　　　　Who comes with her?

STEFANO   None but a holy hermit and her maid.
　I pray you, is my master yet returned?

35　LORENZO   He is not, nor we have not heard from him.
　But go we in, I pray thee, Jessica,
　And ceremoniously let us prepare

5.1 Location: Belmont.
1. Troilus was a Trojan prince whose lover, Cressida, forsook him for the Greek Diomedes after she was sent from Troy to the Greek camp. See *Troilus and Cressida.*
2. Thisbe, going at night to meet her lover, Pyramus, was frightened by a lion and fled. Pyramus, assuming she was dead, killed himself; when she found his body, Thisbe committed suicide too. The story is dra-

matized by "the rude mechanicals" in *A Midsummer Night's Dream.*
3. Dido, Queen of Carthage, was abandoned by her lover, the Trojan hero Aeneas. *willow:* emblem of forsaken love. *waft:* waved to.
4. Medea was a sorceress who loved Jason and helped him win the Golden Fleece; she magically restored Aeson, Jason's father, to youth.

Some welcome for the mistress of the house.
    Enter [LANCELET *the*] *clown.*

LANCELET   Sola, sola! Wo ha, ho sola, sola![5]

40 LORENZO   Who calls?

LANCELET   Sola! Did you see Master Lorenzo and Mistress
Lorenzo? Sola, sola!

LORENZO   Leave hallooing, man! Here!

LANCELET   Sola! Where, where?

45 LORENZO   Here!

LANCELET   Tell him there's a post° come from my master,   *messenger*
with his horn full of good news. My master will be here ere
morning.   [*Exit.*]

LORENZO   Sweet soul, let's in and there expect° their coming.   *await*

50   And yet, no matter. Why should we go in?
My friend Stefano, signify,° I pray you,   *announce*
Within the house, your mistress is at hand,
And bring your music forth into the air.   [*Exit* STEFANO.]
—How sweet the moonlight sleeps upon this bank.

55   Here will we sit and let the sounds of music
Creep in our ears. Soft stillness and the night
Become the touches[6] of sweet harmony.
Sit, Jessica. Look how the floor of heaven
Is thick inlaid with patens° of bright gold;   *disks*

60   There's not the smallest orb which thou behold'st
But in his motion like an angel sings,
Still° choiring to the young-eyed[7] cherubim.   *Continually*
Such harmony[8] is in immortal souls,
But whilst this muddy vesture of decay°   *this mortal body*

65   Doth grossly close it° in, we cannot hear it.°   *(the soul) / (the music)*
—Come, ho! And wake Diana[9] with a hymn.
    [*Enter* MUSICIANS.]
With sweetest touches pierce your mistress'° ear   *(Portia's)*
And draw her home with music.
    [MUSICIANS] *play music.*

JESSICA   I am never merry when I hear sweet music.

70 LORENZO   The reason is, your spirits are attentive;
For do but note a wild and wanton herd
Or race° of youthful and unhandled colts   *group*
Fetching mad bounds, bellowing, and neighing loud,
Which is the hot condition of their blood:

75   If they but hear perchance a trumpet sound,
Or any air of music touch their ears,
You shall perceive them make a mutual° stand,   *simultaneous*
Their savage eyes turned to a modest gaze
By the sweet power of music. Therefore the poet[1]

80   Did feign that Orpheus drew° trees, stones, and floods,   *allured*
Since naught so stockish,° hard, and full of rage   *stolid*
But music for the time doth change his nature.
The man that hath no music in himself,
Nor is not moved with concord of sweet sounds,

85   Is fit for treasons, stratagems,° and spoils;°   *plots / plunder*

---

5. Imitating a messenger's horn.
6. Suit the notes (literally, the fingering of a stringed instrument).
7. Keen-sighted.

8. The music of the spheres.
9. Goddess of the moon and of chastity.
1. Ovid, in *Metamorphoses* 10, tells the story of Orpheus, a legendary musician.

The motions of his spirit are dull as night,
And his affections° dark as Erebus.°   *inclinations / hell*
Let no such man be trusted! Mark the music.

Enter PORTIA *and* NERISSA.

PORTIA   That light we see is burning in my hall;
90   How far that little candle throws his beams!
So shines a good deed in a naughty° world.   *an evil*
NERISSA   When the moon shone we did not see the candle.
PORTIA   So doth the greater glory dim the less.
A substitute° shines brightly as a king   *deputy*
95   Until a king be by, and then his state
Empties itself as doth an inland brook
Into the main of waters.° Music, hark!   *the ocean*
NERISSA   It is your music, madam, of the house.
PORTIA   Nothing is good, I see, without respect;°   *reference to context*
100   Methinks it sounds much sweeter than by day.
NERISSA   Silence bestows that virtue on it, madam.
PORTIA   The crow doth sing as sweetly as the lark
When neither is attended;[2] and I think
The nightingale, if she should sing by day
105   When every goose is cackling, would be thought
No better a musician than the wren.
How many things by season seasoned are[3]
To their right praise and true perfection!
Peace! How the moon sleeps with Endymion[4]
And would not be awaked.
110 LORENZO   That is the voice,
Or I am much deceived, of Portia.
PORTIA   He knows me as the blind man knows the cuckoo—
By the bad voice!
LORENZO   Dear lady, welcome home!
PORTIA   We have been praying for our husbands' welfare,
115   Which speed,° we hope, the better for our words.   *Who prosper*
Are they returned?
LORENZO   Madam, they are not yet,
But there is come a messenger before
To signify their coming.
PORTIA   Go in, Nerissa.
Give order to my servants that they take
120   No note at all of our being absent hence
— Nor you, Lorenzo —Jessica, nor you.

[Trumpet sounds.]

LORENZO   Your husband is at hand. I hear his trumpet.
We are no telltales, madam; fear you not.
PORTIA   This night, methinks, is but the daylight sick;
125   It looks a little paler. 'Tis a day
Such as the day is when the sun is hid.

Enter BASSANIO, ANTONIO, GRAZIANO, *and their followers.*

BASSANIO   We should hold day with the Antipodes,
If you would walk in absence of the sun.[5]

---

2. Is listened to; is accompanied.
3. *by season . . . are:* by proper time are adapted.
4. In classical mythology, a shepherd beloved of the
moon goddess, who caused him to sleep forever.

5. *We . . . sun:* We would share daylight with the
other side of the world (Antipodes) if you habitually
walked when the sun was gone (implying "such is
your radiance").

PORTIA Let me give light, but let me not be light;°   *unfaithful*
130   For a light wife doth make a heavy° husband,   *sad*
    And never be Bassanio so for me—
    But God sort° all. You are welcome home, my lord.   *decide*
BASSANIO I thank you, madam. Give welcome to my friend.
    This is the man; this is Antonio
135   To whom I am so infinitely bound.
PORTIA You should in all° sense be much bound to him,   *every*
    For, as I hear, he was much bound for you.
ANTONIO No more than I am well acquitted° of.   *freed*
PORTIA Sir, you are very welcome to our house.
140   It must appear in other ways than words;
    Therefore I scant this breathing courtesy.[6]
GRAZIANO [*to* NERISSA] By yonder moon I swear you do me wrong.
    In faith, I gave it to the judge's clerk.
    Would he were gelt° that had it, for my part,   *gelded; castrated*
145   Since you do take it, love, so much at heart!
PORTIA A quarrel, ho! Already? What's the matter?
GRAZIANO About a hoop of gold, a paltry ring
    That she did give me, whose posy° was   *motto*
    For all the world like cutler's poetry
150   Upon a knife: "Love me and leave me not."
NERISSA What, talk you of the posy or the value?
    You swore to me when I did give it you
    That you would wear it till your hour of death
    And that it should lie with you in your grave.
155   Though not for me, yet for your vehement oaths,
    You should have been respective° and have kept it.   *careful*
    Gave it a judge's clerk! No, God's my judge,
    The clerk will ne'er wear hair on 's face that had it!
GRAZIANO He will an if he live to be a man.
160 NERISSA Ay, if a woman live to be a man!
GRAZIANO Now, by this hand, I gave it to a youth—
    A kind of boy, a little scrubbèd° boy,   *stunted*
    No higher than thyself—the judge's clerk,
    A prating° boy that begged it as a fee.   *chattering*
165   I could not for my heart deny it him.
PORTIA You were to blame—I must be plain with you—
    To part so slightly with your wife's first gift,
    A thing stuck on with oaths upon your finger
    And so riveted with faith unto your flesh.
170   I gave my love a ring and made him swear
    Never to part with it; and here he stands.
    I dare be sworn for him he would not leave° it,   *part with*
    Nor pluck it from his finger, for the wealth
    That the world masters.° Now, in faith, Graziano,   *possesses*
175   You give your wife too unkind a cause of grief;
    An 'twere to me I should be mad at it.
BASSANIO [*aside*] Why, I were best to cut my left hand off
    And swear I lost the ring defending it!
GRAZIANO My lord Bassanio gave his ring away
180   Unto the judge that begged it, and indeed
    Deserved it, too. And then the boy, his clerk,

6. I make brief this verbal welcome.

That took some pains in writing, he begged mine;
And neither man nor master would take aught
But the two rings.

PORTIA   What ring gave you, my lord?
185   Not that, I hope, which you received of me.
BASSANIO   If I could add a lie unto a fault,
        I would deny it; but you see my finger
        Hath not the ring upon it. It is gone.
PORTIA   Even so void is your false heart of truth.
190   By heaven, I will ne'er come in your bed
        Until I see the ring!
NERISSA   Nor I in yours
        Till I again see mine!
BASSANIO   Sweet Portia,
        If you did know to whom I gave the ring,
        If you did know for whom I gave the ring,
195   And would conceive for what I gave the ring,
        And how unwillingly I left the ring
        When naught would be accepted but the ring,
        You would abate the strength of your displeasure.
PORTIA   If you had known the virtue° of the ring,   *power*
200   Or half her worthiness that gave the ring,
        Or your own honor to contain° the ring,   *retain*
        You would not then have parted with the ring.
        What man is there so much unreasonable,
        If you had pleased to have defended it
205   With any terms of zeal, wanted° the modesty°   *would lack / moderation*
        To urge° the thing held as a ceremony?°   *insist on / sacred symbol*
        Nerissa teaches me what to believe:
        I'll die for't, but some woman had the ring!
BASSANIO   No, by my honor, madam. By my soul,
210   No woman had it, but a civil doctor,°   *doctor of civil law*
        Which did refuse three thousand ducats of me
        And begged the ring, the which I did deny him,
        And suffered° him to go displeased away—   *permitted*
        Even he that had held up the very life
215   Of my dear friend. What should I say, sweet lady?
        I was enforced to send it after him.
        I was beset with shame and courtesy;
        My honor would not let ingratitude
        So much besmear it. Pardon me, good lady,
220   For by these blessed candles of the night,
        Had you been there, I think you would have begged
        The ring of me to give the worthy doctor!
PORTIA   Let not that doctor e'er come near my house.
        Since he hath got the jewel that I loved,
225   And that which you did swear to keep for me,
        I will become as liberal° as you: *generous; licentious*
        I'll not deny him anything I have—
        No, not my body nor my husband's bed!
        Know° him I shall; I am well sure of it.   *(with sexual suggestion)*
230   Lie not a night from home; watch me like Argus.[7]

7. Mythical many-eyed monster.

If you do not, if I be left alone,
Now by mine honor, which is yet mine own,
I'll have that doctor for mine bedfellow.
NERISSA   And I his clerk. Therefore, be well advised
235   How you do leave me to mine own protection!
GRAZIANO   Well, do you so. Let not me take him, then;
For if I do, I'll mar the young clerk's pen.°   *(with sexual suggestion)*
ANTONIO   I am th'unhappy subject of these quarrels.
PORTIA   Sir, grieve not you; you are welcome notwithstanding.
240   BASSANIO   Portia, forgive me this enforcèd wrong,
And in the hearing of these many friends
I swear to thee—even by thine own fair eyes
Wherein I see myself—
PORTIA   Mark you but that?
In both my eyes he doubly sees himself—
245   In each eye one. Swear by your double° self,   *twofold; deceitful*
And there's an oath of credit!⁸
BASSANIO   Nay, but hear me.
Pardon this fault, and by my soul I swear
I never more will break an oath with thee.
ANTONIO   I once did lend my body for his wealth,
250   Which but for him that had your husband's ring
Had quite miscarried. I dare be bound again,
My soul upon the forfeit, that your lord
Will never more break faith advisedly.°   *intentionally*
PORTIA   Then you shall be his surety:° give him this,   *guarantor of a loan*
255   And bid him keep it better than the other.
ANTONIO   Here, Lord Bassanio, swear to keep this ring.
BASSANIO   By heaven, it is the same I gave the doctor!
PORTIA   I had it of him. Pardon me, Bassanio,
For by this ring the doctor lay with me.
260   NERISSA   And pardon me, my gentle Graziano,
For that same "scrubbèd boy," the doctor's clerk,
In lieu of° this last night did lie with me.   *In exchange for*
GRAZIANO   Why, this is like the mending of highways
In summer, where the ways are fair enough!⁹
265   What, are we cuckolds ere we have deserved it?
PORTIA   Speak not so grossly. You are all amazed.°   *confused*
Here is a letter; read it at your leisure.
It comes from Padua from Bellario.
There you shall find that Portia was the doctor,
270   Nerissa there her clerk. Lorenzo here
Shall witness I set forth as soon as you
And even but now returned. I have not yet
Entered my house. Antonio, you are welcome,
And I have better news in store for you
275   Than you expect. Unseal this letter soon.
There you shall find three of your argosies
Are richly come to harbor suddenly.
You shall not know by what strange accident
I chancèd on this letter.
ANTONIO   I am dumb!°   *dumbstruck*

---

8. An oath to be believed (ironic).   9. *where . . . enough:* when repair is not required.

280 BASSANIO   Were you the doctor and I knew you not?

GRAZIANO   Were you the clerk that is to make me cuckold?

NERISSA   Ay, but the clerk that never means to do it,
Unless he live until he be a man.

BASSANIO   Sweet doctor, you shall be my bedfellow.
285 When I am absent, then lie with my wife.

ANTONIO   Sweet lady, you have given me life and living,°   *possessions*
For here I read for certain that my ships
Are safely come to road.°   *harbor*

PORTIA   How now, Lorenzo!
My clerk hath some good comforts too for you.

290 NERISSA   Ay, and I'll give them him without a fee.
There do I give to you and Jessica
From the rich Jew a special deed of gift,
After his death of all he dies possessed of.

LORENZO   Fair ladies, you drop manna in the way
Of starvèd people.

295 PORTIA   It is almost morning,
And yet I am sure you are not satisfied
Of these events at full. Let us go in,
And charge us there upon interrogatories,[1]
And we will answer all things faithfully.

300 GRAZIANO   Let it be so. The first interrogatory
That my Nerissa shall be sworn on is
Whether till the next night she had rather stay,
Or go to bed now, being two hours to day.
But were the day come, I should wish it dark
305 Till I were couching° with the doctor's clerk.   *lying*
Well, while I live I'll fear no other thing
So sore as keeping safe Nerissa's ring.°   *Exeunt.*[2] *(with sexual suggestion)*

---

1. And question us under oath.
2. PERFORMANCE COMMENT While Graziano's speech
suggests a cheerful resolution, the final exit or tableau
offers several possibilities for directors to influence an
audience's interpretation of the action and comment
on the futures of its principals. See Digital Edition
PC 7.

Much Ado About Nothing

There are certain foods whose sweet deliciousness relies upon an undertone of bitterness. The bitterness by itself would be unpalatable; the sweetness alone would be cloying. Everything depends on the way the tastes are braided together, either in nature or by a skilled chef. *Much Ado About Nothing,* first published in 1600 and probably written in 1598, is precisely such a food. The play weaves together two stories: the benevolent luring of the quarreling Beatrice and Benedict into mutual declarations of love, and the villainous luring of Claudio into the mistaken belief that his fiancée, Hero, is unchaste. For the former plot, there seems to be no specific source, though Shakespeare would have encountered stories of scorners of love who fall in love (including Chaucer's *Troilus and Criseyde*). For the story of the virtuous lady falsely accused, sources abound, including Ludovico Ariosto's wonderful version in Canto V of *Orlando Furioso* (1516, translated into English by Sir John Harington in 1591) and Matteo Bandello's twenty-second *Novella* (1554, translated into French by François de Belleforest in 1574). Shakespeare probably knew these and other versions, both dramatic and nondramatic, among them a tragic retelling by Edmund Spenser in Book II of *The Faerie Queene* (1590). By deftly intertwining the two plots, *Much Ado About Nothing* mingles lightheartedness with a certain haunting sadness.

Sadness is a recurrent undertone in Shakespeare's earlier comedies: *The Comedy of Errors* opens with a condemned man's lament, *The Merchant of Venice* is darkened by Antonio's melancholy and Shylock's bitter rage, and *Love's Labor's Lost* (which features in Biron and Rosaline a pair of sparring lovers who strikingly anticipate Benedict and Beatrice) ends with a death. In several later comedies, most notably *Measure for Measure,* the darkness is so intensified as to make the term "comedy" seem a problem. But in *Much Ado About Nothing* Shakespeare creates a balance of laughter, longing, and pain that he equals only in two other great romantic comedies from the same period, *As You Like It* and *Twelfth Night, or What You Will.* The titles of all three plays convey an impression of easy, festive wit, a magical effortlessness that is in fact the product of extraordinary discipline and skill.

This cunning use of effort to produce the effect of effortlessness can be understood in the light of Baldassare Castiglione's famous courtesy manual *The Book of the Courtier* (1528). Castiglione's book, published in an English translation in 1561, depicts a witty and sophisticated group of men and women who, in several extended conversations, discuss the qualities that must be possessed by the ideal courtier. The courtier, as they envisage him, must be equally adept at making war and making love. He must be able to assist the Prince and to dance elegantly, to grasp the subtleties of diplomacy and to sing in a pleasant, unaffected voice, to engage in philosophical speculation and to tell amusing after-dinner stories. In similar fashion, court ladies must be at once modest and spirited, chaste and slyly knowing, unspoiled and elegant. These are, in less idealized and rarefied form, the social roles that Benedict and Beatrice are called upon to play. They are roles that demand exceptionally versatile actors.

Such courtly performances, Castiglione's conversationalists acknowledge, risk seeming stilted and artificial; they will be successful only if they appear entirely spontaneous and natural. However carefully they prepare their parts, courtiers should hide all signs of study and rehearsal. To achieve grace, they must practice what Castiglione calls *sprezzatura,* a cultivated nonchalance. *Sprezzatura* is a technique for the manipulation of appearance, for masking the hard work that underlies successful performances. This masking is an open secret: others know that you are masking, but they must keep this knowledge suspended in the belief that it is a breach of decorum to acknowledge their own knowledge.

The society of *The Book of the Courtier* lives with other open secrets. Dark forces lie just outside the charmed circle of delightful lords and ladies: war, arbitrary power, the high risk of betrayal and double-dealing, the commodification of women, the grinding labor to which the great mass of human beings are condemned. The courtier's artful refusal to acknowledge any of these forces could be a mode of escapism, but Castiglione is alert to reality's harsh demands. For him, fashioning the self is a means not of withdrawing from a treacherous world, but of operating successfully within it.

Like Castiglione's *Courtier, Much Ado About Nothing* (whose title suggests the playwright's own mastery of *sprezzatura*) is pervasively concerned with social performance that seems at once spontaneous and calculated. Beatrice and Benedict, at the play's center, are both exquisitely self-conscious, but their self-consciousness takes the paradoxical form of a jaunty indifference to conventional niceties, an almost reckless exuberance that masks a heightened sensitivity to the social currents in which they swim.

By contrast, Don John, the bastard brother, characterizes himself from the start as a radically antisocial creature: "I had rather be a canker in a hedge than a rose in his grace. And it better fits my blood to be disdained of all than to fashion a carriage to rob love from any" (1.3.22–24). These are the sentiments of the outsider, one who, like the bastard Edmund in *King Lear*, is not properly part of the family and kinship network, and they are sufficient, in this play, to account for Don John's relentless, curiously disinterested villainy. He is a man who refuses to "fashion a carriage"—to observe the appropriate code of manners—and this refusal is itself a sign of rebellion. For manners are the lived texture of social life in *Much Ado*, not in the sense of a compulsory set of rules but rather in the sense of an evolving awareness of mutual obligation and interconnectedness.

There is, to be sure, something like compulsion in the obligations and pressures within which the men and women of *Much Ado* live, but the play frustrates any attempt to strip away the fabric of graciousness, apparent choice, and pretended spontaneity with which the compulsions are dressed. An exchange in the comedy's opening moments exemplifies the perfect balance between obligation and will that governs the play's vision of social life. Leonato, the Governor of Messina, is informed by letter of the imminent arrival of Don Pedro of Aragon. (Sicily was ruled for centuries by Spanish viceroys and governors.) Entertainment must be provided at once, and Don Pedro's first words call attention to the pressure of compulsory courtesy: "Good Signor Leonato, are you come to meet your trouble! The fashion of the world is to avoid cost, and you encounter it." It is obviously the fashion of the world to apologize in just this way for imposition, and such an apology calls for an equally conventional denial that any trouble is involved. Leonato duly produces such a denial, a particularly gracious and well-turned one: "Never came trouble to my house in the likeness of your grace. For trouble being gone, comfort should remain, but when you depart from me, sorrow abides and happiness takes his leave." Don Pedro responds to this exquisite compliment with an elegantly modified renewal of his first words and then a polite turn toward Leonato's daughter, Hero: "You embrace your charge too willingly. I think this is your daughter?" (1.1.77–85).

In a strict calculation of power politics, these words are meaningless: they posture emptily above the "real" social exchange, which involves the obligation of the civilian authority toward the military authority (as it happens, a foreign military) at the close of a successful campaign. But such a view neglects the importance of graceful social performance, performance whose ease signals the elite status of the speakers and tacitly acknowledges the possibility of failure or refusal. With a ceremonial greeting such as this, the possibility may seem merely theoretical, but in fact it comes to hover over the entire play (whose main plot is in effect formally initiated by Don Pedro's polite notice of Leonato's daughter). By the fifth act, after Don Pedro's officer Claudio has publicly humiliated and repudiated his intended bride, all courtesy has withered away, and only bitterness and recrimination exist between the gracious host and his princely guest.

Dogberry's zany sleuthing resolves the crisis, but the crucial point is that there is nothing absolute and automatic about the code of manners. Social rituals are vulnerable to disruption and misunderstanding, and this vulnerability underscores the importance of consciously keeping up appearances, patrolling social perimeters, and fabricating civility. In Casti-

A night watchman. From Thomas Dekker, *The Bellman of London* (1608).

glione's world, a high premium is placed on the concealment of the labor expended in this fabrication, but Shakespeare's comedy gives us glimpses in the frequent references to the support staff and attentiveness involved in entertainment: "Where is my cousin your son? Hath he provided this music?" (1.2.1–2); "Being entertained for a perfumer—as I was smoking a musty room . . ." (1.3.47–48); "The revelers are entering, brother. Make good room" (2.1.71–72). Social labor is still more visible in the diverse kinds of discourse in which the characters participate or to which they refer: greeting, entertainment, embassy, formal letter, conjuration, courtship, epigraph, sonneteering, gossip, legal deposition, aggressive wit, formal denunciation, ritualized apology.

Each of these forms of speech requires a display of skill and hence confers a measure of the honor or shame to which the characters of *Much Ado About Nothing* are intensely attuned. Honor and shame are particularly social emotions, the emotions of those who exist in a world of watching and being watched. "Nothing" in Shakespeare's time was pronounced "noting": this is a play obsessed with characters noting other characters. Hence the special force of *masking*, where the serious business of watching is playfully disrupted by disguise, and hence too the crucial significance of those scenes in which Beatrice and Benedict think they are noting others but are in reality being noted (and tricked). Sensitivity to the possibility of being shamed—which includes being laughed at, rejected, insulted, dishonored, humiliated, and so forth—is never far from the characters of *Much Ado*. It extends from Leonato, who thinks that death is the fairest cover for his daughter's public humiliation; to Benedict, whose intellectual and sexual endurance is ridiculed by Beatrice when he ducks out of their first exchange with "a jade's trick" (1.1.118); to Dogberry, who longs to be writ down an ass. At its core is intense male anxiety about female infidelity, manifested in the constant nervous jokes about cuckoldry and played on viciously by Don John. "If I see anything tonight why I should not marry her," Claudio tells Don John, "tomorrow in the congregation, where I should wed, there will I shame her." Don Pedro promises to join with his friend "to disgrace her" (3.2.104–08).

Honor and shame, as the play develops them, are closely bound up with linguistic performance. Language is society's way of being intimately present in the individual; the characters may adjust to that social presence, may like Beatrice and Benedict playfully resist it, may like Dogberry distort it unintentionally, but the shared codes of language are more powerful than any individual.

Close attention to the language of *Much Ado About Nothing* begins with the observation that the comedy is written largely, though not entirely, in prose, a medium far more familiar to modern audiences than the blank verse that dominates many of Shakespeare's plays. (A relevant contrast would be to *Romeo and Juliet*, which shares some of the comedy's preoccupations with social pressure and the disruptive power of love, but is written largely, though not entirely, in exceptionally intense poetry.) There are moments of verse in *Much Ado*, such as Leonato's ghastly expression of hope in act 4 that his shamed daughter will die, but these quickly give way to the looser, more irregular rhythms of prose. This prose, however, is of a kind to which we are no longer accustomed. Modern prose tends by design to be rather plain and colorless; Elizabethan prose is often playful, rhetorically inventive, and richly metaphorical. *Much Ado About Nothing* at once plays elaborate prose games and pokes fun at them, as when Benedict complains that lovesick Claudio "was wont to speak plain and to the purpose, like an honest man and a soldier; and now is he turned orthography. His words are a very fantastical banquet: just so many strange dishes" (2.3.17–20). Shakespeare was certainly capable of writing what we would regard as clear, uncluttered prose: "I learn in this letter that Don Pedro of Aragon comes this night to Messina" (1.1.1–2). But he could also produce astonishing rhetorical effects:

> She told me, not thinking I had been myself, that I was the Prince's jester; that I was duller than a great thaw—huddling jest upon jest with such impossible conveyance upon me that I stood like a man at a mark with a whole army shooting at me. She speaks poniards and every word stabs. If her breath were as terrible as her terminations, there were no living near her; she would infect to the north star. I would not marry her though she were endowed with all that Adam had left him before he transgressed. She would have made Hercules have turned spit, yea, and have cleft his club to make the fire, too. (2.1.216–26)

The wonderful improvisational piling up of images, each at once subtly linked to the preceding one and yet swerving in a new direction, captures the movement of Benedict's mind: the rush of genuine anger and hurt feelings mingled with the impulse to turn his pain into a comically misogynistic performance to entertain Don Pedro (a performance that, ironically, confirms the charge—that he is the Prince's jester—that originally stung him).

Linguistic performance is the social equivalent of the performance in warfare that is both alluded to and conspicuously excluded from the play's action. Language is violence, and language is the alternative to violence: the play entertains both hypotheses and plays them off against each other. "There is a kind of merry war betwixt Signor Benedict and her," says Leonato of his niece. "They never meet but there's a skirmish of wit between them" (1.1.49–51). If words are the agents of civility, they are also dangerous weapons: "Thy slander hath gone through and through her heart / And she lies buried with her ancestors"; "God knows, I loved my niece, / And she is dead, slandered to death by villains" (5.1.68–69, 87–88). What we glimpse in the symbolic murder of Hero is not only the maligning power of slander, but also the aggressive potential of even polite or playful speech. The "merry war" between Beatrice and Benedict leaves scars.

The more one attends to the language of *Much Ado About Nothing*, the more its whiplash merriment seems saturated with violence. In the lighthearted opening scene alone, there are almost constant comic references to war, plague, betrayal, heresy, burning at the stake, blinding, hanging, spying, poisoning. To be sure, the horrors are not themselves realized dramatically in the play; they are present as mere jokes. Nonetheless, they are present, recalled again and again by the constant threat of disaster, by symbolic death, by public shaming. Even in the tidal rush of the comic resolution, amid the marriages, the music, and the dance, Benedict's final words— the final words of the play—deliberately call attention to the violence that the language has continually, if obliquely, registered. Informed of Don John's capture,

Lovers sparring with torches. From George Wither, *A Collection of Emblems* (1635).

Benedict declares, "Think not on him till tomorrow. I'll devise thee brave punishments for him. Strike up, pipers!" [MUSICIANS *play. They all*] *dance* [*and exeunt*] (5.4.123–24).

Viewed in the light of the close, with its conspicuous deferral of torture, but only until tomorrow, the play does not simply transform human misery and violence into wit, but rather addresses itself to the ways in which society manages to endure, to reproduce, to avoid immersion in its own destructive element, to dance. It does so by conscious and unconscious deferral, by the manipulation of appearances, by the deployment of illusions that are known by at least some of its members (the worst and the best) to be illusions.

Illusions are tricks and deceptions, but they are also the social fictions men and women live by. Claudio and Hero exist in the play almost entirely in and as such fictions: their emotions seem less something they possess inwardly than something constructed for them out of the appropriate conventions and rituals. A more complex manifestation in the play of the primacy of illusion is the relation between Beatrice and Benedict. The plot to trick the celebrated skirmishers into marriage originates with Don Pedro, who promises, if Leonato, Hero, and Claudio cooperate with him, to "fashion" the match (2.1.324). The key to his success is his ability to mobilize the social code of shame and honor to which Beatrice and Benedict are bound and to use this code as a means to discipline—to shape into a plot that will culminate in marriage—the powerful chafing between them. For both Beatrice and Benedict, the force that pushes them toward declarations of love and hence toward marriage vows is as much hearing themselves criticized by their friends as hearing that the other is desperately in love. "Can this be true?" asks Beatrice, her ears burning. "Stand I condemned for pride and scorn so much?" (3.1.107–08). "I hear how I am censured," Benedict declares, resolving that he "must not seem proud" (2.3.198–99, 202).

The conspiratorial fabrication of appearances so as to manipulate the code of shame and honor has the odd effect of establishing a link between the socially approved practices of Don Pedro and the wicked practices of Don John, his bastard brother. Shakespeare seems to go out of his way to call attention to this link: moments after Don Pedro undertakes to "fashion" the affection between Beatrice and Benedict, the villainous Borachio declares that he "will so fashion the matter that Hero shall be absent" and hence can be impersonated by Margaret (2.2.39–40). In effect, the play's term for the social system in which all the characters—evil as well as virtuous—are involved is "fashion." Shakespeare deftly uses the term as both noun and verb—that is, both to designate the images (including the fashionable costumes) that elicit emotions and to describe the process that shapes these images.

Fashion is closely related not only to image but also to verbal style, which in the aesthetics of the period was regarded as a kind of dress. "The body of your discourse," laughs Benedict, "is sometime guarded with fragments, and the guards are but slightly basted on neither" (1.1.242–44). The pervasiveness of fashion allows the possibility of drastic deception, but it is also society's redemptive principle. The movement of the play is not so much the unmasking of fraud to reveal the true, virtuous essence within as it is the refashioning, after a dangerous illusion, of the proper image and the appropriate words: "Sweet Hero," cries Claudio after his eyes have been opened to the deception, "now thy image doth appear / In the rare semblance that I loved it first" (5.1.236–37).

The fashioning with which the play is concerned complicates any simple opposition between authentic inner feelings and social norms. This is, after all, a plot that features a wooing by masked proxy instead of direct wooing, a theatrical ritual of remorse instead of remorse, a declaration of love based upon a set of illusions and motivated by the fear of shame. Near the play's close, we see Benedict struggling to compose the required sonnet to Beatrice—an entirely conventional exercise performed to fulfill the theatrical role in which he has been cast ("myself in love"). And in the final moments, when the deception is revealed, it is this exercise, rather than any feelings of the heart, that confirms the match. "I'll be sworn upon't, that he loves her," declares Claudio:

> For here's a paper written in his hand,
> A halting sonnet of his own pure brain,
> Fashioned to Beatrice.
>
> (5.4.85–88)

When a similar sonnet by Beatrice is produced, Benedict cries, "A miracle! Here's our own hands against our hearts" (5.4.91–92).

Many readers of the play, and most performers, have tried to reverse this formulation: Beatrice and Benedict's conversations may be hostile, the interpretation goes, but in their hearts they are, and have long been, deeply in love. Beatrice seems to refer to an earlier time when she had given her heart to Benedict and had evidently been disappointed: "once before he won it of me with false dice" (2.1.248). If they do not declare their love, it is because they are too defensive or, alternatively, too wise to play society's conventional game. In a world of pervasive conventionality and social control, one clever way to insist upon some spontaneity and hence to achieve some authenticity is to quarrel. Perhaps. But what if we do not dismiss their own words? What if we take the conspiracy against them seriously? Beatrice and Benedict would in that case not "love" each other from the start; it would not at all be clear that they love each other, entirely independent of social manipulation, at the close. They are, at least to some extent, tricked into marriage; without the pressure that moves them to professions of love, they would have remained unmarried. Beatrice and Benedict constantly tantalize us with the possibility of an identity quite different from that of Claudio and Hero, an identity deliberately fashioned to resist the constant pressure of society. But that pressure finally prevails. Marriage is a social conspiracy.

If such a view seems ultimately too unsentimental to be tenable in a romantic comedy, it nonetheless makes possible the brilliant scene in which Benedict asks what he can do to prove his love for Beatrice, and Beatrice replies, "Kill Claudio" (4.1.285). Similarly, it helps to account for the laughter provoked by the disillusioned exchange very near the play's close: "Do not you love me?" "Why, no, no more than reason" (5.4.74). In both cases, where we might expect tender words, we get the opposite. If we feel nonetheless that romantic love triumphs in the end, we do so in effect because we—audience and readers—participate in the conspiracy to gull the pair into marriage by insisting that they love each other more than reason. In doing so, we confer upon the general restoration of civility at the play's close something more deeply pleasurable.

Benedict and Beatrice have rational arguments, grounded in the gender politics of their world, for remaining single. Benedict knows that a married man must put his honor at risk by entrusting it to a woman, while Beatrice knows that a married woman must put her integrity at risk by submitting herself to a man: "Would it not grieve a woman to be overmastered with a piece of valiant dust?" (2.1.51–52). Even when they are manipulated into declaring their love, they cannot settle into the language of conventional courtship: "Thou and I are too wise," Benedict tells Beatrice, "to woo peaceably" (5.2.60). Their union at the close is a triumph of folly over the "wisdom" of the single life, a triumph that recalls Erasmus's *Praise of Folly,* where love is said to be possible only because men and women are induced to put aside their reason and plunge into saving foolishness. Why should they do so? The answer is that it is better to live in illusion than in social isolation and that, as Benedict says, "the world must be peopled" (2.3.213).

In most productions of the play, audiences are made to feel that submission to the discipline of love and marriage—"Taming my wild heart" (3.1.112), as Beatrice so wonderfully puts it—is a magnificent release of love and energy. Shakespeare had already experimented with comparable themes in *The Taming of the Shrew,* but Petruccio's conquest of Katherina seems, at least for many modern viewers, too brutal to accept without a lingering sense of constriction and loss. What keeps the conclusion of *Much Ado About Nothing* from appearing brittle or bitter is a sense that the triumph of illusion is life-affirming, a sense that the friction between Beatrice and Benedict can be turned into mutual pleasure.

A man trapped in the yoke of matrimony. From Henry Peacham, *Minerva Britanna* (1612).

If the Claudio/Hero plot and the Beatrice/Benedict plot are two ways in which Shakespeare's comedy shows the saving necessity of illusion, there is a third manifestation: the illusion that evil manifests itself as Don John—that is, in a supremely incompetent and finally impotent form—and that, although it fools clear-eyed and sophisticated observers like Don Pedro, it may be exposed by a bumbling idiot like Dogberry. Some years later, Shakespeare returned to a ruthlessly disillusioned version of the same story, the lover tricked into believing that his beloved has been unfaithful, and called it not *Much Ado About Nothing* but *Othello.*

STEPHEN GREENBLATT

SELECTED BIBLIOGRAPHY

Berger, Harry, Jr. "Against the Sink-a-Pace: Sexual and Family Politics in *Much Ado About Nothing.*" *Shakespeare Quarterly* 33 (1982): 302–13. Characterizes Messina's gender conventions in terms of virtue, constancy, reputation, deception, and fashion.

Berry, Ralph. *Shakespeare's Comedies: Explorations in Form.* Princeton, NJ: Princeton UP, 1972. 154–74. Argues that by focusing on the difficult reconciliation of sensory experience and judgment, *Much Ado About Nothing* explores the limits of knowledge.

Cook, Carol. "'The Sign and Semblance of Her Honor': Reading Gender Difference in *Much Ado About Nothing.*" *PMLA* 101.2 (1986): 186–202. Explores how the play presents the polysemous threat of women in a world where men are the manipulators and interpreters of signs.

Everett, Barbara. "*Much Ado About Nothing:* The Unsociable Comedy." *English Comedy.* Ed. Michael Cordner, Peter Holland, and John Kerrigan. New York: Cambridge UP, 1994. 68–84. Discusses how Shakespeare's realistic portrait of love in society typically mixes its comic nothings with serious concerns.

Gay, Penny. "*Much Ado About Nothing:* A Kind of Merry War." *As She Likes It: Shakespeare's Unruly Women.* London: Routledge, 1994. 143–77. Presents performance history since the 1950s, spotlighting representations of Beatrice and Benedict.

Howard, Jean. "Renaissance Antitheatricality and the Politics of Gender and Rank in *Much Ado About Nothing.*" *Shakespeare Reproduced: The Text in History and Ideology.* Ed. Jean E. Howard and Marion F. O'Connor. New York: Methuen, 1987. 163–87. Argues that *Much Ado About Nothing* supports Elizabethan ideology, condemning marginal social groups through accusations of illegitimate theatrical practice.

Moisan, Thomas. "Deforming Sources: Literary Antecedents and Their Traces in *Much Ado About Nothing.*" *Shakespeare Studies* 31 (2003): 165–83. Examines how the play's furtive and ambivalent relationship to its sources reflects its depiction of character, politics, power, and representation.

Myhill, Nova. "Spectatorship in/of *Much Ado About Nothing.*" *Studies in English Literature* 39.2 (1999): 291–311. Considers how *Much Ado About Nothing's* unreliable "notings" challenge the theater audience's assumptions of omniscience and invulnerability.

Salingar, Leo. "Borachio's Indiscretion: Some Noting about *Much Ado.*" *The Italian World of English Renaissance Drama: Cultural Exchange and Intertextuality.* Ed. Michele Marrapodi. London: Associated UP, 1998. 225–38. Looks at *Much Ado* as a bittersweet masquerade of social ambiguity and false communications.

Traugott, John. "Creating a Rational Rinaldo: A Study in the Mixture of the Genres of Comedy and Romance in *Much Ado About Nothing.*" *Genre* 15 (1982): 157–81. Shows how comedy and romance contaminate and purify each other, one becoming ennobled and the other cured of cruelty.

MUSIC AND FILMS

Berlioz, Hector. *Béatrice et Bénédict*. Recommended recording: Baker, Allen, Davis, LSO arkivmusic.com. Typically lush operatic reimagining that leaves out the Don John subplot to focus on the gradual, eventually ecstatic union of Beatrice and Benedict.

Much Ado About Nothing. 1993. Dir. Kenneth Branagh. UK/USA. 111 min. Festive romp set in sunny country-house Italy. With Kenneth Branagh and Emma Thompson. (See also Branagh, *"Much Ado About Nothing": Screenplay, Introduction, and Notes on the Making of the Movie* [New York: Norton, 1993].)

Much Ado About Nothing. 2013. Dir. Joss Whedon. USA. 109 min. Benedict slips from Beatrice's bed at the opening of this black-and-white recasting of the play in contemporary Southern California. With Amy Acker as Beatrice, Alexis Denisof as Benedict, and Nathan Fillion as Dogberry.

TEXTUAL INTRODUCTION

The text of *Much Ado About Nothing* is one of the most exciting in the Shakespeare canon because of the opportunity it gives us to see the playwright at work. The play was published once during Shakespeare's lifetime, in London in 1600 by Andrew Wise and William Aspley. This edition, a small quarto (or Q), formed the basis of the text printed in 1623 in the First Folio (F). *The Norton Shakespeare* is based on Q because this text was probably printed from Shakespeare's own working papers. There are several places where we can see that the text from which the printer was working was not the final state of the play. It opens, for example, with an entrance for Innogen, who is described as Leonato's wife. Leonato's wife also enters at the beginning of 2.1, but Innogen does not speak on any occasion and is never referred to again. Leonato's brother is not named in the dialogue until 5.1.92, but is introduced first as *"an old man brother to Leonato"* (1.2.0) and then in speech prefixes and stage directions as *"Brother"* until 5.4, when he becomes *"old man."* Similarly, Prince John is called *"Bastard."* This suggests that Shakespeare was thinking of character-types when he started work on the play and developed the characters' personalities as he went along. Stage directions are adequate for a reader but would not be sufficiently precise for an acting company. In act 5, for example, we have *two or three [Attendants]* (5.4.33), *three or four [Attendants]* (5.3.0), and *Constables* (5.1.195), but are not told the precise number of actors on stage. Although the play is set in Messina, in Sicily, which at the time Shakespeare was writing was part of the Spanish Kingdom of Aragon, the Prince is at first called *"Peter"* before Shakespeare settles into calling him *"Pedro."*

The most complex scenes textually are those involving Dogberry, Verges, and the officers of the watch (3.3, 3.5, 4.2, and 5.1). The number of watchmen, or constables, is not specified. Verges is called the *"Headborough,"* or local constable, in the entrance to 3.5 only. A Sexton appears in 4.2 together with a Town Clerk who, like Innogen, is a ghost character who never speaks: he may be the same as the Sexton. All this suggests that Shakespeare was picturing the characters from a small-town administration as he developed the plot. In 4.2 we come even closer to Shakespeare's creative process, when the speeches for Dogberry's role are labeled *"Kemp,"* for Will Kemp, the comic actor who played this part, and at 4.2.4 *"Andrew,"* meaning a clown's role. Verges's speeches are labeled *"Cowley"* or *"Couley,"* which again was the name of an actor, Richard Cowley. Shakespeare here had in his mind's eye the roles as they would appear on stage, impersonated by his colleagues in the Lord Chamberlain's Men, and these slips of the pen allow us to be certain that the text that we are reading is unusually close to Shakespeare's own draft.

The publishers of the play made their entry in the Stationers' Register on August 23, 1600, giving them the right to print both *Much Ado About Nothing* and *2 Henry IV*. Less than three weeks earlier, on August 4, 1600, the Stationers Company had recorded that *Much Ado* was to be "stayed," or withheld from publishing, but the reason for this is not known.

Wise and Aspley contracted out the production of the book, in quarto format, to the printer Valentine Sims, who also printed *2 Henry IV*. The same compositor set both texts; *Much Ado* was probably printed after *2 Henry IV*. On the first and last pages of sheet G, scenes 4.1 and 4.2, the text is crowded on the page, which suggests that the compositor made a slight error in "casting off" his copy and had too much material. Charlton Hinman argued that *Much Ado* was printed by page rather than by forme (see Glossary) and that the crowded page reflected the actual layout of Shakespeare's papers, but Hinman's studies cannot be fully replicated and it is more likely that Q was printed by formes in the normal way. Several of the textual problems, especially in the Dogberry scenes (e.g., 4.2.61), are apparently the result of the state of Shakespeare's papers and the need to crowd the page.

While sheets D, E, F and G were being printed, some corrections, or "press variants," were made. One surviving copy, Qu, preserves the uncorrected readings, which mostly affect spelling and punctuation.

TRUDI DARBY

TEXTUAL BIBLIOGRAPHY

Ferguson, W. Craig. "The Compositors of *Henry IV, Part 2, Much Ado About Nothing, The Shoemakers' Holiday*, and *The First Part of the Contention.*" *Studies in Bibliography* 13 (1960): 20–31.

Hazel Smith, John. "The Composition of the Quarto of *Much Ado About Nothing.*" *Studies in Bibliography* 16 (1963): 10–27.

Hinman, Charlton. *Much Ado About Nothing.* Shakespeare Quarto Facsimiles No. 15. Oxford: Clarendon, 1971.

PERFORMANCE NOTE

Much Ado About Nothing is rare among Shakespeare's plays for having its star characters, Beatrice and Benedict, occupy places of secondary importance in the main plot. Consequently, productions must address the need for the sparring couple to command the audience's attention without overwhelming the play, either by marginalizing the courtship and eventual union of Claudio and Hero or by rendering Dogberry's comedy, or Don John's villainy, distracting or superfluous. Beatrice and Benedict require actors of considerable versatility: alternating sarcastic banter with moments of humble self-reflection, each graduates from episodes of screwball comedy to solemn expressions of love and fidelity. It can therefore be challenging for productions to succeed on each of these fronts without eclipsing the subplots or obscuring their purposes. Productions must also decide, crucially, whether Beatrice and Benedict's verbal banter is lighthearted or acerbic, the result of genuine distaste or of a need to mask their affections for one another. Benedict often makes his attraction to Beatrice legible to the audience from the start, while Beatrice shows perfect indifference; other productions emphasize Beatrice's account of a failed romance with Benedict to suggest her lingering affection. Either choice complicates their exchanges throughout the play.

Productions must also consider the transition from the lighthearted comedy of the play's first half to the tragic events of the second, determining whether to foreshadow the sobering divisions to come by emphasizing such things as Don Pedro's rejection by Beatrice or Don John's exclusion from his brother's circle. Other prominent staging considerations include the degree of credibility necessary for the deceptions of onstage audiences; whether to introduce Margaret in scenes that highlight her role in Hero's ruin; and the delivery and aftermath of Beatrice's notorious challenge to Benedict: "Kill Claudio" (4.1.285).

BRETT GAMBOA

Much Ado About Nothing

[THE PERSONS OF THE PLAY

PEDRO, Prince of Aragon
JOHN, illegitimate half-brother to Pedro
BENEDICT }
CLAUDIO } accompanying Pedro
BORACHIO }
CONRAD } accompanying John
MESSENGER
LORD

LEONATO, Governor of Messina
Innogen, wife to Leonato
ANTHONY, brother to Leonato
HERO, daughter to Leonato
BEATRICE, niece to Leonato
BALTHASAR }
MARGARET } members of Leonato's household
URSULA }
BOY
FRIAR
MUSICIANS
Kinsmen
Attendants

DOGBERRY, a Constable in charge of the WATCH
VERGES, the Headborough
SEXTON
FIRST WATCHMAN
SECOND WATCHMAN
WATCHMEN
Town Clerk]

1.1

Enter LEONATO *Governor of Messina, Innogen his wife,*
HERO *his daughter, and* BEATRICE *his niece, with a*
MESSENGER.[1]

LEONATO I learn in this letter that Don Pedro of Aragon comes
this night to Messina.

MESSENGER He is very near by this. He was not three leagues
off when I left him.

5 LEONATO How many gentlemen have you lost in this action?°   *campaign*

MESSENGER But few of any sort,° and none of name.°   *rank / distinction*

LEONATO A victory is twice itself when the achiever brings
home full numbers. I find here that Don Pedro hath bestowed
much honor on a young Florentine called Claudio.

1.1 Location: Messina (a city in Sicily). Before the
house of Leonato.
1. TEXTUAL COMMENT Innogen is a ghost, or silent,

character: she never speaks, although she appears
twice in the play. See Digital Edition TC 1.

10   MESSENGER   Much deserved on his part, and equally remem-
bered° by Don Pedro. He hath borne himself beyond the   *rewarded*
promise of his age, doing in the figure of a lamb the feats of
a lion. He hath indeed better bettered° expectation than you   *exceeded*
must expect of me to tell you how.

15   LEONATO   He hath an uncle here in Messina will be very much
glad of it.

    MESSENGER   I have already delivered him letters, and there
appears much joy in him, even so much that joy could not
show itself modest° enough without a badge° of bitterness.°   *moderate / show / grief*

20   LEONATO   Did he break out into tears?

    MESSENGER   In great measure.

    LEONATO   A kind° overflow of kindness.° There are no faces   *natural / tenderness*
truer than those that are so washed. How much better is it
to weep at joy than to joy at weeping!

25   BEATRICE   I pray you, is Signor Mountanto² returned from the
wars or no?

    MESSENGER   I know none of that name, lady. There was none
such in the army of any sort.

    LEONATO   What is he that you ask for, niece?

30   HERO   My cousin means Signor Benedict of Padua.³

    MESSENGER   Oh, he's returned, and as pleasant° as ever he was.   *entertaining*

    BEATRICE   He set up his bills° here in Messina and challenged   *public notices*
Cupid at the flight,⁴ and my uncle's fool,° reading the chal-   *jester*
lenge, subscribed for Cupid and challenged him at the bird-
35   bolt.⁵ I pray you, how many hath he killed and eaten in these
wars? But how many hath he killed? For indeed, I promised
to eat all of his killing.

    LEONATO   Faith, niece, you tax° Signor Benedict too much.   *abuse*
But he'll be meet° with you, I doubt it not.   *even*

40   MESSENGER   He hath done good service, lady, in these wars.

    BEATRICE   You had musty victual, and he hath holp° to eat it. He   *helped*
is a very valiant trencher-man.° He hath an excellent stomach.° *hearty eater / appetite*

    MESSENGER   And a good soldier too, lady.

    BEATRICE   And a good soldier to a lady. But what is he to a lord?

45   MESSENGER   A lord to a lord, a man to a man, stuffed° with all   *well furnished*
honorable virtues.

    BEATRICE   It is so indeed. He is no less than a stuffed man.° But   *mannequin*
for the stuffing—well, we are all mortal.⁶

    LEONATO   You must not, sir, mistake my niece. There is a kind
50   of merry war betwixt Signor Benedict and her. They never
meet but there's a skirmish of wit between them.

    BEATRICE   Alas, he gets nothing by that. In our last conflict,
four of his five wits⁷ went halting° off, and now is the whole   *limping*
man governed with one. So that if he have wit enough to keep
55   himself warm, let him bear it for a difference between himself and his horse, for it is all the wealth that he hath left: to
be known a reasonable creature. Who is his companion now?
He hath every month a new sworn brother.

---

2. In fencing, a montanto is an upright blow or thrust.
3. A city in northern Italy.
4. To an archery match. (Benedict claimed to surpass
Cupid at arousing love.) "Flight" may also suggest
flyte, an archaic word meaning "a contest of insults."
5. To a contest using bird bolts, or blunt, short-range
arrows allowed to fools and children (and thus appro-

priate to young Cupid). *subscribed for*: took up the
challenge on behalf of.
6. But as for what he is made of (his "stuffing"), he is
probably as faulty as the rest of us.
7. *five wits*: mental faculties (memory, imagination,
judgment, fantasy, and common sense).

MESSENGER   Is't possible?

60 BEATRICE   Very easily possible. He wears his faith° but as the   *loyalty*
fashion of his hat: it ever changes with the next block.[8]

MESSENGER   I see, lady, the gentleman is not in your books.°   *favor*

BEATRICE   No. An° he were, I would burn my study. But I pray   *If*
you, who is his companion? Is there no young squarer° now   *boisterous quarreler*
65 that will make a voyage with him to the devil?

MESSENGER   He is most in the company of the right noble
Claudio.

BEATRICE   O Lord! He will hang upon him like a disease. He is
sooner caught than the pestilence,° and the taker° runs   *plague / victim*
70 presently° mad. God help the noble Claudio. If he have caught   *immediately*
the Benedict it will cost him a thousand pound ere 'a° be cured.   *he*

MESSENGER   I will hold friends[9] with you, lady.

BEATRICE   Do, good friend.

LEONATO   You will never run mad,[1] niece.

75 BEATRICE   No, not till a hot January.

MESSENGER   Don Pedro is approached.

> *Enter Don* PEDRO, CLAUDIO, BENEDICT, BALTHASAR,
> *and* JOHN *the bastard.*

PEDRO   Good Signor Leonato, are you come to meet your
trouble! The fashion° of the world is to avoid cost, and you   *custom*
encounter° it.   *go to meet*

80 LEONATO   Never came trouble to my house in the likeness of
your grace. For trouble being gone, comfort should remain,
but when you depart from me, sorrow abides and happiness
takes his leave.

PEDRO   You embrace your charge° too willingly. I think this is   *duty*
85 your daughter?

LEONATO   Her mother hath many times told me so.

BENEDICT   Were you in doubt, sir, that you asked her?

LEONATO   Signor Benedict, no, for then were you a child.[2]

PEDRO   You have it full,[3] Benedict. We may guess by this what
90 you are, being a man. Truly, the lady fathers herself.[4] Be
happy, lady, for you are like an honorable father.

> [*He talks aside with* LEONATO.]

BENEDICT   If Signor Leonato be her father, she would not have
his head[5] on her shoulders for all Messina, as like him as she is.

BEATRICE   I wonder that you will still° be talking, Signor Bene-   *always*
95 dict. Nobody marks you.

BENEDICT   What! My dear Lady Disdain! Are you yet living?

BEATRICE   Is it possible Disdain should die while she hath
such meet° food to feed it as Signor Benedict? Courtesy   *suitable*
itself must convert° to Disdain if you come in her presence.   *turn*

100 BENEDICT   Then is Courtesy a turncoat. But it is certain I am
loved of° all ladies, only you excepted, and I would I could   *by*
find in my heart that I had not a hard heart, for truly I love
none.

BEATRICE   A dear happiness to women; they would else have
105 been troubled with a pernicious suitor. I thank God and my

---

8. Newest mold for a hat; fashion.
9. I will stay on good terms.
1. "Catch the Benedict."
2. Implying facetiously that if he hadn't been a child

at the time Benedict might have cuckolded Leonato.
3. Your sarcasm is fully repaid.
4. She shows by her looks who her father is.
5. The head of an old man.

cold blood, I am of your humor° for that. I had rather hear   *disposition*
my dog bark at a crow than a man swear he loves me.

BENEDICT   God keep your ladyship still in that mind. So some
gentleman or other shall scape a predestinate° scratched   *escape an inevitable*
110   face.

BEATRICE   Scratching could not make it worse, an 'twere such
a face as yours were.

BENEDICT   Well, you are a rare parrot teacher.[6]

BEATRICE   A bird of my tongue is better than a beast of yours.[7]

115   BENEDICT   I would my horse had the speed of your tongue and
so good a continuer.[8] But keep your way,° o'God's name. I   *carry on*
have done.

BEATRICE   You always end with a jade's trick.[9] I know you of
old.

120   PEDRO [*finishing his conversation*] That is the sum of all,
Leonato. —Signor Claudio and Signor Benedict! My dear
friend Leonato hath invited you all. I tell him we shall stay
here at the least a month, and he heartily prays some occasion may detain us longer. I dare swear he is no hypocrite
125   but prays from his heart.

LEONATO   If you swear, my lord, you shall not be forsworn. [*to*
JOHN] Let me bid you welcome, my lord, being° reconciled to   *since you are*
the Prince your brother. I owe you all duty.

JOHN   I thank you. I am not of many words, but I thank you.

130   LEONATO [*to* PEDRO] Please it your grace lead on?

PEDRO   Your hand, Leonato, we will go together.[1]

                  Exeunt all but BENEDICT *and* CLAUDIO.

CLAUDIO   Benedict, didst thou note the daughter of Signor
Leonato?

BENEDICT   I noted her not,[2] but I looked on her.

135   CLAUDIO   Is she not a modest young lady?

BENEDICT   Do you question me as an honest man should do,
for my simple true judgment? Or would you have me speak
after my custom, as being a professed tyrant to° their sex?   *pitiless critic of*

CLAUDIO   No, I pray thee, speak in sober judgment.

140   BENEDICT   Why, i'faith, methinks she's too low° for a high   *short*
praise, too brown for a fair praise, and too little for a great
praise. Only this commendation I can afford her, that were
she other than she is, she were unhandsome; and being no
other but as she is, I do not like her.

145   CLAUDIO   Thou thinkest I am in sport.° I pray thee tell me   *jest*
truly how thou lik'st her.

BENEDICT   Would you buy her, that you inquire after her?

CLAUDIO   Can the world buy such a jewel?

BENEDICT   Yea, and a case to put it into. But speak you this
150   with a sad° brow? Or do you play the flouting jack, to tell us   *serious*

---

6. Chatterer (repetitive, like one who teaches a parrot to speak).
7. A bird with my powers of speech is better than a
dumb beast who, like you, has none.
8. And had your staying power ("continuer," in
horsemanship, means "stayer").

9. A trick worthy of a badly trained horse (here,
dropping out of a race).
1. We will walk out hand in hand (and thus avoid
taking precedence).
2. I paid her no special attention.

Cupid is a good hare-finder, and Vulcan a rare carpenter?[3]
Come, in what key shall a man take° you to go° in the song?   *understand / join*

CLAUDIO   In mine eye she is the sweetest lady that ever I
looked on.

155   BENEDICT   I can see yet without spectacles, and I see no such
matter. There's her cousin, an she were not possessed with a
fury, exceeds her as much in beauty as the first of May doth
the last of December. But I hope you have no intent to turn
husband, have you?

160   CLAUDIO   I would scarce trust myself, though I had sworn the
contrary, if Hero would be my wife.

BENEDICT   Is't come to this? In faith, hath not the world one
man but he will wear his cap with suspicion?[4] Shall I never
see a bachelor of threescore again? Go to,° i'faith. An thou   *Go on*
165   wilt needs thrust thy neck into a yoke, wear the print of it
and sigh away Sundays.[5] Look, Don Pedro is returned to
seek you.

Enter PEDRO.

PEDRO   What secret hath held you here that you followed not
to Leonato's?

170   BENEDICT   I would your grace would constrain me to tell.

PEDRO   I charge thee on thy allegiance.

BENEDICT   You hear, Count Claudio? I can be secret as a dumb°   *mute*
man, I would have you think so, but on my allegiance—mark
you this, on my allegiance—he is in love. "With who?" Now
175   that is your grace's part. Mark how short his answer is:
"With Hero, Leonato's short daughter."

CLAUDIO   If this were so, so were it uttered.[6]

BENEDICT   Like the old tale, my lord, "It is not so, nor 'twas
not so."[7] But indeed, God forbid it should be so.

180   CLAUDIO   If my passion change not shortly, God forbid it
should be otherwise.

PEDRO   Amen, if you love her, for the lady is very well
worthy.

CLAUDIO   You speak this to fetch me in,° my lord.   *trick me*

185   PEDRO   By my troth, I speak my thought.

CLAUDIO   And in faith, my lord, I spoke mine.

BENEDICT   And by my two faiths and troths,[8] my lord, I spoke
mine.

CLAUDIO   That I love her, I feel.

190   PEDRO   That she is worthy, I know.

BENEDICT   That I neither feel how she should be loved, nor
know how she should be worthy, is the opinion that fire cannot melt out of me. I will die in it at the stake.

PEDRO   Thou wast ever an obstinate heretic in the despite° of   *contempt*
200   beauty.

---

3. *play . . . carpenter:* spout praises contrary to fact
and intended satirically. Blind Cupid is poorly suited
to the sharp-sighted sport of hunting hares, while Vulcan, the god of fire, was an excellent ("rare") blacksmith, not a carpenter. *flouting jack:* mocking rogue.
4. *but . . . suspicion:* who will not be suspected of
wearing his cap in order to hide a cuckold's horns
(conventional sign of a wife's infidelity).
5. *thrust . . . Sundays:* take on the burdens and tedium

of marriage, when you might be enjoying yourself as a
bachelor.
6. *so . . . uttered:* This is how Benedict would tell it.
7. In an English fairy tale (a variant on the Blue-
beard story), a man suspected by his bride-to-be of
having killed his former wives denies his guilt with
the refrain Benedict quotes.
8. His loyalty to both Don Pedro and Claudio and,
jokingly, his duplicity.

CLAUDIO   And never could maintain his part° but in the force   *argument*
of his will.[9]

BENEDICT   That a woman conceived me, I thank her; that she
brought me up, I likewise give her most humble thanks. But
205   that I will have a recheat winded in my forehead, or hang
my bugle in an invisible baldric,[1] all women shall pardon
me. Because I will not do them the wrong to mistrust any,[2]
I will do myself the right to trust none. And the fine° is (for   *conclusion*
the which I may go the finer[3]), I will live a bachelor.

210 PEDRO   I shall see thee, ere I die, look pale with love.

BENEDICT   With anger, with sickness, or with hunger, my
lord, not with love. Prove° that ever I lose more blood with   *If you prove*
love than I will get again with drinking,[4] pick out mine eyes
with a ballad-maker's[5] pen and hang me up at the door of a
215   brothel house for the sign of blind Cupid.[6]

PEDRO   Well, if ever thou dost fall from this faith, thou wilt
prove a notable argument.°   *subject of talk*

BENEDICT   If I do, hang me in a bottle like a cat and shoot at
me,[7] and he that hits me, let him be clapped on the shoulder
220   and called Adam.[8]

PEDRO   Well, as time shall try.° In time the savage bull doth   *prove*
bear the yoke.[9]

BENEDICT   The savage bull may, but if ever the sensible°   *rational*
Benedict bear it, pluck off the bull's horns and set them in
225   my forehead. And let me be vilely painted, and in such great
letters as they write, "Here is good horse to hire," let them
signify under my sign, "Here you may see Benedict, the
married man."

CLAUDIO   If this should ever happen, thou wouldst be horn-
230   mad.[1]

PEDRO   Nay, if Cupid have not spent all his quiver in Venice,[2]
thou wilt quake for this shortly.

BENEDICT   I look for an earthquake[3] too, then.

PEDRO   Well, you will temporize with the hours.[4] In the mean-
235   time, good Signor Benedict, repair° to Leonato's. Commend   *go*
me to him, and tell him I will not fail him at supper, for
indeed he hath made great preparation.

BENEDICT   I have almost matter° enough in me for such an   *intelligence*
embassage.° And so I commit you—   *errand*

240 CLAUDIO   To the tuition[5] of God. From my house, if I had it—

9. Through prideful obstinacy rather than reason.

1. *But . . . baldric:* But that I should wear a cuckold's horns. A recheat was a call sounded ("winded") on a horn to recall the hounds. A baldric was a belt to hold a horn ("bugle"); it was invisible, a sign of the cuckold's ignorance.

2. Because I do not wish to wrong women by suspecting any of infidelity.

3. I may dress better (because he will have more money to spare).

4. *lose . . . drinking:* alluding to the belief that sighing like a lover caused the blood to evaporate, and drinking wine renewed it.

5. Popular love poet or satirist.

6. A painted sign, such as might hang before a brothel.

7. *hang . . . me:* Cats in baskets ("bottles") were com-

mon Elizabethan targets for recreational archery.

8. Perhaps Adam Bell, a celebrated archer.

9. Proverbial; here, apparently a variation on a line from Thomas Kyd's *Spanish Tragedy* (ca. 1587): "In time the savage bull sustains the yoke" (2.1.3).

1. Furious; raving like a wild beast (referring to the rage of a cuckolded husband).

2. Venice was famous in Shakespeare's time for its beautiful courtesans. *spent all his quiver:* used all his arrows, with sexual innuendo.

3. An earthquake would be as unlikely as my quaking with love.

4. You will soften as time passes; with perhaps a bawdy pun on "hours," "whores" (pronounced similarly).

5. Protection (Claudio and Don Pedro parody a conventional formula for ending a letter).

PEDRO   The sixth of July, your loving friend, Benedict.
BENEDICT   Nay, mock not, mock not. The body of your dis-
       course is sometime guarded with fragments,[6] and the guards
       are but slightly basted on,[7] neither. Ere you flout° old ends°   *mock / clichés*
245   any further, examine your conscience. And so I leave you.
                                                            Exit.
CLAUDIO   My liege, your highness now may do me good.
PEDRO   My love is thine to teach. Teach it but how,
       And thou shalt see how apt it is to learn
       Any hard lesson that may do thee good.
250   CLAUDIO   Hath Leonato any son, my lord?
PEDRO   No child but Hero. She's his only heir.
       Dost thou affect° her, Claudio?   *love*
CLAUDIO   O my lord,
       When you went onward on this ended action,°   *campaign*
       I looked upon her with a soldier's eye
255   That liked, but had a rougher task in hand
       Than to drive liking to the name of love.
       But now I am returned and that° war thoughts   *now that*
       Have left their places vacant—in their rooms
       Come thronging soft and delicate desires,
260   All prompting me how fair young Hero is,
       Saying, I liked her ere I went to wars—
PEDRO   Thou wilt be like a lover presently°   *shortly*
       And tire the hearer with a book of words.°   *lover's set speeches*
       If thou dost love fair Hero, cherish it,
265   And I will break° with her and with her father,   *speak*
       And thou shalt have her. Was't not to this end
       That thou began'st to twist° so fine a story?   *spin*
CLAUDIO   How sweetly you do minister to love
       That know love's grief by his complexion!°   *by its appearance*
270   But lest my liking might too sudden seem,
       I would have salved° it with a longer treatise.   *smoothed*
PEDRO   What need the bridge much broader than the flood?°   *river*
       The fairest grant is the necessity.[8]
       Look, what° will serve is fit. 'Tis once,° thou lovest,   *whatever / In brief*
275   And I will fit thee with the remedy.
       I know we shall have reveling° tonight.   *festivity; masked ball*
       I will assume thy part° in some disguise   *role*
       And tell fair Hero I am Claudio,
       And in her bosom I'll unclasp my heart[9]
280   And take her hearing prisoner with the force
       And strong encounter of my amorous tale.
       Then after, to her father will I break,
       And the conclusion is, she shall be thine.
       In practice let us put it presently.   *Exeunt.*

---

6. *The body . . . fragments:* The substance (also punning on the dressmaker's "bodice") of what you say is
sometimes ornamented ("guarded") with odds and
ends ("fragments") such as you are mocking me for
using.

7. And the decorative phrases are barely relevant.
8. The best gift is something that is truly needed.
9. And I will privately reveal to her my feelings (as if
I were you).

1.2

Enter LEONATO *and an old man* [ANTHONY], *brother
to* LEONATO.

LEONATO How now, brother? Where is my cousin° your son?   kinsman (nephew)
Hath he provided this music?
ANTHONY He is very busy about it. But brother, I can tell you
strange news that you yet dreamt not of.
5 LEONATO Are they° good?   (the news)
ANTHONY As the event stamps them.[1] But they have a good
cover; they show well outward. The Prince and Count Claudio, walking in a thick pleached[2] alley in mine orchard,°   garden
were thus much overheard by a man of mine. The Prince
10 discovered° to Claudio that he loved my niece, your daugh-   revealed
ter, and meant to acknowledge it this night in a dance. And
if he found her accordant,° he meant to take the present   consenting
time by the top[3] and instantly break° with you of it.   speak
LEONATO Hath the fellow any wit° that told you this?   intelligence
15 ANTHONY A good sharp fellow. I will send for him, and question him yourself.
        [*Enter Attendants.*][4]
LEONATO No, no. We will hold it as a dream till it appear°   manifest
itself. But I will acquaint my daughter withal,° that she may   with it
be the better prepared for an answer if, peradventure,° this   by chance
20 be true. Go you and tell her of it. [*to Attendants*] Cousins,
you know what you have to do. Oh, I cry you mercy,[5] friend.
Go you with me, and I will use your skill. Good cousin, have
a care this busy time.   *Exeunt.*

1.3

Enter Sir JOHN *the bastard, and* CONRAD
his companion.

CONRAD What the good year, my lord! Why are you thus out
of measure[1] sad?
JOHN There is no measure in the occasion that breeds. Therefore the sadness is without limit.
5 CONRAD You should hear reason.
JOHN And when I have heard it, what blessing brings it?
CONRAD If not a present° remedy, at least a patient suffer-   immediate
ance.
JOHN I wonder that thou, being as thou sayest thou art, born
10 under Saturn,[2] goest about to apply a moral medicine to a
mortifying mischief.° I cannot hide what I am. I must be sad   deadly sickness
when I have cause and smile at no man's jests; eat when I
have stomach° and wait for no man's leisure; sleep when I   appetite
am drowsy and tend on° no man's business; laugh when I am   attend to
15 merry and claw° no man in his humor.°   flatter / mood

1.2 Location: Leonato's house.
1. As good as the outcome ("event") proves ("stamps")
them. The image is of news bound in a book with a
handsome cover.
2. Enclosed by trees with intertwining boughs.
3. He meant to seize the opportunity. (Time is proverbially bald except for the "top," or forelock.)
4. The attendants are evidently engaged in preparations for the reveling (2.1). "Cousins" (line 20) may
refer to dependents in Leonato's household.

5. I beg your pardon (perhaps because he has not
initially recognized one of the attendants, or
because he has bumped into him). Leonato's reference to "skill" suggests that he might be talking to a
musician.
1.3 Location: Scene continues.
1. *What the good year*: What the devil. *out of measure*:
disproportionately.
2. Born when Saturn was in the ascendant (therefore "saturnine," meaning melancholy).

CONRAD   Yea, but you must not make the full show of this till
you may do it without controlment.° You have of late stood out°   *restraint / rebelled*
against your brother, and he hath ta'en you newly into his
grace,° where it is impossible you should take true root but   *favor*
20 by the fair weather that you make yourself. It is needful that
you frame the season for your own harvest.

JOHN   I had rather be a canker³ in a hedge than a rose³ in his   *wild rose; weed*
grace. And it better fits my blood° to be disdained of all than   *disposition*
to fashion° a carriage° to rob love from any. In this, though I   *affect; feign / behavior*
25 cannot be said to be a flattering honest man, it must not be
denied but I am a plain-dealing villain. I am trusted with a
muzzle and enfranchised with a clog;⁴ therefore I have
decreed° not to sing in my cage. If I had my mouth, I would   *determined*
bite. If I had my liberty, I would do my liking. In the mean-
30 time, let me be that I am, and seek not to alter me.

CONRAD   Can you make no use of your discontent?

JOHN   I make all use of it, for I use it only.

     Enter BORACHIO.⁵

Who comes here? What news, Borachio?

BORACHIO   I came yonder from a great supper. The Prince
35 your brother is royally entertained by Leonato, and I can
give you intelligence of an intended marriage.

JOHN   Will it serve for any model° to build mischief on? What   *ground plan*
is he for a fool⁶ that betroths himself to unquietness?

BORACHIO   Marry,⁷ it is your brother's right hand.

40 JOHN   Who? The most exquisite Claudio?

BORACHIO   Even he.

JOHN   A proper squire!⁸ And who? And who? Which way looks
he?

BORACHIO   Marry, one Hero, the daughter and heir of
45 Leonato.

JOHN   A very forward March-chick.⁹ How came you to this?

BORACHIO   Being entertained for a perfumer¹—as I was smok-
ing° a musty room—comes me the Prince and Claudio, hand   *perfuming*
in hand, in sad° conference. I whipped me behind the arras°   *serious / wall hanging*
50 and there heard it agreed upon that the Prince should woo
Hero for himself, and, having obtained her, give her to
Count Claudio.

JOHN   Come, come, let us thither. This may prove food to my
displeasure.° That young start-up° hath all the glory of my   *hatred / upstart*
55 overthrow. If I can cross² him any way, I bless myself every
way. You are both sure,° and will assist me?   *reliable*

CONRAD   To the death, my Lord.

JOHN   Let us to the great supper. Their cheer is the greater
that° I am subdued. Would the cook were o'my mind!³ Shall   *since*
60 we go prove° what's to be done?   *find out*

BORACHIO   We'll wait° upon your lordship.   *Exeunt.*   *attend*

---

3. Cultivated rose.
4. I am trusted by being muzzled (in other words, not
trusted at all) and given my freedom with a clog (a
heavy block of wood attached to an animal or man as
a restraint).
5. The name derives from the Spanish for "drunkard" or "wine bottle."
6. What kind of fool is he.

7. By the Virgin Mary (a mild oath).
8. A fine young lover (ironic).
9. Precocious youngster, like a bird hatched early in
the season.
1. Being hired to burn sweet herbs (to mask unpleasant domestic odors).
2. Thwart (punning on "make the sign of the cross").
3. *o'my mind:* inclined to poison the food.

2.1

Enter LEONATO, *his brother* [ANTHONY], *his wife,*
HERO *his daughter, and* BEATRICE *his niece,* [URSULA,
MARGARET,] *and a kinsman.*

LEONATO Was not Count John here at supper?

ANTHONY I saw him not.

BEATRICE How tartly° that gentleman looks! I never can see   *sour*
him, but I am heartburned¹ an hour after.

5 HERO He is of a very melancholy disposition.

BEATRICE He were° an excellent man that were made just in   *would be*
the midway between him and Benedict. The one is too like
an image° and says nothing, and the other too like my lady's   *a statue*
eldest son,² evermore tattling.°   *chattering*

10 LEONATO Then half Signor Benedict's tongue in Count John's
mouth, and half Count John's melancholy in Signor Benedict's face—

BEATRICE With a good leg and a good foot, uncle, and money
enough in his purse, such a man would win any woman in   *he*
15 the world, if 'a° could get her goodwill.

LEONATO By my troth, niece, thou wilt never get thee a husband if thou be so shrewd° of thy tongue.   *shrewish*

ANTHONY In faith, she's too curst.°   *sharp-tongued*

BEATRICE Too curst is more³ than curst. I shall lessen God's
20 sending that way, for it is said, "God sends a curst cow short
horns,⁴ but to a cow too curst, he sends none."

LEONATO So, by being too curst, God will send you no horns?

BEATRICE Just,° if he send me no husband,⁵ for the which   *Just so*
blessing I am at him upon my knees every morning and eve-
25 ning. Lord, I could not endure a husband with a beard on
his face. I had rather lie in the woolen!⁶

LEONATO You may light on a husband that hath no beard.

BEATRICE What should I do with him? Dress him in my
apparel and make him my waiting-gentlewoman? He that
30 hath a beard is more than a youth, and he that hath no
beard is less than a man; and he that is more than a youth is
not for me, and he that is less than a man, I am not for him.
Therefore, I will even take sixpence in earnest of the bear-
ward and lead his apes into hell.⁷

35 LEONATO Well, then, go you into hell?

BEATRICE No, but° to the gate, and there will the devil meet   *only*
me, like an old cuckold with horns on his head, and say,
"Get you to heaven, Beatrice, get you to heaven! Here's no
place for you maids." So deliver I up my apes and away to
40 Saint Peter for the heavens.⁸ He shows me where the bach-
elors⁹ sit, and there live we, as merry as the day is long.

ANTHONY [*to* HERO] Well, niece, I trust you will be ruled by
your father.

2.1 Location: Leonato's house.
1. I suffer from heartburn, caused by Don John's tart
looks.
2. That is, a spoiled child.
3. By one, punning on "too/two."
4. Proverbial: God makes sure that the vicious
("curst") have little power to do harm.
5. That is, if God sent her a husband, she would cuckold him.

6. Sleep between rough blankets (without sheets).
7. *take . . . hell:* take advance payment from the bear-
keeper (who trained bears for the popular sport of
bearbaiting and who usually had charge of other animals; leading apes into hell was the proverbial fate
of old maids.
8. Peter is gatekeeper of heaven. *for the heavens:* as
far as heaven is concerned.
9. Unwed men or women.

BEATRICE Yes, faith. It is my cousin's duty to make curtsy and
45 say, "Father, as it please you." But yet, for all that, cousin, let
him be a handsome fellow or else make another curtsy and
say, "Father, as it please me."

LEONATO Well, niece, I hope to see you one day fitted with a
husband.

50 BEATRICE Not till God make men of some other metal than
earth. Would it not grieve a woman to be overmastered
with° a piece of valiant dust? To make an account of her life   *by*
to a clod of wayward marl?° No, uncle, I'll none. Adam's   *clay*
sons are my brethren, and, truly, I hold it a sin to match in
55 my kindred.¹

LEONATO Daughter, remember what I told you. If the Prince
do solicit you in that kind,² you know your answer.

BEATRICE The fault will be in the music, cousin, if you be not
wooed in good time. If the Prince be too important,° tell   *importunate*
60 him there is measure³ in everything, and so dance out the
answer. For hear me, Hero: wooing, wedding, and repenting is as a Scotch jig, a measure, and a cinquepace.⁴ The
first suit° is hot and hasty like a Scotch jig and full as fantas-   *courtship*
tical; the wedding, mannerly° modest as a measure, full of   *graciously*
65 state and ancientry;° and then comes Repentance, and with   *old-fashioned decorum*
his bad legs falls into the cinquepace, faster and faster, till
he sink into his grave.

LEONATO Cousin, you apprehend passing° shrewdly.   *understand more than*

BEATRICE I have a good eye, uncle. I can see a church by
70 daylight.⁵

LEONATO The revelers are entering, brother. Make good
room.

Enter Prince PEDRO, CLAUDIO, *and* BENEDICT, *and*
BALTHASAR, *and Don* JOHN[, *and* BORACHIO,
wearing masks].

PEDRO Lady, will you walk about with your friend?⁶

HERO So you walk softly, and look sweetly, and say nothing, I
75 am yours for the walk, and especially when I walk away.

PEDRO With me in your company.

HERO I may say so when I please.

PEDRO And when please you to say so?

HERO When I like your favor,° for God defend the lute should   *face*
80 be like the case.⁷

PEDRO My visor° is Philemon's roof. Within the house is   *mask*
Jove.⁸

HERO Why, then, your visor should be thatched.⁹

PEDRO Speak low, if you speak love.
[They step aside.]

---

1. *match in my kindred:* marry incestuously.
2. *in that kind:* that is, to marry him.
3. Moderation (punning on the name of a slow, stately dance [line 62] and continuing the link between dancing and wooing "in good time" [line 59]).
4. A lively five-step dance.
5. That is, see what's in front of me.
6. *friend:* often used to mean "lover." *walk about:*

take a turn (apparently a term in dancing).
7. God forbid your face should be as unappealing as your mask.
8. The peasant Philemon and his wife, Baucis, entertained Jove, disguised, in their humble cottage (Ovid, *Metamorphoses* 8).
9. According to Golding, Philemon's roof was "thatched all with straw"; Hero means that the mask should be fitted with false hair or beard.

85   BALTHASAR [*to* MARGARET]   Well, I would you did like me.[1]

MARGARET   So would not I, for your own sake, for I have
many ill° qualities.   *bad*

BALTHASAR   Which is one?

MARGARET   I say my prayers aloud.

90   BALTHASAR   I love you the better. The hearers may cry
"Amen."

MARGARET   God match me with a good dancer.

BALTHASAR   Amen.

MARGARET   And God keep him out of my sight when the
95   dance is done. Answer, clerk![2]

BALTHASAR   No more words. The clerk is answered.

URSULA [*to* ANTHONY]   I know you well enough. You are Signor
Anthonio.

ANTHONY   At a word,° I am not.   *In short*

100   URSULA   I know you by the waggling of your head.

ANTHONY   To tell you true, I counterfeit him.

URSULA   You could never do him so ill-well[3] unless you were
the very man. Here's his dry hand up and down.[4] You are he!
You are he!

105   ANTHONY   At a word, I am not.

URSULA   Come, come, do you think I do not know you by your
excellent wit? Can virtue° hide itself? Go to! Mum,° you are   *excellence / Be quiet*
he. Graces will appear, and there's an end.[5]

BEATRICE [*to* BENEDICT]   Will you not tell me who told
110   you so?

BENEDICT   No, you shall pardon me.

BEATRICE   Nor will you not tell me who you are?

BENEDICT   Not now.

BEATRICE   That I was disdainful, and that I had my good wit
115   out of the *Hundred Merry Tales*?[6] Well, this was Signor
Benedict that said so.

BENEDICT   What's he?

BEATRICE   I am sure you know him well enough.

BENEDICT   Not I, believe me.

120   BEATRICE   Did he never make you laugh?

BENEDICT   I pray you, what is he?

BEATRICE   Why, he is the Prince's jester. A very dull fool, only
his° gift is in devising impossible° slanders. None but liber-   *his only / unbelievable*
tines delight in him, and the commendation is not in his
125   wit, but in his villainy,° for he both pleases men and angers   *rudeness*
them. And then they laugh at him and beat him. I am sure
he is in the fleet.° I would he had boarded me.[7]   *company (of dancers)*

BENEDICT   When I know the gentleman, I'll tell him what you
say.

---

1. **TEXTUAL COMMENT** In the original quarto, lines
85, 88, and 90 are spoken by Benedict, but because
various problems arise in staging the scene when
Benedict speaks the lines, editors have traditionally
reassigned them to Balthasar. See Digital Edition
TC 2.
2. That is, say "Amen" again. The parish clerk led the

responses in church services.
3. *do him so ill-well:* mime his imperfections so ably.
4. His wrinkled hand exactly.
5. And that is all there is to be said.
6. A famously bad joke-book, first published in 1526.
7. Assaulted me like a ship.

130 BEATRICE Do, do. He'll but break a comparison[8] or two on
me, which, peradventure,° not marked, or not laughed at,   *perhaps*
strikes him into melancholy. And then there's a partridge
wing saved, for the fool will eat no supper that night. We
must follow the leaders.°   *leaders in the dance*

135 BENEDICT In every good thing.

BEATRICE Nay, if they lead to any ill I will leave them at the
next turning.

[They] dance [and all but JOHN, CLAUDIO, *and*
BORACHIO] *exeunt.*

JOHN *[to* BORACHIO] Sure, my brother is amorous on Hero
and hath withdrawn her father to break° with him about it.   *speak*

140 The ladies follow her, and but one visor° remains.   *(man wearing a) mask*

BORACHIO And that is Claudio. I know him by his bearing.

JOHN *[to* CLAUDIO] Are not you Signor Benedict?

CLAUDIO You know me well. I am he.

JOHN Signor, you are very near my brother in his love.° He is   *favor*
145 enamored on Hero. I pray you, dissuade him from her. She
is no equal for his birth. You may do the part of an honest
man in it.

CLAUDIO How know you he loves her?

JOHN I heard him swear his affection.

150 BORACHIO So did I too, and he swore he would marry her
tonight.

JOHN Come, let us to the banquet.°   *after-dinner sweets*

Exeunt JOHN *and* BORACHIO. CLAUDIO *remains.*

CLAUDIO Thus answer I in name of Benedict
But hear these ill news with the ears of Claudio.
155 'Tis certain° so. The Prince woos for himself.   *certainly*
Friendship is constant in all other things
Save in the office° and affairs of love.   *business*
Therefore all° hearts in love use their own tongues.   *let all*
Let every eye negotiate for itself
160 And trust no agent. For beauty is a witch
Against whose charms faith° melteth into blood.°   *loyalty / passion*
This is an accident of hourly proof[9]
Which I mistrusted° not. Farewell, therefore, Hero.   *suspected*

Enter BENEDICT.

BENEDICT Count Claudio?

165 CLAUDIO Yea, the same.

BENEDICT Come, will you go with me?

CLAUDIO Whither?

BENEDICT Even to the next willow[1] about your own business,
County.° What fashion will you wear the garland° of? About   *Count / (of willow)*
170 your neck, like an usurer's chain?[2] Or under your arm, like a
lieutenant's scarf?[3] You must wear it one° way, for the Prince   *some*
hath got your Hero.

CLAUDIO I wish him joy of her.

---

8. He'll only try out, or "crack," a satirical comparison (as one "breaks" a lance).
9. An occurrence demonstrated every hour; a common event.

1. Symbol of unrequited love.
2. A gold chain worn by a moneylender.
3. A sash draped across the chest.

BENEDICT Why, that's spoken like an honest drover;° so they
175 sell bullocks. But did you think the Prince would have
served you thus?   *cattle dealer*

CLAUDIO I pray you, leave me.

BENEDICT Ho, now! You strike like the blind man. 'Twas the
boy that stole your meat, and you'll beat the post.[4]

180 CLAUDIO If it° will not be, I'll leave you.   *Exit.*   *(your departure)*

BENEDICT Alas, poor hurt fowl! Now will he creep into
sedges.[5] But that my lady Beatrice should know me and not
know me! The Prince's fool? Hah! It may be I go under that
title because I am merry. Yea, but so I am apt to do myself
185 wrong. I am not so reputed. It is the base, though bitter,
disposition of Beatrice that puts the world into her person
and so gives me out.[6] Well, I'll be revenged as I may.

    Enter [PEDRO] *the Prince.*

PEDRO Now signor, where's the Count? Did you see him?

BENEDICT Troth, my lord, I have played the part of Lady
190 Fame.° I found him here as melancholy as a lodge in a war-   *Lady Rumor*
ren.[7] I told him, and I think I told him true, that your grace
had got the goodwill of this young lady, and I offered him
my company to a willow tree, either to make him a garland,
as being forsaken, or to bind him up a rod,° as being worthy   *bundle of sticks*
195 to be whipped.

PEDRO To be whipped? What's his fault?

BENEDICT The flat° transgression of a schoolboy, who, being   *stupid*
overjoyed with finding a birds' nest, shows it his companion,
and he steals it.

200 PEDRO Wilt thou make a trust a transgression? The transgression is in the stealer.

BENEDICT Yet it had not been amiss the rod had been made,
and the garland, too. For the garland he might have worn
himself, and the rod he might have bestowed on you, who,
205 as I take it, have stolen his birds' nest.

PEDRO I will but teach them to sing and restore them to the
owner.

BENEDICT If their singing answer your saying, by my faith,
you say honestly.[8]

210 PEDRO The lady Beatrice hath a quarrel to° you. The gentle-   *with*
man that danced with her told her she is much wronged by
you.

BENEDICT Oh, she misused° me past the endurance of a block!   *abused*
An oak but with one green leaf on it[9] would have answered
215 her. My very visor began to assume life and scold with her.
She told me, not thinking I had been myself, that I was the
Prince's jester; that I was duller than a great thaw[1]—huddling
jest upon jest with such impossible conveyance° upon me   *speed*

---

4. Probably alluding to a folktale, which existed in
various forms, of a boy who robbed and played a trick
on his blind master. *post:* pillar (with play on Benedict as the "post," or messenger, who bears bad news).
5. *creep into sedges:* hide to nurse his wounds, as an
injured bird crawls into the tall grass along a
riverbank.
6. It is Beatrice's low but sarcastic disposition that

makes her believe the whole world is of her opinion
and represents me accordingly.
7. A burrow in a rabbit warren. (The rabbit was a traditional symbol of melancholy.)
8. If they sing as you say they will—if you have wooed
Hero for Claudio—then you are talking honorably.
9. An oak with barely any life remaining in it.
1. When the muddy roads kept everyone at home.

that I stood like a man at a mark° with a whole army shoot-   target
220 ing at me. She speaks poniards° and every word stabs. If her   daggers
breath were as terrible as her terminations,° there were no   expressions
living near her; she would infect to the north star.[2] I would
not marry her though she were endowed with all that Adam
had left him° before he transgressed. She would have made   (the whole world)
225 Hercules have turned spit, yea, and have cleft his club to
make the fire, too.[3] Come, talk not of her. You shall find her
the infernal Ate° in good apparel. I would to God some   goddess of discord
scholar would conjure[4] her, for certainly, while she is here a
man may live as quiet in hell as in a sanctuary, and people
230 sin upon purpose because they would go thither. So indeed
all disquiet, horror, and perturbation follows° her.   attends upon
            Enter CLAUDIO *and* BEATRICE[, HERO, *and* LEONATO].
PEDRO   Look! Here she comes.
BENEDICT   Will your grace command me any service to the
235 world's end? I will go on the slightest errand now to the
Antipodes° that you can devise to send me on. I will fetch   other side of the world
you a tooth-picker,° now, from the furthest inch of Asia;   toothpick
bring you the length of Prester John's foot; fetch you a hair
off the great Cham's beard; do you any embassage to the
240 pigmies,[5] rather than hold three words' conference with this
harpy.[6] You have no employment for me?
PEDRO   None, but to desire your good company.
BENEDICT   O God, sir! Here's a dish I love not. I cannot
endure my Lady Tongue.   *Exit.*
PEDRO   Come, lady, come! You have lost the heart of Signor
245 Benedict.
BEATRICE   Indeed, my lord, he lent it me awhile, and I gave
him use° for it: a double heart for his single one. Marry,   interest
once before he won it of° me with false dice. Therefore your   from
grace may well say I have lost it.[7]
250 PEDRO   You have put him down, lady. You have put him down.[8]
BEATRICE   So I would not he should do me, my lord, lest I
should prove the mother of fools. I have brought Count Claudio, whom you sent me to seek.
255 PEDRO   Why, how now, Count? Wherefore are you sad?
CLAUDIO   Not sad, my lord.
PEDRO   How then? Sick?
CLAUDIO   Neither, my lord.
BEATRICE   The Count is neither sad, nor sick, nor merry, nor
well, but civil,° Count, civil as an orange,[9] and something°   serious / somewhat
260 of that jealous complexion.[1]

---

2. Thought to be the remotest star.
3. The Amazon Omphale made Hercules, a Greek
hero, wear her clothes and spin; Benedict imagines
an even greater humiliation and more menial duty—
turning the spit.
4. Conjure the evil spirits out of, or supernaturally
consign to hell. *scholar:* learned person (who could
speak Latin, the language of exorcism).
5. *Prester John's . . . pigmies:* all distant, fantastic figures. In legend, Prester John ruled in Ethiopia, while
the Great Cham (Kublai Khan) reigned in Mongolia,
and a race of dwarfs was said to inhabit the mountains of India.
6. Mythical creature with the face and body of a
woman and the wings and claws of a bird of prey.
7. PERFORMANCE COMMENT How and to whom Beatrice discloses her past romantic attachment to Benedict can influence the tone of a production. See
Digital Edition PC 1.
8. Humiliated him. (Beatrice, in reply, puns on the
physical sense of "put down".)
9. Punning on "Seville," famous for its bitter oranges.
1. Yellow (the traditional color of jealousy).

PEDRO   I'faith, lady, I think your blazon° to be true; though   *formal description*
I'll be sworn, if he be so, his conceit° is false. Here, Claudio,   *imagined idea*
I have wooed in thy name, and fair Hero is won. I have
broke° with her father, and his goodwill obtained. Name the   *negotiated*
265   day of marriage, and God give thee joy.

LEONATO   Count, take of me my daughter, and with her my
fortunes. His grace hath made the match, and all grace say
amen to it.[2]

BEATRICE   Speak, Count. 'Tis your cue.

270   CLAUDIO   Silence is the perfectest herald of joy. I were but
little happy if I could say how much. Lady, as you are mine,
I am yours. I give away myself for you and dote upon the
exchange.

BEATRICE   [*to* HERO]   Speak, cousin! Or if you cannot, stop his
275   mouth with a kiss and let not him speak neither.

PEDRO   In faith, lady, you have a merry heart.

BEATRICE   Yea, my lord, I thank it. Poor fool, it keeps on the
windy° side of care. My cousin tells him in his ear that he is   *windward; safe*
in her heart.

280   CLAUDIO   And so she doth, cousin.

BEATRICE   Good Lord, for alliance![3] Thus goes everyone to
the world but I, and I am sunburnt.[4] I may sit in a corner
and cry, "Heigh ho, for a husband!"[5]

PEDRO   Lady Beatrice, I will get you one.

285   BEATRICE   I would rather have one of your father's getting.°   *begetting*
Hath your grace ne'er a° brother like you? Your father got   *no*
excellent husbands, if a maid could come by them.

PEDRO   Will you have me, lady?

BEATRICE   No, my lord, unless I might have another for work-
290   ing days. Your grace is too costly to wear every day. But I
beseech your grace, pardon me. I was born to speak all
mirth and no matter.°[6]   *substance*

PEDRO   Your silence most offends me, and to be merry best
becomes you. For out o'question, you were born in a merry
295   hour.

BEATRICE   No, sure, my lord, my mother cried. But then there
was a star danced, and under that was I born. Cousins, God
give you joy.

LEONATO   Niece, will you look to those things I told you of?

300   BEATRICE   I cry you mercy,° uncle. [*to* PEDRO] By your grace's   *I beg your pardon*
pardon.   *Exit* BEATRICE.

PEDRO   By my troth, a pleasant-spirited lady.

LEONATO   There's little of the melancholy element in her, my
lord. She is never sad° but when she sleeps, and not ever°   *serious / not always*
305   sad then. For I have heard my daughter say she hath often
dreamt of unhappiness and waked herself with laughing.

PEDRO   She cannot endure to hear tell of a husband.

---

2. May God, the source of all grace, confirm it.
3. Kinship through marriage. (Claudio has just
addressed Beatrice as one of the family.)
4. Unattractive, and therefore unlikely to marry. (Sun-
tans, like dark complexions, were unfashionable.)
goes . . . to the world: gets married.

5. Title of a ballad; probably a catchphrase in Shakespeare's time.
6. **PERFORMANCE COMMENT** Don Pedro's marriage
offer, and Beatrice's quick refusal, can be played sincerely or as repartee. See Digital Edition PC 2.

LEONATO   Oh, by no means. She mocks all her wooers out of
suit.°   *wooing (her)*

310   PEDRO   She were an excellent wife for Benedict.

LEONATO   O Lord! My lord, if they were but a week married
they would talk themselves mad.

PEDRO   County Claudio, when mean you to go to church?

CLAUDIO   Tomorrow, my lord. Time goes on crutches till Love
315   have all his rites.

LEONATO   Not till Monday, my dear son, which is hence a just
seven-night. And a time too brief, too, to have all things
answer° my mind.°   *match / wishes*

PEDRO   Come, you shake the head at so long a breathing,° but   *interval*
320   I warrant° thee, Claudio, the time shall not go dully by us. I   *assure*
will, in the interim, undertake one of Hercules' labors,[7]
which is, to bring Signor Benedict and the lady Beatrice into
a mountain of affection, th'one with th'other. I would fain°   *gladly*
have it a match, and I doubt not but to fashion it, if you
325   three will but minister such assistance as I shall give you
direction.

LEONATO   My lord, I am for you, though it cost me ten nights'
watchings.°   *staying awake*

CLAUDIO   And I, my lord.

330   PEDRO   And you too, gentle Hero?

HERO   I will do any modest office,° my lord, to help my cousin   *task*
to a good husband.

PEDRO   And Benedict is not the unhopefullest° husband that   *least promising*
I know. Thus far can I praise him. He is of a noble strain,° of   *descent*
335   approved° valor, and confirmed honesty.° [*to* HERO] I will   *proven / honor*
teach you how to humor your cousin, that she shall fall in
love with Benedict. [*to* CLAUDIO *and* LEONATO] And I, with
your two helps, will so practice on° Benedict that in despite   *trick*
of his quick wit and his queasy stomach,° he shall fall in love   *qualms (about love)*
340   with Beatrice. If we can do this, Cupid is no longer an
archer. His glory shall be ours, for we are the only love gods.
Go in with me, and I will tell you my drift.°   *Exeunt.*   *scheme*

2.2

Enter JOHN *and* BORACHIO.

JOHN   It is so. The Count Claudio shall marry the daughter of
Leonato.

BORACHIO   Yea, my lord. But I can cross° it.   *thwart*

JOHN   Any bar, any cross, any impediment will be medicinable°   *therapeutic*
5   to me. I am sick in displeasure to him, and whatsoever comes
athwart his affection ranges evenly with mine.[1] How canst
thou cross this marriage?

BORACHIO   Not honestly, my lord, but so covertly that no dishonesty shall appear in me.

10   JOHN   Show me briefly how.

BORACHIO   I think I told your lordship, a year since, how
much I am in the favor of Margaret, the waiting-
gentlewoman to Hero.

---

7. Hercules performed twelve tasks, or labors, of
extraordinary difficulty.
2.2 Location: Scene continues.

1. Whatever frustrates his wishes conforms with
mine.

JOHN   I remember.

15   BORACHIO   I can, at any unseasonable instant° of the night,   *any time whatever*
appoint° her to look out at her lady's chamber window.   *arrange with*

JOHN   What life is in that to be the death of this marriage?

BORACHIO   The poison of that lies in you to temper.° Go you   *concoct*
to the Prince your brother. Spare not to tell him that he

20   hath wronged his honor in marrying the renowned Claudio,
whose estimation° do you mightily hold up,° to a contami-   *reputation / defend*
nated stale,° such a one as Hero.   *prostitute*

JOHN   What proof shall I make of that?

BORACHIO   Proof enough to misuse° the Prince, to vex° Clau-   *deceive / torment*

25   dio, to undo Hero, and kill Leonato. Look you for any other
issue?°   *result*

JOHN   Only to despite° them I will endeavor anything.   *Merely to spite*

BORACHIO   Go, then. Find me a meet hour to draw Don Pedro
and the Count Claudio alone. Tell them that you know that

30   Hero loves me. Intend° a kind of zeal both to the Prince and   *Pretend*
Claudio, as in° love of your brother's honor, who hath made   *as if for*
this match, and his friend's reputation, who is thus like to
be cozened with the semblance of a maid,[2] that you have discovered thus. They will scarcely believe this without trial.°   *proof*

35   Offer them instances, which shall bear no less likelihood
than to see me at her chamber window; hear me call Margaret, Hero; hear Margaret term me, Claudio;[3] and bring them
to see this the very night before the intended wedding. For in
the meantime, I will so fashion the matter that Hero shall be

40   absent, and there shall appear such seeming truth of Hero's
disloyalty that jealousy shall be called assurance,[4] and all
the preparation° overthrown.   *wedding preparation*

JOHN   Grow this° to what adverse issue it can, I will put it in   *Let this lead*
practice. Be cunning in the working this,° and thy fee is a   *of this*

45   thousand ducats.°   *gold coins*

BORACHIO   Be you constant in the accusation, and my cunning
shall not shame me.

JOHN   I will presently go learn their day of marriage.

Exeunt.

2.3

Enter BENEDICT *alone.*

BENEDICT   Boy!

[*Enter* BOY.]

BOY   Signor?

BENEDICT   In my chamber window lies a book. Bring it hither
to me, in the orchard.

5   BOY   I am here already,[1] sir.

BENEDICT   I know that, but I would have thee hence, and here
again.

Exit [BOY].

2. To be cheated with the mere appearance of a virgin.
3. TEXTUAL COMMENT Most editors assume an error in the Quarto here and emend to "Borachio," but this edition follows the Quarto. See Digital Edition TC 3.

4. That suspicion shall be called certainty.
2.3 Location: Leonato's garden.
1. That is, it's as good as done. (Benedict takes him literally.)

I do much wonder that one man, seeing how much another
man is a fool when he dedicates his behaviors to love, will,
after he hath laughed at such shallow follies in others, become
the argument° of his own scorn by falling in love; and such　　　　　　　　*subject*
a man is Claudio. I have known when there was no music
with him but the drum and the fife, and now had he rather
hear the tabor and the pipe.[2] I have known when he would
have walked ten mile afoot to see a good armor,° and now will　　　*suit of armor*
he lie ten nights awake, carving° the fashion of a new dou-　　　　　　*designing*
blet.° He was wont° to speak plain and to the purpose, like　　*jacket / accustomed*
an honest man and a soldier; and now is he turned orthogra-
phy.[3] His words are a very fantastical° banquet: just so many　　　　　*poetic*
strange dishes. May I be so converted and see° with these　　　　　*still see*
eyes? I cannot tell; I think not. I will not be sworn but love
may transform me to an oyster; but I'll take my oath on it, till
he have made an oyster of me, he shall never make me such
a fool. One woman is fair, yet I am well; another is wise, yet
I am well; another virtuous, yet I am well. But till all graces
be in one woman, one woman shall not come in my grace.°　　　　　*favor*
Rich she shall be, that's certain; wise, or I'll none;[4] virtuous,
or I'll never cheapen° her; fair, or I'll never look on her; mild,　　*bargain for*
or come not near me; noble, or not I for an angel;[5] of good
discourse, an excellent musician, and her hair shall be of
what color it please God. Ha! The Prince and Monsieur Love!
I will hide me in the arbor.

　　　Enter Prince [PEDRO], LEONATO, CLAUDIO. [MUSICIANS
　　　play within.][6]
PEDRO　Come, shall we hear this music?
CLAUDIO　Yea, my good lord. How still the evening is,
As° hushed on purpose to grace harmony!　　　　　　　　　　　　*As if*
PEDRO　See you where Benedict hath hid himself?
CLAUDIO　Oh, very well, my lord. The music ended,°　　　*Once the music is over*
We'll fit the kid-fox with a pennyworth.[7]
　　　Enter BALTHASAR *with* [*the* MUSICIANS].
PEDRO　Come, Balthasar, we'll hear that song again.
BALTHASAR　Oh, good my lord, tax° not so bad a voice　　　　　　*task*
To slander music any more than once.
PEDRO　It is the witness still of excellency,
To put a strange face on his own perfection.[8]
I pray thee, sing, and let me woo° no more.　　　　　　　　　　　*cajole*
BALTHASAR　Because you talk of wooing[9] I will sing,
Since many a wooer doth commence his suit
To her he thinks not worthy. Yet he woos,
Yet will he swear he loves.
PEDRO　　　　　　　　　　　Nay, pray thee, come,

---

2. The drum and fife were used by the military; the
tabor (a small drum) and pipe were used in social
festivities.
3. Become overelaborate in his speech.
4. I'll have none (of her).
5. Not I, though she be an angel (punning on coins:
an angel was worth 10 shillings, and a noble 6 shillings 8 pence).
6. TEXTUAL COMMENT The cues for music in the
Quarto edition are somewhat confusing and require
editorial intervention. Examining the original cues

and how editors revise them can help readers think
about how musical performance is staged in this play.
See Digital Edition TC 4.
7. We'll give our young cub more than he bargained
for. *kid-fox*: apparently refers to a young fox; this is
the only listed usage in the *OED*.
8. *It is the witness . . . perfection*: It is always the
mark of great skill to deny its own proficiency.
9. Because you put it in terms of wooing (and so are
likely to continue to flatter me insincerely).

Or if thou wilt hold longer argument,
Do it in notes.°   *music*

50 BALTHASAR   Note this before my notes:
There's not a note of mine that's worth the noting.
PEDRO   Why, these are very crochets[1] that he speaks:
Note notes, forsooth, and nothing.[2]
BENEDICT [*aside*]   Now, divine air, now is his soul ravished. Is

55 it not strange that sheeps' guts[3] should hale° souls out of men's   *drag*
bodies? Well, a horn[4] for my money, when all's done.
                              The Song.
BALTHASAR [*sings*]   Sigh no more, ladies, sigh no more.
                    Men were deceivers ever,
                    One foot in sea, and one on shore,
                    To one thing constant never.
60   Then sigh not so, but let them go,
                    And be you blithe and bonny,°   *beautiful*
                    Converting all your sounds of woe,
                    Into hey nonny nonny.

65   Sing no more ditties, sing no more
                    Of dumps[5] so dull and heavy,
                    The fraud of men was ever so,
                    Since summer first was leafy,
                    Then sigh not so, &c.

70 PEDRO   By my troth, a good song.
BALTHASAR   And an ill singer, my lord.
PEDRO   Ha! No, no, faith, thou sing'st well enough for a shift.°   *to make do*
BENEDICT [*aside*]   An° he had been a dog that should have   *If*
howled thus they would have hanged him, and I pray God
75 his bad voice bode no mischief. I had as lief° have heard the   *gladly*
night raven,° come what plague could have come after it.   *bird of ill omen*
PEDRO   Yea, marry,[6] dost thou hear, Balthasar? I pray thee,
get us some excellent music, for tomorrow night we would
have it at the lady Hero's chamber window.
80 BALTHASAR   The best I can, my lord.
PEDRO   Do so. Farewell.   *Exit* BALTHASAR.
Come hither, Leonato. What was it you told me of today,
that your niece Beatrice was in love with Signor Benedict?
CLAUDIO [*aside*]   Oh, ay, stalk on, stalk on. The fowl sits.[7] [*He*
85 *raises his voice.*] I did never think that lady would have loved
any man.
LEONATO   No, nor I neither. But most wonderful° that she   *astounding*
should so dote on Signor Benedict, whom she hath in all
outward behaviors seemed ever to abhor.
90 BENEDICT [*aside*]   Is't possible? Sits the wind in that corner?
LEONATO   By my troth, my lord, I cannot tell what to think of
it. But that she loves him with an enraged° affection, it is   *violent*
past the infinite° of thought.   *furthest bounds*

---

1. Whimsies; quarter notes (in music).
2. *Note . . . nothing:* Get on with your singing, and
nothing else. ("Nothing" and "noting" sounded the
same in Elizabethan pronunciation. Compare the
same play on words in the comedy's title.)
3. Used to string musical instruments.

4. Military or hunting horn.
5. Melancholy tunes or moods.
6. A mild oath. (Don Pedro is continuing the speech
interrupted by Benedict's aside.)
7. *stalk . . . sits:* go on quietly. Our prey has alighted.

PEDRO   Maybe she doth but counterfeit.

95 CLAUDIO   Faith, like° enough.   *likely*

LEONATO   O God! Counterfeit? There was never counterfeit of passion came so near the life of passion as she discovers° it.   *exhibits*

PEDRO   Why? What effects of passion shows she?

100 CLAUDIO   [*aside*]   Bait the hook well. This fish will bite.

LEONATO   What effects, my lord? She will sit you[8]— [*to* CLAUDIO] You heard my daughter tell you how.

CLAUDIO   She did indeed.

PEDRO   How? How, I pray you? You amaze me. I would have
105 thought her spirit had been invincible against all assaults of affection.

LEONATO   I would have sworn it had, my lord, especially against Benedict.

BENEDICT   [*aside*]   I should think this a gull,° but that the   *trick*
110 white-bearded fellow speaks it. Knavery cannot, sure, hide himself in such reverence.

CLAUDIO   [*aside*]   He hath ta'en th'infection. Hold° it up.   *Keep*

PEDRO   Hath she made her affection known to Benedict?

LEONATO   No, and swears she never will. That's her torment.

115 CLAUDIO   'Tis true indeed, so your daughter says. "Shall I," says she, "that have so oft encountered him with scorn, write to him that I love him?"

LEONATO   This says she now when she is beginning to write to him. For she'll be up twenty times a night, and there will
120 she sit in her smock° till she have writ a sheet of paper. My   *slip*
daughter tells us all.

CLAUDIO   Now you talk of a sheet of paper, I remember a pretty jest your daughter told us of.

LEONATO   Oh, when she had writ it and was reading it over,
125 she found Benedict and Beatrice between the sheet.

CLAUDIO   That.

LEONATO   Oh, she tore the letter into a thousand halfpence;°   *small pieces*
railed at herself, that she should be so immodest to write to one that she knew would flout° her. "I measure him," says   *jeer at*
130 she, "by my own spirit. For I should flout him if he writ to me, yea, though I love him, I should."

CLAUDIO   Then down upon her knees she falls, weeps, sobs, beats her heart, tears her hair, prays, curses, "Oh, sweet Benedict! God give me patience."

135 LEONATO   She doth indeed. My daughter says so. And the ecstasy° hath so much overborne her that my daughter is   *passion*
sometime afeard she will do a desperate outrage° to herself.   *injury*
It is very true.

PEDRO   It were good that Benedict knew of it by some other, if
140 she will not discover° it.   *reveal*

CLAUDIO   To what end? He would make but a sport of it and torment the poor lady worse.

PEDRO   An he should, it were an alms° to hang him. She's an   *charitable deed*
excellent sweet lady, and, out of all suspicion,° she is virtuous.   *doubt*

---

8. She will sit down (i.e., weak with lovesickness).

145 CLAUDIO And she is exceeding wise—

PEDRO In everything but in loving Benedict.

LEONATO O my lord! Wisdom and blood° combating in so ⟶ *passion*
tender a body, we have ten proofs to one that blood hath the
victory. I am sorry for her, as I have just cause, being her
150 uncle and her guardian.

PEDRO I would she had bestowed this dotage° on me. I would ⟶ *infatuation*
have daffed⁹ all other respects° and made her half myself. I ⟶ *considerations*
pray you, tell Benedict of it, and hear what 'a° will say. ⟶ *he*

LEONATO Were it good, think you?

155 CLAUDIO Hero thinks surely she will die. For, she says, she
will die if he love her not; and she will die ere she make her
love known; and she will die if he woo her, rather than she
will bate° one breath of her accustomed crossness.° ⟶ *abate / contrariness*

PEDRO She doth well. If she should make tender° of her love, ⟶ *make an offer*
160 'tis very possible he'll scorn it. For the man, as you know all,
hath a contemptible° spirit. ⟶ *contemptuous*

CLAUDIO He is a very proper° man. ⟶ *handsome*

PEDRO He hath, indeed, a good outward happiness.¹

CLAUDIO Before God, and in my mind, very wise.

165 PEDRO He doth, indeed, show some sparks that are like wit.

CLAUDIO And I take him to be valiant.

PEDRO As Hector,² I assure you. And in the managing of
quarrels you may say he is wise, for either he avoids them
with great discretion, or undertakes them with a most
170 Christianlike fear.

LEONATO If he do fear God, 'a must necessarily keep peace. If
he break the peace, he ought to enter into a quarrel with
fear and trembling.

PEDRO And so will he do, for the man doth fear God, howso-
175 ever it seems not in him by some large° jests he will make. ⟶ *improper*
Well, I am sorry for your niece. Shall we go seek Benedict
and tell him of her love?

CLAUDIO Never tell him, my lord. Let her wear it out with
good counsel.° ⟶ *advice*

180 LEONATO Nay, that's impossible. She may wear her heart out
first.

PEDRO Well, we will hear further of it by° your daughter. Let ⟶ *from*
it cool the while. I love Benedict well, and I could wish he
would modestly examine himself to see how much he is
185 unworthy so good a lady.

LEONATO My lord, will you walk? Dinner is ready.

CLAUDIO [*aside*] If he do not dote on her upon this, I will
never trust my expectation.° ⟶ *predictions*

PEDRO [*aside*] Let there be the same net spread for her, and
190 that must your daughter and her gentlewomen carry.° The ⟶ *manage*
sport will be, when they hold one an opinion of another's
dotage, and no such matter.³ That's the scene that I would
see, which will be merely a dumb show.⁴ Let us send her to
call him in to dinner.   [*Exeunt.* BENEDICT *remains.*]

---

9. Set aside or cast off.
1. He is well endowed with looks and bearing.
2. The noblest and bravest Trojan warrior in Homer's
Iliad.

3. *when . . . matter:* when each believes that the
other is madly in love, without any basis in fact.
4. Pantomime (because words for once will fail
them).

195 BENEDICT   This can be no trick. The conference was sadly
borne.° They have the truth of this from Hero. They seem to   *seriously conducted*
pity the lady; it seems her affections have their full bent.[5]
Love me? Why, it must be requited. I hear how I am censured. They say I will bear myself proudly if I perceive the
200 love come from her. They say, too, that she will rather die
than give any sign of affection. I did never think to marry. I
must not seem proud. Happy are they that hear their detrac-
tions and can put them to mending.° They say the lady is   *amending*
fair. 'Tis a truth; I can bear them witness. And virtuous? 'Tis
205 so, I cannot reprove° it. And wise, but for loving me. By my   *contradict*
troth, it is no addition to her wit,[6] nor no great argument of
her folly, for I will be horribly in love with her. I may chance
have some odd quirks° and remnants of wit broken on° me   *quips / cracked against*
because I have railed so long against marriage; but doth not
210 the appetite alter? A man loves the meat in his youth that he
cannot endure in his age. Shall quips, and sentences,° and   *epigrams*
these paper bullets of the brain awe a man from the career°   *swift course*
of his humor?° No, the world must be peopled. When I said   *liking*
I would die a bachelor, I did not think I should live till I were
215 married.
          Enter BEATRICE.
Here comes Beatrice. By this day, she's a fair lady. I do spy
some marks of love in her.
BEATRICE   Against my will, I am sent to bid you come in to
dinner.
220 BENEDICT   Fair Beatrice, I thank you for your pains.
BEATRICE   I took no more pains for those thanks than you
take pains to thank me. If it had been painful, I would not
have come.
BENEDICT   You take pleasure, then, in the message?
225 BEATRICE   Yea, just so much as you may take upon a knife's
point and choke a daw withal.° You have no stomach,° signor?   *jackdaw with / appetite*
Fare you well.   *Exit.*
BENEDICT   Hah! "Against my will, I am sent to bid you come
in to dinner." There's a double meaning in that. "I took no
230 more pains for those thanks than you took pains to thank me":
that's as much as to say, any pains that I take for you is as easy
as thanks. If I do not take pity of her, I am a villain. If I do not
love her, I am a Jew.[7] I will go get her picture.[8]   *Exit.*

3.1

          Enter HERO *and two gentlewomen,* MARGARET
          and URSULA.
HERO   Good Margaret, run thee to the parlor.
There shalt thou find my cousin Beatrice
Proposing° with the Prince and Claudio.   *Talking*
Whisper her ear,° and tell her I and Ursula   *(in her ear)*
5 Walk in the orchard, and our whole discourse
Is all of her. Say that thou overheard'st us,

---

5. Are stretched to the limit (like a bent bow).
6. No additional proof of her intelligence.
7. That is, lacking in Christian charity (an anti-
Semitic stereotype).

8. *get her picture:* have her portrait painted (for a
love locket) or sketch it himself.
3.1 Location: Leonato's garden.

And bid her steal into the pleachèd[1] bower
Where honeysuckles, ripened by the sun,
Forbid the sun to enter, like favorites
10 Made proud by princes, that advance their pride
Against that power that bred it.[2] There will she hide her
To listen° our propose.° This is thy office.   *hear / conversation*
Bear thee well in it, and leave us alone.
MARGARET I'll make her come, I warrant you, presently. [*Exit.*]
15 HERO Now, Ursula, when Beatrice doth come,
As we do trace° this alley up and down   *pace*
Our talk must only be of Benedict.
When I do name him, let it be thy part
To praise him more than ever man did merit.
20 My talk to thee must be how Benedict
Is sick in love with Beatrice. Of this matter
Is little Cupid's crafty arrow made
That only wounds by hearsay.[3] Now begin,
For look where Beatrice like a lapwing[4] runs
25 Close by the ground to hear our conference.
   Enter BEATRICE.
URSULA [*aside to* HERO] The pleasantest angling is to see the fish
Cut with her golden oars the silver stream
And greedily devour the treacherous bait.
So angle we for Beatrice, who even now
30 Is couchèd° in the woodbine coverture.[5]   *hidden*
Fear you not my part of the dialogue.
HERO [*aside to* URSULA] Then go we near her, that her ear lose
 nothing
Of the false sweet bait that we lay for it.
[*aloud*] No, truly, Ursula, she is too disdainful.
35 I know her spirits are as coy° and wild   *disdainful; shy*
As haggards° of the rock.   *wild female hawks*
URSULA   But are you sure
That Benedict loves Beatrice so entirely?
HERO So says the Prince and my new trothèd lord.
URSULA And did they bid you tell her of it, madam?
40 HERO They did entreat me to acquaint her of it,
But I persuaded them, if they loved Benedict,
To wish him wrestle with affection
And never to let Beatrice know of it.
URSULA Why did you so? Doth not the gentleman
45 Deserve as full° as fortunate a bed   *fully*
As ever Beatrice shall couch upon?
HERO O God of love! I know he doth deserve
As much as may be yielded to a man.
But nature never framed a woman's heart
50 Of prouder stuff than that of Beatrice.
Disdain and scorn ride sparkling in her eyes,
Misprizing° what they look on, and her wit   *Despising*
Values itself so highly that to her

---

1. Screened by intertwining branches.
2. *that advance . . . it:* who presumptuously oppose
the power that created them.
3. Wounds by rumor or gossip.
4. Peewit, a bird that scuttles along the ground.
5. The honeysuckle arbor.

All matter else seems° weak. She cannot love,   *Other topics seem*
55   Nor take no shape nor project of affection,[6]
     She is so self-endeared.
     URSULA   Sure, I think so,
     And therefore, certainly, it were not good
     She knew his love, lest she'll make sport at it.
     HERO   Why, you speak truth. I never yet saw man,
60   How° wise, how noble, young, how rarely° featured,   *However / splendidly*
     But she would spell him backward.[7] If fair-faced,
     She would swear the gentleman should be her sister;
     If black,° why, nature, drawing of an antic,°   *dark / buffoon*
     Made a foul blot;° if tall, a lance ill-headed;   *error*
65   If low, an agate[8] very vilely cut;
     If speaking, why, a vane blown with all winds;
     If silent, why, a block movèd with° none.   *by*
     So turns she every man the wrong side out,
     And never gives to truth and virtue that
70   Which simpleness° and merit purchaseth.°   *integrity / deserve*
     URSULA   Sure, sure, such carping is not commendable.
     HERO   No, not to be so odd and from all fashions,[9]
     As Beatrice is, cannot be commendable.
     But who dare tell her so? If I should speak,
75   She would mock me into air. Oh, she would laugh me
     Out of myself; press me to death with wit.[1]
     Therefore let Benedict, like covered fire,
     Consume away in sighs;[2] waste inwardly.
     It were a better death than die with mocks,
80   Which is as bad as die with tickling.
     URSULA   Yet tell her of it; hear what she will say.
     HERO   No. Rather I will go to Benedict
     And counsel him to fight against his passion.
     And truly, I'll devise some honest° slanders   *harmless*
85   To stain my cousin with. One doth not know
     How much an ill word may empoison liking.
     URSULA   Oh, do not do your cousin such a wrong!
     She cannot be so much without true judgment,
     Having so swift and excellent a wit
90   As she is prized° to have, as to refuse   *esteemed*
     So rare a gentleman as Signor Benedict.
     HERO   He is the only man of Italy,
     Always excepted my dear Claudio.
     URSULA   I pray you, be not angry with me, madam.
95   Speaking my fancy, Signor Benedict,
     For shape, for bearing, argument,[3] and valor,
     Goes foremost in report through Italy.
     HERO   Indeed, he hath an excellent good name.
     URSULA   His excellence did earn it ere he had it.
100   When are you married, madam?

---

6. *Nor take . . . affection:* Nor form the image or even the concept of love.
7. She would speak of his virtues as faults.
8. Tiny figures were carved in agates and used as seals or in rings.
9. *from all fashions:* contrary to normal behavior.
1. Crushing weights were loaded upon accused crim-

inals who refused to enter a plea. Hero suggests that she will be silenced with mockery ("laugh me / Out of myself") and then mocked for her silence ("press me to death with wit").
2. Each sigh was said to draw a drop of blood from the heart.
3. Intellect and rhetorical skill.

HERO   Why, every day! Tomorrow![4] Come, go in.
    I'll show thee some attires and have thy counsel
    Which is the best to furnish° me tomorrow.   *grace*

URSULA [*aside to* HERO]   She's limed,[5] I warrant you. We have
    caught her, madam.

105   HERO [*aside to* URSULA]   If it prove so, then loving goes by haps.°   *chance*
    Some Cupid kills with arrows, some with traps.

                        [*Exeunt* HERO *and* URSULA.]

BEATRICE   What fire is in mine ears?[6] Can this be true?
    Stand I condemned for pride and scorn so much?
    Contempt, farewell, and maiden pride, adieu!

110   No glory lives behind the back of such.[7]
    And Benedict, love on. I will requite thee,
    Taming my wild heart to thy loving hand.[8]
    If thou dost love, my kindness° shall incite thee   *reciprocal love*
    To bind our loves up in a holy band.°   *marriage*

115   For others say thou dost deserve, and I
    Believe it better than reportingly.°   *Exit.*   *as mere rumor*

3.2

Enter Prince [PEDRO], CLAUDIO, BENEDICT,
and LEONATO.

PEDRO   I do but stay till your marriage be consummate, and
    then go I toward Aragon.

CLAUDIO   I'll bring° you thither, my lord, if you'll vouchsafe° me.   *accompany / allow*

PEDRO   Nay. That would be as great a soil in the new gloss of
5   your marriage as to show a child his new coat and forbid
    him to wear it. I will only be bold with° Benedict for his   *ask*
    company, for from the crown of his head to the sole of his
    foot, he is all mirth. He hath twice or thrice cut Cupid's
    bowstring, and the little hangman° dare not shoot at him.   *rogue; executioner*
10   He hath a heart as sound as a bell, and his tongue is the
    clapper: for what his heart thinks, his tongue speaks.

BENEDICT   Gallants, I am not as I have been.

LEONATO   So say I. Methinks you are sadder.°   *more serious*

CLAUDIO   I hope he be in love.

15   PEDRO   Hang him, truant! There's no true drop of blood in
    him, to be truly touched with love. If he be sad, he wants°   *lacks*
    money.

BENEDICT   I have the toothache.[1]

PEDRO   Draw° it.   *Extract*

20   BENEDICT   Hang it.

CLAUDIO   You must hang it first and draw it afterwards.[2]

PEDRO   What? Sigh for the toothache?

LEONATO   Where is but a humor[3] or a worm.

BENEDICT   Well, everyone can master a grief but he that has it.

25   CLAUDIO   Yet, say I, he is in love.

---

4. From tomorrow on, I shall be a married woman
every day.
5. Snared with birdlime, a glue spread on branches
to catch birds.
6. Proverbially, if others were talking about you elsewhere, your ears would burn.
7. No one praises such people behind their backs.
8. In falconry, the bird is tamed by the hand of the

falconer. There is also a pun on "heart/hart."
3.2 Location: Leonato's house.
1. Toothaches supposedly plagued lovers.
2. *hang it:* a mild expletive (like "darn it"). Claudio
plays on the notion of hanging criminals, who were
then cut down and "drawn" (disemboweled).
3. Poisonous fluid in the body (which, along with
worms, was thought to be the cause of toothache).

PEDRO   There is no appearance of fancy° in him, unless it be   *love*
a fancy that he hath to strange disguises, as to be a Dutch-
man today, a Frenchman tomorrow; or in the shape of two
countries at once, as a German from the waist downward,
30   all slops,° and a Spaniard from the hip upward, no doublet.[4]   *baggy breeches*
Unless he have a fancy to this foolery, as it appears he hath,
he is no fool for fancy, as you would have it appear he is.[5]
CLAUDIO   If he be not in love with some woman, there is no
believing old° signs. 'A° brushes his hat o'mornings. What   *time-honored / He*
35   should that bode?
PEDRO   Hath any man seen him at the barber's?
CLAUDIO   No. But the barber's man hath been seen with him,
and the old ornament of his cheek hath already stuffed tennis balls.[6]
40   LEONATO   Indeed, he looks younger than he did, by the loss of
a beard.
PEDRO   Nay, 'a rubs himself with civet.° Can you smell him   *perfume*
out[7] by that?
CLAUDIO   That's as much as to say, the sweet youth's in love.
45   PEDRO   The greatest note of it is his melancholy.
CLAUDIO   And when was he wont to wash[8] his face?
PEDRO   Yea, or to paint himself? For the which, I hear what
they say of him.
CLAUDIO   Nay, but his jesting spirit, which is now crept into a
50   lute string, and now governed by stops.[9]
PEDRO   Indeed, that tells a heavy tale for him. Conclude, conclude! He is in love.
CLAUDIO   Nay, but I know who loves him.
PEDRO   That would I know too. I warrant, one that knows him
55   not.
CLAUDIO   Yes, and his ill conditions,[1] and in despite of all,
dies for him.
PEDRO   She shall be buried with her face upwards.[2]
BENEDICT   Yet is this no charm for the toothache. [*to* LEONATO]
60   Old signor, walk aside with me. I have studied eight or nine
wise words to speak to you, which these hobbyhorses° must   *clowns*
not hear.   [*Exeunt* BENEDICT *and* LEONATO.]
PEDRO   For° my life, to break° with him about Beatrice.   *Upon / speak*
CLAUDIO   'Tis even so. Hero and Margaret[3] have by this° played   *by now*
65   their parts with Beatrice, and then the two bears will not
bite one another when they meet.
         Enter JOHN *the bastard.*
JOHN   My lord and brother, God save you.
PEDRO   Good e'en,° brother.   *Good evening*
JOHN   If your leisure served, I would speak with you.
70   PEDRO   In private?

---

4. His doublet is covered with a Spanish cloak.
5. Unless he enjoys dressing up foolishly, as it seems
he does, he is not in love, as you believe.
6. Benedict has shaved off his beard. Tennis balls
were stuffed with hair.
7. Detect his secret (with play on literal "smell").
8. When was he accustomed to use cosmetic washes
on (compare "paint" in following line).
9. Frets on a lute's fingerboard; restraints. (Lutes
were associated with lovers' serenades.)

1. *Yes . . . conditions:* I.e., You're mistaken; she does
know him and his bad qualities.
2. That is, in Benedict's arms, where she will die
(Elizabethan slang for "have an orgasm") in the act of
love; perhaps a joking reversal of the idea that as one
responsible for her own fate, she should be buried,
like a suicide, with her face downward.
3. Ursula and Hero played the trick on Beatrice with
help from Margaret.

JOHN   If it please you. Yet Count Claudio may hear, for what I
   would speak of concerns him.

PEDRO   What's the matter?

JOHN [*to* CLAUDIO]   Means your lordship to be married
75   tomorrow?

PEDRO   You know he does.

JOHN   I know not that, when he knows what I know.

CLAUDIO   If there be any impediment, I pray you discover° it.   *reveal*

JOHN   You may think I love you not. Let that appear hereafter
80   and aim better at° me by that I now will manifest. For my   *think better of*
   brother, I think he holds you well,° and in dearness° of heart   *in high respect / affection*
   hath holp° to effect your ensuing marriage. Surely, suit ill   *helped*
   spent, and labor ill bestowed.

PEDRO   Why, what's the matter?

85   JOHN   I came hither to tell you. And circumstances short-
   ened,° for she has been too long a-talking of,[4] the lady is   *put simply*
   disloyal.°   *unfaithful*

CLAUDIO   Who? Hero?

JOHN   Even she. Leonato's Hero, your Hero, every man's Hero.

90   CLAUDIO   Disloyal?

JOHN   The word is too good to paint out° her wickedness. I   *fully describe*
   could say she were worse. Think you of a worse title, and I
   will fit her to it. Wonder not till further warrant.° Go but   *evidence*
   with me tonight. You shall see her chamber window entered,
95   even the night before her wedding day. If you love her, then
   tomorrow wed her; but it would better fit your honor to
   change your mind.

CLAUDIO   May this be so?

PEDRO   I will not think it.

100   JOHN   If you dare not trust that you see, confess not that you
   know.[5] If you will follow me, I will show you enough; and
   when you have seen more and heard more, proceed accordingly.

CLAUDIO   If I see anything tonight why I should not marry her,
105   tomorrow in the congregation, where I should wed, there will
   I shame her.

PEDRO   And as I wooed for thee to obtain her, I will join with
   thee to disgrace her.

JOHN   I will disparage her no farther till you are my wit-
110   nesses. Bear it coldly° but till midnight, and let the issue   *calmly*
   show itself.

PEDRO   Oh, day untowardly turned!°   *miserably changed*

CLAUDIO   Oh, mischief strangely thwarting!

JOHN   Oh, plague right well prevented! So will you say when
115   you have seen the sequel.   [*Exeunt.*]

---

4. For we have already talked about her too much.   5. If you won't risk seeing for yourself, don't claim to
know.

3.3

Enter DOGBERRY *and* [VERGES] *his compartner*° *with*   *fellow officer*
the WATCH.[1]

DOGBERRY   Are you good men and true?

VERGES   Yea, or else it were pity but they should suffer salvation,[2] body and soul.

DOGBERRY   Nay, that were a punishment too good for them if
5   they should have any allegiance° in them, being chosen for   *(for "disloyalty")*
the Prince's watch.

VERGES   Well, give them their charge,° neighbor Dogberry.   *instructions*

DOGBERRY   First, who think you the most desertless° man to   *(for "deserving")*
be Constable?[3]

10 FIRST WATCHMAN   Hugh Oatcake, sir, or George Seacoal, for
they can write and read.

DOGBERRY   Come hither, neighbor Seacoal. God hath blessed
you with a good name.[4] To be a well-favored° man is the gift   *good-looking*
of fortune, but to write and read comes by nature.

15 SECOND WATCHMAN   Both which, Master Constable—

DOGBERRY   You have. I knew it would be your answer. Well,
for your favor,° sir, why, give God thanks and make no boast   *looks*
of it. And for your writing and reading, let that appear when
there is no need of such vanity. You are thought here to be
20   the most senseless° and fit man for the Constable of the   *(for "sensible")*
watch: therefore, bear you the lantern. This is your charge.
You shall comprehend all vagrom[5] men. You are to bid any
man stand,° in the Prince's name.   *stop*

SECOND WATCHMAN   How if 'a° will not stand?   *he*

25 DOGBERRY   Why, then, take no note of him, but let him go
and presently° call the rest of the watch together, and thank   *immediately*
God you are rid of a knave.

VERGES   If he will not stand when he is bidden, he is none of
the Prince's subjects.

30 DOGBERRY   True, and they are to meddle with none but the
Prince's subjects. You shall also make no noise in the streets;
for, for the watch to babble and to talk is most tolerable° and   *(for "intolerable")*
not to be endured.

A WATCHMAN   We will rather sleep than talk. We know what
35   belongs° to a watch.[6]   *is appropriate*

DOGBERRY   Why, you speak like an ancient° and most quiet   *experienced*
watchman, for I cannot see how sleeping should offend.
Only have a care that your bills[7] be not stolen. Well, you are
to call at all the alehouses and bid those that are drunk, get
40   them to bed.

A WATCHMAN   How if they will not?

3.3 Location: A street.
1. Watchmen who patrolled the streets, proclaiming the hour and performing police duties. "Verges" probably alludes to a "verge," or wand of office, carried by officials.
2. For "damnation." (Verges and Dogberry repeatedly say the opposite of what they mean.)
3. The leader of the watch. (Dogberry himself is the parish constable.)
4. Sea coal from Newcastle was known for its high

quality (thus the "good name").
5. For "vagrant." *comprehend*: for "apprehend."
6. Textual Comment As with the other scenes involving Dogberry and the watch, the speech prefixes in this scene show clear signs of being work in progress and need editorial intervention. Examining how editors revise the original speech prefixes provides insight into Shakespeare's creative process. See Digital Edition TC 5.
7. Weapons (long shafts with blades or ax heads).

DOGBERRY   Why, then, let them alone till they are sober. If they make you not then the better answer, you may say they are not the men you took them for.

45 A WATCHMAN   Well, sir.

DOGBERRY   If you meet a thief, you may suspect him, by vir-tue of your office, to be no true° man. And for such kind of men, the less you meddle or make° with them, why, the more is° for your honesty.

honest
have to do
the better it is

50 A WATCHMAN   If we know him to be a thief, shall we not lay hands on him?

DOGBERRY   Truly, by your office you may, but I think they that touch pitch will be defiled.[8] The most peaceable way for you, if you do take a thief, is to let him show himself what he 55 is and steal out of your company.

VERGES   You have been always called a merciful man, partner.

DOGBERRY   Truly, I would not hang a dog by my will, much more° a man who hath any honesty in him.

(for "less")

VERGES   If you hear a child cry in the night, you must call to 60 the nurse and bid her still° it.

calm

A WATCHMAN   How if the nurse be asleep and will not hear us?

DOGBERRY   Why, then, depart in peace and let the child wake her with crying. For the ewe that will not hear her lamb when it baas will never answer a calf° when he bleats.

blockhead

65 VERGES   'Tis very true.

DOGBERRY   This is the end of the charge. You, Constable, are to present° the Prince's own person.[9] If you meet the Prince in the night, you may stay° him.

represent
stop

VERGES   Nay, by'r Lady, that I think 'a cannot.

70 DOGBERRY   Five shillings to one on't with any man that knows the statutes, he may stay him. Marry, not without° the Prince be willing. For, indeed, the watch ought to offend no man, and it is an offense to stay a man against his will.

unless

VERGES   By'r Lady, I think it be so.

75 DOGBERRY   Hah, ah, hah! Well, masters, good night. An there be any matter of weight chances,[1] call up me. Keep your fel-lows' counsels, and your own, and good night. [*to* VERGES] Come, neighbor.

A WATCHMAN   Well, masters, we hear our charge. Let us go sit 80 here upon the church bench till two, and then all to bed.

DOGBERRY   One word more, honest neighbors. I pray you, watch about Signor Leonato's door, for the wedding being there tomorrow there is a great coil° tonight. Adieu! Be vigi-tant,° I beseech you.

to-do, bustle
(for "vigilant")

Exeunt [DOGBERRY *and* VERGES].

Enter BORACHIO *and* CONRAD.

85 BORACHIO   What, Conrad!

A WATCHMAN [*aside*]   Peace, stir not.

BORACHIO   Conrad, I say!

CONRAD   Here, man. I am at thy elbow.

---

8. A proverbial saying, derived from the Apocryphal book of Ecclesiasticus (13:1). *pitch:* tar.
9. Dogberry presents a parodic version of the notion that the monarch's authority was in theory separable

from his person (others could represent that author-ity when he was physically absent).
1. *An . . . chances:* If anything important happens.

BORACHIO   Mass,° and my elbow itched![2] I thought there would   *By the mass*
90   a scab[3] follow.

CONRAD   I will owe thee an answer for that. And now, forward with thy tale.

BORACHIO   Stand thee close then under this penthouse,° for it   *overhanging structure*
drizzles rain, and I will, like a true drunkard, utter[4] all to thee.

95   A WATCHMAN [*aside*]   Some treason, masters. Yet stand close.°   *keep hidden*

BORACHIO   Therefore, know, I have earned of Don John a
thousand ducats.

CONRAD   Is it possible that any villainy should be so dear?°   *valuable*

BORACHIO   Thou shouldst rather ask if it were possible any
100   villainy should be so rich. For when rich villains have need
of poor ones, poor ones may make what price they will.

CONRAD   I wonder at it.

BORACHIO   That shows thou art unconfirmed.° Thou knowest   *inexperienced*
that the fashion of a doublet, or a hat, or a cloak is nothing
105   to[5] a man.

CONRAD   Yes; it is apparel.

BORACHIO   I mean the fashion.

CONRAD   Yes; the fashion is the fashion.

BORACHIO   Tush! I may as well say, the fool's the fool. But
110   seest thou not what a deformed° thief[6] this fashion is?   *deforming*

A WATCHMAN [*aside*]   I know that Deformed. 'A° has been a   *He*
vile thief this seven year. 'A goes up and down° like a gentle-   *struts here and there*
man. I remember his name.

BORACHIO   Didst thou not hear somebody?

115   CONRAD   No. 'Twas the vane on the house.

BORACHIO   Seest thou not, I say, what a deformed thief this
fashion is? How giddily 'a turns about all the hot bloods°   *dandies*
between fourteen and five-and-thirty, sometimes fashioning them like Pharaoh's soldiers in the reechy° painting,[7]   *grimy*
120   sometime like god Bel's[8] priests in the old church window,
sometime like the shaven Hercules[9] in the smirched worm-
eaten tapestry, where his codpiece[1] seems as massy as his club?

CONRAD   All this I see, and I see that the fashion wears out
more apparel than the man.[2] But art not thou thyself giddy
125   with the fashion too, that thou hast shifted[3] out of thy tale
into telling me of the fashion?

BORACHIO   Not so, neither. But know that I have tonight wooed
Margaret, the lady Hero's gentlewoman, by the name of Hero.
She leans me° out at her mistress' chamber window; bids me   *leans*
130   a thousand times good night. I tell this tale vilely. I should
first tell thee how the Prince, Claudio, and my master, planted,

---

2. Proverbially, itching elbows alerted you against
shady company.
3. Contemptible person; punning on a literal "scab."
4. The drunken Borachio alludes to the Latin tag *in
vino veritas* ("in wine there is truth").
5. Tells us nothing about (but Conrad takes him to
mean "means nothing to").
6. Used here to mean "rogue"—but also that keeping
up with fashion robs men of their money.
7. Perhaps refers to a painting of the fleeing Israelites pursued by Pharaoh's army.

8. Bel (Baal) was a Babylonian god who had seventy
priests. His story, told in the biblical Apocrypha, is
sometimes depicted in stained-glass windows.
9. Probably referring to the story of Omphale (compare
2.1.225), or perhaps confusing Hercules with Samson.
1. Pouch, often stuffed and ornamented, worn over a
man's breeches, covering the genitals.
2. *fashion . . . man*: fashions change before clothes
wear out.
3. Punning on "changed clothes."

and placed, and possessed[4] by my master Don John, saw afar
off in the orchard this amiable° encounter.   *loving*

CONRAD   And thought they Margaret was Hero?

135   BORACHIO   Two of them did: the Prince and Claudio. But the
devil my master knew she was Margaret. And partly by his
oaths which first possessed them; partly by the dark night
which did deceive them; but chiefly by my villainy, which did
confirm any slander that Don John had made—away went
140   Claudio enraged; swore he would meet her as he was appointed
next morning at the temple;° and there, before the whole   *church*
congregation, shame her with what he saw o'er night and
send her home again without a husband.

FIRST WATCHMAN   We charge you, in the Prince's name, stand!

145   SECOND WATCHMAN   Call up the right[5] Master Constable! We
have here recovered the most dangerous piece of lechery[6]
that ever was known in the commonwealth.

FIRST WATCHMAN   And one Deformed is one of them. I know
him. 'A wears a lock.[7]

150   CONRAD   Masters! Masters!

SECOND WATCHMAN   You'll be made bring Deformed forth, I
warrant you.

CONRAD   Masters!

A WATCHMAN   Never speak, we charge you. Let us obey° you   *(for "compel")*
155   to go with us.

BORACHIO   We are like to prove a goodly° commodity, being   *fine (ironic)*
taken up of these men's bills.[8]

CONRAD   A commodity in question,[9] I warrant you. [*to the*
WATCH] Come, we'll obey you.   *Exeunt.*

3.4

Enter HERO, *and* MARGARET, *and* URSULA.

HERO   Good Ursula, wake my cousin Beatrice and desire her
to rise.

URSULA   I will, lady.

HERO   And bid her come hither.

5   URSULA   Well.°   [*Exit* URSULA.]   *Very well*

MARGARET   Troth, I think your other rebato° were better.   *stiffly wired collar*

HERO   No, pray thee, good Meg, I'll wear this.

MARGARET   By my troth, 's° not so good, and I warrant° your   *it's / am sure*
cousin will say so.

10   HERO   My cousin's a fool and thou art another. I'll wear none
but this.

MARGARET   I like the new tire° within excellently, if the hair   *headdress with wig*
were a thought browner. And your gown's a most rare° fash-   *splendid*
ion, i'faith. I saw the Duchess of Milan's gown that they
15   praise so.

HERO   Oh, that exceeds,° they say.   *surpasses all*

---

4. Informed; but perhaps also controlled (as by the devil).
5. Respectfully, as in "right worshipful."
6. For "treachery." *recovered*: for "discovered."
7. A "lovelock," or curl of hair, worn by courtiers.
8. *being . . . bills:* a multiple pun: after we have been

hoisted on their halberds (weapons); been arrested on their warrants; been obtained on credit ("taken up") in exchange for their bonds ("bills").
9. Of doubtful value; about to be judicially interrogated.
3.4 Location: Leonato's house.

MARGARET   By my troth, 's but a nightgown° in respect of   *dressing gown*
yours. Cloth o'gold and cuts, and laced with silver, set with
pearls, down sleeves, side sleeves, and skirts round, under-
20   borne with a bluish tinsel.¹ But for a fine, quaint,° graceful,   *elegant*
and excellent fashion, yours is worth ten on't.

HERO   God give me joy to wear it, for my heart is exceeding
heavy.

MARGARET   'Twill be heavier soon by the weight of a man.

25   HERO   Fie upon thee! Art not ashamed?

MARGARET   Of what, lady? Of speaking honorably? Is not
marriage honorable in° a beggar? Is not your lord honorable   *even in*
without marriage? I think you would have me say, saving
your reverence,² "a husband." An° bad thinking do not wrest°   *If / pervert*
30   true speaking, I'll offend nobody. Is there any harm in "the
heavier for a husband"? None, I think, an it be the right
husband and the right wife; otherwise, 'tis light° and not   *licentious*
heavy.

    Enter BEATRICE.
Ask my lady Beatrice else. Here she comes.

35   HERO   Good morrow, coz.

BEATRICE   Good morrow, sweet Hero.

HERO   Why, how now? Do you speak in the sick tune?

BEATRICE   I am out of all other tune, methinks.

MARGARET   Clap's° into "Light o'love"; that goes without a   *Let us shift*
40   burden.³ Do you sing it, and I'll dance it.

BEATRICE   Ye light o'love with your heels?⁴ Then if your husband have stables enough, you'll see he shall lack no bairns.⁵

MARGARET   Oh, illegitimate construction!⁶ I scorn that with
my heels.⁷

45   BEATRICE   'Tis almost five o'clock, cousin. 'Tis time you were
ready,° by my troth. I am exceeding ill, heigh-ho.   *dressed*

MARGARET   For a hawk, a horse,⁸ or a husband?

BEATRICE   For the letter that begins them all: H.⁹

MARGARET   Well, an you be not turned Turk,¹ there's no more
50   sailing by the star.²

BEATRICE   What means the fool, trow?°   *I wonder*

MARGARET   Nothing, I, but God send everyone their heart's
desire.

HERO   These gloves the Count sent me—they are an excellent
55   perfume.³

BEATRICE   I am stuffed,⁴ cousin, I cannot smell.

MARGARET   A maid, and stuffed! There's goodly catching of cold.

---

1. *Cloth . . . tinsel:* made of silk or woolen cloth interwoven with gold thread, with ornamental slashes
("cuts") showing the fabric beneath, and decorated
with silver embroidery or lace and with pearls; with
fitted ("down") sleeves and another pair that hung
open from the shoulder; trimmed at the hem or fully
lined ("underborne") with another kind of metallic
fabric.
2. A polite expression of apology (as if "husband" were
an offensive term).
3. Bass part (for a man's voice), with play on heavy
"weight of a man." "Light o' Love" was a popular tune.
4. *Ye . . . heels:* Your dancing toys with love? ("Light-
heeled" was slang for "promiscuous.")
5. Punning on "barns." *bairns:* children.

6. A multiple pun: forced interpretation; making of
bastards; illegal building (of stables and barns).
7. I kick that away (reject it).
8. Responding to Beatrice's ostentatious sigh as a
hunting cry.
9. Punningly: "ache" was pronounced in the same
way.
1. If you have not reneged (on your vows against marriage). "To turn Turk" is, in the Christian proverb, to
become a renegade (by going over to the enemy, the
Muslim Turks).
2. No more navigating by the polestar. (No truths
can be trusted from now on.)
3. Perfumed gloves were fashionable.
4. In the nose; Margaret follows with an obscene pun.

BEATRICE Oh, God help me! God help me! How long have
you professed apprehension?°   *claimed to be witty*

60 MARGARET Ever since you left it. Doth not my wit become me
rarely?°   *excellently*

BEATRICE It is not seen enough. You should wear it in your
cap.[5] By my troth, I am sick.

MARGARET Get you some of this distilled *carduus benedictus*[6]

65 and lay it to your heart. It is the only thing for a qualm.°   *sudden faintness*

HERO There thou prickest her with a thistle.

BEATRICE *Benedictus?* Why *benedictus?* You have some moral[7]
in this *benedictus.*

MARGARET Moral? No, by my troth, I have no moral mean-

70 ing. I meant plain holy thistle. You may think, perchance,°   *perhaps*
that I think you are in love. Nay, by'r Lady, I am not such a
fool to think what I list;° nor I list not to think what I can;   *please*
nor, indeed, I cannot think, if I would think my heart out of
thinking, that you are in love, or that you will be in love, or

75 that you can be in love. Yet Benedict was such another,[8] and
now is he become a man. He swore he would never marry,
and yet now, in despite of his heart, he eats his meat without
grudging.[9] And how you may be converted I know not, but
methinks you look with your eyes as other women do.

80 BEATRICE What pace is this that thy tongue keeps?

MARGARET Not a false gallop.[1]

            Enter URSULA.

URSULA Madam, withdraw. The Prince, the Count, Signor
Benedict, Don John, and all the gallants of the town are come
to fetch you to church.

85 HERO Help to dress me, good coz, good Meg, good Ursula.

                                        [*Exeunt.*]

                        3.5

Enter LEONATO, *and* [DOGBERRY] *the Constable, and*
[VERGES] *the Headborough.*°   *local constable*

LEONATO What would you with me, honest neighbor?

DOGBERRY Marry, sir, I would have some confidence° with you,   *(for "conference")*
that discerns° you nearly.   *(for "concerns")*

LEONATO Brief,° I pray you, for you see it is a busy time with me.   *Be brief*

5 DOGBERRY Marry, this it is, sir.

VERGES Yes, in truth it is, sir.

LEONATO What is it, my good friends?

DOGBERRY Goodman° Verges, sir, speaks a little off the   *(commoner's title)*
matter.° An old man, sir, and his wits are not so blunt° as,   *subject / (for "sharp")*

10 God help, I would desire they were. But, in faith, honest as
the skin between his brows.

VERGES Yes. I thank God, I am as honest as any man living
that is an old man and no honester than I.

DOGBERRY Comparisons are odorous.° Palabras,[1] neighbor   *(for "odious")*

15 Verges!

---

5. Like the coxcomb of a professional fool.
6. Holy thistle, or blessed thistle (a medicinal herb
good for the heart).
7. Hidden meaning (with ensuing pun on "no moral"
as "immoral").
8. Benedict was once an enemy of love.

9. Nonetheless, he has a perfectly good appetite.
1. Not a canter. (I am not speaking at a false pace.)
3.5 Location: Scene continues.
1. Be brief (from a Spanish expression, *pocas palabras,* meaning "few words").

LEONATO   Neighbors, you are tedious.[2]

DOGBERRY   It pleases your worship to say so, but we are the
poor Duke's officers.° But truly, for mine own part, if I were   *the Duke's poor officers*
as tedious as a king, I could find in my heart to bestow it all
20   of your worship.

LEONATO   All thy tediousness on me, ah?

DOGBERRY   Yea, an 'twere a thousand pound more than 'tis,
for I hear as good exclamation[3] on your worship as of any
man in the city. And though I be but a poor man, I am glad
25   to hear it.

VERGES   And so am I.

LEONATO   I would fain° know what you have to say.   *gladly*

VERGES   Marry, sir, our watch tonight, excepting your worship's
presence,[4] ha' ta'en a couple of as arrant knaves as any in
30   Messina.

DOGBERRY   A good old man, sir; he will be talking. As they
say, "When the age is in, the wit is out,"[5] God help us. It is a
world to see.[6] Well said, i'faith, neighbor Verges. Well, God's
a good man. An° two men ride of a horse, one must ride   *If*
35   behind. An honest soul, i'faith, sir, by my troth he is, as ever
broke bread.[7] But God is to be worshipped. All men are not
alike. Alas, good neighbor.

LEONATO   Indeed, neighbor, he comes too short of you.

DOGBERRY   Gifts that God gives.

40   LEONATO   I must leave you.

DOGBERRY   One word, sir! Our watch, sir, have indeed comprehended two aspitious[8] persons, and we would have them
this morning examined before your worship.

LEONATO   Take their examination yourself and bring it me.
45   I am now in great haste, as it may appear unto you.

DOGBERRY   It shall be suffigance.°   *(nonsense word for*
                                                                             "sufficient")

LEONATO   Drink some wine ere you go. Fare you well.

[*Enter* MESSENGER.]

MESSENGER   My lord, they stay° for you, to give your daughter   *wait*
to her husband.

50   LEONATO   I'll wait upon them. I am ready.

[*Exeunt* LEONATO *and* MESSENGER.]

DOGBERRY   Go, good partner, go get you to Francis Seacoal.[9]
Bid him bring his pen and inkhorn to the jail. We are now to
examination° these men.   *(for "examine")*

VERGES   And we must do it wisely.

55   DOGBERRY   We will spare for no wit, I warrant you. Here's that°   *that which*
shall drive some of them to a *non come.*[1] Only get the learned
writer to set down our excommunication,° and meet me at   *(for "examination")*
the jail.   [*Exeunt.*]

---

2. Dogberry takes it to mean "rich."
3. Properly, "accusation"; but Dogberry probably intends "acclamation."
4. For "respecting your worship's presence": an apology for speaking what might displease.
5. Dogberry's version of the proverb "When the wine is in, the wit is out."
6. Dogberry seems to mean "a strange world"; the expression normally meant "wonderful to behold."

7. Dogberry strings together three proverbial sentences, all of which are remembered correctly but irrelevantly.
8. For "suspicious." *comprehended*: for "apprehended."
9. Refers to the Sexton in 4.2, not the George Seacoal of the watch in 3.3.
1. For "nonplus" (bewilderment); perhaps confused by Dogberry with *non compos mentis* (insane).

4.1

Enter [PEDRO *the*] *Prince,* [JOHN *the*] *Bastard,*
LEONATO, FRIAR, CLAUDIO, BENEDICT, HERO, *and*
BEATRICE.[1]

LEONATO Come, Friar Francis, be brief. Only to the plain
form of marriage, and you shall recount their particular
duties afterward.

FRIAR [*to* CLAUDIO] You come hither, my lord, to marry this
5   lady?

CLAUDIO No.

LEONATO To be married to her, Friar. You come to marry her.

FRIAR [*to* HERO] Lady, you come hither to be married to this
Count?

10 HERO I do.

FRIAR If either of you know any inward° impediment why   secret
you should not be conjoined, I charge you on your souls to
utter it.

CLAUDIO Know you any, Hero?

15 HERO None, my lord.

FRIAR Know you any, Count?

LEONATO I dare make his answer. "None!"

CLAUDIO Oh, what men dare do! What men may do! What men
daily do, not knowing what they do!

20 BENEDICT How now? Interjections? Why, then, some be of
laughing, as, "ah, ha, he."[2]

CLAUDIO Stand thee by, Friar. [*to* LEONATO] Father, by your leave,
Will you with free and unconstrainèd° soul   uncompelled
Give me this maid, your daughter?

25 LEONATO As freely, son, as God did give her me.

CLAUDIO And what have I to give you back, whose worth
May counterpoise° this rich and precious gift?   equal

PEDRO Nothing, unless you render her again.°   give her back

CLAUDIO Sweet Prince, you learn° me noble thankfulness.   teach

30   There, Leonato, take her back again.
Give not this rotten orange to your friend.
She's but the sign° and semblance of her honor.   mere appearance
Behold, how like a maid she blushes here!
Oh, what authority and show of truth

35   Can cunning sin cover itself withal!°   with
Comes not that blood° as modest evidence   blush
To witness° simple virtue? Would you not swear,   testify to
All you that see her, that she were a maid
By these exterior shows? But she is none.

40   She knows the heat of a luxurious° bed.   lustful
Her blush is guiltiness, not modesty.

LEONATO What do you mean, my lord?

CLAUDIO   Not to be married;
Not to knit my soul to an approvèd° wanton.   proven

LEONATO Dear my lord, if you, in your own proof,°   endeavor

45   Have vanquished the resistance of her youth

4.1 Location: A church.
1. PERFORMANCE COMMENT Margaret is notably
absent from this scene; some stage directors choose
to include her. See Digital Edition PC 3.

2. Benedict alludes to a passage in William Lily's
Latin grammar, used in all Elizabethan schools:
"Some [interjections] are of laughing; as Ha ha he"
(1567 edition).

And made defeat of her virginity—
CLAUDIO   I know what you would say. If I have known her,
   You will say, she did embrace me as a husband,
   And so extenuate the forehand sin.[3]
50   No, Leonato,
   I never tempted her with word too large°   immodest
   But, as a brother to his sister, showed
   Bashful sincerity and comely love.
HERO   And seemed I ever otherwise to you?
55   CLAUDIO   Out on thee,[4] seeming! I will write against it.
   You seem to me as Dian in her orb,[5]
   As chaste as is the bud ere it be blown.°   blossom
   But you are more intemperate in your blood°   passion
   Than Venus or those pampered animals
60   That rage in savage sensuality.
HERO   Is my lord well, that he doth speak so wide?°   wildly
LEONATO   Sweet prince, why speak not you?
PEDRO   What should I speak?
   I stand dishonored, that have gone about°   tried
   To link my dear friend to a common stale.°   prostitute
65   LEONATO   Are these things spoken, or do I but dream?
JOHN   Sir, they are spoken, and these things are true.
BENEDICT   This looks not like a nuptial.
HERO   "True"? O God!
CLAUDIO   Leonato, stand I here?
   Is this the Prince? Is this the Prince's brother?
70   Is this face Hero's? Are our eyes our own?
LEONATO   All this is so. But what of this, my lord?
CLAUDIO   Let me but move° one question to your daughter,   put
   And by that fatherly and kindly° power   natural
   That you have in her, bid her answer truly.
75   LEONATO   I charge thee do so, as thou art my child.
HERO   Oh, God defend me! How am I beset!
   What kind of catechizing[6] call you this?
CLAUDIO   To make you answer truly to your name.[7]
HERO   Is it not Hero? Who can blot that name
   With any just reproach?
80   CLAUDIO   Marry, that can Hero.
   "Hero" itself[8] can blot out Hero's virtue.
   What man was he talked with you yesternight
   Out at your window betwixt twelve and one?
   Now if you are a maid, answer to this.
85   HERO   I talked with no man at that hour, my lord.
PEDRO   Why, then are you no maiden. Leonato,
   I am sorry you must hear. Upon mine honor,
   Myself, my brother, and this grievèd° Count   wronged
   Did see her, hear her, at that hour last night
90   Talk with a ruffian at her chamber window;
   Who hath, indeed, most like a liberal° villain,   loose-tongued

---

3. And so excuse the sin of having sex before marriage ("the forehand sin").
4. A curse; "thee" could refer to Hero or "seeming" (putting on a false show).
5. Diana (Roman goddess of chastity and of the moon) in her orbit, or sphere of activity.

6. A catechism is a set of formal questions and answers used to teach church doctrine.
7. To make you admit that you are what you have been called.
8. The name (or reputation) of Hero.

Confessed the vile encounters they have had
A thousand times in secret.

JOHN   Fie, fie, they are
Not to be named, my lord; not to be spoke of.
95   There is not chastity enough in language
Without offense to utter them. Thus, pretty lady,
I am sorry for thy much misgovernment.°   *ample misconduct*

CLAUDIO   O Hero! What a Hero hadst thou been,
If half thy outward graces had been placed
100   About thy thoughts and counsels of thy heart!
But fare thee well. Most foul, most fair, farewell!
Thou pure impiety and impious purity.
For° thee I'll lock up all the gates of love,   *Because of*
And on my eyelids shall conjecture° hang   *suspicion*
105   To turn all beauty into thoughts of harm;
And never shall it more be gracious.°   *attractive*

LEONATO   Hath no man's dagger here a point for me?
              [HERO *falls to the ground.*]

BEATRICE   Why, how now, cousin? Wherefore sink you down?

JOHN   Come, let us go. These things come thus to light
Smother her spirits° up.   [*Exeunt* PEDRO, CLAUDIO,   *vital forces*
                                            and JOHN.]

110   BENEDICT   How doth the lady?

BEATRICE   Dead, I think. Help, uncle!
Hero! Why, Hero! Uncle! Signor Benedict! Friar!

LEONATO   O Fate! Take not away thy heavy hand.
Death is the fairest cover for her shame
That may be wished for.

115   BEATRICE   How now? Cousin Hero?

FRIAR   Have comfort, lady.

LEONATO   Dost thou look up?

FRIAR   Yea, wherefore should she not?

LEONATO   Wherefore? Why, doth not every earthly thing
Cry shame upon her? Could she here deny
120   The story that is printed in her blood?°   *blush*
Do not live, Hero. Do not ope thine eyes.
For did I think thou wouldst not quickly die—
Thought I thy spirits were stronger than thy shame—
Myself would on the rearward° of reproaches   *in the wake*
125   Strike at thy life. Grieved I, I had but one?
Chid I for that at frugal nature's frame?°   *plan*
Oh, one too much by thee. Why had I one?
Why ever wast thou lovely in my eyes?
Why had I not with charitable hand
130   Took up a beggar's issue at my gates,
Who, smirchèd thus° and mired with infamy,   *(as you are)*
I might have said, "No part of it is mine.
This shame derives itself from unknown loins."
But mine, and mine I loved, and mine I praised,
135   And mine that I was proud on,° mine so much   *of*
That I myself was to myself not mine[9]
Valuing of her—why, she—oh, she is fallen
Into a pit of ink, that the wide sea

9. That I cared nothing for myself in comparison.

Hath drops too few to wash her clean again
140 And salt too little which may season give[1]
To her foul tainted flesh.

BENEDICT   Sir, sir, be patient.
For my part, I am so attired in wonder
I know not what to say.

BEATRICE   Oh, on my soul, my cousin is belied.°   slandered
145 BENEDICT   Lady, were you her bedfellow last night?

BEATRICE   No, truly, not; although until last night
I have this twelvemonth been her bedfellow.

LEONATO   Confirmed, confirmed! Oh, that is stronger made
Which was before° barred up with ribs of iron.   already
150 Would the two princes lie, and Claudio lie,
Who loved her so that, speaking of her foulness,
Washed it with tears? Hence from her. Let her die.

FRIAR   Hear me a little,
For I have only silent been so long
155 And given way unto this course of fortune[2]
By noting of the lady.[3] I have marked
A thousand blushing apparitions
To start into her face; a thousand innocent shames
In angel whiteness beat away those blushes;
160 And in her eye there hath appeared a fire
To burn the errors° that these princes hold   (like heretics)
Against her maiden truth. Call me a fool,
Trust not my reading nor my observations,
Which with experimental seal doth warrant
165 The tenor of my book;[4] trust not my age,
My reverence, calling, nor divinity,
If this sweet lady lie not guiltless here,
Under some biting error.

LEONATO   Friar, it cannot be.
Thou seest that all the grace that she hath left
170 Is that she will not add to her damnation
A sin of perjury. She not denies it.
Why seek'st thou then to cover with excuse
That which appears in proper° nakedness?   true

FRIAR   Lady, what man is he you are accused of?
175 HERO   They know that do accuse me. I know none.
If I know more of any man alive
Than that which maiden modesty doth warrant,
Let all my sins lack mercy. O my father!
Prove you that any man with me conversed
180 At hours unmeet,° or that I yesternight   improper
Maintained the change° of words with any creature,   exchange
Refuse° me, hate me, torture me to death.   Disown

FRIAR   There is some strange misprision° in the princes.   misunderstanding

---

1. Give renewal. (Salt is a preservative for meat.)
2. Textual Comment The Quarto sets lines 153–55 as prose, but it is likely that this was a result of error by the printer. This edition follows editorial tradition in printing the lines as poetry. See Digital Edition TC 6.

3. By . . . lady: So I could observe, or because I was observing, Hero.
4. Which . . . book: Which guarantees, with the confirmation of experience, the truth of the conclusions I have drawn from my study.

BENEDICT Two of them have the very bent of° honor,   *are wholly devoted to*
185   And if their wisdoms be misled in this
       The practice° of it lives in John the bastard,   *trickery*
       Whose spirits toil in frame of° villainies.   *in plotting*
   LEONATO I know not. If they speak but truth of her,
       These hands shall tear her. If they wrong her honor,
190   The proudest of them shall well hear of it.
       Time hath not yet so dried this blood of mine,
       Nor age so ate up my invention,°   *ingenuity*
       Nor fortune made such havoc of my means,°   *wealth*
       Nor my bad life reft° me so much of friends,   *deprived*
195   But they shall find awaked in such a kind°   *manner*
       Both strength of limb and policy° of mind,   *cunning*
       Ability in means and choice of friends,
       To quit me of⁵ them throughly.°   *thoroughly*
   FRIAR   Pause awhile,
       And let my counsel sway you in this case.
200   Your daughter here the princes left for dead.
       Let her awhile be secretly kept in,
       And publish° it that she is dead indeed.   *announce*
       Maintain a mourning ostentation,°   *formal display*
       And on your family's old monument°   *burial vault*
205   Hang mournful epitaphs, and do all rites
       That appertain unto a burial.
   LEONATO   What shall become of this? What will this do?
   FRIAR   Marry, this well carried° shall on her behalf   *managed*
       Change slander to remorse.° That is some good.   *pity*
210   But not for that dream I on this strange course,
       But on° this travail look for greater birth.⁶   *from*
       She dying, as it must be so maintained,
       Upon the instant that she was accused,
       Shall be lamented, pitied, and excused
215   Of° every hearer. For it so falls out   *By*
       That what we have, we prize not to the worth°   *full value*
       Whiles we enjoy it. But being lacked and lost,
       Why, then we rack⁷ the value. Then we find
       The virtue that possession would not show us
220   Whiles it was ours. So will it fare with Claudio.
       When he shall hear she died upon° his words   *as a result of*
       Th'idea° of her life shall sweetly creep   *The image*
       Into his study of imagination,°   *reverie*
       And every lovely organ° of her life   *aspect*
225   Shall come appareled in more precious habit,
       More moving delicate and full of life,
       Into the eye and prospect° of his soul   *vision*
       Than when she lived indeed. Then shall he mourn,
       If ever love had interest in his liver,⁸
230   And wish he had not so accusèd her.
       No, though he thought his accusation true.
       Let this be so, and doubt not but success°   *what follows*
       Will fashion the event° in better shape   *result*

---

5. To be avenged upon.   7. Stretch (as on a rack, an instrument of torture).
6. Look for a more important consequence (with pun   8. Thought of as the seat of passions, including love.
on "travail" as "labor pains" as well as "effort").

Than I can lay it down in likelihood.
235 But if all aim but this be leveled false,[9]
The supposition of the lady's death
Will quench the wonder of her infamy.
And if it sort° not well, you may conceal her   *turn out*
As best befits her wounded reputation,
240 In some reclusive° and religious life,   *cloistered*
Out of all eyes, tongues, minds, and injuries.°   *calumny*
BENEDICT   Signor Leonato, let the Friar advise you.
And though you know my inwardness° and love   *close friendship*
Is very much unto the Prince and Claudio,
245 Yet, by mine honor, I will deal in this
As secretly and justly as your soul
Should with your body.
LEONATO   Being that I flow in° grief,   *Since I am flooded by*
The smallest twine° may lead me.   *thread*
FRIAR   'Tis well consented. Presently away,°   *Let's leave immediately*
250 For to strange sores, strangely they strain the cure.[1]
Come, lady, die to live. This wedding day
Perhaps is but prolonged.° Have patience and endure.   *postponed*
              Exeunt [all but BEATRICE *and* BENEDICT].
BENEDICT   Lady Beatrice, have you wept all this while?
BEATRICE   Yea, and I will weep a while longer.
255 BENEDICT   I will not desire that.
BEATRICE   You have no reason. I do it freely.
BENEDICT   Surely, I do believe your fair cousin is wronged.
BEATRICE   Ah, how much might the man deserve of me that
would right her!
260 BENEDICT   Is there any way to show such friendship?
BEATRICE   A very even° way, but no such friend.   *clear*
BENEDICT   May a man do it?
BEATRICE   It is a man's office, but not yours.
BENEDICT   I do love nothing in the world so well as you. Is not
265 that strange?
BEATRICE   As strange as the thing I know not. It were as pos-
sible for me to say I loved nothing so well as you. But believe
me not. And yet I lie not. I confess nothing, nor I deny noth-
ing. I am sorry for my cousin.
270 BENEDICT   By my sword, Beatrice, thou lovest me.
BEATRICE   Do not swear and eat it.[2]
BENEDICT   I will swear by it that you love me, and I will make
him eat it that says I love not you.
BEATRICE   Will you not eat your word?
275 BENEDICT   With no sauce that can be devised to it. I protest°   *affirm*
I love thee.
BEATRICE   Why, then, God forgive me.
BENEDICT   What offense, sweet Beatrice?
BEATRICE   You have stayed me in a happy hour.[3] I was about
280 to protest I loved you.
BENEDICT   And do it with all thy heart.

---

9. But if we miss our aim in all but this.
1. Shakespeare's version of the proverb "A desperate disease must have a desperate cure." *strange:* extreme, extraordinary. *sores:* sicknesses. *strain:* employ something beyond its usual use.
2. Eat your words; go back on your oath. Benedict takes it to mean his sword (as does F: "swear by it and eat it").
3. You have stopped me at a fortunate moment.

BEATRICE	I love you with so much of my heart that none is left to protest.	
BENEDICT	Come, bid me do anything for thee.	
285 BEATRICE	Kill Claudio.[4]	
BENEDICT	Ha! Not for the wide world.	
BEATRICE	You kill me to deny° it. Farewell.	*by refusing*
BENEDICT	Tarry, sweet Beatrice.	
BEATRICE	I am gone, though I am here. There is no love in	
290	you. Nay, I pray you, let me go.	
BENEDICT	Beatrice.	
BEATRICE	In faith, I will go.	
BENEDICT	We'll be friends first.	
BEATRICE	You dare easier be friends with me than fight with	
295	mine enemy.	
BENEDICT	Is Claudio thine enemy?	
BEATRICE	Is 'a not approved in the height[5] a villain that hath slandered, scorned, dishonored my kinswoman? Oh, that I were a man! What, bear her in hand[6] until they come to take	
300	hands and then with public accusation, uncovered° slander, unmitigated rancor—O God, that I were a man! I would eat his heart in the marketplace.	*barefaced*
BENEDICT	Hear me, Beatrice.	
BEATRICE	Talk with a man out at a window? A proper saying!°	*A likely story*
305 BENEDICT	Nay, but Beatrice—	
BEATRICE	Sweet Hero! She is wronged. She is slandered. She is undone.	
BENEDICT	Beatrice!	
BEATRICE	Princes and counties! Surely a princely testimony. A	
310	goodly count![7] Count Comfit!° A sweet gallant, surely! Oh, that I were a man for his sake! Or that I had any friend would be a man for my sake! But manhood is melted into curtsies, valor into compliment, and men are only turned into tongue, and trim° ones, too. He is now as valiant as Hercules that°	*Sugarplum* *fine (ironic) / who*
315	only tells a lie and swears it. I cannot be a man with° wishing. Therefore I will die a woman with grieving.	*by*
BENEDICT	Tarry, good Beatrice. By this hand, I love thee.	
BEATRICE	Use it for my love some other way than swearing by it.	
320 BENEDICT	Think you in your soul the Count Claudio hath wronged Hero?	
BEATRICE	Yea, as sure as I have a thought or a soul.	
BENEDICT	Enough; I am engaged.° I will challenge him. I will kiss your hand, and so I leave you. By this hand, Claudio	*pledged*
325	shall render me a dear account.° As you hear of me, so think of me. Go comfort your cousin. I must say she is dead; and so farewell. [*Exeunt.*]	*pay me dearly*

---

4. PERFORMANCE COMMENT In performance, this line can be delivered with gravity or for comic effect. See Digital Edition PC 4.
5. Is he not proved in the highest degree.

6. *bear her in hand:* lead her on with false hopes.
7. Story, tale (with plays on "count" as a legal indictment and as Claudio's title).

4.2

Enter the Constables [DOGBERRY, VERGES, *the* SEXTON],
BORACHIO *and the Town Clerk, in gowns*[1][, *the*
WATCH, *and* CONRAD].

DOGBERRY　Is our whole dissembly° appeared?　　　　　　　*(for "assembly")*

VERGES　Oh, a stool and a cushion for the Sexton.

SEXTON　Which be the malefactors?[2]

DOGBERRY　Marry, that am I and my partner.

5　VERGES　Nay, that's certain. We have the exhibition° to examine.　　*(for "commission")*

SEXTON　But which are the offenders that are to be examined?
Let them come before Master Constable.

DOGBERRY　Yea, marry, let them come before me. What is your
name, friend?

10　BORACHIO　Borachio.

DOGBERRY　Pray write down, "Borachio." Yours, sirrah?[3]

CONRAD　I am a gentleman, sir, and my name is Conrad.

DOGBERRY　Write down, "Master Gentleman Conrad." Masters, do you serve God?

15　CONRAD *and* BORACHIO　Yea, sir, we hope.

DOGBERRY　Write down that they hope they serve God. And
write "God" first, for God defend° but God should go before[4]　　*forbid*
such villains. Masters, it is proved already that you are little
better than false knaves, and it will go near to be thought so

20　shortly. How answer you for yourselves?

CONRAD　Marry, sir, we say we are none.

DOGBERRY　A marvelous witty° fellow, I assure you. But I will　　*clever*
go about with° him. Come you hither, sirrah! A word in your　　*outwit*
ear, sir. I say to you, it is thought you are false knaves.

25　BORACHIO　Sir, I say to you, we are none.

DOGBERRY　Well, stand aside. Fore God, they are both in a tale.°　　*telling the same story*
Have you writ down that they are none?

SEXTON　Master Constable, you go not the way to examine.
You must call forth the watch that are their accusers.

30　DOGBERRY　Yea, marry, that's the eftest° way. Let the watch　　*(nonsense word*
come forth. —Masters, I charge you in the Prince's name,　　*for "aptest")*
accuse these men.

FIRST WATCHMAN　This man said, sir, that Don John the Prince's
brother was a villain.

35　DOGBERRY　Write down, "Prince John a villain." Why, this is
flat perjury:[5] to call a prince's brother "villain."

BORACHIO　Master Constable.

DOGBERRY　Pray thee, fellow, peace! I do not like thy look, I
promise thee.

40　SEXTON　What heard you him say else?

SECOND WATCHMAN　Marry, that he had received a thousand
ducats of Don John for accusing the lady Hero wrongfully.

DOGBERRY　Flat burglary° as ever was committed.　　　　　*(for "perjury")*

4.2 Location: A prison or hearing room in Messina.
1. Constables wore black gowns. The Sexton is presumably Francis Seacoal (3.5.51). Q's direction calls
him the town clerk, an office more appropriate to his
function in the scene than sexton, with which, however, it seems often to have been combined.

2. Dogberry seems to mistake "malefactors" for "factors," or agents.
3. Contemptuous, since "sirrah" is used to address
inferiors, provoking Conrad's claim to be a gentleman.
4. (Punningly) take precedence over.
5. Perhaps a mistake for "treachery" or "slander."

VERGES Yea, by mass,[6] that it is.

45 SEXTON What else, fellow?

FIRST WATCHMAN And that Count Claudio did mean upon° | *on the basis of*
his words to disgrace Hero before the whole assembly, and
not marry her.

DOGBERRY Oh! Villain, thou wilt be condemned into everlast-
50 ing redemption° for this. | *(for "damnation")*

SEXTON What else?

FIRST WATCHMAN *and* SECOND WATCHMAN This is all.

SEXTON And this is more, masters, than you can deny. Prince
John is this morning secretly stolen away. Hero was in this
55 manner accused; in this very manner refused; and upon the
grief of this, suddenly died. Master Constable, let these men
be bound and brought to Leonato's. I will go before and
show him their examination.   [*Exit.*]

VERGES Come, let them be opinioned.° Let them be in the | *(for "pinioned")*
60 hands of—

CONRAD [*pointing to* DOGBERRY] Coxcomb![7]

DOGBERRY God's° my life, where's the Sexton? Let him write | *God save*
down, "The Prince's officer, Coxcomb!" Come, bind them.
—Thou naughty varlet.° | *wicked knave*

65 CONRAD Away! You are an ass. You are an ass.

DOGBERRY Dost thou not suspect° my place? Dost thou not | *(for "respect")*
suspect my years? Oh, that he were here to write me down
an ass! But masters, remember that I am an ass. Though it
be not written down, yet forget not that I am an ass. No,
70 thou villain, thou art full of piety,° as shall be proved upon | *(for "impiety")*
thee by good witness. I am a wise fellow, and which is more,
an officer, and which is more, a householder, and which is
more, as pretty a piece of flesh[8] as any is in Messina, and
one that knows the law, go to, and a rich fellow enough, go
75 to, and a fellow that hath had losses,[9] and one that hath two
gowns and everything handsome about him. Bring him
away. Oh, that I had been writ down an ass!   *Exeunt.*

5.1

Enter LEONATO *and his brother* [ANTHONY].

ANTHONY If you go on thus you will kill yourself,
And 'tis not wisdom thus to second° grief | *assist*
Against yourself.

LEONATO   I pray thee, cease thy counsel,
Which falls into mine ears as profitless
5 As water in a sieve. Give not me counsel,
Nor let no comforter delight mine ear
But such a one whose wrongs do suit° with mine. | *match*
Bring me a father that so loved his child,
Whose joy of° her is overwhelmed like mine, | *in*
10 And bid him speak of patience.
Measure his woe the length and breadth of mine,
And let it answer every strain° for strain— | *intense hardship*

---

6. "By the mass," a common oath.
7. This is an emendation of a corrupt passage, given
in Q as part of the previous speech.
8. *as pretty . . . flesh:* as fine (or gallant) a mortal
man.
9. *hath had losses:* was once richer.
5.1 Location: Near Leonato's house.

As thus for thus, and such a grief for such—
In every lineament, branch, shape, and form.[1]
15 If such a one will smile and stroke his beard,
And sorrow, wag, cry "Hem!" when he should groan[2]—
Patch° grief with proverbs, make misfortune drunk   *Mend*
With candle-wasters[3]—bring him yet to me,
And I of him will gather patience.
20 But there is no such man. For, brother, men
Can counsel and speak comfort to that grief
Which they themselves not feel. But tasting it,
Their counsel turns to passion which before
Would give preceptial° medicine to rage,   *precepts as*
25 Fetter strong madness in a silken thread,
Charm ache with air° and agony with words.   *breath*
No, no! 'Tis all men's office° to speak patience   *business*
To those that wring° under the load of sorrow,   *writhe*
But no man's virtue nor sufficiency°   *ability*
30 To be so moral° when he shall endure   *moralizing*
The like himself. Therefore give me no counsel.
My griefs cry louder than advertisement.°   *advice*
ANTHONY   Therein do men from children nothing differ.
LEONATO   I pray thee, peace! I will be flesh and blood.
35 For there was never yet philosopher
That could endure the toothache patiently,
However they have writ the style of gods
And made a push at chance and sufferance.[4]
ANTHONY   Yet bend° not all the harm upon yourself.   *direct*
40 Make those that do offend you suffer too.
LEONATO   There thou speak'st reason. Nay, I will do so.
My soul doth tell me Hero is belied,
And that shall Claudio know. So shall the Prince
And all of them that thus dishonor her.
           Enter Prince [PEDRO] *and* CLAUDIO.
45 ANTHONY   Here comes the Prince and Claudio hastily.
PEDRO   Good e'en,° good e'en.   *evening*
CLAUDIO   Good day to both of you.
LEONATO   Hear you, my lords?
PEDRO   We have some haste, Leonato.
LEONATO   Some haste, my lord? Well, fare you well, my lord.
Are you so hasty now? Well, all is one.°   *no matter*
50 PEDRO   Nay, do not quarrel with us, good old man.
ANTHONY   If he could right himself with quarreling
Some of us° would lie low.   *(Don Pedro and Claudio)*
CLAUDIO   Who wrongs him?
LEONATO   Marry, thou dost wrong me, thou dissembler, thou![5]
Nay, never lay thy hand upon thy sword.
I fear thee not.

---

1. Leonato moves from the outline of the body to its integral whole. *lineament:* outline. *branch:* limb. *shape:* appearance. *form:* entire body.
2. TEXTUAL COMMENT *wag, cry "Hem!":* talk animatedly, clear his throat (as if about to make a speech). This somewhat baffling line, perhaps reflecting Leonato's anguish, has puzzled editors, who have proposed many emendations. See Digital Edition TC 7.
3. *make misfortune . . . candle-wasters:* forget about

misfortune through tedious philosophy. *drunk:* insensible. *candle-wasters:* philosophers; burners of midnight oil (and their works).
4. *writ . . . sufferance:* written as if they transcended human passion, and expressed themselves scornfully about (said "push" to) bad luck and suffering. *push:* equivalent here to "pish," a noise of disdain.
5. "Thou," which in early modern English is less formal than "you," is used contemptuously here.

55	CLAUDIO Marry, beshrew° my hand	*curse*
	If it should give your age such cause of fear.	
	In faith, my hand meant nothing to⁶ my sword.	
	LEONATO Tush, tush, man! Never fleer° and jest at me.	*sneer; mock*
	I speak not like a dotard nor a fool	
60	As under privilege of age to brag	
	What I have done, being young, or what would do,	
	Were I not old. Know, Claudio, to thy head,°	*face*
	Thou hast so wronged mine innocent child and me	
	That I am forced to lay my reverence by,	
65	And with gray hairs and bruise of many days	
	Do challenge thee to trial of a man.°	*(a duel)*
	I say thou hast belied mine innocent child.	
	Thy slander hath gone through and through her heart	
	And she lies buried with her ancestors,	
70	Oh! in a tomb where never scandal slept	
	Save this of hers, framed° by thy villainy.	*created*
	CLAUDIO My villainy?	
	LEONATO Thine, Claudio, thine I say.	
	PEDRO You say not right, old man.	
	LEONATO My lord, my lord!	
	I'll prove it on his body if he dare,	
75	Despite his nice fence⁷ and his active practice,	
	His May of youth and bloom of lustihood.°	*virility*
	CLAUDIO Away! I will not have to do with you.	
	LEONATO Canst thou so daff me?° Thou hast killed my child.	*brush me off*
	If thou kill'st me, boy, thou shalt kill a man.	
80	ANTHONY He shall kill two of us, and men indeed.	
	But that's no matter. Let him kill one first.	
	Win me and wear me!⁸ Let him answer me.°	*(in a duel)*
	Come, follow me, boy! Come, sir boy, come follow me,	
	Sir boy! I'll whip you from your foining fence.⁹	
85	Nay, as I am a gentleman, I will.	
	LEONATO Brother!	
	ANTHONY Content yourself.° God knows, I loved my niece,	*Don't interfere*
	And she is dead, slandered to death by villains	
	That dare as well answer a man indeed	
90	As I dare take a serpent by the tongue.	
	Boys, apes,° braggarts, jacks,° milksops!	*fools / knaves*
	LEONATO Brother Anthony!	
	ANTHONY Hold you content. What, man! I know them, yea,	
	And what they weigh, even to the utmost scruple.°	*1/24 ounce*
95	Scambling, outfacing, fashion-monging boys¹	
	That lie, and cog,° and flout,° deprave,° and slander,	*cheat / mock / defame*
	Go anticly,° and show outward hideousness,²	*outlandishly dressed*
	And speak of half a dozen dang'rous words,	
	How they might hurt their enemies, if they durst.	
	And this is all.	
100	LEONATO But brother Anthony.	

---

6. My hand had no designs upon.
7. His nimble fencing (said contemptuously).
8. A form of challenge: let him beat me and only then boast of it.
9. Thrusting position in fencing (Anthony probably means that he will compel Claudio to close with him in the duel, or that he will literally take a whip to him).
1. *Scambling . . . boys:* Quarrelsome, insolent, faddish boys.
2. A fearsome exterior.

ANTHONY   Come, 'tis no matter.
 Do not you meddle. Let me deal in this.
PEDRO   Gentlemen both, we will not wake° your patience.   *test*
 My heart is sorry for your daughter's death,
105 But on my honor, she was charged with nothing
 But what was true and very full of proof.
LEONATO   My lord, my lord!
PEDRO   I will not hear you.
LEONATO   No? Come, brother, away. I will be heard.
ANTHONY   And shall, or some of us will smart for it.
       Exeunt LEONATO *and* ANTHONY.
110 PEDRO   See, see! Here comes the man we went to seek.
    Enter BENEDICT.
CLAUDIO   Now, signor, what news?
BENEDICT   Good day, my lord.
PEDRO   Welcome, signor. You are almost come to part almost
 a fray.
115 CLAUDIO   We had liked to have had° our two noses snapped *We nearly had*
 off with° two old men without teeth.   *by*
PEDRO   Leonato and his brother. What thinkest thou? Had we
 fought, I doubt° we should have been too young for them. *suspect*
BENEDICT   In a false quarrel there is no true valor. I came to
120 seek you both.
CLAUDIO   We have been up and down to seek thee, for we are
 high proof° melancholy and would fain have it beaten away. *to a high degree*
 Wilt thou use thy wit?
BENEDICT   It is in my scabbard. Shall I draw it?
125 PEDRO   Dost thou wear thy wit by thy side?
CLAUDIO   Never any did so, though very many have been beside
 their wit.° I will bid thee draw as we do the minstrels:[3] draw *out of their minds*
 to pleasure us.
PEDRO   As I am an honest man, he looks pale. Art thou sick,
130 or angry?
CLAUDIO   What, courage, man! What though care killed a cat?[4]
 Thou hast mettle° enough in thee to kill care.   *spirit; courage*
BENEDICT   Sir, I shall meet your wit in the career.° An you *at full gallop*
 charge° it against me, I pray you, choose another subject. *aim*
135 CLAUDIO   Nay, then, give him another staff.° This last was broke *lance*
 'cross.[5]
PEDRO   By this light, he changes° more and more. I think he *changes color*
 be angry indeed.
CLAUDIO   If he be, he knows how to turn his girdle.[6]
140 BENEDICT   [*to* CLAUDIO]   Shall I speak a word in your ear?
CLAUDIO   God bless° me from a challenge!   *protect*
BENEDICT   [*aside to* CLAUDIO]   You are a villain. I jest not. I will
 make it good how you dare, with what° you dare, and when *whatever weapon*
 you dare. Do me right,[7] or I will protest° your cowardice. *proclaim*
145 You have killed a sweet lady, and her death shall fall heavy
 on you. Let me hear from you.

---

3. *draw . . . minstrels:* draw a sword, the way a minstrel is bidden to draw a bow across his musical
instrument.
4. Proverbial (compare "Curiosity killed the cat").
5. Was snapped in the middle, like a badly handled

lance. (Claudio is mocking Benedict's attempt at wit.)
6. A colloquialism of uncertain derivation, possibly meaning "let him get on with it" or "that's his
problem."
7. Give me satisfaction.

CLAUDIO [*aside to* BENEDICT]   Well, I will meet you, so I may
　　　have good cheer.
PEDRO   What? A feast? A feast?
150　CLAUDIO   I'faith, I thank him, he hath bid me to a calf's head
　　　and a capon, the which if I do not carve most curiously,° say
　　　my knife's naught.° Shall I not find a woodcock[8] too?
BENEDICT   Sir, your wit ambles[9] well. It goes easily.
PEDRO   I'll tell thee how Beatrice praised thy wit the other
155　day. I said thou hadst a fine wit. "True," said she, "a fine little
　　　one." "No," said I, "a great wit." "Right," says she, "a great
　　　gross one." "Nay," said I, "a good wit." "Just," said she, "it
　　　hurts nobody." "Nay," said I, "the gentleman is wise." "Cer-
　　　tain," said she, "a wise gentleman."[1] "Nay," said I, "he hath the
160　tongues."° "That I believe," said she, "for he swore a thing to
　　　me on Monday night which he forswore on Tuesday morning.
　　　There's a double tongue. There's two tongues." Thus did she
　　　an hour together trans-shape° thy particular virtues, yet at
　　　last she concluded, with a sigh, thou wast the properest° man
165　in Italy.
CLAUDIO   For the which she wept heartily and said she cared
　　　not.
PEDRO   Yea, that she did. But yet, for all that, and if she did
　　　not hate him deadly, she would love him dearly. The old man's
170　daughter told us all.
CLAUDIO   All, all, and moreover, God saw him when he was
　　　hid in the garden.[2]
PEDRO   But when shall we set the savage bull's horns on the
　　　sensible Benedict's head?
175　CLAUDIO   Yea, and text underneath, "Here dwells Benedict
　　　the married man"?[3]
BENEDICT   Fare you well, boy. You know my mind. I will leave
　　　you now to your gossip-like° humor. You break° jests as brag-
　　　garts do their blades,[4] which, God be thanked, hurt not. My
180　lord, for your many courtesies I thank you. I must discon-
　　　tinue your company. Your brother the bastard is fled from
　　　Messina. You have among you killed a sweet and innocent
　　　lady. For my lord Lackbeard there, he and I shall meet, and
　　　till then, peace be with him.　　　　　　　　　　　[*Exit.*]
185　PEDRO   He is in earnest.
CLAUDIO   In most profound earnest, and I'll warrant you, for
　　　the love of Beatrice.
PEDRO   And hath challenged thee?
CLAUDIO   Most sincerely.
190　PEDRO   What a pretty thing man is, when he goes in his dou-
　　　blet and hose and leaves off his wit![5]

Marginal glosses:
daintily / useless (lines 151–52)
knows several languages (line 160)
distort / handsomest (lines 163–64)
old-womanish / crack (line 178)

---

8. The calf's head, capon, and woodcock were variet-
ies of food that also symbolize stupidity.
9. Moves slowly (in other words, it does not gallop as
a quick wit would).
1. A phrase often used ironically to mean "an old
fool."
2. Allusion to Genesis 3:8 (Adam attempting to hide
from God in the Garden of Eden); contains a half-
hidden reference to the trick played on Benedict in
the garden.
3. Claudio and Don Pedro recall that Benedict joked
that if he ever fell in love, his friends could set horns
in his forehead, have his picture painted, and title it
"Benedict, the married man" (1.1.223–28).
4. Braggarts secretly dent their swords to make it
appear that they have been dealing fierce blows.
5. When he puts on fine clothes but forgets to wear
his brain.

CLAUDIO   He is then a giant to an ape, but then is an ape a
doctor to such a man.[6]

PEDRO   But soft you,° let me be. Pluck up,° my heart, and be   *wait / Collect yourself*
195   sad.° Did he not say my brother was fled?   *serious*

Enter Constables [DOGBERRY *and* VERGES], CONRAD,
and BORACHIO.

DOGBERRY   Come you, sir, if justice cannot tame you she shall
ne'er weigh more reasons[7] in her balance.° Nay, and you be a   *scales*
cursing hypocrite once,° you must be looked to.   *even once*

PEDRO   How now, two of my brother's men bound? Borachio
200   one?

CLAUDIO   Hearken after° their offense, my lord.   *Inquire into*

PEDRO   Officers, what offense have these men done?

DOGBERRY   Marry, sir, they have committed false report.
Moreover, they have spoken untruths. Secondarily, they are
205   slanders.° Sixth and lastly, they have belied a lady. Thirdly,   *(for "slanderers")*
they have verified° unjust things. And to conclude, they are   *affirmed as true*
lying knaves.

PEDRO   First I ask thee, what they have done? Thirdly I ask
thee, what's their offense? Sixth and lastly, why they are
210   committed?° And to conclude, what you lay to their charge?   *held on arrest*

CLAUDIO   Rightly reasoned and in his own division.° And by   *logical organization*
my troth, there's one meaning well suited.[8]

PEDRO [*to* CONRAD *and* BORACHIO]   Who have you offended,
masters, that you are thus bound to your answer?[9] This
215   learned Constable is too cunning to be understood. What's
your offense?

BORACHIO   Sweet Prince, let me go no farther to mine answer.°   *trial; account*
Do you hear me, and let this Count kill me. I have deceived
even your very eyes. What your wisdoms could not discover
220   these shallow fools have brought to light, who in the night
overheard me confessing to this man how Don John, your
brother, incensed° me to slander the lady Hero; how you were   *incited*
brought into the orchard and saw me court Margaret in
Hero's garments; how you disgraced her when you should
225   marry her. My villainy they have upon record, which I had
rather seal° with my death than repeat over to my shame. The   *confirm; end*
lady is dead upon mine and my master's false accusation, and
briefly, I desire nothing but the reward of a villain.

PEDRO [*to* CLAUDIO]   Runs not this speech like iron through
230   your blood?

CLAUDIO   I have drunk poison whiles he uttered it.

PEDRO [*to* BORACHIO]   But did my brother set thee on to this?

BORACHIO   Yea, and paid me richly for the practice° of it.   *execution*

PEDRO   He is composed and framed° of treachery   *made up*
235   And fled he is upon this villainy.

CLAUDIO   Sweet Hero, now thy image doth appear
In the rare semblance° that I loved it first.   *likeness*

---

6. Such a man is much bigger than an ape, but an
ape is a learned man ("doctor") compared with him.
7. Legal cases. Also, "reason" was pronounced like
"raisin," producing a comic image here.

8. Dressed in several different costumes (with play
on legal "suit").
9. Required to respond (punning on "bound over for
trial" and "bound with ropes").

DOGBERRY   Come, bring away the plaintiffs.° By this time our   (for "defendants")
   Sexton hath reformed° Signor Leonato of the matter. And   (for "informed")
240   masters, do not forget to specify, when time and place shall
   serve, that I am an ass.
VERGES   Here! Here comes master Signor Leonato, and the
   Sexton too.
        Enter LEONATO, *his brother* [ANTHONY], *and*
        the SEXTON.
LEONATO   Which is the villain? Let me see his eyes,
245   That when I note another man like him
   I may avoid him. Which of these is he?
BORACHIO   If you would know your wronger, look on me.
LEONATO   Art thou the slave that with thy breath hast killed
   Mine innocent child?
BORACHIO   Yea, even I alone.
250 LEONATO   No, not so, villain. Thou beliest thyself.
   Here stand a pair of honorable men;
   A third is fled that had a hand in it.
   I thank you, princes, for my daughter's death.
   Record it with your high and worthy deeds.
255   'Twas bravely done, if you bethink you of it.
CLAUDIO   I know not how to pray your patience,
   Yet I must speak. Choose your revenge yourself.
   Impose° me to what penance your invention   *Subject*
   Can lay upon my sin. Yet sinned I not
   But in mistaking.
260 PEDRO   By my soul, nor I.
   And yet, to satisfy this good old man
   I would bend under any heavy weight
   That he'll enjoin me to.
LEONATO   I cannot bid you bid my daughter live;
265   That were impossible. But I pray you both,
   Possess° the people in Messina here   *Inform*
   How innocent she died, and if your love
   Can labor aught in sad invention,[1]
   Hang her an epitaph upon her tomb
270   And sing it to her bones. Sing it tonight.
   Tomorrow morning, come you to my house,
   And since you could not be my son-in-law,
   Be yet my nephew. My brother hath a daughter,
   Almost the copy of my child that's dead,
275   And she alone is heir to both of us.[2]
   Give her the right you should have given her cousin,
   And so dies my revenge.
CLAUDIO   O noble sir!
   Your over-kindness doth wring tears from me.
   I do embrace your offer, and dispose
280   For henceforth° of poor Claudio.   *For the future*
LEONATO   Tomorrow then I will expect your coming.
   Tonight I take my leave. This naughty° man   *evil*
   Shall face to face be brought to Margaret,

---

1. Can produce anything in the way of sad art.
2. Shakespeare (or Leonato) has apparently forgotten Anthony's son mentioned at 1.2.1.

Who, I believe, was packed° in all this wrong,   *confederate*
285   Hired to it by your brother.
   BORACHIO   No, by my soul, she was not,
    Nor knew not what she did when she spoke to me,
    But always hath been just and virtuous
    In anything that I do know by° her.   *of*
290   DOGBERRY   Moreover, sir, which indeed is not under white
    and black, this plaintiff[3] here, the offender, did call me
    "ass." I beseech you, let it be remembered in his punish-
    ment. And also, the watch heard them talk of one Deformed.
    They say he wears a key in his ear and a lock hanging by it,[4]
295   and borrows money in God's name, the which he hath used°   *done habitually*
    so long and never paid that now men grow hard-hearted and
    will lend nothing for God's sake.[5] Pray you, examine him
    upon that point.
   LEONATO   I thank thee for thy care and honest pains.
300   DOGBERRY   Your worship speaks like a most thankful and rev-
    erend youth, and I praise God for you.
   LEONATO [*giving money to* DOGBERRY]   There's for thy pains.
   DOGBERRY   God save the foundation.[6]
   LEONATO   Go. I discharge thee of thy prisoner, and I thank
305   thee.
   DOGBERRY   I leave an arrant knave with your worship, which I
    beseech your worship to correct yourself[7] for the example of
    others. God keep your worship. I wish your worship well.
    God restore you to health. I humbly give you leave to depart,
310   and if a merry meeting may be wished, God prohibit° it.   *(for "permit")*
    Come, neighbor.   [*Exeunt* DOGBERRY *and* VERGES.]
   LEONATO   Until tomorrow morning, lords, farewell.
   ANTHONY   Farewell, my lords. We look for you tomorrow.
   PEDRO   We will not fail.
   CLAUDIO   Tonight I'll mourn with Hero.
315   LEONATO   Bring you these fellows on. We'll talk with Margaret,
    How her acquaintance grew with this lewd° fellow.   *worthless*
                        Exeunt.

5.2

Enter BENEDICT *and* MARGARET.

   BENEDICT   Pray thee, sweet mistress Margaret, deserve well
    at my hands by helping me to the speech of Beatrice.
   MARGARET   Will you then write me a sonnet in praise of my
    beauty?
5   BENEDICT   In so high a style, Margaret, that no man living
    shall come over[1] it. For in most comely truth, thou deservest it.
   MARGARET   To have no man come over me? Why, shall I
    always keep below stairs?[2]

---

3. For "defendant." *under white and black:* in writing.
4. Dogberry's garbled recollection of the lovelock mentioned at 3.3.149.
5. "In God's name" and "for God's sake" were phrases used by beggars.
6. A conventional response to alms from a charitable foundation.
7. Dogberry wishes Leonato himself to punish ("cor-

rect") Borachio, but accidentally says that Leonato should be punished.
5.2 Location: Near Leonato's house or in his garden.
1. Surpass; climb over (punning on "stile": steps over a fence). Margaret humorously takes "come over" in a sexual sense.
2. In the servants' quarters (and therefore never as a "mistress").

BENEDICT Thy wit is as quick as the greyhound's mouth.[3] It
10   catches.
MARGARET And yours as blunt as the fencer's foils,[4] which hit
    but hurt not.
BENEDICT A most manly wit, Margaret. It will not hurt a woman.
    And so, I pray thee, call Beatrice. I give thee the bucklers.[5]
15 MARGARET Give us the swords. We have bucklers of our own.
BENEDICT If you use them, Margaret, you must put in the
    pikes with a vice,° and they are dangerous weapons for maids.   *screw*
MARGARET Well, I will call Beatrice to you, who I think hath
    legs.   *Exit* MARGARET.
20 BENEDICT And therefore will come.[6]
    [*Sings.*] The god of love
               That sits above,
               And knows me, and knows me,
               How pitiful I deserve.[7]
25 I mean in singing. But in loving, Leander the good swimmer,
    Troilus the first employer of panders,[8] and a whole book full
    of these quondam carpet-mongers[9] whose names yet run
    smoothly in the even road of a blank verse—why, they were
    never so truly turned over and over° as my poor self in love.   *head over heels*
30 Marry, I cannot show it in rhyme. I have tried. I can find out
    no rhyme to "lady" but "baby"; an innocent° rhyme. For   *childish*
    "scorn," "horn"; a hard[1] rhyme. For "school," "fool"; a bab-
    bling rhyme; very ominous endings. No, I was not born under
    a rhyming planet,[2] nor I cannot woo in festival terms.°   *fancy rhetoric*
           Enter BEATRICE.
35 Sweet Beatrice, wouldst thou come when I called thee?
BEATRICE Yea, signor, and depart when you bid me.
BENEDICT Oh, stay but till then.
BEATRICE "Then" is spoken. Fare you well now. And yet, ere I
    go, let me go with that° I came, which is with knowing what   *what*
40   hath passed between you and Claudio.
BENEDICT Only foul words, and thereupon I will kiss thee.
BEATRICE Foul words is but foul wind, and foul wind is but
    foul breath, and foul breath is noisome.° Therefore I will   *foul-smelling*
    depart unkissed.
45 BENEDICT Thou hast frighted the word out of his° right sense,°   *its / meaning; wits*
    so forcible is thy wit. But I must tell thee plainly, Claudio
    undergoes° my challenge, and either I must shortly hear   *is subject to*
    from him, or I will subscribe° him a coward. And I pray thee,   *proclaim*
    now tell me, for which of my bad parts didst thou first fall in
50   love with me?
BEATRICE For them all together, which maintained so poli-
    tic° a state of evil that they will not admit any good part to   *cunningly governed*

3. Your wit picks things up as easily as a hunting dog
with its mouth.
4. Practice rapiers, capped at the tip.
5. Benedict offers to surrender by giving up the
bucklers: shields with spikes ("pikes") in the center.
Margaret bawdily interprets this as the female sexual
organ.
6. A popular question and answer of the time was
"How came you hither?" "On my legs."
7. How greatly I deserve pity (but Benedict takes it
as "how pitifully small my deserts are"). These four
lines are the beginning of a popular sentimental

ballad.
8. Troilus, loving Cressida, employed her uncle Pandarus as go-between. Leander swam the Hellespont
nightly to be with his love, Hero.
9. Knights of long ago ("quondam") who avoided
military service and spent their time in ladies' car-
peted boudoirs.
1. Disagreeable, because horns were associated with
cuckoldry.
2. At a time when the stars would influence me to
become a poet.

intermingle with them. But for which of my good parts did
you first suffer° love for me?

55 BENEDICT Suffer love! A good epithet.° I do suffer° love indeed,
for I love thee against my will.

BEATRICE In spite of your heart, I think. Alas, poor heart! If
you spite it for my sake, I will spite it for yours, for I will
never love that which my friend hates.

60 BENEDICT Thou and I are too wise to woo peaceably.

BEATRICE It appears not in this confession.³ There's not one
wise man among twenty that will praise himself.

BENEDICT An old, an old instance,° Beatrice, that lived in the
time of good neighbors.⁴ If a man do not erect in this age his
65 own tomb ere he dies, he shall live no longer in monument°
than the bell rings and the widow weeps.

BEATRICE And how long is that, think you?

BENEDICT Question?⁵ Why, an hour in clamor° and a quarter
in rheum.° Therefore is it most expedient for the wise, if Don
70 Worm, his conscience,⁶ find no impediment to the contrary,
to be the trumpet of his own virtues, as I am to myself. So
much for praising myself, who I myself will bear witness is
praiseworthy. And now tell me, how doth your cousin?

BEATRICE Very ill.

75 BENEDICT And how do you?

BEATRICE Very ill too.

BENEDICT Serve God, love me, and mend.° There will I leave
you, too, for here comes one in haste.

Enter URSULA.

URSULA Madam, you must come to your uncle. Yonder's old
80 coil° at home. It is proved my lady Hero hath been falsely
accused, the Prince and Claudio mightily abused,° and Don
John is the author of all, who is fled and gone. Will you
come presently?

BEATRICE Will you go hear this news, signor?

85 BENEDICT I will live in thy heart, die⁷ in thy lap, and be buried
in thy eyes. And moreover, I will go with thee to thy uncle's.

Exeunt.

	feel
	expression / suffer from
	maxim
	remembrance
	ringing
	tears
	recover
	great disturbance
	deceived

5.3

Enter CLAUDIO, *Prince* [PEDRO, *a* LORD], *and three or
four* [*Attendants*] *with tapers*¹ [*and a* MUSICIAN].²

CLAUDIO Is this the monument° of Leonato?   *family tomb*

LORD It is, my lord.

[*He reads the*] *epitaph.*
"Done to death by slanderous tongues
Was the Hero that here lies.
5   Death, in guerdon° of her wrongs,   *recompense*
Gives her fame which never dies.

3. Since it is not wise to claim to be wise.
4. In the good old days, when neighbors praised each
other.
5. Is that the question?
6. Facetious way of referring to the proverbial gnawing "worm of conscience."
7. With the common Elizabethan connotation of
orgasm.

5.3 Location: A churchyard.
1. Candles or torches carried in token of penitence.
2. TEXTUAL COMMENT Q does not give an entry for a
Musician at the beginning of this scene, which
means it is not clear who sings the song "Pardon,
goddess of the night." To solve the problem, this edition calls for a Musician to enter here. See Digital
Edition TC 8.

So the life that died with° shame   *from*
Lives in death with glorious fame."
[*He hangs up the scroll.*]
Hang thou there upon the tomb,
10   Praising her when I am dead.
CLAUDIO   Now, music, sound and sing your solemn hymn.
Song.
MUSICIAN [*sings*]   Pardon, goddess of the night,[3]
Those that slew thy virgin knight.[4]
For the which, with songs of woe,
15   Round about her tomb they go.
Midnight, assist our moan!
Help us to sigh and groan
Heavily, heavily.
Graves, yawn and yield your dead!
20   Till death be utterèd,°   *fully lamented*
Heavily, heavily.[5]
LORD   Now unto thy bones, goodnight!
Yearly will I do this rite.
PEDRO   Good morrow, masters. Put your torches out.
25   The wolves have preyed,[6] and look, the gentle day,
Before the wheels of Phoebus,[7] round about
Dapples the drowsy East with spots of gray.
Thanks to you all, and leave us. Fare you well.
CLAUDIO   Good morrow, masters. Each his several° way.   *separate*
30   PEDRO   Come! Let us hence, and put on other weeds!°   *garments*
And then to Leonato's we will go.
CLAUDIO   And Hymen now with luckier issue speed 's[8]
Than this° for whom we rendered up this woe.   *Exeunt.*   *this woman*

5.4

Enter LEONATO, BENEDICT, MARGARET, URSULA,
Old Man [ANTHONY], FRIAR, HERO.
FRIAR   Did I not tell you she was innocent?
LEONATO   So are the Prince and Claudio, who accused her
Upon° the error that you heard debated.   *Because of*
But Margaret was in some fault for this,
5   Although against her will,° as it appears   *unintentionally*
In the true course of all the question.°   *investigation*
ANTHONY   Well, I am glad that all things sorts° so well.   *turn out*
BENEDICT   And so am I, being else by faith° enforced   *my pledge*
To call young Claudio to a reckoning for it.
10   LEONATO   Well, daughter, and you gentlewomen all,
Withdraw into a chamber by yourselves,
And when I send for you, come hither masked.
The Prince and Claudio promised by this hour

---

3. Diana, Roman goddess of the moon and patroness   variant. See Digital Edition TC 9.
of virgins.   6. Have finished preying (for the night has passed).
4. Hero (imagined as a knight, or follower, of Diana). 7. The sun god's chariot wheels.
5. TEXTUAL COMMENT In F, the final line of the song   8. And may Hymen (Greek god of marriage) grant us
reads "Heavenly, heavenly." Although this edition fol- more favorable results.
lows Q, it is interpretively rewarding to consider F's 5.4 Location: Leonato's house.

To visit me. You know your office,° brother.   task

15   You must be father to your brother's daughter,
And give her to young Claudio.   *Exeunt ladies.*

ANTHONY   Which I will do with confirmed° countenance.   serious

BENEDICT   Friar, I must entreat your pains, I think.

FRIAR   To do what, signor?

20   BENEDICT   To bind me or undo° me; one of them.   ruin; unbind
Signor Leonato, truth it is, good signor,
Your niece regards me with an eye of favor.

LEONATO   That eye my daughter lent her— 'tis most true.

BENEDICT   And I do with an eye of love requite her.

25   LEONATO   The sight whereof I think you had from me,
From Claudio, and the Prince. But what's your will?

BENEDICT   Your answer, sir, is enigmatical.
But for my will: my will is,° your goodwill   is that
May stand with ours, this day to be conjoined

30   In the state of honorable marriage
In which, good Friar, I shall desire your help.

LEONATO   My heart is with your liking.

FRIAR   And my help.
Here comes the Prince and Claudio.
Enter Prince [PEDRO], and CLAUDIO, *and two or*
three [Attendants].

PEDRO   Good morrow to this fair assembly.

35   LEONATO   Good morrow, Prince. Good morrow, Claudio.
We here attend you. Are you yet° determined   still
Today to marry with my brother's daughter?

CLAUDIO   I'll hold my mind° were she an Ethiope.¹   intention

LEONATO   Call her forth, brother. Here's the Friar ready.
[*Exit* ANTHONY.]

40   PEDRO   Good morrow, Benedict. Why, what's the matter
That you have such a February face?
So full of frost, of storm and cloudiness?

CLAUDIO   I think he thinks upon the savage bull.²
Tush, fear not, man! We'll tip thy horns with gold,

45   And all Europa° shall rejoice at thee   Europe
As once Europa did at lusty Jove,
When he would play the noble beast in love.³

BENEDICT   Bull Jove, sir, had an amiable° low.   amorous
And some such strange bull leaped your father's cow

50   And got a calf° in that same noble feat   begot a blockhead
Much like to you, for you have just his bleat.
Enter Brother [ANTHONY], HERO, BEATRICE,
MARGARET, URSULA[, *the women masked*].

CLAUDIO   For this I owe you.⁴ Here comes other reck'nings.°   accounts to settle
Which is the lady I must seize upon?

LEONATO   This same is she, and I do give you her.

55   CLAUDIO   Why then, she's mine. Sweet, let me see your face.

LEONATO   No, that you shall not, till you take her hand
Before this Friar and swear to marry her.

CLAUDIO   Give me your hand before this holy Friar.

1. In other words, black and therefore, according to   to carry off the princess Europa, who, according to
the Elizabethan racist stereotype, ugly.   the poet Ovid, decked the bull's horns with flowers.
2. Continuing the teasing of 5.1.173.   4. I will pay you back later (for the insults).
3. In Greek mythology, Jove took the form of a bull

I am your husband, if you like of me.°   like me
60 HERO [taking off her mask]   And when I lived I was your other
          wife,
      And when you loved, you were my other husband.
    CLAUDIO   Another Hero?
    HERO   Nothing certainer.
      One Hero died defiled,° but I do live,   slandered
      And surely as I live, I am a maid.
65 PEDRO   The former Hero? Hero that is dead?
    LEONATO   She died, my lord, but whiles her slander lived.
    FRIAR   All this amazement can I qualify.°   lessen
      When after that the holy rites are ended,
      I'll tell you largely° of fair Hero's death.   in full
70   Meantime, let wonder° seem familiar,°   marvels / commonplace
      And to the chapel let us presently.
    BENEDICT   Soft and fair,° Friar. Which is Beatrice?   Wait a minute
    BEATRICE   I answer to that name. What is your will?
    BENEDICT   Do not you love me?
    BEATRICE   Why, no, no more than reason.
75 BENEDICT   Why, then, your uncle, and the Prince, and Claudio
      Have been deceived. They swore you did.
    BEATRICE   Do not you love me?
    BENEDICT   Troth, no, no more than reason.
    BEATRICE   Why, then, my cousin, Margaret, and Ursula
      Are much deceived, for they did swear you did.
80 BENEDICT   They swore that you were almost sick for me.
    BEATRICE   They swore that you were well-nigh dead for me.
    BENEDICT   'Tis no such matter. Then you do not love me?
    BEATRICE   No, truly, but in friendly recompense.
    LEONATO   Come, cousin. I am sure you love the gentleman.
85 CLAUDIO   And I'll be sworn upon't, that he loves her.
      For here's a paper written in his hand,
      A halting sonnet of his own pure brain,
      Fashioned° to Beatrice.   Addressed
    HERO   And here's another,
      Writ in my cousin's hand, stolen from her pocket,
90   Containing her affection unto Benedict.
    BENEDICT   A miracle! Here's our own hands against our
      hearts.[5] Come, I will have thee. But by this light, I take thee
      for pity.
    BEATRICE   I would not deny you. But by this good day, I yield
95   upon great persuasion, and partly to save your life. For I was
      told you were in a consumption.
    LEONATO   Peace! [He gives her hand to BENEDICT.] I will stop
      your mouth.
          [BENEDICT kisses BEATRICE.]
    PEDRO   How dost thou, Benedict the married man?
100 BENEDICT   I'll tell thee what, Prince. A college of wit-crackers[6]
      cannot flout° me out of my humor. Dost thou think I care   jeer
      for a satire or an epigram? No. If a man will be beaten with

---

5. Our own handwritten testimony contradicts the
indifference we claim to feel in our hearts (or proves
our hearts to be guilty of loving).

6. a college of wit-crackers: a whole assembly of
wise-guys.

brains, 'a shall wear nothing handsome about him.[7] In brief,
since I do purpose° to marry, I will think nothing to any   *intend*
105   purpose that the world can say against it. And therefore
never flout at me for what I have said against it; for man is a
giddy thing, and this is my conclusion. For thy part, Claudio, I did think to have beaten thee. But in that thou art
like° to be my kinsman, live unbruised, and love my cousin.   *likely*
110   CLAUDIO   I had well hoped thou wouldst have denied Beatrice, that I might have cudgeled thee out of thy single life to
make thee a double-dealer;° which out of question thou wilt   *married man; adulterer*
be, if my cousin do not look exceeding narrowly° to thee.   *closely*
BENEDICT   Come, come! We are friends. Let's have a dance
115   ere we are married, that we may lighten our own hearts and
our wives' heels.
   [*Enter* MUSICIANS.]
LEONATO   We'll have dancing afterward.
BENEDICT   First, of my word! Therefore play music. Prince,
thou art sad. Get thee a wife! Get thee a wife! There is no
120   staff more reverend than one tipped with horn.[8]
   Enter MESSENGER.
MESSENGER   My lord, your brother John is ta'en in flight
And brought with armed men back to Messina.
BENEDICT   Think not on him till tomorrow. I'll devise thee
brave° punishments for him. Strike up, pipers!   *fine*
   [MUSICIANS *play. They all*] *dance* [*and exeunt*].

7. No, if a man is easily injured by ridicule, he will
never even dare to dress well (since that would provoke attention).
8. A final allusion to the cuckold's horns.

The Merry Wives of Windsor

"The first act of the *Merry Wives* alone contains more life and reality than all German literature." So wrote Friedrich Engels to Karl Marx, his fellow German revolutionary and coauthor with Engels of the *Manifesto of the Communist Party*. Perhaps what he admired in *The Merry Wives of Windsor* (1599) is the dramatization of the middle class as it is being formed out of social tensions and verbal distinctions. Probably Engels also shared the enthusiasm of centuries of theater audiences for the play's elaborate intrigues and stage business. Certainly, this is Shakespeare's most middle-class play in subject matter, setting, and outlook. It is also his most farcical, more so even than early works like *The Comedy of Errors* and *The Taming of the Shrew*. Farce and intrigue establish the comic tone that informs the play's ultimate good-humored reconciliation. They also provide the plot mechanisms through which the characters' self-interest is forged into a social unity where hierarchy, though not eliminated, is temporarily suspended. The fusion of these two elements— the theatrical and the social—produces the play's distinctiveness.

The Merry Wives celebrates the playful but chaste behavior of the titular characters, Mistress Page and Mistress Ford, each married to a prosperous burgher. Mistress Page delivers the overt message: "Wives may be merry and yet honest too" (4.2.92),* where "honest" means sexually faithful to one's husband. Master Page's easy and—from a sexual perspective—justified trust of his wife provides a norm from which Master Ford's irrational jealousy of his wife deviates. The two women's plot against Sir John Falstaff, their would-be seducer, is also designed to dupe and cure Ford. In the subplot, the love marriage between Fenton, the impoverished gentleman, and the Pages' daughter Anne—beneath him socially but above him financially— arguably is also assimilable to citizen values.

The play's time and place reinforce this sense of middle-class community. They create the impression of life in an English provincial town at the moment of the work's first performance. Although *The Comedy of Errors* and *The Merchant of Venice* depict prosperous citizens below the aristocracy, those characters live abroad, in the past, or both. By contrast, *The Merry Wives* retains a contemporary, domestic, and nonaristocratic feel unique in Shakespeare. This feel is not uniform, however. The play refers back to the early fifteenth century, and the closest analogue and most likely source for the main plot are from the Italian writer Ser Giovanni Fiorentino's *Il Pecorone* (1558). This plot and the primary subplot also draw on ancient Roman comedy, medieval farce, and Renaissance Italian drama. Finally, the play includes characters from above and below the middle class. Yet the historical allusions don't evoke a bygone era, the foreign traditions are reworked into English stereotypes, and the upper- and lower-class figures ultimately underscore middle-class inclusiveness.

The play ironizes nearly every character's claim to social standing. Slender's pretensions to gentility are mocked from beginning to end. In the opening scene, his uncle, Justice Shallow, acts not to preserve the peace but to undermine it. Similarly ineffectual are the pacifying efforts of the Welsh parson, Sir Hugh Evans, who agrees to a duel with another foreigner, the well-to-do French Doctor Caius. Most of these characters, moreover, derive their authority from the outside—the church or the royal court.

---

*All quotations are taken from the edited text of the Folio, printed here. The Digital Edition includes edited texts of both the Folio and the Quarto.

Cuckold, his unfaithful wife, and the seducer. From *Roxburghe Ballads* (seventeenth century).

A different kind of conflict pits the wealthy citizens against their social superiors. Page rejects the love suit of Fenton, and Falstaff is abused—in act 5 functioning as a scapegoat against whom the townspeople can unite. This antagonism between citizen and gentleman is given a financial twist appropriate to the dominant ethos of the play. Page believes that Fenton is motivated by money rather than love, a charge that Fenton tells Anne was originally—but is no longer—true:

> I found thee of more value
> Than stamps in gold or sums in sealèd bags,
> And 'tis the very riches of thyself
> That now I aim at.
>
> (3.4.15–18)

Free of romantic concerns, Falstaff's seductions are motivated perhaps by lust and certainly by profit, metaphorically figured as mercantile imperialist treasure. Of Mistress Page he exclaims: "She bears the purse too. She is a region in Guiana, all gold and bounty. I will be cheaters to them both, and they shall be exchequers to me. They shall be my East and West Indies, and I will trade to them both. . . . Sail like my pinnace to these golden shores" (1.3.58–61, 70).

The conclusion resolves this conflict. Page and his wife, although at cross-purposes with each other, each try to marry Anne off to an unsuitable partner. But having been outwitted, both accept their daughter's marriage with good humor. This incorporation of Fenton is extended by Mistress Page to Falstaff as well. Her act reveals the generosity of the citizens' world. The marriage of Fenton to Anne—the main accomplishment of the play, with the exception of the simultaneous duping of Falstaff and curing of Ford—reconciles the middle class with their social betters. Both plots raise the fear of mercenary, sexually threatening aristocratic interlopers only to dispel the concern—because of the predator's comic incompetence or the falseness of the suspicion. Even though the play's language highlights Fenton's lofty rank—he alone speaks primarily in blank verse—he too becomes part of the community. Similarly, the climactic tricking of Falstaff draws on the court masque. But this theatrical form, in which courtiers become the actors, is here recast in a popular, festive mode.

The concluding scene in the fuller Folio text also includes a compliment to the Order of the Garter uttered in blank verse—to reflect the elevated subject matter—by Mistress Quickly disguised as the Queen of Fairies (5.5.52–73). The Order of the Garter was an aristocratic fraternity under the patronage of the Queen that inducted new members at Windsor Castle. This passage has the effect of placing the town of Windsor under the protection of the castle of Windsor, just as the town's Garter Inn evokes the castle's more elevated Order of the Garter. *The Merry Wives* also shares the names of several characters with the two parts of *Henry IV* and with *Henry V*—Falstaff, Mistress Quickly, Shallow, Pistol, Bardolph, Nim. Fenton supposedly "kept company with the wild Prince and Poins" (3.2.64), an allusion to the future Henry V and one of his companions in the *Henry IV* plays. But though the names are the same, the characters are not. The easily duped Falstaff of Windsor lacks the indomitable comic resourcefulness he repeatedly demonstrates in the history plays. Still, the political associations lend a national, monarchical aspect to the more circumscribed events of *The Merry Wives*. The effect is contradictory: royal power is asserted in its absence, but the town's middling sort come to stand for all of England.

The play's generalizing force is further enhanced by an indebtedness to popular culture unusual even for Shakespeare. In keeping with its social milieu, *The Merry Wives* has a far higher percentage of prose than does any other Shakespearean work. Much of it satirically reproduces the language of proverb and cliché; Master Slender and Mistress Quickly in particular depend on language that verges on the meaningless. Shallow's words to Page convey vague goodwill and ineptitude: "Master Page, I am glad to see you. Much good do it your good heart. . . . and I thank you always with my heart, la, with my heart. . . . Sir, I thank you, by yea and no, I do" (1.1.67–72). Similarly, Quickly unleashes a barrage of weakly communicative phrasing that somehow enables her to connect with almost all the other characters: "nobody but has his fault," "the very yea and the no," "that's neither here nor there," "What the goodyear," "thereby hangs a tale," "an honest maid as ever broke bread," "Out upon't" (1.4.12, 84–85, 94–95, 108, 132, 133–34, 147).

The Merry Wives also brings onstage a considerable number of lower-class characters. These are not the clowns and fools of the more aristocratic romantic comedies, but servants: John and Robert, who work for the Fords; Simple, who waits on Slender; John Rugby and Mistress Quickly, who belong to Caius's household; and Falstaff's hangers-on—Bardolph, Pistol, and Nim. In the final scene, when the children of Windsor dress as fairies to punish Falstaff, they mobilize a popular rural belief, evidently shared by their victim, in mischievous immortal spirits who prey upon local inhabitants. Falstaff's insults and injuries—suffocation, dunking in the river, beating, and pinching—belong to the popular tradition of knockabout physical stage action in farce and shaming rituals of the time.

Yet the play's relationship to the lower classes, as to the upper, is mixed. Mistress Quickly is treated with contemptuous condescension. More important, Falstaff and his followers, despite Falstaff's elite connections, engage in the lawlessness that the prosperous middle class of the time attributed to the poor. As the play opens, Shallow charges Falstaff with various crimes, among them stealing his deer. Falstaff then directs his penchant for poaching to the merry wives—unsuccessfully— until he himself becomes the hunted and symbolically cuckolded deer at play's end. Thus, the Pages and Fords define themselves against the social strata both above and below them. This position is modified in the final scene, but only by celebrating a popular culture whose superstitions are viewed with nostalgia but without credulity.

Windsor's sense of community depends in addition on cheerfully casual ethnocentrism. Hostility to foreigners is part of the throwaway language of the play (especially the Host's): "base Hungarian wight," "Base Phrygian Turk," "Flemish drunkard," "Cathayan," "Ethiopian," "Francisco," "Castalian king urinal," "Anthropophaginian" (cannibal), "Bohemian Tartar" (1.3.18, 78; 2.1.19, 127; 2.3.24, 29; 4.5.8, 16). Ford

Elizabeth I and the Knights of the Garter. Engraved by Michael Gheeraerts the Elder (1576).

trades in similar stereotypes: "I will rather trust a Fleming with my butter, Parson Hugh the Welshman with my cheese, an Irishman with my aqua-vitae bottle, or a thief to walk my ambling gelding, than my wife with herself" (2.2.267–70). The same effect is produced by the obscure, satirical treatment of Germans and of a particular German duke, who is accused of horse stealing in the fragmentary third plot of the play, Caius and Evans's revenge on the Host (4.3, 4.5.60–76).

But the chauvinism of *The Merry Wives* appears most prominently in the fractured English of the French Caius and Welsh Evans themselves, and in the good-humored ridicule it evokes. Evans "makes fritters of English" (5.5.134); he and Caius "hack our English" (3.1.68). Their marked accents, as well as Caius's frequent reversion to French, foreground their foreignness. The Host thwarts their silly decision to duel out of affection for the two men and perhaps out of hostility to this aristocratic practice. Their intention and their inability to execute it intensify the other characters' sense of English middle-class superiority. This sense is clear in the First Folio (1623), which the present (print) edition follows. But it is even more consistently emphasized in the 1602 First Quarto, for which see the Digital Edition. (For more on the differences between the Folio and Quarto, see the Textual Introduction.) Nonetheless, the Welshman is more integrated into Windsor life than the truly foreign Frenchman is. At least Evans attempts to make peace; he teaches Latin to one child and prepares others for the final trick on Falstaff; and he participates in the punishment and criticism of the fat intruder. By contrast, Caius instigates a duel, seeks a loveless marriage, and is then duped.

As the title reveals, however, the play's conflicts are fought mainly in terms of gender. But the meaning of these conflicts is unclear. Is the wives' triumph over Falstaff's sexual adventuring and Ford's jealousy a victory for *middle-class* women, for middle-class *women*, for both? The play celebrates the wives' autonomy, their merriness—a merriness, however, that protects their husbands' wealth.

But not entirely. First, the wives, through their self-discipline and disciplining of

others, define the social norm and are given increasingly broad authority to enforce it. Their household tasks—not least laundering—become metaphors for larger projects: Falstaff is dumped in the river to cleanse him of his sins, and Mistress Quickly as the Queen of Fairies orders elves to "scour" Windsor Castle (5.5.58). Second, though Page contrasts his liberal attitude toward his wife with Ford's misogyny, Mistress Page's scheming against her husband's plans for their daughter's marriage reveals that female self-assertion does not necessarily dovetail with male desire. In this sense, Ford's fears are justified, Page's confidence undermined. Neither parent prevails, though a woman does: Anne replicates her parents' companionate marriage, but against their will, by choosing her own husband.

Mistress Quickly's language produces a view of gender and sexuality less tied to middle-class norms. Although that language's sexual innuendo often escapes the speaker herself, she is not alone in her heedless punning. Evans evinces a comparable obliviousness to the sexual implications of his words, an obliviousness that Quickly's comic misunderstandings during the Latin lesson (4.1) reveal. Evans, who doubles as Windsor's schoolmaster, quizzes young William Page on Latin grammar as it was taught in the first school years, asking his pupil for the plural possessive (or "genitive case") of the word for "this" ("of these"). Mistress Quickly comments uncomprehendingly: what she overlooks in her own speech she detects in a language she cannot understand.

> WILLIAM Genitive case?
> EVANS Ay.
> WILLIAM Genitive, *horum, harum, horum.*
> MISTRESS QUICKLY Vengeance of Jenny's case! Fie on her,
>   never name her, child, if she be a whore!
>
> (4.1.51–55)

Here, "genitive" suggests "generative" or even "genital" as well as "Jenny"; "case" is slang for "vagina"; and "*horum,*" a genitive plural, evokes the more obvious "whore."

The scene counterposes Latin and English, literacy and illiteracy, middle class and lower, man and woman.

This is not an isolated moment. Earlier, the language of grammar, here too allied to translation, is sexualized when Falstaff announces his intention to seduce Mistress Ford:

> FALSTAFF I can construe the action of her familiar style, and
>   the hardest voice of her behavior, to be Englished rightly, is "I
>   am Sir John Falstaff's."
> PISTOL He hath studied her will, and translated her will—out of
>   honesty, into English.
>
> (1.3.39–43)

A different pattern of sexual allusion emerges when Falstaff is trapped in Ford's house on his second assignation with Mistress Ford, and the wives have him escape disguised as the "Aunt of Brentford." Although Ford does not detect the trick, he does spew out a torrent of hostile rhetoric—"A witch, a quean, an old cozening quean!" he begins (4.2.150)—before beating up someone he believes to be an old woman. But of course the woman is Falstaff, whose transvestite outfit anticipates the conclusion of *The Merry Wives*. Although neither the Folio nor the Quarto is consistent enough about the colors the characters wear at the end of the play to make clear how Fenton fools the other suitors and elopes with Anne, the central trick is unambiguous. "I came yonder at Eton to marry Mistress Anne Page, and she's a great lubberly boy!" Slender laments. "If I had been married to him, for all he was in woman's apparel, I would not have had him" (5.5.167–68, 174–75). Caius is even more entangled in the deception. "Vere is Mistress Page? By gar, I am cozened! I ha' married *un garçon*, a boy, *un paysan*, by gar! A boy . . ." (5.5.184–85).

This is not the first such sexual tease. Earlier, Ford complains of the intimacy between the merry wives: "I think if your husbands were dead, you two would marry." The charge of what we would now call homosexuality is rejected. "Be sure of that— two other husbands," Mistress Page replies (3.2.11–13). Similarly, the ending entertains the option of man–boy sexual relations only to punish Anne's foolish suitors. Like adultery and financially motivated arranged marriages, these are deviations from the romantic and sexual norm, whose literal issue is emphasized by the unusual prominence of children in the play.

Yet the cross-dressing conclusion points self-referentially beyond the fiction to the actors producing it. Shakespeare wrote for a transvestite theater in which boys performed female parts. The audience might note the distance between the Queen of Fairies—a flattering allusion to Queen Elizabeth—and Mistress Quickly, the fictional character playing the doubly fictional part. It might register the real boy actor impersonating these two fictional figures. And at the very end, Slender and Caius are not alone in their predicament: Fenton, too, goes off with a boy dressed as a girl. This conclusion simultaneously celebrates and subverts the theatrical illusion. Renaissance accounts praise the lifelike persuasiveness of the best boy actors who impersonated women. Here, the boy gets the girl just as the audience would wish, at the very moment Shakespeare reminds it that it has believed in the very falsehood accepted by some of the play's more foolish characters. This belief in turn links up with the many challenges to the normative heterosexuality apparently embodied by the merry wives—the linguistic suggestiveness, the almost complete absence of romantic or sexual attachment between man and woman, the various hints of homosocial bonding or homoerotic desire.

Something similar applies to the setting of this dramaturgical brazenness, Windsor Forest itself. As Shallow's charge that Falstaff has "killed my deer" suggests (1.1.95), the forest is contested space. But though it is a real place, it is also an invented one. The fairies who haunt it are just children performing a play. The story of Herne the Hunter, "with great ragged horns" (4.4.28), is not taken seriously by the perpetrators

A "skimmington," a public rite of humiliation for domestic disorder.
From *English Customs* (1628).

of the trick. The natural world is given its meaning by human activity within it. The
effect is to equate the horned Falstaff first with Herne and then with the oak tree
around which Herne supposedly walks. The fairy children circle Falstaff, and as they
prepare to burn his fingers, Evans asks of him: "Will this wood take fire?" (5.5.86).
Earlier in the scene, Falstaff calls himself "a woodman" (5.5.24). And his name not
only alludes to his sexual failure but also fits with his decision to lie down in terror
(5.5.45 SD), while its second syllable suggests the material of which he is made. He is
the oak in the royal forest felled by the townspeople asserting their (uncertain) rights
to Crown land.

This final scene, like *The Merry Wives* as a whole, is socially suggestive and visually funny. Much of the play's pleasure arises from the physical comedy of plot and
counterplot—Caius discovering Simple in his closet, Ford in disguise urging Falstaff
to seduce his wife, Caius and Evans unknowingly preparing for solo duels, Falstaff
repeatedly escaping Ford only to suffer still greater humiliation, the deluded would-
be bridegrooms stealing off with the wrong fairies. This effective stage business
helps explain the work's success both in the theater and in operatic adaptation (especially Verdi's *Falstaff*, 1893).

Particularly at the end, however, stage business also settles the subplot in a way
that unravels the logic of the main plot. The revenge on Falstaff brings together a
socially and verbally heterogeneous, often antagonistic group—the merry wives and
their servants, their husbands, Evans, Mistress Quickly, and the children of Windsor. Yet the result is not the expected expulsion of the predatory courtier by a unified
town but the undoing of nearly all positions of superiority.

The mechanism for this anti-scapegoating outcome is the decision by the Fords
and Pages to subject Falstaff to one more humiliation. Though they are confident
that he no longer poses a threat, perhaps they believe he needs to make amends to
the whole town. Thus, the main plot, in which Falstaff and Ford are fooled by the
wives, is balanced by the subplot, in which the fun at the expense of Caius and Slender is less important than the thwarting of the Pages, who have plotted against each
other and must endure the humbling reversal of having Ford and Falstaff lecture
them. As Falstaff says: "I am glad, though you have ta'en a special stand to strike at
me, that your arrow hath glanced" (5.5.210–11). Even Anne acknowledges fault:
"Pardon, good father. —Good my mother, pardon!" (line 192). Similarly, in the fragmentary third plot the Host fools Evans and Caius, only to have these two rivals
unite to exact revenge from him.

The pattern is that of the duper duped. The renunciation of plotting and hostility
by a compromised group of characters produces a moral leveling. The hierarchies

and conflicts that separate man from woman, parent from child, sexual normality from sexual deviancy, town from Crown, Englishman from foreigner, upper class from middle class, and middle class from lower are resolved—or evaded—through a good-natured, universal inclusiveness. The middle class is a more encompassing category than at the beginning of the play. Its strength lies in its cheerful capacity to absorb all comers despite the efforts of most of the leading characters, its ability to fashion a unity felt to be more profound than the conflicts dividing the town. When Mistress Page invites the other characters to "laugh this sport o'er by a country fire" (5.5.218), she incorporates within the play an experience the play itself has provided to its audience.

Earlier, however, Ford has disguised himself as Broom ostensibly to aid Falstaff in seducing Mistress Ford, so that he, Broom, will be able to commit adultery with her in turn. Thus, when Ford, undisguised, concludes *The Merry Wives* by informing Falstaff that Broom will in fact sleep with Mistress Ford, we may see either a witty assertion of marital fidelity or a tacit acknowledgment that there is pleasure only in the violation of that norm.

Walter Cohen

SELECTED BIBLIOGRAPHY

Goldberg, Jonathan. "What Do Women Want? *The Merry Wives of Windsor.*" *Criticism* 51 (2009): 367–83. Argues that the play actually undermines the apparently normative heterosexuality embodied by the merry wives, instead presenting homosocial triangles, hostility between the sexes, and same-sex desire.

Helgerson, Richard. "Language Lessons: Linguistic Colonialism, Linguistic Post-colonialism, and the Early Modern English Nation." *Yale Journal of Criticism* 11 (1998): 289–99. Explores Latin versus English versus marginal dialects as colonizing and colonized languages.

Kegl, Rosemary. "'The Adoption of Abominable Terms': Middle Classes, Merry Wives, and the Insults That Shape Windsor." *The Rhetoric of Concealment: Figuring Gender and Class in Renaissance Literature.* Ithaca, NY: Cornell UP, 1994. 77–125. Examines the language of class and gender hierarchy, with attention to issues of ethnocentrism.

Korda, Natasha. *Shakespeare's Domestic Economies: Gender and Property in Early Modern England.* Philadelphia: U of Pennsylvania P, 2002. 76–110. Emphasizes the merry wives' disciplining and self-disciplining management of their households, behavior ratified at the national level through the concluding role of the Queen of Fairies.

Lamb, Mary Ellen. *The Popular Culture of Shakespeare, Spenser, and Jonson.* New York: Routledge, 2006. 125–59. Sees the play's middling sort as defining themselves against both dissolute aristocrats and the criminal poor, both exemplified by Falstaff, with the final scene combining contempt and nostalgia for a popular culture.

Nardizzi, Vin. "Felling Falstaff in Windsor Park." *Ecocritical Shakespeare.* Ed. Lynn Bruckner and Dan Brayton. Farnham, Surrey: Ashgate, 2011. 123–38. Emphasizes, in the final scene, the identification of Falstaff with Herne's oak, whose felling establishes a tenuously unified middle-class community.

Parker, Patricia. "*The Merry Wives of Windsor* and Shakespearean Translation." *Modern Language Quarterly* 52 (1991): 225–61. Focuses on the scene of Latin instruction (4.1) as integral to the play, revealing links between language and sexuality.

Theis, Jeffrey. "The 'ill-kill'd' Deer: Poaching and Social Order in *The Merry Wives of Windsor.*" *Texas Studies in Literature and Language* 43 (2001): 46–73. Argues that the play draws on the class issue of poaching—literally in the opening of the play, metaphorically in Falstaff's sexual designs on the merry wives.

Wall, Wendy. *Staging Domesticity: Household Work and English Identity in Early Modern Drama*. Cambridge: Cambridge UP, 2002. 90–95, 112–26. Places female domesticity (especially cleaning) at the center of local and national community, connecting it to proper English speech, the fabricated popular culture of fairies, and the monarchy.

Zucker, Adam. *The Places of Wit in Early Modern English Comedy*. Cambridge: Cambridge UP, 2011. 23–53. Treats Windsor Forest in the final scene as a socially contested real place and a creation of the townspeople, who show similar social and linguistic mastery throughout the play.

FILM

The Merry Wives of Windsor. 1982. Dir. David Hugh Jones. UK. 170 min. A BBC production with Ben Kingsley as Ford and Judy Davis as Mistress Ford.

TEXTUAL INTRODUCTION

The Merry Wives of Windsor was entered in the Stationers' Register in two separate entries for January 18, 1602 (here modernized):

> JOHN BUSBY   Entered for his copy under the hand of Master
> Seton a book called An excellent and pleasant conceited
> comedy of Sir John Falstaff and the merry wives of Windsor.
> [6 pence]
> ARTHUR JOHNSON   Entered for his copy by assignment from John
> Busby, a book called an excellent and pleasant conceited
> comedy of Sir John Falstaff and the merry wives of Windsor.
> [6 pence]

The reassignment of copyright to produce the printed book was legal and not infrequent among printers. Johnson sold the book "at his shop in Paul's Churchyard at the sign of the Flower-de-luce and the Crown" (title page), but he subcontracted the printing from Thomas Creede, who published many plays between 1594 and 1638.

Normally, the earliest printed text of a play is considered authoritative, but in this case scholars have regarded the 1602 First Quarto (Q1) as a "bad quarto" because of its differences from the 1623 Folio: it is 40 percent shorter, with markedly different treatments of the Anne/Fenton romance plot and of the resolutions of act 5. For a long time, scholars believed Q1 to represent a "memorial reconstruction"—a recollected or reported version of the play, based on a performance and published without the theatrical owner's permission. In 1910, W. W. Greg deduced that the actor who played the Host of the Garter must have pirated the material, largely because Q1 accurately reflects F in most of the Host's lines and those of characters in scenes with him but tends to be sketchy elsewhere. Falstaff's lines are also represented fairly accurately, and possibly the actor playing Falstaff participated in the memorial reconstruction. Like the tradition—invented by John Dennis in 1702 and accepted by various editors since 1709—that Queen Elizabeth asked Shakespeare to write a play about Falstaff in love, theories about Q1 in relation to F have a life of their own. Scholars long accepted Greg's theory, but recently critics have doubted that memorial reconstruction is an adequate explanation for certain anomalies in Q1. Some have argued that Q1 is either a performance-based abridgment or an authorized revision of an even earlier text that eventually became the F version. The differences between the *Merry Wives* texts are not surprising considering the twenty-one-year gap between the printed books. Certainly, Q1 remains the only version printed in Shakespeare's lifetime. Very likely Q1 was performed as well as read; it was reprinted as Q2 in 1619 virtually without change.

Q1 is an important witness to performance practice, which is visible especially in stage directions not present in F. It offers a vivid report of how actors moved on the stage, including entrances and exits, and demonstrates how characters responded to lines with actions (as in the buck-basket scenes and the final scene in Windsor Forest). The Q1 text is more accurate in giving Ford's "alias" as "Brook," a word on which puns and politics depend, rather than F's "Broom," and does not try to hide the jokes about German courtiers. Q1's language tends to be more racy and colloquial, typical of plays printed before the laws against profanity came into force (1606). Q1 has fewer scenes, and they are sequenced differently from F, which transposes the last two scenes of act 3 and adds the first four scenes of act 5. Robin, Falstaff's page, has no lines in Q, and William Page has no role and no Latin lesson; the sole "Garter" reference is to the name of the inn where Falstaff lodges. Windsor references are rare in Q, but the play's energetic representation of middle-class town life establishes *The Merry Wives* as Shakespeare's only citizen comedy.

The 1623 F text is the scribe Ralph Crane's transcription, showing his characteristic division into acts and scenes, use of parentheses and hyphens, and massed entries at the head of each scene. F's text is considerably different and much longer than Q's; nevertheless, approximately five hundred lines of Q find no exact counterpart in F. Q also offers other changes—often delightful rhetorical expansions—that suggest a different overall concept. F's curious omissions and errors include the absence of Q scene 8's "Give me thy hand terrestrial" (3.1.90–91), required by the Host's rhetorical balance; the muddle of speech prefixes in F 4.2.46–58, which assign Mistress Ford two speeches in a row; and the grammatically flawed "him" in F 4.3.5 instead of Q scene 14's "them" (line 5), referring to gentlemen meeting the German duke. F fails to indicate which boy wears which color in the boy-brides sequence of 5.5. The exits and re-entrances for Mistress Ford, Mistress Page, and Falstaff in F 4.2 are not as straightforward as in Q. F notably inserts Pistol in the Herne's Oak entertainment of 5.5, although, in Q and apparently in F as well, Pistol had left Windsor by mid-play.

Textual scholars disagree about which version is the original. Most editors reject the undocumented theory of an urtext and point out that there is no proof that plays were abridged for touring. F may be a version presented at court, possibly as entertainment for a Garter Feast at Windsor Castle between 1597 and 1601; current scholarship dates the play 1599, shortly before *Henry V*. Alternatively, F may have been revised from Q for James's court or for the Garter Feast in 1604, with an elaboration of the fairy queen episode into something like a court masque. Thus, Q might have developed into F through rewriting and improvisation, perhaps by Shakespeare and/or other actors, several times by 1623. Since Shakespeare retired from the stage around 1613 and died in 1616, he may have had no hand in later accretions to the text, the authority of which would then depend on the theatrical traditions of the King's Men.

Helen Ostovich

Textual Bibliography

Grav, Peter. "Money Changes Everything: Quarto and Folio *The Merry Wives of Windsor* and the Case for Revision." *Comparative Drama* 40.2 (2006): 217–40.

Greg, W. W., ed. *Shakespeare's "Merry Wives of Windsor," 1602*. Oxford: Clarendon, 1911.

Johnson, Gerald D. "*The Merry Wives of Windsor*, Q1: Provincial Touring and Adapted Texts." *Shakespeare Quarterly* 38.2 (1987): 154–65.

PERFORMANCE NOTE

Unlike most plays by Shakespeare, *The Merry Wives of Windsor* seems to yield limited rewards to directorial interpretation and ingenuity. Attempts to add tension by darkening the tone of what is essentially "revenge" comedy or to create psychological depth in characters distinguished from one another by their linguistic particularities and cartoonish excesses can actually sap the strength of this play—the essence of which lies precisely in caricature, farce, and the vibrancy and resilience of Falstaff, its central character. Productions sometimes make travesties of Falstaff and Ford, though at the risk of damaging their credibility as "straight men," thereby lessening the stakes of the embarrassments they suffer at the hands of the merry wives. Falstaff's challenge to the actor is to be both the butt of jokes and the play's best joker, distinguished as much for his lordly manner as for his low behavior. Likewise, the Ford actor must invite both condescension and empathy, his irrational jealousy not wholly occluding his humanity.

Though Ford and Falstaff suffer stinging embarrassments during the first four acts, the tone can change in act 5, when Falstaff appears as Herne the Hunter. The fairies' appearance and the subsequent masque present opportunities not only for spectacle and invention, but also for introducing realistic brutality and even terror, depending on how roughly the fairies "pinch the unclean knight" (4.4.54) and how dark and sinister the forest appears. Depending on the production's approach, Falstaff can share in the couples' spirit of forgiveness and reconciliation at play's end, or he can remain ostracized and humiliated, like Shylock or Malvolio at the conclusions of *The Merchant of Venice* and *Twelfth Night*, respectively. The fact that the farce persists until so late in the play can intensify the effect of such a turn. Productions must further decide whether Falstaff pursues the two wives purely for money or for lust as well; how to stage his exit from Ford's house in a buck-basket; how to clarify Evans and Caius's plot to revenge themselves on the Host; and how perceptible characters such as Mistress Quickly and Anne Page are during the masque.

BRETT GAMBOA

The Merry Wives of Windsor

1.1 (Q 1)

Enter Justice SHALLOW, SLENDER, [*and*]
Sir¹ Hugh EVANS.

SHALLOW Sir Hugh, persuade me not. I will make a Star
  Chamber° matter of it. If he were twenty Sir John Falstaffs,   *high court*
  he shall not abuse Robert Shallow, esquire.°   *(just below a knight)*
SLENDER In the county of Gloucester, justice of peace and
5 quorum.²
SHALLOW Ay, cousin° Slender, and *custalorum*.   *kinsman (here, nephew)*
SLENDER Ay, and *ratolorum*³ too; and a gentleman born, Mas-
  ter Parson, who writes himself *Armigero*° in any bill, war-   *esquire; arms bearer*
  rant, quittance,° or obligation—*Armigero*!   *discharge from debt*
10 SHALLOW Ay, that I do, and have done any time these three
  hundred years.

1.1 Location: A street, later moving to the entrance
to Page's house.
1. *Justice*: justice of the peace (line 4), a local judge.
Sir: clergyman's honorary title, not indicating knighthood, as it does with Falstaff (line 2). As 4.1 reveals,
Evans is also the town's schoolmaster.

2. Designating justices who could try a felon if a sufficient number of them (two or more) were present.
3. *"Custalorum"* (line 6) and *"ratolorum"* are blunders for *custos rotulorum* ("keeper of the rolls"), the
principal justice in a county; perhaps a play on "rat."

1474

SLENDER All his successors gone before him hath done't, and
    all his ancestors that come after him may. They may give the
    dozen white luces° in their coat.°   *pike / coat of arms*

15 SHALLOW It is an old coat.

EVANS The dozen white louses do become an old coat[4] well. It
    agrees well passant.[5] It is a familiar° beast to man and signi-   *familial; too intimate*
    fies love.

SHALLOW The luce is the fresh fish; the salt fish is an old cod.[6]

20 SLENDER I may quarter,[7] coz.°   *kinsman*

SHALLOW You may, by marrying.

EVANS It is marring indeed, if he quarter it.

SHALLOW Not a whit.

EVANS Yes, py'r Lady.° If he has a quarter of your coat, there is   *by our Lady (Mary)*

25   but three skirts° for yourself, in my simple conjectures, but   *coattails*
    that is all one. If Sir John Falstaff have committed dispar-
    agements unto you, I am of the church and will be glad to
    do my benevolence to make atonements and compromises
    between you.

30 SHALLOW The council[8] shall hear it. It is a riot.

EVANS It is not meet° the council hear a riot; there is no fear   *fitting that*
    of Got in a riot. The council, look you, shall desire to hear
    the fear of Got, and not to hear a riot. Take your 'visements
    in that.°   *Be advised*

35 SHALLOW Ha! O'my life, if I were young again, the sword
    should end it.

EVANS It is petter that friends is the sword, and end it.[9] And
    there is also another device in my prain, which peradven-
    ture prings goot discretions with it. There is Anne Page,

40   which is daughter to Master George Page, which is pretty
    virginity.

SLENDER Mistress Anne Page? She has brown hair and speaks
    small° like a woman.   *in a soprano voice*

EVANS It is that fery person for all the 'orld, as just as you will

45   desire, and seven hundred pounds of moneys, and gold and
    silver, is° her grandsire upon his death's-bed—Got deliver to   *did*
    a joyful resurrections—give, when she is able to overtake
    seventeen years old. It were a goot motion,° if we leave our   *plan*
    pribbles and prabbles,° and desire a marriage between Mas-   *raving and squabbles*

50   ter Abraham° and Mistress Anne Page.   *(Slender)*

SLENDER Did her grandsire leave her seven hundred pound?

EVANS Ay, and her father is make her a petter penny.°   *will give much more*

SLENDER I know the young gentlewoman. She has good gifts.°   *qualities*

EVANS Seven hundred pounds and possibilities° is goot gifts.   *financial prospects*

---

4. Cod; scrotum. Evans, in what is meant to be a stereotypical Welsh accent, often pronounces "t" for
"d," "p" for "b," and "f" for "v" and omits initial "w."
"Louses" is Evans's comic error for "luces" (line 14), a
term from heraldry, the branch of knowledge concerned with the right to bear arms, with family pedigrees, and with coats of arms. (See also "Armigero"
and "coat," lines 8–9, 15–16.) The error is set up by
the two meanings of "old coat" (noble lineage, worn-
out clothing), and Evans's pronunciation then provokes further uncomprehending wordplay by Shallow
(line 19).
5. Walking, looking to the right with the right paw

raised (heraldic); surpassingly. The heraldic image is
absurd for a fish, only slightly less so for a louse.
6. Perhaps a joke involving Evans's pronunciation
("louses/luces"; "coat/cod"). *fresh*: freshwater, unpre-
served. *salt*: saltwater, salt-cured, obscene.
7. I may add another (family's) coat to one of the four
parts of my heraldic arms (for instance, through marriage); but in Evans's reply, cut up in quarters.
8. Star Chamber (lines 1–2); but Evans understands
it as "church council."
9. The intervention of friends should end the
dispute.

55 SHALLOW   Well, let us see honest Master Page. Is Falstaff there?

EVANS   Shall I tell you a lie? I do despise a liar, as I do despise
one that is false, or as I despise one that is not true. The
knight Sir John is there, and I beseech you be ruled by your
well-willers.° I will peat the door for Master Page.   *well-wishers*
[*He knocks on the door.*]

60 —What ho? Got pless your house here!

PAGE [*within*]   Who's there?

EVANS   Here is Got's plessing and your friend, and Justice
Shallow, and here young Master Slender, that peradventures
shall tell you another tale,° if matters grow to your likings.   *(a marriage proposal)*
[*Enter Master* PAGE.]

65 PAGE   I am glad to see your worships well. I thank you for my
venison, Master Shallow.

SHALLOW   Master Page, I am glad to see you. Much good do it
your good heart. I wished your venison better; it was ill°   *ineptly; unlawfully*
killed—how doth good Mistress Page?—and I thank you

70 always with my heart, la,° with my heart.   *indeed*

PAGE   Sir, I thank you.

SHALLOW   Sir, I thank you, by yea and no,° I do.   *(almost meaningless)*

PAGE   I am glad to see you, good Master Slender.

SLENDER   How does your fallow° greyhound, sir? I heard say   *light-brown*

75 he was outrun on Cotswold.°   *the Cotswold hills*

PAGE   It could not be judged, sir.

SLENDER   You'll not confess, you'll not confess!°   *(that the dog lost)*

SHALLOW [*to* SLENDER]   That he will not. 'Tis your fault,° 'tis   *You're in the wrong*
your fault. [*to* PAGE] 'Tis a good dog.

80 PAGE   A cur, sir.

SHALLOW   Sir, he's a good dog and a fair dog. Can there be
more said? He is good and fair. Is Sir John Falstaff here?

PAGE   Sir, he is within, and I would I could do a good office
between you.

85 EVANS   It is spoke as a Christians ought to speak.

SHALLOW   He hath wronged me, Master Page.

PAGE   Sir, he doth in some sort confess it.

SHALLOW   If it be confessed, it is not redressed. Is not that so,
Master Page? He hath wronged me, indeed he hath, at a

90 word° he hath. Believe me, Robert Shallow, esquire, saith   *in short*
he is wronged.

PAGE   Here comes Sir John.
[*Enter Sir John* FALSTAFF, BARDOLPH, NIM,
and PISTOL.]

FALSTAFF   Now, Master Shallow, you'll complain of me to the
King?

95 SHALLOW   Knight, you have beaten my men, killed my deer,
and broke open my lodge.°   *keeper's house*

FALSTAFF   But not kissed your keeper's daughter?

SHALLOW   Tut, a pin.° This shall be answered.   *trifling comment*

FALSTAFF   I will answer it straight: I have done all this. That

100 is now answered.

SHALLOW   The council shall know this.

FALSTAFF   'Twere better for you if it were known in counsel.°   *kept secret*
You'll be laughed at.

EVANS   *Pauca verba,*° Sir John, good worts.   *Few words*

105 FALSTAFF Good worts?° Good cabbage! —Slender, I broke *words; cabbage*
your head. What matter° have you against me? *complaint*

SLENDER Marry, sir, I have matter in my head against you,
and against your coney-catching° rascals, Bardolph, Nim, *swindling*
and Pistol.

110 BARDOLPH You Banbury cheese.° *thin (like Slender)*

SLENDER Ay, it is no matter.

PISTOL How now, Mephistopheles?[1]

SLENDER Ay, it is no matter.

NIM Slice, I say, *pauca, pauca!* Slice, that's my humor.[2]

115 SLENDER [*to* SHALLOW] Where's Simple, my man? Can you
tell, cousin?

EVANS Peace, I pray you. Now let us understand. There is
three umpires in this matter, as I understand; that is, Master Page (*fidelicet°* Master Page), and there is myself (*fideli-* *namely*
120 *cet* myself), and the three party is (lastly and finally) mine
Host of the Garter.° *(a Windsor inn)*

PAGE We three to hear it and end it between them.

EVANS Fery goot. I will make a prief of it in my notebook, and
we will afterwards 'ork upon the cause with as great dis-
125 creetly as we can.

FALSTAFF Pistol.

PISTOL He hears with ears.

EVANS The tevil and his tam!° What phrase is this? He hears *dam (mother)*
with ear? Why, it is affectations.

130 FALSTAFF Pistol, did you pick Master Slender's purse?

SLENDER Ay, by these gloves, did he—or I would I might never
come in mine own great chamber° again else—of seven *hall; bedroom*
groats in mill sixpences and two Edward shovelboards[3] that
cost me two shilling and two pence apiece of Ed Miller, by
135 these gloves.

FALSTAFF Is this true, Pistol?

EVANS No, it is false, if it° is a pickpurse. *he*

PISTOL Ha, thou mountain foreigner!° Sir John and master *Welshman*
mine,
I combat challenge of this latten bilbo.[4]
140 Word of denial in thy *labras°* here, *lips*
Word of denial! Froth and scum, thou liest!

SLENDER [*pointing to* NIM] By these gloves, then 'twas he.

NIM Be advised, sir, and pass good humors.° I will say marry *behave properly*
trap with you,[5] if you run the nut-hook's humor on me.[6]
145 That is the very note° of it. *fact*

SLENDER [*indicating* BARDOLPH] By this hat, then he in the
red face° had it, for though I cannot remember what I did *(Bardolph)*

---

when you made me drunk, yet I am not altogether an ass.
FALSTAFF What say you, Scarlet and John?[7]
150   BARDOLPH Why, sir, for my part, I say the gentleman had
drunk himself out of his five sentences.
EVANS It is "his five senses." Fie, what the ignorance is!
BARDOLPH And being fap,° sir, was, as they say, cashiered,°   drunk / kicked out
and so conclusions passed the careers.[8]
155   SLENDER Ay, you spake in Latin[9] then too. But 'tis no matter.
I'll ne'er be drunk whilst I live again, but in honest, civil,
godly company, for° this trick. If I be drunk, I'll be drunk   on account of
with those that have the fear of God, and not with drunken
knaves.
160   EVANS So Got 'udge me,° that is a virtuous mind.   judge
FALSTAFF You hear all these matters denied, gentlemen, you
hear it.
[*Enter* MISTRESS FORD, MISTRESS PAGE, *and her*
daughter ANNE *with wine.*][1]
PAGE Nay, daughter, carry the wine in. We'll drink within.
[*Exit* ANNE.]
SLENDER O heaven! This is Mistress Anne Page.
165   PAGE How now, Mistress Ford?
FALSTAFF Mistress Ford, by my troth, you are very well met.
By your leave, good mistress.
[*Sir John kisses* MISTRESS FORD.]
PAGE Wife, bid these gentlemen welcome. —Come, we have
a hot venison pasty to° dinner. Come, gentlemen, I hope we   pie for
170   shall drink down all unkindness.
[*Exeunt all but* SLENDER.]
SLENDER I had rather than forty shillings I had my book of
songs and sonnets here.[2]
[*Enter* SIMPLE.]
How now, Simple, where have you been? I must wait on
myself, must I? You have not the book of riddles about you,
175   have you?
SIMPLE Book of riddles? Why, did you not lend it to Alice
Shortcake upon Allhallowmas last, a fortnight afore
Michaelmas?[3]
[*Enter* SHALLOW *and* EVANS.]
SHALLOW Come, coz, come, coz, we stay° for you. A word   wait
180   with you, coz. [*He draws* SLENDER *aside.*] Marry,° this, coz: Indeed
there is as 'twere a tender,° a kind of tender, made afar   (marriage) proposal
off° by Sir Hugh here. Do you understand me?   indirectly
SLENDER Ay, sir, you shall find me reasonable.° If it be so, I   (with Falstaff)
shall do that that is reason.
185   SHALLOW Nay, but understand me.
SLENDER So I do, sir.

---

7. Robin Hood's accomplices, Will Scarlet and Little
John; alluding to Bardolph's complexion.
8. Things got out of hand; he misinterpreted
things.
9. Slender can't understand Bardolph's slang and so
assumes it must be Latin.
1. TEXTUAL COMMENT For the stage directions and
stage action in lines 161–70, see Digital Edition TC 1

(Folio edited text).
2. Probably Richard Tottel's *Miscellany* (1557), an
out-of-date collection of love poetry on whose quot-
able quotes Slender wishes to draw in wooing Anne
Page.
3. Allhallowmas, or All Saints' Day (November 1), is
actually over a month after Michaelmas, September 29.

EVANS   Give ear to his motions.° Master Slender, I will descrip-   *proposals*
tion the matter to you, if you be capacity of it.
SLENDER   Nay, I will do as my cousin Shallow says. I pray you,
190   pardon me. He's a justice of peace in his country,° simple°   *district / humble; foolish*
though I stand here.
EVANS   But that is not the question. The question is concerning your marriage.
SHALLOW   Ay, there's the point, sir.
195   EVANS   Marry, is it, the very point of it—to Mistress Anne
Page.
SLENDER   Why, if it be so, I will marry her, upon any reason-
able demands.°   *requests*
EVANS   But can you affection the 'oman? Let us command to
200   know that of your mouth, or of your lips, for divers philosophers hold that the lips is parcel° of the mouth. Therefore,   *part and parcel*
precisely, can you carry your good will to the maid?
SHALLOW   Cousin Abraham Slender, can you love her?
SLENDER   I hope, sir, I will do as it shall become one that would
205   do reason.
EVANS   Nay, Got's lords and his ladies, you must speak possit-
able,° if you can carry her your desires towards her.   *positively*
SHALLOW   That you must. Will you, upon good dowry, marry
her?
210   SLENDER   I will do a greater thing than that upon your request,
cousin, in° any reason.   *within*
SHALLOW   Nay, conceive° me, conceive me, sweet coz! What I   *understand*
do is to pleasure you, coz. Can you love the maid?
SLENDER   I will marry her, sir, at your request. But if there be
215   no great love in the beginning, yet heaven may decrease° it   *(for "increase")*
upon better acquaintance, when we are married and have
more occasion to know one another. I hope upon familiarity
will grow more content. But if you say marry her, I will marry
her. That I am freely dissolved° and dissolutely.   *(for "resolved")*
220   EVANS   It is a fery discretion answer, save the faul'° is in the   *fault*
'ord dissolutely. The 'ort is, according to our meaning, reso-
lutely. His meaning is good.
SHALLOW   Ay, I think my cousin meant well.
SLENDER   Ay, or else I would I might be hanged, la.
[*Enter* ANNE *Page.*]
225   SHALLOW   Here comes fair Mistress Anne. —Would I were
young for your sake, Mistress Anne.
ANNE   The dinner is on the table. My father desires your wor-
ships' company.
SHALLOW   I will wait on him, fair Mistress Anne.
230   EVANS   Od's° plessed will, I will not be absence at the grace.   *God's*
[*Exeunt* SHALLOW *and* EVANS.]
ANNE [*to* SLENDER]   Will't please your worship to come in, sir?
SLENDER   No, I thank you, forsooth, heartily. I am very well.
ANNE   The dinner attends° you, sir.   *awaits*
SLENDER   I am not a-hungry, I thank you, forsooth. [*to* SIM-
235   PLE] Go, sirrah, for all you are my man, go wait upon my
cousin Shallow.   [*Exit* SIMPLE.]
A justice of peace sometime may be beholden to his friend
for a man. I keep but three men and a boy yet, till my mother

be dead. But what though?° Yet I live like a poor gentleman   *what of it*
240 born.
ANNE   I may not go in without your worship. They will not sit
till you come.
SLENDER   I'faith, I'll eat nothing. I thank you as much as
though I did.
245 ANNE   I pray you, sir, walk in.
SLENDER   I had rather walk here, I thank you. I bruised my
shin th'other day with playing at sword and dagger with a
master of fence°—three venies° for a dish of stewed prunes⁴—   *fencing / bouts*
and, by my troth, I cannot abide the smell of hot meat° since.   *food; prostitutes*
      [*Dogs bark within.*]
250 Why do your dogs bark so? Be there bears i'th' town?
ANNE   I think there are, sir. I heard them talked of.
SLENDER   I love the sport° well, but I shall as soon quarrel at⁵   *bearbaiting*
it as any man in England. You are afraid if you see the bear
loose, are you not?
255 ANNE   Ay, indeed, sir.
SLENDER   That's meat and drink° to me now. I have seen   *everyday fare*
Sackerson⁶ loose twenty times, and have taken him by the
chain. But, I warrant you, the women have so cried and
shrieked at it that it passed.° But women indeed cannot   *surpassed description*
260 abide 'em. They are very ill-favored° rough things.   *ugly*
      [*Enter* PAGE.]
PAGE   Come, gentle Master Slender, come. We stay for you.
SLENDER   I'll eat nothing, I thank you, sir.
PAGE   By cock and pie,° you shall not choose,° sir. Come, come.   *(mild oath) / you must*
SLENDER   Nay, pray you lead the way.
265 PAGE   Come on, sir.
SLENDER   Mistress Anne, yourself shall go first.
ANNE   Not I, sir. Pray you keep on.°   *go on*
SLENDER   Truly I will not go first, truly, la. I will not do you
that wrong.
270 ANNE   I pray you, sir.
SLENDER   I'll rather be unmannerly than troublesome. You do
yourself wrong, indeed, la.
      Exeunt [SLENDER *first,* PAGE *and* ANNE *following*].

1.2 (Q 2)
Enter EVANS *and* SIMPLE.

EVANS   Go your ways, and ask of° Doctor Caius' house which   *concerning*
is the way. And there dwells one Mistress Quickly, which is
in the manner of his nurse, or his dry-nurse,° or his cook, or   *housekeeper*
his laundry, his washer, and his wringer.
5 SIMPLE   Well, sir.
EVANS   Nay, it is petter yet. Give her this letter, for it is a 'oman
that altogethers acquaintance° with Mistress Anne Page;   *is well acquainted*
and the letter is to desire and require her to solicit your mas-
ter's desires, to Mistress Anne Page. I pray you, begone.
      [*Exit* SIMPLE.]
10 I will make an end of my dinner; there's pippins° and cheese   *apples*
to come.   *Exit.*

---

4. Also slang for "prostitute."   6. Famous bear used in bearbaiting.
5. Object to dispute.   1.2 Location: Scene continues.

1.3 (Q 3)

Enter FALSTAFF, HOST [*of the Garter*], BARDOLPH, NIM,
PISTOL[, *and the boy* ROBIN].

FALSTAFF Mine Host of the Garter.

HOST What says my bully rook?° Speak scholarly and wisely. — *fine fellow*

FALSTAFF Truly, mine Host, I must turn away some of my
followers.

5 HOST Discard, bully Hercules, cashier.° Let them wag.° Trot, — *dismiss / go their ways*
trot.

FALSTAFF I sit° at ten pounds a week. — *lodge*

HOST Thou'rt an emperor—Caesar, kaiser, and vizier.[1] I will
entertain° Bardolph. He shall draw, he shall tap.° Said I — *employ / tend bar*
10 well, bully Hector?[2]

FALSTAFF Do so, good mine Host.

HOST I have spoke. Let him follow. [*to* BARDOLPH] Let me see
thee froth[3] and live. I am at a word.° Follow. [*Exit.*] — *I mean what I say*

FALSTAFF Bardolph, follow him. A tapster is a good trade. An
15 old cloak makes a new jerkin;° a withered servingman a — *jacket*
fresh tapster. Go, adieu.

BARDOLPH It is a life that I have desired. I will thrive. [*Exit.*]

PISTOL O base Hungarian wight,[4] wilt thou the spigot wield?

NIM He was gotten in drink.[5] Is not the humor conceited?° — *idea witty*

20 FALSTAFF I am glad I am so acquit of this tinderbox.[6] His thefts
were too open. His filching was like an unskillful singer: he
kept not time.

NIM The good humor° is to steal at a minute's rest.° — *trick / within a minute*

PISTOL Convey, the wise it call. Steal? Foh, a fico[7] for the
25 phrase!

FALSTAFF Well, sirs, I am almost out at heels.° — *destitute*

PISTOL Why, then, let kibes° ensue. — *sore heels*

FALSTAFF There is no remedy. I must coney-catch,° I must — *swindle*
shift.° — *live by my wits*

30 PISTOL Young ravens must have food.

FALSTAFF Which of you know Ford of this town?

PISTOL I ken the wight.° He is of substance good.° — *know the man / well-off*

FALSTAFF My honest lads, I will tell you what I am about.° — *up to; in girth*

PISTOL Two yards and more.

35 FALSTAFF No quips now, Pistol. Indeed I am in the waist two
yards about, but I am now about no waste. I am about thrift.
Briefly, I do mean to make love to Ford's wife. I spy entertainment[8] in her. She discourses, she carves,[9] she gives the
leer of invitation. I can construe[1] the action of her familiar
40 style, and the hardest voice of her behavior, to be Englished
rightly, is "I am Sir John Falstaff's."

1.3 Location: The Garter Inn.
1. *vizier:* Turkish viceroy. *Caesar:* the name of Julius
Caesar became a title, "emperor."
2. Greatest of the Trojans who fought in the Trojan
War. Similarly, Hercules (line 5) was the most famous
hero of classical mythology.
3. *froth:* cheat the customer—by putting a good head
on the beer (to give short measure).
4. Hungry, contemptible man.
5. Begotten when his parents were drunk (thought to
make one cowardly).
6. Alluding to Bardolph's red complexion and irascible temper. *acquit:* rid.

7. An abusive insult usually accompanied by the gesture of showing the thumb pushed between index
and middle fingers: historically, "fig" (Spanish); allu-
sively, "female genitals."
8. Provision of food, drink, and lodging; ability to
give sexual pleasure.
9. Perhaps: acts courteously; gestures broadly with
her hands; shows pleasing skill in carving meat—
hence, somewhere between ordinary friendliness and
sexual enticement.
1. Interpret (beginning a grammatical pun that
includes "style," "voice," "Englished," and "translated,"
lines 40, 42).

PISTOL He hath studied her will, and translated her will²—
out of honesty,° into English.   *chastity*

NIM The anchor is deep.³ Will that humor pass?°   *phrase pass muster*

45 FALSTAFF Now, the report° goes, she has all the rule of her   *rumor*
husband's purse. He hath legions of angels.°   *gold coins*

PISTOL As many devils entertain,° and to her, boy,° say I.   *employ / (hunting cry)*

NIM The humor rises. It is good—humor me the angels!⁴

FALSTAFF I have writ me here a letter to her, and here another

50 to Page's wife, who even now gave me good eyes too, exam-
ined my parts° with most judicious oeillades:° sometimes the   *sexual capacity / ogling*
beam of her view gilded my foot, sometimes my portly belly.

PISTOL Then did the sun on dunghill shine.

NIM I thank thee for that humor.

55 FALSTAFF Oh, she did so course° o'er my exteriors, with such   *travel*
a greedy intention, that the appetite of her eye did seem to
scorch me up like a burning-glass.⁵ Here's another letter to
her. She bears the purse too. She is a region in Guiana,⁶ all
gold and bounty. I will be cheaters⁷ to them both, and they

60 shall be exchequers to me. They shall be my East and West
Indies, and I will trade to them both. [*He gives a letter to*
PISTOL.] Go, bear thou this letter to Mistress Page; [*giving a*
letter to NIM] and thou this to Mistress Ford. We will thrive,
lads, we will thrive!

65 PISTOL [*returning the letter*] Shall I Sir Pandarus of Troy⁸
become,
And by my side wear steel?° Then Lucifer take all.   *And remain a soldier*

NIM [*returning the letter*] I will run no base humor. Here,
take the humor-letter. I will keep the 'havior of reputation.⁹

FALSTAFF [*to* ROBIN] Hold,° sirrah, bear you these letters   *Take these*
tightly;°   *safely*

70 Sail like my pinnace° to these golden shores.   *small, fast boat*
[*to* PISTOL *and* NIM] Rogues, hence, avaunt!° Vanish like   *begone*
hailstones, go!
Trudge, plod away i'th' hoof,° seek shelter, pack!°   *on foot / be off*
Falstaff will learn the honor of the age,
French thrift, you rogues—myself and skirted page.¹
[*Exeunt* FALSTAFF *and* ROBIN.]

75 PISTOL Let vultures gripe° thy guts, for gourd and fulham²   *seize*
holds,°   *are profitable*
And high and low beguiles the rich and poor!
Tester° I'll have in pouch° when thou shalt lack,   *Sixpence / purse*
Base Phrygian Turk!³

---

2. Intention; sexual desires; legal document (thought of as written in Latin).

3. That's a deep plot; you're out of your depth (?).

4. Perhaps: the plot develops; it's good. Get the money. (Here, as elsewhere in Nim's speech, "humor" means whatever the context demands.)

5. Glass lens used to concentrate the sun's rays and so start a fire.

6. South American country famed for its unexploited wealth and fertility, as were the East and West Indies (lines 60–61).

7. Escheaters, officers of the Exchequer (or Treasury; line 60) responsible for estates that fell forfeit and so came to the Crown; deceivers, robbers.

8. Pandarus is the aristocrat who, as Troy is besieged by the Greeks, serves as go-between (or pander) in

the affair between Troilus and Cressida, Pandarus's niece. Shakespeare's *Troilus and Cressida* is several years later than *The Merry Wives*.

9. I will behave respectfully.

1. Suggesting that French gentlemen were thought to retain few, though well-dressed, followers. *skirted:* wearing a coat with full tails.

2. *gourd and fulham:* false dice and loaded dice— loaded "high" to produce a four, five, or six, or "low" to produce a one, two, or three. See line 76.

3. Terms of abuse. The Turks, Europe's main military foe, were Muslims and hence considered infidels. The Phrygians, early inhabitants of what is now Turkey, were conquered by Europeans; to the classical Greeks, "Phrygian" was equivalent to "slave."

NIM   I have operations° which be humors of revenge.   *plans*
PISTOL   Wilt thou revenge?
80   NIM   By welkin° and her star.   *the sky (poetic)*
PISTOL   With wit or steel?
NIM   With both the humors, I!
I will discuss° the humor of this love to Ford.   *disclose*
PISTOL   And I to Page shall eke° unfold   *also (archaic)*
How Falstaff, varlet vile,
85   His dove will prove,° his gold will hold,   *test; sample*
And his soft couch defile.
NIM   My humor shall not cool. I will incense Ford to deal
with poison; I will possess him with yellowness,[4] for this
revolt of mine° is dangerous. That is my true humor.   *(against Falstaff)*
90   PISTOL   Thou art the Mars of malcontents.[5]
I second thee. Troop on!   *Exeunt.*

1.4 (Q 4)
Enter MISTRESS QUICKLY [*and*] SIMPLE.
MISTRESS QUICKLY   What,° John Rugby!   *(a summoning call)*
[*Enter John* RUGBY.]
I pray thee go to the casement and see if you can see my
master, Master Doctor Caius, coming. If he do, i'faith, and
find anybody in the house, here will be an old° abusing of   *will be lots of*
5   God's patience and the King's English.
RUGBY   I'll go watch.
MISTRESS QUICKLY   Go, and we'll have a posset[1] for't soon at
night,° in faith, at the latter end of a sea-coal[2] fire.   *toward nightfall*
[*Exit* RUGBY.]
An honest, willing, kind fellow, as ever servant shall come in
10   house withal,° and, I warrant you, no telltale, nor no breed-   *with*
bate.° His worst fault is that he is given to prayer; he is   *troublemaker*
something peevish° that way—but nobody but has his fault.   *foolish*
But let that pass. Peter Simple you say your name is?
SIMPLE   Ay, for fault° of a better.   *lack*
15   MISTRESS QUICKLY   And Master Slender's your master?
SIMPLE   Ay, forsooth.
MISTRESS QUICKLY   Does he not wear a great round beard like
a glover's paring knife?
SIMPLE   No, forsooth. He hath but a little wee face with a
20   little yellow beard, a Cain-colored° beard.   *yellow or reddish*
MISTRESS QUICKLY   A softly-sprighted° man, is he not?   *meek-spirited*
SIMPLE   Ay, forsooth. But he is as tall a man of his hands as
any is, between this and his head.[3] He hath fought with a
warrener.°   *gamekeeper*
25   MISTRESS QUICKLY   How, say you? Oh, I should remember him.
Does he not hold up his head, as it were, and strut in his gait?
SIMPLE   Yes, indeed, does he.

---

4. Fill him with jealousy. (An inconsistency: in 2.1,
Nim goes to Page and Pistol to Ford, who is possessed with yellowness.)
5. Most warlike rebel (Mars was the Roman god of war).
1.4 Location: Dr. Caius's house.

1. Restorative drink of hot milk curdled with wine
or ale.
2. Coal brought by sea.
3. But he is as brave a man as any is around here.

MISTRESS QUICKLY Well, heaven send Anne Page no worse
    fortune! Tell Master Parson Evans I will do what I can for
30   your master. Anne is a good girl, and I wish—
        [*Enter* RUGBY.]
RUGBY Out, alas, here comes my master!   [*Exit.*]
MISTRESS QUICKLY We shall all be shent.° Run in here, good   *scolded*
    young man. Go into this closet.
        [SIMPLE *steps into the closet.*]
    [*aside*] He will not stay long. —[*loudly*] What, John Rugby?
35   John? What, John, I say!
        [*Enter* RUGBY.]
    [*loudly*] Go, John, go inquire for my master. I doubt° he be   *suspect*
    not well, that he comes not home.   [*Exit* RUGBY.]
    [*Sings.*]   And down, down, a'down-a (etc.).
        [*Enter Doctor* CAIUS.]
CAIUS Vat is you sing? I do not like dese toys.° Pray you, go   *frivolous tunes*
40   and vetch me in my closet, *une boîte en vert*; a box, a green-a
    box. *Tu entends*° vat I speak? A green-a box.   *Do you hear*
MISTRESS QUICKLY Ay, forsooth, I'll fetch it you. [*aside*] I am
    glad he went not in himself. If he had found the young man,
    he would have been horn-mad.°   *mad as a bull*
        [*She fetches the box from the closet.*]
45 CAIUS Fe, fe, fe, fe! *Ma foi, il fait fort chaud! Je m'en vais à la*
    cour—la grande affaire.[4]
MISTRESS QUICKLY Is it this, sir?
CAIUS *Oui, mets-la à ma* pocket.[5] *Dépêche*, quickly! Vere is
    dat knave, Rugby?
50 MISTRESS QUICKLY [*calling*] What, John Rugby! John!
        [*Enter* RUGBY.]
RUGBY Here, sir.
CAIUS You are John Rugby, and you are Jack° Rugby. Come,   *(connotes knavery)*
    take-a your rapier, and come after my heel to the court.
RUGBY 'Tis ready, sir, here in the porch.
        [*He fetches the rapier.*]
55 CAIUS By my trot,° I tarry too long. Od's me,° *qu'ai-j'oublié*?[6]   *troth / God save me*
    Dere is some simples[7] in my closet dat I vill not for the varld
    I shall leave behind.
        [*He goes to the closet.*]
MISTRESS QUICKLY [*aside*] Ay me, he'll find the young man
    there, and be mad.
60 CAIUS [*discovering* SIMPLE] Oh, *diable*,° *diable*! Vat is in my   *devil*
    closet? Villainy! *Larron!*° —Rugby, my rapier.   *Thief*
MISTRESS QUICKLY Good master, be content.
CAIUS Wherefore shall I be content-a?
MISTRESS QUICKLY The young man is an honest man.
65 CAIUS What shall de honest man do in my closet? Dere is no
    honest man dat shall come in my closet.
MISTRESS QUICKLY I beseech you be not so phlegmatic.[8] Hear
    the truth of it. He came of an errand to me from Parson Hugh.

---

4. French: By my faith, it is very hot. I am going to
court—important business. (The French in this
scene is translated only when Caius fails to do so
himself.)
5. Yes, put it in my pocket.

6. What have I forgotten?
7. Medicines composed of one herb or constituent;
unknown to Caius, also the character's name.
8. Cold and dull (Quickly's mistake for the opposite
temperament—choleric, or angry).

CAIUS Vell.

70 SIMPLE Ay, forsooth, to desire her to—

MISTRESS QUICKLY Peace, I pray you.

CAIUS [*to* MISTRESS QUICKLY] Peace-a your tongue! [*to* SIMPLE]
Speak-a your tale.

SIMPLE To desire this honest gentlewoman, your maid, to

75 speak a good word to Mistress Anne Page for my master in
the way of marriage.

MISTRESS QUICKLY This is all, indeed, la, but I'll ne'er put my
finger in the fire, an need not.⁹

CAIUS Sir Hugh send-a you? —Rugby, *baille*° me some paper.   bring

80 [*to* SIMPLE] Tarry you a little-a while.
        [RUGBY *brings paper. The doctor writes.*]

MISTRESS QUICKLY [*aside to* SIMPLE] I am glad he is so quiet.
If he had been thoroughly moved,° you should have heard   really angered
him so loud and so melancholy!° But notwithstanding, man,   (for "choleric"?)
I'll do you your master what good I can. And the very yea

85 and the no is, the French doctor, my master—I may call him
my master, look you, for I keep his house, and I wash, wring,
brew, bake, scour, dress meat° and drink, make the beds,   prepare food
and do all myself—

SIMPLE 'Tis a great charge° to come under one body's hand.   burden; (sexual)

90 MISTRESS QUICKLY Are you advised o'that?° You shall find it a   You're telling me
great charge, and to be up early and down late. But notwith-
standing—to tell you in your ear, I would have no words of
it—my master himself is in love with Mistress Anne Page.
But notwithstanding that I know Anne's mind, that's neither

95 here nor there.

CAIUS [*giving the letter to* SIMPLE] You, jack'nape,° give-a this   idiot
letter to Sir Hugh. By gar,° it is a shallenge. I will cut his   God
troat in de park, and I will teach a scurvy jackanape priest
to meddle or make°—you may be gone. It is not good you   interfere

100 tarry here. By gar, I will cut all his two stones.° By gar, he   testicles
shall not have a stone to throw at his dog.   [*Exit* SIMPLE.]

MISTRESS QUICKLY Alas, he speaks but for his friend.

CAIUS It is no matter-a ver° dat. Do not you tell-a me dat I   for
shall have Anne Page for myself? By gar, I vill kill de jack-

105 priest!° And I have appointed mine Host of de Jarteer° to   knave-priest / Garter
measure our weapon.° By gar, I will myself have Anne Page.   to referee

MISTRESS QUICKLY Sir, the maid loves you, and all shall be
well. We must give folks leave to prate. What the goodyear!°   What the devil

CAIUS Rugby, come to the court with me. [*to* MISTRESS

110 QUICKLY] By gar, if I have not Anne Page, I shall turn your
head out of my door. —Follow my heels, Rugby.

MISTRESS QUICKLY You shall have An°—   Anne; an
        [*Exit* CAIUS *with* RUGBY.]
fool's head of your own. No, I know Anne's mind for that.
Never a woman in Windsor knows more of Anne's mind than

115 I do, nor can do more than I do with her, I thank heaven.

FENTON [*within*] Who's within there, ho?

MISTRESS QUICKLY Who's there, I trow?° —Come near° the   wonder / Enter
house, I pray you.
        [*Enter* FENTON.]

---

9. I'll never put myself in danger by getting involved if I don't have to.

FENTON How now, good woman, how dost thou?

120 MISTRESS QUICKLY The better that it pleases your good worship to ask!

FENTON What news? How does pretty Mistress Anne?

MISTRESS QUICKLY In truth, sir, and she is pretty, and hon-
est,° and gentle,° and one that is your friend. I can tell you   *chaste / well-bred*
125 that by the way, I praise heaven for it.

FENTON Shall I do any good,° think'st thou? Shall I not lose   *make any progress*
my suit?

MISTRESS QUICKLY Troth, sir, all is in His hands above. But
notwithstanding, Master Fenton, I'll be sworn on a book°   *a Bible*
130 she loves you. Have not your worship a wart above your eye?

FENTON Yes, marry, have I. What of that?

MISTRESS QUICKLY Well, thereby hangs a tale. Good faith, it
is such another Nan!¹ But, I detest,° an honest maid as ever   *(for "protest")*
broke bread.° We had an hour's talk of that wart. I shall   *ate (proverbial)*
135 never laugh but in that maid's company. But, indeed, she is
given too much to allicholy° and musing. But for you—   *(for "melancholy")*
well—go to!°   *come, come*

FENTON Well, I shall see her today. Hold, there's money for
thee. Let me have thy voice in my behalf. If thou seest her
140 before me, commend me—

MISTRESS QUICKLY Will I? I'faith, that we will. And I will tell
your worship more of the wart the next time we have confidence,° and of other wooers.   *private talk*

FENTON Well, farewell. I am in great haste now.

145 MISTRESS QUICKLY Farewell to your worship. [*Exit* FENTON.]
Truly an honest gentleman. But Anne loves him not. For I
know Anne's mind as well as another° does.—Out upon't,²   *anyone else*
what have I forgot?   *Exit.*

2.1 (Q 5)

Enter MISTRESS PAGE [*reading of a letter*].

MISTRESS PAGE What, have I scaped love letters in the holiday
time° of my beauty, and am I now a subject for them? Let me   *heyday*
see: "Ask me no reason why I love you, for though Love use
Reason for his precisian, he admits him not for his coun-
5 selor.¹ You are not young; no more am I. Go to, then, there's
sympathy.° You are merry; so am I. Ha, ha, then there's more   *agreement*
sympathy. You love sack,° and so do I. Would you desire bet-   *Spanish wine*
ter sympathy? Let it suffice thee, Mistress Page, at the least
if the love of soldier can suffice, that I love thee. I will not say
10 'pity me'—'tis not a soldier-like phrase—but I say 'love me':

By me, thine own true knight,
By day or night,
Or any kind of light,
With all his might,
15 For thee to fight.
John Falstaff."

What a Herod of Jewry° is this? Oh, wicked, wicked world!   *bragging stage villain*
One that is well-nigh worn to pieces with age, to show him-

---

1. Nan (Anne) is such an extraordinary (or lively) one.
2. Expression of dismay.
2.1 Location: Outside Page's house.

1. Though Love employs Reason to make strong
arguments, or preach, on Love's behalf (a "precisian"
was a puritan), Love will not accept Reason's advice.

self a young gallant? What an unweighed° behavior hath this   *unbalanced*
20 Flemish° drunkard picked, with the devil's name,° out of my   *(proverbially drunk) / aid*
conversation,° that he dares in this manner assay° me?   *conduct / proposition*
Why, he hath not been thrice in my company. What should
I say° to him? I was then frugal of my mirth. Heaven for-   *should I have said*
give me! Why, I'll exhibit° a bill in the parliament for the   *introduce*
25 putting down² of men. How shall I be revenged on him?
For revenged I will be, as sure as his guts are made of
puddings!°   *gut-encased sausages*

    [*Enter* MISTRESS FORD.]

MISTRESS FORD   Mistress Page, trust me, I was going to your
house.
30 MISTRESS PAGE   And, trust me, I was coming to you. You look
very ill.
MISTRESS FORD   Nay, I'll ne'er believe that. I have° to show to   *have something*
the contrary.
MISTRESS PAGE   Faith, but you do, in my mind.
35 MISTRESS FORD   Well, I do then. Yet I say I could show you to
the contrary. O Mistress Page, give me some counsel.
MISTRESS PAGE   What's the matter, woman?
MISTRESS FORD   O woman, if it were not for one trifling respect,°   *consideration*
I could come to such honor!°   *rank*
40 MISTRESS PAGE   Hang the trifle, woman; take the honor. What
is it? Dispense with trifles. What is it?
MISTRESS FORD   If I would but go to hell for an eternal
moment or so, I could be knighted.³
MISTRESS PAGE   What? Thou liest! Sir Alice Ford? These
45 knights will hack,° and so thou shouldst not alter the article   *(military); (sexual?)*
of thy gentry.°   *terms of your station*
MISTRESS FORD   We burn daylight.° Here, read, read. Perceive   *waste time*
how I might be knighted. [*She gives a letter to* MISTRESS PAGE,
who reads it.] I shall think the worse of fat men, as long as I
50 have an eye to make difference of° men's liking.° And yet he   *judge among / looks*
would not swear, praised women's modesty, and gave such
orderly and well-behaved reproof to all uncomeliness,° that I   *improper behavior*
would have sworn his disposition would have gone to° the   *accorded with*
truth of his words. But they do no more adhere and keep
55 place together than the hundred psalms to the tune of
"Greensleeves."° What tempest, I trow, threw this whale,   *(popular love song)*
with so many tuns° of oil in his belly, ashore at Windsor?   *casks*
How shall I be revenged on him? I think the best way
were to entertain him with hope till the wicked fire of lust
60 have melted him in his own grease. Did you ever hear the
like?
MISTRESS PAGE   Letter for letter, but that the name of Page
and Ford differs. [*She shows her own letter.*] To thy great
comfort in this mystery of ill opinions,⁴ here's the twin
65 brother of thy letter. But let thine inherit first, for I protest
mine never shall. I warrant he hath a thousand of these letters, writ with blank space for different names—sure,
more, and these are of the second edition. He will print

---

2. *putting down:* suppression; perhaps also an
unconscious sexual suggestion that men are to be put
down for the purpose of intercourse.

3. Dubbed a knight; sexually provided with a knight.
4. Falstaff's unfounded and hence mysterious belief
that the wives are promiscuous.

them, out of doubt,° for he cares not what he puts into the   *undoubtedly*
70 press[5] when he would put us two. I had rather be a giantess
and lie under Mount Pelion.[6] Well, I will find you twenty
lascivious turtles[7] ere one chaste man.

MISTRESS FORD [*comparing the two letters*] Why, this is the
very same: the very hand, the very words! What doth he think
75 of us?

MISTRESS PAGE Nay, I know not. It makes me almost ready to
wrangle° with mine own honesty.° I'll entertain° myself like   *argue / chastity / treat*
one that I am not acquainted withal,° for sure, unless he   *with*
know some strain in me that I know not myself, he would
80 never have boarded[8] me in this fury.

MISTRESS FORD Boarding, call you it? I'll be sure to keep him
above deck.

MISTRESS PAGE So will I. If he come under my hatches, I'll
never to sea again. Let's be revenged on him. Let's appoint
85 him a meeting, give him a show of comfort° in his suit, and   *encouragement*
lead him on with a fine-baited° delay, till he hath pawned   *temptingly alluring*
his horses to mine Host of the Garter.[9]

MISTRESS FORD Nay, I will consent to act any villainy against
him that may not sully the chariness° of our honesty. Oh,   *scrupulous integrity*
90 that my husband saw this letter! It would give eternal food
to his jealousy.

[*Enter* MASTER FORD *with* PISTOL, *and* MASTER PAGE
with NIM.]

MISTRESS PAGE Why, look where he comes, and my goodman°   *husband*
too. He's as far from jealousy as I am from giving him cause,
and that, I hope, is an unmeasurable distance.

95 MISTRESS FORD You are the happier woman.

MISTRESS PAGE Let's consult together against this greasy
knight. Come hither.

[*They talk aside.*]

FORD Well, I hope it be not so.

PISTOL Hope is a curtal° dog in some affairs.   *an unreliable*
100 Sir John affects° thy wife.   *loves; aims at*

FORD Why, sir, my wife is not young.

PISTOL He woos both high and low, both rich and poor,
Both young and old, one with another,° Ford.   *indiscriminately*
He loves the gallimaufry,° Ford. Perpend.°   *mixture / Consider*

105 FORD Love my wife?

PISTOL With liver° burning hot. Prevent—   *(seat of the passions)*
Or go thou like Sir Actaeon,[1]
He, with Ringwood[2] at thy heels.
Oh, odious is the name!

110 FORD What name, sir?

PISTOL The horn,° I say. Farewell.   *(of a cuckold)*
Take heed, have open eye, for thieves do foot°   *walk; (sexual)*

---

5. Printing press; what he presses sexually.
6. The giants were the Titans, who in Greek mythology rebelled against the Olympian gods and were
punished by being buried under Mt. Pelion.
7. Turtledoves (proverbially true to their mates).
8. Nautical metaphor: accosted; sexually entered.
9. See note to 4.3.11. The plot does not develop in
exactly the way anticipated: Ford supplies Sir John

with funds, so at first he doesn't have to pawn his
horses to raise money for his courting.
1. In Greek mythology, Actaeon was turned into a
stag and consequently was hunted and killed by his
own dogs. The stag, in particular its horns, was considered an emblem of the cuckold, the man whose
wife was unfaithful to him.
2. Supposed name of one of Actaeon's dogs.

By night. Take heed, ere summer comes, or cuckoo
Birds³ do sing. —Away, Sir Corporal Nim!
115   —Believe it, Page, he speaks sense.   [*Exit.*]
FORD [*aside*]   I will be patient. I will find out° this.   *investigate*
NIM [*to* PAGE]   And this is true. I like not the humor of lying.
He hath wronged me in some humors: I should° have borne   *was supposed to*
the humored letter to her. But I have a sword, and it shall
120   bite upon my necessity.° He loves your wife. There's the short   *when I need it to*
and the long. My name is Corporal Nim. I speak, and I
avouch 'tis true. My name is Nim, and Falstaff loves your
wife. Adieu. I love not the humor of bread and cheese.⁴ Adieu.
                                                              [*Exit.*]
PAGE [*aside*]   The humor of it, quoth 'a?° Here's a fellow   *he*
125   frights English out of his° wits.   *its*
FORD [*aside*]   I will seek out Falstaff.
PAGE [*aside*]   I never heard such a drawling, affecting° rogue.   *affectedly speaking*
FORD [*aside*]   If I do find° it—well.   *ascertain*
PAGE [*aside*]   I will not believe such a Cathayan,° though the   *Chinese; scoundrel*
130   priest o'th' town commended him for° a true man.   *as*
FORD [*aside*]   'Twas a good sensible fellow. Well.
        [MISTRESS PAGE *and* MISTRESS FORD *come forward.*]
PAGE   How now, Meg?
MISTRESS PAGE   Whither go you, George? Hark you.
        [*They talk apart.*]
MISTRESS FORD   How now, sweet Frank? Why art thou
135   melancholy?
FORD   I melancholy? I am not melancholy. Get you home, go.
MISTRESS FORD   Faith, thou hast some crochets° in thy head.   *strange notions*
—Now, will you go, Mistress Page?
MISTRESS PAGE   Have with you.° —You'll come to dinner,   *I'm coming*
140   George?
        [*Enter* MISTRESS QUICKLY.]
[*aside to* MISTRESS FORD] Look who comes yonder. She shall
be our messenger to this paltry knight.
MISTRESS FORD [*aside to* MISTRESS PAGE]   Trust me, I thought
on her. She'll fit it.°   *fit the part*
145   MISTRESS PAGE [*to* MISTRESS QUICKLY]   You are come to see my
daughter Anne?
MISTRESS QUICKLY   Ay, forsooth, and I pray how does good
Mistress Anne?
MISTRESS PAGE   Go in with us and see. We have an hour's talk
150   with you.   [*Exeunt* MISTRESS PAGE, MISTRESS FORD, *and*
                                                        MISTRESS QUICKLY.]
PAGE   How now, Master Ford?
FORD   You heard what this knave told me, did you not?
PAGE   Yes, and you heard what the other told me?
FORD   Do you think there is truth in them?
155   PAGE   Hang 'em, slaves! I do not think the knight would offer°   *attempt*
it. But these that accuse him in his intent towards our wives

---

3. The cuckoo's habit of leaving its eggs to be hatched
by others made it the emblem of cuckolders and made
the sound of its call a taunt to cuckolds. Its song is
prevalent in late spring, after the mating season.

4. Nim's meager fare as Falstaff's retainer, or as now
unemployed; a popular name for wood sorrel, an edi-
ble plant also known as cuckoo-bread or cuckoo-
cheese—hence, an allusion to cuckolding.

are a yoke° of his discarded men—very rogues, now they be   *pair*
out of service.

FORD   Were they his men?

160   PAGE   Marry, were they.

FORD   I like it never the better for that. Does he lie° at the   *lodge*
Garter?

PAGE   Ay, marry, does he. If he should intend this voyage
toward my wife, I would turn her loose to him, and what he

165   gets more of her than sharp words, let it lie on my head.[5]

FORD   I do not misdoubt° my wife, but I would be loath to   *mistrust*
turn them together. A man may be too confident. I would
have nothing lie on my head. I cannot be thus satisfied.

    [*Enter* HOST.]

PAGE   Look where my ranting Host of the Garter comes.

170   There is either liquor in his pate, or money in his purse,
when he looks so merrily. —How now, mine Host?

HOST   How now, bully rook?° Thou'rt a gentleman.   *fine fellow*

    [*Enter* SHALLOW.]

Cavaliero[6] Justice, I say.

SHALLOW   I follow, mine Host, I follow. —Good even° and   *day*

175   twenty,° good Master Page. Master Page, will you go with us?   *twenty times over*
We have sport in hand.

HOST   Tell him, Cavaliero Justice. Tell him, bully rook.

SHALLOW   Sir, there is a fray to be fought, between Sir Hugh,
the Welsh priest, and Caius, the French doctor.

180   FORD   Good mine Host o'th' Garter, a word with you.

HOST   What say'st thou, my bully rook?

    [*They talk aside.*]

SHALLOW   [*to* PAGE]   Will you go with us to behold it? My
merry Host hath had the measuring of their weapons;° and I   *has been named referee*
think hath appointed them contrary° places. For, believe   *different*

185   me, I hear the parson is no jester. Hark, I will tell you what
our sport shall be.

    [*They talk aside.*]

HOST   Hast thou° no suit against my knight, my guest cavaliero?   *Are you sure you have*

FORD   None, I protest. But I'll give you a pottle of burned°   *two quarts of heated*
sack to give me recourse° to him, and tell him my name is   *access*

190   Broom[7]—only for a jest.

HOST   My hand, bully. Thou shalt have egress and regress—
said I well? And thy name shall be Broom. It is a merry
knight. [*to* SHALLOW *and* PAGE] Will you go, mijn'heers?°   *gentlemen (Dutch)*

SHALLOW   Have with you, mine Host.

195   PAGE   I have heard the Frenchman hath good skill in his rapier.

SHALLOW   Tut, sir. I could have told you more. In these times
you stand on distance: your passes, stoccados,[8] and I know
not what. 'Tis the heart, Master Page, 'tis here,° 'tis here. I   *like this (?)*
have seen the time, with my long sword,[9] I would have made

200   you four tall° fellows skip like rats.   *valiant*

---

5. Let it be my responsibility (but Ford hears an allusion to the cuckold's horns).
6. Gallant gentleman (comic).
7. Q: Brook; F: Broom. "Brooke" was the family name of Lord Cobham, who had objected to the characterization of his ancestor Oldcastle in *1 Henry*

IV. The name was changed to "Falstaff." Presumably, another such objection led to the shift from "Brook" to "Broom." See the Textual Introduction.
8. *In . . . stoccados:* Today, people rely on the distance between duelists—lunges, thrusts.
9. Obsolete, heavy weapon.

HOST   Here, boys, here, here. Shall we wag?°   *go*

PAGE   Have with you. I had rather hear them scold than fight.

                 [Exeunt HOST *and* SHALLOW *with* PAGE.]

FORD   Though Page be a secure° fool and stands so firmly on   *an overconfident*

his wife's frailty, yet I cannot put off my opinion so easily. She

205   was in his company at Page's house, and what they made°   *got up to*

there, I know not. Well, I will look further into't, and I have a

disguise to sound¹ Falstaff. If I find her honest, I lose° not my   *waste*

labor. If she be otherwise, 'tis labor well bestowed.   *Exit.*

2.2 (Q 6)

Enter FALSTAFF [*and*] PISTOL.

FALSTAFF   I will not lend thee a penny.

PISTOL [*drawing his sword*] Why, then, the world's mine oyster,

Which I with sword will open.

FALSTAFF   Not a penny. I have been content, sir, you should

5   lay my countenance to pawn.¹ I have grated upon° my good   *harassed*

friends for three reprieves for you and your coach-fellow°   *companion*

Nim, or else you had looked through the grate° like a gemini°   *prison bars / pair*

of baboons. I am damned in hell for swearing to gentlemen

my friends you were good soldiers and tall fellows. And when

10   Mistress Bridget lost the handle of her fan,² I took't° upon   *swore*

mine honor thou hadst it not.

PISTOL   Didst not thou share? Hadst not thou fifteen pence?

FALSTAFF   Reason,° you rogue, reason. Think'st thou I'll endan-   *With good reason*

ger my soul gratis?° At a word, hang no more about me; I am   *for free*

15   no gibbet° for you. Go, a short knife and a throng,° to your   *gallows / thrust*

manor of Pict-hatch, go.³ You'll not bear a letter for me, you

rogue? You stand upon your honor. Why, thou unconfinable

baseness, it is as much as I can do to keep the terms of my

honor precise.° Ay, ay, I myself sometimes, leaving the fear of   *pure*

20   heaven on the left hand⁴ and hiding mine honor in my neces-

sity, am fain to shuffle, to hedge, and to lurch;⁵ and yet you,

rogue, will ensconce° your rags, your cat-a-mountain° looks,   *hide / wildcat*

your red-lattice° phrases, and your bold-beating° oaths under   *alehouse / very bold (?)*

the shelter of your honor? You will not do it? You?

25 PISTOL [*sheathing his sword*] I do relent. What would thou

more of man?

             [Enter ROBIN.]

ROBIN   Sir, here's a woman would speak with you.

FALSTAFF   Let her approach.

         [Enter MISTRESS QUICKLY.]

MISTRESS QUICKLY   Give your worship good morrow.

FALSTAFF   Good morrow, goodwife.

30 MISTRESS QUICKLY   Not so, an't please your worship.

FALSTAFF   Good maid, then.

MISTRESS QUICKLY   I'll be sworn, as my mother was the first

hour I was born.

---

1. To plumb the depths of.

2.2 Location: The Garter Inn.

1. Exploit my reputation (as surety for borrowing money, etc.).

2. Fans were often made with handles of precious metal or ivory.

3. Pickpockets used a short knife to cut purse strings

in a crowd. Pict-hatch was an area of London infamous for its thieves and prostitutes—hence, an unlikely locale for a "manor" (with a possible pun on "manner," or habits).

4. Disregarding the fear of God.

5. Am obliged to cheat, be devious, and steal.

FALSTAFF I do believe the swearer.[6] What° with me?   *What do you want?*

35 MISTRESS QUICKLY Shall I vouchsafe[7] your worship a word or
two?

FALSTAFF Two thousand, fair woman, and I'll vouchsafe thee
the hearing.

MISTRESS QUICKLY There is one Mistress Ford, sir—I pray,

40 come a little nearer this ways.
[*She draws* FALSTAFF *aside.*]
I myself dwell with Master Doctor Caius.

FALSTAFF Well, on. Mistress Ford, you say.

MISTRESS QUICKLY Your worship says very true. I pray your
worship, come a little nearer this ways.

45 FALSTAFF I warrant thee, nobody hears. [*He gestures at* PIS-
TOL *and* ROBIN.] Mine own people,° mine own people.   *(Pistol and Robin)*

MISTRESS QUICKLY Are they so? Heaven bless them and make
them his servants.

FALSTAFF Well, Mistress Ford—what of her?

50 MISTRESS QUICKLY Why, sir, she's a good creature. Lord,
Lord, your worship's a wanton! Well, heaven forgive you,
and all of us, I pray—

FALSTAFF Mistress Ford—come, Mistress Ford—

MISTRESS QUICKLY Marry, this is the short and the long of it.

55 You have brought her into such a canaries° as 'tis wonderful.   *(for "quandaries")*
The best courtier of them all, when the court lay° at Wind-   *resided*
sor, could never have brought her to such a canary. Yet there
has been knights, and lords, and gentlemen, with their
coaches, I warrant you, coach after coach, letter after letter,

60 gift after gift, smelling so sweetly, all musk, and so rustling,
I warrant you, in silk and gold, and in such alligant° terms,   *(for "elegant")*
and in such wine and sugar° of the best and the fairest that   *flattery*
would have won any woman's heart, and, I warrant you, they
could never get an eye-wink of her. I had myself twenty

65 angels° given me this morning, but I defy° all angels in any   *coins (as bribe) / despise*
such sort, as they say, but in the way of honesty. And, I war-
rant you, they could never get her so much as sip on a cup
with the proudest of them all, and yet there has been earls—
nay, which is more, pensioners[8]—but I warrant you, all is

70 one with her.

FALSTAFF But what says she to me? Be brief, my good she-
Mercury.°   *female messenger*

MISTRESS QUICKLY Marry, she hath received your letter, for
the which she thanks you a thousand times, and she gives

75 you to notify° that her husband will be absence from his   *note*
house between ten and eleven.

FALSTAFF Ten and eleven.

MISTRESS QUICKLY Ay, forsooth, and then you may come and
see the picture, she says, that you wot° of. Master Ford her   *know*

80 husband will be from home. Alas, the sweet woman leads an
ill life with him. He's a very jealousy man. She leads a very
frampold° life with him, good heart.   *disagreeable*

---

6. Quickly thinks she is asserting her virginity, but
by confusing the proverbs "as good a maid as her
mother" and "as innocent as a newborn babe," she
actually claims the opposite. Falstaff expresses his
belief in what she has literally, but unintentionally,
said.
7. Grant (error for "be vouchsafed, or granted, by").
8. Gentlemen of the royal bodyguard.

FALSTAFF Ten and eleven. Woman, commend me to her. I
will not fail her.

85 MISTRESS QUICKLY Why, you say well. But I have another
messenger° to your worship. Mistress Page hath her hearty   *(for "message")*
commendations to you too, and, let me tell you in your ear,
she's as fartuous° a civil modest wife, and one, I tell you,   *(for "virtuous"); farting*
that will not miss you° morning nor evening prayer, as any is   *miss*
90 in Windsor, whoe'er be the other, and she bade me tell your
worship that her husband is seldom from home, but she hopes
there will come a time. I never knew a woman so dote upon a
man. Surely I think you have charms,° la—yes, in truth!   *magic powers*
FALSTAFF Not I, I assure thee. Setting the attraction of my
95 good parts° aside, I have no other charms.   *sexual capacities*
MISTRESS QUICKLY Blessing on your heart for't.
FALSTAFF But I pray thee, tell me this: has Ford's wife and
Page's wife acquainted each other how they love me?
MISTRESS QUICKLY That were a jest indeed! They have not so
100 little grace, I hope. That were a trick indeed! But Mistress
Page would desire you to send her your little page, of all
loves.° Her husband has a marvelous infection to⁹ the little   *for love's sake*
page, and truly Master Page is an honest man. Never a wife
in Windsor leads a better life than she does. Do what she will,
105 say what she will, take all, pay all, go to bed when she list,° rise   *wants*
when she list, all is as she will. And truly she deserves it, for if
there be a kind woman in Windsor, she is one. You must send
her your page, no remedy.
FALSTAFF Why, I will.
110 MISTRESS QUICKLY Nay, but do so then, and, look you, he may
come and go between you both. And in any case have a nay-
word,° that you may know one another's mind, and the boy   *password*
never need to understand anything, for 'tis not good that
children should know any wickedness. Old folks, you know,
115 have discretion, as they say, and know the world.
FALSTAFF Fare thee well, commend me to them both. There's
my purse—I am yet thy debtor. —Boy, go along with this
woman.   [*Exit* MISTRESS QUICKLY *with* ROBIN.]
[*aside*] This news distracts° me.   *bewilders (with joy)*
120 PISTOL [*aside*] This punk° is one of Cupid's carriers.°   *whore / messengers*
Clap on° more sails! Pursue! Up with your sights!   *Set*
Give fire! She is my prize,° or ocean whelm° them all. [*Exit.*]   *booty / overwhelm*
FALSTAFF Say'st thou so, old Jack?° Go thy ways. I'll make   *(addressing himself)*
more of thy old body than I have done. Will they yet look
125 after° thee? Wilt thou, after the expense of so much money,   *desire*
be now a gainer? Good body, I thank thee. Let them say 'tis
grossly° done; so it be fairly° done, no matter.   *crudely / successfully*
[*Enter* BARDOLPH *with a cup of sack.*]
BARDOLPH Sir John, there's one Master Broom below would
fain° speak with you, and be acquainted with you; and hath   *be pleased to*
130 sent your worship a morning's draught of sack.
FALSTAFF Broom is his name?
BARDOLPH Ay, sir.

9. For "affection for."

FALSTAFF   Call him in.   [*Exit* BARDOLPH.]
[*He drinks sack.*] Such Brooms are welcome to me, that
135   o'erflows such liquor.[1] Aha, Mistress Ford and Mistress Page,
have I encompassed° you? Go to, *via!*°   *outwitted / On with it*
         [*Enter* FORD *disguised like Broom, ushered in
         by* BARDOLPH.]
FORD   Bless you, sir.
FALSTAFF   And you, sir. Would you speak with me?
FORD   I make bold to press with so little preparation° upon   *prior notice*
140   you.
FALSTAFF   You're welcome. What's your will? Give us leave,
drawer.°   [*Exit* BARDOLPH.]   *Leave us, bartender*
FORD   Sir, I am a gentleman that have spent much. My name
is Broom.
145   FALSTAFF   Good Master Broom, I desire more acquaintance
of you.
FORD   Good Sir John, I sue for yours—not to charge you,° for   *(with an expense)*
I must let you understand I think myself in better plight for
a lender than you are;[2] the which hath something° embold-   *somewhat*
150   ened me to this unseasoned° intrusion. For they say if money   *ill-timed*
go before, all ways do lie open.
FALSTAFF   Money is a good soldier, sir, and will on.°   *get on*
FORD   Troth, and I have a bag of money here troubles me. If
you will help to bear it, Sir John, take all, or half, for easing
155   me of the carriage.°   *burden of carrying it*
FALSTAFF   Sir, I know not how I may deserve to be your porter.
FORD   I will tell you, sir, if you will give me the hearing.
FALSTAFF   Speak, good Master Broom. I shall be glad to be
your servant.
160   FORD   Sir, I hear you are a scholar—I will be brief with you—
and you have been a man long known to me, though I had
never so good means as desire to make myself acquainted
with you. I shall discover° a thing to you, wherein I must   *reveal*
very much lay open mine own imperfection. But, good Sir
165   John, as you have one eye upon my follies, as you hear them
unfolded, turn another into the register° of your own, that I   *catalog*
may pass with a reproof the easier, sith° you yourself know   *since*
how easy it is to be such an offender.
FALSTAFF   Very well, sir, proceed.
170   FORD   There is a gentlewoman in this town—her husband's
name is Ford.
FALSTAFF   Well, sir.
FORD   I have long loved her and, I protest° to you, bestowed   *declare*
much on her; followed her with a doting observance;°   *attentiveness*
175   engrossed° opportunities to meet her; fee'd° every slight   *collected / purchased*
occasion that could but niggardly give me sight of her; not
only bought many presents to give her, but have given largely°   *bountifully*
to many to know what she would have given.° Briefly, I have   *would like to be given*
pursued her as love hath pursued me, which hath been on
180   the wing of all occasions. But, whatsoever I have merited,

---

1. Q's "Brook" produces wordplay with "o'erflows,"   housecleaning.
lost here. See also 3.5.30–31. But Ford's pseudonym   2. I am more able to undertake a risk, an obligation,
of "Broom" in F connects with the play's emphasis on   or a pledge ("plight") as a lender than you are.

either in my mind, or in my means, meed° I am sure I have   *recompense*
received none, unless experience be a jewel that I have purchased at an infinite rate,° and that hath taught me to say   *cost*
this:
185   Love like a shadow flies, when substance Love pursues,
      Pursuing that that flies, and flying what pursues.³

FALSTAFF   Have you received no promise of satisfaction at her
    hands?
FORD   Never.
190   FALSTAFF   Have you importuned her to such a purpose?
FORD   Never.
FALSTAFF   Of what quality was your love, then?
FORD   Like a fair house, built on another man's ground, so
    that I have lost my edifice by mistaking the place where I
195   erected it.
FALSTAFF   To what purpose have you unfolded this to me?
FORD   When I have told you that, I have told you all. Some say
    that, though she appear honest° to me, yet in other places   *chaste*
    she enlargeth° her mirth so far that there is shrewd° con-   *gives rein to / malicious*
200   struction made of her. Now, Sir John, here is the heart of my
    purpose: you are a gentleman of excellent breeding, admira-
    ble discourse, of great admittance,⁴ authentic in your place°   *of respectable rank*
    and person, generally allowed° for your many warlike, court-   *universally approved*
    like, and learned preparations.°   *accomplishments*
205   FALSTAFF   O sir!
FORD   Believe it, for you know it. There is money. [*He offers*
    money.] Spend it, spend it, spend more, spend all I have—only
    give me so much of your time in exchange of it as to lay an
    amiable° siege to the honesty of this Ford's wife. Use your art   *amorous*
210   of wooing; win her to consent to you. If any man may, you
    may as soon as any.
FALSTAFF   Would it apply well to the vehemency of your affec-
    tion that I should win what you would enjoy? Methinks you
    prescribe to yourself very preposterously.
215   FORD   Oh, understand my drift. She dwells so securely° on   *relies so confidently*
    the excellency of her honor that the folly of my soul dares
    not present itself. She is too bright to be looked against.°   *at*
    Now, could I come to her with any detection° in my hand,   *accusation*
    my desires had instance° and argument to commend them-   *precedent*
220   selves. I could drive her then from the ward° of her purity,   *defense*
    her reputation, her marriage vow, and a thousand other her°   *of her*
    defenses, which now are too too strongly embattled against
    me. What say you to't, Sir John?
FALSTAFF   Master Broom, [*accepting the money*] I will first
225   make bold with your money. Next, give me your hand. [*They*
    shake hands.] And last, as I am a gentleman, you shall, if you
    will, enjoy Ford's wife.
FORD   O good sir!
FALSTAFF   I say you shall.

---

3. *Love . . . what pursues:* Like a shadow, love pursues a physical object ("substance")/person/money
that flees, and flees a physical object/person/money

that pursues.
4. Having qualities ensuring ready admittance into
high society.

230   FORD   Want° no money, Sir John, you shall want none.   *Lack*

      FALSTAFF   Want no Mistress Ford, Master Broom, you shall
      want none. I shall be with her, I may tell you, by her own
      appointment. Even as you came in to me, her assistant, or
      go-between, parted from me. I say I shall be with her
235   between ten and eleven, for at that time the jealous rascally
      knave her husband will be forth.° Come you to me at night;   *away*
      you shall know how I speed.°   *do*

      FORD   I am blest in your acquaintance. Do you know Ford,
      sir?

240   FALSTAFF   Hang him, poor cuckoldly knave, I know him not. Yet
      I wrong him to call him poor. They say the jealous wittolly°   *willingly cuckolded*
      knave hath masses of money, for the° which his wife seems   *due to*
      to me well favored.° I will use her as the key of the cuckoldly   *good-looking*
      rogue's coffer, and there's my harvest-home.°   *profitable harvest*

245   FORD   I would you knew Ford, sir, that you might avoid him if
      you saw him.

      FALSTAFF   Hang him, mechanical salt-butter⁵ rogue! I will
      stare him out of his wits. I will awe him with my cudgel: it
      shall hang like a meteor° o'er the cuckold's horns. Master   *an (ill-omened) comet*
250   Broom, thou shalt know I will predominate over the peas-
      ant, and thou shalt lie with his wife. Come to me soon at
      night. Ford's a knave, and I will aggravate his style.⁶ Thou,
      Master Broom, shalt know him for knave and cuckold.
      Come to me soon at night.   [*Exit.*]

255   FORD   What a damned epicurean° rascal is this? My heart is   *sensual*
      ready to crack with impatience. Who says this is improvident°   *baseless*
      jealousy? My wife hath sent to him, the hour is fixed, the
      match is made. Would any man have thought this? See the
      hell of having a false woman! My bed shall be abused, my
260   coffers ransacked, my reputation gnawn at, and I shall not
      only receive this villainous wrong, but stand under° the   *have to put up with*
      adoption of abominable terms, and by him that does me this
      wrong. Terms! Names! Amaimon sounds well; Lucifer, well;
      Barbason, well; yet they are devils' additions,° the names of   *names*
265   fiends. But cuckold? Wittol? Cuckold? The devil himself hath
      not such a name. Page is an ass, a secure ass; he will trust his
      wife, he will not be jealous! I will rather trust a Fleming with
      my butter, Parson Hugh the Welshman with my cheese, an
      Irishman with my aqua-vitae° bottle, or a thief to walk my   *whiskey*
270   ambling gelding, than my wife with herself. Then she plots,
      then she ruminates, then she devises; and what they think
      in their hearts they may effect, they will break their hearts
      but they will effect. Heaven be praised for my jealousy! Eleven
      o'clock the hour. I will prevent this, detect my wife, be
275   revenged on Falstaff, and laugh at Page. I will about it. Better
      three hours too soon than a minute too late. Fie, fie, fie! Cuck-
      old, cuckold, cuckold.   *Exit.*

---

5. *mechanical salt-butter:* lower-class cheap-living; Flemish salt butter was less expensive than domestic butter.

6. Increase (irritate) his titles (by adding the title of "cuckold" to Ford's name).

2.3 (Q 7)

Enter [Doctor] CAIUS *[and his man]* RUGBY.

CAIUS   Jack Rugby.

RUGBY   Sir.

CAIUS   Vat is the clock, Jack?

RUGBY   'Tis past the hour, sir, that Sir Hugh promised to meet.

5   CAIUS   By gar, he has save his soul, dat he is no come. He has
    pray his pible well, dat he is no come. By gar, Jack Rugby, he
    is dead already, if he be come.

RUGBY   He is wise, sir. He knew your worship would kill him
    if he came.

10   CAIUS *[drawing his rapier]*   By gar, de herring is no dead so¹ as
    I vill kill him. Take your rapier, Jack. I vill tell you how I vill
    kill him.

RUGBY   Alas, sir, I cannot fence.

CAIUS   Villain, take your rapier.

15   RUGBY   Forbear. Here's company.

    [CAIUS *sheathes his rapier.*]
    [*Enter* SHALLOW, PAGE, *the* HOST *of the Garter,*
    and SLENDER.]

HOST   Bless thee, bully Doctor.

SHALLOW   Save you, Master Doctor Caius.

PAGE   Now, good Master Doctor.

SLENDER   Give you good morrow, sir.

20   CAIUS   Vat be all you one, two, tree, four, come for?

HOST   To see thee fight, to see thee foin,° to see thee traverse,²   *thrust*
    to see thee here, to see thee there, to see thee pass thy punto,
    thy stock, thy reverse, thy distance, thy montant.³ Is he dead,
    my Ethiopian?° Is he dead, my Francisco?° Ha, bully? What   *black man / Frenchman*

25   says my Aesculapius, my Galen, my heart of elder,⁴ ha? Is he
    dead, bully stale?⁵ Is he dead?

CAIUS   By gar, he is de coward jack-priest° of de vorld. He is   *knave-priest*
    not show his face.

HOST   Thou art a Castalian king urinal,⁶ Hector of Greece,°   *(error for "Troy")*

30   my boy.

CAIUS   I pray you bear witness that me have stay six or seven,
    two, tree hours for him, and he is no come.

SHALLOW   He is the wiser man, Master Doctor. He is a curer
    of souls, and you a curer of bodies. If you should fight, you go

35   against the hair° of your professions. Is it not true, Master   *grain*
    Page?

PAGE   Master Shallow, you have yourself been a great fighter,
    though now a man of peace.

SHALLOW   Bodykins,° Master Page, though I now be old and   *By God's dear body*

40   of the peace, if I see a sword out, my finger itches to make
    one.° Though we are justices, and doctors, and churchmen,   *join in*
    Master Page, we have some salt° of our youth in us. We are   *vigor*
    the sons of women, Master Page.

2.3 Location: Windsor Park (east of Windsor).
1. Not so dead (from the proverbial simile "dead as a herring").
2. Move backward and forward.
3. *pass . . . montant:* use your thrust with the sword point, your thrust, your backhand sword blow, your skill in keeping at the right distance, your upward thrust.
4. Replacing "heart of oak"; as the elder is a soft,

low-growing tree, this is an insult disguised as a compliment. Aesculapius was the classical god of medicine. Galen was a physician of ancient Greece.
5. Decoy or dupe; wine or urine (often used for medical diagnosis).
6. Urine bottle. *Castalian:* of the spring Castalia, which was sacred to the Muses; "cast-stale-ian" (one who diagnoses by inspecting urine); Castilian (Spanish).

PAGE 'Tis true, Master Shallow.

45 SHALLOW It will be found so, Master Page. Master Doctor
  Caius, I am come to fetch you home. I am sworn of the
  peace. You have showed yourself a wise physician, and Sir
  Hugh hath shown himself a wise and patient churchman.
  You must go with me, Master Doctor.

50 HOST Pardon, guest° Justice. [to CAIUS] A word, Monsieur   *(at the Host's inn)*
  Mockwater.[7]

CAIUS Mockvater? Vat is dat?

HOST Mockwater, in our English tongue, is valor, bully.

CAIUS By gar, then I have as much mockvater as de Englishman.

55 Scurvy jack-dog° priest! By gar, me vill cut his ears.   *mongrel*

HOST He will clapperclaw thee tightly,° bully.   *maul thee soundly*

CAIUS Clapper-de-claw? Vat is dat?

HOST That is, he will make thee amends.

CAIUS By gar, me do look° he shall clapper-de-claw me, for,   *anticipate*
60 by gar, me vill have it.

HOST And I will provoke him to't, or let him wag.°   *run away*

CAIUS Me tank you for dat.

HOST And moreover, bully— [aside to the others] but first, Mas-
  ter Guest and Master Page, and eke° Cavaliero Slender, go you   *also*
65 through the town to Frogmore.°   *(village near Windsor)*

PAGE [aside to HOST] Sir Hugh is there, is he?

HOST [aside to PAGE] He is there. See what humor he is in,
  and I will bring the doctor about by the fields. Will it do well?

SHALLOW [aside to HOST] We will do it.

70 PAGE, SHALLOW, SLENDER [to CAIUS] Adieu, good Master
  Doctor.   [Exeunt all but the HOST and Doctor CAIUS;
                                    RUGBY *waits aside.*]

CAIUS By gar, me vill kill de priest, for he speak for a jacka-
  nape° to Anne Page.   *on behalf of an idiot*

HOST Let him die. Sheathe thy impatience; throw cold water
75 on thy choler. Go about the fields with me through Frogmore.
  I will bring thee where Mistress Anne Page is, at a farmhouse
  a-feasting, and thou shalt woo her. Cried game![8] Said I well?

CAIUS By gar, me tank you vor dat. By gar, I love you. And I
  shall procure-a you de good guest: de earl, de knight, de lords,
80 de gentlemen, my patients.

HOST For the which I will be thy adversary[9] toward Anne
  Page. Said I well?

CAIUS By gar, 'tis good. Vell said.

HOST Let us wag, then.

85 CAIUS Come at my heels, Jack Rugby.   *Exeunt.*

3.1 (Q 8)
Enter EVANS [with a Bible in one hand and a rapier in
the other, and] SIMPLE [carrying Evans' gown].

EVANS I pray you now, good Master Slender's servingman and
  friend Simple by your name, which way have you looked for
  Master Caius, that calls himself doctor of physic?°   *medicine*

---

7. Implying that Caius's diagnoses from urine are
quackery, or that Caius is sterile (water being semen)
and so lacking in valor.
8. The chase is on.

9. The Host again makes a joke at the expense of
Caius, who understands "adversary" as "advocate."
3.1 Location: In fields near Frogmore.

SIMPLE   Marry, sir, the Petty Ward, the Park Ward,[1] every
5   way—Old Windsor way[2] and every way but the town way.
EVANS   I most fehemently desire you, you will also look that
   way.
SIMPLE   I will, sir.   [*Exit.*]
EVANS   Pless my soul! How full of cholers° I am, and trempling   *anger*
10   of mind! I shall be glad if he have deceived me. How melan-
   cholies I am! I will knog° his urinals about his knave's cos-   *knock*
   tard,° when I have good opportunities for the 'ork.° Pless my   *head / work*
   soul!
[*Sings.*]   To shallow rivers to whose falls
15   Melodious birds sings madrigals.
         There will we make our peds of roses,
         And a thousand fragrant posies.[3]
         To shallow—
   Mercy on me, I have a great dispositions to cry.
20   [*Sings.*]   Melodious birds sing madrigals.—
         When as I sat in Pabylon[4]—
         And a thousand vagrant posies.
         To shallow, etc.
         [*Enter* SIMPLE.]
SIMPLE   Yonder he° is coming, this way, Sir Hugh.   *(Caius)*
25   EVANS   He's welcome.
   [*Sings.*]   To shallow rivers to whose falls—
   Heaven prosper the right. What weapons is° he?   *has*
SIMPLE   No weapons, sir. There comes my master, Master Shal-
   low, and another gentleman, from Frogmore, over the stile,
30   this way.
EVANS   Pray you give me my gown—or else keep it in your arms.
         [*He seems to read his Bible.*]
         [*Enter* PAGE, SHALLOW, *and* SLENDER.]
SHALLOW   How now, Master Parson? Good morrow, good Sir
   Hugh. Keep a gamester from the dice and a good student
   from his book, and it is wonderful.
35   SLENDER [*aside*]   Ah, sweet Anne Page.
PAGE   Save you, good Sir Hugh.
EVANS   Pless you from° his mercy sake, all of you.   *for*
SHALLOW   What? The sword and the word?° Do you study them   *the Bible*
   both, Master Parson?
40   PAGE   And youthful still in your doublet and hose,[5] this raw
   rheumatic day!
EVANS   There is reasons and causes for it.
PAGE   We are come to you to do a good office, Master Parson.
EVANS   Fery well. What is it?
45   PAGE   Yonder is a most reverend gentleman who, belike,° hav-   *probably*
   ing received wrong by some person, is at most odds with his
   own gravity and patience that ever you saw.
SHALLOW   I have lived fourscore years and upward. I never
   heard a man of his place, gravity, and learning so wide of his
50   own respect.[6]

---

1. Toward the Little Park and the Great Park.
2. Toward Old Windsor (a village near Shakespeare's
Windsor).
3. Somewhat misrecalled lines from "Come live with
me and be my love," a song by Christopher Marlowe.
4. Evans inserts the first line of a metrical version of

Psalm 137 (with "I" for "we"), which describes the
weeping of the exiled Israelites in Babylon.
5. Close-fitting jacket and tights—that is, without a
cloak.
6. Indifferent to his own good reputation.

EVANS What is he?

PAGE I think you know him: Master Doctor Caius, the renowned French physician.

EVANS Got's will and his passion of my heart! I had as lief° *as much wished*
55 you would tell me of a mess of porridge.° *thick soup*

PAGE Why?

EVANS He has no more knowledge in Hibbocrates[7] and Galen, and he is a knave besides—a cowardly knave as you would desires to be acquainted withal.

60 PAGE [*to* SHALLOW] I warrant you, he's the man should fight with him.

SLENDER [*aside*] O sweet Anne Page!

SHALLOW [*to* PAGE] It appears so by his weapons. Keep them asunder—here comes Doctor Caius.

[*Enter the* HOST, CAIUS, *and* RUGBY.]
[CAIUS *and* EVANS *offer to fight.*]

65 PAGE Nay, good Master Parson, keep in your weapon.

SHALLOW So do you, good Master Doctor.

HOST Disarm them, and let them question.° *debate*
[PAGE *and* SHALLOW *take their weapons.*]
Let them keep their limbs whole and hack our English.

CAIUS [*aside to* EVANS] I pray you, let-a me speak a word with
70 your ear. [*aloud*] Vherefore vill you not meet-a me?

EVANS [*aside to* CAIUS] Pray you use your patience. [*aloud*] In good time.

CAIUS By gar, you are de coward, de jack-dog, john-ape!

EVANS [*aside to* CAIUS] Pray you let us not be laughingstocks
75 to other men's humors. I desire you in friendship, and I will one way or other make you amends. [*aloud*] I will knog your urinal about your knave's cogscomb!° *coxcomb; head*

CAIUS *Diable!*° Jack Rugby, mine Host de Jarteer, have I not *Devil*
stay for him to kill him? Have I not? At de place I did
80 appoint?

EVANS As I am a Christians soul, now look you, this is the place appointed! I'll be judgment° by mine Host of the Garter. *judged*

HOST Peace, I say, Gallia and Gaul, French and Welsh, soul-curer and body-curer![8]

85 CAIUS Ay, dat is very good, excellent.

HOST Peace, I say. Hear mine Host of the Garter. Am I politic?° *devious*
Am I subtle?° Am I a machiavel?[9] Shall I lose my doctor? No, *crafty*
he gives me the potions and the motions.° Shall I lose my *bowel movements*
parson, my priest, my Sir Hugh? No, he gives me the prov-
90 erbs and the no-verbs.[1] [*to* CAIUS] Give me thy hand terrestrial.° [*to* EVANS] Give me thy hand celestial—so! Boys of *(as bodily curer)*
art,° I have deceived you both: I have directed you to wrong *learning*
places. Your hearts are mighty, your skins are whole, and let
burned sack be the issue!° [*to* SHALLOW *and* PAGE] Come, lay *outcome*
95 their swords to pawn.[2] [*to* EVANS *and* CAIUS] Follow me, lads
of peace, follow, follow, follow! [*Exit.*]

---

7. Hippocrates (ancient Greek physician).
8. *Gallia and Gaul:* Wales and France. TEXTUAL COMMENT For the possible stage business that accompanies the three paired addresses to the two antagonists, see Digital Edition TC 2 (Folio edited text).
9. Follower of Niccolò Machiavelli, Italian political theorist reviled by the Elizabethans, who was held to epitomize the "politic" and "subtle."
1. Prohibitions; verbal errors (the Welshman's misuse of standard English).
2. As a pledge; because they are not needed.

SHALLOW   Trust me, a mad° host! Follow, gentlemen, follow.   *wildly exuberant*
         [*Exeunt* SHALLOW *and* PAGE.]
SLENDER   O sweet Anne Page!   [*Exit.*]
CAIUS   Ha, do I perceive dat? Have you make-a de *sot*° of us,   *fool*
100   ha, ha?
EVANS   This is well. He has made us his vlowting-stog.³ I desire
      you that we may be friends, and let us knog our prains
      together to be revenge on this same scall,° scurvy, cogging   *scabby*
      companion,° the Host of the Garter.   *cheating rogue*
105   CAIUS   By gar, with all my heart. He promise to bring me where
      is Anne Page. By gar, he deceive me too.
EVANS   Well, I will smite his noddles.° Pray you, follow.   *head*
                                          [*Exeunt.*]

3.2 (Q 9)
         Enter MISTRESS PAGE [*and*] ROBIN.
MISTRESS PAGE   Nay, keep your way,° little gallant. You were   *go on*
      wont° to be a follower,° but now you are a leader. Whether   *accustomed / servant*
      had you rather:° lead mine eyes, or eye your master's heels? *Which would you prefer*
ROBIN   I had rather, forsooth, go before you like a man than
5   follow him° like a dwarf.   *(Falstaff)*
MISTRESS PAGE   Oh, you are a flattering boy! Now I see you'll
      be a courtier.
         [*Enter* FORD.]
FORD   Well met, Mistress Page. Whither go you?
MISTRESS PAGE   Truly, sir, to see your wife. Is she at home?
10   FORD   Ay, and as idle as she may hang together for want¹ of
      company. I think if your husbands were dead, you two would
      marry.
MISTRESS PAGE   Be sure of that—two other husbands.
FORD   [*indicating* ROBIN]   Where had you this pretty weather-
15   cock?°   *(Robin)*
MISTRESS PAGE   I cannot tell what the dickens his name is my
      husband had him of.° —What do you call your knight's   *got him from*
      name, sirrah?
ROBIN   Sir John Falstaff.
20   FORD   Sir John Falstaff?
MISTRESS PAGE   He, he. I can never hit on 's name. There is
      such a league° between my goodman° and he! Is your wife at *friendship / husband*
      home indeed?
FORD   Indeed she is.
25   MISTRESS PAGE   By your leave, sir, I am sick till I see her.
                                    [*Exit with* ROBIN.]
FORD   Has Page any brains? Hath he any eyes? Hath he any
      thinking? Sure they sleep—he hath no use of them! Why, this
      boy will carry a letter twenty mile as easy as a cannon will
      shoot point-blank twelve score.² He pieces out° his wife's   *increases*
30   inclination. He gives her folly motion and advantage.³ And
      now she's going to my wife, and Falstaff's boy with her. A
      man may hear this shower sing in the wind°—and Falstaff's   *hear trouble brewing*

---

3. Flouting-stock (laughingstock).
3.2 Location: A street in Windsor.
1. And as bored as she can stand to be without falling apart, for lack.

2. Will shoot straight 240 yards.
3. He gives her lust ("folly") prompting and
opportunity.

boy with her! Good plots they are laid, and our revolted°   *disloyal*
wives share damnation together. Well, I will take him,° then   *catch him by surprise*
35   torture my wife, pluck the borrowed veil of modesty from
the so-seeming Mistress Page, divulge° Page himself for a   *reveal*
secure° and willful Actaeon,° and to these violent proceed- *overconfident / cuckold*
ings all my neighbors shall cry aim.° [*A clock strikes.*] The   *shall applaud*
clock gives me my cue, and my assurance bids me search.
40   There I shall find Falstaff. I shall be rather praised for this
than mocked, for it is as positive as the earth is firm that Falstaff is there. I will go.

       [*Enter* PAGE, SHALLOW, SLENDER, HOST, EVANS,
       CAIUS, *and* RUGBY.]

SHALLOW, PAGE, SLENDER, HOST, EVANS, CAIUS   Well met, Master Ford.

45 FORD   Trust me, a good knot!° I have good cheer° at home,   *group / food and drink*
and I pray you all go with me.

SHALLOW   I must excuse myself, Master Ford.

SLENDER   And so must I, sir. We have appointed to dine with
Mistress Anne, and I would not break with° her for more   *break my word to*
50   money than I'll speak of.

SHALLOW   We have lingered about° a match between Anne   *delayed in concluding*
Page and my cousin Slender, and this day we shall have our
answer.

SLENDER   I hope I have your good will, Father Page.

55 PAGE   You have, Master Slender. I stand wholly for you, but
my wife, Master Doctor, is for you altogether.

CAIUS   Ay, be gar, and de maid is love-a me. My nursh-a°   *housekeeper*
Quickly tell me so mush.

HOST   What say you to young Master Fenton? He capers,° he   *leaps in dancing*
60   dances, he has eyes of youth. He writes verses, he speaks
holiday,° he smells April and May. He will carry't,° he will   *gaily / succeed*
carry't, 'tis in his buttons,° he will carry't!   *youth*

PAGE   Not by my consent, I promise you. The gentleman is of
no having,° he kept company with the wild prince and Poins.[4]   *property*
65   He is of too high a region;° he knows too much.[5] No, he shall   *rank*
not knit a knot in° his fortunes with the finger of my sub-   *strengthen*
stance.° If he take her, let him take her simply.° The wealth I *wealth / without dowry*
have waits on my consent, and my consent goes not that way.

FORD   I beseech you heartily, some of you go home with me to
70   dinner. Besides your cheer you shall have sport: I will show
you a monster.° Master Doctor, you shall go. So shall you,   *(Falstaff)*
Master Page, and you, Sir Hugh.

SHALLOW   Well, fare you well. [*aside to* SLENDER] We shall
have the freer wooing at Master Page's.

                              [*Exit with* SLENDER.]

75 CAIUS   Go home, John Rugby. I come anon.   [*Exit* RUGBY.]

HOST   Farewell, my hearts. I will to my honest knight Falstaff
and drink canary° with him.   *Canary Islands wine*

FORD [*aside*]   I think I shall drink in pipe-wine first with him.

---

4. Prince Hal (the future Henry V) and Poins (line   than Fenton's, companions.
64) in *1* and *2 Henry IV*—actually Falstaff's, rather   5. *knows too much*: is too sophisticated and courtly.

I'll make him dance.[6] [*aloud*] Will you go, gentles?°   *gentlemen*
80 PAGE, CAIUS, *and* EVANS Have with you° to see this monster!   *We are coming*
                                Exeunt.

3.3 (Q 10)

Enter MISTRESS FORD [*and*] MISTRESS PAGE.

MISTRESS FORD [*calling*] What, John! What, Robert!
MISTRESS PAGE Quickly, quickly! Is the buck-basket°—   *laundry basket*
MISTRESS FORD I warrant.° —What, Robert, I say.   *I'm sure it is*
MISTRESS PAGE Come, come, come!
    [*Enter two* SERVANTS *and a great buck-basket.*]
5 MISTRESS FORD Here, set it down.
MISTRESS PAGE Give your men the charge.° We must be brief.   *instructions*
MISTRESS FORD [*to the* SERVANTS] Marry, as I told you before,
    John and Robert, be ready here hard by in the brewhouse
    and, when I suddenly call you, come forth and without any
10   pause or staggering take this basket on your shoulders. That
    done, trudge with it in all haste, and carry it among the
    whitsters° in Datchet Mead,[1] and there empty it in the   *linen bleachers*
    muddy ditch close by the Thames' side.
MISTRESS PAGE [*to the* SERVANTS] You will do it?
15 MISTRESS FORD [*to* MISTRESS PAGE] I ha' told them over and
    over. They lack no direction.° [*to the* SERVANTS] Begone, and *instructions*
    come when you are called.   [*Exeunt* SERVANTS.]
      [*Enter* ROBIN.]
MISTRESS PAGE Here comes little Robin.
MISTRESS FORD How now, my eyas-musket,° what news with *young sparrow hawk*
20   you?
ROBIN My master Sir John is come in at your back door, Mis-
    tress Ford, and requests your company.
MISTRESS PAGE You little Jack-a-Lent,° have you been true to us? *Lenten puppet*
ROBIN Ay, I'll be sworn! My master knows not of your being
25   here, and hath threatened to put me into everlasting liberty
    if I tell you of it,° for he swears he'll turn me away.[2]   *(Falstaff's visit)*
MISTRESS PAGE Thou'rt a good boy. This secrecy of thine shall
    be a tailor to thee, and shall make thee a new doublet and
    hose. I'll go hide me.
30 MISTRESS FORD Do so. [*to* ROBIN] Go tell thy master I am alone.
                               [*Exit* ROBIN.]
  —Mistress Page, remember you your cue.
MISTRESS PAGE I warrant thee. If I do not act it, hiss me.
                                  [*Exit.*]
MISTRESS FORD Go to, then. We'll use this unwholesome
    humidity,° this gross watery pumpkin. We'll teach him to   *body fluids*
35   know turtles from jays.[3]
      [*Enter* FALSTAFF.]

---

6. *drink . . . dance:* make it uncomfortable for Falstaff. Pipe wine is wine from the cask, with a pun on
"the whine of musical pipes," which are played for a
dance. Ford also puns on "canary" (line 77), which is
also a dance. Drinking becomes a metaphor for
Ford's intention to make Falstaff dance to his tune.

3.3 Location: Ford's house.
1. Meadow situated between Windsor Little Park
and the Thames.
2. He'll dismiss me.
3. Gaudy birds: hence, flirtatious women. *turtles:*
turtledoves, proverbially faithful.

FALSTAFF Have I caught thee, my heavenly jewel? Why, now
let me die,° for I have lived long enough. This is the period°　　*(death); (orgasm) / end*
of my ambition. Oh, this blessed hour!

MISTRESS FORD O sweet Sir John.

40 FALSTAFF Mistress Ford, I cannot cog,° I cannot prate, Mis-　　*lie*
tress Ford. Now shall I sin in my wish: I would thy husband
were dead. I'll speak it before the best lord—I would make
thee my lady.

MISTRESS FORD I, your lady, Sir John? Alas, I should be a piti-
45 ful lady.

FALSTAFF Let the court of France show me such another. I
see how thine eye would emulate the diamond. Thou hast
the right arched beauty of the brow that becomes the ship-
tire, the tire-valiant, or any tire of Venetian admittance.[4]

50 MISTRESS FORD A plain kerchief, Sir John. My brows become
nothing else, nor that well neither.

FALSTAFF Thou art a tyrant° to say so. Thou wouldst make an　　*(punning on "tire")*
absolute° courtier, and the firm fixture of thy foot would give　　*a perfect*
an excellent motion to thy gait in a semicircled farthingale.[5]
55 I see what thou wert° if fortune thy foe were not, nature thy　　*would be*
friend.° Come, thou canst not hide it.　　*nature being thy friend*

MISTRESS FORD Believe me, there's no such thing in me.

FALSTAFF What made me love thee? Let that persuade thee.
There's something extraordinary in thee. Come, I cannot cog
60 and say thou art this and that, like a-many of these lisping
hawthorn buds° that come like women in men's apparel and　　*young perfumed wooers*
smell like Bucklersbury[6] in simple time.[7] I cannot, but I love
thee, none but thee; and thou deserv'st it.

MISTRESS FORD Do not betray° me, sir. I fear you love Mistress　　*deceive*
65 Page.

FALSTAFF Thou mightst as well say I love to walk by the Coun-
ter gate,° which is as hateful to me as the reek of a limekiln.[8]　　*debtors' prison*

MISTRESS FORD Well, heaven knows how I love you, and you
shall one day find it.

70 FALSTAFF Keep in that mind. I'll deserve it.

MISTRESS FORD Nay, I must tell you, so you do, or else I could
not be in that mind.

　　　　　[*Enter* ROBIN.]

ROBIN Mistress Ford, Mistress Ford, here's Mistress Page at
the door, sweating and blowing° and looking wildly, and　　*puffing*
75 would needs speak with you presently!°　　*immediately*

FALSTAFF She shall not see me. I will ensconce me behind the
arras.°　　*wall curtain*

MISTRESS FORD Pray you do so. She's a very tattling woman.

　　　　　[FALSTAFF *stands behind the arras.*]
　　　　　[*Enter* MISTRESS PAGE.]

—What's the matter? How now?

80 MISTRESS PAGE O Mistress Ford, what have you done? You're
shamed, you're overthrown, you're undone forever!

---

4. Fancifully extravagant headdresses ("tires"), the
"ship-tire" in the form of a ship, that were acceptable
in Venice. "Tire" is from "attire."
5. Skirt shaped with covered hoops at the back.
6. London street where herbs were sold.

7. Summer (when medicinal herbs, or "simples,"
were available).
8. *reek of a limekiln:* smoke of a furnace used to produce lime by heating limestone.

MISTRESS FORD What's the matter, good Mistress Page?

MISTRESS PAGE Oh, welladay,° Mistress Ford, having an honest   *alas*
man to° your husband, to give him such cause of suspicion!   *as*

85 MISTRESS FORD What cause of suspicion?

MISTRESS PAGE What cause of suspicion? Out upon you!° How   *(a reproach)*
am I mistook in you!

MISTRESS FORD Why, alas, what's the matter?

MISTRESS PAGE Your husband's coming hither, woman, with
90 all the officers in Windsor, to search for a gentleman that he
says is here now in the house, by your consent, to take an ill
advantage of his absence. You are undone.

MISTRESS FORD 'Tis not so, I hope.

MISTRESS PAGE Pray heaven it be not so, that you have such a
95 man here. But 'tis most certain your husband's coming with
half Windsor at his heels to search for such a one. I come
before to tell you. If you know yourself clear,° why, I am glad   *innocent*
of it. But if you have a friend° here, convey, convey him out!   *lover*
Be not amazed,° call all your senses to you, defend your   *bewildered*
100 reputation, or bid farewell to your good° life forever.   *respectable*

MISTRESS FORD What shall I do? There is a gentleman, my
dear friend, and I fear not mine own shame so much as his
peril. I had rather than a thousand pound he were out of the
house.

105 MISTRESS PAGE For shame, never stand° "you had rather" and   *waste time over*
"you had rather"! Your husband's here at hand. Bethink you
of some conveyance.° In the house you cannot hide him. Oh,   *trick; transport*
how have you deceived me! Look, here is a basket. If he be of
any reasonable stature, he may creep in here and throw foul
110 linen upon him, as if it were going to bucking.° Or it is whit-   *washing*
ing° time—send him by your two men to Datchet Mead.   *bleaching*

MISTRESS FORD He's too big to go in there: what shall I do?

FALSTAFF [*rushing forward*] Let me see't, let me see't, oh, let
me see't! I'll in, I'll in. —Follow your friend's counsel—I'll in!

115 MISTRESS PAGE What, Sir John Falstaff? [*aside to him*] Are
these your letters, knight?

FALSTAFF [*aside to her*] I love thee. Help me away! Let me
creep in here. I'll never—
[*Sir John goes into the basket; they put clothes
over him.*]

MISTRESS PAGE [*to* ROBIN] Help to cover your master, boy.
120 —Call your men, Mistress Ford. [*aside to* FALSTAFF] You dissembling knight!

MISTRESS FORD What John, Robert! John!
[*Enter the two* SERVANTS.]
Go, take up these clothes here, quickly. Where's the cowl-
staff?° Look how you drumble!° Carry them to the laun-   *basket pole / dawdle*
125 dress in Datchet Mead. Quickly, come.
[SERVANTS *carry the basket away.*]
[*Enter* FORD, PAGE, CAIUS, EVANS *to meet it.*]

FORD [*to the gentlemen*] Pray you come near. If I suspect
without cause, why then make sport at me, then let me be
your jest—I deserve it. [*to* SERVANTS] How now? Whither
bear you this?

130 SERVANTS To the laundress, forsooth.

MISTRESS FORD   Why, what have you to do° whither they bear   *to do with*
it? You were best° meddle with buck-washing.[9]   *(sarcastic)*
FORD   Buck? I would I could wash myself of the buck! Buck,
buck, buck, ay, buck! I warrant you, buck! And of the season
135   too, it shall appear.
                    [*Exeunt* SERVANTS *with the buck-basket and* ROBIN.]
Gentlemen, I have dreamed tonight;° I'll tell you my dream.   *last night*
Here, here, here be my keys, ascend° my chambers, search,   *go up to*
seek, find out! I'll warrant we'll unkennel° the fox. Let me   *dislodge*
stop this way° first. [*He locks the door.*] So, now uncase!   *passage*
140   PAGE   Good Master Ford, be contented. You wrong yourself
too much.
FORD   True, Master Page. —Up, gentlemen, you shall see
sport anon. Follow me, gentlemen.   [*Exit.*]
EVANS   This is fery fantastical humors and jealousies.
145   CAIUS   By gar, 'tis no the fashion of France. It is not jealous in
France.
PAGE   Nay, follow him, gentlemen. See the issue of his search.
                              [*Exeunt all the gentlemen.*]
MISTRESS PAGE   Is there not a double excellency in this?
MISTRESS FORD   I know not which pleases me better, that my
150   husband is deceived, or Sir John.
MISTRESS PAGE   What a taking° was he in, when your husband   *panic*
asked who was in the basket!
MISTRESS FORD   I am half afraid he will have need of washing.[1] So throwing him into the water will do him a benefit.
155   MISTRESS PAGE   Hang him, dishonest rascal! I would all of the
same strain were in the same distress.
MISTRESS FORD   I think my husband hath some special suspicion of Falstaff's being here, for I never saw him so gross in
his jealousy till now.
160   MISTRESS PAGE   I will lay a plot to try° that, and we will yet   *test*
have more tricks with Falstaff. His dissolute disease will
scarce obey° this medicine.   *be cured by*
MISTRESS FORD   Shall we send that foolish carrion,° Mistress   *rotten flesh*
Quickly, to him, and excuse his throwing into the water, and
165   give him another hope, to betray him to another punishment?
MISTRESS PAGE   We will do it. Let him be sent for tomorrow
eight o'clock to have amends.
                    [*Enter* FORD, PAGE, CAIUS, *and* EVANS.]
FORD   I cannot find him. Maybe the knave bragged of that he
could not compass.°   *accomplish*
170   MISTRESS PAGE [*aside to* MISTRESS FORD]   Heard you that?
MISTRESS FORD   You use me well, Master Ford, do you?
FORD   Ay, I do so.
MISTRESS FORD   Heaven make you better than your thoughts.
FORD   Amen.
175   MISTRESS PAGE   You do yourself mighty wrong, Master Ford.
FORD   Ay, ay, I must bear it.
EVANS   If there be anypody in the house, and in the cham-
bers, and in the coffers, and in the presses,° heaven forgive   *large recessed cupboards*
my sins at the day of judgment!

---

9. Washing that needs bleaching (but Ford thinks of   meaning "to copulate").
"buck" as "stag," the horned cuckold, and as a verb   1. Fear will have made him urinate.

180 CAIUS Begar, nor I too. There is nobodies.

PAGE Fie, fie, Master Ford, are you not ashamed? What spirit,
what devil suggests this imagination? I would not ha' your
distemper in this kind for the wealth of Windsor Castle.

FORD 'Tis my fault, Master Page. I suffer for it.

185 EVANS You suffer for a pad conscience. Your wife is as honest
a 'omans as I will desires among five thousand, and five hundred too.

CAIUS By gar,° I see 'tis an honest woman.   *By God*

FORD Well, I promised you a dinner. Come, come, walk in
190 the park. I pray you pardon me. I will hereafter make known
to you why I have done this. —Come, wife. Come, Mistress
Page. I pray you pardon me, pray heartily pardon me.

PAGE Let's go in, gentlemen, [*aside to* CAIUS *and* EVANS] but,
trust me, we'll mock him. —[*aloud*] I do invite you tomorrow
195 morning to my house to breakfast. After, we'll a-birding°   *go bird hunting*
together. I have a fine hawk for[2] the bush. Shall it be so?

FORD Anything.

EVANS If there is one, I shall make two in the company.

CAIUS If there be one, or two, I shall make-a the turd.

200 FORD Pray you go, Master Page.

[*Exeunt all but* EVANS *and* CAIUS.]

EVANS I pray you now, remembrance tomorrow on the lousy
knave, mine Host.[3]

CAIUS Dat is good, by gar—with all my heart!

EVANS A lousy knave, to have his gibes and his mockeries.

Exeunt.

3.4 (Q 12)

Enter FENTON [*and*] ANNE *Page.*

FENTON I see I cannot get thy father's love;
Therefore no more turn me to him, sweet Nan.

ANNE Alas, how then?

FENTON   Why, thou must be thyself.°   *in charge of yourself*
He doth object I am too great of birth
5 And that, my state being galled with° my expense,   *estate being hurt by*
I seek to heal it only by his wealth.
Besides these, other bars he lays before me—
My riots past, my wild societies°—   *companionships*
And tells me 'tis a thing impossible
10 I should love thee but as a property.

ANNE Maybe he tells you true.

FENTON No, heaven so speed° me in my time to come!   *as heaven may prosper*
Albeit I will confess thy father's wealth
Was the first motive that I wooed thee, Anne,
15 Yet wooing thee, I found thee of more value
Than stamps in gold° or sums in sealèd bags,   *stamped gold coins*
And 'tis the very riches of thyself
That now I aim at.

ANNE   Gentle Master Fenton,[1]
Yet seek my father's love, still seek it, sir.

---

2. For driving birds into.
3. A cryptic reference to the "revenge" proposal at
3.1.101–04.

3.4 Location: Outside Page's house.
1. For a very different handling of this moment, see
Q 12.11–31.

20   If opportunity and humblest suit
      Cannot attain it, why then—

                [Enter SHALLOW, SLENDER, *and* MISTRESS QUICKLY.]
                          Hark you hither.

              [She whispers to him aside.]

SHALLOW Break their talk, Mistress Quickly. My kinsman
    shall speak for himself.

SLENDER I'll make a shaft or a bolt on't.[2] 'Slid,° 'tis but   *By God's eyelid*
25   venturing.

              *[*MISTRESS QUICKLY *approaches* ANNE.]

SHALLOW Be not dismayed.

SLENDER No, she shall not dismay me. I care not for that, but
    that I am afeared.

MISTRESS QUICKLY *[to* ANNE*]* Hark ye, Master Slender would
30   speak a word with you.

ANNE I come to him. *[aside to* FENTON*]* This is my father's
    choice.
    Oh, what a world of vile ill-favored° faults   *ugly*
    Looks handsome in three hundred pounds a year!°   *(moderate wealth)*

           *[*ANNE *moves toward* SHALLOW *and* SLENDER.]

MISTRESS QUICKLY *[drawing* FENTON *aside]* And how does
35   good Master Fenton? Pray you, a word with you.

SHALLOW She's coming. To her, coz! O boy, thou hadst a
    father°—   *be manly; you're manly*

SLENDER I had a father, Mistress Anne; my uncle can tell you
    good jests of him. —Pray you, uncle, tell Mistress Anne the
40   jest how my father stole two geese out of a pen, good uncle.

SHALLOW Mistress Anne, my cousin loves you.

SLENDER Ay, that I do, as well as I love any woman in
    Gloucestershire.

SHALLOW He will maintain you like a gentlewoman.

45 SLENDER Ay, that I will, come cut and long tail,° under the   *no matter what*
    degree° of a squire.   *in the rank*

SHALLOW He will make you a hundred and fifty pounds
    jointure.°   *widowhood settlement*

ANNE Good Master Shallow, let him woo for himself.

50 SHALLOW Marry, I thank you for it. I thank you for that good
    comfort. *[withdrawing]* —She calls you, coz. I'll leave you.

ANNE Now, Master Slender.

SLENDER Now, good Mistress Anne.

ANNE What is your will?

55 SLENDER My will? 'Od's heartlings,° that's a pretty jest indeed.   *By God's little hearts*
    I ne'er made my will yet, I thank heaven. I am not such a
    sickly creature, I give heaven praise.

ANNE I mean, Master Slender, what would you with me?

SLENDER Truly, for mine own part, I would little or nothing
60   with you. Your father and my uncle hath made motions.° If it   *proposals*
    be my luck, so; if not, happy man be his dole.[3] They can tell
    you how things go better than I can. You may ask your father.
    Here he comes.

              [Enter PAGE *and* MISTRESS PAGE.]

---

2. I'll do it one way or another (with possible sexual   3. Good luck to the successful suitor.
connotation).

PAGE   Now, Master Slender. —Love him, daughter Anne.

65   Why, how now? What does Master Fenton here?

[*to* FENTON] You wrong me, sir, thus still to haunt my house.

I told you, sir, my daughter is disposed of.

FENTON   Nay, Master Page, be not impatient.

MISTRESS PAGE   Good Master Fenton, come not to my child.

PAGE   She is no match for you.

70   FENTON   Sir, will you hear me?

PAGE   No, good Master Fenton.

—Come, Master Shallow. Come, son Slender, in.

—Knowing my mind, you wrong me, Master Fenton.

             [*Exit* PAGE *with* SHALLOW *and* SLENDER.]

MISTRESS QUICKLY [*aside to* FENTON]   Speak to Mistress Page.

75   FENTON   Good Mistress Page, for that° I love your daughter   *because*

In such a righteous fashion as I do,

Perforce,° against all checks,° rebukes, and manners,   *Of necessity / reproofs*

I must advance the colors° of my love   *military banners*

And not retire. Let me have your good will.

80   ANNE   Good mother, do not marry me to yond fool.

MISTRESS PAGE   I mean it not. I seek you a better husband.

MISTRESS QUICKLY   That's my master, Master Doctor.

ANNE   Alas, I had rather be set quick i'th' earth°   *half-buried alive*

And bowled to death with turnips!

85   MISTRESS PAGE [*to* ANNE]   Come, trouble not yourself. —Good

      Master Fenton,

I will not be your friend, nor enemy.

My daughter will I question how she loves you,

And, as I find her, so am I affected.°   *inclined*

Till then, farewell, sir. She must needs go in,

90   Her father will be angry.

FENTON   Farewell, gentle Mistress. Farewell, Nan.

             [*Exeunt* MISTRESS PAGE *and* ANNE.]

MISTRESS QUICKLY   This is my doing now. "Nay," said I, "will

you cast away your child on a fool and a physician? Look on

Master Fenton." This is my doing.

95   FENTON   I thank thee, and I pray thee, [*handing her a ring*]

      once° tonight   *at some time*

Give my sweet Nan this ring. [*He gives her money.*] There's

      for thy pains.

MISTRESS QUICKLY   Now heaven send thee good fortune!

                      [*Exit* FENTON.]

A kind heart he hath. A woman would run through fire and

water for such a kind heart. But yet I would my master had

100   Mistress Anne, or I would Master Slender had her. Or, in

sooth, I would Master Fenton had her. I will do what I can

for them all three, for so I have promised, and I'll be as good

as my word, but speciously[4] for Master Fenton. Well, I must

of° another errand to Sir John Falstaff from my two mis-   *run*

105   tresses. What a beast am I to slack° it!   *Exit.*   *to be remiss in*

---

4. *speciously*: error for "specially," but Quickly's mistake inadvertently reveals the truth that she is playing
falsely with Fenton.

3.5 (Q 11)

Enter FALSTAFF.

FALSTAFF   Bardolph, I say!
        [*Enter* BARDOLPH.]
BARDOLPH   Here, sir.
FALSTAFF   Go, fetch me a quart of sack. Put a toast° in't.   *piece of hot toast*
        [*Exit* BARDOLPH.]
Have I lived to be carried in a basket like a barrow° of   *wheelbarrow*
5   butcher's offal?° And to be thrown in the Thames? Well, if I   *waste meat*
    be served such another trick, I'll have my brains ta'en out and
    buttered,¹ and give them to a dog for a New Year's gift. The
    rogues slighted° me into the river with as little remorse as   *slid; dumped scornfully*
    they would have drowned a blind bitch's° puppies, fifteen   *bitch's blind*
10   i'th' litter. And you may know by my size that I have a kind
    of alacrity in sinking. If the bottom were as deep as hell, I
    should down.° I had been drowned but that the shore was   *reach the bottom*
    shelvy° and shallow: a death that I abhor. For the water   *made of sandbanks*
    swells a man, and what a thing should I have been when I
15   had been swelled! I should have been a mountain of mummy.°   *dead flesh*
        [*Enter* BARDOLPH *with sack.*]
BARDOLPH   Here's Mistress Quickly, sir, to speak with you.
FALSTAFF   Come, let me pour in some sack to the Thames
    water, for my belly's as cold as if I had swallowed snowballs
    for pills to cool the reins.° [*He drinks.*] Call her in.   *kidneys*
20   BARDOLPH   Come in, woman.
        [*Enter* MISTRESS QUICKLY.]
MISTRESS QUICKLY   By your leave, I cry you mercy.² Give your
    worship good morrow.
FALSTAFF [*to* BARDOLPH]   Take away these chalices. Go, brew°   *prepare*
    me a pottle° of sack finely.   *two quarts*
25   BARDOLPH   With eggs, sir?
FALSTAFF   Simple of itself.° I'll no pullet°-sperm in my brewage.   *Pure / young hen*
        [*Exit* BARDOLPH.]
    —How now?
MISTRESS QUICKLY   Marry, sir, I come to your worship from
    Mistress Ford.
30   FALSTAFF   Mistress Ford? I have had Ford enough. I was
    thrown into the ford; I have my belly full of ford.
MISTRESS QUICKLY   Alas the day, good heart, that was not her
    fault. She does so take on with her men; they mistook their
    erection.³
35   FALSTAFF   So did I mine, to build upon a foolish woman's
    promise.
MISTRESS QUICKLY   Well, she laments, sir, for it, that it would
    yearn° your heart to see it. Her husband goes this morning   *grieve*
    a-birding; she desires you once more to come to her, between
40   eight and nine. I must carry her word° quickly. She'll make   *your reply*
    you amends, I warrant you.
FALSTAFF   Well, I will visit her. Tell her so, and bid her think
    what a man is. Let her consider his frailty, and then judge of
    my merit.

3.5 Location: The Garter Inn.
1. "Buttered" brains may have meant "foolish."
2. *I cry you mercy:* Excuse me.

3. Quickly means that Mistress Ford "does take on"
(scold) her servants, who misunderstood her direction,
but there's an obvious, unintentional sexual pun.

45   MISTRESS QUICKLY   I will tell her.
     FALSTAFF   Do so. Between nine and ten, say'st thou?
     MISTRESS QUICKLY   Eight and nine, sir.
     FALSTAFF   Well, be gone. I will not miss° her.   *fail*
     MISTRESS QUICKLY   Peace be with you, sir.   [*Exit.*]
50   FALSTAFF   I marvel I hear not of Master Broom; he sent me
     word to stay° within. I like his money well. Oh, here he comes.   *wait for him*
           [*Enter* FORD *disguised as Broom.*]
     FORD   Bless you, sir.
     FALSTAFF   Now, Master Broom, you come to know what hath
     passed between me and Ford's wife.
55   FORD   That indeed, Sir John, is my business.
     FALSTAFF   Master Broom, I will not lie to you. I was at her
     house the hour she appointed me.
     FORD   And sped you,° sir?   *did you succeed*
     FALSTAFF   Very ill-favoredly,° Master Broom.   *badly*
60   FORD   How so, sir? Did she change her determination?
     FALSTAFF   No, Master Broom, but the peaking cornuto° her   *sneaking cuckold*
     husband, Master Broom, dwelling in a continual 'larum° of   *alarm*
     jealousy, comes me° in the instant of our encounter, after we   *comes*
     had embraced, kissed, protested, and, as it were, spoke the
65   prologue of our comedy; and at his heels, a rabble of his
     companions, thither provoked and instigated by his distem-
     per, and, forsooth, to search his house for his wife's love.
     FORD   What? While you were there?
     FALSTAFF   While I was there.
70   FORD   And did he search for you and could not find you?
     FALSTAFF   You shall hear. As good luck would have it, comes
     in one Mistress Page, gives intelligence of Ford's approach,
     and in her invention, and Ford's wife's distraction, they con-
     veyed me into a buck-basket.
75   FORD   A buck-basket?
     FALSTAFF   Yes. A buck-basket. Rammed me in with foul shirts
     and smocks, socks, foul stockings, greasy napkins,° that,°   *cloths / so that*
     Master Broom, there was the rankest compound of villain-
     ous smell that ever offended nostril.
80   FORD   And how long lay you there?
     FALSTAFF   Nay, you shall hear, Master Broom, what I have
     suffered to bring this woman to evil for your good. Being
     thus crammed in the basket, a couple of Ford's knaves, his
     hinds,° were called forth by their mistress to carry me in the   *servants (pejorative)*
85   name of foul clothes to Datchet Lane. They took me on their
     shoulders; met the jealous knave their master in the door,
     who asked them once or twice what they had in their basket!
     I quaked for fear lest the lunatic knave would have searched
     it. But fate, ordaining he should be a cuckold, held° his hand.   *held back*
90   Well, on went he for a search, and away went I for foul
     clothes. But mark the sequel, Master Broom. I suffered the
     pangs of three several° deaths: first, an intolerable fright, to   *different*
     be detected with° a jealous rotten bellwether;[4] next, to be   *by*
     compassed like a good bilbo in the circumference of a peck,[5]

---

4. Leader of the flock, with a bell around its neck and a horn like a cuckold's on its head.
5. To be bent double (encompassed) like a flexible

sword from Bilbao; see note to 1.1.139) in the cramped space of a laundry basket (in a receptacle holding a peck, or a quarter of a bushel).

95   hilt to point, heel to head; and then, to be stopped° in like a   *stoppered*
      strong distillation° with stinking clothes that fretted[6] in their   *liquid*
      own grease. Think of that—a man of my kidney°—think of   *constitution*
      that, that am as subject to heat as butter; a man of continual
      dissolution° and thaw. It was a miracle to scape suffocation.   *melting*
100   And in the height of this bath—when I was more than half
      stewed in grease, like a Dutch dish—to be thrown into the
      Thames and cooled, glowing hot, in that surge like a
      horseshoe! Think of that—hissing hot—think of that, Master
      Broom!
105   FORD   In good sadness,° sir, I am sorry that for my sake you   *seriousness*
      have suffered all this. My suit then is desperate. You'll under-
      take her no more?
      FALSTAFF   Master Broom, I will be thrown into Etna,° as I have   *Sicilian volcano*
      been into Thames, ere I will leave her thus. Her husband is
110   this morning gone a-birding. I have received from her another
      embassy° of meeting. Twixt eight and nine is the hour, Mas-   *message*
      ter Broom.
      FORD   'Tis past eight already, sir.
      FALSTAFF   Is it? I will then address me to my appointment.
115   Come to me at your convenient leisure, and you shall know
      how I speed. And the conclusion shall be crowned with your
      enjoying her. Adieu. You shall have her, Master Broom.
      Master Broom, you shall cuckold Ford.   [*Exit.*]
      FORD   Hum! Ha! Is this a vision? Is this a dream? Do I sleep?
120   Master Ford, awake! Awake, Master Ford! There's a hole
      made in your best coat,[7] Master Ford. This 'tis to be married;
      this 'tis to have linen and buck-baskets! Well, I will proclaim
      myself what I am. I will now take° the lecher. He is at my   *catch*
      house. He cannot scape me. 'Tis impossible he should. He
125   cannot creep into a halfpenny purse, nor into a pepperbox.
      But lest the devil that guides him should aid him, I will
      search impossible places. Though what I am I cannot avoid;
      yet to be what I would not shall not make me tame. If I have
      horns to make one mad, let the proverb go with me. I'll be
130   horn-mad.[8]   *Exit.*

4.1[1]

Enter MISTRESS PAGE, MISTRESS QUICKLY, [*and*]
     WILLIAM.

MISTRESS PAGE   Is he at Master Ford's already, think'st thou?
MISTRESS QUICKLY   Sure he is by this,° or will be presently,°   *now / immediately*
      but truly he is very courageous° mad about his throwing into   *(for "ragingly")*
      the water. Mistress Ford desires you to come suddenly.°   *at once*
5   MISTRESS PAGE   I'll be with her by and by.° I'll but bring my   *right away*
      young man here to school. Look where his master comes;
      'tis a playing day, I see.
      [*Enter* EVANS.]
      How now, Sir Hugh, no school today?
      EVANS   No. Master Slender is let° the boys leave° to play.   *asked that / be allowed*
10   MISTRESS QUICKLY   Blessing of his heart!

---

6. Fermented.
7. Proverbial for "Your reputation is spoiled."
8. I'll be as furious as a horned animal in breeding

season; furious to be a cuckold.
4.1 Location: Outdoors.
1. This scene is not present in Q.

MISTRESS PAGE Sir Hugh, my husband says my son profits
nothing in the world[2] at his book. I pray you, ask him some
questions in his accidence.°   *Latin grammar*

EVANS Come hither, William. Hold up your head, come.

15 MISTRESS PAGE Come on, sirrah. Hold up your head. Answer
your master—be not afraid.

EVANS William, how many numbers is in nouns?

WILLIAM Two.°   *(singular and plural)*

MISTRESS QUICKLY Truly, I thought there had been one num-
20 ber more, because they say " 'od's 'ouns."[3]

EVANS Peace your tattlings. —What is "fair," William?

WILLIAM *Pulcher.*

MISTRESS QUICKLY Polecats?° There are fairer things than   *Smelly animals; whores*
polecats, sure.

25 EVANS You are a very simplicity 'oman. I pray you, peace.
—What is *lapis*, William?

WILLIAM A stone.

EVANS And what is a stone, William?

WILLIAM A pebble.

30 EVANS No, it is *lapis*. I pray you remember in your prain.

WILLIAM *Lapis.*

EVANS That is a good William. What is he, William, that does
lend articles?

WILLIAM Articles are borrowed of the pronoun, and be thus
35 declined: *singulariter nominativo, hic, haec, hoc.*[4]

EVANS *Nominativo, hig, hag, hog.*[5] Pray you, mark: *genitivo,*°   *genitive*
huius. Well, what is your accusative case?

WILLIAM *Accusativo, hinc.*°   *(for "hunc")*

EVANS I pray you, have your remembrance, child. *Accusativo,*
40 *hing, hang, hog.*

MISTRESS QUICKLY Hang-hog[6] is Latin for bacon, I warrant
you.

EVANS Leave your prabbles, 'oman. —What is the focative°   *vocative; (obscene)*
case, William?

45 WILLIAM Oh . . . *vocativo* . . . oh—

EVANS Remember, William, focative is *caret.*[7]

MISTRESS QUICKLY And that's a good root.

EVANS 'Oman, forbear.

MISTRESS PAGE [*to* MISTRESS QUICKLY] Peace.

50 EVANS What is your genitive case plural, William?

WILLIAM Genitive case?

EVANS Ay.

WILLIAM Genitive, *horum, harum, horum.*

MISTRESS QUICKLY Vengeance of° Jenny's case! Fie on her,   *A plague on*
55 never name her, child, if she be a whore![8]

EVANS For shame, 'oman.

MISTRESS QUICKLY You do ill to teach the child such words.

---

2. My son fails to improve.
3. God's wounds; three is an odd ('od's) number.
4. William recites by memory from his textbook.
Singulariter nominativo is "in the nominative singular" (in which William gives the masculine, feminine, and neuter forms of the pronoun "this").
5. The pronunciation in Evans's accent.
6. Alluding to the saying "Hog is not bacon until it
be hanged."

7. Missing. Quickly understands "carrot," whose slang
sense "penis" is supported by a suggestion of "fuck" in
"focative."
8. *Jenny's case . . . whore:* "Genitive" is perhaps mis-
understandable as Latin for "generative" or even
"genital"—as well as "Jenny"; "case" is understood by
Quickly to mean "situation" and also the slang term
for "vagina."

[*to* MISTRESS PAGE] He teaches him to hick and to hack;
which they'll do fast enough of themselves, and to call
60 whore'm. [*to* EVANS] Fie upon you![9]

EVANS 'Oman, art thou lunatics? Hast thou no understand-
ings for thy cases, and the numbers of the genders? Thou art
as foolish Christian creatures as I would desires.

MISTRESS PAGE [*to* MISTRESS QUICKLY] Prithee, hold thy peace.

65 EVANS Show me now, William, some declensions of your
pronouns.

WILLIAM Forsooth, I have forgot.

EVANS It is *qui, que, quod*; if you forget your *quis*, your *ques*,
and your *quods*,[1] you must be preeches.° Go your ways and   *flogged*
70 play, go.

MISTRESS PAGE He is a better scholar than I thought he was.

EVANS He is a good sprag° memory. Farewell, Mistress Page.   *sprack (lively)*

MISTRESS PAGE Adieu, good Sir Hugh.   [*Exit* EVANS.]
Get you home, boy.   [*Exit* WILLIAM.]

75 Come, we stay too long.
               Exeunt [MISTRESS PAGE *and* MISTRESS QUICKLY].

4.2 (Q 13)

Enter FALSTAFF [*and*] MISTRESS FORD.

FALSTAFF Mistress Ford, your sorrow hath eaten up my sufferance.[1] I see you are obsequious° in your love, and I pro-   *devoted*
fess requital to a hair's breadth,° not only, Mistress Ford, in   *in full*
the simple office of love, but in all the accoutrement, com-
5 pliment, and ceremony of it. But are you sure of your husband now?

MISTRESS FORD He's a-birding, sweet Sir John.

MISTRESS PAGE [*within*] What ho, gossip° Ford! What ho!   *friend*

MISTRESS FORD Step into the chamber, Sir John.
        [*Enter* MISTRESS PAGE.]

10 MISTRESS PAGE How now, sweetheart, who's at home besides
yourself?

MISTRESS FORD Why, none but mine own people.°   *servants*

MISTRESS PAGE Indeed?

MISTRESS FORD No, certainly. [*aside to her*] Speak louder.

15 MISTRESS PAGE [*loudly*] Truly, I am so glad you have nobody
here.

MISTRESS FORD Why?

MISTRESS PAGE Why, woman, your husband is in his old lines°   *role*
again. He so takes on° yonder with my husband, so rails   *raves*
20 against all married mankind, so curses all Eve's daughters,°   *women*
of what complexion° soever, and so buffets himself on the   *temperament*
forehead, crying, "Peer out,[2] peer out!" that any madness I
ever yet beheld seemed but tameness, civility, and patience
to this his distemper he is in now. I am glad the fat knight is
25 not here.

9. *to hick and to hack:* to hiccup (from drinking) and
slash to pieces (perhaps sexual). TEXTUAL COMMENT
On Quickly's misunderstanding of Latin as English in
this scene, see Digital Edition TC 3 (Folio edited text).
1. Possibly pronounced as "keys, case, cods," with
"keys" a euphemism for "penis," "case" a term for

"vagina," and "cods" slang for "testicles."
4.2 Location: Ford's house.
1. Your sorrow has made the memory of my suffering
disappear.
2. Emerge (addressed to imagined cuckold's horns).

MISTRESS FORD Why, does he talk of him?

MISTRESS PAGE Of none but him, and swears he was carried
out, the last time he searched for him, in a basket. Protests
to my husband he is now here, and hath drawn him and the
rest of their company from their sport to make another
experiment° of his suspicion. But I am glad the knight is not
here. Now he shall see his own foolery.

    trial

MISTRESS FORD How near is he, Mistress Page?

MISTRESS PAGE Hard by, at street end. He will be here anon.

MISTRESS FORD I am undone. The knight is here.

MISTRESS PAGE Why, then you are utterly shamed, and he's
but a dead man. What a woman are you? Away with him,
away with him! Better shame than murder.

MISTRESS FORD Which way should he go? How should I
bestow° him? Shall I put him into the basket again?

    dispose of

[*Enter* FALSTAFF.]

FALSTAFF No, I'll come no more i'th' basket. May I not go out
ere he come?

MISTRESS PAGE Alas, three of Master Ford's brothers watch
the door with pistols, that none shall issue out. Otherwise
you might slip away ere he came. But what make you° here?

    are you doing

FALSTAFF What shall I do? I'll creep up into the chimney.

MISTRESS FORD[3] There they always use to discharge their
birding-pieces.°

    bird guns

MISTRESS PAGE Creep into the kiln-hole.°

    oven

FALSTAFF Where is it?

MISTRESS FORD He will seek there, on my word! Neither press,°
coffer, chest, trunk, well, vault, but he hath an abstract° for
the remembrance of such places, and goes to them by his
note. There is no hiding you in the house.

    cupboard
    a list

FALSTAFF I'll go out then.

MISTRESS FORD If you go out in your own semblance, you die,
Sir John—unless you go out disguised.

MISTRESS PAGE How might we disguise him?

MISTRESS FORD Alas the day, I know not. There is no woman's gown big enough for him. Otherwise he might put on a
hat, a muffler,° and a kerchief, and so escape.

    face scarf

FALSTAFF Good hearts, devise something! Any extremity rather
than a mischief.°

    calamity

MISTRESS FORD My maid's aunt, the fat woman of Brentford,[4]
has a gown above.

MISTRESS PAGE On my word, it will serve him. She's as big as
he is! And there's her thrummed° hat and her muffler too.
Run up, Sir John.

    fringed

MISTRESS FORD Go, go, sweet Sir John. Mistress Page and I
will look° some linen for your head.

    look for

MISTRESS PAGE Quick, quick! We'll come dress you straight.
Put on the gown the while.   [*Exit* FALSTAFF.]

---

3. TEXTUAL COMMENT For the assigning of speeches
to Mistresses Ford and Page in this scene, see Digital
Edition TC 4 (Folio edited text).
4. Gillian of Brentford, a scurrilous comic figure,
perhaps historically based, best known for her will,
in which she supposedly "bequeathed a score of farts
amongst her friends" (Thomas Nashe, prologue to his
Summer's Last Will and Testament). Brentford was a
village halfway between Windsor and London.

MISTRESS FORD   I would my husband would meet him in this
shape! He cannot abide the old woman of Brentford; he
75   swears she's a witch, forbade her my house, and hath threatened to beat her.

MISTRESS PAGE   Heaven guide him to thy husband's cudgel,
and the devil guide his cudgel afterwards.

MISTRESS FORD   But is my husband coming?

80   MISTRESS PAGE   Ay, in good sadness,° is he, and talks of the   *in all seriousness*
basket, too, howsoever[5] he hath had intelligence.°   *information*

MISTRESS FORD   We'll try° that, for I'll appoint my men to carry   *test*
the basket again, to meet him at the door with it, as they did
last time.

85   MISTRESS PAGE   Nay, but he'll be here presently. Let's go dress
him like the witch of Brentford.

MISTRESS FORD   I'll first direct my men what they shall do
with the basket. Go up. I'll bring linen for him straight.°   *immediately*

MISTRESS PAGE   Hang him, dishonest° varlet, we cannot mis-   *lewd*
90   use him enough.
We'll leave a proof by that which we will do,
Wives may be merry and yet honest° too.   *chaste*
We do not act that° often jest and laugh;   *misbehave who*
'Tis old, but true: "Still swine eats all the draff."[6]
        [*Exeunt* MISTRESS FORD *and* MISTRESS PAGE.]
        [*Enter the two* SERVANTS *with* MISTRESS FORD.]

95   MISTRESS FORD   Go, sirs, take the basket again on your shoulders. Your master is hard at° door. If he bid you set it down,   *close to the*
obey him. Quickly, dispatch.   [*Exit.*]

FIRST SERVANT   Come, come, take it up.

SECOND SERVANT   Pray heaven it be not full of knight again.

100   FIRST SERVANT   I hope not. I had lief° as bear so much lead.   *I would rather*
        [*Enter* FORD, PAGE, EVANS, CAIUS, *and* SHALLOW.]

FORD   Ay, but if it prove true, Master Page, have you any way
then to unfool me again?[7] [*to* SERVANTS] Set down the basket, villains. —Somebody call my wife. [*to* SERVANTS] Youth
in a basket!° Oh, you panderly rascals! [*to his guests*] There's   *Fortunate lover*
105   a knot,° a ging,° a pack, a conspiracy against me! Now shall   *group / gang*
the devil be shamed.° —What, wife, I say! Come, come forth!   *truth be known*
Behold what honest clothes you send forth to bleaching.

PAGE   Why, this passes,° Master Ford. You are not to go loose   *goes beyond all bounds*
any longer; you must be pinioned.

110   EVANS   Why, this is lunatics. This is mad as a mad dog.

SHALLOW   Indeed, Master Ford, this is not well, indeed.
        [*Enter* MISTRESS FORD.]

FORD   So say I too, sir. —Come hither, Mistress Ford, Mistress
Ford, the honest woman, the modest wife, the virtuous creature, that hath the jealous fool to° her husband. I suspect   *for*
115   without cause, mistress, do I?

MISTRESS FORD   Heaven be my witness, you do, if you suspect
me in any dishonesty.

FORD   Well said, brazen-face, hold it out!° [*He kicks the bas-*   *keep it up*
ket.] Come forth, sirrah.

5. By whatever means.
6. Proverbial: "The quiet swine eats all the hogwash."
In other words, quietness conceals sexual immorality
(whereas playfulness is innocent; see line 92).

7. Page has evidently accused Ford of making a fool
of himself; Ford wants to know if Page will withdraw
the charge if Ford is proved correct in his suspicions.

[*He opens the basket and begins to toss out
the laundry.*]

120 PAGE This passes.

MISTRESS FORD Are you not ashamed? Let the clothes alone.

FORD [*into the basket*] I shall find you anon.

EVANS 'Tis unreasonable! Will you take up your wife's clothes?
Come, away.

125 FORD Empty the basket, I say.

MISTRESS FORD Why, man, why?

FORD Master Page, as I am a man, there was one conveyed
out of my house yesterday in this basket. Why may not he be
there again? In my house I am sure he is. My intelligence° is   *information*
130 true. My jealousy is reasonable. Pluck me out all the linen!

MISTRESS FORD If you find a man there, he shall die a flea's
death.⁸

PAGE Here's no man.

SHALLOW By my fidelity, this is not well, Master Ford. This
135 wrongs you.°   *You shame yourself*

EVANS Master Ford, you must pray, and not follow the imaginations of your own heart. This is jealousies.

FORD Well, he's not here I seek for.

PAGE No, nor nowhere else but in your brain.

140 FORD Help to search my house this one time. If I find not
what I seek, show no color° for my extremity.° Let me for-   *excuse / excesses*
ever be your table-sport.° Let them say of me, "As jealous as   *laughingstock*
Ford, that searched a hollow walnut for his wife's leman."°   *lover*
Satisfy me once more! Once more search with me!

[*Exeunt the* SERVANTS *with the refilled basket.*]

145 MISTRESS FORD [*calling*] What ho, Mistress Page, come you
and the old woman down. My husband will come into the
chamber.

FORD Old woman? What old woman's that?

MISTRESS FORD Why, it is my maid's aunt of Brentford.

150 FORD A witch, a quean, an old cozening quean!° Have I not   *cheating hussy*
forbid her my house? She comes of errands, does she? We are
simple men, we do not know what's brought to pass under
the profession° of fortune-telling. She works by charms, by   *claim*
spells, by th' figure,⁹ and such daubery° as this is beyond our   *trickery*
155 element.° We know nothing. Come down, you witch, you hag   *knowledge*
you, come down, I say!

MISTRESS FORD Nay, good sweet husband! —Good gentlemen, let him not strike the old woman.

[*Enter* MISTRESS PAGE *bringing* FALSTAFF *disguised
as an old woman.*]

MISTRESS PAGE Come, Mother Pratt.° Come, give me your   *Buttocks*
160 hand.

FORD I'll prat° her! [FORD *beats* FALSTAFF *with a cudgel.*] Out   *beat; trick*
of my door, you witch, you rag, you baggage, you polecat, you
runion,° out, out! I'll conjure you! I'll fortune tell you!   *contemptible woman*

[*Exit* FALSTAFF, *running.*]

8. Anyone hiding there must be insignificantly small.
9. Astrological or magical diagrams, or wax effigies used by witches.

MISTRESS PAGE   Are you not ashamed? I think you have killed
the poor woman.

MISTRESS FORD   Nay, he will do it. [*to* FORD] 'Tis a goodly credit
for you.

FORD   Hang her, witch!

EVANS   By yea and no, I think the 'oman is a witch indeed. I
like not when a 'oman has a great peard; I spy a great peard
under his muffler.

FORD   Will you follow, gentlemen? I beseech you, follow. See
but the issue° of my jealousy. If I cry out° thus upon no trail,   *outcome / bark*
never trust me when I open° again.   *start barking*

PAGE   Let's obey his humor° a little further. Come, gentlemen.   *indulge him*
          [*Exeunt* FORD, PAGE, EVANS, CAIUS, *and* SHALLOW.]

MISTRESS PAGE   Trust me, he beat him most pitifully.

MISTRESS FORD   Nay, by the mass, that he did not. He beat
him most unpitifully, methought.

MISTRESS PAGE   I'll have the cudgel hallowed and hung o'er
the altar. It hath done meritorious service.

MISTRESS FORD   What think you? May we, with the warrant of
womanhood and the witness of a good conscience, pursue
him with any further revenge?

MISTRESS PAGE   The spirit of wantonness is sure scared out of
him. If the devil have him not in fee simple with fine and
recovery, he will never, I think, in the way of waste attempt us
again.[1]

MISTRESS FORD   Shall we tell our husbands how we have
served him?

MISTRESS PAGE   Yes, by all means, if it be but to scrape the
figures° out of your husband's brains! If they can find in   *fantasies*
their hearts the poor unvirtuous fat knight shall be any fur-
ther afflicted, we two will still be the ministers.

MISTRESS FORD   I'll warrant they'll have him publicly shamed,
and methinks there would be no period° to the jest should   *conclusion*
he not be publicly shamed.

MISTRESS PAGE   Come, to the forge with it, then shape it! I
would not have things cool.   *Exeunt.*

4.3 (Q 14)

Enter HOST *and* BARDOLPH.

BARDOLPH   Sir, the German desires to have three of your horses.
The Duke himself will be tomorrow at court, and they° are   *(the Germans)*
going to meet him.

HOST   What duke should that be, comes° so secretly? I hear   *who comes*
not of him in the court. Let me speak with the gentlemen.
They speak English?

BARDOLPH   Ay, sir! I'll call them to you.

HOST   They shall have my horses, but I'll make them pay. I'll
sauce them.° They have had my houses a week at command.[1]   *make them pay dearly*
I have turned away my other guests. They must come off,° I'll   *pay up*
sauce them. Come.[2]   *Exeunt.*

4.4 (Q 15)

Enter PAGE, FORD, MISTRESS PAGE, MISTRESS FORD,
and EVANS.

EVANS 'Tis one of the best discretions of a 'oman[1] as ever I
did look upon.

PAGE And did he send you both these letters at an instant?°   *at the same time*

MISTRESS PAGE Within a quarter of an hour.

5   FORD Pardon me, wife. Henceforth do what thou wilt.
    I rather will suspect the sun with° cold   *of*
    Than thee with wantonness. Now doth thy honor stand,
    In him that was of late an heretic,
    As firm as faith.

PAGE   'Tis well, 'tis well, no more.

10   Be not as extreme in submission as in offense,
    But let our plot go forward. Let our wives
    Yet once again—to make us public sport—
    Appoint a meeting with this old fat fellow
    Where we may take him and disgrace him for it.

15   FORD There is no better way than that they spoke of.

PAGE How? To send him word they'll meet him in the park at
midnight? Fie, fie, he'll never come.

EVANS You say he has been thrown in the rivers, and has
been grievously peaten as an old 'oman. Methinks there
20   should be terrors in him that he should not come! Methinks
his flesh is punished. He shall have no desires.

PAGE So think I too.

MISTRESS FORD Devise but how you'll use° him when he comes,   *treat*
    And let us two devise to bring him thither.

25   MISTRESS PAGE There is an old tale goes that Herne the
      Hunter,
    Sometime° a keeper here in Windsor Forest,   *Once*
    Doth all the winter time, at still midnight,
    Walk round about an oak, with great ragged° horns,   *jagged*
    And there he blasts° the tree, and takes° the cattle,   *blights / bewitches*
30   And makes milch kine° yield blood, and shakes a chain   *dairy cattle*
    In a most hideous and dreadful manner.
    You have heard of such a spirit, and well you know
    The superstitious idle-headed eld°   *people of olden times*
    Received and did deliver to our age
35   This tale of Herne the Hunter for a truth.

PAGE Why, yet there want not° many that do fear   *are*
    In deep of night to walk by this Herne's oak.
    But what of this?

MISTRESS FORD   Marry, this is our device:
    That Falstaff at that oak shall meet with us.

40   PAGE Well, let it not be doubted but he'll come,
    And, in this shape, when you have brought him thither,
    What shall be done with him? What is your plot?

MISTRESS PAGE That likewise have we thought upon, and
      thus:
    Nan Page, my daughter, and my little son,
45   And three or four more of their growth,° we'll dress   *size*
    Like urchins,° ouphes,° and fairies, green and white,   *goblins / elf children*

4.4 Location: Ford's house.   1. Mistress Page is one of the most discreet women.

With rounds of waxen tapers° on their heads   *crowns of candles*
And rattles in their hands. Upon a sudden,
As Falstaff, she, and I are newly met,
50   Let them from forth a sawpit² rush at once
With some diffusèd° song. Upon their sight   *disordered*
We two, in great amazèdness, will fly.
Then let them all encircle him about,
And fairy-like to pinch the unclean knight,
55   And ask him why that hour of fairy revel,
In their so sacred paths, he dares to tread
In shape profane.
FORD   And till he tell the truth,
Let the supposèd fairies pinch him sound°   *soundly*
And burn him with their tapers.
MISTRESS PAGE   The truth being known,
60   We'll all present ourselves, dishorn the spirit,
And mock him home to Windsor.
FORD   The children must
Be practiced well to this, or they'll ne'er do't.
EVANS   I will teach the children their behaviors, and I will be
like a jackanapes° also, to burn the knight with my taber.   *tame monkey; trickster*
65   FORD   That will be excellent. I'll go buy them vizards.°   *masks*
MISTRESS PAGE   My Nan shall be the queen of all the fairies,
Finely attired in a robe of white.
PAGE [*aside*]   That silk³ will I go buy, and in that time
Shall Master Slender steal my Nan away
70   And marry her at Eton.⁴ [*aloud*] Go send to Falstaff straight.
FORD   Nay, I'll to him again in name of Broom.
He'll tell me all his purpose. Sure, he'll come.
MISTRESS PAGE   Fear not you that. Go get us properties°   *props*
And tricking° for our fairies.   *costumes*
75   EVANS   Let us about it! It is admirable pleasures and ferry hon-
est knaveries.   [*Exeunt* EVANS, FORD, *and* PAGE.]
MISTRESS PAGE   Go, Mistress Ford,
Send quickly to Sir John to know his mind.
                        [*Exit* MISTRESS FORD.]
I'll to the doctor. He hath my good will,
80   And none but he, to marry with Nan Page.
That Slender, though well landed,° is an idiot;   *owning much land*
And he° my husband best of all affects.°   *him / likes most*
The doctor is well moneyed, and his friends
Potent at court. He, none but he, shall have her,
85   Though twenty thousand worthier come to crave her.
                              [*Exit.*]

4.5 (Q 16)

Enter [the] HOST *[and]* SIMPLE.

HOST   What wouldst thou have, boor? What, thickskin?° Speak,   *dullard*
breathe, discuss; brief, short, quick, snap!
SIMPLE   Marry, sir, I come to speak with Sir John Falstaff
from Master Slender.

---

2. A pit over which wood was sawed.
3. A sign of Page's financial means.

4. Across the Thames from Windsor.
4.5 Location: The Garter Inn.

5   HOST   There's his chamber, his house, his castle, his standing
bed and truckle bed.[1] 'Tis[2] painted about with the story of
the prodigal,° fresh and new. Go, knock, and call. He'll speak   *prodigal son (Luke 15)*
like an Anthropophaginian° unto thee. Knock, I say!   *cannibal*

SIMPLE   There's an old woman, a fat woman, gone up into his
10   chamber. I'll be so bold as stay, sir, till she come down. I come
to speak with her, indeed.

HOST   Ha? A fat woman? The knight may be robbed. I'll call.
—Bully knight! Bully Sir John! Speak from thy lungs military! Art thou there? It is thine Host, thine Ephesian,° calls.   *mate*

15   FALSTAFF [*within*]   How now, mine Host?

HOST   Here's a Bohemian Tartar tarries° the coming down of   *Here a savage awaits*
thy fat woman. Let her descend, bully, let her descend! My
chambers are honorable. Fie! Privacy?° Fie!   *secret goings-on*
    [*Enter* FALSTAFF.]

FALSTAFF   There was, mine Host, an old fat woman even now
20   with me, but she's gone.

SIMPLE   Pray you, sir, was't not the wise woman° of Brentford?   *woman skilled in magic*

FALSTAFF   Ay, marry, was it, mussel shell.° What would you   *empty head (?); gaper (?)*
with her?

SIMPLE   My master, sir, my Master Slender, sent to her, seeing
25   her go through the streets, to know, sir, whether one Nim,
sir, that beguiled° him of a chain, had the chain or no.   *cheated*

FALSTAFF   I spake with the old woman about it.

SIMPLE   And what says she, I pray, sir?

FALSTAFF   Marry, she says that the very same man that
30   beguiled Master Slender of his chain cozened° him of it.   *tricked*

SIMPLE   I would I could have spoken with the woman herself.
I had other things to have spoken with her too from him.

FALSTAFF   What are they? Let us know.

HOST   Ay, come! Quick!

35   SIMPLE   I may not conceal° them, sir.   *(for "reveal")*

HOST   Conceal them, or thou diest.

SIMPLE   Why, sir, they were nothing but about Mistress Anne
Page, to know if it were my master's fortune to have her
or no.

40   FALSTAFF   'Tis, 'tis his fortune.

SIMPLE   What, sir?

FALSTAFF   To have her or no. Go, say the woman told me so.

SIMPLE   May I be bold to say so, sir?

FALSTAFF   Ay, sir. Like who more bold?°   *As bold as they come*

45   SIMPLE   I thank your worship. I shall make my master glad
with these tidings.   [*Exit.*]

HOST   Thou art clerkly,° thou art clerkly, Sir John. Was there   *learned*
a wise woman with thee?

FALSTAFF   Ay, that there was, mine Host, one that hath taught
50   me more wit than ever I learned before in my life. And I paid
nothing for it neither, but was paid° for my learning.   *thrashed*
    [*Enter* BARDOLPH *in filthy wet clothes.*]

BARDOLPH   Out, alas, sir! Cozenage, mere° cozenage!   *utter*

HOST   Where be my horses? Speak well of them, varletto.°   *varlet*

---

1. Trundle bed, which could be stored under the larger standing bed.   2. The "it" in "'Tis" refers to either the wall hanging or the bed hanging.

BARDOLPH   Run away with the cozeners! For so soon as I came
55   beyond Eton, they threw me off from behind one of them in
a slough of mire, and set spurs and away, like three German
devils, three Doctor Faustaffs![3]

HOST   They are gone but to meet the Duke, villain. Do not say
they be fled. Germans are honest men.

     [*Enter* EVANS.]
60 EVANS   Where is mine Host?

HOST   What is the matter, sir?

EVANS   Have a care of your entertainments.° There is a friend   *guests*
of mine come to town tells me there is three cozen°-Germans   *related; cheating*
that has cozened all the hosts of Reading, of Maidenhead, of
65   Colnbrook,° of horses and money. I tell you for good will, look   *nearby villages*
you. You are wise and full of gibes and vlouting-stocks,° and   *laughingstocks*
'tis not convenient° you should be cozened. Fare you well.   *appropriate*

         [*Exit.*]

     [*Enter* CAIUS.]

CAIUS   Vere is mine Host *de* Jarteer?

HOST   Here, Master Doctor, in perplexity and doubtful dilemma.
70 CAIUS   I cannot tell vat is dat, but it is tell-a me dat you make
grande préparation for a duke *de* Jamanie.° By my trot,° der   *Germany / troth*
is no duke that the court is know to come. I tell you for good
will. *Adieu.*   [*Exit.*]

HOST [*to* BARDOLPH]   Hue and cry,° villain! Go! [*to* FALSTAFF]   *Raise the alarm*
75   Assist me, knight! I am undone. [*to* BARDOLPH] Fly, run! Hue
and cry, villain! —I am undone.

         [*Exeunt* HOST *and* BARDOLPH.]

FALSTAFF   I would all the world might be cozened, for I have
been cozened and beaten too. If it should come to the ear of
the court how I have been transformed, and how my trans-
80   formation hath been washed and cudgeled, they would melt
me out of my fat, drop by drop, and liquor° fishermen's boots   *grease*
with me. I warrant they would whip me with their fine wits
till I were as crestfallen° as a dried pear. I never prospered   *shriveled*
since I forswore myself at primero.° Well, if my wind were   *cards*
85   but long enough,° I would repent.   *(to list all my sins)*

     [*Enter* MISTRESS QUICKLY.]
Now, whence come you?

MISTRESS QUICKLY   From the two parties, forsooth.

FALSTAFF   The devil take one party and his dam° the other, and   *mother*
so they shall be both bestowed. I have suffered more for their
90   sakes, more than the villainous inconstancy of man's disposition is able to bear.

MISTRESS QUICKLY   And have not they suffered? Yes, I war-
rant, speciously° one of them. Mistress Ford, good heart, is   *(for "specially")*
beaten black and blue, that you cannot see a white spot
95   about her.

FALSTAFF   What tell'st thou me of black and blue? I was beaten
myself into all the colors of the rainbow, and I was like to be
apprehended for the witch of Brentford! But that my admi-

---

3. Bardolph alludes to Marlowe's *Doctor Faustus*, whose titular hero makes a pact with the devil. In one scene, three devils are conjured to "horse" Benvolio, Frederick, and Martino on their backs and throw them in "some lake of mud and dirt" (1616 Quarto; scene 13). In the following scene, the three appear muddy and, anticipating Falstaff's punishment, with horns on their heads.

rable dexterity of wit, my counterfeiting the action of an old
100   woman, delivered me, the knave constable had set me i'th'
stocks—i'th' common stocks—for a witch!

MISTRESS QUICKLY   Sir, let me speak with you in your chamber.
You shall hear how things go and, I warrant, to your content.
Here is a letter will say somewhat. Good hearts, what ado
105   here is to bring you together! Sure, one of you does not serve
heaven well, that you are so crossed.°   *thwarted*

FALSTAFF   Come up into my chamber.   *Exeunt.*

4.6 (Q 17)

Enter FENTON [*and the*] HOST.

HOST   Master Fenton, talk not to me. My mind is heavy. I will
give over° all.   *give up*

FENTON   Yet hear me speak. Assist me in my purpose
And, as I am a gentleman, I'll give thee
5   A hundred pound in gold, more than your loss.

HOST   I will hear you, Master Fenton, and I will at the least
keep your counsel.°   *secret*

FENTON   From time to time, I have acquainted you
With the dear love I bear to fair Anne Page,
10   Who mutually hath answered my affection—
So far forth as herself might be her chooser¹—
Even to my wish. I have a letter from her
Of such contents as you will wonder at;
The mirth whereof, so larded with my matter,°   *mixed with my concern*
15   That neither singly can be manifested
Without the show of both. Fat Falstaff
Hath a great scene. The image° of the jest   *idea*
I'll show you here at large. Hark, good mine Host.
Tonight at Herne's Oak, just twixt twelve and one,
20   Must my sweet Nan present° the Fairy Queen.   *play the part of*
The purpose why is here—[*showing a letter*]—in which
disguise,
While other jests are something rank on foot,°   *somewhat thick afoot*
Her father hath commanded her to slip
Away with Slender and with him at Eton
25   Immediately to marry. She hath consented. Now, sir,
Her mother, even strong against that match
And firm for Doctor Caius, hath appointed
That he shall likewise shuffle her away,
While other sports are tasking of° their minds,   *engaging*
30   And at the dean'ry,² where a priest attends,
Straight marry her. To this her mother's plot
She, seemingly obedient, likewise hath
Made promise to the doctor. Now, thus it rests:°   *things stand thus*
Her father means she shall be all in white,
35   And in that habit,° when Slender sees his time   *dress*
To take her by the hand and bid her go,
She shall go with him. Her mother hath intended—
The better to denote her to the doctor,

4.6 Location: Scene continues.   the staff of certain churches); (loosely) a parsonage.
1. Insofar as she might choose her own husband.   Here, Fenton refers to the deanery attached to St.
2. Residence of the dean (the head of the clergy on   George's Chapel on the property of Windsor Castle.

For they must all be masked and vizarded—
40 That, quaint° in green, she shall be loose enrobed,   *elegantly*
With ribbons pendent flaring° 'bout her head;   *waving down*
And when the doctor spies his vantage ripe,
To pinch her by the hand, and on that token
The maid hath given consent to go with him.
45 HOST Which means she to deceive, father or mother?
FENTON Both, my good Host, to go along with me.
And here it rests, that you'll procure the vicar
To stay for me at church twixt twelve and one,
And, in the lawful name of° marrying,   *name of lawful*
50 To give our hearts united ceremony.
HOST Well, husband° your device. I'll to the vicar.   *manage well; (pun)*
Bring you the maid, you shall not lack a priest.
FENTON So shall I evermore be bound to thee.
Besides, I'll make a present° recompense.   *immediate*
[FENTON *gives him money.*]
                                                              Exeunt [*severally*].

5.1

Enter FALSTAFF *and* MISTRESS QUICKLY.

FALSTAFF Prithee, no more prattling. Go. I'll hold.° —This   *keep the appointment*
is the third time. I hope good luck lies in odd numbers.
—Away, go! —They say there is divinity° in odd numbers,   *divine power*
either in nativity, chance, or death. —Away!
5 MISTRESS QUICKLY I'll provide you a chain, and I'll do what I
can to get you a pair of horns.
FALSTAFF Away, I say! Time wears!° Hold up your head and   *passes*
mince.°   [*Exit* MISTRESS QUICKLY.]   *walk affectedly*
[*Enter* FORD *disguised as Broom.*]
How now, Master Broom? Master Broom, the matter will be
10 known tonight or never. Be you in the park about midnight
at Herne's Oak, and you shall see wonders.
FORD Went you not to her yesterday, sir, as you told me you
had appointed?
FALSTAFF I went to her, Master Broom, as you see,° like a   *as I am now*
15 poor old man, but I came from her, Master Broom, like a
poor old woman. That same knave Ford, her husband, hath
the finest mad devil of jealousy in him, Master Broom, that
ever governed frenzy. I will tell you, he beat me grievously in
the shape of a woman—for in the shape of man, Master
20 Broom, I fear not Goliath with a weaver's beam,[1] because I
know also life is a shuttle.[2] I am in haste. Go along with me.
I'll tell you all, Master Broom. Since I plucked geese,° played   *(child's prank)*
truant, and whipped top,° I knew not what 'twas to be beaten   *spun a top*
till lately. Follow me. I'll tell you strange things of this knave
25 Ford, on whom tonight I will be revenged, and I will deliver
his wife into your hand. Follow. Strange things in hand,
Master Broom! Follow.   *Exeunt.*

5.1 Location: The Garter Inn.   2. From Job 7:6: "My days are swifter than a weaver's
1. The biblical simile for Goliath's spear handle   shuttle."
(1 Samuel 17:7).

5.2

Enter PAGE, SHALLOW, [*and*] SLENDER.

PAGE Come, come. We'll couch° i'th' castle ditch till we see   *lie*
the light of our fairies. Remember, son Slender, my—

SLENDER Ay, forsooth, I have spoke with her, and we have a nay-
word° how to know one another. I come to her in white and cry   *password*
5   "mum"; she cries "budget"°; and by that we know one another.   *mumbudget (silence)*

SHALLOW That's good, too. But what needs either your "mum"
or her "budget"? The white will decipher her well enough.
—It hath struck ten o'clock.

PAGE The night is dark. Light and spirits will become it well.
10   Heaven prosper our sport! No man means evil but the devil,
and we shall know him by his horns. Let's away. Follow me.
Exeunt.

5.3

Enter MISTRESS PAGE, MISTRESS FORD, [*and*] CAIUS.

MISTRESS PAGE Master Doctor, my daughter is in green.
When you see your time, take her by the hand, away with
her to the deanery, and dispatch it quickly. Go before into
the park. We two must go together.

5   CAIUS I know vat I have to do. Adieu.

MISTRESS PAGE Fare you well, sir.   [*Exit* CAIUS.]
My husband will not rejoice so much at the abuse of Falstaff
as he will chafe at the doctor's marrying my daughter. But
'tis no matter. Better a little chiding than a great deal of
10   heartbreak.

MISTRESS FORD Where is Nan now, and her troop of fairies,
and the Welsh devil, Hugh?

MISTRESS PAGE They are all couched in a pit hard by Herne's
Oak with obscured lights which, at the very instant of Fal-
15   staff's and our meeting, they will at once display to the night.

MISTRESS FORD That cannot choose but amaze° him.   *That is bound to frighten*

MISTRESS PAGE If he be not amazed, he will be mocked. If he
be amazed, he will every way be mocked.

MISTRESS FORD We'll betray him finely.

20   MISTRESS PAGE Against such lewdsters and their lechery,
Those that betray them do no treachery.

MISTRESS FORD The hour draws on. To the oak, to the oak!
Exeunt.

5.4

Enter EVANS *and* FAIRIES.

EVANS Trib,° trib, fairies! Come, and remember your parts.   *Trip (move nimbly)*
Be pold, I pray you! Follow me into the pit and, when I give
the watch-'ords, do as I pid you. Come, come—trib, trib!
Exeunt.

5.5 (Q 18)

Enter FALSTAFF [*with a buck's head upon him*].

FALSTAFF The Windsor bell hath struck twelve. The minute
draws on. Now the hot-blooded gods assist me! Remember,

5.2 Location: An approach to Windsor Park.   **5.4** Location: Scene continues.
5.3 Location: Scene continues.   **5.5** Location: Windsor Park.

Jove, thou wast a bull for thy Europa.¹ Love set on thy horns.
O powerful Love, that in some respects makes a beast a
5 man; in some other, a man a beast. You were also, Jupiter, a
swan for the love of Leda.² O omnipotent Love, how near
the god drew to the complexion of a goose! A fault done first
in the form of a beast—O Jove, a beastly fault!—and then
another fault in the semblance of a fowl. Think on't, Jove, a
10 foul fault! When gods have hot° backs, what shall poor men   *lustful*
do? For me, I am here a Windsor stag, and the fattest, I
think, i'th' forest. Send me a cool rut-time,° Jove, or who can   *mating season*
blame me to piss my tallow?³ —Who comes here? My doe?
[*Enter* MISTRESS FORD.]

MISTRESS FORD   Sir John? Art thou there, my dear? My male
15 deer?

FALSTAFF   My doe with the black scut?° Let the sky rain pota-   *tail; pubic hair*
toes; let it thunder to the tune of "Greensleeves,"° hail   *popular love song*
kissing-comfits, and snow eringoes!⁴ Let there come a tem-
pest of provocation,° I will shelter me here.   *sexual incitement*
[*He clutches her.*]
[*Enter* MISTRESS PAGE.]

20 MISTRESS FORD   Mistress Page is come with me, sweet hart.°   *deer; (pun on "heart")*

FALSTAFF   Divide me like a bribed° buck, each a haunch. [*They*   *stolen*
sit on his lap.] I will keep my sides to myself, my shoulders for
the fellow of this walk,° and my horns° I bequeath your hus-   *woods keeper* / *(cuckold's)*
bands. Am I a woodman,⁵ ha? Speak I like Herne the Hunter?
25 Why, now is Cupid a child of conscience. He makes restitution.° As I am a true spirit, welcome!   *repays my suffering*
[*There is a noise of horns.*]

MISTRESS PAGE   Alas, what noise?

MISTRESS FORD   Heaven forgive our sins!

FALSTAFF   What should this be?

30 MISTRESS FORD *and* MISTRESS PAGE   Away, away!
[*The two women run away.*]

FALSTAFF   I think the devil will not have me damned, lest the
oil that's in me should set hell on fire. He would never else
cross me thus.
Enter [MISTRESS QUICKLY *like the Queen of Fairies,*
PISTOL *as Hobgoblin,*⁶ EVANS *like a satyr, and boys*
dressed like] FAIRIES [*carrying tapers, including*
ANNE *Page*].

MISTRESS QUICKLY   Fairies black, gray, green, and white,
35 You moonshine revelers and shades° of night,   *spirits*
You orphan heirs of fixèd destiny,⁷
Attend° your office° and your quality.°   *Perform* / *duty* / *calling*
Crier° Hobgoblin, make the fairy oyes.°   *Town crier* / *hear ye*

---

1. In classical mythology, Jupiter turned himself into
a bull and abducted Europa by swimming across the
sea with her on his back.
2. Jupiter turned himself into a swan in order to rape
Leda.
3. If I urinate or sweat away my fat (as stags were
thought to do at rutting time).
4. Candied roots of sea holly that, like sweet "pota-
toes" (lines 16–17), were considered an aphrodisiac.
kissing-comfits: breath sweeteners ("comfits" are

candies).
5. *Woodman:* hunter; lecher; wooden man.
6. Anne, who was assigned the part of the Queen of
Fairies at 4.4.66, is here replaced by Quickly, either as
part of the marital scheming or simply as an indication
that the boy actor who played Quickly also is to play
this role. Similarly, Hobgoblin may have been played
by Pistol or simply by the actor who played Pistol.
7. You parentless inheritors of fixed duties (?). (Fairies were supposed to be parentless.)

PISTOL   Elves, list° your names. Silence, you airy toys!°   *listen for / trifles*

40   Cricket,° to Windsor chimneys shalt thou leap.   *(elf's name)*

         Where fires thou find'st unraked° and hearths unswept,   *(hence, likely to die out)*

         There pinch the maids as blue as bilberry!°   *blueberry*

         Our radiant queen hates sluts and sluttery.°   *dirtiness*

FALSTAFF [*aside*]   They are fairies. He that speaks to them
         shall die!

45   I'll wink° and couch.° No man their works must eye.   *shut my eyes / lie down*

         [FALSTAFF *lies down and covers his eyes.*]

EVANS   Where's Bede?

         [*Second boy steps forward.*]

                        Go you and, where you find a maid

         That ere she sleep has thrice her prayers said,

         Raise up° the organs of her fantasy;°   *Stimulate / imagination*

         Sleep she[8] as sound as careless° infancy.   *carefree*

50   But those as° sleep and think not on their sins,   *who*

         Pinch them—arms, legs, backs, shoulders, sides, and shins.

MISTRESS QUICKLY   About,° about!°   *To work*

         Search Windsor Castle, elves, within and out.

         Strew good luck, ouphes,° on every sacred room,   *elves*

55   That it may stand till the perpetual doom°   *Judgment Day*

         In state° as wholesome as in state° 'tis fit,   *condition / dignity*

         Worthy° the owner and the owner it.   *Worthy of*

         The several chairs of order[1] look you scour

         With juice of balm and every precious flower.

60   Each fair installment,° coat, and sev'ral crest,[2]   *stall or seat*

         With loyal blazon,[3] evermore be blest.

         And nightly, meadow fairies, look you sing

         Like to the Garter's compass,° in a ring.   *circle*

         Th'expressure° that it bears, green let it be,   *image*

65   More fertile fresh than all the field to see,

         And *Honi soit qui mal y pense*[4] write

         In emerald tufts, flowers purple, blue, and white,

         Like sapphire, pearl, and rich embroidery,

         Buckled below fair knighthood's bending knee.

70   Fairies use flowers for their charactery.°   *lettering*

         Away, disperse! But till 'tis one o'clock,

         Our dance of custom° round about the oak   *customary dance*

         Of Herne the Hunter let us not forget.

EVANS   Pray you lock hand in hand; yourselves in order set;

75   And twenty glowworms shall our lanterns be

         To guide our measure° round about the tree.   *dance*

         But stay! I smell a man of middle earth.°   *a mortal*

FALSTAFF [*aside*]   Heavens defend me from that Welsh fairy,
         lest he transform me to a piece of cheese!

80 PISTOL [*to* FALSTAFF]   Vile worm, thou wast o'erlooked° even   *destined to evil*
         in thy birth.

---

8. Though she is sleeping; may she sleep.

9. TEXTUAL COMMENT For this speech's courtly account of the Order of the Garter, given a more popular tone in Q, see Digital Edition TC 5 (Folio edited text).

1. The various stalls assigned, in St. George's Chapel, Windsor, to members of the Order of the Garter (a high dignity that the monarch conferred, marked by a garter worn below the knee).

2. *crest:* heraldic device on top of the helmet. *coat:* coat of arms displayed on the stall or seat.

3. *With loyal blazon:* Together with the coat of arms on a banner.

4. Evil to him who evil thinks (the motto of the Order of the Garter).

MISTRESS QUICKLY With trial-fire touch me° his finger end.   *touch*
 If he be chaste, the flame will back descend
 And turn him to no pain. But if he start,
85 It is the flesh of a corrupted heart.
PISTOL A trial, come!
EVANS   Come! Will this wood° take fire?⁵   *(Falstaff's fingers)*
 [*The* FAIRIES *variously burn Falstaff's fingers and
 then pinch him.*]
FALSTAFF [*startled*] Oh, oh, oh!
MISTRESS QUICKLY Corrupt, corrupt, and tainted in desire!
 About him, fairies, sing a scornful rhyme
90 And, as you trip, still° pinch him to your time.   *continually*

The Song.

FAIRIES [*sing*]
   Fie on sinful fantasy! Fie on lust and luxury!°   *lechery*
   Lust is but a bloody fire,° kindled with unchaste   *fire of the blood*
    desire,
   Fed in heart whose flames aspire°   *rise up*
   As thoughts do blow them higher and higher.
95   Pinch him, fairies, mutually.° Pinch him for his   *all together*
    villainy.
   Pinch him, and burn him, and turn him about,
   Till candles, and starlight, and moonshine be out!
 [*Here they pinch him, and sing about him, and the
 *DOCTOR *comes one way and steals away first boy in
 white.*⁶ *And* SLENDER *another way he takes second boy
 in green. And* FENTON *steals Mistress* ANNE, *being in
 red. And a noise of hunting is made within: and all
 the* FAIRIES *run away.* FALSTAFF *pulls off his buck's
 head and rises up. And enter Master* PAGE, *Master
 *FORD, *and their wives* MISTRESS PAGE *and* MISTRESS
 FORD, *with Master* SHALLOW.]
PAGE [*to* FALSTAFF] Nay, do not fly. I think we have watched
 you° now.   *caught you in the act*
 Will none but Herne the Hunter serve your turn?
100 MISTRESS PAGE [*to* PAGE] I pray you, come, hold up° the jest   *prolong*
 no higher.°   *further*
 [*to* FALSTAFF] Now, good Sir John, how like you Windsor
 wives?
MISTRESS FORD See you these, husband? [*She points to the
 buck-horns.*] Do not these fair yokes°   *horns*
 Become the forest better than the town?
FORD [*to* FALSTAFF] Now, sir, who's a cuckold now? Master
105 Broom, Falstaff's a knave, a cuckoldly knave. Here are his
 horns, Master Broom. And, Master Broom, he hath enjoyed
 nothing of Ford's but his buck-basket, his cudgel, and twenty
 pounds of money, which must be paid to Master Broom. His
 horses are arrested° for it,⁷ Master Broom.   *seized as security*

---

5. Here and elsewhere in the scene, Falstaff is almost
equated with Herne's oak and hence treated like a
piece of wood—as the second syllable of his name
suggests. His entire name suggests his repeated sexual failures.

6. TEXTUAL COMMENT For the color-coding of the
fairies in this SD, absent in F but present in Q, see
Digital Edition TC 6 (Folio edited text).
7. See note to 4.3.11.

110 MISTRESS FORD   Sir John, we have had ill luck. We could never
meet. I will never take you for my love again, but I will always
count you my deer.

FALSTAFF   I do begin to perceive that I am made an ass.

FORD   Ay, and an ox too. Both the proofs are extant.[8]

115 FALSTAFF   And these are not fairies. I was three or four times
in the thought they were not fairies, and yet the guiltiness of
my mind, the sudden surprise of my powers,° drove the   (of reason)
grossness of the foppery° into a received belief, in despite of   deceit
the teeth of° all rhyme and reason, that they were fairies.   against
120 See now how wit may be made a Jack-a-Lent° when 'tis upon   butt
ill employment.

EVANS   Sir John Falstaff, serve Got and leave your desires,
and fairies will not pince you.

FORD   Well said, fairy Hugh.

125 EVANS   And leave you your jealousies too, I pray you.

FORD   I will never mistrust my wife again, till thou art able to
woo her in good English.

FALSTAFF   Have I laid my brain in the sun and dried it, that it
wants° matter to prevent so gross o'erreaching as this? Am I   lacks
130 ridden with° a Welsh goat too? Shall I have a coxcomb° of   harassed by / jester's cap
frieze? 'Tis time I were choked with a piece of toasted cheese.[9]

EVANS   Seese is not good to give putter; your belly is all putter.

FALSTAFF   Seese and putter? Have I lived to stand at the taunt
of one that makes fritters of English? This is enough to be
135 the decay of lust and late-walking° through the realm.   (for sexual purposes)

MISTRESS PAGE   Why, Sir John, do you think though° we would   even if
have thrust virtue out of our hearts by the head and shoulders, and have given ourselves without scruple to hell, that
ever the devil could have made you our delight?

140 FORD   What, a hodge-pudding?° A bag of flax?   sausage

MISTRESS PAGE   A puffed° man?   inflated

PAGE   Old, cold, withered, and of intolerable entrails?

FORD   And one that is as slanderous as Satan?

PAGE   And as poor as Job?

145 FORD   And as wicked as his wife?[1]

EVANS   And given to fornications, and to taverns, and sack,
and wine, and metheglins,° and to drinkings, and swear-   Welsh spiced drink
ings, and starings? Pribbles and prabbles?°   Raving and squabbles

FALSTAFF   Well, I am your theme. You have the start° of me. I   advantage
150 am dejected.° I am not able to answer the Welsh flannel.   humbled
Ignorance itself is a plummet o'er me.[2] Use me as you will.

FORD   Marry, sir, we'll bring you to Windsor to one Master
Broom, that you have cozened of money, to whom you should
have been° a pander. Over and above that° you have suffered,   intended to be / what
155 I think to repay that money will be a biting affliction.

---

8. "Ox" (fool, cuckold) is inspired by "yokes" (line 102).
The "proofs" are either the horns, which are "extant"
(existing), or the "ass" and the "ox."
9. "Welsh goat" (line 130) refers to the large number
of goats in Wales, "frieze" (line 131) to a coarse wool
made there, and "toasted cheese" to what was supposedly a favorite Welsh food.
1. Satan slanders Job (Job 1:9–11, 2:4–5); Job's wife
tempts him to curse God (2:9).

2. A "plummet" is a "plumb line," used for measuring
depths, with a pun on "plumbet," a woolen fabric and,
hence, connected with "Welsh flannel," one of Falstaff's names here for Evans (along with "Ignorance").
The ignorant Evans, the "Welsh flannel," is a woolen
fabric over Falstaff, by which Falstaff means that
even the ignorant Evans can plumb Falstaff's depths,
can see his true motives.

PAGE Yet be cheerful, knight. Thou shalt eat a posset³ tonight
at my house, where I will desire thee to laugh at my wife,
that now laughs at thee. Tell her Master Slender hath married her daughter.

160 MISTRESS PAGE [aside] Doctors doubt that.° If Anne Page be   (expresses disbelief)
my daughter, she is, by this,° Doctor Caius' wife.   now
     Enter SLENDER.

SLENDER Whoa, ho, ho, father Page!

PAGE Son? How now? How now, son, have you dispatched?°   settled the business

SLENDER Dispatched? I'll make the best in Gloucestershire
165 know on't°—would I were hanged, la, else!°   of it / otherwise

PAGE Of what, son?

SLENDER I came yonder at Eton to marry Mistress Anne
Page, and she's a great lubberly° boy! If it had not been i'th'   loutish
church, I would have swinged° him, or he should have   beaten
170 swinged me. If I did not think it had been Anne Page, would
I might never stir, and 'tis a postmaster's boy.°   stableboy

PAGE Upon my life, then, you took the wrong.

SLENDER What need you tell me that? I think so, when I took
a boy for a girl! If I had been married to him, for all° he was   even though
175 in woman's apparel, I would not have had him.

PAGE Why, this is your own folly! Did not I tell you how you
should know my daughter by her garments?

SLENDER I went to her in green, and cried "mum," and she cried
"budget," as Anne and I had appointed, and yet it was not
180 Anne, but a postmaster's boy.

MISTRESS PAGE [to PAGE] Good George, be not angry. I knew
of your purpose; turned my daughter into white, and indeed
she is now with the doctor at the deanery, and there married.
     Enter CAIUS.

CAIUS Vere is Mistress Page? By gar, I am cozened! I ha' mar-
185 ried un garçon, a boy, un paysan,° by gar! A boy, it is not Anne   a peasant
Page, by gar! I am cozened.

MISTRESS PAGE Why? Did you take her in white?

CAIUS Ay, by gar, and 'tis a boy! By gar, I'll raise all Windsor.

FORD This is strange. Who hath got the right Anne?

190 PAGE My heart misgives me. Here comes Master Fenton.
     [Enter FENTON and ANNE.]
How now, Master Fenton?

ANNE Pardon, good father. —Good my mother, pardon!

PAGE Now, mistress, how chance you went not with Master
Slender?

195 MISTRESS PAGE Why went you not with Master Doctor, maid?

FENTON You do amaze° her. Hear the truth of it.   confuse
You would have married her most shamefully
Where there was no proportion° held in love.   balance
The truth is, she and I, long since contracted,°   betrothed
200 Are now so sure° that nothing can dissolve° us.   united / separate
Th'offense is holy that she hath committed,
And this deceit loses the name of craft,
Of disobedience, or unduteous title,°   undutifulness
Since therein she doth evitate° and shun   avoid

3. Take a restorative drink of hot milk curdled with wine or ale.

205   A thousand irreligious cursèd hours
       Which forcèd marriage would have brought upon her.
       FORD [*to* PAGE *and* MISTRESS PAGE]   Stand not amazed. Here is
          no remedy.
       In love, the heavens themselves do guide the state:
       Money buys lands, and wives are sold by fate.
210   FALSTAFF   I am glad, though you have ta'en a special stand° to   *hunter's station*
       strike at me, that your arrow hath glanced.°   *missed*
       PAGE   Well, what remedy? —Fenton, heaven give thee joy. What
         cannot be eschewed must be embraced.
       FALSTAFF   When night-dogs run, all sorts of deer are chased.[4]
215   MISTRESS PAGE   Well, I will muse° no further. —Master Fenton,   *complain*
       Heaven give you many many merry days.
       Good husband, let us everyone go home,
       And laugh this sport o'er by a country fire,
       Sir John and all.
       FORD   Let it be so. Sir John,
220   To Master Broom you yet shall hold your word,
       For he tonight shall lie with Mistress Ford.   *Exeunt.*

---

4. When "dogs" (the failed suitors) run out of control at night, they may catch "all sorts of deer" (the disguised boys, rather than Anne). In other words, you can't control nocturnal intrigue.

Henry the Fifth

What makes somebody a great leader? The brief, brilliant life of King Henry V provides a good opportunity to reflect on that question. From a military point of view, Henry V was perhaps the most capable king England ever had. In 1414, reviving an English royal claim on the French throne, he invaded France. The following year, he won the Battle of Agincourt against impossible odds—a victory so surprising and decisive that it is still studied by military historians and strategists. Forced to sue for peace, the King of France signed a treaty declaring Henry heir to the French throne and consenting to a marriage between Henry and the French princess Katherine. Not surprisingly, Henry's story was a favorite with his English compatriots. It was lovingly chronicled by the historians Raphael Holinshed (died ca. 1580) and Edward Hall (d. 1547), and it was probably dramatized once or more by other playwrights before Shakespeare brought his own version to the stage in 1599.

In Shakespeare's play, Henry's impressive leadership is repeatedly emphasized by the Chorus, by his followers, and even occasionally by his enemies. He not merely copes with but triumphs over the difficult political situation he inherits when he comes to the throne. He unites his disputatious people against an external enemy, expends their aggressions abroad instead of at home, and gains himself a kingdom to boot. He displays unshakable personal courage in the campaign in France, in the smaller skirmishes as well as in the desperate moments before Agincourt. His "Once more unto the breach" speech (3.1.1–34)* and his prophetic vision of aged veterans boasting to their compatriots on St. Crispin's Day (4.3.18–67) have often been held up as models of inspirational eloquence.

However, *Henry V* clear-sightedly acknowledges that the factors that render someone an effective king are not necessarily morally admirable ones. Even while Shakespeare displays Henry's charisma to the full, he refuses to be entirely dazzled by his allure. In the early sixteenth century, Niccolò Machiavelli had introduced Renaissance political thinkers to the notion that success as a ruler might be separable from, or even inimical to, what was conventionally considered virtuous behavior. A successful leader, Machiavelli argued, needed the traits of both the fox and the lion; in other words, he had to know how to use deception and violence to achieve his ends. Shakespeare's Henry is certainly no monster of iniquity, but his career poses some of the same questions that Machiavelli raised in *The Prince*. What is the relationship of political success to personal goodness? Should princes be judged by moral rules different from those that apply to the rest of humankind?

In Shakespeare's play, such questions arise in a dramatic framework that complicates the answers it might offer. *Henry V* is the last written of a set of eight plays on medieval English history. Shakespeare's first four history plays had dealt with the tumultuous years between 1422 and 1485, when England was first at war with France and then, after 1455, embroiled in a civil war—the Wars of the Roses. Shakespeare wrote another four plays several years later, presenting the events of 1398 to 1420 that led up to these long wars over the royal succession. *Richard II* depicts Henry Bolingbroke's successful rebellion against Richard II and his coronation as Henry IV. The next two plays describe the troubled reign of the usurper, whose former allies turn

*All quotations are taken from the edited text of the Folio, printed here. The Digital Edition includes edited texts of both the Folio and the Quarto.

Henricus v. From John Rastell, *The Pastime of People* (1529).

against him and whose son keeps company with thieves. At the end of *2 Henry IV,* the King dies and young Prince Harry ascends the throne as Henry V. In the play that bears his name, Henry V belies his wastrel reputation and proves himself an astute ruler and canny military commander. In the final lines of *Henry V,* however, the Chorus foresees Henry's imminent death, after which civil strife will break out once again.

Henry V is, therefore, one of a group of plays rather than a free-standing work. It refers constantly to events before and after its own temporal limits, events familiar to Shakespeare's audience from plays they had already seen performed. Surely our awareness of the internecine strife that precedes and follows Henry's reign reinforces our admiration for him. Where others have failed and will again fail, miserably, Henry magnificently triumphs. At the same time, *Henry V* is haunted by problems merely deferred, not resolved. The Chorus's final prediction of imminent disaster darkens an otherwise straightforwardly triumphal conclusion; in the long view, the success of the play's hero looks transitory, even futile.

In 1599, such complexities may have seemed especially pertinent. England was mobilizing for a major campaign against Ireland to be led by Elizabeth's dashing young favorite, the Earl of Essex. *Henry V* registers both the patriotic excitement generated by the prospect of a military venture in foreign parts and the dread of war in a notoriously difficult environment (in the event, Essex's expedition was a disaster). These acutely mixed feelings were symptomatic of more general disputes about England's foreign policy at the turn of the seventeenth century. For much of the sixteenth century, England had attempted merely to defend its borders, but as it became wealthier and more powerful, expansion seemed feasible again. Ireland and the Netherlands beckoned; so did the New World, where France and Spain had already established colonies. Henry V's foray into France typified the kind of aggressive enterprise that some of Shakespeare's contemporaries wished their nation to underwrite and that others denounced as wasteful and dangerous.

Given these dramatic and historical complexities, it is not surprising that *Henry V* has generated striking interpretive disagreements, nor that the play continues to be viewed through the lens of contemporary events. In Laurence Olivier's film version, made during World War II, *Henry V* is a vindication of England's excellence, and the victory at Agincourt a hopeful precedent for success in a justified European war. Kenneth Branagh's 1989 film, on the other hand, reflects the murkier experience of more recent conflicts: the U.S. intervention in Vietnam, the British in the Falkland Islands. Did Shakespeare intend the play as a paean to militarism or as an exposé of war's pointless brutality? Is Henry supposed to be a heroic or a repellent character? Is the war in France justified or purely expedient?

A closer look at *Henry V* reveals a play not only deeply equivocal but self-consciously so. The capstone of Shakespeare's years of experimentation in the genre of history play, *Henry V* seems profoundly aware of the way generic constraints bear in upon its hero. Comedy and tragedy form themselves upon the rhythms of an individual life, ending in marriage or in death. History plays, by contrast, even when they seem to concentrate on the fortunes of a single character, dramatize the life of a nation, or at least its governing class. Characters in history plays are conceived as an endless generational succession, inheriting a political and historical situation from their ancestors and passing it down to their descendants. When one person dies, another steps into his place. A king's marriage or death represents not merely a natural culmination of his personal story, but one episode in an ongoing, unending sequence of events.

The young King Henry V is, therefore, both more and less than a talented and intelligent individual. One of a series, like the play that bears his name, he must come to terms with what it means to be part of a family line, what it means for one's "career" to begin before birth and end long after death. And Henry's family line is, of course, a tangled matter. His dubious title to the English throne reflects some of the instabilities in the concept of inheritance: what can it mean to acquire name and title "legitimately" from a man who stole the throne? The passing of property and title from one generation to the next might seem to reflect facts of nature, but it is also, as the Archbishop of Canterbury's discussion of "Salic law" reveals in 1.2, a matter of custom, a cultural construction. Inheritance can be altered as well by force or by negotiation: Henry IV compelled Richard to abdicate, and Henry V's victory at Agincourt requires the French King to recognize an English conqueror rather than his own son as heir to the French throne.

Troubles over the way proper generational sequence ought to be defined resonate throughout the play. War, in particular, seems intimately tied up with questions of lineage. Battlefield heroics can reinforce and clarify the relationship between fathers and sons. King Charles of France, for instance, describes Henry's belligerence as his birthright:

> The kindred of him hath been fleshed upon us,
> And he is bred out of that bloody strain
> That haunted us in our familiar paths.
> Witness our too much memorable shame
> When Cressy battle fatally was struck,
> And all our princes captived by the hand
> Of that black name, Edward, Black Prince of Wales,
> Whiles that his mountain sire, on mountain standing
> Up in the air, crowned with the golden sun,
> Saw his heroical seed, and smiled to see him
> Mangle the work of nature and deface
> The patterns that by God and by French fathers
> Had twenty years been made.
>
> (2.4.50–62)

Henry's great-uncle, Edward the Black Prince, butchers the French while the Prince's father, King Edward III, proudly looks on. There seem to be no mothers in this entirely male domain, merely God and fathers in alliance, so that Edward III himself seems rather improbably deified, "[u]p in the air, crowned with the golden sun." Henry, in his stirring speech to his troops at Harfleur, evidences a similar pattern of assumptions:

> On, on, you noblest English,
> Whose blood is fet from fathers of war-proof,
> Fathers that like so many Alexanders
> Have in these parts from morn till even fought,
> And sheathed their swords for lack of argument.
> Dishonor not your mothers; now attest
> That those whom you called fathers did beget you.
>
> (3.1.17–23)

Mothers get a mention from Henry, as they did not from the French King, but they contribute nothing of their own nature to their offspring: their function is merely to duplicate the fathers in the next generation. Any discrepancy between the achievement of the fathers and the achievement of the sons, in fact, "dishonors" the mothers by implying that they must have slept with men other than their husbands, because the only explanation for such an inconsistency is that the biological father must be different from the acknowledged one. Once again, fathers set demanding precedents for sons eager to emulate their exploits but inevitably threatened by the possibility of falling short. The French King and Henry imagine inheritance, which might seem a passive process, as a strenuous endeavor.

If battle clarifies the pedigrees of winners, it simultaneously obscures those of the losers. In practical terms, of course, Henry's victory debars the Dauphin, the French King's son and heir apparent, from assuming his father's title. More generally, however, as both Henry and the French King insist, defeat in battle disrupts familial affinity, defacing paternal patterns, dishonoring mothers. Negotiating with Harfleur's governor, Henry predicts the consequences of the town's refusal to surrender quietly:

> why, in a moment look to see
> The blind and bloody soldier with foul hand
> Defile the locks of your shrill-shrieking daughters;
> Your fathers taken by the silver beards
> And their most reverend heads dashed to the walls;
> Your naked infants spitted upon pikes,
> Whiles the mad mothers with their howls confused
> Do break the clouds, as did the wives of Jewry
> At Herod's bloody-hunting slaughtermen.
> (3.4.33–41)

On the face of it, it might seem surprising for a general to characterize his own troops as rapists and murderers, or implicitly to compare himself with the infanticidal King Herod, one of the Bible's wickedest villains. Yet Henry's rhetorical tactics are entirely deliberate: by describing his soldiers' potential victims as members of families—as daughters, fathers, infants, mothers—he heightens the impact of their violence. The rampaging army, he implies, will shatter not merely individuals but whole networks of affiliation. The speech effectively intimidates his auditors, who give up without a fight.

The difficulties of succession and inheritance are issues for Shakespeare the playwright as well as for the characters in his play. Just as the protagonist Henry V must strive to match and excel the patterns set by his ancestors, so the play Henry V must concern itself with what it means to be a sequel in two different senses: the way in which it re-presents actual historical events in a necessarily diminished theatrical form, and the way in which it must struggle to gratify an audience whose expectations had been formed by three exceedingly popular plays in the same series. At the beginning of every act, a Chorus pointedly emphasizes the play's self-conscious lack of realism:

> Can this cockpit hold
> The vasty fields of France? Or may we cram
> Within this wooden O the very casques
> That did affright the air at Agincourt?
> (Prologue, lines 11–14)

Of course, Henry V is no more implausible than most other Renaissance plays. But in a sense, the theatrical anxieties of Henry V are cognate with the personal anxieties of its hero; the play is afraid of degenerating from its precursors, proving an inadequate replica of a distinguished original. And just as Henry V seems to overcompensate, not merely living up to his illustrious predecessors but going beyond them, so too Henry V, like many sequels, copes with its belatedness by a strategy of overstatement. It exaggerates some of the themes and issues of the earlier plays. In

Soldiers using a battering ram. From Flavius Vegetius
Renatus, *The Four Books of Flavius Vegetius Renatus:
Briefly Containing a Plain Form, and Perfect Knowledge of
Martial Policy* . . . (1572).

1 Henry IV, Hotspur, Prince Harry's valiant antagonist, epitomized many of the traditional ideals of chivalry—a word derived from the French *cheval,* "horse." In *Henry V,*
the Dauphin, Henry's new rival, writes a sonnet to his horse that begins "Wonder of
nature!"—for, he says, "my horse is my mistress" (3.8.37, 40). Hotspur's chivalry,
caricatured to the point of ridiculousness, degenerates in *Henry V* into bestiality
jokes made at the expense of a blustering fop.

Shakespeare dramatizes Henry's success, in other words, not merely by magnifying
his exploits but by minimizing the threat from possible competitors. Although the
enemies of Henry's adulthood are technically more formidable than the enemies of his
adolescence, they are characterized as bumbling and laughable, so that Henry's victory
over them seems virtually preordained. Henry's allies seem similarly diminished. Falstaff, who dominated much of *1* and *2 Henry IV,* dies without reappearing in *Henry V,*
leaving his cronies Bardolph, Nym, and Pistol to accompany Henry to France. They
are joined by Fluellen, a Welsh soldier; MacMorris, an Irish one; Jamy, a Scots one; and
Williams, a rural English one. This miscellany is proof of Henry's charisma; while in
the previous plays the Irish, Scots, and Welsh were up in arms, *Henry V* successfully
enlists them in his cause—not by homogenizing their differences, but by inspiring their
allegiance to him even as they quarrel furiously with one another. Henry's triumph at
Agincourt, Shakespeare claims, involves all the peoples of the British Isles. At the same
time, these loyal adherents are given little of Falstaff's subversive wit, presumably
because Falstaff's wholesale critique of military valor would undercut too thoroughly
the premises of Henry's royal magnetism. Even the bluff yeoman Williams, who complains of the disproportionate suffering that common people undergo to satisfy the
ambitions of their betters, does not dissent from the fundamental principle of social and
military hierarchy: to disobey one's superiors, he claims, "were against all proportion of

subjection" (4.1.135). For better or worse, everyone seems to agree, the subject's life is at the ruler's disposal.

Shakespeare's excision of Falstaff's skeptical intelligence from *Henry V* means that there is no one within the play to point out the ironies of many of the turns of the plot. Presumably, though no one comments explicitly upon it, the venality of the clerics who finance Henry's expedition to France is sufficiently clear to the audience. Likewise, when Gower loyally remarks that Henry, unlike Alexander, never killed any of his friends, we are likely to think back to Falstaff's death, attributed earlier to Henry's neglect, and also to reflect that of Henry's other Eastcheap chums only Pistol has survived the "great victory" at Agincourt. For Henry's self-assertion necessarily occurs not merely at the expense of the French Dauphin, whom he displaces, but at the expense of civilians and allies. Henry's soldiers are wasted by disease, hanged, occasionally even killed in battle. In 4.1, the common soldier worries, in an age without veteran's benefits, of dying with "wives left poor behind them" and "children rawly left" (lines 129–31). Just before the Battle of Agincourt, Henry inspires his outnumbered men by calling them a "band of brothers" striving as one, despite ethnic and class differences, toward a glorious shared goal.

> For he today that sheds his blood with me
> Shall be my brother. Be he ne'er so vile,
> This day shall gentle his condition.
>   (4.3.60–63)

The speech is a famously stirring one, yet after the victory at Agincourt, Henry apparently forgets his promise to "gentle" the lowborn soldiers who fought on his behalf. As we have seen, when kings talk about inheritance, the mothers crucial for reproduction seem to disappear; likewise, the victories of an army are attributed to the king who leads them, and the followers required for the great man's "glorious victory" do not necessarily share in its benefits.

Neither we nor Henry can be certain whether, or to what extent, his exceptional situation and abilities should afford him special privileges. In fact, Henry's unusual gifts as a leader of men render the uncertainty more pointed. Richard II disregarded common folk, and Henry IV deliberately avoided them; but Henry V inspires them by his capacity to immerse himself sympathetically in their lives. His insistence upon his ordinariness becomes a strategy of rule—part of what he is loved for during his lifetime and what becomes legendary after his death. But then, when he insists on seeing himself as a unique case nonetheless, he seems not merely to be asserting a king's usual prerogatives, but to be inconsistently or hypocritically making special allowances for himself.

This unresolved ambivalence becomes obvious in 4.1, when Henry disguises himself as a commoner and ventures among his rank and file. Initially, he argues for the essential similarity between himself and his followers:

> I think the King is but a man, as I am. The violet smells to him as it doth to me; the element shows to him as it doth to me. All his senses have but human conditions. His ceremonies laid by, in his nakedness he appears but a man. And though his affections are higher mounted than ours, yet when they stoop, they stoop with the like wing. (lines 98–103)

The ordinary soldiers, Williams and Bates, are unconvinced, pointing out that if they lose the battle, the King will be ransomed while they will be killed. And yet, they note, because they are required to obey the King under any circumstances, they need not concern themselves with the justice of his cause: their blood will be on Henry's head if he is waging an unjust war. The common soldiers see the King as unlike themselves, with special responsibilities that compensate for his special privileges. Henry responds indignantly:

The King is not bound to answer the particular endings of his soldiers, the father of his son, nor the master of his servant, for they purpose not their death when they purpose their services. Besides, there is no king, be his cause never so spotless, if it come to the arbitrement of swords, can try it out with all unspotted soldiers. Some, peradventure, have on them the guilt of premeditated and contrived murder; some, of beguiling virgins with the broken seals of perjury; some, making the wars their bulwark, that have before gored the gentle bosom of peace with pillage and robbery. (lines 143–52)

Henry resists accepting the extraordinary moral burden his followers would confer upon him. Yet his refusal is based not on his earlier assertion of the shared humanity of king and subject, but on a conviction of the king's special position. He distinguishes sharply and problematically between the king's "superior" violence—the violence of war—and the violence of individual subjects, which is merely criminal. After the soldiers leave, Henry exclaims bitterly:

> Upon the King! "Let us our lives, our souls,
> Our debts, our careful wives,
> Our children, and our sins, lay on the King!"
> We must bear all. O hard condition,
> Twin-born with greatness, subject to the breath
> Of every fool whose sense no more can feel
> But his own wringing. What infinite heartsease
> Must kings neglect that private men enjoy!
> (lines 207–14)

It is hard to take this self-pity seriously, given that Henry attempts to deflect all blame for his actions onto enemies and inferiors, even while accepting as his due the rewards that accrue to him by virtue of his exceptional status.

However, Shakespeare also shows effectively the King's genuine isolation from ordinary pleasures of work and play that normal people can take for granted. Though he repudiates Falstaff, the King retains a distinctly sportive quality; but the moral and practical gap that yawns between the ascendant Henry and his correspondingly diminished associates complicates the effect of his playfulness. In 2.2, with a typical flourish, he pretends to hand the traitors Scrope, Grey, and Cambridge their military commissions, after feigning to inquire about mercy for traitors. Actually, he gives them letters showing that he knows of their plot. This is splendid theater, but it is also quite chilling: Henry plays with his guilty victims as a cat plays with a mouse. His joke signifies not true contest, but absolute control.

Elsewhere, too, Henry's power tips the balance of hostility and affection that usually characterizes practical jokes in a markedly aggressive direction. In disguise on the eve of the Battle of Agincourt, he argues with the commoner Williams, as we have already seen, over the question of the king's responsibility for his subjects. He and Williams exchange gloves so they will be able to resume the quarrel after the battle. In 4.7, with victory assured, Henry gives Williams's glove to Fluellen to see what Williams will do when he sees it again. When Williams attacks Fluellen, Henry stops the fight, pretending to be angry at the insult to himself. Williams—technically guilty of the capital crime of mutiny—defends himself boldly enough, and Henry, thinking to be generous, returns Williams's glove to him filled with coins. Yet Williams fails to thank Henry, and when Fluellen attempts to add to the gift, Williams spurns it angrily. It is unclear from the script whether Williams eventually accepts the gold; either way, Henry's power contaminates what he wants to see as a game. While in the earlier plays Prince Harry always had the advantage of rank, it was still possible for Falstaff to give him almost as good as he got. Now that Henry is king and Falstaff is dead, Henry is always the winner, and so the game is no game at all. Arguably, in fact, Henry goes to war with

Game of tennis (see 1.2.262–67). From Johann Amos Comenius, *Orbis Sensualium Pictus* (1659).

France because he misses a sense of *competition*—because the fate of the effective king is that he cannot find real opposition at home.

Henry's wooing of Katherine in 5.2 is typified by the same dubious sense of fun. This scene, often quite endearing onstage, is also entirely beside the point. We hear from the Chorus in 3.0 that the French King suggested marrying Katherine to Henry before his forces arrived in France, but Henry rejected the offer because the suggested dowry—some "petty and unprofitable dukedoms"—did not suffice. Nonetheless, in 5.2, Henry calls Katherine his "capital demand" and presents himself to her as a wooer. He pretends that Katherine is free to reject him, even though the marriage is already arranged as part of the peace treaty. Rather like Williams, Katherine refuses to play along: when he asks, "Canst thou love me?" she replies, "I cannot tell" (lines 182–83). Then "wilt thou have me?" "Dat is as it shall please *le roi mon père*" (lines 228–29). Is Katherine being coy, or is she simply speaking the literal truth? In the game as Henry constructs it, Katherine's refusals can as easily be interpreted as coquettishness as real denial. In other words, even if she refuses to play Henry's game, she necessarily plays it anyhow. In *Henry V*, Shakespeare must cope with a knotty dramatic problem: how to interest an audience in a man who has, or wins, everything—whose life seems an unbroken series of successes. In the final scene as in the rest of the play, Shakespeare fascinates us by exhibiting the inevitably equivocal nature of kingly glory.

KATHARINE EISAMAN MAUS

SELECTED BIBLIOGRAPHY

Altman, Joel. "'Vile Participation': The Amplification of Violence in the Theatre of *Henry V*." *Shakespeare Quarterly* 42 (1991): 1–32. Explores *Henry V* in the context of contemporary political and religious issues—in particular, the debate over the nature of Communion.

Barton, Anne. "The King Disguised: Shakespeare's *Henry V* and the Comical History." *The Triple Bond: Plays, Mainly Shakespearean, in Performance*. Ed. Joseph G. Price. University Park: Pennsylvania State UP, 1975. 92–117. Sees *Henry V* in a tradition of Elizabethan plays that combine history and comedy.

Cormack, Bradin. "'If We Be Conquered': Legal Nationalism and the France of Shakespeare's English Histories." *A Power to Do Justice: Jurisdiction and Early English Literature.* Chicago: U of Chicago P, 2007. 177–226. Examines Shakespeare's treatment of France and the French language in terms of sixteenth-century English anxieties about national identity.

Daniel, Drew. "Scambling Harry and Sampling Hal." *Shakesqueer: A Queer Companion to the Complete Works of Shakespeare.* Durham, NC: Duke UP, 2011. 121–29. Discusses modern electronic digital sampling as an analogy for King Henry's ability to appropriate and repurpose the rhetoric of others.

Danson, Lawrence. "*Henry V:* King, Chorus, and Critics." *Shakespeare Quarterly* 34 (1983): 27–43. Examines King Henry as an actor and the Chorus as a means of drawing attention to the relationship between history and theater.

Dollimore, Jonathan, and Alan Sinfield. "History and Ideology, Masculinity and Miscegenation." *Faultlines: Cultural Materialism and the Politics of Dissident Reading.* Berkeley: U of California P, 1992. 109–42. Asserts that imperialist and masculinist attitudes reinforce one another in the play.

Dutton, Richard. "Methinks the Truth Should Live from Age to Age: The Dating and Contexts of *Henry V.*" *Huntington Library Quarterly* 68 (2005): 173–204. Reviews the different political contexts of the Quarto and Folio versions of the play.

Greenblatt, Stephen. "Invisible Bullets: Renaissance Authority and Its Subversion, *Henry IV* and *Henry V.*" *Political Shakespeare: New Essays in Cultural Materialism.* Ed. Jonathan Dollimore and Alan Sinfield. Manchester: Manchester UP, 1985. 18–47. Explores theater and the glamour of a royal power that incorporates what seems to undermine it.

Kerrigan, John. "Oaths, Threats, and *Henry V.*" *Review of English Studies,* n.s. 63 (2012): 551–71. Examines binding language and speech acts in the play.

Quint, David. "Alexander the Pig: Shakespeare on History and Poetry." *Boundary* 2.10 (1982): 49–63. Discusses Shakespeare's relation to Renaissance humanists' conceptions of history.

Rabkin, Norman. "Rabbits, Ducks, and *Henry V.*" *Shakespeare Quarterly* 28 (1977): 279–96. Presents *Henry V* as an unresolvably ambiguous play.

FILMS

Henry V. 1944. Dir. Laurence Olivier. UK. 137 min. Colorful, patriotic version made near the end of World War II, with Olivier as a very sympathetic king. Intelligently translates the play's theatrical self-consciousness to the medium of film.

Henry V. 1979. Dir. David Giles. UK. 163 min. This BBC-TV production retains more features of a stage production than do the elaborate Olivier and Branagh versions. David Gwillim is a pleasant but resolute hero.

Henry V. 1989. Dir. Kenneth Branagh. UK. 137 min. Harsher and more violent than the Olivier version, with an elaborate reenactment of the Battle of Agincourt. Branagh stars as a grimly driven Henry.

Henry V. 2012. Dir. Thea Sharrock. UK. An abridged version, the fourth in the BBC *Hollow Crown* series. Tom Hiddleston, who played Prince Hal in *1* and *2 Henry IV,* stars as Henry V.

TEXTUAL INTRODUCTION

Henry V exists in two distinct forms, with distinct titles: the 1623 First Folio version, *The Life of Henry the Fifth* (F), and the Quarto version, *The Chronicle History of Henry the Fifth* (Q1), published in 1600, just one year after the play's first performance on the London stage. There was also a Second Quarto, published in 1602, but apart from a very few emendations, this text is virtually a reprint of Q1. The play was published in quarto a third time (Q3) in 1619, though the title page bears the incorrect date of 1608; in addition to having corrected a number of errors in Q1, Q3 seems to have been consulted in the setting of F. For its part, F, which runs to slightly more than twice the length of the Quarto versions, has been the preferred text for virtually every modern edition—and every modern staging—of the play. Most scholars and editors agree that even though it was printed more than two decades earlier, Q1 actually represents a later state of the play than appears in F. While F is generally thought to derive from Shakespeare's "foul papers," and thus to enjoy a high degree of authority, Q1 is derived from F and, some have argued, may therefore represent (at least in part) Shakespeare's subsequent revisions of the play. But even if Q1's revisions and cuts and abridgments are not strictly Shakespearean, to the extent that they may represent the play as it was actually staged at one moment they nevertheless can lay claim to a certain playhouse authority.

The major differences between F and Q1 are easily summarized. To begin with the most conspicuous differences, the Chorus appears only in F, and the Dauphin who appears in F has a larger role than in the Quarto version, as Q1 seems to heed the French King's command (in F 3.6 and Q1 Scene 9) that his son remain with him in Rouen while the other French nobles ride out to engage Henry in the field of battle. F ahistorically (and in contradiction to one of Shakespeare's main historical source texts, Raphael Holinshed's *Chronicles of England, Scotland, and Ireland*) places the Dauphin at the Battle of Agincourt. Additionally, Q1 frequently cuts or transposes scenes, abridges a number of the longer speeches (Henry's St. Crispin's Day speech, most notably), and eliminates certain characters altogether, including Captains Mac-Morris and Jamy (figures who, in F, represent the Irish and the Scots), as well as a number of nonspeaking parts. Q1 also offers a slightly modified list of characters: the Bedford in F becomes Q1's Clarence, the Westmorland of F is Warwick in Q1, and Q1's Bourbon is given lines in the Agincourt scenes that in F are assigned to Bretagne or the Dauphin.

There are a number of competing theories to account for the relationship between Q1 and F, including the suggestion that Q1 was based on an incomplete or less-than-successful memorial reconstruction of the F text in which those actors who played the roles of Exeter and Gower transcribed the play from memory (which would account for the higher degree of reliability for those scenes in which they appeared onstage). Alternatively, it has been argued that Q1 represents a trimmed and abridged version of the F text, prepared, perhaps, for performance on one of the company's provincial tours (which would account for the relative brevity of Q1, as well as for the decrease in the number of speaking parts). Of course, it is possible that both theories may be correct: the company of players may have entrusted the abridgment of the maximal text (represented in F) to those players who had the roles of Exeter and Gower, whose work was based largely—though perhaps not exclusively—on their recollection and reconstruction of the play. Taken together, these hypotheses, as well as the nature of the text itself, might encourage readers and editors to consider Q1 as differently authoritative, rather than as nonauthoritative or as one of the so-called "bad quartos" that have reached us through a process of degradation and corruption. Although this is indeed the way in which Q1 has been historically understood (not unlike the situation one finds with the Q1 *Hamlet*, for example), some important recent textual scholarship on Shakespeare as reviser of his plays, for instance, or on the play text's proximity to an actual theatrical staging, has enabled a new approach to Q1 that accepts it as a later—though not as a wholly corrupted—version of the F text that is valuable on its own aesthetic and historical terms.

Howard Marchitello

PERFORMANCE NOTE

All productions of *Henry V* must address the dissonance between the Chorus's ideal-ized presentation of events and the thorny realities that Shakespeare describes. Some take the Chorus as a guide and strive to present Henry as "the mirror of all Christian kings," the brave, genial, pious hero that audiences expect. Such a Henry earnestly proclaims the common soldiers his brothers, seems troubled when acquiescing to Bardolph's execution, and appears genuinely smitten with Katherine. Others present a ruthless, role-playing machiavel who woos out of policy rather than passion, orates rather than prays, and affects humility among his soldiers while treating their lives and deaths with cool indifference. The text can be adapted to suit the chosen char-acterization: directors can, for example, omit (or emphasize) Henry's threat to defile the French daughters at Harfleur, or rearrange scenes so that Henry's unmotivated killing of his French prisoners seems to revenge the lives of the slain English boys. Nevertheless, even the most idealized Henrys tend to provoke contrary feelings.

The two popular film versions (Olivier, 1944; Branagh, 1989) have influenced subse-quent productions significantly. Many directors follow Branagh in depicting war as an unglamorous enterprise, ennobling the King as an isolated, war-weary figure forced into unpleasant choices. Each film's Chorus has been likewise influential by initially fore-grounding the play's theatricality, making any ensuing attempts at realism more affect-ing by contrast. Today's directors must decide whether to take the Chorus's disavowals of theater's representational power as a challenge to present realistic armies, horses, and cities, or as a license for minimalism and stylization. They also must decide whether Pistol, Bardolph, and Nym should alienate or engage audiences, their vices motivated by greed or by a will to survive after Henry abandons them in *2 Henry IV*. Meanwhile, the prelates can be savvy statesmen or fools; the French self-satisfied dandies or aggrieved patriots; Michael Williams a reasonable *vox populi* or an inveterate cynic. Other consid-erations include whether the multinational British soldiers are unified or fragmented, whether to give the French wars contemporary relevance, and whether to stage the deaths of Pistol's Boy, Bardolph, and Le Fer.

BRETT GAMBOA

The Life of Henry the Fifth

[THE PERSONS OF THE PLAY

CHORUS

The English:
KING Henry the Fifth
Duke of BEDFORD ⎫
Duke of GLOUCESTER ⎬ brothers to King Henry
Duke of CLARENCE ⎭
Duke of EXETER, uncle to King Henry
Duke of YORK
Earl of HUNTINGDON
Earl of SALISBURY
Earl of WARWICK
Earl of WESTMORLAND
Richard, Earl of CAMBRIDGE ⎫
Henry, Lord SCROPE of Masham ⎬ traitors
Sir Thomas GREY ⎭
Archbishop of CANTERBURY
Bishop of ELY
Sir Thomas ERPINGHAM
Captain FLUELLEN ⎫
Captain GOWER ⎬ officers
Captain JAMY ⎪
Captain MACMORRIS ⎭
John BATES ⎫
Alexander COURT ⎬ soldiers
Michael WILLIAMS ⎭
HERALD

BARDOLPH
NYM
PISTOL
BOY
HOSTESS Quickly

The French:
Charles the Sixth, KING OF FRANCE
QUEEN ISABEL, Queen of France
The DAUPHIN, son to the King of France and Queen Isabel
Princess KATHERINE, daughter to the King of France and Queen Isabel
ALICE, attending on Princess Katherine
Duke of BERRY
Duke of BOURBON
Duke of BRETAGNE
Duke of ORLÉANS
CONSTABLE of France
Lord RAMBURES
Earl of GRANDPRÉ

Duke of BURGUNDY
MONTJOY, the French herald
GOVERNOR of Harfleur
French AMBASSADORS to England
Monsieur Le Fer, a FRENCH SOLDIER
French MESSENGER
Attendants, Lords, Soldiers, Citizens of Harfleur, Prisoners]

Prologue

Enter CHORUS.[1]

CHORUS   Oh, for a muse of fire that would ascend
    The brightest heaven of invention,°   *imagination*
    A kingdom for a stage, princes to act,
    And monarchs to behold the swelling° scene.   *expansive; splendid*
5   Then should the warlike Harry, like himself,
    Assume the port° of Mars,° and at his heels,   *bearing / god of war*
    Leashed in like hounds, should famine, sword, and fire
    Crouch for employment. But pardon, gentles° all,   *gentlefolk*
    The flat unraisèd° spirits that hath dared   *uninspired*
10   On this unworthy scaffold° to bring forth   *platform*
    So great an object. Can this cockpit° hold   *small cockfighting arena*
    The vasty fields of France? Or may we cram
    Within this wooden O° the very casques°   *round theater / helmets*
    That did affright the air at Agincourt?[2]
15   Oh, pardon, since a crooked figure[3] may
    Attest° in little place a million,   *Represent*
    And let us, ciphers° to this great account,°   *zeroes / sum; story*
    On your imaginary forces° work.   *powers of imagination*
    Suppose within the girdle of these walls
20   Are now confined two mighty monarchies,
    Whose high, uprearèd, and abutting fronts°   *frontiers*
    The perilous narrow ocean° parts asunder.   *(English Channel)*
    Piece out our imperfections with your thoughts;
    Into a thousand parts divide one man
25   And make imaginary puissance.°   *power*
    Think, when we talk of horses, that you see them
    Printing their proud hooves i'th' receiving earth.
    For 'tis your thoughts that now must deck° our kings,   *equip*
    Carry them here and there, jumping o'er times,
30   Turning th'accomplishment of many years
    Into an hourglass: for the which supply,°   *to supplement which*
    Admit me Chorus to this history,
    Who Prologue-like your humble patience pray,
    Gently to hear, kindly to judge our play.[4]   *Exit.*

1.1

Enter the [Archbishop] of CANTERBURY *and [the*
Bishop of] ELY.

CANTERBURY   My lord, I'll tell you, that self° bill is urged   *same*

---

1. TEXTUAL COMMENT For a short account of the role of
the Chorus, who is present in the Folio text but not
in the shorter Quarto, see Digital Edition TC 1 (Folio
edited text).
2. Site of Henry's famous victory over the French
in 1415.
3. A zero, which multiplies a digit's value by ten.

crooked: curved.
4. PERFORMANCE COMMENT Different productions
have interpreted the role of the Chorus in widely varying ways. For a discussion of some options, see Digital
Edition PC 1.
1.1 Location: In Henry's court.

Which in th'eleventh year of the last king's reign
Was like,° and had indeed against us passed,   *likely*
But that the scambling and unquiet time
5   Did push it out of farther question.°   *consideration*
ELY   But how, my lord, shall we resist it now?
CANTERBURY   It must be thought on. If it pass against us
We lose the better half of our possession,
For all the temporal lands[1] which men devout
10   By testament have given to the Church
Would they strip from us, being valued thus:
As much as would maintain, to the king's honor,
Full fifteen earls and fifteen hundred knights,
Six thousand and two hundred good esquires,[2]
15   And to relief of lazars° and weak age,   *lepers*
Of indigent faint souls past corporal° toil,   *bodily*
A hundred almshouses, right well supplied;
And to the coffers of the King beside,
A thousand pounds by th' year. Thus runs the bill.
ELY   This would drink deep.
20   CANTERBURY   'Twould drink the cup and all.
ELY   But what prevention?
CANTERBURY   The King is full of grace and fair regard.°   *kindly inclination*
ELY   And a true lover of the holy Church.
CANTERBURY   The courses of his youth promised it not.
25   The breath no sooner left his father's body
But that his wildness, mortified° in him,   *struck dead*
Seemed to die too; yea, at that very moment
Consideration° like an angel came   *Spiritual reflection*
And whipped th'offending Adam° out of him,   *innate depravity*
30   Leaving his body as a paradise
T'envelop and contain celestial spirits.
Never was such a sudden scholar made;
Never came reformation in a flood
With such a heady currence° scouring faults,   *headlong current*
35   Nor never Hydra-headed[3] willfulness
So soon did lose his seat°—and all at once—   *throne*
As in this King.
ELY   We are blessèd in the change.
CANTERBURY   Hear him but reason in divinity°   *theology*
And, all-admiring, with an inward wish
40   You would desire the King were made a prelate.°   *an important clergyman*
Hear him debate of commonwealth affairs,
You would say it hath been all in all his study.
List° his discourse of war and you shall hear   *Listen to*
A fearful battle rendered you in music.
45   Turn him to any cause of policy,°   *political issue*
The Gordian knot[4] of it he will unloose,
Familiar° as his garter, that when he speaks,   *Offhandedly*

1. Land devoted to secular uses. Parliament is attempting in this bill to transfer much of the wealth of the
Catholic Church into the King's hands. The claim that
the Church mismanaged its resources was one pretext
for Henry VIII's confiscation of them in the 1530s, a bit
more than a century after the reign of Henry V and
about sixty years before Shakespeare wrote this play.

2. Gentlemen below knightly rank.
3. Many-headed (the Hydra was a monstrous snake,
killed by Hercules).
4. It was foretold that whoever untied the intricate
Gordian knot would rule Asia; Alexander the Great
cut it with his sword.

The air, a chartered libertine,° is still,   *licensed freedman*
And the mute wonder lurketh in men's ears
50 To steal his sweet and honeyed sentences.
So that the art and practic part of life
Must be the mistress to this theoric[5]—
Which is a wonder how his grace should glean it,
Since his addiction° was to courses vain,   *inclination*
55 His companies° unlettered, rude, and shallow,   *companions*
His hours filled up with riots,° banquets, sports,   *reveling*
And never noted in him any study,
Any retirement, any sequestration°   *removal*
From open haunts and popularity.[6]
60 ELY The strawberry grows underneath the nettle,
And wholesome berries thrive and ripen best
Neighbored by fruit of baser quality;
And so the Prince obscured his contemplation
Under the veil of wildness, which, no doubt,
65 Grew like the summer grass, fastest by night,
Unseen, yet crescive in his faculty.[7]
CANTERBURY It must be so, for miracles are ceased,[8]
And therefore we must needs admit the means°   *natural causes*
How things are perfected.
ELY   But, my good lord,
70 How now for mitigation of this bill
Urged by the Commons? Doth his majesty
Incline to it, or no?
CANTERBURY   He seems indifferent,
Or rather swaying more upon our part
Than cherishing th'exhibitors[9] against us.
75 For I have made an offer to his majesty,
Upon our spiritual convocation,[1]
And in regard of causes now in hand
Which I have opened° to his grace at large,   *expounded*
As touching France, to give a greater sum
80 Than ever at one time the clergy yet
Did to his predecessors part withal.°   *with*
ELY How did this offer seem received, my lord?
CANTERBURY With good acceptance of his majesty,
Save that there was not time enough to hear,
85 As I perceived his grace would fain° have done,   *gladly*
The severals[2] and unhidden passages°   *channels of descent*
Of his true titles to some certain dukedoms,
And generally to the crown and seat of France,
Derived from Edward,° his great-grandfather.   *(King Edward III)*
90 ELY What was th'impediment that broke this off?
CANTERBURY The French ambassador upon that instant
Craved audience, and the hour I think is come
To give him hearing. Is it four o'clock?
ELY It is.

---

5. *the art . . . theoric:* practical experience must have taught him the theory.
6. From public places and unrefined companions.
7. Yet growing according to its natural ability.
8. Protestants believed that no miracles occurred after scriptural times (anachronistic in the mouth of a medieval archbishop).
9. Parliamentary sponsors of the bill.
1. On behalf of the assembled clergy.
2. Legal means by which land is conveyed in separate parts to different heirs.

95 CANTERBURY Then go we in, to know his embassy,°   *message*
         Which I could with a ready guess declare
         Before the Frenchman speak a word of it.
    ELY I'll wait upon you, and I long to hear it.   *Exeunt.*

                          1.2 (Q Scene 1)
         Enter the KING, [GLOUCESTER,] BEDFORD, CLARENCE,
           WARWICK, WESTMORLAND, EXETER[, *and Attendants*].
    KING Where is my gracious lord of Canterbury?
    EXETER Not here in presence.
    KING   Send for him, good uncle.
                                    [*Exit Attendant.*]
    WESTMORLAND Shall we call in th'ambassador, my liege?
    KING Not yet, my cousin.¹ We would be resolved,
5   Before we hear him, of some things of weight
         That task° our thoughts concerning us and France.   *exercise*
              Enter [*Archbishop of* CANTERBURY *and Bishop*
              of ELY].
    CANTERBURY God and his angels guard your sacred throne,
         And make you long become° it.   *adorn*
    KING   Sure we thank you.
         My learnèd lord, we pray you to proceed,
10   And justly and religiously unfold
         Why the law Salic² that they have in France
         Or° should or should not bar us in our claim.   *Either*
         And God forbid, my dear and faithful lord,
         That you should fashion, wrest, or bow your reading³
15   Or nicely charge° your understanding soul   *foolishly burden*
         With opening titles miscreate,⁴ whose right
         Suits not in native colors° with the truth.   *Does not accord*
         For God doth know how many now in health
         Shall drop their blood in approbation°   *confirmation*
20   Of what your reverence shall incite us to.
         Therefore take heed how you impawn° our person,   *pledge*
         How you awake our sleeping sword of war;
         We charge you in the name of God, take heed.
         For never two such kingdoms did contend
25   Without much fall of blood, whose guiltless drops
         Are every one a woe, a sore complaint
         'Gainst him whose wrongs gives edge unto the swords
         That makes such waste in brief mortality.°   *short-lived humankind*
         Under this conjuration° speak, my lord,   *injunction*
30   For we will hear, note, and believe in heart
         That what you speak is in your conscience washed
         As pure as sin with baptism.
    CANTERBURY Then hear me, gracious sovereign, and you peers
         That owe yourselves, your lives, and services
35   To this imperial throne. There is no bar
         To make against your highness' claim to France
         But this which they produce from Pharamond:°   *(legendary French king)*
         In terram Salicam mulieres ne succedant—

───

1.2 Location: The royal court.   2. Explained below, lines 35ff.
1. Kinsman; complimentary form of address from   3. Should shape, pervert, or bend your interpretation.
King to nobles.   4. With explicating false property rights.

"No woman shall succeed in Salic[5] land"—
40   Which Salic land the French unjustly gloze°   *interpret*
To be the realm of France, and Pharamond
The founder of this law and female bar.[6]
Yet their own authors faithfully affirm
That the land Salic is in Germany,
45   Between the floods° of Sala and of Elbe,   *rivers*
Where Charles the Great, having subdued the Saxons,
There left behind and settled certain French
Who, holding in disdain the German women
For some dishonest° manners of their life,   *unchaste*
50   Established then this law: to wit, no female
Should be inheritrix in Salic land—
Which Salic, as I said, twixt Elbe and Sala,
Is at this day in Germany called Meissen.
Then doth it well appear the Salic law
55   Was not devisèd for the realm of France.
Nor did the French possess the Salic land
Until four hundred one-and-twenty years
After defunction° of King Pharamond,   *death*
Idly° supposed the founder of this law,   *Foolishly*
60   Who died within the year of our redemption°   A.D.
Four hundred twenty-six. And Charles the Great°   *Charlemagne*
Subdued the Saxons and did seat° the French   *establish*
Beyond the River Sala in the year
Eight hundred five. Besides, their writers say,
65   King Pépin, which deposèd Childéric,
Did as heir general[7]—being descended
Of Blithild, which was daughter to King Clothair—
Make claim and title to the crown of France.
Hugh Capet also, who usurped the crown
70   Of Charles the Duke of Lorraine, sole heir male
Of the true line and stock of Charles the Great,
To fine° his title with some shows of truth,   *complete; purify*
Though in pure truth it was corrupt and naught,
Conveyed himself as heir to th' Lady Lingard,
75   Daughter to Charlemagne, who was the son
To Louis the Emperor, and Louis the son
Of Charles the Great. Also King Louis the Ninth,[8]
Who was sole heir to the usurper Capet,
Could not keep quiet in his conscience,
80   Wearing the crown of France, till satisfied
That fair Queen Isabel, his grandmother,
Was lineal of° the Lady Ermengarde,   *descended from*
Daughter to Charles the foresaid Duke of Lorraine,
By the which marriage the line of Charles the Great
85   Was reunited to the crown of France.
So that, as clear as is the summer's sun,
King Pépin's title and Hugh Capet's claim,

---

5. Referring to an ancient Frankish tribe that lived beside the Rhine River.
6. And prohibition of female inheritance.
7. One who inherits through either the male or the female line.

8. TEXTUAL COMMENT In F, "Louis the Tenth," corrected in modern editions to reflect the historical facts. Shakespeare's error has enabled scholars to identify his source text, which makes the same mistake. See Digital Edition TC 2 (Folio edited text).

King Louis his° satisfaction, all appear   *(Louis')*
To hold in right and title of the female.
90   So do the kings of France unto this day,
Howbeit they would hold up this Salic law
To bar your highness claiming from the female,
And rather choose to hide them in a net°   *complexities*
Than amply to embar° their crooked titles,   *frankly to rule out*
95   Usurped from you and your progenitors.
     KING   May I with right and conscience make this claim?
     CANTERBURY   The sin upon my head, dread sovereign.
For in the Book of Numbers° is it writ,   *Numbers 27:8*
"When the man dies, let the inheritance
100   Descend unto the daughter." Gracious lord,
Stand for your own; unwind your bloody flag;
Look back into your mighty ancestors.
Go, my dread lord, to your great-grandsire's tomb,
From whom you claim.[9] Invoke his warlike spirit,
105   And your great-uncle's, Edward the Black Prince,
Who on the French ground played a tragedy,
Making defeat° on the full power of France,   *(at Crécy, in 1346)*
Whiles his most mighty father° on a hill   *(Edward III)*
Stood smiling to behold his lion's whelp
110   Forage in blood of French nobility.
O noble English, that could entertain°   *encounter*
With half their forces the full pride of France
And let another half stand laughing by,
All out of work and cold for° action.   *for want of*
115   ELY   Awake remembrance of these valiant dead,
And with your puissant° arm renew their feats.   *powerful*
You are their heir, you sit upon their throne;
The blood and courage that renownèd them°   *made them famous*
Runs in your veins—and my thrice-puissant liege
120   Is in the very May-morn of his youth,
Ripe for exploits and mighty enterprises.
     EXETER   Your brother kings and monarchs of the earth
Do all expect that you should rouse yourself
As did the former lions of your blood.
125   WESTMORLAND   They know your grace hath cause and means
       and might;
So hath your highness. Never king of England
Had nobles richer and more loyal subjects,
Whose hearts have left their bodies here in England
And lie pavilioned° in the fields of France.   *encamped*
130   CANTERBURY   Oh, let their bodies follow, my dear liege,
With blood and sword and fire, to win your right—
In aid whereof, we of the spirituality°   *clergy*
Will raise your highness such a mighty sum
As never did the clergy at one time
135   Bring in to any of your ancestors.
     KING   We must not only arm t'invade the French,
But lay down our proportions[1] to defend

---

9. Edward III claimed the French throne through his   1. Decide the distribution of our forces.
mother, Isabella.

Against the Scot, who will make road upon us
With all advantages.°   *Given any opportunity*
140 CANTERBURY   They of those marches,° gracious sovereign,   *borderlands*
Shall be a wall sufficient to defend
Our inland from the pilfering borderers.
KING   We do not mean the coursing snatchers° only,   *mounted raiders*
But fear the main intendment° of the Scot,   *hostile intention*
145 Who hath been still a giddy° neighbor to us.   *always an unreliable*
For you shall read that my great-grandfather
Never went with his forces into France
But that the Scot on his unfurnished° kingdom   *unprotected*
Came pouring like the tide into a breach,°   *gap in a dike*
150 With ample and brim fullness of his force
Galling° the gleanèd° land with hot assays,°   *Hurting / depleted / attacks*
Girding with grievous siege castles and towns,
That England, being empty of defense,
Hath shook and trembled at th'ill neighborhood.
155 CANTERBURY   She hath been then more feared than harmed,
     my liege.
For hear her but exampled° by herself: *given an example*
When all her chivalry hath been in France
And she a mourning widow of her nobles,
She hath herself not only well defended
160 But taken and impounded as a stray
The King of Scots,[2] whom she did send to France
To fill King Edward's fame with prisoner kings
And make her chronicle as rich with praise
As is the ooze and bottom of the sea
165 With sunken wreck° and sumless treasuries.[3]   *shipwrecks*
WESTMORLAND[4]   But there's a saying very old and true:
     "If that you will France win,
     Then with Scotland first begin."
For once the eagle England being in prey,°   *out hunting*
170 To her unguarded nest the weasel Scot
Comes sneaking, and so sucks her princely eggs,
Playing the mouse in absence of the cat,
To 'tame[5] and havoc° more than she can eat.   *spoil*
EXETER   It follows then the cat must stay at home;
175 Yet that is but a crushed° necessity,   *forced*
Since we have locks to safeguard necessaries
And pretty° traps to catch the petty thieves.   *clever*
While that the armèd hand doth fight abroad,
Th'advisèd° head defends itself at home.   *The well-advised*
180 For government, though high and low and lower,[6]
Put into parts,[7] doth keep in one consent,°   *harmony*
Congreeing° in a full and natural close°   *Coming together / cadence*
Like music.
CANTERBURY   True. Therefore doth heaven divide

---

2. David II of Scotland, taken prisoner in 1346, when Edward III was in France; actually, he was imprisoned in London.
3. Incalculable riches.
4. TEXTUAL COMMENT In F, this speech is assigned to the Bishop of Ely, in Q to "A Lord," but most editors assign it to Westmorland. For the rationale for the emendation, see Digital Edition TC 3 (Folio edited text).
5. Attame, or meddle with.
6. That is, composed of three social classes.
7. Divided into different functions.

The state of man in diverse functions,
185 Setting endeavor in continual motion,
To which is fixèd, as an aim or butt,°   target
Obedience. For so work the honeybees,
Creatures that by a rule in nature teach
The act of order to a peopled kingdom.
190 They have a king[8] and officers of sorts,
Where some like magistrates correct at home,
Others like merchants venture trade abroad;
Others like soldiers, armèd in their stings,
Make boot upon° the summer's velvet buds,   Plunder
195 Which pillage they with merry march bring home
To the tent-royal of their emperor,
Who busied in his majesty surveys
The singing masons building roofs of gold;
The civil citizens kneading° up the honey;   weighing
200 The poor mechanic° porters crowding in   menial
Their heavy burdens at his narrow gate;
The sad-eyed justice with his surly hum
Delivering o'er to executors° pale   executioners
The lazy yawning drone. I this infer:
205 That many things, having full reference
To one consent,[9] may work contrariously.°   disparately
As many arrows loosèd several ways°   shot from different places
Come to one mark,
As many ways meet in one town,
210 As many fresh streams meet in one salt sea,
As many lines close in the dial's° center,   sundial's
So may a thousand actions, once afoot,
End in one purpose, and be all well borne
Without defeat. Therefore to France, my liege.
215 Divide your happy England into four,
Whereof take you one quarter into France,
And you withal shall make all Gallia° shake.   France
If we with thrice such powers left at home
Cannot defend our own doors from the dog,
220 Let us be worried,° and our nation lose   savaged
The name° of hardiness and policy.[1]   reputation
KING   Call in the messengers sent from the Dauphin.[2]
                                        [*Exeunt Attendants.*]
Now are we well resolved, and by God's help
And yours, the noble sinews of our power,
225 France being ours, we'll bend it to our awe,°   make it submit to us
Or break it all to pieces. Or° there we'll sit,   Either
Ruling in large and ample empery°   sovereignty
O'er France and all her almost kingly dukedoms,
Or lay these bones in an unworthy urn,
230 Tombless, with no remembrance over them.
Either our history shall with full mouth
Speak freely of our acts, or else our grave,
Like Turkish mute,[3] shall have a tongueless mouth,

---

8. The queen bee was thought to be male.
9. *having . . . consent:* united by a common purpose.
1. Political discernment.

2. Title of the French heir apparent.
3. Turkish harem attendants were reportedly castrated and deprived of speech.

Not worshipped with a waxen epitaph.[4]
  Enter AMBASSADORS *of France [with Attendants,*
  carrying a tun°].   *chest; barrel*

235 Now are we well prepared to know the pleasure
  Of our fair cousin Dauphin, for we hear
  Your greeting is from him, not from the King.
  AMBASSADOR May't please your majesty to give us leave
  Freely to render what we have in charge,
240 Or shall we sparingly show you far off[5]
  The Dauphin's meaning and our embassy?
  KING We are no tyrant, but a Christian king,
  Unto whose grace our passion is as subject
  As is our wretches fettered in our prisons.
245 Therefore with frank and with uncurbèd plainness,
  Tell us the Dauphin's mind.
  AMBASSADOR   Thus then in few:°   *short*
  Your highness lately sending into France
  Did claim some certain dukedoms in the right
  Of your great predecessor, King Edward the Third.
250 In answer of which claim the Prince our master
  Says that you savor° too much of your youth, *show traces*
  And bids you be advised there's naught in France
  That can be with a nimble galliard° won: *lively dance*
  You cannot revel into dukedoms there.
255 He therefore sends you, meeter° for your spirit, *more appropriate*
  This tun of treasure, and in lieu of this
  Desires you let the dukedoms that you claim
  Hear no more of you. This the Dauphin speaks.
  KING What treasure, uncle?
  EXETER   Tennis balls, my liege.
260 KING We are glad the Dauphin is so pleasant° with us. *jocular*
  His present and your pains we thank you for.
  When we have matched our rackets to these balls,
  We will in France, by God's grace, play a set
  Shall strike his father's crown° into the hazard.[6] *royal crown; coin*
265 Tell him he hath made a match with such a wrangler
  That all the courts of France will be disturbed
  With chases.[7] And we understand him well,
  How he comes o'er° us with our wilder days, *taunts*
  Not measuring what use we made of them.
270 We never valued this poor seat° of England, *throne*
  And therefore living hence° did give ourself *away from court*
  To barbarous license, as 'tis ever common
  That men are merrier when they are from home.
  But tell the Dauphin I will keep my state,° *dignity; territory*
275 Be like a king, and show my sail of greatness
  When I do rouse me in° my throne of France. *about*
  For that have I laid by my majesty
  And plodded like a man for working days.
  But I will rise there with so full a glory

---

4. Not dignified with (even) a perishable memorial.
5. Show you in an abridged and roundabout way.
6. Jeopardy; aperture in the back wall of an Elizabethan tennis court.

7. Military pursuit; in tennis, the second impact of a missed return, rated by its proximity to the back wall (a disputable point, hence, "wrangler" in line 265).

280	That I will dazzle all the eyes of France,
	Yea, strike the Dauphin blind to look on us.
	And tell the pleasant Prince this mock of his
	Hath turned his balls to gun-stones,° and his soul	cannonballs
	Shall stand sore charged° for the wasteful vengeance	heavily burdened
285	That shall fly with them. For many a thousand widows
	Shall this his mock mock out of their dear husbands,
	Mock mothers from their sons, mock castles down,
	And some are yet ungotten and unborn
	That shall have cause to curse the Dauphin's scorn.
290	But this lies all within the will of God,
	To whom I do appeal, and in whose name
	Tell you the Dauphin I am coming on
	To venge me° as I may and to put forth	avenge myself
	My rightful hand in a well-hallowed cause.
295	So get you hence in peace. And tell the Dauphin
	His jest will savor but of shallow wit
	When thousands weep more than did laugh at it.
	—Convey them with safe conduct. —Fare you well.

Exeunt AMBASSADORS [*and Attendants*].

EXETER   This was a merry message.

300   KING   We hope to make the sender blush at it.
Therefore, my lords, omit no happy hour
That may give furth'rance to our expedition,
For we have now no thought in us but France,
Save those to God that run before our business.

305   Therefore let our proportions for these wars
Be soon collected and all things thought upon
That may with reasonable swiftness add
More feathers to our wings, for, God before,[8]
We'll chide this Dauphin at his father's door.

310   Therefore let every man now task his thought,
That this fair action may on foot be brought.

Flourish. Exeunt.

2.0

Enter CHORUS.

	CHORUS Now all the youth of England are on fire,
	And silken° dalliance in the wardrobe lies.	luxurious
	Now thrive the armorers, and honor's thought
	Reigns solely in the breast of every man.
5	They sell the pasture now to buy the horse,
	Following the mirror° of all Christian kings	exemplar
	With wingèd heels, as English Mercuries.[1]
	For now sits expectation in the air
	And hides a sword from hilts unto the point
10	With crowns imperial, crowns,° and coronets,	titles; coins
	Promised to Harry and his followers.
	The French, advised by good intelligence°	espionage
	Of this most dreadful preparation,
	Shake in their fear, and with pale policy°	feeble intrigue

8. With God leading us; if God leads us.

2.0
1. Messenger of the gods; patron of thieves.

15   Seek to divert the English purposes.
       O England, model° to thy inward greatness,   *small replica*
       Like little body with a mighty heart,
       What mightst thou do that honor would thee do,
       Were all thy children kind and natural!
20   But see, thy fault France hath in thee found out:
       A nest of hollow² bosoms, which he fills
       With treacherous crowns; and three corrupted men,
       One, Richard, Earl of Cambridge, and the second,
       Henry, Lord Scrope of Masham, and the third,
25   Sir Thomas Grey, knight, of Northumberland,
       Have for the gilt³ of France—oh, guilt indeed!—
       Confirmed conspiracy with fearful° France,   *frightened*
       And by their hands this grace of kings must die—
       If hell and treason hold° their promises—   *keep*
30   Ere he take ship for France, and in Southampton.
       Linger your patience on, and we'll digest
       Th'abuse of distance, force—perforce—a play.⁴
       The sum is paid, the traitors are agreed,
       The King is set from London, and the scene
35   Is now transported, gentles, to Southampton.
       There is the playhouse now, there must you sit,
       And thence to France shall we convey you safe
       And bring you back, charming the narrow seas
       To give you gentle pass. For if we may,
40   We'll not offend one stomach⁵ with our play.
       But till the King come forth, and not till then,
       Unto Southampton do we shift our scene.   *Exit.*

2.1 (Q Scene 2)
Enter Corporal NYM *and Lieutenant* BARDOLPH.

BARDOLPH   Well met, Corporal Nym.

NYM   Good morrow, Lieutenant Bardolph.

BARDOLPH   What, are Ensign° Pistol and you friends yet?   *flag bearer*

NYM   For my part, I care not. I say little, but when time shall
5   serve, there shall be smiles—but that shall be as it may. I dare
not fight, but I will wink° and hold out mine iron.° It is a   *close my eyes / sword*
simple one, but what though?° It will toast cheese, and it will   *of that*
endure cold, as another man's sword will, and there's an end.

BARDOLPH   I will bestow a breakfast to make you friends, and
10   we'll be all three sworn brothers to France. Let't be so, good
Corporal Nym.

NYM   Faith, I will live so long as I may, that's the certain of it,
and when I cannot live any longer, I will do as I may. That is
my rest, that is the rendezvous° of it.   *last word (?)*

15 BARDOLPH   It is certain, Corporal, that he is married to Nell
Quickly, and certainly she did you wrong, for you were troth-
plight° to her.   *betrothed*

---

2. Hypocritical; empty (as receptacles for money).
3. Gold; gold leaf (suggesting superficiality).
4. TEXTUAL COMMENT *digest . . . play:* incorporate (and make acceptable) a violation of the unity of place, and, by necessity, stuff a play with events. The Folio version of the line—"Th'abuse of distance; force a play"—is metrically awkward and fails to make sense, so it is generally considered to be corrupt. Modern editors

emend in various ways; for the options, see Digital Edition TC 4 (Folio edited text).
5. Offend anyone; make anyone seasick.
2.1 Location: Eastcheap, a slum section of London, site of the tavern scenes in *1* and *2 Henry IV*. Bardolph, Pistol, and Hostess Quickly were featured in the *Henry IV* plays; Nym (slang for "thief") is a new character.

NYM   I cannot tell. Things must be as they may. Men may sleep,
and they may have their throats about them at that time, and
20   some say knives have edges. It must be as it may. Though
Patience be a tired mare, yet she will plod. There must be conclusions. Well, I cannot tell.
          Enter PISTOL *and* [HOSTESS] *Quickly.*
BARDOLPH   Here comes Ensign Pistol[1] and his wife. Good Corporal, be patient here.

25   NYM   How now, mine host° Pistol?   *tavern keeper; pimp*
PISTOL   Base tyke, call'st thou me host?
Now by this hand I swear, I scorn the term.
Nor shall my Nell keep lodgers.
HOSTESS   No, by my troth, not long. For we cannot lodge and
30   board a dozen or fourteen gentlewomen that live honestly
by the prick° of their needles, but it will be thought we keep   *(unwittingly obscene)*
a bawdy house straight.
          [NYM *draws his sword.*]
Oh, welladay,° Lady![2] If he be not hewn now we shall see   *alas*
willful adultery° and murder committed.   *(for "assault")*
          [PISTOL *draws his sword.*]
35   BARDOLPH   Good Lieutenant, good Corporal, offer nothing° here.   *don't fight*
NYM   Pish.
PISTOL   Pish for thee, Iceland dog.° Thou prick-eared cur of   *small, hairy breed*
Iceland.
HOSTESS   Good Corporal Nym, show thy valor and put up° your   *away*
40   sword.
          [PISTOL *and* NYM *sheathe their swords.*]
NYM   Will you shog off?° I would have you *solus.*[3]   *move along*
PISTOL   *Solus,* egregious dog? O viper vile!
The *solus* in thy most marvelous face,
The *solus* in thy teeth, and in thy throat,
45   And in thy hateful lungs, yea in thy maw, perdy.[4]
And which is worse, within thy nasty mouth!
I do retort° the *solus* in thy bowels,   *send back*
For I can take,° and Pistol's cock is up,[5]   *take fire; strike*
And flashing fire will follow.
50   NYM   I am not Barbason,° you cannot conjure me.[6] I have an   *(the name of a devil)*
humor° to knock you indifferently well. If you grow foul with   *inclination*
me, Pistol, I will scour you with my rapier, as I may, in fair
terms.° If you would walk off, I would prick your guts a little,   *pretty thoroughly*
in good terms, as I may, and that's the humor of it.
55   PISTOL   O braggart vile, and damnèd furious wight!°   *creature*
The grave doth gape and doting death is near.
Therefore exhale.°   *draw (your sword)*
          [PISTOL *and* NYM *draw their swords.*]
BARDOLPH   Hear me, hear me what I say.
          [*He draws his sword.*]
He that strikes the first stroke, I'll run him up to the hilts, as
60   I am a soldier.
PISTOL   An oath of mickle° might, and fury shall abate.   *great*

---

1. Sixteenth-century pistols were notoriously noisy
and inaccurate.
2. By our Lady, a mild oath.
3. Alone; unmarried.

4. *in thy maw, perdy:* in your stomach, indeed (old-
fashioned).
5. Pistol's trigger is cocked (unwittingly obscene).
6. Frighten me with big words.

[*They sheathe their swords.*]

[*to* NYM] Give me thy fist,° thy forefoot to me give.   (*i.e., hand*)

Thy spirits are most tall.°   *valiant*

NYM   I will cut thy throat one time or other, in fair terms, that
65   is the humor of it.

PISTOL   *Couple a gorge,*[7]

That is the word. I thee defy again.

O hound of Crete, think'st thou my spouse to get?

No, to the spital[8] go,

70   And from the powd'ring tub[9] of infamy

Fetch forth the lazar kite of Cressid's kind,[1]

Doll Tearsheet[2] she by name, and her espouse.

I have and I will hold the quondam° Quickly   *former*

For the only she, and—*pauca,*° there's enough.   *few (words); in short*

75   Go to.

        Enter the BOY.

BOY   Mine host Pistol, you must come to my master,° and you,   (*Sir John Falstaff*)
    Hostess. He is very sick and would to bed. Good Bardolph,
    put thy face between his sheets and do the office of a warm-
    ing pan.[3] Faith, he's very ill.

80   BARDOLPH   Away, you rogue!

HOSTESS   By my troth, he'll yield the crow a pudding[4] one of
    these days. The King has killed his heart.[5] Good husband,
    come home presently.°   *Exit* [*with* BOY].   *right away*

BARDOLPH   Come, shall I make you two friends? We must to
85   France together. Why the devil should we keep knives to cut
    one another's throats?

PISTOL   Let floods o'erswell[6] and fiends for food howl on!

NYM   You'll pay me the eight shillings I won of you at betting?

PISTOL   Base is the slave that pays.

90   NYM   That now I will have, that's the humor of it.

PISTOL   As manhood shall compound.° Push home.   *valor will determine*

        [*They*] *draw* [*their swords*].

BARDOLPH [*drawing his sword*]   By this sword, he that makes
    the first thrust, I'll kill him. By this sword, I will.

PISTOL   Sword is an oath,[7] and oaths must have their course.

        [*He sheathes his sword.*]

95   BARDOLPH   Corporal Nym, an° thou wilt be friends, be friends.   *if*
    An thou wilt not, why, then, be enemies with me too. Prithee,
    put up.

NYM   I shall have my eight shillings?

PISTOL   A noble° shalt thou have, and present pay,[8]   *6 shillings 8 pence*
100   And liquor likewise will I give to thee,

And friendship shall combine, and brotherhood.

I'll live by Nym and Nym shall live by me.

Is not this just? For I shall sutler[9] be

Unto the camp, and profits will accrue.

7. Corrupt French for "Cut the throat."
8. Hospital; in Elizabethan times, a filthy, disease-ridden place occupied by indigents near death.
9. Sweat bath, used in treating syphilis.
1. The diseased, scavenging whore (Cressida, a faithless Trojan woman, was a pattern of female wickedness).
2. A prostitute who appears in *2 Henry IV*.

3. Referring to Bardolph's "fiery" complexion.
4. He'll feed the crows (after his death).
5. By rejecting him, in the last scene of *2 Henry IV*.
6. Let destruction reign (perhaps an unidentified quotation).
7. Punning on "'s word," by God's word.
8. And immediate payment.
9. Seller of provisions (notoriously dishonest).

105   Give me thy hand.

NYM   I shall have my noble?

PISTOL   In cash, most justly paid.

NYM   Well, then, that's the humor of't.

[NYM *and* BARDOLPH *sheathe their swords.*]

Enter HOSTESS.

HOSTESS   As ever you come of women, come in quickly to Sir
110   John. Ah, poor heart, he is so shaked of a burning quotidian
tertian[1] that it is most lamentable to behold. Sweet men, come
to him.   [*Exit.*]

NYM   The King hath run bad humors on° the knight, that's the   *showed ill will toward*
even° of it.   *truth*

115   PISTOL   Nym, thou hast spoke the right,
His heart is fracted° and corroborate.[2]   *broken*

NYM   The King is a good king, but it must be as it may. He
passes some humors and careers.°   *behaves strangely*

PISTOL   Let us condole° the knight, for, lambkins, we will live.   *console*

[*Exeunt.*]

2.2 (Q Scene 3)

Enter EXETER, BEDFORD, *and* WESTMORLAND.

BEDFORD   Fore God, his grace is bold to trust these traitors.

EXETER   They shall be apprehended by and by.

WESTMORLAND   How smooth and even they do bear themselves,
As if allegiance in their bosoms sat,
5   Crownèd with faith and constant loyalty.

BEDFORD   The King hath note of all that they intend,
By interception which they dream not of.

EXETER   Nay, but the man that was his bedfellow,[1]
Whom he hath dulled and cloyed° with gracious favors—   *tired and sated*
10   That he should for a foreign purse so sell
His sovereign's life to death and treachery!

Sound trumpets. Enter the KING, SCROPE, CAMBRIDGE,
and GREY.

KING   Now sits the wind fair, and we will aboard.
My lord of Cambridge, and my kind lord of Masham,
And you, my gentle knight, give me your thoughts:
15   Think you not that the powers we bear with us
Will cut their passage through the force of France,
Doing the execution° and the act   *destruction*
For which we have in head° assembled them?   *an army*

SCROPE   No doubt, my liege, if each man do his best.

20   KING   I doubt not that, since we are well persuaded
We carry not a heart with us from hence
That grows not in a fair consent with ours,
Nor leave not one behind that doth not wish
Success and conquest to attend on us.

25   CAMBRIDGE   Never was monarch better feared and loved
Than is your majesty; there's not, I think, a subject
That sits in heart-grief and uneasiness

---

1. Dangerous fever (the Hostess conflates quotidian
fever, which recurs daily, with tertian fever, which
recurs every third day).
2. Confirmed (error for "corrupted").

2.2 Location: Southampton, a port in the south of
England.
1. It was common for men to share a bed.

Under the sweet shade of your government.

GREY   True. Those that were your father's enemies
30   Have steeped their galls° in honey and do serve you   *bitterness*
With hearts create of duty and of zeal.

KING   We therefore have great cause of thankfulness,
And shall forget the office° of our hand   *use*
Sooner than quittance° of desert and merit,   *payment*
35   According to the weight and worthiness.

SCROPE   So service shall with steelèd sinews toil,
And labor shall refresh itself with hope
To do your grace incessant services.

KING   We judge no less. —Uncle of Exeter,
40   Enlarge° the man committed° yesterday   *Release / imprisoned*
That railed against our person. We consider
It was excess of wine that set him on,
And on his more advice° we pardon him.   *sober reconsideration*

SCROPE   That's mercy, but too much security.°   *complacency*
45   Let him be punished, sovereign, lest example
Breed, by his sufferance,° more of such a kind.   *by pardoning him*

KING   Oh, let us yet be merciful.

CAMBRIDGE   So may your highness, and yet punish too.

GREY   Sir, you show great mercy if you give him life,
50   After the taste of much correction.

KING   Alas, your too much love and care of me
Are heavy orisons° 'gainst this poor wretch.   *weighty pleas*
If little faults proceeding on distemper°   *from drunkenness*
Shall not be winked at,° how shall we stretch our eye   *overlooked*
55   When capital crimes, chewed, swallowed, and digested,[2]
Appear before us? We'll yet° enlarge that man,   *nonetheless*
Though Cambridge, Scrope, and Grey, in their dear° care   *loving*
And tender preservation of our person,
Would have him punished. And now to our French causes.
Who are the late[3] commissioners?

60   CAMBRIDGE   I one, my lord.
Your highness bade me ask for it° today.   *(the commission)*

SCROPE   So did you me, my liege.

GREY   And I, my royal sovereign.

KING   Then, Richard, Earl of Cambridge, there is yours;
65   There yours, Lord Scrope of Masham; and sir knight,
Grey of Northumberland, this same is yours.
Read them, and know I know your worthiness.
—My lord of Westmorland, and Uncle Exeter,
We will aboard tonight. —Why, how now, gentlemen?
70   What see you in those papers that you lose
So much complexion? —Look ye, how they change!
Their cheeks are paper. —Why, what read you there
That have so cowarded and chased your blood
Out of appearance?°   *sight*

CAMBRIDGE   I do confess my fault
75   And do submit me to your highness' mercy.

GREY *and* SCROPE   To which we all appeal.

KING   The mercy that was quick° in us but late   *alive*

---

2. That is, crimes thoroughly premeditated.   3. Newly appointed (to govern during Henry's absence).

By your own counsel is suppressed and killed.
You must not dare, for shame, to talk of mercy,
80 For your own reasons turn into your bosoms,
As dogs upon their masters, worrying° you.   *tearing*
—See you, my princes and my noble peers,
These English monsters!⁴ My lord of Cambridge here,
You know how apt our love was to accord°   *agree*
85 To furnish with all appertinents°   *privileges*
Belonging to his honor; and this man
Hath for a few light crowns lightly conspired
And sworn unto the practices° of France   *plots*
To kill us here in Hampton. To the which
90 This knight,° no less for bounty bound to us   *(Grey)*
Than Cambridge is, hath likewise sworn. —But oh,
What shall I say to thee, Lord Scrope, thou cruel,
Ingrateful, savage, and inhuman creature?
Thou that didst bear the key of all my counsels,
95 That knew'st the very bottom of my soul,
That almost mightst have coined me into gold,
Wouldst thou have practiced on° me for thy use?   *conspired against*
May it be possible that foreign hire
Could out of thee extract one spark of evil
100 That might annoy my finger? 'Tis so strange
That though the truth of it stands off as gross°   *clearly*
As black on white, my eye will scarcely see it.
Treason and murder ever kept together,
As two yoke-devils sworn to either's purpose,
105 Working so grossly in a natural° cause   *(for devils)*
That admiration° did not whoop° at them,   *astonishment / cry out*
But thou, 'gainst all proportion,° didst bring in   *natural order*
Wonder to wait on° treason and on murder.   *consort with*
And whatsoever cunning fiend it was
110 That wrought upon thee so preposterously°   *unnaturally*
Hath got the voice° in hell for excellence.   *vote*
And other devils that suggest° by treasons   *seduce*
Do botch and bungle up° damnation   *clumsily conceal*
With patches, colors,° and with forms being fetched°   *pretexts / derived*
115 From glist'ring semblances of piety;
But he that tempered° thee, bade thee stand up,°   *molded / rebel*
Gave thee no instance° why thou shouldst do treason,   *motive*
Unless to dub thee with the name⁵ of traitor.
If that same demon that hath gulled° thee thus   *duped*
120 Should with his lion-gait walk the whole world,
He might return to vasty Tartar° back   *to huge hell*
And tell the legions,° "I can never win   *armies of devils*
A soul so easy as that Englishman's."
Oh, how hast thou with jealousy° infected   *suspicion*
125 The sweetness of affiance!° Show men dutiful?   *trust*
Why, so didst thou. Seem they grave and learned?
Why, so didst thou. Come they of noble family?
Why, so didst thou. Seem they religious?
Why, so didst thou. Or are they spare in diet,

---

4. "Monsters" were usually imported freaks.   5. To knight you with the title.

130 Free from gross passion, or° of mirth or anger,   *either*
Constant in spirit, not swerving with the blood,°   *passion*
Garnished and decked in modest complement,°   *appearance*
Not working with the eye without the ear,
And but in purgèd° judgment trusting neither?   *purified*
135 Such, and so finely bolted,° didst thou seem.   *sifted*
And thus thy fall hath left a kind of blot
To mark the full-fraught° man and best endued   *packed (with excellences)*
With some suspicion. I will weep for thee,
For this revolt of thine, methinks, is like
140 Another fall of man. —Their faults are open.°   *obvious*
Arrest them to the answer of the law,
And God acquit them of their practices.

EXETER   I arrest thee of high treason, by the name of Richard,
Earl of Cambridge.
145 I arrest thee of high treason, by the name of Henry,
Lord Scrope of Masham.
I arrest thee of high treason, by the name of Thomas
Grey, knight of Northumberland.

SCROPE   Our purposes God justly hath discovered,°   *revealed*
150 And I repent my fault more than my death,
Which I beseech your highness to forgive,
Although my body pay the price of it.

CAMBRIDGE   For me, the gold of France did not seduce,
Although I did admit it as a motive
155 The sooner to effect what I intended.[6]
But God be thanked for prevention,
Which I in sufferance° heartily will rejoice,   *suffering punishment*
Beseeching God and you to pardon me.

GREY   Never did faithful subject more rejoice
160 At the discovery of most dangerous treason
Than I do at this hour joy o'er myself,
Prevented from a damned enterprise.
My fault, but not my body, pardon, sovereign.

KING   God quit° you in his mercy. Hear your sentence.   *acquit*
165 You have conspired against our royal person,
Joined with an enemy proclaimed and fixed,
And from his coffers
Received the golden earnest of° our death,   *advance payment for*
Wherein you would have sold your king to slaughter,
170 His princes and his peers to servitude,
His subjects to oppression and contempt,
And his whole kingdom into desolation.
Touching our person seek we no revenge,
But we our kingdom's safety must so tender,°   *regard*
175 Whose ruin you have sought, that to her laws
We do deliver you. Get ye therefore hence,
Poor miserable wretches, to your death,
The taste whereof God of his mercy give
You patience to endure, and true repentance

6. The Earl of Cambridge was heir of Edmund Mortimer through his wife, Edmund's sister, and Mortimer arguably had a better claim to the English throne than did Henry himself. Henry's adherence to a principle of inheritance "in right and title of the female" (1.2.89) is hardly absolute.

180 Of all your dear° offenses. —Bear them hence.   *grievous*
         Exeunt [SCROPE, CAMBRIDGE, GREY, *and Attendants*].
Now, lords, for France, the enterprise whereof
Shall be to you, as us, like° glorious.   *equally*
We doubt not of a fair and lucky war,
Since God so graciously hath brought to light
185 This dangerous treason lurking in our way
To hinder our beginnings. We doubt not now
But every rub° is smoothèd on our way.   *obstacle*
Then forth, dear countrymen. Let us deliver
Our puissance° into the hand of God,   *power*
190 Putting it straight in expedition.°   *at once in action*
Cheerly to sea. The signs° of war advance.   *flags*
No king of England, if not king of France.

                 Flourish. [*Exeunt.*]

2.3 (Q Scene 4)
Enter PISTOL, NYM, BARDOLPH, BOY, *and* HOSTESS.

HOSTESS   Prithee, honey-sweet husband, let me bring° thee to   *accompany*
Staines.[1]
PISTOL   No, for my manly heart doth erne.°   *grieve*
Bardolph, be blithe; Nym, rouse thy vaunting veins;
5   Boy, bristle thy courage up.
For Falstaff he is dead, and we must earn therefore.
BARDOLPH   Would I were with him, wheresome'er he is, either
in heaven or in hell.
HOSTESS   Nay, sure he's not in hell. He's in Arthur's bosom,[2] if
10   ever man went to Arthur's bosom. 'A° made a finer end, and   *He*
went away an° it had been any christom[3] child. 'A parted e'en   *as if*
just between twelve and one, e'en at the turning o'th' tide. For
after I saw him fumble with the sheets, and play with flowers,°   *(on the bedclothes)*
and smile upon his fingers' ends, I knew there was but one
15   way. For his nose was as sharp as a pen, and 'a babbled of
green fields.[4] "How now, Sir John?" quoth I. "What, man! Be
o'good cheer." So 'a cried out, "God, God, God," three or four
times. Now I, to comfort him, bid him 'a should not think of
God; I hoped there was no need to trouble himself with any
20   such thoughts yet. So 'a bade me lay more clothes on his feet.
I put my hand into the bed and felt them, and they were as
cold as any stone. Then I felt to his knees, and so up'ard and
up'ard, and all was as cold as any stone.
NYM   They say he cried out of sack.[5]
25 HOSTESS   Ay, that 'a did.
BARDOLPH   And of women.
HOSTESS   Nay, that 'a did not.
BOY   Yes, that 'a did, and said they were devils incarnate.
HOSTESS   'A could never abide carnation, 'twas a color he never
30   liked.

2.3 Location: Eastcheap.
1. Town on the road to Southampton.
2. Mistake for "Abraham's bosom," heaven.
3. Error for "chrisom," just christened.
4. TEXTUAL COMMENT Falstaff was reciting the Twenty-Third Psalm ("The Lord is my shepherd"), but Hostess Quickly does not recognize it. The Folio

is corrupt at this point, reading "a Table of green fields," and was corrected by the eighteenth-century editor Lewis Theobald in a famous emendation. For a discussion of the textual issue, see Digital Edition TC 5 (Folio edited text).
5. *of sack*: against wine, formerly one of Falstaff's great indulgences.

BOY 'A said once the devil would have him about women.

HOSTESS 'A did in some sort, indeed, handle° women; but then   *discuss*
he was rheumatic,[6] and talked of the Whore of Babylon.[7]

BOY Do you not remember 'a saw a flea stick upon Bardolph's
35   nose and 'a said it was a black soul burning in hell-fire.

BARDOLPH Well, the fuel[8] is gone that maintained that fire;
that's all the riches I got in his service.

NYM Shall we shog?° The King will be gone from Southampton.   *be off*

PISTOL Come, let's away. —My love, give me thy lips.
      [*He kisses her.*]

40   Look to my chattels and my movables.°   *personal property*
Let senses rule. The word is "Pitch and pay."°   *Cash down, no credit*
Trust none, for oaths are straws, men's faiths are wafer-cakes,°   *fragile*
And Holdfast is the only dog,[9] my duck,°   *darling*
Therefore *caveto*° be thy counselor.   *"beware"*
45   Go, clear thy crystals.° —Yokefellows in arms,   *wipe your eyes*
Let us to France, like horse-leeches, my boys,
To suck, to suck, the very blood to suck!

BOY And that's but unwholesome food, they say.

PISTOL Touch her soft mouth, and march.

50   BARDOLPH Farewell, hostess.
      [*He kisses her.*]

NYM I cannot kiss, that is the humor of it, but adieu.

PISTOL Let housewifery appear. Keep close,° I thee command.   *Stay indoors; be thrifty*

HOSTESS Farewell! Adieu!   *Exeunt.*

2.4 (Q Scene 5)

Flourish. Enter the KING OF FRANCE, *the* DAUPHIN,
[*the* CONSTABLE,] *the Dukes of* BERRY *and* BRETAGNE.

KING OF FRANCE Thus comes the English with full power
      upon us,
And more than carefully it us concerns
To answer royally in our defenses.
Therefore the Dukes of Berry and of Bretagne,
5   Of Brabant and of Orléans shall make forth,
And you, Prince Dauphin, with all swift dispatch,
To line° and new repair our towns of war   *garrison*
With men of courage and with means defendant.°   *of defense*
For England° his approaches makes as fierce   *the King of England*
10   As waters to the sucking of a gulf.°   *whirlpool*
It fits us then to be as provident
As fear may teach us, out of late° examples   *recent*
Left by the fatal and neglected[1] English
Upon our fields.

DAUPHIN   My most redoubted° father,   *formidable*
15   It is most meet° we arm us 'gainst the foe,   *proper*
For peace itself should not so dull a kingdom—
Though war nor no known quarrel were in question—
But that defenses, musters, preparations,

---

6. Error for "lunatic," delirious.
7. The scarlet woman of Revelation, identified by
Protestants with the Catholic Church.
8. That is, Falstaff's liquor.
9. Alluding to the proverb "Brag is a good dog, but

Holdfast is better."
2.4 Location: France, where the remainder of the play
takes place. The king's court at Rouen.
1. The fatally underestimated, at the Battles of Crécy
(1346) and Poitiers (1356).

Should be maintained, assembled, and collected
20 As° were a war in expectation.   *As if*
Therefore, I say, 'tis meet we all go forth
To view the sick and feeble parts of France.
And let us do it with no show of fear,
No, with no more than if we heard that England
25 Were busied with a Whitsun morris dance.²
For, my good liege, she is so idly° kinged,   *frivolously*
Her scepter so fantastically° borne   *irrationally*
By a vain, giddy, shallow, humorous° youth,   *capricious*
That fear attends her not.
  CONSTABLE   Oh, peace, Prince Dauphin.
30 You are too much mistaken in this king.
Question your grace the late° ambassadors   *recent*
With what great state he heard their embassy,
How well supplied with noble counselors,
How modest in exception,° and withal   *objecting*
35 How terrible° in constant resolution,   *fearsome*
And you shall find his vanities forespent°   *his former follies*
Were but the outside of the Roman Brutus,³
Covering discretion with a coat of folly,
As gardeners do with ordure° hide those roots   *manure*
40 That shall first spring and be most delicate.
DAUPHIN   Well, 'tis not so, my lord High Constable.
But though° we think it so, it is no matter.   *if*
In cases of defense, 'tis best to weigh°   *consider*
The enemy more mighty than he seems.
45 So the proportions of defense are filled,⁴
Which, of a weak and niggardly projection,°   *scale*
Doth like a miser spoil his coat with scanting°   *skimping*
A little cloth.
KING OF FRANCE   Think we King Harry strong.
And, princes, look you strongly arm to meet him.
50 The kindred of him hath been fleshed⁵ upon us,
And he is bred out of that bloody strain
That haunted us in our familiar paths.
Witness our too much memorable shame
When Cressy battle fatally was struck,°   *fought*
55 And all our princes captived by the hand
Of that black name, Edward, Black Prince of Wales,
Whiles that his mountain° sire, on mountain standing   *ascendant*
Up in the air, crowned with the golden sun,
Saw his heroical seed, and smiled to see him
60 Mangle the work of nature and deface
The patterns that by God and by French fathers
Had twenty years been made. This is a stem
Of that victorious stock, and let us fear
The native° mightiness and fate° of him.   *hereditary / fortune*
       Enter a MESSENGER.
65 MESSENGER   Ambassadors from Harry, King of England,

---

2. Folk dance celebrating Whitsuntide, a summer holiday.
3. Lucius Junius Brutus pretended idiocy to disarm the tyrant Lucius Tarquinius Superbus, against whom he led a successful revolt.
4. A proper defense is mounted.
5. Have been given their first taste of blood.

Do crave admittance to your majesty.

KING OF FRANCE   We'll give them present audience. Go and
　　bring them.   [*Exit* MESSENGER.]
You see this chase is hotly followed, friends.

DAUPHIN   Turn head[6] and stop pursuit, for coward dogs
70　Most spend their mouths° when what they seem to threaten   bark the loudest
　　Runs far before them. Good my sovereign,
　　Take up the English short and let them know
　　Of what a monarchy you are the head.
　　Self-love, my liege, is not so vile a sin
　　As self-neglecting.

　　　　　Enter EXETER [*with Attendants*].

75　KING OF FRANCE   From our brother of England?

EXETER   From him, and thus he greets your majesty:
　　He wills you, in the name of God Almighty,
　　That you divest yourself and lay apart°   aside
　　The borrowed glories that by gift of heaven,
80　By law of nature and of nations, 'longs°   belongs
　　To him and to his heirs, namely the crown
　　And all wide-stretched honors that pertain
　　By custom and the ordinance of times°   laws of ages
　　Unto the crown of France. That you may know
85　'Tis no sinister° nor no awkward° claim,   illegitimate / oblique
　　Picked from the wormholes of long-vanished days,
　　Nor from the dust of old oblivion raked,
　　He sends you this most memorable line,°   pedigree
　　In every branch truly demonstrative,°   conclusive
90　Willing you overlook° this pedigree.   Wishing you to look over
　　And when you find him evenly derived°   directly descended
　　From his most famed of famous ancestors,
　　Edward the Third, he bids you then resign
　　Your crown and kingdom, indirectly° held   unjustly
95　From him, the native and true challenger.°   claimant

KING OF FRANCE   Or else what follows?

EXETER   Bloody constraint, for if you hide the crown
　　Even in your hearts, there will he rake for it.
　　Therefore in fierce tempest is he coming,
100　In thunder and in earthquake, like a Jove,
　　That if requiring° fail, he will compel.   requesting
　　And bids you, in the bowels° of the Lord,   compassion
　　Deliver up the crown, and to take mercy
　　On the poor souls for whom this hungry war
105　Opens his vasty jaws; and on your head
　　Turning the widows' tears, the orphans' cries,
　　The dead men's blood, the pining maidens' groans,
　　For husbands, fathers, and betrothèd lovers
　　That shall be swallowed in this controversy.
110　This is his claim, his threatening, and my message—
　　Unless the Dauphin be in presence here,
　　To whom expressly I bring greeting too.

KING OF FRANCE   For us, we will consider of this further.

6. Make a stand (a hunting term).

Tomorrow shall you bear our full intent
Back to our brother of England.

115 DAUPHIN   For the Dauphin,
I stand here for him. What to him from England?

EXETER   Scorn and defiance, slight regard, contempt,
And anything that may not misbecome
The mighty sender, doth he prize° you at.   *assess*
120 Thus says my king: an if° your father's highness   *an if = if*
Do not, in grant° of all demands at large,°   *concession / in full*
Sweeten the bitter mock you sent his majesty,
He'll call you to so hot an answer for it
That caves and womby vaultages° of France   *hollow caverns*
125 Shall chide your trespass and return your mock
In second accent° of his ordnance.°   *echo / artillery*

DAUPHIN   Say if my father render fair return
It is against my will, for I desire
Nothing but odds° with England. To that end,   *strife*
130 As matching to his youth and vanity,°   *frivolity*
I did present him with the Paris°-balls.   *tennis*

EXETER   He'll make your Paris Louvre° shake for it,   *(French royal palace)*
Were it the mistress° court of mighty Europe.   *principal (in tennis)*
And be assured, you'll find a diff'rence,
135 As we his subjects have in wonder found,
Between the promise of his greener° days   *younger*
And these he masters now. Now he weighs time
Even to the utmost grain.° That you shall read   *smallest unit*
In your own losses, if he stay in France.

140 KING OF FRANCE   Tomorrow shall you know our mind at full.
            Flourish.[7]

EXETER   Dispatch us with all speed, lest that our king
Come here himself to question our delay,
For he is footed° in this land already.   *come ashore*

KING OF FRANCE   You shall be soon dispatched with fair
        conditions.
145 A night is but small breath° and little pause   *small time*
To answer matters of this consequence. [*Flourish.*] *Exeunt.*

3.0
        Flourish. Enter CHORUS.

CHORUS   Thus with imagined wing° our swift scene flies   *wings of imagination*
In motion of no less celerity
Than that of thought. Suppose that you have seen
The well-appointed° King at Hampton pier   *well-equipped*
5 Embark his royalty, and his brave fleet
With silken streamers the young Phoebus fanning.[1]
Play with your fancies,° and in them behold   *imagination*
Upon the hempen tackle ship-boys climbing;
Hear the shrill whistle° which doth order give   *(of the ship's captain)*
10 To sounds confused; behold the threaden° sails,   *woven of thread*

---

7. Fanfare (to signal the end of the interview; Exeter   3.0
unceremoniously continues).   1. *the . . . fanning:* fluttering toward the rising sun.
                                                   Phoebus was the sun god.

Borne with th'invisible and creeping wind,
Draw the huge bottoms° through the furrowed sea,   *hulls*
Breasting the lofty surge. Oh, do but think
You stand upon the rivage° and behold   *shore*
15 A city on th'inconstant billows dancing,
For so appears this fleet majestical,
Holding due course to Harfleur.² Follow, follow!
Grapple° your minds to sternage° of this navy,   *Fasten / the sterns*
And leave your England as dead midnight still,
20 Guarded with grandsires, babies, and old women,
Either past or not arrived to pith° and puissance.   *strength*
For who is he, whose chin is but enriched
With one appearing hair, that will not follow
These culled° and choice-drawn cavaliers to France?   *select*
25 Work, work your thoughts, and therein see a siege.
Behold the ordnance° on their carriages,   *cannons*
With fatal mouths gaping on girded° Harfleur.   *encircled*
Suppose th'ambassador from the French comes back,
Tells Harry that the King doth offer him
30 Katherine his daughter, and with her, to° dowry,   *as*
Some petty and unprofitable dukedoms.
The offer likes° not; and the nimble gunner   *pleases*
With linstock° now the devilish cannon touches,   *lighting stick*
    Alarum, and chambers° go off.   *small cannons*
And down goes all before them. Still be kind,
35 And eke out our performance with your mind.   *Exit.*

3.1

Alarum. Enter the KING, EXETER, BEDFORD, *and*
GLOUCESTER [*and Soldiers with*] *scaling ladders
at Harfleur.*

KING Once more unto the breach,¹ dear friends, once more,
Or close the wall up with our English dead.
In peace there's nothing so becomes a man
As modest stillness and humility;
5 But when the blast of war blows in our ears,
Then imitate the action of the tiger:
Stiffen the sinews, conjure up the blood,
Disguise fair nature with hard-favored rage.
Then lend the eye a terrible aspect;
10 Let it pry° through the portage² of the head   *peer*
Like the brass cannon; let the brow o'erwhelm° it   *overhang*
As fearfully as doth a gallèd° rock   *worn*
O'erhang and jutty° his confounded° base,   *jut out over / ruined*
Swilled° with the wild and wasteful° ocean.   *Washed / destructive*
15 Now set the teeth and stretch the nostril wide,
Hold hard the breath and bend up every spirit
To his full height. On, on, you noblest English,
Whose blood is fet° from fathers of war-proof,°   *fetched / proven in war*
Fathers that like so many Alexanders³

---

2. French port on the mouth of the Seine.
3.1 Location: Before Harfleur.
1. Gap in the fortifications, created by artillery bombardment.

2. Portholes (that is, eye sockets).
3. Alexander the Great was said to have wept because no worlds remained for him to conquer.

20 Have in these parts from morn till even fought,
And sheathed their swords for lack of argument.°   *opposition*
Dishonor not your mothers; now attest
That those whom you called fathers did beget you.
Be copy° now to men of grosser° blood   *example / less noble*
25 And teach them how to war. And you, good yeomen,°   *men below noble rank*
Whose limbs were made in England, show us here
The mettle° of your pasture; let us swear   *quality*
That you are worth your breeding—which I doubt not,
For there is none of you so mean and base
30 That hath not noble luster in your eyes.
I see you stand like greyhounds in the slips,°   *leashes*
Straining upon the start. The game's afoot.
Follow your spirit, and upon this charge
Cry, "God for Harry! England and Saint George!"°   *(patron saint of England)*

Alarum, and chambers go off. [Exeunt.]

3.2 (Q Scene 6)

Enter NYM, BARDOLPH, PISTOL, *and* BOY.

BARDOLPH   On, on, on, on, on! To the breach, to the breach!
NYM   Pray thee, Corporal, stay. The knocks are too hot, and
for mine own part I have not a case° of lives. The humor of   *set*
it is too hot, that is the very plain-song° of it.   *plain truth*
5 PISTOL   The plain-song is most just,° for humors do abound.   *apt*
Knocks go and come, God's vassals drop and die,
[*Sings.*]   And sword and shield
                  In bloody field
                  Doth win immortal fame.
10 BOY   Would I were in an alehouse in London. I would give all
my fame for a pot of ale and safety.
PISTOL   And I.
[*Sings.*]   If wishes would prevail with me°   *in my case*
                  My purpose should not fail with me,
15   But thither would I hie.°   *go*
BOY [*sings*]   As duly,
                  But not as truly,
                  As bird doth sing on bough.

Enter FLUELLEN [*and beats them in*].

FLUELLEN   Up to the breach, you dogs! Avaunt, you cullions!¹
20 PISTOL   Be merciful, great duke, to men of mold!²
Abate thy rage, abate thy manly rage,
Abate thy rage, great duke! Good bawcock,³ bate
Thy rage! Use lenity,° sweet chuck!   *leniency*
NYM   These be good humors!⁴ Your honor runs bad humors!°   *is ill tempered*

Exeunt [all but BOY].

25 BOY   As young as I am, I have observed these three swashers.°   *swashbucklers*
I am boy to them all three, but all they three, though they
would serve me, could not be man⁵ to me, for indeed three
such antics° do not amount to a man. For Bardolph, he is   *buffoons*
white livered° and red faced, by the means whereof 'a° faces it   *cowardly / he*

3.2 Scene continues.
1. Be off, you wretches! *cullions:* testicles.
2. Earth (that is, mortal men).

3. Fine chap (French *beau coq*).
4. This is fine behavior (sarcastic).
5. Punning on the sense "personal servant."

30 out but fights not. For Pistol, he hath a killing tongue and a
quiet sword, by the means whereof 'a breaks words and keeps
whole weapons. For Nym, he hath heard that men of few
words are the best men, and therefore he scorns to say his
prayers lest 'a should be thought a coward. But his few bad
35 words are matched with as few good deeds, for 'a never broke
any man's head but his own, and that was against a post when
he was drunk. They will steal anything and call it purchase.[6]
Bardolph stole a lute case, bore it twelve leagues,° and sold it   *about 36 miles*
for three halfpence. Nym and Bardolph are sworn brothers in
40 filching,° and in Calais[7] they stole a fire-shovel. I knew by that   *stealing*
piece of service the men would carry coals.[8] They would have
me as familiar with men's pockets as their gloves or their
handkerchiefs, which makes° much against my manhood if I   *offends*
should take from another's pocket to put into mine, for it is
45 plain pocketing up of wrongs.[9] I must leave them and seek
some better service. Their villany goes against my weak stom-
ach, and therefore I must cast it up.°   *Exit.*   *vomit it; leave it*

3.3 (Q Scene 6)

Enter GOWER [*and* FLUELLEN, *meeting*].

GOWER   Captain Fluellen, you must come presently° to the   *immediately*
mines.[1] The Duke of Gloucester would speak with you.

FLUELLEN   To the mines? Tell you the Duke it is not so good to
come to the mines. For, look you, the mines is not according
5 to the disciplines° of the war. The concavities° of it is not suf-   *tactics; art / depth*
ficient. For, look you, th'athversary, you may discuss unto the
Duke, look you, is digt° himself four yard under the counter-   *digged (dug)*
mines.[2] By Cheshu,° I think 'a will plow° up all, if there is not   *Jesu / blow*
better directions.

10 GOWER   The Duke of Gloucester, to whom the order° of the   *supervision*
siege is given, is altogether directed by an Irishman, a very
valiant gentleman, i'faith.

FLUELLEN[3]   It is Captain MacMorris, is it not?

GOWER   I think it be.

15 FLUELLEN   By Cheshu, he is an ass, as[4] in the world. I will verify
as much in his beard.° He has no more directions in the true   *to his face*
disciplines of the wars, look you, of the Roman disciplines,
than is a puppy dog.

Enter MACMORRIS *and Captain* JAMY.

GOWER   Here 'a comes, and the Scots captain, Captain Jamy,
20 with him.

FLUELLEN   Captain Jamy is a marvelous falorous° gentleman,   *valorous*
that is certain, and of great expedition° and knowledge in   *quick-wittedness*
th'ancient wars, upon my particular knowledge of his direc-
tions. By Cheshu, he will maintain his argument as well as

---

6. Booty (seized in combat).
7. French port town.
8. Do dirty work; tolerate insults.
9. Pocketing stolen goods; putting up with insults (unmanly behavior).
3.3 Location: Outside Harfleur.
1. Tunnels dug to undermine a besieged fortress.
2. Tunnels dug to undermine enemy "mines."

3. TEXTUAL COMMENT The Folio speech prefix is "Welch" [Welsh], and Fluellen is thus identified until the end of the scene; likewise, MacMorris becomes "Irish," and Jamy becomes "Scot." Modern editors emend for the sake of consistency, but the shift in speech prefixes reflects this scene's interest in national identity. See Digital Edition TC 6 (Folio edited text).
4. *he is an ass, as:* he is as big an ass as there is.

25 any military man in the world, in the disciplines of the pristine wars of the Romans.

JAMY I say gud day, Captain Fluellen.

FLUELLEN God-den to your worship, good Captain James.

GOWER How now, Captain MacMorris, have you quit the
30 mines? Have the pioneers given o'er?° *diggers stopped work*

MACMORRIS By Chrish, la,[5] 'tish ill done. The work ish give
over, the trumpet sound the retreat. By my hand I swear, and
my father's soul, the work ish ill done. It ish give over. I would
have blowed up the town, so Chrish save me, la, in an hour.
35 Oh, 'tish ill done, 'tish ill done. By my hand, 'tish ill done.

FLUELLEN Captain MacMorris, I beseech you now, will you
vouchsafe° me, look you, a few disputations with you as partly *allow*
touching or concerning the disciplines of the war, the Roman
wars, in the way of argument, look you, and friendly com-
40 munication? Partly to satisfy my opinion and partly for the
satisfaction, look you, of my mind, as touching the direction
of the military discipline, that is the point.

JAMY It sall be vary gud, gud feith, gud captains bath,° and I *both*
sall quit° you, with gud leave, as I may pick occasion. That *requite; answer*
45 sall I, marry.

MACMORRIS It is no time to discourse, so Chrish save me. The
day is hot, and the weather, and the wars, and the King, and
the dukes. It is no time to discourse. The town is besieched,
and the trumpet call us to the breach, and we talk and, be
50 Chrish, do nothing. 'Tis shame for us all, so God sa'° me, 'tis *save*
shame to stand still, it is shame, by my hand. And there is
throats to be cut, and works to be done, and there ish nothing
done, so Christ sa' me, la.

JAMY By the mess,° ere these eyes of mine take themselves to *By the mass (an oath)*
55 slumber, ay'll de gud service, or I'll lig° i'th' grund for it. Ay *lie*
owe God a death, and I'll pay't as valorously as I may, that
sall I surely do, that is the breff and the long. Marry, I wad
full fain heard° some question 'tween you twae.° *eagerly have heard / two*

FLUELLEN Captain MacMorris, I think, look you, under your
60 correction, there is not many of your nation—

MACMORRIS Of my nation? What ish my nation? Ish a villain,
and a bastard, and a knave, and a rascal? What ish my
nation? Who talks of my nation?

FLUELLEN Look you, if you take the matter otherwise than is
65 meant, Captain MacMorris, peradventure I shall think you
do not use me with that affability as in discretion you ought
to use me, look you, being as good a man as yourself, both in
the disciplines of war and in the derivation of my birth, and
in other particularities.

70 MACMORRIS I do not know you so good a man as myself. So
Chrish save me, I will cut off your head.

GOWER Gentlemen both, you will mistake each other.

JAMY Ah, that's a foul fault.

A parley[6] *[is sounded].*

GOWER The town sounds a parley.

---

5. "La" adds force to an utterance.   6. Trumpet call requesting negotiation.

75 FLUELLEN Captain MacMorris, when there is more better
opportunity to be required, look you, I will be so bold as to tell
you I know the disciplines of war. And there is an end.

Exeunt.

3.4 (Q Scene 7)

[*The* GOVERNOR *and others upon the walls.*] *Enter the*
KING *and all his train before the gates.*

KING   How yet resolves the Governor of the town?
This is the latest parle° we will admit.   *last parley*
Therefore to our best mercy give yourselves,
Or like to men proud of° destruction   *glorying in*
5   Defy us to our worst. For as I am a soldier,
A name that in my thoughts becomes me best,
If I begin the batt'ry° once again,   *bombardment*
I will not leave the half-achieved Harfleur
Till in her ashes she lie burièd.
10   The gates of mercy shall be all shut up,
And the fleshed° soldier, rough and hard of heart,   *inflamed*
In liberty of bloody hand shall range
With conscience wide° as hell, mowing like grass   *permissive*
Your fresh fair virgins and your flow'ring infants.
15   What is it then to me if impious war,
Arrayed in flames like to the prince of fiends,
Do with his smirched complexion all fell° feats   *cruel*
Enlinked to waste° and desolation?   *destruction*
What is't to me, when you yourselves are cause,
20   If your pure maidens fall into the hand
Of hot and forcing violation?
What rein can hold licentious wickedness
When down the hill he holds° his fierce career?°   *maintains / gallop*
We may as bootless° spend our vain command   *unprofitably*
25   Upon th'enragèd soldiers in their spoil
As send precepts° to the leviathan°   *summons / sea monster*
To come ashore. Therefore, you men of Harfleur,
Take pity of your town and of your people
Whiles yet my soldiers are in my command,
30   Whiles yet the cool and temperate wind of grace
O'erblows° the filthy and contagious clouds[1]   *Disperses*
Of heady° murder, spoil, and villany.   *headstrong*
If not, why, in a moment look to see
The blind and bloody soldier with foul hand
35   Defile the locks of your shrill-shrieking daughters;
Your fathers taken by the silver beards
And their most reverend heads dashed to the walls;
Your naked infants spitted° upon pikes,   *impaled*
Whiles the mad mothers with their howls confused
40   Do break the clouds, as did the wives of Jewry[2]
At Herod's bloody-hunting slaughtermen.
What say you? Will you yield and this avoid?
Or, guilty in defense, be thus destroyed?

3.4 Location: Scene continues.   2. Judea; see Matthew 2:16–18.
1. Pestilence was believed to drop from the sky.

GOVERNOR   Our expectation hath this day an end.

45 The Dauphin, whom of succours we entreated,
Returns° us that his powers are yet not ready   *Replies to*
To raise so great a siege. Therefore, dread King,
We yield our town and lives to thy soft mercy.
Enter our gates, dispose of us and ours,

50 For we no longer are defensible.

KING   Open your gates.   [*Exit* GOVERNOR.]
Come, Uncle Exeter,
Go you and enter Harfleur. There remain,
And fortify it strongly 'gainst the French.
Use mercy to them all. For us, dear uncle,

55 The winter coming on and sickness growing
Upon our soldiers, we will retire to Calais.
Tonight in Harfleur will we be your guest;
Tomorrow for the march are we addressed.°   *ready*

Flourish, and enter the town.

3.5 (Q Scene 8)
Enter KATHERINE *and* [ALICE,] *an old gentlewoman.*

KATHERINE   *Alice, tu as été en Angleterre, et tu bien parles le
langage.*[1]

ALICE   *Un peu, madame.*

KATHERINE   *Je te prie m'enseigner. Il faut que j'apprenne à*
5 *parler. Comment appelez-vous la main en anglais?*

ALICE   *La main? Elle est appelée* de hand.

KATHERINE   De hand. *Et les doigts?*

ALICE   *Les doigts? Ma foi, j'oublie les doigts, mais je me souvien-
drai. Les doigts, je pense qu'ils sont appelés* de fingres. *Oui,* de
10 fingres.

3.5 Location: The French King's palace.
1. A translation of this French scene follows, with editorial comments in brackets.

KATHERINE   Alice, you've been in England, and you speak the language well.
ALICE   A little, madam.
KATHERINE   Please teach me. I must learn to speak it. What do you call *la main* in English?
ALICE   *La main?* It is called de hand.
KATHERINE   De hand. And *les doigts?*
ALICE   *Les doigts?* Faith, I forget *les doigts,* but I'll remember. *Les doigts*—I think they're called de fingres. Yes, de fingres.
KATHERINE   *Le main,* de hand; *les doigts,* de fingres. I think I'm a good student. I've learned two words of English quickly. What do you call *les ongles?*
ALICE   *Les ongles?* We call them de nails.
KATHERINE   De nails. Listen; tell me if I speak well: de hand, de fingres, and de nails.
ALICE   That's well said, madam. It is very good English.
KATHERINE   Tell me the English for *le bras.*
ALICE   De arm, madam.
KATHERINE   And *le coude?*
ALICE   D'elbow.
KATHERINE   D'elbow. I'll repeat all the words you have taught me so far.
ALICE   It is too difficult, madam, in my opinion.
KATHERINE   Excuse me, Alice. Listen: d'hand, de fingres, de nails, d'arm, de bilbow.
ALICE   D'elbow, madam.

KATHERINE   O Lord God, I forgot. D'elbow. What do you call *le col?*
ALICE   De nick, madam.
KATHERINE   De nick. And *le menton?*
ALICE   De chin.
KATHERINE   De sin. *Le col,* de nick; *le menton,* de sin.
ALICE   Yes. Saving your honor, to tell the truth, you pronounce the words just as properly as the native English.
KATHERINE   I don't doubt that I'll learn, with God's help, and in a short time.
ALICE   Haven't you already forgotten what I have taught you?
KATHERINE   No, and I shall recite to you right now: d'hand, de fingres, de mails—
ALICE   De nails, madam.
KATHERINE   De nails, de arm, de ilbow—
ALICE   Saving your honor, d'elbow.
KATHERINE   That's what I said. D'elbow, de nick, and de sin. What do you call *le pied* and *la robe?*
ALICE   De foot, madam, and de coun [gown].
KATHERINE   De foot, and de coun? O Lord God, those are evil-sounding words, easily misconstrued, vulgar, and immodest, and not for respectable ladies to use. [They sound like the French *foutre,* "fuck," and *con,* "cunt."] I wouldn't speak those words in front of French gentlemen for all the world. Ugh! De foot and de coun! Still, I shall recite my entire lesson once more. D'hand, de fingres, de nails, d'arm, d'elbow, de nick, de sin, de foot, de coun.
ALICE   Excellent, madam!
KATHERINE   That's enough for one time. Let's go to dinner.

KATHERINE *La main,* de hand; *les doigts,* de fingres. *Je pense que je suis la bonne écolière. J'ai gagné deux mots d'anglais vitement. Comment appelez-vous les ongles?*

ALICE *Les ongles? Nous les appelons* de nails.

15 KATHERINE De nails. *Écoutez; dites-moi si je parle bien:* de hand, de fingres, *et* de nails.

ALICE *C'est bien dit, madame. Il est fort bon anglais.*

KATHERINE *Dites-moi l'anglais pour le bras.*

ALICE De arm, *madame.*

20 KATHERINE *Et le coude?*

ALICE D'elbow.

KATHERINE D'elbow. *Je m'en fais la répétition de tous les mots que vous m'avez appris dès à présent.*

ALICE *Il est trop difficile, madame, comme je pense.*

25 KATHERINE *Excusez-moi, Alice. Écoutez:* d' hand, de fingres, de nails, de arm, de bilbow.

ALICE D'elbow, *madame.*

KATHERINE *O Seigneur Dieu, je m'en oublie!* D'elbow. *Comment appelez-vous le col?*

30 ALICE De nick, *madame.*

KATHERINE De nick. *Et le menton?*

ALICE De chin.

KATHERINE De sin. *Le col,* de nick; *le menton,* de sin.

ALICE *Oui. Sauf votre honneur, en vérité, vous prononcez les mots aussi droit que les natifs d'Angleterre.*

35 KATHERINE *Je ne doute point d'apprendre, par la grâce de Dieu, et en peu de temps.*

ALICE *N'avez-vous déjà oublié ce que je vous ai enseigné?*

KATHERINE *Non, et je réciterai à vous promptement:* d'hand, de fingres, de mails—

40 ALICE De nails, *madame.*

KATHERINE De nails, de arm, de ilbow—

ALICE *Sauf votre honneur,* d'elbow.

KATHERINE *Ainsi dis-je,* d'elbow, de nick, *et* de sin. *Comment appelez-vous le pied et la robe?*

45 ALICE De foot, *madame, et* de coun.

KATHERINE De foot, *et* de coun? *O Seigneur Dieu, ils sont les mots de son mauvais, corruptible, gros, et impudique, et non pour les dames d'honneur d'user. Je ne voudrais prononcer ces mots devant les seigneurs de France pour tout le monde! Foh!* De foot *et* de coun! *Néanmoins, je réciterai une autre fois ma leçon ensemble:* d'hand, de fingres, de nails, d'arm, d'elbow, de nick, de sin, de foot, de coun.

ALICE *Excellent, madame!*

55 KATHERINE *C'est assez pour une fois. Allons-nous à dîner.*

Exeunt.

3.6 (Q Scene 9)

Enter the KING OF FRANCE, *the* DAUPHIN, *the* CONSTABLE *of France,* [*the Duke of* BRETAGNE,] *and others.*

KING OF FRANCE 'Tis certain he hath passed the River Somme.

CONSTABLE An if he be not fought withal,° my lord,   °with

3.6 Location: The French King's court.

Let us not live in France; let us quit all
And give our vineyards to a barbarous people.
5   DAUPHIN   *O Dieu vivant!*° Shall a few sprays[1] of us,   *O living God*
The emptying of our fathers' luxury,[2]
Our scions,° put in wild and savage stock,   *grafts*
Spirt° up so suddenly into the clouds   *Sprout*
And overlook their grafters?
10 BRETAGNE   Normans, but bastard Normans, Norman bastards!
Mort de ma vie,° if they march along   *Death of my life*
Unfought withal, but I will sell my dukedom
To buy a slobbery° and a dirty farm   *muddy*
In that nook-shotten[3] isle of Albion.°   *England*
15 CONSTABLE   *Dieu de batailles,*° where° have they this mettle?   *God of battles / whence*
Is not their climate foggy, raw, and dull,
On whom, as in despite,° the sun looks pale,   *contempt*
Killing their fruit with frowns? Can sodden° water,   *boiled (to make ale)*
A drench for sur-reined jades,[4] their barley broth,
20 Decoct° their cold blood to such valiant heat?   *Boil (to purify)*
And shall our quick blood, spirited with wine,
Seem frosty? Oh, for honor of our land,
Let us not hang like roping° icicles   *ropelike*
Upon our houses' thatch, whiles a more frosty people
25 Sweat drops of gallant youth in our rich fields!
Poor may we call them° in their native lords.   *(the fields)*
DAUPHIN   By faith and honor,
Our madams mock at us and plainly say
Our mettle is bred out,° and they will give   *is exhausted*
30 Their bodies to the lust of English youth,
To new-store France with bastard warriors.
BRETAGNE   They bid us to the English dancing-schools
And teach lavoltas° high and swift corantos,[5]   *leaping dance*
Saying our grace is only in our heels,
35 And that we are most lofty runaways.
KING OF FRANCE   Where is Montjoy the herald? Speed° him hence.   *Quickly send*
Let him greet England with our sharp defiance.
Up, princes, and with spirit of honor edged
More sharper than your swords, hie° to the field.   *go*
40 Charles Delabreth, High Constable of France,
You Dukes of Orléans, Bourbon, and of Berry,
Alençon, Brabant, Bar, and Burgundy,
Jaques Chatillion, Rambures, Vaudemont,
Beaumont, Grandpré, Roussi, and Fauconbridge,
45 Foix, Lestrelles, Boucicault, and Charolais,
High dukes, great princes, barons, lords, and knights,
For your great seats now quit you[6] of great shames.
Bar Harry England, that sweeps through our land
With pennons° painted in the blood of Harfleur.   *banners*
50 Rush on his host as doth the melted snow
Upon the valleys, whose low vassal seat
The Alps doth spit and void his rheum° upon.   *empty its moisture*

---

1. Offshoots (bastards).
2. The discharge ("emptying") of our forefathers' lust.
3. With an indented shore.
4. A tonic for overworked horses.
5. Running dance.
6. *For . . . you:* In defense of your high ranks, now revenge yourselves.

Go down upon him—you have power enough—
And in a captive chariot into Rouen
Bring him our prisoner.
55 CONSTABLE   This becomes the great.°   *befits noblemen*
 Sorry am I his numbers are so few,
 His soldiers sick and famished in their march,
 For I am sure when he shall see our army
 He'll drop his heart into the sink° of fear   *pit*
60 And for achievement° offer us his ransom.   *instead of battle*
KING OF FRANCE Therefore, Lord Constable, haste on Montjoy,
 And let him say to England that we send
 To know what willing ransom he will give.
 —Prince Dauphin, you shall stay with us in Rouen.
65 DAUPHIN Not so, I do beseech your majesty.
KING OF FRANCE Be patient, for you shall remain with us.
 —Now forth, Lord Constable and princes all,
 And quickly bring us word of England's fall.   *Exeunt.*

3.7 (Q Scene 10)

Enter [the] English and Welsh Captains, GOWER and
FLUELLEN[, *meeting*].

GOWER How now, Captain Fluellen, come you from the bridge?
FLUELLEN I assure you there is very excellent services committed at the bridge.
GOWER Is the Duke of Exeter safe?
5 FLUELLEN The Duke of Exeter is as magnanimous as Agamemnon,[1] and a man that I love and honor with my soul, and my
 heart, and my duty, and my life, and my living, and my uttermost power. He is not, God be praised and blessed, any hurt
 in the world, but keeps the bridge most valiantly, with excel-
10 lent discipline. There is an ensign lieutenant there at the
 pridge, I think in my very conscience he is as valiant a man as
 Mark Antony, and he is a man of no estimation° in the world, *fame*
 but I did see him do as gallant service—
GOWER What do you call him?
15 FLUELLEN He is called Ensign Pistol.
GOWER I know him not.

Enter PISTOL.

FLUELLEN Here is the man.
PISTOL Captain, I thee beseech to do me favors.
 The Duke of Exeter doth love thee well.
20 FLUELLEN Ay, I praise God, and I have merited some love at
 his hands.
PISTOL Bardolph, a soldier firm and sound of heart,
 Of buxom° valor, hath by cruel fate   *lively*
 And giddy Fortune's furious fickle wheel,
25 That goddess blind
 That stands upon the rolling restless stone—
FLUELLEN By your patience, Ensign Pistol: Fortune is painted
 blind, with a muffler° afore her eyes, to signify to you that *blindfold*
 Fortune is blind. And she is painted also with a wheel, to
30 signify to you, which is the moral of it, that she is turning,

---

3.7 Location: The English camp.   1. Greek general in the Trojan War.

and inconstant, and mutability, and variation. And her foot,
look you, is fixed upon a spherical stone, which rolls and
rolls and rolls. In good truth, the poet makes a most excel-
lent description of it. Fortune is an excellent moral.°   *symbolic emblem*

35 PISTOL Fortune is Bardolph's foe, and frowns on him,
For he hath stol'n a pax,[2] and hanged must 'a° be.   *he*
A damnèd death!
Let gallows gape for dog, let man go free,
And let not hemp[3] his windpipe suffocate!

40 But Exeter hath given the doom° of death   *sentence*
For pax of little price.
Therefore go speak—the Duke will hear thy voice—
And let not Bardolph's vital thread be cut
With edge of penny cord and vile reproach.

45 Speak, Captain, for his life, and I will thee requite.
FLUELLEN Ensign Pistol, I do partly understand your meaning.
PISTOL Why, then rejoice therefor.
FLUELLEN Certainly, Ensign, it is not a thing to rejoice at. For
if, look you, he were my brother, I would desire the Duke to

50 use his good pleasure and put him to execution, for discipline
ought to be used.
PISTOL Die and be damned, and *fico*[4] for thy friendship!
FLUELLEN It is well.
PISTOL The fig of Spain!   *Exit.*

55 FLUELLEN Very good.
GOWER Why, this is an arrant counterfeit rascal, I remember
him now—a bawd, a cutpurse.°   *thief*
FLUELLEN I'll assure you, 'a uttered as prave words at the pridge
as you shall see in a summer's day. But it is very well. What he

60 has spoke to me, that is well, I warrant you, when time is serve.
GOWER Why, 'tis a gull,° a fool, a rogue, that now and then goes   *simpleton*
to the wars to grace himself at his return into London under
the form of a soldier. And such fellows are perfect in the great
commanders' names, and they will learn° you by rote where   *teach*

65 services were done—at such and such a sconce,° at such a   *fortification*
breach, at such a convoy; who came off bravely, who was shot,
who disgraced, what terms the enemy stood on. And this they
con° perfectly in the phrase of war, which they trick up° with   *memorize / adorn*
new-tuned° oaths. And what a beard of the General's cut and   *newly coined*

70 a horrid suit of the camp[5] will do among foaming bottles and
ale-washed wits is wonderful to be thought on. But you must
learn to know such slanders° of the age, or else you may be   *disgraces*
marvelously mistook.
FLUELLEN I tell you what, Captain Gower, I do perceive he is

75 not the man that he would gladly make show to the world he
is. If I find a hole in his coat,° I will tell him my mind.   *means of exposing him*
[*A drum is heard.*]
Hark you, the King is coming, and I must speak with him
from the pridge.
Drum and Colors.° Enter the KING [*and*   *Drummer and flag bearer*
GLOUCESTER] *and his poor Soldiers.*

---

2. Small tablet with a crucifix stamped on it.
3. Fiber of which ropes were made.
4. Spanish for "fig"; obscene gesture made by thrusting the thumb between two fingers.
5. *horrid . . . camp:* frightening soldier's attire.

FLUELLEN   God pless your majesty.

80   KING   How now, Fluellen, cam'st thou from the bridge?

FLUELLEN   Ay, so please your majesty. The Duke of Exeter has
very gallantly maintained the pridge. The French is gone off,
look you, and there is gallant and most prave passages.° Marry,   *altercations*
th'athversary was have possession of the pridge, but he is

85   enforced to retire, and the Duke of Exeter is master of the
pridge. I can tell your majesty, the Duke is a prave man.

KING   What men have you lost, Fluellen?

FLUELLEN   The perdition° of th'athversary hath been very great,   *loss*
reasonable great. Marry, for my part I think the Duke hath

90   lost never a man, but one that is like to be executed for robbing
a church, one Bardolph, if your majesty know the man. His
face is all bubuncles, and whelks,° and knobs, and flames   *abscesses and pimples*
o'fire, and his lips blows at his nose, and it is like a coal of fire,
sometimes plue, and sometimes red. But his nose is exe-

95   cuted,[6] and his fire's out.

KING   We would have all such offenders so cut off. And we give
express charge that in our marches through the country there
be nothing compelled from the villages, nothing taken but°   *unless*
paid for, none of the French upbraided or abused in disdain-

100   ful language. For when lenity° and cruelty play for a king-   *leniency*
dom, the gentler gamester is the soonest winner.

Tucket.° Enter MONTJOY.   *Trumpet call*

MONTJOY   You know me by my habit.°   *herald's coat*

KING   Well, then, I know thee. What shall I know of thee?

MONTJOY   My master's mind.

105   KING   Unfold it.

MONTJOY   Thus says my king: "Say thou to Harry of England,
though we seemed dead, we did but sleep. Advantage° is a   *Circumspection*
better soldier than rashness. Tell him we could have rebuked
him at Harfleur, but that we thought not good to bruise

110   an injury° till it were full ripe. Now we speak upon our   *squeeze a pimple*
cue,° and our voice is imperial. England shall repent his   *at the proper time*
folly, see his weakness, and admire our sufferance.° Bid him   *wonder at our patience*
therefore consider of his ransom, which must proportion the
losses we have borne, the subjects we have lost, the disgrace

115   we have digested,° which in weight to re-answer,° his petti-   *endured / compensate*
ness would bow under. For our losses, his exchequer° is too   *the King's treasury*
poor; for th'effusion of our blood, the muster[7] of his kingdom
too faint a number; and for our disgrace, his own person
kneeling at our feet but a weak and worthless satisfaction. To

120   this add defiance, and tell him for conclusion, he hath betrayed
his followers, whose condemnation is pronounced." So far my
king and master; so much my office.

KING   What is thy name? I know thy quality.°   *rank*

MONTJOY   Montjoy.

125   KING   Thou dost thy office fairly. Turn thee back
And tell thy king I do not seek him now,
But could be willing to march on to Calais
Without impeachment.° For to say the sooth,°   *hindrance / truth*
Though 'tis no wisdom to confess so much

6. Slit (in the pillory before he is hanged).   7. Entire population, assembled for military service.

130　Unto an enemy of craft and vantage,°　　　　　　　*cunning and superiority*
　　My people are with sickness much enfeebled,
　　My numbers lessened, and those few I have
　　Almost no better than so many French;
　　Who when they were in health, I tell thee, herald,
135　I thought upon one pair of English legs
　　Did march three Frenchmen. Yet forgive me, God,
　　That I do brag thus. This your air of France
　　Hath blown that vice in me. I must repent.
　　Go, therefore, tell thy master here I am.
140　My ransom is this frail and worthless trunk;°　　　　　*body*
　　My army but a weak and sickly guard.
　　Yet, God before, tell him we will come on,
　　Though France himself and such another neighbor
　　Stand in our way. There's for thy labor, Montjoy.[8]
145　Go bid thy master well advise himself.
　　If we may pass, we will: if we be hindered,
　　We shall your tawny ground with your red blood
　　Discolor. And so, Montjoy, fare you well.
　　The sum of all our answer is but this:
150　We would not seek a battle as we are,
　　Nor as we are we say we will not shun it.
　　So tell your master.
MONTJOY　I shall deliver so. Thanks to your highness.　　*[Exit.]*
GLOUCESTER　I hope they will not come upon us now.
155　KING　We are in God's hand, brother, not in theirs.
　　March to the bridge. It now draws toward night.
　　Beyond the river we'll encamp ourselves,
　　And on tomorrow bid them march away.　　　　　*Exeunt.*

3.8 (Q Scene 11)

Enter the CONSTABLE *of France, the Lord* RAMBURES,
ORLÉANS, [*and the*] DAUPHIN,[1] *with others.*

CONSTABLE　Tut, I have the best armor of the world. Would it
　　were day.
ORLÉANS　You have an excellent armor, but let my horse have
　　his due.
5　CONSTABLE　It is the best horse of Europe.
ORLÉANS　Will it never be morning?
DAUPHIN　My lord of Orléans, and my lord High Constable,
　　you talk of horse and armor?
ORLÉANS　You are as well provided of both as any prince in
10　the world.
DAUPHIN　What a long night is this! I will not change my horse
　　with any that treads but on four pasterns.° Ch' ha! He bounds　　*hooves*
　　from the earth as if his entrails were hairs—*le cheval volant*,
　　the Pegasus, *qui a les narines de feu!*[2] When I bestride him, I
15　soar, I am a hawk. He trots the air. The earth sings when he

8. Henry generously "tips" the enemy herald.
3.8 Location: The French camp near Agincourt.
1. TEXTUAL COMMENT Although in 3.6 the French
king ordered the Dauphin to "stay with us in Rouen"
(3.6.64), in the Folio text the Dauphin appears here
and in subsequent Agincourt scenes. In the Quarto,

his speeches are given to Bourbon. There are various
explanations for this inconsistency; see Digital Edition
TC 7 (Folio edited text).
2. The flying horse . . . with nostrils of fire. Pegasus
was a mythological flying horse, ridden by the hero
Perseus.

touches it;[3] the basest horn° of his hoof is more musical than the pipe of Hermes.[4] *lowest part (with pun)*

ORLÉANS   He's of the color of the nutmeg.

DAUPHIN   And of the heat of the ginger.[5] It is a beast for Per-
20   seus. He is pure air and fire, and the dull elements of earth and water never appear in him, but only in patient stillness while his rider mounts him. He is indeed a horse, and all other jades° you may call beasts. *nags*

CONSTABLE   Indeed, my lord, it is a most absolute° and excel- *perfect*
25   lent horse.

DAUPHIN   It is the prince of palfreys.° His neigh is like the bid- *warhorses*
ding of a monarch, and his countenance enforces homage.

ORLÉANS   No more, cousin.

DAUPHIN   Nay, the man hath no wit that cannot from the rising
30   of the lark to the lodging of the lamb vary deserved praise on my palfrey. It is a theme as fluent° as the sea. Turn the sands *flowing; abundant*
into eloquent tongues and my horse is argument° for them *subject*
all. 'Tis a subject for a sovereign to reason on, and for a sovereign's sovereign to ride on, and for the world, familiar to us
35   and unknown, to lay apart their particular functions and
wonder at him. I once writ a sonnet in his praise, and began
thus, "Wonder of nature!"

ORLÉANS   I have heard a sonnet begin so to one's mistress.

DAUPHIN   Then did they imitate that which I composed to my
40   courser, for my horse is my mistress.

ORLÉANS   Your mistress bears well.[6]

DAUPHIN   Me well, which is the prescript praise and perfection
of a good and particular° mistress. *private*

CONSTABLE   Nay, for methought yesterday your mistress
45   shrewdly° shook your back. *severely*

DAUPHIN   So perhaps did yours.

CONSTABLE   Mine was not bridled.

DAUPHIN   Oh, then belike she was old and gentle, and you rode
like a kern° of Ireland, your French hose° off and in your strait *soldier / wide breeches*
50   strossers.° *tights*

CONSTABLE   You have good judgment in horsemanship.

DAUPHIN   Be warned by me, then: they that ride so, and ride
not warily, fall into foul bogs. I had rather have my horse to
my mistress.

55   CONSTABLE   I had as lief have my mistress a jade.° *horse; whore*

DAUPHIN   I tell thee, Constable, my mistress wears his own hair.[7]

CONSTABLE   I could make as true a boast as that if I had a sow
to my mistress.

DAUPHIN   *"Le chien est retourné à son propre vomissement, et*
60   *la truie lavée au bourbier."*[8] Thou mak'st use of anything.

CONSTABLE   Yet do I not use my horse for my mistress, or any
such proverb so little kin to the purpose.

---

3. When Pegasus struck Mount Helicon with his hoof, the fountain of the Muses sprang forth.
4. Greek messenger god, whose sweet playing on the pipe charmed the many-eyed guard Argus, enabling the imprisoned Io to escape.
5. Horses' colors supposedly suggested their disposi-tions: "nutmeg" meant "pleasant and nimble"; "ginger"

meant "hot and skittish."
6. Carries weight (with obscene innuendo).
7. Implying that the constable's mistress does not, having lost it to syphilis.
8. "The dog is turned to his own vomit again and the sow that was washed to her wallowing in the mire" (quoting 2 Peter 2:22).

RAMBURES My lord Constable, the armor that I saw in your
tent tonight, are those stars or suns upon it?

65 CONSTABLE Stars, my lord.

DAUPHIN Some of them will fall tomorrow, I hope.

CONSTABLE And yet my sky shall not want.

DAUPHIN That may be, for you bear a many superfluously,
and 'twere more honor some were away.

70 CONSTABLE E'en as your horse bears your praises, who would
trot as well were some of your brags dismounted.

DAUPHIN Would I were able to load him with his desert! Will
it never be day? I will trot tomorrow a mile, and my way shall
be paved with English faces.

75 CONSTABLE I will not say so, for fear I should be faced out of
my way.° But I would it were morning, for I would fain° be   *turned aside / gladly*
about the ears of the English.

RAMBURES Who will go to hazard° with me for twenty prisoners?   *wager*

CONSTABLE You must first go yourself to hazard ere you have
80 them.

DAUPHIN 'Tis midnight. I'll go arm myself.   *Exit.*

ORLÉANS The Dauphin longs for morning.

RAMBURES He longs to eat the English.

CONSTABLE I think he will eat all he kills.

85 ORLÉANS By the white hand of my lady, he's a gallant prince.

CONSTABLE Swear by her foot, that she may tread out° the oath.   *erase with her foot*

ORLÉANS He is simply the most active gentleman of France.

CONSTABLE Doing is activity, and he will still be doing.

ORLÉANS He never did harm that I heard of.

90 CONSTABLE Nor will do none tomorrow. He will keep that good
name still.

ORLÉANS I know him to be valiant.

CONSTABLE I was told that by one that knows him better than
you.

95 ORLÉANS What's he?

CONSTABLE Marry, he told me so himself, and he said he cared
not who knew it.

ORLÉANS He needs not; it is no hidden virtue in him.

CONSTABLE By my faith, sir, but it is: never anybody saw it but
100 his lackey.⁹ 'Tis a hooded valor, and when it appears it will
bate.¹

ORLÉANS "Ill will never said well."

CONSTABLE I will cap that proverb with, "There is flattery in
friendship."

105 ORLÉANS And I will take up that with, "Give the devil his due."

CONSTABLE Well placed! There stands your friend for the
devil. Have at the very eye° of that proverb with "A pox of the   *bull's-eye*
devil."

ORLÉANS You are the better at proverbs by how much "A
110 fool's bolt° is soon shot."   *short, blunt arrow*

CONSTABLE You have shot over.°   *overshot the target*

ORLÉANS 'Tis not the first time you were overshot.°   *defeated*

    Enter a MESSENGER.

---

9. That is, the only person he is brave enough to beat
is his servant.

1. Beat its wings (like a hawk, which was kept "hooded"
until prey was sighted); also, abate.

MESSENGER   My lord High Constable, the English lie within
fifteen hundred paces of your tents.

115   CONSTABLE   Who hath measured the ground?

MESSENGER   The Lord Grandpré.

CONSTABLE   A valiant and most expert gentleman.

[*Exit* MESSENGER.]

Would it were day! Alas, poor Harry of England! He longs
not for the dawning as we do.

120   ORLÉANS   What a wretched and peevish fellow is this King of
England, to mope° with his fat-brained followers so far out   *wander*
of his knowledge.

CONSTABLE   If the English had any apprehension° they would   *sense*
run away.

125   ORLÉANS   That they lack, for if their heads had any intellectual armor they could never wear such heavy headpieces.

RAMBURES   That island of England breeds very valiant creatures: their mastiffs are of unmatchable courage.

ORLÉANS   Foolish curs, that run winking° into the mouth of a   *with closed eyes*
130   Russian bear² and have their heads crushed like rotten apples.
You may as well say that's a valiant flea that dare eat his breakfast on the lip of a lion.

CONSTABLE   Just,° just. And the men do sympathize with the   *True*
mastiffs in robustious and rough coming on, leaving their wits
135   with their wives. And then give them great meals of beef,³ and
iron, and steel: they will eat like wolves and fight like devils.

ORLÉANS   Ay, but these English are shrewdly° out of beef.   *badly*

CONSTABLE   Then shall we find tomorrow they have only stom-
achs° to eat and none to fight. Now is it time to arm. Come,   *appetite*
140   shall we about it?

ORLÉANS   It is now two o'clock. But let me see—by ten
We shall have each a hundred English men.   *Exeunt.*

4.0

[*Enter*] CHORUS.

CHORUS   Now entertain conjecture of° a time   *imagine*
When creeping murmur and the poring° dark   *pouring; eye-straining*
Fills the wide vessel of the universe.
From camp to camp, through the foul womb of night,
5   The hum of either army stilly sounds,
That° the fixed sentinels almost receive   *So that*
The secret whispers of each other's watch.
Fire answers fire, and through their paly° flames   *pale*
Each battle sees the other's umbered° face.   *shadowed*
10   Steed threatens steed, in high and boastful neighs
Piercing the night's dull ear; and from the tents
The armorers accomplishing° the knights,   *equipping*
With busy hammers closing rivets up,
Give dreadful note of preparation.
15   The country cocks do crow, the clocks do toll,
And the third hour of drowsy morning name.
Proud of their numbers and secure in soul,

2. Referring to the sport of bearbaiting, in which   3. A traditional English food.
dogs were set upon a bear chained to a post.

The confident and over-lusty French
Do the low-rated° English play at dice, *underrated*
20 And chide the cripple tardy-gated night,
Who like a foul and ugly witch doth limp
So tediously away. The poor condemnèd English,
Like sacrifices, by their watchful fires
Sit patiently and inly° ruminate *inwardly*
25 The morning's danger; and their gesture sad,
Investing° lank-lean cheeks and war-worn coats, *Accompanying*
Presenteth them unto the gazing moon
So many horrid ghosts. Oh, now, who will behold
The royal captain of this ruined band
30 Walking from watch to watch, from tent to tent,
Let him cry, "Praise and glory on his head!"
For forth he goes and visits all his host,° *army*
Bids them good morrow with a modest smile,
And calls them brothers, friends, and countrymen.
35 Upon his royal face there is no note° *sign*
How dread an army hath enrounded° him. *encircled*
Nor doth he dedicate° one jot of color *lose*
Unto the weary and all-watched night,
But freshly looks and overbears attaint[1]
40 With cheerful semblance and sweet majesty,
That every wretch, pining and pale before,
Beholding him, plucks comfort from his looks.
A largess universal,° like the sun, *wealth available to all*
His liberal eye doth give to everyone,
45 Thawing cold fear, that mean and gentle° all *lowborn and noble*
Behold, as may unworthiness define,[2]
A little touch of Harry in the night.
And so our scene must to the battle fly,
Where, oh, for pity, we shall much disgrace,
50 With four or five most vile and ragged foils° *swords*
Right ill-disposed in brawl ridiculous,
The name of Agincourt. Yet sit and see,
Minding° true things by what their mockeries be. *Exit.* *Imagining*

4.1 (Q Scene 12)

Enter the KING, GLOUCESTER, [*and then*] BEDFORD.
KING Gloucester, 'tis true that we are in great danger;
The greater therefore should our courage be.
Good morrow, brother Bedford. God Almighty!
There is some soul of goodness in things evil,
5 Would men observingly distill it out.
For our bad neighbor makes us early stirrers,
Which is both healthful and good husbandry.° *economy*
Besides, they are our outward consciences
And preachers to us all, admonishing
10 That we should dress us fairly° for our end. *prepare adequately*
Thus may we gather honey from the weed
And make a moral of the devil himself.
  Enter ERPINGHAM.

4.0
1. And suppresses signs of exhaustion.

2. As far as their limited capacities permit.
4.1 Location: The English camp at Agincourt.

Good morrow, old Sir Thomas Erpingham.
A good soft pillow for that good white head
15 Were better than a churlish turf of France.

ERPINGHAM   Not so, my liege. This lodging likes° me better,   *pleases*
Since I may say, "Now lie I like a king."

KING   'Tis good for men to love their present pains
Upon example:[1] so the spirit is eased,
20 And when the mind is quickened, out of doubt
The organs, though defunct and dead before,
Break up their drowsy grave and newly move
With casted slough[2] and fresh legerity.°   *nimbleness*
Lend me thy cloak, Sir Thomas. —Brothers both,
25 Commend me to the princes in our camp;
Do my good morrow° to them, and anon   *Say good morning*
Desire them all to my pavilion.

GLOUCESTER   We shall, my liege.

ERPINGHAM   Shall I attend your grace?

KING   No, my good knight;
30 Go with my brothers to my lords of England.
I and my bosom must debate awhile,
And then I would no other company.

ERPINGHAM   The Lord in heaven bless thee, noble Harry.

KING   God-a-mercy,° old heart, thou speak'st cheerfully.   *Thank you*

Exeunt [all but KING].

Enter PISTOL.
35 PISTOL   *Che vous là?*°   *Who goes there? (unidiomatic)*

KING   A friend.

PISTOL   Discuss unto me: art thou officer,
Or art thou base, common, and popular?°   *plebeian*

KING   I am a gentleman of a company.

40 PISTOL   Trail'st thou the puissant pike?°   *Are you an infantryman?*

KING   Even so. What are you?

PISTOL   As good a gentleman as the Emperor.

KING   Then you are a better than the King.

PISTOL   The King's a bawcock,° and a heart of gold,   *fine fellow*
45 A lad of life, an imp of Fame,°   *a scion of noble stock*
Of parents good, of fist most valiant.
I kiss his dirty shoe, and from heartstring
I love the lovely bully.° What is thy name?   *lovable swashbuckler*

KING   Harry le Roy.°   *the King*

50 PISTOL   Le Roy? A Cornish name. Art thou of Cornish crew?

KING   No, I am a Welshman.

PISTOL   Know'st thou Fluellen?

KING   Yes.

PISTOL   Tell him I'll knock his leek about his pate
55 Upon Saint Davy's day.[3]

KING   Do not you wear your dagger in your cap that day, lest
he knock that about yours.

PISTOL   Art thou his friend?

KING   And his kinsman too.

60 PISTOL   The *fico*[4] for thee then!

---

1. By the pattern provided by others.
2. Old skin having been cast off (like a snake's).

3. March 1, Welsh national holiday celebrating St.
David's victory over the Saxons.
4. See 3.7.52.

KING   I thank you. God be with you.

PISTOL   My name is Pistol called.   *Exit.*

KING   It sorts° well with your fierceness.   agrees

      Enter FLUELLEN *and* GOWER[*, separately*].

GOWER   Captain Fluellen!

65   FLUELLEN   'So!° In the name of Jesu Christ, speak fewer! It is   Gadso (an oath)
the greatest admiration° in the universal° world when the true   wonder / whole
and ancient prerogatifs and laws of the wars is not kept. If you
would take the pains but to examine the wars of Pompey the
Great⁵ you shall find, I warrant you, that there is no tiddle-
70   taddle nor pibble-babble° in Pompey's camp. I warrant you,   chattering
you shall find the ceremonies of the wars, and the cares of it,
and the forms of it, and the sobriety of it, and the modesty of
it, to be otherwise.

GOWER   Why, the enemy is loud. You hear him all night.

75   FLUELLEN   If the enemy is an ass and a fool and a prating cox-
comb,° is it meet,° think you, that we should also, look you, be   yammering fool / proper
an ass and a fool and a prating coxcomb, in your own con-
science now?

GOWER   I will speak lower.

80   FLUELLEN   I pray you and beseech you that you will.

      Exeunt [FLUELLEN *and* GOWER].

KING   Though it appear a little out of fashion,°   unconventional
There is much care and valor in this Welshman.

      Enter three Soldiers, John BATES, *Alexander* COURT,
      and Michael WILLIAMS.

COURT   Brother John Bates, is not that the morning which
breaks yonder?

85   BATES   I think it be. But we have no great cause to desire the
approach of day.

WILLIAMS   We see yonder the beginning of the day, but I think
we shall never see the end of it. —Who goes there?

KING   A friend.

90   WILLIAMS   Under what captain serve you?

KING   Under Sir Thomas Erpingham.

WILLIAMS   A good old commander and a most kind gentleman.
I pray you, what thinks he of our estate?°   situation

KING   Even as men wrecked upon a sand, that look to be washed
95   off the next tide.

BATES   He hath not told his thought to the King?

KING   No, nor it is not meet he should. For though I speak it to
you, I think the King is but a man, as I am. The violet smells
to him as it doth to me; the element shows° to him as it doth to   the sky appears
100   me. All his senses have but human conditions.° His ceremo-   limitations
nies laid by, in his nakedness he appears but a man. And
though his affections° are higher mounted than ours, yet   desires
when they stoop,⁶ they stoop with the like wing. Therefore,
when he sees reason of fears° as we do, his fears, out of doubt,   to fear
105   be of the same relish° as ours are. Yet, in reason, no man   taste; kind
should possess him with⁷ any appearance of fear, lest he by
showing it should dishearten his army.

---

5. Roman general, defeated by Julius Caesar.   7. Induce him to experience.
6. Plummet down (term from falconry).

BATES He may show what outward courage he will, but I believe, as cold a night as 'tis, he could wish himself in Thames up to
110 the neck. And so I would he were, and I by him, at all adventures,[8] so we were quit° here. *away from*

KING By my troth,° I will speak my conscience of the King. I *oath*
think he would not wish himself anywhere but where he is.

BATES Then I would he were here alone. So should he be sure
115 to be ransomed, and a many poor men's lives saved.

KING I dare say you love him not so ill to wish him here alone,
howsoever you speak this to feel° other men's minds. Methinks *test*
I could not die anywhere so contented as in the King's company, his cause being just and his quarrel honorable.

120 WILLIAMS That's more than we know.

BATES Ay, or more than we should seek after. For we know
enough if we know we are the King's subjects. If his cause
be wrong, our obedience to the King wipes the crime of it
out of us.

125 WILLIAMS But if the cause be not good, the King himself hath
a heavy reckoning to make when all those legs and arms and
heads chopped off in a battle shall join together at the latter
day[9] and cry all, "We died at such a place"—some swearing,
some crying for a surgeon, some upon their wives left poor
130 behind them, some upon the debts they owe, some upon their
children rawly° left. I am afeard there are few die well that die *abruptly; poorly*
in a battle, for how can they charitably dispose of anything
when blood is their argument?° Now, if these men do not die *business*
well, it will be a black matter for the King that led them to it—
135 who° to disobey were against all proportion of subjection.[1] *whom*

KING So, if a son that is by his father sent about merchandise
do sinfully miscarry upon the sea, the imputation of° his *blame for*
wickedness, by your rule, should be imposed upon his father
that sent him. Or if a servant, under his master's command
140 transporting a sum of money, be assailed by robbers and die
in many irreconciled iniquities,° you may call the business of *unatoned sins*
the master the author of the servant's damnation. But this is
not so. The King is not bound to answer the particular endings of his soldiers, the father of his son, nor the master of his
145 servant, for they purpose not their death when they purpose
their services. Besides, there is no king, be his cause never so
spotless, if it come to the arbitrement° of swords, can try it out *settlement*
with all unspotted° soldiers. Some, peradventure,° have on *unblemished / perhaps*
them the guilt of premeditated and contrived murder; some,
150 of beguiling virgins with the broken seals of perjury; some,
making the wars their bulwark,° that have before gored the *defense (against the law)*
gentle bosom of peace with pillage and robbery. Now, if these
men have defeated the law and outrun native° punishment, *at home*
though they can outstrip men, they have no wings to fly from
155 God. War is his beadle.° War is his vengeance. So that here *police officer*
men are punished for before-breach° of the King's laws in *earlier breaking*
now the King's quarrel. Where they feared the death, they

---

8. Whatever might happen.
9. Last Judgment, when it is believed that human beings are to be resurrected in the body.

1. *against . . . subjection:* to defy all proper relationships of authority and subordination.

have borne life away; and where they would be safe, they perish. Then if they die unprovided,° no more is the King guilty
160 of their damnation than he was before guilty of those impi-
eties for the which they are now visited.° Every subject's duty
is the King's, but every subject's soul is his own. Therefore
should every soldier in the wars do as every sick man in his
bed: wash every mote° out of his conscience. And dying so,
165 death is to him advantage;° or not dying, the time was bless-
edly lost wherein such preparation was gained. And in him
that escapes, it were not sin to think that, making God so free
an offer, he° let him outlive that day to see his greatness and
to teach others how they should prepare.
170 WILLIAMS 'Tis certain, every man that dies ill,° the ill upon
his own head. The King is not to answer it.
BATES I do not desire he should answer for me, and yet I determine to fight lustily for him.
KING I myself heard the King say he would not be ransomed.
175 WILLIAMS Ay, he said so to make us fight cheerfully. But when
our throats are cut he may be ransomed and we never the
wiser.
KING If I live to see it, I will never trust his word after.
WILLIAMS You pay him then! That's a perilous shot out of an
180 elder-gun,° that a poor and a private displeasure can do against
a monarch. You may as well go about to turn the sun to ice
with fanning in his face with a peacock's feather! You'll never
trust his word after! Come, 'tis a foolish saying.
KING Your reproof is something too round;° I should be angry
185 with you if the time were convenient.
WILLIAMS Let it be a quarrel between us, if you live.
KING I embrace it.
WILLIAMS How shall I know thee again?
KING Give me any gage° of thine and I will wear it in my bon-
190 net. Then if ever thou dar'st acknowledge it, I will make it my
quarrel.
WILLIAMS Here's my glove. Give me another of thine.
KING There.
       [*They exchange gloves.*]
WILLIAMS This will I also wear in my cap. If ever thou come to
195 me and say after tomorrow, "This is my glove," by this hand I
will take thee a box on the ear.
KING If ever I live to see it, I will challenge it.
WILLIAMS Thou dar'st as well be hanged.
KING Well, I will do it, though I take thee in the King's company.
200 WILLIAMS Keep thy word. Fare thee well.
BATES Be friends, you English fools, be friends! We have
French quarrels enough, if you could tell how to reckon.°
KING Indeed, the French may lay twenty French crowns° to
one they will beat us, for they bear them on their shoulders.
205 But it is no English treason to cut French crowns,[2] and
tomorrow the King himself will be a clipper.
                                    Exeunt Soldiers.

Glosses (right margin):

159 unprepared
161 punished
164 speck
165 profit
168 (God)
170 in sin
180 a popgun
184 blunt
189 token
202 count
203 coins; heads

---

2. "Clipping" (line 206), or shaving, precious metal off coins was punishable as treason.

Upon the King! "Let us our lives, our souls,
Our debts, our careful wives,
Our children, and our sins, lay on the King!"
210 We must bear all. Oh, hard condition,
Twin-born with greatness, subject to the breath
Of every fool whose sense no more can feel
But his own wringing.° What infinite heartsease   *pain*
Must kings neglect that private men enjoy!
215 And what have kings that privates have not too,
Save ceremony, save general ceremony?
And what art thou, thou idol ceremony?
What kind of god art thou, that suffer'st more
Of mortal griefs than do thy worshippers?
220 What are thy rents?° What are thy comings-in?°   *revenues / income*
O ceremony, show me but thy worth.
What is thy soul of adoration?[3]
Art thou aught° else but place, degree, and form,   *anything*
Creating awe and fear in other men,
225 Wherein thou art less happy, being feared,
Than they in fearing?
What drink'st thou oft, instead of homage sweet,
But poisoned flattery? O be sick, great greatness,
And bid thy ceremony give thee cure!
230 Think'st thou the fiery fever will go out
With titles blown from adulation?
Will it give place to flexure° and low bending?   *bowing*
Canst thou, when thou command'st the begger's knee,
Command the health of it? No, thou proud dream
235 That play'st so subtly with a king's repose.
I am a king that find° thee, and I know   *expose*
'Tis not the balm, the scepter, and the ball,°   *orb (royal accessory)*
The sword, the mace, the crown imperial,
The intertissued robe of gold and pearl,
240 The farcèd° title running fore the king,   *stuffed*
The throne he sits on, nor the tide of pomp
That beats upon the high shore of this world—
No, not all these, thrice-gorgeous ceremony,
Not all these, laid in bed majestical,
245 Can sleep so soundly as the wretched slave
Who, with a body filled and vacant mind,
Gets him to rest, crammed with distressful bread;
Never sees horrid night, the child of hell,
But like a lackey,° from the rise to set,   *servant*
250 Sweats in the eye of Phoebus,° and all night   *the sun*
Sleeps in Elysium;° next day after dawn   *classical paradise*
Doth rise and help Hyperion° to his horse,   *(the sun's charioteer)*
And follows so the ever-running year
With profitable labor to his grave.
255 And but for ceremony such a wretch,
Winding up days with toil and nights with sleep,
Had the forehand° and vantage of a king.   *advantage*
The slave, a member of the country's peace,

---

3. What is the secret of the adoration you inspire?

Enjoys it, but in gross brain little wots°   *thinks*
260   What watch the king keeps to maintain the peace,
Whose hours the peasant best advantages.°   *profits most from*
      Enter ERPINGHAM.

ERPINGHAM   My lord, your nobles, jealous of° your absence,   *concerned about*
Seek through your camp to find you.

KING   Good old knight,
Collect them all together at my tent.
I'll be before thee.

265   ERPINGHAM   I shall do't, my lord.   *Exit.*

KING   O God of battles, steel my soldiers' hearts.
Possess them not with fear. Take from them now
The sense of reck'ning° if th'opposed numbers   *ability to count*
Pluck their hearts from them. Not today, O Lord,
270   Oh, not today, think not upon the fault
My father made in compassing the crown.[4]
I Richard's body have interrèd new,°   *buried anew*
And on it have bestowed more contrite tears
Than from it issued forcèd drops of blood.
275   Five hundred poor I have in yearly pay,
Who twice a day their withered hands hold up°   *(in prayer)*
Toward heaven to pardon blood. And I have built
Two chantries,[5] where the sad and solemn priests
Sing still for Richard's soul. More will I do,
280   Though all that I can do is nothing worth,
Since that my penitence comes after all,
Imploring pardon.
      Enter GLOUCESTER.

GLOUCESTER   My liege!

KING   My brother Gloucester's voice? Ay.
285   I know thy errand; I will go with thee.
The day, my friend, and all things stay° for me.   *Exeunt.*   *wait*

4.2

Enter the DAUPHIN, ORLÉANS, [*and*] RAMBURES.

ORLÉANS   The sun doth gild our armor. Up, my lords!

DAUPHIN   *Monte cheval!*° My horse! *Varlet lacquais,*° ha!   *To horse / valet*

ORLÉANS   O brave spirit!

DAUPHIN   *Via, les eaux et terre!*

5   ORLÉANS   *Rien puis? L'air et feu?*[1]

DAUPHIN   *Cieux,*° cousin Orléans!   *To the heavens*
      Enter CONSTABLE.

Now my lord Constable!

CONSTABLE   Hark how our steeds for present° service neigh.   *immediate*

DAUPHIN   Mount them and make incision in their hides,
That their hot blood may spin in English eyes
10   And dout° them with superfluous courage. Ha!   *extinguish*

RAMBURES   What, will you have them weep our horses' blood?

---

4. Henry's father usurped the throne from its rightful possessor, Richard II.
5. Chapels where masses for the dead were sung.
4.2. Location: The French camp.

1. Away, over water and earth!
   No more? Air and fire? (Playing on the four elements, of which fire was the highest.)

How shall we then behold their natural tears?
    Enter MESSENGER.
MESSENGER   The English are embattled,[2] you French peers.
CONSTABLE   To horse, you gallant princes, straight to horse!

15   Do but behold yond poor and starvèd band,
    And your fair show° shall suck away their souls,   *appearance*
    Leaving them but the shales and husks of men.
    There is not work enough for all our hands,
    Scarce blood enough in all their sickly veins
20   To give each naked curtle ax° a stain   *cutlass*
    That our French gallants shall today draw out
    And sheathe for lack of sport. Let us but blow on them,
    The vapor of our valor will o'erturn them.
    'Tis positive against all exceptions,° lords,   *'Tis definitely true*
25   That our superfluous lackeys and our peasants,
    Who in unnecessary action swarm
    About our squares of battle, were enough
    To purge this field of such a hilding° foe,   *worthless*
    Though we upon this mountain's basis by°   *foot nearby*
30   Took stand° for idle speculation,   *Stood still*
    But that our honors must not. What's to say?
    A very little little let us do
    And all is done. Then let the trumpets sound
    The tucket sonance° and the note to mount,   *trumpet signal*
35   For our approach shall so much dare the field
    That England shall couch down in fear and yield.
        Enter GRANDPRÉ.
GRANDPRÉ   Why do you stay so long, my lords of France?
    Yond island carrions,° desperate of their bones,   *cadavers*
    Ill-favoredly become the morning field.
40   Their ragged curtains° poorly are let loose,   *banners*
    And our air shakes them passing scornfully.
    Big Mars° seems bankrupt in their beggared host   *(god of war)*
    And faintly through a rusty beaver° peeps.   *visor*
    The horsemen sit like fixèd candlesticks
45   With torch-staves° in their hands, and their poor jades   *tapers*
    Lob° down their heads, drooping the hides and hips,   *Hang*
    The gum down-roping° from their pale-dead eyes,   *mucus dripping*
    And in their palled° dull mouths the gimmaled° bit   *pale / jointed*
    Lies foul with chewed grass, still and motionless.
50   And their executors,[3] the knavish crows,
    Fly o'er them all, impatient for their hour.
    Description cannot suit itself in words,
    To demonstrate the life of° such a battle   *depict realistically*
    In life so lifeless as it shows itself.
55 CONSTABLE   They have said their prayers, and they stay° for   *wait*
    death.
DAUPHIN   Shall we go send them dinners and fresh suits
    And give their fasting horses provender,°   *food*
    And after° fight with them?   *afterward*
CONSTABLE   I stay but for my guidon.° To the field!   *pennant*

---

2. Drawn into lines of battle.
3. Administrators of wills (who dispose of the remains of the dead).

60   I will the banner from a trumpet° take   *trumpeter*
      And use it for my haste. Come, come away!
      The sun is high and we outwear° the day.   *Exeunt.*   *waste*

4.3 (Q Scene 13)

Enter GLOUCESTER, BEDFORD, EXETER, ERPINGHAM
with all his host, SALISBURY, *and* WESTMORLAND.[1]

GLOUCESTER   Where is the King?
BEDFORD   The King himself is rode to view their battle.°   *army*
WESTMORLAND   Of fighting men they have full threescore
      thousand.°   *60,000*
EXETER   There's five to one. Besides, they all are fresh.
5   SALISBURY   God's arm strike with us! 'Tis a fearful odds.
      God be wi' you, princes all. I'll to my charge.°   *command post*
      If we no more meet till we meet in heaven,
      Then joyfully, my noble lord of Bedford,
      My dear lord Gloucester, and my good lord Exeter,
10   And my kind kinsman, warriors all, adieu.
BEDFORD   Farewell, good Salisbury, and good luck go with thee.
EXETER   Farewell, kind lord. Fight valiantly today.
      And yet I do thee wrong to mind° thee of it,   *remind*
      For thou art framed of the firm truth of valor.

                                      [*Exit* SALISBURY.]

15   BEDFORD   He is as full of valor as of kindness,
      Princely in both!

        Enter the KING.

WESTMORLAND   Oh, that we now had here
      But one ten thousand of those men in England
      That do no work today.
KING   What's he that wishes so?
      My cousin Westmorland? No, my fair cousin:
20   If we are marked to die, we are enough
      To do our country loss,° and if to live,   *For our country to lose*
      The fewer men, the greater share of honor.
      God's will, I pray thee wish not one man more.
      By Jove, I am not covetous for gold,
25   Nor care I who doth feed upon my cost;
      It ernes° me not if men my garments wear;   *grieves*
      Such outward things dwell not in my desires.
      But if it be a sin to covet honor
      I am the most offending soul alive.
30   No, faith, my coz,° wish not a man from England.   *kinsman*
      God's peace, I would not lose so great an honor
      As one man more methinks would share° from me,   *deprive*
      For the best hope I have. Oh, do not wish one more!
      Rather proclaim it, Westmorland, through my host°   *army*
35   That he which hath no stomach° to this fight,   *appetite; courage*
      Let him depart; his passport shall be made
      And crowns for convoy° put into his purse.   *money for transport*
      We would not die in that man's company

4.3 Location: The English camp.
1. TEXTUAL COMMENT In historical fact, the Earl of
Westmorland remained in England, charged with
securing the border with Scotland; the Quarto text
substitutes Warwick in this scene. The Norton edition
based on the Folio retains the Folio reading; for a
fuller discussion, see Digital Edition TC 8 (Folio edited
text).

That fears his fellowship° to die with us.   *duty as our companion*
40   This day is called the feast of Crispian.[2]
He that outlives this day and comes safe home
Will stand a-tiptoe when this day is named
And rouse him at the name of Crispian.
He that shall see this day and live old age
45   Will yearly on the vigil° feast his neighbors   *eve of the saint's day*
And say, "Tomorrow is Saint Crispian."
Then will he strip his sleeve and show his scars
And say, "These wounds I had on Crispin's day."
Old men forget; yet all shall be forgot
50   But he'll remember, with advantages,°   *embellishments*
What feats he did that day. Then shall our names,
Familiar in his mouth as household words—
Harry the King, Bedford and Exeter,
Warwick and Talbot, Salisbury and Gloucester—
55   Be in their flowing cups freshly remembered.
This story shall the good man teach his son,
And Crispin Crispian shall ne'er go by
From this day to the ending of the world
But we in it shall be rememberèd,
60   We few, we happy few, we band of brothers—
For he today that sheds his blood with me
Shall be my brother. Be he ne'er so vile,°   *lowborn*
This day shall gentle his condition.[3]
And gentlemen in England now abed
65   Shall think themselves accursed they were not here,
And hold their manhoods cheap whiles any speaks
That fought with us upon Saint Crispin's day.
        Enter SALISBURY.
SALISBURY   My sovereign lord, bestow yourself° with speed.   *take your positions*
The French are bravely in their battles° set   *battle lines*
70   And will with all expedience° charge on us.   *speed*
KING   All things are ready, if our minds be so.
WESTMORLAND   Perish the man whose mind is backward now!
KING   Thou dost not wish more help from England, coz?
WESTMORLAND   God's will, my liege, would you and I alone,
75   Without more help, could fight this royal battle!
KING   Why, now thou hast unwished five thousand men,
Which likes° me better than to wish us one.   *pleases*
—You know your places. God be with you all!
        Tucket. Enter MONTJOY.
MONTJOY   Once more I come to know of thee, King Harry,
80   If for thy ransom thou wilt now compound,°   *make terms*
Before thy most assurèd overthrow.
For certainly thou art so near the gulf
Thou needs must be englutted.° Besides, in mercy   *swallowed*
The Constable desires thee thou wilt mind°   *remind*
85   Thy followers of repentance, that their souls
May make a peaceful and a sweet retire
From off these fields where, wretches, their poor bodies

2. October 25, dedicated to the martyred brothers   3. Shall raise him to gentlemanly rank.
Crispin and Crispianus (or Crispinian).

Must lie and fester.

KING   Who hath sent thee now?

MONTJOY   The Constable of France.

90   KING   I pray thee bear my former answer back:
Bid them achieve° me and then sell my bones.   *get*
Good God, why should they mock poor fellows thus?
The man that once did sell the lion's skin
While the beast lived, was killed with hunting him.[4]
95   A many of our bodies shall no doubt
Find native° graves, upon the which, I trust,   *(English)*
Shall witness live in brass of this day's work.
And those that leave their valiant bones in France,
Dying like men, though buried in your dunghills,
100   They shall be famed. For there the sun shall greet them
And draw their honors reeking° up to heaven,   *steaming; stinking*
Leaving their earthly parts to choke your clime,
The smell whereof shall breed a plague in France.
Mark then abounding valor in our English,
105   That being dead, like to the bullets crazing,°   *ricocheting*
Break out into a second course of mischief,
Killing in relapse of mortality.°   *another fatal outbreak*
Let me speak proudly. Tell the Constable
We are but warriors for the working day;°   *workaday warriors*
110   Our gayness and our gilt are all besmirched
With rainy marching in the painful field.
There's not a piece of feather° in our host—   *decorative plume*
Good argument, I hope, we will not fly—
And time hath worn us into slovenry.°   *filth*
115   But by the mass, our hearts are in the trim,°   *fine shape*
And my poor soldiers tell me, yet ere night
They'll be in fresher robes, or they will pluck
The gay new coats o'er the French soldiers' heads
And turn them out of service.[5] If they do this,
120   As, if God please, they shall, my ransom then
Will soon be levied.[6] Herald, save thou thy labor:
Come thou no more for ransom, gentle herald.
They shall have none, I swear, but these my joints,
Which if they have as I will leave 'em them,
125   Shall yield them little. Tell the Constable.

MONTJOY   I shall, King Harry. And so fare thee well.
Thou never shalt hear herald any more.   *Exit.*

KING   I fear thou wilt once more come again for a ransom.
      Enter YORK.

YORK   My lord, most humbly on my knee I beg
130   The leading of the vaward.°   *vanguard*

KING   Take it, brave York. —Now soldiers, march away,
And how thou pleasest, God, dispose the day!   *Exeunt.*

4.4 (Q Scene 15)

Alarum. Excursions.° Enter PISTOL, FRENCH   *Skirmishes*
SOLDIER, [*and*] BOY.

PISTOL   Yield, cur!

---

4. *The man . . . him:* alluding to one of Aesop's fables.   6. Collected (from the French themselves).
5. Dismiss them, stripped of their servant's uniforms.   **4.4.** Location: The battlefield.

FRENCH SOLDIER *Je pense que vous êtes le gentilhomme de*
  bon qualité.[1]

PISTOL Qualité? "Calin o custore me!"[2]

5 Art thou a gentleman? What is thy name? Discuss.

FRENCH SOLDIER *O Seigneur Dieu!*°   O Lord God

PISTOL O Signieur Dew should be a gentleman.—
  Perpend° my words, O Signieur Dew, and mark: Weigh
  O Signieur Dew, thou diest on point of fox,°   sword

10 Except, O Signieur, thou do give to me
  Egregious° ransom.   Extraordinary

FRENCH SOLDIER *Oh, prenez miséricorde! Ayez pitié de moi!*[3]

PISTOL Moy shall not serve, I will have forty moys,[4]
  Or I will fetch thy rim° out at thy throat   stomach lining

15 In drops of crimson blood.

FRENCH SOLDIER *Est-il impossible d'échapper la force de ton bras?*[5]

PISTOL Brass, cur?
  Thou damned and luxurious° mountain goat,   lecherous
  Offer'st me brass?

20 FRENCH SOLDIER *Oh, pardonnez-moi!*

PISTOL Say'st thou me so? Is that a ton of moys?
  —Come hither, boy. Ask me this slave in French
  What is his name.

BOY *Écoutez. Comment êtes-vous appelé?*[6]

25 FRENCH SOLDIER *Monsieur Le Fer.*

BOY He says his name is Master Fer.

PISTOL Master Fer? I'll fer him, and firk° him, and ferret° him.   beat / savage
  Discuss the same in French unto him.

BOY I do not know the French for fer, and ferret, and firk.

30 PISTOL Bid him prepare, for I will cut his throat.

FRENCH SOLDIER *Que dit-il, monsieur?*°   What does he say, sir?

BOY *Il me commande à vous dire que vous faites vous prêt, car ce*
  soldat ici est disposé tout à cette heure de couper votre gorge.°   (translates Pistol)

PISTOL Owy, cuppele gorge, permafoy,[7]

35 Peasant, unless thou give me crowns, brave crowns;
  Or mangled shalt thou be by this my sword.

FRENCH SOLDIER *Oh, je vous supplie, pour l'amour de Dieu,*
  me pardonner! Je suis le gentilhomme de bonne maison. Gar-
  dez ma vie, et je vous donnerai deux cents écus.°   (translated by the Boy)

40 PISTOL What are his words?

BOY He prays you to save his life. He is a gentleman of a good
  house, and for his ransom he will give you two hundred crowns.

PISTOL Tell him my fury shall abate, and I
  The crowns will take.

45 FRENCH SOLDIER *Petit monsieur, que dit-il?*[8]

BOY *Encore qu'il est contre son jurement de pardonner aucun*
  prisonnier; néanmoins, pour les écus que vous lui ici prom-
  ettez, il est content à vous donner la liberté, le franchisement.

FRENCH SOLDIER [*to* PISTOL] *Sur mes genoux je vous donne*

50 *mille remerciements, et je m'estime heureux que j'ai tombé*

---

1. I think you are a gentleman of high rank.
2. The Irish refrain of a popular ballad, meaning "I
am a girl from beside the Suir."
3. Oh, take pity! Have pity on me!
4. Pistol mistakes *moi* for the name of a coin.

5. Is it impossible to escape the strength of your arm?
6. Listen. What's your name?
7. Yes, cut your throat, by my faith.
8. Little sir, what says he?

entre les mains d' un chevalier, comme je pense, le plus brave,
valliant, et très distingué seigneur d'Angleterre.°   (translated by the Boy)

PISTOL   Expound unto me, boy.

BOY   He gives you upon his knees a thousand thanks, and he
55   esteems himself happy that he hath fallen into the hands of
one, as he thinks, the most brave, valorous, and thrice-worthy
seigneur of England.

PISTOL   As I suck blood, I will some mercy show.
Follow me.

60   BOY   *Suivez-vous le grand capitaine.*⁹

[*Exeunt* PISTOL *and* FRENCH SOLDIER.]

I did never know so full a voice issue from so empty a heart.
But the saying is true, "The empty vessel makes the greatest
sound." Bardolph and Nym had ten times more valor than
this roaring devil i'th' old play, that everyone may pare his
65   nails with a wooden dagger,¹ and they are both hanged, and
so would this be if he durst steal anything adventurously.° I   recklessly
must stay with the lackeys with the luggage of our camp.
The French might have a good prey of us if he knew of it, for
there is none to guard it but boys.   *Exit.*

4.5 (Q Scene 14)

Enter CONSTABLE, ORLÉANS, BOURBON, [*the*] DAUPHIN,
and RAMBURES.

CONSTABLE   *O diable!*

ORLÉANS   *O Seigneur! Le jour est perdu, tout est perdu!*

DAUPHIN   *Mort de ma vie!*¹ All is confounded,° all!   lost
Reproach and everlasting shame
5   Sits mocking in our plumes.

A short alarum.

O méchante Fortune!° Do not run away!   evil fate

CONSTABLE   Why, all our ranks are broke.

DAUPHIN   Oh, perdurable shame! Let's stab ourselves!
Be these the wretches that we played at dice for?

10   ORLÉANS   Is this the king we sent to for his ransom?

BOURBON   Shame, and eternal shame, nothing but shame!
Let us die instant. Once more back again!
And he that will not follow Bourbon now,
Let him go hence and, with his cap in hand,
15   Like a base pandar° hold the chamber door   pimp
Whilst by a slave no gentler° than my dog   better born
His fairest daughter is contaminated.

CONSTABLE   Disorder that hath spoiled° us friend° us now.   ruined / befriend
Let us on heaps go offer up our lives.

20   ORLÉANS   We are enough yet living in the field
To smother up the English in our throngs,
If any order might be thought upon.

BOURBON   The devil take order now! I'll to the throng.
Let life be short, else shame will be too long.   *Exeunt.*

---

9. Follow the great captain.
1. Allegorical Vice characters in old-fashioned morality
plays were typically armed with wooden daggers.
4.5 Location: Scene continues.

1. O the devil!
O God! The day is lost, all is lost!
Death of my life!

4.6 (Q Scene 16)

Alarum. Enter the KING *and his train,°* *with Prisoners.*   *followers*

KING Well have we done, thrice-valiant countrymen.
But all's not done; yet keep the French the field.
    [*Enter* EXETER.]

EXETER The Duke of York commends him to your majesty.

KING Lives he, good uncle? Thrice within this hour

5 I saw him down, thrice up again and fighting.
From helmet to the spur all blood he was.

EXETER In which array, brave soldier, doth he lie,
Larding° the plain, and by his bloody side,   *Moistening*
Yokefellow to his honor-owing° wounds,   *honorable*

10 The noble Earl of Suffolk also lies.
Suffolk first died, and York, all haggled over,°   *hacked up*
Comes to him where in gore he lay insteeped,°   *soaked*
And takes him by the beard, kisses the gashes
That bloodily did yawn upon his face.

15 He cries aloud, "Tarry, my cousin Suffolk!
My soul shall thine keep company to heaven.
Tarry, sweet soul, for mine; then fly abreast,
As in this glorious and well-foughten field
We kept together in our chivalry."

20 Upon these words I came and cheered him up.
He smiled me in the face, raught° me his hand,   *reached*
And with a feeble grip says, "Dear my lord,
Commend my service to my sovereign."
So did he turn, and over Suffolk's neck

25 He threw his wounded arm and kissed his lips,
And so espoused to death, with blood he sealed
A testament of noble-ending love.
The pretty and sweet manner of it forced
Those waters from me which I would have stopped,

30 But I had not so much of man in me,
And all my mother° came into mine eyes   *(feminine) tenderness*
And gave me up to tears.

KING   I blame you not,
For hearing this I must perforce compound°   *come to terms*
With mistful eyes, or they will issue° too.   *weep*
    Alarum.

35 But hark, what new alarum is this same?
The French have reinforced their scattered men.
Then every soldier kill his prisoners!¹
Give the word through.   *Exeunt.*

4.7 (Q Scene 17)

Enter FLUELLEN *and* GOWER.

FLUELLEN Kill the poys and the luggage! 'Tis expressly against
the law of arms. 'Tis as arrant a piece of knavery, mark you
now, as can be offert. In your conscience now, is it not?

GOWER 'Tis certain there's not a boy left alive. And the cow-
5 ardly rascals that ran from the battle ha' done this slaughter.
Besides, they have burned and carried away all that was in

4.6 Location: Scene continues.
1. PERFORMANCE COMMENT This may or may not be

done onstage. See Digital Edition PC 2.
4.7 Location: Before Henry's pavilion.

the King's tent, wherefore the King most worthily hath caused
every soldier to cut his prisoner's throat. Oh, 'tis a gallant king!

FLUELLEN   Ay, he was porn at Monmouth,° Captain Gower.   *(in Wales)*
10   What call you the town's name where Alexander the Pig was
born?

GOWER   Alexander the Great.

FLUELLEN   Why, I pray you, is not "pig" great? The pig, or the
great, or the mighty, or the huge, or the magnanimous, are
15   all one reckonings, save the phrase is a little variations.°   *(for "varied")*

GOWER   I think Alexander the Great was born in Macedon.
His father was called Philip of Macedon, as I take it.

FLUELLEN   I think it is in Macedon where Alexander is porn.
I tell you, Captain, if you look in the maps of the world I
20   warrant you sall find in the comparisons between Macedon
and Monmouth that the situations, look you, is both alike.
There is a river in Macedon, and there is also moreover a
river at Monmouth. It is called Wye at Monmouth, but it is
out of my prains what is the name of the other river—but 'tis
25   all one, 'tis alike as my fingers is to my fingers, and there is
salmons in both. If you mark Alexander's life well, Harry of
Monmouth's life is come after it indifferent well.¹ For there
is figures° in all things. Alexander, God knows, and you know,   *comparisons*
in his rages, and his furies, and his wraths, and his cholers,°   *angers*
30   and his moods, and his displeasures, and his indignations, and
also being a little intoxicates in his prains, did in his ales and
his angers, look you, kill his best friend Clytus—

GOWER   Our King is not like him in that. He never killed any
of his friends.

35   FLUELLEN   It is not well done, mark you now, to take the tales
out of my mouth ere it is made an end and finished. I speak
but in the figures and comparisons of it. As Alexander killed
his friend Clytus, being in his ales and his cups, so also
Harry Monmouth, being in his right wits and his good judg-
40   ments, turned away the fat knight with the great belly doublet; he was full of jests, and gipes,° and knaveries, and   *gibes*
mocks—I have forgot his name.

GOWER   Sir John Falstaff.

FLUELLEN   That is he. I'll tell you, there is good men porn at
45   Monmouth.

GOWER   Here comes his majesty.

> *Alarum. Enter* KING HARRY [*with*] BOURBON [*as his
> prisoner,* EXETER, GLOUCESTER, WARWICK, *a Herald,
> and others,*] *with Prisoners.*² *Flourish.*

KING   I was not angry since I came to France
Until this instant. Take a trumpet, herald;
Ride thou unto the horsemen on yond hill.
50   If they will fight with us, bid them come down,
Or void° the field: they do offend our sight.   *leave*
If they'll do neither, we will come to them
And make them skirr° away as swift as stones   *scurry*
Enforced° from the old Assyrian slings.   *Driven*
55   Besides, we'll cut the throats of those we have,

---

1. *is . . . well:* resembles it fairly well.
2. This is a second batch of prisoners, captured after the French counterattack.

And not a man of them that we shall take
Shall taste our mercy. Go and tell them so.
   Enter MONTJOY.
EXETER Here comes the herald of the French, my liege.
GLOUCESTER His eyes are humbler than they used to be.
60 KING How now, what means this, herald? Know'st thou not
  That I have fined° these bones of mine for ransom?   *pledged*
  Com'st thou again for ransom?
MONTJOY   No, great King.
  I come to thee for charitable license°   *permission*
  That we may wander o'er this bloody field
65 To book° our dead and then to bury them;   *register*
  To sort our nobles from our common men.
  For many of our princes, woe the while,
  Lie drowned and soaked in mercenary blood;[3]
  So do our vulgar° drench their peasant limbs   *common people*
70 In blood of princes, and their wounded steeds
  Fret fetlock°-deep in gore and with wild rage   *ankle*
  Yerk out their armèd heels at their dead masters,
  Killing them twice. O give us leave, great King,
  To view the field in safety and dispose
  Of their dead bodies.
75 KING   I tell thee truly, herald,
  I know not if the day be ours or no,
  For yet a many of your horsemen peer°   *appear*
  And gallop o'er the field.
MONTJOY   The day is yours.
  KING Praised be God, and not our strength, for it!
80 What is this castle called that stands hard by?
MONTJOY They call it Agincourt.
  KING Then call we this the field of Agincourt,
  Fought on the day of Crispin Crispian.
FLUELLEN Your grandfather of famous memory, an't° please *if it*
85 your majesty, and your great-uncle Edward the Plack Prince
 of Wales, as I have read in the chronicles, fought a most
 prave pattle here in France.
  KING They did, Fluellen.
FLUELLEN Your majesty says very true. If your majesty is
90 remembered of it, the Welshmen did good service in a garden where leeks did grow, wearing leeks in their Monmouth
 caps,[4] which your majesty know to this hour is an honorable
 badge of the service. And I do believe your majesty takes no
 scorn to wear the leek upon Saint Tavy's day.
95 KING I wear it for a memorable honor,
  For I am Welsh, you know, good countryman.
FLUELLEN All the water in Wye° cannot wash your majesty's *(Welsh river)*
 Welsh plood out of your pody, I can tell you that. God pless
 it and preserve it, as long as it pleases his grace, and his
100 majesty too!
  KING Thanks, good my countryman.
FLUELLEN By Jeshu, I am your majesty's countryman, I care
 not who know it. I will confess it to all the world. I need not

---

3. Common soldiers, unlike noblemen, fought for pay. 4. Tall, tapering caps without brims.

to be ashamed of your majesty, praised be God, so long as
105   your majesty is an honest man.
  KING   God keep me so.
        Enter WILLIAMS.
                  Our herald go with him.
  Bring me just notice° of the numbers dead   *accurate record*
  On both our parts.
      [*Exeunt* MONTJOY, GOWER, *and the English Herald*.]
          Call yonder fellow hither.
  EXETER   Soldier, you must come to the King.
110   KING   Soldier, why wear'st thou that glove in thy cap?
  WILLIAMS   An't please your majesty, 'tis the gage° of one that   *token*
  I should fight withal, if he be alive.
  KING   An Englishman?
  WILLIAMS   An't please your majesty, a rascal that swaggered
115   with me last night, who if 'a lived and ever dare to challenge
  this glove, I have sworn to take him a box o'th' ear. Or if I can
  see my glove in his cap, which he swore as he was a soldier
  he would wear if 'a lived, I will strike it out soundly.
  KING   What think you, Captain Fluellen? Is it fit this soldier
120   keep his oath?
  FLUELLEN   He is a craven° and a villain else, an't please your   *coward*
  majesty, in my conscience.
  KING   It may be his enemy is a gentleman of great sort, quite
  from the answer of his degree.[5]
125   FLUELLEN   Though he be as good a gentleman as the devil is,
  as Lucifer and Belzebub° himself, it is necessary, look your   *Satan*
  grace, that he keep his vow and his oath. If he be perjured,
  see you now, his reputation is as arrant a villain and a jack-
  sauce° as ever his black shoe trod upon God's ground, and   *saucy knave*
130   his earth, in my conscience, la!
  KING   Then keep thy vow, sirrah, when thou meet'st the fellow.
  WILLIAMS   So I will, my liege, as I live.
  KING   Who serv'st thou under?
  WILLIAMS   Under Captain Gower, my liege.
135   FLUELLEN   Gower is a good captain, and is good knowledge
  and literature° in the wars.   *well read*
  KING   Call him hither to me, soldier.
  WILLIAMS   I will, my liege.   *Exit.*
  KING   Here, Fluellen, wear thou this favor for me and stick it
140   in thy cap. When Alençon and myself were down together, I
  plucked this glove from his helm. If any man challenge this,
  he is a friend to Alençon and an enemy to our person. If thou
  encounter any such, apprehend° him, an° thou dost me love.   *arrest / if*
  FLUELLEN   Your grace does me as great honors as can be
145   desired in the hearts of his subjects. I would fain° see the   *gladly*
  man that has but two legs that shall find himself aggriefed
  at this glove, that is all. But I would fain see it once, an't
  please God of his grace that I might.
  KING   Know'st thou Gower?
150   FLUELLEN   He is my dear friend, an't please you.
  KING   Pray thee, go seek him and bring him to my tent.

---

5. Quite above responding to a challenge from one of Williams's rank.

FLUELLEN   I will fetch him.   *Exit.*

KING   My lord of Warwick and my brother Gloucester,
Follow Fluellen closely at the heels.
155 The glove which I have given him for a favor
May haply purchase him a box o'th' ear.
It is the soldier's. I by bargain should
Wear it myself. Follow, good cousin Warwick.
If that the soldier strike him, as I judge
160 By his blunt bearing he will keep his word,
Some sudden mischief may arise of it.
For I do know Fluellen valiant
And touched with choler,° hot as gunpowder,   *made angry*
And quickly will return an injury.°   *insult*
165 Follow, and see there be no harm between them.
Go you with me, uncle of Exeter.   *Exeunt.*

4.8 (Q Scene 18)

Enter GOWER and WILLIAMS.

WILLIAMS   I warrant° it is to knight you, Captain.   *I'm sure*

Enter FLUELLEN.

FLUELLEN   God's will and his pleasure, Captain. I beseech you
now, come apace° to the King. There is more good toward   *quickly*
you, peradventure,° than is in your knowledge to dream of.   *perhaps*
5 WILLIAMS   Sir, know you this glove?
FLUELLEN   Know the glove? I know the glove is a glove.
WILLIAMS   I know this, and thus I challenge it.
[*He*] *strikes him.*
FLUELLEN   'Sblood, an arrant traitor as any's in the universal
world, or in France, or in England!
10 GOWER   How now, sir, you villain!
WILLIAMS   Do you think I'll be forsworn?
FLUELLEN   Stand away, Captain Gower. I will give treason his
payment into plows, I warrant you.
WILLIAMS   I am no traitor.
15 FLUELLEN   That's a lie in thy throat! I charge you in his maj-
esty's name, apprehend him. He's a friend of the Duke
Alençon's.
Enter WARWICK and GLOUCESTER.
WARWICK   How now, how now, what's the matter?
FLUELLEN   My lord of Warwick, here is, praised be God for it,
20 a most contagious° treason come to light, look you, as you   *noxious*
shall desire in a summer's day.
Enter KING and EXETER.
Here is his majesty.
KING   How now, what's the matter?
FLUELLEN   My liege, here is a villain and a traitor that, look
25 your grace, has struck the glove which your majesty is take
out of the helmet of Alençon.
WILLIAMS   My liege, this was my glove—here is the fellow° of   *mate*
it—and he that I gave it to in change promised to wear it in his
cap. I promised to strike him if he did. I met this man with my
30 glove in his cap, and I have been as good as my word.

4.8 Location: Scene continues.

FLUELLEN Your majesty hear now, saving your majesty's manhood, what an arrant, rascally, beggarly, lousy knave it is. I
hope your majesty is pear° me testimony, and witness, and   *(for "will bear")*
will avouchment° that this is the glove of Alençon that your   *(for "vouch")*
35 majesty is give me, in your conscience now.
KING Give me thy glove, soldier.
Look, here is the fellow of it.
'Twas I indeed thou promised'st to strike.
And thou hast given me most bitter terms.°   *words*
40 FLUELLEN An't please your majesty, let his neck answer for it,
if there is any martial law in the world.
KING How canst thou make me satisfaction?
WILLIAMS All offenses, my lord, come from the heart. Never
came any from mine that might offend your majesty.
45 KING It was ourself thou didst abuse.
WILLIAMS Your majesty came not like yourself. You appeared
to me but as a common man. Witness the night, your garments, your lowliness. And what your highness suffered
under that shape, I beseech you take it for your own fault
50 and not mine. For had you been as I took you for, I made no
offense. Therefore I beseech your highness pardon me.
KING Here, Uncle Exeter, fill this glove with crowns
And give it to this fellow. —Keep it, fellow,
And wear it for an honor in thy cap
55 Till I do challenge it. —Give him the crowns.
—And Captain, you must needs be friends with him.
FLUELLEN By this day and this light, the fellow has mettle
enough in his belly. —Hold, there is twelve pence for you,
and I pray you to serve God, and keep you out of prawls and
60 prabbles, and quarrels and dissensions, and I warrant you it
is the better for you.
WILLIAMS I will none of your money.
FLUELLEN It is with a good will. I can tell you, it will serve
you to mend your shoes. Come, wherefore should you be so
65 pashfull? Your shoes is not so good. 'Tis a good shilling, I
warrant you, or I will change it.[1]
           Enter HERALD.
KING Now, herald, are the dead numbered?
HERALD Here is the number of the slaught'red French.
KING What prisoners of good sort° are taken, uncle?   *high rank*
70 EXETER Charles, Duke of Orléans, nephew to the King,
John, Duke of Bourbon, and Lord Boucicault.
Of other lords and barons, knights and squires,
Full fifteen hundred, besides common men.
KING This note doth tell me of ten thousand French
75 That in the field lie slain. Of princes in this number
And nobles bearing banners,° there lie dead   *coats of arms*
One hundred twenty-six. Added to these,
Of knights, esquires, and gallant gentlemen,
Eight thousand and four hundred, of the which
80 Five hundred were but yesterday dubbed knights.
So that in these ten thousand they have lost
There are but sixteen hundred mercenaries;

---

1. Williams may or may not take the money.

The rest are princes, barons, lords, knights, squires,
And gentlemen of blood and quality.
85   The names of those their nobles that lie dead:
Charles Delabreth, High Constable of France;
Jaques of Chatillion, Admiral of France;
The Master of the Crossbows, Lord Rambures;
Great Master of France, the brave Sir Guiscard Dauphin;
90   John, Duke of Alençon; Anthony, Duke of Brabant,
The brother to the Duke of Burgundy;
And Edward, Duke of Bar; of lusty earls,
Grandpré and Roussi, Fauconbridge and Foix,
Beaumont and Marle, Vaudemont and Lestrelles.
95   Here was a royal fellowship of death.
Where is the number of our English dead?
　　　[HERALD *gives him another paper.*]
Edward the Duke of York; the Earl of Suffolk;
Sir Richard Keighley; Davy Gam, esquire;
None else of name,° and of all other men   high rank
100   But five-and-twenty. O God, thy arm was here;
And not to us but to thy arm alone
Ascribe we all. When, without stratagem,
But in plain shock° and even play of battle,   confrontation
Was ever known so great and little loss
105   On one part and on tother? Take it, God,
For it is none but thine.
EXETER   'Tis wonderful.
KING   Come, go we in procession to the village,
And be it death proclaimèd through our host
To boast of this, or take that praise from God
110   Which is his only.
FLUELLEN   Is it not lawful, an't please your majesty, to tell
how many is killed?
KING   Yes, Captain, but with this acknowledgment,
That God fought for us.
115 FLUELLEN   Yes, in my conscience, he did us great good.
KING   Do we all holy rites.
Let there be sung *Non nobis,* and *Te Deum,*[2]
The dead with charity enclosed in clay,°   buried with pious love
And then to Calais, and to England then,
120   Where ne'er from France arrived more happy° men.   *Exeunt.*   more fortunate

5.0

Enter CHORUS.
CHORUS   Vouchsafe° to those that have not read the story   Allow
That I may prompt them—and of such as have,
I humbly pray them to admit th'excuse
Of time, of numbers, and due course of things
5   Which cannot in their huge and proper life
Be here presented. Now we bear the King
Toward Calais. Grant him there; there seen,
Heave him away upon your wingèd thoughts

---

2. *Non nobis* is Psalm 115, beginning "Not unto us, O Lord, not unto us, but unto thy name give the glory." *Te Deum* is a canticle of thanks beginning "We praise thee, O God."

Athwart the sea. Behold, the English beach
10 Pales in° the flood with men, wives, and boys,   *Fences in*
Whose shouts and claps outvoice the deep-mouthed sea,
Which like a mighty whiffler¹ fore the King
Seems to prepare his way. So let him land,
And solemnly see him set on to London.
15 So swift a pace hath thought that even now
You may imagine him upon Blackheath,²
Where that his lords desire him to have borne
His bruisèd helmet and his bendèd sword
Before him through the city. He forbids it,
20 Being free from vainness and self-glorious pride,
Giving full trophy, signal, and ostent°   *honor for the victory*
Quite from himself to God. But now behold,
In the quick forge and working-house of thought,
How London doth pour out her citizens.
25 The Mayor and all his brethren in best sort,°   *clothing*
Like to the senators of th'antique Rome
With the plebeians° swarming at their heels,   *commoners*
Go forth and fetch their conqu'ring Caesar in—
As, by a lower but by loving likelihood,³
30 Were now the General of our gracious Empress,⁴
As in good time he may, from Ireland coming,
Bringing rebellion broachèd° on his sword,   *impaled*
How many would the peaceful city quit
To welcome him! Much more, and much more cause,
35 Did they this Harry. Now in London place him.
As yet the lamentation of the French
Invites the King of England's stay at home.
The Emperor's coming⁵ in behalf of France,
To order peace between them [
40   ]⁶ and omit
All the occurrences, whatever chanced,
Till Harry's back return again to France.⁷
There must we bring him; and myself have played
The interim, by remembering° you 'tis past.   *reminding*
45 Then brook° abridgement and your eyes advance   *tolerate*
After your thoughts, straight back again to France.   *Exit.*

5.1 (Q Scene 19)

Enter FLUELLEN *and* GOWER.

GOWER Nay, that's right. But why wear you your leek today?
Saint Davy's day is past.
FLUELLEN There is occasions and causes why and wherefore
in all things. I will tell you ass my friend, Captain Gower.
5 The rascally, scald,° beggarly, lousy, pragging knave Pistol,   *scabby*
which you and yourself and all the world know to be no pet-
ter than a fellow, look you now, of no merits, he is come to
me and prings me pread and salt yesterday,° look you, and   *(on St. Davy's Day)*

5.0
1. Official who cleared the way for a procession.
2. Open space outside London.
3. Lovingly anticipated probability.
4. *General . . . Empress:* Earl of Essex.
5. Sigismund, the Holy Roman Emperor, attempted—

and failed—to negotiate a peace between France and
England.
6. A line is evidently missing here.
7. Henry invaded France a second and third time, in
1417 and 1421; act 5 begins in the latter year.
5.1 Location: The English camp.

bid me eat my leek. It was in a place where I could not breed
10 no contention with him, but I will be so bold as to wear it in
my cap till I see him once again, and then I will tell him a
little piece of my desires.
      Enter PISTOL.
GOWER   Why, here he comes, swelling like a turkey-cock.
FLUELLEN   'Tis no matter for his swellings nor his turkey-cocks.
15 —God pless you, Ensign Pistol, you scurvy, lousy knave, God
pless you.
PISTOL   Ha, art thou bedlam?° Dost thou thirst, base Trojan,°   *crazy / villain*
To have me fold up Parca's[1] fatal web?
Hence! I am qualmish° at the smell of leek.   *nauseated*
20 FLUELLEN   I peseech you heartily, scurvy, lousy knave, at my
desires, and my requests, and my petitions, to eat, look you,
this leek. Because, look you, you do not love it, nor your
affections, and your appetites, and your disgestions does not
agree with it, I would desire you to eat it.
25 PISTOL   Not for Cadwallader° and all his goats.   *(last Welsh king)*
FLUELLEN *(strikes him)*   There is one goat for you. Will you be
so good, scald° knave, as eat it?   *worthless*
PISTOL   Base Trojan, thou shalt die.
FLUELLEN   You say very true, scald knave, when God's will is.
30 I will desire you to live in the meantime and eat your victuals.°   *food*
Come, there is sauce for it.
      [*He strikes him.*]
You called me yesterday mountain-squire,° but I will make   *(Wales is mountainous)*
you today a squire of low degree. I pray you, fall to. If you
can mock a leek you can eat a leek.
35 GOWER   Enough, Captain, you have astonished° him.   *stunned*
FLUELLEN   I say I will make him eat some part of my leek or I
will peat his pate° four days. —Bite, I pray you. It is good for   *head*
your green° wound and your ploody coxcomb.°   *fresh / head*
PISTOL   Must I bite?
40 FLUELLEN   Yes, certainly, and out of doubt and out of question too, and ambiguities.
PISTOL   By this leek, I will most horribly revenge—
      [FLUELLEN *threatens him.*]
I eat and eat—I swear—
FLUELLEN   Eat, I pray you. Will you have some more sauce to
45 your leek? There is not enough leek to swear by.
PISTOL   Quiet thy cudgel,° thou dost see I eat.   *wooden club*
FLUELLEN   Much good do you, scald knave, heartily. Nay,
pray you, throw none away. The skin is good for your broken
coxcomb. When you take occasions to see leeks hereafter, I
50 pray you mock at 'em, that is all.
PISTOL   Good.
FLUELLEN   Ay, leeks is good. Hold you, there is a groat° to   *fourpence*
heal your pate.
PISTOL   Me a groat?
55 FLUELLEN   Yes, verily,° and in truth you shall take it, or I have   *truly*
another leek in my pocket which you shall eat.
PISTOL   I take thy groat in earnest° of revenge.   *advance payment*

1. The Parcae were the mythological Fates who spun and cut the thread of life.

FLUELLEN If I owe you anything, I will pay you in cudgels. You
shall be a woodmonger and buy nothing of me but cudgels.
60 God b'wi' you, and keep you, and heal your pate. *Exit.*
PISTOL All hell shall stir for this.
GOWER Go, go, you are a counterfeit cowardly knave. Will you
mock at an ancient tradition, begun upon an honorable
respect and worn as a memorable trophy of predeceased valor,
65 and dare not avouch° in your deeds any of your words? I have   *prove*
seen you gleeking and galling at° this gentleman twice or   *jesting and annoying*
thrice. You thought because he could not speak English in the
native garb, he could not therefore handle an English cudgel.
You find it otherwise. And henceforth let a Welsh correction
70 teach you a good English condition. Fare ye well.   *Exit.*
PISTOL Doth Fortune play the hussy with me now?
News have I that my Nell² is dead
I'th' spital of a malady of France,°   *venereal disease*
And there my rendezvous° is quite cut off.   *refuge*
75 Old I do wax, and from my weary limbs
Honor is cudgeled. Well, bawd° I'll turn,   *pimp*
And something lean to cutpurse of quick hand.
To England will I steal, and there I'll steal;
And patches will I get unto these cudgeled scars,
80 And swear I got them in the Gallia° wars.   *Exit.*   *French*

5.2 (Q Scene 20)

Enter at one door KING HENRY, EXETER, BEDFORD,
WARWICK, *and other Lords* [GLOUCESTER, WESTMORLAND,
CLARENCE, *and* HUNTINGDON]. *At another,* QUEEN
ISABEL, *the* KING [OF FRANCE], *the Duke of* BURGUNDY,
[KATHERINE, ALICE,] *and other French.*

KING Peace to this meeting, wherefor° we are met.   *for which*
Unto our brother France and to our sister,
Health and fair time of day. Joy and good wishes
To our most fair and princely cousin Katherine.
5 And as a branch and member of this royalty,
By whom this great assembly is contrived,
We do salute you, Duke of Burgundy.
And princes French, and peers, health to you all.
KING OF FRANCE Right joyous are we to behold your face,
10 Most worthy brother England, fairly met.
So are you, princes English, every one.
QUEEN ISABEL So happy be the issue,° brother England,¹   *outcome*
Of this good day and of this gracious meeting,
As we are now glad to behold your eyes—
15 Your eyes which hitherto have borne in them,
Against the French that met them in their bent,°   *glance*
The fatal balls° of murdering basilisks.²   *eyeballs; cannonballs*

2. TEXTUAL COMMENT The Folio and Quarto have
"my Doll," emended in most modern texts to "my
Nell" (that is, Mistress Quickly, Pistol's wife); for the
rationale, see Digital Edition TC 9 (Folio edited text).
5.2 Location: The French court.
1. TEXTUAL COMMENT The Folio has "brother Ireland," clearly a mistake; it is emended here to

"brother England." The slip is suggestive of the play's
persistent interest in Ireland and the Irish, and of
analogies between Henry's activities in France and
the Earl of Essex's expedition in Ireland in 1599. For
a discussion, see Digital Edition TC 10 (Folio edited
text).
2. Fabulous animals able to kill with a glance.

The venom of such looks we fairly hope
Have lost their quality,° and that this day   *nature*
20 Shall change all griefs and quarrels into love.
    KING   To cry amen to that, thus we appear.
    QUEEN ISABEL   You English princes all, I do salute you.
    BURGUNDY   My duty to you both, on equal love,
      Great Kings of France and England. That I have labored
25 With all my wits, my pains, and strong endeavors,
    To bring your most imperial majesties
    Unto this bar° and royal interview   *court*
    Your mightiness on both parts best can witness.
    Since then my office hath so far prevailed
30 That face to face and royal eye to eye
    You have congreeted,° let it not disgrace me   *met*
    If I demand before this royal view
    What rub° or what impediment there is   *hindrance*
    Why that the naked, poor, and mangled peace,
35 Dear nurse of arts, plenties, and joyful births,
    Should not in this best garden of the world,
    Our fertile France, put up her lovely visage?
    Alas, she hath from France too long been chased,
    And all her husbandry° doth lie on heaps,   *agriculture*
40 Corrupting in it° own fertility.   *its*
    Her vine, the merry cheerer of the heart,
    Unpruned dies; her hedges even-pleached,°   *interwoven*
    Like prisoners wildly overgrown with hair,
    Put forth disordered twigs; her fallow leas°   *unplanted fields*
45 The darnel, hemlock, and rank fumitory°   *(kinds of weeds)*
    Doth root upon, while that the coulter° rusts   *plow*
    That should deracinate° such savagery.   *root out*
    The even mead,° that erst brought sweetly forth   *meadow*
    The freckled cowslip, burnet, and green clover,
50 Wanting the scythe, all uncorrected, rank,
    Conceives by idleness,° and nothing teems   *Breeds worthless things*
    But hateful docks, rough thistles, kecksies, burrs,°   *(all are weeds)*
    Losing both beauty and utility.
    And° as our vineyards, fallows, meads, and hedges,   *And if*
55 Defective in their natures, grow to wildness,
    Even so our houses and ourselves and children
    Have lost, or do not learn for want of time,
    The sciences° that should become° our country,   *knowledge / adorn*
    But grow like savages, as soldiers will
60 That nothing do but meditate on blood,
    To swearing and stern looks, diffused° attire,   *disordered*
    And everything that seems unnatural.
    Which to reduce into our former favor³
    You are assembled, and my speech entreats
65 That I may know the let° why gentle peace   *impediment*
    Should not expel these inconveniences
    And bless us with her former qualities.
    KING   If, Duke of Burgundy, you would the peace
      Whose want gives growth to th'imperfections

---

3. To revert to our old appearance.

70   Which you have cited, you must buy that peace
     With full accord to all our just demands,
     Whose tenors° and particular effects   *general principles*
     You have enscheduled briefly in your hands.
    BURGUNDY The King hath heard them, to the which, as yet
     There is no answer made.
75 KING   Well, then, the peace
     Which you before so urged lies in his answer.
    KING OF FRANCE I have but with a cursitory° eye   *cursory*
     O'erglanced the articles. Pleaseth your grace
     To appoint some of your council presently
80   To sit with us once more, with better heed
     To re-survey them, we will suddenly
     Pass our accept and peremptory° answer.   *approved and definite*
    KING Brother, we shall. —Go, Uncle Exeter,
     And brother Clarence, and you, brother Gloucester,
85   Warwick, and Huntingdon, go with the King,
     And take with you free power to ratify,
     Augment, or alter, as your wisdoms best
     Shall see advantageable for our dignity,
     Anything in or out of our demands,
90   And we'll consign° thereto. —Will you, fair sister,   *agree*
     Go with the princes, or stay here with us?
    QUEEN ISABEL Our gracious brother, I will go with them.
     Haply° a woman's voice may do some good   *Perhaps*
     When articles too nicely° urged be stood on.   *punctiliously*
95 KING Yet leave our cousin Katherine here with us.
     She is our capital° demand, comprised   *chief*
     Within the fore-rank of our articles.
    QUEEN ISABEL She hath good leave.
             Exeunt all but KING *and* KATHERINE [*and* ALICE].
    KING   Fair Katherine, and most fair,
     Will you vouchsafe to teach a soldier terms
100   Such as will enter at a lady's ear
     And plead his love-suit to her gentle heart?
    KATHERINE Your majesty shall mock at me. I cannot speak
     your England.
    KING O fair Katherine, if you will love me soundly with your
105   French heart, I will be glad to hear you confess it brokenly
     with your English tongue. Do you like me, Kate?
    KATHERINE *Pardonnez-moi,*° I cannot tell vat is "like me."   *Excuse me*
    KING An angel is like you, Kate, and you are like an angel.
    KATHERINE [*to* ALICE] *Que dit-il, que je suis semblable à les*
110   *anges?*
    ALICE *Oui, vraiment, sauf votre grâce, ainsi dit-il.*[4]
    KING I said so, dear Katherine, and I must not blush to affirm it.
    KATHERINE *O bon Dieu,*° *les langues des hommes sont pleines*   *O good God*
    de tromperies!°   *(translated in line 115)*
115 KING What says she, fair one? That the tongues of men are
     full of deceits?
    ALICE *Oui,* dat de tongues of de mans is be full of deceits—
     dat is de Princess.

---

4. What does he say, that I am like an angel? Yes, truly, save your grace, he says that.

KING　The Princess is the better Englishwoman. I'faith, Kate,
120　my wooing is fit for thy understanding. I am glad thou canst
speak no better English, for if thou couldst, thou wouldst
find me such a plain king that thou wouldst think I had sold
my farm to buy my crown. I know no ways to mince it in love
but directly to say, "I love you." Then if you urge me farther
125　than to say, "Do you, in faith?," I wear out my suit. Give me
your answer, i'faith do, and so clap° hands and a bargain.　*shake*
How say you, lady?
KATHERINE　*Sauf votre honneur,°* me understand well.　*Saving your honor*
KING　Marry, if you would put me to verses or to dance for
130　your sake, Kate, why, you undid me. For the one I have neither words nor measure,° and for the other I have no strength　*meter*
in measure°—yet a reasonable measure in strength. If I　*talent for dancing*
could win a lady at leapfrog, or by vaulting into my saddle
with my armor on my back, under the correction of bragging
135　be it spoken, I should quickly leap into a wife. Or if I might
buffet° for my love, or bound my horse for her favors, I could　*box*
lay on like a butcher and sit like a jackanapes,° never off.　*monkey*
But before God, Kate, I cannot look greenly,° nor gasp out　*abashed*
my eloquence. Nor I have no cunning in protestation, only
140　downright oaths, which I never use till urged, nor never
break for urging. If thou canst love a fellow of this temper,°　*makeup*
Kate, whose face is not worth sunburning, that never looks
in his glass° for love of anything he sees there, let thine eye　*mirror*
be thy cook. I speak to thee plain soldier: if thou canst love
145　me for this, take me. If not, to say to thee that I shall die is
true—but for thy love, by the Lord, no. Yet I love thee, too.
And while thou liv'st, dear Kate, take a fellow of plain and
uncoined° constancy, for he perforce must do thee right,　*not in common use*
because he hath not the gift to woo in other places. For
150　these fellows of infinite tongue, that can rhyme themselves
into ladies' favors, they do always reason themselves out
again. What, a speaker is but a prater,° a rhyme is but a bal-　*chatterer*
lad! A good leg will fall, a straight back will stoop, a black
beard will turn white, a curled pate will grow bald, a fair
155　face will wither, a full eye will wax° hollow; but a good　*become*
heart, Kate, is the sun and the moon—or rather the sun and
not the moon, for it shines bright and never changes, but
keeps his course truly. If thou would have such a one, take
me; and take me, take a soldier; take a soldier, take a king.
160　And what say'st thou then to my love? Speak, my fair, and
fairly, I pray thee.
KATHERINE　Is it possible dat I sould love de enemy of France?
KING　No, it is not possible you should love the enemy of
France, Kate. But in loving me you should love the friend of
165　France. For I love France so well that I will not part with a
village of it; I will have it all mine. And Kate, when France is
mine, and I am yours, then yours is France, and you are mine.
KATHERINE　I cannot tell vat is dat.
KING　No, Kate? I will tell thee in French, which I am sure will
170　hang upon my tongue like a new-married wife about her husband's neck, hardly to be shook off. *Je quand je suis le possession de France, et quand vous avez le possession de moi*—let
me see, what then? Saint Denis be my speed!—*donc votre est*

France, et vous êtes mienne.[5] It is as easy for me, Kate, to con-
175 quer the kingdom as to speak so much more French. I shall
     never move° thee in French, unless it be to laugh at me.   *persuade*
KATHERINE *Sauf votre honneur, le français que vous parlez, il*
     est meilleur que l'anglais lequel je parle.[6]
KING No, faith, is't not, Kate. But thy speaking of my tongue,
180 and I thine, most truly-falsely, must needs be granted to be
     much at one.° But Kate, dost thou understand thus much   *alike; united*
     English? "Canst thou love me?"
KATHERINE I cannot tell.
KING Can any of your neighbors tell, Kate? I'll ask them.
185 Come, I know thou lovest me, and at night when you come
     into your closet° you'll question this gentlewoman about me;   *bedchamber*
     and I know, Kate, you will to her dispraise those parts° in   *qualities*
     me that you love with your heart. But good Kate, mock me
     mercifully, the rather, gentle Princess, because I love thee
190 cruelly. If ever thou beest mine, Kate, as I have a saving
     faith within me tells me thou shalt, I get thee with scam-
     bling,° and thou must therefore needs prove a good soldier-   *fighting*
     breeder. Shall not thou and I, between Saint Denis and Saint
     George,[7] compound a boy, half French, half English, that
195 shall go to Constantinople and take the Turk by the beard?
     Shall we not? What say'st thou, my fair flower-de-luce?[8]
KATHERINE I do not know dat.
KING No, 'tis hereafter to know, but now to promise. Do but
     now promise, Kate, you will endeavor for your French part
200 of such a boy, and for my English moiety° take the word of a   *half*
     king, and a bachelor. How answer you, *la plus belle Kather-*
     ine du monde, mon très cher et divin déesse?[9]
KATHERINE Your majesty 'ave *fausse*° French enough to deceive   *false*
     de most *sage demoiselle*° dat is *en France.*   *wise maiden*
205 KING Now fie upon my false French! By mine honor, in true
     English, I love thee, Kate. By which honor I dare not swear
     thou lovest me, yet my blood° begins to flatter me that thou   *instinct*
     dost, notwithstanding the poor and untempering° effect of   *uningratiating*
     my visage. Now beshrew° my father's ambition! He was   *curse*
210 thinking of civil wars when he got me; therefore was I cre-
     ated with a stubborn outside, with an aspect° of iron, that   *a face*
     when I come to woo ladies I fright them. But in faith, Kate,
     the elder I wax, the better I shall appear. My comfort is that
     old age, that ill layer-up° of beauty, can do no more spoil   *preserver*
215 upon my face. Thou hast me, if thou hast me, at the worst;
     and thou shalt wear me, if thou wear me, better and better.
     And therefore tell me, most fair Katherine, will you have
     me? Put off your maiden blushes, avouch the thoughts of
     your heart with the looks of an empress, take me by the
220 hand and say, "Harry of England, I am thine," which word
     thou shalt no sooner bless mine ear withal but I will tell
     thee aloud, "England is thine, Ireland is thine, France
     is thine, and Henry Plantagenet is thine," who, though I

5. Translation of the last part of his previous speech 7. Patron saints of France and England.
(lines 166–67).   8. Fleur-de-lis, the French national emblem.
6. Saving your honor, the French you speak is better 9. The most beautiful Katherine in the world, my
than the English I speak.   very dear and divine goddess.

speak it before his face, if he be not fellow° with the best   *equal*
225 king, thou shalt find the best king of good fellows. Come,
your answer in broken music,° for thy voice is music and thy   *music in parts*
English broken. Therefore, queen of all, Katherine, break
thy mind to me in broken English: wilt thou have me?

KATHERINE   Dat is as it shall please *le roi mon père.°*   *the King my father*

230 KING   Nay, it will please him well, Kate. It shall please him, Kate.

KATHERINE   Den it sall also content me.

KING   Upon that I kiss your hand, and I call you my queen.

KATHERINE   *Laissez, mon seigneur, laissez, laissez! Ma foi, je
ne veux point que vous abaissez votre grandeur en baisant la*
235   *main d'une de votre seigneurie indigne serviteur. Excusez-
moi, je vous supplie, mon très-puissant seigneur.*[1]

KING   Then I will kiss your lips, Kate.

KATHERINE   *Les dames et demoiselles pour être baisées devant
leurs noces, il n'est pas la coutume de France.°*   *(translated in lines 241–46)*

240 KING   Madam my interpreter, what says she?

ALICE   Dat it is not be de fashion *pour les°* ladies of France—I   *for the*
cannot tell vat is *baiser en°* Anglish.   *"kiss" in*

KING   To kiss.

ALICE   Your majesty *entend* bettre *que moi.*[2]

245 KING   It is not a fashion for the maids in France to kiss before
they are married, would she say?

ALICE   *Oui, vraiment.°*   *Yes, truly*

KING   O Kate, nice° customs curtsy to great kings. Dear Kate,   *fastidious*
you and I cannot be confined within the weak list° of a   *barrier*
250 country's fashion. We are the makers of manners, Kate, and
the liberty that follows our places stops the mouth of all
find-faults, as I will do yours for upholding the nice fashion
of your country in denying me a kiss. Therefore, patiently,
and yielding. [*He kisses her.*] You have witchcraft in your
255 lips, Kate. There is more eloquence in a sugar touch of them
than in the tongues of the French Council, and they should
sooner persuade Harry of England than a general petition of
monarchs. Here comes your father.

Enter the French Power, and the English Lords.

BURGUNDY   God save your majesty. My royal cousin,
260 Teach you our Princess English?

KING   I would have her learn, my fair cousin, how perfectly I
love her, and that is good English.

BURGUNDY   Is she not apt?

KING   Our tongue is rough, coz,° and my condition is not   *kinsman*
265 smooth, so that, having neither the voice nor the heart of
flattery about me, I cannot so conjure up the spirit of love in
her that he will appear in his true likeness.

BURGUNDY   Pardon the frankness of my mirth if I answer you
for that. If you would conjure in her, you must make a circle;[3]
270 if conjure up love in her in his true likeness, he must appear
naked and blind.° Can you blame her then, being a maid yet   *(like Cupid, god of love)*
rosed over with the virgin crimson of modesty, if she deny the

---

1. Stop, my lord, stop, stop! My faith, I do not want
you to lower your grandeur by kissing the hand of one
of your humble servants. Excuse me, I beseech you,
my very powerful lord.

2. Your majesty understands better than I.
3. By embracing her (sorcerers drew circles to call up
devils).

appearance of a naked blind boy in her naked seeing self? It
were, my lord, a hard condition for a maid to consign to.

275 KING   Yet they do wink° and yield, as love is blind and enforces.   *close their eyes*

BURGUNDY   They are then excused, my lord, when they see
not what they do.

KING   Then, good my lord, teach your cousin to consent
winking.

280 BURGUNDY   I will wink on her to consent, my lord, if you will
teach her to know my meaning. For maids well summered
and warm kept are like flies at Bartholomew-tide,° blind,   *August 24*
though they have their eyes; and then they will endure handling, which before would not abide looking on.

285 KING   This moral ties me over to time and a hot summer; and
so I shall catch the fly, your cousin, in the latter end,[4] and
she must be blind too.

BURGUNDY   As love is, my lord, before that it loves.

KING   It is so. And you may some of you thank love for my
290 blindness, who cannot see many a fair French city for one
fair French maid that stands in my way.

KING OF FRANCE   Yes, my lord, you see them perspectively,[5]
the cities turned into a maid—for they are all girdled with
maiden walls that war hath never entered.

295 KING   Shall Kate be my wife?

KING OF FRANCE   So please you.

KING   I am content, so the maiden° cities you talk of may wait   *unconquered*
on her: so the maid that stood in the way for my wish shall
show me the way to my will.

300 KING OF FRANCE   We have consented to all terms of reason.

KING   Is't so, my lords of England?

WESTMORLAND   The King hath granted every article:
His daughter first, and so in sequel all,
According to their firm proposed natures.

305 EXETER   Only he hath not yet subscribed° this: where your   *signed to*
majesty demands that the King of France, having any occa-
sion to write for matter of grant,° shall name your highness   *in formal documents*
in this form and with this addition: [*reading*] in French:
"*Notre très cher fils Henri, Roi d'Angleterre, Héritier de France*";
310 and thus in Latin: "*Praeclarissimus filius noster Henricus,
Rex Angliae et Haeres Franciae.*"[6]

KING OF FRANCE   Nor this I have not, brother, so denied
But your request shall make me let it pass.

KING   I pray you then, in love and dear alliance,
315 Let that one article rank with the rest,
And thereupon give me your daughter.

KING OF FRANCE   Take her, fair son, and from her blood raise up
Issue° to me, that the contending kingdoms   *Offspring*
Of France and England, whose very shores look pale
320 With envy of each other's happiness,
May cease their hatred, and this dear conjunction°   *loving union*
Plant neighborhood° and Christian-like accord   *neighborliness*
In their sweet bosoms, that never war advance

---

4. At last; in the backside.
5. In a lens that produces optical illusions.

6. Our very dear son Henry, King of England and
heir of France.

His bleeding sword twixt England and fair France.
325 LORDS Amen.
KING Now welcome, Kate, and bear me witness all
That here I kiss her as my sovereign queen.
    Flourish.
QUEEN ISABEL God, the best maker of all marriages,
Combine your hearts in one, your realms in one!
330 As man and wife, being two, are one in love,
So be there twixt your kingdoms such a spousal
That never may ill office° or fell° jealousy,   *bad action / cruel*
Which troubles oft the bed of blessèd marriage,
Thrust in between the paction° of these kingdoms   *agreement*
335 To make divorce of their incorporate league;
That English may as French, French Englishmen,
Receive each other. God speak this amen.
ALL Amen.
KING Prepare we for our marriage, on which day,
340 My lord of Burgundy, we'll take your oath,
And all the peers', for surety of our leagues.
Then shall I swear to Kate, and you to me,
And may our oaths well kept and prosp'rous be!
    Sennet.° Exeunt.   *Ceremonial trumpet call*

Epilogue

    Enter CHORUS.[1]
CHORUS Thus far, with rough and all-unable pen,
Our bending° author hath pursued the story,   *(over a desk)*
In little room confining mighty men,
Mangling by starts the full course of their glory.
5 Small time, but in that small most greatly lived
This star of England. Fortune made his sword,
By which the world's best garden he achieved,
And of it left his son imperial lord.
Henry the Sixth, in infant bands° crowned King   *swaddling clothes*
10 Of France and England, did this king succeed,
Whose state so many had the managing
That they lost France and made his England bleed,
Which oft our stage hath shown[2]—and for their sake,
In your fair minds let this acceptance take.°   [*Exit.*]   *this play find favor*

Epilogue
1. The following lines form a sonnet.
2. In *1 Henry VI, 2 Henry VI (The First Part of the Contention), 3 Henry VI (Richard Duke of York),* and *Richard III.*

As You Like It

Most of *As You Like It* occurs in a forest that Shakespeare transforms into a place for thought experiments, debates, and disguises. In the forest, time slows down. As one character famously says: "There's no clock in the forest" (3.2.278–79). As a result, those who live there or visit have the leisure to talk, sing, jest, and try out new social roles. In the spirit of serious play, *As You Like It* invites its characters and its audiences to suspend the rules of everyday existence and to imagine different realities. What could the world look like if, for example, women had the same freedoms as men? Or if rank did not matter in determining a person's worth? As a clown figure in the play says: "Much virtue in 'if'" (5.4.94). What if we could have the world "as [we] like it?" Shakespeare's title invites us to contemplate that very question. What do we like? What do we desire? And, by extension, how could the world be rearranged to accommodate those desires and wishes?

Because of its setting and its themes, *As You Like It* is usually called a pastoral comedy—that is, a comic play that juxtaposes (1) a corrupt world of the city or the court and (2) what is imagined as the simpler existence of the fields and forest. The pastoral mode had its origins in ancient Greece, where the poet Theocritus used rural settings and rustic shepherds to explore the pain of love and the harsh injustices of daily life. The Roman poet Virgil expanded this tradition, elaborating in particular the opposition between city and country life. In England, many of Shakespeare's contemporaries worked in pastoral forms, particularly Edmund Spenser, whose *Shepheardes Calender* (1579) was modeled on Virgil's *Eclogues,* and Sir Philip Sidney, whose vast prose romance *The Countess of Pembrokes Arcadia* was first published in revised form in 1590. These works often juxtaposed a corrupt court and rural innocence.

As a literary mode, pastoral can take many forms. There are pastoral lyrics, dialogues, prose romances, and dramas. Certain topics and situations, however, recur in many kinds of pastoral. Often, for example, people in flight from urban or courtly life temporarily retreat to the country, where, sometimes disguising themselves as shepherds, they converse with those native to the place. In this rural setting talk abounds. Characters complain about unresponsive lovers, hold singing contests, and debate the relative merits of country and court life, whether nature is improved or spoiled by art, and whether "gentleness" (meaning both "nobility" and "a virtuous nature") is a condition one can achieve or to which one must be born. The rural setting also affords the opportunity for serious social critique. The greed of landlords, the deceit of courtiers, and the corruption of the clergy are common topics of complaint.

The relationship of the "natural" to the "artificial" is a topic fundamental to pastoral; that is, are what human beings have made—cities, gardens, systems of social hierarchy—preferable to the simplicity and lack of artifice supposedly found in rural settings and communities? Such debates continue today, as we frequently long for simpler, slower lives but find it hard to wean ourselves from all the sophisticated conveniences of modern life. The choices weren't easier in the early modern period, when courts and cities had pleasures and attractions as well as vices and corruptions. Moreover, while pastoral frequently celebrates simplicity, it does so in a highly artful manner, drawing on conventions that have been part of the Western literary tradition for at least two thousand years; and the characters who most praise

First page of the *Gest of Robin Hood*, one of the most important sixteenth-century renditions of the Robin Hood legend.

rural life are frequently "just visiting" and playing an elaborate game of "let's pretend." Hence, many disguises are found in pastoral, where courtiers pose as rustic shepherds, men as women, women as men, and dukes as forest outlaws. As all those who take rural vacations know, however, retreating to a green world—even if one does not stay—can offer a much-needed change of perspective and an opportunity to see oneself and others in a new way, and perhaps to grow and change. This is, of course, the challenge facing the many courtly characters who end up in *As You Like It*'s green world.

In writing the play, Shakespeare fully embraced the serious concerns of pastoral while reveling in its potential for high-spirited fun. In the main action, a good ruler, Duke Senior, has been ousted from his throne by a usurping younger brother, Duke Frederick. The banished Duke takes refuge in the Forest of Arden, where he lives like Robin Hood with a band of loyal followers. When his daughter, Rosalind, companion to Frederick's daughter, Celia, is likewise banished, she disguises herself as a young man named Ganymede and also journeys to Arden. Celia, posing as a lowborn woman named Aliena, goes with her, as does Touchstone the Clown. A second line of action concerns two other brothers: Orlando, the youngest son, and Oliver, the oldest son of Sir Roland de Bois. The inheritor of his father's estate, Oliver treats Orlando cruelly, denying him the education befitting a gentleman. In danger both from Duke Frederick and from his brother, Orlando also flees to the forest, accompanied by Adam, a family servant who long ago had served Orlando's father. By act 2, all of these refugees from court life find themselves in a natural world, which, in spite of its considerable hardships, they prefer to the treachery of court. Arden, however, is not Edenic. There are lions and snakes in this pastoral retreat, and real shepherds like Corin who speak matter-of-factly about the hard and dirty labor that tending real sheep entails. But in Arden there is also time to mock infatuated lovers, to jest, and to sing. In fact, *As You Like It* contains more songs than any other Shakespearean play. In their song-filled green world, the characters hunt deer, tend sheep, and converse endlessly about exile, love, and other matters of the heart.

The broad outlines of the *As You Like It* story are taken from Thomas Lodge's enormously popular prose romance *Rosalynde,* written in 1586–87 and published in 1590, although Shakespeare also changed what he drew from Lodge. In *Rosalynde,* for example, the Duke Senior and Duke Frederick characters are not brothers, but in both the ducal and the Orlando-Oliver plots Shakespeare makes the enmity of brothers the principal sign of the corruption of "civilized" life. In Lodge, moreover, the father in the Orlando-Oliver plot does not follow the English custom of primogeniture, by which all property is settled on the oldest son; instead, he divides his property among his male offspring according to their merits. By having Oliver inherit almost everything, Shakespeare evokes an English social practice that caused great hardship to many younger brothers. Furthermore, Shakespeare's Orlando, unlike his counterpart in Lodge's story, writes exceptionally bad love poetry, contributing to the sense that love makes people foolish even as it exalts them. The court women are handled differently as well by Shakespeare: he reduces the Celia character's centrality and instead emphasizes Rosalind and her love affair with Orlando. Throughout, Shakespeare tempers the violence of Lodge's romance and elaborates its comic potential. In *Rosalynde*, for example, the exiled Duke defeats the usurper in battle, but Shakespeare's Frederick has a religious conversion and voluntarily relinquishes the dukedom. Shakespeare also added to Lodge's cast of characters. Oliver Martext, William, Audrey, Touchstone the Clown, and Jaques the melancholy satirist are all Shakespeare's creations. Jaques, in particular, adds a touch of caustic salt and Touchstone a dash of earthy realism to the play's exploration of competing value systems.

In fact, *As You Like It* is poised carefully on the razor's edge separating fantasy from harsh reality. Shakespeare's use of place is a case in point. Lodge's romance is set in the Forest of Ardennes, an ancient woodland comprising part of what are now France, Belgium, and Luxembourg. Shakespeare also uses a French setting, but in the First Folio (1623) this woodland is called the Forest of Arden, an anglicized spelling that also happens to be the name of an English forest near Shakespeare's birthplace in Warwickshire. This fortuitous overlapping of French and English place-names is indicative of the play's double vision. Overtly set in a fantastical foreign kingdom, *As You Like It* nonetheless alludes to places (such as the Forest of Arden), people (such as Robin Hood), and practices (such as primogeniture) native to Shakespeare's own England. Through the distancing artifice of pastoral, the play deals with problems close to home.

The Englishness of Shakespeare's *As You Like It* is enhanced by allusions to the popular folk hero Robin Hood. In the opening scene of *As You Like It*, Charles the wrestler reports that the banished Duke is "already in the forest of Arden, and a many merry men with him; and there they live like the old Robin Hood of England. They say many young gentlemen flock to him every day and fleet the time carelessly as they did in the golden world" (1.1.100–104). Shakespeare could count on his audience to know the story of Robin Hood, and its evocation carried certain associations. The legendary figure and his band of men stood not only for the community and brotherhood characteristic of the Golden Age and absent in modern life, but also for resistance to tyranny. The great forests of England were the king's own preserves. To kill the deer in those forests was a crime against the monarch. Yet Robin Hood lived in the forest, dined on the king's deer, and opposed King John's unjust reign. In the 1590s, many of those resisting the enclosure of farmland for sheep grazing took refuge in forest areas, and poaching the king's deer had long been one way by which the poor defied the law to feed themselves when food was short, as it often was because of bad harvests in the late 1590s.

As You Like It only obliquely alludes to this immediate social context, but act 1 depicts a world of injustice and social disorder that both motivates the flight to Arden and evokes the tradition of opposition to tyranny associated with Robin Hood. Orlando's situation speaks to the peculiarly English plight of younger brothers who, under the system of primogeniture, inherited little from their fathers and were often at the mercy of elder siblings. Oliver is a nightmare version of an eldest son: he deprives Orlando of a gentleman's education, connives with the Duke's professional wrestler to have his brother injured, and throws his father's old servant, Adam, out of the house. His cruelty is echoed by the tyranny of Duke Frederick. The play's opening scenes underscore the inhumanity and tyrannical willfulness in the court and in the household of old Sir Roland's eldest son. Less clear is whether this corruption stems from human institutions, particularly the system of primogeniture, or from the "naturally" evil natures of Frederick and Oliver. The play does not answer this or other thorny questions directly. In fact, it seems organized to provoke thought rather than to urge conclusions, and the ending does not so much lay out a plan for social reform as celebrate a utopian moment of forgiveness, reconciliation, and hope—the latter symbolized by the multiple marriages it energetically stages.

The play's most sustained examination of human folly focuses on the behavior of those who succumb to love. There are many lovers in Arden, and for almost none does the course of love run smooth. Lovesickness was a recognized malady in early modern culture, a condition that so disordered those who endured it that it could cause paleness, sighing, tears, fainting, melancholy, palpitations, and a host of other symptoms. In *As You Like It,* all lovers are slightly mad, and the play approaches their tribulations with a mixture of sympathy, detached amusement, and analytical curiosity. Shakespeare draws on the critical capacities of pastoral to explore the causes of lovers' unhappiness and to probe the surprisingly complex issue of what is natural in matters of love and sexual desire. In this regard, the play takes little for granted—neither the stability of gender difference nor the naturalness of heterosexuality nor the invariant nature of being in love.

Rosalind and Orlando are the play's most prominent lovers, and through their courtship the play explores the problems of loving well. Orlando, for example, loves by the book—that is, in imitation of the conventions employed by the fourteenth-century Italian poet Petrarch, whose love poems to a woman named Laura established one of the paradigmatic love rhetorics of Renaissance culture. Conventionally, the Petrarchan lover worships and idealizes a woman who is inaccessible to him, either because of her rank or because of her cold heart. He burns with passion; he wastes from despair; she does not respond. Orlando, rushing through the forest pinning bad love poems on trees, is a sendup of a Petrarchan lover. Touchstone makes fun of his verses; Rosalind, dressed as a man but pretending to be "Rosalind" in order to cure Orlando of his lovesickness, delights in showing how exaggerated and unrealistic are the Petrarchan lover's claims for the perfection of his mistress and the vastness of his suffering. As she caustically says to him, when he protests that he will die for his passion: "men have died from time to time, and worms have eaten them, but not for love" (4.1.92–94). She is equally hard on the idealization of women, insisting that real women can be fickle and bad-tempered as easily as they can seem like goddesses. One way to interpret Orlando and Rosalind's prolonged interactions is to see her slowly educating him in a more realistic and egalitarian approach to the relationship of man to woman than that offered by the Petrarchan tradition. Yet the self-mockery, realism, and genuine regard for the other that come to characterize their relationship are hardly in themselves natural behaviors, but ones in which Orlando must be tutored. Other critics argue that the lengthy byplay between Orlando and his "Rosalind" indicates Rosalind's desire to retain her maidenly independence as long as possible, since as a wife her freedom of speech and movement would in all likelihood be more curtailed than when she is cross-dressed as a saucy boy.

Rosalind and Orlando, however, are not the only lovers in the forest. There is also the mooning shepherd, Silvius, who believes no one has ever loved with his intensity, and his proud mistress, Phoebe, who thinks much too well of her own limited charms and throws herself quite inappropriately into the part of the disdainful Petrarchan mistress. As Rosalind informs her: "I must tell you friendly in your ear, / Sell when you can; you are not for all markets" (3.5.59–60). Even Touchstone, ever ready to puncture the romantic ravings of Orlando and Rosalind, Silvius and Phoebe, cannot escape love's call. Functioning as the clown figure often does, to provide a detached commentary on the action around him, Touchstone is nonetheless a participant as well as an observer. His "love" is about as natural—in the sense of urgently physical—and as far removed from Petrarchan idealizations as can be imagined. His intended, Audrey, does not know what "poetical" means, and Touchstone laments that she has such a rudimentary command of language that she often cannot understand what he says to her. And yet, as he confides to Jaques, "As the ox hath his bow, sir, the horse his curb, and the falcon her bells, so man hath his desires" (3.3.67–68)—that is, as each creature has some restraint placed on his movement, so a man's sexual desires constrain him to accommodate himself to a woman, even one like Audrey, and to the marriage yoke. If Orlando and Silvius live too much in the thrall of poetic idealizations, Touchstone and Audrey starkly reveal what love looks like when it is reduced to a matter of pure desire and when all artfulness, all poetry, and all sweet amorous delay are eschewed.

The delightful Rosalind, however, is the play's most intriguing lover. Her importance is signaled by the fact that she is given more lines to speak than any other female character in any of Shakespeare's plays. Articulate and witty, she is at once an observer and a critic of others and herself a full participant in the whirligig of love. In this, she resembles Touchstone the Clown and differs from the melancholy Jaques, who persistently catalogs the follies of others but holds back from full participation in the life around him. (Fittingly, Jaques remains in the forest at the end of the play, when most of the others return to their lives outside the pastoral retreat.) Rosalind is at the center of nearly everything that happens in *As You Like It*, and the complexity of her role is enhanced by the fact that for much of four acts she dresses like a man and successfully passes for one. In the 1590s, Shakespeare wrote a number of other comedies (*The Two Gentlemen of Verona, The Merchant of Venice, Twelfth Night*) in which women dress as men to protect themselves from danger, to pursue a lover, or temporarily to acquire the prerogatives of the socially dominant gender. Rosalind's is arguably the most complicated of these cases of cross-dressing because she not only passes as a man, but while in her male disguise plays the role of Rosalind in her forest encounters with Orlando. A woman disguised as a man thus makes her own identity into a fiction she performs!

Rosalind's complex cross-dressing has many consequences. For one thing, it makes problematic the "natural" gender distinctions that supposedly separate man from woman. In a literal sense, clothes here make the man—or woman. A doublet and hose and a swaggering demeanor effectively create the illusion of masculinity, and Rosalind uses her disguise to try on the privileges of the supposedly superior sex. Far from a passive object of Petrarchan adoration, she takes charge of her escape from Frederick's court and her encounters with Orlando in the forest. Typically, Renaissance women remained under the control of their fathers and mothers until marriage bequeathed them to the care of a husband. Rosalind's special circumstances—a father banished, an uncle who wants her gone from court—put her in an unusual situation. Her decision to cross-dress further sets her apart. Mobile, loquacious, and bossy, Rosalind confutes the idea that women are by nature passive, silent, and in need of masculine supervision. At the same time, she exhibits certain stereotypically "female" behavior: to Celia she confesses how much she is in love with Orlando, and when he is wounded she faints from seeing his blood on a cloth. The cross-dressed Rosalind keeps open the question of what a woman (or a man) "really" is.

To the question of how men and women differ, some Renaissance anatomical theory gave answers unlike those we now take for granted. According to Galen, an ancient Greek anatomist whose work on the body was widely influential in the early modern period, men and women had similar anatomical structures; women were simply less perfect than men, there having been less heat present when they were conceived. This meant, among other things, that women's genitalia were just like men's—with the vagina and ovaries corresponding to the penis and scrotum—except that they had not been pushed outside the body as men's had been. Because by this account male-female difference was less grounded in ideas of absolute bodily difference than is typical today, much emphasis was placed on behavioral differences and on distinctions of dress. Preachers enjoined women to be chaste, silent, and obedient and forbade them to wear the clothes of the opposite sex. In such a context, female cross-dressing, however playfully undertaken, always threatened to expose the artifice of gender distinctions by showing how easily one sex could assume the clothes and ape the behavior of the other.

The particularities of Rosalind's disguise, moreover, complicate her representation even further. When cross-dressed, Rosalind calls herself Ganymede, a name that had long-standing and unmistakable associations with homoerotic love. In Greek mythology, Ganymede was a beautiful boy whom Jove desired and whom he seized and carried to Mount Olympus to be cupbearer to the gods. A number of early modern paintings, woodcuts, and engravings depict the moment when Jove, in the

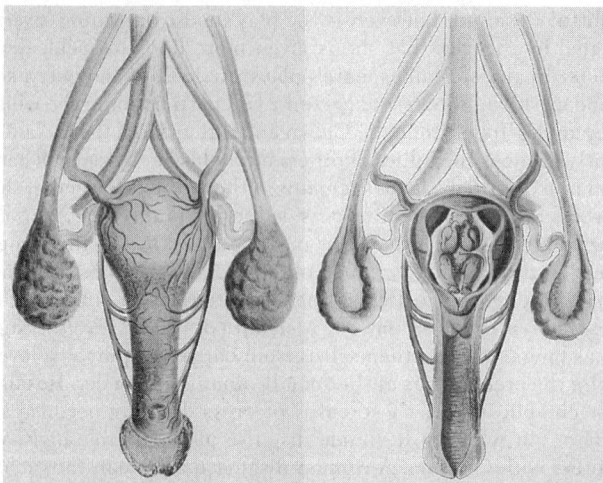

Typical sixteenth-century anatomy-book illustration of the female organs of generation.
Left: The vagina and uterus are almost indistinguishable from the male penis and
scrotum. *Right:* They have been cut open to reveal a tiny fetus in the uterus.
From Fritz Weindler, *Geschichte der Gynäkologisch-anatomischen Abbildung* (1908).
(Originally appeared in George Bartisch, *Kunstbuch,* 1575.)

form of an eagle, sweeps the boy away from earth and into the heavens. In Shakespeare's day, the word "Ganymede" commonly signified a young boy who was the
lover of another (usually older) man. Shakespeare could hardly have been unaware of
these associations when he had Rosalind choose this name as her alias. Consequently, when the cross-dressed heroine commands Orlando to woo his "Rosalind,"
he woos a figure who is dressed like a man and who bears a name signifying his status as a homoerotic love object. In performance, what the audience *sees* is one "man"
flirting with another, even while the audience *knows* that one of these "men" is a
woman. Provocatively, Shakespeare uses Orlando and Rosalind's encounters to over-
lay a story of male-female desire with traces of another tale of a man's love for a boy.

Long before *As You Like It* was penned, pastoral had been used to depict the
beauty of both male friendship and homoerotic love. Edmund Spenser, in the January Eclogue of *The Shepheardes Calender,* describes the passion of Hobbinol for
Colin Cloute, who in turn loves an unresponsive woman named Rosalind. Commenting on this passage, E.K., the anonymous annotator of *The Shepheardes Calender,*
drew on classical precedent to defend pederastic love (love of an older man for a
younger boy) as less dangerous than gynerastic love (love of man for woman). Since
women were generally considered men's intellectual and moral inferiors, love for a
woman was—so the argument went—less likely to be a rational passion than was
love for a boy or a man. In the 1580s, Richard Barnfield wrote a pastoral work called
The Affectionate Shepherd in which the male speaker celebrates his love for a beautiful young man named Ganymede.

Shakespeare is therefore not unique in introducing a Ganymede figure into the
pastoral landscape, though he does so with a difference. In *As You Like It,* Ganymede
is a disguise, a persona assumed and eventually discarded by Rosalind. As with much
else in this play, Shakespeare thus presents two opposing outcomes as simultaneously possible. For several acts, Orlando seems to pursue in one person both a boy
and a woman, but in the final scene Rosalind reassumes her female clothes and
Ganymede disappears, thus ending the play with an emphasis on the culmination of
male-female love in marriage. But this is not quite the whole story. On the Renaissance
stage, women's parts were played by boy actors. In the Epilogue, which Rosalind

Ganymede being abducted by Jupiter in the form of an eagle.
Woodcut by Virgil Solis. From *Metamorphosis Ovidii . . .* (1563).

speaks, she calls attention to this fact, making it clear that if Orlando has finally won his Rosalind, the two players who enact this union are a young boy and a man. Man has married woman; man has simultaneously embraced boy.

In *As You Like It,* other erotic possibilities flourish as well. The friendship between Rosalind and Celia, for example, is remarkably close. Charles the wrestler says: "never two ladies loved as they do" (1.1.98). Celia readily gives up her father, her fortune, and her position at the court to follow Rosalind to Arden, where the two women in effect set up household together. Although they are yoked in love like Juno's swans, from the beginning Celia is afraid that Rosalind does not love her as much as she loves Rosalind (1.2.6–11). Quite quickly, Rosalind's primary interest becomes her pursuit of Orlando. Yet in the midst of her love games with him, Rosalind also dallies with the ambitious and amorous Phoebe, who has taken the disguised Rosalind for a man. Overtly, Rosalind scorns Phoebe and directs her to love Silvius, but she also takes care to tell Phoebe where she lives (3.5.73–74) and encourages her attentions even while denying them. As with other relationships in the play, it is not altogether clear whom Phoebe really desires: is it the man she thinks she sees or the woman beneath? Though the play eventually deposits Rosalind, Celia, and Phoebe all within the circle of Hymen, the god of marriage, it does so only after raising the possibility of other erotic conjunctions, including woman's love for woman.

In part, *As You Like It* can play so freely with various erotic possibilities because in the early modern period people were not assumed, as they often are today, to have a fixed sexual identity—to *be*, that is, a lesbian or a heterosexual. Often, one could engage in a range of sexual practices without contradiction. Depending on life stage and social circumstance, a man might have sex with a dependent man, such as a servant, and with a woman, such as his wife. The point is that performing a specific sexual act did not presume—or guarantee—a particular sexual identity. And yet Shakespeare's comedy, like many others, also acknowledges the social weight that the early modern period placed on marriage, the institution through which political alliances were forged, property passed, and lineage established. *As You Like It* both celebrates and pokes fun at the social importance of marriage by having Hymen, god of marriage, appear onstage in the last act to preside over a veritable spate of betrothals—four, to be exact. As Jaques suggests (5.4.35–36), it is indeed as if the beasts were proceeding, two by two, into Noah's ark.

Besides yoking individual man to individual woman, marriage in this play helps to resolve seemingly intractable social problems. For example, Orlando's situation as younger brother is miraculously ameliorated through his marriage to Rosalind. As her husband, he becomes Duke Senior's heir, thus achieving a fortune equal to his gentle nature. Again, the play has things two ways at once. Duke Senior is restored to his dukedom, which confirms the prerogatives of older brothers, but Orlando does not have to suffer permanently the disadvantages of being a younger son. Primogeniture is simultaneously affirmed and circumvented. Moreover, when Oliver reforms, that reformation is sealed by his marriage to Celia, an indication that he now takes part in the communal life of his culture without the willful displays of indifference and selfishness that marked his earlier behavior.

Yet as this comedy celebrates marriage, it also registers a certain resistance to it and persistently maps alternative routings of desire. Rosalind registers that resistance when she complains of how avidly men court women before marriage and how indifferently they treat them afterward: "men are April when they woo, December when they wed" (4.1.127–28). Marriage, she implies, can dull a man's desire and lessen a woman's emotional power over him. It also, of course, made women legally subject to their husbands. When Rosalind doffs her man's disguise to become a wife, she relinquishes many kinds of freedom. But the play also records *men's* resistance to marriage, partly through its many cuckold jokes. These jokes acknowledge that marriage may not fully circumscribe or satisfy a woman's sexual desires, that a man's control of his wife's sexuality may be more fiction than fact, leaving him vulnerable to public mockery. As the Duke's men sing as they bring home a slaughtered deer:

> Take thou no scorn to wear the horn.
> It was a crest e'er thou wast born.
> Thy father's father wore it,
> And thy father bore it.
>
> (4.2.14–17)

The song transforms cuckold anxiety into entertainment, but it cannot erase that anxiety.

Consider, as well, the strange moment when Orlando comes across his brother, Oliver, lying asleep under an old oak. As Oliver sleeps, a female snake approaches his open mouth, threatening his life. Though the snake is frightened off, it is immediately replaced in this fantastic, dreamlike scenario by a hungry female lion with whom Orlando fights in order to save his brother's life (4.3.97–131). Twice, danger is represented in female form, and the reconciliation of the two brothers occurs only when Orlando spills his own blood to beat back these threats. In *As You Like It,* as marriage is both desired and feared, so the feminine is represented as both an attraction and a source of danger.

In pastoral, little is immune from critique. Yet the remarkable thing about *As You Like It* is that critique does not cancel affirmation. The play anatomizes court life and exposes its treachery, but many characters leave Arden to journey back to the court when Frederick has repented and the benevolent Duke Senior has returned to power. The play likewise dissects the problems of marriage, yet many marry at the end. Pastoral has a utopian as well as a critical dimension. The green world of shepherds holds traces of the simplicity of a lost Golden Age, and a sojourn in that world can prompt transformations in the everyday world to which the sojourners return. *As You Like It* is to a remarkable degree open to the infinite malleability of human beings and their social practices. A duke can become a forest outlaw and embrace the change; a tyrannical usurper can be touched by the words of a holy man, relinquish his power, and retire from the world. What men and women have marred, they may also mend.

It is through the heroine, however, that *As You Like It* offers its richest dramatization of a figure who plays endlessly with the limits and possibilities of her circumstances. This is true even in the Epilogue, when Rosalind, now in woman's clothing, steps forward to address the audience and solicit their applause. The persona of Ganymede cast aside, the heroine appears as the woman she "really" is. But it is precisely at this moment of closure that she breaks the dramatic frame to remind the audience of *another* reality: that "she" is played by a "he." Dressed like a woman but declaring she is not, this unpredictable figure, this he/she, continues to the end to defy the fixed identities and the exclusionary choices of the everyday world, offering instead a world of multiple possibilities and transformable identities, a world as perhaps we might come to like it.

JEAN E. HOWARD

SELECTED BIBLIOGRAPHY

Colie, Rosalie L. "Perspectives on Pastoral: Romance, Comic and Tragic." *Shakespeare's Living Art*. Princeton, NJ: Princeton UP, 1974. 243–83. Analyzes the many pastoral conventions found in *As You Like It* and how they contribute to the play's perspectivism—that is, its juxtaposition of competing viewpoints.

Crane, Mary. "Theatrical Practice and the Ideologies of Status in *As You Like It*." *Shakespeare's Brain: Reading with Cognitive Theory*. Princeton, NJ: Princeton UP, 2001. 67–93. Examines how, through its emphasis on words like "villain" and "clown," *As You Like It* explores possibilities for upward and downward mobility in the world of the play and in the social world at large, including the theatrical community of which Shakespeare was a part.

Fisher, Will. "Home Alone: The Place of Women's Homoerotic Desire in Shakespeare's *As You Like It*." *Feminisms and Early Modern Texts: Essays for Phyllis Rackin*. Ed. Rebecca Anne Bach and Gwynne Kennedy. Selinsgrove, PA: Susquehanna UP, 2010. 99–118. Explores how Rosalind and Celia mimic aspects of heterosexual marriage, including a concern with acquiring property, and establish a household beyond the boundaries of masculine control.

Howard, Jean E. "Power and Eros: Crossdressing in Dramatic Representation and Theatrical Practice." *The Stage and Social Struggle in Early Modern England*. London: Routledge, 1994. 93–128. Examines cross-dressing as a convention through which *As You Like It* and other comedies explore the politics of early modern gender relations and the fluidity of sexual desire.

Marshall, Cynthia. "The Doubled Jaques and Constructions of Negation in *As You Like It*." *Shakespeare Quarterly* 49 (1998): 375–92. Argues that in *As You Like It* the repression of melancholia, registered as a trace in the figure of Jaques, allows for the release of the high spirits and verbal fireworks proper to comedy.

Montrose, Louis. "'The Place of a Brother' in *As You Like It*: Social Process and Comic Form." *Shakespeare Quarterly* 32 (1981): 28–54. Argues that in *As You Like It* the process of comedy repairs the negative consequences of primogeniture for younger sons as Orlando finds a surrogate father in Duke Senior and a fortune through marriage.

Theis, Jeffrey S. "Shakespeare's Green Plot: The Stage as Forest and the Forest as Stage in *As You Like It*." *Writing the Forest in Early Modern England: A Sylvan*

Pastoral Nation. Pittsburgh, PA: Duquesne UP, 2009. 35–89. Explores the forest of Arden as a malleable stage where characters experiment with new or altered social roles and test pastoral conventions.

Traub, Valerie. "The Homoerotics of Shakespearean Comedy." *Desire and Anxiety: Circulations of Sexuality in Shakespearean Drama*. London: Routledge, 1992. 117–44. Explores the role of the boy actor in the production and circulation of homoerotic desire and argues that *As You Like It* playfully refuses the binary distinction between the heteroerotic and the homoerotic.

Watson, Robert N. "As You Liken It: Simile in the Forest." *Back to Nature: The Green and the Real in the Late Renaissance*. Philadelphia: U of Pennsylvania P, 2006. 77–107. Argues for the importance of similes in *As You Like It* as they show humanity's attempts to comprehend and become one with a natural world from which it is fundamentally alienated.

Wilson, Richard. "Like the Old Robin Hood: *As You Like It* and the Enclosure Riots." *Will Power: Essays on Shakespearean Authority*. London: Harvester Wheatsheaf, 1993. 63–82. Connects *As You Like It* to the social disturbances and food shortages of the 1590s but argues that the play pulls back from lodging a radical critique of social injustice.

FILMS

As You Like It. 1936. Dir. Paul Czinner. UK. 96 min. This black-and-white film features Laurence Olivier, in his first Shakespeare performance on film, as the dashing but moody Orlando with Elisabeth Bergner as an insipid Rosalind. Charming woodland scenes in a significantly cut production.

As You Like It. 1978. Dir. Basil Coleman. UK. 150 min. Lively performances in this BBC-TV production by Helen Mirren as Rosalind, Angharad Rees as Celia, and Victoria Plucknett as Phoebe. Playing Jaques, Richard Pasco brings poignant understatement to the famous "seven ages of man" speech.

As You Like It. 2006. Dir. Kenneth Branagh. UK. 127 min. In this gorgeous production, the action is relocated from medieval France to nineteenth-century Japan. With Bryce Dallas Howard (Rosalind), David Oyelowo (Orlando), Rowola Garai (Celia), Brian Blessed (Duke Senior and Duke Frederick), and Alfred Molina (Touchstone).

TEXTUAL INTRODUCTION

The text of *As You Like It* presents few difficulties. There are no early quarto versions—at least none are known to have survived—and thus we have only one authoritative early text, that preserved in the First Folio (F). Unlike many other plays in the Folio, *As You Like It* is well printed by the standards of its time. It has a full set of act and scene divisions. It is fairly reliable in terms of speech prefixes and lineation that signals the difference between verse and prose. Its stage directions are spare but for the most part not problematic. One major difference between F and most modern editions is that, with one exception, throughout F in entrances, exits, and speech prefixes Touchstone is called only "*Clown*," a generic label that emphasizes his role as the play's official fool-figure rather than his individuality. Even in the one entrance that does give his name (at 2.4.0), he is referred to in F as "*Clowne, alias Touchstone*." Aside from that mention, the only way we know his name in F is that he is addressed as "Touchstone" three times by other characters (2.4.15, 3.2.11, and 3.2.40). In *The Norton Shakespeare*, in keeping with our faithfulness to the early texts on which the edition is based, we have followed F and identified this character as "*Clown*" rather than "*Touchstone*" in all speech prefixes. (See also Digital Edition TC 2.)

There are other small difficulties with casting, since the Folio does not include a list of "The Persons of the Play." For example, how many Lords attend on Duke Senior in the forest or on the usurping Duke Frederick at court? Does the Forest of Arden have "Foresters" in addition to the "Lords," or do the Lords simply function at times as foresters? The F stage direction at the beginning of 2.1 specifies the entrance of "*two or three Lords like Forresters*," suggesting that in this scene the Lords simply habit themselves as foresters. But at the beginning of 4.2, the stage direction reads "*Enter Iaques and Lords, Forresters*," leaving open the question of whether there are separate Foresters on stage. Here, the fluidity of the stage directions may tell us something about performance: how many Lords were in attendance and the extent to which some of them dressed as foresters would depend on the availability of extra actors for any given performance.

This edition does not preserve another "error" in the Folio—its use of male pronouns for female actors and persons. At several points, Rosalind is referred to as the "wrong" gender—most notably, in the final scene. Hymen in F seems to construct a tableau of same-sex marriage by inviting the Duke to "receive thy daughter" and Orlando so that he can "join his hand with his" (5.4.105), where we would expect "her hand with his." Since in Shakespeare's company women's parts were all played by men or boys, Hymen's speech gestures toward the sexual identity of the boy actor playing the part of Rosalind. In a play so rife with gender confusion, the mistake is perhaps not surprising, and most editors have emended one of the occurrences of "his" to "her." If this were the only case of pronoun gender confusion in the play, we might chalk it up to a printer's error, but similar errors, mostly in connection with Rosalind, occur at several other points in the text: see 1.1.95 (discussed in Digital Edition TC 1), 3.2.133, 5.2.17, and as a confirmation to the audience of the male identity of the youth playing her part, Rosalind's "Epilogue." *As You Like It* plays with gender confusion in hilarious, outrageously excessive ways, such as having a heroine who is a boy actor playing the part of a young woman who goes on to play the part of a young man who then enacts the part of the woman, Rosalind, he really "is" beneath his disguise. In such a dizzying array of possibilities for gender confusion, we should not be surprised to see a similar confusion in the play's language relating to gender identity, and we should not assume that it is an error on Shakespeare or someone else's part.

In this edition we have preserved a few wordings that are usually modernized in recent editions. For example, in Rosalind's derisive speech at 4.1.33, does she refer to Jaques as having "swum" in a "gondola," as the word is modernized in most recent editions, or in a "gundello," as here and in F? *The Norton Shakespeare* has kept the Folio reading on the grounds that it signals Rosalind's ridicule of Jaques (see Digital Edition TC 7). Added stage directions are usually implied by the play's language. For example, in 1.1.46, when Orlando responds to Oliver's attack, this edition adds "*He grabs* OLIVER *by the throat*" because Orlando states in his next speech: "Wert thou not my brother I would not take this hand from thy throat till this other [hand] had pulled out thy tongue." Stage directions are added in 3.3 to clarify that Jaques is not at first visible to the Clown and Audrey, and at 3.5 to clarify a speech in which Rosalind addresses alternately Silvius and Phoebe. Similarly, at several points F is confusing about speech prefixes. In 2.5.41–50, for example, three speeches in a row are attributed to "*Amiens*" with a song in between. Does he speak them all, and does he sing the song? In this edition he does, because that seems the most likely interpretation of the Folio speech prefixes.

LEAH S. MARCUS

PERFORMANCE NOTE

Shakespeare constantly sought to enrich the fundamental attraction of acting—namely, that actors clearly are, and as clearly are not, the characters they play. Rosalind is like every character in that she is represented by an actor, but she is unique in Shakespeare for portraying a second character that plays (represents) a version of the first, thus ultimately playing both characters and genders simultaneously. Productions of *As You Like It* often seek to extend the paradoxes of person and gender exemplified in Rosalind—for instance, by casting the Forest of Arden as an idyllic approximation of the court; by redeploying Duke Frederick, Le Beau, and Charles as Duke Senior, Jaques, and Amiens; or by indicating that Orlando is sexually attracted to the indeterminate figure Ganymede, thereby possibly posing a barrier to the play's generic resolution. These rich potential gender dynamics may explain why the play continues to inspire directors to employ all-male or all-female casts.

Even relative to other Shakespeare plays, *As You Like It* offers companies an unusual number and range of choices respecting characterization. Actors and directors must decide, for instance, whether Rosalind begins the play morose at her father's banishment or fierce before an unjust usurper, whether she passes easily as a boy or forever seems moments from discovery, whether she is confident in her hold on Orlando or continuously jealous and alert. Jaques can appear misanthropic or simply melancholy, while the merry men might seem at ease in their new lifestyle or merely to be smiling through their misery. Orlando, meanwhile, may present as a Petrarchan lover or as aggressive and immature; Touchstone the Clown can be a loyal confidante or a parasite; Corin, Silvius, Phoebe, and the other Arden dwellers can be attractive in their simplicity or tedious and filthy. Other considerations in performance include the relative heights of Rosalind and Celia; staging the wrestling and other set pieces; the depiction and mood of the Forest of Arden; and the ontological status of Hymen.

Brett Gamboa

As You Like It

[THE PERSONS OF THE PLAY

ROSALIND, daughter to the banished Duke Senior, later disguised as Ganymede
CELIA, daughter to Duke Frederick and cousin to Rosalind; later disguised as Aliena
ORLANDO, youngest son to Sir Roland de Bois
OLIVER, eldest son to Sir Roland de Bois
JAQUES DE BOIS, second son to Sir Roland de Bois
ADAM, servant to Oliver, later to Orlando
DENNIS, servant to Oliver

DUKE SENIOR, now living in exile
AMIENS
JAQUES
FIRST LORD   ⎫
SECOND LORD   ⎬ courtiers attending on Duke Senior
FIRST PAGE   ⎭
SECOND PAGE

DUKE FREDERICK, younger brother to Duke Senior
Touchstone the CLOWN, court jester to Duke Frederick
CHARLES, wrestler attached to Duke Frederick's court
LE BEAU
FIRST LORD   ⎫ courtiers attending on Duke Frederick
SECOND LORD   ⎭

CORIN, an old shepherd
SILVIUS, a young shepherd, in love with Phoebe
PHOEBE, a shepherdess
WILLIAM, a countryman, in love with Audrey
AUDREY, a country wench
SIR OLIVER MARTEXT, a country vicar

HYMEN, god of marriage

Attendants, Musicians]

1.1

Enter ORLANDO *and* ADAM.

ORLANDO As I remember, Adam, it was upon this fashion bequeathed me by will: but poor° a thousand crowns[1] and, as thou say'st, charged° my brother on his blessing[2] to breed me° well—and there begins my sadness. My brother Jaques he keeps at school° and report speaks goldenly of his profit. For my part, he keeps me rustically at home or, to speak more properly, stays° me here at home unkept.° For call you

°*only*
°*he (my father) charged*
°*bring me up*
°*university*

°*detains / uncared for*

1.1 Location: The orchard of Oliver's house, in the vicinity of Duke Frederick's court in France.
1. Equivalent to about 25,000 English pounds in today's currency. Orlando's inheritance is worth twice as much as Adam's life savings (see 2.3.38).
2. On pain of losing his blessing.

that keeping for a gentleman of my birth that differs not
from the stalling of an ox? His horses are bred better: for
10 besides that they are fair with° their feeding, they are taught
their manège,[3] and to that end riders dearly° hired. But I,
his brother, gain nothing under him but growth, for the which
his animals on his dunghills are as much bound to him as I.
Besides this nothing that he so plentifully gives me, the some-
15 thing that nature gave me his countenance° seems to take
from me. He lets me feed with his hinds,° bars me[4] the place
of a brother, and as much as in him lies, mines my gentility
with my education.[5] This is it, Adam, that grieves me; and
the spirit of my father, which I think is within me, begins to
20 mutiny against this servitude. I will no longer endure it,
though yet I know no wise remedy how to avoid it.

      Enter OLIVER.

ADAM Yonder comes my master, your brother.
ORLANDO Go apart, Adam, and thou shalt hear how he will
shake me up.°
25 OLIVER Now, sir, what make you° here?
ORLANDO Nothing. I am not taught to make anything.
OLIVER What mar you° then, sir?
ORLANDO Marry,[6] sir, I am helping you to mar that which God
made—a poor unworthy brother of yours—with idleness.
30 OLIVER Marry, sir, be better employed and be naught° awhile.
ORLANDO Shall I keep your hogs and eat husks with them?
What prodigal portion have I spent that I should come to
such penury?[7]
OLIVER Know you where you are, sir?
35 ORLANDO O sir, very well: here in your orchard.
OLIVER Know you before whom, sir?
ORLANDO Ay, better than him I am before knows me. I know
you are my eldest brother and, in the gentle condition of
blood, you should so know me.[8] The courtesy of nations[9]
40 allows you my better in that you are the first born, but the same
tradition takes not away my blood, were there twenty brothers
betwixt us. I have as much of my father in me as you, albeit I
confess your coming before me is nearer to his reverence.[1]
OLIVER What, boy?
      [*He attacks* ORLANDO.]
45 ORLANDO Come, come, elder brother—you are too young° in
this!
      [*He grabs* OLIVER *by the throat.*]
OLIVER Wilt thou lay hands on me, villain?°
ORLANDO I am no villain. I am the youngest son of Sir Roland
de Bois. He was my father, and he is thrice a villain that says
50 such a father begot villains. Wert thou not my brother I would
not take this hand from thy throat till this other had pulled
out thy tongue for saying so: thou hast railed on° thyself.

Glosses (right margin):
- handsome because of / expensively
- conduct / farmworkers
- insult me
- are you doing
- are you destroying
- get lost
- inexperienced
- lowborn man; scoundrel
- abused

3. Paces and actions of a trained horse.
4. Excludes me from.
5. Undermines my gentility by my (poor) education.
6. An oath, derived from the name of the Virgin Mary.
7. Alluding to the biblical parable of the prodigal son (Luke 15:11–32), who after squandering his share of his father's fortune envied the swine he tended and wished to eat their fodder.
8. And because of the noble blood that we share, you should acknowledge me as a brother.
9. Customs of civil society. Referring to the English system of primogeniture, which allowed for the transmission of all property to the eldest son.
1. Your being older than I am makes you more worthy of the respect that he commanded.

ADAM Sweet masters, be patient! For your father's remembrance, be at accord.

55 OLIVER Let me go, I say!

ORLANDO I will not till I please. You shall hear me. My father charged you in his will to give me good education. You have trained me like a peasant, obscuring and hiding from me all gentleman-like qualities.° The spirit of my father grows   *accomplishments*

60 strong in me, and I will no longer endure it. Therefore allow me such exercises° as may become a gentleman, or give me   *pursuits* the poor allottery° my father left me by testament. With that   *portion* I will go buy my fortunes.

OLIVER And what wilt thou do—beg when that is spent? Well,

65 sir, get you in. I will not long be troubled with you. You shall have some part of your will. I pray you leave me.

ORLANDO I will no further offend you than becomes me for my good.

OLIVER Get you with him, you old dog.

70 ADAM Is "old dog" my reward? Most true—I have lost my teeth in your service. God be with my old master; he would not have spoke such a word.   *Exeunt* ORLANDO [*and*] ADAM.

OLIVER Is it even so? Begin you to grow upon me?² I will physic your rankness³ and yet give no thousand crowns neither.

75 Holla, Dennis!
          Enter DENNIS.

DENNIS Calls your worship?

OLIVER Was not Charles, the duke's wrestler, here to speak with me?

DENNIS So please you, he is here at the door and importunes

80 access to you.

OLIVER Call him in. 'Twill be a good way, and tomorrow the wrestling is.   [*Exit* DENNIS.]
          Enter CHARLES.

CHARLES Good morrow to your worship.

OLIVER Good Monsieur Charles, what's the new news at the

85 new court?

CHARLES There's no news at the court, sir, but the old news: that is, the old Duke is banished by his younger brother, the new Duke; and three or four loving lords have put themselves into voluntary exile with him, whose lands and revenues

90 enrich the new Duke; therefore he gives them good leave° to   *full permission* wander.

OLIVER Can you tell if Rosalind, the Duke's daughter, be banished with her father?

CHARLES Oh, no, for the Duke's daughter, her cousin, so loves

95 her, being ever from their cradles bred° together, that she⁴   *brought up* would have followed her exile or have died to stay behind her. She is at the court and no less beloved of her uncle than his own daughter, and never two ladies loved as they do.

OLIVER Where will the old Duke live?

---

2. To grow so big you crowd upon me.
3. Remedy your overgrowth (as with vegetation); apply a purgative to your diseased blood.
4. TEXTUAL COMMENT The Folio (F) prints "hee"

instead of "she," perhaps referring to the sex of the boy actor who would have played Celia on the early modern stage. See Digital Edition TC 1.

100 CHARLES   They say he is already in the Forest of Arden,[5] and
        a many merry men with him; and there they live like the old
        Robin Hood[6] of England. They say many young gentlemen
        flock to him every day and fleet° the time carelessly° as they   pass / without worries
        did in the golden world.[7]
105 OLIVER   What, you wrestle tomorrow before the new Duke?
     CHARLES   Marry, do I, sir, and I came to acquaint you with a
        matter: I am given, sir, secretly to understand that your
        younger brother Orlando hath a disposition to come in dis-
        guised against me to try a fall.° Tomorrow, sir, I wrestle for my   bout
110   credit,° and he that escapes me without some broken limb   reputation
        shall acquit him well. Your brother is but young and tender,
        and for your love I would be loath to foil° him, as I must for   defeat
        my own honor, if he come in. Therefore, out of my love to you
        I came hither to acquaint you withal,° that either you might   with this
115   stay° him from his intendment° or brook° such disgrace well   keep / intent / endure
        as he shall run into, in that it is a thing of his own search° and   seeking
        altogether against my will.
     OLIVER   Charles, I thank thee for thy love to me, which thou
        shalt find I will most kindly requite. I had myself notice of
120   my brother's purpose herein, and have by underhand° means   subtle
        labored to dissuade him from it, but he is resolute. I'll tell
        thee, Charles, it° is the stubbornest young fellow of France: (Orlando)
        full of ambition, an envious emulator of every man's good
        parts,° a secret and villainous contriver against me, his natu-   qualities
125   ral brother. Therefore use thy discretion: I had as lief° thou   willingly
        didst break his neck as his finger. And thou wert best look
        to't, for if thou dost him any slight disgrace, or if he do not
        mightily grace° himself on thee, he will practice° against   win credit for / plot
        thee by poison, entrap thee by some treacherous device, and
130   never leave thee till he hath ta'en thy life by some indirect
        means or other. For I assure thee, and almost with tears I
        speak it, there is not one so young and so villainous this day
        living. I speak but brotherly[8] of him, but should I anatomize°   dissect; fully reveal
        him to thee as he is, I must blush and weep and thou must
135   look pale and wonder.
     CHARLES   I am heartily glad I came hither to you. If he come
        tomorrow I'll give him his payment. If ever he go alone°   walks without aid
        again, I'll never wrestle for prize more. And so God keep
        your worship!
140 OLIVER   Farewell, good Charles.   Exit [CHARLES].
        Now will I stir this gamester.° I hope I shall see an end of   (Orlando)
        him, for my soul—yet I know not why—hates nothing more
        than he. Yet he's gentle,° never schooled and yet learned,   of noble character
        full of noble device,° of all sorts enchantingly beloved,[9] and   purposes
145   indeed so much in the heart of the world, and especially of

---

5. TEXTUAL COMMENT F anglicizes the spelling of the
French Ardennes, the name of an ancient forest encompassing parts of France, Belgium, and Luxembourg,
thus evoking the English forest of Arden near Shakespeare's birthplace in Warwickshire. Some editions
emend "Arden" to "Ardennes." See Digital Edition TC 2.
6. A legendary English outlaw, associated with Not-
tingham's Sherwood Forest, who robbed from the
rich and gave his plunder to the poor.
7. Alluding to the classical myth of an earlier world
of perpetual spring, abundance, and ease from which
humankind had degenerated (Ovid, *Metamorphoses*
1). This golden world was often identified with a pastoral life.
8. In a manner proper to a brother.
9. Beloved of all ranks as if by enchantment.

my own people, who best know him, that I am altogether misprized.° But it shall not be so long—this wrestler shall clear all.° Nothing remains but that I kindle° the boy thither,° which now I'll go about.   *Exit.*

despised
fix everything
urge / (to the court)

1.2

Enter ROSALIND *and* CELIA.

CELIA   I pray thee, Rosalind, sweet my coz,° be merry.   *cousin*

ROSALIND   Dear Celia, I show more mirth than I am mistress of, and would you yet I were merrier? Unless you could teach me to forget a banished father, you must not learn° me   *teach*
5   how to remember any extraordinary pleasure.

CELIA   Herein I see thou lov'st me not with the full weight that I love thee. If my uncle, thy banished father, had banished thy uncle, the Duke my father, so° thou hadst been   *provided*
still with me I could have taught my love to take thy father
10   for mine. So wouldst thou if the truth of thy love to me were so righteously tempered° as mine is to thee.   *properly constituted*

ROSALIND   Well, I will forget the condition of my estate° to   *circumstances*
rejoice in yours.

CELIA   You know my father hath no child but I, nor none is
15   like to have. And truly, when he dies, thou shalt be his heir; for what he hath taken away from thy father, perforce° I will   *as a matter of course*
render thee again in affection. By mine honor I will, and when I break that oath let me turn monster. Therefore, my sweet Rose, my dear Rose, be merry.

20   ROSALIND   From henceforth I will, coz, and devise sports.°   *entertainments*
Let me see—what think you of falling in love?

CELIA   Marry, I prithee do—to make sport withal.° But love   *to provide amusement*
no man in good earnest, nor no further in sport neither than with safety of a pure blush thou mayst in honor come off
25   again.[1]

ROSALIND   What shall be our sport then?

CELIA   Let us sit and mock the good housewife Fortune[2] from her wheel, that her gifts may henceforth be bestowed equally.

30   ROSALIND   I would we could do so, for her benefits are mightily misplaced, and the bountiful blind woman° doth most   *(Fortune)*
mistake in her gifts to women.

CELIA   'Tis true, for those that she makes fair she scarce makes honest,° and those that she makes honest she makes   *chaste*
35   very ill-favoredly.°   *ugly*

ROSALIND   Nay, now thou goest from Fortune's office° to   *function*
Nature's: Fortune reigns in° gifts of the world, not in the   *presides over*
lineaments of Nature.[3]

Enter CLOWN.[4]

1.2 Location: The grounds of Duke Frederick's court.
1. *than . . . again:* than, with the protection afforded by your innocence ("pure blush"), you may honorably escape ("come off again").
2. Referring to the blind goddess of classical mythology who directed human destiny with the movements of her wheel, here likened to the mistress of a household with a spinning wheel.

3. *lineaments of nature:* one's natural features.
4. TEXTUAL COMMENT Although most modern editions refer to this character as "Touchstone" from his first entrance, it is only at the beginning of 2.4 that the stage directions of F name him as such. He is otherwise called only "*Clown*" in the stage directions and speech prefixes of F, a designation that links him with the stock fool-figures of other plays. See Digital Edition TC 3.

CELIA No, when Nature hath made a fair creature, may she
40   not by Fortune fall into the fire? Though Nature hath given
us wit to flout at Fortune, hath not Fortune sent in this fool
to cut off the argument?

ROSALIND Indeed, there is Fortune too hard for Nature,
when Fortune makes Nature's natural° the cutter-off of   *fool*
45   Nature's wit.

CELIA Peradventure° this is not Fortune's work neither, but   *Perhaps*
Nature's, who perceiveth our natural wits too dull to reason
of such goddesses, hath sent this natural for our whetstone.⁵
For always the dullness of the fool is the whetstone of the
50   wits. —How now, wit, whither wander you?⁶

CLOWN Mistress, you must come away to your father.

CELIA Were you made the messenger?

CLOWN No, by mine honor, but I was bid to come for you.

ROSALIND Where learned you that oath, fool?

55 CLOWN Of a certain knight that swore by his honor they
were good pancakes and swore by his honor the mustard
was naught.° Now I'll stand to it° the pancakes were naught   *worthless / affirm*
and the mustard was good, and yet was not the knight
forsworn.°   *perjured*

60 CELIA How prove you that in the great heap of your knowledge?

ROSALIND Ay, marry, now unmuzzle your wisdom.

CLOWN Stand you both forth now: stroke your chins and
swear by your beards that I am a knave.

65 CELIA By our beards, if we had them, thou art.

CLOWN By my knavery, if I had it, then I were. But if you
swear by that that is not you are not forsworn. No more was
this knight swearing by his honor, for he never had any; or if
he had, he had sworn it away before ever he saw those pancakes or that mustard.

CELIA Prithee, who is't that thou mean'st?

CLOWN One that old Frederick, your father, loves.

ROSALIND⁷ My father's love is enough to honor him enough.
Speak no more of him: you'll be whipped for taxation° one of   *slander*
75   these days.

CLOWN The more pity that fools may not speak wisely what
wise men do foolishly.

CELIA By my troth thou sayest true, for since the little wit
that fools have was silenced,⁸ the little foolery that wise men
80   have makes a great show. Here comes Monsieur the Beau.

    Enter LE BEAU.

ROSALIND With his mouth full of news.

CELIA Which he will put on° us as pigeons feed their young.   *force upon*

ROSALIND Then shall we be news-crammed.⁹

---

5. Celia suggests the Clown's function by describing him as a "whetstone" (a stone for sharpening tools), a word that also plays on his name (a touchstone was a stone that was used to test the purity of gold and silver). Touchstone tests and sharpens the wits of those he encounters.
6. Alluding to the catchphrase "wandering wits."
7. TEXTUAL COMMENT Most modern editors assign this speech to Celia on the grounds that she asked the question to which the Clown has just responded

and because the Clown has referred to her father. F, however, assigns this speech to Rosalind, who might be asserting the preeminence of her father's love over Frederick's. See Digital Edition TC 4.
8. This is a possible allusion to the Bishop of London's order for the burning of satirical books in June 1599.
9. Forced to digest news, also suggesting "mews" as meaning the cages in which pigeons were kept before being fattened, or "crammed," for the table.

CELIA All the better: we shall be the more marketable.°   *fit to be sold*

85   —Bonjour,° Monsieur Le Beau. What's the news?   *Good day*

LE BEAU Fair princess, you have lost much good sport.

CELIA Sport? Of what color?°   *kind*

LE BEAU What color, madam? How shall I answer you?

ROSALIND As wit and fortune will.°   *desire*

90   CLOWN Or as the destinies decrees.

CELIA Well said—that was laid on with a trowel.[1]

CLOWN Nay, if I keep not my rank—[2]

ROSALIND Thou losest thy old smell.

LE BEAU You amaze° me, ladies. I would have told you of good   *confuse*

95   wrestling, which you have lost the sight of.

ROSALIND Yet tell us the manner of the wrestling.

LE BEAU I will tell you the beginning, and if it please your

ladyships, you may see the end. For the best is yet to do,°   *to come*

and here, where you are, they are coming to perform it.

100   CELIA Well, the beginning? That is dead and buried.[3]

LE BEAU There comes an old man and his three sons—

CELIA I could match this beginning with an old tale.[4]

LE BEAU —Three proper° young men, of excellent growth   *handsome*

and presence—

105   ROSALIND With bills° on their necks: "Be it known unto all   *proclamations*

men by these presents"[5]—

LE BEAU —The eldest of the three wrestled with Charles, the

Duke's wrestler, which Charles in a moment threw him and

broke three of his ribs, that there is little hope of life in him.

110   So he served the second and so the third. Yonder they lie,

the poor old man, their father, making such pitiful dole°   *mourning*

over them that all the beholders take his part with weeping.

ROSALIND Alas!

CLOWN But what is the sport, monsieur, that the ladies have

115   lost?

LE BEAU Why, this that I speak of.

CLOWN Thus men may grow wiser every day. It is the first

time that ever I heard breaking of ribs was sport for ladies.

CELIA Or I, I promise thee.

120   ROSALIND But is there any else° longs to see this broken   *anyone else who*

music[6] in his sides? Is there yet another dotes upon rib-

breaking? Shall we see this wrestling, cousin?

LE BEAU You must if you stay here, for here is the place

appointed for the wrestling and they are ready to perform it.

125   CELIA Yonder, sure, they are coming. Let us now stay and

see it.

      Flourish.[7] *Enter* DUKE [FREDERICK], LORDS, ORLANDO,

      CHARLES, *and Attendants.*

---

1. Bluntly; excessively. With a reference to a builder's heavy application of mortar.
2. My status (as a jester). Rosalind then puns on the meaning of "rank" as "foul smelling."
3. *the beginning . . . buried*: Over and done with; gone. (Referring to the start of the wrestling, with a possible jab at Le Beau's longwindedness.)
4. *old tale*: Celia suggests that the motif of a father and his three sons is the starting point for many familiar folktales.
5. That is, by these legal documents—a legal phrase that appears at the start of formal documents, with a pun on "presence."
6. Literally, a musical composition for a variety of instruments; here, referring to the labored breathing caused by the broken ribs.
7. The sounding of horns or trumpets to signal the arrival of an important person.

DUKE FREDERICK   Come on! Since the youth will not be
entreated,° his own peril on his forwardness.[8]   *persuaded (to desist)*
ROSALIND   Is yonder the man?
130   LE BEAU   Even he, madam.
CELIA   Alas, he is too young! Yet he looks successfully.°   *as if he would do well*
DUKE FREDERICK   How now, daughter and cousin[9]—are you
crept hither to see the wrestling?
ROSALIND   Ay, my liege, so please you give us leave.
135   DUKE FREDERICK   You will take little delight in it, I can tell
you: there is such odds° in the man. In pity of the challeng-   *superiority*
er's youth I would fain° dissuade him, but he will not be   *willingly*
entreated. Speak to him, ladies; see if you can move him.
CELIA   Call him hither, good Monsieur Le Beau.
140   DUKE FREDERICK   Do so. I'll not be by.
LE BEAU   Monsieur the challenger, the princess calls for you.
ORLANDO   I attend them with all respect and duty.
ROSALIND   Young man, have you challenged Charles the
wrestler?
145   ORLANDO   No, fair princess. He is the general challenger. I
come but in, as others do, to try with him the strength of my
youth.
CELIA   Young gentleman, your spirits are too bold for your
years. You have seen cruel proof of this man's strength: if
150   you saw yourself with your eyes or knew yourself with your
judgment,[1] the fear° of your adventure would counsel you to   *danger*
a more equal enterprise. We pray you for your own sake to
embrace your own safety and give over this attempt.
ROSALIND   Do, young sir. Your reputation shall not therefore
155   be misprized.° We will make it our suit to the Duke that the   *undervalued*
wrestling might not go forward.
ORLANDO   I beseech you, punish me not with your hard
thoughts,° wherein I confess me much guilty to deny so fair   *displeasure*
and excellent ladies anything. But let your fair eyes and
160   gentle wishes go with me to my trial, wherein if I be foiled°   *defeated*
there is but one shamed that was never gracious;° if killed,   *in favor*
but one dead that is willing to be so. I shall do my friends no
wrong, for I have none to lament me; the world no injury, for
in it I have nothing. Only in the world I fill up a place, which
165   may be better supplied when I have made it empty.
ROSALIND   The little strength that I have, I would it were with
you.
CELIA   And mine to eke out° hers.   *add to*
ROSALIND   Fare you well! Pray heaven I be deceived in you.
170   CELIA   Your heart's desires be with you.
CHARLES   Come, where is this young gallant that is so desirous to lie with his mother earth?[2]
ORLANDO   Ready, sir, but his will° hath in it a more modest   *(sexual) desire*
working.°   *undertaking*
175   DUKE FREDERICK   You shall try but one fall.

---

8. *his own . . . forwardness:* let the danger he encounters be blamed on his own rashness.
9. *cousin:* a term used to signify many kinship
relations.
1. If you used your discernment and judgment upon

yourself.
2. To fall to the ground. The words echo biblical
descriptions of the body's return to earth at death
and pun on "lie with" as slang for "have sexual relations with."

CHARLES   No, I warrant your grace, you shall not entreat him
　　to a second that have so mightily persuaded him from a first.
ORLANDO   You mean to mock me after. You should not have
　　mocked me before—but come your ways.°　　　　　　　　　　　　*let's begin*
180　ROSALIND   Now Hercules be thy speed,[3] young man!
CELIA   I would I were invisible, to catch the strong fellow by
　　the leg.
　　　　　　　[CHARLES *and* ORLANDO] *wrestle.*
ROSALIND   O excellent young man!
CELIA   If I had a thunderbolt in mine eye, I can tell who
185　should down.
　　　　　　　Shout. [ORLANDO *throws* CHARLES.]
DUKE FREDERICK   No more, no more!
ORLANDO   Yes, I beseech your grace—I am not yet well
　　breathed.°　　　　　　　　　　　　　　　　　　　　　　　　　　　*exercised*
DUKE FREDERICK   How dost thou, Charles?
LE BEAU　　　　　　　　　　　　　　He cannot speak, my lord.
DUKE FREDERICK   Bear him away.
　　　　　　　[*Attendants carry* CHARLES *off.*]
190　　　　　　　　　　　　　　—What is thy name, young man?
ORLANDO   Orlando, my liege, the youngest son of Sir Roland
　　de Bois.
DUKE FREDERICK   I would thou hadst been son to some man else.
　　The world esteemed thy father honorable,
195　But I did find him still° mine enemy.　　　　　　　　　　　　　*always*
　　Thou shouldst have better pleased me with this deed
　　Hadst thou descended from another house.
　　But fare thee well! Thou art a gallant youth.
　　I would thou hadst told me of another father.
　　　　　　　Exeunt DUKE [FREDERICK, LORDS, *and* LE BEAU].
200　CELIA   Were I my father, coz, would I do this?
ORLANDO   I am more proud to be Sir Roland's son,
　　His youngest son, and would not change that calling°　　　　*title*
　　To be adopted heir to Frederick.
ROSALIND   My father loved Sir Roland as his soul,
205　And all the world was of my father's mind.
　　Had I before known this young man his son
　　I should have given him tears unto° entreaties　　　　　　　*as well as*
　　Ere he should thus have ventured.
CELIA　　　　　　　　　　　　Gentle° cousin,　　　　　　　　　*Noble; kind*
　　Let us go thank him and encourage him.
210　My father's rough and envious° disposition　　　　　　　　　*spiteful*
　　Sticks° me at heart. —Sir, you have well deserved.　　　　　*Stabs*
　　If you do keep your promises in love
　　But justly,° as you have exceeded all promise,　　　　　*to the same degree*
　　Your mistress shall be happy.
ROSALIND　　　　　　　　　　　Gentleman,
　　Wear this for me,
　　　　　　　[*giving him a chain from her neck*]
215　　　　　　　　　　　　one out of suits° with fortune,　　　　　*favor*

---

3. May Hercules bring you luck. The phrase alludes to a mythological wrestling match in which Hercules, whose name was synonymous with physical strength, vanquished Antaeus.

That could° give more but that her hand lacks means.   *would*
—Shall we go, coz?

CELIA   Ay. —Fare you well, fair gentleman.

ORLANDO   Can I not say I thank you? My better parts
Are all thrown down, and that which here stands up
220   Is but a quintain,[4] a mere lifeless block.

ROSALIND   He calls us back. My pride fell with my fortunes:
I'll ask him what he would. —Did you call, sir?
Sir, you have wrestled well and overthrown
More than your enemies.

CELIA   Will you go, coz?

225 ROSALIND   Have with you.° —Fare you well.   *I'll go with you*

               Exeunt [CELIA, ROSALIND, *and* CLOWN].[5]

ORLANDO   What passion hangs these weights upon my tongue?
I cannot speak to her, yet she urged conference.°   *conversation*

            Enter LE BEAU.

O poor Orlando, thou art overthrown!
Or° Charles or something weaker masters thee.   *Either*

230 LE BEAU   Good sir, I do in friendship counsel you
To leave this place. Albeit you have deserved
High commendation, true applause, and love,
Yet such is now the Duke's condition°   *state of mind*
That he misconsters° all that you have done.   *misconstrues*
235 The Duke is humorous:[6] what he is indeed
More suits° you to conceive than I to speak of.   *Is more fitting for*

ORLANDO   I thank you, sir, and pray you tell me this:
Which of the two was daughter of the Duke
That here was at the wrestling?

240 LE BEAU   Neither his daughter if we judge by manners,
But yet indeed, the taller is his daughter.[7]
The other is daughter to the banished Duke,
And here detained by her usurping uncle
To keep his daughter company, whose loves
245 Are dearer than the natural bond of sisters.
But I can tell you that of late this Duke
Hath ta'en displeasure 'gainst his gentle niece—
Grounded upon no other argument°   *reason*
But that the people praise her for her virtues
250 And pity her for her good father's sake—
And on my life, his malice 'gainst the lady
Will suddenly break forth. Sir, fare you well.
Hereafter, in a better world than this,
I shall desire more love and knowledge of you.

255 ORLANDO   I rest much bounden° to you. Fare you well.   *obliged*

              [*Exit* LE BEAU.]

---

4. A wooden post used as a target in jousts and other aristocratic sports. Orlando suggests that his reason and speech (his "better parts") have been "thrown down," or defeated, in his encounter with Rosalind, leaving him standing speechless, like a post.
5. F marks only an exit for Rosalind here, but Celia almost certainly accompanies her offstage. The Clown, whose stage exit is not indicated in F, likely leaves with Rosalind and Celia, rather than (as many editors assume) with the Duke's party.

6. Moody. The term derives from Renaissance medical theory, which held that good mental and physical health depended on the proper balance of four bodily fluids, or humors.
7. TEXTUAL COMMENT Le Beau suggests here that Celia is taller than Rosalind, but other moments in the text (1.3.111; 4.3.86) indicate that Rosalind is the taller of the two. Le Beau's mistake is characteristic of his tendency to become easily confused. See Digital Edition TC 5.

Thus must I from the smoke into the smother—[8]
From tyrant duke unto a tyrant brother.
But heavenly Rosalind! *Exit.*

1.3

Enter CELIA *and* ROSALIND.

CELIA Why cousin, why Rosalind—Cupid have mercy![1] Not a word?

ROSALIND Not one to throw at a dog.

CELIA No, thy words are too precious to be cast away upon
5 curs. Throw some of them at me; come, lame me with reasons.[2]

ROSALIND Then there were two cousins laid up, when the one should be lamed with reasons and the other mad without any.

10 CELIA But is all this for your father?

ROSALIND No, some of it is for my child's father.[3] Oh, how full of briars is this working-day world!

CELIA They are but burrs, cousin, thrown upon thee in holiday foolery; if we walk not in the trodden paths our very
15 petticoats will catch them.

ROSALIND I could shake them off my coat; these burrs are in my heart.

CELIA Hem[4] them away.

ROSALIND I would try if I could cry "hem" and have him.

20 CELIA Come, come—wrestle with thy affections.

ROSALIND Oh, they take the part of a better wrestler than myself.

CELIA Oh, a good wish upon you:° you will try in time in   *good luck to you*
despite of a fall.[5] But turning these jests out of service,° let   *dismissing these jokes*
25 us talk in good earnest. Is it possible on such a sudden you should fall into so strong a liking with old Sir Roland's youngest son?

ROSALIND The Duke my father loved his father dearly.

CELIA Doth it therefore ensue that you should love his son
30 dearly? By this kind of chase° I should hate him, for my   *logic*
father hated his father dearly; yet I hate not Orlando.

ROSALIND No, faith, hate him not, for my sake.

CELIA Why should I not? Doth he not deserve well?

Enter DUKE [FREDERICK] *with* LORDS.

ROSALIND Let me love him for that, and do you love him
35 because I do. Look, here comes the Duke.

CELIA With his eyes full of anger.

DUKE FREDERICK Mistress, dispatch you with your safest haste[6]
And get you from our court.

ROSALIND   Me, uncle?

---

8. Out of the frying pan into the fire. *smother:* thick, suffocating smoke.
1.3 Location: Duke Frederick's court.
1. May Cupid (god of love) be compassionate.
2. Throw so many reasons (for your silence) at me that if they were stones, I would be made lame.
3. That is, for one who will be father to my child.

4. Cough, with a pun on "burrs" (lines 13, 16) as meaning "something that sticks in your throat."
5. You are destined to wrestle with him eventually even though it will cause you to fall, with a pun on "fall" as "lapse from chastity."
6. Leave quickly, which is your best safety.

DUKE FREDERICK   You, cousin.
　　　Within these ten days if that thou beest found
40　So near our public court as twenty miles,
　　　Thou diest for it.
ROSALIND   I do beseech your grace,
　　　Let me the knowledge of my fault bear with me.
　　　If with myself I hold intelligence°　　　　　　　　　　　*I communicate*
　　　Or have acquaintance with mine own desires;
45　If that I do not dream or be not frantic°—　　　　　　　　　*insane*
　　　As I do trust I am not—then, dear uncle,
　　　Never so much as in a thought unborn
　　　Did I offend your highness.
DUKE FREDERICK   Thus do all traitors:
　　　If their purgation° did consist in words,　　　　　　　　*exoneration*
50　They are as innocent as grace itself.
　　　Let it suffice thee that I trust thee not.
ROSALIND   Yet your mistrust cannot make me a traitor.
　　　Tell me whereon the likelihood depends.
DUKE FREDERICK   Thou art thy father's daughter—there's enough.
55　ROSALIND   So was I when your highness took his dukedom;
　　　So was I when your highness banished him.
　　　Treason is not inherited, my lord;
　　　Or if we did derive it from our friends,°　　　　　　　　*relatives*
　　　What's that to me? My father was no traitor.
60　Then, good my liege, mistake me not so much
　　　To think my poverty is treacherous.
CELIA   Dear sovereign, hear me speak.
DUKE FREDERICK   Ay, Celia, we stayed° her for your sake;　　　　*detained*
　　　Else had she with her father ranged° along.　　　　　　　*roamed*
65　CELIA   I did not then entreat to have her stay:
　　　It was your pleasure and your own remorse.°　　　*pity; sense of guilt*
　　　I was too young that time to value her,
　　　But now I know her: if she be a traitor,
　　　Why, so am I. We still° have slept together,　　　　　　　*always*
70　Rose at an instant,° learned, played, ate together,　　*at the same moment*
　　　And wheresoe'er we went, like Juno's swans,
　　　Still we went coupled and inseparable.[7]
DUKE FREDERICK   She is too subtle° for thee, and her　　　　*cunning*
　　　　smoothness,
　　　Her very silence and her patience,
75　Speak to the people, and they pity her.
　　　Thou art a fool. She robs thee of thy name,°　　　　*reputation; fame*
　　　And thou wilt show more bright and seem more virtuous
　　　When she is gone. Then open not thy lips.
　　　Firm and irrevocable is my doom,°　　　　　　　　　　　　*judgment*
80　Which I have passed upon her: she is banished.
CELIA   Pronounce that sentence then on me, my liege.
　　　I cannot live out of her company.
DUKE FREDERICK   You are a fool. —You, niece, provide
　　　　yourself:°　　　　　　　　　　　　　　　　　　　　　*make preparation*
　　　If you out-stay the time, upon mine honor

---

7. That is, yoked together inseparably like the swans that draw the chariot of Juno (queen of the gods). According to Ovid, swans were associated with Venus (goddess of love), not with Juno.

85   And in the greatness of my word,[8] you die.

Exeunt DUKE [FREDERICK *and* LORDS].

CELIA O my poor Rosalind, whither wilt thou go?
        Wilt thou change° fathers? I will give thee mine.   *exchange*
        I charge thee, be not thou more grieved than I am.
ROSALIND I have more cause.
CELIA   Thou hast not, cousin.
90   Prithee, be cheerful. Know'st thou not the Duke
        Hath banished me, his daughter?
ROSALIND   That he hath not.
CELIA No, hath not? Rosalind lacks then the love
        Which teacheth thee that thou and I am one.
        Shall we be sundered? Shall we part, sweet girl?
95   No, let my father seek another heir.
        Therefore devise with me how we may fly,
        Whither to go and what to bear with us;
        And do not seek to take your change upon you,[9]
        To bear your griefs yourself and leave me out.
100   For by this heaven, now at our sorrows pale,
        Say what thou canst, I'll go along with thee.
ROSALIND Why, whither shall we go?
CELIA To seek my uncle in the Forest of Arden.
ROSALIND Alas, what danger will it be to us,
105   Maids as we are, to travel forth so far!
        Beauty provoketh thieves sooner than gold.
CELIA I'll put myself in poor and mean° attire   *lowly*
        And with a kind of umber[1] smirch my face;
        The like do you. So shall we pass along
        And never stir° assailants.   *provoke*
110 ROSALIND   Were it not better
        Because that I am more than common tall,
        That I did suit° me all points° like a man: *dress / ways*
        A gallant curtal ax° upon my thigh,   *short sword*
        A boar-spear[2] in my hand, and—in my heart
115   Lie there what hidden woman's fear there will—
        We'll have a swashing° and a martial outside,   *swaggering*
        As many other mannish cowards have
        That do outface it with their semblances.[3]
CELIA What shall I call thee when thou art a man?
120 ROSALIND I'll have no worse a name than Jove's own page,
        And therefore look you call me Ganymede.[4]
        But what will you be called?
CELIA Something that hath a reference to my state:
        No longer Celia, but Aliena.°   *"the estranged one"*

---

8. And in accordance with the power of my decree as
Duke.
9. To bear alone the burden of your change of
fortunes.
1. Brown pigment. Rubbing umber on their faces
would give Rosalind and Celia the dark or sunburned
complexion that in Elizabethan society marked the
low social status of those who labored outside. Ladies
wore masks to keep their complexions white. The text
at 4.3.87 describes Celia as "browner" than Rosalind, suggesting that perhaps she is the only one of

the two women to use the umber (or, possibly, that
her hair is darker than Rosalind's).
2. A long-bladed spear used to impale boar.
3. Who brazenly defy the world with the mere
appearance of bravery.
4. The name of a beautiful young man who, according to classical mythology, was so beloved by Jove
(king of the gods) that Jove carried him off to heaven
and made him his cupbearer. Also a slang term for a
young man who sold his sexual services to or was
kept by an older man.

125 ROSALIND   But cousin, what if we assayed° to steal   *tried*
       The clownish fool out of your father's court—
       Would he not be a comfort to our travel?⁵
     CELIA   He'll go along o'er the wide world with me.
       Leave me alone to woo him. Let's away
130   And get our jewels and our wealth together,
       Devise the fittest time and safest way
       To hide us from pursuit that will be made
       After my flight. Now go we in content
       To liberty and not to banishment.   *Exeunt.*

2.1

Enter DUKE SENIOR, AMIENS,¹ *and two or three* LORDS
    like° *Foresters.*   *dressed as*

     DUKE SENIOR   Now, my co-mates and brothers in exile,
       Hath not old custom° made this life more sweet   *longstanding tradition*
       Than that of painted pomp?° Are not these woods   *artificial splendor*
       More free from peril than the envious court?
5   Here feel we not the penalty of Adam²—
       The season's difference,° as° the icy fang   *change / such as*
       And churlish° chiding of the winter's wind,   *rough*
       Which when it bites and blows upon my body
       Even till I shrink with cold, I smile and say,
10   "This is no flattery: these are counselors
       That feelingly° persuade me what I am."   *through my senses*
       Sweet are the uses° of adversity,   *benefits*
       Which like the toad, ugly and venomous,
       Wears yet a precious jewel in his head.³
15   And this our life exempt from public haunt°   *free from crowds*
       Finds tongues in trees, books in the running brooks,
       Sermons in stones, and good in everything.
     AMIENS   I would not change it. Happy is your grace
       That can translate the stubbornness of fortune
20   Into so quiet and so sweet a style.
     DUKE SENIOR   Come, shall we go and kill us venison?
       And yet it irks me the poor dappled fools,°   *innocent creatures*
       Being native burghers° of this desert° city,   *citizens / unpeopled*
       Should in their own confines,° with forkèd heads,°   *bounds / arrows*
       Have their round haunches gored.
25   FIRST LORD   Indeed, my lord,
       The melancholy Jaques⁴ grieves at that,
       And in that kind° swears you do more usurp   *vein*
       Than doth your brother that hath banished you.
       Today my lord of Amiens and myself
30   Did steal behind him as he lay along°   *stretched out*
       Under an oak, whose antic° root peeps out   *old; oddly shaped*
       Upon the brook that brawls° along this wood,   *loudly flows*

---

5. F's spelling of "travel" as "travail" (suffering)
emphasizes the hardship of the journey.
2.1 Location: The Forest of Arden.
1. The name of a town in northern France with
which this character is perhaps associated.
2. In Genesis 3, Adam's punishment for disobeying
God involved expulsion from Eden and the laying of
a curse upon the earth. This was frequently interpreted as the end of the temperate climate associated

with paradise.
3. The toad was popularly believed to be poisonous
and to have in its head a jewel, the toadstone.
4. Jaques's name, usually pronounced with two syllables, puns on "jakes," the word for "privy" (toilet). He
is a stock figure of the melancholic man prone to solitude and black thoughts because of an excess of
black bile, one of the four humors.

To the which place a poor sequestered° stag | *cut off from the herd*
That from the hunter's aim had ta'en a hurt
35 Did come to languish. And indeed, my lord,
The wretched animal heaved forth such groans
That their discharge did stretch his leathern coat
Almost to bursting; and the big round tears
Coursed° one another down his innocent nose | *Pursued*
40 In piteous chase. And thus the hairy fool,
Much markèd of° the melancholy Jaques, | *observed by*
Stood on th'extremest verge° of the swift brook, | *farthest edge*
Augmenting it with tears.

DUKE SENIOR But what said Jaques?
Did he not moralize° this spectacle? | *draw a moral from*

45 FIRST LORD Oh, yes—into a thousand similes.
First, for his weeping into the needless° stream, | *needing no more water*
"Poor deer," quoth he, "thou mak'st a testament
As worldlings do, giving thy sum of more° | *your supplement*
To that which had too much." Then, being there alone,
50 Left and abandoned of° his velvet friend,[5] | *by*
"'Tis right," quoth he, "thus misery doth part° | *separate from*
The flux° of company." Anon° a careless[6] herd, | *flow / Just then*
Full of the pasture,° jumps along by him | *Full from grazing*
And never stays to greet him. "Ay," quoth Jaques,
55 "Sweep on, you fat and greasy citizens!
'Tis just the fashion: wherefore do you look
Upon that poor and broken bankrupt there?"
Thus most invectively he pierceth through
The body of country, city, court—
60 Yea, and of this our life—swearing that we
Are mere usurpers, tyrants, and what's worse° | *whatever is worse*
To fright the animals and to kill them up° | *off*
In their assigned and native dwelling place.

DUKE SENIOR And did you leave him in this contemplation?
65 SECOND LORD We did, my lord, weeping and commenting
Upon the sobbing deer.

DUKE SENIOR Show me the place.
I love to cope° him in these sullen fits, | *contend with*
For then he's full of matter.° | *material for thought; pus*

FIRST LORD I'll bring you to him straight.° | *immediately*

Exeunt.

2.2

Enter DUKE [FREDERICK] *with* LORDS.

DUKE FREDERICK Can it be possible that no man saw them?
It cannot be! Some villains of my court
Are of consent and sufferance in this.[1]

FIRST LORD I cannot hear of any that did see her.
5 The ladies, her attendants of her chamber,
Saw her abed, and in the morning early
They found the bed untreasured of their mistress.

SECOND LORD My lord, the roynish° clown at whom so oft | *vulgar*

---

5. Smooth-coated companion. The phrase alludes
both to the velvet covering the male deer's antlers
and to an expensive fabric worn by the prosperous.

6. Carefree, unconcerned; thoughtless.
2.2 Location: Duke Frederick's court.
1. Have agreed to and tolerated this.

Your grace was wont° to laugh is also missing.   *accustomed*

10 Hisperia, the princess' gentlewoman,
Confesses that she secretly o'erheard
Your daughter and her cousin much commend
The parts° and graces of the wrestler   *qualities*
That did but lately foil the sinewy Charles;

15 And she believes, wherever they are gone,
That youth is surely in their company.

DUKE FREDERICK   Send to his brother.° Fetch that gallant   *(Oliver)*
    hither.
If he° be absent, bring his brother° to me.   *(Orlando) / (Oliver)*
I'll make him find him. Do this suddenly,

20 And let not search and inquisition quail°   *fail*
To bring again° these foolish runaways.   *Exeunt.*   *back*

2.3

Enter ORLANDO *and* ADAM [*from different doors*].

ORLANDO   Who's there?

ADAM   What, my young master? O my gentle master,
O my sweet master, O you memory
Of old Sir Roland, why, what make you° here?   *what are you doing*

5 Why are you virtuous? Why do people love you?
And wherefore° are you gentle, strong, and valiant?   *why*
Why would you be so fond° to overcome   *foolish*
The bonny prizer° of the humorous° Duke?   *robust champion / moody*
Your praise is come too swiftly home before you.

10 Know you not, master, to some kind of men
Their graces° serve them but as enemies?   *virtues*
No more° do yours: your virtues, gentle master,   *No better*
Are sanctified and holy traitors to you.
Oh, what a world is this, when what is comely

15 Envenoms° him that bears it!   *Poisons*

ORLANDO   Why, what's the matter?

ADAM   O unhappy youth,
Come not within these doors. Within this roof
The enemy of all your graces lives.
Your brother—no, no brother, yet the son—

20 Yet not the son, I will not call him son—
Of him I was about to call his father—
Hath heard your praises, and this night he means
To burn the lodging where you use° to lie,   *are accustomed*
And you within it. If he fail of that

25 He will have other means to cut you off.
I overheard him and his practices.°   *plots*
This is no place;° this house is but a butchery.°   *home / slaughterhouse*
Abhor it, fear it, do not enter it!

ORLANDO   Why, whither, Adam, wouldst thou have me go?

30 ADAM   No matter whither, so you come not here.

ORLANDO   What, wouldst thou have me go and beg my food,
Or with a base and boisterous° sword enforce   *violent*
A thievish living on the common road?
This I must do or know not what to do.

35 Yet this I will not do, do how I can:

2.3 Location: Oliver's house.

I rather will subject me to the malice
Of a diverted blood[1] and bloody° brother.   *murderous*
ADAM But do not so. I have five hundred crowns,[2]
The thrifty hire I saved[3] under your father,
40 Which I did store to be my foster nurse[4]
When service should in my old limbs lie lame°   *be lamely performed*
And unregarded age in corners thrown.°   *be thrown*
Take that, and he that doth the ravens feed,
Yea, providently caters for the sparrow,[5]
45 Be comfort to my age. Here is the gold.
All this I give you. Let me be your servant.
Though I look old, yet I am strong and lusty,°   *robust*
For in my youth I never did apply
Hot and rebellious° liquors in my blood,   *unhealthful*
50 Nor did not with unbashful forehead° woo   *bold countenance*
The means of weakness and debility.
Therefore my age is as a lusty winter:
Frosty but kindly.° Let me go with you.   *pleasant; benign*
I'll do the service of a younger man
55 In all your business and necessities.
ORLANDO O good old man, how well in thee appears
The constant° service of the antique world,   *faithful*
When service sweat° for duty, not for meed!°   *labored / reward*
Thou art not for the fashion of these times,
60 Where none will sweat but for promotion
And having that, do choke their service up,°   *cease service*
Even with the having. It is not so with thee.
But poor old man, thou prun'st a rotten tree
That cannot so much as a blossom yield
65 In lieu of° all thy pains and husbandry.°   *In return for / gardening*
But come thy ways; we'll go along together
And ere we have thy youthful wages spent,
We'll light upon some settled low content.°   *humble contentment*
ADAM Master, go on and I will follow thee
70 To the last gasp with truth and loyalty.
From seventeen years till now almost fourscore
Here livèd I, but now live here no more.
At seventeen years many their fortunes seek,
But at fourscore it is too late a week.°   *a time*
75 Yet fortune cannot recompense me better
Than to die well and not my master's debtor.   *Exeunt.*

2.4

Enter ROSALIND *for°* Ganymede, CELIA *for Aliena, and*   *as*
CLOWN, *alias Touchstone.*
ROSALIND O Jupiter,[1] how merry are my spirits!
CLOWN I care not for my spirits if my legs were not weary.

---

1. Of a kinship diverted from its natural course.
2. Approximately 12,500 English pounds in today's currency.
3. The wages I thriftily saved.
4. Caretaker. A foster nurse was a woman hired to breast-feed and care for other people's children.
5. Alluding to various biblical passages (especially

Luke 12:6 and 22–24 and Psalm 147:9) that characterize God as the caretaker of all creatures.
2.4 Location: The remainder of act 2 takes place in the Forest of Arden.
1. Another name for Jove, king of the gods in classical mythology and Ganymede's master.

ROSALIND   I could find in my heart to disgrace my man's
apparel and to cry like a woman, but I must comfort the
5   weaker vessel,° as doublet and hose[2] ought to show itself   *woman*
courageous to petticoat; therefore, courage, good Aliena!
CELIA   I pray you, bear with me; I cannot go no further.
CLOWN   For my part, I had rather bear with you than bear
you; yet I should bear no cross[3] if I did bear you, for I think
10   you have no money in your purse.
ROSALIND   Well, this is the Forest of Arden.[4]
CLOWN   Ay, now am I in Arden, the more fool I. When I was
at home I was in a better place, but travelers must be
content.
       Enter CORIN *and* SILVIUS.
15   ROSALIND   Ay, be so good, Touchstone.[5] Look you, who comes
here—a young man and an old in solemn talk.
CORIN   That is the way to make her scorn you still.
SILVIUS   O Corin, that thou knew'st how I do love her!
CORIN   I partly guess, for I have loved ere now.
20   SILVIUS   No, Corin, being old, thou canst not guess,
Though in thy youth thou wast as true a lover
As ever sighed upon a midnight pillow.
But if thy love were ever like to mine—
As sure I think did never man love so—
25   How many actions most ridiculous
Hast thou been drawn to by thy fantasy?°   *imagination*
CORIN   Into a thousand that I have forgotten.
SILVIUS   Oh, thou didst then never love so heartily.
If thou rememb'rest not the slightest folly
30   That ever love did make thee run into,
Thou hast not loved.
Or if thou hast not sat as I do now,
Wearing° thy hearer in thy mistress' praise,   *Wearying*
Thou hast not loved.
35   Or if thou hast not broke from company
Abruptly, as my passion now makes me,
Thou hast not loved.
O Phoebe, Phoebe, Phoebe!   *Exit.*
ROSALIND   Alas, poor shepherd! Searching of° thy wound,   *Probing*
40   I have by hard adventure° found mine own.   *unlucky chance*
CLOWN   And I mine. I remember when I was in love I broke
my sword upon a stone and bid him "Take that!" for coming
a-night to Jane Smile;[6] and I remember the kissing of her
batler[7] and the cow's dugs° that her pretty chapped hands   *udders*
45   had milked; and I remember the wooing of a peascod instead
of her, from whom I took two cods and, giving her them
again, said with weeping tears, "Wear these for my sake."[8]

2. That is, as manhood (signified by male attire, close-fitting jacket and breeches).
3. Trouble; money—specifically, Elizabethan coins stamped with the image of a cross.
4. PERFORMANCE COMMENT Production decisions about representing the Forest of Arden involve set design as well as the creation of an atmosphere. For example, do Rosalind and Celia look upon their arrival in Arden with wonder, or with fear? See Digital Edition PC 1.
5. F reads "be so good Touchstone." Most modern editors emend to "be so, good Touchstone." In either case, Rosalind is urging Touchstone to be content.
6. *I broke . . . Smile:* I struck a stone as though it were a rival to me in my nocturnal visits to Jane Smile.
7. A wooden bat for beating clothes while washing them.
8. *wooing . . . sake":* referring to English country courtship rituals in which a pea pod ("peascod") and its husks ("cods") were considered lucky gifts. "Peascod" and "cods" were also slang terms for male genitalia, suggesting the implicit sexual import of these gifts.

We that are true lovers run into strange capers; but as all is
mortal in nature, so is all nature in love mortal in folly.[9]

50 ROSALIND Thou speak'st wiser than thou art ware° of.   *aware*

CLOWN Nay, I shall ne'er be ware° of mine own wit till I   *wary*
break my shins against it.

ROSALIND Jove, Jove! This shepherd's passion
Is much upon my fashion.°   *of my sort*

55 CLOWN And mine, but it grows something° stale with me.   *somewhat*

CELIA I pray you, one of you question yond man
If he for gold will give us any food.
I faint almost to death.

CLOWN [*to* CORIN]   Holla, you clown!°   *peasant; yokel*

ROSALIND Peace, fool—he's not thy kinsman.

CORIN Who calls?

CLOWN   Your betters, sir.

60 CORIN   Else are they very wretched.

ROSALIND Peace, I say! —Good even° to you, friend.   *evening*

CORIN And to you, gentle sir, and to you all.

ROSALIND I prithee, shepherd, if that love or gold
Can in this desert place buy entertainment,°   *accommodation*

65 Bring us where we may rest ourselves and feed.
Here's a young maid with travel much oppressed,
And faints for succor.°   *for lack of aid (food)*

CORIN   Fair sir, I pity her
And wish, for her sake more than for mine own,
My fortunes were more able to relieve her.

70 But I am shepherd to another man
And do not shear the fleeces that I graze.
My master is of churlish° disposition   *miserly*
And little recks° to find the way to heaven   *thinks*
By doing deeds of hospitality.

75 Besides, his cot,° his flocks, and bounds of feed°   *cottage / grazing rights*
Are now on sale; and at our sheepcote° now,   *cottage*
By reason of his absence, there is nothing
That you will feed on. But what is, come see,
And in my voice[1] most welcome shall you be.

80 ROSALIND What° is he that shall buy his flock and pasture?   *Who*

CORIN That young swain that you saw here but erewhile,°   *just now*
That little cares for buying anything.

ROSALIND I pray thee, if it stand with honesty,
Buy thou the cottage, pasture, and the flock,

85 And thou shalt have to pay° for it of us.   *the money to pay*

CELIA And we will mend° thy wages. I like this place   *improve*
And willingly could waste° my time in it.   *spend*

CORIN Assuredly the thing is to be sold.
Go with me: if you like upon report

90 The soil, the profit, and this kind of life,
I will your very faithful feeder° be   *servant*
And buy it with your gold right suddenly.   *Exeunt.*

---

9. So all lovers show their humanity in their foolishness.

1. And insofar as my authority stretches.

2.5
Enter AMIENS, JAQUES, *and* [*other* LORDS].

Song.

AMIENS [*sings*]¹   Under the greenwood tree
     Who loves to lie with me
     And turn° his merry note   *tune*
     Unto the sweet bird's throat:°   *voice*
5   Come hither, come hither, come hither.
       Here shall he see
       No enemy
       But winter and rough weather.

JAQUES   More, more—I prithee, more!
10 AMIENS   It will make you melancholy, Monsieur Jaques.

JAQUES   I thank it. More, I prithee, more! I can suck melan-
    choly out of a song as a weasel sucks eggs.² More, I prithee,
    more!

AMIENS   My voice is ragged;° I know I cannot please you.   *harsh*
15 JAQUES   I do not desire you to please me, I do desire you to sing.
    Come, more—another stanzo. Call you 'em stanzos?³

AMIENS   What you will, Monsieur Jaques.

JAQUES   Nay, I care not for their names;⁴ they owe me nothing.
    Will you sing?
20 AMIENS   More at your request than to please myself.

JAQUES   Well, then, if ever I thank any man I'll thank you. But
    that° they call compliment is like th'encounter of two dog-   *what*
    apes;° and when a man thanks me heartily, methinks I have *dog-faced baboons*
    given him a penny and he renders me the beggarly thanks.⁵
25   Come, sing—and you that will not, hold your tongues.

AMIENS   Well, I'll end the song. —Sirs, cover the while.⁶ The
    Duke will drink under this tree. —He hath been all this day
    to look° you.   *searching for*

JAQUES   And I have been all this day to avoid him. He is too
30   disputable° for my company. I think of as many matters as   *argumentative*
    he, but I give heaven thanks and make no boast of them.
    Come, warble, come!

Song.

ALL (*together here*⁷)   Who doth ambition shun
         And loves to live i'th' sun,
35   Seeking the food he eats
       And pleased with what he gets:
       Come hither, come hither, come hither.
       Here shall he see, etc.

JAQUES   I'll give you a verse to this note° that I made yesterday   *tune*
40   in despite of my invention.⁸
        [*He hands* AMIENS *a paper.*]

AMIENS   And I'll sing it. Thus it goes:

2.5
1. F does not indicate who sings this song. Traditionally, it has been assigned to Amiens, whose part may
have been played by Robert Armin, a clown who
joined Shakespeare's company in 1599 and who was
known for his fine singing voice.
2. *as a weasel sucks eggs*: referring to the belief that
weasels sucked the yolks out of birds' eggs.
3. A relatively new, and Italianate, word at the time

of the play's composition.
4. Punning on the legal sense of "names" as "signatures of borrowers."
5. Excessive thanks, like that given by a beggar.
6. Set the table in the meantime.
7. F's direction before this song reads: "Song. Altogether here."
8. Even though I have little power of creativity.

If it do come to pass
That any man turn ass,
Leaving his wealth and ease
A stubborn will to please,
45   Ducdame,⁹ ducdame, ducdame:
Here shall he see
Gross fools as he
An if° he will come to me.   *If only*
50   What's that "ducdame"?
JAQUES   'Tis a Greek¹ invocation to call fools into a circle. I'll
go sleep if I can; if I cannot I'll rail against all the firstborn
of Egypt.²
AMIENS   And I'll go seek the Duke. His banquet³ is prepared.
                                                                 Exeunt.

2.6
Enter ORLANDO *and* ADAM.
ADAM   Dear master, I can go no further. Oh, I die for food!
Here lie I down and measure out my grave. Farewell, kind
master.
ORLANDO   Why, how now, Adam? No greater heart in thee?
5   Live a little, comfort° a little, cheer thyself a little. If this   *be comforted*
uncouth° forest yield anything savage I will either be food   *wild*
for it or bring it for food to thee. Thy conceit° is nearer death   *imagination*
than thy powers. For my sake, be comfortable; hold death
awhile at the arm's end. I will here be with thee presently,°   *soon*
10   and if I bring thee not something to eat, I will give thee
leave to die; but if thou diest before I come thou art a
mocker of my labor. Well said—thou look'st cheerily,° and   *cheerfully*
I'll be with thee quickly. Yet thou liest in the bleak air.
Come, I will bear thee to some shelter, and thou shalt not
15   die for lack of a dinner if there live anything in this desert.°   *uninhabited place*
Cheerily, good Adam!   *Exeunt.*

2.7
Enter DUKE SENIOR *and* LORD[s], *like*° *outlaws.*   *dressed as*
DUKE SENIOR   I think he be transformed into a beast,
For I can nowhere find him like° a man.   *in the shape of*
FIRST LORD   My lord, he is but even now gone hence.
Here was he merry, hearing of a song.
5   DUKE SENIOR   If he, compact of jars,° grow musical,   *full of discords*
We shall have shortly discord in the spheres.¹
Go seek him; tell him I would speak with him.
Enter JAQUES.
FIRST LORD   He saves my labor by his own approach.
DUKE SENIOR   Why how now, monsieur, what a life is this
10   That your poor friends must woo your company?
What? You look merrily.

9. A word of unknown meaning. Possibly a variation on a Welsh phrase meaning "Come hither" or on a Gypsy phrase meaning "I foretell."
1. "Greek" was used to signify anything unintelligible.
2. According to Exodus 11 and 12, the Hebrew God caused the deaths of all firstborn Egyptian children after Pharaoh would not let the Israelites leave his country. Jaques may be vowing to denounce all first-born sons, which would include Duke Senior.
3. A light meal of sweetmeats and wine.
2.7
1. Alluding to the Pythagorean belief that the earth was the center of eight concentric spheres whose movements created a heavenly harmony (the music of the spheres) inaudible to humans.

JAQUES   A fool, a fool! I met a fool i'th' forest—
A motley fool![2] A miserable world!
As I do live by food, I met a fool,
15   Who laid him down and basked him in the sun,
And railed on Lady Fortune in good terms,
In good set° terms, and yet a motley fool.   *outspoken; rhetorical*
"Good morrow, fool," quoth I. "No, sir," quoth he,
"Call me not fool till heaven hath sent me fortune."[3]
20   And then he drew a dial[4] from his poke,°   *pocket; pouch*
And looking on it with lackluster eye,
Says very wisely, "It is ten o'clock.
Thus we may see," quoth he, "how the world wags.°   *moves on*
'Tis but an hour ago since it was nine,
25   And after one hour more 'twill be eleven.
And so from hour to hour we ripe and ripe,
And then from hour to hour we rot and rot,
And thereby hangs a tale."[5] When I did hear
The motley fool thus moral on the time,
30   My lungs began to crow like chanticleer°   *a rooster*
That fools should be so deep° contemplative;   *profoundly*
And I did laugh sans° intermission   *without*
An hour by his dial. O noble fool,
A worthy fool! Motley's the only wear.°   *garb worth wearing*
35 DUKE SENIOR   What fool is this?
JAQUES   O worthy fool! One that hath been a courtier
And says if ladies be but young and fair,
They have the gift to know it. And in his brain,
Which is as dry[6] as the remainder° biscuit   *last*
40   After a voyage, he hath strange places° crammed   *sites; commonplaces*
With observation, the which he vents
In mangled forms. Oh, that I were a fool!
I am ambitious for a motley coat.
DUKE SENIOR   Thou shalt have one.
JAQUES   It is my only suit,°   *request; costume*
45   Provided that you weed your better judgments
Of all opinion that grows rank° in them   *wild*
That I am wise. I must have liberty
Withal—as large a charter° as the wind   *license*
To blow on whom I please—for so fools have.
50   And they that are most gallèd° with my folly,   *vexed*
They most must laugh. And why, sir, must they so?
The why is plain as way to parish church:[7]
He that a fool doth very wisely hit
Doth very foolishly, although he smart,

2. Someone wearing "motley," the multicolored costume conventionally associated with fools and jesters.
3. Referring to the proverbial notion that fortune favored fools.
4. A portable sundial about the size of a napkin ring, or possibly an early version of the watch, which would have been carried in a pocket in the seventeenth century.
5. 'Tis . . . tale: the puns and sexual wordplay in these lines suggest a story of male sexual activity leading to debility: "hour" puns on "whore" (they were pronounced similarly); "ripe" means "to come of age sexually"; "rot" puns on "rut," which means "to have sex in an animal-like state of excitement"; and "tale" puns on "tail," slang for "penis." "And thereby hangs a tale" was an Elizabethan commonplace.
6. According to Renaissance medical theory, dry brains signified slow wits and strong memories.
7. plain . . . church: simple and easy to see, like the footpaths that often connected English parish churches with the surrounding rural areas.

55	Seem senseless of the bob.° If not,	*unaware of the taunt*
	The wise man's folly is anatomized°	*dissected; laid open*
	Even by the squand'ring glances° of the fool.	*random hits*
	Invest° me in my motley. Give me leave	*Dress; establish*
	To speak my mind, and I will through and through	
60	Cleanse the foul body of th'infected world	
	If they will patiently receive my medicine.	
	DUKE SENIOR Fie on thee! I can tell what thou wouldst do.	
	JAQUES What, for a counter,[8] would I do but good?	
	DUKE SENIOR Most mischievous foul sin in chiding sin:	
65	For thou thyself hast been a libertine,°	*(sexually) unrestrained person*
	As sensual as the brutish sting° itself;	*lust*
	And all th'embossèd sores and headed evils[9]	
	That thou with license of free foot° hast caught	*travel*
	Wouldst thou disgorge° into the general world.	*vomit*
70	JAQUES Why, who cries out on pride°	*extravagance*
	That can therein tax° any private party?°	*blame / one person*
	Doth it not flow as hugely as the sea,	
	Till that the weary very means° do ebb?	*source itself*
	What woman in the city do I name	
75	When that I say the city woman bears	
	The cost° of princes on unworthy shoulders?	*costly attire*
	Who can come in and say that I mean her,	
	When such a one as she, such is her neighbor?	
	Or what is he of basest function°	*lowliest social status*
80	That says his bravery° is not on° my cost,	*fine attire / at*
	Thinking that I mean him, but therein suits	
	His folly to the mettle° of my speech?	*spirit*
	There then, how then, what then—let me see wherein	
	My tongue hath wronged him. If it do him right,°	*describe him justly*
85	Then he hath wronged himself. If he be free,°	*guiltless*
	Why then my taxing° like a wild goose flies—	*reproof*
	Unclaimed of any man. But who comes here?	

Enter ORLANDO [*with sword drawn*].

	ORLANDO Forbear and eat no more!	
	JAQUES Why, I have ate° none yet.	*eaten*
90	ORLANDO Nor shalt not till necessity be served.	
	JAQUES Of what kind° should this cock come of?	*lineage; stock*
	DUKE SENIOR Art thou thus boldened, man, by thy distress?	
	Or else a rude despiser of good manners,	
	That in civility thou seem'st so empty?	
95	ORLANDO You touched my vein° at first—the thorny point	*assessed my condition*
	Of bare distress hath ta'en from me the show	
	Of smooth civility. Yet am I inland bred,[1]	
	And know some nurture. But forbear, I say!	
	He dies that touches any of this fruit	
100	Till I and my affairs are answerèd.°	*satisfied*
	JAQUES An° you will not be answered with reason, I must die.	*If*
	DUKE SENIOR What would you have? Your gentleness° shall force	*gentility; kindness*
	More than your force move us to gentleness.	

---

8. In return for a coin of no value (normally used for reckoning sums).
9. Swollen sores and boils that have come to a head. Both were symptoms of venereal disease.

1. Brought up in a civilized way—that is, raised in the country's interior regions rather than near its supposedly savage borders.

ORLANDO   I almost die for food, and let me have it.
105   DUKE SENIOR   Sit down and feed, and welcome to our table.
ORLANDO   Speak you so gently? Pardon me, I pray you.
I thought that all things had been savage here,
And therefore put I on the countenance
Of stern commandment. But whate'er you are
110   That in this desert inaccessible
Under the shade of melancholy boughs,
Lose and neglect the creeping hours of time:
If ever you have looked on better days,
If ever been where bells have knolled° to church,   *summoned*
115   If ever sat at any good man's feast,
If ever from your eyelids wiped a tear,
And know what 'tis to pity and be pitied,
Let gentleness my strong enforcement be,²
In the which hope I blush and hide my sword.
120   DUKE SENIOR   True it is that we have seen better days,
And have with holy bell been knolled to church,
And sat at good men's feasts and wiped our eyes
Of drops that sacred pity hath engendered;
And therefore, sit you down in gentleness
125   And take upon command° what help we have   *at your will*
That to your wanting may be ministered.
ORLANDO   Then but forbear your food a little while,
Whiles like a doe I go to find my fawn
And give it food. There is an old poor man,
130   Who after me hath many a weary step
Limped in pure love; till he be first sufficed°—   *satisfied*
Oppressed with two weak° evils, age and hunger—   *enfeebling*
I will not touch a bit.
DUKE SENIOR   Go find him out
And we will nothing waste° till your return.   *consume*
135   ORLANDO   I thank ye, and be blest for your good comfort!
                                                    [*Exit.*]
DUKE SENIOR   Thou seest we are not all alone unhappy:
This wide and universal theater
Presents more woeful pageants° than the scene   *spectacles*
Wherein we play in.
JAQUES   All the world's a stage,
140   And all the men and women merely players.
They have their exits and their entrances,
And one man in his time plays many parts,
His acts being seven ages. At first the infant,
Mewling° and puking in the nurse's arms;   *Crying*
145   Then the whining schoolboy with his satchel
And shining morning face, creeping like snail
Unwillingly to school. And then the lover,
Sighing like furnace,³ with a woeful ballad
Made to his mistress' eyebrow. Then a soldier,
150   Full of strange oaths and bearded like the pard,⁴
Jealous in honor,⁵ sudden and quick in quarrel,

---

2. Let natural kindness or gentility be what compels your compassion.
3. Emitting sighs as a furnace emits smoke.
4. Leopard. The soldier's bristling mustache is compared to the leopard's whiskers.
5. Vigilant in matters of honor.

Seeking the bubble reputation
Even in the cannon's mouth. And then the justice,
In fair round belly with good capon[6] lined,°   *filled; stuffed*
155 With eyes severe and beard of formal cut,
Full of wise saws° and modern instances,°   *sayings / trite examples*
And so he plays his part. The sixth age shifts
Into the lean and slippered pantaloon,[7]
With spectacles on nose and pouch on side,
160 His youthful hose, well saved, a world too wide
For his shrunk shank;° and his big manly voice,   *calf*
Turning again toward childish treble, pipes
And whistles in his° sound. Last scene of all,   *its*
That ends this strange eventful history,
165 Is second childishness and mere° oblivion,   *complete*
Sans° teeth, sans eyes, sans taste, sans everything.   *Without*
　　　　Enter ORLANDO [*carrying*] ADAM.
DUKE SENIOR　Welcome! Set down your venerable burden
And let him feed.
ORLANDO　　　　　　I thank you most for him.
ADAM　So had you need:
170 I scarce can speak to thank you for myself.
DUKE SENIOR　Welcome! Fall to; I will not trouble you
As yet to question you about your fortunes.°   *circumstances*
—Give us some music and, good cousin, sing.
　　　　　　　　Song.
AMIENS [*sings*][8]　Blow, blow, thou winter wind.
175 　　　　Thou art not so unkind
　　　　As man's ingratitude.
　　　　Thy tooth is not so keen
　　　　Because thou art not seen,
　　　　Although thy breath be rude.°   *rough*
180 　　　　Heigh-ho, sing heigh-ho unto the green holly.[9]
　　　　Most friendship is feigning, most loving mere folly.
　　　　Then heigh-ho, the holly:
　　　　This life is most jolly.

　　　　Freeze, freeze, thou bitter sky
185 　　　　That dost not bite so nigh°   *closely*
　　　　As benefits forgot.
　　　　Though thou the waters warp,°   *cause to contract; freeze*
　　　　Thy sting is not so sharp
　　　　As friend remembered not.
190 　　　　Heigh-ho, sing, etc.

DUKE SENIOR　If that you were the good Sir Roland's son,
As you have whispered faithfully you were,
And as mine eye doth his effigies° witness   *likeness*
Most truly limned° and living in your face,   *portrayed*
195 Be truly welcome hither. I am the Duke
That loved your father. The residue of your fortune
Go to my cave and tell me. —Good old man,

6. A cock, castrated and fattened as a delicacy (proverbially, a bribe for magistrates).
7. A foolish old man named after a figure in *commedia dell'arte,* Italian popular comedy.

8. Again, F does not indicate who sings this song. It
is usually assigned to Amiens.
9. The evergreen associated with English holiday
festivities.

Thou art right welcome, as thy master is.
—Support him by the arm. —Give me your hand,
200   And let me all your fortunes understand.   *Exeunt.*

3.1

Enter duke [frederick], lords, *and* oliver.

duke frederick   Not see him since? Sir, sir, that cannot be.
But were I not the better part made° mercy,   composed of
I should not seek an absent argument°   subject
Of my revenge, thou present. But look to it:
5   Find out thy brother, wheresoe'er he is.
Seek him with candle;° bring him dead or living   diligently
Within this twelvemonth, or turn° thou no more   return
To seek a living in our territory.
Thy lands and all things that thou dost call thine
10   Worth seizure do we seize into our hands
Till thou canst quit° thee by thy brother's mouth   acquit
Of what we think against thee.
oliver   Oh, that your highness knew my heart in this!
I never loved my brother in my life.
15   duke frederick   More villain thou. —Well, push him out of
doors,
And let my officers of such a nature°   whose job it is
Make an extent° upon his house and lands.   a writ of seizure
Do this expediently° and turn° him going.   *Exeunt.*   quickly / set

3.2

Enter orlando [*holding a sheaf of papers*].

orlando   Hang there, my verse, in witness of my love.
And thou, thrice-crownèd queen of night,[1] survey
With thy chaste eye from thy pale sphere above
Thy huntress' name,° that my full life doth sway.°   (Rosalind) / rule
5   O Rosalind, these trees shall be my books,
And in their barks my thoughts I'll character,°   inscribe
That every eye which in this forest looks
Shall see thy virtue witnessed everywhere.
Run, run, Orlando—carve on every tree
10   The fair, the chaste and unexpressive° she!   *Exit.*[2]   inexpressible
Enter corin *and* clown.

corin   And how like you this shepherd's life, Master Touchstone?
clown   Truly, shepherd, in respect of° itself, it is a good life;   with regard to
but in respect that it is a shepherd's life, it is naught.° In   worthless
15   respect that it is solitary, I like it very well; but in respect that
it is private, it is a very vile life. Now in respect it is in the
fields, it pleaseth me well; but in respect it is not in the court,
it is tedious. As it is a spare° life, look you, it fits my humor°   frugal / temperament

---

3.1 Location: Duke Frederick's court.
3.2 Location: The remaining scenes of the play take place in the Forest of Arden.
1. The goddess who ruled on earth as Diana, patron of chastity and of the hunt; in the heavens as Cynthia, Phoebe, or Luna, goddess of the moon; and in the underworld as Hecate.
2. Orlando's appearance at lines 1–10 is self-

contained and could form a separate scene. However, the ensuing conversation between Corin and Touchstone appears to take place on the same spot where Orlando has just stood, making the action continuous. This edition, like F, makes Orlando's lines part of the longer scene involving Corin, Touchstone, and eventually Rosalind and others.

well; but as there is no more plenty in it, it goes much against
20 my stomach.° Hast any philosophy in thee, shepherd?   *inclination*

CORIN   No more but that I know the more one sickens, the
worse at ease he is; and that he that wants° money, means,   *lacks*
and content, is without three good friends; that the property
of rain is to wet and fire to burn; that good pasture makes fat
25 sheep and that a great cause of the night is lack of the sun;
that he that hath learned no wit by nature nor art may com-
plain° of good breeding, or comes of a very dull kindred.   *lament his lack*

CLOWN   Such a one is a natural philosopher.[3] Wast ever in
court, shepherd?

30 CORIN   No, truly.

CLOWN   Then thou art damned.

CORIN   Nay, I hope.

CLOWN   Truly thou art damned, like an ill-roasted egg all on
one side.[4]

35 CORIN   For not being at court? Your reason?

CLOWN   Why if thou never wast at court thou never saw'st
good manners.° If thou never saw'st good manners, then thy   *etiquette; morals*
manners must be wicked, and wickedness is sin, and sin is
damnation. Thou art in a parlous° state, shepherd!   *perilous*

40 CORIN   Not a whit, Touchstone—those that are good manners
at the court are as ridiculous in the country as the behavior
of the country is most mockable at the court. You told me
you salute not at the court but° you kiss your hands. That   *unless*
courtesy would be uncleanly if courtiers were shepherds.

45 CLOWN   Instance,° briefly; come, instance.   *An example*

CORIN   Why, we are still° handling our ewes, and their fells,°   *constantly / skins*
you know, are greasy.

CLOWN   Why, do not your courtiers' hands sweat? And is not
the grease of a mutton as wholesome as the sweat of a man?
50 Shallow, shallow! A better instance, I say—come!

CORIN   Besides, our hands are hard.

CLOWN   Your lips will feel them the sooner. Shallow again—a
more sounder instance, come!

CORIN   And they are often tarred over with the surgery of our
55 sheep,[5] and would you have us kiss tar? The courtiers' hands
are perfumed with civet.[6]

CLOWN   Most shallow man, thou worm's meat in respect of° a   *in comparison with*
good piece of flesh, indeed! Learn of the wise and perpend:°   *consider*
civet is of a baser birth than tar—the very uncleanly flux° of   *discharge*
60 a cat. Mend° the instance, shepherd.   *Improve*

CORIN   You have too courtly a wit for me; I'll rest.

CLOWN   Wilt thou rest damned? God help thee, shallow man!
God make incision in thee: thou art raw.[7]

CORIN   Sir, I am a true laborer: I earn that° I eat, get° that I   *what / make*
65 wear, owe no man hate, envy no man's happiness, glad of
other men's good, content with my harm;° and the greatest   *misfortune*
of my pride is to see my ewes graze and my lambs suck.

---

3. A born philosopher; a philosopher who studies
natural phenomena; a fool.
4. *ill-roasted . . . side*: referring to the practice of
roasting eggs on a spit over a wood fire.
5. Referring to the practice of treating sheep wounds
with tar.

6. A musk-scented substance obtained from the anal
glands of certain cats.
7. Make a cut to let blood (and thus cure you of your
"raw"ness, or inexperience); make a cut to score you,
as raw meat was scored in preparation for cooking.

CLOWN   That is another simple° sin in you: to bring the ewes   *foolish; plain*
and the rams together and to offer° to get your living by the   *undertake*
70   copulation of cattle, to be bawd to a bellwether[8] and to
betray a she-lamb of a twelvemonth to a crooked-pated old
cuckoldy ram,[9] out of all reasonable match. If thou beest not
damned for this, the devil himself will have no shepherds.[1] I
cannot see else how thou shouldst scape.°   *escape*
75   CORIN   Here comes young Master Ganymede, my new mistress's brother.
          Enter ROSALIND[, *as Ganymede, reading a paper*].
ROSALIND   "From the east to western Inde,°   *Indies*
No jewel is like Rosalind.
Her worth, being mounted on the wind,
80   Through all the world bears Rosalind.
All the pictures fairest lined°   *drawn*
Are but black to° Rosalind.   *compared to*
Let no face be kept in mind
But the fair of Rosalind."
85   CLOWN   I'll rhyme you so eight years together, dinners and
suppers and sleeping-hours excepted; it is the right butter-
women's rank to market.[2]
ROSALIND   Out, fool!
CLOWN   For a taste:
90   If a hart° do lack a hind,°   *male deer / female deer*
Let him seek out Rosalind.
If the cat will after kind,°   *act naturally; mate*
So, be sure, will Rosalind.
Wintered garments must be lined,[3]
95   So must slender Rosalind.
They that reap must sheaf and bind,
Then to cart[4] with Rosalind.
Sweetest nut hath sourest rind:
Such a nut is Rosalind.
100   He that sweetest rose will find
Must find love's prick° and Rosalind.   *thorn; penis*
This is the very false gallop of verses.° Why do you infect   *way verses canter on*
yourself with them?
ROSALIND   Peace, you dull fool! I found them on a tree.
105   CLOWN   Truly, the tree yields bad fruit.
ROSALIND   I'll graft it with you° and then I shall graft it with   *(punning on "yew")*
a medlar:[5] then it will be the earliest fruit i'th' country, for
you'll be rotten ere you be half ripe, and that's the right°   *true*
virtue of the medlar.

8. The leading sheep of a flock, who usually wore a
bell.
9. Cuckolds, men whose wives were sexually unfaithful, supposedly wore horns to signify their shame.
The ram may *make* cuckolds—that is, be lecherous.
crooked-pated: with crooked horns.
1. It will be because the devil refuses to admit shepherds into hell.
2. *It . . . market*: The rhymes are truly like a stream
of dairywomen going to market at the same time.
Such women were proverbially talkative.
3. Clothes worn in winter must be stuffed with

material, with a pun on "lined" as meaning "copu-
lated with," used especially of female animals. The
implication is that "slender Rosalind" will be impreg-
nated and thus grow larger.
4. A cart on which harvests were transported to the
market; a cart on which women accused of prostitution
or other forms of disorderly conduct were transported
and exposed to public abuse.
5. A tree whose fruit was not ripe until it was so soft
as to be rotten, with a pun on "meddler," one who
meddles.

110 CLOWN You have said—but whether wisely or no, let the forest
　　　judge.
　　　　　　　Enter CELIA *[as Aliena] with a writing.*
　　ROSALIND Peace! Here comes my sister reading—stand aside.
　　CELIA "Why should this a desert be—
　　　　For it is unpeopled? No.
115　　Tongues I'll hang on every tree
　　　　That shall civil° sayings show:　　　　　　　　　　　　　*civilized*
　　　　Some, how brief the life of man
　　　　Runs his erring° pilgrimage,　　　　　　　　　　　　　*wandering*
　　　　That the stretching of a span
120　　Buckles in his sum of age;[6]
　　　　Some of violated vows
　　　　Twixt the souls of friend and friend.
　　　　But upon the fairest boughs,
　　　　Or at every sentence end,
125　　Will I Rosalinda write,
　　　　Teaching all that read to know
　　　　The quintessence of every sprite°　　　　　　　　　　*spirit; soul*
　　　　Heaven would in little show.[7]
　　　　Therefore heaven nature charged
130　　That one body should be filled
　　　　With all graces wide enlarged:[8]
　　　　Nature presently° distilled　　　　　　　　　　　　　*at once*
　　　　Helen's cheek but not her heart,[9]
　　　　Cleopatra's[1] majesty,
135　　Atalanta's better part,[2]
　　　　Sad Lucretia's modesty.[3]
　　　　Thus Rosalind of many parts,
　　　　By heavenly synod° was devised　　　　　　　　　　*assembly*
　　　　Of many faces, eyes, and hearts
140　　To have the touches° dearest prized.　　　　　　　　*traits*
　　　　Heaven would that she these gifts should have,
　　　　And I to live and die her slave."
　　ROSALIND O most gentle Jupiter! What tedious homily of love
　　　have you wearied your parishioners withal, and never cried,
145　　"Have patience, good people."
　　CELIA How now? Back, friends. Shepherd, go off a little; go
　　　with him, sirrah.
　　CLOWN Come, shepherd, let us make an honorable retreat,
　　　though not with bag and baggage, yet with scrip and scrippage.[4]

---

6. *the stretching . . . age:* the width of an open hand
(a "span") encompasses an entire lifetime. A comparison derived from verses appearing in Elizabethan
prayer books.
7. In classical and medieval philosophy, the quintessence of a thing is its purest part or most essential
characteristic. Orlando's poem suggests that heaven
and nature have extracted all the best virtues of
other women and embodied and portrayed them "in
little"—that is, in only one person, Rosalind.
8. Graces that otherwise have been widely
distributed.
9. The features, but not the false heart, of Helen of
Troy. Supposedly, Helen's abduction by Paris from
her husband, Menelaus, was the event that precipitated the Trojan War. In some accounts, Helen is

blamed for her abduction and so could be said to
have a false heart.
1. Queen of Egypt and the tragic heroine of Shakespeare's *Antony and Cleopatra.*
2. In Greek myth, Atalanta was a fleet-footed and
chaste hunter who challenged her suitors to a race.
She was only defeated when one of them dropped
three golden apples, which she stopped to pick up.
The reference here is possibly to her beauty or her
speed, rather than her greed.
3. Lucretia killed herself to save her honor after
being raped by Tarquin (a story told by Shakespeare
in *The Rape of Lucrece*).
4. *though . . . scrippage:* though not with the belongings retained by an army in retreat, yet with a shepherd's pouch and its contents.

Exeunt [CLOWN *and* CORIN].

150 CELIA Didst thou hear these verses?

ROSALIND Oh, yes, I heard them all and more too, for some of
them had in them more feet° than the verses would bear. · · · · · · · · · · *metrical units*

CELIA That's no matter; the feet might bear° the verses. · · · · · · · · · · · · · *carry*

ROSALIND Ay, but the feet were lame and could not bear
155 themselves without° the verse, and therefore stood lamely in · · · · · · · · *out of*
the verse.

CELIA But didst thou hear without wondering how thy name
should be° hanged and carved upon these trees? · · · · · · · · · · · · · *came to be*

ROSALIND I was seven of the nine days out of the wonder⁵
160 before you came; for look here what I found on a palm tree.
I was never so be-rhymed since Pythagoras' time that I was
an Irish rat,⁶ which I can hardly remember.

CELIA Trow you° who hath done this? · *Can you imagine*

ROSALIND Is it a man?

165 CELIA And a chain, that you once wore, about his neck.
Change you color?

ROSALIND I prithee, who?

CELIA O Lord, Lord—it is a hard matter for friends to meet,
but mountains may be removed with° earthquakes and so · · · · · · · · · · *moved by*
170 encounter.

ROSALIND Nay, but who is it?

CELIA Is it possible?

ROSALIND Nay, I prithee now with most petitionary vehe-
mence, tell me who it is.

175 CELIA Oh, wonderful, wonderful, and most wonderful—
wonderful and yet again wonderful, and after that out of all
hooping!⁷

ROSALIND Good my complexion!⁸ Dost thou think though I
am caparisoned° like a man I have a doublet and hose in my · · · · · · · · *dressed*
180 disposition? One inch of delay more is a South Sea of dis-
covery.⁹ I prithee, tell me who is it quickly, and speak apace.° · · · · · · · *quickly*
I would thou couldst stammer, that thou mightst pour this
concealed man out of thy mouth as wine comes out of a
narrow-mouthed bottle: either too much at once or none at
185 all. I prithee, take the cork out of thy mouth that I may
drink thy tidings.

CELIA So you may put a man in your belly.° · · · · · · · · · · · · · *stomach; womb*

ROSALIND Is he of God's making? What manner of man? Is
his head worth a hat or his chin worth a beard?

190 CELIA Nay, he hath but a little beard.

ROSALIND Why, God will send more if the man will be thank-
ful. Let me stay° the growth of his beard if thou delay me · · · · · · · · · · *wait for*
not the knowledge of his chin.

---

5. Referring to the proverbial "nine days' wonder," a novelty that caused amazement.

6. I was never so overwhelmed with rhyme since the days of the ancient Greeks, when I was an Irish rat. Alluding to Pythagoras's doctrine of the transmigration of souls and to the popular belief in England that Irish bards were capable of rhyming rats to death.

7. After that, beyond what can be contained, with a

pun on "whooping": beyond what all shouts of astonishment can express.

8. An expression of impatience. "Complexion" means "temperament," believed to be caused by the particular mixture of the four humors in one's body. Rosalind's meaning seems to be: Pay attention to my womanly temperament (which is impatient)!

9. More delay will seem as infinite as a voyage of discovery to the South Seas.

CELIA   It is young Orlando, that tripped up the wrestler's
195   heels and your heart both in an instant.
ROSALIND   Nay, but the devil take mocking: speak sad brow
and true maid.[1]
CELIA   I'faith, coz, 'tis he.
ROSALIND   Orlando?
200   CELIA   Orlando!
ROSALIND   Alas the day! What shall I do with my doublet and
hose? What did he when thou saw'st him? What said he?
How looked he? Wherein went he?°   What makes he here?   *What was he wearing?*
Did he ask for me? Where remains he? How parted he with
205   thee? And when shalt thou see him again? Answer me in
one word.
CELIA   You must borrow me Gargantua's[2] mouth first: 'tis a
word too great for any mouth of this age's size. To say ay
and no to these particulars is more than to answer in a
210   catechism.[3]
ROSALIND   But doth he know that I am in this forest and in
man's apparel? Looks he as freshly as he did the day he
wrestled?
CELIA   It is as easy to count atomies° as to resolve the proposi-   *specks (of dust)*
215   tions[4] of a lover. But take a taste of my finding him and relish
it with good observance:[5] I found him under a tree, like a
dropped acorn—
ROSALIND   It may well be called Jove's tree,[6] when it drops
forth fruit.
220   CELIA   Give me audience, good madam.
ROSALIND   Proceed.
CELIA   There lay he, stretched along like a wounded knight—
ROSALIND   Though it be pity to see such a sight, it well
becomes the ground.
225   CELIA   Cry "holla"° to the tongue, I prithee; it curvets° unsea-   *hold / leaps about*
sonably. He was furnished° like a hunter—   *dressed*
ROSALIND   Oh, ominous: he comes to kill my heart![7]
CELIA   I would sing my song without a burden.° Thou bring'st   *refrain*
me out of tune.
230   ROSALIND   Do you not know I am a woman? When I think I
must speak. Sweet, say on.
Enter ORLANDO *and* JAQUES.
CELIA   You bring me out.° Soft, comes he not here?   *make me lose the tune*
ROSALIND   'Tis he! Slink by and note him.
JAQUES   I thank you for your company, but good faith, I had as
235   lief° have been myself alone.   *as willingly*
ORLANDO   And so had I; but yet, for fashion sake, I thank you
too for your society.
JAQUES   God b'wi' you,° let's meet as little as we can.   *Good-bye*

---

1. Speak seriously and as a virtuous woman or on
your honor as a virgin.
2. A voracious giant famous in French folklore and
from the writings of Rabelais.
3. A summary, in question-and-answer form, of
basic tenets of religious doctrine. In Shakespeare's
time, all members of the Church of England learned
to recite such a catechism.
4. *resolve the propositions:* answer the questions.

5. And enhance its flavor by paying careful
attention.
6. The oak was traditionally viewed as sacred to
Jove, the god of thunder, and was said therefore to be
often struck by lightning.
7. TEXTUAL COMMENT F reads "Hart" (a male deer).
In the forest scenes, the pursuit of love (seeking
hearts) is often compared to the hunting of deer. See
Digital Edition TC 6.

ORLANDO   I do desire we may be better strangers.

240 JAQUES   I pray you, mar no more trees with writing love songs
in their barks.

ORLANDO   I pray you, mar no more of my verses with reading
them ill-favoredly.°   *unsympathetically*

JAQUES   Rosalind is your love's name?

245 ORLANDO   Yes, just.

JAQUES   I do not like her name.

ORLANDO   There was no thought of pleasing you when she
was christened.

JAQUES   What stature is she of?

250 ORLANDO   Just as high as my heart.

JAQUES   You are full of pretty answers. Have you not been
acquainted with goldsmiths' wives and conned them out of
rings?[8]

ORLANDO   Not so. But I answer you right painted cloth,[9] from
255 whence you have studied your questions.

JAQUES   You have a nimble wit: I think 'twas made of Atalanta's
heels.[1] Will you sit down with me, and we two will rail
against our mistress, the world, and all our misery?

ORLANDO   I will chide no breather° in the world but myself,   *person*
260 against whom I know most faults.

JAQUES   The worst fault you have is to be in love.

ORLANDO   'Tis a fault I will not change for your best virtue. I
am weary of you.

JAQUES   By my troth, I was seeking for a fool when I found
265 you.

ORLANDO   He is drowned in the brook. Look but in and you
shall see him.

JAQUES   There I shall see mine own figure.

ORLANDO   Which I take to be either a fool or a cipher.[2]

270 JAQUES   I'll tarry no longer with you. Farewell, good Signor
Love.

ORLANDO   I am glad of your departure. Adieu, good Monsieur
Melancholy.   [*Exit* JAQUES.][3]

ROSALIND   I will speak to him like a saucy lackey,° and under   *insolent servant*
275 that habit° play the knave with him. —Do you hear, forester?   *guise; disguise*

ORLANDO   Very well. What would you?

ROSALIND   I pray you, what is't o'clock?

ORLANDO   You should ask me what time o'day. There's no
clock in the forest.

280 ROSALIND   Then there is no true lover in the forest, else sighing every minute and groaning every hour would detect° the   *reveal*
lazy foot of time as well as a clock.

ORLANDO   And why not the swift foot of time? Had not that
been as proper?

---

8. Romantic verses were often inscribed on rings
sold in shops managed by the wives of goldsmiths;
with a pun on "rings" as a slang term for "vaginas."

9. I answer you in the style of the pithy sayings issuing from the mouths of figures in painted wall hangings (a popular and inexpensive form of interior
decoration).

1. See note to 3.2.135.

2. A zero; punning on "figure" (line 268) as meaning
"numeral."

3. Editors usually give Jaques an exit here, although
none is indicated in F. It would not be out of character, however, for Jaques to remain onstage in the
background during Orlando and Rosalind's exchange
(as he does during Touchstone's courting of Audrey
in 3.3) and to exit with them at the end of the scene.

285 ROSALIND By no means, sir. Time travels in divers paces with
divers persons. I'll tell you who Time ambles withal,° who   *with*
Time trots withal, who Time gallops withal, and who he
stands still withal.

ORLANDO I prithee, who doth he trot withal?

290 ROSALIND Marry, he trots hard° with a young maid between   *uncomfortably*
the contract of her marriage and the day it is solemnized. If
the interim be but a se'nnight,° Time's pace is so hard that it   *week*
seems the length of seven year.

ORLANDO Who ambles Time withal?

295 ROSALIND With a priest that lacks Latin and a rich man that
hath not the gout: for the one sleeps easily because he cannot study, and the other lives merrily because he feels no
pain—the one lacking the burden of lean and wasteful°   *illness-inducing*
learning, the other knowing no burden of heavy tedious
300 penury.° These Time ambles withal.   *poverty*

ORLANDO Who doth he gallop withal?

ROSALIND With a thief to the gallows, for though he go as
softly° as foot can fall, he thinks himself too soon there.   *slowly*

ORLANDO Who stays it still withal?

305 ROSALIND With lawyers in the vacation, for they sleep
between term[4] and term and then they perceive not how
Time moves.

ORLANDO Where dwell you, pretty youth?

ROSALIND With this shepherdess, my sister, here in the
310 skirts° of the forest like fringe upon a petticoat.   *edges*

ORLANDO Are you native of this place?

ROSALIND As the coney° that you see dwell where she is   *rabbit*
kindled.°   *born*

ORLANDO Your accent is something finer than you could pur-
315 chase° in so removed° a dwelling.   *acquire / remote*

ROSALIND I have been told so of many. But indeed, an old
religious uncle of mine taught me to speak, who was in his
youth an inland man, one that knew courtship° too well, for   *court life; wooing*
there he fell in love. I have heard him read many lectures
320 against it, and I thank God I am not a woman, to be touched
with so many giddy offenses as he hath generally taxed their
whole sex withal.

ORLANDO Can you remember any of the principal evils that
he laid to the charge of women?

325 ROSALIND There were none principal; they were all like one
another as halfpence are, every one fault seeming monstrous till his fellow-fault came to match it.

ORLANDO I prithee, recount some of them.

ROSALIND No, I will not cast away my physic but° on those   *my medicine except*
330 that are sick. There is a man haunts the forest that abuses
our young plants with carving "Rosalind" on their barks,
hangs odes upon hawthorns and elegies on brambles—all,
forsooth, deifying the name of Rosalind. If I could meet that
fancy-monger,° I would give him some good counsel, for he   *dealer in love*
335 seems to have the quotidian[5] of love upon him.

---

4. *term:* a limited period of time in which the courts
were in session and when lawyers were therefore

busy. Vacation came between terms.
5. Daily recurring fever said to be a sign of love.

ORLANDO   I am he that is so love-shaked. I pray you tell me
your remedy.

ROSALIND   There is none of my uncle's marks upon you. He
taught me how to know a man in love, in which cage of
340   rushes[6] I am sure you are not prisoner.

ORLANDO   What were his marks?

ROSALIND   A lean cheek, which you have not; a blue eye[7] and
sunken, which you have not; an unquestionable° spirit, which   *a taciturn*
you have not; a beard neglected, which you have not—but
345   I pardon you for that, for simply your having in beard° is   *such beard as you have*
a younger brother's revenue.[8] Then your hose should be
ungartered, your bonnet unbanded,° your sleeve unbut-   *lacking a band*
toned, your shoe untied, and everything about you demonstrating a careless desolation. But you are no such man; you
350   are rather point-device° in your accoutrements, as loving   *extremely precise*
yourself than seeming the lover of any other.

ORLANDO   Fair youth, I would I could make thee believe I love.

ROSALIND   Me believe it? You may as soon make her that you
love believe it, which I warrant she is apter to do than to
355   confess she does: that is one of the points in the which
women still° give the lie to their consciences. But in good   *always*
sooth,° are you he that hangs the verses on the trees,   *truth*
wherein Rosalind is so admired?

ORLANDO   I swear to thee, youth, by the white hand of Rosa-
360   lind, I am that he—that unfortunate he.

ROSALIND   But are you so much in love as your rhymes speak?

ORLANDO   Neither rhyme nor reason can express how much.

ROSALIND   Love is merely a madness and, I tell you, deserves
as well a dark house and a whip as madmen do;[9] and the
365   reason why they° are not so punished and cured is that the   *(lovers)*
lunacy is so ordinary that the whippers are in love too. Yet I
profess curing it by counsel.

ORLANDO   Did you ever cure any so?

ROSALIND   Yes, one—and in this manner: he was to imagine
370   me his love, his mistress, and I set him every day to woo me.
At which time would I, being but a moonish° youth, grieve,   *changeable*
be effeminate,[1] changeable, longing and liking, proud, fan-
tastical,° apish,° shallow, inconstant, full of tears, full of   *capricious / affected*
smiles; for every passion something and for no passion truly
375   anything, as boys and women are for the most part cattle of
this color; would now like him, now loathe him, then enter-
tain him,° then forswear him, now weep for him, then spit   *treat him kindly*
at him; that I drave° my suitor from his mad humor of love   *drove*
to a living humor° of madness, which was to forswear the   *an actual condition*
380   full stream of the world and to live in a nook merely monastic.°   *as a hermit*
And thus I cured him, and this way will I take upon me to
wash your liver[2] as clean as a sound sheep's heart, that there
shall not be one spot of love in't.

---

6. A prison easy to escape from.
7. An eye ringed with dark circles (suggesting
insomnia).
8. Younger brothers traditionally received small
inheritances; here, suggesting that Orlando's beard is
likewise thin or small.
9. Confinement in a dark room and whipping, com-

mon treatments for insanity, were believed to rid the
insane of the devils that possessed them.
1. Like a woman; sensual or self-indulgent; a term
often used to deride men perceived as excessive in
their sexual interest in women.
2. In Renaissance medical theory, the seat of the
passions.

ORLANDO   I would not be cured, youth.

385 ROSALIND   I would cure you if you would but call me Rosalind
and come every day to my cot° and woo me.   *cottage*

ORLANDO   Now, by the faith of my love, I will. Tell me where
it is.

ROSALIND   Go with me to it and I'll show it you, and by the way
390 you shall tell me where in the forest you live. Will you go?

ORLANDO   With all my heart, good youth.

ROSALIND   Nay, you must call me Rosalind. —Come, sister,
will you go?   *Exeunt.*

3.3
Enter CLOWN [*and*] AUDREY; *and* JAQUES [*apart*].

CLOWN   Come apace, good Audrey. I will fetch up your goats,
Audrey. And how, Audrey—am I the man yet? Doth my simple
feature° content you?   *appearance*

AUDREY   Your features! Lord warrant° us, what features?   *defend*

5 CLOWN   I am here with thee and thy goats as the most capri-
cious° poet, honest Ovid, was among the Goths.[1]   *witty; lascivious*

JAQUES [*aside*]   Oh, knowledge ill-inhabited—worse than Jove
in a thatched house![2]

CLOWN   When a man's verses cannot be understood nor a
10 man's good wit seconded with° the forward child under-   *supported by*
standing, it strikes a man more dead than a great reckoning°   *tavern bill*
in a little room.[3] Truly, I would the gods had made thee
poetical.

AUDREY   I do not know what "poetical" is. Is it honest in deed
15 and word? Is it a true thing?

CLOWN   No, truly—for the truest poetry is the most feigning°   *imaginative; false*
and lovers are given to poetry; and what they swear in poetry
may be said, as lovers, they do feign.

AUDREY   Do you wish then that the gods had made me
20 poetical?

CLOWN   I do, truly. For thou swear'st to me thou art honest.°   *chaste*
Now if thou wert a poet I might have some hope thou didst
feign.

AUDREY   Would you not have me honest?

25 CLOWN   No, truly, unless thou wert hard-favored;° for honesty   *ugly*
coupled to beauty is to have honey a sauce to sugar.

JAQUES [*aside*]   A material° fool!   *full of matter or sense*

AUDREY   Well, I am not fair, and therefore I pray the gods
make me honest.

30 CLOWN   Truly, and to cast away honesty upon a foul slut were
to put good meat into an unclean dish.[4]

AUDREY   I am not a slut, though I thank the gods I am foul.[5]

CLOWN   Well, praised be the gods for thy foulness—sluttishness
may come hereafter. But be it as it may be, I will marry thee;

3.3
1. Punning on "goats / Goths," which were similarly
pronounced, and referring to the Roman poet's exile
among the Goths.
2. In *Metamorphoses* 8, Ovid tells how the king of
the gods was given shelter for a time in the humble
dwelling of Philemon and Baucis.
3. These lines have been taken to refer to the death

in 1593 of Christopher Marlowe, a contemporary
playwright, in a quarrel in a tavern over a bill.
4. The term "slut" was used to describe a woman of
dirty or untidy habits and appearance, as well as one
whose character and behavior were considered loose.
5. Ugly. Audrey apparently takes "foul" as a term of
praise.

35   and to that end I have been with Sir Oliver Martext, the
vicar of the next village, who hath promised to meet me in
this place of the forest and to couple us.

JAQUES [*aside*]   I would fain° see this meeting.   *gladly*

AUDREY   Well, the gods give us joy!

40 CLOWN   Amen. A man may, if he were of a fearful heart, stag-
ger° in this attempt: for here we have no temple but the wood,   *hesitate*
no assembly but horn-beasts.[6] But what though? Courage!
As horns are odious, they are necessary. It is said many a
man knows no end of his goods:[7] right—many a man has

45 good horns and knows no end of them. Well, that is the
dowry of his wife: 'tis none of his own getting.[8] Horns? Even
so. Poor men alone? No, no—the noblest deer hath them as
huge as the rascal.° Is the single man therefore blessed? No,   *young or lean deer*
as a walled town is more worthier than a village, so is the

50 forehead of a married man more honorable than the bare
brow of a bachelor. And by how much defense° is better   *skill in self-defense*
than no skill, by so much is a horn more precious than to
want.°   *to lack (one)*

       Enter SIR OLIVER MARTEXT.

Here comes Sir Oliver. —Sir Oliver Martext, you are well
55 met. Will you dispatch us here under this tree, or shall we
go with you to your chapel?

SIR OLIVER   Is there none here to give the woman?

CLOWN   I will not take her on gift of any man.

SIR OLIVER   Truly, she must be given, or the marriage is not
60 lawful.

JAQUES [*coming forward*]   Proceed, proceed. I'll give her.

CLOWN   Good even, good Master What-ye-call't. How do you,
sir? You are very well met. God 'ield you for your last com-
pany.[9] I am very glad to see you. Even a toy° in hand here,   *trifling matter*
65 sir. Nay, pray be covered.°   *replace your hat*

JAQUES   Will you be married, motley?

CLOWN   As the ox hath his bow,° sir, the horse his curb,[1] and   *yoke*
the falcon her bells,[2] so man hath his desires; and as pigeons
bill,° so wedlock would be nibbling.   *rub bill to bill*

70 JAQUES   And will you, being a man of your breeding, be married under a bush like a beggar? Get you to church and have
a good priest that can tell you what marriage is; this fellow
will but join you together as they join wainscot.° Then one   *wood paneling*
of you will prove a shrunk panel and, like green timber,
75 warp,° warp.   *go wrong; shrink*

CLOWN   I am not in the mind but° I were better to be married   *not sure but that*
of° him than of another; for he is not like to marry me well,   *by*
and not being well married it will be a good excuse for me
hereafter to leave my wife.

---

6. Horned beasts such as deer, goats, and the like
that inhabited the forest, with an allusion to the
horns of the cuckolded husband.
7. A proverbial expression suggesting a man so
wealthy he can't count all his money.
8. *'tis . . . getting:* he is not responsible for the horns;
he is not responsible for conceiving his children
(since his wife has been sexually unfaithful).

9. God yield you (a salutation meaning "May God
reward you") for your recent companionship.
1. A bit placed in the horse's mouth to control its
movements.
2. Bells attached to a falcon's legs before releasing
it for the hunt so that it might be easily reclaimed
afterward.

80 JAQUES Go thou with me
And let me counsel thee.
CLOWN Come, sweet Audrey—
We must be married,° or we must live in bawdry.°   *(properly wed) / in sin*
Farewell, good Master Oliver—not
85   "O sweet Oliver,
O brave Oliver,
Leave me not behind thee!"[3]
but
Wind° away,   *Go*
90   Begone I say.
I will not to wedding with thee.
SIR OLIVER 'Tis no matter. Ne'er a fantastical knave of them
all shall flout me out of my calling.   *Exeunt.*

3.4

Enter ROSALIND [*as Ganymede*] *and* CELIA [*as Aliena*].
ROSALIND Never talk to me—I will weep!
CELIA Do, I prithee, but yet have the grace to consider that
tears do not become a man.
ROSALIND But have I not cause to weep?
5 CELIA As good cause as one would desire; therefore, weep.
ROSALIND His very hair is of the dissembling color.[1]
CELIA Something° browner than Judas's; marry, his kisses are   *Somewhat*
Judas's own children.
ROSALIND I'faith, his hair is of a good color.
10 CELIA An excellent color: your chestnut was ever the only
color.
ROSALIND And his kissing is as full of sanctity as the touch of
holy bread.[2]
CELIA He hath bought a pair of cast° lips of Diana.[3] A nun of   *cast-off; sculpted*
15 winter's sisterhood° kisses not more religiously: the very ice   *devoted to coldness*
of chastity is in them.
ROSALIND But why did he swear he would come this morning
and comes not?
CELIA Nay, certainly there is no truth in him.
20 ROSALIND Do you think so?
CELIA Yes, I think he is not a pickpurse nor a horse-stealer,
but for his verity° in love—I do think him as concave° as a   *truthfulness / hollow*
covered goblet or a worm-eaten nut.
ROSALIND Not true in love?
25 CELIA Yes, when he is in, but I think he is not in.
ROSALIND You have heard him swear downright he was.
CELIA Was is not is. Besides, the oath of lover is no stronger
than the word of a tapster:° they are both the confirmer of   *tavern-keeper*
false reckonings. He attends° here in the forest on the Duke   *waits*
30 your father.
ROSALIND I met the Duke yesterday and had much question°   *conversation*
with him. He asked me of what parentage I was; I told him

---

3. Lines from a popular Elizabethan ballad.
3.4
1. Alluding to the tradition that Judas, the disciple
who betrayed Jesus, had red hair.

2. Referring to bread blessed after the Eucharist
during Christian religious services and distributed to
those who did not take Communion.
3. The goddess of chastity. See note to 3.2.2.

of as good as he, so he laughed and let me go. But what talk
we of fathers when there is such a man as Orlando?

35 CELIA   Oh, that's a brave° man: he writes brave verses, speaks   *splendid*
brave words, swears brave oaths, and breaks them bravely—
quite traverse,[4] athwart the heart of his lover, as a puny°   *an unskilled*
tilter that spurs his horse but° on one side breaks his staff   *only*
like a noble goose.° But all's brave that youth mounts and   *fool*
40 folly guides. Who comes here?

        Enter CORIN.

CORIN   Mistress and master, you have oft enquired
After the shepherd that complained of love,
Who you saw sitting by me on the turf,
Praising the proud disdainful shepherdess
That was his mistress.
45 CELIA   Well, and what of him?
CORIN   If you will see a pageant truly played
Between the pale complexion of true love
And the red glow of scorn and proud disdain,[5]
Go hence a little and I shall conduct you,
If you will mark° it.   *observe*
50 ROSALIND   Oh, come, let us remove.
The sight of lovers feedeth those in love.
Bring us to this sight and you shall say
I'll prove a busy actor in their play.   *Exeunt.*

3.5
        Enter SILVIUS *and* PHOEBE.
SILVIUS   Sweet Phoebe, do not scorn me; do not, Phoebe.
Say that you love me not, but say not so
In bitterness. The common executioner,
Whose heart th'accustomed sight of death makes hard,
5 Falls not° the ax upon the humbled neck   *Does not let fall*
But first begs° pardon. Will you sterner be   *Without first begging*
Than he that dies and lives by bloody drops?
        Enter ROSALIND [*as Ganymede*], CELIA [*as Aliena*],
        and CORIN.
PHOEBE   I would not be thy executioner.
I fly thee, for I would not injure thee.
10 Thou tell'st me there is murder in mine eye.
'Tis pretty, sure, and very probable
That eyes, that are the frail'st and softest things,
Who shut their coward gates on atomies,°   *dust motes*
Should be called tyrants, butchers, murderers.
15 Now I do frown on thee with all my heart,
And if mine eyes can wound, now let them kill thee.
Now counterfeit to swoon; why now, fall down;
Or if thou canst not, oh, for shame, for shame,
Lie not to say mine eyes are murderers!
20 Now show the wound mine eye hath made in thee.
Scratch thee but with a pin and there remains
Some scar of it; lean upon a rush,

---

4. Crossways. The term from jousting was used to
designate the dishonorable practice of breaking one's
lance across, rather than directly against, an opponent's shield.

5. Referring to the paleness of Silvius, the true lover,
and the red cheeks of the disdainful Phoebe.

The cicatrice and capable impressure[1]
Thy palm some moment keeps. But now mine eyes,
25   Which I have darted at thee, hurt thee not;
Nor, I am sure, there is no force in eyes
That can do hurt.

SILVIUS   O dear Phoebe,
If ever—as that ever may be near—
You meet in some fresh cheek the power of fancy,°   *love*
30   Then shall you know the wounds invisible
That love's keen arrows make.

PHOEBE   But till that time
Come not thou near me. And when that time comes,
Afflict me with thy mocks; pity me not,
As till that time I shall not pity thee.

35   ROSALIND   And why, I pray you? Who might be your mother
That you insult, exult, and all at once°   *all in one breath*
Over the wretched? What though you have no beauty—
As, by my faith, I see no more in you
Than without candle may go dark to bed[2]—
40   Must you be therefore proud and pitiless?
Why, what means this? Why do you look on me?
I see no more in you than in the ordinary°   *common run*
Of nature's sale-work.° —'Ods my little life,[3]   *ready-made goods*
I think she means to tangle° my eyes too!   *entrap*
45   —No, faith, proud mistress, hope not after it;
'Tis not your inky brows, your black silk hair,
Your bugle° eyeballs, nor your cheek of cream   *like black glass beads*
That can entame my spirits to your worship.°   *the worship of you*
—You foolish shepherd, wherefore do you follow her
50   Like foggy south,° puffing with wind and rain?[4]   *south wind*
You are a thousand times a properer° man   *more attractive*
Than she a woman. 'Tis such fools as you
That makes the world full of ill-favored° children.   *ugly*
'Tis not her glass° but you that flatters her,   *mirror*
55   And out of you° she sees herself more proper   *from you (as mirror)*
Than any of her lineaments can show her.
—But mistress, know yourself: down on your knees
And thank heaven, fasting, for a good man's love.
For I must tell you friendly in your ear,
60   Sell when you can; you are not for all markets.
Cry the man mercy,° love him, take his offer.   *Beg his pardon*
Foul is most foul, being foul, to be a scoffer.[5]
—So take her to thee, shepherd. Fare you well.

PHOEBE   Sweet youth, I pray you, chide a year together.°   *without interruption*
65   I had rather hear you chide than this man woo.

ROSALIND   He's fallen in love with your foulness [*to* SILVIUS]
and she'll fall in love with my anger. If it be so, as fast as she
answers thee with frowning looks, I'll sauce° her with bitter   *sharply rebuke*
words. [*to* PHOEBE] Why look you so upon me?

70   PHOEBE   For no ill will I bear you.

3.5
1. The scarlike mark and the impression that the
skin receives.
2. *I see . . . bed:* I see you have not enough beauty to
light your way to bed without a candle.

3. An abbreviated version of the oath "God save my
life."
4. That is, with sighs and tears.
5. The ugly seem most ugly when they are abusive.

ROSALIND I pray you, do not fall in love with me,
For I am falser than vows made in wine.°   *when drinking*
Besides, I like you not. If you will know my house,
'Tis at the tuft of olives,° here hard by.   *olive trees*
75 Will you go, sister? Shepherd, ply her hard.°   *assail her vigorously*
Come, sister. —Shepherdess, look on him better
And be not proud: though all the world could see
None could be so abused in sight as he.
—Come, to our flock.

Exeunt [ROSALIND, CELIA, *and* CORIN].[6]

80 PHOEBE Dead shepherd,[7] now I find thy saw of might:°   *your saying powerful*
"Who ever loved that loved not at first sight?"
SILVIUS Sweet Phoebe—
PHOEBE   Ha? What say'st thou, Silvius?
SILVIUS Sweet Phoebe, pity me.
PHOEBE Why, I am sorry for thee, gentle Silvius.
85 SILVIUS Wherever sorrow is, relief would be.
If you do sorrow at my grief in love,
By giving love your sorrow and my grief
Were both extermined.°   *Would both be ended*
PHOEBE Thou hast my love—is not that neighborly?[8]
SILVIUS I would have you.
90 PHOEBE   Why, that were covetousness.[9]
Silvius, the time was that I hated thee,
And yet it is not° that I bear thee love.   *it has not yet happened*
But since that thou canst talk of love so well,
Thy company, which erst° was irksome to me,   *formerly*
95 I will endure, and I'll employ thee too.
But do not look for further recompense
Than thine own gladness that thou art employed.
SILVIUS So holy and so perfect is my love,
And I in such a poverty of grace,[1]
100 That I shall think it a most plenteous crop
To glean the broken ears° after the man   *(of corn)*
That the main harvest reaps. Loose now and then
A scattered° smile, and that I'll live upon.   *stray*
PHOEBE Know'st thou the youth that spoke to me erewhile?
105 SILVIUS Not very well, but I have met him oft,
And he hath bought the cottage and the bounds°   *pastures*
That the old Carlot once was master of.
PHOEBE Think not I love him though I ask for him.
'Tis but a peevish boy, yet he talks well.
110 But what care I for words? Yet words do well
When he that speaks them pleases those that hear.
It is a pretty youth—not very pretty—
But sure, he's proud, and yet his pride becomes him.
He'll make a proper° man. The best thing in him   *handsome*
115 Is his complexion; and faster than his tongue

6. F marks a single exit for Rosalind here, but it is
unlikely that Celia and Corin remain.
7. Referring to Christopher Marlowe, poet and playwright who died in 1593. Line 81 is taken from his
poem *Hero and Leander*.
8. With a reference to Romans 13:9: "Thou shalt love
thy neighbor as thyself."

9. With a reference to Exodus 20:17: "Thou shalt not
covet thy neighbor's house, thou shalt not covet thy
neighbor's wife, nor his manservant, nor his maid
servant, nor his ox, nor his ass, nor any thing that is
thy neighbor's."
1. And I so lacking in (your) favor.

Did make offense, his eye did heal it up.
He is not very tall, yet for his years he's tall.
His leg is but so-so, and yet 'tis well.
There was a pretty redness in his lip—
120 A little riper and more lusty red
Than that mixed in his cheek; 'twas just the difference
Betwixt the constant red and mingled damask.[2]
There be some women, Silvius, had they marked him
In parcels° as I did, would have gone near   *Item by item*
125 To fall in love with him. But for my part,
I love him not, nor hate him not, and yet
Have more cause to hate him than to love him.
For what had he to do to chide at me?
He said mine eyes were black and my hair black
130 And, now I am remembered, scorned at me.
I marvel why I answered not again.
But that's all one; omittance is no quittance.[3]
I'll write to him a very taunting letter,
And thou shalt bear it. Wilt thou, Silvius?
SILVIUS Phoebe, with all my heart.
135 PHOEBE   I'll write it straight.°   *immediately*
The matter's in my head and in my heart.
I will be bitter with him and passing° short.   *extremely*
Go with me, Silvius.   *Exeunt.*

4.1

Enter ROSALIND [*as Ganymede*], CELIA [*as Aliena*],
       and JAQUES.

JAQUES I prithee, pretty youth, let me be better acquainted
   with thee.
ROSALIND They say you are a melancholy fellow.
JAQUES I am so: I do love it better than laughing.
5 ROSALIND Those that are in extremity of either are abominable fellows and betray themselves to every modern censure
   worse than drunkards.
JAQUES Why, 'tis good to be sad° and say nothing.   *serious*
ROSALIND Why, then 'tis good to be a post.
10 JAQUES I have neither the scholar's melancholy, which is
   emulation;° nor the musician's, which is fantastical;° nor the   *envy / overly fanciful*
   courtier's, which is proud; nor the soldier's, which is ambi-
   tious; nor the lawyer's, which is politic; nor the lady's, which
   is nice;° nor the lover's, which is all these; but it is a melan-   *fastidious*
15 choly of mine own, compounded of many simples,° extracted   *ingredients*
   from many objects,° and indeed the sundry contemplation   *sights*
   of my travels,[1] in° which by often° rumination wraps me in a   *upon / frequent*
   most humorous° sadness.   *moody*
ROSALIND A traveler? By my faith, you have great reason to
20   be sad! I fear you have sold your own lands to see other
   men's; then to have seen much and to have nothing is to
   have rich eyes and poor hands.

---

2. *constant . . . damask:* uniform red and a mixture
of red and white characteristic of certain kinds of
roses.
3. A proverbial expression meaning that a debt is not

canceled simply because one fails ("omits") to exact it.
4.1
1. The various thoughts arising during my travels,
with a pun on "travails," meaning "labors."

JAQUES   Yes, I have gained my experience.
          Enter ORLANDO.
ROSALIND   And your experience makes you sad. I had rather
25   have a fool to make me merry than experience to make me
     sad—and to travel for it too!
ORLANDO   Good day and happiness, dear Rosalind.
JAQUES   Nay then, God b'wi' you an° you talk in blank verse.   *if*
ROSALIND   Farewell, Monsieur Traveler. Look you lisp² and
30   wear strange° suits, disable° all the benefits of your own   *foreign / disparage*
     country, be out of love with your nativity,° and almost chide   *birthplace*
     God for making you that countenance you are; or I will scarce
     think you have swum in a gundello.³   [*Exit* JAQUES.]⁴
     Why, how now, Orlando, where have you been all this while?
35   You, a lover? An you serve me such another trick, never
     come in my sight more.
ORLANDO   My fair Rosalind, I come within an hour of my
     promise.
ROSALIND   Break an hour's promise in love? He that will
40   divide a minute into a thousand parts and break but a part
     of the thousand part of a minute in the affairs of love, it may
     be said of him that Cupid hath clapped him o'th' shoulder,
     but I'll warrant him heart-whole.⁵
ORLANDO   Pardon me, dear Rosalind.
45   ROSALIND   Nay, an you be so tardy, come no more in my sight.
     I had as lief° be wooed of a snail.   *as gladly*
ORLANDO   Of a snail?
ROSALIND   Ay, of a snail: for though he comes slowly, he car-
     ries his house on his head—a better jointure,° I think, than   *marriage settlement*
50   you make a woman. Besides, he brings his destiny with him.
ORLANDO   What's that?
ROSALIND   Why, horns, which such as you are fain to be
     beholden to your wives for.⁶ But he comes armed in his for-
     tune⁷ and prevents the slander of his wife.
55   ORLANDO   Virtue is no horn-maker, and my Rosalind is
     virtuous.
ROSALIND   And I am your Rosalind.
CELIA   It pleases him to call you so. But he hath a Rosalind of
     a better leer° than you.   *more attractive*
60   ROSALIND   Come—woo me, woo me, for now I am in a holiday
     humor and like enough to consent. What would you say to
     me now an I were your very, very Rosalind?
ORLANDO   I would kiss before I spoke.
ROSALIND   Nay, you were better speak first, and when you
65   were graveled° for lack of matter, you might take occasion to   *at a loss*
     kiss. Very good orators, when they are out,° they will spit;   *speechless*
     and for lovers lacking (God warn° us) matter, the cleanliest   *defend*
     shift° is to kiss.   *cleverest device*
ORLANDO   How if the kiss be denied?

---

2. Speak with an affected (foreign) accent.
3. TEXTUAL COMMENT Ridden in a gondola—that is, seen Venice, a popular destination for English travelers. See Digital Edition TC 7.
4. F marks no exit for Jaques here, but he and Rosalind have formally parted, and Jaques enters with a new group of characters at the beginning of 4.2.
5. Cupid has tapped him (as in an arrest) or wounded him (with his arrow), but I'll guarantee he left his heart intact.
6. An allusion to the cuckold's horns.
7. Equipped with the insignia of his destined future.

70 ROSALIND Then she puts you to entreaty, and there begins
new matter.
ORLANDO Who could be out, being before his beloved mistress?
ROSALIND Marry, that should you if I were your mistress, or I
should think my honesty ranker than my wit.[8]
75 ORLANDO What, of my suit?[9]
ROSALIND Not out of your apparel, and yet out of your suit.
Am not I your Rosalind?
ORLANDO I take some joy to say you are because I would be
talking of her.
80 ROSALIND Well, in her person, I say I will not have you.
ORLANDO Then in mine own person, I die.
ROSALIND No, faith, die by attorney.° The poor world is   *proxy*
almost six thousand years old,[1] and in all this time there was
not any man died in his own person, *videlicet*° in a love   *namely*
85 cause. Troilus[2] had his brains dashed out with a Grecian
club; yet he did what he could to die before, and he is one of
the patterns of love. Leander,[3] he would have lived many a
fair year though Hero had turned nun, if it had not been for
a hot midsummer night; for, good youth, he went but forth
90 to wash him in the Hellespont and, being taken with the
cramp, was drowned, and the foolish chroniclers of that age
found° it was Hero of Sestos. But these are all lies: men   *claimed*
have died from time to time, and worms have eaten them,
but not for love.
95 ORLANDO I would not have my right° Rosalind of this mind,   *true*
for I protest her frown might kill me.
ROSALIND By this hand, it will not kill a fly. But come—now
I will be your Rosalind in a more coming-on° disposition,   *agreeable*
and ask me what you will, I will grant it.
100 ORLANDO Then love me, Rosalind.
ROSALIND Yes, faith, will I—Fridays and Saturdays and all.
ORLANDO And wilt thou have me?
ROSALIND Ay, and twenty such.
ORLANDO What sayest thou?
105 ROSALIND Are you not good?
ORLANDO I hope so.
ROSALIND Why, then, can one desire too much of a good thing?
—Come, sister, you shall be the priest and marry us.
—Give me your hand, Orlando. What do you say, sister?
110 ORLANDO Pray thee, marry us.
CELIA I cannot say the words.
ROSALIND You must begin, "Will you, Orlando,"—
CELIA Go to![4] Will you, Orlando, have to wife this Rosalind?
ORLANDO I will.
115 ROSALIND Ay, but when?
ORLANDO Why now, as fast as she can marry us.

8. I would think my chastity was fouler than my intelligence; with a pun on "out" (lines 66, 72) as meaning "not permitted sexual entrance."
9. My petition. Orlando asks if he will be at a loss for words ("out") in furthering his courtship ("suit"). Rosalind puns on "suit" as meaning "clothing."
1. Elizabethan divines generally dated the world's creation somewhere around 4000 B.C.E.
2. The forsaken Trojan lover of Cressida, killed by the Greek warrior Achilles.
3. In Greek mythology, the lover of Hero; he swam the Hellespont nightly to visit her and was drowned.
4. An expression of mild impatience.

ROSALIND Then you must say, "I take thee, Rosalind, for wife."

ORLANDO I take thee, Rosalind, for wife.[5]

120 ROSALIND I might ask you for your commission,° but I do take | authority
thee, Orlando, for my husband. There's a girl goes before° | who anticipates
the priest, and certainly a woman's thought runs before her
actions.

ORLANDO So do all thoughts: they are winged.

ROSALIND Now tell me how long you would have her after
125 you have possessed her.

ORLANDO Forever and a day.

ROSALIND Say "a day" without the "ever." No, no, Orlando: men
are April when they woo, December when they wed; maids are
May when they are maids, but the sky changes when they are
130 wives. I will be more jealous of thee than a Barbary cock-
pigeon[6] over his hen, more clamorous than a parrot against° | in expectation of
rain, more newfangled° than an ape, more giddy in my desires | in love with novelty
than a monkey. I will weep for nothing, like Diana in the
fountain,[7] and I will do that when you are disposed to be
135 merry. I will laugh like a hyen,° and that when thou art | hyena
inclined to sleep.

ORLANDO But will my Rosalind do so?

ROSALIND By my life, she will do as I do.

ORLANDO Oh, but she is wise.

140 ROSALIND Or else she could not have the wit to do this: the
wiser the waywarder. Make° the doors upon a woman's wit | Close
and it will out at the casement;° shut that and 'twill out at | window frame
the keyhole; stop that, 'twill fly with the smoke out at the
chimney.

145 ORLANDO A man that had a wife with such a wit, he might
say, "Wit, whither wilt?"[8]

ROSALIND Nay, you might keep that check° for it, till you met | rebuke
your wife's wit going to your neighbor's bed.

ORLANDO And what wit could wit have to excuse that?

150 ROSALIND Marry, to say she came to seek you there. You shall
never take her without her answer unless you take her without her tongue. Oh, that woman that cannot make her fault
her husband's occasion,[9] let her never nurse her child herself, for she will breed it like a fool.

155 ORLANDO For these two hours, Rosalind, I will leave thee.

ROSALIND Alas, dear love, I cannot lack thee two hours!

ORLANDO I must attend the Duke at dinner. By two o'clock I
will be with thee again.

ROSALIND Ay, go your ways, go your ways! I knew what you
160 would prove:° my friends told me as much, and I thought no | turn out to be
less. That flattering tongue of yours won me. 'Tis but one
cast away° and so, come, death! Two o'clock is your hour? | one lover jilted

ORLANDO Ay, sweet Rosalind.

---

5. PERFORMANCE COMMENT Some directors have
Orlando and Rosalind kiss here to seal their compact. Many productions suggest either that Orlando
recognizes Rosalind or that he experiences a same-sex
attraction to Ganymede. See Digital Edition PC 2.
6. An ornamental bird, traditionally an emblem of
jealousy. It was introduced into Europe from Asia by
Turks, whom Elizabethans associated with North
Africa's Barbary Coast. Turkish husbands were imagined by the English to be excessively vigilant about
the sexual fidelity of their wives.
7. Referring to the figures of the goddess Diana used
as centerpieces for ornamental fountains in London
and elsewhere.
8. Wit, where would you go? A catchphrase
addressed to one who talks too much.
9. Who cannot make her error a means of putting
her husband in the wrong.

ROSALIND By my troth, and in good earnest, and so God
mend me, and by all pretty oaths that are not dangerous—if
you break one jot of your promise or come one minute
behind your hour, I will think you the most pathetical°
break-promise, and the most hollow lover, and the most
unworthy of her you call Rosalind that may be chosen out of
the gross° band of the unfaithful. Therefore beware my censure and keep your promise!

ORLANDO With no less religion° than if thou wert indeed my
Rosalind. So, adieu.

ROSALIND Well, Time is the old justice that examines all such
offenders, and let Time try.° Adieu. *Exit* [ORLANDO].

CELIA You have simply misused° our sex in your love-prate: we
must have your doublet and hose plucked over your head and
show the world what the bird hath done to her own nest.

ROSALIND O coz, coz, coz, my pretty little coz, that thou didst
know how many fathom deep I am in love! But it cannot be
sounded: my affection hath an unknown bottom, like the
Bay of Portugal.

CELIA Or rather bottomless, that° as fast as you pour affection in, it runs out.

ROSALIND No, that same wicked bastard of Venus¹ that was
begot of thought, conceived of spleen,° and born of
madness—that blind rascally boy that abuses° everyone's
eyes because his own are out—let him be judge how deep I
am in love. I'll tell thee, Aliena, I cannot be out of the sight
of Orlando. I'll go find a shadow° and sigh till he come.

CELIA And I'll sleep. *Exeunt.*

Margin glosses:
- *pathetic* (line 167)
- *entire* (line 170)
- *faith* (line 172)
- *determine* (line 175)
- *completely slandered* (line 176)
- *so that* (line 183)
- *caprice* (line 186)
- *deceives* (line 187)
- *shady place* (line 190)

4.2

Enter JAQUES *and* LORDS [*dressed as*] *foresters.*¹

JAQUES Which is he that killed the deer?

FIRST LORD Sir, it was I.

JAQUES Let's present him to the Duke like a Roman conqueror.
And it would do well to set the deer's horns upon his head for
a branch° of victory. Have you no song, forester, for this
purpose?

SECOND LORD Yes, sir.

JAQUES Sing it. 'Tis no matter how it be in tune, so it make
noise enough.

Music. Song.

SECOND LORD [*sings*]² What shall he have that killed the deer?
His leather skin and horns to wear.
Then sing him home. The rest shall bear°
This burden:°
Take thou no scorn° to wear the horn.
It was a crest³ e'er thou wast born.
Thy father's father wore it,
And thy father bore it.

Margin glosses:
- *wreath* (line 5)
- *carry; sing* (line 12)
- *(the deer); refrain* (line 13)
- *Do not disdain* (line 14)

1. Cupid, the son of Venus by her lover Mercury, not
by her husband, Vulcan.
4.2
1. F's stage direction—"*Enter Jaques and Lords,
Foresters*"—leaves ambiguous whether Jaques and
the lords are dressed as foresters or are accompanied
by them.
2. F does not assign this song to anyone. The stage
direction reads: "*Music, Song.*"
3. A coat of arms; a head ornament.

> The horn, the horn, the lusty horn
> Is not a thing to laugh to scorn.

Exeunt.

4.3

Enter ROSALIND *[as Ganymede] and* CELIA *[as Aliena].*

ROSALIND   How say you now, is it not past two o'clock? And
here much Orlando!

CELIA   I warrant you, with pure love and troubled brain, he
hath ta'en his bow and arrows and is gone forth to sleep.

Enter SILVIUS *[with a letter].*

5   Look who comes here.

SILVIUS   My errand is to you, fair youth.
My gentle Phoebe did bid me give you this.
I know not the contents, but as I guess
By the stern brow and waspish action

10   Which she did use as she was writing of it,
It bears an angry tenor. Pardon me.
I am but as a guiltless messenger.

ROSALIND *[reads]*   Patience herself would startle at this letter
And play the swaggerer.[1] Bear this, bear all!

15   She says I am not fair, that I lack manners;
She calls me proud and that she could not love me,
Were man as rare as phoenix.[2] 'Od's° my will,   *God's*
Her love is not the hare that I do hunt!
Why writes she so to me? Well, shepherd, well—

20   This is a letter of your own device.

SILVIUS   No, I protest I know not the contents.
Phoebe did write it.

ROSALIND   Come, come—you are a fool
And turned° into the extremity of love.   *brought*
I saw her hand. She has a leathern hand,

25   A freestone°-colored hand. I verily did think   *yellow-brown limestone*
That her old gloves were on, but 'twas her hands.
She has a housewife's hand. But that's no matter.
I say she never did invent this letter;
This is a man's invention and his hand.

30 SILVIUS   Sure, it is hers.

ROSALIND   Why, 'tis a boisterous and a cruel style—
A style for challengers. Why, she defies me
Like Turk to Christian.[3] Women's gentle brain
Could not drop forth such giant rude invention,

35   Such Ethiope[4] words, blacker in their effect
Than in their countenance! Will you hear the letter?

SILVIUS   So please you, for I never heard it yet—
Yet heard too much of Phoebe's cruelty.

ROSALIND   She "Phoebes" me.[5] Mark how the tyrant writes:

4.3
1. *Patience . . . swaggerer*: even patience would be
surprised by the contents of this letter and respond
with defiance.
2. A legendary bird of Arabia, supposedly unique,
which lived five hundred years, died in flames, and
was reborn from its own ashes.
3. Alluding to medieval plays in which Turks and

Christians appeared as bitter enemies or to a common Elizabethan perception of the Turk as an enemy
to the Christian countries of western Europe.
4. Ethiopian. In Elizabethan racial discourse, the
term signified blackness and evil.
5. She addresses me as Phoebe would—that is, in a
disdainful manner.

40 (*Reads.*) "Art thou god to shepherd turned,
That a maiden's heart hath burned?"
—Can a woman rail thus?

SILVIUS Call you this railing?

ROSALIND (*reads*) "Why, thy godhead laid apart,°   set aside
45 Warr'st thou with a woman's heart?"
—Did you ever hear such railing?
"Whiles the eye of man did woo me,
That could do no vengeance° to me."   harm
—Meaning me a beast.
50 "If the scorn of your bright eyne°   eyes
Have power to raise such love in mine,
Alack, in me what strange effect
Would they work in mild aspect?°   if they looked kindly
Whiles you chid me I did love:
55 How then might your prayers move?
He that brings this love to thee
Little knows this love in me;
And by him seal up thy mind,[6]
Whether that thy youth and kind°   nature
60 Will the faithful offer take
Of me and all that I can make.°   offer you
Or else by him my love deny,
And then I'll study how to die."

SILVIUS Call you this chiding?

65 CELIA Alas, poor shepherd!

ROSALIND Do you pity him? No, he deserves no pity. —Wilt
thou love such a woman? What, to make thee an instrument
and play false strains upon thee? Not to be endured! Well,
go your way to her, for I see love hath made thee a tame
70 snake, and say this to her: that if she love me, I charge her to
love thee; if she will not, I will never have her unless thou
entreat for her. If you be a true lover, hence and not a word,
for here comes more company.   *Exit* SILVIUS.

Enter OLIVER.

OLIVER Good morrow, fair ones. Pray you, if you know,
75 Where in the purlieus° of this forest stands   outskirts
A sheepcote fenced about with olive trees?

CELIA West of this place, down in the neighbor bottom:°   next valley
The rank of osiers° by the murmuring stream,   row of willows
Left on your right hand, brings you to the place.
80 But at this hour the house doth keep itself:
There's none within.

OLIVER If that an eye may profit by a tongue,
Then should I know you by description,
Such garments and such years: "The boy is fair,
85 Of female favor,° and bestows° himself   appearance / behaves
Like a ripe° sister; the woman low°   mature / short
And browner than her brother." Are not you
The owner of the house I did inquire for?

CELIA It is no boast, being asked, to say we are.

90 OLIVER Orlando doth commend him to you both,

---

6. And by means of him (Silvius), send your thoughts to me (in a letter).

And to that youth he calls his Rosalind
He sends this bloody napkin.° Are you he?   *handkerchief*
ROSALIND   I am. What must we understand by this?
OLIVER   Some of my shame, if you will know of me
95   What man I am, and how and why and where
This handkerchief was stained.
CELIA   I pray you, tell it.
OLIVER   When last the young Orlando parted from you
He left a promise to return again
Within an hour; and pacing through the forest,
100   Chewing the food of sweet and bitter fancy,
Lo, what befell: he threw his eye aside,
And mark what object° did present itself.   *spectacle*
Under an old oak, whose boughs were mossed with age
And high top bald with dry antiquity,
105   A wretched, ragged man, o'ergrown with hair,
Lay sleeping on his back. About his neck
A green and gilded snake had wreathed itself,
Who with her head, nimble in threats, approached
The opening of his mouth. But suddenly,
110   Seeing Orlando, it unlinked° itself   *uncoiled*
And with indented° glides did slip away   *undulating*
Into a bush, under which bush's shade
A lioness with udders all drawn dry[7]
Lay couching, head on ground, with catlike watch
115   When that° the sleeping man should stir. For 'tis   *In readiness for when*
The royal disposition of that beast
To prey on nothing that doth seem as dead.
This seen, Orlando did approach the man,
And found it was his brother, his elder brother.
120   CELIA   Oh, I have heard him speak of that same brother,
And he did render him the most unnatural
That lived amongst men.
OLIVER   And well he might so do,
For well I know he was unnatural.
ROSALIND   But to Orlando: did he leave him there,
125   Food to the sucked and hungry lioness?
OLIVER   Twice did he turn his back and purposed so;
But kindness, nobler ever than revenge,
And nature, stronger than his just occasion,°   *fair opportunity*
Made him give battle to the lioness,
130   Who quickly fell before him, in which hurtling,°   *conflict*
From miserable slumber I awaked.
CELIA   Are you his brother?
ROSALIND   Was't you he rescued?
CELIA   Was't you that did so oft contrive° to kill him?   *plot*
OLIVER   'Twas I, but 'tis not I: I do not shame
135   To tell you what I was, since my conversion
So sweetly tastes, being the thing I am.
ROSALIND   But for° the bloody napkin?   *What about*
OLIVER   By and by.

---

7. Having been nursed dry, the lion would be ferociously hungry.

When from the first to last, betwixt us two,
Tears our recountments° had most kindly bathed—   *narratives*
140 As how I came into that desert place—
In brief, he led me to the gentle Duke,
Who gave me fresh array and entertainment,°   *hospitality*
Committing me unto my brother's love,
Who led me instantly unto his cave,
145 There stripped himself; and here upon his arm
The lioness had torn some flesh away,
Which all this while had bled; and now he fainted
And cried in fainting upon Rosalind.
Brief, I recovered° him, bound up his wound;   *revived*
150 And after some small space, being strong at heart,
He sent me hither, stranger as I am,
To tell this story, that you might excuse
His broken promise, and to give this napkin,
Dyed in this blood, unto the shepherd youth
155 That he in sport doth call his Rosalind.
            [ROSALIND *faints.*]
CELIA   Why, how now, Ganymede? Sweet Ganymede!
OLIVER   Many will swoon when they do look on blood.
CELIA   There is more in it. —Cousin Ganymede!
OLIVER   Look, he recovers.
ROSALIND   I would I were at home.
160 CELIA   We'll lead you thither.
        —I pray you, will you take him by the arm?
OLIVER   Be of good cheer, youth. You a man?
        You lack a man's heart.
ROSALIND   I do so, I confess it.
        Ah, sirrah, a body would think this was well counterfeited!
165 I pray you, tell your brother how well I counterfeited.
        Heigh-ho!
OLIVER   This was not counterfeit: there is too great testimony
        in your complexion that it was a passion of earnest.°   *a genuine fit*
ROSALIND   Counterfeit, I assure you.
170 OLIVER   Well, then, take a good heart and counterfeit to be a
        man.
ROSALIND   So I do, but i'faith, I should have been a woman by
        right.
CELIA   Come, you look paler and paler. Pray you, draw home-
175 wards. —Good sir, go with us.
OLIVER   That will I, for I must bear answer back
        How you excuse my brother, Rosalind.
ROSALIND   I shall devise something; but I pray you, commend
        my counterfeiting to him. Will you go?   *Exeunt.*

5.1
Enter CLOWN *and* AUDREY.
CLOWN   We shall find a time, Audrey. Patience, gentle Audrey!
AUDREY   Faith, the priest was good enough, for all the old
        gentleman's° saying.   *(Jaques's)*
CLOWN   A most wicked Sir Oliver, Audrey, a most vile Mar-
5 text. But Audrey, there is a youth here in the forest lays claim
        to you.

AUDREY   Ay, I know who 'tis: he hath no interest in me° in the   *no right to me*
   world. Here comes the man you mean.
     Enter WILLIAM.

CLOWN   It is meat and drink to me to see a clown,° by my   *peasant; yokel*
10   troth. We that have good wits have much to answer for: we
   shall be flouting; we cannot hold.°   *refrain*

WILLIAM   Good ev'n, Audrey.

AUDREY   God ye° good ev'n, William.   *God give you*

WILLIAM   And good ev'n to you, sir.
    [*He takes off his hat.*]

15 CLOWN   Good ev'n, gentle friend. Cover thy head,[1] cover thy
   head—nay, prithee, be covered! How old are you, friend?

WILLIAM   Five and twenty, sir.

CLOWN   A ripe age. Is thy name William?

WILLIAM   William, sir.

20 CLOWN   A fair name. Wast born i'th' forest here?

WILLIAM   Ay, sir, I thank God.

CLOWN   "Thank God"—a good answer. Art rich?

WILLIAM   Faith, sir, so-so.

CLOWN   "So-so" is good, very good, very excellent good. And
25   yet it is not; it is but so-so. Art thou wise?

WILLIAM   Ay, sir. I have a pretty wit.

CLOWN   Why, thou say'st well. I do now remember a saying:
   "The fool doth think he is wise, but the wise man knows
   himself to be a fool." The heathen philosopher, when he had
30   a desire to eat a grape, would open his lips when he put it
   into his mouth, meaning thereby that grapes were made to
   eat and lips to open.[2] You do love this maid?

WILLIAM   I do, sir.

CLOWN   Give me your hand. Art thou learned?

35 WILLIAM   No, sir.

CLOWN   Then learn this of me: to have is to have. For it is a
   figure in rhetoric° that drink, being poured out of a cup into *rhetorical commonplace*
   a glass, by filling the one doth empty the other. For all your
   writers do consent that *ipse* is he.[3] Now you are not *ipse*, for
40   I am he.

WILLIAM   Which "he," sir?

CLOWN   He, sir, that must marry this woman. Therefore, you
   clown, abandon—which is in the vulgar "leave"—the
   society—which in the boorish is "company"—of this
45   female—which in the common is "woman." Which together
   is, abandon the society of this female or, clown, thou
   perishest—or to thy better understanding, diest—or, to wit,
   I kill thee: make thee away, translate thy life into death, thy
   liberty into bondage. I will deal in poison with thee, or in
50   bastinado,° or in steel. I will bandy with thee in faction; I will   *beating with a club*
   o'errun thee with policy;[4] I will kill thee a hundred and fifty
   ways. Therefore tremble and depart!

AUDREY   Do, good William.

5.1
1. Evidently William has taken off his hat in a gesture of deference.
2. Touchstone's speech may be a response to William's gaping mouth.

3. For all authorities agree that *ipse* is translated as "he himself." The Latin word was proverbially applied to wooers who won the favor of their lovers.
4. I will contend ("bandy") with you in argument; I will overwhelm you with craftiness.

WILLIAM   God rest you merry, sir.   *Exit.*
      Enter CORIN.
55   CORIN   Our master and mistress seeks you. Come away, away!
    CLOWN   Trip, Audrey, trip, Audrey! I attend, I attend.
                                                          Exeunt.

5.2

      Enter ORLANDO *and* OLIVER.
    ORLANDO   Is't possible that on so little acquaintance you
    should like her? That but seeing, you should love her? And
    loving, woo? And wooing, she should grant? And will you
    persevere to enjoy her?
5   OLIVER   Neither call the giddiness° of it in question, the pov-   *foolish haste*
    erty of her, the small acquaintance, my sudden wooing, nor
    sudden consenting, but say with me, "I love Aliena." Say
    with her that she loves me. Consent with both, that we may
    enjoy each other. It shall be to your good, for my father's
10 house and all the revenue that was old Sir Roland's will I
    estate° upon you, and here live and die a shepherd.   *settle*
      Enter ROSALIND [*as Ganymede*].
    ORLANDO   You have my consent. Let your wedding be tomor-
    row. Thither will I invite the Duke and all 's contented fol-
    lowers. Go you and prepare Aliena; for look you, here comes
15 my Rosalind.
    ROSALIND   God save you, brother.
    OLIVER   And you, fair sister.   [*Exit.*]
    ROSALIND   O my dear Orlando, how it grieves me to see thee
    wear thy heart in a scarf!°   *sling*
20 ORLANDO   It is my arm.
    ROSALIND   I thought thy heart had been wounded with the
    claws of a lion.
    ORLANDO   Wounded it is, but with the eyes of a lady.
    ROSALIND   Did your brother tell you how I counterfeited to
25 swoon when he showed me your handkerchief?
    ORLANDO   Ay, and greater wonders than that.
    ROSALIND   Oh, I know where you are. Nay, 'tis true. There was
    never anything so sudden but the fight of two rams and Cae-
    sar's thrasonical° brag of "I came, saw, and overcome."[1] For   *boastful*
30 your brother and my sister no sooner met but they looked,
    no sooner looked but they loved, no sooner loved but they
    sighed, no sooner sighed but they asked one another the
    reason, no sooner knew the reason but they sought the rem-
    edy. And in these degrees have they made a pair° of stairs   *flight*
35 to marriage, which they will climb incontinent° or else be   *hastily*
    incontinent[2] before marriage. They are in the very wrath of
    love° and they will together. Clubs cannot part them.   *heat of passion*
    ORLANDO   They shall be married tomorrow, and I will bid the
    Duke to the nuptial. But oh, how bitter a thing it is to look
40 into happiness through another man's eyes! By so much the
    more shall I tomorrow be at the height of heart-heaviness by

---

5.2
1. Caesar's well-known announcement of military
victory, made famous as "I came, I saw, I overcame"
in Thomas North's translation of Plutarch's *Lives*
(1579).
2. Be sexually unrestrained.

how much I shall think my brother happy in having what he
wishes for.
ROSALIND   Why, then, tomorrow I cannot serve your turn[3] for
45   Rosalind?
ORLANDO   I can live no longer by thinking.
ROSALIND   I will weary you, then, no longer with idle talking.
Know of me then, for now I speak to some purpose, that I
know you are a gentleman of good conceit.° I speak not this   *understanding*
50   that you should bear a good opinion of my knowledge, inso-
much° I say I know you are. Neither do I labor for a greater   *inasmuch as*
esteem than may in some little measure draw a belief from
you, to do yourself good[4] and not to grace me. Believe then,
if you please, that I can do strange things. I have since I was
55   three year old conversed° with a magician most profound in   *associated*
his art, and yet not damnable.[5] If you do love Rosalind so
near the heart as your gesture° cries it out, when your brother   *behavior*
marries Aliena shall you marry her. I know into what straits
of fortune she is driven, and it is not impossible to me, if it
60   appear not inconvenient to you, to set her before your eyes
tomorrow—human as she is and without any danger.
ORLANDO   Speak'st thou in sober meanings?
ROSALIND   By my life, I do—which I tender° dearly, though I   *value*
say I am a magician. Therefore put you in your best array;
65   bid° your friends. For if you will be married tomorrow you   *invite*
shall, and to Rosalind if you will.
         Enter SILVIUS *and* PHOEBE.
Look, here comes a lover of mine and a lover of hers.
PHOEBE   Youth, you have done me much ungentleness°   *discourtesy*
To show the letter that I writ to you.
70   ROSALIND   I care not if I have. It is my study°   *objective*
To seem despiteful° and ungentle to you.   *contemptuous*
You are there followed by a faithful shepherd.
Look upon him, love him; he worships you.
PHOEBE   Good shepherd, tell this youth what 'tis to love.
75   SILVIUS   It is to be all made of sighs and tears,
And so am I for Phoebe.
PHOEBE   And I for Ganymede.
ORLANDO   And I for Rosalind.
ROSALIND   And I for no woman.
80   SILVIUS   It is to be all made of faith and service,
And so am I for Phoebe.
PHOEBE   And I for Ganymede.
ORLANDO   And I for Rosalind.
ROSALIND   And I for no woman.
85   SILVIUS   It is to be all made of fantasy,
All made of passion and all made of wishes,
All adoration, duty, and observance,°   *devotion*
All humbleness, all patience and impatience,
All purity, all trial, all observance,
90   And so am I for Phoebe.

---

3. Substitute for Rosalind; satisfy you sexually in
Rosalind's place.
4. *Neither . . . good:* Nor am I attempting to enhance
my reputation more than is necessary to persuade
you to do yourself some good.
5. That is, not meriting execution for heresy. Elizabethan statutes made certain forms of witchcraft and
black magic punishable by death.

PHOEBE And so am I for Ganymede.

ORLANDO And so am I for Rosalind.

ROSALIND And so am I for no woman.

PHOEBE If this be so, why blame you me to love you?

95 SILVIUS If this be so, why blame you me to love you?

ORLANDO If this be so, why blame you me to love you?

ROSALIND Why do you speak too, "Why blame you me to love you?"

ORLANDO To her that is not here, nor doth not hear.

ROSALIND Pray you, no more of this—'tis like the howling of
100 Irish wolves against the moon.⁶ [*to* SILVIUS] I will help you
if I can. [*to* PHOEBE] I would love you if I could. Tomorrow
meet me all together. I will marry you if ever I marry woman,
and I'll be married tomorrow. [*to* ORLANDO] I will satisfy you
if ever I satisfied man, and you shall be married tomorrow.
105 [*to* SILVIUS] I will content you if what pleases you contents
you, and you shall be married tomorrow. [*to* ORLANDO] As
you love Rosalind, meet. [*to* SILVIUS] As you love Phoebe,
meet. And as I love no woman, I'll meet. So fare you well. I
have left you commands.

110 SILVIUS I'll not fail, if I live.

PHOEBE Nor I.

ORLANDO Nor I.   *Exeunt.*

5.3

Enter CLOWN *and* AUDREY.

CLOWN Tomorrow is the joyful day, Audrey; tomorrow will
we be married.

AUDREY I do desire it with all my heart, and I hope it is no
dishonest° desire to desire to be a woman of the world.¹   *unchaste*
5 Here come two of the banished Duke's pages.

Enter two PAGES.

FIRST PAGE Well met, honest gentleman!

CLOWN By my troth, well met! Come, sit, sit—and a song.

SECOND PAGE We are for you.° Sit i'th' middle.   *That suits us*

FIRST PAGE Shall we clap into't roundly, without hawking² or
10 spitting or saying we are hoarse—which are the only° pro-   *best; sole*
logues to a bad voice?

SECOND PAGE I'faith, i'faith—and both in a tune° like two   *in unison*
gypsies on a horse.

Song.

PAGES [*sing*]³ It was a lover and his lass,
15   With a hey and a ho and a hey nonny-no,
         That o'er the green cornfield° did pass   *field of wheat*
         In the springtime, the only pretty ring time,°   *time for weddings*
         When birds do sing, hey ding-a ding, ding,
         Sweet lovers love the spring.

---

6. That is, it is barbaric. The howling of wolves at the
moon was a proverbial way of referring to an irrational or futile course of action. Irish wolves might be
perceived as especially disorderly, for Ireland's abundance of wolves was for many Elizabethan writers a
mark of that country's lack of civility.
5.3
1. A married woman.

2. Shall we begin energetically and at once, without
clearing our throats?
3. F does not include this speech prefix, simply the
world "song." This is one of the few Shakespeare
songs for which contemporary music survives. It is
set for a single voice with lute accompaniment in
Thomas Morley's *First Book of Airs* (1600).

20   And therefore take° the present time,   *seize*
           With a hey and a ho and a hey nonny-no,
           For love is crownèd with the prime°   *spring; perfection*
           In springtime, etc.

           Between the acres of the rye,
25   With a hey and a ho and a hey nonny-no,
           These pretty country folks would lie
           In springtime, etc.

           This carol they began that hour,
           With a hey and a ho and a hey nonny-no,
30   How that a life was but a flower
           In springtime, etc.[4]

CLOWN Truly, young gentlemen, though there was no great
matter° in the ditty, yet the note was very untunable.[5]   *sense*
FIRST PAGE You are deceived, sir. We kept time; we lost not
35 our time.
CLOWN By my troth, yes. I count it but time lost to hear such
a foolish song. God b'wi' you and God mend your voices.
Come, Audrey.   *Exeunt.*

5.4

Enter DUKE SENIOR, AMIENS, JAQUES, ORLANDO,
OLIVER, [*and*] CELIA [*as Aliena*].
DUKE SENIOR Dost thou believe, Orlando, that the boy
Can do all this that he hath promisèd?
ORLANDO I sometimes do believe and sometimes do not.
As those that fear they hope[1] and know they fear.
Enter ROSALIND [*as Ganymede*], SILVIUS, *and* PHOEBE.
5 ROSALIND Patience once more whiles our compact is urged.°   *declared*
You say if I bring in your Rosalind,
You will bestow her on Orlando here?
DUKE SENIOR That would I, had I° kingdoms to give with her.   *even if I had*
ROSALIND And you say you will have her when I bring her?
10 ORLANDO That would I, were I of all kingdoms king.
ROSALIND You say you'll marry me if I be willing?
PHOEBE That will I, should I die the hour after.
ROSALIND But if you do refuse to marry me,
You'll give yourself to this most faithful shepherd?
15 PHOEBE So is the bargain.
ROSALIND You say that you'll have Phoebe if she will?
SILVIUS Though to have her and death were both one thing.
ROSALIND I have promised to make all this matter even.°   *smooth; right*
Keep you your word, O Duke, to give your daughter;
20 You yours, Orlando, to receive his daughter.
Keep you your word, Phoebe, that you'll marry me
Or else, refusing me, to wed this shepherd.
Keep your word, Silvius, that you'll marry her
If she refuse me; and from hence I go
25 To make these doubts all even.

---

4. TEXTUAL COMMENT The order of these stanzas   5. Yet the music was disagreeable.
differs from that found in Morley's *First Book of Airs.*   **5.4**
See Digital Edition TC 8.   1. Fear that their hope will not be fulfilled.

Exeunt ROSALIND *and* CELIA.

DUKE SENIOR   I do remember in this shepherd boy
          Some lively° touches of my daughter's favor.°   *vivid / appearance*
ORLANDO   My lord, the first time that I ever saw him
          Methought he was a brother to your daughter.
30   But my good lord, this boy is forest-born
          And hath been tutored in the rudiments
          Of many desperate° studies by his uncle,   *dangerous*
          Whom he reports to be a great magician
          Obscurèd in the circle of this forest.²

          Enter CLOWN *and* AUDREY.

35   JAQUES   There is, sure, another flood toward,° and these cou-   *at hand*
          ples are coming to the ark.³ Here comes a pair of very
          strange beasts, which in all tongues are called fools.
     CLOWN   Salutation and greeting to you all!
     JAQUES   Good my lord, bid him welcome. This is the motley-
40   minded° gentleman that I have so often met in the forest.   *foolish-brained*
          He hath been a courtier, he swears.
     CLOWN   If any man doubt that, let him put me to my purga-
          tion.⁴ I have trod a measure,° I have flattered a lady, I have   *danced*
          been politic with my friend, smooth with mine enemy. I
45   have undone° three tailors, I have had four quarrels, and   *made bankrupt*
          like to have fought° one.   *came close to fighting*
     JAQUES   And how was that ta'en up?°   *settled*
     CLOWN   Faith, we met and found the quarrel was upon the
          seventh cause.
50   JAQUES   How seventh cause? Good my lord, like this fellow!
     DUKE SENIOR   I like him very well.
     CLOWN   God 'ield you, sir, I desire you of the like. I press
          in here, sir, amongst the rest of the country copulatives,⁵ to
          swear and to forswear, according as marriage binds and
55   blood breaks:° a poor virgin, sir, an ill-favored thing, sir, but   *passion rebels*
          mine own; a poor humor° of mine, sir, to take that that no   *whim*
          man else will. Rich honesty° dwells like a miser, sir, in a   *chastity*
          poor house as your pearl in your foul oyster.
     DUKE SENIOR   By my faith, he is very swift and sententious.°   *witty and wise*
60   CLOWN   According to the fool's bolt,⁶ sir, and such dulcet
          diseases.°   *sweet afflictions*
     JAQUES   But for the seventh cause—how did you find the
          quarrel on the seventh cause?
     CLOWN   Upon a lie seven times removed —bear your body
65   more seeming,° Audrey —as thus, sir: I did dislike⁷ the cut of   *becomingly*
          a certain courtier's beard; he sent me word if I said his beard
          was not cut well, he was in the mind it was. This is called
          the Retort Courteous. If I sent him word again it was not
          well cut, he would send me word he cut it to please himself.
70   This is called the Quip Modest. If again it was not well cut,

---

2. Concealed within the boundaries of this forest.
This may be a reference to the magic circle within
which magicians were supposed to be able to practice
their art safely.
3. Alluding to a biblical account in Genesis 7:2 in
which pairs of male and female animals shelter on
Noah's ark to escape the flood that covers the earth.

4. Let me be put to trial to clear myself (of the
charge of lying).
5. People who are about to copulate.
6. And his wittiness quickly disappears. The comment alludes to the proverb "A fool's bolt (or arrow) is
soon shot."
7. Show my dislike of.

he disabled° my judgment. This is called the Reply Churlish.
If again it was not well cut, he would answer I spake not
true. This is called the Reproof Valiant. If again it was not
well cut, he would say I lie. This is called the Countercheck°

75 Quarrelsome, and so to Lie Circumstantial° and the Lie
Direct.

JAQUES   And how oft did you say his beard was not well cut?

CLOWN   I durst go no further than the Lie Circumstantial;
nor he durst not give me the Lie Direct, and so we measured

80 swords⁸ and parted.

JAQUES   Can you nominate° in order, now, the degrees of the
lie?

CLOWN   O sir, we quarrel in print, by the book,⁹ as you have
books for good manners.¹ I will name you the degrees: the

85 first, the Retort Courteous; the second, the Quip Modest;
the third, the Reply Churlish; the fourth, the Reproof Valiant; the fifth, the Countercheck Quarrelsome; the sixth,
the Lie with Circumstance; the seventh, the Lie Direct. All
these you may avoid but the Lie Direct, and you may avoid

90 that too with an "if." I knew when seven justices could not take
up° a quarrel; but when the parties were met themselves,
one of them thought but of an "if"—as, "if you said so then
I said so"—and they shook hands and swore brothers.° Your
"if" is the only peacemaker: much virtue in "if."

95 JAQUES   Is not this a rare fellow, my lord? He's as good at anything, and yet a fool.

DUKE SENIOR   He uses his folly like a stalkinghorse,² and
under the presentation° of that he shoots his wit.

Enter HYMEN,³ [*god of marriage,*] ROSALIND, *and*
CELIA [*as themselves*].
Still° *music.*

HYMEN   Then is there mirth in heaven

100 When earthly things, made even,°
Atone° together.
Good Duke, receive thy daughter;
Hymen from heaven brought her—
Yea, brought her hither

105 That thou mightst join her hand with his,⁴
Whose heart within his bosom is.

ROSALIND [*to* DUKE SENIOR]   To you I give myself, for I am yours.
[*to* ORLANDO] To you I give myself, for I am yours.

DUKE SENIOR   If there be truth in sight, you are my daughter.

110 ORLANDO   If there be truth in sight, you are my Rosalind.

PHOEBE   If sight and shape be true,
Why then my love adieu!

---

glosses (right margin):

disparaged

Rebuff
Indirect

name

settle

became sworn brothers

appearance

Soft

set right
Are at one; unite

---

8. We checked that our swords were of the same length (as was customary prior to a duel).
9. According to the rules as set down in books on the etiquette of dueling. Touchstone's speech exposes the absurd aspects of the elaborate codes of behavior set forth in such books.
1. Elizabethan England witnessed an outpouring of courtesy literature aimed at both social aspirants and established courtiers.
2. A real or imitation horse used as a means of cam-

ouflage in hunting.
3. The god of marriage in classical mythology, conventionally depicted as a young man who carried a veil and a bridal torch. PERFORMANCE COMMENT Directors must decide whether to make Hymen a heavenly deity or one of Rosalind's friends recruited to help her. See Digital Edition PC 3.
4. TEXTUAL COMMENT F prints "his hand with his," here emended to "her hand with his." For the possible reasons for this, see Digital Edition TC 9.

ROSALIND   I'll have no father if you be not he.
　—I'll have no husband if you be not he,
115　　—Nor ne'er wed woman if you be not she.
HYMEN   Peace, ho! I bar° confusion.　　　　　　　　　　　*forbid*
　'Tis I must make conclusion
　Of these most strange events.
　Here's eight that must take hands
120　To join in Hymen's bands°　　　　　　　　　*bonds of marriage*
　If truth hold true contents.⁵
　[*to* ROSALIND *and* ORLANDO.] You and you no cross° shall part.　　*adversity*
　[*to* CELIA *and* OLIVER] You and you are heart in heart.
　[*to* PHOEBE] You to his love must accord,°　　　　　*consent*
125　Or have a woman to° your lord.　　　　　　　　　*as*
　[*to* CLOWN *and* AUDREY] You and you are sure together,°　　*tightly bound*
　As the winter to foul weather.
　Whiles a wedlock hymn we sing,
　Feed° yourselves with questioning,　　　　　　　　*Satisfy*
130　That reason wonder may diminish
　How thus we met, and these things finish.
　　　　　　　　　Song.
　　Wedding is great Juno's° crown.　　　　*goddess of marriage*
　　O blessèd bond of board and bed!
　　'Tis Hymen peoples every town;
135　　High° wedlock then be honorèd.　　　　　　*Solemn*
　　Honor, high honor, and renown
　　To Hymen, god of every town.
DUKE SENIOR   O my dear niece, welcome thou art to me!
　Even daughter, welcome in no less degree.⁶
140　PHOEBE   I will not eat my word: now thou art mine,
　Thy faith my fancy° to thee doth combine.　　　　　*love*
　　　　Enter [JAQUES DE BOIS, *the*] *second brother.*
JAQUES DE BOIS   Let me have audience for a word or two.
　I am the second son of old Sir Roland,
　That bring these tidings to this fair assembly.
145　Duke Frederick, hearing how that every day
　Men of great worth resorted to this forest,
　Addressed a mighty power,° which were on foot　　　　　*army*
　In his own conduct,° purposely to take　　　　*Under his command*
　His brother here and put him to the sword.
150　And to the skirts° of this wild wood he came,　　　　*outskirts*
　Where, meeting with an old religious man,
　After some question° with him, was converted　　　*conversation*
　Both from his enterprise and from the world,
　His crown bequeathing to his banished brother
160　And all their lands restored to him⁷ again
　That were with him exiled. This to be true
　I do engage° my life.　　　　　　　　　　*pledge*
DUKE SENIOR　　　　　　　Welcome, young man.
　Thou offer'st fairly° to thy brothers' wedding:　　*You bring fine gifts*
　To one° his lands withheld and to the other°　　*(Oliver) / (Orlando)*

---

5. If truth is true; if truth please you.
6. Daughter, you are no less welcome.

7. Although F has "him," many modern editions emend to "them."

160	A land itself at large,[8] a potent° dukedom.	*powerful*
	First in this forest let us do° those ends	*accomplish*
	That here were well begun and well begot;°	*conceived*
	And after, every° of this happy number	*every one*
	That have endured shrewd° days and nights with us	*evil*
165	Shall share the good of our returnèd fortune,	
	According to the measure of their states.°	*ranks*
	Meantime, forget this new-fall'n° dignity	*newly acquired*
	And fall into our rustic revelry.	
	Play music, and you brides and bridegrooms all,	
170	With measure heaped in joy to th' measures fall.[9]	
	JAQUES Sir, by your patience.° If I heard you rightly,	*with your permission*
	The duke hath put on a religious life	
	And thrown into neglect the pompous° court?	*ceremonious*
	JAQUES DE BOIS He hath.	
175	JAQUES To him will I: out of these convertites°	*converts*
	There is much matter to be heard and learned.	
	[*to* DUKE SENIOR] You to your former honor I bequeath—	
	Your patience and your virtue well deserves it;	
	[*to* ORLANDO *and* ROSALIND] You to a love that your true faith	
	doth merit,	
180	[*to* OLIVER *and* CELIA] You to your land and love and great	
	allies,°	*relatives*
	[*to* SILVIUS *and* PHOEBE] You to a long and well-deservèd bed,	
	[*to* CLOWN *and* AUDREY] And you to wrangling, for thy loving	
	voyage	
	Is but for two months victualed.° So—to your pleasures!	*supplied with food*
	I am for other than for dancing measures.	
185	DUKE SENIOR Stay, Jaques, stay!	
	JAQUES To see no pastime, I! What you would have°	*like (from me)*
	I'll stay to know at your abandoned cave. *Exit.*	
	DUKE SENIOR Proceed, proceed! We'll begin these rites,	
	As we do trust they'll end in true delights.	
	[*Dancing, then exeunt all but* ROSALIND.][1]	

[*Epilogue.*]

190	ROSALIND It is not the fashion to see the lady the epilogue,[2]	
	but it is no more unhandsome than to see the lord the pro-	
	logue. If it be true that good wine needs no bush,[3] 'tis true	
	that a good play needs no epilogue. Yet to good wine they do	
	use good bushes, and good plays prove the better by the help	
195	of good epilogues.	
	What a case° am I in, then, that am neither a good epi-	*plight; costume*
	logue nor cannot insinuate° with you in the behalf of a good	*ingratiate myself*
	play? I am not furnished like a beggar; therefore to beg will	
	not become me. My way is to conjure° you, and I'll begin	*charge; bewitch*
200	with the women: I charge you, O women, for the love you	

---

8. An entire country. As Rosalind's husband, Orlando is heir to the dukedom returned to Duke Senior.

9. With a measure of overflowing joy, begin your dances ("measures").

1. TEXTUAL COMMENT F indicates only a single exit for Duke Senior, but most editors assume that Rosalind remains alone onstage to deliver the Epilogue.

See Digital Edition TC 10.
Epilogue

2. In the vast majority of Elizabethan plays, the Epilogue is spoken by a male character.

3. Advertisement. The proverb derived from the practice of hanging a branch of ivy in tavern windows to indicate that wine was for sale.

bear to men, to like as much of this play as please you. And
I charge you, O men, for the love you bear to women—as I
perceive by your simpering, none of you hates them—that
between you and the women, the play° may please. If I were   *drama; love play*
205   a woman[4] I would kiss as many of you as had beards that
pleased me, complexions that liked° me, and breaths that I   *pleased*
defied° not. And I am sure, as many as have good beards or   *disdained*
good faces or sweet breaths will for my kind offer, when I
make curtsey, bid me farewell.°   *Exit.*   *(with applause)*

4. A pointed reference to the fact that women's roles in the Elizabethan theater were played by boys.

Julius Caesar

In *Julius Caesar*, Shakespeare dramatizes incidents of world-historical significance. As the events of the play unfold, the characters are constantly aware that the eyes of the world are, and will remain, upon them. Indeed, one of the protagonists, Caius Cassius, eagerly anticipates his own impersonated presence on Shakespeare's stage:

> How many ages hence
> Shall this our lofty scene be acted over
> In states unborn and accents yet unknown!
> (3.1.112–14)

Cassius correctly forecasts that his own actions, although they will eventually become ancient history, will nonetheless remain compelling to people far removed in time, place, and language from the original events. Implicit in Cassius's prediction, moreover, may be a sly conjecture on Shakespeare's part about the power of his own drama to echo down the centuries. For most modern readers and playgoers, Shakespeare's vivid re-presentation of Julius Caesar's assassination has become much more familiar than the history that inspired it.

What was that history? By 44 B.C.E., an astonishing sequence of conquests had made Rome, once an unremarkable Italian town, the center of a vast empire that stretched from North Africa to Britain, from Babylon to Spain. Yet eventually Rome's outsized ambitions threatened to destroy it. For hundreds of years, Rome had been governed not by a king or a dictator, but by elected officers, and its republican traditions had been a source of fierce civic pride. Yet as the city's military endeavors grew increasingly ambitious, Rome's generals, with the might of their armies behind them, came to wield more power than the factionalized Senate to which they supposedly owed allegiance. Of these generals, the charismatic and enterprising Julius Caesar, who had subdued much of northwest Europe even while consolidating his popularity among the poorer classes at home, seemed particularly dangerous. When legal and military attempts to curb Caesar's growing power failed, a group of conspirators led by Caius Cassius and Marcus Brutus assassinated him. Yet the death of Caesar did not, as his killers had hoped, restore Rome to its tradition of republican government. Instead, civil war ensued, in which Caesar's friend Mark Antony and Caesar's adopted heir, Octavius, defeated the forces of the conspirators. Eventually, after a power struggle among the victors (recounted in Shakespeare's *Antony and Cleopatra*), Octavius was enthroned as the Emperor Augustus. His ascendancy, consolidating immense power in a single individual, completed the political transformation that Julius Caesar's assassins had tried to prevent.

Virtually from the moment the conspirators pulled their swords from Caesar's bleeding corpse, the events that Shakespeare treats in *Julius Caesar* were amply documented and their rationale debated. Different commentators from antiquity to the Renaissance, depending on their own political convictions, viewed the assassination as an act of heroism or villainy and celebrated or denounced its perpetrators accordingly. While Michelangelo and Milton idealize Brutus as a selfless defender of human liberty, Dante plunges him, with Cassius, into the deepest pit of hell. It is not surprising that Shakespeare, ever alive to the dramatic possibilities inherent in multiple, conflicting perspectives, should choose to stage an incident that had been provoking debate for more than sixteen hundred years.

Julius Caesar. From Plutarch,
*The Lives of the Noble
Grecians and Romans* (1595).

For Shakespeare's contemporaries, the questions raised by Caesar's career were not merely of antiquarian interest. Throughout early modern Europe, strong rulers were attempting, with varying degrees of success, to consolidate their power. In England, these efforts threatened the traditional prerogatives of the aristocracy and of elected representatives in the House of Commons. For thinkers and writers saturated by their classical education in the antique past, it was easy to see the shift toward strong monarchy as replaying the shift from republican to imperial Rome. In England in 1599, moreover, concerns over this general trend were exacerbated by more specific anxieties. Queen Elizabeth I had proven a remarkably durable and effective queen, but at sixty-six, she was an old woman by Renaissance standards. Since she had never begotten children nor named an heir, it was unclear who would succeed her or how the new monarch would be selected. Conceivably England would plunge, upon her death, into civil chaos. In a state in which censorship made direct commentary on contemporary political affairs virtually impossible, the story of Caesar's death and its calamitous aftermath provided an opportunity to reflect, at a suitably prudent distance, upon what might happen when accepted methods of allocating and transferring sovereign power disintegrated.

Although the consequences of Julius Caesar's assassination took years to unfold, the event is historically important because it seems to mark the end of one epoch and the beginning of another. Similarly, Shakespeare's *Julius Caesar*, first performed in 1599, marks a watershed in his career as a playwright. On the one hand, his foray into Roman history seems to look back to, and develop further, some of the central political concerns of the English history plays that Shakespeare had written in the 1590s. *Julius Caesar*, like the history plays, grapples with such questions as: Who constitutes a political community—everybody in the state, both rich and poor, or only the elite and powerful among them? What traits make a person fit to rule, and how is power conferred upon him or her? Are citizens allowed, or even obliged, to defend the rule of law by resorting to extralegal violence? When the demands of civic responsibility apparently conflict with those of personal loyalty, which ought to prevail? In *Julius Caesar,* these are questions not about individuals, but about the life of an entire society.

Yet in the English history plays, especially the "second tetralogy" consisting of *Richard II, 1* and *2 Henry IV,* and *Henry V,* Shakespeare had dramatized political change in a way that highlighted the significance of individual characters. And in *Julius Caesar,* the problem of individual character figures even more profoundly. In the conflicted, articulate, highly self-conscious Brutus, Shakespeare invents a kind of hero who forecasts those of the tragedies that he will begin to write at the turn of the seventeenth century: the brooding Hamlet, the self-destructive Othello, the murderous but self-analytical Macbeth. Of course, distinctions between "personal" and "political" matters tend to be fuzzy and suspect, and, in a play about an assassination, are likely to be impossible to disentangle. Nonetheless, for all its acute analysis of human beings in groups, *Julius Caesar* turns on a question that seems more personal than social: What brings a man to destroy what he claims to love?

Shakespeare's source materials may well have encouraged this simultaneous attention to political dilemmas and psychological complexity. The most important sources for *Julius Caesar* were the biographies of Caesar and Brutus in Plutarch's *Lives of the Noble Grecians and Romans,* translated into English by Thomas North. Writing in the first century C.E., Plutarch had construed the biographer's task as inextricable from the historian's, since in his view history recorded the achievements of great men. Shakespeare followed Plutarch in stressing the decisive roles played by the acknowledged leaders of Roman society, rather than dwelling on the frictions among larger social groups. Not that he was unaware of the latter: the testiness of *Julius Caesar's* opening scene makes the internal divisions in Roman society abundantly clear. But throughout the play, commoners are largely imagined from an upper-class perspective, as a politically unsophisticated mob. The capacity for conscious and reflective political decision making rests in the hands of a small elite.

Marc Antony. From Plutarch, *The Lives of the Noble Grecians and Romans* (1595).

Plutarch's "great man" view of history lends itself to compelling dramas involving a manageable number of psychologically complex characters. And Shakespeare's drastic condensation of narrative time frame in *Julius Caesar* has the effect of exaggerating Plutarch's emphases. In Plutarch, Caesar's triumph over Pompey's sons occurs in October, but Shakespeare makes it coincide with the mid-February festival of Lupercalia, so that the assassination on the Ides (15th) of March seems a direct response to a specific display of arrogance. Likewise, in Plutarch, Brutus and Cassius withdraw from Rome more than a year after Caesar's funeral, but in Shakespeare, their flight follows immediately upon Antony's brilliant incitement of the Roman mob. The effect is not only to escalate dramatic momentum but also to make the personal strengths and weaknesses of Rome's leaders seem matters of titanic consequence.

In the Roman Republic, Plutarch claimed, there was always more than one powerful person, but there were rarely more than a few. Shakespeare depicts the last days of the Republic in a drama that no single protagonist appropriates wholly to himself. Instead, *Julius Caesar* divides its attention among several characters, setting them off against one another, while the titular hero makes less claim upon the audience's attention than might be expected. Plutarch's biography emphasizes Caesar's military genius, his ruthless executive skill, and his astonishing capacity to rescue himself repeatedly from crushing adversity. Shakespeare's Caesar seems less outsized. His accomplishments are not shown or much alluded to, and much of what we do hear is filtered through the hostile reports of resentful observers. He wants supremacy less, apparently, because he has any particular vision for the Roman polity than because he yearns for the unqualified homage of others. His egotism seems a bit ridiculous: despite his physical frailties, he imagines himself as embodying a godlike permanence, "unshaked of motion" (3.1.71):

> I am constant as the Northern Star,
> Of whose true-fixed and resting quality
> There is no fellow in the firmament.
> (3.1.61–63)

Shakespeare loads this moment of self-description with dramatic irony: even as Caesar speaks these lines, the conspirators encircle him, daggers in hand. Yet Caesar's weaknesses also make the conspirators' fears seem less plausible. Deaf and epileptic, he seems an unlikely aspirant to tyrannical power.

Brutus, Caesar's friend and killer, is far more fully elaborated, and in fact the originality of Shakespeare's play lies in its concentration of attention on the complicated Brutus instead of upon the play's titular hero. Unlike the other characters, Brutus appears to us in several guises: as a public figure, a husband, a master of servants, a military leader. Thus he experiences painfully in his own person the value conflicts that are elsewhere dispersed among various antagonists. How is Brutus—and how are we—to reconcile his tender regard for his wife and servant with his willingness to commit political murder? Does Brutus's intimacy with Caesar make his decision to assassinate him truly noble, since it cannot be said to stem from self-interest? Or does it suggest a troubling insensitivity to the claims of friendship and to Caesar's genuinely exceptional character? Does he "love the name of honor" so much that he betrays it?

The soliloquies in which Brutus carefully deliberates upon his reasons for, and the possible consequences of, his actions provide abundant insight into his turbulent inner life. Yet the soliloquies raise as many questions about his motives as they resolve. They force the audience to wonder how Brutus's idealism and his commitment to principle are to be evaluated. Surely his habit of appealing to abstract moral and political tenets is an admirable trait, especially in a city in which selfishness seems the dominant passion. But repeatedly, this practice leads him to commit disastrous tactical errors. Concerned to minimize bloodshed, he refuses to countenance Cassius's suggestion that Antony be killed along with Caesar. Then—once again ignoring Cassius's advice— he permits Antony to deliver an unsupervised eulogy at Caesar's funeral, thereby losing the "spin" on Caesar's death and unleashing the rage of the crowd against himself and his allies. Later, his indignation at what he believes to be Cassius's corrupt practices seriously endangers their alliance.

In all these cases, Brutus tries to diminish the extent to which any of his actions might conceivably serve his own self-interested ends, even though by doing so he risks and eventually dooms the cause he is attempting to serve. Brutus shares Caesar's admiration for the Stoic virtue of "constancy," framing it, however, less in terms of power over others than in terms of personal self-control. By behaving according to immovable principles, he tries to give his life a stern but reassuring integrity. Like Caesar, Brutus ends up paying for this aspiration with his life, and even before he does so, the desire to be, in Caesar's words, "constant as the Northern Star" seems misplaced in a play in which character seems complex and highly mutable.

In comparison, the impulsive, unscrupulous Cassius is far more alert to the way the world really works, willingly stooping to expediency to get what he wants and what his cause needs. The contrast with Antony likewise clarifies the way in which Brutus's principles incapacitate him. Antony emerges as a formidable opponent not despite but because of traits that Brutus can see only as weaknesses: love of sensual indulgence, lack of principle, a tendency to live in the present without sufficient care for past or future. Antony's uninhibited, improvisatory nature suits him beautifully for swaying the plebeians. A marvelous actor, Antony exploits gestures, cunning rhetoric, props, and any other means that fully serve the particular moment in which he finds himself. In fact, his political astuteness seems to arise directly from his personal familiarity with passion, since much of politics is, as Brutus never quite realizes, a matter of assessing and responding to group desire. While Brutus naively believes that Caesar's death simply restores the Republic to its status quo ante, Antony immediately understands that the future of Rome and its institutions rests in the hands of Rome's populace and thus—since that populace is fickle and violent—ultimately in the hands of whoever can sway the populace to his will.

Even while Shakespeare vividly differentiates his characters, he shows clearly how they derive from the particular social and intellectual culture they inhabit. Shakespeare was no antiquarian: he imagines the characters of *Julius Caesar* wearing Elizabethan doublet and hose, and he notoriously equips ancient Rome with a medieval invention, the mechanical clock. Nonetheless, his Romans share a set of distinctive values, ideals, and assumptions. When Antony, at the end of the play, calls Brutus "the noblest Roman of them all," he is not simply praising Brutus as an individual. Instead, he is locating Brutus in a tradition of specifically "Roman" virtue, a virtue associated with the particular strengths of the republican form of government that Brutus died attempting to defend.

What does this virtue entail? Brutus's willingness to identify his abstract principles with the common good, as well as his intense suspicion of anyone who appears self-aggrandizing, is wholly characteristic of an ethos that distinguishes sharply between duty and pleasure, between public good and private self-enrichment. The heroes of the Roman Republic had always been celebrated for their incorruptibility and for their preference for public service, however thankless, over private goods such as marriage, friendship, sensual pleasure, and personal enrichment. Many of them adhered to a

Stoic code of personal conduct that mandated emotional self-control and self-sacrifice. At the same time, Rome was in fact a hotbed of nepotism and unscrupulousness, and its venality grew along with its power. Thus, pillars of the Roman Republic like Lucius Junius Brutus, Marcus Cato, Scipio Africanus, and Marcus Brutus himself were admired not merely because their civic-mindedness was socially valuable, but because such exemplars were rarer and more surprising than Romans liked to admit.

The sharp distinction that Roman culture made between public and private domains has important consequences in *Julius Caesar*. The public world is an all-male affair. Bonds and rivalries among men provide both the glue that holds the Roman Republic together and a competitive petulancy that ordinarily precludes a single individual's gaining too much power. We are given a vivid picture of this complex interpersonal dynamic in Cassius's account of his swimming contest with Caesar. In an incident of pure bravado, friends test their toughness against one another, and one ends up saving the other's life; but because all neediness is imagined to be shameful, what seems like generosity or charity is shot through with contempt. A similar rivalrous emotional intensity characterizes the highly charged quarrel and reconciliation between Brutus and Cassius in 4.2. For these men, loving someone does not preclude wanting to kill him.

Compared to the fraught ambivalence of the relationships between men, the heterosexual connections in the play seem rather pallid. Although Brutus is deeply attached to Portia, it does not occur to him to take her into his confidence until she struggles mightily for the privilege on the eve of the assassination; even then, all she requests is information, not permission to offer advice. Similarly, Decius easily shames Caesar into ignoring Calphurnia's foreboding dream:

> it were a mock
> Apt to be rendered, for someone to say,
> "Break up the Senate till another time
> When Caesar's wife shall meet with better dreams."
> (2.2.96–99)

Even the most powerful man in the Roman Empire, apparently, cannot risk being seen by other men to be influenced by a mere wife, no matter how intelligent or prescient she may be. Most telling, in what is perhaps a sign of textual corruption but more probably an instance of Shakespearean skill in delineating character, we are given two successive accounts of the way Brutus learns of Portia's suicide. In the first, Brutus divulges the loss himself to Cassius, expressing his grief in solitary conference with an old friend. Shortly thereafter, however, he tells his military subordinates that he has not received any news of Portia at all. Once informed that she has died "in strange manner," he affects a studied indifference, insisting that the tidings merely interfere with more important matters at hand. His apparent ability to sequester domestic concerns from public and military ones elicits the admiration of those around him: for true "Romans" are willing to incur huge emotional costs for what they imagine is the greater good.

Since honor, in this conceptual system, is supposed to involve fierce commitment to the public sphere, and since that sphere is exclusively the domain of men, the women in *Julius Caesar* are marginalized. Even within the confines of the household, they seem unable to cultivate an alternative form of social value. Maternity, for instance, is not a source of power here: Calphurnia is barren and Portia, too, is apparently childless. Their intuitive concern for their husbands has no practical effect. "Nobility" requires them to internalize values that for them have little use. Portia proves what she calls her masculine courage to her husband by the bizarre means of stabbing herself deliberately in the thigh, a gesture that suggests a self-castration, as if a woman were at best a slashed man. For the virtue that she claims to possess is not truly her own possession; rather, it is a quality reflected from her male relatives that makes her superior to ordinary women. "Think you I am no stronger than my sex, / Being so fathered and so husbanded?" (2.1.296–97). Portia kills herself, typically, in an exceptionally painful way, by swallowing hot coals. While the fabled hardihood of

Brutus falling on his sword. From Geffrey Whitney, A *Choice of Emblems* (1586).

Portia's father, Cato, or her husband, Brutus, has at least some military rationale, Portia's imitation of their fortitude seems pointlessly self-punishing, serving neither their ends nor her own.

The pressure of Roman values on the characters of *Julius Caesar* suggests that its protagonists are not entirely free to invent themselves; they are limited to the cultural materials at hand. Moreover the complexity of the situation in which they find themselves makes it difficult for them to know exactly why they behave as they do. Often in *Julius Caesar*, the same scene provides a character with a variety of motives, permitting alternative descriptions of a single action. Thus, when Brutus decides to participate in the conspiracy to kill Caesar, he believes that he has carefully sequestered his self-interest from his convictions about the common good. But Cassius has meanwhile been tossing flattering messages through his window, so the theater audience must consider the possibility that Brutus's appeal to principle is a rationalization, and that he is swayed by a personal ambition of which he may not be entirely aware.

Elsewhere, Shakespeare complicates his portraits by what might be called a technique of gradual release. By slowly making details available to the audience, he forces it to revise its previous impressions to take account of new information. For instance, Antony's bravura eulogy reaches a climax when he reads Caesar's will, thus harnessing the plebeians' greed to the end of revenging Caesar's death. A mere two scenes later, he is shown in conference with Lepidus and Octavius, giving brisk orders to minimize the cost of Caesar's generosity. The incongruity between the first scene and the second makes Antony's original celebration of his friend's magnanimity seem, in retrospect, less sincere or spontaneous. Nonetheless, the two scenes do not force the audience to a single obvious conclusion. Does Antony's later parsimony indicate that he was simply hypocritical when he used Caesar's will to provoke a riot? Perhaps, but not necessarily; he could simply have been caught up in a wave of loyalty to Caesar and in the pathos of the situation, or he could have had vaguely ambitious but not yet fully articulated plans. In such cases, Shakespeare's cunning dramatic presentation enhances the complexity of his characterizations. The realistic illusion depends as much on what he withholds from the audience as on what he provides it.

On other grounds, too, a reading focusing purely on character seems finally inadequate. In oft-cited lines, Cassius pronounces: "The fault, dear Brutus, is not in our stars, / But in ourselves, that we are underlings" (1.2.140–41). It is not at all clear, however, that he is right. Plutarch emphasizes how the fates of his biographical subjects fail to reflect their virtues. Caesar, who had miraculously survived so many strange adventures in hostile foreign lands, can be dispatched in a few minutes by his erstwhile friends just moments after leaving his own house. Cicero, whose oratory had held sway in Rome for so many years, is obliterated by Antony and Octavius practically as an afterthought. The gifted and honorable Brutus meets death after a military defeat that seems almost accidental. Cassius's suicide is even more haphazard. The inscrutable workings of fate play at least as great a role as personality does in determining the outcome of the action.

For this reason, virtually all the characters find it impossible to achieve a reliable perspective on events in which they are immersed. In the play's most literal case of limited vision, the "thick-sighted" Cassius misinterprets victory as defeat and kills himself moments before his triumphant soldiers arrive, hoping to congratulate him. Here and elsewhere, Shakespeare drums home the difference between the perspective of the theater audience, for whom the killing of Julius Caesar is an act centuries old, now replayed for its entertainment value, and the perspective of the characters within the play, for whom it is unfolding in the present moment, its consequences both dire and unknown. From our point of view, ironies are everywhere. Caesar pronounces upon his immovable constancy moments before being dispatched. His murderers, attempting to eliminate a potential tyrant, open the way for centuries of despotism. As Antony plots with Octavius to eliminate Lepidus, the audience knows, as Antony cannot, that the apparently modest, noncommittal Octavius will ultimately annihilate both his triumviral associates.

To be alive to such ironies, the characters would need to be able to look into the future. Struggling to understand their own place in history, they continually resort to augury, attempting—usually incorrectly—to comprehend the omens that shadow forth their fates. In *Julius Caesar*, omens are always telling, but they are rarely intelligible except in retrospect. No one knows what to make of the lions loose in the streets; the soothsayer arrives too late; Calphurnia's dream is misinterpreted; Cassius notices carrion birds on his standards but decides to disregard them. By emphasizing the analogies among personal, political, and natural forms of disruption, omens on the one hand intensify the significance of the play's characters: their decisions, quirks, and flaws affect the structure of the universe itself. They are indeed, as they have imagined themselves to be, persons of unprecedented and enormous significance. On the other hand, the reliability of omens challenges the notion that history is the product of personal effort. Augury implies restrictions on free will, suggesting that individuals are caught in the toils of a historical process they cannot possibly control or understand. Undergirding the other questions of authority and responsibility in *Julius Caesar* are two unanswerable questions: Who creates history? And what can that history possibly mean?

KATHARINE EISAMAN MAUS

SELECTED BIBLIOGRAPHY

Bloom, Harold, ed. *William Shakespeare's "Julius Caesar."* New York: Chelsea House, 1988. Anthology of critical essays.

Burckhardt, Sigurd. "How Not to Murder Caesar." *Shakespearean Meanings.* Princeton: Princeton UP, 1968. 3–21. Examines *Julius Caesar* and historical change.

Lucking, D. "Brutus' Reasons: *Julius Caesar* and the Mystery of Motive." *English Studies* 91 (2010): 119–32. Presents a detailed discussion of Brutus's enigmatic motives.

Miles, Gary B. "How Roman Are Shakespeare's 'Romans'?" *Shakespeare Quarterly* 40 (1989): 257–83. Analyzes Shakespeare's adaptation and revision of his classical sources.

Miola, Robert S. "*Julius Caesar* and the Tyrannicide Debate." *Renaissance Quarterly* 38 (1985): 271–89. Notes that Renaissance political theorists disagreed over whether the killing of a king was ever justified, and asserts that *Julius Caesar* shows Shakespeare's knowledge of this dispute.

Paster, Gail Kern. "'In the Spirit of Men There Is No Blood': Blood as a Trope of Gender in *Julius Caesar*." *Shakespeare Quarterly* 40 (1989): 284–98. Looks at manliness and bloody bodies in the play.

Rebhorn, Wayne. "The Crisis of the Aristocracy in *Julius Caesar*." *Renaissance Quarterly* 43 (1990): 75–111. Argues that Shakespeare's Romans resemble sixteenth-century English aristocrats in their desire for self-mastery and competitiveness with one another.

Visser, Nicholas. "Plebeian Politics in *Julius Caesar*." *Shakespeare in Southern Africa* 7 (1994): 22–31. Looks at how contemporary South African performances offer insights into the play's concept of class relations and of the mob.

Wilson, Richard, ed. *Julius Caesar*. New York: Palgrave, 2002. Excellent collection of critical essays on the play.

Zander, Horst, ed. *Julius Caesar: New Critical Essays*. New York: Routledge, 2005. A collection of twenty-one essays on the politics, plot, and language of *Julius Caesar*, on current critical debates, and on the play's performance history.

FILMS

Julius Caesar. 1953. Dir. Joseph L. Mankiewicz. USA. 120 min. This black-and-white Hollywood production features James Mason as a brooding, intense Brutus, John Gielgud as Cassius, and the young Marlon Brando, in an Oscar-nominated performance, as a charismatic Antony.

Julius Caesar. 1970. Dir. Stuart Burge. UK. 117 min. A brisk production, enlivened by colorful street and battle scenes. Jason Robards plays Brutus, Charlton Heston is Antony, John Gielgud is Caesar, and Diana Rigg is Portia.

Julius Caesar. 1979. Dir. Herbert Wise. UK. 161 min. A BBC-TV production. Textually faithful but blandly acted. David Collings is, however, effective as Cassius.

TEXTUAL INTRODUCTION

Shakespeare's *Julius Caesar* exists in a single early version, that of the First Folio of 1623. The Folio entitles the play "The Tragedie of Ivlivs Caesar" (also calling it "The Life and death of Julius Caesar" in the "Catalogve," or Table of Contents) and divides it into five acts (without scene divisions). The play presents few textual difficulties. In fact, it is nearly free of the minor inconsistencies in names and confusions of speech attribution that typically occur in most early Shakespeare texts. Thus, whatever the exact nature of the manuscript that furnished copy for the printed version, it must have been quite clearly written out, although no editor has detected any of the usual signs that would suggest the involvement of a professional scribe in the process.

The relatively high number and unusual detail of the play's stage directions (e.g., "*Thunder and lightning. Enter Julius Caesar in his nightgown*" [2.2.0]) have suggested to some that the manuscript may have been based on performance practice. The frequent, but seemingly inconsistent, spelling of names as if they were Italian rather than Latin ("Antonio" for Antonius or Antony, "Octavio" rather than Octavius, etc.) may indicate Shakespearean preference. By the time of its publication in 1623, more than twenty years had passed since the play's probable first staging at the (then newly built) Globe in 1599, and there is no reason to doubt that it was in performance during those years, yet the printed text shows very few inconsistencies in roles or action that might signal alteration or revision. Some editors have questioned whether the double disclosure of Portia's death in 4.3 (4.3.146–57 and 4.3.180–94) might represent alternative versions of the scene, but most have retained both disclosure sequences as integral to a full portrayal of Brutus's character under the stress of the moment. In general, the Folio printers treated the text with some care, leaving very few typesetting errors such as misplaced or turned letters or obvious misspellings (a few examples of such errors remaining uncorrected by the Folio are noted at 2.1.267, 4.3.115, 4.3.271) and correcting three substantive errors on one page of text during the print run (at 5.3.97, 5.3.101, 5.5.23 SD).

The Folio text of the play is somewhat unusual in Shakespeare's canon for the high number of its short lines. Some of these are simply instances of the typesetters' typical interventions to avoid overrunning the margins (e.g., 1.1.31 appears arbitrarily divided in F as "Wherefore rejoice? / What conquest brings he home?"). Many appear as verse lines shared between speakers (e.g., 3.1.10, 3.1.85, 3.1.121, 3.1.144), while some occur within individual speeches that are otherwise lined as pentameter (e.g., at 1.3.71).

Subsequent early reprints of the First Folio text appear in the Second Folio (1632), Third Folio (1663), and Fourth Folio (1685), and these texts correct certain minor errors as noted in the Textual Variants. The play also appeared in six separately printed late seventeenth-century quarto versions derived from the Folio; two of these can be dated to 1684 and 1691.

JAMES R. SIEMON

PERFORMANCE NOTE

Julius Caesar tempts most directors to make stark choices: Is Rome a place of heroic ideals and grandeur, or of pettiness and infighting? Are the conspirators freedom fighters or jealous malcontents? Is Caesar a compassionate leader or a tyrant? The inclination to find answers for these questions helps explain a stage history largely split between productions that strive to make Caesar and Antony worthy of their generic statuses (one a more sympathetic tragic center for gaining psychological depth, the other a more welcome revenger for shedding callousness and opportunism), and those that place Caesar at the head of fascist versions of Rome that recall the regimes of Pinochet, Mugabe, and Mussolini—contemporary analogues that help to justify those who rebel against him. Yet a central challenge for directors is in fact to resist such dichotomies, since the text generates a great deal of its energy through a string of paradoxes. Caesar clearly is and is not ambitious; Brutus is eminently loyal, high-minded, *and* traitorous; Cassius alternates as the play's most sinister and most sensitive character; Antony weeps over Caesar one moment and orders the execution of a friend in the next. Casca, too, is sardonic and assured in 1.2, timid and superstitious in 1.3, while Portia is roundly hailed as a model of perseverance, yet kills herself soon after Brutus departs for battle.

Retaining such inconsistencies while taking both Caesar's and the conspirators' sides is a continuous challenge for productions, but the result can enrich a play built on a fundamental dissonance between the historical personages the audience has reason to expect and the ambivalent characters that Shakespeare delivers. Contemporary productions have increasingly moved away from heroism and nobility on either side, privileging the domestic dramas and internal turmoil and hesitation of the major players. Though the affect, interiority, and relationships of Brutus, Cassius, Antony, and Caesar are key concerns, productions must also consider the size and composition of the crowd of plebeians; the staging of the storm in 1.3 and the third-act assassinations of Caesar and Cinna; whether the play's engagement with the supernatural is sincere or superficial; the nature and extent of Caesar's infirmities; and the threat of anticlimax after Antony's funeral oration.

BRETT GAMBOA

The Tragedy of Julius Caesar

[THE PERSONS OF THE PLAY

Julius CAESAR
CALPHURNIA, wife to Caesar
SERVANT to them

Marcus BRUTUS
PORTIA, wife to Brutus
LUCIUS, servant to them

Caius CASSIUS ⎫
CASCA ⎪
CINNA ⎪
DECIUS Brutus ⎬ patricians who join with Brutus against Caesar
Caius LIGARIUS ⎪
METELLUS Cimber ⎪
TREBONIUS ⎭

CICERO ⎫
PUBLIUS ⎬ senators
POPILIUS Lena ⎭

FLAVIUS ⎫ tribunes
MURELLUS ⎭

Mark ANTONY ⎫
LEPIDUS ⎬ triumvirs who rule Rome after Caesar's death
OCTAVIUS ⎭

LUCILIUS ⎫
TITINIUS ⎪
MESSALA ⎪
VARRUS ⎪
CLAUDIO ⎪
Young CATO ⎬ officers and soldiers in the armies of Brutus and Cassius
STRATO ⎪
VOLUMNIUS ⎪
DARDANIUS ⎪
CLITUS ⎪
Flavius ⎭

CARPENTER
COBBLER
SOOTHSAYER
ARTEMIDORUS
PLEBEIANS
CINNA the Poet
Another POET
PINDARUS, slave to Cassius

MESSENGER
SOLDIERS
SERVANTS
Commoners]

1.1

Enter FLAVIUS, MURELLUS, *and certain Commoners*
[including a CARPENTER *and* COBBLER] *over the stage.*[1]

FLAVIUS Hence! Home, you idle creatures, get you home!
   Is this a holiday? What, know you not,
   Being mechanical,° you ought not walk   *of the artisan class*
   Upon a laboring day without the sign°   *tools and garments*
5   Of your profession? —Speak, what trade art thou?
CARPENTER Why, sir, a carpenter.
MURELLUS Where is thy leather apron and thy rule?
   What dost thou with thy best apparel on?
   —You, sir, what trade are you?
10 COBBLER Truly, sir, in respect of° a fine workman, I am but,   *in comparison with*
   as you would say, a cobbler.[2]
MURELLUS But what trade art thou? Answer me directly.
COBBLER A trade, sir, that I hope I may use with a safe con-
   science, which is indeed, sir, a mender of bad soles.°   *(punning on "souls")*
15 FLAVIUS What trade, thou knave? Thou naughty° knave, what trade?   *wicked*
COBBLER Nay, I beseech you, sir, be not out[3] with me. Yet if
   you be out, sir, I can mend you.
MURELLUS What mean'st thou by that? Mend me, thou saucy fellow?
COBBLER Why, sir, cobble you.
20 FLAVIUS Thou art a cobbler, art thou?
COBBLER Truly, sir, all that I live by is with the awl. I meddle
   with no tradesman's matters nor women's matters,° but withal[4]   *(a bawdy joke)*
   I am indeed, sir, a surgeon to old shoes: when they are in great
   danger, I recover° them. As proper° men as ever trod upon   *resole; cure / fine*
25   neat's leather° have gone° upon my handiwork.   *cowhide / walked*
FLAVIUS But wherefore art not in thy shop today?
   Why dost thou lead these men about the streets?
COBBLER Truly, sir, to wear out their shoes, to get myself into
   more work. But indeed, sir, we make holiday to see Caesar
30   and to rejoice in his triumph.[5]
MURELLUS Wherefore rejoice? What conquest brings he home?
   What tributaries° follow him to Rome   *ransom payers*
   To grace in captive bonds his chariot wheels?[6]
   You blocks, you stones, you worse than senseless° things!   *inanimate*
35   O you hard hearts, you cruel men of Rome,
   Knew you not Pompey?[7] Many a time and oft
   Have you climbed up to walls and battlements,
   To towers and windows, yea, to chimney tops,
   Your infants in your arms, and there have sat

1.1 Location: A street in Rome.
1. PERFORMANCE COMMENT The crowd scenes in
Julius Caesar are important for framing the political
implications of the action. For a discussion of the
performance options, see Digital Edition PC 1.
2. Mender of shoes; bungler (the sense Murellus
understands).
3. Angry; worn out, like shoes.
4. Nevertheless; punning on "awl."

5. Triumphal procession in honor of victory (by Roman
custom, over foreign enemies, but here over Caesar's
political adversaries, Pompey's sons).
6. Captives were tied to their conquerors' chariots.
7. Pompey the Great, who had shared rule of Rome
with Caesar and Crassus; he was defeated by Caesar after their alliance disintegrated and was later
assassinated.

40 The livelong day with patient expectation
 To see great Pompey pass the streets of Rome.
 And when you saw his chariot but appear,
 Have you not made an universal shout,
 That Tiber[8] trembled underneath her banks

45 To hear the replication° of your sounds   *echo*
 Made in her concave shores?
 And do you now put on your best attire?
 And do you now cull out° a holiday?   *choose*
 And do you now strew flowers in his way

50 That comes in triumph over Pompey's blood?°   *offspring*
 Begone!
 Run to your houses, fall upon your knees,
 Pray to the gods to intermit[9] the plague
 That needs must light on this ingratitude.

55 FLAVIUS Go, go, good countrymen, and for this fault
 Assemble all the poor men of your sort,°   *rank*
 Draw them to Tiber banks, and weep your tears
 Into the channel, till the lowest stream
 Do kiss the most exalted shores of all.°   *tops of the riverbanks*
     Exeunt all the Commoners.

60 See whe'er° their basest mettle be not moved.   *whether*
 They vanish tongue-tied in their guiltiness.
 Go you down that way towards the Capitol;[1]
 This way will I. Disrobe the images
 If you do find them decked with ceremonies.[2]

65 MURELLUS May we do so?
 You know it is the Feast of Lupercal.[3]
 FLAVIUS It is no matter. Let no images
 Be hung with Caesar's trophies.° I'll about   *ornaments*
 And drive away the vulgar° from the streets;   *commoners*

70 So do you too, where you perceive them thick.
 These growing feathers plucked from Caesar's wing
 Will make him fly an ordinary pitch,[4]
 Who else° would soar above the view of men   *otherwise*
 And keep us all in servile fearfulness.   *Exeunt.*

1.2

Enter CAESAR, ANTONY *for the course,*[1] CALPHURNIA,
PORTIA, DECIUS, CICERO, BRUTUS, CASSIUS, CASCA,
a SOOTHSAYER; *after them* MURELLUS *and* FLAVIUS.

CAESAR Calphurnia.
CASCA   Peace ho, Caesar speaks.
CAESAR   Calphurnia.
CALPHURNIA Here, my lord.
CAESAR Stand you directly in Antonio's way
 When he doth run his course. —Antonio.

---

8. River that flows through Rome.
9. Withhold (plague was considered a divine punishment).
1. Hill on whose top was the Temple of Jupiter, where victorious generals in a triumph offered sacrifice.
2. Caesar's followers had put imperial crowns ("ceremonies") on his statues.

3. Lupercalia, a festival celebrated on February 15. Historically, Caesar's triumph took place in October.
4. At a medium height (an image from falconry).
1.2 Location: A public place in Rome.
1. During the Lupercalia, two celebrants ran naked through Rome, striking those they met with goatskin thongs.

5 ANTONY Caesar, my lord.

CAESAR Forget not in your speed, Antonio,
To touch Calphurnia, for our elders say
The barren touchèd in this holy chase
Shake off their sterile curse.

ANTONY   I shall remember.

10 When Caesar says, "Do this," it is performed.

CAESAR Set on° and leave no ceremony out.   *Proceed*

SOOTHSAYER Caesar.

CAESAR Ha? Who calls?

CASCA Bid every noise be still. Peace yet again.

15 CAESAR Who is it in the press° that calls on me?   *crowd*
I hear a tongue shriller than all the music
Cry "Caesar." Speak, Caesar is turned to hear.

SOOTHSAYER Beware the Ides[2] of March.

CAESAR   What man is that?

BRUTUS A soothsayer bids you beware the Ides of March.

20 CAESAR Set him before me. Let me see his face.

CASSIUS Fellow, come from the throng. Look upon Caesar.

CAESAR What say'st thou to me now? Speak once again.

SOOTHSAYER Beware the Ides of March.[3]

CAESAR He is a dreamer; let us leave him. Pass.°   *Onward*
            Sennet.° Exeunt all but BRUTUS *and* CASSIUS.   *Trumpet flourish*

25 CASSIUS Will you go see the order of the course?°   *running of the race*

BRUTUS Not I.

CASSIUS I pray you, do.

BRUTUS I am not gamesome.° I do lack some part   *fond of sport*
Of that quick° spirit that is in Antony.   *lively*

30 Let me not hinder, Cassius, your desires;
I'll leave you.

CASSIUS Brutus, I do observe you now of late.
I have not from your eyes that gentleness
And show of love as I was wont° to have.   *accustomed*

35 You bear too stubborn and too strange° a hand[4]   *unfriendly*
Over your friend that loves you.

BRUTUS   Cassius,
Be not deceived. If I have veiled my look,°   *seemed less outgoing*
I turn the trouble of my countenance°   *my troubled looks*
Merely° upon myself. Vexèd I am   *Wholly*

40 Of late with passions of some difference,°   *conflicting kinds*
Conceptions only proper° to myself,   *suitable*
Which give some soil,° perhaps, to my behaviors;   *blemish*
But let not therefore my good friends be grieved—
Among which number, Cassius, be you one—

45 Nor construe any further° my neglect   *make any more of*
Than that poor Brutus, with himself at war,
Forgets the shows of love to other men.

CASSIUS Then, Brutus, I have much mistook your passion,°   *feelings*
By means whereof[5] this breast of mine hath buried°   *concealed*

---

2. The ides marked roughly the midpoint of every Roman month (usually the 13th); in March, the 15th.
3. TEXTUAL COMMENT Short lines like this one, followed by complete iambic pentameter lines, may sometimes suggest a pause in performance, but Shakespeare uses short lines quite variously. See Digital Edition TC 1 for a fuller explanation.
4. Management of horse's reins (figurative).
5. In consequence of which mistake.

50 Thoughts of great value, worthy cogitations.
Tell me, good Brutus, can you see your face?
BRUTUS No, Cassius, for the eye sees not itself
But by reflection, by some other things.
CASSIUS 'Tis just,°   true
55 And it is very much lamented, Brutus,
That you have no such mirrors as will turn
Your hidden worthiness into your eye,
That you might see your shadow.° I have heard   reflection
Where many of the best respect° in Rome,   repute
60 Except immortal Caesar, speaking of Brutus
And groaning underneath this age's yoke,
Have wished that noble Brutus had his eyes.[6]
BRUTUS Into what dangers would you lead me, Cassius,
That you would have me seek into myself
65 For that which is not in me?
CASSIUS Therefore,° good Brutus, be prepared to hear;   As to that
And since you know you cannot see yourself
So well as by reflection, I, your glass,°   mirror
Will modestly discover° to yourself   reveal
70 That of yourself which you yet know not of.
And be not jealous on° me, gentle Brutus.   suspicious of
Were I a common laughter,° or did use   object of ridicule
To stale° with ordinary° oaths my love   debase / cheap
To every new protester;° if you know   declarer of friendship
75 That I do fawn on men and hug them hard
And after scandal° them; or if you know   defame
That I profess myself° in banqueting   declare friendship
To all the rout,° then hold me dangerous.   mob
            Flourish and shout.
BRUTUS What means this shouting? I do fear the people
Choose Caesar for their king.
80 CASSIUS   Ay, do you fear it?
Then must I think you would not have it so.
BRUTUS I would not, Cassius, yet I love him well.
But wherefore do you hold me here so long?
What is it that you would impart to me?
85 If it be aught toward the general good,
Set honor in one eye and death i'th' other
And I will look on both indifferently;°   impartially
For let the gods so speed me as[7] I love
The name of honor more than I fear death.
90 CASSIUS I know that virtue to be in you, Brutus,
As well as I do know your outward favor.°   appearance
Well, honor is the subject of my story.
I cannot tell what you and other men
Think of this life; but, for my single self,
95 I had as lief not be as° live to be   I had rather be dead than
In awe of such a thing as I myself.
I was born free as Caesar, so were you;
We both have fed as well, and we can both
Endure the winter's cold as well as he.

---

6. That is, could see properly.   7. Make me fortunate insofar as.

100	For once, upon a raw and gusty day,	
	The troubled Tiber chafing with° her shores,	*raging against*
	Caesar said to me, "Dar'st thou, Cassius, now	
	Leap in with me into this angry flood	
	And swim to yonder point?"° Upon the word,	*promontory*
105	Accoutered° as I was, I plungèd in	*Fully dressed*
	And bade him follow; so indeed he did.	
	The torrent roared, and we did buffet it	
	With lusty sinews, throwing it aside	
	And stemming° it with hearts of controversy.°	*confronting / rivalry*
110	But ere we could arrive° the point proposed,	*reach*
	Caesar cried, "Help me, Cassius, or I sink!"	
	I, as Aeneas,[8] our great ancestor,	
	Did from the flames of Troy upon his shoulder	
	The old Anchises bear, so from the waves of Tiber	
115	Did I the tired Caesar; and this man	
	Is now become a god, and Cassius is	
	A wretched creature and must bend his body°	*must bow*
	If Caesar carelessly but nod on him.	
	He had a fever when he was in Spain,	
120	And when the fit was on him, I did mark	
	How he did shake. 'Tis true, this god did shake.	
	His coward lips did from their color fly,[9]	
	And that same eye whose bend° doth awe the world	*glance*
	Did lose his° luster. I did hear him groan.	*its*
125	Ay, and that tongue of his that bade the Romans	
	Mark him and write his speeches in their books,	
	"Alas," it cried, "Give me some drink, Titinius,"	
	As a sick girl. Ye gods, it doth amaze me	
	A man of such a feeble temper° should	*constitution*
130	So get the start of° the majestic world	*advantage over*
	And bear the palm° alone.	*be victor*
	Shout. Flourish.	
	BRUTUS Another general shout?	
	I do believe that these applauses are	
	For some new honors that are heaped on Caesar.	
135	CASSIUS Why, man, he doth bestride the narrow world	
	Like a Colossus,[1] and we petty men	
	Walk under his huge legs and peep about	
	To find ourselves dishonorable graves.	
	Men at some time are masters of their fates.	
140	The fault, dear Brutus, is not in our stars,	
	But in ourselves, that we are underlings.	
	"Brutus" and "Caesar"—what should be in that "Caesar"?	
	Why should that name be sounded more than yours?	
	Write them together, yours is as fair a name;	
145	Sound them, it doth become the mouth as well;	
	Weigh them, it is as heavy; conjure with 'em,	
	"Brutus" will start[2] a spirit as soon as "Caesar."	

8. Legendary Trojan warrior and founder of Rome; when the Greeks burned Troy, he carried his father, Anchises, out on his back.
9. Did turn pale; did desert their flag (Caesar suffered epileptic seizures).

1. Giant statue of Apollo, which straddled the harbor of Rhodes.
2. Raise (only the names of the gods were thought to be able to raise the dead).

Now, in the names of all the gods at once,
Upon what meat° doth this our Caesar feed   *food*
150   That he is grown so great? Age, thou art shamed!
Rome, thou hast lost the breed of noble bloods!
When went there by an age, since the great flood,[3]
But it was famed with° more than with one man?   *renowned for*
When could they say, till now, that talked of Rome,
155   That her wide walks encompassed but one man?
Now is it Rome indeed, and room° enough,   *(pronounced like "Rome")*
When there is in it but one only man.
Oh, you and I have heard our fathers say
There was a Brutus once[4] that would have brooked°   *endured*
160   Th'eternal devil to keep his state° in Rome   *hold court*
As easily as a king.
BRUTUS   That you do love me, I am nothing jealous.°   *not at all uncertain*
What you would work° me to, I have some aim.°   *persuade / idea*
How I have thought of this, and of these times,
165   I shall recount hereafter. For this present,°   *present time*
I would not, so with love° I might entreat you,   *if in friendship*
Be any further moved.° What you have said,   *persuaded*
I will consider; what you have to say,
I will with patience hear, and find a time
170   Both meet° to hear and answer such high things.   *Fitting both*
Till then, my noble friend, chew upon this:
Brutus had rather be a villager
Than to repute himself a son of Rome
Under these hard conditions as this time
175   Is like to lay upon us.
CASSIUS   I am glad that my weak words
Have struck but thus much show of fire from Brutus.
        Enter CASSIUS and his train.°   *retinue*
BRUTUS   The games are done, and Caesar is returning.
CASSIUS   As they pass by, pluck Casca by the sleeve,[5]
180   And he will, after his sour fashion, tell you
What hath proceeded worthy° note today.   *worthy of*
BRUTUS   I will do so. But look you, Cassius,
The angry spot doth glow on Caesar's brow,
And all the rest look like a chidden° train: *scolded*
185   Calphurnia's cheek is pale, and Cicero
Looks with such ferret[6] and such fiery eyes
As we have seen him in the Capitol,
Being crossed in conference° by some senators.   *opposed in debate*
CASSIUS   Casca will tell us what the matter is.
190   CAESAR   Antonio.
ANTONY   Caesar.
CAESAR   Let me have men about me that are fat,
Sleek-headed men, and such as sleep a-nights.
Yond Cassius has a lean and hungry look.
195   He thinks too much; such men are dangerous.

---

3. A great flood was recorded in classical as well as
biblical accounts.
4. Lucius Junius Brutus, an ancestor of Marcus Brutus and a founder of the Roman Republic, famed for
his role in expelling the Tarquins, who had ruled Rome

as kings.
5. Like "cloak" (line 215), "doublet" (line 261), and
"unbraced" (1.3.48), this suggests a performance in
Elizabethan dress.
6. Ferretlike (red and darting).

ANTONY Fear him not, Caesar; he's not dangerous.
 He is a noble Roman and well given.°   *well disposed*
CAESAR Would he were fatter! But I fear him not.
 Yet if my name[7] were liable to fear,
200 I do not know the man I should avoid
 So soon as that spare Cassius. He reads much,
 He is a great observer, and he looks
 Quite through[8] the deeds of men. He loves no plays,
 As thou dost, Antony; he hears no music.[9]
205 Seldom he smiles, and smiles in such a sort°   *manner*
 As if he mocked himself and scorned his spirit
 That could be moved to smile at anything.
 Such men as he be never at heart's ease
 Whiles they behold a greater than themselves,
210 And therefore are they very dangerous.
 I rather tell thee what is to be feared
 Than what I fear; for always I am Caesar.
 Come on my right hand, for this ear is deaf,
 And tell me truly what thou think'st of him.
     Sennet. Exeunt CAESAR *and his train*
       [*leaving* CASCA *behind*].
215 CASCA You pulled me by the cloak.° Would you speak with me? *pulled me aside*
 BRUTUS Ay, Casca. Tell us what hath chanced today
 That Caesar looks so sad.°   *serious*
 CASCA Why, you were with him, were you not?
 BRUTUS I should not then ask Casca what had chanced.
220 CASCA Why, there was a crown offered him; and being offered
 him, he put it by with the back of his hand, thus, and then
 the people fell a-shouting.
 BRUTUS What was the second noise for?
 CASCA Why, for that, too.
225 CASSIUS They shouted thrice. What was the last cry for?
 CASCA Why, for that, too.
 BRUTUS Was the crown offered him thrice?
 CASCA Ay, marry,° was't, and he put it by thrice, every time *indeed*
 gentler than other; and at every putting-by, mine honest° *(sarcastic)*
230 neighbors shouted.
 CASSIUS Who offered him the crown?
 CASCA Why, Antony.
 BRUTUS Tell us the manner of it, gentle° Casca.   *noble*
 CASCA I can as well be hanged as tell the manner of it. It was
235 mere foolery;° I did not mark it. I saw Mark Antony offer him *utter absurdity*
 a crown—yet 'twas not a crown neither, 'twas one of these
 coronets—and, as I told you, he put it by once; but for all that,
 to my thinking, he would fain° have had it. Then he offered it *gladly*
 to him again; then he put it by again; but to my thinking, he
240 was very loath to lay his fingers off it. And then he offered it
 the third time; he put it the third time by, and still° as he *continually*
 refused it the rabblement hooted and clapped their chopped° *chapped*
 hands, and threw up their sweaty nightcaps,[1] and uttered such

---

7. One of my name (that is, myself).
8. Completely into the motives of.
9. Dislike of music was regarded as a sign of wicked-

ness; see *The Merchant of Venice*.
1. Artisans wore felt hats on holidays.

a deal of stinking breath because Caesar refused the crown
245 that it had—almost—choked Caesar, for he swooned and fell
down at it; and for mine own part, I durst not laugh for fear of
opening my lips and receiving the bad air.
CASSIUS   But soft, I pray you. What, did Caesar swoon?
CASCA   He fell down in the marketplace, and foamed at mouth,
250 and was speechless.
BRUTUS   'Tis very like; he hath the falling sickness.[2]
CASSIUS   No, Caesar hath it not, but you and I,
And honest Casca, we have the falling sickness.
CASCA   I know not what you mean by that, but I am sure Cae-
255 sar fell down. If the tag-rag people° did not clap him and   *riffraff*
hiss him, according as he pleased and displeased them, as
they use° to do the players in the theater, I am no true man.   *are accustomed*
BRUTUS   What said he when he came unto himself?
CASCA   Marry, before he fell down, when he perceived the
260 common herd was glad he refused the crown, he plucked me
ope[3] his doublet° and offered them his throat to cut; an° I had   *jacket / if*
been a man of any occupation,° if I would not have taken him   *workingman*
at a° word, I would I might go to hell among the rogues. And   *his*
so he fell. When he came to himself again, he said if he had
265 done or said anything amiss, he desired their worships to
think it was his infirmity. Three or four wenches where I
stood cried, "Alas, good soul!" and forgave him with all their
hearts. But there's no heed to be taken of them; if Caesar
had stabbed their mothers, they would have done no less.
270 BRUTUS   And after that, he came thus sad away?
CASCA   Ay.
CASSIUS   Did Cicero say anything?
CASCA   Ay, he spoke Greek.
CASSIUS   To what effect?
275 CASCA   Nay, an I tell you that, I'll ne'er look you i'th' face again.
But those that understood him smiled at one another and
shook their heads; but, for mine own part, it was Greek to me.
I could tell you more news, too: Murellus and Flavius, for
pulling scarves[4] off Caesar's images, are put to silence.° Fare   *deprived of office*
280 you well. There was more foolery yet, if I could remember it.
CASSIUS   Will you sup with me tonight, Casca?
CASCA   No, I am promised forth.°   *elsewhere*
CASSIUS   Will you dine with me tomorrow?
CASCA   Ay, if I be alive, and your mind hold,° and your dinner   *does not change*
285 worth the eating.
CASSIUS   Good. I will expect you.
CASCA   Do so. Farewell both.   *Exit.*
BRUTUS   What a blunt fellow is this grown to be!
He was quick mettle° when he went to school.   *of energetic spirit*
290 CASSIUS   So is he now in execution
Of any bold or noble enterprise,
However he puts on this tardy form.[5]
This rudeness° is a sauce to his good wit,°   *harshness / intelligence*

---

2. Epilepsy (Cassius then puns on "collapse from   4. Decorations (see 1.1.63–64).
power").   5. Although he feigns this indolent manner.
3. Pulled open ("me" is colloquial).

        Which gives men stomach° to digest his words   *relish*

295   With better appetite.

    BRUTUS   And so it is. For this time I will leave you.

        Tomorrow, if you please to speak with me,

        I will come home to you; or, if you will,

        Come home to me, and I will wait for you.

300   CASSIUS   I will do so. Till then, think of the world.°   *Exit* BRUTUS.   *state of affairs*

        Well, Brutus, thou art noble. Yet I see

        Thy honorable mettle may be wrought

        From that it is disposed.⁶ Therefore it is meet°   *fitting*

        That noble minds keep ever with their likes;

305   For who so firm that cannot be seduced?

        Caesar doth bear me hard,° but he loves Brutus.   *ill will*

        If I were Brutus now, and he were Cassius,

        He should not humor° me. I will this night   *influence*

        In several hands° in at his windows throw,   *various handwritings*

310   As if they came from several citizens,

        Writings, all tending to° the great opinion   *intimating*

        That Rome holds of his name, wherein obscurely°   *cryptically*

        Caesar's ambition shall be glancèd° at.   *hinted*

        And after this, let Caesar seat him sure,⁷

315   For we will shake him or worse days endure.   *Exit.*

1.3

Thunder and lightning. Enter CASCA *and* CICERO.

    CICERO   Good even,° Casca. Brought° you Caesar home?   *evening / Escorted*

        Why are you breathless? And why stare you so?

    CASCA   Are not you moved, when all the sway° of earth   *realm*

        Shakes like a thing unfirm? O Cicero,

5   I have seen tempests when the scolding winds

        Have rived° the knotty oaks, and I have seen   *split*

        Th'ambitious ocean swell, and rage, and foam

        To be exalted with° the threat'ning clouds;   *raised as high as*

        But never till tonight, never till now,

10   Did I go through a tempest dropping fire.

        Either there is a civil strife in heaven,

        Or else the world, too saucy° with the gods,   *insolent*

        Incenses them to send destruction.

    CICERO   Why, saw you anything more° wonderful?   *else*

15   CASCA   A common slave—you know him well by sight—

        Held up his left hand, which did flame and burn

        Like twenty torches joined; and yet his hand,

        Not sensible of° fire, remained unscorched.   *Not feeling*

        Besides—I ha' not since put up° my sword—   *sheathed*

20   Against° the Capitol I met a lion,¹   *Next to*

        Who glazed° upon me and went surly by   *stared*

        Without annoying° me. And there were drawn   *harming*

        Upon a heap² a hundred ghastly° women   *terrified*

---

6. *wrought . . . disposed:* changed from its natural property (alluding to the alchemical transmutation of metals).
7. Establish himself securely.
1.3 Location: A street in Rome.
1. African beasts were brought to Rome in large quan-
tities for display and for spectacular staged games; kept in an enclosure outside the city, they occasionally escaped. Casca's encounter is thus unusual but not impossible.
2. Huddled in a crowd.

Transformèd with their fear, who swore they saw
25 Men all in fire walk up and down the streets.
And yesterday the bird of night° did sit   screech owl
Even at noonday upon the marketplace,
Hooting and shrieking. When these prodigies°   abnormalities
Do so conjointly meet,° let not men say,   happen together
30 "These are their reasons, they are natural,"
For I believe they are portentous things
Unto the climate° that they point upon.   region
CICERO   Indeed, it is a strange-disposèd time;
But men may construe things after their fashion,°   in their own way
35 Clean° from the purpose of the things themselves.   Completely different
Comes Caesar to the Capitol tomorrow?
CASCA   He doth; for he did bid Antonio
Send word to you he would be there tomorrow.
CICERO   Good night then, Casca. This disturbèd sky
Is not to walk in.
40 CASCA   Farewell, Cicero.   *Exit* CICERO.
            Enter CASSIUS.
CASSIUS   Who's there?
CASCA   A Roman.
CASSIUS   Casca, by your voice.
CASCA   Your ear is good. Cassius, what night is this?
CASSIUS   A very pleasing night to honest men.
CASCA   Who ever knew the heavens menace so?
45 CASSIUS   Those that have known the earth so full of faults.
For my part, I have walked about the streets,
Submitting me unto the perilous night,
And thus unbracèd,° Casca, as you see,   with open doublet
Have bared my bosom to the thunder-stone;°   thunderbolt
50 And when the cross° blue lightning seemed to open   forked; hostile
The breast of heaven, I did present myself
Even° in the aim and very flash of it.   Exactly
CASCA   But wherefore did you so much tempt the heavens?
It is the part of men to fear and tremble
55 When the most mighty gods by tokens° send   signs
Such dreadful heralds to astonish° us.   dismay
CASSIUS   You are dull, Casca, and those sparks of life
That should be in a Roman you do want,°   lack
Or else you use not. You look pale, and gaze,
60 And put on fear, and cast yourself in wonder
To see the strange impatience of the heavens.
But if you would consider the true cause
Why all these fires, why all these gliding ghosts,
Why birds and beasts from quality and kind,[3]
65 Why old men, fools, and children calculate,°   prophesy
Why all these things change from their ordinance,°   usual order
Their natures, and pre-formèd faculties,
To monstrous° quality—why, you shall find   unnatural
That heaven hath infused them with these spirits
70 To make them instruments of fear and warning

---

3. *from quality and kind:* behaving contrary to their nature.

Unto some monstrous state.[4]
Now could I, Casca, name to thee a man
Most like this dreadful night
That thunders, lightens, opens graves, and roars
75 As doth the lion in the Capitol;[5]
A man no mightier than thyself or me
In personal action, yet prodigious° grown,   *ominous*
And fearful,° as these strange eruptions° are.   *terrifying / upheavals*
    CASCA 'Tis Caesar that you mean, is it not, Cassius?
80   CASSIUS Let it be who it is; for Romans now
Have thews° and limbs like to their ancestors,   *sinews*
But, woe the while,° our fathers' minds are dead,   *alas for these times*
And we are governed with our mothers' spirits.
Our yoke and sufferance° show us womanish.   *servitude and patience*
85   CASCA Indeed, they say the senators tomorrow
Mean to establish Caesar as a king,
And he shall wear his crown by sea and land
In every place save here in Italy.
    CASSIUS I know where I will wear this dagger then;
90 Cassius from bondage will deliver Cassius.
Therein, ye gods, you make the weak most strong;
Therein, ye gods, you tyrants do defeat.
Nor stony tower, nor walls of beaten brass,
Nor airless dungeon, nor strong links of iron,
95 Can be retentive to° the strength of spirit;   *Can imprison*
But life, being weary of these worldly bars,°   *hindrances*
Never lacks power to dismiss itself.
If I know this, know all the world besides,
That part of tyranny that I do bear
I can shake off at pleasure.
             Thunder still.
100 CASCA   So can I.
So every bondman in his own hand bears
The power to cancel his captivity.
    CASSIUS And why should Caesar be a tyrant then?
Poor man, I know he would not be a wolf
105 But that he sees the Romans are but sheep;
He were no lion, were not Romans hinds.°   *female deer; servants*
Those that with haste will make a mighty fire
Begin it with weak straws. What trash is Rome!
What rubbish and what offal,° when it serves   *waste product*
110 For the base° matter to illuminate   *underlying; despicable*
So vile a thing as Caesar! But, O grief,
Where hast thou led me? I perhaps speak this
Before a willing bondman; then I know
My answer must be made.[6] But I am armed,° *(physically and morally)*
115 And dangers are to me indifferent.°   *insignificant*
    CASCA You speak to Casca, and to such a man
That is no fleering° telltale. Hold.° My hand. *sneering / Enough*
Be factious° for redress of all these griefs,   *Form a group*

---

4. Abnormal situation; atrocious government.
5. Possibly the lion of line 20; or Shakespeare may imagine that the Romans kept a live lion or two at the

Capitol as the English did at the Tower of London, where they were a popular attraction.
6. I must pay the penalty.

And I will set this foot of mine as far
As who° goes farthest.   *whoever*

120 CASSIUS   There's a bargain made.
Now know you, Casca, I have moved° already   *persuaded*
Some certain of the noblest-minded Romans
To undergo° with me an enterprise   *undertake*
Of honorable, dangerous consequence;

125 And I do know by this° they stay° for me   *this time / wait*
In Pompey's Porch.[7] For now, this fearful night,
There is no stir or walking in the streets;
And the complexion of the element°   *disposition of the sky*
In favor's° like the work we have in hand,   *In appearance is*

130 Most bloody, fiery, and most terrible.
          Enter CINNA.
CASCA   Stand close° awhile, for here comes one in haste.   *concealed*
CASSIUS   'Tis Cinna; I do know him by his gait.
He is a friend. —Cinna, where haste you so?
CINNA   To find out you. Who's that? Metellus Cimber?

135 CASSIUS   No, it is Casca, one incorporate°   *a party*
To our attempts. Am I not stayed for,° Cinna?   *awaited*
CINNA   I am glad on't.[8] What a fearful night is this!
There's two or three of us have seen strange sights.
CASSIUS   Am I not stayed for? Tell me.

140 CINNA   Yes, you are. O Cassius, if you could
But win the noble Brutus to our party—
CASSIUS   Be you content. Good Cinna, take this paper,
And look you lay it in the praetor's[9] chair,
Where Brutus may but° find it; and throw this   *must surely*

145 In at his window; set this up with wax
Upon old Brutus'° statue. All this done,   *Lucius Junius Brutus's*
Repair° to Pompey's Porch, where you shall find us.   *Proceed*
Is Decius Brutus and Trebonius there?
CINNA   All but Metellus Cimber, and he's gone

150 To seek you at your house. Well, I will hie°   *hasten*
And so bestow these papers as you bade me.
CASSIUS   That done, repair to Pompey's Theater.
                                        Exit CINNA.
Come, Casca, you and I will yet ere day
See Brutus at his house. Three parts° of him   *quarters*

155 Is ours already, and the man entire
Upon the next encounter yields him ours.
CASCA   Oh, he sits high in all the people's hearts;
And that which would appear offense in us,
His countenance, like richest alchemy,[1]

160 Will change to virtue and to worthiness.
CASSIUS   Him, and his worth, and our great need of him,
You have right well conceited.° Let us go,   *understood*
For it is after midnight, and ere day
We will awake him and be sure of him.   *Exeunt.*

---

7. Portico of a theater commissioned by Pompey.
8. Cinna is responding to Cassius's information about Casca.
9. Brutus was one of sixteen praetors, or chief magistrates, subordinate only to the two consuls.
1. Alchemy attempted to change base metals into gold. *countenance:* approval; noble appearance.

2.1

Enter BRUTUS *in his orchard.*

BRUTUS   What, Lucius, ho!
  —I cannot by the progress of the stars
  Give guess how near to day. —Lucius, I say!
  —I would it were my fault to sleep so soundly.
5 —When, Lucius, when?° Awake, I say. What, Lucius!   *(expressing impatience)*
        Enter LUCIUS.
LUCIUS   Called you, my lord?
BRUTUS   Get me a taper° in my study, Lucius.   *candle*
  When it is lighted, come and call me here.
LUCIUS   I will, my lord.   *Exit.*
10 BRUTUS   It must be by his° death; and for my part   *(Caesar's)*
  I know no personal cause to spurn° at him   *kick*
  But for the general.° He would be crowned: *common good*
  How that might change his nature, there's the question.
  It is the bright day that brings forth the adder,
15 And that craves° wary walking. Crown him that,   *calls for*
  And then I grant we put a sting in him
  That at his will he may do danger with.
  Th'abuse of greatness is when it disjoins
  Remorse° from power; and to speak truth of Caesar,   *Conscience*
20 I have not known when his affections swayed°   *passions ruled*
  More than his reason. But 'tis a common proof°   *experience*
  That lowliness° is young ambition's ladder,   *humility*
  Whereto the climber upward turns his face;
  But when he once attains the upmost round°   *rung*
25 He then unto the ladder turns his back,
  Looks in the clouds, scorning the base degrees[1]
  By which he did ascend. So Caesar may;
  Then, lest he may, prevent. And since the quarrel
  Will bear no color for the thing he is,[2]
30 Fashion° it thus: that what he is, augmented,   *Describe*
  Would run to these and these extremities.
  And therefore think him as a serpent's egg
  Which, hatched, would as his kind° grow mischievous,°   *by its nature / harmful*
  And kill him in the shell.
        Enter LUCIUS.
35 LUCIUS   The taper burneth in your closet,° sir.   *private room*
  Searching the window for a flint, I found
  This paper, thus sealed up, and I am sure
  It did not lie there when I went to bed.
        [He] gives him the letter.
BRUTUS   Get you to bed again; it is not day.
40 Is not tomorrow, boy, the first of March?[3]
LUCIUS   I know not, sir.
BRUTUS   Look in the calendar and bring me word.
LUCIUS   I will, sir.   *Exit.*
BRUTUS   The exhalations° whizzing in the air   *meteors*
45 Give so much light that I may read by them.

2.1 Location: Outside Brutus's house.
1. Low rungs; contemptible means; lowly social ranks.
2. Will find no plausible pretext in his conduct so far.

3. TEXTUAL COMMENT Some editors emend "first" to "Ides." For the rationale behind retaining the Folio "first," see Digital Edition TC 2.

        [He] opens the letter and reads.
        "Brutus, thou sleep'st. Awake, and see thyself.
        Shall Rome, et cetera?[4] Speak, strike, redress!"
        "Brutus, thou sleep'st. Awake."
        Such instigations have been often dropped
50   Where I have took them up.
        "Shall Rome, et cetera?" Thus must I piece it out:
        Shall Rome stand under one man's awe? What, Rome?
        My ancestors did from the streets of Rome
        The Tarquin drive when he was called a king.[5]
55   "Speak, strike, redress!" Am I entreated
        To speak and strike? O Rome, I make thee promise,
        If the redress will follow,[6] thou receivest
        Thy full petition at the hand of Brutus.
            Enter LUCIUS.
    LUCIUS   Sir, March is wasted fifteen days.
            Knock within.
60   BRUTUS   'Tis good. Go to the gate; somebody knocks.
                         [Exit LUCIUS.*]*
        Since Cassius first did whet° me against Caesar,   *incite*
        I have not slept.
        Between the acting of a dreadful thing
        And the first motion,° all the interim is   *impulse*
65   Like a phantasma° or a hideous dream: *nightmare*
        The genius° and the mortal instruments[7]   *immortal spirit*
        Are then in council, and the state of man,
        Like to a little kingdom, suffers then
        The nature of an insurrection.[8]
            Enter LUCIUS.
70   LUCIUS   Sir, 'tis your brother Cassius[9] at the door,
        Who doth desire to see you.
    BRUTUS   Is he alone?
    LUCIUS   No, sir, there are more with him.
    BRUTUS   Do you know them?
    LUCIUS   No, sir. Their hats are plucked about their ears,
        And half their faces buried in their cloaks,
75   That by no means I may discover° them   *identify*
        By any mark of favor.°   *distinctive feature*
    BRUTUS   Let 'em enter.   *[Exit* LUCIUS.*]*
        They are the faction. O conspiracy,
        Sham'st thou to show thy dang'rous brow by night
        When evils are most free?° Oh, then, by day   *uninhibited*
80   Where wilt thou find a cavern dark enough
        To mask thy monstrous visage? Seek none, conspiracy.
        Hide it in smiles and affability;
        For if thou path, thy native semblance on,°   *walk undisguised*

---

4. TEXTUAL COMMENT "Et cetera" might be a word
in the note Brutus is reading, or it might indicate
that he is not bothering to read the entire note
because he knows its contents in advance. Digital
Edition TC 3 explains why the first possibility is the
more likely: the note implies rather than states a
dangerous proposition.

5. See note to 1.2.159.
6. That is, if killing Caesar will restore the Republic.
7. Bodily powers.
8. *the state . . . insurrection:* referring to a commonplace analogy between disorder in man, in the body
politic, and in nature.
9. Cassius was married to Brutus's sister.

Not Erebus° itself were dim enough   *dark underworld region*
85   To hide thee from prevention.[1]

Enter the conspirators, CASSIUS, CASCA, DECIUS,
    CINNA, METELLUS, *and* TREBONIUS.

CASSIUS   I think we are too bold[2] upon your rest.
  Good morrow, Brutus. Do we trouble you?
BRUTUS   I have been up this hour, awake all night.
  Know I these men that come along with you?
90   CASSIUS   Yes, every man of them; and no man here
  But honors you; and every one doth wish
  You had but that opinion of yourself
  Which every noble Roman bears of you.
  This is Trebonius.
BRUTUS   He is welcome hither.
CASSIUS   This, Decius Brutus.
95   BRUTUS   He is welcome too.
CASSIUS   This, Casca; this, Cinna; and this, Metellus Cimber.
BRUTUS   They are all welcome.
  What watchful° cares do interpose themselves   *sleep-preventing*
  Betwixt your eyes and night?
CASSIUS   Shall I entreat a word?

They whisper.
100   DECIUS   Here lies the east. Doth not the day break here?
CASCA   No.
CINNA   Oh, pardon, sir, it doth; and yon gray lines
  That fret° the clouds are messengers of day.   *interlace*
CASCA   You shall confess that you are both deceived.
105   Here, as I point my sword, the sun arises,
  Which is a great way growing° on the south,   *encroaching*
  Weighing° the youthful season of the year.   *On account of*
  Some two months hence up higher toward the north
  He first presents his fire, and the high° east   *due*
110   Stands, as the Capitol, directly here.
BRUTUS   Give me your hands all over, one by one.
CASCA   And let us swear our resolution.
BRUTUS   No, not an oath. If not the face° of men,   *(grave) expressions*
  The sufferance° of our souls, the time's abuse[3]—   *suffering*
115   If these be motives weak, break off betimes,°   *at once*
  And every man hence to his idle° bed.   *unused; lazy*
  So let high-sighted° tyranny range on   *arrogant*
  Till each man drop by lottery.[4] But if these,°   *these reasons*
  As I am sure they do, bear fire enough
120   To kindle cowards and to steel with valor
  The melting spirits of women, then, countrymen,
  What need we any spur but our own cause
  To prick us to redress? What other bond
  Than secret Romans[5] that have spoke the word
125   And will not palter?° And what other oath   *equivocate*
  Than honesty° to honesty engaged   *integrity*
  That this shall be or we will fall for it?

---

1. From being recognized and thwarted.
2. We intrude too presumptuously.
3. The corruption of the present time.
4. Chance (the tyrant's caprice).
5. Than that we are Romans capable of secrecy.

Swear° priests and cowards and men cautelous,°   *Let swear / crafty; wary*
Old feeble carrions,° and such suffering souls   *corpselike men*
130 That welcome wrongs.[6] Unto bad causes swear
Such creatures as men doubt,° but do not stain   *suspect*
The even° virtue of our enterprise,   *just; straightforward*
Nor th'insuppressive° mettle of our spirits,   *the indomitable*
To think that or° our cause or our performance   *either*
135 Did need an oath, when every drop of blood
That every Roman bears, and nobly bears,
Is guilty of a several bastardy[7]
If he do break the smallest particle
Of any promise that hath passed from him.
140 CASSIUS But what of Cicero? Shall we sound him?°   *find out his thoughts*
I think he will stand very strong with us.
CASCA Let us not leave him out.
CINNA   No, by no means.
METELLUS Oh, let us have him, for his silver hairs
Will purchase us a good opinion°   *reputation*
145 And buy men's voices to commend our deeds.
It shall be said his judgment ruled our hands;
Our youths and wildness shall no whit appear,
But all be buried in his gravity.
BRUTUS Oh, name him not. Let us not break with° him,   *disclose our plans to*
150 For he will never follow anything
That other men begin.
CASSIUS Then leave him out.
CASCA Indeed, he is not fit.
DECIUS Shall no man else be touched, but only Caesar?
155 CASSIUS Decius, well urged.° I think it is not meet°   *suggested / proper*
Mark Antony, so well beloved of Caesar,
Should outlive Caesar. We shall find of him
A shrewd° contriver; and you know, his means,   *malicious*
If he improve° them, may well stretch so far   *make the most of*
160 As to annoy° us all. Which to prevent,   *harm*
Let Antony and Caesar fall together.
BRUTUS Our course[8] will seem too bloody, Caius Cassius,
To cut the head off and then hack the limbs,
Like wrath in death and envy° afterwards;   *malice*
165 For Antony is but a limb of Caesar.
Let's be sacrificers, but not butchers, Caius.
We all stand up against the spirit of Caesar,
And in the spirit of men there is no blood.
Oh, that we then could come by° Caesar's spirit   *obtain*
170 And not dismember Caesar! But, alas,
Caesar must bleed for it. And, gentle friends,
Let's kill him boldly, but not wrathfully;
Let's carve him as a dish fit for the gods,
Not hew him as a carcass fit for hounds.
175 And let our hearts, as subtle° masters do,   *cunning*
Stir up their servants° to an act of rage   *(that is, our hands)*
And after seem to chide 'em. This shall make
Our purpose necessary and not envious,°   *malicious*

---

6. That gladly submit to oppression.   non-Roman blood.
7. Will show itself individually to be adulterated by 8. Punning on "corse," meaning "corpse."

Which so appearing to the common eyes,
180   We shall be called purgers,° not murderers.   *purifiers*
And for Mark Antony, think not of him,
For he can do no more than Caesar's arm
When Caesar's head is off.
CASSIUS   Yet I fear him,
For in the engrafted° love he bears to Caesar—   *deep-rooted*
185 BRUTUS   Alas, good Cassius, do not think of him.
If he love Caesar, all that he can do
Is to himself: take thought° and die for Caesar.   *succumb to melancholy*
And that were much he should,[9] for he is given
To sports, to wildness, and much company.
190 TREBONIUS   There is no fear° in him; let him not die,   *nothing to fear*
For he will live and laugh at this hereafter.
         Clock strikes.
BRUTUS   Peace, count the clock.[1]
CASSIUS   The clock hath stricken three.
TREBONIUS   'Tis time to part.
CASSIUS   But it is doubtful yet
Whether Caesar will come forth today or no,
195 For he is superstitious grown of late,
Quite from the main° opinion he held once   *Contrary to the strong*
Of fantasy, of dreams, and ceremonies.
It may be these apparent° prodigies,   *manifest*
The unaccustomed terror of this night,
200 And the persuasion of his augurers[2]
May hold him from the Capitol today.
DECIUS   Never fear that. If he be so resolved,
I can o'ersway° him. For he loves to hear   *prevail upon*
That unicorns may be betrayed with trees,[3]
205 And bears with glasses,[4] elephants with holes,°   *pits*
Lions with toils,° and men with flatterers;   *nets*
But when I tell him he hates flatterers,
He says he does, being then most flattered.
Let me work,
210 For I can give his humor the true bent,[5]
And I will bring him to the Capitol.
CASSIUS   Nay, we will all of us be there to fetch him.
BRUTUS   By the eighth hour. Is that the uttermost?°   *latest*
CINNA   Be that the uttermost, and fail not then.
215 METELLUS   Caius Ligarius doth bear Caesar hard,°   *ill will*
Who rated° him for speaking well of Pompey;   *rebuked*
I wonder none of you have thought of him.
BRUTUS   Now, good Metellus, go along by him.°   *to his house*
He loves me well, and I have given him reasons;
220 Send him but hither and I'll fashion° him.   *work upon*
CASSIUS   The morning comes upon's. We'll leave you, Brutus.
And, friends, disperse yourselves; but all remember
What you have said, and show yourselves true Romans.
BRUTUS   Good gentlemen, look fresh and merrily.

---

9. And that is more than he is likely to do.
1. The clock is an anachronism, like sleeves and doublets.
2. Priests who interpreted "auguries," or omens.

3. The unicorn could supposedly be caught by tricking it into impaling its horn on a tree.
4. Mirrors (imagined to bewilder bears).
5. Give his disposition the right direction.

225   Let not our looks put on° our purposes,   *display*
      But bear it as our Roman actors do,
      With untired spirits and formal constancy.°   *decorous self-possession*
      And so good morrow to you every one.

                    Exeunt all but BRUTUS.

      Boy! Lucius! Fast asleep? It is no matter.
230   Enjoy the honey-heavy dew of slumber.
      Thou hast no figures° nor no fantasies   *imaginings*
      Which busy care draws in the brains of men;
      Therefore thou sleep'st so sound.

         Enter PORTIA.

PORTIA   Brutus, my lord.
BRUTUS   Portia, what mean you? Wherefore rise you now?
235   It is not for° your health thus to commit   *good for*
      Your weak condition to the raw cold morning.
PORTIA   Nor for yours neither. You've ungently,° Brutus,   *unkindly*
      Stole from my bed. And yesternight at supper
      You suddenly arose and walked about,
240   Musing and sighing, with your arms across;[6]
      And when I asked you what the matter was,
      You stared upon me with ungentle looks.
      I urged you further; then you scratched your head
      And too impatiently stamped with your foot.
245   Yet I insisted; yet you answered not,
      But with an angry wafture° of your hand   *gesture*
      Gave sign for me to leave you. So I did,
      Fearing to strengthen that impatience
      Which seemed too much enkindled, and withal°   *besides*
250   Hoping it was but an effect of humor,°   *moodiness*
      Which sometime hath his° hour with every man.   *its*
      It will not let you eat, nor talk, nor sleep;
      And could it work so much upon your shape
      As it hath much prevailed on your condition,°   *disposition*
255   I should not know you[7] Brutus. Dear my lord,
      Make me acquainted with your cause of grief.
BRUTUS   I am not well in health, and that is all.
PORTIA   Brutus is wise, and were he not in health,
      He would embrace the means to come by it.
260 BRUTUS   Why, so I do. Good Portia, go to bed.
PORTIA   Is Brutus sick? And is it physical°   *curative*
      To walk unbracèd° and suck up the humors[8]   *with open doublet*
      Of the dank morning? What, is Brutus sick,
      And will he steal out of his wholesome bed
265   To dare the vile contagion of the night,
      And tempt the rheumy and unpurgèd° air   *moist and impure*
      To add unto his sickness? No, my Brutus,
      You have some sick offense° within your mind,   *disturbance*
      Which by the right and virtue° of my place°   *prerogative / (as a wife)*

---

6. Crossed (a sign of melancholy).
7. "know you": recognize you as. TEXTUAL COMMENT There is no comma in the Folio text between "you" and "Brutus," indicating that the name is the object of "know." In his behavior, in other words, Brutus lives up to the reputation for wisdom that he has already established for himself. For this way of using names in *Julius Caesar,* see Digital Edition TC 4.
8. Inhale the mists.

270	I ought to know of. And upon my knees	
	I charm° you, by my once-commended beauty,	*conjure*
	By all your vows of love, and that great vow	
	Which did incorporate and make us one,	
	That you unfold to me, your self, your half,	
275	Why you are heavy,° and what men tonight	*dejected*
	Have had resort to you; for here have been	
	Some six or seven who did hide their faces	
	Even from darkness.	

BRUTUS   Kneel not, gentle Portia.

PORTIA   I should not need, if you were gentle Brutus.

280	Within the bond of marriage, tell me, Brutus,	
	Is it excepted[9] I should know no secrets	
	That appertain to you? Am I your self	
	But, as it were, in sort or limitation?[1]	
	To keep with you at meals, comfort your bed,	
285	And talk to you sometimes? Dwell I but in the suburbs[2]	
	Of your good pleasure? If it be no more,	
	Portia is Brutus' harlot, not his wife.	

BRUTUS   You are my true and honorable wife,

	As dear to me as are the ruddy drops	
290	That visit° my sad heart.	*afflict; come to*

PORTIA   If this were true, then should I know this secret.

	I grant I am a woman, but withal°	*still*
	A woman that Lord Brutus took to wife.	
	I grant I am a woman, but withal	
295	A woman well reputed, Cato's daughter.[3]	
	Think you I am no stronger than my sex,	
	Being so fathered and so husbanded?	
	Tell me your counsels;° I will not disclose 'em.	*secrets*
	I have made strong proof of my constancy,	
300	Giving myself a voluntary wound	
	Here, in the thigh. Can I bear that with patience	
	And not my husband's secrets?	

BRUTUS   O ye gods,

	Render me worthy of this noble wife!	

       Knock.

	Hark, hark, one knocks. Portia, go in awhile,	
305	And by and by thy bosom shall partake	
	The secrets of my heart.	
	All my engagements° I will construe° to thee,	*commitments / explain*
	All the charactery[4] of my sad brows.	
	Leave me with haste. *Exit* PORTIA.	

     Enter LUCIUS *and* LIGARIUS.

          Lucius, who's that knocks?

310	LUCIUS Here is a sick man that would speak with you.	

BRUTUS   Caius Ligarius, that Metellus spake of.

	Boy, stand aside. —Caius Ligarius, how?°	*how are you*

LIGARIUS   Vouchsafe° good morrow from a feeble tongue.   *Deign to accept*

---

9. Is it stipulated as a qualification that.
1. *in sort or limitation*: after a fashion or with restrictions (like "excepted," "limited" is a legal term).
2. Outlying areas (where brothels were located in Shakespeare's time).

3. Marcus Portius Cato was renowned for his strict moral integrity; after Caesar's victory over Pompey, he killed himself rather than submit to Caesar's rule.
4. Handwriting (the lines of care "inscribed" on his forehead).

BRUTUS   Oh, what a time have you chose out, brave Caius,
315   To wear a kerchief![5] Would you were not sick!

LIGARIUS   I am not sick, if Brutus have in hand
Any exploit worthy the name of honor.

BRUTUS   Such an exploit have I in hand, Ligarius,
Had you a healthful ear to hear of it.

320   LIGARIUS   By all the gods that Romans bow before,
I here discard my sickness. Soul of Rome,
Brave son derived from honorable loins,
Thou like an exorcist° hast conjured up   *a magician*
My mortifièd° spirit. Now bid me run,   *deadened*
325   And I will strive with things impossible,
Yea, get the better of them. What's to do?

BRUTUS   A piece of work that will make sick men whole.°   *healthy*

LIGARIUS   But are not some whole that we must make sick?

BRUTUS   That must we also. What it is, my Caius,
330   I shall unfold to thee as we are going
To whom it must be done.

LIGARIUS   Set on° your foot,   *Advance*
And with a heart new fired I follow you
To do I know not what; but it sufficeth
That Brutus leads me on.
                Thunder.

BRUTUS   Follow me then.   *Exeunt.*

2.2

Thunder and lightning. Enter Julius CAESAR *in his
nightgown.°*   *dressing gown*

CAESAR   Nor heaven nor earth have been at peace tonight.
Thrice hath Calphurnia in her sleep cried out,
"Help ho, they murder Caesar!" —Who's within?
                Enter a SERVANT.

SERVANT   My lord.

5   CAESAR   Go bid the priests do present° sacrifice,   *immediate*
And bring me their opinions of success.[1]

SERVANT   I will, my lord.   *Exit.*
                Enter CALPHURNIA.

CALPHURNIA   What mean you, Caesar? Think you to walk forth?
You shall not stir out of your house today.

10   CAESAR   Caesar shall forth. The things that threatened me
Ne'er looked but on my back. When they shall see
The face of Caesar, they are vanishèd.

CALPHURNIA   Caesar, I never stood on ceremonies,°   *heeded omens*
Yet now they fright me. There is one within,
15   Besides the things that we have heard and seen,
Recounts most horrid sights seen by the watch.[2]
A lioness hath whelpèd in the streets,
And graves have yawned and yielded up their dead.
Fierce fiery warriors fight[3] upon the clouds

---

5. Kerchiefs were commonly worn by the sick in Elizabethan England.
2.2 Location: Caesar's house.
1. Of the outcome (good or bad), as determined by
reading the entrails of the sacrificial animals.
2. Night watchmen (another anachronism).

3. TEXTUAL COMMENT Some editors change Folio's
"fight" to "fought," but between lines 13 and 26, past
and present tenses are variable, suggesting perhaps
Calphurnia's panic and trepidation. See Digital Edition TC 5 for a fuller explanation.

20 In ranks and squadrons and right form of war,°   *regular battle formation*
Which drizzled blood upon the Capitol.
The noise of battle hurtled in the air;
Horses do neigh, and dying men did groan,
And ghosts did shriek and squeal about the streets.
25 O Caesar, these things are beyond all use,°   *all normal experience*
And I do fear them.
CAESAR   What can be avoided
Whose end is purposed by the mighty gods?
Yet Caesar shall go forth, for these predictions
Are to° the world in general as to Caesar.   *Are as applicable to*
30 CALPHURNIA   When beggars die there are no comets seen;
The heavens themselves blaze forth° the death of princes.   *flame out; proclaim*
CAESAR   Cowards die many times before their deaths;
The valiant never taste of death but once.
Of all the wonders that I yet have heard,
35 It seems to me most strange that men should fear,
Seeing that death, a necessary end,
Will come when it will come.
            Enter a SERVANT.
                              What say the augurers?
SERVANT   They would not have you to stir forth today.
Plucking the entrails of an offering forth,
40 They could not find a heart within the beast.
CAESAR   The gods do this in shame of cowardice.°   *to put cowardice to shame*
Caesar should be a beast without a heart
If he should stay at home today for fear.
No, Caesar shall not. Danger knows full well
45 That Caesar is more dangerous than he.
We are two lions littered in one day,
And I the elder and more terrible;
And Caesar shall go forth.
CALPHURNIA   Alas, my lord,
Your wisdom is consumed in confidence.°   *overconfidence*
50 Do not go forth today. Call it my fear
That keeps you in the house, and not your own.
We'll send Mark Antony to the Senate House,
And he shall say you are not well today.
Let me upon my knee prevail in this.
55 CAESAR   Mark Antony shall say I am not well,
And for thy humor° I will stay at home.   *whim*
            Enter DECIUS.
Here's Decius Brutus. He shall tell them so.
DECIUS   Caesar, all hail! Good morrow, worthy Caesar.
I come to fetch you to the Senate House.
60 CAESAR   And you are come in very happy° time   *opportune*
To bear my greeting to the senators
And tell them that I will not come today.
Cannot is false; and that I dare not, falser;
I will not come today. Tell them so, Decius.
CALPHURNIA   Say he is sick.
65 CAESAR   Shall Caesar send a lie?
Have I in conquest stretched mine arm so far
To be afeard to tell graybeards the truth?
Decius, go tell them Caesar will not come.

DECIUS   Most mighty Caesar, let me know some cause,
70   Lest I be laughed at when I tell them so.
CAESAR   The cause is in my will: I will not come.
      That is enough to satisfy the Senate.
      But for your private satisfaction,
      Because I love you, I will let you know.
75   Calphurnia here, my wife, stays° me at home.   *keeps*
      She dreamt tonight° she saw my statue,   *last night*
      Which, like a fountain with an hundred spouts,
      Did run pure blood; and many lusty° Romans   *joyful*
      Came smiling and did bathe their hands in it.
80   And these does she apply° for warnings and portents   *interpret*
      And evils imminent, and on her knee
      Hath begged that I will stay at home today.
DECIUS   This dream is all amiss interpreted;
      It was a vision fair and fortunate.
85   Your statue spouting blood in many pipes,
      In which so many smiling Romans bathed,
      Signifies that from you great Rome shall suck
      Reviving blood, and that great men shall press
      For tinctures, stains, relics, and cognizance.[4]
90   This by Calphurnia's dream is signified.
CAESAR   And this way have you well expounded it.
DECIUS   I have, when you have heard what I can say,
      And know it now: the Senate have concluded
      To give this day a crown to mighty Caesar.
95   If you shall send them word you will not come,
      Their minds may change. Besides, it were a mock
      Apt to be rendered,[5] for someone to say,
      "Break up the Senate till another time
      When Caesar's wife shall meet with better dreams."
100   If Caesar hide himself, shall they not whisper,
      "Lo, Caesar is afraid"?
      Pardon me, Caesar, for my dear dear love
      To your proceeding° bids me tell you this,   *advancement*
      And reason to my love is liable.[6]
105 CAESAR   How foolish do your fears seem now, Calphurnia!
      I am ashamèd I did yield to them.
      Give me my robe, for I will go.

            Enter BRUTUS, LIGARIUS, METELLUS, CASCA,
            TREBONIUS, CINNA, *and* PUBLIUS.

      And look where Publius is come to fetch me.
PUBLIUS   Good morrow, Caesar.
CAESAR   Welcome, Publius.
110   —What, Brutus, are you stirred so early too?
      —Good morrow, Casca. —Caius Ligarius,
      Caesar was ne'er so much your enemy
      As that same ague° which hath made you lean.   *fever*
      What is't o'clock?
BRUTUS   Caesar, 'tis strucken eight.

4. Heraldic colors and emblems ("tinctures," "stains," and "cognizance"); venerated properties of saints ("tinctures," "stains," and "relics").

5. *a mock . . . rendered*: a sarcastic reply likely to be made.

6. And prudence is subordinate to my affection.

115 CAESAR I thank you for your pains and courtesy.
    Enter ANTONY.
  See, Antony that revels long a-nights
  Is notwithstanding up. —Good morrow, Antony.
ANTONY So to most noble Caesar.
CAESAR Bid them prepare within.
120   —I am to blame to be thus waited for.
  —Now, Cinna. —Now, Metellus. —What, Trebonius,
  I have an hour's talk in store for you.
  Remember that you call on me today;
  Be near me that I may remember you.
125 TREBONIUS Caesar, I will. [*aside*] And so near will I be
  That your best friends shall wish I had been further.
CAESAR Good friends, go in and taste some wine with me,
  And we, like⁷ friends, will straightway go together.
BRUTUS [*aside*] That every like is not the same, O Caesar,
130   The heart of Brutus earns° to think upon. *Exeunt.*   grieves

2.3

    Enter ARTEMIDORUS [*reading*].
ARTEMIDORUS "Caesar, beware of Brutus, take heed of Cassius,
  come not near Casca, have an eye to Cinna, trust not Trebonius, mark well Metellus Cimber. Decius Brutus loves thee
  not. Thou hast wronged Caius Ligarius. There is but one mind
5   in all these men, and it is bent against Caesar. If thou beest
  not immortal, look about you. Security gives way to° conspir- *Overconfidence permits*
  acy. The mighty gods defend thee. Thy lover,° Artemidorus."   *friend*
  Here will I stand till Caesar pass along,
  And as a suitor° will I give him this.   *petitioner*
10   My heart laments that virtue cannot live
  Out of the teeth of emulation.¹
  If thou read this, O Caesar, thou mayest live;
  If not, the fates with traitors do contrive.° *Exit.*   *conspire*

2.4

    Enter PORTIA *and* LUCIUS.
PORTIA I prithee, boy, run to the Senate House.
  Stay not to answer me, but get thee gone.
  Why dost thou stay?
LUCIUS   To know my errand, madam.
PORTIA I would have had thee there and here again
5   Ere I can tell thee what thou shouldst do there.
  [*aside*] O constancy, be strong upon my side;
  Set a huge mountain 'tween my heart and tongue.
  I have a man's mind but a woman's might;
  How hard it is for women to keep counsel.°   *a secret*
  —Art thou here yet?
10 LUCIUS   Madam, what should I do?
  Run to the Capitol, and nothing else?
  And so return to you, and nothing else?

---

7. As becomes (but Brutus plays on the senses "resembling" and "equal to").
2.3 Location: A street near the Capitol.

1. Beyond the danger of ambitious envy.
2.4 Location: Brutus's house.

PORTIA   Yes, bring me word, boy, if thy lord look well;
         For he went sickly forth. And take good note
15   What Caesar doth, what suitors press to him.
         Hark, boy, what noise is that?
LUCIUS   I hear none, madam.
PORTIA   Prithee, listen well.
         I heard a bustling rumor° like a fray,   *disturbed clamor*
         And the wind brings it from the Capitol.
20 LUCIUS   Sooth,° madam, I hear nothing.   *In truth*
         Enter the SOOTHSAYER.
PORTIA   Come hither, fellow. Which way hast thou been?
SOOTHSAYER   At mine own house, good lady.
PORTIA   What is't o'clock?
SOOTHSAYER   About the ninth hour, lady.
25 PORTIA   Is Caesar yet gone to the Capitol?
SOOTHSAYER   Madam, not yet. I go to take my stand
         To see him pass on to the Capitol.
PORTIA   Thou hast some suit to Caesar, hast thou not?
SOOTHSAYER   That I have, lady, if it will please Caesar
30   To be so good to Caesar as to hear me:
         I shall beseech him to befriend himself.
PORTIA   Why, know'st thou any harms intended towards him?
SOOTHSAYER   None that I know will be, much that I fear may chance.
         Good morrow to you. —Here the street is narrow.
35   The throng that follows Caesar at the heels,
         Of senators, of praetors, common suitors,
         Will crowd a feeble man almost to death.
         I'll get me to a place more void° and there   *empty*
         Speak to great Caesar as he comes along.   *Exit.*
40 PORTIA   I must go in. Ay me! How weak a thing
         The heart of woman is! O Brutus,
         The heavens speed thee in thine enterprise!
         Sure the boy heard me. —Brutus hath a suit
         That Caesar will not grant. —Oh, I grow faint.
45   —Run, Lucius, and commend me to my lord.
         Say I am merry.° Come to me again   *in good spirits*
         And bring me word what he doth say to thee.   *Exeunt.*

3.1

         Flourish. Enter CAESAR, BRUTUS, CASSIUS, CASCA,
         DECIUS, METELLUS, TREBONIUS, CINNA, ANTONY,
         LEPIDUS, ARTEMIDORUS, PUBLIUS, [POPILIUS,] *and*
         the SOOTHSAYER.
CAESAR   The Ides of March are come.
SOOTHSAYER   Ay, Caesar, but not gone.
ARTEMIDORUS   Hail, Caesar. Read this schedule.°   *document*
DECIUS   Trebonius doth desire you to o'erread,
5   At your best leisure, this his humble suit.
ARTEMIDORUS   O Caesar, read mine first, for mine's a suit
         That touches° Caesar nearer. Read it, great Caesar.   *concerns*
CAESAR   What touches us ourself shall be last served.°   *attended to*
ARTEMIDORUS   Delay not, Caesar; read it instantly.

3.1 Location: At the Capitol.

CAESAR   What, is the fellow mad?

10 PUBLIUS   Sirrah, give place.

CASSIUS   What, urge you your petitions in the street?
   Come to the Capitol.

   [CAESAR *moves away, others following.*]

POPILIUS [*to* CASSIUS]   I wish your enterprise today may thrive.

CASSIUS   What enterprise, Popilius?

15 POPILIUS   Fare you well.

BRUTUS   What said Popilius Lena?

CASSIUS   He wished today our enterprise might thrive.
   I fear our purpose is discoverèd.

BRUTUS   Look how he makes to° Caesar. Mark him.   *goes toward*

20 CASSIUS   Casca, be sudden,° for we fear prevention.   *swift*
   —Brutus, what shall be done? If this be known,
   Cassius or Caesar never shall turn back,°   *return alive*
   For I will slay myself.

BRUTUS   Cassius, be constant.°   *resolute*
   Popilius Lena speaks not of our purposes:

25 For look, he smiles, and Caesar doth not change.

CASSIUS   Trebonius knows his time, for look you, Brutus,
   He draws Mark Antony out of the way.

                         [*Exeunt* TREBONIUS *and* ANTONY.]

DECIUS   Where is Metellus Cimber? Let him go
   And presently prefer° his suit to Caesar.   *at once present*

30 BRUTUS   He is addressed.° Press near and second him.   *ready*

CINNA   Casca, you are the first that rears your hand.

CAESAR   Are we all ready? What is now amiss
   That Caesar and his Senate must redress?

METELLUS   Most high, most mighty, and most puissant° Caesar,   *powerful*

35 Metellus Cimber throws before thy seat
   An humble heart.

CAESAR   I must prevent° thee, Cimber: *thwart*
   These couchings° and these lowly courtesies°   *stoopings / bows*
   Might fire the blood° of ordinary men,   *passions*
   And turn preordinance and first decree¹

40 Into the lune of children.² Be not fond³
   To think that Caesar bears such rebel° blood   *lawless*
   That will be thawed from the true quality°   *proper constancy*
   With that which melteth fools—I mean sweet words,
   Low-crookèd° curtsies, and base spaniel fawning.   *Obsequious; dishonest*

45 Thy brother by decree is banishèd.⁴
   If thou dost bend and pray and fawn for him,
   I spurn thee like a cur out of my way.
   Know, Caesar doth not wrong, nor without cause
   Will he be satisfied.

50 METELLUS   Is there no voice more worthy than my own
   To sound more sweetly in great Caesar's ear
   For the repealing of my banished brother?

---

1. Established precedent and original rulings.
2. TEXTUAL COMMENT "Lane" in Folio, emended to "lune" (whim or caprice) in this and other modern editions. For the rationale behind this change, see

Digital Edition TC 6.
3. Do not be so foolish as.
4. Shakespeare's sources do not indicate why Publius Cimber was banished.

BRUTUS   I kiss thy hand, but not in flattery, Caesar,
    Desiring thee that Publius Cimber may
55   Have an immediate freedom of repeal.°   *release from banishment*
CAESAR   What, Brutus?
CASSIUS   Pardon, Caesar; Caesar, pardon.
    As low as to thy foot doth Cassius fall
    To beg enfranchisement° for Publius Cimber.   *liberation*
CAESAR   I could be well moved, if I were as you;
60   If I could pray to move,° prayers would move me.   *make pleas*
    But I am constant as the Northern Star,°   *polestar*
    Of whose true-fixed and resting° quality   *stationary*
    There is no fellow° in the firmament.   *equal*
    The skies are painted with unnumbered sparks;
65   They are all fire, and every one doth shine.
    But there's but one in all doth hold his place.
    So in the world: 'tis furnished well with men,
    And men are flesh and blood, and apprehensive;°   *capable of understanding*
    Yet in the number I do know but one
70   That unassailable holds on his rank,°   *maintains his place*
    Unshaked of motion;[5] and that I am he
    Let me a little show it, even in this:
    That I was constant° Cimber should be banished   *resolute*
    And constant do remain to keep him so.
CINNA   O Caesar—
75 CAESAR   Hence. Wilt thou lift up Olympus?[6]
DECIUS   Great Caesar—
CAESAR   Doth not Brutus bootless° kneel?   *in vain*
CASCA   Speak, hands, for me.[7]
    They stab CAESAR.[8]
CAESAR   *Et tu, Brutè?*[9] —Then fall, Caesar.
    [*He*] *dies.*
CINNA   Liberty! Freedom! Tyranny is dead!
80   Run hence, proclaim, cry it about the streets.
CASSIUS   Some to the common pulpits° and cry out,   *public platforms (rostra)*
    "Liberty, freedom, and enfranchisement."
BRUTUS   People and senators, be not affrighted.
    Fly not, stand still. Ambition's debt is paid.
CASCA   Go to the pulpit, Brutus.
85 DECIUS   And Cassius too.
BRUTUS   Where's Publius?°   *(an elderly senator)*
CINNA   Here, quite confounded° with this mutiny.°   *confused / tumult*
METELLUS   Stand fast together, lest some friend of Caesar's
    Should chance—
90 BRUTUS   Talk not of standing. —Publius, good cheer.
    There is no harm intended to your person,
    Nor to no Roman else. So tell them, Publius.
CASSIUS   And leave us, Publius, lest that the people
    Rushing on us should do your age some mischief.°   *injury*

---

5. Completely steady; unmoved by persuasion.
6. High mountain in Greece where the gods were supposed to dwell.
7. Let my hands beseech in prayer; let violent action take over where speech has failed.
8. PERFORMANCE COMMENT Caesar's assassination can be staged as a quasi-ritual "sacrifice" or as a bloody slaughter, and there are a variety of options

for the actors who play Brutus and Caesar. See Digital Edition PC 2 for a discussion of how the staging of Caesar's death affects an audience's understanding of the play.
9. Latin: You too, Brutus? According to the historian Suetonius, Caesar spoke these words in Greek and stopped defending himself when he saw Brutus among the conspirators, saying, in Greek, "You too, child?"

95 BRUTUS   Do so, and let no man abide° this deed   *pay the penalty for*
But we the doers.

        Enter TREBONIUS.

CASSIUS   Where is Antony?

TREBONIUS   Fled to his house amazed.
Men, wives, and children stare, cry out, and run
As° it were doomsday.   *As if*

BRUTUS   Fates, we will know your pleasures.

100 That we shall die, we know; 'tis but the time
And drawing days out that men stand upon.[1]

CASCA   Why, he that cuts off twenty years of life
Cuts off so many years of fearing death.

BRUTUS   Grant that, and then is death a benefit:

105 So are we Caesar's friends, that have abridged
His time of fearing death. Stoop, Romans, stoop,
And let us bathe our hands in Caesar's blood
Up to the elbows and besmear our swords.
Then walk we forth, even to the marketplace,°   *the Roman Forum*

110 And, waving our red weapons o'er our heads,
Let's all cry, "Peace, freedom, and liberty!"

CASSIUS   Stoop then, and wash. How many ages hence
Shall this our lofty scene be acted over
In states unborn and accents° yet unknown!   *languages*

115 BRUTUS   How many times shall Caesar bleed in sport,°   *for entertainment*
That now on Pompey's basis lies along[2]
No worthier than the dust!

CASSIUS   So oft as that shall be,
So often shall the knot° of us be called   *group*

120 The men that gave their country liberty.

DECIUS   What, shall we forth?

CASSIUS   Ay, every man away.
Brutus shall lead, and we will grace° his heels   *honor*
With the most boldest and best hearts of Rome.

        Enter a SERVANT.

BRUTUS   Soft,° who comes here? A friend of Antony's.   *Wait*

125 SERVANT [*kneeling*]   Thus, Brutus, did my master bid me kneel.
Thus did Mark Antony bid me fall down,
And, being prostrate, thus he bade me say:
"Brutus is noble, wise, valiant, and honest;°   *honorable*
Caesar was mighty, bold, royal, and loving.

130 Say, I love Brutus, and I honor him;
Say, I feared Caesar, honored him, and loved him.
If Brutus will vouchsafe that Antony
May safely come to him and be resolved°   *learn for certain*
How Caesar hath deserved to lie in death,

135 Mark Antony shall not love Caesar dead
So well as Brutus living, but will follow
The fortunes and affairs of noble Brutus
Thorough° the hazards of this untrod state[3]   *Through*
With all true faith." So says my master Antony.

140 BRUTUS   Thy master is a wise and valiant Roman.

---

1. *'tis . . . upon:* it is but the specific time of death and the possibility of extending their lives with which men concern themselves.

2. Lies stretched out on the pedestal ("basis") of Pompey's statue.
3. These unprecedented circumstances.

I never thought him worse.
Tell him, so° please him come unto this place,   *if it should*
He shall be satisfied and, by my honor,
Depart untouched.

SERVANT   I'll fetch him presently.°   *Exit.*   *at once*

145 BRUTUS   I know that we shall have him well to friend.°   *as a friend*
CASSIUS   I wish we may, but yet have I a mind
That fears him much; and my misgiving still
Falls shrewdly to the purpose.[4]

      Enter ANTONY.

BRUTUS   But here comes Antony. —Welcome, Mark Antony.

150 ANTONY   O mighty Caesar! Dost thou lie so low?
Are all thy conquests, glories, triumphs, spoils,
Shrunk to this little measure? Fare thee well.
—I know not, gentlemen, what you intend,
Who else must be let blood, who else is rank.[5]

155 If I myself, there is no hour so fit
As Caesar's death's hour, nor no instrument
Of half that worth as those your swords, made rich
With the most noble blood of all this world.
I do beseech ye, if you bear me hard,°   *bear me ill will*

160 Now, whilst your purpled° hands do reek° and smoke,   *bloody / steam*
Fulfill your pleasure. Live° a thousand years,   *If I live*
I shall not find myself so apt° to die.   *ready*
No place will please me so, no mean° of death,   *manner*
As here by Caesar and by you cut off,

165 The choice° and master spirits of this age.   *most select*
BRUTUS   O Antony! Beg not your death of us.
Though now we must appear bloody and cruel,
As by our hands and this our present act
You see we do, yet see you but our hands

170 And this the bleeding business they have done.
Our hearts you see not. They are pitiful;°   *full of pity*
And pity to the general wrong of Rome—
As fire drives out fire, so pity pity[6]—
Hath done this deed on Caesar. For your part,°   *As for you*

175 To you our swords have leaden° points, Mark Antony.   *blunt*
Our arms in strength of malice[7] and our hearts
Of brothers' temper,° do receive you in   *disposition*
With all kind love, good thoughts, and reverence.
CASSIUS   Your voice° shall be as strong as any man's   *opinion*

180 In the disposing of new dignities.[8]
BRUTUS   Only be patient till we have appeased°   *calmed*
The multitude, beside themselves with fear,
And then we will deliver you the cause
Why I, that did love Caesar when I struck him,
Have thus proceeded.

185 ANTONY   I doubt not of your wisdom.
Let each man render me his bloody hand.

---

4. *my . . . purpose:* my suspicions always turn out to
be unfortunately pertinent.
5. Festering with disease; overgrown. *let blood:* have
blood drawn off medically (but here, killed).

6. That is, pity for the state has driven out pity for
Caesar.
7. Although strong in their apparent enmity.
8. Conferring new offices of state.

First, Marcus Brutus, will I shake with you;
—Next, Caius Cassius, do I take your hand;
—Now, Decius Brutus, yours; —now yours, Metellus;
190   —Yours, Cinna; —and, my valiant Casca, yours;
—Though last, not least in love, yours, good Trebonius.
Gentlemen all, alas, what shall I say?
My credit° now stands on such slippery ground   *credibility*
That one of two bad ways you must conceit° me: *judge*
195   Either a coward or a flatterer.
—That I did love thee, Caesar, oh, 'tis true.
If then thy spirit look upon us now,
Shall it not grieve thee dearer° than thy death   *more keenly*
To see thy Antony making his peace,
200   Shaking the bloody fingers of thy foes,
Most noble, in the presence of thy corpse?
Had I as many eyes as thou hast wounds,
Weeping as fast as they stream forth thy blood,
It would become me better than to close°   *agree*
205   In terms of friendship with thine enemies.
Pardon me, Julius. Here wast thou bayed,° brave hart,[9]   *brought to bay*
Here didst thou fall, and here thy hunters stand
Signed° in thy spoil° and crimsoned in thy Lethe.[1]   *Marked / slaughter*
O world! Thou wast the forest to this hart,
210   And this indeed, O world, the heart of thee.
How like a deer strucken by many princes
Dost thou here lie!
CASSIUS   Mark Antony—
ANTONY   Pardon me, Caius Cassius.
The enemies of Caesar shall say this;
215   Then, in a friend, it is cold modesty.°   *moderation*
CASSIUS   I blame you not for praising Caesar so,
But what compact° mean you to have with us?   *agreement*
Will you be pricked in number of° our friends,   *be counted among*
Or shall we on° and not depend on you?   *proceed*
220   ANTONY   Therefore I took your hands, but was indeed
Swayed from the point by looking down on Caesar.
Friends am I with you all and love you all,
Upon this hope, that you shall give me reasons
Why and wherein Caesar was dangerous.
225   BRUTUS   Or else were this a savage spectacle.
Our reasons are so full of good regard°   *sound considerations*
That were you, Antony, the son of Caesar,
You should be satisfied.
ANTONY   That's all I seek;
And am, moreover, suitor° that I may   *petitioner*
230   Produce° his body to the marketplace   *Bring out*
And in the pulpit,° as becomes a friend,   *rostrum*
Speak in the order° of his funeral.   *ceremony*
BRUTUS   You shall, Mark Antony.
CASSIUS   Brutus, a word with you.

---

9. Stag (punning on "heart").
1. Lost lifeblood (Lethe was the river of forgetfulness in the classical underworld).

[*aside to* BRUTUS] You know not what you do. Do not consent
235   That Antony speak in his funeral.
Know you how much the people may be moved
By that which he will utter?
BRUTUS [*aside to* CASSIUS]   By your pardon:°   *With your permission*
I will myself into the pulpit first
And show the reason of our Caesar's death.
240   What Antony shall speak I will protest°   *proclaim*
He speaks by leave and by permission,
And that we are contented Caesar shall
Have all true° rites and lawful ceremonies.   *proper*
It shall advantage° more than do us wrong.   *benefit*
245 CASSIUS [*aside to* BRUTUS]   I know not what may fall.° I like it not.   *happen*
BRUTUS   Mark Antony, here, take you Caesar's body.
You shall not in your funeral speech blame us,
But speak all good you can devise of Caesar
And say you do't by our permission,
250   Else shall you not have any hand at all
About° his funeral. And you shall speak   *In*
In the same pulpit whereto I am going,
After my speech is ended.
ANTONY   Be it so.
I do desire no more.
255 BRUTUS   Prepare the body, then, and follow us.
                        Exeunt all but ANTONY.
ANTONY   O pardon me, thou bleeding piece of earth,
That I am meek and gentle with these butchers.
Thou art the ruins of the noblest man
That ever livèd in the tide of times.°   *flow of history*
260   Woe to the hand that shed this costly° blood.   *precious*
Over thy wounds now do I prophesy,
Which like dumb mouths do ope their ruby lips
To beg the voice and utterance of my tongue,
A curse shall light upon the limbs of men;
265   Domestic fury and fierce civil strife
Shall cumber° all the parts of Italy;   *oppress*
Blood and destruction shall be so in use°   *so customary*
And dreadful objects so familiar
That mothers shall but smile when they behold
270   Their infants quartered° with the hands of war,   *cut in pieces*
All pity choked with custom of fell° deeds;   *familiarity with cruel*
And Caesar's spirit, ranging° for revenge,   *roving like a wild beast*
With Ate° by his side come hot from hell,   *goddess of discord*
Shall in these confines° with a monarch's voice   *regions*
275   Cry havoc[2] and let slip° the dogs of war,   *unleash*
That this foul deed shall smell above the earth
With carrion men groaning for burial.
          Enter Octavius' SERVANT.
You serve Octavius Caesar, do you not?
SERVANT   I do, Mark Antony.
280 ANTONY   Caesar did write for him to come to Rome.

---

2. Military order for slaughter and pillage.

SERVANT   He did receive his letters and is coming,
And bid me say to you by word of mouth—
O Caesar!
ANTONY   Thy heart is big.° Get thee apart and weep.   *swollen with grief*
285   Passion,° I see, is catching, for mine eyes,   *Sorrow*
Seeing those beads of sorrow stand in thine,
Began to water. Is thy master coming?
SERVANT   He lies° tonight within seven leagues° of Rome.   *stays / twenty miles*
ANTONY   Post° back with speed and tell him what hath chanced.   *Ride quickly*
290   Here is a mourning Rome, a dangerous Rome,
No Rome of safety for Octavius yet.
Hie° hence and tell him so. Yet stay awhile;   *Hasten*
Thou shalt not back till I have borne this corpse
Into the marketplace. There shall I try°   *test*
295   In my oration how the people take
The cruel issue° of these bloody men;   *deed*
According to the which thou shalt discourse
To young Octavius of the state of things.
Lend me your hand.   *Exeunt [with Caesar's body]*.

3.2

Enter BRUTUS *and goes into the pulpit, and* CASSIUS,
with the PLEBEIANS.

PLEBEIANS   We will be satisfied!° Let us be satisfied!   *given an explanation*
BRUTUS   Then follow me, and give me audience, friends.
Cassius, go you into the other street
And part the numbers.°   *divide the multitude*
5   —Those that will hear me speak, let 'em stay here;
Those that will follow Cassius, go with him;
And public reasons shall be renderèd
Of Caesar's death.
FIRST PLEBEIAN   I will hear Brutus speak.
SECOND PLEBEIAN   I will hear Cassius and compare their reasons
10   When severally° we hear them renderèd.   *separately*
                    [Exit CASSIUS, *with some* PLEBEIANS.]
THIRD PLEBEIAN   The noble Brutus is ascended. Silence.
BRUTUS   Be patient till the last.°   *end of my address*
Romans, countrymen, and lovers,° hear me for my cause, and   *dear friends*
be silent that you may hear. Believe me for° mine honor, and   *on account of*
15   have respect to° mine honor that you may believe. Censure°   *regard for / Judge*
me in your wisdom, and awake your senses° that you may the   *understanding*
better judge. If there be any in this assembly, any dear friend
of Caesar's, to him I say that Brutus' love to Caesar was no
less than his. If then that friend demand why Brutus rose
20   against Caesar, this is my answer: not that I loved Caesar less,
but that I loved Rome more. Had you rather Caesar were living and die all slaves, than that Caesar were dead, to live all
freemen? As Caesar loved me, I weep for him; as he was fortunate, I rejoice at it; as he was valiant, I honor him; but, as
25   he was ambitious, I slew him. There is tears for his love; joy
for his fortune; honor for his valor; and death for his ambition. Who is here so base that would be a bondman? If any,

3.2 Location: The Forum.

speak, for him have I offended.° Who is here so rude° that   *wronged / barbarous*
would not be a Roman? If any, speak, for him have I offended.
30 Who is here so vile that will not love his country? If any,
speak, for him have I offended. I pause for a reply.

ALL   None, Brutus, none.

BRUTUS   Then none have I offended. I have done no more to
Caesar than you shall do[1] to Brutus. The question of° his   *reasons for*
35 death is enrolled° in the Capitol, his glory not extenuated°   *recorded / diminished*
wherein he was worthy, nor his offenses enforced° for which   *unduly stressed*
he suffered death.

     Enter MARK ANTONY [*and others*] *with Caesar's body.*

Here comes his body, mourned by Mark Antony, who, though
he had no hand in his death, shall receive the benefit of his
40 dying—a place in the commonwealth—as which of you shall
not? With this I depart, that, as I slew my best lover° for the   *friend*
good of Rome, I have the same dagger for myself when it shall
please my country to need my death.

ALL   Live, Brutus, live, live.

45 FIRST PLEBEIAN   Bring him with triumph home unto his house.

SECOND PLEBEIAN   Give him a statue with his ancestors.

THIRD PLEBEIAN   Let him be Caesar.

FOURTH PLEBEIAN   Caesar's better parts°   *qualities*
Shall be crowned in Brutus.

FIRST PLEBEIAN   We'll bring him to his house with shouts and
    clamors.

BRUTUS   My countrymen—

50 SECOND PLEBEIAN   Peace, silence! Brutus speaks.

FIRST PLEBEIAN   Peace, ho!

BRUTUS   Good countrymen, let me depart alone,
    And, for my sake, stay here with Antony.
    Do grace° to Caesar's corpse and grace[2] his speech   *Pay respect*
55   Tending° to Caesar's glories, which Mark Antony—   *Relating*
    By our permission—is allowed to make.
    I do entreat you, not a man depart,
    Save I alone, till Antony have spoke.   *Exit.*

FIRST PLEBEIAN   Stay, ho, and let us hear Mark Antony.

60 THIRD PLEBEIAN   Let him go up into the public chair.
    We'll hear him. —Noble Antony, go up.

      [ANTONY *ascends to the pulpit.*]

ANTONY   For Brutus' sake, I am beholden to you.

FOURTH PLEBEIAN   What does he say of Brutus?

THIRD PLEBEIAN   He says for Brutus' sake
65 He finds himself beholden to us all.

FOURTH PLEBEIAN   'Twere best he speak no harm of Brutus here.

FIRST PLEBEIAN   This Caesar was a tyrant.

THIRD PLEBEIAN   Nay, that's certain.
We are blest that Rome is rid of him.

SECOND PLEBEIAN   Peace, let us hear what Antony can say.

ANTONY   You gentle Romans—

70 ALL   Peace, ho! Let us hear him.

ANTONY   Friends, Romans, countrymen, lend me your ears.[3]

---

1. Should do (in such circumstances).
2. Courteously hear.
3. PERFORMANCE COMMENT Antony's bravura funeral oration can be played as a sincerely mournful funeral eulogy of a dead friend, as a deliberate attempt to instigate violence against Caesar's assassins, or as something in between. For a discussion of the possibilities, see Digital Edition PC 3.

I come to bury Caesar, not to praise him.
The evil that men do lives after them;
The good is oft interrèd with their bones.
75 So let it be with Caesar. The noble Brutus
Hath told you Caesar was ambitious.
If it were so, it was a grievous fault,
And grievously hath Caesar answered° it.   paid the penalty for
Here, under leave° of Brutus and the rest—   by permission
80 For Brutus is an honorable man;
So are they all, all honorable men—
Come I to speak in Caesar's funeral.
He was my friend, faithful and just to me;
But Brutus says he was ambitious,
85 And Brutus is an honorable man.
He hath brought many captives home to Rome,
Whose ransoms did the general coffers° fill.   public treasury
Did this in Caesar seem ambitious?
When that the poor have cried, Caesar hath wept;
90 Ambition should be made of sterner stuff.
Yet Brutus says he was ambitious,
And Brutus is an honorable man.
You all did see that on the Lupercal
I thrice presented him a kingly crown,
95 Which he did thrice refuse. Was this ambition?
Yet Brutus says he was ambitious,
And sure he is an honorable man.
I speak not to disprove what Brutus spoke,
But here I am to speak what I do know.
100 You all did love him once, not without cause.
What cause withholds you, then, to mourn for him?
—O judgment! Thou art fled to brutish beasts,
And men have lost their reason. —Bear with me;
My heart is in the coffin there with Caesar,
105 And I must pause till it come back to me.
FIRST PLEBEIAN Methinks there is much reason in his sayings.
SECOND PLEBEIAN If thou consider rightly of the matter,
     Caesar has had great wrong.
THIRD PLEBEIAN   Has he, masters?
     I fear there will a worse come in his place.
110 FOURTH PLEBEIAN Marked ye his words? He would not take the
          crown;
     Therefore 'tis certain he was not ambitious.
FIRST PLEBEIAN If it be found so, some will dear abide° it.   pay dearly for
SECOND PLEBEIAN Poor soul, his eyes are red as fire with
          weeping.
THIRD PLEBEIAN There's not a nobler man in Rome than Antony.
115 FOURTH PLEBEIAN Now mark him. He begins again to speak.
ANTONY But° yesterday the word of Caesar might   Only
     Have stood against the world. Now lies he there,
     And none so poor to do him reverence.[4]
     O masters! If I were disposed to stir
120 Your hearts and minds to mutiny° and rage,   rebellion

---

4. And no one is so lowly as to owe obeisance to him.

I should do Brutus wrong and Cassius wrong,
Who, you all know, are honorable men.
I will not do them wrong; I rather choose
To wrong the dead, to wrong myself and you,
125   Than I will wrong such honorable men.
But here's a parchment with the seal of Caesar;
I found it in his closet.° 'Tis his will.   *study*
Let but the commons° hear this testament—   *commoners*
Which, pardon me, I do not mean to read—
130   And they would go and kiss dead Caesar's wounds
And dip their napkins⁵ in his sacred blood,
Yea, beg a hair of him for memory,
And, dying, mention it within their wills,
Bequeathing it as a rich legacy
135   Unto their issue.°   *children*
FOURTH PLEBEIAN   We'll hear the will. Read it, Mark Antony.
ALL   The will, the will! We will hear Caesar's will.
ANTONY   Have patience, gentle friends: I must not read it.
It is not meet° you know how Caesar loved you.   *fitting*
140   You are not wood, you are not stones, but men;
And being men, hearing the will of Caesar,
It will inflame you, it will make you mad.
'Tis good you know not that you are his heirs,
For if you should, oh, what would come of it?
145   FOURTH PLEBEIAN   Read the will! We'll hear it, Antony.
You shall read us the will, Caesar's will.
ANTONY   Will you be patient? Will you stay awhile?
I have o'ershot myself⁶ to tell you of it.
I fear I wrong the honorable men
150   Whose daggers have stabbed Caesar; I do fear it.
FOURTH PLEBEIAN   They were traitors. "Honorable men"!
ALL   The will! The testament!
SECOND PLEBEIAN   They were villains, murderers. The will! Read
the will!
155   ANTONY   You will compel me then to read the will?
Then make a ring about the corpse of Caesar,
And let me show you him that made the will.
Shall I descend? And will you give me leave?
ALL   Come down.
160   SECOND PLEBEIAN   Descend.
THIRD PLEBEIAN   You shall have leave.
[ANTONY *comes down*.]
FOURTH PLEBEIAN   A ring; stand round.
FIRST PLEBEIAN   Stand from the hearse.° Stand from the body.   *bier*
SECOND PLEBEIAN   Room for Antony, most noble Antony.
165   ANTONY   Nay, press not so upon me. Stand far° off.   *farther*
ALL   Stand back! Room! Bear back!
ANTONY   If you have tears, prepare to shed them now.
You all do know this mantle. I remember
The first time ever Caesar put it on:
170   'Twas on a summer's evening in his tent,

---

5. Handkerchiefs (implying that Caesar is a martyr   6. I have gone too far (an image from archery).
whose bloody relics should be regarded as holy).

That day he overcame the Nervii.[7]
Look, in this place ran Cassius' dagger through.
See what a rent the envious° Casca made.   spiteful
Through this the well-belovèd Brutus stabbed,
175   And as he plucked his cursèd steel away,
Mark how the blood of Caesar followed it,
As° rushing out of doors to be resolved[8]   As if
If Brutus so unkindly° knocked or no;   cruelly; unnaturally
For Brutus, as you know, was Caesar's angel.[9]
180   Judge, O you gods, how dearly Caesar loved him!
This was the most unkindest cut of all;
For when the noble Caesar saw him stab,
Ingratitude, more strong than traitors' arms,
Quite vanquished him. Then burst his mighty heart,
185   And in his mantle muffling up his face,
Even at the base of Pompey's statue,
Which all the while ran blood, great Caesar fell.
Oh, what a fall was there, my countrymen!
Then I, and you, and all of us fell down,
190   Whilst bloody treason flourished[1] over us.
Oh, now you weep, and I perceive you feel
The dint° of pity. These are gracious drops.   impression
Kind souls, what, weep you when you but behold
Our Caesar's vesture° wounded? Look you here,   garment
195   Here is himself, marred as you see with traitors.
            [ANTONY lifts Caesar's mantle.]
FIRST PLEBEIAN   O piteous spectacle!
SECOND PLEBEIAN   O noble Caesar!
THIRD PLEBEIAN   O woeful day!
FOURTH PLEBEIAN   O traitors, villains!
200   FIRST PLEBEIAN   O most bloody sight!
SECOND PLEBEIAN   We will be revenged!
ALL   Revenge! About!° Seek! Burn! Fire! Kill! Slay! Let not a   To work
   traitor live!
ANTONY   Stay, countrymen.
205   FIRST PLEBEIAN   Peace there! Hear the noble Antony.
SECOND PLEBEIAN   We'll hear him, we'll follow him, we'll die
   with him!
ANTONY   Good friends, sweet friends, let me not stir you up
   To such a sudden flood of mutiny.
210   They that have done this deed are honorable.
What private griefs° they have, alas, I know not,   personal grievances
That made them do it. They are wise and honorable,
And will no doubt with reasons answer you.
I come not, friends, to steal away your hearts.
215   I am no orator, as Brutus is,
But, as you know me all, a plain blunt man
That love my friend, and that they know full well
That gave me public leave to speak[2] of him.

---

7. Gallic tribe conquered by Caesar in 57 B.C.E.; it
was an important victory, extravagantly celebrated in
Rome.
8. To find out for sure.

9. Attendant spirit (that is, dearest friend).
1. Shook its sword; triumphed.
2. Permission to speak in public.

For I have neither wit,° nor words, nor worth,°   *intelligence / stature*
220 Action,° nor utterance, nor the power of speech   *Gesture*
To stir men's blood. I only speak right on.°   *straightforwardly*
I tell you that which you yourselves do know,
Show you sweet Caesar's wounds, poor poor dumb mouths,
And bid them speak for me. But were I Brutus,
225 And Brutus Antony, there were an Antony
Would ruffle° up your spirits and put a tongue   *stir*
In every wound of Caesar that should move
The stones of Rome to rise and mutiny.°   *riot*
ALL   We'll mutiny.
FIRST PLEBEIAN   We'll burn the house of Brutus.
230 THIRD PLEBEIAN   Away, then. Come, seek the conspirators.
ANTONY   Yet hear me, countrymen; yet hear me speak.
ALL   Peace, ho! Hear Antony, most noble Antony.
ANTONY   Why, friends, you go to do you know not what.
Wherein hath Caesar thus deserved your loves?
235 Alas, you know not. I must tell you then.
You have forgot the will I told you of.
ALL   Most true, the will! Let's stay and hear the will.
ANTONY   Here is the will, and under Caesar's seal:
To every Roman citizen he gives,
240 To every several° man, seventy-five drachmas.[3]   *individual*
SECOND PLEBEIAN   Most noble Caesar! We'll revenge his death.
THIRD PLEBEIAN   O royal Caesar!
ANTONY   Hear me with patience.
ALL   Peace,° ho!   *Silence*
245 ANTONY   Moreover, he hath left you all his walks,
His private arbors, and new-planted orchards,°   *gardens*
On this side Tiber. He hath left them you,
And to your heirs forever: common pleasures°   *public parks*
To walk abroad and recreate yourselves.
250 Here was a Caesar! When comes such another?
FIRST PLEBEIAN   Never, never! —Come, away, away!
We'll burn his body in the holy place
And with the brands fire the traitors' houses.
Take up the body.
255 SECOND PLEBEIAN   Go fetch fire.
THIRD PLEBEIAN   Pluck down benches.
FOURTH PLEBEIAN   Pluck down forms,° windows,° anything.   *benches / shutters*
               Exeunt PLEBEIANS [*with the body*].
ANTONY   Now let it work. Mischief, thou art afoot;
Take thou what course thou wilt.
        Enter SERVANT.
                How now, fellow?
260 SERVANT   Sir, Octavius is already come to Rome.
ANTONY   Where is he?
SERVANT   He and Lepidus are at Caesar's house.
ANTONY   And thither will I straight° to visit him.   *at once*
He comes upon a wish.° Fortune is merry   *just as I wished*
265 And in this mood will give us anything.

---

3. Greek silver coins.

SERVANT   I heard him say Brutus and Cassius
   Are rid° like madmen through the gates of Rome.   *Have ridden*
ANTONY   Belike° they had some notice° of the people,   *Probably / warning*
   How I had moved them. Bring me to Octavius.   *Exeunt.*

3.3
Enter CINNA *the poet, and after him the* PLEBEIANS.

CINNA   I dreamt tonight° that I did feast with Caesar,   *last night*
   And things unluckily charge my fantasy.[1]
   I have no will to wander forth of doors,
   Yet something leads me forth.
5   FIRST PLEBEIAN   What is your name?
   SECOND PLEBEIAN   Whither are you going?
   THIRD PLEBEIAN   Where do you dwell?
   FOURTH PLEBEIAN   Are you a married man or a bachelor?
   SECOND PLEBEIAN   Answer every man directly.[2]
10   FIRST PLEBEIAN   Ay, and briefly.
   FOURTH PLEBEIAN   Ay, and wisely.
   THIRD PLEBEIAN   Ay, and truly, you were best.°   *you'd better*
   CINNA   What is my name? Whither am I going? Where do I
      dwell? Am I a married man or a bachelor? Then to answer
15   every man directly and briefly, wisely and truly: wisely I say,
      I am a bachelor.
   SECOND PLEBEIAN   That's as much as to say they are fools that
      marry. You'll bear me a bang° for that, I fear. Proceed directly.   *get a blow from me*
   CINNA   Directly, I am going to Caesar's funeral.
20   FIRST PLEBEIAN   As a friend or an enemy?
   CINNA   As a friend.
   SECOND PLEBEIAN   That matter is answered directly.
   FOURTH PLEBEIAN   For your dwelling—briefly.
   CINNA   Briefly, I dwell by the Capitol.
25   THIRD PLEBEIAN   Your name, sir, truly.
   CINNA   Truly, my name is Cinna.
   FIRST PLEBEIAN   Tear him to pieces! He's a conspirator.
   CINNA   I am Cinna the poet, I am Cinna the poet!
   FOURTH PLEBEIAN   Tear him for his bad verses, tear him for his
30   bad verses!
   CINNA   I am not Cinna the conspirator.
   FOURTH PLEBEIAN   It is no matter, his name's Cinna. Pluck
      but his name out of his heart, and turn him going.°   *send him packing*
   THIRD PLEBEIAN   Tear him, tear him! Come, brands, ho, fire-
35   brands! To Brutus', to Cassius', burn all! Some to Decius'
      house, and some to Casca's, some to Ligarius'. Away, go!
                     Exeunt all the PLEBEIANS *[carrying off* CINNA*]*.

4.1
Enter ANTONY, OCTAVIUS, *and* LEPIDUS.

ANTONY   These many, then, shall die; their names are pricked.°   *marked down*
OCTAVIUS   Your brother too must die. Consent you, Lepidus?
LEPIDUS   I do consent.

3.3 Location: A street in Rome.
1. And bad omens oppress my imagination.

2. At once; speaking straightforwardly.
4.1 Location: Antony's house in Rome.

OCTAVIUS   Prick him down, Antony.

LEPIDUS   Upon condition° Publius shall not live,   *Provided that*

5   Who is your sister's son, Mark Antony.

ANTONY   He shall not live; look, with a spot I damn him.[1]

    But, Lepidus, go you to Caesar's house;

    Fetch the will hither, and we shall determine

    How to cut off some charge in legacies.[2]

10   LEPIDUS   What, shall I find you here?

OCTAVIUS   Or° here, or at the Capitol.   *Exit* LEPIDUS.   *Either*

ANTONY   This is a slight unmeritable° man,   *undeserving*

    Meet° to be sent on errands. Is it fit,   *Fit*

    The threefold world divided,[3] he should stand

    One of the three to share it?

15   OCTAVIUS   So you thought him

    And took his voice° who should be pricked to die   *accepted his opinion*

    In our black° sentence and proscription.[4]   *death*

ANTONY   Octavius, I have seen more days than you,

    And though we lay these honors on this man

20   To ease ourselves of divers sland'rous loads,°   *burdens of reproach*

    He shall but bear them as the ass bears gold,

    To groan and sweat under the business,

    Either led or driven as we point the way;

    And having brought our treasure where we will,

25   Then take we down his load and turn him off,

    Like to the empty° ass, to shake his ears   *unladen*

    And graze in commons.[5]

OCTAVIUS   You may do your will,

    But he's a tried and valiant soldier.

ANTONY   So is my horse, Octavius, and for that

30   I do appoint° him store of provender.   *provide*

    It is a creature that I teach to fight,

    To wind,° to stop, to run directly on,   *turn*

    His corporal° motion governed by my spirit;   *bodily*

    And in some taste° is Lepidus but so.   *measure*

35   He must be taught and trained and bid go forth—

    A barren-spirited fellow, one that feeds

    On objects, arts, and imitations[6]

    Which, out of use and staled° by other men,   *made uninteresting*

    Begin his fashion.[7] Do not talk of him

40   But as a property.° And now, Octavius,   *tool*

    Listen° great things. Brutus and Cassius   *Give ear to*

    Are levying powers.° We must straight make head.[8]   *armies*

    Therefore let our alliance be combined,

    Our best friends made,° our means stretched;[9]   *mustered*

45   And let us presently go sit in council

    How covert matters° may be best disclosed   *dangers*

---

1. With a mark I condemn him to death.
2. Reduce the amount paid out to beneficiaries of Caesar's will.
3. Antony, Octavius, and Lepidus, in the second triumvirate, or joint rule of three, parceled out rule of Rome's empire among themselves.
4. A "proscribed" person had a price on his head, his property was confiscated, and his children were prevented from holding office.
5. In the public pasture; among the common people.
6. On curiosities, contrivances, and counterfeits.
7. He then takes up as fashionable.
8. We must raise an army at once.
9. Our bands of followers augmented.

And open perils surest answerèd.°   most safely confronted
OCTAVIUS   Let us do so, for we are at the stake[1]
And bayed about with many enemies;
50   And some that smile have in their hearts, I fear,
Millions of mischiefs.°   *Exeunt.*   evils

4.2

Drum. Enter BRUTUS, LUCILIUS, [LUCIUS,] *and the army.*
TITINIUS *and* PINDARUS *meet them.*
BRUTUS   Stand ho!°   Halt
LUCILIUS   Give the word, ho, and stand![1]
BRUTUS   What now, Lucilius, is Cassius near?
LUCILIUS   He is at hand, and Pindarus is come
5   To do you salutation from his master.
BRUTUS   He greets me well.° Your master, Pindarus,   with a worthy man
In his own change or by ill officers,[2]
Hath given me some worthy° cause to wish   justifiable
Things done, undone; but if he be at hand
I shall be satisfied.[3]
10   PINDARUS   I do not doubt
But that my noble master will appear
Such as he is, full of regard[4] and honor.
BRUTUS   He is not doubted.
          [BRUTUS *and* LUCILIUS *speak apart.*]
                              A word, Lucilius,
How he received you: let me be resolved.°   informed
15   LUCILIUS   With courtesy and with respect enough,
But not with such familiar instances°   tokens of friendship
Nor with such free and friendly conference°   conversation
As he hath used of old.
BRUTUS   Thou hast described
A hot friend cooling. Ever note, Lucilius,
20   When love begins to sicken and decay
It useth an enforcèd ceremony.°   a strained formality
There are no tricks° in plain and simple faith,   artifices
But hollow° men, like horses hot at hand,[5]   insincere
Make gallant show and promise of their mettle;
          Low march[6] *within.*
25   But when they should endure the bloody spur,
They fall their crests° and like deceitful jades°   lower their necks / nags
Sink° in the trial. Comes his army on?   Fail
LUCILIUS   They mean this night in Sardis to be quartered.
The greater part, the horse in general,°   all the cavalry
Are come with Cassius.
          Enter CASSIUS *and his powers.*°   armies
30   BRUTUS   Hark, he is arrived.
March gently° on to meet him.   slowly
CASSIUS   Stand ho!

---

1. That is, like bears in the sport of bearbaiting, tied to a stake and surrounded by baying hounds.
4.2 Location: Sardis, in what is now western Turkey. Outside Brutus's tent in his army's camp.
1. Pass the word, and halt.
2. By his own altered feelings or through the actions of bad subordinates.
3. I shall receive a full explanation.
4. Respect for you; renown (for his own abilities).
5. Eager at the outset.
6. Soft drumbeat (as from a distance; the sound becomes louder as the army enters).

BRUTUS   Stand ho! Speak the word along.

FIRST SOLDIER   Stand!

35   SECOND SOLDIER   Stand!

THIRD SOLDIER   Stand!

CASSIUS   Most noble brother, you have done me wrong.

BRUTUS   Judge me, you gods! Wrong I mine enemies?
        And if not so, how should I wrong a brother?

40   CASSIUS   Brutus, this sober form of yours hides wrongs,
        And when you do them—

BRUTUS   Cassius, be content.°   *keep calm*
        Speak your griefs° softly. I do know you well.   *grievances*
        Before the eyes of both our armies here,
        Which should perceive nothing but love from us,
45   Let us not wrangle. Bid them move away;
        Then in my tent, Cassius, enlarge° your griefs,   *express fully*
        And I will give you audience.

CASSIUS   Pindarus,
        Bid our commanders lead their charges° off   *troops*
        A little from this ground.

50   BRUTUS   Lucilius, do you the like, and let no man
        Come to our tent till we have done our conference.
        Let Lucius and Titinius guard our door.

                        Exeunt all but BRUTUS *and* CASSIUS.

4.3

CASSIUS   That you have wronged me doth appear in this:
        You have condemned and noted° Lucius Pella   *publicly disgraced*
        For taking bribes here of the Sardians,
        Wherein my letters, praying on his side
5   Because I knew the man, was slighted off.°   *contemptuously ignored*

BRUTUS   You wronged yourself to write in such a case.

CASSIUS   In such a time as this it is not meet°   *appropriate*
        That every nice° offense should bear his comment.°   *trivial / be criticized*

BRUTUS   Let me tell you, Cassius, you yourself
10   Are much condemned to have° an itching palm,   *for having*
        To sell and mart° your offices for gold   *traffic in*
        To undeservers.

CASSIUS   I, an itching palm?
        You know that you are Brutus that speaks this,
        Or, by the gods, this speech were else° your last.   *otherwise*

15   BRUTUS   The name of Cassius honors this corruption,[1]
        And chastisement doth therefore hide his head.

CASSIUS   Chastisement?

BRUTUS   Remember March, the Ides of March remember:
        Did not great Julius bleed for justice' sake?
20   What villain touched his body that did stab
        And not for justice?[2] What, shall one of us
        That struck the foremost man of all this world
        But for supporting robbers,[3] shall we now
        Contaminate our fingers with base bribes,

4.3 Location: Sardis, in what is now western Turkey.
Scene continues in Brutus's tent.
1. Makes this corruption appear honorable.
2. *What . . . justice?*: Who was so villainous as to

stab Caesar for any motive other than justice?
3. Caesar was accused of permitting, even encouraging, corruption among his subordinates.

25	And sell the mighty space of our large honors°	*impressive reputations*
	For so much trash° as may be graspèd thus?	*money (contemptuous)*
	I had rather be a dog and bay° the moon	*howl at*
	Than such a Roman.	
	CASSIUS Brutus, bait° not me.	*howl at; harass*
	I'll not endure it. You forget yourself	
30	To hedge me in.° I am a soldier, I,	*limit my authority*
	Older in practice, abler than yourself	
	To make conditions.°	*manage affairs*
	BRUTUS Go to! You are not, Cassius.	
	CASSIUS I am.	
	BRUTUS I say you are not.	
35	CASSIUS Urge° me no more; I shall forget myself.	*Provoke*
	Have mind upon your health. Tempt me no farther.	
	BRUTUS Away, slight man.	
	CASSIUS Is't possible?	
	BRUTUS Hear me, for I will speak.	
	Must I give way and room to your rash choler?[4]	
40	Shall I be frighted when a madman stares?	
	CASSIUS O ye gods, ye gods! Must I endure all this?	
	BRUTUS All this? Ay, more. Fret till your proud heart break.	
	Go show your slaves how choleric° you are	*enraged*
	And make your bondmen tremble. Must I budge?°	*flinch*
45	Must I observe° you? Must I stand and crouch°	*defer to / cringe*
	Under your testy humor?° By the gods,	*irritable temper*
	You shall digest[5] the venom of your spleen°	*anger*
	Though it do split you; for, from this day forth,	
	I'll use you for my mirth, yea, for my laughter,	
	When you are waspish.	
50	CASSIUS Is it come to this?	
	BRUTUS You say you are a better soldier.	
	Let it appear so; make your vaunting° true,	*boasting*
	And it shall please me well. For mine own part,	
	I shall be glad to learn of° noble men.	*from*
55	CASSIUS You wrong me every way; you wrong me, Brutus.	
	I said an elder soldier, not a better.	
	Did I say "better"?	
	BRUTUS If you did, I care not.	
	CASSIUS When Caesar lived he durst not thus have moved° me.	*angered*
	BRUTUS Peace, peace, you durst not so have tempted him.	
60	CASSIUS I durst not?	
	BRUTUS No.	
	CASSIUS What, durst not tempt him?	
	BRUTUS For your life you durst not.	
	CASSIUS Do not presume too much upon my love;	
	I may do that I shall be sorry for.	
65	BRUTUS You have done that you should be sorry for.	
	There is no terror, Cassius, in your threats,	
	For I am armed so strong in honesty°	*rectitude*
	That they pass by me as the idle wind,	
	Which I respect not.° I did send to you	*pay no attention to*
70	For certain sums of gold, which you denied me;	

---

4. Must I allow free passage to your rash anger?   5. Swallow (not give vent to).

For I can raise no money by vile means.
By heaven, I had rather coin my heart
And drop my blood for drachmas than to wring
From the hard hands of peasants their vile trash
75 By any indirection.° I did send   *devious means*
To you for gold to pay my legions,
Which you denied me. Was that done like Cassius?
Should I have answered Caius Cassius so?
When Marcus Brutus grows so covetous
80 To lock such rascal counters from his friends,
Be ready, gods, with all your thunderbolts;
Dash him to pieces!
CASSIUS   I denied you not.
BRUTUS   You did.
CASSIUS   I did not. He was but a fool
That brought my answer back. Brutus hath rived° my heart.   *broken*
85 A friend should bear his friend's infirmities,
But Brutus makes mine greater than they are.
BRUTUS   I do not, till you practice them on me.
CASSIUS   You love me not.
BRUTUS   I do not like your faults.
CASSIUS   A friendly eye could never see such faults.
90 BRUTUS   A flatterer's would not, though they do appear
As huge as high Olympus.
CASSIUS   Come, Antony, and young Octavius, come,
Revenge yourselves alone on Cassius,
For Cassius is aweary of the world:
95 Hated by one he loves, braved° by his brother,   *defied*
Checked° like a bondman, all his faults observed,   *Rebuked*
Set in a notebook, learned, and conned by rote°   *memorized*
To cast into my teeth. Oh, I could weep
My spirit from mine eyes! There is my dagger,
100 And here my naked breast; within, a heart
Dearer° than Pluto's[6] mine, richer than gold.   *More valuable*
If that thou beest a Roman, take it forth.
I that denied thee gold will give my heart.
Strike as thou didst at Caesar; for I know,
105 When thou didst hate him worst, thou loved'st him better
Than ever thou loved'st Cassius.
BRUTUS   Sheathe your dagger.
Be angry when you will, it shall have scope;°   *room for exercise*
Do what you will, dishonor shall be humor.[7]
O Cassius, you are yokèd° with a lamb   *allied*
110 That carries anger as the flint bears fire,
Who, much enforcèd,° shows a hasty spark   *struck*
And straight° is cold again.   *immediately*
CASSIUS   Hath Cassius lived
To be but mirth and laughter to his Brutus
When grief and blood ill-tempered[8] vexeth him?
115 BRUTUS   When I spoke that, I was ill-tempered too.

6. Roman god of riches (Plutus; often conflated with Pluto, god of the underworld).
7. Dishonorable actions shall be ascribed to moodi-

ness.
8. Literally, badly mixed blood (thought to produce anger and melancholy).

CASSIUS   Do you confess so much? Give me your hand.
BRUTUS   And my heart, too.
CASSIUS   O Brutus!
BRUTUS   What's the matter?
CASSIUS   Have not you love enough to bear with me
    When that rash humor° which my mother gave me   *temperament*
    Makes me forgetful?
120 BRUTUS   Yes, Cassius, and from henceforth
    When you are over-earnest with your Brutus,
    He'll think your mother chides and leave you so.°   *let you alone*
      Enter a POET [*with* LUCILIUS *and* TITINIUS].
POET   Let me go in to see the generals.
    There is some grudge between 'em; 'tis not meet
    They be alone.
125 LUCILIUS   You shall not come to them.
POET   Nothing but death shall stay me.
CASSIUS   How now? What's the matter?
POET   For shame, you generals; what do you mean?
    Love and be friends, as two such men should be;
130   For I have seen more years, I'm sure, than ye.
CASSIUS   Ha, ha, how vilely doth this cynic[9] rhyme!
BRUTUS   Get you hence, sirrah.° Saucy fellow, hence!   *(contemptuous address)*
CASSIUS   Bear with him, Brutus. 'Tis his fashion.
BRUTUS   I'll know his humor when he knows his time:[1]
135   What should the wars do with these jigging° fools?   *incompetently versifying*
    —Companion,° hence!   *(contemptuous)*
CASSIUS   Away, away, be gone.   *Exit* POET.
BRUTUS   Lucilius and Titinius, bid the commanders
    Prepare to lodge their companies tonight.
CASSIUS   And come yourselves, and bring Messala with you
140   Immediately to us.   [*Exeunt* LUCILIUS *and* TITINIUS.]
BRUTUS [*calls*]   Lucius, a bowl of wine.
CASSIUS   I did not think you could have been so angry.
BRUTUS   O Cassius, I am sick of° many griefs.   *suffering from*
CASSIUS   Of your philosophy you make no use
145   If you give place to accidental evils.[2]
BRUTUS   No man bears sorrow better. Portia is dead.
CASSIUS   Ha? Portia?
BRUTUS   She is dead.
CASSIUS   How scaped I killing° when I crossed you so?   *being killed*
150   O insupportable and touching loss!
    Upon what sickness?
BRUTUS   Impatient of° my absence,   *Inability to tolerate*
    And grief that young Octavius with Mark Antony
    Have made themselves so strong—for with° her death   *with the news of*
    That tidings came—with this she fell distract
155   And, her attendants absent, swallowed fire.[3]
CASSIUS   And died so?

---

9. Member of a philosophical school that refused to respect differences in social class.
1. I'll tolerate his eccentricity when he finds an appropriate time for it.
2. Brutus admired the Stoics, who taught that the wise man should remain unaffected by circumstances outside himself. *evils:* misfortunes.
3. Portia committed suicide by swallowing live embers.

BRUTUS   Even so.
CASSIUS   O ye immortal gods!
          Enter LUCIUS *with wine and tapers.°*   candles
BRUTUS   Speak no more of her. —Give me a bowl of wine.
     —In this I bury all unkindness, Cassius.
          [He] drinks.
CASSIUS   My heart is thirsty for that noble pledge.
160   —Fill, Lucius, till the wine o'erswell° the cup.   overflow
     I cannot drink too much of Brutus' love.   *[Exit* LUCIUS.*]*
          Enter TITINIUS *and* MESSALA.
BRUTUS   Come in, Titinius. —Welcome, good Messala.
     Now sit we close about this taper here
     And call in question° our necessities.   discuss
CASSIUS   Portia, art thou gone?
165 BRUTUS   No more, I pray you.
     —Messala, I have here receivèd letters
     That young Octavius and Mark Antony
     Come down upon us with a mighty power,
     Bending their expedition° toward Philippi.⁴   Pressing hastily
170 MESSALA   Myself have letters of the selfsame tenor.
BRUTUS   With what addition?
MESSALA   That by proscription⁵ and bills of outlawry
     Octavius, Antony, and Lepidus
     Have put to death an hundred senators.
175 BRUTUS   Therein our letters do not well agree:
     Mine speak of seventy senators that died
     By their proscriptions, Cicero being one.
CASSIUS   Cicero one?
MESSALA   Cicero is dead,
     And by that order of proscription.
180 Had you your letters from your wife, my lord?
BRUTUS   No, Messala.
MESSALA   Nor nothing in your letters writ of her?
BRUTUS   Nothing, Messala.
MESSALA   That methinks is strange.
BRUTUS   Why ask you? Hear you aught of her in yours?
185 MESSALA   No, my lord.
BRUTUS   Now, as you are a Roman, tell me true.
MESSALA   Then like a Roman bear the truth I tell,
     For certain she is dead, and by strange manner.
BRUTUS   Why, farewell, Portia.⁶ We must die, Messala.
190 With meditating that she must die once,°   at some time
     I have the patience to endure it now.
MESSALA   Even so great men great losses should endure.
CASSIUS   I have as much of this in art⁷ as you,
     But yet my nature could not bear it so.
195 BRUTUS   Well, to our work alive.⁸ What do you think
     Of marching to Philippi presently?°   at once
CASSIUS   I do not think it good.
BRUTUS   Your reason?

---

4. City in northeastern Greece.
5. See note to 4.1.17.
6. Brutus claims not to have heard any news of Portia, though earlier (lines 146–55) he describes her

death to Cassius; see the Introduction for a discussion of this conflict.
7. I have learned as much of this philosophy.
8. *alive:* of concern to those now living.

CASSIUS This it is:
200 'Tis better that the enemy seek us.
So shall he waste his means, weary his soldiers,
Doing himself offense, whilst we, lying still,
Are full of rest, defense, and nimbleness.

BRUTUS Good reasons must of force° give place to better: *of necessity*
205 The people twixt Philippi and this ground
Do stand but in a forced affection,
For they have grudged us contribution.⁹
The enemy, marching along by them,
By them shall make a fuller number up,
210 Come on refreshed, new-added,° and encouraged;   *reinforced*
From which advantage shall we cut him off
If at Philippi we do face him there,
These people at our back.

CASSIUS   Hear me, good brother.

BRUTUS Under your pardon.° You must note beside   *Allow me to continue*
215 That we have tried the utmost of our friends;
Our legions are brimful, our cause is ripe.
The enemy increaseth every day;
We, at the height, are ready to decline.
There is a tide in the affairs of men
220 Which, taken at the flood, leads on to fortune;
Omitted,° all the voyage of their life   *Once missed*
Is bound in° shallows and in miseries.   *confined to*
On such a full sea are we now afloat,
And we must take the current when it serves
Or lose our ventures.¹

225 CASSIUS   Then, with your will,° go on.   *as you wish*
We'll along ourselves and meet them at Philippi.

BRUTUS The deep of night is crept upon our talk,
And nature must obey necessity,
Which we will niggard° with a little rest.   *stint*
There is no more to say.

230 CASSIUS   No more. Good night.
Early tomorrow will we rise and hence.°   *depart*

BRUTUS Lucius.
    [*Enter* LUCIUS.]
                    My gown.°   [*Exit* LUCIUS.]   *dressing gown*
                    Farewell, good Messala.
—Good night, Titinius. —Noble, noble Cassius,
Good night, and good repose.

CASSIUS   O my dear brother,
235 This was an ill beginning of the night.
Never come such division tween our souls!
Let it not, Brutus.
        Enter LUCIUS *with the gown.*

BRUTUS Everything is well.

CASSIUS Good night, my lord.

240 BRUTUS Good night, good brother.

TITINIUS *and* MESSALA Good night, Lord Brutus.

BRUTUS Farewell, everyone.

---

9. Money to support the army.   1. Investments (in trading voyages).

Exeunt [all but BRUTUS *and* LUCIUS].

Give me the gown. Where is thy instrument?°   *(probably a lute)*

LUCIUS   Here in the tent.

BRUTUS   What, thou speak'st drowsily?

245   Poor knave,° I blame thee not; thou art o'erwatched.²   *lad*
     Call Claudio and some other of my men;
     I'll have them sleep on cushions in my tent.

LUCIUS   Varrus and Claudio.

Enter VARRUS *and* CLAUDIO.

VARRUS   Calls my lord?

250 BRUTUS   I pray you, sirs, lie in my tent and sleep.
     It may be I shall raise you° by and by   *get you up*
     On business to my brother Cassius.

VARRUS   So please you, we will stand and watch your pleasure.³

BRUTUS   I will not have it so. Lie down, good sirs.

255   It may be I shall otherwise bethink me.°   *change my mind*
     —Look, Lucius, here's the book I sought for so;
     I put it in the pocket of my gown.

LUCIUS   I was sure your lordship did not give it me.

BRUTUS   Bear with me, good boy, I am much forgetful.

260   Canst thou hold up thy heavy eyes awhile
     And touch thy instrument a strain or two?

LUCIUS   Ay, my lord, an't° please you.   *if it*

BRUTUS   It does, my boy.
     I trouble thee too much, but thou art willing.

LUCIUS   It is my duty, sir.

265 BRUTUS   I should not urge thy duty past thy might;
     I know young bloods° look for a time of rest.   *youthful spirits*

LUCIUS   I have slept, my lord, already.

BRUTUS   It was well done, and thou shalt sleep again;
     I will not hold thee long. If I do live,

270   I will be good to thee.

Music and a song.

     This is a sleepy tune. —O murd'rous slumber!
     Layest thou thy leaden mace° upon my boy   *heavy staff of office*
     That plays thee music? —Gentle knave, good night;
     I will not do thee so much wrong to wake thee.

275   If thou dost nod, thou break'st thy instrument;
     I'll take it from thee and, good boy, good night.
     Let me see, let me see; is not the leaf turned down
     Where I left reading? Here it is, I think.

Enter the GHOST OF CAESAR.

     How ill this taper burns.⁴ Ha! Who comes here?

280   I think it is the weakness of mine eyes
     That shapes this monstrous apparition.
     It comes upon° me. —Art thou any thing?   *toward*
     Art thou some god, some angel, or some devil,
     That mak'st my blood cold and my hair to stare?°   *stand on end*

285   Speak to me what thou art.

GHOST OF CAESAR   Thy evil spirit, Brutus.

BRUTUS   Why com'st thou?

---

2. You have stayed up too long.
3. And stay awake to attend to your wishes.

4. The dimming of a flame was held to indicate a ghost's presence.

GHOST OF CAESAR   To tell thee thou shalt see me at Philippi.
BRUTUS   Well, then I shall see thee again?
GHOST OF CAESAR   Ay, at Philippi.
290   BRUTUS   Why, I will see thee at Philippi, then.
                                        [*Exit* GHOST OF CAESAR.]
Now I have taken heart, thou vanishest.
Ill spirit, I would hold more talk with thee.
—Boy, Lucius! —Varrus, Claudio, sirs, awake!
Claudio!
295   LUCIUS   The strings, my lord, are false.°   *out of tune*
BRUTUS   He thinks he still is at his instrument.
Lucius, awake.
LUCIUS   My lord.
BRUTUS   Didst thou dream, Lucius, that thou so cried'st out?
300   LUCIUS   My lord, I do not know that I did cry.
BRUTUS   Yes, that thou didst. Didst thou see anything?
LUCIUS   Nothing, my lord.
BRUTUS   Sleep again, Lucius. —Sirrah Claudio.
[*to* VARRUS] Fellow, thou, awake.
305   VARRUS   My lord.
CLAUDIO   My lord.
BRUTUS   Why did you so cry out, sirs, in your sleep?
BOTH   Did we, my lord?
BRUTUS   Ay. Saw you anything?
VARRUS   No, my lord, I saw nothing.
CLAUDIO   Nor I, my lord.
310   BRUTUS   Go and commend me° to my brother Cassius.   *send my regards*
Bid him set on his powers betimes before,[5]
And we will follow.
BOTH   It shall be done, my lord.   *Exeunt.*

5.1
Enter OCTAVIUS, ANTONY, *and their army.*
OCTAVIUS   Now, Antony, our hopes are answerèd.
You said the enemy would not come down
But keep the hills and upper regions.
It proves not so: their battles° are at hand;   *forces*
5   They mean to warn° us at Philippi here,   *challenge*
Answering before we do demand of them.
ANTONY   Tut, I am in their bosoms,[1] and I know
Wherefore they do it: they could be content
To visit other places° and come down   *To go elsewhere*
10   With fearful bravery,[2] thinking by this face°   *pretense; defiance*
To fasten in our thoughts that they have courage;
But 'tis not so.
                    Enter a MESSENGER.
MESSENGER   Prepare you, generals.
The enemy comes on in gallant show.
Their bloody sign° of battle is hung out,   *red flag*
15   And something to° be done immediately.   *is to*
ANTONY   Octavius, lead your battle softly° on   *your army warily*

---

5. March off with his army before me.
5.1 Location: The remainder of the play takes place
on the battlefield near Philippi.

1. I know their secret thoughts.
2. With a show of courage that conceals fear; with a
terrifying display.

Upon the left hand of the even field.

OCTAVIUS   Upon the right hand, I. Keep thou the left.

ANTONY   Why do you cross° me in this exigent?°   thwart / critical moment

20   OCTAVIUS   I do not cross you,³ but I will do so.
          March.
          Drum. Enter BRUTUS, CASSIUS, and their army
          [including LUCILIUS, TITINIUS, and MESSALA].

BRUTUS   They stand and would have parley.

CASSIUS   Stand fast, Titinius. We must out° and talk.   go forward

OCTAVIUS   Mark Antony, shall we give sign of battle?

ANTONY   No, Caesar, we will answer on their charge.⁴

25   Make forth.° The generals would have some words.   Go forward

OCTAVIUS [to his officers]   Stir not until the signal.
          [The generals step toward one another.]

BRUTUS   Words before blows. Is it so, countrymen?

OCTAVIUS   Not that we love words better, as you do.

BRUTUS   Good words are better than bad strokes, Octavius.

30   ANTONY   In your° bad strokes, Brutus, you give good words.   As you deliver
          Witness the hole you made in Caesar's heart,
          Crying, "Long live! Hail, Caesar."

CASSIUS   Antony,
          The posture° of your blows are yet unknown;   quality
          But for your words, they rob the Hybla⁵ bees
          And leave them honeyless.

35   ANTONY   Not stingless too?

BRUTUS   Oh, yes, and soundless too,
          For you have stol'n their buzzing, Antony,
          And very wisely threat before you sting.

ANTONY   Villains, you did not so when your vile daggers

40   Hacked one another in the sides of Caesar.
          You showed your teeth like apes,° and fawned like hounds,   You pretended to smile
          And bowed like bondmen, kissing Caesar's feet,
          Whilst damnèd Casca, like a cur, behind
          Struck Caesar on the neck. O you flatterers!

45   CASSIUS   Flatterers? —Now, Brutus, thank yourself.
          This tongue had not offended so today
          If Cassius might have ruled.°   had his way

OCTAVIUS   Come, come, the cause.° If arguing make us sweat,   matter in hand
          The proof° of it will turn to redder drops: testing

50   Look, I draw a sword against conspirators.
          [He draws.]
          When think you that the sword goes up again?
          Never, till Caesar's three-and-thirty wounds
          Be well avenged, or till another Caesar⁶
          Have added slaughter to⁷ the sword of traitors.

55   BRUTUS   Caesar, thou canst not die by traitors' hands
          Unless thou bring'st them with thee.°   (Unless by your hand)

OCTAVIUS   So I hope.
          I was not born to die on Brutus' sword.

BRUTUS   Oh, if thou wert the noblest of thy strain,°   family

---

3. March on the right side; dispute with you in the
future.
4. We will meet them when they attack.

5. Sicilian town famous for honey.
6. That is, Octavius Caesar himself.
7. Has increased the slaughter committed by.

Young man, thou couldst not die more honorable.
60 CASSIUS   A peevish° schoolboy, worthless of such honor,   silly
Joined with a masquer and a reveler.[8]
ANTONY   Old Cassius still.
OCTAVIUS   Come, Antony, away.
—Defiance, traitors, hurl we in your teeth.
If you dare fight today, come to the field;
65 If not, when you have stomachs.°   inclination; courage
               Exeunt OCTAVIUS, ANTONY, *and [their] army.*
CASSIUS   Why now, blow wind, swell billow, and swim bark!°   ship
The storm is up, and all is on the hazard.°   at risk
BRUTUS   Ho, Lucilius! Hark, a word with you.
               LUCILIUS *and* MESSALA *stand forth.*°   come forward
LUCILIUS   My lord.
               [BRUTUS *and* LUCILIUS *step aside together.*]
70 CASSIUS   Messala.
MESSALA   What says my general?
CASSIUS   Messala,
This is my birthday, as° this very day   on
Was Cassius born. Give me thy hand, Messala.
75 Be thou my witness that against my will,
As Pompey was, am I compelled to set
Upon one battle all our liberties.
You know that I held Epicurus strong
And his opinion.[9] Now I change my mind
80 And partly credit things that do presage.
Coming from Sardis, on our former ensign°   foremost banner
Two mighty eagles fell,° and there they perched,   alighted
Gorging and feeding from our soldiers' hands,
Who to Philippi here consorted° us.   accompanied
85 This morning are they fled away and gone,
And in their steads do ravens, crows, and kites[1]
Fly o'er our heads and downward look on us
As° we were sickly prey. Their shadows seem   As if
A canopy most fatal,° under which   ominous
90 Our army lies, ready to give up the ghost.
MESSALA   Believe not so.
CASSIUS   I but believe it partly,
For I am fresh of spirit and resolved
To meet all perils very constantly.°   resolutely
BRUTUS   Even so, Lucilius.
               [*He rejoins* CASSIUS.]
95 CASSIUS   Now, most noble Brutus,
The gods° today stand friendly that we may,   May the gods
Lovers° in peace, lead on our days to age.   Close friends
But since the affairs of men rests still° incertain,   always remain
Let's reason with° the worst that may befall.   consider
100 If we do lose this battle, then is this
The very last time we shall speak together.
What are you then determinèd to do?

---

8. That is, Antony, who was noted for his love of
extravagant entertainments and banquets.
9. Epicurus, a Greek philosopher, thought the gods
indifferent to human affairs and therefore disbelieved
omens.
1. These are all scavenger birds, considered bad omens.

BRUTUS Even by the rule of that philosophy[2]
By which I did blame Cato[3] for the death
105 Which he did give himself—I know not how,
But I do find it cowardly and vile,
For fear of what might fall,° so to prevent° *happen / anticipate*
The time° of life—arming myself with patience *natural limit*
To stay° the providence of some high powers *await*
110 That govern us below.
CASSIUS Then, if we lose this battle,
You are contented to be led in triumph[4]
Thorough° the streets of Rome? *Through*
BRUTUS No, Cassius, no. Think not, thou noble Roman,
115 That ever Brutus will go bound to Rome;
He bears too great a mind. But this same day
Must end that work the Ides of March begun,
And whether we shall meet again, I know not.
Therefore our everlasting farewell take:
120 Forever and forever farewell, Cassius.
If we do meet again, why, we shall smile;
If not, why then this parting was well made.
CASSIUS Forever and forever farewell, Brutus.
If we do meet again, we'll smile indeed;
125 If not, 'tis true this parting was well made.
BRUTUS Why, then, lead on. Oh, that a man might know
The end of this day's business ere it come.
But it sufficeth that the day will end,
And then the end is known. —Come, ho, away. *Exeunt.*

5.2

Alarum.° Enter BRUTUS *and* MESSALA. *Offstage call to battle*
BRUTUS Ride, ride, Messala, ride, and give these bills° *written orders*
Unto the legions on the other side.° *(Cassius's wing)*
Loud alarum.
Let them set on° at once; for I perceive *advance*
But cold demeanor° in Octavio's wing, *lack of fighting spirit*
5 And sudden push gives them the overthrow.
Ride, ride, Messala! Let them all come down. *Exeunt.*

5.3

Alarums. Enter CASSIUS [*carrying a standard*°] *and* *a banner*
TITINIUS.
CASSIUS Oh, look, Titinius, look, the villains° fly! *(Cassius's own men)*
—Myself have to mine own turned enemy.
This ensign° here of mine was turning back; *standard-bearer*
I slew the coward and did take it° from him. *(the standard)*
5 TITINIUS O Cassius, Brutus gave the word too early,
Who having some advantage on Octavius,
Took it too eagerly. His soldiers fell to spoil,° *looting*
Whilst we by Antony are all enclosed.
Enter PINDARUS.
PINDARUS Fly further off, my lord, fly further off!

---

2. Brutus admired Plato, who rejected suicide.
3. See note to 2.1.295.
4. As a captive in a triumphal procession; see note to 1.1.30.

10   Mark Antony is in your tents, my lord.
    Fly therefore, noble Cassius, fly far off.
    CASSIUS   This hill is far enough. —Look, look, Titinius,
    Are those my tents where I perceive the fire?
    TITINIUS   They are, my lord.
    CASSIUS   Titinius, if thou lovest me,
15   Mount thou my horse and hide thy spurs in him
    Till he have brought thee up to yonder troops
    And here again, that I may rest assured
    Whether yond troops are friend or enemy.
    TITINIUS   I will be here again even with° a thought.   *Exit.*   *as fast as*
20   CASSIUS   Go, Pindarus, get higher on that hill.
    My sight was ever thick.° Regard Titinius,   *dim*
    And tell me what thou not'st about the field.
    —This day I breathèd first. Time is come round,
    And where I did begin, there shall I end.
25   My life is run his compass.° —Sirrah, what news?   *its circuit*
    PINDARUS *(above°)*   O my lord!   *(on the stage balcony)*
    CASSIUS   What news?
    PINDARUS   Titinius is enclosèd round about
    With horsemen that make to him on the spur,[1]
30   Yet he spurs on. Now they are almost on him.
    Now, Titinius! Now some light.° Oh, he lights too.   *alight*
    He's ta'en.° *(Shout.)* And hark, they shout for joy.   *taken*
    CASSIUS   Come down, behold no more.
    —O coward that I am, to live so long
35   To see my best friend ta'en before my face.
        Enter PINDARUS.
    —Come hither, sirrah.
    In Parthia° did I take thee prisoner,   *(modern Iran)*
    And then I swore thee, saving of[2] thy life,
    That whatsoever I did bid thee do,
40   Thou shouldst attempt it. Come now, keep thine oath.
    Now be a freeman, and with this good sword
    That ran through Caesar's bowels, search° this bosom.   *penetrate*
    Stand° not to answer. Here, take thou the hilts,°   *Delay / sword handle*
    And when my face is covered, as 'tis now,
45   Guide thou the sword. —Caesar, thou art revenged,
    Even with the sword that killed thee.
        [He dies.]
    PINDARUS   So, I am free, yet would not so have been
    Durst° I have done my will. —O Cassius,   *Dared*
    Far from this country Pindarus shall run,
50   Where never Roman shall take note of him.   *[Exit.]*
        Enter TITINIUS *and* MESSALA.
    MESSALA   It is but change,° Titinius; for Octavius   *an even exchange*
    Is overthrown by noble Brutus' power,
    As Cassius' legions are by Antony.
    TITINIUS   These tidings will well comfort Cassius.
    MESSALA   Where did you leave him?
55   TITINIUS   All disconsolate,

5.3
1. Who approach him at a gallop.

2. I made you swear, when I spared.

With Pindarus his bondman on this hill.
MESSALA   Is not that he that lies upon the ground?
TITINIUS   He lies not like the living. O my heart!
MESSALA   Is not that he?
TITINIUS   No, this was he, Messala,
60 But Cassius is no more. O setting sun,
As in thy red rays thou dost sink to night,
So in his red blood Cassius' day is set.
The sun of Rome is set. Our day is gone.
Clouds, dews, and dangers come; our deeds are done.
65 Mistrust of my success³ hath done this deed.
MESSALA   Mistrust of good success hath done this deed.
O hateful Error, Melancholy's child,⁴
Why dost thou show to the apt° thoughts of men   *impressionable*
The things that are not? O Error, soon conceived,
70 Thou never com'st unto a happy birth
But kill'st the mother° that engendered thee.   *(the melancholy person)*
TITINIUS   What, Pindarus! Where art thou, Pindarus?
MESSALA   Seek him, Titinius, whilst I go to meet
The noble Brutus, thrusting this report
75 Into his ears. I may say "thrusting" it,
For piercing steel and darts° envenomèd   *spears*
Shall be as welcome to the ears of Brutus
As tidings of this sight.
TITINIUS   Hie you, Messala,
And I will seek for Pindarus the while.   [*Exit* MESSALA.]
80 Why didst thou send me forth, brave Cassius?
Did I not meet thy friends, and did not they
Put on my brows this wreath of victory
And bid me give it thee? Didst thou not hear their shouts?
Alas, thou hast misconstrued everything.
85 But hold thee, take this garland on thy brow.
Thy Brutus bid me give it thee, and I
Will do his bidding. —Brutus, come apace,°   *quickly*
And see how I regarded° Caius Cassius.   *esteemed*
—By your leave, gods. This is a Roman's part.
90 —Come, Cassius' sword, and find Titinius' heart.
          [*He*] *dies.*
          Alarum. Enter BRUTUS, MESSALA, *young* CATO,⁵
          STRATO, VOLUMNIUS, *and* LUCILIUS.
BRUTUS   Where, where, Messala, doth his body lie?
MESSALA   Lo, yonder, and Titinius mourning it.
BRUTUS   Titinius' face is upward.
CATO   He is slain.
BRUTUS   O Julius Caesar, thou art mighty yet;
95 Thy spirit walks abroad and turns our swords
In our own proper° entrails.   *our very own*
          Low° alarums.   *Soft*
CATO   Brave Titinius!
—Look whe'er° he have not crowned dead Cassius.   *whether*
BRUTUS   Are yet two Romans living such as these?

---

3. Doubt about the outcome of my mission.   5. The son of Marcus Portius Cato.
4. That is, bred from melancholy thoughts.

The last of all the Romans, fare thee well!
100   It is impossible that ever Rome
Should breed thy fellow. —Friends, I owe more tears
To this dead man than you shall see me pay.
—I shall find time, Cassius; I shall find time.
—Come therefore, and to Thasos° send his body.   *an island near Philippi*
105   His funerals shall not be in our camp,
Lest it discomfort° us. —Lucilius, come.   *dishearten*
—And come, young Cato, let us to the field.
Labio and Flavio set our battles° on.   *forces*
'Tis three o'clock, and, Romans, yet ere night
110   We shall try fortune in a second fight.   *Exeunt.*

5.4

Alarum. Enter BRUTUS, MESSALA, [*young*] CATO,
LUCILIUS, *and Flavius.*

BRUTUS   Yet, countrymen, oh, yet hold up your heads.
              [*Exeunt* BRUTUS, MESSALA, *and Flavius.*]

CATO   What bastard° doth not? Who will go with me?   *untrue Roman*
   I will proclaim my name about the field.
   I am the son of Marcus Cato, ho!
5   A foe to tyrants and my country's friend.
   I am the son of Marcus Cato, ho!
       Enter SOLDIERS, *and fight.*

LUCILIUS   And I am Brutus, Marcus Brutus, I!
   Brutus, my country's friend! Know me for Brutus!
   O young and noble Cato, art thou down?
10   Why now thou diest as bravely as Titinius
   And mayst be honored, being Cato's son.

FIRST SOLDIER   Yield, or thou diest.

LUCILIUS   Only I yield to die.[1]
   There is so much[2] that thou wilt kill me straight;°   *immediately*
   Kill Brutus and be honored in his death.

15 FIRST SOLDIER   We must not. A noble prisoner.

SECOND SOLDIER   Room, ho! Tell Antony, Brutus is ta'en.

FIRST SOLDIER   I'll tell the news.
       Enter ANTONY.
                 Here comes the general.
   —Brutus is ta'en, Brutus is ta'en, my lord.

ANTONY   Where is he?

20 LUCILIUS   Safe, Antony, Brutus is safe enough.
   I dare assure thee that no enemy
   Shall ever take alive the noble Brutus.
   The gods defend him from so great a shame!
   When you do find him, or° alive or dead,   *either*
25   He will be found like Brutus, like himself.°   *true to his noble nature*

ANTONY [*to* FIRST SOLDIER]   This is not Brutus, friend,
     but I assure you,
   A prize no less in worth. Keep this man safe;
   Give him all kindness. I had rather have
   Such men my friends than enemies. —Go on,
30   And see whe'er Brutus be alive or dead;

5.4
1. I yield only so that I may die.

2. There is enough inducement.

And bring us word unto Octavius' tent
How everything is chanced.°   *has happened*
        Exeunt [in different directions].

5.5

        Enter BRUTUS, DARDANIUS, CLITUS, STRATO, *and*
        VOLUMNIUS.

BRUTUS   Come, poor remains of friends, rest on this rock.
CLITUS   Statilius[1] showed the torchlight, but, my lord,
        He came not back: he is or ta'en° or slain.   *either captured*
BRUTUS   Sit thee down, Clitus. Slaying is the word;
5   It is a deed in fashion. Hark thee, Clitus.
        [*He whispers.*]
CLITUS   What, I, my lord? No, not for all the world.
BRUTUS   Peace then, no words.
CLITUS   I'll rather kill myself.
BRUTUS   Hark thee, Dardanius.
        [*He whispers.*]
DARDANIUS   Shall I do such a deed?
CLITUS   O Dardanius!
10   DARDANIUS   O Clitus!
CLITUS   What ill request did Brutus make to thee?
DARDANIUS   To kill him, Clitus. Look, he meditates.
CLITUS   Now is that noble vessel full of grief,
        That it runs over even at his eyes.
15   BRUTUS   Come hither, good Volumnius. List° a word.   *Listen to*
VOLUMNIUS   What says my lord?
BRUTUS   Why this, Volumnius:
        The ghost of Caesar hath appeared to me
        Two several° times by night—at Sardis once,   *different*
        And this last night here in Philippi fields.
        I know my hour is come.
20   VOLUMNIUS   Not so, my lord.
BRUTUS   Nay, I am sure it is, Volumnius.
        Thou seest the world, Volumnius, how it goes:
        Our enemies have beat° us to the pit.[2]   *driven*
                Low alarums.
        It is more worthy to leap in ourselves
25   Than tarry till they push us. Good Volumnius,
        Thou know'st that we two went to school together;
        Even for that our love of old, I prithee,
        Hold thou my sword hilts whilst I run on it.
VOLUMNIUS   That's not an office for a friend, my lord.
                Alarum still.
30   CLITUS   Fly, fly, my lord! There is no tarrying here.
BRUTUS   Farewell to you, —and you, —and you, Volumnius.
        —Strato, thou hast been all this while asleep.
        Farewell to thee too, Strato. —Countrymen,
        My heart doth joy that yet in all my life
35   I found no man but he was true to me.
        I shall have glory by this losing day
        More than Octavius and Mark Antony

5.5
1. A soldier sent ahead with instructions to signal by   torchlight if all is well.
                                                                2. Animal trap; grave.

By this vile conquest shall attain unto.
So fare you well at once, for Brutus' tongue
40 Hath almost ended his life's history.
Night hangs upon mine eyes; my bones would rest,
That have but labored³ to attain this hour.
        Alarum. Cry within, "Fly, fly, fly!"
CLITUS Fly, my lord, fly!
BRUTUS   Hence, I will follow.
        [*Exeunt* CLITUS, DARDANIUS, *and* VOLUMNIUS.]
I prithee, Strato, stay thou by thy lord.
45 Thou art a fellow of a good respect;°   *reputation*
Thy life hath had some smatch° of honor in it.   *relish*
Hold, then, my sword and turn away thy face
While I do run upon it. Wilt thou, Strato?
STRATO Give me your hand first. Fare you well, my lord.
50 BRUTUS Farewell, good Strato.
        [*He runs on his sword.*]
                        —Caesar, now be still.
I killed not thee with half so good a will.
        [*He*] *dies.*
        *Alarum. Retreat.*⁴ Enter ANTONY, OCTAVIUS, MESSALA,
        LUCILIUS, *and the army.*
OCTAVIUS What man is that?
MESSALA My master's man. —Strato, where is thy master?
STRATO Free from the bondage you are in, Messala.
55 The conquerors can but make a fire of him,°   *burn his body*
For Brutus only overcame himself,⁵
And no man else hath honor by his death.
LUCILIUS So Brutus should be found. —I thank thee, Brutus,
That thou hast proved Lucilius' saying true.
60 OCTAVIUS All that served Brutus, I will entertain them.°   *take them into service*
        —Fellow, wilt thou bestow° thy time with me?   *spend*
STRATO Ay, if Messala will prefer° me to you.   *recommend*
OCTAVIUS Do so, good Messala.
MESSALA How died my master, Strato?
65 STRATO I held the sword, and he did run on it.
MESSALA Octavius, then take him to follow° thee,   *serve*
That did the latest° service to my master.   *last*
ANTONY This was the noblest Roman of them all.
All the conspirators save only he
70 Did that° they did in envy of great Caesar;   *what*
He only in a general honest thought⁶
And common good to all⁷ made one of them.
His life was gentle,° and the elements⁸   *noble*
So mixed in him that Nature might stand up
75 And say to all the world, "This was a man."
OCTAVIUS According to° his virtue, let us use him   *In accordance with*
With all respect and rites of burial.
Within my tent his bones tonight shall lie,
Most like a soldier, ordered° honorably.   *treated*
80 So call the field to rest, and let's away
To part° the glories of this happy day.   *Exeunt all.*   *share*

---

3. Labored for no other purpose than.
4. Trumpet signal to cease pursuit.
5. For only Brutus conquered Brutus.
6. With a virtuous, principled conviction.

7. And desire for the common good.
8. The four bodily humors, different combinations of which supposedly affected temperament; in the ideal individual, no single humor predominated.

Twelfth Night

Shakespeare's contemporary Thomas Coryat wrote that he witnessed something quite remarkable when he went to the theater in Venice: "I saw women act, a thing that I never saw before." That an Englishman had to travel abroad to see women actors for the first time is not surprising. All the great women's roles in Elizabethan and Jacobean plays were written to be performed by trained adolescent boys, and boys played the female parts as well in all grammar school and university productions. But what struck Coryat in Venice was neither the gratifying naturalness of finally seeing women play women's parts nor the comparative inadequacy of English boy actors. Rather, he was impressed that the women actors managed to hold their own in representing the female sex: "They performed it," he writes, "with as good a grace, as ever I saw any masculine Actor."

Recent scholars have observed that there were in fact occasions in which audiences in England could have seen women performing: troupes from abroad, including women actors, occasionally toured England, and English women performed in the theatrical spectacles known as masques and in other entertainments. But in England, women did not perform on the public stage (the word "actress" had not yet entered the English language), and the remarks of Coryat and others suggest that their absence was rarely if ever lamented. The boy actors were evidently extraordinarily skillful, and the audiences were sufficiently immersed in the conventions both of theater and of social life in general to accept gesture, makeup, and above all dress as a convincing representation of femininity.

Twelfth Night, or What You Will, written for Shakespeare's all-male company, plays brilliantly with these conventions. The comedy depends on an actor's ability to transform himself, through costume, voice, and gesture, into a young gentlewoman, Viola, who transforms herself, through costume, voice, and gesture, into a young man, Cesario. The play's delicious complications follow from the emotional turbulence that Viola's transformation engenders. Shipwrecked on a strange coast and bereft of her twin brother, the disguised Viola finds a place in the service of the powerful Duke Orsino, with whom she promptly falls in love. Orsino is in love with Lady Olivia, a wealthy countess whose household includes, among its servants and dependents, a steward or house manager, a waiting-gentlewoman, a professional entertainer, and a down-at-the-heels, perpetually drunken uncle. When Orsino sends Cesario to help him woo the proud Olivia, Olivia not only rejects the Duke's suit but falls in love with his messenger. Discomfited to learn that she is the object of Olivia's love, Viola reflects on the plot's impassioned triangle:

> My master loves her dearly,
> And I, poor monster, fond as much on him.
> And she, mistaken, seems to dote on me.
> What will become of this?
>
> (2.2.32–35)

"Poor monster": in *Twelfth Night*, clothes do not simply reveal or disguise identity; they partly constitute identity—or so Viola playfully imagines—making her a strange, hybrid creature. To be sure, she understands perfectly well the narrow biological definition of her sex (though in the characteristically male-centered language of Shakespeare's culture, she phrases that definition in terms of what she "lack[s]" [3.4.272]). Yet there is something almost magical in this play about costume, so that even at the close, when identities have been sorted out and the couples happily matched, Orsino cannot bring himself to call his bride-to-be by her rightful name or to address her as a woman:

> Cesario, come—
> For so you shall be while you are a man—
> But when in other habits you are seen,
> Orsino's mistress and his fancy's queen.
> (5.1.371–74)

It would have been simple for Shakespeare to devise a concluding scene in which Viola appears in women's "habits," but he goes out of his way to leave her in men's clothes and hence to disrupt with a delicate comic touch the return to the "normal." The transforming power of costume unsettles fixed categories of gender and social class; it allows characters to explore emotional territory that a culture officially hostile to same-sex desire and cross-class marriage would ordinarily have ruled out of bounds. Longing, intimacy, and desire do not conform comfortably to social norms. Formal speeches take on a startling intensity, service slides into aching love, friendship turns into self-abnegating adoration, the pursued becomes the pursuer. In *Twelfth Night*, conventional expectations repeatedly give way to a different way of perceiving the world.

Shakespeare wrote *Twelfth Night* around 1601. He had already written such comedies as *A Midsummer Night's Dream*, *Much Ado About Nothing*, and *As You Like It*, with their playful, subtly ironic investigations of the ways in which heterosexual couples precipitate from the murkier crosscurrents of male and female friendships; as interesting, perhaps, he had probably just recently completed *Hamlet*, with its unprecedented exploration of mourning, betrayal, antic humor, and tragic isolation. *Twelfth Night* would prove to be, in the view of many critics, both the most perfect and in some sense the last of the great festive comedies. Shakespeare returned to comedy later in his career, but always with more insistent overtones of bitterness, loss, and grief. There are dark notes in *Twelfth Night* as well: Olivia is in mourning for her brother; Viola thinks that her brother, too, is dead; Antonio believes that he has been betrayed by the man he loves; Orsino threatens to kill Cesario. Desire is repeatedly linked to frustration and loss. The servants who devote themselves tirelessly to pleasing the wealthy aristocrats on whose whims they depend anxiously compete with one another for signs of favor and live in fear of the contempt or indifference of their masters. But these notes are swept up in the current of sweet music that pervades the play, drawing the characters into a giddy, carnivalesque dance of illusion, disguise, folly, and clowning. And for at least the heroine, selfless devotion is magically rewarded, as the intimacy between master and trusted servant is transmuted into reciprocal love and desire.

The play's subtitle, *What You Will*, underscores the celebratory spirit associated with Twelfth Night, the Feast of the Epiphany (January 6), which in Elizabethan England marked the culminating night of the traditional Christmas revels. On Twelfth Night 1601, the Queen's guest of honor was a twenty-eight-year-old Italian nobleman, Don Virginio Orsino, Duke of Bracciano. Orsino wrote to his wife that he was entertained that night with "a mingled comedy, with pieces of music and dances." Since the company that performed was the Lord Chamberlain's Men—Shakespeare's company—it has been argued that the comedy was *Twelfth Night*, but there is no scholarly consensus on this hypothesis. The title, in any case, would for Shakespeare's contemporaries have conjured up a whole series of time-honored festivities associated with the midwinter season. A rigidly hierarchical social order that ordinarily demanded deference, sobriety, and strict obedience to authority temporarily gave way to raucous rituals of inversion: young boys were crowned for a day as bishops and carried through the streets in mock religious processions; abstemiousness was toppled by bouts of heavy drinking and feasting; the spirit of parody, folly, and misrule reigned briefly in places normally reserved for stern-faced moralists and sober judges.

That these festivities were associated with Christian holidays—the Epiphany marked the visit of the Three Kings to Bethlehem to worship the Christ child—did not altogether obscure the continuities with pagan winter rituals such as the Roman Saturnalia, with its comparably explosive release from everyday discipline into a disorderly realm of belly laughter and belly cheer. Puritans emphasized these continuities in launching a fierce attack on the Elizabethan festive calendar and its whole ethos, just as they attacked the theater for what they saw as its links with paganism, idleness, and sexual license. Elizabethan and Jacobean authorities in the church and the state had their own concerns about idleness and subversion, but they generally protected and patronized both festive ritual and theater on the grounds that these provided a valuable release from tensions that might otherwise prove dangerous. Sobriety, piety, and discipline were no doubt admirable virtues, but most human beings were not saints. "Dost thou think because thou art virtuous," the drunken Sir Toby asks the censorious steward Malvolio, "there shall be no more cakes and ale?" (2.3.106–08).

Fittingly, the earliest firm record of a performance of *Twelfth Night,* as noted in the diary of John Manningham, was "at our feast" in the Middle Temple (one of London's law schools) in February 1602. Manningham wrote observantly that the play was "much like the *Comedy of Errors,* or *Menaechmi* in Plautus, but most like and near to that in Italian called *Inganni.*" That is, *Twelfth Night* resembles Shakespeare's own earlier play on identical twins (along with that play's Roman source) and still more resembles a series of sixteenth-century Italian comedies built around the intertwining themes of love, fraud (*inganno*), and mistaken identity. Several of these comedies feature the plot device of a female twin who takes service as a page with the man she loves. Closest of these to Shakespeare's comedy is *Gl'Ingannati* (The Deceived), written for performance at Carnival time in Siena in 1531 and translated into French in 1543. It seems likely that Shakespeare knew this play or one that derived from it, and he may have picked up several details in addition to the overall plot line. But the tone of *Gl'Ingannati,* with its bawdy jokes about nuns and old men, its sly, sardonic servants, and its farcical intrigues, is far from *Twelfth Night*'s blend of melancholy and delight, its bittersweet mingling of divided and contradictory desires. Tellingly, in the Italian comedy, the heroine is all along plotting to win the love of the man she serves; she has disguised herself in order to dissuade him from wooing elsewhere. Viola's predicament—her attempt to serve Orsino even at the cost of her own deepest longings—represents a wholly different emotional register.

That predicament is not Shakespeare's invention; he found it, with many other elements of his plot, in an English story, Barnabe Riche's tale "Apollonius and Silla" in *Riche His Farewell to Military Profession* (1581), which was in turn based on French and Italian sources. Riche is too addicted to moralizing to explore his heroine's character with much subtlety, but he does underscore how painful it is for her to hide her feelings while acting as go-between, and hence he anticipates, if only woodenly, the mood that Shakespeare exquisitely captures in Viola's lines about one who "sat like Patience on a monument, / Smiling at grief" (2.4.111–12). There is less precedent, in Riche or in any of the known sources, for the aspect of *Twelfth Night* that Manningham found particularly memorable and that has continued to delight audiences: the gulling of Malvolio.

Malvolio (It. *male voglio:* "I wish ill") is explicitly linked to those among Shakespeare's contemporaries most hostile to the theater and to such holidays as Twelfth Night: "sometimes," says Lady Olivia's waiting-gentlewoman Maria, "he is a kind of puritan" (2.3.129). When we first see Malvolio, he is harshly critical of the Clown, who is attempting to win back Olivia's favor. "Unless you laugh and minister occasion to him," Malvolio sourly observes, "he is gagged" (1.5.78–79). Though ungenerous, the observation is canny, for comedy does seem to depend on a collaborative spirit from which Malvolio conspicuously excludes himself. He is a man without friends. More dangerously, he is a man in a socially dependent position with a gift for acquiring enemies, as he does when he tries to silence the noisy revelry of that classic carnivalesque

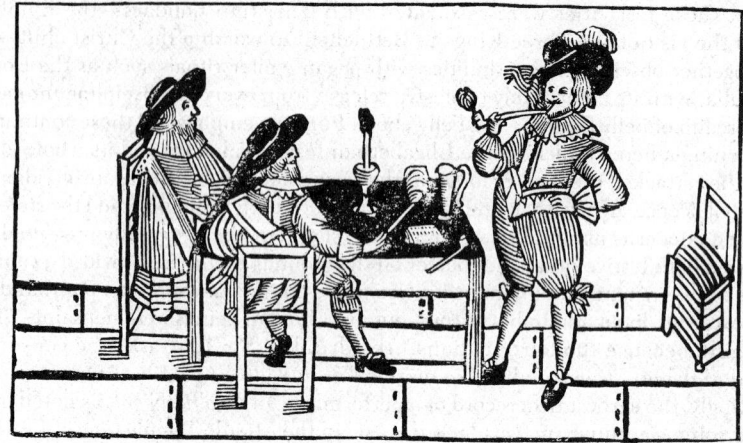

Gentlemen drinking and smoking. From Phillip Stubbes, *The Anatomy of Abuses* (1583).

threesome of a drunkard, a blockhead, and a professional fool: Olivia's uncle Sir Toby, his boon companion Sir Andrew Aguecheek, and the Clown.

Olivia remarks to Malvolio that he is "sick of self-love" (1.5.82), and it is this narcissism that his enemies exploit to undo him. When Malvolio finds Maria's forged letter, he is in the midst of a deliciously self-gratifying fantasy that he has married Olivia, a fantasy less of erotic bliss than of social domination. The dream of rising above his station fuels his credulous eagerness to interpret the letter according to his fondest wishes and to comply with its absurd suggestions for his festive dress and demeanor. This compliance, by making it seem to Olivia that he has gone mad, renders Malvolio vulnerable to a further humiliation. In a parody of the age's brutal "therapy" for insanity, he is clapped into a dark room and subjected to a mock exorcism. Finally, he suffers what is perhaps the cruelest punishment for someone who dreams that greatness will be thrust upon him: he is simply forgotten. When in the play's final moments he is released, Malvolio is in no mood to join in the general air of communal wonder and rejoicing. More alone than ever, he introduces into the comedy's resolution an extraordinary note of vindictive bitterness: "I'll be revenged on the whole pack of you" (5.1.364). Shakespeare does not hide the cruelty of the treatment to which Malvolio has been subjected—"He hath been most notoriously abused" (5.1.365), says Olivia— nor does he shrink from showing the audience other disagreeable qualities in Sir Toby and his companions. But while the close of the comedy seems to embrace these failings in a tolerant, bemused, aristocratic recognition of human folly, it can find no place for Malvolio's blend of puritanism and social climbing.

Malvolio is scapegoated for indulging in a fantasy that colors several of the key relationships in *Twelfth Night*: the fantasy of winning the hand of one of the noble and enormously wealthy aristocrats who reign over the social world of the play. The beautiful heiress Olivia, mistress of a great house, is a glittering prize that lures not only Malvolio but also the foolish Sir Andrew and the elegant, imperious Duke Orsino. In falling in love with the Duke's graceful messenger (and, as she thinks she has done, in marrying him), Olivia seems to have made precisely the kind of match that had fueled Malvolio's social-climbing imagination. As it turns out, the match is not between unequals: "Be not amazed," the Duke tells her when she realizes that she has married someone she scarcely knows. "Right noble is his blood" (5.1.254). The social order, then, has not been overturned: as in a carnival, when the disguises are removed, the revelers resume their "proper" socially and sexually approved positions.

Yet there is something decidedly improper about the perverse erotic excitement that the play discovers in disguise, displacement, indirection, and deferral, and something irreducibly strange about the marriages with which *Twelfth Night* ends. The drunken aristocrat Sir Toby has married the lady-in-waiting Maria as a reward for devising the plot against Malvolio. Olivia has entered into a "contract of eternal bond of love" (5.1.149) with someone whose actual identity is only revealed to her after the marriage ceremony. (In Riche's version of the story, she is pregnant and her marriage saves her from social disgrace; but Shakespeare omits this plot twist, thereby raising the tone but heightening the irrationality of the finale.) The strangeness of the bond between virtual strangers is matched by the strangeness of Orsino's instantaneous decision to marry his page Cesario—as soon as "he" can become Viola by changing into women's clothes. Only a few minutes earlier, in a fit of jealous rage at Olivia's love for Cesario, Orsino had threatened to kill "the lamb that I do love" (5.1.123); now he will wed that lamb.

Lutenist. By Jost Amman (1568).

The sudden transformation is prepared for in part by Orsino's passionate insistence that he loves the boy he intends to kill and in part by the earlier signs of intimacy between them: "I have," he tells Cesario, "unclasped / To thee the book even of my secret soul" (1.4.12–13). But this intimacy between master and servant has been formed around Orsino's grand passion for Olivia, a passion that is reiterated through virtually the entire play. The revelation at the play's climax—"One face, one voice, one habit, and two persons" (5.1.206)—forces a realignment of all the relationships. With Sebastian married to Olivia, Viola becomes Olivia's "sister" (or, as we would say, sister-in-law); and by marrying Viola, Orsino likewise makes Olivia his "sweet sister" (5.1.370). Orsino then will continue in a sense to "love" Olivia, but only through the bond of kinship formed by the linked twins—a strangely appropriate fate for someone who tried to woo by proxy!

That this solution does not seem entirely zany—that it seems a fit ending for a romantic comedy—depends on several key features in *Twelfth Night*'s emotional landscape. It is significant that Orsino's love for Olivia, though poetically intense, is detached from any direct personal encounter. Not only does her vow of a seven-year seclusion compel Orsino to delegate his passion to a messenger, but also this passion seems largely self-regarding and self-indulgent. His famous opening lines on the paradoxes of love—its close intertwining of fulfillment and decline, stealing and giving, freshness and decay—revolve around the contemplation less of the lady than of his own solitary, self-gratifying imagination: "So full of shapes is fancy / That it alone is high fantastical" (1.1.14–15). The play does not ridicule Orsino's aristocratic reveries, although they seem at moments like elegant versions of what is cruelly mocked in Malvolio, but it does invite the audience to treat them with a certain ironic detachment.

Orsino's love seems to circle all too readily back upon himself: he is fascinated by his role as melancholy lover. That self-absorption is not the only shape of passion is made clear by several contrasting figures, of whom the most selfless is the sea captain Antonio, consumed with desire for his friend Sebastian. In a play full of coy allusions to same-sex desire, Antonio's "willing love" (3.3.11) is the most explicit representation of passion as absolute devotion, a willingness to sacrifice everything in the service of the beloved. The mistaken belief that this devotion has been callously betrayed is one of the play's most poignant moments, a moment perhaps only partially redeemed by the manifest relief and joy with which the newly wed Sebastian greets his friend in the last act.

Intense, intimate bonding between men is a recurrent theme in Shakespeare's culture. (A comparable interest in female friendship is reflected in the love between Hermia and Helena in *A Midsummer Night's Dream* and Rosalind and Celia in *As You Like It.*) Shakespeare explores the pleasures and perils of male friendship in such plays as *The Two Gentlemen of Verona, The Merchant of Venice,* and *Much Ado About Nothing* and, most famously, in the sonnets to the fair young man whom he calls "the master-mistress of my passion" (Sonnet 20). Orsino expresses doubt that a woman can love with an intensity equal to a man's:

> There is no woman's sides
> Can bide the beating of so strong a passion
> As love doth give my heart. No woman's heart
> So big, to hold so much. They lack retention.
> (2.4.90–93)

It is perhaps this misogynistic belief (which the play proves to be utterly wrong) that conditions the only authentic emotional bond that we see Orsino forge, the bond with his devoted young servant Cesario. In conversation with Cesario, the haughty Duke manages for a few moments at least to escape from his languid self-absorption and express interest in someone else's thoughts and feelings: "What dost thou know?"; "And what's her history?"; "But died thy sister of her love, my boy?" (2.4.101, 106, 116). These simple questions, modest in themselves, are a marked departure from Orsino's usual manner of speech; they signal both a curiosity and a responsiveness that he does not manifest with anyone else. Part of the quirky delight of the play's resolution is to give to the union between Orsino and Viola something of the intimacy that had only seemed possible between men.

This resolution depends principally on the remarkable qualities of the play's central character, Viola. Like Antonio, Viola is prepared to sacrifice herself for her beloved: "And I most jocund, apt, and willingly," she tells Orsino, "To do you rest a thousand deaths would die" (5.1.125–26). But where Antonio experiences passion as tragic compulsion—he speaks of Sebastian's beauty as "witchcraft" drawing him into danger—Viola's spirit, as her word "jocund" suggests, is extraordinarily resilient. No sooner does she sadly observe that her brother must have perished in the shipwreck than she remarks, "Perchance he is not drowned" (1.2.5); no sooner does she find herself isolated and unprotected than she determines to serve Lady Olivia; and no sooner does she learn that this route is blocked than she resolves to disguise herself as a man and serve Orsino instead. Here and throughout the play, Viola seems to draw on an inward principle of hope. That principle, along with an improvisational boldness, an eloquent tongue, and a keen wit, enables her to keep afloat in an increasingly mad swirl of misunderstandings and cross-purposes.

Those misunderstandings, of course, are largely her creation in the sense that they mainly derive from a disguise that confounds the distinction between male and female. "they shall yet belie thy happy years / That say thou art a man," Orsino says to Cesario (1.4.29–30). The description that follows seems to imagine that boys begin almost as girls and only subsequently become males:

> Diana's lip
> Is not more smooth and rubious. Thy small pipe
> Is as the maiden's organ, shrill and sound,
> And all is semblative a woman's part.
> (1.4.30–33)

This perception of ambiguity, rooted in early modern ideas about sexuality and gender, is one of the elements that enabled a boy actor in this period convincingly to mime "a woman's part." According to one ancient anatomical tradition, contested but still highly influential in Shakespeare's time, sexual difference is not absolute: males and females share a single physiological structure whose differentiation only occurs over time. Such a theory implies a prolonged period of indistinction upon which *Twelfth Night* continually plays, and that helps to account for the emotional tangle that the cross-dressed Viola inspires.

Having, in her role as intermediary, aroused Olivia's love, Viola does not see how to disabuse the enamored Countess without abandoning the disguise. For all her lively resolution, she is passive in the face of the complexities she has engendered, counting on time and chance to sort out what she cannot: "O time, thou must untangle this, not I. / It is too hard a knot for me t'untie" (2.2.39–40). Perhaps this passivity, or more accurately this trust in time, is a form of wisdom in a world where everything seems topsy-turvy. If so, it is a wisdom that links Viola to the Clown, who exults at the play's close in what he calls "the whirligig of time" (5.1.363).

The Clown does not have a major part in the comedy's plot, but he shares with Viola a place at its imaginative center. A few years before the creation of *Twelfth Night*, the famous, boisterous clown Will Kemp quit Shakespeare's company in a huff and was replaced by Robert Armin, a comic actor of unusual sensitivity and subtlety. In paying handsome tribute to the Clown's intelligence, Viola seems to acknowledge Armin's special gift: "This fellow is wise enough to play the fool / And to do that well craves a kind of wit" (3.1.53–54). His wit often takes the form of a perverse literalism that slyly calls attention to the play's repeated confounding of such simple binaries as male and female, outside and inside, role and reality. The paradox of the wise fool, celebrated by Erasmus in his famous *Praise of Folly* (1509), is one that fascinated Shakespeare, who returned to it in plays as diverse as *As You Like It* and *King Lear*. More clearly than his equivalents elsewhere in Shakespeare's work, the Clown is a professional entertainer, paid for his services and finding employment now in one noble house and now in another. He can be unreliable, irresponsible, and importunate, but he also understands, as he teasingly shows Olivia, that it is foolish to bewail forever a loss that cannot be recovered. And he understands that it is important to take such pleasures as life offers and not to wait: "In delay there lies no plenty," he sings. "Then come kiss me, sweet and twenty. / Youth's a stuff will not endure" (2.3.48–50). There is in this wonderful song, as in all of his jests, a current of sadness. The Clown knows, as the refrain of the last of his songs puts it, that "the rain it raineth every day" (5.1.378). His counsel is for "present mirth" and "present laughter" (2.3.46). This is, of course, the advice of a fool. But do the Malvolios of the world have anything wiser to suggest?

STEPHEN GREENBLATT

SELECTED BIBLIOGRAPHY

Auden, W. H. "Music in Shakespeare." *The Dyer's Hand, and Other Essays*. New York: Random House, 1948. Analyzing songs from the plays, Auden reflects on music as a social exercise, dramatic convention, and supernatural signifier.

Callaghan, Dympna. "'And all is semblative a woman's part': Body Politics and *Twelfth Night*." *Shakespeare without Women: Representing Gender and Race on the Renaissance Stage*. New York: Routledge, 2000. 26–48. Argues that the misogynistic ridicule of Olivia's genitals in the Malvolio letter is an assertion of male control over the female body.

Gay, Penny. "*Twelfth Night*: Desire and Its Discontents." *As She Likes It: Shakespeare's Unruly Women*. London: Routledge, 1994. 17–47. Describes key postwar English stage productions.

Greenblatt, Stephen. "Fiction and Friction." *Shakespearean Negotiations: The Circulation of Social Energy in Renaissance England*. Berkeley: U of California P, 1988. 66–93. In light of contemporary anatomical theories, relates sexual chafing to verbal sparring and the generation of identity.

Malcolmson, Cristina. "'What You Will': Social Mobility and Gender in *Twelfth Night*." *The Matter of Difference: Materialist Feminist Criticism of Shakespeare*. Ed. Valerie Wayne. Ithaca, NY: Cornell UP, 1991. 29–57. Argues that *Twelfth Night* dramatizes the superiority of women to men in order to call into question the rigid structures of the traditional social order governing both gender and status.

Neely, Carol Thomas. *Distracted Subjects: Madness and Gender in Shakespeare and Early Modern Culture*. Ithaca, NY: Cornell UP, 2004. Asserts that *Twelfth Night's* displaced erotic choices cohere with changing medical discourse about pathological female lovesickness.

Orgel, Stephen. *Impersonations: The Performance of Gender in Shakespeare's England*. Cambridge: Cambridge UP, 1996. Approaches paradoxes in English playacting practice through contemporary notions of gender construction and sexual desire.

Schalkwyk, David. "Love and Service in *Twelfth Night* and the Sonnets." *Shakespeare Quarterly* 56 (2005): 76–100. Explores how intimacy between masters and servants complicates and enriches depiction of love.

Schiffer, James, ed. *"Twelfth Night": New Critical Essays*. New York: Routledge, 2011. Presents fifteen contemporary essays covering a range of topics from performance history and editing to queer theory and social class.

Wells, Stanley, ed. *"Twelfth Night": Critical Essays*. New York: Garland, 1986. Twenty essays from the nineteenth century onward treat mainly formal and structural aspects and early twentieth-century productions.

FILMS

Twelfth Night [*Dvenadsataia 'noch*]. 1956. Dir. Y. Fried. USSR. 90 min. This Soviet version celebrates the triumph of carnivalesque optimism over turmoil.

Twelfth Night: Shakespeare: The Animated Tales. 1992. Dir. Marcia Muat. UK/Russia. 20 min. This animated version was produced in joint Welsh-Russian collaboration.

Twelfth Night. 1996. Dir. Trevor Nunn. UK. 134 min. With Ben Kingsley, Helena Bonham Carter, and Nigel Hawthorne. Romantic Celtic coastlines combine with a poignant musical score, a stuffy Malvolio, and a gravely wise Feste.

Twelfth Night. 2003. Dir. Tim Supple. UK. 125 min. Parminder Nagra as Viola. A contemporary, multicultural update.

She's the Man. 2006. Dir. Andy Fickman. USA. 105 min. An updated American high-school romantic comedy.

TEXTUAL INTRODUCTION

Twelfth Night was first printed in the First Folio of 1623, which thus serves as the only authority for its text. Though it was common for plays to be set by two compositors, the whole of *Twelfth Night* was set by the workman identifiable by his idiosyncratic habits of spelling and composition and known to scholars as Compositor B.

Of the twenty-one Folio pages (numbered 255 to 275, with 265 misnumbered as 273) that constitute *Twelfth Night*, only three show any evidence of proofreading, and none of the corrections on those pages is substantive. But even without proofreading, the text is unusually clean. There are appropriate act and scene divisions throughout (which have been followed for this edition). Except for act 3, the ends of acts are marked with "*Finis*." Characters' entrances and exits are mostly noted and usually timely, and speech prefixes are generally correct. The accuracy of the presswork improves as it progresses, and what mistakes there are seem to be simple typos, misreading of the copy, or dropped or misattributed speech prefixes. In the original text at 1.3.88–89, Sir Toby Belch tells Sir Andrew Aguecheek nonsensically that his hair will not "coole my nature." Editors, emending the line to "curl by nature," infer that the compositor simply misread his copy. In 3.4.23–24, Malvolio clearly does not utter the line

"Why, how dost thou, man? What is the matter with thee?" and this edition, like others, attributes it to Olivia, though the speech might also belong to Maria. A more interesting case involves the famous speech in 2.5.126–28 in which Malvolio reads from the letter, "Some are born great, some achieve greatness, and some have greatness thrust upon 'em." The Folio text, however, begins the sequence with "Some are become great," which makes sense and therefore should not require emendation. But when Malvolio repeats the words of the letter to Olivia at 3.4.36–40, he uses the more familiar "Some are born great." Editors have adopted that reading as an emendation in the first instance, assuming both that the compositor misread his copy and that the sentence makes better sense as a progression from "born great" to "achieve greatness." Another mistake may be compositorial misremembering. At the entrance of Viola as Cesario in 1.5.155, the Folio text reads *"Enter Violenta,"* the name of a ghost character in *All's Well That Ends Well*, which Compositor B had just been working on. Perhaps, scholars have suggested, his copy text read *"Vio."* and he supplied the spelling of that play's character. Such mistakes are both minor and relatively rare in *Twelfth Night*.

Even so, textual scholars debate what kind of manuscript Compositor B was working from—a theatrical promptbook (or transcript thereof) or a scribal copy not of playhouse origin but derived instead from Shakespeare's working papers. Theatrical manuscripts are said to be characterized by the occasional insertion of actors' names instead of characters' names—which does not occur in *Twelfth Night*—or by technical stage directions. These might include the direction *"Enter* VIOLA *[as Cesario] and* MALVOLIO *at several doors"* that opens act 2, scene 2; or the direction "MALVOLIO *(within)"* in act 4, scene 2; or even *"Clock strikes"* in act 3, scene 1.

But such evidence is too slight to prove a theatrical origin for the manuscript behind the Folio text of *Twelfth Night*. Instead, the manuscript shows signs of being the scribal transcript of authorial papers, often called "foul papers" from their supposed messiness. Evidence for this theory is the Latin explicit—such as *"Finis Actus Primus"*—that ends all of the acts but act 3. In a stage tradition of continuous action, as at the public theaters where *Twelfth Night* was first performed, such act-scene divisions would be considered merely decorative or editorial in nature rather than functional. But this evidence, too, is slight and conjectural, based on speculations about what features manuscripts of different origins should and should not have. The manuscript's evident tidiness suggests that it was a transcript, but its origins—theatrical, authorial, or other—will never be known. Since Shakespeare left behind no dramatic manuscripts and cannot have been involved with the printing of the First Folio, we will probably never know exactly what kind of manuscript provided the working copy for Compositor B, except that it was clearly in good shape and hence relatively easy for him to read.

More interesting is the question of when—in the sequence of printing the First Folio—*Twelfth Night* was printed. In the book's divisions by genre, the play is the penultimate of the Comedies—appearing between *All's Well That Ends Well* and *The Winter's Tale*. A blank page—itself highly unusual at a time when paper constituted the highest cost in publishing—comes between the end of *Twelfth Night* and the beginning of *Winter's Tale*, suggesting that *Twelfth Night* was originally intended to conclude the Comedies. Even more perplexing is that the printing—heretofore proceeding in an unbroken sequence—was interrupted before *Twelfth Night*, with Compositor B jumping ahead from the not-quite-finished *All's Well* to the Histories section. He then composed the whole of *King John* and part of *Richard II* before returning to complete *All's Well* and set type for *Twelfth Night*. There can have been no problem in securing the right to print the play. *Twelfth Night* was entered properly in the Stationers' Register and appeared in the Folio for the first time. Perhaps there was a delay in securing the manuscript—a scribe not having finished transcribing it. But an answer to that question would depend on knowing what kind of text the compositor was working from, and as discussed above, evidence for that too can never be conclusive.

GAIL KERN PASTER

PERFORMANCE NOTE

Given its evenhanded distribution of lines and variety of substantial secondary roles, *Twelfth Night* calls for an ensemble with extraordinary depth and versatility. Its casting challenges include finding at least six talented comic actors, as well as a credible pair of "twins" for Viola and Sebastian, but the most notable issue may be the absence of a clear male lead. Orsino's pursuit of Olivia is the plot's first matter of business; Toby Belch has the play's largest role; and Sebastian's marriage to Olivia and reunion with Viola are central concerns of the last act—yet none of the roles tends to dominate the audience's attention like those of Viola, Malvolio, and the Clown. Each production, then, must establish its particular balance between the three star parts—each capable of overshadowing the others as well as the production—while accommodating the play's repeated efforts to advance more traditional protagonists in their stead.

The uncertainty of the main plot and the absence of a clear male lead allow directors to tell starkly different stories without substantially altering the text. Whether a production exposes or understates Orsino's self-importance; whether Toby is a good-natured friend to Andrew or purely mercenary; whether Malvolio's tyranny or his tragedy is emphasized; whether Antonio's feud with Orsino and love for Sebastian are featured or downplayed—all are choices that can shift the play's focus as well as the audience's sense of allegiance. Productions must also address the tension created by the farcical below-stairs comedy that grows darker and more complicated than the play's genre anticipates. In recent years, directors have often explored the comedy's darker matter, both by intensifying Malvolio's (and sometimes Antonio's) plight and by accenting the strains of melancholy and cynicism that are potential in the Clown.

BRETT GAMBOA

Twelfth Night, or What You Will

[THE PERSONS OF THE PLAY

ORSINO, Duke of Illyria
VALENTINE }
CURIO } members of Orsino's court

VIOLA, a shipwrecked lady from Messaline, later disguised as Cesario
CAPTAIN, rescuer of Viola
SEBASTIAN, twin brother to Viola
ANTONIO, sea captain, rescuer of Sebastian

Lady OLIVIA, a Countess
MARIA, waiting-gentlewoman to Olivia
MALVOLIO, steward to Olivia
FABIAN, member of Olivia's household
CLOWN, Olivia's jester, also called Feste
SIR TOBY Belch, kinsman to Olivia
SIR ANDREW Aguecheek, a visiting knight
PRIEST

FIRST OFFICER
SECOND OFFICER
SERVANTS
Lords, Sailors, Musicians, Attendants]

1.1

Enter ORSINO, *Duke of Illyria,* CURIO, *and other
Lords [with Musicians playing].*

ORSINO   If music be the food of love, play on.
Give me excess of it that, surfeiting,
The appetite may sicken and so die.
That strain again—it had a dying fall.°   *cadence*
5   Oh, it came o'er my ear like the sweet sound
That breathes upon a bank of violets,
Stealing and giving odor. Enough, no more!
'Tis not so sweet now as it was before.
O spirit of love, how quick and fresh° art thou   *lively and eager*
10   That, notwithstanding thy capacity
Receiveth as the sea,° naught enters there   *Receives without limit*
Of what validity° and pitch° soe'er,   *value / height; excellence*
But falls into abatement° and low price   *lesser value*
Even in a minute. So full of shapes is fancy°   *love; desire*
15   That it alone is high fantastical.°   *uniquely imaginative*
CURIO   Will you go hunt, my lord?
ORSINO   What, Curio?
CURIO   The hart.

ORSINO   Why, so I do, the noblest that I have.[1]
Oh, when mine eyes did see Olivia first,
Methought she purged the air of pestilence.[2]
20   That instant was I turned into a hart,
And my desires, like fell° and cruel hounds,   savage
E'er since pursue me.[3]
         Enter VALENTINE.
                        How now, what news from her?
VALENTINE   So please my lord, I might not be admitted,
But from her handmaid do return this answer:
25   The element itself, till seven years' heat,[4]
Shall not behold her face at ample° view,   full
But, like a cloistress,° she will veilèd walk   nun
And water once a day her chamber round
With eye-offending brine.° All this to season   stinging tears
30   A brother's dead love,[5] which she would keep fresh
And lasting in her sad remembrance.
ORSINO   Oh, she that hath a heart of that fine° frame   exquisitely made
To pay this debt of love but to a brother,
How will she love, when the rich golden shaft[6]
35   Hath killed the flock of all affections else°   other emotions
That live in her; when liver, brain, and heart,[7]
These sovereign thrones, are all supplied, and filled
Her sweet perfections[8] with one self° king!   one and the same
Away before me to sweet beds of flowers.
40   Love thoughts lie rich when canopied with bowers.
                                                    Exeunt.

1.2

                Enter VIOLA, *a* CAPTAIN, *and Sailors.*
VIOLA[1]   What country, friends, is this?
CAPTAIN   This is Illyria, lady.
VIOLA   And what should I do in Illyria?
My brother, he is in Elysium.[2]
5   Perchance° he is not drowned. What think you, sailors?   *Perhaps*
CAPTAIN   It is perchance° that you yourself were saved.   *by chance*
VIOLA   Oh, my poor brother! And so perchance may he be.
CAPTAIN   True, madam. And, to comfort you with chance,[3]
Assure yourself, after our ship did split,
10   When you and those poor number saved with you
Hung on our driving boat,[4] I saw your brother,
Most provident in peril, bind himself
(Courage and hope both teaching him the practice)
To a strong mast that lived° upon the sea.   remained afloat

1.1 Location: Illyria, the Greek and Roman name for
the eastern Adriatic coast; probably not suggesting a
real country to Shakespeare's audience.
1. Orsino plays on "hart/heart."
2. Plague and other illnesses were thought to be
caused by bad air.
3. Alluding to the classical legend of Actaeon, who
was turned into a stag and hunted by his own hounds
for having seen the goddess Artemis naked.
4. The sky itself / for seven summers.
5. *All . . . love:* All this to preserve (by the salt of the
tears) the love of a dead brother.

6. Of Cupid's golden-tipped arrow, which caused
desire.
7. In Elizabethan psychology, these were the seats of
passion, intellect, and feeling.
8. *and filled . . . perfections:* and all her flawless qualities are governed by.
1.2 Location: The coast of Illyria.
1. Viola is not named in the dialogue until 5.1.231.
2. The heaven of classical mythology.
3. With what may have happened.
4. The ship's boat. *driving:* being driven by the
wind.

15   Where, like Arion[5] on the dolphin's back,
      I saw him hold acquaintance with the waves,
      So long as I could see.
VIOLA [*giving him money*]   For saying so, there's gold.
      Mine own escape unfoldeth to° my hope,   *encourages*
      Whereto thy speech serves for authority°   *support*
20   The like of him.[6] Know'st thou this country?
CAPTAIN   Ay, madam, well, for I was bred and born
      Not three hours' travel from this very place.
VIOLA   Who governs here?
CAPTAIN   A noble duke in nature, as in name.
25   VIOLA   What is his name?
CAPTAIN   Orsino.
VIOLA   Orsino. I have heard my father name him.
      He was a bachelor then.
CAPTAIN   And so is now, or was so very late.°   *lately*
30   For but a month ago I went from hence,
      And then 'twas fresh in murmur° (as you know,   *newly rumored*
      What great ones do, the less will prattle of)
      That he did seek the love of fair Olivia.
VIOLA   What's she?
35   CAPTAIN   A virtuous maid, the daughter of a count
      That died some twelvemonth since, then leaving her
      In the protection of his son, her brother,
      Who shortly also died. For whose dear love,
      They say, she hath abjured the sight
      And company of men.
40   VIOLA   Oh, that I served that lady,
      And might not be delivered° to the world   *revealed*
      Till I had made mine own occasion mellow°   *ripe (to be revealed)*
      What my estate° is.   *social rank*
CAPTAIN   That were hard to compass,°   *achieve*
      Because she will admit no kind of suit,°   *petition*
45   No, not the Duke's.
VIOLA   There is a fair behavior[7] in thee, Captain.
      And though that nature with a beauteous wall
      Doth oft close in pollution, yet of thee
      I will believe thou hast a mind that suits
50   With this, thy fair and outward character.[8]
      I prithee (and I'll pay thee bounteously)
      Conceal me what I am, and be my aid
      For such disguise as haply shall become
      The form of my intent.[9] I'll serve this duke.
55   Thou shalt present me as an eunuch[1] to him.
      It may be worth thy pains, for I can sing
      And speak to him in many sorts of music
      That will allow° me very worth his service.   *prove*

---

5. A legendary Greek musician who, in order to save himself from being murdered on a voyage, jumped overboard and was carried to land by a dolphin.
6. That he too has survived.
7. Outward appearance; conduct.
8. Appearance (suggesting moral qualities).

9. *as . . . intent:* that perhaps may be fitting to my purpose. *form:* shape.
1. Castrati (hence, "eunuchs") were prized as male sopranos; the disguise would have explained Viola's feminine voice. Viola (or perhaps Shakespeare) seems to have changed plans: she presents herself instead as a young page.

What else may hap, to time I will commit.
60   Only shape thou thy silence to my wit.°   *imagination; plan*
CAPTAIN   Be you his eunuch, and your mute[2] I'll be.
When my tongue blabs, then let mine eyes not see.
VIOLA   I thank thee. Lead me on.   *Exeunt.*

1.3

Enter SIR TOBY *and* MARIA.

SIR TOBY   What a plague means my niece to take the death of
    her brother thus? I am sure care's an enemy to life.
MARIA   By my troth, Sir Toby, you must come in earlier a-nights.
    Your cousin,[1] my lady, takes great exceptions to your ill
5   hours.
SIR TOBY   Why, let her except before excepted.[2]
MARIA   Ay, but you must confine yourself within the modest°   *moderate*
    limits of order.
SIR TOBY   Confine! I'll confine myself no finer[3] than I am.
10   These clothes are good enough to drink in, and so be these
    boots, too. An° they be not, let them hang themselves in their   *If*
    own straps.
MARIA   That quaffing and drinking will undo you. I heard my
    lady talk of it yesterday and of a foolish knight that you brought
15   in one night here to be her wooer.
SIR TOBY   Who, Sir Andrew Aguecheek?
MARIA   Ay, he.
SIR TOBY   He's as tall a man as any's[4] in Illyria.
MARIA   What's that to th' purpose?
20 SIR TOBY   Why, he has three thousand ducats a year.
MARIA   Ay, but he'll have but a year in all these ducats.[5] He's
    a very° fool and a prodigal.   *an absolute*
SIR TOBY   Fie, that you'll say so! He plays o'th' viol-de-
    gamboys,[6] and speaks three or four languages word for word
25   without book,° and hath all the good gifts of nature.   *from memory*
MARIA   He hath, indeed, almost natural.[7] For besides that he's
    a fool, he's a great quarreler. And but that he hath the gift°   *talent; present*
    of a coward to allay the gust° he hath in quarreling, 'tis   *gusto*
    thought among the prudent he would quickly have the gift
30   of a grave.
SIR TOBY   By this hand, they are scoundrels and substractors[8]
    that say so of him. Who are they?
MARIA   They that add, moreover, he's drunk nightly in your
    company.
35 SIR TOBY   With drinking healths to my niece. I'll drink to her
    as long as there is a passage in my throat and drink in
    Illyria. He's a coward and a coistrel° that will not drink   *horse groom; lout*

---

2. In Turkish harems, eunuchs served as guards and were assisted by "mutes" (usually, servants whose tongues had been cut out).
1.3 Location: The Countess Olivia's house.
1. Term used generally of kinsfolk.
2. Playing on the legal jargon *exceptis excipiendis,* "with the previously stated exceptions." Sir Toby refuses to take Olivia's displeasure seriously.
3. Suggesting both "a refined manner of dress" and

"narrowly" (referring to his girth).
4. Any (man who) is. *tall:* brave; worthy. (Maria takes it in the modern sense of height.)
5. He'll spend his fortune in a year.
6. A facetious corruption of "viola da gamba," a bass viol held between the knees.
7. Idiots and fools were called "naturals."
8. Corruption of "detractors." (In reply, Maria puns on "substract" as "subtract.")

to my niece till his brains turn o'th' toe like a parish top.
What, wench! *Castiliano vulgo,*[9] for here comes Sir Andrew
40 Agueface.

Enter SIR ANDREW *Aguecheek.*

SIR ANDREW Sir Toby Belch. How now, Sir Toby Belch?
SIR TOBY Sweet Sir Andrew.
SIR ANDREW Bless you, fair shrew.[1]
MARIA And you too, sir.
45 SIR TOBY Accost, Sir Andrew, accost.[2]
SIR ANDREW What's that?
SIR TOBY My niece's chambermaid.[3]
SIR ANDREW Good Mistress Accost, I desire better acquaintance.
MARIA My name is Mary, sir.
50 SIR ANDREW Good Mistress Mary Accost—
SIR TOBY You mistake, knight. "Accost" is front° her, board   confront
her, woo her, assail[4] her.
SIR ANDREW By my troth, I would not undertake[5] her in this
company.° Is that the meaning of "accost"?   the audience
55 MARIA Fare you well, gentlemen.
SIR TOBY An thou let part so,[6] Sir Andrew, would thou mightst
never draw sword again.
SIR ANDREW An you part so, mistress, I would I might never
draw sword again. Fair lady, do you think you have fools in
60 hand?°   to deal with
MARIA Sir, I have not you by th' hand.
SIR ANDREW Marry, but you shall have, and here's my hand.
MARIA [*taking his hand*] Now, sir, thought is free.[7] I pray you,
bring your hand to th' buttery bar,[8] and let it drink.
65 SIR ANDREW Wherefore, sweetheart? What's your metaphor?
MARIA It's dry,[9] sir.
SIR ANDREW Why, I think so. I am not such an ass, but I can
keep my hand dry.[1] But what's your jest?
MARIA A dry jest,[2] sir.
70 SIR ANDREW Are you full of them?
MARIA Ay, sir, I have them at my fingers' ends.[3] Marry, now
I let go your hand, I am barren.°   *Exit.*   empty of jokes
SIR TOBY O knight, thou lack'st a cup of canary.[4] When did I
see thee so put down?[5]
75 SIR ANDREW Never in your life, I think, unless you see canary
put me down. Methinks sometimes I have no more wit than

---

9. Variously interpreted, but may mean "Speak of the
devil," since Castilians were considered devilish, and
vulgo refers to the common tongue. *parish top:* parishes kept large tops that were spun by whipping them,
for the parishioners' amusement and exercise.
1. Andrew possibly confuses "shrew" (ill-tempered
woman) with "mouse," an endearment.
2. Address (her); originally a naval term meaning "go
alongside; greet."
3. Lady-in-waiting; not a menial servant, but a gentlewoman in attendance on a great lady.
4. *board:* speak to; tackle. *assail:* greet (also nautical).
5. Take her on (with sexual implication).
6. If you let her go without protest or without bidding her farewell.

7. The customary retort to "Do you think I am a
fool?"
8. Ledge on the half-door to a buttery or a wine cellar
on which drinks were served.
9. Thirsty; but a dry hand was also thought to be a
sign of impotence.
1. Alluding to the proverb "Even fools have enough
wit to come in out of the rain."
2. A stupid joke (referring to Andrew's stupidity); an
ironic quip; a joke about dryness.
3. Always ready; or "by th' hand" (line 61).
4. A sweet wine, like sherry, originally from the Canary
Islands.
5. Defeated in repartee; "put down" with drink.

a Christian° or an ordinary man has. But I am a great eater
of beef,[6] and I believe that does harm to my wit.   *an average man*

SIR TOBY No question.

80   SIR ANDREW An I thought that, I'd forswear it. I'll ride home
      tomorrow, Sir Toby.

SIR TOBY *Pourquoi,*° my dear knight?   *Why*

SIR ANDREW What is *pourquoi?* Do, or not do? I would I had
bestowed that time in the tongues[7] that I have in fencing,
85   dancing, and bearbaiting. Oh, had I but followed the arts.

SIR TOBY Then hadst thou had an excellent head of hair.

SIR ANDREW Why would that have mended° my hair?   *improved*

SIR TOBY Past question, for thou seest it will not curl by
nature.[8]

90   SIR ANDREW But it becomes me well enough, does't not?

SIR TOBY Excellent, it hangs like flax on a distaff.[9] And I hope
to see a housewife[1] take thee between her legs and spin it
off.[2]

SIR ANDREW Faith, I'll home tomorrow, Sir Toby. Your niece
95   will not be seen. Or, if she be, it's four to one she'll none of
me. The Count himself here hard by woos her.

SIR TOBY She'll none o'th' Count. She'll not match above her
degree,° neither in estate,[3] years, nor wit. I have heard her   *social rank*
swear't. Tut, there's life in't,[4] man.

100   SIR ANDREW I'll stay a month longer. I am a fellow o'th' strangest mind i'th' world. I delight in masques and revels sometimes altogether.

SIR TOBY Art thou good at these kickshawses,[5] knight?

SIR ANDREW As any man in Illyria, whatsoever he be, under
105   the degree of my betters, and yet I will not compare with an
old man.[6]

SIR TOBY What is thy excellence in a galliard,[7] knight?

SIR ANDREW Faith, I can cut a caper.[8]

SIR TOBY And I can cut the mutton to't.

110   SIR ANDREW And I think I have the back-trick[9] simply as strong
as any man in Illyria.

SIR TOBY Wherefore are these things hid? Wherefore have
these gifts a curtain[1] before 'em? Are they like to take dust
like Mistress Mall's[2] picture? Why dost thou not go to church
115   in a galliard and come home in a coranto?[3] My very walk
should be a jig. I would not so much as make water but in a
cinquepace.[4] What dost thou mean? Is it a world to hide
virtues in? I did think by the excellent constitution of thy
leg, it was formed under the star of a galliard.[5]

---

6. Contemporary medicine held that beef dulled the
intellect.
7. Foreign languages; Toby takes him to mean "curling tongs."
8. To contrast with Andrew's "arts" (line 85).
9. In spinning, flax would hang in long, thin, yellowish
strings on the "distaff," a pole held between the knees.
1. Housewives spun flax; the pronunciation, "hus-
wife," also suggests the meaning "prostitute."
2. Make him bald (as a result of venereal disease).
3. Status; possession.
4. Proverbial: "While there's life, there's hope."
5. Trifles; trivialities (from the French *quelque chose*).
6. An expert (perhaps a backhanded compliment).

7. A lively, complex dance, including the caper.
8. Leap. (Toby puns on the pickled flower buds used
in a sauce served with mutton.)
9. Probably a dance movement, a kick of the foot
behind the body (also suggesting sexual prowess, with
later reference to "mutton" as "prostitute").
1. Used to protect paintings from dust.
2. Like "Moll[y]," "Mall" was a nickname for "Mary."
3. An even more rapid dance than the galliard.
4. Galliard, or, more properly, the steps joining the
figures of the dance; punning on "cinque" pronounced
as "sink," as in "sewer."
5. Astrological influences favorable to dancing.

120   SIR ANDREW   Ay, 'tis strong, and it does indifferent° well in a   *moderately*
     dun-colored[6] stock.° Shall we set about some revels?   *stocking*
     SIR TOBY   What shall we do else? Were we not born under
     Taurus?[7]
     SIR ANDREW   Taurus? That's sides and heart.
125   SIR TOBY   No, sir, it is legs and thighs. Let me see thee
     caper. [SIR ANDREW *dances a caper.*] Ha, higher! Ha, ha,
     excellent!   *Exeunt.*

1.4

Enter VALENTINE *and* VIOLA [*as Cesario*] *in man's attire.*[1]

VALENTINE   If the Duke continue these favors towards you,
     Cesario, you are like to be much advanced. He hath known
     you but three days, and already you are no stranger.
VIOLA   You either fear his humor° or my negligence that you   *moodiness*
5   call in question the continuance of his love. Is he incon-
     stant, sir, in his favors?
VALENTINE   No, believe me.
               Enter DUKE, CURIO, *and Attendants.*
VIOLA   I thank you. Here comes the Count.
ORSINO   Who saw Cesario, ho?
10   VIOLA   On your attendance,° my lord, here.   *Waiting at your service*
ORSINO [*to* CURIO *and Attendants*]   Stand you awhile aloof.°   *aside*
     —Cesario,
     Thou know'st no less, but all.° I have unclasped   *than everything*
     To thee the book even of my secret soul.
     Therefore, good youth, address thy gait° unto her,   *go*
15   Be not denied access, stand at her doors,
     And tell them, there thy fixèd foot shall grow°   *take root*
     Till thou have audience.
VIOLA   Sure, my noble lord,
     If she be so abandoned to her sorrow
     As it is spoke, she never will admit me.
20   ORSINO   Be clamorous and leap all civil bounds[2]
     Rather than make unprofited° return.   *unsuccessful*
VIOLA   Say I do speak with her, my lord, what then?
ORSINO   Oh, then unfold the passion of my love,
     Surprise[3] her with discourse of my dear° faith.   *heartfelt*
25   It shall become thee well to act my woes.
     She will attend it better in thy youth
     Than in a nuncio's° of more grave aspect.°   *messenger's / appearance*
VIOLA   I think not so, my lord.
ORSINO   Dear lad, believe it.
     For they shall yet belie thy happy years
30   That say thou art a man. Diana's lip
     Is not more smooth and rubious.° Thy small pipe°   *ruby red / voice*

---

6. TEXTUAL COMMENT The Folio's "dam'd color'd"
does not make much sense as a modifier for stockings
and has prompted a variety of emendations. For more
on this issue, see Digital Edition TC 1.
7. The astrological sign of the bull was usually thought
to govern the neck and throat (appropriate to heavy
drinkers).

1.4 Location: Orsino's palace.
1. PERFORMANCE COMMENT How to stage Viola's first
appearance in masculine attire is one of many important decisions related to twinning and cross-dressing
in this play. For more, see Digital Edition PC 1.
2. All constraints of polite behavior.
3. Capture by unexpected attack (of military origin).

Is as the maiden's organ, shrill and sound,[4]
And all is semblative° a woman's part. [5]   *like*
I know thy constellation[6] is right apt
35   For this affair. —Some four or five, attend him,
All if you will. For I myself am best
When least in company. [*to* VIOLA] Prosper well in this,
And thou shalt live as freely as thy lord
To call his fortunes thine.
VIOLA   I'll do my best
40   To woo your lady. [*aside*] Yet a barful strife;[7]
Whoe'er I woo, myself would be his wife.   *Exeunt.*

1.5

Enter MARIA *and* CLOWN.

MARIA   Nay, either tell me where thou hast been, or I will not
open my lips so wide as a bristle may enter in° way of thy   *by*
excuse. My lady will hang thee for thy absence.
CLOWN   Let her hang me. He that is well hanged in this world
5   needs to fear no colors.[1]
MARIA   Make that good.°   *Explain that*
CLOWN   He shall see none to fear.
MARIA   A good lenten[2] answer. I can tell thee where that saying
was born, of "I fear no colors."
10   CLOWN   Where, good Mistress Mary?
MARIA   In the wars,[3] and that may you be bold to say in your
foolery.
CLOWN   Well, God give them wisdom that have it. And those
that are fools, let them use their talents.[4]
15   MARIA   Yet you will be hanged for being so long absent. Or to
be turned away,[5] is not that as good as a hanging to you?
CLOWN   Many a good hanging prevents a bad marriage.[6] And
for turning away, let summer bear it out.°   *make it endurable*
MARIA   You are resolute then?
20   CLOWN   Not so, neither, but I am resolved on two points.
MARIA   That if one break, the other will hold. Or if both break,
your gaskins fall.[7]
CLOWN   Apt in good faith, very apt. Well, go thy way. If Sir
Toby would leave drinking, thou wert as witty a piece of
25   Eve's flesh[8] as any in Illyria.
MARIA   Peace, you rogue, no more o'that. Here comes my lady.
Make your excuse wisely, you were best.°   *you had better*
Enter Lady OLIVIA *with* MALVOLIO° [*and Attendants*].   *"ill will"*
CLOWN   Wit,[9] an't° be thy will, put me into good fooling.   *if it*
Those wits that think they have thee do very oft prove fools,

---

4. High pitched and uncracked.
5. PERFORMANCE COMMENT Orsino's attention to
feminine qualities in Cesario is particularly charged
in performance. For more on the dramatic possibilities this moment affords, see Digital Edition PC 2.
6. *Nature* and abilities (as supposedly determined by
the stars).
7. An undertaking full of impediments.
1.5 Location: Olivia's house.
1. Proverbial for "fear nothing." *colors:* worldly deceptions, with a pun on "collars" as "hangman's noose."
2. Thin or meager (like Lenten fare).
3. *In the wars:* "colors" in line 9 refers to military flags.
4. Alluding to the parable of the talents, Matthew

25. The comic implication is that a fool should strive
to increase his measure of folly. Since "fool" and
"fowl" had similar pronunciations, there may also be
a play on "talents/talons."
5. Dismissed; also, perhaps, turned off or hanged.
6. *Many . . . marriage:* Proverbial. *hanging:* execution;
sexual prowess.
7. Maria puns on "points" as the laces used to fasten
gaskins—wide breeches—to a man's jacket.
8. A woman. The Clown may imply both that Maria
and Toby would make a good match and that Maria is
as witty as Toby is sober.
9. Intelligence, which is often contrasted with will.

30   and I that am sure I lack thee may pass for a wise man. For
what says Quinapalus?[1] "Better a witty fool than a foolish
wit." —God bless thee, lady.[2]

OLIVIA   Take the fool away.

CLOWN   Do you not hear, fellows? Take away the lady.

35 OLIVIA   Go to, you're a dry[3] fool. I'll no more of you. Besides,
you grow dishonest.°   *unreliable*

CLOWN   Two faults, madonna,° that drink and good counsel   *my lady*
will amend. For give the dry fool drink, then is the fool not
dry. Bid the dishonest man mend° himself; if he mend, he is   *reform*

40   no longer dishonest. If he cannot, let the botcher° mend him.   *tailor; cobbler*
Anything that's mended is but patched. Virtue that trans-
gresses is but patched with sin, and sin that amends is but
patched with virtue. If that this simple syllogism will serve,
so. If it will not, what remedy? As there is no true cuckold

45   but calamity, so beauty's a flower.[4] The lady bade, take away
the fool. Therefore I say again, take her away.

OLIVIA   Sir, I bade them take away you.

CLOWN   Misprision[5] in the highest degree. Lady, *Cucullus
non facit monachum.*[6] That's as much to say as I wear not

50   motley[7] in my brain. Good madonna, give me leave to prove
you a fool.

OLIVIA   Can you do it?

CLOWN   Dexteriously,° good madonna.   *Dexterously*

OLIVIA   Make your proof.

55 CLOWN   I must catechize[8] you for it, madonna. Good my mouse
of virtue,° answer me.   *My good virtuous mouse*

OLIVIA   Well, sir, for want of other idleness,° I'll bide° your   *pastime / await*
proof.

CLOWN   Good madonna, why mourn'st thou?

60 OLIVIA   Good fool, for my brother's death.

CLOWN   I think his soul is in hell, madonna.

OLIVIA   I know his soul is in heaven, fool.

CLOWN   The more fool, madonna, to mourn for your brother's
soul, being in heaven. Take away the fool, gentlemen.

65 OLIVIA   What think you of this fool, Malvolio? Doth he not
mend?[9]

MALVOLIO   Yes, and shall do, till the pangs of death shake
him. Infirmity° that decays the wise doth ever make the bet-   *(Old) age*
ter fool.[1]

70 CLOWN   God send you, sir, a speedy infirmity, for the better
increasing your folly. Sir Toby will be sworn that I am no
fox, but he will not pass his word for twopence that you are
no fool.

OLIVIA   How say you to that, Malvolio?

---

1. The Clown frequently invents his own authorities.
2. TEXTUAL COMMENT Editors sometimes mark this speech of the Clown's as an aside. But this apostrophe to wit, for a character as bold and outspoken as the Clown, does not seem to require this editorial intervention. For more on the issue of asides, see Digital Edition TC 2.
3. Dull, but the Clown interprets the term as "thirsty." *Go to:* an expression of impatience.
4. *As . . . flower:* In taking her vow (1.2.38–40), Olivia has wedded herself to calamity but must be

unfaithful, or let pass her moment of beauty.
5. Misapprehension; wrongful arrest.
6. The cowl does not make the monk (a Latin proverb).
7. The multicolored costume of a fool.
8. Question (as in catechism, which tests the orthodoxy of belief).
9. Improve, but Malvolio takes "mend" to mean "grow more foolish."
1. Make the fool more foolish.

75 MALVOLIO I marvel your ladyship takes delight in such a bar-
ren rascal. I saw him put down° the other day with an ordi- *defeated in repartee*
nary fool that has no more brain than a stone. Look you
now, he's out of his guard° already. Unless you laugh and *defenseless*
minister occasion² to him, he is gagged. I protest I take
80 these wise men that crow so at these set° kind of fools no *artificial*
better than the fools' zanies.° *stooges*

OLIVIA Oh, you are sick of self-love, Malvolio, and taste with
a distempered³ appetite. To be generous, guiltless, and of
free° disposition is to take those things for bird-bolts⁴ that *magnanimous*
85 you deem cannon bullets. There is no slander in an allowed
fool, though he do nothing but rail, nor no railing in a
known discreet man, though he do nothing but reprove.

CLOWN Now Mercury endue thee with leasing,⁵ for thou
speak'st well of fools.
Enter MARIA.

90 MARIA Madam, there is at the gate a young gentleman much
desires to speak with you.

OLIVIA From the Count Orsino, is it?

MARIA I know not, madam. 'Tis a fair young man and well
attended.

95 OLIVIA Who of my people hold him in delay?

MARIA Sir Toby, madam, your kinsman.

OLIVIA Fetch him off, I pray you. He speaks nothing but
madman.° Fie on him.   [*Exit* MARIA.] *madman's talk*
—Go you, Malvolio. If it be a suit from the Count, I am sick
100 or not at home. What° you will to dismiss it.   *Exit* MALVOLIO. *Say whatever*
—Now you see, sir, how your fooling grows old,° and people *stale*
dislike it.

CLOWN Thou hast spoke for us, madonna, as if thy eldest son
should be a fool. Whose skull Jove cram with brains, for—
105 here he comes—
Enter SIR TOBY.
one of thy kin has a most weak *pia mater*.⁶

OLIVIA By mine honor, half drunk. What is he at the gate,
cousin?° *kinsman*

SIR TOBY A gentleman.

110 OLIVIA A gentleman? What gentleman?

SIR TOBY 'Tis a gentleman here. [*He belches*.] A plague o'these
pickle herring! [*to* CLOWN] How now, sot?° *fool; drunkard*

CLOWN Good Sir Toby.

OLIVIA Cousin, cousin, how have you come so early by this
115 lethargy?

SIR TOBY Lechery? I defy lechery. There's one° at the gate. *someone*

OLIVIA Ay, marry, what is he?

SIR TOBY Let him be the devil an° he will, I care not. Give me *if*
faith,⁷ say I. Well, it's all one.°   *Exit.* *it doesn't matter*

120 OLIVIA What's a drunken man like, fool?

CLOWN Like a drowned man, a fool, and a madman. One

---

2. And give opportunity.
3. An unbalanced; a sick.
4. Blunt arrows for shooting birds.
5. May Mercury, the god of deception, endow you

with the talent of tactful lying.
6. Brain; or literally, the membrane enclosing it.
7. To defy the devil by faith alone.

draught above heat[8] makes him a fool, the second mads him,
and a third drowns him.

OLIVIA Go thou and seek the crowner° and let him sit o'[9] my
125 coz,° for he's in the third degree of drink. He's drowned. Go
look after him.

CLOWN He is but mad yet, madonna, and the fool shall look
to the madman.   [*Exit.*]

Enter MALVOLIO.

MALVOLIO Madam, yond young fellow swears he will speak
130 with you. I told him you were sick; he takes on him to
understand so much, and therefore° comes to speak with
you. I told him you were asleep; he seems to have a fore-
knowledge of that too, and therefore comes to speak with
you. What is to be said to him, lady? He's fortified against
135 any denial.

OLIVIA Tell him he shall not speak with me.

MALVOLIO He's been told so. And he says he'll stand at your
door like a sheriff's post,[1] and be the supporter to a bench,
but he'll speak with you.

140 OLIVIA What kind o'man is he?

MALVOLIO Why, of mankind.°

OLIVIA What manner of man?

MALVOLIO Of very ill manner. He'll speak with you, will you
or no.

145 OLIVIA Of what personage° and years is he?

MALVOLIO Not yet old enough for a man, nor young enough
for a boy; as a squash[2] is before 'tis a peascod, or a codling°
when 'tis almost an apple. 'Tis with him in standing water°
between boy and man. He is very well favored,° and he speaks
150 very shrewishly.° One would think his mother's milk were
scarce out of him.

OLIVIA Let him approach. Call in my gentlewoman.

MALVOLIO Gentlewoman, my lady calls.   *Exit.*

Enter MARIA.

OLIVIA Give me my veil, come, throw it o'er my face.
155 We'll once more hear Orsino's embassy.

Enter VIOLA [*as Cesario*].[3]

VIOLA The honorable lady of the house, which is she?

OLIVIA Speak to me; I shall answer for her. Your will?

VIOLA Most radiant, exquisite, and unmatchable beauty—I
pray you, tell me if this be the lady of the house, for I never
160 saw her. I would be loath to cast away° my speech. For
besides that it is excellently well penned, I have taken great
pains to con° it. Good beauties, let me sustain no scorn. I
am very comptible° even to the least sinister usage.[4]

OLIVIA Whence came you, sir?

165 VIOLA I can say little more than I have studied,[5] and that
question's out of my part. Good gentle one, give me modest°

Glosses (right margin):
- coroner (line 124)
- cousin; uncle (line 125)
- for that very reason (line 131)
- like any other (line 141)
- appearance (line 145)
- an unripe apple (line 147)
- at the turn of the tide (line 148)
- handsome (line 149)
- sharply (line 150)
- waste (line 160)
- memorize (line 162)
- sensitive (line 163)
- adequate (line 166)

8. One drink ("draught") beyond the quantity necessary to warm him.
9. *sit o'*: hold an inquest for.
1. A decorative post set before a sheriff's door, as a sign of authority.
2. An undeveloped pea pod.
3. TEXTUAL COMMENT The stage direction in F reads

"*Enter Violenta*," so editors invariably emend to read "*Viola*." For discussion of how this mistake might have happened, see Digital Edition TC 3 and the Textual Introduction.
4. To the slightest discourteous treatment.
5. Learned by heart (a theatrical term).

assurance if you be the lady of the house, that I may proceed
in my speech.

OLIVIA   Are you a comedian?°   *an actor*

170   VIOLA   No, my profound heart.[6] And yet, by the very fangs of
malice, I swear I am not that I play. Are you the lady of the
house?

OLIVIA   If I do not usurp myself, I am.

VIOLA   Most certain, if you are she, you do usurp yourself. For

175   what is yours to bestow is not yours to reserve. But this is
from my commission.° I will on with my speech in your   *beyond my instructions*
praise, and then show you the heart of my message.

OLIVIA   Come to what is important in't. I forgive you° the   *excuse you from*
praise.

180   VIOLA   Alas, I took great pains to study it, and 'tis poetical.

OLIVIA   It is the more like to be feigned. I pray you keep it in.
I heard you were saucy at my gates, and allowed your
approach rather to wonder at you than to hear you. If you
be not mad,° be gone. If you have reason,° be brief. 'Tis not   *utterly mad / any sanity*

185   that time of moon with me to make one in so skipping a
dialogue.[7]

MARIA   Will you hoist sail, sir? Here lies your way.

VIOLA   No, good swabber, I am to hull[8] here a little longer.
—Some mollification for your giant,[9] sweet lady.

190   OLIVIA   Tell me your mind.

VIOLA   I am a messenger.[1]

OLIVIA   Sure you have some hideous matter to deliver, when
the courtesy° of it is so fearful. Speak your office.°   *introduction / business*
                                                                declaration
VIOLA   It alone concerns your ear. I bring no overture° of war,

195   no taxation of homage.[2] I hold the olive[3] in my hand. My
words are as full of peace as matter.°   *meaning*

OLIVIA   Yet you began rudely. What are you? What would you?

VIOLA   The rudeness that hath appeared in me have I learned
from my entertainment.° What I am, and what I would, are   *reception*

200   as secret as maidenhead.° To your ears, divinity; to any oth-   *virginity*
ers, profanation.

OLIVIA   Give us the place alone. We will hear this divinity.°   *religious discourse*

[*Exeunt* MARIA *and Attendants.*]
—Now sir, what is your text?[4]

VIOLA   Most sweet lady—

205   OLIVIA   A comfortable° doctrine, and much may be said of it.   *comforting*
Where lies your text?

VIOLA   In Orsino's bosom.

OLIVIA   In his bosom? In what chapter of his bosom?

VIOLA   To answer by the method,° in the first of his heart.   *in the same style*

210   OLIVIA   Oh, I have read it; it is heresy. Have you no more
to say?

VIOLA   Good madam, let me see your face.

---

6. My most wise lady; upon my soul.
7. *'Tis . . . dialogue:* I am not lunatic enough to take
part in so flighty a conversation. (Lunacy was thought
to be influenced by the phases of the moon.)
8. To lie unanchored with lowered sails. *swabber:* a
cleaner of boat decks.
9. Mythical giants guarded ladies; here, also mocking Maria's diminutive size. *Some . . . for:* Please

pacify.
1. From Orsino; Olivia pretends she understands her
to mean a king's messenger, or a messenger-at-arms,
employed on important state affairs.
2. Demand for dues paid to a superior.
3. Olive branch (as a symbol of peace).
4. Quotation (as a theme of a sermon, in keeping
with "divinity," "doctrine," "heresy," etc.).

OLIVIA   Have you any commission from your lord to negotiate
with my face? You are now out of° your text. But we will   *straying from*
215   draw the curtain and show you the picture. [*She unveils.*]
Look you, sir, such a one I was this present.[5] Is't not well
done?
VIOLA   Excellently done, if God did all.[6]
OLIVIA   'Tis in grain,° sir, 'twill endure wind and weather.   *genuine*
220   VIOLA   'Tis beauty truly blent,[7] whose red and white
Nature's own sweet and cunning° hand laid on.   *skillful*
Lady, you are the cruel'st she° alive   *woman*
If you will lead these graces to the grave
And leave the world no copy.[8]
225   OLIVIA   O sir, I will not be so hardhearted. I will give out div-
ers schedules° of my beauty. It shall be inventoried and   *various inventories*
every particle and utensil labeled[9] to my will. As *item*, two
lips, indifferent° red; *item*, two gray eyes, with lids[1] to them;   *moderate*
item, one neck, one chin, and so forth. Were you sent hither
230   to praise° me?   *appraise; flatter*
VIOLA   I see you what you are, you are too proud.
But if° you were the devil, you are fair.   *Even if*
My lord and master loves you. Oh, such love
Could be but recompensed though[2] you were crowned
235   The nonpareil of beauty.°   *An unequaled beauty*
OLIVIA   How does he love me?
VIOLA   With adorations, fertile° tears,   *ever-flowing*
With groans that thunder love, with sighs of fire.
OLIVIA   Your lord does know my mind. I cannot love him.
240   Yet I suppose him virtuous, know him noble,
Of great estate, of fresh and stainless youth,
In voices well divulged,° free,° learned, and valiant,   *spoken of / generous*
And in dimension and the shape of nature[3]
A gracious person. But yet I cannot love him.
245   He might have took his answer long ago.
VIOLA   If I did love you in° my master's flame,°   *with / passion*
With such a suffering, such a deadly° life,   *deathlike*
In your denial I would find no sense.
I would not understand it.
OLIVIA   Why, what would you?
250   VIOLA   Make me a willow[4] cabin at your gate
And call upon my soul° within the house;   *(Olivia)*
Write loyal cantons of contemnèd° love   *songs of rejected*
And sing them loud even in the dead of night;
Halloo[5] your name to the reverberate° hills   *echoing*
255   And make the babbling gossip of the air[6]
Cry out, "Olivia!" Oh, you should not rest

5. Portraits usually gave the year of painting. "This present" was a term used to date letters.
6. If it is natural (without the use of cosmetics).
7. Blended, or mixed (of paints). Shakespeare uses the same metaphor in Sonnet 20, lines 1–2, and Viola's next lines recall Sonnet 11, lines 13–14. As Cesario, Viola is playing with established conventions of poetic courtship.
8. Viola means "child"; Olivia takes her to mean "list" or "inventory."
9. Every single part and article added as a codicil (parodying the legal language of a last will and testament).
1. Eyelids, but also punning on "pot lids" (punning on "utensil" as a household implement).
2. *Could . . . though:* Would have to be requited even if.
3. *dimension . . . shape of nature:* The two terms are synonymous, meaning "bodily form."
4. Traditional symbol of rejected love.
5. Shout; or perhaps "hallow," as in "bless."
6. For the love of Narcissus, the nymph Echo wasted away to a mere voice, only able to repeat whatever she heard spoken.

Between the elements of air and earth
But you should pity me.

OLIVIA   You might do much.
What is your parentage?

260 VIOLA Above my fortunes, yet my state° is well.   social status
I am a gentleman.

OLIVIA   Get you to your lord.
I cannot love him. Let him send no more
Unless, perchance, you come to me again
To tell me how he takes it. Fare you well.

265 I thank you for your pains. Spend this for me.
          [*She offers a purse.*]

VIOLA I am no fee'd post,° lady. Keep your purse.   hired messenger
My master, not myself, lacks recompense.
Love make his heart of flint that you shall love,[7]
And let your fervor, like my master's, be

270 Placed in contempt. Farewell, fair cruelty.   *Exit.*

OLIVIA "What is your parentage?"
"Above my fortunes, yet my state is well.
I am a gentleman." I'll be sworn thou art.
Thy tongue, thy face, thy limbs, actions, and spirit

275 Do give thee five-fold blazon.[8] Not too fast. Soft,° soft,   *Wait*
Unless the master were the man.[9] How now?
Even so quickly may one catch the plague?
Methinks I feel this youth's perfections
With an invisible and subtle stealth

280 To creep in at mine eyes. Well, let it be.
What ho, Malvolio!
          Enter MALVOLIO.

MALVOLIO   Here, madam, at your service.

OLIVIA Run after that same peevish messenger,
The County's° man. He left this ring behind him,   *Count's*
Would I° or not. Tell him I'll none of it.   *Whether I wished it*

285 Desire him not to flatter with° his lord,   *encourage*
Nor hold him up with hopes. I am not for him.
If that the youth will come this way tomorrow,
I'll give him reasons for't. Hie thee,° Malvolio.   *Hurry*

MALVOLIO Madam, I will.   *Exit.*

290 OLIVIA I do I know not what, and fear to find
Mine eye too great a flatterer for my mind.[1]
Fate, show thy force. Ourselves we do not owe.°   *own*
What is decreed must be, and be this so.   [*Exit.*]

2.1

          Enter ANTONIO *and* SEBASTIAN.

ANTONIO Will you stay no longer? Nor will° you not that I go   *wish*
with you?

SEBASTIAN By your patience, no. My stars shine darkly over
me. The malignancy of my fate[1] might perhaps distemper°   *infect*

---

7. *Love . . . love:* May love make the heart of the man
you love as hard as flint.
8. Formal description of a gentleman's coat of arms.
9. If Orsino were Cesario (*man:* servant).
1. My eye (through which love has entered my heart)

has seduced my reason.
2.1 Location: Near the coast of Illyria.
1. Evil influence of the stars; "malignancy" also signifies a deadly disease.

5 yours. Therefore I shall crave of you your leave that I may
bear my evils alone. It were a bad recompense for your love
to lay any of them on you.

ANTONIO Let me yet know of you whither you are bound.

SEBASTIAN No, sooth,° sir. My determinate° voyage is mere   *truly / destined*
10 extravagancy.° But I perceive in you so excellent a touch of   *idle wandering*
modesty° that you will not extort from me what I am willing   *politeness*
to keep in. Therefore it charges me in manners² the rather
to express° myself. You must know of me then, Antonio, my   *reveal*
name is Sebastian, which I called Roderigo. My father was
15 that Sebastian of Messaline³ whom I know you have heard
of. He left behind him myself and a sister, both born in an°   *within the same*
hour. If the heavens had been pleased, would we had so
ended. But you, sir, altered that, for some hour before you
took me from the breach° of the sea was my sister drowned.   *surf*

20 ANTONIO Alas the day!

SEBASTIAN A lady, sir, though it was said she much resembled
me, was yet of many accounted beautiful. But though I
could not with such estimable° wonder overfar believe that,   *appreciative*
yet thus far I will boldly publish° her: she bore a mind that   *proclaim*
25 envy could not but call fair. She is drowned already, sir, with
salt water, though I seem to drown her remembrance again
with more.

ANTONIO Pardon me, sir, your bad entertainment.⁴

SEBASTIAN O good Antonio, forgive me your trouble.

30 ANTONIO If you will not murder me⁵ for my love, let me be
your servant.

SEBASTIAN If you will not undo what you have done—that is,
kill him whom you have recovered°—desire it not. Fare ye   *rescued*
well at once. My bosom is full of kindness,° and I am yet° so   *tender emotion / still*
35 near the manners of my mother⁶ that upon the least occa-
sion more mine eyes will tell tales of me.° I am bound to the   *betray my feelings*
Count Orsino's court. Farewell.   *Exit.*

ANTONIO The gentleness° of all the gods go with thee.   *favor*
I have many enemies in Orsino's court,
40 Else would I very shortly see thee there.
But come what may, I do adore thee so
That danger shall seem sport, and I will go.   *Exit.*

2.2

Enter VIOLA [*as Cesario*] *and* MALVOLIO *at*
several° doors.   *separate*

MALVOLIO Were not you e'en° now with the Countess Olivia?   *just*

VIOLA Even now, sir. On° a moderate pace I have since arrived   *At*
but hither.°   *come only this far*

MALVOLIO [*giving her a ring*] She returns this ring to you, sir.
5 You might have saved me my pains to have taken° it away   *by taking*
yourself. She adds, moreover, that you should put your lord

---

2. Therefore courtesy requires.
3. Possibly Messina, Sicily.
4. Your poor reception at my hands.
5. Murder him by insisting that they part.

6. So near woman's readiness to weep.
2.2 Location: Between Olivia's house and Orsino's
palace.

into a desperate assurance° she will none of him. And one   *hopeless certainty*
thing more, that you be never so hardy° to come again in his   *bold*
affairs unless it be to report your lord's taking of this.[1]
10   Receive it so.
VIOLA   She took the ring of me.[2] I'll none of it.
MALVOLIO   Come, sir, you peevishly threw it to her, and, her
will is, it should be so returned. [*He throws down the ring.*] If
it be worth stooping for, there it lies, in your eye.° If not, be   *sight*
15   it his that finds it.   *Exit.*
VIOLA [*picking up the ring*]   I left no ring with her. What means
    this lady?
Fortune forbid my outside° have not charmed her.   *appearance*
She made good view of° me, indeed so much   *looked carefully at*
That methought her eyes had lost° her tongue,   *made her lose*
20   For she did speak in starts distractedly.°   *madly*
She loves me, sure. The cunning of her passion
Invites me in° this churlish messenger.   *by means of*
None of my lord's ring? Why, he sent her none.
I am the man.[3] If it be so, as 'tis,
25   Poor lady, she were better love a dream.
Disguise, I see thou art a wickedness
Wherein the pregnant enemy[4] does much.
How easy is it for the proper false[5]
In women's waxen hearts to set their forms.[6]
30   Alas, our frailty is the cause, not we,
For such as we are made of, such we be.[7]
How will this fadge?° My master loves her dearly,   *turn out*
And I, poor monster,[8] fond° as much on him.   *dote*
And she, mistaken, seems to dote on me.
35   What will become of this? As I am man,
My state is desperate° for my master's love.   *hopeless*
As I am woman, now, alas the day,
What thriftless° sighs shall poor Olivia breathe!   *unprofitable*
O time, thou must untangle this, not I.
40   It is too hard a knot for me t'untie.   [*Exit.*]

2.3

Enter SIR TOBY *and* SIR ANDREW.

SIR TOBY   Approach, Sir Andrew. Not to be abed after midnight is to be up betimes,° and "*diluculo surgere*,"[1] thou   *early*
know'st.
SIR ANDREW   Nay, by my troth,° I know not. But I know to be   *faith*
5   up late is to be up late.
SIR TOBY   A false conclusion; I hate it as an unfilled can.° To   *tankard*
be up after midnight and to go to bed then is early. So that
to go to bed after midnight is to go to bed betimes. Does not
our lives consist of the four elements?[2]

---

1. Reception of this rejection.
2. Viola pretends to believe Olivia's story. *of*: from.
3. The man with whom she has fallen in love.
4. The devil, who is always quick and ready ("pregnant") to deceive.
5. Handsome, but deceitful (men).
6. *In . . . forms*: To impress their images on women's
affections (as a seal stamps its image in wax).

7. For being made of frail flesh, we are frail.
8. Since she is both man and woman.
2.3 Location: Olivia's house.
1. Part of a Latin proverb, meaning "to rise at dawn
(is most healthy)."
2. The four elements, thought to make up all matter,
were earth, air, fire, and water.

10 SIR ANDREW Faith, so they say. But I think it rather consists
 of eating and drinking.
 SIR TOBY Thou'rt a scholar. Let us therefore eat and drink.
 —Marian, I say, a stoup° of wine!   *two-pint tankard*
  Enter CLOWN.
 SIR ANDREW Here comes the fool, i'faith.
15 CLOWN How now, my hearts. Did you never see the picture of
 We Three?[3]
 SIR TOBY Welcome, ass, now let's have a catch.[4]
 SIR ANDREW By my troth, the fool has an excellent breast.° I   *singing voice*
 had rather than forty shillings I had such a leg,° and so   *(for dancing)*
20 sweet a breath to sing, as the fool has. In sooth, thou wast in
 very gracious fooling last night when thou spok'st of Pigrogromitus of the Vapians passing the equinoctial of Queu-
 bus.[5] 'Twas very good, i'faith. I sent thee sixpence for thy   *sweetheart*
 leman.° Hadst it?
25 CLOWN I did impeticos thy gratility.[6] For Malvolio's nose is
 no whipstock. My lady has a white hand, and the Myrmi-
 dons are no bottle-ale houses.[7]
 SIR ANDREW Excellent! Why, this is the best fooling when all
 is done. Now, a song.
30 SIR TOBY Come on, there is sixpence for you. Let's have a
 song.
 SIR ANDREW There's a testril[8] of me too. If one knight
 give a—[9]
 CLOWN Would you have a love song or a song of good life?
35 SIR TOBY A love song, a love song.
 SIR ANDREW Ay, ay. I care not for good life.
 CLOWN (*sings*) O mistress mine, where are you roaming?
   Oh, stay and hear, your true love's coming
   That can sing both high and low.
40   Trip° no further, pretty sweeting.   *Go*
   Journeys end in lovers meeting,
   Every wise man's son doth know.[1]
 SIR ANDREW Excellent good, i'faith.
 SIR TOBY Good, good.
45 CLOWN [*sings*] What is love? 'Tis not hereafter.
   Present mirth hath present laughter.
   What's to come is still° unsure.   *always*
   In delay there lies no plenty,
   Then come kiss me, sweet and twenty.°   *twenty times sweet*
50   Youth's a stuff will not endure.
 SIR ANDREW A mellifluous voice, as I am true knight.
 SIR TOBY A contagious breath.[2]
 SIR ANDREW Very sweet and contagious, i'faith.

---

3. A trick picture portraying two fools' or asses'
heads, the third being that of the viewer.
4. A round: a simple song for several voices.
5. *Pigrogromitus . . . Queubus:* the Clown's mock
learning. *equinoctial:* equator of the astronomical
heavens.
6. Comic jargon for "impocket (or impetticoat) your
gratuity."
7. *for . . . houses:* Perhaps it is the sheer inscrutabil-
ity of the Clown's foolery that so impresses Sir
Andrew (lines 28–29). *whipstock:* handle of a whip.

bottle-ale houses: cheap taverns.
8. Sir Andrew's version of "tester" (sixpence).
9. In F, "give a" appears at the end of a justified line;
an omission is possible.
1. *O mistress . . . know:* The words are not certainly
Shakespeare's; they fit the tune of an instrumental
piece printed in Thomas Morley's *First Book of Consort Lessons* (1599). *wise man's son:* wise men were
thought to have foolish sons.
2. A catchy voice; with a play on "disease-causing
air."

SIR TOBY   To hear by the nose, it is dulcet in contagion.[3] But
55   shall we make the welkin° dance indeed? Shall we rouse the   *sky*
      night owl in a catch that will draw three souls out of one
      weaver?[4] Shall we do that?
SIR ANDREW   An° you love me, let's do't. I am dog° at a catch.   *If / clever*
CLOWN   By'r lady, sir, and some dogs will catch well.
60   SIR ANDREW   Most certain. Let our catch be "Thou knave."
CLOWN   "Hold thy peace, thou knave,"[5] knight. I shall be con-
      strained in't to call thee knave, knight.
SIR ANDREW   'Tis not the first time I have constrained one to
      call me knave. Begin, fool. It begins, "Hold thy peace."
65   CLOWN   I shall never begin if I hold my peace.
SIR ANDREW   Good, i'faith. Come, begin.
            Catch sung.
            Enter MARIA.
MARIA   What a caterwauling do you keep here! If my lady
      have not called up her steward Malvolio and bid him turn
      you out of doors, never trust me.
70   SIR TOBY   My lady's a Cathayan,[6] we are politicians,° Malvolio's   *schemers*
      a Peg-o-Ramsey,[7] and [*singing*] "Three merry men be we."
      Am not I consanguineous?[8] Am I not of her blood? Tilly-
      vally!° "Lady"! [*He sings.*] "There dwelt a man in Babylon,   *Fiddlesticks*
      lady, lady."[9]
75   CLOWN   Beshrew° me, the knight's in admirable fooling.   *Curse*
SIR ANDREW   Ay, he does well enough if he be disposed, and
      so do I too. He does it with a better grace, but I do it more
      natural.[1]
SIR TOBY [*sings*]   "O'the twelfth day of December"[2]—
80   MARIA   For the love o'God, peace!
            Enter MALVOLIO.
MALVOLIO   My masters, are you mad? Or what are you? Have
      you no wit,° manners, nor honesty° but to gabble like tinkers   *sense / decency*
      at this time of night? Do ye make an alehouse of my lady's
      house, that ye squeak out your coziers'° catches without any   *cobblers'*
85   mitigation or remorse[3] of voice? Is there no respect of place,
      persons, nor time in you?
SIR TOBY   We did keep time, sir, in our catches. Sneck up!°   *Go hang yourself*
MALVOLIO   Sir Toby, I must be round° with you. My lady bade   *plainspoken*
      me tell you that, though she harbors you as her kinsman,
90   she's nothing allied to your disorders. If you can separate
      yourself and your misdemeanors, you are welcome to the
      house. If not, an it would please you to take leave of her,
      she is very willing to bid you farewell.
SIR TOBY [*sings*]   "Farewell, dear heart, since I must needs be
      gone."[4]

---

3. If one could hear through the nose, the sound would be sweetly ("dulcet") infectious.

4. Weavers were traditionally addicted to psalm singing, so to move them with popular catches would be a great triumph. Music was said to be able to draw the soul from the body.

5. The words of the catch are "Hold thy peace, I prithee hold thy peace, thou knave." Each singer repeatedly calls the others knaves and tells them to stop singing.

6. A Cathayan (or Chinese); also, from travelers' tales, someone who misleads or exaggerates. (See T. Billings, "Caterwauling Cataians: The Genealogy of a Gloss," in SQ 54 [2003]: 1–28.)

7. Name of a dance and popular song; here, used contemptuously.

8. A blood relative of Olivia's. "Three . . . we": a refrain from a popular song.

9. The opening and refrain of a popular song called "Constant Susanna."

1. Effortlessly; but unconsciously playing on "natural" as in "fool" or "idiot."

2. Snatch of a ballad; or possibly a drunken version of "twelfth day of Christmas"—that is, Twelfth Night.

3. Without any abating or softening.

4. Part of another song that Sir Toby and the Clown adapt for the occasion.

95 MARIA Nay, good Sir Toby.
CLOWN [sings] "His eyes do show his days are almost done."
MALVOLIO Is't even so?
SIR TOBY [sings] "But I will never die."
CLOWN [sings] "Sir Toby, there you lie."
100 MALVOLIO This is much credit to you.
SIR TOBY [sings] "Shall I bid him go?"
CLOWN [sings] "What an if° you do?"   an if = if
SIR TOBY [sings] "Shall I bid him go, and spare not?"
CLOWN [sings] "Oh, no, no, no, no, you dare not."
105 SIR TOBY Out o'tune, sir, ye lie. [to MALVOLIO] Art any more
than a steward? Dost thou think because thou art virtuous,
there shall be no more cakes and ale?[5]
CLOWN Yes, by Saint Anne, and ginger[6] shall be hot i'th'
mouth, too.
110 SIR TOBY Thou'rt i'th' right. [to MALVOLIO] Go, sir, rub your
chain with crumbs.[7] —A stoup of wine, Maria.
MALVOLIO Mistress Mary, if you prized my lady's favor
at anything more than contempt, you would not give
means° for this uncivil rule.° She shall know of it, by this   drink / behavior
115 hand.   Exit.[8]
MARIA Go shake your ears!°   (like an ass)
SIR ANDREW 'Twere as good a deed as to drink when a man's
a-hungry to challenge him the field,° and then to break   to a duel
promise with him, and make a fool of him.
120 SIR TOBY Do't, knight. I'll write thee a challenge, or I'll deliver
thy indignation to him by word of mouth.
MARIA Sweet Sir Toby, be patient for tonight. Since the youth
of the Count's was today with my lady, she is much out of
quiet. For Monsieur Malvolio, let me alone with him. If I do
125 not gull him into a nay-word[9] and make him a common recreation,° do not think I have wit enough to lie straight in my   sport; jest
bed. I know I can do it.
SIR TOBY Possess° us, possess us. Tell us something of him.   Inform
MARIA Marry, sir, sometimes he is a kind of puritan.[1]
130 SIR ANDREW Oh, if I thought that, I'd beat him like a dog.
SIR TOBY What, for being a puritan? Thy exquisite° reason,   ingenious
dear knight?
SIR ANDREW I have no exquisite reason for't, but I have reason good enough.
135 MARIA The devil a puritan that he is, or anything constantly
but a time-pleaser,° an affectioned° ass that cons state with-   bootlicker / affected
out book and utters it by great swaths.[2] The best persuaded
of himself[3]—so crammed, as he thinks, with excellencies—
that it is his grounds of faith° that all that look on him love   his creed
140 him. And on that vice in him will my revenge find notable
cause to work.

---

5. *cakes and ale:* traditionally associated with church
festivals, and therefore disliked by puritans.
6. Used to spice ale. *Saint Anne:* mother of the Virgin; the oath would be offensive to puritans who
attacked her cult.
7. Clean your steward's chain; mind your own business.
8. TEXTUAL COMMENT Although F has Malvolio exit
by himself here, some editors choose to have the
Clown exit here as well. For more on the implications

of this decision, see Digital Edition TC 4.
9. If I do not trick ("gull") him into making his name
a byword (for "dupe").
1. Could mean "morally strict and censorious," as
well as "a follower of the puritan religious faith."
2. *cons . . . swaths:* memorizes dignified and high-
flown language and utters it in great sweeps (like hay
falling under a scythe).
3. Having the highest opinion of himself.

SIR TOBY   What wilt thou do?

MARIA   I will drop in his way some obscure epistles of love,
wherein by the color of his beard, the shape of his leg, the
145   manner of his gait, the expressure° of his eye, forehead, and   *expression*
complexion he shall find himself most feelingly personated.°   *represented*
I can write very like my lady, your niece. On a forgotten°   *bygone*
matter we can hardly make distinction of our hands.°   *handwriting*

SIR TOBY   Excellent, I smell a device.

150   SIR ANDREW   I have't in my nose too.

SIR TOBY   He shall think by the letters that thou wilt drop that
they come from my niece, and that she's in love with him.

MARIA   My purpose is indeed a horse of that color.

SIR ANDREW   And your horse now would make him an ass.

155   MARIA   Ass,° I doubt not.   *(punning on "as")*

SIR ANDREW   Oh, 'twill be admirable.

MARIA   Sport royal, I warrant you. I know my physic° will work   *medicine*
with him. I will plant you two, and let the fool make a third,
where he shall find the letter. Observe his construction° of it.   *interpretation*
160   For this night, to bed, and dream on the event.° Farewell.   *outcome*
                                                              Exit.

SIR TOBY   Good night, Penthesilea.[4]

SIR ANDREW   Before me,[5] she's a good wench.

SIR TOBY   She's a beagle true bred, and one that adores me.
What o'that?

165   SIR ANDREW   I was adored once too.

SIR TOBY   Let's to bed, knight. Thou hadst need send for more
money.

SIR ANDREW   If I cannot recover° your niece, I am a foul way   *win*
out.°   *out of money*

170   SIR TOBY   Send for money, knight. If thou hast her not i'th'
end, call me cut.[6]

SIR ANDREW   If I do not, never trust me, take it how you will.

SIR TOBY   Come, come, I'll go burn some sack.[7] 'Tis too late to
go to bed now. Come, knight; come, knight.   *Exeunt.*

2.4

Enter DUKE, VIOLA [*as Cesario*], CURIO, *and others.*

ORSINO   Give me some music. Now good morrow,° friends.   *morning*
Now, good Cesario, but° that piece of song,   *just*
That old and antique° song we heard last night.   *quaint*
Methought it did relieve my passion° much,   *suffering*
5   More than light airs and recollected° terms°   *artificial / lyrics*
Of these most brisk and giddy-pacèd times.
Come, but one verse.

CURIO   He is not here, so please your lordship, that should sing it.

ORSINO   Who was it?

10   CURIO   Feste the jester,[1] my lord, a fool that the Lady Olivia's
father took much delight in. He is about the house.

---

4. Queen of the Amazons (a joke about Maria's small size).
5. On my soul (a mild oath).
6. A dock-tailed horse; also, slang for "gelding" or for "female genitals."
7. I'll go warm and spice some Spanish wine.
2.4 Location: Orsino's palace.

1. TEXTUAL COMMENT This is the only time in the play that Olivia's household entertainer is ever given a proper name, yet editorial tradition has often preferred "Feste" over any other speech prefix. This edition follows F and denominates him by his status and profession as "Clown." For more on the issue of speech prefixes and names, see Digital Edition TC 5.

ORSINO Seek him out and play the tune the while.

                         [*Exit* CURIO.]

        Music plays.

  —Come hither, boy. If ever thou shalt love,

  In the sweet pangs of it remember me.

15 For such as I am, all true lovers are,

  Unstaid° and skittish in all motions° else   *Unstable / emotions*

  Save in the constant image of the creature

  That is beloved. How dost thou like this tune?

VIOLA It gives a very echo to the seat

  Where love is thronèd.[2]

20 ORSINO   Thou dost speak masterly.°   *expertly*

  My life upon't, young though thou art, thine eye

  Hath stayed upon some favor° that it loves.   *face*

  Hath it not, boy?

VIOLA   A little, by your favor.°   *leave; face*

ORSINO What kind of woman is't?

VIOLA   Of your complexion.

25 ORSINO She is not worth thee then. What years, i'faith?

VIOLA About your years, my lord.

ORSINO Too old, by heaven. Let still° the woman take   *always*

  An elder than herself. So wears° she to him,   *adapts*

  So sways she level[3] in her husband's heart.

30 For, boy, however we do praise ourselves,

  Our fancies° are more giddy and unfirm,   *affections*

  More longing, wavering, sooner lost and worn,°   *exhausted*

  Than women's are.

VIOLA   I think° it well, my lord.   *believe*

ORSINO Then let thy love be younger than thyself,

35 Or thy affection cannot hold the bent.[4]

  For women are as roses whose fair flower,

  Being once displayed,° doth fall that very hour.   *opened*

VIOLA And so they are. Alas, that they are so,

  To die even° when they to perfection grow!   *just*

       Enter CURIO *and* CLOWN.

40 ORSINO [*to* CLOWN] O fellow, come, the song we had last night.

  Mark it, Cesario, it is old and plain.

  The spinsters° and the knitters in the sun   *spinners*

  And the free° maids that weave their thread with bones[5]   *carefree*

  Do use to chant it. It is silly sooth°   *simple truth*

45 And dallies with° the innocence of love,   *lingers lovingly on*

  Like the old° age.   *golden*

CLOWN Are you ready, sir?

ORSINO Ay, prithee, sing.

       Music. The Song.

CLOWN [*sings*] Come away,° come away, death,   *Come hither*

50 And in sad cypress[6] let me be laid.

  Fly away, fly away, breath,

  I am slain by a fair cruel maid.

---

2. *It . . . thronèd*: It reflects the feelings of the heart.
3. So does she balance influence and affection.
4. Cannot remain at full stretch (like the tautness of a bowstring).

5. Spools made from bone on which lace (called "bone lace") was woven.
6. Cypress-wood coffin. Like yews, cypresses were emblematic of mourning.

My shroud of white stuck all with yew,°   *sprigs of yew*
Oh, prepare it.
55   My part of death, no one so true
Did share it.[7]
Not a flower, not a flower sweet
On my black coffin let there be strewn.
Not a friend, not a friend greet
60   My poor corpse where my bones shall be thrown.
A thousand thousand sighs to save,
Lay me, oh, where
Sad true lover never find my grave,
To weep there.
65 ORSINO [*giving money*]   There's for thy pains.
CLOWN   No pains, sir. I take pleasure in singing, sir.
ORSINO   I'll pay thy pleasure, then.
CLOWN   Truly, sir, and pleasure will be paid° one time or   *paid for*
another.
70 ORSINO   Give me now leave° to leave° thee.   *permission / dismiss*
CLOWN   Now the melancholy god[8] protect thee, and the tailor
make thy doublet of changeable taffeta,[9] for thy mind is a very
opal.[1] I would have men of such constancy put to sea, that their
business might be everything and their intent° everywhere, for   *destination*
75 that's it that always makes a good voyage of nothing.[2] Farewell.
                                              Exit.
ORSINO   Let all the rest give place.°   [*Exeunt* CURIO *and others.*]   *withdraw*
                    Once more, Cesario,
Get thee to yond same sovereign cruelty.
Tell her my love, more noble than the world,
Prizes not quantity of dirty lands.
80 The parts° that Fortune hath bestowed upon her,[3]   *possessions*
Tell her I hold as giddily[4] as Fortune,
But 'tis that miracle and queen of gems
That nature pranks° her in attracts my soul.   *adorns*
VIOLA   But if she cannot love you, sir?
ORSINO   It cannot be so answered.
85 VIOLA   Sooth,° but you must.   *In truth*
Say that some lady, as perhaps there is,
Hath for your love as great a pang of heart
As you have for Olivia. You cannot love her.
You tell her so. Must she not then be answered?
90 ORSINO   There is no woman's sides
Can bide° the beating of so strong a passion   *withstand*
As love doth give my heart. No woman's heart
So big, to hold so much. They lack retention.°   *constancy*
Alas, their love may be called appetite,
95 No motion of the liver, but the palate,[5]

---

7. *My part . . . it:* No one has died so true to love as I.
8. Saturn (thought to control the melancholic).
9. Shot silk, whose color changes with the angle of vision. *doublet:* close-fitting jacket.
1. An iridescent gemstone that changes color depending on the angle from which it is seen.
2. *that's . . . nothing:* This fickle lack of direction can make a voyage in the notoriously changeful sea carefree and consonant with one's desires.
3. TEXTUAL COMMENT F does not capitalize "for-

tune" in line 80, though "Fortune" does appear in the very next line. Since the word seems to refer to the allegorical figure of Fortuna, both instances have been capitalized here. For more on the issue of capitalization, see Digital Edition TC 6.
4. Lightly (fortune being fickle).
5. *appetite . . . palate:* Appetite, like the palate, is easily sated and thus lacks the emotional depth and complexity of real love, whose seat is the liver. *motion:* impulse.

That suffer surfeit, cloyment,° and revolt.°   *satiety / revulsion*
But mine is all as hungry as the sea
And can digest as much. Make no compare
Between that love a woman can bear me
And that I owe° Olivia.   *have for*

100 VIOLA   Ay, but I know—
ORSINO   What dost thou know?
VIOLA   Too well what love women to men may owe.
   In faith, they are as true of heart as we.
   My father had a daughter loved a man
105   As it might be perhaps, were I a woman,
   I should your lordship.
ORSINO   And what's her history?
VIOLA   A blank, my lord. She never told her love
   But let concealment, like a worm i'th' bud,
   Feed on her damask[6] cheek. She pined in thought,
110   And, with a green and yellow° melancholy,   *pale and sallow*
   She sat like Patience on a monument,[7]
   Smiling at grief. Was not this love indeed?
   We men may say more, swear more, but indeed
   Our shows are more than will.[8] For still° we prove   *always*
115   Much in our vows, but little in our love.
ORSINO   But died thy sister of her love, my boy?
VIOLA   I am all the daughters of my father's house,
   And all the brothers too, and yet I know not.
   Sir, shall I to this lady?
ORSINO   Ay, that's the theme,
120   To her in haste. Give her this jewel. Say
   My love can give no place, bide no denay.[9]   *Exeunt.*

2.5

Enter SIR TOBY, SIR ANDREW, *and* FABIAN.

SIR TOBY   Come thy ways,° Signior Fabian.   *Come along*
FABIAN   Nay, I'll come. If I lose a scruple° of this sport, let me   *miss a scrap*
   be boiled to death with melancholy.[1]
SIR TOBY   Wouldst thou not be glad to have the niggardly ras-
5   cally sheep-biter[2] come by some notable shame?
FABIAN   I would exult, man. You know he brought me out
   o'favor with my lady about a bearbaiting[3] here.
SIR TOBY   To anger him we'll have the bear again, and we will
   fool° him black and blue, shall we not, Sir Andrew?   *mock*
10 SIR ANDREW   An° we do not, it is pity of our lives.   *If*

Enter MARIA [*with a letter*].

SIR TOBY   Here comes the little villain. How now, my metal of
   India?[4]
MARIA   Get ye all three into the box tree.°[5] Malvolio's coming   *hedge of boxwood*
   down this walk. He has been yonder i'the sun practicing

---

6. Pink and white, like a damask rose.
7. A memorial statue symbolizing patience.
8. Our displays of love are greater than our actual feelings.
9. My love cannot be bated, nor tolerate refusal.
2.5 Location: Olivia's garden.
1. Melancholy was a cold humor; "boiled" puns on "bile," the surplus of which produced melancholy.
2. Literally, a dog that attacks sheep; here, a mali-
cious sneak.
3. Puritans disapproved of blood sports like bear-baiting.
4. A woman worth her weight in gold.
5. PERFORMANCE COMMENT The exact onstage location where Toby, Andrew, and Fabian hide while spying on Malvolio can make a significant difference in productions. For more, see Digital Edition PC 3.

15 behavior to his own shadow this half hour. Observe him, for
the love of mockery, for I know this letter will make a con-
templative° idiot of him. Close,° in the name of jesting!   *vacuous / Keep close; hide*
    [*The men hide. She places the letter.*]
Lie thou there, for here comes the trout that must be caught
with tickling.[6]   *Exit.*
    Enter MALVOLIO.

20 MALVOLIO   'Tis but fortune, all is fortune. Maria once told me
    she° did affect° me, and I have heard herself come thus   *(Olivia) / care for*
    near, that should she fancy,° it should be one of my complex-   *fall in love*
    ion. Besides, she uses me with a more exalted respect than
    anyone else that follows her. What should I think on't?

25 SIR TOBY   Here's an overweening rogue.
    FABIAN   Oh, peace! Contemplation makes a rare turkeycock[7]
    of him. How he jets° under his advanced° plumes!   *struts / raised*
    SIR ANDREW   'Slight,[8] I could so beat the rogue.
    SIR TOBY   Peace, I say.

30 MALVOLIO   To be Count Malvolio.
    SIR TOBY   Ah, rogue.
    SIR ANDREW   Pistol him, pistol him!
    SIR TOBY   Peace, peace.
    MALVOLIO   There is example° for't. The Lady of the Strachy   *precedent*
35   married the yeoman of the wardrobe.[9]
    SIR ANDREW   Fie on him, Jezebel.[1]
    FABIAN   Oh, peace, now he's deeply in. Look how imagination
    blows him.°   *puffs him up*
    MALVOLIO   Having been three months married to her, sitting
40   in my state°—   *chair of state*
    SIR TOBY   Oh, for a stone-bow[2] to hit him in the eye!
    MALVOLIO   Calling my officers° about me, in my branched[3]   *household attendants*
    velvet gown, having come from a daybed° where I have left   *couch*
    Olivia sleeping.
45 SIR TOBY   Fire and brimstone!
    FABIAN   Oh, peace, peace.
    MALVOLIO   And then, to have the humor of state[4] and, after a
    demure travel of regard,[5] telling them I know my place as I
    would they should do theirs, to ask for my kinsman Toby—
50 SIR TOBY   Bolts and shackles!
    FABIAN   Oh, peace, peace, peace! Now, now.
    MALVOLIO   Seven of my people with an obedient start make°   *go*
    out for him. I frown the while, and perchance wind up my
    watch, or play with my[6]—some rich jewel. Toby approaches,
55   curtsies° there to me—   *bows*
    SIR TOBY   Shall this fellow live?
    FABIAN   Though our silence be drawn from us with cars,[7] yet
    peace.

6. Flattery; trout can be caught by stroking them
under the gills.
7. Proverbially proud; they display their feathers like
peacocks.
8. By God's light (an oath).
9. Perhaps an allusion to a noblewoman who had
married her manservant, but there is no certain identification. *yeoman of the wardrobe:* keeper of clothes
and linen.
1. Biblical allusion to the proud wife of Ahab, king of
Israel.

2. A catapult, or a crossbow for stones.
3. Embroidered with branch patterns.
4. To adopt the grand air of exalted greatness.
5. After casting my eyes gravely about the room.
6. Malvolio momentarily forgets that he will have
abandoned his steward's chain; watches were an
expensive luxury at this time.
7. A prisoner might be tied to two carts or chariots
("cars") and pulled by horses in opposite directions to
extort information.

MALVOLIO   I extend my hand to him thus, quenching my famil-
60   iar smile with an austere regard of control.
SIR TOBY   And does not Toby take° you a blow o'the lips, then?   *give*
MALVOLIO   Saying, "Cousin Toby, my fortunes having cast me
on your niece, give me this prerogative of speech."
SIR TOBY   What, what?
65   MALVOLIO   "You must amend your drunkenness."
SIR TOBY   Out, scab.
FABIAN   Nay, patience, or we break the sinews of our plot.
MALVOLIO   "Besides, you waste the treasure of your time with
a foolish knight."
70   SIR ANDREW   That's me, I warrant you.
MALVOLIO   "One Sir Andrew."
SIR ANDREW   I knew 'twas I, for many do call me fool.
MALVOLIO [*seeing the letter*]   What employment° have we here?   *business*
FABIAN   Now is the woodcock near the gin.[8]
75   SIR TOBY   Oh, peace, and the spirit of humors intimate[9] reading aloud to him.
MALVOLIO [*picking up the letter*]   By my life, this is my lady's
hand. These be her very c's, her u's, and her t's,[1] and thus
makes she her great P's. It is in contempt of° question her   *beyond*
80   hand.
SIR ANDREW   Her c's, her u's, and her t's. Why that?
MALVOLIO   "To the unknown beloved, this and my good
wishes"—her very phrases! By your leave, wax.[2] [*He opens the*
letter.] Soft°—and the impressure her Lucrece[3] with which   *Wait*
85   she uses to seal.° 'Tis my lady! To whom should this be?   *habitually seals*
FABIAN   This wins him, liver and all.
MALVOLIO   "Jove knows I love,
        But who?
        Lips, do not move.
90   No man must know."
     "No man must know." What follows? The numbers altered.°   *meter changed*
     "No man must know." If this should be thee, Malvolio!
SIR TOBY   Marry, hang thee, brock.[4]
MALVOLIO   "I may command where I adore,
95   But silence, like a Lucrece knife,[5]
        With bloodless stroke my heart doth gore.
        M.O.A.I. doth sway my life."
FABIAN   A fustian° riddle.   *bombastic*
SIR TOBY   Excellent wench, say I.
100   MALVOLIO   "M.O.A.I. doth sway my life." Nay, but first let me
see, let me see, let me see.
FABIAN   What dish o'poison has she dressed° him!   *prepared*
SIR TOBY   And with what wing the staniel checks at it.[6]
MALVOLIO   "I may command where I adore." Why, she may
105   command me. I serve her, she is my lady. Why, this is evident

---

8. Snare. *woodcock*: a proverbially foolish bird.
9. And may a capricious impulse suggest.
1. Malvolio unwittingly spells out "cut," slang for
"female genitals"; the meaning is compounded by
"great P's." In fact, these letters do not appear on the
outside of the letter.
2. *By . . . wax*: addressed to the sealing wax.

3. The figure of Lucrece, a Roman model of chastity,
is the device ("impressure") imprinted on the seal.
4. Badger (proverbially stinking).
5. The knife with which Lucrece killed herself after
she was raped.
6. And with what alacrity the sparrow hawk goes
after it.

to any formal capacity.° There is no obstruction in this. And *normal intelligence*
the end—what should that alphabetical position° portend? If I *arrangement*
could make that resemble something in me. Softly, "M.O.A.I."

SIR TOBY   Oh, ay,[7] make up that. He is now at a cold scent.

110   FABIAN   Sowter will cry upon't for all this, though it be as rank
as a fox.[8]

MALVOLIO   "M"—Malvolio. M—why, that begins my name.

FABIAN   Did not I say he would work it out? The cur is excellent at faults.[9]

115   MALVOLIO   M. But then there is no consonancy in the sequel.[1]
That suffers under probation.[2] A should follow, but O does.

FABIAN   And "O"[3] shall end, I hope.

SIR TOBY   Ay, or I'll cudgel him, and make him cry "Oh!"

MALVOLIO   And then "I" comes behind.

120   FABIAN   Ay, an you had any eye behind you, you might see
more detraction° at your heels than fortunes before you. *defamation*

MALVOLIO   "M.O.A.I." This simulation° is not as the former. *disguise; riddle*
And yet to crush° this a little, it would bow° to me, for every *force / yield; point*
one of these letters are in my name. Soft, here follows prose.

125   "If this fall into thy hand, revolve.° In my stars° I am above *consider / fortunes*
thee, but be not afraid of greatness. Some are born great,
some achieve greatness, and some have greatness thrust upon
'em.[4] Thy fates open their hands.° Let thy blood and spirit *bestow gifts*
embrace them, and to inure° thyself to what thou art like° to *accustom / likely*

130   be, cast thy humble slough[5] and appear fresh. Be opposite° *contrary*
with a kinsman, surly with servants. Let thy tongue tang
arguments of state.[6] Put thyself into the trick of singularity.° *Cultivate eccentricity*
She thus advises thee that sighs for thee. Remember who
commended thy yellow stockings and wished to see thee

135   ever cross-gartered.[7] I say remember, go to,[8] thou art made if
thou desir'st to be so. If not, let me see thee a steward still,
the fellow of servants, and not worthy to touch Fortune's
fingers. Farewell, she that would alter services[9] with thee,
the Fortunate Unhappy." Daylight and champaign discov-

140   ers[1] not more. This is open.° I will be proud, I will read *clear*
politic° authors, I will baffle[2] Sir Toby, I will wash off gross *political*
acquaintance, I will be point-device, the very man.[3] I do not
now fool myself to let imagination jade° me, for every reason *trick*
excites to this—that my lady loves me! She did commend my

145   yellow stockings of late; she did praise my leg being cross-
gartered. And in this, she manifests herself to my love and
with a kind of injunction drives me to these habits° of her *clothes*
liking. I thank my stars, I am happy. I will be strange,° stout,° *aloof / proud*

---

7. *Oh, ay:* playing on "O.I."
8. "Sowter" (the name of a hound), having lost the
scent, will start to bay loudly as he picks up the new,
rank (stinking) smell of the fox. *though:* as though.
9. At picking up a scent after it is momentarily lost.
A "fault" is a "cold scent" (line 109).
1. There is no consistency in what follows.
2. That weakens upon being put to the test.
3. As in the hangman's noose; the last letter of Malvolio's name; or "O" as a lamentation.
4. TEXTUAL COMMENT In F's version of this scene,
this oft-quoted sentence begins differently, with
"Some are become great." For more details, see Digital Edition TC 7.

5. A snake's old skin, which peels away.
6. Let your tongue ring out arguments of statecraft
or politics.
7. An antiquated way of adjusting a garter—going
once below the knee, crossing behind it, and knot-
ting above the knee at the side.
8. An emphatic expression, like "I tell you."
9. Change places (of servant and mistress or master).
1. *champaign discovers:* open countryside reveals.
2. Term used to describe the formal unmaking of a
knight; hence, "disgrace."
3. I will be in every detail the identical man
(described in the letter).

150 in yellow stockings, and cross-gartered even with the swift-
    ness of putting on. Jove and my stars be praised. Here is yet
    a postscript: "Thou canst not choose but know who I am. If
    thou entertainest° my love, let it appear in thy smiling. Thy   accept
    smiles become thee well. Therefore in my presence still° smile,   constantly
    dear my sweet, I prithee." Jove, I thank thee! I will smile, I
155 will do everything that thou wilt have me.   *Exit.*

FABIAN   I will not give my part of this sport for a pension of
    thousands to be paid from the Sophy.°   *Shah of Persia*
SIR TOBY   I could marry this wench for this device.
SIR ANDREW   So could I too.
160 SIR TOBY   And ask no other dowry with her, but such another jest.
        Enter MARIA.
SIR ANDREW   Nor I neither.
FABIAN   Here comes my noble gull-catcher.°   *trickster*
SIR TOBY   Wilt thou set thy foot o'my neck?
SIR ANDREW   Or o'mine either?
165 SIR TOBY   Shall I play my freedom at tray-trip⁴ and become thy
    bond slave?
SIR ANDREW   I'faith, or I either?
SIR TOBY   Why, thou hast put him in such a dream that, when
    the image of it leaves him, he must run mad.
170 MARIA   Nay, but say true: does it work upon him?
SIR TOBY   Like aqua vitae° with a midwife.   *spirits; liquor*
MARIA   If you will then see the fruits of the sport, mark his
    first approach before my lady. He will come to her in yellow
    stockings, and 'tis a color she abhors, and cross-gartered, a
175 fashion she detests. And he will smile upon her, which will
    now be so unsuitable to her disposition, being addicted to a
    melancholy as she is, that it cannot but turn him into a
    notable contempt.⁵ If you will see it, follow me.
SIR TOBY   To the gates of Tartar,° thou most excellent devil   *hell*
180 of wit.
SIR ANDREW   I'll make one° too.   *Exeunt.*   *go along*

                        3.1
        Enter VIOLA [*as Cesario*] *and* CLOWN [*with a tabor*].¹
VIOLA   Save° thee, friend, and thy music. Dost thou live by thy   *God save*
    tabor?
CLOWN   No, sir, I live by° the church.   *near*
VIOLA   Art thou a churchman?
5 CLOWN   No such matter, sir. I do live by² the church, for I do
    live at my house, and my house doth stand by the church.
VIOLA   So thou mayst say, the king lies by³ a beggar if a beggar
    dwell near him. Or the church stands° by thy tabor, if thy   *is maintained*
    tabor stand by the church.
10 CLOWN   You have said, sir. To see this age! A sentence° is but   *saying*
    a chev'rel° glove to a good wit. How quickly the wrong side   *kidskin*
    may be turned outward.

---

4. A game of dice in which the winner throws a three
("tray" is from the Spanish *tres*). *play:* wager.
5. A notorious object of contempt.
3.1 Location: Olivia's garden.
1. The dialogue demands only a tabor, but jesters
commonly played a pipe with one hand while tapping

a tabor (a small drum, hanging from the neck) with
the other.
2. Viola understands "by" to mean "earn my keep
through," but the Clown explains "by" as merely
"close to."
3. Lives near; punning on "goes to bed with."

VIOLA Nay, that's certain. They that dally nicely° with words   *play subtly*
may quickly make them wanton.[4]

15 CLOWN I would therefore my sister had had no name, sir.

VIOLA Why, man?

CLOWN Why, sir, her name's a word, and to dally with that
word might make my sister wanton. But, indeed, words are
very rascals since bonds disgraced them.[5]

20 VIOLA Thy reason, man?

CLOWN Troth, sir, I can yield you none without words, and
words are grown so false, I am loath to prove reason with them.

VIOLA I warrant thou art a merry fellow and car'st for nothing.

CLOWN Not so, sir, I do care for something. But in my con-
25 science, sir, I do not care for you. If that be to care for nothing, sir, I would it would make you invisible.

VIOLA Art not thou the Lady Olivia's fool?

CLOWN No indeed, sir, the Lady Olivia has no folly. She will
keep no fool, sir, till she be married, and fools are as like hus-
30 bands as pilchers[6] are to herrings—the husband's the bigger.
I am indeed not her fool, but her corrupter of words.

VIOLA I saw thee late° at the Count Orsino's.   *lately*

CLOWN Foolery, sir, does walk about the orb[7] like the sun. It
shines everywhere. I would be sorry, sir, but the fool should
35 be as oft with your master as with my mistress.[8] I think I
saw your wisdom[9] there.

VIOLA Nay, an thou pass upon[1] me, I'll no more with thee.
Hold, there's expenses for thee.
[*She gives him a coin.*]

CLOWN Now Jove in his next commodity° of hair send thee a   *shipment*
40 beard.

VIOLA By my troth, I'll tell thee, I am almost sick for one,[2]
though I would not have it grow on my chin. Is thy lady within?

CLOWN Would not a pair of these have bred,[3] sir?

VIOLA Yes, being kept together and put to use.[4]

45 CLOWN I would play Lord Pandarus[5] of Phrygia, sir, to bring
a Cressida to this Troilus.

VIOLA I understand you, sir. 'Tis well begged.
[*She gives him another coin.*]

CLOWN The matter I hope is not great, sir, begging but a beggar. Cressida was a beggar.[6] My lady is within, sir. I will
50 conster° to them whence you come. Who you are and what   *explain*
you would are out of my welkin. I might say "element," but
the word is overworn.[7]   *Exit.*

VIOLA This fellow is wise enough to play the fool
And to do that well craves a kind of wit.°   *intelligence*
55 He must observe their mood on whom he jests,
The quality of persons, and the time,
And, like the haggard, check at every feather
That comes before his eye.[8] This is a practice°   *skill*
As full of labor as a wise man's art.
60 For folly that he wisely shows is fit,[9]
But wise men, folly-fall'n, quite taint[1] their wit.

      Enter SIR TOBY *and* SIR ANDREW.

SIR TOBY Save you, gentleman.
VIOLA And you, sir.
SIR ANDREW *Dieu vous garde,*[2] *monsieur.*
65 VIOLA *Et vous aussi. Votre serviteur.*[3]
SIR ANDREW I hope, sir, you are, and I am yours.
SIR TOBY Will you encounter[4] the house? My niece is desirous
    you should enter, if your trade be to her.
VIOLA I am bound to° your niece, sir. I mean, she is the list° of   *for / destination*
70   my voyage.
SIR TOBY Taste° your legs, sir, put them to motion.   *Try*
VIOLA My legs do better understand° me, sir, than I understand   *stand under*
    what you mean by bidding me taste my legs.
SIR TOBY I mean, to go, sir, to enter.
75 VIOLA I will answer you with gate and entrance, but we are
    prevented.°   *anticipated*

      Enter OLIVIA *and* [MARIA, *her*] *gentlewoman.*

    Most excellent accomplished lady, the heavens rain odors on
    you.
SIR ANDREW [*to* SIR TOBY] That youth's a rare° courtier. "Rain   *an excellent*
80   odors," well.°   *well put*
VIOLA My matter hath no voice,° lady, but to your own most   *must not be spoken*
    pregnant° and vouchsafed° ear.   *receptive / proffered*
SIR ANDREW [*to* SIR TOBY] "Odors," "pregnant," and "vouch-
    safed." I'll get 'em all three all ready.[5]
85 OLIVIA Let the garden door be shut, and leave me to my hearing.

             [*Exeunt* SIR TOBY, SIR ANDREW, *and* MARIA.]

    Give me your hand, sir.
VIOLA My duty, madam, and most humble service.
OLIVIA What is your name?
VIOLA Cesario is your servant's name, fair princess.
90 OLIVIA My servant, sir? 'Twas never merry world[6]
    Since lowly feigning° was called compliment.   *pretended humility*
    You're servant to the Count Orsino, youth.
VIOLA And he is yours, and his must needs be yours.
    Your servant's servant is your servant, madam.
95 OLIVIA For° him, I think not on him. For his thoughts,   *As for*
    Would they were blanks rather than filled with me.

---

8. *And . . . eye:* As a wild hawk ("haggard") must be sensitive to its prey's disposition.
9. For folly that he skillfully displays is proper.
1. Discredit; spoil. *folly-fall'n:* fallen into folly.
2. God protect you (French).
3. And you also. (I am) your servant. (Sir Andrew's awkward reply demonstrates that his French is limited.)
4. Pedantry for "enter." (Toby mocks Viola's courtly language.)
5. *I'll . . . ready:* I'll commit them all to memory for later use.
6. *'Twas . . . world:* the proverbial "Things have never been the same."

VIOLA   Madam, I come to whet your gentle thoughts
        On his behalf.
OLIVIA   Oh, by your leave,[7] I pray you.
        I bade you never speak again of him.
100   But would you undertake another suit,
        I had rather hear you to solicit that
        Than music from the spheres.[8]
VIOLA   Dear lady—
OLIVIA   Give me leave, beseech you. I did send,
        After the last enchantment you did here,
105   A ring in chase of you. So did I abuse°   deceive; dishonor
        Myself, my servant, and I fear me you.°   and, as I fear, you
        Under your hard construction[9] must I sit
        To force° that on you in a shameful cunning   For forcing
        Which you knew none of yours. What might you think?
110   Have you not set mine honor at the stake,
        And baited it with all th'unmuzzled thoughts[1]
        That tyrannous heart can think? To one of your receiving°   perception
        Enough is shown. A cypress,[2] not a bosom,
        Hides my heart. So let me hear you speak.
VIOLA   I pity you.
115 OLIVIA   That's a degree to° love.   toward
VIOLA   No, not a grece,° for 'tis a vulgar proof°   step / common experience
        That very oft we pity enemies.
OLIVIA   Why, then methinks 'tis time to smile again.[3]
        O world, how apt° the poor are to be proud!   ready
120   If one should be a prey, how much the better
        To fall before the lion than the wolf.[4]
            Clock strikes.
        The clock upbraids me with the waste of time.
        Be not afraid, good youth, I will not have you.
        And yet when wit and youth is come to harvest,
125   Your wife is like to reap a proper° man.   handsome; worthy
        There lies your way, due west.
VIOLA   Then westward ho![5]
        Grace and good disposition° attend your ladyship.   peace of mind
        You'll nothing, madam, to my lord by me?
OLIVIA   Stay. I prithee, tell me what thou[6] think'st of me?
130 VIOLA   That you do think you are not what you are.[7]
OLIVIA   If I think so, I think the same of you.[8]
VIOLA   Then think you right. I am not what I am.
OLIVIA   I would you were as I would have you be.
VIOLA   Would it be better, madam, than I am?
135   I wish it might, for now I am your fool.[9]

---

7. Permit me to interrupt (polite expression).
8. Exquisite music thought to be made by the planets
as they moved, but inaudible to mortal ears.
9. Your unfavorable interpretation (of my behavior).
1. *set . . . thoughts*: as bears that were tied up at the
stake and baited with dogs.
2. Veil of transparent silken gauze; the cypress tree
was also emblematic of mourning.
3. Time to discard love's melancholy.
4. *If . . . wolf*: If I had to fall prey to love, it would
have been better to succumb to the noble Orsino

than to the hard-hearted Cesario.
5. Thames watermen's cry to attract passengers for
the court at Westminster from London.
6. Olivia changes from "you" to the familiar "thou."
7. In other words, that you think you are in love with
a man, but in fact you are in love with a woman.
8. Olivia may think that Cesario has suggested that
she is mad; or she may imply that she thinks that
Cesario, despite his subordinate position, is noble.
9. You have made a fool of me.

OLIVIA [*aside*]   Oh, what a deal of scorn looks beautiful
In the contempt and anger of his lip!
A murd'rous guilt shows not itself more soon
Than love that would seem hid. Love's night is noon.[1]
140 —Cesario, by the roses of the spring,
By maidhood, honor, truth, and everything,
I love thee so that, maugre° all thy pride,   *despite*
Nor° wit nor reason can my passion hide.   *Neither*
Do not extort thy reasons from this clause,[2]
145 For that° I woo thou therefore hast no cause.   *That because*
But rather reason thus with reason fetter;[3]
Love sought is good, but given unsought is better.
VIOLA   By innocence I swear, and by my youth,
I have one heart, one bosom, and one truth,
150 And that no woman has, nor never none
Shall mistress be of it, save I alone,
And so adieu, good madam. Never more
Will I my master's tears to you deplore.°   *lament*
OLIVIA   Yet come again. For thou perhaps mayst move
155 That heart, which now abhors, to like his love.   *Exeunt.*

3.2

Enter SIR TOBY, SIR ANDREW, *and* FABIAN.

SIR ANDREW   No, faith, I'll not stay a jot longer.
SIR TOBY   Thy reason, dear venom,° give thy reason.   *venomous one*
FABIAN   You must needs yield your reason, Sir Andrew.
SIR ANDREW   Marry, I saw your niece do more favors to the
5   Count's servingman than ever she bestowed upon me. I saw't
i'th' orchard.°   *garden*
SIR TOBY   Did she see thee the while, old boy, tell me that?
SIR ANDREW   As plain as I see you now.
FABIAN   This was a great argument° of love in her toward you.   *proof*
10 SIR ANDREW   'Slight,° will you make an ass o'me?   *By God's light*
FABIAN   I will prove it legitimate, sir, upon the oaths of judgment and reason.
SIR TOBY   And they have been grand-jury men[1] since before
Noah was a sailor.
15 FABIAN   She did show favor to the youth in your sight only to
exasperate you, to awake your dormouse° valor, to put fire in   *meek; timid*
your heart and brimstone in your liver. You should then have
accosted her and, with some excellent jests, fire-new from
the mint,° you should have banged the youth into dumbness.   *newly minted*
20 This was looked for at your hand and this was balked.° The   *neglected*
double gilt[2] of this opportunity you let time wash off, and
you are now sailed into the north of my lady's opinion,[3]
where you will hang like an icicle on a Dutchman's[4] beard,
unless you do redeem it by some laudable attempt either of
25 valor or policy.°   *cunning*

---

1. Love, though attempting secrecy, still shines out
as bright as day.
2. Do not take the position that just because I woo
you, you are under no obligation to reciprocate.
3. But instead constrain your reasoning with this
argument.
3.2 Location: Olivia's house.

1. Grand-jury men were supposed to be good judges
of evidence.
2. Twice gilded, and as such, Sir Andrew's "golden
opportunity" to prove both love and valor.
3. Into Olivia's cold disfavor.
4. Perhaps an allusion to navigator Willem Barents,
who led an expedition to the Arctic in 1596–97.

SIR ANDREW   An't° be any way, it must be with valor, for policy   *If it*
I hate. I had as lief° be a Brownist as a politician.[5]   *as soon*

SIR TOBY   Why, then, build me thy fortunes upon the basis of
valor. Challenge me° the Count's youth to fight with him,   *for me*
30   hurt him in eleven places. My niece shall take note of it, and,
assure thyself, there is no love-broker in the world can more
prevail in man's commendation with woman than report of
valor.

FABIAN   There is no way but this, Sir Andrew.

35   SIR ANDREW   Will either of you bear me a challenge to him?

SIR TOBY   Go, write it in a martial hand. Be curst° and brief. It   *sharp*
is no matter how witty, so it be eloquent and full of invention.°   *imagination; untruth*
Taunt him with the license of ink.[6] If thou thou'st[7] him
some thrice, it shall not be amiss, and as many lies° as will   *accusations of lying*
40   lie in thy sheet of paper, although the sheet were big enough
for the bed of Ware[8] in England, set 'em down, go about it.
Let there be gall[9] enough in thy ink, though thou write with
a goose-pen,[1] no matter. About it.

SIR ANDREW   Where shall I find you?

45   SIR TOBY   We'll call thee at the cubiculo.° Go.   *little chamber*

                    Exit SIR ANDREW.

FABIAN   This is a dear manikin° to you, Sir Toby.   *puppet*

SIR TOBY   I have been dear° to him, lad, some two thousand   *costly*
strong or so.

FABIAN   We shall have a rare letter from him. But you'll not
50   deliver't?

SIR TOBY   Never trust me, then. And by all means stir on the
youth to an answer. I think oxen and wain-ropes[2] cannot hale°   *drag*
them together. For Andrew, if he were opened and you find
so much blood in his liver[3] as will clog° the foot of a flea, I'll   *weigh down*
55   eat the rest of th'anatomy.°   *cadaver*

FABIAN   And his opposite° the youth bears in his visage no   *adversary*
great presage of cruelty.

                    Enter MARIA.

SIR TOBY   Look where the youngest wren of mine comes.

MARIA   If you desire the spleen° and will laugh yourselves into   *a laughing fit*
60   stitches, follow me. Yon gull° Malvolio is turned heathen, a   *fool*
very renegado.[4] For there is no Christian that means to be
saved by believing rightly can ever believe such impossible
passages of grossness.[5] He's in yellow stockings.

SIR TOBY   And cross-gartered?

65   MARIA   Most villainously,° like a pedant° that keeps a school   *abominably / teacher*
i'th' church.[6] I have dogged him like his murderer. He does
obey every point of the letter that I dropped to betray him.
He does smile his face into more lines than is in the new

---

5. A schemer. A Brownist was a member of the puritan sect founded in 1581 by Robert Browne.
6. *license of ink:* freedom taken in writing, but not risked in conversation.
7. Call him "thou" (an insult to a stranger).
8. Famous Elizabethan bedstead, nearly eleven feet square, now in the Victoria and Albert Museum, London.
9. Oak gall, an ingredient in ink; bitterness or rancor.
1. A quill made of a goose feather. (The goose was proverbially cowardly and foolish.)
2. Wagon ropes pulled by oxen.
3. Supposed to be the source of blood, which engendered courage.
4. Renegade (Spanish); a Christian converted to Islam.
5. Such patent absurdities (in the letter).
6. Because no schoolroom is available in a small rustic community.

map with the augmentation of the Indies.[7] You have not
70   seen such a thing as 'tis. I can hardly forbear hurling things
at him. I know my lady will strike him. If she do, he'll smile
and take't for a great favor.

SIR TOBY   Come, bring us, bring us where he is.   *Exeunt.*

3.3

Enter SEBASTIAN *and* ANTONIO.

SEBASTIAN   I would not by my will have troubled you,
    But, since you make your pleasure of your pains,
    I will no further chide you.

ANTONIO   I could not stay behind you. My desire,
5   More sharp than filèd steel, did spur me forth.
    And not all° love to see you, though so much   *only*
    As might have drawn one to a longer voyage,
    But jealousy° what might befall your travel,   *apprehension*
    Being skill-less in° these parts which, to a stranger   *unfamiliar to*
10   Unguided and unfriended, often prove
    Rough and unhospitable. My willing love,
    The rather° by these arguments of fear,   *more willingly*
    Set forth in your pursuit.

SEBASTIAN   My kind Antonio,
    I can no other answer make but thanks
15   And thanks. And ever oft,° good turns   *very often*
    Are shuffled off° with such uncurrent[1] pay.   *shrugged off*
    But were my worth as is my conscience° firm,   *sense of indebtedness*
    You should find better dealing. What's to do?
    Shall we go see the relics° of this town?   *sights*

20 ANTONIO   Tomorrow, sir. Best first go see your lodging.

SEBASTIAN   I am not weary, and 'tis long to night.
    I pray you, let us satisfy our eyes
    With the memorials and the things of fame
    That do renown this city.

ANTONIO   Would you'd pardon me.
25   I do not without danger walk these streets.
    Once in a sea-fight 'gainst the Count his° galleys   *(the Count's)*
    I did some service, of such note indeed
    That were I ta'en° here it would scarce be answered.[2]   *captured*

SEBASTIAN   Belike° you slew great number of his people?   *Perhaps*

30 ANTONIO   Th'offense is not of such a bloody nature,
    Albeit the quality° of the time and quarrel   *circumstances*
    Might well have given us bloody argument.°   *cause for bloodshed*
    It might have since been answered in repaying
    What we took from them, which for traffic's° sake   *trade's*
35   Most of our city did. Only myself stood out,
    For which, if I be lapsèd° in this place,   *caught*
    I shall pay dear.

SEBASTIAN   Do not then walk too open.

ANTONIO   It doth not fit me. Hold, sir, here's my purse.

---

7. Possibly refers to a map published in 1599 showing the East Indies more fully than in earlier maps
and crisscrossed by many rhumb lines.
3.3 Location: A street scene.

1. Out of currency; worthless.
2. It would be difficult for me to make reparation
(and thus my life would be in danger).

In the south suburbs at the Elephant[3]
40 Is best to lodge. I will bespeak our diet°   *order our meals*
Whiles you beguile° the time and feed your knowledge   *pass*
With viewing of the town. There shall you have me.
SEBASTIAN   Why I your purse?
ANTONIO   Haply° your eye shall light upon some toy°   *Perhaps / trifle*
45 You have desire to purchase, and your store,°   *resources*
I think, is not for idle markets,[4] sir.
SEBASTIAN   I'll be your purse-bearer and leave you
For an hour.
ANTONIO   To th'Elephant.
SEBASTIAN   I do remember.   *Exeunt.*

3.4

Enter OLIVIA *and* MARIA.

OLIVIA [*aside*]   I have sent after him. He says he'll come.
How shall I feast him? What bestow of° him?   *on*
For youth is bought more oft than begged or borrowed.[1]
I speak too loud.
5 —Where's Malvolio? He is sad,° and civil,°   *sober / respectful*
And suits well for a servant with my fortunes.
Where is Malvolio?
MARIA   He's coming, madam, but in very strange manner. He
is sure possessed,° madam.   *(by the devil); insane*
10 OLIVIA   Why, what's the matter? Does he rave?
MARIA   No, madam, he does nothing but smile. Your ladyship
were best to have some guard about you if he come, for sure
the man is tainted in 's wits.
OLIVIA   Go, call him hither.   [*Exit* MARIA.]
                    I am as mad as he,
15 If sad and merry madness equal be.
          Enter MALVOLIO [*with* MARIA].
How now, Malvolio?
MALVOLIO   Sweet lady, ho, ho.
OLIVIA   Smil'st thou? I sent for thee upon a sad occasion.°   *about a serious matter*
MALVOLIO   Sad, lady? I could be sad. This does make some
20 obstruction in the blood, this cross-gartering. But what of
that? If it please the eye of one, it is with me as the very true
sonnet° is: "please one, and please all."[2]   *song*
OLIVIA   Why, how dost thou, man? What is the matter with
thee?
25 MALVOLIO   Not black in my mind, though yellow[3] in my legs.
It did come to his hands, and commands shall be executed.
I think we do know the sweet Roman hand.°   *italic calligraphy*
OLIVIA   Wilt thou go to bed,[4] Malvolio?
MALVOLIO   To bed? "Ay, sweetheart, and I'll come to thee."[5]
30 OLIVIA   God comfort thee! Why dost thou smile so and kiss
thy hand so oft?

---

3. An inn with this name did in fact exist on Bank-
side, near the Globe. The area was notorious for its
many brothels.
4. Not large enough to spend on luxuries.
3.4 Location: The garden of Olivia's house.
1. "Better to buy than to beg or borrow" was
proverbial.
2. If I please one, I please all I care to please (words

of a popular bawdy ballad).
3. Black and yellow bile indicated choleric and melancholic dispositions, respectively. "Black and yellow" was the name of a popular song; to "wear yellow
hose" was to be jealous.
4. In order to cure his madness with sleep.
5. A line from a popular song.

MARIA How do you, Malvolio?

MALVOLIO At your request. Yes, nightingales answer daws.[6]

MARIA Why appear you with this ridiculous boldness before
35 my lady?

MALVOLIO "Be not afraid of greatness." 'Twas well writ.

OLIVIA What mean'st thou by that, Malvolio?

MALVOLIO "Some are born great."

OLIVIA Ha?

40 MALVOLIO "Some achieve greatness."

OLIVIA What say'st thou?

MALVOLIO "And some have greatness thrust upon them."

OLIVIA Heaven restore thee.

MALVOLIO "Remember who commended thy yellow
45 stockings"—

OLIVIA Thy yellow stockings?

MALVOLIO "And wished to see thee cross-gartered."

OLIVIA Cross-gartered?

MALVOLIO "Go to. Thou art made, if thou desir'st to be so."

50 OLIVIA Am I made?

MALVOLIO "If not, let me see thee a servant still."

OLIVIA Why, this is very midsummer madness.

    Enter SERVANT.

SERVANT Madam, the young gentleman of the Count Orsino's is returned. I could hardly entreat him back. He attends
55 your ladyship's pleasure.

OLIVIA I'll come to him.   [*Exit* SERVANT.]
Good Maria, let this fellow be looked to. Where's my cousin
Toby? Let some of my people have a special care of him. I
would not have him miscarry° for the half of my dowry.   *come to harm*

    Exeunt [OLIVIA *and* MARIA].

60 MALVOLIO Oh, ho, do you come near° me now? No worse man   *appreciate*
than Sir Toby to look to me. This concurs directly with the
letter. She sends him on purpose that I may appear stubborn
to him, for she incites me to that in the letter. "Cast thy
humble slough," says she. "Be opposite with a kinsman, surly
65 with servants, let thy tongue tang with arguments of state,
put thyself into the trick of singularity." And consequently°   *subsequently*
sets down the manner how—as a sad face, a reverend car-
riage, a slow tongue, in the habit of some sir of note,° and so   *gentleman*
forth. I have limed[7] her. But it is Jove's doing, and Jove make
70 me thankful. And when she went away now—"let this fellow
be looked to." "Fellow"![8] Not "Malvolio," nor after my degree,
but "fellow." Why, everything adheres together, that no dram
of a scruple, no scruple of a scruple,[9] no obstacle, no incredulous or unsafe circumstance—what can be said? Nothing
75 that can be can come between me and the full prospect of
my hopes. Well, Jove, not I, is the doer of this, and he is to be
thanked.

    Enter SIR TOBY, FABIAN, *and* MARIA.

SIR TOBY Which way is he, in the name of sanctity? If all the

---

6. Shall I deign to reply to you? Yes, since even the
nightingale sings in response to the crowing of the
jackdaw.
7. Birds were caught by smearing sticky birdlime on
branches.

8. Malvolio takes the word to mean "companion."
9. *no dram . . . scruple:* both phrases mean "no scrap
of a doubt." *dram:* one-eighth of a fluid ounce. *scruple:* one-third of a dram.

devils of hell be drawn in little,[1] and Legion[2] himself pos-
80 sessed him, yet I'll speak to him.

FABIAN Here he is, here he is. [*to* MALVOLIO] How is't with
you, sir? How is't with you, man?

MALVOLIO Go off, I discard you. Let me enjoy my private.° Go   *privacy*
off.

85 MARIA Lo, how hollow° the fiend speaks within him. Did not   *resonantly*
I tell you? Sir Toby, my lady prays you to have a care of him.

MALVOLIO Ah ha, does she so?

SIR TOBY Go to, go to. Peace, peace, we must deal gently with
him. Let me alone.° —How do you, Malvolio? How is't with   *Leave him to me*
90 you? What, man, defy the devil. Consider, he's an enemy to
mankind.

MALVOLIO Do you know what you say?

MARIA La° you, an you speak ill of the devil, how he takes it   *Look*
at heart. Pray God he be not bewitched.

95 FABIAN Carry his water to th' wise woman.[3]

MARIA Marry, and it shall be done tomorrow morning if I
live. My lady would not lose him for more than I'll say.

MALVOLIO How now, mistress?

MARIA O Lord.

100 SIR TOBY Prithee, hold thy peace. This is not the way. Do you
not see you move° him? Let me alone with him.   *anger*

FABIAN No way but gentleness, gently, gently. The fiend is
rough° and will not be roughly used.   *violent*

SIR TOBY Why, how now, my bawcock?[4] How dost thou, chuck?

105 MALVOLIO Sir.

SIR TOBY Ay, biddy,° come with me. What, man, 'tis not for grav-   *hen*
ity° to play at cherry-pit[5] with Satan. Hang him, foul collier.[6]   *for a man of dignity*

MARIA Get him to say his prayers, good Sir Toby. Get him to
pray.

110 MALVOLIO My prayers, minx?°   *impertinent girl*

MARIA No, I warrant you, he will not hear of godliness.

MALVOLIO Go, hang yourselves all. You are idle° shallow things.   *foolish*
I am not of your element.° You shall know more hereafter.   *social sphere*

                                    Exit.

SIR TOBY Is't possible?

115 FABIAN If this were played upon a stage now, I could condemn it as an improbable fiction.

SIR TOBY His very genius° hath taken the infection of the   *spirit*
device,° man.   *trick*

MARIA Nay, pursue him now, lest the device take air and taint.[7]

120 FABIAN Why, we shall make him mad indeed.

MARIA The house will be the quieter.

SIR TOBY Come, we'll have him in a dark room and bound.[8] My
niece is already in the belief that he's mad. We may carry it

---

1. Be contracted into a small space (punning on
"painted in miniature").
2. Alluding to a scene of exorcism in Mark 5:8–9:
"For he [Jesus] said unto him, Come out of the man,
thou unclean spirit. And he asked him, What is thy
name? And he answered saying, My name is Legion:
for we are many."
3. *water*: urine (for medical diagnosis). *wise woman*:
local healer, "good witch."

4. Fine fellow (from the French *beau coq*, "fine bird").
5. A children's game in which cherrystones were
thrown into a hole.
6. Dirty coal man (the devil was supposed to be
black).
7. Spoil (like leftover food) by exposure to air; become
known (and thus ruined).
8. Customary treatments for madness.

125 thus° for our pleasure and his penance till our very pastime,   *continue the pretense*
tired out of breath, prompt us to have mercy on him. At which
time, we will bring the device to the bar[9] and crown thee for
a finder of madmen.[1] But see, but see.

Enter SIR ANDREW.

FABIAN   More matter for a May morning.[2]

SIR ANDREW [*presenting a paper*]   Here's the challenge. Read
130 it. I warrant there's vinegar and pepper in't.

FABIAN   Is't so saucy?

SIR ANDREW   Ay, is't. I warrant him. Do but read.

SIR TOBY   Give me. [*He reads.*] "Youth, whatsoever thou art,
thou art but a scurvy fellow."

135 FABIAN   Good and valiant.

SIR TOBY   "Wonder not, nor admire° not in thy mind why I do   *marvel*
call thee so, for I will show thee no reason for't."

FABIAN   A good note, that keeps you from the blow of the law.[3]

SIR TOBY   "Thou com'st to the Lady Olivia, and in my sight she
140 uses thee kindly. But thou liest in thy throat.° That is not   *deeply*
the matter I challenge thee for."

FABIAN   Very brief and to exceeding good sense—less.[4]

SIR TOBY   "I will waylay thee going home, where if it be thy
chance to kill me—"

145 FABIAN   Good.

SIR TOBY   "Thou kill'st me like a rogue and a villain."

FABIAN   Still you keep o'th' windy side[5] of the law. Good.

SIR TOBY   "Fare thee well, and God have mercy upon one of
our souls. He may have mercy upon mine, but my hope is
150 better,[6] and so look to thyself. Thy friend, as thou usest him,
and thy sworn enemy, Andrew Aguecheek."

SIR TOBY   If this letter move° him not, his legs cannot. I'll   *provoke*
give't him.

MARIA   You may have very fit occasion for't. He is now in some
155 commerce° with my lady, and will by and by depart.   *conversation*

SIR TOBY   Go, Sir Andrew, scout me° for him at the corner of   *look out*
the orchard like a bumbaily.[7] So soon as ever thou seest him,
draw and, as thou draw'st, swear horrible. For it comes to
pass oft that a terrible oath, with a swaggering accent sharply
160 twanged off, gives manhood more approbation° than ever   *credit*
proof° itself would have earned him. Away.   *trial*

SIR ANDREW   Nay, let me alone for swearing.[8]   *Exit.*

SIR TOBY   Now will not I deliver his letter. For the behavior of
the young gentleman gives him out to be of good capacity°   *ability*
165 and breeding. His employment between his lord and my
niece confirms no less. Therefore, this letter, being so excellently ignorant, will breed no terror in the youth. He will
find it comes from a clodpoll.° But, sir, I will deliver his   *blockhead*
challenge by word of mouth, set upon Aguecheek a notable

9. Into the open court (to be judged).
1. *finder of madmen*: one of a jury "finding," or
declaring, a man to be mad.
2. More pastime fit for a holiday.
3. That protects you from a charge of a breach of
peace.
4. F's "sence-lesse" appears to use the hyphen to signal an aside.

5. To windward (and therefore safe, not exposed to
the law's blasts).
6. *my hope is better*: Andrew means that he expects
to survive, but he ineptly implies that he expects to
be damned.
7. A petty sheriff's officer employed to arrest debtors.
8. Have no doubts as to my swearing ability.

170 report of valor, and drive the gentleman—as I know his
youth will aptly receive it[9]—into a most hideous opinion of
his rage, skill, fury, and impetuosity. This will so fright
them both that they will kill one another by the look, like
cockatrices.[1]

    Enter OLIVIA *and* VIOLA [*as Cesario*].

175 FABIAN Here he comes with your niece. Give them way° till   *Stand aside*
he take leave and presently after him.
    SIR TOBY I will meditate the while upon some horrid message
for a challenge.   [*Exeunt* SIR TOBY, MARIA, *and* FABIAN.]
    OLIVIA I have said too much unto a heart of stone
180 And laid mine honor too unchary° on't.   *carelessly*
There's something in me that reproves my fault,
But such a headstrong potent fault it is
That it but mocks reproof.
    VIOLA With the same 'havior that your passion bears[2]
185 Goes on my master's griefs.
    OLIVIA Here, wear this jewel[3] for me. 'Tis my picture.
Refuse it not. It hath no tongue to vex you.
And I beseech you come again tomorrow.
What shall you ask of me that I'll deny,
190 That honor, saved, may upon asking give?[4]
    VIOLA Nothing but this: your true love for my master.
    OLIVIA How with mine honor may I give him that
Which I have given to you?
    VIOLA   I will acquit you.[5]
    OLIVIA Well, come again tomorrow. Fare thee well.
195 A fiend like thee might bear my soul to hell.   [*Exit.*]

    Enter SIR TOBY *and* FABIAN.

    SIR TOBY Gentleman, God save thee.
    VIOLA And you, sir.
    SIR TOBY That defense thou hast, betake thee to't. Of what
nature the wrongs are thou hast done him I know not, but
200 thy intercepter, full of despite,° bloody as the hunter, attends°   *defiance / awaits*
thee at the orchard end. Dismount thy tuck,[6] be yare° in thy   *prompt*
preparation, for thy assailant is quick, skillful, and deadly.
    VIOLA You mistake, sir, I am sure. No man hath any quarrel
to me. My remembrance° is very free and clear from any   *memory*
205 image of offense done to any man.
    SIR TOBY You'll find it otherwise, I assure you. Therefore, if
you hold your life at any price, betake you to your guard. For
your opposite° hath in him what youth, strength, skill, and   *opponent*
wrath can furnish man withal.
210 VIOLA I pray you, sir, what is he?
    SIR TOBY He is knight dubbed with unhatched[7] rapier and on
carpet consideration,[8] but he is a devil in private brawl.
Souls and bodies hath he divorced three, and his incense-

9. As I know his inexperience will readily believe the
report.
1. Basilisks; mythical creatures supposed to be able
to kill at a glance.
2. *'havior . . . bears:* behavior that characterizes your
lovesickness.
3. Jeweled ornament; here, a brooch or a locket with
Olivia's picture.

4. That honor may grant without compromising
itself.
5. I will release you from your promise.
6. Draw your rapier.
7. Unhacked, or undented; never used in battle.
8. A "carpet knight" obtained his title through connections at court rather than valor on the battlefield.

ment at this moment is so implacable that satisfaction can
215 be none but by pangs of death and sepulcher. "Hob, nob,"⁹ is
his word,° "give't or take't."   *motto*
VIOLA   I will return again into the house and desire some con-
duct° of the lady. I am no fighter. I have heard of some kind   *escort*
of men that put quarrels purposely on others to taste° their   *test*
220 valor. Belike this is a man of that quirk.
SIR TOBY   Sir, no. His indignation derives itself out of a very
competent° injury. Therefore, get you on and give him his   *sufficient*
desire. Back you shall not to the house, unless you undertake that° with me which with as much safety you might   *(a duel)*
225 answer him. Therefore on, or strip your sword stark naked.
For meddle° you must, that's certain, or forswear to wear   *engage in a duel*
iron about you.¹
VIOLA   This is as uncivil as strange. I beseech you do me this
courteous office, as to know of° the knight what my offense   *ascertain from*
230 to him is. It is something of my negligence, nothing of my
purpose.
SIR TOBY   I will do so. Signor Fabian, stay you by this gentleman till my return.   *Exit.*
VIOLA   Pray you, sir, do you know of this matter?
235 FABIAN   I know the knight is incensed against you even to a
mortal arbitrament,° but nothing of the circumstance more.   *deadly duel*
VIOLA   I beseech you, what manner of man is he?
FABIAN   Nothing of that wonderful promise to read him by his
form² as you are like to find him in the proof of his valor. He
240 is indeed, sir, the most skillful, bloody, and fatal opposite that
you could possibly have found in any part of Illyria. Will you
walk towards him? I will make your peace with him, if I can.
VIOLA   I shall be much bound to you for't. I am one that had
rather go with Sir Priest³ than Sir Knight. I care not who
245 knows so much of my mettle.°   *Exeunt.*   *disposition*
    Enter SIR TOBY *and* SIR ANDREW.
SIR TOBY   Why, man, he's a very devil. I have not seen such a
virago.⁴ I had a pass° with him, rapier, scabbard, and all, and   *fencing bout*
he gives me the stuck-in⁵ with such a mortal motion that it
is inevitable. And on the answer,° he pays you as surely as   *return hit*
250 your feet hits the ground they step on. They say he has been
fencer to the Sophy.°   *Shah of Persia*
SIR ANDREW   Pox on't, I'll not meddle with him.
SIR TOBY   Ay, but he will not now be pacified. Fabian can
scarce hold him yonder.
255 SIR ANDREW   Plague on't, an° I thought he had been valiant   *if*
and so cunning in fence, I'd have seen him damned ere I'd
have challenged him. Let him let the matter slip and I'll give
him my horse, gray Capilet.
SIR TOBY   I'll make the motion.° Stand here, make a good show   *offer*
260 on't. This shall end without the perdition of souls.° [*aside*]   *loss of lives*
Marry, I'll ride your horse as well as I ride you.
    · *Enter* FABIAN *and* VIOLA [*as Cesario*].

---

9. Have or have not ("all or nothing").
1. Or forfeit your right to wear a sword.
2. *Nothing . . . form:* From his outward appearance,
you cannot perceive him to be as remarkable.

3. Priests were often addressed as "sir."
4. A woman warrior (suggesting great ferocity with a
feminine appearance).
5. The thrust (from the Italian *stoccata*).

[*aside to* FABIAN]   I have his horse to take up° the quarrel. I   settle
have persuaded him the youth's a devil.
FABIAN [*aside*]   He is as horribly conceited[6] of him, and pants
265   and looks pale as if a bear were at his heels.
SIR TOBY   There's no remedy, sir, he will fight with you for 's
oath sake. Marry, he hath better bethought him of his quarrel, and he finds that now scarce to be worth talking of.
Therefore, draw for the supportance of his vow. He protests
270   he will not hurt you.
VIOLA [*aside*]   Pray God defend me. A little thing would make
me tell them how much I lack of a man.
FABIAN   Give ground if you see him furious.
SIR TOBY   Come, Sir Andrew, there's no remedy. The gentleman
275   will for his honor's sake have one bout with you. He cannot by
the duello° avoid it. But he has promised me, as he is a gentle-   code of dueling
man and a soldier, he will not hurt you. Come on, to't.
SIR ANDREW [*drawing his sword*]   Pray God he keep his oath.
          Enter ANTONIO.
VIOLA [*drawing her sword*]   I do assure you 'tis against my will.
280   ANTONIO [*drawing his sword*]   Put up your sword. If this young
          gentleman
Have done offense, I take the fault on me.
If you offend him, I for him defy you.
SIR TOBY   You, sir? Why, what are you?
ANTONIO   One, sir, that for his love dares yet do more
285   Than you have heard him brag to you he will.
SIR TOBY [*drawing his sword*]   Nay, if you be an undertaker,[7]
I am for you.
          Enter OFFICERS.
FABIAN   O good Sir Toby, hold. Here come the officers.
SIR TOBY [*to* ANTONIO]   I'll be with you anon.
290   VIOLA [*to* SIR ANDREW]   Pray, sir, put your sword up, if you please.
SIR ANDREW   Marry, will I, sir. And for that° I promised you, I'll   as for that
be as good as my word. He will bear you easily and reins well.
FIRST OFFICER   This is the man; do thy office.
SECOND OFFICER   Antonio, I arrest thee at the suit of Count
295   Orsino.
ANTONIO   You do mistake me, sir.
FIRST OFFICER   No, sir, no jot. I know your favor° well,   face
Though now you have no sea cap on your head.
—Take him away. He knows I know him well.
300   ANTONIO   I must obey. [*to* VIOLA] This comes with seeking you.
But there's no remedy, I shall answer° it.   answer for
What will you do now my necessity
Makes me to ask you for my purse? It grieves me
Much more for what I cannot do for you
305   Than what befalls myself. You stand amazed,
But be of comfort.
SECOND OFFICER   Come, sir, away.
ANTONIO   I must entreat of you some of that money.
VIOLA   What money, sir?

6. He has as terrifying an idea.   7. One who would take upon himself a task (here, a
                                        challenge).

For the fair kindness you have showed me here,
310 And part° being prompted by your present trouble,   *in part*
Out of my lean and low ability
I'll lend you something. My having is not much.
I'll make division of my present° with you.   *ready money*
Hold, there's half my coffer.
[*She offers him money.*]
ANTONIO   Will you deny me now?
315 Is't possible that my deserts to you
Can lack persuasion?[8] Do not tempt my misery,
Lest that it make me so unsound° a man   *morally weak*
As to upbraid you with those kindnesses
That I have done for you.
VIOLA   I know of none,
320 Nor know I you by voice or any feature.
I hate ingratitude more in a man
Than lying, vainness, babbling drunkenness,
Or any taint of vice whose strong corruption
Inhabits our frail blood.
ANTONIO   Oh, heavens themselves!
325 SECOND OFFICER Come, sir, I pray you go.
ANTONIO   Let me speak a little. This youth that you see here,
I snatched one half out of the jaws of death,
Relieved him with such sanctity° of love,   *great devotion*
And to his image,[9] which methought did promise
330 Most venerable worth,[1] did I devotion.
SECOND OFFICER What's that to us? The time goes by. Away!
ANTONIO   But oh, how vile an idol proves this god!
Thou hast, Sebastian, done good feature° shame.   *physical beauty*
In nature there's no blemish but the mind.
335 None can be called deformed but the unkind.
Virtue is beauty, but the beauteous evil
Are empty trunks, o'er-flourished[2] by the devil.
FIRST OFFICER The man grows mad, away with him. —Come,
come, sir.
ANTONIO   Lead me on.   *Exeunt* [ANTONIO *and* OFFICERS].
340 VIOLA [*aside*]   Methinks his words do from such passion fly
That he believes himself. So do not I.[3]
Prove true, imagination, oh, prove true,
That I, dear brother, be now ta'en for you.
SIR TOBY   Come hither, knight; come hither, Fabian. We'll
345 whisper o'er a couplet or two of most sage saws.°   *sayings; maxims*
[*They step aside.*]
VIOLA   He named Sebastian. I my brother know
Yet living in my glass.° Even such and so   *mirror*
In favor° was my brother, and he went   *appearance*
Still° in this fashion, color, ornament,   *Always*
350 For him I imitate. Oh, if it prove,
Tempests are kind, and salt waves fresh in love!   [*Exit.*]

---

8. *Is't . . . persuasion:* Is it possible that my past kindness can fail to persuade you?
9. Appearance (with a play on "religious icon").
1. *did . . . worth:* was worthy of veneration.

2. Chests decorated with carving or painting; beautified bodies.
3. *So do not I:* I do not entirely believe the passionate
hope (for my brother's rescue) that is arising in me.

SIR TOBY A very dishonest° paltry boy, and more a coward   *dishonorable*
    than a hare. His dishonesty appears in leaving his friend
    here in necessity and denying him. And for his cowardship,
355   ask Fabian.
FABIAN A coward, a most devout coward, religious in it.
SIR ANDREW 'Slid,° I'll after him again, and beat him.   *By God's eyelid*
SIR TOBY Do, cuff him soundly, but never draw thy sword.
SIR ANDREW An I do not—   [*Exit.*]
360 FABIAN Come, let's see the event.°   *outcome*
SIR TOBY I dare lay any money, 'twill be nothing yet.°   *after all*

                     Exeunt.

4.1

Enter SEBASTIAN *and* CLOWN.

CLOWN Will you° make me believe that I am not sent for you?   *Are you trying to*
SEBASTIAN Go to, go to, thou art a foolish fellow. Let me be
    clear° of thee.   *rid*
CLOWN Well held out,° i'faith. No, I do not know you, nor I   *kept up*
5   am not sent to you by my lady to bid you come speak with
    her, nor your name is not Master Cesario, nor this is not my
    nose neither. Nothing that is so, is so.
SEBASTIAN I prithee vent° thy folly somewhere else. Thou   *utter; excrete*
    know'st not me.
10 CLOWN "Vent my folly." He has heard that word of some great
    man and now applies it to a fool. "Vent my folly." I am afraid
    this great lubber° the world will prove a cockney.° —I prithee   *lout / sissy*
    now, ungird thy strangeness[1] and tell me what I shall vent to
    my lady? Shall I vent to her that thou art coming?
15 SEBASTIAN I prithee, foolish Greek,° depart from me. There's   *buffoon*
    money for thee. If you tarry longer, I shall give worse
    payment.
CLOWN By my troth, thou hast an open hand. These wise men
    that give fools money get themselves a good report,° after   *reputation*
20   fourteen years' purchase.[2]

Enter SIR ANDREW, SIR TOBY, *and* FABIAN.

SIR ANDREW Now, sir, have I met you again. There's for you.
    [*He strikes* SEBASTIAN.]
SEBASTIAN Why, there's for thee, and there, and there. [*He*
    strikes SIR ANDREW.] Are all the people mad?
SIR TOBY Hold, sir, or I'll throw your dagger o'er the house.
25 CLOWN This will I tell my lady straight.° I would not be in   *straightaway*
    some of your coats for twopence.   [*Exit.*]
SIR TOBY Come on, sir, hold.
SIR ANDREW Nay, let him alone. I'll go another way to work
    with him. I'll have an action of battery° against him, if there   *a lawsuit for assault*
30   be any law in Illyria. Though I struck him first, yet it's no
    matter for that.
SEBASTIAN [*to* SIR TOBY] Let go thy hand.
SIR TOBY Come, sir, I will not let you go. Come, my young
    soldier, put up your iron. You are well fleshed.[3] Come on.

4.1 Location: Near Olivia's house.
1. *I . . . strangeness:* Stop pretending not to know me.
(The Clown mocks Sebastian's affected language.)
2. *after . . . purchase:* at a high price. The purchase

price of land was normally twelve times its annual
rent.
3. Experienced in combat. Hunting hounds were said
to be "fleshed" after being fed part of their first kill.

35 SEBASTIAN   I will be free from thee. [*He draws his sword.*] What
wouldst thou now? If thou dar'st tempt me further, draw thy
sword.
   SIR TOBY   What, what? [*He draws his sword.*] Nay, then, I must
have an ounce or two of this malapert° blood from you.   *impudent*
       Enter OLIVIA.
40 OLIVIA   Hold, Toby, on thy life, I charge thee hold!
   SIR TOBY   Madam.
   OLIVIA   Will it be ever thus? Ungracious wretch,
Fit for the mountains and the barbarous caves
Where manners ne'er were preached, out of my sight!
45 Be not offended, dear Cesario.
—Rudesby,° be gone.   *Ruffian*
       [*Exeunt* SIR TOBY, SIR ANDREW, *and* FABIAN.]
              I prithee, gentle friend,
Let thy fair wisdom, not thy passion, sway
In this uncivil and unjust extent°   *assault*
Against thy peace. Go with me to my house,
50 And hear thou there how many fruitless pranks
This ruffian hath botched up,° that thou thereby   *clumsily contrived*
Mayst smile at this. Thou shalt not choose but go.
Do not deny. Beshrew° his soul for me,   *Curse*
He started one poor heart of mine in thee.[4]
55 SEBASTIAN [*aside*]   What relish° is in this? How runs the   *task; meaning*
stream?
Or° I am mad, or else this is a dream.   *Either*
Let fancy° still my sense in Lethe[5] steep.   *imagination*
If it be thus to dream, still let me sleep.
   OLIVIA   Nay, come, I prithee. Would thou'dst be ruled by me!
   SEBASTIAN   Madam, I will.
60 OLIVIA   Oh, say so, and so be.   *Exeunt.*

4.2

      Enter MARIA [*carrying a costume*] *and* CLOWN.
   MARIA   Nay, I prithee put on this gown and this beard. Make
him believe thou art Sir Topas[1] the curate. Do it quickly. I'll
call Sir Toby the whilst.°   [*Exit.*]   *in the meantime*
   CLOWN   Well, I'll put it on, and I will dissemble[2] myself in't.
5 [*He puts on gown and beard.*] And I would I were the first
that ever dissembled in such a gown. I am not tall enough to
become the function well[3] nor lean enough to be thought a
good student.° But to be said° an honest man and a good   *(of divinity) / reputed*
housekeeper° goes as fairly as[4] to say a careful man and a   *host*
10 great scholar. The competitors° enter.   *associates*
      Enter SIR TOBY [*and* MARIA].
   SIR TOBY   Jove bless thee, Master Parson.

---

4. *He . . . thee:* By attacking Sebastian, Sir Toby frightened Olivia, who has exchanged hearts with Sebastian.
started: an allusion to hunting, creating a pun on
"hart/heart."
5. The mythical river of oblivion.
4.2 Location: Olivia's house, where Malvolio will be
found "in a dark room and bound" (3.4.122).

1. The comical hero of Chaucer's *Rime of Sir Topas.*
Also alluding to the mineral topaz, which was thought
to have special curative qualities for insanity.
2. Disguise; with a subsequent play on "lie."
3. To grace the priestly office. *tall:* stout, rather than
of great height.
4. *goes as fairly as:* sounds as well as.

CLOWN   *Bonos dies*,[5] Sir Toby. For, as the old hermit of Prague[6]
that never saw pen and ink very wittily° said to a niece of King   *intelligently*
Gorboduc,° "That that is, is." So I, being Master Parson, am   *legendary British king*
15   Master Parson. For what is "that" but "that," and "is" but "is"?
SIR TOBY   To him, Sir Topas.
CLOWN   What ho, I say, peace in this prison!
SIR TOBY   The knave counterfeits well. A good knave.
MALVOLIO (*within*)[7]   Who calls there?
20   CLOWN   Sir Topas the curate, who comes to visit Malvolio the
lunatic.
MALVOLIO   Sir Topas, Sir Topas, good Sir Topas, go to my lady.
CLOWN   Out, hyperbolical fiend,[8] how vexest thou this man!
Talkest thou nothing but of ladies?
25   SIR TOBY [*aside*]   Well said, Master Parson.
MALVOLIO   Sir Topas, never was man thus wronged. Good Sir
Topas, do not think I am mad. They have laid me here in
hideous darkness.
CLOWN   Fie, thou dishonest Satan. I call thee by the most
30   modest° terms, for I am one of those gentle ones that will   *mildest*
use the devil himself with courtesy. Say'st thou that house°   *room*
is dark?
MALVOLIO   As hell, Sir Topas.
CLOWN   Why, it hath bay windows transparent as barricadoes
35   and the clerestories[9] toward the south-north are as lustrous
as ebony.[1] And yet complainest thou of obstruction?
MALVOLIO   I am not mad, Sir Topas. I say to you this house is
dark.
CLOWN   Madman, thou errest. I say there is no darkness but
40   ignorance, in which thou art more puzzled than the Egyptians in their fog.[2]
MALVOLIO   I say this house is as dark as ignorance, though
ignorance were as dark as hell. And I say there was never
man thus abused. I am no more mad than you are. Make the
45   trial of it in any constant question.°   *logical discussion*
CLOWN   What is the opinion of Pythagoras[3] concerning wild
fowl?
MALVOLIO   That the soul of our grandam might haply° inhabit   *perhaps*
a bird.
50   CLOWN   What think'st thou of his opinion?
MALVOLIO   I think nobly of the soul and no way approve his
opinion.
CLOWN   Fare thee well. Remain thou still in darkness. Thou
shalt hold th'opinion of Pythagoras ere I will allow of thy
55   wits,° and fear to kill a woodcock[4] lest thou dispossess the   *certify your sanity*
soul of thy grandam. Fare thee well.
MALVOLIO   Sir Topas, Sir Topas.

---

5. Good day (false Latin).
6. Probably an invented authority.
7. PERFORMANCE COMMENT Malvolio's prison has
taken many different forms onstage. For examples
as well as information on how the scene may have
been performed on Shakespeare's stages, see Digital
Edition PC 4.
8. The Clown treats Malvolio as a man possessed by
vehement ("hyperbolical") evil spirits.
9. Upper windows, usually in a church or great hall.

barricadoes: barricades (subsequent paradoxes are
equivalent to "as clear as mud").
1. A dense and naturally dull black wood.
2. One of the plagues of Egypt was a "black darkness"
lasting for three days (Exodus 10:21–23).
3. An ancient Greek philosopher who held that
the same soul could successively inhabit different
creatures.
4. A traditionally stupid bird.

SIR TOBY   My most exquisite Sir Topas.

CLOWN   Nay, I am for all waters.[5]

60   MARIA   Thou mightst have done this without thy beard and
gown; he sees thee not.

SIR TOBY   To him in thine own voice and bring me word how
thou find'st him. I would we were well rid of this knavery. If
he may be conveniently delivered, I would he were, for I am

65   now so far in offense with my niece that I cannot pursue
with any safety this sport to the upshot.° Come by and by to   climax; limit
my chamber.   Exeunt [SIR TOBY and MARIA].

CLOWN [sings][6]   "Hey, Robin, jolly Robin,
                Tell me how thy lady does."

70   MALVOLIO   Fool.

CLOWN [sings]   "My lady is unkind, pardie."[7]

MALVOLIO   Fool.

CLOWN [sings]   "Alas, why is she so?"

MALVOLIO   Fool, I say.

75   CLOWN [sings]   "She loves another." Who calls, ha?

MALVOLIO   Good fool, as ever thou wilt deserve well at my
hand, help me to a candle, and pen, ink, and paper. As I am
a gentleman, I will live to be thankful to thee for't.

CLOWN   Master Malvolio?

80   MALVOLIO   Ay, good fool.

CLOWN   Alas, sir, how fell you besides° your five wits?[8]   out of

MALVOLIO   Fool, there was never man so notoriously° abused.   outrageously
I am as well in my wits, fool, as thou art.

CLOWN   But as well? Then you are mad indeed, if you be no

85   better in your wits than a fool.

MALVOLIO   They have here propertied me,[9] keep me in darkness, send ministers to me—asses—and do all they can to
face me[1] out of my wits.

CLOWN   Advise you° what you say. The minister is here. [He   Be careful

90   disguises his voice.] Malvolio, Malvolio, thy wits the heavens
restore. Endeavor thyself to sleep, and leave thy vain bibble-
babble.

MALVOLIO   Sir Topas.

CLOWN [as Sir Topas]   Maintain no words with him, good fel-

95   low. [as himself] Who I, sir? Not I, sir. God buy you,° good   God be with you
Sir Topas. [as Sir Topas] Marry, amen. [as himself] I will, sir,
I will.

MALVOLIO   Fool, fool, fool, I say.

CLOWN   Alas, sir, be patient. What say you, sir? I am shent°   scolded

100   for speaking to you.

MALVOLIO   Good fool, help me to some light and some paper.
I tell thee I am as well in my wits as any man in Illyria.

CLOWN   Well-a-day,° that you were, sir.   Alas

MALVOLIO   By this hand, I am. Good fool, some ink, paper, and

105   light. And convey what I will set down to my lady. It shall
advantage thee more than ever the bearing of letter did.

---

5. I am able to turn my hand to anything.
6. The Clown's song, which makes Malvolio aware of
his presence, is traditional. There is a version by Sir
Thomas Wyatt.
7. A corruption of the French *pardieu,* "by God."

8. Usually regarded as common sense, fantasy, memory, judgment, and imagination.
9. Treated me as a piece of property.
1. *face me*: brazenly construe me as.

CLOWN   I will help you to't. But tell me true, are you not mad
  indeed, or do you but counterfeit?
MALVOLIO   Believe me, I am not, I tell thee true.
110 CLOWN   Nay, I'll ne'er believe a madman till I see his brains. I
  will fetch you light, and paper, and ink.
MALVOLIO   Fool, I'll requite it in the highest degree. I prithee,
  be gone.
CLOWN [sings]   I am gone, sir, and anon, sir,
115   I'll be with you again,
            In a trice, like to the old Vice,[2]
            Your need to sustain.
            Who with dagger of lath,
            In his rage and his wrath,
120   Cries, "Aha" to the devil,
            Like a mad lad,
            "Pare thy nails, dad.
            Adieu, goodman[3] devil."   *Exit.*

4.3

Enter SEBASTIAN.

SEBASTIAN   This is the air, that is the glorious sun.
  This pearl she gave me, I do feel't and see't,
  And though 'tis wonder that enwraps me thus,
  Yet 'tis not madness. Where's Antonio then?
5 I could not find him at the Elephant.
  Yet there he was,° and there I found this credit,°   *had been / report*
  That he did range the town to seek me out.
  His counsel now might do me golden service
  For, though my soul disputes well with my sense[1]
10 That this may be some error but no madness,
  Yet doth this accident and flood of fortune
  So far exceed all instance,° all discourse,°   *precedent / reasoning*
  That I am ready to distrust mine eyes
  And wrangle with my reason that persuades me
15 To any other trust° but that I am mad—   *belief*
  Or else the lady's mad. Yet if 'twere so,
  She could not sway° her house, command her followers,   *rule*
  Take and give back affairs and their dispatch[2]
  With such a smooth, discreet, and stable bearing
20 As I perceive she does. There's something in't
  That is deceivable.° But here the lady comes.   *deceptive*
      Enter OLIVIA *and* PRIEST.
OLIVIA   Blame not this haste of mine. If you mean well,
  Now go with me and with this holy man
  Into the chantry by.° There, before him   *nearby chapel*
25 And underneath that consecrated roof,
  Plight me the full assurance of your faith,[3]
  That my most jealous° and too doubtful soul   *anxious*
  May live at peace. He shall conceal it
  Whiles° you are willing it shall come to note,   *Until*

---

2. A stock comic figure in the old morality plays; the
Vice often carried a wooden dagger.
3. Yeoman; a title given to one not of gentle birth,
hence a parting insult to Malvolio.

4.3 Location: Near Olivia's house.
1. For though my reason and my sense both concur.
2. Undertake business and ensure that it is carried out.
3. Enter into the solemn contract of betrothal.

30   What° time we will our celebration keep   *At which*
      According to my birth.° What do you say?   *rank*
      SEBASTIAN   I'll follow this good man and go with you
      And, having sworn truth, ever will be true.
      OLIVIA   Then lead the way, good father, and heavens so shine,
35   That they may fairly note° this act of mine.   *Exeunt.*   *look favorably upon*

5.1

Enter CLOWN *and* FABIAN.

FABIAN   Now, as thou lov'st me, let me see his letter.
CLOWN   Good Master Fabian, grant me another request.
FABIAN   Anything.
CLOWN   Do not desire to see this letter.
5   FABIAN   This is to give a dog and in recompense desire my dog
      again.[1]

Enter DUKE, VIOLA [*as Cesario*], CURIO, *and Lords.*

ORSINO   Belong you to the Lady Olivia, friends?
CLOWN   Ay, sir, we are some of her trappings.°   *ornaments*
ORSINO   I know thee well. How dost thou, my good fellow?
10   CLOWN   Truly, sir, the better for my foes and the worse for my
      friends.
ORSINO   Just the contrary, the better for thy friends.
CLOWN   No, sir, the worse.
ORSINO   How can that be?
15   CLOWN   Marry, sir, they praise me and make an ass of me.
      Now my foes tell me plainly, I am an ass. So that by my foes,
      sir, I profit in the knowledge of myself, and by my friends I
      am abused.° So that, conclusions to be as kisses, if your four   *deceived*
      negatives make your two affirmatives,[2] why then, the worse
20   for my friends and the better for my foes.
ORSINO   Why, this is excellent.
CLOWN   By my troth, sir, no. Though it please you to be one of
      my friends.
ORSINO   Thou shalt not be the worse for me. There's gold.
25   CLOWN   But° that it would be double dealing,[3] sir, I would you   *Except for the fact*
      could make it another.
ORSINO   Oh, you give me ill counsel.
CLOWN   Put your grace in your pocket,[4] sir, for this once, and
      let your flesh and blood obey it.[5]
30   ORSINO   Well, I will be so much a sinner to° be a double dealer.   *as to*
      There's another.
CLOWN   *Primo, secundo, tertio*[6] is a good play,°° and the old   *game*
      saying is, the third pays for all.[7] The triplex,° sir, is a good *triple time in music*
      tripping measure, or the bells of Saint Bennet,[8] sir, may put
35   you in mind. One, two, three.

ORSINO   You can fool no more money out of me at this throw.°   *throw of the dice*
        If you will let your lady know I am here to speak with her
        and bring her along with you, it may awake my bounty
        further.
40   CLOWN   Marry, sir, lullaby to your bounty till I come again. I
        go, sir, but I would not have you to think that my desire of
        having is the sin of covetousness. But, as you say, sir, let
        your bounty take a nap, I will awake it anon.   *Exit.*
            Enter ANTONIO *and* OFFICERS.
     VIOLA   Here comes the man, sir, that did rescue me.
45   ORSINO   That face of his I do remember well.
        Yet, when I saw it last, it was besmeared
        As black as Vulcan⁹ in the smoke of war.
        A baubling° vessel was he captain of,   *trifling*
        For shallow draught and bulk unprizeable,¹
50   With which such scatheful° grapple did he make   *destructive*
        With the most noble bottom° of our fleet   *ship*
        That very envy° and the tongue of loss°   *even enmity / the losers*
        Cried fame and honor on him. What's the matter?
     FIRST OFFICER   Orsino, this is that Antonio
55   That took the Phoenix and her fraught from Candy.²
        And this is he that did the Tiger board
        When your young nephew Titus lost his leg.
        Here in the streets, desperate of shame and state,³
        In private brabble° did we apprehend him.   *brawl*
60   VIOLA   He did me kindness, sir, drew on my side,⁴
        But in conclusion put strange speech upon° me.   *spoke strangely to*
        I know not what 'twas but distraction.°   *if not insanity*
     ORSINO   Notable° pirate, thou saltwater thief,   *Notorious*
        What foolish boldness brought thee to their mercies,
65   Whom thou in terms so bloody and so dear°   *dire*
        Hast made thine enemies?
     ANTONIO   Orsino, noble sir,
        Be pleased that I shake off these names you give me.
        Antonio never yet was thief or pirate,
        Though I confess, on base° and ground enough,   *foundation*
70   Orsino's enemy. A witchcraft drew me hither.
        That most ingrateful boy there by your side
        From the rude sea's enraged and foamy mouth
        Did I redeem. A wrack past hope he was.
        His life I gave him and did thereto add
75   My love without retention° or restraint,   *reservation*
        All his in dedication. For his sake
        Did I expose myself, pure° for his love,   *only*
        Into the danger of this adverse° town,   *hostile*
        Drew to defend him when he was beset;
80   Where, being apprehended, his false cunning,
        Not meaning to partake with me in danger,
        Taught him to face me out of his acquaintance⁵
        And grew a twenty years' removèd thing

9. Blacksmith of the Roman gods.
1. Of no value because of its small size. *draught:*
water displaced by a vessel.
2. Candia, capital of Crete.
3. *desperate . . . state:* recklessly oblivious of the danger

to his honor and his position (as a free man and public
enemy).
4. Drew his sword in my defense.
5. To brazenly deny my acquaintance.

While one would wink,[6] denied me mine own purse,

85 Which I had recommended° to his use   *consigned*

Not half an hour before.

VIOLA   How can this be?

ORSINO   When came he to this town?

ANTONIO   Today, my lord. And, for three months before,

No int'rim, not a minute's vacancy,°   *interval*

90 Both day and night did we keep company.

        Enter OLIVIA *and Attendants.*

ORSINO   Here comes the countess. Now heaven walks on

    earth.

—But for thee, fellow. Fellow, thy words are madness.

Three months this youth hath tended upon me.

But more of that anon. [*to* FIRST OFFICER] Take him aside.

95 OLIVIA   What would my lord, but that he may not have,[7]

Wherein Olivia may seem serviceable?

—Cesario, you do not keep promise with me.

VIOLA   Madam?

ORSINO   Gracious Olivia.

OLIVIA   What do you say, Cesario? —Good my lord.

100 VIOLA   My lord would speak, my duty hushes me.

OLIVIA   If it be aught° to the old tune, my lord,   *anything*

It is as fat and fulsome° to mine ear   *gross and offensive*

As howling after music.

ORSINO   Still so cruel?

OLIVIA   Still so constant, lord.

105 ORSINO   What, to perverseness? You uncivil lady,

To whose ingrate and unauspicious° altars   *unfavorable*

My soul the faithful'st off'rings have breathed out

That e'er devotion tendered, what shall I do?

OLIVIA   Even what it please my lord that shall become° him.   *be fitting for*

110 ORSINO   Why should I not, had I the heart to do it

Like to th'Egyptian thief at point of death

Kill what I love?[8]—A savage jealousy

That sometime savors nobly.° But hear me this.   *of nobility*

Since you to non-regardance° cast my faith,   *oblivion*

115 And that I partly know the instrument

That screws° me from my true place in your favor,   *wrenches*

Live you the marble-breasted tyrant still.

But this your minion,° whom I know you love   *darling*

And whom, by heaven I swear, I tender° dearly,   *regard*

120 Him will I tear out of that cruel eye

Where he sits crownèd in his master's spite.[9]

Come, boy, with me. My thoughts are ripe in mischief.

I'll sacrifice the lamb that I do love

To spite a raven's heart within a dove.

125 VIOLA   And I most jocund,° apt,° and willingly   *cheerfully / readily*

To do you rest a thousand deaths would die.

OLIVIA   Where goes Cesario?

---

6. *And . . . wink:* In the wink of an eye, pretended we had been estranged for twenty years.
7. Except that which he may not have (my love).
8. In Heliodorus of Emesa's *Ethiopica*, a Greek prose romance translated into English in 1569 and popular in

Shakespeare's day, the Egyptian robber chief Thyamis tries to kill his captive Chariclea, whom he loves, when he is in danger from a rival band.
9. To the mortification of his master.

VIOLA   After him I love
More than I love these eyes, more than my life,
More by all mores¹ than e'er I shall love wife.
130 If I do feign, you witnesses above,
Punish my life for tainting of my love.
OLIVIA Ay me detested, how am I beguiled?
VIOLA Who does beguile you? Who does do you wrong?
OLIVIA Hast thou forgot thyself? Is it so long?
Call forth the holy father.   [*Exit Attendant.*]
135 ORSINO [*to* VIOLA]   Come, away.
OLIVIA Whither, my lord? Cesario, husband, stay.
ORSINO Husband?
OLIVIA   Ay, husband. Can he that deny?
ORSINO Her husband, sirrah?²
VIOLA   No, my lord, not I.
OLIVIA Alas, it is the baseness of thy fear
140 That makes thee strangle thy propriety.³
Fear not, Cesario, take thy fortunes up.
Be that thou know'st thou art, and then thou art
As great as that° thou fear'st.   him whom
        Enter PRIEST.
                        Oh, welcome, Father.
Father, I charge thee by thy reverence
145 Here to unfold—though lately we intended
To keep in darkness what occasion° now   necessity
Reveals before 'tis ripe—what thou dost know
Hath newly passed between this youth and me.
PRIEST A contract of eternal bond of love,
150 Confirmed by mutual joinder° of your hands,   joining
Attested by the holy close° of lips,   meeting
Strengthened by interchangement of your rings,
And all the ceremony of this compact
Sealed in my function⁴ by my testimony.
155 Since when, my watch hath told me, toward my grave
I have traveled but two hours.
ORSINO O thou dissembling cub! What wilt thou be
When time hath sowed a grizzle on thy case?⁵
Or will not else thy craft° so quickly grow   craftiness
160 That thine own trip shall be thine overthrow?⁶
Farewell and take her, but direct thy feet
Where thou and I henceforth may never meet.
VIOLA My lord, I do protest.
OLIVIA   Oh, do not swear.
Hold little° faith though thou hast too much fear.   Preserve some
        Enter SIR ANDREW.
165 SIR ANDREW For the love of God, a surgeon! Send one
presently° to Sir Toby.   immediately
OLIVIA What's the matter?

---

1. More beyond all comparison.
2. Contemptuous form of address to an inferior.
3. That makes you deny your identity (as my husband).
4. Ratified by priestly authority.

5. A gray hair ("grizzle") on your hide (sustaining the metaphor of "cub").
6. That your attempt to trip someone else will be the cause of your downfall.

SIR ANDREW   He's broke° my head across, and has given Sir   cut
    Toby a bloody coxcomb[7] too. For the love of God, your help!
170   I had rather than forty pound I were at home.
OLIVIA   Who has done this, Sir Andrew?
SIR ANDREW   The Count's gentleman, one Cesario. We took
    him for a coward, but he's the very devil incardinate.[8]
ORSINO   My gentleman Cesario?
175   SIR ANDREW   Odd's lifelings,° here he is. You broke my head   By God's little lives
    for nothing, and that that I did, I was set on to do't by Sir
    Toby.
VIOLA   Why do you speak to me? I never hurt you.
    You drew your sword upon me without cause,
180   But I bespake you fair[9] and hurt you not.
        Enter SIR TOBY *and* CLOWN.
SIR ANDREW   If a bloody coxcomb be a hurt, you have hurt
    me. I think you set nothing by° a bloody coxcomb. Here   *think nothing of*
    comes Sir Toby halting.° You shall hear more, but if° he had   *limping / if only*
    not been in drink, he would have tickled° you othergates°   *chastised / in other ways*
185   than he did.
ORSINO   How now, gentleman? How is't with you?
SIR TOBY   That's all one.° He's hurt me, and there's th'end on't.   *No matter*
    [*to* CLOWN] Sot,° didst see Dick Surgeon, sot?   *Fool; drunkard*
CLOWN   Oh, he's drunk, Sir Toby, an hour agone. His eyes were
190   set[1] at eight i'th' morning.
SIR TOBY   Then he's a rogue, and a passy-measures pavan.[2] I
    hate a drunken rogue.
OLIVIA   Away with him! Who hath made this havoc with them?
SIR ANDREW   I'll help you, Sir Toby, because we'll be dressed[3]
195   together.
SIR TOBY   Will you help? An ass-head and a coxcomb,° and a   *fool*
    knave, a thin-faced knave, a gull!°   *dupe*
OLIVIA   Get him to bed, and let his hurt be looked to.
        Enter SEBASTIAN.
SEBASTIAN   I am sorry, madam, I have hurt your kinsman.
200   But, had it been the brother of my blood,
    I must have done no less with wit and safety.[4]
    You throw a strange regard upon me,° and by that   *regard me strangely*
    I do perceive it hath offended you.
    Pardon me, sweet one, even for the vows
205   We made each other but so late ago.
ORSINO   One face, one voice, one habit, and two persons—
    A natural perspective,[5] that is and is not.
SEBASTIAN   Antonio, O my dear Antonio,
    How have the hours racked and tortured me
210   Since I have lost thee!
ANTONIO   Sebastian are you?
SEBASTIAN   Fear'st thou° that, Antonio?   *Do you doubt*

---

7. Head; also, a fool's cap, which resembles the crest
of a cock.
8. Sir Andrew's blunder for "incarnate" (in the flesh).
9. But I spoke courteously to you.
1. Closed (as the sun sets).
2. A variety of the slow dance known as "pavane"

(from the Italian *passamezzo pavana*). Sir Toby may
think its swaying movements suggest drunkenness.
3. We'll have our wounds dressed.
4. With any sense of my welfare.
5. An optical illusion produced by nature (rather
than by a mirror or a "perspective glass").

ANTONIO   How have you made division of yourself?
　　An apple cleft in two is not more twin
　　Than these two creatures. Which is Sebastian?
215　OLIVIA   Most wonderful!°　　　　　　　　　　　　　　　　　*full of wonder*
　　SEBASTIAN   Do I stand there? I never had a brother,
　　Nor can there be that deity° in my nature　　　　　　　　*divine power*
　　Of here and everywhere.° I had a sister　　　　　　　　*Of omnipresence*
　　Whom the blind waves and surges have devoured.
220　Of charity,° what kin are you to me?　　　　　　　　　　*Please*
　　What countryman? What name? What parentage?
　　VIOLA   Of Messaline. Sebastian was my father;
　　Such a Sebastian was my brother too.
　　So went he suited[6] to his watery tomb.
225　If spirits can assume both form and suit,°　　　　　　　*appearance and dress*
　　You come to fright us.
　　SEBASTIAN　　　　　　　　A spirit I am indeed,
　　But am in that dimension grossly clad
　　Which from the womb I did participate.[7]
　　Were you a woman, as the rest goes even,°　　　　　　　*the rest suggests*
230　I should my tears let fall upon your cheek
　　And say, thrice welcome, drownèd Viola.
　　VIOLA   My father had a mole upon his brow.
　　SEBASTIAN   And so had mine.
　　VIOLA   And died that day when Viola from her birth
235　Had numbered thirteen years.
　　SEBASTIAN   Oh, that record is lively[8] in my soul.
　　He finished indeed his mortal act
　　That day that made my sister thirteen years.
　　VIOLA   If nothing lets° to make us happy both　　　　　　*hinders*
240　But this my masculine usurped attire,
　　Do not embrace me till each circumstance
　　Of place, time, fortune do cohere and jump°　　　　　　*agree*
　　That I am Viola. Which to confirm,
　　I'll bring you to a captain in this town
245　Where lie my maiden weeds,° by whose gentle help　　　*clothes*
　　I was preserved to serve this noble count.
　　All the occurrence of my fortune since
　　Hath been between this lady and this lord.
　　SEBASTIAN   So comes it, lady, you have been mistook.
250　But Nature to her bias drew in that.[9]
　　You would have been contracted° to a maid.　　　　　　*betrothed*
　　Nor are you therein, by my life, deceived:
　　You are betrothed both to a maid and man.[1]
　　ORSINO   Be not amazed. Right noble is his blood.
255　If this be so, as yet the glass seems true,[2]
　　I shall have share in this most happy wrack.
　　—Boy, thou hast said to me a thousand times,
　　Thou never shouldst love woman like to me.

---

6. Dressed just like you he went.
7. *But . . . participate*: But I am clad, like all mortals, in the flesh in which I was born.
8. The memory of that is vivid.
9. But Nature followed her inclination. (The image is from the game of bowls, in which players use a ball

with an off-centered weight that causes it to curve away from a straight course.)
1. *maid and man*: a man who is a virgin.
2. *the glass seems true*: the "natural perspective" (line 207) continues to seem real.

VIOLA　And all those sayings will I overswear,°   *swear again*
260　　And all those swearings keep as true in soul
　　　　As doth that orbèd continent[3] the fire
　　　　That severs day from night.

ORSINO　　　　　　　　　　　Give me thy hand,
　　　　And let me see thee in thy woman's weeds.

VIOLA　The captain that did bring me first on shore
265　　Hath my maid's garments. He upon some action°   *legal charge*
　　　　Is now in durance° at Malvolio's suit,   *prison*
　　　　A gentleman and follower of my lady's.

OLIVIA　He shall enlarge° him. [*to Attendant*] Fetch Malvolio   *release*
　　　　hither.
　　　　And yet, alas, now I remember me,
270　　They say, poor gentleman, he's much distract.°   *insane*

Enter CLOWN *with a letter and* FABIAN.

　　　　A most extracting° frenzy of mine own   *distracting*
　　　　From my remembrance clearly banished his.
　　　　How does he, sirrah?

CLOWN　Truly, madam, he holds Beelzebub at the stave's end[4]
275　　as well as a man in his case may do. He's here writ a letter to
　　　　you. I should have given't you today morning. But, as a mad-
　　　　man's epistles are no gospels,[5] so it skills° not much when they   *matters*
　　　　are delivered.

OLIVIA　Open't, and read it.

280　CLOWN　Look then to be well edified, when the fool delivers°   *speaks the words of*
　　　　the madman. [*He reads.*] "By the Lord, madam—"

OLIVIA　How now, art thou mad?

CLOWN　No, madam, I do but read madness. An your ladyship
　　　　will have it as it ought to be, you must allow *vox*.[6]

285　OLIVIA　Prithee, read i'thy right wits.

CLOWN　So I do, madonna. But to read his right wits[7] is to
　　　　read thus. Therefore, perpend,° my princess, and give ear.   *pay attention*

OLIVIA　[*taking the letter and giving it to* FABIAN]　Read it you,
　　　　sirrah.

290　FABIAN　(*reads*)　"By the Lord, madam, you wrong me, and the
　　　　world shall know it. Though you have put me into darkness
　　　　and given your drunken cousin rule over me, yet have I the
　　　　benefit of my senses as well as your ladyship. I have your own
　　　　letter that induced me to the semblance I put on, with the
295　　which I doubt not but to do myself much right or you much
　　　　shame. Think of me as you please. I leave my duty a little
　　　　unthought of, and speak out of my injury.[8]

　　　　　　　　　　　　　　The madly used Malvolio."

OLIVIA　Did he write this?

300　CLOWN　Ay, madam.

ORSINO　This savors not much of distraction.°   *insanity*

OLIVIA　See him delivered.° Fabian, bring him hither.   *released*

　　　　　　　　　　　　　　[*Exit* FABIAN.]

---

3. Referring to either the sun or the sphere within which the sun was thought to be fixed.
4. He holds the devil (who threatens to possess him) at a distance (proverbial).
5. Gospel truths. *epistles*: letters (playing on the sense of apostolic accounts of Christ in the New Testament).
6. The appropriate voice (Latin).
7. To accurately represent his mental state.
8. I neglect the formality I owe you as your servant and speak as an injured person.

My lord, so please you, these things further thought on,
To think me as well a sister as a wife,[9]
305   One day shall crown th'alliance[1] on't, so please you,
Here at my house and at my proper cost.°   *own expense*
ORSINO   Madam, I am most apt° t'embrace your offer.   *ready*
      [*to* VIOLA]   Your master quits° you and, for your service   *releases*
         done him
So much against the mettle° of your sex,   *disposition*
310   So far beneath your soft and tender breeding,
And since you called me master for so long,
Here is my hand. You shall from this time be
Your master's mistress.
OLIVIA   A sister, you are she.
                    Enter [FABIAN *with*] MALVOLIO.
ORSINO   Is this the madman?
OLIVIA   Ay, my lord, this same.
315   —How now, Malvolio?
MALVOLIO   Madam, you have done me wrong, notorious wrong.
OLIVIA   Have I, Malvolio? No.
MALVOLIO [*handing her a letter*]   Lady, you have. Pray you
         peruse that letter.
You must not now deny it is your hand.°   *handwriting*
320   Write from° it if you can, in hand or phrase,   *differently from*
Or say, 'tis not your seal, not your invention.°   *composition*
You can say none of this. Well, grant it then,
And tell me, in the modesty of honor,[2]
Why you have given me such clear lights° of favor,   *signs*
325   Bade me come smiling and cross-gartered to you,
To put on yellow stockings, and to frown
Upon Sir Toby and the lighter° people.   *lesser*
And, acting° this in an obedient hope,   *upon doing*
Why have you suffered me to be imprisoned,
330   Kept in a dark house, visited by the priest,
And made the most notorious geck° and gull   *fool*
That e'er invention° played on? Tell me, why?   *trickery*
OLIVIA   Alas, Malvolio, this is not my writing,
Though I confess much like the character.°   *handwriting*
335   But out of question, 'tis Maria's hand.
And, now I do bethink me, it was she
First told me thou wast mad, then cam'st° in smiling,   *you came*
And in such forms which here were presupposed°   *previously suggested*
Upon thee in the letter. Prithee, be content.
340   This practice hath most shrewdly passed[3] upon thee,
But, when we know the grounds and authors of it,
Thou shalt be both the plaintiff and the judge
Of thine own cause.
FABIAN   Good madam, hear me speak,
And let no quarrel nor no brawl to come
345   Taint the condition of this present hour,
Which I have wondered° at. In hope it shall not,   *marveled*
Most freely I confess myself and Toby
Set this device against Malvolio here,

---

9. To think as well of me as a sister-in-law as you
would have thought of me as a wife.
1. The impending double-marriage ceremony.

2. Tell me with the propriety that becomes a
noblewoman.
3. This trick has most mischievously played.

350	Upon° some stubborn and uncourteous parts°
	We had conceived against him.[4] Maria writ
	The letter at Sir Toby's great importance,°
	In recompence whereof he hath married her.
	How with a sportful malice it was followed°
	May rather pluck on° laughter than revenge,
355	If that the injuries be justly weighed
	That have on both sides passed.

Because / behavior

importunity

followed through
incite

OLIVIA [to MALVOLIO] Alas, poor fool, how have they baffled° thee!   *disgraced*

CLOWN Why, some are born great, some achieve greatness, and some have greatness thrown upon them. I was one, sir, in
360 this interlude,° one Sir Topas, sir. But that's all one. "By the   *comedy*
Lord, fool, I am not mad." But do you remember, "Madam, why
laugh you at such a barren rascal. An you smile not, he's
gagged." And thus the whirligig° of time brings in his revenges.   *spinning top*

MALVOLIO I'll be revenged on the whole pack of you.   [*Exit.*]
365 OLIVIA He hath been most notoriously abused.

ORSINO Pursue him and entreat him to a peace.
                                   [*Exit Attendant.*]

	He hath not told us of the captain yet.
	When that is known, and golden time convents,°
	A solemn combination shall be made
370	Of our dear souls. Meantime, sweet sister,
	We will not part from hence.° Cesario, come—
	For so you shall be while you are a man—
	But when in other habits you are seen,
	Orsino's mistress and his fancy's° queen.

summons; is convenient

(Olivia's house)

love's; imagination's

                          Exeunt [*all but* CLOWN].

375 CLOWN (*sings*)   When that I was and a little tiny boy,
            With hey, ho, the wind and the rain,
            A foolish thing was but a toy,
            For the rain it raineth every day.

            But when I came to man's estate,
380   With hey, ho, etc.
            'Gainst knaves and thieves men shut their gate,
            For the rain, etc.

            But when I came, alas, to wive,
            With hey, ho, etc.
385   By swaggering could I never thrive,
            For the rain, etc.

            But when I came unto my beds,
            With hey, ho, etc.
            With tosspots° still had drunken heads,   *drunkards*
390   For the rain, etc.

            A great while ago the world begun,
            Hey, ho, etc.
            But that's all one, our play is done,
            And we'll strive to please you every day.   [*Exit.*]

---

4. *We . . . him:* To which we took exception.

The Phoenix and Turtle

"The Phoenix and Turtle" was one of several poems—others were by George Chapman, Ben Jonson, and John Marston—appended to Robert Chester's *Love's Martyr* (1601). An abstruse philosophical composition, "The Phoenix and Turtle" may represent Shakespeare's effort to refashion himself as a different kind of poet from the one who appeared two years earlier in unauthorized form in *The Passionate Pilgrim*. Literary innovation here may also have an element of poetic competition with his three fellow contributors to Chester's volume, all of whom were dramatists as well. With two of them, Jonson and Marston, Shakespeare was then probably engaged in the satirical Poets' War, a battle of rival playwrights.

"The Phoenix and Turtle" is composed in trochaic tetrameter with the final (unstressed) syllable dropped—an otherwise atypical meter in the period that, however, Shakespeare employs in his plays for incantations and epitaphs. The poem can be divided into either two or three parts, depending on whether one goes by rhyme scheme or poetic speaker (see Digital Edition TC 1). A tripartite division may ultimately derive from Plato. The first five quatrains, or "requiem" (line 16), may be indebted to Chaucer's late fourteenth-century *Parliament of Fowls* and, behind it, to the elegy on a dead parrot of the classical Latin poet Ovid. In a language of elaborate circumlocution, these lines merely call the birds together to mourn the deaths of two remarkably constant lovers—the proverbially faithful turtledove (here, male) and the legendary phoenix (here, female). Supposedly, only one phoenix was alive at any given moment, and the bird died only to be reborn from its own ashes. Neither of the two birds is named yet, however.

The "anthem" (line 21), which constitutes the next eight stanzas, is presumably intoned by the birds. In a reversal of the procedure of the opening twenty lines, this combination of burial hymn, possibly with Catholic overtones, and epithalamion (marriage celebration) turns to a deceptively simple vocabulary that conceals dense argumentation. As marriage poem, it invokes the work of Shakespeare's older contemporary, Edmund Spenser. Behind the emphasis on the paradoxical unity of two separate beings lies the mystery of the Christian Trinity as understood in Scholastic theology—medieval Europe's assimilation beginning in the twelfth century of the recently translated writings of Aristotle. The ideal love of the two birds ultimately defies the efforts at comprehension by Reason, which cannot understand how

> love in twain,
> Had the essence but in one,
> Two distincts, division none:
> (lines 25–27)

or how

> the self was not the same:
> Single nature's double name,
> Neither two nor one was called.
> (lines 38–40)

In other words, the rationalist vocabulary of this section ultimately undermines its own legitimacy. Perhaps the lines vindicate the more mystical understanding of ideal love that Renaissance thought derived from Plato, whose doctrines Aristotle had sought to answer. In any case, the heterosexual love praised in this self-contradictory fashion parallels the celebration of homoerotic love in the sonnets to the young man: "Let me confess that we two must be twain, / Although our undivided loves are one" (36.1–2).

Following the anthem, Reason delivers the final section of the poem, the *Threnos*, or mourning song. These lines retain the straightforwardly abstract diction of the anthem and the trochaic-tetrameter meter of all that has preceded, but they abandon quatrains (rhyming *abba*) for tercets (rhyming *aaa*). Like the three-part structure, this particular rhyme scheme perhaps alludes to the Trinity. Similarly, the division of the poem into two rhyme schemes may be an effort to replicate formally the rationally incomprehensible unity of the phoenix and turtle. The last five stanzas emphasize the finality of the death of the couple, which apparently excludes both rebirth (even on the part of the immortal phoenix) and "posterity"—the latter as a result of a "married chastity" (lines 59, 61) that has the same (lack of) consequences as the love for the young man in the sonnets. The result is the diminution of life: the only authentic or perhaps ideal "[t]ruth and beauty buried be" (line 64). Here, the poem is of a piece with Shakespearean tragedy in its refusal to find transcendence in death. In this sense, the poem reenacts English literary history, moving from Shakespeare's two most important predecessors, Chaucer and Spenser, to Shakespeare himself.

"The Phoenix and Turtle" raises all sorts of interpretive problems. Since the *Threnos* is spoken by Reason, who has been defeated by the phoenix and turtle, should the concluding stanzas be seen not as authorial statement but as the position of a fallible character who lets fly a crow of triumph at the couple's death? Moreover, the concluding summons of all "[t]hat are either true or fair" (line 66) sits oddly with the immediately preceding insistence that genuine truth and beauty no longer exist: perhaps now they exist only separately. And why does Shakespeare, through Reason, insist on the lack of offspring and, apparently rejecting a central feature of the legend, on the mortality of the phoenix? This last question is only emphasized by the circumstances of publication. All of the poems with which "The Phoenix and Turtle" were printed are on the subject of the phoenix and turtle, and all but Shakespeare's deny the finality of the phoenix's death. "The Phoenix and Turtle" alone forgoes the possibility of exploiting the standard treatment of the phoenix as the intersection of the temporal and the timeless.

The title page of the volume advertises Chester's long poem as "[a]llegorically shadowing the truth of Love, in the constant Fate of the Phoenix and Turtle." This claim, the abstract language of "The Phoenix and Turtle," and the avowed purpose of the volume—to honor Sir John Salusbury of Lleweni, knighted by the Queen in June 1601—have all encouraged a search in Shakespeare's poem for allegorical meaning (beyond the praise of ideal human union through a tale of two birds). The marriage of phoenix and turtle has been seen as the joining of the literal and the metaphorical in poetry, so that the poem self-referentially becomes a metaphor for metaphor itself. Historical readings have found candidates for the parts of the turtle and the phoenix in Salusbury and his wife, as well as in the Earl of Essex, Salusbury, or the English people in relation to Queen Elizabeth. Although none of these theories is convincing, in part because of a failure to explain what real "tragic scene" is being allegorically represented by the couple's deaths (line 52), all testify to the poem's ability to hint at hidden meanings. The most plausible of these possibilities links Salusbury to Elizabeth—and, in more broadly political and religious terms, Catholic Wales to Protestant England. In the aftermath of the Reformation, funeral rites and prayers turned from intercession to commemoration. Recourse to the classical tradition perhaps offered a secular form of intercession, in which the poem itself, represented as the "urn" (line 65), promises a different kind of immortality. In any case, "The Phoenix and Turtle" labors to construct an ideal image of love while simultaneously circumscribing the real utility of that ideal. Marriage and funeral, celebration and dirge, ideal affirmation and pragmatic denial—the poem is a characteristically Shakespearean venture in having it both ways.

WALTER COHEN

SELECTED BIBLIOGRAPHY

Bednarz, James P. "*The Passionate Pilgrim* and 'The Phoenix and Turtle.'" *The Cambridge Companion to Shakespeare's Poetry.* Ed. Patrick Cheney. New York: Cambridge UP, 2007. 108–24. Locates these works in the context of late Elizabethan poetic publication and literary and theatrical competition.

———. *Shakespeare and the Truth of Love: The Mystery of "The Phoenix and Turtle."* London: Palgrave Macmillan, 2012. Rejects topical readings in favor of seeing the poem as a mythmaking, metaphysical work drawing on the mystery of the Trinity to investigate the intersubjective nature of love.

Cheney, Patrick. "The Voice of the Author in 'The Phoenix and Turtle': Chaucer, Shakespeare, Spenser." *Shakespeare and the Middle Ages.* Ed. Curtis Perry and John Watkins. Oxford: Oxford UP, 2009. 103–25. Traces the poem's three-part structure back to Plato and especially to Chaucer's *Parliament of Fowls,* and sees a movement in it from Spenserian romance epic through Chaucerian complaint to Shakespearean tragedy.

Davies, H. Neville. "*The Phoenix and Turtle:* Requiem and Rite." *Review of English Studies* 46 (1995): 525–30. Ties the poem's funeral rite to the Elizabethan Book of Common Prayer.

Enterline, Lynn. "'The Phoenix and the Turtle,' Renaissance Elegies and the Language of Grief." *Early Modern English Poetry: A Critical Companion.* Ed. Patrick Cheney, Andrew Hadfield, and Garrett A. Sullivan, Jr. New York: Oxford UP, 2007. 147–59. Locates the poem in the post-Reformation transition from intercession to commemoration in mourning the dead, with the return to the classical tradition, especially Ovid, self-referentially converting the poem itself into a secular afterlife.

Kerrigan, John. "Reading 'The Phoenix and Turtle.'" *The Oxford Handbook of Shakespeare's Poetry.* Ed. Jonathan F. S. Post. Oxford: Oxford UP, 2013. 540–59. Offers a detailed commentary on the poem attentive to its multiple possible meanings, seeing it as a post-Reformation funeral ritual with Catholic and heraldic elements, and with connections to Elizabeth.

———. "Shakespeare, Elegy, and Epitaph 1557–1640." *The Oxford Handbook of Shakespeare's Poetry.* Ed. Jonathan F. S. Post. Oxford: Oxford UP, 2013. 225–44. Links "The Phoenix and Turtle" to the elegies attributed to Shakespeare, to the volume in which the poem appeared, to the period's competition—in poetry and in stone—in constructing memorials, and to the relationship between Catholic Wales and Protestant England.

Klause, John. "'The Phoenix and Turtle' in Its Time." *In the Company of Shakespeare.* Ed. Thomas Moisan and Douglas Bruster. Madison, NJ: Fairleigh Dickinson UP, 2002. 206–30. Reads "The Phoenix and Turtle" as an ironic critique of Salusbury as well as of the other poets who contributed to the collection, and as a covert defense of Catholicism.

Schoenfeldt, Michael. *The Cambridge Introduction to Shakespeare's Poetry.* Cambridge: Cambridge UP, 2010. 122–29. Focuses on the simple but elusive language of "The Phoenix and Turtle."

Steel, Karl. "*The Phoenix and the Turtle:* 'Number There in Love Was Slain.'" *Shakesqueer: A Queer Companion to the Complete Works of Shakespeare.* Ed. Madhavi Menon. Durham, NC: Duke UP, 2011. 271–77. Ties the undermining of Reason to the multiple possible relationships the poem imagines between the phoenix and the turtle.

TEXTUAL INTRODUCTION

"The Phoenix and Turtle" was printed in 1601 as part of Robert Chester's *Love's Martyr: or, Rosalin's Complaint*, a voluminous work not entered in the Stationers' Register. Like *Venus and Adonis* and *The Rape of Lucrece*, Chester's book was printed by Richard Field, although in this case the publisher was Edward Blount. The Quarto volume of ninety-eight leaves is a curious amalgamation, including Chester's own long narrative poem but also what the title page to the book advertises as "some new compositions, of several modern writers whose names are subscribed to their several works, upon the first subject: viz. the *Phoenix and Turtle*." The "modern writers," who appear in a section of their own marked by the heading "Diverse Poetical Essays," contribute fourteen poems, the first two by a "Vatum Chorus" (Chorus of Poets), with several signed by authors' names: John Marston, George Chapman, Ben Jonson, "Ignoto," and William Shakespeare (the fifth poem in the collaborative sequence). Only three copies of the first edition of *Love's Martyr* are extant, with only two of them complete (the Folger and Huntington copies; a third copy, in the National Library of Wales, is imperfect). In 1611, a reissue was printed, with only one copy extant (in the British Library, London).

Shakespeare's poem appears on signatures Z3v–4v but is curiously printed in two parts. On Z3v–4r, there is no title ("The Phoenix and Turtle" is a modern invention), just the first part of the poem (lines 1–52, or the first thirteen stanzas, all rhyming *abba*). Then, at the top of Z4v, a heading appears, *Threnos* (Mourning song), followed by the second part of the poem (lines 53–67, or the last five stanzas, rhyming *aaa*). Beneath this second part, the name "William Shake-speare" appears. Some scholars want to read the sixty-seven-line poem as two poems, although all recent editors print it as a single composition, signed, like *Venus* and *Lucrece*, by the author.

Shakespeare's poem has no textual cruxes or substantive variants. The syntax of a single line has produced some division among editors. For line 39, the Quarto reads "Single Natures double name," which most editors modernize as "Single Nature's double name"; but some editors read the line differently, as "Single natures, double name," making this elliptical poem even more elliptical here. Although this remains an intriguing intervention, it is not adopted for the present edition, which suggests that the "double name" is that of "[s]ingle nature."

PATRICK CHENEY

The Phoenix and Turtle[1]

Let the bird of loudest lay[2]
On the sole Arabian tree,[3]
Herald sad and trumpet be:
To whose sound chaste wings° obey.   *virtuous birds*

5 But thou, shrieking harbinger,°   *(the screech owl)*
Foul precurrer of the fiend,[4]
Augur of the fever's end,°   *Prophet of death or cure*
To this troop[5] come thou not near.

From this session° interdict°   *(of a court) / forbid*
10 Every fowl of tyrant wing,°   *bird of prey*
Save the eagle, feathered king:
Keep the obsequy° so strict.   *funeral rite*

Let the priest in surplice white,[6]
That defunctive music can,[7]
15 Be the death-divining swan,
Lest the requiem lack his right.°   *its due; its rite*

And thou, treble-dated° crow,   *long-lived*
That thy sable gender mak'st
With the breath thou giv'st and tak'st,[8]
20 'Mongst our mourners shalt thou go.

Here the anthem doth commence:
Love and constancy is dead,
Phoenix and the Turtle fled
In a mutual flame from hence.

---

1. *Phoenix:* a legendary, self-resurrecting bird believed to live in cycles of several centuries, dying in flames and being reborn from its own ashes—here, regarded as female. *Turtle:* turtledove, symbol of constancy—here, regarded as male. TEXTUAL COMMENT For the two main ways of understanding the structure of the poem, see Digital Edition TC 1.
2. Song. It is unclear which bird this refers to—possibly the phoenix, unless one reads "Death is now the Phoenix' nest" (line 56) not as part of a cycle but as a final resting place. Alternatively, it might be some other bird (the rooster?) known for its loud voice.
3. Supposedly, a unique tree on which sits the phoenix, which is similarly unique: only one exists at any given time.

4. Precursor of the devil: screech owls were thought to foretell death.
5. The mourning birds called forth by "the bird of loudest lay" (line 1).
6. The swan. A "surplice" is a loose clerical outer garment.
7. That is skilled in funereal music. Swans were thought to sing beautifully just before (their own) death (hence, the phrase "swan song").
8. *That . . . tak'st:* crows were believed to conceive by billing (kissing)—hence, "With the breath." *giv'st and tak'st:* Job 1:21: "The Lord giveth and the Lord taketh away." Also used in the Anglican funeral rite. *sable gender:* black offspring.

25 So they loved as° love in twain,   *that*
Had the essence but in one,
Two distincts, division none:
Number there in love was slain.[9]

Hearts remote,° yet not asunder;   *separate*
30 Distance and no space was seen
Twixt this Turtle and his queen:
But in them it were a wonder.[1]

So° between them love did shine   *So much*
That the Turtle saw his right°   *due; possession; nature*
35 Flaming in the Phoenix' sight;°   *eyes; appearance*
Either was the other's mine.°   *self; wealth*

Property was thus appalled
That the self was not the same:[2]
Single nature's double name,[3]
40 Neither two nor one was called.

Reason in itself confounded°   *thoroughly destroyed*
Saw division grow together;
To themselves yet either neither,[4]
Simple were so well compounded,[5]

45 That it cried, "How true a twain
Seemeth this concordant one!
Love hath reason, reason none,
If what parts can so remain."[6]

Whereupon it made this threne[7]
50 To the Phoenix and the Dove,
Co-supremes° and stars of love,   *Joint rulers*
As chorus to their tragic scene.

Threnos

Beauty, truth, and rarity,
Grace in all simplicity,
55 Here enclosed, in cinders lie.

---

9. The stanza toys with the commonplace paradox of lovers' simultaneous unity and separateness, ending with the hyperbolic claim that being neither one nor two, the love of the phoenix and the turtle killed the very notion of "number" (line 28).
1. It would have seemed extraordinary in any creatures but them.
2. The notion of an essential self was thus weakened by the fact that the self was not identical to itself.
3. An indivisible essence with two separate names. TEXTUAL COMMENT For the different possible meanings of the line, depending on how one punctuates it,

see Digital Edition TC 2.
4. Saw separate entities paradoxically become one, but each one was neither single nor united. *division*: things divided.
5. Single elements were so perfectly combined (appearing to remain "simple" rather than "compounded").
6. Love represents a higher reason than reason itself because of this embodiment of the paradox of unity of separate elements.
7. Reason made this threnody (a mourning song or epitaph).

Death is now the Phoenix' nest,[8]
And the Turtle's loyal breast
To eternity doth rest.[9]

Leaving no posterity,
60　'Twas not their infirmity:° 　　　　　　　　　　　　　　*sterility*
It was married chastity.

Truth may seem, but cannot be;
Beauty brag but 'tis not she:[1]
Truth and beauty buried be.

65　To this urn let those repair° 　　　　　　　　　　　　　　*go*
That are either true or fair:
For these dead birds sigh a prayer.

---

8. The phoenix's nest, ordinarily a site of regenera-
tion, is finally a place of death; alternatively, the
regenerative qualities of the phoenix's nest will overcome death.

9. Rests eternally; endures forever.
1. Any appearances of fidelity or beauty will only be
illusions.

APPENDICES

Attributed Poems

None of the attributed poems is incontrovertibly by Shakespeare, though the case is much better for some than for others. (See the Textual Introduction.) "A song, 'Shall I die?'"—probably not by Shakespeare—is noteworthy mainly as a virtuoso display of rhyming: there are usually eight pairs of rhyme words in each eight-line stanza, with the rhymes occurring as often as every three syllables and on occasion every two syllables ("Being set, lips met," line 31). Several of the other poems are, like the last part of "The Phoenix and Turtle," elegies—compositions in memory of the dead, though sometimes written while the subject was still alive. The first of the two epitaphs on the usurer John Combe reveals a conventional hostility to usury. The second, however, deploys the complex, sometimes positive, metaphorical relationship between usury and breeding characteristic of the early sonnets. Combe

> did gather [wealth from usury]
> To make the poor his issue [heirs]; he, their father,
> . . . [made] record of his tilth and seeds.
>
> (lines 3–5)

Urging marriage and a family, Sonnet 3 speaks of "the tillage of thy husbandry" (line 6). And Sonnet 6 argues:

> That use is not forbidden usury
> Which happies those that pay the willing loan:
> That's for thyself to breed another thee,
> Or ten times happier, be it ten for one.
>
> (lines 5–8)

Thus, in the sonnets, the language of usury helps clarify paternity, whereas in the second epitaph the language of paternity helps clarify usury. In both, however, the two terms are mutually illuminating. The last line quoted from Sonnet 6 is also reminiscent of the opening of the first epitaph: "Ten in the hundred here lies engraved; / A hundred to ten his soul is ne'er saved." Both refer to the highest legal interest rate—ten in a hundred, or 10 percent. But where the sonnet converts the allusion into a positive image, the elegy reverses the interest rate to denote the long odds against the usurer's salvation.

Similarly, "Verses on the Stanley Tomb at Tong" closely parallels the language of some of Shakespeare's sonnets concerned with the destructive power of time. The "register" and the "sky-aspiring pyramids" (East end 3, West end 2) also appear in Sonnet 123 ("pyramids built up," "registers," lines 2, 9). Closer still is the connection to Sonnet 55: "Not marble nor the gilded monuments / Of princes shall outlive this powerful rhyme" (lines 1–2). Stanley's "fame is more perpetual than these stones" (East 4); "Not monumental stone preserves our fame" (West 1). Stanley's "memory," however, "[s]hall outlive marble and defacers' hands" as well as "time's consumption" (West 3, 4, 5), just as "memory" need not worry that "war shall statues overturn" and is not dependent on "unswept stone besmeared with sluttish time" in Sonnet 55 (lines 8, 5, 4). Although the guarantee of immortality seems to rest on Stanley's life rather than the "powerful rhyme" of the sonnet (line 2), the end is the same: Stanley "is not dead; he doth but sleep" (East 2), while in the sonnet, "'[g]ainst death and all oblivious enmity / Shall you pace forth" (lines 9–10). Ultimately, poetic fame in the sonnet lasts only "till the judgment that yourself arise" (on Judgment Day, line 13); analogously, "Stanley for whom this stands shall stand in heaven" (West 6). The pun on the name in this concluding line ("Stanley/stands/stand") is similar to the sign of the author's hand left in "Upon a Pair of Gloves that Master Sent to his Mistress," where "[t]he will is all" recalls Shakespeare's emphatic references to his first name in Sonnets 135 and 136.

"Upon a Pair of Gloves" seems to reveal the poet intruding himself into a composition ostensibly from Alexander Aspinall to his (future?) wife; the "Epitaph on Himself" is strikingly impersonal. The lack of specificity may in this case be a poetic signature, however. By 1616, perhaps only Shakespeare could have written about Shakespeare without reference to his theatrical or literary career. This modesty coincides with an open threat: "cursed be he that moves my bones" (line 4). The apparently conventional warning was designed to forestall the very real danger of his body being dug up to make room for fresh corpses; in this case, it proved successful.

WALTER COHEN

SELECTED BIBLIOGRAPHY

Kerrigan, John. "Shakespeare, Elegy, and Epitaph 1557–1640." *The Oxford Handbook of Shakespeare's Poetry.* Ed. Jonathan F. S. Post. Oxford: Oxford UP, 2013. 225–44. Links "The Phoenix and Turtle" to the elegies attributed to Shakespeare, to the volume in which the poem appeared, to the period's competition—in poetry and in stone—in constructing memorials, and to the relationship between Catholic Wales and Protestant England.

Schoenfeldt, Michael. *The Cambridge Introduction to Shakespeare's Poetry.* Cambridge: Cambridge UP, 2010. 135–43. Focuses on the "fantasies of Shakespearean authorship" in the attributed poems.

TEXTUAL INTRODUCTION

The present edition prints nine poems attributed to William Shakespeare in the seventeenth century. None of them can be confirmed as written by the author. Nonetheless, scholars have made compelling cases for the funeral verse (Poems 3, 4, 5, 6, 7, 9), with circumstantial evidence supporting attribution for the epitaph on Elias James (Poem 5), that on the Stanley tomb at Tong (Poem 3), and especially the second of the two poems on John Combe (Poem 7).

James was a brewer whose establishment was located near Shakespeare's accommodation in Puddle Dock Hill, London, and Combe was a noted usurer in Stratford-upon-Avon, while Shakespeare himself is known to have had links with the Stanley family. It is also not impossible that he wrote the epitaph upon himself (Poem 9); it has become hard to think about this wry poem as being written by someone other than the Bard. Of course, Shakespeare was a friend and rival of Ben Jonson, even if the capping of verses here (Poem 4) feels apocryphal. The gift poem to Alexander Aspinall (Poem 2), a schoolmaster in Stratford, is a smaller matter, however charming, while the verse on James I (Poem 8)—by the leading playwright of the King's Men—feels appropriately weighty. The longest of the poems, "A Song, 'Shall I Die?'" (Poem 1), is now believed by few to have been written by Shakespeare.

The texts for the nine attributed poems come from a variety of sources: manuscripts, books, engravings, funeral monuments themselves. "A Song, 'Shall I die?'" exists in two manuscripts: one at Yale University and one in the Bodleian Library (dating to the 1630s). Since only the latter attributes the poem to Shakespeare, it is used here as control text; its readings also tend to be preferred, although, as the list of variants indicates, in a few cases recent editors have found the Yale version preferable. Consensus continues to build denying Shakespeare's authorship.

Only one contemporary attribution exists for "Upon a Pair of Gloves"—in a manuscript miscellany compiled around 1629 by Sir Francis Fane and now in the Shakespeare Birth Place Trust Records Office, Stratford. This manuscript also includes an inscription of "Epitaph on Himself" and a version of the first epitaph on Combe. Aspinall was married to Anne Shaw, the widow of Ralph Shaw; the Shaws were neighbors of the Shakespeares, and in 1616 their son July (or Julianus) was a witness of Shakespeare's will. It was conventional to write a poem and include it with the gift of a pair of gloves, and the poem is so slight that it does not secure authorship one way or another, even though critics have been attracted to the word "will" in line 2 as a personal signature.

The text for the "Verses on the Stanley Tomb at Tong" come directly from the inscription at St. Bartholomew Church, so there are no textual variants. The tomb, as well as its inscription, is undated. A manuscript dating to the 1630s is the first to assign authorship to Shakespeare, although Milton in his 1630 memorial poem to Shakespeare (first published in the 1632 Folio) shows evidence that he understood the poem to be by Shakespeare. The link between Shakespeare and the Stanley family—especially Ferdinando Stanley, Lord Strange, patron of Lord Strange's Men—has been reasonably well established. Of all the nine poems, this one feels the most like William Shakespeare. It includes several verbal echoes of such freestanding poems as the sonnets and *The Rape of Lucrece*.

"On Ben Jonson" comes from a manuscript in the Bodleian Library compiled by Nicholas Burghe, perhaps in the mid-seventeenth century.

"An Epitaph on Elias James" is first printed by John Stow in his 1633 *Survey of London*, where it was unattributed. Originally, however, it appeared in the church of St. Andrews by the Wardrobe, London, at the lower end of the south aisle, but the church was destroyed by the Great Fire in 1666. A manuscript version in the Bodleian Library attributes the epitaph to Shakespeare, the same manuscript that attributes to him "A Song, 'Shall I die?'" James worked close to the Blackfriars Theatre; the church where he is buried is opposite to the Blackfriars Gate-House, which Shakespeare owned. Scholars are uncertain whether Shakespeare wrote the epitaph.

The two epitaphs on John Combe are not created equal. Shakespeare almost certainly knew the Stratford moneylender, who died on July 10, 1614: in 1602, Combe and his uncle sold Old Stratford land to Shakespeare; and in his will of 1616 the author left Combe's brother Thomas his sword. The epitaph on the tomb in Holy Trinity Church has disappeared, but in 1673 Robert Dobyns transcribed it in a manuscript preserved at the Folger Library. Despite the connection with Combe, scholars do not think Shakespeare wrote "An Extemporary Epitaph on John Combe, a Noted Usurer." The case is stronger for "Another Epitaph on John Combe," which is attributed to Shakespeare in a manuscript in the Bodleian Library.

"Upon the King" has a complicated transmission history that is still being tracked, but the four-line verse appears beneath a picture of James I in the 1616 edition of his own *Works*, from which the text for the present edition comes. The poem was attributed to Shakespeare in two manuscripts, now in the Folger Library, dating to ca. 1633–34 and ca. 1650, respectively, perhaps simply because he was the leading writer for the King's Men. While the dating of the poem is widely disputed, it may have been written around 1611, making Shakespeare's authorship possible.

Shakespeare's "Epitaph on Himself" comes from the inscription on his grave in Holy Trinity Church, Stratford.

PATRICK CHENEY

Attributed Poems

1
A song, "Shall I die?"[1]

[1]

Shall I die? Shall I fly
Lovers' baits and deceits, sorrow breeding?
Shall I tend?° Shall I send?   *wait passively*
Shall I shew,° and not rue my proceeding?°   *appear / (as in a lawsuit)*
5   In all duty her beauty
Binds me her servant forever.
       If she scorn, I mourn,
I retire to despair, joining° never.   *(sexually; militarily)*

[2]

       Yet I must vent my lust
10 And explain inward pain by my love breeding.[2]
       If she smiles, she exiles
All my moan; if she frown, all my hope's deceiving.
       Suspicious doubt,° oh, keep out,   *fear (of rejection)*
For thou art my tormentor.
15   Fly away, pack away;
I will love, for hope bids me venture.

[3]

       'Twere abuse to accuse
My fair love, ere I prove° her affection.   *test*
       Therefore, try! Her reply
20 Gives thee joy or annoy or affliction.[3]
       Yet howe'er, I will bear
Her pleasure with patience, for beauty
       Sure will not seem to blot
Her deserts; wronging him doth her duty.[4]

[4]

25   In a dream it did seem
(But alas, dreams do pass as do shadows)
       I did walk, I did talk
With my love, with my dove, through fair meadows.
       Still° we passed till at last   *Continually*
30 We sat to repose us for pleasure.
       Being set, lips met,
Arms twined, and did bind my heart's treasure.

1
1. Textual Comment For differences between the two manuscript versions of this poem (lines 4, 8, 10, 15, 54), see Digital Edition TC 1.
2. Yet I must give expression to my lust by explaining (in poetry) the pain caused by my love.

3. "Affliction" may also suggest a sexually transmitted disease.
4. *for beauty . . . duty:* for true beauty will not allow her reputation to appear tarnished; wronging him serves her well.

[5]

Gentle wind sport did find
Wantonly° to make fly her gold tresses.   *Capriciously*
35   As they shook, I did look,
But her fair° did impair all my senses.   *beauty*
As amazed, I gazed
On more than a mortal complexion.
You that love can prove[5]
40   Such force in beauty's inflection.°   *bending*

[6]

Next° her hair, forehead fair,   *Next to*
Smooth and high; next doth lie, without wrinkle,
Her fair brows;° under those,   *forehead*
Star-like eyes win love's prize when they twinkle.
45   In her cheeks who° seeks   *whoever*
Shall find there displayed beauty's banner.°   *(a blush)*
Oh, admiring desiring
Breeds, as I look still upon her.

[7]

Thin lips red, fancy's[6] fed
50   With all sweets when he meets, and is granted
There to trade,[7] and is made
Happy, sure, to endure still undaunted.
Pretty chin doth win
Of all that's called commendations;[8]
55   Fairest neck, no speck.
All her parts merit high admirations.

[8]

Pretty bare, past compare,
Parts, those plots which besots still asunder.[9]
It is meet naught but sweet
60   Should come near that so rare 'tis a wonder.[1]
No mishap, no scape°   *transgression*
Inferior to nature's perfection.
No blot, no spot:
She's beauty's queen in election.

[9]

65   Whilst I dreamt, I exempt
From all care, seemed to share pleasure's plenty.
But awake, care take,
For I find to my mind pleasures scanty.
Therefore I will try
70   To compass° my heart's chief contenting.   *accomplish*
To delay, some say,
In such a case causeth repenting.

---

5. You who are in love are able to test.
6. *Affection is; imagination is.*
7. *granted / There to trade:* allowed to kiss there.
8. Wins praise from all people.
9. *Pretty . . . asunder:* Incomparably pretty "bare"

skin and breasts (exposed above a low neckline),
those nipples ("plots") that, always separated,
(always) cause infatuation.
1. It is proper that nothing but good should come
near that which is so wonderfully valuable.

2
Upon a Pair of Gloves That Master Sent to His Mistress

The gift is small,
The will is all:[1]
Alexander Aspinall[2]

3
Verses on the Stanley Tomb at Tong

[East end]
Ask who lies here, but do not weep.
He is not dead; he doth but sleep.
This stony register° is for his bones;   *record*
His fame is more perpetual than these stones,
5   And his own goodness, with himself being gone,
Shall live when earthly monument is none.

[West end]
Not monumental stone preserves our fame,
Nor sky-aspiring pyramids our name.
The memory of him for whom this stands
Shall outlive marble and defacers' hands.
5   When all to time's consumption shall be given,
Stanley for whom this stands shall stand in heaven.

4
On Ben Jonson[1]

Master Ben Jonson and Master William Shakespeare, being
merry at a tavern, Master Jonson having begun this for his
epitaph:
        Here lies Ben Jonson
5   That was once one,°   *alive*
he gives it to Master Shakespeare to make up who presently
writes:
        Who while he lived was a slow thing,[2]
        And now, being dead, is no thing.

5
An Epitaph on Elias James

When God was pleased, the world unwilling yet,[1]
Elias James to nature paid his debt,
And here reposeth. As he lived, he died,
The saying strongly in him verified:
5   "Such life, such death."° Then, a known truth to tell,   *One dies as one lives*
He lived a godly life, and died as well.

2
1. With a characteristic pun on the poet's name: the
goodwill behind the gift is all-encompassing; it's the
thought that counts.
2. Stratford schoolmaster from 1582 to 1624.
4

1. One of the best known of Shakespeare's fellow
playwrights (1572–1637).
2. Jonson was a notoriously slow writer.
5
1. Though the world was still unwilling.

6
An Extemporary Epitaph on John Combe, a Noted Usurer

Ten in the hundred[1] here lies engraved;
A hundred to ten° his soul is ne'er saved.   *(odds)*
    If anyone ask who lies in this tomb,
    "O ho!" quoth the devil, "'tis my John-a-Combe."

7
Another Epitaph on John Combe

    Howe'er he livèd judge not,
    John Combe shall never be forgot
    While poor hath memory, for he did gather[1]
    To make the poor his issue;° he, their father,   *offspring; heirs*
5   As record of his tilth and seeds[2]
    Did crown° him in his latter deeds.   *honor; praise*

8
Upon the King

Crowns have their compass,° length of days their date,°   *boundaries / limit*
Triumphs their tombs, felicity her fate:
Of more than earth, can earth make none partaker,[1]
But knowledge makes the King most like his maker.

9
Epitaph on Himself

Good friend, for Jesus' sake forbear
To dig the dust enclosèd here.
Blessed be the man that spares these stones,
And cursed be he that moves my bones.

6
1. *Ten . . . hundred*: a slang term for "usurer," suggesting one who lends money at 10 percent interest.
7
1. Accumulate wealth (through usury).

2. Tillage and planting (offspring).
8
1. No earthly power (not even a king) has power over the afterlife.

Early Modern Map Culture

In the early modern period, maps were often considered rare and precious objects, and seeing a map could be an important and life-changing event. This was so for Richard Hakluyt, whose book *The Principal Navigations, Voyages, Traffics and Discoveries of the English Nation* (1598–1600) was the first major collection of narratives describing England's overseas trading ventures. Hakluyt tells how, as a boy still at school in London, he visited his uncle's law chambers and saw a book of cosmography lying open there. Perceiving his nephew's interest in the maps, the uncle turned to a modern map and "pointed with his wand to all the knowen Seas, Gulfs, Bayes, Straights, Capes, Rivers, Empires, Kingdomes, Dukedomes, and Territories of ech part, with declaration also of their speciall commodities and particular wants, which by the benefit of traffike, and entercourse of merchants, are plentifully supplied. From the Mappe he brought me to the Bible, and turning to the 107 Psalme, directed mee to the 23 and 24 verses, where I read, that they which go downe to the sea in ships, and occupy [work] by the great waters, they see the works of the Lord, and his woonders in the deepe." This event, Hakluyt records, made so deep an impression on him that he vowed he would devote his life to the study of this kind of knowledge. *The Principal Navigations* was the result, a book that mixes a concern with the profit to be made from trade and from geographical knowledge with praise for the Christian god who made the "great waters" and, in Hakluyt's view, looked with special favor on the English merchants and sailors who voyaged over them.

In the early modern period, access to maps was far less easy than it is today. Before the advent of printing in the late fifteenth century, maps were drawn and decorated by hand. Because they were rare and expensive, these medieval maps were for the most part owned by the wealthy and the powerful. Sometimes adorned with pictures of fabulous sea monsters and exotic creatures, maps often revealed the Christian worldview of those who composed them. Jerusalem appeared squarely in the middle of many maps (called T and O maps), with Asia, Africa, and Europe, representing the rest of the known world, arranged symmetrically around the Holy City. Because they had not yet been discovered by Europeans, North and South America were not depicted.

Mapping practices changed markedly during the late fifteenth and sixteenth centuries both because of the advent of print and also because European nations such as Portugal and Spain began sending ships on long sea voyages to open new trade routes to the East and, eventually, to the Americas. During this period, monarchs competed to have the best cartographers supply them with accurate maps of their realms and especially of lands in Africa, Asia, or the Americas, where they hoped to trade or plant settlements. Such knowledge was precious and jealously guarded. The value of such maps and the secrecy that surrounded them are indicated by a story in Hakluyt's *Principal Navigations*. An English ship had captured a Portuguese vessel in the Azores, and a map was discovered among the ship's valuable cargo, which included spices, silks, carpets, porcelain, and other exotic commercial objects. The map was "inclosed in a case of sweete Cedar wood, and lapped up almost an hundred fold in fine calicut-cloth, as though it had been some incomparable jewell." The value of the map and an explanation for the careful way in which it was packed lay in the particular information it afforded the English about Portuguese trading routes. More than beautiful objects, maps like this one were crucial to the international race to find safe sea routes to the most profitable trading centers in the East.

In the sixteenth century, books of maps began to be printed, making them more affordable for ordinary people, though some of these books, published as big folio volumes, remained too dear for any but wealthy patrons to buy. Yet maps were increasingly a part of daily life, and printing made many of them more accessible. Playgoers in Shakespeare's audiences must have understood in general the value and uses of maps, for they appear as props in a number of his plays. Most famously, at the beginning of *King Lear*, the old king has a map brought onstage showing the extent of his kingdom. He then points on the map to the three separate parts into which he intends to divide his realm to share among his daughters. The map, often unfurled with a flourish on a table or held up for view by members of Lear's retinue, signals the crucial relationship of the land to the monarch. He is his domains, and the map signifies his possession of them. To divide the kingdom, in essence to tear apart the map, would have been judged foolish and destructive by early modern political theorists. Similarly, in *1 Henry IV*, when rebels against the sitting monarch, Henry IV, plot to overthrow him, they bring a map onstage in order to decide what part of the kingdom will be given to each rebel leader. Their proposed dismemberment of the realm signifies the danger they pose. Treasonously, they would rend in pieces the body of the commonwealth.

Maps, of course, had other uses besides signifying royal domains. In some instances, they were used pragmatically to help people find their way from one place to another. A very common kind of map, a portolan chart, depicted in minute detail the coastline of a particular body of water. Used by sailors, these maps frequently were made by people native to the region they described. Many world or regional maps, because they were beautifully decorated and embellished with vivid colors, were used for decorative purposes. John Dee, a learned adviser to Queen Elizabeth and a great book collector, wrote that some people used maps "to beautifie their Halls, Parlers, Chambers, Galeries, Studies, or Libraries." He also spoke of more scholarly uses for these objects. They could, for example, be useful aids in the study of history or geography, enabling people to locate "thinges past, as battels fought, earthquakes, heavenly fyringes, and such occurents in histories mentioned." Today we make similar use of maps, like those included in this volume, when, in reading Shakespeare's plays, we resort to a map to find out where the Battle of Agincourt took place or where Othello sailed when he left Venice for Cyprus.

The print edition of *The Norton Shakespeare* includes five maps; the Digital Edition seven. Four of these maps, found in both editions, are modern ones drawn specifically to show the location of places important to Shakespeare's plays. They depict the British Isles and western France, London, and the Mediterranean world, in addition to a map of England showing the typical routes the Chamberlain's Men followed when they went on tour outside of London. The print and digital editions also both contain a period map of the Christian Holy Lands at the eastern tip of the Mediterranean Sea. This map was included in what was known as the Bishops' Bible, first printed in London in 1568. Put together under the leadership of the Archbishop of Canterbury, Matthew Parker, working with a committee of Anglican bishops, the 1568 edition featured beautiful typography and illustrations. The text continued to undergo revisions, and twenty editions of it were published between 1568 and 1602.

This last map shows places mentioned in the first four Gospels (Matthew, Mark, Luke, and John), which collectively tell of the life and deeds of Jesus. It indicates, for example, the location of Bethlehem, where he was born; Nazareth, where he spent his youth; and Cana of Galilee, where he turned water into wine at a marriage. It suggests that, to the English reader, this particular territory was overwritten by and completely intertwined with Christian history. Yet in the Mediterranean Sea, on the left of the map, several large ships are visible, reminders of another fact about this region: it was a vigorous trading arena where European Christian merchants did business with local merchants—Christian, Jew, and Muslim—and with traders bringing luxury goods by overland routes from the East. A number of Shakespeare's plays are set in this complex eastern Mediterranean region where several religious traditions laid claim to territory and many commercial powers competed for preeminence. *Pericles,* for example, has a hero who is the ruler of Tyre, a city on the upper right side of the map. In the course of his wanderings, Pericles visits many cities along the eastern coasts of the Mediterranean. The conclusion of the play, in which the hero is reunited both with his long-lost daughter and with the wife he believes dead, has seemed to many critics to share in a sense of Christian miracle, despite its ostensibly pagan setting. *The Comedy of Errors* and parts of *Othello* and of *Antony and Cleopatra* are also set in the Eastern Mediterranean. One of Shakespeare's earliest plays, *The Comedy of Errors,* is an urban comedy in which the protagonists are merchants deeply involved in commercial transactions. It is also the first play in which Shakespeare mentions the Americas, which he does in an extended joke in which he compares parts of a serving woman's body to the countries on a map including Ireland, France, and the Americas. In *Othello,* the eastern Mediterranean island of Cyprus is represented as a tense Christian outpost defending Venetian interests against the Muslim Turks. In *Antony and Cleopatra,* Egypt figures as the site of Eastern luxury and also of imperial conquest, an extension of the Roman Empire. Clearly, this region was to Shakespeare and his audiences one of the most complex and highly charged areas of the world: a site of religious, commercial, and imperial significance.

Two other maps occur only in the Digital Edition, where their colors and their details can be appreciated. The first is a map of London that appeared in a 1574 edition of a famous German atlas, *Civitates Orbis Terrarum (Cities of the World)*, compiled by George Braun with engravings by Franz Hogenberg. This remarkable atlas includes maps and information on cities throughout Europe, Asia, and North Africa; the first of its six volumes appeared in 1572, the last in 1617. Being included in the volume indicated a city's status as a recognized metropolitan center. In a charming touch, Braun added to his city maps pictures of figures in local dress. At the bottom of the map of London, for example, there are four figures who appear to represent the city's prosperous citizens. In the center, a man in a long robe holds the hand of a soberly dressed matron. On either side of them are younger and more ornately dressed figures. The young man sports a long sword and a short cloak, the woman a dress with elaborate skirts. In the atlas, the map is colored, and the clothes of the two young people echo one another in shades of green and red.

At the time the map was made, London was a rapidly expanding metropolis. In 1550, it contained about 55,000 people; by 1600, it would contain nearly 200,000. The map shows the densely populated old walled city north of the Thames River, in the middle of which was Eastcheap, the commercial district where, in Shakespeare's plays about the reign of Henry IV, Falstaff holds court in a tavern. The map also shows that by 1570 London was spreading westward beyond the wall toward Westminster Palace. This medieval structure, which appears on the extreme left side of the map, was where English monarchs resided when in London and where, at the end of *2 Henry IV,* the king dies in the fabled Jerusalem Chamber of the Westminster complex. On the far right of the map, one can see the Tower of London, where Edward IV's young sons were imprisoned by Richard III, an event depicted in Shakespeare's *The Tragedy of King Richard the Third.* The map also indicates the centrality of the Thames to London's commercial life. It shows the river full of boats; some of those on the east side of London Bridge are large oceangoing vessels with several masts. South of the river, where many of the most famous London theaters, including Shakespeare's Globe, were to be constructed in the 1590s, there are relatively few buildings. By 1600, this would change, as Southwark, as it was known, came to be an increasingly busy entertainment, residential, and commercial district.

The final map, of Great Britain and Ireland, comes from a 1612 edition of John Speed's *The Theatre of the Empire of Great Britain,* an innovative atlas containing individual maps of counties and towns in England and Wales, as well as larger maps that include Scotland and Ireland. Speed was by trade a tailor who increasingly devoted his time to the study of history and cartography. Befriended by the antiquarian scholar William Camden, he eventually won patronage from Sir Fulke Greville, who gave him a pension that allowed him to devote himself full-time to his scholarly endeavors. *The Theatre* was one product of this newfound freedom. The map included here, one of his most ambitious, shows the entire British Isles, nominated by Speed as "The Kingdome of Great Britaine and Ireland," though at this time Ireland was far from under the control of the English crown and Scotland was still an independent kingdom. James I, a Scot by birth, had unsuccessfully tried to forge a formal union between England and Scotland. This problem of the relationship of the parts of the British Isles to one another, and England's assertion of power over the others, is treated in *Henry V*, in which officers from Wales, Ireland, and Scotland are sharply delineated yet all depicted as loyal subjects of the English king.

One striking aspect of Speed's map is the balance it strikes between the two capital cities, London on the left, prominently featuring the Thames and London Bridge, and Edinburgh on the right. This would have pleased James, whose interest in his native country Shakespeare played to in his writing of *Macbeth*, which is based on material from Scottish history. Speed's map acknowledges the claims of the monarch to the territory it depicts. In the upper left corner, the British lion and the Scottish unicorn support a roundel topped with a crown. When James became king of England in 1603, he created this merged symbol of Scottish-English unity. The motto of the Royal Order of the Garter, "*Honi soit qui mal y pense*" (Shamed be he who thinks ill of it), is inscribed around the circumference. In the bottom left corner of the map, another locus of authority is established. Two cherubs, one holding a compass, the other a globe, sit beneath a banner on which is inscribed "Performed by John Speed." If the territory is the monarch's, the craft that depicts it belongs to the tailor turned cartographer.

Today, maps are readily available from shops or on the Internet, but in early modern England they were rare and valuable objects that could generate great excitement in those who owned or beheld them. Along with other precious items, maps were sometimes put on display in libraries and sitting rooms, but they had functions beyond the ornamental. They helped to explain and order the world, indicating who claimed certain domains, showing where the familiar stories of the Bible or of English history occurred, helping merchants find their way to distant markets. As John Dee, the early modern map enthusiast concluded, "Some, for one purpose: and some, for an other, liketh, loveth, getteth, and useth, Mappes, Chartes, and Geographicall Globes."

JEAN E. HOWARD

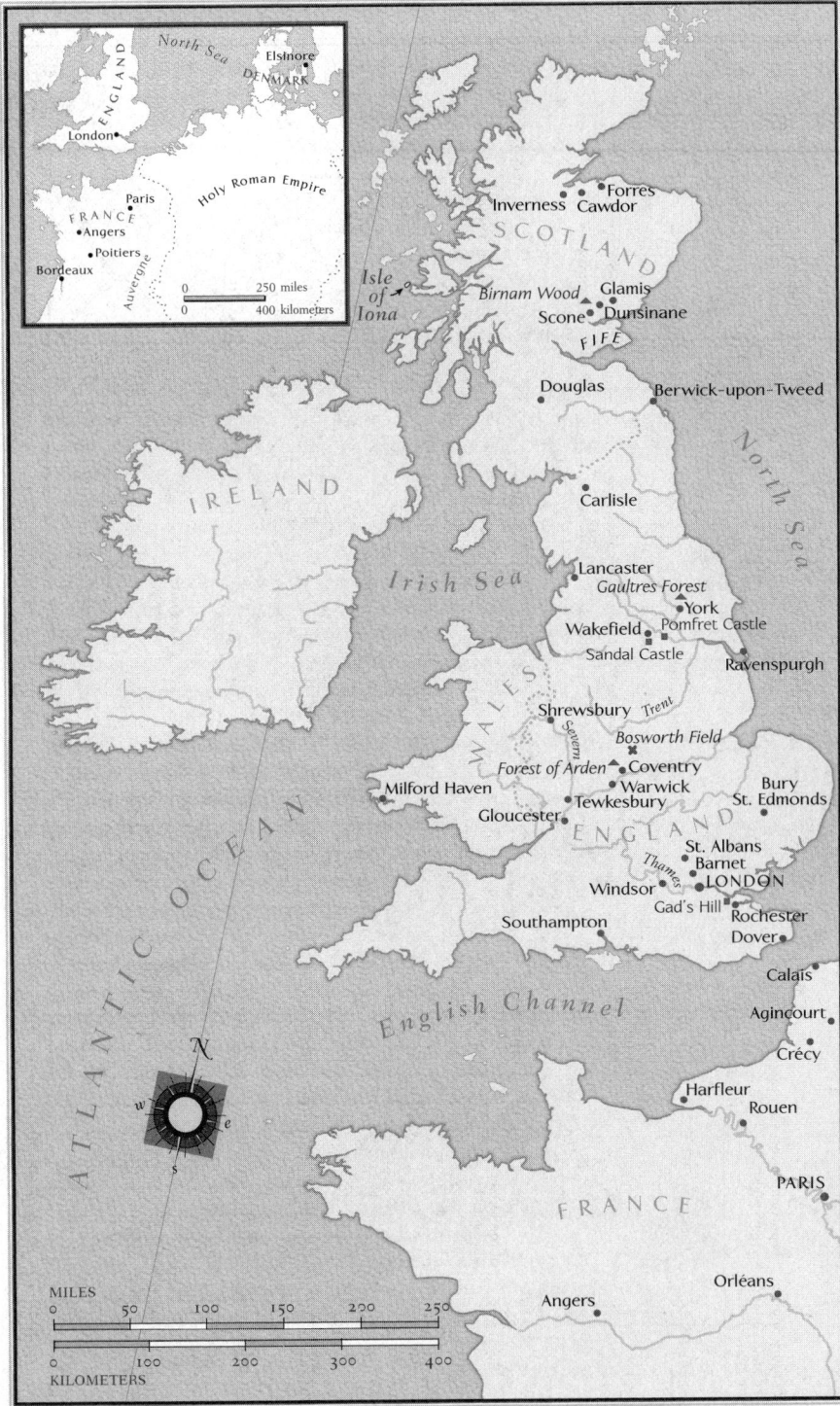

Ireland, Scotland, Wales, England, and Western France: Places Important to Shakespeare's Plays

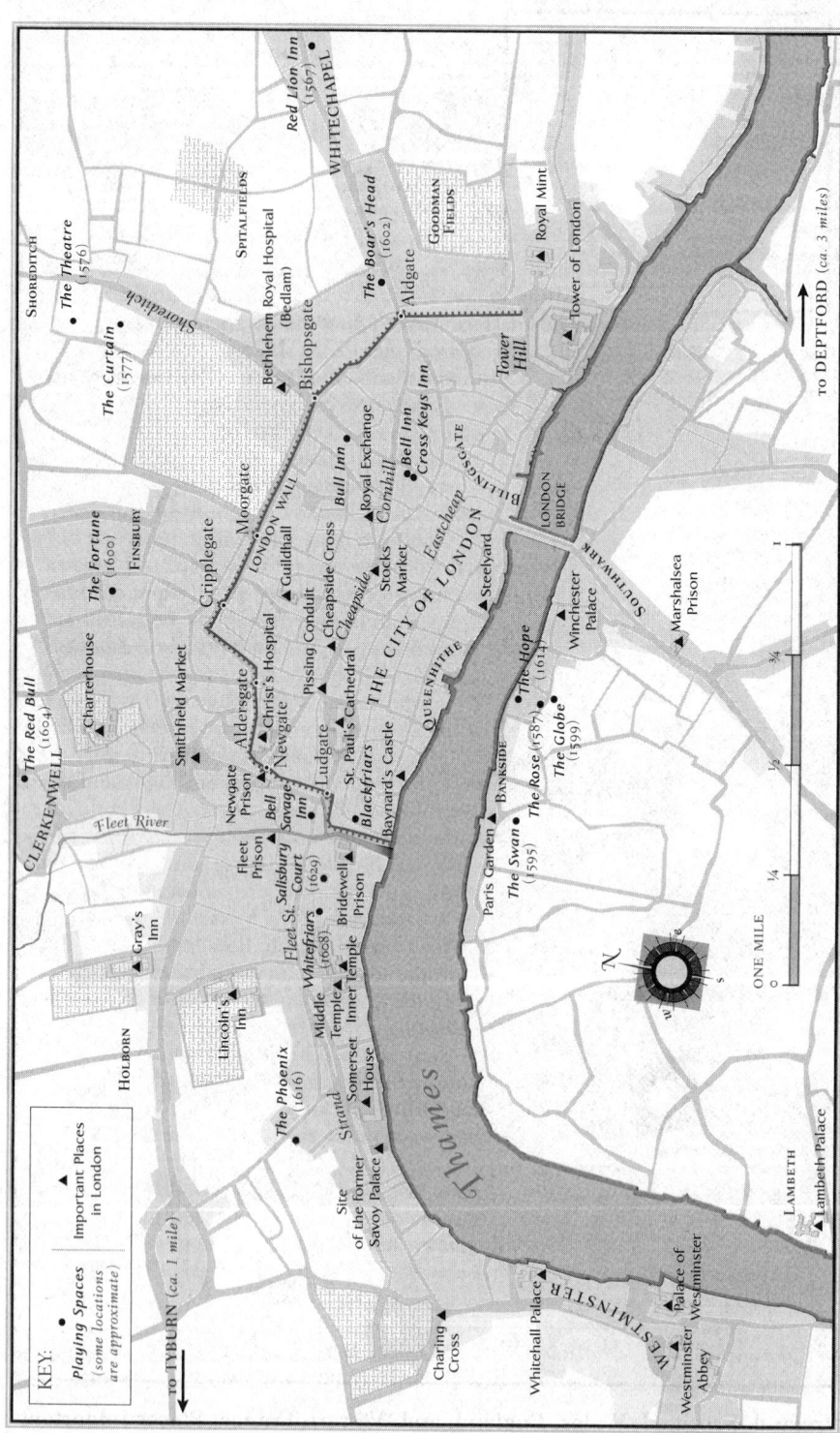

London: Places Important to Shakespeare's Plays and London Playgoing

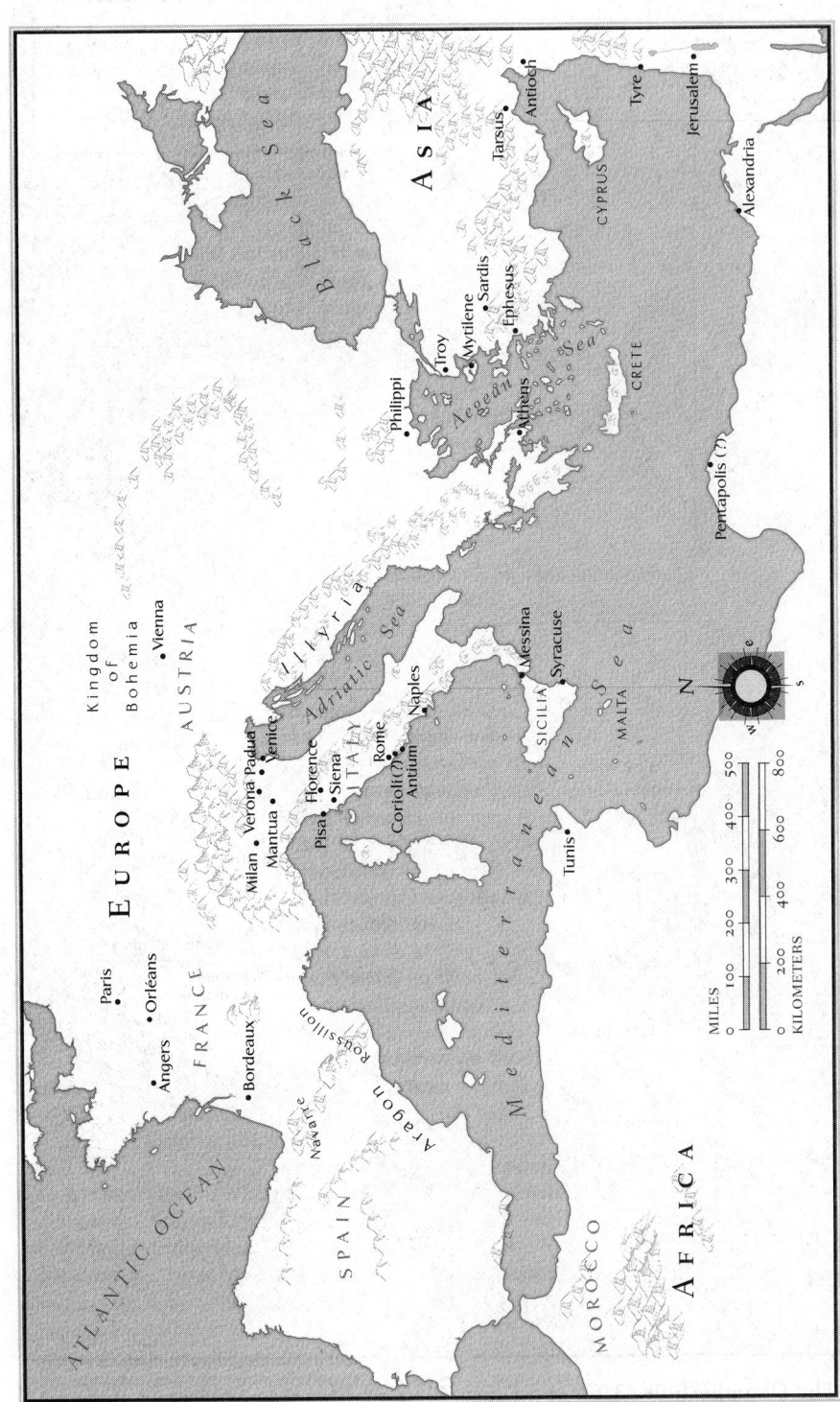

The Mediterranean World: Places Important to Shakespeare's Plays

The Chamberlain's Men and King's Men on Tour (adapted from a map first published by Sally-Beth MacLean in "Tour Routes: 'Provincial Wanderings' or 'Traditional Circuits'?" *Medieval and Renaissance Drama in England* 6 [1992]: 1–14).

Map of the Holy Land, from the Bishops' Bible, printed in London, 1568

Documents

This selection of documents illustrates three pivotal moments: Shakespeare's first recorded appearance on the London literary scene, an appreciation by one of his most enthusiastic early critics, and the canonization of his dramatic works in the First Folio, the single most important Shakespearean document that survives today. A much more extensive selection of documents can be found in the Digital Edition of *The Norton Shakespeare*, providing a broad range of contemporary testimony about Shakespeare's character, his art, and the social and institutional conditions under which it was produced. The first digital section, "Shakespeare and His Works," includes records of Shakespeare's life and career, evidence of his reputation in the literary community, and a variety of reactions to his plays and poems. The second section, "The Theater Scene," takes a wider view of Shakespeare's professional world with playhouse documents that offer a behind-the-scenes glimpse of companies acquiring scripts and properties, actors rehearsing their parts, and new theaters being constructed, while government documents show dramatic patronage, regulation, and censorship in action.

MISHA TERAMURA

Robert Greene on Shakespeare (1592)

[Robert Greene (1558–1592), a prolific author of plays, romances, and pamphlets, attacked Shakespeare in his *Greenes, Groats-worth of witte, bought with a million of Repentance*. Greene had studied at Cambridge, and his "M.A." was prominently displayed on his title pages. Shakespeare's lack of a university education is clearly one motive for the professional resentment expressed in the following excerpt. Another is probably that Greene was poor and very ill and felt forsaken while writing the *Groats-worth of witte*; the preface refers to it as his "swan-like song," and the narrative is framed as the repentance of a dying man. (Some scholars have held that the posthumously published work contains fabrications by a publisher attempting to capitalize on Greene's name.) The three colleagues Greene addresses are likely to be Christopher Marlowe, Thomas Nashe, and George Peele. The text is modernized from the first edition of *Greenes, Groats-worth of witte* (London, 1592).]

> *To those gentlemen, his quondam acquaintance,*
> *that spend their wits in making plays, R.G.*
> *wisheth a better exercise, and wisdom*
> *to prevent his extremities.*[1] . . .

Base-minded men, all three of you, if by my misery you be not warned, for unto none of you (like me) sought those burs to cleave—those puppets[2] (I mean) that spake from our mouths, those antics garnished in our colors. Is it not strange that I, to whom they all have been beholding—is it not like that you, to whom they all have been beholding, shall (were ye in that case as I am now) be both at once of

---

1. Adversity.
2. Actors.

them forsaken? Yes, trust them not: for there is an upstart crow, beautified with our feathers, that with his *tiger's heart wrapped in a player's hide*[3] supposes he is as well able to bombast out a blank verse as the best of you, and, being an absolute *Johannes factotum*,[4] is in his own conceit the only Shake-scene in a country. Oh, that I might entreat your rare wits to be employed in more profitable courses, and let those apes imitate your past excellence and nevermore acquaint them with your admired inventions! I know the best husband of you all will never prove an usurer,[5] and the kindest of them all will never prove a kind nurse. Yet, whilst you may, seek you better masters, for it is pity men of such rare wits should be subject to the pleasure of such rude grooms.

Francis Meres on Shakespeare (1598)

[Francis Meres (1565–1647) was educated at Cambridge and was active in London literary circles in 1597–98, after which he became a rector and schoolmaster in the country. The descriptions of Shakespeare are taken from a section on poetry in *Palladis Tamia. Wits Treasury*, a work largely consisting of translated classical quotations and *exempla*. Unlike the main body of the work, the subsections on poetry, painting, and music include comparisons of English artists to figures of antiquity. Meres goes on after the extract below to list Shakespeare among the best English writers of lyric, tragedy, comedy, and love poetry. The text is modernized from the first edition of *Palladis Tamia* (London, 1598).]

As the Greek tongue is made famous and eloquent by Homer, Hesiod, Euripides, Aeschylus, Sophocles, Pindarus, Phocylides, and Aristophanes, and the Latin tongue by Virgil, Ovid, Horace, Silius Italicus, Lucanus, Lucretius, Ausonius, and Claudianus, so the English tongue is mightily enriched and gorgeously invested in rare ornaments and resplendent habiliments[1] by Sir Philip Sidney, Spenser, Daniel, Drayton, Warner, Shakespeare, Marlowe, and Chapman. . . .

As the soul of Euphorbus was thought to live in Pythagoras, so the sweet witty soul of Ovid lives in mellifluous and honey-tongued Shakespeare. Witness his *Venus and Adonis*, his *Lucrece*, his sugared sonnets among his private friends, etc.

As Plautus and Seneca are accounted the best for comedy and tragedy among the Latins, so Shakespeare among the English is the most excellent in both kinds for the stage. For comedy, witness his *Gentlemen of Verona*, his *Errors*, his *Love Labor's Lost*, his *Love Labor's Won*,[2] his *Midsummer's Night Dream*, and his *Merchant of Venice*; for tragedy, his *Richard the 2*, *Richard the 3*, *Henry the 4*, *King John*, *Titus Andronicus*, and his *Romeo and Juliet*.

As Epius Stolo said that the Muses would speak with Plautus' tongue if they would speak Latin, so I say that the Muses would speak with Shakespeare's fine-filed phrase if they would speak English.

---

3. A parody of *Richard Duke of York* (*3 Henry VI*) 1.4.138: "O tiger's heart wrapped in a woman's hide!" This obvious allusion and the following pun on Shakespeare's name make it certain that Shakespeare is the "crow" described here.
4. Jack-of-all-trades. *conceit:* imagination.
5. Even the thriftiest among you will never commit usury.
1. Sumptuous clothing.
2. Either the play has not survived, or it is now known by a different name. However, this title is recorded elsewhere, in a bookseller's jottings of 1603, where it again appears following *Love's Labor's Lost*.

Front Matter from the First Folio
of Shakespeare's Plays (1623)

After Shakespeare's death in 1616, his friends and colleagues John Heminges and Henry Condell organized this first publication of his collected (thirty-six) plays. Eighteen of the plays had not appeared in print before, and for these the First Folio is the sole surviving source. Only *Pericles, The Two Noble Kinsmen, Sir Thomas More,* and *Edward III* are not included in the volume. Reproduced below in reduced facsimile are the title page (which includes Droeshout's famous portrait of Shakespeare), Heminges and Condell's prefatory address "To the great Variety of Readers," the book's table of contents, and the first page of text from *The Tempest*. Following the facsimile images is a commendatory poem by Shakespeare's great contemporary Ben Jonson (1572–1637), which was also published in the First Folio's front matter.

Mr. WILLIAM
SHAKESPEARES
COMEDIES,
HISTORIES, &
TRAGEDIES.

Published according to the True Originall Copies.

Martin Droeshout sculpsit London.

LONDON
Printed by Isaac Iaggard, and Ed. Blount. 1623.

To the great Variety of Readers.

Rom the moſt able, to him that can but ſpell: There you are number'd. We had rather you were weighd. Eſpecially, when the fate of all Bookes depends vpon your capacities : and not of your heads alone, but of your purſes. Well ! It is now publique, & you wil ſtand for your priuiledges wee know : to read, and cenſure. Do ſo, but buy it firſt. That doth beſt commend a Booke, the Stationer ſaies. Then, how odde ſoeuer your braines be, or your wiſedomes, make your licence the ſame, and ſpare not. Iudge your ſixe-pen'orth, your ſhillings worth, your fiue ſhillings worth at a time, or higher, ſo you riſe to the iuſt rates, and welcome. But, what euer you do, Buy. Cenſure will not driue a Trade, or make the Iacke go. And though you be a Magiſtrate of wit, and ſit on the Stage at *Black-Friers*, or the *Cock-pit*, to arraigne Playes dailie, know, theſe Playes haue had their triall alreadie, and ſtood out all Appeales ; and do now come forth quitted rather by a Decree of Court, then any purchas'd Letters of commendation.

It had bene a thing, we confeſſe, worthie to haue bene wiſhed, that the Author himſelfe had liu'd to haue ſet forth, and ouerſeen his owne writings ; But ſince it hath bin ordain'd otherwiſe, and he by death departed from that right, we pray you do not enuie his Friends, the office of their care, and paine, to haue collected & publiſh'd them; and ſo to haue publiſh'd them, as where (before) you were abuſ'd with diuerſe ſtolne, and ſurreptitious copies, maimed, and deformed by the frauds and ſtealthes of iniurious impoſtors, that expoſ'd them : euen thoſe, are now offer'd to your view cur'd, and perfect of their limbes; and all the reſt, abſolute in their numbers, as he conceiued thē. Who, as he was a happie imitator of Nature, was a moſt gentle expreſſer of it. His mind and hand went together: And what he thought, he vttered with that eaſineſſe, that wee haue ſcarſe receiued from him a blot in his papers. But it is not our prouince, who onely gather his works, and giue them you, to praiſe him. It is yours that reade him. And there we hope, to your diuers capacities, you will finde enough, both to draw, and hold you : for his wit can no more lie hid, then it could be loſt. Reade him, therefore ; and againe, and againe : And if then you doe not like him, ſurely you are in ſome manifeſt danger, not to vnderſtand him. And ſo we leaue you to other of his Friends, whom if you need, can bee your guides : if you neede them not, you can leade your ſelues, and others. And ſuch Readers we wiſh him.

A 3   *Iohn Heminge.*
        Henrie Condell.

Line 8. *Stationer:* bookseller.
Line 13. *Iacke:* machine.
Lines 13–14. *And though . . . dailie:* addressed in particular to men of fashion who occupied seats onstage so they could be seen while watching the play.
Lines 15–17. *these Playes . . . commendation:* The legal puns that began with "Magistrate of wit" (fashionable playgoer) in line 13 continue here. The "purchas'd Letters of commendation" refer to escaping the conse-quences of a crime by means of bribery or other undue influence; Shakespeare's plays, by contrast, have been acquitted after a proper and rigorous trial (approved by theater audiences and not insinuated into the public favor by some outside influence).
Line 27. *absolute in their numbers:* correct in their versification. *thē:* them.
Line 28. *a happie:* an apt; a successful.

A CATALOGVE

of the seuerall Comedies, Histories, and Tragedies contained in this Volume.

Troilus and Cressida, despite its absence from the "Catalogue," was in fact printed in the First Folio. Due to negotiations over printing rights, it was included only at the last minute and placed between the histories and tragedies.

1

THE
TEMPEST.

Actus primus, Scena prima.

A tempestuous noise of Thunder and Lightning heard: Enter a Ship-master, and a Botesvvaine.

Master.

BOte-swaine.

Botes. Heere Master: What cheere?

Mast. Good: Speake to th'Mariners: fall too't, yarely, or we run our selues a ground, bestirre, bestirre. *Exit.*

Enter Mariners.

Botes. Heigh my hearts, cheerely, cheerely my harts: yare, yare: Take in the toppe-sale: Tend to th'Masters whistle: Blow till thou burst thy winde, if roome enough.

Enter Alonso, Sebastian, Anthonio, Ferdinando, Gonzalo, and others.

Alon. Good Botesswaine haue care: where's the Master? Play the men.

Botes. I pray now keepe below.

Anth. Where is the Master, Boson?

Botes. Do you not heare him? you marre our labour, Keepe your Cabines: you do assist the storme.

Gonz. Nay, good be patient.

Botes. When the Sea is: hence, what cares these roarers for the name of King? to Cabine; silence: trouble vs not.

Gon. Good, yet remember whom thou hast aboord.

Botes. None that I more loue then my selfe. You are a Counsellor, if you can command these Elements to silence, and worke the peace of the present, wee will not hand a rope more, vse your authoritie: If you cannot, giue thankes you haue liu'd so long, and make your selfe readie in your Cabine for the mischance of the houre, if it so hap. Cheerely good hearts: out of our way I say. *Exit.*

Gon. I haue great comfort from this fellow: methinks he hath no drowning marke vpon him, his complexion is perfect Gallowes: stand fast good Fate to his hanging, make the rope of his destiny our cable, for our owne doth little aduantage: If he be not borne to bee hang'd, our case is miserable. *Exit.*

Enter Boteswaine.

Botes. Downe with the top-Mast: yare, lower, lower, bring her to Try with Maine-course. A plague——

A cry within. *Enter Sebastian, Anthonio & Gonzalo.*

vpon this howling: they are lowder then the weather, or our office: yet againe? What do you heere? Shal we giue ore and drowne, haue you a minde to sinke?

Sebas. A poxe o'your throat, you bawling, blasphemous incharitable Dog.

Botes. Worke you then.

Anth. Hang cur, hang, you whoreson insolent Noysemaker, we are lesse afraid to be drownde, then thou art.

Gonz. I'le warrant him for drowning, though the Ship were no stronger then a Nutt-shell, and as leaky as an vnstanched wench.

Botes. Lay her a hold, a hold, set her two courses off to Sea againe, lay her off.

Enter Mariners wet.

Mari. All lost, to prayers, to prayers, all lost.

Botes. What must our mouths be cold?

Gonz. The King, and Prince, at prayers, let's assist them, for our case is as theirs.

Sebas. I'am out of patience.

An. We are meerly cheated of our liues by drunkards, This wide-chopt-rascall, would thou mightst lye drowning the washing of ten Tides.

Gonz. Hee'l be hang'd yet, Though euery drop of water sweare against it, And gape at widst to glut him. *A confused noyse within.* Mercy on vs.

We split, we split, Farewell my wife, and children, Farewell brother: we split, we split, we split.

Anth. Let's all sinke with' King

Seb. Let's take leaue of him. *Exit.*

Gonz. Now would I giue a thousand furlongs of Sea, for an Acre of barren ground: Long heath, Browne firrs, any thing; the wills aboue be done, but I would faine dye a dry death. *Exit.*

Scena Secunda.

Enter Prospero and Miranda.

Mira. If by your Art (my deerest father) you haue Put the wild waters in this Rore; alay them: The skye it seemes would powre down stinking pitch, But that the Sea, mounting to th' welkins cheeke, Dashes the fire out. Oh! I haue suffered With those that I saw suffer: A braue vessell

A   (Who

To the memory of my beloved,
The AUTHOR
Mr. William Shakespeare:
And
what he hath left us.[*]

To draw no envy, Shakespeare, on thy name,
  Am I thus ample to° thy book and fame,   *copious in praising*
While I confess thy writings to be such
  As neither man nor muse can praise too much:
5 'Tis true, and all men's suffrage.° But these ways   *agreement*
  Were not the paths I meant° unto thy praise,   *(to take)*
For seeliest¹ ignorance on these may light,
  Which, when it sounds, at best, but° echoes right;   *merely*
Or blind affection, which doth ne'er advance
10   The truth, but gropes, and urgeth all by chance;
Or crafty malice might pretend this praise,
  And think° to ruin, where it seemed to raise.   *intend*
These are as° some infamous bawd or whore   *as though*
  Should praise a matron: what could hurt her more?
15 But thou art proof against° them, and indeed   *impervious to*
  Above th' ill fortune of them, or the need.
I therefore will begin. Soul of the age!
  The applause, delight, the wonder of our stage!
My Shakespeare, rise! I will not lodge thee by
20   Chaucer or Spenser, or bid Beaumont lie
A little further to make thee a room;²
  Thou art a monument without a tomb
And art alive still while thy book doth live,
  And we have wits to read and praise to give.
25 That I not mix thee so, my brain excuses,
  I mean with great but disproportioned° muses.   *not comparable*
For if I thought my judgment were of years°   *mature*
  I should commit° thee surely with thy peers,   *compare*
And tell how far thou didst our Lyly outshine,
30   Or sporting Kyd, or Marlowe's mighty line.³
And though thou hadst small Latin and less Greek,⁴
  From thence to honor thee I would not seek°   *lack*

* By Ben Jonson.
1. Silliest; blindest (falcons' eyelids were "seeled," or stitched shut, while they were being tamed).
2. Geoffrey Chaucer, Edmund Spenser, and Francis Beaumont were all buried near each other in Westminster Abbey (known today as the "Poets' Corner"), while Shakespeare was buried in Stratford-upon-Avon. An earlier elegy for Shakespeare had begun: "Renownèd Spenser, lie a thought more nigh / To learned Chaucer, and, rare Beaumont, lie / A little nearer Spenser to make room / For Shakespeare . . ."
3. John Lyly, Thomas Kyd, and Christopher Marlowe were all celebrated Elizabethan playwrights. *sporting:* gamesome; frolicking (like a young goat, or "kid").
4. The underrating of Shakespeare's Latin was likely influenced by Jonson's pride in his own impressive classical learning.

For names, but call forth thund'ring Aeschylus,
    Euripides, and Sophocles to us,
35 Pacuvius, Accius, him of Cordova dead,[5]
    To life again, to hear thy buskin tread
And shake a stage; or, when thy socks were on,[6]
    Leave thee alone for the comparison
Of all that insolent Greece or haughty Rome
40   Sent forth, or since did from their ashes come.
Triumph, my Britain; thou hast one to show
    To whom all scenes° of Europe homage owe.   *stages*
He was not of an age, but for all time!
    And all the Muses still were in their prime
45 When like Apollo° he came forth to warm   *god of poetry*
    Our ears, or like a Mercury° to charm!   *god of eloquence*
Nature herself was proud of his designs,
    And joyed to wear the dressing of his lines,
Which were so richly spun and woven so fit
50   As, since, she will vouchsafe° no other wit.   *grant*
The merry Greek, tart Aristophanes,
    Neat Terence, witty Plautus[7] now not please,
But antiquated and deserted lie,
    As they were not of Nature's family.
55 Yet must I not give Nature all; thy art,
    My gentle Shakespeare, must enjoy a part.
For though the poet's matter° nature be,   *raw material*
    His art doth give the fashion.° And that he°   *form / that he = he*
Who casts° to write a living line must sweat   *intends*
60   (Such as thine are) and strike the second heat
Upon the Muses' anvil, turn the same,
    And himself with it, that he thinks to frame,
Or for the laurel he may gain a scorn;[8]
    For a good poet's made as well as born,
65 And such wert thou. Look how the father's face
    Lives in his issue;° even so, the race   *offspring*
Of Shakespeare's mind and manners brightly shines
    In his well-turnèd and true-filèd° lines,   *truly polished*
In each of which he seems to shake a lance,[9]
70   As brandished at the eyes of ignorance.
Sweet swan of Avon, what a sight it were
    To see thee in our waters yet appear,
And make those flights upon the banks of Thames
    That so did take° Eliza and our James![1]   *transport*
75 But stay; I see thee in the hemisphere
    Advanced and made a constellation there.[2]

---

5. While the Latin tragedians Marcus Pacuvius and Lucius Accius were known to Jonson only by reputation, Seneca the Younger ("him of Cordova") was a major influence on Renaissance revenge tragedies.
6. The boots ("buskins") and shoes ("socks") worn by classical actors were symbolic of tragedy and comedy, respectively.
7. Aristophanes was a Greek writer of satirical comedies; Terence and Plautus were Roman comic

dramatists.
8. Or else, instead of the laurel (the symbol of poetic accomplishment), he may gain derision.
9. Punning on Shakespeare's name.
1. Queen Elizabeth and King James.
2. It was a commonplace in classical literature that those who lived glorious lives became constellations after death.

Shine forth, thou star of poets, and with rage
  Or influence,[3] chide or cheer the drooping° stage,   *dejected*
Which, since thy flight from hence, hath mourned like night,
80   And despairs day, but for thy volume's light.

BEN: JONSON.

---

3. Stars and planets were thought to affect human affairs. "Rage" suggests poetic inspiration.

Timeline

Dates for plays by Shakespeare and others are conjectural dates of composition, based on current understanding of the evidence. Works of poetry and prose are listed by date of publication.

TEXT	CONTEXT
	1558 Queen Mary I, a Roman Catholic, dies; her sister, Elizabeth, raised Protestant, is proclaimed queen.
	1559 Church of England is reestablished under the authority of the sovereign with the passage of the Act of Uniformity and the Act of Supremacy.
1562 *The Tragedy of Gorboduc*, by Thomas Norton and Thomas Sackville; the first English play in blank verse.	**1563** The Church of England adopts the Thirty-nine Articles of Religion, detailing its points of doctrine and clarifying its differences both from Roman Catholicism and from more radical forms of Protestantism.
	1564 William Shakespeare is born in Stratford to John and Mary Arden Shakespeare; he is christened a few days later, on April 26.
	1565 John Shakespeare is made an alderman of Stratford.
	1567 Mary Queen of Scots is imprisoned on suspicion of the murder of her husband, Lord Darnley. Their infant son, Charles James, is crowned James VI of Scotland. John Brayne builds the first English professional theater in the garden of a farmhouse called the Red Lion on the outskirts of London.
	1568 John Shakespeare is elected Bailiff of Stratford, the town's highest office. Performances in Stratford by the Queen's Players and the Earl of Worcester's men.
	1572 An act is passed that severely punishes vagrants and wanderers, including actors not affiliated with a patron. Performances in Stratford by the Earl of Leicester's men.

TEXT	CONTEXT
	1574 The Earl of Warwick's and Earl of Worcester's men perform in Stratford.
	1576 James Burbage, father of Richard, later the leading actor in Shakespeare's company, builds The Theatre in Shoreditch, a suburb of London.
1577 First edition of Holinshed's *Chronicles*.	**1577** The Curtain Theater opens in Shoreditch.
	1577–80 Sir Francis Drake circumnavigates the globe.
	1578 Mary Shakespeare pawns her lands, suggesting that the family is in financial distress. Lord Strange's Men and Lord Essex's Men perform at Stratford.
1579 Sir Thomas North's English translation of Plutarch's *Lives*.	**1580** A Jesuit mission is established in England with the aim of reconverting the nation to Roman Catholicism. Francis Drake returns from circumnavigation of globe.
	1582 Shakespeare marries Anne Hathaway.
	1583 The birth of Shakespeare's older daughter, Susanna.
	1584 Sir Walter Ralegh establishes the first English colony in the New World at Roanoke Island in modern North Carolina; the colony fails.
	1585 The birth of Shakespeare's twin son and daughter, Hamnet and Judith. John Shakespeare is fined for not going to church.
	1586 Sir Philip Sidney dies from battle wounds.
1587 Thomas Kyd, *The Spanish Tragedy*; Christopher Marlowe, *Tamburlaine*.	**1587** Mary Queen of Scots is executed for treason against Elizabeth I. Francis Drake, leading a daring raid at Cádiz, destroys many Spanish naval vessels and materiel. John Shakespeare loses his position as an alderman. Philip Henslowe builds the Rose theater at Bank-side, on the Thames.
	1588 The Spanish Armada attempts an invasion of England but is defeated.

TEXT	CONTEXT
1589 Robert Greene, *Friar Bacon and Friar Bungay.* Thomas Kyd(?), *Hamlet* (not extant; perhaps a source for Shakespeare's *Hamlet*). Christopher Marlowe, *The Jew of Malta.* Anonymous, *The True Chronicle History of King Leir, and His Three Daughters.*	**1589** Shakespeare is possibly affiliated with Strange's men, Pembroke's men, or both between this time and 1594.
1590 Edmund Spenser, *The Faerie Queene* (1st edition, Books 1–3). Sir Philip Sidney, *Arcadia.*	**1590** James VI of Scotland marries Anne of Denmark. James believes that witches raised a magical storm in an attempt to sink the ship carrying him home with his bride. Witch trials in Scotland.
1591–92 *Two Gentlemen of Verona.* *2 and 3 Henry VI.* *The Taming of the Shrew.* *1 Henry VI.*	**1592** The theatrical entrepreneur and financial manager of the Admiral's Men, Philip Henslowe, begins a diary—an important source for theater historians—recording his business transactions; continued until 1604.
1592–93 *Titus Andronicus.* *Richard III.* *Edward III.* *Venus and Adonis.*	From June 1592 to June 1594, London theaters are frequently shut down because of the plague; acting companies tour the provinces.
1594 *The Rape of Lucrece.* *The Comedy of Errors.*	**1594** Roderigo Lopez, a Christian physician of Portuguese Jewish descent, is executed on slight evidence for having plotted to poison Elizabeth I. The birth of James VI's first son, Henry.
1594–96 *Love's Labor's Lost.* *Richard II.* *Romeo and Juliet.* *A Midsummer Night's Dream.* *King John.*	**1595** Shakespeare lives in St. Helen's Parish, Bishopsgate, London. Shakespeare apparently becomes a sharer in (provides capital for) the newly formed Lord Chamberlain's Men. The Swan Theater is built in Bankside. Hugh O'Neill, Earl of Tyrone, rebels against English rule in Ireland. Walter Ralegh explores Guiana, on the north coast of South America.
1596 Edmund Spenser, *The Faerie Queene* (2nd edition, with Books 4–6). **1596–97** *1 Henry IV.* *The Merchant of Venice.*	**1596** John Shakespeare is granted a coat of arms; hence the title of "gentleman." William Shakespeare's son Hamnet dies. James Burbage buys a medieval hall in the former Blackfriars monastery and transforms it into an indoor theater.
	1597 The landlord refuses to renew the lease on the land under The Theatre in Shoreditch.

TEXT	CONTEXT
1598 *2 Henry IV.* *Much Ado About Nothing.* George Chapman begins to publish his translation of Homer. Ben Jonson, *Every Man in His Humor,* which lists Shakespeare as one of the actors.	**1598** Unable to renew the lease, the Chamberlain's Men move from The Theatre to the nearby Curtain Theater. The Edict of Nantes ends the French civil wars, granting toleration to Protestants. Materials from the demolished Theatre in Shoreditch are transported across the Thames to be used in building the Globe Theater, which opens in the following year.
1599 *The Merry Wives of Windsor.* *Henry V.* *As You Like It.* *Julius Caesar.* *The Passionate Pilgrim*, attributed entirely to Shakespeare. Michael Drayton and several collaborators, who object to Shakespeare's depiction of Oldcastle-Falstaff in the *Henry IV* plays, write *The First Part of the True and Honorable History of the Life of Sir John Oldcastle, the Good Lord Cobham.*	**1599** The Queen's favorite, Robert Devereux, Earl of Essex, leads an expedition to Ireland in March, but returning home without royal permission in September, is rebuked by the Queen and imprisoned. Satires and other offensive books are prohibited by ecclesiastical order. Extant copies are gathered and burned. Two notorious satirists, Thomas Nashe and Gabriel Harvey, are forbidden to publish.
1600–1601 *Hamlet.* *Twelfth Night.*	**1600** The Earl of Essex is suspended from some of his offices and confined to house arrest. The birth of James VI's second son, Charles. The founding of the East India Company. Edward Alleyn and Philip Henslowe build the Fortune Theater for the Lord Admiral's Men.
1601 "The Phoenix and Turtle" published in Robert Chester's *Love's Martyr.* In the "War of the Theaters," Ben Jonson, John Marston, and Thomas Dekker write a series of satiric plays mocking one another.	**1601** The Earl of Essex leads a rebellion against the principal adviser to Elizabeth I and possibly against the Queen herself. The previous afternoon, hoping to enlist support, some of the rebels pay for a performance of *Richard II*. Implicated in the uprising, which is quickly quelled, Shakespeare's patron, the Earl of Southampton, is imprisoned. The Earl of Essex is convicted of treason and beheaded, along with several of his chief supporters. Shakespeare's father dies.
1601–02 *Troilus and Cressida.*	**1602** Shakespeare makes substantial real-estate purchases in Stratford. The opening of the Bodleian Library in Oxford.

TEXT	CONTEXT
1601–03 *Othello.*	
1603 John Florio's translation of Montaigne's *Essays.* Ben Jonson, *Sejanus,* which lists Shakespeare as one of the actors.	**1603** Queen Elizabeth dies; she is succeeded by her cousin, James VI of Scotland (now James I of England).
1603–04 *Sir Thomas More* (revised version).	
	Plague closes the London theaters from mid-1603 to April 1604. Hugh O'Neill surrenders in Ireland.
1604 *Measure for Measure.*	**1604** The conclusion of a peace with Spain makes travel across the Atlantic safer, encouraging plans for English colonies in the Americas.
1605 *The History of King Lear.*	**1605** The discovery of the Gunpowder Plot by some radical Catholics to blow up the Houses of Parliament during its opening ceremonies, when the royal family, Lords, and Commons are assembled in one place. The Red Bull Theater built.
1606–07 *Timon of Athens.* *All's Well That Ends Well.* *Macbeth.* *Antony and Cleopatra.* Middleton(?), *The Revenger's Tragedy.*	**1606** The London and Plymouth Companies receive charters to colonize Virginia. Parliament passes "An Act to Restrain Abuses of Players," prohibiting oaths or blasphemy onstage.
1607–08 *Pericles.*	**1607** An English colony is established in Jamestown, Virginia. Shakespeare's daughter Susanna marries John Hall. Shakespeare's brother Edmund (described as a player) dies.
1608 *Coriolanus.*	
1609 *Shakespeare's Sonnets.*	
1610 *Cymbeline.* Ben Jonson, *The Alchemist.*	**1610** Henry is made Prince of Wales. Shakespeare probably returns to Stratford and settles there. The King's Men begin using Blackfriars Theater as a second, indoor venue.

TEXT	CONTEXT
1611 *The Winter's Tale.* *The Tempest.* Francis Beaumont and John Fletcher, *A King and No King.* Publication of the Authorized (King James) Bible.	**1611** Plantation of Ulster in Ireland, a colony of English and Scottish Protestants settled on land confiscated from Irish rebels.
1612–13 *Cardenio,* with John Fletcher (not extant). *Henry VIII,* with John Fletcher. John Webster, *The White Devil.*	**1612** Prince Henry dies.
1613–14 *The Two Noble Kinsmen,* with John Fletcher.	**1613** Princess Elizabeth marries Frederick V, Elector Palatine. The Globe Theater burns down during a performance of *Henry VIII.*
1614 Ben Jonson, *Bartholomew Fair.* John Webster, *The Duchess of Malfi.*	**1614** Philip Henslowe and Jacob Meade build the Hope Theater, used both for play performances and as a bearbaiting arena. The Globe Theater reopens.
1616 Ben Jonson publishes his *Works,* including the first collection of plays by a commercial English dramatist.	**1616** William Harvey describes the circulation of the blood. Shakespeare's daughter Judith marries. Shakespeare dies on April 23.
1623 Members of the King's Men publish the First Folio of Shakespeare's plays.	

Glossary

STAGE TERMS

"above" The gallery on the upper level of the stage's back wall (see *frons scenae*). In open-air theaters, such as the Globe, this space may have included the lords' rooms. The central section of the gallery was sometimes used by the players for short scenes. Indoor theaters such as Blackfriars featured a curtained alcove for musicians above the stage.

"aloft" See *"above."*

amphitheater An open-air theater, such as the Globe.

arras See *curtain.*

cellarage See *trap.*

chorus In the works of Shakespeare and other Elizabethan playwrights, a single individual (not, as in Greek tragedy, a group) who speaks before the play (and sometimes before each act or, in *Pericles*, at other times), describing events not shown on stage as well as commenting on the action witnessed by the audience.

curtain Curtains, or arras (hanging tapestries), probably covered a part of the stage's back wall (see *frons scenae*), thus concealing the discovery space, and may also have been draped around the edge of the stage to conceal the open area underneath.

discovery space A central opening or alcove concealed behind a curtain in the center of the stage's back wall (see *frons scenae*). The curtain could be drawn aside to "discover" tableaux such as Portia's caskets, the body of Polonius, or the statue of Hermione. Shakespeare appears to have used this stage device only sparingly.

doubling The common practice of having one actor play multiple roles, so that a play with a large cast of characters might be performed by a relatively small company.

dumb shows Mimed scenes performed before a play or as part of the play itself, summarizing or foreshadowing the plot. Dumb shows were popular in early Elizabethan drama; although they already seemed old-fashioned in Shakespeare's time, they were employed by writers up to the 1640s.

epilogue A brief speech or poem addressed to the audience by an actor after the play. In some cases, as in *2 Henry IV*, the epilogue could be combined with, or could merge into, the jig.

frons scenae The wall at the back of the stage, behind which lay the players' tiring house. The *frons scenae* of the Globe featured two doors flanking the central discovery space, with a gallery "above."

gallery Covered seating area surrounding the open yard of the public amphitheater. There were three levels of galleries at the Globe; admission to these seats cost an extra penny (in addition to the basic admission fee of one penny to the yard), and seating in the higher galleries another penny yet.

gatherers Persons employed by the playing company to take money at the entrances to the theater.

groundlings Audience members who paid the minimum price of admission (one penny) to stand in the yard of the open-air theaters; also referred to as "understanders." "Groundling" is an unusual word, possibly coined by Shakespeare; it is unclear whether it was in common usage at the time.

heavens The canopied roof over the stage in the open-air theaters, protecting the players and their costumes from rain. The "heavens" may have been brightly decorated with sun, moon, and stars, and perhaps the signs of the zodiac.

jig A song-and-dance performance by the clown and other members of the company at the conclusion of a play. These performances were frequently bawdy and were officially banned in 1612.

lords' rooms Partitioned sections of the gallery above the stage, or just to the left and right of the stage, where the most prestigious and expensive seats in the public playhouses were located. These rooms did not provide the best view of the action on the stage below. They were designed to make their privileged occupants conspicuous to the rest of the audience.

open-air theaters Unroofed public playhouses in the suburbs of London, such as The Theatre, the Rose, and the Globe.

part The character played by an actor. In Shakespeare's theater, actors were given a roll of paper called a "part" containing all of the speeches and all of the cues belonging to their character. The term "role," synonymous with "part," is derived from such rolls of paper.

patrons Important nobles and members of the royal family under whose protection the theatrical companies of London operated; players not in the service of patrons were punishable as vagabonds. The companies were referred to as their patrons' "Men" or "Servants." Thus the company to which Shakespeare belonged for most of his career was first known as the Lord Chamberlain's Servants, then became the King's Men in 1603, when James I became their patron.

pillars The "heavens" were supported by two tall painted pillars or posts near the front of the stage. These occasionally played a role in stage action, allowing a character to "hide" while remaining in full view of the audience.

pit The area in front of the stage in indoor theaters such as Blackfriars; unlike an open-air playhouse's yard, the pit was designed for a seated audience.

posts See *pillars*.

proscenium The arch that divides the stage, scenery, and backstage area from the auditorium in many theaters built in and after the eighteenth century. It also separates actors and audiences, potentially creating the so-called fourth wall. The stages on which Shakespeare's plays were first performed had no proscenium.

repertory The stock of plays a company had ready for performance at a given time. Companies generally performed a different play each day, often more than a dozen plays in a month and more than thirty in the course of the season.

role See *part*.

sharers Senior actors holding shares in a joint-stock theatrical company; they paid for costumes, hired hands, and new plays, and they shared profits and losses equally. Shakespeare was not only a longtime "sharer" of the Lord Chamberlain's Men but, from 1599, a "housekeeper," the holder of a one-eighth share in the Globe playhouse.

tiring house The players' dressing (attiring) room, a structure located at the back of the stage and connected to the stage by two or more doors in the *frons scenae*.

trap A trapdoor near the front of the stage that allowed access to the cellarage beneath and was frequently associated with hell's mouth. Another trapdoor in the heavens opened for the descent of gods to the stage below.

"within" The tiring house, from which offstage sound effects such as shouts, drums, and trumpets were produced.

yard The central space in open-air theaters such as the Globe, into which the stage projected and in which audience members stood. Admission to the yard in the public theaters cost a penny, the cheapest admission available.

TEXTUAL TERMS

aside See *stage direction*.

autograph Text written in the author's own hand. With the possible exception of a few pages of the collaborative play *Sir Thomas More*, no dramatic works or poems written in Shakespeare's hand are known to survive.

"bad quartos" A polemical term for a group of Shakespeare quartos that are different from and often demonstrably inferior to other versions of the plays in question as they are found in later quartos or in the First Folio. Some of these texts are very short; others include notable distortions of language. Explanations for the "bad quartos" (or, more neutrally, "short quartos") include the possibility that they were Shakespeare's early drafts, abbreviated scripts prepared for performance under circumstances such as touring, or "memorial reconstructions."

base text The early text upon which a modern edition is based, also known as a "control text."

canonical Of an author, the writings generally accepted as authentic. In the case of Shakespeare's dramatic works, only two plays that are not among the thirty-six plays contained in the First Folio, *Pericles* and *The Two Noble Kinsmen*, have won widespread acceptance into the Shakespearean canon, but recent scholarship suggests that he wrote parts of a number of others, including *Edward III* and *Sir Thomas More*.

casting off The practice of dividing up a manuscript to anticipate the number of pages needed to contain it in print. Errors in casting off sometimes led compositors to crowd lines, abbreviate spellings, and print verse as prose. If on the contrary a compositor found he had too much space remaining, he might leave spaces around stage directions, add ornaments, or break prose up into short "verse" lines.

catchword A word printed below the text at the bottom of a page, matching the first word on the following page. The catchword enabled the printer to keep the pages in their proper sequence. Where the catchword fails to match the word at the top of the next page, there is reason to suspect that something has been lost or misplaced.

collaboration   The practice of two or more writers working together to create a play (or other literature). More than half of the plays in Shakespeare's period were collaborative. Shakespeare collaborated with John Fletcher on *Henry VIII*, *The Two Noble Kinsmen*, and the missing *Cardenio*; with George Wilkins on *Pericles*; and with Thomas Middleton on *Timon of Athens*. Shakespeare plays that probably have sections composed by others include *Titus Andronicus*, *1 Henry VI*, and *Macbeth*; in turn, Shakespeare seems to have contributed a section to *Sir Thomas More*.

compositor   A person employed in a print shop to set type. To speed the printing process, most of Shakespeare's plays were set by more than one compositor. Compositors were expected to adjust spelling and provide punctuation and can often be identified by their different habits and preferences (e.g., *been/beene* or *O/Oh* and speech prefixes such as *Que./Queene*). They invariably introduced errors into the texts—for instance, by selecting the wrong letter from the type case or by setting the correct letter upside down.

conflation   A version of a play created by combining readings from more than one substantive text. Since the early eighteenth century, for example, most versions of *King Lear* and of several other plays by Shakespeare have been conflations of quarto and First Folio texts.

deus ex machina   Literally, "god from a machine," the term can refer to any plot device introduced to resolve a seemingly insurmountable problem.

dramatis personae (or The Persons of the Play)   A list of the characters that appear in the play. In the First Folio such lists, called "The Names of the Actors," were printed at the end of some but not all of the plays. In 1709 the editor Nicholas Rowe first provided lists of dramatis personae for all of Shakespeare's dramatic works.

emendation   A correction made in a text by an editor where he or she believes on the basis of evidence and/or inference that it has been corrupted in transmission and needs to be altered for coherence or sense.

exeunt / exit   See *stage direction*.

fair copy   A transcript of the "foul papers" made either by a scribe or by the playwright.

folio   A bookmaking format in which each large sheet of paper is folded once, making two leaves (a leaf is part of a folded sheet of paper with a page on each side). This format produced large volumes, generally handsome and expensive. The First Folio of Shakespeare's plays was printed in 1623.

forme   A body of type secured in a chase, or wooden frame, ready for printing. The forme would be placed into the press and inked and a sheet of paper lowered onto it for imprinting.

foul papers   A term for a playwright's working draft of a play, which is presumed to have contained "false starts," blotted-out passages, ghost characters, and revisions. To judge by apparent errors in the printed texts, several of Shakespeare's plays appear to have been printed from foul papers rather than fair copy; however, no clearcut instance of his foul papers survives, though certain pages in the manuscript of *Sir Thomas More* may represent this stage of the writing process.

ghost characters   Characters named in a stage direction who have no lines during the ensuing action. They may represent a "false start" as the author composed the play, and may not have actually appeared onstage in performance.

licensing By an order of 1581, new plays could not be performed until they had received a license from the Master of the Revels. A separate license, granted by the Court of High Commission, was required for publication, though in practice plays were often printed without license. From 1610, the Master of the Revels had the authority to license plays for publication as well as for performance.

manent / manet See *stage direction*.

massed entry The grouping of all characters who will appear at any point in a scene into a single opening direction. Playwrights such as Ben Jonson preferred this style because of its conformity with classical practice, and it was followed by certain scribes. Modern editors write entry directions to show the point in the scene at which each character enters.

memorial reconstruction The theory that some texts may have been reconstructed from memory by one or more actors, either because a promptbook had been destroyed or because it was not available—for example, while touring. It has been proposed that memorial reconstruction might explain the existence of "bad" or inferior quartos of some of Shakespeare's plays, though this is no longer universally accepted.

octavo A bookmaking format in which each large sheet of paper is folded three times, making eight leaves (sixteen pages front and back). Only one of Shakespeare's plays, *3 Henry VI* (1595), was published in octavo format.

playbook See *promptbook*.

press variants Minor textual variations among pages in books of the same edition, resulting from corrections made in the course of printing or from damaged or slipped type.

promptbook A manuscript of a play (either foul papers or fair copy) annotated and adapted for performance by the theatrical company. The promptbook incorporated stage directions, notes on properties and special effects, and revisions, sometimes including those required by the Master of the Revels. Promptbooks may be identifiable by the replacement of characters' names with actors' names.

quarto A bookmaking format in which each large sheet of paper is folded twice, making four leaves (eight pages front and back). Quarto volumes were smaller and less expensive than books printed in the folio format.

recto Literally, the right-hand page; in a quarto volume, each signature consisted of four leaves each of which had a recto and a verso; the pages were then numbered 1r[ecto], 1v[erso], 2r, 2v, 3r, 3v, 4r, 4v.

scribal copy A transcript of a play produced by a professional scribe (or "scrivener"). Scribes tended to employ their own preferred spellings, abbreviations, and punctuation and could be responsible for introducing a variety of errors.

signature A section of an early book consisting of one group of folded pages (e.g., in a quarto, four leaves or eight pages). Early modern printers indicated each signature by a letter (e.g., A) to assist them in keeping track of the parts of the book to bind together.

single-text editing Editing a work by staying as close as possible to a single early authoritative base text, emending only where necessary for sense and without either conflating by incorporating words or passages from other cognate texts or by reconstructing passages from source materials or other forms of inference.

speech prefix (SP)   The indication of the identity of the speaker of the following line or lines. Early editions of Shakespeare's plays often use different prefixes at different points to designate the same person. On occasion, the name of the actor who was to play the role appears in place of the name of the character.

stage direction (SD)   The part of the text that is not spoken by any character but that indicates actions to be performed onstage. Stage directions in the earliest editions of Shakespeare's plays are sparse; some necessary directions, most notably exits, are missing, and others may appear earlier or later than the plot requires. Directions for action (e.g., "Pray you, undo this button") may be implied in the dialogue but are not necessarily followed in a given production. By convention, the most basic stage directions were written in Latin. "Exit" indicates the departure of a single actor from the stage, "exeunt" the departure of more than one. "Manet" indicates that a single actor remains onstage, "manent" that more than one remains. Lines accompanied by the stage direction "aside" are spoken so as not to be heard by the others onstage. This stage direction appeared in some early editions of Shakespeare plays, but other means were also used to indicate such speech (such as placing the words within parentheses), and sometimes no indication was provided.

Stationers' Register   The account books of the Company of Stationers (the guild of printers, publishers, and booksellers that controlled the London book trade), recording the fees paid by publishers to secure their rights to certain texts, as well as the transfer of these rights between publishers. The Stationers' Register thus provides a valuable if incomplete record of publication in England.

substantive text   The text of an edition based upon access to a manuscript, as opposed to a derivative text based only on an earlier edition.

typecase   The compartmentalized box in which movable type (metal letters, punctuation, etc.) was stored; capital, or "upper-case," letters were traditionally stored at the top of the typecase, "lower-case" letters at the bottom. Compositors drew individual type from the typecase for placing into a "compositor's stick" that held one line of type; from there the type would be transferred to a chase and secured to create a forme. Mistakes in sorting used type back into the typecase may account for some textual errors.

variorum editions   Comprehensive editions of a work or works in which the various views of previous editors and commentators are compiled.

verso   See *recto*

Essential Reference Books

Bate, Jonathan, and Russell Jackson, eds. *Shakespeare: An Illustrated Stage History.* New York: Oxford UP, 1996.

Bullough, Geoffrey, ed. *Narrative and Dramatic Sources of Shakespeare.* 8 vols. New York: Columbia UP, 1957–75.

Chambers, E. K. *The Elizabethan Stage.* 4 vols. Oxford: Clarendon, 1923.

———. *William Shakespeare: A Study of Facts and Problems.* 2 vols. Oxford: Clarendon, 1930.

Crystal, David. *Pronouncing Shakespeare: The Globe Experiment.* Cambridge: Cambridge UP, 2005.

Dent, R. W. *Shakespeare's Proverbial Language: An Index.* Berkeley: U of California P, 1981.

Dessen, Alan C., and Leslie Thomson. *A Dictionary of Stage Directions in English Drama, 1580–1642.* New York: Cambridge UP, 1999.

Dobson, E. J. *English Pronunciation, 1500–1700.* 2nd ed. 2 vols. Oxford: Clarendon, 1968.

Dobson, Michael, and Stanley Wells, eds. *The Oxford Companion to Shakespeare.* Oxford: Oxford UP, 2001.

Duffin, Ross W. *Shakespeare's Songbook.* New York: Norton, 2004.

Foakes, R. A. *Illustrations of the English Stage, 1580–1642.* Stanford: Stanford UP, 1985.

Greenblatt, Stephen, and Peter G. Platt, eds. *Shakespeare's Montaigne: The Florio Translation of the Essays, a Selection.* New York: New York Review Books, 2014.

Greg, W. W., ed. *Dramatic Documents from the Elizabethan Playhouses: Stage Plots: Actors' Parts: Prompt Books.* 2 vols. Oxford: Clarendon, 1931.

Gurr, Andrew. *Playgoing in Shakespeare's London.* 3rd ed. New York: Cambridge UP, 2004.

———. *The Shakespearean Stage, 1574–1642.* 4th ed. New York: Cambridge UP, 2009.

Henslowe, Philip. *Henslowe's Diary.* Ed. R. A. Foakes. 2nd ed. New York: Cambridge UP, 2002.

Hosley, Richard, ed. *Shakespeare's Holinshed: An Edition of Holinshed's Chronicles, 1587.* New York: Putnam, 1968.

Murphy, Andrew. *Shakespeare in Print: A History and Chronology of Shakespeare Publishing.* New York: Cambridge UP, 2003.

Oxford Dictionary of National Biography. Oxford: Oxford UP, 2004. www.oxforddnb.com/

Oxford English Dictionary. Oxford: Clarendon, 1989. www.oed.com/

Partridge, A. C. *Orthography in Shakespeare and Elizabethan Drama.* London: E. Arnold, 1964.

Partridge, Eric. *Shakespeare's Bawdy: A Literary and Psychological Essay and a Comprehensive Glossary.* 3rd ed. New York: Routledge, 2001.

Schoenbaum, Samuel. *William Shakespeare: A Documentary Life.* New York: Oxford UP, 1975.

Spevack, Marvin. *A Complete and Systematic Concordance to the Works of Shakespeare.* 9 vols. Hildesheim: George Olms, 1968–80.

Stern, Tiffany. *Documents of Performance in Early Modern England.* Cambridge: Cambridge UP, 2009

Tilley, Morris Palmer. *A Dictionary of the Proverbs in England in the Sixteenth and Seventeenth Centuries*. Ann Arbor: U of Michigan P, 1950.

Wells, Stanley. *A Dictionary of Shakespeare*. 2nd ed. New York: Oxford UP, 2005.

——. *Re-Editing Shakespeare for the Modern Reader*. New York: Oxford UP, 1984.

Wickham, Glynne. *Early English Stages, 1300 to 1660*. 4 vols. New York: Routledge, 2002.

Williams, Gordon. *A Dictionary of Sexual Language and Imagery in Shakespearean and Stuart Literature*. 3 vols. London: Athlone, 1994.

For a much fuller bibliography, including critical and historical works bearing on the study of Shakespeare, see the Digital Edition of *The Norton Shakespeare*.

ILLUSTRATION ACKNOWLEDGMENTS

The House of Lancaster

EDWARD III

John of Gaunt, Duke of Lancaster   m. Katherine Swynford
m. Blanche of Lancaster

Henry Bollingbroke
(HENRY IV)

Thomas Beaufort,
Duke of Exeter

Henry Beaufort,
Bishop of Winchester

John Beaufort,
Earl of Somerset

Joan Beaufort m. Ralph Neville,
Earl of Westmoreland

Henry of Monmouth
(HENRY V)
m. Catherine of France

Thomas,
Duke of Clarence

John of Lancaster,
Duke of Bedford

Humphrey,
Duke of Gloucester

John Beaufort,
Duke of Somerset

Edmund Beaufort,
Duke of Somerset

Richard Neville,
Earl of Salisbury

HENRY VI m. Margaret of Anjou

Margaret Beaufort
m. Edmund Tudor,
Earl of Richmond

Henry Beaufort,
Duke of Somerset

John Neville,
Marquess of Montague

Richard Neville,
Earl of Warwick

Edward, Prince of Wales m. Anne Neville

Henry Tudor, Earl of Richmond (HENRY VII) m. Elizabeth of York

THE HOUSE OF YORK

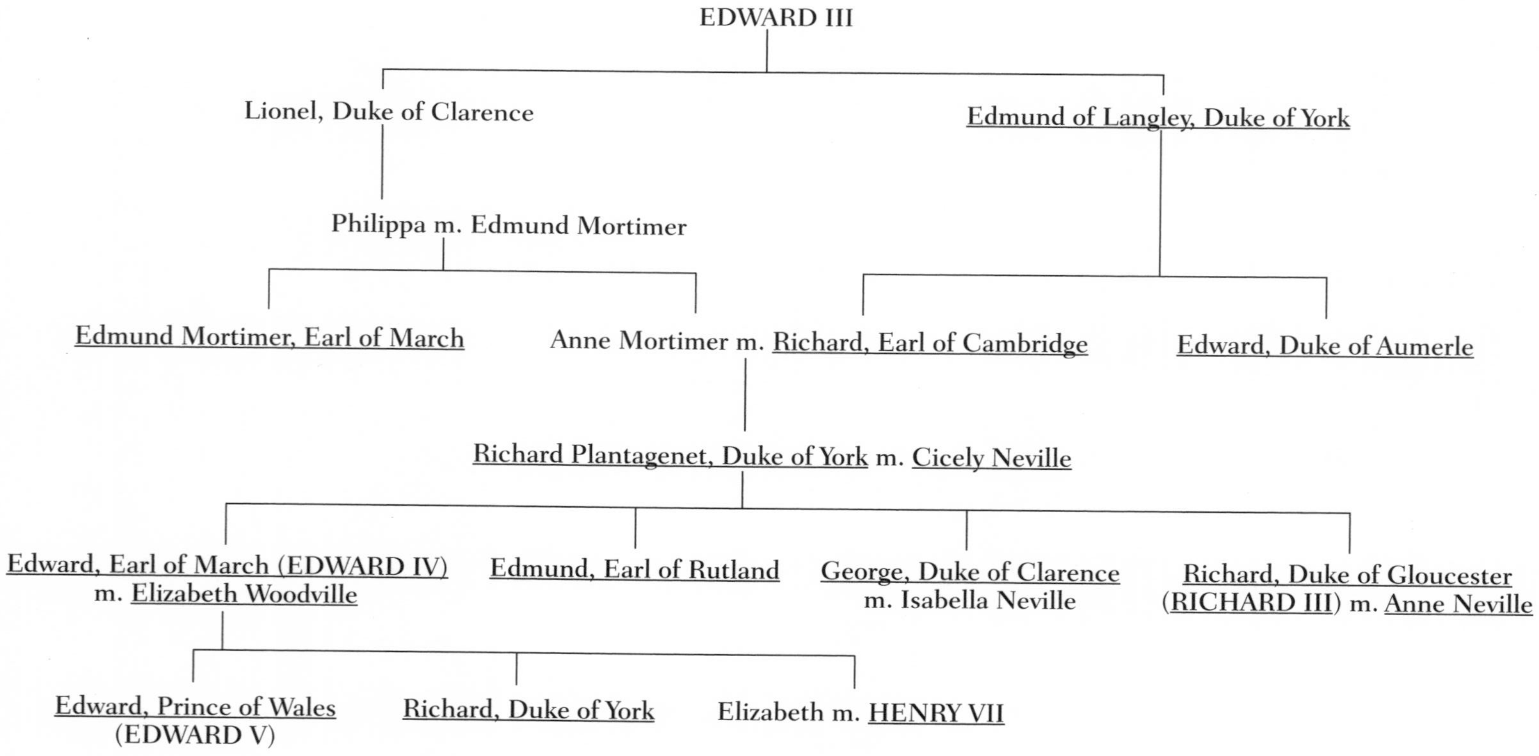

EDWARD III

Lionel, Duke of Clarence

Philippa m. Edmund Mortimer

Edmund Mortimer, Earl of March

Anne Mortimer m. Richard, Earl of Cambridge

Edmund of Langley, Duke of York

Edward, Duke of Aumerle

Richard Plantagenet, Duke of York m. Cicely Neville

Edward, Earl of March (EDWARD IV)
m. Elizabeth Woodville

Edmund, Earl of Rutland

George, Duke of Clarence
m. Isabella Neville

Richard, Duke of Gloucester
(RICHARD III) m. Anne Neville

Edward, Prince of Wales
(EDWARD V)

Richard, Duke of York

Elizabeth m. HENRY VII